To Trevor on his 11th Birthday

Love from

      Mummy and Daddy xxx

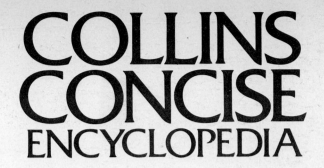

COLLINS CONCISE ENCYCLOPEDIA

COLLINS CONCISE ENCYCLOPEDIA

Collins London & Glasgow

First Published 1977
© 1977 William Collins Sons & Co. Ltd.
ISBN 0 00 434317 4
Typeset by C. R. Barber and Partners, Wrotham, Kent
Printed in Great Britain
by Jarrold and Sons Ltd, Whitefriars, Norwich
for William Collins Sons & Co. Ltd.

PREFACE

Preface

The *Collins Concise Encyclopedia* is completely new, providing a record of all fields of human knowledge and experience in the final quarter of the 20th century. It presents that record in a condensed form in order to make it accessible to as many people as possible. These two aims of comprehensiveness and accessibility have been carried out with the needs of an English-speaking readership in mind.

The *Encyclopedia's* coverage ranges from the ancient Greeks, and the European debt to them in such fields as philosophy and literature, to recent developments in subatomic theory. It encompasses prehistoric cave painting, and rock music in the 1960s and 1970s, as well as tribal rites in the Pacific and medieval Islamic scholarship in the Mediterranean. However, human experience has been heightened through ever-improving communications to such an extent that most of us learn of contemporary events almost as they happen. It is now possible for us to see the death of an American president or the tumultuous events often accompanying the birth of an African nation. Technology has given us access to the experience of people whose existence was unknown to our ancestors. Our knowledge has expanded and the *Collins Concise Encyclopedia* reflects the different directions in which this knowledge has moved.

The book is in one volume to make it easy to pick up and consult. The A to Z treatment enables the reader to gain information as simply as possible. Cross-references link articles and have been used only when the reader can find out more about the subject under another heading. Abbreviations are used to make space available for more information.

Illustrations form an integral part of the book: the photographs, drawings and maps have been chosen both to supplement the text and to give further visual insights into the subject.

Finally, in increasing the extent of worldwide coverage, we have not neglected the particular demands of the English-speaking readership. The *Collins Concise Encyclopedia* maintains the balance between the considerable influences which Britain, the United States and the Commonwealth have had and continue to have on each other.

J. Mallory

Editorial Staff

General Editor	James Mallory
Editorial Team	R. Gow
	Chris Gravell
	Michael Knowling
	Donald McFarlan
	Kay Macpherson
Illustrations	Danielle McGrath
	Ronald Mongredien
Contributors	Neil Ardley
	Michael Hughes
	John Thorne

Abbreviations used in the Encyclopedia

AD	anno domini	Jan.	January
admin.	administration, administrated	Jap.	Japanese
agric.	agricultural, agriculture	jct.	junction
alt.	altitude	kg	kilogram
anc.	ancient	km	kilometre, kilometres
anon.	anonymous	kmh	kilometres per hour
Arab.	Arabic	L.	Lake
at. no.	atomic number	lat.	latitude
at. wt.	atomic weight	lb	pound (unit of weight)
Aug.	August	long.	longitude
autobiog.	autobiography	max.	maximum
auton.	autonomous, autonomy	mfg.	manufacture, manufacturing
av.	average	mi	mile, miles
b.	born	min.	minimum, minute
BC	before Christ	mm	millimetre
biog.	biography	MP	Member of Parliament
bor.	borough	mph	miles per hour
C	central	Mt.	Mount
c	about	Mts.	Mountains
cap.	capital	mun. bor.	municipal borough
cent.	century	N	north
cm	centimetre, centimetres	Nov.	November
co.	county, company	NT	New Testament
co. bor.	county borough	Oct.	October
coll.	college	orig.	originally
co. town	county town	OT	Old Testament
d.	died	penin.	peninsula
Dec.	December	PM	Prime Minister
dept.	department	Pol.	Polish
dist.	district	pop.	population
E	east	Port.	Portuguese
eg	for example	prehist.	prehistoric
Eng.	English	prob.	probably
esp.	especially	protect.	protectorate
est.	estimated	prov.	province
estab.	established	pseud.	pseudonym
etc	and so on	pub.	published
excl.	excludes, excluding	R.	River
Feb.	February	RC	Roman Catholic
Finn.	Finnish	Russ.	Russian
fl	flourished	S	south
Flem.	Flemish	sec	second
Fr.	French	Sept.	September
ft	foot, feet	Span.	Spanish
Ger.	German	sq km	square kilometres
Gk.	Greek	sq mi	square miles
gm	gram	St	Saint
govt.	government	St.	Street
ha.	hectare, hectares	str.	strait
Heb.	Hebrew	Swed.	Swedish
h.e.p.	hydro-electric power	territ.	territory
hist.	historical	Turk.	Turkish
hr	hour	TV	television
hq.	headquarters	UK	United Kingdom
Hung.	Hungarian	UN	United Nations
ie	that is	univ.	university
in.	inch, inches	US	United States
incl.	include, including, included	v	against
indust.	industrial, industry	vol.	volume
isl.	island	WW	World War
Ital.	Italian	W	west
		yd	yard, yards

A

Aachen (Fr. *Aix-la-Chapelle*), city of W West Germany. Pop. 177,000. Indust. centre in coalmining area, railway jct. Thermal baths from Roman times. N cap. of Holy Roman Empire, cathedral (10th cent.) has Charlemagne's tomb. Badly damaged in WWII.

Aalborg, city of NE Jutland, Denmark, on Lim Fjord. Pop. 100,000. Port, shipbuilding; cement; textiles.

Aalst (Fr. *Alost*), town of C Belgium on R. Dender. Pop. 46,000. Textiles, brewing. Hist. printing centre; church (15th cent.).

Aalto, Alvar (1899-1976), Finnish architect, furniture designer. Pioneer of modern architecture, he was noted for his imaginative use of materials, esp. wood and brick, and for relating buildings to the landscape.

Aardvark

aardvark, *Orycteropus afer,* nocturnal burrowing mammal of C and S Africa, order Tubulidentata. Long snout, extensile sticky tongue; diet of ants, termites. Also known as antbear, earth pig.

Aardwolf

aardwolf, *Proteles cristatus,* burrowing hyaena-like mammal of Protelidae family, inhabiting scrubland of S Africa. Diet of termites, carrion.

Aargau, canton of N Switzerland. Area 1404 sq km (542 sq mi); cap. Aarau (Helvetic cap., 1789-1803). Crossed by fertile valley of R. Aare. Cereals, fruit. Mineral springs.

Aarhus, city of E Jutland, Denmark, on Kattegat. Pop. 199,000. Port; trade, transport centre; oil refining.

Aaron, in OT, elder brother of Moses and leader with him of Israelites in march into 'promised land'. First high priest of Hebrews.

Aasen, Ivar Andreas (1813-96), Norwegian philologist. Created from various dialects literary language 'Landsmaal' using it in his own poetry.

abacá, *see* Manila hemp.

Abacus

abacus, calculating device consisting of frame with beads which slide back and forward on parallel wires or in slots. Widely used in Middle East, Orient and Russia.

Abadan, city of SW Iran, on Abadan isl. at head of Persian Gulf. Pop. 306,000. Oil refining and export centre.

Abakan, city of USSR, cap. of Khakass auton. region, SC Siberian RSFSR. Pop. 107,000. Produces textiles, metal products. Founded in 1707 as fortress.

abalone, gastropod mollusc, genus *Haliotis,* found mainly on Californian coast. Shell, resembling human ear, source of mother-of-pearl; flesh commonly eaten. Ormer, *H. tuberculata,* found in Channel Islands.

Abbas [II] Hilmi (1874-1944), last Turkish viceroy (khedive) of Egypt (1892-1914). Deposed when Britain declared Egypt a British protect. following Turkish entry into WWI on German side.

Abbasids, Arab dynasty of caliphs. Overthrew Omayyad dynasty (750) and moved cap. from Damascus to Baghdad. Achieved great fame and splendour under Harun al-Rashid. Destroyed (1258) by Mongols under Hulagu Khan.

Abbas [I] the Great (1557-1628), Persian shah (1587-1628). Greatly enlarged empire at expense of Turks and, with help of English, Portuguese.

Abbaye, group of French writers, artists incl. Georges Duhamel, Charles Vildrac, Albert Gleizes, who estab. short-lived community (1906) in 'L'Abbaye', a house in Créteil. Ideas formulated in Jules Romains' *La Vie unanime* as *Unanisme.*

Abbe, Cleveland (1838-1916), American meteorologist. Using telegraph reports, originated daily weather forecasting (1869); helped found US Weather Bureau.

Abbeville, town of Picardy, N France, on R. Somme. Pop. 25,000. Textiles, carpet mfg., sugar refining.

Abbevillian culture, phase of Lower Palaeolithic period associated with the earliest hand axe industs. in Europe. Evidence found in gravel pits at Abbeville, France.

abbey, in Christian religion, monastic house in which a community of at least 12 monks or nuns live, ruled by an abbot or abbess. First abbey founded (c 529) by St Benedict at Monte Cassino, Italy.

Abbey Theatre, Dublin home of Irish National Theatre Society, founded during Irish literary revival of early 1900s, by W.B. Yeats, G.W. Russell (A.E.), Lady Gregory. Works by Synge, O'Casey received 1st presentation.

Abd el-Krim (*c* 1882-1963), Moroccan tribal chief. Leader of Berber revolt at Rif, until defeated (1925) by French-Spanish forces. Deported to Réunion isl.; escaped 1947.

Abd el-Rahman III (891–961), Omayyad caliph of Córdoba 929-61. Built powerful, prosperous caliphate; made Córdoba leading centre of learning in W Europe.

abdication, formal renunciation of high public office or authority, usually by monarch. In UK requires consent of Parliament, most famous example being Edward VIII (1936).

abdomen, in mammals, part of body below the thorax and above the pelvis; separated from thorax by the diaphragm. Contains stomach, intestines, liver, kidney, *etc.* In insects and crustaceans, hind part of body beyond thorax.

Abdul Hamid II (1842-1918), Ottoman sultan (1876-1909). Dismissed Midhat Pasha whose newly-framed constitution he then suspended (1876). Pursued pro-German policy after CONGRESS OF BERLIN. Deposed by Young Turks.

Abdullah ibn Hussein (1882-1951), Arab leader, b. Mecca, 1st king of Jordan (1946-51). Incorporated Arab Palestine into kingdom after Arab-Israeli war (1948-9), in which he fought. Assassinated.

Abel, in OT, second son of Adam and Eve. Killed by his brother CAIN. A shepherd, his offerings were accepted by God when those of Cain (a tiller of the soil) were refused.

Abel, Sir Frederick Augustus (1827-1902), English chemist, an authority on explosives. Developed smokeless explosives; with Dewar (1889), invented explosive powder, cordite.

Abel, Niels Henrik (1802-29), Norwegian mathematician. Independently of Galois, showed impossibility of solving general polynomial of 5th degree by algebraic means. Noted for pioneering work on elliptic functions.

Abelard, Peter or **Pierre Abélard** (1079-1142), French scholar. Held universals to exist only in thought but based in particular objects. Applied Aristotelian logic to faith in *Sic et Non.* Charged with heresy (1121). Remembered through their letters for tragic romance with Héloïse, provoking his castration by her uncle. Regarded as founder of Univ. of Paris. Works incl. autobiog. *Historia calamitatum.*

Abeokuta, city of SW Nigeria. Pop. 226,000. On Lagos-Kano railway; centre of agric. region, producing yams, palm oil. Cap. of independent Egba state from *c* 1830-1914.

Abercromby, Sir Ralph (1734-1801), British general. Commanded ably in campaigns against French in Europe (1794-5) and West Indies (1795-7). Killed while defeating French at Aboukir Bay.

Aberdare, urban dist. of Mid Glamorgan, S Wales. Pop. 38,000. Coalmining; cables, electrical goods mfg.

Aberdeen, George Hamilton-Gordon, 4th Earl of (1784-1860), British statesman, PM (1852-5). Helped bring Austria into coalition against Napoleon with Treaty of Töplitz (1813). Failed to keep Britain out of Crimean War, resigned as PM after censure.

Aberdeenshire, former county of NE Scotland, now in Grampian region. Grampian Mts. in SW. Crops, livestock (esp. beef cattle); fishing, granite quarrying. Has offshore oil indust. Co. town was **Aberdeen,** city on R. Dee. Pop. 182,000. Chief Scottish fishing port, tourism, shipbuilding, oil rig service industs. Became royal burgh (1179). Has univ. (colls. 1494, 1593); cathedral (14th cent.). Called 'Granite City'.

aberration, in astronomy, apparent displacement of position of star or other heavenly body, caused by motion of earth. During earth's annual motion about sun, star appears to move in small ellipse. Effect discovered by Bradley 1725, who used it to estimate speed of light.

aberration, in optics, failure of lens or mirror to form perfect image. In spherical aberration, light rays from a point source are focused at different points. In chromatic aberration, edges of images are coloured because refractive index of lens varies for light of different wavelengths.

Aberystwyth, mun. bor. of Dyfed, W Wales. Pop. 11,000. Tourist resort. Has coll. of Univ. of Wales (1872); National Library of Wales (1911).

Abidjan, cap. of Ivory Coast, on Ebrie Lagoon. Pop. 510,000. Admin., commercial centre; railway terminus; exports coffee, cocoa, timber, fruit via outport at Port Bouet; univ.

Abilene, town of WC Texas, US. Pop. 90,000. Grew as shipping point for cattle; centre of oil indust. Produces cottonseed oil, oil field equipment, electronic instruments.

Abo, see TURKU, Finland.

abolitionists, in US history, advocates of end to Negro slavery. Influenced by British anti-slavery campaign success (1833). Leaders incl. W.L. Garrison and Wendel Phillips. Fugitive State Law (1850) strengthened UNDERGROUND RAILROAD, activities culminating in John Brown's abortive raid (1859) on Harpers Ferry. Unyielding attitude of abolitionists helped bring about Civil War.

Abomey, town of S Benin. Pop. 42,000. Agric. market. Cap. of native kingdom of Dahomey 17th cent.-1892.

abominable snowman, *see* YETI.

aborigine (Lat. *ab origine,* from the beginning), inhabitants of a country who are believed to be original natives of the region. Term used esp. to refer to AUSTRALIAN ABORIGINES.

abortion, in medicine, spontaneous or induced expulsion of foetus from the womb before 28th week of pregnancy. Sometimes referred to medically as miscarriage if it occurs after 16th week; this term popularly refers to accidental premature birth at any stage.

Aboukir or **Abukir,** village of N Egypt, on Aboukir Bay. Scene of Nelson's victory (1798) over French fleet in the 'Battle of the Nile'.

Abraham, regarded as father of Jewish nation. In OT received Jehovah's promise of Canaan as land for his descendants. Prob. historical figure, but more important in Bible as archetype of the man of faith. *See* ISAAC.

Abraham, Plains of, see QUÉBEC (city).

abrasive, material used for scouring, grinding or polishing. Natural forms incl. corundum, emery and diamond. Artificial forms incl. carborundum (silicon carbide), boron carbide and synthetic diamond.

Abravanel, Judah Léon, called Leone Ebreo (*c* 1460-1523), Jewish philosopher, b. Portugal. Expounded classic interpretation of Platonic love in *Dialogues of Love* (1535) describing union of the lover with the idea of the beautiful.

Abruzzi e Molise, region of SC Italy, in Apennine Mts. Sparsely populated, no large towns. Agric. (livestock, cereals, grapes) in fertile valleys.

Absalom, in OT, King David's favourite son. Instigated revolt against his father. After defeat, was killed by Joab while caught in a tree.

Absalon or **Axel** (*c* 1128-1201), Danish churchman, soldier. Archbishop of Lund 1178-1201; adviser to Waldemar I, Canute IV. Defeated Wends, extended Denmark's Baltic territs.; also patron of learning.

abscess, swollen area in body tissue in which pus collects as a result of infection. Occurs in tooth sockets, inner ear, skin, *etc.* Treated by antibiotics, but may require surgical drainage.

absinthe, green-coloured liqueur flavoured with wormwood, anise and other aromatics; contains from 60% to 80% alcohol. Now banned in most countries because of toxic effect of wormwood on nervous system.

absolute zero, temperature zero point on absolute or Kelvin scale, corresponding to $-273.15°$ C. Theoretically lowest possible temperature, when molecular motion ceases.

absolutism, doctrine or system of govt. under which the ruler has unlimited power. Absolute monarchy *fl* in Europe 16th-18th cent., was defended by HOBBES.

abstract art, non-representational painting and sculpture, relying on form and colour to achieve aesthetic and emotional impact. Abstract art of 20th cent. derives from fauvism and cubism; early exponents incl. Kandinsky (1st abstract work 1910), whose early work emphasizes expressive use of colour, and Mondrian, who developed pure geometric style out of cubism. Brancusi was noted exponent of abstract sculpture.

abstract expressionism, school of American painting which developed after WWII; characterized by emphasis on artist's spontaneous and self-expressive application of paint in creating abstract work. Leading exponents incl. Pollock, Franz Kline and Rothko.

absurd, philosophical term used by CAMUS to describe meaninglessness of human existence in an irrational world. Precondition of much existentialist philosophy and literature as in novels of SARTRE, plays of Beckett, Ionesco. More personally experienced than SCEPTICISM.

Abu l-Ala al-Maarri (973–1058), Arab poet. Known for early innovative verse, *eg Sparks from Flint and Steel,* and later harsh asceticism of *Luzumiyyat* (translated 1904).

Abu Bakr or **Abu Bekr** (573–634), Arab leader. Important early convert to Islam, became devoted follower of Mohammed, who married his daughter. Succeeded Mohammed as 1st caliph (632); expansion of Islam into major world religion began under his rule.

Abu Dhabi, isl. sheikdom of United Arab Emirates, on Persian Gulf. Area *c* 67,300 sq km (26,000 sq mi); pop. 46,000; cap. Abu Dhabi. Has rich oil reserves.

Abu Nuwas, orig. Hasan ibn Hani (762–*c* 815), Arab poet. Favourite of Harun al-Rashid, known for lyric verse, satire, hunting songs. Appears as character in ARABIAN NIGHTS.

Abu Simbel, village of S Egypt, on R. Nile. Site of 2 temples built *c* 1250 BC by Rameses II, rebuilt in sections 1964-8 above flood waters of Aswan High Dam.

Abydos, ancient city of C Egypt, on R. Nile. Former religious centre, with temples to Osiris; burial place of many kings. Remains date from 3100-500 BC.

Abyssinia, *see* ETHIOPIA.

Abyssinian cat

Abyssinian cat, breed of short-haired domesticated cat with ruddy coat. Resembles sacred cats of ancient Egypt.

acacia, genus of tropical and subtropical trees of Leguminosae family. Pinnate leaves with clusters of yellow or white flowers. Many cultivated as ornamentals; yields gum arabic, dyes, tanning aids, furniture woods. Species incl. cooba, *Acacia salicina,* an Australian wattle.

Académie Française, institute estab. 1635 for protection and perfection of French language. Began compilation of definitive dictionary 1639. Awards annual literary prizes.

academies of art, official organizations of artists. First academy, founded by Vasari in Florence (1563) under patronage of Cosimo de' Medici, was concerned with raising social status of artists. French Academy of Painting and Sculpture founded (1648), later achieved monopoly of teaching and public exhibition, served as organ of official taste and standards. By 1790 over 100 academies throughout Europe, incl. Royal Academy, London (founded 1768). Romantic movement brought opposition to formal 'academism'.

academy, originally olive grove near Athens where Plato and followers met. Modern academy is learned society promoting arts, sciences, often publicly financed.

Academy Awards, prizes awarded annually since 1927 by US Academy of Motion Picture Arts and Sciences for outstanding achievements in cinema, incl. awards for best film, actor, music, *etc,* of year. Prizes in form of statuette known as Oscar.

Acadia (Fr. *Acadie), hist.* region of E Canada, comprising Nova Scotia, Prince Edward Isl., part of New Brunswick. French founded Port Royal, its chief town, in 1605; ceded to British 1713.

acanthus, genus of perennial herbs of Mediterranean region. White or coloured flowers with deeply cut spiny leaves. Stylized form of leaf used as architectural ornament, esp. on capitals of Corinthian columns, from *c* 5th cent. BC.

Acapulco, winter seaside resort of SW Mexico, on Pacific. Pop. 235,000. Has many hotels, excellent beaches; facilities for deep-sea diving, fishing. Fruit, cotton trading.

acceleration, rate of change of velocity. Gravitational acceleration is acceleration of free-falling body caused by gravitational attraction of Earth. Assumed constant near Earth's surface, equals *c* 981 cm/sec^2. Varies with altitude and longitude.

accelerator, in physics, device used to impart high velocities to charged particles by accelerating them in electric fields. Linear and cyclic are used in nuclear research, esp. investigation of elementary particles of matter. Examples incl. bevatron, betatron, cyclotron, synchrotron.

accentor, sparrow-like Eurasian bird, genus *Prunella.* Species incl. hedge sparrow or dunnock, *P. modularis.*

accessory, in law, a person who, although absent, helps another to break or escape the law. May be an accessory before (or after) the fact, *ie* one who aids the accused before (or after) the commission of the crime.

accipiter, any of genus *Accipiter* of small hawks with short wings, long tails. Species incl. goshawk, *A. gentilis,* and sparrow hawk, *A. nisus.*

accordion, portable reed organ. Wind is supplied by bellows and is directed to the reeds by keys and buttons, which sound accompanying chords. Invention variously attributed to Buschmann of Berlin (1822), Damien of Vienna (1829) and Bouton of Paris (1852).

accountancy, keeping or inspecting of financial data concerning persons and organizations. Data should incl. specific assets, liabilities, income, expenses, net receipts. First chartered body, Society of Accountants in Edinburgh (1854); American Association of Accountants chartered in 1887.

Accra, cap. of Ghana, on Gulf of Guinea. Pop. 738,000. Admin., commercial centre; railway terminus and port, exports cocoa, hardwoods, gold; Univ. of Ghana nearby. Grew round 2 17th cent. forts; cap. of Gold Coast colony from 1876.

accumulator or **secondary cell,** device used to store electricity. Current is passed between 2 plates in a liquid, causing chemical changes by electrolysis. When plates are electrically connected, reverse chemical changes cause current flow.

acetaldehyde (CH_3CHO), colourless liquid, formed by oxidation of ethanol. Used in dye and hypnotic drug mfg. Occurs in body during decomposition of ingested alcohol.

acetic acid (CH_3COOH), organic acid contained in vinegar. Colourless liquid with pungent smell, obtained by destructive distillation of wood or oxidation of acetaldehyde. Its esters incl. cellulose acetate, used to make plastics.

acetone (CH_3COCH_3), inflammable colourless liquid, the simplest KETONE. Obtained commercially from isopropanol. Used as paint and varnish remover and organic solvent.

acetylcholine, organic chemical secreted at ends of nerve fibres; stimulates adjacent nerve cells, thus transmitting impulses through nervous system.

acetylene (C_2H_2), colourless gas, produced by action of water on calcium carbide or from natural gas. Used in welding and organic synthesis; burns with intense flame when mixed with oxygen in oxyacetylene burner.

acetylsalicylic acid, *see* ASPIRIN.

Achad Haam, pseud. of Asher Ginzberg (1856-1927), Jewish philosopher, b. Ukraine. Founder of cultural Zionism, believed concern for justice forms basis of Judaism.

Achaea, admin. dist. of S Greece, in Peloponnese, cap. Patras. Currants, olives; sheep, goats. Cities formed powerful Achaean League 280-146 BC, until conquered by Rome.

Achard, Franz Karl (1753-1821), German chemist. Founder of 1st sugar beet factory in Germany, using Marggraf's methods of extracting sugar from beet roots.

Achebe, Chinua (1930-), Nigerian novelist. Works, incl. *Things Fall Apart* (1958), *Arrow of God* (1964), deal with the unsettling impact of European values on Nigerian village life.

Acheson, Dean Gooderham (1893-1969), American govt. official. Secretary of state (1949-53), developed policy of Communist containment through aid to W Europe; helped estab. NATO.

Acheson, Edward Goodrich (1856-1931), American inventor. Helped develop electric arc furnace and experimented in production of artificial diamonds. Discovered carborundum and did research on graphite and lubricants.

Acheulian culture, phase of Lower Palaeolithic period in Europe following Abbevillian, associated with use of flaking tools to make hand axes. In Africa, name refers to entire hand axe period, beginning *c* 1.3 million years ago.

Achilles, in Greek legend, warrior and Greek leader in Trojan War. As child, was dipped in R. Styx by his mother, Thetis, to make him invulnerable, but water did not touch heel she held him by. At Troy, killed Hector but was killed by Paris with an arrow which struck his only vulnerable spot, his heel. Hero of Homer's *Iliad.*

Achill Island, Co. Mayo, W Irish Republic. Area 148 sq km (57 sq mi). Mountainous; agric., fishing, tourism. Bridge from mainland.

acid, substance which liberates hydrogen ions in aqueous solution (Arrhenius' theory). Reacts with base to form salts. Strength measured by concentration of hydrogen ions (pH scale); those undergoing complete ionization (eg hydrochloric acid) are strong. Most acids corrode metals, turn litmus red and taste sour.

acidosis, condition in which alkalinity of human blood is less than normal. May be caused by failure of lungs to eliminate carbon dioxide, kidney failure, malnutrition, diabetes.

acne, skin disease caused by abnormal activity of sebaceous (grease) glands; common among adolescents and young adults. Characterized by pimples on face, back and chest; alleviated by ultraviolet light (which occurs in sunlight).

Aconcagua, mountain of W Argentina, highest of Andes Mts., close to Chile border and Uspallata Pass. Height 6960 m (22,835 ft).

aconite, *see* MONKSHOOD.

Acorn

acorn, ovoid fruit or nut of OAK. Consists of nut itself in cup-shaped base. Formerly used as food for pigs.

acorn worm, burrowing marine hemichordate, genus *Balanoglossus,* with acorn-shaped proboscis and gill-slits. Represents link between vertebrates and invertebrates, showing similarities with echinoderms.

Acosta, Uriel (1585-1640), Jewish philosopher, b. Portugal. A Catholic who reverted to Judaism but criticized rabbinical Judaism on rationalist grounds. Committed suicide after excommunication for rejecting belief in immortality.

acoustics, branch of physics dealing with propagation and detection of sound.

Acre (Heb. *Acco*), port of N Israel, on Bay of Haifa. Pop. 339,000. Steel, chemical indust. Christian centre during 13th cent. Crusades. Mainly Turkish rule (1517-1918), British (1918-48).

acropolis, elevated fortified citadel of ancient Greek cities. Surviving buildings of Acropolis in Athens incl. PROPYLAEA, PARTHENON, Erectheum and temple of Athena Nike, mostly constructed under Cimon and Pericles in 5th cent. BC.

acrostic, composition, usually in verse, in which certain letters in each line (eg first or last) spell out a word or words. Used notably by Latin and 16th-17th cent. English poets.

acrylic paint, emulsion paint used by artists, formed by adding pigment to acrylic resin. Can be applied with water to obtain thin washes or directly in thick impasto, imitating oil paint.

Actaeon, in Greek myth, a hunter. Angered Artemis by watching her bathe. She changed him into a stag and he was torn to pieces by his own hounds.

actinides, name given to group of elements with at. nos. from 89 to 103. Incl. uranium, actinium, thorium and 11 man-made transuranic elements. All radioactive and metallic.

actinium (Ac), radioactive metallic element; at. no. 89, at. wt. 227. Discovered (1899) by Debierne in pitchblende.

Actinozoa or **Anthozoa,** class of solitary or colonial coelenterates without free-swimming medusa stage. Incl. corals and sea anemones.

Actium, promontory of NW Greece, opposite modern Préveza. Site of Octavian's naval defeat of Antony and Cleopatra (31 BC).

act of God, in law, unforeseeable, unavoidable accident caused by extraordinary natural event. Injured party cannot normally claim damages.

Acton, John Emerich Edward Dalberg Acton, Baron (1834-1902), English historian. Prominent Liberal and RC, became professor of modern history at Cambridge (1895). Planned *Cambridge Modern History,* wrote many celebrated essays.

Acts of the Apostles, fifth book of NT. Written in Greek *c* AD 60, traditionally ascribed to Luke. Describes growth of early church, incl. missionary journeys of Paul.

acupuncture, form of medical treatment of ancient Chinese origin. Consists of insertion of needles into determined parts of body to relieve pain and treat disease.

Adalbert or **Adelbert** (*c* 1000-72), German churchman, statesman. Archbishop of Hamburg and Bremen; friend and adviser to emperors Henry III and IV.

Adam and **Eve,** first man and woman in creation story of OT book, Genesis. Adam was formed from dust; Eve from one of Adam's ribs taken while he slept. *See* EDEN, GARDEN OF.

Adam, Adolphe (1803-56), French composer. Wrote comic operas, but best known for ballet *Giselle* (1841).

Adam, Robert (1728-92), Scottish architect. With brother, **James Adam** (1730-94), designed numerous public buildings, houses and interiors, in highly refined style derived from Classical architecture. Works incl. London's Adelphi (now destroyed), Syon House, Osterley Park. Also applied principles to furniture design.

Adam de la Halle or **le Bossu** (*c* 1240-88), French poet, dramatist, musician. Works incl. *Le Jeu de Robin et Marion,* dramatized poem of pastoral seduction, with interludes for song. Also composed *rondeaux* of great originality.

Adamov, Arthur (1908-), French dramatist, b. Russia. Plays, *eg Ping-Pong* (1955), *Paolo Paoli* (1957), are satirical indictments of capitalist society.

Robert Adam

Addax

Adder

Adams, prominent American family from Massachusetts. **John Adams** (1735-1826) was president (1797-1801). A Patriot leader, defended Declaration of Independence (1776) as representative at Continental Congress. Served as vice-president (1789-97) under Washington. As president, retained his political integrity despite Federalist-dominated Congress' attempts (eg ALIEN AND SEDITION ACTS) to discredit Jeffersonian Republicans. His son, **John Quincy Adams** (1767-1848), was also president (1825-9). While secretary of state (1817-25), promulgated Monroe Doctrine (1823) on foreign policy in the Americas. A Federalist, elected president by House of Representatives over Jackson after neither candidate had obtained majority of electoral coll. votes. Congressman from Massachusetts (1831-48). His son, **Charles Francis Adams** (1807-86), was a diplomat. Minister to Great Britain (1861-8), aided Union cause in Civil War in negotiations over incidents involving *Trent, Alabama* ships. One of his sons, **Henry Brooks Adams** (1838-1918), was a historian. Works incl. study of medieval times, *Mont-Saint-Michel and Chartres* (1913).

Adams, John Couch (1819-92), English astronomer. Independently of Leverrier, predicted position of previously unknown planet Neptune (1845-6) by calculations accounting for perturbations in motion of Uranus.

Adams, Richard (1920-), English author. Known for bestselling children's novel, *Watership Down* (1972). Other works incl. *Shardik* (1974).

Adams, Samuel (1722-1803), American Revolutionary leader. Advocated total separation from Britain, instigated BOSTON TEA PARTY (1773). Signatory to Declaration of Independence. Second cousin of John Adams.

Adana, city of S Turkey, on R. Seyhan. Pop. 383,000. Trade centre; cotton goods, tobacco. Colonized by Romans; revived under Harun al-Rashid c 782.

Addams, Jane (1860-1935), American social worker, feminist, pacifist. Known for co-founding of (1889) and work at Hull House, social settlement in Chicago. Shared Nobel Peace Prize (1931).

addax, *Addax nasomaculatus,* large antelope of N Africa, esp. Sahara. Has whitish-grey coat, long spiralling horns.

adder, *Vipera berus,* poisonous European snake; bite painful but rarely fatal. Variable colour pattern, normally zigzag band edged by dark spots. Name also applied to African puff adder and various harmless American snakes.

addiction, compulsive uncontrolled use of habit-forming substances, eg alcohol or drugs; marked by physical dependence on drug, tolerance to it, and harmful effects on user and society. Sudden cessation may cause withdrawal symptoms, characterized by acute physical and mental distress.

Addington, Henry, see SIDMOUTH, HENRY ADDINGTON, VISCOUNT.

Addinsell, Richard (1904-), British composer. Best known for *Warsaw Concerto,* written for the film *Dangerous Moonlight* (1941).

Addis Ababa, cap. of Ethiopia. Pop. 881,000. Admin., communications centre, railway to Djibouti; coffee trade, food processing. Hq. of OAU. Cap. of Ethiopia from 1806; cap. of Italian E Africa 1936-41. Has Imperial palace, 2 univs.

Addison, Joseph (1672-1719), English poet, essayist, moralist, politician. Contributed to *Tatler,* collaborated with STEELE in *Spectator* developing Augustan ideals of culture in masterly prose style. Also wrote hymn 'The Spacious Firmament on High', poetry, blank-verse tragedy *Cato* (1713), literary criticism.

Addison's disease, disease of the adrenal glands, identified by English pathologist Thomas Addison (1793-1860). Characterized by anaemia, bronze coloration of skin, loss of weight and low blood pressure.

additive, inclusive term for wide range of chemicals added to substances to produce desired effect, eg anti-knock agents in petrol, food preservers, mould inhibitors.

Adelaide, city of SC Australia, on Torrens R., cap. of South Australia. Pop. 842,000. Commercial, indust. centre; exports (via Port Adelaide) wheat, wool, wattle bark, fruit, animal products; univ. Settled (1836) by free immigrants. Museum; Anglican, RC cathedrals.

Adélie Land, region of Antarctica, S of 60°S and between 136° and 142° E. Part of French Southern and Antarctic Territs. Discovered 1840. Site of research station.

Aden, port of SW Southern Yemen, on Gulf of Aden. Pop. 225,000. Free port since 1850; oil refining, salt mfg. British colony from 1839, joined Federation of South Arabia (1959) with British protect. of Emirates of South. Became cap. of independent Southern Yemen (1970).

Aden, Gulf of, arm of W Arabian Sea, between Southern Yemen and Somali Republic.

Adobe used in building in Mexico

Konrad Adenauer

Adenauer, Konrad (1876-1967), West German statesman, chancellor (1949-63). Twice arrested during Nazi regime. Took part in founding (1945) Christian Democratic Union. Championed W European cooperation esp. through formation (1957) of EEC. Advocated German reunification through free elections and supported De Gaulle's policy of European independence of US.

adenoids, masses of lymphoid tissue in upper part of throat behind the nose. Nasal infection in children resulting from overgrowth sometimes necessitates surgical removal.

adenosine triphosphate (ATP), organic compound important in storage and transfer of energy in living cells. Necessary for muscle contraction, chemical synthesis.

Adige (anc. *Athesis,* Ger. *Etsch*), river of N Italy. Flows *c* 360 km (225 mi) from Resia Pass on Austrian border via Trento, Verona, to Adriatic N of R. Po. Irrigation, h.e.p.

Adirondack Mountains, range of NE New York, US; in S extension of Laurentian Plateau. Rise to 1629 m (5344 ft). Many lakes, waterfalls; extensively forested. Tourist resort area.

Adler, Alfred (1870–1937), Austrian psychologist. After studying with Freud, founded own school of individual psychology. Rejected Freud's emphasis on sexual motive in behaviour in favour of drive for power; believed inferiority complex fundamental to personality problems.

Adler, Felix (1851-1933), American educator, b. Germany. Estab. New York Society for Ethical Culture (1876) and several schools. Works incl. *Creed and Deed* (1877). *See* ETHICAL CULTURE.

administrative law, laws and judicial decisions made by executive under powers given it by legislature of state. In 20th cent., govts. have increased such powers. In US, Administrative Procedure Act (1946) provided safeguards against them. In UK, ministers of the Crown may make orders, *etc,* amending or overriding statutes. Select Committee on Statutory Instruments acts as watchdog on executive.

admiral, brilliantly coloured butterfly of Nymphalidae family. Species incl. red admiral, *Vanessa atalanta,* common in Europe and North America.

Admiralty, in UK, former govt. dept. for admin. of naval affairs. Absorbed by ministry of defence (1964). Also refers to its hq. (1723-5, with modern additions) in Whitehall.

Admiralty Islands, group of small isls. of SW Pacific, in Bismarck Archipelago, NE of New Guinea. Area *c* 2070 sq km (800 sq mi); pop. *c* 22,000. Chief isl. Manus.

adobe, sun-dried brick made of sandy and silty clay mixed with straw. Used for building in Spain, Latin America and SW US.

Adonis, in Greek myth, handsome youth disputed by Aphrodite and Persephone. When killed by wild boar, Zeus arranged for him to spend summer above ground with Aphrodite and winter in underworld with Persephone. Hence celebrated as symbolic of yearly cycle of vegetation.

Adowa, *see* ADUWA, Ethiopia.

adrenal gland, either of 2 endocrine glands against upper ends of each kidney. Consists of inner part (medulla) which secretes noradrenaline and adrenaline, and outer layer (cortex) which secretes steroid hormones that influence CARBOHYDRATE formation, sexual development, and control salt and water balance in body.

adrenaline, hormone secreted by medulla of adrenal gland. Stimulates heart action and sympathetic nervous system, raises blood pressure and blood sugar level; used to treat asthma.

Adrian IV, orig. Nicholas Breakspear (*c* 1115-59), English churchman. Only English pope (1154-9); defended papal supremacy against opponents, incl. Frederick Barbarossa. Prob. gave Ireland as fief to Henry II of England.

Lord Adrian

Adrian, Edgar Douglas Adrian, Baron (1889-), English physiologist. Authority on nervous system; developed electrical methods to investigate sense organs. Shared Nobel Prize for Physiology and Medicine (1932) with Sherrington for work on nerve impulses.

Adrianople, *see* EDIRNE.

Adriatic Sea, arm of Mediterranean Sea between Italy (W) and Yugoslavia, Albania (E). Length *c* 800 km (500 mi); W coast is straight, low-lying; E coast is steep, rocky. Many ports, tourist resorts.

Aduwa or **Adowa,** town of N Ethiopia. Pop. 10,000. Scene of decisive defeat (1896) of Italians by Ethiopians under Menelik II, securing Ethiopian independence.

Adventists, evangelical sects who believe that Second Coming of Christ to Earth is imminent. Largest body is

Adriatic Sea

Seventh Day Adventists, formally organized in US in 1863. Observe Saturday as Sabbath.

advertising, informing public of products, services, needs, *etc*, through media of mass communication. Esp. important in 20th cent. commerce, giving rise to specialist agencies. 'Madison Avenue' synonymous with American advertising indust.

advocate, in law, person appointed to plead another's cause, esp. in court or court-martial, *ie* English barrister or counsel, Scottish and French advocate, American attorney. Lord advocate of Scotland is senior law-officer of the Crown responsible for criminal prosecutions; retires with govt. by which appointed.

A.E., *see* RUSSELL, GEORGE WILLIAM.

Aegean Sea

Aegean Sea, arm of Mediterranean Sea between Greece and Asia Minor. Linked by Dardanelles with Sea of Marmara and Black Sea. Many isls. incl. Cyclades, Dodecanese, Euboea, Sporades. Ports, tourism.

Aegina (mod. *Aigina*), small isl. of Greece, in Saronic Gulf. Sponge fishing, olives, vines. Ancient commercial centre (struck 1st Greek coins) until pop. expelled by Athens (431 BC).

aegis, in Greek myth, shield of Zeus and later of his daughter Athena. Represented as goatskin cloak worn over shoulders or over left arm.

Aegisthus, in Greek myth, incestuous son of THYESTES and his daughter Pelopia. Killed his uncle ATREUS to allow his father to regain throne. Lover of Clytemnestra, he slew her husband, Agamemnon, on his return from Troy. Killed in revenge by Orestes.

Aelfric (*c* 955-1020), English churchman, grammarian, homilist. Greatest English scholar and chief Old English prose stylist of period. Many works incl. free vernacular version of 1st 7 books of OT, *Lives of Saints* (996-7), a grammar.

Aeneas, Trojan leader in Homer's *Iliad* and classical legend. Vergil's *Aeneid,* epic poem in 12 books (30–19 BC) develops him into exemplar of Roman virtues and forefather of Rome's founders, using story to celebrate Augustus' empire. After fall of Troy, Aeneas sets out to find new home, is delayed in Carthage by love for DIDO, but eventually reaches Italy to found Alba Longa.

aeolian harp, zither-like instrument made from strings of varying thickness, all tuned to the same note. Placed out of doors, produces series of rising and falling harmonies when the wind blows over it.

Aeolian Islands, *see* LIPARI ISLANDS, Italy.

Aeolus, in Greek myth, ruler of the winds which he kept in cave on isl. of Aeolia. Gave Odysseus winds adverse to him tied in leather bag.

aerial or **antenna,** in electronics, a conductor used to transmit or receive radio waves. In transmitter, signal from circuit causes electrons in antenna to oscillate, producing electromagnetic radiation. This radiation induces oscillations in receiving aerial, which are then amplified.

aerodynamics, branch of fluid mechanics dealing with forces (resistance, pressure, *etc*) exerted by air or other gases in motion. Concerned with principles governing flight of aircraft, wind resistance of vehicles, buildings, bridges. One of the basic tools is the wind tunnel.

aeroembolism or **bends,** bodily disorder caused by formation of nitrogen bubbles in blood and body tissues following too rapid decrease in atmospheric pressure. Characterized by nausea, pain in muscles, paralysis. Most commonly suffered by deep-sea divers who return to surface too quickly.

aeronautics, science of the design, construction and operation of all heavier-than-air aircraft. *See* AERODYNAMICS, AVIATION.

aeroplane [UK] or **airplane** [US], powered heavier-than-air aircraft which derives lift from action of air against (normally) fixed wings and is driven forward by a screw propeller or by JET PROPULSION. Stability is provided by vertical and horizontal tailpieces; control by flaps (ailerons) on trailing edge of wings. Designs range from early biplane (double-winged) types, monoplanes incl. delta-wing shapes, and swing-wing types suitable for supersonic flight. For history, *see* AVIATION.

aerosol dispenser, container in which gas under pressure is used to aerate and dispense liquid through a valve in the form of spray or foam. Used for insecticides, paints, polishes, *etc*.

Aeschylus (525-456 BC), Greek tragic poet. Founded classical Greek TRAGEDY, introducing 2nd actor and thereby dramatic dialogue. Only 7 of *c* 90 plays survive, of which masterpiece is trilogy *Oresteia*. Also wrote *The Persians, Seven against Thebes*.

Aesculapius, *see* ASCLEPIUS.

Aesop (6th cent. BC), semi-legendary fabulist. Body of native Greek fable ascribed to him. Moral conveyed through stories of animals, *eg The Tortoise and the Hare*. Said to have been freed slave.

aesthetic movement, British artistic movement of 1870s and 1880s, noted for its exaggerated emphasis on artistic sensibility ('art for art's sake'). Influenced by Pre-Raphaelitism, Japanese art, Pater's writing, it sought to improve dress design, book illustration, interior decoration, *etc*.

aesthetics, branch of philosophy concerned with nature of art. Plato contended that beauty lay in object itself; Epicurus that it lay in eye of beholder.

Aethelbert, *see* ETHELBERT.

Aethelred the Unready, *see* ETHELRED THE UNREADY.

Aetius, Flavius (*c* 396-454), Roman general. Strengthened N borders of empire. Defeated Attila and Huns at Châlons (451). Murdered on return to Rome.

Aetolia, region of WC Greece, N of Gulf of Patras. Part of admin. dist. of Aetolia and Acarnania, cap. Missolonghi. Mainly mountainous. Formed Aetolian League 4th cent. BC against Achaea, Macedonia; defeated by Rome 189 BC.

Afars and the Issas, French Territory of the, territ. of E Africa, on Str. of Bab-el-Mandeb. Area 22,000 sq km (8500 sq mi); pop. 101,000; cap. Djibouti. Official language: French. Religion: Islam. Mainly stony desert; nomadic pastoralism, exports cattle, hides, salt. Colony from 1896 as French Somaliland; voted in referendum (1977) in favour of independence. Due to become independent as Djibouti (1977).

affinity, in law, relationship by marriage which is not a blood relationship. May affect legal or canonical status of marriage, *eg* person cannot marry stepchild legally; may not marry deceased spouse's sibling in church.

Afghan hound, breed of large hunting dog. Long narrow head, prominent hip bones, silky thick hair. Stands *c* 68cm/27 in. at shoulder.

Afghanistan, republic of SC Asia. Area 647,500 sq km (250,000 sq mi); pop. 18,796,000; cap. Kabul. Language: Afghan. Religion: Islam. Mainly mountainous, dominated by Hindu Kush; agric., stock rearing (karakul) in river valleys and plains. Dry continental climate, cold in winter, hot in summer. Modern Afghanistan estab. in 18th cent; kingdom created 1926. Republic proclaimed after military coup (1973).

AFL-CIO, *see* AMERICAN FEDERATION OF LABOR AND CONGRESS OF INDUSTRIAL ORGANIZATIONS.

Africa, second largest continent of the world. Area *c* 30,262,000 sq km (11,684,000 sq mi); pop. *c* 352,000,000. Bounded by Mediterranean (N), Red Sea (NE), Indian Ocean (SE, S), Atlantic (W); incl. Madagascar, Cape Verde, Ascension, St Helena isls. Largely ancient plateau; Great Rift Valley in E; mountain ranges incl. Atlas, Ethiopian Highlands, Ruwenzori, Drakensberg; highest point Mt. Kilimanjaro (5892 m/19,340 ft). Main rivers Congo, Limpopo, Niger, Nile, Zambezi; main lakes Albert, Chad, Nyasa, Victoria. Has vast inland deserts, incl. Sahara, Libyan, Kalahari; extensive tropical savannah; jungle, rain forests along equator. Widespread subsistence agric., export crops incl. cocoa, groundnuts, cotton, hardwoods. Mineral resources incl. gold, diamonds, copper, petroleum, iron ore. Earliest prehist. man may have lived in E Africa; advanced civilization developed in Egypt before 3000 BC. N coast colonized by Romans after fall of Carthage (146 BC); Arabs introduced Islam from 7th cent. European exploration began 15th cent., led to extensive colonization in 19th cent. by UK, France, Germany, Italy, Belgium; most colonies became independent in mid-20th cent.

Afrikaans, language of West Germanic group of Indo-European family. Developed from Dutch of 17th cent. Boer settlers in S Africa. Contains many Hottentot, Bantu, English loan-words.

Afro-Asiatic, major Near East and N African language family. Formerly known as Hamito-Semitic, but term abandoned as it misleadingly implied non-Semitic languages were as closely interrelated as Semitic. Incl. Berber, Chad, Cushitic, Egyptian in non-Semitic group, divides Semitic into NW and SW branches.

Agadir, town of SW Morocco, on Atlantic Ocean. Pop. 45,000. Port for fertile agric. dist., exports fruit, vegetables; fishing. Visit by German gunboat *Panther* (1911) caused diplomatic crisis with France. Devastated by earthquake (1960).

Aga Khan III, real name Aga Sultan Sir Mahomed Shah (1877-1957), Indian leader. Hereditary head of Ismaili Moslem sect, founded All-India Moslem League (1906). Member of wealthy family, renowned for extravagant life style.

Agamemnon, legendary leader of Greek forces in Trojan War; king of Mycenae. On his return from Troy, was murdered by his wife, Clytemnestra, and her lover, Aegisthus.

agamid, any of Agamidae family of Old World lizards. East Indian water lizard only aquatic species (also largest, *c* 90 cm/3 ft long); others arboreal or burrowing. Mainly insectivorous; capable under stress of colour change.

Agana, cap. of Guam. Pop. 2000. Admin. centre; large US naval base at nearby Apra Harbor. Rebuilt after WWII.

agaric, any fungus of Agaricaceae family, esp. of genus *Agaricus*. Blade-shaped gills on underside of the cap. Incl. common edible field mushroom, *A. campestris.*

Agartala, cap. of Tripura state, NE India. Pop. 60,000. Market centre.

Agassiz, Jean Louis Rodolphe (1807-73), Swiss zoologist, geologist. Authority on fish, particularly fossil forms; discovered evidence of glacial ages. Taught at Harvard after 1848, his collections forming basis for

Museum of Comparative Zoology. Son, **Alexander Agassiz** (1835-1910), was oceanographer and marine biologist; financed expeditions.

agate, hard, semi-precious gemstone. Chalcedonic variety of silica, formed mainly of fine-grained quartz. Has bands of 2 or more colours. Major sources in US, Brazil, Mexico, India.

Agave

agave, genus of plants native to tropical America and SW US of family Amaryllidaceae. Spirituous liquor (mescal) distilled from agave sap. Some cultivated for their fibre, *eg* sisal.

Agee, James (1909-55), American poet, novelist, film critic. Works incl. *Let Us Now Praise Famous Men* (1941), bitter exposé of Southern poor-white life (with Walker Evans' photographs) and novel, *A Death in the Family* (1957).

Agence France-Presse, French news agency with world-wide coverage. Developed from Agence Havas (formed 1835 by Charles Havas), taken over by Vichy govt. in 1940 and renamed.

aggression, in social psychology, form of behaviour characterized by unprovoked attacks or acts of self-defence. In psychoanalysis, used in special sense by Adler as the manifestation of the 'will to power' over others. In international law, important concept with, as yet, no satisfactory general definition, but used for certain specific acts, *eg* invasion, by one state against another.

Agincourt (mod. *Azincourt*), village of N France. Scene of victory (1415) of Henry V of England over French during Hundred Years War.

Agnew, Spiro Theodore (1918-   ), American politician. Governor of Maryland (1966-9). Elected vice-president (1968) on Republican ticket with Nixon. Resigned (1973) after corruption charges brought against him; pleaded guilty to tax evasion.

Agnon, Shmuel Yosef, orig. Czaczkes (1888-1970), Israeli writer, b. Galicia. Author of novel trilogy *Bridal Canopy* (1931-5) reflecting E European Jewish life. Shared Nobel Prize for Literature (1966) with Nelly Sachs.

agnosticism, maintenance of position that the human mind cannot know anything beyond material phenomena. Term coined by T.H. Huxley (1869); other agnostics incl. Kant, Comte, Herbert Spencer.

Agouti

agouti, rabbit-sized rodent, genus *Dasyprocta,* of forests of Central and South America. Tailless, short-haired; destructive of sugar cane.

Agra, city of Uttar Pradesh, NC India, on R. Jumna. Pop. 595,000. Founded 1566, Mogul cap. until 1658; hist. buildings incl. Taj Mahal and Akbar's fort.

Agricola, Georgius, Latinized form of Georg Bauer (1494-1555), German physician, mineralogist. Explored connections of medicine with mineralogy, was first to classify minerals systematically. Wrote *De re metallica* (pub. 1556).

Agricola, Gnaius Julius (*c* AD 37-93), Roman general. Elected consul in 77. Became governor in Britain (*c* 78-*c* 85) and extended Roman rule into Scotland.

Agricola, Johann, orig. Johannes Schnitter (*c* 1494-1566), German Protestant leader in Reformation. Broke with Luther (1536) to support antinomianism.

agriculture, science and art of farming, incl. the cultivation of soil, production of crops and raising of livestock. Use of chemical fertilizers, herbicides and insecticides, fast-ripening and disease-resistant crops with high yields, specialized animal breeding, advanced mechanization leading to large-scale production, have revolutionized modern agriculture.

Agrigento (anc. *Agrigentum*), town of S Sicily, Italy. Pop. 48,000. Formerly called Girgenti. Harbour at Porto Empedocle; sulphur trade. Founded *c* 580 BC by Greek colonists; taken by Romans 210 BC. Many Greek, Roman remains.

agrimony, plant of genus *Agrimonia* of rose family. Aromatic pinnate leaves with small yellow flowers. Grows wild in N temperate regions and cultivated in herb gardens.

Agrippa, Marcus Vipsanius (*c* 63-12 BC), Roman general. Adviser of Augustus, helped in defeat (31 BC) of Antony at Actium.

Aguascallentes, town of NC Mexico, cap. of Aguascalientes state. Pop. 173,000. Health resort with mineral springs. Important railway workshops; textile mills, potteries.

Agulhas, Cape, headland of W Cape Prov., South Africa. Most S point of Africa. Danger to shipping; lighthouse.

Ahab (d. *c* 853 BC), Israelite king (*c* 874-*c* 853 BC). In OT, provoked Hebrew prophet, Elijah, by allowing his wife, Jezebel, to encourage worship of Baal. Politically, consolidated empire; Syrian wars ended with his death in battle.

Ahaggar or **Hoggar Mountains,** highland region of S Algeria, in WC Sahara. Rises to Mt. Tahat (3000 m/9850 ft). Annual rainfall up to 25 cm (10 in); many wadis. Most important oasis town, Tamanrasset.

Ahmedabad, city of Gujarat state, W India. Pop. 1,588,000. Cotton textiles. Cultural and religious centre; buildings incl. Jama Masjid mosque, Jain temple (1848).

Ahmed III (1673-1736), Ottoman sultan (1703-30). Harboured fugitive Charles XII of Sweden, persuaded to declare war on Russia (1710-11). Recovered Azov, signed Treaty of Passarowitz (1718) after defeat by Austrians. Overthrown by Janissaries.

Ahriman, see ZOROASTRIANISM.

Ahura Mazdah, see ZOROASTRIANISM.

Ahvenanmaa, see ALAND ISLANDS, Finland.

Ahwaz, city of SW Iran, cap. of Khuzistan prov., on R. Karun. Pop. 286,000. Railway jct.; petro-chemical indust. An ancient city, revived recently with development of oilfields.

Aidan, St (d. 651), Irish missionary. Estab. monastery on Lindisfarne. Christianized Northumbria under patronage of King Oswald.

Aigina, see AEGINA, Greece.

Aiken, Conrad Potter (1889-1973), American author. In tradition of Poe, work reflects concern with musicality of poetry, psychological subjects. Also wrote novels.

Ailsa Craig, small granite isl. in Firth of Clyde, W Scotland. Seabird sanctuary.

Aintab, see GAZIANTEP.

Ainu, hairy, European-like aboriginal inhabitants of Japan. Language unrelated to any known linguistic stock. Driven to N islands, fewer than 17,000 remain, supporting themselves by hunting and fishing.

aircraft, any machine designed to travel through the air, whether heavier or lighter than air, incl. AEROPLANE, AIRSHIP, AUTOGYRO, BALLOON, HELICOPTER, glider.

air-cushion vehicle, see HOVERCRAFT.

Airdrie, town of Strathclyde region, C Scotland. Pop. 38,000. Engineering, heavy industs.

Airedale, breed of dog, largest of terrier group. Wiry black and tan coat; stands 58 cm/23 in. at shoulder.

airplane, see AEROPLANE.

air plant, see EPIPHYTE.

The Shenandoah, first airship to use helium

airship or **dirigible balloon,** any self-propelled aircraft that is lighter than air and can be steered. Usually a large gas-filled container with attached means of propulsion and steering, and suspended compartment for passengers or freight. German Zeppelin type with rigid gas-carrying hull used for bombing in WWI. After WWI, British and American types used for passenger-carrying, until destruction by fire of several incl. British R101 (1930), German *Hindenburg* (1937). Non-rigid types (blimps) using non-flammable helium rather than hydrogen continue in use.

Airy, Sir George Biddell (1801-92), English astronomer. Astronomer Royal (1835-81), his reorganization and modernization of Greenwich Observatory made it an important centre.

Aisne, river of N France. Flows *c* 240 km (150 mi) from Argonne via Soissons to R. Oise near Compiègne. Scene of heavy fighting in WWI.

Aix-en-Provence, town of Provence, SE France. Pop. 94,000. Commercial centre, agric. market. Roman *Aquae Sextiae,* founded 123 BC near thermal springs. Cap. and cultural centre of Provence in Middle Ages. Univ. (1409), town hall, cathedral. Birthplace of Cézanne.

Aix-la-Chapelle, see AACHEN, West Germany.

Aix-la-Chapelle, Treaty of, settlement (1668) ending French invasion of Spanish Netherlands (War of Devolution). France retained most conquests in Flanders. Also name of treaty (1748) concluding War of AUSTRIAN SUCCESSION (1740-8). Chief result was ceding of Silesia to Prussia. Pragmatic Sanction upheld, confirming Maria Theresa's right to inherit Habsburg possessions.

Aix-les-Bains (anc. *Aquae Gratianae*), town of Savoy, SE France, on Lac du Bourget. Pop. 21,000. Spa from Roman times.

Ajaccio, town of W Corsica, France, on Gulf of Ajaccio. Pop. 42,000. Port, resort, fishing. Birthplace of Napoleon.

Ajanta, village of Maharashtra state, SC India. Buddhist cave temples dating from *c* 200 BC-AD 700 nearby.

Ajax, legendary Greek hero of Trojan War, second only to Achilles in bravery. Killed himself when beaten by Odysseus in contest for Achilles' armour.

Ajmer, city of NW India, railway jct. and trade centre of Rajasthan. Pop. 263,000. Tomb of famous Moslem saint; cap. of hist. Ajmer state.

Akbar, orig. Jalal ed-Din Mohammed (1542-1605), Mogul emperor of India (1556-1605). Grandson of BABER. Expanded territ. by conquest of Afghanistan and all N India. Introduced admin. reforms and promoted religious tolerance.

Akhenaton, see IKHNATON.

Akhmatova, Anna, pseud. of Anna Gorenko (1889-1967), Russian poet. Major influence on 20th cent. Russian poetry through brief, lucid, concrete style; founded Acmeism. Works incl. *Requiem* for Stalin's victims.

Akkad, ancient kingdom on N bank of Euphrates, Iraq. Flourished under Sargon *c* 2340-*c* 2305 BC. Later absorbed by 3rd Ur dynasty.

Akmolinsk, see TSELINOGRAD.

Akron, city of NE Ohio, US, on Little Cuyahoga R.; at highest point of Ohio and Erie Canal. Pop. 275,000. Rubber indust. (major tyre producer); car parts, machinery, chemicals mfg. Founded 1825.

Aksakov, Sergei Timofeyevich (1791-1859), Russian author. Friend of Gogol; works incl. autobiog. *The Family Chronicle* (1856), *Years of Childhood of Bagrov's Grandson* (1858), prose classics describing life of gentry.

Aksum or **Axum,** ancient town of N Ethiopia. Pop. 10,000. Coffee trade. Cap. of Aksumite empire 1st-8th cent.; religious centre, Ark of the Covenant reputedly brought here by descendant of Solomon.

Aktyubinsk, city of USSR, NW Kazakh SSR. Pop. 164,000. Metallurgical centre; ferro-alloy and chromium plants.

Akureyri, town of N Iceland, on Eyjafjorour. Pop. 11,000. Port; fishing, commercial centre.

Alabama, state of SE US. Area 133,667 sq km (51,609 sq mi); pop. 3,444,000; cap. Montgomery; chief city Birmingham. Plateau in N; plain in S (cotton, corn production) stretches to Gulf of Mexico. Drained by Alabama, Tombigbee rivers. Coal mining, quarrying, iron and steel, petroleum industs. Spanish exploration in 16th cent.; French settlement 1702; ceded by French to British 1765. Seat of Confederate govt. 1861-5. Admitted to Union as 22nd state (1819).

Alabama dispute (1871-2), US claim for damages from UK after Civil War losses to Union shipping caused by British-built confederate warships *Florida, Alabama,* and *Shenandoah.* Arbitration at Geneva awarded considerable damages to US.

alabaster, fine-grained, translucent variety of gypsum. Light-coloured or white, often streaked. Softer than marble, often used for statues, ornaments. Major sources in Mexico, Italy, France, US.

Alain-Fournier, pseud. of Henri Alban Fournier (1886-1914), French author. Reputation based on novel, nostalgic fantasy *Le Grand Meaulnes* (1913). Killed in WWI.

Alamein, El, village of N Egypt, W of Alexandria. Scene of decisive defeat (1942) of Germans under Rommel by British under Montgomery; prevented Axis occupation of Egypt.

Alamo, see SAN ANTONIO.

Alanbrooke, Alan Francis Brooke, 1st Viscount (1883-1963), British general. Commander-in-chief of British Home Forces (1940-1), he was chief of Imperial General Staff (1941-6).

Aland Islands (*Ahvenanmaa*), archipelago of SW Finland, at mouth of Gulf of Bothnia. Area 1505 sq km (581 sq mi); main town Mariehamn. Fishing; barley, flax growing. Incl. *c* 6000 isls., 80 inhabited. Held by Finland from WWI. Pop. Swedish-speaking.

Alarcón, Pedro Antonio de (1833-91), Spanish novelist. Works incl. *The Three Cornered Hat* (1874), basis of de Falla's ballet.

Alarcón y Mendoza, Juan Ruiz de (*c* 1581-1639), Spanish dramatist, b. Mexico. Known for comedies of ethics, esp. *The Truth Suspected* (*c* 1619) adapted by Corneille as *Le Menteur.*

Alaric I (*c* 370-410), Visigothic king. Served with Visigothic troops of Roman emperor Theodosius I; proclaimed their leader in 395. Invaded and plundered Greece (395-6). Invaded Italy (401, 408); sacked Rome 410.

Alaska, state of US, in NW North America. Area 1,518,776 sq km (586,400 sq mi); pop. 302,000; cap. Juneau; largest town Anchorage. Arctic Ocean in N, Pacific in S. Polar climate in N; tundra region drained by Yukon R.; S volcanic ranges stretch W to Aleutian Isls. Scattered Eskimo pop. Fish, fur, timber, minerals are main resources. Important oil strike in late 1960s. Of strategic importance; has D.E.W. line radar system. Settled by Russians in 18th cent.; bought by US 1867. Gold strikes 1899, 1902. Admitted to Union as 49th state (1959).

Alaska Range, mountain system of SC Alaska, US. Incl. North America's highest peak, Mt. McKinley (6194 m/20,320 ft).

Alba, Fernando, Duque de, see ALVA, FERNANDO ALVAREZ DE TOLEDO, DUQUE DE.

Albacete, town of SE Spain, cap. of Albacete prov. Pop. 93,000. Agric. market; produces cutlery, daggers.

albacore, see TUNNY.

Alba Iulia, town of WC Romania, on R. Mures. Pop. 84,000. In vine-growing dist. Roman *Apulum*; former seat of Transylvanian princes; site of union of Transylvania and Romania (1918).

Alba Longa, ancient city of C Italy, near Castel Gandolfo. Founded 12th cent. BC, reputed birthplace of Romulus and Remus. Destroyed 7th cent. BC by Rome.

Albania (*Shqipnija*), republic of SE Europe, on Adriatic. Area *c* 28,500 sq km (11,000 sq mi); pop. 2,416,000; cap. Tirana. Language: Albanian. Religions: Islam, Eastern Orthodox. Mainly mountainous; lower marshy but fertile areas near coast. Cereals, tobacco, olives; slow indust. development. Turkish until 1912; Italian occupation in WWII, communist govt. estab. 1946 under Hoxha.

Albany, town of SW Western Australia, on King George Sound. Pop. 13,000. Fishing port; exports wheat, fruit. Founded (1826) as Frederickstown.

Albany, cap. of New York state, US; on Hudson R. Pop. 116,000. Port and shipping centre; printing and publishing, varied mfg. industs. One of oldest US cities. Dutch settlement estab. 1614; English control 1664; became cap. 1797.

Albany Congress, meeting (1754) of delegates from 7 American colonies at Albany, New York. Benjamin Franklin's Plan of Union, for unifying colonies, later rejected by colonial legislature and Britain. Treaty signed with Iroquois.

Galápagos or waved albatross (Diomedea irrorata)

albatross, large sea bird of genus *Diomedea,* found in S hemisphere. Long narrow wings, hooked beak; excels in sustained flight. Largest species is wandering albatross, *D. exulans.*

Albee, Edward Franklin (1928-), American playwright. Known for one-act absurdist plays, incl. *The Zoo Story* (1958), and first full length play *Who's Afraid of Virginia Woolf?* (1962).

Albéniz, Isaac (1860-1909), Spanish pianist, composer. One of the 1st Spanish composers to write in a national style, he produced much piano music, incl. suite *Iberia*, songs and operas.

Alberoni, Giulio (1664-1752), Italian churchman. Created chief minister of Spain (1715). Attempted to rescind Treaty of Utrecht and gain control of Austrian possessions in Italy; Spanish claims resisted by QUADRUPLE ALLIANCE. Dismissed in 1719.

Albert I (1875-1934), Belgian king (1909-34). Sponsored resistance to German invasion during WWI. Initiated social reforms in Belgium and Belgian Congo. Killed in climbing accident.

Alberta, Prairie prov. of W Canada. Area 661,188 sq km (255,285 sq mi); pop. 1,627,000; cap. Edmonton; other major city Calgary. Scenic Rocky Mts. in W; mainly forested in N; agric. plains (wheat, cattle) in S. Drained N by Peace, Athabaska rivers. Leading oil, coal producer; large natural gas reserves. Ceded by Hudson's Bay Co. to Canada 1869; became prov. 1905.

Albert Canal, Belgium. Length 130 km (81 mi); connects R. Meuse at Liège with R. Scheldt at Antwerp. Opened 1939.

Alberti, Leone Battista (1404-72), Italian architect. His *De re aedificatoria*, inspired by Vitruvius, was 1st Renaissance treatise on architecture and influenced Renaissance style. Emphasized use of Classical forms, and scientific methods to obtain perfect proportion.

Alberti, Rafael (1902-), Spanish author. Poems reveal interest in folklore, subsequently surrealism. Popular plays incl. *El hombre deshabitado* (1931).

Albert Nile, see BAHR-EL-JEBEL, Sudan.

Albert Nyanza or **Lake Albert,** lake between W Uganda and NE Zaïre. Area 5345 sq km (2064 sq mi); part of Great Rift Valley. Fed by Victoria Nile, Semliki rivers; drained by Albert Nile. Discovered 1864, named after Prince Consort.

Albert of Brandenburg (1490-1568), German military-religious leader, grand master of Teutonic Knights (1511-25). Converted to Protestantism and estab. Prussia as hereditary duchy (1525).

Albert [Francis Charles Augustus Emmanuel] of Saxe-Coburg-Gotha, Prince (1819-61), German prince, consort of Queen Victoria of Britain. Promoted arts and scientific developments, notably Great Exhibition of 1851. Exercised strong influence on foreign policy.

Albertus Magnus, St (*c* 1200-80), Dominican scholastic philosopher, teacher of Aquinas. Attempted to reconcile Aristotelian thought and Christian doctrine in *Summa theologiae*.

Albertville, see KALEMIE, Zaïre.

Albi (anc. *Albiga*), town of S France, on R. Tarn, cap. of Tarn dept. Pop. 47,000. Food processing, textiles, glass mfg. Gave name to Albigensian heresy of 12th-13th cent. Cathedral (13th cent.). Birthplace of Toulouse-Lautrec.

Albigensians, religious group of S France, *fl* 12th-13th cent. Regarded as heretics, adopted Manichaean doctrine of duality of good and evil, held that Jesus lived only in semblance. Supported by Raymond VI of Toulouse; movement killed by Albigensian Crusade proclaimed by Pope Innocent III (1208), and by Inquisition.

albinism, condition in humans, animals and plants, characterized by deficiency of pigmentation. In humans, manifested by white skin, white hair and pink eyes; inherited as a recessive genetic character.

Albinoni, Tommaso (1671-1750), Italian composer, violinist. Wrote over 50 operas and many concertos for solo violin. Work was admired by Bach, who used some of Albinoni's themes.

Alboin (d. 573), Lombard king. Invaded Italy from N of Alps (568); took Milan (569) and Pavia (572). Estab. Lombard rule over most of N and C Italy.

albumin or **albumen,** in biochemistry, one of group of water-soluble proteins occurring in animal and vegetable fluids and tissues. Found in blood, milk, muscles, egg-white (albumen).

Albuquerque, Alfonso de (1453-1515), Portuguese admiral, administrator. Founded Portuguese empire in East (1503-15), conquering Goa, Malacca, Ceylon. Died at sea after being superseded in office.

Albuquerque, health resort of C New Mexico, US; on Rio Grande. Pop. 244,000; state's largest city. Railway jct.; railway engineering, food processing. Founded 1706.

Albury, city of SE New South Wales, Australia, on Murray R. Pop. 27,000. Railway jct.; meat processing; trade in wheat, wool, fruit.

Alcaeus (b. *c* 620 BC), Greek lyric poet. Prolific and varied writer, greatly influenced Horace among others. Associate of SAPPHO

Alcalá Zamora, Niceto (1877-1949), Spanish statesman. Jailed for republican activities before becoming 1st president of republic (1931-6) on overthrow of monarchy.

Alcamenes (5th cent. BC), Athenian sculptor. Pupil of Phidias, his *Aphrodite of the Gardens* was one of the masterpieces of the ancient world.

Alcántara, town of W Spain, on R. Tagus. Pop. 5000. Roman remains incl. large bridge. Military-religious Order of Alcántara founded here (13th cent.) to fight Moors.

Alcatraz, rocky isl. of W California, US; in San Francisco Bay. Military prison from 1859; federal prison 1933-63, now closed.

Alcázar at Seville

alcázar, fortress or palace built by the Moors in Spain. Best known are those in Seville and Toledo.

alchemy, early form of chemistry, with philosophical and magical associations. Came to Europe through Islamic science, which used methods and traditions of Egyptians, Babylonians, and philosopy of Greeks. Based on Aristotelian idea of one 'prime matter' for all substances, sought to change one substance into another. Best known for attempts to make gold from base metals. Developed complex symbolism.

Alcibiades (*c* 450-404 BC), Athenian statesman. Helped form alliance of Argos, Mantinea and Athens against Sparta; defeated at Mantinea (418). Led Sicilian expedition of 415; accused of sacrilegious mutilation of statues of Hermes in Athens before embarkation, fled to Sparta. Returned to Athens (411), won several battles before naval defeat at Notium (407). Murdered in Phrygia.

Alcmaeonidae, powerful Athenian family, 6th-5th cent. BC. Its members incl. ALCIBIADES, PERICLES and CLEISTHENES.

Alcock, Sir John William (1892-1919), English aviator. With **Sir Arthur Whitten Brown** (1886-1948), made 1st Atlantic crossing in an aeroplane (1919).

alcohol, organic compound obtained from HYDROCARBON by replacement of 1 or more hydrogen atoms with hydroxyl (-OH) radicals. Name applies esp. to ETHANOL (ethyl alcohol). Other alcohols incl. METHANOL, GLYCOL, GLYCEROL.

alcoholism, pathological condition caused by excessive consumption of ethyl alcohol. Chronic form leads to vitamin deficiency, gastritis, cirrhosis of liver, brain damage. May be treated by drugs, psychotherapy or by organizations such as Alcoholics Anonymous.

Alcott, Louisa May (1832-88), American author. Semiautobiog. novels *Little Women* (1868-9), *Little Men* (1871), *Jo's Boys* (1886), describing her unconventional upbringing, are now children's classics.

Alcuin (*c* 735-804), English churchman and scholar at Charlemagne's court. Estab. study of the 7 liberal arts, the curriculum of medieval W Europe.

Aldabra Island, small atoll group in Indian Ocean, NW of Madagascar. Formerly part of British Indian Ocean Territ., now admin. by Seychelles. Noted for rare plants and animals, esp. giant land tortoises.

Aldanov, Mark, pseud. of Mark Aleksandrovich Landau (1886-1957), Russian émigré author. Major works incl. tetralogy *The Thinker* (1921-7) on social conflict of period 1793-1821, *The Fifth Seal* (1939) portraying decay of revolutionary idealism in Spanish Civil War.

aldehyde, organic compound of form RCHO where R is an ALKYL or ARYL group. Examples incl. benzaldehyde, C_6H_5CHO, used in perfume and dye mfg., ACETALDEHYDE and FORMALDEHYDE.

Black alder

alder, deciduous shrub or tree of genus *Alnus* of cool temperate regions. Toothed leaves and cone-like fruit. Wood is water resistant; used for pumps, millwheels, bridges, *etc.* Bark yields brownish dye. Species incl. black alder, *A. glutinosa.*

alder fly, slender 4-winged fly with long antennae, order Neuroptera. Larvae aquatic, pupating in land burrows.

Alderney, northernmost of Channel Islands, UK. Area 8 sq km (3 sq mi). Main town St Anne. Cattle rearing, potato growing.

Aldershot, mun. bor. of Hampshire, S England. Pop. 33,000. Has large military training centre, estab. 1854.

Aldington, Richard (1892-1962), English writer. Member of early group of poets who introduced IMAGISM. Bitterly anti-war novels incl. *The Colonel's Daughter* (1931). Also wrote lives of T.E. Lawrence and D.H. Lawrence.

Aldridge-Brownhills, town of West Midlands met. county, WC England. Pop. 88,000. Formed from union of 2 towns (1966). Engineering indust.; bricks, tiles mfg.

Aldrin, Edwin, *see* ARMSTRONG, NEIL.

Aldus Manutius (1450-1515), Venetian printer, humanist. Printed works of classical authors, *eg* Aristotle, in inexpensive editions for scholars. Designed a Greek alphabet and introduced italic type (1501). Founded Aldine Press.

Alegría, Ciro (1909-67), Peruvian novelist. Wrote mainly about exploitation of Indian communities, esp. *Broad and Alien is the World* (1941).

Alemán, Mateo (1547-*c* 1615), Spanish writer. Wrote picaresque *Guzmán de Alfarache* (2 parts 1599, 1604).

Alemanni, Germanic tribe occupying Rhenish lands in 5th cent. Dialects of SW Germany and Switzerland called Alemannic.

Alembert, Jean le Rond d' (1717-83), French mathematician, philosopher. Enunciated D'Alembert's principle (1742), which he used to solve problems in fluid motion. Assisted in writing of Diderot's *Encyclopédie.*

Alençon, town of NW France, on R. Sarthe, cap. of Orne dept. Pop. 33,000. Market town; famous from 17th cent. for lace production.

Aleppo (Arab. *Haleb*), city of NW Syria. Pop. 639,000. Trade in wool; produces silk and cotton goods. Once a centre of caravan trade with East, taken by Turks (1517) and held until WWI.

Alessandria, town of Piedmont, NW Italy, on R. Tanaro. Cap. of Alessandria prov. Pop. 105,000. Railway jct., engineering, hat mfg. Founded 11th cent. as stronghold of Lombard League.

Alesund or **Aalesund,** town of W Norway. Pop. 39,000. Major fishing port; whaling, sealing.

Aletsch Glacier, C Switzerland, in Bernese Oberland. Largest glacier in Europe, length *c* 26 km (16 mi). Nearby is Aletschhorn peak (4180 m/13,721 ft).

Aleutian Islands

Aleutian Islands, chain of *c* 150 isls. in Bering Sea, between USSR and Alaska, US; extension of Aleutian Range. Pop. *c* 8000. Incl. Unimak, Unalaska, Andreanof Isls. Mainly mountainous with several volcanoes. Small groups of Russo-Eskimo fishers and fur trappers.

Alewife

alewife, *Alosa pseudoharengus,* North American fish of herring family. Used in manufacture of oil and fertilizer. Also called sawbelly.

Alexander III, orig. Orlando Bandinelli (d. 1181), Italian churchman, pope (1159-81). Opposed by 3 successive antipopes, forced to seek refuge in France 1162-5; supported by Lombard League in contest with Frederick Barbarossa, who was defeated at Legnano (1176). Supported Becket against Henry II of England. Summoned Third Lateran Council (1179), which estab. rules for future papal elections.

Alexander VI, orig. Rodrigo Lanzol y Borja (1431-1503), Spanish-Italian churchman, pope (1492-1503). Elected pope by bribery, his papacy was notorious for political intrigue and favouritism shown to his illegitimate children (incl. Cesare and Lucrezia Borgia).

Alexander I (1777-1825), tsar of Russia (1801-25). Succeeded his father, Paul I, at whose murder he prob. connived. Early attempts at domestic reform failed. Joined alliance against Napoleon in 1805; series of defeats resulted in peace with Treaty of Tilsit (1807). Successfully countered Napoleon's invasion of Russia (1812); attended Congress of Vienna (1814-15) to map out political settlement of Europe. Fearing liberalism, promoted Holy Alliance with Austria, Prussia to retain European status quo.

Alexander II (1818-81), tsar of Russia (1855-81). Son of Nicholas I, initiated reform programme that incl. Edict of Emancipation (1861), freeing serfs; failure of changes resulted in increasing terrorism. Adopted expansionist foreign policy in Asia. Assassinated by anarchist.

Alexander III (1845-94), tsar of Russia (1881-94). Son of Alexander II, he took measures, particularly by increasing police powers, to crush liberalism, enforce persecution of Jews and minorities. Advocated peace in foreign policy.

Alexander [III] the Great (356-323 BC), Macedonian king. Son of Philip II of Macedon, succeeded father in 336. After subduing an uprising in Thebes, began conquest of Persian Empire (334). Gained control of most of Asia Minor, defeating Darius III at Issus (333). Occupied Egypt, where he founded Alexandria. Returning to Mesopotamia, destroyed Persian army at Gaugamela on Tigris (331). Pushed on into Bactria and India, reaching Punjab by 326. Army refused to go beyond R. Hyphasis and Alexander returned to Susa (324). Attempted to fuse Greek and Asian cultures by marrying his officers to Asian wives (he married Bactrian princess ROXANA). Died of fever in Babylon.

Alexander III (1241-86), king of Scotland (1249-86). Victory over Haakon IV of Norway at Largs (1263) led to acquisition of Western Isles and Isle of Man.

Gold medallion showing the head of Alexander the Great

Alexander (1888-1934), king of Yugoslavia (1921-34). Ruled dictatorially after 1929 in effort to overcome internal strife among Croats, Serbs, Slovenes. Assassinated by Croatian terrorist in France.

Alexander, Harold Rupert Leofric George, Earl Alexander of Tunis (1891-1969), British field marshal. In WW II, directed retreats from Dunkirk (1940) and Burma (1942); led invasion of Italy through Sicily, becoming Allied commander-in-chief of Mediterranean forces. Governor-general of Canada (1946-52).

Alexander, Sir William, *see* STIRLING, WILLIAM ALEXANDER, EARL OF.

Alexander Archipelago, group of *c* 1000 isls. off SE Alaska, US; part of Alaska Panhandle. Consists of summits of submerged mountain system; densely forested. Pop. mainly Indian.

Alexander Nevski, St (1220-63), Russian national hero. Grand duke of Vladimir-Suzdal, acquired name Nevski after defeating Swedes on the Neva (1240). Victorious over Livonian Knights near L. Peipus (1242).

Alexander Obrenovich (1876-1903), king of Serbia (1889-1903). Took over govt. (1893), abolished liberal constitution. Scandalous marriage (1900) to Draga Mashin

Lord Alexander of Tunis

and repressive political measures ended in royal couple's assassination by army group.

Alexander of Hales (d. 1245), English scholastic philosopher. His *Summa universae theologiae* was first exposition of Christian doctrine to cite Aristotle as authority, and incl. elements of Arabic thought. A Franciscan; taught at Univ. of Paris.

Alexandra Feodorovna (1872-1918), Russian empress, consort of Nicholas II. Granddaughter of Queen Victoria. Dominated by RASPUTIN, who encouraged royal couple's opposition to reform. Shot with husband and family by Bolsheviks.

Alexandretta, *see* ISKENDERUN.

Alexandria (*El Iskandarîya*), city of N Egypt, between L. Mareotis and Mediterranean Sea. Pop. 2,032,000. Major port, railway jct., air terminal; exports cotton; cotton industs. Founded 332 BC by Alexander the Great, partly on former Pharos isl. Ancient Jewish, Greek, Arab cultural and educational centre (libraries, univ.); Roman prov. cap. Declined after taken by Arabs (7th cent.); revived 19th cent. when joined to Nile by canal. Remains of ancient city incl. Pompey's Pillar, ruins at Pharos, catacombs.

Alexandrian Codex, Greek manuscript of the Scriptures believed written 5th cent. Presented by patriarch of Constantinople to Charles I of England (1628). Contains Septuagint version of OT. Now in British Museum.

Alexius [I] Comnenus (1048-1118), Byzantine emperor (1081-1118). Withstood Norman and Turkish attacks; defeated the Petchenegs (1091). Negotiated with leaders of 1st Crusade to return to him all former Byzantine territs. conquered. Father of ANNA COMNENA.

alfalfa or **lucerne,** *Medicago sativa,* European leguminous forage plant. Trifoliate leaves, purple clover-like flowers. Naturalized in most temperate regions and used extensively in US for fodder, pasture and as a cover crop.

Alfieri, Vittorio, Conte (1749-1803), Italian writer. Tragedies show hatred of tyranny, *eg Saul* (1782), *Antigone* (1783). Other works incl. sonnets, political pamphlets, autobiog.

Alfonso VIII (1155-1214), king of Castile (1158-1214). Son and successor of Sancho III. Defeated Moors at Navas de Tolosa (1212).

Alfonso [X] the Wise (1221-84), king of Castile and León (1252-84). Son and successor of Ferdinand III. Main ambition to become Holy Roman emperor, failed in election (1257). Took Cádiz from Moors (1262). Patron of learning; systematized legal code with work *Las Siete Partidas.*

Alfonso XIII (1886-1941), king of Spain (1886-1931). Reigned during dictatorship (1923-30) of Primo de Rivera. Estab. of republic under Alcalá forced him into exile.

Alfred the Great (849-99), king of Wessex (871-99). Most of reign spent fighting Danish invaders. Retreat to Somerset (878) gave rise to legend of Alfred and the cakes.

Later routed Danes at Ethandun, enabling him to bring in reforms, legal code based on strong centralized monarchy. Created navy. Great interest in culture led to revival of clerical learning, estab. of Old English prose. Translated many Latin works, inspired others. ANGLO-SAXON CHRONICLE begun at his command.

algae, chlorophyll-containing plants of division Thallophyta. Found in fresh and salt water. Range from unicellular forms, usually microscopic, to multicellular forms up to 30 m/100 ft in length. Incl. pond scum, seaweeds.

Algardi, Alessandro (1595-1654), Italian sculptor. Superseded Bernini as leading sculptor in Rome during reign of Pope Innocent X (1644-55); executed numerous statues and portrait busts in Bolognese Classical style.

Algarve, coastal region and prov. of S. Portugal, cap. Faro. Tourism; fruit, fishing. Last Moorish stronghold in Portugal, reconquered 1249.

algebra, branch of mathematics which generalizes operations of ordinary arithmetic by allowing letters or other symbols to stand for unknown quantities. Modern abstract algebra develops axiomatically systems that arise in many branches of mathematics; incl. ring theory and group theory.

Algeciras, town of Andalusia, S Spain, on Algeciras Bay. Pop. 82,000. Port; fishing, tourism. Founded 711 by Moors; new town built 1760. Scene of European powers' conference (1906) on Morocco.

Alger, Horatio (1834-99), American children's author. Themes usually of poor boys succeeding through effort and good behaviour. Best-sellers incl. 'Ragged Dick', 'Tattered Tom' series.

Algeria, republic of N Africa. Area 2,388,000 sq km (922,000 sq mi); pop. 15,772,000; cap. Algiers. Languages: Arabic, French. Religion: Islam. Sahara in S; coastal plain, Atlas Mts. in N. Cereals, dates, wine production; fishing; mineral resources incl. major oil, natural gas fields. Incl. ancient region of Numidia. Arabs introduced Islam in 7th cent.; stronghold of Barbary pirates 16th-18th cent.; occupied by French from 1830. Violent campaign fought by FLN in 1950s, led to independence (1962) after referendum.

Algiers (Arab. *Al-jezair,* Fr. *Alger*), cap. of Algeria, on Bay of Algiers. Pop. 943,000. Major port, exports wine, fruit; admin., commercial centre, univ. (1879). Founded 10th cent.; base for Barbary pirates 16th-18th cent. Taken by French (1830). Allied N African hq. in WWII. Badly damaged during independence conflict. Has 16th cent. fortress.

Algonkin, *see* ALGONQUIN.

Algonquian, North American Indian linguistic family, largest within Algonquian-Mosan stock. Incl. Blackfoot, Cheyenne, Cree, Ojibwa, Micmac, Mohegan tribes.

Algonquian-Mosan, widespread North American Indian linguistic stock. Incl. Algonquian, Ritwan, and Mosan families.

Algonquin or **Algonkin,** North American Indian tribe of Algonquian linguistic stock. Among first tribes to make alliance with French settlers (early 17th cent.). Dispersed by Iroquois, remnants in Québec, Ontario. Little remains of their culture.

algorithm, in mathematics, systematic procedure for solution of a problem in a finite number of steps. Computers may be programmed to use algorithms to solve complicated equations quickly.

Algren, Nelson (1909-), American novelist. Works, *eg Never Come Morning* (1942), *The Man with the Golden Arm* (1949), extract a poetic nihilism from the brutality of Chicago street life.

Alhambra, fortified palace of Moorish rulers of Granada, Spain. Built largely in 14th cent., its interior is richly decorated with geometric ornament and fine honeycomb vaulting.

Ali (*c* 600-61), 4th caliph (656-61). Married Fatima, daughter of Mohammed. His rule was opposed by Muawiya, who became caliph on abdication of Ali's son, Hasan. Murdered by fanatics. Shiite-Sunnite division in Islam began after his reign.

Ali, Muhammad, orig. Cassius Marcellus Clay (1942-), American boxer. Famous for his unorthodox style and colourful personality, he won world heavyweight title (1964). Refused to serve in US Armed Forces because of Black Muslim faith; licence to box withdrawn (1967-70). Regained title with defeat of George Foreman (1974).

Alicante, city of SE Spain, on Mediterranean Sea, cap. of Alicante prov. Pop. 185,000. Port, exports wine, fruit, tobacco; tourist resort. Castle on hilltop site fortified from Greek times.

Alice Springs, town of SC Northern Territ., Australia, on Todd R. Pop. 11,000. Railway to Adelaide; centre for surrounding cattle raising, mining industs.; tourism; base of Royal Flying Doctor Service. Founded (1889) as Stuart; cap. (1926-31) of former Central Australia.

alien, in law, resident of a country who owes political allegiance to another country. Subject to laws limiting entry to countries, conditions of residence. British Nationality Act (1948) defined as alien anyone unrecognized as British subject in any part of the Commonwealth. May only enter UK by permission of an immigration officer; since 1970, Commonwealth citizens' entry limited by patrial rule. In US, entry subject to scrutiny by Immigration and Naturalization Service. Alien may claim intercession by home country.

Alien and Sedition Acts (1798), legislation passed by Congress of US empowering president to expel aliens. Also provided for prosecution of those conspiring against or defaming govt. Sponsored by Federalists to counter Jeffersonian strength among immigrant voters.

alienation, in social sciences, term used to refer to estrangement of part or whole of personality from experience. Used as important concept by Marx for effects of economic production and class system on workers ('alienated labour').

Aligarh, city of Uttar Pradesh, NC India. Pop. 254,000. Trade centre; cotton milling. Important Moslem university (1920).

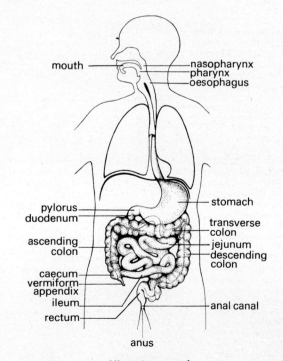

mouth — nasopharynx pharynx oesophagus

pylorus duodenum — stomach

transverse colon

ascending colon — jejunum descending colon

caecum vermiform appendix ileum — anal canal

rectum

anus

Alimentary canal

alimentary canal, in mammals, tubular passage from mouth to anus, concerned with intake of food, its digestion, and disposal of residual waste products. Incl. pharynx, oesophagus, stomach, intestines, rectum.

alimony, in law, allowance ordered by court to be paid by husband to separated wife. Temporary alimony may be ordered pending divorce, nullity suit, *etc.* After decree, permanent alimony may be ordered usually until remarriage of ex-wife.

Ali Pasha (c 1744-1822), Turkish governor of Yannina (1787-1820); known as 'Lion of Yannina'. Began as Albanian brigand leader. Ruled as despot until ordered deposed (1820); rebelled against Turkish troops. Assassinated by Turkish agent.

aliphatic compounds, organic compounds containing only straight or branched open chains of carbon atoms, as opposed to closed rings of carbon atoms in AROMATIC compounds. Incl. paraffins, olefines, fatty acids.

alkali, soluble hydroxide of a metal, esp. an alkali metal. Term also applies to any strong BASE. Alkalis neutralize acids and turn litmus blue. Used in manufacture of soap, paper, glass.

alkali metals, the univalent metallic elements lithium, sodium, potassium, rubidium and caesium.

alkaloid, any of group of organic bases containing nitrogen, often of plant origin and having medicinal or poisonous effects. Examples are morphine, quinine, caffeine.

Al-Khwarizmi (fl 820), Arabian mathematician. Wrote treatise on algebraic methods and work on arithmetic in which he introduced Hindu numerals; these were adopted as familiar 'Arabic' numerals after work was translated into Latin in Middle Ages.

Al-Kindi (fl 9th cent.), Arabian philosopher. Used Islamic philosophy to reconcile thoughts of Plato and Aristotle.

Alkmaar, town of NW Netherlands, on North Holland canal. Pop. 51,000. Commercial centre, famous cheese market.

Al-Kuwait, see KUWAIT.

alkyl group, in chemistry, univalent hydrocarbon RADICAL of form C_nH_{2n+1}.

Allah, Arabic name for God used by Moslems and Arabic-speaking Christians.

Allahabad, city of Uttar Pradesh, NC India, near confluence of Jumna and Ganges. Pop. 514,000. Hindu pilgrimage centre.

Allegheny Mountains, W range of Appalachian system, NE US. Extend from N Pennsylvania to Virginia; rise to 1480 m (c 4860 ft) at highest point. Rich coal, iron ore deposits.

allegory, narrative or description in which characters, objects, incidents, form extended metaphor for system of religious, political or social ideas. Characters often treated as universal 'types'. Very strong in medieval Europe, more recent examples range from Bunyan's *Pilgrim's Progress* to Orwell's *Animal Farm.*

Allen, Ethan (1738-89), American Revolutionary leader. Organized Vermont militia, known as Green Mountain Boys; defended region against New York control in boundary dispute. Captured Fort Ticonderoga (1775); seized by British during attempt to invade Canada. Advocated independence for Vermont.

Allen, Hervey (1889-1949), American writer. Known for best-selling romance of Napoleonic times *Anthony Adverse* (1933).

Allen, William (1532-94), English churchman. Refused to take oath of supremacy on accession of Elizabeth I. Founded seminary at Douai. Became cardinal (1587) and encouraged English RCs to rise against Elizabeth.

Allen, Bog of, peat bog of EC Irish Republic, between rivers Shannon and Liffey. Peat used to fuel power stations.

Allenby, Edmund Henry Hynman, 1st Viscount Allenby of Megiddo (1861-1936), British field marshal. Commander of British Expeditionary Force (1917-19), invaded Palestine and decisively defeated Turks at Megiddo (1918). High commissioner for Egypt (1919-25).

Allende, Salvador (1909-73), Chilean statesman. Elected president (1970), becoming 1st Marxist head of govt. in South America. Withdrawal of financial credit by West followed agrarian reforms and nationalizing foreign investments. Subversion by CIA and US indust. fuelled domestic discontent. Allende died in military coup.

Allenstein, see OLSZTYN, Poland.

Allentown, town of E Pennsylvania, US; on Lehigh R. Pop. 110,000. Indust. and commercial centre; textiles, cement mfg. On edge of Pennsylvania anthracite field.

allergy, hypersensitivity to usually harmless specific substance, *eg* pollen, hair, various foods, or physical conditions (heat and cold). Believed to be caused by antibodies which cause local tissue inflammation by release of histamine while providing little immune protection. Allergic disorders incl. skin rashes, asthma, hay fever.

Alleyn, Edward ('Ned') (1566-1626), English actor-manager. Main rival of BURBAGE. Played in several of Marlowe's plays incl. *Tamburlaine, Doctor Faustus, The Jew of Malta.*

Allier, river of C France. Flows c 435 km (270 mi) from Cévennes via fertile Limagne to R. Loire near Nevers.

alligator, large aquatic reptile of crocodile family; 2 species: *Alligator mississippiensis* of S US, and smaller *A. sinensis* of Yangtze valley, China. Leather greatly valued, leading to diminution of species; now protected in US.

allium, genus of bulbous plants of lily family. Strong-smelling leaves; umbellate white, yellow or red flowers. Found in Europe, N Africa, Asia, North America. Species incl. onion, garlic, chives, leek, shallot, all with characteristic odour.

Alloa, town of Central region, C Scotland, on R. Forth. Pop. 14,000. Brewing, distilling.

allosaur, extinct carnivorous dinosaur of Jurassic period, genus *Allosaurus.* Over 9.2 m/30 ft long with small forelegs, massive hind legs.

allotropy, property that certain chemical elements have of existing in 2 or more forms, with different crystalline structures and physical properties. Carbon, sulphur and phosphorus exhibit allotropy.

alloy, metallic substance composed of 2 or more metals or of metallic and non-metallic elements. May be a compound, mixture or solid solution. Common alloys are brass (copper, zinc) and steel (iron, carbon).

All Saints' Day, in RC and Anglican churches, feast day (1 Nov.) instituted by Pope Gregory IV in honour of all saints, known and unknown. One of principal feasts in RC calendar.

All Souls' Day, in RC calendar, feast day (2 Nov.) on which church prays for faithful still suffering in purgatory.

allspice, berry of allspice tree, *Pimenta officinalis,* of myrtle family. Yields pungent aromatic spice.

Allston, Washington (1779-1843), American painter. First important American Romantic painter, he did large dramatic works, *eg Belshazzar's Feast,* and, later, more lyrical landscapes.

alluvium, sand, silt or gravel transported and deposited by running water. Provides excellent crop-growing conditions on river flood plains or in delta areas, *eg* Nile, Ganges rivers.

Alma-Ata, city of USSR, cap. of Kazakh SSR. Pop. 794,000. Cultural and indust. centre; machinery, textile mfg. Seat of Kazakh Academy of Sciences (1946). Formerly called Verny.

Almadén, town of New Castile, C Spain. Pop. 14,000. Rich mercury mines, worked from Roman times.

almanac, yearly calendar originally containing astronomical, meteorological and ecclesiastical data, often incl. astrological and prophetic material. Now usually refers to book of useful facts and statistics.

Al-Mansur, see MANSUR.

Almeida, Francisco de (c 1450-1510), Portuguese admiral. First viceroy of Portuguese India (1505-9). Took control of spice trade in Indian Ocean by defeating Arabs and their allies off Diu (1509).

Almería, city of S Spain, on Gulf of Almería, cap. of Almeria prov. Pop. 115,000. Port, exports minerals, fruit (esp. grapes). *Fl* under Moors (8th-15th cent.) as naval base. Medieval castle, cathedral.

Almond blossom

almond, *Prunus amygdalus,* tree of warm temperate regions, native to W Asia. Fruit has nut-like edible stone or kernel which yields oil. Sweet almonds used in cooking and confectionery. Bitter almonds used in manufacture of flavouring extracts, cosmetics, medicine.

Aloe

aloe, genus of plants of lily family. Fleshy leaves, red or yellow flowers. Found chiefly in S Africa. Yields bitter laxative drug and hemp-like fibre.

Alost, see AALST, Belgium.

Alpaca

alpaca, *Lama pacos,* domesticated South American mammal, related to llama. Bred for its fleecy brown or black wool.

Alp Arslan (1029-72), sultan of Seljuk Turks (1063-72). Invaded Georgia, Armenia (1065); defeated Byzantines at Manzikert (1071), thereby gaining control of Asia Minor. Succeeded by son Malik Shah.

alphabet, any system of characters used to record a language in which there is (theoretically) a one-to-one relationship between each character and phoneme. Developed by Phoenicians (c 1400 BC) possibly from signs derived from Egyptian hieroglyphic writing. Transmitted from NW Semites to Greece (first recorded c 8th cent. BC),

used in ancient Rome. Forms basis of alphabets in W European and several recently written African and Asian languages. Cyrillic alphabet, also developed from Greek, used in Russian. Hebrew and Arabic alphabets are also still in use.

Alpha Centauri, brightest star of constellation Centaurus, visible in S hemisphere. Has 3 components, incl. Proxima Centauri, nearest star to Earth beyond Sun (4.3 light years away).

alpha particle, positively charged helium nucleus, consisting of 2 neutrons and 2 protons, emitted during spontaneous decay of nucleus of certain radioactive elements, *eg* uranium 238. Relatively low penetrating power.

alpine rose, any of various European and Asiatic alpine RHODODENDRONS.

Alps, mountain system of SC Europe. Extend from Franco-Italian border through Switzerland, Germany, Austria to Yugoslavia. Many glaciers, valleys, snow-capped peaks. C Alps incl. Mont Blanc (highest), Monte Rosa, Matterhorn, Jungfrau. Crossed by many passes incl. Brenner, Great St Bernard, Mont Cenis, Simplon. Dairying, timber, h.e.p., tourism esp. winter sports.

Als (Ger. *Alsen*), isl. of Denmark, in Little Belt; separated from S Jutland by Als Sound. Area 313 sq km (121 sq mi); main town Sönderborg. Bridge to mainland (1930). Held by Prussia (1864-1920).

Alsace (Ger. *Elsass*), region of NE France, between Vosges Mts. and R. Rhine. Main towns Colmar, Mulhouse, Strasbourg. Agric. in Rhine plain, vineyards on Vosges foothills, potash mining. Long disputed by France and Germany. Annexed by France in 17th cent.; incorporated, with part of Lorraine, into Germany (1871) as imperial territ. of Alsace-Lorraine. Restored to France after WWI.

Alsatian dog

alsatian or **German shepherd,** sheepdog of wolf-like appearance, used in police work and as guide dog for blind. Stands *c* 63 cm/25 in. at shoulder.

Altai, mountain system of USSR (S Siberia), W Mongolia and N China. Reaches 4506 m (14,783 ft) at Belukha. Rich mineral deposits incl. lead, zinc, silver.

Altaic, major European and Asian family of languages. Divided into W and E groups, incl. Turkic, Mongolian and Manchu languages.

Altamira, cave site of Santander prov., N Spain. Cave contains drawings of animals made in late Magdalenian period; discovered 1879.

Altdorf, town of C Switzerland, on L. Lucerne, cap. of Uri canton. Pop. 7000. Scene of William Tell legend, commemorative statue and theatre.

Altdorfer, Albrecht (*c* 1480-1538), German painter. First European to stress romantic use of landscape. Early works show insignificant figures set in mysterious landscapes; later works incl. pure landscapes.

alternating current (AC), electric current that periodically reverses its direction of flow, changing continuously to reach a maximum in one direction, then in the other. Used extensively because of ease of changing voltage; transmitted at high voltages to minimize energy loss.

alternation of generations, in biology, occurrence of generations of an organism in alternate order, one of which reproduces sexually, the other asexually. Phenomenon exhibited by many coelenterates, which alternate between sedentary asexual polyps and free-swimming sexual medusae (jellyfish).

Althing, legislature of Iceland. Oldest European assembly, convened 930. Dissolved 1800-74 during period of direct rule by Denmark.

altimeter, device used to measure altitude. Types in use incl. aneroid barometer. Absolute altimeter, used by aircraft, works by reflecting radio signals from Earth's surface.

Altman, Robert (1922-), American film director. Achieved international success with *M.A.S.H.* (1970), other films incl. *Nashville* (1976).

alto, in singing, term used for highest male voice; also lowest female voice. In instruments of similar range, usually pitched between soprano and tenor.

alto flute, see FLUTE.

alum, hydrated double sulphate of potassium and aluminium, used as mordant in dyeing and fireproofing agent.

alumina or **aluminium oxide** (Al_2O_3), chemical compound occurring naturally in clay, and as main component of bauxite. Also found in almost pure form as corundum.

aluminium or **aluminum** (Al), silvery metallic element; at. no. 13, at. wt. 26.98. Ductile and malleable; good conductor of heat and electricity. Obtained commercially by electrolysis of bauxite and cryolite. Used pure or alloyed where lightness is required, *eg* in aircraft or cooking utensils.

alum root, any of several herbs of genus *Heuchera,* esp. North American *H. americana,* of saxifrage family. Heart-shaped leaves and clusters of tiny purplish flowers. Roots have astringent properties.

Alva, Fernando Alvarez de Toledo, Duque de (1508-82), Spanish general, administrator. Commanded armies of Charles V, Philip II. As regent (1567-73) in Netherlands for Philip II, instituted 'Court of Blood' (Alva boasted of *c* 18,000 executed) to crush rebellion against Spanish tyranny. Conquered Portugal (1580).

Alvarado, Pedro de (1486-1541), Spanish conquistador. Accompanied Cortés in conquest of Mexico (1519), acting as his principal officer. Subjugated Guatemala, Salvador (1523-4); governor of Guatemala until his death fighting Mexican Indians.

alyssum, genus of plants of Cruciferae or mustard family. Greyish leaves, small yellow or white flowers. Native to Eurasia.

AM (amplitude modulation), see MODULATION.

Amadeus, Lake, salt lake of S Northern Territ., Australia. Area *c* 880 sq km (340 sq mi). In cattle raising area; natural gas found nearby.

Amadis of Gaul, medieval chivalric romance. Composed in Spain or Portugal (13th or 14th cent.) but draws on ARTHURIAN LEGEND to present ideal knight.

Amagasaki, port of Japan, on Osaka Bay, Honshu isl. Pop. 553,000. Indust. centre; iron and steel works, chemical and textile mfg.

Amalfi, town of Campania, W Italy, on Gulf of Salerno. Pop. 12,000. Resort. Prosperous medieval republic until taken by Pisa (12th cent.). Produced maritime code (*Tavole Amalfitane*).

amalgam, alloy containing mercury. Gold and silver amalgams occur naturally; tin, copper and other amalgams are man-made. Used in dentistry, mirror mfg.

Amalric or **Amaury,** two Latin kings of Jerusalem. **Amalric I** (*c* 1135-74), king 1162–74, fought unsuccessfully against Nur-ad-Din to retain control of Egypt. **Amalric II** (1144-1205), king 1197–1205, became king by marrying daughter of Amalric I. Also king of Cyprus 1194-1205.

Amalthea, in Greek myth, nurse of infant Zeus on Crete. Often described as a she-goat, one of whose horns was known as Cornucopia (Horn of Plenty).

amanita, genus of widely distributed fungi. Most species have russet cap with white markings and are poisonous. Incl. *Amanita muscaria* or fly agaric.

amaranth, any of genus *Amaranthus* of plants of worldwide distribution. Garden species cultivated for colourful foliage and showy flowers, *eg* Joseph's coat, love-lies-bleeding. Some species are weeds, *eg* pigweed, tumbleweed.

Amarillo, town of N Texas, US; in Texas Panhandle. Pop. 127,000. Railway jct.; oil refining, meat packing. Grew up as wheat, cattle market.

Amarna, Tel-el-, see TEL-EL-AMARNA.

amaryllis, genus of bulbous plants native to S Africa. Several white, purple or pink flowers on single stem. Species incl. belladonna lily, *Amaryllis belladonna.*

Amaterasu, sun goddess in SHINTO pantheon. She shut herself in the cave of heaven because of her brother's cruelty. Grandmother of Jimmu Tenno, mythical first ruler of Japan.

Amati, family of Italian violin makers in Cremona in 16th and 17th cents. Founded by **Andrea Amati** (*c* 1505-*c* 1575), who estab. basic design used by his descendants. Most famous member was **Niccolò Amati** (1596-1684), who taught Antonio Stradivari and Andrea Guarneri.

Amazon

Amazon, river of South America; main stream of largest river system in world. Formed in N Peru by confluence of Marañón, Ucayali; flows E 6280 km (*c* 3900 mi) across Brazil to the Atlantic. Main tributaries incl. Negro in N, Tocantins, Xingu, Tapajos in C Brazil. Tropical jungle along banks; major source of rubber during late 19th cent.; inhabited by primitive Indian tribes. Recent economic development in region.

Amazons, in Greek legend, nation of female warriors living around Euxine Sea (Black Sea). As 9th labour Heracles was required to obtain girdle of Amazon queen, Hippolyte. She was captured by Theseus, and bore him Hippolytus.

amber, yellow, often transparent fossil resin, derived from now extinct conifers. In highly polished form, used since prehist. times for beads, amulets, *etc.* Found mainly in Tertiary estuarine deposits on Baltic coast.

ambergris, waxy substance secreted from intestine of sperm whale, found floating in tropical seas. Physiological significance undecided. Used as perfume fixative.

Ambler, Eric (1909-), English thriller writer. Set new standard in genre, with anti-heroes, documentary settings. Works incl. *The Mask of Dimitrios* (1939), *Journey into Fear* (1940).

Ambleside, tourist resort of Cumbria, NW England. Pop. 2000. In Lake Dist. at head of L. Windermere. Nearby is Grasmere, home of Wordsworth.

Amboina or **Ambon,** isl. of Indonesia, in S Moluccas. Area *c* 820 sq km (315 sq mi); chief town Ambon, pop. 56,000. Exports spices, copra. Taken (1605) from Portuguese by Dutch; scene of massacre of British settlement (1623).

Ambrose, St (*c* 340-97), Roman churchman. Elected bishop of Milan (374), denounced Arianism at Synod of Aquileia (381). Wrote doctrinal instructions and reformed ritual; encouraged use of hymns in worship (Ambrosian chant).

ambrosia and **nectar,** in Greek myth, the food and drink of the gods, giving immortality and eternal youth.

ambrosia beetle, beetle of Scolytidae family, abundant in tropics. Bores into wood, introducing ambrosia mould, which it cultivates as food.

Amenhotep III (*fl* 14th cent. BC), Egyptian pharaoh (*c* 1410-1372 BC). Ruled during an age of great splendour, his empire at peace. Built great monuments at Thebes, incl. temples at Luxor and Karnak. Succeeded by IKHNATON.

America, *see* NORTH AMERICA, CENTRAL AMERICA, SOUTH AMERICA.

American Federation of Labor and Congress of Industrial Organizations (AFL-CIO), federation of auton. labour unions in US. Estab. by merger (1955) of American Federation of Labor (AFL) and Congress of Industrial Organizations (CIO). AFL formed (1881) as loose-knit association of craft unions, against radicalism of KNIGHTS OF LABOR. This tradition continued until 1935 split, when dissidents set up Congress of Industrial Organizations (CIO), led by J.L. LEWIS. Merger (1955) created AFL-CIO.

American football, eleven-a-side team game played with oval leather ball. Developed from English rugby in 1870s into major college sport. Professional form was organized into leagues in 1920 (National Football League, comprising 28 teams from large cities, dates from 1922).

American Friends Service Committee, organization estab. (1917) by SOCIETY OF FRIENDS in US. Provides for overseas relief and reconstruction; shared Nobel Peace Prize (1947) with Service Council of British Society of Friends.

American Indians, pre-European inhabitants of the Americas. South American cultures incl. MAYA, TOLTEC, AZTEC, INCA, CHIBCHA, some of which reached high cultural level; all fell during Spanish conquest. North American Indian tribes driven back by westward expansion into Indian Territories. Some 400,000 remain in US and Canada. Extremely diverse culture, but divides loosely into NW coast, Plains, Plateau, E woodlands, Northern, and SW groups. Most tribes were relatively settled farmers, food gatherers or hunters but the advent of the horse in late 17th cent. revolutionized Plains culture; led to nomadic hunting of buffalo from horseback with bow and arrow, and the last serious resistance to white hegemony. Although largely assimilated into Western culture, 20th cent. has seen movement towards preserving Indian culture throughout Americas.

American League, US professional baseball league founded 1901. Comprises 8 charter members, with 6 more teams added by 1977.

American Revolution (1775-83), uprising resulting in independence from Britain of Thirteen Colonies of North America. By mid-18th cent., colonists had begun demands for limited self-govt.; Stamp Act (1765) caused colonial opposition to 'taxation without representation'. Further resentment after Townshend Acts (1767), levying duty on British manufactured goods, resulted in Boston Massacre (1770) and BOSTON TEA PARTY (1773). Parliament subsequently passed Intolerable Acts (1774); representatives of colonies listed grievances at Continental Congress of 1774. Conflict began (April, 1775) at Lexington. Washington appointed to lead Continental Army; Declaration of Independence adopted July, 1776. Badly prepared volunteer forces of colonists defeated in Québec campaign (1775-6); fighting inconclusive until British defeat (Oct. 1777) at Saratoga, followed by hard winter for colonial army at Valley Forge. French gave rebels crucial aid and British were pushed N from Carolinas (1780-1), leading to Cornwallis' surrender (Oct. 1781) and conclusion of hostilities. Treaty of Paris (1783) formally recognized independence of US. Conflict also known as American War of Independence.

American Samoa, *see* SAMOA.

America's Cup, international yachting trophy. Cup first awarded by Royal Yacht Squadron to schooner *America*

after race round Isle of Wight (1851). Presented (1857) to New York Yacht Club as international challenge trophy. Every competition for it has been won by US.

americium (Am), man-made radioactive element, at. no. 95, mass no. of most stable isotope 243. Silvery-white metal, discovered (1944) by bombarding plutonium with neutrons.

Amersfoort, town of C Netherlands, in Utrecht prov. Pop. 76,000. Chemicals, carpet mfg. Water gate (14th cent.).

amethyst, semi-precious gemstone, a variety of quartz. Violet or purple in colour. Major sources in Brazil, Uruguay, Sri Lanka, Siberia, US.

Amharic, official language of Ethiopia, belonging to SW Semitic branch of Afro-Asiatic family.

Amherst, Jeffrey Amherst, Baron (1717-97), British army officer. Captured Louisburg (1758), Montréal (1760) from French during Seven Years War in North America.

amides, organic compounds obtained by replacing hydrogen atoms of ammonia, NH_3, by organic acid radicals, *eg* acetamide, CH_3CONH_2.

Amiens, city of N France, on R. Somme, cap. of Somme dept. Pop. 118,000. Agric. market; textile centre from 16th cent. Cap. of Picardy until 1790. Scene of Treaty of Amiens (1802) ending French Revolutionary Wars. Cathedral (13th cent.).

Amiens, Treaty of (1802), settlement between Britain, France, Spain and Batavian Republic in which Britain returned most of its gains from French Revolutionary Wars; France agreed to evacuate Naples.

Idi Amin

Amin, Idi (1925-), Ugandan political leader. Seized power in 1971 military coup. Nationalized UK-owned firms. Expelled Uganda Asians and ruthlessly suppressed opponents. Head of Organization of African Unity (1975).

amines, compounds obtained by replacing hydrogen atoms of ammonia, NH_3, by organic radicals. Divided into primary, secondary or tertiary amines according to whether 1, 2 or 3 hydrogen atoms are replaced.

amino acids, organic compounds in which carboxyl (COOH) and amino (NH_2) groups are linked to central carbon atom. Essential to living tissue as they link to form proteins; 22 occur in animal proteins. In man, 8 cannot be synthesized and must be incl. in diet.

Amirante Islands, dependency of the Seychelles in Indian Ocean. Pop. *c* 100. Exports copra.

Amis, Kingsley (1922-), English writer. One of ANGRY YOUNG MEN. Works incl. satirical novel *Lucky Jim* (1954) attacking academic establishment.

Amman, cap. of Jordan. Pop. 570,000. Commercial, indust. centre. Textile mfg.; noted marble quarries nearby. As Rabbath Ammon, cap. of Ammonites; named Philadelphia in 3rd cent. BC. Great pop. increase after Israeli wars (1949).

Ammanati, Bartolomeo (1511-92), Italian sculptor, architect. Works incl. Santa Trinita bridge and court facade of Pitti Palace in Florence. Sculpture incl. Neptune fountain, also in Florence.

ammeter, instrument used for measuring strength of electric current in ampères. DC ammeter contains pivoted coil, which carries current to be measured, and permanent magnet.

ammonia (NH_3), pungent-smelling highly soluble gas. Forms weak base ammonium hydroxide NH_4OH when dissolved in water. Produced from atmospheric nitrogen by Haber process. Used in manufacture of explosives and fertilizers and as refrigerant.

ammoniac or **gum ammoniac,** gum resin prepared from milky exudation from stem of plant, *Dorema ammoniacum,* native to Iran, India, Siberia. Used in perfumes, manufacture of porcelain cements and in medicine as an expectorant.

ammonite, coiled fossil mollusc of class Cephalopoda. Has elaborately chambered shell. Common in Mesozoic era, extinct by end of Cretaceous period.

amnesia, temporary or prolonged loss of memory. Suppression of memory may be caused by neurosis; permanent loss may result from head injuries.

amoeba, microscopic one-celled animal of class Rhizopoda. Consists of naked mass of protoplasm. Moves and feeds in water by action of pseudopodia (false feet); reproduces by fission. Species incl. *Entamoeba histolytica,* cause of amoebic dysentery.

Amon, in ancient Egyptian pantheon, creator of universe. Represented as ram or man with ram's head and horns. Had oracle (Jupiter Amon) at Siwa in Libyan desert. Identified with Greek Zeus and Roman Jupiter.

Amor, in Roman pantheon, god of love. Merely a translation of Greek EROS, had little place in Roman religion.

Amos, prophetic book of OT, written by shepherd Amos *c* 750 BC. Attacks hypocritical worship, social injustice. Made up of 3 parts, God's judgment on Gentiles and Israel; sermons on fate of Israel; visions of destruction. Final promise of redemption is prob. by later writer.

Amoy (*Hsiamen*), seaport of Fukien prov., SE China. Pop. 400,000. Fishing, food processing, chemical mfg. Opened to trade with West as treaty port (1842).

Ampère, André Marie (1755-1836), French physicist. Extended Oersted's findings on interaction of electricity and magnetism; showed that electric currents exert forces on one another. Formulated Ampère's law on strength of magnetic field induced by current flowing in conductor.

ampère or **amp,** SI unit of electric current; defined as current in pair of infinitely long, infinitely thin, parallel wires that produces force of 2×10^{-7} newtons per metre of length.

amphetamine, colourless liquid, used in form of sulphate to stimulate central nervous system. Used to overcome depression, aid slimming by suppression of appetite. Addiction to amphetamines can cause heart damage and mental disturbance.

Amphibia (amphiblans), class of cold-blooded vertebrates comprising frogs, salamanders and legless, worm-like caecilians. Larva is aquatic, breathing through gills; undergoes rapid metamorphosis to terrestrial lung-breathing adult.

amphibole, any of various rock-forming silicate minerals. Found widely among igneous and metamorphic rocks; group incl. hornblende, asbestos.

Amphineura, class of marine molluscs with elongated symmetrical bodies, minute heads and primitive nervous systems. Found mainly on rocks; chiton is best-known example.

amphioxus, small fish-like chordate animal of subphylum Cephalochordata. Found with head protruding from burrows it makes in sea bottom. Believed to be an ancestor of vertebrates. Also called lancelet.

amphitheatre, circular or oval theatre with an open space surrounded by rising rows of seats. Earliest dates from 1st cent. BC; used by Romans for staging gladiatorial contests. Examples incl. ruined Colosseum in Rome and those in Nîmes and Arles, France.

Amphitrite, in Greek myth, one of the NEREIDS. Wife of Poseidon, by whom she was mother of Triton.

amplitude, in physics, the maximum departure from equilibrium of an oscillatory phenomenon, *eg* alternating current or swinging pendulum.

Amritsar, city of Punjab state, N India. Pop. 433,000. Carpet mfg.; trade in cotton, skins. Sikh religious centre, site of Golden Temple. Scene of 1919 nationalist massacre by British.

Amsterdam, cap. of Netherlands, at confluence of Ij and Amstel rivers. Pop. 808,000. Major port, indust. centre (shipbuilding, chemicals, diamond cutting and polishing). Built on piles, with radial and concentric canal system, many bridges. Canal links to North Sea, Rhine delta. Chartered *c* 1300, Hanseatic trade centre; at cultural, commercial height in 17th cent. Taken by French 1795; cap. from 1815 (admin. sits at The Hague). German occupation in WWII. Churches (13th, 15th cent.), Rijksmuseum (1808, with priceless Dutch, Flemish paintings), van Gogh museum, univs. (1632, 1882). Airport at Schiphol.

Amsterdam Island, isl. of S Indian Ocean, forming part of French Southern and Antarctic Territs. Area 60 sq km (25 sq mi). Site of research station.

Amu Darya (anc. *Oxus*), river of C Asia. Length *c* 2500 km (1550 mi). Rises in Pamir Mts., flows W along Afghanistan-USSR border and NW through Turkmen SSR and Uzbek SSR to enter Aral Sea by long delta.

amulet, object worn as charm to ward off evil influences, sometimes hung on doors or walls. Believed to be source of impersonal power, inherent in object rather than that of deity working through object. Common to many cultures; may be engraved with symbols or magic formulae.

Roald Amundsen

Amundsen, Roald (1872-1928), Norwegian explorer. First to reach South Pole (1911), 35 days ahead of R.F. Scott. First to navigate Northwest Passage (1903-6). Flew over North Pole (1926) with Umberto Nobile, whom he tried to rescue from polar air crash (1928); died in search.

Amundsen Sea, part of S Pacific Ocean, E of Ross Sea, extending into Ellsworth Highlands, Antarctica.

Amur (*Heilung-kiang*), river of NE Asia. Length *c* 2900 km (1800 mi). Flows SE forming much of Soviet-Chinese (Manchuria) border before turning NE to Tartar Str. Navigable, ice-free May-Oct.

amylase, enzyme which helps convert starch into sugar. Found in saliva, pancreatic juices and in some plants.

Amyot, Jacques (1513-93), French humanist. Translated Plutarch's *Lives* (1559), providing basis of North's English translation.

Anabaptists, originally pejorative name for various Protestant sects which deny validity of infant baptism. Applied historically to German followers of Thomas Münzer (d. 1525), who preached separation of church and state, and were persecuted as heretics.

anaconda, *Eunectes murinus,* semi-aquatic constrictor snake of boa family from tropical South America. Olive green with black spots; reaches lengths of 7.5 m/25 ft.

Anacreon (*c* 570-*c* 485 BC), Greek lyric poet. Poems mostly celebrate love and wine.

Anaconda

anaemia, disease resulting from reduction in number, or in haemoglobin content, of red blood cells. Caused by loss of blood by bleeding, excessive destruction of red cells, iron deficiency, *etc.* Characterized by paleness, weakness, breathlessness.

anaesthetics, drugs which produce loss of sensation, either in restricted area (local anaesthetic) or whole body (general anaesthetic). General anaesthetics in use incl. ether, cyclopropane, sodium pentothal, nitrous oxide. Local anaesthetic acts on peripheral nerve endings in region of application; drugs used incl. procaine and novocaine. Early experimenters in use of anaesthetics incl. C.W. Long (ether, 1842) and J.Y. Simpson (chloroform, 1847).

Anaheim, town of S California, US; SE of Los Angeles. Pop. 167,000. Indust. centre; tourist resort based on Disneyland (opened 1955).

analgesic, drug used to relieve pain. Those used incl. derivatives of salicylic acid (*eg* aspirin), phenacetin, phenylbutazone.

analog computer, *see* COMPUTER.

analysis, in chemistry, decomposition of a substance into its elements or constituent parts to determine either their nature (qualitative analysis) or proportion (quantitative analysis).

analytical or **coordinate geometry,** branch of geometry in which position is defined by reference to coordinate axes and curves described by algebraic equations.

anarchism, in politics, theory that all forms of authority interfere with individual freedom and that state should be replaced by freely-associating communities. Early principles outlined by Zeno of Citium; modern anarchist theories developed by WILLIAM GODWIN, PROUDHON and BAKUNIN, who introduced terrorism as strategic means of resisting organized govt. Theories influenced syndicalists, esp. in Spanish Civil War.

Anastasia (b. 1901), Russian princess. Daughter of Nicholas II, believed assassinated with rest of royal family (1918) after Russian Revolution. Several women, notably Anna Anderson, have since claimed her identity without conclusive proof.

Anatolia, *see* ASIA MINOR.

anatomy, branch of science concerned with structure of plants and animals, and with their dissection. Pioneers in its study incl. Galen, whose findings dominated medical thought until 16th cent., and Vesalius, who founded modern descriptive anatomy.

Anaxagoras (*c* 500–*c* 428 BC), Greek philosopher. Developed dualistic theory of universe composed of particles arranged by an omnipresent intelligence (*nous*). Also studied astronomy, correctly explaining eclipses.

Anaximander (*c* 611–547 BC), Greek philosopher. Held that world consists of primary matter (*apeiron*) which is eternal and indestructible. Invented sundial, map. Known as 1st Greek author to write in prose.

ancestor worship, religious practices based on belief that souls of the dead continue to be involved with their living descendants. Occurs in many societies, incl. ancient Greeks and Romans.

Anchises, in Greek myth, member of royal house of Troy, father of Aeneas, by Aphrodite. Carried from burning remains of Troy by Aeneas, whom he accompanied on his voyages.

Anchorage, town of SC Alaska, US; at head of Cook Inlet. Pop. 48,000; state's largest, most important town. Transport jct.; fishing, oil, mining centre. Military bases estab. in WWII. Badly damaged by earthquake (1964).

anchovy, small herring-like marine fish of Engraulidae family. *Engraulis encrasicholus,* found in Mediterranean, used as food.

Ancona, city of the Marches, EC Italy, on the Adriatic Sea; cap. of Ancona prov. Pop. 113,000. Port, shipbuilding, sugar refining. Founded 4th cent. BC by Greeks from Syracuse; *fl* under Romans (triumphal arch erected AD 115 to Trajan). Romanesque cathedral.

Andalusia (*Andalucía*), region and former prov. of S Spain. Incl. Sierra Morena (N), Guadalquivir basin (C), Sierra Nevada (S). Irrigated agric., fruit growing, bull breeding; rich mineral resources, fishing, tourism. Widespread poverty among rural pop. Settled 11th cent. BC by Phoenicians; *fl* under Moorish rule (8th-15th cent.) esp. at Córdoba, Granada, Seville.

Andaman and Nicobar Islands, union territ. of India, in SE Bay of Bengal. Area: Andaman Isls. 6500 sq km (2500 sq mi); Nicobar Isls. 1830 sq km (700 sq mi). Pop. 115,000; cap. Port Blair (pop. 26,000). Timber, copra exports.

Andamawa-Eastern, subgroup of Niger-Congo branch of Niger-Kordofanian language family. Languages spoken in Nigeria, Cameroon, C Africa; incl. Sango, Zande.

Andean condor, *Vultur gryphus,* vulture of high peaks of Andes. Black plumage, bare head and neck; one of largest flying birds with wingspan of *c* 3 m/10 ft.

Andean-Equatorial, mainly South American linguistic stock. Incl. Quechu-Maran, Arawakan, Tucanoan groups.

Andersen, Hans Christian (1805-75), Danish author. His 168 fairy tales (pub. 1835-72), incl. 'The Ugly Duckling', 'The Emperor's New Clothes', 'The Red Shoes', children's classics combining symbolic significance with humour and whimsy. Also wrote plays, poetry, novel *Improvisatoren* (1835).

Andersen-Nexö, Martin (1869-1954), Danish novelist. Author of epic of the Danish proletariat, *Ditte, Daughter of Mankind* (5 vols., 1917-21).

Anderson, Carl David (1905-   ), American physicist. With Hess, awarded Nobel Prize for Physics (1936) for discovery of positron while researching cosmic radiation. Also discovered muon (mu-meson) in 1935, produced in upper atmosphere by cosmic rays.

Anderson, Dame Judith (1898-   ), Australian actress, appeared mainly in US. Roles incl. Lavinia in O'Neill's *Mourning Becomes Electra,* Gertrude to Gielgud's *Hamlet, Medea.*

Anderson, Marian (1902-   ), American contralto. Pioneered acceptance of black singers in concert and opera worlds. In 1955 she became 1st black singer to appear at the Metropolitan Opera, New York.

Anderson, Maxwell (1888-1959), American dramatist. Works incl. blank verse *Winterset* (1935), *High Tor* (1936), *Lost in the Stars* (1950), the last with music by Weill and based on Alan Paton's *Cry the Beloved Country.*

Anderson, Sherwood (1876-1941), American author. Themes show pathos of individuals in industrial society reflected in related short stories of *Winesburg, Ohio* (1919) and novels *Poor White* (1920), *Dark Laughter* (1925).

Andes, major mountain system of South America, extending N-S 8000 km (5000 mi) from Venezuela to Cape Horn. Rises to highest point at Aconcagua (6960 m/22,835 ft) on Chile-Argentina border. Forms volcanic plateau in Bolivia, narrow ranges in Ecuador, Colombia. Peruvian Andes was centre of ancient Inca civilizations. Indian pop. in high basins; important deposits of copper, silver, tin. Region subject to earthquakes.

Andhra Pradesh, state of SE India. Area 275,000 sq km (106,000 sq mi); pop. 43,400,000; cap. Hyderabad. Largely plains; mountains (Eastern Ghats) in E. Rice, sugar cane grown. Formed in 1956 to unite Telugu-speaking peoples of Madras and Hyderabad states.

Andorra, republic of SW Europe, in E Pyrenees. Area 495 sq km (191 sq mi); pop. 19,000; cap. Andorra la Vella. Language: Catalan. Religion: RC. Under nominal Franco-

Andorra

Wood anemone (Anemone nemorosa)

Spanish suzerainty. Many high peaks, up to *c* 3050 m (10,000 ft). Pasture (cattle, sheep), tobacco, fruit; tourism.

Andrassy, Julius, Count (1823-90), Hungarian statesman. Supported KOSSUTH during Revolution of 1848-9, exiled until 1858. Helped form AUSTRO-HUNGARIAN MONARCHY (1867); premier of Hungary (1867-71), encouraged Magyar supremacy over Slavs.

André, John (1751-80), British soldier. As adjutant-general to Clinton, negotiated with BENEDICT ARNOLD to betray West Point to British in 1780. Caught and hanged as spy.

Andreanof Islands, *see* ALEUTIAN ISLANDS.

Andrew, St (*fl* 1st cent. AD), fisherman, one of Twelve Disciples of Jesus. Traditionally, missionary to Gentiles, crucified on X-shaped cross. Patron saint of Russia, Scotland.

Andrewes, Lancelot (1555-1626), English churchman, scholar. Bishop of Chichester (1605), Ely (1609), Winchester (1619). Opposed Puritanism; helped translate Authorized (King James) Version of Bible. Noted for both learning and piety.

Andrews, Roy Chapman (1884-1960), American naturalist, explorer, author. Specialist on aquatic mammals of Alaska, Asiatic coast. Led expeditions to C Asia, discovering fossil plants and animals, dinosaur eggs.

Andreyev, Leonid Nikolayevich (1871-1919), Russian author. Novels, *eg The Red Laugh* (1904), treat sensational themes in complex, symbolic way, as do plays, *Life of Man* (1906), *He Who Gets Slapped* (1914).

Andrić, Ivo (1892-1975), Yugoslav author. Known for chronicle novel, *The Bridge on the Drina* (1945), relating history of Bosnian bridge. Nobel Prize for Literature (1961).

androgen, name given to any male sex hormone which gives rise to secondary sexual characteristics. Natural androgens are steroids produced in testes and adrenal cortex.

Andromache, in Greek myth, wife of Hector of Troy and mother of Astyanax. At fall of Troy Greeks killed her child and she became slave of Neoptolemus, son of Achilles. Later married Helenus, brother of Hector.

Andromeda, in Greek myth, daughter of Cepheus by Cassiopeia. Rescued from sea monster by Perseus, who subsequently married her. Andromeda, Cassiopeia, Cepheus were placed among the stars at their death.

Andromeda Galaxy, spiral galaxy in constellation Andromeda, *c* 2 million light years away; visible to naked eye as dim patch of light.

Andros, Aegean isl. of Greece, northernmost of Cyclades. Area 375 sq km (145 sq mi); main town Andros. Famous for wines from ancient times.

Aneirin (*fl c* AD 600), Welsh poet. Long heroic poem *Y Gododdin* is contained in *Llyfr Aneirin* ('Book of Aneirin'), 13th cent. manuscript.

anemone, genus of plants of buttercup family, widely distributed in temperate and subarctic regions. Species incl. *Anemone patens,* blue flower of North American prairies, *A. quinquefolia,* spring wild flower with slender stem and delicate whitish blossoms. Cultivated garden varieties have showy variously coloured flowers, *eg* European pasqueflower *A. pulsatilla.*

aneroid barometer, instrument for measuring atmospheric pressure. Consists of partially evacuated metal container, thin lid displaced by changes in atmospheric pressure, thus causing a pointer to move.

aneurism or **aneurysm,** abnormal bulge of weakened wall of an artery; caused by syphilis, atheroma, injury, high blood pressure. Bulge may burst, resulting in serious internal bleeding; treatment by surgery, *eg* insertion of tube of synthetic material.

Angara, river of USSR. Flows N *c* 1850 km (1150 mi) from SW corner of L. Baikal through Irkutsk, then W to join R. Yenisei. Used for h.e.p.

Angarsk, city of USSR, SC Siberian RSFSR; on R. Angara. Pop. 219,000. Produces petrochemicals.

angel (Gk.,= messenger), in theology, immortal being. According to traditions of Judaism, Christianity and Islam, intermediate between God and man. Classified by Dionysius the Areopagite into 3 choirs: seraphim, cherubim, thrones; dominions, virtues, powers; principalities, archangels, angels. Angels of hell are followers of Satan and tempt mankind.

Angel Falls, waterfall of SE Venezuela, on Caroní tributary. Prob. highest waterfall in world. Height 979 m (3212 ft).

angelfish, brightly-coloured fish of Chaetodontidae family. Spiny headed, with laterally-compressed body; inhabits tropical reefs.

angelica or **archangel,** plant of genus *Angelica*, esp. *A. archangelica*. Cultivated in Europe for aromatic odour and root stalks which are candied and eaten, and for roots and seeds yielding oil used in perfume and liqueurs.

Angelico, Fra, orig. Guido di Pietro (1387-1455), Italian painter, Dominican friar. Work, intended to serve religion, is characterized by simple direct style, and purity of line and colour. Painted frescoes *c* 1440 in convent of San Marco, Florence, and in chapel of Pope Nicholas V in Vatican.

Angell, Sir Norman, orig. Ralph Norman Angell Lane (1872-1967), British writer. In *The Great Illusion* (1910), argued that common economic interest of nations makes war futile. Nobel Peace Prize (1933).

Angers (anc. *Juliomagus*), city of W France, on R. Maine, cap. of Maine-et-Loire dept. Pop. 129,000. Wine, glass, textiles; largest French slate quarries nearby. Hist. cap. of Anjou from 9th cent. Castle, cathedral (both 13th cent.).

Angevin, noble family of medieval Europe. Descended from Fulk the Red, 1st count of Anjou, France, whence the name. Comprised 2 main lines: 1) rulers of parts of France (from 9th cent.), Jerusalem (1131-86), PLANTAGENET kings of England (from 1154); 2) branch of CAPETIANS, incl. rulers of parts of France (from 1246), kings of Naples and Sicily (from 1266), Hungary (from 1308), Poland (from 1370).

angina pectoris, disease characterized by sudden attacks of chest pain extending down left arm. Caused by obstruction of coronary arteries, resulting in lack of oxygen to heart muscles.

angiosperm, any plant of class Angiospermae, incl. all the flowering plants, characterized by having the seeds enclosed in an ovary. Opposed to GYMNOSPERM.

Angkor, ruins in W Cambodia. Incl. Angkor Thom, ancient cap. of Indo-Chinese Khmer empire, and Angkor Wat temple. Discovered by French in 1861.

anglerfish, any of Lophiidae family of bottom-dwelling marine fish. Worm-like filament growing from head lures prey to its mouth. Species incl. *Lophius piscatorius,* found in European waters.

Angles, Teutonic people originally inhabiting what is now Schleswig-Holstein (S Denmark, N Germany). Settled in late 5th cent. in E, N and C England in area of later kingdoms of East Anglia, Northumbria and Mercia.

Anglesey, isl. of Gwynedd, NW Wales, separated from mainland by Menai Strait. Area 705 sq km (272 sq mi); main town Holyhead. Agric., *eg* livestock rearing. Tourist industs.

Anglican Communion, informal organization of the Church of England and derived churches with closely related faith and forms, incl. Church of Ireland, Episcopal Church of Scotland, Protestant Episcopal Church in US. Representatives meet every 10 years at Lambeth Conference with archbishop of Canterbury presiding. *See* ENGLAND, CHURCH OF.

angling, sport of fishing with rod and line. Freshwater fish sought by anglers incl. salmon, trout, bass and pike; saltwater varieties prized incl. tuna, marlin and swordfish. Izaak Walton's *Compleat Angler* (1653) is famous account of angling.

Anglo-Catholicism, *see* OXFORD MOVEMENT.

Anglo-Saxon Chronicle, annals of English history, begun under Alfred the Great *c* 891, written in Old English. Simultaneous compilation at 7 different places gives varied picture of English history, incl. Danish invasions, clerical corruption, stories, *eg* 'Cynewulf and Cyneheard'. Peterborough Chronicle continues to 1154.

Anglo-Saxon language, *see* ENGLISH.

Anglo-Saxon literature, written works in Old English. Poetry unrhymed, using 4-stress line broken into 2 halves, each with internal alliteration, suited to narrative, not lyric. Heroic epic BEOWULF, *Battle of Maldon, etc,* reveal Germanic pagan heritage and oral tradition, although recorded in Christian era. Elegaic verse incl. *Deor, The Wanderer.* Hymn of CAEDMON 1st Christian poem, others incl. *The Dream of the Road,* versions of pieces from Bible, *eg Judith,* lives of saints. Literary prose begun in reign of ALFRED with translations from Latin and the ANGLO-SAXON CHRONICLE.

Anglo-Saxons, Teutonic peoples who settled in England in 5th-6th cent. Incl. ANGLES, SAXONS and JUTES. Term also used generally for non-Celtic inhabitants of British Isles before Norman Conquest; recent use for Anglo-American society, its values and attitudes.

Angola

Angola, formerly Portuguese West Africa, republic of WC Africa. Area (incl. CABINDA) 1,246,600 sq km (481,300 sq mi); pop. 5,812,000; cap. Luanda. Languages: Bantu, Portuguese. Religions: native, Christian. Narrow coastal strip, interior tableland; main river Cunene. Livestock, fishing; exports coffee, diamonds, oil. Colonized 16th cent. by Portuguese, centre for slave trade until 19th cent. Civil uprisings in 1960s ruthlessly suppressed. Independent

1975; war between competing liberation groups ended in victory (1976) for Marxist forces.

Angora, *see* ANKARA.

angostura bark, bitter aromatic bark of 2 South American trees, *Galipea officinalis* and *G. cusparia.* Used in medicine and in preparation of liqueurs and bitters.

Angoulême, town of W France, on R. Charente, cap. of Charente dept. Pop. 51,000. Road and rail jct., wine, paper mfg. Seat of counts of Angoumois from 9th cent. Cathedral (12th cent.).

Angry Young Men, applied to several British authors of 1950s, incl. John Osborne, Kingsley Amis, John Braine. Work characterized by resentment of establishment.

Angström, Anders Jons (1814-74), Swedish physicist. Pioneer in spectroscopy, he investigated solar spectrum, and discovered hydrogen in Sun. Unit of measurement of wavelength of light named after him (1 angstrom = 10^{-10} m).

Anguilla, isl. of E West Indies, in Leeward Isls. Area 91 sq km (35 sq mi); pop. 6000. Exports cotton, salt. Former British colony with ST KITTS, Nevis; associate state of St Kitts-Nevis-Anguilla; nationalist unrest led to landing of British troops (1969).

Angus, former county of E Scotland, now in Tayside region. Co. town was Forfar. Grampian Mts. in N; Sidlaw Hills in S; fertile Strathmore in C. Barley, potato growing; livestock rearing. Known as Forfarshire until 1928.

Anhwei, prov. of E China. Area *c* 142,450 sq km (55,000 sq mi); pop. (est.) 35,000,000; cap. Hofei. Watered by Yangtze in S (rice, barley); soya beans, wheat in N.

anhydride, in chemistry, non-metallic oxide or organic compound (*eg* sulphur trioxide) which reacts with water to form an acid; or metallic oxide (*eg* calcium oxide) which reacts with water to form a base.

aniline ($C_6H_5NH_2$), colourless oily liquid, obtained from coal tar or by reduction of nitrobenzene. Used in manufacture of dyes, plastics and drugs.

animal, any member of animal kingdom, as opposed to plant kingdom. Distinction between plants and animals is largely based on means of feeding; most plants manufacture food from inorganic substances, whereas animals must eat food containing necessary proteins. Animals are also usually capable of independent movement and have nervous systems. Some unicellular organisms, *eg Euglena,* possess chlorophyll but have certain animal characteristics. Animals are classified into *c* 20 phyla ranging from unicellular Protozoa to Chordata, which incl. all vertebrates. *See* CLASSIFICATION.

animism, in primitive religion, belief that material objects and natural phenomena contain a spiritual force which governs their existence. In philosophy, doctrine that the essential force of life is irreducible to the mechanistic laws of natural science.

anise, *Pimpinella anisum,* herbaceous plant of Mediterranean regions. Small white or yellow flowers. Its seed (aniseed) is used medicinally to expel intestinal gas and in cookery for its liquorice-like flavour.

Anjou

Anjou, hist. region of NW France, cap. Angers. Drained by R. Loire. County from 9th cent., finally annexed (1481) to

French crown by Louis XI. Plantagenet rulers of England descended from counts of Anjou.

Ankara, cap. of Turkey, in C Anatolia; formerly Angora. Pop. 1,461,000. Commercial centre; trade in mohair from Angora goats; leather goods, textile mfg. Cap. of Roman province of Galatia in 1st cent AD; has ruined marble temple. Replaced Constantinople (1923) as Turkish cap. Ataturk mausoleum is notable building.

Annaba, city of NE Algeria, on Mediterranean Sea. Pop. 169,000. Formerly called Bône. Port, exports phosphates, iron ore; iron, chemical industs. Important city of ancient Numidia, Roman *Hippo Regius.* Episcopal see of St Augustine 396-430.

Anna Comnena (1083-*c* 1148), Byzantine princess, daughter of Emperor Alexius I (Comnenus). Conspired to overthrow brother, Emperor John II. Forced to retreat into convent where she wrote *Alexiad,* history of her father's reign and 1st Crusade.

Anna Ivanovna (1693-1740), tsarina of Russia (1730-40), successor of Peter II. Ruled autocratically using German favourites. Intervened in War of Polish Succession (1733-5). Warred with Turkey (1736-9).

Annam, hist. kingdom and French protect. of SE Asia. Dominated by Annam Highlands. Part of VIETNAM after 1954.

Annapolis, cap. of Maryland, US; near mouth of Severn R. Pop. 30,000. In fruit- and vegetable-growing region. Became colonial cap. 1694; US cap. 1783-4. Mainly residential with many hist. buildings; has US Naval Academy.

Annapurna, mountain range in Nepalese Himalayas. Has 2 high peaks: Annapurna I, height 8078 m (26,502 ft), and Annapurna II, height 7938 m (26,041 ft).

Ann Arbor, town of SE Michigan, US; on Huron R. Pop. 100,000. Research, educational, indust. centre in farming, fruit-growing region. Varied mfg. industs. Has Univ. of Michigan (1841).

Anne (1665-1714), queen of England, Scotland and Ireland (1702-14). Daughter of James II, last Stuart monarch. Act of Union (1707) made her 1st queen of Great Britain and Ireland. Reign dominated by War of Spanish Succession (1701-14), in which British forces were commanded by MARLBOROUGH, a leading favourite. Succeeded by George I under Act of Settlement (1701), none of her children having survived her.

annealing, process by which materials, esp. metals, are relieved of strains, rendering them less brittle. Involves application of heat and slow controlled cooling.

Anne Boleyn, see BOLEYN, ANNE.

Annecy, town of SE France, on L. Annecy, cap. of Haute-Savoie dept. Pop. 57,000. Resort, textiles, paper mfg.; bell foundry at nearby Annecy-le-Vieux. Birthplace of St Francis of Sales.

Annelida (annelids), phylum of worms, incl. earthworms, leeches and aquatic worms, *eg* ragworm, lugworm. Body made of jointed segments.

Anne of Austria (1601-66), queen of France, daughter of Philip III of Spain. Wife of Louis XIII, acted as regent (1643-61) for son Louis XIV. Regency dominated by MAZARIN, whom she may have married secretly.

Anne of Cleves (1515-57), English queen, fourth wife of Henry VIII. Marriage (1540), arranged by Thomas Cromwell to build alliance with Germany, nullified 6 months later.

annual, plant which germinates, flowers, seeds and dies within 1 year, *eg* zinnia. Biennial completes life cycle in 2 years, flowering in 2nd year. Many crop vegetables are biennials which are harvested after 1 year when they have produced a food store but have not yet run to flower, *eg* cabbage, carrot. Perennial has life cycle of more than 2 years, *eg* tulip.

Annunciation, Feast of the, or **Lady Day,** holy day (25 March) commemorating announcement to the Virgin Mary, by angel Gabriel, that she was to be the mother of Jesus.

Anne of Cleves

anoa, *Anoa depressicornus,* smallest member of buffalo family, found in Celebes. Stands *c* 1 m/40 in. high at shoulder; horns almost straight.

anode, *see* ELECTRODE.

anole, arboreal lizard of iguana family of the Americas, noted for colour changes. Species incl. green anole, *Anolis carolinensis.*

anomie or **anomy,** individual's lack of ethical values, rules, resulting from personal disorganization or from inability to find solution to contradictory norms in society (*see* DURKHEIM). Also applied to social structure without norms.

Anouilh, Jean (1910-), French dramatist. Plays revolve on problem of purity *v* worldly maturity, *eg Antigone* (1942), *L'Alouette* (1953) on Joan of Arc, *Becket* (1959) on Becket's relationship with Henry II.

Ansbach, town of SC West Germany. Pop. 33,000. Textiles, machinery mfg. Grew around 8th cent. abbey. Residence of Hohenzollerns 1331-1791.

Anschluss (Ger.,=joining), term referring to German annexation of Austria (1938). Policy developed by Hitler and advocated in Austria by National Socialists although contravening peace treaties of 1919.

Anselm, St (*c* 1033-1109), Italian churchman, theologian, archbishop of Canterbury (1093-1109). Denied right to appoint bishops claimed by William II, Henry I of England. Exiled; reconciled in compromise agreed by pope. First to incorporate Aristotelian logic into theology, promulgated ontological proof of God's existence.

Ansermet, Ernest (1883-1969), Swiss conductor. Associated with Diaghilev's Ballets Russes from 1915. Founded L'Orchestre de la Suisse Romande in Geneva (1918).

Anshan, city of Liaoning prov., NE China. Pop. 1,500,000. Metallurgical centre; major iron and steel plant, chemicals mfg. Developed under Japanese in 1930s.

Anson, George Anson, Baron (1697-1762), British admiral. Circumnavigated world (1740-4), inflicting heavy damage on Spanish ships. Instigated admin. reform in navy as first lord of the Admiralty in 1750s.

ant, insect of Formicidae family, comprising thousands of widely-distributed species. Lives mainly in underground colonies with various castes maintaining division of social activities, *eg* cultivating fungi, 'milking' aphids, guarding colony. Most ants wingless sterile workers; adult males winged and short-lived. Fertile females (queens) shed wings and start colonies after nuptial flight.

Antakya or **Antioch,** town of S Turkey, on R. Orontes. Pop. 58,000. Founded *c* 300 BC, became important commercial city under Romans and early centre of Christianity. Changed hands often; fell to Crusaders (1098) and Mamelukes (1268). Declined in importance; attached to Syria after 1919, restored to Turkey in 1939.

'Milking' aphids: ants extracting sweet nutritious fluid from greenfly by stroking them

Antar (*fl* 6th cent.), Arabian warrior and poet. Of slave origin, became popular hero, subject of Arabian romance *Antar*; represented in MUALLAQAT.

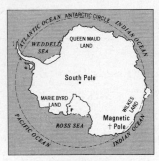

Antarctica

Antarctica, continent surrounding South Pole, completely covered by ice shelf. Area *c* 13,000,000 sq km (5,000,000 sq mi). Comprises 2 geologically distinct regions, E and W Antarctica, joined by immensely thick ice cap. Ellsworth Highlands rise to 5140 m (16,860 ft) at Vinson Massif, highest point on continent. Early explorations made by Bellingshausen (1819-21), Weddell (1823), Ross (1841-2); Amundsen reached South Pole first (1911), month before Scott; Byrd first flew over Pole (1929). Area S of 60°S reserved for international scientific research. *See* AUSTRALIAN ANTARCTIC TERRITORY, BRITISH ANTARCTIC TERRITORY, NORWEGIAN ANTARCTIC TERRITORY, ROSS DEPENDENCY, ADÉLIE LAND. Chile, Argentina, USSR and US also maintain bases. Unassigned area incl. Ellsworth Highlands, Marie Byrd Land, Bellingshausen and Amundsen seas.

antbear or **giant anteater,** *Myrmecophaga jubata,* South American mammal, order Edentata. Shaggy grey coat, long snout; diet of ants, termites.

antbird, any of Formicariidae family of birds of Central and South America, most resembling thrushes. Often feeds on insects displaced by columns of ants.

anteater, one of several mammals, *eg* pangolin, echidna, antbear, characterized by long snout, sticky tongue and ant diet.

antelope, hoofed ruminant of Bovidae family, found mainly in Africa. Species incl. bushbuck, bongo; largest is giant eland. Horns hollow and unbranched.

antenna, *see* AERIAL.

antennae, in zoology, flexible jointed appendages on heads of most arthropods. Function mainly sensory (touch, smell), but used by some crustaceans for swimming or attachment.

Antheil, George (1900-59), American composer. Known for unorthodox music using mechanical sound sources. His *Ballet Mécanique* (1927), featuring aircraft propellers and automobile horns, attempted to symbolize the machine age.

Anthony, St or **Anthony of Egypt** (*c* 251-*c* 356), Egyptian ascetic. Traditionally, founder of 1st Christian monastery.

Anthony, Susan Brownell (1820-1906), American abolitionist, feminist, temperance advocate. Helped organize women's suffrage movement in US and secure laws giving women rights over property and children. President (1892-1900) of the Woman Suffrage Association.

Anthozoa, *see* ACTINOZOA.

anthracene, solid hydrocarbon derived from coal tar. Colourless with blue fluorescence, darkens in sunlight. Derivatives form alizarin dyes.

anthracite, hard, shiny black variety of COAL. Has high carbon content, burns with smokeless flame and has good heat-producing capacity; widely used as domestic fuel. Dates mainly from Carboniferous period.

anthrax, infectious disease of cattle, sheep, *etc*; can be transmitted to man as localized inflammation of skin producing pustules, or as fulminating pneumonia. Caused by *Bacillus anthracis*; treated by penicillin and other antibiotics. Vaccine developed by Pasteur.

anthropology, scientific study of man and his societies. Developed in early 19th cent. Deals with evolution, distribution, social organization, cultural relationships. Distinguished from sociology in its tendency to concentrate on data from non-literate peoples, and historical emphasis.

Antibes, town of SE France, on Côte d'Azur. Pop. 48,000. Port, resort, flower-growing centre; perfume, chocolate mfg. Greek colony founded 4th cent. BC. Roman remains; Château Grimaldi has works by Picasso.

antibiotic, chemical substance, produced by bacteria, moulds, fungi, *etc,* which in dilute solution has capacity of inhibiting growth of or destroying bacteria or other micro-organisms. First observed and named was penicillin (by Alexander Fleming, 1928); those used to treat infectious diseases incl. streptomycin, aureomycin, chloromycetin.

antibody, protein produced in vertebrate cells to counteract presence in body of specific antigens (enzyme, toxin) associated with invading bacteria or viruses. By combining chemically with antigens, antibodies form defence mechanism against disease-producing organisms and provide immunity to later attacks.

Anti-Comintern Pact, agreement between Germany and Japan (1936). Stated policy of opposition to international communism. Enlarged (1941) to incl. most AXIS countries.

Anti-Corn Law League, *see* CORN LAWS.

anticyclone, area of relatively high atmospheric pressure, normally creating dry, cloudless conditions, warm in summer, cold in winter. Air moves spirally outwards to areas of lower pressure; deflection by Earth's rotation causes clockwise wind circulation in N hemisphere, anti-clockwise in S hemisphere.

antifreeze, substance of low freezing point added to a liquid to depress its freezing point. Ideally should be stable, non-corrosive, non-volatile and good conductor of heat but not of electricity. Ethylene glycol is used in cooling systems of water-cooled engines.

Antigone, in Greek myth, daughter of OEDIPUS and Jocasta; sister of Polynices and Eteocles. Accompanied her father in exile to Colonus, returned to Thebes after his death. Despite prohibition of Creon, she performed funerary rites over Polynices. As punishment, buried alive where she committed suicide.

Antigonus [I] Cyclops (382-301 BC), Macedonian soldier, ruler. Served under Alexander the Great, after whose death he attempted to gain control of all Asia. Held Asia Minor and Syria by 316. Failed to conquer Egypt. Defeated and killed at Ipsus in Phrygia.

Antigua, town of SC Guatemala. Pop. 22,000. Commercial centre in coffee-growing region. Hist. cap. (1542-1776); frequent earthquakes led to shifting of cap. to Guatemala City.

Antigua, isl. of E West Indies, in Leeward Isls. Area 280 sq km (108 sq mi); pop. 70,000; cap. St John's (pop. 24,000). Sugar cane, cotton growing; exports sugar, molasses, rum. Has important tourist industs. Discovered by Columbus (1493). Settled by British in 17th cent.; became associate state (1967) with dependencies Barbuda, Redonda.

antihistamine, name given to drugs which neutralize effects of histamine in human body. Used in treatment of allergies.

Anti-Lebanon, mountain range on Syria-Lebanon border. Highest point Mt. Hermon 2814 m (9232 ft). Once noted for timber, now barren.

Antilles, isl. group of Caribbean, incl. all West Indies except Bahamas. Greater Antilles consist of Cuba, Jamaica, Hispaniola, Puerto Rico. Lesser Antilles consist of Leeward and Windward Isls., Netherlands Antilles.

anti-matter, hypothetical matter composed of ANTI-PARTICLES. Ordinary matter and anti-matter brought in contact should annihilate each other, liberating radiation energy. Thus anti-matter cannot exist long in our universe.

antimony (Sb), brittle silver-grey semi-metallic element; at. no. 51, at. wt. 121.75. Occurs as oxide or as stibnite Sb_2S_3. Produced by roasting ore and reducing oxide with iron. Used in making alloys, esp. type metal, and in medicine.

antinomianism, in Christian theology, doctrine that faith alone, not obedience to moral law, is necessary for salvation. Heresy prevalent in Middle Ages; upheld by Anabaptists.

Antioch, see ANTAKYA.

Antiochus [III] the Great (d. 187 BC), Syrian king (223-187 BC). Reconquered much of earlier Seleucid empire. Invaded Greece but was defeated by Romans at Thermopylae (191). Following him into Asia Minor, Romans destroyed his army at Magnesia (190).

anti-particles, particles analogous to ELEMENTARY PARTICLES of matter but having opposite charge and magnetic moment. Brought into contact, an elementary particle and its anti-particle annihilate each other, producing radiation and other elementary particles. Anti-particle of electron is POSITRON.

antipodes, places diametrically opposite in location on the globe, ie separated by 180° of longitude and by the Equator. Term commonly used in UK to refer to Australia or New Zealand.

Antipodes Islands, rocky, uninhabited isl. group of New Zealand, to SE of South Island in S Pacific Ocean. Nearest land to antipodean point of London, England.

antipope, pope set up by a group within RC church against the one chosen by church laws and whose election has subsequently been declared uncanonical. *See* SCHISM, GREAT.

anti-Semitism, antipathy towards Jews. Manifested from Roman times to 19th cent. through persecution and restriction (*see* GHETTO). Religious cause stressed until 19th cent., subsequently practised for political, social or economic gains, reaching its height in Nazi Germany. Hitler instigated extermination of c 6 million Jews (1939-45). In E Europe, esp. USSR, Poland, Jews have suffered restrictive laws, recurrent violence, eg Kishinev massacre (1903), pogroms.

antiseptic, chemical used to curb growth of or destroy micro-organisms, usually on living tissue, and thus to prevent infection. LISTER introduced use in surgery following Pasteur's research. Modern development is

technique of asepsis, *ie* production of germ-free conditions for surgery.

Antisthenes (c 444-c370 BC), Greek philosopher. Sophist in early life, but subsequently disciple of Socrates. Founded school of CYNICS at Athens.

antitoxin, antibody formed in body to neutralize poisons (toxins) released into bloodstream by bacteria. Can be given by injection for short-term effect against toxins, eg those of diphtheria and tetanus.

anti-trust legislation, *see* MONOPOLY.

Antlion larva with prey

antlion, larva of several species of winged insects of Myrmeleonidae family. Digs pits in sand and feeds on insects that fall in.

Antofagasta, port of N Chile, on Pacific coast. Pop. 126,000. Nitrates, copper exports. Its occupation by Chileans initiated war (1879-84) with Bolivia, which ceded territ. to Chile. Has artificial harbour; railway link with Bolivia.

Antoine, André (1858-1943), French actor-manager. Founded (1887) Théâtre Libre, Paris, to promote naturalistic drama in France; incl. plays of Ibsen, Hauptmann, Strindberg.

Antonello da Messina (c 1430-79), Italian painter. Influenced by detailed realism of Flemish oil-painting technique. Works incl. bust portraits and religious works, *eg St Sebastian* (Dresden).

Antonescu, Ion (1882-1946), Romanian military and political leader. Became premier (1940) before estab. dictatorship. Allied Romania with Axis powers in WWII, but was overthrown 1944. Executed for war crimes.

Antonine Wall, Roman wall, C Scotland. Length 60 km (37 mi), extending from R. Forth to R. Clyde; marked Empire's northern frontiers. Abandoned c 185; remains still visible.

Antoninus Pius (AD 86-161), Roman emperor (138-161). Adopted by Hadrian as his successor in 138. Encouraged art, science and building during peaceful reign. Had Antonine Wall built between firths of Clyde and Forth in Scotland (142).

Antony, Mark or **Marcus Antonius** (c 83-30 BC), Roman soldier, political leader. Served with Caesar in Gaul, taking his side during civil war. After Caesar's assassination (44), aroused the mob to expel conspirators from Rome. After conflict with Octavian, joined him and Lepidus in 2nd Triumvirate, which ruled the empire for 5 years. He and Octavian defeated Brutus and Cassius at Philippi (42). While in Asia Minor, fell in love with Cleopatra. Deprived of power by senate, was defeated by Octavian at Actium (31). Joined Cleopatra in Egypt, where he killed himself.

Antrim, former county of NE Ireland, co. town was Belfast. Low basalt plateau; scenic valleys ('Glens of Antrim'); Giant's Causeway on N coast. Main industs., agric., fishing, linen mfg., shipbuilding. **Antrim,** town on Lough Neagh. Pop. 2000. Has 10th cent. round tower. **Antrim,** district; area 563 sq km (217 sq mi); pop. 27,000. Created in 1973, formerly part of Co. Antrim.

Antung, city of Liaoning prov., NE China. Pop. 450,000. Seaport near mouth of R. Yalu opposite Korea. Indust. centre; silk, paper, textiles mfg. Former treaty port, opened 1907.

Antwerp (Fr. *Anvers*), city of N Belgium, cap. of Antwerp prov. Pop. 234,000. Port and commercial centre on R. Scheldt. Sugar, oil refining; shipbuilding, textiles; diamond trade. Gothic cathedral (1352). Trade centre of 16th cent. Europe, declined after sack by Spaniards (1576), closure of Scheldt (1648-1795). Prosperity regained from 19th cent. Damaged in both WWs.

Wall painting of Anubis at Thebes

Anubis, in ancient Egyptian pantheon, god who led the dead to judgment. Depicted with head of a jackal. Sometimes identified with Greek Hermes.

Anura, order of amphibians, comprising toads and frogs. Hind legs enlarged for jumping, feet webbed for swimming.

Anuradhapura, town of N Sri Lanka. Pop. 29,000. Site of ancient cap. of Ceylon, founded in 5th cent. BC. Buddhist pilgrimage centre with numerous ruins and sacred botree (scion of that at Buddh Gaya).

anus, in mammals, posterior opening of alimentary canal, through which waste is excreted.

Anville, Jean Baptiste Bourguignon d' (1697-1782), French geographer, cartographer. Leading map-maker of 18th cent., used original sources to improve accuracy. Works incl. maps of China (1735), *Atlas général* (from 1737).

anxiety, in psychology, reaction ranging from uneasiness to complete panic when individual is faced with real or apparent threat. Classified normal and neurotic; latter often said to be core of neuroses, characterized by helpless response to threat.

Anyang, city of Honan prov., EC China. Pop. 225,000. Coal mining, cotton textile mfg. Ancient cultural centre of Shang dynasty. Excavations begun 1928 revealed royal tombs of *c* 1350 BC.

Anzengruber, Ludwig (1839-89), Austrian dramatist. Known for his naturalistic dialect plays, *eg The Double Suicide* (1876), *The Fourth Commandment* (1877), depicting rustic and family problems.

Anzio (anc. *Antium*), town of WC Italy, on Tyrrhenian Sea. Pop. 16,000. Fishing port. Birthplace of Caligula, Nero. Scene of Allied landings (1944).

Aomori, seaport of Japan, N Honshu isl. Pop. 240,000. Exports rice, timber, esp. to Hokkaido.

Aorangi, *see* COOK, MOUNT.

aorta, main artery of body, conveying blood from left ventricle of the heart to all parts of body except the lungs.

Aosta, town of NW Italy, in the Alps, on R. Dora Baltea. Cap. of Valle d'Aosta prov. Pop. 39,000. Tourist centre; metals, chemicals. Roman ruins, medieval cathedral.

aoudad or **Barbary sheep,** *Ammotragus lervia,* wild N African sheep with large curved horns. Resembles goat; highly adaptable to climatic extremes.

Apache, North American Indian tribes of Nadene linguistic stock. Warlike hunters of SW. Successfully resisted advance of Spanish colonization but inter-tribal warfare reduced numbers. Some 80,000 still live in reservations, mainly in Arizona.

apartheid, racial segregation on grounds of colour, practised in South Africa from 1948. In Afrikaans, word means 'apartness'; policy aimed at achieving separate development of races, effectively restricting residence, movements, occupations of non-whites. Rather than change its racist policy, South Africa withdrew from Commonwealth (1961).

apatite, calcium phosphate mineral, usually containing chlorine and fluorine. Commonly green or brown with white streaks; found in igneous rocks and metamorphosed limestones. Used in production of phosphate fertilizers. Major sources in USSR, US, N Africa.

ape, any of Pongidae family of Old World tailless monkeys, particularly those most closely related to man (gibbon, orangutan, gorilla and chimpanzee).

Apeldoorn, city of EC Netherlands. Pop. 128,000. Railway jct. Paper mfg. Royal family summer residence nearby.

Apelles (*fl* 4th cent. BC), Greek painter. Reputed to be leading painter of antiquity, none of his work survives. Court painter in Macedon to Philip and Alexander; his portrait of Alexander holding a thunderbolt was in Temple of Diana at Ephesus.

Apennines, mountain range of Italy. Extends *c* 1300 km (800 mi) from Maritime Alps to Calabria and Sicily. Livestock, agric. on lower slopes; marble quarries. Formerly widely forested. Highest peak Monte Corno (2913 m/9560 ft) in Gran Sasso d'Italia, C Italy. Earthquakes, esp. in S; volcanoes, incl. Vesuvius.

aphelion, point furthest from Sun in orbit of planet about Sun. Opposite is perihelion.

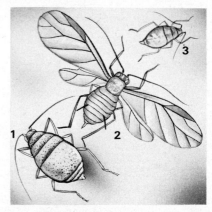

Aphid: 1. wingless viviparous female; 2. winged viviparous female; 3. oviparous female

aphid or **plant louse,** small soft-bodied insect of Aphididae family. Causes much damage to plants by sucking sap and carrying virus disease. Common greenfly, pest of roses, is an aphid.

Aphrodite, in Greek myth, goddess of love, beauty, fertility. Daughter of Zeus and Dione, or sprung from sea into which a severed member of Uranus had been thrown. Unfaithful wife of Hephaestus, being variously connected with Ares, Dionysus, Hermes, Poseidon and the mortals Anchises, Adonis. Had power of granting beauty and charm. Identified by Romans with Venus.

Apia, cap. of Western Samoa, on Upolu Isl. Pop. 28,000. Admin. centre; port, exports fruit, copra, cocoa. Burial place of R.L. Stevenson.

Apis, in ancient Egyptian myth, sacred bull in which OSIRIS was believed to be incarnate.

apocalypse, form of prophetic writing common in ancient Hebrew and Christian literature. Depicts end of the world in visions of triumph of good over evil; characterized by rich and obscure symbolism. NT book of REVELATION is often known as the Apocalypse.

Apocrypha, Jewish writings of *c* 300 BC - *c* AD 100 not incl. in the canon of sacred scripture by the Council of

Jamnia (AD 90) and now excluded by most Protestant churches. Consists of 14 books included in SEPTUAGINT and VULGATE.

apogee, point furthest from Earth in orbit of Moon or satellite about Earth. Opposite is perigee.

Apollinaire, Guillaume, orig. Wilhelm Apollinaris de Kostrowitski (1880-1918), French poet, b. Rome. His art criticism established CUBISM as a movement, which influenced poetry *Alcools* (1913), *Calligrammes* (1918). Also wrote surrealist drama *Les Mamelles de Tirésias* (1917), modernist manifesto, *L'esprit nouveau et les poètes.*

Apollo or **Phoebus Apollo,** in Greek myth, son of Zeus and Leto, born with his sister Artemis at Delos. God of social and intellectual attributes of Greek civilization, *eg* prophecy, healing, purification, music, archery. Represented as ideal of youthful beauty. Cult centred at Delphi where oracular utterances were given by his priestess, Pythia.

Apollodorus (*fl* 415 BC), Athenian painter. First painter to use light and shade to model figures, step towards illusionistic painting.

Apollonius of Perga (*fl* 247-205 BC), Greek mathematician. Wrote treatise on conic sections, extending work of Euclid; it is a high point of Greek geometry. No other works extant.

Apollonius Rhodius (*c* 295 BC–after 247 BC), Alexandrian scholar, poet. Librarian of Museum in Alexandria, wrote epic *Argonautica* about Jason and the Golden Fleece.

Apollo programme, *see* SPACE EXPLORATION.

apologetics, the branch of theology which deals with the formal defence of a religious belief. Major Christian apologists incl. Augustine, Aquinas, Pascal, Karl Barth. Since 19th cent., principal attacks on belief have come from psychology, Darwinism, historical criticism of Gospels.

apoplexy or **stroke,** sudden paralysis with total or partial loss of consciousness and sensation, possible loss of speech, and other after-effects of varying severity. Caused by bleeding from arteries in brain, thrombosis or embolism.

apostle, name given to TWELVE DISCIPLES of Jesus (sometimes excluding Judas Iscariot), and also to other early missionaries of Christian church, *eg* St Paul, St Barnabas.

Apostles' Creed, one of the three basic statements of Christian faith. Used in RC and various Protestant churches. Formerly ascribed to the Apostles; prob. dates in present form from 6th cent.

apostolic succession, doctrine that the religious authority and mission conferred by Jesus on St Peter has come down through an unbroken succession of bishops. Basis of religious authority in RC, Eastern Orthodox and Anglican churches, but not accepted by Presbyterian churches.

Appalachian Mountains, system of E North America. Extend 2570 km (*c* 1600 mi) from Québec (Canada) to C Alabama. Incl. White, Green, Catskill, Allegheny, Blue Ridge, Black Mts. Mt. Mitchell is highest point (2037 m/6684 ft). Rich in mineral resources, esp. coal.

appeasement, policy of acceding to demands of hostile power in attempt to maintain peace. Used by British, French towards AXIS powers in late 1930s; culminated in MUNICH PACT.

appendix or **vermiform appendix,** in man, outgrowth of large intestine in lower right abdomen. No known function. Infection may result in appendicitis which usually necessitates removal of appendix.

Appert, Nicolas (1750-1841), French pioneer of food canning. Awarded (1810) prize by French govt. for discovering method of preserving food in sealed containers.

Appian Way (anc. *Via Appia*), ancient road of Italy, begun 312 BC, extending *c* 560 km (350 mi) from Rome to Brindisi. Part of Roman route to Greece, Asia.

apple, any tree of genus *Malus* of rose family. The common apple *M. sylvestris* has hard, round, red, yellow or green edible fruit. Economically important esp. in North America, Europe and Australasia. Several thousand varieties of cultivated apples incl. eating, cooking and cider types.

Appian Way, Rome

Appleby, mun. bor. of Cumbria, NW England, on R. Eden. Pop. 2000. Former co. town of Westmorland. Has annual horse fair (June).

apple of discord, in Greek myth, golden apple inscribed 'for the fairest' thrown among guests at wedding of Peleus and Thetis by Eris. Claimed by Athena, Hera and Aphrodite, and awarded by PARIS to Aphrodite who in return helped him kidnap Helen, thus starting the Trojan War.

Apples of the Hesperides, *see* HESPERIDES.

Appleton, Sir Edward Victor (1892-1965), English physicist. Investigated reflection of radio waves by ionized particles in upper atmosphere; located Kennelly-Heaviside layer and discovered Appleton layers above this. Awarded Nobel Prize for Physics (1947).

Appomattox Courthouse, building near Appomattox S Virginia, US. Scene of Confederate General Lee's surrender to Union on 9 April, 1865, marking end of Civil War.

apprenticeship, period of instruction in which pupil learns trade by working with skilled tradesmen. Originally part of medieval guild system, now survives in highly skilled trades. After apprenticeship, worker becomes journeyman, then master.

apricot, *Prunus armeniaca,* tree with downy, orange-coloured edible fruit. Native to Far East, introduced into Europe and US.

a priori, in logic, term denoting that which comes before experience, as opposed to *a posteriori* denoting that which comes after experience. Hence formal logic is *a priori* while scientific information is *a posteriori.*

apse, vaulted semicircular or polygonal projection at sanctuary end of church.

Apuleius, Lucius (*fl* 2nd cent. BC), Roman writer, orator. Known for *Metamorphoses* or *Golden Ass,* prose romance which greatly influenced development of novel in post-Renaissance fiction.

Apulia (*Puglia*), region of SE Italy. Hilly in C, plains in N and S; cereals, olives, vines, almonds. Prone to drought. Part of medieval Norman kingdom of Sicily.

Aqaba, Gulf of, thin arm of NE Red Sea. Jordan's only sea outlet. Blockade by Egypt in 1967 war failed on Israeli capture of Sinai Penin.

aquamarine, semi-precious gemstone, a variety of beryl. Transparent, blue or blue-green in colour; used in jewellery. Major sources in US, Brazil, Siberia, Malagasy Republic.

Aquarius, *see* ZODIAC.

aquatint, method of etching by tone rather than line, giving effect similar to water colour or wash drawing. Transparent tones are obtained by biting printing plate with acid through porous ground. Much used by Goya.

aqueduct, artificial channel constructed for conducting water. Name often applies to bridge built in series of arches to carry water across a river or valley, *eg* Pont du Gard, Nîmes.

aquilegia, genus of herbs of buttercup family. Species incl. COLUMBINE.

Aquinas, Thomas, see THOMAS AQUINAS, ST.

Aquitaine, region of SW France. Fertile plain drained by R. Garonne; main cities Bordeaux, Toulouse. Cereals, vineyards, fruit and vegetable growing. Roman prov. from 56 BC; powerful medieval duchy (name corrupted to *Guienne*) under English rule from 1152; retaken by France (1451).

Arabia

Arabia, penin. of SW Asia, between Red Sea and Persian Gulf. Mainly desert inhabited by pastoral nomads; rich oil deposits in E. Tribes united (6th cent.) by Mohammed who founded Islamic religion. Under control of OTTOMAN Turks until 1918, Saudi Arabia emerged as dominant country of region after 1925.

Arabian Nights, also known as *The Thousand and One Nights,* series of stories in Arabic, linked by story of Scheherazade, who keeps her husband in suspense by telling him stories over 1001 nights, thus escaping death, fate of all his previous wives. Incl. tales of Ali Babi and Aladdin. Only partly Arab in origin, the collection draws on all leading Eastern cultures. First European translation into French 1704-17, English translations incl. Burton's unexpurgated version (16 vols., 1885–8).

Arabian Sea, part of NW Indian Ocean; lies between Arabia and India.

Arabic, SW Semitic language of Afro-Asiatic family. Spoken in most of N Africa, Sudan, Arabian peninsula, Lebanon, Syria and Iraq.

Arabic literature, began with lyric poetry in pre-Islamic period (4th cent.). Only form was ode, 30-100 lines long, on love, fighting, hunting, as in MUALLAQAT. 8th–9th cent. saw change of subject to town life, abandonment of ode form by leading poets, *eg* ABU NUWAS. Poetry superseded by prose romances, *eg* ARABIAN NIGHTS. Also historical, geographical, theological and philosophical writing, latter esp. by Spanish Arab writers. Little writing of world note since 1300.

Arabic numerals, number signs 0 1 2 3 4 5 6 7 8 9; of Hindu origin, they were introduced into Europe by translation of Arabic texts during Middle Ages.

arabis, genus of herbs of Cruciferae family with white or purple flowers. Species incl. North American rock cress, *A. canadensis,* with long curved pods, and tower mustard, *A. glabra,* a widely distributed cress.

Arab-Israeli wars, series of conflicts, culminating on 4 occasions in outright war between Israel and Arab countries over existence in Palestine of independent Jewish state of Israel. Its proclamation (1948) led to immediate invasion by neighbouring Arab states; ended (1949) by UN armistice. Resulted in increased territ. for Israel, Egypt and Jordan. Egyptian seizure (1956) of Suez Canal precipitated Sinai campaign in which Israel succeeded in occupying Gaza Strip and most of Sinai; Israel gave these up on agreeing to UN cease-fire (Nov. 1956). Third war broke out in June, 1967, after Egypt blockaded Gulf of Aqaba to Israeli shipping. Israel extended frontiers to control W R. Jordan, E bank of Suez Canal, Sinai and Jordanian sector of Jerusalem. Fourth war (Yom Kippur war), Oct. 1973, involved Israeli crossing of Suez Canal after early Egyptian successes, as well as repulse of Syria at Golan Heights. UN supervised ceasefire following intervention by KISSINGER. Israel withdrew from Egyptian side of Suez Canal and relinquished control of Sinai strategic positions to UN.

Arab League, organization of Arab states formed (1945) to promote cooperation, esp. in defence and economic affairs; attempted joint Arab action against existence of state of Israel. Original members were Egypt, Syria, Lebanon, Jordan, Iraq, Saudi Arabia, Yemen; 11 more subsequently joined. Collective security agreement came into force 1952; failures in 1960s, esp. 1967 war, resulted in decline in League's importance as unifying force in Arab world.

Arabs, name given to large group of Arabic-speaking people in W Asia and N Africa bound by common tradition, Islamic religion and Arabic language. Main Arab countries are Egypt, Saudi Arabia, Iraq, Lebanon, Syria, Sudan, Libya, Tunisia and Yemen. Divided into settled Arabs and Bedouin nomad herdsmen.

Aracajú, port of NE Brazil, on Sergipe R. near Atlantic. Pop. 183,000. Sugar, rice, cotton exports. Sugar refining, textile mfg.

Arachne, in Greek myth, Lydian girl who challenged Athena to contest in weaving. Depicted love of the gods, thus angering Athena who destroyed the work. Hanged herself and was turned into spider by Athena.

Arachnida (arachnids), class of arthropods incl. spiders, scorpions, mites, ticks, king crabs. Mainly terrestrial, but king crab is aquatic. Characterized by 2 body sections and 6 pairs of appendages, 4 being locomotory.

Arad, city of W Romania, on R. Mureş. Pop. 143,000. Railway jct.; commercial, indust. centre in agric. area. Turkish fortress (16th-17th cent.); Austro-Hungarian until 1919.

Arafura Sea, extension of W Pacific Ocean, between Australia and New Guinea. Linked to Coral Sea by Torres Str.

Aragon, Louis (1897-), French writer. After early associations with DADA, wrote surrealist novel *Le Paysan de Paris* (1926). Became Communist; later works incl. poetry, *eg Le Crève-Coeur* (1941) inspired by participation in Resistance.

Aragón, region and former prov. of NE Spain. Incl. Pyrenees foothills, Ebro valley, part of C plateau; arid, sparsely pop. Main towns Saragossa, Huesca. Sheep rearing, irrigated agric., mineral deposits. Independent kingdom from 1035; united with Catalonia 1137, with Castile 1479 by marriage of Ferdinand and Isabella.

Araguaia, river of C Brazil. Rises on Mato Grosso plateau. Flows NE 2100 km (*c* 1300 mi) to join Tocantins R. Fork in middle course encloses large Bananal Isl.

Arakan, coastal region of Burma on Bay of Bengal. Bounded by Arakan Yoma Mts. Heavy monsoon rainfall; rice grown.

Aral Sea

Aral Sea, inland sea of USSR, on Kazakh-Uzbek SSR border; 4th largest lake in world. Area *c* 67,000 sq km

(26,000 sq mi). Slightly saline; no outlet. Fished for carp, perch.

Aram, Eugene (1704-59), English philologist. Notorious for murder (1745) of friend, for which he was acquitted, then, after discovery of skeleton, tried and hanged. Subject of poem by Thomas Hood, novel by Bulwer-Lytton.

Aramaic, language of Syria belonging to NW Semitic branch of Afro-Asiatic family. Now dead, widely spoken in centuries before and after Christ. Superseded by Arabic.

Aran Islands, small, rocky isl. group of Co. Galway, W Irish Republic, in Galway Bay. Largest is Inishmore. Fishing.

Arany, János (1817-82), Hungarian poet. Known for satirical *The Lost Constitution* (1846). Also wrote epic 'Toldi' trilogy (1846-79), ballads.

Ararat, Mount (*Agri Dagi*), mountain of NE Turkey, near border with Iran and Soviet Armenia. Has 2 main peaks; higher is Great Ararat, height 5156 m (16,916 ft), traditional resting place of Noah's Ark.

Araucanian Indians, South American peoples who occupied much of present-day Chile. Strongly resisted Spanish colonization from 1540 until final subjugation in 1883.

araucaria, genus of coniferous trees of S hemisphere. Species incl. Chile pine or monkey puzzle, *Araucaria araucana,* with stiff pointed leaves, edible nuts, widely grown as ornamental.

arbitration, *see* CONCILIATION, INDUSTRIAL.

arborvitae, any of several evergreen trees or shrubs of genus *Thuja* of cypress family. Flattened sprays of scale-like leaves. Species incl. American northern white cedar, *T. occidentalis.* Western red cedar, *T. plicata,* is source for interior woodwork.

Arbroath, town of Tayside region, E Scotland. Pop. 23,000. Formerly Aberbrothock. Fishing indust. (famous for smoked haddock); tourist resort; cloth mfg. Has 12th cent. abbey; scene of Robert I's Declaration of Independence (1320).

Arbuthnot, John (1667-1735), Scottish satirist and scientific writer, court physician to Queen Anne. Founded Scriblerus Club with Pope and Swift. Principal author of the *Memoirs of Martinus Scriblerus* (1741), satire on false taste. Political satire, the *History of John Bull* (5 pamphlets, 1712) estab. John Bull as national type.

arbutus, genus of trees or shrubs of the heath family with dark-green leaves, clusters of pinkish flowers and strawberry-like berries. Widely grown as ornamental.

arc, electric, luminous and intensely hot discharge produced when current flows through a gap between 2 electrodes; characterized by high current and low voltage. Carbon arcs used as sources of very bright light; heating effect utilized in electric arc furnace.

Arcadia, admin. dist. of S Greece, in C Peloponnese. Mainly mountainous. Isolated; pastoral farming from ancient times.

Arch, Joseph (1826-1919), English labour leader. Farm labourer and Methodist preacher, formed union of agric. labourers (1872).

arch, curved structure, *eg* of bricks or stone blocks, which supports weight of material over an open space. Keystone (inserted in centre of arch) pushes stress outwards. Types used incl. pointed arch, characteristic of Gothic buildings, and semi-circular arch, employed by Romans and revived in Renaissance.

Archaean era, *see* PRECAMBRIAN.

archaeology, the study of human past by systematic examination and tabulation of excavated relics. Little interest was shown in ancient remains until Renaissance, when Greek and Roman pottery, coins became highly prized. Systematic classification dates from concept of THREE AGE SYSTEM, introduced in 1818 by Thomsen. Scientific contributions to modern archaeology incl. radioactive dating methods.

archaeopteryx, earliest known fossil bird (Jurassic period), probably descended from dinosaur. Feathers on tail and wings; possession of teeth and claws on wings indicates reptilian origin. Flightless.

Archangel (*Arkhangelsk*), city of USSR, port of NW European RSFSR; at mouth of N R. Dvina. Pop. 355,000. Port icebound much of year, kept open by icebreakers; exports timber. Sawmilling and fishery centre. Founded 1553 with estab. of Muscovy Co.; only Russian seaport until St Petersburg founded (1703).

archangel, chief ANGEL. Best known are Michael, Gabriel, Raphael.

archbishop, high dignitary in episcopal churches. The archbishops of Canterbury and York are principal dignitaries of Church of England.

Archerfish

archerfish, *Toxotes jaculator,* freshwater fish of East Indies. Captures insect prey by spitting jets of water at them.

archery, art of shooting with bow and arrow, formerly practised in hunting and warfare, today solely a sport. Origins prob. reach back over 50,000 years; bow-making techniques were improved in Near East from *c* 2500 BC. Decisive in battles in Middle Ages (Crécy, Agincourt) until introduction of gunpowder. Official sport at Olympic Games since 1972.

Archimedes (*c* 287-212 BC), Greek mathematician, physicist, inventor. Created science of hydrostatics and worked out the principle of the lever. Determined areas under curves and volumes of solids by methods akin to calculus; obtained accurate approximation for π. Enunciated Archimedes' principle – upward thrust exerted on body immersed in fluid equals weight of fluid displaced.

archipelago, group or chain of islands. Ancient name for Aegean Sea and formerly used for any sea with many isls.

Archipenko, Aleksandr (1887-1964), American sculptor, b. Russia. Influenced by cubism, he made use of holes and concave surfaces to create new forms. Employed unusual materials, *eg* glass, plastic.

architecture, art of designing and constructing buildings, ideally aiming for maximum beauty and utility. Styles are influenced by climate, materials and techniques available, social and cultural settings. History of architecture is largely concerned with religious buildings, reaching back beyond 3000 BC to tombs of ancient Egypt. In 20th cent. techniques such as steel frame and reinforced concrete have revolutionized architecture.

arctic fox, *Alopex lagopus,* small fox of Arctic region. Valued for slate-grey fur which turns white in winter.

Arctic Ocean, ocean surrounding North Pole, lying entirely above Arctic Circle (66½° N). Area *c* 14,300,000 sq km (5,500,000 sq mi). Connected to Atlantic by Greenland Sea, to Pacific by Bering Strait. Largely covered by ice, which breaks into drifting pack-ice in summer.

Ardebil, town of NW Iran, near USSR border. Pop. 88,000. Agric. market centre; carpet mfg. Home of Safi ad-Din (14th cent.), leader of Sufi sect; his mausoleum is pilgrimage centre.

Arctic

Argentina

Arden, John (1930-), English playwright. Works, incl. *Live like Pigs* (1958), *Serjeant Musgrave's Dance* (1959), reflect ambivalent sympathies by mingling song, prose and verse dialogue.

Arden, Forest of, Warwickshire, WC England. Remnant of once extensive Midlands forest. Scene of Shakespeare's *As You Like It.*

Ardennes, plateau of SE Belgium, NE France, Luxembourg. Extensive woodland, some agric. Battlefield in both WWs.

Ardizzone, Edward Jeffrey Irving (1900-), British artist. Has written and illustrated numerous books, esp. for children, incl. *Tim All Alone* (1956). Official War Artist (1940-6).

Ards, dist. of E Northern Ireland. Area 361 sq km (129 sq mi); pop. 50,000. Created 1973, formerly part of Co. Down.

areca, genus of palm trees native to tropical Asia, Malaya, Australia. Smooth, slender trunk and feathery leaves. Species incl. betel palm, *Areca catechu,* bearing a nut.

Areopagus, Athenian council of elders with political and judicial powers in 6th and 5th cents. BC. Power reduced to jurisdiction in homicide cases by 462 BC. Named after hill near Acropolis where council met.

Arequipa, town of S Peru, alt. 2380 m (*c* 7800 ft). Pop. 195,000. Wool market; tourism. Founded (1540) by Pizarro on ancient Inca site. Damaged by frequent earthquakes.

Ares, in Greek myth, son of Zeus and Hera; god of war. Loved by Aphrodite. Appears as instigator of violence or as tempestuous lover. Identified by Romans with Mars.

Arethusa, in Greek myth, nymph loved by a river god, Alpheus, who pursued her to Syracuse where she was changed into a spring by Artemis. Alpheus flowed under the sea from Greece and joined her.

Aretino, Pietro (1492-1557), Italian writer, adventurer. Known for venomous and bawdy satire, called by Ariosto 'scourge of princes'. *Letters* give uninhibited picture of 16th cent. Italy.

Arezzo, city of NC Italy, cap. of Arezzo prov. Pop. 89,000. Agric. market, textiles. Etruscan, then Roman settlement. Red clay vases made in Roman times. Medieval cultural centre; Gothic cathedral, church (frescoes). Birthplace of Petrarch.

Argenteuil, suburb of Paris, N France, on right bank of R. Seine. Aero and vehicle industs., market gardens. Grew around convent founded 7th cent. by Charlemagne, at which Héloise was abbess (12th cent.).

Argentina, federal republic of S South America, on Atlantic. Area 2,776,889 sq km (1,072,157 sq mi); pop. 23,364,000; cap. Buenos Aires. Language: Spanish. Religion: RC. W boundary formed by Andes; cotton growing in Chaco plain (N); pop. and wealth in Pampas (beef, wheat produce); arid Patagonia plateau in S (sheep rearing, oil); indust. concentrated in Buenos Aires. Spanish colonization in 16th cent.; independence struggle led by San Martín (achieved 1816); republic estab. 1852. Ruled by successive dictatorships in 20th cent., esp. Perón (1946-55, 1973-4).

argentite, silver ore mineral. Dark grey in colour; composed of silver sulphide. Major sources in US, USSR, Australia.

Argolis, admin. dist. of SE Greece, in NE Peloponnese, cap. Nauplia. Wine, fruit. Ancient region, incl. Argos, Mycenae.

argon (Ar), inert gaseous element; at. no. 18, at. wt. 39.95. Found in air (0.9%); obtained by distillation of liquid air. Used to fill electric lamps, fluorescent tubes and as inert atmosphere for welding. Discovered (1894) by Rayleigh, Ramsay.

argonaut or **paper nautilus,** marine cephalopod mollusc, genus *Argonauta,* related to octopus. Female builds itself thin translucent shell to incubate eggs.

Argonauts, in Greek myth, band of heroes led by JASON, sent to bring GOLDEN FLEECE from king of Colchis to Greece. Sailed in ship *Argo* suffering many trials on outward and homeward journey, *eg* the Symplegades (clashing rocks), Scylla and Charybdis.

Argonne, hilly woodland of NE France, in Champagne and Lorraine. Strategic WWI battleground.

Argos, ancient city of S Greece, in NE Peloponnese. Pop. 17,000. Occupied from Bronze Age; 'Diomed' of Homer's *Iliad.* Centre of Argolis, dominated Peloponnese from 7th cent. BC; taken by Sparta *c* 494 BC, by Rome 146 BC. Heraeum temple nearby.

Argun, river of NE Asia, Length *c* 1530 km (950 mi). Rises in Heilungkiang prov., China, forms part of Soviet-Chinese border. Joins R. Shilka to form Amur. Fertile valley; corn, sugar beet grown.

Argus or **Argos,** in Greek myth, many-eyed herdsman charged by Hera to watch over Io, whom she had changed into a heifer. Slain by Hermes, his eyes were taken by Hera to deck the peacock's tail.

Argyll, Archibald Campbell, 8th Earl of (1607–61), Scottish nobleman. Led Covenanting forces against royalists in Civil War. After execution of Charles I, supported Charles II who had agreed to introduce Presbyterianism to England. Submitted to Cromwell (1652); beheaded after Restoration. His son, **Archibald Campbell, 9th Earl of Argyll** (1629-85), was beheaded for aiding Monmouth's rebellion. **John Campbell, 2nd Duke of Argyll and Duke of Greenwich** (1678-1743), was general responsible for quelling Jacobite rebellion of 1715.

Argyllshire, former county of W Scotland, now in Strathclyde region. Incl. some of Inner Hebrides; co. town was Inveraray. Mountainous; indented coast. Sheep, forestry, fishing, distilling, tourism.

aria, in music, composition for voice, esp. solo with orchestral accompaniment. A feature of operas, cantatas, oratorios since 1600.

Ariadne, in Greek myth, daughter of King Minos and Pasiphaë, who gave THESEUS the skein of thread by which he found his way out of the labyrinth after slaying the Minotaur. Fled with Theseus, but deserted by him on Naxos, was found by Dionysus who married her.

Arianism, see ARIUS.

Arica, port of extreme N Chile, on Pacific. Pop. 92,000. Important oil terminal. Taken in war with Peru (1884); now free trade zone for Bolivian, Peruvian mineral exports.

Aries, see ZODIAC.

Arion (*fl* late 7th cent. BC), semi-legendary Greek poet, credited with invention of dithyramb.

Ariosto, Ludovico (1474-1533), Italian poet. Famous for epic poem *Orlando Furioso* (1532) on Roland, sometimes called greatest Renaissance poem. Also wrote lyrics, satires, dramas.

Aristarchus of Samos (3rd cent. BC), Greek astronomer. Reputed to be 1st to hold theory that Earth revolves about Sun. Devised trigonometrical methods to determine relative distances of Sun and Moon from Earth.

Aristarchus of Samothrace (*c* 217-*c* 143 BC), Greek scholar. Librarian at Alexandria (*c*160-145), known as 'Great Grammarian' for scientific textual analysis, as shown by work on Homer.

Aristides [the Just] (*c* 530-*c* 468 BC), Athenian statesman, general. Ostracized (483 BC) by Themistocles, he fought at Salamis and commanded army in victory over Persians at Plataea (479 BC). Organized Delian League against Persia.

Aristippus (*c* 435-*c* 356 BC), Greek philosopher. Pupil of Socrates. Founder of Cyrenaics, holding pleasure to be the greatest good, virtue to be the ability to enjoy. Thus opposed to Cynics in first coherent statement of HEDONISM.

aristocracy, in political theory, term used for govt. by elite, usually hereditary, designated as best equipped to rule. Usage has widened to denote class from which governing elite is drawn, or those who by birth or wealth occupy privileged position compared with rest of community.

Aristophanes (*c* 450–*c* 385 BC), BC), Greek comic poet. Although not innovative, plays are greatest of Greek comedies, mixing political, social and literary satire, vigorous rather than savage. Only 11 plays extant, incl. *The Clouds, The Wasps, The Birds, Lysistrata,* and *The Frogs.*

Aristotle

Aristotle (384-322 BC), Greek philosopher. Pupil of Plato, tutor of Alexander the Great. Founded Peripatetic school of Athens (335 BC). Established the methods of Western philosophy in *eg, Analytics, Metaphysics, Ethics, Politics, Poetics.* Believed in Divine Being, but unlike Plato did not posit separate world of ideal essences. Held that happiness, goodness in man come from use of reason, *ie* fulfilment of intended function. Enlightened monarchy with aristocracy was his political ideal.

arithmetic, branch of mathematics dealing with real numbers, their addition, subtraction, multiplication, and division. Term also applies to study of whole numbers (integers), esp. prime numbers.

Arius (*c* 256-336), Libyan theologian. Advanced theory (Arianism) that Christ was not co-equal or co-eternal with God, thus renouncing Trinity. Condemned as heretic at 1st Council of Nicaea (325). Arianism persisted in N Africa and Spain until 6th cent.

Arizona, state of SW US. Area 295,024 sq km (113,909 sq mi); pop. 1,771,000; cap. Phoenix; other major city Tucson. Forested Colorado Plateau in C (incl. Grand Canyon), desert in S. Agric. irrigated by several dams (*eg* Roosevelt,

Coolidge); fruit, vegetables, wheat, beef, cotton farming. Copper, silver mining. Largest Indian pop. in US (many reservations). First explored in 16th cent. by Spanish; purchased by US (1848). Admitted to Union as 48th state (1912).

ark, in OT, *see* NOAH.

Arkansas, state of SC US. Area 137,539 sq km (53,104 sq mi); pop. 1,923,000; cap. Little Rock; other major cities Fort Smith, Hot Springs. Ozark Mts. in NW; Mississippi R. forms E border; crossed by White, Arkansas, Ouachita rivers. Agric. incl. cotton, soya bean growing, livestock farming; important bauxite mines. Part of French Louisiana Purchase (1803). Admitted to Union as state (1836).

Arkansas, river of C US. Rises in Rocky Mts. of C Colorado. Flows SE 2330 km (*c* 1450 mi) through Kansas, Oklahoma, Arkansas to Mississippi. Chief tributary Canadian R.

Arklow, town of Co. Wicklow, E Irish Republic, at mouth of R. Avoca. Pop. 7000. Fishing; fertilizers; tourism.

ark shell, marine bivalve mollusc of Arcidae family with boat-shaped shell.

Arkwright, Sir Richard (1732-92), English inventor. Developed mechanical spinning process (patent, 1769) which provided basis for mass-production in cotton indust.

Arlberg Pass, W Austria. Height 1801 m (5912 ft); links Vorarlberg (W) and Tyrol (E) by road and rail (latter uses tunnel, built 1884).

Arlen, Michael (1895-1956), English novelist, b. Bulgaria. Known for best-selling novel *The Green Hat* (1924) set in fantasy London society.

Arles, town of Provence, SE France, on Rhône delta. Pop. 46,000. Agric. market, wines, silk mfg. Important Roman, Gaulish centre; archbishopric from 4th cent. Cap. of kingdom of Arles (933-1378). Roman remains incl. arena, theatre; has cathedral (11th cent.).

Arlington National Cemetery, burial ground of US war dead (estab. 1864). Opposite Washington, DC, on Potomac R. Incl. tomb of Unknown Soldier and also notable citizens, *eg* J.F. Kennedy.

arm, in man, upper limb of body, extending from shoulder to wrist. Skeleton is formed by humerus in upper arm, radius and ulna in forearm.

Armada, Spanish, fleet of 130 ships sent (1588) by Philip II of Spain to carry invasion force against England. Attacked by English fleet under Howard off Plymouth, and later broken up by fire ships off Calais. Suffered heavy losses through storm damage while escaping via Scotland and W coast of Ireland; less than half of fleet reached Spain.

Three-banded armadillo (*Tolypeutes tricinctus*)

armadillo, burrowing mammal of Dasypodidae family found from S US to South America. Body armour-plated with bony discs; rolls up into ball when threatened. Species incl. nine-banded armadillo, *Dasypus novemcinctus,* found in Texas.

Armageddon, in Bible, esp. Book of Revelation, scene of last, decisive battle between forces of good and evil, to be fought before the Day of Judgment. Name prob. refers to the 'hill of Megiddo' which was a proverbial symbol of war because of its many ancient battles.

Armagh, former county of S Northern Ireland. Low-lying in N; hilly in S. Agric.; cattle rearing; linen mfg. Co. town was **Armagh.** Pop. 12,000. Ecclesiastical cap. of Ireland from 5th cent. Has Protestant, RC cathedrals. **Armagh,**

district; area 675 sq km (260 sq mi); pop. 47,000. Created 1973, formerly part of Co. Armagh.

Armenian SSR

Armenia, hist. region and former kingdom, now divided between Turkey, Iran and USSR. Mainly plateau, incl. Mt. Ararat and sources of Tigris and Euphrates. Embraced Christianity (303); changed hands repeatedly, with Russia taking what is now Armenian SSR from Persia in 19th cent. Turkish attempts to suppress Armenian nationalism led to massacres (1894-1915).

Armenian, language in Thraco-Phrygian branch of Indo-European family. Spoken mainly in Armenian SSR. Although ancient, not written until 5th cent. AD. Modern form known as Ashksarhik.

Armenian Soviet Socialist Republic, constituent republic of SW USSR, bounded on S and W by Iran and Turkey. Area 29,800 sq km (11,500 sq mi); pop. 2,493,000. Cap. Yerevan. Mainly mountainous with high plateaux; produces cotton, tobacco, wine; minerals incl. copper, molybdenum, zinc. Region seized by Russia from Persia (1828); incorporated by USSR (1920).

Arminius (d. AD 21), German chieftain. Organized rebellion against Romans and destroyed (AD 9) legions under Quintilius Varus. Defeat led Romans to withdraw from territ. E of Rhine.

Arminius, Jacobus, orig. Jacob Harmensen (1560-1609), Dutch Reformed theologian. Opposed Calvinist teaching of absolute predestination. Teachings formulated (1622) by Simon Episcopus became known as Arminianism.

armistice, truce before signing of peace treaty; temporary stopping of hostilities by mutual agreement. Armistice Day (11 Nov.) anniversary of WWI armistice (1918), commemorated by National Day of Remembrance (UK), Veterans Day (US).

Armory Show, international art exhibition held at 69th Regiment Armory, New York, in 1913. Introduced modern European art into US ; cubist, fauvist, post-impressionist and symbolist works were shown.

Louis Armstrong

Armstrong, Louis ('Satchmo') (1900-71), American jazz trumpeter, band leader, singer. First musician to develop a solo style in jazz, he created stunning improvisations that defined the role of the soloist. Known internationally for his ability to entertain audiences.

Neil Armstrong, first man on the Moon

Armstrong, Neil (1930-), American astronaut. As member of *Apollo XI* mission (July, 1969), became 1st man to set foot on Moon; accompanied by **(Edwin) 'Buzz' Aldrin** (1930-), while **Michael Collins** (1930-) remained in Moon orbit in command module.

army, organized body of men, trained and armed for military combat on land. Professional standing army developed with growth of Roman Empire. In feudal Europe, military service was obligatory among knights and yeomanry. System declined with increased use of mercenaries. CONSCRIPTION was introduced during French Revolutionary Wars. During peacetime, modern army often made up of enlisted volunteers.

army ant or **driver ant,** nomadic ant, esp. of genus *Eciton* found in South American tropics. Travels in long columns, devouring animals in its path.

army worm, larva of noctuid moth, *Pseudaletia unipuncta.* Can move in large groups, devouring crops. Major pest in US.

Arnauld, Antoine (1612-94), French theologian. Wrote pro-Jansenist *De la fréquente communion* (1643), attacking Jesuits. Collaborated on Port-Royal textbooks. His sister, **Jacqueline Marie Arnauld** (1591-1661), was abbess of Port-Royal convent from 1599, adopting name Marie-Angélique de Ste Madeleine. Introduced Jansenist teaching to Port-Royal, making it famous for strict discipline, piety of nuns.

Arne, Thomas Augustine (1710-78), English composer. Wrote many operas, but best known for his tuneful songs, incl. 'Rule Britannia' and several Shakespeare settings.

Arnhem, city of EC Netherlands, on R. Rhine, cap. of Gelderland prov. Pop. 134,000. Railway jct., engineering, textiles. Scene of defeat (1944) of British airborne assault.

Arnhem Land, aboriginal reserve of NE Northern Territ., Australia. Pop. *c* 4000; white settlement confined to mission stations. Mainly swamp and grassland; monsoon climate. Bauxite development at Gove.

Arnim, Elizabeth von, pseud. of Countess Russell, née Mary Annette Beauchamp (1856-1941), English novelist, b. Australia. Known for *Elizabeth and Her German Garden* (1898), whimsical account of her marriage to Count von Arnim.

Arnim, Ludwig Joachim von (1781-1831), German poet. With brother-in-law Brentano, pub. folksong collection *The Boy's Magic Horn* (1805-8). Wife, **Bettina von Arnim** (1785-1859), pub. *Goethe's Correspondence with a Child* (1835), semi-fictitious memoir of her childhood correspondence with Goethe.

Arno, river of NC Italy. Flows 240 km (150 mi) from Apennines via Florence, Pisa to Ligurian Sea. Fertile, scenic valley.

Thomas Arne

Arnold, Benedict (1741-1801), American general. Held commands during American Revolution, but plotted to betray West Point garrison. Discovered but escaped and later fought for British.

Arnold, Sir Edwin (1832-1904), English orientalist. Wrote blank-verse epic on life of Buddha, *The Light of Asia* (1879). Translated many Oriental literary works.

Arnold, Thomas (1795–1842), English educator. As headmaster of Rugby (1827-42), he reformed English public school system, creating modern pattern. Also a classical scholar, historian. His son, **Matthew Arnold** (1822-88), was a poet and critic. Held that poetry should be 'criticism of life', saw culture as the only means to save society from Victorian materialism. Poems incl. 'The Scholar Gypsy' (1853), 'Thyrsis' (1866), criticism incl. *Essays in Criticism* (2 series 1865, 18888). Major figure in English critical tradition.

Arnold of Brescia (c 1090-1155), Italian religious reformer. Attacked clerical corruption, esp. possession of property by the Church. Condemned with Abelard by Synod of Sens (1140). Became leader of republican commune in Rome, but was executed as a political rebel when Adrian IV restored papal power.

aromatic compounds, in chemistry, organic compounds derived from benzene. Many such compounds, esp. those discovered first, have recognizable odours.

Arp, Jean or **Hans** (1887-1966), French sculptor and painter. Associated with dada and surrealist groups. Produced 2-dimensional works, incl. collages, flat reliefs, and sculpture in the round; sculpture of 1930s suggests organic forms while remaining abstract.

arquebus or **harquebus,** small-calibre gun operated by matchlock, precursor of the musket. Prominent in 16th cent. Italian wars.

arrack, alcoholic liquor made mainly in Asian countries from fermented rice, molasses or coconut palm juice.

Arran, isl. of Strathclyde region, W Scotland. Area 430 sq km (166 sq mi); pop. 4000; main town Brodick. Tourism, hill-walking.

Arras, town of N France, on canalized R. Scarpe, cap. of Pas-de-Calais dept. Pop. 54,000. Agric. market, engineering. Medieval tapestry indust. Hist. cap. of Artois, under Spanish rule 1493-1640. Birthplace of Robespierre.

Arras, Treaty of, agreement (1482) between Louis XI of France and Maximilian of Austria. Maximilian was to cede duchy of Burgundy, Artois and Franche-Comté (inherited at death of his wife, Mary of Burgundy) to France.

Arrebo, Anders Kristensen (1587-1637), Danish poet, bishop of Trondheim (1618-22). Best known for Creation epic *Hexaëmeron rhythmico-danicum* (1630-7), introducing Alexandrine into N Europe.

arrest, seizure and taking into custody of person by authority of law. In civil law, can only take place on issue of court order. Arrest may be made with or without warrant when a crime is thought to have been committed; both law officers and private individuals are empowered and have duty to arrest person suspected of committing felony or breach of the peace in their presence.

Arrhenius, Svante August (1859-1927), Swedish chemist. Awarded Nobel Prize for Chemistry (1903) for his theory of electrolytic dissociation (ionization), explaining ability of certain solutions to conduct electricity.

arrowhead, any aquatic perennial of genus *Sagittaria* of water plantain family. Arrow-shaped leaves, small, white, cup-like flowers.

arrowroot, several tropical plants with starchy roots; esp. *Maranta arundinacea* with large leaves, white flowers, whose roots yield easily-digestible starch.

arrow wood, any of several shrubs, esp. of honeysuckle family. Several North American species formerly used by Indians to make arrows.

arrow-worm, *see* CHAETOGNATHA.

arsenic (As), chemical element; at. no. 33, at. wt. 74.92. Exists in 3 allotropic forms, commonest being grey crystalline arsenic. Occurs as realgar (As_2S_3), white arsenic (AS_2O_3) and arsenopyrite (FeAsS). Its extremely poisonous compounds used in weed and insect killers, also medicinally.

arsphenamine, organic compound of arsenic discovered (1910) by Paul Ehrlich. Formerly used to treat syphilis, it was 1st drug to be prepared specifically for treatment of a particular disease.

art, visual, branch of human activity, divided into PAINTING, SCULPTURE and ARCHITECTURE. Individual articles in this encyclopedia on styles of painting incl.: MANNERISM, IMPRESSIONISM, FAUVISM, CUBISM, POP and OP ART, FUTURISM, ABSTRACT EXPRESSIONISM, POST-IMPRESSIONISM, ABSTRACT ART, SOCIAL REALISM. For various articles on architectural styles *see*: BAROQUE, ROCOCO, ROMANESQUE, NORMAN ARCHITECTURE, GOTHIC, EARLY ENGLISH, PERPENDICULAR, DECORATED STYLE, NEO-CLASSICISM, GOTHIC REVIVAL.

Artaud, Antonin (c 1895-1948), French avant-garde dramatic theorist, producer. In *The Theatre of Cruelty* (1935), *The Theatre and Its Double* (1938) stressed that theatre should interpret experience in primitive images.

art deco, decorative style of late 1920s and 1930s, deriving its name from Exposition Internationale des Arts Décoratifs et Industriels Modernes (1925) in Paris. Characterized by geometric design, bright metallic surfaces, it attempted to express 'machine' aesthetic. Popular again in 1970s.

Artemis, in Greek myth, daughter of Zeus and Leto; sister of Apollo. Virgin goddess of hunting, wildlife, chastity, childbirth. Associated with the moon because of its supposed influence on organic life. Identified by Romans with Diana.

artemisia, genus of perennial herbs of Compositae family. Native to temperate and arctic regions. Scented foliage and small rayless flowers. Species incl. wormwood, mugwort, sagebrush, tarragon.

arteriosclerosis, hardening and thickening of walls of the arteries. Usually caused by deposition of fatty material, *eg* cholesterol, in linings of arteries. Frequently occurs in old age.

artery, any vessel carrying blood from heart to body tissues. Arteries have thick walls, lined with elastic fibres and muscles to withstand blood pressure.

artesian well, drilled well which relies on hydrostatic pressure to force water to surface. Pressure created within syncline, which comprises water-bearing layer (aquifer) sandwiched between impermeable strata. Named after Artois, France, where 1st such well was drilled.

Artevelde, Jacob van (c 1290-1345), Flemish statesman. Nicknamed 'Brewer of Ghent'. Head of Ghent govt. during Anglo-French war; negotiated agreement on Flemish neutrality, and commercial treaty with England. His son,

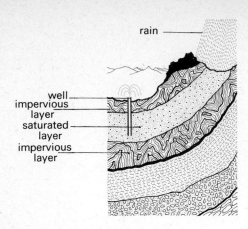

Artesian well

Philip van Artevelde (c 1340-82), led weavers' revolt (1381) against Count of Flanders; defeated after French intervention, killed.

arthritis, inflammation of joints. Rheumatoid arthritis, most severely crippling form, is characterized by inflammation of connective tissue around joints, esp. those of wrist and hand; often leads to deformity of joints. Cause unknown. Osteoarthritis is degeneration of joints, with loss of cartilage lining and growth of bone. Occurs mainly in elderly people, esp. in joints of leg and spine.

Arthropoda (arthropods), largest phylum of animal kingdom, incl. arachnids, crustaceans, insects, centipedes, millipedes. Segmented body, horny outer skeleton, primitive brain; various jointed appendages serve as limbs, gills or jaws.

Arthur, see ARTHURIAN LEGEND.

Arthur I (1187-c 1203), duke of Brittany (1196-c 1203). Posthumous son of Geoffrey, 4th son of Henry II of England. Rival to Prince John in claim for English throne after death of Richard I (1199). Captured by John; imprisoned at Rouen, prob. murdered there.

Arthur, Chester Alan (1830-86), American statesman, Republican president (1881-5). Nominated and elected vice-president (1880), acceded on Garfield's assassination. Supported civil service reform (1883), prosecuted corruption in civil service.

Arthurian legend, mass of interrelated stories prob. drawn from Celtic legend centring on King Arthur and his court. Arthur first mentioned in Celtic literature, c 600, as leader of Britons. GEOFFREY OF MONMOUTH's *Historia* (c1135) portrayed Arthur as conqueror of W Europe. Wace's *Roman de Brut* (c1155) first treated story as courtly romance, introduced Round Table. CHRÉTIEN DE TROYES (12th cent.) wrote 5 romances dealing with Arthur's knights. First treatment of Tristram and Isolde story was by German poet GOTTFRIED VON STRASSBURG. After 1225 literary tradition continued only in England, with anon. *Sir Gawain and the Green Knight* (c1370) and MALORY's *Morte d'Arthur.* Full story makes Arthur illegitimate son of King Uther Pendragon, who demonstrates royal blood by removing sword from stone. Later receives invincible sword Excalibur from Lady in the Lake, and estab. court at Camelot, marrying Guinevere and gathering around his Round Table best knights of Christendom. Decline begins with Holy Grail quest (dispersing knights), with Sir Lancelot's love for Guinevere, and ends with Sir Mordred (Arthur's son) fatally wounding Arthur. He is taken to Avalon, whence he will return in time of national peril. Other figures incl. Sir Galahad and Sir Percival, pure heroes of Holy Grail quest; Sir Gawain, Arthur's nephew; Merlin, magician and adviser to Arthur; Morgan le Fay, Arthur's half-sister and enchantress.

artichoke, name for 2 different garden vegetables of Compositae family. *Cynara scolymus,* native to Africa, is French or globe artichoke. Jerusalem artichoke, *Helianthus tuberosus,* is perennial sunflower with tuberous roots used as vegetable or livestock feed.

Articles of Confederation, see CONFEDERATION, ARTICLES OF.

artificial insemination, method of introducing semen from male into female artificially to facilitate fertilization. Widely used in propagation of animals, esp. livestock. Sometimes used in humans when normal fertilization impossible.

artificial kidney, mechanical device which substitutes for lost kidneys. Blood is led from arteries by cellophane tube and waste products removed by DIALYSIS. Used 2 or 3 times per week.

artificial respiration, restoration or maintenance of breathing by manual or mechanical means. Mechanical devices used incl. IRON LUNG. Mouth-to-mouth method involves forcing breath into patient's mouth, while holding his nostrils shut.

artillery, originally any form of armament involving discharge of a projectile, incl. bow, catapult. Now any type of heavy firearm fired from carriage or platform.

Artiodactyla, order of herbivorous mammals, distinguished by possession of 2 or 4 hoofed toes. Incl. camel, deer, sheep, cattle.

Art nouveau jewellery

art nouveau, term used to describe style of decorative art, at its height in Europe and North America c 1890-1910. Characterized by flat curvilinear designs based on natural forms. Applied in architecture and interior design (by Horta, van de Velde, Mackintosh), jewellery, book illustration (by Beardsley), glassware (by Louis Tiffany).

Artois, region and former prov. of N France, cap. Arras. Mainly agric., incl. part of Franco-Belgian coalfield. Disputed by France and the Habsburgs, finally taken by France 1640. Scene of many battles in WWI. Gave name to artesian wells, first sunk here in 12th cent.

arts and crafts movement, artistic and social movement, originating in late 19th cent. England, which tried to revive standard of decorative arts and restore creative dignity of craftsmen in reaction to debased quality of manufactured goods. Influenced by work and theories of William Morris, cooperative workshops were founded to produce furniture, textiles, wallpaper, pottery.

Artsybashev, Mikhail Petrovich (1870-1927), Russian novelist, dramatist. Created sensation with novels *Sanin* (1907), *Breaking-point* (1912), for their frank, disillusioned treatment of sex. Exiled 1921.

Aruba, see NETHERLANDS ANTILLES.

arum, any plant of Araceae family. Has thick fleshy leaves with spathe at base, small flowers. Native mainly to tropical swamps and temperate Eurasia.

Arundel, Thomas Howard, 2nd Earl of (1585-1646), English art collector. Carried out excavations in Italy and had antiquities sought out for him abroad; his collection of ancient sculptures was donated to Oxford Univ. (1667). Formed noted manuscript and painting collection, incl. works of Holbein.

Arundel, mun. bor. of West Sussex, SE England, on R. Arun. Has 11th cent. castle, seat of dukes of Norfolk.

Arvida, town of EC Québec, Canada; on Saguenay R. Pop. 18,000. H.e.p. from river provides power for large aluminium smelter.

Aryan, Sanskrit word used for peoples speaking Indo-European languages. The Aryans originally spread (from *c* 2000 BC) throughout Mesopotamia from S Russia and Turkestan. Term used, with little scientific basis, in Nazi ideology to designate Indo-European race.

aryl group, in chemistry, organic RADICAL or group of atoms derived from aromatic compounds, *eg* phenyl radical C_6H_5.

asafetida, soft brown gum resin obtained from roots of various Asiatic plants of genus *Ferula*. Bitter acrid taste and unpleasant odour. Formerly used in medicine as a carminative and antispasmodic.

Asahikawa, city of Japan, WC Hokkaido isl. Pop. 288,000. Indust. centre; sake brewing, wood products and textile mfg.

asbestos, silicate mineral with fibrous structure. Common forms are chrysotile (type of SERPENTINE), crocidolite; often found as veins in other rock. Resistant to fire and acid, fibres may be pressed into plasterboard, woven into ropes, clothing, pipe insulation, *etc*. Major sources in Canada, South Africa, Rhodesia.

Asbury, Francis (1745-1816), American clergyman, b. England. Sent as missionary by John Wesley in 1771. Estab. 'circuit rider' system of itinerant preachers on frontier. First American Methodist-Episcopal bishop.

Ascension, isl. in S Atlantic, NW of St Helena. Area 88 sq km (34 sq mi). Site of American satellite tracking station. Dependency of St Helena since 1922.

Ascension, Christian festival, celebrating the bodily ascent of Jesus into heaven on the 40th day after Resurrection.

asceticism, doctrine that man can reach a higher spiritual state by rigorous self-discipline and self-denial. Has been common in the major monotheistic religions, also Hinduism, Buddhism and among the CYNICS. May involve prolonged fasting, self-mutilation, flagellation.

Asch, Sholem (1880-1957), American author, b. Poland. Important figure in modern Yiddish literature. Biblical novels incl. *The Nazarene* (1939), *The Prophet* (1955). Interpreted Christianity as an extension of Judaism.

Ascham, Roger (1515-68), English classical scholar and humanist. Tutor, subsequently Latin secretary to Elizabeth I. Wrote *Toxophilus* (1545) on virtues of English long-bow, *The Schoolmaster* (1570), an unfinished treatise on education.

Asclepius, mythical Greek physician, son of Apollo. Learned art of medicine from CHIRON. Killed by Zeus for raising Hippolytus from the dead. Worshipped as god of healing, esp. at Epidaurus. Serpent was sacred to him. Known as Aesculapius by Romans.

ascorbic acid or **vitamin C,** crystalline water-soluble solid, occurring in fruit and vegetables. Necessary in diet of humans and guinea pigs to form fibres of connective tissue (absence causes scurvy). Identified 1932. Held to be effective in counteracting colds.

Ascot, village of Berkshire, S England. Has famous racecourse at Ascot Heath estab. 1711.

Asgard, in Norse myth, home of the gods (Aesir) and slain heroes. Consisted of many great banqueting halls, incl. VALHALLA. Entered via rainbow bridge, Bifrost, guarded by Heimdal, watchman of the gods.

ash, any tree of genus *Fraxinus*. Pinnate leaves, winged fruit, tough elastic wood. Source of valuable timber. Incl. common European ash, *F. excelsior*, as well as white ash *F. americana* and black ash *F. nigra* of US.

Ashanti, admin. region of S Ghana. Hilly and forested, produces cocoa, hardwoods; noted for gold working. Hist. stronghold of Ashanti tribe, cap. Kumasi; wars against British in 19th cent. led to annexation by Gold Coast colony (1901), break-up of Ashanti confederation. Region of Ghana from 1957.

Ashby de la Zouch, urban dist. of Leicestershire, C England. Pop. 7000. In coalmining area. Castle, where Mary Queen of Scots imprisoned (1569), appears in Scott's *Ivanhoe*.

ashcan school, popular name for group of American painters, called 'The Eight', who exhibited in New York in 1908. Attempted to portray contemporary scene in realistic terms. Led by Robert Henri, group incl. Arthur Davies, William Glackens. Organized ARMORY SHOW.

Ashcroft, Dame Edith Margaret Emily ('Peggy') (1907-), English actress. Notable in Shakespearian roles and as Margaret in *Dear Brutus*, Miss Madrigal in *The Chalk Garden*.

Ashdod, port of SW Israel. Pop. 40,000. Construction indust. Ancient city of Philistines.

Ashes, the, mythical cricket trophy said to be held by the winning team of test series between England and Australia. Name derives from mock obituary of English cricket written in *Sporting Times* (1882), stating that 'the body will be cremated and the ashes taken to Australia'.

Ashkenazim, term applied to Jews who settled in N and C Europe. Distinguished from Sephardim, those who settled in Iberian penin.

Ashkhabad, town of USSR, cap. of Turkmen SSR; near Iran border. Pop. 266,000. Textile mfg. Founded 1881, almost destroyed by earthquake in 1948.

Ashtart, *see* ASTARTE.

Ashton, Sir Frederick William Mallandaine (1906-), British choreographer, dancer, b. Ecuador. Founder choreographer to the Royal Ballet, director (1963-70). Ballets incl. *Façade, Enigma Variations, Tales of Beatrix Potter* (film, 1971).

Ash Wednesday, first day of Christian LENT, seventh Wednesday before Easter. Name derived from custom of sprinkling ashes on the forehead as sign of penitence.

Asia, largest and most populous continent of the world. Bounded by Pacific (E), Arctic (N), Indian (S) oceans; stretches from Ural Mts. (USSR) and Asia Minor in W to Bering Str., Japan and Indonesia in E. Area *c* 43,300,000 sq km (16,700,000 sq mi). Pop. *c* 2,060,000,000. Mountain ranges incl. Himalayas, whose peaks, *eg* MT. EVEREST, are highest in world. Major rivers Yenisei, Ob in Siberia; Yangtze, Mekong, Amur (S, SE); Indus, Ganges (S), Tigris, Euphrates (SW), centres of earliest known civilizations. Cold Siberian tundra merges in S with coniferous forestland; wooded steppes merge into desert regions of W China. In SE are fertile monsoon coastlands and river valleys of China, Japan, India, Indonesia and Indo-China, all densely populated and supported by rice crops. Vast oil reserves in SW desert regions (Arabia) now exploited; mineral resources in Siberia being developed.

Asia Minor or **Anatolia,** penin. of W Asia, between Black Sea, Mediterranean and Aegean; comprises Asiatic Turkey. High plateau crossed by Taurus Mts. in S; dry interior with many salt lakes. Scene of ancient cultures and numerous invasions; fell to Ottoman Turks 13th-15th cent.

Asimov, Isaac (1920-), American scientist and writer, b. Russia. Author of science fiction, *eg I, Robot* (1950), and scientific books for layman, *eg The Intelligent Man's Guide to Science* (1960).

Aske, Robert (d. 1537), English lawyer. Leader of PILGRIMAGE OF GRACE. Although tried to prevent 2nd revolt, was arrested and executed for high treason.

Asmara, city of N Ethiopia, cap. of Eritrea prov. on plateau. Pop. 241,000. Trade centre in agric. region; textiles, ceramics mfg.; univ. (1958). Railway link to Massawa. Cap. of Italian colony of Eritrea from 1890 until taken in 1941 by British.

Asoka (d. *c* 230 BC), Indian emperor of Maurya dynasty. Extended his empire over Afghanistan, Baluchistan and most of India. Abandoned wars after conversion to Buddhism, which he made state religion. Sent Buddhist missionaries abroad.

asp, one of several species of small poisonous snakes incl. *Vipera aspis* of S Europe, and Egyptian cobra.

asparagus, *Asparagus officinalis,* perennial garden vegetable native to Eurasia, cultivated in Britain, US. Tender shoots considered delicacy. Decorative species incl. *A. plumosus.*

Aspasia (fl 5th cent. BC), Greek courtesan. Mistress of Pericles, who could not marry her as she was a foreigner. Held important position in Athenian intellectual life.

aspen, any of several species of poplars with flattened leaves. Incl. *Populus tremula* of Europe as well as *P. tremuloides* and *P. grandidentata* of North America. Soft wood of some species is source of pulp.

asphalt, brown or black tar-like substance composed of various hydrocarbons. Occurs in asphalt lakes; obtained as residue of petroleum distillation. Used in road making and water-proofing.

asphodel, hardy stemless plant of genera *Asphodelus* and *Asphodeline* of lily family, native to Eurasia. Has showy flower spikes.

Aspidistra

aspidistra, genus of Asiatic herbs of lily family. Has stiff, glossy, evergreen leaves, dark inconspicuous flowers near ground. Cultivated as house plant.

aspirin or **acetylsalicylic acid,** white crystalline solid used to reduce fever and relieve pain. Dangerous in excessive doses as it may cause bleeding in stomach.

Asquith, Herbert Henry, 1st Earl of Oxford and Asquith (1852-1928), British statesman, PM (1908-16). Headed Liberal govt. which introduced national insurance scheme after depriving Lords of veto power in 1911 PARLIAMENT ACT. Attempt to estab. Irish Home Rule failed. Resigned in favour of Lloyd George following WWI reverses.

ass, small horse-like mammal, genus *Equus,* found wild in semi-desert areas of Africa and Asia. Species incl. African ass, *E. asinus,* and Asian ass, *E. hemionus.* Noted for endurance; domesticated varieties, incl. donkey, used as pack animals. Mule is offspring of jackass with horse mare, hinny offspring of she-ass with horse stallion; both sterile.

Assam, state of NE India. Area *c* 77,700 sq km (30,000 sq mi); pop. 14,952,000; cap. Shillong. Almost enclosed by mountains; pop. concentrated in fertile river valleys, *eg* Brahmaputra. Heavy rainfall; produces timber, tea, rice. Incl. Northeast Frontier Agency union territ.

assassination, murder (esp. of politically important person) by surprise attack. Word derives from Moslem secret sect, the Assassins.

Assassins, members of a secret sect in Islam, founded *c* 1090 by Hasan Sabbah in Persia. Distinguished by total obedience to their leader, supposedly while under the influence of hashish. Regarded murder as sacred duty to eliminate enemies, incl. Crusaders. Purged by Mongols (from 1256).

Assent, Royal, in UK law, formal consent given by sovereign to bill after its passage through Parliament, condition of its becoming an act of Parliament. Last refused by Queen Anne (1702).

Assiniboine, river of Canada. Rises in E Saskatchewan, flows SE 950 km (590 mi) into Manitoba to join Red R. at Winnipeg.

Assisi, town of Umbria, C Italy. Pop. 24,000. Religious, tourist centre, overlooking Spoleto valley. Birthplace of St Francis; churches (frescoed by Cimabue, Giotto) built (13th cent.) over his tomb.

assizes, in England, court sessions held periodically by judges of High Court in regions to try civil and criminal cases. Assize towns grouped in 7 circuits, with 2 judges travelling each circuit.

The convent of St Francis, Assisi

Associated Press (AP), American news agency. Founded (1848) as New York Associated Press, cooperative venture by several newspapers to cover Mexican War; international offices, hq. still New York.

association, in psychology, principle according to which ideas, feelings are connected in mind of the individual because of their previous occurrence together. In sociology, basic social unit, esp. one with common goal(s).

Association football or **soccer,** eleven-a-side team game played with round leather ball. Follows rules set down by Football Association in London (1863). Played worldwide, esp. on professional basis in Europe and South America. First professionals in England (1880s), League estab. 1888. International competition is controlled by FIFA (founded 1904) which organizes World Cup every 4 years (first held 1930).

Assuan, *see* ASWAN, Egypt.

Assurbanipal (d. *c* 626 BC), Assyrian king (669-626 BC). Completed conquest of Egypt begun under his father Esarhaddon, but lost control of country in 660. Suppressed revolt in Babylonia and sacked Babylon (648). Known for his palace and library of cuneiform tablets, excavated at Nineveh. Empire declined after his death.

Assurnasirpal II, king of Assyria, one of the earliest Assyrian conquerors

Assyria, ancient empire of SW Asia, centred on Ashur on upper R. Tigris. *Fl* 9th-7th cents. BC when it gained ascendancy in Middle East esp. under Sargon II and Sennacherib. Conquered Egypt 671 BC under Esarhaddon and reached height of its power under Assurbanipal. Empire declined rapidly and cap. Nineveh was destroyed 612 BC by Medes and Babylonians.

Fred Astaire and Ginger Rogers in *Top Hat*

Astaire, Fred, pseud. of Frederick Austerlitz (1899-   ), American dancer, singer, film actor. Known for films, esp. with Ginger Rogers, expressing 1930s' elegance, wit, *eg Top Hat* (1935), *Swing Time* (1936).

Astarte or **Ashtart,** Semitic goddess of fertility and love. Associated with planet Venus. Identified with Babylonian Ishtar and Greek Aphrodite.

astatine (At), radioactive element of halogen group; at. no. 85, mass no. of most stable isotope 210. Half-life 8.3 hrs. First prepared 1940 by bombarding bismuth with alpha particles.

aster, large genus of perennial plants of Compositae family. Purplish, blue, pink or white daisy-like flowers. Most garden varieties derived from North American fall-blooming species. Cultivated as Michaelmas daisies in Europe.

asteroid or **planetoid,** minor planet of Solar System. Over 1600 recognized, most of which lie in belt between Mars and Jupiter. Largest and 1st discovered (1801) is Ceres, diameter 686 km (427 mi).

Asteroidea, see STARFISH.

asthma, chronic disorder characterized by difficulty in breathing. Results from spasm of muscles in bronchial tubes and is accompanied by accumulation of mucus. Often caused by allergy or emotional stress.

Asti, town of Piedmont, NW Italy, cap. of Asti prov. Pop. 77,000. Distilleries; famous for sparkling wines (Asti Spumante).

astigmatism, irregularity in curvature of lens (incl. eye lens); results in light rays from mutually perpendicular planes being brought to different focal points. Use of cylindrical lens corrects astigmatism of eye.

Aston, Francis William (1877-1945), English chemist. Used mass spectrograph to show existence of isotopes in non-radioactive elements, *eg* neon. Awarded Nobel Prize for Chemistry (1922).

Astor, John Jacob (1763-1848), American millionaire, b. Germany. Amassed immense fortune after start as fur trader, estab. family as prominent New Yorkers. Great-grandson, **William Waldorf Astor, 1st Viscount Astor** (1848-1919), moved to England in 1890, founded English branch of family, known for philanthropy. His daughter-in-law, **Nancy Witcher Astor,** née Langhorne (1879-1964), was 1st woman to sit in House of Commons (1919-45). Famous political hostess, influenced govt. policy through 'Cliveden set', Conservative group who met at her Cliveden house parties.

Astrakhan, city of USSR, SE European RSFSR; on Volga Delta. Pop. 427,000. Centre of river transport; shipbuilding, fish processing (esp. caviare). Cap. of Tartar khanate, taken by Ivan the Terrible 1556.

astringent, drug used to contract body tissue and check bleeding, mucus secretion, *etc.* Examples incl. aluminium salts, tannin, silver nitrate.

astrolabe, ancient and medieval scientific instrument used to measure altitude of heavenly bodies. Consisted of graduated metal disc with pivoted sighting arm. Replaced by quadrant and sextant.

astrology, form of divination based on theory that all events on Earth are determined by movements of heavenly bodies. Basis of ancient astronomy, from which it diverged after Copernicus. Individual's fate predicted by use of horoscope, map of heavens at time of birth, drawing on chart of ZODIAC.

astronomy, scientific study of nature, position and motion of heavenly bodies. Of ancient origin, *fl* under Greeks; their findings, summarized by Ptolemy, were displaced by Copernican theory in 16th cent. Newton's laws of motion and gravitation provided basis for later study. Branches incl. astrophysics, cosmology, radio and X-ray astronomy.

astrophysics, branch of astronomy dealing with physical properties of heavenly bodies and also their origin and evolution.

Asturias, Miguel Angel (1899-1974), Guatemalan author, diplomat. Novels incl. *El Señor Presidente* (1946), *Mulata de tal* (1963, *The Mulatta and Mr Fly*), use technique of 'magical realism'. Nobel Prize for Literature (1967).

Asturias, region and former kingdom of NW Spain, hist. cap. Oviedo. Cantabrian Mts. in S; hilly woodland, pasture. Coalmining from Roman times, metal industs.; cattle raising, apple orchards. Christian stronghold during Moorish conquest; kingdom joined with León 866, later with Castile. Principality 1388-1931.

Astyanax, in Greek myth, son of Hector and ANDROMACHE.

Asunción, cap. of Paraguay, port on Paraguay R. Pop. 437,000. Major commercial, transport centre; food processing, textile mfg. Founded *o* 1536. Centre of Spanish colonization in S of continent.

Aswan or **Assuan** (anc. *Syene*), city of S Egypt, just below First Cataract of the Nile. Pop. 202,000. Trade, tourist centre; chemicals indust.; syenite quarries. Nearby are Aswan Dam (completed 1902); Aswan High Dam (completed 1970), 111 m (365 ft) high, 4.8 km (3 mi) wide, has created L. Nasser, resevoir (area *c* 5180 sq km/2000 sq mi) providing irrigation, h.e.p. for Egypt and Sudan. Construction required raising of ABU SIMBEL temples.

Asyût (anc. *Lycopolis*), city of C Egypt, on R. Nile. Pop. 176,000. Trade and transport centre, noted for pottery, ornamental carving; cotton. Asyût barrage across Nile (1902) provides irrigation.

Atacama Desert, arid region of N Chile-S Peru, between Andes and Pacific coast. Alt. 610 m (*c* 2000 ft). Has rich nitrate, copper, iron ore deposits. One of driest areas in world, with almost no vegetation.

Atahualpa (d. 1533), last Inca ruler of Peru. Seized whole empire after defeating half-brother Huáscar. Captured (1532) by Spanish conquistador Pizarro, who had him killed.

Atalanta, in Greek myth, huntress famed for speed and skill. Took part in Calydonian hunt, was first to wound the boar. Ran race with suitors on condition that she would marry first man to outstrip her; the others would be killed. Hippomenes, or Melanion, won race by dropping 3 golden apples which Atalanta stopped to pick up.

Ataturk, Kemal, orig. Mustafa Kemal Pasha (1881-1938), Turkish military and political leader. Participated in Young Turks revolt (1908). Estab. rival govt. in Asia Minor (1919) against Allied-controlled Constantinople regime after Turkey's collapse in WWI. Repulsed Greek invasion from Anatolia (1919-22); re-estab. Turkish sovereignty over occupied territs. First president of Turkey (1923-38), ruled as dictator. Introduced Westernizing reform programme.

Kemal Ataturk

ataxia, lack of coordination of muscles resulting in erratic body movements. May be caused by damage to central nervous system.

Atbara, town of NE Sudan, at confluence of Nile and Atbara. Pop. 53,000. Major railway jct., railway engineering.

Ate, in Greek myth, personification of moral blindness and infatuation.

Athabascan or **Athapascan,** linguistic family of North American Indians of W Canada and W US, of Nadene stock.

Athabaska, river of NC Alberta, Canada. Rises in Rocky Mts., flows NE 1230 km (765 mi) to **Lake Athabaska** (on N Alberta-Saskatchewan border); area 8100 sq km (c 3120 sq mi). Rich oil-bearing sands along lower course of river.

Athanasian Creed, statement of Christian belief maintaining belief in the Trinity, as opposed to Arianism (see ARIUS). Formerly attributed to Athanasius, now believed to date from 6th cent.

Athanasius, St (c 296-373), Egyptian theologian, patriarch of Alexandria. Maintained consubstantiality of Jesus with God, opposing ARIUS at 1st Council of Nicaea (325) and in Defence against the Arians (348). Influential in shaping Catholic doctrine.

atheism, denial of existence of God or gods. Occurs in ancient times, eg in Socrates' attack on religious orthodoxy of Athens; again in 19th cent. with belief in an inherent conflict between science and religion. See AGNOSTICISM.

Athelstan (c 895-939), king of England (924-39). Consolidated and built upon work of his grandfather, Alfred; defeated union of Scots, Danes and Welsh at Brunanburh (937).

Athena or **Pallas Athena,** in Greek myth, patron goddess of Athens, personification of wisdom, patron of intellectual and practical skills. Represented as warlike virgin goddess, having sprung fully-armed from the head of Zeus. PARTHENON erected to her on Acropolis. Identified by Romans with Minerva.

Athenagoras, orig. Aristokles Spirou (1886-1971), Greek churchman. Became ecumenical patriarch of Eastern Orthodox Church in 1949. Met Pope Paul VI (1964, 1967), thus advancing reconciliation of Orthodox and RC churches.

Athens (Athinai), cap. of Greece, on Plain of Attica. Pop. 2,540,000 (incl. Piraeus). Admin., indust., cultural centre; univ.; Greek Orthodox archbishopric. Foremost Greek city state from 5th cent. BC, esp. under Pericles. Won Persian Wars, but defeated by Sparta (404 BC); decline followed defeat by Philip of Macedon (338 BC); sacked by Rome (86 BC). Fell to Turks 1458, rebuilt as cap. of independent Greece (1834). Buildings incl. Acropolis, Parthenon, Erechtheum. Now forms one city with **Piraeus,** largest Greek port. Exports wine, olive oil. Built c 450 BC, once linked to Athens by Long Walls, destroyed by Sulla (86 BC).

atherosclerosis, type of arteriosclerosis associated with deposits of fatty material, usually cholesterol, in lining of arteries. Factors linked to its cause incl. eating of animal fat, tobacco smoking, lack of exercise.

athlete's foot, see RINGWORM.

athletics, physical games and contests, divided into field (throwing, jumping, vaulting) and track (running) events. History can be traced as far as Greek games of 13th cent. BC. Modern athletics date from 19th cent. and received considerable impetus from estab. of international competitions, esp. Olympic Games (1896).

Athlone, town of Co. Westmeath, C Irish Republic, on R. Shannon. Pop. 10,000. Military station; broadcasting centre.

Athos or **Akti,** penin. of NE Greece, easternmost part of Chalcidice penin., Macedonia. Rises to Mt. Athos (Hagion Oros: 'Holy Mountain'), 2032 m (6670 ft) high; incl. 20 Basilian monasteries (founded 10th cent.), created an autonomous state 1927.

Atkinson, Sir Harry Albert (1831-92), New Zealand political leader, b. England. Premier of colony (1876-7, 1883-4, 1887-91).

Atlanta, cap. of Georgia, US. Pop. 497,000. Transport and commercial centre; textiles, steel products. Founded 1837 as Terminus, renamed 1843. City burned by W. T. Sherman during Civil War.

Atlantic Cable, submarine telegraph cable linking Britain and US. Successfully laid (1866) through efforts of C. FIELD. Telephone cable link between UK and Canada completed 1961.

Atlantic Charter, programme drawn up (Aug. 1941) by Churchill (Britain) and F.D. Roosevelt (US), stating general aims for post-WWII peace. Goals incl. in UN declaration (1942).

Atlantic City, resort of SE New Jersey, US; on Absecon Beach (sand bar). Pop. 48,000. Has board walks, luxury hotels, auditorium; holds political conventions.

Atlantic Ocean, world's 2nd largest ocean. Area 82,362,000 sq km (c 31,800,000 sq mi). Extends from Arctic to Antarctic, between Americas and Europe and Africa. Greatest depth at Milwaukee Deep (8530 km /28,000 ft) just N of Puerto Rico. Chief ocean currents Equatorials and subsidiaries: Gulf Stream and Labrador in N, Brazil and Guinea in S. N Atlantic is world's busiest passenger and freight waterway.

Atlantis, legendary large island in western sea. Plato describes it as a Utopia, destroyed by earthquake. Solon identified it with Santorin in Cyclades isls., which erupted c 1500 BC causing destruction of Minoan civilization by fire and tidal wave.

Atlas, in Greek myth, a Titan, son of Iapetus and Clymene. For his part in Titans' revolt against Olympans, condemned to hold up sky. Identified with Atas Mts. in N Africa.

Atlas Mountains, system of NW Africa. Extend c 2400 km (1500 mi) from SW Morocco to N Tunisia. Incl. Tell Atlas, Saharan Atlas (Algeria); High Atlas (Morocco) rise to 4163 m/13,664 ft at Djebel Toubkal. Resources incl. phosphates, coal, oil, iron ore.

atmosphere, combination of gases surrounding a celestial body. For Earth, it consists mainly of nitrogen (78%), oxygen (21%). Extends up to c 950 km (600 mi), becomes rarer with distance from Earth's surface, 99% of mass of atmosphere being within 80 km (50 mi). Layers, in ascending order, are TROPOSPHERE, STRATOSPHERE, mesosphere, thermosphere, exosphere. Atmosphere forms protective shield; absorbs and scatters harmful radiation, causes solid matter to burn up. Also see IONOSPHERE

atoll, form of CORAL REEF. Circular or horseshoe-shaped, encloses a lagoon.

atom, in chemistry, smallest particle of an element which can take part in chemical reaction. Atom consists of positively charged nucleus, where its mass is concentrated, surrounded by orbiting electrons; nucleus is composed of protons and neutrons, the number of protons equal to number of electrons. See ELEMENT.

atomic bomb, weapon deriving explosive force from nuclear fission. Detonated by rapidly bringing together 2 subcritical masses of fissile material (eg uranium 235 or plutonium 239), with total mass exceeding critical mass.

Ensuing chain reaction releases nuclear energy, yielding intense heat and shock waves, gamma and neutron radiation. Developed during WWII and first used on Hiroshima.

atomic clock, extremely accurate clock utilizing vibrations of atoms and molecules. Originally ammonia and caesium used; now hydrogen maser gives accuracy of c 1 part in 10^{13}.

atomic energy, see NUCLEAR ENERGY.

Atomic Energy Commission, US body set up (1946) to supervise peaceful uses of atomic energy. Five members appointed by president, subject to Senate's approval.

atomic mass unit or **amu,** unit of mass, 1/12 of mass of most abundant isotope of carbon (mass no. 12). Equals c 1.66×10^{-27} kg.

atomic number, number of protons in atomic nucleus of an element.

atomic theory, study of structure of fundamental components of matter. Early contributors incl. DEMOCRITUS (5th cent. BC) who held that matter is composed of minute indivisible particles (atoms) in motion. Modern theory began with John DALTON (1808) who held that elements are made of identical atoms, whose physical and chemical properties are different from those of atoms of other elements. A theory of internal structure of atoms was formulated by RUTHERFORD and improved by BOHR, who used quantum theory to describe electron orbits about central nucleus. Most recent theories rely on probabilistic methods of WAVE MECHANICS.

atomic weight, average mass of atom of specified isotopic composition of an element, measured in atomic mass units. Usually natural isotopic composition taken.

atonality, in music, absence of a key or tonal centre. Much of modern 'classical' music has moved away from definite tonal centres. Developed in work of Ives, Schoenberg, Webern, Bartók.

atonement, in Christian theology, the effect of Jesus' sufferings and death in bringing about the reconciliation of man to God. First made explicit by St Anselm in *Cur Deus Homo?*

Atonement, Day of (Heb. *Yom Kippur*), most important Jewish holy day on 10th day of 7th month, Tishri (late Sept. or Oct). Day of prayer for forgiveness; liturgy begins with Kol Nidre prayer.

Atreus, in Greek myth, king of Mycenae; father of Agamemnon and Menelaus. To avenge treachery of his brother, THYESTES, he killed Thyestes' sons and served their flesh to him at a banquet. Killed by AEGISTHUS.

atrium, in anatomy, either of two upper chambers on each side of heart. Left atrium receives oxygenated blood from lungs; right atrium receives venous blood from rest of body.

atrium, in architecture, inner central court of Roman house, usually open to sky and surrounded by dwelling rooms. Name also applies to open court in front of early Christian and medieval churches.

atropine, poisonous alkaloid obtained from deadly nightshade and other plants. Depresses parasympathetic nerves and accelerates heart; used in moderate doses to dilate pupil of eye.

Atropos, see FATES.

Attenborough, Sir Richard (1923-), English actor, film producer. Roles incl. Pinkie in *Brighton Rock* (1947); directed and produced *Oh What a Lovely War* (1969).

Attica (*Attiki*), admin. dist. of EC Greece, cap. Athens. Cereals, olive oil, wine. In legend, ancient state formed by Theseus; dominated by Athens from 5th cent. BC.

Attila (c 406-53), 406–53), king of the Huns (434–53). Ruled over most of area between the Rhine and Caspian. Forced Rome to pay tribute and invaded Gaul when tributes ceased. Defeated at Châlons (451). Later invaded Italy but withdrew N after abandoning plan to capture Rome (452).

Attis, in Phrygian pantheon, god of vegetation. After death, caused by self-castration, spirit passed into pine tree; violets grew from his blood, symbolizing rebirth of plant life. Spring festival celebrated death and resurrection.

Attlee, Clement Richard Atlee, 1st Earl (1883-1967), British statesman, PM (1945-51). Rose to Labour Party

Lord Attlee

leadership (1935), after serving in 1924 and 1929 Labour govts. Deputy leader in Churchill's wartime coalition cabinet (1942-5). His own admin. inaugurated nationalization of major industs., created National Health Service; concluded Palestinian mandate and granted independence to India. After 1951 election loss, led opposition until retirement (1955).

attorney, in law, person empowered to act as agent for or in behalf of another, esp. a lawyer. *See* ADVOCATE.

Aube, river of NE France. Flows c 240 km (150 mi) NW from Langres Plateau to R. Seine.

aubergine, deep purple fruit of eggplant, *Solanum melongena*, native to India. Cultivated widely esp. in Mediterranean region.

Aubigné, Théodore Agrippa d' (1552-1630), French poet, historian. Satirical epic poem *Les Tragiques* (1616) propounded Huguenot view of the religious wars. Helped estab. Alexandrine as sophisticated French verse form.

aubretia, genus of plant of Cruciferae family. Showy purplish flowers, often cultivated in rock gardens. Native to Middle East.

Aubrey, John (1626-97), English writer. Known for his collection of vivid biog. sketches, pub. (1813) as *Brief Lives*.

Aubusson, town of Marche, C France, on R. Creuse. Pop. 7000. Noted from 15th cent. for tapestries and carpets.

Aucassin et Nicolette, anon. French romance written c 1200, alternating prose and verse. Verse sung to music which is still extant.

Auch, town of SW France, on R. Gers, cap. of Gers dept. Pop. 24,000. Agric. market, wine, brandy. Major city (*Auscorum*) of Roman Gaul; cap. of Armagnac from 10th cent., of Gascony from 17th cent. Cathedral (15th cent.).

Auchinleck, Sir Claude John Eyre (1884-), British field marshal. Commander-in-chief in Middle East (1941-2); forced back to Egyptian frontier by Rommel. Commander-in-chief in India (1943-7).

Auckland, city of N North Isl., New Zealand, on isthmus between 2 harbours. Pop. 152,000. Major port for overseas trade; exports dairy produce, fruit, timber. Shipbuilding, engineering industs.; food processing. Has major airport; univ. (1882); RC, Anglican cathedrals. Former cap. of New Zealand (1840-65). Seven extinct volcanoes in area.

Auden, W[ystan] H[ugh] (1907-73), English poet. Led left-wing literary movement in 1930s. Plays with Isherwood incl. *The Dog Beneath the Skin* (1935), *The Ascent of F.6* (1937). *Collected Poetry* (1945) contains best-known verse. Also wrote opera libretti (incl. text for Stravinsky's *The Rake's Progress*) and criticism; edited anthologies and lectured. Settled in US 1939.

Audenarde, see OUDENAARDE, Belgium.

Audubon, John James (c 1785-1851), American ornithologist, artist. Conducted first bird-banding experiments in US. Visited Britain (1826) to obtain

W.H. Auden

Coin showing head of Augustus

publication of *The Birds of America* and *Ornithological Biography* (with William MacGillivray), works featuring his drawings of bird life.

Augier, Emile (1820-89), French dramatist. Reacting against romantic drama, wrote comedies affirming bourgeois values, *eg Gabrielle* (1849).

Augsburg, city of S West Germany, on R. Lech. Pop. 213,000. Railway jct., textile centre. Roman colony founded 14 BC by Augustus. Important commercial centre 15th-16th cent., home of Fugger banking family.

Augsburg, League of, European alliance (1686) against Louis XIV of France formed by Habsburgs, Sweden and various German states. Joined by England and Holland (1689) to form Grand Alliance which fought France until 1697. *See* RYSWICK, TREATY OF.

Augsburg, Peace of, settlement (1555) of problems created within Holy Roman Empire by Reformation. Estab. principle that choice between Lutheranism and Catholicism was to be made by individual princes.

Augsburg Confession, official statement of Lutheran beliefs. Presented to Charles V at Diet of Augsburg (1530). Mainly the work of Melanchthon and endorsed by Luther.

Augurs or **Augures,** college of officials in ancient Rome who interpreted signs (*auspicia*) of divine approval or disapproval in natural phenomena, *eg* eclipse, meteors, flight or feeding of birds.

Augusta, town of E Georgia, US; on Savannah R. Pop. 60,000. Cotton market; indust., trade centre. Estab. as trading post 1735; state cap. 1785-95.

Augusta, cap. of Maine, US; on Kennebec R. Pop. 22,000. Trading post estab. 1628. Mfg. industs. developed with damming of river (1837).

Augustine, St (354-430), Numidian churchman, theologian. Brought up as Christian, but not baptized until 387 after period of great doubt recorded in spiritual autobiog. *Confessions.* Bishop of Hippo in N Africa (396-430), defended Christianity against heretical beliefs incl. Manichaeism, Pelagianism. Other works incl. *City of God,* defending Christianity against pagan critics and giving Christian view of history.

Augustine of Canterbury, St (d. *c* 605), Roman Benedictine missionary, 1st archbishop of Canterbury. Sent (596) by Pope Gregory I to England, converted Ethelbert of Kent and introduced Roman doctrines, calendar into England.

Augustinians, religious orders in RC church which live according to Rule of St Augustine of Hippo. First organized in 11th cent. Most famous house is hospice on Great St Bernard Pass.

Augustus, full name Gaius Julius Caesar Octavianus (63 BC–AD 14), 1st Roman emperor. Adopted as son and heir by Julius Caesar. On Caesar's death, entered into ruling coalition (2nd Triumvirate) with Lepidus and ANTONY. Subsequent conflict with Antony and Cleopatra culminated in his victory at Actium (31 BC), leaving him master of Rome. Assumed leadership (28 BC), given title Augustus. Took control of the army and estab. frontiers of the empire. Reorganized admin. of the provinces. Rule marked by prosperity, flourishing of the arts.

auk, diving bird of Alcidae family of N hemisphere, with webbed feet, short wings. Flightless great auk, *Pinguinus impennis,* was largest species; became extinct in mid-19th cent. through hunting.

Auld Lang Syne, Scots song, words of which were reworked by Robert Burns. The tune prob. originated as a folk song.

Aulis, ancient port of Boeotia, EC Greece. Greek fleet sailed from here against Troy. Site of ruined temple of Artemis.

Aurangzeb (1618-1707), Mogul emperor of India (1658-1707). Seized throne by imprisoning father, Shah Jehan. Extended empire through military conquests. Fanatical supporter of Islam, destroyed Hindu temples and antagonized Sikhs.

Aurelian, full name Lucius Domitius Aurelianus (*c* 212-75), Roman emperor (270-5). Successful military leader, acclaimed emperor by his troops. Secured Danube and Rhine frontiers against barbarians and defeated ZENOBIA of Palmyra; recaptured Gaul.

Aurelius, Marcus, *see* MARCUS AURELIUS ANTONINUS.

Auric, Georges (1899-), French composer. Wrote much music for ballet, incl. *Phèdre,* and films, incl. René Clair's *A Nous la liberté.* A member of the group of composers known as 'les Six'.

auricula, *Primula auricula,* yellow primrose, native to Alpine Europe. Also called bear's-ear because of shape of leaves.

Aurignac, village of S France, at foot of Pyrenees. Pop. 1000. Gave name to Aurignacian culture after Palaeolithic remains found in caves; excavated *c* 1860.

Aurora, in Roman religion, goddess of dawn, identified with Greek Eos.

aurora, coloured light phenomenon visible at night in near-polar regions. Aurora borealis (northern lights) seen in N hemisphere, aurora australis in S. Believed to be caused by collisions of air molecules and charged particles from Sun, deflected towards poles by Earth's magnetic field. Occurs esp. during periods of sunspot activity.

Auschwitz, *see* OŚWIĘCIM, Poland.

Austen, Jane (1775-1817), English novelist. Works reflect experience as unmarried daughter of a country rector, but her ironically witty analysis of character and moral problems is profound and universal. *Emma* (1816) and *Pride and Prejudice* (1813) are most popular, but *Sense and Sensibility* (1811), *Mansfield Park* (1814), *Northanger Abbey* and *Persuasion* (both pub. 1818) all show the same skilful construction.

Jane Austen

Austerlitz (*Slavkov*), town of SC Czechoslovakia. Pop. 4000. Scene of battle (1805) in which French under Napoleon defeated combined Austro-Russian force.

Austin, Alfred (1835-1913), English writer. Editor of *National Review* (1887-95), poet laureate from 1896. Also wrote prose, *eg The Garden that I Love* (1894).

Austin, Herbert Austin, 1st Baron (1866-1941), English pioneer automobile manufacturer. Designed 1st Wolseley automobile (1895); began production of Austin in 1906.

Austin, John Langshaw (1911-60), English philosopher. Influenced analytic philosophy by advocating investigation of ordinary linguistic usage. Works incl. *Sense and Sensibilia* (1962).

Austin, Stephen Fuller (1793-1836), American pioneer. Pursued plans of his father, Moses Austin, to develop settlement of Texas. Estab. communities between Colorado and Brazos rivers. Opposition to Mexican rule helped precipitate separation of Texas from Mexico.

Austin, cap. of Texas, US; on Colorado R. Pop. 250,000. In irrigated agric. region; food processing industs. Educational and artistic centre. Estab. as cap. 1839. Has Univ. of Texas (1883).

Australasia, term referring normally to Australia, New Zealand, New Guinea and adjacent isls. May also refer to all Oceania.

Australia, smallest continent, between Indian Ocean (W) and Pacific Ocean (E). Forms, with Tasmania, Commonwealth of Australia. Area 7,690,000 sq km (2,970,000 sq mi); pop. 12,728,000; cap. Canberra. Language: English. Religions: Anglican, RC. Comprises 6 states: New South Wales, Queensland, South Australia, Tasmania, Victoria, Western Australia; also Capital Territ., Northern Territ. Narrow coastal lowlands, except for Nullarbor Plain in S; Great Dividing Range in E; vast arid tableland in W. Climate varies from tropical monsoon in N to temperate in S. Isolation led to distinct flora and fauna *eg* giant eucalyptus, marsupials. Agric. incl. sheep rearing, wheat and fruit growing; minerals incl. gold, lead, copper, zinc, uranium, bauxite, oil, iron, coal; industs. incl. iron and steel, chemicals. E coast claimed (1770) for Britain by Cook. Originally used as penal settlement; pop. increased greatly after gold discoveries *c* 1850. Separate colonies federated 1901 to form Commonwealth.

Australian aborigines, ethnic group of Australian mainland (mainly N and NE). Nomadic hunters, they have primitive material culture but complex social system with totemic worship. Weapons incl. boomerang. Est. pop. is 70,000 mostly on reservations, largest being Arnhem Land, Northern Territ.

Australian Alps, mountain range of SE New South Wales and NE Victoria, Australia. Incl. Snowy Mts.; highest peak Mt. Kosciusko. Winter sports area.

Australian Antarctic Territory, all isls. and mainland S of 60°S and between 45° and 160°E (with exception of Adélie Land); comprises almost half of Antarctica. Incl. Enderby, MacRobertson, Princess Elizabeth, Wilhelm II, Queen Mary, Wilkes, George V lands and parts of Victoria Land.

Australian Capital Territory (ACT), territ. of SE Australia, enclave within New South Wales. Area, incl. Jervis Bay port, 2432 sq km (939 sq mi); pop. 144,000; cap. Canberra. Mainly grassy or forested upland; drained by Molonglo R. ACT created 1911 to incl. site of new federal cap.

Australian rules football, eighteen-a-side team game played with an oval ball. Dates from 1858, rules being revised in 1866. Derived from soccer, rugby and Gaelic football. Most popular in S and W states.

Australopithecus, extinct genus of hominid family from which modern man may have evolved. Earliest discovered was *Australopithecus africanus,* (South Africa, 1925). Tool-making form *A. boisei* (formerly known as *Zinjanthropus*), *c* 1.8 million years old, was discovered (1959) by Leakey in OLDUVAI GORGE.

Austria

Austria (*Osterreich*), republic of C Europe. Area 83,851 sq km (32,375 sq mi); pop. 7,521,000; cap. Vienna. Language: German. Religion: RC. Mainly mountainous, fertile Danube plain in NE. Agric. (cereals, cattle, pigs), timber, coal, iron ore, h.e.p. Indust. centres Vienna, Graz, Linz. Ruled by Habsburgs 1282-1918, centre of Holy Roman Empire; incorporated Hungary, expanded with Partitions of Poland (18th cent.). Became Austrian empire (1804); unrest in Hungary led to dual monarchy (1867), collapsed 1918. Forcibly made part of Nazi Germany 1938-45; occupied by Allies 1945-55.

Austrian Succession, War of the (1740-8), European conflict precipitated by Maria Theresa's succession to Habsburg lands, by PRAGMATIC SANCTION, challenged by Bavarian elector (later Emperor Charles VII). Frederick II of Prussia, by claiming and invading Silesia, started war; withdrew (1745) after obtaining most of Silesia, through Treaty of Dresden. Bavaria withdrew from war after death of Charles VII (1745) when it was overrun by Austrians. Subsequent hostilities inconclusive, war concluded by TREATY OF AIX-LA-CHAPELLE.

Austro-Hungarian Monarchy or **Dual Monarchy,** reorganized form of Habsburg empire, estab. (1867) to placate Hungarian nationalist aspirations. Hungary given control of internal affairs, union of crowns of Hungary and Austria maintained. Dissolved 1918.

Austro-Prussian War, conflict (June-Aug. 1866), between Prussia, supported by Italy, and Austria, allied with several German states. Prussia won quick victory over German states and defeated Austrians at Sadowa. Peace of Prague resulted in Austria ceding Venetia to Italy; Prussia annexed Frankfurt, Hanover and Hesse-Kassel. War provided 2nd stage in estab. of German Empire in 1871. Also known as Seven Weeks War.

authoritarianism, in psychology, tendency in individual to be obsequious to those hierarchically superior, and to be dominant over those inferior. In sociology, the theory and practice of administration by means of commands,

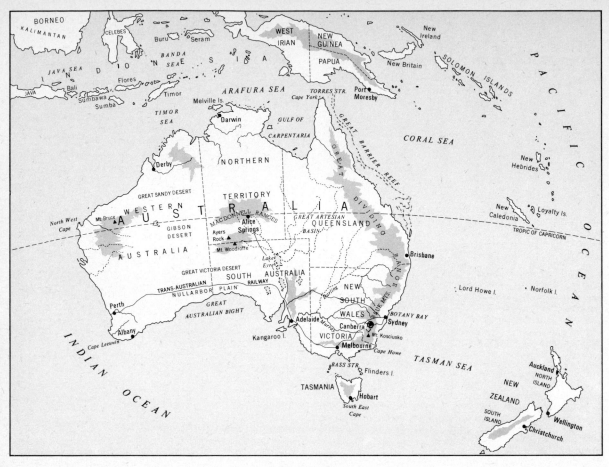

Australasia

punishment, without recourse to justification, consultation, persuasion.

Authorized Version, English translation of the Bible, pub. in 1611 with the authorization of King James I (also called King James Bible). Prepared by committee of Protestant scholars under direction of Lancelot Andrewes.

autism, psychosis, esp. of children, characterized by withdrawal from contact with other humans and disregard for external reality.

autobiography, person's account of own life. Mainly a post-Renaissance form, *Confessions* of St Augustine could be regarded as a precursor. Later exponents incl. Casanova, Ben Franklin, Rousseau. Forms range from poetry (Wordsworth's *Prelude*) to Hitler's political *Mein Kampf.*

auto da fé (Port.,=act of faith), ceremonial burning of heretics in public. In widest use during Inquisition in Spain and Portugal; last known use in Mexico (1815). Also refers to trial and sentencing of alleged heretics by Inquisition.

autogiro or **gyroplane,** aircraft that moves forward by means of a powered propeller and is supported in air mainly by a revolving horizontal aerofoil turned by air pressure and not motor power. Used for its ability to make short take-offs and landings.

autoimmunity, abnormal condition occurring when body produces antibodies reacting against its own tissues. Diseases prob. resulting from autoimmunity incl. rheumatoid arthritis, haemolytic anaemia, lupus, *etc.*

Autolycus, in Greek myth, grandfather of Odysseus. Accomplished thief and trickster with special powers.

automation, in industry, automatic control of processes by self-regulating machinery. Such machinery makes use of part of its output effect to modify and correct input (feedback), using *eg* electronic sensing devices.

automobile or **motor car,** self-propelling passenger vehicle usually powered by INTERNAL COMBUSTION ENGINE. Wheels driven via GEARBOX and DIFFERENTIAL. Developed in Germany by Karl Benz (*c* 1885), Gottlieb Daimler, and in US by Henry Ford.

Automobile Association (AA), organization estab. (1905) to protect and uphold rights of motorists in UK. Largest body of its kind in the world.

autonomy, in politics, freedom to act without external constraint, specifically referring to limited self-determination; often granted as prelude to complete independence, *eg* UK granted extensive internal legislative powers to Canada, Australia before their independence.

autumn crocus, *see* MEADOW SAFFRON.

Auvergne, region and former prov. of C France, in Massif Central, cap. Clermont-Ferrand. Cereals, livestock, cheese mfg.; mineral springs. Mainly mountainous, range of extinct volcanoes runs N-S. Hist. part of Aquitaine, part of France from 1527.

Auxerre, town of NC France, on R. Yonne, cap. of Yonne dept. Pop. 38,000. Centre for Chablis wines. Church of St Germain has 6th cent. crypt; Gothic cathedral (13th cent.).

auxin, plant hormone, produced in actively growing parts, which regulates amount, type and direction of plant growth. Synthetic auxins are important in agriculture to promote growth, *etc.*

avalanche, swiftly descending mass of ice and snow, often with accumulated rock and vegetation, common in mountain areas. Causes incl. melting of base of snow mass, sudden shocks (*eg* noise, earth tremors).

Avalon, in Celtic myth, isle of blest or paradise, sometimes identified with Glastonbury (Somerset). *See* ARTHURIAN LEGEND.

Avebury, John Lubbock, 1st Baron, *see* LUBBOCK, JOHN.

Avebury, village in Wiltshire, England, SW of Swindon. Site of Neolithic stone circle, older and larger than that at Stonehenge. Many stones removed in earlier times for building material.

Aveiro, town of NW Portugal. Pop. 16,000. Fishing port, salt indust. Built over water.

Ave Maria (Lat.,=hail, Mary), prayer to Virgin Mary, fixed in present form by Pope Pius V (16th cent.). Main prayer of the ROSARY.

Averroës, Arabic name Ibn Rushd (1126-98), Spanish Moslem philosopher. Made Aristotle known in Europe by commentaries which were translated into Latin. Dealt with the demarcation of faith and reason, but felt that they were not opposed.

Avesta or **Zend-Avesta,** collection of writings sacred to Zoroastrians and Parsees. Incl. creation myth, litanies, laws of ritual purification. Written in old Iranian and survives only in fragmentary and much corrupted form. *See* ZOROASTRIANISM.

aviation, operation of heavier-than-air aircraft. History of aviation highlighted by Wright brothers' 1st flight in heavier-than-air craft (US, 1903); Louis Blériot's flight across English Channel (1909); Alcock and Brown's trans-atlantic flight (1919); Charles Lindbergh's solo Atlantic crossing (1932). First transatlantic passenger service begun by Pan American Airways (1939). Years following WWII saw development of jet propulsion and supersonic flight for military and civilian purposes.

Avicebron, *see* IBN GABIROL, SOLOMON BEN JUDAH.

Avicenna, Arabic name Ibn Sina (980-1037), Persian philosopher, physician. Estab. classification of sciences used in medieval schools of Europe. Known for his *Canon of Medicine.*

Avignon, town of Provence, S France, on R. Rhône. Cap. of Vaucluse dept. Pop. 89,000. Wine trade, silk mfg., tourist centre. Papal see during 'Babylonian Captivity' (1309-77), remained under papal control until 1791. Town walls, papal palace (both 14th cent.); ruins of 12th cent. bridge.

Avila, town of C Spain, on R. Adaja, cap. of Avila prov. Pop. 25,000. Tourist and religious centre. Cathedral, town walls (both 11th cent.). Birthplace of St Teresa.

avocado or **avocado pear,** tropical American tree, *Persea americana,* esp. cultivated varieties originating in West Indies, Guatemala, Mexico. Yields pulpy, green or purple, pear-shaped edible fruit. Also called alligator pear.

avocet, long-legged wading bird related to snipe, genus *Recurvirostra,* with worldwide distribution. Feeds by sweeping upward-curving bill through water.

Avogadro, Amadeo, Conte di Quaregna (1776-1856), Italian physicist. Formulated Avogadro's hypothesis, that equal volumes of gases at same temperature and pressure contain equal numbers of molecules, thus explaining Gay-Lussac's law of combining volumes.

avoirdupois, systems of weights used in UK and US: 16 drams = 1 ounce, 16 ounces = 1 pound, 28 pounds = 1 quarter, 4 quarters = 1 hundredweight, 20 hundredweights = 1 ton.

Avon, county of SW England, on Bristol Channel. Area 1337 sq km (516 sq mi); pop. 914,000; co. town Bristol. Created 1974, incl. parts of Gloucestershire, Wiltshire, Somerset.

Avon, several rivers of UK. **1,** flows 154 km (96 mi) from Northamptonshire via Stratford into R. Severn at Tewkesbury. **2,** flows 120 km (75 mi) from Gloucestershire via Bath, Bristol into Bristol Channel at Avonmouth. Also name of other rivers in Scotland, Wales.

Axis, coalition of states (1936-45), active in WWII. Grew out of German-Italian alliance (1936); joined by Japan in Berlin Pact of 1940. Later incl. Hungary, Romania, Bulgaria, Slovakia, Croatia. Also *see* ANTI-COMINTERN PACT.

Axminster, town in Devon, SW England, on R. Axe. Pop. 14,000. Once famous for carpet mfg.

Axolotl

axolotl, aquatic larval salamander, genus *Ambystoma,* of SW US and Mexico. Does not develop into terrestrial adult amphibian, but can breed. *See* NEOTENY.

Axum, *see* AKSUM, Ethiopia.

Ayacucho, town of C Peru. Pop. 28,000. In rich mining region. Sucre's victory over Spanish nearby (1824) led to Peru's independence.

aye-aye, *Daubentonia madagascariensis,* nocturnal arboreal mammal of lemur family, found in Madagascar. Gnawing teeth and long fingers with claws. Feeds on insects, fruit.

Ayer, Sir A[lfred] J[ules] (1910-), English philosopher. Brought LOGICAL POSITIVISM to attention of English readership in *Language, Truth and Logic* (1936). Other works incl. *The Foundations of Empirical Knowledge* (1940), *The Problem of Knowledge* (1956).

Ayesha (*c* 611-678), favourite wife of Mohammed. Helped father, Abu Bakr, succeed to caliphate on Mohammed's death. Fomented revolt against ALI, 4th caliph.

Aylesbury, mun. bor. of C England, co. town of Buckinghamshire. Pop. 41,000. Main indust. food processing.

Aymará, South American Indians of Titicaca Basin in Peru and Bolivia. Thought to have built ruined city of Tiahuanaco. They survived 15th cent. domination by Incas.

Ayrshire, former county of SW Scotland, now in Strathclyde region. Hills in SE. Dairying (Ayrshire cattle) potato growing; coalmining industs. Co. town was Ayr, royal burgh on R. Ayr. Pop. 48,000. Small port, resort; textile, engineering industs. Alloway, birthplace of Burns, is nearby.

Aytoun, William Edmonstoune (1813-65), Scottish writer. Professor of Rhetoric at Edinburgh Univ. from 1845, remembered for *Lays of the Scottish Cavaliers* (1849) and parodies *The Bon Gaultier Ballads* (1855).

Ayub Khan, Mohammed (1907-74), Pakistani army officer, statesman. Became president after military coup (1958). Introduced land reforms; ended martial law (1962). Resigned 1969 amidst mounting opposition.

Ayutthaya or **Ayuthia,** town of SC Thailand, on R. Chao Phraya. Pop. 33,000. Centre of rice growing area. Cap. of Siam (1350-1767) until destroyed by Burmese; has many temples, pagodas.

azalea, widely distributed genus of shrubs or trees, now usually considered a subgenus of genus *Rhododendron.* Deciduous leaves and funnel-shaped flowers of various colours. Many varieties cultivated as house plants. Species incl. American flame azalea, *R. calendulaceum.*

Azaña, Manuel (1880-1940), Spanish statesman. Premier of republic (1931-3, 1936), attempted to introduce social reform. President (1936-9), fled to France on Franco's victory in Civil War.

Azerbaijan

Azerbaijan Soviet Socialist Republic, constituent republic of SW USSR; on Iran border. Area *c* 86,600 sq km (33,400 sq mi); pop. 5,111,000; cap. Baku. Crossed by Caucasus Mts. in N; C plain watered by R. Kura and tributaries. Produces cotton, wheat; major oil deposits in Apsheron penin., centred on Baku. Territ. ceded to Russia in 19th cent. by Persia, incorporated by USSR (1920).

Azhar, El, in Cairo, Egypt, main theological seminary of Islamic world (founded *c* 970).

azimuth, in astronomy, arc of horizon between its N or S point and vertical circle passing through zenith and centre of heavenly body.

Azores (*Açores*), archipelago of N Atlantic, admin. dist. of Portugal *c* 1450 km (900 mi) W of Lisbon. Area 2300 sq km (888 sq mi); largest isl. São Miguel, has chief town Ponta Delgada. Volcanic, rises to 2315 m (7600 ft). Fruit, vegetables grown; winter resort. Settled by Portuguese mid-15th cent.

Azorín, pseud. of José Martínez Ruíz (1873-1967), Spanish author. Essays *El alma castellana* (1900) deal with theme of recurrence of time. Also wrote autobiog. novels, *eg Antonia Azorín* (1903).

Azov, Sea of (Latin *Palus Maeotis*), N arm of Black Sea, to which it is connected by Kerch str. Area *c* 37,700 sq km (14,500 sq mi). Shallow, with many sandbanks and low salinity; receives R. Don near town of Azov. Important fisheries.

Aztec, American Indian people of C Mexico. Ruling group at time of Spanish conquest (16th cent.). Noted for highly sophisticated civilization, centred on cap. Tenochtitlán on site of modern Mexico City. Spoke a Uto-Aztecan language.

Aztec civilization, culture of Aztec people developed (from 12th cent.) on Mayan and Toltec foundations. Characterized by use of irrigation for agriculture, fine weaving, intricate metalwork (esp. gold), massive buildings erected by slave labour. Religion was pantheistic, latterly involving human sacrifice.

Azteco-Tanoan, NW American and Mexican linguistic stock. Largest family within it is Uto-Aztecan, incl. Nahuatl (Aztec), Hopi, Shoshone, Yaqui, Paiute languages; other families are Kiowan, Tanoan and possibly Zuni.

Azuela, Mariano (1873-1952), Mexican novelist. *Los de abajo* (1915; *The Underdogs*) based on medical experiences during Revolution. *Los caciques* (1917), *Las moscas* (1918) are both indictments of economic oppression.

azurite, copper ore mineral. Azure blue in colour, it is a carbonate of copper, often found associated with malachite. Major sources in US, France.

B

Baalbek, town of N Lebanon. Pop. 12,000. Associated with Phoenician sun god Baal. Ancient Heliopolis. Prominent in Roman times, its ruins incl. temples of Jupiter and Bacchus.

Baal-Schem-Tov, orig. Israel ben Eliezer (1700-60), Russian Jewish teacher. Founded HASIDISM movement, preaching belief in joyous religious expression rather than academic rabbinical formalism.

Babbage difference machine

Babbage, Charles (1792-1871), English mathematician. Devised mechanical calculating machine (1834), forerunner of modern computers; it was never completed because of inadequate engineering techniques.

Babbitt, Irving (1865-1933), American critic, essayist. One of founders of early 20th cent. 'New Humanism' movement, influencing T.S. Eliot through advocacy of return to classical ideals. Works incl. *The New Laokoön* (1910), *Rousseau and Romanticism* (1919), *Democracy and Leadership* (1924).

Babel, Isaak Emmanuelovich (1894-*c* 1939), Russian short-story writer. Known for collections *Red Cavalry* (1926) about his experiences in Revolution and *Odessa Tales* (1927) based on his early life. Prob. executed.

Babel, Tower of, in OT, structure erected by Noah's descendants in Babylonia. Symbol of pride of city-dwellers who sought to rebel against God by building a tower to heaven. Thwarted by God's confusing their language so that they could not understand each other.

Bab-el-Mandeb, strait connecting Red Sea with Gulf of Aden. Width *c* 32 km (20 mi); separates SW Arabia from NE Africa.

Baber or **Babar,** title given to Zahir ed-Din Mohammed (*c* 1482-1530), Indian emperor, founder of Mogul dynasty. Conquered most of N India (1526), invading from Afghanistan. Distinguished for his writings, cultural interests.

Babeuf, François Noël (1760-97), French revolutionary. Advocate of economic equality and early form of communism. Leader of cell-based group which plotted overthrow of the DIRECTORY. Betrayed and executed.

Babirussa

babirussa, *Babirussa babirussa,* wild pig of Celebes. Has backward-curving tusks; inhabits marshy forest.

Baboon

baboon, large short-tailed monkey, genus *Papio*, found mainly in Africa. Fierce, with dog-like teeth and snout; lives in large social groups. Arabian baboon, *P. hamadryas*, once sacred to Egyptians.

Babylon, ancient city of Babylonia, on N bank of Euphrates. Its ruins are in C Iraq, S of Baghdad. Important under Hammurabi (*c* 1750 BC) who made it cap. of Babylonia. Destroyed *c* 689 BC by Assyrians, rebuilt and achieved great splendour under Nebuchadnezzar. Its Hanging Gardens were one of the Seven Wonders of the World.

Babylonia, ancient empire of S Mesopotamia. Grew to power in 18th cent. BC under Hammurabi, who took Babylon as his cap. Conquered and ruled by the Kassites until *c* 1150. Recovered under Assyrian rule, which it later overthrew with capture of Nineveh (612). Under Nebuchadnezzar, empire was extended over Mesopotamia, Egypt, Palestine. Absorbed into Persian empire after Cyrus' conquest (539 BC).

Babylonian Captivity, in history of Israel, period from fall of Jerusalem to Babylonians (586 BC) until creation of new Jewish state (538 BC) in Palestine. Many Jews were removed to Mesopotamia at this time. Term also applied to period in Middle Ages when papacy moved from Rome to Avignon, France. Began (1309) under Clement V, ended (1377) under Gregory XI; all popes of this period were French.

Bacchanalia, ancient Roman festivals in honour of Bacchus, god of wine. Excesses caused them to be banned by the Senate (186 BC), although they were continued secretly.

Bacchus, Roman name for Greek god DIONYSUS.

J.S. Bach

Bach, Johann Sebastian (1685-1750), German composer, leading member of family of musicians. Music director in several royal courts, supreme organist of his time. Bach's music came when the adoption of equal temperament made great harmonic movement possible; combined this with immense contrapuntal skill to produce some of the most assured music ever composed. His work consists mainly of keyboard works, pieces for instruments and orchestra, and religious music. Works incl. *Magnificat, Mass in B minor, St John Passion, The Well-tempered Clavier, Brandenburg Concertos.* His son, **Carl Philipp Emanuel Bach** (1714-88), was also a composer, as well as a noted keyboard player and improviser. Compositions characteristic of mid-18th cent., in reaction against his father's polyphonic style. His half-brother, **Johann Christian Bach** (1735-82), lived in London from 1762, where he enjoyed royal patronage. First to play piano as solo instrument in Britain. Wrote operas, symphonies, piano concertos.

backgammon, game played on a special board by two people. Each has 15 pieces which are moved according to the throw of dice. Played by Greeks and Romans and still common in countries of E Mediterranean; enjoyed popularity in West in mid-20th cent.

backswimmer, water bug of Notonectidae family, found worldwide. Swims on back using long oar-like legs. Voracious predator; sucks body fluids of tadpoles, small fish, insects.

Bacolod, commercial town of Philippines. Pop. 212,000. Seaport and sugar-processing centre.

Francis Bacon

Bacon, Francis (1910-), British painter, b. Dublin. Works, characterized by lurid colour, distorted figures and use of photographs, emphasize repulsiveness and horror of human condition. Incl. *Velázquez' Innocent X* and *Three Studies for Figures at the Base of a Cruxifixion* (1944).

Bacon, Francis, Baron Verulam (1561-1626), English philosopher, statesman. In *The Advancement of Learning* (1605), *Novum Organum* (1620), developed INDUCTIVE METHOD as replacement for deduction from Aristotelian authority. Also known for *Essays* (1597-1625) on religious, ethical matters. Lord Chancellor (1618); removed from office (1621) for corruption.

Bacon, Roger (*c* 1215- *c* 1292), English scholar, scientist. Believed scientific experiment and learning necessary complement to faith. Credited with discovery of gunpowder; worked in optics. Wrote encyclopedic *Opus majus, Opus minor* and *Opus tertium*, written for Pope Clement IV.

Baconian theory, argument first advanced in mid-18th cent. by W.H. Smith that Shakespeare lacked the education to write plays attributed to him, proposing Francis Bacon as true author. Now generally discredited.

Bacon's Rebellion (1676), uprising of English colonists in Virginia, led by Nathaniel Bacon (1647-76), over exploitation of small farmers. Revolt collapsed following Bacon's death from fever.

bacteria, large group of usually one-celled micro-organisms, found in soil, water, plants and animals. Considered plant-like, they lack chlorophyll and multiply rapidly by simple fission. Of 3 typical shapes: rod-shaped (*bacillus*), spherical (*coccus*) and spiral (*spirillum*). Many are active in fermentation, promotion of decay of dead organic material and fixing of atmospheric nitrogen. Pathogenic (parasitic) bacteria, 'germs', produce wide range of plant and animal diseases.

bacteriophage, virus that is parasitic upon certain bacteria, whose synthetic machinery it uses to replicate itself.

Bactrian camel, *see* CAMEL.

Badajoz, city of W Spain, on R. Guadiana, cap. of Badajoz prov. Pop. 102,000. Food processing, border trade centre. Former seat of Moorish emirate. Moorish citadel, 13th cent. cathedral.

Badalona, city of Catalonia, NE Spain. Pop. 163,000. Forms conurbation with Barcelona; textiles, chemicals, glass industs. Nearby 15th cent. monastery.

Baden, region of SW West Germany. Former state, from 1952 part of Baden-Württemberg. Incl. picturesque Black Forest and part of Jura; vineyards, minerals, tourism.

Baden, town of NC Switzerland. Pop. 14,000. Hot saline and sulphur therapeutic springs. Seat of Confederation Diet (1424-1712).

Baden-Baden, town of SW West Germany, in Black Forest. Pop. 40,000. Tourism; thermal springs in use from Roman times.

Baden-Powell, Robert Stephenson Smyth, 1st Baron Baden-Powell of Gilwell (1857-1941), British army officer. Defended Mafeking (1899-1900) during Boer War. Founded BOY SCOUTS.

badger, *Meles meles,* nocturnal burrowing carnivore of Europe and N Asia, with black and white striped head. Diet of rodents, insects. American badger, *Taxidea taxus,* is smaller species.

Bad Homburg, *see* HOMBURG VON DER HÖHE.

Badminton, village of Gloucestershire, W England. Seat of dukes of Beaufort. Game named after it. Has annual horse trials.

badminton, game played by volleying a light shuttle, either of feathers or nylon, over a net using gut-strung rackets. Played by 2 or 4 persons. Rules were drawn up in 1870s; said to have originated at Badminton, seat of duke of Beaufort.

Badoglio, Pietro (1871-1956), Italian field marshal. Commanded conquest (1935-6) of Ethiopia. After fall of Mussolini (1943) formed non-fascist govt. Signed armistice with Allies, declared war on Germany.

Baedeker, Karl (1801-59), German publisher. Introduced famous series of Baedeker travel guides, reliability of which based on his own observations.

Baekeland, Lee Hendrik (1863-1944), American chemist, b. Belgium. Developed photographic paper using Velox process. Synthesized bakelite, phenol-formaldehyde resin used for electrical insulation.

Baer, Karl Ernst von (1792-1876), Estonian naturalist. Regarded as founder of comparative embryology, he discovered notochord and mammalian egg. Originated theory of embryonic germ layers which develop to form various vertebrate organs and tissues.

Baffin Bay

Baffin, William (c 1584-1622), English explorer. Piloted 2 unsuccessful expeditions (1615-16) to find Northwest Passage. Baffin Bay and Baffin Isl. named after him.

Baffin Island, largest and most E island in Canadian Arctic; in SE Franklin Dist., Northwest Territs. Area 476,068 sq km (c 183,810 sq mi). Eskimo pop.; whaling, fur trapping. Separated from Greenland by Baffin Bay, connected by Davis Str. to Atlantic.

Bagehot, Walter (1826-77), English economist, social and literary critic. Author of classic interpretation of govt., *The English Constitution* (1867); other works incl. *Physics and Politics* (1872). Editor (1860-77) of *The Economist.*

Baghdad, cap. of Iraq; on R. Tigris. Pop. 2,970,000. Road, rail, air route jct.; produces textiles and cement. Founded 763, *fl* under caliph Harun al-Rashid as centre of commerce and learning. Declined after sack by Mongols (1258). Became cap. of independent Iraq (1921).

Baghdad railway, railway linking Istanbul with Baghdad, Iraq. Financed by German capital, Turkish section to Konya was completed by 1896. Because of its strategic importance, German plans to extend line to Baghdad were opposed by Britain (1911). Completed in 1940.

Bagnold, Enid (1889-), English author. Known for novel *National Velvet* (1935), also wrote plays incl. *The Chalk Garden* (1956).

bagpipe, musical wind instrument consisting of bag inflated by either bellows or by player's breath blown through pipe; bag is squeezed by arm to force air out into several reed-pipes. Chanter pipe has finger holes to produce melody; drones produce continuous bass notes. Of ancient Asiatic origin, bagpipes were introduced to Europe by Romans. Bagpipe playing as art form is esp. developed in Scotland.

Baguio, summer cap. of Philippines, mountain resort in NC Luzon isl. Pop. 85,000. Gold mining centre.

Bahaism, religion founded in 19th cent. by Baha Ullah (1817-92), Persian religious leader. Bahaists believe in the unity of all religions, universal education, equality of the sexes and world peace.

Bahamas, coral isl. state of c 700 isls. in N West Indies; member of British Commonwealth. Incl. Andros (largest), New Providence, SAN SALVADOR. Area 11,404 sq km (4403 sq mi); pop. 168,000, mostly Negro; cap. Nassau. Subsistence agric.; some timber, fish, salt, exports. Important tourist industs. Subject to hurricane damage. Settled by English in 17th cent.; crown colony until independence in 1973.

Bahawalpur, town of EC Pakistan. Pop. 134,000. Cotton goods, soap mfg. Cap. of former princely state of Bahawalpur.

Bahia, see SALVADOR, Brazil.

Bahía Blanca, seaport of E Argentina. Pop. 192,000. Railway jct.; exports beef, grain, wool; meat packing, oil refining industs. Estab. as fort and trading post (1828).

Bahrain or **Bahrein,** isl. group of E Arabia, in Persian Gulf. Area c 595 sq km (230 sq mi); pop. 225,000; cap. Manama. Important oil reserves; dates grown. Sheikdom under British protection until 1971; allied with United Arab Emirates.

Bahr-el-Jebel, section of R. White Nile, S Sudan. Called Albert Nile from L. Albert (Uganda) to Sudan border, flows c 960 km (600 mi) N to join Bahr-el-Ghazal at L. No

Baia-Mare, city of NW Romania, mountain resort. Pop. 109,000. Mining, smelting indust. (gold, silver, lead, zinc); chemicals. Hungarian minority pop.

Baikal, Lake, freshwater lake of USSR, SC Siberian RSFSR. Area c 31,500 sq km (12,200 sq mi). World's deepest lake, reaching depth of 1742 m (5714 ft). R. Angara only outlet.

Baikonour, town of USSR, C Kazakh SSR. Site of Soviet rocket centre.

bail, in law, temporary release of an arrested person on giving bond to court, with assurance that he will appear at subsequent proceedings. Usually granted in civil cases, may be withheld in criminal.

Bain, Alexander (1818-1903), Scottish philosopher. Associate of J. S. Mill. Works on speculative psychology incl. *Mind and Body* (1872). Founded psychological journal *Mind* (1886).

Baird, John Logie (1888-1946), Scottish inventor. Pioneer of television, gave 1st transmission demonstration (1926) using mechanical scanning disc. Demonstrated colour television 1939.

Baja California (Lower California), narrow penin. of NW Mexico, between Gulf of California and Pacific. Mainly mountainous, arid climate; vegetation and pop. concentrated in irrigated region near US border.

bakelite, see BAEKELAND.

Baker, Sir Benjamin (1840-1907), English civil engineer. Helped in design and construction of Forth Rail Bridge (1890), London underground railway, and 1st Aswan Dam.

Baker, George Pierce (1866-1935), American educator. Pioneered use of drama in education through estab. 47 Workshop at Harvard (1906). Wrote *Dramatic Technique* (1919).

Baker, Sir Samuel White (1821-93), English explorer. Explored Nile and tributaries from 1861, met J.H. Speke at Gondokoro (1863). First European to reach Albert Nyanza (1864). Later worked to suppress slave trade on upper Nile.

Bakewell, Robert (1725-95), English livestock breeder. Bred livestock for meat quality; developed new breeds of sheep and cattle by selection and inbreeding.

Bakst, Léon, orig. Lev Nikolayevich Rosenberg (1868-1924), Russian painter. Gained international reputation for stage and costume design while working with Diaghilev's Ballets Russes. His work, noted for exotic motifs and intense colour, was influenced by Russian folk art.

Baku, city of USSR, cap. of Azerbaijan SSR; on Caspian Sea. Pop. 1,314,000. Centre of oil producing area of Apsheron penin. from 1870s; importance has diminished since WW II. Under Persian control 16th-18th cent., incorporated by Russia (1806).

Bakunin, Mikhail Aleksandrovich (1814-76), Russian anarchist. An aristocrat, active in Revolution of 1848; eventually exiled in Siberia but escaped 1861. Expelled (1872) from First INTERNATIONAL for opposition to Marxists. Believed in complete freedom, with violence as revolutionary means.

Balakirev, Mili Alekseyevich (1837-1910), Russian composer. Leader of nationalist Russian school of music; founded group of composers called 'the Five'. Works incl. symphonic poem *Tamara* and overture *King Lear.*

Costume design by Bakst showing Nijinsky in
L'Après-midi d'un faune

Balaklava, suburb of Sevastopol, USSR, Ukrainian SSR; on Crimean penin. Scene of charge of Light Brigade on 25 Oct. 1854 during battle of Crimean War.

balalaika, Russian guitar, usually with three strings, fretted fingerboard and triangular body.

balance of payments, statement of account of a country comprising record of all public and private transactions between that country and all other countries. Takes into account all gifts, foreign aid, loans, interest on debts, payments for goods and received payments for exports, shipping and commercial services abroad, interest on overseas investments.

balance of power, policy of preventing one nation from gaining sufficient power to threaten security of other nations. Formulated by Metternich at Congress of Vienna (1815), served as basis for 19th cent. foreign policy of European nations. Again underlay post-WWII relations between US and USSR.

Balanchine, George, orig. Georgi Melitonovich Balanchivadze (1904-), American choreographer, dancer, teacher, b. Russia. Co-director with Diaghilev of Ballets Russe in Paris (1924-8). Directed New York City Ballet from 1948. Known for choreography of Stravinsky's music.

Balaton (Ger. *Plattensee*), shallow lake of WC Hungary, largest in C Europe. Area 596 sq km (230 sq mi). Vineyards around shores; tourism.

Balboa, Vasco Nuñez de (c 1475-1519), Spanish conquistador. Joined in conquest of Darién; crossed isthmus (1513) accompanied by Indians, becoming first to reach Pacific. Claimed coast for Spain. Beheaded for treason.

Balboa, port of Panama Canal Zone, at Pacific end of Canal. Pop. 3000. Admin. hq. of zone and canal. Has extensive docks, ship repairing industs; US naval base.

Balchin, Nigel Marlin (1908-70), English novelist. Wrote psychological thrillers, *eg The Small Back Room* (1943) about wartime research, *Mine Own Executioner* (1945).

bald eagle, *Haliaeetus leucocephalus,* North American bird of prey. Black, with white head, neck and tail. Feeds on dead fish, rodents. National emblem of US.

Balder, in Norse myth, son of Odin, god of light, peace, virtue, wisdom. Killed by the trickery of Loki after attempt by his mother to make him invulnerable.

Baldwin I (c 1058-1118), king of Jerusalem (1100-18). Succeeded as ruler his brother, Godfrey of Bouillon, both having taken part in 1st Crusade.

Baldwin, James (1924-), American author. Best known for first novel, *Go Tell it on the Mountain* (1953), but essays on Negro problems incl. equally important *Notes of a Native Son* (1955). Also wrote plays, *eg Amen Corner* (1955).

Baldwin, Robert (1804-58), Canadian statesman. Co-leader with LaFontaine of ministry (1848-51) which achieved responsible govt. for Prov. of Canada (modern Québec and Ontario).

Stanley Baldwin

Baldwin, Stanley Baldwin, 1st Earl (1867-1947), British statesman, PM (1923-4, 1924-9, 1935-7). Leader of Conservative Party (1923-37). First term ended on protectionist tariff issue; later instrumental in ending General Strike (1926). Rise of fascism in Europe and constitutional crisis over Edward VIII's abdication marked 3rd term.

Bâle, *see* BASLE, Switzerland.

Balearic Islands

Balearic Islands (*Islas Baleares*), archipelago of W Mediterranean Sea, forming Baleares prov. of Spain. Area 5012 sq km (1935 sq mi); cap. Palma. Incl. Majorca, Minorca, Iviza, Formentera. Tourism, agric., fishing. Inhabited from prehist. times; under Moorish rule 10th cent.-1235; united with Aragón 1349.

Balewa, Alhaji Sir Abubakar Tafawa, *see* TAFAWA BALEWA.

Balfour, Arthur James Balfour, 1st Earl of (1848-1930), British statesman, PM (1902-5). His Conservative govt. resigned after cabinet split over Joseph Chamberlain's proposals for tariff reform (1905); party heavily defeated in 1906 election. As foreign secretary, drew up BALFOUR DECLARATION (1917).

Balfour Declaration (1917), assurance of British protection for Jewish settlement of Palestine after its capture by British forces. Drawn up by foreign secretary Balfour and contained in letter to Rothschild of British Zionist Federation. Jews allowed into Palestine under limited quota system between world wars.

Bali

Bali, isl. of Indonesia, just off E Java. Area *c* 5700 sq km (2200 sq mi); pop. 2,250,000. Mountainous, with fertile soil and good climate; produces rice, copra, coffee. Balinese are Hindus, having been converted in 7th cent.

Balikesir, town of NW Turkey. Pop. 69,000. Cereal, opium trade; rug mfg.

balkanization, breakup of territ. into small, mutually hostile political units. Term derived from post-WWI treaties of Trianon and Sèvres, in which Allies estab. new boundaries for Balkan countries.

Balkan Peninsula, SE Europe. Extends S from rivers Danube, Sava. Comprises Albania, Bulgaria, Greece, Turkey (Europe), Yugoslavia. Includes Balkan Mts. (Bulg. *Stara Planina*), range of C Bulgaria. Rise to 2372 m (7785 ft); crossed by Shipka Pass.

Balkan Wars (1912-13), two short wars for possession of Ottoman Empire's European territ. Serbo-Bulgarian alliance (1912) led to First War (Oct.), in which Turkey lost all European possessions except Constantinople area. Austria, Hungary and Italy, at a meeting of Great Powers in London, created (1913) an independent Albania, thwarting ambitions of Serbia, which then demanded greater share of Macedonia from Bulgaria. Latter attacked Serbia (June,1913), only to be attacked by Romania, Greece and Turkey. Second Balkan War ended with Treaty of Bucharest (Aug. 1913), in which Bulgaria lost territ. to all its enemies. Serbian territ. ambitions contributed to outbreak of WWI.

Balkhash, Lake, shallow lake of USSR, in SE Kazakh SSR. Area *c* 18,200 sq km (7000 sq mi). E part saline; W part, fed chiefly by R. Ili, fresh; no outlet. On N shore, **Balkhash,** is copper-mining centre. Pop. 70,000.

Ball, John (d. 1381), English priest. Expounded Wycliffe's doctrines; excommunicated (1376) and imprisoned. Released by rebels, became leader of PEASANTS' REVOLT (1381); caught and executed.

ballad, orig. (medieval British) narrative song in short stanzas, often with refrain, usually of popular origin, and orally transmitted, though sometimes composed by minstrels for noble audience. Now incl. narrative poems, *eg* Rossetti's *Sister Helen.*

ballade, poetic form set to music, *fl* 13th and 14th cent. in Provence and Italy. Composers, esp. Chopin and Brahms, used term for dramatic piano pieces.

Ballance, John (1839-93), New Zealand politician, b. Ireland, premier (1891-3). His Liberal govt. introduced widespread constitutional and social reforms.

Ballantyne, R[obert] M[ichael] (1825-94), Scottish writer of boy's adventure stories. Works incl. *Martin Rattler* (1858) and *Coral Island* (1858).

Ballarat, city of S Victoria, Australia. Pop. 58,000. Railway engineering, indust. centre; trade in wool, wheat, fruit. Mining town from 1851 gold rush; scene of 'Eureka Stockade' miners' revolt (1854).

ballet, dramatic entertainment combining music, dance, mime, spectacle. Ballet as known today descends from court festivities of French, Italian Renaissance. Developed by French, esp. at Louis XIV's court where Lully and Molière created *comédies-ballets,* combination of dance and speech. The 5 classical feet positions were adopted in 18th cent., classical white dress and *en pointe* style in 19th cent. In 20th cent., rigid traditions attacked by Isadora Duncan and Diaghilev's Ballets Russes. With latter were associated Fokine, Nijinsky, Pavlova, Massine, Balanchine. Modern choreographers incl. Martha Graham, Frederick Ashton, and companies incl. New York City Ballet, Bolshoi (Moscow), Royal Ballet (London).

balloon, non-powered aircraft obtaining lift from bag filled with lighter-than-air gas or hot air. Montgolfier brothers credited with invention (hot-air type, 1783). Hydrogen type first flown (1783) by J. Charles. Used for military observation since Napoleonic Wars; in WWII, balloons anchored by cables were used to obstruct low-flying aircraft. Now used for meteorological research, normally filled with helium for its non-flammability.

Ballymena, town of E Northern Ireland, in former Co. Antrim. Pop. 16,000. Linen mfg. **Ballymena,** district; area 637 sq km (246 sq mi); pop. 50,000. Created 1973, formerly part of Co. Antrim.

Ballymoney, dist. of NC Northern Ireland. Area 418 sq km (161 sq mi); pop. 23,000. Created 1973, formerly part of Co. Antrim.

balm or **bee balm,** *Melissa officinalis,* many branched lemon-scented perennial of thyme family with white, lipped flowers. Favourite plant of bees.

balsa or **corkwood,** *Ochroma lagopus,* tree of Central and South America and West Indies. Strong, light wood used in model-making. Raft in Kontiki expedition (1947) was made of balsa trunks.

balsam, several trees, shrubs and plants of family Balsaminaceae which yield aromatic balsam. Species incl. orange balsam, *Impatiens capenis,* of North America; Himalayan balsam, *I. grandulifera,* showiest of the genus, grows wild beside rivers.

Baltic, branch of Indo-European family of languages, close to Slavic. Incl. Lettish (Latvian), Lithuanian, Old Prussian; last now dead. Said to be closest of modern Indo-European languages to ancient parent tongue.

Baltic Sea

Baltic Sea (Ger. *Ostsee*), sea of N Europe. Bordered by Denmark, Germany, Finland, Poland, Sweden, USSR. Linked to North Sea by Oresund, Great and Little Belt, Kiel Canal. Shallow; small tides. Hist. area of Hanseatic trade. Intensive fishing.

Baltic States, hist. name for countries on E shores of Baltic Sea, incl. LIVONIA, Estonia, Latvia, Lithuania (all now in USSR).

Baltimore, port of N Maryland, US; on Chesapeake Bay inlet. Pop. 906,000. Has natural harbour; exports coal and grain. Commercial, indust., railway centre; shipbuilding, steel indust., oil refining. Built 1729, with growth based on shipbuilding ('Baltimore' clippers famous in 19th cent.). Terminus of 1st US railway. RC bishopric (Primate of US); Johns Hopkins Univ. (1876).

Baltimore oriole, *Icterus galbula,* North American insectivorous bird. Male black and orange; nest is woven hanging bag.

Baluchi, *see* IRANIAN.

Baluchistan, region of SW Pakistan bounded by Iran, Afghanistan and Arabian Sea. Arid and mountainous;

inhabited by Baluchis, Pathans. N controlled by British after Afghan wars of 19th cent.

Balzac, Honoré de (1799-1850), French novelist. Best known for *La Comédie humaine*, extensive series of novels incl. *Eugénie Grandet* (1833), *Père Goriot* (1834), *Cousine Bette* (1846), which attempted to represent contemporary French society by creating a complete, detailed fictional world.

Balzac, Jean-Louis Guez de (*c* 1597-1654), French writer. *Lettres* (1624) had great influence on French prose style.

Bamako, cap. of Mali, on R. Niger. Pop. 197,000. Admin., commercial centre; river port, railway to Dakar. Former cap. of French Sudan.

Bamberg, town of EC West Germany, on R. Regnitz. Pop. 71,000. Textiles, engineering, beer industs. Seat of powerful ecclesiastical state 1007-1802. Cathedral (13th cent.) has tombs of Emperor Henry II, Pope Clement II.

bamboo or **cane,** semitropical or tropical grasses of the genera *Bambusa, Arundinaria, Phyllostachys.* Rapidly growing clump plant propagated by spreading underground roots. Some attain 35 m/120 ft. *Bambusa arundinacea,* hard, durable, with hollow stems, is used in buildings, furniture, utensils, paper making. Young bamboo shoots of some species are edible.

Bananas growing on palm

banana, *Musa sapientum,* large perennial Asian plant, now widely cultivated in tropical regions of W hemisphere. Simple leaves, clustered flowers with edible fruits growing in large pendent bunches. Rich in carbohydrates.

Banat of Temesvár, plain of Romania and Yugoslavia, between Transylvanian Alps and R. Tisza. Fertile, agric.; main town Timişoara. Hungarian from 11th cent., divided between Romania, Yugoslavia after WWI.

Banbridge, dist. of S Northern Ireland. Area 445 sq km (172 sq mi); pop. 30,000. Created 1973, formerly part of Co. Down.

Banbury, mun. bor. of Oxfordshire, C England. Pop. 29,000. Market town; food processing industs. Famous for cakes. Has Banbury Cross of nursery rhyme.

band, a group of musicians, usually smaller than an orchestra. A brass band consists principally of brass instruments; a percussion or rhythm band mainly of percussion instruments. Bands are also named by the kind of music they play, *eg* dance band, military band. A 'big band' is large dance band consisting of sections of saxophones, trombones and trumpets overlying a rhythm section; it developed with the swing music of the 1930s.

Banda, Hastings Kamuzu (1902-), Malawi statesman. Campaigned against Federation of Rhodesia and Nyasaland; imprisoned 1959-60. Became PM (1963), and president (1966) after Nyasaland had become republic as Malawi.

Bandar, *see* MASULIPATNAM.

Bandaranaike, Sirimavo (1916-), Sri Lankan politician, PM (1960-5, 1970-). Entered politics following her husband Solomon Bandaranaike's assassination (1959) while PM. She hosted Conference of Non-aligned Nations (1976).

Bandicoot

bandicoot, nocturnal Australasian marsupial of Peramelidae family, comprising *c* 20 species. Rat-like, with pointed muzzle; digs for insects, worms, roots.

Bandung, city of W Java, Indonesia. Pop. 1,202,000. Textile, rubber product mfg. Resort in beautiful surroundings.

Banff, resort town of SW Alberta, Canada. Pop. 4000. Nearby is Banff National Park; area 6641 sq km (2564 sq mi). Scenic lakes, glaciers, hot springs.

Banffshire, former county of NE Scotland, now in Grampian region. Cairngorm Mts. in S, fertile coastal plain in N. Cattle, fishing, distilling. Co. town was **Banff,** royal burgh (chartered 1163) on Moray Firth. Pop. 8000. Resort.

Bangalore, city of S India, cap. and railway jct. of Karnataka state. Pop. 1,648,000. Textile indust., electrical apparatus, machinery mfg. Tata Institute of Science (1911). Founded 16th cent.; ruins of Tippoo Sahib's palace.

Bangka, isl. of Indonesia, separated from SE Sumatra by Bangka Strait. Area *c* 11,900 sq km (4600 sq mi). Major tin producer.

Bangkok (*Krung Thep*), cap. of Thailand, port near mouth of R. Chao Phraya. Pop. 1,867,000. Exports teak, rice, rubber; rice milling, oil refining. Transport in old city mainly by canal boats. Became cap. 1782; royal temple (1785) has famous image of Buddha.

Bangladesh

Bangladesh, republic of SC Asia, at N end of Bay of Bengal. Area *c* 143,000 sq km (55,200 sq mi); pop. 71,614,000; cap. Dacca. Language: Bengali. Religion: Islam. Consists mainly of deltas of Ganges, Brahmaputra and Meghna rivers; densely populated. Agric. economy based on rice, tea and esp. jute. Subject to flooding and cyclones. Was East PAKISTAN from 1947 until civil war led to independence (1971).

Bangor, port of E Northern Ireland, on Belfast Lough. Pop. 35,000. Tourist resort; former shipbuilding indust. Has ruins of 6th cent. abbey.

Bangor, city of Gwynedd, NW Wales, on Menai Strait. Pop. 15,000. Tourist resort. Has Univ. of Wales coll. (1893); 16th cent. cathedral.

Bangui, cap. of Central African Republic, on R. Ubangi. Pop. 187,000. Port and trade centre, textile indust. Univ. (1970). Founded 1889, formerly cap. of Ubangi-Shari territ.

Bangweulu, Lake, shallow lake of N Zambia. Area c 9840 sq km (3800 sq mi); bordered by swamps. Discovered (1868) by Livingstone.

Banjermasin or **Bandjarmasin,** cap. of Kalimantan prov. (Borneo), Indonesia. Pop. 282,000. Port near mouth of R. Barito. Exports oil, rubber.

banjo, stringed musical instrument with a circular parchment resonator and open back. Of African origin but developed in US, where it was brought by black slaves.

Banjul, cap. of Gambia, at mouth of R. Gambia. Pop. 39,000. Admin., commercial centre; port, exports groundnuts, hides. Founded 1816, known as Bathurst until 1973.

Bankhead, Tallulah Brockman (1903-68), American actress. Known as radio, screen and stage star, esp. in *Private Lives.*

banking, conduct of financial transactions through institutions primarily devoted to accepting deposits (subject to transfer and withdrawal by cheque) and making loans. Thus banks do not necessarily own the total of the funds they may use. Practised in classical times; large-scale banking in Middle Ages dominated by Italian families. Modern banking developed during 18th-19th cent. in W Europe and US with expansion of trade and indust. *See* BANK OF ENGLAND, FEDERAL RESERVE SYSTEM.

Bank of England, central bank of Britain, founded (1694) as commercial bank. Bank Charter Act (1844) estab. present system. Responsible for issue of bank notes, funding of national debts, *etc.* Nationalized 1946.

bank rate [UK] or **discount rate** [US], minimum rate at which Bank of England or US Federal Reserve Bank makes loans to commercial banks and other prime borrowers. As other lending rates are closely related to bank rate, high rate restricts borrowing and lending, low rate encourages expansion of credit. Thus used as instrument of monetary control.

Banks, Sir Joseph (1743-1820), English naturalist. Accompanied Cook in expedition around the world (1768-71), accumulating remarkable plant collection. Leading figure in development of Kew Gardens. President of the Royal Society (1778-1820).

banksia or **bottle brush,** genus of evergreen trees and shrubs of Protraceae family named after Sir Joseph Banks. Widely distributed in S hemisphere, esp. Australia.

Banks Island, SW Franklin Dist., Northwest Territs., Canada. Area 67,340 sq km (c 26,000 sq mi). First explored 1851.

Bannister, Sir Roger Gilbert (1929-), English physician. First man to run the mile in under 4 min. (Oxford, 1954). Best time was 3 min. 58.8 sec.

Bannockburn, town of Central region, C Scotland. Site of battle (1314) in which Robert the Bruce's victory over Edward II of England secured Scottish independence.

banteng, *Bos sondaicus,* rare species of wild cattle of SE Asia, widely domesticated. Has white rump and legs; related to gaur.

Banting, Sir Frederick Grant (1891-1941), Canadian physician. With C.H. Best, isolated (1921) insulin from pancreas; later purified it for use in treating human diabetes. Shared Nobel Prize for Physiology and Medicine (1923).

Bantry Bay, inlet of SW Irish Republic, 40 km (25 mi) long. Anchorage; oil storage. Scene of attempted French landing (1796). At head is port, Bantry (pop. 2000).

Bantu, African ethnic and linguistic group, c 70 million. Stretch from Equator south, except for extreme SW Africa. Physically diverse, classified mainly on language. Highly developed pre-European conquest; developed protective confederations in 19th cent., incl. ZULU and Basuto. Name, meaning 'the people', commonly used in South Africa for all native people. *See* BANTU LANGUAGES.

Bantu in ceremonial attire

Bantu languages, group of African languages, most important within NIGER-CONGO branch, although considered part of Benue-Congo subgroup. Contains hundreds of languages, spoken throughout C and S Africa; incl. SWAHILI, Zulu, Xhosa, Sotho, Kikuyu.

Banville, Théodore Faullain de (1823-91), French poet. Known for contribution to *Parnasse contemporain* (1866) and collections *Les Stalactites* (1846), *Les Exilés* (1867).

Banyan tree in Sri Lanka

banyan, E Indian fig tree, *Ficus benghalensis.* Branches send out aerial roots which reach ground to form new trunks, creating large sheltered area. Sacred among Hindus.

Baobab tree in Ethiopia

baobab or **boojum,** *Adansonia digitata,* large tree native to Africa, India. Broad trunk adaptable to storage of water. Yields edible fruit (monkey bread). Bark used in making paper, cloth, rope. Leaves used medicinally.

baptism, in most Christian churches, sacrament admitting a person into Christianity. Involves ritual purification with water and invocation of grace of God to free the soul from sin. Baptism of Jesus by John the Baptist is considered part of founding of Christian church.

Baptists, Christian denomination holding that BAPTISM should be given only to believers after confession of faith, and by immersion in water rather than by sprinkling. First English Baptist congregation formed (*c* 1608) in Amsterdam under John Smyth. Baptist World Alliance (1905) holds regular congresses.

Barabbas, in NT, prisoner chosen by the mob, in accordance with Passover custom, to be released by Pilate in place of Jesus.

Baranof Island, off SE Alaska, US; in Alexander Archipelago. Area 4162 sq km (1607 sq mi). Largest town Sitka.

Barbados, low-lying isl. state, in British Commonwealth. Most E of West Indies. Area 430 sq km (166 sq mi); pop. 238,000; cap. Bridgetown. Has fertile agric. soil; sugar cane growing; molasses, rum mfg. Winter tourist resort. Claimed by English 1605; independence 1966. Subject to severe hurricanes.

barbary ape, *Macaca sylvanus,* tailless monkey of N Africa, S Spain and Gibraltar. Only monkey native to Europe.

Barbary Coast, coast of N Africa from Morocco to Libya. Named after Berbers, the chief inhabitants. Notorious for piracy on European shipping (16th-19th cent.), ended by French capture of Algiers (1830). Name also applied to waterfront dist. of San Francisco, US, after 1849 gold rush.

barbastelle, *Barbastella barbastellus,* common European bat, with almost black fur. Roosts in large colonies.

barbel, freshwater fish of carp family, genus *Barbus,* found in Asia, Africa, Europe. Thread-like growths (barbels) hanging from jaws act as organs of touch. European variety, *B. barbus,* is coarse fish.

Barber, Samuel (1910-), American composer. Work inclines to contemporary European idioms and is written mainly in traditional forms. Best-known piece is *Adagio For Strings.*

barberry, any deciduous shrub of genus *Berberis.* Spiny leaves, sour red berries, yellow flowers. Ornamental species, often used in hedges, incl. Japanese barberry, *B. thunbergii.* The common European barberry, *B. vulgaris,* is also found in North America.

barbet, brightly coloured bird of Capitonidae family of Old World tropical forests. Thick solid beak with whiskers growing at base.

Barbirolli, Sir John (1899-1970), British conductor. Gained renown in 1936 on succeeding Toscanini as conductor of the New York Philharmonic Orchestra; best known as the conductor of the Hallé Orchestra (Manchester) from 1943 to 1968.

barbiturates, group of drugs derived from barbituric acid, used to promote sleep and as sedatives. Overuse may lead to addiction.

Barbizon School, group of French landscape painters who made their centre at Barbizon in Forest of Fontainebleau in 1840s. Members incl. Millet, Daubigny. Aimed at exact rendering of country life and scenery, painted directly from nature.

Barbour, John (*c* 1316-95), Scottish poet and churchman. Known for chronicle-poem *The Bruce* (1375).

Barbuda, *see* ANTIGUA.

Barbusse, Henri (1873-1935), French novelist. Known for *Under Fire* (1916) a realistic indictment of war. Other novels incl. *The Inferno* (1908), *Chains* (1925).

Barcelona, city of Catalonia, NE Spain, on Mediterranean Sea. Cap. of Barcelona prov. Pop. 1,745,000. Major port; indust., commercial centre; univ. (1430). Founded by Carthaginians; taken (801) by Charlemagne, independent countship from 9th cent. *Fl* after union (1137) of Aragón and Catalonia. Catalan cultural centre, focus of radical movements. Seat of govt. (1938-9) in Civil War. Cathedral (13th cent.), palaces.

Barclay de Tolly, Mikhail, Prince (1761-1818), Russian field marshal. Commanded Russian forces in Finland (1808-9) and against Napoleon during the retreat to Moscow.

Bardia, town of of NE Libya, in Cyrenaica. Pop. 4000. Scene of heavy fighting in WWII, base for Italian campaign against Egypt, taken from Italians by British 1942.

Baréa, Arturo (1897-1957), Spanish novelist. Exiled after Civil War, best known for autobiog. trilogy *The Forging of a Rebel* (1951). Also wrote essay on Lorca.

Barebone, Praise-God (*c* 1596-1679), English noncon-formist lay preacher. Member of provisional assembly (Barebone's Parliament) nominated by Cromwell (1653) after dissolution of Rump Parliament.

Bareilly, city of Uttar Pradesh, N India. Pop. 326,000. Trade centre; carpet, furniture mfg.

Barents or **Barentz, Willem** (d. 1597), Dutch explorer. Made 3 unsuccessful attempts to find Northeast Passage, reached Spitsbergen and Novaya Zemlya. Barents Sea named after him.

Barents Sea, extension of Arctic Ocean, lying N of Norway and bounded in part by Franz Josef Land and Novaya Zemlya. Ice-free ports, *eg* Murmansk, and fisheries in S.

barge, large boat, usually flat-bottomed, used for transportation on sheltered waters. Common on Nile in ancient Egypt. Modern barges towed by tugs. Self-propelled steel barges used on Great Lakes of North America for bulk transport. Recent developments incl. ships which can take barges aboard to unload them.

Barham, Richard Harris (1788-1845), English antiquary. Known for verse tales, *The Ingoldsby Legends* (1840).

Bari, city of Apulia, SE Italy, on Adriatic Sea. Cap. of Bari prov. Pop. 365,000. Major port; oil refining, textiles; univ. (1924). Roman colony (*Barium*); taken (1071) by Normans, embarkation point for medieval Crusades. Cathedral (12th cent.), basilica with relics of St Nicholas.

Baring, Maurice (1874-1945), English author. As journalist in Russia wrote on its culture. Works incl. poetry, plays, novels, *eg C* (1924), and autobiog. *The Puppet Show of Memory* (1922).

Baring-Gould, Sabine (1834-1924), English writer. Wrote many religious and hist. works, children's fiction, hymns, *eg* 'Onward Christian Soldiers'.

barite, barytes or **heavy spar** (BaSO₄), heavy, white or colourless mineral. Consists of orthorhombic-shaped crystals; occurs in massive or granular forms. Uses incl. paint pigment, medical radiology. Major deposits in England, Romania, US.

barium (Ba), silvery metallic element; at. no. 56, at. wt. 137.34. Occurs as BARYTES and as carbonate; prepared industrially by reduction of barium oxide. Compounds used in glass, paint and fireworks; sulphate taken internally to help obtain X-ray pictures of digestive tract.

bark, outer covering of the stems and roots of trees and woody plants. Consists of 2 layers; the inner of living flexible cork-like material, the outer a dead inflexible shell. Many barks have economic uses *eg* as in hemp, flax, jute or as flavourings, *eg* cinnamon or drugs, *eg* quinine, cocaine.

bark beetle or **engraver beetle,** insect of Scolytidae family. Tunnels between bark and wood of trees, creating elaborate gallery system; major pest of timber.

Barker, George Granville (1913-), English poet. Contemporary of Auden and wrote on Spanish Civil War, but more akin to Dylan Thomas. Many works incl. *Collected Poems* (1957).

Barker, Harley Granville, *see* GRANVILLE-BARKER

Barking, bor. of NE Greater London, England. Pop. 160,000. Has large power station. Motor vehicles indust. Created 1965 from Barking, Dagenham.

Bar-le-Duc, town of Lorraine, NE France, on R. Ornain and Rhine-Marne canal. Cap. of Meuse dept. Pop. 20,000. Metal goods, textiles, jams. Seat of medieval Bar duchy.

Barletta, town of Apulia, SE Italy, on Adriatic Sea. Pop. 76,000. Port, indust. centre; wine, fruit market. Saltworks nearby. Taken (12th cent.) by Normans; *fl* 15th cent. with large merchant fleet.

barley, genus *Hordeum* of grass family, probably originating in Asia Minor. Cultivated since prehistoric times. Most common cultivated form is *H. vulgare.* Unbranched stems rise in clumps and bearded seed heads extend from the grains. Used to make malt and to feed livestock.

Barlow, Joel (1754-1812), American poet. Known for epic, *The Columbiad* (1807), on the discovery of America. Also wrote political tracts.

Barna, Victor (1911-72), British table tennis player, b. Hungary. Known for the artistry of his play, he was 5 times men's singles world champion and 8 times men's doubles champion (1930-9).

barnacle, sedentary crustacean of subclass Cirripedia, found on rocks, piers and boat hulls. In some species, *eg* acorn barnacle, *Balanus,* body enclosed in limy plates. Other naked varieties parasitic on marine invertebrates.

Barnacle goose

barnacle goose, *Branta leucopsis,* European goose with black and white plumage. Eaten on fast days in Middle Ages, as it was believed to be fish, hatching from barnacle.

Barnard,, Christiaan Neethling (1922-   ), South African surgeon. Performed 1st human heart transplant operation (Cape Town, Dec. 1967); patient died after 18 days.

Barnard, Frederick Augustus Porter (1809-89), American educator. President of Columbia Coll. (1864–89), which he reformed and extended. Advocated equal educational opportunities for women.

Barnardo, Thomas John (1845-1905), British social reformer, b. Ireland. Known for founding 'Dr Barnardo's Homes', refuges for destitute children. Also instrumental in securing legislation to protect children.

Barnato, Barnett, orig. Barney Isaacs (1852-97), South African financier, b. London. Made fortune in South African diamond mining, but company merged (1888) with Cecil Rhodes's De Beers concern. Committed suicide.

Barnaul, city of USSR, SC Siberian RSFSR. Pop. 459,000. Railway jct. and port on R. Ob. Textile, machinery mfg. Founded in 18th cent. as mining centre.

Barnes, see RICHMOND-UPON-THAMES, England.

Barnet, bor. of W Greater London, England. Pop. 304,000. Created 1965 from parts of Middlesex, Hertfordshire. Scene of Yorkist victory (1471) in which Warwick the Kingmaker was killed.

Barnett, Samuel Augustus (1844-1913), English clergyman, social reformer. Founded (1884) Toynbee Hall settlement, London, to study problems of the poor.

barn owl, long-legged pale owl of Tytonidae family with worldwide distribution, esp. *Tyto alba.* Lives in farm buildings; hunts mainly by sound.

Barnsley, town of South Yorkshire met. co., N England, on R. Dearne. Pop. 75,000. Coalmining; engineering, textiles industs.

Barnstaple, mun. bor. of Devon, SW England, on R. Taw. Pop. 17,000. Lace, gloves, pottery mfg. Has 15th cent. stone bridge.

Barn owl *(Tyto alba)*

Barnum, Phineas T[aylor] (1810-91), American showman. Exploited public taste for sensational, *eg* exhibiting midget Tom Thumb. Estab. circus 'The Greatest Show on Earth' (1871).

Baroda, city of Gujarat state, W India. Pop. 467,000. Railway jct.; textile mfg. Cap. of former princely state of Baroda.

Baroja y Nessi, Pío (1872-1956), Spanish novelist. Known for *The Tree of Knowledge* (1911) a pessimistic account of the intellectual life.

barometer, instrument used to measure atmospheric pressure. Comprises mercury-filled tube closed at upper end and held inverted in mercury-filled vessel. Height of mercury in tube gives atmospheric pressure. *See* also ANEROID barometer.

Barons' War (1263-7), in English history, war between Henry III and his barons, led by DE MONTFORT. Henry's defeat at Lewes (1265) led to summoning of Great Parliament. De Montfort was defeated and killed at Evesham (1265).

Baroque, in art and architecture, style characterized by much dramatic ornamentation and use of curved, rather than straight lines. Flourished from *c* 1580-1730; high Baroque style of Bernini was designed to impress beholders both physically and emotionally by enormity and vigour of its figures.

Barquisimeto, city of NW Venezuela. Pop. 291,000. In agric. region (coffee, sugar, cattle exports); textile, cigarettes, leather mfg. Founded (1552) as Nueva Segovia.

Barra, isl. of Outer Hebrides, W Scotland. Chief town Castlebay.

barracuda, voracious tropical fish of Sphyraenidae family. Great barracuda, *Sphyraena barracuda,* is largest, *c* 1.8 m/6 ft long. Popular game fish.

Barranquilla, port of N Colombia, near mouth of Magdalena R. Pop. 656,000. Sugar refining, textile, chemical mfg.

Barras, Paul François Jean Nicolas, Vicomte de (1755-1829), French Revolutionary. Jacobin activist, later helped overthrow Robespierre during THERMIDOR, ending Reign of Terror (1794). Leading member of Directory, lost power after supporting Napoleon's coup of 18 Brumaire (1799).

Barrault, Jean-Louis (1910-   ), French actor-director. Renowned mime, director of Théâtre de France (1959-68); films incl. *Les Enfants du Paradis* (1944), *La Ronde* (1950).

barrel organ, mechanical organ in which a barrel armed with pins rotates and trips levers that admit air to organ pipes, to produce a single piece of music. Barrel is usually turned by hand as in the mobile street piano, often wrongly called a barrel organ because it has a similar barrel-and-pin mechanism.

Jean-Louis Barrault

Barrès, [Augustin-] Maurice (1862-1923), French novelist. Known for trilogies *Le Culte du moi* (1888-91) about an egoist who discovers his need for others, *Le Roman de L'énergie national* (1897-1903) based on his public life.

Barrett Browning, Elizabeth, *see* BROWNING, ROBERT.

Sir James Barrie

Barrie, Sir J[ames] M[atthew] (1860-1937), Scottish author. Plays incl. classic nostalgic fantasy *Peter Pan* (1904), also *The Admirable Crichton* (1902), *Dear Brutus* (1917). Wrote novels *eg The Little Minister* (1891), *Sentimental Tommy* (1896).

barrister, in England, qualified member of legal profession who presents and pleads cases in courts. In higher courts has exclusive right to appear on behalf of litigant, but (with few exceptions) can do so only on solicitor's instructions. To qualify, student must join one of four INNS OF COURT; becomes 'junior', then King's (or Queen's) Counsel. *See* ADVOCATE.

barrow, in archaeology, mound erected over burial place. European barrows, dating from Neolithic times, are usually long or round. Building of barrows for burial of important people lasted into Saxon and Viking times.

Barrow-in-Furness, bor. in Furness area of Cumbria, NW England. Pop. 64,000. Iron and steel mfg., shipbuilding, engineering industs.

Barry, Sir Charles (1795-1860), English architect. With Pugin, designed Houses of Parliament at Westminster (1840-6).

Barry, Sir Gerald Reid (1899-1968), English journalist. Editor of *News Chronicle* (1936-47) and co-founder of Political and Economic Planning (P.E.P.).

Barry, mun. bor. and port of S Glamorgan, S Wales, on Bristol Channel. Pop. 42,000. Exports coal, steel.

Barrymore, Lionel (1878-1954), American stage and film actor. Film roles incl. Rasputin in *Rasputin and the Empress* (1932). His sister, **Ethel Barrymore** (1879-1959), was a leading American actress, appearing on Broadway stage until 1944, then moved to Hollywood to play 'character' parts in films. Their brother, **John Barrymore** (1882-1942), also acted on stage (*Richard III, Hamlet*), and in film. Known for 'profile' as young matinée idol, then romantic star of 1920s (*Raffles*, 1917, *Beau Brummell*, 1924).

Bart, Jean (*c* 1650-1702), French sailor. Began as privateer, elevated to rear admiral (1696) by Louis XIV after exploits during wars of 1690s against European Allies.

Barth, Heinrich (1821-65), German explorer. Appointed by UK govt. to accompany trans-Saharan expedition (1850); explored Niger, L. Chad, upper R. Benue areas. Wrote *Travels and Discoveries in North and Central Africa* (1857-8).

Barth, John (1930-), American author. Known for fanciful philosophical fiction *eg The Sotweed Factor* (1960) an extravagant historical novel, *Giles Goat-Boy* (1966) satirizing the concept of education.

Barth, Karl (1886-1968), Swiss Protestant theologian. Believed authority of God is revealed in Jesus and biblical study is superior to philosophy. Early opponent of Nazism. Works incl. *The Word of God and the Word of Man* (1924).

Bartholdi, Frédéric Auguste (1834-1904), French sculptor. Works incl. Statue of Liberty in New York harbour and *Lion of Belfort*.

Bartlett, John (1820-1905), American editor, publisher. Known for his collection of *Familiar Quotations* (1855), also wrote Shakespeare concordances, books on chess.

Béla Bartók

Bartók, Béla (1881-1945), Hungarian composer, pianist. Collected folk music, which influenced much of his work; compositions subsequently became more dissonant. His 6 string quartets greatly extended quartet medium; other works incl. *Concerto for Orchestra*, opera *Bluebeard's Castle*.

Bartolommeo [del Fattorino], Fra (1475-1517), Italian painter of Florentine school. Worked with Raphael in development of high Renaissance style; influenced Raphael in handling of drapery and colouring. Works incl. *Pietà* (Florence).

Barton, Clara (1821-1912), American philanthropist. Organized American National Red Cross Society (1881), and was its president until 1904.

Barton, Sir Edmund (1849-1920), Australian statesman, PM (1901-3). Leader of movement for federation of Australian colonies, became 1st PM with independence.

Barton, Elizabeth (*c* 1506-34), English nun, called the Maid of Kent. Uttered 'prophecies' denouncing Henry VIII's proposed divorce of Catherine of Aragon. Executed for treason.

Baruch, Bernard Mannes (1870-1965), American financier, economic adviser. Held govt. posts under Wilson, F.D. Roosevelt. Representative for US to United Nations Atomic Energy Commission (1946-7), formulated proposals for control of atomic energy.

baryon, in physics, one of class of elementary particles, comprising protons, neutrons, and HYPERONS. All experience STRONG NUCLEAR INTERACTION and obey Fermi-Dirac statistics, *ie* are FERMIONS.

barytes, *see* BARITE.

basalt, fine-grained igneous rock, occurring abundantly in volcanic lava. Usually black or dull grey in colour. Basalt flows underly sediments beneath all oceans, and form many land masses,*eg* Deccan of India, Columbia R. plateau of US.

base, in chemistry, substance which yields hydroxyl (OH) ions if dissolved in water. Reacts with acids to form salt and water. Inorganic bases obtained by adding water to metal oxide; strength depends on degree of ionization. More generally, base defined as substance that accepts protons (thus amines are organic bases).

baseball, nine-a-side team game played with bat and ball, mainly in US. Invention is sometimes attributed to Abner Doubleday (1839). First organized team was New York Knickerbockers (1845); 1st professional team Cincinnati Red Stockings (1869). Major League baseball is played by 26 teams divided between National and American Leagues. Leading teams from the 2 leagues meet annually in World Series to determine champion.

Basel, *see* BASLE, Switzerland.

Bashkir, auton. republic of E European RSFSR, USSR. Area *c* 144,000 sq km (55,000 sq mi); pop. 3,820,000; cap. Ufa. Plateau and mountainous area in S Urals; extensively forested. Forms E part of Volga-Ural oilfields, connected by pipeline to refineries at Omsk. Natural gas, coal, metal ores (iron, copper, manganese).

Basic English, acronym for British American Scientific International Commercial English. Artificial international language, formulated by C.K. Ogden and I.A. Richards (*c* 1928). It is claimed that its vocabulary of 850 English words is capable of expressing any concept and is intended to be an auxillary language.

basil, several aromatic, perennial herbs or shrubs of Labiatae (mint) family, native to Asia. Leaves of sweet basil, *Ocimum basilicum,* and bush basil, *O. suave,* are used in cookery.

Basildon, urban dist. of Essex, SE England. Pop. 129,000. Engineering, printing industs. Designated new town (1955) incorporating 4 Essex bors.

basilica, large Roman building used as public meeting place; usually rectangular with an interior colonnade and aisles on each side. With advent of Christianity, many were converted into churches.

basilisk, tropical American lizard of iguana family, genus *Basiliscus.* Semi-aquatic, can walk in upright position. Male is crested.

Basingstoke, mun. bor. of Hampshire, S England. Pop. 53,000. Market town, transport jct.

Baskerville, John (1706-65), English printer. Important designer of typefaces; produced books of quality using high-grade paper and specially prepared black ink. Pub. quarto edition of Vergil (1757) and a Bible (1763).

basketball, five-a-side team ball game. Devised 1891 by James Naismith at Springfield, Mass., US, as an indoor game for YMCA. Extremely popular sport in US colleges;

professional National Basketball Association was formed 1949. Olympic event since 1936.

basking shark, *Cetorhinus maximus,* large shark, reaching length of 9.7 m/35 ft; common to N Atlantic. Harmless, feeds on plankton. Cruises on ocean surface.

Basle (Fr. *Bâle,* Ger. *Basel),* city of NW Switzerland, on R. Rhine. Pop. 213,000. Commercial, indust. centre at head of Rhine navigation; railway jct. Roman *Basilia;* joined Swiss Confederation 1501. Oldest Swiss univ. (1460). Cathedral is burial-place of Erasmus.

Basle, Council of, RC reform council (1431-49). Beginning at Basle, with splinter groups moving to Ferrara and Florence, it attempted and failed to replace papal authority with that of the council.

Basque Provinces (Basque *Euzkadi),* region of NE Spain, incl. Alava, Guipúzcoa, Vizcaya provs. Name sometimes incl. Basque areas of Navarre, Gascony (France). Chief cities Bilbao, San Sebastian, Guernica (hist. seat of Basque parliaments). Iron, lead, zinc mining, engineering, fishing. Basques are an ancient people of obscure origin; unique language, distinctive customs. Settled here 9th cent., estab. kingdom of Navarre; later lost independence to Castile. Autonomous Basque govt. in Civil War defeated (1937) after Guernica bombed. Basque nationalism remains source of unrest.

Basra (Arab. *Al Basrah),* city of SE Iraq. Pop. 371,000. Port on Shatt-al-Arab. Oil refining. Exports petroleum products, dates. Cultural centre under Harun al-Rashid.

bass, marine and freshwater fish, incl. sea bass (Serranidae) and sunfish (Centrarchidae) families, found in North America, Europe. Popular game and food fish.

basset, breed of short-legged long-eared hound, used in hunting. Stands *c* 36 cm/14 in. at shoulder.

Basse-Terre, *see* GUADELOUPE.

Basseterre, cap. of ST KITTS.

basset horn, musical wind instrument of clarinet family. Invented *c* 1770, now largely displaced by bass clarinet.

bassoon, orchestral woodwind instrument of oboe family. Wooden or metal tube is bent back on itself, double reed being brought within reach of player's mouth by curved metal tube. Contrabassoon is lower in pitch.

Bass Strait, channel between Tasmania and mainland Australia; greatest width *c* 240 km (150mi). Furneaux Isls. at E end. Has major oil, natural gas deposits.

basswood, tree of genus *Tilia* of linden family, esp. *T. glabra.* Soft, strong wood is valued for furniture building.

Bast, in ancient Egyptian pantheon, goddess of fire. Represented as cat or cat-headed. Known by Greeks as Bubastis.

Bastia, town of NE Corsica, France, on Tyrrhenian Sea. Pop. 50,000. Port, exports wine, fish, timber; cigarette mfg.; tourist centre. Founded 14th cent. by Genoese, cap. of Corsica until 1791. Citadel (16th cent.).

Bastille, former state prison in Paris. Long used as prison, inmates incl. Voltaire, Fouquet. Stormed as 1st act of French Revolution by Parisian mob (1789) and razed to ground. Anniversary of destruction, 14 July, is national holiday.

Basutoland, *see* LESOTHO.

Mouse-eared bat (*Myotis myotis*)

bat, noctural mammal of order Chiroptera, found in tropical and temperate regions. Only true flying mammal, elongated fingers are joined by membranous wing. Some tropical species are fruit-eating; most others insectivorous, locating prey and navigating by echo sounding. Blood-sucking varieties, *eg* vampire bat, in South America. Gregarious, living in groups in caves, *etc*; sleeps upside down suspended by claws.

Batavia, see DJAKARTA.

Bates, Daisy Mary, née O'Dwyer Hunt (1861-1951), Australian journalist, b. Ireland. Lived among Aborigines; accumulated knowledge in *The Passing of The Aborigines* (1938), which revealed long neglect of inherent race problems.

Bates, Henry Walter (1825-92), English naturalist. Explored upper Amazon (1848-59), collecting 8000 new animal species. Investigated protective resemblance of harmless animal to poisonous one. *See* MIMICRY.

Bates, H[erbert] E[rnest] (1905-74), English author. Known for novels of rural life, incl. *My Uncle Silas* (1939), *The Darling Buds of May* (1958). Also wrote short-stories of service life under pseud. 'Flying Officer X'.

batfish, tropical fish of anglerfish family, with flattened body. Seeks prey by crawling on sea bed.

Bath: The Royal Crescent

Bath, city of Avon, SW England, on R. Avon. Pop. 85,000. Roman *Aquae Sulis* built *c* AD 50 on site of thermal springs. Medieval wool indust. Fashionable 18th cent. spa. Famous Georgian architecture of Nash, Wood, *eg* Royal, Lansdown Crescents.

batholith or **bathylith,** mass of intrusive igneous rock. Usually granite, forms substructure to many mountain or upland regions. Steep-sided, descends to unknown depths. Examples incl. Idaho, US, and Dartmoor, England.

Bathsheba, in OT, wife of Uriah the Hittite. David sent Uriah to death in battle and then married her. She bore him Solomon.

Bathurst, city of N New South Wales, Australia, on Macquarie R. Pop. 17,000. In stock raising and wheat growing area. Founded 1815, grew with 1851 gold rush.

Bathurst, see BANJUL, Gambia.

bathysphere, see SUBMERSIBLE.

batik, Indonesian method of applying coloured designs to cloth. Parts not to be dyed are coated with wax which can be removed after immersion of cloth in dye. Introduced into Europe in 19th cent. by Dutch.

Batista [y Zaldívar], Fulgencio (1901-73), Cuban political leader. Military coup (1933) brought him to power; became president 1940. Exiled to US (1945), reinstated after leading 2nd coup 1952. Discontent and corrupt regime resulted in overthrow (1959) by CASTRO. Fled to Dominican Republic.

Baton Rouge, cap. of Louisiana, US; port and indust. town on Mississippi R. Pop. 166,000. Cotton, sugar exports; oil refining. Fort estab. by French (1719). Became cap. 1849.

Battambang, town of W Cambodia. Pop. 43,000. Marketing centre of rice growing area. Textile mfg.

Battersea, part of Wandsworth bor., S London, England, on S bank of R. Thames. Has power station, amusement park, famous dogs' home.

battery, group of cells used as source of electric power. Common dry battery usually consists of Leclanché cells.

Battle, town of East Sussex, S England. Pop. 5000. Site of Battle of Hastings (1066). Abbey founded by William the Conqueror to commemorate it.

battle cruiser, see CRUISER.

battleship, large, armoured warship equipped with heavy guns. Evolved from ironclad warship of 19th cent., built of steel by 1870s. Britain's *Dreadnought* (1906) introduced the 'all-big-gun' class of warship. Extensively used during WWI, became obsolete in WWII with development of aerial tactics, esp. dive-bombing.

Batumi or **Batum,** town of USSR, cap. of Adzhar auton. republic, Georgian SSR. Pop. 106,000. Port on SE Black Sea. Exports petroleum, manganese. Oil refining centre, connected by pipeline to Baku.

Baudelaire, Charles Pierre (1821-67), French poet, important SYMBOLIST. His single collection *Les Fleurs du Mal* (1857) in nuances of imagery attempts to evoke the mystery of life and temper morality with aesthetics. Known also for doctrine of correspondences, *ie* interrelation of senses. Also translated his great influence, Poe.

Baudouin (1930-), king of Belgium (1951-). Son of Leopold III, on whose abdication he became king.

Bauhaus, school of design, architecture and craftsmanship, founded (1919) by Walter Gropius in Weimar, Germany; aimed at union of creative arts and technology of modern mass-production. Artists associated with Bauhaus incl. Klee, Kandinsky, Moholy-Nagy. Moved to Dessau, then to Berlin; closed by the Nazis (1933). Its ideas and teaching influenced both art and industrial design.

Bautzen, town of SE East Germany, on R. Spree. Pop. 44,000. Textiles, railway engineering. Cathedral (15th cent.).

bauxite, clay-like mineral deposit, a mixture of hydrated aluminium oxides. Colour varies from white to reddish-brown. Chief source of aluminium and its compounds; major deposits in France, USSR, West Indies.

Bavaria

Bavaria (*Bayern*), state of SE West Germany. Area 70, 531 sq km (27,232 sq mi); cap. Munich. Uplands, plains, valleys; principal rivers Danube, Main. Agric., forestry, tourism. Indust. centred in Munich, Nuremberg, Augsburg. As duchy then kingdom, under Wittelsbach dynasty 1180-1918. Stronghold of Nazi party before WWII. Hist. separatist region, joined Federal Republic 1949.

Bax, Sir Arnold (1883-1953), British composer. Master of King's Musick (1942-53). Work shows Celtic influence;

incl. *The Garden of Fand, Tintagel* and *A Garland for the Queen.*

Baxter, Richard (1615-91), English nonconformist clergyman. Served as chaplain in Cromwell's army (1645-7), modified views at Restoration. Left Church of England after Act of Uniformity (1662), believing that a place should be found for moderate dissenters within Church.

Bayard, Pierre du Terrail (*c* 1474-1524), French military hero. Known as 'the knight without fear or blame'. Commander of French forces in Italian wars.

Bayern, see BAVARIA, West Germany.

Bayeux, town of Normandy, N France. Pop. 13,000. Lace, pottery mfg. Museum contains 'Bayeux Tapestry'. Cathedral (12th cent.).

Bayeux Tapestry, piece of embroidery depicting invasion of England by William the Conqueror (1066). Length *c* 70 m/230 ft; prob. made in 11th cent. Preserved in Bayeux Museum, France.

Bay Islands (*Sp. Islas de la Bahia*), archipelago off N Honduras, in Caribbean. Area 373 sq km (144 sq mi). Agric., esp. coconut, banana, pineapple growing. British colony 1852-9, ceded to Honduras.

Bayle, Pierre (1647-1706), French philosopher. Advocated religious tolerance, holding morality to be independent of religion. Major work, *Dictionnaire historique et critique* (1697-1706) influenced Encyclopedists.

Baylis, Lilian Mary (1874-1937), English theatre manager. Founded Old Vic Theatre Co., making it a centre of Shakespearian plays, Sadler's Wells Opera, Vic-Wells Ballet.

Bay of Pigs, see PIGS, BAY OF.

bayonet, blade clipped on to end of musket or rifle. Introduced in late 17th cent. Said to have originated at Bayonne.

Bayonne, town of SW France, at confluence of Adour and Nive. Pop. 45,000. Port; metals and chemicals industs., brandy. Centre of sword mfg. (16th-17th cent.), gave name to bayonet. Cathedral (13th cent.), Basque museum.

Bay Psalm Book (1640), full title *The Whole Booke of Psalmes Faithfully Translated in English Metre,* first bound book printed in America. Edited from translations by ministers of Massachusetts.

Bayreuth, town of EC West Germany. Pop. 65,000. Textiles, metals, pottery mfg. Home of Wagner, who designed the opera house (built 1876); annual Wagner festival.

bay tree or **bay laurel,** see LAUREL.

Bazaine, Achille François (1811-88), French marshal. Surrendered entire force at Metz (1870) during Franco-Prussian War after being out-manoeuvred. Imprisoned (1873) for treason, escaped to Spain.

BBC, see BROADCASTING.

Beadle, George Wells (1903-), American geneticist. Shared Nobel Prize for Medicine and Physiology (1958) with E.L. Tatum for work on bread mould which showed that genes control cell's synthesis of enzymes and other proteins.

beagle, small hound with short legs and drooping ears, developed in England to hunt hares. Stands *c* 33 cm/13 in. at shoulder.

Beale, Dorothea (1831-1906), British educator. Pioneered women's education, esp. as head of Cheltenham Ladies' Coll. (1858-1906).

bean, large kidney-shaped edible seed of several plants of Leguminosae family. Inexpensive source of protein. Species incl. runner bean, soya bean, haricot or navy bean.

bear, large mammal of Ursidae family of Europe, Asia, America. Shaggy fur, short tail; walks flat on soles of feet. Solitary, sleeps through winter in cold climates. Eats little flesh, diet mainly vegetable. Varieties incl. BROWN, BLACK, POLAR bears.

Bear, Great and Little, see URSA MAJOR and URSA MINOR.

bearberry, *Arctostaphylos uva-ursi,* American trailing shrub with small leathery leaves, pinkish or white flowers, glossy red berries. Bears are said to be fond of the fruit, hence the name.

Beard, Charles Austin (1874-1948), American historian. Co-founder of New School for Social Research (1917). Wrote *An Economic Interpretation of the Constitution* (1913), study of economic interests involved in framing of US Constitution.

bearded lizard, *Amphibolurus barbatus,* agamid lizard of Australia. Inflates beardlike membrane of scales around throat when aroused.

Aubrey Beardsley

Beardsley, Aubrey Vincent (1872-98), English artist, illustrator. His highly stylized, often grotesque, black and white drawings epitomized art nouveau. Art editor of *Yellow Book* (1894-6); illustrated *Rape of the Lock* and Wilde's *Salomé.*

beard worm, see POGONOPHORA.

beat generation, in literature, term for certain US writers active in the 1950s, incl. Kerouac, Burroughs, Ginsberg. Characterized by anarchic life-style, use of drugs, rejection of middle-class values; influenced by Zen Buddhism, music of Charlie Parker, poetry of Whitman.

Beatitudes, in NT, eight blessings given by Jesus at the opening of the Sermon on the Mount.

Beatles, the, British rock musicians, one of most successful groups ever. Comprised John Lennon (1940-), Paul McCartney (1942-), George Harrison (1943-) and Ringo Starr, orig. Richard Starkey (1940-). Gained world-wide following in the 1960s, developing rock music to new musical heights, esp. in *Sergeant Pepper's Lonely Hearts Club Band.* Disbanded *c* 1970, subsequently active individually.

Beaton, Sir Cecil Walter Hardy (1904-), English photographer, designer, writer. Noted for portrait-studies; designs for theatre, cinema, incl. *My Fair Lady.*

Beaton or **Bethune, David** (1494-1546), Scottish churchman, cardinal-archbishop of St Andrews. On basis of a dubious will of James V, attempted to assume regency for Mary Queen of Scots. As chancellor (1543), opposed Henry VIII's plans for subjugation of Scotland. His persecution of Protestants led to burning of George Wishart. Murdered in revenge.

Beatty, David Beatty, 1st Earl (1871-1936), British admiral. Led squadron in defeat of German navy at Jutland (1916). Commander of British fleet (1916-19). First sea lord at the Admiralty (1919-27).

Beauce, fertile limestone plain of N France, SW of Paris. Main town Chartres. Cereal production, esp. wheat; called 'granary of France'.

Beaufort, Henry (*c* 1377-1447), English prelate, statesman; half-brother of Henry IV of England. Chancellor to Henry IV (1403-4), Henry V (1413-17) and during regency of Henry VI (1424-26). Made cardinal 1426, he attempted to lead a crusade against the Hussites (1429).

Beaufort Scale, measure of wind velocity; varies from 0 for calm to 12 for hurricane force. Devised in 1805 by Sir Francis Beaufort.

Beaufort Sea, part of Arctic Ocean, bounded by Banks Isl. (N Canada) in E and N Alaska in S.

Beauharnais, Alexandre, Vicomte de (1760-94), French general. Served in American and French revolutionary wars; executed in reign of terror. His wife later (1796) married Napoleon (*see* JOSEPHINE). Their son, **Eugène de Beauharnais** (1781-1824), was created Italian viceroy (1805) by Napoleon after serving in his army.

Beaumarchais, assumed name of Pierre Augustin Caron (1732-99), French dramatist. Best known for comedies *The Barber of Seville* (1775), *The Marriage of Figaro* (1784).

Beaumaris, mun. bor. of Gwynedd, NW Wales, former co. town of Anglesey. Pop. 2000. Tourist resort. Has ruined 14th cent. castle.

Beaumont, Francis (1584-1616), English dramatist. Wrote mainly in collaboration with FLETCHER; thought to be sole author of *The Woman Hater* (1606), burlesque *The Knight of the Burning Pestle* (1607).

Beaumont, port of SE Texas, US; on Neches R. with canal access to sea. Pop. 116,000. Oil refining and shipping.

Beaune, town of Burgundy, E France. Pop. 17,000. Agric. market, centre of Burgundy wine trade. Hôtel-Dieu (1443) contains van der Weyden polyptch *Last Judgment*.

Beauregard, Pierre Gustave Toutant (1818-93), Confederate general during US Civil War. As commander at Charleston, ordered firing on Fort Sumter (1861). Reinforced Lee in 1864 Virginia campaigns.

Beauvais, town of N France, cap. of Oise dept. Pop. 49,000. Agric. market. Scene of heroic defence (1472) against Charles the Bold. Centre of Gobelins tapestry indust. until WWII. Cathedral (1227) has highest Gothic choir vault.

Beauvoir, Simone de (1908-), French novelist, essayist, member of EXISTENTIALIST movement. Works incl. *Les Mandarins* (1954) fictionalized account of Sartre circle, *Le Deuxième Sexe* (1949) analyzing position of women in society.

Beaver

beaver, large rodent of Europe and North America, genus *Castor*. Amphibious; webbed hind feet and broad flattened tail. Colonial, lives in 'lodges' in river banks; constructs dams in rivers, streams. Species incl. Canadian *C. canadensis* and European *C. fiber*. Numbers depleted by fur hunters.

Beaverbrook, William Maxwell Aitken, 1st Baron (1879-1964), British statesman, newspaper owner, b. Canada. Already wealthy on arrival in England, bought *Daily Express, Evening Standard,* founded *Sunday Express*. Advocate of imperialism; later organized munitions production while in Churchill's war cabinet (1940-5).

Bebington, mun. bor. of Merseyside met. county, NW England, port on Wirral penin. Pop. 61,000. Incl. Port Sunlight model town, estab. 1888 for Lever Bros. workers.

Beccaria, Cesare Bonesana, Marchese di (1738-94), Italian economist, jurist. First writer to attack fundamentally death penalty, torture, as well as reasoning behind harsh punishments. Influenced Voltaire, English utilitarians.

Bechuanaland, *see* BOTSWANA.

Beckenbauer, Franz (1945-), German footballer. Played for West Germany over 100 times, captaining them in 1974 World Cup victory. Captained Bayern Munich team to 3 successive European Cup wins (1974-6).

Becket, Thomas à, *see* THOMAS À BECKET, ST.

Samuel Beckett

Beckett, Samuel (1906-), Irish author, settled in France 1932; works in English and French. Best known for tragicomedy *Waiting for Godot* (1954). Also wrote novels *eg Murphy* (1938), *Molloy* (1951). Nobel Prize for Literature (1969).

Beckford, William (1759-1844), English writer. Known for Gothic romance *Vathek: An Arabian Tale* (1786). Also wrote travel books.

Beckmann, Max (1884-1950), German painter. Painted large allegorical pictures in 1930s, often savage in form, depicting hopelessness and brutality of human situation. Works incl. 9 large triptychs.

Becquerel, Antoine Henri (1852-1908), French physicist. Discovered radioactivity (1896) when he observed clouding of photographic film by uranium salt. Shared Nobel Prize for Physics (1903) with the Curies.

Bedbug (*Cimex lectularius*)

bedbug, small parasitic insect of Cimicidae family with flattened wingless body. Infests beds, walls, feeding on warm blood of mammals, birds. Extremely resistant, can withstand months of fasting.

Beddoes, Thomas Lovell (1803-49), English writer. Works incl. verse tales *The Improvisatore* (1821), macabre tragedy *Death's Jest Book* (1850).

Bede or **Baeda** (c 673-735), English historian, theologian. Known as the Venerable Bede, spent life as Benedictine monk teaching and writing. Best known for *Ecclesiastical History of the English Nation*, in Latin, often translated.

Bedfordshire, county of SC England. Area 1234 sq km (476 sq mi); pop. 481,000. Wheat growing, market gardening; indust. centre Luton. Co. town **Bedford,** mun. bor. on R. Ouse. Pop. 73,000. Agric. equipment mfg., light industs.

Bédier, Joseph (1864-1938), French literary historian. Known for reconstruction in modern French of the *Roman de Tristan et Iseult* (1900), writing on origin of medieval epic.

Bedlam, popular name for oldest English lunatic asylum (St Mary of Bethlehem). Founded *c*1400 in London; removed to near Croydon 1930.

Bedouin, nomadic ARABS of Saudi Arabia, Syria, Jordan, Iraq, N Africa. Dependent on camel, sheep breeding. Land divided into tribal orbits under a sheik.

bedstraw, any plant of genus *Galium.* Square stem, stalkless whorled leaves, small white or coloured flowers. Formerly used as straw for beds.

Bumble bee and honey bees collecting nectar

bee, four-winged hairy insect of worldwide distribution, order Hymenoptera. Bees are social or solitary. Solitary bees nest in soil or hollow stems. Social bees, incl. bumble bee, cuckoo bee, honey bee, live in colonies, usually operating caste system of queen, workers (infertile females) and male drones. Agents of flower pollination when seeking nectar.

bee balm, *see* BALM.

Beebe, Charles William (1877-1962), American naturalist, explorer. Became ornithological curator (1899) at New York Zoological Society, later director of tropical research. Conducted pioneer research of ocean depths in bathysphere (1934).

beech, large, widespread family of trees incl. the beeches, oaks and chestnuts, but esp. genus *Fagus* with smooth, grey bark, hard wood, pale green leaves and edible 3-corned nuts. Wood is used in furniture and building. Common species are European *F. sylvatica,* copper beech, *F. atropunicea,* and American *F. grandifolia.*

Beecham, Sir Thomas (1879-1961), English conductor. Founded London Philharmonic Orchestra (1932) and Royal Philharmonic Orchestra (1947). Popularized works of Richard Strauss, Delius. Remembered for his boisterous personality.

Beecher, Lyman (1775-1863), American Congregationalist clergyman, father of Harriet Beecher STOWE. Founded American Bible Society (1816). His son, **Henry Ward Beecher** (1813-87), was also a clergyman. Championed anti-slavery cause, female suffrage, theory of evolution. Aquitted in famous adultery trial.

bee-eater, small brightly-coloured coloured bird of Meropidae family, found in tropical areas of Old World. Feeds on bees, other insects; nests in holes in river bank, road cuttings, *etc.*

beefwood, hard, heavy, dark red wood from tropical tree, *Manilkara bidentata,* used in flooring and furniture.

beer, alcoholic beverage made by brewing aqueous extract of cereals, esp. malted barley, with hops. Malted barley is crushed and mixed with warm water, which allows enzymes present in malt to convert its starch into sugar. Solution obtained (wort) is boiled with hops, which provide flavouring. Liquid is cooled, mixed with yeast and allowed to ferment. Quantity of malt and water, as well as length of fermenting, determine alcoholic content (usually from 3% to 6%). Britain, Germany, Czechoslovakia and US are major beer producers.

Beerbohm, Sir [Henry] Max[imilian] (1872-1956), English writer, caricaturist. Known for witty theatre criticism, only novel *Zuleika Dobson* (1911) fantasy set in Oxford.

Beersheba, commercial town of SC Israel. Pop. 84,000. Trade centre for tribes of Negev desert. Pottery, glass mfg. Hist. associated with Abraham, Elijah.

beet, several varieties of biennial plants of genus *Beta* with edible leaves, thick fleshy white or red roots, widely cultivated as food crop. The sugar beet, *B. vulgaris,* native to Europe and grown in North America, provides *c* 30% of world's sugar. The garden beet or beetroot has red-veined leaves, edible root. Variety *cicla* is cultivated for leaves, known as beet spinach or Swiss chard.

Statue of Beethoven at Bonn

Beethoven, Ludwig van (1770-1827), German composer, pianist. In early life, had some teaching from Mozart, Haydn; concert debut 1795. One of most original and influential composers, bridged Classical and Romantic eras in creating music of great emotional impact and formal qualities. Suffered increasing deafness from 1801 onwards. Among best-known works are orchestral, choral, chamber works and piano sonatas, *eg Third (Eroica), Fifth, Sixth (Pastoral)* and *Ninth (Choral)* symphonies, as well as *Moonlight Sonata, Mass in D,* string quartets and opera *Fidelio.*

beetle, any insect of order Coleoptera (comprising *c* 250,000 species). Biting mouthparts; horny forewings cover membranous hind wings and protect body. Undergoes complete METAMORPHOSIS.

Mrs Beeton

Beeton, Isabella Mary, née Mayson (1836-65), English writer on cookery. Best remembered for *Mrs Beeton's Book* *of Household Management* (1859-60), guide to cookery and domestic economy.

begonia, genus of succulent herbs with ornamental leaves and clustered red, pink or white flowers. Native of tropics. Cultivated varieties are divided into fibrous-rooted types which are mainly houseplants for winter blooming, and bulbous, tuberous and rhizomatous begonias.

Behan, Brendan (1923-64), Irish playwright. Known for black comedies, *The Quare Fellow* (1956), *The Hostage* (1959). Autobiog. *Borstal Boy* (1958) describes his formative years in IRA.

behaviourism, in psychology, doctrine that valid data consists only of the observable and measurable in individual's responses, not valuing subjective or introspective accounts.

Behistun, village of W Iran. Monument of Darius I carved in rock above village. Cuneiform inscriptions on it in Old Persian, Susian and Babylonian deciphered by Rawlinson (1846); provided key for study of Mesopotamian culture.

Behn, Aphra (1640-89), first English woman professional writer. Works incl. exotic romances and plays, *eg* novel *Oroonoko* (1688). Spy for Charles II in Antwerp (1666-7).

Behrens, Peter (1868-1940), German architect. Pioneer in evolution of modern architectural style and industrial design. Designed factories, houses, offices in functionalist manner employing modern materials. Taught Gropius, Mies van der Rohe, Le Corbusier.

Beida, town of NE Libya in Cyrenaica. Pop. 32,000. Govt. offices, univ. Built from 1961, designated as future national cap.

Beira, town of SC Mozambique, on Mozambique Channel. Pop. 50,000. Port, exports copper, tobacco, tea; large transit trade, rail links with Malawi, Rhodesia (closed 1976), Zambia.

Beirut, cap. of Lebanon. Pop. 720,000. Port on Mediterranean. Trade centre since Phoenician times. Focus of foreign education; 4 univs. Financial centre; food processing. Became cap. of Lebanon under French mandate (1920).

Beith, John Hay, *see* HAY, IAN.

Beit-Lahm, transliteration of Arabic form of BETHLEHEM.

Bejaïa, town of N Algeria, on Gulf of Bejaïa. Pop. 63,000. Formerly called Bougie. Port, exports fruit, olive oil, phosphates; terminal of oil pipeline from Hassi Messaoud. Cap. of Vandals in 5th cent.; stronghold of Barbary pirates.

Belasco, David (1859-1931), American actor, producer. Productions influenced American theatre. Also wrote plays, *eg The Girl of the Golden West* (1905).

Belém, seaport of NE Brazil, cap. of Pará state, on Pará R. Pop. 603,000. Exports nuts, timber, jute. Centre of early 20th cent. rubber export boom.

Belfast, cap. and port of Northern Ireland, on Belfast Lough. Pop. 359,000. Admin., commercial centre. Shipbuilding; linen, tobacco mfg. Has Queen's Univ. (1845). Severely damaged by bombs and fires in religious conflict from 1969. **Belfast,** district; area 115 sq km (44 sq mi); pop. 404,000. Created 1973, formerly part of Cos. Antrim, Down.

Belfort, town of E France, cap. of Territ. of Belfort dept. Pop. 56,000. Commands Belfort Gap between Vosges and Jura. Cotton mills, metal working. Successful resistance of Prussian siege (1870-1) commemorated by *Lion of Belfort* statue; remained French when Alsace ceded (1871) to Germany.

Belgae, tribes of mixed Celtic-Germanic origin, described by Julius Caesar. Occupied parts of Belgium and NE France, whence they spread to S England *c* 100 BC. Introduced coinage, potter's wheel, improved standards of agric. in England.

Belgaum, town of Mysore state, SW India. Pop. 214,000. Textile mfg.

Belgian Congo, *see* ZAÏRE.

Belgium (Fr. *Belgique,* Flem. *België*), kingdom of NW Europe. Area 30,510 sq km (11,780 sq mi); pop. 9,756,000; cap. Brussels. Languages: Flemish (N), Walloon French (S). Religion: RC. Main rivers Meuse, Scheldt. Sandy area in N (Flanders), fertile plain in C; forested plateau in SE (Ardennes). Intensive agric. (cereals, flax, livestock).

Extensive trade along North Sea coast and canal network. Heavy indust. (metals, textiles) on SC coalfield. Named after Celtic *Belgae*; divided into independent duchies, counties in Middle Ages. Ruled by Burgundy, Habsburgs, Spain, France, Netherlands; independent monarchy from 1830. Colonized Congo (*see* ZAÏRE). German occupation in both WWs.

Belgrade (*Beograd*), cap. of Yugoslavia and of Serbia, at confluence of Danube and Sava. Pop. 770,000. River port, railway jct.; commercial, indust. centre, esp. textiles, chemicals, electrical goods; univ. (1863). Fortified (3rd cent. BC) by Celts. Held by Turks 1521-1867; became cap. of Serbia 1882, of Yugoslavia 1918. Has Turkish citadel.

Belinski, Vissarion Grigoryevich (1811-48), Russian critic. Seminal influence on Russian 'natural' school, urged social reform as literature's goal. Encouraged Dostoyevski, Gogal, Turgenev.

Belisarius (*c* 505-65), Byzantine general. Served under Justinian I, for whom he suppressed the Nika revolt (532). Defeated Vandals in Africa (534). Fought against Goths in Italy, capturing Ravenna (540). Thwarted Bulgarian attack on Constantinople (559).

Belize

Belize, British crown colony of Central America, on Caribbean. Area 22,965 sq km (8867 sq mi); pop. 120,000; cap. Belmopan. Mainly flat with dense forests (valuable timber exports); Maya Mts. in interior. Tropical climate. Sugar cane, citrus fruit growing. English settlement (17th cent.) disputed by Spanish; colony estab. 1884; name changed from British Honduras (1973). Former cap. **Belize,** port at mouth of Belize R. Pop. 39,000. Timber exports; fish packing.

Bell, Alexander Graham (1847-1922), American scientist, inventor, b. Scotland. Gave 1st successful transmission of sound by telephone (1876). Patented device (1876) and organized Bell Telephone Co. (1877). Estab. laboratory which produced 1st successful phonograph record.

Bell, Gertrude Margaret Lowthian (1868-1926), English traveller, writer. Journeyed widely in Near East; contributed to founding of modern Iraq. Works incl. *The Desert and the Sown* (1907), *The Arab of Mesopotamia* (1917).

bell, (1) orchestral percussion instrument made of long tubes of brass, suspended in same arrangement as a keyboard; struck with mallet; (2) hollow cup-like vessel, usually made of metal, which rings when struck by an internal clapper or external hammer. Bells are often hung in sets and can be played by mechanical means to produce tunes (*see* CARILLON) or by groups of ringers who go through permutations of the diatonic scale, called change-ringing.

belladonna, *see* NIGHTSHADE.

Bellay, Joachim du (1522-60), French poet. Wrote manifesto of PLÉIADE, *Défense et illustration de la langue française* (1549).

Bellerophon, in Greek myth, hero who slew the CHIMAERA with help of winged horse, Pegasus. Angered Zeus by attempting to fly to heaven on Pegasus. Was thrown to earth and crippled or killed.

bellflower, *see* CAMPANULA.

Bellingshausen, Fabian Gottlieb von (1778-1852), Russian naval officer, explorer. Circumnavigated Antarctica (1819-21), possibly being 1st to sight continental Antarctica.

Bellingshausen Sea, part of S Pacific Ocean, W of British Antarctic Territ. Named after leader of Russian expedition (1819-21).

Giovanni Bellini: *The Doge Leonardo Loredan*

Bellini, Jacopo (*c* 1400-70), Italian painter. Few of his paintings survive, but his 2 surviving sketchbooks were used by his 2 sons and Mantegna. **Gentile Bellini** (*c* 1429-1507) was prominent portraitist and painter of processions and ceremonies. Worked at court in Constantinople (1479-81). **Giovanni Bellini** (*c* 1430-1516) taught Giorgione and Titian. Works, characterized by lyrical handling of landscape, influenced subsequent Venetian artists. Painted many large altarpieces, small devotional works and portraits.

Bellini, Vincenzo (1801-35), Italian composer. Known for lyrical operas *Norma* and *La sonnambula*.

Bellinzona, town of S Switzerland, on R. Ticino, cap. of Ticino canton. Pop. 17,000. Railway jct., engineering. Tourism (15th cent. castles).

Belloc, [Joseph] Hilaire [Pierre] (1870-1953), English writer, b. France. Known for collections of gruesome humorous verse, *eg The Bad Child's Book of Beasts* (1896), *Cautionary Tales* (1908). Also wrote novels, historical biog.

Bellona, Roman goddess of war, identified with Greek Enyo and cult partner of Mars. Temple in the Campus Martius was used to receive foreign ambassadors.

Bellotto, Bernardo, *see* CANALETTO.

Bellow, Saul (1915-), American novelist, b. Canada. Works incl. *The adventures of Augie March* (1953), *Herzog* (1964), estab. him as major figure. Deals with individual's problems in urban democratic society. Nobel Prize for Literature (1976).

bell-ringing, *see* BELL.

Belo Horizonte, city of E Brazil, cap. of Minas Gerais state. Pop. 1,235,000. Centre of mining area (iron, manganese); agric. centre (cotton, cattle); steel indust., textile mfg., diamond cutting. Brazil's 1st planned city, built at end of 19th cent.

Belorussia, *see* BYELORUSSIAN SOVIET SOCIALIST REPUBLIC.

Belsen, village of NE West Germany, in Lower Saxony. Site of concentration camp under Nazi regime.

Belt, Great and **Little,** strs. of Denmark, linking Kattegat with Baltic Sea. Great Belt (*Store Baelt*) separates Zealand and Fyn Isl.; Little Belt (*Lille Baelt*) separates Fyn Isl. and Jutland.

Beltane, *see* MAY DAY.

beluga or **white whale,** *Delphinapterus leucas,* whale of Arctic seas, *c* 4.6 m/15 ft long. Diet of fish, crustaceans; skin of excellent quality.

Bely, Andrei, pseud. of Boris Nikolayevich Bugayev (1880-1934), Russian poet, novelist. One of SYMBOLISTS, friend of BLOK; known for long mystical poem *Christ is Risen* (1918). Also wrote novels, *eg The Silver Dove* (1910), memoires.

Bembo, Pietro (1470-1547), Italian churchman, humanist. Edited Petrarch, Dante. Helped estab. Tuscan as literary language of Italy.

Benares, *see* VARANASI.

Benavente [y Martínez], Jacinto (1866-1954), Spanish playwright. Social satirist esp. in farce, *Los intereses creados* (1907, *Bonds of Interest* 1917). Nobel Prize for Literature (1922).

Ben Bella, Ahmed (1919-), Algerian political leader. Joined Algerian nationalist movements, founder (1954) of FLN in Cairo. Twice arrested by the French, returned to become premier (1962). Elected president (1963), ousted in coup (1965).

Benbow, John (1653-1702), English naval officer. Hero of 4-day fight with French in Caribbean (1702) when his flagship was deserted by rest of squadron. Died of his wounds.

Benda, Julien (1867-1956), French critic. Strict rationalist, critical of Bergson. *The Treason of the Intellectuals* (1927) attacks surrender of abstract thought for ideology.

Bendigo, city of NC Victoria, Australia. Pop. 46,000. Agric. market, armaments mfg. Founded (1851) as Sandhurst; formerly centre of extensive goldmining area.

bends, in medicine, *see* AEROEMBOLISM.

Benedetti, Vincent, Comte (1817-1900), French diplomat. Ambassador to Prussia (1864-70). Public release by Bismarck of much altered version of Benedetti's interview at Ems with William I helped precipitate Franco-Prussian War.

Benedict, St (*c* 480-*c* 547), Italian monk. Founded BENEDICTINES, formulating chief rule of Western monasticism, based on communal living with time for work and prayer.

Benedict XV, orig. Giacomo della Chiesa (1854-1922), Italian churchman, pope (1914-22). Maintained strict Vatican neutrality in WWI, concentrated on relief of war suffering.

Benedict, Ruth Fulton (1887-1948), American anthropologist. Extended scope of anthropology through work on concept of culture motif. Works incl. *Patterns of Culture* (1934).

Benedictines, RC monastic order, estab. by ST BENEDICT at Monte Cassino (*c* 529). Stressing communal living and physical labour, they also did much to preserve learning in early Middle Ages. Notable Benedictines were St Gregory the Great and St Augustine of Canterbury who introduced the order into England.

Benelux, economic union of Belgium, Netherlands, Luxembourg. Estab. (1958) after customs union ratified in 1948.

Beneš, Eduard (1884-1948), Czech statesman, president (1935-8, 1945-8). Served as foreign minister under Masaryk; architect of Czech-French alliances after WWI. Exiled during WWII, headed provisional govt. in London, re-elected president after Czech liberation. Resigned after Communist coup of 1948.

Benét, Stephen Vincent (1898-1943), American poet. Epic poems, *John Brown's Body* (1928), *Western Star* (1943), examine roots of American culture. Other works incl. famous 'American Names' (1927), short stories, novels. Brother, **William Rose Benét** (1886-1950), was poet and journalist. Founded *Saturday Review of Literature,* wrote verse autobiog. *The Dust which is God* (1941).

Benevento, town of Campania, SC Italy, cap. of Benevento prov. Pop. 60,000. Tobacco, confectionery, wine and liqueur mfg. Roman trade centre on Appian Way; under papal rule 11th-19th cent.

Bengal, region of NE India and Bangladesh in Ganges-Brahmaputra delta. Under British control following victory at Plassey (1757). Divided (1947) into largely Hindu West Bengal and Moslem East Bengal (now in BANGLADESH). **Bay of Bengal** is arm of Indian ocean between E India and Burma.

Bengali, Indic language belonging to Indo-Iranian branch of Indo-European. Spoken in Bangladesh, Calcutta region.

Benghazi or **Bengasi,** city of NE Libya, in Cyrenaica on Gulf of Sidra. Pop. 170,000. Port, admin. centre, railway jct. Founded by Greeks. Centre of Italian colonization from 1911 until taken by British in WWII. Cap. of Cyrenaica prov. 1951-63; joint cap. (with Tripoli) of Libya 1951-72.

Benguela or **Benguella,** town of W Angola, on Atlantic Ocean. Pop. 35,000. Port, railway from Mozambique. Founded 17th cent.; former slave trade centre.

David Ben-Gurion

Ben-Gurion, David (1886-1973), Israeli statesman, b. Poland. Supported British pledges to help Jewish settlement of Palestine. Leader of Mapai party, 1st premier (1948-53) of Israel; returned for 2nd term (1955-63). Broke away from Mapai (1965).

Benin or **Dahomey,** republic of W Africa. Area 112,700 sq km (43,500 sq mi); pop. 2,912,000; cap. Porto Novo. Official language: French. Religions: native, RC. Mainly subsistence agric.; exports coffee, cotton, palm oil. Native kingdom 17th-19th cent. with cap. at Abomey, promoted slave trade. Colonized (1892-3) by French; territ. of French West Africa from 1899. Independent from 1960, has had unstable govt.

Benin, city of S Nigeria. Pop. 122,000. Centre of rubber, palm and timber producing area. *Fl* 14th-17th cents. as cap. of Benin kingdom; famous for iron, ivory, bronze carvings. Taken (1898) by Britain.

Benjamin, in OT, youngest son of Jacob and Rachel. His descendants (tribe of Benjamin) incl. Israel's 1st king, Saul, and St Paul.

Benjamin, Judah Philip (1811-84), Confederate statesman. Led defence of Southern policy before and during US Civil War (1861-5); known as 'the brains of the Confederacy'. After defeat of South, escaped to England; became prominent barrister.

Benn, Gottfried (1886-1956), German poet, critic. Collections of expressionist verse incl. *Flesh* (1916), *Rubble* (1919). Autobiog. (1950) reflects agony of Nazi era.

Bennett, [Enoch] Arnold (1867-1931), English author. Known for realistic novels set in industrial Staffordshire, *eg Anna of the Five Towns* (1902), *The Old Wives' Tale* (1908).

Bennett, James Gordon (1795-1872), American journalist, b. Scotland. Founded *New York Herald* (1835), changing image of newspapers with pictures, crime, sport. Son, **James Gordon Bennett** (1841-1918), succeeded him as editor (1867), advocated sensational reporting *eg* financed Stanley's search for Livingstone.

Bennett, R[ichard] B[edford] Bennett, 1st Viscount (1870-1947), Canadian statesman, Conservative PM (1930-5). Successfully advocated adoption of preferential imperial tariff.

Ben Nevis, *see* NEVIS, BEN, Scotland.

Benoni, city of S Transvaal, South Africa. Pop. 163,000. Goldmining, engineering centre in Witwatersrand.

Benson, Sir Frank (1858-1939), British actor-manager. Estab. Stratford-on-Avon Shakespeare festival.

Jeremy Bentham

Bentham, Jeremy (1748-1832), English philosopher. Trained in law, early exponent of UTILITARIANISM in *Introduction to the Principles of Morals and Legislation* (1789); taught that govt. should consider 'the greatest good for the greatest number'. Founded (1824) *Westminster Review* with James Mill.

Bentley, E[dmund] C[lerihew] (1875-1956), English author. Wrote classic detective novel *Trent's Last Case* (1912). Invented 4-line doggerel verse, 'clerihew'.

Bentley, Richard (1662-1742), British philologist. Pioneered close textual criticism in classical studies, using it to prove *Letters of Phalaris* were forgeries.

Benton, Thomas Hart (1782-1858), American politician. Senator from Missouri (1821-51). Drew up President Jackson's Specie Circular (1836), advocating hard money purchases. Supported development of West, financing several explorations.

Benue, river of N Cameroon and E Nigeria. Flows *c* 1450 km (900 mi) W from Adamawa Highlands via Makurdi to R. Niger at Lokoja.

Benue-Congo, subgroup of Niger-Congo branch of Niger-Kordofanian language family. Incl. BANTU LANGUAGES, as well as others, *eg* Bute, Tiv, Efik.

Early Benz automobile

Benz, Karl (1844-1929), German engineer. Credited with building 1st automobile with internal combustion engine (*c* 1885). Engine was water-cooled and had electric ignition. In 1926 his company merged as Daimler-Benz.

benzene (C_6H_6), colourless liquid hydrocarbon; found in coal tar and produced from petroleum by cracking. Structure as hexagonal ring of 6 carbon atoms, linked by alternate double and single bonds, with hydrogen atom joined to each carbon atom, described by Kekulé. Used as solvent and as starting point of numerous aromatic compounds.

benzoin or **gum benjamin,** resin obtained from pierced bark of certain East Indian trees of genus *Styrax.* Used in preparation of incense, medicine and perfumes.

Ben-Zvi, Izhak (1884-1963), Israeli historian and statesman, b. Russia. Worked with BEN-GURION in Zionist activities. President of Israel (1952-63).

Beograd, *see* BELGRADE, Yugoslavia.

Beowulf, Old English epic. Composed 8th cent., tells story derived from folk tale and Scandinavian history. In first part, young Beowulf rescues Danish court from water monster Grendel and Grendel's mother. In second part, after long and honourable life, Beowulf is called on to defend country from dragon, does so but dies and is given hero's funeral. Celebrates both Germanic pagan and Christian values.

Béranger, Pierre Jean de (1780-1857), French folk poet. Wrote songs satirizing glory, reflecting popular desire for peace, *eg Le Roi d'Yvetot* (1813).

Berber horseman

Berber, non-Semitic language group within Afro-Asiatic family. Incl. Berber, Tuareg, Rif, *etc,* and is spoken over wide area of N Africa.

Berbera, town of N Somalia, on Gulf of Aden. Pop. 40,000. Port, exports livestock, hides.

Berbers, Hamitic peoples of N Africa, of unknown origin. Previously Christian they became Moslem by 10th cent. under Arab domination. Apart from the TUAREG they are now settled agriculturists with local industries, *eg* metalwork, pottery, weaving.

Berchtesgaden, town of SE West Germany, in Bavarian Alps. Pop. 5000. Tourism, salt mining, woodcarving. Site of Hitler's mountain retreat.

Berdyaev, Nikolai Aleksandrovich (1874-1948), Russian religious philosopher. Initially Marxist, came to believe in the necessity of spiritual support. Attacked dehumanizing power of technology. Exiled 1922.

Bérenger or **Berengarius of Tours** (*c* 998-1088), French ecclesiastic, head of Tours Cathedral school. Held radical views on Eucharist, rejected transubstantiation. Accused of heresy after quarrel with Lanfranc; eventually reconciled with Church.

Berenson, Bernard (1865-1959), American art critic, b. Lithuania. Expert on Italian art, he advised collectors and authenticated works for dealers. Writings incl. *Italian Painters of the Renaissance* (1930).

Berezniki, town of USSR, E European RSFSR. Pop. 150,000. Centre of chemical indust., based on local potash.

Berg, Alban (1885-1935), Austrian composer. Disciple of Schoenberg; developed 12-note technique to greater heights of expression than his master. Works incl. 2 operas, *Wozzeck* and *Lulu,* violin concerto and *Lyric Suite* for string quartet.

Bergamo, city of Lombardy, N Italy, cap. of Bergamo prov. Pop. 131,000. Engineering, textiles. Incl. old walled hilltop town, with 12th cent. cathedral, Renaissance chapel.

bergamot, several plants incl. species of *Monarda,* native to North America, with oval leaves aromatic when crushed. Sweet bergamot, *M. didyma,* is common in gardens and used to make infusion, Oswego tea. European bergamot is *Mentha aquitica.* Bergamot also designates a type of pear-shaped orange, *Citrus bergamia,* rind of which yields an oil used in perfumery.

Bergen, city of SW Norway. Pop. 113,000. Port, fishing, shipbuilding, tourism. Founded 1070, *fl* in Middle Ages, member of Hanseatic League. Rebuilt after fire (1916); German naval base in WWII, severely damaged.

Bergen-op-Zoom, town of SW Netherlands, on R. Zoom near confluence with Scheldt. Pop. 40,000. River port; food processing, iron, steel. Strongly fortified in 16th cent., frequently besieged.

Bergius, Friedrich (1884-1949), German chemist. Awarded Nobel Prize for Chemistry (1931) for production of light fuel oil by hydrogenation under pressure of paste of coal and heavy oil. Subsequent manufacture of synthetic fuel developed by Germany in WWII.

Bergman, [Ernst] Ingmar (1918-), Swedish stage, film, TV writer-director, producer. Internationally famous from late 1950s for expressionist films with themes of alienation of individual from God, problems of personal relationships. Films incl. *The Seventh Seal* (1956), *Wild Strawberries* (1957), *Persona* (1966).

Bergman, Ingrid (1917-), Swedish actress. Best known for films made after move to Hollywood (1938), incl. *Casablanca* (1943); career broken by public reaction to affair with ROSSELLINI (1948), returned to Hollywood (1956).

Bergman, Torbern Olof (1735-84), Swedish chemist, mineralologist. Developed theory of chemical affinity, purporting to predict outcome of reactions. Improved methods of chemical analysis; worked in mineral classification.

Bergson, Henri (1859-1941), French philosopher. Anti-rationalist, believed in direct intuition as basis of knowledge. Saw evolution as opposition of 'life-force' (*élan vital*) to intransigence of matter. Influenced Proust in theories of memory. Nobel Prize for Literature (1927). Works incl. *Matter and Memory* (1896), *Creative Evolution* (1907).

Beria, Lavrenti Pavlovich (1899-1953), Soviet political leader. Powerful head of Russian secret police (1938-53); tried and executed during post-Stalin power struggle.

beriberi, deficiency disease caused by lack of vitamin B₁ (thiamin) in diet. Characterized by neuritis, swelling of body, *etc.* Occurs mostly in Far East where diet is largely of polished rice.

Bering, Vitus Jonassen (1681-1741), Danish explorer. Employed by Peter I to explore N Siberia; proved that Asia and America not connected. Died on Bering Isl. while leading Great Northern Expedition (1733-41). Bering St. and Sea also named after him.

Bering Sea

Bering Sea, extension of N Pacific, between E Siberia and Alaska. Navigable only in summer. Explored by Dane, Vitus Bering *c* 1728. Bering Strait connects it to Arctic Ocean.

Berio, Luciano (1925-), Italian composer. His avant-garde music employs indeterminacy, electronic effects.

Works incl. *Sequenze,* series of virtuoso pieces for various solo instruments.

Busby Berkeley: example of his choreography from *Dames*

Berkeley, Busby, orig. William Berkeley Enos (1895-1976), American song-and-dance director. Known for spectacular, kaleidoscopic sequences, using great many chorus girls, in 1930s films, incl. *Gold Diggers* series (1933-8), *Dames* (1934).

Berkeley, George (1685-1753), Irish philosopher. Leading anti-materialist, saw the existence of perceived world as dependent on act of the perceiver ('being is being perceived'). Major work, *Treatise concerning the Principles of Human Knowledge* (1710).

Berkeley, Sir Lennox (1903-), English composer. Has written works in traditional forms, esp. for human voice. Compositions incl. chamber music, operas, symphonies.

Berkeley, residential town of W California, US; on E San Francisco Bay. Pop. 117,000. Mfg. industs. Has most famous part of Univ. of California (1873).

berkelium (Bk), transuranic element of actinide series; at. no. 97, mass no. of most stable isotope 247. First prepared 1949 by bombarding americium with alpha particles.

Berkhampstead, urban dist. of Hertfordshire, SC England. Pop. 15,000. Has public school (1541).

Berkshire, county of SC England. Area 1255 sq km (484 sq mi); pop. 645,000; co. town Reading. In Thames basin; rich agric. incl. dairying, pigs, wheat, oats. Chalk downs cross C.

Berlichingen, Götz von (c 1480-1562), German knight. Led rebel peasants against S German nobility in PEASANTS' WAR (1524-5). Drama by Goethe based on his memoirs.

Berlin, Irving, orig. Israel Baline (1888-), American composer, b. Russia. Popular songs and musicals incl. 'Alexander's Ragtime Band', 'I'm Dreaming of a White Christmas', *Annie Get Your Gun, Call Me Madam.*

Berlin, city of NE Germany, on R. Spree, divided into East and West Berlin. East Berlin (pop. 1,088,000) is cap. of East Germany; West Berlin (pop. 2,122,000) is West German enclave, connected to west by specified land routes and air 'corridors'. Indust. and mfg. centre. City was cap. of Prussia, then of United Germany 1871-1945. Severely damaged in WWII, military occupation divided city after 1945. Soviet blockade of W sectors (1948-9), erection of Berlin wall (1961).

Berlin, Congress of (1878), called to review terms imposed on Turkey by Russia at end of RUSSO-TURKISH WARS; chaired by Bismarck, incl. Disraeli, Andrassy. Revised boundary between Greece and Turkey, placed

East Berlin: The Brandenburg Gate

Bosnia and Hercegovina under Austro-Hungary; Serbia, Montenegro, Romania recognized as independent.

Berlin airlift, supply by Western powers of foodstuffs, *etc,* to, and removal of exports from, Berlin in 1948. Followed imposition of blockade by USSR during period of increasing tension. Blockade ended 1949.

Berliner Ensemble, state theatre company of German Democratic Republic estab. (1948) by BRECHT.

Berlinguer, Enrico (1922-), Italian politician. Secretary of Communist party from 1972, his attempts to redefine party role within Western democracy resulted in electoral gains.

Berlin Pact, see AXIS.

Berlin Wall, division between East and West Berlin, erected by East Germany (1961). Followed failure of USSR to gain withdrawal of Allies from city. Use of 12 crossing points requires authorization.

Hector Berlioz

Berlioz, [Louis] Hector (1803-69), French composer. Wrote many large-scale works, often with a literary basis, in which he made innovations in orchestration. Works incl. *Symphonie fantastique, Romeo et Juliet, La Damnation de Faust.*

Bermondsey, see SOUTHWARK, England.

Bermuda, coral isl. group of *c* 300 isls. in NC Atlantic. British crown colony, Bermuda largest isl. Area 52 sq km (20 sq mi); pop. 53,000; cap. Hamilton. Indust. based on year-round US tourism. Discovered by Spanish (1515); settled by English (1609).

Bern (Fr. *Berne*), cap. of Switzerland and Bern canton, on R. Aare. Pop. 162,000. Knitwear, chocolate mfg.; printing,

Bermuda

publishing. Hq. of Universal Postal Union; univ. (1834). Founded 1191, medieval town remains. Cap. from 1848.

Bernadette, St, orig. Marie Bernarde Soubirous (1844-79), French visionary. As a girl claimed to see visions of Virgin Mary at Lourdes, now a centre of RC pilgrimage. Canonized in 1933.

Bernadotte, Count Folke (1895-1948), Swedish diplomat, nephew of King Gustavus V. Appointed (1948) UN mediator in Palestine, assassinated in Jerusalem by Jewish extremist.

Bernadotte, Jean Baptiste Jules, see CHARLES XIV, king of Sweden.

Bernanos, Georges (1888-1948), French novelist. Works incl. *Diary of a Country Priest* (1936), deal with struggle between good and evil in exceptional souls. Also known for anti-Vichy essays, *eg Lettre aux Anglais* (1942).

Bernard, Claude (1813-78), French physiologist. Considered founder of experimental medicine, his numerous investigations incl. work on chemistry of digestion and functions of pancreas. Discovered function of glycogen in liver. Wrote *Introduction à l'étude de la médecine expérimentale* (1865).

Bernard, Tristan, pseud. of Paul Bernard (1866-1947), French dramatist. Known for popular comedies, *eg Le Petit Café* (1911), *Jules, Juliette et Julien* (1929).

Bernardin de Saint-Pierre, Jacques Henri (1737-1814), French writer. Disciple of Rousseau. *Etudes de la Nature* (1784), incl. novel *Paul et Virginie,* reflect horror of civilization.

Bernard of Clairvaux, St (1090-1153), French churchman, scholar. Founded Cistercian monastery of Clairvaux (1115). Influential in contemporary politics, securing recognition for Pope Innocent II. Mystical in theology, opposed rationalism of Abelard, Arnold of Brescia. Inspired 2nd Crusade (1146).

Bernard of Menthon or **Montjoux, St** (*c* 996-*c* 1081), Savoyard churchman. Founded hospices in St Bernard passes to aid travellers. Patron saint of mountaineers.

Berne Convention, see COPYRIGHT.

Bernhard of Saxe-Weimar (1604-39), German Protestant soldier. Contributed to defeat of Holy Roman Empire during Thirty Years War with victories at Regensburg (1633), Breisach (1638). Routed at Nördlingen (1634).

Bernhardt, Sarah, pseud. of Rosine Bernard (1844-1923), French actress. Famous for performances at Comédie Française. Best-known roles incl. Phèdre, Hamlet; played latter with wooden leg.

Bernini, Giovanni Lorenzo (1598-1680), Italian sculptor, architect. Greatest practitioner of Italian Baroque style; under papal patronage in Rome he designed churches, tombs, statues, fountains, *etc.* Appointed architect to St Peter's (1629), he created colonnades and piazza in front of the church. Works incl. *Ecstasy of St Theresa* (1645-52) and tomb of Urban VIII.

Bernoulli, Jacob or **Jacques** (1654-1705), Swiss mathematician. Developed Leibnitz's calculus; contributed to calculus of variations; estab. principles of probability theory in *Ars Conjectandi*; discovered Bernoulli numbers. His brother **Johann Bernoulli** (1667-1748), was a pioneer

of calculus of variations. His son, **Daniel Bernoulli** (1700-82), worked on fluid motion (Bernoulli's principle), kinetic theory of gases and probability theory. Wrote *Hydrodynamica* (1738).

Bernstein, Eduard (1850-1932), German political theorist. In exile (1878-1901); leader of 'revisionist' faction of Social Democratic party after writing *Evolutionary Socialism* (1898), a denial of Marxist prognosis of revolution.

Bernstein, Leonard (1918-), American pianist, composer, conductor. Music makes fresh use of American idioms, esp. musicals *On the Town, West Side Story.* Works also incl. religious music, *eg Chichester Psalms* and *Mass,* fusing contemporary serious and popular idioms.

Berry, Charles, Duc de (1778-1820), French prince, younger son of Charles X. His assassination led to reaction against French liberals during the reign of Louis XVIII.

Berry, hist. region of C France, cap. Bourges. Plateau, agric. in fertile Indre and Cher river valleys. Purchased (1101) by French crown; duchy (1360-1601).

Berthelot, [Pierre Eugène] Marcelin (1827-1907), French chemist. Pioneer of modern organic chemistry; synthesized acetylene, ethanol, *etc,* thus dispelling notion of vital force necessary for organic synthesis. Later worked in thermochemistry, devising special calorimeter.

Berthollet, Claude Louis, Comte (1748-1822), French chemist. Collaborated with Lavoisier in devising new chemical nomenclature. Discovered bleaching action of chlorine. Worked on rate of chemical reactions, anticipating law of mass action.

Bertillon, Alphonse (1853-1914), French criminologist. Devised Bertillon system, method of criminal identification by classification of body measurements.

Bertran de Born (*c* 1140-*c* 1214), French troubadour. Involved in struggles between Henry II and his sons, known for verses in praise of war.

Berwick, James Fitzjames, Duke of (1670-1734), French marshal. Illegitimate son of James II of England, whom he supported at Battle of the Boyne (1690). Fought in Wars of Spanish and Polish Succession. Killed in latter.

Berwick-on-Tweed, mun. bor. of Northumberland, NE England, at mouth of Tweed. Pop. 11,000. Salmon fishing. Long disputed by Scotland, became neutral territ. 1551; incorporated 1885.

Berwickshire, former county of SE Scotland, now in Borders region. Lammermuir Hills in N (sheep); Merse lowland in S (cereal growing). Co. town was Duns.

beryl, very hard mineral, silicate of beryllium and aluminium. Comprises hexagonal crystals which may be extremely large. Gem forms are EMERALD, AQUAMARINE.

beryllium (Be), hard corrosion-resisting metallic element; at. no. 4, at. wt. 9.01. Occurs as BERYL; obtained by electrolysis of fused salts. Used for making light alloys and in windows for X-ray tubes.

Berzelius, Jöns Jakob, Baron (1779-1848), Swedish chemist. Worked in several branches of chemistry; gave composition of numerous compounds and compiled table of atomic weights. Discovered selenium, thorium, cerium. Introduced modern chemical symbols and formulae.

Bes, in ancient Egyptian pantheon, god of music, pleasure and fashion, guardian of the home, children. Represented as bandy-legged dwarf.

Besançon, city of E France, on R. Doubs, cap. of Doubs dept. Pop. 116,000. Watchmaking centre, textiles; univ. (1691). Hist. cap. of Franche-Comté. Roman remains, 12th cent. cathedral, palace. Birthplace of Victor Hugo.

Besant, Annie, née Wood (1847-1933), English theosophist, social reformer. Tried, but acquitted, for immorality after pub. birth control pamphlet (1877). Disciple of Helena BLAVATSKY; went to India, where she helped further nationalist cause. President of Theosophical Society (1907-33), wrote much on THEOSOPHY.

Besant, Sir Walter (1836-1901), English author. Novels, incl. *All Sorts and Conditions of Men* (1882), deal with social evils in E London. Also wrote on history, French literature.

Annie Besant

Besier, Rudolph (1878-1942), English playwright, b. Java. Known for *The Barretts of Wimpole Street* (1930) on romance of Robert and Elizabeth Barrett Browning.

Bessarabia, hist. region of Moldavian SSR and W Ukrainian SSR. Disputed by Russia and Turkey; ceded to Russia (1812). Declared itself independent (1918) and joined in union with Romania; recovered by USSR in WW II.

Bessel, Friedrich Wilhelm (1784-1846), German astronomer. In 1838, was 1st to determine accurately parallax of a star (61 Cygni), thus finding its distance from Earth. Compiled star catalogue and introduced Bessel's function in mathematics.

Bessemer, Sir Henry (1813-98), English industrialist, inventor. Developed (*c* 1856) Bessemer process in mfg. of steel in which impurities (*eg* carbon, manganese, silicon) are removed by oxidation when air is blown through molten pig iron.

bestiary, medieval allegorical prose or verse catalogue of animals, real and mythical. Descriptions convey Christian or moral message. In later Middle Ages often richly illustrated. Name also applied to early popular treatises on natural history.

beta particle, electron or positron emitted by radioactive nucleus. Electron emitted when neutron spontaneously decays into proton, an anti-neutrino being produced as well. Penetration power *c* 100 times that of alpha particle.

betatron, cyclic accelerator used to obtain high energy beam of electrons by accelerating them in rapidly increasing magnetic field.

Betelgeuse, red supergiant star in constellation Orion. Of variable brightness, due to pulsation; *c* 500 light years away.

betel palm, *Areca catechu,* palm native to SE Asia. Source of betel nut, an astringent, orange, nut-like fruit, widely chewed in E for its stimulant effect.

Bethe, Hans Albrecht (1906-   ), American physicist, b. Germany. Described thermonuclear mechanism (carbon cycle) by which Sun converts hydrogen to helium, thereby creating solar energy. Awarded Nobel Prize for Physics (1967).

Bethlehem (Arab. *Beit-Lahm*), town of W Jordan. Pop. 24,000. Considered birthplace of Jesus. Emperor Constantine built basilica (333) on traditional site of Nativity; rebuilt by Justinian in 6th cent.

Bethlehem, town of E Pennsylvania, US; on Lehigh R. Pop. 73,000. Important steel, cement mfg. Settled by Moravians (1741).

Bethnal Green, *see* TOWER HAMLETS, England.

Betjeman, Sir John (1906-   ), English poet and architectural authority. Known for light, witty verse, *eg New Bats in Old Belfries* (1940), autobiog. *Summoned by Bells* (1960). Works on architecture, *eg Ghastly Good Taste* (1933) reflect love of Victoriana. Poet laureate (1972).

betony, *Stachys officinalis,* European perennial of thyme family with spike of red-purple flowers. Once used as remedy for many ills and thought to be good for soul as well as body. Wood betony is lousewort.

Betterton, Thomas (*c* 1635-1710), English actor. Member, subsequently manager of Davenant's company. Most famous actor of Restoration stage esp. in Shakespearian roles.

Betti, Ugo (1892-1953), Italian dramatist, poet. Known for plays on problems of justice and religious faith, *eg The Queen and the Rebels* (1951), *The Burnt Flowerbed* (1953).

Beuthen, *see* BYTOM, Poland.

Aneurin Bevan

Bevan, Aneurin (1897-1960), British politician. As minister of health (1945-51), inaugurated nationalized health service. Resigned over social services cuts, became leader of the left within Labour Party; later, advocated nuclear disarmament.

bevatron, cyclic accelerator used to accelerate protons and other particles up to 6 GeV. Used at Univ. of California (Berkeley) to discover anti-proton.

Beveland, North, isl. of SW Netherlands, in Scheldt estuary. **South Beveland,** formerly an isl., is now penin. following reclamation. Both produce wheat, sugar beet.

Beveridge, William Henry (1879-1963), British economist, b. India. Supervised estab. of labour exchanges, wartime food rationing while in civil service (1908-19). Director of London School of Economics (1919-37). Prepared govt. report proposing social security system (1942), planned spending for full employment (1944).

Beverley, mun. bor. of Humberside, N England. Pop. 17,000. Former co. town of East Riding of Yorkshire. Has 13th cent. minster.

Beverley Hills, town of S California, US; suburb of Los Angeles. Pop. 33,000. Home of Hollywood film stars.

Bevin, Ernest (1881-1951), British politician and labour leader. Instrumental in union merger creating Transport and General Workers' Union. Minister of labour in wartime cabinet (1940-5); foreign secretary (1945-51), worked for closer ties with US through anti-Soviet policy.

Bewick, Thomas (1753-1828), English wood engraver. Illustrated natural history books, *eg History of British Birds* (pub. 1797 and 1804). Helped revive standards of wood engraving, introducing new expressive techniques.

Bexley, bor. of SE Greater London, England. Pop. 216,000. Created 1965 from several Kent towns.

Beza, Theodore (1519-1605), French Protestant theologian. Friend and biographer of Calvin whom he succeeded in chair of theology at Geneva (1564). Worked on Greek and Latin editions of NT.

Béziers, town of Languedoc, S France, on Canal du Midi. Pop. 82,000. Wine, brandy trade; cork, barrel mfg. Inhabitants massacred (1209) by Simon de Montfort for harbouring Albigensian heretics.

Bhagavad-Gita (Sanskrit,=song of the blessed one), philosophical dialogue contained in the Mahabharata epic. Sacred text incl. much of basis of Hindu thought and philosophy.

Bhamo, town of NE Burma, head of navigation on the Irrawaddy. Pop. *c* 16,000. Market centre, trade with China; ruby mining.

Bharat, ancient Hindi name for India, now used officially.

Bhave, [Acharya] Vinoba (1895-), Indian social worker, religious figure, Sanskrit scholar. Disciple of Gandhi, he founded Bhoodan ('land gift') movement (1951) to promote voluntary distribution of land by wealthy to poor.

Bhavnagar, city of Gujarat state on Gulf of Cambay, W India. Pop. 226,000. Port; exports cotton; textile mfg. Cap. of former princely state of Bhavnagar.

Bhopal, cap. of Madhya Pradesh, C India. Pop. 392,000. Textile mfg. Cap. of former princely state of Bhopal. Had women leaders (19th cent.).

Bhubaneswar or **Bhuvaneswar,** cap. of Orissa state, E India. Pop. 106,000. Many Hindu and Buddhist temples; pilgrimage centre.

Bhutan, kingdom of SC Asia. Area *c* 47,000 sq km (18,000 sq mi); pop. 1,146,000; cap. Thimbu. Language: Tibetan variant. Religion: Mahayana Buddhism. In E Himalayas, bordered by India, Tibet. Parts of S annexed by British in 19th cent; British, then Indian protect.

Bhutto, Zulfikar Ali (1928-), Pakistani political leader. Succeeded to presidency (1971) on overthrow of YAHYA KHAN. PM (1973-), effected reconciliation with independent Bangladesh. Re-elected 1977 amidst allegations of rigged voting.

Biafra, *see* NIGERIA.

Bialik, Haggim Nahman (1873-1934), Russian poet. Work in Hebrew, *eg* 'In the City of Slaughter' (1903), influential in renaissance of the language. Also translated classics from many languages. Lived in Berlin and Israel.

Bialystok, city of NE Poland, cap. of Bialystok prov. Pop. 170,000. Railway jct.; textile mfg., machinery. Founded 14th cent.; under Russian rule 1807-1919.

Biarritz, town of SW France, on Bay of Biscay. Pop. 30,000. Developed in 19th cent. from fishing village into fashionable resort, through patronage of Napoleon III, Queen Victoria.

Bible, sacred book of Christianity. The canon, or standard list, of books making up OLD TESTAMENT is accepted by most churches and is also sacred book of Judaism. The APOCRYPHA, some books of which are accepted by the Eastern Orthodox church, is recognized by the RC church apart from 2 books of Esdras and the Prayer of Manasses. The canon of 27 books of NEW TESTAMENT is same for all Christian churches. Bible was 1st book to be printed by GUTENBERG, in Latin (*see* VULGATE). Translators into English incl. WYCLIFFE, TYNDALE; AUTHORIZED VERSION most famous translation. RC scholars pub. DOUAY version (1582-1610).

bibliography, study of editions, dates, authorship *etc,* of books and other literature, or book containing such study; list of books or other literature related to particular author or subject. National bibliographies incl. literature pub. in one language or country, often in specified time period, *eg British National Bibliography* (1950-), *Cumulative Book Index* (US, 1898-) and *Bibliographie de la France* (1811-). Universal bibliographies attempt listing of all printed material, usually as catalogues of biggest libraries, *eg Catalogue général des livres imprimés* (1900-49, Bibliothèque Nationale, Paris), *Catalogue of Printed Books* (1881-1900, British Museum), *Library of Congress Catalog* (1942-).

Bichat, Marie François Xavier (1771–1802), French anatomist, physiologist. Introduced concept of tissue and, working without a microscope, identified 21 types of it. Findings provided basis of modern histology.

bicycle, light, two-wheeled vehicle driven by pedals. First bicycle (with treadles and driving rods) built (1840) in Scotland by Kirkpatrick MacMillan. The 'boneshaker' with rotary cranks built (*c* 1865) in Paris. Subsequently, light spoked wheels with rubber tyres introduced. Pennyfarthing had large, driven front wheel (up to 163 cm/64 in. diameter) giving higher gear ratio, with rear wheel as small as 30 cm (12 in.). Safety bicycle with equal-sized wheels and sprocket-chain drive first manufactured

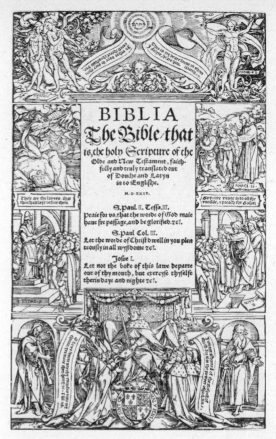

Bible: title page of the first printed English Bible, Coverdale's translation

by James Starley (*c* 1885) in Coventry. Developments incl. free-wheeling rear hub, variable ratio gears.

Bidault, Georges (1899-), French political leader. Fought in French underground. Premier (1949-50) and foreign minister. Exiled 1962-8 for participating in terrorist opposition to Algerian independence.

Biddle, John (1615-62), English religious leader, founder of UNITARIANISM. Despite official attempts to suppress his work, continued to publish and preach. Died in prison.

Biddle, Nicholas (1786-1844), American banker. President of Bank of US (1823-36), advocated theory of central banking. Opposed by President Jackson, who refused to renew bank charter (1836). *See* INDEPENDENT TREASURY SYSTEM.

Biedermeier style, name given to German style of furniture and decoration of period 1818-48. Resembled French Empire style, but simpler and more suited to bourgeois needs.

Biel, *see* BIENNE, Switzerland.

Bielefeld, city of N West Germany. Pop. 168,000. Indust. centre, esp. linen, silk, sewing machines, vehicles.

Bielsko-Biala, city of S Poland. Pop. 106,000. Textile (esp. woollens) indust., machinery. Formed (1950) from merger of Bielsko and Biala Krakowska.

Bienne (Ger. *Biel*), town of NW Switzerland, on L. Bienne. Pop. 64,000. Watch mfg.; machine tools. Ancient lake dwellings nearby. Funicular railway to Jura resorts.

biennial, *see* ANNUAL.

Bierce, Ambrose Gwinett (1842-*c* 1914), American author. Known for collections of short stories, *In the Midst of Life* (1892), macabre *Can Such Things Be?* (1893), and for cruelly witty journalism.

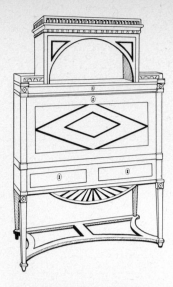

Biedermeier cabinet

big-bang theory, in cosmology, hypothesis that universe evolved from highly dense concentration of matter which underwent enormous explosion. This accounts for expansion of universe observed by Hubble. Its plausibility increased with observation in 1960s of uniform background radiation emanating from outer space. Opposed by STEADY-STATE THEORY.

Bighorn, river of Wyoming, US; tributary of Yellowstone R. Battle between Colonel Custer and Sioux forces took place at jct. of Bighorn and Little Bighorn rivers (1876).

bighorn or **Rocky Mountain sheep,** large wild sheep of NW North America, incl. *Ovis canadensis.* Male has heavy curling horns, female small upright horns.

bignonia, small genus of American and Japanese woody vines, named after Abbé Bignon, librarian of Louis XV. *Bignonia capreolata* or cross vine is a partial evergreen of SE US.

Bihar, state of NE India. Area 174,000 sq km (67,000 sq mi); pop. 56,332,000; cap. Patna. N fertile plain crossed by Ganges; rice grown. Important producer of coal, iron ore. Buddhist centre (*see* BUDDH GAYA).

Bijagós or **Bissagos Islands,** archipelago of Guinea-Bissau. Area *c* 1550 sq km (600 sq mi); main town Bolama. Low-lying; produce rice, coconuts.

Bijapur, town of Karnataka state, SE India. Pop. 103,000. Cotton ginning. Hist. cap. of Moslem Bijapur kingdom; numerous ruins, mosques, palaces and Gol Gumbaz (17th cent. tomb).

Bikaner, town of Rajasthan, NW India, on edge of Thar desert. Pop. 189,000. Blanket, carpet mfg. Surrounded by stone wall.

Bikini Atoll, in Marshall Isls., C Pacific Ocean. Uninhabited; pop. removed prior to US atomic bomb tests (1946-58).

Bilbao, city of N Spain, at mouth of R. Nervión, cap. of Vizcaya prov. Pop. 410,000. Port, exports wine, iron ore; shipbuilding, iron and steel indust. Seat of Basque autonomous govt. (1936-7) in Civil War.

bilberry, blaeberry or **whortleberry,** *Vaccinium myrtillus,* small shrub native to N Europe and Britain. Has small, globular, bluish-black, edible fruit. Similar species are cultivated in US (*see* BLUEBERRY).

Bildungsroman (Ger., = novel of education), novel tracing development of hero, *eg* Goethe's seminal *Wilhelm Meister,* Mann's *The Magic Mountain.*

bile, bitter yellow-brown fluid secreted by the liver. Found in gall bladder, from which it is discharged into duodenum to aid digestion, esp. of fats. Colour results from carrying waste products of haemoglobin destruction.

bilharzia or **schistosomiasis,** disease caused by infestation of veins by flukes of genus *Schistosoma.* Larvae in water penetrate skin and adult worms settle in urinary bladder. Eggs cause inflammation of tissue, leading to degeneration of bladder, liver, *etc.*

billiards, game played with cue and 3 balls (1 white cue ball, 1 red and 1 white object ball) on oblong cloth-covered slate table, edges of which are cushioned. Scoring is by pocketing object or cue ball, or by cannons (striking the 2 object balls successively with cue ball). Played in England and France from 16th cent.

Billings, Josh, pseud. of Henry Wheeler Shaw (1818-85), American humorist. Known for volumes of *Sayings* (1865-6), annual *Farmer's Allminax* (1869-80) satirizing govt. policy from rustic standpoint.

Billings, town of S Montana, US; on Yellowstone R. Pop. 62,000; state's largest town. Agric. and livestock market; sugar refining.

bimetallic strip, strip of 2 different metals bonded together in such a way that strip buckles when heated (as metals expand at different rates). Used in thermostats.

bimetallism, use of two metals (usually gold and silver) as monetary standard with fixed values in relation to each other. Both metals circulate as legal tender. Term does not apply to systems where other metals (*eg* copper, nickel) are used as token coinage.

binary number system, representation of integers by powers of 2, using only digits 0 and 1. In this system, 2 is represented by 10, 3 by 11, *etc.* Used in computers.

binary star, star consisting of 2 components, revolving about common centre of gravity under effect of mutual gravitation. Very common; *c* 50% of stars in our galaxy are binaries.

binding energy, in physics, energy required to decompose atomic nucleus into constituent protons and neutrons. Binding energy of neutron is energy required to remove neutron from nucleus.

bindweed, widely distributed family of plants with long climbing stems. Species incl. greater bindweed, *Calystegia sepium,* and lesser or field bindweed, *Convolvulus arvensis* with white or pink flowers. Black bindweed, *Polygonum convolvulus,* of dock family is widespread.

Binet, Alfred (1857-1911), French psychologist. With Théodore Simon, developed Binet-Simon scales (1905-11), series of tests of intelligence forming basis of modern intelligence testing.

binocular, optical instrument for viewing distant objects. Consists of 2 telescopes (binoculars) mounted so that a separate image enters each of viewer's eyes giving greater perception of depth than single image. Normally uses prisms to reduce length.

binomial theorem, in mathematics, theorem giving expansion of powers of $x + y$ in terms of powers of x and y.

Binyon, [Robert] Laurence (1869-1943), English poet. Known for translation of Dante's *Divine Comedy* into English *terza rima.* Other works incl. *The Burning of the Leaves* (1944), essays on Far Eastern art.

Bío-Bío, longest river of Chile, rising in Andes. Flows NW 390 km (*c* 240 mi) to Pacific near Concepción. H.e.p. supplies in upper reaches.

biochemistry, chemistry of living things. Two main branches: determination of structure of organic compounds present in living organisms, *eg* plant pigments, vitamins, proteins; elucidation of chemical means by which substances are utilized or made in living organisms.

biography, account of person's life by another. Classical biographies incl. Xenophon, Suetonius, Plutarch; medieval writers adapted biog. to give account of miracles performed by saints (hagiography); Renaissance emphasized concern for individual and realism, *eg* Roper's life of Thomas More, Vasari's lives of Italian artists (1550); biog. at height in 18th cent., *eg* Boswell's *Life of Samuel Johnson* (1791), Johnson's own *Lives of the Poets* (1779-81). New developments in 20th cent. incl. use of psychology (*eg* Strachey's *Eminent Victorians*) and fictional biog., combining hist. and creative writing, *eg* Maurois' works on

Shelley, Byron *etc,* Irving Stone on Michelangelo, van Gogh.

biology, science and study of living things, comprising BOTANY and ZOOLOGY. Study of form and structure of an organism is morphology; of the functions, physiology; of reproduction and early growth, embryology; of fossil remains, palaeontology. For division of plants and animals into series according to similarities and relationships, *see* CLASSIFICATION.

biosphere, that part of the Earth's crust and atmosphere which contains living organisms.

birch, family of deciduous trees comprising ALDERS and birches, genus *Betula.* Latter is hardy, with papery white bark; yields hard wood. Aromatic oil from sweet birch, *B. lenta,* used as wintergreen oil.

bird, any of class Aves of warm-blooded, egg-laying, feathered vertebrates, with forelimbs modified into wings; *c* 8700 living species. Believed to have evolved from reptiles; *see* ARCHAEOPTERYX.

bird of paradise, bird of Paradisaeidae family of New Guinea and adjacent isls. Males brightly coloured with elongated tail feathers, brilliant ruffs.

Birdum, town of N Northern Territ., Australia. Terminal of railway from Darwin. Centre of extensive cattle raising region.

Birkenhead, Frederick Edwin Smith, 1st Earl of (1872-1930), British politician. Led Conservative opposition to Irish Home Rule, later prosecuted CASEMENT as attorney general (1915-19). Served as lord chancellor (1919-22).

Birkenhead, co. bor. of Merseyside met. county, NW England, on Wirral penin. Pop. 138,000. Port on R. Mersey, docks opened 1847. Has tunnel link with Liverpool.

Birmingham, city of West Midlands met. county, WC England. Pop. 1,013,000; 2nd largest British city. Transport centre; metal working, esp. vehicles, firearms. Main expansion during Indust. Revolution. Has 2 univs.

Birmingham, city of NC Alabama, US; at S end of Appalachian Mts. Pop. 301,000; state's largest city. Iron and steel centre; cement, textile, chemical mfg. Railway jct. Founded 1871.

Birobidzhan or **Birobijan,** town of USSR, Khabarovsk territ., RSFSR. Pop. 56,000. Sawmilling, clothing mfg. Cap. of Birobidzhan Jewish auton. region, formed 1928 as centre for Soviet Jews. Mainly agric., with mining and forestry.

birth control, *see* CONTRACEPTION.

birthmark, congenital skin blemish. Types incl. pigmented naevus or mole, caused by cluster of pigment cells; strawberry mark and port-wine stain, composed of small blood vessels.

Biscay, Bay of, inlet of N Atlantic Ocean, lying between Ushant Isl., NW France, and Cape Ortegal, NW Spain. Noted for strong currents, heavy seas.

Bishop Auckland, urban dist. of Durham, N England. Pop. 33,000. Seat of Durham bishopric from 12th cent.

Biskra, town and oasis of NE Algeria, at foot of Aurès Mts. Pop. 59,000. Winter resort and major date producer. Former French military post.

Bismarck, Otto Eduard Leopold, Fürst von (1815-98), German statesman, chief minister of Prussia (1862-90), architect of German Empire. War with Denmark (1864) resulted in acquisition of Schleswig; friction over Holstein led to Austro-Prussian War (1866), in which Prussian leadership in Germany was consolidated. Provoked French into Franco-Prussian War (1870-1), in which Prussia annexed Alsace-Lorraine. With formation (1871) of German Empire, he became its 1st chancellor. Ruled autocratically (known as 'iron chancellor'), controlling domestic and foreign policies. Engaged in struggle (*Kulturkampf*) between state and Catholic church, but, as with his opposition to socialism, it eventually failed. Resented by William II; dismissed 1890.

Bismarck, cap. of North Dakota, US; railway jct. on Missouri R. Pop. 35,000. Agric. market (esp. spring wheat). Cap. from 1883.

Bismarck

Bismarck Archipelago

Bismarck Archipelago, volcanic isl. group in SW Pacific; part of Papua New Guinea. Area *c* 49,700 sq km (19,200 sq mi). Incl. New Britain, New Ireland, Admiralty Isls.

bismuth (Bi), metallic element; at. no. 83, at. wt. 208.98. Occurs as metal or as oxide Bi_2O_3; obtained by reducing oxide with carbon. Used in metal castings and making alloys of low melting point; compounds used in medicine.

bison, hoofed mammal of cattle family with shaggy mane, short horns, humped back. American bison or buffalo, *Bison bison,* once numerous on Great Plains; now protected after over-hunting. European bison or WISENT very rare.

Bissagos Islands, *see* BIJAGÓS ISLANDS.

Bissau (Port. *Bissão*), cap. of Guinea-Bissau, on Geba estuary. Pop. 62,000. Admin. centre; port, exports hardwoods, copra, palm oil. Cap. of Portuguese Guinea from 1942.

Bitolj (Turk. *Monastir*), town of Macedonia, S Yugoslavia. Pop. 66,000. Agric. centre, carpet mfg. Near Roman *Heraclea Lyncestis*; under Turks from 1395. Taken by Serbia 1913. Has mosques, churches, bazaar.

bittern, wading bird of heron family, with speckled plumage, long pointed bill. Species incl. nocturnal common European bittern, *Botaurus stellaris,* and American *B. lentiginosus.* Male emits booming call.

bittersweet, *see* NIGHTSHADE.

bitumen, name given to various mixtures of hydrocarbons, esp. solid or tarry mixtures obtained as residues on distilling coal tar, petroleum, *etc.*

Bivalvia (bivalves), aquatic molluscs of class Lamellibranchiata. Shell formed from 2 hinged halves. Incl. oysters, mussels, clams.

Bizerte (Arab. *Banzart*), town of N Tunisia, on Mediterranean Sea. Pop. 95,000. Port; steelworks nearby. German naval base in WWII, badly damaged. Evacuated by France (1963).

Bizet, Georges, orig. Alexandre César Léopold Bizet (1838-75), French composer. Best known for orchestral pieces *L'Arlésienne* and *Jeux d'Enfants,* and opera *Carmen.* Bizet's lyrical qualities were unrecognized in his lifetime.

spectral distribution of black body radiation led to quantum theory.

Georges Bizet

Blackbuck

Bjerknes, Vilhelm Frimann Koren (1862-1951), Norwegian physicist, meteorologist. Applied hydrodynamic and thermodynamic theories to weather prediction. With son, **Jakob Aall Bonnevie Bjerknes** (1897-   ), evolved polar-front theory of cyclones, basis of modern weather forecasting.
Björneborg, see PORI, Finland.
Björnson, Björnstjerne (1832-1910), Norwegian author. Known for novels reflecting interest in Norwegian people and legends, *eg The Fisher Maiden* (1868). Also wrote poetry, incl. words of Norwegian national anthem, social dramas. Nobel Prize for Literature (1903).
Black, Joseph (1728-99), Scottish physician and chemist, b. France. Showed that carbon dioxide is produced when calcium carbonate is heated and investigated its properties. Investigated specific and latent heat.
Black-and-Tans, nickname of irregular force in UK, enlisted for service in Ireland as auxiliaries to Royal Irish Constabulary during disturbances of 1919-22. Name arose from khaki colour of uniform worn with black accessories of Royal Irish Constabulary.
black bear, *Ursus americanus,* most widespread and numerous North American bear, smaller than brown bear. Lives in forests; diet of roots, berries. Himalayan black bear, *Sclenarctos thibetanus,* forest-dwelling bear found from Persia to Himalayas.
Blackbeard, see TEACH, EDWARD.
blackberry or **bramble,** *Rubus fructicosus,* low, rambling shrub with white flowers and black fruit. North American species incl. *R. allegheniensis.* Edible berries made into jam or jelly. Once valued for orange dye yielded by roots, and as remedy for swellings and burns.

European blackbird

blackbird, one of various thrush-like birds, males black with yellow beak. Common European variety is *Turdus merula.* Redwinged blackbird most abundant bird of America.
black body, in physics, ideal surface or body which absorbs completely all radiation falling on it. Must also be perfect emitter of radiation, total depending only on absolute temperature. Planck's attempts to explain

blackbuck, *Antilope cervicapra,* long-horned antelope of W India. Male black above, white on belly. Female fawn and white.
Blackburn, co. bor. of Lancashire, NW England. Pop. 102,000. Cotton weaving, textile machinery, chemicals, paint mfg.
Black Country, indust. area of WC England, centred in S Staffordshire. Formerly affected by smoke and soot from foundries, factories, *etc.*
Black Death, outbreak of plague which affected Europe *c* 1346-9. Catastrophic effect on pop., killing over ⅓ of inhabitants of many areas.
black earth or **chernozem,** fertile black or dark brown soil. Consists of modified form of LOESS, rich in HUMUS. High nutrient content, good structure make it very suitable for agric., as in *eg* USSR, NC North America.
Blackett, Baron Patrick Maynard Stuart (1897-1974), English physicist. Used cloud chamber to photograph nuclear disintegration (1925). Awarded Nobel Prize for Physics (1948) for this work and for subsequent improvements of Wilson cloud chamber.
black-eyed susan, *Rudbeckia hirta,* species of cornflower native to North America. Biennial, *c* 60 cm/2 ft high with dark-centred golden flowers.
black fly, small biting fly of Simuliidae family, found worldwide. Larvae inhabit running water. Females persistent blood-suckers; in Africa transmit roundworm to humans, causing 'river blindness'.
Blackfoot, North American Indian tribes of Algonquian linguistic stock. Settled in 19th cent. on upper Missouri and N Saskatchewan rivers and W to Rocky Mts. Plains buffalo hunters, noted for hostility to settlers and complex ritual. A few remain on reservations in Alberta, Montana.
Black Forest (*Schwarzwald*), wooded mountain region of SW West Germany. Highest peak is Feldberg (*c* 1490 m/4900 ft). Tourism, forestry, woodcarving, clock mfg. Source of Danube, Neckar rivers.
black-headed gull, see GULL.
Black Hills, mountains of NC US, in SW South Dakota, and NE Wyoming. Rise to 2207 m (7242 ft). Forestry, tourism, mineral resources (esp. gold). Gold rush in 1873. Famous sculptures of 4 US presidents at Mt. Rushmore.
black hole, hypothetical state of sufficiently massive star that undergoes gravitational collapse within a certain (Schwarzchild) radius. Region of space around black hole is so distorted that light cannot escape from black hole and so it can never be observed. Certain X-ray stars are believed to be binary companions of black holes.
Black Hole of Calcutta, name given to small room in which British garrison of Calcutta were imprisoned overnight (1756) after successful attack by nawab of Bengal. Most prisoners died of suffocation.

blackjack, see VINGT-ET-UN.

Blackmore, Richard Doddridge (1825-1900), English novelist. Known for classic historical romance, *Lorna Doone* (1869).

Blackpool, co. bor. of Lancashire, NW England. Pop. 151,000. Leading English coastal resort; has famous tower (158 m/520 ft), illuminations.

black power, economic and political power sought by American blacks in struggle for civil rights. Incl. variety of specific movements. Arose as reaction to limited success of non-violent civil rights movement in 1950s and 60s. Increasingly radical, violent action advocated by black urban groups. Militants incl. Black Panther party (estab. 1966), MALCOLM X, Eldridge Cleaver.

Black Prince, see EDWARD THE BLACK PRINCE.

black rat, *Rattus rattus,* common rat of Middle Ages in Europe, largely displaced by brown rat. Carried plague from Asia.

Black Sea (anc. *Pontus Euxinus*), inland sea of SE Europe, bounded by USSR, Turkey, Bulgaria, Romania. Area *c* 414,000 sq km (160,000 sq mi). Linked to Sea of Azov (NE) by Kerch Str.; to Aegean (SW) by Dardanelles. Almost tideless; marine life in upper levels only.

blackshirts, members of fascist organization. Refers specifically to militant units of Italian Fascist party (estab. 1919) which had black-shirted uniform. March on Rome (1922) brought MUSSOLINI to power. Term also refers to Hitler's elite bodyguard (*Schutz staffel* or SS).

Blackstone, Sir William (1723-80), English jurist. Wrote *Commentaries on the Laws of England* (1765-9), long used both in UK and US as standard work.

black swan, *Cygnus atratus,* only swan native to Australia, unique to that country.

blackthorn or **sloe,** *Prunus spinosa,* European deciduous spiny shrub of rose family. Short spikes of small, white flowers are followed by small, astringent fruits (sloes or sloe plums) which are used to flavour sloe gin. Stems used to make shillelaghs in Ireland.

Blackwell, Elizabeth (1821-1910), American physician, b. England. First woman in US to obtain a medical degree (1849). Helped found (1857) New York Infirmary for Women and Children and its coll. for training women doctors.

black widow, black venomous spider of tropics and subtropics, genus *Latrodectus.* Female, much larger than male, often eats it after mating. Bite of female intensely painful, rarely fatal.

Blackwood, Algernon (1869-1951), English author. Known for short stories, *eg Tales of the Uncanny and Supernatural* (1949).

Blackwood's Magazine, British literary magazine, first pub. Edinburgh (1817) by William Blackwood (1776-1834). Known for strong Tory feeling and savagery towards 'Cockney School' of poets, *eg* Keats, Hazlitt. Editors incl. John Gibson Lockhart, James Hogg.

bladder, see GALL BLADDER and URINARY BLADDER.

bladderwort, plant of genus *Utricularia* of Eurasia and N America, esp. *U. vulgaris,* water bladderwort with finely-divided leaves and small bladders. These capture minute water animals and digest them.

blaeberry, see BILBERRY.

Blagonravov, Anatoli Arkadyevich (1894-   ), Russian rocketry expert. Head of Soviet Academy of Artillery Science. Believed to have directed early part of Sputnik programme.

Blaine, James Gillespie (1830-93), American politician. Twice defeated as Republican presidential nominee (1876, 1884). As secretary of state (1889-92), set up 1st Pan-American Congress.

Blake, Robert (*c* 1599-1657), English admiral. Defeated Prince Rupert's fleet (1650), Tromp and Dutch navy (1653). Estab. English sea power in the Mediterranean (1654) with victory at Tunis. Captured Spanish treasure fleet (1657). Helped organize Commonwealth's navy.

Blake, William (1757-1827), English poet, engraver, artist. Known for intensely personal vision, abandonment of conventions in poetry and engravings. Translated Biblical

symbolism into his own mythology, in works incl. *Songs of Innocence* (1789), *Songs of Experience* (1794), and long, complex 'prophetic books', *eg The Marriage of Heaven and Hell* (1793). Precursor of Romanticism in belief in imagination, individual liberty, simplicity. Illustrated own work but most famous for etchings for Book of Job.

Blanc, Louis (1811-82), French political leader. A socialist, he advocated system of cooperative workshops in *Organisation du travail* (1840). Fled to England, after fall of provisional govt. (of which he had been a member) of 1848, remaining until estab. of Third Republic (1871).

Blanc, Mont, see MONT BLANC.

Blanchard, Jean Pierre or **François** (1753-1809), French balloonist. With John Jeffries, made 1st crossing by air (1785) of English Channel in a balloon.

Fanny Blankers-Koen at the 1948 Olympic Games

Blankers-Koen, Fanny (1918-   ), Dutch athlete. Won 4 Olympic titles in 1948: 100 and 200 m sprints, 80 m hurdles and 4 × 100 m relay.

blank verse, unrhymed verse; in English usually of iambic pentameters. Used in dramatic and epic poetry from Shakespeare and Milton to present.

Blanqui, Louis Auguste (1805-81), French revolutionary socialist. Leader in Revolution of 1848, Paris Commune (1871). Social theories, *eg* dictatorship of proletariat, influenced Marx; wrote *Critique sociale* (1885).

Blantyre, city of S Malawi, in Shiré Highlands. Pop. 169,000. Commercial, indust. centre on L. Malawi-Mozambique railway. Founded (1876) as mission by Livingstone, named after his birthplace. Joined to nearby Limbe in 1956.

Blarney, village of Co. Cork, S Irish Republic. Castle (15th cent.) contains Blarney Stone, kissing of which reputedly gives one persuasive speech ('blarney').

Blasco Ibañez, Vicente (1867-1928), Spanish novelist. Known for *The Four Horsemen of the Apocalypse* (1916) about WWI, but early naturalistic novels, *eg The Cabin* (1898), possibly of greater merit.

blast furnace, tower-like furnace used to smelt metals, esp. iron, from their ores. Mixture of ore, coke and limestone is placed in furnace and heated by a blast of air introduced from below. Molten metal separates from slag produced and both are drained off from bottom of furnace.

Blaue Reiter, Der, name given to group of expressionist painters, incl. Marc, Kandinsky, Macke and Klee, working in Munich 1911-14.

Blavatsky, Helena Petrovna, née Hahn (1831-91), Russian occultist. Founded Theosophical Society in New York (1875). Her *Isis Unveiled* (1887) is the textbook of THEOSOPHY.

blazing star, several American plants with purple or white flower clusters, *eg* the lily *Chamaelirium luteum* and the daisy *Liatris scariosa.*

bleaching, decolorization of coloured matter by chemicals. Common bleaches incl. sodium hypochlorite solution

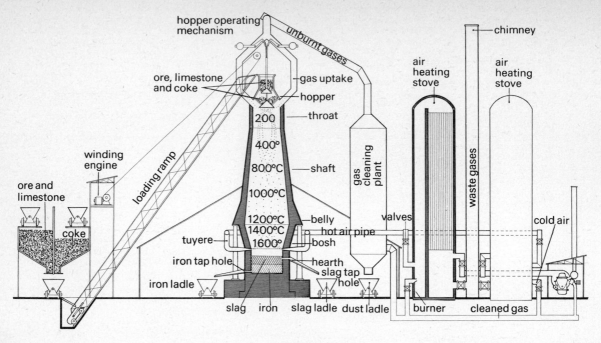

Blast furnace

(NaOCl), which acts by oxidation, and sulphur dioxide (SO_2), which acts by reduction.

bleeding heart, any plant of genus *Dicentra* with fern-like leaves and drooping clusters of pink, heart-shaped flowers, esp. *D. spectabilis,* a widely cultivated garden variety, native to Japan.

Blenheim (*Blindheim*), village of SC West Germany. Scene of defeat (1704) of French by Prince Eugène and Marlborough in War of Spanish Succession.

blenny, small fish of Bleniidae family, with numerous species, found worldwide. Elongated, often scaleless body. Shanny, *Blennius pholis,* common European variety. Some blennies capable of colour mimicry.

Blériot, Louis (1872-1936), French aviator, inventor. Designed monoplane in which he made (1909) 1st English Channel crossing in heavier-than-air machine.

blesbok, *Damaliscus albifrons,* small South African antelope, red-brown with white patch on face; found only in nature reserves.

Blessington, Marguerite, Countess of (1789-1849), Irish writer, beauty. Estab. literary salon in Kensington (W London). Known for *Conversations with Lord Byron* (1834).

Blest Gana, Alberto (1830-1920), Chilean novelist. Wrote naturalistic *Martin Rivas* (1862, translated 1918), in emulation of Balzac.

Bligh, William (1754-1817), British admiral. Remembered for mutiny (1789) on his ship, *Bounty,* while on an expedition in Pacific. Governor of New South Wales (1805-8). Deposed during Rum Rebellion.

blight, general term for many diseases of plants esp. those caused by fungi of family Erysiphaceae which are seen as a white dust on leaves of plant. Also refers to attack by bacteria or insects, *eg* greenfly.

blimp, *see* AIRSHIP.

blindness, partial or complete loss of sight. Often results from degenerative diseases associated with ageing; other causes incl. glaucoma, cataracts, *etc.* Trachoma is a common cause of blindness in tropical countries.

blindworm, *see* SLOW-WORM.

Bliss, Sir Arthur (1891-1975), British composer. Master of the Queen's Musick (1953-75). His music, vigorous and romantic, incl. *Colour Symphony,* ballets *Checkmate, Miracle in the Gorbals* and film music.

blister beetle, soft-bodied beetle of Meloidae family, often of bright metallic colouring. Some varieties harmful to crops. Cantharides, a blistering agent, formerly extracted from wings of Spanish fly, a S European species.

Blitzkrieg (Ger.,=lightning war), form of large-scale surprise attack involving motorized forces with air support. Developed by Germans in WWII.

Blixen, Karen, Baroness (1885-1962), Danish author. Short-stories incl. *Seven Gothic Tales* (pub. under pseud. Isak Dinesen, 1934), *Out of Africa* (1937), *Winter's Tales* (1942).

Ernest Bloch

Bloch, Ernest (1880-1959), American composer, b. Switzerland. Often used Jewish themes in compositions, *eg* rhapsody *Schelomo.* Other works incl. opera *Macbeth.*

Blocksberg, *see* BROCKEN, East Germany.

Bloemfontein, judicial cap. of South Africa and cap. of Orange Free State. Pop. 180,000. Commercial, transport, educational centre; univ. (1855). Founded 1846.

Blois, town of Orléanais, NC France, on R. Loire. Cap. of Loir-et-Cher dept. Pop. 45,000. Wine and brandy trade. Château (13th cent.) was residence of counts of Blois, and later of French kings.

Blok, Aleksandr Aleksandrovich (1880-1921), Russian poet; leader of Russian SYMBOLISTS. Works incl. mystical celebration of eternal feminine, *Songs of the Beautiful Lady* (1904), masterpiece of Revolution *The Twelve* (1918). Also wrote increasingly pessimistic plays.

Blondel, Maurice (1861-1949), French philosopher. Anti-rationalist, but accepted rationalist proofs of God's existence. Claimed no finite good can satisfy action, only infinite God.

Blondin, Charles, pseud. of Jean François Gravelet (1824-97), French tightrope walker. Famous for crossing of Niagra Falls on rope at height of *c* 50 m (160 ft).

blood, principal fluid of circulatory system in higher vertebrates. Carries oxygen and cell-building material to body tissues and disposes of carbon dioxide and other wastes. Composed of plasma (55%) and cells (45%). Red blood cells (erythrocytes) contain haemoglobin which combines with oxygen in lungs and thus enables oxygen to circulate to tissues. White blood cells (leucocytes) destroy bacteria and form antibodies to neutralize poisons. Smaller blood platelets (thrombocytes) help initiate blood clotting.

blood groups, classification of human blood into groups according to compatibility of red cells of one group with plasma of another. Incompatibility results in agglutination (clumping) of cells which must be avoided in transfusions. Four main groups, A, AB, B and O, used in system devised by LANDSTEINER (1900).

bloodhound, large black and tan dog, with drooping ears, wrinkled forehead, keen sense of smell. Stands *c* 69 cm/27 in. at shoulder. Used in tracking fugitives.

blood poisoning, name given to 3 conditions: toxaemia, presence in bloodstream of toxin produced by pathogenic bacteria; septicaemia, spread of bacteria through bloodstream; cellulitis, spread of bacteria from a wound to nearby tissue.

blood pressure, pressure exerted by blood on walls of arteries. Varies with heartbeat between *c* 120 mm/4.72 in. of mercury (systolic pressure) and 80 mm/3.15 in. (diastolic pressure); increases with age. Obesity, arteriosclerosis cause high blood pressure.

bloodstone or **heliotrope,** semi-precious gemstone, a variety of chalcedony. Mostly dark green, speckled with red jasper. Major sources in US, Brazil, India, Australia.

blood transfusion, transfer of blood from one mammal to another of same species. BLOOD GROUPS of donor and patient must be determined to avoid destroying transferred red cells. Tests should also be made for organisms causing disease, *eg* malaria, serum hepatitis.

blood vessels, in higher vertebrates, system of vessels through which blood circulation takes place. They comprise: arteries, carrying blood away from heart; veins, carrying blood towards heart; capillaries, minute vessels which form subdivisions of arteries and then form first small veins. Exchange of material between blood and tissue occurs through thin walls of capillaries.

Bloody Assizes, see JEFFREYS, GEORGE.

Bloomer, Amelia Jenks (1818-94), American social reformer and feminist. Editor of the journal *Lily*, devoted to women's rights and temperance. She advocated wearing of short skirt and loose trousers gathered at the ankles (known as 'bloomers').

Bloomfield, Leonard (1887-1949), American linguist. In major work, *Language* (1933), held that linguistic phenomena should be studied as a formal whole in isolation from their environment or history.

Bloomsbury group, name given to group of English writers, artists, intellectuals who met in Bloomsbury district of London from 1906. Incl. Virginia and Leonard Woolf, Lytton Strachey, E.M. Forster, Duncan Grant,

Contemporary illustration of 'bloomers'

Keynes, Bertrand Russell. 'Bloomsbury' values represented an elitist sensitivity to art and friendship.

Blow, Susan Elizabeth (1843-1916), American educator. Influenced by Froebel, she estab. 1st successful public kindergarten in US.

blowfly, two-winged fly of Calliphoridae family, commonly called bluebottle or greenbottle. Maggots develop in and feed on living tissue or decaying matter.

Blücher, Gebhard Leberecht von (1742-1819), Prussian field marshal. Contributed to Allied victories against Napoleon at Leipzig (1813), Waterloo (1815).

Bluebeard, villain of traditional tale best known in Perrault's version (1697), prob. based on murderer, Gilles de Rais. Many versions of tale incl. Maeterlinck's *Ariane et Barbe-bleue* (1901) and operas by Offenbach, Bartók.

bluebell, plant of many species, esp. of genera *Campanula* and *Mertensia,* bearing blue, drooping, bell-shaped flowers. Species incl. *C. rotundifolia,* bluebell of Scotland or harebell and *Endymion nonscriptus* or wild hyacinth, found in Europe and North America. *See* SQUILL.

blueberry, several plants of genus *Vaccinium,* esp. the high-bush blueberry, *V. corymbosum,* a profusely-branched North American shrub with sweet, edible berry.

bluebird, small North American songbird of thrush family, genus *Sialia.* Male has blue plumage, red breast.

bluebonnet, *Lupinus subcarnosus,* annual plant of the lupin family, generally limited to Texas. The state flower, it is a protected plant.

bluebottle fly, blue-coloured BLOWFLY, notorious for spreading dirt and germs.

blue collar, grouping of workers in semi-skilled or unskilled occupations, usually manual labour. Term derived from traditional colour of workshirts. *See* WHITE COLLAR.

Bluefields, port of SE Nicaragua, on Caribbean near mouth of Escondido R. Pop. 23,000. Hardwood, banana exports. Cap. of British protectorate of Mosquito Coast until 1860.

bluefish, *Pomatomus saltatrix,* food fish common to Atlantic coast of North America; occurs also in Indian Ocean, Mediterranean. Travels in dense, voracious shoals.

bluegrass, several grasses of the genus *Poa,* important in lawns and pastures. Known as meadow grass in Britain. Kentucky bluegrass, *P. pratensis,* is particularly valuable as food for horses.

blue-green algae, any of the division Cyanophyta of microscopic ALGAE that contain a blue pigment which masks the green chlorophyll. Widely distributed in unicellular or colonial bodies on moist soil, rocks and trees and in fresh or salt water. Help maintain soil fertility by fixing atmospheric nitrogen and preventing erosion.

blue laws, American legislation minutely regulating public, private conduct. Term originally used of 17th cent. Connecticut laws, typical of colonies' strict proscription of drunkenness, sexual misconduct. Now seldom enforced.

Blue Nile, see NILE.

blues, fundamental form of American vocal music, deriving from Negro work songs, and usually melancholy and reflective in mood. Its melodic inflections (blue notes) have influenced much of today's popular music.

bluestocking, female intellectual, esp. with literary tastes and often pedantic. Originally applied c 1750 to social circle incl. Elizabeth Montagu.

bluet or **innocence,** *Houstonia caerulea,* of the madder family, native to North America. Delicate, perennial plant with four-petalled bluish flowers with yellow eyes and small leaves at base of stem. Esp. common in New England.

Blue tit

blue tit or **tom tit,** *Parus caeruleus,* European titmouse with yellow underparts and blue cap. Acrobatic when feeding, mainly insectivorous.

blue whale, *Balaenoptera musculus,* whalebone whale of worldwide distribution, now rare from over-fishing. Plankton diet. Largest known mammal, reaching length of 30 m/100 ft.

Blum, Léon (1872-1950), French statesman. Headed 1st POPULAR FRONT govt. (1936-7), instituted sweeping labour reforms. Arrested (1940) by Vichy govt., imprisoned by Germans (1942-5). Again premier 1946-7.

Blunden, Edmund Charles (1896-1974), English poet and critic. Known for prose and verse memories, *Undertones of War* (1928), collections, *The Shepherd* (1922), *Shells by a Stream* (1944).

Blunt, Wilfrid Scawen (1840-1922), English author, diplomat, explorer. Known for poetry, *eg Love Sonnets of Proteus* (1880). Bitter anti-imperialist propaganda caused by travels in Egypt, Arabia.

Blyton, Enid (1885-1968), English writer. Wrote many best-selling children's books, incl. 'Noddy', 'The Famous Five', 'The Secret Seven' series.

boa, large tropical constrictor snake of Boidae family. Best known is boa constrictor, *Constrictor constrictor,* of Central and South America. Arboreal, terrestrial, burrowing varieties exist. Young are born live.

Boadicea, see BOUDICCA.

boar, strictly, male pig. Wild boar, *Sus scrofa,* of Europe, N Africa, Asia, probably forerunner of domestic pig; coarse hair and enlarged canine tusk.

Boas, Franz (1858-1942), American anthropologist, b. Germany. Developed rigorous methodology in cultural and physical anthropology. Pioneered linguistics. Wrote classic studies of Eskimos, North American Indians.

boatbilled heron, bird of Cochleariidae family of Central and South America. Resembles ordinary heron but distinguished by large flattened bill.

Boa Vista, town of N Brazil, cap. of Roraima territ.; on Rio Branco. Pop. 36,000. Centre for processing and shipping minerals (gold, bauxite, quartz, *etc*) from surrounding area.

bobcat or **wildcat,** *Felix rufa,* small lynx of North America, with reddish-brown coat. Nocturnal hunter. Also called bay lynx.

Bob cat

Bobo-Dioulasso, city of SW Upper Volta. Pop. 102,000. Commercial centre; groundnuts trade. On Ouagadougou-Abidjan railway.

bobolink, *Dolichonyx oryzivorus,* North American songbird, related to blackbird, oriole. Plumage black and white. Winters in South America; may eat rice crops on flight south.

bobsledding, winter sport in which two or four persons descend course of icy, steeply-banked twisting inclines aboard a bobsled, an open, steel-bordered vehicle with sled-like runners. A development of tobogganing, it originated (19th cent.) in Switzerland. Olympic event since 1924.

bobwhite, *Colinus virginianus,* small North American quail, often called a partridge. Favourite game bird.

Boccaccio, Giovanni (1313-75), Italian poet, b. France. Friendship with PETRARCH influenced him greatly. Best known for secular classic Decameron, also wrote prose romance *Filocolo* (c 1340), verse tales *Filostrato* (c 1335), *Teseida* (1339-40).

Boccherini, Luigi (1743-1805), Italian composer, cellist. Prolific composer, noted for chamber music; wrote over 100 each of string quartets and quintets. Best-known piece is a minuet that comes from one of the string quartets.

Boccioni, Umberto (1882-1916), Italian sculptor, painter. One of the original futurists; work, influenced by cubism, attempted to translate motion, light and sound into form. Works incl. painting *The City Rises* (1910), sculpture *Unique Forms of Continuity in Space* (1913).

Bochum, city of W West Germany, in Ruhr. Pop. 342,000. Indust. centre, esp. iron, steel, engineering, chemicals. Badly damaged in WWII.

Bode, Johann Elert (1747-1826), German astronomer. Compiled *Uranographia* (1801), catalogue of stars and nebulae with star maps. Known for law giving approximate relative distances of planets from Sun.

Bodensee, see CONSTANCE, LAKE, Switzerland.

Bodh Gaya, see BUDDH GAYA.

Bodhisattva, in Mahayana Buddhism, a potential Buddha who, despite enlightenment, postpones his apotheosis to assist others.

Bodin, Jean (1530-96), French philosopher. Wrote *Six livres de la république* (1576), advocating strong monarchy to restore order to war-torn France; early study of political economy.

Bodleian Library, Oxford Univ., England, library famous for collection of rare books and manuscripts. Named after Sir Thomas Bodley, who restored it in late 16th cent. after original library (estab. 15th cent.) destroyed. Receives copy of every book pub. in UK under Copyright Act (1911).

Bodley, Sir Thomas (1545-1613), English scholar, diplomat. Best know as organizer of Bodleian Library, also went on missions for Elizabeth I.

Bodmin, mun. bor. of Cornwall, SW England. Pop. 6000. Former co. town, replaced by Truro. Bodmin Moor nearby.

Bodoni, Giambattista (1740-1813), Italian printer. Working in Parma, he produced editions of the classics famous for their typographical elegance. Designed many new typefaces.

Boeotia (*Voiotía*), region of EC Greece. Ancient cap. Thebes, led Boeotian League 6th cent. BC. Modern admin. dist., cap. Levadia.

Boerhaave, Hermann (1668-1738), Dutch physician. Estab. method of clinical teaching at Leiden Univ., helping to make it leading medical centre in Europe.

Boer War or **South African War** (1899-1902), conflict between Britain and Transvaal Republic-Orange Free State alliance; result of protracted dispute between British and Boers over British territ. ambitions. Aggravated by discovery of gold (1886) and arrival of prospectors. Immediate cause was Britain's refusal to withdraw troops from Transvaal following Jameson Raid (1895). British forces were besieged at Ladysmith, Kimberley and Mafeking by superior Boer army. Ascendant after arrival of heavy reinforcements under Roberts and Kitchener, British relieved Mafeking, invaded Transvaal and occupied Pretoria by July, 1900. Boers adopted guerrilla tactics, led by Botha and Smuts, but were forced to submit (1902). Peace signed May, 1902, in Treaty of Vereeniging.

Boethius, Anicius Manlius Severinus (*c* 480-*c* 525), Roman philosopher. Minister under Emperor Theodoric; wrote *The Consolation of Philosophy* while awaiting execution for treason. Greatly influential in transmitting Greek philosophy to Middle Ages.

Bogarde, Dirk, pseud. of Derek Niven van den Bogaerde (1921-   ), British film actor. Known for roles in films such as *The Servant* (1963) and *The Damned* (1969).

Bogart, Humphrey [De Forest] (1899-1957), American film actor. Famous in tough, cynical roles of 1940s, esp. as private eye in *The Maltese Falcon* (1941), *The Big Sleep* (1946), and as Rick in *Casablanca* (1942). Later films incl. *The African Queen* (1952).

Boghazkeui or **Bogazkoy**, village of NC Turkey. Cap. of Hittite empire (1400-1200 BC) with numerous ruins. Records of Hittite culture discovered here on clay tablets in early 20th cent.

Bognor Regis, mun. bor. of West Sussex, S England. Pop. 34,000. Seaside resort; many small hotels, convalescent homes.

Bogotá, cap. of Colombia, in E Andean valley; alt. 2610 m (*c* 8560 ft). Pop. 1,966,000. Cultural, financial centre; textile, chemical mfg.; tobacco, food products. Has international airport. Founded by Spanish (1538) on Chibcha Indian site; cap. from time of Colombian independence. Has Univ. (1572), OAS hq.

Bohemia (*Cechy*), region and former prov. of W Czechoslovakia. Mainly plateau; chief rivers Elbe, Moldau. Agric. (cereals, fruit); minerals (esp. uranium); spas. Indust. centred in Prague, Plzeň (beer). Hist. kingdom; Czech from 1918.

Böhme, Jakob (1575-1624), German mystic. Described all existence as a manifestation of the creative will of God. Evil results from effort to make single element assume the whole. Influenced Hegel. Works incl. *De signatura rerum*.

Böhmerwald or **Bohemian Forest** (*Ceský Les*), wooded mountain range of Czech-West German border. Highest peak Mt. Arber, alt. 1456 m (4780 ft). Timber; coal, lignite deposits.

Bohr, Niels Henrik David (1885-1962), Danish physicist. Used quantum theory to explain hydrogen atom spectrum, postulating that electron moves in restricted orbits about atomic nucleus. Theory superseded by wave mechanics. Awarded Nobel Prize for Physics (1922). His son, **Aage Bohr** (1922-   ), shared Nobel Prize for Physics (1975) for work on ellipsoidal shape of atomic nucleus.

Boiardo, Matteo Maria, Conte (1441-94), Italian poet. Author of unfinished epic *Orlando Innamorato*, based on Roland legend, continued by ARIOSTO in *Orlando Furioso*.

boil, in medicine, inflamed nodule around root of a hair or in a sweat gland. Often caused by infection with *Staphylococcus aureus*. Can be treated by antibiotics.

Boileau [-Despréaux], Nicolas (1636-1711), French critic, poet. Most famous critic of neoclassical age. Works incl. verse treatise *L'Art poétique* (1674). *Satires* after Juvenal.

Boise, cap. of Idaho, on Boise R. Pop. 75,000; state's largest city. Trade, transport centre. Grew after 1863 gold rush; became agric. centre after building of Arrowrock Dam (1911-15).

Boito, Arrigo (1842-1918), Italian composer, poet. Works incl. opera *Mefistofele* and libretti for Verdi's *Falstaff* and *Otello*.

Bok, Edward William (1863-1930), American editor, b. Holland. Influential as campaigning editor (1889-1919) of popular *Ladies' Home Journal*.

Bokhara, see BUKHARA.

Boksburg, city of S Transvaal, South Africa. Pop. 105,000. Major gold and coalmining centre in Witwatersrand.

Boldrewood, Rolf, pseud. of Thomas Alexander Browne (1826-1915), Australian novelist. Known for adventure stories, esp. *Robbery Under Arms* (1888), celebrating outback.

Boleslaus [I] the Brave (*c* 966-1025), king of Poland (992-1025). First Polish ruler to call himself king. Greatly extended and consolidated Polish territ. by military campaigns and by Peace of Bautzen (1018) with emperor Henry II.

boletus, genus of fleshy fungi, with thick stems and caps, often brightly coloured. Widely distributed; several species are poisonous but the cèpe, *Boletus edulis*, is edible.

Anne Boleyn

Boleyn, Anne (*c* 1507-36), English queen, 2nd wife of Henry VIII. Mother of Elizabeth I; she was executed for alleged adultery.

Bolingbroke, Henry St John, Viscount (1678-1751), English politician. Tory secretary of state under Robert Harley, whom he ousted (1714). Opposed George I's accession, was impeached and fled to France. Helped plan Jacobite uprising of 1715. Pardoned (1723), intrigued against Walpole.

Bolívar, Simón (1783-1830), South American revolutionary, b. Caracas; called the 'Liberator'. Rose to leadership during revolution against Spain (1810). After victory at Boyacá (1819), elected president of Greater Columbia. After meeting with SAN MARTÍN at Guayaquil, helped liberate Ecuador (1822), Peru (1824), created Bolivia. His vision of united Spanish America was promoted at meeting in Panama (1826), which accomplished little. Resigned from presidency (1830).

Bolivia, landlocked republic of C South America. Area 1,098,580 sq km (424,162 sq mi); pop. 5,250,000; cap. Sucre; admin. cap. La Paz. Languages: Spanish, Quechua, Aymará, Guaraní. Religion: RC. Andes and tableland (incl. L. Titicaca) in W; tropical rain forests in NE, Chaco plain in SE. Important tin, silver, copper mines (esp. at Potosí) are main source of wealth. Native Indians (Inca ruled) overrun by Spanish (16th cent.); gained independence under Sucre (1824). Wars with Chile, Brazil, Paraguay reduced territ.

Simón Bolívar

Böll, Heinrich (1917-   ), German author. Works critical of modern society incl. *Letter to a Young Catholic* (1958), novels *eg Billiards at Nine-thirty* (1959). Nobel Prize for Literature (1972).

boll weevil, *Anthonomus grandis,* grey weevil which lays eggs in cotton bolls; larvae feed on cotton fibres. Major pest of S US, Mexico.

Bologna, Giovanni da (1529-1608), Flemish sculptor. Leading sculptor in Florence after death of Michelangelo, his *Rape of the Sabines* (1579-83) is considered a high point of mannerism. Other works incl. *Flying Mercury* (1564).

Bologna, city of Emilia-Romagna, N Italy, cap. of Bologna prov. Pop. 502,000. Engineering, printing, foodstuffs. Roman *Bononia,* on Aemilian Way. Leading medieval centre of learning, with law school, univ. (1200); scholars incl. Dante, Petrarch. Under papal rule from 1560, united with Sardinia 1860. Many medieval buildings.

Bolshevism, Russian revolutionary movement which seized power (Oct. 1917). Term originated at Russian Social Democratic Congress (1903) in London, when radical wing led by LENIN prevailed in dispute over strategy and split from moderates headed by PLEKHANOV, whose followers were called Mensheviks. Russian word *bolshe* means larger; Menshevism, contending faction, comes from *menshe,* smaller. Bolsheviks became Russian Communist party (1918), Mensheviks losing all support by 1921.

Bolshoi Theatre, principal opera, ballet theatre in Moscow.

Bolt, Robert Oxton (1924-   ), English playwright. Best known for *A Man for All Seasons* (1960, filmed 1967) on the martyrdom of Sir Thomas More, and screenplays.

Bolton, bor. of Greater Manchester met. county, NW England. Pop. 154,000. Cotton spinning, woollens, textile machinery mfg.

Boltwood, Bertram Borden (1870-1927), American chemist. Worked on radioactive dating of minerals and geological strata. Investigated radioactive decay of uranium, showing that radium and ionium are intermediate products.

Boltzmann, Ludwig (1844-1906), Austrian physicist. Developed statistical mechanics, esp. kinetic theory of gases, independently of Maxwell. Gave mathematical treament of Stefan's law of black body radiation.

Bolzano (Ger. *Bozen*), city of Trentino-Alto Adige, NE Italy, on R. Isarco. Cap. of Bolzano prov. Pop. 105,000. Tourist centre on route to Brenner Pass; textiles, engineering. Passed to Italy from Austria (1919).

Boma, town of W Zaïre, on Congo estuary. Pop. 79,000. Port, exports palm oil, timber, coffee. Former slave trade centre. Cap. of Congo Free State (1866-1908), of Belgian Congo until 1929.

bombardier beetle, *Brachinus crepitans,* blue-grey and orange beetle. Emits volatile fluid with explosive crack when irritated.

Bombay, cap. of Maharashtra state, W India, on Arabian Sea. Pop. of greater city 5,969,000. Indust. centre, major port; exports cotton, cotton goods. Under Portuguese control (1534), ceded to Charles II of England; passed to East India Co. Has extensive university (1857).

Bon, Cape or **Ras Addar,** headland of NE Tunisia, projecting *c* 80 km /50 mi into Mediterranean Sea. Hilly, fertile; fruit, vineyards, tobacco. Last German forces in N Africa surrendered here (1943).

Bonaparte, Corsican family, from which NAPOLEON I was descended. His father, **Carlo Buonaparte** (1746-85), was pro-French Corsican lawyer; married Letizia Ramolino (1750-1836). Among their children were: **Joseph Bonaparte** (1768-1844), king of Naples (1806-8) and of Spain (1808-13), forced to abdicate; **Lucien Bonaparte** (1775-1840), contributor to Napoleon's success in coup d'état of 18 Brumaire (1799); **Louis Bonaparte** (1778-1846), king of Holland (1806-10), removed by Napoleon for defying anti-English Continental System; **Caroline Bonaparte** (1782-1839), wife of French marshal MURAT and queen of Naples (1808-15); **Jérôme Bonaparte** (1784-1860), king of Westphalia (1807-13). His marriage (1803) to an American was annulled by Napoleon.

Bonar Law, Andrew, *see* LAW, ANDREW BONAR.

Bonaventure, St, orig. Giovanni di Fidanza (1221-74), Italian philosopher, called the Seraphic Doctor. Influential head of Franciscan order. Attempted to reconcile Aristotelian philosophy with Christianity but placed emphasis on the mystical. Works incl. *The Journey of the Mind to God.*

Bondfield, Margaret Grace (1873-1953), British politician, trade unionist. First woman in British cabinet, as minister of labour (1929-31).

bonds, *see* SHARES.

Bône, *see* ANNABA, Algeria.

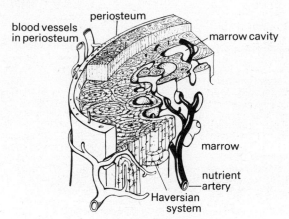

Section of long bone

bone, hard tissue which forms skeleton in vertebrates. Consists of cells held in a matrix of protein fibres and inorganic salts (mainly calcium phosphate). Cells are connected by network of blood vessels and nerves (Haversian canals). Blood-forming marrow is contained in cavities of long bones.

boneset, *Eupatorium perfoliatum,* perennial herb of daisy family native to North America, with white-rayed flowers and leaves pierced by the stem. The Indians first discovered its medicinal properties.

bongo, *Boocerus eurycerus,* large spiral-horned antelope of equatorial African forests. Elusive, travels in small groups; favourite big-game.

Bonhoeffer, Dietrich (1906-45), German Lutheran theologian. Led Church's resistance to Nazism; headed secret theological school (1935-40). Hanged.

Boniface, St, orig. Winfrid (*c* 675 - *c* 754), English Benedictine monk, missionary in Germany. Created arch-

Bongo

bishop of Mainz (745). Estab. bishoprics, abbeys; checked growth of Celtic Christianity. Killed by pagans in Friesland.

Boniface VIII, orig. Benedetto Caetani (*c* 1235-1303), Italian churchman, pope (1295-1303). Quarrelled with Philip IV of France over taxation of clergy and papal supremacy; issued bulls *Clericis laicos* (1296), *Unam sanctam* (1302). Attacked by Philip's supporters at Anagni (1303), died soon after.

Bonington, Richard Parkes (1802-28), English painter. Known for landscapes in water colour and historical scenes, influenced artists in France and England.

Bonin Islands (*Ogasawara-gunto*), volcanic isl. group of Japan, in Pacific *c* 960 km (600 mi) S of Tokyo. Japanese military base in WWII; occupied by US (1945-1968).

bonito, saltwater fish of mackerel family, found in Atlantic, Mediterranean. Incl. *Sarda sarda,* large game, food fish.

Bonn (anc. *Castra Bonnensia*), cap. of West Germany, on R. Rhine. Pop. 279,000. Admin. centre; publishing, pharmaceuticals, furniture, univ. (1784). Became cap. 1949; has Bundeshaus (Parliament building). Birthplace of Beethoven.

Bonnard, Pierre (1867-1947), French painter. Member of the Nabis group; his early work, influenced by Gauguin and Japanese prints, was characterized by decorative colour and simplified flat form. Later work often depicts intimate domestic interiors and landscapes, using heavier paint, bright colours.

bonsai, art of dwarfing trees in small containers by pruning roots and branches. Technique, first practised in China, pre-dates 13th cent. Specimens can be 300-400 years old and are heirlooms in Japan.

bontebok, *Damaliscus pygargus,* large dark brown antelope of South Africa. No longer found in wild, but preserved in parks.

Blue-faced boobies *(Sula dactylatra)* on the Galápagos Islands

booby, large tropical seabird of Sulidae family, related to gannet. Dives underwater to catch fish. Peruvian booby, *Sula variegata,* is principal producer of guano.

boogie woogie, type of piano jazz style popular in 1930s in US. The left hand keeps up a constant rhythmic phrase while the right executes series of simple variations, often improvised.

boojum tree, *see* BAOBAB.

bookkeeping, systematic recording of money transactions. In double entry bookkeeping, assets are recorded in one column with liabilities in another.

booklouse, small soft-bodied insect, order Psocoptera. Usually wingless, with biting mouth parts. Feeds on dried paste of books.

Book of Changes, *see* I CHING.

Book of the Dead, ancient Egyptian religious text, collection of incantations, prayers and spells. Prob. intended as guide for the dead on their journey through the underworld.

Boole, George (1815-64), English mathematician, logician. Known for *An Investigation of the Laws of Thought* (1854), in which logic is treated symbolically, using operations akin to those of algebra. Ideas influenced subsequent work in mathematical philosophy and are important in computer technology.

Daniel Boone

Boone, Daniel (1734-1820), American frontiersman. Explored and settled Kentucky in 1770s. His adventures became part of American folklore.

Booth, Charles (1840-1916), English social investigator. Pioneered social survey methods through immense, scrupulous work, *Life and Labour of the People in London* (17 vols., 1889-1903).

Booth, John Wilkes (1838-65), American actor. Confederate sympathizer, shot President Lincoln in Ford's Theatre, Washington; killed 2 weeks later. His brother, **Edwin Booth** (1833-93), was a well known actor in Shakespearian roles.

Booth, William (1829-1912), English evangelist preacher. Developed Salvation Army (1878) from missionary work among poor in London. Eldest son, **Bramwell Booth** (1856-1929), succeeded him in 1912 as general of Salvation Army. Fought white slave trade; promoted Criminal Law Amendment Act (1885). Daughter, **Evangeline Cory Booth** (1865-1950), directed Salvationist movement in Canada and US. General of international movement (1934-9).

Boothia, low-lying penin. of S Franklin Dist., Northwest Territs., Canada. Area 32,331 sq km (12,483 sq mi). Most N part of mainland; has magnetic N pole. First explored (1829-33) by Sir James Ross.

Bootle, bor. of Merseyside met. county, NW England. Pop. 74,000. Seaport on R. Mersey; extensive timber trade.

bootleggers, persons, esp. during PROHIBITION in US, engaged in illegal trade in alcoholic beverages.

Bopp, Franz (1791-1867), German philologist. Author of *Comparative Grammar* (1833-52) demonstrating relationship of Indo-European languages.

borage, any of Boraginaceae family of hairy herbs, shrubs and trees of Asia and Europe, esp. Mediterranean region.

William Booth

Esp. *Borago officinalis,* annual herb with deep blue flowers. Leaves are used in salads.

Boras, town of SW Sweden, on R. Viske. Pop. 73,000. Textiles centre. Founded (1632) by Gustavus Adolphus.

borax or **sodium tetraborate** ($Na_2B_4O_7.10H_2O$), crystalline salt, found naturally as tincal. Used in borax bead test to detect the presence of certain metals, as antiseptic and in glass mfg.

Bordaberry [Arocena], Juan María (1928-), Uruguayan politician, president (1972-). Succeeded Pacheco as president at time of intense activity by Tupamaro urban guerrillas. Tenure marked by increasing military involvement in govt. and outlawing of Marxist parties.

Bordeaux, city of SW France, on R. Garonne, cap. of Gironde dept. Pop. 267,000. Port, centre of Bordeaux wine trade; univ. (1441). Hist. cap. of Aquitaine and Guienne, under English rule (1154-1453). Hq. of Girondists in French Revolution. Has attractive 18th cent. architecture.

Borden, Lizzie [Andrew] (1860-1927), American woman, notorious through trial for murder of her father, stepmother (1892), which ended in her acquittal.

Borden, Sir Robert Laird (1854-1937), Canadian statesman, Conservative PM (1911-20). Led Canada through WWI, introducing conscription 1917.

Borders, region of SE Scotland. Area 4670 sq km (1803 sq mi); pop. 99,000. Created 1975, incl. former Berwickshire, Peeblesshire, Selkirkshire, Roxburghshire.

Bordet, Jules (1870-1961), Belgian serologist and immunologist, b. France. Investigated action of antibodies on bacteria and discovered process of complement fixation. Also discovered whooping cough bacillus. Awarded Nobel Prize for Physiology and Medicine (1919).

bore, tidal wave found in many river estuaries. Caused by inrush of water, opposed by river current, into progressively narrower and shallower channel. Occurs in *eg* Seine, Severn, Hooghly, Bay of Fundy.

Borges, Jorge Luis (1899-), Argentinian author. Known for personal form of semi-fictional essay 'Ficcione' reflecting interest on philosophical subjects, collected in translated *Labyrinths* (1962). Also wrote verse, criticism.

Borgia, Cesare (1476-1507), Italian political leader. Son of Rodrigo y Borja (later Pope Alexander VI), who made him a cardinal at age of 17. Resigned after murder (1498) of brother at which he prob. connived. Schemed with the French to capture cities of Romagna and estab. his own principality. Fell ill (1503), then lost power as Julius II forced him to restore possessions to papacy. Died fighting for king of Navarre. Considered archetype of Renaissance prince. His sister, **Lucrezia Borgia** (1480–1519), was alleged to be involved in her brother's intrigues. Married

Alfonso d'Este (1501) who became duke of Ferrara; made court centre of artistic and intellectual life.

Borglum, [John] Gutzon [de la Mothe], (1867-1941), American sculptor. Carved faces of Washington, Jefferson, Lincoln and Theodore Roosevelt on Mt. Rushmore, South Dakota.

boric or **boracic acid** (H_3BO_3), crystalline soluble solid, with weak acid properties. Used in eyewash and in making enamels.

Boris III (1894-1943), Bulgarian ruler (1918-43). Ruled dictatorially from 1935; brought Bulgaria into Axis group (1941). Died mysteriously shortly after visit to Hitler.

Boris Godunov, *see* GODUNOV, BORIS.

Borlaug, Norman Ernest (1914-), American agric. scientist. Awarded Nobel Peace Prize (1970) for developing high-yield crop varieties for use in underdeveloped countries.

Bormann, Martin (1900-45), German political leader. One of Hitler's chief associates, gained prominence in Nazi party, esp. after 1941. Disappeared at end of WWII, long sought for war crimes. Declared dead (1973) by West German govt.

Born, Max (1882-1970), British physicist, b. Germany. Shared Nobel Prize for Physics (1954) for work on statistical interpretation of wave functions, which helped describe electron behaviour.

Borne, [Karl] Ludwig, orig. Löb Baruch (1786-1837), German journalist. *Letters from Paris* (1830-3), criticizing Prussia, were banned. His liberal views were shared by Heine, with whom he led Young Germany movement.

Borneo

Borneo, largest isl. of Malay Archipelago. Area c 743,000 sq km (287,000 sq mi). Largely dense jungles and mountains; interior sparsely populated by Dyaks. Important oilfields; rubber and copra exports. Divided into 4 sections: Indonesian Kalimantan, former British colonies of Sabah and Sarawak (now part of Malaysia), and British protect. of Brunei.

Bornholm, isl. of Denmark, in Baltic Sea off S Sweden. Area 588 sq km (227 sq mi); main town Rönne. Mainly hilly; tourism, agric., fishing. Danish since 1660.

Borobudur, extensive ruined Buddhist monument in W Java; built between 750 and 850 in form of truncated pyramid and decorated with bas-reliefs depicting life of Buddha.

Borodin, Aleksandr Porfirevich (1833-87), Russian composer. Member of Russian nationalist group of composers 'the Five'. Works incl. 2 symphonies, opera *Prince Igor,* from which came 'Polovtsian Dances', 3 string quartets. Was also professor of chemistry.

Borodino, Battle of, fought (Sept. 1812) during Napoleonic Wars, at Borodino, near Moscow. Russian forces under Kutuzov engaged Napoleon's army in defence of Moscow. French entered Moscow one week later.

boron (B), non-metallic element, existing as brown amorphous powder or dark crystals; at. no. 5, at. wt. 10.81. Occurs in borax and boric acid. Steel alloy used as moderator in nuclear reactors. Borazon (BN), prepared at high temperature and pressure, used in indust. grinding; harder than diamond and more resistant to heat.

Borromean Islands, NW Italy. Group of 4 isls. in L. Maggiore. Isola Bella has palace, terraced gardens (17th cent.).

Borromini, Francesco (1599-1667). Italian architect. With Bernini, leading architect of Roman Baroque style. Works in Rome incl. San Carlo alle Quattro Fontane, noted for its dynamic spatial composition, and Sant' Ivo della Sapienza. Influenced subsequent work in Italy, Austria and S Germany.

Borrow, George Henry (1803-81), English writer. Known for part fantasy, part biog. works on travel and Gypsies, *eg The Bible in Spain* (1843), *The Romany Rye* (1857). Also wrote Romany lexicon, translations.

borzoi, long-haired Russian wolfhound. Silky whitish coat, narrow head. Stands *c* 76 cm/30 in. at shoulder.

Bosanquet, Bernard (1848-1923), English philosopher. Idealist, reacted against English empiricism. Works incl. *The Philosophical Theory of the State* (1899), *Value and Destiny of the Individual* (1913).

Bosch, Carl (1874-1940), German chemist. Adapted HABER process to indust. production. Invented Bosch process for large scale production of hydrogen. Shared Nobel Prize for Chemistry (1931).

Bosch, Hieronymus (*c* 1450-1516), Flemish painter. Famous for his fantastic allegorical and religious scenes, painted in minute detail and bright colour; depicted grotesque half animal, half human creatures and strange plants. His symbolism remains obscure. Works incl. *Seven Deadly Sins* (Madrid).

Bose, Sir Jagadis Chandra (1858-1937), Indian physicist, botanist. Demonstrated that plants respond to stimull in similar way to animals. Invented crescograph to measure plant growth.

Bosnia and Hercegovina, auton. republic of WC Yugoslavia. Area 51,115 sq km (19,735 sq mi); cap. Sarajevo. Mountainous, mainly within Dinaric Alps; main river Sava. Agric. (cereals, fruit, tobacco) in valleys. Bosnia annexed Hercegovina (14th cent.), fell to Turks 1463; ceded to Austria-Hungary 1878; focus of pre-WWI conflict with Serbia, Russia. Part of Yugoslavia from 1918.

boson, in physics, elementary particle, *eg* photon and certain mesons, that does not obey Pauli exclusion principle. Said to obey Bose-Einstein statistics.

Bosporus or **Bosphorus,** narrow str. separating European and Asiatic Turkey; 32 km (20 mi) long, links Black Sea with Sea of Marmara. One of its inlets, the Golden Horn, forms harbour of Istanbul. Of great strategic importance, controlled by Turks since 1452.

Bossuet, Jacques Bénigne (1627-1704), French churchman, noted orator. Attacked Protestantism, quietism (esp. that of FÉNELON) and the Jesuits. In *Histoire universelle* (1681), defended divine authority of civil institutions.

Boston, mun. bor. of Lincolnshire, E England, on R. Witham. Pop. 26,000. Market town; fishing indust.; medieval seaport. Has church tower, 'Boston Stump', height 83 m/273 ft.

Boston, cap. of Massachusetts, US; on Massachusetts Bay. Pop. 641,000. Atlantic seaport; financial, trade, cultural, education centre. Machinery, textiles, publishing indust. Settled by Puritans 1630. Focus of pre-Revolution activity (Boston Massacre 1770; Boston Tea Party 1773; Bunker Hill 1775); Lexington and Concord battles fought nearby (1776); Boston anti-slavery movement (1831). Indust. growth with 19th cent. shipping. Has many hist. buildings incl. State Capitol, Christ Church, Boston Museum of Fine Arts. Symphony Orchestra.

Boston Tea Party, pre-American Revolution incident (1773) caused by British govt.'s retention of tea tax after repeal of Townshend Acts imposing duty on specified goods. Group of angry Boston citizens, disguised as Indians, threw tea from ships into harbour.

Boston terrier, small dog, bred in US from bulldog and bull terrier. Brindle or black coat. Stands *c* 41 cm/16 in. at shoulder.

Boswell, James (1740-95), Scottish author. Known for masterly biog. of friend Dr Samuel Johnson (1791). Also

wrote many miscellaneous articles, *eg Private Papers,* discovered in 20th cent.

Bosworth Field, scene of last battle of Wars of Roses (1485) in which Richard III was defeated and killed by forces of Henry of Richmond, later Henry VII. Near Market Bosworth, Leicestershire.

botany, branch of BIOLOGY, science that deals with plants, their life, structure, growth and classification. Systematic plant CLASSIFICATION begun by Aristotle and his pupil Theophrastus, and improved upon by Linnaeus. Studies of plant anatomy, embryology and reproduction made by 18th cent. Classification now made according to structure, environment and functions.

Botany Bay, inlet of Tasman Sea, E New South Wales, Australia. Site of landing (1770) by Cook and Banks. Now surrounded by Sydney suburbs; oil refinery, airport on shores.

botfly, common name of hairy fly of several families. Larvae are endoparasites of horses, sheep, humans; may migrate through skin, causing serious damage. Incl. horse botfly (family Gasterophilidae), sheep botfly and warble fly (family Oestridae), and human botfly (family Cuterebridae).

Botha, Louis (1862-1919), South African soldier and statesman. Commanded Boers in war with Britain (1899-1902). Premier of Transvaal (1907-10), 1st PM of Union of South Africa (1910-19). During WWI, conquered German South West Africa.

Bothe, Walter Wilhelm Georg (1891-1957), German physicist. Devised method for studying cosmic rays using Geiger counters (coincidence counting) and for measuring minute intervals of time. Shared Nobel Prize for Physics (1954).

Bothnia, Gulf of, N arm of Baltic Sea between Sweden (W) and Finland (E). Aland Isls. at mouth. Ice-bound in winter.

Bothwell, James Hepburn, 4th Earl of (*c* 1536-78), Scottish nobleman, 3rd husband of Mary Queen of Scots. Mary's confidant after murder of RIZZIO (1566), responsible for assassination (1567) of DARNLEY. After abducting and marrying Mary, he was forced by Scottish nobles to flee to Denmark.

bo tree, name given by Buddhists to *Ficus religiosa,* the pipal or sacred fig tree under which Buddha was enlightened.

Botswana

Botswana, republic of S Africa; formerly Bechuanaland. Area 600,000 sq km (231,000 sq mi); pop. 709,000; cap. Gaborone. Languages: Tswana, English. Religions: native, Christian. Mainly dry plateau, Okavango Swamp in N, Kalahari Desert in S; nomadic pastoralism, exports cattle, hides. Main food crops maize, millet. Created Bechuanaland Protect. 1885; independent as Botswana from 1966; member of British Commonwealth.

Botticelli, Sandro, orig. Alessandro dei Filipepi (*c* 1445-1510), Italian painter. One of the leading Florentine painters of the Renaissance, his work is noted for delicacy, expressive line and its slight archaism. Most famous works are *Primavera* and *Birth of Venus.*

bottle brush, *see* BANKSIA.

bottlenosed dolphin, *Tursiops truncatus,* Atlantic cetacean, with short snout. Larger than common dolphin, *c*

Botticelli: detail from the *Adoration of the Magi*. presumed to be a self-portrait

3.6 m/12 ft long. Sociable, responsive to human contact; has been much studied.

bottlenosed whale, *Hyperoodon rostratus,* N Atlantic beaked whale, related to sperm whale. Eats mainly cuttlefish; *c* 6.4 m/21 ft long.

botulism, rare type of food poisoning caused by toxin produced by bacterium *Clostridium botulinum,* sometimes found in improperly preserved or canned food. Characterized by muscular paralysis; often fatal.

Botvinnik, Mikhail Moiseyevich (1911-), Russian chess player. World champion (1948-56, 1958-60, 1961); defeated by T. Petrosian in 1963 world contest.

Bouaké or **Bwake,** city of Ivory Coast. Pop. 161,000. Agric. market on Abidjan-Ougadougou railway; trade in coffee, cocoa, tobacco, sisal.

Boucher, François (1703-70), French painter. His work is considered the embodiment of French 18th cent. rococo taste. Made many tapestry designs and paintings of mythological scenes; director of Gobelins factory from 1755.

Boucher de Crèvecoeur de Perthes, Jacques (1788-1868), French archaeologist. Discovered (1837) in Somme valley evidence of man-made tools among remains of extinct animals of Pleistocene epoch. Argued that ancient culture existed before previously accepted date; conclusions were unrecognized for *c* 20 years.

Boudicca or **Boadicea** (d. AD 62), British queen of Iceni in East Anglia. Led revolt (61) against Romans following brutal annexation of her dead husband's territ. Burned Colchester and London. Her army was defeated by Paulinus; she took poison.

Boudin, Eugène Louis (1824-98), French painter. Painted numerous coastal and harbour scenes, noted for their luminous skies. Advocate of painting directly from nature, influenced Monet.

Bougainville, Louis Antoine de (1729-1811), French navigator. Circumnavigated globe 1767-9, after which he wrote *Description d'un Voyage autour du Monde*. Largest of Solomon Isls. and bougainvillea plant named after him.

Bougainville, largest of Solomon Isls., SW Pacific; part of Papua New Guinea. Area *c* 10,050 sq km (3880 sq mi). Mountainous, rises to *c* 2590 m (8500 ft) at Mt. Balbi, an active volcano.

bougainvillea, small genus of ornamental, tropical American evergreen vines with brilliant red or purple flowers. Named after French explorer Bougainville.

Bougie, *see* BEJAÏA, Algeria.

Boulanger, Georges Ernest Jean Marie (1837-91), French general. War minister (1886-7); gained great popular support as leader of Boulangist movement. Suspected of dictatorial ambitions, fled to Belgium and London (1889). Settled in Jersey where he committed suicide.

Boulanger, Nadia (1887-), French music teacher. Her analytical gifts and insistence on creativity have spurred many modern composers, incl. Copland, Berkeley.

boulder clay or **till,** unstratified mixture of clay, sand, gravel and boulders, transported and deposited by retreating glacier. Type of DRIFT, laid down directly from glacier without water transport.

Boulez, Pierre (1925-), French composer. Extended 12-note technique of Schoenberg to fixed organization of all musical elements, *eg* in *Le Marteau sans maître.* Also a noted conductor, esp. of 20th cent. composers.

Boulle or **Buhl, André Charles** (1642-1732), French cabinet maker. Made furniture for palaces, esp. Versailles, of Louis XIV. Developed form of marquetry (Buhl work) in which layers of tortoiseshell inlaid with brass were applied to furniture.

Boulogne (-sur-Mer), town of Picardy, N France, on English Channel. Pop. 50,000. Port, ferry services to Dover and Folkestone (England); fishing indust. Badly damaged in WWII.

Boult, Sir Adrian Cedric (1889-), British conductor. Formed BBC Symphony Orchestra in 1930 and was its principal conductor until 1949; moved to London Philharmonic Orchestra until 1957. Championed music of Holst, Vaughan Williams, Elgar.

Boulton, Matthew (1728-1809), English engineer, manufacturer. Financed Watt's steam engine, becoming (1775) his partner in its production. In 1797 he produced new copper coinage for Britain.

Boumedienne, Houari (*c* 1932-), Algerian political leader. Became chief of staff in FLN in fight for Algerian independence (achieved 1962). Overthrew Ben Bella (1965), became chief of state as head of revolutionary council.

bouncing Bet, *see* SOAPWORT.

Bounty, naval ship, *see* BLIGH, WILLIAM.

Bourbon, royal house of Europe. Ruled France, Spain, Two Sicilies and Parma. Line traced from Robert of Clermont's marriage (1272) into Bourbon family, his son becoming 1st duke of Bourbon. Title died with CHARLES, DUC DE BOURBON, but branch of family founded line of Bourbon-Vendôme. **Antoine de Bourbon** (1518-62) became king of Navarre; his son became Henry IV, 1st Bourbon king of France, whose descendants reigned until 1830 (except 1792-1814). Line of Bourbon-Spain started in 1700 with accession of grandson of Louis XIV, Philip V of Spain. Bourbon-Sicily came from Spanish house, founded (1759) by Ferdinand I of the Two Sicilies, ending with Francis II in 1861. Bourbon-Parma (1748-1860) was founded by younger son of Philip V of Spain.

Bourbon, Charles, Duc de (1490-1527), French nobleman. Created Constable of France after victory at Marignano (1515). Later joined Emperor Charles V; helped drive French from Italy, killed while leading attack on Rome.

bourgeoisie, the mercantile or shopkeeping middle class of any country. Prominent from end of medieval period, when they successfully opposed feudal nobility. In Marxist theory, class which, since end of Middle Ages, rose to power, overcoming nobles, monarchs, to reach exclusive political sway in modern state. Thus is one of two elements, the other being the proletariat, in modern dialectical struggle.

Bourges, town of C France, cap. of Cher dept. Pop. 74,000. Route centre, armaments mfg. Hist. cap. of Berry. Cathedral (13th cent.).

Bourget, Paul Charles Joseph (1852-1935), French novelist. Works, *eg Cruelle Enigme* (1885), *Le Disciple* (1889), important in development of psychological novel. Also wrote criticism.

Bourguiba, Habib ben Ali (1903-), Tunisian political leader. Led struggle for independence from France, involved in peace negotiations (1954). Elected premier (1956), then president (1959).

Bournemouth, co. bor. of Dorset, S England (formerly in Hampshire). Pop. 153,000. Resort on Poole Bay; has many hotels, convalescent homes.

Bournville, suburb of Birmingham, WC England. Founded 1879 by G. Cadbury for workers at chocolate factory. Early example of town planning.

Bouts, Dierick or **Dirk** (*c* 1410-75), Netherlandish painter. Noted for his sense of colour and the beauty of his landscape backgrounds. Works incl. *Justice of the Emperor Otto* (Brussels).

Bouvet Island, isl. in S Atlantic, *c* 2900 km (1800 mi) SSW of Cape Town. Discovered 1739, Norwegian dependency since 1930.

Bovet, Daniele (1907-), Italian pharmacologist, b. Switzerland. Discovered (1937) antihistamine drugs used to treat allergies and developed method to use curare as muscle relaxant; also worked on sulfa drugs. Awarded Nobel Prize for Physiology and Medicine (1957).

Bovidae, family of even-toed UNGULATES, order Artiodactyla, incl. cattle, sheep, goats, antelopes.

bow, *see* ARCHERY.

Bowdler, Thomas (1754-1825), English physician, editor. Expurgated literary texts, esp. those of Shakespeare, of anything 'which cannot with propriety be read aloud in a family'; hence to 'bowdlerize'.

Bowen, Elizabeth Dorothea Cole (1899-1973), Irish novelist. Best known for sensitive novels esp. *The Death of the Heart* (1938). Also wrote short-stories, essays.

bowerbird, small bird of Australia, New Guinea, family Ptilonorhynchidae. Male builds bower, decorated with feathers, shells, to attract female.

bowfin, *Amia calva,* freshwater fish of eastern North America. Primitive, shows features of fish of Mesozoic era. Voracious predator, lives in overgrown backwaters.

bowling, tenpin, indoor game played by rolling a ball at 10 wooden 'pins'. Game consists of 10 frames, a player being allowed to bowl twice if necessary in a frame. Modernized form of game believed to have been originally introduced into America by Dutch settlers in 17th cent.

bowls or **lawn bowling,** outdoor game dating at least from 13th cent. in England. Played on green, divided into 6 rinks. Opponents alternately roll balls close to small white ball and attempt to dislodge those previously rolled. Rules governed by International Bowling Board (founded 1905), comprising 18 countries.

Bowra, Sir [Cecil] Maurice (1898-1971), English Classical scholar and critic. Known for wit and wide learning. Works incl. *Heroic Poetry* (1952), *Primitive Song* (1962).

box, evergreen shrub of genus *Buxus* of Europe and N Asia. Common variety, *B. sempervirens,* is slow growing and used for clipped hedges.

boxer, short-coated dog of German origin. Fawn or brindle coloured, with protruding jaw. Stands *c* 58 cm/23 in. high at shoulder.

Boxer Rebellion (1898-1900), uprising in China by the Boxers, secret society dedicated to removal of foreign influence. Encouraged by dowager empress Tzu Hsi. Revolt crushed by joint European, Japanese, American forces. China forced to pay heavy indemnities (1901), to allow foreign troops to be stationed in Peking and to alter trade agreements to advantage of foreign nations.

boxing, sport of fighting with the fists. Boxing with bare fists was incl. in ancient Olympic games. Revived in 18th cent. in England in form of prize fighting. Rules for boxing with gloves were devised *c* 1867 under patronage of marquess of Queensberry. In modern Olympics since 1908; has also become a major professional sport in Europe and America.

box tortoise or **turtle,** North American land turtle, genus *Terrapene.* Can withdraw entirely into hinged shell, which it closes tightly.

Boyacá, town of NC Colombia, in E Andes. Pop. 8000. Scene of Bolívar's defeat of Spanish in 1819, led to independence of Colombia, Venezuela.

Boyce, William (1711-79), English composer. Master of the King's Musick from 1755. Wrote several symphonies, church and stage music; songs incl. 'Hearts of Oak'.

Boyd Orr, John Boyd Orr, 1st Baron (1880-1971), Scottish biologist. First director-general (1945-8) of UN Food and Agriculture Organization. Awarded Nobel Peace Prize (1949) for contributions to study of nutrition and world food problems.

Boyle, Robert (1627-91), Irish chemist. Enunciated Boyle's law, that volume of a gas kept at constant temperature is inversely proportional to its pressure, following experiments with air. Published *The Sceptical Chymist* (1661), in which he forwarded atomic view of matter, and distinguished between elements and compounds.

Boyne, river of NE Irish Republic, flows 130 km (80 mi) from Bog of Allen via Kildare, Meath to Irish Sea near Drogheda. Scene of battle (1690) in which William III of England defeated Jacobites under James II.

Boy Scouts, non-military, non-political international organization of boys over 12 years old. Estab. (1908) in UK by Baden- Powell, whose book *Scouting for Boys* (1908) led to incorporation of association by royal charter (1912), and spread of movement worldwide. Introduced into US (1910) by W. Boyce. Parallel organizations for girls are Girl Guides (UK; estab. 1922) and Girl Scouts (US; estab. 1912).

Brabant, area of Belgium and Netherlands. Former prov. of Low Countries, duchy from 12th cent. Prosperous medieval wool, textiles trade centred in Antwerp, Brussels, Louvain. Ruled from 15th cent. by Habsburgs. Divided 1830; Brabant, Antwerp are Belgian provs., North Brabant is Dutch prov.

Bracegirdle, Anne (*c* 1663-1748), English actress. Protegée of Betterton, friend of Congreve becoming famous in his plays, esp. as Millamant in *The Way of the World.*

Brachiopoda (brachiopods), phylum of marine invertebrates, often called lampshells (resemble ancient Roman lamp). Brachiopod has bivalve shell enclosing soft body; feeds by means of lopophore. Fossil species of Palaeozoic, Mesozoic eras are common; *c* 250 living species, *c* 30,000 extinct.

bracken or **brake,** several species of FERN, esp. European and American *Pteridium aquilinum,* with coarse, sharp stem and branched spreading fronds. In some places a pernicious weed. Roots once used in tanning and the fronds in thatching.

Bracton, Henry de (d. 1268), English jurist. Wrote *De legibus et consuetudinibus Angliae,* 1st account of English laws and customs.

Bradbury, Ray Douglas (1920-), American science fiction writer. Works incl. novels *eg Fahrenheit 451* (1953), short stories *eg The Martian Chronicle* (1950), and poetry.

Braddock, Edward (1695-1755), British general. During French and Indian War, commanded expedition (1755) to capture Fort Duquesne, losing more than half his troops and his own life.

Bradford, William (1590-1657), English colonist. Founder and long-time governor of Plymouth Colony. Author of *History of Plimoth Plantation.*

Bradford, city of West Yorkshire met. county, N England. Pop. 294,000. Woollens, worsteds, textiles, engineering industs. Church (15th cent.) now cathedral.

Bradlaugh, Charles (1833-91), English social reformer. Championed women's suffrage, birth control, trade unionism. Associate of ANNIE BESANT.

Bradley, Andrew Cecil (1851-1935), English literary critic. Best known for *Shakespearean Tragedy* (1904) stressing an understanding of Shakespeare's characters as a key to the plays.

Bradley, Francis Herbert (1846-1924), English philosopher. Opposed logical empiricism by differentiating between the psychological event and formal meaning in thought. Works incl. *Ethical Studies* (1876), *Appearance and Reality* (1893).

Bradley, Omar Nelson (1893-), American general. Led US troops in Normandy invasion (1944). Chairman joint chiefs of staff (1949-53).

Bradman, Sir Donald George (1908-), Australian cricketer. A prolific run scorer, he played for Australia (1928-48), captain from 1936. His aggregate of 974 runs (1930) is highest for England-Australia test series.

Bradshaw, George (1801-53), English map engraver. Originated railway guides, first pub. 1839.

Sir Donald Bradman

Johannes Brahms

Bradstreet, Anne (*c* 1612-72), American poet, b. England. Wrote first book of original verse published in Massachusetts Bay Colony, *The Tenth Muse Lately Sprung Up in America* (1650); best known for expression of sexual tenderness.

Brady, Mathew B. (1823–96), American photographer. Known for photographic record of Civil War and portraits of Lincoln.

Braga (anc. *Bracara Augusta*), town of NW Portugal. Pop. 41,000. Ecclesiastical centre from Middle Ages; seat of RC primate. Shrine of Bom Jesus do Monte nearby.

Bragança, town of NE Portugal. Pop. 8000. Castle was seat of royal house of Braganza.

Requiem, piano and violin concertos, choral and orchestral compositions, and chamber music.

Braid, James (*c* 1795-1860), Scottish surgeon. First to use term hypnotism, rather than mesmerism or animal magnetism; recognized that hypnotism arises from suspension of conscious mind.

Brăila, city of E Romania, on lower Danube. Pop. 161,000. Port, exports grain; railway workshops. Held by Turkey (1544-1828).

Braille, Louis (*c* 1809-52), French inventor. Blind from the age of three, he devised (1829) the system of raised point writing and printing named after him, enabling the blind to read and write.

Sir William H. Bragg

Bragg, Sir William Henry (1862-1942), English physicist. Researched into penetrating power of alpha particles. Shared Nobel Prize for Physics (1915) with his son, **Sir William Lawrence Bragg** (1890-1971), for working out theory of X-ray diffraction and using it to determine X-ray wavelengths and crystal structure.

Brahe, Tycho (1546-1601), Danish astronomer. Improved astronomical instruments, thus obtaining positions of heavenly bodies with unprecedented accuracy. Built 2 observatories on isl. of Hven. Kepler made extensive use of Brahe's observations in formulating laws of planetary motion.

Brahma, in Hinduism, supreme and eternal spirit of the universe. Personified as creator in divine triad (*see also* VISHNU, SIVA).

Brahman or **Brahmin,** in Hinduism, member of priestly (highest) Hindu CASTE. Only Brahmans may interpret the sacred Vedic texts.

Brahmaputra, river of NE India, *c* 2900 km (1800 mi) long. Rises in Himalayas of SW Tibet as Tsangpo, flows through fertile Assam valley; merges with Ganges in Bangladesh.

Brahms, Johannes (1833-97), German composer, pianist. Helped by Joachim and Liszt; close friend of Schumann. Settled in Vienna (1863). Despite romantic inclinations, he worked in classical forms. Works incl. 4 symphonies, a

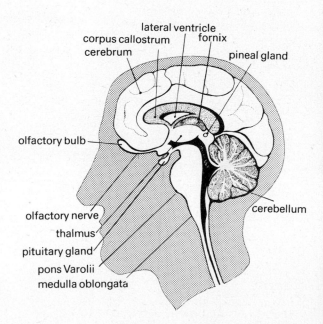

Section of the brain

brain, in vertebrates, that part of central nervous system enclosed in skull. Divided into 3 main sections: hindbrain, midbrain and forebrain. Hindbrain contains brain stem, extending from spinal chord; anterior to this is cerebellum, which coordinates muscular movements. Midbrain contains control network for senses of sight and hearing. Forebrain contains: thalamus, which receives and distributes incoming sensations and perceives sensation of pain; hypothalamus, which regulates body temperature, heart beat, metabolic rate, *etc*; relatively huge cerebrum, divided into 2 hemispheres with 4 paired lobes. Cerebrum controls sensations of vision, hearing, touch, *etc*, and higher mental processes.

Braine, John Gerard (1922-), English novelist. Known for *Room at the Top* (1957) a pessimistic view of provincial life. One of the ANGRY YOUNG MEN.

brake, *see* BRACKEN.

Brakpan, city of S Transvaal, South Africa. Pop. 113,000. At height of 1650 m (5400 ft); goldmining centre in Witwatersrand.

Bramah, Joseph (1748-1814), English inventor. Patented hydraulic press (1795). Also suggested possibilities of screw propeller, hydraulic transmission.

Bramante, Donato (1444-1514), Italian architect. Major architect of high Renaissance; engaged by Julius II to rebuild St Peter's, Rome (1503). Other works in Rome incl. Tempietto in courtyard of San Pietro in Montorio.

bramble, *see* BLACKBERRY.

Branchiopoda, subclass of primitive aquatic crustaceans, with many pairs of flattened, leaf-like limbs. Well-known example is daphnia or waterflea.

Brancusi, Constantin (1876-1957), Romanian sculptor. Pioneer of abstract sculpture; his work, in wood, stone and highly-polished metal, is noted for its simplification of natural forms. Works incl. *Bird in Space*.

Brandenburg, town of C East Germany, on R. Havel. Pop. 90,000. Agric. machinery, textiles. Cathedral, town hall (both 14th cent.). Cap. of former Brandenburg prov. of Prussia.

Brandes, Georg Morris Cohen (1842-1927), Danish literary critic. Formulator of Scandinavian naturalism, esp. in *Critical Studies* (1899) incl. study of Ibsen.

Brando, Marlon (1924-), American stage and film actor. First known for 'primitive male' roles, as in play *A Streetcar Named Desire* (1947), film *On the Waterfront* (1954). Later developed range in films with *The Godfather* (1972), *Last Tango in Paris* (1973).

Brandon, town of Canada, SW Manitoba; on Assiniboine R. Pop. 31,000. Centre of wheat-growing region; agric. implement mfg.

Willy Brandt

Brandt, Willy, orig. Herbert Ernst Karl Frahm (1913-), German statesman. Active in Norwegian resistance during WWII. Mayor of West Berlin (1957-66) until joined coalition govt. First Social Democrat chancellor (1969-74). Awarded Nobel Peace Prize (1971) for policies of seeking to improve relations with E European countries.

brandy, name for alcoholic spirit distilled from any wine. Best-known grape wine brandy is cognac, made from white grapes in Charente (France). Kirsch is distilled from fermented cherry juice, and slivovitz, of E Europe, from

plums. Characteristic light tawny colour acquired when left to mature in oak casks.

Brant, Joseph, Indian name Thayendanegea (1742-1807), Mohawk Indian chief. During American Revolution, aided British and later settled his people in Canada.

Brantford, town of S Ontario, Canada; on Grand R. Pop. 64,000. Electrical equipment mfg., agric. implements. Alexander Graham Bell developed 1st telephone here (1876).

brant goose, *see* BRENT GOOSE.

Branting, [Karl] Hjalmar (1860-1925), Swedish statesman. Formed 1st Social Democrat ministry, premier 3 times (1920, 1921-3, 1924-5). Shared Nobel Peace Prize (1921).

Georges Braque

Braque, Georges (1882-1963), French painter. Early work was in fauve style. Collaborated with Picasso in development of cubism until 1914; originated use of collage in his paintings. Later work incl. still lifes and landscapes in more realistic style.

Bras d'Or, tidal lake of E Nova Scotia, Canada. Area 930 sq km (*c* 360 sq mi). Almost divides Cape Breton Isl.

Brasilia, cap. of Brazil, in C federal dist. Pop. 538,000. Built as cap. with intention of stimulating growth in undeveloped interior; inaugurated 1960.

Braşov, city of SC Romania, in Transylvanian Alps. Pop. 193,000. Commercial, indust. centre (textiles, machinery); tourism. Founded (1211) by Teutonic Knights; passed from Hungary to Romania in 1920.

brass, name applied to various alloys of zinc and copper; sometimes containing other metal components. Ductile, resists corrosion.

brassica, *see* CABBAGE; TURNIP.

brass instruments, instruments in which sound is produced by vibration of the lips within a mouthpiece, *eg* FRENCH HORN; TROMBONE; TRUMPET; TUBA.

Bratislava (Ger. *Pressburg*), city of S Czechoslovakia, on R. Danube. Pop. 284,000. River port; agric. market, oil refinery (pipeline from Ukraine 1962). Cap. of Hungary 1541-1784 and Slovakia 1918-45. Gothic cathedral, town hall (13th cent.).

Braunschweig, *see* BRUNSWICK, West Germany.

Brautigan, Richard (1935-), American author. Novels reflecting the life of the Pacific coast incl. *Trout Fishing in America* (1967), *In Watermelon Sugar* (1968).

Bravo, Rio, Mexican name for RIO GRANDE.

Bray, Thomas (1656-1730), English clergyman, philanthropist. Founded (1699) the Society for Promoting Christian Knowledge (SPCK).

Brazil (*Brasil*), republic of E South America. Area 8,511,965 sq km (3,286,470 sq mi); pop. 79,000,000; cap. Brasilia; major cities Rio de Janeiro; São Paulo. Language: Portuguese. Religion: RC. Covers nearly ½ of South Ameri-

Brazil

can continent. Has extensive Atlantic coastline; mainly agric. esp. coffee, cotton, sugar cane growing. Tropical forested Amazon basin produces rubber. Mato Grosso plateaux in undeveloped interior (mineral resources eg iron ore, manganese). Drained by Amazon (W), Paraná-Paraguay (S), São Francisco river systems. Indust. concentrated in São Paulo, Minas Gerais regions (esp. cotton, steel, chemicals, engineering). Portuguese settlement began in 16th cent.; pop. gradually mixed. Independence gained (1822); republic estab. 1889. Govt. instability of 20th cent. broken by Vargas' dictatorship (1930-45).

brazilnut, edible seeds of tree *Bertholletia excelsa,* of nettle family, native to Brazil. Large woody fruits contain *c* 20 three-sided edible oily nuts.

Brazos, river of SC US. Rises in E New Mexico, flows SE 1410 km (870 mi) to Gulf of Mexico. Provides irrigation, h.e.p. for N Texas.

Brazza, Pierre Paul François Camille Savorgnan de, Comte (1852-1905), French explorer and colonial official, b. Italy. Explored W and C Africa from 1874, esp. Congo basin; founded Brazzaville (1880). Added much territ. to French empire in C Africa.

Brazzaville, cap. of the Congo, on Stanley Pool of R. Congo, opposite Kinshasa (Zaïre). Pop. 250,000. Admin., commercial centre. River port, railway to Pointe Noire; trade in wood, rubber, minerals from interior to coast. Founded by Brazza (1880); cap. of French Equatorial Africa 1910-60.

bread, food baked from kneaded dough made from flour, water and yeast (used as raising agent). Unleavened bread contains no raising agent. Wheat flour is generally used, but rye is sometimes employed. White bread is made from grain from which husk has been removed.

breadfruit, large, round, pulpy fruit of Malayan tree, *Artocarpus altilis,* found throughout S Pacific and tropical America. When baked the fruit can be used as bread substitute.

Breakspear, Nicholas, *see* ADRIAN IV.

bream, *Abramis brama,* European freshwater food fish of carp family. Protruding mouth used for feeding on bottom.

breast, in human female, either of 2 milk-secreting (mammary) glands. Develops with onset of puberty, increasing in size and shape. Towards end of pregnancy, hormones from pituitary gland stimulate secretion of milk. Corresponding male glands are undeveloped.

breccia, rock composed of small angular fragments, bound together in matrix of cementing material. Normally formed close to origin of constituent fragments, unlike CONGLOMERATE. Examples incl. cemented scree deposits, fault breccias, volcanic breccias.

Brecht, [Eugen Friedrich] Bertolt (1898-1956), German dramatist. Early work expressionist; best known for Marxist dramas, *eg The Threepenny Opera* (1928) with music by Weill, *Mother Courage and Her Children* (1939), *The Caucasian Chalk Circle* (1945). Applied anti-illusionistic 'alienation' theory in own theatre company, the Berliner Ensemble from 1948.

Breckinridge, John Cabell (1821-75), American politician. Vice-president (1857-61), presidential candidate (1860) of South's Democratic faction. Confederate general in Civil War.

Breconshire or **Brecknockshire,** former county of SC Wales, now in Powys. Mountainous in S, incl. Brecon Beacons (National Park). Coalmining; agric. **Brecon** or **Brecknock,** mun. bor. and co. town of Powys. Pop. 6000. Has cathedral (1923) formerly Priory Church.

Breda, town of SW Netherlands, in North Brabant. Pop. 122,000. Food processing, textiles. Strategic site, Spanish capture (1625) shown in Velázquez' *Surrender of Breda.*

breeder reactor, nuclear reactor which, in addition to creating atomic energy, produces more nuclear fuel by neutron bombardment of suitable radioactive elements, *eg* uranium 238.

breeding, attempt to improve genetic strains of plants and animals by careful selection of parent stock. Cattle are bred to improve meat or milk yield; cereals are bred to be more disease resistant and give larger and more rapid yields.

Bregenz (anc. *Brigantium*), town of NW Austria, on L. Constance, cap. of Vorarlberg prov. Pop. 23,000. Tourism, h.e.p.

Bremen, city of N West Germany, on R. Weser, cap. of Bremen state. Pop. 595,000. Major port; indust., commercial centre. Hanseatic League member from 1358; has medieval cathedral, town hall. Badly damaged in WWII.

Bremerhaven, city of N West Germany, at mouth of R. Weser. Pop. 145,000. Outport for Bremen; major fishing, ferry port. Founded 1827.

Brennan, Christopher John (1870-1932), Australian poet. Known for idiosyncratic melancholic verse, *eg* 'The Wanderer'. *The Verse of Christopher Brennan* (1958) is definitive collection.

Brenner Pass (Ital. *Passo Brennero*), on Austro-Italian border. Height 1370 m (4500 ft); road (1772), railway (1867) connect Innsbruck with Bolzano.

Brent, bor. of W Greater London, England. Pop. 279,000. Created 1965 from Wembley, Willesden mun. bors.

Brentano, Clemens Maria (1778-1842), German poet. Created 'legend' of 'Lorelei' in novel *Godwi* (1800-1). Collaborated with Achim von ARNIM in *The Boy's Magic Horn* (1805-8). Wrote much romantic verse, novellas.

Brentano, Ludwig Joseph ('Lujo') (1844-1931), German economist. Known for study of guilds and trade unions in England. Leading opponent of German militarism. Awarded Nobel Peace Prize (1927).

brent goose or **brant goose,** *Branta bernicla,* small, dark goose with black head. Breeds in Arctic, winters along Atlantic coast of North America.

Brescia, city of Lombardy, N Italy, cap. of Brescia prov. Pop. 215,000. Indust. centre; iron, munitions, textiles. Roman *Brixia,* has temple of Vespasian (AD 73); medieval cathedrals.

Breslau, *see* WROCLAW, Poland.

Brest, city of Brittany, NW France, on Atlantic Ocean. Pop. 154,000. Port, fishing; major French naval base. Harbour built (1631) by Richelieu. German submarine base in WWII, town badly damaged by Allied bombing.

Brest, city of USSR, transport centre of SW Byelorussian SSR. Pop. 128,000. Cap. of Polish-Lithuanian state from 1569, passed to Russia 1795. Formerly Brest-Litovsk; site of Soviet-German treaty (1918) in WWI. Belonged to Poland (1921-45).

Brest-Litovsk, Treaty of, peace treaty in WWI, signed (1918) by Soviet Russia and Central powers at Brest, after 1917 armistice. Russia recognized independence of Ukraine and Georgia, confirmed independence of Finland, gave up Poland, Baltic states and part of Byelorussia to Germany and Austro-Hungary; also made some concessions to Turkey. Terms renounced at end of WWI.

Brétigny, Treaty of (1360), concluded second phase of Hundred Years War between England and France. King John II was to be ransomed, Edward III was granted countships in France but abandoned claim to French throne.

Breton, André (1896-1966), French author. Involved in DADA, later founded SURREALISM in 3 manifestoes (1924-42). Also wrote novel, *Nadja* (1928), love poetry.

Breton, language, *see* CELTIC.

Bretonneau, Pierre (1778-1862), French surgeon. Performed 1st successful tracheotomy (1825) and identified diphtheria. His theory of origin and communication of infectious diseases anticipated Pasteur's germ theory.

Bretton Woods Conference, name given to UN Monetary and Financial Conference (July, 1944), held at Bretton Woods, New Hampshire, US. Resulted in creation of INTERNATIONAL MONETARY FUND and INTERNATIONAL BANK FOR RECONSTRUCTION AND DEVELOPMENT.

Breuer, Josef (1842-1925), Austrian physician. Developed hypnosis method of questioning to alleviate mental illness; later developed by Freud into psychoanalysis. With Freud, wrote *Studien über Hysterie* (1895).

Breuil, Henri (1877-1961), French archaeologist. One of first to study and interpret Palaeolithic cave art. Suggested that depiction of animals constituted system of sympathetic magic designed to ensure successful hunting.

Brewer, Ebenezer Cobham (1810-97), English clergyman. Best known for *Dictionary of Phrase and Fable* (1870).

brewing, *see* BEER.

Brewster, Sir David (1781-1868), Scottish physicist. Noted for discovery that beam of light reflected from glass is completely polarized when reflected and refracted rays are at right angles.

Leonid Brezhnev

Brezhnev, Leonid Ilyich (1906-), Soviet political leader. President (1960-4) until he succeeded Khrushchev as first secretary of Communist party's Central Committee. Policies incl. DÉTENTE with US, growing estrangement from China, extension of Soviet influence in developing countries. Supported invasion (1968) of Czechoslovakia. Formally acknowledged as head of state after changes to Soviet constitution (1977).

Briand, Aristide (1862-1932), French statesman. Began as Socialist, heading several govts. (1909-29). Foreign minister (1925-32), helped conclude Locarno (1925) and Kellogg-Briand (1928) pacts, aimed at maintaining European peace. Shared Nobel Peace Prize (1926) with Stresemann.

Briansk, *see* BRYANSK.

briar, sweetbriar or **eglantine,** *Rosa eglanteria,* European species of bush rose. Hooked white or pink single flowers, scarlet fruit (hips) which are rich in vitamin C. Now naturalized in North America.

bridge, card game for four players derived from WHIST. Most popular form is contract bridge, invention of which is credited to Harold Vanderbilt (1925); popularized by CULBERTSON, Charles Goren. Rules governing tournament play determined by Portland Club, London, European Bridge League, and American Contract Bridge League.

bridge, structure to carry road, railway or canal over gap or barrier. Most common types are cantilever, suspension and arch bridges. Some of world's best-known bridges incl. Forth Railway Bridge, Scotland (cantilever); Brooklyn Bridge, New York (suspension); Sydney Harbour Bridge, Australia (steel arch); Golden Gate Bridge, San Francisco (suspension).

Bridgeport, town of SW Connecticut, US; on Long Isl. Sound. Pop. 157,000. Munitions mfg., engineering, plastics indust. First settled as fishing community (1639).

Bridges, Calvin Blackman (1889-1938), American geneticist. His work on *Drosophila* (common fruit fly) proved vital role played by chromosomes in conveying hereditary characteristics of living organisms.

Bridges, Robert Seymour (1844-1930), English poet. Friend of G.M. Hopkins, editor of his work. Own work incl. *Shorter Poems* (1890), *The Testament of Beauty* (1929). Poet laureate (1913).

Bridget or **Birgitta of Sweden, St** (*c* 1300-73), Swedish nun, patron saint of Sweden. On death of her husband founded Order of the Holy Saviour (Bridgettines). Went to Rome (1349), where she became famous for advocating reform. Visions famous in Middle Ages.

Bridget, St (*c* 453-*c*523), Irish abbess. Regarded as founder of 1st women's religious community in Ireland at Kildare. Also called Brigid, Bride.

Bridgetown, cap. and seaport of Barbados, on Carlisle Bay. Pop. 9000. Popular tourist resort. Exports sugar, rum, molasses.

Bridgewater, Francis Egerton, 3rd Duke of (1736-1803), pioneer of British inland navigation. Had canal constructed to carry coal from his Worsley estate to Manchester; later had canal extended to the Mersey (1772).

Bridie, James, pseud. of Osborne Henry Mavor (1888-1951), Scottish playwright. Known for *The Anatomist* (1931) on Burke and Hare, *A Sleeping Clergyman* (1933) on heredity, and *Daphne Laureola* (1949).

Brie, region of N France, E of Paris. Cereals, cattle rearing; noted for dairy produce, esp. cheese. Early medieval county, cap. Meaux.

Brieux, Eugène (1858-1932), French dramatist. Known for plays dealing with morality of family and society incl. *Les Trois Filles de M. Dupont* (1899), *La Femme seule* (1913).

Brighouse, Harold (1882-1958), English playwright. Known for Lancashire dialect play *Hobson's Choice* (1916).

Bright, John (1811-89), British politician. Noted orator, joined by COBDEN in leading Anti-Corn Law League, advocating free trade; Corn Laws repealed (1846). Championed middle classes on basis of laisser-faire doctrines.

Bright, Richard (1789-1858), English physician. Described (1827) Bright's disease, kidney inflammation characterized by retention of water in body, albumin in urine.

Brighton, co. bor. of East Sussex, S England. Pop. 166,000. Seaside resort, popular since Royal Pavilion built 1817 by Prince Regent (George IV). Has Roedean School for girls; Univ. of Sussex (1959) is nearby.

brill, *Scophthalmus rhombus,* European marine flatfish of turbot family. Valued as food.

Brillat-Savarin, Anthelme (1755-1826), French gastronomist and lawyer. Famous for *La Physiologie du goût* (1825), an entertaining account of the joys of dining.

Brindisi, town of Apulia, SE Italy, on Adriatic Sea, cap. of Brindisi prov. Pop. 85,000. Port; petrochemicals, engineering. As Roman *Brundisium* was naval station, terminus of Appian Way. Medieval castle, cathedral.

Brisbane, city of E Australia, cap. of Queensland; on Brisbane R. Pop. 866,000. Admin., commercial centre; port, exports wool, wheat, fruit, minerals. Founded (1824) as penal colony; first free settlers came 1838; state cap. from 1859. Univ. of Queensland (1909).

Brissot de Warville, Jacques Pierre (1754-93), French revolutionary, journalist. Girondist leader, executed during Reign of Terror.

bristletail, primitive, wingless insect with long antennae. Divided into 2 orders: 1) Diplura, eyeless with 2 long tail filaments, represents link with ancestral insect type; 2) Thysanura, with compound eye, body scales, lives among stones, dead leaves. Species incl. SILVERFISH.

Bristol, city of Avon, SW England, on R. Avon. Pop. 425,000. Seaport, food processing, aircraft mfg., tobacco indust. Medieval wool trade; 17th-18th cent. slave trade. Has Church of St Mary Redcliffe (14th cent.), univ. (1909). Bombed in WWII.

Bristol Channel, inlet of Atlantic between SW England and Wales, c 136 km (85 mi) long. Chief river is Severn; extreme tidal range.

Britain, Battle of, German air offensive (Aug.-Oct. 1940), intended to destroy British defences prior to invasion. Luftwaffe lost 1733 aircraft and abandoned tactic in mid-Oct., though night raids continued.

British Antarctic Territory, all isls. and mainland S of 60° S and between 20° and 80° W. Incl. Graham Land, parts of Coats Land and Weddell Sea, South Shetland and South Orkney Isls.

British Cameroons, *see* CAMEROON.

British Columbia, coastal prov. of W Canada; incl. Vancouver, Queen Charlotte Isls. Area 948,600 sq km (366,255 sq mi); pop. 2,185,000; cap. Victoria; major city Vancouver. Mainly mountainous. Coast Mts. rise to Rockies in interior; main rivers Fraser, Columbia; h.e.p. Major timber indust; dairy, fruit, mixed farming; fisheries; copper, lead, zinc mining; aluminium smelting. Acquired by Hudson's Bay Co. (1821), became prov. 1871; linked with E by railway (1885).

British Commonwealth of Nations, *see* COMMONWEALTH, BRITISH.

British Guiana, *see* GUYANA.

British Honduras, *see* BELIZE.

British Indian Ocean Territory, colony formed (1965) from Chagos archipelago, Des Roches, Farquhar and Aldabra isls. Pop. 2000. Last 3 isls. part of Seychelles from 1976.

British Isles, archipelago of NW Europe in Atlantic Ocean, comprising GREAT BRITAIN, IRELAND. Incl. Hebrides, Orkneys, Shetland, Isle of Man, Isle of Wight, Scilly Isles, Channel Isls.

British Museum, national museum in London, founded (1753) on basis of Sir Hans Sloane's collection; opened to public 1759. Collection incl. coins and stamps, books and manuscripts, *eg* Lindisfarne Gospels, Egyptian antiquities, *eg* Rosetta Stone, classical sculpture, *eg* Elgin Marbles.

British North America Act (1867), constitution of Canada, passed by British Parliament, embodying plans for federal govt. agreed at Québec Conference (1864). Provided for division of provincial (enumerated) and federal (residual) legislative powers; safeguarded independence of courts and special language and educational status for Québec prov. Also allowed for admission of further provs.

British Standards Institution (BSI), originally Engineering Standards Committee, formed by various engineering bodies (1901, granted charter 1929) who voluntarily prepared and pub. agreed mfg. standards for their products. The BSI now covers over 60 major industs. in UK.

British thermal unit (BTU), quantity of heat required to raise temperature of 1 pound of water by 1° F; equals c 252 calories.

Brittain, Vera Mary (1896-1970), English author. Wrote novels, autobiog. *eg Testament of Youth* (1933) on work as nurse in WWI.

Brittany (*Bretagne*), region of NW France, occupying penin. between English Channel and Bay of Biscay; hist. cap. Rennes. Rocky coast, natural harbours (*eg* Brest), interior largely moorland. Agric., esp. fruit, vegetables; fishing, tourism. Ancient *Armorica*; settled by Celts from Britain *c* 500 AD. Medieval duchy, incorporated (1532) into France. Breton language still spoken in rural areas, distinctive customs retained.

Britten, [Edward] Benjamin (1913-76), English composer. Highly personal composer, worked in traditional idioms and forms, principally opera and vocal music. Works incl. operas *Peter Grimes* and *Billy Budd,* oratorio *A War Requiem,* symphonic work *The Young Person's Guide to the Orchestra.*

Brittany

Benjamin Britten

brittle star, any echinoderm of class Ophiuroidea. Star-shaped, with long narrow arms emanating from central disc; all species marine. Can regenerate arms thrown off when under attack.

Brixham, part of Torbay, Devon, SW England. Former co. bor.; resort, fishing port. William of Orange landed here (1688).

Brno (Ger. *Brünn*), city of C Czechoslovakia. Pop. 336,000. Commercial and indust. centre, esp. textiles, engineering. Produced Bren gun. Besieged by Swedish (1645). Hist. hilltop prison-fortress until 1857. Cap. of Moravia (1938-45).

broadbill, perching bird of Eurylaimidae family of African and Asian tropical forests. Green or black and yellow plumage, with short wide bill.

broadcasting, public transmission of sound and images by radio and television. Sound broadcasting began c 1920 in US; 1st public TV service begun by British Broadcasting Corporation (1936). Developments since incl. use of high frequencies (VHF) to increase available radio space, and colour TV, begun in US (1953), in Europe later.

Broads, The, *see* NORFOLK, England.

Broadway, street of New York City. Passes through theatre district, hence synonymous with American commercial theatre. Off Broadway, term used for small N.Y. theatres putting on 'art' productions.

broccoli, *Brassica oleracea,* plant related to the cauliflower but bearing tender shoots with greenish buds cooked as vegetable. Native to S Europe and cultivated widely in N temperate zones.

Broch, Hermann (1886-1951), Austrian novelist. Known for complex trilogy *The Sleepwalkers* (1931-2), *The Death of Vergil* (1945). Settled in US (1938).

broch, circular dry-stone tower, up to 15 m (50 ft) high, found mostly in N and NW Scotland. Used as fortified homestead in early Christian times.

Brocken or **Blocksberg,** mountain of East Germany, highest of Harz Mts. (1142 m/3747 ft). Traditional meeting place of witches on Witches' Sabbath (May 1). Scene in Goethe's *Faust.*

Broglie, Louis Victor, Prince de (1892-), French physicist. Awarded Nobel Prize for Physics (1929) for theory of wave nature of electron, starting point of wave mechanics.

Broken Hill, city of W New South Wales, Australia. Pop. 30,000. Silver, lead, zinc, gold mining; market town for large pastoral area.

Broken Hill, see KABWE, Zambia.

Bromberg, see BYDGOSZCZ, Poland.

bromine (Br), reddish-brown volatile liquid element of halogen family; at. no. 35, at. wt. 79.91. Vapour has choking, irritating smell. Occurs in salts found in sea water and mineral deposits. Used in organic synthesis; compounds used in photography (silver bromide) and formerly in medicine.

Bromley, bor. of SE Greater London, England. Pop. 304,000. Created 1965 from Bromley, Beckenham mun. bors., 4 NW Kent towns incl. Orpington.

bronchitis, inflammation of air-passages (bronchial tubes) in lungs. Acute form may be caused by viral or bacterial infection. Chronic form, characterized by regular coughing with mucus, may be caused by smoking, air pollution, fog.

Bronowski, Jacob (1908-74), English scientist, writer, b. Poland. Attempted to fuse cultural, scientific history, esp. in *The Ascent of Man* (1973).

Brontë sisters, three English novelists. Although daughters of a Yorkshire clergyman, living circumscribed lives, produced some of most famous fiction of early 19th cent. **Charlotte Brontë,** pseud. Currer Bell (1816-55), wrote semi-autobiog. works incl. *Jane Eyre* (1847), *Villette* (1853), *The Professor* (1857). **Emily Jane Brontë,** pseud. Ellis Bell (1818-48), wrote single novel, masterpiece *Wuthering Heights* (1847), imaginative verse. **Anne Brontë,** pseud. Acton Bell (1820-49), known for *The Tenant of Wildfell Hall* (1848), also collaborated with sisters in poetry and juvenilia. Their works show effect on powerful imaginations of wild surroundings and intense isolated family life.

brontosaurus, extinct semi-aquatic herbivorous dinosaur, genus *Apatosaurus.* Over 21.3 m/70 ft long, with long neck and tail, it weighed *c* 30 tons. Bones have been found in Jurassic strata of US.

Bronx, see NEW YORK CITY.

bronze, alloy consisting mainly of copper and tin; may contain zinc and aluminium. Used to make medals, bells, *etc;* phosphor bronze used in springs, aluminium bronze in bearings.

Bronze Age, archaeological period characterized by use of bronze weapons and tools. Dates from before 3500 BC in Middle East, is associated with beginning of recorded history. Placed between Stone and Iron Ages.

Bronzino, Angelo, real name di Cosimo Allori (1503-72), Italian painter. Noted for his portraits in mannerist style; his sitters were rendered in unemotional, elegant manner. Works incl. *Venus, Cupid, Time and Folly.*

Brook, Peter Stephen Paul (1925-), English director. Known for innovative productions using stage and actors to full, *eg The Persecution and Assassination of Marat ...* (1964), *A Midsummer Night's Dream* (1970).

Brooke, Alan Francis, see ALANBROOKE, ALAN FRANCIS BROOKE, 1ST VISCOUNT.

Brooke, Sir James (1803-68), British colonial administrator. Famous as 'white rajah' of Sarawak, which he became (1841) after helping sultan to suppress revolt. His nephew, **Sir Charles Anthony Johnson Brooke** (1829-1917), succeeded him, abolishing slavery during rule. His son, **Sir Charles Vyner Brooke** (1874-1963), transferred Sarawak to British crown (1946).

Brooke, Rupert Chawner (1887-1915), English poet. Known for romantic, patriotic (often on war) verse, esp.

Rupert Brooke

'Grantchester' and *1914 and Other Poems* (1915). Also wrote perceptive criticism. Died of septicaemia on Dardanelles expedition.

Brookeborough, Basil Stanlake Brooke, 1st Viscount (1888-1973), Irish statesman, PM of Northern Ireland (1943-63). Advocated strong links with Britain.

Brook Farm, experimental community estab. (1841-7) near West Roxbury, Mass. Founded by G. Ripley, members incl. Hawthorne and other writers, scholars. Adhered to communist theories.

Brooklyn, see NEW YORK CITY.

Brooks, Van Wyck (1886-1963), American literary historian. Works, *eg The Wine of the Puritans* (1909), *America's Coming of Age* (1915), *Makers and Finders* (series 1936-52), helped estab. sense of autonomy and unity in American culture.

broom, shrubs of 3 related genera *Cytisus, Genista, Spartium* of Leguminosae family, with yellow, white or purple flowers. Common or Scotch broom is native to temperate Europe, Asia and is naturalized in North America.

Brouwer, Adriaen (*c* 1605-38), Flemish painter. Known for genre scenes of peasant life, often set in taverns; later work was usually monochromatic.

Brown, Sir Arthur Whitten, see ALCOCK, SIR JOHN WILLIAM.

Brown, Ford Madox (1821-93), English painter, b. France. Associated with the Pre-Raphaelites, and profoundly influenced by them. Works incl. *Work* and *The Last of England.*

Brown, George (1818-80), Canadian journalist, statesman, b. Scotland. Founded *Toronto Globe* (1844), campaigning for representation by population.

Brown, James ('Jimmy') (1936-), American football player. Renowned runner in college and professional game. Retired to become film actor (1965).

John Brown

Brown, John (1800-59), American abolitionist. Belief in need for armed intervention to free slaves led to his capture of govt. arsenal at HARPERS FERRY (1859). It was retaken and Brown was hanged.

Brown, Lancelot ('Capability') (1716-83), English landscape gardener. Laid out gardens at Chatsworth, Blenheim, *etc*, using clumps of trees, serpentine lakes, undulating lawns to achieve informal effect.

Brown, Robert (1773-1858), Scottish botanist. Botanical collector on Australian expedition (1801-5), studied fossil botany. Discovered gymnospermism and cell nucleus in plants. Described movements of microscopic particles in fluid medium (Brownian motion).

brown algae, any of the division Phaeophyta of large ALGAE that contain a brown pigment which masks the green chlorophyll. Often have air bladders and a gelatinous surface, *eg* bladder wrack, *Fucus vesiculosus*. Mainly marine group abundant in colder latitudes. Some species are 70 m/230 ft long.

brown bear, *Ursus arctos,* omnivorous bear of Europe, Asia, North America. Variations in size of species, with Kodiak bear of Alaska largest; also incl. GRIZZLY BEAR. Gives birth to 1 or 2 tiny helpless cubs. Rare in Europe, now protected.

Browne, Hablot Knight, pseud. Phiz (1815-82), English illustrator. Works incl. illustrations for many of novels by Charles Dickens and cartoons for *Punch* magazine.

Browne, Robert (*c* 1550-1633), English preacher. Led separatist group (Brownists) opposed to Established church. Pub. tracts regarded as basis of CONGREGATIONALISM.

Browne, Sir Thomas (1605-82), English author. Known for individual, sonorous prose style, esp. in *Religio Medici* (1643), *Hydriotaphia, Urn Burial* (1658), ranging over science, philosophy, mysticism.

brown earth or **brown forest soil,** widely distributed group of soils associated with deciduous forests.

Brownian motion, unceasing random movement of small particles suspended in fluid. Described by Scottish botanist Robert Brown (1827) when observing motion of pollen grains in water. Caused by bombardment of particles by continuously moving fluid molecules; theoretical explanation given by Einstein (1905).

Robert Browning

Browning, Robert (1812-89), English poet. Known for long poem, *The Ring and the Book* (1868-9), earlier poetry 'Pippa Passes', 'My Last Duchess'. Work notable for metric innovation, dramatic monologue allowing shifting viewpoint. His wife, **Elizabeth Barrett Browning** (1806-61), was also a poet, known for *Sonnets from the Portuguese* (1850), addressed to husband. Known for their love affair, overcoming her jealous father and her own invalidism.

brown rat, *Rattus norvegicus,* large rodent of Muridae family. Of Asian origin, reached Europe, US in 18th cent. Destruction of foodstuffs, spread of disease make it major pest.

brownshirts (*Sturm Abteilung* or SA), paramilitary force (storm troops) of Nazi party, founded in 1922. Wore brown uniform, distinct from black of the *Schutz staffel* (SS) or elite corps.

Bruce, Sir David (1855-1931), British bacteriologist, b. Australia. Specialist in tropical diseases, discovered bacterium causing undulant fever (named brucellosis after him). Also an authority on sleeping sickness and nagana.

Bruce, James (1730-94), Scottish explorer. Journeyed through Ethiopia 1768-73, visiting source of Blue Nile and following it to confluence with White Nile. Wrote *Travels to Discover the Source of the Nile.*

Bruce, Robert, *see* ROBERT THE BRUCE.

Bruce, Stanley Melbourne, 1st Viscount Bruce of Melbourne (1883-1967), Australian statesman, PM (1923-9). Treasurer (1921-3) before becoming leader of National Party, headed coalition govt. with Country Party.

brucellosis, *see* UNDULANT FEVER.

Bruch, Max (1838-1920), German composer. Best known for violin concerto in G minor, still popular in concert repertory. Also wrote *Kol Nidre* for cello and orchestra.

Brücke, Die ('the bridge'), group of German expressionist painters, incl. Kirchner, Schmidt-Rottluff and Heckel, founded in Dresden (1905). Work, characterized by vivid symbolic colour, distortion, was influenced by primitive art and van Gogh, Gauguin, Munch, *etc*. Disbanded 1913.

Bruckner, Anton (1824-96), Austrian composer. Influenced by Wagner in producing grandiose works, albeit principally for orchestra in classic forms. Major compositions incl. 9 symphonies, several masses and *Te Deum.*

Brueghel or **Bruegel,** family of Flemish painters. **Pieter Brueghel** (*c* 1525-69) was noted for his painting of landscape, peasant village scenes and religious subjects; in allegorical works, made use of fantastic images of Bosch. Works incl. series *The Months*. His son, **Pieter Brueghel** (1564-1638), known as 'Hell Brueghel' copied many of his father's works. Another son, **Jan Brueghel** (1568-1625), known as 'Velvet Brueghel', painted landscapes and still life.

Brugge (Fr. *Bruges*), town of NW Belgium, cap. of West Flanders prov. Pop. 51,000. Agric. market, lace mfg.; ship canal to Zeebrugge. Prosperous medieval wool trade, Hanseatic centre. Cloth Hall, belfry (13th cent.) with carillon; art treasures incl. works of Michelangelo, van Eyck.

Brugmann, [Friedrich] Karl (1849-1919), German linguist. Maintained scientific rules of linguistics allow no exceptions. Wrote standard comparative grammar of Indo-European languages.

bruise, bleeding into injured skin following a blow, *etc*. Discoloration results when red blood pigment loses its oxygen and later breaks down into bile pigments.

Brumaire, second month of French Revolutionary Calendar (officially operating 1793-1805). Coup of 18 Brumaire (9-10 Nov. 1799) overthrew DIRECTORY and created consulate under Napoleon.

Brummell, George Bryan ('Beau') (1778-1840), English dandy. Close associate of the prince regent (later George IV), he became recognized arbiter of fashionable dress in Regency period. Died in squalor following quarrel with the prince and loss of his fortune through gambling.

Brunei

'Beau' Brummell

Brunei, sultanate of N Borneo. Area *c* 5760 sq km (2200 sq mi); pop. 136,000. Cap. and main seaport, Bandar Seri Begawan (formerly Brunei), pop. 37,000. Rubber, fruit grown; rich oil deposits. Became British protect. 1888.

Isambard Kingdom Brunel

Brunel, Sir Marc Isambard (1769-1849), British engineer, b. France. Built old Bowery Theatre, New York, Thames tunnel, London (1825-43). His son, **Isambard Kingdom Brunel** (1806–59), an authority on rail traction, steam navigation and civil engineering, was responsible for building of much of Great Western Railway. Designed steamships *Great Western* (1838), *Great Eastern* (1858).

Brunelleschi, Filippo (1377-1446), Italian architect. Pioneer in scientific study of perspective and the creation of controlled space, based on mathematical proportion. Most famous for design of dome of Florence cathedral (1420).

Brunhild, Brynhild or **Brünnhilde,** in Germanic myth, great female warrior. In NIBELUNGENLIED defeated by SIEGFRIED, and causes his death. In *Volsungsaga*, is chief of Valkyries, loved by Sigurd, whom she kills for infidelity, then commits suicide. Story adapted by Wagner in *Ring of the Nibelung.*

Brüning, Heinrich (1885-1970), German politician. Leader of Catholic Centre party, chancellor (1930-2) during economic crisis stemming from unemployment and inflation. Introduced harsh financial measures, disbanded Hitler's storm troops. Dismissed by Hindenburg, in exile (1934-52).

Bruno, Giordano (1548-1600), Italian philosopher. Rejected dogma on grounds that knowledge is infinite and final truth cannot be established. Formulated monadic theory of universe. Influenced Spinoza, Leibnitz. A Dominican, burned as heretic.

Bruno of Cologne, St (*c* 1030-1101), German monk. Founded order of CARTHUSIANS.

Brunswick (*Braunschweig*), city of NE West Germany, on R. Oker. Pop. 223,000. Food processing, machinery, publishing industs. Hanseatic League member from 13th cent. Has medieval cathedral, town hall, fountain.

brush turkey, *Alectura lathami,* large bird of E Australia. Eggs laid in mound of plant matter and hatched by heat of fermentation.

Brussels (Fr. *Bruxelles*), cap. of Belgium, on R. Senne. Pop. 1,075,000. Commercial, indust. centre (textiles, esp. lace); railway jct. Gothic cathedral, Grand' Place, town hall (15th cent.), Atomium (1958); univ. (1834). Hq. of EEC, NATO. Cap. of Brabant from 15th cent., of Belgium from independence (1830), German occupation in WWs.

Brussels sprouts, *Brassica oleracea gemmifera,* vegetable of CABBAGE family. Small edible heads are borne on stem.

Brutus, Marcus Junius (*c* 85-42 BC), Roman political leader. Sided with Pompey against Caesar in civil war; pardoned after battle of Pharsala. Joined Cassius in assassination of Caesar (44), but had to flee to Macedonia. Defeated by Antony and Octavian at Philippi (42); committed suicide.

Bryan, William Jennings (1860-1925), American politician. Leading advocate of free silver movement. His 'Cross of Gold' speech led to Democratic presidential nomination (1896); he was nominated again in 1900, 1908. Great orator, later defended religious conservatism notably in SCOPES TRIAL (1925).

Bryansk or **Briansk,** city of USSR, WC European RSFSR. Pop. 338,000. Railway jct.; machine mfg., ironworks. Founded 1146, passed to Russia in 17th cent.

Bryant, William Cullen (1794-1878), American poet. Known for early work, *eg* 'Thanatopsis', 'To a Waterfowl', in *Poems* (1832); found metaphysical consolation in nature. Editor of New York *Evening Post* from (1829).

Bryce, James Bryce, Viscount (1838-1922), British statesman, historian and jurist. Ambassador to US (1907-13). Works incl. *The American Commonwealth* (1888), classic observation of American lifestyle, and *Studies in History and Jurisprudence* (1901).

bryony, any of a genus, *Bryonia,* of perennial vines of the gourd family with large fleshy roots and greenish flowers.

Bryophyta, small phylum of plant kingdom comprising mosses and liverworts. Widely distributed on moist soil and rocks. Reproduction is normally by spores.

Bubastis, see BAST.

bubble chamber, vessel filled with superheated transparent liquid used to study nature and motion of charged atomic particles. Passage of particle through liquid causes string of bubbles to appear, which are then photographed.

Buber, Martin (1878-1965), Austrian philosopher. Exponent of religious existentialism; influenced by Kierkegaard and HASIDISM. Works, esp. *I and Thou* (1923), explore the individual's personal dialogue with God. Worked to infuse political Zionism with ethical values. Settled in Jerusalem (1938).

Bucaramanga, city of NC Colombia, in E Andes. Pop. 250,000. In coffee, cotton, tobacco growing region; has associated industs. Founded 1622.

Bucer or **Butzer, Martin,** orig. Kuhhorn (1491-1551), German Protestant theologian. Attempted to unite Lutheran and Zwinglian doctrines. Refused to sign Augsburg Interim (1548) and settled in England on invitation of Cranmer.

Buchan, John, 1st Baron Tweedsmuir (1875-1940), British author, statesman, b. Scotland. Best known for adventure novels, esp. *The Thirty Nine Steps* (1915), *Greenmantle* (1916). Governor-general of Canada (1935-40).

Buchanan, James (1791-1868), American statesman. As Democratic president (1857-61), pursued moderate policy on slavery issue. Efforts to achieve compromise met with suspicion by both North and South, and Civil War followed end of his admin.

Bucharest (*Bucureşti*), cap. of Romania, on R. Dambrovita. Pop. 1,529,000. Cultural, commercial, indust. centre. Orthodox patriarchal see. Cathedral (17th cent.), former royal palace, univ. (1864). Cap. of Walachia from 1698; of Romania from 1861.

Buchenwald, village of SW East Germany, near Weimar. Site of Nazi concentration camp in WWII.

Buchman, Frank Nathan Daniel (1878-1961), American evangelist. Stressed 'world-changing through life-changing', advocated group confessions; founded Oxford Group (1921). Campaigned from 1938 for Moral Re-Armament (MRA).

Büchner, Eduard (1860-1917), German chemist. Awarded Nobel Prize for Chemistry (1907) for discovery that yeast enzymes, rather than intact yeast cells, cause alcoholic fermentation of sugar.

Büchner, Georg (1813-37), German dramatist. Inspired by French Revolution, wrote 2 stark, realistic tragedies, *Danton's Death* (1835), *Wozzeck* (pub. 1879). Latter made into opera by Berg.

Buck, Pearl S[ydenstricker] (1892-1973), American novelist. Wrote novels based on experiences as daughter of missionaries in China, *eg* trilogy *The House of Earth* (1935), translations from Chinese. Nobel Prize for Literature (1938).

buckeye, American shrubs and trees of genus *Aesculus* similar to horse chestnut but without sticky winter buds. Red buckeye, *A. pavia,* native to E US is small shrub with red flowers and smooth brown fruit. Ohio buckeye, *A. glabra,* is a popular ornamental tree.

Buckingham, George Villiers, 1st Duke of (1592-1628), English courtier. Royal favourite under James I, arranged Charles I's marriage to Henrietta Maria of France. Expeditions against France during Charles' reign met with little success. Assassinated. His son, **George Villiers, 2nd Duke of Buckingham** (1628-87), was powerful courtier under Charles II. Member of CABAL ministry.

Buckingham Palace, official London residence of British sovereigns since Queen Victoria's reign. Built (1703) for the dukes of Buckingham; bought as private residence by George III. Reconstructed (1825-36) by John Nash.

Buckinghamshire, county of SC England. Area 1882 sq km (726 sq mi); pop. 496,000; co. town Aylesbury. Chiltern Hills in S; fertile valley in N. Cereals, fruit, vegetable growing, livestock rearing. **Buckingham,** mun. bor. on R. Ouse. Pop. 5000. Market town, dairy produce. Stowe House public school (1923) nearby.

buckthorn, family of deciduous and evergreen trees and shrubs, Rhamnaceae, native to Europe and N Asia. Some species have thorny branches. Fruit has purgative properties and yields dye, Chinese green. Common buckthorn, *Rhamnus cathartica,* is hedge plant in America.

buckwheat, any of several plants of genus *Fagopyrum,* grown for their black tetrahedral grains from which a dark nutritious flour can be made.

Budaeus, *see* BUDÉ, GUILLAUME.

Budapest, cap. of Hungary, on R. Danube. Pop. 2,027,000. Admin., commercial centre; heavy industs.; food processing, agric. market (grain, wine, cattle). Formed from union of Buda and Pest (1872). Roman *Aquincum*; 13th cent. church, univ. (1635), 19th cent. basilica. Damaged during Russian siege (1945) and in revolution (1956).

Buddha (Sanskrit,=the enlightened one), title given to Siddhartha Gautama (*c* 563-483 BC), Indian ascetic, founder of BUDDHISM. Renounced luxury for asceticism following prophetic vision and after 6 years' contemplation found perfect enlightenment under sacred bo tree in Buddh

Buddha: bronze statuette from 8th century Kashmir

Gaya, thus becoming the Buddha. Life then devoted to teaching of path to enlightenment.

Buddh Gaya or **Bodh Gaya,** village of Bihar state, NE India, S of Gaya. Site of Buddha's enlightenment under sacred botree.

Buddhism, religion of followers of BUDDHA, widespread in SE Asia, China and Japan; originally related to Hinduism, it was in part reaction against its formalism. The 'four noble truths' are: life is sorrow; origin of sorrow is desire; sorrow ceases when desire ceases; desire is ended by following the 'noble eightfold path'. That path comprises: right belief, right resolve, right speech, right conduct, right occupation, right effort, right contemplation, right meditation. Final goal is Nirvana, the annihilation of all desires and passions and cessation of rebirth. *See* MAHAYANA and ZEN BUDDHISM.

Budé, Guillaume (1467-1540), French scholar, known by Latinized name Budaeus. Leading humanist and scholar of Renaissance. Persuaded Francis I of France to found Collège de France, furthered classical scholarship both by teaching and writing.

Budge, [John] Donald (1915-), American tennis player. First man to achieve the 'grand slam' of tennis by winning British, US, French and Australian singles championships (1938).

budgerigar, *Melopsittacus undulatus,* Australian parakeet, with many domestic varieties. In wild, green with yellow head. Colour variations produced by selective breeding. Lives in nomadic flocks; diet of seed, grain. Popular pet and excellent mimic, introduced to Europe in 1840s.

budget, govt. statement (usually issued annually) of revenue and expenditure of previous year and estimated revenue and expenditure of forthcoming year. In UK, presented by chancellor of the exchequer to Commons, sitting as Committee of Ways and Means. In US, executive budget recommendations supervised by Bureau of the Budget (estab. 1921) after Congressional approval.

Budweis, see CESKÉ BUDEJOVICE, Czechoslovakia.

Buenaventura, seaport of W Colombia, on Pacific. Pop. 179,000. Coffee, hides, sugar, platinum and gold exports. Founded *c* 1540, grew with building of railway to Cali (1914).

Buenos Aires, cap. of Argentina, on W Rio de la Plata estuary. Pop. 2,972,000, greater city pop. 8,353,000; incl. suburbs La Matanza, Lanús, Morón, General San Martín, Lomas de Zamóra, Quilmes, Vicente López. Railway terminus; country's chief port, indust., commercial centre. Beef, wheat, wool exports. Settled permanently 1580; became cap. 1880. Prospered with development of Pampas in 19th cent. Has San Martín's tomb, opera house, cathedral, univ. (1827).

Buffalo, city of W New York, US; on L. Erie and Niagara R. Pop. 463,000. Major Great Lakes port and transport jct.

serving Middle West. Grain, iron, coal shipping; iron and steel, chemical mfg., flour milling. First settled 1803; burned by British in War of 1812. President W. McKinley assassinated here (1901).

buffalo, any of various large forms of cattle. Species incl. CAPE BUFFALO, and Indian WATER BUFFALO. Name also popularly applied to American bison.

Buffalo Bill, *see* CODY, WILLIAM FREDERICK.

Buffet, Bernard (1928-), French painter. Known for his austere portrayal of figures, religious scenes and city life; work characterized by cold tonality and prominent black lines.

Buffon, Georges Louis Leclerc, Comte de (1707-88), French naturalist, author. Wrote encyclopedia of natural history, *Histoire naturelle* (1749-1804, 44 volumes).

Bug or **Western Bug,** river of E Europe. Rises in NW Ukrainian SSR, flows *c* 800 km (500 mi) NW into Poland to join R. Vistula below Warsaw. Forms part of Poland-USSR frontier. **Southern Bug** flows *c* 850 km (530 mi) SE through Ukrainian SSR into Black Sea.

bug, any insect of suborder Heteroptera of order Hemiptera. Sucking mouthparts; front wings half membranous, half thickened. Wingless varieties also exist. Term also popularly applied to any insect or insect-like animal.

Buganda, *see* UGANDA.

bugle, any plant of genus *Ajuga*. Perennial, with numerous running stems and spikes of white, pink or blue flowers.

bugle, valveless form of trumpet which produces only notes of the harmonic series; all bugle calls are confined to these notes.

building society [UK] or **savings and loan association** [US], financial organization that accepts savings from the public to be placed in share accounts on which dividends are paid and from which mortgage loans on homes are made. Early examples directly controlled building of houses. First estab. Birmingham, England (1781), first in US estab. 1831.

Bujumbura, cap. of Burundi, on L. Tanganyika. Pop. 107,000. Admin. centre; port, exports coffee, cotton, hides. Estab. as German military post (1889). Formerly called Usumbura, was cap. of Ruanda-Urundi.

Bukavu, city of E Zaïre, on L. Kivu, cap. of Kivu prov. Formerly called Costermansville. Pop. 156,000. Port, commercial centre; coffee, pharmaceuticals indust.

Bukhara or **Bokhara,** town of USSR, S Uzbek SSR. Pop. 114,000. Centre of cotton producing area; once famous for carpets. Centre of Islamic learning under Arab rule in 8th cent. Cap. of emirate of Bukhara until 1920.

Bukharin, Nikolai Ivanovich (1888-1938), Soviet political leader. Leading Bolshevik theorist after Lenin's death, advocated gradualist policies on collectivizing agric. Executed in Stalinist party purges.

Bukovina, region of NE Romania and SW USSR (Ukraine), in Carpathian foothills. Main town Chernovtsy; main rivers Siret, Prut. Ceded by Turkey to Austria (1775); Romanian from 1918, N part to USSR (1940).

Bulawayo, city of SW Rhodesia. Pop. 297,000. Indust., commercial centre, agric. market, railway engineering. Founded 1893. Cecil Rhodes tomb in nearby Matopo Hills.

bulb, underground storage and reproductive structure of certain plants. Formed by swelling of leaf bases, constructing sheath round embryo flower. Distinct from corm which is formed by swelling of stem, as in crocus; rhizome which is an elongated underground swelling of stem, as in iris; and tuber which is a swollen underground branch, as in potato, or root as in dahlia.

bulbul, songbird of Pycnonotidae family, of Africa, S Asia. Dull green, yellow, grey or brown plumage; mainly fruit-eating. Popular as cage bird, it is related to thrush, lark.

Bulgakov, Mikhail Afanasyevich (1891-1940), Russian author. Known for *The White Guard* (1925) which he dramatized as *The Days of the Turbins* (1926) portraying a family hostile to the revolution, *The Master and Margarita* (pub. 1967) a fantasy set in modern Moscow.

Bulganin, Nikolai Aleksandrovich (1895-1975), Russian military and political leader. Helped plan 1941

defence of Moscow against German invasion. Armed forces minister (1947-9), premier (1953-8), succeeded by KHRUSHCHEV.

Bulgaria, republic of SE Europe, on Balkan Penin. Area 110,899 sq km (42,818 sq mi); pop. 8,619,000; cap. Sofia. Languages: Bulgarian, Turkish. Religions: Eastern Orthodox, Islam. Balkan Mts. run E-W across C, Rhodope Mts. in SW. Lowland in N (Danube basin), SE; Black Sea in E. Continental climate; cereals, tobacco, wine, attar of roses. Agric. increasingly mechanized. Coal, oil industs. developing. Invaded 7th cent. AD by Bulgars from Russia; Turkish rule (1395-1878) ended by Russia; independent monarchy (1908). Lost territ. in Balkan Wars (1912-13), WWs. Communist govt. estab. (1946).

Bulge, Battle of the, popular name for last German offensive (in the Ardennes) of WWII on Western Front (Dec. 1944-July, 1945).

Bull, Olaf (1883-1933), Norwegian poet. One of most important of 20th cent., known for introspective, concretely-realized verse, *eg Metope* (1927).

bull, papal pronouncement, more solemn than a brief or encyclical, traditionally sealed with lead. Famous bulls incl. *Exsurge Domine* (1520) against Luther, *Pastor aeternus* (1871) on papal infallibility. Also used to proclaim canonization of a saint.

Bulldog

bulldog, breed of dog once used in bull-baiting. Square-jawed, with powerful grip. Stands between 33-38 cm/13-15 in. at shoulder.

bullfighting, national spectacle of Spain (where it is known as *corrida de toros*), also popular in S France and Latin America. Matador, aided by banderilleros and picadors, makes passes with cape and manoeuvres bull to tire it for the kill. Earliest dated public bullfight in Spain was in 1080.

bullfinch, *Pyrrhula pyrrhula,* timid bird of finch family found in woodlands of Europe, North America, Asia. Male has pink breast, black wings.

bullfrog, *Rana catesbeiana,* largest North American frog, up to 20 cm/8 in. long. Catches prey (mice, frogs, insects) with tongue. Male emits deep croak as mating call.

bullhead, any of several marine and freshwater fish of Cottidae family, found in N hemisphere. European bullhead or miller's thumb, *Cottus gobio,* is mainly nocturnal river species. Often called sculpin in North America.

Bull Moose Party, *see* PROGRESSIVE PARTY.

Bull Run, stream of N Virginia, US; SW of Washington DC. Scene of 2 Confederate victories during Civil War (1861, 1862).

Bülow, Hans von (1830-94), German pianist, conductor. Considered 1st virtuoso conductor; advocated Liszt, Wagner, Brahms. Directed premieres of Wagner's *Tristan*, and *Die Meistersinger*, after which his wife Cosima, daughter of Liszt, left him for Wagner.

bulrush, several species of perennial sedge of genus *Scirpus,* growing in wet land or water. Slender, round or triangular stems tipped with brown spikelets of minute flowers. Species incl. *S. lacustris* of Europe, and *S. validus* of US.

Bulwer-Lytton, Edward George Earle Lytton, 1st Baron Lytton (1803-73), English author. Known for novels, *eg Pelham* (1828), *The Last Days of Pompeii* (1834), plays incl. *Richelieu* (1839).

bumble bee, social bee of worldwide distribution, usually of genus *Bombus*. Yellow and black hairy body, rounder than honey bee. Often nests in holes in ground; in temperate regions, only queen survives winter. Also called humble bee.

Bunau-Varilla, Philippe Jean (1859-1940), French engineer. Worked on Panama Canal, forming new company (1894) after bankruptcy of Lesseps' project. Negotiated treaty (1903), which gave US control of Panama Canal Zone.

Bunbury, town of SW Western Australia, on Indian Ocean. Pop. 18,000. Market town and port, exports timber, wheat; superphosphate mfg.

Bunche, Ralph Johnson (1904-71), American govt. official. First Black to be division head in Dept. of State (1945). Director of UN Trusteeship Division (1946-54). He mediated in Palestine (1948-9), for which he was awarded Nobel Peace Prize (1950).

Bundaberg, city of SE Queensland, Australia, on Pacific Ocean. Pop. 27,000. Originally a timber port, now refines and exports sugar. Deepwater terminal built 1958.

Bunin, Ivan Alekseyevich (1870-1953), Russian author. Known for short story, *The Gentleman from San Fransisco* (1916); novels esp. *The Village* (1910) depicting brutality of peasant life. Settled in France (1919). Awarded Nobel Prize for Literature (1933).

Bunker Hill, Battle of (June, 1775), in American Revolution, conflict in which British victory failed to break colonists' siege of Boston. Actually fought on nearby Breed's Hill (Charleston, Mass.).

Bunsen, Robert Wilhelm (1811-99), German scientist. With Kirchhoff, pioneered spectrum analysis, thus discovering elements caesium and rubidium. Worked on arsenic-containing organic compounds. Contributions to chemical apparatus incl. Bunsen burner and zinc-carbon battery.

bunting, any of various small, brightly coloured birds of Emberizidae family. Species incl. YELLOWHAMMER, SNOW BUNTING. Name applied in US to birds of finch family.

Buñuel, Luis (1900-), Spanish film writer-director. First known for surrealist films (using Dali's sets), incl. *Un Chien andalou* (1928); later films mock bourgeois and religious hypocrisy, *eg Viridiana* (1961), *The Discreet Charm of the Bourgeoisie* (1972).

Bunyan, John (1628-88), English author and preacher. Known for classic religious allegory *The Pilgrim's Progress* (1678) which exerted great influence on English prose. Imprisoned (1660-72) for unlicensed preaching.

Burbage, Richard (*c* 1567-1619), English actor-manager. First to play many major parts in plays of Shakespeare, Jonson, Fletcher, incl. Hamlet, Othello, Lear. With his brother, Cuthbert, estab. Globe Theatre at Southwark, London.

Burbank, Luther (1849-1926), American plant breeder. Developed new varieties of flowers, fruits and vegetables, notably potato. Works incl. *How Plants Are Trained to Work for Man* (1921).

burbot, *Lota lota,* freshwater fish of cod family, widely distributed in Europe, Asia, North America. Barbels on nose and chin; broad, flat head. Sometimes called ling.

Burckhardt, Jacob Christoph (1818-97), Swiss historian. Author of classic *The Civilization of the Renaissance in Italy* (1860), expressing view that each culture is peculiar to its era.

Burckhardt, Johann Ludwig (1784-1817), Swiss explorer. Supported by the African Association (London), he visited Syria and Egypt, rediscovering Petra (1812). Joined pilgrimage to Medina and Mecca, disguised as Moslem. Works incl. *Travels in Arabia* (pub. 1829).

burdock, *Arctium lappa,* tall spreading largeleaved perennial plant native to Europe, found in North America. Purple flower heads are surrounded by hooked bristles which dry to form burrs. An essence made from plant is used in a soft drink and formerly in medicine.

Burdwan, town of West Bengal, NE India. Pop. 145,000. Rice trade centre. Numerous temples dedicated to Hindu god Shiva.

bureaucracy, literally 'rule by officials', used in sociology to describe a form of administrative organization, typified, according to WEBER, by rational decision-making, impersonal social relations, routinization of tasks, and centralized authority.

Burgas, town of E Bulgaria, on Black Sea. Pop. 142,000. Port, exports wool, tobacco; chemicals indust., oil refining. Founded 18th cent.

Burgenland, prov. of E Austria. Area 3963 sq km (1530 sq mi); cap. Eisenstadt. Low-lying in N (incl. L. Neusiedler); hilly in C, S. Ruled by Austria 1491-1647 and Hungary 1647-1918. Part, incl. Sopron, returned to Hungary after 1921 plebiscite.

Bürger, Gottfried August (1747-94), German poet. Member of STURM UND DRANG movement, known for folk-style ballads esp. *Lenore* (1774).

Burgess, Anthony, pseud. of John Burgess Wilson (1917-), English novelist, critic. Best known for novels criticizing modern society, *eg A Clockwork Orange* (1962), *Inside Mr Enderby* (1966).

Burgh, Hubert de (d. 1243), English statesman. Chamberlain to King John, became chief justiciar (1215) until charged with treason (1231). Later pardoned, restored to earldom of Kent.

Burghley, William Cecil, 1st Baron (1520-98), English statesman. Chief adviser as member of privy council to Elizabeth I, instrumental in consolidation of Protestantism and in execution of Mary Queen of Scots (1587).

burglary, in law, breaking and entering any building with intent to commit a FELONY. 'Breaking' is not limited to forcible entry, but can incl. entry by use of threat, fraud, *etc.*

Burgos, city of N Spain, cap. of Burgos prov. Pop. 120,000. Textiles, leather goods; tourism. Founded 9th cent., cap. of Castile until 11th cent. Franco's cap. during Civil War (1936-9). Famous Gothic cathedral (1221) contains tomb of El Cid.

Burgoyne, John (1722-92), British army officer, playwright. During American Revolution led poorly trained troops in invasion from Canada, was forced to surrender at Saratoga (1777). Wrote several comedies, *eg The Heiress* (1786).

Burgundy (*Bourgogne*), region of E France, hist. cap. Dijon. Famous for wines (esp. in Chablis, Côte d'Or). Medieval duchy, at cultural and commercial height in 14th-15th cent.; ruled most of NE France, Low Countries. Passed to France (1477).

Edmund Burke: detail of portrait by Reynolds

Burke, Edmund (1729-97), British statesman, writer, b. Ireland. Prominent Whig orator, pamphleteer, wrote *Thoughts on the Present Discontents* (1770), attacking George III's influence in politics, and *Conciliation with*

America (1775). Instigated impeachment and trial (1787-94) of HASTINGS. Broke with party (1791) over French Revolution, which he denounced in *Reflections on the Revolution in France* (1790).

Burke, John (1787-1848), Irish genealogist. Published dictionary of peerage, baronetage which became British annual, widely known as *Burke's Peerage.*

Burke, Robert O'Hara (1820-61), Irish soldier, policeman, explorer. With W.J. Wills, crossed Australia from Melbourne to Gulf of Carpentaria as leader of Victorian expedition (1860-1). Both died of starvation on return journey.

Burke, William (1792-1829), Irish murderer. Notorious for killing, with fellow-Irishman William Hare, at least 15 people to sell bodies to Edinburgh anatomist. Burke was hanged on Hare's evidence.

Burlington, Richard Boyle, 3rd Earl of (1694-1753), English architect and patron. Leading advocate of Palladianism in English architecture, he patronized Kent, Campbell, *etc* and encouraged their writings on the style. Own work incl. his villa at Chiswick.

Burlington, city of NW Vermont, US; on L. Champlain. Pop. 39,000; state's largest city. Major indust. centre. First settled 1773.

Burma, Union of, republic of SE Asia. Area *c* 678,000 sq km (262,000 sq mi); pop. 30,310,000; cap. Rangoon. Official language: Burmese. Religion: Buddhism. Agric. concentrated around Irrawaddy valley; major rice growing area separated from India and Bangladesh by mountain ranges. Exports incl. teak, petroleum, rubies. Annexed by Britain in 19th cent.; became prov. of India (1885-1937); independent republic (1948).

Burmese, language belonging to Tibetan-Burman branch of Sino-Tibetan family. It is both main vernacular and official language of Burma.

Burmese cat, breed of short-haired domesticated cats. Originally brown, now blue and cream varieties bred.

Burne-Jones, Sir Edward Coley (1833-98), English painter. Known for his paintings of medieval subjects, which have a dream-like romantic quality. Designed tapestry and stained glass for William Morris' company.

Burnet, Sir Frank Macfarlane (1899-), Australian physician. Authority on virus diseases. Shared Nobel Prize for Physiology and Medicine (1960) with Medawar for work on formation of antibodies following transplantation of foreign living tissue.

Burnett, Frances [Eliza] Hodgson (1849-1924), American novelist, b. England. Known for popular children's fiction esp. *Little Lord Fauntleroy* (1886), *The Secret Garden* (1911).

Burney, Fanny, pseud. of Mrs Frances Burney D'Arblay (1752-1840), English author. Known for *Early Diary: 1768-78* (1889) with sketches of Dr Johnson, Reynolds, *etc,* and *Diary and Letters: 1778-1840* (pub. 1842-6) giving account of Court. Also wrote domestic novels, *eg Evelina* (1778).

Burnham, [Linden] Forbes [Sampson] (1923-), Guyanese politician, PM (1964-). Succeeded Jagan as PM of British Guiana (1964) and led country to independence as Guyana (1966).

burning bush, *Euonymus atropurpureas,* North American tree widely cultivated as ornamental for its brightly coloured autumn foliage.

burning bush, in OT, bush out of which voice of God spoke to Moses on Mt. Horab (Exodus 3: 2), assuring Moses of deliverance of Israel from Egypt. Emblem of Presbyterian church in remembrance of its early persecution.

Burnley, co. bor. of Lancashire, NW England. Pop. 76,000. In coalmining area; cotton weaving, textiles; machinery mfg.

Burns, John (1858-1943), British labour leader. Helped lead London dock strike (1889) for higher wages. Socialist advocate, served as Independent Labour MP (1892-1918).

Burns, Robert (1759-96), Scottish poet. Gained fame with *Poems, Chiefly in the Scottish Dialect* (1786). Best known works incl. 'Tam o'Shanter', 'The Jolly Beggars', 'Holy Willie's Prayer', 'To a mouse', reflect background as tenant-

farmer's son but encompass witty anti-clericalism, political radicalism.

Burr, Aaron (1756-1836), American political leader. Tied with JEFFERSON in 1800 presidential election, elected vice-president by House of Representatives. Killed HAMILTON in duel (1804) after being defeated in election for governor of New York. Involved in plan to invade Mexico, tried for treason (1807) and acquitted.

Burroughs, Edgar Rice (1875-1950), American novelist. Created Tarzan in *Tarzan of the Apes* (1914). Also wrote science fiction.

William Burroughs

Burrourghs, William (1914-), American novelist. Works incl. *Junkie* (1953), *The Naked Lunch* (1959), using experimental forms to convey a world at mercy of technology, drugs.

Bursa, city of NW Turkey. Pop 318,000. Agric. trade; textile, carpet mfg. Cap. of Ottoman Turks (1326-1402), until sacked by Tamerlane. Has mosques and tombs of early sultans.

Burslem, part of Stoke-on-Trent, WC England. Oldest of 'Five Towns' in Potteries. Has Wedgwood Institute (1863).

Burt, Sir Cyril Lodowic (1883-1971), English psychologist. Pioneer in use of intelligence tests to predict achievement in schoolchildren. Recent doubt about validity of data he used to support his theories.

Burton, Sir Richard Francis (1821-90), English explorer, writer. Visited Mecca and Medina (1853) in Moslem disguise. Attempted, with J.H. Speke, to find source of Nile; reached L. Tanganyika (1858). Later explored W Africa, Brazil. Wrote accounts of travels, translated *Arabian Nights* (1885-8).

Burton, Robert (1577-1640), English author. Known for compendium of wide-ranging erudition, *The Anatomy of Melancholy* (1621), cataloguing every cause and form of melancholy, written under pen-name of Democritus Junior.

Burundi

Burundi, republic of EC Africa. Area 27,800 sq km (10,750 sq mi); pop. 3,615,000; cap. Bujumbura. Languages: Bantu,

French. Religions: native, Christian. Mainly high broken plateau; L. Tanganyika in SW. Cattle rearing, tin mining, exports coffee. Formerly a kingdom, part of German East Africa from 1899, of Belgian colony of Ruanda-Urundi after WWI. UN Trust territ. from 1946; independent 1962, became republic 1966. Has traditional rivalry between Tutsi and Hutu.

Bury, co. bor. of Lancashire, NW England, on R. Irwell. Pop. 68,000. Cotton indust., textile machinery mfg. Medieval woollen indust.

Buryat, auton. republic of SE Siberian RSFSR, USSR; borders on Mongolia. Area c 351,000 sq km (136,000 sq mi); pop. 812,000; cap. Ulan-Ude. Largely plateau and mountain ranges; extensively forested. Stock rearing; grain grown in river valleys. Coal, iron, molybdenum deposits.

burying beetle, brightly coloured insect of Necrophoridae family. Buries small dead animals, laying eggs on corpses. Larvae feed on decaying flesh.

Bury St Edmunds, mun. bor. of Suffolk, E England. Pop. 26,000. Market town; sugar refining, brewing industs. Ruined abbey is burial place of St Edmund (d. 870). Has two 15th cent. churches, one now cathedral.

bus, public passenger-carrying vehicle of large seating capacity. Horse-drawn form originated in France in early 19th cent. and was introduced to London in 1829. Motorized form dates from early 20th cent.

Bush, Alan Dudley (1900-), English composer. Works characterized by thorough construction and a lyricism often deriving from English folk music. Known for chamber piece *Dialectic,* reflecting Marxist sympathies.

Bushbaby

bushbaby, small arboreal mammal of tropical Africa, genus *Galago.* Nocturnal, with large eyes, bushy tail; capable of great leaps. Mainly insectivorous; some species make good pets.

bush buck, *Tragelaphus scriptus,* small antelope of savannahs of C and W Africa. Dark red with white spots or stripes; males have horns with single spiral.

Bushehr or **Bushire,** chief seaport of SW Iran, on Persian Gulf. Pop. 26,000. Founded 1736; exports wool, rugs, cotton.

bushido (Jap., = way of the warrior), ancient code of honour, conduct of Japanese nobility. Emphasizes loyalty, courage, self-sacrifice, preferring death to dishonour. Scorned commerce, profit. Code of the SAMURAI.

bushmaster, *Lachesis muta,* large poisonous snake of pit viper family, found in Central and South America. Unlike other pit vipers, lays eggs. Reaches lengths of 3.7 m/12 ft.

Bushmen, remnants of aboriginal race of S Africa, now confined to C and N Kalahari Desert. Nomadic hunters living in groups of 50-100. Noted for cave paintings. Language has same 'clicks' as that of Hottentots.

bushrangers, Australian robbers of 19th cent. Originally escaped convicts living in bush, raiding settlements. Later, gold discoveries led to incentive for organized gangs raiding highways, banks, eg KELLY gang.

Ferruccio Busoni

Busoni, Ferruccio Benvenuto (1866-1924), Italian pianist and composer. Best known for his music editing, eg of Bach and Liszt, and teaching, notably of Kurt Weill. Made piano transcriptions, esp. of Bach; wrote opera *Doktor Faust.*

Bustamante, Sir [William] Alexander, orig. Clarke (1884-), Jamaican statesman. As Labour Party leader, was chief minister (1953-5). First PM (1962-7) of fully independent Jamaica.

bustard, any of Otididae family of Old World birds, related to crane. Ground-living, can run quickly. Large size makes flight difficult. The great bustard, *Otis tarda,* largest European land bird.

butane (C_4H_{10}), gaseous hydrocarbon of paraffin series. Obtained from natural gas and petroleum. Used as fuel, stored under pressure.

butcherbird, any of genus *Cracticus* of Australasian birds with strong hooked bills. Preys on insects, birds, lizards; impales bodies on thorns to store them.

Bute, John Stuart, 3rd Earl of (1713-92), British statesman, PM (1761-3). George III's chief exponent of Tory policies against Whig supremacy. Resigned after unpopular treaty ending Seven Years War (1763).

Buteshire, former county of W Scotland, now in Strathclyde region. Incl. isls. in Firth of Clyde (Bute, Arran, Great and Little Cumbrae). Agric., tourism. Isl. of **Bute** (area 145 sq km/ 56 sq mi) has the former co. town, Rothesay.

Butler, James, see ORMONDE, JAMES BUTLER, 1ST DUKE OF.

Butler, Joseph (1692-1752), English theologian. Bishop of Durham (1750). Known for *Analogy of Religion, Natural and Revealed, to the Constitution and Course of Nature* (1736), which attempted to refute deism by demonstrating inherent probability of Christian belief.

Butler, Reg (1913-), English sculptor. His bronzes are concerned with the human figure and have emphasized its sensuous quality. Won prize for monument to Unknown Political Prisoner (1953).

Butler, R[ichard] A[usten], Baron Butler of Saffron Walden (1902-), British politician. Minister of education (1941-5), sponsored 1944 Education Act. In Conservative govts. (1951-64), he was chancellor of the exchequer (1951-5), foreign secretary (1963-4).

Butler, Samuel (1612-80), English poet. Known for *Hudibras,* mock-epic satirizing Puritan cant and hyprocrisy.

Butler, Samuel (1835-1902), English author. Known for autobiog. novel, *The Way of all Flesh* (1903), condemning his Victorian upbringing; *Erewhon* (1872) satirizing received opinions.

Butor, Michel (1926-), French novelist. Novels, eg *Passage de Milan* (1954), *L'Emploi du Temps* (1956), deal with phenomenological experience of objects in time. *Le Génie du Lieu* (1958) explains his literary theories.

Butte, town of SW Montana, US. Pop. 23,000. Major copper, gold, silver producer (Anaconda mines); produces ⅓ of US copper. Estab. 1862.

butter-and-eggs, *see* TOADFLAX.

buttercup, herbs of Ranunculaceae family with alternate leaves and glossy yellow flowers. Native to cooler regions of N hemisphere. Pernicious weed, species incl. tall perennial meadow or bitter buttercup, *Ranunculus acris*; creeping buttercup, *R. repons,* and bulbous buttercup, *R. bulbosus.*

butterfly, insect of group comprising, with moths, order Lepidoptera. Scales on body, wings (2 pairs, often brightly coloured). Uses proboscis to suck nectar. Four stage life cycle: egg, larva, pupa, adult. Larva is caterpillar, usually herbivorous. Mainly diurnal, unlike moth.

butternut, oily, edible fruit of white walnut tree, *Juglans cinerea,* of E North America. Kernel is used in candy, ice cream, and is pickled.

buttress, projecting structure of brick or masonry, built against a wall to give additional strength. Flying buttresses are arches or parts of arches, which support distant walls and are themselves supported by buttresses.

Buxtehude, Dietrich (1637-1707), Danish composer, organist. Organist at Lübeck from 1668. Organ compositions influenced Bach, who walked over 320 km (200 mi) to hear Buxtehude play.

buzzard, any of numerous heavily-built hawks, esp. genus *Buteo,* with short broad wings, soaring flight. Species incl. European buzzard, *Buteo buteo.* In US, name applied to various hawks and vultures.

Byblos, chief city of Phoenicia in 2nd millennium BC. Trade centre with Egypt as early as 2800 BC. Gave name to Greek word for book *biblos,* on account of papyrus fields. At site of modern Jebail.

Bydgoszcz (Ger. *Bromberg*), city of NC Poland, on R. Brda and Bydgoszcz canal, cap. of Bydgoszcz prov. Pop. 283,000. River port, railway jct.; textile mfg., machinery. Founded 14th cent.; under Prussian rule 1772-1919.

Byelorussian or **Belorussian Soviet Socialist Republic,** constituent republic of W USSR. Area *c* 208,000 sq km (80,000 sq mi); pop. 9,003,000; cap. Minsk. Mainly low-lying, with Pripet marshes in S; large areas forested. Peat major source of power. Region disputed by Poland, Russia until it passed to Russia (1795); joined USSR 1922. Area greatly increased by acquisitions from Poland in 1945. Has seat in UN. Also called White Russia.

byliny, heroic songs of Russia, orally transmitted and sung by professional reciters. Feature either legendary or historic heroes, often with superhuman qualities; usual setting 11th-15th cent. N Russia.

Byng, John (1704-57), British admiral. Failure to relieve Minorca (1756) from French siege resulted in his court martial and execution.

Byng, Julian Hedworth George, 1st Viscount Byng of Vimy (1862-1935), British general. Commanded capture of Vimy Ridge (1917) during WWI. Governor-general of Canada (1921-6), refused to grant Mackenzie King's request to dissolve Parliament, precipitating constitutional crisis.

Byrd, Richard Evelyn (1888-1957), American explorer, aviator. Made 1st flight to North Pole (1926), to South Pole (1929). Led 5 US expeditions to Antarctica 1928–56. Writings incl. *Skyward* (1928), *Alone* (1938).

Byrd, William (*c* 1543-1623), English composer. Composed both Anglican and RC music, incl. motets and 3 Masses. Also wrote string and keyboard music, madrigals. A master of polyphony, regarded as one of foremost early English composers.

Lord Byron

Byron, Lord George Gordon Noel, 6th Baron Byron of Rochdale (1788-1824), English poet. Best known for *Childe Harold's Pilgrimage* (1912-17), 'Vision of Judgment' (1822), *Don Juan* (1819-24). Regarded as embodiment of Romanticism, left England (1816) for Italy. Died at Missolonghi while aiding Greek fight for independence.

Bytom (Ger. *Beuthen*), city of S Poland. Pop. 187,000. Lead and zinc mining from 12th cent., metal works. Under Prussian rule 1742-1945.

Byzantine Empire, former empire of SE Europe and Asia Minor. Named after Byzantium, rebuilt as cap. and renamed Constantinople (AD 330) after Constantine I. Territ. incl. (at various times) Asia Minor, Balkan Penin. incl. Macedonia, Thrace, Greece, Illyria. Main language Greek; main religion Orthodox Christianity. State estab. as direct successor to Roman Empire; suffered barbarian invasions 4th-6th cents. *Fl* as centre of art, architecture, education, law, esp. under JUSTINIAN I. Involved in political schism with West (800), religious schism (1054); suffered Turkish, Norman attacks in 11th cent. Fourth Crusade diverted to sack Constantinople (1204). Empire partially recovered under Palaeologus family; finally fell (1453) to Turks.

Byzantium, *see* ISTANBUL.

C

cabal, term for secret group of policy-makers, originating from Charles II of England's advisers. Name from initials of members Clifford, Arlington, Buckingham, Ashley and Lauderdale.

cabala, cabbala or **kabbala,** occult religious philosophy developed by certain Jewish rabbis in Middle Ages. Adherents believed that every letter and number in Scripture was part of a significant mystical system, accessible only to the initiate. Became basis of letter and number formulae of medieval magic. Chief works incl. *Zohar* and *Sefer Yezira.*

Cabbage

cabbage, *Brassica oleracea capitata,* leafy vegetable of mustard family from which cauliflower, broccoli, kohlrabi, Brussels sprouts and KALE are derived. Native to E Europe, it has been cultivated for more than 4000 years. Varieties are green, white or red, with various leaf forms.

cabbage white butterfly, *Pieris brassicae,* insect whose larvae feed on cabbage, other plants. Commonest British butterfly.

cabbala, *see* CABALA.

Cabell, James Branch (1879-1958), American novelist. Known for epic novels about mythical state, Poictesme, *eg The Cream of the Jest* (1917), *Jurgen* (1919).

Cabet, Etienne (1788-1856), French writer, reformer. While exiled in England (1834-9), wrote *Voyage en Icarie* (1840) advocating total state control of society. Estab. communes in US, members of which were called Icarians.

Cabinda, exclave of Angola, W Africa. Area 7250 sq km (2800 sq mi); pop. 51,000; main town Cabinda. Exports coffee, hardwoods, oil. Separated from Angola (1886) when mouth of R. Congo ceded to Belgian Congo (now Zaïre).

cabinet, in govt., group of advisers responsible to head of state, who themselves usually head executive depts. of govt. Evolved out of English PRIVY COUNCIL to become a body of ministers selected by prime minister from major party in House of Commons. Cabinet is responsible for executing govt. policy, and is answerable to Parliament. Also, it coordinades activities of state's depts. In UK, depts. represented incl. Foreign Office, Home Office, Treasury. Most Commonwealth countries have imitated system. In US, cabinet comprises heads of the 12 executive depts. of govt. and ambassador to UN. Appointed by and responsible to president alone. Members of US cabinet not drawn from either house of Congress.

Cable, George Washington (1844-1925), American author. Known for short stories dealing with Creole culture, esp. *Old Creole Days* (1879). Also wrote history *The Creoles of Louisiana* (1884).

Cabot, John, English form of Giovanni Caboto (*c* 1450-98), Italian navigator, explorer. Led English expedition (1497) in search of W sea route to Orient. Landed in E Canada, laying basis for English claims to North America. His son, **Sebastian Cabot** (*c* 1485-1557), explored Rio de la Plata region (1526-30) for Spain; later entered service of Henry VIII. Founded 'Merchant Adventurers' which estab. trade with Russia.

Cabrini, St Frances Xavier (1850-1917), American nun, b. Italy. Founded Missionary Sisters of the Sacred Heart of Jesus (1880), specifically to work among the poor and sick. Settled in US (1889) to help arriving Italian immigrants; 1st US citizen to be canonized (1946).

cacao, *see* COCOA.

Caccini, Giulio (*c* 1545-1618), Italian composer. His settings of drama, *eg Euridice* (composed with Peri in 1600), helped introduce opera into the West.

cachalot, *see* SPERM WHALE.

Cactus in flower

cactus, plant of family Cactaceae comprising several hundred species, mainly native to tropical regions of North and South America. Most species adapt to drought by storing water in fleshy stem. Largest genus is the *Opuntia,* distinguished by its jointed pads, sharp spines. Other genera incl. night-blooming cactus, *Cereus;* Christmas cactus, *Zygocactus;* orchid cactus, *Epiphyllum.*

cactus moth, *Cactoblastis cactorum,* South American moth of Pyralididae family. Successfully introduced to Australia (1925) from Argentina to control prickly pear cactus.

Cadbury, George (1839-1922), English chocolate manufacturer, social reformer. Assumed control of father's Birmingham factory, and, with his brother Richard, greatly expanded its business. Moved factory to Bournville (1879), where he set up model workers' village.

caddis fly, any insect of Trichoptera order with hairy wings and body, very reduced mouth-parts. Nocturnal, resembles moth. Larvae aquatic, living in tubular cases of twigs, sand, *etc.*

Cade, Jack (d. 1450), English rebel. Leader of Kentish uprising (1450) against Henry VI. Rebels defeated royal force and occupied London, but were pardoned and dispersed. Cade was hunted down and killed.

cadenza, an interlude in a piece of music, usually a concerto, in which a soloist plays unaccompanied to demonstrate his virtuosity. Cadenzas were once improvised but now most performers play standard written cadenzas.

Cadiz, city of SW Spain, on Bay of Cadíz, cap. of Cadíz prov. Pop. 136,000. Port, exports wine, fruit; shipyards, naval base. Founded *c* 1100 BC by Phoenicians; held 8th-13th cent. by Moors; *fl* in colonial era (16th-18th cent.), centre of New World trade. Has 2 cathedrals (13th, 18th cent.).

cadmium (Cd), soft silvery-white metallic element; at. no. 48, at. wt. 112.4. Occurs in zinc ores and as greenockite (yellow sulphide); obtained during production of zinc. Used in alloys, accumulators and as moderator in nuclear reactors; compounds used as pigments in paint.

Caecilia (caecilians), *see* GYMNOPHIONA.

Caedmon (*fl* 7th cent. AD), English poet. First English Christian poet to be known by name, his story is told by BEDE, who gives Latin translation of only extant poem, on the Creation.

Caen, city of Normandy, N France, on R. Orne. Cap. of Calvados dept. Pop. 110,000. Port; agric. market, textiles (esp. lace) mfg. Important medieval centre; has three 11th cent. churches. Much destruction, incl. univ. (1432), during WWII.

Caerleon, urban dist. of Gwent, SE Wales, on R. Usk. Pop. 4000. Has remains of Roman fortress (*Isca*); associated with Arthurian legend.

Caernarvonshire, former county of NW Wales, now in Gwynedd. Mountainous except for Lleyn Penin. in SW; incl. SNOWDON. Sheep farming, slate quarries; tourism.

Caernarfon, mun. bor. and co. town of Gwynedd, on Menai Strait. Pop. 9000. Port, tourist resort. Castle (13th cent.) was site of investiture of Prince of Wales (1969).

Caerphilly, urban dist. of S Glamorgan, S Wales. Pop. 41,000. Coalmining; cheese mfg. Has largest Welsh castle (13th cent.).

Caesalpinus, Andreas, orig. Cesalpino (15191603), Italian botanist, physician. Anticipated Linnaean system by devising classification of plants based on comparative study of fruit and flowers. Described a theory of blood circulation.

Caesar, [Gaius] Julius (*c* 102–44 BC, Roman soldier, statesman. Governor of Further Spain (61), estab. military reputation. Formed 1st Triumvirate with Crassus and Pompey on return to Rome (60). Appointed ruler of Gaul, greatly enlarged the empire by subjugating the Gauls (58-51). Struggle for power with Pompey and the senate culminated in civil war (49) when Caesar's armies crossed the Rubicon into Italy. Routed Pompey at Pharsala (48) and pursued him into Egypt; there he met Cleopatra, by whom he had a son. Created dictator for 10 years (46), began to restore order to empire. Appointed dictator for life (44), he was assassinated by group of former supporters under Brutus, Cassius. Wrote *Gallic Wars, Civil War.*

Caesarean section, surgical operation for delivery of baby by cutting through mother's abdominal wall and front of uterus. In legend, Julius Caesar was said to have been born this way.

caesium or **cesium** (Cs), soft metallic element, at. no. 55, at. wt. 132.91. Highly reactive; ignites in air and combines vigorously with water to form powerful alkali. Used in photoelectric cells. Discovered (1860) by Bunsen and Kirchhoff.

Caetano, Marcello (1906-   ), Portuguese political leader. Succeeded Salazar as premier (1968). Exiled 1974 following military coup under Spinola.

caffeine, alkaloid drug present in coffee, tea, *etc*; stimulates heart and increases alertness when subject is tired.

Cage, John (1912-   ), American composer, writer, mycologist. Known for experimental, controversial works, esp. those using random elements, *eg Music of Changes*, electronic and silent music. Created 1st 'happening' (Black Mountain Coll. in 1952).

Cagliari, town of S Sardinia, Italy, on Gulf of Cagliari. Cap. of Cagliari prov. Pop. 232,000. Port, exports salt, metal ores, fish; univ. (1626). Carthaginian city, taken (238 BC) by Romans. Held by Pisa 11th-14th cent. Roman remains incl. amphitheatre; 2 Pisan towers.

Cagliostro, Alessandro, Conte di, real name Giuseppe Balsamo (1743-95), Italian adventurer. Travelled in Europe and Near East, posing as occultist. Imprisoned (1789) after heresy trial by Roman Inquisition.

Cagney, James (1899-   ), American film actor. Known for mannered playing in gangster roles, esp. in *The Public Enemy* (1931), *The Roaring Twenties* (1939).

Cahors, town of SC France, on R. Lot, cap. of Lôt dept. Pop. 21,000. Hist. cap. of Quercy; medieval banking centre. Fortified 14th cent. bridge.

Caicos Islands, *see* TURKS AND CAICOS.

Caillaux, Joseph (1863-1944), French politician, premier (1911-12). Five times finance minister, introduced income tax (1906). Resigned 1914 after his wife shot a journalist. Held pacifist views, imprisoned after trial for treason during WWI; pardoned 1924. Later became senator.

caiman, reptile of alligator family of Central and South America. Species incl. black caiman, *Melanosuchus niger*; can reach length of 4.6m/15ft.

Cain, in OT, elder son of Adam and Eve. Killed his brother ABEL in jealousy when Abel's offerings were accepted by God. Condemned to wander the earth.

Cainozoic era, *see* CENOZOIC.

Cairngorms, mountain range of NE Scotland, in GRAMPIANS. Highest point Ben Macdhui (1309 m/ 4296 ft). Has nature reserve; tourist industs., incl. climbing, winter sports (esp. at Aviemore).

Cairns, city of NE Queensland, Australia, on Trinity Bay. Pop. 33,000. Originally gold and tin port, now exports sugar, timber; tourist centre for Barrier Reef isls.

cairn terrier, small shaggy dog of Scottish origin. Bred to chase vermin from burrows. Stands 25 cm/10 in. high at shoulder.

Cairo (*El Qâhira*), cap. of Egypt, at head of Nile delta. Pop. 4,961,000, largest city in Africa. Admin., commercial, indust. centre; cement, textile mfg., brewing. Site of Roman *Babylon;* Old Cairo (*El Fustât*) founded 7th cent., New Cairo founded 969. Ruled by Ottoman Turks 1517-1798. Hist. Islamic religious, educational centre, has *c* 200 mosques, El Azhar Univ. (972), Saladin's citadel (12th cent.), many museums, *eg* Museum of Antiquities. Pyramids of Giza nearby.

Caithness, former county of N Scotland, now in Highland region. Has infertile moorland and hills. Sheep farming, crofting, fishing. Co. town was Wick.

Cajamarca, town of NW Peru, alt. 2740 m (*c* 9000 ft). Pop. 28,000. In gold, silver mining region; agric. market. Site of Pizarro's execution of Atahualpa, last Inca ruler. Thermal springs, Inca ruins.

Calabria, region of SW Italy, penin. between Tyrrhenian, Ionian seas. Main town Reggio, cap. Catanzaro. Underdeveloped region, mainly mountainous, partly forested. Vines, fruits, olives; h.e.p. in La Sila mountains. Ancient *Bruttium*; part of medieval Norman kingdom of Sicily, of kingdom of Naples from 1822.

Calais, town of N France, on English Channel. Pop. 75,000. Port, fishing, ferry service to Dover (England). Under English rule (1347-1558) following long siege by Edward III. Badly damaged in WWII.

calceolaria, large genus of South American plants of the figwort family, bearing colourful, slipper-shaped flowers.

calcite ($CaCO_3$), mineral form of calcium carbonate. Consists of hexagonal crystals; white, often slightly coloured by impurities. Forms incl. chalk, limestone, marble. Used in building, cement and fertilizer mfg.

calcium (Ca), soft white metallic element; at. no. 20, at. wt. 40.08. Occurs as carbonate (limestone, marble, chalk) and sulphate (gypsum). Obtained by electrolysis of fused calcium chloride. Essential constituent of living organisms, found in bones and teeth.

calculator, electronic, numerical calculating device employing a microprocessor incorporated into a single chip of semiconducting material. Series of keys are used to enter numbers or commands into the calculator; results of calculations usually appear on electronic display panel. More advanced calculators possess keys for special mathematical functions, have memories and can be programmed.

calculus, branch of mathematical analysis dealing with continuously varying functions and their rates of change. Concerned with such problems as drawing tangents, calculating velocity, determining area and volume, *etc.* Divided into DIFFERENTIAL and INTEGRAL CALCULUS.

Calcutta, cap. of West Bengal, E India. Pop. 7,005,000. Major port, exports raw materials; indust. centre, jute milling, textiles. Founded *c* 1690 by East India Co.; scene of 'Black Hole' massacre of British garrison (1756). Cap. of India 1833-1912. Univ. (1857).

Calder, Alexander (1898-1976), American sculptor. Invented the mobile, form of kinetic sculpture, consisting of cut-out shapes connected by wire. His static sculpture uses simple shapes of flat metal welded together.

Calder, Ritchie Calder, Baron Ritchie- (1906-), Scottish scientific journalist, author. Known for works proposing technological solutions of Third World problems.

Calderón [de la Barca], Pedro (1600-81), Spanish playwright. Known for classic of Spanish theatre, *Life is a Dream* (*c* 1636). Also wrote many classical comedies, religious plays.

Caldwell, Erskine [Preston] (1903-), American author. Novels, *eg Tobacco Road* (1932), *God's Little Acre* (1933), deal with poverty in South, as dramatic but accurate social documentaries.

Caledonia, Roman name (from 1st cent. AD) for Britain N of Antonine Wall. Now used poetically for whole of Scotland.

Caledonian Canal, waterway of N Scotland. Length 97 km (60 mi), connects Loch Linnhe with Moray Firth via lochs Lochy, Oich and Ness. Completed 1847, now of little importance.

calendar, systematic division of year into months and days. Ancient Chinese and Egyptian calendars based on phases of moon with adjustments to fit solar year. Julius Caesar introduced Julian calendar (45 BC), dividing year into 365 days and inserting additional day every 4th year. Inaccurate by 10 days in 1582 when Pope Gregory XIII ordered readjustment, not adopted by British colonies until 1752.

Calgary, city of S Alberta, Canada; on Bow R., in foothills of Rockies. Pop. 403,000. Railway jct.; oil refining, meat packing, flour milling. Founded 1883. Has annual Calgary Stampede.

Calhoun, John Caldwell (1782-1850), American statesman, political theorist. Leading spokesman for South in STATES' RIGHTS controversy. Vice-president (1825-32), split with Jackson over NULLIFICATION, involving South Carolina's refusal to enforce federal tariff acts.

Cali, city of SW Colombia, in W Andean valley. Pop. 951,000. Indust., agric. centre; sugar refining, textiles, footwear, soap mfg. Founded 1536; grew after railway to Buenaventura built (1914).

calico, form of plain weave cotton cloth, originating in Calicut, India. Imported into England in 17th cent., it was produced there in large quantities in 18th cent.

Calicut, *see* KOZHIKODE.

California, state of W US. Area 411,000 sq km (158,690 sq mi); pop. 19,953,000; cap. Sacramento; chief cities Los Angeles, San Francisco, San Diego. Most populous state in US. Bounded by Pacific in W, Sierra Nevada in E, Coast Range shelters fertile Central Valley. Varied climate. Irrigation widely used for agric.; fruit, cotton, vegetables, cattle and dairy produce. Seasonal labour, mostly Mexican, employed for picking and packing. Fisheries, defence industs; fuel minerals esp. oil. Spanish settled in 18th cent.; republic estab. after Mexican War (1846); ceded to US (1848); gold rush (1849) resulted in great pop. increase. Admitted to Union as 31st state (1850).

California, Gulf of, narrow arm of Pacific, separating Lower California from W Mexico. Fishing, pearl diving.

California, University of, univ. under state support since estab. (1868). On 9 campuses, incl. Berkeley, Los Angeles, San Diego, Santa Barbara, Santa Cruz.

California Institute of Technology, Pasadena, California, US. Privately supported college, founded (1891) as the Throop Polytechnic Institute. Incl. Jet Propulsion Laboratory and Guggenheim Aeronautical Laboratory.

Californian sea lion, *Zalophus californianus,* species of sea lion of NE Pacific coast, Galapagos. Agile, often trained as juggler in zoos and circuses.

californium (Cf), transuranic element; at. no. 98, mass no. of most stable isotope 251. First prepared (1950) at Univ. of California by bombarding curium with alpha particles.

Caligula, real name Gaius Caesar Germanicus (AD 12-41), Roman emperor (37-41). Ruled tyrannically after an illness which is believed to have left him insane. Said to have made his horse a consul. Assassinated by one of his guards.

caliph, name given to successors of Mohammed who assumed leadership of Islam. First caliph was ABU BAKR. Dispute over right of descendants of ALI to succeed to caliphate led to split between SHIITES and SUNNITES. Muawiya estab. Omayyad dynasty in Damascus; it was destroyed by Shiites (750), who set up Abbasid dynasty in Baghdad. Abbasid rule lasted until capture of Baghdad (1258) by Mongols.

Calixtus II, orig. Guy de Vienne (d. 1124), Burgundian churchman, pope (1119-24). Expelled antipope Gregory VIII. Settled investiture dispute with Emperor Henry V by Concordat of Worms (1122), called 1st Lateran Council.

Calixtus III, orig. Alonso de Borja (1378-1458), Spanish churchman, pope (1455-8). Estab. Borgia family in Italy through nepotism. Sponsored partly successful crusade against Turks.

James Callaghan

Callaghan, [Leonard] James (1912-), British statesman, PM (1976-). Posts in Labour govt. incl. chancellor of the exchequer (1964-7), foreign secretary (1974-6). Succeeded Wilson as PM in Labour leadership election. Term marked by efforts to combat high inflation.

Callao, major seaport of W Peru. Pop. 335,000. Pacific depot for Lima, handling most of Peru's imports. Fish processing, agric. related industs. Founded 1537; occupied by Chile (1881-3). Destroyed by earthquake (1746).

Callas, Maria, née Calogeropoulou (1923-), American soprano. Born in New York of Greek parents, trained in Athens. Became internationally renowned opera singer in 1950s. Famous roles in *Madame Butterfly, Norma, Aïda.*

Calles, Plutarco Elias (1877-1945), Mexican military and political leader, president (1924-8). During admin., reversed many of his earlier measures taken to consolidate 1910 revolution. Exiled 1936.

Callicrates (5th cent. BC), Greek architect. With Ictinus, built the Parthenon at Athens (447-432 BC). Also designed temple of Athena Nike on the Acropolis.

calligraphy, art of fine writing. Practised by Chinese from 5th cent. BC, it was regarded as equal to painting; also important in Japanese art from 7th cent. AD. In Islamic art, which forbids portrayal of living forms, decoration of Koran represents highly refined development of calligraphy.

Callimachus (*c* 305–*c* 240 BC), Greek poet and scholar. Prolific writer, best known for *Aetia*, elegiac verse account of religious practices. Profound influence on later writers.

Calliope, in Greek and Roman myth, Muse of epic poetry. Represented as carrying a writing tablet and stylus.

Callot, Jacques (*c* 1592-1635), French engraver. Famous for his *Grandes Misères de la Guerre*, which documents horrors of Cardinal Richelieu's invasion of Lorraine in 1633. Specialized in pictures of beggars and hunchbacks.

Calmette, Léon Charles Albert (1863-1933), French physician, bacteriologist. Founded and directed Pasteur Institute in Lille. With Alphonse Guérin, discovered BCG vaccine used against tuberculosis.

calomel or **mercurous chloride** (Hg_2Cl_2), white insoluble powder, once used as purgative and in treatment of syphilis.

calorie, unit of heat energy; defined as quantity of heat required to raise temperature of 1 gram of water by 1° C. Equals 4.1855 joules.

Calvary (Lat., *calvaria* = skull; translation of Aramaic *golgotha*), scene of Jesus' crucifixion outside walls of Jerusalem. Traditionally, believed to be near site of the Holy Sepulchre.

Calvin

Calvin, John (1509-64), French theologian, Reformation leader. Converted to Protestantism (*c* 1533); systematized Protestant theology in *Institutes of the Christian Religion* (1536), rejecting papal authority. Estab. theocratic republic in Geneva as centre of CALVINISM. Taught doctrine of predestination, salvation for the elect, justification by faith alone and subservience of state to church. Encouraged thrift, industry and sobriety.

Calvinism, Protestant doctrine formulated by CALVIN. Distinguished from Lutheranism by doctrine of PREDESTINATION. Adopted by Huguenots in France, spread to Scotland through teachings of John Knox and influenced Puritans in England and New England. Associated with PRESBYTERIANISM.

Calypso, in Greek myth, nymph, daughter of Atlas. In Homer's *Odyssey* she entertained ODYSSEUS for 7 years when he was shipwrecked on Ogygia.

calypso, humorous song, often extemporized on topical or amatory theme, sung to traditional Caribbean melody and accompaniment.

Camaguey, town of EC Cuba. Pop. 197,000. Railway jct., agric. trade centre, esp. cattle, sugar. Founded in 16th cent. Has 17th cent. cathedral.

Camargue, La, region of Rhône delta, S France. Mainly marsh, lagoons in S. Fishing, marine salt indust.; horse and bull rearing, some agric. (incl. rice) on reclaimed land. Frequented by many species of wild bird.

Cambacérès, Jean Jacques Régis de (1753-1824), French revolutionary, statesman, legislator. Second consul (1799-1804); helped prepare Code Napoléon (1800-4),

developing and codifying civil law. Created duke of Parma (1808).

Camberwell, *see* SOUTHWARK, England.

Cambodia

Cambodia, state of SE Asia. Area *c* 181,300 sq km (70,000 sq mi); pop. 8,100,000; cap. Phnom Penh. Language: Khmer. Religion: Hinayana Buddhism. Large plain drained by Mekong. Mainly agric. (rice); Tonlé Sap is base for fisheries. Formerly French protect. of Cambodia (1863-1955), part of INDO-CHINA. Independent constitutional monarchy (1955), Khmer republic estab. 1970. Involved in Vietnam War with US invasion (1970). Five year civil war ended in 1975 by victory of Communist Khmer Rouge forces.

Cambrai, town of Nord, NE France, on R. Escaut (Scheldt). Pop. 40,000. Hist. textile centre, gave name to cambric. Scene of formation of League of Cambrai (1508) against Venice. Under Spanish rule 1595-1677.

Cambrian Mountains, mountain system of Wales. Runs N-S, incl. SNOWDON, Cader Idris, Plynlimmon.

Cambrian period, first geological period of Palaeozoic era; began *c* 570 million years ago, lasted *c* 70 million years. Extensive seas. Typified by trilobites, graptolites, brachiopods; some algae, lichens. Also *see* GEOLOGICAL TABLE.

Cambridge, city of E Massachusetts, US; near Boston on Charles R. Pop. 100,000. Has Harvard and Radcliffe Univs., Massachusetts Institute of Technology. Industs. incl. scientific instruments, printing and publishing. First settled 1630.

Cambridgeshire, county of E England. Area 3409 sq km (1316 sq mi); pop. 533,000. Incl. Isle of Ely. Fertile fens, artificial drainage; cereals, sugar beet, fruit, vegetable growing. Co. town **Cambridge,** city on R. Cam. Pop. 99,000. Univ. has 23 residential colls. (oldest Peterhouse, 1284). Medieval trading centre. Electronics indust.

Cambridge University, Cambridge, UK, one of two oldest English univs. Estab. (*c* 1209) by dissident Oxford scholars. Since 1st college, Peterhouse, founded (1284), the univ. has grown to comprise 23 residential colleges for undergraduates, 3 of which are women's. Women were only allowed full membership in 1948. Has led in modern literature, philosophy, science, with Cavendish Laboratory for experimental physics. Also noted are King's College Chapel, Fitzwilliam Museum.

Cambyses (d. 522 BC), Persian king. Succeeded his father, Cyrus the Great, in 529. Conquered Egypt 525. Said to have murdered brother Smerdis. Killed himself after unsuccessful attempt to regain kingdom from a usurper who claimed to be Smerdis.

Camden, William (1551-1623), English antiquary. Wrote *Britannia* (1586), a pioneering topographical survey of England. Edited medieval manuscripts and wrote history of Elizabethan times.

Camden, bor. of NW Greater London, England. Pop. 201,000. Created 1965 from Hampstead, Holborn, St Pancras met. bors.

Camden, port of W New Jersey, US; opposite Philadelphia on Delaware R. Pop. 103,000. Shipping, oil refining centre, food canning. First settled by Quakers (1681).

Bactrian camels : mother and baby

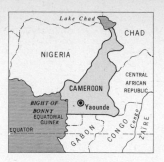

Cameroon

camel, mammal of Camelidae family, related to llama, order Artiodactyla. Arabian camel or dromedary, *Camelus dromedarius,* has 1 hump; Bactrian camel, *Camelus bactrianus,* of C Asian deserts, has 2 humps, shaggy coat. Fat stored in humps helps desert survival. Strong pack animal, but some dromedaries used only for riding.

camellia, genus of flowering evergreen shrubs and small trees of Theaceae family, native to Asia. Cultivated in warm climates and greenhouses. Most important economically is tea plant, *Camellia chinensis,* from India and China. Garden varieties belong to *C. japonica* and *C. reticulata,* and incl. greenhouse and outdoor species.

Camelot, *see* ARTHURIAN LEGEND.

Camembert, village of Normandy, N France. Gave name to a cheese, first made here in 18th cent.

Cameo in ivory relief (1736)

cameo, carving in relief on hard or precious stones or on shells. Agate and sardonyx are used so that raised design can be cut in a lighter layer than background. Cameos, esp. portrait heads, were highly developed in ancient Greek and Roman eras.

camera, light-proof container with lens that focuses optical image to be recorded on light-sensitive FILM. Developments incl. adjustable focus lens to allow objects at various distances to be recorded sharply, variable aperture settings (*f* stop) to control amount of light entering camera, high-speed shutters to photograph moving objects and linked light meters to control these variables automatically. The motion picture camera takes a series of photographs (usually 24 per sec) which when projected at same rate gives impression of movement.

Cameron, Richard (d. 1680), Scottish leader of extreme sect of COVENANTERS. Strongly opposed efforts to re-estab. Episcopal church in Scotland after Restoration. Denied the authority of Charles II. Killed by royalist forces. Followers (Cameronians) became Reformed Presbyterian Church (1743).

Cameroon (Fr. *Cameroun*), republic of WC Africa, on Bight of Biafra. Area 474,000 sq km (183,000 sq mi); pop. 6,282,000; cap. Yaoundé. Languages: French, English. Religions: Christianity, Islam. Savannah in N; tropical forest in W; elsewhere mainly plateau. Produces cocoa, coffee, bananas, groundnuts; bauxite mining. Formerly German (Kamerun); taken by Allies in WWI. Divided (1919) into British, French Cameroons; both UN Trust Territs. from 1946. French Cameroons independent from 1960; S part of British Cameroons joined to form federal republic (1961); N part joined Nigeria.

Cameroon, Mount, volcano of W Cameroon. Highest peak of W Africa, reaches 4067 m/ 13,350 ft. Rainfall on W slopes exceeds 1016 cm/400 in. per year.

Camões or **Camoens, Luis Vaz de** (*c* 1524-80), Portuguese poet. Best known for epic *The Lusiads* (1572) celebrating Portuguese history and exploits of Vasco da Gama. Also wrote sonnets and lyrics.

camomile or **chamomile,** any plant of genera *Anthemis* or *Matricaria* of aster family. Common European species, *A. nobilis,* is used for the astringent and bitter camomile tea.

camouflage, in warfare, diguise of military objectives (incl. troops) by making them blend with their surroundings. Greatly developed in WWI, subsequently declined in importance with development of radar, although retains usefulness in guerrilla campaigns.

Campanella, Tommaso (1568-1639), Italian author. Most of life spent in prison as political radical. Wrote philosophical prose, love lyrics. Known for Platonic utopia, *City of the Sun* (1623).

Campania, region of S Italy, main town Naples. Largely fertile, produces hemp, fruit, tobacco; mountainous interior. Many coastal resorts. Roman region much smaller, incl. sites of Pompeii, Herculaneum.

campanile, in architecture, Italian bell-tower usually built separately from main building, *eg* church or town hall. Examples incl. that of Florence, built by Giotto (1334), and the leaning tower of Pisa.

campanula, genus of plants of bellflower family with bell-shaped flowers. Found in temperate parts of N hemisphere and widely cultivated. Harebell, *Campanula rotundifolia,* and Canterbury bell, *C. medium,* are well-known species.

Campbell, Scottish noble family, *see* ARGYLL, ARCHIBALD CAMPBELL, 8TH EARL OF.

Campbell, Alexander (1788-1866), American clergyman, b. Ireland. Broke with Presbyterian church to found Disciples of Christ (Campbellites), advocating return to Christian simplicity.

Campbell, Sir Colin *see* CLYDE, COLIN CAMPBELL, 1ST BARON.

Campbell, John, 1st Earl of Breadalbane (*c* 1635-1717), Scottish chieftain. Led massacre (1692) of Macdonald clan at Glencoe for delay in swearing allegiance to William III.

Campbell, Sir Malcolm (1885-1949), British motor racing enthusiast. Broke world speed record on land (1935) in *Bluebird* car and on water (1939) in boat of same name. His son, **Donald Malcolm Campbell** (1921-67), broke world water record in turbo-jet hydroplane and land record (both 1964). Died in attempt on water record.

Campbell, Mrs Patrick, née Beatrice Stella Tanner (1865-1940), English actress, friend of Wilde, Shaw. Known for role of Eliza Doolittle in Shaw's *Pygmalion*.

Campbell, Roy Dunnachie (1901-57), South African poet. Known for poetry celebrating danger, vitality *eg Flaming Terrapin* (1924), and *Flowering Rifle* (1939), satire celebrating Franco in whose army he fought.

Campbell, Thomas (1777-1844), Scottish poet. Remembered for war songs, *eg* 'Ye Mariners of England'. Also wrote discursive verse essay *The Pleasures of Hope* (1799), criticism.

Campbell-Bannerman, Sir Henry (1836-1908), British statesman, PM (1905-8). Liberal leader, his admin. was marked by self-govt. for South African colonies and growth of conflict between Commons and Lords.

Campbeltown, town of Strathclyde region, W Scotland, on Kintyre penin. Pop. 6000. Port; distilling.

Campeche, port of E Mexico, cap. of Campeche state; on Gulf of Campeche. Pop. 70,000. Cigars, leather, footwear mfg., fish canning. Importance of shallow harbour diminished after colonial times.

Camperdown (*Kamperduin*), village of North Holland prov., NW Netherlands. Naval battle fought offshore (1797) in which British defeated Dutch.

camphor, volatile, crystalline substance with strong, characteristic odour, derived from wood of camphor laurel, *Cinnamomum camphora*. Used to protect fabrics from moths, in manufacturing cellulose plastics, and in medicine as an irritant and stimulant.

Campi, Giulio (*c* 1502-72), Italian painter and architect. Founded school of painters at Cremona. Specialized in frescoes and altarpieces. Taught his brothers Antonio and Vincenzo.

Campinas, town of SC Brazil in São Paulo state. Pop. 376,000. Agric. (sugar refining), transport, indust. centre; coffee exports.

Campion, Edmund (*c* 1540-81), English Jesuit martyr. Favourite of Elizabeth I before his conversion to Catholicism. Became Jesuit (1573) after studying at Douai. Returned to England as missionary (1580), preached with effect until captured; executed for treason.

Campion, Thomas (1567-1620), English poet, musician. Best known for songs for the lute.

campion, various flowering plants of genera *Lychnis* and *Silene* of the pink family. Species incl. red campion, *L. dioica*, pink-flowered hairy perennial of Britain, moss campion, *S. acaulis*, perennial alpine plentiful in Scotland, and sea campion, *S. maritima*.

Campo Formio, Treaty of (Oct. 1797), French-Austrian settlement of Napoleon's campaign in Italy. Austria ceded Austrian Netherlands to France and secretly promised left bank of Rhine; Venetian Republic dissolved and most of it ceded to Austria, the rest to France and Cisalpine Republic (N Italy).

Campos, market town of SE Brazil, near Paraíba R. mouth. Pop. 319,000. In rich agric. region; large-scale sugar refining, distilling.

Camus, Albert (1913-60), French writer, b. Algeria. In essay *Le Mythe de Sisyphe* (1942), outlined theory of ABSURD which permeates novels, *eg L'Etranger* (1942), *La Peste* (1947). Member of SARTRE circle but parted from him on thinking. Awarded Nobel Prize for Literature (1957).

Canaan, OT name for region W of R. Jordan. The 'promised land' occupied by Israelites after Exodus from Egypt. Subsequently known as Palestine.

Canada, federal country of N North America, independent member of British Commonwealth. Area 9,976,128 sq km (3,851,787 sq mi); pop. 21,568,000; cap. Ottawa; major cities Montréal, Toronto. Languages: English, French. Religions: Protestant, RC. Stretches from Pacific to Atlantic, from Arctic to the Great Lakes; extreme climate. Comprises 10 provs. as well as Yukon and Northwest Territs. Rocky Mts. divide coastal British Columbia (timber, wood pulp, h.e.p.) and agric. Prairies (wheat); Ontario, Québec (major concentrations of pop, and

indust.); Maritimes, Newfoundland (fisheries); C Laurentian Plateau (copper, nickel, oil). Explored 1534 by Cartier, settled by French in 17th cent.; competing claims to sovereignty resolved by British victory at Québec (1759). Independence (1867) uniting Upper (Ontario) and Lower (Québec) Canada with Nova Scotia, New Brunswick; subsequently enlarged by W expansion.

Canadian, river of SC US. Rises in E New Mexico, flows 1458 km (906 mi) across Texas Panhandle and Oklahoma to join Arkansas R. H.e.p. at Eufaula reservoir. **North Canadian,** river of SC US. Flows SE from N New Mexico through Oklahoma to join Canadian R. at Eufaula.

Canadian Pacific Railway (CPR), privately owned and operated railway system. First Canadian transcontinental railway, completed in 1885. Built as one of conditions on which British Columbia agreed to enter confederation in 1871.

canal, artificial waterway used for transportation, drainage and irrigation. GRAND CANAL of China, completed in 13th cent., is longest in world. Transportation canals may be provided with locks so that level of water can be changed to raise or lower boats. St Lawrence Seaway network of canals connects Great Lakes with Atlantic.

Canaletto's *Venice: the basin of S. Marco*

Canaletto, properly Antonio Canale (1697-1768), Italian painter. Specialized in topographically accurate views of Venice; visited England (1746-55) where he produced several fine landscapes and views of London. Nephew and pupil **Bernardo Bellotto** (1720-80) assumed uncle's name; painted accurate views of Warsaw, Dresden, *etc*.

canary, *Serinus canarius*, small singing finch of Canary Islands, Azores. Grey or green in wild; yellow varieties bred in captivity. Popular pet.

Canary Islands

Canary Islands, isl. group of Atlantic Ocean, off NW Africa, comprising 2 provs. of Spain. Isls. incl. Grand Canary, Lanzarote, Tenerife. Area 7270 sq km (2807 sq mi); main towns Las Palmas, Santa Cruz de Tenerife. Volcanic, rise to *c* 3700 m (12,100 ft). Banana, tobacco growing, fishing, tourism. Possibly the ancient 'Fortunate Islands'; Spanish from 1476.

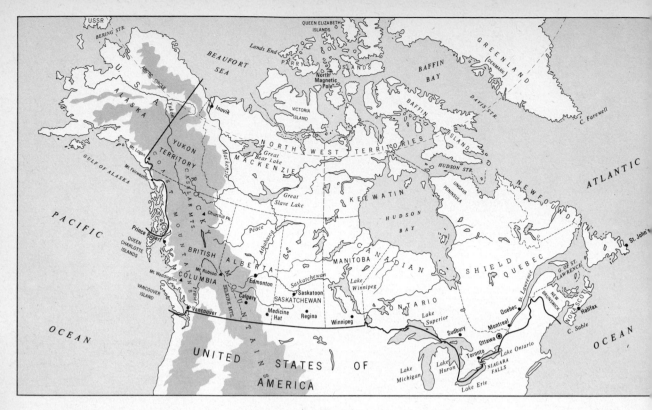

Canada

canasta, card game, a variation of rummy, for two to six players, using a double deck of cards. Originated in Montevideo (1949).

Canaveral, Cape, E Florida, US. Missile-testing centre, launch point of satellites, space craft. Known as Cape Kennedy 1963-73.

Canberra, cap. of Australia, in Australian Capital Territory, on Molonglo R. Pop. 159,000. Admin. centre; national library, univ. (1929). Founded 1913, replaced Melbourne as cap. 1927.

Cancer, see ZODIAC.

cancer, group of diseases resulting from disorder of cell growth. Cancer cells grow without control or need, locally at first, but later they may spread to other parts of body via lymph vessels or veins. Causes incl. chemical agents, *eg* dyes and hydrocarbons, cigarette smoke, radiation, viruses, hereditary factors. Treatments incl. X-rays and radioactive sources, hormones, surgery and chemotherapy.

Cancer, Tropic of, parallel of latitude 23½°N of Equator. Marks most N position at which Sun appears vertically overhead at noon. At this line, Sun shines directly overhead at June solstice (summer in N hemisphere).

Candela [Outeriño], Félix (1910-), Mexican architect, b. Spain. Known for his shell-like structures in reinforced concrete; designed Church of Our Lady, Mexico City.

Candia, see IRÁKLION, Greece.

candle, mass of tallow or wax surrounding a wick, used as source of light when burned. Known since Roman times, candles, usually of tallow, became widespread in Europe during Middle Ages. Modern candles are usually machine-moulded from paraffin wax.

Candy, see KANDY.

candytuft, annual or perennial herb of cabbage family, native to S and W Europe. Globe candytuft, *Iberis umbellata,* is cultivated species.

cane, see BAMBOO; RATTAN; SUGAR CANE.

Canea (*Khania*), town of NW Crete, Greece, on Canea Bay. Pop. 38,000. Port; fruit, wine trade. Ancient *Cydonia*;

thrived under Venetians (13th-17th cent.). Cap. of Crete from 1840.

Canidae, the dog family. Carnivorous mammals, incl. wolf, fox, jackal, dog.

canna or **Indian shot,** genus of plants of Cannaceae family, native to tropical America and Asia. Many varieties cultivated for striking foliage and brilliant flowers. *Canna indica* and *C. edulis* yield kind of arrowroot.

cannabis, see HEMP.

Cannae (modern *Canna*), town of Apulia, S Italy, on R. Aufidus (modern *Ofanto*). Scene of Hannibal's victory (216 BC) over Romans.

Cannes, town of Provence, SE France, on Côte d'Azur. Pop. 68,000. Resort, casinos; fruit and flower growing, perfume mfg. Annual international film festival.

cannibalism, practice in certain societies of eating human flesh. Has occurred among many peoples at many times. Normally associated with the ritual attempt to transfer properties of victim to other members of group.

Canning, George (1770-1827), British statesman, PM (1827). Tory foreign secretary (1807-9), planned capture of Danish fleet (1807). Supported Spanish American and Greek independence movements after succeeding CASTLEREAGH as foreign secretary (1822). Advocated free trade and Catholic Emancipation. His son, **Charles John Canning, Earl Canning** (1812-62), was noted for clemency as governor-general of India during Mutiny of 1857. First viceroy of India (1858-62).

canning, process of preserving cooked food by sealing it in airtight containers, afterwards subjected to heat. Method was invented in early 19th cent. France by N. Appert, who used glass bottles. Use of tin cans was patented in 1810, but mass-production of tin-coated steel cans began in 1840s.

cannon, a smooth-bore piece of artillery, used until the 19th cent., firing shot of 24-47 lb (11-21 kg). The term also now refers to large machine guns carried by fighter aircraft.

Cano, Juan Sebastian del (c 1476-1526), Spanish navigator. Sailed (1519-22) with Magellan, on whose death he took command, becoming first to circumnavigate globe.

canoe, narrow, light boat ending in a point at each end. Usually propelled by paddles but sail or motor may be used. Important in the culture of several primitive peoples, eg in South Pacific, among North American Indians. The Indian birchbark canoe was adopted by Europeans for explorations and trapping expeditions in North America. See CANOEING, KAYAK.

canoeing, sport of propelling a canoe through water. Divided into various activities: slalom, down river or white-water racing, long distance and sprint racing. Popularized by John McGregor who founded Canoe Club in England (1866). Olympic event since 1936.

canon, musical form in which a melody is repeated note for note so that it overlaps itself. A catch or round is a simple vocal canon.

canonization, process by which RC church gives official sanction to veneration of dead person as a saint. Formal canonization dates from enactments of Pope Urban VIII in 1634. After careful investigation of a candidate's life, case may be brought by Church with objections raised by the *promotor fidei* (popularly known as 'devil's advocate'). Case for canonization consists of proof of 4 miracles and evidence of an exemplary life.

canon law, body of laws governing the ecclesiastical affairs of a Christian church. In RC church, systematized in *Codex juris canonici* (1918). In Church of England, based on canons pub. in 1604 and subsequently revised. Only clergy are bound by it, unless laws are authorized by Parliament or declared old custom. Rejected in Scotland after Reformation, but retained in laws of marriage, legitimacy and succession.

Canova, Antonio (1757-1822), Italian sculptor. Leading neo-Classical sculptor, he was patronized by the popes and later by the Bonaparte family. Works incl. 2 colossal nude statues of Napoleon.

Cantabrian Mountains, range of N Spain, extending c 480 km (300 mi) E-W parallel to Bay of Biscay coast. Rise to 2648 m (8687 ft) at Peña Cerredo. Rich in coal and iron. Source of R. Ebro.

cantaloupe, see MELON.

cantata, sacred or secular piece of music of several movements for chorus and orchestra, usually with vocal soloists; similar to oratorio but shorter.

Canterbury, city of Kent, SE England, on R. Stour. Pop. 33,000. Roman *Durovernum;* hist. cap. of Saxon Kent. Abbey founded 597 by St Augustine who was 1st archbishop. Seat of Anglican primate. Pilgrimage centre since Becket's murder in cathedral (1170). Focus of Chaucer's *Canterbury Tales.* King's School (c 600, refounded 1541).

Canterbury, region of EC South Isl., New Zealand. Area 36,000 sq km (13,900 sq mi); pop. 398,000; chief city Christchurch. Extends from Pacific coast (E) to Southern Alps foothills (W). Sheep, dairy farming on Canterbury Plains; tourism, h.e.p. in mountains.

cantilever, in architecture, horizontal beam supported at one end only and carrying a load at free end or evenly distributed along exposed portion. Used in bridge building for large spans, eg Forth Railway Bridge, Scotland.

Canton, China, see KWANGCHOW.

Canton, indust. town of NE Ohio, US. Pop. 110,000. Iron and steel, varied mfg. industs.

Canton and Enderbury Islands, in Phoenix Isls., C Pacific Ocean. Jointly admin. from 1939 by US, UK; others of Phoenix Isls. part of Gilbert and Ellice Isls. colony. Originally source of guano for US, also export copra. Canton was air refuelling base, now disused.

Cantonese, see CHINESE.

Canute or **Knut [II] the Great** (c 995-1035), king of England, Denmark and Norway. Invaded England 1015, sole ruler from 1016; estab. more efficient admin., codified law. King of Denmark from 1018, of Norway after invasion in 1028.

canvasback, *Aythya valisneria,* North American duck. Brown head, dark back; hunted as game.

canyon, deep, narrow gorge, often with steep sides. Usually formed in arid areas by rivers cutting into soft rock, low rainfall preventing erosion of canyon walls. Grand Canyon, US, is largest in world.

capacitance, in electronics, property of CAPACITOR which determines how much charge can be stored in it for given potential difference between its terminals; measured, in farads, as amount of charge required to increase potential by 1 unit.

capacitor, device for storing electric charge, usually consisting of 2 or more conducting plates separated by insulating material (dielectric). Used in electrical devices, eg radios. Formerly called condenser.

Cape Breton, isl. of Canada, forms E part of Nova Scotia. Area 10,282 sq km (c 3970 sq mi). Rugged terrain, fishing, lumbering, coal mining at Sydney-Glace Bay, steel production. French colony 1713-58; joined with Nova Scotia 1820.

Cape buffalo, *Syncerus caffer,* species of African cattle, widespread S of Sahara. Small red variety or forest buffalo, found in forests; large black variety in grassland.

Cape Coast, town of S Ghana, on Gulf of Guinea. Pop. 72,000. Port, exports cocoa, hardwoods; fishing. Fort estab. (1652) by Swedes; British from 1664. Cap. of Gold Coast until 1876.

Cape hunting dog, *Lycaon pictus,* wild dog of S and E Africa. Hunts in packs; can kill much larger animals.

Capek, Karel (1890-1938), Czech playwright. Known for *R.U.R.* (1921) about a fantasy state where robots revolt against man. Also wrote novels, short stories. Collaborated with his brother, **Josef Capek** (1887-1945), in social allegory *The Insect Play* (1921).

Cape of Good Hope, see GOOD HOPE, CAPE OF.

Cape [of Good Hope] Province, prov. (largest) of SW South Africa. Area 720,000 sq km (278,000 sq mi); pop. 4,235,000; cap. Cape Town. Plateau, drained by R. Orange. Produces cereals, tobacco, fruit, vines; diamond (Kimberley), copper (Okiep) mining. Settled from 1652 by Dutch at Table Bay, by Huguenots (1689). Annexed 1806 by Britain; became prov. of Union of South Africa (1910).

caper, any plant of genus *Capparis,* esp. a prickly, trailing Mediterranean bush, *C. spinosa,* tiny green flower buds of which are pickled and used to flavour sauces.

capercaillie or **capercailzie,** *Tetrao urogallus,* large grouse-like bird of N Europe. Grey-coloured; usually seen on ground.

Capernaum, ancient town of N Israel, on Sea of Galilee. Associated with Jesus' teachings.

Capet, Hugh (c 938-96), French king (987-96). Son of Hugh the Great; elected successor to Louis V in preference to Charles, duke of Lorraine. First of Capetians.

Capetians, dynasty of French kings, named after Hugh Capet (c 938-96), 1st Capetian ruler. Direct descendants of his ruled 987-1328, last was Charles IV. Throne then passed to House of Valois.

Cape Town or **Capetown,** legislative cap. of South Africa and cap. of Cape Prov. Pop. 1,096,000. Port on Table Bay, at foot of Table Mt. Admin., commercial centre, univ. (1918). Founded (1652) by Dutch; cap. of Cape Colony until 1910. Dutch colonial architecture, botanic gardens. Oldest South African white settlement.

Cape Verde Islands, country of EC Atlantic. Area 4040 sq km (1560 sq mi); pop. 300,000; cap. Praia. Incl. 10 isls. of volcanic origin. Stock raising, fishing; exports coffee, fruit. Colonized 15th cent. by Portuguese. Independent 1975, retains links with Guinea-Bissau.

Cape York Peninsula, penin. of N Queensland, Australia, between Coral Sea and Gulf of Carpentaria. Aboriginal reserves; cattle ranching, bauxite mining. First part of Australia sighted by Europeans (Jansz, 1606).

Cap-Haïtien, seaport of N Haiti. Pop. 46,000. Coffee, sugar, banana exports. Cap. of French colony (1670-1770). Almost destroyed by earthquake (1842).

capillaries, in physiology, see BLOOD VESSELS.

Cape Town: Town Hall with Table Mountain in background

capillary action, force resulting from adhesion, cohesion and surface tension in liquids which are in contact with solids. Accounts for water rising in capillary tube, because adhesive force between glass and water exceeds cohesive force between water molecules.

capital, in architecture, the top part of a column, pilaster or pier, which transmits the weight of the superstructure to the supporting column. Gothic and Romanesque capitals were often richly carved with animal forms, grotesque heads, *etc.*

capital, in economics, originally interest-bearing money; now all means of production and distribution, *eg* land, plant, transport, raw materials, potentially yielding income. Ownership of capital is both private and public in most indust. countries, although in Communist countries nearly all capital is state-owned. *See* CAPITALISM, CORPORATE STATE.

capitalism, economic system in which means of production and distribution (land, factories, transport) are privately owned and operated for profit. Importance dates from Industrial Revolution, characterized by free competition and great concentrations of wealth; later by large corporations and varying degrees of govt. regulation, often as technocratic state capitalism (*see* CORPORATE STATE). As term, capitalism developed by Marx in historical analysis (DIALECTICAL MATERIALISM) as stage in evolution of society.

capital punishment, legally sanctioned taking of life as punishment for crime. Once recognized penalty for sacrilege and offences against property, in 20th cent. usually reserved for treason, murder. In 1970s only W European countries retaining it were France, Spain. In US, Supreme Court ruled (1972) that death penalty violated 8th, 14th Amendments, but left way open for it to be imposed by new legislation passed by Congress or specific states, as it was in same year by Congress (for hijacking) and by most states.

Capone, Al[fonso] (1899-1947), American gangster, b. Italy. Notorious for leadership of crime syndicate in Chicago during prohibition era of 1920s.

Caporetto, see KOBARID, Yugoslavia.

Capote, Truman (1924-   ), American author. Early work, *eg Other Voices, Other Rooms* (1928), has gothic elements. *Breakfast at Tiffany's* (1958) reflects New York chic; *In Cold Blood* (1966) is leading example of 'documentary fiction'.

Capp, Al (1909-   ), American cartoonist, known for burlesque, satirical strip cartoon, 'Li'l Abner'.

Al Capone

Cappadocia, mountainous region of Asia Minor, in C Turkey. Independent kingdom in 3rd cent. BC, with cap. at Mazaca; became Roman prov. in AD 17.

Capra, Frank (1897-   ), American film writer-director, b. Sicily. Known for stylish comedies of 1930s–40s, conveying belief in redeemable human nature, incl. *Platinum Blonde* (1932), *It Happened One Night* (1934), *Mr Deeds Goes to Town* (1936).

Capri, isl. of S Italy, in Bay of Naples. Area 10 sq km (4 sq mi). Tourist centre with famous Blue Grotto. Site of ruined villas of emperors Augustus, Tiberius.

Capricorn, see ZODIAC.

Capricorn, Tropic of, parallel of latitude $23\frac{1}{2}°$ S of Equator. Marks most S position at which Sun appears vertically overhead at noon. At this line, Sun shines directly overhead at December solstice (summer in S hemisphere).

Caprivi, Georg Leo, Graf von (1831-99), German statesman. Bismarck's successor as chancellor (1890-4), pursued conservative policies.

Caprivi Strip, narrow extension of South West Africa to R. Zambezi. Length *c* 480 km (300 mi); obtained (1890) by German chancellor von Caprivi in negotiations with UK.

capsicum, see CAYENNE.

Capua (anc. *Casilinum*), town of Campania, S Italy, on R. Volturno. Pop. 18,000. Strategic Roman site on Appian Way; sacked by Arabs (AD 841), inhabitants moved to present site.

Capuana, Luigi (1839-1915), Italian novelist and critic. Introduced Zolaesque naturalism to Italy, laying foundation for *verismo*. Drama editor of *La Nazione*, novels incl. *Giacinta* (1879), *Il Marchese di Roccaverdina* (1901).

capuchin, commonest monkey of Central and South America, genus *Cebus*, incl. *c* 12 species. Hair resembles monk's cowl. Lives in troops led by dominant male.

Capybara

capybara, *Hydrochoerus hydrochoeris,* largest rodent, up to 1.2 m/4 ft long, resembling giant guinea pig. Lives in groups, good swimmer; found on river banks of South America.

car, *see* AUTOMOBILE.

Caracalla, real name Marcus Aurelius Antoninus (186–217), Roman emperor (211-17). Ruled alone after murdering his brother Geta (212) who was co-emperor with him. Granted Roman citizenship to all free inhabitants of empire. Extravagant reign ended with his assassination by Macrinus.

Caracas, cap. of Venezuela, linked to Caribbean port La Guaira. Pop. 2,175,000; alt. 945 m (*c* 3100 ft). Oil refining, textile mfg. Founded 1567. Scene of declaration of Venezuelan independence (1811); birthplace of Bolivar. Cap. from 1829. Wealth derived from oil has facilitated growth of modern city.

Caractacus or **Caradoc** (*fl* AD 50), British chieftain. Led resistance against Romans (43-51). Captured and taken to Rome, where his life was spared by Claudius.

carat, unit describing quantity of gold in an alloy: 1 carat is 24th part of pure gold, thus 15 carat gold contains 15 parts gold and 9 parts alloy.

Caravaggio, Michelangelo Amerighi da (1573-1610), Italian painter. Famous for his revolutionary use of light and shade, contemporary costume and rejection of idealization to achieve previously unknown degree of realism. Had great influence on subsequent artists. Works incl. *Martyrdom of St Matthew.*

Caraway

caraway, white-flowered biennial herb, *Carum carvi,* of parsley family with spicy, strong-smelling seeds which are used as flavouring and a carminative. Leaves are eaten as vegetables and in soup.

carbide, compound of an element, usually metal, with carbon. Incl. calcium carbide (CaC₂), used to make acetylene and silicon carbide or carborundum (SiC₂), used as abrasive.

carbohydrate, organic compound of carbon, hydrogen and oxygen with general formula C_x $(H_2O)_y$, incl. sugars, starches and cellulose. Formed in green plants by PHOTOSYNTHESIS; starch essential to human diet, providing energy during its oxidation.

carbolic acid, *see* PHENOLS.

carbon (C), non-metallic element; at. no. 6, at. wt. 12.01. Exists in 3 allotropic forms: crystalline diamond and graphite, and amorphous carbon (charcoal, lampblack, coke). Numerous compounds subject of organic chemistry. Used in electrodes; activated charcoal, specially treated to remove hydrocarbons, absorbs gases.

Carbonari ('charcoal burners'), Italian political secret society originating in Naples. Aimed at expulsion of foreign rulers and estab. of democracy. Active in uprisings (1820, 1831), later merged with Young Italy movement of MAZZINI.

carbon dioxide (CO₂), colourless gas, found in atmosphere; formed by combustion of carbon or heating carbonates. Dissolves in water to form weak unstable carbonic acid. Exhaled by animals and absorbed by plants, which convert it into carbohydrates and oxygen by photosynthesis. Used in production of mineral water, in fire extinguishers; solid carbon dioxide known as 'dry ice' used as refrigerant.

carbon fibre, material composed of extremely fine filaments of pure carbon bonded together. Great strength-to-weight ratio and heat resistance; valuable in reinforcing components of jet engines.

Carboniferous period, fifth geological period of Palaeozoic era; began *c* 345 million years ago, lasted *c* 65 million years. Divided into Lower Carboniferous, or Mississippian and Upper Carboniferous, or Pennsylvanian. Many crinoids, brachiopods; increasing amphibians, fish, insects, 1st reptiles. Club mosses, horsetails led to development of vast COAL seams. Also *see* GEOLOGICAL TABLE.

carbon monoxide (CO), colourless inflammable gas, formed by incomplete combustion of carbonaceous fuels. Extremely poisonous, as it combines with haemoglobin of blood, making this unavailable to carry oxygen. Occurs in exhaust fumes of petrol engines, coal gas.

carborundum, *see* CARBIDE.

carboxylic acid, organic acid containing 1 or more carboxyl (COOH) groups, *eg* formic acid.

carbuncle, inflammation of tissue beneath the skin, of same kind as a BOIL, but larger and with several heads through which pus is discharged.

Carcassonne, town of Languedoc, S France, on R. Aude. Cap. of Aude dept. Pop. 46,000. Tourist centre, wine trade. Divided by R. Aude into ancient hilltop 'Cité' (castle, cathedral, town walls) and 'Ville Basse' (founded 1247).

Carchemish, ancient city of S Turkey, on Euphrates near Syrian border. Centre of neo-Hittite culture *c* 1000 BC; scene of victory of Nebuchadnezzar II over Necho II (605 BC) which ended Egyptian power in Asia.

carcinogen, any substance that produces cancer. In 1775 Pott showed that soot causes cancer in chimney sweeps. Isolation of carcinogens started (1915) when Yamagima and Ichikawa showed that repeated applications of coal tar to skin of rabbits produces cancer.

Carco, Francis, pseud. of François Marie Alexandre Carcopino-Tusoli (1886-1958), French author. Known for sketches of bohemian life in poetry, *eg La Bohème et mon coeur* (1912), and novels, memoirs.

cardamom or **cardamon,** spice from seed capsules of E Indian plant, *Elettaria cardamomum,* used in curries and pickling.

Cárdenas, Lázaro (1895-1970), Mexican political leader. President (1934-40); his policy incl. land reform reallocating private holdings to individuals and collectives, expropriation of foreign assets.

Cardiff, cap. city and port of Wales, in S Glamorgan. Near Bristol Channel on R. Taff. Pop. 278,000. Major coal, iron, steel exports. Admin., commercial centre; has coll. of Univ. of Wales. Site of Roman station; 11th cent. castle.

Cardigan, James Thomas Brudenell, 7th Earl of (1797-1868), British army officer. Led the disastrous cavalry charge at Balaklava (1854) in the Crimean War, immortalized by Tennyson. The woollen garment called a cardigan is named after him.

Cardiganshire, former county of W Wales, now in Dyfed. Main town Aberystwyth. Plateau in E (livestock rearing), lowland along coast (oats, barley growing). Has many British, Roman remains. Co. town was **Cardigan,** mun. bor. on R. Teifi. Pop. 4000. Agric. market.

cardinal, any of several North American crested songbirds of scarlet plumage, esp. *Richmondena cardinalis* of E US.

Carducci, Giosuè (1835-1907), Italian poet, critic. Works reflect aims of *Risorgimento, eg Hymn to Satan,* rebelling against traditional religion, endorsing material progress. Nobel Prize for Literature (1906).

Carew, Thomas (*c* 1594-1640), English poet. Known for Cavalier lyric verse in manner of Jonson, *eg* 'Ask me no more where Jove bestows', 'Mediocrity in love rejected'.

Carey, William (1761-1834), English missionary in India. A founder of Baptist Missionary Society (1792). Translated Bible into *c* 40 Indian dialects.

Carib, South American Indians of separate Carib language family, formerly inhabiting Lesser Antilles. Named by

Columbus, noted for their ferocity (a corruption of Carib gives English word 'cannibal'); also expert navigators. Some 500 pure-blooded Caribs remain on Dominica.

Caribbean Sea and Islands

Caribbean, sea of W Atlantic Ocean, bounded by Venezuela, Colombia, Central America. Area 1,942,500 sq km (*c* 750,000 sq mi). Linked with Gulf of Mexico by Yucatán Channel. Has many isls. *eg* West Indies, Greater and Lesser Antilles. Named after Carib Indians who once inhabited coastal areas.

Barren-ground caribou in Alaska

caribou, large North American deer, resembling reindeer, genus *Rangifer.* Native of Arctic and subarctic. Both sexes have antlers. Two main types: barren-ground group of Alaska, N Canada; woodland group of E Canada.

carillon, set of bells worked by keyboard and pedals, or automatically. The world's largest carillon, at Cincinnati, Ohio, contains 83 bells in a tower 91m (300 ft) high.

Carinthia (*Kärnten*), prov. of S Austria. Area 9531 sq km (3680 sq mi); cap. Klagenfurt. Mountainous, incl. GROSSGLOCKNER, many lakes. Timber, mining. Incorporated into Austria 14th cent.

Carlisle, city and co. bor. of Cumbria, N England, on R. Eden. Pop. 71,000. Railway jct., textile mfg. Roman *Luguvallum;* hist. strategic site in border wars; has castle (1092), cathedral (12th cent.).

Carlists, supporters of descendants of Don Carlos de Bourbon (1788-1855), 2nd son of Charles IV of Spain, as pretenders to Spanish throne. Defeated in civil war (1833-9) by forces of Isabella II, and failed in uprisings (1860, 1869, 1872). Also lost civil war of 1873-6 despite gains in Basque provs., Catalonia. Supported fascists under FRANCO in Spanish Civil War (1936-9).

Carlos (1545-68), Spanish prince. Imprisoned by his father, Philip II, for involvement in assassination plot (1567). Hero of Schiller's tragedy, *Don Carlos.*

Carlow, county of Leinster prov., SE Irish Republic. Area 896 sq km (346 sq mi); pop. 34,000. Mountains in SE. Agric., dairying, livestock. Co. town **Carlow,** pop. 9000. Market town. Theological coll. (18th cent.), RC cathedral (19th cent.).

Carlsbad, *see* KARLOVY VARY, Czechoslovakia.

Thomas Carlyle

Carlyle, Thomas (1795-1881), Scottish writer. Translated Goethe, Schiller. Distrust of democracy, belief in divinely-informed hero expressed in *French Revolution* (1837), *On Heroes, Hero-Worship* (1841). Also wrote biog. *Frederick the Great* (1858-65). *Sartor Resartus* (1833-4) is spiritual autobiog.

Carman, [William] Bliss (1861-1929), Canadian poet. Known for bohemian 'vagabond' verse, esp. *Low Tide on Grand Pré* (1893). Also wrote essays, *The Kinship of Nature* (1906).

Carmarthenshire, former county of S Wales, now in Dyfed. Mountainous in NE (livestock rearing), agric. in lowlands. Coalmining, metal industs. centred on Llanelli in SE. **Carmarthen,** mun. bor. and co. town of Dyfed, on R. Towy. Pop. 13,000. Dairy centre, on site of Roman town *Maridunum.*

Carmel, Mount, mountain of NW Israel, rising 546 m (1792 ft) from Haifa. Associated in Bible with prophet Elijah. Carmelite order was founded here in 12th cent.

Carmelites, in RC church, mendicant friars of the order of Our Lady of Mt. Carmel. Founded as order of hermits in Palestine *c* 1150. Stress contemplative aspects of religious life and have incl. several mystics, *eg* ST THERESA OF AVILA, St John of the Cross. Known as White Friars.

Carmen Sylva, *see* ELIZABETH, Romanian queen consort.

Carnac, town of Brittany, NW France, on Quiberon Bay. Pop. 4000. Site of *c* 3000 menhirs arranged in rows, among which are ancient burial chambers.

Carnap, Rudolf (1891-1970), German philosopher, settled in US 1936. Pioneer of LOGICAL POSITIVISM, claiming object of philosophy is description and criticism of language. Works incl. *The Logical Syntax of Language* (1934).

Carnarvon, *see* CAERNARVONSHIRE, Wales.

carnation, *Dianthus caryophyllus,* perennial herbaceous plant with many cultivated varieties. White, pink or red flowers popular as buttonholes. *See* PINK.

Carné, Marcel (1903-), French film director. Known for subtly-characterized films, incl. *Le Jour se lève* (1939), *Les Enfants du Paradis* (1944).

Carnegie, Andrew (1835-1919), American industrialist, b. Scotland. Estab. steel business based in Pittsburgh which produced by 1900 one quarter of total US steel. Sold out (1901) to US Steel Corporation and devoted his fortune to funding of libraries, univs.

Carnegie, Dale (1888-1955), American writer. Famous for self-improvement manuals, esp. *How to Win Friends and Influence People* (1936).

Carniola (*Kranj*), region of NW Yugoslavia, in Slovenia. Former crownland of Austria, hist. cap. Ljubljana. Divided 1919 between Yugoslavia and Italy; all within Yugoslavia by 1947.

Carnivora (carnivores), order of flesh-eating mammals with large canine teeth. Terrestrial group, Fissipedia, incl.

dog, cat, otter, bear, lion. Marine group, Pinnipedia, incl. seal, walrus.

Carnot, Lazare Nicolas Marguerite (1753-1823), French revolutionary soldier. Organized republican armies, reforming methods and supply systems. Exiled (1815) after restoration. His son, **Nicolas Léonard Sadi Carnot** (1796-1832), was a physicist. Helped found thermodynamics with work on heat, mechanical energy. His nephew, **[Marie François] Sadi Carnot** (1837-94), was a statesman. President (1887-94), countered Boulanger's populist movement. Assassinated by Italian anarchist at Lyons.

carob, leguminous tree, *Ceratonia siliqua,* of E Mediterranean, bearing leathery brown pods with sweet pulp which are sometimes used as fodder.

Carol I (1839-1914), king of Romania (1881-1914). Elected prince of Romania (1866). Obtained independence at CONGRESS OF BERLIN, after siding with Russia in war with Turkey (1877-8).

Carol II (1893-1953), king of Romania (1930-40). Renounced right to succession (1925), but deposed son Michael (1930) and took throne. Overthrown by ANTONESCU (1940), fled to Mexico.

carol, song of annual religious festivals, esp. Christmas. Some of the tunes originate in folk song while others are borrowed from secular music or specially composed.

Caroline Islands

Caroline Islands, archipelago of W Pacific Ocean. Area 900 sq km (350 sq mi); chief isls. PALAU, Ponape, Truk, Yap. Main crops copra, sugar cane, tapioca; also produce bauxite, phosphate, guano. Discovered 1526 by Spain, bought (1899) by Germany. Occupied by Japanese from WWI; part of US Trust Territ. of the Pacific Isls. from 1947.

Caroline of Brunswick (1768-1821), German princess, consort of George IV of England. Married (1795) prince of Wales, but they were separated 1796. She refused to renounce her rights at his accession; George's subsequent divorce proceedings were abandoned.

Carolingians, dynasty of Frankish rulers, succeeding Merovingians (751) through Pepin the Short. His son, Charlemagne, crowned Western emperor (800); empire split by Treaty of Verdun (843) among his grandsons who founded dynasties ruling Germany until 911 and France until 987. Succeeded by Capetians.

Carossa, Hans (1878-1956), German novelist. Stylish autobiog. novels incl. *Childhood* (1922), *A Romanian Diary* (1924).

carotenoids, group of orange, yellow or red plant pigments; found in parts of plant where chlorophyll is absent, they assist in photosynthesis. Carotene, found in carrots, certain other vegetables, and butter, is converted to vitamin A in body.

carp, freshwater fish of Cyprinidae family, esp. *Cyprinus carpio,* of worldwide distribution. May be cultivated as food fish. Goldfish is domestic variety of golden carp.

Carpaccio, Vittore (c 1460-1526), Italian painter. Influenced by Gentile Bellini, his narrative paintings, filled with anecdotal detail, describe pageantry of Venice. Works incl. *Legend of St Ursula* series.

Carpathians, mountain range of EC Europe, curving from Czechoslovakia through SW Ukraine to Romania. Rise to 2662 m (8737 ft) in Tatra Mts. (Czechoslovakia). Forests; minerals; tourism.

Carpentaria, Gulf of, shallow inlet of Arafura Sea, N Australia, between Arnhem Land and Cape York Penin.

17th century Turkish carpet

carpet or **rug,** thick fabric, usually of wool, used as a floor covering, *etc.* Carpet making reached a high point of artistry in Turkey, Persia and C Asia in 16th cent. European production dates from 17th cent. at such centres as the Savonnerie in Paris. In England, Axminster, Wilton and Kidderminster were important centres. Power loom introduced 1841 made mass-production possible.

carpetbagger, American political term popularized in post-Civil War period. Referred to speculators and entrepreneurs who started business in devastated Southern states with no more than they could carry in a carpetbag.

carpet beetle, any of several beetles of Dermestidae family, whose larvae feed on wool, furs, *etc.* Larder beetle, *Dermestes lardarius,* is related pest of stored food.

Carpini, Giovanni de Piano (c 1180-1252), Italian Franciscan monk. Sent by Pope Innocent IV in 1245 to Mongol court of Karakorum. Crossed Russia and Asia in c 106 days. Journal was 1st European record of Mongols.

Carracci, Ludovico (1555-1619), Italian artist. Founded teaching Academy in Bologna with cousins, **Agostino Carracci** (1557-1602) and **Annibale Carracci** (1560-1609). Annibale's decoration of Farnese Gallery in Rome is esp. famous for its use of illusionism and feigned architectural, sculptural forms.

carrageen, *Chondrus crispus,* reddish-brown edible seaweed of N Europe and North America. Extract used in jellies, lotions, surgical dressings.

Carrantuohill, mountain of Co. Kerry, SW Irish Republic. Highest in Ireland (1040 m/3414 ft).

Carranza, Venustiano (1859-1920), Mexican political leader, president (1914-20). Contested leadership with Huerta, Villa and Zapata after overthrow of Díaz (1911). Reform programme of nationalization of mineral assets (1917) was never implemented.

Carrara, town of Tuscany, NC Italy. Pop. 68,000. Centre of Italian marble indust. Has medieval cathedral.

Carrel, Alexis (1873-1944), American surgeon, biologist, b. France. Developed technique of sewing blood vessels together (suturing) for use in organ and tissue transplants; awarded Nobel Prize for Physiology and Medicine (1912).

carriage, non-self-propelling wheeled vehicle, esp. for carrying passengers; strictly refers to 4-wheel types. Covered horse- or mule-drawn carriage dates from c 15th cent. Public stagecoach much used in 17th and 18th cent. Hansom cab (2-wheel) plying for hire introduced in London (1834). Other 2-wheeled carriages incl. stanhope, tilbury, gig, sulky, dog-cart. Private 4-wheeled carriages widely used in 19th cent. incl. brougham, landau, victoria. Open 4-wheeled carriages incl. phaeton, wagonette, brake.

Carrickfergus, town of E Northern Ireland, on Belfast Lough. Pop. 15,000. In former Co. Antrim. Fishing port; linen mfg. **Carrickfergus,** district; area 77 sq km (30 sq mi); pop. 27,000. Created 1973, formerly part of Co. Antrim.

Carrick-on-Shannon, co. town of Leitrim, NW Irish Republic, on R. Shannon. Pop. 2000. Agric. market; fishing.

carrion crow, *see* CROW.

Carroll, John (1735-1815), American churchman. Jesuit, friend of Ben Franklin, supported patriot cause in American Revolution. Secured toleration for Catholicism in US.

Lewis Carroll

Carroll, Lewis, pseud. of Charles Lutwidge Dodgson (1832-98), English writer, mathematician. Known for classics of inverted logic, ostensibly for childern, *eg Alice's Adventures in Wonderland* (1865), *Through the Looking-glass* (1872). Also wrote nonsense verse incl. *The Hunting of the Snark* (1876).

Carroll, Paul Vincent (1900-68), Irish playwright. Comedies reflect struggles of Irish village life, as in *Shadow and Substance* (1937), *The Wayward Saint* (1955).

carrot, *Daucus carota,* widely distributed biennial plant of parsley family, with fleshy, orange-coloured edible roots. Derived from Queen Anne's lace or wild carrot.

Carson, Christopher ('Kit') (1809-68), American frontiersman. Renowned Indian fighter, acted as guide in Frémont's Western expeditions in 1840s. Aided in Mexican War (1846).

Carson, Edward Henry Carson, Baron (1854-1935), Irish politician. Opposed Irish Home Rule and rallied Ulster in support of British govt. during WWI, serving in wartime cabinets. Denounced creation (1921) of independent Irish Free State.

Carson, Rachel Louise (1907-64), American biologist, writer. Works, incl. *The Sea around Us* (1951) and *Silent Spring* (1962), deal with danger to wild life from fertilizers and pesticides.

Carson City, cap. of Nevada, US; near California border. Pop. 15,000. Grew in late 19th cent. after nearby silver strike at Comstock Lode. Resort town. Named after Kit Carson.

Cartagena, seaport of N Colombia, on Caribbean. Pop. 257,000. Has canal link to Magdalena R. Oil pipeline terminus; exports agric. produce. Founded (1533) by Spanish, it was shipping centre for precious stones and metals of New World; frequently sacked and invaded.

Cartagena, city of Murcia, SE Spain, on Mediterranean Sea. Pop. 147,000. Port, exports iron and lead; metallurgical centre, naval base. Founded *c* 225 BC by Hasdrubal; major port under Romans. *Fl* 16th-18th cent. with New World trade.

Cartago, town of C Costa Rica. Pop. 22,000. In livestock rearing, coffee growing region. Founded 1563; admin. centre until 1821. Destroyed by volcanic eruption (1723). Annual pilgrimages.

Carte, Richard D'Oyly, *see* D'OYLY CARTE, RICHARD.

cartel, in economics, association of manufacturers or traders to fix prices, sales quotas or to divide markets. Shares many characteristics of MONOPOLY.

Carter, Elliott (1908-), American composer. His complex works usually employ traditional forms; esp. noted for chamber music. Compositions incl. *Variations for Orchestra,* 3 string quartets.

Carter, Howard (1873-1939), English archaeologist. Working with Lord Carnarvon in Valley of Kings in Egypt, discovered (1922) tomb of Tutankhamen, only Egyptian royal tomb to be discovered intact with all its treasure.

Jimmy Carter

Carter, James Earl ('Jimmy') (1924-), American statesman, president (1977-). Governor of Georgia (1970-4). As Democratic presidential candidate, defeated Gerald Ford in 1976 election.

Carteret, John, 1st Earl Granville (1690-1763), British statesman. Foreign minister (1721-4), clashed with Walpole. Leader of opposition (1730-42), instrumental in Walpole's downfall; became virtual head of govt. (1742-4). Supported George II's unpopular Hanoverian policy.

Carthage, ancient city of N Africa, near modern Tunis. Founded 9th cent. BC by Phoenicians; estab. colonies in Sardinia, Sicily, Spain. Trade rivalry with Rome led to PUNIC WARS, city finally destroyed 146 BC. New colony founded 44 BC by Romans; Vandal cap. from AD 439. Totally destroyed (698) by Arabs.

Carthusians, order of monks in RC church. Most austere order, each member living in individual cell, scarcely meeting others unless in public worship. Founded (1084) by St Bruno at Chartreuse, France. Chartreuse liqueur first made here.

Cartier, Sir George Etienne (1814-73), Canadian statesman. First minister (1858-62) of Lower Canada in Cartier-Macdonald ministry, largely responsible for French-Canadian interest in confederation.

Cartier, Jacques (1491-1557), French navigator, explorer. In search of Northwest Passage, made 2 voyages (1534, 1535-6) exploring E Canada, Gulf of St Lawrence. Reached St Lawrence R.; visited Stadacona (now Québec), Hochelaga (now Montréal); proclaimed French sovereignty. Colonizing expeditions (1541, 1543) failed.

Carthage

Cartier-Bresson, Henri (1908-   ), French photographer. Known for extreme naturalism, as well as news photographs of important international events. Worked with Jean Renoir, founded Magnum-Photos (1947).

cartilage or **gristle,** tough whitish tissue which forms part of skeletal systems. Lines moving surfaces of joints and forms external ear, nose, *etc.* Skeletons of embryos are largely formed of cartilage, which gradually turns to bone.

cartography, the art and science of map making, now generally applied to all stages from field survey to finished map. Ancient Babylonians produced earliest known map (c 2500 BC); Greeks, esp. Eratosthenes and Ptolemy, estab. principles of cartography little altered until 17th cent. First world atlas produced by Mercator (1569). Modern cartography founded by Delisle and d'Anville; 1st systematic national survey pub. 1756 in France, followed 1801 by British Ordnance Survey.

cartoon, in art, full-size preliminary drawing of a design or painting, usually worked out in detail. Name also applies to drawing with humorous or satirical intention.

Cartwright, John (1740-1824), English reformer. Refused to fight American colonists. Campaigned for abolition of slavery, vote by secret ballot, other reforms. His brother, **Edmund Cartwright** (1743-1823), invented the powerloom (1785) and wool-combing machines.

Caruso, Enrico (1873-1921), Italian operatic tenor. Achieved fame in Europe and America. One of 1st singers to exploit gramophone recording successfully.

Carver, George Washington (c 1864-1943), American agricultural chemist. Devoted himself to improvement of the economy of the South. Encouraged growth of peanuts and sweet potatoes to enrich the soil, and devised numerous uses for these crops.

Cary, [Arthur] Joyce [Lunel] (1888-1957), English novelist, b. Ireland. Early works, *eg Mister Johnson* (1939) reflect experiences in Nigerian colonial services, later novels, *eg The Horse's Mouth* (1944), *A Prisoner of Grace* (1952), deal comically with individual's isolation, with artist, politician as hero.

caryatid, in Greek architecture, supporting column in form of draped female figure (said to represent woman of Caryae). Famous examples found on porch of Erechtheum, Athens.

Casablanca (Arab. *Dar-al-Baida*), city of N Morocco, on Atlantic Ocean. Pop. 1,371,000. Indust., commercial centre; major port, exports phosphates, manganese. Founded 16th cent. by Portuguese on site of ancient *Anfa.* Scene of Roosevelt-Churchill meeting (1943).

Casals, Pablo or **Pau** (1876-1973), Spanish cellist, conductor. Founder and musical director of Barcelona orchestra (1919-36). Renowned for interpretation of Bach's cello pieces, he raised status of cello as a solo instrument.

Casanova de Seingalt, Giovanni Giacomo (1725-98), Italian adventurer, writer. Known for *Mémoires* (1826-38) which recount his fluctuating affairs, both financial and sexual, on travels across Europe.

Cascade Range, N extension of mountain system of W US; from California through Oregon, Washington to S British Columbia (Canada). Mt. Rainier in Washington is highest point (4392 m/14,410 ft). Heavily forested on slopes.

casein, main protein of milk, precipitated by addition of acid or rennet. Chief constituent of cheese; used to make plastics, adhesives.

Roger Casement

Casement, Roger David (1864-1916), Irish nationalist. Served in British consular service in Belgian Congo and Peru. Attempted to gain German aid for Irish rebellion (1916), returning to Ireland in German submarine. Captured and hanged for treason. Regarded as martyr by Irish.

Caserta, town of Campania, S Italy, cap. of Caserta prov. Pop. 67,000. Agric. market. Has royal palace (1774). Scene of surrender (1945) of German forces in Italy.

Casey, Richard Gardiner Casey, Baron (1890-1976), Australian statesman. Liberal minister (1949-60) in Menzies govt. Governor-general of Australia (1965-9).

Casimir [III] the Great (1310-70), king of Poland (1333-70). Estab. peace by diplomacy with Teutonic Knights and king of Bohemia. Codified laws of Poland and founded Univ. of Kraków (1364).

Caslon, William (1692-1766), English typefounder. Designed 'old-style' types, legibility of which made their use widespread with printers until end of 18th cent.

Caspian Sea

Caspian Sea, salt lake between Europe and Asia, world's largest inland sea. Area *c* 373,000 sq km (144,000 sq mi). Almost entirely in USSR, part of S shore in Iran. Receives

R. Volga and R. Ural, no outlet; 27m (90 ft) below sea level, its level decreases by evaporation. Sturgeon fisheries.

Cassander (c 350-297 BC), Macedonian king. Son of Antipater, fought against Polyperchon who had succeeded Antipater as regent of Macedonia. Master of Macedonia by 316, strengthened his position by murdering Alexander the Great's widow and son. Defeated Antigonus I at Ipsus (301).

Cassandra, in Greek legend, daughter of King Priam of Troy. Prophetess of Apollo, who caused her prophecies never to be believed. After fall of Troy, captive of Agamemnon; killed with him by his wife Clytemnestra.

Cassatt, Mary (1845-1926), American painter, etcher. Allied to impressionist group, she was influenced by Degas. Later work, influenced by Japanese prints, relied on line and pattern. Excelled in mother-and-child scenes.

cassava or **manioc,** any of several tropical American plants of genus *Manihot* of the spurge family, having edible starchy roots used to make tapioca.

Cassel, see KASSEL, West Germany.

cassia, the bark of a tree, *Cinnamomum cassia,* of the laurel family, native to SE Asia. Used as a cinnamon substitute. Also a genus, *Cassia,* of herbs, shrubs and trees of Leguminosae family, common in tropical countries. The cathartic drug senna is prepared from the leaves of *C. acutifolia* and *C. angustifolia.*

Cassini, Giovanni (1625-1712), French astronomer, b. Italy. Organized observatory in Paris. Discovered 4 satellites of Saturn and division of its rings into 2 concentric parts. Ascertained rotation period of Mars and Jupiter.

Cassino, town of Latium, C Italy, at foot of Monte Cassino. Pop. 19,000. Monastery on summit founded 529 by St Benedict; used as stronghold by Germans (1944), destroyed by Allied bombing. Restored 1964.

Cassirer, Ernst (1874-1945), German philosopher. Known for Kantian critique of culture leading to conception of man as the 'symbolic animal'. Works incl. *Philosophy of Symbolic Forms* (1923-9).

cassiterite or **tinstone** (SnO₂), tin ore mineral. Consists of tin dioxide; very hard and heavy, dark brown or black in colour. Commercial source of tin. Major sources in East Indies, Nigeria, Bolivia.

Cassius [Longinus], Gaius (d. 42 BC), Roman soldier. Pardoned by Caesar after supporting Pompey in civil war (48 BC). He became a leading figure in the conspiracy to assassinate Caesar (44 BC). With Brutus, he was defeated by Mark Antony at Philippi, where he committed suicide.

Cassivellaunus (fl c 55 BC), British chieftain. Led resistance against Roman invasion under Caesar, but was defeated and forced to pay tribute.

Casson, Sir Hugh Maxwell (1910-   ), British architect. Director of Architecture for Festival of Britain (1948-51). Works incl. *Homes by the Million, An Introduction to Victorian Architecture* (1947). President of the Royal Academy (1975).

cassowary, *Casuarius casuarius,* large flightless bird of N Australia, New Guinea, with brightly coloured neck and head, capped by bony crest; related to emu. Male incubates eggs.

castanets, percussion instrument consisting of a pair of shell-shaped wooden blocks joined by a piece of string; held between thumb and fingers and clicked rapidly together. A pair is usually held in each hand. Characteristic to Spain.

caste, in Hindu population of India, exclusive social grouping. Classified by Brahmans (c AD 200) into 4 divisions with Untouchables below these; now c 3000 castes. Traditionally, no member of any caste may marry outside it; rules may also regulate occupation and diet. Discrimination against castes made illegal (1947).

Castel Gandolfo, village of Latium, C Italy, in Alban Hills. Castle (17th cent.) is papal summer residence; Vatican astronomical observatory estab. 1936.

Castellammare di Stabia, town of Campania, S Italy, on Bay of Naples. Pop. 69,000. Resort (mineral springs), naval dockyard, engineering. Roman *Stabiae,* destroyed by Vesuvius eruption AD 79. Ruined 13th cent. castle.

Castellani, Sir Aldo (1877-1971), British bacteriologist, b. Italy. Authority on tropical medicine, he discovered cause and means of transmission of sleeping sickness. Also discovered spirochaete causing yaws.

Castellón de la Plana, town of E Spain, cap. of Castellón de la Plana prov. Pop. 94,000. Agric. market, exports almonds, oranges via outport at El Gráo. Has church (14th cent.).

Castelo Branco, Camilo (1825-90), Portuguese novelist. Known for autobiog. novel *Amor de Perdição* (1862). Noted as prose stylist.

Castiglione, Baldassare, Conte (1478-1529), Italian author. Wrote *Libro del Cortegiano* (1528; English translation, *The Courtier,* 1561), lively collection of dialogues on Renaissance courtly morals and manners.

Castile (*Castilla*), region and former kingdom of C Spain. Largely arid plateau, drained by Douro, Tagus rivers; divided by mountains into Old (N) and New (S) Castile. Limited agric. incl. cereals, fruit, sheep; mining. Independent from 10th cent.; led fight against Moors. United with León (1230), Aragón (1479) to found Spain. Language became standard Spanish.

castle, fortified dwelling characteristic of medieval times. Principal features of Norman castle were: rectangular donjon or keep, which served as living quarters; inner bailey (courtyard) surrounding the keep and separated from outer bailey by a wall; outer walls of masonry, from which round towers (bastions) projected; moats, crossed by drawbridges, which protected outer walls.

Castlebar, co. town of Mayo, NW Irish Republic. Pop. 6000. Agric. market. Scene of French-Irish rout of English garrison ('Races of Castlebar' 1798).

Castlereagh, Robert Stewart, 2nd Viscount (1769-1822), British statesman, b. Ireland. As Irish secretary crushed French-backed revolt (1795). Secretary of war during Napoleonic wars, helped plan Peninsular campaign. Fought duel with George CANNING after alleged political betrayal, resigned 1803. Foreign secretary (1812-22), helped organize 'Concert of Europe' opposing Napoleon. Favoured moderate settlement at Congress of VIENNA (1814-15), maintenance of conservative interests in Europe. Committed suicide.

Castlereagh, dist. of E Northern Ireland. Area 84 sq km (33 sq mi); pop. 67,000. Created 1973, formerly part of Co. Down.

Castor and **Pollux,** in classical myth, see DIOSCURI.

castor oil, extracted from seeds of Palma Christi shrub, *Ricinus communis,* native to subtropical regions, but widely cultivated as ornamental. The oil is used medicinally as a quick-acting laxative; also used in paint and varnish indust.

castration, removal of sex glands (testicles) of male animal. Results in sterility and curbing of secondary sex characteristics when practised on children. Used to improve meat quality and decrease aggressiveness of farm animals.

Castries, cap. of ST LUCIA.

Castro [Ruz], Fidel (1927-   ), Cuban revolutionary and political leader, premier (1959-   ). Chief figure in '26th of July' movement; organized Cuban revolutionary forces while in Mexico and returned to lead successful guerrilla campaign (1956-9), which overthrew BATISTA. Proclaimed (1961) allegiance to Communist bloc; supported revolutionary movements in Latin America. Collectivized agriculture, expropriated industs.

casuistry, originally, branch of ethics which deals with delicate moral questions by applying general principles. Term also refers to arguing away of ambiguous acts with hair-splitting subtleties.

cat, any animal of Felidae family, incl. lion, leopard, tiger. Carnivorous, with sharp claws used for climbing trees, holding prey. Numerous varieties of domestic cat, *Felis catus,* probably derived from African wildcat, *F. lybica.*

catacombs, early Christian subterranean cemeteries arranged in vaults and galleries; those in Rome date mainly from 3rd and early 4th cents. and cover c 600 acres. Also served as places of refuge during Christian persecutions;

Fidel Castro

later became shrines of pilgrimage. Others, besides Rome, were in Naples, Syracuse, Paris, *etc.*

Catalan, Romance language of Italic branch of Indo-European family. Spoken in Catalonia, Valencia, Balearic Islands, Roussillon region of SE France, and is Andorran official language.

catalepsy, unconscious fit, resulting in temporary loss of feeling and rigidity of muscles. May occur in epilepsy, schizophrenia, hysteria.

Çatal Huyuk, ancient town standing on edge of Konya plateau, SC Turkey. Excavated in 1950s and 1960s, building levels dating back to 6000 BC were discovered. Evidence of developed agric. and definite site planning was found.

Catalonia (*Cataluña*), region of NE Spain, hist. cap. Barcelona. Hilly, drained by R. Ebro. Almond, fruit growing, wine mfg.; metal, textile industs. based on h.e.p. Frankish county from 9th cent.; united with Aragón (12th cent.), with Castile (15th cent.). Autonomous govts. (1932-4, 1936-9) reflect hist. strong Catalan nationalism. Catalan language suppressed after 1939.

catalpa, small genus of deciduous American and Asiatic trees of Bignoniaceae family. Large heart-shaped leaves, showy clusters of trumpet-shaped flowers, slender pods.

catalyst, any substance which speeds up or slows down rate of chemical reaction, but is itself unchanged at end of reaction. Plays important role in indust. preparation of ammonia, sulphuric acid, *etc.* Platinum, nickel, manganese dioxide are catalysts.

Catania, city of E Sicily, Italy, on Gulf of Catania. Cap. of Catania prov. Pop. 402,000. Port, shipbuilding, sulphur refining, food processing; univ. (1434). Founded 8th cent. BC by Greek colonists. Often damaged by eruptions of Mt. Etna.

Catanzaro, town of SW Italy, cap. of Catanzaro prov. and (from 1971) of Calabria. Pop. 86,000. Citrus fruit production. Famous until 17th cent. for velvet, damask.

catapult, an ancient and medieval weapon with retractable arms attached to cords. The arms were drawn back and spears, arrows, or stones were propelled forward.

cataract, in medicine, disease of eye in which lens becomes opaque, causing partial or total blindness. Commonly results from ageing; treated by surgery.

catarrh, obsolete term for inflammation of mucous membrane, esp. of nose, causing a discharge of mucus. RHINITIS now describes such inflammation of nose.

catastrophism, in geology, theory that features of Earth's crust change by means of isolated catastrophes. Rejects theory of evolution implicit in UNIFORMITARIANISM. Widely held from ancient times, upheld by Cuvier in early 19th cent.; now generally discarded.

catchment area, area in which all water drains into a particular river, lake or reservoir. Separated from adjacent catchment area by high land forming a WATERSHED. Term

now also applied to area served by any given facility, *eg* shop, library, airport.

catechu, extract of leaves of an E Indian acacia, *Acacia catechu.* Rich in tannin, it is used medicinally as an internal astringent and in dyeing and tanning.

caterpillar, worm-like, segmented, larva of butterfly or moth. Usually herbivorous, has strong jaws. Moults skin *c* 5 times to allow growth. Pupates in cocoon spun from silk thread.

catfish, any of a large group of scaleless freshwater and marine fish, abundant in New World. Whisker-like sensory barbels around mouth.

Cathari, generic name for adherents of dualistic heresies in medieval Europe, esp. ALBIGENSIANS.

Cather, Willa Sibert (1873-1947), American author. Known for novels of pioneering life *My Antonia* (1918), *One of Ours* (1922). Also wrote critical essays on her literary influences.

Catherine I (*c* 1683-1727), tsarina of Russia (1725-7). Originally Martha Skavronskaya, a Livonian peasant girl; became mistress of Peter the Great and married him (1711). Chosen as his successor.

Catherine the Great

Catherine [II] the Great (1729-96), tsarina of Russia (1762-96), b. Germany. Married (1744) the future Peter III, whom she had deposed by conspiracy headed by the Orlovs shortly after his accession. Reforming zeal unfulfilled after peasant rebellion (1773-5) and French Revolution. Her reign was marked by territ. expansion at expense of Poland, ascendancy in Near East after wars (1768-74, 1787-92) with Turkey and annexation of Crimea. A monarch of the Enlightenment, encouraged development of Russian literature. Lovers incl. Orlov, Potemkin.

Catherine de' Medici, *see* MEDICI.

Catherine of Alexandria, St (d. *c* 307), Alexandrian martyr. Traditionally, broke spiked wheel on which she was being tortured; subsequently beheaded. Patron saint of virgins.

Catherine of Aragon (1485-1536), queen of England, 1st wife of Henry VIII. Daughter of Ferdinand and Isabella of Spain. Discontent with their marriage and lack of a male heir led Henry to seek annulment on grounds of illegality. Pope's refusal led to English Reformation.

Catherine of Braganza (1638-1705), Portuguese princess, consort of Charles II of England. Dowry for marriage (1662) incl. Bombay, Tangier. Lived away from court, but protected by Charles when accused of complicity in Popish Plot (1678).

Catherine of Genoa, St (1447-1510), Genoese mystic. Broke from life of society in order to nurse sick. Thoughts contained in *Treatise on Purgatory* and *Spiritual Dialogue*.

Catherine of Siena, St (1347-80), Italian Dominican nun, mystic. After vision of united Church, convinced Pope

Gregory XI to leave Avignon for Rome; subsequently defended Urban VI against antipope Clement VII. Teachings contained in *A Treatise on Divine Providence.*

Catherine of Valois (1401-37), French princess, consort of Henry V of England. Gave birth to Henry VI (1421). Secret marriage to Owen Tudor after Henry V's death (1422) provided basis for subsequent Tudor claims to English throne.

cathode, see ELECTRODE.

cathode rays, stream of electrons emitted from cathode when electrical discharge takes place in tube containing gas at very low pressure.

cathode ray tube, vacuum tube in which cathode rays are directed by electric fields to strike fluorescent screen and produce illuminated traces, visible outside tube. Used in oscilloscopes and television picture tubes.

Catholic Emancipation, name given to series of acts passed in Britain. Culminated in Catholic Emancipation Act (1829) which relieved British RCs from the legal and civil disabilities accumulated since time of Henry VIII, *eg* restrictions on land inheritance, debarment from forces, judiciary, univs.

Catiline, full name Lucius Sergius Catilina (*c* 108-62 BC), Roman politician. Twice failed to be elected consul (66, 63); after his 2nd failure, when defeated by Cicero, formed scheme to take power by force. Conspiracy exposed by Cicero in 4 orations; Catiline killed in subsequent battle.

Catlin, George (1796-1872), American artist, chronicler. Specialized in painting American Indian scenes; wrote *Manners, Customs and Condition of the North American Indians* (1841).

catmint or **catnip,** *Nepeta cataria,* plant of mint family, with downy leaves, spikes of bluish flowers. Native to Britain and Europe. Tea, made of leaves and flowers is old medicinal remedy.

Cato, Marcus Porcius or **Cato the Elder** (234-149 BC), Roman statesman. Appointed censor (184), tried to restrict entry to senate to those he considered worthy. Opposed introduction of Greek culture in favour of ancient Roman simplicity. Campaigned for the destruction of Carthage. Wrote *De Re Rustica,* treatise on agric.

Cato Street conspiracy, see THISTLEWOOD, ARTHUR.

Catskill Mountains, range of E New York, US; part of Appalachian Mts. Rise to 1231 m (4040 ft). Area provides water for New York City. Incl. locale of Rip van Winkle tale. Popular tourist area.

cattail or **reed mace,** any of genus *Typha* of tall marsh plants with reed-like leaves and long, brown, fuzzy, cylindrical flower spikes. Incl. species *T. latifolia, T. angustifolia* which are used in making baskets and matting.

Cattaro, see KOTOR, Yugoslavia.

cattle, ruminant mammals of genus *Bos.* In particular domestic cattle, *Bos taurus,* used for dairy products, meat, hides. Milk breeds incl. Ayrshire (brown and white), Friesian and Holstein (black and white), Guernsey (fawn and white), Jersey. Meat producers incl. Aberdeen Angus (black), Hereford (red with white face). Normandy and short horn are dual purpose.

Catullus, Gaius Valerius (*c* 84-*c* 54 BC), Roman poet. Describes unhappy love for 'Lesbia' in superb lyrics. Other poems incl. satires, epigrams. Personal approach, intense feeling and colloquial style make him major influence on European literature.

Caucasus, mountain system of SW USSR, between Black and Caspian seas. Its peaks incl. Mt. Elbrus. Separates N Caucasia from Transcaucasia.

Cauchy, Augustin Louis, Baron (1789-1857), French mathematician. Gave rigorous treatment of foundations of calculus; developed theory of functions of complex variable. Also contributed to astronomy, hydrodynamics, optics.

cauliflower, variety of cabbage, *Brassica oleracea botrytis.* Has a dense white mass of fleshy flower stalks which form edible head. Introduced from Cyprus in 16th cent., now grown extensively as commercial or garden crop.

Cavafy, Constantinos (1863-1933), Greek poet, b. Egypt. Works incl. ironic narrative poems on Greek past, homosexual love lyrics, collected in *The Complete Poems of Cavafy* (pub. 1961).

Cavalcanti, Guido (*c* 1255-1300), Italian poet. Friend of Dante, wrote *canzoni,* ballads and sonnets, all on theme of love, notably in *Canzone d'amore.*

Cavaliers, in English Civil War (1642-8), supporters of Charles I in his struggle with Parliament's forces (Roundheads).

Cavalli, Pietro Francesco (1602-76), Italian composer. Active in the early development of opera. He composed over 40 operas, in which song achieved greater importance.

cavalry, mounted soldiers, important from classical times down to the 18th cent. because of their speed and mobility. Declined during the 19th cent. but were still used for reconnaissance and skirmishing in the early part of WWI. Now all UK cavalry regiments are armoured units except for the Household Cavalry, retained for ceremonial purposes.

Cavan, county of Ulster prov., NC Irish Republic. Area 1891 sq km (730 sq mi); pop. 53,000. Hilly moorland, largely infertile; many lakes. Some agric., livestock; distilling. Co. town **Cavan,** pop. 3000. Ruined abbey; modern RC cathedral.

Cave, Edward (1691-1754), English publisher. Founded *The Gentleman's Magazine* (1731-1914), first modern magazine, giving Johnson a vehicle for essays.

cave, natural chamber or cavity in Earth's crust. Sea-caves formed by wave action or by abrasion due to pebbles, boulders, *etc* being hurled against cliff. Inland caves usually found in limestone areas, formed by running water dissolving rock.

Cavell, Edith (1865-1915), English nurse. Matron of nurses' training institute in Brussels. Shot by the Germans for helping Allied soldiers to escape over Dutch frontier in WWI.

Cavendish, pseud. of Henry Jones (1831-99), English card game expert. Formulated rules for playing whist. Wrote *Principles of Whist* (1862).

Cavendish, Henry (1731-1810), English scientist, b. France. Investigated properties of hydrogen ('inflammable air') and carbon dioxide. Researched into composition of water and air. Measured density of Earth.

Cavendish, Thomas (*c* 1555-92), English navigator. Commanded 3rd circumnavigation of globe (1586-8), destroying Spanish shipping and settlements on W coast of South America. Died attempting similar voyage.

cave paintings, see ALTAMIRA; LASCAUX.

caviare, salted eggs of sturgeon prepared, mainly in USSR and Iran, as a table delicacy. Black Sea and Caspian are major areas for catching the sturgeon.

Cavour, Camillo Benso, Conte di (1810-61), Italian statesman. Premier of Sardinia (1852-9, 1860-1), secured French alliance which brought Sardinia's union with Lombardy after war with Austria (1859). Sponsored Garibaldi's campaign leading to unification (*Risorgimento*) of Italy under VICTOR EMMANUEL II.

cavy, any of various species of South American tailless rodents of Caviidae family. Guinea pig is domesticated form of Brazilian cavy, *Cavia aperea.*

Cawnpore, see KANPUR.

Caxton, William (*c* 1422-91), first English printer. Learned printing trade in Cologne and then printed in Bruges (1475) his own translation of *Recuyell of the Historyes of Troye,* 1st book pub. in English. Returned to England to set up press in Westminster, where he printed 1st dated book in England, *Dictes or Sayengis of the Philosophres* (1477).

Cayenne, cap. of French Guiana, Atlantic port on isl. at mouth of Cayenne R. Pop. 20,000. Original source of Cayenne pepper. Exports rum, gold. Had penal settlement 1854-1938.

cayenne, very hot red pepper made from dried pods of several species of *Capsicum,* native to South America.

Cayman Islands, coral group of West Indies, NW of Jamaica. Area 260 sq km (100 sq mi); pop. 10,000; cap.

Georgetown. Comprise Grand Cayman, Little Cayman, Cayman Brac. Famous for turtles; turtle products, shark skin exports. Admin. by Jamaica until 1962; British colony.

Ceará, state of NE Brazil. Area 148,015 sq km (757,149 sq mi); pop. 4,367,000. Cap. Fortaleza. In irrigated agric. region; exports cotton, sugar, carnauba wax.

Ceauşescu, Nicolae (1918-), Romanian political leader, president (1974-). Succeeded Gheorghiu-Dej as Communist Party general secretary (1965), continued policy of independence within Soviet bloc.

Cebu, isl. of Philippines. Area c 4400 sq km (1700 sq mi). Grows corn, sugar cane, peanuts; coal and copper mined. **Cebu** is chief town and port; pop. 385,000. Cap. of Spanish colony (1565-71). Has cross erected by Magellan (1521).

Cecil, Edgar Algernon Robert, 1st Viscount Cecil of Chelwood (1864-1958), British statesman. Helped draft Covenant of League of Nations. Awarded Nobel Peace Prize (1937).

Cecil, Lord [Edward Christian] David [Gascoyne] (1902-), English literary critic and biographer. Works incl. biog. of Cowper *The Stricken Deer* (1929), *Early Victorian Novelists* (1934), *The Young Melbourne* (1939).

Cecil, Robert, *see* SALISBURY, ROBERT CECIL, 1ST EARL OF.

Cecil, William, *see* BURGHLEY, WILLIAM CECIL, 1ST BARON.

cedar, coniferous tree of genus *Cedrus* of pine family, with short needle leaves arranged in close spiral on spine-like branches. Has durable wood with characteristic fragrance. Species incl. notable cedar of Lebanon, *C. libani.*

Cedar Rapids, town of E Iowa, US; on Cedar R. Pop. 111,000. Maize, livestock market; related agric. industs.

celandine, name of 2 unrelated plants. Lesser celandine, *Ranunculus ficaria,* of buttercup family is small herb with heart-shaped leaves and yellow flowers. Greater celandine, *Chelidonium majus,* of poppy family is erect, branched herb with divided leaves and yellow flowers.

Celebes

Celebes or **Sulawesi,** isl. of Indonesia. Area c 186,000 sq km (72,000 sq mi); pop. c 9,000,000. Irregular shape comprises 4 penins; largely mountainous with forests. Exports coffee, timber, copra, spices. Under Dutch control by 1670.

celery, *Apium graveolens,* biennial plant of parsley family, native to Europe and America. Blanched stem used in salads and as vegetable, dried leaves as flavouring.

celesta, orchestral keyboard instrument invented (1886) by Auguste Mustel in Paris. Hammers strike steel bars attached to wooden resonators.

Celestina, La, anon. Spanish prose work, original title *Comedia de Calisto y Melibea* (1499). In dramatic form, tells story of young gentleman who uses bawd Celestina to seduce young gentlewoman. Considerably influenced Spanish theatre and novel.

Céline, Louis-Ferdinand, pseud. of L.-F. Destouches (1894-1961), French novelist. Known for violently pessimistic *Voyage au bout de la nuit* (1932), *Mort à crédit* (1936). Renounced earlier communism in *Mea Culpa* (1937), turning to anti-Semitic fascism in *Bagatelles pour un massacre* (1937).

cell, fundamental unit of living matter. Consists of mass of protoplasm bounded by a membrane and, in case of plants, additional rigid cell wall. Usually contains central NUCLEUS

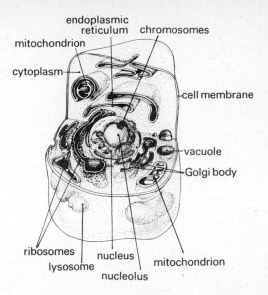

Animal cell

surrounded by cytoplasm, in which enzyme systems which control cell's metabolism are situated. Plant cells also contain chloroplasts in which photosynthesis takes place. Cells reproduce themselves by various methods of division. *See* MEIOSIS and MITOSIS.

cell, voltaic, device for producing electric current by chemical action. Two main types: primary cell and secondary cell or ACCUMULATOR. Primary cell usually irreversible in action. Variety of Leclanché cell, in which electrodes are carbon and zinc and electrolyte is ammonium chloride, used in common dry cell.

Cellini, Benvenuto (1500-71), Florentine sculptor, goldsmith. Famous works incl. gold salt-cellar and bronze statue *Perseus.* Best known for *Autobiography* giving vivid picture of artistic life in Rome and Florence.

cello or **violoncello,** low-pitched member of violin family. Developed in 17th cent., it gradually replaced bass viol as bass line in orchestras and chamber groups, and as solo instrument.

cellulose, chief constituent of cell walls or fibres of all plant tissue. White polymeric carbohydrate, insoluble in water. Nearly pure in the fibre of cotton, linen, hemp. Basis of nitrocellulose, celluloid, collodion and guncotton. Used in manufacture of rayon, plastics, explosives.

Celsius, Anders (1701-44), Swedish inventor, astronomer. Devised (1742) Celsius or centigrade temperature scale. Took boiling point of water as O° and freezing point as 100°; order later reversed.

Celtic, branch of Indo-European language family. Spoken throughout Europe before Roman conquest, now exists as 2 subgroups: Brythonic (Breton, Welsh, and extinct Cornish); Goidelic or Gaelic (Irish Gaelic, Scottish Gaelic and extinct Manx). Continental, 3rd subgroup, now extinct.

Celts, ancient people who inhabited W and C Europe. Associated with La Tène culture (beginning in 5th cent. BC), which saw development of iron working and characteristic linear art. Invaded N Italy in early 4th cent. BC and later reached Greece and Asia Minor. Romans gained control of their territs. in Italy by 222 BC and most of their territ. in France and Belgium during Gallic Wars (58-51 BC).

cement, material which bonds together 2 surfaces. Portland cement made by mixing powdered limestone and clay and heating product; mixed with water and sand to make mortar, or with sand, gravel and water to make concrete.

Cenozoic or **Cainozoic era,** fourth and most recent geological era, incl. time from end of Mesozoic era to present day. Began *c* 65 million years ago. Comprises Tertiary and Quaternary periods. Alpine, Himalayan mountain building; extensive glaciation; formation of deserts. Typified by evolution of modern flora and fauna; dominance of mammals, emergence of *Homo sapiens*. Also *see* GEOLOGICAL TABLE.

censorship, system in which circulation of writings, presentation of plays, films, TV programmes, works of art, *etc*, may in whole or part be prohibited. In UK, films are voluntarily submitted to British Board of Film Censors, sale of publications may be banned under Obscene Publications Act (1857); in US, there is film censorship in some states. Censorship is feature of totalitarian states.

census, official, usually periodic, count of population and recording of economic status, age, sex, *etc*. Estab. in ancient times amongst Jews, Romans for tax purposes. Census of England and Scotland first took place in 1801, has been done every 10 years since. In US, federal census began 1790, Bureau of Census estab. 1902.

centaur, in Greek myth, one of race of beings with upper body of human, lower of horse. Represented as tending to riotous living and wine, as in fight with Lapiths. *See* CHIRON.

centigrade temperature, *see* TEMPERATURE.

West Indian giant centipede

centipede, any carnivorous many-legged arthropod of class Chilopoda. Flat segmented body with poison claws on first segment; *c* 35 pairs of legs. Widely distributed; largest species *c* 30 cm/12 in. long.

CENTO, *see* CENTRAL TREATY ORGANIZATION.

Central, region of C Scotland. Area 2621 sq km (1012 sq mi); pop. 263,000. Created 1975, incl. former Stirlingshire, Clackmannanshire, SW Perthshire.

Central African Republic

Central African Republic, republic of C Africa. Area 623,000 sq km (241,000 sq mi); pop. 1,716,000; cap. Bangui. Languages: Sangho, French. Religions: native, Christian. Largely savannah-covered plateau, tropical forest in S; drained by Ubangi, Shari rivers. Cotton, coffee growing; diamond, uranium mining. Formerly Ubangi-Shari territ. of French Equatorial Africa, independent from 1960. Member of French Community.

Central America, isthmus connecting North and South America, comprising Guatemala, Costa Rica, Nicaragua, Honduras, Belize, El Salvador, Panama, and some Mexican states. Area 584,000 sq km (*c* 230,000 sq mi). Has many volcanic mountains, coastal plains; tropical climate. Subject to earthquakes. Bananas, coffee, cotton produce. Panama Canal links Caribbean, Pacific. Had ancient Maya

Central America

civilizations. Region comprised Central American Federation (1825-38).

Central American Common Market (CACM), body estab. (1960) by treaty to facilitate trade between members. Members originally Honduras, Nicaragua, Guatemala, Salvador, later joined by Costa Rica. Honduras withdrew after 1969.

Central Committee of the Communist Party, in USSR, executive, possessing real power over Supreme Soviet legislative structure. Its members elected from Party Congress, who, in turn, elect Politburo and Secretariat. Central Committee role reduced during Stalinist era.

Central Intelligence Agency (CIA), independent executive bureau of govt. of US estab. by National Security Act (1947) as centre for all foreign intelligence operations. Allen Dulles, director (1953-61), strengthened CIA and emboldened tactics. Scandal broke (1974) with discovery that CIA had been massively involved in illegal domestic espionage. Senate Intelligence Committee found (1975) CIA, from 1950s, had policy to assassinate foreign leaders, also attempted to block Allende's accession to power in Chile.

Central Treaty Organization (CENTO), defensive military alliance, formed 1955 by Iraq (withdrew 1958), Iran, Turkey, Pakistan and UK on basis of Baghdad Pact; US interests represented. Also provides for social and economic cooperation. Known as Middle East Treaty Organization until 1959.

centre of gravity, in physics, point on body where its weight can be considered as concentrated. Centre of mass defined similarly. These correspond in constant gravitational field.

centrifugation, means of separating solid, whose particles are too fine to be filtered, from a liquid. Liquid spun at high velocity so that centrifugal force moves denser material, *eg* suspended solids, to sides of tube containing liquid. Ultracentrifuge, working at greater speeds, used to determine particle size and molecular weights in polymers.

century plant, *Agave americana*, tropical American plant with fleshy leaves and tall stalk that bears greenish flowers only once after 10-30 years and then dies. Once mistakenly thought to bloom only once a century.

Cephalonia (*Kefallinia*), isl. of Greece, largest of Ionian Isls. Area 925 sq km (357 sq mi); main town Argostolion. Mountainous; fruit, wine. Disastrous earthquake 1953.

Cephalopoda (cephalopods), class of molluscs, incl. squid, octopus, cuttlefish, with prehensile tentacles around mouth. Usually no shell (*see* ARGONAUT). Numerous fossil species.

Ceram, isl. of Indonesia, in S Moluccas. Area *c* 17,000 sq km (6600 sq mi). Mountainous with dense forests in interior; produces copra, sago.

ceramics, art and science of making POTTERY.

Cerberus, in Greek myth, three-headed dog which guarded passage to and from the underworld (Hades). Dead were buried with honey cake to appease him on their journey. Last labour of Heracles was to capture him.

cereal, variety of annuals of grass family cultivated for edible fruit, known as grain. Cereal crops cover *c* ½ world's

Century plant

arable land, chief in order of acreage being wheat, rice, millet, sorghum, maize, barley, oats, rye. Some cereals fermented to make alcohol.

Ceres, Roman fertility goddess of the earth and growing corn, identified with Greek goddess DEMETER. Her temple on the Aventine Hill was centre of a plebeian cult.

cerium (Ce), soft metallic element of lanthanide group; at. no. 58, at. wt. 140.12. Alloyed with iron, used in lighter flints. Compounds used to make gas mantles.

Cerro de Pasco, town of WC Peru, alt. 4270 m (14,000 ft), one of world's highest towns. Pop. 21,000. Hist. famous silver mines (struck 1630); copper, vanadium now mined.

Cervantes

Cervantes [Saavedra], Miguel de (1547-1616), Spanish novelist. Known for satire of chivalric romance, *Don Quixote* (1605-15), influential in development of novel. Also wrote pastoral romances, *eg Novelas ejemplares* (1613), many plays.

cervix, see UTERUS.

Ceské Budejovice (Ger. *Budweis*), town of SW Czechoslovakia, on R. Moldau. Pop. 78,000. Beer mfg.; timber, graphite industs. Noted for Baroque architecture.

Cestoda (cestodes), class of ribbon-like flatworms without gut or mouth. Body divided into numerous segments. Parasitic in intestinal canals of vertebrates. Species incl. TAPEWORM.

Cetacea (cetaceans), order of aquatic fish-like mammals. No hind limbs; front limbs modified into flippers. Divided into toothed whales, *eg* dolphin, porpoise, sperm whale, and toothless whales, *eg* blue whale.

Cetewayo or **Ketchwayo** (*c* 1836-84), Zulu chieftain. Led determined resistance to British advances into his territ. until defeated (1879) at Ulundi.

Cetinje, town of SE Yugoslavia. Pop. 9000. Grew around monastery (1485); cap. of Montenegro until WWII.

Ceuta, Spanish enclave in NW Morocco. Area 18 sq km (7 sq mi); pop. 88,000. Free port and military post. Spanish from 1580, now part of Cádiz prov.

Cévennes, mountain range of S France, SE of Massif Central. Runs SW-NE for *c* 240 km (150 mi), highest peak Mont Mézenc (1754 m/ 5755 ft). Source of many rivers, incl. Loire, Allier, Lot. Largely barren limestone. Sheep rearing.

Ceylon, *see* SRI LANKA.

Cézanne: still life

Cézanne, Paul (1839-1906), French painter. Encouraged by Pissarro, he abandoned a violent romantic style for impressionist landscape technique. Later work was distinguished from impressionism by emphasis on structural analysis and use of tone and colour to express form. His attempts to reduce forms to their geometric equivalents influenced cubism. Works incl. sequence of bathers, portraits, still life.

c.g.s. system of units, system of physical units based on centimetre, gram and second. Superseded by SI units for scientific works.

Chabrier, [Alexis] Emmanuel (1841-94), French composer. Best-known work is the rhapsody *España*, written after a visit to Spain in 1882. His opera *Le Roi malgré lui* is still performed.

Chabrol, Claude (1930–), French film director, critic. Credited with starting *nouvelle vague* cinema technique. Early films incl. *Le Beau Serge* (1958), later ones, often centred around murder, incl. *The Beast Must Die* (1969), *The Butcher* (1970).

Chaco or **Gran Chaco,** large lowland plain of C South America, stretching from S Bolivia through Paraguay to N Argentina. Sparse pop.; unexploited resources. Bolivia and Paraguay warred for regional control (1932-5).

Chad, republic of NC Africa. Area 1,284,000 sq km (495,000 sq mi); pop. 3,868,000; cap. Ndjamena. Official language: French. Religions: native, Christian, Islam. Savannah in S; desert, Tibesti Mts. in N. Main river Shari, flows into L. Chad in SW. Cotton, peanut growing in S; nomadic pastoralism in N. Crossed by trans-Saharan caravan routes. Former territ. of French Equatorial Africa, independent from 1960. Member of French Community.

Chad, non-Semitic language group within Afro-Asiatic family. Incl. languages spoken in Nigeria, Cameroon, Chad, Central African Republic; most widespread language of group is Hausa.

Chad, Lake, lake of NC Africa. Mainly in SW Chad, partly in NE Nigeria, SE Niger, NW Cameroon. Area varies with season, up to *c* 26,000 sq km (10,000 sq mi); fed by R. Shari, no outlets. Now much smaller than when discovered (1823).

Chad

Chadwick, Sir Edwin (1800-90), British social reformer. Influenced by Bentham in reforms to poor law, public health, esp. through responsibility for Public Health Act (1848) and as commissioner to Board of Health (1848-54).

Chadwick, Sir James (1891-1974), English physicist. Discovered neutron during bombardment of beryllium by alpha particles (1932); awarded Nobel Prize for Physics (1935).

Chadwick, Lynn (1914-), English sculptor. Began sculpting career with mobiles. Later produced 'balanced sculpture' consisting of figures with thin legs, bulky bodies and bird-like heads.

Chaeronea, ancient town of Boeotia, EC Greece. Athens and Thebes defeated here (338 BC) by Philip II of Macedon; Mithradates VI defeated (86 BC) by Sulla. Birthplace of Plutarch.

Chaetognatha, phylum of transparent marine invertebrates (arrow-worms). Prey seized by bristle-like jaws.

Chaetopoda, class of annelid worms with bristles (chaetae) on body. Divided into 2 orders: mainly marine Polychaeta, incl. lugworm, ragworm, and terrestrial Oligochaeta.

chafer, insect of scarab beetle family. Herbivorous, destructive of plants. Species incl. COCKCHAFER.

chaffinch, *Fringilla coelebs,* finch common in European woodlands. Male has pinkish breast, white bars on brown wings.

Chagall, Marc (1889-), Russian painter. His imaginative, richly coloured art is based on reminiscences of Russian-Jewish village life; has designed stained glass and murals. Fantasies influenced surrealists. Lived mainly in France from 1910.

Chagos Archipelago, isl. group in C Indian Ocean, NE of Mauritius; part of British Indian Ocean Territ. Exports copra.

Chaillu, Paul Belloni du (*c* 1835-1903), American explorer, prob. b. Paris. Made 2 expeditions to Gabon (1855-9, 1863-5), returning to US with many new zoological and botanical specimens. Works incl. *Explorations in Equatorial Africa* (1861), *Journey to Ashango-Land* (1867).

Chain, Sir Ernst Boris (1906-), British biochemist, b. Germany. Shared Nobel Prize for Physiology and Medicine (1945) with Fleming and Florey for initiating work on penicillin.

chain reaction, in physics, self-sustaining nuclear reaction of FISSION type. Occurs when neutrons emitted from uranium 235 cause fission of further uranium nuclei. Basis of atomic bomb and nuclear reactors.

chalcedony, variety of silica, consisting mainly of extremely fine quartz crystals. Occurs in many different forms, some semi-precious, *eg* agate, bloodstone, chrysoprase, onyx.

Chalcidice (*Khalkidiki*), penin. of NE Greece, on Aegean Sea; modern admin. dist., cap. Polygyros. Incl. ATHOS. Wheat, olives, wine; magnesite mining. Colonized 7th cent. BC from Chalcis (whence name).

Chalcis (*Khalkis*), town of E Greece, cap. of Euboea admin. dist. Pop. 24,000. Port, agric. trade. Active colonizer (*eg*

Chalcidice, Sicily) from 8th cent. BC. Called Negropont in Middle Ages.

chalcopyrite ($CuFeS_2$), copper ore mineral. Sulphide of copper and iron; brass yellow in colour, tarnishes easily. Occurs in igneous and metamorphic rocks; widely distributed.

Chaldaeans, Semitic people who inhabited S Babylonia from *c* 1000 BC. Empire flourished under Nebuchadnezzar II but fell to Cyrus the Great (539 BC). Astrology reached high development in this period, hence term used loosely to denote astrologers.

Chaliapin, Feodor Ivanovich (1873-1938), Russian bass singer. Famous as Boris Godunov in Mussorgsky's opera. Also known for his recitals, at which he popularized the famous Russian folk song 'Song of the Volga Boatmen'.

chalk, soft, fine-grained limestone, white in colour. Consists mainly of calcareous skeletal material, laid down in Cretaceous period. Used to make putty, plaster, quicklime, cement.

Challoner, Richard (1691-1781), English RC churchman. Revised Douay Bible, his version becoming standard for English-speaking Catholics. Attacks by Protestant opponents culminated in flight from London during Gordon riots (1780).

Chalmers, Thomas (1780-1847), Scottish theologian. Leader of seceding Church of Scotland ministers who broke (1843) to form Free Church.

Châlons-sur-Marne, town of Champagne, NE France, on R. Marne. Cap. of Marne dept. Pop. 54,000. Centre of Champagne wine trade, brewing. Medieval textile indust. Scene of Aetius' and Theodoric's victory over Attila the Hun (451).

Chalon-sur-Saône, town of Burgundy, EC France, on R. Saône and Canal du Centre. Pop. 53,000. River port, wine and grain trade. Cap. of kingdom of Burgundy in 6th cent.

Chamberlain, Houston Stewart (1855-1927), Anglo-German writer, b. England. Known for *Foundations of the Nineteenth Century* (1899), forming doctrine of Teutonic superiority and anti-Semitism. Son-in-law of Richard Wagner.

Chamberlain, Joseph (1836-1914), British politician. Reform mayor of Birmingham (1873-6). Resigned (1886) from Gladstone's cabinet over Irish Home Rule policy, leading Liberal Unionist revolt. Colonial secretary (1893-1903), his imperial expansionist policies helped precipitate Boer War. Championed imperial preference tariffs, resigned 1903; this split coalition with Conservatives, leading to 1906 election defeat. His son, **Sir [Joseph] Austen Chamberlain** (1863-1937), was Conservative chancellor of exchequer (1903-6, 1919-21). Helped negotiate Irish settlement (1921). Foreign secretary (1924-9), instrumental in signing of LOCARNO PACT (1925) guaranteeing German borders; awarded Nobel Peace Prize (1925). His half-brother, **[Arthur] Neville Chamberlain** (1869-1940), was PM (1937-40). Chancellor of exchequer before succeeding Baldwin at head of National govt. Used 'appeasement' policy in attempting to limit Hitler in E Europe, signing MUNICH PACT (1938) over Czechoslovakia. Led Britain into WWII, resigning (1940) after German invasion of Norway.

Chamberlain, Wilt [on Norman] (1936-), American basketball player. Held all major scoring records, incl. 31,419 points during career (1959-73) in National Basketball Association. Stood 216 cm (7ft 1in.).

chamber music, music for performance by a small number of singers or players, *eg* a string quartet. Originally intended for performance in a private house but now mainly to be heard in smaller concert halls.

Chambers, Sir William (1723-96), British architect. Leading official architect of his day, his works incl. Somerset House, London (1776-86), and the pagoda in Kew Gardens.

Chambéry, town of SE France, cap. of Savoie dept. Pop. 54,000. Tourist centre; vermouth, silk mfg. Hist. cap. of Savoy. Cathedral (14th cent.).

chameleon, any of Chamaeleontidae family of lizard-like Old World reptiles. Long prehensile tail, eyes capable of

Common chameleon

independent movement. Extends tongue to catch insects. Undergoes colour change to match surroundings.

Chaminade, Cécile Louise Stéphanie (1857-1944), French composer and pianist. Known mainly for her graceful songs and piano pieces.

chamois, *Rupicapra rupicapra,* ruminant mammal intermediate between antelope and goat. Agile jumper, found in mountains of Europe and SW Asia. Name also applied to leather of animal.

chamomile, see CAMOMILE.

Chamonix, town of Savoy, E France, in Chamonix valley. Pop. 8000. Alpine resort, base for ascent of mountains in Mont Blanc region.

Champagne

Champagne, region and former prov. of NE France, cap. Troyes. Divided into 3 by parallel ridges; dairying in E, sheep rearing in C, champagne in W (esp. around Rheims, Epernay). Main rivers Aisne, Marne, Seine. Powerful medieval county, scene of famous trade fairs, *eg* Provins, Troyes. Incorporated into France (1314). Battleground in many wars.

champagne, sparkling white wine produced around Rheims and Epernay in Champagne district of France. Sparkling quality is obtained by adding cane sugar to wine which has been bottled following initial fermentation; this induces a secondary fermentation in the bottle.

Champaigne, Philippe de (1602-74), French painter. Court painter to Marie de' Medici and patronized by Richelieu, he was prominent painter of portraits and frescoes. Influenced by Jansenism after 1643, his work became simpler and more austere.

Champlain, Samuel de (1567-1635), French explorer. Made several voyages to E Canada and NE US; sailed up St Lawrence R. (1603), founded Port Royal (1605) and led 1st colonists to Québec (1608). Initiated fur trade; laid basis for French claims in North America.

Champlain, Lake, on New York-Vermont border, NE US; extends into S Québec (Canada). Length 201 km (125 mi). Fishing resort. Strategic region in Seven Years War, American Revolution (Fort Ticonderoga). Named after French explorer.

Champollion, Jean François (1790-1832), French archaeologist. Regarded as founder of science of Egyptology, deciphered Egyptian hieroglyphics (1822) with aid of ROSETTA STONE.

chancel, part of E end of church around altar, reserved for clergy and choir. Often separated by railings or screen from main body of church.

Chancellorsville, E Virginia, US. Site of Confederate General Lee's last great victory of American Civil War (1863) which led to his invasion of North in Gettysburg Campaign.

Chandigarh, joint cap. of Punjab and Haryana states, N India. Pop. 233,000. Built in 1950s to designs by Le Corbusier.

Chandler, Raymond Thornton (1888-1959), American detective story writer. Created cynical private detective, Philip Marlowe. Crime novels incl. *The Big Sleep* (1939), *Farewell, My Lovely* (1940).

Chandragupta Maurya (*fl* 321-296 BC), founder of Maurya dynasty in India. Conquered Magadha (321) and took control of most of N India. Defeated (305) Seleucus 1, who had invaded NW India to regain Alexander the Great's conquests.

Chanel, Gabrielle ('Coco') (1883-1971), French fashion designer. Founded fashion house in Paris (1914), dominating fashion world by 1924. Noted for successful scent (Chanel No. 5) and design of comfortable clothes.

Chaney, Lon (1883-1930), American film actor. Known for macabre disguises in horror films, *eg The Hunchback of Notre Dame* (1923), *The Phantom of the Opera* (1925).

Changchow, city of Kiangsu prov., E China. Pop. 300,000. Port on Grand Canal; important market centre; produces motor vehicles.

Changchun, cap. of Kirkin prov., NE China. Pop. 1,500,000. Railway jct.; major motor vehicle production centre, esp. trucks, tractors; film studios. Cap. of Manchukuo under Japanese (1934-45).

Changkiakow (*Kalgan*), city of Inner Mongolia auton. region, N China. Pop. 1,000,000. Trade centre, food processing. Military centre in Manchu dynasty, on caravan route between Peking and Ulan Bator.

Changsha, cap. of Hunan prov. SC China. Pop. 850,000. Port on R. Siang. Trade centre (rice, tea, timber), handicrafts (porcelain, embroidery). Treaty port in 19th cent.

Chankiang, see TSAMKONG.

Channel Islands (Fr. *Iles Normandes*), UK isl. group in S English Channel. Area 194 sq km (75 sq mi); pop. 126,000. Main isls. Jersey, Guernsey, Alderney, Sark; main town St Helier (Jersey). Separate laws, taxes; languages incl. English, French, Norman dialects. Market gardening, dairying, tourism. Isls. English from Norman Conquest (1066). German occupation (1940-5).

Channel swimming, sport of swimming across English Channel, first accomplished by M. WEBB (1875). First to make two-way crossing was Argentinian Antonio Abertondo (1961).

chansons de geste, medieval French epic poems (late 11th-early 14th cent.). More than 80 survive of which most important are in cycle *Geste du Roi*, on Charlemagne and vassals. Best known and oldest is *Chanson de Roland* (c 1098-1100). See ROLAND.

chant, a vocal melody usually sung as part of a ritual, often religious and often unaccompanied. The melody is usually sung in unison. PLAINSONG is a medieval religious chant from which Western art music grew.

Chantilly, town of Picardy, N France. Pop. 10,000. Horse racing centre; popular Parisian resort near Forest of Chantilly. Former lace mfg. centre. Hist. château.

Chao Phraya or **Menam,** river of Thailand. Rises in N highland near Laos, flows c 1200 km (750 mi) S to Gulf of Siam. Valley is rich rice growing area. Chief port Bangkok.

Chaos, in Greek myth, disordered void from which sprang GAEA, mother of all things earthly and divine.

Chapala, Lake, WC Mexico. Length 80 km (c 50 mi). On C plateau; largest lake in Mexico. Important tourism in surrounding area and isls. Waters are rapidly receding.

Chaplin, Sir Charles Spencer ('Charlie') (1889-), British film actor, producer, director. Famous for creation

Charlie Chaplin with 1972 Oscar

of tramp-like clown figure, with baggy pants, toothbrush moustache, distinctive walk. Worked first with Mack Sennett's Keystone Cops, later appeared in full-length features, *eg The Gold Rush* (1924).

Chapman, George (*c* 1560-1634), English poet, dramatist, translator. Best known for sophisticated verse translation *The Whole Works of Homer* (1616) which inspired Keats's sonnet. Also wrote philosophical tragedies, *eg Bussy d'Ambois* (1604), comedies.

char, food fish of salmon family, genus *Salvelinus,* inhabiting deep cold lakes. Arctic char, *S. alpinus,* is European variety, found in Norway. Also incl. brook trout of North America.

characin, predatory fish of Characinidae family of tropical Africa, America. Popular aquarium fish, often brightly coloured. Piranha is well-known species.

charcoal, *see* Carbon.

Charcot, Jean Martin (1825-93), French neurologist. Estab. major neurological clinic in Paris. Studied treatment of hysteria by hypnosis and influenced Freud, his pupil, in his early thinking on subject.

Chardin: *Vase of Flowers*

Chardin, Jean Baptiste Siméon (1699-1779), French painter. Noted for his still lifes and genre scenes of simple domestic interiors, devoid of sentimentality. Developed exceptional use of light and colour. Works incl. 2 self-portraits in pastel.

Charente, river of WC France. Flows *c* 355 km (220 mi) from Haute-Vienne dept. via Angoulême to Bay of Biscay opposite Oléron Isl. Region of cattle raising, cognac production.

charge, electric, fundamental attribute of elementary particles of matter. By convention, electron carries 1 negative unit of electric charge, proton 1 positive unit; matter containing excess of electrons is negatively charged, *etc.* Like charges repel each other, unlike charges attract each other. Measured in coulombs.

Chari, *see* Shari.

Chari-Nile, chief branch of Nilo-Saharan language family. Comprises languages spoken in Sudan, Zaïre, Uganda, Cameroon, Chad, Central African Republic, Kenya, Tanzania, Ethiopia.

Charites or **Graces,** in Greek myth, three sister goddesses, daughters of Zeus. Personification of charm and beauty in human life and nature. They are Aglaea (Brilliance), Euphrosyne (Joy), Thalia (Bloom).

Charlemagne or **Charles I** (742–814), king of the Franks (771-814), emperor of the West Romans (800-14). Son of Pepin the Short. Sole ruler of Franks on death of brother Carloman (771). In support of pope, defeated Lombards and became their king (774). Led campaign aginst Moors of NE Spain (778); subjugated Saxons (772-804), forced their conversion to Christianity. Crowned emperor by Leo III, whose papal ambitions he had supported; created strong empire by estab. marches, efficient admin. His court at Aachen (Fr. *Aix-la-Chapelle*) became centre of learning, classical studies; famous scholars incl. Alcuin, Einhard. Life became centre of medieval cycle of romance and legend, notably in the *Chanson de Roland* (prob. written 11th cent.).

Charles I : detail of Honthorst's portrait

Charleroi, town of S Belgium, on R. Sambre. Pop. 24,000. Coalmining, steel mfg. Canal link with Brussels.

Charles [II] the Bald (823-77), king of West Franks (843-77), Holy Roman emperor (875-7). With brother, Louis the German, defeated Lothair I at Fontenoy (841); became West Frankish king by Treaty of Verdun (843). Succeeded Louis II as emperor (875).

Charles [III] the Fat (839-888), king of West Franks (884-7), Holy Roman emperor (881-7). Son of Louis the German; also king of Italy from 879. Deposed 886 by Arnulf following weakness in fighting Norse invaders.

Charles IV or **Charles of Luxembourg** (1316-78), king of Bohemia (1346-78), king of Germany (1347-78), Holy Roman emperor (1355-78). Son of John of Luxembourg. Founded univ. at Prague (1348); issued Golden Bull (1356) on matter of imperial elections.

Charles V (1500-58), Holy Roman emperor (1519-58), king of Spain as Charles I (1516-56). Son of Philip I of Castile, became greatest Habsburg and most powerful ruler in Europe. Wars against France during 1520s ended in consolidation of influence over papacy. Promoted Catholic reform with Council of Trent (1545). Enlarged Spanish empire in Americas, conquering Mexico and Peru. After 1530, increasingly delegated powers in Germany to his brother, later Ferdinand I. Fierce opponent of Protestantism, broke power of Reformation princes in Germany (1547), but later signed Peace of Augsburg (1555) allowing choice of religion to be made by individual princes. Retired to monastery (1556).

Charles VI (1685-1740), Holy Roman emperor (1711-40), king of Hungary as Charles III. Unsuccessfully claimed Spanish throne, instigating war (1701-14). Had no male heir, circumvented succession problem by issuing PRAGMATIC SANCTION, passing Habsburg lands on to his daughter, Maria Theresa.

Charles VII (1697-1745), Holy Roman emperor (1742-5). Elector of Bavaria as Charles Albert (1726-45). Disputed succession (1740) under PRAGMATIC SANCTION; joined alliance against Maria Theresa, elected to throne (1742), losing his own Bavarian territ.

Charles (1887-1922), emperor of Austria (1916-18), also king of Hungary (as Charles IV). Succeeded great uncle Francis Joseph; deposed after unsuccessful attempt to make separate peace with Allies in WWI. Twice failed in coups to regain Hungary. Died in exile.

Charles I (1600-49), king of England, Scotland and Ireland (1625-49). Succeeding father James I, offended public by Catholic marriage. Struggle with Puritan-dominated Parliament led to Petition of Right (1628) asserting Parliament's supremacy. Charles ruled repressively without Parliament (1629-40) until Scottish wars forced him to recall it. Long Parliament of 1640 had STRAFFORD beheaded and ended arbitrary taxation and Star Chamber courts. Defeated in ensuing CIVIL WAR (1642-6), captured 1646. Tried by Puritan-controlled court, convicted of treason and beheaded.

Charles II (1630-85), king of England, Scotland and Ireland (1660-85). Fled to France (1646), crowned king in Scotland (1651) after father Charles I's death; escaped again when defeated by Cromwell. Restored as king (1660), aided by CLARENDON, his chief minister. CABAL ministry replaced Clarendon in 1667. Charles entered 2 Dutch wars to assert commercial supremacy. Secretly allied with France (1670), promising to restore Catholicism. Forced to approve TEST ACT (1673), directed against Catholics; later blocked Exclusion Act (1681) against his brother James by dissolving Parliament, after which he ruled absolutely. No legitimate heirs, succeeded by brother. Important features of reign incl. development of political parties, advances in trade and sea power, territ. expansion and growth of Parliament's power.

Charles [V] the Wise (1337-80), king of France (1364-80). Served as regent during father John II's captivity, suppressing JACQUERIE uprising. Reformed taxation, strengthened army and navy; his general, du GUESCLIN, warred successfully against Navarre, English forces in France.

Charles [VI] the Well Beloved (1368-1422), king of France (1380-1422). Under power of regent until 1388; insane after 1392. Rival factions fought for power, leading to civil war between houses of Orléans (Armagnacs) and Burgundy. Invasion and victory of Henry V of England at Agincourt (1415) led to Treaty of Troyes (1420) recognizing Henry as Charles's successor.

Charles VII (1403-61), king of France (1422-61). Excluded from succession by father Charles VI, ruled from Bourges until Joan of Arc raised siege of Orléans and had him crowned at Rheims (1429). During reign, English expelled from all France except Calais, ending Hundred Years War.

Charles X (1757-1836), king of France (1824-30). Led ultra-royalist group before following his brother, Louis XVIII, to throne. Abdicated after liberal-inspired July Revolution. Died in exile.

Charles I, orig. Charles Robert of Anjou (1288-1342), king of Hungary (1308-42). Son-in-law of Stephen V of Hungary, his election as king initiated Hungarian branch of Angevin dynasty. Reorganized army; secured succession of son Louis I to Polish throne.

Charles I, orig. Charles of Anjou (1226-85), king of Naples and Sicily (1266-85). Initiated Angevin dynasty in Naples; gained political hegemony over Italy as leader of Guelphs.

Conquered Albania. Sicilian Vespers revolt (1282) led to war with Peter III of Aragon over throne of Sicily.

Charles II (1661-1700), king of Spain (1665-1700). Last of Spanish Habsburgs, constantly at war with Louis XIV. Died childless, precipitating WAR OF THE SPANISH SUCCESSION.

Charles III (1716-88), king of Spain (1759-88). King of Naples and Sicily after 1735, succeeded Ferdinand VI on Spanish throne. Brought Spain into SEVEN YEARS WAR and American Revolution against British (1779).

Charles IV (1748-1819), king of Spain (1788-1808). Reign dominated by chief minister, Godoy, who favoured involvement in French Revolutionary Wars; Spain withdrew 1795. Alliance with France (1796) led to disastrous Peninsular War (1807). Forced to abdicate in favour of his son, Ferdinand, after which both were held captive by Napoleon until 1814.

Charles [Gustavus] X (1622-60), king of Sweden (1654-60). Invaded Poland (1655), captured Warsaw and Kraków; forced to withdraw after unsuccessful siege of Czestochowa. Wars with Denmark (1658-60) resulted in territ. expansion into Danish lands in Sweden.

Charles XII (1682-1718), king of Sweden (1697-1718). Challenged by alliance of Denmark, Poland and Russia, routed Danes and defeated Peter the Great at Narva (1700), crushed Poland. Campaign in Russia (1708-9) ended in defeat at Poltava; fled to Turkey, failed to gain continued support from Ahmed III after Russo-Turkish peace (1711). Invaded Norway (1716), killed during siege of Fredrikssten. Despite strategic flair, failed to consolidate successes and Sweden entered decline as major power.

Charles XIV (1763-1844), king of Sweden and Norway (1818-44). Born in France as Jean Baptiste Jules Bernadotte, became one of Napoleon's marshals. Adopted (1810) as heir to Swedish throne by Charles XIII, for whom he ruled. Joined alliance against Napoleon; secured union of Sweden and Norway (1814) before ascending throne. Economic progress during his reign; lost popular support through anti-liberal policy.

Charles [Philip Arthur George], Prince of Wales (1948-   ), heir to British throne. Son of Elizabeth II and Prince Philip.

Charles, Jacques Alexandre César (1746-1823), French physicist. Evolved Charles' law: at constant pressure volume of gas is directly proportional to its absolute temperature. Made 1st successful ascent in hydrogen balloon.

Charles Albert (1798-1849), king of Sardinia (1831-49). Avoided revolution by granting constitution (1848). Warred with Austria in Italy; defeated at Novara, abdicated in favour of his son, Victor Emmanuel II.

Charles Martel (c 688-741), Frankish ruler. Grandfather of Charlemagne. United Merovingian kingdoms of Austrasia, Neustria under his rule. Thwarted Moslem invasion of Europe with victory at Poitiers (732).

Charles the Bold (1433-77), last duke of Burgundy (1467-77). Son of Philip the Good, father of Mary of Burgundy. Confirmed opponent of Louis XI of France. Aimed to restore Lotharingian kingdom; killed while fighting Swiss after he had annexed Lorraine.

Charleston, port of S South Carolina, US; on Atlantic inlet. Pop. 67,000. Naval depot; timber, fruit, cotton exports. Settled by English (1670). Civil War opened with Confederates firing on Fort Sumter (1861); besieged by Union forces (1863-5). Has famous botanical gardens.

Charleston, cap. of West Virginia, US; on Kanawha R. Pop. 230,000. Rail, trade and indust. centre. Oil refining; chemical, glass mfg. Expanded around Fort Lee; became permanent state cap. 1885. Home of Daniel Boone.

Charlevoix, Pierre François Xavier de (1682-1761), French Jesuit missionary. Travels in Canada and S to Louisiana recorded in *Histoire de la Nouvelle France* (1744), 1st detailed description of C North America.

charlock, *Brassica arvensis*, plant of mustard family with yellow flowers, seedpods. Pernicious weed in Britain. Seeds can lie dormant for c 50 years.

Charles XII of Sweden

Charlotte, city of SC North Carolina, US; in Piedmont region. Pop. 241,000; state's largest city. Transport jct.; cotton, textiles, chemical mfg.

Charlottetown, seaport of Canada; cap. of Prince Edward Isl., on S coast. Pop. 19,000. Exports dairy produce, potatoes. Settled 1768; scene of Canadian confederate conference (1864). Has RC St Dunstan's Univ. (1855).

Charlton, Robert ('Bobby') (1937-), English footballer. Outstanding forward for Manchester United and England; played 106 times for England (1958-70). Renowned for sportsmanship.

charm, in nuclear physics, supposed fundamental attribute of elementary particles, manifested by non-zero charm quantum number. First predicted theoretically, its status was enhanced by discovery (1974) of the psi (J) particle, believed to be composed of a new type of charmed QUARK and corresponding anti-quark.

Charon, in Greek myth, boatman of R. Styx who ferried souls of the dead to underworld (Hades). A coin was placed in the mouth of the dead to pay for this service.

Charpentier, Gustave (1860-1956), French composer. Best known for orchestral piece *Impressions of Italy* and opera *Louise*.

Chartier, Alain (c 1385-c 1433), French poet. Known for anti-English prose pamphlet *Le Quadrilogue invectif* (1422) and poem 'La Belle Dame sans mercy' (1424). Secretary to Charles VI.

Chartism, movement in Britain for social and political reform, estab. 1838. Roots lay in decline in working class conditions during economic depression of 1830s. Principles contained in 'People's Charter', submitted to Parliament: universal manhood suffrage, equal election dists., vote by ballot, annual parliaments, abolition of property qualification for MPs, payment of MPs. Petition's rejection followed by riots; movement declined in 1840s, esp. after 1848. Brought about some legislation but important indust. reform was to come with development of trade unions.

Chartres, town of N France, on R. Eure, cap. of Eure-et-Loir dept. Pop. 37,000. Market town; tourist and pilgrimage centre. Medieval county, duchy from 1528. Famous Gothic cathedral (12th-13th cent.) with 2 spires, 13th cent. stained-glass windows.

Chartreuse, Grande, mountain group of SE France, in Dauphiné Alps. Highest peak Chamechaude (2085 m/6847 ft). Monastery (1084), principal seat of Carthusian order until 1903, produces famous liqueur.

Charybdis, in Greek myth, *see* SCYLLA.

Chase, Salmon Portland (1808-73), American statesman. Opposed slavery while serving in Senate. As treasury secretary (1861-4), originated national bank system. Chief justice of Supreme Court (1864-73), presided over impeachment trial of President Johnson (1868).

chat, insectivorous bird of thrush family, esp. of genera *Cercomela* and *Saxicola*. Whinchat and stonechat are species. Yellow-breasted chat is largest North American warbler.

château, term originally denoting a French medieval castle. With development of castles into places of residence rather than defence in 15th and 16th cents., name came to describe large country houses and estates. Famous examples found in Loire valley.

Chateaubriand, François René, Vicomte de (1768-1848), French author, diplomat. Forerunner of French romanticism through egoism, impassioned prose, interest in the exotic. Works incl. novels *Atala* (1801), *Les Natchez* (1826) dealing with Red Indians, autobiog. *Mémoires d'Outre-tombe* (1848-50).

Châteauroux, town of Berry, C France, on R. Indre. Cap. of Indre dept. Pop. 51,000. Agric. market, woollens mfg., brewing. Grew around 10th cent. castle, seat of medieval lords of Déols.

Château-Thierry, town of Brie, N France, on R. Marne. Pop. 12,000. Produces musical and scientific instruments. Scene of many battles, esp. in WWI.

Chatham, 1st Earl of, *see* PITT, WILLIAM.

Chatham, mun. bor of Kent, SE England. Pop. 57,000. Naval base, estab. by Henry VIII; has naval barracks (1897), hospital (1907).

Chatham Islands, isl. group of New Zealand, in SW Pacific Ocean. Area 965 sq km (372 sq mi). Small Maori pop. with main occupations sheep farming, fishing. Discovered (1791) by British.

Chattanooga, town of SE Tennessee, US; on Tennessee R. Pop. 119,000. Timber products, machinery mfg. Centre of Tennessee Valley Authority irrigation and h.e.p. schemes. Strategic area (1863) during Civil War.

Chattanooga campaign, a series of engagements (1863) in the American Civil War, notably Chickamauga, Lookout Mt., and Missionary Ridge (Nov.) where Grant defeated the Confederates, who withdrew to Georgia.

Chatterji, Bankim Chandra (1838-94), Indian novelist. Works, esp. *Durges-Nandini* (1864), found favour with nationalists. Wrote Indian national song 'Bande-Mataram'.

The Death of Thomas Chatterton by Henry Wallis

Chatterton, Thomas (1752-70), English poet. Known for 'forgeries' of poetry by imaginary 15th cent. priest, Thomas Rowley. Work has considerable imaginative, poetic power, eg 'An Excelente Balade of Charitie'. His suicide made him a hero of later Romantics.

Chaucer, Geoffrey (c 1340-1400), English poet. Member of king's household, holder of various official posts, employed on missions to Continent. First important poems derived from French works, in content or style, eg *Romaunt of the Rose* (c 1370) and *Boke of the Duchesse* (1369). After visiting Italy influenced by Dante (*House of Fame,* c 1379-80) and Boccaccio, whose *Filostrato* he used for *Troilus and Criseyde* (c 1385-6). Best known for unfinished cycle *Canterbury Tales* (c 1387), collection of 23 tales narrated by pilgrims en route from London to Canterbury. Works preeminent in estab. of modern English as literary language.

Cheboksary, town of USSR, cap. of Chuvash auton. republic, E European RSFSR. Pop. 227,000. Agric. centre on Volga; h.e.p. station.

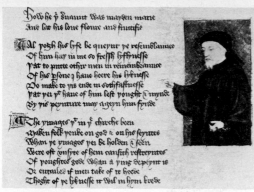

Portrait of Chaucer in a 15th century manuscript by Hoccleve

check, see CHEQUE.
checkers, see DRAUGHTS.
cheese, food made from curds of soured milk. Numerous varieties of cheese are usually divided into hard cheeses, *eg* Cheddar, Edam and Gouda, and soft cheeses, *eg* Brie and Camembert. Various micro-organisms introduced into cheese produce characteristic flavours, *eg* those of Stilton. Leading cheese producers incl. England, Holland, Switzerland, Italy.

Cheetah

cheetah, *Acinonyx jubatus,* dog-like cat of grasslands and semi-deserts of Africa, SW Asia. Small head, long legs, black-spotted tawny coat. Fastest of all land mammals, reaching speeds of 95 km/60 mph.
Chefoo, port of Shantung prov., NE China; formerly Yentai. Pop. 180,000. Fishing port; orchards; produces wine, brandy. Treaty port in 19th cent., opened to foreign trade in 1858.
Chekhov, Anton Pavlovich (1860-1904), Russian dramatist and short story writer. Known for plays dealing with hopelessness of communication, *eg The Seagull* (1896), *Uncle Vanya* (1899), *Three Sisters* (1901), *The Cherry Orchard* (1904), now classics. Stories incl. *Ward No. 6* (1892), and *The Lady with the Dog* (1899).
Chekiang, maritime prov. of E China. Area *c* 103,600 sq km (40,000 sq mi); pop. (est.) 31,000,000; cap. Hangchow. Contains fertile Yangtze delta (rice). Mountainous, densely populated. Rice, tea, wheat, cotton grown.
Chelmsford, mun. bor. and co. town of Essex, SE England. Pop. 58,000. Light industs. Church (1424, rebuilt 19th cent.) now cathedral.
Chelonia, order of reptiles, comprising tortoises and turtles. Body encased in firm shell of polygonal dermal plates.
Chelsea, see KENSINGTON AND CHELSEA, England.
Cheltenham, mun. bor. of Gloucestershire, W England. Pop. 70,000. Spa from 18th cent.; has famous racecourse, public school (1841).
Chelyabinsk, city of USSR, SW Siberian RSFSR. Pop. 910,000. Railway jct.; indust. centre; produces steel, zinc, agric. machinery.

chemical engineering, branch of ENGINEERING dealing with design, construction and operation of plants and machinery for industrial mfg. of chemicals, *eg* acids, dyes, synthetic plastics.
chemical warfare, the use of POISON GAS or liquids as a weapon, started by the ancient Greeks with sulphur fumes. Prohibited by the Hague Declaration (1899) but employed with deadly effect by the Germans in WWI, using chlorine, phosgene and mustard gas. Again outlawed at the Washington Conference (1922) it was not used in WWII.
chemistry, science concerned with composition of substances and their reactions with one another. Usually divided into organic, inorganic and physical chemistry. Organic chemistry deals with compounds of carbon, excluding metal carbonates and oxides and sulphides of carbon. Inorganic chemistry deals with elements and their compounds, excluding organic carbon compounds. Physical chemistry is application of physical measurements and laws to chemical systems and their changes.
Chemnitz, see KARL-MARX-STADT, East Germany.
Chengchow, cap. of Honan prov., EC China. Pop. 1,500,000. Rail jct.; textile centre; meat packing, fertilizer mfg.
Chengteh, city of Hopeh prov., NE China. Pop. 200,000. Lumber, pharmaceuticals. Former summer capital of Ching dynasty with palaces, gardens, Lamaist temple.
Chengtu, cap. of Szechwan prov., SC China. Pop. 2,000,000. Port on R. Min. Textile, paper mfg. Cultural, commercial centre; 2 univs. Ancient cap. of Shu Han dynasty 3rd cent.
Chénier, André Marie de (1762-94), French poet, b. Istanbul. *Bucoliques, Elégies,* reflect love of Greek antiquity. Also wrote philosophical poetry, *eg L'Invention* (1819). Supporter of Revolution but executed during Reign of Terror.
Chennault, Claire Lee (1890-1958), American general, airman. Pioneered fighter tactics in WWI. Organized Chiang Kai-shek's air defences; estab. (1941) American Volunteer Group of airmen ('Flying Tigers').
Cheops, see KHUFU.
Chepstow, urban dist. of Gwent, SE Wales on R. Wye. Pop. 6000. Market town. Tubular bridge built by Brunel (1852). Tintern Abbey is nearby.
cheque or **check,** written order to a bank to pay the stated amount of money from one's account. Used in Italy in 15th cent., now principal medium of exchange.
Chequers, Tudor mansion and estate near Wendover, Buckinghamshire, England. Official country residence of UK prime minister. Presented to nation in 1921.
Cherbourg, town of Normandy, N France, on N coast of Cotentin penin. Pop. 40,000. Transatlantic port; major fortified naval base from 17th cent.
Cheremkhovo, city of USSR, SC Siberian RSFSR. Pop. 127,000. Centre of coal mining area; chemicals mfg., oil refining.
Cherenkov, Pavel Alekseyich (1904-), Soviet physicist. Discovered Cherenkov effect when high energy charged particles move through medium at velocity exceeding that of light in the medium; used in detection of subatomic particles. Shared Nobel Prize for Physics (1958).
Cherepovets, town of USSR, NW European RSFSR. Pop. 205,000. Supplies iron and steel to Leningrad area; chemicals mfg.
Cheribon, see TJIREBON.
Cherkasov, Nikolai Konstantinovich (1903-66), Russian actor. Known in West for title roles of films *Alexander Nevsky* (1938), *Ivan the Terrible* (1945).
Chernigov, city of USSR, N Ukrainian SSR. Pop. 177,000. Port on R. Desna; transport hub. Cap. of principality in 11th cent., has Byzantine cathedral dating from this time.
Chernovtsy (Romanian *Cernauti*), town of USSR, W Ukrainian SSR. Pop. 196,000. Textile, machinery mfg. Grew under Austro-Hungarian rule (1775-1918) as cap. of Bukovina; in Romania (1918-40).
chernozem, see BLACK EARTH.

Cherokee, North American Indian tribe of Hokan-Siouan linguistic stock. Largest tribe in SE US. Settled farmers with advanced culture. Frequently fought Iroquois and were valuable allies of British against the French. Estab. (1827) Cherokee Nation with govt. modelled on that of white colonists. Became US citizens (1906), a few remain in North Carolina.

cherry, tree of genus *Prunus* of rose family. Smooth stone enclosed in fleshy, usually edible fruit. Native to Asia Minor. Most varieties are derived from sweet-cherry, *P. avium.*

Cherubini

Cherubini, [Maria] Luigi (1760-1824), Italian composer. Lived in Paris from 1788 and became director of Paris Conservatoire in 1822. Composed several operas, incl. *Medea* and *The Water-carrier* (French title *Les deux journées*).

chervil, *Anthriscus cerefolium,* annual herb of parsley family with sweet, aromatic leaves used for flavouring in cookery. Native to Russia, reaching Mediterranean area *c* 300 BC.

Chesapeake Bay, largest Atlantic inlet of US; separates E Maryland and part of Virginia from mainland. Length 320 km (*c* 200 mi). Important oyster, crab fisheries.

Cheshire, county of NW England. Area 2322 sq km (896 sq mi); pop. 896,000; co. town Chester. Wirral penin. in NW; low-lying, drained by Mersey, Dee. Dairying, esp. cheese; shipbuilding; salt, chemical industs.

chess, game for 2 players, each with 16 pieces, played on a board divided into 64 squares, alternately black and white. Pieces are moved according to conventional rules. Prob. originated in India, later spreading to Persia and Middle East. Popular in W Europe by 13th cent.

chest, in human anatomy, same as THORAX.

Chester, city and co. town of Cheshire, NW England, on R. Dee. Pop. 63,000. Railway jct.; metal goods mfg. Roman *Devana Castra;* only English city with medieval walls intact. Cathedral dates from Norman times; has 16th-17th cent. timbered houses.

Chesterfield, Philip Dormer Stanhope, 4th Earl of (1694-1773), English statesman, man of letters. Remembered for *Letters to His Son* (pub. 1774), written to his bastard son.

Chesterfield, mun. bor. of Derbyshire, NC England. Pop. 70,000. Indust. centre in coalmining area. Has 14th cent. church with twisted spire.

Chesterton, G[ilbert] K[eith] (1874-1936), English author. Known for novels of ideas, *eg The Napoleon of Notting Hill* (1904), *The Man Who Was Thursday* (1908); 'Father Brown' detective stories. Also wrote literary criticism, RC apologia, *eg St Thomas Aquinas* (1933).

chestnut, tree of genus *Castanea* of beech family found in N temperate regions. Species incl. edible sweet or Spanish chestnut, *C. sativa,* American chestnut, *C. dentata,* and

G.K. Chesterton

Japanese chestnut *C. crenata.* Fruit is burr-like, containing 2-3 nuts. Wood is strong and durable. *See* HORSE CHESTNUT.

Chevalier, Maurice (1888-1972), French film actor, singer. Achieved fame in Paris revues of 1920s, became international film star in 1930s; known for accent, boater, charm. Films incl. *Love Me Tonight* (1932), *Gigi* (1958).

Cheviot Hills, range on Scotland-England border, rising to 815 m (2676 ft) on The Cheviot. Sheep rearing (Cheviot breed).

Chevreul, Michel Eugène (1786-1889), French chemist. Researched into colour contrasts and animal fats. Isolated stearic, oleic and palmitic acids, important in modern manufacture of soap and candles.

chevrotain or **mouse deer,** mammal of Tragulidae family of forests of Asia, Africa. Resembles deer, but has no antlers. Smallest of ruminants, reaches heights of 30 cm/1 ft.

chewing gum, gummy substance usually made from chicle, with added flavouring and sweeteners. Patented in US in 1869.

Whirlwind, a Cheyenne chief

Cheyenne, North American Indian tribe of Algonquian linguistic stock. Originally farmers on Cheyenne R., became nomadic buffalo hunters after introduction of horse (*c* 1760). Colorado gold discovery (1858) forced Cheyenne into reservation where govt. neglect provoked raids by the Indians, who were then massacred by US army at Sand Creek (1864). A few remain in Montana.

Cheyenne, cap. of Wyoming, US; in extreme S of state. Pop. 41,000. Transport jct., commercial centre in cattle rearing region. Territ. cap. 1869; grew with cattle, gold booms of 1870s.

Chiang Kai-shek

Chickpea

Chiang Kai-shek (1887-1975), Chinese military and political leader. Emerged as head of revolutionary Kuomintang in 1920s, leading expedition (1926-8) in N resulting in overthrow of Peking govt. Leader (1928-48), ruled with extensive power. Fought local warlords and, with Communists, resisted Japanese invasions; later driven from mainland (1950) in civil war with Communists. After 1950, challenged Communists from Taiwan-based Nationalist govt., pledged to return to mainland.

Chianti, Monti, small mountain range of Tuscany, C Italy, W of R. Arno. Grapes for Chianti wine grown on slopes.

Chiba, city of Japan, on Tokyo Bay, Honshu isl. Pop. 482,000. Steel, paper and textile mfg. Has Buddhist temple (8th cent.).

Chibcha, South American Indians of E Andes of Colombia. Most populous and highly developed state between Mexico and Peru at time of Spanish conquest. Conquered by 1541. Probable source of the legend of El Dorado; rulers covered in gold dust in annual ceremony.

Chicago, port of NE Illinois, US; on SW shore of L. Michigan. Transport and indust. hub of US Middle West. Pop. 3,369,000. Shipping, railway centre; important grain market; large meatpacking indust., machinery mfg. Growth began after completion of Erie Canal. Became a city (1837); devastated by fire (1871). Has Univ. of Chicago (1892); Art Institute.

Chichén Itzá, ruin of E Mexico, ancient Mayan city state on Yucatán penin. Founded in 6th cent. by the Itzá. Important archaelogical site with pyramids, temples, statues.

Chichester, Sir Francis (1901-72), English yachtsman, aviator. Made 1st E-W solo flight across Tasman Sea (1931). Best known for sailing around world single-handed in *Gipsy Moth IV* (1966-7).

Chichester, city and co. town of West Sussex, SE England, Pop. 21,000. Agric. market. Roman remains incl. amphitheatre; has church (11th cent.) with separate bell tower. Goodwood racecourse nearby.

chickadee, small North American tit of Paridae family. Black-capped chickadee, *Parus atricapillus,* found in E US.

chicken, see FOWL.

chickenpox, infectious virus disease, usually of young children. Characterized by eruption of small spots which later become blisters. Incubation period of 2 to 3 weeks.

chickpea, bushy annual plant, *Cicer arietinum,* of Leguminosae family. Cultivated in India for edible seeds contained in pods.

chickweed, low annual or perennial herb of genus *Stellaria* of pink family, native to temperate regions. Small, white flowers. Old World weed, *S. media,* is well-known species of lawns and gardens.

Chiclayo, town of NW Peru, on Pacific coastal plain. Pop. 135,000. In agric. region, producing sugar cane, rice; related industs.

chicle, gum-like substance derived from latex of tropical American trees, esp. sapodilla, *Achras sapota,* of Yucatán and Guatemala. Introduced into US as rubber substitute and basis of chewing gum.

chicory, *Cichorium intybus,* European annual plant, also grown in US. Leaves used in salads; root ground and roasted as coffee substitute. *See* ENDIVE.

Chicoutimi, port and lumber town of EC Québec, Canada; at confluence of Saguenay and Chicoutimi rivers. Pop. 34,000. Pulp and paper centre (with nearby Jonquière; pop. 28,000).

Chiemsee, lake of Bavaria, SE West Germany. Area 83 sq km (32 sq mi); alt. 518 m (1700 ft). Palace built in imitation of Versailles on isl. by Ludwig II.

chiffchaff, *Phylloscopus collybita,* European bird of warbler family. Olive-green and brown; distinctive song, giving rise to name.

chiffon, sheer lightweight fabric made of silk, rayon or cotton. Delicate and transparent, it is used in scarves and blouses, *etc.*

Chifley, Joseph Benedict (1885-1951), Australian statesman, PM (1945-9). Railway union activist, entered Parliament 1928. Held several Labor cabinet posts incl. treasurer from 1941 before becoming leader. His govt. strengthened position of central bank as means of countering depression.

chigger, minute reddish larva of certain mites. Parasitic on vertebrates, its saliva causes severe itch. *Trombicula irritans* is American species.

chigoe or **jigger,** *Tunga penetrans,* small flea parasitic on humans, domestic animals. Female bores into flesh, feeding on blood; causes serious sores. Widespread in tropics.

Chihli, see HOPEH and POHAI, GULF OF.

Chihuahua, town of N Mexico, cap. of Chihuahua state. Pop. 289,000. On C plateau in cattle-raising, mining region; textile mfg., smelting indust.

chihuahua, small dog, probably descended from the Techichi of the Toltecs of Mexico. Large pointed ears; stands 13 cm/5 in. high at shoulder.

chilblain, painful inflammation of skin of hands and feet, caused by contraction of blood vessels in response to cold.

Childe, Vere Gordon (1892-1957), British archaeologist, b. Australia. Known for study of European prehistory, *Dawn of European Civilization* (1939). Excavated Skara Brae in Orkney (1928-30).

Chile, republic of W South America. Area 756,945 sq km (292,256 sq mi); pop. 10,045,000; cap. Santiago. Language: Spanish. Religion: RC. Comprises narrow coastal strip W of Andes extending S to Tierra del Fuego, with outlying Easter, Juan Fernández isls. Important mining in Atacama Desert region (copper, nitrates, iron ore). Agric. in SC valleys (sheep, cattle rearing). Conquered by Spanish in

Smooth Chihuahua

Chile

16th cent.; Indian resistance until 19th cent. Independence gained under San Martín (1818); gained N region in war with Bolivia, Peru (1879-84). First South American country to elect Marxist govt. (1970); fell in military coup (1973).

chili, *see* PEPPER.

Chillon, fortress at E end of L. Geneva, Switzerland. Mainly built 13th cent.; scene of Byron's *Prisoner of Chillon.*

Chiloé Island, forested isl. off SW Chile. Area 8394 sq km (3241 sq mi). Largest of Chilean isls. Exports timber.

Chilopoda, *see* CENTIPEDE.

Chiltern Hills, SC England. Chalk range *c* 88 km (55 mi) long, running SW-NE through Oxfordshire, Buckinghamshire, Hertfordshire.

Chilung or **Keelung,** seaport and naval base of N Taiwan. Pop. 334,000. Chemical mfg., shipbuilding.

Chimaera, in Greek myth, fire-breathing monster with lion's head, goat's body, dragon's tail. Killed by Bellerophon.

chimaera, cartilaginous fish of Holocephali group, with worldwide distribution. Long thread-like tail, large pectoral fins; closely resembles shark.

Chimborazo, inactive volcano with snow-capped cone; highest peak in Ecuadorian Andes. Height 6272 m (20,577 ft). Explored by von Humboldt (1802), first climbed by Whymper (1880).

chimes, set of bells, usually sounded as a signal, *eg* of the hour. The chimes heard in an orchestra consist of a set of tubular bells which are struck with hammer.

Chimkent, town of USSR, SE Kazakh SSR. Pop. 265,000. Lead and zinc refining; chemical, textile mfg.

chimpanzee, *Pan troglodytes,* ape of African tropical forests. Black hair, naked face; diet of fruit, small animals. Walks on all fours. Most intelligent ape, can use simple tools. Stands *c* 1.5 m/5 ft tall.

China, People's Republic of, state of E Asia. Area *c* 9,561,000 sq km (3,691,500 sq mi); pop. (est.) 800,000,000; cap. Peking, largest city Shanghai. Official language: Peking Chinese; religions: Confucianism, Buddhism, Taoism. Comprises 21 provs., 5 auton. regions. Mountainous in N (Manchuria) and W (TIBET), descends to fertile valleys, plains in E. Chief rivers incl. Hwang Ho, Yangtze. Climate extreme in N, subtropical in S. Agric. economy,

China

esp. rice, wheat; textile mfg. Great mineral potential, coal mining. China ruled by succession of imperial dynasties until 1912. Chiang Kai-shek's rule (1928-49) ended by estab. of Communist govt. under Mao Tse-tung. Joined UN 1971.

china clay or **kaolin,** fine, whitish clay. Consists mainly of kaolinite (hydrous aluminium silicate). Used in pottery, paper, rubber mfg., medicine. Major sources in US, France, England.

chinchilla, small squirrel-like rodent of Chinchillidae family found in South American Andes. Bred on farms in North America, Europe for its valuable fur.

Chindwin, river of N Burma. Chief tributary of Irrawaddy; *c* 880 km (550 mi) long.

Chinese, chief language group of Sino-Tibetan family. Has largest number of speakers in world. Official language of China is Mandarin, from N China, on which is based new 'national tongue', *Kno-yu,* renamed by Communists *p'u t'ung hua.* Other forms incl. Wu (Kiangsu and Chekiang provs.), Fukienese (Fukien prov., Taiwan, SE Asia), Cantonese (Kwangsi, Kwangtung provs., Hong Kong, SE Asia, US), Hakka (Kwangtung, Kiangsi provs.). Debatable whether mutually unintelligible forms are dialects or languages. All variants share literary language *wenyen,* which is very different from vernaculars, and *paihua,* vernacular adopted by Communist regime for all writing.

Chinese lantern or **winter cherry,** *Physalis alkekengi,* plant of nightshade family of Eurasian origin. Bears fruit in inflated orange calyx which is dried to form floral decoration.

Chinese literature, oldest extant works written in late Chou dynasty (*c* 1027-256 BC), although written records date from *c* 1400 BC. Important early works incl. *Wu Ching,* traditionally attributed to Confucius, made up of 5 books on chronology, divination (I CHING), ritual, history, poetry; *Shih Ching; Tao Te Ching* and *Chuang-Tze,* both associated with TAOISM. Greatest poetry written in T'ang period (AD 618-906) using special literary language; poets incl. Wang Wei, Li Po, Tu Fu, Po Chü-I; poems short, allusive, non-intellectual, influenced IMAGISTS. Narrative vernacular prose begun in T'ang, developing through drama of Yüan period (AD 1260-1368) to great novels of Ming, *eg Hsi Yu Chi* (translated as *Monkey,* 1943), and later works, *eg Hung Lou Meng* (18th cent.). Post-1949 literature governed by criterion of socialist realism, although some early works used as political allegory, esp. those attacking Confucius.

Chingford, *see* WALTHAM FOREST, England.

Chinghai, *see* TSINGHAI.

Chingkiang, city of Kiangsu prov., E China. Pop. 250,000. Commercial centre; flour and rice mills. Former treaty port on R. Yangtze-Grand Canal jct., its importance has declined.

Chinook, North American Indian tribe of Penutian linguistic stock. Sea-going traders of Columbia valley, W US. Practised head flattening, potlatch.

Chinwangtao, port of Hopeh prov., NE China, on Pohai. Pop. 200,000. Ice-free port in major coal area.

Chioggia, town of Veneto, NE Italy, on isl. in lagoon of Venice. Pop. 48,000. Port, resort; fishing, metal indust.

Scene of naval battles (1379-80) between Venice and Genoa.

Chios (*Khíos*), isl. of Greece, in Aegean Sea off Turkey. Area 870 sq km (336 sq mi). Wine, figs, mastic. Pop. massacred by Turks 1822. Main town, **Chios,** is a port; pop. 24,000. Ancient Ionian city state; Turkish held 1566-1912, taken by Greece. Traditional birthplace of Homer.

Chipmunk

chipmunk, burrowing North American rodent of squirrel family. Common chipmunk of E North America, *Tamias striatus,* has cheek pouches, striped markings on head, back. Diet of nuts, berries. Chipmunks of genus *Eutamias* found in W North America, Asia.

Chippendale, Thomas (1718-79), English cabinet maker. Pub. *The Gentleman and Cabinet Maker's Director* (1754), important book of furniture designs, primarily in the rococo style, but sometimes inspired by contemporary taste for Gothic or Chinese style. Worked mainly with dark mahogany.

Chippewa, see OJIBWA.

Chirac, Jacques (1932-), French political leader. Gaullist leader, was PM (1974-6) under Giscard d'Estaing. Elected mayor of Paris (1977), first since THIERRY.

Chirico, Giorgio de (1888-), Italian painter, b. Greece. Precursor of surrealism, his early work conveys mood of mystery and unease by use of empty spaces, steep perspective and objects taken out of context. Adopted more romantic realistic style after WWI.

Chiron, in Greek myth, wisest and kindliest of the CENTAURS. Skilled in medicine, prophecy, taught Asclepius, Achilles, Jason.

chiropractic, system of treatment of disease based on theory that disease is caused by interference of normal nerve function, which can be restored by manipulation, esp. of backbone. Originated by D.D. Palmer (1895).

Chiroptera, order of mammals, consisting of bats.

Chita, town of USSR, SE Siberian RSFSR. Pop. 258,000. Centre of rich mineral region, producing tungsten, molybdenum. Grew with arrival of Trans-Siberian railway (1897).

chiton, any marine mollusc of order Polyplacophora. Shell composed of 8 overlapping plates. Herbivorous; lives on rock surfaces.

Chittagong, cap. of Chittagong division, SE Bangladesh. Pop. 469,000. Major seaport on R. Karnaphuli. Exports jute, tea. Oil refinery, iron and steel works. Hindu temples, Buddhist ruins.

chivalry, system of organization and code of personal conduct pertaining to medieval knighthood. Reached zenith at time of Crusades (12th-13th cents.). In ideal form involved knightly class in strict observance of qualities of loyalty, piety, valour, honour; also emphasized nobility of womanhood. Battlefields and tournaments served as arenas for displaying these virtues. Mixture of military and Christian ideals, seen most clearly in formation of military-religious orders, *eg* Knights Templars, Knights Hospitallers. Large body of literature grew around chivalric ideals, *eg* CHANSONS DE GESTE, epic poems of the TROUBADOURS. Also *see* ARTHURIAN LEGEND, CHRÉTIEN DE TROYES.

chives, *Allium schoenoprasum,* perennial plant of onion family. Tubular leaves used in salads and as flavouring.

Chkalov, see ORENBURG.

chloramphenicol, antibiotic used in treatment of infectious diseases, *eg* typhoid, typhus fever. Originally obtained from cultures of *Streptomyces venezuelae;* now synthesized.

chlorella, genus of unicellular green algae. Several species are rich sources of proteins, carbohydrates and fats.

chlorine (Cl), greenish-yellow gaseous element; at. no. 17, at. wt. 35.45. Occurs in sodium chloride (common salt) in sea water and rocks; obtained by electrolysis of brine. Used in manufacture of hydrochloric acid, bleaches, and much organic synthesis; also used to purify water.

chloroform ($CHCl_3$), volatile liquid with sweet smell. Produced by action of chlorine on methane. Used as industrial solvent and formerly as anaesthetic.

chlorophyll, complex pigment existing only in plants which make their own food by PHOTOSYNTHESIS, *ie* autotrophs. Molecule similar to blood pigment, haemoglobin. Chlorophyll is green, but colour may be masked by other pigments. Absent from all heterotrophs, *eg* fungi, animals.

chocolate, see COCOA.

Choctaw, North American Indian tribe of Hokan-Siouan linguistic stock. Similar in culture to their enemies the CREEK and Chickasaw. Formerly occupied C and S Mississippi. Friendly with French, moved to reserve in Oklahoma (1832).

Chodowiecki, Daniel Nikolaus (1726-1801), German painter, etcher. Noted for his sketches of bourgeois life and book illustrations. Painted *The Departure of Jean Calas,* illustrated *Don Quixote.*

choir, trained body of singers. A full choir is divided into 4 ranges of voices (sopranos, altos, tenors and basses) and each group normally sings a separate line from the others.

cholera, acute infectious disease caused by bacterium *Vibrio cholerae;* contracted from food or water contaminated by human faeces. Characterized by severe diarrhoea, muscular cramps, dehydration. Controlled by proper sanitation.

cholesterol, white fatty alcohol of STEROID group, found in body tissue, blood and bile. Assists in synthesis of vitamin D and various hormones. Excessive deposits of cholesterol on inside of arteries are associated with arteriosclerosis and coronary heart disease.

Cholon, see HO CHI MINH CITY.

Chomsky, [Avram] Noam (1928-), American linguist. In *Syntactic Structures* (1957) set out theory of transformational-generative grammar. Theory began revolution in linguistics by positing a 'deep structure' (possibly common for all languages) from which innumerable syntactic combinations may be generated using transformational rules resulting in 'surface structure' (different for each language). Later wrote political commentaries.

Chopin, Frédéric François (1810-49), Polish composer, pianist. Lived in France from 1831. A leader of the Romantic movement, Chopin composed almost entirely for piano. Expanded harmonic concepts in his mazurkas, ballades, nocturnes, études, *etc.* Lived with George Sand from 1838 to 1847.

chorale, hymn of Protestant church, usually written in 4 parts for choir but generally sung in unison by congregation. Tunes often used in German Baroque music as themes for larger choral works. Chorale prelude, for organ, is based on chorale tune.

chord, in music, any group of notes that are heard at the same time, but usually 3 or more. The formation of chords is studied in HARMONY.

Chordata (chordates), phylum of animals possessing a NOTOCHORD at any stage of development. Incl. vertebrates, hemichordates, tunicates.

Chorzów (Ger. *Königshütte*), city of S Poland. Pop. 152,000. Coalmining, iron and steel works, nitrate plant, engineering. Under Prussian rule 1794-1921.

Chopin

Chou En-lai

Chou En-lai (1898-1976), Chinese political leader, premier (1949-76). Helped found (1922) Chinese Communist Party. Cooperated with Chiang Kai-shek against Japanese invasions, but fought against him (1930) after split with Kuomintang. Participated in LONG MARCH (1934-5). First premier and also foreign minister (1949-58), remaining in power despite ideological differences with Chairman Mao Tse-tung.

chough, mainly European bird of crow family, genus *Pyrrhocorax,* with black plumage and red feet. Species incl. *P. pyrrhocorax,* with long red beak, and yellow-billed Alpine chough, *P. graculus,* of mountain habitat.

chow chow, breed of dog developed in China. Thick brown or black coat, black tongue. Stands 50 cm/20 in. high at shoulder.

Chrétien de Troyes or **Chrestien de Troyes** (*fl* 1170), French poet. Wrote verse romances, 1st treatments of ARTHURIAN LEGEND, *eg Yvain, Erec et Enide, Lancelot, Perceval,* using elements of legend, Christian thought, code of courtly love.

Christ, see JESUS CHRIST.

Christadelphians, religious sect founded (1848) by John Thomas in Brooklyn, US. Members adhere to literal interpretation of Bible, have no ordained ministers, await estab. of Christ's theocracy on earth and avoid participation in civil life.

Christchurch, city of E South Isl., New Zealand, on Canterbury Plains. Pop. 165,000. Outport at Lyttelton exports wool, meat, dairy produce; food processing. Founded 1850 as church settlement. Has Anglican cathedral, univ. (1873).

Christian I (1426-81), king of Denmark (1448-81). United Norway with Denmark (1450); union lasted until 1814. King of Sweden (1457-64), but defeated in his attempts to subdue the country (1471).

Christian IV (1577-1648), king of Denmark and Norway (1588-1648). Championed Protestant cause during Thirty Years War; invaded Germany (1625), defeated (1626) and signed separate peace in 1629. Re-entered war (1643-5) opposing Sweden, lost 2 Norwegian territs.

Christian IX (1818-1906), king of Denmark (1863-1906). Annexed Schleswig (1863), precipitating war against Prussia and Austria in which Denmark lost Schleswig and Holstein.

Christian X (1870-1947), king of Denmark (1912-47). Figurehead of national resistance during German occupation of WWII. Lost Iceland (1944) after public referendum.

Christiania, see OSLO, Norway.

Christianity, religion of those who believe that Jesus is the realization of the Messiah prophesied in OT and who base their faith on his life and teachings, as recorded in the NT and on Jewish myth and history of OT. Early Church tended to be highly organizational and this tendency, coupled with geographic spread of Christianity, soon resulted in variety of churches (*eg* RC, Eastern Orthodox, Coptic). Subsequent reformed churches (*see* REFORMATION) were reaction against what was felt to be formalism and authoritarianism of traditional RC church.

Christian Science, religion founded by MARY BAKER EDDY and practised by the Church of Christ, Scientist. Adherents believe that evil and disease can only be overcome by the individual's awareness of spiritual truth in his own mind. Promulgated in international daily paper, *Christian Science Monitor.*

Christie, Agatha Mary Clarissa, Lady Mallowan (1891-1976), English author. Known for *c* 50 works of detective fiction, *eg The Murder of Roger Ackroyd* (1926), and plays, esp. *The Mousetrap* (1952). Created private detective Hercule Poirot.

Christie's, popular name for Christie, Manson and Woods, Ltd., London firm of art auctioneers and appraisers. Estab. by James Christie (1766).

Christina (1626-89), queen of Sweden (1632-54). Succeeded her father Gustavus II, OXENSTIERNA ruling during her minority. Patronized arts and scholars, but ruled extravagantly. Refused to marry, abdicated (1654) in favour of cousin Charles X. Settled in Rome, became a Catholic; failed in attempts to regain throne.

Christmas, in Christian calendar, celebration (on 25 Dec.) of the birth of Jesus Christ. Not widely celebrated until Middle Ages, although its near coincidence with the winter solstice links it with many ancient festivals.

Christmas Island, territ. of Australia, in Indian Ocean S of Sunda Trench. Area 142 sq km (55 sq mi); pop. 3500. Large phosphate deposits. British from 1888; admin. from Singapore after 1900; transferred to Australia 1958.

Christmas Island, one of Line Isls., C Pacific Ocean, part of Gilbert and Ellice Isls. colony. Area 577 sq km (223 sq mi); largest atoll in the Pacific. Produces copra. Sovereignty disputed by US.

Christmas rose, see HELLEBORE.

Christophe, Henri (1767-1820), Haitian king (1811-20). Born a slave, became one of leaders of Haiti's revolt against France (1790). Elected president (1806). Declared himself king (1811), shot himself after revolt of troops.

Christopher, St (Gk.,=Christ bearer), possibly a Christian martyr of Asia Minor (3rd cent.). Legendary carrier of infant Jesus over a river, sins of the world borne by Jesus making burden almost impossible. Patron saint of travellers, often represented on medallions.

chromatography, method of analysis or separation of chemical mixtures by allowing solution of mixture to flow through column of adsorbent material. Components are adsorbed in different layers, appearing as distinct bands or spots.

chromium (Cr), hard white metallic element; at. no. 24, at. wt. 51.996. Occurs as chrome iron ore (chromite); obtained by reducing oxide with aluminium. Used in manufacture of stainless steel and as protective coating on steel.

chromosome, microscopic thread-like structure found in nucleus of living cells. Consists of linear arrangement of genes, which control hereditary characteristics of organism; DNA is basic constituent. Body cells in each species contain same number of chromosomes, usually occurring in pairs. There are 46 in human cells.

chromosphere, see SUN.

Chronicles 1 and **2,** in OT, books detailing history of David, thus paralleling and supplementing Kings 1 and 2. Incl. detailed descriptions of worship in the Temple.

chronometer, highly accurate clock, used esp. at sea to determine longitude. First successful marine chronometer constructed by John Harrison (1761).

chrysanthemum, genus of annual or perennial herbs of daisy family. Native to Orient, but widely cultivated. Late blooming red, yellow, or white flowers. Floral emblem of Japan.

Chrysler, Walter Percy (1875-1940), American industrialist. Starting as machinist's apprentice, became (1919) vice-president of General Motors. Founded Chrysler Corporation (1924).

chrysoprase (SiO_2), semi-precious gemstone, a variety of chalcedony. Apple-green in colour, due to nickel impurities. Major sources in Silesia, Australia, US.

Chrysostom, John, see JOHN CHRYSOSTOM, ST.

Chuang Chou (c 369-c 286 BC), Chinese philosopher. Leading Taoist, stressed the relativity of ideas. Advocated union with universal Tao or nature principle.

chub, fish of carp family. Species incl. *Leuciscus cephalus,* European freshwater fish; in America, river chub, *Hybopsis kentuckiensis.*

chuckwalla, *Sauromalus obesus,* herbivorous lizard of iguana family of NW Mexico, W US desert regions. Reaches lengths of 40 cm/16 in.

Chukiang, Canton or **Pearl,** river of Kwangtung prov. S. China. Length 177 km (110 mi). Links Kwangchow (Canton) with South China Sea, forming estuary between Hong Kong and Macao.

Chungking, city of Szechwan prov., SC China on jct. of Yangtze-Chialing rivers. Pop. 3,500,000. Major commercial, indust. centre; shipyards; produces steel, motor vehicles, textiles. Cap. of China during Sino-Japanese War (1937). Former treaty port, opened 1891.

Chur (Fr. *Coire),* town of E Switzerland, cap. of Graubünden canton, Pop. 31,000. Wine market, tourist centre. Roman *Curia Rhaetorum;* cathedral, town hall.

Churchill, Charles (1731-64), English satirist. Known as contributor to John Wilkes' *North Briton.* Political satires incl. *The Prophecy of Famine* (1763), an attack on Scots at court.

Churchill, John, see MARLBOROUGH, JOHN CHURCHILL, 1ST DUKE OF.

Winston Churchill in 1939

Churchill, Lord Randolph Henry Spencer (1849-95), British statesman. Drafted Conservative policy for increased democracy, but resigned (1886) as chancellor of the exchequer over high military expenditure. His son, **Sir Winston Leonard Spencer Churchill** (1874-1965), was PM (1940-5, 1951-5). Journalist and soldier before election to Parliament (1900), he headed Admiralty ministry (1911-15) until failure of Dardanelles campaign in WWI discredited him. Served in Lloyd George's govt. (1917-21), Conservative chancellor of the exchequer (1924-9). Regained influence by opposing 'appeasement' policies towards Germany and replaced Neville Chamberlain at head of wartime coalition govt. Became symbol of British resistance during WWII; attended series of international conferences (Yalta, Potsdam, *etc)* to oversee settlement of the War. After 1945 leader of the Opposition until returned to power in 1951; retired 1955. Written works incl. *The Second World War* (6 vols., 1948-53), for which he was awarded Nobel Prize for Literature (1953).

Churchill, port of N Manitoba, Canada; on Hudson Bay at mouth of Churchill R. Pop. 2000. Railway terminus; grain shipping. Estab. as Hudson's Bay Co. trading post (1688).

Churchill: 1, river of WC Canada. Rises in NW Saskatchewan, flows E 1600 km (1000 mi) through Manitoba to Hudson Bay. Main tributary, Beaver R. H.e.p. at Island Falls. **2,** river of S Labrador, E Canada. Flows 970 km (c 600 mi) from Grand Falls to L. Melville; Churchill Falls is site of one of world's largest h.e.p. plants. Formerly called Hamilton R., renamed after Sir Winston Churchill (1965).

Church of England, see ENGLAND, CHURCH OF.

Church of Scotland, see SCOTLAND, CHURCH OF.

Churriguera, José (1665-1725), Spanish architect and sculptor. Designed catafalque of Queen Maria Luisa; his altar of San Esteban at Salamanca is decorated with twisted columns and elaborate leafwork. Gave name to style of Baroque architecture and decoration in Spain in late 17th and early 18th cent.

Chu Teh (c 1886-1976), Chinese military and political leader. With Mao Tse-tung led the Long March (1934-5). Commanded Chinese Communist forces during WWII and ensuing civil war. Appointed deputy chairman of People's Republic 1949. Denounced during 1967 'cultural revolution'.

Chuvash, auton. republic of EC RSFSR, USSR; in middle Volga valley. Area c 18,300 sq km (7070 sq mi); pop. 1,244,000; cap. Cheboksary. Wooded steppeland; main occupations agric. and forestry; notable woodworking. Chuvashes, descended from ancient Bulgars, are Finno-Tartar people.

CIA, See CENTRAL INTELLIGENCE AGENCY.

Ciano, Galeazzo (1903-44), Italian political leader. Joined Fascist movement, married (1930) Mussolini's daughter, Edda. Foreign minister 1936-43; helped depose Mussolini (1943), arrested and shot by Fascists.

Cibber, Colley (1671-1757), English actor-manager, playwright. Wrote *Love's Last Shift* (1690), first of the 'sentimental comedies'. Known for foppish roles, as manager of Drury Lane and for brilliant autobiog. Created poet laureate (1730).

cicada, any 4-winged insect of Cicadidae family of warm areas. Eggs laid in holes bored in twigs or plant stems; larvae live several years in ground. Males make loud noise by vibrating tymbal organ.

Cicero, Marcus Tullius (106-43 BC), Roman orator, statesman. Appointed consul (63) in opposition to CATILINE. Exposed Catiline's conspiracy to seize power by force in 4 famous orations. Sided with Pompey during civil war; pardoned by Caesar. Attacked Antony in 2 *Philippics;* on reconciliation of Octavian and Antony he was executed on orders of Antony. Famous for series of letters, giving picture of Roman life. Philosophical and rhetorical works are masterpieces of Latin prose.

cichlid, freshwater fish of Cichlidae family of tropical regions. Spiny finned; some species carry their eggs in mouth. Found particularly in Lake Tanganyika.

Cid, El, see DÍAZ DE VIVAR, RODRIGO.

cider, fermented apple juice containing from 4% to 7% alcohol. Major areas of production are Normandy and Brittany in France, Norfolk and SW of England. In US, cider refers to unfermented apple juice (hard cider is fermented form).

Cienfuegos, port of C Cuba, on Caribbean. Pop. 85,000. Has large scenic harbour. Tobacco, sugar exports. Rum distilleries. Founded 1819 by French colonists from Louisiana.

cigar, compact roll of tobacco leaves for smoking. Indians of West Indies and parts of South America smoked cured tobacco leaves in pre-Columbian times; cigar smoking was introduced into Spain and rest of Europe in late 16th cent. Cigars have been machine-made since *c* 1900 but finest cigars, *eg* those of Havana, are hand-made.

cigarette, roll of finely cut tobacco wrapped in thin paper. Popular tobaccos are those grown in Virginia, Georgia, the Carolinas in US, and in Turkey, Syria and Greece. Cigarette smoking has grown enormously in popularity in 20th cent. but its links with lung cancer have led to anti-smoking campaigns.

Cilicia, region of Asia Minor, in SE Turkey between Taurus Mts. and Mediterranean. Cilician Gates is pass through mountains important for access to interior. Armenian state (Little Armenia) founded here 1080; taken by Turks 1375.

Ciliophora, class of Protozoa, possessing protoplasmic filaments (cilia), used for movement, feeding.

Cimabue, Giovanni, orig. Cenni di Pepo (*c* 1240-*c* 1302), Italian painter. Regarded as founder of modern painting; fame due to mention in Dante's *Divine Comedy*. Forms link between Byzantine style and more realistic style of early Renaissance. Works incl. frescoes, mosaics.

Cimarron, river of SC US. Rises in NE New Mexico, flows E 1123 km (698 mi) into S Kansas, across Oklahoma to Arkansas R.

cinchona, genus of tropical South American trees from the bark of which quinine and related medicinal alkaloids are obtained. Widely cultivated in Asia and East Indies.

Cincinnati, city of SW Ohio, US; on Ohio R. Pop. 453,000. Transport jct., commercial centre. Industs. incl. machine tools, chemical mfg., meat packing. Founded 1788; focus of shipping in 19th cent.

Cincinnatus, Lucius Quinctius (*fl* 5th cent. BC), Roman soldier. Appointed dictator (458 BC) he defeated the Aequi, then resumed life as a farmer 16 days later.

cinema, art and business of making films or motion pictures; term often used for motion pictures alone. Nineteenth cent. developments in CAMERA, FILM, projectors resulted in public screening by 1896. First film theatre built (1905) in Pittsburgh, US. Film-making in US at first estab. in New York, with Hollywood becoming centre after 1913. Films were silent, accompanied by piano or organ, until *The Jazz Singer* (1927) introduced dialogue. Colour perfected with Technicolor (1932). Genres of Hollywood's 'golden age' (1930s and 1940s) incl. westerns, musicals, detective thrillers. Post-war developments incl. Italian social realism (late 1940s), *nouvelle vague* (France, late 1950s), Western appreciation of Japanese film and maturation of film criticism.

cineraria, ornamental blooming plants of genus *Senecio*. Varieties incl. popular garden plant, dusty miller and greenhouse *S. cruentus*.

Cinna, Lucius Cornelius (d. 84 BC), Roman politician. Consul (87-84), expelled from Rome when he tried to introduce reforms during Sulla's absence. Captured Rome with Marius and ruled alone when Marius died. Killed in mutiny when embarking to fight Sulla.

cinnabar (HgS), mercury ore mineral. Heavy, red or brown in colour; consists of mercuric sulphide. Major sources in Spain, Italy, US.

cinnamon, sweet spice from dried inner bark of E Indian evergreen tree, *Cinnamomum zeylanicum,* used in cookery and medicine.

cinquefoil, plant of genus *Potentilla* of rose family, with yellow or white flowers and fruit like small, dry strawberry. Most species are perennial herbs from N temperate and

Creeping cinquefoil

subarctic regions. Species incl. creeping cinquefoil, *P. reptans,* and silvery cinquefoil, *P. argenta.*

Cinque Ports, originally ports of Hastings, Romney, Hythe, Dover, Sandwich, S England. From 11th cent. given extensive Crown privileges for supplying warships. Winchelsea, Rye, others added later.

Cintra (*Sintra*), town of SC Portugal. Pop. 8000. Beauty celebrated by many poets incl. Byron. Moorish castle, royal palace (15th cent.).

CIO, see AMERICAN FEDERATION OF LABOR AND CONGRESS OF INDUSTRIAL ORGANIZATIONS.

circulation (blood), see BLOOD VESSELS; HEART; LUNGS.

Cirencester, urban dist. of Gloucestershire, W England. Pop. 13,000. Agric. market. Roman *Corinium,* remains incl. amphitheatre. Has ruined 12th cent. abbey.

cirrhosis, degenerative disease of liver, marked by excessive formation of fibrous scar tissue. Often caused by chronic alcoholism or malnutrition.

Cirripedia (cirripedes), subclass of crustaceans, incl. barnacle and parasitic *Sacculina.*

cirrus cloud, see CLOUD.

Cisalpine Republic, state (1797-1805) of N Italy on both sides of R. Po; protect. created by Napoleon. Called Italian Republic from 1802 until merging with Venetia.

Cistercians, in RC church, monks of order founded (1098) by St Robert of Molesme and St Stephen Harding. Derived from Benedictine order, stressed asceticism. Influential in introducing new agric. techniques in Europe. Made great use of lay brothers in their farms. Notable members incl. St Bernard of Clairvaux. See TRAPPISTS.

citric acid, soluble crystalline organic acid, found in lemons, oranges, *etc.* Obtained by fermentation of glucose. Used in flavouring effervescent drinks.

citrus, genus of evergreen trees and shrubs of family Rutaceae, native to Asia. Bear oranges, lemons, limes, citron, grapefruit, *etc.*

Città Vecchia (*Mdina*), town of Malta. Cap. until 1570; severely damaged by earthquake 1693. Cathedral (12th cent.), palace of Knights Hospitallers, catacombs.

Ciudad Bolívar, port of E Venezuela, on Orinoco R. Pop. 110,000. Cattle, gold exports. Hist. mfg. of Angostura bitters. Founded as Angostura (1764).

Ciudad Juárez, see JUÁREZ.

Ciudad Real, town of C Spain, cap. of Ciudad Real prov. Pop. 42,000. Agric. market, textile mfg., brandy distilling. Founded 13th cent.; Gothic cathedral.

Ciudad Trujillo, see SANTO DOMINGO.

civet, small cat-like carnivore of Viverridae family of Africa, SE Asia. Species incl. Indian civet, *Viverra zibetta.* Possesses scent producing glands, secretion used in perfume mfg.

civil disobedience, non-violent opposition to law or govt. policy by refusing to comply with it, usually on the grounds of conscience. Advocated by M.L. King while leading black civil rights movement in US (1950s, 1960s). More extreme form of opposition pursued by GANDHI in campaign of passive resistance, involving fastings and mass public demonstrations in Indian struggle for independence.

civil engineering, branch of ENGINEERING dealing with planning, designing and construction of *eg* bridges, harbours, tunnels. Also incl. alteration of landscape to suit particular needs. Professional institutions estab. in UK (1818), US (1852).

African civet *(Civettictis civetta)*

civil law, body of codified law governing individual's private rights, distinct from public and CRIMINAL LAW. Based on Roman law, esp. as laid down in *Corpus juris civilis* and revived 11th-12th cent. Adopted by continental Europe, Latin America, some Asian states. Most English-speaking countries have COMMON LAW.

civil rights, rights guaranteed to individual by law. Universal Declaration of Human Rights, passed (1948) by UN, incl. list of basic civil rights which should be available to all people in world. In US, set out in 13th, 14th, 15th and 19th Amendments to Constitution. Extended by acts of Congress to give minority groups, esp. blacks, equal rights. Four acts passed 1866-75, further three in 1957, 1960, 1964, latter three as result of civil rights movement's opposition to racial discrimination. Voting Rights Act (1965), originally aimed at protection of blacks' voting rights, extended to foreign-language minorities (1975). Feminists have since taken advantage of 1964 Civil Rights Act's provisions on employment, *etc.* In UK, Race Relations Acts (1965, 1968), set up Race Relations Board, to which cases of discrimination made illegal by acts can be referred. Equal Pay Act (1970), Sex Discrimination Act (1975) gave women rights in employment, education, services.

civil service, body of those employed by central govt. other than those in armed forces, judiciary. Term originally applied to part of East India Co.'s administration, later (mid-19th cent.) assumed modern meaning. US Civil Service Commission estab. (1883) as result of anti-patronage reform movement. Governs entry into service through examinations, as in UK civil service (since 1855).

Civil War, in English history, conflict (1642-6, 1648) between supporters of Charles I (Royalists or Cavaliers) and of Parliament (Roundheads). Struggle was culmination of Parliament's attempt to limit king's powers, *eg* by PETITION OF RIGHT (1628); central to dispute was Charles' belief in divine right to rule as opposed to Parliament's legislative rights, esp. over taxation. King was supported by majority of nobles, Catholics, Anglicans, and Parliament by merchants, gentry, Puritan movement and initially by Scottish Presbyterians. Parliamentary forces, organized (1644-5) into New Model Army, gained decisive victories at Marston Moor (1644), Naseby (1645) under CROMWELL and Fairfax. First phase of war ended with king's surrender to Scots (1646). Second phase, following king's escape and Scottish intervention on his side, ended with Cromwell's victory at Preston (1648).

Civil War, in US history, conflict (1861-5) between Union (Northern states) and Confederacy (Southern states). Causes incl. disagreement over prohibition of slavery in W territs. (*see* KANSAS-NEBRASKA BILL), also issue of STATES' RIGHTS. Southern states seceded from Union (1860-1), during which time LINCOLN was elected president; fighting started with Confederates firing on Fort Sumter (April, 1861). Early Southern successes, esp. under R.E. LEE, reversed in Gettysburg campaign (June-July, 1863). Gradual Union military ascendancy under U.S. GRANT culminated in retreat of Southern troops towards Richmond and Sherman's advance into Georgia (May-Sept. 1864). Lee eventually surrendered at Appomattox Courthouse (April, 1865). Union victory marred by assassination of Lincoln, whose EMANCIPATION PROCLAMATION (1862) abolishing slavery was upheld; seceding states were readmitted to Union under RECONSTRUCTION.

Civitavecchia, town of Latium, WC Italy, on Tyrrhenian Sea. Pop. 38,000. Port of Rome from 1st cent. AD; fishing, cement. Citadel designed by Michelangelo.

Clackmannanshire, former county of Scotland, now in Central region. Ochil Hills in N; plain of R. Forth in S. Coalmining, brewing, distilling. Co. town was **Clackmannan,** pop. 2000.

Clair, René, orig. René Chomette (1898-   ), French film director known for sophisticated comedy, *eg Sous les Toits de Paris* (1929), *A Nous la Liberté* (1931), *Les Belles de nuit* (1952).

clam, one of various bivalve molluscs, living in sand or mud. Round clam or quahog, *Venus mercenaria,* of NW Atlantic coast, common edible species.

clan, form of social group whose members trace descent from common ancestor. Term originally used in Scottish Highlands but extended to similar groups elsewhere. The clan includes several families but traces descent through one line only and is exogamous.

Clapham, part of Wandsworth, SC London, England. Incl. Clapham (railway) Jct.

Clare or **Clara, St** (*c* 1193-1253), Italian nun. Disciple of St Francis of Assisi, founded (*c* 1212) order of Franciscan nuns, 'Poor Clares', strictly upholding ideal of poverty. Proclaimed patron saint of television (1958).

Clare, John (1793-1864), English poet. Known for *Poems Descriptive of Rural Life and Scenery* (1820), *The Shepherd's Calendar* (1827) on changing countryside, vanishing customs. Went insane in middle age, died in asylum.

Clare, county of Munster prov., W Irish Republic. Area 3188 sq km (1231 sq mi); pop. 75,000; co. town Ennis. Hilly in E, N; rugged coast. Many bogs, lakes; low-lying, fertile along Shannon estuary. Agric., salmon fishing; prehist. remains.

Clarendon, Edward Hyde, 1st Earl of (1609-74), English statesman. After death of Charles I, became Charles II's chief adviser in exile. Appointed lord chancellor at Restoration (1660), favoured religious toleration; later, however, enforced Clarendon Code (1661-5), statutes strengthening Church of England. Lived in exile after dismissal (1667). Wrote *History of the Rebellion.*

clarinet, single-reed woodwind instrument with cylindrical bore, invented late 17th cent. Usually pitched in B flat and A. Occasionally used as a solo instrument. Also found in military bands; plays a very characteristic role in traditional jazz.

Clark, Jim (1937-68), Scottish racing driver. Twice world champion (1963, 1965), he won Indianapolis 500 (1965). His total of major Grand Prix wins exceeded that of Fangio. Died in crash at Hockenheim circuit.

Clark, Kenneth Mackenzie Clark, Lord (1903-   ), British art historian. His writings incl. *Leonardo da Vinci* (1939), *Landscape into Art* (1949), and *Civilisation* (1970), based on popular lecture series for television.

Clark, Mark Wayne (1896-   ), American general. In WWII, commanded in N African and Italian invasions. Supreme commander of UN forces in Korea (1952-3).

Clarkson, Thomas (1760-1846), English philanthropist. Supported Wilberforce in obtaining passage of bill abolishing British slave trade (1807). Helped found Anti-Slavery Society (1823).

class, social, *see* SOCIAL CLASS.

Classicism, in the arts, adherence to qualities regarded as characteristic of ancient Greece, Rome, incl. rationality, restraint, formal precision. *See* ROMANTICISM.

classification, in biology, systematic grouping of animals and plants into categories according to similarities and evolutionary relationships. Broadest division is into 2 kingdoms, Plantae (plants) and Animalia (animals); 3rd kingdom, Protista, consisting of all protozoans, algae, fungi and bacteria, is sometimes used. Kingdoms are divided into 6 taxa: phylum (division in botany), class, order, family, genus, species (from most to least inclusive). Species is smallest unit of classification, usually defined as those animals or plants capable of interbreeding only among themselves. Closely related species are grouped into same genus. Binomial nomenclature used in international scientific descriptions of animals employs genus name, whose initial letter is capitalized, followed by specific name, uncapitalized. Man belongs to species *Homo sapiens*, genus *Homo*, family Hominidae, order Primates, class Mammalia, phylum Chordata.

Claudel, Paul [Louis Charles Marie] (1868-1955), French dramatist, poet and diplomat. Known for poetic dramas with religious inspiration, *eg Tête d'Or* (1890), *La Ville* (1890), showing symbolist influence, *Le Soulier de Satin* (1929), using Japanese no conventions. Also wrote lyric verse, prose impressions of China.

Claude Lorrain, pseud. of Claude Gellée (1600-82), French painter. Famous for his poetic treatment of landscape, depicting mythical seaports and country around Rome. Works incl. *Liber Veritatis,* book of drawings of his own paintings.

Claudian (*c* AD 370-404), Latin poet. Last major classicist of Rome, wrote epic *Rape of Proserpine,* idylls, epigrams.

Claudius I (10 BC–AD 54), Roman emperor (AD 41-54). Nephew of Tiberius, succeeded Caligula as emperor through support of Praetorian guard. Reign marked by territ. expansion; made Britain a province (43). Poisoned, prob. at instigation of wife Agrippina, who persuaded him to accept her own son Nero as his heir.

Clausewitz, Karl von (1780-1831), Prussian army officer and military strategist. Author of influential *On War* (pub. from 1832), expounding tactics involved in waging total warfare.

Clausius, Rudolf Julius Emanuel (1822-88), German mathematician, physicist. Developed concept of entropy and introduced 2nd law of thermodynamics: heat does not flow of itself from colder to hotter bodies. Contributed to kinetic theory of gases.

Claverhouse, John Graham of, see DUNDEE, JOHN GRAHAM OF CLAVERHOUSE, 1ST VISCOUNT.

clavichord, small keyboard instrument, developed in 15th cent. Small tangents (blades) of brass, activated by keys, press against strings, simultaneously sounding them and stopping them.

clawed frog, amphibian of genus *Xenopus,* with webbed, clawed feet; found in Africa S of Sahara.

clawed toad, *Xenopus laevis,* tropical African toad with webbed, clawed feet. Female used to test for pregnancy; urine of pregnant woman produces enlargement of toad's ovary.

Clay, Cassius, see ALI, MUHAMMAD.

Clay, Henry (1777-1852), American politician. Congressman from Kentucky, leader of 'war hawks' before War of 1812. Instrumental in passages of Compromises (1820, 1850), maintaining balance of slave and free states. Opposed extremists in N and S, supported claims of Union. Unsuccessful presidential candidate (1832, 1844).

clay, fine-grained earth, consisting mainly of hydrous aluminium silicate. May be residual (found in place of origin) or transported. Sticky and plastic when wet, hardens when dry or fired. Used for making bricks, tiles, pottery, drainage pipes.

Cleanthes (*c* 300-220 BC), Greek philosopher. Pupil of Zeno, subsequently leader of Stoics. See STOICISM.

clearwing, day-flying moth, resembling wasp, with transparent wings. Species incl. currant clearwing, *Sesia tipuliformis,* a fruit pest.

clef, sign at the beginning of a staff of music that defines the pitches of the lines and spaces making up the staff.

cleft palate, congenital defect caused by failure of 2 halves of palate to unite; often associated with divided or hare lip. Repair may be effected by surgery carried out in infancy.

cleg, see HORSEFLY.

Cleisthenes (*fl* 510 BC), Athenian statesman. Member of Alcmaeonidae family, continued work of Solon in making Athens a democracy. Divided citizens into 10 tribes, each tribe subdivided into demes. Introduced system of ostracism.

Cleland, John (1709-89), British author. Known for *Fanny Hill - Memoirs of a Woman of Pleasure* (1749), which was suppressed as pornography.

clematis, genus of perennial plants and woody vines of the buttercup family usually with brightly coloured flowers. Garden varieties incl. Jackman clematis and Japanese clematis. Wild variety, *Clematis vitalba.*

Georges Clemenceau

Clemenceau, Georges (1841-1929), French statesman, premier (1906-9, 1917-20), known as the 'Tiger'. Headed coalition govt. that helped secure victory in WWI. Opposed President Wilson in post-war settlement at Versailles (1919); resigned amidst criticism for his moderate stand towards Germany.

Clement V, orig. Bertrand de Got (1264-1314), French churchman, pope (1305-14). Estab. papal seat at Avignon (1308). Dominated by Philip IV of France, he supported dissolution of the Knights Templars.

Clement VII, orig. Giulio de' Medici (1478-1534), Italian churchman, pope (1523-34). Supported Francis I of France against Emperor Charles V, who besieged Rome (1527) and imprisoned him. Refused to sanction Henry VIII's divorce from Catherine of Aragon.

Clement XI, orig. Giovanni Francesco Albani (1649-1721), Italian churchman, pope (1700-21). Renowned in youth for his learning. As pope, prosecuted Jansenism in the Church, esp. in bull *Unigenitus* (1713).

Clementi, Muzio (1752-1832), Italian composer, pianist. Lived mainly in England. First composer to write specifically for the piano, composing a famous collection of studies, *Gradus ad Parnassum,* and many sonatas.

Clement of Alexandria, orig. Titus Flavius Clemens (*c* 150-*c* 215), Greek Christian theologian. Taught at Alexandrian catechetical school, where ORIGEN was his pupil. Attempted to reconcile Christianity with Greek thought by showing Christ to be culmination of all philosophies.

Cleopatra (69-30 BC), Egyptian queen. At age of 17, became joint ruler with brother, Ptolemy XII. Deprived of power, she was reinstated with aid of Julius Caesar, by whom she bore a son in Rome. Returned to Egypt after Caesar's death, later to become mistress of Mark Antony. Their union was opposed by Octavian, who destroyed their fleet at Actium (31 BC). They retired into Egypt and both committed suicide.

Cleopatra's Needles, popular name for 2 ancient Egyptian obelisks in red granite, originally erected at Heliopolis (*c* 1475 BC). Later removed to Alexandria (*c* 14 BC), one was presented to Britain (1878), the other to America (1880); they stand on Thames Embankment, London, and in Central Park, New York.

clerihew, form of verse invented by Edward Clerihew Bentley, having two couplets humorously characterizing person whose name is one of the rhymes.

Clermont-Ferrand, city of SC France, in Massif Central, cap. of Puy-de-Dôme dept. Pop. 149,000. Rubber mfg. centre, metal goods; univ. (1808). Hist. cap. of Auvergne; scene of church council (1095) leading to the Crusades. Gothic cathedral (13th cent.).

Cleveland, [Stephen] Grover (1837-1908), American statesman, president (1885-9, 1893-7). Reform mayor of Buffalo (1882-3) and New York governor (1883-5) before assuming presidency. Alienated radical Democrats in 2nd term by upholding gold standard. Sent troops into Illinois to break Pullman railway strike (1894).

Cleveland, county of NE England. Area 583 sq km (225 sq mi); pop. 567,000; co. town Middlesbrough. Centred on R. Tees. Iron, steel mfg.; heavy indust. Created 1974 incl. parts of N Yorkshire, Durham.

Cleveland, port of NE Ohio, US; on L. Erie at mouth of Cuyahoga R. Pop. 751,000; state's largest city. Major iron ore shipping centre; steel mfg., oil refining (Rockefeller), chemicals mfg. First settled 1796. Canal and railway spurred growth in 19th cent.

Cleves, see KLEVE, West Germany.

click beetle, any beetle of Elateridae family. Jumps in air with clicking noise when placed on back. Larvae, called wireworms, are agricultural pests, feeding on roots, grass.

climate, average meteorological conditions of a place or region, taken over a period of years. Dependent on many factors, eg latitude, nearness to sea. Studied as climatology.

Clio, in Greek and Roman myth, Muse of history. Represented as carrying an open scroll.

Clitheroe, mun. bor. of Lancashire, NW England, on R. Ribble. Pop. 13,000. Weaving, paper mfg. Has ruined Norman castle.

Clive, Catherine ('Kitty'), née Rafter (1711-85), English actress. Known for comedy roles. Friend of Horace Walpole.

Robert Clive

Clive, Robert, Baron Clive of Plassey (1725-74), British soldier, administrator. In military service of East India Co., won series of victories, notably at Arcot (1751), Calcutta, Plassey (1757). Consolidated British power in India, ousting French. As governor of Bengal promoted reform. On return to England (1767), charged with accepting bribes; acquitted but committed suicide.

cloisonné, enamel decoration, esp. used in Chinese and Japanese art, in which solid metal outlines are filled with enamel paste or powder, baked, and finally ground smooth.

Clonmel, co. town of Tipperary, S Irish Republic, on R. Suir. Pop. 12,000. Sporting centre (hunting, horseracing); livestock market.

closed shop, organization hiring only labour union members as employees, either throughout or for particular jobs. Subject of indust. and political conflict in US and UK. In former, unions adopted closed shop policy c 1840, but strikes to support it were declared illegal until 1935 Wagner Act. Many states passed 'right-to-work' laws

Cloisonné: Chinese incense-burner

outlawing closed shop. In UK, Industrial Relations Act (1971) made closed shop agreement void at law, but law overturned by following Labour govt.

clothes moth, small moth of Tineidae family. Lays eggs on articles of wool, fur, etc, which larvae eat.

Clotho, see FATES.

Cloth of Gold, Field of, place near Calais, France, where Henry VIII of England met Francis I of France (1520) to discuss possible alliance against Charles V. Name given because of lavish display of wealth by both retinues.

cloud, mass of water droplets or ice crystals suspended in the atmosphere. Formed by condensation of water vapour, normally at considerable height. The 3 primary cloud types (cirrus, cumulus, stratus) first recognized by Luke Howard (1803). International classification now identifies 10 basic forms, distinguished by height. High clouds (over c 6100 m/20,000 ft) incl. cirrus, cirrostratus, cirrocumulus. Intermediate clouds (c 2000 m/6500 ft to c 6100 m/20,000 ft) incl. altocumulus, altostratus. Low clouds (below c 2000 m/6500 ft) incl. stratus, nimbostratus, stratocumulus. Clouds growing vertically upwards incl. cumulus, cumulonimbus. Certain clouds are associated with particular weather conditions, eg nimbostratus with continuous rain or snow, cumulus with fair weather, cumulonimbus with thunderstorms.

cloud chamber, in physics, enclosed chamber containing supersaturated vapour used to detect paths of charged particles. Particle produces ions as it passes through chamber; path seen as row of droplets formed by condensation of liquid on these ions.

clouded leopard, Neofelis nebulosa, nocturnal carnivore of cat family of SE Asian forests. Arboreal, with long heavy tail.

Clough, Arthur Hugh (1819-61), English poet. Known for hexameter verse Bothie of Toper-na-Fuosich (1848), lyrics, esp. 'Say not the struggle nought availeth'. Arnold's Thyrsis commemorates his death.

clove, pungent dried flower bud of evergreen shrub, Eugenia caryophyllata, of myrtle family, native to East Indies. Used whole for pickling and flavouring, ground for confectionery; oil used medicinally.

clover, any plant of genus Trifolium of Leguminosae family. Low-growing trifoliate plant with small flowers in dense heads. Widespread in temperate regions. Used as forage crop and to allow NITROGEN FIXATION in soil.

Clovis I (c 466-511), Frankish king (481-511). Son of Childeric I; founded Merovingian monarchy in Gaul and SW Germany. Defeated Romans at Soissons (486), Alemanni at Tolbiarum (496), Visigoths at Vouillé (507). Converted to Christianity (496), estab. court at Paris; thus laid foundations of Charlemagne's empire and modern France.

club moss, low evergreen plant of genera Lycopodium and Selaginella, with scale-like leaves and club-shaped cones containing spores. Found in tropical and subtropical forests. L. clavatus used for manufacture of vegetable sulphur (lycopodium powder).

club root, disease of plants of cabbage family, caused by a slime mould, Plasmodiophora brassicae, and characterized by swellings of the roots.

Cluj (Hung. Kolozsvár), city of WC Romania. Pop. 213,000. Commercial, indust. centre of Transylvania. Prob. dates from Roman times. Gothic church (14th cent.); seat of 4 bishoprics.

Clover

Cluny, town of Burgundy, E France. Pop. 4000. Grew around large Benedictine abbey (founded 910) which became major religious and cultural centre in Middle Ages.

Clwyd, county of NE Wales. Area 2425 sq km (936 sq mi); pop. 354,000; co. town Mold. Created 1974, incl. former Denbighshire, Flintshire.

Clyde, Colin Campbell, 1st Baron (1792-1863), British army officer, b. Scotland. Led Highland Brigade in Crimea, notably at Balaklava (1854). Instrumental in quelling Indian Mutiny (1857).

Clyde, river of W Scotland. Flows 170 km (105 mi) from S Lanarkshire via fruit-growing areas (Lanark, Carluke) and heavy indust. areas (Glasgow, Clydebank) to Firth of Clyde. Has shipbuilding industs., ports, tourist resorts.

Clydebank, town of Strathclyde region, W Scotland, on R. Clyde. Pop. 48,000. *Queen Mary, Queen Elizabeth, QE2* built in shipyards. Sewing machine mfg. Damaged in WW II air raids.

Clytemnestra, in Greek myth, daughter of Leda and Tyndareus. Unfaithful wife of Agamemnon, whom she murdered on his return from Troy; lover of Aegisthus. Mother by Agamemnon of Orestes, Electra and Iphigenia. Killed with Aegisthus when Orestes avenged his father's death.

Cnossus, see KNOSSOS, Greece.

coal, dark brown or black combustible mineral. Occurs in bands or seams in sedimentary rock. Formed over millions of years by heating and compaction of partly decayed vegetable matter; various stages, in order of increasing carbon content, are peat, lignite, bituminous coal, anthracite. Coals occur from Devonian period on, with max. in Carboniferous. Used as fuel, also in production of coke, coal gas, plastics. Major sources in US, UK, France, Australia, China, USSR.

coal gas, gas made by destructive distillation of coal. Main constituents are hydrogen (50%), methane (30%). Used for heating, illumination. Poisonous, as it contains carbon monoxide.

coal tar, thick black liquid obtained by destructive distillation of coal. Distillation and purification yield such compounds as xylene, toluene, benzene, phenol. Pitch remains as a residue.

coastguard, govt. organization employed to defend nation's coasts, aid vessels in distress, prevent smuggling, *etc.* In UK was estab. after Napoleonic Wars to prevent smuggling, but now concerned mainly with lifesaving. In US, is special naval branch, formed (1915) with wide duties, incl. maintenance of lighthouses, enforcement of law and order at sea.

Coast Mountains, range of W British Columbia, Canada. Run parallel to Pacific Coast for 1610 km (1000 mi). Rise to highest point at Mt. Waddington 4042 m (13,260 ft). Extensively wooded; heavy rainfall; h.e.p.

Coast Range, volcanic mountain range of W US, parallel to Pacific coastline. Extends S from Washington, Oregon to California.

Coatbridge, town of Strathclyde region, WC Scotland. Pop. 52,000. Coalmining; iron and steel industs.

Ring-tailed coati (*Nasua nasua*)

coati, any of genus *Nasua* of arboreal mammals, related to raccoon, found in Central and South America. Long snout; omnivorous.

cobalt (Co), hard silvery-white metallic element; at. no. 27, at. wt. 58.93. Occurs combined with arsenic and sulphur; obtained by reducing oxide with carbon or aluminium. Used in alloys; radioactive cobalt 60 used to treat cancer. Compounds used in pigments (esp. blue).

Cobb, Ty[rus Raymond] (1886-1961), American baseball player. Estab. many records, incl. 4191 hits and .367 batting average, during career mainly with Detroit. Won 12 batting championships.

William Cobbett

Cobbett, William (1762-1835), English political journalist. Campaigned for social, economic reform in his *Weekly Political Register* (1802-35). Best known for *Rural Rides* (1830) describing conditions in the country.

Cobden, Richard (1804-65), British politician. With John Bright, leader of Anti-Corn Law League; fought for repeal of Corn Laws, achieved (1846) under Peel. Negotiated tariff treaty (1859-60) with French.

Cóbh, town of Co. Cork, S Irish Republic. Pop. 6000. Port of Cork; yachting. Formerly called Queenstown.

Coblenz, see KOBLENZ, West Germany.

cobra, highly venomous snake of Elapidae family, found in Africa and Asia. Opens hood of skin around neck when angered. Species incl. Indian cobra, *Naja naja,* and Egyptian cobra, *N. haja,* often used by snake charmers. Largest is king cobra, *N. hannah,* reaching 5.5 m/18 ft.

Coburg, town of EC West Germany. Pop. 43,000. Metals, glass, toy mfg. Former cap. of Saxe-Coburg. Ducal palace (16th cent.). Nearby is birthplace of Albert, consort of Queen Victoria.

coca, tropical South American shrub, *Erythroxylon coca,* dried leaves of which are the source of the alkaloid drug, cocaine.

cocaine, white crystalline alkaloid obtained from leaves of coca plant. Formerly used as local anaesthetic, it is a habit-forming drug, causing temporary elation and hallucinations.

Cochabamba, town of WC Bolivia, cap. of Cochabamba dept. Pop. 160,000. In grain, fruit-growing region. Oil refining, furniture, footwear, tyre mfg. Has univ. (1832).

Cochin, seaport of Kerala state, SW India, on Arabian Sea. Pop. 438,000. Exports coconut products. Chief port of former princely state of Cochin. Earliest European settlement in India (1503) following visit of Vasco da Gama.

Cochin China, former French colony of SE Asia. Contained within South VIETNAM after 1954.

Cochran, C[harles] B[lake] (1872-1951), British theatrical impresario. Introduced Diaghilev's Russian Ballet to London; best known for 'young ladies', many of whom became musical comedy stars.

cockatoo, easily domesticated crested parrot of Australia, New Guinea, Philippines. Plumage mainly white, edged with yellow or pink.

cockchafer, *Melolontha melolontha,* European species of beetle with black head, thorax and reddish-brown wing cases. Lifespan of *c* 3 years. Larvae are root feeders.

Cockcroft, Sir John Douglas (1897-1967), English physicist. With E.T.S. Walton built 1st particle accelerator and used it in 1st successful transmutation of atomic nuclei. They shared Nobel Prize for Physics (1951).

Cocker spaniel

cocker spaniel, small dog, developed in England. Silky hair, drooping ears. Stands 36 cm/14 in. at shoulder.

cock-fighting, sport of setting trained cocks, usually bearing metal spurs, to fight against each other. Can be traced back as far as 12th cent. in England. Banned in Britain and America in mid-19th cent. Still popular in parts of Asia and Latin America.

cockle, one of group of edible bivalve molluscs, genus *Cardium.* Body enclosed by 2 heart-shaped ribbed shells with scalloped edges.

cockroach, any insect of suborder Blattaria, found worldwide, esp. in tropics. Flat, brownish body, long antennae; emits unpleasant odour. Omnivorous, pest of foodstores. *Blatta orientalis* is cosmopolitan domestic species.

cocoa or **cacao,** *Theobroma cacao,* spreading tree of Sterculia family, found in forests of South America. Grows to av. height of 10 m/30 ft and has large, round fruits each containing 20-40 seeds or beans (cacao). These when roasted and powdered (cocoa) are used in chocolate and as a beverage.

coconut, *Cocos nucifera,* tropical tree bearing large, brown, hard-shelled fruit. Edible white kernel (copra) and

'milk' used in confectionery. Yields oil used in soap; husk provides fibre for matting; leaves used as roof covering.

Cocos or **Keeling Islands,** group of 27 small coral isls., S of Sumatra; under Australian admin. since 1955. Area 13 sq km (5 sq mi); pop. 600. Discovered (1609) by Captain Keeling of East India Co. Exports copra.

Jean Cocteau

Cocteau, Jean (1889-1963), French author, film director. Avant-garde works deal with theme of poet as defier of destiny, risking destruction. Known for ballets for Diaghilev; novels, *eg Les Enfants terribles* (1929, film 1950); plays, *eg La Machine infernale* (1934) on Oedipus myth; films, *eg Le Sang d'un Poète* (1932); autobiog., poetry.

Cod, Cape, narrow sandy penin. of SE Massachusetts, US. Famous holiday resort, fishing area. Pilgrim Fathers landed here (1620).

cod, food fish of Gadidae family of N Atlantic, N Pacific. Atlantic cod, *Gadus morhua,* found esp. off coasts of Newfoundland and Iceland, commercially important. Cod-liver oil source of vitamins A, D.

codeine, alkaloid drug derived from opium and similar to morphine. Used medicinally to relieve pain and suppress coughs.

Code Napoléon, first modern law code, promulgated (1804) by Napoleon I. Important in development of CIVIL LAW, model for many nations' codes.

cod liver oil, oil obtained from liver of cod and other fish. Rich in vitamins A and D, it was much used in treatment of vitamin deficiency diseases, *eg* rickets.

Cody, William Frederick (1846-1917), American showman. Known as 'Buffalo Bill'. Worked as frontier scout. After 1883 toured US, Europe with his 'Wild West Show'.

coeducation, system of education in which students of both sexes are instructed together. Early examples in Scotland and American colonies (17th cent.), spread with W expansion in US (*c* 1840s) and extension of public education. Elsewhere, widespread coeducation, esp. in univs. and colleges, did not come until early 20th cent. with increasing participation of women in indust., professions.

Head of coelacanth

Poster for 'Buffalo Bill' Cody's Wild West Show

Coelacanthidae (coelacanths), order of primitive marine fish, known from fossils of Devonian period. Believed to be ancestors of land animals. Living specimen of genus *Latimeria* discovered (1938) off E Africa; other species found since then.

Coelenterata (coelenterates), phylum of aquatic, mainly marine, animals. Life cycle generally involves alternation between asexual sedentary polyp and free-swimming sexual medusa (jellyfish). Polyp stage dominant in some members, *eg* corals, sea anemones, but medusa stage in others, *eg* true jellyfish. Many polyps colonial; some solitary, *eg* HYDRA.

coffee, *Coffea arabica,* evergreen shrub native to Arabia, grown extensively in Brazil, Africa and Asia. Seeds roasted and ground to make beverage. Unknown in Europe until 17th cent. World production *c* 4,000,000 metric tons.

Cognac, town of W France, on R. Charente. Pop. 23,000. Produces famous brandy; barrel mfg., bottling.

cognac, *see* BRANDY.

Cohn, Ferdinand Julius (1828-98), German botanist. Regarded as founder of bacteriology. Studied plant pathology, investigating the lower algae, fungi and bacteria.

Coimbatore, town of Tamil Nadu state, S India. Pop. 353,000. Rice and flour milling, textile mfg. Commands pass through Western Ghats.

Coimbra, city of C Portugal. Pop. 46,000. Wine, grain market. Univ. (1537), 2 cathedrals. Flourished from Roman times; cap. of Portugal 1139-1260.

coins, *see* NUMISMATICS.

Coke, Sir Edward (1552-1634), English jurist, statesman. Appointed attorney-general (1594); as chief justice of Common Pleas (1606-16), championed Parliament, common law, principles of personal liberty against James I's assertion of royal prerogative. Leader of parliamentary opposition from 1620, under Charles I drew up Petition of Right (1628). Wrote *Institutes*, a legal classic.

Coke, Thomas William, Earl of Leicester of Holkham (1754-1842), English agriculturist. Remembered for systematic improvement of methods of arable farming and of breeding livestock, esp. sheep.

coke, residue from destructive distillation of coal; contains *c* 80% carbon. Used as smokeless fuel and in preparation of metals from their ores in blast furnaces.

cola or **kola,** *Cola acuminata,* tree of W tropical Africa, West Indies and Brazil. Nuts yield caffeine and extract used in flavouring soft drinks.

Colbert, Jean Baptiste (1619-83), French statesman. Chief adviser to Louis XIV after 1661, leading exponent of mercantilist policies to develop nation's wealth. Protected indust. with subsidies and tariffs, price regulation. Had

road and canal network built, encouraged trade and colonization.

Colchester, mun. bor. of Essex, SE England, on R. Colne. Pop. 76,000. Market town, famous oyster fisheries; has Univ. of Essex (1961). Ancient British cap. Roman *Camulodunum,* part of town wall remains; has Norman castle, now museum.

cold, common, acute inflammation of mucous membranes of nose and throat; believed to be caused by any of *c* 50 different viruses. Most common human ailment. Lack of immunity to common cold prob. caused by new strains of virus developing from earlier ones.

Coldstream, town of Borders region, SE Scotland, on R. Tweed. Pop. 1000. Bridge to Cornhill, England. Gen. Monck's army raised to restore Charles II (1660) led to naming of Coldstream Guards.

Cold War, economic and political rivalry between nations, without actual military conflict. Popularly used for post-WWII struggle between Communist nations and West. Also term for ideological split between USSR and China, and competition with West for prestige in developing countries by use of aid programmes.

Cole, G[eorge] D[ouglas] H[oward] (1889-1959), English economist. Chairman of Fabian Society (1939-46); president from 1952. Also leading advocate of guild socialism. Author of many works, *eg The Simple Case for Socialism* (1935), *History of Socialist Thought* (1953-8).

cole, *see* KALE.

Coleoptera, largest order of insects; *see* BEETLE.

Coleraine, town of N Northern Ireland, on R. Bann. Pop. 15,000. In former Co. Londonderry. Fishing; whiskey distilling. Has seat of Univ. of Ulster (1968). **Coleraine,** district; area 484 sq km (187 sq mi); pop. 46,000. Created 1973, formerly part of Co. Londonderry.

Samuel Taylor Coleridge

Coleridge, Samuel Taylor (1772-1834), English poet, critic. Estab. English Romanticism in publication, with Wordsworth, of *Lyrical Ballads* (1798) incl. 'The Rime of the Ancient Mariner'. Other works incl. 'Kubla Khan' (1816), philosophical, critical reflections in *Biographia Literaria* (1817).

Coleridge-Taylor, Samuel (1875-1912), British composer. Born of English mother and W African father. Best known for his 3 choral works on the subject of Longfellow's *Hiawatha*.

Colet, John (*c* 1467-1519), English humanist. Noted for his exegesis of Pauline theology at Oxford (1497-1504). Dean of St Paul's (1505); refounded and endowed St Paul's School (1509).

Colette, [Sidonie Gabrielle] (1873-1954), French novelist. Known for analytical studies of women, *eg* 'Claudine' series (1900-3) of semi-autobiog. novels written with 1st husband, and for *Chéri* (1920), *Gigi* (1945).

Coligny, Gaspard de (1519-72), French naval officer. Protestant leader with CONDÉ in religious wars, gained favourable peace (1570). Adviser to Charles IX, antagonized Catherine de' Medici; he was 1st victim of St Bartholomew's Day massacre.

collage, art form in which bits of paper, cloth or other objects are stuck to a canvas or other surface. Much used by cubists, who introduced strips of newspaper into otherwise conventionally painted compositions.

collar bone or **clavicle,** part of shoulder extending from shoulder blade (scapula) to breastbone (sternum).

collective bargaining, in indust. relations, term for negotiations between employer and employees' representatives, usually labour union, to agree pay, conditions of work, union rights. Term coined by Beatrice Webb for process first used in 19th cent. Britain.

collective farming, agric. cooperative movement. In USSR, Stalin instituted (1929) *kolkhoz* method in which land, farm equipment were pooled and profits shared among members. Although almost all Soviet agric. was collectivized by 1938, state farms, paying the workers, were later introduced. Chinese cooperatives place greater emphasis on communal living and encourage participation of indust. workers.

college, institution of higher education. Generally, smaller in size and spread of curriculum than UNIVERSITY; several colleges may constitute university. Earliest were in Paris (12th cent.), preceding famous centres of learning at Oxford and Cambridge univs. Industrial Revolution led to need for scientific and technical training (technical colleges); late 19th cent. brought colleges of education (teachers' training). In US, colleges may grant degrees in specialized courses of study, *eg* liberal arts, law, medicine, architecture.

Collège de France, institution of higher learning estab. (1529) in Paris by Francis I. Has no fees, no examinations, no degrees, and no state supervision.

collie, breed of long-haired sheepdog, developed in Scotland. Long narrow head; stands 56-66 cm/22-26 in. at shoulder. Kelpie is Australian sheepdog developed from collie or dingo-collie cross.

Collier, Jeremy (1650-1726), English clergyman. Refused to swear allegiance to William III (1688). Wrote *Short View of the Immorality and Profaneness of the English Stage* (1698).

collimator, device used to obtain parallel beam of light. Consists of tube containing convex lens at 1 end; at other end is adjustable slit, placed at focus of lens.

Collingwood, Cuthbert Collingwood, Baron (1750–1810), British admiral. Distinguished himself at St Vincent (1797) and took command at Trafalgar (1805) after Nelson's death.

Collingwood, Robin George (1889-1943), English philosopher. Believed philosophy originates in history, not science. Works incl. *Principles of Art* (1937), *The Idea of History* (1945).

Collins, Michael (1890-1922), Irish Sinn Fein leader. Organized guerrilla warfare against British. With Arthur Griffith, estab. (1921) Irish Free State. Briefly (1922) head of state and army, before he was assassinated.

Collins, Michael, see ARMSTRONG, NEIL.

Collins, [William] Wilkie (1824-89), English novelist, associate of Dickens. Known for thriller *The Woman in White* (1860), *The Moonstone* (1868), regarded as 1st English detective novel. Also wrote plays.

Collodi, pseud. of Carlo Lorenzini (1826-90), Italian journalist. Known for *The Adventures of Pinocchio* (1883), made into animated cartoon by Disney (1943).

colloid, solid, liquid or gaseous substance made up of very small insoluble particles that remain in suspension in solid, liquid or gas medium of different matter. Examples incl. solutions of starch and albumen. Suspension of colloidal particles in gas is called an aerosol, *eg* fog and smoke.

collotype, method of printing by which inked reproductions are transferred directly to paper from an image formed on a gelatine-coated glass plate. Used for printing high quality colour illustrations.

Colman, George, ('the Elder') (1732-94), English dramatist. Known for comedies, esp. *The Clandestine*

Marriage (1766) written with Garrick, *The Jealous Wife* (1761).

Colman, Ronald (1891-1958), British actor. Played 'English gentleman' roles in films, as in *Bulldog Drummond* (1929), *The Prisoner of Zenda* (1937), *A Double Life* (1948).

Colmar or **Kolmar,** town of Alsace, E France, cap. of Haut-Rhin dept. Pop. 63,000. Major textile mfg. centre, wine trade. Free imperial city from 1226, annexed by France (1681). Many medieval buildings, incl. 13th cent. convent.

colobus monkey, genus of slender African monkeys, usually with long black and white fur, and no thumbs. Treetop dwelling; diet of leaves, fruit. Fur hunting has diminished numbers.

Cologne cathedral

Cologne (*Köln*), city of NW West Germany, on R. Rhine. Pop. 846,000. River port, railway jct.; indust., banking centre; univ. (1388). Perfume mfg., incl. 'eau-de-Cologne'. Roman *Colonia Agrippinensis*; powerful medieval archbishopric, Hanseatic League member from 1201. Gothic cathedral (begun 1248). Badly damaged in WWII.

Colomb-Béchar, town and oasis of W Algeria. Pop. 47,000. Produces dates. On projected trans-Saharan railway; nearby are Kenadsa coal mines.

Colombia, republic of NW South America. Area 1,138,900 sq km (439,700 sq mi); pop. 22,750,000; cap. Bogotá. Language: Spanish. Religion: RC. Has Pacific and Caribbean coasts; Andes in W; tropical forests, grasslands in E; uninhabited lowland in interior. Chief rivers are Cauca, Magdalena. Coffee, bananas are chief crops; important mineral resources incl. platinum, oil. Spanish colony from 16th cent. Independence gained under Bolívar in 1819; known as New Granada until 1863. Panama seceded in 1903; civil war 1949-53.

Colombo, cap. and chief port of Sri Lanka. Pop. 562,000. Commercial centre; exports rubber, tea. Univ. (1870). Under Dutch control in 17th cent., ceded to British (1796). Site of Colombo Plan conference (1950), on Commonwealth-US aid to S and SE Asia.

Colón, town of Panama, at Caribbean end of Panama Canal; on Manzanillo Isl. Pop. 68,000. Exports tropical fruit, wood. Neighbouring Cristóbal is in Canal Zone.

Colorado, state of WC US. Area 270,000 sq km (104,247 sq mi); pop. 2,207,000; cap. Denver. Mainly in Rocky Mts., mean alt. 2070 m (*c* 6800 ft), plains in E. Has sources of Rio Grande, Arkansas, Colorado rivers. Agric. incl. potato, sugar beet, alfalfa, wheat growing, stock raising. Coal, uranium, molybdenum mining. Part of Louisiana Purchase of 1803; had gold, silver strikes in 19th cent. Admitted to Union as 38th state (1876).

Colorado, two rivers of SW US, **1,** rises in Rocky Mts., N Colorado, flows SW 2334 km (1450 mi) through Utah, Arizona (Grand Canyon). Forms much of Californian border. Continues into Mexico to Gulf of California. Provides h.e.p. and irrigation from numerous dams, *eg* Hoover. **2,** rises in NW Texas, flows SE 1439 km (894 mi) to Gulf of Mexico. Also has several dams.

Colorado beetle

Colorado beetle or **potato beetle,** *Leptinotarsa decemlineata,* leaf-eating beetle originally of W North America, now found wherever potatoes cultivated. Yellow, with black stripes. Serious pest of potatoes, other garden vegetables.

Colorado Springs, town of C Colorado, US; at foot of Pikes Peak. Pop. 135,000. Health and holiday resort (nearby is Garden of the Gods sandstone region). Has US Airforce Academy.

Colosseum or **Coliseum,** largest amphitheatre of ancient Rome, built *c* AD 75-80. A 4-storied oval building, it held *c* 45,000 people on tiers around the arena. Still largely extant.

Colossians, Epistle to the, NT book, traditionally attributed to St Paul while in prison at Rome (*c* AD 62). Warns the church at Colossae of dangers of false teaching.

Colossus of Rhodes, bronze statue of sun god, Helios, which stood in Rhodes harbour. Built by Chares *c* 292-280 BC, it was *c* 30 m (100 ft) high. One of seven wonders of the ancient world, it was destroyed by an earthquake (224 BC).

colour, sensation resulting from stimulation of retina of the eye by light of certain wavelengths. Any colour can be produced by combining beams of primary colours, red, green and blue. Pigmented objects produce colour by absorbing certain wavelengths and reflecting others; primary pigment colours are red, yellow and blue.

colour blindness, inability to distinguish between certain colours, esp. red and green. Red-green form is a sex-linked character, being transmitted from women to their sons; thus it is much more common in men. *See* SEX CHROMOSOME.

Colt .45 army revolver (1873); known as the 'peacemaker'

Colt, Samuel (1814-62), American inventor. Patented the revolving-breech pistol (1836) and set up a large arms factory at Hartford, Conn.

coltsfoot, *Tussilago farfara,* plant of daisy family. Common weed of N temperate regions. Large heart-shaped leaves, hairy, scaly stalk, yellow spring flower.

Colum, Padraic (1881-1972), Irish poet. Associated with Irish Renaissance. Works incl. *Wild Earth* (1907), autobiog.

Our Friend James Joyce (1959), classic song 'She Passed through the Fair'.

Columba or **Columcille, St** (*c* 521-97), Irish missionary. Estab. Celtic monasteries in Ireland at Derry, Durrow, Kells. Set up monastery on Iona (563) as centre for the conversion of N Scotland. Made extensive and successful missionary journeys among the Picts.

Columban, St (*c* 540-615), Irish missionary, scholar. Founded Celtic monasteries at Luxeuil and Bobbio (614), noted centres of learning. Incurred hostility of ecclesiastical and civil authorities through his austerity and Celtic ecclesiastical customs.

Columbia, cap. of South Carolina, US; on Congaree R. Pop. 114,000. Cultural, education centre. Agric. industs. esp. cotton, textile mills. Founded 1786. Chosen as cap. 1786.

Columbia, river of W US and Canada. Rises in Rocky Mts. (SE British Columbia). Flows 1950 km (*c* 1210 mi) to US border; then SW through Washington, which lower course separates from Oregon, before reaching Pacific. Snake R. is chief tributary. Supplies irrigation for surrounding agric. regions from Grand Coulee, Bonneville dams. Source of h.e.p.

Columbia, District of, *see* DISTRICT OF COLUMBIA.

Columbia University, New York City, US. Estab. (1754) as King's College by grant of George II. Became Columbia Univ. (1896) after additions and enlargements. Incl. Barnard Coll. for Women, many graduate and research schools.

columbine, plant of genus *Aquilegia* of buttercup family, incl. *c* 70 species found in temperate regions. Native European species, *A. vulgaris,* is purple or white. *A. caerulia,* a blue and white variety, is state flower of Colorado.

columbium, *see* NIOBIUM.

Columbus, Christopher, English form of Cristoforo Colombo (1451-1506), Italian navigator, b. Genoa. Engaged for many years in Portuguese sea trade; sailed westward (1492) for Ferdinand and Isabella of Spain in *Santa María, Niña,* and *Pinta,* landing on Watling Isl. in Bahamas. On 3 subsequent voyages reached Leeward Isls., Puerto Rico, Cuba, Jamaica, Hispaniola, and American mainland from Orinoco to Panama, believed by him to be East Indies.

Columbus, town of W Georgia, US; on Chattahoochee R. Pop. 155,000. Indust., transport centre; cotton, textiles, agric. implement mfg. Founded as trading post (1828).

Columbus, cap. of Ohio, US; on Scioto R. Pop. 533,000. Indust. and transport centre; produces aircraft, car parts, mining machinery. Founded as state cap. 1812.

column, in architecture, slender upright structure generally consisting of cylindrical or polygonal shaft, with base and capital; used as a support or ornamental member in a building. Greeks perfected design of columns in temples, *eg* Parthenon. *See* ORDERS OF ARCHITECTURE.

Colwyn Bay, mun. bor. of Clwyd, N Wales. Pop. 26,000. Seaside resort.

coma, state of complete and prolonged unconsciousness from which patient cannot be aroused. Caused by brain disturbance, *eg* injury, poisoning, lack of oxygen.

Comanche, North American Indian tribe of Uto-Aztecan linguistic stock. Separated from SHOSHONE and settled (*c* 1680) in S Texas and W Oklahoma. Nomadic plains warriors, fiercely opposed to white man. Greatly reduced by war and disease to *c* 1500 (1904), when confined to Oklahoma reserve.

Combination Acts (1799, 1800), in UK, laws outlawing trade unions. Unions went underground until laws were repealed 1824.

comb jelly, *see* CTENOPHORA.

COMECON, *see* COUNCIL FOR MUTUAL ECONOMIC ASSISTANCE.

Comédie-Française, French national theatre in Paris estab. 1681 from a company of Molière's actors. Renamed *Théâtre Française* (1791).

comedy, originally drama or narrative with happy ending and non-tragic theme (*eg* Dante's *Divine Comedy*), now usually given humorous treatment. In England, tradition goes back through Latin writers, *eg* Plautus, to Greek dramas of Aristophanes, Menander. In France, Molière combined *commedia dell'arte* with classical influence in Comedy of Manners, which developed in England into Restoration comedy (Congreve), and later into satirical character comedies of Goldsmith, Sheridan, Wilde; 20th cent. social comedies written by G.B. Shaw, Noël Coward.

Comenius, Johann Amos, Latinized form of Jan Amos Komenský (1592-1670), Czech educator, Moravian churchman. Advocate of universal education, coeducation. Revolutionized Latin teaching, relating it to everyday life, through textbook *The Visible World in Pictures* (1658).

comet, heavenly body moving under influence of Sun. Consists of bright nucleus, surrounded by hazy gaseous mass (coma). When passing near Sun, tail of gaseous material may be formed, pointing away from Sun. Generally follows elongated elliptical orbit, returning at calculable intervals, *eg* Halley's comet. Others have completely disintegrated, *eg* Biela's comet.

Comines, Commines or **Commynes, Philippe de** (*c* 1447–*c* 1511), French historian, diplomat. Served Charles the Bold of Burgundy, Louis XI and Charles VIII of France. His *Mémoires* (1524) are valuable for objective analysis of characters of contemporary figures.

Cominform (Communist Information Bureau), coordinating organ of Communist parties of USSR, its E European allies, France and Italy. Estab. in Belgrade (1947), hq. moved to Bucharest after expulsion of Yugoslavia (1948). Became instrument of oppression for Stalin, dissolved in 1956.

Comintern (Communist International), also known as Third International, association of world Communist parties estab. by Lenin (1919). Leading members incl. Zinoviev, Trotsky, Radek, Bukharin. Founded to give leadership to more extreme elements of world socialist movements, dominated by Russian Communists. Anti-Comintern Pact formed (1936) by Germany and Japan. USSR dissolved Comintern in 1943 as goodwill gesture to Allies in WWII.

commedia dell'arte, Italian dramatic genre dating from 16th cent. Travelling actors improvised on stock characters (Harlequin, Scaramouche, *etc*). Conventions influenced Shakespeare, Jonson, Mollère, de Vega, Goldoni, later developed into pantomime.

commerce, the buying and selling of goods, esp. on large scale, *eg* between countries. Carried on in ancient times around Mediterranean by Egyptians, Sumerians, Phoenicians. Crusades stimulated European trading aspirations, trade superiority eventually passing to cities of N Italy. Exploitation of New World by Spain gave her brief hegemony. The 18th cent. was marked by rivalry between Dutch, British and (later) French. Industrial Revolution gave Britain superiority in 19th cent. Recent developments incl. European Economic Community and growing trade between Communist and capitalist blocs. *See* MERCANTILISM, FREE TRADE.

Commines, Philippe de, *see* COMINES.

commodity, in economics, term for anything which is limited in supply and thus has a value in exchange.

Commodus, Lucius Aelius Aurelius (AD 161-92), Roman emperor (180-92). Son of Marcus Aurelius, his wasteful gladiatorial contests led to popular unrest. Strangled by a wrestler.

common law, law of nation based on custom, usage, and legal precedent. Distinct from but complementary to statute law. Important in England where it became estab. in 13th cent., influenced English-speaking countries.

Common Market, Central American, *see* CENTRAL AMERICAN COMMON MARKET.

Common Market, European, *see* EUROPEAN COMMUNITIES.

Commons, House of, *see* HOUSE OF COMMONS.

Commonwealth, govt. of England under Cromwell and Parliament (1649-60); also *see* PROTECTORATE.

Commonwealth, British, free association of UK and ex-colonies. Evolved from dominions, estab. as autonomous by STATUTE OF WESTMINSTER (1931) after Imperial Conference (1926). Commonwealth Relations Office estab.

1947, with which Colonial Office was merged (1966). Member states incl. Canada, Australia, New Zealand, India, many African, Asian, Caribbean states. South Africa withdrew (1961), Pakistan (1972). Territs. dependent on UK incl. Hong Kong, Gibraltar, Bermuda.

Commune of Paris, (18 March-29 May, 1871), Parisian revolutionary govt. Set up at end of FRANCO-PRUSSIAN WAR after premier Adolphe Thiers' attempt to crush armed national guard of Paris. Socialist govt. elected (26 March). Thiers' siege succeeded, and *c* 20,000 prisoners killed.

Communion, Holy, *see* EUCHARIST.

Communism, Mount, highest peak of USSR, in Pamir Mts., Tadzhik SSR; height 7495 m (24,590 ft).

Communism, modern, international movement advocating revolutionary overthrow of capitalism (*see* MARXISM), arising out of Marx and Engels' *Communist Manifesto* (1848). Guided by principles of communal ownership of means of production, everyone receiving according to his need and working according to his capacity. Marxian Communism spread through founding of First INTERNATIONAL and rise of Social Democratic parties in Europe. Radical form taken (1903) in Russia when Bolsheviks, under Lenin, urged immediate violent revolution to overthrow CAPITALISM and estab. world socialist state. Bolsheviks triumphed in RUSSIAN REVOLUTION (1917). Leninists urged workers' union for international revolution; stateless, universal Communism with no class distinction would theoretically follow 'dictatorship of proletariat'. Stalin consolidated Communist power in USSR during 1930s. Soviet victory in WWII brought addition of E European satellites to Communist bloc. Links with China after estab. of Communist state (1949) under Mao Tse-tung; in early 1960s China's accusations of Soviet conciliation with West brought rift. Western powers involved in conflicts in attempts to contain spread of Communism, esp. Korea (1950-3), and US in Vietnam (1965-73).

communism, social or economic system or theory in which property (esp. means of production) is held in common by all members of society, not by individuals. As theory of govt. and social reform, communism can be attributed to Plato who in *Republic* outlined society with communal property. In England, forms of communism manifested in Sir Thomas More's *Utopia* and the DIGGERS. Recent attempts based upon principles of communism incl. Israeli *kibbutzim,* 'drop-out' settlements in US. Movement tends toward agric. based communities, although modern COMMUNISM developed as reaction to capitalist enterprise following Industrial Revolution, in protest against appalling labour conditions.

Communist Manifesto, *see* MARX, KARL.

Communist Party, a political organization based on principles of Communism, as developed by Marx and Engels; modified by Lenin, Stalin and others, dedicated to estab. state socialism. In USSR developed from Bolshevik-Menshevik split (1903), gained power during Russian Revolution (1917). Later centralized, wielding real power through CENTRAL COMMITTEE. In China founded 1921, developed under Mao Tse-tung; protracted struggle with Kuomintang, interrupted by WWII, civil war, ended with Communist triumph and estab. of People's Republic (1949). In Americas, Communist Party govts. incl. that under Castro in Cuba and short-lived one under Allende in Chile. Communist parties in West have attempted to gain power through electoral process and trade union activities.

Commynes, Philippe de, *see* COMINES.

Como, town of Lombardy, N Italy, at S end of L. Como. Cap. of Como prov. Pop. 99,000. Tourist resort. Famous in Middle Ages for craftsmen (silk, *etc*). Marble cathedral, Gothic town hall.

Comodoro Rivadavia, port of SE Argentina, on Atlantic. Pop. 78,000. Major oil centre; has natural gas pipeline to Buenos Aires.

Comorin, Cape, southernmost point of India, near Nagercoil (Tamil Nadu).

Comoro Islands, republic in Indian Ocean, at N end of Mozambique Channel; comprise group of volcanic isls.

Area 2170 sq km (838 sq mi); pop. 250,000; cap. Moroni. Language: French. Religions: Islam, Christianity. Produce vanilla, copra, cocoa, coffee. Formerly French overseas territ., became independent 1975.

company, limited, in UK, organization, public or private, and legally registered, formed to carry out activities (usually on profit basis). Each partner is liable under 1855 Limited Liabilities Act for only the amount of his investment. Act brought British practice in line with that of Continent. In US, corporations are functionally and legally similar.

compass, name given to 2 instruments: mathematical compass is used to draw circles and measure distance; magnetic compass is used to determine direction by allowing magnetic needle to swing freely on a pivot.

competition, in economics, term for the degree to which the market can be influenced by buyers and sellers. Perfect competition is a theoretical model, in which many producers with no control over price produce goods which are sold to competing buyers. In fact, market limited by industrial cooperation, patents, *etc. See* MONOPOLY, SUPPLY AND DEMAND.

Compiègne, town of Ile-de-France, N France, on R. Oise. Pop. 33,000. Tourist resort, sawmilling, glassworks. Scene of siege (1430) in which Joan of Arc captured by English. Armistice of 1918 and French surrender of 1940 both signed in nearby forest.

complex, in psychology, idea or group of ideas arising in the mind as result of highly emotional experience, and repressed partly or wholly, as result of conflict with other ideas accepted by individual. Most famous is Oedipus complex.

complex number, in mathematics, number expressed as formal sum $a + bi$, where a and b are real numbers and i is square root of -1. Complex numbers form an extension of real number system in which all polynomials have roots.

Compositae, largest and most highly advanced family of flowering plants. Characterized by flower heads composed of dense clusters of small flowers surrounded by a ring of small leaves, *eg* daisy, thistle, artichoke, chrysanthemum.

comprehensive education, system of state-financed education combining various types of SECONDARY SCHOOL, drawing all pupils from surrounding catchment area. Its implementation in UK by local authorities from 1960s aroused opposition in many areas among advocates of separation of pupils by ability(*see* GRAMMAR SCHOOL).

Compromise of 1850, measures passed by US Congress balancing interests of slave and free states. Provided for California's admission as free state, abolished slavery in Dist. of Columbia. Estab. strict fugitive slave law, boundary of Texas. Bills failed ultimately to resolve slavery question.

Compton, Arthur Holly (1892-1962), American physicist. Discovered Compton effect, describing loss of energy (increase of wavelength) of photon striking a free electron. Shared Nobel Prize for Physics (1927).

Compton-Burnett, Dame Ivy (1892-1969), English novelist. Known for stylized, formal dialogue novels, *eg Brothers and Sisters* (1929), *Elders and Betters* (1944), *Mother and Son* (1955), dealing with claustrophobic family power struggles.

computer, device which, by means of stored instructions and information, performs large numbers of calculations at great speed or may be used to compile, correlate and select data (data processing). Two types; digital, which processes information in numerical form, usually in BINARY SYSTEM, and analog, which represents information in terms of quantities (*eg* current or voltage) rather than by digital counting. Sequence of calculations controlled by program, *ie* series of precisely defined instructions fed into machine. Specialized programming 'languages' evolved to describe operations which machine will carry out. Early examples incl. calculating machines designed by BABBAGE.

Comte, [Isidore] Auguste [Marie François Xavier] (1798-1857), French philosopher. Disciple of Saint-Simon. Founder of POSITIVISM. Delineated 3 stages (theological, metaphysical, positive) in all fields of knowledge; rejected

Auguste Comte

metaphysics in favour of modern science. Works incl. *Cours de Philosophie Positive* (1830-42).

Conakry or **Konakry,** cap. of Guinea, on Tombo Isl. Pop. 197,000. Admin., commercial centre; railway terminus and deepwater port, exports alumina, iron ore, bananas.

Conan Doyle, *see* DOYLE, SIR ARTHUR CONAN.

Conant, James Bryant (1893-   ), American educator. Known for investigations into American education, pub. in, *eg Slums and Schools* (1961), *The Comprehensive High School* (1967).

concentration camp, institution for detention of elements of population deemed dangerous by regime. Term first applied to British examples in Boer War. Used esp. by Germans during WWII against 'undesirables', *eg* Jews, Poles; notorious examples incl. Buchenwald, Dachau, Oswiecim. Associated with single-party state.

Concepción, town of SC Chile, near mouth of Bío-Bío R. Pop. 190,000. Textile, leather, glass mfg. Export centre through port of Talcahuano. Major coalfields nearby. Founded 1550. Has suffered many earthquakes.

concertina, a form of accordion in which both sets of fingers operate buttons or studs, so that the hands do not have to move over a keyboard while squeezing and expanding the bellows. Invented by the scientist Sir Charles Wheatstone in 1829.

concerto, music for one or more soloists and orchestra, usually in 3 movements or sections. A *concerto grosso* features a group of instrumentalists with orchestra. A concerto for orchestra is a display piece to demonstrate virtuosity of the entire orchestra.

conch, marine mollusc, with spiral one-piece shell. Species incl. *Strombus gigas* of West Indies. Shell used for ornaments or as simple trumpet.

conciliation, industrial, means of settling labour disputes by means of seeking involvement and recommendations of 3rd party, often govt. agency, *eg* UK Advisory Conciliation and Arbitration Service, US Federal Mediation and Conciliation Service. If parties do not come to voluntary settlement, arbitration may follow to impose compulsory decision.

Concord, *see* BOSTON, Massachusetts.

Concord, cap. of New Hampshire, US; on Merrimack R. Pop. 30,000. Granite quarrying nearby; printing indust. Settled *c* 1725.

concordance, alphabetical list of important words used in a book or by a particular writer, with references to the passages in which they occur. First examples inspired by conviction of thematic links between passages of Bible, *eg Concordantiae Morales* on Vulgate, attributed to Anthony of Padua. Notable examples of Biblical concordances incl. those of Alexander CRUDEN.

Concorde, first supersonic (Mach 2.2) passenger aircraft developed jointly by France and UK. Maiden flight,

Toulouse (March, 1969). Services inaugurated (1976), despite protests in US, UK by environmentalists, because of excessive noise.

concrete, building material made of sand and gravel, bonded with cement; dries to form hard stone-like substance. May be strengthened by introducing steel rods (reinforced concrete). Used by Romans for construction of roads and buildings. Modern concrete dates from discovery of portland cement in early 19th cent.

Condé, Louis [I] de Bourbon, Prince de (1530-69), French nobleman. Huguenot leader, led Protestant forces in religious wars of 1560s. Army defeated by Catholic forces, killed at Jarnac. His great-grandson, **Louis [II] de Bourbon, Prince de Condé** (1621-86), known as the 'Great Condé', won major battles at Nördlingen (1645), Lens (1648) during Thirty Years War. Led FRONDE uprising, commanding army of princes (1651) and Spanish forces (1653-9) against Louis XIV; defeated in battle of the Dunes by Turenne (1658). Pardoned, later fought successfully for Louis against the Dutch.

condenser, in chemistry, device for condensing vapour into liquid, consisting of glass tubes cooled by air or water.

condenser, in electricity, see CAPACITOR.

Condillac, Etienne Bonnot de (1715-80), French philosopher. Believed thoughts arise from sensations, mediated by language; developed theory in *Traité des sensations* (1745), which influenced later psychologists. Also contributed to *Encyclopédie* (1751-72).

condor, New World vulture, inhabiting high mountain regions. Black plumage with white markings on wings, neck. Feeds mainly on carrion. Two species: nearly extinct Californian condor, *Gymnogyps californianus,* and ANDEAN CONDOR.

Condorcet, [Marie Jean] Antoine Nicolas de Caritat, Marquis de (1743-94), French philosopher, mathematician. Girondist member of legislative assembly, laid foundation for state education. Outlawed by Jacobins. Wrote *Esquisse d'un tableau historique de progrès de l'esprit humain,* describing man's progress and heralding perfection of human state to follow French Revolution. His concept of progress influenced later social theorists, esp. Comte.

conduction, thermal, transfer of heat from hotter parts of a medium to colder parts by passage of energy from particle to particle. In metals, heat flow is largely due to motion of energetic free electrons towards colder regions.

THE UNION STATES

Confederacy

Confederacy or **Confederate States of America** (1861-5), govt. estab. by Southern states of US which seceded from Union. After election of Lincoln as president, 7 states left Union (early 1861) followed by 4 more after Lincoln's declaration of war. Jefferson Davis was elected president; Judah P. Benjamin was outstanding cabinet member. For subsequent history, see CIVIL WAR (US).

Confederation, Articles of (1781), pre-constitutional formulation of how American colonies were to be governed. Proved unsatisfactory as central govt. too dependent on states for money, executive powers. Superseded by Constitution (1789). Confederation in Canada embodied in BRITISH NORTH AMERICA ACT (1867).

Confederation of the Rhine, see RHINE, CONFEDERATION OF THE.

confession, in RC, Orthodox and High Anglican churches, disclosure of sin to priest to obtain absolution. *See* PENANCE.

Confucius, latinized form of K'ung Fu-tzu (c 551-c 479 BC), Chinese philosopher and social reformer. Advocate of ethical system founded on absolute justice and moderation with the aim of stabilizing society. Teachings became basis of Confucianism, developed as state religion with adherence to traditional values.

conger eel, any of Congridae family of scaleless saltwater eels. Long dorsal fin, sharp teeth, powerful jaws. European conger, *Conger conger,* reaches length of 2.1 m/7 ft. *C. oceanica,* of Atlantic coast of North America, is smaller.

conglomerate, in geology, rock composed of rounded fragments, bound together in matrix of cementing material. Normally formed of transported pebbles, unlike breccia. Examples incl. single pebble type, mixed pebble type, and glacial conglomerates.

Congo (Brazzaville), republic of WC Africa. Area 342,000 sq km (132,000 sq mi); pop. 1,004,000; cap. Brazzaville. Languages: Bantu, French. Religions: native, Christian. Mainly tropical forest, exports hardwoods, sugar, tobacco, coffee; main food crops cassava, yams. Lead, potash mining; aluminium indust. Coast explored 15th cent. by Portuguese, interior 19th cent. by de Brazza. Base of French trading (17th-19th cent.). Territ. (Middle Congo) of French Equatorial Africa from 1910; independent 1960. Member of French Community.

Congo (Kinshasa), see ZAÏRE.

Congo or **Zaïre,** river of WC Africa, 2nd longest (c 4800 km/3000 mi) in Africa. Rises in SE Zaïre, called R. Lualaba until reaching Stanley Falls; middle course curves SW, forming part of Zaïre-Republic of Congo border, widening at Stanley Pool. Enters Atlantic by wide estuary, forms part of Zaïre-Angola border. Navigable for ocean-going vessels to Matadi. Mouth discovered (1482), explored by Livingstone (1871); 1st descent made by Stanley (1874-7).

Congregationalism, faith and form of organization of a Protestant denomination in which each member church is self-governing. Based on belief that each congregation has Christ alone at its head. First appeared in 16th cent. England as revolt against state control of Established church; principles formulated by ROBERT BROWNE. Important in development of New England. Congregations now loosely organized in unions.

Congress of Industrial Organizations, see AMERICAN FEDERATION OF LABOR AND CONGRESS OF INDUSTRIAL ORGANIZATIONS.

Congress of Racial Equality (CORE), American organization for civil rights. Estab. (1942) by James Farmer and others.

Congress of the United States, legislature of US federal govt., as distinct from executive and judiciary, estab. (1789) by Article I of Constitution. Comprises an upper house (SENATE) and a lower house (HOUSE OF REPRESENTATIVES).

Congress Party (Indian), see INDIAN NATIONAL CONGRESS.

Congreve, William (1670-1729), English playwright. Known for Restoration comedies, esp. *Love for Love* (1695), *The Way of the World* (1700). Tragedy *The Mourning Bride* (1697) was his most popular play in own day.

conic sections, in geometry, curves produced by intersection of a plane with a right circular cone. Consist of ellipse, circle, parabola, hyperbola and degenerate cases of these. Much studied by ancient Greek geometers.

conifer, class of woody perennials comprising 6 families, c 500 species. Mainly evergreen trees bearing cones. Trees cultivated for timber, pulp, resin and turpentine. Incl. PINE, cypress, yew, sequoia.

Coniston Water, lake of Cumbria, NW England. In Lake Dist. at foot of Old Man of Coniston. Length 8 km (5 mi). Scene of Campbells' water speed records (1939, 1959).

Conjeeveram, see KANCHIPURAM.

conjunctivitis, inflammation of membrane covering inside of eyelids and front of eye. Caused by infection with viruses or bacteria; usually treated by antibiotics.

Connacht or **Connaught,** prov. of W Irish Republic. Area 17,122 sq km (6611 sq mi); pop. 390,000. Comprises cos. Galway, Leitrim, Mayo, Roscommon, Sligo.

Connecticut, New England state of US. Area 12,973 sq km (5009 sq mi); pop. 3,032,000; cap. Hartford. Mainly lowland with indented coastline; divided by Connecticut R. Agric. incl. tobacco growing, dairy, poultry farming. Granite, sandstone quarrying. Mfg. industs. incl. machinery, tools, firearms, textiles, clocks and watches; defence industs. First settled by Dutch, later by Puritans from Massachusetts in 17th cent. One of original 13 colonies of US.

Connelly, Marc[us Cook] (1890-), American dramatist. Known for *The Green Pastures* (1930), enactment of Old Testament stories in lives of Deep South negroes. Also collaborated with G.S. Kaufman, *eg Dulcy* (1921).

Connemara, region of Co. Galway, W Irish Republic. Lakes, mountains (incl. 'Twelve Pins'). Tourism.

Connolly, Cyril Vernon (1903-74), English author, critic. Known for essays in *Enemies of Promise* (1938), *Ideas and Places* (1953). *The Unquiet Grave* (1944) explores his theme of the 'will-to-failure'.

Connolly, James (1870-1916), Irish nationalist. A Socialist, he supported labour movements in US and Ireland. Captured and shot helping to lead 1916 Easter Rebellion.

Connolly, Maureen ('Little Mo') (1934-69), American tennis player. First woman to achieve 'grand slam' of winning all 4 major tennis championships (1953). Won Wimbledon and US titles 3 times, French twice.

Conquistador (Span., = conqueror), name given Spanish leaders in conquest of Americas. Suppressed and exploited Indian pop. in search for gold and silver, esp. during Pizarro's conquest of Inca empire. Expeditions estab. Spanish empire and Golden Age of late 16th and 17th cent.

Conrad III (*c* 1093-1152), German king (1138-52). Founded Hohenstaufen dynasty. Anti-king to Lothair of Saxony 1127-35; never crowned by pope as Holy Roman emperor. Joint leader, with Louis VII of France, of 2nd Crusade (1147-9). Reign marked by opposition of Guelphs, esp. Henry the Lion.

Joseph Conrad

Conrad, Joseph, orig. Teodor Józef Konrad Nalecz Korzeniowski (1857-1924), English novelist, b. Poland. Works, often set at sea, concerned with man's ability to cope with testing situations, *eg Lord Jim* (1900), *Typhoon* (1903), *Victory* (1915). Short stories, *eg* 'Heart of Darkness' (1902), often contain his most intense work.

Conradin (1252-68), duke of Swabia. Son of Conrad IV, last of Hohenstaufen line. Claimed Sicilian throne but was defeated by Charles of Anjou at Tagliacozzo; beheaded at Naples.

consanguinity, relationship by descent from same ancestor. Of legal importance in laws relating to marriage (*see* INCEST) and inheritance.

Conscience, Hendrik (1812-83), Flemish novelist. First novel *In the Year of Marvels, 1566* (1837) was first book published in modern Flemish. Other works incl. *The Lion of Flanders* (1838).

conscientious objector, a term first used in WWI for those who objected to combatant service for moral or religious reasons. They were given legal status in UK by the Military Service Act (1916) and in WWII the Military Training Act (1939) prescribed alternative forms of service. Similar schemes exist in US.

conscription, compulsory enrolment of citizens for military purposes. Recorded in Greece and Rome, it was first used in modern times by Napoleon in 1798. Most European states have invoked it at some time, incl. Britain (1947-62). Introduced in US during Civil War.

conservation laws, in physics, laws stating that total value of some quantity does not change during physical processes, *eg* total electrical charge of a system remains constant. Laws of conservation of mass and of energy have been combined into single mass-energy law following Einstein's demonstration of equivalence of mass and energy.

conservatism, tendency to preserve and to oppose changes in estab. institutions or practices. In politics, manifested in parties advocating policies founded on belief in free enterprise, distrust of state intervention, and conservation in particular of sovereign and religious institutions. In UK, **Conservative Party** replaced TORY Party after Reform Bill of 1832. Survived splits in 1846 and 1905, became champion of propertied democracy and imperialism. Shared major party status with Liberals until 1922, after which alternated with Labour Party in govt. Prominent figures incl. Peel, Disraeli, the Chamberlains, Baldwin, Churchill. Most important Commonwealth counterpart is Canada's Progressive Conservative Party (named 1942), founded 1854 as Conservatives. In European democracies, conservative policies often promoted by Christian Democrat parties.

Constable, John (1776-1837), English painter. With Turner, leading English landscape painter of 19th cent.; his direct observations of nature, capturing effects of changing light, influenced French Romantic painters, incl. Delacroix, and later Barbizon school. *The Hay Wain* and *View on the Stour* won gold medals at Paris Salon of 1824.

Constance (*Konstanz*), town of S West Germany, on R. Rhine at exit from L. Constance. Pop. 61,000. Port; produces textiles, chemicals. Held by Austria 1548-1805. Hist. buildings incl. minster (11th cent.), Dominican monastery. Scene of Council of Constance (1414-18) where Hus was condemned.

Constance, Lake (Ger. *Bodensee*), on Swiss-Austro-German border. Rhine enters at SE, leaves NW. Area 531 sq km (205 sq mi). Tourism, fishing. Ancient lake dwellings.

Constanta, city of SE Romania, on Black Sea. Pop. 186,000. Resort; main Romanian port, exports grain, timber, petroleum (pipeline from Ploeşti). Founded by Greeks; rebuilt by Emperor Constantine 4th cent. Ceded by Turkey to Romania (1878).

Constant [de Rebecque], [Henri] Benjamin (1767-1830), French author, politician, b. Switzerland. Known for short introspective novel, *Adolphe* (1816), prob. based on liaison with Mme de Staël.

Constantine [I] the Great (*c* 288-337), Roman emperor (306-37). Proclaimed emperor by troops in Britain on death of his father Constantius (306). Defeated rival Maxentius (312) in battle before which he is said to have had vision of Christ's cross. Legally recognized Christianity in empire with Edict of Milan (313). Gained control of E part of empire by 324 with defeat of rival Licinius. Consolidated and rebuilt empire; moved capital to Constantinople on Bosporus (330). Became a Christian 337.

Constantine [XI] Palaeologus (1404-53), last Byzantine emperor (1448-53). Proclaimed union of Eastern and Western churches in attempt to obtain aid against Turks. Died defending Constantinople against Turks.

Constantine II (1940-), king of Greece (1964-8). Formally cooperated with military junta that took power (1967), exiled 1968. Monarchy abolished by junta (1973); decision confirmed by popular vote (1974) after overthrow of junta.

Constantine (anc. *Cirta*), city of NE Algeria. Pop. 254,000. Grain, leather, wool trade. Ancient cap. of Numidia; destroyed AD 311, rebuilt AD 313 by Constantine I. Taken by French 1837.

Constantinople, see ISTANBUL.

Constantius II (317-61), Roman emperor (337-61). Son of Constantine I, shared rule with his 2 brothers, being given control of E part of empire. United empire with defeat of usurper Magnentius (351) and ruled alone.

constellation, in astronomy, name given to groups of stars. In N hemisphere, names largely mythological, *eg* Orion; in S hemisphere (mapped 16th - 18th cent.) named after animals or scientific equipment, *eg* Telescopium. Greeks recognized 48 constellations; now 88 are recognized.

constitution, whole system of govt. of a country. In wide sense, applied to both laws and customs which estab. and regulate govt.; more narrowly, to selection of these which are codified in document. Most nations have written constitutions, UK being notable exception.

Constitution of the United States (1789), codification of system of federal govt. Consists of 7 articles, preamble, 26 amendments. Basis estab. (1787) by Federal Constitutional Convention, held in Philadelphia. Provided separation of powers into executive, judicial, legislative branches. First 10 amendments (Bill of Rights) guarantee individual liberties.

constructivism, artistic movement in Russia during years 1917-22, characterized by abstract and geometric design, massive structural form and use of modern materials. Principal exponents were brothers Antoine Pevsner and Naum Gabo.

consul, title of two chief magistrates of ancient Rome. Most powerful office of republic, controlling army, treasury, civil affairs. Became nominal under empire. Term also used (1799-1804) for one of three highest officials of French republic; Napoleon Bonaparte was first consul.

consumption, see TUBERCULOSIS.

contact lens, thin lens of glass or plastic used to correct defective vision. Usually covers only cornea and floats on tears of wearer.

continent, large continuous land mass on Earth's surface. Seven usually distinguished: Africa, Asia, Australia, North America, South America, Europe and Asia (sometimes taken as one, *ie* Eurasia). Upper level of Earth's crust, forming continents, consists of SIAL; lower level, underlying continents and ocean floors, of SIMA. Prob. formed at time crust first solidified, each continent has Precambrian shield at centre. Over ⅔ area of continents lies in N hemisphere.

Continental Congress (1774-89), legislature of Thirteen Colonies of America. First Congress sent petition of grievances to king, abolished trade with Britain. Second issued Declaration of Independence (4 July, 1776), created Continental Army, conducted American Revolution. Estab. Articles of Confederation, governed under them until Constitution adopted (1789).

continental drift, theoretical process by which continents on Earth's surface have changed their position through time. Alfred Wegener suggested (1912) that in Palaeozoic era all land masses were joined as 1 continent (called 'Pangaea'), later splitting into 2 ('Laurasia' and 'Gondwanaland') which slowly split and drifted into present positions. Also see SIAL, SIMA.

continental shelf, submarine ledge bordering most continents. Covered by shallow water, usually less than *c* 180 m/600 ft deep. May show continental features, *eg* cliffs, river valleys. Commercially important, *eg* most fishing grounds, petroleum found there.

Continental System, policy devised (1806) by Napoleon I to curtail British power by economic boycott and unify European states under his rule. All trade with Britain forbidden. Its failure was result of British naval superiority. Russia's withdrawal (1810) from System provoked Napoleon's disastrous Russian campaign (1812).

contour, line on a map joining all points at same height above sea level. Set of contours thus shows relief of the mapped area.

contrabassoon, see BASSOON.

contraception or **birth control,** prevention of conception. Methods used incl. sterilization, abstinence during certain phases of female ovulation, hormone preparations (the 'Pill'), prevention of sperm entry into uterus, or intra-uterine devices. Modern movements for birth control began in 19th cent. following predictions of overpopulation by Malthus. Widely opposed on religious grounds, (*eg* by RC church) and in certain underpopulated countries, it has greatly reduced birth rate in many countries.

convection, transference of heat in liquids or gases by actual motion of fluid. Fluid in contact with heat source expands, becoming less dense; it rises and its place is taken by colder, denser fluid. Resulting circulation of fluid is called convection current.

convolvulus, see BINDWEED.

Conway (*Aberconway*), mun. bor. of Gwynedd, N Wales, at mouth of R. Conway. Pop. 12,000. Seaside resort. Has remains of 13th cent. castle and town walls; bridges by Telford (1826), Stephenson (1848).

cony, name given to mammals of order Hyracoidea, incl. damans, dassies and hyraxes.

Cook, James (1728-79), English naval officer, explorer. Commanded *Endeavour* on scientific expeditions to S Pacific (1768-71), mainly to observe transit of planet Venus; reached Tahiti, explored coasts of New Zealand and E Australia, claiming latter for UK. Landed at Botany Bay (1770). On 2nd voyage (1772-5) crossed Antarctic Circle, explored S Pacific, discovering Norfolk Isl. (1774). On 3rd voyage (1777-9) failed to find passage to Atlantic from N Pacific; killed by natives on Hawaii.

Cook, Thomas (1808-92), English travel agent. Organized railway excursions, starting 1841. Later conducted tours around Europe (1856) and arranged tours in America (1866). Founded travel agency bearing his name.

Cook, Mount, or **Aorangi,** highest mountain of New Zealand; in Southern Alps, South Isl. Height 3762 m (12,349 ft); part of Mt. Cook National Park.

Cooke, [Alfred] Alistair (1908-), American journalist, b. England. Known in Britain for radio broadcasts 'Letter from America' (1938-), TV series 'America' (1972-3, pub. 1973).

Cook Islands, isl. group of SC Pacific Ocean. Area 240 sq km (93 sq mi); pop. 19,000; main isl. Rarotonga. Produce fruit, copra. Admin. by New Zealand from 1901, self-governing from 1965; formerly called Hervey Isls.

Cookstown, dist. of C Northern Ireland. Area 611 sq km (236 sq mi); pop. 26,000. Created 1973, formerly part of Cos. Tyrone, Londonderry.

Coolidge, [John] Calvin (1872-1933), American statesman, president (1923-9). Gained prominence by using militia to end 1919 Boston police strike as governor of Massachusetts. Vice-president (1921-3), took office on death of Harding and pursued conservative policies.

Cooper, Alfred Duff, Viscount Norwich of Aldwick (1890-1954), British statesman. Conservative first lord of the Admiralty (1937-8), resigned over Munich Pact. Member of Churchill's war cabinet before becoming ambassador to France (1944-7). Wrote biographies of Talleyrand and Haig.

Cooper, Gary, pseud. of Frank J. Cooper (1901–61), American film actor. Famous for roles as reticent man of conscience, often cowboy, in such films as *A Farewell to Arms* (1932), *Mr Deeds Goes to Town* (1936), *Sergeant York* (1941), *High Noon* (1952).

Cooper, James Fenimore (1789-1851), American novelist. First American novelist to acquire international fame, known for 'Leatherstocking' series about frontiersmen, creating characters incl. Natty Bumppo. Novels, greatly influenced by Scott, incl. *The Deerslayer* (1841), *The Last of the Mohicans* (1826), *The Pathfinder* (1840).

Cooper, Peter (1791-1883), American inventor, industrialist. Designed and constructed (1830) *Tom Thumb*, 1st American steam locomotive. Promoted laying of 1st Atlantic telegraph cable; leader in iron indust. Helped secure public school system for New York City and opened (1859) pioneer school, Cooper Union.

Cooper, Samuel (1609-72), English miniaturist. Painted portraits of numerous English notables, incl. Cromwell, Charles II, *etc*; enjoyed European reputation. His brother, **Alexander Cooper** (d. 1660), painted for Queen Christina of Sweden.

Cooperative Commonwealth Federation, see NEW DEMOCRATIC PARTY.

cooperative movement, term covering variety of socio-economic organizations. Main type is consumer cooperative, which people join for purchase of goods in retail stores owned by cooperative, or to organize wholesale trade. Producers' cooperatives are rarer, comprise workers joined for common ownership and management of production. Movement began in 19th cent. Britain, developed variously, throughout Europe. Consumers' cooperatives important in Britain, estab. (1844) permanently by followers of Robert Owen at Rochdale. Producers' cooperatives esp. important in Scandinavia, France.

Cooper's hawk, *Accipiter cooperi*, small North American hawk with long rounded tail and short wings.

coot, freshwater bird of Rallidae family, genus *Fulica*. Black with white forehead; unwebbed feet. Species incl. common European *F. atra*, American *F. americana*.

Copenhagen (*Köbenhavn*), cap. of Denmark, on E Zealand and N Amager Isls.; port on Oresund. Pop. 1,380,000. Admin., commercial, cultural centre. Shipbuilding, fishing, brewing, porcelain mfg. Exports dairy produce. Cap. from 1443; British defeated Danes in naval battle (1801). Univ. (1479); Christiansborg Palace (18th cent.), museums.

Copepoda, subclass of crustaceans, with single eye and no carapace. Six pairs of legs on thorax. CYCLOPS is well-known example.

Copernicus, Nicolas (1473-1543), Polish astronomer. Set down in *De revolutionibus orbium coelestium* (pub. 1543) principles of Earth's axial rotation and position of Sun at centre of solar system, with planets in orbit around it. Provided foundation for work of Kepler and Newton.

Copland, Aaron (1900-), American composer. Some of his work is abstract, but much displays American idioms grafted on to European tradition, *eg* the ballets *Rodeo* and *Appalachian Spring*.

copper (Cu), reddish-brown malleable ductile metallic element; at. no. 29, at. wt. 63.54. Occurs free and as sulphide and oxide ores. Excellent conductor of electricity and heat; resists corrosion. Used in electrical wire, boilers, numerous alloys (bronze, brass, *etc*). Compounds used as fungicides and pesticides.

copperhead, *Ancistrodon contortrix*, poisonous snake of pit viper group of E North America and Canada. Name also applied to poisonous Australian *Denisonia superba*.

Coppermine, river in N Mackenzie Dist., Northwest Territs., Canada. Flows N 845 km (525 mi) to Coppermine village, on Coronation Gulf.

copra, see COCONUT.

coprolite, fossilized excrement of animals, usually containing phosphate.

Coptic, non-Semitic language of Afro-Asiatic family. With Ancient Egyptian formed Egyptian branch of family. Both languages now dead. Coptic *fl* during early Christian era, still used in Coptic church ritual.

Copts, native Christian minority (*c* 10%) of Egypt. Culturally rather than ethnically distinct, they belong to the Coptic Church which was isolated when declared heretical in 451. See MONOPHYSITISM.

copyright, exclusive right granted by law to authors, composers, artists, *etc*, to print, publish and sell their works for specified time. Agreement reached (Bern Convention, 1887) by many countries (excluding US) to safeguard rights internationally. Universal Copyright Convention came into force in US (1955), UK (1957).

Coquelin, Benoit Constant (1841-1909), French actor, known as Coquelin Aine. Associated with Comédie-Française (1860-86), formed own company 1892. Greatest role Cyrano de Bergerac in Rostand's play.

coral, small marine coelenterate usually living in colonies in warm seas. Individuals (polyps) consist of jelly-like body surrounded by calcareous skeleton. With death of polyp, skeletons accumulate to build reefs.

coral reef, chain of calcareous rocks found in warm, shallow seas. Consists of skeletal material, mainly coral polyps, accumulated *in situ* over long period, together with transported and chemically precipitated organic debris. Forms incl. fringing reefs, barrier reefs, ATOLLS.

Coral Sea, arm of SW Pacific Ocean, between E Papua New Guinea and NE Australia. Incl. Great Barrier Reef. Scene of US-Australian victory (1942) over Japanese.

coral snake, one of various highly poisonous burrowing snakes of S US, subtropical America; related to cobra. Red, yellow and black bands around body.

cor anglais, see OBOE.

Corbusier, Le pseud. of Charles Edouard Jeanneret (1887-1965), French architect, b. Switzerland. Influential innovator, he employed pure geometrical forms in his work, and industrial methods to mass-produce housing, *eg* Citrohan project (1921). Designed chapel at Ronchamp, Villa Savoye at Poissy, typical of later anti-rational style, and UN building. Devised town-planning schemes and wrote important *Towards a New Architecture* (1923).

Corby, urban dist. of Northamptonshire, C England. Pop. 48,000. Designated new town (1950); iron, steel industs.

Corday, Charlotte (1768-93), French political assassin. A Girondist sympathizer, she stabbed Marat in his bath, and was guillotined 4 days later.

Cordeliers, radical political club during French Revolution. Estab. 1790, active in overthrow of GIRONDISTS (1792-3). At first led by DANTON, Desmoulins, later by Marat, Hébert. Fell apart after Hébert's execution (1794).

Córdoba, city of C Argentina, cap. of Córdoba prov. Pop. 799,000. Railway jct., commercial and cultural centre; cars, tractors, textiles, glass mfg. Supplied with h.e.p. from Río Primero. Founded 1573. Old buildings incl. cathedral, univ. (1613).

Córdoba or **Cordova,** city of S Spain, on R. Guadalquivir, cap. of Córdoba prov. Pop. 236,000. Tourism; industs. incl. textile mfg., engineering. Cap. of independent Moorish emirate, later caliphate, from 756; famous gold, silver, leather crafts. Taken by Castile 1236. Much Moorish architecture, esp. mosque (8th cent.) now a cathedral.

corduroy, see VELVET.

Corelli, Arcangelo (1653-1713), Italian composer, violinist. In his sonatas and *concerti grossi*, he developed characteristic style of writing for violin, both as solo and orchestral instrument.

Corelli, Marie, pseud. of Mary Mackay (1855-1924), Scottish novelist. Sentimental works, *eg Barabbas* (1893), *The Mighty Atom* (1896), attempted to reconcile science, religion.

coreopsis, genus of annual or perennial plants of daisy family, native to North America. Yellow or crimson daisy-like flowers.

Corfu (*Kérkira*), isl. of W Greece, in Ionian Sea. Area 637 sq km (246 sq mi). Olives, wine; tourism. Ancient *Corcyra*; settled by Corinth *c* 734 BC. Under Venetian rule 1386-1797, British 1815-64. Cap. is **Corfu,** pop. 27,000. Port, resort.

corgi, small Welsh dog of 2 varieties: Pembrokeshire, short-tailed and red or red and white; Cardiganshire, long-tailed and any colour except white. Stands *c* 30 cm/12 in. at shoulder.

coriander, *Coriandrum sativum*, annual herb of parsley family native to Mediterranean countries. Grown in Europe and US. Seeds used as flavouring, oil formerly used medicinally.

Corfu

Corinth, Lovis (1858-1925), German painter. Early work was naturalistic in style; after a stroke in 1911 his work became more violent and expressionistic in character. Paintings incl. landscapes, portraits and religious subjects.

Corinth (*Kórinthos*), town of SC Greece, on Gulf of Corinth. Pop. 16,000. Port; raisin, wine trade. Founded *c* 1350 BC; traditional rival of Athens. Colonized Syracuse, Corfu; joined Achaean League. Remains incl. citadel (Acrocorinthus). Refounded (1858) after earthquake.

Corinth, Gulf of, Greece. Inlet of Ionian Sea between mainland and Peloponnese. Joined to Saronic Gulf by canal (1881-93) across Isthmus of Corinth.

Corinthian order, most elaborate of the Greek orders of architecture, similar to Ionic, but distinguished by its bell-shaped capital decorated with design of acanthus leaves and volutes. Oldest known example is at Bassae, *c* 420 BC; order was little used.

Corinthians 1 and **2,** epistles of NT, written by St Paul (*c* AD 55) prob. from Ephesus (1) and Macedonia (2). Admonish the people of Corinth for their notorious immorality.

Cork (*Corcaigh*), county of Munster prov., S Irish Republic. Area 7462 sq km (2881 sq mi); pop. 358,000. Crossed E-W by mountains; fertile valleys; indented coast incl. Bantry Bay. Agric., dairying; fishing. Co. town **Cork,** co. bor. with Cóbh, on R. Lee. Pop. 128,000. Exports agric. produce. Woollen mfg.; distilling. Protestant, RC cathedrals.

cork, outer tissue produced by evergreen cork oak, *Quercus suber,* of the Mediterranean region to replace epidermis as a protective layer. Impervious, compressible and elastic, used for stoppers, floor-coverings, floats, *etc.* Trees can be stripped about every 10 years for *c* 150 years.

corkwood, see BALSA.

corm, see BULB.

Australian pied cormorant (Phalacrocorax varius)

cormorant, diving seabird of Phalacrocoracidae family. Long neck and body, hooked bill, mainly black plumage; breeds in colonies. Tamed and used to catch fish in Japan, China. Species incl. widespread *Phalacrocorax carbo* common on N Atlantic coast.

corn, see MAIZE; WHEAT; OATS.

corncrake, *Crex crex,* brown short-billed European game bird of rail family. Timid, frequents long grass.

Corneille, Pierre (1606-84), French dramatist. Principal formulator of French Classical theatre. Portrayed tragedy within man rather than in external events. Major works incl. *Le Cid* (1637), *Polyeucte* (1641). Finally eclipsed by Racine.

Cornelius, Peter von (1783-1867), German painter. Worked with the Nazarenes in Rome until 1819; returned to Munich where he was active in revival of monumental fresco painting. Executed frescoes from Greek mythology in Munich Glyptothek.

Cornell, Katharine (1898-1974), American actress-manager, b. Germany. Established reputation in *The Green Hat, The Barretts of Wimpole Street*, directed by husband Guthrie McClintic.

Corner Brook, town of W Newfoundland, Canada; on Humber R. Pop. 27,000. Important paper mills, newsprint export.

cornet, brass wind instrument created in France (*c* 1825) by adding valves to post horn, although a modern cornet resembles a squat trumpet. Sound more mellow than trumpet; used mainly in brass bands.

cornet fish or **flutemouth,** marine fish of Fistulariidae family, found in tropical seas. Scaleless, with long rounded snout.

cornflower, *Centaurea cyanus,* hardy annual of daisy family native to Mediterranean regions. Formerly weed in European grainfields, now popular garden flower, esp. blue variety.

Cornish, see CELTIC.

Corn Laws, in Britain, restrictions placed on exports or imports of grain. Acts (1791, 1813) forced up price of grain by protective tariffs on imports, serving interests of landowners. Opposition, esp. among new industrial classes over high food prices, culminated in formation of Anti-Corn Law League (1839), leaders of which incl. Bright, Cobden. Laws repealed 1846 by Peel under mounting public pressure during Irish famine (1845-6).

Cornwall, town of SE Ontario, Canada; on St Lawrence R. Pop. 47,000. Textile mfg., chemicals, paper. Linked with US (Rooseveltown) by bridge.

Cornwall, county of SW England. Area 3546 sq km (1369 sq mi); pop. 377,000; co. town Truro. Interior moorland, *eg* Bodmin Moor in E; rocky, rugged coastline; mild climate. Tourism; dairy farming, fruit, vegetable growing; kaolin indust. has replaced tin, copper mining.

Cornwallis, Charles Cornwallis, 1st Marquess (1738-1805), British general. During American Revolution, led retreat from Carolinas to Virginia; his surrender at Yorktown (1781) marked end of fighting. As governor-general of India, quelled Tippoo Sahib.

Coromandel Coast, see TAMIL NADU.

corona, see SUN.

Corot, Jean Baptiste Camille (1796-1875), French landscape painter. Sketches from nature noted for their simplicity of form and clarity of light. Later misty landscapes, grey-green in tone, were popular successes.

corporate state, system in which state controls economy, comprised mainly of privately-owned businesses. Political and economic power vested in organization controlling corporations of employers and workers; dates from medieval guild system. Modified form under virtual dictatorships operated in Fascist Italy from 1920s and in Portugal until 1974. Collectivist in principle, use of private capital justified in capitalist context on grounds of national priorities. Post-war Western indust. states have taken on some corporate state characteristics.

Corpus Christi, port of S Texas, US; on Corpus Christi Bay, channel access to Gulf of Mexico. Pop. 205,000. Exports cotton, petroleum, fish. Natural gas, oil refining, shipping. Tourist resort.

Correggio, Antonio Allegri da (*c* 1494-1534), Italian painter. Known for his soft painterly style and use of extreme illusionism in his decorations; late works foreshadow Italian Baroque. Works incl. fresco *Assumption of the Virgin* in dome of Parma Cathedral.

Corregidor, fortified isl. of Philippines, at entrance to Manila Bay, Luzon. Taken by US (1898); courageously defended by US forces against Japanese in WWII, surrendered 1942.

Corrientes, town of NE Argentina, cap. of Corrientes prov., on Paraná R. Pop. 138,000. Agric. trade (esp. cotton). Founded 1588.

Corsica

Corsica (*Corse*), isl. dept. of France, in Mediterranean Sea, N of Sardinia. Area 8721 sq km (3367 sq mi); cap. Ajaccio. Plains along E coast, mountainous elsewhere, highest peak Monte Cinto (2709 m/8891 ft); extensive scrubland (*maquis*). Tourism, limited agric. (olives), fishing. Settled from Etruscan times, ceded (1768) to France by Genoa. Banditry and blood feuds rife until early 20th cent. Napoleon born in Ajaccio.

Cort, Henry (1740-1800), English ironmaster. Invented puddling process to remove carbon from pig iron. Introduced rollers to finish iron.

Cortés, Hernán or **Hernando Cortez** (1485-1547), Spanish conquistador. Led force of 600 men in conquest of Mexico. Entered Tenochtitlán (Mexico City) in 1519, where he was received by emperor Montezuma as god Quetzalcoatl. Recaptured Tenochtitlán (1521) after Spaniards had been expelled by Aztec revolt during his absence; victory marked fall of Aztec empire. Gradually lost political power in Mexico, failing to be appointed viceroy.

cortisone, crystalline steroid hormone produced by cortex of adrenal gland. Used to treat inflammatory diseases and allergies, *eg* arthritis, asthma; dangerous side-effects incl. muscle weakness, kidney damage.

Cortona, Pietro Berrettini da (1596-1669), Italian painter, architect. Major exponent of Roman high baroque style, painted huge illusionistic fresco *Allegory of Divine Providence and Barberini Power* (1633-9) on ceiling of Barberini Palace, Rome.

Cortona, town of Tuscany, NC Italy. Pop. 27,000. Etruscan, Roman remains; palace (13th cent.) now museum of Etruscan Academy.

Cortot, Alfred (1877-1962), French pianist and conductor. A propagandist for Wagner, he was also known for the famous trio he formed with violinist Jacques Thibaud and cellist Pablo Casals in 1905. Noted interpreter of Chopin.

Coruña, La, or **Corunna,** city of NW Spain, on Atlantic Ocean, cap. of La Coruña prov. Pop. 190,000. Sardine fishing, cigar mfg. Armada sailed from here 1588. Scene of Peninsular War battle (1809) in which Sir John Moore was killed.

corundum, very hard mineral, form of aluminium oxide. Found chiefly among metamorphosed limestones, shales. Coarser varieties used as abrasives, *eg* EMERY; finer as gems, *eg* RUBY, SAPPHIRE. Major sources in Burma, Thailand, Australia, US.

corvette, originally, a full-rigged sloop of war, below a frigate in size, carrying up to 20 guns on upper deck. In WWII a small anti-submarine escort vessel.

Corvo, Baron, pseud. of Frederick William Rolfe (1860-1913), English novelist, historian. Known for eccentric, paranoid works, *eg Hadrian the Seventh* (1904), *The Desire and Pursuit of the Whole* (1934). Contributed to the YELLOW BOOK.

Cos (*Kos*), isl. of Greece, in the Dodecanese off Turkey. Area 282 sq km (109 sq mi), main town Cos. Cereals, fruit, wine; Cos lettuce originated here. Ancient literary, medical centre (birthplace of Hippocrates).

Cosenza, city of Calabria, SW Italy, on R. Crati. Cap. of Cosenza prov. Pop. 103,000. Furniture, textiles; fruit market. Cathedral (12th cent.), castle (13th cent.).

Cosgrave, William Thomas (1880-1965), Irish statesman. After 1922 split of Sinn Fein, headed Irish Free State govt. (1922-32) until defeat by De Valéra. Resigned 1944 as opposition leader. His son, **Liam Cosgrave** (1920-   ), became PM in 1973 at head of Fine Gael govt. Introduced (1976) measures to prevent IRA activities in Republic supporting conflict in Northern Ireland. Defeated in 1977 election.

cosmetics, substances used to enhance personal appearance, *eg* by cleansing skin and covering blemishes. Use of cosmetics first recorded in ancient Egypt, and became common in imperial Rome. Oils and perfumes were brought to Europe from the East in 11th and 12th cents. In 20th cent. large-scale production of cosmetics on scientific basis began.

cosmic rays, high energy radiation reaching Earth from outer space. Primary cosmic rays consist largely of protons and alpha particles; these collide with particles in upper atmosphere to produce secondary cosmic rays containing mesons, neutrons, electrons, *etc.* Various subatomic particles, incl. positron, discovered in cosmic rays. Source unknown, but some rays originate in solar flares.

cosmology, science of nature, origin and history of universe. Modern cosmology theories assume that universe looks same in all directions and from all positions. General theory of relativity provides framework for study of gravitation and its shaping effect on universe. Theories of origin of universe incl. BIG-BANG and STEADY-STATE theories.

cosmos, genus of autumn-blooming annual plants of Compositae family native to tropical America. Feathery leaves, pink or purple flowers. Cultivated varieties derive from Mexican *Cosmos bipinnatus.*

Cossa, Baldassarre (*c* 1370–1419), Neapolitan churchman, antipope as John XXIII (1410-15). Elected pope after attempt to end GREAT SCHISM at Council of Pisa. Most powerful of resulting 3 rival popes. Abdicated under pressure, with rivals at Council of Constance.

Cossacks, people of S Russia and Siberia, famous as horsemen and cavalry. Settled in Don and Dnepr areas in 15th and 16th cents., held privileges of auton. govt. in return for military service. Participation in unsuccessful peasant revolts in 18th cent. led to loss of some auton. In 19th cent., organized by Russian govt. into 11 communities spread throughout country. Deprived of privileges after many fought against Bolsheviks (1918-20).

cossid moth, moth of Cossidae family, whose larvae bore galleries in tree trunks. Species incl. European goat moth, *Cossus cossus.*

Costa Rica, republic of Central America, between Nicaragua and Panama. Area 50,700 sq km (19,575 sq mi); pop. 1,710,000; cap. San José. Language: Spanish. Religion: RC. Dormant volcanic mountains with jungle in N; plains on Caribbean, Pacific coasts. Mainly agric., coffee, bananas; timber exports. Part of Guatemala under Spanish rule until 1821; part of Central American Federation (1823-38).

Costermansville, *see* BUKAVU, Zaïre.

cost of living index, measurement of cost of goods and services needed to maintain a specific standard of living. Originally used to indicate incidence of poverty, now used by govt. as guide to fiscal policy, and as basis for wage negotiations. In US, Consumer Price Index (1945) compiled by Bureau of Labor Statistics; in UK, Index of Retail Prices (1947) compiled by Cost of Living Advisory Committee.

Côte d'Or, range of hills in Burgundy, E France. Wine-producing region, main centres Dijon, Nuits St Georges, Beaune.

Cotentin, penin. of Normandy, N France. Main town Cherbourg. Sheep rearing, dairying, apple growing.

Cotman, John Sell (1782-1842), English painter. Leading member of Norwich School; his landscape watercolours are noted for simplicity of design and geometric composition.

cotoneaster, genus of shrubs of rose family native to Asia. Most species have glossy green leaves, small pink or white flowers and abundant crimson berries. *Cotoneaster horizontalis* is popular garden variety.

Cotonou, city of S Benin, on Bight of Benin. Pop. 120,000. Commercial centre; port, exports palm oil, groundnuts.

Cotopaxi, mountain of NC Ecuador; world's highest active volcano. Height 5897 m (19,347 ft). First climbed by Reiss (1872).

Cotswold Hills, W England, limestone range mainly in Gloucestershire. Form Severn-Thames watershed. Attractive stone villages. Wool centre until 17th cent.

Cottbus, see KOTTBUS, East Germany.

Cotton, [Thomas] Henry (1907-   ), English professional golfer. Won British Open championship 3 times.

Cotton, John (1584-1652), English Puritan clergyman. Fled (1633) from England to Massachusetts where Boston was named to honour his native English town. Responsible for banishment of ANNE HUTCHINSON and ROGER WILLIAMS. Estab. Congregationalism in colony.

Cotton, Sir Robert Bruce (1571-1631), English antiquary. Formed collection of manuscripts, books and Anglo-Saxon documents, many of which came from suppressed monasteries. Library was presented to nation (1700), later became part of British Museum.

cotton, soft white seed hairs filling pods of various shrubs of genus *Gossypium* of mallow family, native to tropics. Cheapest and most widely used natural fibre. Has been spun, woven and dyed since prehistoric times. Cotton mfg. has been a major industry, esp. in Britain and US (18th and 19th cents.). USSR, India, China, Mexico are other chief producers.

cottonmouth, see WATER MOCCASIN.

cottontail, one of several common non-burrowing American rabbits, genus *Sylvilagus,* with short fluffy tails, white underneath.

couch grass, *Agropyron repens,* troublesome perennial weed on arable land, with creeping rhizomes of which each broken piece is capable of reproduction. Native to Europe, now common in North America.

cougar, see PUMA.

Coulomb, Charles Augustin de (1736-1806), French physicist. Used torsion balance to deduce Coulomb's law: force of attraction or repulsion between charged bodies is proportional to product of magnitude of charges and inversely proportional to square of distance between them. SI unit of charge named after him.

council, ecumenical, in Christianity, convocation of duly constituted authorities of whole church. Modern RC, canonists recognize 21 such councils incl. Nicaea (325), Ephesus (431), BASLE (1431), TRENT (1545), Vatican II (1962). Eastern Orthodox churches recognize the first 7 of these 21.

Council for Mutual Economic Assistance (COMECON), E European organization estab. (1949) to coordinate economic policy in Communist bloc. Its 1959 charter gave it same status as European Economic Community, expanded scope to regulate indust. production. Albania expelled (1961) from membership. Mongolian People's Republic joined (1962).

Council of Europe, organization of European states. Estab. (1949) to secure greater unity between its members; to safeguard common political, cultural heritage; facilitate economic, social progress. Members mainly from W and N Europe. European Commission investigates alleged violations of European Convention on Human Rights (signed 1950), submits findings to European Court of Human Rights (estab. 1958).

counterpoint, in music, art of combining two or more independent melodies so that they form a harmonious whole. Dominant feature of much Renaissance and Baroque music; esp. developed in 16th cent. choral work by such masters as Palestrina.

Counter-Reformation, see REFORMATION, CATHOLIC.

countertenor or **male alto,** adult male singer with unusually high voice, produced by developing falsetto or head voice. Most often to be heard in early classical music.

Country Party, Australian political party. Origins in 19th cent. arose out of rural discontent among wealthy. In 20th cent., has often held 3rd party balance of power in alliance with Liberal party, esp. during and after WWI.

county, in England and Wales, main political, social and admin. division. As 'shire', unit of govt. before Norman Conquest (1066); form for most of 20th cent. estab. by Local Government Act (1888). Restructured by new act (1972) resulting in county and district councils. Now 45 counties in England, 6 in Wales. Scottish counties, by extension of legislation (1973), replaced by 9 regions, 3 island areas. In US, county is principal geographic and political subdivision of all states except Alaska.

coup d'état, in politics, sudden (usually forcible) overthrow of govt. by contending faction for power. Differs from revolution, involving radical restructuring of society, in that top level only of govt. or admin. is replaced. Hist. precedents range from Napoleon's rise to power in France to Amin in Uganda (1971) and Pinochet in Chile (1973).

François Couperin

Couperin, François (1668-1733), French composer, harpsichordist. Noted organist; wrote 4 books of harpsichord suites, also *L'Art de toucher le clavecin* on keyboard technique. Best known of distinguished musical family.

Couperus, Louis Marie Anne (1863-1923), Dutch novelist. Known for realistic novels, esp. the 'Small Souls' tetralogy (1901-3), chronicle of a Dutch family.

Gustave Courbet: self-portrait

Courbet, Gustave (1819-77), French painter. Leader of realist school of French painting, his unidealized scenes from daily life incl. *Funeral at Ornans* (1850). Imprisoned after destruction of Vendôme Column during Paris Commune, he lived in Switzerland from 1873.

courgette or **zucchini,** *Cucurbita pepo,* small marrow, 5-20 cm/2-8 in. long. Ridged outer skin; used as vegetable, baked, fried or stuffed.

courser, long-legged insectivorous bird, genus *Cursorius,* found in arid areas of Africa and S Asia. Species incl. well camouflaged cream-coloured courser, *C. cursor.* Also called desert runner; can run at high speed.

coursing, hunting of game, usually hares, by hounds trained to follow by sight rather than scent. In competitions, 2 dogs chase a hare and are tested for qualities of speed and agility.

court, in law, person or persons appointed to try cases, make investigation, render judgment. Secular, complex system developed in ancient Rome. In UK, High Court of Justice (estab. by Judicature Act, 1873) comprises chancery; King's (or Queen's) Bench; probate, divorce and admiralty; court of appeal. Two systems in US are federal and state. Supreme Court is at head of federal system.

Courtrai, *see* KORTRIJK, Belgium.

Cousin, Jean (*c* 1490-*c* 1560), French painter and engraver. Known for designs of stained glass and tapestries. His son, **Jean Cousin** (*c* 1522-*c* 1590), was book illustrator and designer of stained glass.

Cousin, Victor (1792-1867), French philosopher. Regarded as founder of Eclectic school, believing truth of various systems can be extracted by intuition. Introduced German philosophies into France. Minister of education (1840), reorganized primary education system.

Cousteau, Jacques Yves (1910-   ), French naval officer, underwater explorer. Invented aqualung (1943); helped develop bathyscaphe, underwater filming. Founder of French naval underwater research; has produced many books, films on sea life.

Covenanters, in Scottish history, members of groups bound by oath to defend Presbyterianism. Covenant of 1581 sought to combat RC church in Scotland; National Covenant of 1638 opposed Archbishop Laud's attempts to introduce Book of Common Prayer into Scotland. Supported Puritan Revolution only after English Parliament's acceptance of Solemn League and Covenant (1643), promising estab. of Presbyterianism in England. Resisted coercion after Restoration; movement ended with Glorious Revolution (1688).

Covent Garden, Royal Opera House, originally site of London Theatre; later of Royal Italian Opera House (opened 1732). Present house (opened 1858) home of Royal Opera Co. and Royal Ballet Co.

Coventry, city of West Midlands met. county, WC England. Pop. 335,000. Cars, aircraft, hosiery, rayon industs. Medieval weaving town. Centre destroyed in WWII bombing. New cathedral, incorporating old, completed 1962.

Coverdale, Miles (1488-1569), English translator of Bible. Pub. English translation of entire Bible (1535). Collaborated in Great Bible (1539); edited 'Cranmer's Bible' (1540).

cow, mature female of domestic cattle. Name also applied to mature female of other animals, *eg* buffalo, moose, whale.

Coward, Sir Noël (1899-1973), English actor, playwright, composer, film director. Best known for witty comedies incl. *Private Lives* (1930), *Blithe Spirit* (1941), *Present Laughter* (1943), also wrote revues, songs incl. 'Mad Dogs and Englishmen', film scripts *eg In Which We Serve* (1942), *Brief Encounter* (1945).

Cowes, urban dist. of Isle of Wight, England, on R. Medina. Pop. 19,000. Yachting centre, has famous annual regatta. Osborne House nearby.

Cowley, Abraham (1618-67), English poet. Metaphysical works incl. Biblical epic *Davideis* (1656). Introduced Pindaric ode to England.

Noël Coward in 1972

Cowper, William (1731-1800), English poet. Known for religious *Olney Hymns* (1779) incl. 'God moves in a mysterious way'; *John Gilpin's Ride* (1782), *The Castaway* (1803). Subject of Cecil's biog., *The Stricken Deer* (1928).

cowrie, gastropod mollusc of Cypraeidae family, abundant in tropical seas. Shells, shiny and brightly coloured, sometimes used as money or decoration.

cowslip, *Primula veris,* European plant of primrose family. Has yellow bell flowers.

Cox, David (1783-1859), English painter. Best known for his watercolours of N Wales, painted in broad manner.

coyote or **prairie wolf,** *Canis latrans,* small wolf of plains of W North America. Thick fur, bushy tail; largely nocturnal. Omnivorous, hunts singly or in packs.

Coypu

coypu, *Myocastor coypus,* large herbivorous aquatic rodent of South America, *c* 90 cm/3 ft in length. Introduced into other countries for cultivation of fur (nutria).

Cozens, Alexander (*c* 1717-86), English painter, b. Russia. Best known for his 'blot drawings', means of building landscapes from haphazard arrangement of ink blots. His son, **John Robert Cozens** (1752-96), painted poetic watercolour landscapes in subdued tones of blue, grey and green; influenced Turner, Girtin.

crab, one of various crustaceans of suborder Brachyura with 4 pairs of legs, pair of pincers and flattened shell; abdomen reduced and folded under thorax. Many species edible, incl. European *Cancer pagurus.*

crab apple, *Malus pumila,* tree of apple family of Europe and W Asia. Small reddish-yellow fruit with bitter flavour used in preserves. Parent of all cultivated apples.

Crabbe, George (1754-1832), English poet. Known for realistic, anti-pastoral heroic verse, *eg The Village* (1783), *The Borough* (1810) incl. 'Peter Grimes', used by Benjamin

Britten as theme of opera. Marks transition from 18th cent. Classicism to Romanticism.

Crab nebula, gaseous nebula in constellation Taurus, remnant of supernova explosion seen in 1054. Emits radio waves and X-rays; at its centre is a PULSAR.

Cracow, see KRAKÓW, Poland.

Craig, [Edward] Gordon (1872-1966), English actor, producer. Illegitimate son of Ellen Terry. Staged productions in Europe, incl. *Hamlet* in Moscow. Pub. *On the Art of the Theatre* (1911).

Craigavon, James Craig, 1st Viscount (1871-1940), Irish statesman. Helped organize (1914) Ulster Volunteers to resist Irish Home Rule. First PM of Northern Ireland (1921-40).

Craigavon, dist. of C Northern Ireland. Area 388 sq km (150 sq mi); pop. 66,000. Created 1973, formerly part of Cos. Armagh, Down.

Craigie, Sir William Alexander (1867-1957), British lexicographer, b. Scotland. Joint editor (1901-33) of *New English Dictionary* ('Oxford English Dictionary'). Chief editor of *A Dictionary of American English on Historical Principles* (1938-43).

Craik, Dinah Maria, née Mulock (1826-87), English author. Wrote children's stories, poetry, travel books. Known for novel, *John Halifax, Gentleman* (1856).

Craiova, city of SW Romania, on R. Jiu. Pop. 188,000. Textiles; food processing; leather goods. Roman *Castra Nova*; hist. cap. of Lesser Walachia.

crake, small marsh bird of rail family; short bill, stout body. Species incl. European spotted crake, *Porzana porzana*, and little crake, *P. parva*.

Cranach, Lucas, real name Müller (1472-1553), German artist; known as 'The Elder'. Early works of religious subjects noted for their handling of landscape. Later associated with Luther, he was prolific producer of woodcuts, portraits and mythological figures, developing own style in painting erotic female nudes. Portraits incl. Luther, Charles V.

Cranberry

cranberry, *Vaccinium oxycoccus*, vine-like shrub with bitter, crimson berries, native to Europe and US. Traditional sauce with venison and turkey.

Crane, [Harold] Hart (1899-1932), American poet. Known for *White Buildings* (1926), influenced by Rimbaud, and *The Bridge* (1930). Rejected cultural pessimism of T.S. Eliot. Major influence on post-1946 American poetry.

Crane, Stephen Townley (1871-1900), American author. Best known for Civil War novel, *The Red Badge of Courage* (1895). Other works incl. *Maggie: A Girl of the Streets* (1893), classic short story 'The Open Boat' (1898), poetry.

Crane, Walter (1845-1915), English illustrator and painter. Known for colourful illustrations of children's books. Designed stained glass, textiles and wallpapers and did illustrations for William Morris' Kelmscott Press.

crane, any of Gruidae family of long-necked, long-legged wading birds, found everywhere except South America. Species incl. grey European common crane, *Grus grus*, American whooping crane, *G. americana*, and only Australian crane (brolga), *G. rubicunda*.

Crane fly

crane fly or **daddy-long-legs,** slender harmless long-legged fly of Tipulidae family. Larvae, known as leatherjackets, live in ground and are pests of crops.

cranesbill, see GERANIUM.

Craniata, subphylum of chordates having definite head. Incl. vertebrates, but not hemichordates or protochordates.

Cranmer, Thomas (1489-1556), English churchman, archbishop of Canterbury (1533-56). Annulled Henry VIII's marriage to Catherine of Aragon despite papal opposition (1533). Encouraged translation of Bible into English and its circulation throughout churches. Under Edward VI, compiled 2 Anglican Prayer Books (1549, 1552). Under Mary I, condemned as traitor and heretic, burned at stake.

crannog, in archaeology, lake dwelling built on artificial island of stones, earth, timber. Often surrounded by wooden stockade. Most date from late Bronze Age in Ireland, Scotland.

craps, see DICE.

Crashaw, Richard (c 1612-49), English poet. Known for extreme metaphysical conceits, often regarded as tasteless, esp. in 'St Mary Magdalene, or The Weeper'. Best works incl. 'Hymn to St Teresa', in *Steps to the Temple* (1646).

Crassus, Marcus Licinius (c 108-53 BC), Roman soldier and political leader. Amassed fortune by buying confiscated estates. Crushed revolt of slaves under Spartacus (71). Formed 1st Triumvirate with Caesar and Pompey. Given charge of prov. of Syria, killed after defeat by Parthians in Mesopotamia.

crater, bowl-shaped depression in Earth's surface. May be formed by explosion, *eg* at summit of volcanic cone, or impact, *eg* by meteor striking Earth's surface, as at Meteor Crater, Arizona, US. Craters may be lake-filled.

Crawford, Joan, orig. Lucille le Sueur (1906-77), American film actress. Films incl. *Rain* (1932), *A Woman's Face* (1941), *Whatever Happened to Baby Jane?* (1962).

Crawford, Osbert Guy Stanhope (1886-1957), British archaeologist. Introduced aerial photography into study of archaeology; used mapping techniques, photographs to locate sites.

crayfish or **crawfish,** freshwater crustacean, esp. of genus *Astacus*, resembling small lobster; many edible species. Term also applied to crustaceans of Palinuridae family, *eg* Australian spiny crayfish, *Palinurus cygnus*.

Crécy (-en-Ponthieu), village of Picardy, NE France, near Abbeville. Scene of victory (1346) of Edward III of England over Philip VI of France.

credit card, card allowing user to charge bills to credit account. May be issued by retailer, *eg* department store, oil company, or by bank. Some systems allow payment to be delayed at cost of monthly interest charge.

Cree, North American Indian tribe of Algonquian linguistic stock, formerly inhabiting Manitoba. Plains Cree were buffalo hunters of prairies. Woodland Cree (related to OJIBWA) although warlike were friendly to early French and British fur traders around Hudson Bay.

creed, brief statement of religious belief. Examples incl. Nicene, a revised form of that adopted by 1st Council of Nicaea (325) to combat Arianism, used in RC and Eastern Orthodox churches; Apostles', dating from 650 and similar to Nicene, used in RC and Protestant churches; Augsburg

Confession (1530) is official Lutheran statement; THIRTY-NINE ARTICLES, basic creed of Church of England, dates from reign of Elizabeth I; Westminster Confession (1645-7) is creed of Calvinist Presbyterian churches.

Creek, group of North American Indian tribes, mostly of Hokan-Siouan linguistic stock. Settled farmers in Alabama and Georgia, allied by confederation against N tribes. Rebelled against whites in Creek War (1813-14); defeated by Andrew Jackson at Horseshoe Bend. Ceded their autonomy, became US citizens (1906).

Crefeld, see KREFELD, West Germany.

cremation, ceremonial burning of the dead. Practice in ancient world was prob. based on belief in purifying power of fire. Discontinued in Europe because of Christian belief in resurrection of the body. Subsequently revived with problems of disposal in large cities. First crematorium in US opened 1876; legalized in UK 1884. Forbidden in RC church.

Cremazie, Octave (1827-79), French-Canadian poet. Settled in France (1862). Known for patriotic verse incl. *Chant du vieux soldat canadien* (1855).

Cremona, town of Lombardy, N Italy, on R. Po. Cap. of Cremona prov. Pop. 84,000. Indust., commercial centre; foodstuffs, textiles. Famous for violin mfg. by Amati, Guarneri, Stradivari. Cathedral (12th cent.), tallest campanile in Italy.

creole, person of European parentage born in West Indies, Central America, tropical South America, or descendant of such a person. In linguistics, creolized language is the form which develops when speakers of mutually unintelligible languages live in close and long-term contact with each other, with one of the contributing languages typically dominant. Examples incl. Haitian creole, Gullah of South Carolina, and Georgia.

crepe, thin fabric with crinkled texture, originally woven from raw silk. Black crepe is used for mourning, softer crepe de Chine is used for blouses, lingerie, etc.

Crespi, Giuseppe Maria (1665-1747), Italian painter. Specialized in genre subjects, painted in strong chiaroscuro; influenced later 18th cent. Venetians. Works incl. *The Seven Sacraments* series.

cress, *Lepidium sativum,* tiny plant of mustard family, native to Persia. Used as a garnish. Different genus from WATERCRESS.

crested grebe, *Podiceps cristatus,* largest grebe, found in Africa, Asia, Australia. About size of gull with 2 stiff tufts of black head feathers, long white neck.

Cretaceous period, final geological period of Mesozoic era; began c 135 million years ago, lasted c 70 million years. Widespread inundation; extensive chalk formation esp. in latter (upper) half of period. Echinoderms, lamellibranchs, last ammonites; mammals still small and rare, dinosaurs extinct by end of period. Also see GEOLOGICAL TABLE.

Crete

Crete (*Kriti*), largest isl. of Greece, in E Mediterranean. Area 8332 sq km (3217 sq mi); cap. Iráklion. Mostly mountainous, highest point Mt Ida. Olives, fruit, wine; tourism. Home of Minoan civilization (*fl* 2000-1400 BC); remains incl. KNOSSOS. Turkish from 1669, passed to Greece 1912.

cretinism, congenital deficiency of thyroid hormone secretion, with resulting retardation of physical and mental growth.

Creusot, Le, see LE CREUSOT, France.

Crewe, mun. bor. of Cheshire, NW England. Pop. 51,000. Major railway jct.; railway engineering.

cribbage, old English card game for two players. Scores are marked with pegs on a board. Invention credited to Sir John Suckling (1609-42).

Crichton, James (1560-c 1582), Scottish scholar and adventurer, known as the 'Admirable Crichton'. Travelled in France and Italy, admired for his charm, learning. Died in street fight.

Crick, Francis Harry Compton (1916-   ), English biochemist. Shared Nobel Prize for Physiology and Medicine (1962) with Maurice Wilkins and James Watson for work establishing double helix structure of DNA molecule.

cricket, insect of Gryllidae family, related to grasshopper and locust, but with long antennae. Often lives in human habitations, being active at night. Male produces chirping sound by rubbing forewings.

cricket, eleven-a-side game played with bat, ball and wickets. Marylebone Cricket Club (MCC), founded 1787, was governing body of game in England until formation of Cricket Council in 1969. Organized county cricket dates from 1873. Test matches, dating from 1877, played between England, Australia, New Zealand, West Indies, India, Pakistan and, formerly, South Africa.

Crimea, penin. of USSR, in S Ukrainian SSR; extending into N Black Sea. Taken from Turks by Russia (1783); scene of Crimean War (1853-6). Coast is tourist centre.

Crimean War (1853-6), conflict between Russia and Britain, France and Turkey. General cause was Anglo-Russian dispute, esp. over control of Dardanelles. Pretext was Russian-French quarrel over guardianship of Palestinian holy places. Turkey's rejection of Russian territ. demands prompted latter's occupation of Moldavia and Walachia. Turkey declared war (1853), France and Britain joined (1854), Sardinia (1855). Main campaign, centring on siege of SEVASTOPOL in Crimea, was marked by futile gallantry (eg charge of the Light Brigade at battle of BALAKLAVA) and heavy casualties; hospital work by FLORENCE NIGHTINGALE. Settlement at Congress of Paris checked Russian influence in SE Europe.

criminal law, body of law dealing with crimes punishable by state. In Britain developed out of COMMON LAW; in US, each state has own body of criminal law, based on English customs brought by colonists. Usually, test of criminal liability is intention to commit, so that children (ie under 14 years), insane persons, etc, are not liable.

criminology, scientific study of crime, criminal(s), subfield of sociology; 19th cent. attempts at definition of criminal 'type' gave way to work of, eg William Healy (early 20th cent.), Gluecks (1940s), showing environmental factors. Others have studied crime as business, or as normal learned behaviour.

Crinoidea, class of echinoderms consisting of sea lilies and feather stars. Usually sedentary, supported by stalk. Many fossil varieties from Cambrian period.

Crippen, Hawley Harvey (1861-1910), English murderer, b. US. Known as 1st criminal captured through use of radio. Was arrested on board ship attempting to escape to US with mistress after murdering wife.

Cripps, Sir [Richard] Stafford (1889-1952), British politician. Expelled by Labour Party (1939) for urging 'Popular Front' with Communists against Chamberlain's 'appeasement' policy; readmitted 1945. Served in Churchill's war cabinet from 1942 and in Labour cabinet (1945-50); chancellor of exchequer from 1947.

Crispi, Francesco (1819-1901), Italian politician, premier (1887-91, 1893-6). Encouraged colonial expansion, esp. in Ethiopia. Lost office after Italian defeat by Ethiopians under Menelik II at Aduwa (1896).

critical mass, in nuclear physics, minimum mass of fissile material, eg uranium, that can sustain a chain reaction. If less than critical mass of material is present, reaction dies away.

Stafford Cripps

critical pressure, minimum pressure required to liquefy a gas at its critical temperature.

critical temperature, temperature above which gas cannot be liquefied, regardless of the pressure applied.

Crivelli, Carlo (c 1430-after 1493), Venetian painter. Work is noted for its fantastic ornamentation and hard linear form. Worked in cities of the Italian Marches and settled in Ascoli.

Croaghpatrick, mountain of Co. Mayo, NW Irish Republic. Height 765 m (2510 ft). Traditionally where St Patrick first preached.

croaker, food fish of Sciaenidae family, of tropical and temperate seas. Uses swim bladder to make croaking sound. Related to grunt and drum.

Croatia

Croatia (*Hrvatska*), autonomous republic of NW Yugoslavia. Area 56,524 sq km (21,824 sq mi); cap. Zagreb. Incl. Dalmatia, Istria, Slavonia. Dinaric Alps in W, fertile plain in NE drained by Drava, Sava. Timber, coal, bauxite, most developed region of Yugoslavia; coastal tourism. United with Hungary 1091-1918, part of Yugoslavia from 1918. Strong nationalist sentiment.

Croce, Benedetto (1866-1952), Italian philosopher, historian. Believed ideas are reality, not merely representations. Idealism reflected in *The Philosophy of the Spirit* (1902-17). Minister of education (1920-1) before rise of Fascism.

Crockett, David ('Davy') (1786-1836), American frontiersman. Democrat Congressman from Tennessee. Died at the Alamo fighting for independence of Texas.

Crockett, Samuel Rutherford (1860-1914), Scottish novelist. Wrote sentimental novels of provincial life, *eg The Lilac Sunbonnet* (1894).

crocodile, large carnivorous reptile of order Crocodilia, found throughout tropics. Lives in rivers, swamps and on

Australian saltwater crocodile (*Crocodylus porosus*)

river banks. Species incl. Nile crocodile, *Crocodylus niloticus,* Australian *C. johnstoni* and American *C. acutus.*

Crocodilia (crocodilians), order of large reptiles with powerful jaws, elongated snout. Four-chambered heart, unique among reptiles. Body covered with scales, bony plates. Order incl. crocodile, gavial, alligator.

crocus, genus of spring-flowering plants of iris family with fleshy corms and yellow, purple or white flowers. Over 80 species, native to S Europe. Saffron crocus, *Crocus sativus,* cultivated for use as flavouring and for saffron yellow dye.

Croesus (d. *c* 546 BC), king of Lydia. Completed conquest of Ionian cities of Asia Minor. Allied himself with Babylonia and Egypt to resist Persia, but was defeated and captured by Cyrus the Great. Proverbial figure of great wealth.

crofting, system used esp. in highlands and islands of Scotland, where tenant rents and cultivates small holding or croft, producing food and raising animals for his own needs.

Cro-Magnon man, prehist. human being of Upper Palaeolithic period (*c* 30,000 years ago). Remains found (1868) in rock shelter of Cro-Magnon in Dordogne area of France. Of same species as modern *Homo Sapiens,* but taller.

Cromarty, see ROSS AND CROMARTY, Scotland.

Crome, John (1768-1821), English landscape painter, called 'Old Crome'. A leader of the Norwich school. Influenced by Gainsborough and Dutch 17th cent. painters, esp. Hobbema, he painted Norfolk scenes with fidelity to nature.

Cromer, Evelyn Baring, 1st Earl of (1841-1917), British colonial administrator. As consul-general of Egypt (1883-1907) acted as real ruler, reformed finances, administration.

Crompton, Samuel (1753-1827), English inventor. Devised (1779) spinning mule, an improvement of Hargreaves' spinning jenny, which spun fine yarn suitable for muslin.

Oliver Cromwell

Cromwell, Oliver (1599-1658), English soldier and statesman. Leading Puritan in Parliament before Civil War, assumed command of anti-royalist forces after victories at Edgehill (1642), Marston Moor (1644). Demanded execution of Charles I after Naseby (1645). Cromwell declared republic after king's execution (1649) and crushed Irish resistance; defeated royalist Scots under Charles II (1651). Dissolved 'Rump' Parliament (1653) and estab. Protectorate, which he ruled as lord protector (1653-8). Refused crown (1657), introduced constitution to strengthen his powers. Warred with Dutch (1652-4) after 1651 Navigation Act, and Spain (1655-8). Military genius but his govt. was marked by cruelty and intolerance. Succeeded by his son, **Richard Cromwell** (1626-1712), as lord protector; he resigned 1659 when Commonwealth was re-estab.

Cromwell, Thomas, Earl of Essex (c 1485-1540), English statesman. Secretary to Cardinal Wolsey, whom he succeeded as Henry VIII's chief adviser and lord chamberlain (1539). Instrumental in split with papacy, carried out suppression of monasteries. Failure of Henry's marriage to Anne of Cleves, which he had negotiated to secure German alliance, resulted in his execution for treason.

Cronin, A[rchibald] J[oseph] (1896-), Scottish novelist. Gave up career as doctor after success of *Hatter's Castle* (1931); other novels incl. *The Citadel* (1937). Works usually involve problems of social responsibility. Creator of Dr Finlay.

Cronus, in Greek myth, youngest of the TITANS. Led revolt against Uranus, became ruler of the world. Married his sister Rhea, fathered the OLYMPIAN GODS. Despite attempt to avoid fate by destroying his own children, was overthrown by ZEUS. Identified with Roman Saturn.

Crookes, Sir William (1832-1919), English physicist, chemist. Studied electrical discharges through rarefied gases, developing Crookes tube in process. Discovered thallium and devised radiometer for measuring intensity of radiation.

croquet, outdoor game in which players use mallets to drive wooden balls through a series of hoops placed in the ground. Believed to have originated in France, where it had become popular by 17th cent.

Crosby, Harry Lillis ('Bing') (1904-), American singer, actor. World's most successful singer in terms of record sales, made 1st recording in 1926; famous for relaxed style. Also appeared in many films, esp. with Bob Hope.

Runic cross in Ruthwell Church, Scotland

cross, symbol found in many societies, *eg* in ancient India, among American Indians, but esp. important in Christianity in remembrance of Jesus' crucifixion. May take several forms, *eg* Latin, St Andrew's, Iona. Crucifix is cross with a representation of the dying Jesus used in RC church.

crossbill, bird of finch family. European crossbill, *Loxia curvirostra,* inhabits coniferous forests, as does white-winged crossbill, *L. leucoptera.* Crossed bill used to extract seeds from fruit, cones.

European crossbill

crossbow, a bow fixed to a wooden butt and fired like a musket, the string being pulled back by a lever or winding gear and released by a trigger. Used mainly in the 12th-13th cent.

croton, genus of tropical plants of spurge family. Seeds of spurging croton, *Croton tiglium,* native to India, yield powerful purgative extract, croton oil.

Crotone (anc. *Crotona*), town of Calabria, S Italy, on Gulf of Taranto. Pop. 43,000. Chemicals, zinc smelting using h.e.p. from La Sila. Founded c 710 BC by Achaean colonists. Inhabitants won fame at Olympic Games. Site of Pythagoras' school.

Crow, North American Indian tribe of Hokan-Siouan linguistic stock. Nomadic hunters in Yellowstone R. area. Allied with whites *v* Sioux in 1870s.

crow, any of Corvidae family of perching birds. Often intelligent, with thick beak, mainly black plumage; worldwide distribution. Species incl. carrion crow, *Corvus corone,* hooded crow, *C. corone cornix,* of Europe, and RAVEN, ROOK, MAGPIE.

crowberry, *Empetrum nigrum,* small prostrate trailing shrub. Found on moorland in N temperate regions. Black edible berries.

crowfoot, name loosely applied to many species of plants of genus *Ranunculus* of buttercup family. Deeply divided leaves resembling crow's foot. Water crowfoot, *R. aquatalis,* has white flowers.

Crown, the, in UK govt., monarch as head of state. Formal powers incl. royal assent, needed for all parliamentary legislation, and royal prerogative. Latter incl. domestic duties, *eg* appointment of ministers, creation of peers, summoning and dissolution of Parliament, pardoning criminals; foreign duties, *eg* right to make war, treaties, receive and send ambassadors *etc.* Royal prerogative extends to other Commonwealth countries, and to colonial governors in certain areas. Most Crown powers, in practice, delegated to ministers.

crown jewels or **regalia,** symbols of British royal authority, kept in Tower of London. Present set dates from Restoration; incl. replica of crown of St Edward the Confessor (used at coronation), imperial state crown (worn on state occasions), swords of state, orb and sceptre.

crown land, in UK, land owned by Crown. Since George III, income surrendered to Parliament, which allots payment annually to certain members of royal family.

Croydon, bor. of S Greater London, England. Pop. 332,000. Created 1965 from former co. bor. and residential areas of N Surrey.

Crozet Islands, archipelago of c 20 isls. in SW Indian Ocean, forming part of French Southern and Antarctic Territs. Area 300 sq km (116 sq mi). Site of meteorological station.

Cruciferae, family of flowering plants, with c 220 genera incl. the mustards, cabbages, cresses. Cross-like arrangement of 4 petals. Annuals or biennials.

crucifixion, death imposed by hanging from wooden cross, used widely in Near East, adopted by Romans for slaves and most despised criminals. Romans used T-shaped cross until abolition when Christianity became a lawful religion in empire under Constantine I. JESUS CHRIST died by crucifixion.

Cruden, Alexander (1701-70), Scottish scholar. A London bookseller, he compiled the *Complete Concordance to the Holy Scriptures* (1737), on which later concordances were based.

Cruikshank, George (1792-1878), English caricaturist and illustrator. Popular political cartoonist, he satirized politicians, Prince Regent, *etc.* Illustrated Grimm's *German Popular Stories* (1823) and works of Dickens.

cruiser, originally a ship of war larger than a frigate. In modern navies, a fast, lightly armoured but heavily armed vessel used mainly for engaging enemy raiders and escorting convoys.

Crusades, series of wars by W European Christians (11th-14th cent.) to recover Holy Land from Moslems, so called from cross worn as badge by crusaders. **First Crusade** (1095-9) followed speech by Pope Urban II urging Christians to fight to recover Holy Sepulchre. Preached by wandering preachers, incl. Peter the Hermit and Walter the Penniless, who led disorderly bands of followers to Holy Land. Organized campaign, led by great nobles, monarchs of Europe, culminated in capture of Jerusalem (1099); followed by estab. of Latin Kingdom of Jerusalem, and orders of Knights Hospitallers and Knights Templars. These orders were mainstay of later crusades. Turkish reconquests of Christian territ. occasioned later Crusades, beginning with unsuccessful **Second Crusade** (1147-9). Capture of Jerusalem by Saladin (1187) provoked **Third Crusade** (1189-92), led by Richard I of England, Philip II of France and Emperor Frederick I. Ended without recapture of Jerusalem, but trucial rights. **Fourth Crusade** (1202-4), proclaimed by Innocent III, was diverted from purpose by political ambitions of Venetians and ended in sacking of Constantinople by Crusaders and estab. of Latin Kingdom thereof. **Children's Crusade** (1212) followed, ending in children being enslaved, or dying of hunger, disease. Innocent III preached **Fifth Crusade** (1217-21), directed at Egypt, with no positive conclusion. **Sixth Crusade** (1228-9) led by Emperor Frederick II, gained truce, partial surrender of Jerusalem, crowning of emperor as king thereof. Moslems soon reoccupied Jerusalem, and wars broke out again. **Seventh, Eighth** and **Ninth Crusades** were abortive attempts to stem decline of Christian power in Holy Land, ending with fall of last Christian stronghold, Acre (1291). There were also crusades, proclaimed by pope, against pagans, heretics, *eg* Wends, Hussites, Albigenses.

Crustacea (crustaceans), class of arthropods, incl. crabs, lobsters, barnacles, shrimps, water fleas. Mainly aquatic; 2 pairs of antennae, pair of mandibles, other appendages for walking, swimming, *etc.* Body sometimes covered by chitinous carapace.

Cruyff, Johann (1947-), Dutch footballer. Skilful goalscorer for Ajax team which won 3 successive European Cup finals (1971-3). Later joined Barcelona. Captained Dutch team defeated in 1974 World Cup final.

cryogenics, study of production of very low temperatures and of their effect on properties of matter.

cryolite, rare mineral, a fluoride of sodium and aluminium. Colourless or snow-white, has icy appearance; occurs in vein-like masses in granite. Used in electrolytic production of aluminium. Only major source in Greenland.

crypt, subterranean chamber or vault, esp. under a church floor. Crypts developed when early Christians built churches over tombs of martyrs or saints.

crystal, solidified form of a substance in which atoms or molecules are arranged in ordered geometrical patterns repeated regularly in space. Structure can be studied by examining diffraction patterns produced by passing beams of X-rays through specimens.

Crystal Palace, building of glass and iron, designed by Joseph Paxton to house Great Exhibition of 1851. Erected in Hyde Park, London, it was moved to Sydenham (1852-3); destroyed by fire (1936).

Ctenophora (ctenophores), phylum of freeswimming marine organisms, usually called comb jellies or sea

gooseberries. Body often transparent, globular; bears 8 rows of comb-like plates with cilia to aid swimming.

Ctesibius (*fl* 2nd cent. BC), Greek inventor. Said to be first to discover and use energy of expanding air. Developed water clock, hydraulic organ and force pump.

Cuba

Cuba, isl. republic, largest of West Indies; incl. Isle of Pines. Area 114,524 sq km (44,218 sq mi); pop. 8,553,000; cap. Havana. Language: Spanish. Religion: RC. Mainly low-lying; mountainous in interior and SE. Sugar is main crop and export; tobacco growing (cigar mfg.), fruit growing; timber from inland forested mountains. Settled by Spanish in 16th cent. after Columbus' discovery (1492). Spanish-American War (1898) led to independence in 1902. Castro estab. Communist govt. after 1958 revolt; US-Soviet confrontation over missile installation in Cuba (1962).

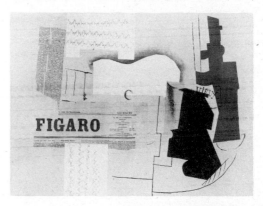

Example of cubism: Picasso's *Guitar, glass and bottle*

cubism, art movement of early 20th cent., derived from work of Cézanne; subjects were portrayed, not as they appear, but by analysis into series of planes. Traditional perspective was abandoned and several different views of subject were often combined. Originated by Picasso and Braque, its formative period was 1907-14.

Cuchulain, hero of Celtic myth. Central to cycle based on exploits, in association with uncle, Conchobar, king of Ulster. Most famous deeds told in *Táin Bó Cúalnge* (the cattle-raid of Cooley).

cuckoo, any of Cuculidae family of mainly insectivorous birds. Long slender body, greyish-brown on top, curved beak. Some species parasitic, laying eggs in other birds' nests, *eg* common European cuckoo, *Cuculus canorus.* American cuckoos, *eg* yellow-billed *Coccyzus americanus,* not parasitic.

cuckoo bee, name for bee of genus *Psithyrus,* parasitic on bumble bee.

cuckoo flower, *Cardamine pratensis,* bitter cress bearing white or purple flowers. Common in N temperate marshes.

cuckoo-spit, see FROGHOPPER.

European cuckoo

cucumber, *Cucumis sativus,* creeping plant of gourd family, native to NW India. Widely grown in temperate regions for elongated, edible fruit. Gherkin is one of 30 related species.

cucumber tree, name for MAGNOLIA.

Cúcuta, town of NE Colombia, in E Andes near Venezuela border. Pop. 167,000. Coffee trade centre. Founded 1734. Badly damaged by earthquake (1875).

Cudworth, Ralph (1617-88), English philosopher. Leading Cambridge Platonist. Attempted to reconcile rational and mystical, opposed Hobbes' materialism. Known for *The True Intellectual System of the Universe* (1678).

Cuenca, town of S Ecuador, in Andes. Alt. 2440 m (*c* 8000 ft). Pop. 77,000. In agric. region (grain production); tyres, textiles, Panama hat mfg. Founded 1557. Has univ. (1868).

Cuenca, town of EC Spain, cap. of Cuenca prov. Pop. 34,000. Agric. market. Medieval textile centre. Cathedral (13th cent.).

Cuernavaca, town of C Mexico, cap. of Morelos state. Pop. 160,000. Health, tourist resort. Has beautiful churches, monasteries and mural decoration by Diego Rivera.

Cuiabá, town of WC Brazil, cap. of Mato Grosso state at navigable head of Cuiabá R. Pop. 101,000. Transport, distribution centre for cattle, hides, dried meat. Founded (1719) during gold rush.

cuirass, originally a leather jerkin. From medieval times, metal armour protecting the body above the waist, esp. in the 'cuirassiers' or heavy cavalry of the 17th cent.

Culbertson, Ely (1891-1955), American bridge expert, b. Romania. Introduced system of bidding into contract bridge; wrote widely on the game and did much to popularize it in 1930s.

Culdees, ancient order of monks of Ireland and Scotland. Renowned for extreme laxness. Last community, at Armagh, disbanded in 1541.

Culiacán, town of NW Mexico, cap. of Sinaloa state. Pop. 359,000. In irrigated agric. region producing maize, beans, sugar cane. Founded 1531.

Culloden Moor, near Inverness, Highland region, N Scotland. Scene of defeat (1746) of Bonnie Prince Charlie's Jacobite forces by Duke of Cumberland's English army.

Cultural Revolution (1966-9), period of ferment in China initiated under Mao Tse-tung, resulting in purge of leadership within Communist Party and state bureaucracies in effort to recreate revolutionary spirit. Top officials removed incl. Chu Teh, Teng Hsiao-ping; radicals in army and youth (*see* RED GUARD), led by Lin Piao, Chiang Ching (Mao's wife), sparked open conflict, mass rallies. Continuing chaos led Chou En-lai to restore order under army.

cultured pearl, semi-precious pearl formed within certain molluscs, *eg* oyster, after introduction of irritant. Mainly produced in Japan.

Cumae, ancient city of Campania, W Italy, near Naples. Strabo calls it earliest Greek colony in Italy (founded *c* 750 BC). Taken 5th cent. BC by Samnites. Many remains, incl. cavern of Cumaean Sybil.

Cumaná, port of NE Venezuela, near Caribbean. Pop. 120,000. Coffee, cacoa exports; fisheries. Founded as Nueva Toledo (*c* 1521); oldest European settlement in South America. Has suffered severe earthquakes.

Cumans, Turkic people, known in Russia as the Polovtsi, who settled in steppes N of Black Sea in 11th cent. Made continued war against Kiev, Byzantine Empire and Hungary. Defeated and dispersed, mainly into Bulgaria and Hungary, by Mongols in mid-13th cent.

Cumberland, William Augustus, Duke of (1721-65), British army officer, son of George II. Commanded the allied forces in the Netherlands in the War of the Austrian Succession, and crushed the 1745 rebellion at Culloden with notorious severity, earning himself the title 'Butcher'.

Cumberland, former county of NW England, now in Cumbria; co. town Carlisle. Lake Dist. in S, incl. Scafell Pike; drained by Derwent, Esk. Plain of Carlisle in N. Dairying, livestock farming; granite, slate quarries. Scene of border warfare until 1603.

Cumberland, river of EC US. Flows from E Kentucky 1106 km (687 mi) SW into Tennessee then NW through Kentucky to Ohio R. at Smithland. Rises in mountains of Cumberland Plateau (incl. Cumberland Gap, strategic frontier and Civil War position).

Cumbernauld, town of Strathclyde, C Scotland. Pop. 32,000. Created as 'new town' 1955; well-designed layout.

Cumbria, county of NW England. Area 6808 sq km (2628 sq mi); pop. 476,000; co. town Carlisle. Created 1974, incl. Cumberland, Westmorland, N Lancashire.

Cumin

cumin, *Cuminum cyminum,* small annual plant of parsley family grown in Egypt and Syria. Umbels of small white or pink flowers. Aromatic seeds used to flavour pickles, curries esp. in Oriental cooking.

Cummings, E[dward] E[stlin] (1894-1962), American poet, painter. Known for poems of typographical experiment, novel *The Enormous Room* (1922) on his imprisonment in French prison camp.

cumulus cloud, *see* CLOUD.

Cunard, Sir Samuel (1787-1865), Canadian shipping magnate. With others, founded (1840) steamship company (later to become Cunard Line) to carry mail from Liverpool to North America.

cuneiform, from Latin meaning 'wedge-shaped', writing developed in Tigris-Euphrates basin, consisting of wedge-like marks impressed on clay tablets. Used by Babylonians and Assyrians, key finds have been made at Nineveh, Lagash and Susa.

Cunene, river of WC Africa. Flows *c* 960 km (600 mi) SW from C Angola via series of cataracts to Atlantic Ocean. Large irrigation, h.e.p. scheme. Forms part of Angola-South West Africa border.

Cuneiform inscription from Turkey

Cunninghame-Graham, Robert Bontine (1852-1936), Scottish writer. Known for travel books, *eg A Vanished Arcadia* (1907) on Latin America. Involved in politics as liberal, socialist; first president Scottish Nationalist Party (1928).

Cuoco, Vincenzo (1770-1823), Italian political theorist. Foresaw gradual reunification of Italy, ideas becoming basis of RISORGIMENTO movement. Exiled from Venice after 1799 republican revolution.

Cupar, town of Fife region, EC Scotland. Pop. 7000. Former royal burgh and co. town of Fife. Tanning, fertilizer industs.

Cupid, Roman god of love, identified with Greek Eros and Roman Amor. Represented as irresponsible cherub with bow and arrow.

cupro-nickel, alloy of copper and nickel; ductile, resists corrosion. Used in coinage.

Curaçao, largest isl. of Netherlands Antilles, in S Caribbean. Area 461 sq km (178 sq mi); pop. 144,000. Has cap. of isl. group, Willemstad. Agric., incl. sisal, citrus fruit growing; famous liqueur mfg.; refining of oil from Venezuela. Discovered by Spanish (1499); Dutch occupation from 1634.

curare, alkaloid from bark of plants of genus *Strychnos.* Used by Amazon Indians as arrow poison. Causes paralysis. Limited medicinal use to relax muscles.

Helmeted curassow (Crax pauxi)

curassow, any of Cracidae family of arboreal birds of tropical America. Black or brown plumage, erect crest; resembles chicken. Species incl. great curassow, *Crax rubra.*

Curie, Pierre (1859-1906), and **Marie Curie,** née Sklodowska (1867-1934), French scientists. Pierre studied effect of heat on magnetic substances, showing that magnetic properties are lost above certain temperature (Curie point); investigated PIEZOELECTRIC effect. Marie worked on uranium, radioactive element in pitchblende. Together they discovered radium and polonium and shared Nobel Prize for Physics (1903) with Becquerel. Later Marie pioneered medicinal use of radioactivity; isolated metallic radium, winning Nobel Prize for Chemistry (1911).

Curitiba, city of SC Brazil, cap. of Paraná state. Pop. 608,000. Agric. market (coffee, timber, maté); centre of immigration influx from 19th cent.

curium (Cm), transuranic element of actinide series; at. no. 96, mass no. of most stable isotope 247. Prepared 1944 at Univ. of California by bombarding plutonium with alpha particles.

curlew, large wading bird with downward-curved bill, brownish-grey plumage. *Numenius arquata* is largest European wader.

curling, game played on ice, usually by two teams of four players, in which heavy stones are slid towards a target circle at far end of rink. Rules controlled by Royal Caledonian Curling Club (founded 1838). Played in Scotland, North America and parts of Europe.

Curran, John Philpot (1750-1817), Irish politician, lawyer. Opponent of British policy in Ireland, defended Irish rebels, incl. Wolfe Tone, against repressive British regime.

currant, shrub of genus *Ribes* of saxifrage family, native to W Europe. Fruit of black currant, *R. nigrum,* and red currant, *R. rubrum,* eaten fresh or made into conserves.

currency, *see* MONEY.

current, *see* ELECTRICITY.

curry, condiment originating in India made from turmeric, coriander, black and cayenne pepper, *etc.* Usually eaten with rice, meat, vegetables.

Curtin, John Joseph (1885-1945) Australian statesman, PM (1941-5). Leader of Labor Party from 1935. As head of wartime govt., organized Australian defence forces to oppose Japanese advances in Pacific.

Curwen, John (1816-80), English musician. Introduced tonic sol-fa system for singing music at sight.

Curzon, George Nathaniel, 1st Marquess Curzon of Kedleston (1859-1925), British statesman. Reform viceroy of India (1899-1905), pacified North West. Conservative foreign secretary, presided at Lausanne Conference (1922-3), resolving Turkey's objections to post-WWI settlement.

Cushing, Harvey Williams (1869-1939), American neurosurgeon. Pioneer in brain surgery, and noted teacher and author. Described Cushing's disease, caused by hyperactivity of adrenal glands; characterized by obesity, hypertension.

Cushitic, non-Semitic language group of Afro-Asiatic family. Spoken mainly in Ethiopia, Sudan, Somalia, Kenya and Tanzania. Most important language of group is Somali.

Custer, George Armstrong (1839-76), American army officer. Fought with distinction in the Civil War. Commanded a cavalry unit against the Indians and was killed with all his men by the Sioux at Little Bighorn.

customs, *see* TARIFFS.

Cuthbert, St (*c* 634-87), English bishop. Preached in Northumberland and Scottish borders. Bishop of Lindisfarne (685-7).

Cuttack, port of Orissa state, E India, on R. Mahanadi. Pop. 194,000. Trade in rice, jute; engineering. Former cap. of Orissa.

cuttlefish, any cephalopod mollusc of Sepioidea family. Ten tentacles around head, parrot-like beak. Flattened shell, or cuttlebone, is internal. Protects itself by ejecting cloud of brown 'ink'.

cutworm, larva of certain owlet moths. Nocturnal caterpillar feeding on roots, shoots of plants; hides in soil by day.

Cuvier, Georges Léopold Chrétien Frédéric Dagobert, Baron, (1769-1832), French zoologist, geologist. Regarded as founder of comparative anatomy and palaeontology. Proposed 4-phylum system of animal classification based on inner structure. Identified and named pterodactyl.

Cuxhaven, town of N West Germany, on Elbe estuary. Pop. 45,000. Outport for Hamburg; fishing, shipbuilding, resort.

Cuyp, Aelbert (1620-91), Dutch painter. Son of Jacob Cuyp and leading member of family of painters. Did landscapes, still lifes, town and river scenes; noted for his handling of light and atmosphere. Works incl. *View of Dordrecht.*

Cuzco, town of SC Peru, alt. 3400 m (11,200 ft). Pop. 105,000. Sugar cane, rice products from irrigated region; woollen textiles mfg. Cap. of Inca empire, its numerous palaces and temples, incl. Temple of the Sun, were destroyed by Spaniards under Pizarro. Many ruins remain.

Cwmbran, urban dist. of Gwent, SE Wales. Pop. 41,000. Designated 'new town' in 1949. Steel, metal working industs.; bricks, tiles mfg.

cyanide, salt of hydrocyanic acid (hydrogen cyanide or prussic acid, HCN). Potassium and sodium cyanide are intensely poisonous white crystalline solids, with odour of bitter almonds; used in extracting gold from low-grade ores, electroplating, steel hardening.

Cybele, in Greek and Roman myth, 'mother of the gods'. Nature goddess, often associated with ATTIS.

cybernetics, science dealing with comparative study of operations of electronic computers and human nervous system. Defined by Norbert Wiener (1948) as 'the study of control and communication in the animal and the machine'.

Cycadales, order of tropical shrubs and trees resembling thick-stemmed palms, with crowns of leathery fern-like leaves and large cones containing fleshy seeds.

cyclamate, salt of organic cyclamic acid, esp. calcium or sodium salt, which has very sweet taste. Formerly used as artificial sweetener; use discouraged because of possible carcinogenic properties.

cyclamen, genus of plants of primrose family, native to Mediterranean region. Heart-shaped leaves, flowers white to deep red with reflexed petals. Species *Cyclamen persicum* is popular houseplant.

cycling, sport of bicycle riding. Various competitive events incl. road racing, time trialling, pursuit racing and sprints. Esp. popular in France, Belgium, Netherlands, where professional long-distance races such as Tour de France are held. Olympic event since 1896.

cyclone, area of relatively low atmospheric pressure together with surrounding wind system. Tropical cyclone is violent storm, *eg* hurricane, typhoon; temperate latitude cyclone now referred to as a DEPRESSION. Wind circulation is clockwise in S hemisphere, anti-clockwise in N hemisphere.

Cyclopes, in Greek myth, gigantic one-eyed beings. In Homer, race of shepherds, one of whom Odysseus blinds (*see* POLYPHEMUS). In Hesiod, they are craftsmen, sons of Uranus and Gaea.

cyclops, small freshwater crustacean of subclass Copepoda. Enlarged antennae used as oars; single median eye.

Cyclostomata (cyclostomes), class of marine chordates with eel-like body, jawless sucking mouth; no bone or scales. Attach themselves by mouth to fish, rasping flesh and sucking blood. Incl. LAMPREY and HAGFISH.

cymbals, orchestral untuned percussion instrument, of oriental origin; made of 2 concave metal discs which are clashed together or struck with a stick.

Cynewulf (*fl* late 8th-9th cent.), Old English poet. Large body of religious verse attributed to him, but only 4 poems certainly his, incl. masterpiece *Elene.*

Cynics, Greek school of philosophy founded (4th cent. BC) by Antisthenes. Held desires to be impediment to happiness, hence self-sufficient ascetic life of followers, *eg* DIOGENES. Basis of STOICISM.

cypress, family of coniferous trees, Cupressaceae, native to Mediterranean region, Asia and North America. Dark green needle leaves in overlapping pairs, woody cones. Distinctive symmetrical form. Lawson cypress, *Chamaecyparis lawsoniana,* grows to *c* 60 m/200 ft.

Cyprus (Gk. *Kypros),* isl. republic of British Commonwealth, in E Mediterranean. Area 9270 sq km (3572 sq mi); pop. 634,000, 80% being Greek Cypriots; cap. Nicosia. Languages: Greek, Turkish. Religions: Eastern Orthodox, Islam. Irrigated plain between 2 mountain ranges. Pastoral economy; grain, wine, olives grown. Minerals incl. iron, copper. Ancient Bronze Age culture; subsequently ruled by Assyria, Persia, Rome, Turkey, Britain (1878-independence in 1960). Bitter conflict (1950-

Cyprus

64, 1974) between Greek, Turkish Cypriots; Turkish invasion 1974.

Cyrano de Bergerac, Savinien (1619-55), French author. Satirized society in *Histoire comique des états et empires de la lune* (1657-62). Inspiration for Rostand's dramatic hero, as longnosed poet-soldier, skilled dueller.

Cyrenaica, region of E Libya. Incl. fertile coastal strip, Libyan Desert, Kufra oasis. First settled 7th cent. BC by Greeks, who founded Cyrene. Under Romans, Arabs prior to Turkish rule from 16th cent.; colonized by Italy 1911-42. Federal prov. (cap. Benghazi) 1951-63.

Cyrenaics, *see* ARISTIPPUS.

Cyril, St (*c* 827-69), Greek Christian missionary. With his brother, **St Methodius** (*c* 815-84), sent (863) to convert Moravians despite opposition of German rulers. Cyrillic alphabet, used in Bulgaria, Russia, Serbia, possibly invented by Cyril.

Cyril of Alexandria, St (*c* 380-444), Egyptian churchman, patriarch of Alexandria. Attacked heretics, condemning Nestorians at Council of Ephesus (431). His own orthodox view of Trinity influenced Monophysite heresy.

Cyrus the Great (d. 529 BC), founder of Persian empire. Overthrew Astyages of Media (551) and gained control of Asia Minor with defeat of Croesus (546). Captured Babylon (539). Ruled with toleration, respecting local customs; allowed exiled Jews to return to Palestine.

czar, *see* TSAR.

Czechoslovakia

Czechoslovakia (*Ceskoslovensko*), republic of EC Europe. Area 127,842 sq km (49,360 sq mi); pop. 14,578,000; cap. Prague. Languages: Czech, Slovak. Religion: RC. Comprises plateau of Bohemia (W); lowland of Moravia (C); highlands of Slovakia (E) incl. W Carpathians, High Tatra. Agric. in fertile valleys (esp. cereals, sugar beet, hops); timber, coal, iron industs.; textiles, engineering. Formed (1918) from parts of Austria-Hungary. Occupied in stages by Germans (1938-45). Coup estab. Communist state (1948); liberalization movement suppressed by Soviet invasion (1968).

Czestochowa, city of S Poland, on R. Warta. Pop. 189,000. Iron and steel works, chemicals indust. Monastery on Jasna Góra hill is pilgrimage centre.

D

dab, *Limanda limanda,* food fish of flounder family, found in N Atlantic.

dabchick, bird of grebe family. Name applied to pied-billed grebe, *Podylimbus podiceps,* of North America. European species, *Podiceps ruficollis,* is diving bird.

Dacca, cap. of Bangladesh. Pop. 1,311,000. Commercial, indust. centre on R. Dhaleswari. Textiles, jute products, chemicals; muslin mfg. centre until late 19th cent. Mogul cap. of Bengal in 17th cent.; cap. of East Pakistan.

dace, *Leuciscus vulgaris,* small freshwater fish of carp family with silver colouring.

Dachau, town of S West Germany, near Munich. Pop. 30,000. Paper, textiles, machinery mfg. Site of concentration camp under Nazi regime.

dachshund, small German dog, with long body, drooping ears and short legs. Short-haired coat; stands 20-25 cm/8-10 in. at shoulder.

dada or **dadaism,** literary, artistic movement of period 1916-22. *Dada* review proclaimed intention to replace rationality with deliberate madness, chaos in art. Dadaists incl. poet Breton, artists Arp, Duchamp. Developed into SURREALISM.

daddy-long-legs, *see* CRANE FLY.

Daedalus, in Greek myth, craftsman and inventor. Built Labyrinth for Minotaur in Crete (*see* MINOS). Made wings of feathers and wax to escape from Crete with son Icarus. Icarus flew too near the sun, the wax melted and he was drowned in the sea.

daffodil, various plants of genus *Narcissus* of amaryllis family with trumpet-like flower. Name usually restricted to common yellow daffodil or lent lily, *N. pseudonarcissus,* found growing wild in woods and fields of temperate countries.

Dagenham, part of Barking, E Greater London, England. Former mun. bor. of Essex. Has Ford motor plant, clothing, chemical mfg.

Dagestan, auton. republic of S European RSFSR, USSR; between E Great Caucasus and Caspian Sea. Area *c* 50,250 sq km (19,400 sq mi); pop. 1,430,000; cap. Makhachkala. Mainly mountainous, with coastal plain along Caspian. Stock raising; grain, cotton, fruit cultivated. Minerals largely undeveloped; some oil, natural gas.

Daguerre, Louis Jacques Mandé (1789-1851), French scene painter, physicist. Invented daguerrotype, photograph produced on copper plate treated with silver iodide; 1st practical method of photography. Also invented diorama, series of pictorial views seen in changing light.

Dahl, Roald (1916-), American writer, b. England. Known for macabre short stories, *eg Kiss Kiss* (1960), also children's books.

dahlia, genus of perennial, tuberous-rooted lateflowering plants of daisy family. Native to Mexico and Central America. Widely cultivated for brightly coloured showy flowers. Well-known species incl. *Dahlia coccinea, D. pinnata* and *D. juarezii.*

Dáil Eireann, legislative, popularly-elected assembly of Republic of Ireland. First assembled (1919) in Dublin. After creation of Irish Free State (1921), upper house, Seanad Eireann, created, which, with Dáil (lower house) constitutes state legislature.

Daimler, Gottlieb (1834-1900), German engineer, inventor. Improved internal combustion engine, furthering car indust. Founded (1890) Daimler Motor Company.

Dairen, Japanese form of Talien, now LU-TA.

dairying, business of producing and distributing milk and milk products. In most countries, milk is consumed in liquid form. In others, *eg* Denmark, New Zealand, transportable milk products such as butter, cheese and dried milk dominate dairy indust.

daisy, *Bellis perennis,* small perennial herb of COMPOSITAE family, native to Europe and W Asia. Other species incl. *Chrysanthemum leucanthemum,* ox-eye daisy.

Dakar

Dakar, cap. of Senegal, on Cape Verde penin. Pop. 581,000. Admin., commercial centre; port, exports groundnuts, animal products; univ. (1949), Pasteur Institute. Former centre of slave trade. Cap. of French West Africa from 1902, of Senegal from 1958.

Dakota, Indians, *see* SIOUX.

Daladier, Edouard (1884-1970), French statesman. Premier (1933, 1933-4, 1938-40), forced to resign (1934) after Stavisky affair; signed Munich Pact (1938) enabling Germany to occupy Sudetenland. Interned by Vichy govt. (1940), deported to Germany (1943-5).

Dalai Lama, head of Lamaist religion of Tibet and Mongolia. Considered divine, reincarnation of his predecessor; 5th Dalai Lama was given (1640) temporal rule over all Tibet and built monastery near Lhasa. During 1959 Tibetan revolt against Chinese Communists 14th Dalai Lama went into exile in India.

Dale, Sir Henry Hallett (1875-1968), English scientist. Shared Nobel Prize for Physiology and Medicine (1930) for studying acetylcholine's role in chemical transmission of nerve impulses.

Daley, Richard Joseph (1902-76), American politician. Mayor of Chicago from 1955, headed Democratic party machine which dominated Chicago politics. Notorious for Chicago police's use of violent methods to disperse demonstrators at Democratic National Convention (1968).

Dalhousie, James Andrew Broun Ramsay, 1st Marquess of (1812-60), British statesman. Governor-general of India (1847-56), annexed (1849) Punjab after 2nd Sikh War. Promoted public works, education and social reform. Annexation of Oudh (1856) contributed to INDIAN MUTINY.

Dali, Salvador (1904-), Spanish surrealist painter. Influenced by Freudian psychology, he painted irrational dream world in a detailed academic style; later work, in more traditional style, incl. religious subjects. Collaborated with Luis Buñuel on surrealist films *Un Chien Andalou* and *L'Age d'Or.*

Dallas, city of NE Texas, US; on Trinity R. Pop. 844,000. Commercial, indust. centre. Oil refining; important cotton market; aircraft, electronic equipment, chemical mfg. Settled 1841; grew up as cotton market. President J. F. Kennedy assassinated here (1963).

Dalmatia

Dalmatia, region of Yugoslavia, in Croatia, on Adriatic coast. Mountainous, incl. Dinaric Alps. Resorts incl. Dubrovnik, Split, Zadar. Passed from Austria to Yugoslavia (1919); Zadar and isls. ceded by Italy (1947).

dalmatian, breed of dog developed in Dalmatia (Yugoslavia). Short-haired, black spots on white coat; stands 48-55 cm/ 19-23 in. at shoulder.

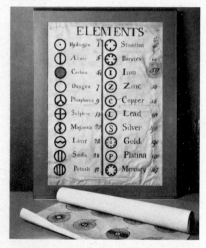

Dalton's diagram of atomic weights

Dalton, John (1766-1844), English chemist. Proposed theory that all matter is composed of indestructible atoms; atoms of same element were identical and differed from those of other elements only in weight. Prepared table of atomic weights and devised law of partial pressures of gases (Dalton's law).

Dam, Henrik (1895-1976), Danish biochemist. Discovered and studied vitamin K, important in clotting of blood, for which he shared Nobel Prize in Physiology and Medicine (1943).

dam, barrier built across river to store water or regulate its flow for irrigation or to supply power. (*See* HYDRO-ELECTRIC POWER.) Notable dams incl. Aswan Dam across R. Nile, Fort Peck Dam (largest capacity in US) in Montana, Indus barrage in Pakistan.

Daman (*Damao*), former Portuguese enclave in W India. Pop. 69,000. Captured by Portuguese (1559), seized by India in 1961. Part of union territ. of Goa, Daman and Diu.

Damanhûr, city of N Egypt, on Nile delta. Pop. 161,000. Trade centre in cotton, rice growing dist.; on Alexandria-Cairo railway.

Damascus (Arab. *Esh-Sham*), cap. of Syria. Pop. 837,000. Famous for silks and metalware. Early Christian centre

under Romans; taken by Arabs (635), seat of caliph (661-750). Cap. of independent republic from 1941.

damask, reversible fabric of silk, cotton, wool, *etc,* with figured pattern formed by weaving. Name derives from city of Damascus where mfg. of fine coloured silk fabrics reached high point in *c* 12th cent.

Damien, Father Joseph, orig. Joseph de Veuster (1840-89), Belgian RC missionary. Worked until death from leprosy in leper colony on Molokai, Hawaii. Made famous through tract by R.L. Stevenson.

Damietta (*Dumyat*), town of N Egypt, on Damietta branch of Nile delta. Pop. 72,000. In rice, cotton growing dist.; gave name to 'dimity' cloth.

Damocles, in classical legend, courtier of Syracuse who, to show him the perils of a ruler's life, was seated at a banquet by Dionysius I under a sword suspended by a single hair.

Damodar, river of EC India, flowing 595 km (370 mi) from E Bihar to meet R. Hooghly in West Bengal. Damodar valley scheme provides h.e.p. for Calcutta; coalfields in valley.

Dampier, William (*c* 1651-1715), English buccaneer, explorer. Took part in several buccaneering expeditions to Africa, Spanish America (1679-91). Commanded naval expedition to W and N Australia, New Guinea, New Britain (1699-1701). Later piloted voyage round world (1708-11).

Common damsel fly

damsel fly, slender type of dragonfly, usually brightly coloured, of suborder Zygoptera. Wings held vertically when at rest.

damson, *see* PLUM.

Dana, Richard Henry (1815-82), American author, lawyer. Known for classic *Two Years before the Mast* (1840) based on experience as sailor. Subsequently campaigned for seamen's rights.

Danaë, in Greek myth, daughter of Acrisius, king of Argos. Imprisoned by her father because of an oracle that she would bear a son who would kill him. Zeus entered the prison as a shower of gold and fathered PERSEUS.

Danang, port of N South Vietnam on S China Sea. Pop. 438,000. Major US military base during Vietnam war.

Danby, Thomas Osborne, Earl of (1631-1712), English statesman. Impeached for treasonable negotiations with France (on Charles II's behalf); imprisoned (1679-84). Joined Whigs in inviting William of Orange to replace James II; served as king's chief minister (1690-5).

dance, the art of rhythmical, expressive movement of the body, often to music. Developed from early ritual, *eg* fertility dances and mimetic dances illustrating movements of planets, events in battle, *etc.* Dancing is still part of the ritual of several ecstatic religious groups, *eg* dervishes, Hasidic Jews. In Greece, became part of drama, *eg* choral dances in honour of Dionysus. Allegorical forms developed in medieval Europe, *eg* dance of death (possibly inspired by outbreaks of hysterical mass dancing during plague epidemics). Division into court and folk dances stemmed from late Middle Ages with the *volta* becoming source of modern ballroom dances. BALLET first appeared in 16th cent. Italian courts. In 20th cent. many dance crazes have been associated with jazz and rock music.

dandelion, several plants of genus *Taraxacum,* esp. *T. officinale,* wild, European plant, cultivated in Asia and North America. Leaves used in salads and as diuretic.

Daniel, apocalyptic book of OT, prob. written *c* 168 BC. Story of Daniel, a Jew living in 6th cent. BC. Captured and taken to Nebuchadnezzar's court, where he was famous for his wisdom. Written to encourage the Jews to keep the faith under persecutions of Antiochus IV of Syria.

Daninos, Pierre (1913-   ), French novelist. Known for humorous caricature of English officer in *Les Carnets du Major Thompson* (1954).

Danish, language of N Germanic group of Indo-European family. Official language of Denmark, spoken also in Greenland, Faeroes, Iceland, Virgin Isls. Developed from Old Norse. Literature in existence since *c* 850.

D'Annunzio, Gabriele (1863-1938), Italian author, soldier. Belief that sensual pleasure alone gives meaning to life reflected in works, *eg* play *La Gioconda* (1898), novel *Il Fuoco* (1900), poetry. Hero of nationalism, held Fiume for 15 months (1919-20), later pro-Fascist.

Dante Alighieri

Dante [Alighieri] (1265-1321), Italian poet. Best known for *Divine Comedy,* long epic poem giving comprehensive view of human destiny, temporal and eternal; divided into journeys through Hell and Purgatory (guided by Vergil) and Paradise (guided by Beatrice). Other works incl. *La Vita Nuova* (1292), prose-linked lyrics addressed to idealized love, Beatrice.

Danton, Georges Jacques (1759-94), French revolutionary. Influential orator, took part in overthrow of Louis XVI (1792). Leader of revolutionaries in new National Convention, advocated spread of Revolution's ideas throughout Europe by war. Member of Committee of Public Safety (1793), eventually opposed REIGN OF TERROR. Guillotined after power struggle with extremists led by Robespierre.

Danube, river of C and SE Europe. Flows 2815 km (1750 mi) from Black Forest (West Germany) to Black Sea (Romania). Tributaries incl. Inn, Sava, Tisza, Prut. Ports incl. Vienna, Belgrade. Navigable below Ulm, passage controlled by commission based in Budapest.

Danzig, see GDAŃSK, Poland.

Daphne, in Greek myth, nymph loved by Apollo. In trying to flee from him, she was changed into a laurel tree.

daphne, genus of small evergreen flowering shrubs, native to Europe and Asia. *Daphne mezereum* and *D. laureola* or spurge laurel are found in Britain and Europe. Chinese *D. odora* and *D. retusa* are widely cultivated for fragrant flowers.

Daphnia, see WATER FLEA.

Da Ponte, Lorenzo, orig. Emanuele Conegliano (1749-1838), Italian poet. Wrote libretti for Mozart's *Marriage of*

Danube

Figaro (1786), *Don Giovanni* (1787), *Così fan Tutte* (1790). Settled in US (1805).

Dardanelles

Dardanelles (anc. *Hellespont*), narrow str. separating European and Asiatic Turkey; 64 km (40 mi) long, connects Aegean Sea and Sea of Marmara. Of great strategic and commercial importance; Troy stood nearby. Crossed by Xerxes I in 480 BC and Alexander The Great in 334 BC. In Turkish hands by 1402, it controlled entrance to Constantinople. Focus of conflict in decay of Ottoman Empire in 19th cent. and also in WWI (*see* GALLIPOLI).

Dar-es-Salaam, cap. of Tanzania, on Indian Ocean. Pop. 344,000. Admin., commercial centre; port, exports sisal, cotton, diamonds; oil refining. Railway links to Kigoma and Zambia; univ. (1961). Founded 1862; cap. of German East Africa 1891-1916.

Darién, Gulf of, inlet of Caribbean, between Panama and Colombia. Scots settlers failed in attempts to colonize Darién isthmus in E Panama (*c* 1700).

Darién scheme, Scottish plan to set up a colony on Darién Isthmus, Panama, and gain access to trade in Pacific. Suggested by WILLIAM PATERSON. Two expeditions (1698, 1699) to Darién failed through illness and Spanish opposition; great losses suffered by Scottish investors hastened Act of Union (1707).

Dario, Rubén, orig. Félix Rubén García Sarmiento (1867-1916), Nicaraguan poet. Coined term 'modernism' for aesthetic values standing outside society. Known for *Azul* (1888), Parnassian-inspired *Prosas profanas* (1896); immense influence on Spanish prose and poetry.

Darius [I] the Great (d. 486 BC), Persian king (521-486). Estab. authority by suppressing revolts of usurpers in early years of reign, then organized personal representatives (satraps) to administer vast empire. Sent unsuccessful expedition to punish Greeks for supporting revolt of Ionian city states (492). Second expedition defeated at Marathon (490).

Darjeeling, resort town of West Bengal, NE India. Pop. 43,000. In Himalayan foothills at alt. of over 1830 m (6000 ft). Nearby tea plantations. Fine views of Kanchenjunga.

darkling beetle, flightless nocturnal beetle of Tenebrionidae family, destructive of plants. Mealworms, larvae of certain species, eat stored foodstuff; also reared as bird food.

Darlan, Jean François (1881-1942), French admiral. Appointed to Pétain's Vichy govt. (1940), received armed forces command (1942). Joined Allies after their landing in N Africa (1942). Assassinated.

Darling, river of E Australia. Flows c 2750 km (1700 mi) SW from W Great Dividing Range to Murray R. at Wentworth. Flow variable; Menindee Lakes storage scheme controls water supply, irrigation, h.e.p.

Darlington, co. bor. of Durham, NE England. Pop. 86,000. Woollens, engineering industs. Stockton-Darlington was 1st passenger railway line (1825).

Darmesteter, Arsène (1846-88), French lexicographer. With Adolphe Hatzfeld, compiled *Dictionnaire général de la langue française* (1890-1900).

Darmstadt, city of WC West Germany. Pop. 142,000. Indust. centre, esp. railway engineering, chemicals. Former cap. of Hesse-Darmstadt duchy.

Darnley, Henry Stuart, Lord (1545-67), English nobleman, 2nd husband of Mary Queen of Scots, father of James VI of Scotland. Joined in murder (1566) of David Rizzio, Mary's favourite. Murdered, prob. at instigation of Earl of Bothwell, Mary's next husband.

Darrow, Clarence Seward (1857-1938), American lawyer. Known for defences of labour leaders (*eg* Eugene Debs, 1894), appearances in murder trials, and in SCOPES TRIAL.

darter, any of Anhingidae family of swimming and diving birds, related to cormorant. Inhabits tropical lakes and swamps. Species incl. *Anhinga anhinga* of S US. Name also applied to various brightly coloured fish of perch family of North America.

Dartford, mun. bor. of Kent, SE England, on R. Darent. Pop. 50,000. Has first English paper mill. Cement, chemical mfg. Tunnel under Thames to Purfleet (1963). Peasants' Revolt (1381) began here.

Dartmoor, moorland area of Devon, SW England; features large granite masses ('tors'). Mostly in national park; livestock rearing; wild ponies. Prison estab. 1806 from French captives, used for convicts from 1850.

Dartmouth, indust. town of S Nova Scotia, Canada. Pop. 65,000. Naval base across harbour from Halifax. Shipbuilding, sugar refining. Linked by suspension bridge with Halifax. Settled 1750.

Dartmouth, mun. bor. of Devon, SW England. Pop. 6000. Port; Royal Naval Coll. (1905).

Charles Darwin

Darwin, Erasmus (1731-1802), English physician, naturalist. Author of *Zoonomia* (1794-6), anticipating Lamarck's evolutionary theories. His grandson, **Charles Robert Darwin** (1809-82), was a naturalist. His observations and explorations during the *Beagle*'s voyages in the Pacific led to theory of evolution known as Darwinism, recorded in *On the Origin of Species* (1859) and

The Descent of Man (1871). Theories on man's ancestry and principle of natural selection bitterly contested by contemporaries on theological grounds.

Darwin, cap. of Northern Territ., Australia, on N shore of Port Darwin. Pop. 35,000. Port, exports uranium, iron ore; major airport. Settled (1869) as Palmerston; renamed 1911, when passed under federal control. Severely damaged in 1942 Japanese air raids, again by storms (1974).

dasyure, any of family Dasyuridae of nocturnal marsupials found in Australia. Carnivorous or insectivorous; large variations in size, appearance. Species incl. TASMANIAN DEVIL.

date palm, *Phoenix dactylifera,* tree grown widely in N Africa and W Asia. Now cultivated in S California and Mexico. Nutritious brown fruit eaten raw.

dating, in archaeology, assessment of age of remains. Methods incl. RADIOACTIVE DATING, dendrochronology.

Daubigny, Charles François (1817-78), French landscape painter. Associated with Barbizon school, was early exponent of painting in open air; influenced Monet and Sisley. Best known for scenes of Seine and Oise.

Daudet, Alphonse (1840-97), French author. Portrayed Provençal life in humorous, naturalistic short stories, *eg Lettres de mon Moulin* (1866), 'Tartarin' series. Also wrote novels of Parisian society, *eg Le Nabob* (1877).

Daumier, Honoré (1808-79), French artist. Caricatured bureaucrats, politicians, bourgeoisie; imprisoned for representing Louis Philippe as 'Gargantua'. Paintings, describing contemporary life or on Don Quixote theme, incl. *Third Class Carriage*.

dauphin, title of eldest son of kings of France. Prob. derives from dolphin device adopted (12th cent.) by counts of Vienne, first to bear the title. Title passed to French royal family in 1350.

Dauphiné

Dauphiné, region and former prov. of SE France, cap. Grenoble. Mountainous in E; main rivers Drôme, Isère. Tourism, h.e.p., vines, silk mfg. Part of kingdom of Arles (10th-13th cent.), annexed by France (1456). Rulers took title *dauphin,* adopted by sons of French kings.

Davao, seaport of Philippines, on Davao Gulf, SE Mindanao isl. Pop. 464,000. Centre of region producing hemp, timber, coffee. Underwent great indust. growth in 1960s.

Davenant, Sir William (1606-68), English dramatist, poet. Possibly illegitimate son of Shakespeare. Wrote first English opera *The Siege of Rhodes* (1659). Better known as reviver of English theatre after Cromwell's Commonwealth.

David or **Dewi, St** (d. c 588), patron saint of Wales. First abbot of Menevia (now St David's). Founded several monasteries in Wales. Feast day is 1 March.

David (c 1060-c 970 BC), king of Israel; Hebrew national hero. Traditionally, harpist to King Saul and slayer of Philistine giant Goliath. Anointed king after death of Saul and Jonathan (c 1012). Captured Jerusalem, making it his cap. in place of Hebron.

David I (1084-1153), king of Scotland (1124-53). Supported his niece, Matilda, in her struggle with Stephen for the English crown. Invaded England in 1138, defeated by

Stephen. Promoted Anglo-Norman aristocracy in Scotland, encouraged trade, church.

David, Gerard (d. 1523), Flemish painter of Bruges school. Influenced by earlier Flemish masters, he painted religious scenes in a style which became obsolete in his lifetime. Works incl. *The Judgment of Cambyses.*

David, Jacques Louis (1748-1825), French painter. Treated heroic and republican themes in austere neo-Classical manner; ardent supporter of Napoleon, he painted pictures glorifying his exploits. Works incl. *Oath of the Horatii* (1785), *Death of Marat, Napoleon crossing the Alps.*

Davies, W[illiam] H[enry] (1871-1940), Welsh poet. Best known for prose *Autobiography of a Super-Tramp* (1907), reflecting life as a tramp in US and UK. *Complete Poems* (1943) are simple descriptions of nature.

da Vinci, see LEONARDO DA VINCI.

Davis, Bette, orig. Ruth Elizabeth Davis (1908-), American film actress. Known for intense, dramatic roles in, *eg Dark Victory* (1939), *Now Voyager* (1942), *All About Eve* (1950), *Whatever Happened to Baby Jane?* (1962).

Jefferson Davis

Davis, Jefferson (1808-89), American statesman. Secretary of war (1853-7); withdrew as senator for Mississippi at state's secession (1861). President of Confederacy (1861-5), criticized for centralizing policies which contradicted Southern cause of states' rights. Captured and confined by Federal troops (1865-7), never prosecuted.

Davis or **Davys, John** (1550–1605), English navigator. Made 3 voyages (1585-7) in search of Northwest Passage, reached Baffin Bay via strait named after him. Killed while fighting Japanese pirates in East Indies.

Davis, Miles (1926-), American jazz musician. Noted for cool style in playing trumpet and flügelhorn, working with small groups in 1950s and 1960s. Compositions incl. *Sketches of Spain.*

Davis, William Morris (1850-1934), American geographer, geologist. His theory of landscape evolution, involving cycles of erosion leading to peneplain ('almost plain'), form basis of modern geomorphology. Founded Association of American Geographers (1904).

Davis Strait, arm of N Atlantic between Baffin Isl. and W Greenland. Length 640 km (*c* 400 mi); width at narrowest point 290 km (*c* 180 mi). Named after explorer John Davis.

Davos, town of E Switzerland, in Graubünden canton. Pop. 10,000. Health resort; winter sports.

Davy, Sir Humphrey (1778-1829), English chemist. Studied electrolysis, isolating sodium, potassium, boron, calcium, magnesium and barium. Discovered use of nitrous oxide as anaesthetic and identified chlorine as an element. Invented miner's safety lamp and electric arc.

Dawes, Charles Gates (1865-1951), American statesman. Author of Dawes plan (1924) to facilitate German payment of reparations after WWI; shared Nobel Peace Prize (1925). Vice-president under Coolidge (1925-9).

Sir Humphrey Davy

Dawson, town of W Yukon Territ., Canada; on Yukon R. Pop. 760. Tourist centre. Founded 1896 during Klondike gold rush, when pop. rose to *c* 20,000. Territ. cap. until 1951.

Day, Thomas (1748-89), English writer. Known for *History of Sandford and Merton* (1783-9), contrasting educational principles.

Dayan, Moshe (1915-), Israeli military leader. Army chief of staff (1953-8). As defence minister (1967-74), largely responsible for Israeli victory over Arab states (1967). Blamed for early reverses in 1973 October War. Resigned.

Day-Lewis, C[ecil] (1904-72), English poet, b. Ireland. Member of left-wing literary movement of 1930s. Collections incl. *The Magnetic Mountain* (1933), *Overtures to Death* (1938). Wrote detective novels under pseud. Nicholas Blake. Created poet laureate 1968.

daylight saving time, time reckoned (usually 1 hour) later than standard time. Adopted in many countries as wartime measure; continued after WWII as 'summer' time by turning clocks ahead in spring and back in autumn.

Dayton, city of SW Ohio; on Great Miami R. Pop. 247,000. Machine tools, refrigerators, aircraft mfg. Wright brothers estab. aircraft research centre (1911). Centre of US military aviation development.

Daytona Beach, resort town of NE Florida, US; on Atlantic Ocean. Pop. 45,000. Has motor speed trials on beach. Founded 1870.

Dazai Osamu, pseud. of Tsushima Shuji (1909-48), Japanese novelist. Wrote pessimistic novels, *eg The Setting Sun* (1947), *No Longer Human* (1948). Committed suicide.

D-Day, term for the day in WWII on which the Allied invasion of Europe began; 6th June, 1944.

DDT, dichloro-diphenyl-trichloroethane, white powder used as insecticide, effective on contact. Developed during 1940s, it helps control insect-borne diseases, *eg* malaria, typhus, yellow fever. Use has been restricted because of harmful effects on animals caused by its accumulation in plants.

deadly nightshade, see NIGHTSHADE.

dead men's fingers, *Alyconium digitarum,* coral polyp possessing 8 feathery tentacles, found on coasts of Britain.

Dead Sea, salt lake on Jordan-Israel border, *c* 70 km (45 mi) long. Lies in Ghor depression with surface 394 m (1292 ft) below sea level. Evaporation yields potash, bromide. Dead Sea biblical scrolls found nearby at Qumran.

Dead Sea Scrolls, collection of ancient Jewish religious writings, found in caves NW of Dead Sea (1947 and later). Written during 1st cents. BC and AD, possibly by a com-

Allied landing on D-Day

Dead Sea Scrolls

munity of ESSENES, they are of importance in study of origins of Christianity.

deafness, total or partial inability to hear. May be caused by accumulated wax, growth of bone in middle ear, diseases affecting foetus in early pregnancy, injury. Electronic hearing aids are used to amplify sound and alleviate deafness.

Deakin, Alfred (1856-1919), Australian statesman, PM (1903-4, 1905-8, 1909-10). Liberal leader, advocated social reform, imperial trade preference and federation of Australian states.

Deal, mun. bor. of Kent, SE England. Pop 25,000. One of Cinque Ports. Julius Caesar prob. landed nearby (55 BC).

Dean, Forest of, Gloucestershire, W England. Ancient royal forest. Early indust. region (wood, coal, iron ore exploitation); largely deforested by 17th cent.

Dearborn, town of SE Michigan, US: on Rouge R., W of Detroit. Pop. 105,000. Birthplace of Henry Ford, who estab. his 1st motor car factory here.

death, end of life and cessation of all vital functions in animal or plant. Heart may beat after cessation of breathing and resuscitation is sometimes possible through stimulation of nervous system shortly after cessation of heartbeat. In humans there is danger of brain damage if delay exceeds 20 mins.

death cap or **death cup,** *Amanita phalloides,* toadstool with pale yellow cap, white gills. Appears in autumn in deciduous woods. Deadly poisonous with no known antidote.

death penalty, *see* CAPITAL PUNISHMENT.

death's head hawk moth, *Acherontia atropos,* brown and yellow moth with skull-like mark on abdomen. Found in Europe, Africa; largest British moth with wingspan 13-15 cm/5-6 in. Larvae eat potato leaves.

Death Valley, arid basin of SE California, US; part of Great Basin region. Very high temperature in summer. Badwater is W hemisphere's lowest point (*c* 86 m/282 ft below sea level).

death watch beetle, *Xestobium refovillosum,* small brown beetle of Anobiidae family which attacks seasoned wood. Noted for sound made by head knocking against hard surface.

Deauville, town of Normandy, N France, at mouth of R. Touques. Pop. 6000. Fashionable resort with casino, racecourse.

Debrecen, city of E Hungary. Pop. 168,000. Railway jct.; agric. market, machinery. Calvinist coll. (1550), now univ. Seat of revolutionary govt. (1849).

Debrett, John (1753-1822), English publisher. Compiled and pub. *Peerage of England, Scotland and Ireland* (1802). Revised editions bearing his name still appear.

Debs, Eugene V[ictor] (1855-1926), American trade unionist, socialist leader. President of American Railway Union, imprisoned (1894) for disobeying court order in Pullman strike. Pacifist, imprisoned (1918) under Espionage Act.

Debureau, Jean-Gaspard (1796-1846), French pantomimist. Created white-faced Pierrot character; enormously popular in Paris.

Debussy, Claude (1862-1918), French composer. Works incl. piano music, *eg Clair de Lune,* orchestral pieces, *eg La Mer, L'Après-midi d'un faune, Nocturnes* and opera *Pelléas et Mélisande.* Although impressionistic, his works are innovative harmonically.

Debye, Peter Joseph Wilhelm (1884-1966), American physicist, b. Netherlands. Awarded Nobel Prize for Chemistry (1936) for work on molecular structure. Used X-rays to study powders of crystalline substances; devised theory to explain anomalous behaviour of strong electrolytes.

Decalogue, *see* TEN COMMANDMENTS.

decathlon, ten-event athletic contest, comprising 100, 400, 1500 m runs, 110 m hurdles, javelin and discus throws, shot put, high jump, long jump and pole vault. Olympic event since 1912.

Decatur, Stephen (1779-1820), American naval officer. Won fame for his incursion into the port of Tripoli (1804) to burn the captured US frigate *Philadelphia.* Led a successful expedition against Algiers (1815).

Deccan, triangular plateau of SC India, enclosed by Eastern and Western Ghats.

Decembrist Revolt, uprising in St Petersburg, Russia, on accession of Nicholas I in Dec. 1825. Group mainly of army officers plotted to replace Nicholas by his brother Constantine and obtain a constitution. Its failure ended with hanging of some leaders, but revolutionary ideas intensified despite repression.

decibel, in acoustics, numerical expression of relative loudness of a sound: difference in decibels of 2 sounds is 10 times the common logarithm of the ratio of their power levels.

decimal system, system of computation based on powers of 10. Decimal fractions are fractions having some power of 10 as denominator; denominator is not usually written but is expressed by decimal point. Thus 25.03 is $\frac{2503}{100}$. Used in metric system of weights and measures, most national currencies.

Decius, Gaius Messius Quintus (AD 201-51), Roman emperor (249-51). Proclaimed emperor by his troops on the

Danube, organized persecution of Christians throughout the empire. Killed trying to repel invasion of Goths.

Declaration of Independence, *see* INDEPENDENCE, DECLARATION OF.

decorated style, name given to second period of English Gothic architecture, which followed Early English in late 13th and 14th cents. Characterized by use of bar tracery in window design, and complicated vaulting. Wells Cathedral, near Bristol, exemplifies style.

decorations, civil or military reward for service. Originated in medieval practice of conferring KNIGHTHOOD. British civilian orders incl. GARTER, Thistle, Bath. Others incl. Red and Black Eagle (Prussia), Legion of Honour (France). Military orders incl. Iron Cross (Germany), Croix de Guerre (France), VICTORIA CROSS (UK), PURPLE HEART (US), Red Star (USSR).

Dee, several rivers of UK. **1,** NE Scotland, flows 140 km (87 mi) from Cairngorms to North Sea at Aberdeen. **2,** In Wales and England, flows 113 km (70 mi) from Gwynedd to Irish Sea via Cheshire.

Daniel Defoe

composition and cut-off views. Themes incl. racecourses, ballet scenes, women washing.

Hog deer

De Gaulle in London in 1940

deer, any of Cervidae family of ruminant mammals, incl. deer, elks, reindeer, moose. Worldwide distribution except Australia. Antlers, confined to males except for reindeer and caribou, usually branched and shed annually.

defence mechanism, in psychiatry, unconscious behaviour pattern designed to avert painful or anxiety-provoking feelings. Forms incl. repression of distress or its sublimation into useful forms, regression to infantile behaviour, *etc.*

deflation, *see* INFLATION.

Defoe, Daniel (1660-1731), English author. Best known as author of novels *Robinson Crusoe* (1719), *Moll Flanders* (1722) among 500 works, mainly non-fiction. Also wrote prolifically on politics, economics in his thrice-weekly *Review* (1704-13).

De Forest, Lee (1873-1961), American inventor. Innovator of developments in wireless telegraphy, TV, sound pictures, *eg* De Forest Phonofilm of 1920s, early sound synchronization experiment.

Deganawidah or **Dekanawideh** ('heavenly messenger'), North American Indian prophet. With disciple Hiawatha founded (*c* 1570) Iroquois Five Nations confederacy in E Canada and US.

Degas, [Hilaire Germain] Edgar (1834-1917), French painter, sculptor. Associated with the impressionists, he sought to unite Classical art with immediacy of impressionism. Influenced by photography and Japanese prints, work achieves spontaneity by asymmetric

De Gaulle, Charles André Joseph Marie (1890-1970), French military and political leader, president (1958-69). Opposed armistice with Germany (1940) and formed Free French forces in Britain. Served as interim president (1945-6). Recalled (1958) as premier, elected 1st president of newly-created Fifth Republic. Ended French colonial power in Algeria; withdrew French forces from NATO (1966); vetoed British attempts to join EEC. Policies marked by nationalism and desire for European economic and military independence from US. Resigned after referendum defeat.

De Havilland, Sir Geoffrey (1882-1965), English aircraft designer. Designed WWI fighters, WWII *Mosquito* fighter-bomber and the post-war *Comet,* 1st jet airliner.

De Havilland, Olivia (1916-   ), American film actress, b. Japan. Known for comic or romantic roles in 1930s-40s, as in *Gone with the Wind* (1939), later developed range to appear in, *eg, Hush Hush Sweet Charlotte* (1964).

Dehra Dun, town of Uttar Pradesh, N India. Pop. 199,000. Founded in late 17th cent. by Ram Rai, leader of Hindu ascetic sect; his temple (1699) notable building. Site of Indian Military Academy.

deists, those who believe in the existence of God on purely rational grounds without reliance on revelation or authority. Term esp. used for 17th and 18th cent. rationalists, *eg* Voltaire, Rousseau, Ben Franklin, who held that proof of existence of God was to be found in nature. Also known as freethinkers.

Dekker or **Decker, Thomas** (*c* 1572-1632), English dramatist. Known for comedies of London life, esp. *The Shoemaker's Holiday* (1600), *The Roaring Girl* (*c* 1610) in collaboration with Middleton. Collaborated with John Ford on *The Witch of Edmonton*. Also wrote pamphlets on London low life.

Delacroix, [Ferdinand Victor] Eugène (1798- 1863), French painter. Major painter of Romantic movement in France, he was a noted colourist. Painted historical subjects, scenes of Arab life, themes from Shakespeare, Byron, *etc.* Works incl. *Massacre at Chios, Liberty Leading the People, Women of Algiers.*

Delagoa Bay, inlet of Indian Ocean, on SE coast of Mozambique. Maputo situated on inner bay. Discovered 1502 by Vasco da Gama's expedition.

De La Mare, Walter (1873-1956), English author. Known for fantasy and children's verse, *eg The Listeners* (1912), *Peacock Pie* (1913), and novels, esp. *Memoirs of a Midget* (1921).

Delane, John Thaddeus (1817-79), English journalist. Edited *The Times* (1841-77), giving it international status.

Delaunay, Robert (1885-1941), French painter. Founder of orphism, attempt to introduce more colour into austere forms of cubism; painted abstract colour discs, suggestive of movement. Influenced many artists, incl. Marc and Klee.

Delaware, group of closely-related North American Indian tribes of Algonquian linguistic stock. Called Lenape until 18th cent. Migrated to Atlantic from NW. Made treaty with William Penn (1682), but Iroquois attacks drove them into Ohio. Survivors of massacre (1782) in Pennsylvania fled to Ontario, where their descendants now live.

Delaware, state of E US, on Atlantic. Area 5328 sq km (2057 sq mi); pop. 548,000; cap. Dover; largest city Wilmington. Mainly low-lying, hilly in N. Agric. incl. fruit, vegetable growing; poultry rearing, fishing important. Chemical indust. English settlement (1664); one of original 13 colonies of US. Remained in Union during Civil War (1861-5) despite being slave state.

De la Warr, Thomas West, Baron (1577-1618), English colonial governor. Became 1st governor of Virginia colony (1609); on arrival, persuaded desperate colonists not to leave. State of Delaware named after him.

Delcassé, Théophile (1852-1923), French statesman. As foreign minister (1898-1905), negotiated amicable settlements of colonial differences with Britain, *eg* in FASHODA INCIDENT. Paved way for Entente Cordiale with Britain; also strengthened alliance with Russia.

Deledda, Grazia (1875-1936), Italian novelist. Wrote novels, short stories about peasants of native Sardinia, *eg Elias Portoliu* (1903), *Ashes* (1904), *The Mother* (1920). Nobel Prize for Literature (1926).

Delescluze, Charles (1809-71), French journalist. Leader of Paris Commune in 1871, allowed himself to be shot on barricades after realizing that defeat was at hand.

Delft, town of W Netherlands, on Schie canal. Pop. 81,000. Ceramics ('delftware') mfg. begun 16th cent. Prinsenhof museum; Gothic churches, tomb of William the Silent. Birthplace of Vermeer.

Delhi, union territ. of N India. Area 1484 sq km (573 sq. mi); pop. 3,630,000. Old Delhi, on R. Jumna, important railway centre; textile mfg., gold and silver filigree work. Reconstructed in 17th cent. by Shah Jehan; fort contains Imperial Palace (1638-48) and Jama Masjid mosque. Interim cap. of India (1912-31), succeeded by neighbour **New Delhi,** which became cap. of republic (1947). Pop. 293,000. Univ. (1922).

Delian League, union of Greek states founded at Delos (478 BC) under Athenian leadership; later developed into an Athenian empire. Disbanded at end of Peloponnesian War (404 BC). Confederation revived to resist Spartan aggression (378 BC); lasted until defeat by Philip of Macedon (338 BC).

Delibes, [Clément Philibert] Léo (1836-91), French composer. Wrote ballet music and operas known for lyricism. Works include *Coppélia, Silvia* and *Lakmé.*

delirium, brain disturbance marked by extreme excitement, hallucinations, confused speech. May result from disease, high fever, *etc.* Delirium tremens is form of delirium associated with chronic alcoholism; symptoms incl. sweating, trembling, vivid hallucinations.

Delisle, Guillaume (1675-1726), French geographer, cartographer. Pioneer of modern cartography, used astronomical observations to improve accuracy of maps. His world map in 2 hemispheres was pub. 1700.

Delius

Delius, Frederick (1862-1934), English composer. Work is both romantic and impressionist with an individual harmonic quality. Best-known pieces incl. orchestral works *On Hearing the First Cuckoo in Spring* and *Brigg Fair,* and choral work *Sea Drift.*

della Robbia, see ROBBIA, LUCA DELLA.

De Long, George Washington (1844-81), American explorer. Attempted, with George Melville, to reach North Pole (1879-81); caught in pack ice and forced to abandon ship, he died on return journey. Expedition added much to geographical knowledge of area N of Siberia.

Delorme or **de l'Orme, Philibert** (*c* 1510-70), French architect. Court architect to Francis I and Henry II, he designed Renaissance château of Diane de Poitiers at Anet and the Tuileries in Paris. Little of his work remains.

Delos (*Dhilos*), small isl. of SE Greece, in Cyclades. Traditional birthplace of Apollo, Artemis, important religious remains. Treasury of Delian League 478-454 BC.

Delphi

Delphi (*Delphoi*), ancient city of C Greece, in Phocis, at foot of Mt. Parnassus. Site of Delphic oracle and Pythian games. Excavated 19th cent., many remains found, esp. temple to Apollo.

delphinium, genus of hardy plants of buttercup family. Spikes of spurred, irregular flowers, usually blue, on tall spike. Widely distributed in N hemisphere. Also called larkspur.

delta, roughly triangular area of alluvial deposits formed at mouth of a river. Consists of complex of distributary channels, lagoons, marshes. Usually very fertile, many support large agric. pop. Name derived from Greek letter *delta* (△); applied originally to Nile delta, now to any similar feature, *eg* Hwang-Ho, Mississippi.

Delvaux, Paul (1897-), Belgian painter. Known for his meticulous surrealist works, in which nude or semi-clothed women wander dreamily through architectural settings.

Demerara, river of Guyana. Rises in Guiana Highlands, flows N *c* 320 km (200 mi) to enter Atlantic at Georgetown. Used to transport bauxite.

Demeter, in Greek myth, earth goddess of corn, harvest, fruitfulness. Daughter of Cronus and Rhea; mother by Zeus of PERSEPHONE. She and her daughter were leading figures in Eleusinian mystery cults, representing seasonal cycle. Identified with Roman Ceres.

De Mille, Cecil B[lount] (1881-1959), American film producer-director. Pioneer, later grand old man of Hollywood, known for adventure films in 1930s-40s, *eg The Plainsman* (1936), and later for biblical epics, *eg The Ten Commandments* (1956).

democracy, govt. in which the people hold power either directly or through elected representatives, rather than by class, group or individual. In Greek city states, democracy took direct form of plebiscite or popular assembly, with exclusion of slaves. Modern democracy evolved out of demands for political and legal equality, later economic and social equality; such demands provoked American and French revolutions. Locke, Montesquieu, Rousseau were chief theorists in 17th and 18th cents. Modern Western democracy is based on competing party system, with emphasis on rule of law and freedom of expression.

Democratic Party, in US, one of the two major political parties. Origins in Democratic Republican Party founded by Jefferson (1800) in opposition to Hamilton's Federalists. Name changed to present one under Jackson (1828). Splits, created by slavery issue and Civil War, led to eclipse of party; revived with support of South after RECONSTRUCTION (1876). Radical ascendancy under Bryan brought wider base, support from rural and urban working classes, although irreconcilable factions caused electoral defeat; in 20th cent., attracted Negro and ethnic minorities. Identified with reform, esp. after F.D. Roosevelt's NEW DEAL (1932), thereafter dominated Republicans except for periods 1953-61, 1969-77.

Democritus (*c* 460-*c* 370 BC), Greek philosopher. Developed atomistic theory of matter originally suggested by Leucippus. Held that truth could be discovered by thought and that perceptions lead to confusion.

demography, science of statistics dealing with distribution, density, data of birth, marriage, death of populations. Used to determine rates of birth, death, *etc*, in analysis of social systems.

De Morgan, William Frend (1839-1917), English craftsman, novelist. Designed tiles and plates; rediscovered secrets of medieval ceramics. Worked with William Morris. Now known for novels, esp. *Joseph Vance* (1906).

Demosthenes (*c* 384-322 BC), Greek statesman, orator. Advocated resistance to growing power of Philip of Macedon in series of orations, *Philippics* and *Olynthiacs,* but Philip triumphed at battle of Chaeronea (338). After death of Alexander the Great, organized unsuccessful revolt against Antipater; took poison to avoid capture.

demotic writing, Egyptian flowing (cursive) script, derived from HIERATIC in 7th cent. BC and lasting until 5th cent. AD. Written from right to left.

Dempsey, William Harrison ('Jack'), (1895-), American boxer. World heavyweight champion (1919-26). Fight with Carpentier (1921) was first to produce gate of million dollars. Lost title to Gene Tunney (1926); controversial re-match (1927) again won by Tunney.

Denbighshire, former county of N Wales, now in Clwyd. Mountainous in S; scenic, fertile valleys. Coalmining (centred on Wrexham); slate quarrying; agric. Co. town was **Denbigh,** mun. bor. in Vale of Clwyd. Pop. 8000.

dengue or **breakbone fever,** tropical virus infection, transmitted by mosquitoes. Characterized by fever, rash, and severe pain in joints and back.

Den Helder, town of NW Netherlands. Pop. 58,000. Port, naval base, N terminus of North Holland canal. Fortified (1811) by Napoleon.

Denikin, Anton Ivanovich (1872-1947), Russian army officer. Leader of the anti-revolutionary 'White Army', defeated in 1919. He died in exile in US.

denim, strong coarse twill-weave cotton fabric, first made in Nîmes, France. Name derives from *serge de Nîmes.* Important feature of 20th cent. 'casual' clothing.

Denis or **Dionysius of Paris, St** (d. *c* 258), patron saint of France. First bishop of Paris. Traditionally a missionary sent into Gaul *c* 250 and martyred at Montmartre ('Martyr's Hill').

Denis, Maurice (1870-1943), French painter. Member of the Nabis, he is remembered for his theoretical writings on symbolist painting. Sought to revive religious painting after 1919.

Denmark

Denmark (*Danmark*), kingdom of NC Europe. Area 43,022 sq km (16,611 sq mi); pop. 5,025,000; cap. Copenhagen. Language: Danish. Religion: Lutheranism. Comprises Jutland penin., Baltic isls. incl. Zealand, Laaland, Fyn, Bornholm. Overseas territs. incl. Greenland, Faeroes. Agric., esp. dairying, livestock; fishing. United with Sweden (1397-1523), with Norway (1397-1814); lost Norway in Napoleonic wars, Schleswig-Holstein to Prussia (1864). Under German occupation (1940-5). Joined EEC in 1973.

density, in physics, mass per unit volume of a substance; usually measured in grams per cubic cm. Density of water is 1 gram per cc at 4°C.

dentistry, care and treatment of teeth and gums. Egyptian writings of *c* 16th cent. BC describe dental care, but professional dentistry dates from 19th cent. Important developments incl. use of X-rays, high speed drills, local anaesthetics and taking of fluoride to reduce dental caries.

dentition, number and kind of teeth and their arrangement in mouths of vertebrates. Most lower vertebrates are homodonts (teeth are all similar); in heterodonts, several different types of teeth are present (incisors, canines, premolars and molars).

Dent(s) du Midi, mountain group of SW Switzerland, in the Alps. Rise to 3259 m (10,696 ft) at Haute Cime.

Denver, cap. of Colorado, US; on South Platte R. Alt. 1609 m (5280 ft). Pop. 515,000. Transport jct.; mining machinery, meat produce, air defence indust. Has many parks; health and recreation centre. Founded 1859. Cap. from 1867; grew during gold, silver strikes in 1870s.

deodar, *Cedrus deodara,* species of cedar native to Himalayas with fragrant, durable, light-red wood. Cultivated as ornamental because of graceful drooping branches and soft green foliage.

depreciation, in accounting, reduction in value of CAPITAL through wear, deterioration or obsolescence. Allowance is made for this in book-keeping so that income is not overestimated.

depression, in economics, period of crisis characterized by falling prices, contraction of production, restricted credit, unemployment, bankruptcies. Usually interpreted as overproduction of goods linked with decreased demand; the resulting fall in consumer purchasing power tends to

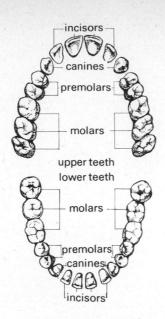

Dentition of a human adult

De Quincey

give cumulative effect. Before 18th cent. usually had non-economic causes, *eg* crop failure. Subsequently, causes mainly indust. or commercial. The Great Depression followed 1929 crash of New York stock market.

depression, in meteorology, area of relatively low atmospheric pressure, characteristic of temperate latitudes. Formed by warm tropical air meeting and rising above cold polar air, with associated formation of fronts. May be very extensive; brings unsettled, rainy weather. Also *see* CYCLONE.

depression, in psychiatry, emotional condition characterized by feeling of hopelessness, inadequacy, loss of vigour. May be neurotic or psychotic, *eg* manic-depressive psychosis. Some forms are treated by drugs or electric shock therapy.

Deptford, part of Lewisham, SE Greater London, England. Engineering industs., chemicals, soap mfg. Naval dockyard estab. by Henry VIII, closed 1869.

De Quincey, Thomas (1785-1859), English essayist. Known for *Confessions of an English Opium Eater* (1822). Pieces for journals, *eg Murder Considered as One of the Fine Arts* (1827), *The English Mail Coach* (1849), reflect ability to create dream experiences.

Derain, André (1880-1954), French painter. Prominent member of fauve group, his early work is characterized by use of patches of vibrant pure colour. Later influenced by Cézanne and cubism, reverted to sombre neo-Classical style.

Derby, Edward George Geoffrey Smith Stanley, 14th Earl of (1799-1869), British statesman, PM (1852, 1858-9, 1866-8). As Whig colonial secretary, sponsored bill abolishing slavery in British Empire (1833). Joined Tories under Peel; later headed protectionist Tories after split over Peel's free trade policies (1846).

Derby, English horse race, founded (1780) by Earl of Derby, run over course 1.5 mi (2.4 km) long at Epsom, Surrey, in May or June. Also *see* KENTUCKY DERBY.

Derbyshire, county of NC England. Area 2631 sq km (1015 sq mi); pop. 886,000; co. town Matlock. Peak Dist. in NW; lowland in S, E. Mineral springs (*eg* Buxton); stock rearing; coalmining. Co. bor. **Derby,** former co. town, on R. Derwent. Pop. 219,000. Railway jct.; aircraft engines; famous porcelain mfg.

Derg, Lough, lake of C Irish Republic. In Shannon basin, separates Galway, Clare, Tipperary. Isl. has ecclesiastical ruins. Also small lake of Co. Donegal, with isl. cave, scene of St Patrick's purgatory.

dermatitis, inflammation of skin. Atopic dermatitis or eczema, characterized by an itchy rash, is often associated with allergies such as hay fever. Contact dermatitis is allergic reaction to substances touching skin.

Derna, oasis town of NE Libya, in Cyrenaica. Pop. 26,000. Former caravan centre. Captured by US 1805 from Barbary pirates; held by Turkey from 1835 until taken by Italy (1911) and British (1942).

Derry, *see* LONDONDERRY, Northern Ireland.

dervish, mendicant monk of ISLAM. Various sects are characterized by extreme methods of producing ecstatic states, *eg* whirling and howling dervishes. Strongly antinomian, claiming special favour with God. Theology based on SUFISM.

Derwent, several rivers of England. **1,** in Cumbria, flows 56 km (35 mi) from Lake Dist. via Derwentwater to Irish Sea. **2,** in Derbyshire, flows 96 km (60 mi) from Peak Dist. to R. Trent; supplies N Midlands reservoirs. **3,** in North Yorkshire, flows 112 km (70 mi) from N York Moors to R. Ouse.

Derwentwater, lake of Cumbria, NW England. In Lake Dist.; length 5 km (3 mi). Lodore Falls at S end. Tourism.

Desai, [Shri] Morarji Ranchhodji (1896-), Indian political leader, PM (1977-). Member of Gandhi's civil disobedience movement (1930s), imprisoned several times. Acted as minister in govts. (1956-69). Leader of opposition to Mrs Gandhi (1969-77), imprisoned under emergency powers. Led Janata coalition to 1977 election win.

Descartes, René (1596-1650), French philosopher, mathematician. Started from position of universal doubt, tempered only by dictum 'I think, therefore I am'. Created system known as Cartesian dualism, based on distinction between spirit and matter, in *Discours de la Méthode* (1637). Also regarded as founder of analytical geometry, developed algebraic notation. Contributed much to science of optics.

desert, any barren, unproductive region where rainfall is less than 25 cm/10 in. per year. Surface may be sandy or stony, sometimes with poor scrub vegetation; pop. is scant, specially adapted. Deserts may be hot (*eg* Sahara, Arabian), cool mid-latitude (*eg* Gobi) or cold and perpetually ice-covered (as in N Canada, Siberia).

De Sica, Vittorio (1901-74), Italian film director, actor. Achieved world fame with compassionate, realistic films in

Descartes

1940s, *eg Shoeshine* (1946), *Bicycle Thieves* (1948), continued skilful, intelligent work with *Two Women* (1961).

Des Moines, cap. of Iowa, US; at confluence of Des Moines and Raccoon rivers. Pop. 201,000. Commercial, transport centre in Corn Belt. Coal mining, printing and publishing industs., agric. machinery mfg. Became cap. 1857.

Desmoulins, Camille (1760-94), French revolutionary, journalist. Exhorted mob to storm Bastille (July, 1789). Author of pamphlets attacking Girondists. Later adopted moderate stance with Danton; guillotined.

De Soto, Hernando (*c* 1500-42), Spanish explorer. Served under Pizarro in Peru before leading expedition (1538-42) through Florida and SE North America. Prob. 1st white man to see and cross Mississippi R.

Despenser, Hugh le (1262-1326), English courtier. Chief adviser to Edward II, joined at court by his son, **Hugh le Despenser** (d. 1326). Both were banished by the barons (1321-2), but on return held real power over England, dominating Edward until his overthrow (1326) by ISABELLA and MORTIMER. Despensers then executed.

Des Prés or **Desprez, Josquin** (*c* 1440-1521), Flemish composer. He developed counterpoint to great expressive ends in his works, which incl. Masses, motets and secular songs.

Dessalines, Jean Jacques (*c* 1758-1806), emperor of Haiti (1804-6). Originally a slave, joined Toussaint L'Ouverture's war of liberation (1791). Drove out French (1803), proclaimed himself emperor. Murdered during revolt against his despotic regime.

Dessau, town of C East Germany, on R. Mulde. Pop. 96,000. Produces machinery (Junkers aircraft until 1945). Former cap. of Anhalt state.

destroyer, a warship originally built (1893) as a defence against fast boats carrying the newly-invented torpedo. Used in WWII for anti-submarine work, escort and reconnaissance, it has now been largely superseded by the smaller frigate.

detective fiction, story in which clues systematically examined lead to solving a crime, usually murder. First true detective story was Poe's 'The Murders in the Rue Morgue' (1841), with W. Collins' *The Moonstone* (1868) first in England. Genre estab. in 1880s by Conan DOYLE and his hero Sherlock Holmes. Subsequent exponents incl. Chesterton, Agatha Christie, Simenon. Hammett, Chandler initiated tough 'private eye' school in US in 1930s.

détente, relaxation of international tensions and hostilities, manifested in treaties or trade agreements. Détente was estab. as policy between US and USSR in mid-1970s, esp. in fields of strategic arms and influence in Third World.

detergent, substance used to improve cleansing power of water, *eg* soap. Acts by emulsifying oil on dirty surfaces, thus allowing water to dislodge exposed dirt particles. Synthetic detergents produce no scum, but phosphate present in some is source of pollution.

determinant, in mathematics, number obtained from square MATRIX by specified sequence of additions and multiplications. Usually represented by square array of numbers. Wide use, particularly in solution of systems of linear equations.

determinism, in philosophy, doctrine that phenomena are conditioned by preceding data, *eg* denial of moral choice in ethics. Also finds support in psychoanalysis, which denies existence of causeless acts. See FREE WILL.

Detmold, town of N West Germany. Pop. 63,000. Furniture, brewing. Former cap. of Lippe. Nearby monument commemorates Arminius' victory (AD 9) over Romans.

detonator, explosive compound, *eg* mercuric fulminate, capable of rapid decomposition. Shock waves created used to set off more inert explosives.

Detroit, port of SE Michigan, US: on Detroit R. between L. St Clair and L. Erie. Pop. 1,511,000. Major shipping, rail centre. World's leading automobile producer (Ford, General Motors, Chrysler). Other industs. incl. food processing, chemicals, steel mfg., shipyards, oil refining. Settled by French (1701).

Dettifoss, waterfall of NE Iceland, on R. Jokulsa á Fjollum. Iceland's most spectacular falls.

Dettingen, village of Bavaria, SC West Germany, on R. Main. Scene of Allies' victory (1743) over French in War of Austrian Succession.

Deucalion, in Greek myth, son of Prometheus. With wife Pyrrha, survived flood sent by Zeus. Told by oracle to throw behind them the 'bones of their mother' (*ie* stones) which became new generation.

deuterium (D), isotope of hydrogen; mass no. 2. Constituent of HEAVY WATER (D_2O). Deuteron is name given to deuterium nucleus.

Deuteronomy (Gk., ‑second law), in OT, fifth book of Pentateuch. Contains core of Jewish law, ascribed traditionally to Moses.

De Valéra, Eamon (1882-1975), Irish statesman, b. US. Participant in Easter Rebellion, imprisoned (1916). Became head of Sinn Fein (1917) and of revolutionary Dáil. Left Dáil (1922) over exclusion of Northern Ireland after creation of Irish Free State; returned (1927) at head of Fianna Fáil party. PM (1937-48, 1951-4, 1957-9), kept Ireland neutral in WWII; president (1959-73).

devaluation, lowering of value of currency in terms of gold or other currencies, so that its exchange rate falls. Resulting increase in cost of imports and fall in price of exports may check deficit in BALANCE OF PAYMENTS through sale of more goods abroad.

Deventer, town of EC Netherlands, on R. Ijssel. Pop. 63,000. Textiles, chemicals; famed gingerbread (*Deventer koek*). Medieval educational and religious Hanseatic centre, where Erasmus and Thomas à Kempis studied.

devil fish, name given to manta ray and type of American octopus.

devil's coach horse, *Staphylinus olens,* large carnivorous beetle of W Europe. Holds abdomen erect; emits offensive odour when threatened.

Devil's Island, see SALUT, ILES DU.

devil's paintbrush, *Hieracium aurantiacum,* C European weed of daisy family with flame-coloured flowers. Now a common weed in N US and Canada.

De Vinne, Theodore Low (1828-1914), American printer. Founded and managed company, later known as De Vinne Press, famous for its excellent printing. Authority on practice and history of typography.

devolution, delegation of specific powers or authority by nation's central govt. to local governing units. Devolved powers restricted to education, health, transport, *etc.* Often adopted as constitutional response to national self-determination movements. Differs from FEDERALISM in that sovereignty in all areas remains with central govt. and legislature.

Devolution, War of (1667-8), war arising out of Louis XIV's claim to Spanish Netherlands. France opposed by Triple Alliance of United Provinces, Sweden, England. Peace concluded with Treaty of Aix-la-Chapelle.

Devon, county of SW England. Area 6715 sq km (2592 sq mi); pop. 921,000; co. town Exeter. Hilly, over 610 m (2000 ft) on Dartmoor; rich agric. lowlands. Livestock rearing, dairy farming (esp. cream); fishing; mining; tourism. Sea ports were hist. important (esp. Plymouth).

Devonian period, fourth geological period of Palaeozoic era; began c 395 million years ago, lasted c 50 million years. Formation of Old Red Sandstone, shales; climax of Caledonian mountain building period. Fauna incl. ammonoid cephalopods, jawed fish, crinoids, last graptolites; flora incl. treefern forests. Also see GEOLOGICAL TABLE.

Devon Island, E Franklin Dist., Northwest Territs., Canada; between Ellesmere and Baffin isls. Area 54,100 sq km (20,900 sq mi). Most E of Parry Isls.

Devonshire, Spencer Compton Cavendish, 8th Duke of (1833-1908), British statesman. Held several posts in Liberal cabinets until 1885. Split with Gladstone over Irish Home Rule bill (1886), leading new Liberal Unionist party.

dew, water deposited on surfaces when decreasing temperature causes saturation of water vapour in air. Dew point is temperature at which dew forms; if below freezing point, dew freezes and hoar frost results.

Dewar, Sir James (1842-1923), Scottish chemist. Researched in low temperature physics; first to liquefy and solidify hydrogen. Developed vacuum flask for insulating fluids, forerunner of Thermos.

dewberry, trailing shrub of genus *Rubus.* Similar to blackberry but with earlier and larger fruit.

De Wet, Christian Rudolf (1854-1922), Boer general, statesman. Led short-lived revolt in opposition to entry into WWI in support of Britain; suppressed by Botha.

Dewey, George (1837-1917), American naval officer. Commanded in decisive victory over Spanish fleet in Manila Bay (1898) during Spanish-American War.

Dewey, John (1859-1952), American philosopher and educator. His philosophy, 'instrumentalism', held truth to be evolutionary and human activities to be instruments for resolving human problems. In education, advocated 'learning by doing' over authoritarian methods. Works incl. *The School and Society* (1899).

Dewey, Melvil (1851-1931), American librarian. Known for Dewey decimal system, by which books can be classified according to subject. Estab. 1st school of librarianship, was one of the founders of American Library Association.

De Wint, Peter (1784-1849), English landscape painter. Noted for watercolours, painted in broad washes of colour and conveying an atmosphere of calm.

Dewsbury, bor. of West Yorkshire met. county, N England, on R. Calder. Pop. 51,000. Textiles, clothing, shoddy mfg.

diabetes, disease characterized by excessive secretion of urine. *Diabetes mellitus,* caused by insulin deficiency, leads to excess glucose in blood and urine. Marked by loss of weight; acidosis and coma may follow. Treatment by controlled diet and insulin injections.

Diadochi (Gk., = successors), Macedonian generals, incl. Antigonus, Antipater, Seleucus and Lysimachus, who fought series of civil wars for control of Alexander's empire after his death (323 BC). Empire broke up at finish of wars (281 BC).

Diaghilev, Serge Pavlovich (1872-1929), Russian ballet impresario. Revived Russian ballet, making it serious art involving leading dancers, musicians, artists of day, incl. Pavlova, Nijinsky, Stravinsky, Fokine, Bakst; put on new ballets, *eg Les Sylphides, L'Après-midi d'un faune, Sacré du Printemps.* Founded Ballets Russes (1909) which toured in W Europe, Americas, profoundly influencing ballet everywhere except Russia.

dialect, form of speech peculiar to a locality, community, or social group which is considered to deviate in a characteristic way from the postulated standard speech of users' native language. While contiguous dialects of same language are usually mutually intelligible, with increasing distance differences accumulate so that the dialects of same language become mutually unintelligible.

dialectical materialism, method of hist. analysis, formulated by Marx and Engels, which applies Hegel's dialectic method to observable social processes and natural phenomena. Following FEUERBACH, they substituted materialism for ideas as the basis of the thesis-antithesis-synthesis process. In society, control of means of production determines social structure of classes; conflict between them results in hist. change.

dialysis, in chemistry, separation of colloidal particles from substances in true solution. Technique involves dissolved molecules passing through a membrane more rapidly than larger colloid molecules. Artificial kidney purifies blood by dialysis.

diamagnetism, property of certain substances, *eg* bismuth, of being repelled by magnetic fields. Results from substance being weakly magnetized in direction opposite to external field.

Diamantina, town of E Brazil, in Minas Gerais state, on E plateau. Pop. 25,000. Former diamond centre, textile, tanning industs.

diamond, hardest known mineral, a crystalline form of carbon. Occurs in alluvial deposits and ultrabasic igneous rocks. Gem forms are transparent, brilliant and colourless; others may be yellow, blue, black, *etc.* Flawless crystals used in jewellery; largest is 'Cullinan' in British crown; indust. diamonds used in cutting tools, abrasives, record player styli. Major source of gem diamonds is South Africa; indust. diamonds mainly from Zaïre, Brazil, Ghana.

Diana, in early Roman myth, goddess of the moon, hunting, women in childbirth. Identified with Greek Artemis. Worshipped in Rome as Virgin goddess; her temple at Aricia associated with fertility cult.

diarrhoea, frequent discharge of watery faeces. Often caused by inflammation of intestine by bacteria, viruses, *etc,* or by nervous stress. May be treated by drugs or absorbents such as kaolin.

diastase, enzyme which converts starch into maltose and later into dextrose. Occurs in seeds of grain and in malt.

diatom, microscopic plant of ALGAE group with silica-containing shell, found in fresh or salt water in Arctic and other cold regions. Diatomaceous earth and diatomite, formed from shells of dead diatoms, are used industrially, esp. for insulating against heat.

Diaz or **Dias, Bartolomeu** (d. 1500), Portuguese navigator. First European to voyage around Cape of Good Hope (1488), opening up sea route to India.

Díaz, Porfirio (1830-1915), Mexican statesman. President (1877-80, 1884-1911) in period of growing prosperity based upon foreign investment. Neglected welfare and education of poor. Lost power during revolt under Madero, went into exile.

Díaz de Vivar, Rodrigo (c 1040–99), Spanish soldier, national hero, called 'El Cid Campeador' (Lord Champion). Banished from Castile (1081) by Alfonso VI; became soldier of fortune, fighting both Moors and Christians. Captured Valencia (1094), ruling it until his death. Subsequently celebrated in literature, folklore; adopted as heroic leader of *reconquista* of Spain from Moors.

dice, small cubes usually of ivory or bone, sides of which are marked by different numbers of dots (so that opposite faces total 7). Several games of chance, incl. craps, poker dice and backgammon, are played with dice.

Dickens, Charles [John Huffam] (1812-70), English novelist. Began as journalist, soon started serial works attacking social abuses, often blending sentiment with humorous caricature, *eg Pickwick Papers* (1836-7), *Oliver Twist* (1838), *Nicholas Nickleby* (1838-9). Major works incl. *David Copperfield* (1849-50), *Great Expectations* (1860-1), *Our Mutual Friend* (1864-5). Other works incl. 'A Christmas Carol' (1853), hist. *A Tale of Two Cities* (1859). Known for detailed, realistic creation of world and inhabitants.

Dickinson, Emily [Elizabeth] (1830-86), American poet. Lived in seclusion, dominated by Calvinist father. Poetry (first pub. 1890) noted for intense, idiosyncratic style, often deals with problems of faith.

Charles Dickens

dicotyledon, any of the class Dicotyledoneae of angiosperms with 2 seed leaves in embryo plant. Class incl. many forest and fruit trees, food plants, *eg* potato, bean and ornamentals, *eg* rose, clematis.

dictator, in ancient Rome, magistrate appointed in times of emergency to rule with absolute power. In modern usage denotes ruler with absolute power, authority, esp. one exercising it tyrannically. Characteristically, rule tends to TOTALITARIANISM. Examples incl. MUSSOLINI, STALIN, HITLER, military juntas, esp. in Latin America.

dictionary, book of alphabetically listed words in a language, with definitions, derivations, pronunciations, *etc.* Bilingual dictionaries provide equivalents of words in another language. Early English dictionaries incl. Nathan Bailey's *Dictionarium Britannicum* (1730), Samuel Johnson's *Dictionary of the English Language* (1755). In America, Noah Webster's *Dictionary of the English Language* (1806) is 1st example. French Academy has published a dictionary which attempts to be prescriptive since 17th cent.

Diderot, Denis (1713-84), French philosopher. Chief editor of *Encyclopédie* (1747-72), also wrote 1st French 'bourgeois drama', *eg Le Neveu de Rameau.* Forerunner of modern art criticism in *Salons* (1759-71). Anti-clerical, imprisoned for some works, *eg Lettres sur les aveugles* (1749), revealing scepticism and materialism.

Dido, founder-queen of Carthage in Roman legend. Best known through Vergil's use of legend in *Aeneid,* in which love between her and AENEAS almost causes him to betray his duty to found Rome. When he leaves, she kills herself.

Didot, François Ambroise (1730-1804), French printer. Acclaimed as best printer of his age, he designed a number of modern types. His sons, **Pierre Didot** (1761-1853) and **Firmin Didot** (1764-1836), pub. carefully edited, inexpensive books for students. Firmin invented stereotyping process.

Diefenbaker, John George (1895-), Canadian statesman, PM (1957-63). Leader of Progressive Conservatives (1956-67), won large victory at 1958 election.

dielectric, substance which does not conduct electricity but can sustain an electric field. Used to separate plates in capacitors.

Diels, Otto Paul Hermann (1876-1954), German chemist. Shared Nobel Prize for Chemistry (1950) with Kurt Alder for developing system of synthesizing benzene ring hydrocarbons (Diels-Alder reaction).

Diem, Ngo Dinh (1901-63), Vietnamese political leader. Premier (1954), became president (1955) of South Vietnam when it was declared a republic. Favoured Catholics over Buddhists. Killed during military coup.

Diemen, Anton van (1593-1645), Dutch naval officer. As governor-general of Dutch East Indian Company, sent TASMAN on expedition (1642) which discovered Van Diemen's Land (now Tasmania).

Dienbienphu, town of W North Vietnam. Vietminh victory (1954) marked end of French Indo-China.

Dieppe, town of Normandy, N France, on English Channel. Pop. 30,000. Port, ferry service to Newhaven (England); resort, fishing, shipbuilding. Scene of Allied commando raid (1942).

diesel engine, type of INTERNAL COMBUSTION ENGINE invented by German engineer Rudolf Diesel (1858-1913). Air drawn into cylinder is heated by compression, then ignites fuel oil injected into cylinder; resulting explosion provides power stroke. Though initially more expensive than equivalent petrol (gasoline) engine, uses cheaper fuel. Patented 1892.

Marlene Dietrich in *The Blue Angel*

Dietrich, Marlene, orig. Maria Magdalene von Losch (*c* 1904-), German film actress, cabaret singer. Moved to US in 1920s. Achieved fame in *The Blue Angel* (1930), developing stereotype as husky-voiced, arrogant *femme fatale,* esp. with director von Sternberg, as in *The Scarlet Empress* (1934).

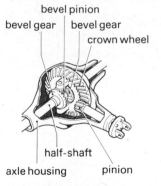

Differential

differential, in automobile, arrangement of gears in driven axle allowing driving force to be distributed to both wheels, yet allowing wheels to turn at different speeds relative to each other (*eg* when vehicle rounds corner, outer wheel must travel further).

differential calculus, mathematical study of rates of change of continuously varying functions. Devised independently by Newton and Leibnitz to study problems in dynamics and geometry. Important applications in physics where many phenomena are described by laws dealing with rate of change; leads to study of differential equations.

diffraction, breaking up of ray of light into bright and dark bands or coloured bands, observable after ray has passed through narrow slit or over sharp edge of opaque object. Caused by INTERFERENCE. Effect used in diffraction grating to produce spectra; grating usually consists of glass plate or polished metal surface ruled with equidistant parallel lines.

diffusion, in chemistry, intermingling of liquids or gases by continuous thermal motion of their molecules or ions. Gases spread out and mix by diffusion.

digestion, process by which food is broken down by enzymes into forms which can be used in METABOLISM. In man, carbohydrates are broken down by ptyalin in saliva and by amylase in intestine; protein by pepsin in stomach; fats by action of lipase and bile salts.

Diggers, members of 17th cent. English socio-religious sect, offshoot of LEVELLERS; *fl* 1649-50. Led by Gerrard Winstanley, combined communistic and egalitarian principles; estab. colony on common land in Surrey, destroyed (1650) by a mob.

digital computer, see COMPUTER.

digitalis, genus of Old World plants of figwort family. Incl. FOXGLOVE.

Dijon, city of Burgundy, E France, cap. of Côte-d'Or dept. Pop. 145,000. Road and railway jct., engineering, food processing, wine trade; univ. (1722). Hist. cap. of Burgundy, passed to France (1477). Medieval cultural centre. Gothic cathedral (13th cent.), ducal palace (14th cent.).

Dill

dill, *Anethum graveolens,* European annual or biennial herb of parsley family. Aromatic seeds used in flavouring.

Dilthey, Wilhelm (1833-1911), German philosopher. Estab. methodology of 'psychical sciences' (descriptive and analytic psychology) influencing later studies.

diminishing returns, law of, in economics, prediction that, after a certain point, an increase in one factor of production (other factors being constant) will yield relatively decreasing returns. Applied to indust. production and exploitation of land.

Dimitrov, Georgi (1882-1949), Bulgarian political leader. Arrested in Berlin on charge of setting fire to REICHSTAG (1933). Acquitted, went to Soviet Union; secretary-general

of Comintern (1934-43). Returned to Bulgaria (1944) to lead Communist Party; premier (1946-9).

Dimitrovo, see PERNIK, Bulgaria.

Dinan, town of Brittany, NW France, on R. Rance. Pop. 17,000. Resort, hosiery mfg., cider, beer. Medieval walls, castle; Church of St Sauveur.

Dinant, town of S Belgium, on R. Meuse, in the Ardennes. Pop. 10,000. Famous for brass, bronze, copperware in Middle Ages; tourist centre. Sacked by Charles the Bold (1466), badly damaged in WWI.

Dinaric Alps (*Dinara Planina*), mountain range of W Yugoslavia. Separates Dalmatia from Bosnia and Hercegovina. Name also applied to all limestone ranges between Julian Alps (NW) and Balkan system (SE).

Dinesen, Isak, see BLIXEN, KAREN, BARONESS.

dingo, *Canis dingo,* wolf-like wild dog, only indigenous carnivore of Australia. Erect ears, bushy tail; preys on sheep herds. Probably descended from domestic dogs introduced to Australia in prehist. times.

Dingwall, town of Highland region, N Scotland. Pop. 4000. Former royal burgh and co. town of Ross and Cromarty. Market town, railway jct.

Dinoflagellata (dinoflagellates), order of green, yellow or brown single-celled organisms. Cellulose shell, 2 flagella; mainly marine. Considered to be link between plants and animals. Incl. *Noctiluca* causing phosphorescence at sea.

dinosaur, any of large group of extinct, mainly terrestrial reptiles of Mesozoic era. Reached lengths of 27.5 m/90 ft. Mainly herbivorous; later species of Cretaceous period carnivorous, with larger brains, *eg* tyrannosaur.

Diocletian, full name Gaius Valerius Diocletianus (245-313), Roman emperor (284-305), b. Dalmatia. Appointed Maximian joint emperor (286) and Galerius and Constantius sub-emperors (292) to help defend empire. Persecuted Christians severely. Abdicated in favour of Galerius.

diode, in electronics, thermionic valve consisting of evacuated tube containing 2 electrodes. Electrons are emitted by heated cathode and migrate to positively charged plate (anode). Used in conversion of alternating current to direct current, *eg* in radio and television receivers.

Diogenes (*c* 412-323 BC), Greek philosopher. Cynic and ascetic, pupil of Antisthenes. Said to have searched Athens for an honest man and to have lived in a tub.

Diomedes, in Greek myth, Thracian king, son of Ares. Fed his horses on human flesh. Killed by Heracles (8th Labour).

Diomedes, in Greek myth, son of Tydeus; one of principal Greek heroes in Trojan War. In some stories, helped Odysseus remove the PALLADIUM from Troy; settled in Italy after Trojan War.

Dion, Albert de, Comte (1856-1946), French automobile pioneer. With Bouton produced light cars incorporating many developments esp. in running gear.

Dionysia, festivals of DIONYSUS.

Dionysius the Areopagite, St (*fl* 1st cent), Athenian churchman. Converted by St Paul. Traditionally 1st bishop of Athens; martyred. Several theological writings falsely attributed to him in Middle Ages; now attributed to 'Pseudo-Dionysius'.

Dionysius the Elder (*c* 430-367 BC), Greek political leader in Sicily. Became tyrant of Syracuse (405) and carried out 2 successful wars against Carthage. Defeated disastrously in 3rd war. Succeeded by his son **Dionysius the Younger** (*fl* 350BC), who was driven out of Syracuse by Dion. Returned after latter's murder (354) but expelled 344.

Dionysus (Roman name Bacchus), Greek god of wine, fertility, son of Zeus and Semele. His worship originated in Thrace and Asia Minor, accompanied by ecstasy in worshippers (esp. women) called Maenads or Bacchantes. Worshipped with Apollo at Delphi, and in countryside as god of vegetation.

Diophantus of Alexandria (*fl* 3rd cent.), Greek algebraist. Noted for his work on integer solutions of indeterminate (Diophantine) equations and work on theory of numbers; only 6 of 13 vols. of his *Arithmetica* survive.

Dior, Christian (1905-57), French fashion designer. Estab. fashion houses in Paris (1946) and New York (1948). Introduced 'New Look' (1947), extravagant style contrasting sharply with wartime fashions. Major influence in world fashion.

Dioscuri, in Greek and Roman myth, joint name for Castor and Polydeuces (Lat. Pollux), according to Homer, twin sons of LEDA by Zeus. Placed by him among stars as constellation Gemini.

diphtheria, acute infectious disease of throat and other mucous membranes caused by bacteria. Characterized by formation of membranous crust in air passages; toxin produced by bacteria can produce local paralysis.

diplomatic service, body of representatives of a govt. responsible for conduct of relations with foreign govts. Estab. systematically by Italians in 15th cent., esp. by Venice. Soon imitated by leading European states. By 1815 classes, *ie* ambassadors, envoys, ministers resident and chargés d'affaires, recognized. Diplomatic immunity, *ie* diplomat being placed outside law of land, estab. 16th-17th cent. Diplomat is responsible to his own foreign minister, negotiates with foreign ministry of country to which he is accredited.

Diplopoda, *see* MILLIPEDE.

dipper or **water ouzel,** any of Cinclidae family of aquatic perching birds. Lives near mountain streams; able to walk under water in pursuit of insects, larvae. Species incl. European *Cinclus cinclus.*

Diptera, order of 2-winged flies. Mouthparts lengthened into proboscis for piercing, sucking. *See* FLY.

Dirac, Paul Adrien Maurice (1902-), English physicist. Introduced relativity theory into study of wave mechanics, extending de Broglie's ideas of wave nature of electron. Predicted existence of positron (discovered 1932). Shared Nobel Prize for Physics (1933) with Schrödinger.

direct current (DC), electric current flowing always in same direction. Produced by batteries.

Directory, executive body of five men, appointed by the two legislative chambers, which governed France (1795-9). Overthrown by coup of 18 Brumaire by which Bonaparte became first consul.

Dire Dawa, town of EC Ethiopia. Pop. 50,000. On Addis Ababa-Djibouti railway; trade in hides, coffee; textile, cement mfg.

dirigible balloon, *see* AIRSHIP.

disarmament, reduction of armed forces and armaments, *eg* to limit set by treaty. Since WWI international attempts have been made to restrict weapons, *eg* Disarmament Conference (1932-7). After 1945, nuclear weapons made problem more serious. Charter of United Nations provided for disarmament planning in Security Council. Commission set up (1946), reached impasse (1948). Geneva Conference (1955) led to conferences on test-ban treaty and moratorium on testing until 1961. Moscow Agreement (1963) banned tests in atmosphere, under water, outer space. USSR and US drafted non-proliferation treaty (1968), approved by UN. *See* also STRATEGIC ARMS LIMITATION TALKS (SALT).

Disciples, Twelve, *see* TWELVE DISCIPLES.

discount rate, *see* BANK RATE.

discrimination, accordance of differential or prejudicial treatment, esp. actions or policies directed against welfare of certain groups, minorities. Can be on racial, religious, sexual or class grounds. Racial discrimination provoked CIVIL RIGHTS movement in US, clashes in Africa (esp. in Rhodesia, South Africa in 1970s), passing of Race Relations Act in UK. Sexual discrimination, *eg* against women, homosexuals, became object of protest in 1960s and 1970s.

disinfectant, substance used to destroy harmful microbes. First used was phenol (carbolic acid), introduced by Lister (1867). Disinfectant applied to living things usually called an antiseptic.

Disney, Walt[er Elias] (1901-66), American film producer, famous for animated cartoons. Created character Mickey Mouse in 1928, Donald Duck in 1936. First full-length cartoon was *Snow White and the Seven Dwarfs* (1938). Studio (estab. 1923) made innovations in

Disney's Mickey Mouse in *Steamboat Willy*

animation techniques. Also produced documentaries on animals, *eg The Living Desert* (1953), and children's films with human casts, *eg Treasure Island* (1950).

dispersion of light, breaking up of light into its component colours, *eg* by a prism. Spectrum produced by shining white light through prism results from refractive index of glass differing for light of different wavelengths (different colours).

Disraeli: detail of painting by Millais

Disraeli, Benjamin, 1st Earl of Beaconsfield (1804-81), British statesman, PM (1868, 1874-80). Member of Young England Tories, opposed repeal of Corn Laws and helped defeat Peel's ministry after their repeal (1846). Chief figure in revitalized Conservatives after passage of 1867 Reform Bill extending franchise; succeeded Derby as PM (1868). Second term (1874-80) marked by aggressive imperial and military policy, esp. in S Africa, Balkans and Mediterranean; secured controlling interest in Suez Canal for Britain (1875). Had Victoria crowned empress of India (1876). Also known for novels, *eg Coningsby* (1844), *Sybil* (1845).

dissenter or **nonconformist,** in UK, one who adheres to the form of a religion other than that of the Established Church. Applied esp. to those who failed to accept Act of Uniformity (1662). Denotes more popularly the Protestant dissenter, *eg* Presbyterians, Baptists, Methodists, referred to in Toleration Act (1689).

Di Stefano, Alfredo (1926-), Argentinian footballer. Renowned centre-forward, he is remembered for his goal-scoring achievements for Spain's Real Madrid, leading teams which won 1st 5 European Champions Cups.

distemper, in veterinary medicine, any of several infectious catarrhal diseases of animals, esp. canine distemper, virus disease of young dogs. Controlled by vaccination.

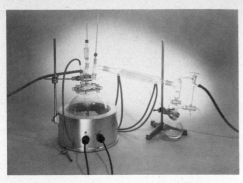

Apparatus for vacuum distillation

distillation, vaporization of a liquid followed by condensation back into liquid form. Used to separate mixtures of liquids of different boiling points or to purify liquid contaminated by non-volatile impurities.

distribution, in economics, proportion of goods and services which each economic group receives from total production. Group may be social, geographical, *etc.* Redistribution of wealth often used by radicals as basis of argument for political change.

District of Columbia (DC), federal admin. dist. of E US; on Potomac R. Area 180 sq km (*c* 70 sq mi); pop. 757,000. Co-extensive with cap. Washington.

Diu, former Portuguese enclave in W India. Pop. 20,000. Taken by Portuguese (1534), seized by India (1961). Part of union territ. of Goa, Daman and Diu.

diver, fish-eating bird of N hemisphere of Gavidae family. Short legs, webbed feet; inhabitant of lakes, bays. Great Northern diver, *Gavia immer,* called loon in North America, found also in N Europe.

divine right, doctrine supporting hereditary kingship on grounds that it is according to divine and natural law, and cannot be set aside without breaking such law. Claimed by James I and Charles I of England, lost importance with 1688 Revolution and Parliament's growing power.

diving, sport in which competitor projects himself into water from an elevated position, possibly executing somersaults before entering water. Divided into springboard and platform or high diving. Olympic event for men since 1904, for women since 1912.

division of labour, in economics, organization of workers so that different groups have specialized roles in production. May be geographical, *eg* region concentrates on one product, or occupational, *eg* on modern production line. First examined as concept by Adam Smith.

divorce, decree of dissolution of marriage granted by court. Distinct from nullity, decree that marriage was originally illegal. In UK, irretrievable breakdown of marriage is only ground; in US, grounds vary from state to state, but main ones are adultery, desertion, cruelty. Also *see* ALIMONY.

Diyarbakir, city of EC Turkey, on R. Tigris. Pop. 180,000. Commercial centre; trade in wool, grain. Became Roman colony AD 230, then under Persian and Arab rule. Taken by Turks (1515). Devastated by earthquake (1966).

Djailolo, *see* HALMAHERA.

Djajapura, cap. of Irian Jaya (West Irian), Indonesia. Pop. 16,000. Formerly known as Hollandia, Kotabaru and Sukarnapura.

Djakarta or **Jakarta,** cap. of Indonesia, on coast of NW Java. Pop. 4,576,000. Commercial, transport and cultural centre. Major export port at nearby Tanjungpriok. Founded (1619) as Batavia by Dutch, renamed 1949.

Djenné or **Jenné,** town of S Mali, on R. Bani. Pop. 9000. Agric. market. Founded 8th cent., *fl* 12th-16th cent. on salt, gold, slave trade.

Djerba or **Jerba,** isl. of SE Tunisia, on Gulf of Gabès. Area 510 sq km (197 sq mi). Tourist resort; olive, date growing;

sponge fishing. Traditionally Homer's isl. of the lotus-eaters.

Djibouti or **Jibuti,** cap. of French Territ. of the Afars and the Issas, on Gulf of Tadjoura. Pop. 62,000. Port, railway to Addis Ababa (Ethiopia); transit trade, exports cattle, hides, salt. Cap. of French Somaliland from 1892.

Dmitri (1582-91), Russian prince, son of Ivan the Terrible. Heir to his brother Feodor I, he was murdered prob. at instigation of regent, Boris Godunov. Claims to succession were made by Polish-backed impostors (false Dmitris), who invaded Russia but all were eventually killed.

DNA or **deoxyribonucleic acid,** fundamental genetic material found in the chromosomes of cell nuclei. Molecule consists of 2 interwound helical strands, each strand composed of long chain of nucleotides (derived from a nitrogenous base, a sugar and phosphate group). Sequence of bases in molecule constitutes genetic code which determines proteins and enzymes to be synthesized by cell. At cell division, DNA replicates itself, thus ensuring that hereditary information is passed to new cells.

Dnepr

Dnepr or **Dnieper,** river of USSR. Rises in Smolensk region, flows *c* 2250 km (1400 mi) generally S through Byelorussian and Ukrainian SSR into N Black Sea. Navigable above Zaporozhye (Dneproges dam).

Dneprodzerzhinsk, city of USSR, EC Ukrainian SSR; port on R. Dnepr. Pop. 235,000. Iron and steel mfg., chemicals.

Dneproges, see ZAPOROZHYE.

Dnepropetrovsk, city of USSR, EC Ukrainian SSR; on R. Dnepr. Pop. 903,000. Indust. centre, producing iron, steel and manganese. Grew with completion of Dneproges dam (1932).

Dnestr or **Dniester,** river of USSR. Rises in Carpathian Mts. of W Ukrainian SSR; follows winding course SE through Moldavian SSR to Black Sea. Length *c* 1350 km (850 mi).

Dnieper, see DNEPR.

Dobell, Sir William (1899-1970), Australian painter. Noted for his portraits, which convey keen sense of character perception; works incl. portrait *Joshua Smith.*

Doberman pinscher, breed of large dog, used as police or guard dog. Short-haired, smooth coated; stands 61-71 cm/24-28 in. at shoulder.

Dobruja (*Dobrogea*), region of SE Romania and NE Bulgaria. Forests; agric. Part of Roman Moesia, Byzantine, Ottoman empires. Divided after Congress of Berlin (1878); N to Romania, S to Bulgaria. S part became Romanian (1913-40), returned to Bulgaria.

dock or **sorrel,** any of genus *Rumex* of perennial herbs native to temperate regions. Large leaves, stout taproots, small green or brown flowers; popular antidote to nettle stings. Common sorrel, *R. acetosa,* is used in salads.

docks, berthing spaces in ports for ships. Two basic types: dry docks, which may be floating or fixed, used for building or cleaning and repairing ships; wet docks, usually equipped with wharves and quays, used for loading and unloading cargo. Floodgates may be necessary to maintain water levels in docks if there is a wide range in tides.

dodder, several species of *Cuscuta,* a parasitic genus of morning glory family. Native to tropical and temperate regions. Lack leaves, roots and chlorophyll; draw nourishment from host through suckers.

Dodecanese

Dodecanese (*Dhodhekánisos*), isl. group of Greece, in SE Aegean Sea. Area 2720 sq km (1050 sq mi); cap. Rhodes. Incl. Rhodes, Cos, Kárpathos. Olives, fruit, sponges. Turkish from 1522, taken by Italy 1912; passed to Greece 1947.

Dodge, Mary Mapes (1831-1905), American editor, author. Wrote children's classic *Hans Brinker, or the Silver Skates* (1865).

Dodge City, SW Kansas, US; on Arkansas R. Pop. 15,000. Hist. trading post on Santa Fé trail and wild cattle town (Wyatt Earp). Wheat, livestock distribution centre.

Dodgson, C. L., *see* CARROLL, LEWIS.

dodo, *Raphus cucullatus,* flightless bird of Mauritius, resembling turkey. Became extinct in 17th cent. through persecution by man.

Dodoma, town of EC Tanzania. Pop. 15,000. Agric. centre; designated (1975) future national cap.

Dodona, in Greek religion, seat of earliest oracle. Sacred to Zeus and Dione; oracle based on an oak tree's rustling of leaves as interpreted by priests.

Dodsley, Robert (1703-64), English publisher. Pub. works of Pope, Samuel Johnson and Goldsmith. Edited *Select Collection of Old Plays* (12 vols., 1744) and *A Collection of Poems by Several Hands* (3 vols., 1748). With Burke, founded *Annual Register* (1758), which still appears.

dog, *Canis familiaris,* domestic carnivore of Canidae family, to which wolf, jackal belong. Numerous varieties developed from wolf by selective breeding since *c* 8000 BC. Dogs classified as sporting, non-sporting, hounds, terriers, working or toys.

doge, chief magistrate in medieval and Renaissance Venice and Genoa. In 14th cent. held office for life; later office made elective for 2 year terms.

dogfish, small shark of several families of warm and temperate seas. Lesser spotted dogfish, *Scyliorhinus canicula,* found in European waters. Spiny dogfish, *Squalus acanthias,* is commonest.

Dogger Bank, large sand bank in North Sea, off Northumberland, England. Cod fisheries; scene of WWI naval battle (1915).

dogtooth violet, any plant of genus *Erythronium* of lily family. Species incl. American *E. americanum* and European *E. denscanis.*

dogwood, any of genus *Cornus* of trees and shrubs. Esp. *C. sanguinea,* a European flowering shrub and *C. florida,* a small tree of E US.

Dohnányi, Erno (1877-1960), Hungarian composer. Best known for his *Variations on a Nursery Song* for piano and orchestra. Wrote in more traditional style than his nationalist contemporaries Bartók and Kodály.

Dôle, town of E France, on R. Doubs. Pop. 29,000. Agric. market, cheese and wine trade. Hist. cap. of Franche-Comté, taken by French crown (1674).

Dolet, Etienne (1509-46), French scholar, printer. Wrote and printed many works on grammar, history, philosophy, esp. *Commentaries on the Latin Language.* Often accused of heresy, was eventually convicted and burned in Paris.

Dogwood

Dolgellau or **Dolgelly,** urban dist. of Gwynedd, NW Wales. Pop. 2000. Former co. town of Merionethshire. Slate quarrying; tourism. Hist. wool indust.

Dollard des Ormeaux, Adam (1635-60), French adventurer in Canada. Heavily outnumbered, he and a small band of companions withstood an Iroquois attack at Long Sault rapids (1660); all were eventually killed. May have delayed Iroquois attack on Montréal. Ensuing legend was later questioned.

Dollfuss, Engelbert (1892-1934), Austrian statesman. Christian Socialist chancellor (1932-4), in conflict with German-backed National Socialists over maintenance of Austrian independence. Assumed dictatorial powers (1933), estab. corporate state (1934). Assassinated by group of Austrian Nazis.

Döllinger, Johann Joseph Ignaz von (1799-1890), German theologian. Excommunicated (1871) for rejecting papal infallibility, originating movement from which Old Catholic Church emerged 1874.

Dolmetsch, Arnold (1858-1940), Swiss musicologist, resident in Britain from 1914. Revived interest in old and neglected instruments, esp. the recorder.

dolomite, greyish-white mineral, carbonate of calcium and magnesium. Also a rock, consisting of over 20% mineral dolomite; formed by replacement of calcium by magnesium in limestone. Rock may be metamorphosed into dolomitic marble. Used as building stone. Widespread; major sources in N Italy, US, Brazil.

Dolomites, range of NE Italy, in the Alps. Highest point Marmolada (3340 m/10,965 ft). Named from rock which forms them. Tourist area, chief resort Cortina d'Ampezzo.

dolphin, any of Delphinidae family of toothed whales, of worldwide distribution. Incl. common dolphin, *Delphinus delphis,* and KILLER WHALE. Bottle-nosed dolphin, genus *Tursiops,* highly intelligent; capable of communicating by sound.

Domagk, Gerhard (1895-1964), German chemist and pathologist. Discovered effect of dye Prontosil in treating streptococcal infections; its active constituent, sulphanilamide, was 1st sulphonamide drug. Awarded Nobel Prize for Physiology and Medicine (1939).

dome, vaulted roof, usually hemispherical in shape and circular in plan. Ancient domes incl. Mycenaean 'Treasury of Atreus' of 14th cent. BC, constructed in concentric rings of stones. Romans developed concrete dome, *eg* Pantheon in Rome. Other famous domes incl. those of St Peter's, Rome, and St Paul's, London.

Dolphins

Domenichino, orig. Domenico Zampieri (1581-1641), Italian artist of Bolognese school. A leading pupil of the Carracci, he maintained their Classical doctrines and was an influential landscapist. Executed numerous decorations in palaces, villas and chapels of Rome and Naples.

Domesday Book (1085-6), record of intensive survey of England made by order of William I (the Conqueror). Main aim was to aid taxation through knowledge of economic resources. Covered ownership of land and its value, and pop. Outstanding for speed with which it was compiled and thoroughly, and as basic source in medieval history.

Dominic, St, orig. Dominigo de Guzmán (c 1170-1221), Spanish churchman, founder of DOMINICANS. He and his bishop were sent by Innocent III to S France to preach to the Albigenses, 1st RC missionaries to be successful there.

Dominica, largest isl. of SE West Indies, in Windward Isls. Area 750 sq km (290 sq mi); pop. 70,000; cap. Roseau. Mainly mountainous with much volcanic activity (hot springs, gases). Fruit growing; rum, copra exports. Successive French, British occupation, then British colony; became associate state 1967.

Dominican Republic, republic of West Indies, occupying E Hispaniola. Area 48,734 sq km (18,816 sq mi); pop. 4,012,000; cap. Santo Domingo. Language: Spanish. Religion: RC. Mountains in interior; agric. land in E; sugar, coffee, cacao, tobacco produce. Bauxite, rock salt mining. Discovered by Columbus (1492); settled by Spanish; independence gained 1844; US military rule 1916-24; dictatorship under Trujillo (1930-61).

Dominicans, in RC church, order of preaching friars founded (1216) by St Dominic. Emphasize study; prominent in medieval universities. Officially the Order of Preachers, popularly called Black Friars because of black mantle and scapular worn over white habit. Aquinas was most notable Dominican theologian.

Domitian, full name Titus Flavius Domitianus (AD 51-96), Roman emperor (81-96). Son of Vespasian, succeeded brother Titus. After crushing revolt of Roman troops in Upper Germany (89), ruled despotically until stabbed to death.

Don, rivers of UK. **1,** in Yorkshire, flows 112 km (70 mi) from Pennines via Sheffield to R. Ouse. **2,** in Scotland, flows 129 km (80 mi) from Grampians to North Sea; famous for salmon fishing.

Don, river of USSR. Rises in C European RSFSR, flows SE and then SW, c 1900 km (1200 mi) to Sea of Azov. Joined by canal to R. Volga near Volgograd.

Donatello, orig. Donato di Niccolo di Betto Bardi (c 1386-1466), Italian painter and sculptor. Most influential sculptor of 15th cent., early work was in Gothic style. Sculptures *St Mark* and *St George* show new humanist expression. Pioneer in use of perspective, he introduced shallow relief technique into sculpture. Other masterpieces incl. bronze *David* and equestrian statue *Gattamelata*.

Donati, Giovanni Battista (1826-73), Italian astronomer. Made early spectral analysis of comets, finding that their structure is partly gaseous. Discovered 6 comets, incl. Donati's comet (1858).

Donatus (*fl* AD 333), Roman grammarian. *Ars Grammatica* became standard elementary Latin text-book during Middle Ages. Taught St Jerome.

Donbas or **Donets Basin,** region of USSR in plain of R. Donets, E Ukrainian SSR. Largest coalfields of USSR support major indust., incl. iron and steel mfg.

Doncaster, bor. of West Yorkshire met. county, N England, on R. Don. Pop. 83,000. Coalmining; railway engineering; has famous racecourse. On Roman site (*Danum*).

Donegal, county of Ulster prov., N Irish Republic. Area 4830 sq km (1865 sq mi); pop. 108,000; co. town Lifford. Rocky, indented coast incl. Malin Head, most N point of Ireland; hilly interior. Fishing; livestock; woollen, tweed mfg.; h.e.p. **Donegal,** town on Donegal Bay. Pop. 2000. Ruined 15th cent. monastery.

Donets, river of USSR. Flows c 1050 km (650 mi) from S European RSFSR, through Ukrainian SSR, to join R. Don. *See* DONBAS.

Donetsk, city of USSR, E Ukranian SSR. Pop. 905,000. Indust. centre of Donbas; coal mining, iron and steel industs. Named Yuzovka then Stalino before 1961.

Dönitz, Karl (1891-), German naval officer. In WWII, commanded submarine activity; chief of naval staff (1943). Named to succeed Hitler, ordered German surrender to Allies (May, 1945). Imprisoned (1946-56) after Nuremberg trials.

Donizetti

Donizetti, Gaetano (1797-1848), Italian composer. Wrote tuneful operas, incl. *Lucia di Lammermoor, La Fille du régiment* and *Don Pasquale.*

donkey, see ASS.

Donleavy, J[ames] P[atrick] (1926-), American author, living mainly in Ireland. Novels, *eg The Ginger Man* (1955), *The Beastly Beatitudes of Balthazar B* (1969), combine bawdy humour with self-pity.

Donne, John (c 1572-1631), English poet, divine. Greatest of metaphysical school. Work, characterized by irony, intellectual 'conceits', incl. early love poetry, *eg Songs and Sonnets*, later religious verse, *eg* 'Death be not proud', 'Batter my heart three-person'd God', 'At the round earth's imagined corners'. Noted for sermons preached as Dean of St Paul's from 1621.

Donnybrook, suburb of Dublin, Irish Republic. Formerly village, site of riotous fairs, suppressed (1855).

John Donne

Doolittle, Hilda, pseud. H.D. (1886-1961), American poet. Known as IMAGIST for verse, wife of Richard Aldington. Attained new reputation with *Helen in Egypt* (1961).

Doppler, Christian Johann (1803-53), Austrian physicist. Predicted Doppler effect: apparent change in frequency of sound or electromagnetic radiation caused by relative motion of source and observer. Observed frequency is higher than emitted frequency as observer and source approach, lower as they recede. Effect used by astronomers to determine relative velocity of heavenly body and Earth.

Dorcas gazelle, *Gazella dorcas,* one of smallest of gazelles, standing less than 60 cm/2 ft. Found N of Sahara; numbers diminished by hunting.

Dorchester, mun. bor. and co. town of Dorset, S England, on R. Frome. Pop. 14,000. Maiden Castle prehist. hill fort nearby. Roman *Durnovaria,* many remains. 'Casterbridge' of Hardy's novels.

Dordogne, river of WC France. Flows *c* 465 km (290 mi) from Auvergne Mts. to R. Garonne, forming the Gironde estuary. Tourism, vineyards (incl. St Emilion), h.e.p.

Dordrecht or **Dort,** city of SW Netherlands, on R. Oude Maas. Pop. 102,000. Shipbuilding, marine engineering. Chief Dutch port until 17th cent.; 1st meeting place of United Provs. (1572). Church (14th cent.).

Doré, Gustave (1832-83), French book illustrator. Illustrated Dante's *Inferno, Don Quixote,* the Bible; drew pictures of poor quarters of London (1869-71). Work is noted for his love of the grotesque.

Doric order, earliest and most used of the Greek orders of architecture. Characterized by its lack of base, massive tapering shaft with 20 flutes, simple capital. Parthenon in Athens shows the perfected order.

Dormouse

dormouse, small squirrel-like arboreal rodent of Gliridae family, widely distributed in Old World. Diet of seed, berries, *etc.* European species undergo long hibernation. Species incl. edible dormouse, *Glis glis,* garden dormouse,

Eliomys quercinus, and common dormouse, *Muscardinus avellanarius,* only British variety.

Dornoch, town of Highland region, N Scotland, on Dornoch Firth. Pop. 1000. Former royal burgh and co. town of Sutherland.

Dorpat, see TARTU.

Dorset, county of S England. Area 2654 sq km (1024 sq mi); pop. 566,000; co. town Dorchester. Chalk downs (sheep); lowlands (dairying); Portland stone quarried. Coastal resorts *eg* Weymouth. Ancient remains incl. Maiden Castle hill fort. Setting of Hardy's Wessex novels.

Dortmund, city of W West Germany, in Ruhr. Pop. 642,000. Port, connected by Dortmund-Ems canal to North Sea; brewing, coal, steel, engineering industs. Member of Hanseatic League. Badly damaged in WWII.

dory, marine fish of Zeidae family. John dory, *Zeus faber,* yellow or golden with spiny dorsal fin, is common in Mediterranean.

Dos Passos, John Roderigo (1896-1970), American novelist. Works incl. *Manhattan Transfer* (1925), trilogy *U.S.A.* (1930-7); mixed 'newsreel', biog. techniques to form composite picture of society. Also wrote reportage, plays.

Dostoyevski

Dostoyevski, Feodor Mikhailovich (1821-81), Russian novelist. Combined vivid realistic narrative with psychological insight. Major works, incl. *Crime and Punishment* (1866), *The Idiot* (1868), *The Brothers Karamazov* (1879-80), reflect concern with guilt, religious faith.

Dou or **Douw, Gerard** or **Gerrit** (1613-75), Dutch portrait and genre painter. Pupil of Rembrandt, he developed a minute detailed technique. His works incl. *Dropsical Woman.*

Douai, town of N France, on R. Scarpe. Pop. 49,000. On Nord coalfield, iron and steel indust. Under Spanish rule (1477-1667). English, Scottish RC colleges estab. in 16th cent., 'Douay Bible' pub. 1610.

Douala, city of Cameroon, on Bight of Biafra. Pop. 250,000. Railway terminus and port, exports tropical hardwoods, cocoa, bananas. Former cap. of German colony of Kamerun.

Douay Bible, English version of the Bible translated from the Latin Vulgate edition for the use of RCs. NT pub. at Rheims (1582); OT at the RC college for English priests in Douai (1610).

double bass, four-stringed low-pitched instrument, considered either a survivor of VIOL family or lowest member of violin family. Played with bow in orchestra and plucked to supply bass line in popular music.

Doubs, river of E France. Flows *c* 430 km (270 mi) from E Jura Mts. via NW Switzerland and Besançon to R. Saône near Chalon. Forms part of Franco-Swiss border.

Doughty, C[harles] M[ontagu] (1843-1926), English traveller, author. Known for *Travels in Arabia Deserta* (1888) revealing passion for Arab culture. Poetry incl. *Mansoul, or The Riddle of the World* (1920).

Douglas, Lord Alfred Bruce (1870-1945), English poet. Friendship with Oscar Wilde precipitated latter's eventual prosecution for homosexual practices.

Douglas, Clifford Hugh (1879-1952), Scottish economist, engineer. Early theorist of SOCIAL CREDIT. Chief reconstruction adviser to Social Credit govt. of Alberta (1935-6).

Douglas, Gavin (*c* 1474-1522), Scottish poet. Known for version of *Aeneid* (1513), most sustained poetic achievement in Scots language.

Douglas, George, pseud. of George Brown (1869-1902), Scottish novelist. Wrote *The House with Green Shutters* (1901), effectively ending sentimental picture of village life drawn by Barrie, Crockett.

Douglas, Sir James de Douglas, Lord of (*c* 1286-1330), Scottish nobleman, called Black Douglas. After losing estates by order of Edward I, terrorized borders. Later joined Robert the Bruce, with whom he fought at Bannockburn. Died in Spain on way to Palestine to bury Robert's heart.

Douglas, Lloyd Cassell (1877-1951), American novelist. Known for best-selling sentimental novels on religious themes, esp. *The Robe* (1942).

Douglas, [George] Norman (1868-1952), Scottish novelist. Known for *South Wind* (1917), a celebration of Mediterranean hedonism. *Old Calabria* (1915) combines travel, philosophy, autobiog.

Douglas, Stephen Arnold (1813-61), American politician. Democratic senator from Illinois (1847-61), introduced KANSAS-NEBRASKA BILL (1854) in attempt to settle slavery issue. Later asserted doctrine of territ. rights to exclude slavery during famous election campaign debates (1858) with Lincoln.

Douglas, cap. of Isle of Man, UK. Pop. 20,000. Seaport, resort on E coast. Admin. and legislative buildings.

Douglas fir, *Pseudotsuga taxifolia,* evergreen tree of W North America. Timber exported in large quantities as lumber and plywood.

Douglas-Home, Alexander Frederick, Baron Home of the Hirsel (1903-), British statesman, PM (1963-4). Conservative foreign secretary (1960-3), renounced titles (originally 14th earl of Home) to become PM in succession to Macmillan. Lost ensuing election. Again foreign secretary (1970-4), made life peer (1974).

Doukhobors, *see* DUKHOBORS.

Doumer, Paul (1857-1932), French statesman. Elected president (1931), assassinated by a Russian émigré.

Dounreay, village of Highland region, N Scotland. Site of UK's first large-scale nuclear reactor.

Douro (Span. *Duero*), river of Spain and Portugal. Flows *c* 770 km (480 mi) from NC Spain, W to Atlantic Ocean near Oporto. Used for irrigation, h.e.p.

douroucouli, *Aotus trivirgatus,* monkey of Central and South America. Only nocturnal species of monkey.

Douw, Gerrit, *see* DOU, GERARD.

dove, medium-sized bird of same family (Columbidae) as pigeon. Short neck and legs, cooing cry; seed eater. Species incl. rock dove, *Columba livia,* ancestor of domestic pigeons; turtle dove, *Streptopelia turtur,* of S Europe, Africa.

Dover, mun. bor. of Kent, SE England. Pop. 34,000. Ferry port, shortest cross-Channel route (to Calais, 35 km/22 mi). Has Roman lighthouse; Norman castle; one of Cinque Ports.

Dover, cap. of Delaware, US. Pop. 17,000. Fruit canning indust. Settled 1683; became cap. 1777.

Dover, Strait of (Fr. *Pas de Calais*), between SE England and NE France, links English Channel with North Sea. At narrowest only 34 km (21 mi) wide.

Dowding, Hugh Caswall Tremenheere Dowding, 1st Baron (1882-1970), British air marshal. During Battle of Britain, he was chief of Fighter Command (1939-42).

Dowland, John (1563-1626), English composer and lutanist. Remembered for his plaintively beautiful lute songs and solos. Lutanist to Christian IV of Denmark and to James I and Charles I of England.

Down, former county of SE Northern Ireland. Hilly, incl. Mourne Mts. in SE; Ards Penin., Strangford Lough in E. Agric., linen mfg., tourism. Co. town was Downpatrick. **Down,** district; area 646 sq km (249 sq mi); pop. 49,000. Created 1973, formerly part of Co. Down.

Downing Street, London street off Whitehall, in which are located official residences of British PM (number 10) and chancellor of exchequer (number 11).

Downpatrick, town of SE Northern Ireland. Pop. 8000. Former co. town of Down. Its cathedral is reputed to have remains of Irish saints Patrick, Columba, Bridget.

Downs, S England. Chalk ranges running W-E. North Downs (up to 294 m/965 ft) of Surrey and Kent end at white cliffs of Dover. South Downs (up to 264 m/865 ft) of Sussex end at Beachy Head. Sheep pasture land. Hampshire, Berkshire, Marlborough downs further W.

Dowson, Ernest Christopher (1867-1900), English poet. Lived mainly in France, influenced by 'decadent' poets esp. Verlaine. Known for 'Cynara' (1896).

Doyle, Sir Arthur Conan (1859-1930), English author, b. Scotland. Created detective Sherlock Holmes in *A Study in Scarlet* (1887). Along with many Holmes stories, also wrote historical romances, *eg The White Company* (1891). Knighted for defence of British policy in Boer War.

D'Oyly Carte, Richard (1844-1901), English theatrical impresario. Known for productions of Gilbert and Sullivan operettas. Built Savoy Theatre, London (1881).

Drabble, Margaret (1939-), English author. Novels, *eg A Summer Birdcage* (1963), *The Millstone* (1966), deal with the problem of conflicting female roles.

Draco (*fl c* 623 BC), Athenian statesman. Devised code of laws noted for their severity, as almost all crimes carried death penalty.

dragon, fabulous monster of Christian, Chinese, Japanese and other folklore. Usually represented as huge, fire-breathing, winged reptilian quadruped. Sometimes used in Christian art, literature to symbolize forces of evil.

dragonet, any of Callionymidae family of small brightly coloured fish, related to goby. Scaleless, with large pectoral fins.

dragon fish, any of Pegasidae family of small flying fish of Indian, Pacific oceans. Long snout, body covered with bony plates.

Dragonfly

dragonfly, any of Odonata order of insects with 2 pairs of membranous wings, large eyes and long thin brightly-coloured body. Feeds on small insects seized in flight. Wingspan of some fossil varieties *c* 60 cm/2 ft.

dragoon, cavalry soldier trained to fight on foot. The name comes from the short musket, called a dragon, carried by the French cavalry of Marshal Bussac (1600).

Drake, Sir Francis (*c* 1540-96), English naval officer. In 1570-3 took part in raiding expeditions to the Spanish Main and in the *Golden Hind* was 1st English mariner to circumnavigate the globe (1577-80), for which he was knighted by Elizabeth I. In 1585 he commanded a marauding fleet off Spanish America, and in 1587 destroyed the Spanish fleet at Cádiz.

Drakensberg Mountains or **Quathlamba,** range of South Africa. Extends c 1125 km (700 mi) SW-NE from Cape Prov. to Transvaal; rises to 3481 m (11,425 ft) in Lesotho. Forms SE escarpment of C plateau.

drama, artistic form traditionally combining speech and action to tell story, but also incl. monologue, mime. Western drama originated in Greek Dionysiac festivals, leading to classical TRAGEDY. Popular COMEDY developed alongside using stock characters. Renaissance revived classical theories while in Italy popular COMMEDIA DELL'ARTE flourished. Fusion of classical and popular traditions led to Elizabethan and Jacobean drama in England. Classical models were more rigidly observed in France. Restoration drama was largely artificial and gave way to sentimental and then romantic drama. Realism introduced in 19th cent. leading to deeper psychological interest. See NO PLAY, JAPANESE LITERATURE.

Drammen, town of SE Norway, at head of Drammen Fjord. Pop. 48,000. Port, exports wood pulp, paper.

Draper, John William (1811-82), American scientist, b. England. Contributed to fields of photochemistry and radiant energy, anticipating development of spectrum analysis. Author of *Human Physiology* (1856), which contained 1st photographs reproducing what is seen under microscope.

draughts or **checkers,** game of skill for 2 persons played with 24 round pieces on a board divided into 64 alternate light and dark squares. Played in Europe from 16th cent.

Drava, river of EC Europe. Flows c 725 km (450 mi) from S Austria through Yugoslavia to Danube near Osijek. Forms part of Yugoslav-Hungarian border.

Dravidian, major group of inhabitants of India, before Aryan invasion, therefore name for S India group possibly descended from pre-Aryan stock. Also name for family of languages mainly in S India and Sri Lanka, incl. Telugu, Tamil, Kannada and Malayalam.

Drayton, Michael (1563-1631), English poet. Remembered for *Polyolbion* (1612), a patriotic description of British countryside. Also wrote shorter poems, incl. sonnet beginning, 'Since there's no help, come let us kiss and part'.

dreams, sequences of sensations, images, thoughts, *etc,* occurring during SLEEP. Shown to be necessary in restorative process of sleep. Considered important in ancient times and among primitive peoples. Interest revived by Freud (who distinguished latent content and manifest content) and Jung.

Dred Scott Case (1856-7), test case brought before US Supreme Court. Decision rejected Negro slave's plea for freedom on ground that he had lived several years in free territ., decreed that Negro 'whose ancestors . . . were sold as slaves' was not entitled to rights of Federal citizen. Declared MISSOURI COMPROMISE unconstitutional, further aggravated North-South dispute.

Dreiser, Theodore (1871-1945), American novelist. Known for naturalistic *Sister Carrie* (1900), *An American Tragedy* (1925) attacking the 20th cent. American dream. Also wrote plays, essays, autobiog. *A Hoosier Holiday* (1916).

Drenthe, prov. of NE Netherlands. Area 2644 sq km (1021 sq mi); cap. Assen. Infertile heathland, reclamation in W. Rye, potatoes, cattle; oil, natural gas.

Dresden, city of SE East Germany, on R. Elbe. Pop. 504,000. River port, railway jct.; produces machine tools, optical instruments. 'Dresden' pottery made at Meissen. Cap. of Saxony 1485-1918. Cultural centre with noted art collections, Baroque buildings; many destroyed in WWII.

Dreyfus affair (1894-1906), scandal arising out of trial of French army officer, **Alfred Dreyfus** (1859-1935), for treason. Accused of selling military secrets to Germany, he became centre of case arousing anti-Semitic tirades in press and dividing France into groups of royalists, militarists, Catholics on one side, and republicans, socialists, anti-clerics on the other. Dreyfus, a Jew, was

imprisoned on Devils Isl.; pardoned (1899) after long struggle by supporters, incl. Zola, to show evidence against him was based on forgery. Affair discredited monarchists and army, united left wing.

drift, in geomorphology, transported material deposited during glaciation of a region. Consists of clay, sand, gravel, boulders. Fluvio-glacial drift is laid down by water run-off from glacier's edge; BOULDER CLAY is laid down directly from ice.

drill, *see* MANDRILL.

Drin, river of Albania. Formed from union of Black and White Drin; flows 282 km (175 mi) to Adriatic. Not navigable.

Drinkwater, John (1882-1937), English poet, dramatist. Wrote poems, *eg Poems of Men and Hours* (1911), verse plays *Mary Stuart* (1921), *Oliver Cromwell* (1921).

drive, in psychology, *see* LIBIDO.

Drogheda, town of Co. Louth, NE Irish Republic, on R. Boyne. Pop. 20,000. Exports cattle; linen, cotton mfg. Captured (1649) by Cromwell, massacre followed.

dromedary, *see* CAMEL.

drongo, any of Dicruridae family of insectivorous birds, with black iridescent plumage, arched bill. Commonest in S Asia, also found in Australia, Africa. Species incl. king crow, *Dicrurus macrocerus,* of India.

dropsy, *see* OEDEMA.

drosophila, any of genus *Drosophila* of fruit flies. Subject of much genetic research because of short life cycle.

Droste-Hülshoff, Annette von (1797-1848), German poet. Wrote nature and religious poetry, *eg The Spiritual Year* (1851), ironic novella *The Jews' Beech Tree* (1842).

drugs, chemical substances taken for prevention or alleviation of disease. Types in use incl. antibiotics, sulphonamides, barbiturates, amphetamines. Name also applies to habit-forming narcotics, *eg* heroin, opium.

Druids, ancient religious body of priests, soothsayers, poets in Celtic Gaul and Britain. Taught immortality of soul; held oak and mistletoe sacred. Important in education of young; exercised political power through federation extending across tribal divisions. Druidism declined in Gaul by 1st cent. and soon after in Britain. Prehist. remains, *eg* Stonehenge, once attributed to Druids.

drum, percussion instrument; consists of a skin stretched over a hollow cylinder, which resonates when the skin is struck. Timpani or kettledrums produce notes of definite pitch and can be tuned, but other drums are of indefinite pitch.

drumlin, elongated, oval ridge consisting of BOULDER CLAY. Formed by deposition and moulding of material by ice-sheet flowing over area. Aligned parallel to direction of ice flow. Commonly occurs in swarms, *eg* Down, Northern Ireland and Wisconsin, US.

Drummond, William Henry (1854-1907), Canadian poet, b. Ireland. Known for poems in French-Canadian dialect on rural Québec life.

Drummond of Hawthornden, William (1585-1649), Scottish poet. Wrote melancholic sonnets, prose work *The Cypress Grove, or Philosophical Reflections against the Fear of Death* (1630).

Drury Lane, street in London, site of several theatres. First built in 1663, destroyed by fire (1672). Present theatre dates from 1812.

Druses, secret religious sect in S Syria and Lebanon. Basically Moslem, but believe in the divinity of the Caliph Hakim (11th cent.). Fiercely resisted Ottoman rule. Perpetrated several massacres of Christians, esp. in 1860s.

Dryads, in Greek myth, NYMPHS who lived in trees. Died together with trees which had been their home.

dry cell, *see* CELL, VOLTAIC.

Dryden, John (1631-1700), English poet. Literary arbiter of Restoration. Known for *Absalom and Achitophel* (1681) written in heroic couplets, plays esp. *All for Love* (1678), prose criticism, translations of Vergil. Poet laureate (1668-89).

dry farming, system of farming without irrigation in an almost rainless region. Involves conserving natural moisture in soil and planting drought-resistant crops. Widely used in arid regions of, *eg* US, USSR, India.

drypoint, method of engraving by drawing on metal printing plate with sharp hard needle. Quality of drypoint lies in 'burr' of metal shavings turned up at side of furrow made by needle; ink collects in burr and gives richness to the print. Technique was used by Dürer, Whistler, Rembrandt.

dry rot, fungous disease of seasoned timber resulting in its softening and eventual crumbling to powder; often occurs in humid unventilated conditions. Prevented by application of creosote or fungicides.

Drysdale, George Russell (1912-), Australian artist. Known for his paintings of the harsh Australian outback and loneliness and isolation of its people.

Dual Monarchy, see AUSTRO-HUNGARIAN MONARCHY.

Dubai, seaport of Dubai sheikdom, United Arab Emirates, on Persian Gulf. Pop. 70,000.

Du Barry, Marie Jeanne Bécu, Comtesse (1743-93), French courtesan. Last of Louis XV's mistresses, extravagant but not politically ambitious. Banished from court at his death (1774). Guillotined in the Revolution.

Dubček, Alexander (1921-), Czechoslovakian political leader. First secretary of Communist Party (1968-9), chief figure in 'liberalizing' movement in Czech politics, soon crushed by Soviet military intervention (1968). Later deprived of political office, succeeded by pro-Soviet govt. under Gustav Husák (1969).

Du Bellay, Joachim (1522-60), French poet. Formulated doctrine of PLEIADE in *Défense et Illustration de la Langue Française* (1549). Advocated return to classical standards in poetry. Associate of Ronsard.

Dublin, county of Leinster prov., E Irish Republic. Area 922 sq km (356 sq mi); pop. 850,000; co. town DUBLIN. Mountainous in S; elsewhere lowland. Agric., livestock.

Dublin (*Baile Atha Cliath*), cap. of Irish Republic, co. town of Dublin, on R. Liffey and Irish Sea. Pop. 566,000. Admin. and commercial centre, seaport; brewing, distilling, textile mfg. Trinity Coll. (1591), Univ. Coll. Has RC pro-cathedral, 2 Protestant cathedrals, Abbey Theatre (1904). Hist. focus of Irish political unrest, culminated in Easter Rising (1916).

Dubna, town of USSR, C European RSFSR. Pop. 44,000. Founded 1956 as seat of Joint Institute of Nuclear Research whose members incl. most Communist nations.

Du Bois, William Edward Burghardt (1868-1963), American writer, civil rights leader. Works, incl. *Souls of Black Folk* (1903), *Black Reconstruction* (1935), claimed immediate equality for US Blacks. Died in Ghana.

Dubrovnik (Ital. *Ragusa*), town of Dalmatia, SE Yugoslavia, on Adriatic Sea. Pop. 23,000. Port, resort. Founded 7th cent. by Greeks; rich medieval republic rivalling Venice until 16th cent. Cathedral (17th cent.), ancient walls.

Du Cange, Charles du Fresne, Sieur (1610-88), French scholar. Compiled *Glossarium mediae et infimae Latinitatis,* biggest collection of early medieval Latin and ancient Romance word forms.

Duccio di Buoninsegna (*fl* 1278-1318), Italian painter. Leading painter of Siena, he is known for his mastery of linear design and narrative skill. Masterpiece is altarpiece for Siena Cathedral (1308-11).

Duchamp, Marcel (1887-1968), French painter. Pioneer of the DADA group, he is known for his 'ready-mades', *eg* bottle rack, mounted bicycle wheel. Most famous work is *Nude Descending a Staircase,* which combines cubism and futurism.

duck, aquatic bird of Anatidae family with webbed feet, long neck and long flat bill. Plumage waterproofed by oil from gland near tail.

duckbilled platypus, *Ornithorhynchus anatinus,* semi-aquatic, egg-laying mammal of Australia, Tasmania. Thick fur, webbed feet, duck-like bill; poison spur on heel. Most reptile-like of mammals.

ductless glands, see ENDOCRINE GLANDS.

Dudintsev, Vladimir Dmitryevich (1918-), Russian novelist. Created sensation with *Not by Bread Alone* (1956)

A diving duck, the scaup

Duckbilled platypus

attacking Soviet bureaucracy. Exonerated by Khrushchev (1959).

Dudley, John, see NORTHUMBERLAND, JOHN DUDLEY, DUKE OF.

Dudley, Robert, see LEICESTER, ROBERT DUDLEY, EARL OF.

Dudley, co. bor. of West Midlands met. county, WC England. Pop. 186,000. Wrought iron indust.; metal goods.

duel, combat with swords or pistols, arranged by challenge and fought under conventional rules, usually to resolve personal quarrel or decide point of honour. Duelling is illegal in most countries and killing an opponent considered murder.

due process of law, in law, principle protecting individuals from state power. Common to modern democratic states, demands that no one may be deprived of life, liberty, property except by estab. practices of law. In US, guaranteed by 14th Amendment.

Duero, see DOURO.

Dufay, Guillaume (*c* 1400-74), Flemish composer. Travelled widely, serving in papal choir (1428-33, 1435-7) and at court of Burgundy. Leading composer of *chansons* and church music; works incl. Mass based on his song 'Se la face ay pale'.

Dufy, Raoul (1877-1953), French artist. Influenced by fauvism, he adopted style of simplified form and bright colour. Later work marked by calligraphic style and brilliant colour; also designed textiles.

dugong, *Dugong dugon,* whale-like herbivorous mammal of Red Sea and Indian Ocean. Brownish or greyish, reaches lengths of *c* 3 m/10 ft. Slow-moving and defenceless; much hunted, now rare. Also called sea cow.

Duhamel, Georges (1884-1966), French author. Leader of ABBAYE. Subsequently wrote plays, *eg The Light* (1911), novel cycles *Salavin* (1920-32), *Pasquier Chronicles* (1933-45), and essay *The Heart's Domain* (1919) urging cultivation of inner life.

duiker, any of several small antelopes of African bush S of Sahara. Species incl. common grey duiker, *Sylvicapra grimmia,* with short horns on both sexes.

Duisburg, city of W West Germany, at confluence of Rhine and Ruhr. Pop. 449,000. Major port; steel, engineering, textile industs. Member of Hanseatic League. Heavy bombing in WWII.

Dukas, Paul (1865-1935), French composer. Best known for scherzo *The Sorcerer's Apprentice* (1897), opera *Ariane et Barbe-Bleue*.

Dufy: *Pier at Deauville*

Dukhobors or **Doukhobors,** Russian religious sect widespread 17th-19th cent., officially called Christians of the Universal Brotherhood. Believed in complete equality of man, denied authority of state and church. Persecuted, they emigrated (1890s) and settled in W Canada. Clashes with govt. and neighbours over social unorthodoxies of sect have continued.

dulcimer, a musical instrument in which strings stretched over a wooden frame are struck by mallets held in the hands. Originated in East in medieval times, lives on in E European folk music.

Dulles, John Foster (1888-1959), American statesman. Eisenhower's secretary of state (1953-9), pursued foreign policy based on collective security of US and Allies and development of nuclear weapons to retaliate in event of attack. His brother, **Allen Welsh Dulles** (1893-1969), was director of Central Intelligence Agency (1953-61).

Dulong, Pierre Louis (1785-1838), French scientist. Discovered explosive nitrogen trichloride. With A.T. Petit, formulated Dulong-Petit law: product of specific heat and atomic weight is approximately same for all solid elements.

dulse, *Rhodymenia palmata,* edible seaweed. Solitary or tufted red fronds grow on rocks, shellfish or other seaweeds.

Duluth, indust. town and port of NE Minnesota; at W end of L. Superior. Pop. 101,000. Shipping route esp. iron ore, coal, grain. Flour milling, sawmilling industs.

duma, Russian house of representatives, granted by Nicholas II after Revolution of 1905. Legislative powers restricted by tsar's prerogative. Last duma (1912-17) ended by March revolution.

Dumas, Alexandre, (père) (1802-70), French author. Known for *c* 300 vols. of swashbuckling romance, esp. *The Three Musketeers* (1844), *Count of Monte Cristo* (1845), plays, *eg La Tour de Nesle* (1832). His son, **Alexandre Dumas (fils)** (1824-95) known for plays esp. *La Dame aux Camélias* (1852), basis of Verdi's opera *La Traviata,* film *Camille.*

Du Maurier, George Louis Palmella Busson (1834-96), English novelist, illustrator, b. Paris. Remembered for cartoons in *Punch,* novels *Peter Ibbetson* (1892), *Trilby* (1894). His granddaughter, **Daphne Du Maurier** (1907-),

known for romantic novels often set in Cornwall, *eg Jamaica Inn* (1936).

Dumbarton, town of Strathclyde region, W Scotland, on R. Clyde. Pop. 26,000. Former royal burgh and co. town of Dunbartonshire. Shipbuilding, engineering industs.; whisky distilling. Cap. of ancient Strathclyde kingdom.

Dumfries and Galloway, region of SW Scotland. Area 6369 sq km (2459 sq mi); pop. 144,000. Created 1975, incl. former Dumfriesshire, Kirkcudbrightshire, Wigtownshire.

Dumfriesshire, former county of S Scotland. Southern Uplands in N; plain of R. Solway in S; Annan, Nith valleys run N-S. Sheep, cattle rearing, root crops; coalmining. Co. town was **Dumfries,** former royal burgh on R. Nith. Pop. 29,000. Tweed mfg. Old Bridge (1280); Burns' Mausoleum (1815).

Dumouriez, Charles François du Périer (1739-1823), French general. Commanded French Revolutionary forces against Austria at Jemappes (1792). Intrigued with and deserted to Austrians (1793). Settled in England (1800).

Dunant, Jean Henri (1828-1910), Swiss philanthropist. Horrified by experience of tending wounded at battle of Solferino, promoted estab. of International Red Cross (1863). Shared 1st Nobel Peace Prize (1901).

Dunbar, William (*c* 1460-*c* 1520), Scottish poet. Influenced by Chaucer and Scottish traditions, but with vigorous personal voice expressed in technically innovative verse. Poems incl. 'Lament for the Makaris'.

Dunbar, town of Lothian region, E Scotland. Pop. 5000. Fishing port, resort. Scene of battle (1650) in which Cromwell defeated Scots.

Dunbartonshire, former county of W Scotland, now in Strathclyde region. Mountainous in N; incl. Loch Lomond (tourism); industs. along Clyde estuary and Vale of Leven, incl. shipbuilding, bleaching, dyeing.

Duncan, Isadora (1878-1927), American dancer. Toured Europe, US, performing own concept of dance, inspired by ancient Greek art, with long loose robes and bare feet, free and expressive movements.

Dundalk, co. town of Louth, E Irish Republic, on Dundalk Bay. Pop. 22,000. Exports agric. produce. Railway engineering; linen, hosiery mfg.

Dundee, John Graham of Claverhouse, 1st Viscount (*c* 1649-89), Scottish nobleman, known as 'Bonnie Dundee'. Hated by Covenanters, whom he attempted to suppress (1678-88), earning name 'Bloody Clavers'. Raised force to restore James II, killed in victory of Jacobites at Killiecrankie.

Dundee, city of Tayside region, E Scotland, on Firth of Tay. Pop. 182,000. Seaport; jute indust., clocks, cash registers, confectionery mfg., publishing. Bridges (railway 1888, road 1966).

Dundonald, Thomas Cochrane, 10th Earl of (1775-1860), British naval officer. After a successful early career against the French, was dismissed from the navy and imprisoned for fraud. Served Chile, Brazil, and Greece in wars of independence until reinstated in 1832.

Dunedin, city of SE South Isl., New Zealand, on Otago Harbour. Pop. 82,000. Port, exports wool, meat; engineering, woollen mills. Founded 1848 by Scottish settlers; grew rapidly in 1861 gold rush. Has Anglican, RC cathedrals; Univ. of Otago (1869).

Dunfermline, town of Fife, E Scotland. Pop. 50,000. Silk, rayon mfg.; engineering. Has palace of Scottish kings; royal tombs in 11th cent. abbey. Park, library donated by Carnegie, born here.

Dungannon, town of C Northern Ireland. Pop. 8000. In former Co. Tyrone. Hist. seat of O'Neills. **Dungannon,** district; area 780 sq km (301 sq mi); pop. 42,000. Created 1973, formerly part of Co. Tyrone.

dung beetle, insect of scarab beetle family that rolls ball of dung in which to lay eggs and provide food for larvae. Important agent in disposal of animal dung.

Dunkirk (*Dunkerque*), town of Nord, N France, on Str. of Dover. Pop. 28,000. Port, shipbuilding, major iron and steel indust. Under English rule (1658-62). Scene of evacuation (1940) of *c* 300,000 Allied troops.

Dún Laoghaire, bor. of Co. Dublin, E Irish Republic, on Dublin Bay. Pop. 53,000. Resort; port, ferry service to Holyhead (Wales). Formerly called Kingstown.

Dunlop, John Boyd (1840-1921), Scottish veterinary surgeon. Patented (1888) Dunlop version of pneumatic tyre, producing it commercially in Belfast.

Dunne, John William (1875-1949), English philosopher. Posited theory of time (serialism) to account for telepathic phenomena, arguing that all time exists simultaneously. Works incl. *An experiment with Time* (1927), *The New Immortality* (1938).

Dunois, Jean, Comte de (c 1403-68), French soldier, called the 'Bastard of Orléans'. Commanded besieged forces at Orléans until relieved (1429) by Joan of Arc, whom he aided in ensuing campaign against English.

Dunoon, town of Strathclyde region, W Scotland, on Firth of Clyde. Pop. 10,000. Resort; nearby is US nuclear submarine base at Holy Loch.

Duns, town of Borders region, SE Scotland. Pop. 2000. Former co. town of Berwickshire.

Dunsany, Lord Edward John Moreton Drax Plunkett (1878-1957), Irish author. Known for short stories, *eg* in *The Gods of Pagana* (1905), plays *The Glittering Gate* (1909) produced by Yeats at Abbey Theatre.

Duns Scotus, John (c 1265-1308), Scottish philosopher. A Franciscan, opposed nominalism of Aquinas. Challenged harmony of reason and faith by showing limits of human reason. Known as 'Doctor Subtilis'.

Dunstable, John (d. 1453), English composer. Travelled abroad in service of English regent of France. Compositions, mainly for the Church, influenced composers of Burgundian school, *eg* Dufay. Works incl. song 'O rosa bella'.

Dunstable, mun. bor. of Bedfordshire, S England. Pop. 32,000. Printing, engineering industs., motor vehicles. Whipsnade Zoo nearby. On Watling St.

Dunstan, St (c 924-88), English prelate, statesman. Became abbot of Glastonbury, where he began revival of regularized monasticism in England. As archbishop of Canterbury from 961, drew up national code for monasteries based on Benedictine rule. Principal adviser to all contemporary Wessex kings, virtual ruler of England under Edred and Edgar.

Dupleix, Joseph François (1697-1763), French colonial administrator. Governor of French possessions in India (1742-54), planned to estab. French supremacy through military and political measures. Initially successful until thwarted by CLIVE. Recall to France marked collapse of French colonial ambitions in India.

Du Pont, Eleuthère Irénée (1772-1834), American chemicals manufacturer, b. France. Founded (1802) powder mill near Wilmington, Delaware, expanding Du Pont firm into one of largest explosives makers. Firm developed numerous chemical manufactures, incl. nylon, and acquired other industs. under **Pierre Samuel Du Pont** (1870-1954), long-time president of business.

Durango, town of NC Mexico, cap. of Durango state; alt. 1980 m (c 6500 ft). Pop. 193,000. In rich mining region producing silver, gold, iron ore, copper; iron ore foundries, textile, glass mfg. Founded 1563.

Duras, Marguerite (1914-), French novelist. Works incl. *Sea Wall* (1950), film scenario *Hiroshima mon amour* (1959).

Durazzo (*Durrës*), town of W Albania, on Adriatic. Pop. 53,000. Country's main seaport, exports olive oil, tobacco. Founded 7th cent. BC; important Roman port (*Dyrrachium*).

Durban, city of Natal, South Africa, on Indian Ocean. Pop. 721,000, incl. large Asian community. Major port, exports minerals, grain, fruit; indust. centre, resort. Has part of Univ. of Natal (1909). Founded 1835. Scene of African-Indian riots (1949).

Dürer, Albrecht (1471-1528), German artist. Prolific master of woodcuts, copper engravings and drawings; following visits to Italy, he was largely instrumental in introducing discoveries of Italian Renaissance into North. Works incl. series of woodcuts for *Apocalypse,*

Drawing of a hare by Dürer

watercolours of alpine scenery; few paintings incl. *Four Apostles.* Influenced by writings of Luther.

Durham, John George Lambton, 1st Earl of (1792-1840), British statesman. Promoted liberal measures, *eg* 1832 Reform Bill, earning nickname 'Radical Jack'. Governor-general of Canada, prepared *Report on the Affairs of British North America* (1839) advocating responsible self-govt.

Durham, county of NE England. Area 2435 sq km (940 sq mi); pop. 608,000. Pennines in W (sheep), fertile valleys; coastal plain in E, coalfield. Coalmining, iron and steel, shipbuilding industs., chemicals mfg. Co. town **Durham,** city on R. Wear. Pop. 25,000. Castle (1072) now site of univ. (1832). Cathedral (1093) has Bede's remains.

Durham, town of NC North Carolina, US. Pop. 95,000. Tobacco market, cigarette mfg. Seat of Duke Univ. (1924).

Durkheim, Emile (1858-1917), French sociologist. Stressed importance of collective mind of society in creating personal morality, with loss of social controls leading to deep unhappiness (*anomie*). Works incl. *Suicide* (1897), *The Elementary Forms of Religious Life* (1912).

Durrell, Lawrence George (1912-), English author, b. India. Best known for 'The Alexandria Quartet' of *Justine* (1957), *Balthazar* (1958), *Mountolive* (1958), *Clea* (1960), using multiple viewpoints. Also wrote poetry celebrating Mediterranean.

Dürrenmatt, Friedrich (1921-), Swiss playwright. Known for ironic tragicomedies *The Marriage of Mr Mississippi* (1952), *The Visit of the Old Lady* (1956). Stage technique similar to Brecht's in disruption of illusion.

Durrës, see DURAZZO, Albania.

Duse, Eleonora (1859-1924), Italian actress. Known for tragic roles, *eg* Hedda Gabler, Magda in *The Seagull*. Appeared in Europe, America. Had intimate relationship with D'Annunzio.

Dushanbe, city of USSR, cap. of Tadzhik SSR. Pop. 400,000. Cotton and silk mfg.; meat packing. Called Stalinabad (1929-61).

Düsseldorf, city of W West Germany, on R. Rhine, cap. of North Rhine-Westphalia. Pop. 650,000. Has international airport. Iron, steel, vehicles, textiles mfg. Cultural centre, art academy (18th cent.). Chartered 1288, residence (14th-16th cent.) of dukes of Berg.

dust bowl, area where exposed top soil is raised by strong winds into dust storms and blown away. Occurs after removal of protective vegetation cover by ploughing. Term applied in particular to W prairies of US, severely affected in late 1930s.

Dutch, language of W Germanic group of Indo-European family. Written and spoken language diverge greatly, since former developed from sophisticated Flemish of 15th cent. Flanders, Brabant, latter from vernacular of Holland.

Dutch East Indies, see INDONESIA.

Dutch elm disease, virulent and widespread disease of elms caused by a fungus, *Ceratocystis ulmi,* carried by the AMBROSIA BEETLE. Produces wilting and drying of the leaves and ultimately death of the tree. First appeared in Netherlands.

Dutch Guiana, see SURINAM.

Dutchman's-pipe, *Aristolochia durior,* woody climbing vine native to E US. Yellow-brown flowers have shape of tobacco pipe.

Dutch Reformed Church, see REFORMED CHURCH IN AMERICA.

Dutch Wars, three naval wars, arising from commercial rivalry, fought between England and Netherlands. First war (1652-4) was precipitated by seizure of Dutch merchant fleet and passage of Navigation Act (1651). English blockaded Dutch coast, defeated fleet under Tromp (1653). Second conflict (1664-7) sparked by continued threat to English sea power and trade. English raided Dutch colonies in Africa and North America. Dutch inflicted heavy losses on English fleet in raid on Thames (1667). Settlement of Treaty of Breda incl. favourable change in trade laws for Dutch. Third war (1672-4) formed part of Louis XIV's campaign against Netherlands (1672-8). England allied with France by terms of Treaty of Dover (1670); made peace 1674.

Duvalier, François ('Papa Doc') (1907-71), dictator of Haiti (1957-71). Estab. dictatorship after becoming president (1957); used personal police force (Tonton Macoutes) to enforce brutal repression of opponents. Succeeded by his son, Jean-Claude Duvalier (1951-   ), as president for life.

Duveen, Joseph, 1st Baron Duveen of Millbank (1869-1939), English art dealer. Instrumental in formation of art collections of many wealthy Americans. Benefactor of National Gallery and Tate Gallery, London.

Dvina, two rivers of W USSR. **Northern Dvina** flows *c* 750 km (470 mi) NW through N European RSFSR to Dvina Bay at Archangel. **Western Dvina** flows *c* 1020 km (640 mi) from Valdai Hills to Gulf of Riga in Latvian SSR.

Dvořák, Antonin (1841-1904), Czech composer. Encouraged by Brahms, much of his work was influenced by Czech folksong. Taught in America (1892-5). Compositions incl. 9 symphonies (best known is 9th, *From the New World),* string quartets, choral works.

dwarf, in plants and animals, term applied to specimens which do not attain normal height. In humans, dwarfism may result from deficiency of pituitary hormone or from achondroplasia, hereditary disorder resulting in defective growth of limbs.

Dyak, non-Moslem peoples of Borneo. Divided into Sea Dyaks of coasts and rivers, and Land Dyaks of interior. Fishers, hunters (with poison darts) hardly influenced by modern civilization, retaining stringent taboos and custom of head hunting. Society organized around 'long houses' which contain whole village.

dyestuffs, materials used to impart colour to textiles or other substances. Originally obtained from natural materials, *eg* plant roots, best known being indigo and

Antonin Dvořák

alizarin. Synthetic dyes manufactured from distillation products of coal tar and known as aniline colours.

Dyfed, county of SW Wales. Area 5765 sq km (2226 sq mi); pop. 319,000; co. town Carmarthen. Created 1974, incl. former Pembrokeshire, Cardiganshire, Carmarthenshire.

Dylan, Bob, orig. Robert Zimmerman (1941-   ), American singer, composer. Leading exponent in 1960s of 'folk rock' fusing folk and rock idioms, *eg Highway 61 Revisited.* Songs, often social commentaries, influenced many young singers and musicians.

dynamics, branch of physics dealing with the motion of bodies under the action of given forces. Also *see* STATICS.

dynamite, powerful explosive discovered by Alfred Nobel (1866). Consists of NITROGLYCERINE absorbed in porous substance, *eg* kieselguhr or wood pulp; varying amounts of ammonium or sodium nitrate added. Activated by detonator.

dynamo, device for converting mechanical energy into electrical energy. Simplest type consists of powerful magnet between whose poles an armature (laminated iron core with wire wound around it) is rotated. *See* ELECTROMAGNETIC INDUCTION.

dyne, unit of force in C.G.S. SYSTEM; 1 dyne acting on mass of 1 gram will produce acceleration of $1 \, cm/sec^2$.

dysentery, any of various intestinal inflammations, characterized by intense diarrhoea, usually accompanied by blood and mucus. Amoebic dysentery is caused by parasitic protozoon *Entamoeba histolytica*; bacterial by a bacillus of *Shigella* group.

Dyson, Sir Frank Watson (1868-1939), English astronomer. Director of Greenwich Observatory (1910-33). Studied stellar motions and solar eclipses. Inaugurated radio transmission of Greenwich time.

dysprosium (Dy), soft metallic element of lanthanide group; at. no. 66, at. wt. 162.5. Discovered (1886) by Lecoq de Boisbaudran.

Dzhambul, city of USSR, SC Kazakh SSR. Pop. 205,000. Food processing, chemical mfg. Founded in 7th cent., passed to Russia 1864.

Dzungaria, region of Sinkiang prov., NW China. Area *c* 777,000 sq km (300,000 sq mi). Semi-desert plateau; agric. where irrigated. Oilfields, mineral deposits.

E

Ea, water god of Sumerian origin. Benefactor of mankind in Babylonian creation myth. Also god of purity, wisdom.

eagle, carnivorous bird of Accipitridae family with long talons, feathered neck and head. Powerful flier, with keen eyesight; usually nests in inaccessible places (cliffs, mountains).

eagle ray, any of Myliobatidae family of large, flat cartilaginous fish. Long whip-like tail, large wing-like pectoral fins. Species incl. *Myliobatus aquila* of Mediterranean and African coasts.

Ealing, bor. of W Greater London, England. Pop. 299,000. Created 1965 from Ealing, Acton, Southall mun. bors. (all formerly in Middlesex).

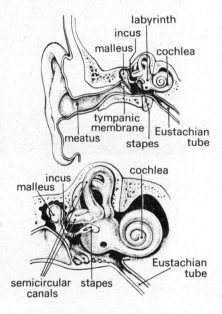

Structure of human ear; lower diagram shows inner ear in more detail

ear, organ of hearing. Human ear consists of: external ear and auditory canal, ending at ear drum; middle ear, cavity containing 3 small bones which communicate vibrations of ear drum to inner ear, a labyrinthine structure in temporal bone; cochlea, containing auditory nerve endings, and 3 fluid-containing semicircular canals, important for balance, are found in inner ear.

Earhart, Amelia (1897-1937), American aviator. First woman to make solo flight of Atlantic (1932). Lost in Pacific during attempt to fly around the world.

Early English, name given to first period of English Gothic architecture (13th cent.). Characterized by pointed arches, long narrow windows without mullions. Salisbury Cathedral exemplifies the style.

Earth, the, fifth largest planet of solar system, third in distance from Sun; mean distance from Sun *c* 150,000,000 km (93,000,000 mi). Revolves in elliptical orbit about Sun, taking 365¼ days to complete orbit, its inclination producing change of seasons. Earth is slightly flattened at poles; equatorial radius *c* 6378 km (3963 mi), polar radius *c* 6357 km (3950 mi). Believed to have central core of iron and nickel, surrounded by mantle of silicate rocks which support thin outer crust.

earthquake, shaking or trembling of the Earth's crust originating naturally below the surface. Consists of series of shock waves generated at focus or foci, which may cause changes in level, cracking or distortion of surface. Often accompanied by volcanic activity, landslides, giant sea waves (*tsunamis*). Associated with younger fold-mountain regions of Earth, esp. fault lines; prob. the result of stresses caused by movement of crustal plates (*see* PLATE TECTONICS). Severity measured by various scales, *eg* Richter, Mercalli. Main zones of activity: (1) Pacific area incl. W coast of America, Alaska, Japan, Philippines, New Zealand; (2) S Europe, NE Africa, Iran, Himalayas, East Indies; (3) mid-oceanic ridges. Recent severe earthquakes incl. Skopje, Yugoslavia (1963), Managua, Nicaragua (1972), Tangshan, China (1976).

earthworm, any of number of round, segmented worms that burrow in soil, class Oligochaeta. Common species of N hemisphere is *Lumbricus terrestris,* important for aerating and fertilizing soil. Giant earthworm of Australia, *Megascolides australis,* reaches lengths of 3.3 m/11 ft.

earwig, any of Dermaptera order of widely distributed insects. Short stiff forewings, conspicuous forceps at end of abdomen; omnivorous. European earwig, *Forficula auricularia,* introduced into America, Australia.

easement, in law, right or privilege that a person may have in another's land. Most usual example is right of way; others incl. bringing water over land, drainage, prevention of building on the land to exclude neighbour's light.

East Anglia, E England. Rich agric. area incl. Norfolk, Suffolk; flat, artificially drained. Crops incl. wheat, barley, sugar beet. Ancient kingdom (6th cent.) of Angles. Earldom from 10th cent.

East Bengal, *see* BENGAL.

Eastbourne, co. bor. of East Sussex, S England. Pop. 70,000. Coastal resort.

East China Sea, arm of Pacific Ocean, bordering on China and extending from Taiwan to Japan.

Easter, annual Christian festival commemorating resurrection of Jesus. Instituted *c* AD 68, named after Anglo-Saxon goddess of spring. In the West, falls on 1st Sunday after full moon after vernal equinox, between 22nd March and 25th April. In Eastern Orthodox Church, calculated from Julian calendar.

Easter Island (Span. *Isla de Pascua*), pastoral isl. off Chile, in E Pacific. Area 199 sq km (46 sq mi); pop. 1600. Agric. incl. livestock rearing, tobacco, sugar cane growing. Has mysterious statues, undeciphered wooden tablets. Discovered 1722; annexed by Chile 1888.

Eastern Orthodox Church, collective name for independent Christian churches of E Europe and W Asia. Rejected authority of Roman See under Pope Leo IX in 1054. Originally made up of 4 patriarchates (Constantinople, Alexandria, Antioch, Jerusalem), now also incl. certain autonomous churches of USSR, Greece, Romania.

Easter Rebellion, uprising in Dublin (24-29 April, 1916) against British rule in Ireland. Forcibly suppressed, leaders executed. Hardened split between loyalist and nationalist factions.

East Germany, *see* GERMANY.

Stone statue on Easter Island

East India Company, English company chartered (1600) by Elizabeth I for trade with East. Activities largely confined to India after 1623, where it thrived on export of textiles. After Clive's victories over French rivals, became virtual ruler of India. Trade monopoly withdrawn by govt. acts of 1813, 1833. British govt. assumed direct control after Indian Mutiny (1858), company dissolved 1874.

East Indies, vague term which once referred to SE Asia, incl. India, Malay and Indo-Chinese archipelagos; later referred to Netherlands East Indies (now Indonesia).

East Kilbride, town of Strathclyde region, WC Scotland. Pop. 64,000. Created 'new town' in 1947. Aircraft equipment, electronics, printing industs.

East London, city of SE Cape Prov., South Africa, on Indian Ocean. Pop. 123,000. Port, exports grain, fruit; fishing; indust. centre, resort. Founded 1847, formerly called Port Rex.

East Lothian, former county of E Scotland, now in Lothian region. Formerly known as Haddingtonshire. Low-lying in N; Lammermuir Hills in S. Agric., mainly sheep rearing; coalmining. Coastal resorts incl. North Berwick. Co. town was Haddington.

Eastman, George (1854-1932), American inventor, founder of Eastman Kodak. Invented a dry-plate film process, Kodak camera, roll film and form of colour photography. Amassed large fortune from production of these; spent est. 100 million dollars on philanthropic projects.

East Pakistan, *see* BANGLADESH.

East Riding, *see* YORKSHIRE, England.

East Sussex, *see* SUSSEX, England.

Eastwood, Clint (1930-), American actor. After TV success, became famous in Italian 'spaghetti' westerns (esp. 'Dollars' series) as amoral gunfighter hero; later acted, directed in US, as in *Play Misty for Me* (1971).

eau de Cologne, perfume made from alcohol and aromatic oils. Believed to have been invented by F.M. Farina, who began production in Cologne *c* 1709.

Ebbw Vale, urban dist. of Gwent, SE Wales, on R. Ebbw. Pop. 26,000. Coalmining; iron, steel industs.

Ebert, Friedrich (1871-1925), German statesman. Social Democrat, headed provisional govt. after kaiser's abdication (1918). Elected 1st president of republic (1919),

put down Spartacist uprising (1919) and Kapp putsch (1920).

ebony, trees or shrubs of genus *Diospyros* of Ebenaceae family. Grows in tropical and subtropical climates. Black hardwood used for cabinet work is derived largely from *D. ebenum* of S India and Sri Lanka. *D. kaki* (E Asia) and *D. virginiana* (W US) are other well-known species with edible plum-like fruit known as persimmons.

Ebro, river of NE Spain. Flows *c* 925 km (575 mi) from Cantabrian Mts., N Spain, via Saragossa to Mediterranean Sea near Tortosa. Used for irrigation, h.e.p. Ancient *Iberus,* gave name to Iberian penin.

Eccles, Sir John Carew (1903-), Australian physiologist. Shared Nobel Prize for Physiology and Medicine (1963) for explaining communication in body's nervous system.

Ecclesiastes, book of OT, written (prob. 3rd cent. BC) by a man of high station in Jerusalem (formerly ascribed to Solomon). Finds philosophical consolation in futility of the world.

Ecclesiasticus or **The Wisdom of Jesus,** apocryphal book of OT written (*c* 200-175 BC) by Jesus, son of Sirach. Celebrates value of wisdom.

Echegaray [y Eizaguirre], José (1832-1916), Spanish dramatist, mathematician. Works deal with theme of melancholic passion *eg El Gran Galeoto* (1881). Awarded Nobel Prize for Literature (1904).

Echidna

echidna or **spiny anteater,** spiny-backed burrowing monotreme of Australasia. Long, toothless snout; extensile tongue used to catch ants, termites. Eggs hatched in pouch. Species incl. *Tachyglossus setosus* of Tasmania.

Echinodermata (echinoderms), phylum of marine invertebrates, incl. starfish, brittle star, sea urchin, sea lily, sea cucumber. Radially symmetric body, generally pentagonal in shape; calcareous exoskeleton of plates or spines.

Echinoidea (echinoids), *see* SEA URCHIN.

Echo, in Greek myth, mountain nymph whose speech Hera caused to be limited to the repetition of the last words of others. Wasted away through unrequited love for Narcissus until only voice left.

echo, in physics, repetition of sound by reflection of sound waves from a surface. Ships measure depth of water with an echo sounder which indicates time taken for sound pulse to echo off sea bed. *See* SONAR.

Eckhart, Johannes (*c* 1260-*c* 1328), German Dominican theologian, mystic; known as 'Meister'. Evolved popular mystical system with Aristotelian, scholastic elements. Theories condemned as heretical.

eclecticism, method or system of thought gathered from various doctrines. Differs from syncretism in that no attempt is made to resolve possible conflicts in the source doctrines, *eg* the medieval attempts to combine Christianity and Aristotelian philosophy.

eclipse, in astronomy, partial or complete obscuring of one celestial body by another as viewed from a fixed point. Solar eclipses occur when shadow of Moon falls on Earth; *c*

2 or 3 seen per year. Lunar eclipses occur when shadow of Earth falls on Moon; at most 2 seen per year.

ecology, interdisciplinary study of plants and animals in relation to their environment. Examines all sequences in development of these relationships up to final, stable or *climax* community. Term first used by Haeckel (1869).

econometrics, use of mathematical and statistical methods in field of economics to verify and develop economic theories, forecasting and planning.

economics, study of production, distribution and consumption of commodities. First attempts at analysis were by ancient Greeks, *eg* Plato (*Republic*) and Aristotle. Development of modern economics began with advocacy of LAISSER-FAIRE by physiocrats, and was elaborated by classical economists, *eg* Adam Smith (*Wealth of Nations*, 1776), Ricardo and J.S. Mill; founded on belief in inflexible natural laws governing exchange and production of goods. Challenged in 19th cent. by socialists, esp. Karl Marx (*Das Kapital,* 1867), who believed in societal change on moral and social grounds as well as economic, and threw light on weaknesses of classical market economy such as crisis recurrence. Classical form re-estab. (1870s) and applied mathematically by Alfred Marshall. KEYNES' theories on planning and spending increased govt. interventionist role in West's national economies; resisted in 1970s by monetarists who believed in controlling money supply.

Ecuador, republic of NW South America, incl. offshore Galápagos Isls. Area 283,561 sq km (109,483 sq mi); pop. 6,600,000; cap. Quito, chief port Guayaquil. Language: Spanish. Religion: RC. Pacific coast plain rises to volcanic Andes. Bananas, coffee are main crops; subsistence agric. in mountains. Spanish colony from 16th cent.; part of viceroyalty of Peru until liberated 1822; independence 1830 at dissolution of Greater Columbia.

ecumenism, term for movement aimed at unification of Christian churches. Early attempts incl. the Evangelical Alliance (UK 1846, US 1867). World Council of Churches (1948) brought together more than 200 Protestant, Orthodox and Old Catholic churches. Since 2nd Vatican Council (1962), RC Church has been increasingly involved in quest for Christian unity.

eczema, see DERMATITIS.

Edam, town of NW Netherlands. Pop. 8000. Market for Edam cheese; earthenware mfg.

Edda, title given to two distinct Icelandic works in Old Norse. *Poetic* or *Elder Edda* (late 13th cent.) is a collection of 34 anon. mythological heroic lays, most valuable set of texts in OLD NORSE LITERATURE. *Prose* or *Younger Edda,* by SNORRI STURLUSON, sets down rules for scaldic poetry and gives account of Scandinavian mythology.

Eddington, Sir Arthur Stanley (1882-1944), English astronomer and physicist. Made theoretical study of structure of stars, predicting enormous temperatures in their interiors. Early exponent of theory of relativity and gravitation.

Eddy, Mary Baker (1821-1910), American religious leader. Founder and 1st pastor of Church of Christ, Scientist, in Boston. CHRISTIAN SCIENCE doctrine, inspired by belief in divine healing, formulated in her *Science and Health* (1875).

Eddystone Rocks, English Channel, group of rocks 23 km (14 mi) SSW of Plymouth. Site of several lighthouses from 1698.

edelweiss, *Leontopodium alpinum,* small perennial flowering plant of daisy family. Native to high mountains of Europe and C Asia. Dense woolly white flowers.

Eden, [Robert] Anthony, 1st Earl of Avon (1897-1977), British statesman, PM (1955-7). Conservative foreign secretary (1935-8), resigned over Chamberlain's 'appeasement' policy of Germany. Again foreign secretary (1940-5, 1951-5). Resigned as PM after SUEZ CRISIS.

Eden, Garden of, in OT, first home of man. Created by God as home for ADAM and Eve; contained trees of life and knowledge. They were banished after tasting the forbidden fruit of the tree of knowledge (Genesis 2 : 3).

Edelweiss

Edentata (edentates), order of primitive mammals without teeth or with only enamelless molars. Incl. sloths, anteaters, armadillos of South America.

Edessa (*Edhessa*), town of Macedonia, N Greece. Pop. 16,000. Agric. market, textiles. Ancient *Aegea*; earliest seat of Macedonian kings.

Edessa, see URFA.

Edgar (*c* 943-75), king of all England (959-75). Called the Peaceful, allowed Danes limited autonomy in Danelaw. Restored monasticism with Dunstan. Danish-English peace ended with his death.

Edgeworth, Maria (1767-1849), Irish novelist, b. England. Known for Irish regional novels of manners *eg Castle Rackrent* (1800), *Ormond* (1817). Influenced Scott.

Edinburgh, Philip [Mountbatten], Duke of (1921-), consort of Elizabeth II of Great Britain, b. Greece. Son of Prince George of Greece and Princess Alice, daughter of George I of Greece. Married Elizabeth in 1947.

Edinburgh, cap. city of Scotland, in Lothian region, on S side of Firth of Forth. Pop. 453,000. Admin., commercial centre; printing, publishing; brewing, distilling. Has univ. (1583). Seaport at Leith. Annual arts festival from 1947. Buildings incl. castle (with Norman chapel), St. Giles Church (12th cent.), Holyrood Palace (royal residence from time of James IV); Royal Scottish Academy; National Gallery. Georgian architecture (esp. Adam) in 18th-19th cent. New Town.

Edirne, town of Turkey, in Thrace; formerly Adrianople. Pop. 46,000. Silk, cotton mfg. Founded by Hadrian in AD 125; scene of decisive defeat of Romans by Visigoths (378). Twice fell to Russians in 19th cent.; taken by Turks in 1913. Has 16th cent. mosque of Sultan Selim II.

Edison, Thomas Alva (1847-1931), American inventor. Contributed to wireless telegraphy, telephony and generation of electricity. Invented phonograph (1878) and 1st practicable electric light. Developed 1st distribution system for electric lighting (built in New York, 1881-2). His companies, holding *c* 1300 patents, were consolidated as General Electric Company.

Edmonton, prov. cap. of Alberta, Canada; on N Saskatchewan R. Pop. 438,000. Transport, indust. centre in agric. and oil producing region; furs, oil refining, meat packing. Major airport. Has Univ. of Alberta (1906).

Edmund Ironside (d. 1016), king of England (1016). Led English opposition to Canute, coming to terms, after battle of Assandun, and partitioning England. Canute gained whole kingdom on Edmund's death.

Edrisi, see IDRISI.

education, process of training and developing knowledge, skill, mind, character, *etc,* esp. by formal schooling or study. Formal education began in Greece, with training in mathematics, music, Homer, philosophy. During Dark Ages, learning preserved by monks; became more general with estab. of monastic schools and univs. (11th-13th cents.). Education limited to clergy, nobility (training in chivalry), and future craftsmen. Renaissance brought widening of whom and what was taught, introducing classics to curriculum. After Reformation many more schools were estab. Important extension of popular education was a feature of late 19th cent. By late 20th cent., most countries in world provided universal, free education, often with private or religious organizations paralleling state-run schools. Also *see* COMPREHENSIVE EDUCATION.

Education Act (1944), legislation governing education in England and Wales; estab. Ministry of Education with centralized control and funding of state education. Divided school system into 2 levels, primary and secondary, making secondary education compulsory, and allowed for great expansion of education provided by state.

Edward I (1239-1307), king of England (1272-1307). Fought for father Henry III against rebel barons 1264-7, was chief agent in their defeat. Conquered Wales, but failed in long campaigns to subdue Scots. Noted for legal reforms, esp. Statutes of Westminster. His Model Parliament (1295) gave greater representation to barons, clergy, merchants, estab. their right to approve king's collection of taxes.

Edward II (1284-1327), king of England (1307-27). Continued father Edward I's attempts to subjugate Scotland, but defeated by Robert the Bruce (1314). Favours to Piers Gaveston led to barons' revolt, and alienated his wife, Isabella. Later favourites, the Despensers, were virtual rulers until Isabella and lover Mortimer invaded from France. They defeated, deposed and later murdered Edward, executed the Despensers.

Edward III (1312-77), king of England (1327-77). Son of Edward II, overthrew (1330) rule of his mother Isabella and her lover Mortimer, who had been regents. Reign dominated by Hundred Years War, beginning 1337, in which he and son Edward the Black Prince were prominent. Expenses of war allowed Parliament to win concessions from king by withholding money. Reign also marked by Black Death (1347), consequent social changes, and religious unrest, esp. through teachings of Wycliffe.

Edward VII when Prince of Wales

Edward IV (1442-83), king of England (1461-70, 1471-83). Son of Richard, duke of York, became king on defeat of Lancastrians at Mortimer's Cross. Fled to Holland after quarrel with Warwick, who briefly restored Henry VI. Recovered throne with victories at Barnet and Tewkesbury (1471).

Edward V (1470-83), king of England (1483). Son of Edward IV, imprisoned with brother Richard, duke of York, in the Tower of London by their uncle, Gloucester.

Gloucester took throne as Richard III when they were declared illegitimate; he is believed to have had them murdered.

Edward VI (1537-53), king of England (1547-53). Son of Henry VIII and Jane Seymour. Succeeded father under council of regents controlled by uncle, EDWARD SEYMOUR. Reign saw growth of Protestantism and introduction of Book of Common Prayer. Seymour was overthrown by NORTHUMBERLAND who gained right of succession for Lady JANE GREY, a Protestant.

Edward VII (1841-1910), king of Great Britain and Ireland (1901-10). Eldest son of Queen Victoria, known for his involvement in fashionable society, love affairs and sporting activities. Promoted Entente Cordiale with France.

Edward VIII (1894-1972), king of Great Britain and Ireland (1936). Son of George V, created prince of Wales (1910). Following opposition of Baldwin's cabinet, forced to abdicate to avoid constitutional crisis over proposed marriage to American divorcée, Wallis Warfield Simpson. Married her (1937) after becoming duke of Windsor.

Edward Nyanza or **Lake Edward,** lake on border of Uganda and Zaïre. Area 2150 sq km (830 sq mi); part of Great Rift Valley. Drained by R. Semliki into Albert Nyanza. Discovered 1889, named after Prince of Wales.

Edwards, Jonathan (1703-58), American theologian. Orthodox Calvinist preaching resulted in religious revival ('Great Awakening') in New England. Developed metaphysical defence of determinism in *The Freedom of the Will* (1754).

Edward the Black Prince (1330-76), eldest son of Edward III of England. Notable as protagonist in Hundred Years War, esp. in victory at Poitiers (1356) when he captured John II of France. Held large parts of France under father. Opposed brother, John of Gaunt, who held power at end of Edward's reign. Died before father, who was succeeded by Black Prince's son, Richard II.

Edward the Confessor (d. 1066), king of England (1042-66). Grew up in Normandy until he succeeded Harthacanute. Showed favours to Normans, thereby increasing strife with Earl Godwin of Wessex, whose son, Harold, he recognized as heir after Godwin and family returned from exile. During their exile, prob. promised William of Normandy succession. Succession crisis resolved by Norman Conquest.

Edward the Elder (d. 924), king of S Wessex (899-924). Son of Alfred, with whom he ruled and fought in wars with Danes. Extended kingdom to reach Humber.

Edwin (*c* 585-632), king of Northumbria. Seized throne (616) from Ethelfrith and extended kingdom over all of England except Kent. Converted to Christianity 627. Encouraged conversion of his people by Paulinus.

EEC, *see* EUROPEAN COMMUNITIES.

Common eel travelling overland

eel, any of order Anguilliformes of snake-like bony fish. Naked skin or minute scales; no pelvic fins. Species incl. common eel, *Anguilla anguilla,* born in Sargasso Sea; crosses Atlantic in larval state to mature in European rivers.

eel grass, *Zostera marina,* flowering plant of the pondweed family. Grows underwater with long grass-like leaves. Found in Europe and North America in shallow salt water.

Egbert (d. 839), king of Wessex (802-39). United most of England under his rule by 829 with his victories in Cornwall and Mercia and by forcing Kent and Northumbria to submit to him.

Eger (Ger. *Erlau*), town of N Hungary, on R. Eger. Pop. 44,000. Wine market. Medieval ecclesiastical centre, associated with St Stephen. Many churches, called 'Rome of Hungary'.

Egeria, in Roman religion, nymph of spring from which VESTAL VIRGINS drew water. Goddess of childbirth. Legendary lover and instructress of King Numa.

Egerton, Thomas, Baron Ellesmere (1540-1617), English statesman. Adviser to Elizabeth I. Testified against former friend Essex (1601). Lord chancellor (1603-17), supported James I's use of royal prerogative; obtained dismissal of his opponent, Sir THOMAS COKE.

egg, in biology, *see* OVUM.

eggplant, *see* AUBERGINE.

Egham, urban dist. of Surrey, S England. Pop. 31,000. Incl. RUNNYMEDE; has Holloway Coll. (1886).

eglantine, *see* BRIAR.

Egmont, Lamoral, Count of (1522-68), Flemish statesman. Supported overlord Philip II of Spain against France (1557-8). Stadholder of Flanders and Artois (1559-67), he protested against governorship of Netherlands by Cardinal Granvelle. Arrest and execution by duke of Alva aroused Netherlands to revolt, and was subject of Goethe's tragedy *Egmont,* for which Beethoven wrote overture, incidental music.

ego, in psychoanalysis, term used in narrow sense to denote that part of the personality which mediates between the ID, the SUPEREGO and the outside world.

Snowy egret *(Egretta thula)*

egret, slender heron-like wading bird with white plumage. Species incl. great white egret, *Egretta alba*, and little egret, *E. garzetta.*

Egypt

Egypt (*Misr*), republic of NE Africa. Area 1,001,000 sq km (386,500 sq mi); pop. 35,619,000; cap. Cairo, chief port Alexandria. Language: Arabic. Religion: Islam. Largely desert (incl. Eastern, Libyan), Qattara Depression in NW, Sinai penin. in NE. Pop. concentrated in fertile Nile valley (Upper Egypt), delta (Lower Egypt). Produces cotton, rice, cereals; petroleum, phosphates. Ancient Egypt ruled by 30 dynasties grouped into 3 'kingdoms' 3100-332 BC. Conquered by Alexander the Great; ruled successively by Ptolemys, Rome, Arabs, Mamelukes, Ottoman Turks. Home of early Christian leaders 1st-6th cent.; Islam introduced 7th cent. by Arabs. Dominated by British, French in 19th cent.; made British protect. (1914). Constitutional monarchy from 1923, sovereign state from 1936. Republic proclaimed 1953; formed United Arab Republic 1958 with Syria, Yemen, disintegrated 1961; called Arab Republic of Egypt after 1971. Has led 4 Arab wars against Israel (1948, 1956, 1967, 1973) without success, leaving most of Sinai penin. under Israeli occupation.

Egyptian, *see* COPTIC.

Ehrenburg, Ilya Grigoryevich (1891-1967), Russian author. Covered Spanish Civil War for Soviet papers (1936-7). Novel *The Thaw* (1954-6) gave name to post-Stalin relaxation.

Paul Ehrlich

Ehrlich, Paul (1854-1915), German bacteriologist. Discovered means of staining and identifying tuberculosis bacilli; also discovered drug arsphenamine, 1st effective treatment against syphilis. Shared Nobel Prize for Physiology and Medicine (1908) for theory of antibodies' role in immunity.

Eichendorff, Joseph, Freiherr von (1788-1857), German poet. Known for lyrical poetry celebrating Silesian countryside, much of it set to music by Schumann, Brahms. Friend of late romantics, incl. Brentano. Also wrote novels.

Eichmann, [Karl] Adolf (1902-62), German Nazi official. Chief of Gestapo's Jewish section (from 1939); promoted use of gas chambers. Escaped after WWII. Abducted (1960) from Argentina by Israeli agents, executed in Israel.

eider duck, *Somateria mollissima,* large sea duck of N regions. Eider down used for stuffing quilts, pillows.

Eiffel, Alexandre Gustave (1832-1923), French engineer. Built bridges and viaducts. Contributed to aerodynamics. Designed Eiffel Tower, 400 m (984 ft) high, built for 1889 Paris Exhibition.

Eiger, mountain of SC Switzerland, height 3973 m (13,042 ft). Notorious North Face, where many climbers have died.

Eight, The, *see* ASHCAN SCHOOL.

Eilat, port of S Israel, at head of Gulf of Aqaba. Pop. 12,800. Oil pipeline (opened 1957) bypasses Suez Canal. Biblical Elath.

Eindhoven, town of S Netherlands. Pop. 190,000. Rapid 20th cent. growth from radio, television indust.; also produces vehicles, plastics.

Einhorn, David (1809-79), American Jewish theologian, b. Bavaria. Leader of movement for reform in practice of Judaism. Campaigned against slavery during Civil War.

Einstein, Albert (1879-1955), American physicist, b. Germany. In 1905, enunciated special theory of relativity and gave theoretical explanation of Brownian motion and photoelectric effect. Published (1916) general theory of

Albert Einstein

RELATIVITY, a geometric theory of gravitation superseding that of Newton. Awarded Nobel Prize for Physics (1921). Attempted to find unified theory of gravitation and electromagnetism.

einsteinium (Es), transuranic element of actinide group; at. no. 99, mass no. of most stable isotope 254. Discovered (1952) in debris of thermonuclear explosion.

Eire, see IRELAND, REPUBLIC OF.

Eisenach, town of SW East Germany. Pop. 50,000. Rock salt mining; cars, chemicals. Wartburg castle on hilltop. Birthplace of J.S. Bach.

Eisenhower, Dwight David (1890-1969), American general and statesman, president (1953-61). During WWII, chief of Allied forces in N Africa (1942-3), supreme commander of Allied invasion of Europe (1944). Army chief of staff (1945-8); commanded NATO forces (1950-2). Elected Republican president, defeating Adlai Stevenson. Fostered anti-Communist alliances in SE Asia, Latin America.

Eisenstadt, town of E Austria, cap. of Burgenland prov. Pop. 10,000. Hist. home of Esterhazys.

Eisenstein, Sergei Mikhailovich (1898-1948), Russian film director. Outstanding in history of film, pioneering cinematic techniques, *eg* montage. Won fame with *Battleship Potemkin* (1925), later made impressive epics on Russian history, *eg Alexander Nevsky* (1938), *Ivan the Terrible* (1942-6).

Eisleben, town of W East Germany, near Harz Mts. Pop. 33,000. Copper mining from 13th cent.; textiles. Birthplace of Luther.

Eisteddfod, traditional Welsh festival for the encouragement of bardic arts, esp. music, poetry, by competition. Dates from before 12th cent. but discontinued 17th-19th cents. Now meets annually in August.

El-Aaiún, see SPANISH SAHARA.

eland, either of 2 large antelopes. Giant eland, *Taurotragus derbianus,* of C and S Africa, is largest species of antelope. Cape eland, *T. oryx,* found in grassland of S Africa.

elasticity, in physics, property in materials of returning to their original shape and dimensions after being deformed by external forces. Material is permanently distorted if applied forces exceed elastic limit.

Elath, see EILAT.

Elba, isl. of W Italy, separated from Tuscany by Str. of Piombino. Area 223 sq km (86 sq mi). Fishing, tourism; iron ore mining from Etruscan times. Principality (1814-15) under exiled Napoleon.

Elbe (Czech. *Labe*), river of C Europe. Flows 1167 km (725 mi) from NW Czechoslovakia via East and West Germany to North Sea at Hamburg. Navigable for *c* 800 km (500 mi); canal links with Rhine, Weser rivers.

Elba

Elberfeld, see WUPPERTAL, West Germany.

Elbert, Mount, peak of C Colorado, US; highest of US Rocky Mts. Height 4399 m (14,433 ft).

Elblag (Ger. *Elbing*), town of N Poland, on R. Elblag near Vistula Lagoon. Pop. 90,000. Port; shipbuilding, textile mfg. Founded 13th cent.; member of Hanseatic League. Polish from *c* 1460; under Prussian rule 1772-1945.

Elbrus or **Elbruz, Mount,** massif in Caucasus Mts., USSR, W Georgian SSR. Comprises 2 peaks of volcanic origin, one of which, at height of 5633 m (18,481 ft) is highest in Europe.

Elburz Mountains, mountain range in N Iran, running parallel to S Caspian Sea. Rise to 5771 m (18,934 ft) at Mt. Demavend. N slopes rainy and forested, S slopes arid.

Elche, city of Valencia, SE Spain. Pop. 123,000. Noted for date palms; also footwear mfg. Held by Moors 8th-13th cent.

Leaves, flowers and berries of elder (*Sambucus nigra*)

elder, any of genus *Sambucus* of deciduous bushy trees of honeysuckle family. Esp. *S. nigra,* common in Europe, with small, strong-smelling white flower and red or black berries, used to make wine.

Eldon, John Scott, 1st Earl of (1751-1838), English statesman. Tory lord chancellor (1801-6, 1807-27), often dominating cabinet. Introduced repressive legislation, opposing liberal reform, Catholic Emancipation.

Eleanor of Aquitaine (*c* 1122-1204), queen of Henry II of England. Married Henry after annulment of marriage to Louis VII of France. Her sons, Richard I, John, became kings of England. Estab. own court at Poitiers and aided sons in unsuccessful revolt (1173) against Henry. After many years' confinement by Henry, she helped Richard secure throne (1189).

Eleanor of Castile (d. 1290), queen of Edward I of England. Remembered for 12 crosses Edward reputedly erected to mark stages of her funeral procession, *eg* at Lincoln, St Albans, Charing Cross.

elecampane, *Inula helenium,* tall perennial plant of daisy family with toothed leaves and clusters of yellow flower heads.

election, selection of persons for office by vote. Used occasionally in ancient Greece, regularly in Rome to appoint tribunes. Elections regularized in England (1688) although Commons elected in some manner since 14th cent. SUFFRAGE extended by REFORM BILL (1832). Ballot Act (1872) introduced secret ballot. In UK, general (*ie* national) election always follows dissolution of Parliament, at least every 5 years. In US, elections take place every 2, 4, 6 years.

electoral college, in US politics, body of electors from each state with formal duty of choosing president and vice-president. Electors of each state, equal in number to its members in Congress, expected to vote for candidates selected by popular vote in state. President need not obtain majority of popular vote in country.

electors, number of princes within Holy Roman Empire who had theoretical right to elect head of empire; in reality, in all elections after 1438 except one, a Habsburg became emperor. In 1356 number set at 7, usually archbishops of Mainz, Trier, Cologne, king of Bohemia, duke of Saxony, margrave of Bradenburg and electors of the Palatinate. Dismissed on dissolution of Empire (1806).

Electra, in Greek myth, daughter of AGAMEMNON and Clytemnestra. Helped brother ORESTES avenge Agamemnon's death in tragedies of Aeschylus, Sophocles, Euripides.

Electra complex, *see* OEDIPUS COMPLEX.

electrical engineering, branch of ENGINEERING dealing with generation and transmission of electrical power and with the devices that use it. *See* ELECTRONICS.

electric eel, *Electrophorus electricus,* large eel-like fish of pools, streams of NE South America. Capable of generating shock of *c* 500 volts, which will kill other fish and severely injure man.

electric fish, one of various fish capable of generating electricity by muscular contraction. Uses shocks for navigation, defence or killing prey. Incl. electric eel, electric ray, stargazer.

electricity, general term for physical phenomena associated with electric CHARGE. Flow of electric charge in conductors constitutes electric current. Charge can be generated by friction, by chemical means (*eg* in a cell) or by electromagnetic induction.

electric light, light produced by electrical means. Electric light bulb contains inert gas (*eg* nitrogen) and wire filament; current passing through filament heats it to white heat. First practical form developed by Edison (1879).

electric motor, device for converting electrical energy into mechanical energy. Simplest type consists of current-carrying coil or armature placed between poles of powerful magnet; mechanical force acting on armature causes it to rotate.

electrocardiograph, instrument used to diagnose heart disorders by tracing changes in electric current and voltage produced by contractions of heart. Invented by Dutch physiologist Willem Einthoven (1860-1927) who was awarded Nobel Prize for Physiology and Medicine (1924).

electrochemistry, science dealing with effect of electrical energy on chemical reactions or with production of electrical energy by chemical means.

electrode, terminal by which electric current enters or leaves conducting substances, *eg* liquid in electrolytic cell or gas in electrical discharge tube. Positive electrode is the anode, negative is the cathode.

electroencephalograph, instrument used to record electrical activity of nerve cells in the brain. Used to diagnose brain disorders, esp. epilepsy. Recorded results called EEGs.

electrolysis, decomposition of chemical compound (electrolytes) by passage of electric current through compound in solution or in molten state. Electrolyte dissociates into positive and negative ions; ions move to electrodes of opposite charge and give up their charge. Technique used in electroplating of metals.

electromagnetic induction, production of electromotive force in a circuit by variation of a magnetic field. Effect observed independently by Faraday and Henry. Phenomenon forms basis of DYNAMO.

electromagnetic radiation, radiation propagated through space by variation in electric and magnetic fields. Such radiation consists of waves travelling at speed of light, nature of which depends on frequency. Incl. heat rays, radio waves, light, gamma rays and X-rays.

electromotive force, force of electric pressure that causes electric current to flow in circuits. Equivalent to difference in potential between points in circuit.

electron, elementary particle of matter which by convention carries one negative unit of charge. Electrons are constituents of atoms, assumed to move in orbits about the atomic nucleus; number of protons in nucleus equals number of circulating electrons. Movement of free (*ie* detached from their atomic orbit) electrons constitutes electric current.

electronic music, *see* MUSIC, ELECTRONIC.

electronics, branch of electrical engineering dealing with controlled movement of electrons through thermionic valves and semiconductors and with the devices that use them. Incl. technology of computers, radio circuitry, *etc.*

electron microscope, microscope using beam of electrons to obtain greatly enlarged images of objects. Electron beam passes through thin film of material under investigation and is focused by magnetic or electrostatic fields to form image on fluorescent screen.

electron tube, US term for THERMIONIC VALVE.

electron-volt, unit of energy used in nuclear physics; equals work done on an electron to pass it through potential difference of 1 volt. 1 GeV (BeV in US) = 10^9 electron-volts.

electroscope, device used to detect electric charge. Gold leaf electroscope consists of 2 thin strips of gold leaf attached to metallic conducting rod. Leaves diverge under repelling action of like charges when rod acquires electric charge.

elegy, lyrical poem in contemplative tone lamenting the dead. Examples incl. Milton's 'Lycidas', Gray's 'Elegy Written in a Country Churchyard', Arnold's 'Thyrsis'.

element, in chemistry, substance which cannot be decomposed by chemical means into simpler substances. Elements consist of atoms of same atomic number; traditionally 92 occur in nature and 11 more have been made in the laboratory.

elementary particles, in physics, subatomic particles which are basic components of matter. Incl. electron, proton, neutrino which are stable, and neutron, various mesons and many other particles which are unstable. Each elementary particle has corresponding anti-particle, with same mass but opposite charge, spin, *etc.* Recent theories suggest that all elementary particles are composed of QUARKS and LEPTONS.

elementary school, *see* PRIMARY SCHOOL.

elephant, thick-skinned mammal of order Proboscidea, with flexible, strong trunk. Indian elephant, *Elephas maximus,* often domesticated, is used for heavy work in India, Burma, Sri Lanka; female without tusks. African elephant, *Loxodonta africana,* larger than Indian, with larger ears. Both species live in itinerant herds.

elephantiasis, chronic disease characterized by gross thickening of skin and connective tissue, esp. of legs and genitals. Caused by blockage of lymphatic vessels, usually by infestation with filaria worms.

Eleusis, ancient city near Athens with shrine of DEMETER. Home of Eleusinian mystery cults celebrating cycle of fertility and death through worship of Demeter, Persephone.

El Ferrol, *see* FERROL, EL, Spain.

Elgar, Sir Edward (1857-1934), English composer. First major figure in British music since Purcell. *Enigma Variations* estab. him in 1899. Other works incl. oratorio *The Dream of Gerontius* and marches *Pomp and Circumstance,* a tune from which was used for song *Land of Hope and Glory.*

African elephants

Elgin, Thomas Bruce, 7th Earl of (1766-1841), British soldier, diplomat. Brought Elgin Marbles from Athens to England. His son, **James Bruce, 8th Earl of Elgin** (1811-63), was governor-general of Canada (1847-54). Carried out Earl of Durham's plan for govt. reform.

Elgin, town of Grampian region, N Scotland, on R. Lossie. Pop. 16,000. Former royal burgh and co. town of Morayshire. Market town, distilling; port at Lossiemouth. Has ruined cathedral (13th cent.).

Elgin Marbles: horsemen preparing for the Panathenaic procession

Elgin Marbles, ancient sculptures removed from the Parthenon, Athens and acquired by Lord Elgin from the Turks. Brought to England (1803-12), bought by govt. and deposited in British Museum (1816).

Elgon, Mount, peak of Kenya-Uganda border, NE of L. Victoria. Extinct volcano; height 4319 m (14,176 ft). Former cave dwellings on slopes.

El Greco, see GRECO, EL.

Elijah, Hebrew prophet of 9th cent. BC. Violently censured the spread of idolatrous worship during reign of King Ahab. Major prophet of Jewish tradition.

Eliot, Charles W[illiam] (1834-1926), American educator. As president of Harvard Univ. (1869-1909), made many changes, expanding it and raising standards. Aided development of Radcliffe Coll. for women.

Eliot, George, pseud. of Mary Ann or Marian Evans (1819-80), English novelist. Works deal with moral, social problems of her day, eg *The Mill on the Floss* (1860), *Silas Marner* (1861), *Middlemarch* (1872). Influenced by rationalist theology, sociology of Herbert Spencer.

Eliot, Sir John (1592-1632), English parliamentary leader. Led impeachment proceedings against duke of Buckingham (1626). Pressed Charles I to accept Petition of Right (1628). His further opposition to king led to his imprisonment; died in prison.

Eliot, T[homas] S[tearns] (1888-1965), English poet, b. US. Early works, eg *Prufrock and Other Observations* (1917), *The Waste Land* (1922), reflect classical, intellectually conservative attitude to culture. Verse dramas incl. *Murder in the Cathedral* (1935), *The Cocktail Party* (1949), on religious themes. Wrote influential criticism esp. on metaphysical poets, Dante. Awarded Nobel Prize for Literature (1948).

Elisabethville, see LUBUMBASHI, Zaïre.

Elisha, Hebrew prophet, disciple of ELIJAH. Sent messenger to anoint Jehu when he was in rebellion against house of Ahab.

Elizabeth I: portrait attributed to Gheeraerts

elixir, hypothetical substance capable of turning base metals into gold, sought by alchemists. Elixir of life to prolong life was also thought to exist.

Elizabeth I (1533-1603), queen of England (1558-1603). Daughter of Henry VIII and Anne Boleyn, succeeded to throne after perilous early life. Re-estab. Protestantism by acts of Supremacy and Uniformity (1559). Persecuted Catholics in later years of reign after series of plots which aimed to replace her by MARY QUEEN OF SCOTS; signed Mary's death warrant (1587). Reign marked by growth of commerce, beginning of colonization of North America, defeat of Spanish Armada (1588), flourishing of drama, literature, music.

Elizabeth II (1926-), queen of Great Britain and Northern Ireland (1952-). Daughter of George VI, married (1947) Philip Mountbatten, duke of EDINBURGH. Eldest son and heir apparent is CHARLES. Other children are Anne (1950-), Andrew (1960-), Edward (1964-).

Elizabeth (1843-1916), queen consort of Carol I of Romania, b. Germany. Under pseud. Carmen Sylva, wrote books in several languages, incl. *Pensées d'une reine* (1882).

Elizabeth, town of NE New Jersey, US; on Newark Bay. Pop. 113,000. Shipbuilding, Singer sewing machine mfg. First settled 1664. American Revolution battleground.

Elizabethan drama, name given to plays written between c 1570 and 1600 combining traditions of English comedies, chronicle plays with Renaissance classicism. Examples incl. blank verse plays of Shakespeare, Marlow, Jonson, ranging from tragedy to comedy of sophisticated construction and wit.

Elizabethan style, in architecture, transitional style of English Renaissance; combined aspects of perpendicular Gothic with Italian Renaissance ideas and Flemish decoration. Exemplified by many country houses, *eg* Longleat and Hardwick Hall.

elk, *Alces alces,* largest deer of Europe and Asia. Inhabitant of marshland. American variety is WAPITI.

Ellesmere, most N isl. of Canada, in NE Franklin Dist., Northwest Territs; largest of Queen Elizabeth Isls. Area 213,000 sq km (82,000 sq mi). Ice-cap in S and E; mountainous. Eskimo pop. Discovered by William Baffin (1616).

Ellesmere Port, mun. bor. of Cheshire, NW England. Pop. 62,000. On Manchester Ship Canal; oil refinery, petroleum, engineering industs.

Ellice Islands, group of 9 atolls, colony of UK. Area 23 sq km (9 sq mi); cap. Funafuti. Produce copra. Sovereignty over 4 of group disputed by US. Formerly called Lagoon Isls. Withdrew from Gilbert and Ellice Isls. colony (1976), formed separate colony of Tuvalu.

Ellington, Edward Kennedy ('Duke') (1899-1974), American pianist, composer. Major composer in jazz music, he also wrote many famous songs, incl. *Mood Indigo, Solitude.*

ellipse, in geometry, curve traced by point which moves so that sum of its distances from 2 fixed points (its foci) is constant. One of the CONIC SECTIONS.

Ellis, [Henry] Havelock (1859-1939), English writer, psychologist. Known for *Studies in the Psychology of Sex* (7 vols., 1898-1928), one of 1st scientific examinations of sexuality.

Ellora, village of Maharashtra state, WC India. Famous Hindu, Buddhist and Jain rock temples carved in hillside, esp. Hindu Kailasa temple.

Ellsworth, Lincoln (1880-1951), American engineer, explorer. Flew with Amundsen from Spitsbergen to Alaska over North Pole (1926). First to fly over Antarctica (1935), claiming vast territ. for US.

Ellsworth Highlands, region of Antarctica, in unallocated area between Ross Dependency and British Antarctic Territ. Named after American explorer Lincoln Ellsworth (1880-1951).

English elm (*Ulmus procera*)

elm, family (Ulmaceae) of deciduous trees with rough oval leaves, native to N temperate regions. Esp. denotes genus *Ulmus,* incl. wych elm, *U. glabra,* which reaches 35 m/120 ft in height, and English elm, *U. procera.* North American species incl. smooth-leaved elm, *U. carpinifolia,* and slippery elm, *U. rubra. See* DUTCH ELM DISEASE.

El Paso, border city of SW Texas, US; opposite Juárez (Mexico) on Rio Grande. Pop. 322,000. Travel jct., tourist and commercial centre. Copper smelting, oil refining. Settled 1827.

El Salvador, republic of Central America. Area 21,393 sq km (8260 sq mi); pop. 3,534,000; cap. San Salvador. Language: Spanish. Religion: RC. Pacific coastline rises to fertile plain (coffee, cotton growing; cattle rearing);

El Salvador

volcanic mountains. World's main source of balsam. Spanish rule (1524-1821); member of Central American Federation until independence in 1838.

Elsheimer, Adam (1578-1610), German painter. Painted small pictures on copper of biblical and mythological scenes set in ideal landscapes; noted for his light effects.

Elsinore, see HELSINGÖR, Denmark.

Eluard, Paul, pseud. of Eugène Grindel (1895-1952), French poet. After interest in dada, became a founder of SURREALISM. Works incl. *Les Nécessités d'une vie et les conséquences des rêves* (1921), *Les Yeux fertiles* (1936). Later poetry reflects political interests.

Ely, Isle of, region of Cambridgeshire, EC England, former admin. county. Fen drained to yield agric. land. **City of Ely,** on R. Ouse. Pop. 10,000. Agric. market. Cathedral (11th cent.) has Norman nave.

Elysée, palace in Paris, built 1718; once home of Madame de Pompadour, it became official residence of French president in 1873.

Elysium or **Elysian Fields,** in Greek myth, paradise for heroes favoured by the gods. In Homer, it lies on the most W edge of the world. Later tradition had it as part of underworld for all blessed dead.

Elzevir, Louis (*c* 1540-1617), Dutch publisher. Founded firm at Leiden (1583), which was continued by his descendants until 1712. Produced good inexpensive editions of Latin, French and Greek classics. Special type, known as 'old style' or Elzevir, was designed for firm by Christopher van Dyck.

Emancipation, Edict of (1861), proclamation freeing all Russian serfs (*c* ⅓ of pop.) issued by Alexander II. Complex procedures for land purchases by peasants and abuse of edict by landlords helped provoke Russian Revolution.

Emancipation Proclamation, in US history, edict freeing slaves in rebellious Confederate states. Issued by Lincoln (Sept. 1862), became law 1 Jan. 1863. Intended to deplete Confederacy's reserves of slave labour and improve Union cause in Europe.

embroidery, art of decorating cloth with varied stitches of coloured or metallic thread. Use is recorded in ancient Egypt, Babylon and China. From 12th to 14th cents., England was famous for its embroidered church vestments and altar-cloths.

embryo, in zoology, animal in earliest stages of its development, before it emerges from egg membranes, or in viviparous animals, from uterus of mother. Name foetus is often applied to later stages of embryo's development. Also *see* SEED.

Emden, town of NW West Germany, on Ems estuary. Pop. 46,000. Port, canal link with Dortmund. Exports coal; oil refining, shipbuilding. Dates from 10th cent.

emerald, gem form of BERYL. Green colour is due to presence of chromium compounds. Major sources in Colombia, Brazil, US.

Emerson, Ralph Waldo (1803-82), American philosopher, poet. Influenced by Carlyle. Founded transcendentalism, *ie* belief that man has intuitive knowledge of 'world soul'. Ideas formulated in *Nature* (1836). Wrote essays, lyrics, often in free verse form.

Embroidery: Japanese gift cover

Gowns in the Empire style

emery, finely granular form of CORUNDUM, containing some magnetite. Used as an abrasive. Major sources in Greece, Asia Minor.

Emilia-Romagna, region of N Italy, cap. Bologna. Apennines in S; fertile Po valley in C and N. Agric., food processing. Adriatic resorts, *eg* Rimini.

Eminence Grise, *see* JOSEPH, FATHER.

Emin Pasha, name adopted by Eduard Schnitzer (1840-90), German explorer. Medical officer under C.G. Gordon in Khartoum from 1875, succeeded him as governor of Equatoria (S Egyptian Sudan) in 1878. Murdered by Arab slave traders while exploring region of L. Tanganyika.

Emmet, Robert (1778-1803), Irish nationalist. Went to France (1800) to enlist support for an Irish uprising. Led small group of followers in insurrection (July, 1803). Captured and hanged.

emotion, in psychology, complex response to stimulus, with both physiological and psychological effects, *eg* changes in rate of breathing, gland secretion, strong feelings of excitement, which usually involve impulse to definite action.

Empedocles (*c* 495-*c* 435 BC), Greek philosopher. Held matter to be composed of 4 elements: earth, water, fire, air. Explained motion as resolution of opposed forces of harmony and discord.

emperor moth, *Saturnia pavonia,* large European moth with 4 eye-like spots on wing; branched antennae.

emphysema, disease involving abnormal distention of air sacs of lungs. Occurs with old age or at an advanced stage of chronic bronchitis. Symptoms incl. difficulty in breathing, coughing with sputum.

Empire State Building, New York City, formerly tallest building in world, 380 m (1250 ft) high. Built 1930-1, it has 102 storeys and is a tourist attraction in Manhattan. *See* SKYSCRAPER.

Empire style, mode of furniture design and interior decoration popular in France *c* 1804-30. Originated by architects Percier and Fontaine who decorated state apartments for Napoleon; combined neo-Classical designs with Egyptian motifs. In women's costume, term refers to high-waisted gowns with flowing skirt and short, puffed sleeves.

empiricism, philosophical belief, opposed to RATIONALISM, that all knowledge is derived from experience. Denies innate ideas and *a priori* truth. Dominant tradition in British philosophy since Locke.

Empson, William (1906-   ), English critic, poet. Known for influential *Seven Types of Ambiguity* (1930), arguing that effects of poetry come from multiple meanings. Also wrote criticism on Milton, Joyce; poetry *eg The Gathering Storm* (1940).

Ems, river of NW Germany. Flows *c* 370 km (230 mi) from Westphalia to North Sea near Emden. Linked to Ruhr by Dortmund-Ems canal. Oil, natural gas in surrounding area.

Ems dispatch (July, 1870), communication between William I of Prussia and his premier Bismarck which led to Franco-Prussian War. William refused to assure French ambassador Benedetti that no Hohenzollern would seek Spanish throne. Bismarck successfully provoked French govt. to declare war by publishing version of William's reply.

Emu

emu, *Dromaius novaehollandiae,* second largest living bird; flightless, capable of running fast. Found in Australian inland areas. Brown body; reaches height of 1.5 m/5 ft.

emulsion, colloidal suspension of 2 immiscible fluids, *eg* milk. Emulsions may be stabilized by emulsifying agents; milk is stabilized by casein.

enamel, vitreous glaze, coloured by metallic oxides, which can be fused to surfaces of metals, glass or pottery. Of ancient origin, art of enamelling, esp. *cloisonné* technique, was perfected by Byzantines in 10th cent. Limoges, France, was main centre of European enamelling from 12th to 16th cents.

Encarnación, town of SE Paraguay, on Alto Paraná R. opposite Posadas (Argentina). Pop. 24,000. Maté, timber, tobacco, cotton exports.

encaustic, method of painting in which colours mixed in wax are fused to a surface by hot irons. Used by ancient Greeks, Romans and Egyptians.

encephalitis, name for viral inflammation of the brain, *eg* rabies, poliomyelitis. *Encephalitis lethargica* or sleepy sickness was widespread epidemic during WWI but vanished in 1920s.

Encke, Johann Franz (1791-1865), German astronomer. Investigated motion of comets, particularly Encke's comet, orbit of which he calculated; its period of revolution of 3.3 years is shortest yet observed.

enclosure, in English history, practice of fencing off land formerly subject to common rights (open field system). Arose out of demand at end of 14th cent. for wool to supply Flemish trade. Caused serious hardship, leading to rebellions in Tudor period. New wave of enclosures from 1750 to 1800 forced landless workers to move to cities, where they were to supply the labour for the Industrial Revolution.

encyclopedia, a book, or set of books, containing articles, usually arranged alphabetically, covering a general or specific area of knowledge. Earliest extant example is Pliny the Elder's *Historia Naturalis* (1st cent. AD). John Harris' *Lexicon Technicum* (1704) is first alphabetical example in English. *The Encyclopaedia Britannica* dates from 1768.

Encyclopedists, 18th cent. contributors to Diderot's *Encyclopédie,* incl. Voltaire, Montesquieu, Rousseau.

Enderbury Island, *see* CANTON AND ENDERBURY ISLANDS.

Enders, John Franklin (1897-), American microbiologist. With T. H. Weller and F.C. Robbins, shared Nobel Prize for Physiology and Medicine (1954) for growing poliomyelitis virus on embryonic tissue.

endive, *Cichorium endiva,* plant of daisy family, similar to dandelion. Native to Europe but widely cultivated in US, where it is known as chicory. Leaves used in salads.

concerned with metabolism, growth and sexual functions. Principal glands are thyroid, pituitary, parathyroid, adrenals, testicles and ovaries, parts of pancreas.

endorphins, class of pain-killers, incl. ENKEPHALIN, found naturally in the brain and pituitary gland. May play a role in mental disorders, acupuncture and behaviour associated with addiction to opiates.

Endymion, in Greek myth, handsome shepherd of Mt. Latmos. Loved by the moon goddess Selene, she imposed eternal sleep on him so that she might visit him each night.

energy, in physics, the ability to do WORK. A body may have potential energy because of its position or kinetic energy because of its motion. It was believed that energy can neither be created nor destroyed, but can be converted from one form into another, *eg* electrical energy into heat energy. Einstein's law $E = mc^2$ now shows that mass and energy are equivalent; energy obtained from annihilation of mass accounts for nuclear energy and power of stars.

Enfield, bor. of N Greater London, England. Pop. 267,000. Created 1965 from mun. bor. of Middlesex. Small arms; cables mfg.

Friedrich Engels

Engels, Friedrich (1820-95), German philosopher. Collaborated with Marx in evolving Communist doctrine, notably in *The Communist Manifesto* (1848). Lived in England after 1850, edited much of Marx's *Das Kapital.* His own works incl. *The Origin of the Family, Private Property and the State* (1884).

Enghien, Louis Antoine Henri de Bourbon-Condé, Duc d' (1772-1804), French prince. Held a command in army of French émigrés which unsuccessfully invaded France. Falsely accused of plotting to overthrow Napoleon, court-martialled and shot.

engineering, science of putting scientific knowledge to practical use esp. in design and construction of engines, machines and public works. Field divided into civil, mechanical, chemical.

England, constituent country of UK, in S part of GREAT BRITAIN. Area 130,357 sq km (50,331 sq mi); pop. 45,870,000; cap. London. Major cities Birmingham, Liverpool, Manchester. Comprises 39 counties, 6 met. counties, Greater London. Main rivers Thames, Severn, Humber, Tees, Tyne. Pastoral uplands in NW (Pennines, Lake Dist.); lowland (agric., dairying) in SE. Indust. centred in Midlands (coal, iron), Lancashire, Yorkshire (textiles), NE (shipbuilding, engineering). Roman occupation (AD 43-5th cent.) followed by Saxon, Viking, Norman invasions. Successive royal dynasties Plantagenet, Lancaster, York, Tudor, Stuart, Orange, Hanover, Windsor. Church of England split from Rome under Henry VIII. Indust. Revolution began here (18th cent.), made England world's

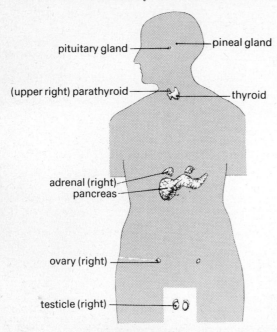

pituitary gland — pineal gland

(upper right) parathyroid — thyroid

adrenal (right) —
pancreas —

ovary (right) —

testicle (right) —

Endocrine glands

endocrine glands or **ductless glands,** organs in body which secrete hormones directly into bloodstream;

England

leading indust. nation in 19th cent. Estab. large overseas Empire (Commonwealth after 1931). United with Wales 1536, with Scotland 1707, with Ireland 1801 (partition 1921) to form UNITED KINGDOM.

England, Church of, established church in England. Henry VIII withdrew allegiance to Pope and declared sovereign to be head of English church; confirmed by Act of Supremacy (1543). Under Mary, England was again RC, but Elizabeth I restored Protestantism, Thirty-nine Articles adopted as basic doctrine. Act of Supremacy (1559) restored ecclesiastical jurisdiction to the crown. Presbyterianism substituted for episcopacy by Long Parliament (1646); episcopacy restored (1660). High Church tradition emphasizes ritualism and apostolic succession, Low Church stresses Bible and preaching. Archbishop of Canterbury is chief primate of Church of England and of unestablished Episcopal Church in Scotland, Church of Ireland, Church in Wales, Anglican Church of Canada, Church of England in Australia and Church of the Province of New Zealand.

English, language of W Germanic group of Indo-European family. Second only to Mandarin Chinese in number of speakers in world. First language in Britain, US, Australia, New Zealand. One of two working languages of United Nations. Incl. many dialects, *eg* American, Scots, Standard (received pronunciation) English. Developed from languages of 5th cent. Germanic invaders of Britain, which became regional dialects. West Saxon (of Wessex) became dominant in 9th cent. (*see* ANGLO-SAXON LITERATURE). Language of this period termed Old English. Norman Conquest (1066) brought change, Norman French being used as official, polite language. Development continued, Middle English (*c*1150–*c*1500) becoming standard in 14th cent. Important literature incl. *Gawayne and the Greene Knight, Piers Plowman.* Modern English developed from London dialect pre-1500, language of CHAUCER. Subsequent change mainly loss of inflections, gain of loan-words from French.

English Channel (Fr. *La Manche*), arm of Atlantic between England and France; length 563 km (350 mi), width varies from 160 km (100 mi) to 34 km (21 mi) at STRAIT OF DOVER. Many resorts on both coasts; ferry services. First balloon crossing 1785, first swum 1875, first aircraft crossing 1909.

engraving, process of cutting, etching or drawing marks on metal plates, wooden blocks, *etc,* for purpose of reproducing prints. Three main types: relief, incl. woodcutting; intaglio, incl. ETCHING, DRYPOINT; surface printing, *eg* LITHOGRAPHY.

enkephalin, pain-killer, similar in action to morphine, found naturally in the brain. Destroyed rapidly by enzymes in the brain; addictive if this destructive enzyme action is inhibited. May play a role in mechanism of addiction to morphine.

Enlightenment or **Age of Reason,** European movement of 18th cent., characterized by rationalism, learning, 'scientific' (*ie* sceptical), empirical approach. Based on work of Newton, Descartes, Locke in 17th cent. and expressed esp. in Diderot's *Encyclopédie,* and writings of Voltaire, Rousseau, Hume, Kant. Manifested by social reforms of 'enlightened despots', *eg* Frederick II of Prussia, Catherine II of Russia, and revolutionary movements in France, America.

Ennis, co. town of Clare, W Irish Republic. Pop. 6000. Agric. market, food processing, whiskey distilling. RC pro-cathedral; abbey ruins.

Enniskillen, town of SW Northern Ireland. Pop. 7000. Former co. town of Fermanagh. Agric. market. Hist. Protestant stronghold.

Ennius, Quintus (239–*c* 169 BC), Roman author. First major Latin classical poet, admired and imitated by later writers. Works incl. epic *Annales.*

Enosis, name given to Greek Cypriot movement for union of Cyprus with Greece. Esp. favoured by EOKA organization led by George Grivas both before and after independence from Britain.

Enschede, town of EC Netherlands. Pop. 143,000. Centre of cotton indust.; canal links to Ijssel, Rhine rivers. Rebuilt after 1862 fire.

Ensor, James Ensor, Baron (1860-1949), Belgian painter. Work has fantastic and macabre quality; used masks, skeletons, ghosts to depict everyday life. Precursor of expressionism. Works incl. *Entry of Christ into Brussels in 1889* (1888).

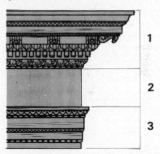

Corinthian entablature: 1. cornice; 2. frieze; 3. architrave

entablature, in classical architecture, horizontal superstructure supported by columns. Consists of architrave, surmounted by frieze, with cornice on top.

Entebbe, town of S Uganda, on N shore of Victoria Nyanza. Pop. 11,000. Commercial centre, international airport. Cap. of British Uganda (1894-1962).

Entente Cordiale, see TRIPLE ALLIANCE and TRIPLE ENTENTE.

enteritis, inflammation of the intestine, esp. small intestine. Common form is gastro-enteritis, characterized by abdominal pains, diarrhoea, vomiting; caused by bacterial food poisoning, viruses.

entomology, branch of zoology dealing with insects. Important aspect of entomology is need to control insects which spread disease to man and animals or destroy crops, and stored produce. Other aspects incl. taxonomy (classification of insects), ecology (place of insects in food webs).

entrepreneur, in economics, person who assumes risk and management of a business organization. Fully differentiated from ordinary capitalist by 19th cent. economists who saw him as coordinator and innovator necessary for corporate indust. Entrepreneurial class achieved prominence during Industrial Revolution.

entropy, in thermodynamics, term introduced to describe degree of disorder of a system. Entropy never decreases in an isolated system. When it increases the ability of the total energy in system to do useful work diminishes.

Enugu, city of SE Nigeria. Pop. 167,000. Indust. centre on railway to Port Harcourt; coalmining, engineering, sawmilling. Former cap. of Eastern Region; cap. of Biafra (1967-70) in civil war.

Enver Pasha (1881-1922), Turkish general, political leader. Leader in Young Turks' revolution (1908); became virtual dictator after coup (1913). Instrumental in bringing

Turkey into WWI. Killed leading anti-Soviet forces in Bukhara.

enzymes, large group of proteins, produced by plant and animal cells, which act as catalysts in specific chemical reactions vital to life. A few are found in natural secretions, such as digestive juices pepsin and trypsin.

Eocene epoch, second geological epoch of Tertiary period. Alpine mountain building continued. Further evolution of primitive mammals which began in Palaeocene epoch. Increase in temperature, causing widespread subtropical conditions. Also *see* GEOLOGICAL TABLE.

Eos (Gk., = dawn), in Greek myth, goddess of dawn. Daughter of Hyperion, sister of Helios (sun) and Selene (moon). Identified by Romans with Aurora.

Epaminondas (*c* 418-362 BC), Theban soldier, statesman. Defeated Spartans at Leuctra (371 BC); died while crushing them again at Mantinea. Renowned as a military strategist, he influenced Alexander the Great.

Epernay, town of NE France, on R. Marne. Pop. 28,000. Centre of Champagne wine indust., has large underground cellars; cask mfg., bottling.

ephedrine, alkaloid drug extracted from certain Chinese plants or synthesized. Used to relieve nasal congestion and asthma.

Ephesians, epistle of NT, traditionally written to Christians at Ephesus by St Paul (*c* AD 60) during his Roman imprisonment, but possibly by a later writer. Uses metaphor of mystical body of Christ as a plea for Christian unity.

Ephesus, ancient Ionian city, on W coast of Asia Minor. Taken by Romans (133 BC), became cap. of Roman Asia. Had famous temple of Diana (Artemis); site of St Paul's epistle. Destroyed (262) by Goths, never recovered its importance.

epic, long narrative poem dealing with exploits of one or more heroic individuals, historical or legendary, usually in exalted style and moral tone. Examples incl. Iliad, Odyssey, Aeneid (classical); BEOWULF (Old English); *Chanson de Roland* (French); *Gerusalemme Liberate* (Italian); *The Lusiads* (Portuguese); *Paradise Lost* (English).

Epictetus, (*fl c* AD 100), Greek Stoic philosopher. An emancipated slave, taught in Rome before being banished. Advocated life free of desires, trust in providence.

Head of statue of Epicurus

Epicurus (*c* 340-*c* 270 BC), Greek philosopher. Founder of the Epicurean school of philosophy. Advocated reliance on the senses. Saw freedom from pain or anxiety as greatest good, achieved by simple living.

Epidaurus, ancient city of Greece, in NE Peloponnese. Site of temple of Asclepius. Greek independence proclaimed (1822) at nearby Nea Epidhavros.

epiglottis, triangular flap of cartilage behind the tongue. Folds back over windpipe during swallowing, thus preventing food from entering lungs.

epigram, short poem, developed from Greek by Roman writers who estab. distinct satirical character, *eg* Martial.

epilepsy, group of chronic disorders of the brain characterized by fits. Classified as *petit mal,* in which there is momentary loss of consciousness, or *grand mal,* in which there is loss of consciousness and muscle stiffening for a few minutes. Treatment by sedatives and drugs.

Epinal, town of Lorraine, E France, on R. Moselle. Cap. of Vosges dept. Pop. 40,000. Textile indust., liqueur mfg. Famous from 16th cent. for engravings (*images d'Epinal*).

Epiphany (Gk., = showing), Christian feast, celebrated on 6th Jan. Commemorates baptism of Jesus, visit of wise men to Bethlehem, miracle of changing water to wine at Cana. More ancient and technically more important than Christmas. Eve of feast is Twelfth Night.

epiphyte or **air plant,** general name for plant which grows on another plant but is not a parasite and produces its own food by photosynthesis, drawing water from atmosphere. Incl. orchids, Spanish moss.

Epirus (*Ipiros*), region of NW Greece and SW Albania, between Pindus Mts. and Ionian Sea. Famed for cattle, horses. *Fl* 3rd cent. BC under Pyrrhus. Turkish from 15th cent., later divided between Greece and Albania.

episcopacy, system of church govt. by bishops, used in all pre-Reformation, and some post-Reformation churches. Estab. by end of 1st cent. and not challenged until Luther's rejection of the supernatural powers of bishops in ordaining priests and ruling clergy. Calvin rejected system as major abuse. Degrees of authority are pope, patriarch, archbishop, bishop.

Episcopal Church (Protestant), *see* ANGLICAN COMMUNION.

epistles, in NT, traditionally ascribed to the Apostles, 21 letters addressed to some of the new churches and individual members of them.

Epping, urban dist. of Essex, SE England. Pop. 12,000. On N edge of Epping Forest, park from 1882.

Epsom and Ewell, mun. bor. of Surrey, SE England. Pop. 72,000. Epsom Downs racecourse nearby (Derby) has 17th cent. spa (Epsom salts).

Epsom salts, hydrated magnesium sulphate ($MgSO_4.7H_2O$), used as a purgative.

Epstein, Sir Jacob (1880-1959), British sculptor of Russo-Polish descent, b. New York. Works frequently aroused violent criticism; influenced by African art and vorticist movement. Sculpture incl. *The Rock Drill* and *Christ in Majesty* for Llandaff Cathedral (S Wales).

equation, in chemistry, expression of chemical reaction by means of formulae and symbols. The equation $2H_2 + O_2 = 2H_2O$ states that 2 molecules of hydrogen combine with 1 oxygen molecule to form 2 of water.

Equator, imaginary line around the Earth, equidistant from both poles and perpendicular to axis. Forms a GREAT CIRCLE; divides globe into N and S hemispheres.

Equatorial Guinea, republic of WC Africa, on Gulf of Guinea. Area 28,000 sq km (10,800 sq mi); pop. 305,000; cap. Rey Malabo. Languages: Bantu, Spanish. Religions: native, RC. Comprises Río Muni (mainland), Macias Nguema Biyoga isl. Hot, wet climate: exports coffee, cocoa, hardwoods. Colony as Spanish Guinea from 18th cent.; independent from 1968.

equestrianism, competitive sport for horse and rider. Divided into 3 events: dressage, which tests horse's training; show jumping; 3-day event, consisting of show jumping, dressage and cross-country phases. Olympic event since 1912.

Equidae, family of odd-toed ungulates with single large hoof on each foot. Comprises horses, asses and zebras.

equinox, time of year when Sun appears directly overhead at the Equator at noon. Night and day are thus of equal length throughout the world. Occurs twice a year: 21 March (vernal equinox), 22 Sept. (autumnal equinox).

equity, in law, resort to general principles of fairness and justice when existing law is inadequate. In UK, developed to supplement COMMON LAW. In US, system of rules and doctrines supplementing common and statute law. Distinction between common law and equity removed by their amalgamation.

equivalent weight, in chemistry, number of grams of an element which will combine with or replace 1 gram of hydrogen or 8 grams of oxygen. Product of equivalent weight and valency of element equals its atomic weight. Equivalent weight of an acid is weight of acid containing 1 gram of hydrogen replaceable by a metal.

Erasistratus (*fl* 3rd cent. BC), Greek physician and anatomist. With Herophilus, leader of school of medicine in Alexandria. Investigated functions of nerves, veins and arteries; devised reverse theory of blood circulation.

Erasmus: detail of portrait by Holbein

Erasmus, Desiderius (*c* 1466-1536), Dutch philosopher, humanist. Wrote Latin translation of New Testament (1516), satire *The Praise of Folly*. Believed in rational piety, took critical attitude to superstition. Opponent of religious bigotry, supported Luther's aims but hostile to results of Reformation which caused war. Influenced English humanists, esp. Thomas More.

Erastus, Thomas, orig. Lüber or Liebler (1524-83), Swiss Protestant theologian, physician. In *Explicatio* (pub. 1589) he opposed punitive powers of church, held that punishment of sin should be left to civil authorities; doctrine known as Erastianism.

Erato, in Greek and Roman myth, Muse of love lyric. Represented with lyre.

Eratosthenes (*c* 276-194 BC), Greek geographer, astronomer, mathematician, b. Cyrene. Worked mainly at Alexandria; calculated circumference of Earth. His *Geographica* laid basis of mathematical geography.

erbium (Er), metallic element of lanthanide group; at. no. 68, at. wt. 167.26. Discovered (1843) by C.G. Mosander.

Erebus, in Greek myth, son of Chaos and father by his sister Nyx of Aether (clear air) and Hemera (day). Personification of darkness, esp. represents gloom around Hades.

Erebus, Mount, active volcano on Ross Isl., in Ross Sea, Antarctica. Height 4024m (13,202 ft). Discovered (1841) by James Ross.

Erfurt, city of SW East Germany, on R. Gera. Pop. 198,000. Machinery, electrical goods, agric. market. Founded by St Boniface 741; former univ. (1392-1816), cathedral (15th cent.).

erg, unit of work or energy in c.g.s. system: 1 erg represents work done when force of 1 dyne acts through distance of 1 cm.

ergonomics, the study of relationship between people and their environment, esp. the science that seeks to adapt work or working conditions to the worker.

ergot, parasitic fungus, *Claviceps purpurea,* of cereal grains, esp. rye. Contains toxic alkaloids which cause hallucinations but can be used medicinally to limit bloodflow.

Erhard, Ludwig (1897-1977), West German statesman. As minister of economics, laid foundation of German 'economic miracle' with currency reforms of 1948.

Succeeded Adenauer as Christian Democrat chancellor (1963-6).

Ericaceae, family of flowering plants. Mostly evergreen, with woody, creeping stems. Incl. heaths and rhododendrons.

Eric IX (d. 1160), king of Sweden, called 'Eric the Saint'. Converted Finland to Christianity by force; after murder by pagan Dane, became patron saint of Sweden.

Ericsson, Leif, *see* LEIF ERICSSON.

Eric the Red (*fl* 10th cent.), Norse chieftain. Discovered and colonized Greenland. Unsuccessful in resistance to son Leif Ericsson's conversion of Greenland to Christianity.

Erie, North American Indian tribe of Hokan-Siouan linguistic stock. Sedentary farmers of area SE of L. Erie in 17th cent. Traditional enemies of Iroquois Confederacy, were almost exterminated in 1656 after one of the most destructive Indian wars. A few descendants live on reservations in Oklahoma.

Erie, port of NW Pennsylvania, US; on L. Erie. Pop. 264,000. Coal, timber, grain, petroleum shipping; paper, electrical equipment mfg. Estab. by French as Fort Presque (1753); passed to US (1785).

Erie, Lake, shallowest of Great Lakes, C Canada-US. Area 25,745 sq km (9940 sq mi). Trade route connecting L. Huron and L. Ontario. Chief ports Cleveland, Buffalo, Toledo. Discovered by French in 17th cent. Ice-bound from December-March.

Erigena, Johannes Scotus (*c* 810-*c* 877), Irish philosopher. Identified philosophy with theology. Attempted to combine Christianity with neoplatonism. Taught at Carolingian court of Emperor Charles II.

Erin, poetic name for Ireland.

Erinyes, *see* EUMENIDES.

Eritrea, prov. of N Ethiopia, on Red Sea. Area 118,500 sq km (45,750 sq mi); cap. Asmara, chief port Massawa. Arid, rugged region with narrow coastal strip. Nomadic pastoralism, hides, coffee, cereal products. Colonized 1890 by Italy, base for Italian invasions of Ethiopia 1896, 1935. Under British military rule from 1941; united federally with Ethiopia 1952, fully integrated 1962. Terrorist separation movement in 1970s.

Erivan, *see* YEREVAN.

Erlander, Tage Fritiof (1901-), Swedish political leader, Social Democrat premier (1946-69). Expert on social welfare and education, he extended scope of welfare state and maintained Sweden's neutrality in cold war.

Erlangen, town of SC West Germany, at confluence of Regnitz and Schwabach. Pop. 84,000. Indust. centre, esp. textiles, beer; univ. (1743). Rebuilt after fire (1706).

ermine, *see* STOAT.

Ernst, Max (1891-1976), German painter. A founder of DADA in Cologne (1919) and surrealist movement in Paris (1924). Developed *frottage* technique (similar to brass rubbing) and used collage and photomontage. Works incl. 'collage novel' *Une Semaine de Bonté*.

Eros, in Greek myth, god of love, son of Aphrodite. Represented as beautiful but irresponsible in his infliction of passion. Also worshipped as fertility god. Identified by Romans with CUPID.

erosion, process by which features of Earth's surface are worn away. With weathering and transportation, forms one of constituent processes of denudation, although erosion is often used loosely as synonymous with latter. Results from mechanical action of transported debris, *eg* windborne particles may erode a cliff. Types incl. wind, river, marine, glacial erosion.

Erse, *see* GAELIC.

Erskine, Thomas Erskine, 1st Baron (1750-1823), British jurist, b. Scotland. Known for defending radicals at time of French Revolution, esp. Thomas Paine against accusation of sedition over *The Rights of Man*. Secured reform of libel laws.

Ervine, St John Greer (1883-1971), Irish dramatist. Manager of ABBEY THEATRE (1915). Plays incl. *Mixed Marriage* (1911) on RC, Protestant bitterness, comedies *eg* *The First Mrs Fraser* (1928). Also wrote novels, lives of Wilde, Shaw.

erythrocyte, *see* BLOOD.

Erzberger, Matthias (1875-1921), German statesman. Leader of Catholic Centre party, chief delegate at signing of armistice (1918). Minister of finance (1919-20), centralized taxation and nationalized railways. Murdered.

Erzerum, *see* ERZURUM.

Erzgebirge or **Ore Mountains,** range on NW Czechoslovakia-SE East Germany border, rising to 1243 m (4081 ft). Silver, copper, lead ores now virtually exhausted; uranium mined from WWII. Spas, winter sports.

Erzurum or **Erzerum,** city of NE Turkey, in Armenia, at an alt. of 1920 m (6300 ft). Pop. 152,000. Of strategic importance, held by Armenians, Byzantines and Persians; taken by Turks (1515).

Esarhaddon (d. 668 BC), Assyrian king (681-668 BC). Succeeded his father Sennacherib. Brought Assyria to zenith of power, extending empire over Media, Palestine and Egypt. Restored Babylon, destroyed by his father.

Esau, in OT, son of Isaac, older twin brother of JACOB, who tricked him into selling his birthright. Represented as man of the open air and skilful hunter. Ancestor of Edomites.

Esbjerg, town of W Jutland, Denmark, on North Sea. Pop. 68,000. Chief Danish fishing port; exports dairy produce. Ferry services to England.

escape velocity, minimum velocity required by a body to escape gravitational influence of a planet. Depends on mass and diameter of planet. For Earth, escape velocity is *c* 11.2 km/sec.

Eschenbach, Wolfram von, *see* WOLFRAM VON ESCHENBACH.

Esch(-sur-l'Alzette), town of Luxembourg, on R. Alzette. Pop. 27,000. Iron and steel indust.

Escorial or **Escurial,** town of C Spain, near Madrid. Site of building complex incl. monastery, palace and mausoleum built 1563-84 by Philip II; contains many art treasures.

Esdras 1 and **2,** apocryphal books of OT dating from *c* 100 BC-*c* AD 100. Mainly transcripts of EZRA. Esdras 2 is apocalyptic account of Ezra's revelation. In some canons, term is used for books of Ezra and Nehemiah, the apocryphal books then being Esdras 3 and 4.

Esenin, Sergei Aleksandrovich, *see* YESENIN, SERGEI ALEKSANDROVICH.

Esfahan, *see* ISFAHAN.

Eshkol, Levi, orig. Shkolnik (1895-1969), Israeli statesman, premier (1963-9), b. Ukraine. Emigrated to Palestine (1931). Minister of finance (1952-63), succeeded Ben-Gurion as premier.

Eskilstuna, town of SE Sweden. Pop. 69,000. Iron and steel centre; cutlery, hardware, precision engineering. Chartered 17th cent.

Eskimo, people of Arctic and Labrador coasts, of Eskimo-Aleut linguistic stock. Pop. (1963) *c* 55,000, incl. *c* 1600 Chukchi Eskimos of NE Siberia. Six main cultural groups: MacKenzie; Copper or Blond Eskimos, thought to be of mixed descent from Norse colonists of Greenland; Caribou; Central; Labrador; East and West Greenlanders. Culture varies, but most build stone or earth winter huts (igloos are comparatively rare) and have skin summer tents. Economy depends on hunting (seal, bear, walrus, caribou). Live in loose, voluntary association under most skilled hunter. Origins thought to be Asian via Aleutian Isls.

Eskimo-Aleut, linguistic family comprising Aleut, spoken on Aleutian and Kodiak isls. Language of ESKIMO people. Steadily declining number of speakers.

Eskisehir (anc. *Dorylaeum*), city of WC Turkey, in Asia Minor. Pop. 243,000. Railway jct.; agric. trade, textile mfg. Has meerschaum deposits and sulphur springs nearby.

Espartero, Baldomero, Duque de la Victoria (*c* 1792-1879), Spanish general. Defeated CARLISTS in civil war (1833-9). Ruled dictatorially for Isabella until ousted by rebellion (1843). Returned as premier (1854-6).

esparto, two kinds of tall, coarse grass, *Stipa tenacissima* and *Lygeum spartum,* native to S Spain and N Africa. Used to make cordage and paper.

Esperanto, artificial language for international (chiefly European) use. Invented (1887) by Polish oculist, Dr L.L.

Eskimo hunter

Zamenhof (1859-1917). Uses word bases common to main European languages. Has self-evident parts of speech (*eg* all nouns end in -*o,* all adjectives in -*a*), single and regular conjugation of verbs and simplified inflections.

espionage, clandestine procuring of information, esp. military intelligence. Not illegal under international law. Origins of modern military intelligence attributed to Frederick II of Prussia; by WWI, European powers had developed espionage systems. Recent trends incl. increased use of diplomatic officials, reconnaissance from satellites.

essay, short literary composition dealing in discursive way with its subject from a personal point of view. Genre estab. by Montaigne (1580), Bacon (1597), developed in periodicals of Addison, Steele (18th cent.). Now generally adopted as vehicle of literary criticism or political, economic reflection.

Essen, city of W West Germany, in Ruhr. Pop. 692,000. Major indust. centre from estab. of Krupp steelworks (early 19th cent.); coal, chemicals, engineering, h.e.p. Grew around 9th cent. convent. Badly damaged in WWII.

Essenes, Jewish community (2nd cent. BC-2nd cent. AD). Condemned slavery, trading; emphasized ceremonial purity. Subsisted by simple agric., handicrafts. Possibly referred to in Dead Sea Scrolls.

essential oils, volatile substances of vegetable origin, which impart characteristic flavour or odour to plant of origin. Mostly benzene derivatives or terpenes. Used as perfumes and flavouring agents.

Essex, Robert Devereux, 2nd Earl of (1567-1601), English nobleman. Distinguished himself as cavalry officer at battle of Zutphen (1586). Favourite of Elizabeth I; incurred royal displeasure through secret marriage (1590). Politically ambitious but failed to take power from Burghley; lord lieutenant of Ireland (1599), unable to quell Irish revolt under Tyrone. Excluded from court after unauthorized return to England. Executed for intriguing against govt. His son, **Robert Devereux, 3rd Earl of Essex** (1591-1646), was restored to father's estates by James I. Fought in Civil War, resigning (1645) after disastrous command of parliamentary forces in Cornwall.

Essex, county of SE England. Area 3673 sq km (1418 sq mi); pop. 1,398,000; co. town Chelmsford. Mainly lowland, low hills in N. Agric. (N), dairying (S), fishing, oysters. Coastal resorts *eg* Southend-on-Sea; seaports *eg* Tilbury.

Oil refineries. Ancient Saxon kingdom, later English earldom.

Esslingen, town of SW West Germany, on R. Neckar. Pop. 87,000. Textiles, metal goods, furniture; noted wines. Scene of founding (1488) of Swabian League. Passed to Württemburg 1802.

estate, in law, degree, nature, extent and quality of interest or ownership person has in land. Real estate is interest in freehold land, personal estate any other kind of property. Since feudal times, term also used to refer to each of 3 social classes having specific political powers: 1st estate was Lords Spiritual (clergy); 2nd estate was Lords Temporal (nobility); 3rd estate was Commons (bourgeoisie).

Estates-General or **States-General,** French national assembly (1302-1789). Three ESTATES were represented as separate bodies in it. Summoned first by Philip IV, powers were never clearly defined; merely approved monarch's legislation. Did not meet (1614-1789) until Louis XVI called it to resolve govt. financial crisis. Commons and radicals in other 2 estates dominated it in move to make it legislative body. In June, 1789, declared themselves National Assembly, defying king. See FRENCH REVOLUTION.

Este, Alfonso d' (1476-1534), Italian nobleman, duke of Ferrara and Modena. Married Lucrezia Borgia (1501); upheld family tradition of art patronage. In Italian wars, fought against papacy.

ester, organic compound formed by replacing hydrogen of an acid by an organic radical. Many fats and oils are esters; others used as artificial fruit flavours.

Esther, historical book of OT. Story of Esther, Jewish wife of Ahasuerus (Xerxes I), king of Persia (486-465 BC), who prevented massacre of Jews.

Estienne or **Etienne,** family of printers in Paris and Geneva. Firm was founded in Paris by **Henri Estienne** (d. 1520). His son, **Robert Estienne** (d. 1559) was the royal printer; produced classics, dictionaries and lexicons, eg his own Latin thesaurus (1531). Forced to move business to Geneva (1550) on becoming a Protestant. His brother, **Charles Estienne** (c 1504-64), a scholar, wrote and printed many works, incl. a French encyclopedia. Robert's son, **Henri Estienne** (c 1531-98), also a scholar, pub. linguistically accurate critical editions of classical texts, also own Thesaurus graecae linguae (1572). Advocated use of French as literary language.

ethane (C_2H_6), gaseous hydrocarbon of paraffin series. Found in natural gas; used as fuel and in organic synthesis.

ethanol or **ethyl alcohol** (C_2H_5OH), colourless inflammable liquid, the active ingredient of alcoholic drinks. Prepared by fermentation of sugar or by various indust. processes. Used as fuel and in organic synthesis. See PROOF SPIRIT.

Ethelbert or **Aethelbert** (c 552-616), Anglo-Saxon ruler. Became king of Kent (560). Married Christian princess, Berta, and was converted to Christianity by St Augustine. Made Canterbury a great Christian centre.

Ethelred or **Aethelred the Unready** (956-1016), king of England (978-1016). Rule constantly threatened by Danes after 991, when he began levies of Danegeld. Fled country after defeat (1013) on Sweyn's death (1014), succeeded by his son Edmund Ironside.

ether, in chemistry, organic compound in which two hydrocarbon radicals are linked by an oxygen atom. Name usually refers to diethyl ether ($C_2H_5OC_2H_5$), prepared by action of concentrated sulphuric acid on ethanol; used as anaesthetic and solvent.

ether, in physics, hypothetical medium, pervading all space, once believed necessary for transmission of electromagnetic radiation, eg light. Following failure of Michelson-Morley experiment to detect its existence, Einstein's relativity theory showed ether was unnecessary concept.

Etherege, Sir George (c 1635-91), English playwright, poet. Known for complex Restoration comedies, eg Love in a Tub (1664); masterpiece The Man of Mode, or Sir Fopling Flatter (1676).

Ethical Culture, movement originated in New York by FELIX ADLER. Members accept as supreme the ethical factor in all relations of life (personal, social, international) apart from any theological or metaphysical considerations. Stresses importance of education.

ethics, in philosophy, the study of standards of conduct and moral judgement. Classical works incl. Plato's Republic, Aristotle's Nicomachean Ethics. Christian ethics draw mainly on New Testament and Aristotle. Subsequently, debate was centred on extent to which morality is imposed from outside individual, with 'intuitionists' (eg Rousseau) holding that conscience is innate and 'empiricists' (eg Locke) holding that it is acquired.

Estonia

Ethiopia

Estonian Soviet Socialist Republic (Eesti), constituent republic of W USSR. Area c 45,000 sq km (17,400 sq mi); pop. 1,357,000; cap. Tallinn. Bounded by Gulf of Finland to N; generally low-lying, with extensive forests. Agric., dairying. Under Swedish control in 17th cent., Estonia passed to Russia in 1721. Independent 1920-40; Occupied by Germany (1941-4).

Esztergom (Ger. Gran), town of N Hungary, on R. Danube. Pop. 25,000. Spa resort. Birthplace of St Stephen; domed cathedral (1870).

etching, process of engraving a metal plate, usually of copper. Plate is covered with acid-resistant resin and design is drawn on this with a needle, exposing underlying metal. Plate is bathed in acid so that its exposed parts are eaten away, thus transferring design to plate.

Ethiopia or **Abyssinia,** republic of NE Africa. Area 1,222,000 sq km (472,000 sq mi); pop. 26,076,000; cap. Addis Ababa. Language: Amharic. Religions: Coptic Christianity, Islam. High plateau, bisected from NE-SW by Great Rift Valley, incl. L. Tana, source of Blue Nile. Subsistence agric.; exports coffee, hides; gold mining, salt indust. Aksumite empire fl 1st-7th cent.; declined after Moslem incursions, dissolved into rival principalities. Reunited 19th cent., defeated invading Italians 1896. Occupied by Italy 1936; taken by British 1941, regained independence. United federally with ERITREA 1952, fully integrated 1962. Emperor Haile Selassie I deposed 1974 by military coup.

Ethiopic, minor Semitic language group of Afro-Asiatic family. Incl. Ge'ez (classical Ethiopic, now dead), AMHARIC, Tigre, Tigrinya.

ethnology, branch of anthropology which deals comparatively with cultures, their distribution, social systems, *etc.*

ethyl alcohol, *see* ETHANOL.

ethylene (C₂H₄), colourless inflammable gas of olefine series. Obtained by catalytic cracking of petroleum. Used as an anaesthetic, in manufacture of polythene and to speed ripening of fruit.

Etienne, family of printers, *see* ESTIENNE.

Etna, volcano of E Sicily, Italy. Height 3261 m (10,705 ft); isolated peak with *c* 200 minor cones. Lower slopes densely pop., used for growing fruit, olives, almonds. Encircled by railway, road. Major eruptions 1669, 1928, 1971; Catania twice destroyed.

Eton, urban dist. of Buckinghamshire, SC England. Pop. 4000. On Thames opposite Windsor. Has Eton Coll. public school (1440).

Etruria, ancient region of NW Italy, incl. Tuscany, part of Umbria. Home of ancient Etruscans.

Etruscans, ancient people of NC Italy, believed to have emigrated from Asia Minor in 12th cent. BC. Distinctive culture emerged in 8th cent. BC; at height of civilization in 6th cent. BC. Wealth partly based on knowledge of metalworking; noted for sculpture, tomb paintings and architecture. Declined in 5th and 4th cents. BC in face of Gallic invasion from N and Roman conquests. Spoke non-Indo-European language, which has not been interpreted.

Etsch, *see* ADIGE, Italy.

Etty, William (1787-1849), English painter. He is remembered for his voluptuous nudes, presented as religious and classical subjects.

etymology, branch of LINGUISTICS that deals with the origin and development of words. Concerned with changes in both meaning and sound. In 19th cent. study of sound changes in Indo-European languages revealed laws (*eg* Grimm's law) governing phonetic development. Subsequent linguists have tended to study language at a given time (synchronistically) without reference to development (diachronistically).

Euboea (*Evvoia*), isl. of E Greece, in Aegean Sea. Area 3800 sq km (1467 sq mi); cap. Chalcis. Mountainous, highest point Mt. Delphi (1742 m/5718 ft). Cereals, vines, livestock. Road bridge to mainland. Greek from 1830.

Eucalyptus leaves (*Eucalyptus dalrympleana*)

eucalyptus, genus of evergreen trees of myrtle family, native to W Australia. Pendent leaves, pink or white flowers. Yields timber, gums and aromatic oils. Common species is blue gum, *Eucalyptus globulus.*

Eucharist, Christian SACRAMENT in which bread and wine are consecrated and received as body and blood of Jesus. In RC and Orthodox churches, the elements are regarded as miraculously becoming the substance of God (transubstantiation); in most Protestant churches, the rite is regarded as symbolic and is known as the Lord's Supper. Also known as Holy Communion.

Eucken, Rudolf Christoph (1846-1926), German philosopher. Developed system (activism) which stressed ethical effort rather than intellectual idealism. Awarded Nobel Prize for Literature (1908).

Euclid (*fl c* 300 BC), Greek mathematician. Compiler of *Elements,* collection of all geometric knowledge of his time. Esp. noted for its emphasis on deductive reasoning; definitions are given, axioms stated and theorems deduced logically. Also contains important results in number theory. Taught at Alexandria; little else known of his life.

Eugène de Savoie-Carignan, Prince [François] (1663–1736), Austrian general, b. France. Joined Marlborough in War of Spanish Succession, defeating the French at Blenheim (1704), Oudenarde (1708), Malplaquet (1709). He fought with further success against the Turks in 1716-17, winning decisive victory at Belgrade.

Eugénie, née Eugenia María de Montijo de Guzmán (1826-1920), empress of the French, consort of Napoleon III; b. Spain. Married Napoleon III (1853); acted as regent when he was at war. Supported war against Prussia. Fled to England on husband's fall (1870).

euglenoids, members of division, Euglenophyta, of colourless ALGAE common in fresh water, esp. in ponds rich in organic substance.

Euler, Leonhard (1707-83), Swiss mathematician. Made numerous contributions to all branches of mathematics, esp. calculus of variations, number theory, hydrodynamics, mechanics and lunar motion. Many theorems bear his name.

Eumenides (Gk.,=kindly ones), in Greek religion, the Furies who tortured conscience of evil-doers, esp. those who killed their own kindred. Born by Earth after Uranus' blood fell on her, named Alecto, Tisiphone, Megaera. 'Eumenides' is a propitiatory euphemism for Erinyes ('Terrible Ones').

Eupen and Malmédy, areas of E Belgium, near German border. Ceded to Belgium by Treaty of Versailles (1919).

euphonium, low-pitched brass instrument with 4 valves, used in brass bands.

Euphrates, river of SW Asia. Length *c* 2740 km (1700 mi). Rises in E Turkey, flows SE through Syria, Iraq; merges with R. Tigris to form Shatt-al-Arab. Irrigated ancient Mesopotamia. Dam at Tabqa, Syria, irrigates large agric. area.

euphuism, English literary style of late 16th, early 17th cent., named after Lyly's didactic novel, *Euphues* (1578), characterized by exaggerated refinement, neat antitheses.

Euratom, *see* EUROPEAN COMMUNITIES.

Eureka Stockade (1854), armed rebellion of miners on Ballarat goldfield, Australia. Causes were resentment of high cost of mining licences, lack of political representation, Chinese competition on field. Rebellion put down swiftly, but legislation followed to satisfy miners' main grievances. Incident since acclaimed as beginning of democracy in Australia, but also seen as birth of 'White Australia' policy, as consequences incl. poll-tax on Chinese immigrants.

eurhythmics, method of training response to music through harmonious movement of the body. Developed by Jaques-Dalcroze, influenced ballet, acting.

Euric (*fl* 5th cent.), Visigothic king in Spain (466-*c* 484). Subjugated Iberia, parts of Gaul and made Toulouse his cap. Drew up codified Visigothic law.

Euripides (*c* 484-406 BC), Greek tragic poet. Noted for innovations, incl. sympathetic portrayal of common people and women, social criticism, religious unorthodoxy, realistic characterization and language. Wrote over 80 plays, 18 extant, incl. *Alcestis, Medea, Hippolytus, Trojan Women, Electra* and *Bacchae.*

Europa, in Greek myth, daughter of Phoenician King Agenor. Zeus, in the shape of a bull, abducted her to Crete, where she bore him Minos, Rhadamanthus and Sarpedon.

Europe, smallest mainland continent. Area *c* 10,360,000 sq km (4,000,000 sq mi); pop. *c* 690,000,000. Forms penin. of Eurasia projecting into Atlantic, separated from Asia by Ural and Caucasus Mts., Black and Caspian Seas. Crossed W-E by ranges incl. Pyrenees, Alps, Carpathians, Balkans, Caucasus (highest peak Mt. Elbrus 5631 m/18,481 ft). Main rivers Don, Dnepr, Danube, Oder, Elbe, Rhine, Rhône,

Loire, Tagus, Volga. Many isls. incl. Iceland, Great Britain, Ireland, Corsica, Sicily, Sardinia. Main penins. incl. Balkan, Italian, Iberian. Fertile N European plain extends France-Poland. Major focus of civilization from *c* 1500 BC. Greek, Roman empires followed by spread of Christianity, agric., commerce in Middle Ages, Renaissance (centred in N Italy), rise of nation states. Rapid indust. progress in 18th-19th cents. spurred colonialism, spreading European culture to America, Africa, India. Scene of many wars throughout hist.; focus of 2 WWs in 20th cent. Basic political division from 1945 into communist (E), capitalist (W) blocs.

European Atomic Energy Community, *see* EUROPEAN COMMUNITIES.

European Coal and Steel Community, *see* EUROPEAN COMMUNITIES.

European Communities, international organization with aims of economic integration, political unity. Originally 6 W European countries (Belgium, France, West Germany, Italy, Luxembourg, Netherlands) under Treaty of Rome (1957) estab. 3 communities: European Coal and Steel Community (ECSC), European Economic Community (EEC or Common Market), European Atomic Energy Community (Euratom). Merged executives in 1967 to form one Commission. UK, Denmark, Irish Republic joined 1973. Governed by Commission, Council of Ministers, European Parliament. Court of Justice regulates treaties' application, advisory committees monitor social, labour conditions, consumer affairs, *etc*. EEC estab. (1958) with goals of customs union (achieved 1968), common policies on trade, agric.; talks on foreign policy initiated 1970. ECSC estab. 1952 to achieve common market for coal, iron ore, scrap, steel. Harmonized external tariff, regulated internal competition, aided workers in contracting coal indust.; has eventual goal (with Euratom) of Common Energy Policy. Euratom estab. 1958 to promote peaceful uses of nuclear energy; coordinates and promotes research, pools information, promotes training of scientists, technicians.

European Economic Community, *see* EUROPEAN COMMUNITIES.

European Free Trade Association (EFTA), customs union and trading group estab. 1960 by Austria, Denmark, Norway, Portugal, Sweden, Switzerland, UK. Finland became associate member (1961), Iceland joined 1970. UK and Denmark left 1972 to join EEC.

europium (Eu), metallic element of lanthanide series; at. no. 63, at. wt. 151.96. Occurs in monazite. Discovered (1896) by spectroscopic analysis.

Europoort, *see* ROTTERDAM, Netherlands.

Eurydice, *see* ORPHEUS.

Eurynome, in Pelasgian myth, woman who emerged from chaos, created Ophion and mated with him. Thus regarded as mother of all living things. In Greek myth, daughter of Oceanus; mother by Zeus of Graces.

Eustachio, Bartolommeo (d. 1574), Italian anatomist. His descriptions and drawings of various organs were completed in 1552 but not published until 1714. Discovered Eustachian tube, narrow canal connecting middle ear and throat.

Euterpe, in Greek myth, Muse of lyric poetry. Represented as having a flute.

Eutheria, suborder of mammals in which embryo develops in uterus, drawing nourishment through placenta. Incl. all mammals except monotremes, marsupials.

Evans, Sir Arthur John (1851-1941), English archaeologist. Began excavations at Knossos, Crete, in 1899; in course of 30 years' work, he revealed an ancient culture which he named MINOAN CIVILIZATION.

Evans, Dame Edith (1888-1976), English actress. Estab. reputation as Millamant in *The Way of the World*. Known in many major roles incl. Nurse in *Romeo and Juliet*.

Evans, Maurice (1901-   ), English actor-manager. Roles incl. Hamlet, Richard II, Macbeth. Became US citizen (1941).

Evansville, city of SW Indiana, US; on Ohio R. Pop. 139,000. Shipping; meat packing, flour milling, agric. machinery mfg.

evaporation, conversion of a liquid into vapour, without boiling point of liquid necessarily being reached. Rate of evaporation increased by application of heat and by lowering pressure above liquid.

Evatt, Herbert Vere (1894-1965), Australian statesman. Justice of high court of Australia (1930-40); foreign minister (1941-9). Promoted interests of smaller nations as president of UN General Assembly (1948-9).

Eve, *see* ADAM.

Evelyn, John (1620-1706), English diarist. Known for *Diary* of 1641-1706 (pub. 1818) containing sketches of contemporaries. Also wrote on various topics, incl. gardening, pollution.

evening primrose, any of genus, *Oenothera,* of plants native to North America, with yellow, white or pink flowers which open in evening.

Everest, Mount, highest mountain in world, on Nepal-Tibet border; height 8848 m (29,028 ft). First climbed in 1953, by Hillary and Tensing.

Everglades, subtropical swampy region of S Florida US. Area 12,950 sq km (*c* 5000 sq mi). Notable plants, wildlife, esp. water birds, in National Park.

evergreen, tree or plant which remains in foliage throughout the year. In the tropics many broadleaved angiosperms are evergreen, whereas in colder areas evergreens are mainly conifers.

everlasting flowers, blossoms which keep colour and shape when dried by hanging upside down. Often of Compositae family. Incl. flowers of *Xeranthemum, Helipterum, Waitzia* genera.

Everyman (*c* 1500), anon. English morality play. Dramatizes late medieval Christian view of human nature and destiny. Protagonist Everyman, summoned to last journey by Death, seeks help from friends, incl. Kindred, Worldly Goods, Beauty, but only Good Deeds stays with him to end.

Evesham, mun. bor. of Hereford and Worcester, WC England, on R. Avon. Pop. 14,000. In fertile Vale of Evesham; fruit, vegetable growing. Agric. market, canning. Simon de Montfort killed in battle here (1265).

evolution, in biology, theory that all species of animals and plants developed from earlier forms by hereditary transmission of slight variations in genetic composition to successive generations. Theory of evolution by natural selection is due to Darwin (1859); earlier theories incl. Lamarck's inheritance of acquired characteristics. Opposed by theory of special creation, which supposes that each organism is created in its final form and has not undergone successive evolutionary changes.

Evora (anc. *Ebora*), town of S Portugal. Pop. 24,000. Textile mfg., agric. market. Roman 'temple of Diana' ruins. Moorish until 1166.

Evreux, town of Normandy, N France, cap. of Eure dept. Pop. 46,000. Metal, chemical industs. Medieval cathedral noted for stained-glass windows. Extensively damaged in WWII.

Excalibur, *see* ARTHURIAN LEGEND.

exchange, foreign, rate at which currency of one country is exchanged for that of another. Varies with supply and demand of foreign currency, (*see* BALANCE OF PAYMENTS). Apart from speculation, foreign currency is bought by importers and investors in foreign stocks.

excise, tax or duty on the manufacture, sale or consumption of various commodities within a country. Distinct from customs, paid on goods entering country from abroad. Developed in 17th cent. by Holland. Usual goods subject to such tax are tobacco, alcoholic beverages, luxury goods, *etc*.

excommunication, act of formally excluding a person from the sacraments, rights and privileges of a religious body, usually to punish the person expelled and to protect remaining members from his influence. Retained esp. in RC church which teaches that the offender separates himself on commission of the offence (*eg* heresy). Excommunicates are free to return to the church on repentance.

excretion, elimination of useless or harmful metabolic products; organs mainly concerned being kidneys and large intestines of vertebrates, Malpighian tubes of insects, nephridia of invertebrates and stomata of plants.

Exe, river of SW England, flows *c* 88 km (55 mi) from Exmoor to English Channel at Exmouth.

executive, in politics, that part of govt. concerned with admin. of laws, incl. bureaucracy and officials who direct it. In US, theory distinguishes between making of policy decisions and carrying them out. Also *see* SEPARATION OF POWERS.

executor, in law, person appointed by testator to carry out provisions and directions of will. May be appointed by court if deceased died intestate to collect assets, settle debts.

Exeter, city and co. town of Devon, SW England, on R. Exe. Pop. 96,000. Railway jct.; agric. market. Has 11th cent. cathedral, guildhall, univ. (1955).

existentialism, philosophical movement which holds that there is no fixed human nature, that man is free to act as he will and that this is the source of his anguish. Derived from Kierkegaard, exponents incl. SARTRE, Jaspers.

Exmoor, moorland of SW England, national park in Devon, Somerset. Formerly forested; sheep, wild deer, ponies. Scene of Blackmore's *Lorna Doone.*

Exmouth, urban dist. of Devon, SW England, on R. Exe. Pop. 26,000. Resort, fishing port.

Exodus (Gk., = going out), in OT, 2nd book of Pentateuch. Covers period of Jewish history during which Israelites, under Moses, escaped from bondage in Egypt. Deals with founding of the Jewish nation, incl. Moses receiving the TEN COMMANDMENTS and other laws.

exorcism, ritual act of driving evil spirits from person, places or things in which they are believed to dwell. Occurs in primitive societies and in sophisticated religious practice. Scriptural justification is found in the instances of Christ's driving out of devils in NT. Officially recognized in RC church.

explosive, substance which, when heated or otherwise excited, undergoes rapid decomposition with production of large volume of gas; rapid increase of pressure in confined space caused by gas produces explosion. High explosives, incl. TNT, dynamite and nitroglycerine, require detonators to set them off.

expressionism, term for art which tries to give objective expression to inner experience. In 20th cent. painting, associated with artists such as Soutine, Kokoschka, Rouault and the Blaue Reiter, Brücke movements; characterized by distortion of form, violent non-naturalistic colour. Precursors of style incl. van Gogh, Munch. In drama, Strindberg was important forerunner.

extreme unction, sacrament in RC and Orthodox churches of anointing and giving absolution of sins to the dying.

extroversion and **introversion,** in psychology, terms coined by JUNG to denote opposite types of personality. Extrovert personality directs his interest and activity outwards, depends on environment, other people, while an introvert directs his activity inwards to self, and is less affected by surroundings.

extrusive rock, any rock formed by solidification of molten material forced out at Earth's surface. All extrusive rocks are thus IGNEOUS ROCKS; they incl. volcanic lava and pyroclastic material.

Eyck, Hubert van (*c* 1370-1426) and **Jan van Eyck** (*c* 1390-1441), Dutch painters, brothers, who founded Flemish school. Little is known of Hubert; altarpiece of Ghent Cathedral *Adoration of the Lamb* was completed after his death by Jan. Work is characterized by descriptive realism conveyed in minute detail. Jan was court painter to Philip the Good of Burgundy; he is famous for his portraits, incl. *Arnolfini and his Wife.*

eye, organ of sight. Human eyeball has opaque white outer layer (sclera) with transparent bulge (cornea) in front. IRIS is located behind cornea and lens behind this; watery

Jan van Eyck: detail of *Arnolfini and his Wife*

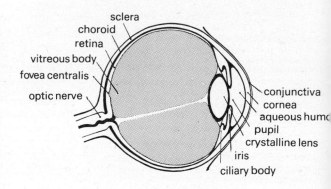

Human eye

aqueous humour fills space between these and jelly-like vitreous humour rest of eye. Light-sensitive RETINA lines inner surface of sclera and transmits sensation of light through optic nerves to brain.

Eyre, Lake, salt lake of NE South Australia. Area *c* 9100 sq km (3500 sq mi); falls to 12m (39 ft) below sea level. Much of it is perennially dry.

Eysenck, Hans Jurgen (1916-   ), British psychologist, b. Germany. Known for advocacy of behaviour therapy rather than Freudian psychoanalysis, and for belief in absolute measurability of intelligence. Works incl. *Race Intelligence and Education* (1971).

Ezekiel, prophetical book of OT. Recounts visions of priest, Ezekiel (*fl* 592 BC). Focuses on fall of Jerusalem, but foretells restoration of its glory.

Ezra, historical book of OT, opening with return of Jews from exile in Babylon to Jerusalem (538 BC) and covering 80 years of Hebrew prophet and scribe Ezra's life and teachings; incl. rebuilding of Temple.

F

Fabergé, Peter Carl (1846-1920), Russian goldsmith. His workshops were famous for exquisite masterpieces, incl. flowers, animals and series of imperial Easter eggs, commissioned by Alexander III for his wife.

Fabian Society, British socialist organization, founded 1884. Aimed to achieve socialism through gradual reformist strategy rather than revolutionary action. Instrumental in estab. British Labour Party. Prominent members have incl. G.B. Shaw, Sidney and Beatrice Webb. Continues political research and publication.

Fabius Maximus, Quintus (d. 203 BC), Roman soldier. Called *Cunctator* ('Delayer') for his successful delaying tactics employed against Hannibal after defeat at L. Trasimene. Romans were routed at Cannae (216 BC) after his recall to Rome.

fable, short moral tale, with animals, inanimate objects as characters. Best-known exponents incl. Aesop, La Fontaine.

fabliau, popular comic tale, usually bawdy or scurrilous, burlesquing human foolishness. Chaucer's *Miller's Tale* has many elements of fabliau.

Fabre, Jean Henri (1823-1915), French entomologist. Author of many works incl. *Souvenirs entomologiques* (1879-1907), based on detailed observations of insect life.

Fabricius, Hieronymus (c 1537-1619), Italian anatomist and embryologist. Described embryonic development of mammals, birds, *etc.* His discovery of valves in veins influenced his pupil William Harvey.

Factory Acts, legislation enacted by British Parliament to regulate conditions and hours of work, safety and sanitary provisions in factories and workshops. First was Health and Morals of Apprentices Act (1802); Cotton Mills Act (1819) forbade employment of children under 9 and reduced hours of labour for under-16s. Act of 1845 banned night-work for women, and that of 1847 introduced 10 hour working day. Factory inspectors appointed 1833. Offices, shops, *etc,* covered 1963.

Fadeyev, Aleksandr Aleksandrovich (1901-56), Russian novelist. Extended socialist realism with psychological insight of *The Nineteen* (1927), *The Young Guard* (1945). Committed suicide.

faeces, waste matter expelled from intestines. Consists of undigested food, bacteria, water and mucus. Colour is due to bile pigment, smell due to nitrogen compounds produced by bacteria.

Faenza (anc. *Faventia),* town of Emilia-Romagna, NC Italy. Pop. 55,000. Ceramics (majolica or *faience)* produced from 12th cent. Cathedral (15th cent.), museum of ceramics.

Faeroes, isl. group of Denmark, in N Atlantic. Area 1399 sq km (540 sq mi); pop. 42,000; cap. Thorshavn. Rugged, treeless. Sheep; fishing. Passed from Norway to Denmark (1380); auton. legislature from 1948.

Fahrenheit, Gabriel Daniel (1686-1736), German meteorological instrument maker. Pioneered use of mercury in thermometers and devised Fahrenheit scale of temperature.

fainting, temporary unconsciousness caused by inadequate flow of blood to brain. May be treated by stretching out victim or lowering his head.

Fairbanks, Douglas (1889-1939), American film actor. Famous for roles as gallant swashbuckler, as in *The Mark of Zorro* (1920), *The Thief of Baghdad* (1923), and for marriage to Mary PICKFORD. Their son, **Douglas Fairbanks, Jnr** (1907-), also became a film star, known for debonair roles. Films incl. *The Prisoner of Zenda* (1937).

Fairbanks, town of C Alaska, US; on Tanana R. Pop. 15,000. Terminus of Alaska Highway. Founded after 1902 gold strike.

Fairfax, Thomas, 3rd Baron Fairfax of Cameron (1612-71), English general. Commanded New Model Army which defeated Charles I at Naseby (1645). Refused to preside over trial of Charles as he doubted the judges' impartiality. Resigned command rather than invade Scotland (1650).

Fair Isle, small isl. in Shetlands, N Scotland. Famous knitwear mfg. Has bird observatory.

fairy, in folklore, supernatural being with magical powers. Concept has existed from earliest times but has greatly varied: described as demonic, mischievous, loving, bountiful. National variations incl. Arab djinns, SW English pixies, German elves, Scandinavian trolls.

Faisal, *see* FEISAL.

Faiyûm, El, city of N Egypt, in fertile El Faiyûm oasis. Pop. 151,000. Trade centre in cotton, sugar producing region. Archaeological remains at nearby Birket Qarun (ancient L. Moeris).

Faizabad or **Fyzabad,** town of Uttar Pradesh, N India. Pop. 110,000. Railway jct; sugar refining. Incl. hist. site of Jain religious centre.

Falange, orig. *Falange Española,* fascist movement and party in Spain. Founded (1933) by José Antonio Primo de Rivera; became only legal party in Spain under leadership of Franco (1937). Power waned, esp. after Franco enacted new constitution (1966).

falcon, bird of prey of Falconidae family. Long pointed wings, powerful hooked beak; diet of birds, insects, small mammals. Some falcons trained for hunting small game. Species incl. peregrine, kestrel, merlin, South American caracara.

falconry, *see* HAWKING.

Falkirk, town of Central region, C Scotland. Pop. 38,000. Large iron foundries. Scene of Edward I of England's victory over Wallace (1298).

Falkland, Lucius Cary, 2nd Viscount (c 1610-43), English statesman, patron of literature. Entered Parliament (1640), supported impeachment of Strafford. Later sided with Charles I and took part in king's peace negotiations with Parliament (1642). Killed in battle, supposedly in despair of civil war.

Falkland Islands (Span. *Islas Malvinas),* crown colony of UK, in S Atlantic Ocean. Comprise East and West Falkland, c 200 small isls. Area 12,100 sq km (4700 sq mi); pop. 2500; cap. Stanley. Sheep rearing. Dependencies incl. South Georgia, South Orkney, South Shetland, South Sandwich Isls., Graham Land. Entire area claimed by Argentina.

Falla, Manuel de (1876-1946), Spanish composer. Influenced by Spanish folk music. His few compositions incl. opera *La Vida breve, Nights in the Gardens of Spain* for piano and orchestra, ballets *El Amor brujo* and *The Three-cornered Hat.*

Fallada, Hans, pseud. of Rudolf Ditzen (1893-1947), German novelist. Influenced by expressionism, later known for sympathetic portrayal of working classes, *eg* in *Little Man, What Now?* (1932) set in depression of 1920s.

fall line, line joining waterfalls or rapids on a number of rivers flowing roughly parallel to each other. Marks sudden increase in slope, *eg* at edge of plateau; forms head of navigation, source of h.e.p. Applied in particular to boundary between piedmont plateau and coastal plain of E US, fall line cities incl. Trenton, Philadelphia, Richmond.

Fallopius or **Gabriele Fallopio** (1523–62), Italian anatomist. Noted member of Paduan school of anatomists. Discovered Fallopian tubes, leading from ovaries to the uterus, in which fertilization takes place.

fall-out, radioactive material deposited on Earth's surface following nuclear explosions. May cause genetic damage or various diseases, *eg* leukaemia. Strontium 90 present in fall-out is very dangerous as it may replace calcium in body.

Fallow deer

fallow deer, *Dama dama,* European deer of Mediterranean region, rare in wild state. Usually reddish-brown with white spots; also dark varieties. Introduced into many parts of N Europe, North America as park animal.

Falmouth, mun. bor. of Cornwall, SW England. Pop. 18,000. Ship repairs, fishing port, resort.

Falster, isl. of S Denmark, in Baltic Sea. Area 513 sq km (198 sq mi); main town Nyköbing. Bridges to Zealand, Laaland. Dairying, pig farming.

Famagusta, port of E Cyprus. Pop. *c* 40,000. Exports citrus fruits, potatoes; holiday resort. Near ancient Salamis on site of Arsinoë.

family, social unit consisting of parental couple and children ('nuclear family'). Other close relatives may be included, *eg* grandparents, aunts, uncles, *etc* ('extended family'). Depends on stability of parental relationship, obligations and bonds between blood relations, satisfaction of personal and social needs.

Fanfani, Amintore (1908-), Italian statesman. A Christian Democrat, he held premiership for 3 terms (1954, 1958-9, 1960-3). President of UN General Assembly (1965-6).

Fangio [y Cia], Juan Manuel (1911-), Argentinian racing driver. World champion 5 times (1951, 1954-7). Retired 1958.

Fanon, Frantz Omar (1925-61), Algerian revolutionary, b. Martinique. Involved in revolt against French rule in 1950s. Leading exponent of peasant revolution in Africa. Works incl. *Black Skin, White Masks* (1952), *Wretched of the Earth* (1961).

Fantin-Latour, [Ignace] Henri (1836-1904), French painter. Painted still lifes, flower pieces and romantic figure subjects. Best known for his portrait groups of famous contemporaries, *eg Hommage à Delacroix*.

FAO, *see* FOOD AND AGRICULTURE ORGANIZATION.

Faraday, Michael (1791-1867), English chemist and physicist. Studies in electrochemistry led to discovery of 2 quantitative laws of electrolysis (Faraday's laws). Discovered principle of electromagnetic induction, effect utilized in dynamo. His concept of electric and magnetic fields of force became basis of Maxwell's electromagnetic theory. Discovered benzene (1825).

Michael Faraday

Far East, vague term for countries of E Asia, incl. China, Japan, Korea and Mongolia. Sometimes also taken to incl. countries of SE Asia and Malay Archipelago.

Farewell, Cape, headland, most S point of Greenland on Egger Isl.

Fargo, William George (1818-81), American expressman. A founder of American Express Co. (1850). Joined Henry Wells to form (1852) Wells-Fargo to handle New York-San Francisco express traffic.

Fargo, town of E North Dakota, US; on Red R. Pop. 53,000; state's largest town. Transport jct.; livestock, wheat market; agric. machinery mfg. Named after stage coach system organizer.

Farnborough, urban dist. of Hampshire, S England. Pop. 41,000. Has Royal Aircraft Estab. research centre.

Farne Islands, *c* 30 isls. off Northumberland, NE England. Chapel to St Cuthbert (d. 687). Scene of Grace Darling's rescue of survivors from the *Forfarshire* (*1838*).

Farnese, Alessandro (1545-92), Italian general, duke of Parma and Piacenza. Nephew of John of Austria, whom he succeeded as Spanish governor of Netherlands (1578). Recovered S Netherlands from rebels. Sent to France to support Catholics against Henry IV.

Faro, town of S Portugal, cap. of Algarve prov. Pop. 19,000. Port, exports wine, figs, cork; sardine, tuna fishing; tourism.

Faroe Islands, *see* FAEROES, Denmark.

Farouk I (1920-65), king of Egypt (1936-52). Exiled after military coup under Naguib and Nasser (1952). Succeeded by son Fuad, who was deposed in 1953.

Farquhar, George (1678-1707), English dramatist, b. Ireland. Developed Restoration comedy into more sentimental mode. Works incl. *The Recruiting Officer* (1706), *The Beaux' Stratagem* (1707). Former adapted by Brecht as *Trumpets and Drums* (1956).

Farragut, David Glasgow (1801-70), American admiral. Led naval action which captured New Orleans from Confederates (1862). Effectively ended Confederate blockade-running by capturing Mobile Bay (1864).

Farrar, Frederick William (1831-1903), English clergyman, author, b. India. Best known for school stories extolling Christian virtues, esp. *Eric, or Little by Little* (1858). Also wrote sermons, theological works.

Farrell, James T[homas] (1904-), American novelist. Known for naturalistic novels esp. 'Studs Lonigan' trilogy (1932-5). Also wrote short stories, and criticism, *A Note on Literary Criticism* (1936) being statement of proletarian aesthetics.

Fars, province of S Iran, on Persian Gulf. As ancient *Persis*, was area from which Persians created their empire. Incl. towns of Persepolis and Pasargadae.

far sight [US], *see* HYPERMETROPIA.

fasces, bundle of rods bound about an axe with projecting blade. Carried before Roman magistrates as symbol of their authority; later became symbol of Italian fascism.

fascism, political ideology of totalitarian, militarist and nationalistic character. Advocates govt. by one-party dictatorship and centralized control of private economic enterprise (*see* CORPORATE STATE). Nationalism most extreme in racist suppression of minorities, *eg* anti-Semitism; strong police measures used to maintain law and order, oppose democracy, Communism. Originated with Mussolini's Fascist party which held power in Italy (1922-43). Fascism had spread by 1936 to Germany (Nazis), Japan, Spain (Falange), most of E Europe.

Fashoda, *see* KODOK, Sudan.

Fashoda Incident (1898-9), Anglo-French dispute over control of upper Nile region. French forces took Fashoda (now Kodok) in S Sudan, but, fearing war, withdrew upon British insistence. Peaceful settlement marked end of French claims in area.

Fates (Gk. *Morai*), in Greek myth, three goddesses who controlled course of human life; Clotho spun the thread of life, Lachesis measured it, Atropos cut it. The Roman Fates (*Parcae*) were Nona, Decuma, Morta.

Fathers of the Church, term for Christian teachers and writers of the early Church whose work is considered orthodox. In West, incl. those up to and incl. St Gregory the Great, and to St John of Damascus in East.

Fatimites or **Fatimids,** Moslem dynasty, claiming descent from Mohammed's daughter, Fatima, which ruled in N Africa and Egypt (909-1171). Founded by Obaidallah, whose cap. was in Tunisia. Successors conquered Sicily, W Arabia, Palestine and Syria. Cairo became Fatimite cap. (969). Rule ended with Saladin's conquest of Egypt.

fats, group of naturally occurring substances found in plants and animals. Consist of mixtures of esters of glycerol with higher fatty acids, *eg* stearic, palmitic, oleic acids. Excellent source of energy in food.

Faulkner, John Meade (1858-1932), English author. Best known for classic adventure story *Moonfleet* (1898).

Faulkner or **Falkner, William** (1897-1962), American novelist, short story writer. Created imaginary county in Deep South, populated with vivid characters in complex, decaying society. Novels incl. *The Sound and the Fury* (1929), *Sanctuary* (1931), *Light in August* (1932). Awarded Nobel Prize for Literature (1949).

fault, in geology, fracture in rock strata along which movement has occurred to displace sides relative to each other. Movement may be upward, sideways, or both; uplift on one side of fault can result in steep cliff or 'fault scarp'.

Faunus, in Roman myth, god of forests, patron of herdsmen. Attended by fauns, creatures with body of a man, legs of a goat. Identified with Greek Pan.

Fauré, Gabriel (1845-1924), French composer. Wrote delicate and sensitive music. Works incl. nocturnes for piano, chamber music, operas, a Requiem, songs. A great teacher (of Ravel among others); director of Paris Conservatoire (1905-20).

Faust, hero of several medieval legends. Based on historical figure (d. *c* 1540), a philosopher who was said to have sold his soul to the Devil in exchange for knowledge and power. Story, first pub. in the *Faustbuch* of 1587, inspired Marlowe, Goethe, Thomas Mann, Gounod and many others.

fauvism, short-lived modern art movement (*c* 1905-8). Used bold distortion of form and brilliant pure colour. Exponents incl. Matisse, Derain, Vlaminck, Marquet; given name ('Les Fauves' = wild beasts) by critic at controversial 1st showing.

Fawkes, Guy (1570-1606), English conspirator. Catholic convert, served with Spanish armies in Netherlands. Involved in Gunpowder Plot (5 Nov. 1605) to blow up Houses of Parliament during opening of new session by James I. Plot exposed, Fawkes and other leaders executed.

FBI, *see* FEDERAL BUREAU OF INVESTIGATION.

feather star, free-swimming marine invertebrate of class Crinoidea. Mouth uppermost; 5 feather-like arms used for swimming. Capable of regeneration.

Guy Fawkes with conspirators

February Revolution (1848), revolution in France which overthrew Louis Philippe and estab. Second Republic; provoked REVOLUTION OF 1848 in much of Europe. After uprising, moderate provisional govt. granted demands for indust. reforms, but sabotage caused failure of policies and further revolt. Louis Napoleon elected president after formulation of new constitution.

Fécamp, town of Normandy, N France, on English Channel. Pop. 22,000. Fishing, boatbuilding industs. From 16th cent. noted for production, originally by monks, of benedictine liqueur.

Federal Bureau of Investigation (FBI), branch of US Dept. of Justice. Estab. (1908) to investigate all violations of Federal laws except those, as of currency, tax, postal laws, dealt with by other Federal agencies. Drew criticism during WATERGATE AFFAIR.

federalism, system of govt. dividing nation's sovereign powers between central (federal) authority and constituent subdivisions (states, provinces). Central govt. powers usually incl. foreign relations, defence, commerce, coinage; states usually control their internal affairs. Arbitration of disputes often delegated to courts with reference to written constitution and precedents. US, West Germany, USSR, Canada, Australia have federal govt. structures.

Federalist Papers, series of 85 essays written (1787-8) by Alexander Hamilton, James Madison and John Jay analyzing Federal Constitution and urging its adoption by American states.

Federalist Party, in US history, political party (estab. *c* 1791) under leadership of Alexander Hamilton and John Adams. Advocated strong central govt., expansion of commerce, anti-French foreign policy. Lost power to Jeffersonians after 1800. National significance lost by 1817.

Federal Reserve System, central banking system of US (estab. 1913). Each of 12 regional reserve banks serves each Federal Reserve district. National banks maintain reserves on deposit with regional banks. Money supply and credit conditions regulated by Federal Reserve Board.

Federal Trade Commission (FTC), govt. agency of US estab. (1915) to maintain fair practice in commercial competition, check growth of monopolies, *etc.* Successive legislation gave FTC legal power, *eg* in preventing false advertising, to issue cease-and-desist orders.

feedback, *see* AUTOMATION.

Feiffer, Jules (1927-), American satirical strip cartoonist, screen writer. Preoccupied with personal inadequacies, petty corruptions, of 'typical' Americans. Filmscripts incl. *Carnal Knowledge* (1971).

Feininger, Lyonel (1871-1956), American painter, graphic artist. Trained in Germany, he was associated with later forms of cubism. Specialized in architectural and marine subjects. Taught at Bauhaus 1919-32.

Feisal I or **Faisal I** (1885-1933), king of Iraq (1921-33). Joined with T.E. Lawrence in revolt against Turkey (1916). Proclaimed king of Syria (1920), deposed by French mandatory powers. British, who held mandate in Iraq, supported him in fight for Iraqi throne.

Feisal II or **Faisal II** (1935-58), king of Iraq (1939-58). Succeeded his father, Ghazi I; ruled through regent until 1953. Killed in military coup which estab. republic.

Feisal, Ibn Al-Saud (1905-75), king of Saudi Arabia (1964-75). Succeeded brother Saud as king. Reign marked by pro-Western policies, increasing wealth and technological advances, based on vast oil exports. Assassinated by a nephew.

feldspars or **felspars,** group of rock-forming aluminium silicate minerals. Distinct types contain calcium, potassium, sodium or, very rarely, barium. Comprise *c* 50% of Earth's crust; found in igneous rocks, *eg* granite, basalt. Clay is product of weathering of feldspars.

Felidae, the cat family, incl. cats, lions, tigers, leopards and extinct sabre-toothed tiger.

Felixstowe, urban dist. of Suffolk, E England. Pop. 19,000. Resort, major container port.

Fellini, Federico (1920-   ), Italian film director. Noted for sympathy for victims of violence, greed or apathy. Films incl. *La Strada* (1954), *Notte di Cabiria* (1957) (both won Oscars), *8½* (1963), *Satyricon* (1969).

felony, serious crime, as distinct from MISDEMEANOUR. In UK law, distinction only historically valid. In US, both federal and state law maintain it, usually trying felony by jury, with serious penalty.

femur, in man, same as thigh bone.

fencing, sport of combat with swords. Three types of sword used: foil, a light weapon; épée, derived from duelling sword; sabre, a cut-and-thrust weapon. Olympic event for men since 1896, for women since 1924.

Fénelon, François de Salignac de la Mothe (1651-1715), French theologian. Archbishop of Cambrai from 1695. Defended quietism in *Maximes des saints* (1697). Wrote utopian novel, *Télémaque* (1699), to instruct young prince.

Feng Yu-hsiang (1880-1948), Chinese army officer, called the 'Christian general'. Fought in N China, Manchuria during civil war. Joined Nationalist govt. (1928), later led group opposing Chiang Kai-shek.

Fenians, secret revolutionary society formed (*c* 1858) to secure Irish independence from Britain. Promoted risings and terrorism suppressed by British, thus drawing attention to Irish problems. Group of Irish emigrants in US attempted invasion of Canada (1866); invasion ended in failure but encouraged Canadian confederation. *See also* SINN FEIN.

fennec, *Fennecus zerda,* small fawn-coloured fox of desert areas of N Africa, Arabia. Large ears and eyes; diet of insects, rodents.

fennel, name for several herbs, esp. those of genus *Foeniculum* in parsley family, used to flavour fish sauces and salad dressings. Wild fennel, *F. vulgare,* is used in stuffing.

Fens, The, flat low-lying area of E England, W and S of The Wash, within Cambridgeshire, Lincolnshire, Norfolk. Formerly bay of North Sea, silting created marsh. Draining begun 1621 by Vermuyden (Dutch). Now fertile, rich agric. incl. cereals, sugar beet, fruit.

fer-de-lance, *Bothrops atrox,* highly venomous snake of pit viper group of tropical America, West Indies. Reaches lengths of *c* 1.8 m/6 ft.

Ferdinand (1793-1875), emperor of Austria (1835-48). Subject to fits of insanity; dominated by foreign minister METTERNICH. Fled country during Revolution of 1848; abdicated in favour of nephew Francis Joseph.

Ferdinand I (1503-64), Holy Roman emperor (1558-64). Claimed kingdoms of Bohemia and Hungary on death of brother-in-law, Louis II (1526). Claim to Hungary opposed by John Zapolya and Turkish allies, leading to war until 1538. Negotiated Peace of Augsburg (1555) before succeeding his brother, Charles V, as emperor.

Ferdinand II (1578-1637), Holy Roman emperor (1619-37). A fervent Catholic, his deposition as king of Bohemia (1619) by Bohemian Protestants marked beginning of THIRTY YEARS WAR. Reimposed Catholicism in Bohemia by force after victory at White Mountain (1620). Failed to sustain early successes of Tilly and Wallenstein.

Ferdinand (1861-1948), king of Bulgaria (1908-18). German prince, elected prince of Bulgaria (1887), although not recognized by European powers until 1896. Proclaimed Bulgarian independence from Ottoman Empire (1908), taking title 'tsar' of Bulgaria. Defeated in 2nd Balkan War (1913); joined Central Powers in WWI. Abdicated in favour of his son, Boris III.

Ferdinand II (1816-85), king consort of Maria II of Portugal (1837-53). Regent for sons Pedro V and Louis I. Refused crowns of Greece (1862) and of Spain (1869).

Ferdinand (1865-1927), king of Romania (1914-27). Joined Allies in WWI; acquired territ. from Hungary and Russia after war. Reign marked by agrarian reform and introduction of universal suffrage.

Ferdinand I [the Great] (d. 1065), king of Castile (1035-65) and León (1037-65). Began reconquest of Spain, making Moorish emirs of Saragossa, Seville, Toledo, Badajoz his vassals.

Ferdinand V [the Catholic] (1452-1516), king of Aragón and Castile. Married his cousin Isabella of Castile (1469); they ruled Castile jointly (1474-1504) until her death. Became Ferdinand II of Aragón (1479), thus uniting all of Spain except Granada. In 1492, reconquered Granada and expelled Jews from Spain. Rivalled Portuguese colonial expansion, notably by financing Columbus.

Ferdinand VII (1784-1833), king of Spain (1808-33). Imprisoned in France (1808-14) by Napoleon. Restored (1814), precipitated revolt (1820) by revoking liberal constitution. Restored to absolute power by French military intervention. Reign saw loss of Spanish colonies in North and South America.

Ferdinand I (1751-1825), king of the Two Sicilies (1816-25). Became king of Naples and Sicily (1759). Influenced by wife Marie Caroline, opposed French in Revolutionary Wars. Lost Naples to France (1806-15). On restoration, he ruled despotically.

Fermanagh, former county of SW Northern Ireland. Hilly in NE, SW; bisected by Upper and Lower Lough Erne. Agric.; cattle rearing. Co. town was Enniskillen.

Fermanagh, district; area 1876 sq km (724 sq mi); pop. 51,000. Created 1973, formerly Co. Fermanagh.

Fermat, Pierre de (1601-65), French mathematician. Anticipated Descartes' discovery of analytical geometry and certain features of differential calculus. Famed for work on number theory; his famous 'last theorem' remains unproved, despite his claims. Enunciated principle that path taken by light ray between 2 points is that taking least time.

fermentation, chemical change caused by enzyme action. Yeast enzyme system causes alcoholic fermentation of sugar, with production of ethyl alcohol and carbon dioxide.

Fermi, Enrico (1901-54), American physicist, b. Italy. Awarded Nobel Prize for Physics (1938) for work on neutron bombardment, esp. use of absorbing materials to slow down neutrons. Headed Univ. of Chicago group which achieved first controlled nuclear reaction (1942).

fermions, in physics, elementary particles, incl. electron, proton, which conform to Fermi-Dirac statistics and obey Pauli exclusion principle. Divided into baryons and leptons. Number of fermions taking part in nuclear interactions appears to be conserved.

fermium (Fm), transuranic element; at. no. 100, mass no. of most stable isotope 257. Discovered in debris of nuclear explosion (1953) and named after E. Fermi.

fern, any of a class, Filicineae, of flowerless perennial plants. Distinctive frond-shaped leaves. Reproduces by spores rather than seeds. More than 6000 species, widely distributed esp. in tropics. Fossils indicate many early varieties.

Fernandel, stage name of Fernand Constantin (1903-1971), French comedian. Known for role as priest in film of

Fern

The Little World of Don Camillo (1953), as quins (playing all five) in *The Sheep has Five Legs* (1953).

Fernando da Noronha, isl. group of Brazil, off NE coast. Area *c* 10 sq km (26 sq mi). Penal colony from 18th cent.; military base.

Fernando Póo, see MACIAS NGUEMA BIYOGA.

Ferrar, Nicholas (1592-1637), English theologian. Retired from Parliament and founded (1625) austere Anglican monastic community at Little Gidding, Cambridgeshire. Disbanded by Parliament (1647).

Ferrara, city of Emilia-Romagna, NC Italy, cap. of Ferrara prov. Pop. 155,000. Agric. market, food processing; univ. (1391). Cultural centre 13th-16th cent. under Este family; incorporated 1598 into Papal States. Moated castle (14th cent.).

Ferrel, William (1817-91), American meteorologist. Studied winds, tides and currents, formulating 'Ferrel's law' on deflection of moving bodies by rotation of the Earth.

Ferret

ferret, domesticated albino variety of polecat, genus *Mustela*. Tamed to hunt rabbits and rats.

Ferrier, Kathleen (1912-53), British contralto. Her rich, full voice rapidly brought her international fame after WW II; career cut short by cancer. Title role of Britten's *The Rape of Lucretia* written for her.

Ferrol (del Caudillo), El, town of Galicia, NW Spain, on Atlantic Ocean. Pop. 88,000. Chief Atlantic naval base; fish processing. Birthplace of Franco ('El Caudillo').

ferromagnetism, property of certain metals, esp. iron, cobalt and nickel, of having high susceptibility to acquiring magnetism. Such materials exhibit HYSTERESIS and may be used as permanent magnets.

Ferry, Jules François (1832-93), French statesman. As minister of education, estab. free, compulsory, secular education at elementary level (1882). As premier (1880-1, 1883-5) pursued expansionist colonial policies in Africa, Indo-China.

fertility drugs, substances used to increase possibility of conception. Male infertility sometimes treated by thyroid and pituitary hormones. Failure to ovulate in female can be treated by drug clomiphene, but this may cause multiple births.

fertility rites, ceremonies to ensure abundance of food and birth of children. Usually rituals involving personification of natural phenomena, *eg* seed, Sun, Earth, and invoking sympathetic magic.

fertilization, union of male sperm cell with female egg cell (ovum) to form a zygote, which develops to form new individual. *See* also POLLINATION.

fertilizer, substance put on soil to improve quantity and quality of plant growth, usually by supplying necessary nitrogen, phosphorus and potassium. Organic fertilizers incl. animal manure and bone meal; inorganic incl. nitrates and ammonium compounds, superphosphates and basic slag.

fescue, any of genus *Festuca* of perennial grasses. Many used in temperate regions for lawns or pasture, *eg* meadow fescue, *F. elatior.*

Festival of Lights, see HANUKKAH.

fetishism, worship of inanimate object believed to have supernatural power. *See* TABOO, TOTEMISM.

feudalism, economic, political, social system of medieval Europe. In ideal system, ownership of all land was vested in king, who granted it to highest nobles in return for military, personal service; they in turn granted land to lesser nobles, and so on, until lowest level (serf) reached. Local unit was manor, whose lord (seigneur) granted land to and protected peasants, villeins, serfs, in return for service. Church ownership of land worked in parallel. System declined with growth of money economy, rise of mercantile classes.

Feuerbach, Ludwig Andreas von (1804-72), German philosopher. Abandoned Hegelian idealism for naturalistic materialism. In *The Essence of Christianity* (1841) analyzed religion anthropologically, asserting God to be man's projection of his own nature.

fever, abnormally high body temperature, usually a symptom of infection or disease. Believed to be caused by stimulation of temperature-control centre of brain during destruction of bacteria.

Feverfew

feverfew, *Chrysanthemum parthenium*, perennial herb of daisy family. Dried leaves and flowers used to make medicinal tea.

Feydeau, Georges (1862-1921), French playwright. Known for ingeniously contrived farces, incl. *La dame de chez Maxim* (1899), *Un fil à la patte* (1899).

Feynman, Richard Phillips (1918-), American physicist. Shared Nobel Prize for Physics (1965) for work on quantum electrodynamics. Devised Feynman diagram to describe particle transformations.

Fez

Fez (Fr. *Fès*), city of N Morocco, Pop. 321,000. Route centre; carpet mfg., leather goods. Founded 808; sacred city of Islam with *c* 100 mosques, has ancient Moslem univ.

Fezzan, region of SW Libya. Mainly desert, some oases; produces dates. Formerly crossed by many caravan routes. Taken by Turks 1842, by Italy 1911; under French military govt. 1943-51. Federal prov. (cap. Sebha) 1951-63.

Ffestiniog, urban dist. of Gwynedd, NW Wales. Pop. 6000. Blaenau Ffestiniog is nearby, major slate quarrying centre; h.e.p. station (1963).

Fianna Fáil, Irish political party, estab. 1926 by opponents of Irish Free State. Under leadership of DE VALÉRA, controlled govt. from 1932, demanding separation from Britain. Opposed by FINE GAEL.

fiat money, *see* FIDUCIARY ISSUE.

fibre, thread-like tissue capable of being spun into yarn. Animal fibres, composed mainly of protein, incl. silk, wool, hair of goats, rabbits, *etc*; vegetable fibres, composed mostly of cellulose, incl. cotton, kapok, hemp. Modern synthetic fibres are usually polymers, *eg* nylon and various polyesters.

fibre optics, branch of optics dealing with transmission of light along very narrow flexible glass cables. Technique used to locate faults in machinery, investigate human body.

Fichte, Johann Gottlieb (1762-1814), German philosopher. Wrote *Critique of Religious Revelation* (1792), developing Kantian ethics. *Addresses to the German People* (1808) stirred national feeling against Napoleon's domination.

Fiddler crab

fiddler crab, small burrowing crab, genus *Uca,* of salt marshes and sandy beaches. Male has one claw much larger than other.

fiduciary issue or **fiat money,** in banking, the portion of an issue of currency notes which is not backed by gold or other tangible assets available on demand. Normally backed by bills of exchange or govt. securities.

Field, Cyrus West (1819-92), American paper manufacturer. Promoted 1st Atlantic cable (1866) and cable from US to Australia via Hawaii.

Field, John (1782-1837), Irish composer, pianist. Worked mainly in Russia as teacher and performer. Devised *nocturne* form, later developed by Chopin. Compositions influenced several Romantic composers.

Field, Marshall (1834-1906), American merchant. From clerk, rose to make great personal fortune; estab. many modern methods of retailing. Gave land, money to Chicago Art Institute, Univ., Museum of Natural History. His grandson, **Marshall Field III** (1893-1956), devoted himself to social projects. Supported liberal newspapers, charities.

Fieldfare

fieldfare, *Turdus pilaris,* European bird of thrush family, with grey head, brown back. Breeds in colonies in N Europe.

field hockey, *see* HOCKEY.

Fielding, Henry (1707-54), English author. Important in development of English novel. First novels, *eg Joseph Andrews* (1742), burlesqued trials of virginity of Richardson's *Pamela,* as well as using powerful social satire. Best known for *Tom Jones* (1749), complex comic masterpiece. Also wrote plays, political satire, criticism.

field mouse, *see* MOUSE.

Fields, Gracie, orig. Grace Stansfield (1898-), English comedienne, music-hall singer. Songs associated with her incl. 'The Biggest Aspidistra in the World', 'Sally'.

Fields, W. C., orig. Claude William Dukenfield (1880-1946), American film actor. Famous as gravel-voiced, alcoholic, intolerant comedian, who improvised many of his films. Starred in films from 1915, incl. *The Bank Dick* (1940), *Never Give a Sucker an Even Break* (1941).

field theory, in physics, means of representing effect of physical phenomena throughout space. Magnetic, electric and gravitational forces may all be represented by fields.

Fiesole (anc. *Faesulae),* town of Tuscany, NC Italy, on hill overlooking Florence. Mainly residential; tourism. Etruscan, then Roman settlement; many remains, incl. amphitheatre.

Fife, region of E Scotland, between firths of Tay and Forth. Area 1305 sq km (504 sq mi); pop. 328,000. Created 1975 from former Fife county. Lomond Hills in W. Rich agric. (esp. cereals); coalmining; fishing. Ancient Pictish kingdom.

fifth column, collaborationist group, native to one country but working for another. Term first used by Spanish Nationalist General Mola (1936) who, besieging Madrid with 4 columns, boasted of having a 'fifth column' already within.

Fig

fig, any of genus *Ficus* of mulberry family, esp. *F. carica,* broad-leaved cultivated tree bearing soft, many-seeded, edible fruit. Prob. grown first in Arabia; spread to Mediterranean countries and US.

fighting fish, *Betta splendens,* small brightly coloured freshwater fish of S Asia. Males, very aggressive to each other, bred in Siam for fighting.

figwort, perennial plant of genus *Scrophularia* with square stem. Species incl. common figwort, *S. nodosa,* with tuberous roots and water figwort, *S. aquatica.*

Fiji Islands, country of SW Pacific Ocean, comprising *c* 320 isls of which *c* 100 inhabited. Area 18,350 sq km (7080 sq mi); pop. 560,000; cap. Suva. Main isls. Viti Levu, Vanua Levu. Produces sugar cane, rice, fruit and gold; tourist centre. Discovered (1643) by Abel Tasman; British colony from 1874 until independence 1970. Large Indian pop., descendants of plantation workers imported 19th cent. Member of British Commonwealth.

filbert, two deciduous HAZEL trees, *Corylus maxima* and *C. avellana.* Native to W Asia, widely cultivated for nut crop.

Fillmore, Millard (1800-74), American statesman, president (1850-3). Whig vice-president, succeeded Zachary Taylor as president. Supported 'compromise' view on slavery issue. Presidential candidate (1856) for Know-Nothing party.

filtration, separation of suspended undissolved solids from liquids. Filters incl. absorbent paper, fabrics, sands and charcoal.

finch, any of Fringillidae family of small short-beaked, seed-eating birds. Incl. canary, sparrow, goldfinch.

Fine Gael, Irish political party, estab. 1933. Has held power three times, only in coalition with Labour Party. Opposed by FIANNA FÁIL.

Fingal's Cave, cavern in Staffa, (isl. of Inner Hebrides), W Scotland. Associated with legends.

fingerprint, impression of lines, whorls on inner surface of end joint of finger. Used by police for identification, impression being thought unique and permanent for each individual.

Finisterre, Cape, headland of La Coruña prov., most W point of Spanish mainland. Scene of two English naval victories (1747, 1805) over French.

Finland (*Suomi*), republic of NE Europe. Area 337,010 sq km (130,120 sq mi); pop. 4,668,000; cap. Helsinki. Languages: Finnish, Swedish. Religion: Lutheran. Tundra

Finland

in N (Lapland), mainly within Arctic Circle; lakes, forests in S. Mostly low-lying; main rivers Torne, Kemi, Oulu. Forestry (pulp, paper), h.e.p., some agric. Conquered (12th cent.) by Eric IX of Sweden, Swedish culture estab. in Middle Ages. Ceded to Russia 1809. Independence followed Russian Revolution (1917), republic estab. 1919. Lost territ. (incl. Karelia) after war with USSR (1939-40).

Finland, Gulf of, arm of Baltic Sea, between Finland and USSR. Frozen in winter. Main ports Helsinki, Leningrad, Tallinn, Vyborg.

Finno-Ugric or **Finno-Ugrian,** language group within URALIC family. Incl. Estonian, Finnish, Lapp, Hungarian (Magyar).

Finsteraarhorn, peak of WC Switzerland, highest in Bernese Oberland, 4273 m (14,026 ft).

fir, general name for any of the tall, widely distributed, coniferous, evergreen trees of genus *Abies,* and for other similar trees, *eg* Douglas fir.

Firbank, [Arthur Annesley] Ronald (1886-1926), English novelist. Known for artificial, fantastic novels of delicate wit *eg Vainglory* (1915), *Caprice* (1917).

Firdausi or **Ferdusi, Mansur Abu'l-Qasim** (*c* 935-*c* 1020), Persian poet. Famed for classic epic *Shah-nama* (book of the kings), relating traditional history of Iranian kings; model for most later Moslem epic poetry.

firearms, weapons discharging projectiles by use of explosives. Primitive cannon were first used *c* 1300; handguns followed half a century later. The most rapid improvements came with the invention of the percussion cap, breech loading and the magazine in the 19th cent. Automatic weapons appeared *c* 1900.

fireclay, clay composed mainly of alumina and silica, capable of resisting intense heat. Used to make firebrick for lining kilns and metallurgical furnaces. Often found under coal seams.

firefly, any of Lampyridae family of luminescent beetles, most numerous in tropics. Light, produced by chemical action in special organs on abdomen, used as communication between sexes. Larvae, wingless females called glow-worms.

Firenze, see FLORENCE, Italy.

Fire of London (1666), fire which swept through city, devastating almost all of medieval London. In 4 days, it destroyed *c* 13,000 buildings, incl. St Paul's Cathedral. Rebuilding undertaken by Christopher Wren.

fire salamander, *Salamandra salamandra,* European amphibian with dark skin and yellow markings. Feeds at dusk; diet of worms, insects.

fireworks, preparations of explosives used for display purposes. Thought to have originated in China, introduced to Europe (13th cent.). Potassium nitrate and potassium chlorate commonly used with various metal salts to give range of colours.

First World War, see WORLD WAR I.

Fischer, Emil (1852-1919), German organic chemist. Awarded Nobel Prize for Chemistry (1902) for research on structure of sugars and purines. Analyzed way in which amino acids combine to form proteins and devised methods of synthesizing proteins.

Fischer, Robert James ('Bobby') (1943-), American chess player. First American world champion, he defeated Russian Boris Spassky amidst worldwide publicity in Reykjavik (1972). Resigned title 1974.

Fischer-Dieskau, Dietrich (1925-), German baritone. Known particularly for his interpretation of *lieder*. Also sings in opera.

Fish, Hamilton (1808-93), American statesman. Secretary of state (1869-77), negotiated settlement of *Alabama* claim with Britain (1871). Negotiated settlement with Spain after seizure of American ship *Virginius* in Cuba, thus averting potential war.

fish (Pisces), cold-blooded aquatic vertebrate. Gill-breathing, finned; body usually covered with scales. Diet of plankton, plants and aquatic animals. Divided into cartilagincus fish (shark, ray, *etc*) and bony fish (with bone in skeleton). Largest is whale shark, *c* 17.2 m/50 ft. long. *see* ICHTHYOLOGY.

Fisher, Andrew (1862-1928), Australian statesman, b. Scotland. Labor Party leader; PM (1908-9, 1910-13, 1914-15). Terms marked by reforms in taxation and land policy.

Fisher, Geoffrey Francis, Baron Fisher of Lambeth (1887-1972), English churchman. Archbishop of Canterbury (1945-61). Promoted ecumenical movement, visiting pope in 1960; president of World Council of Churches (1946-54).

Fisher, St John (1459-1535), English churchman, scholar. Imprisoned (1534) for opposing Henry VIII's divorce from Catherine of Aragon; Pope Paul III consequently made him cardinal (1535). Henry had him beheaded.

Fisher, John Arbuthnot, 1st Baron (1841–1920), British admiral. As first sea lord (1904-10) introduced the *Dreadnought* class of battleships. Recalled to the same office in 1914, but resigned because of differences with Churchill over the Dardanelles campaign (1915).

fisher or **pekan,** *Martes pennanti,* large North American carnivore of marten family. Nocturnal; forest dweller.

fisheries, pursuit and capture of aquatic animals. Most fish are caught by trawling, seining, drifting or by baited lines. Most highly developed fisheries are those of N Atlantic, esp. around Iceland, Newfoundland and Labrador. Modern intensive methods of fishing incl. use of factory ships which quickly freeze or can their catch. Major fishing nations are Japan, USSR, China, Peru, Norway and US.

Fishguard and Goodwick, urban dist. of Dyfed, SW Wales. Pop. 5000. Railway terminus; ferry services to Cork, Rosslare (Ireland).

fish louse, crustacean with sucking mouthparts, of subclass Branchiura. External parasite of fish.

Fisk, James *see* GOULD, JAY.

fission, in biology, form of asexual reproduction occurring in various plants, protozoa, bacteria, *etc,* in which parent organism splits into 2 or more approximately equal parts, each becoming an independent individual.

fission, nuclear, splitting of heavy atomic nuclei (*eg* uranium or plutonium) into 2 fragments of approximately equal mass, accompanied by release of nuclear energy and neutrons. May occur spontaneously or be caused by impact of neutrons. *See* CHAIN REACTION.

Fitzgerald, Edward (1809-83), English author. Best known for creative verse translation, *The Rubaiyat of Omar Khayyam* (1859).

Fitzgerald, F[rancis] Scott [Key] (1896-1940), American author. Works reflect despair of 'lost generation' in 1920s America, *eg* novels *The Beautiful and the Damned* (1922), *The Great Gatsby* (1925), *Tender is the Night* (1934). Short stories incl., 'The Diamond as Big as the Ritz', collected in *Tales of the Jazz Age* (1922).

Fitzherbert, Maria Anne, née Smythe (1756-1837), wife of George, Prince of Wales. Married George (1785); marriage deemed illegal as she was a Catholic and he a minor. Relationship continued until 1803, despite his marriage to Caroline of Brunswick (1795).

Fitzroy, Robert (1805–65), British naval officer, meteorologist. Commanded *Beagle* on voyages to Tierra del Fuego (1828-30, 1831-6), accompanied on 2nd by Charles Darwin. Began system of storm warnings issued by Board of Trade. Gave name to Fitzroy barometer; wrote *Weather Book* (1863).

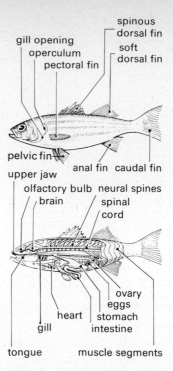

Organs of a bony fish (striped bass)

Labels: gill opening, operculum, pectoral fin, spinous dorsal fin, soft dorsal fin, pelvic fin, anal fin, caudal fin, upper jaw, olfactory bulb, brain, neural spines, spinal cord, ovary, eggs, stomach, intestine, heart, gill, tongue, muscle segments

Fiume, *see* RIJEKA-SUSAK, Yugoslavia.

Five, the, group of Russian composers, founders of nationalist school of music that drew on Russian history and literature as well as folk music. Comprised BALAKIREV, BORODIN, César Cui (1835-1918), MUSSORGSKY and RIMSKY-KORSAKOV. Also known as 'the Mighty Handful'.

fives, handball game played by 2 or 4 competitors in a special court. Chiefly confined to Britain, esp. to public schools. Three main forms: Rugby, Eton and Winchester.

Five Year Plan, Soviet economic programme, first introduced in USSR by Stalin (1928) to impose collectivization of agric. and enhance industrialization. Ruthlessly enforced, caused much suffering. Other programmes followed; practice has been adopted elsewhere, *eg* Cuba, China.

flagellants, term applied to severely ascetic Christian groups who practised public flagellation as a penance. Widespread in 12th cent. Europe. Prohibited (1349) by Pope Clement VI, but heretical groups persisted. Still survive in South America.

Flagellata (flagellates), class of Protozoa possessing 1 or more flagella, giving mobility. Incl. both plant and animal forms. Also called Mastigophora.

Flaherty, Robert J[oseph] (1884-1951), American explorer and film producer. Explored NE Canada. He made 1st full-length documentary film, *Nanook of the North* (1920). Later documentaries incl. *Man of Aran* (1934).

flame, region where chemical interaction between gases heated above kindling temperature takes place, with accompaniment of heat and light.

flamenco, Spanish style of singing and guitar-playing, often danced to. It is vigorous and may be extemporized along set patterns. Practised mainly in Andalusia; reflects Moorish influence.

flamingo, any of Phoenicopteridae family of large gregarious wading birds. Long thin legs, webbed feet, sinuous neck; red or pink plumage. Found in tropical and temperate zones.

Lesser flamingo *(Phoeniconaias minor)*

Flax

Human flea *(Pulex irritans)*

Flaminius, Titus Quinctius (*c* 228-174 BC), Roman soldier. Defeated Philip V of Macedon at Cynoscephalae (197) and declared independence of Greek cities (196).

Flamsteed, John (1646-1719), English astronomer. First Astronomer Royal, appointed 1675; compiled accurate star catalogue.

Flanders (Flem. *Vlaanderen*), region of SW Belgium and NE France. Former county of Low Countries. Medieval cloth centre (Bruges, Ghent); now indust. area based on coalfields. Battleground in many wars. In Belgium, divided into East, West Flanders provs.; in France, part of NORD region. Distinct Flemish language.

flatfish, any of order Pleuronectiformes of fish with compressed, asymmetric bodies. Larvae normal, but during growth, eyes migrate to same side of head. Eyed side of fish camouflaged, other side unpigmented. Species incl. turbot, halibut, flounder, sole, plaice.

flat foot, condition in which entire sole of human foot rests upon ground. Caused by weakness of muscles of the arches and consequent stretching of ligaments.

Flathead or **Salish,** North American Indian tribe of Bitterroot R. valley, W Montana. Buffalo hunters after introduction of horse. Wars with Blackfoot, concluded by peace treaty (1872), reduced numbers to *c* 350. Now settled near Flathead L., NW Montana.

flatworm, *see* PLATYHELMINTHES.

Flaubert, Gustave (1821-80), French novelist. Famous works, *eg Madame Bovary* (1857), *L'Education sentimentale* (1869), *Three Tales* (1877), reveal perfection of form, extreme impersonality of style, despite tragic material.

flax, any plant of genus *Linum,* esp. *L. usitatissimum* with slender leaves and small blue flowers, of worldwide distribution. Stems are source of LINEN and seeds of LINSEED oil.

Flaxman, John (1755-1826), English neo-classical sculptor. At first a designer for Wedgwood, devoted himself to monumental sculpture after visit to Rome. Works incl. *Mansfield* in Westminster Abbey. Gained reputation for series of outline drawings illustrating Homer, Dante, *etc.*

flea, any of Aphaniptera order of wingless, flattened insects. Long hind legs adapted for jumping. Adult sucks blood of mammals, birds; transmits disease, esp. bubonic plague and endemic typhus.

fleabane, any plant of genus *Erigeron,* of Compositae family. Formerly thought to drive away flies.

Flecker, [Herman] James Elroy (1884-1915), English poet. Work reflects Eastern travels as diplomat. Best known for exotically lyrical *The Golden Journey to Samarkand* (1913).

Fleet Street, term for British national newspapers, since most are located in or around street of that name in London.

Sir Alexander Fleming

Fleming, Sir Alexander (1881-1955), Scottish bacteriologist. Discovered penicillin in a mould contaminating bacterial culture, but did not develop its large-scale antibiotic use. Shared Nobel Prize for Physiology and Medicine (1945) with Chain and Florey for work on penicillin.

Fleming, Ian Lancaster (1908-65), English novelist. Known for 'James Bond' 'spy' novels, *eg Casino Royale* (1953), *From Russia with Love* (1957), *Goldfinger* (1959).

Fleming, Sir John Ambrose (1849-1945), English electrical engineer. Devised thermionic valve, used to rectify alternating current.

Flemish, language of W Germanic group of Indo-European family. Usually thought to be Belgian variant of DUTCH, not distinct language. Spoken in N Belgium, France.

Flensburg, town of N West Germany, on inlet of Baltic Sea. Pop. 95,000. Port; fishing, shipbuilding, paper mfg. Chartered 1284; passed from Denmark to Prussia 1867.

Fletcher, John (1579-1625), English dramatist. Wrote majority of 52 plays pub. with BEAUMONT. True collaborations incl. tragi-comedies *Philaster, A King and No King.* Wrote comedies, *eg The Wild Goose Chase,* alone. Also collaborated with Massinger, Shakespeare.

Flinders, Matthew (1774-1814), English naval officer, hydrographer. Surveyed and charted Australian coasts. First to circumnavigate Tasmania (1798), also circumnavigated Australia (1801-3). Wrote *Voyage to Terra Australis* (1814).

Flinders Island, *see* FURNEAUX ISLANDS.

Flint, town of EC Michigan, US; on Flint R. Pop. 193,000. Has major motor vehicle indust.

flint, hard, fine-grained rock, a variety of quartz. Dark grey or black in colour. Often found in chalk and limestone, dates from upper Cretaceous and Tertiary periods. May be shaped by flaking; widely used in Stone Age for making tools, weapons.

Flintshire, former county of NE Wales, now in Clwyd. Clwydian Hills in W, Dee estuary to E. Coalmining; agric.; coastal resorts. Main indust. centre **Flint,** mun. bor. on R. Dee. Pop. 15,000. Artificial silk mfg.

FLN, *see* NATIONAL LIBERATION FRONT.

Flodden, hill of Northumberland, NE England. Scene of battle in which James IV of Scotland defeated, killed by English under Earl of Surrey (1513).

flood, inundation of land by overflow of a body of water, usually a river. Often caused by melting of snow and ice into headwaters, but brief 'flash floods' may follow short, torrential downpours of rain. Natural flood plains of rivers, normally inundated annually, are rich in alluvium. Flood control performed by dams, locks, levées, *eg* Tennessee Valley Authority, US; seawater controlled by dykes, behind which reclamation is possible, *eg* Zuider Zee, Netherlands.

Flora, Roman goddess of flowers and fertility. Her festival (28th April - 3rd May) was celebrated with licentious farces.

Florence Cathedral

Florence (*Firenze*), city of NC Italy, on R. Arno, cap. of Tuscany. Pop. 482,000. Indust., tourist centre; railway jct. Etruscan, then Roman settlement. Scene of Guelph-Ghibelline conflict (12th-13th cent.). Under Medici family became centre of Renaissance art, architecture; its famous artists incl. da Vinci, Donatello, Giotto, Michelangelo,

Raphael. Birthplace of Dante. Buildings incl. Pitti palace, Ponte Vecchio, Uffizi gallery, domed cathedral. Cap. of Italy 1865-70. Damaged in WWII, 1966 floods.

Flores, isl. of Indonesia, in Lesser Sundas. Area *c* 17,000 sq km (6600 sq mi). Mountainous with many active volcanoes; interior forested.

Florey, Howard Walter, Baron Florey (1898-1968), British pathologist, b. Australia. With E.B. CHAIN, developed methods of purifying penicillin and producing it on a large scale for use during WWII. Shared Nobel Prize for Physiology and Medicine (1945).

Florianópolis, seaport of S Brazil, cap. of Santa Catarina state; on Santa Catarina Isl. Pop. 139,000. Exports sugar, tobacco, fruit. Linked to mainland by suspension bridge.

Florida, state of SE US; mainly on penin. separating Atlantic and Gulf of Mexico. Area 151,670 sq km (58,560 sq mi); pop. 6,789,000; cap. Tallahassee; chief cities Jacksonville, Miami. Generally low-lying, swampy (Everglades); subtropical climate. Agric. esp. citrus fruits; fishing; aero-space industs. Major tourist region, resorts incl. Miami, Palm Beach. Spanish colonized area in 16th cent.; purchased by US 1821. Admitted to Union as 27th state (1845).

Florida Keys, chain of small isls., S of Florida, US. Largest are Key West and Key Largo. Linked by highway. Resort for game fishing.

flotsam, jetsam and **lagan,** goods lost at sea. Jetsam refers to goods cast overboard which sink; flotsam to goods which continue to float; lagan to sunken goods marked by a buoy so that they may be reclaimed. Goods washed ashore are referred to as wreck.

flounder, *see* FLATFISH.

flour, finely ground and sifted meal of cereal, esp. wheat and rye, consisting mainly of starch and gluten. Different grades of flour make bread, pastry, macaroni, *etc.*

flower, part of seed plant containing reproductive organs, *ie* the male stamens bearing pollen in anthers, and the ovary or gynaecium, the whole surrounded by petals and sepals.

flügelhorn, brass instrument similar in shape to bugle, with 3 valves like a trumpet, but producing a fuller, more mellow sound. Played in brass bands but most characteristically in jazz.

fluidics, technology of building equivalents of electronic circuits using flow of fluid instead of electrons. Systems use valves which take place of transistors in logic circuits. Used when conditions (*eg* heat, ionizing radiation) make electronics unreliable.

fluke, any of order Trematoda of parasitic flatworms, with 2 suckers used for adhesion. Life cycle involves several larval forms and one or more hosts. Species incl. liver fluke of sheep, *Fasciola hepatica,* and Chinese liver fluke, *Clonorchis sinensis,* parasitic in humans.

fluorescence, property of certain materials of absorbing light of short wavelength (*eg* violet or ultra violet) and emitting light of longer wavelength (such as visible light). In fluorescent lamp, ultra violet light, produced by passing current through mercury vapour, is converted to visible light by fluorescent substance on walls of glass tube.

fluoridation, addition of metallic fluorides, esp. sodium fluoride, to drinking water to reduce incidence of dental decay.

fluorine (F), pale yellow gaseous element of halogen family; at. no. 9, at. wt. 18.998. Very chemically active, not found free; occurs in cryolite and fluorspar. First prepared by Moissan (1886) by electrolysis. Used in manufacture of FLUOROCARBONS.

fluorite or **fluorspar,** crystalline mineral, composed of calcium fluoride. Transparent, sometimes fluorescent; colourless but tinted by impurities. Used in glassmaking, as flux in metallurgy; source of fluorine; 'Blue John' is blue, ornamental form. Major sources in US, Mexico, Germany, England.

fluorocarbons, group of synthetic organic compounds obtained by replacing some or all of the hydrogen atoms of hydrocarbons by fluoride atoms. Chemically stable, used in manufacture of oils, plastics (*eg* Teflon), refrigerants and aerosols propellants.

fluorspar, *see* FLUORITE.

Flushing (*Vlissingen*), town of SW Netherlands, on Walcheren Isl. at mouth of Western Scheldt. Pop. 39,000. Oil refining, fishing, shipbuilding. First Dutch city to rebel against Spain (1572). Strategic site, scene of Allied invasion (1944).

flute, woodwind instrument of metal or wood with range of 3 octaves, played by blowing across small aperture near one end. Alto flute sounds a fourth lower than concert flute and bass flute an octave lower. The piccolo sounds an octave higher.

fly, any of order Diptera of insects with 1 pair of functional membranous wings. Many flies transmit disease by blood-sucking or carrying germs on body. Species incl. MOSQUITO, HORSEFLY, TSETSE FLY. Name applied esp. to HOUSE FLY and also to other orders of insect.

flycatcher, any of Muscicapidae family of small birds with thin curved beak. Catches insects while in flight. Species incl. spotted flycatcher, *Muscicapa striata,* widespread in Europe.

Flying Dutchman, legendary spectral ship, believed to haunt Cape of Good Hope. Captain is doomed to sail forever. Subject of opera by Wagner.

flying fish, any fish capable of leaping from water, using enlarged pectoral fins to glide through air; mainly tropical. Species incl. Atlantic flying fish, *Exocoetus volitans.*

flying fox, one of several fruit-eating bats, found in tropics from Asia to Australia, genus *Pteropus.* Malayan kalong, *P. vampyrus,* is *c* 1.5 m/5 ft long, largest of all bats.

flying lemur, any of order Dermoptera of arboreal nocturnal mammals of SE Asia. Membrane stretched between legs enables it to make gliding leaps. Also called colugo.

flying squirrel, any of several nocturnal species of squirrel. Uses fold of skin stretched from forelegs to hind legs to glide from tree to tree. Species incl. American *Glaucomys volans,* European *Pteromys volans.*

Flynn, Errol (1909-59), Australian film actor. Known for roles as adventurous womanizer, as in *Captain Blood* (1935), *The Sea Hawk* (1940), *Too Much Too Soon* (1958).

FM (frequency modulation), *see* MODULATION.

Marshal Foch

Foch, Ferdinand (1851–1929), French general. Fore-stalled the initial German advance at the Marne (1914) and distinguished himself at the battles of Ypres (1915) and the Somme (1916). His appointment as Allied supreme commander in 1918 marked the beginning of the German decline.

focus, in optics, point at which rays of light reflected by a mirror or refracted by a lens meet (real focus), or would meet if continued back through lens or mirror (virtual focus). Focal length of thin lens is distance from its optical centre to point at which rays of light parallel to its principal axis are focused.

foetus, mammalian embryo in later stages of its development when main features of fully developed animal are recognizable; in man, embryo is considered as foetus after 2 months of gestation.

fog, mass of water droplets suspended in the air, obscuring vision for any distance up to 1 km/0.62 mi. Formed by water vapour condensing on minute dust particles. Mixture of smoke and fog, common in indust. areas, results in smog.

Fogazzaro, Antonio (1842-1911), Italian novelist. Works, *eg The Politician* (1885), *The Patriot* (1896), attempt to reconcile traditional RC dogma with scientific rationalism.

Foggia, city of Apulia, SE Italy, cap. of Foggia prov. Pop. 139,000. Major wheat market; flour, cheese. Cathedral (12th cent.); palace gateway (13th cent.).

Fokine, Michel (1880-1942), American choreographer, dancer, b. Russia. One of founders of modern ballet, working with Diaghilev in most brilliant period of Ballets Russes (1909-14). Created *The Firebird, Le Spectre de la rose, Petrouchka.*

Fokker, Anton Herman Gerard (1890-1939), Dutch aircraft manufacturer, b. Java. Built WWI bi-planes and tri-planes in German factories. Developed device to allow machine gun to be fired through moving propeller. Settled in US in 1922.

Folkestone, mun. bor. of Kent, SE England. Pop. 44,000. Cross-Channel ferry services. One of Cinque Ports.

folklore, term coined (1846) by W. T. Thoms to denote traditional beliefs, legends, customs, *etc,* of a people. Regarded as important by anthropologists as the imaginative expression of a society's cultural values.

Folsom culture, early North American culture associated with arrow points found with bones of extinct bison near Folsom, New Mexico. Believed to date from *c* 9000 BC; some argue that they date from *c* 23,000 BC.

Fonda, Henry (1905-   ), American actor. Appeared in films as gauche young rustic, *eg Young Mr Lincoln* (1939), *The Grapes of Wrath* (1940), later expressing likeable wisdom in *Twelve Angry Men* (1957). His daughter, **Jane Fonda** (1937-   ), is a film actress. Appeared in *Klute* (1971) and in political films, *eg Tout va bien* (1972). His son, **Peter Fonda** (1939-   ), is best known as actor-producer of *Easy Rider* (1969), expressing mood of late 1960s American youth.

Fonseca, Gulf of, Pacific inlet bordered by El Salvador, Honduras and Nicaragua.

The palace at Fontainebleau

Fontainebleau, town of Ile-de-France, N France, in forest of Fontainebleau. Pop. 20,000. Resort; NATO hq. (1945-67). Château, built by Francis I, was former residence of French kings; scene of revocation of Edict of Nantes (1685), of 1st abdication of Napoleon (1814).

Fontana, Domenico (1543-1607), Italian architect. Under patronage of Sixtus V, completed dome of St Peter's, built Lateran Palace and Vatican library.

Fontane, Theodor (1819-98), German author. Turned from poetry to novel late in life. Known for masterpiece, *Effi Briest* (1895) on theme of advance of bourgeoisie at expense of aristocracy.

Fontanne, Lynn (*c* 1887-), American actress, b. England. Known for roles in intimate comedy with her husband Alfred Lunt (1893-), esp. *Design for Living* (1933).

Fontenoy, village of Hainaut prov., Belgium. Scene of French victory (1745) over British, Dutch, and Austrian forces.

Fonteyn, Dame Margot, orig. Margaret Hookham (1919-), English ballerina. Long-time *prima ballerina assoluta* of the Royal Ballet. Acclaimed for roles in such ballets as *The Sleeping Beauty, Giselle.* Famed for partnership with Rudolf Nureyev.

Foochow, cap. of Fukien prov., SE China on R. Min. Pop. 900,000. Fishing port; steel, chemical mfg. One of 5 original treaty ports, formerly major tea exports. Educational centre, summer resort.

food, any substance taken into and assimilated by a plant or animal, which enables it to grow and repair tissue and provides source of energy. Human food should contain: protein, necessary for building and repairing tissue; carbohydrates and fats, which provide energy; minerals, *eg* iron, calcium and phosphorus; vitamins.

Food and Agriculture Organization (FAO), specialized agency of UN, estab. 1945; hq. in Rome. Aims to help nations increase efficiency of farming, forestry and fisheries. Operations incl. research and development, financial and technical assistance, information services.

food poisoning, sickness caused by eating food contaminated by bacteria, *eg* salmonellae, or by toxin produced by bacteria, *eg* staphylococci, present on food before cooking. Also caused by inorganic compounds, *eg* those of lead, or organic compounds present in certain animals and plants, *eg* toadstools.

foot, end part of leg on which person or animal stands or moves. Human foot has 26 bones: 14 phalanges in toes, 7 tarsal bones forming the heel and 5 metatarsals in the ball of foot.

foot, in measurement, British unit of length: 1 ft = 0.3048 m.

foot-and-mouth disease, contagious virus disease of cloven-footed animals *eg* cattle, deer. Characterized by fever and blisters in mouth and around hoofs. Controlled by slaughter and strict quarantine.

football, *see* AMERICAN FOOTBALL; ASSOCIATION FOOTBALL; AUSTRALIAN RULES FOOTBALL; GAELIC FOOTBALL; RUGBY FOOTBALL.

Forbes-Robertson, Sir Johnston (1853-1937), English actor-manager. Known as Hamlet and the Stranger in *The Passing of the Third-Floor Back* (1908).

force, in mechanics, agency which alters state of rest or motion of a body, producing acceleration in it. SI unit of force is the newton. By Newton's law of motion, force is proportional to rate of change of momentum of body.

Ford, Ford Madox, pseud. of Ford Madox Hueffer (1873-1939), English novelist, editor. Known for *The Good Soldier* (1915), *Parade's End* tetralogy (1924-8). Founded *English Review* (1908).

Ford, Gerald Rudolph, orig. Leslie Lynch King (1913-), American statesman, president (1974-7). Republican leader in House of Representatives (1965-73). Vice-president (1973-4) after Agnew's resignation, president after Nixon's. Pardoned Nixon of any criminal acts committed during his presidency. Defeated by Carter in 1976 election.

Ford, Henry (1863-1947), American industrialist. Pioneer automobile manufacturer, developed mass-production techniques. Ford Motor Company by *c* 1915 was world's largest automobile producer. Controversial in his anti-union policy. Founded (1936) philanthropic Ford Foundation with his son, Edsel.

Henry Ford

Ford, John (1586-*c* 1640), English dramatist. Collaborated with Dekker in early plays. Best known for *'Tis Pity She's a Whore* (*c* 1627), *The Broken Heart* (*c* 1629), reflecting typical Jacobean concern with sexual corruption.

Ford, John, orig. Sean O'Fearna (1895-1973), American film director. From 1917 made over 125 feature films; known for human dramas in 1930s, *eg The Informer* (1935), but famous for westerns, from 1940s onwards, incl. *She Wore a Yellow Ribbon* (1949).

foreign aid, financial, technical and military assistance, usually given to another country at govt. level. Aims incl. reconstructing economies of countries after war, strengthening defences of allies, promoting economic growth of underdeveloped countries. US aid began with Lend-Lease (WWII), and European Recovery Program (Marshall Plan, 1948). UN, US, French and UK programmes aid underdeveloped nations.

foreign exchange, *see* EXCHANGE, FOREIGN.

Foreign Legion, French force of foreign mercenaries under French officers and senior NCOs. Formed by Louis Philippe mainly to keep the peace in Algeria, with hq. at Sidi-bel-Abbès. It withdrew after Algeria became independent.

Forel, Auguste (1848-1931), Swiss psychiatrist, entomologist. From studies of ants, begun in boyhood, extrapolated ideas to apply them to psychiatry. Advocated humane treatment of insane, use of hypnotism in therapy; also studied sexual problems, alcoholism.

Foreland, North and **South,** two chalk headlands of Kent, SE England. Former N of Broadstairs; latter NE of Dover. Both have lighthouses.

Foreman, Carl (1914-) American film writer, producer, director. Films incl. *High Noon* (1952), *The Bridge on the River Kwai* (1957).

Forester, C[ecil] S[cott] (1899-1966), English novelist. Best known for 'Horatio Hornblower' novels about British naval officer in Napoleonic wars. Other novels incl. *The African Queen* (1935), *The Ship* (1943).

forestry, science of planting, tending and managing timber as a crop. Trees are classified as coniferous, often called softwoods, and broadleaved, called hardwoods. Major producers of coniferous wood, used for construction, pulp and paper, are USSR, US, Canada, Sweden and Finland. Broadleaved woods are important in Brazil, Indonesia, India, China.

Forfar, town of Tayside region, E Scotland. Pop. 11,000. Former royal burgh and co. town of Angus. Jute, linen mfg.

forgery, act of imitating documents, signatures, works of art, *etc*, with intent to deceive. In law, crime limited to written documents.

Common forget-me-not

forget-me-not, any annual or perennial plant of widely-distributed genus *Myosotis*. Oval leaves with blue, white, or yellow flowers. Species incl. common forget-me-not, *M. arvensis* and water forget-me-not, *M. scorpoides*.

Forli, city of Emilia-Romagna, NC Italy, cap. of Forli prov. Pop. 106,000. Textiles, furniture. Roman *Forum Livii*; part of Papal States from 1504. Medieval cathedral, citadel.

formaldehyde (HCHO), pungent gas, produced by oxidation of methanol. Dissolves readily in water, 40% solution being known as formalin. Used as disinfectant and preservative, and in manufacture of plastics.

Forman, Milos (1932-   ), Czech film director. Known for acutely observed comedies, *eg The Firemen's Ball* (1968). Became famous for *One Flew Over the Cuckoo's Nest* (1976).

formic acid (HCOOH), colourless liquid, found in nettles and ant and bee stings. Manufactured from steam and carbon monoxide by catalysis. Used in dyeing.

Formosa, *see* TAIWAN.

formula, in chemistry, representation of nature and number of atoms which constitute single molecule of chemical compound by means of letters and figures. Structural formula indicates arrangement of atoms and nature of chemical bonds linking them. Empirical formula indicates only relative proportions of atoms and not necessarily their actual numbers.

Forres, town of Grampian region, NE Scotland. Pop. 5000. Market town, distilling. Ancient castle is traditionally scene of Macbeth's murder of Duncan. Has 11th cent. carved monolith.

Forrest, Edwin (1806-72), American tragic actor. Major roles incl. Lear, Hamlet, Othello. Appeared in London (1836,1845).

Forrest, John Forrest, 1st Baron (1847-1918), Australian explorer, politician. Led expedition from Perth to Adelaide (1870). Served as surveyor-general, then as premier (1890-1901) of Western Australia.

Forster, E[dward] M[organ] (1879-1970), English author. Novels, *eg Where Angels Fear to Tread* (1905), *Howard's End* (1910), *A Passage to India* (1924), contrast spontaneity of paganism with deficiencies of British middle class sensibility. Later abandoned novels for essays on politics and criticism.

forsythia, *Forsythia suspensa*, deciduous shrub with olive-brown twigs and yellow flowers which appear before leaves. Hybrids widely cultivated.

Fortaleza, Atlantic port of NE Brazil, cap. of Ceará state. Pop. 859,000. Important sugar refining, flour milling; carnauba wax, cotton exports; textile, soap mfg. Founded 1609.

Fort-de-France, cap. of MARTINIQUE.

Fortescue, Sir John (*c* 1394-1476), English jurist. Chief justice of King's Bench (1442-61). Known as one of earliest English constitutional lawyers. Wrote *De laudibus legum Angliae* (pub. 1537).

Fort George, river of WC Québec, Canada. Flows W 770 km (*c* 480 mi) into James Bay at Fort George trading post.

Forth, river of C Scotland. Flows 105 km (65 mi) from Central region into Firth of Forth. Ports incl. Grangemouth, Leith. Estuary crossed by rail bridge (1890), 2 road bridges (1936, 1964). Linked to W coast by disused Forth and Clyde Canal.

Fort Lamy, *see* NDJAMENA, Chad.

Fort Lauderdale, resort town of SE Florida, US; on Atlantic. Pop. 140,000. Market gardening, fruit produce.

Fortuna, Roman goddess of fortune. Originally associated with fertility, later identified with Greek Tyche (chance). Represented with cornucopia and ship's rudder.

Fortunate Isles, in classical and Celtic legend, isls. in far west where the souls of favoured dead lived in paradise. Sometimes identified with Madeira or Canaries.

Fort Wayne, town of NE Indiana, US; on Maumee R. Pop. 178,000. Railway jct.; shipping point, electrical equipment mfg. Fort estab. 1794; grew as fur-trading centre.

Fort William, *see* THUNDER BAY, Canada.

Fort William, town of Highland region, NW Scotland, on Loch Linnhe. Pop. 4000. Near Ben Nevis; tourist centre. Aluminium works, distilling. Pulp mill nearby. Fort dismantled 1866.

Fort Worth, city of NE Texas, US; on Trinity R. tributary. Pop. 393,000. Railway jct.; grain, livestock market; meat packing, aircraft mfg., oil and gas industs. Army fort estab. 1847.

forum, market and meeting place of Roman towns, usually surrounded by public buildings and colonnades. Forum in Rome extended from Capitoline Hill almost to Colosseum and contained various triumphal arches, basilicas, temples.

Foscolo, Ugo (1778-1827), Italian author, patriot. Works incl. epistolary novel *Last Letters of Jacopo Ortis* (1802); poem *I Sepolcri* (1807) combines romantic spirit with classical style.

Fosdick, Harry Emerson (1878-1969), American Baptist minister. Minister of inter-denominational Riverside Church, New York (1926-46). Adopted Modernist view in fundamentalist controversies.

fossil, remains or impressions of animal or plant life preserved in rocks of Earth's crust. Study of fossils is called palaeontology. Can aid dating and correlating of geological strata, and study of evolution. Common fossils incl. amber, ammonite, coal.

Foster, Stephen Collins (1826-64), American composer. Wrote many famous songs, principally about life in the American South, incl. 'Oh! Susannah', 'My Old Kentucky Home', 'Camptown Races', 'Swannee River', 'Jeannie with the Light Brown Hair'.

Foucauld, Charles Eugène, Vicomte de (1858-1916), French explorer and Trappist monk. Worked among the Tuareg in Sahara, producing study of their culture. Murdered during Senussi revolt.

Foucault, Jean Bernard Léon (1819-68), French physicist. Calculated speed of light through air and other media by arrangement of stationary and rotating mirrors. Demonstrated rotation of Earth by turning of plane of oscillation of long pendulum.

Fouché, Joseph (1759-1820), French political leader. As Consulate's and Napoleon's police minister (1799-1802, 1804-10), ran spy network; discovered Cadoudal plot (royalist conspiracy, 1804) against Napoleon. Organized ruthless political and police system. Created duke of Otranto (1809); eventually exiled from France.

Fouqué, Friedrich Heinrich Karl, Baron de la Motte (1777-1843), German poet. Known for romantic tales from legend, esp. *Undine* (1811). Prominent in German romanticism.

Fouquet, Nicolas, Marquis de Belle-Isle (1615-80), French statesman. Superintendent of finance (1653-61) during Louis XIV's minority, acquired great personal wealth by embezzlement. Imprisoned for life (1664) after trial beginning in 1661. Patron of La Fontaine, Molière.

four-eyed fish, any fish of Anablepidae family of Central and South American rivers. Each eye divided into 2 halves, with separate retinas; upper half used for aerial vision, lower for aquatic vision.

Four-H or **4-H Clubs,** service of US Dept. of Agriculture for rural youth between ages of 9 and 19. Estab. (1914), derives name from aim to improve use of 'head, heart, hands and health'.

Fourier, [François Marie] Charles (1772-1837), French social philosopher. Evolved system of utopian communism in *Théorie des quatre mouvements* (1808). Aimed to reorganize society into small, self-sufficient cooperative units (phalansteries). Influenced American communities, *eg* Brook Farm.

Fourier, Jean Baptiste Joseph, Baron (1768-1830), French mathematician. Famed for *Théorie analytique de la Chaleur,* in which he developed Fourier series (representation of functions by infinite series of sines and cosines). This method is of fundamental mathematical importance.

Fournier, Henri Alban, *see* ALAIN-FOURNIER.

Fournier, Pierre Simon (1712-68), French typefounder. Devised 1st point system for measuring type. Author of *Manuel typographique* (1764-6), dealing with engraving, typefounding and printing.

four o'clock, *Mirabilis jalapa,* perennial plant of tropical America. Red, yellow or striped tubular flowers, up to 5 cm/2 in. long, which open in late afternoon. Cultivated as temperate garden plant. Also called marvel of Peru.

four stroke (cycle) engine, *see* INTERNAL COMBUSTION ENGINE.

Fourteen Points, *see* WILSON, THOMAS WOODROW.

Fourteenth Amendment, US constitutional amendment (1868). Estab. basis of US citizenship and forbade states to curtail individual privileges, to deprive person of rights of life, liberty or property without 'due process of law', or to deny equal protection of law. Used extensively and broadly interpreted by Supreme Court, *eg* on issue of racial discrimination (1954).

Fouta Djallon or **Futa Jallon,** highland area of W Africa, mainly in Guinea. Av. height *c* 910 m/3000 ft. Mostly grassland; cattle raising, rice and banana growing. Source of Niger, Senegal, Gambia rivers.

fowl, domestic bird used for food, esp. chicken, turkey, goose, duck, pheasant.

Fowler, H[enry] W[atson] (1858-1933), English lexicographer. Compiler of *A Dictionary of Modern English Usage* (1926). Collaborated with his brother, **F[rancis] G[eorge] Fowler** (1870-1918), on *The King's English* (1906) and *The Concise Oxford Dictionary of Current English* (1911).

Fowles, John (1926-   ), English novelist. Works, *eg The Collector* (1963), *The French Lieutenant's Woman* (1969), combine erudition and experiment with form of novel.

Fowliang or **King-te-chen,** town of Kiangsi prov., SE China. Pop. 300,000. Famous for porcelain produced since Han dynasty.

Fox, Charles James (1749-1806), English statesman, orator. Disliked by George III, who secured his dismissal as lord of the treasury (1774). Opposed Lord North's policy in America. Demanded British abstention during French Revolution. Advocated political rights for dissenters and Catholics; as foreign secretary (1806), urged abolition of slave trade (achieved 1807).

Fox, George (1624-91), English religious leader. Founded SOCIETY OF FRIENDS (Quakers), spreading doctrine in journeys to Scotland, North America, Holland. *Journal* (pub. 1694) was edited by William Penn.

fox, wild carnivore of dog family, common in N hemisphere. Nocturnal predator, diet of small animals, fruit; lives in burrows. European red fox, *Vulpes vulpes,* red-brown above, white below; hunted for fur and sport. American red fox, *V. fulva,* is related species.

Foxe, John (1516-87), English Protestant clergyman. Famous for *Actes and Monuments* (1563), known as *Book*

European red fox

Charles James Fox

of Martyrs, celebrating piety and heroism of Protestants martyred under Mary Tudor.

Foxglove

foxglove, *Digitalis purpurea,* perennial of figwort family, native to W and C Europe. Tapering spikes with purple, pink or white, bell-shaped flowers. Popular garden varieties developed. Leaves yield poisonous alkaloid, digitalin, used in medicine.

fox terrier, small terrier with smooth or wire-haired coat, originally bred for chasing foxes from hiding. Stands 38 cm/15 in. at shoulder.

Foyle, river of Northern Ireland. Flows through former Co. Tyrone to Atlantic via Lough Foyle (navigable inlet c 24 km/15 mi long), below Londonderry. Fishing.

f.p.s. system of units, British system of physical units based on fundamental units of foot, pound and second.

fractions, in mathematics, see RATIONAL NUMBER.

Fra Diavolo, pseud. of Michele Pezza (1771-1806), Italian brigand. Leader of robber band employed by British against French in Naples. Captured and hanged by French. Auber's opera, *Fra Diavolo* (1830), based loosely on his exploits.

Fragonard, Jean Honoré (1732-1806), French painter. Painted frivolous, gallant and sentimental subjects which typified court life of Louis XV; career was ruined by the Revolution. Works incl. *The Swing.*

France, Anatole, pseud. of Jacques Anatole François Thibault (1844-1924), French author. Arbiter of French taste as literary editor of *Le Temps* in late 19th cent. Novels incl. *Le Crime de Sylvestre Bonnard* (1881), political satires *L'Ile des pingouins* (1908), *La Révolte des anges* (1914). Awarded Nobel Prize for Literature (1921).

France, republic of W Europe. Area c 547,000 sq km (211,000 sq mi); pop. 52,360,000; cap. Paris. Language: French. Religion: RC. Comprises 95 admin. depts., incl. Corsica. Mountainous regions incl. Vosges, Jura (E), Alps (SE), Massif Central (SC), Pyrenees (SW); fertile lowlands in Aquitaine, Paris Basin. Main rivers Seine, Loire, Rhône. Mainly agric. until recently, esp. cereals, livestock, vineyards. Indust. centred on NE coal and iron ore deposits (Nord, Lorraine). Tourism, esp. along S coast. Exports wines, luxury goods, motor cars. Roman prov. of Gaul until 5th cent.; Frankish kingdom estab. 9th cent. under Charlemagne, consolidated 10th-14th cent. by Capet dynasty. Regained much territ. from England in Hundred Years War; Louis XIV defeated in War of Spanish Succession. Revolution (1789) and Napoleonic Wars followed by brief restorations of monarchy, succession of republics. Fifth Republic created 1958 by De Gaulle. Suffered heavy losses in WWI, German occupation (Vichy regime) in WWII. Retains close ties with former overseas possessions, formed French Community (1958). Member of EEC.

Francesca, Piero della, see PIERO DELLA FRANCESCA.

Franche-Comté, region and former prov. of E France, hist. cap. Besançon (Dôle until 1678). Incl. parts of Jura, Vosges; forests, agric. esp. dairying. United in 9th cent. as Free County of Burgundy, part of Holy Roman Empire from 1034; under Spanish Habsburgs in 16th-17th cent. Ceded to France (1678).

Francia, José Gaspar Rodríguez (c 1766-1840), Paraguayan political leader. Chief architect of national independence, known as 'El Supremo'. Took part in revolution of 1811, became dictator (1814-40). Encouraged internal growth, ardent nationalism.

Francis I (1768-1835), emperor of Austria (1804-35). Succeeded father Leopold II as Holy Roman emperor (1792). Unsuccessful in wars with France (1792-1809). After assuming Austrian title, forced to dissolve Holy Roman Empire (1806). Daughter, Marie Louise, married (1810) Napoleon. Joined Allies against Napoleon (1813); presided over Congress of Vienna.

Francis I (1708-65), Holy Roman emperor (1745-65). Married MARIA THERESA (1736), to whom he left exercise of power. Ceded duchy of Lorraine to STANISLAUS Leszczynski (1735) after War of Polish Succession. Father of Joseph II, Leopold II, Marie Antoinette.

Francis I (1494-1547), king of France (1515-47). Succeeded father-in-law, Louis XII. Continually at war in Italy with Emperor Charles V, who had won imperial election over Francis (1519). Campaigns largely unsuccessful; captured at Pavia (1525). Renaissance patron, invited Leonardo da Vinci, Benvenuto Cellini to France.

Francis II (1836-94), king of the Two Sicilies (1859-61). Opposed movement for Italian unification. Driven from Naples by Garibaldi. Went into exile after defeat at Gaeta (1861).

Francis, Duc d'Alençon (c 1554-84), French prince, youngest son of Henry II. Suitor of Elizabeth I of England. Invited to rule Low Countries by William the Silent (1580), forced to leave (1583). His death led to Henry IV's succession.

Francis Borgia, St (1510-72), Spanish Jesuit leader. Member of Borgia family. Renounced his duchy (Candia) and joined Jesuits under St Ignatius Loyola. General of Order (1565-72); endowed Roman College, promoted foreign missions and edited Jesuit rule.

Francis Ferdinand (1863-1914), Austrian archduke. Heir apparent to Francis Joseph; assassinated with wife in Sarajevo by Gavrilo Princip, Serbian nationalist. Death led to Austrian ultimatum to Serbia and outbreak of WWI.

Franciscans or **Grey Friars,** in RC church, members of several orders following the rule of ST FRANCIS OF ASSISI, incl. Capuchins and Conventuals. Noted missionaries, educators and preachers. Famous members incl. St Anthony of Padua.

Francis Joseph or **Franz Josef** (1830-1916), emperor of Austria (1848-1916). Succeeded on abdication of his uncle, Ferdinand. Subdued independence movements in Hungary, Sardinia (1849). Lost Lombardy (1859), Venetia (1866) to Italy. Reorganized empire into Austro-Hungarian Monarchy to placate Hungarian nationalists, becoming king of Hungary (1867). Reign saw growth of Slav nationalism in empire.

Francis of Assisi, St, orig. Giovanni di Bernardone (c 1182-1226), Italian friar. Attracted following by preaching, founded Fransiscan order of friars in Rome (1209); its rule based on brotherhood, absolute poverty and concern for poor and sick. Many stories told of his simple life, gentleness with animals.

Francis of Sales, St (1567-1622), French Jesuit preacher. Bishop of Geneva (1602); converted many Huguenots. With St Jane Frances of Chantal, founded Order of the Visitation for women unable to undergo the austerity of the established orders.

Francis Xavier, St (1506-52), Basque Jesuit missionary, called 'Apostle to the Indies'. With ST IGNATIUS OF LOYOLA, founded Society of Jesus (Jesuits). Estab. missions in India, Japan and China, where he died.

francium (Fr), extremely unstable radioactive element of alkali metal group; at. no. 87, mass no. of most stable isotope 223. Discovered (1939) as decay product of actinium.

Franck, César Auguste (1822-90), Belgian composer. Lived mostly in Paris as teacher and organist. Leader of 19th cent. French Romantic school. Best known for *Symphony in D minor* and organ works.

Franco [Bahamonde], Francisco (1892-1975), Spanish military and political leader. Rose to power before SPANISH CIVIL WAR, led Fascist revolt with German and Italian support, becoming head of insurgent govt. (1936). Dissolved all political parties but FALANGE and began authoritarian rule. Despite agreements with Hitler, Mussolini, kept Spain neutral in WWII. Restored monarchy by law of succession (1947), retaining post of regent until his death. Chose JUAN CARLOS as successor and king.

francolin, gamebird related to partridge, genus *Francolinus,* found mainly in African grasslands. Many species, eg yellow-necked francolin, *F. leucoscepus,* have spurs on legs.

Franconia (*Franken*), hist. region of SC West Germany, extending E from Rhine along Main valley. Cities incl. Frankfurt, Speyer, Würzburg. Medieval duchy, divided (939) into W (Rhenish), E. Name revived 1837, applied to 3 divisions of Bavaria. Homeland of Franconian (Salian) dynasty.

Franco-Prussian War (1870-1), conflict between German states and France. Napoleon III provoked into declaring war by Bismarck's EMS DISPATCH. France lost

General Franco

Benjamin Franklin

decisive battle of Sedan, Napoleon captured. French resistance continued briefly, peace concluded with Treaty of Versailles (1871); Paris Commune held out against Prussian siege until suppressed by French army. Results of war incl. German unification under Prussia, French loss of Alsace-Lorraine, estab. of Third Republic in France.

Frank, Anne (1929-*c* 1945), Dutch author of *The Diary of a Young Girl* (1947), recording experiences while hiding from Nazis in Amsterdam warehouse 1942-44. Died in Belsen concentration camp.

Frank, Ilya Mikhailovich (1908-   ), Soviet physicist. Explained cause of CHERENKOV effect. Shared Nobel Prize for Physics (1958) with Cherenkov and I.Y. Tamm.

Frankfort, cap. of Kentucky, US; on Kentucky R. Pop. 22,000. Whisky distilling, trade.

Frankfurt (-am-Main), city of W West Germany, on R. Main. Pop. 658,000. Transport, commercial centre; publishing, chemicals, vehicles. Trade fairs held from *c* 1240. Founded 1st cent. by Romans; free imperial city 1372-1806. Seat of German Confederation (1815-66); treaty ending Franco-Prussian War signed here (1871). Cathedral, 15th cent. town hall (*Römer*). Birthplace of Goethe.

Frankfurt-an-der-Oder, town of E East Germany, on R. Oder. Pop. 58,000. Railway jct.; food processing, esp. frankfurter sausages. Hanseatic League member; univ. moved to Breslau (Wroclaw) 1811. Lost suburb on E bank to Poland (1945).

Frankfurter, Felix (1882-1965), American lawyer, b. Austria. Associate justice of US Supreme Court (1939-62). In writings and teaching, important contributor to liberal legal tradition.

frankincense, aromatic resin from NE African trees of genus *Boswellia*. Used by ancient Egyptians and Jews as incense in religious rites.

Frankland, Sir Edward (1825-99), English chemist. First to study organo-metallic compounds; his research led him to devise theory of valency.

Franklin, Benjamin (1706-90), American statesman, scientist, writer. His common sense and wit were popularized in his *Poor Richard's Almanack* (1732-57). Colonial leader, presented plan for union at Albany Congress (1754), helped draft Declaration of Independence (1776). Ambassador in Europe (1776-85), negotiated French recognition of new republic (1778) and peace with Britain (1781-3). Active in Federal Constitutional Congress (1787). Among many scientific experiments, flew kite in thunderstorm, proving presence of electricity in lightning; invented lightning rod.

Franklin, Sir John (1786-1847), English naval officer, explorer. Led 2 expeditions to Canadian Arctic (1819-22, 1825-7). Searched for Northwest Passage (1845), but entire expedition was lost; rescue parties found evidence that ships had become ice-bound.

Franklin, admin. dist. of N Northwest Territs., Canada. Area 1,422,565 sq km (549,253 sq mi); pop. 8000. Comprises Arctic archipelago (*c* 80 isls.); Melville and Boothia penins. Has Baffin Isl. National Park. Fur trapping; Eskimo pop. Named after British explorer, Sir John Franklin.

Franks, group of Germanic tribes who settled along lower Rhine in 3rd cent. Salian Franks invaded Gaul in 4th-5th cents. under their leader Clovis, who accepted Christianity and united all the Franks. Frankish empire expanded to incl. much of France, W Germany, Switzerland, Austria and parts of Italy by 9th cent.

Franz Josef Land, Arctic archipelago of USSR, N of Novaya Zemlya. Comprises *c* 80 uninhabited isls., largely ice covered; site of meteorological stations. Discovered (1873) by Austrian expedition, annexed by USSR (1926).

Frasch process, method of mining sulphur by pumping superheated steam into underground deposits; molten sulphur is forced to surface by compressed air.

Fraser, Dawn (1937-   ), Australian swimmer. Won 100m freestyle at 3 successive Olympics (1956, 1960, 1964). Held 27 individual world records during career (1956-64).

Fraser, [John] Malcolm (1930-   ), Australian politician, PM (1975-   ). Became leader of Liberal Party (1975). Appointed PM of interim govt. (Nov. 1975) by governor-general, Sir John Kerr, replacing Whitlam's Labor admin. Won ensuing election.

Fraser, Simon (1776-1862), Canadian explorer and fur trader, b. US. Entered service of North West Co. (1792); explored S Canadian Rockies from 1805, estab. trading posts. Reached Pacific (1808) via Fraser R.

Fraser, chief river of British Columbia, Canada. Rises in E Rocky Mts., flows NW, then SW 1370 km (*c* 850 mi) to Str. of Georgia, S of Vancouver. Salmon; scenic canyon in lower course. Navigable to Yale *c* 130 km (*c* 80 mi) from mouth. Named after Canadian explorer, Simon Fraser.

Fraserburgh, town of Grampian region, NE Scotland. Pop. 11,000. Major herring fishing port; offshore oil service industs.

fraud, in law, intentional deception to cause person to give up property or other legal right. If contract is based on fraud, injured party may void it and claim damages.

Fraunhofer, Joseph von (1787-1826), German optician, physicist. Improved telescopes and other optical instruments. Known for investigation of dark lines of solar spectrum (Fraunhofer lines), caused by absorption of certain wavelengths of light by elements present in Sun's chromosphere.

Fray Bentos, port of SW Uruguay, on Uruguay R. Pop. 21,000. Commercial, indust. centre; has important meat packing, canning industs.

Frazer, Sir James George (1854-1941), Scottish classicist, anthropologist. Best known for *The Golden Bough* (1890), an exhaustive study of magic, superstition, primitive religion.

Fréchette, Louis Honoré (1839-1908), French-Canadian poet. Known for epic of French-Canadian history, *La légende d'un peuple* (1887). Other works incl. *Les fleurs boréales* (1879).

Frederick I [Barbarossa] (*c* 1122-90), German king (1152-90), Holy Roman emperor (1155-90). As king, pacified Germany. When emperor, conducted 4 Italian campaigns against Lombard League and papacy. At first successful, was defeated at Legnano (1176), conceded Lombard League's demands at Peace of Constance (1183); excommunicated by Pope Alexander III. Drowned in Cilicia on Third Crusade.

Frederick II (1194-1250), Holy Roman emperor (1220-50). Received (1197) Sicily from Pope Innocent III. Crusade, really state visit, resulted in cession of Jerusalem, Nazareth, Bethlehem to Christians, and his crowning (1229) as king of Jerusalem. Latter gave rise to long conflict with papacy, and his excommunication (1245).

Frederick III (1415-93), Holy Roman emperor (1452-93). Succeeded to German throne (1440). Allowed wars to rage around him but outlived most of his enemies and rivals. Extended Habsburg power through marriages of his relatives.

Frederick IX (1899-1972), king of Denmark (1947-72). Married Princess Ingrid of Sweden (1935). Succeeded by his daughter Margarethe.

Frederick VI (1768-1839), king of Norway (1808-14), of Denmark (1808-39). Allied himself with Napoleon after British attack on Copenhagen (1807). As result of peace settlement, lost kingdom of Norway to Sweden.

Frederick I (1657-1713), king of Prussia (1701-13). Succeeded father Frederick William as elector of Brandenburg (1688). Became 1st king of Prussia.

Frederick [II] the Great (1712-86), king of Prussia (1740-86). Initiated (1740) War of Austrian Succession against Maria Theresa, securing Silesia. His leadership and military genius in wars during rule made Prussia a leading European power. Further enlarged kingdom through 1st partition of Poland (1772). Prolific writer, composer, patron of arts, had noted association with Voltaire. Became symbol of German nationalism.

Frederick III (1831-88), emperor of Germany (1888). Son of William I. A liberal, often disagreed with Bismarck's aggressive policies. Died 3 months after accession.

Frederick Barbarossa, *see* FREDERICK I.

Frederick Henry (1584-1647), prince of Orange. Son of William the Silent, stadholder of Netherlands (1625-47; title made hereditary, 1631). Captured several frontier forts from Spaniards. During his rule, art, science and commerce flourished.

Fredericksburg, town of E Virginia, US; on Rappahannock R. Pop. 14,000. Settled 1671; Civil War battleground (Chancellorsville nearby). Has many hist. buildings.

Frederick the Winter King (1596-1632), king of Bohemia (1619-20). Elector palatine (1610-20), chosen by Bohemian Protestants to replace Ferdinand II as king of Bohemia. Defeated at White Mountain (1620), lost Bohemia.

Frederick William (1620-88), elector of Brandenburg (1640-88), known as the 'Great Elector'. Rebuilt army and territ. after Thirty Years War, enlarging possessions at Peace of Westphalia (1648). Laid foundation of powerful Prussian state.

Frederick William I (1688-1740), king of Prussia (1713-40). Laid foundations of efficient admin. and army; avoided

Frederick the Great of Prussia

wars, built up treasury by careful economy. Father of Frederick the Great, whose talent he did not appreciate.

Frederick William III (1770-1840), king of Prussia (1797-1840). Tried to remain neutral in Napoleonic Wars. Defeated by Napoleon at Jena (1806); forced to accept Treaty of Tilsit (1807), which greatly reduced his territ. Later advised by Hardenberg, Scharnhorst, rebelled against Napoleon's domination (1813-14).

Frederick William IV (1795-1861), king of Prussia (1840-61). At first, gave in to 1848 revolutionaries' demands, later crushed them. Belief in divine right to rule led him to refuse offer of imperial crown from Frankfurt parliament (1849). Mental disturbance (1857) led to regency of his brother William I.

Fredericton, cap. of New Brunswick, Canada; on St John R. Pop. 25,000. Timber, leather products. Founded by United Empire Loyalists (1783); became cap. 1788.

Frederikshaab, town of SW Greenland. Pop. *c* 1000. Radio, meteorological station. Danish colony founded 1742.

free enterprise, economic practice in which relationship of supply and demand is allowed to regulate economy without govt. control. *See* LAISSER-FAIRE.

Freemasonry, principles and rituals of Free and Accepted Masons, international secret society practising brotherliness, charity and mutual aid. Masons claim roots in ancient times but order prob. derives from English and Scottish fraternities of stonemasons and cathedral builders in Middle Ages. Organized in self-governing national authorities known as grand lodges; first opened in London (1717), others in all European countries by 1800. Members must be male and believe in a higher being.

free port, port or zone within port free of customs regulation (*see* TARIFF). Estab. in late Middle Ages, *eg* by Hanseatic League. Present ones incl. Hong Kong, Singapore, parts of most international airports.

freesia, genus of bulbous plants of iris family, native to South Africa. Fragrant, usually white or yellow, funnel-shaped flowers.

freethinkers, *see* DEISTS.

Freetown, cap. of Sierra Leone, on Sierra Leone Penin. Pop. 179,000. Admin., commercial centre; good natural harbour, exports diamonds, iron ore, palm products. Settled (1787-92) by freed slaves. Cap. of British colony of Sierra Leone from 1808.

Freesia

free trade, international trade conducted without restrictions, *eg* quotas on imports, protective tariffs, export bounties. Advocates hold that system allows each country to specialize in goods it can produce most cheaply. European Economic Community aims to abolish protective tariffs between members.

free will, in theology, doctrine that man can choose between good and evil independently of the will of God. Problematic when held alongside belief in God's omniscience. Aquinas argued that foreknowledge did not imply intervention. Calvin held the opposite belief, *ie* predestination.

freeze drying, technique of drying food, vaccines, *etc,* by rapid freezing, followed by removal of frozen water by evaporation at low temperature and pressure.

freezing, conversion of liquid into solid form. For given pressure, freezing occurs at fixed temperature; this temperature may be lowered by dissolving substances in fluid.

Frege, Gottlob (1848-1925), German philosopher, mathematician. Founder of modern symbolic logic. Held all mathematics to be derivable from logical principles, and all verbal concepts expressible as symbolic functions.

Freiburg, see FRIBOURG, Switzerland.

Freiburg (-im-Breisgau), city of SW West Germany, on W edge of Black Forest. Pop. 168,000. Textiles, paper mfg. Held by Austria 1368-1805. Scene of battle (1644) between French and Bavarians. Gothic cathedral, univ. (1457).

Fréjus (anc. *Forum Julii*), town of Provence, SE France, on Côte d'Azur. Pop. 26,000. Resort. Former Roman naval base, port long silted up; remains incl. amphitheatre.

Fremantle, city of SW Western Australia, at mouth of Swan R. Pop. 25,000. Outport for Perth, exports oil, wheat, wool, minerals. Founded 1829.

Frémont, John Charles (1813-90), American explorer, politician. Explored Rocky Mts., Oregon, Nevada, California. Helped free California from Mexico (1846); governor of Arizona Territ. (1878-83).

French, John Denton Pinkstone, Earl of Ypres (1852–1925), British general. During Boer War, captured Bloemfontein. Chief of Imperial General Staff (1911-14), he commanded the British Expeditionary Force to France (1915). Lord-lieutenant of Ireland (1918-21).

French, Romance language belonging to Italic branch of Indo-European family. One of official languages of United Nations. Developed from vernacular Latin, with Celtic and Germanic elements in vocabulary. Historically divided into Old French (9th–13th cent.), Middle French (14th–16th cent.), Modern French (17th cent.–). French Academy aims to preserve language against foreign influences, slang.

French and Indian War (1754-60), North American conflict between Britain and France, part of SEVEN YEARS WAR. Aided by Iroquois Indians, British attacked French forts and cities, finally taking Québec by victory on Plains of Abraham (1759). Treaty of Paris (1763) ended French claims to Canada.

French Cameroons, *see* CAMEROON.

French Community, political union (estab. 1958) comprising France, its overseas depts. and territs., and 6 independent African republics: Central African Republic, Chad, Congo (Brazzaville), Gabon, Malagasy Republic, Senegal. Promotes economic, defensive and cultural cooperation. Originally incl. all former French colonies in Africa; most withdrew in 1962.

French Equatorial Africa, former French overseas territ. Comprised present-day CENTRAL AFRICAN REPUBLIC, CHAD, People's Republic of the CONGO, GABON. Estab. 1910, cap. Brazzaville; dissolved 1958.

French Guiana, overseas dept. of France, NE South America. Area 91,000 sq km (35,135 sq mi); pop. 50,000; cap. Cayenne. Rises from Atlantic coast to tropical forests and mountains of Inini territ. Largely undeveloped; main exports gold, timber, rum. Site of former penal colonies incl. Devil's Isl. Became French dept. 1946.

French Guinea, *see* GUINEA.

French horn, brass instrument of coiled tubing, whose bore widens into a flared bell-shape. Well-known concertos have been written for it by Mozart and R. Strauss.

French India, group of 5 former French settlements in India, incl. Pondicherry on E coast, Mahe on W coast. All transferred to India by 1954.

French Polynesia, overseas territ. of France, in S Pacific Ocean. Comprises Gambier, Marquesas, Society, Tuamotu, Tubuai isl. groups. Area 4000 sq km (1550 sq mi); pop. 124,000; cap. Papeete (Tahiti). Produce fruit, copra, pearl shell; tourist indust. Acquired by France during 19th cent.

French Revolution, political uprising, begun 1789. Product of 18th cent. liberalism and assertion of capitalist class against outdated feudal system. Immediate cause was state's vast debt. To raise money, LOUIS XVI convened ESTATES-GENERAL (May, 1789), which demanded sweeping political, social and fiscal reforms and declared itself National Assembly. Louis yielded, but dismissal of NECKER led to mob's storming of Bastille. National Guard organized, feudal privileges abolished, and commune estab. as govt. of Paris. Louis imprisoned (1791) after attempt to flee country, forced to accept new constitution. Republican GIRONDISTS and extremists controlled legislative assembly; their desire to spread revolutionary ideas and Austrian threats to restore Louis to absolute power served as pretext for FRENCH REVOLUTIONARY WARS. After abortive insurrections, National Convention (estab. 1792) abolished monarchy, set up First Republic (Sept. 1792), convicted and executed Louis for treason (Jan. 1793). Royalist backlash led to REIGN OF TERROR. DIRECTORY estab. 1795; corrupt admin. led to Napoleon's coup d'état of 18 Brumaire and Consulate (1799).

French Revolutionary Calendar, official calendar of France (1793-1805), dividing year into 12 months of 30 days, with 5 or 6 leap days. Month was divided into 3 weeks of 10 days, day into 10 hours. Computed from 22 Sept. 1792, date of overthrow of monarchy.

French Revolutionary Wars, general European conflict (1792-1802), precipitated by French Revolution. Austrian and Prussian intention to restore Louis XVI to former power, and French desire to spread revolution throughout Europe, led France to declare war on Austria. After early reverses, France invaded Germany, Netherlands and Italy (where Napoleon came to prominence). By beginning of 19th cent., Austria and its Russian allies had withdrawn from war, leaving Britain alone against France. Short-lived peace (1802) followed by Napoleonic Wars (1803-15). *See* NAPOLEON I.

French Southern and Antarctic Territories, French overseas territ. Area 410,000 sq km (158,000 sq mi). Formed 1955 from Adélie Land (Antarctica) and Kerguelen, Amsterdam, St Paul and Crozet isls. (Indian Ocean).

French Sudan, *see* MALI.

French West Africa, former French overseas territ. Comprised present-day BENIN, GUINEA, IVORY COAST, MALI, MAURITANIA, NIGER, SENEGAL, UPPER VOLTA. Estab. 1895, cap. Dakar; dissolved 1958.

Freneau, Philip Morin (1752-1832), American poet, journalist. Known for anti-British verse, *eg The British*

Prison Ship (1781), nature lyrics incl. 'The Wild Honeysuckle', 'The Indian Burying Ground'.

frequency, in physics, number of periodic oscillations, vibrations or waves per unit of time; usually measured in cycles per second. For wave motion, frequency equals wave velocity divided by wavelength.

fresco, method of wall-painting with watercolours on ground of wet plaster. Technique was perfected in Italy in 16th cent.; Raphael's frescoes in Stanze of Vatican are esp. fine.

Fresnel, Augustin Jean (1788-1827), French physicist. His investigations on diffraction of light and double refraction gave support to transverse wave theory of light. Designed lenses to replace mirrors in lighthouses.

Fresno, town of SC California, US. Pop. 166,000. Agric. produce esp. raisins; fruit drying, packing.

Sigmund Freud

Freud, Sigmund (1856-1939), Austrian psychiatrist, founder of PSYCHOANALYSIS. His work on hysteria led him to believe that symptoms were caused by early trauma, and were expressions of repressed sexual energy. Devised 'free association' technique and dream interpretation to discover repressed experiences. Emphasized importance of infantile sexuality in personality's development in later life. Influenced Jung and Adler, who later opposed him. Works incl. *The Interpretation of Dreams* (1900), *The Psychopathology of Everyday Life* (1904), *The Ego and the Id* (1923).

Freytag, Gustav (1816-95), German novelist, playwright. Known for novel sequence covering German history *The Ancestors* (6 vol., 1873-80). Plays incl. *The Journalists* (1854), a comedy of international politics.

Fribourg (Ger. *Freiburg*), town of W Switzerland, cap. of Fribourg canton. Pop. 40,000. Chocolate mfg. Cathedral (13th cent.); univ. (1889).

friction, force opposing motion of one surface over another; heat produced by friction accounts for inefficiency of machinery.

Friedman, Milton (1912-), American economist. A leading monetarist, he rejected Keynesian thesis that govt. spending leads to economic improvement; advocated strict control of money supply. Awarded Nobel Prize for Economics (1976).

Friedrich, Caspar David (1774-1840), German romantic painter. Specialized in melancholy forest and mountain scenes, portrayed in strange light of dusk or moonlight. Works incl. *Cross in the Mountains* (1807).

Friedrichshafen, town of SW West Germany, on L. Constance. Pop. 39,000. Port, resort; tanning. Former site of Zeppelin plant, heavily bombed in WWII.

Friendly Islands, see TONGA.

Friesland (anc. *Frisia*), prov. of N Netherlands. Area 3432 sq km (1325 sq mi); cap. Leeuwarden. Incl. W Frisian Isls.

Noted for Friesian cattle. Distinct dialect, still widely spoken. Medieval region under counts of Holland, joined United Provs. 1579. East Friesland (N West Germany) separate from 1454.

frigate, originally a narrow-hulled oared sailing vessel in the Mediterranean. In the 18th cent. a full-rigged warship of up to 50 guns. In WWII a ship specially designed for convoy and anti-submarine work, superseding the destroyer.

Frigate bird

frigate bird, any of Fregatidae family of large tropical seabirds with webbed feet, large hooked beak. Frequently robs other birds of their food.

Frigg or **Frigga,** in Germanic myth, mother goddess, wife of Odin, mother of Balder. Worshipped as deity of household and love.

Frisian Islands, offshore group of *c* 30 isls. in North Sea, stretching from Wadden Zee to Jutland. Comprise W Frisians (Netherlands), E Frisians (West Germany), N Frisians (Denmark, West Germany). Low-lying, sandy; cattle, fishing.

Friuli-Venezia Giulia, region of NE Italy. Alps in N, fertile plain in S; chief city Venice, cap. Trieste. Part (Istria) ceded to Yugoslavia 1947.

Frobisher, Sir Martin (*c* 1535-94), English navigator. Made 3 unsuccessful attempts (1567-8) to find Northwest Passage; discovered Frobisher Bay. Joined Drake in West Indies expedition (1585). Knighted for part in defeating Spanish Armada (1588).

Froebel, Friedrich Wilhelm August (1782-1852), German educator. Founded kindergarten system, estab. 1st kindergarten in 1837, 1st kindergarten training school in 1849. His theories had strong spiritual element; stressed pleasurable environment. Works incl. *The Education of Man* (1826).

Marsh frog (*Rana ridibunda*)

frog, tailless amphibian of order Anura. Mainly aquatic or semi-aquatic, with webbed feet; arboreal forms have enlarged webbed hands, feet. Sticky tongue used to seize prey. Young, known as tadpoles, have fish-like form. Species incl. common frog, *Rana temporaria*; hind legs of edible frog, *R. esculenta*, eaten in France, S US.

frogbit, *Hydrocharis morsus-ranae*, floating pond weed with kidney shaped leaves, white flowers. Sinks to bottom during winter. Common in N Europe.

frogfish, any of Antennariidae family of rounded scaleless fish with flipper-like pectoral fins. Body camouflaged with numerous fleshy flaps and warts. Lives in floating seaweed of tropical seas.

froghopper, any of Cercopidae family of leaping insects. Larvae enveloped in froth (cuckoo-spit) secreted from anus; often seen on plants. Also called spittle bug.

Froissart, Jean (*c* 1338-*c* 1410), French chronicler, poet, traveller. Wrote *Chronicles,* lively and invaluable, though sometimes inaccurate, record of Europe 1325-1400, covering 1st half of Hundred Years War.

Fromm, Erich (1900-   ), American psychoanalyst, writer, b. Germany. Works, dealing with alienation of people in indust. society, incl. *Escape from Freedom* (1941), *The Sane Society* (1955).

Fronde, name given to French civil wars during Louis XIV's minority (1648-53). First, caused by quarrels between Parlement of Paris and royal authority over taxation, was suppressed by MAZARIN and CONDÉ. Second, caused by attempt of nobles to limit power of Mazarin, was led by Condé. Condé, allied with Spain, continued fighting until 1659 although Fronde had collapsed by 1653.

front, in meteorology, line at Earth's surface marking boundary between cold and warm air masses. As warm air is lighter, it ascends the frontal plane or surface above cold air. Cold front results from advancing cold air mass; warm front from advancing warm air mass. Associated with DEPRESSIONS.

Frontenac, Louis de Buade, Comte de (*c* 1622-98), French governor of New France in Canada (1672-82, 1689-98). Helped promote fur trade, exploration. Authority disputed by Jesuits; recalled to France (1682). Reappointed 1689 to counter Iroquois aggression.

Frost, Robert Lee (1874-1963), American poet. Lyrics dealing with New England life incl. 'Mending Wall', 'The Death of the Hired Man', 'Stopping by Woods on a Snowy Evening'. Most famous verse in *North of Boston* (1914), *West-running Brook* (1928). Known for clear, simple, moral poetry, close to rural life and nature, which can also express irony, bitterness, despair.

frost, weather condition occurring when air temperature falls to 0°C or below. Exists in 2 main forms: (1) hoarfrost, produced when water vapour crystallizes directly as white coating on ground; (2) ground or black frost, produced when sub-zero temperatures cause water to freeze. Latter type important in growing season available to crops, and in weathering rock.

frostbite, damage to skin and tissues resulting from exposure to intense cold. Caused by lack of blood circulation and formation of ice crystals; nose, hands, feet, and ears most often affected.

fructose or **fruit sugar,** crystalline sugar found in ripe fruit and honey.

fruit, mature, fertilized ovary of flower, varying in form from dandelion tufted seed to cultivated apple. Edible fruit classified as tree, *eg* apple, orange; bush, *eg* strawberry, blackcurrant; stone, *eg* plum; pip, *eg* grape; berry, *eg* raspberry; and nut, *eg* walnut.

fruit bat, any of suborder Megachiroptera of large fruit-eating bats of Old World tropics. Species incl. FLYING FOX.

fruit fly, insect of Trypetidae family, whose larvae bore into fruit, other plants. Mediterranean fruit fly, *Ceratitis capitata,* is serious pest of citrus fruit.

Frunze, city of USSR, cap. of Kirghiz SSR. Pop. 452,000. Centre of fertile agric. region; produces machinery, textiles. Renamed (1925) in honour of revolutionary hero M. V. Frunze.

Fry, Christopher (1907-   ), English dramatist. Known for witty verse plays, *eg The Lady's Not for Burning* (1949), *A Phoenix Too Frequent* (1949), *Venus Observed* (1950).

Fry, Elizabeth, née Gurney (1780-1845), English prison reformer, philanthropist. A Quaker, she improved conditions for women in Newgate and other prisons.

Fry, Roger Eliot (1866-1934), English art critic, painter. Arranged influential 'Manet and the Post-Impressionists' exhibition (1910) which introduced post-impressionist art

Elizabeth Fry

into Britain. Writings on art incl. *Vision and Design* (1920) and *Cézanne* (1927).

Frye, Northrop (1912-   ), Canadian literary critic. Best known for *Anatomy of Criticism* (1957), advocating a scientific theory of criticism.

Fuad I, orig. Ahmed Fuad Pasha (1868-1936), king of Egypt (1922-36). Ruled as sultan (1917-22) before becoming king when British protect. in Egypt ended. Autocracy opposed in parliament by anti-colonialist Wafd party.

Vivian Fuchs (with pipe) and other members of the Commonwealth Trans-Antarctic Expedition

Fuchs, Sir Vivian Ernest (1908-   ), English geologist, explorer. Directed Falkland Isls. Dependencies Survey (1950-5). Led, with Sir Edmund Hillary, Commonwealth Trans-Antarctic Expedition (1957–8), 1st overland crossing of Antarctic.

fuchsia, genus of colourful shrubs of willow herb family with red or purple flowers. Most species native to tropical America. Widely cultivated ornamental.

fuel cell, cell which produces electricity by oxidation of fuel. Simplest type uses hydrogen and oxygen, with catalytic electrodes. Used in space flights.

Fugger, Jacob (1459-1525), German merchant, member of great Augsburg trading family. Brought family fortune to height through near monopolies in mining and trading of copper, mercury, silver. Owned fleets, vast land holdings, great houses. Helped finance Maximilian I, and to secure election of Charles V. Family patronized arts, learning. Fortune drained after his death by support for Habsburg wars.

fugue, piece of music in a set number of parts or voices, each of which follows separate yet interrelated melodic line. A fugue begins with each voice stating a theme in turn but thereafter is not confined to a set pattern. J.S. Bach achieved highest development of fugue composition.

Fujiyama or **Fuji-san,** highest mountain of Japan, in C Honshu isl.; alt. 3776 m (12,390 ft). A dormant volcano, last active in 1707. Place of pilgrimage, sacred to Japanese.

Fukien, prov. of SE China on Formosa Str. Area 119,000 sq km (46,000 sq mi); pop. (est.) 17,000,000; cap. Foochow. Mountainous, forested; lumber resources. Formerly great tea exports, famous preserved fruit. Troop bases because of strategic proximity of Taiwan.

Fukuoka, seaport of Japan, on Kyushu isl. Pop. 853,000. Shipbuilding, textile mfg. Scene of attempted invasions by Kublai Khan (1274, 1281).

Fulani, pastoralists of W Africa, found throughout area between Upper Nile and Senegal. Moslem; reached height of power in 19th cent., during which they conquered Hausa states of Nigeria.

Fulda, town of EC West Germany, on R. Fulda. Pop. 45,000. Agric. market, textiles. Christianity spread throughout C Germany from abbey (744); St Boniface buried in cathedral.

Fulham, part of Hammersmith, WC Greater London, England. Met. bor. until 1965. Fulham Palace is residence of bishop of London.

Fuller, Richard Buckminster (1895-), American architect, engineer. Constructor of geodesic dome, spherical structure of light but extremely strong triangular members. Exponent of *Dymaxion* principle of maximum effectiveness with minimum outlay of materials.

Fuller, Roy Broadbent (1912-), English poet. Works, *eg Counterparts* (1954), *Brutus's .Orchard* (1957), often reflect discontent with English society. Also wrote novels, *eg The Ruined Boys* (1959).

fulmar, *Fulmarus glacialis,* large grey seabird of petrel family of Arctic and subarctic regions. Visits land only to breed.

Fulton, Robert (1765-1815), American engineer, inventor. Built *Clermont* (1807), 1st successful steamship in American waters.

fumitory, any plant of Fumariaceae family, esp. widely distributed species *Fumaria officinalis* with fern-like leaves and pink, spurred flowers. Formerly used in medicine.

Funchal, cap. of Madeira Isls., Portugal. Pop. 100,000. Commercial centre; port, exports Madeira wines; tourism.

function, in modern mathematics, rule which associates to each member of a set a member of another set. More familiarly, functions are expressed by formulae which express variation of 1 quantity (dependent variable) in terms of variation of other quantities (independent variables).

functionalism, in art and architecture, 20th cent. principle emphasizing unity of form and purpose, and rejecting all inessential ornament. Prominent exponents of the style were members of Bauhaus school and Le Corbusier.

fundamentalism, conservative, mainly Protestant, religious movement of 20th cent. Upholds traditional interpretations of Bible against modern textual criticism and scientific theory (*eg* Darwinism). Movement organized in 1909, esp. influential in US.

Fundy, Bay of, arm of N Atlantic, SE Canada; 270 km (*c* 170 mi) long; separates New Brunswick from Nova Scotia

penin. Has tides up to 12-15 m (40-50 ft) high.

Fünen, see FYN, Denmark.

fungus, any of many plants of division Thallophyta. Lacking CHLOROPHYLL, they depend on organic matter for growth. Saprophytes feed on dead organisms, parasites on living. Reproduction by SPORE rather than seed. Incl. mushrooms, toadstools, yeasts.

fur, soft thick hair covering the skin of many mammals, *eg* sable, mink, ermine, chinchilla. Valued for both warm and luxurious clothing. Fur trade encouraged exploration of Asia and North America (17th-19th cents.). In Canada, Hudson's Bay Co. was largely instrumental in opening up country during the pursuit of beaver pelts.

Furies, see EUMENIDES.

Furneaux Islands, isl. group in Bass Str., off Tasmania, SE Australia. Largest is Flinders Isl. (area 2072 sq km/800 sq mi). Intensive cattle and sheep raising.

Furness, penin. of Cumbria, NW England. N partly in Lake Dist. Shipbuilding at BARROW-IN-FURNESS.

Fürth, town of SC West Germany. Pop. 95,000. Toys, glass mfg. Fürth-Nuremberg was 1st railway in Germany (1835). Prospered from 14th cent. as refuge for Jews from persecution in Nuremberg.

Furtwängler, Wilhelm (1886-1954), German conductor. Conductor of Berlin Philharmonic Orchestra (1922-45). Known for interpretation of Wagner's operas and orchestral work of Beethoven, Brahms, Bruckner.

furze, see GORSE.

Fuseli, Henry, orig. Johann Heinrich Füssli (1741-1825), Anglo-Swiss painter, b. Zurich. He produced highly imaginative works, depicting horrific and fantastic scenes. Works incl. *The Nightmare* and illustrations of Milton and Shakespeare. Influenced William Blake.

Fushun, city of Liaoning prov., NE China. Pop. 1,700,000. Major indust. centre; extensive open cast coal mines, oil shale refining; engineering, automobile mfg.

Fusin, city of Liaoning prov., NE China. Pop. 500,000. Indust. centre, coal mining.

fusion, nuclear, nuclear reaction in which two light atomic nuclei fuse to form heavier nucleus, with release of enormous energy, *eg* deuterium and tritium nuclei fuse to form helium nucleus. Nuclei must have sufficient kinetic energy to overcome repulsive forces; extremely high temperatures provide this energy. Potential source of useful energy; basis of stellar energy and hydrogen bomb.

Fust, Johann (*c* 1400-66), German printer. Lent money to Gutenberg to help finance his printing experiments; received Gutenberg's press and type for non-payment of debt. Printed (1457) 1st dated book, a psalter.

Futa Jallon, see FOUTA DJALLON.

Futuna Island, see WALLIS AND FUTUNA ISLANDS.

futurism, artistic and literary movement inaugurated by publication of Futurist Manifesto in Paris (1909) by Italian poet Marinetti. 'Manifesto of Futurist Painting' (1910) was signed by group of Italian painters incl. Boccioni, Balla, Carra. They sought to eliminate conventional form and to express vital dynamism of machine age.

Fyn (Ger. *Fünen*), isl. of Denmark. Area 2976 sq km (1149 sq mi); main town Odense. Dairying. Separated by Little Belt from Jutland (W), by Great Belt from Zealand (E).

Fyne, Loch, sea loch of Strathclyde region, W Scotland. Length 64 km (40 mi). Noted for herring, kippers.

Fyzabad, see FAIZABAD.

G

gabbro, coarse-grained, plutonic igneous rock. Consists of plagioclase feldspar plus one or more varieties of pyroxene, *eg* augite. Dark coloured and heavy; formed by slow cooling of large underground masses. Common in Europe, US, South Africa.

Gaberones, *see* GABORONE, Botswana.

Gabès, town of SE Tunisia, on Gulf of Gabès. Pop. 77,000. Fishing port, railway to Tunis; exports dates, fruit from surrounding oasis.

Gable, Clark (1901-60), American film actor. Star for nearly 30 years, known as 'king' of Hollywood. Best-known for *Gone With the Wind* (1939).

Gabo, Naum (1890-), American sculptor, b. Russia. Uses modern synthetic materials in space-constructions; pioneer of kinetic art. With brother, Antoine Pevsner, wrote *Realistic Manifesto of Constructivism* (1920).

Gabon

Gabon, republic of WC Africa. Area 268,000 sq km (103,500 sq mi); pop. 520,000; cap. Libreville. Languages: Bantu, French. Religions: native, RC. Coastal plain, interior plateau; largely tropical rain-forest. Exports petroleum, manganese, hardwoods. Reached *c* 1485 by Portuguese; slave trade 17th-19th cent. Part of French Congo from 1886; territ. of French Equatorial Africa from 1908; independent republic from 1960. Member of French Community.

gaboon viper, *Bitis gabonica,* short, thick, brightly patterned snake of W African forests. Sluggish, it bites swiftly when disturbed.

Gabor, Dennis (1900-), British physicist, b. Hungary. Awarded Nobel Prize for Physics (1971) for invention of principle of holography (1948), a 3-dimensional lensless system of photography, used in many fields. Practical applications began following invention of laser in 1960s.

Gaborone, cap. of Botswana. Pop. 26,000. Admin. centre. Small village until chosen (1964) as cap. of new republic from 1966; formerly Gaberones, renamed 1969.

Gabriel, archangel, messenger of God. Appears several times in Bible, notably to tell Virgin Mary she will bear child to be called Jesus. In Islam, revealed Koran to Mohammed. Christian tradition regards him as trumpeter of Last Judgment.

Gadafy, Muammar al-, *see* QADDHAFI, MUAMMAR AL-.

Gadames, *see* GHADAMES, Libya.

Gaddi, Taddeo (d. 1366), Florentine painter. Follower of Giotto, became leader of Florentine painting after Giotto's death. Works incl. fresco cycle *Life of the Virgin*. His son, **Agnolo Gaddi** (*c* 1350-96), also painted frescoes incl. *Legend of True Cross* cycle.

gadfly, name used for various blood-sucking flies, *eg* horsefly, that attack livestock.

gadolinium (Gd), metallic element of lanthanide series; at. no. 64, at. wt. 157.25. Some isotopes used in nuclear reactors to absorb neutrons.

Gadsden, James (1788-1858), American railway promoter, diplomat. Advocate of railway link between South and Pacific. Minister to Mexico (1853-6), negotiated Gadsden Purchase of land to build line along Mexican border.

Gaea, in Greek myth, goddess of earth. In Hesiod's *Theogony,* she emerged from primeval chaos and gave birth to Uranus, the sky. Her children by Uranus were the TITANS.

Gaelic or **Goidelic,** subgroup of CELTIC branch of Indo-European language family. Incl. Irish Gaelic, Scottish Gaelic, extinct Manx. Irish Gaelic divided into Old (7th–9th cent.), Middle (10th–16th cent.) and Modern periods. Revived in 20th cent. as national language of Eire. Scottish Gaelic identical with Irish until 17th cent.

Gaelic football, fifteen-a-side team game played with a round ball, combining aspects of soccer and rugby. Mainly confined to Ireland. Rules drawn up by Gaelic Athletic Association, founded 1884.

Gaelic literature, literature of Gaelic-speaking Ireland and Scotland. Not separated nationally until 17th cent., therefore divided into Old Irish (before 900), Middle Irish (until 1350), Late Middle or Early Modern Irish (until 1650) and Modern Irish and Scottish Gaelic (from 1650). Old Irish works incl. Book of Leinster. Middle Irish works divided into 2 cycles of heroic tales, *ie* Red Branch or Ulster cycle (pagan), and Fenian (later, more complex, Christian), incl. work by poet OSSIAN. Modern Irish period saw rise of prose, less formal poetry. Scottish Gaelic poetry stimulated by events of 1745, as in poetry of Alexander MacDonald, and by *Ossian* of James MACPHERSON. Gaelic revival in late 19th cent. Ireland.

Gaeta, town of Latium, WC Italy, on Bay of Gaeta. Pop. 22,000. Port, resort. Scene of final defeat (1861) of Francis II of Naples by Victor Emmanuel II.

Gafsa (anc. *Capsa*), town of WC Tunisia. Pop. 30,000. Phosphate mines; oasis produces dates, olives. Hot springs important in Roman times. Nearby prehist. remains.

Gagarin, Yuri Alekseyevich (1934-68), Russian cosmonaut. First man to orbit Earth (April, 1961). His flight in satellite, *Vostok,* lasted *c* 89 mins. Killed in aeroplane acccident.

gaillardia, genus of chiefly W US herbs of composite family with hairy foliage and large flower heads with yellow or red rays and purple disks. Species incl. blanket flower, *Gaillardia aristata.*

Gainsborough, Thomas (1727-88), English painter. Influenced by Van Dyck, painted elegant portraits, *eg Blue Boy, Mrs Siddons,* members of Royal Family; also first authentically English landscapes; *Mr and Mrs Andrews in a Landscape* combines genres.

Gainsborough, urban dist. of Lincolnshire, E England, on R. Trent. Pop. 17,000. Identified with St Ogg's in Eliot's *Mill on the Floss.*

Gaiseric or **Genseric** (*c* 390–477), king of the Vandals (428-77). Invaded Roman Africa from Spain, captured Carthage (439) and made it his cap. Sacked Rome (455). Controlled Roman Africa, Sicily, Corsica, Sardinia at his death.

Yuri Gagarin

Gaitskell, Hugh Todd Naylor (1906-63), British politician. Labour chancellor of exchequer (1950-1). Leader of parliamentary Labour Party (1955-63), adopted moderate stance on nationalization and disarmament issues.

galago, *see* BUSHBABY.

Galahad, *see* ARTHURIAN LEGEND.

Galápagos Islands or **Colón Archipelago,** isl. group of Ecuador, in E Pacific Ocean. Area *c* 7800 sq km (3000 sq mi); chief isls. San Cristóbal (Eng. Chatham) and Isabela (Albemarle). Unique flora and fauna (isls. named after giant tortoise, Span. *galápago*); visited (1835) by Darwin; now nature reserve.

Galatea, *see* PYGMALION.

Galati or **Galatz,** city of E Romania, on R. Danube. Pop. 191,000. Naval base; port, exports grain, timber.

Galatia, ancient region of C Asia Minor, around modern Ankara. Invaded by Gauls in 3rd cent. BC (hence name). Came under Roman rule in 2nd cent. BC; Roman prov. 25 BC.

Galatians, St Paul's Epistle to the, book of NT, possibly written *c* AD 48 at Ephesus. Exposition of how Christianity superseded law of Moses.

Galatz, *see* GALATI, Romania.

galaxy, large grouping of stars, gas and dust held together by mutual gravitational attraction. Milky Way is galaxy containing solar system. Most galaxies are elliptical or spiral shaped, a few being irregular in shape; *c* 10⁹ are thought to exist.

Galbraith, J[ohn] K[enneth] (1908-), American economist, b. Canada. Adviser to J.F. Kennedy; US ambassador to India (1961-3). Advocate of using nation's wealth for public projects rather than consumer goods; early critic of dependence on economic growth. Works incl. *The Affluent Society* (1958), *The New Industrial State* (1967).

Galen (*c* 130-*c* 200), Greek physician. Wrote extensively on human anatomy, basing his work on dissection of animals. Systematized contemporary medical knowledge in series of treatises; authority remained unchallenged until 16th cent.

galena (PbS), lead ore mineral. Grey in colour, heavy; consists of lead sulphide. Chief source of lead; also often contains silver. Major sources in US, Australia, Germany, England.

Galerius (d. AD 310), Roman emperor (305-10). Created Caesar (sub-emperor) by Diocletian (293). Defeated Persians 297. Became joint emperor with Constantine I. Ruled Eastern empire until his death.

Galiani, Ferdinando (1728-87), Italian economist. Works, *eg Della Moneta* (1750), attacked theory that money has no intrinsic value and that land is source of all wealth.

Galicia (Pol. *Galicja,* Ukr. *Halychyna*), region of SE Poland and W Ukraine. Incl. plains in N, N Carpathians in S; main rivers Dnestr, Vistula. Chief cities Kraków, Lvov. Hist. duchy, part of Poland from 14th cent.; ceded to Austria by 1772 partition.

Galicia, region and former kingdom of NW Spain. Mountainous with deep valleys, indented coast; drained by R. Miño. Stock raising, fishing. Main towns La Coruña, Vigo, Santiago de Compostela. Taken from Moors by Asturias (9th cent.).

Galilee, Sea of, lake of NE Israel, Length 23 km (14 mi), area *c* 166 sq km (64 sq mi). Lies below sea level, fed by hot mineral springs. Fisheries since Biblical times. Also known as L. Tiberias.

Galileo

Galileo Galilei (1564-1642), Italian astronomer and physicist. Constructed first astronomical telescope (1609) and discovered 4 brightest satellites of Jupiter. Investigated motion of falling bodies, his findings contradicting Aristotle's teaching. Supported Copernican theory; later forced by Inquisition to renounce this belief. His use of observation, experiment and mathematics helped lay foundation of modern science.

gall, growths on plants caused by insects, esp. of Cynipidae family. The common oak apple gall is produced through a chemical irritant deposited by the gall wasp when it lays its eggs on the underside of a leaf. Each gall contains a wasp larva.

Gallatin, Albert (1761-1849), American politician, financier, b. Switzerland. Secretary of the treasury (1801-14), curtailed US military expenditure and reshaped federal financial policies. Led negotiations concluding War of 1812 between US and Britain.

gall bladder, membranous sac which stores and concentrates bile from liver in most vertebrates. In humans, attached to underside of liver; contracts to eject bile into duodenum to aid digestion.

Galle, seaport of SW Sri Lanka. Pop. 72,000 Exports tea, coconut products. Chief port of Sri Lanka under Portuguese and Dutch, declined with improvement of Colombo harbour (1885).

galleon, a square-rigged warship of the 16th cent. with narrow hull, beaked bow and rectangular forecastle, carrying usually 2 tiers of guns. Used by Spanish to bring treasure from Americas.

galley, long, low-built vessel propelled by oars and sail. Used in ancient and medieval times, esp. in Mediterranean. Rowers were generally slaves or prisoners.

Gallicanism, term for movement in French RC church claiming limited autonomy from pope; opposed to ULTRAMONTANISM. Important principles enunciated in the 4 Gallican Articles of 1682, *ie* kings, general councils not subject to pope. Lost legitimacy with Vatican Council's enunciation of papal infallibility (1869).

Gallico, Paul William (1897-1976), American author. Known for popular novels, *eg The Adventures of Hiram Holliday* (1939), *The Snow Goose* (1941), *Love of Seven Dolls* (1954).

Gallic Wars, campaigns of Julius Caesar during his proconsulship in Gaul (58-51 BC). Defeated the Helvetii and the German king Ariovistus (58), then the Belgae (57). Invaded Britain twice (55, 54). Quelled revolt of Ambiorix (53). Conquest of Gaul was completed when Caesar crushed rebellion led by Vercingetorix (52).

Gallienus (d. AD 268), Roman emperor (253-68). Shared power with his father, Valerian, until Valerian was captured by the Persians (260). Rebellions occurred in most of the provs. during his reign. Murdered by his troops.

Gallipoli (*Gelibolu*), penin. of European Turkey, between Gulf of Saros and Dardanelles. Scene of unsuccessful landings by Allies to capture Constantinople via Dardanelles (1915-16).

gallium (Ga), soft metallic element; at. no. 31, at. wt. 69.72. Used to make high temperature thermometers and alloys of low melting point. Existence predicted by Mendeleev; discovered spectroscopically in 1875.

gallon, unit of liquid measure. British Imperial gallon is volume occupied by 10 pounds of water under specified conditions; equals *c* 4.546 litres. US gallon is *c* 5/6 of Imperial gallon.

Galloway, area of SW Scotland, in Dumfries and Galloway region. Rhinns of Galloway penin. in SW, with Mull of Galloway at S end (most S point in Scotland). Dairying; black Galloway cattle.

Gallup, George Horace (1901-), American statistician. Founded Gallup Poll and American Institute of Public Opinion (1935).

gall wasp, small narrow-waisted insect of Cynipidae family. Lays eggs in plants, introducing irritant simultaneously. Larvae develop in swellings (galls) which appear on plant. Galls often seen on oak trees.

Galois, Evariste (1811-32), French mathematician. Pioneer in use of modern techniques in algebra, he showed impossibility of solving general polynomial of 5th degree by algebraic means.

Galsworthy, John (1867-1933), English author. Known for the 'Forsyte Saga' (1906-22) portraying Edwardian moneyed class. Also wrote Ibsenesque plays of ideas dealing with social injustice, *eg Strife* (1909), *The Skin Game* (1920). Awarded Nobel Prize for Literature (1932).

Galt, John (1779-1839), Scottish novelist. Known for chronicle novel of Scots provincial life *Annals of the Parish* (1821). Other works incl. *The Provost* (1822), *The Entail* (1823).

Galton, Sir Francis (1822-1911), English scientist. Founded and coined term for eugenics, movement to improve species through control of hereditary factors. Developed statistical correlation and questionnaire techniques.

Galvani, Luigi (1737-98), Italian physician. Discovered contraction of frog's muscles produced by contact with 2 different metals. Ascribed source of electricity to animal tissue; theory discredited by Volta.

galvanization, plating of iron or steel sheets with zinc to protect them from atmospheric corrosion. Sheets usually immersed in molten zinc; zinc can also be deposited by electrolysis.

galvanometer, device used to measure or detect small electric currents. Usually consists of current-carrying coil suspended between poles of permanent magnet; magnetic field produced by current interacts with field of magnet, causing coil to move.

Galveston, port and tourist resort of SE Texas, US; on Galveston Isl. in Gulf of Mexico inlet. Pop. 62,000. Shipyards; exports sulphur, cotton, wheat. Oil, cotton processing; chemical, hardware mfg. Damaged by hurricanes (1900, 1961).

Galway, county of Connacht prov., W Irish Republic. Area 5939 sq km (2293 sq mi); pop. 148,000. Indented coast,

mountains in W; incl. scenic Connemara, Aran Isls. Agric., fishing; marble quarrying. Co. town **Galway,** on Galway Bay. Pop. 27,000. Fishing port, esp. salmon; univ. coll. (1849).

Gama, Vasco da (*c* 1469-1524), Portuguese navigator. Discovered sea route to India via Cape of Good Hope (1497-9), opening up East Indian trade and leading to development of Portuguese empire. Made 2 further voyages to India; briefly viceroy (1524).

Gambetta, Léon Michel (1838-82), French statesman, premier (1881-2). Organized resistance in Franco-Prussian War; escaped from siege of Paris by balloon. Played important part in estab. of Third Republic.

Gambia

Gambia, republic of W Africa. Area 10,360 sq km (4000 sq mi); pop. 493,000; cap. Banjul. Official language: English. Religions: native, Islam. Smallest country in Africa, surrounded by Senegal; extends *c* 320 km (200 mi) along R. Gambia. Exports groundnuts, hides. First discovered in 15th cent. by Portuguese. British colony from 1843; independent (1965). Member of British Commonwealth.

Gambier Islands, archipelago of S Pacific Ocean, part of French Polynesia. Main isl. Mangareva. Produce copra, coffee, pearl shell. Acquired by France (1881).

Gamelin, Maurice Gustave (1872-1958), French general. As commander of the Allied armies in France at the outset of WWII, bore responsibility for the disastrous defeat of June 1940, and was replaced by Weygand. Imprisoned for treason in 1943, he was released by the Allies (1945).

gamete, in biology, reproductive cell, haploid and usually sexually differentiated. Male gamete (spermatozoon) unites with female gamete (ovum) to form the cell (zygote) which develops into new individual.

game theory, use of mathematical analysis to select best available strategy in order to maximize one's winnings or minimize opponent's winnings in a game, war, business, *etc.* Important in mathematical economics. Founded by VON NEUMANN.

gamma globulin, fraction of protein in human blood plasma containing most antibodies. Can be separated from blood and used to provide temporary immunity against disease, *eg* hepatitis.

gamma rays, high frequency electromagnetic radiation, similar to X-rays. Emitted by atomic nuclei during radioactive decay; great penetrating power.

Gander, town of NE Newfoundland, Canada; N of Gander L. Pop. 8000. Grew up round airport from 1935; important air base in WWII.

Gandhi, Indira (1917-), Indian stateswoman, PM (1966-77). Daughter of Nehru, succeeded Shastri as leader of Congress Party and PM. Declared war on Pakistan (1971) in support of Bangladesh independence (estab. 1971). Proclaimed state of emergency (1975-7); retained premiership, suspending most democratic processes, imprisoning opponents. Lost ensuing election.

Gandhi, Mohandas Karamchand (1869-1948), Indian political and religious leader. Known as *Mahatma* (great souled). Studied law in England; went to Africa (1893), where he championed rights of Indians. Returned to India (1915), began campaign for independence. Asserted Hindu

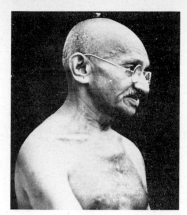

Gandhi

ethics by abstaining from Western ways, practising asceticism. Imprisoned (1930) by British for civil disobedience campaigns, employing passive resistance and fasting as political weapons. Prominent in conferences leading to independence (1947), disappointed by partition into Hindu and Moslem states. Shot by Hindu nationalist fanatic.

Ganesa, in Hindu religion, god of wisdom and patron of literature. Son of Siva and Parvati; usually represented with head of an elephant.

Ganges, river of N India and Bangladesh. Rises in Himalayan Uttar Pradesh, flows *c* 2500 km (1560 mi) through Allahabad, Varanasi and Patna to form delta at Bay of Bengal. Major irrigation source. Sacred to Hindus.

ganglion, mass of nerve cells serving as centre from which nerve impulses are transmitted. Name also applies to small cystic tumour growing on tendon sheath.

gangrene, decay of tissue in injured part of body caused by loss of blood supply to that part. Gas gangrene occurs when certain bacteria invade wounds, destroying nearby healthy tissue and forming gas. Damaged tissue must be removed surgically.

Gangtok, cap. of SIKKIM.

Northern gannet

gannet, marine bird of Sulidae family, found on all coasts except Antarctica. Nests in colonies on cliffs. Commonest species is northern gannet or solan goose, *Sula bassana.*

Ganymede, in Greek myth, son of Tros, king of Troy. Because of his great beauty, Zeus, in the form of an eagle, carried him to Mt. Olympus to be cup-bearer of the gods.

gar, *see* GARPIKE.

Garamond or **Garamont, Claude** (d. 1561), French type designer. Perfected Roman typeface which was to replace Gothic as dominant form in European typography. Designed influential Greek type for Estienne printing firm.

Garbo, Greta, orig. Greta Gustafsson (1905-), Swedish film actress. Spent most of her career in US. Became symbol of aloof allurement, enhancing this by early retirement. Films incl. *Queen Christina* (1933), *Camille* (1936), *Ninotchka* (1939).

Garcia Lorca, Federico (1898-1936), Spanish poet. Major poet of his generation, murdered by Falangists in

Civil War. Revived Spanish ballad form with *Romancero gitano* (1929), expressing preoccupation with death in intensely sensual imagery. Also known for plays, esp. tragedy *Blood Wedding* (1933).

Garda, Lake, N Italy, mainly in Lombardy. Largest lake in Italy, area 370 sq km (149 sq mi). Fishing; resorts, fruit growing on shores.

garden city, planned residential and indust. town designed to combine advantages of town and country. Features incl. encircling rural belt, predetermined max. pop., community ownership of land. Term first used (1869) by A.T. Stewart in US; adopted and greatly modified by Sir Ebenezer Howard (1898) in England. Led to development of Letchworth and Welwyn Garden City.

gardenia, genus of evergreen trees and shrubs of madder family. Native to subtropical S Africa and Asia. Glossy leaves, highly fragrant white or yellow, waxy flowers.

Garden of the Gods, *see* COLORADO SPRINGS.

Gardiner, Stephen (*c* 1493-1555), English churchman. Secretary to Wolsey before gaining royal favour through attempts to obtain Henry VIII's divorce from Catherine of Aragon. Appointed bishop of Winchester (1531), supported royal supremacy in Church of England. Lord high chancellor under Mary I.

Gardner, Erle Stanley (1889-1970), American author. Known for over 100 crime novels, creating detective Perry Mason.

Gardner, Dame Helen Louise (1908-), British scholar. Known for influential criticism on metaphysical poets, *eg The Divine Poems of John Donne* (1952).

Garfield, James [Abram] (1831-81), American statesman, president (1881). Republican congressman from Ohio (1863-80), nominated as compromise candidate for presidency (1880). Fatally shot by disappointed office-seeker.

garfish or **needlefish,** any of Belonidae family of long slender fish with elongated jaws and many sharp teeth. Widely distributed in tropical and warm temperate seas. Species incl. European garfish, *Belone belone.*

Gargoyle on Notre Dame, Paris

gargoyle, water spout in form of grotesque figure, human or animal, projecting from the gutter of a building. Many examples found on Gothic cathedrals.

Garibaldi, Giuseppe (1807-82), Italian soldier and patriot. Fought in South American wars (1836-48) after involvement in unsuccessful republican plot. Returned to Italy, fought for Sardinia against Austria (1848) and for Roman Republic against France (1849). With 1000 volunteer 'Red Shirts', conquered Sicily and Naples (1860), making Victor Emmanuel king of Italy. Twice attempted (1862, 1867) to unite Papal States with new kingdom.

Garibaldi

Garland, Judy, orig. Frances Gumm (1922-69), American film actress, singer. Started as juvenile star, as in *The Wizard of Oz* (1939), later films incl. *Easter Parade* (1948), *A Star is Born* (1954).

Garlic

garlic, *Allium sativum,* perennial plant of lily family, native to Asia. Pungent, bulbous root is used to flavour meat and salad dishes.

garnet, crystalline silicate mineral. Hard, colours incl. red, white, green, brown, yellow. Found in metamorphic rocks, esp. gneiss, mica, hornblende schists. Red, transparent variety is semi-precious gemstone; others used as abrasives. Major sources in India, Brazil, US.

Garonne, river of SW France. Flows *c* 645 km (400 mi) from Spanish Pyrenees via Toulouse to join R. Dordogne near Bordeaux, forming Gironde estuary.

garpike, any of Lepisosteidae family of primitive long, thin fish. Long snout, diamond-shaped scales; found in fresh water of North and Central America. Species incl. longnose gar, *Lepisosteus osseus,* a voracious predator.

Garrick, David (1717-79), English actor-manager. Manager of Drury Lane Theatre (1747-76). Did much to revive Shakespeare's popularity. Also wrote comedies. Most popular actor of day.

Garter, [Most Noble] Order of the, oldest British order of knighthood, estab. *c* 1344. Limited to 25 knights and members of royal family. Has motto, *Honi soit qui mal y pense.*

garter snake, small, harmless, striped snake of genus *Thamnophis,* common in North America.

Gary, Romain (1914-), French novelist, b. Russia. Best known for *A European Education* (1945), *The Roots of Heaven* (1956).

Gary, town of NW Indiana, US; on L. Michigan. Pop. 175,000. Major world steel producer; tinplate, cement, chemicals mfg.

gas, state of matter in which molecules move freely, causing matter to expand indefinitely to fill its container.

Gascony (*Gascogne*), region and former prov. of SW France, hist. cap. Auch. Incl. sandy Landes, hilly

Armagnac, part of Pyrenees; agric., vineyards, brandy. Duchy created 7th cent., incorporated (11th cent.) into Aquitaine. Under English rule (1154-1453). Basque language and customs survive in some areas.

Gaskell, Elizabeth Cleghorn, née Stevenson (1810-65), English novelist. Works, incl. *Mary Barton* (1848), *Cranford* (1853), *Sylvia's Lovers* (1863), deal with social, moral problems of Victorian age. Wrote life of Charlotte Brontë (1857).

gas mask, protective face covering with absorption system to remove toxic gases from inhaled air. Filters usually made of activated charcoal and soda lime. Used against poison gas in warfare and in industry.

gasoline, see PETROLEUM.

Gasparri, Pietro (1852-1934), Italian churchman. Created cardinal (1907) for codification of canon law. Representing Pius XI, signed LATERAN TREATY (1929) which estab. independent Vatican City.

Gaspé, penin. of E Québec, Canada, extending into Gulf of St Lawrence. Mountainous interior; wooded. Coastal fishing, lumbering, pulp milling; tourism.

Gasperi, Alcide de (1881-1954), Italian statesman, premier (1945-53). Helped found Christian Democrat party, representing centre-right. As premier, worked for European unity.

gas plant, *Dictamnus albus,* Eurasian perennial herb. Fragrant white or pink flowers give off flammable vapour in hot weather. Formerly reputed to have healing powers.

Gastein, valley of C Austria, in Höhe Tauern. Resort area; spas incl. Bad Gastein, which has thermal radium springs.

Gastropoda (gastropods), class of molluscs with distinct head, eyes and tentacles. Large flattened foot used for motion. Incl. snail, limpet, with one-piece spiral shell, and slug, with reduced shell.

Gastrotricha, phylum of minute hermaphroditic aquatic worm-like animals that swim by means of cilia. Sometimes classed with roundworms and rotifers.

Gates, Horatio (1727-1806), American army officer, b. England. During American Revolution, defeated British under Burgoyne at Saratoga (1779). Rival of Washington but plan to replace him with Gates failed. Commander in Carolina campaign.

Gateshead, co. bor. of Tyne and Wear met. county, NE England, on R. Tyne. Pop. 94,000. Opposite Newcastle, linked by tunnel, bridges. Shipbuilding, engineering industs., chemicals mfg. Rebuilt after 1854 fire.

Gatling gun

Gatling, Richard Jordan (1818-1903), American inventor. Developed the Gatling revolving battery gun (1861-2), precursor of MACHINE GUN.

Gatun, Lake, see PANAMA CANAL.

Gaudier-Brzeska, Henri (1891-1915), French sculptor. Member of vorticist group, he worked in London from 1911. Work incl. fluid drawings of animals and sculpture influenced by African art.

Gaudí i Cornet, Antonio (1852-1926), Spanish architect. His art nouveau buildings are known for their undulating

Gaudi's Sagrada Familia, Barcelona

façades and decorations of ceramics. Designed church of Sagrada Familia in Barcelona, which remains unfinished.

Gauguin: detail from *Three Tahitians*

Gauguin, [Eugène Henri] Paul (1848-1903), French painter. Began painting in impressionist manner, became leading artist of synthetist style, his work is characterized by use of pure unnaturalistic colours applied in flat areas. Rejecting Western civilization, he sought simplicity of primitive life in Tahiti. Works incl. *The Yellow Christ*. Great influence on 20th cent. art.

Gaul (anc. *Gallia*), hist. region of W Europe, mainly coextensive with modern France. Originally comprised Cisalpine Gaul (Italy N of Apennines) conquered 3rd cent. BC by Romans, and Transalpine Gaul (modern France) conquered by Julius Caesar in Gallic Wars (58-51 BC).

gaur, *Bibos gaurus,* wild ox of forested hills of India, Burma. Largest of wild cattle. Gayal, *B. frontalis*, considered a domesticated form of gaur.

Gauss, Karl Friedrich (1777-1855), German mathematician. Made numerous contributions to mathematics, incl. number theory, algebra, geometry; discovered a form of non-Euclidean geometry. Calculated orbit of asteroid Ceres (1801). Worked on terrestrial magnetism, electromagnetism; invented an electric telegraph with Weber (1833). Works incl. *Disquisitiones arithmeticae* (1801).

Gautier, Théophile (1811-72), French author. Poetry, with its emphasis on form, provided model for Parnassians,

esp. *Emaux et Camées* (1852). Novels incl. *Mlle de Maupin* (1835), *Le Capitaine Fracasse* (1863).

Gaveston, Piers (d. 1312), courtier, favourite of Edward II of England. The king allowed him great power, incl. regency in own absence, which roused anger of barons. They banished Gaveston twice, and finally had him beheaded.

gavial, *Gavialis gangeticus,* animal of crocodile group, distinguished by long, narrow snout. Diet of fish; not dangerous to man. Found in large rivers of India, Burma.

Gävle, town of E Sweden, on Gulf of Bothnia. Pop. 65,000. Port, exports iron ore, timber; fish canning. Formerly called Gefle.

Gawain or **Gawaine,** *see* ARTHURIAN LEGEND.

Gay, John (1685-1732), English poet, playwright. Remembered as author of *The Beggar's Opera* (1728) satirizing literary conventions, political figures, and as friend of Pope, Arbuthnot. Also wrote miscellaneous satirical verse, essays.

Gaya, city of Bihar state, NE India. Pop. 180,000. Trade in rice, sugar cane. BUDDH GAYA nearby.

gayal, *see* GAUR.

Gay-Lussac, Joseph Louis (1778-1850), French chemist, physicist. Discovered independently Charles' law of expansion of gases. Stated law of combining gas volumes: volumes of gases which combine to give gaseous product are in ratio of small whole numbers to each other and to volume of product. First to make ascent by balloon to collect scientific data.

Gaza, city of NE Egypt, on Mediterranean Sea. Pop. 118,000. Port; admin., commercial centre of Gaza Strip coastal region. Formerly one of chief cities of Philistines, taken by Alexander the Great 332 BC. Battlefield in WW I (1917). Under Egypt from 1949; occupied by Israel from 1967 war.

Grant's gazelle

gazelle, small swift-running antelope of Africa, Asia, genus *Gazella*. Usually fawn coloured, with backward-pointing horns. Species incl. DORCAS GAZELLE.

Gaziantep, city of S Turkey, near Syrian border. Pop. 275,000. Agric. centre; textile mfg. Strategically important, taken by Saladin in 1183. Fell to French (1921) after siege during their Syrian mandate; returned (1922). Formerly called Aintab.

Gdańsk, city of N Poland, on Gulf of Gdańsk, cap. of Gdańsk prov. Pop. 370,000. Port, exports coal, timber, grain; shipbuilding, food processing. Hist. known as Danzig. Hanseatic League member; under Prussian rule 1793-1919. Free city under League of Nations from 1919; annexed by Germany 1939, returned 1945.

Gdynia, city of N Poland, on Gulf of Gdańsk. Pop. 192,000. Port, exports coal, timber, grain; naval base, shipbuilding. Developed after 1924 from fishing village to replace free city of Danzig (Gdańsk) as major Polish port.

gearbox, box containing system of toothed wheels which are used to transmit motion from one part of a machine to another. Different ratios of diameters of driving and driven wheels can be used to vary speed and torque. In automobile, ratios may be changed while in motion to allow engine to operate near its most efficient speed for a wide range of road speeds.

Geber or **Jabir ibn Haiyan** (*fl* 8th cent.), Arabian alchemist, physician. Works attributed to him provided the basis of medieval alchemy, incl. chemical theory and laboratory investigation.

gecko, any of Gekkonidae family of harmless lizards of tropical and subtropical regions. Many can walk vertically on smooth surfaces, using adhesive pads on feet. Catches insects with extensile tongue. Tail can break off when seized; new one grows.

Geddes, Sir Patrick (1854-1932), Scottish biologist, sociologist. Pioneered human geography; applied biological training to civic welfare, planning. Replanned many cities, incl. Edinburgh and several in India. Writings incl. *City Development* (1904).

Geelong, city of S Victoria, Australia, on Corio Bay. Pop. 115,000. Port, exports wheat, wool, meat products; textile mfg., oil refining. Founded 1838, grew after 1851 gold rush.

Geiger counter, device used to detect and measure ionizing radiation, esp. alpha, beta and gamma rays. Consists of positively charged wire inside negatively charged metal cylinder. Ions, formed by incoming radiation, migrate to electrodes and produce electrical pulse.

Geisel, Ernesto (1907-   ), Brazilian general, political leader, president (1974-   ). Estab. as president by chiefs of armed services after managing state oil monopoly for 4 years. Term marked by economic difficulties, suppression of dissidents.

gel, in chemistry, solid, jelly-like material formed by coagulation of colloidal solution.

Gela, town of S Sicily, Italy. Pop. 66,000. Founded *c* 690 BC by Greeks, *fl* 5th cent. BC under Hippocrates. Scene of Allied landing (1943).

Gelderland, prov. of EC Netherlands. Area 5017 sq km (1937 sq mi); cap. Arnhem. Drained by Ijssel, Waal, Lower Rhine. Fertile Betuwe in SW. Medieval duchy. E part incl. Geldern, ducal cap., ceded to Prussia (1715).

Gelibolu, see GALLIPOLI.

gelignite, blasting explosive consisting of nitroglycerine, nitrocellulose, wood pulp and potassium nitrate.

Gell-Mann, Murray (1929-   ), American physicist. Awarded Nobel Prize for Physics (1969) for contributions and discoveries concerning elementary particles and their interactions. Worked on theory of 'strange' particles; devised system of particle classification ('eight-fold way'). Introduced concept of QUARK as building block for elementary particles.

Gelsenkirchen, city of W West Germany, on Rhine-Herne canal. Pop. 345,000. Major coalmining centre of Ruhr coalfield; grew rapidly after 1850. Heavily bombed in WWII.

Gemini, see ZODIAC.

gemsbok, *Oryx gazella,* large antelope of desert regions of S Africa. Generally grey, with long horns, tufted tail.

gemstone, mineral which when cut and polished may be used as a gem. Hard, normally transparent and crystalline. Precious varieties incl. diamond, emerald, ruby, sapphire; semi-precious incl. amethyst, aquamarine, garnet.

gene, unit of hereditary material. Genes are arranged into linear sequence to form chromosomes, each gene occurring at a specific point. Composed of DNA; changes in structure of DNA cause mutation of genes, leading to changes in inheritable characteristics.

General Agreement in Trades and Tariffs (GATT), United Nations agency estab. (1948) as interim arrangement in advance of International Trade Organization. Since latter never effected, GATT remained only international body laying down code of conduct for trade and acting as forum for solving related problems. Aims to reduce tariffs *etc,* assist trade of developing countries. Notable GATT negotiations incl. Kennedy Round (1964-7), Tokyo conference from 1973.

General Assembly of United Nations, *see* UNITED NATIONS.

General Strike (1926): volunteers driving a tram

general strike, withdrawal of labour by workers in an entire indust. or throughout a region or country. Often politically motivated in that it seeks govt. concessions or overthrow of govt. Examples incl. that in Russia (Oct. 1905), resulting in granting of democratically-elected DUMA, and in Northern Ireland (May, 1974) which brought down power-sharing executive. In Britain, the **General Strike** (May, 1926) was called by TUC in response to national lockout of coalminers. Less than half the workers responded and govt. was able to keep most services running. TUC capitulated, miners remained on strike until Nov.

Genesis, in OT, 1st book giving an account of the creation of the world and of man. Traces Hebrew history from Abraham to Joseph. Generally thought to have been compiled after the Exile, but contains much Babylonian and Egyptian folklore, *eg* Flood, Creation myths.

Genet, Jean (1910-   ), French dramatist. Convicted criminal, became leading exponent of ABSURD drama. Plays incl. *The Maids* (1948), *The Balcony* (1956). Other works incl. novel *Our Lady of the Flowers* (1949).

genet, cat-like carnivore of Viverridae family, related to civet. Preys nocturnally on rodents, birds; most abundant in africa. common genet, *Genetta genetta,* found in S Europe.

genetics, branch of biology dealing with heredity and variation in similar or related animals and plants. Documented studies on sweet pea by Mendel were foundation of genetics. Modern developments are based on genetic code, which describes various arrangements of nitrogenous bases that constitute DNA, the fundamental genetic material.

Geneva (Fr *Genève,* Ger. *Genf),* city of SW Switzerland, on R. Rhône and L. Geneva, cap. of Geneva canton. Pop. 174,000. Cultural, commercial centre; watches, optical instruments; confectionery. Prehist. then Roman site; part of Holy Roman Empire during Middle Ages. Joined Swiss Confederation 1815. Centre of Reformation; Calvin's Academy (1559) became univ. (1873). Palais des Nations was seat of League of Nations 1920-46, now used by UN agencies. Red Cross hq.

Geneva, Lake (Fr. *Lac Léman,* Ger. *Genfersee),* on Swiss-French border. Rhône enters at E, leaves SW. Area 578 sq km (223 sq mi). Attractive scenery, tourism.

Geneva or **'Breeches' Bible,** version produced (1560) as Protestant propaganda against Queen Mary. Annotated and financed by English Calvinist exiles at Geneva. Gained its popular name from the account of Adam and Eve in Genesis 3:7, *ie* 'made themselves breeches'.

Geneva Conference, name given to two meetings held in Geneva (April-July, 1954, July, 1955) to discuss peace solutions for Indo-Chinese and Korean wars. In Vietnam, set up international commission to supervise ceasefire and partition of country. Failed to achieve permanent solution to armistice position in Korea. Second meeting became 'summit conference' between leaders of US, Britain, France and USSR. Resulted in suggestions for supervision of military installations, armaments. Name also given to DISARMAMENT talks, *etc,* held at various times in Geneva.

Geneva Convention, an international agreement (1864) regulating the treatment of wounded in war. Later extended to cover treatment of sick and prisoners and protection of civilians in war-time. Revised (1906, 1929, 1949).

Genghis Khan or **Jenghiz Khan** (*c* 1167–1227), Mongol chieftain. Conquered Mongolia (1206), most of Chin empire in China (1213-15), Turkestan, Transoxania, and Afghanistan (1218-24), and invaded SE Europe. He ruled finally over all lands between the Yellow and the Black seas. His grandson Kublai Khan conquered the rest of China.

Genoa (*Genova*), town of NW Italy, on Ligurian Sea, cap. of Liguria and of Genoa prov. Pop. 822,000. Port, shipbuilding; engineering; univ. (1243). Medieval maritime republic, *fl* during Crusading era. Birthplace of Columbus, John Cabot. Has fine palaces and churches.

genre, style of painting in which subjects or scenes from everyday life are treated realistically. Genre painting was prominent in 17th cent. Dutch art; its exponents incl. Steen, Vermeer, de Hooch.

Gent, see GHENT, Belgium.

gentian, family, Gentianaceae, of low-growing plants of worldwide distribution, esp. those of genus *Gentiana* with many species popular in rock gardens. *G. lutea* contains a bitter component used as a tonic.

Gentile da Fabriano (*c* 1370-1427), Italian painter. A leading exponent of International Gothic style, his masterpiece is *Adoration of the Magi* (Florence). Painted frescoes in Lateran Basilica, Rome (now destroyed).

genus, in biology, *see* CLASSIFICATION.

geodesy, science of measuring shape and size of the Earth, and of locating points on its surface. Geodetic Survey deals with such large areas that curvature of Earth's surface must be taken into account.

Geoffrey IV, called Geoffrey Plantagenet (1113-51), count of Anjou (1129-51). After marrying MATILDA, daughter of Henry I of England, he claimed and won (1144) Normandy in her name. Son became Henry II of England.

Geoffrey of Monmouth (*c* 1100-54), British chronicler. Wrote *Historia Regum Britanniae* (modern edition, 1929), which provided basis for the Arthurian cycles, and was treated as history well into 17th cent.

geography, study of the similarities, differences, and relationships between regions of the Earth's surface. Falls into 2 sections: physical geography (incl. study of climate, landforms, soils) and human geography (incl. economic, political, urban, historical geography). First developed by Greeks, *eg* Thales, Eratosthenes, Ptolemy; regional description advanced by Strabo in Roman times. Arabs, *eg* Idrisi, Ibn Khaldun, maintained study through Middle Ages until new impetus came from Spanish, Portuguese exploration of 15th–16th cents. Modern systematic (*ie* topical) and regional approaches to geography estab. by Humboldt and Ritter respectively. In 19th cent., regional tradition dominated through work of Vidal de la Blache and French school; 20th cent. has seen ascendancy of systematic approach and quantitative techniques in analyzing geographical data.

geology, study of the composition, structure and history of the Earth, and the processes resulting in its present state. Study of composition incl. crystallography, mineralogy, petrology and geochemistry; study of structure incl. structural geology and geophysics; study of history incl. historical geology, stratigraphy and palaeontology. Physical geology studies processes of change. Term first used in 18th cent. by Swiss geologists, although study of Earth dates back to Greek times. Georgius Agricola studied minerals in 16th cent.; modern geology pioneered by Hutton's theory of uniformitarianism (1795); 20th cent. research in atomic structure, radioactivity, *etc,* has greatly advanced geology.

geometry, branch of mathematics that deals with points, lines, surfaces and solids. Elementary geometry is based on exposition given by EUCLID. Analytic geometry uses algebraic methods to study geometry. Later developments incl. differential geometry, which uses calculus to study surfaces, projective geometry and non-Euclidean geometry.

George III

geomorphology, study of landforms, esp. their character, origin and evolution. Employs both geographical and geological knowledge. Current ideas rest on 'cycles of erosion' theory of W.M. DAVIS.

George, St (*c* 4th cent.), patron saint of England. Traditionally, Palestinian soldier martyred in Asia Minor. In art, literature represented as slayer of a dragon. Cult brought to England in Crusades. His red cross is on the Union Jack. No longer considered saint by RC church.

George I (1660-1727), king of Great Britain and Ireland (1714-27). Elector of Hanover (1698-1727), became king under terms of ACT OF SETTLEMENT. Left admin. of govt. to ministers, practice which initiated cabinet govt. in Britain.

George II (1683-1760), king of Great Britain and Ireland (1727-60). Son of George I, whose policy of ministerial govt. he continued. Last British king to lead troops in battle (Dettingen, 1743).

George III (1738-1820), king of Great Britain and Ireland (1760-1820). Ruled through sympathetic ministers (Bute, North) in attempt to assert authority until younger Pitt's ministry curbed ambitions. Chief event of reign was AMERICAN REVOLUTION, result of North's coercive policies. Intermittent insanity led to regency of his son (later George IV).

George IV (1762-1830), king of Great Britain and Ireland (1820-30). Served as prince regent during insanity of his father, George III (1811-20); leader of dissolute social set. Personally unpopular, esp. through attempts to divorce his wife, Caroline of Brunswick.

George V (1865-1936), king of Great Britain and Ireland (1910-36). Second son of Edward VII. Played role as moderator in constitutional crisis over Parliament Act of 1911. His wife, Mary of Teck (1867-1953), bore him 5 sons and a daughter. During WWI, changed name of royal house from Saxe-Coburg-Gotha to Windsor.

George VI (1895-1952), king of Great Britain and Northern Ireland (1936-52). Became king when his brother, Edward VIII, abdicated. Married Elizabeth Bowes-Lyon (1900-), now known as the Queen Mother. Elder daughter succeeded him as Elizabeth II.

George II (1890-1947), king of Greece (1922-3, 1935-47). Deposed, went into exile. After restoration, allowed METAXAS to take dictatorial powers. Exiled during German occupation, returned after plebiscite (1946) in favour of monarchy.

George, Henry (1839-97), American economist. Proposed 'single tax' on land to cover full cost of govt. Works incl. *Progress and Poverty* (1879).

George, Stefan (1868-1933), German poet. Influenced by Nietzsche and French symbolists, saw poet as priest with

GEOLOGICAL TABLE: TIME SCALE

Estimated ages in millions of years

	ERA	PERIOD	EPOCH	TIME BEGAN	MAJOR EVENTS	ANIMAL AND PLANT LIFE
PHANEROZOIC EON	CENOZOIC	Quaternary	Holocene Pleistocene	c 10,000 yrs c 2	Retreat of ice; present landscape formed. Major Ice Ages; pluvials	Rise of man; beginning of extinction of mammals *eg* mammoths, sabre-tooth carnivores.
		Tertiary	Pliocene Miocene Oligocene Eocene Palaeocene	c 13 c 25 c 36 c 58 c 65	Alpine-Himalayan mountain building. Shallow seas in Europe; extensive clay plains formed.	Proliferation of mammals; ancestors of modern fauna. Vegetation of modern types.
	MESOZOIC	Cretaceous		c 135	Extensive inundation; chalk formation.	Echinoderms, lamellibranchs, last ammonites. Dinosaurs become extinct.
		Jurassic		c 195	Widespread limestone formation.	Ammonites, brachiopods, lamellibranchs, insects. 1st birds. Dinosaurs reach max. size.
		Triassic		c 225	Extensive arid, semi-arid areas. Red sands in North America.	Ammonites, crinoids, lamellibranchs. 1st mammals, dinosaurs.
	PALAEOZOIC	Permian		c 280	Increasing aridity; salt beds formed. Marls, sandstones, evaporites developed.	Last trilobites. Increasing ammonites, reptiles. More advanced conifers.

		Carboniferous
		  Pennsylvanian
		  Mississippian
				c 345	Formation of coal measures. Shallow seas over continents, vast swamps.	Crinoids, brachiopods; increasing fish, amphibians, insects. 1st reptiles. Club mosses, horsetails.

		Devonian		c 395	Climax of Caledonian mountain building; formation of Old Red Sandstone.	Cephalopods, jawed fish, crinoids, last graptolites. Treefern forests.
		Silurian		c 435	Extensive seas; Caledonian mountain building continues.	Graptolites, trilobites, brachiopods, cephalopods. Jawless fish. 1st land plants.
		Ordovician		c 500	Extensive seas; beginning of Caledonian mountain building.	Graptolites dominant; also trilobites, crinoids, corals. 1st vertebrates (fish) in North America.
		Cambrian		c 570	Europe largely submerged. Large shallow seas covered North America.	Trilobites dominant; also graptolites, brachiopods. Some algae, lichens.
	PRECAMBRIAN ERA			c 4500	Formation, consolidation of continental shields *eg* Canadian, African, Australian.	Rare traces of rudimentary life, found only in Late Precambrian. Forerunners of trilobites, worms, sponges, jellyfish. Some algae, fungi.

duty to people as well as self. Collections incl. *The Year of the Soul* (1897), *The New Kingdom* (1928).

George Cross, highest British civilian award for acts of courage. Instituted 1940.

George of Podebrad (1420-71), king of Bohemia (1458-71). Leader of the moderate Utraquists during Hussite wars, he seized Prague (1448); held power in Bohemia during minority and reign of Ladislaus. After excommunication (1466), resisted invasion of MATTHIAS CORVINUS of Hungary, who had himself crowned king of Bohemia (1469).

George Town, Malaysia, *see* PENANG.

Georgetown, cap. of CAYMAN ISLANDS.

Georgetown, cap. of Guyana, Atlantic port at mouth of Demerara R. Pop. 166,000. Sugar, rice, bauxite exports. Famous botanical gardens (palms, orchids). Devastated by fire (1945, 1951).

Georgia, state of SE US. Area 152,489 sq km (58,876 sq mi); pop. 4,590,000; cap. Atlanta. Large areas of swamp and forest; Atlantic coastal plain rises gradually to Appalachians. Subtropical climate. Agric. produce incl. peanuts, cotton, maize, tobacco. Minerals esp. kaolin clay. Cotton milling, wood processing. British colony estab. after struggle with Spanish (1754). One of original 13 colonies of US. Devastated by Union forces during Civil War (1864).

Georgian Bay, arm of NE L. Huron, E Ontario, Canada. Separated from L. Huron by Manitoulin Isl. Georgian Bay Isls. National Park estab. 1929; summer resort.

Georgian Soviet Socialist Republic, constituent republic of W USSR. Area *c* 69,700 sq km (26,900 sq mi); pop. 4, 688,000; cap. Tbilisi. Bounded by Black Sea in W, Greater Caucasus in N and Lesser Caucasus in S. Tea, citrus fruit, tobacco grown on Black Sea coast; rich manganese deposits. Region contained ancient kingdom of Colchis, legendary home of Golden Fleece. As independent kingdom, *fl* in 12th and 13th cent., but accepted Russian protection in 18th cent. Joined USSR (1922), becoming constituent republic (1936).

Georgian style, name given to English architecture during reigns of George I, II and III (1714-1820). Revival of Palladianism, led by Campbell, Earl of Burlington and W. Kent, dominated first half of period. Neo-Classicism of Adam, Soane, *etc*, dominated second half.

Gera, city of SC East Germany, on R. White Elster. Pop. 111,000. Railway jct.; produces textiles, machinery. Town hall (16th cent.).

Geraldton, town of W Western Australia, on Champion Bay. Pop. 15,000. Port, exports minerals, wheat, wool, crayfish; superphosphate mfg.

geranium, family, Geraniaceae, of widely distributed plants, esp. those of genera *Geranium* and *Pelargonium* native to S Africa. Cranesbill geranium grows wild in Americas. Many species yield extracts used in pharmacy.

Gérard, François Pascal, Baron (1770-1837), French painter, b. Rome. Pupil of David; leading portraitist, court painter to Napoleon, Louis XVIII. Historical scenes incl. *Battle of Austerlitz.*

gerbil, small burrowing rodent of desert regions of Africa, Asia. Large hind legs used for leaping. Mainly nocturnal, with large eyes and long tail; diet of seeds, grain. Popular as pet.

gerenuk, *Litocranius walleri,* long-legged gazelle of E Africa. Also called giraffe-necked gazelle, uses long neck to eat leaves of high branches.

geriatrics, branch of medicine dealing with diseases and care of old people. Diseases associated with old age incl. degeneration of arteries (arteriosclerosis), osteoarthritis, and weakening of bone tissue (osteoporosis), which makes old people prone to bone fractures.

Géricault, [Jean Louis André] Théodore (1791-1824), French painter. Regarded as a founder of French Romantic school; painted many horse and racing subjects. Realistic treatment of *The Raft of the Medusa* (1819) provoked public protest.

German, Sir Edward, orig. Edward German Jones (1862-1936), British composer. Wrote light operas, *eg Merrie England,* incidental music for theatrical productions.

German, W Germanic language of Indo-European family. Official language of Federal Republic of Germany, German Democratic Republic, Austria, and most common language in Switzerland. First language for many elsewhere, important as second esp. in commerce. Divided into High German (spoken in southern areas), Low German (northern lowlands). Latter can incl. Dutch, Flemish, English. Modern standard German descends from German used for Luther's translation of Bible, a High German dialect.

germander, any plant of genus *Teucrium* of mint family. Worldwide distribution; common North American forms, *T. canadense* and *T. accidentale,* and British, *T. scorodonia,* are known as wood sage.

Germanic languages, branch of Indo-European family of languages. Divided into East, North and West Germanic groups. East incl. Gothic, Burgundian, Vandalic , all dead. North, also called Scandinavian, incl. Danish, Norwegian, Swedish, Icelandic; all descend from Old Norse. West incl. English, Dutch, German.

Germanic religion, *see* TEUTONIC MYTHOLOGY.

germanium (Ge), soft metalloid element; at. no. 32, at. wt. 72.59. Semiconductor, used in transistors; also used as a rectifier.

German measles, *see* RUBELLA.

German shepherd, *see* ALSATIAN.

Germany

Germany (*Deutschland*), country of NC Europe, now divided into East and West Germany. Language: German. Religions: Protestant, RC. Low, sandy plain in N; block mountains, forests in C; Rhine valley in W; Bavarian Alps in S. Main rivers Rhine, Elbe, Oder, Danube; extensive canal system. Industs. centred in Ruhr (W), Saxony (E). Separated from France on death of Charlemagne (AD 814), principalities formed Holy Roman Empire (962-1806). Confederation from 1815 under Prussian hegemony, empire estab. 1871. Colonial expansion in late 19th cent. Nationalist, expansionist aims contributed to WWI, after which Weimar Republic proclaimed. Rise of Hitler led to WWII; much territ. lost (incl. E Prussia), occupation by 4 allied powers 1945 followed by partition 1949. **East Germany** (*Deutsche Demokratische Republik*), occupied by USSR after WWII; communist govt., member of Warsaw Treaty Organization, COMECON. Area *c* 108,000 sq km (42,000 sq mi); pop. 16,980,000; cap. East Berlin. **West Germany** (*Bundesrepublik Deutschland*), occupied by UK, USA, France after WWII; federal govt., member of NATO, EEC. Area *c* 249,000 sq km (96,000 sq mi); pop. 61,967,000; cap. Bonn.

germination, process whereby plant embryo within seed resumes growth after period of dormancy. This period varies from a few days (most grasses) to over 400 years (Indian lotus). Process requires water, oxygen and in many cases light. Temperature is also critical.

Germiston, city of S Transvaal, South Africa. Pop. 281,000. Railway jct., important goldmining and refining, indust. centre in Witwatersrand. Founded 1887, after discovery of gold.

germ warfare, the use of disease bacteria, biological poisons, hormones, *etc* as a weapon of war. Employed in crude forms (pollution of water supplies, deliberate planting of contaminated material, *etc*) for many years. It has been avoided in modern warfare despite much research.

Gerona, town of NE Spain, cap. of Gerona prov. Pop. 50,000. Food processing, textile mfg. Held by Moors 8th-11th cent.; resisted French siege (1809). Gothic cathedral (14th cent.).

gerrymander, in politics, rearranging of voting areas to advantage of one party. Derived from its practice in Massachusetts by state governor Elbridge Gerry (1744-1814), who was US vice-president (1813-14).

Gershwin, George (1898-1937), American composer. Treated jazz idiom in symphonic form. Works incl. *Rhapsody in Blue, An American in Paris* and Negro opera *Porgy and Bess.* Also composed many tuneful songs for Broadway musicals.

Gerson, Jean Charlier de (1363-1429), French churchman, writer. Advanced conciliar theory at Council of Pisa (1409), attempting to end Great Schism by asserting council's supremacy over pope.

Gesenius, Wilhelm (1786-1842), German theologian, Hebrew scholar. Opened Hebrew to scientific study, esp. with his grammar and dictionary.

Gesner, Konrad von (1515-65), Swiss naturalist, philologist. Wrote plant dictionary *Historia plantarum* (1541). His *Historia animalium* (1551-8) is considered basis of modern zoology.

Gestalt, in psychology, affirmation that experience consists of organized wholes (*gestalten*) rather than of sum of distinct parts. Developed in Germany, exponents incl. Kurt Koffka.

Gestapo (*Geheime Staatspolizei*), secret police in Nazi Germany (1933-45). Combined with Hitler's SS after 1936 under Himmler. Carried out ruthless policy of investigation, torture and extermination. Infiltrated and destroyed organizations opposed to Nazism. Indicted as one body at Nuremberg war crimes trials (1945-6).

Gethsemane, traditional site of Jesus' betrayal in garden at foot of Mount of Olives near Jerusalem. In Jordanian territ. since 1948.

Getty, [Jean] Paul (1892-1976), American businessman. Long considered richest man in world, controlled empire of *c* 200 businesses.

Gettysburg, bor. of S Pennsylvania, US. Pop. 7000. Scene of Federal repulse of Confederate's advance into North during Civil War; also of Lincoln's famous Address (1863).

Gettysburg Address (19 Nov. 1863), brief speech delivered by President Lincoln at dedication of cemetery on site of Battle of Gettysburg. Contained famous statement of the principles of American govt. 'of the people, by the people, for the people'.

Gettysburg campaign (June-July, 1863), episode in American Civil War. After Confederate victory at Chancellorsville, R.E. Lee invaded S Pennsylvania. Met Union forces W of Gettysburg; driven to Cemetery Hill, where Confederates were decisively defeated. Marked turning point of war.

Geulincx, Arnold (1624-69), Flemish philosopher. Resolved problems of Cartesian dualism by positing doctrine of occasionalism, *ie* that although mind and matter cannot interact God intervenes in each instance where an act of mind seems coordinated with a movement of the body.

geyser, spring from which columns of superheated water and steam are intermittently ejected. Caused by hot lava heating water which has percolated into geyser's central tube; found in active or recently active volcanic areas. Famous geyser regions are Iceland, New Zealand, and Yellowstone Park, Wyoming, US.

Gezira, triangular plain of EC Sudan. Lies between White Nile and Blue Nile, S of Khartoum; irrigated from Sennar Dam. Major cotton-growing region.

Ghadames or **Gadames,** town of NW Libya, Tripolitania, on border with Algeria, Tunisia. Pop. 3000. In Ghadames oasis; former caravan centre.

Ghana, republic of W Africa, on Gulf of Guinea. Area 238,500 sq km (92,100 sq mi); pop. 9,607,000; cap. Accra. Language: English. Religions: native, Christianity. Largely

'Old Faithful': geyser in Yellowstone Park, Wyoming, US.

forest, with savannah in N; main river Volta. Cocoa, hardwoods, palm products; also gold, diamonds, manganese. Former centre of slave trade; British Gold Coast colony estab. 1874. Ghana formed as independent state (1957) from Gold Coast, Ashanti, Togoland, Northern territs. Republic from 1960; Nkrumah's rule ended by coup (1966). Member of British Commonwealth.

Ghats, two mountain ranges of S India: Eastern Ghats (E coast), av. height *c* 450 m (1500 ft); Western Ghats, av. height *c* 900 m (3000 ft). Together enclose Deccan plain. Joined at highest peak, Anai Mudi (2695 m/8840 ft).

Ghent (Flem. *Gent,* Fr. *Gand),* city of WC Belgium, on R. Scheldt, cap. of East Flanders prov. Pop. 153,000. Port, canal to Terneuzen; industs. incl. textiles, steel. Hist. cap., cultural centre of Flanders. Castle, cathedral (12th cent.); Cloth Hall (14th cent.); univ. (1816).

Gheorghiu-Dej, Gheorghe (1901-65), Romanian political leader. Premier (1952-5), became first secretary of Communist Party (1955) and was president (1961-5). Began policy of securing economic independence from Soviet Union.

gherkin, see CUCUMBER.

ghetto, section of a city inhabited mainly by members of racial or religious minority group and characterized by poverty and social deprivation. Originally applied to early medieval European cities in which segregation of Jews into autonomous community was voluntary. First compulsory segregation began late 14th cent. in Spain and Portugal; others incl. Frankfurt (1460), Venice (1516). Nazis estab. Jewish ghettos, *eg* in Warsaw.

Ghibellines, see GUELPHS AND GHIBELLINES.

Ghiberti, Lorenzo (1378-1455), Florentine sculptor. Best known for bronze doors of Baptistery in Florence, which took him 23 years to complete. Commissioned to make 2nd pair of doors (1425-52). His workshop was centre of artistic activity.

Ghirlandaio or **Girlandaio, Domenico** (1449-94), Florentine fresco painter. Noted for his ability to portray contemporary life and manners, as in his *Calling of the Apostles* (Sistine Chapel, Rome). Michelangelo was apprenticed to him.

ghost dance, central ritual of North American Indian religion of 19th cent. Originated among PAIUTE (*c* 1870), rapidly spread through W tribes. Danced on the nights of 5 successive days, inducing hypnotic trances.

ghost swift moth, *Hepialus humuli,* moth of swift group. White males fly around together at dusk to attract females.

Giacometti, Alberto (1901-66), Swiss sculptor, painter. Member of surrealist group in 1930s; work from this period incl. *The Palace at 4 am.* Returned to realistic single figures, usually elongated and emaciated, in plaster of paris on a wire foundation.

giant panda, *see* PANDA.

giants, in myth and folklore, man-like beings of more than human size and strength, but lacking supernatural status of gods, civilization of men. In Greek myth, attempted unsuccessfully to conquer Olympian gods; in Scandinavian myth, regarded as first of world's inhabitants. Perpetuated in allegories and children's stories, *eg* 'Jack the Giant Killer'.

Giant's Causeway, headland of N Northern Ireland, in former Co. Antrim. Comprises many levels of hexagonal basalt columns. In legend, built as giant's route to Scotland.

Gibbon, Edward (1737-94), English historian. Author of panoramic *The History of the Decline and Fall of the Roman Empire* (6 vol., 1776-88), inspired by visit to Rome. Attacked for criticism of rise of early Christianity.

Gibbon, Lewis Grassic, pseud. of James Leslie Mitchell (1901-35), Scottish novelist. Known for trilogy *A Scots Quair* (1932-4) about Aberdeenshire life before and after WWI.

gibbon, smallest of anthropoid apes, genus *Hylobates,* found in SE Asia. Arboreal, uses long arms to swing through branches. Only monkey to walk upright.

Gibbon

Gibbons, Grinling (1648-1721), English woodcarver, sculptor, b. Rotterdam. Famous for carvings of fruit, flowers, and animals; employed by Wren to decorate choir stalls of St Paul's Cathedral, London. Royal master carver from reign of Charles II to George I.

Gibbons, Orlando (1583-1625), English organist, composer. Finest keyboard player of his day, organist at Westminster Abbey. Composed anthems, madrigals, *eg Silver Swan,* instrumental pieces.

Gibbons, Stella Dorothea (1902-), English novelist. Known for burlesque of genre of rural pessimism, *Cold Comfort Farm* (1932).

Gibbs, Josiah Willard (1839-1903), American physicist. Applied principles of thermodynamics to physical chemistry, developing concept of free energy and chemical potential as driving mechanisms of chemical reactions.

Gibraltar, British crown colony of S Iberian penin., on Str. of Gibraltar. Area 6.5 sq km (2.5 sq mi); pop. 29,000; rises to 425 m (1400 ft). Free port, heavily fortified naval base, tourist resort. Rock of Gibraltar was one of the ancient 'Pillars of Hercules'. Held by Moors from 8th cent., by Spain 1462-1704. British control long challenged by Spain.

Gibraltar

Gibraltar, Strait of, channel connecting Mediterranean Sea and Atlantic Ocean. Narrowest width *c* 13 km (8 mi); separates S Spain from N Africa. Headlands at Rock of Gibraltar (N) and Ceuta (S) formerly called Pillars of Hercules.

Gibson, Charles Dana (1867-1944), American illustrator. Created 'Gibson Girl', idealized type of American young woman; illustrated Hope's *Prisoner of Zenda.*

Gide, André (1869-1951), French author. Works reflect own struggle for self-development balancing hedonism with asceticism. Novels incl. *La Porte étroite* (1909), *Les Faux-monnayeurs* (1926). Founded *La Nouvelle Revue Française* (1909). Nobel Prize for Literature (1947).

Gielgud, Sir [Arthur] John (1904-), English stage, film actor, producer. Played many leading roles in Sheridan and Shakespeare (esp. Hamlet).

Giessen, town of NC West Germany, on R. Lahn. Pop. 76,000. Machine tools, leather, rubber; iron mines nearby. Protestant univ. (1607).

Gifu, city of Japan, C Honshu isl. Pop. 386,000. Textile and paper ware mfg. Fishing with trained cormorants on R. Nagara is tourist attraction.

Gijón, city of Asturias, NW Spain, on Bay of Biscay. Pop. 188,000. Port, exports coal and iron ore; iron and steel, glass industs. Defeated Armada took refuge here 1588.

gila monster, *Heloderma suspectum,* venomous lizard of deserts of SW US and Mexico. Body covered with bead-like scales arranged in bands of orange and black.

Gilbert, Grove Karl (1843-1918), American geologist. First senior geologist of US Geological Survey (1879). Worked mainly in W US; formed influential theories of denudation, river development, glaciation. Works incl. *Lake Bonneville* (1890).

Gilbert, Sir Humphrey (*c* 1539-83), English navigator. First to argue existence of Northwest Passage in *Discourse* (1576). Made expedition to Newfoundland (1583), which he claimed for England; drowned during voyage home.

Gilbert or **Gilberd, William** (1544-1603), English scientist, physician. Known for studies of magnetism, particularly idea that Earth behaves as large magnet; findings described in *De magnete* (1600).

Gilbert, Sir W[illiam] S[chwenck] (1836-1911), English author. Known as librettist of SULLIVAN's light operas, *eg Trial by Jury* (1875), *H.M.S. Pinafore* (1878), *The Pirates of Penzance* (1879), *Iolanthe* (1882) *The Mikado* (1885). Also wrote humorous, cynical *Bab Ballads* (1869).

Gilbert and Ellice Islands, two colonies of UK, in WC Pacific Ocean. Incl. Gilbert Isls., Ellice Isls., some of Line, Phoenix Isls. Area 930 sq km (360 sq mi); pop. 64,000; cap. Tarawa (Gilbert Isl.). Produce copra, phosphates; fishing, tourist industs. Gilbert, Ellice groups became protectorate 1892; colony formed 1915. Line, Phoenix groups joined 20th cent. Ellice Isls. withdrew, formed separate territ. of Tuvalu (1976).

Gilgamesh, hero of Babylonian epic. Earliest known written epic (*c* 2000 BC) found on clay tablets in ruins of Nineveh. Gilgamesh story prob. much older, of Sumerian origin, tells of his search for immortality after friend Enkidu dies. Some parallels with OT, *eg* Noah figure, Flood.

Gill, [Arthur] Eric [Rowland] (1882-1940), English sculptor, engraver, type designer. Attempted to revive religious attitude to art; sculpture incl. *Stations of the Cross* in Westminster Cathedral. Illustrated books and designed 'Gill Sans-serif' alphabet.

gill, organ in aquatic animals for absorption of oxygen dissolved in water. Consists of membrane or outgrowth of body surface through which oxygen passes into blood and carbon dioxide into water. Fish have internal gills; external gills found on amphibian larvae, molluscs, *etc.*

Gillen, Francis James (1856-1912), Australian anthropologist. Known for studies of Arunta aboriginal tribe. Works incl. *The Native Tribes of Central Australia* (1899).

Gillingham, mun. bor. of Kent, SE England on R. Medway. Pop. 87,000. Dockyards; fruit growing.

Gillray, James (1757-1815), English caricaturist. Satirized family of George III in *A New Way to Pay the National Debt* (1786); lampooned the French, politicians and social customs of his day.

Gilson, Etienne (1884-), French historian of philosophy. Leader in RC neo-Thomist movement. Works incl. *Le Thomisme* (1919), *L'Esprit de la philosophie médiévale* (1932).

gin, alcoholic spirit distilled from grain and flavoured with juniper berries. Major producers are Netherlands, where it originated in 17th cent., Britain and US.

ginger, *Zingiber officinale,* perennial plant. Originally from S China but known to ancient Greeks, Romans and Indians. Hot, spicy root is sliced and preserved in syrup as confection. Ground ginger is used as spice.

ginkgo or **maidenhair tree,** *Ginkgo biloba,* deciduous tree, native to China. Fan-shaped leaves, fleshy seeds in edible kernel. Survivor of prehistoric era. Widely cultivated as ornament.

Ginsberg, Allen (1926-), American poet. Leader of BEAT GENERATION. Best known for *Howl* (1956) lamenting sickness of American society. Other works incl. *Reality Sandwiches* (1965), *Ankor Wat* (1968).

ginseng, aromatic plant of genus *Panax.* Species incl. Chinese, *P. schinseng* and *P. quinquefolius* of North American woodlands. Aromatic root has sweetish taste and was valued medicinally in China.

Giolitti, Giovanni (1842-1928), Italian politician. Five times premier between 1892 and 1921, introduced social reforms and encouraged labour unions. Opposed Italian involvement in WWI.

Giono, Jean (1895-1970), French novelist. Works, *eg Colline* (1928), *Regain* (1930), celebrate peasant paganism of Provence.

Giorgione [da Castelfranco], orig. Giorgio Barbarelli (*c* 1477-1510), Venetian painter. His *Tempest* is considered 1st example of 'landscape of mood'; work has poetic, evocative quality, based on new effects of light and colour. Formative influence on work of Titian and other Venetian artists; little is known of his life.

Giotto [di Bondone] (*c* 1266-*c* 1337), Florentine artist. Regarded as founder of modern painting, he broke with formula of Byzantine art and introduced new naturalism into his figures. Works incl. fresco cycle in Arena Chapel, Padua, depicting life and passion of Christ. Probably painted fresco cycle of *Life of St Francis* in Upper Church at Assisi.

gipsy, *see* GYPSY.

gipsy moth, *Lymantria dispar,* European moth, extinct in Britain since *c* 1850. Introduced into North America, has become serious pest in forests; caterpillars eat so many leaves that trees die.

giraffe, hoofed long-legged mammal of African grasslands. Tallest of animals (reaches height of 5.5 m/18 ft), uses long neck to eat leaves of trees. Two species, genus *Giraffa.*

Giraudoux, [Hippolyte] Jean (1882-1944), French author, diplomat. Known for highly stylized, verbal plays, *eg Judith* (1931), *La Guerre de Troie n'aura pas Lieu* (1935),

Giraffe

often adapted from classical myth. Novels incl. *Suzanne et le Pacifique* (1921). Diplomatic career recalled in memoirs.

Girl Guides and **Girl Scouts,** *see* BOY SCOUTS.

Gironde, estuary of W France, *c* 72 km (45 mi) long, formed by jct. of Garonne and Dordogne rivers near Bordeaux. Major artery of wine trade.

Girondists, French political party during Revolution. Moderate republicans, instrumental in estab. of First Republic (1792-3). Favoured European war to spread revolutionary ideas. Overthrown by extremist Jacobins and Cordeliers.

Girtin, Thomas (1775-1802), English landscape painter. Revolutionized watercolour technique in England, abandoning topographical style of 18th cent.; introduced bold style, using broad washes of strong colour. Works incl. *White House at Chelsea* (1800).

Gisborne, town of E North Isl., New Zealand, on Poverty Bay. Pop. 27,000. Port, exports wool, meat, dairy produce; food processing.

Valéry Giscard d'Estaing

Giscard d'Estaing, Valéry (1926-　), French statesman, president (1974-　). Finance minister (1962-6, 1969-74). Leader of Independent Republicans (allied with Gaullists), defeated Mitterrand in presidential election.

Gish, Dorothy, orig. Dorothy de Guiche (1898–1968), American silent film actress. Famous for roles in D.W. Griffith's films from 1912. Appeared with her sister, **Lillian Gish,** orig. Lillian de Guiche (1896-　), in *Orphans of the Storm* (1922).

Gissing, George Robert (1857-1903), English novelist. Works describe crushing effects of poverty, esp. in *New Grub Street* (1891), upon writers. Also wrote *By the Ionian Sea* (1901).

Gîza, El, or **Gizeh,** city of N Egypt, on R. Nile opposite Cairo. Pop. 712,000. Produces cotton textiles, cigarettes, footwear. Nearby are Great Pyramid of Khufu (Cheops), one of Seven Wonders of the World, and the Sphinx.

Glace Bay, town of NE Nova Scotia, Canada; on Cape Breton Isl. Pop. 23,000. Important coal mines; fishing harbour.

Fox glacier, New Zealand

glacier, moving mass of snow and ice formed in high mountains and polar regions. Compaction turns snow into névé then to granular ice. Types incl. mountain or valley glacier, piedmont glacier, ice sheet.

gladiators, the professional fighters of ancient Rome, who engaged in mortal combat as a public spectacle, using sword and shield or sometimes trident and net.

gladiolus, genus of corm-based plants native to S Africa. Member of Iridaceae family. Widely cultivated as garden plant. Sword-like leaves in flat vertical fans, spikes of funnel-shaped flowers.

Gladstone: cartoon by Phil May

Gladstone, William Ewart (1809-98), British statesman, PM (1868-74, 1880-5, 1886, 1892-4). Renowned orator,

policies based upon strong religious and moral convictions. As chancellor of the exchequer, promoted free trade and progressive taxation policy. Headed Liberal govts. which achieved Irish land acts, civil service and army reforms, development of education. Last ministry, dominated by Irish problems, ended after defeat of HOME RULE bill.

Glamis, village of Tayside region, E Scotland. Glamis Castle (17th cent.) on site of older castle of Macbeth.

Glamorgan, county of S Wales. Area 2250 sq km (869 sq mi); pop. 1,299,000; co. town Cardiff. Mountainous in N; fertile Vale of Glamorgan in S; Gower Penin. in SW. Main rivers Taff, Neath. Major indust. area; rich coal deposits (Rhondda, Merthyr Tydfil); iron and steel works (Swansea, Port Talbot). Admin. divided (1974) into West, Mid, South Glamorgan.

gland, organ which builds up chemical compounds from the blood and secretes them. Most glands discharge through ducts either to outer surface of skin, *eg* sweat glands, or to an inner surface, *eg* digestive glands secreting into gut. Ductless or ENDOCRINE GLANDS secrete hormones directly into the blood.

Glanvill, Ranulf de (d. 1190), English jurist. He served Henry II of England, finally as chief justiciar. Known for commissioning treatise on laws and customs of England, which bears his name.

Glaser, Donald Arthur (1926-　), American scientist. Awarded Nobel Prize for Physics (1960) for inventing bubble chamber to observe trajectories of subatomic particles.

Glasgow, Ellen Anderson Gholson (1874-1945), American novelist. Works, *eg Barren Ground* (1925), *In This Our Life* (1941), deal with development of the post-Reconstruction South.

Glasgow, largest city of Scotland, in Strathclyde region, on R. Clyde. Pop. 897,000. Major port; industs. incl. shipbuilding, engineering, textiles, brewing, whisky distilling. Founded 6th cent. by St Kentigern; royal burgh, grew mainly 18th-19th cents. through tobacco, cotton trade; R. Clyde first deepened 1768. Has 12th cent. cathedral; 2 univs. (1451, 1964); noted art gallery.

glass, hard brittle substance, usually made by fusing sand (silica) with lime and soda or potash; molten mass is rapidly cooled to prevent crystallization. Other metallic oxides, *eg* lead, barium or aluminium, are added to increase durability, impart colour or provide special optical properties.

glass fibre, fine filaments of glass which may be woven into a cloth and impregnated with hard-setting resins. The resulting material is extremely strong, lightweight and corrosion resistant. Used in boat and vehicle-body construction.

glass snake, lizard of genus *Ophisaurus* of slow-worm family. Legless or with vestigial limbs; diet of insects, small animals. Tail breaks easily, hence name. Species incl. *O. apodus* of Asia Minor and Balkans.

Glastonbury, mun. bor. of Somerset, SW England. Pop. 7000. In legend, site of 1st English Christian church estab. by Joseph of Arimathea; burial place of King Arthur. Has ruined 8th cent. abbey. Ancient lake villages nearby.

Glauber, Johann Rudolf (1604-68), German chemist. Discovered sodium sulphate (Glauber's salt) in mineral stream and wrote on its medicinal uses. Studied and prepared many compounds, esp. metal salts.

glaucoma, disease of the eye characterized by abnormally high pressure within eyeball; often results in impaired vision or blindness. Usually requires surgery or treatment by drugs.

Glazunov, Aleksandr Konstantinovich (1865-1936), Russian composer. Wrote in romantic rather than nationalist style of his teacher Rimsky-Korsakov. Composed 8 symphonies.

Gleiwitz, *see* GLIWICE, Poland.

Glencoe, valley of R. Coe, Strathclyde region, W Scotland. Scene of massacre (1692) of clan Macdonald by Campbells and English.

Glendower, Owen (c 1359-c 1416), Welsh chieftain. Led series of revolts in Wales against Henry IV, defeating king's forces in campaigns of 1400-2. Lost ground after 1405, the revolt being effectively over by 1409.

Glenn, John Herschel (1922-), American astronaut. First American to orbit Earth (Feb. 1962), achieved aboard *Mercury* space capsule.

gliding, sport of flying heavier-than-air machine without engine power, using air currents to gain height, and gravity to maintain forward motion. First gliders were developed by Otto Lilienthal in 1890s and also by the Wright brothers. Sport first organized in 1920s.

Glinka, Mikhail Ivanovich (1804-57), Russian composer. One of founders of Romantic movement, he also created a characteristic 'Russian' style. Best-known works are operas *A Life for the Tsar* and *Russlan and Ludmilla.*

Gliwice (Ger. *Gleiwitz*), city of S Poland.Pop. 171,000. Coalmining, steel works, engineering. Under Prussian rule 1742-1945.

globe fish, any of several tropical fish that can inflate themselves into globular form as defence measure by swallowing air. Incl. PUFFER fish.

Globe Theatre, Elizabethan playhouse in London. Built in 1599, destroyed by fire (1613) during first night of Shakespeare's *Henry VIII.* Rebuilt but finally demolished in 1644 by Puritans. Most of Shakespeare's plays first staged here.

glockenspiel, tuned percussion instrument consisting of set of steel bars of different lengths, which player hits with hammers. Produces high but penetrating bell-like sound.

Glomma (*Glama*), longest river of Norway. Flows *c* 605 km (375 mi) from Dovrefjell plateau S via Sarpsborg to Skagerrak at Fredrikstad. H.e.p., timber transport.

Glorious Revolution (1688-9), in English history, overthrow of Catholic James II by united Whig and Tory opposition. William of Orange was petitioned by Whig and Tory leaders to rule as William III jointly with Mary, James' Protestant daughter. Their acceptance of Bill of Rights assured Parliament's authority in place of 'divine right of kings'.

glottis, opening between vocal chords in larynx, which controls production of sound.

Gloucester, Gilbert de Clare, 8th Earl of (1243–95), English nobleman. Joined de Montfort in defeat of Henry III at Lewes (1264). Took royalist side in defeat of de Montfort at Evesham (1265). Captured London (1267) and eventually became reconciled to Henry III.

Gloucester, Humphrey, Duke of (1391-1447), English nobleman. Served as regent (1420-1) while his brother Henry V fought in France. Patronized scholars and learning; his gift of books to Oxford Univ. formed part of later Bodleian Library.

Gloucester, Thomas of Woodstock, Duke of (1355-97), English nobleman. Led baronial opposition to Richard II. Forced dismissal of Richard's chancellor (1386) and defeated (1387) his adviser, de Vere, leaving the king powerless. Reconciled to Richard (1389), later arrested for further intrigues and prob. murdered.

Gloucestershire, county of W England. Area 2638 sq km (1018 sq mi); pop. 482,000. Cotswold Hills in E (sheep); lower Severn valley in C (dairying, fruit); Forest of Dean in W (coal). Co. town **Gloucester,** on R. Severn. Pop. 90,000. City, river port; timber trade. Hist. Roman town; has cathedral (15th cent.) on site of abbey (681).

glow-worm, larva or wingless female of various luminescent beetles of Lampyridae family, esp. *Lampyris noctiluca.* Organs on abdomen produce greenish light by enzyme action.

Glubb, Sir John Bagot (1897-), British soldier, known as 'Glubb Pasha'. Commander of Arab legion from 1939. Dismissed as result of anti-British public opinion (1956).

Gluck, Christoph Willibald von (1714-87), German composer, active in Paris, Vienna. Reformed opera by stressing importance of drama, simplicity. Works incl. *Orfeo ed Euridice, Alcestis, Iphigénie en Tauride.*

glucose, crystalline sugar, occurring in fruit and honey. Sugars and other carbohydrates are converted into glucose in body; its oxidation to carbon dioxide and water is major energy source. Produced commercially by hydrolysis of starch.

gluten, sticky protein substance, found in wheat and other grain; gives dough its elastic consistency.

glutton, *see* WOLVERINE.

glycerol or **glycerin[e],** colourless viscous alcohol, obtained by hydrolysis of fats during manufacture of soap. Glycerides, its esters with fatty acids, are chief constituents of fats and oils. Used in manufacture of explosives, resins, foodstuffs, toilet preparations and as antifreeze.

glycogen or **animal starch,** carbohydrate formed from glucose and stored in animal tissues, esp. liver and muscles. Can be reconverted into glucose to supply body's energy needs.

glycol or **ethylene glycol,** colourless viscous liquid, used in manufacture of polyester fibres (Dacron, Terylene) and as antifreeze.

Gmelin, Leopold (1788-1853), German chemist. Studied chemistry of digestion and discovered potassium ferricyanide (Gmelin's salt), used to detect bile pigments. Published textbook *Handbuch der Theoretischen Chemie* (9 vols., 1843).

gnat, two-winged fly of mosquito family with piercing mouthparts and long antennae. Name applied to mosquito in Britain, to smaller flies in US.

gnatcatcher, small insectivorous American warbler of genus *Polioptila.*

gnateater, small South American bird, genus *Conopophaga,* found in Amazon forests.

gneiss, coarse-grained, crystalline rock, resembling granite. Formed by metamorphism of igneous and sedimentary rock; displays alternate bands of constituents, *eg* feldspar, hornblende, mica. Major sources in Scotland, Scandinavia, Canada.

Gniezno (Ger. *Gnesen*), town of WC Poland. Pop. 50,000. Railway jct.; food processing. First cap. of Poland, kings crowned here until 1320. Under Prussian rule 1793-1919. Cathedral contains relics of St Adalbert, patron saint of Poland.

Gnosticism, system of belief combining ideas from Christian theology, Greek philosophy and diverse mystic cults. Arose during 1st cent. Followers believed in salvation through direct spiritual knowledge rather than faith. Influenced early Christianity by forcing it to define its doctrine in declaring Gnosticism heretical.

White-tailed gnu

gnu or **wildebeest,** large antelope of E and S Africa, with buffalo-like head, hairy mane, beard and tail. Two species, genus *Connochaetes;* white-tailed gnu, *C. gnu,* nearly extinct but now protected.

Goa, former Portuguese enclave of W India. Area *c* 3500 sq km (1350 sq mi); pop. 537,000; cap. Panjim. Captured by Portuguese (1510), seized by India (1961). Has tomb of missionary St Francis Xavier. Part of union territ. of Goa, Daman and Diu.

goat, hollow-horned ruminant, genus *Capra,* related to sheep. Usually coarse-haired, males bearded. Domesticated varieties kept for nutritious milk, flesh, hair; wild goats incl. IBEX, MARKHOR.

goat moth, large grey-brown moth of cossid family. Larvae, said to have goat-like smell, burrow into wood, feeding on pulp; take 3 years to develop. Species incl. European *Cossus cossus.*

goatsucker, see NIGHTJAR.

Gobelins, Manufacture Nationale des, French tapestry manufactory. Founded in 15th cent. as dye works, purchased 1662 by Louis XIV. Now state-controlled.

Gobi Desert, sandy region of C Asia (China, Mongolia). Area c 1,295,000 sq km (500,000 sq mi); av. alt. 1200 m (4000 ft). Grassy fringes inhabited by pastoral Mongols. Several sites where dinosaur eggs have been found.

goby, any of Gobiidae family of spiny-finned carnivorous fish. Pelvic fins joined to form suction disc, used to cling to rocks. Freshwater and saltwater varieties. Species incl. giant goby, *Gobius cobitis*.

God, in the three major monotheistic religions (Judaism, Christianity, Islam), creator and ruler of the universe. Regarded as eternal, infinite, immanent, omniscient. Often given attributes of goodness, love, mercy. In Christianity, believed to have lived on earth in person of Jesus Christ. *See* TRINITY.

Godard, Jean-Luc (1930-), French film writer-director. After semi-surrealist *A Bout de Souffle* (1960), *Alphaville* (1965), made political films, *eg Tout va bien* (1972).

Godavari, river of SC India. Flows c 1440 km (900 mi) SE from Western Ghats (Maharashtra) across the Deccan to Bay of Bengal. Sacred to Hindus.

Godden, Rumer (1907-), English novelist. *Black Narcissus* (1939), *The River* (1946), draw on childhood experiences in India. *Take Three Tenses* (1945) experiments with handling of time.

Gödel, Kurt (1906-), American mathematical logician, b. Czechoslovakia. Noted for work on foundations of mathematics. Showed that, beginning with any set of axioms, there will always be statements, within a system governed by these axioms, that are neither provable nor disprovable in the system; thus mathematics cannot be proved consistent.

Godesberg or **Bad Godesberg,** town of W West Germany, on R. Rhine. Mineral springs; embassies, diplomats' residences. Site of meeting (1938) between Chamberlain and Hitler prior to Munich Pact. Incorporated (1969) into Bonn.

Godfrey of Bouillon (c 1059-1100), duke of Lower Lorraine, leader of the 1st Crusade (1096). After conquest of Jerusalem (1099), was elected its ruler, but refused the title of king, preferring 'protector of the Holy Sepulchre'.

Godiva (fl c 1040–80), wife of Leofric, earl of Mercia. According to legend, she rode naked through the streets of Coventry so that her husband would grant her request to relieve the people of his heavy taxes.

Godolphin, Sidney Golodphin, 1st Earl of (1645-1712), English statesman. Noted for financial expertise, served as first lord of treasury (1684-9, 1700-1, 1702-10). Close associate of Marlborough. Dismissed (1710) by Queen Anne.

Godoy, Manuel de (1767-1851), Spanish statesman. Royal favourite, became (1792) chief minister to Charles IV. Opposed revolutionary France, but made peace (1795). Subsequent dependence on France and corrupt regime led to his overthrow (1808).

God Save the King/Queen, British national anthem. Of obscure origin, its 1st public performance was during Jacobite rebellion of 1745. Same tune is also used for songs 'God Save America' and 'My Country 'Tis Of Thee'.

Godthaab, cap. of Greenland, on Godthaab Fjord. Pop.6000. Port; founded 1721, first Danish colony on Greenland.

Godunov, Boris (c 1551-1605), tsar of Russia (1598-1605). Favourite of Ivan IV; ruled as regent during reign of Feodor I (1584-98) before succeeding him. Prob. had Dmitri, Feodor's brother and heir, murdered. Died while opposing pretender who claimed to be Dmitri.

Godwin (d. 1053), earl of Wessex, chief adviser to Canute and Edward the Confessor. Helped Edward to the throne (1042) and married his daughter Edith to him. Led opposition to king's French favourites, for which he and sons were exiled. Invaded England (1052), forced Edward to reinstate him. His son Harold succeeded Edward for 4 months.

Godwin, William (1756-1836), English writer. Best known for *An Enquiry Concerning Political Justice* (1793) arguing that best society would be one of rational individualists. Theories influenced Romantic poets. Wrote novel, *Caleb Williams, on Things as They Are* (1794). Husband of MARY WOLLSTONECRAFT.

Godwin-Austen, Mount, see K2.

godwit, migrant wading bird of sandpiper family, genus *Limosa*. European species incl. black-tailed godwit, *L. limosa*, with chestnut breast, and bar-tailed godwit, *L. lapponica*.

Goebbels, Paul Joseph (1897-1945), German political leader. Nazi propaganda minister (1933-45), took control of press, radio and cinema to further Nazi ideals; noted orator. Committed suicide during fall of Berlin.

Hermann Goering

Goering or **Göring, Hermann Wilhelm** (1893-1946), German political leader. Took part in Munich 'putsch' (1923). Air minister under Hitler (1933); controlled German economy (1937-43). Responsible for expansion of Luftwaffe and air war against Britain (1940-1). Committed suicide after being sentenced to death at Nuremberg trials.

Goes, Hugo van der (d. 1482), Flemish painter. Famous for *Portinari Altarpiece* (Florence), large work depicting the Adoration of the Shepherds. Other works incl. *Monforte Altarpiece* (Berlin).

Goethe: detail of portrait

Goethe, Johann Wolfgang von (1749-1832), German author. Leading figure in STURM UND DRANG movement, also held important cabinet post at Weimar and researched into plant biology and optics. Known for romantic novel *The*

Sorrows of Young Werther (1774). Later classical works incl. plays *Iphigenia in Tauris* (1787), *Torquato Tasso* (1790), novel *Wilhelm Meister* (2 vols., 1796). Later works indicate regained sympathy with Romanticism. *Faust* (Part I, 1808; Part II, 1832) remains his masterpiece, a symbolic representation of the human search for knowledge and experience.

Gogarty, Oliver St John (1878-1957), Irish poet. Known as Dublin wit at time of Irish renaissance, prototype of Buck Mulligan in Joyce's *Ulysses*. Works incl. autobiog. *As I Was Going Down Sackville Street* (1936).

Van Gogh: *Sunflowers*

Gogh, Vincent van (1853-90), Dutch painter. Early work, dark and heavy in form, replaced by lighter impressionist technique in Paris (1886). Settled at Arles (1888), where he was briefly joined by Gauguin. From 1888, subject to fits of insanity, he produced portraits and landscapes, painted in bold colour with swirling brushstrokes. Committed suicide in Auvers. Work, which influenced later expressionists, incl. *Sunflowers* and *Starry Night.*

Gogol, Nikolai Vasilyevich (1809-52), Russian author. Works mix stark realism with grotesque caricature and fantasy as in short story 'The Overcoat' (1842), satirical comedy *The Inspector General* (1836) about provincial bureaucracy. Novel *Dead Souls* (1842) is about trickster who mortgages dead serfs to make fortune.

Goiânia, town of C Brazil, cap. of Goiás state. Pop. 389,000. Commercial centre, livestock market, coffee exports. Modern planned city, built to replace Goiás City as state cap. (1937).

Goiás, state of WC Brazil. Area 642,092 sq km (247,912 sq mi); pop. 2,941,000; cap. Goiânia. Forests in N; savannah in S. Crops incl. coffee, tobacco, rice. Contains Federal Dist. of Brasilia.

goitre, enlargement of thyroid gland producing swelling on front of neck. Simple goitre is caused by iodine deficiency; incidence is reduced by adding iodine to table salt. Exophthalmic goitre or Grave's disease, caused by over-activity of thyroid, is accompanied by protrusion of eyeballs.

gold (Au), ductile, malleable metallic element; at. no. 79, at. wt. 196.97. Chemically inert; resists corrosion; found free. Used in coinage, jewellery and dentistry (alloyed with silver or copper).

Goldberg, Arthur Joseph (1908-), American lawyer, diplomat. Specialist in labour law, believer in settling disputes by mediation. Labor secretary (1961-2), associate justice of Supreme Court (1962-5), ambassador to UN (1965-8).

Gold Coast, see GHANA.

goldcrest, *Regulus regulus,* smallest European bird, with yellow crown, olive green upper-parts. Found in coniferous woods.

Golden Bull, name for important imperial charter. Chief one was Charles IV's (1356), which provided the constitution for the HOLY ROMAN EMPIRE.

golden eagle, *Aquila chrysaetos,* large eagle of mountainous regions of N hemisphere. Dark plumage with golden tinge on head. Diet of birds, rodents.

Golden Fleece, in Greek myth, fleece of winged ram which carried Phrixus and Helle from the intrigues of their father's concubine. Phrixus sacrificed ram; fleece guarded by dragon at Colchis. Later recovered by JASON.

Golden Gate Bridge, suspension bridge over Golden Gate waterway, San Francisco, US. Opened 1937, its total length is 2824 m (9266 ft); main span 1280 m (4200 ft) is one of world's longest bridges.

Golden Horde, Mongol warriors of Batu Khan, so-called from the splendour of his camp. Their empire was estab. in mid-13th cent. and comprised most of Russia. They took part in Kublai Khan's Chinese conquests. Empire broke up into autonomous khanates after 1405, finally crushed by IVAN III (1487).

Golden Horn, see BOSPORUS.

golden mole, any of Chrysochloridae family of burrowing insectivorous mammals of C and S Africa. Has conical muzzle, glossy fur and reduced eyes.

Goldenrod *(Solidago nemoralis)*

goldenrod, any of genus *Solidago* of perennial plants of Compositae family, with spikes of yellow flowers. Native to Europe and North America. Species incl. *S. virgaurea* and *S. canadensis.* Formerly thought to have medicinal properties.

goldfinch, *Carduelis carduelis,* Eurasian finch with scarlet face, black and yellow wings. Sociable, found in gardens, orchards, *etc.*

goldfish, *Carassius auratus,* small freshwater fish of carp family, of Asiatic origin. Many domestic varieties obtained by controlled breeding; often kept in ponds, fishbowls.

Golding, William Gerald (1911-), English novelist. Best known for first novel, moral allegory *Lord of the Flies* (1954). Other novels incl. *Pincher Martin* (1956), *The Spire* (1964).

Goldoni, Carlo (1707-93), Italian dramatist. Turned from *commedia dell'arte* to realistic, everyday subjects for comedies *La Bottega del caffè* (1751), *La Locandiera* (1753). *Memoirs* (1787) written in French.

Goldsmith, Oliver (1730-74), English author, b. Ireland. Known for humorous pastoral novel *The Vicar of Wakefield* (1766). Also wrote poem *The Deserted Village,* regretting rural enclosures, and comedy *She Stoops to Conquer* (1773).

gold standard, system whereby a unit of currency is equal to and redeemable in a specified quantity of gold. Used as international reference for currencies in late 19th cent. International gold standard broke down in WWI. Many currencies now fixed to US dollar.

Goldwyn, Samuel, orig. Samuel Goldfish (1882-1974), American film producer, b. Poland. Leading producer since *The Squaw Man* (1913), other films incl. *Wuthering Heights* (1939), *The Best Years of Our Lives* (1946). With L.B. MAYER, formed Metro-Goldwyn-Mayer (MGM) (1924).

golem, in medieval Jewish legend, a robot servant artificially created by cabalistic rites. Often associated with rabbis in European countries, esp. Rabbi Löw in 16th cent. Prague.

golf, game played with ball and clubs over outdoor course. Origins can be traced back to 15th cent. in Scotland. Original 13 rules were drawn up by Royal and Ancient Club, St Andrews, Scotland (1754). Great growth as leisure activity and as professional sport, esp. in US, dates from 1920s. Standard golf course comprises 18 holes of varying length (total *c* 4500-5000 m/5000-6000 yd).

Golgi, Camillo (1844-1926), Italian histologist and neurologist. Developed method of staining nerve tissue with silver salts; discovered Golgi apparatus in cytoplasm of cells. Shared Nobel Prize for Physiology and Medicine (1906).

Golgotha, Aramaic name for CALVARY.

Goliath, in OT, giant champion of Philistines, enemies of Israel. Killed by David with a stone from his sling (1 Samuel 17).

Gollancz, Sir Hermann (1852-1930), English rabbi, b. Germany. A noted Hebrew scholar, he taught at Univ. College, London (1902-24).

Gollancz, Sir Victor (1893-1967), English writer, publisher. Founded Left Book Club (1936).

Gomel, city of USSR, SE Byelorussian SSR. Pop. 289,000. Produces machinery, textiles. Alternately belonged to Poland and Russia, until finally taken by Russians 1772.

Gómez, Juan Vicente (1857-1935), Venezuelan political leader. Ruled as virtual dictator (1908-35) after seizing power from Cipriano Castro. Maintained popularity of regime by encouraging foreign investment.

Gompers, Samuel (1850-1924), American labour leader, b. England. Instrumental in founding American Federation of Labor (1886), serving as its president (1886-94, 1896-1924). Opposed to radical or socialist programmes, goals incl. less working hours and higher wages.

Gomulka, Wladyslaw (1905-), Polish political leader. Became leader of Polish Communist Party (1943), expelled (1949) for 'nationalist deviations'. Reinstated after Poznań riots (1956). Resigned during 1970 riots over massive food price increases.

Gonaïves, port of NW Haiti, on Gulf of Gonaïves. Pop. 29,000. Agric. exports. Site of proclamation of Haiti's independence (1804).

Goncharov, Ivan Aleksandrovich (1812-91), Russian novelist. Known for classic realist novel *Oblomov* (1859) creating prototype of rich, idle 'superflous man'.

Goncourt, Edmond [Huot] de (1822-96) and **Jules de Goncourt** (1830-70), French writers, brothers. Novels *Renée Mauperin* (1864), *Germinie Lacerteux* (1869) anticipate Naturalism. Best known for *Journal,* kept from 1851-70, recording French literary life. Edmond left sum in will to found Académie Goncourt which awards annual Prix Goncourt for best piece of imaginative prose.

Gondar, town of NW Ethiopia. Pop. 35,000. Road, rail, trade centre, tourist resort. Cap. of Ethiopia 17th cent.-1837. Last Italian stronghold in Ethiopia in WWII.

gong, percussion instrument of Oriental origin, consisting of free-hanging metal disc with turned-in edges; struck with mallet.

gonorrhoea, acute infectious inflammation of mucous membranes of genital passages; caused by a gonococcus transmitted during sexual intercourse. Symptoms are pain in passing water and discharge of pus from urethra. Treated by antibiotics, *eg* penicillin.

Good Friday, the Friday before Easter Sunday, observed by Christians as commemoration of Jesus' crucifixion.

Good Hope, Cape of, headland of SW Cape Prov., South Africa, on W side of False Bay. Rounded (1488) and named 'Cape of Storms' by Bartolomeu Dias; renamed by Henry the Navigator.

Goodman, Benjamin David ('Benny') (1909-), American band leader, clarinettist. Organized his own orchestra from 1933, and contributed to development of swing music. First American band leader to employ both black and white musicians.

Goodman, Nelson (1906-), American philosopher. Worked on theories of inductive logic. Believes that philosophy should give precise descriptions of the world. Works incl. *Fact, Fiction and Forecast* (1955).

Goodwin Sands, sandbars off Kent, SE England. Length 16 km (10 mi); marked by lightships, shipping hazard.

Goodyear, Charles (1800-60), American inventor. Developed vulcanization process for rubber (1839) which prevents it melting in hot weather.

Goole, mun. bor. of Humberside, E England, on R. Ouse. Pop. 18,000. Port; shipbuilding indust., chemicals mfg.

Canada goose

goose, long-necked web-footed bird, related to duck and swan. Two genera, *Anser* being grey, *Branta* black. Domestic goose bred from greylag goose, *Anser anser.* Wild goose is migratory, breeding in tundra regions of N hemisphere. Species incl. Canada goose, *Branta canadensis,* of North America.

Gooseberry

gooseberry, shrub of genus *Ribes* of saxifrage family. Esp. *R. uva-crispa,* native to cool, moist climates. Berry used in preserves.

gopher, small burrowing rodent of Geomyidae family of North America. Carries food in fur-lined cheek pouches. Also called pocket gopher.

goral, bovine animal of genus *Naemorhedus,* found in Himalayan mountains; intermediate between goat and antelope.

Gorchakov, Aleksandr Mikhailovich, Prince (1798-1883), Russian statesman. Foreign minister (1856-82), maintained Russian neutrality during Prussian expansionist wars with Austria and France.

Gordimer, Nadine (1923-), South African author. Works, incl. short story collection *The Soft Voice of the Serpent* (1953); novels, *eg Occasion for Loving* (1963), explore psychology of emotional crises.

Gordon, Adam Lindsay (1833-70), Australian poet, b. Azores. Known for spirited *Bush Ballads and Galloping Rhymes* (1870).

Gordon, Charles George (1833-85), British soldier and administrator, known as 'Chinese' Gordon. Commanded 'ever victorious army' which suppressed TAIPING REBELLION in China. Governor of Sudan (1877-80); killed after 10-month siege of Khartoum, having been sent to evacuate it during MAHDI's revolt.

Gordon, Lord George (1751-93), English politician. Led mob which marched on Houses of Parliament to petition for repeal of Catholic Relief Act, which had lifted civil restrictions on Catholics. March degenerated into week-long destructive 'Gordon Riots' (1780). Tried for treason, acquitted.

Gorgons, in Greek myth, three sisters (Euryale, Medusa, Stheno) with snakes instead of hair. Their gaze turned people to stone. Medusa, only mortal one, slain by Perseus.

Gorilla

gorilla, *Gorilla gorilla,* largest of anthropoid apes, reaching height of 1.8 m/6 ft; found in forest of W equatorial Africa. Terrestrial, walks on all fours using knuckles; vegetarian diet.

Gorizia (Ger. *Görz*), town of Friuli-Venezia Giulia, NE Italy, on R. Isonzo. Pop. 42,000. Resort; textiles, machinery. Former duchy, passed (1508) to Habsburgs. Battleground in WWI.

Gorki, Maksim, pseud. of Aleksei Maksimovich Peshkov (1868-1936), Russian author. Early works, *eg* short stories *Twenty-six Men and a Girl* (1899), play *The Lower Depths* (1902), autobiog. *Childhood* (1913-14), draw on wide variety of experiences to express humanist ideals convincingly. After Revolution, formulated conceptual 'socialist realism'.

Gorky, Arshile (1904-48), American painter, b. Armenia. Influenced by cubism of Picasso and surrealism of Miró, he was pioneer of abstract expressionism, using flowing colour to achieve emotional effect.

Gorky or **Gorki,** city of USSR, C European RSFSR; major port at confluence of Volga and Oka. Pop. 1,213,000. Indust. centre, producing textiles, automobiles, chemicals. Founded as Nizhni Novgorod, famous for its fair in 19th cent.; renamed 1932 after novelist Gorki.

Görlitz, town of SE East Germany, on R. Neisse. Pop. 89,000. On Polish border; engineering, textiles. Church has 15th cent. replica of Holy Sepulchre.

Gorlovka, city of USSR, indust. centre of E Ukrainian SSR. Pop. 337,000. In Donets coal mining region; chemical mfg.

gorse or **furze,** spiny evergreen bush of Leguminosae family. Fragrant yellow flowers followed by black, hairy seed pods. Species incl. common *Ulex europaeus.*

Gort, John Vereker Gort, 1st Viscount (1886-1946), British army officer. Commanded the British Expeditionary Force at the beginning of WWII and organized the Dunkirk evacuation. Governor of Gibraltar (1941) and of Malta (1942–4) where he organized its defences against constant air attack.

Gorton, John Grey (1911-), Australian statesman, PM (1968-71). Resigned to be succeeded as Liberal leader by W. McMahon.

Gorzów Wielkopolski (Ger. *Landsberg-an-der-Warthe*), town of NW Poland, on R. Warta. Pop. 70,000. Textiles, footwear mfg., chemicals. Founded 13th cent.; in Brandenburg until 1945.

Goshawk

goshawk, *Accipiter gentilis,* hawk of Eurasia, North America. Feeds on birds, small mammals; trained for falconry.

Goslar, town of NE West Germany, at foot of Harz Mts. Pop. 41,000. Mining centre (iron, lead, sulphur); textiles, chemicals mfg.; tourism. Hanseatic League member. Has Imperial palace (11th cent.), round tower (1517).

Gospels of Matthew, Mark, Luke and **John,** first 4 books of NT. First 3 (known as Synoptic Gospels) agree in subject matter and order of events of life, death and teachings of Jesus. Gospel according to John is a more philosophical book demonstrating Jesus as the vital force in the world.

Gosport, mun. bor. of Hampshire, S England. Pop. 76,000. Port on Portsmouth Harbour; yacht building; has naval barracks.

Gosse, Sir Edmund William (1849-1928), English author. Known for account of his fanatically religious upbringing, *Father and Son* (1907), biog., esp. of Donne, translations of Ibsen influential in bringing the 'new drama' to England.

Göta Canal, waterway of S Sweden. Length *c* 385 km (240 mi), from Göteborg via R. Göta, Lakes Vänern, Vättern to Baltic Sea near Söderköping. Opened 1832.

Göteborg or **Gothenburg,** city of SW Sweden, icefree port on Kattegat at mouth of R. Göta. Pop. 486,000. Fishing; marine engineering. Founded (1619) by Gustavus Adolphus; cathedral, 17th cent. town hall, univ. (1891).

Gotha, town of SW East Germany. Pop. 57,000. Engineering, food products. Hist. publishing centre. Cap. of Saxe-Gotha 1640-1918.

Gotha, Almanach de, reference book on European royalty and nobility, pub. annually (1863-1944) at Gotha, Germany. Incl. details of admin. and statistics on most countries.

Gothenburg, see GÖTEBORG, Sweden.

Gothic, style of architecture which developed in France (12th cent.) and was dominant in W Europe until 16th cent. Characterized by use of flying buttresses, ribbed vaulting, pointed arches. Early examples of style incl. St Denis

Abbey (1140) and Notre Dame in Paris (1163). English Gothic is divided into Early English (*eg* Salisbury Cathedral), decorated (*eg* Exeter Cathedral) and perpendicular (*eg* Gloucester Cathedral).

Gothic revival, in architecture, revival of Gothic style in late 18th and 19th cents., esp. in Britain and US. Horace Walpole's Strawberry Hill (1750-70) is early example of style. Influential writings of Pugin and Ruskin made it dominant in Victorian era, esp. for design of churches.

Goths, Germanic people, originally inhabiting the Vistula basin, who invaded E parts of Roman empire in 3rd and 4th cents. Divided into 2 branches: West Goths or VISIGOTHS; East Goths or OSTROGOTHS.

Gotland, Baltic isl. of SE Sweden. Area 3173 sq km (1225 sq mi); cap. Visby. Cereals, sugar beet; tourism. Trade centre from Stone Age. Taken by Sweden (1280); held by Danish (1570-1645).

Gottfried von Strassburg (*fl* 13th cent.), German poet. Wrote major epic, *Tristan* (*c* 1210), on which Wagner based opera *Tristan und Isolde.*

Göttingen, city of NE West Germany, on R. Leine. Pop. 111,000. Precision instruments, machinery mfg. Hanseatic League member from 1351. Univ. (1724), famous for expulsion (1837) of brothers Grimm; now noted for maths, physics.

Gottsched, Johann Christoph (1700-66), German literary theorist, dramatist. Influenced by French Classicism, wrote *The Dying Cato* (1732); acted as literary dictator of his age, prepared way for serious national theatre.

Gottwald, Klement (1896-1953), Czechoslovak political leader. Premier in provisional govt. (1946-8), replaced (1948) Beneš as president after Communist coup. Supported Soviet Union and satellite status of country, purged party of liberal elements.

Gottwaldov, town of C Czechoslovakia. Pop. 65,000. Wood products; centre of Bata footwear indust. estab. 1913. Known as Zlín until 1949.

gouache, method of painting which mixes watercolours with gum arabic, thus rendering them opaque.

Gouda, town of W Netherlands. Pop. 46,000. Market for Gouda cheese; pottery. Gothic town hall.

Goudy, Frederic William (1865-1947), American type designer. A prolific designer, with over 100 typefaces to his credit, he also wrote books about his craft.

Goujon, Jean (*c* 1510-68), French sculptor. Collaborated with Lescot on rood screen of St Germain-l'Auxerrois and decorations for the Louvre. Finest work was relief ornamentation of *Fontaine des Innocents* (1547-9).

Goulburn, town of SE New South Wales, Australia, on Hawkesbury R. Pop. 22,000. Agric. market, food processing, chenille mfg. Founded 1833.

Gould, Jay (1836-92), American financial speculator. With James Fisk (1834-72), gained control over Erie Railroad, defeating Cornelius Vanderbilt, and ruined it through stock manipulation. Also with Fisk, caused Black Friday stock speculation scandal (1868). Controlled Union Pacific and other railways.

Gounod, Charles (1818-93), French composer. Outstanding works are operas *Faust* and *Romeo and Juliet;* also wrote church music, *eg La Rédemption.*

gourami, *Osphronemus goramy,* freshwater food fish of SE Asia. Brightly coloured varieties popular as aquarium fish.

gourd, member of Cucurbitaceae, family of trailing plants with succulent, usually edible fruit *eg* squash, melon, pumpkin; mostly of Asian and Mexican origin. Esp. *Cucurbita maxima,* a globular yellow gourd which weighs up to 110 kg/240 lb.

gout, metabolic disease confined mainly to males. Characterized by excess of uric acid in blood and deposition of sodium urate crystals in joints. Results in painful and tender inflammation of affected parts (often big toe). Treatment by drugs and dietary control.

Gower, John (d. 1408), English poet. Friend of Chaucer, known for moral and didactic works, *eg Confessio Amantis*

(1390), series of tales illustrating Seven Deadly Sins. Also wrote French, Latin, other English poems.

Gowon, Yakubu (1934-   ), Nigerian military, political leader. Emerged as head of federal military govt. after 1966 coups. Crushed Biafran attempt to secede (1967-70). Overthrown by coup (1975) after period of economic mismanagement.

Goya [y Lucientes], Francisco José de (1746-1828), Spanish painter. Court painter to the king (1786), his paintings of royal family show his contempt for their stupidity. Produced series of etchings incl. 'Caprices', 'Bull-fight', 'Disasters of War'. Macabre 'black paintings' of later years incl. *Saturn Devouring his Children.* Work influenced 19th cent. French painters, esp. Manet.

Gozon, Marquis de (1712-59), French general. Commanded French forces in Canada after 1756, capturing Fort William and defending Ticonderoga (1758). He was defeated and mortally wounded at Québec by British under Wolfe.

Gozzi, Count Carlo (1720-1806), Italian playwright. Ignored theatrical reforms of age, attempted to revive COMMEDIA DELL'ARTE in plays, *eg King Turandot* (1762, basis of operas by Weber, Puccini), *Fable of the Love of Three Oranges* (1761, basis of Prokofiev's opera).

Graaf, Reinier de (1641-73), Dutch physician. Studied and wrote on generative organs and pancreas. Graafian follicles of ovaries, containing maturing ovum, named after him.

Grable, Betty (1916-73), American film actress. Most famous pin-up of WWII, films incl. *Million Dollar Legs* (1939), *Tin Pan Alley* (1940).

Gracchus, Tiberius Sempronius (163-133 BC), Roman politician. As tribune (133), introduced law to redistribute state land held by the rich among small land-holders. Attempt to be re-elected tribune was declared illegal by the senate and he was killed during subsequent riots. His brother, **Gaius Sempronius Gracchus** (153-121 BC), was elected tribune (123, 122), reintroduced Tiberius' agrarian reforms and reduced power of aristocracy. Failed in re-election bid (121) and was killed during election riots.

W.G. Grace

Grace, W[illiam] G[ilbert] (1848-1915), English cricketer. Greatest cricketer of his times, he scored over 54,000 runs, incl. 126 centuries, and took over 2800 wickets in his first-class career. Captained England 13 times.

grace, in Christian theology, the unmerited love and favour of God towards man, which redeems his original sin and allows him to enjoy eternal life. Most theologies retain man's freedom in accepting grace, but CALVINISM holds that grace is irresistible but only offered to those whose salvation is predestined.

Graces, see CHARITES.

grackle, any of several North American blackbirds, esp. purple grackle, *Quiscalus quiscula,* common in cities.

Graeae or **Graiae,** in Greek myth, Deino, Enyo and Pemphredo, sisters of the GORGONS. Personification of old age; born with grey hair and only one eye and one tooth between them.

graft, in surgery, *see* TRANSPLANTATION.

grafting, in horticulture, practice of uniting two plants and growing them as one. The stock may be a mature plant or a root, the scion (part to be grafted on) may be a bud or a cutting.

Graham, Martha (1895-), American choreographer, dancer. One of most important figures in modern dance, creating new forms and her own highly developed technique. Works incl. *Appalachian Spring* (1944).

Graham, Thomas (1805-69), Scottish chemist. Evolved Graham's law on relationship between diffusion rates and densities of gases. Pioneered study of colloid chemistry and developed dialysis process to separate crystalloids from colloids.

Graham, William Franklin ('Billy') (1918-), American evangelist. Has used revivalist techniques with success in US and abroad from 1949.

Grahame, Kenneth (1859-1932), British author. Remembered for children's classic *The Wind in the Willows* (1908).

Graham Land, mountainous penin. of Antarctica, lying between Bellingshausen and Weddell seas. Part of British Antarctic Territ. from 1962.

Grahamstown, town of SE Cape Prov., South Africa. Pop. 41,000. Site of Rhodes Univ. (1904). Founded 1812 as British military outpost against Kaffir tribesmen.

Grail, Holy, in medieval legend and literature, variously depicted as chalice, dish, stone, or cup. Many pagan elements in legend, but best-known version is Christian one, identifying Grail as cup used in Last Supper, later used by Joseph of Arimathea to catch crucified Christ's blood. Carried by Joseph to England, handed down from generation to generation. Became subject of quest by Arthur's knights, would be revealed only to pure knight. *See* ARTHURIAN LEGEND.

Grainger, Percy Aldridge (1882-1961), Australian composer, pianist. Known for arrangements of folk music, *eg Shepherd's Hey, Country Gardens.* Settled in US (1914).

gram, unit of mass in c.g.s. system; 1000 grams = 1 kilogram = 2.20462 pounds.

grammar school, in England, state-financed secondary school, attended by pupils selected on academic ability. Also *see* COMPREHENSIVE EDUCATION. Elsewhere, formerly used to refer to some primary or elementary schools.

gramophone or **phonograph,** instrument for reproducing sound that has been mechanically transcribed in a spiral groove on a disc or cylinder. Needle following the groove in rotating disc or cylinder picks up and transmits the sound vibrations. First built (1878) by Thomas Edison; use of discs introduced (1887) by Emile Berliner. Subsequent developments incl. electronic reproduction, stereo.

Grampian, region of NE Scotland. Area 8702 sq km (3360 sq mi); pop. 437,000. Created 1975, incl. former Morayshire, Banffshire, Aberdeenshire, Kincardineshire.

Grampians, mountain system of Scotland, N of line joining Helensburgh and Stonehaven, and S of Great Glen. Incl. Ben Nevis, Cairngorms.

grampus, *see* KILLER WHALE.

Gram's method, method of staining and classifying bacteria. Those which retain gentian violet dye after treatment with iodine solution and alcohol are said to be Gram positive, the others Gram negative. Devised by Danish pathologist, Hans Gram (1853-1938).

Granada, city of SW Nicaragua, on L. Nicaragua. Pop. 51,000. Coffee, sugar cane trade; clothing, furniture mfg. Founded 1524. Raided by pirates (17th cent.); partly burned (1856).

Granada, city of S Spain, cap. of Granada prov. Pop. 190,000. Agric. market, tourist centre, univ. (1531). Cap. of Moorish Kingdom from 1238; last Moorish stronghold in Spain, fell to Castile 1492. Moorish architecture incl. Alhambra palace (13th cent.) and Generalife gardens; cathedral (16th cent.) contains tombs of Ferdinand and Isabella.

Granados [y Campiña], Enrique (1867-1916), Spanish composer. Known for piano pieces, *Goyescas* (1911), later made into opera (1916), inspired by work of Goya. Nationalist influence reflected in *Twelve Spanish Dances.*

Granby, John Manners, Marquess of (1721-70), British soldier. Became a popular hero as leader of the victorious cavalry at Warburg (1760). Celebrated in many inn signs.

Granby, town of SE Québec, Canada. Pop. 34,000. Textiles, rubber, furniture mfg.

Gran Chaco, see CHACO.

Grand Alliance, War of the (1688-97), conflict between France and European coalition known as League of Augsburg (Grand Alliance after 1689), begun when Louis XIV invaded Palatinate. England had sea victories, but Alliance was defeated in land battles. Concluded by TREATY OF RYSWICK.

Grand Banks, see LABRADOR CURRENT.

Grand Canal (*Yun-ho*), waterway of E China. Extends from Peking to Hangchow, c 1600 km (1000 mi) long. Navigable throughout year by junks, small steamers. Begun in 6th cent. BC taking 2000 years to complete. Economic importance now reduced after silting.

Grand Canyon, gorge of NW Arizona, US; on Colorado R. Length 349 km (217 mi); width 6.4-29 km (4-18 mi); depth 1.6 km (c 1 mi). Has spectacular scenery. Popular tourist region of geological importance. Part of Grand Canyon National Park.

Grand Coulee, dam on Columbia R., US. Provides h.e.p. and irrigation over wide area. Built 1933-44.

Grand Falls, town of C Newfoundland, Canada, on Exploits R. Pop. 8000. Paper mills; h.e.p.

Grand National, annual English steeplechase, run since 1839 in March or April at Aintree, Liverpool, over course 4.5 mi (7.2 km) long. Considered world's greatest steeplechase.

Grand Rapids, town of WC Michigan, US; on Grand R. Pop. 198,000. Agric. market in fruit-growing area; furniture, paper, electrical goods mfg. Estab. as lumber town in 1820s.

Grand Remonstrance, list of protests against autocratic rule of Charles I of England, drawn up by Long Parliament (1641). Demanded parliamentary control of appointment of royal ministers, church reform.

Grangemouth, town of Central region, C Scotland; on Firth of Forth at E end of Forth and Clyde Canal. Pop. 25,000. Port; oil refining, chemicals mfg.

Granger movement (1867-75), American agrarian grouping estab. to further educational and social ideals. Organized in local units, called granges; became politicized in protest against economic abuses. Ceased political action after 1875.

granite, coarse-grained, crystalline, igneous rock. Whitish-grey in colour, hard; consists mainly of quartz, feldspar, mica. Formed at depth, occurs as dykes, sills, batholiths; often exposed by erosion of overlying rocks. Used in building. Commonest of plutonic rocks; major sources in US, Canada.

Gran Paradiso, mountain of NW Italy, in Graian Alps. Highest peak (4059 m/13,323 ft) in Italy.

Gran Sasso d'Italia, mountain group of C Italy. Highest part of Apennines, rising to 2913 m (9560 ft) at Monte Corno.

Grant, Cary, orig. Archibald Leach (1904-), British film actor. Star since early 1930s as suave, often humorous, hero of such films as *Bringing up Baby* (1938), *Arsenic and Old Lace* (1944), *Indiscreet* (1958), *Charade* (1963).

Grant, Duncan (1885-), British artist. Member of Bloomsbury group; work influenced by Cézanne, Matisse and African art. Output incl. portraits, landscapes, textile designs, stage scenes.

Grant, Ulysses Simpson (1822-85), American general and statesman, president (1869-77). Commanded Union

Ulysses Grant in 1864

army (1864-5) in Civil War after success of his Vicksburg campaign. Wore down Confederate army by sustained war of attrition, forcing Lee's surrender at Appomattox Courthouse (1865). Republican admin. characterized chiefly by bitter partisan politics and corruption.

Grantham, mun. bor. of Lincolnshire, E England. Pop. 28,000. Has medieval Angel Hotel; 13th cent. church.

Granvelle, Antoine Perrenot de (1517-86), French churchman. In service of Philip II of Spain, appointed cardinal (1561). Sent to Netherlands to advise regent, Margaret of Parma. Alienated nobles by retaining Spanish troops, introducing Inquisition. Recalled 1564.

Granville, John Carteret, 1st Earl, see CARTERET, JOHN, 1ST EARL GRANVILLE.

Granville-Barker, Harley (1877-1946), English dramatist, director, critic, actor. Known for critical *Prefaces to Shakespeare* (1923-47), plays, *eg The Voysey Inheritance* (1905). Stagings of Shakespeare (1911-13) radically changed production techniques.

Grape

grape, smooth-skinned juicy berry of many vines of genus *Vitis*. Globular or oblong shaped, colours vary from green to white, black to purple; grows in clusters. Numerous hybrids and varieties of Old and New World types. Species incl. *V. vinifera* and *V. rotundifolia*. Since ancient times eaten both fresh and dried as fruit, and fermented to produce wine.

grapefruit, *Citrus paradisi,* edible fruit widely cultivated in tropical areas. Round in shape, growing in clusters, with bitter yellow rind and acid juicy pulp.

grape hyacinth, any plant of genus *Muscari* which is hardy bulbous perennial of lily family. Spikes of small blue flowers. Over 40 species native to Europe and Asia Minor.

graphite, soft crystalline form of carbon, known as plumbago or blacklead. Occurs naturally. Used as lubricant, in electrical machinery and in making 'lead' pencils.

Grape hyacinth (*Muscari armeniacum*)

graptolites, extinct colonial animals, whose skeletons are found as fossils in Cambrian, Ordovician and Silurian rocks. Classified among Protochordata.

Grasmere, *see* AMBLESIDE, England.

Grass, Günter (1927-   ), German author, sculptor. Novels incl. *The Tin Drum* (1959), *Dog Years* (1963), *Local Anaesthetic* (1969), reflect political concerns. Also wrote plays, poetry.

grass, any plant of Gramineae family. Long, narrow leaves, jointed stems, flowers in spikelets, seed-like fruit, *eg* wheat, sugar cane, bamboo. Also incl. hay and pasture grasses. Worldwide distribution.

Grasse, town of Provence, SE France. Pop. 32,000. Resort, flower growing; perfume mfg.

grasshopper, insect of order Orthoptera, with hind legs adapted for jumping, thickened forewings, membranous hind wings. Two families: short-horned grasshoppers (Acrididae) and long-horned grasshoppers (Tettigoniidae). Males make chirping noise by rubbing body parts.

grass of parnassus, *Parnassia palustris,* perennial plant with solitary, delicate, white buttercup-like flower. Found in European marshland.

Grass snake

grass snake, *Natrix natrix,* harmless snake common in Europe. Good swimmer, often found near water; diet of mice, fish, frogs. Normally greenish-brown with yellow collar.

grass tree, several Australian trees of *Xanthorrhoea* genus. Woody trunk with tuft of grass-like leaves, white flowers, protruding spike *c* 3 m/10 ft tall. Some species yield aromatic resins.

Gratian (AD 359-83), Roman emperor (375–83). Ruled Western empire with his brother Valentinian II. Became Eastern emperor (378) but appointed Theodosius in his place (379). Influenced by Ambrose, bishop of Milan, he vigorously attacked paganism in Rome. Assassinated by followers of rebel Maximus.

Gratian (fl 1140), Italian monk. Estab. study of CANON LAW. His treatise, *Decretum* (*c* 1140), became basis of papal *Corpus juris canonici* (1500).

Grattan, Henry (1746-1820), Irish politician, patriot. Led opposition which secured (1782) right of Irish parliament to initiate legislation; gained vote for Catholics in Ireland. Supported Catholic Emancipation; opposed Act of Union (1800) ending Irish parliament.

Graubünden, see GRISONS, Switzerland.

gravel, coarse sediment, precisely defined in geology as having particle size between 2 mm and 4 mm. Commonest constituent is quartz. Term also used loosely for mixture of pebbles and rock fragments, used in roadbuilding *etc.*

Graves, Robert Ranke (1895-   ), English author. Known for autobiog. *Good-bye to All That* (1929) giving account of WWI experiences, historical novels of classical Rome, *eg I, Claudius* (1934), mythography, esp. *The White Goddess* (1948), and poetry in *Collected Poems* (1965).

Gravesend, mun. bor. of Kent, SE England, on R. Thames. Pop. 54,000. Yachting centre; customs and pilot station. Tomb of POCAHONTAS (d. 1617).

gravitation, universal force of attraction between bodies. Newton's law of gravitation states that any 2 particles attract each other with force proportional to product of their masses and inversely proportional to distance between them. Gravity is gravitational force between Earth and bodies near its surface; accounts for weight of a body and its tendency to fall to earth. Modern gravitational theories are based on Einstein's general theory of relativity, in which distribution of matter determines the structure of SPACE-TIME CONTINUUM.

gravitational collapse, in astronomy, tendency of a star to contract under influence of its own gravitation as its store of nuclear fuel becomes depleted. Depending on mass of star, may become white dwarf, supernova or neutron star; for sufficiently large mass, BLACK HOLE may be formed.

Gray, Thomas (1716-71), English poet. Famous for 'Ode on a Distant Prospect of Eton College' (1747), 'Elegy Written in a Country Churchyard' (1751). Other works, mainly Pindaric odes, incl. 'Ode on the Death of a Favourite Cat' (1748).

grayling, *Thymallus thymallus,* grey-coloured freshwater fish of salmon family, widely distributed in Europe.

Gray's Inn, see INNS OF COURT.

Graz, city of SE Austria, on R. Mur, cap. of Styria prov. Pop. 249,000. Produces iron, steel, textiles, paper. Built around Schlossberg, ruined hilltop fortress. Gothic cathedral, univ. (1586).

Great Artesian Basin, artesian water-bearing basin of E Australia. Largest in world, area c 1,735,000 sq km (670,000 sq mi); mainly in SW Queensland. Provides water for stock raising.

Great Australian Bight, large bay of S coast of South and Western Australia, part of Indian Ocean. Extends *c* 1125 km (700 mi) E-W.

Great Barrier Reef, coral reef off NE coast of Australia, extends *c* 2000 km (1250 mi) from Torres Str. to Tropic of Capricorn. Incl. *c* 350 types of coral colony; area of tourism.

Great Bear Lake, W Mackenzie Dist., Northwest Territs., Canada. Area 31,800 sq km (*c* 12,275 sq mi). Drained by Great Bear R. into Mackenzie R. Navigable only 4 months of year.

Great Belt, see BELT, GREAT and LITTLE, Denmark.

Great Britain, largest isl. of British Isles, comprising ENGLAND, SCOTLAND, WALES, isls. governed with mainland (but not N Ireland, Isle of Man, Channel Isls.). Area 230,608 sq km (89,038 sq mi). Bounded by Atlantic, Irish Sea (N, W), English Channel (S), North Sea (E). Highland in N, W (Scottish Highlands, Lake Dist., Pennines, Wales); lowlands in SE. Maritime temperate climate. Political unit from 1707, extended to Ireland 1801. UNITED KINGDOM formed by partition of Ireland (1921).

great circle, circle described on surface of a sphere by a plane which passes through centre of sphere. Shortest distance between 2 points on a sphere lies on great circle passing through them.

Great Dane, breed of large powerful dog with short dense coat. Stands *c* 76 cm/30 in. at shoulder.

Great Dividing Range, mountain system of E Australia, running parallel to coast from Cape York Penin. to S Victoria. Comprises series of ranges, incl. Blue Mts., Snowy Mts. Forms major watershed.

Great Exhibition, first modern, international indust. exhibition. Held (May-Oct. 1851) under patronage of Prince Albert in CRYSTAL PALACE. Had aim of encouraging craftmanship, indust. design. Incl. *c* 100,000 exhibits from *c*

14,000 exhibitors. Surplus funds were used to estab. Victoria and Albert Museum, Science Museum, Royal College of Art.

Great Glen, fault valley of N Scotland. Length *c* 97 km (60 mi) runs SW-NE from Loch Linnhe to Moray Firth.

Great Lakes, in C North America; 5 freshwater lakes between Canada and US. They are lakes Superior, Michigan, Huron, Erie, Ontario. Form important transport route with St Lawrence Seaway to E. Main cargoes iron ore, coal, grain. Also have important commercial fisheries, tourist resorts.

Great Plains, grassy plateau region of WC US-Canada. Extend from Rocky Mts. to prairies of Mississippi valley, S to Texas-Oklahoma. Mainly stock-grazing land.

Great Rift Valley, fault system of SW Asia and E Africa. Extends *c* 4800 km/3000 mi from R. Jordan valley (Syria) to C Mozambique; divides into W, E sections in E Africa, filled by many lakes. Ranges from 396 m/1300 ft below sea level (Dead Sea) to 1830 m/6000 ft above sea level (S Kenya).

Great Salt Lake, inland salt lake of N Utah, US. Area 2590 sq km (*c* 1000 sq mi). Salt extracts; size has varied greatly. Is remnant of hist. L. Bonneville.

Great Schism, see SCHISM, GREAT.

Great Slave Lake, S Mackenzie Dist., Northwest Territs., Canada. Area 28,400 sq km (*c* 10,980 sq mi). Drained by Mackenzie R. Gold deposits at Yellowknife. Named after Slave Indians who once lived on its shores.

great tit, *Parus major,* largest Eurasian tit, with blue-black head, yellow under-parts and black stripe on breast.

Great Trek, see TREK, GREAT.

Great Wall of China

Great Wall of China, fortification across N China running *c* 2400 km (1500 mi) along S edge of Mongolian plain from Kansu prov. to Hopeh prov. on Yellow Sea. First built in 3rd cent BC as protection against hostile nomadic tribes.

Great Yarmouth, co. bor. of Norfolk, E England. Pop. 50,000. Coastal resort; herring indust. ('bloaters' once famous). Large 12th cent. church rebuilt after WWII.

grebe, any of Podicipedidae family of freshwater diving birds with short tail, partially webbed feet; worldwide distribution. Nests in floating vegetation. Largest species is CRESTED GREBE.

Greco, El, pseud. of Domenicos Theotocopoulos, (*c* 1541-1614), Greek-Spanish painter, b. Crete. Trained in Venice, was influenced by Titian, Michelangelo and Byzantine art. In Toledo, painted visionary religious works in highly mannerist style, characterized by vivid colour, harsh light, twisting of natural shapes. Works incl. *Burial of Count Orgaz, View of Toledo.*

Greco, Emilio (1913-   ), Italian sculptor. Specializes in bronze portrait busts and life-size nude figures, generally shown in twisted poses.

Greece (*Ellas, Hellas*), republic of SE Europe, incl. S Balkan penin., Aegean and Ionian isls. Area 132,000 sq km (50,900 sq mi); pop. 8,950,000; cap. Athens. Language: Greek. Religion: Eastern Orthodox. Pindus Mts. run N-S; fertile valleys. Agric. backward (tobacco, currants, olives); tourist indust. Home of Minoan, Mycenaean civilizations; powerful city-states (*eg* Athens, Sparta, Corinth) from 6th cent. BC. Centre of literature, art, science. Weakened by city state rivalry (*eg* Peloponnesian War), conquered 338 BC by Philip II of Macedon. Fell to Romans 146 BC. Turkish from 1453, revolts led to independence 1829, monarchy from 1832. Territ. gained in Balkan Wars (1913), WWI. Influx of refugees from Turkey in 1920s. Coup (1967) exiled king, estab. military govt. until 1974.

Greek, branch of Indo-European language family. Ancient Greek language associated with major civilization, literature. Its dialects incl. Aeolic, Arcadian, Attic, Ionic, Doric, Cyprian, of which Attic (dialect of Athens) was dominant. From Attic, *koinē* (common language) developed, used all over Mediterranean. NT written in *koinē*, and Modern Greek descended from it. Latter divided into *katharevousa* (written form), and *dēmotikē* (vernacular).

Greek Church, see EASTERN ORTHODOX CHURCH.

Greek myths, legends and literature revolving around themes in Greek religion. Taken from many sources, some indigenous, others Minoan, Mycenaean, Egyptian and Asian, so that the classical Greek pantheon drew deities from all the cultures involved. First consistent picture of resultant blend found in *Iliad*; fullest conscious attempt to connect myths in Hesiod's *Theogony*. As told by Homer, OLYMPIAN GODS were represented as being in charge of natural forces but were not omnipotent and were subject to fate. By time of the tragic dramatists and Plato (*c* 5th cent. BC) the importance of myth was declining in Greek thought.

Greeley, Horace (1811-72), American newspaper editor, political leader. Founded New York *Tribune* (1841) as responsible, cheap paper for working class. Advocate of social reforms, coined phrase, 'Go West, young man'. Supported Liberal Republican Party, after earlier encouraging U.S. Grant. Unsuccessful presidential candidate (1872).

Green, Henry, pseud. of Henry Vincent Yorke (1905-73), English novelist. Works, *eg Living* (1929), *Loving* (1945), *Concluding* (1948), expose man's inadequacies in a gently comic light.

Green, Julien (1900-), French author of American parentage. Novels, *eg Le Visionnaire* (1934), *Chaque Homme dans sa nuit* (1960), reflect obsession with sin, fear of madness and death.

Green, Thomas Hill (1836-82), English philosopher. Hegelian idealist, critical of prevailing empiricism of Spencer, J. S. Mill. Wrote influential *Prolegomena to Ethics* (1883).

Green, river of W US. Flows 1175 km (730 mi) from W Wyoming through NW Colorado and E Utah to join Colorado R.

green algae, any of the division Chlorophyta of ALGAE in which the chlorophyll is not masked by any other pigment. Considered ancestral type from which higher green plants evolved. Aquatic, mainly freshwater, or terrestrial in moist areas.

Greenaway, Kate (1846-1901), English watercolour painter. Illustrated children's books, *eg Mother Goose, Birthday Book;* her depiction of children in quaint early 19th cent. costume influenced children's fashions.

Greenback Party, political party in US promoting currency expansion (1874-84). Members, mainly farmers, wanted inflated currency to wipe out farm debts from period of high prices. As Greenback Labor Party, enjoyed some success in 1878 congressional election.

Green Bay, port of E Wisconsin, US; at head of inlet of L. Michigan. Pop. 88,000. Shipping centre for dairy produce. Paper mills, engineering works. French trading post estab. in 18th cent.

green belt, tract of open land surrounding a town or city. Involves restrictions on development to preserve area for farming, woodland, recreational purposes.

Greene, [Henry] Graham (1904-), English author. Novels, concerned with individuals faced with moral dilemmas, incl. *Brighton Rock* (1938), *The Power and the Glory* (1940). Also wrote 'literary thrillers', esp. *The Third*

Man (1950), 'entertainments', *eg Our Man in Havana* (1958), essays and plays.

Greenfinch

greenfinch, *Carduelis chloris,* common European songbird. Male is olive-green, with yellow on wings and tail.

greengage, small round variety of plum. Sweet and golden-green in colour. Native to France, introduced into England in 18th cent.

greenhouse effect, the retention of heat from sunlight at the Earth's surface, caused by atmospheric carbon dioxide that admits shortwave radiation but traps longwave radiation emitted by the Earth. Some posit that, because of enormous amounts of carbon dioxide released through man's activities, Earth will suffer continuous heating-up.

Greenland, isl. of Denmark, in N Atlantic, mostly N of Arctic Circle. Area 2,176,000 sq km (840,000 sq mi); pop. 51,000; cap. Godthaab. Ice-cap (incl. Humboldt Glacier of NW) covers most of interior, up to 2450 m (8000 ft) thick. Cryolite mining at Ivigtut; sheep in SW; cod, halibut industs. US air bases at Thule, Sondre Stromfjord. Discovered (*c* 982) by Eric the Red, modern colonization begun *c* 1721. Danish colony until 1953.

Greenland Sea, arm of Arctic Ocean, connecting it with the Atlantic; lies between Greenland and Spitsbergen. Largely covered with drifting pack-ice.

Greenland shark, *Somniosus microcephalus,* large shark of colder N Atlantic; reaches length of 6.5 m/21 ft. Appears sluggish but is active predator.

Green Mountain Boys, see ALLEN, ETHAN.

Greenock, town of Strathclyde region, WC Scotland. Pop. 69,000. Container port, shipbuilding, sugar refining.

Greensboro, town of N North Carolina, US. Pop. 144,000. Important insurance, educational, trade centre; textile, chemical mfg.

green turtle, *Chelonia mydas,* edible turtle, widely distributed in tropics; feeds on algae. Flesh and eggs highly prized, leading to rarity of species.

Greenwich, bor. of SE Greater London, England, on R. Thames. Pop. 216,000. Created 1965, incl. former Greenwich, Woolwich met. bors. Original site of Royal Observatory (1675) now in Herstmonceux; on prime meridian (long. 0°), source of Greenwich Mean Time. Has Royal Naval Coll.; maritime museum.

Greenwich Village, see NEW YORK CITY.

Greenwood, Walter (1903-), English novelist. Known for first novel *Love on the Dole* (1933), which publicized suffering of working classes during Depression.

Gregorian chant, see PLAINSONG.

Gregory [I] the Great, St (*c* 540-604), Roman monk, pope (590-604). Extended and defined papal authority, promoting monasticism, missions to England. Refusal to recognize patriarch of Constantinople furthered split with Eastern Church. Responsible for major doctrinal pronouncements, changes in liturgy and contribution to development of plainsong (Gregorian chant).

Gregory VII, St, orig. Hildebrand (d. 1085), pope (1073-85). First known as Benedictine monk for Hildebrandine reform, attacking simony, lay investiture, clerical unchastity. Carried on reforms as pope, causing strife with Henry IV of Germany, who sided with party which resented papacy's domination in temporal sphere. Henry, excommunicated twice, captured (1083) Rome, forcing Gregory into exile.

Gregory XI, orig. Pierre Roger de Beaufort (1330-78), French churchman, pope (1370-8). Encouraged by prophecies of Catherine of Siena, he removed the papacy, after much struggle, to Rome from Avignon (1376-7). He condemned Wycliffe's teachings. Elections following death led to Great SCHISM.

Gregory XII, orig. Angelo Corrario (c 1327-1417), Italian pope (1406-15). Attempted to end Great SCHISM by agreeing to resign if Avignon antipope Benedict XIII did so too. Agreement was broken, and later Council of Pisa (1409) deposed both him and antipope. After being pronounced canonical pope by Council of Constance (1415), Gregory resigned.

Gregory XIII, orig. Ugo Buoncompagni (1502-85), Italian churchman, pope (1572-85). Prominent in Council of Trent (1562-3), became cardinal 1565. Supported Jesuits. Introduced Gregorian calendar.

Gregory, Lady [Isabella] Augusta, née Persse (1852-1932), Irish author. A founder manager, director of Abbey Theatre, Dublin. Friend and patron of Yeats, and influential in awakening of self-consciously Irish literary movement.

Gregory of Nyssa, St (d. AD 394), Cappadocian churchman, theologian. Consecrated bishop of Nyssa (371) by his brother, St Basil the Great. Opposed Arianism in writings and missions; hailed as pillar of orthodoxy by council at Constantinople (381).

Gregory of Tours, St (c 538-c 594), French bishop, historian. Remembered for *History of the Franks*, source book for Dark Ages in W Europe.

Grenada, isl. state of SE West Indies, in Windward Isls. Area 311 sq km (120 sq mi); pop. 87,000; cap. St. George's. Cacao, limes, fruit, spice exports; cotton, rum mfg. British colony from 1783, became independent (1974).

Hand grenade

grenade, a metal container filled with explosive, thrown by hand or special launcher and detonated by a short time-fuse.

Grenadines, isl. group of SE West Indies, in Windward Isls. Admin. by Grenada and St Vincent.

Grenoble, city of SE France, on R. Isère, cap. of Isère dept. Pop. 162,000. Tourist, winter sports centre; glove mfg., metals indust. based on h.e.p., nuclear research; univ. (1339). Hist. cap. of Dauphiné. Medieval cathedral, 16th cent. Palais de Justice.

Grenville, George (1712-70), British statesman, PM (1763-5). Began (1763) prosecution of JOHN WILKES. His policy of internally taxing America (Stamp Act, 1765) antagonized colonists. His son, **William Wyndham Grenville, Baron Grenville** (1759-1834), was also PM (1806-7). Served as foreign secretary (1791-1801) before forming coalition of 'all the talents' which secured abolition of slave trade.

Grenville, Sir Richard (c 1542-91), English admiral. Commanded (1585) fleet carrying 1st colonists to Virginia. As commander of the *Revenge* he continued to engage a large Spanish fleet off the Azores although mortally wounded and deserted by rest of squadron.

Gresham, Sir Thomas (c 1519-79), English financier. Founder of Royal Exchange; endowed Gresham College, London. Name given to Gresham's law, ie that 'bad' money tends to drive 'good' money from circulation.

Gretna Green, village of Dumfries and Galloway region, S Scotland. Formerly popular for marriages of runaway couples from England.

Greuze, Jean Baptiste (1725-1805), French portrait and genre painter. Produced sentimental genre scenes charged with moral and social import, incl. *The Broken Pitcher.* His portraits are more highly prized.

Greville, Sir [Charles Cavendish] Fulke, 1st Baron Brooke (1554-1628), English author, courtier. Remembered for memoir of friend, *The Life of the Renowned Sir Philip Sidney* (1652). Also wrote love lyrics, philosophical treatises.

Grey, Charles Grey, 2nd Earl (1764-1845), British statesman, PM (1830-4). Foreign secretary (1806-7), resigned over George III's opposition to measure of Catholic Emancipation. His admin. was noted for REFORM BILL of 1832.

Grey, Edward, 1st Viscount Grey of Fallodon (1862-1933), British statesman. Liberal foreign secretary (1905-16), worked in vain to prevent war. Achieved accord with Russia (1907), completing TRIPLE ENTENTE.

Grey, Sir George (1812-98), British colonial administrator. Governor of South Australia (1841-5), then of New Zealand (1845-53, 1861-8), where he helped placate Maoris. Premier of New Zealand (1877-9).

Grey, Lady Jane (c 1537-54), English noblewoman. Married Lord Guildford Dudley, son of NORTHUMBERLAND, who persuaded Edward VI to make Jane his successor, rather than Mary Tudor. She was actually proclaimed queen (July, 1553), imprisoned after 9 days and beheaded.

Grey, Zane (1875-1939), American author. Known for best-selling 'Western' novels incl. *The Last of the Plainsmen* (1908), *Riders of the Purple Sage* (1912), doing much to estab. genre.

grey heron, *Ardea cinerea,* large heron with yellowish bill, black crest. Powerful flier.

greyhound, breed of tall, slender hound, once used to hunt small game; racing of greyhounds popularized in 20th cent. Stands c 66 cm/26 in. at shoulder.

greyhound racing, sport in which greyhounds chase mechanically-propelled 'hare' around an oval track. Derived from coursing, it originated in US (1919-20); 1st English track opened 1926.

grey whale, *Eschritius glaucus,* migratory whalebone whale of Arctic; winters on N Pacific coast. Reaches lengths of 13.7 m/45 ft. Almost extinct in 19th cent., now protected.

Grieg, Edvard Hagerup (1843-1907), Norwegian composer. Work combines romantic with national idioms. His *Piano Concerto in A minor* is among the most popular of all concertos; also known for *Peer Gynt* suite.

Griffenfeld, Peder Schumacher, Count (1635-99), Danish statesman. Secretary to Frederick III and chief minister to Christian V (1671-6). Made crown more autocratic, promoted trade. Tried and sentenced to life imprisonment at instigation of nobles.

griffin, mythical creature with body and hind legs of a lion and head and wings of an eagle. Originated in ancient Middle Eastern legend, possibly as protective device representing vigilance.

Griffith, Arthur (1872-1922), Irish statesman. Founder of journal *The United Irishman* (estab. 1899), which he used to campaign for a separate Irish parliament. Leader of SINN FEIN separatist movement. Became 1st president of Irish Free State (1922).

Griffith, D[avid] W[ark] (1880-1948), American film director-producer. First major US director. Pioneered cinematic techniques, eg flashback, cross-cutting, close-up; best remembered for *Birth of a Nation* (1915), *Intolerance* (1916).

D.W. Griffith instructing an actress in *Battle of the Sexes* (1928)

Grignard, François Auguste Victor (1871-1935), French chemist. Awarded Nobel Prize for Chemistry (1912) for discovery of Grignard reagents, organic compounds of magnesium with alkyl halides; of great importance in organic synthesis.

Grigualand, *see* TRANSKEI.

Grillparzer, Franz (1791-1872), Austrian dramatist. Works, influenced by Shakespeare, incl. historical tragedy *King Ottocar's Success and Downfall* (1825). Also wrote sentimental novella *The Poor Minstrel* (1831).

Grimaldi, Francesco Maria (1618-63), Italian physicist. First to discover diffraction of light and evolve wave theory of light. Also studied and named Moon's dark areas.

Grimaldi, Joseph (1779-1837), English clown. Prob. most popular of all clowns, who are called 'Joey' after him. Master of comic song, dance, acrobatics, mime, management of props. Songs long outlived him.

Grimm, Jakob Ludwig (1785-1863) and his brother, **Wilhelm Karl Grimm** (1786-1859), German philologists and literary scholars. Famous for collection of folk tales *Grimm's Fairy Tales* (1812-15). Jakob considered founder of comparative philology, famous for Grimm's law, theory of sound changes in Indo-European languages, formulated in *Deutsche Grammatik* (1819-37).

Grimmelshausen, Hans Jakob Christoffel von (c 1622-76), German author. Defended peasants, satirized Thirty Years War in picaresque novel *Simplicissimus* (1668).

Grimsby, co. bor. of Humberside, E England, at mouth of Humber. Pop. 96,000. Major fishing port; boat building.

Gris, Juan, pseud. of José Victoriano González (1887-1927), Spanish painter. Associated with Picasso; pioneered synthetic cubism, non-representational phase of cubism. Wrote *Les Possibilités de la peinture* (1924).

Grisons (Ger. *Graubünden*), canton of E Switzerland. Largest Swiss canton, area 7110 sq km (2745 sq mi); cap. Chur. Forested mountains; glaciers; headwaters of Inn, Rhine; resorts. Joined Swiss Confederation 1803.

Grivas, George (1898-1974), Greek Cypriot revolutionary. Under the name 'Dighenis' led the EOKA terrorist movement against British rule in Cyprus from 1954 until the settlement of 1959. Launched further terrorist campaign (1971).

grizzly bear, *Ursus horribilis,* brown bear of Alaska, W Canada and Rocky Mts. Most carnivorous of bears, nearly exterminated for attacking livestock.

Grodno, city of USSR, W Byelorussian SSR; on R. Neman. Pop. 139,000. Agric. machinery, textile mfg. Cap. of Lithuania 14th cent.; passed to Russia (1795). Part of Poland (1920-39).

Gromyko, Andrei Andreyevich (1909-   ), Soviet diplomat. Held several ambassadorial posts before becoming foreign minister (1957).

Groningen, prov. of NE Netherlands. Area 2328 sq km (899 sq mi). Dairying, large natural gas deposits. Cap.

Groningen, pop. 171,000. Railway jct., agric. market, chemicals. Hanseatic town; did not join Dutch revolt against Spain, taken by Dutch 1594. Univ. (1614).

Groote Eylandt, isl. of Northern Territ., Australia, in Gulf of Carpentaria. Area c 2460 sq km (950 sq mi). Part of ARNHEM LAND reserve; 2 mission stations. Manganese deposits.

Gropius, Walter (1883-1969), German architect. Leading functionalist architect, his early factory designs, constructed with modern industrial materials, were pioneering works in modern style. Founder-director of the Bauhaus (1919-28). Lived in UK, then US from 1930s.

Gros, Antoine Jean, Baron (1771-1835), French painter. Pupil of David; travelled with Napoleonic armies as official war artist. Best known for his depiction of exploits of Napoleon, incl. *The Battle of Eylau* and *The Plague-stricken at Jaffa.*

grosbeak, any of various birds of finch family characterized by thick conical beak. Species incl. pine grosbeak, *Pinicola enucleator,* of Arctic forests.

Groseilliers, Médard Chouart, Sieur des (c 1618-c 1690), French trader. Explored Canada in search of furs with brother-in-law PIERRE RADISSON. His success influenced English to estab. Hudson's Bay Co.

Grosseteste, Robert (c 1175-1253), English churchman. Chancellor of Oxford University and bishop of Lincoln (1235-53). Supported de Montfort and defended papal prerogatives. His work on Aristotle laid foundations for Albertus Magnus and Aquinas. Also wrote treatises on physics.

Grossglockner, highest mountain of Austria, in Höhe Tauern. Height 3796 m (12,460 ft); Grossglocknerstrasse, mountainside road (1935), reaches 2346 m (7700 ft).

Grossmith, George (1847-1912) and his brother, **Weedon Grossmith** (1853-1919), English actors. Known for their collaboration in *Diary of a Nobody* (1892), affectionately satirizing lower middle class life.

Grosz, George (1893-1959), German artist. Associated with dadaism, satirized bourgeoisie, militarism. Later painted symbolic anti-war pieces. Lived in US after 1933.

Grotefend, Georg Friedrich (1775-1853), German philologist. An authority on classical languages, he began decipherment of Persian cuneiform script (1802).

Grotius, Hugo (1583-1645), Dutch jurist, statesman. Wrote *De jure belli ac pacis* (1625), on natural law, regarded as 1st definition of international law.

Ground beetle (*Speomolops sardous*)

ground beetle, any of Carabidae family of carnivorous beetles. Larvae and adults found in debris, under rocks, *etc;* feed on insects, slugs, snails. Some have bright metallic colouring, eg *Carabus nitens.* Violet ground beetle, *C. violaceus,* commonest species.

ground ivy, *Glechoma hederacea,* creeping aromatic perennial plant of mint family. Originally European, naturalized in North America.

groundnut, *see* PEANUT.

groundsel or **ragwort,** any plant of *Senecio* genus of Compositae family. Esp. *S. vulgaris* of temperate areas of Europe, with small yellow flowers and deeply cut leaves.

ground squirrel, one of various burrowing mammals of temperate zones of N hemisphere, genus *Citellus.*

grouse, gamebird of moorlands of N hemisphere with mottled feathers, round body. Species incl. PTARMIGAN, CAPERCAILLIE, and red grouse, *Lagopus lagopus,* common in Scotland.

Grove, Sir George (1820-1900), English musicographer. His *Dictionary of Music and Musicians* (1879-89) is a standard reference work. First director of Royal College of Music (1882-94).

Grozny, city of USSR, cap. of Chechen Ingush auton. republic, S European RSFSR. Pop. 355,000. Major oil centre; connected by pipeline to Caspian and Black seas. Oil discovered here (1893).

Grundtvig, Nikolai Frederik Severin (1783-1872), Danish educator, minister, writer. Founded Danish folk high school system, emphasized teaching of national history and literature.

Grünewald, Matthias (c 1470-1528), German painter. Famous for *Isenheim Altarpiece,* a dramatic depiction of the Crucifixion painted in late Gothic style; work is noted for its portrayal of intense suffering of Christ.

Gruyères (Ger. *Greierz*), town of W Switzerland. Pop. 1000. Famous cheese first made here; cattle.

Guadalajara, city of WC Mexico, cap. of Jalisco state. Pop. 1,196,000. Commercial and route centre, famous glass, pottery industs. Settled 1542. Has 17th cent. colonial architecture; univ. (1792), 16th-17th cent. cathedral. Popular health resort on plateau c 1500 m (5000 ft) high.

Guadalajara, town of C Spain, cap. of Guadalajara prov. Pop. 32,000. Agric. market. Scene of Republican victory (1937) in Civil War. Infantado palace (15th cent.).

Guadalcanal, largest of Solomon Isls., in SW Pacific. Area c 6500 sq km (2500 sq mi); pop. 24,000; main town Honiara. Copra exports. Discovered 1788; occupied by Japan in WWII, retaken by US (1943) after intensive fighting.

Guadalupe Hidalgo, *see* MEXICO CITY.

Guadalupe Hidalgo, Treaty of (1848), settlement, signed in suburb of Mexico City, ending war between Mexico and US. Texas and much of SW US recognized as American territ. US paid compensation and settled claims against Mexico.

Guadeloupe, overseas isl. dept. of France, in Leeward Isls., West Indies. Area 1779 sq km (687 sq mi); pop. 327,000; cap. Basse-Terre (pop. 16,000). Comprises 2 islands (Guadeloupe, Grande-Terre), 3 dependencies and N half of St MARTIN. Fruit, coffee, rum, cacao products. Settled by French in 17th cent.; dept. from 1946.

Guam, largest of Mariana Isls., W Pacific Ocean, territ. of US. Area 540 sq km (210 sq mi); pop. 97,000; cap. Agana. Subsistence farming; economy dominated by US military base. Discovered (1521) by Magellan; taken from Spain by US (1898). Occupied by Japanese (1941-4).

guanaco, *Lama huanacos,* American mammal of camel family, found in arid regions of Andes. Thought by some to be ancestor of domesticated llama; woolly, resembles long-legged sheep.

guano, accumulated excrement of seabirds, found esp. on isls. off coast of Peru. Rich in phosphate and nitrogen, it was formerly an important fertilizer.

Guantánamo, port of SE Cuba. Pop. 130,000. Sugar refining, coffee roasting, chocolate, liqueur mfg. Founded by French (1822). Nearby Guantánamo Bay has US naval base.

Guaraní, South American Indians of Paraguay and S Brazil. Originally semi-nomadic farmers, intermarried with early Spanish settlers and adopted Spanish customs. Known as Tupí in Amazonian Brazil.

Guardi, Francesco (1712-93), Venetian painter. Specialized in Venetian scenes in manner of Canaletto, although his treatment of light is more impressionistic. Collaborated with his brother on religious subjects.

guards, the elite regiments of an army, generally originating from the sovereign's bodyguard. The British guards comprise 2 sections: the Household Cavalry (Life Guards and Horse Guards) and the Foot Guards (Grenadiers, Coldstream, Scots, Irish and Welsh).

Guareschi, Giovanni (1908-68), Italian journalist. Known for humorous stories, *eg The Little World of Don Camillo*

(1950), about friendly feud between parish priest and communist mayor.

Guarini, Giovanni Battista (1538-1612), Italian poet. Best known for seminal pastoral play *Il Pastor Fido* (1590), imitating Tasso's *Aminta,* but combining tragedy, comedy.

Guarini, Guarino (1624-83), Italian architect, philosopher, mathematician. His Sindone Chapel and Church of San Lorenzo, Turin, with their complex domes, are major examples of later Baroque.

Guarneri or **Guarnerius,** family of Italian violin makers in Cremona. Founded by **Andrea Guarneri** (c 1626-98), a pupil of AMATI. Most famous member was **Giuseppe Guarneri** (1687-1744), known as 'del Gesu' from cross and letters IHS which appear on his labels.

Guatemala, republic of Central America. Area 108,889 sq km (42,042 sq mi); pop. 5,110,000, mostly Indian; cap. Guatemala City. Languages: Spanish, Indian dialects. Religion: RC. Volcanic mountains near Pacific coast; jungle in N (Péten). Agric. economy; coffee, cotton, banana growing. Hist. civilizations incl. Maya-Quiché; Spanish conquest 1524; gained independence 1821; basis of Central American Federation (1825-38). Frequent earthquakes, esp. 1976.

Guatemala City, cap. of Guatemala, alt. 1520 m (c 5000 ft). Pop. 731,000, largest city in Central America. Coffee exports, textiles, cement, soap mfg. Founded 1776 as cap., rebuilt after 1917-18 earthquakes, badly damaged in 1976 earthquake. Has Univ. of San Carlos (1676).

guava, *Psidium guajava,* small tree of tropical America. Yellowish, pear-shaped, edible fruit is used in preserves.

Guayaquil, port of W Ecuador, at mouth of Guayas R. Pop. 794,000. Bananas, cacao, coffee exports; iron founding, textile mfg. Linked by rail and road with Quito. Founded c 1535; site of hist. Bolívar-San Martín meeting (1822). Suffered from fire and earthquake damage.

Gubbio (anc. *Iguvium*), town of Umbria, EC Italy. Pop. 33,000. Agric. market, pottery. Iguvine Tables found here detailing Umbrian life in 1st, 2nd cents. AD. Medieval cathedral, palace.

Gudbrandsdal, valley of S Norway, extends NW-SE from Dovrefjell to L. Mjosa. Agric., livestock, timber, h.e.p. Hist. trade, invasion route. Associated with Peer Gynt legend.

gudgeon, *Gobio gobio,* small European freshwater fish with 2 barbels; used for bait.

Guelder rose

guelder rose or **snowball,** *Viburnum opulus,* bush of honeysuckle family. Native to N temperate regions. Grows to c 2 m/6 ft, with spherical clusters of white flowers.

Guelph, town of S Ontario, Canada; on Speed R. Pop. 60,000. In rich agric. region; electrical goods mfg. Founded 1827.

Guelphs and Ghibellines, rival political factions in late medieval Europe. Rivalry began with strife between Guelphs or Welfs and the Hohenstaufen emperors, to whom Ghibellines were loyal, in 12th cent. Germany. Continued in 13th–14th cent. Italy after Hohenstaufen line died out, with Guelphs at first loyal to papacy and Ghibellines to Holy Roman emperor; later broke up into petty feuds.

Guercino, pseud. of Gian-Francesco Barbieri (1591-1666), Italian painter. Early work, influenced by Ludovico Carracci, incl. ceiling fresco *Aurora* in Villa Ludovisi,

Rome. Became leading artist in Bologna after death of Guido Reni.

Guernica, town of Basque prov., N Spain. Pop. 15,000. Hist. meeting place of Basque parliament. Destruction (1937) by German bombing during Civil War inspired painting by Picasso.

Guernsey, second largest of Channel Isls., UK. Area 62 sq km (24 sq mi); pop. incl. dependencies 54,000; cap. St Peter Port. Fruit, vegetables, flower growing; Guernsey cattle; tourism.

guerrilla warfare, harassing action by small bands of men in enemy-occupied territ. Significant in Communist strategy in SE Asia from 1950s.

Guesclin, Bertrand du (*c* 1320-80), French soldier. Relieved and defended Rennes against the English (1356-7). Constable of France (1370-80), he recovered much of territ. held by the English in S and W of France.

Che Guevara

Guevara, Ernesto ('Che') (1928-67), Cuban revolutionary, b. Argentina. Guerrilla leader in Cuban invasion (1956), economic adviser in Castro govt. (1959-65). Went to Bolivia to further Communist revolution; captured while leading guerrilla band, executed. Exploits inspired many left-wing revolutionary movements.

Guggenheim, Meyer (1828-1905), American industrialist, b. Switzerland. Amassed fortune in metal processing. His son, **Daniel Guggenheim** (1956-1930), was instrumental in merging (1901) smelting interests with American Smelting and Refining Co., of which he was made president. Another of Meyer's sons, **Simon Guggenheim** (1867-1941) estab. (1925), with his wife, the John Simon Guggenheim Memorial Foundation (1925). Another son, **Solomon Guggenheim** (1861-1949), estab. foundation which founded Solomon R. Guggenheim Museum for modern art (1937).

Guiana, region of NE South America, bounded by Negro, Orinoco, Amazon rivers and Atlantic in E. Mainly highlands, with humid coastal strip. Incl. Guyana, Surinam, French Guiana, parts of Venezuela, N Brazil.

Guicciardini, Francesco (1483-1540), Italian historian, statesman. Wrote important history of Italy, relating events of Italian wars (1492-1534).

guided missile, type of ROCKET or jet-propelled missile with explosive warhead, controlled in flight by radio or automated guidance system. Developed by Germans in WWII (esp. V-2, using gyroscopic control). Advances in electronics have led to great accuracy in control over thousands of miles. US Minuteman and Polaris missiles are key strategic weapons.

Guido d'Arezzo or **Guido Aretinus** (*c* 990-1050), Italian Benedictine monk and musical innovator. His simple system of learning to read music was adopted in the 19th cent. as the basis of tonic sol-fa.

Guienne, *see* GUYENNE, France.

Guildford, mun. bor. of Surrey, SE England. Pop. 57,000. Has hospital, guildhall (both 17th cent.); cathedral (1936); Univ. of Surrey (1966). Medieval cloth trade.

guilds or **gilds,** associations of people within same craft or trade, powerful in medieval W Europe. They had local control over craft or trade, set standards for craftsmen to work to, prices of goods, protected trade from taxation and estab. status of members in society. Merchant guilds were oldest, craft guilds grew in importance in 12th cent. Disappeared with Industrial Revolution.

guillemot, long-billed diving bird, abundant on N Atlantic coasts. Nests in large colonies on cliffs. Species incl. common guillemot, *Uria aalge,* and black guillemot, *Cepphus grylle.*

Guimarães or **Guimarãis,** town of NW Portugal. Pop. 24,000. Hist. royal residence; scene of siege (1127) by Alfonso VII of León.

Guimard, Hector (1867-1942), French architect, furniture designer. Leading art nouveau architect, he designed decorative metal arches for entrances to Paris Métro stations.

Guinea, republic of W Africa. Area 246,000 sq km (95,000 sq mi); pop. 4,312,000; cap. Conakry. Language: French. Religion: Islam. Humid, marshy coastal plain rises to interior highlands, esp. Fouta Djallon dist. in N. Cattle raising important; exports bananas, iron ore, alumina. Former French Guinea estab. 1895; part of French West Africa from 1904; became independent 1958.

Guinea, Equatorial, see EQUATORIAL GUINEA.

Guinea, Gulf of, inlet of Atlantic Ocean off W Africa. Extends from Cape Palmas (Liberia) to Cape Lopez (Gabon). Incl. bights of Benin and Bonny.

Guinea-Bissau

Guinea-Bissau, republic of W Africa. Area 36,130 sq km (13,950 sq mi); pop. 517,000; cap. Bissau. Language: Portuguese. Religions: native, Islam. Coastal mangrove swamp, tropical forest; produces palm oil, hardwoods, copra, groundnuts. Centre of slave trade 17th-18th cent.; became Portuguese colony (1879), overseas prov. (1951). Independence gained 1974. Claims right to Cape Verde Isls.

guinea fowl, *Numida meleagris,* turkey-like domestic fowl of African origin. Flesh considered delicacy by Greeks and Romans.

guinea pig, domesticated form of CAVY. Popular as pet, also used in laboratories for testing serums, *etc.*

Guinness, Sir Alec (1914-   ), English stage, film actor. Best known for parts in films, *eg Kind Hearts and Coronets, The Lavender Hill Mob, The Bridge on the River Kwai.* On stage, remembered for modern-dress Hamlet (1958).

Guise, Claude de Lorraine, 1st Duc de (1496-1550), French nobleman. Given title by Francis I; founder of Guise family. His daughter, Mary of Guise, married James V of Scotland and was mother of Mary Queen of Scots. His sons, **François de Lorraine, 2nd Duc de Guise** (1519-63) and **Charles de Lorraine, Cardinal de Guise** (*c* 1525-74), shared control of France during reign of Francis II, husband of Mary Queen of Scots. Led militant Catholic party which provoked civil war with Huguenots. François was assassinated. His son, **Henri de Lorraine, 3rd Duc de Guise** (1550-88), was largely responsible for Saint Bartholomew's Day Massacre. Formed Catholic League

Claude de Lorraine, Duc de Guise

(1576) to oppose Huguenots. Assassinated at king's instigation after leading revolt against HENRY III.

guitar, six-stringed, flat-backed instrument with frets on the fingerboard. Popular in 17th-18th cent., interest in guitar music renewed in 20th cent. Electric guitar, introduced to amplify the sound, has become an instrument in its own right in the hands of rock musicians.

guitar fish, any of Rhinobatidae family of shark-like rays, with long tail and broad guitar-shaped body. Species incl. spotted guitar fish, *Rhinobatus lentiginosus,* of W Atlantic.

Guitry, Sacha [Alexandre Pierre Georges] (1885-1957), French dramatist, b. Russia. Wrote light comedies, films which he directed himself, *eg Roman d'un Tricheur* (1936).

Guizot, François Pierre Guillaume (1787-1874), French statesman, historian. Controlled Louis Philippe's cabinet after 1840, premier (1847-8). Resisted reforms; his conservative policies contributed to unrest leading to Revolution of 1848.

Gujarat, state of W India. Area 190,000 sq km (72,000 sq mi); pop. 26,687,000; cap. Ahmedabad. Mainly fertile plain; incl. Kathiawar penin. and marshy Rann of Kutch. Cereals, cotton grown. Formed (1960) from N and W parts of former Bombay state.

Gujarati, Indic language in Indo-Iranian branch of Indo-European family. Leading West Indic tongue, spoken mainly in Gujarat, Maharashtra states.

Gujranwala, town of N Pakistan. Pop. 366,000. Cereals trade, textile mfg. Birthplace of Ranjit Singh, Sikh leader; centre of Sikh power until 2nd Sikh War (1848-9) with British.

Gulbenkian, Calouste Sarkis (1869-1955), British industrialist, diplomat, b. Turkey. He made a vast fortune in oil, becoming known as 'Mr Five Per Cent' through holding 5% of shares in each firm in which he was interested. He estab. the Calouste Gulbenkian Foundation, leaving it most of his fortune, incl. a valuable art collection.

Gulf Stream, warm ocean current of N Atlantic. Flows from Gulf of Mexico NE up US coast. Off Newfoundland merges with the North Atlantic Drift, tempering climate of W and N Europe.

gull, any of Laridae family of web-footed seabirds. White or grey in colour; usually nests on cliffs, rocky coasts. Black-headed gull, *Larus ridibundus,* breeds inland on marshes, moors. HERRING GULL is commonest coastal gull.

gullet, see OESOPHAGUS.

gumbo, see OKRA.

gum tree, see EUCALYPTUS.

gun, see ARTILLERY, SMALL ARMS, PISTOL, MACHINE GUN.

gunboat, originally a small, shallow-draught fighting ship built to operate on rivers. Since WWII a high-speed coastal patrol vessel.

gunpowder, an explosive made from potassium nitrate, sulphur and carbon. Believed to have been invented in 9th cent. China and introduced to Europe in 14th cent., its use as a propellant revolutionized warfare, but it is now seldom used except in fireworks.

Gunpowder Plot, see FAWKES, GUY.

Guntur, city of Andhra Pradesh, SE India. Pop. 270,000. Trade in cotton, tobacco. Ceded to British by French (1788).

guppy, *Lebistes reticulatus,* small tropical freshwater fish of South America and Caribbean. Many brightly coloured varieties bred for aquaria.

Gur or **Voltaic,** subgroup of Niger-Congo branch of Niger-Kordofanian language family. Several language groups within it, incl. Mossi (Upper Volta), Dagomba and Mamprusi (N Ghana).

Gurkha, certain predominantly Hindu tribes of Nepal. Famed for their fighting qualities, they provided the British army with 10 regiments in WWI, and in WWII fought with distinction in N Africa, Malaya and Burma.

gurnard or **sea robin,** any of Triglidae family of marine fish, with finger-like pectoral fins used for locomotion on sea bottom. Produces sound by vibrating swimbladder.

Guryev, town of USSR, SW Kazakh SSR; port on Caspian Sea near mouth of R. Ural. Pop. 114,000. Oil refining, fishing.

Gustavus I (1496-1560), king of Sweden (1523-60). Elected king after leading peasant rebellion which achieved Swedish independence from Denmark. Estab. Lutheran National Church (1527), gained economic freedom from German-dominated Hanseatic League, made crown hereditary in Vasa family.

Gustavus [II] Adolphus (1594-1632), king of Sweden (1611-32). Championed Protestant cause in THIRTY YEARS WAR. Brilliant commander, gained series of victories while campaigning in Germany (1630-2). Defeated WALLENSTEIN at Lützen, but was killed.

Gustavus V (1858-1950), king of Sweden (1907-50). Maintained Sweden's neutrality in WWI, WWII. Reign marked by further democratization and strong economy.

Gutenberg, Johann (*c* 1397-1468), German printer. Regarded as inventor of printing from movable type (*c* 1437). Entered partnership in Mainz with Johann Fust (1455) to finance publishing of *Mazarin Bible.* Lost press to Fust for defaulting in payment of debt; Fust may have completed printing of this bible (dated 1456).

Guthrie, Sir [William] Tyrone (1900-71), English actor, producer. Administrator of Old Vic and Sadler's Wells theatres (1939-45). Helped found Canada's Shakespeare Festival at Stratford, Ontario (1953).

gutta-percha, rubber-like gum produced from LATEX of several SE Asian trees of *Palaquium* and *Payena* genera. Used in electrical insulation, manufacture of golf balls.

Guyana, country of NE South America, member of British Commonwealth; formerly British Guiana. Area 215,000 sq km (83,000 sq mi); pop. 714,000; cap. Georgetown. Language: English. Religions: Hinduism, Islam, Christianity. Mainly jungle with cultivable coastal strip. Chief products sugar (demerara), rice, bauxite. Settled by Dutch in 17th cent.; British occupation (1796); independence (1966) as Guyana.

Guyenne or **Guienne,** hist. region of SW France, cap. Bordeaux. Formed, with Gascony, duchy of Aquitaine; under English rule (1154-1453).

Guyon, Jeanne Marie Bouvier de la Motte, (1648-1717), French mystic. Denounced as heretic and imprisoned for preaching doctrines of quietism.

Guys, Constantin (1802-92), French illustrator. Described by Baudelaire as the 'painter of modern life', he is remembered for drawings of all facets of Parisian life during Second Empire.

Guzmán Blanco, Antonio (1829-99), Venezuelan political leader, president (1870-88). Ruled as virtual dictator until overthrown and exiled. Encouraged public works, education and own personality cult.

Gwalior, city of Madhya Pradesh, NC India. Pop. 406,000. Indust. centre; flour milling, cotton goods. Overlooked by Hindu fort containing temples, palaces. Cap. of former princely state of Gwalior.

Gwelo, town of C Rhodesia. Pop. 55,000. Agric. market, footwear mfg., chrome and asbestos industs. Founded 1894.

Gwent, county of SE Wales. Area 1376 sq km (531 sq mi); pop. 442,000; co. town Newport. Created 1974, formerly known as Monmouthshire.

Gwyn or **Gwynne, Eleanor ('Nell')** (1650-87), English comic actress. Principally remembered as favourite and mistress of Charles II, by whom she had 2 sons.

Gwynedd, county of NW Wales. Area 3868 sq km (1493 sq mi); pop. 221,000; co. town Caernarfon.Created 1974, incl. former counties Anglesey, Caernarvonshire, Merionethshire.

gymnastics, performance of athletic exercises, whose competitive form can be traced to ancient Greek Olympics. Modern form was developed in early 19th cent. in Germany, esp. by Ludwig Jahn. First international competition held at 1896 Olympics. Events incl. vaulting and pommel horse, rings, parallel and asymmetric bars, beam and floor exercises.

Gymnophiona (gymnophions), order of limbless, worm-like amphibians. Functionless eyes hidden under skin. Found in Asia, Africa, Central America. Order formerly called Caecilia.

gymnosperm, botanical term for seed plants in which ovules are not enclosed in an ovary. They incl. cycads and conifers.

gynaecology, branch of medicine concerned with ailments specific to women, esp. those of reproductive system.

Győr (Ger. *Raab*), city of NW Hungary, on R. Raba. Pop. 107,000. River port; indust. centre. Nearby is abbey founded by St Stephen.

gypsum, hydrous calcium sulphate mineral. Soft, white or grey; found among clays and limestones. Occurs in various forms, *eg* alabaster, selenite. Used in cement, fertilizers, plaster of Paris. Major sources in US, Mexico, France, Italy.

gypsy, gipsy or **Romany,** member of nomadic tribe, believed to have originated in NW India. Entered Europe in

English gypsy

early 15th cent. Spread throughout Europe and North America but mostly found in Balkans, Spain, Italy. Have their own language (Romany) which belongs to Indo-Iranian group. Traditionally earned living by metalworking, fortune telling, horse trading. Est. numbers *c* 5 million.

gyroscope, wheel mounted so that it is free to rotate about any axis. When wheel is spun, its support may be turned in any direction without altering wheel's original plane of motion. Used in gyrocompass, as control device for guided missiles, and, in large form, as ship stabilizer.

H

Haag, Den, *see* HAGUE, THE, Netherlands.

Haakon IV (1204-63), king of Norway (1223-63). Won throne after dispute over succession. Acquired Greenland, Iceland, reformed laws, held splendid court. He died on invasion of Orkney Isls.

Haakon VII (1872-1957), king of Norway (1905-57). Second son of Frederick VIII of Denmark. Elected king after Norway achieved independence from Sweden. Led resistance to German occupation (1940-5) from Britain.

Haarlem, city of W Netherlands, on R. Spaarne, cap. of North Holland prov. Pop. 173,000. Centre of bulb, flower indust.; printing, chocolate. Sacked by Spanish 1573; centre of painting 16th-17th cents. Church (15th cent.), town hall, Frans Hals museum.

Habakkuk, prophetic book of OT, possibly written *c* 600 BC. Consists of set of poems on triumph of divine justice and mercy over evil.

habeas corpus (Lat., = you must have the body), in law, writ or order from judge to custodian of detained person requiring that person be brought before court at stated time, place, for decision on legality of his detention. In UK and US, serves as chief safeguard against illegal detention.

Haber, Fritz (1868-1934), German chemist. Known for Haber process by which ammonia is produced catalytically from hydrogen and nitrogen at high pressures; used in fertilizer manufacture. Awarded Nobel Prize for Chemistry (1918).

Habsburg or **Hapsburg,** ruling house of Austria (1282-1918), also of Hungary and Bohemia (1526-1918), Spain (1516-1700). Austria became hereditary possession under RUDOLPH, count of Habsburg. From 1438, all Holy Roman emperors but one belonged to Habsburg house. Acquired Low Countries through Maximilian I's marriage (1477) to Mary of Burgundy. Reached greatest height as world power under Emperor CHARLES V, who brought Spain into Habsburg dominions. Hungary and Bohemia incorporated (1526) through marriage of Charles' brother, FERDINAND I. Habsburgs lost some territ., *eg* Spain, through wars of succession in 18th cent. With FRANCIS II's assumption of title emperor of Austria (1804), family history became synonymous with that of Austria (AUSTRO-HUNGARIAN MONARCHY after 1867). After death of Charles I, who abdicated 1918, claims to dynasty passed to his son, Archduke Otto.

hackberry, *Celtis occidentalis,* deciduous tree of elm family. Native to E US. Has small edible fruit.

Hackney, bor. of NC Greater London, England. Pop. 217,000. Created 1965, former met. bor. Incl. Shoreditch, Stoke Newington. Hackney Marsh once highwaymen's haunt.

Haddington, town of Lothian region, SE Scotland. Pop. 7000. Former royal burgh and co. town of East Lothian. Market town; woollens mfg.

haddock, *Melanogrammus aeglefinus,* marine fish of Gadidae family, similar to cod but smaller; conspicuous black lateral line. Found on N Atlantic coasts of Europe, North America. Eaten fresh or smoked.

Hades, in Greek myth, home of the dead, ruled by Pluto (or Hades) and Persephone. Separated from living world by rivers Styx (hateful), Lethe (forgetfulness), Phlegethon (fiery), Cocytus (wailing), Acheron (woeful). Dead ferried across Styx by CHARON. Entrance was guarded by CERBERUS.

Hadhramaut, region of E Southern Yemen. Arid coastal plain extending *c* 640 km (400 mi) W-E along Gulf of Aden. Dates, millet grown.

Hadrian (AD 76–138), Roman emperor (117-38), b. Spain. Estab. Euphrates as E frontier of empire, abandoning Trajan's conquests in Mesopotamia. Adopted defensive policy, building walls in Germany and across Solway Firth in Britain (126).

hadrons, class of ELEMENTARY PARTICLES which experience the STRONG NUCLEAR INTERACTION. Incl. protons, neutrons, mesons. Hadrons are held to be composed of QUARKS, unlike LEPTONS, the other basic class of elementary particles.

Haeckel, Ernst Heinrich (1834-1919), German biologist. Principal German exponent of Darwinism; his biogenetic law, that each organism in its development repeats stages through which its ancestors passed in course of evolution, was influential in 19th cent. First to construct genealogical trees of living organisms.

haematite or **hematite** (Fe_2O_3), iron ore mineral. Consists of ferric oxide; occurs as reddish-brown earthy masses or dark grey crystals. Found among all types of rocks, often causing reddish colour. Important source of iron. Major sources in US, Canada, Australia.

haemoglobin, red colouring matter of red blood cells of vertebrates. Consists of protein (globin) combined with iron-containing haem. Carries oxygen from lungs to tissues in form of easily decomposed oxy-haemoglobin and carries carbon dioxide back to lungs.

haemophilia, condition in which one of normal blood-clotting factors is absent. Characterized by prolonged bleeding from minor injuries and spontaneous internal bleeding. Inherited only by males through mother.

haemorrhage, escape of large quantities of blood from blood vessels. Blood from cut artery is bright red and comes in spurts; blood from veins is much darker and flows smoothly.

haemorrhoids or **piles,** painful swelling of veins in region of the anus. May occur during pregnancy, as a result of constipation, *etc.* Treated by suppositories or surgery.

Hafiz, Shams al-Din Mohammed (*c* 1326-90), Persian poet. Famed for *c* 500 short lyrics on themes of love and wine.

hafnium (Hf), metallic element; at. no. 72, at. wt. 178.49. Resembles zirconium; found in zirconium minerals. Used in manufacture of tungsten filaments. Discovered (1923) by X-ray spectroscopy.

Hagen, Walter (1892-1969), American golfer. Twice won US Open championship, 4 times winner of British Open and 5 times of Professional Golfers' Association championship. Did much to popularize game by his showmanship.

Hagen, city of W West Germany, in Ruhr. Pop. 200,000. Indust. centre (iron, steel, chemicals, vehicles), formerly noted for textile mfg.

hagfish, any of Myxinidae family of saltwater CYCLOSTOMES, with worm-like body; reaches lengths of 60 cm/2 ft. Lives in mud on sea bottom, feeding on worms, crustaceans; parasitic on fish. Secretes mucus for protection.

haggada, *see* TALMUD.

Haggai, prophetic book of OT, written *c* 520 BC in Jerusalem after return from the Exile. Consists of exhortations to rebuild the Temple; gives picture of conditions in Palestine.

Haggard, Sir [Henry] Rider (1856-1925), English novelist. Known for adventure stories in African setting, esp. *King Solomon's mines* (1885), *Allan Quatermain* (1887).

Hagia Sophia, domed basilica in Istanbul, built (532-7) as Christian church for Justinian by Anthemius of Tralles and

Isidore of Miletus. A masterpiece of Byzantine art, it was converted into a mosque following Turkish conquest (1453). Now a museum.

Hague, The (*Den Haag, 's-Gravenhage*), city of W Netherlands, cap. of South Holland prov., seat of Dutch govt. Pop. 525,000. Site of 1899, 1907 Peace Conferences; seat of International Court of Justice (1913). Residence of Stadholders 17th-18th cents. Buildings incl. Binnenhof (legislature), Mauritshuis (art gallery).

Hague Conferences, two international peace conferences held 1899, 1907. Failed to achieve aim of arms reduction, but set up arbitration procedures, conventions respecting rules of war. First conference estab. Hague Tribunal, Permanent Court of Arbitration on international disputes. Superseded (1945) by International Court of Justice.

Hahn, Kurt [Matthias Robert Martin] (1886-1974), British educator, b. Germany. Best known for association with Outward Bound schools, stressing training for leadership through physical hardship, danger. Estab. Gordonstoun School (1933).

Hahn, Otto (1879-1968), German physical chemist. Discovered several radioactive isotopes, incl. protactinium (with Lise Meitner). Awarded Nobel Prize for Chemistry (1944) for inducing nuclear fission in uranium by bombardment with neutrons.

Haifa, port of NW Israel, on Mediterranean. Pop. 335,000. Indust. centre; oil refining, chemicals, textiles. Rail jct. and international airport. Seat of Technion (Israel Institute of Technology).

Haig, Douglas Haig, 1st Earl (1861-1928), British army officer, b. Scotland. Commanded 1st Army Corps in France (1914); commander-in-chief of British forces (1915-17). His costly strategy of prolonged trench warfare provoked criticism, but he was architect of final victory.

hail, hard pellets of ice, often associated with thunderstorms. Nucleus, *eg* dust particle, is carried upward by air current until layer of ice coats it; gathers further layers on descent. Hailstones can cause damage, *eg* to crops, property, aircraft.

Haile Selassie

Haile Selassie, orig. Tafari Makonnen (1891-1975), emperor of Ethiopia (1930-74). Led resistance to Italian invasion (1935), fled to England (1936). Regained throne (1941). Leader of pan-African movement. Deposed (1974) by military coup.

Hainan, isl. of Kwangtung prov., S China. Area *c* 33,670 sq km (13,000 sq mi); pop. 2,800,000; main port Hoihow. Produces timber, rubber, coffee, iron ore. Large naval base at Yulin.

Hainaut, region and prov. of SW Belgium. Main rivers Sambre, Sheldt; main towns Mons, Charleroi. Fertile in N; important coalmining, steel industs. in S.

Haiphong, chief seaport of NE North Vietnam. Pop. 390,000. Naval base near mouth of R. Red. Commercial, indust. centre; cement, textile, chemical industs. Heavily bombed by US in Vietnam war.

hair, filamentous outgrowth of the skin, consisting mainly of keratin. Grows from small depression (follicle) at whose side is a sebaceous gland, providing oil for skin. Hair is characteristic of mammals.

Haiti, republic of West Indies, occupying W HISPANIOLA. Area 27,713 sq km (10,700 sq mi); pop. 4,315,000, mainly Negro; cap. Port-au-Prince. Languages: French, Creole dialect. Religion: RC. Consists of 2 penins and 2 isls. Largely wooded mountains; tropical climate. Subsistence agric.; commercial crops incl. coffee, sugar, sisal; timber, bauxite. Spanish ceded possession in 17th cent. to French sugar planters. Independence 1804; hist. ruled by despots, esp. Duvalier (1957-71).

hake, marine food fish of Merlucciidae family, related to the cod; long-bodied, with projecting lower jaw. Species incl. European *Merluccius merluccius,* now scarce through overfishing.

Hakka, see CHINESE.

Hakluyt, Richard (*c* 1552-1616), English geographer. Encouraged exploration, esp. in North America; translated foreign accounts of journeys, voyages. Best known as author of *The Principal Navigations, Voyages, Traffics and Discoveries of the English Nation* (1 vol. 1589, 3 vols. 1600).

Hakodate, port of Japan, on Tsugaru Str., SW Hokkaido isl. Pop. 242,000. Shipbuilding, fishing indust.

halakah, see TALMUD.

halberd, combined spear and battleaxe, of German origin, used by foot-soldier in the 15th–17th cents.

Halberstadt, town of WC East Germany. Pop. 46,000. Food processing, machinery, textiles. Cathedral, town hall (both 14th cent.).

Halcyone, (Gk.,= kingfisher), in Greek myth, daughter of Aeolus. Drowned herself in sea when husband died in shipwreck. Out of pity, the gods turned the couple into kingfishers and forbade the winds to blow during the 'halcyon days' of their breeding season at the winter solstice.

Haldane, John Scott (1860-1936), British scientist, b. Scotland. Studied regulation of breathing by carbon dioxide in blood. Investigated physiological effects of working in mines and of deep-sea diving. His son, **J[ohn] B[urdon] S[anderson] Haldane** (1892-1964) worked in genetics and wrote popular scientific essays.

Hale, George Ellery (1868-1938), American astronomer. Founded and directed Yerkes, Mt. Wilson and Mt. Palomar observatories. Invented spectroheliograph, and found magnetic fields in sunspots.

Hale, Sir Matthew (1609-76), English jurist. Chief justice of Court of King's Bench (1671), author of many works on criminal law, *eg Pleas of the Crown* (1678).

Halévy, Jacques François (1799-1862), French composer. Known mainly for his opera *La Juive.* Taught Bizet, who married his daughter.

half-life, time taken for half the atoms of a radioactive substance to disintegrate. Uranium 238 has half-life of 4.5 × 10^9 years.

half-tone, see PHOTOENGRAVING.

Haliburton, Thomas Chandler (1796-1865), Canadian author, jurist. Created Yankee 'Sam Slick' in satirical sketches in *The Novascotian* journal, later collected as *The Clockmaker* (1836).

halibut, *Hippoglossus hippoglossus,* largest flatfish, reaching lengths of 2.4 m/8 ft; found in N Atlantic. Popular food fish. Related species in N Pacific.

Halicarnassus, ancient city of SW Asia Minor (modern Turkey). Site of mausoleum, built (*c* 350 BC) in memory of King Mausolus of Caria by his wife. White marble structure, decorated with sculpture, it was one of Seven Wonders of the World.

Halifax, Charles Montagu, Earl of (1661-1715), English statesman. Instrumental in estab. national debt (1692), Bank of England (1694). Chancellor of the exchequer (1694), first lord of the treasury (1697-9).

Halifax, Edward Frederick Lindley Wood, 1st Earl of (1881-1959), British statesman. Viceroy of India (1926-31). As foreign secretary (1938-40) instrumental in 'appeasement' policy which led to Munich Pact (1938).

Halifax, cap. of Nova Scotia, Canada; largest port in Maritimes; Canada's principal ice-free Atlantic port. Pop. 122,000. Railway terminus. Shipbuilding, oil refining, food processing (fish). Founded 1749 as naval base; important during both WWs. Has Citadel fortress, Dalhousie Univ. (1818).

Halifax, co. bor. of West Yorkshire met. county, N England. Pop. 91,000. Woollens, carpets mfg. Former centre of Flemish immigration.

Hall, Charles Martin (1863-1914), American chemist. Independently of Héroult, devised process for large-scale manufacture of aluminium by electrolysis of alumina dissolved in cryolite.

Hall, Edwin Herbert (1855-1938), American physicist. Discovered Hall effect, in which an electric potential is produced across a current-carrying wire by application of magnetic field perpendicular to current.

Hall, [Margaret] Radclyffe (1886-1943), English author. Known for controversial novel *The Well of Loneliness* (1928), a sympathetic treatment of female homosexuality.

Halle, town of SC East Germany, on R. Saale. Pop. 254,000. Railway jct.; salt (saline springs), lignite mining. Former Hanseatic League member; univ. (1694). Birthplace of Handel.

Edmund Halley

Halley, Edmund (1656-1742), English astronomer. Astronomer Royal after 1720. Studied motion of comets and predicted return of comet of 1682 (Halley's comet); it returns every 75 or 76 years (expected again in 1986). Indicated how transit of Venus could be used to determine solar parallax. Financed publication of Newton's *Principia*.

Halloween, eve of ALL SAINTS' DAY. Esp. celebrated in countries with strong Celtic influence; prob. derives from pre-Christian feasts to mark beginning of winter. Modern customs incl. bobbing for apples, telling tales of witches, ghosts, 'trick-or-treat' (US).

Hallstatt, village of C Austria. Salt mined from prehist. times. Site of late Bronze, early Iron Age remains; given name to Hallstatt culture in archaeology.

hallucination, false sensory impression which invents or misinterprets external phenomena. May occur during schizophrenia or be induced by certain drugs, *eg* mescaline, cannabis or LSD.

Halmahera or **Djailolo,** isl. of Indonesia, in N Moluccas. Area *c* 18,200 sq km (7000 sq mi). Mountainous, with active volcanoes. Produces nutmeg, sago.

halogens, in chemistry, the 5 elements fluorine, chlorine, bromine, iodine and astatine (unstable). Chemically similar, monovalent and highly reactive.

Hals, Frans (*c* 1580-1666), Dutch genre and portrait painter. His bold brushstrokes give impression of gaiety to individual portraits, *eg Laughing Cavalier*; captures fleeting expressions in his large groups of archers and musketeers.

Halsey, William Frederick (1882-1959), American naval officer. Commander of Third Fleet during WWII, defeated Japanese off the Solomons (Nov. 1942). Admiral of the fleet (1945-7).

Hälsingborg or **Helsingborg,** town of S Sweden, on Oresund. Pop. 82,000. Port, ferry service to Helsingör (Denmark). Copper refining; textiles. Contested by Denmark until 1710.

Halsted, William Stewart (1852-1922), American surgeon. Pioneer in use of cocaine as local anaesthetic. Initiated use of rubber gloves in surgery.

Hama, city of WC Syria, on R. Orontes. Pop. 137,000. Market centre; textile mfg. Noted for enormous wooden waterwheels used for irrigation. Ancient city of Hittite origin, often mentioned in Bible as Hamath.

Hamadan (anc. *Ecbatana*), city of WC Iran. Pop. 141,000. Produces rugs, leather goods. Hist. cap. of Media. Has tomb of philosopher Avicenna.

Hamamatsu, indust. city of Japan, SC Honshu isl. Pop. 432,000. Musical instrument, motorcycle and textile mfg.

Hamburg, city of N West Germany, on R. Elbe, cap. of Hamburg state. Pop. 1,782,000. Major port (outport at Cuxhaven), transshipment trade, shipbuilding, chemicals industs.; cultural, broadcasting centre. Founded by Charlemagne, archbishopric from 834. Alliance (1241) with Lübeck formed basis of Hanseatic League. Rapid growth in 19th cent., incorporated Altona 1938. Severely damaged in 1842 fire, WWII. Birthplace of Brahms, Mendelssohn.

Hameln (Eng. *Hamelin*), town of NW West Germany, on R. Weser. Pop. 49,000. Food processing indust. Scene of the legend of the Pied Piper, depicted in 'Ratcatcher's House' (built 1603).

Hamersley Range, mountain range of NW Western Australia. Highest peak Mt. Bruce (1226 m/4024 ft). Extensive high-quality iron ore deposits.

Hamilcar Barca (d. 228 BC), Carthaginian soldier. Commander in Sicily during First Punic War (247-241), but was defeated and forced to withdraw. Virtual dictator of Carthage after 237. Led successful invasion of Spain (237-228) but was killed. Father of Hannibal.

Hamilton, Alexander (1755-1804), American statesman, b. West Indies. Instrumental in ratification of Constitution esp. through contribution to *Federalist Papers*. Dominated President Washington's cabinet as 1st secretary of the treasury (1789-95), pursued centralization of finances, stabilization of economy. Leader of FEDERALIST PARTY. Supported Jefferson in presidential ballot (1800) against AARON BURR, who later killed him in duel.

Hamilton, Lady Emma, née Lyon (1765-1815), English courtesan. Became mistress, later wife (1791), of Sir William Hamilton, British ambassador to Naples. Became mistress (1798) to Horatio Nelson, bearing (1801) him a daughter. Died in poverty.

Hamilton, Iain Ellis (1922-), Scottish composer. Has written abstract works in 12-note technique. Compositions incl. operas, concertos, *Sinfonia* for 2 orchestras.

Hamilton, James Hamilton, 1st Duke of (1606-49), Scottish nobleman. As adviser to Charles I on Scottish affairs, attempted to appease Covenanters; failed and led army (1639) against them. Fought for Charles at Preston (1648), captured and executed.

Hamilton, Sir William (1788-1856), Scottish philosopher. Influential in introducing Kant and Hegel into British thought.

Hamilton, Sir William Rowan (1805-65), Irish mathematician. Known for his development of quaternions, noncommutative algebra used in geometric problems. His work in dynamics was influential in later quantum mechanics.

Hamilton, cap. and chief port of Bermuda, on Bermuda isl. Pop. 2000. Tourist resort. Founded 1790; succeeded St George as cap. (1815).

Hamilton, port of S Ontario, Canada; at W end of L. Ontario. Pop. 309,000. Railway jct.; mfg. centre; steel works, auto and rail machinery. Founded 1813. Has McMaster Univ. (1930).

Hamilton, town of N North Isl., New Zealand, on Waikato R. Pop. 75,000. Agric. market, food processing; agric. research stations.

Hamilton, town of Strathclyde region, WC Scotland. Pop. 46,000. Coalmining area; engineering, textiles industs. Rudolf Hess landed nearby (1941).

Hamilton, river of E Canada, *see* CHURCHILL (2).

Hamm, town of W West Germany, on R. Lippe. Pop. 71,000. Railway jct., marshalling yards; coalmining, iron, steel. Badly damaged in WWII.

Hammarskjöld, Dag (1905-61), Swedish statesman. As secretary-general of the UN (1953-61) increased its influence. Influential in Suez Crisis (1956), active in attempts to solve Congo problem (1960-1) until his death in plane crash. Nobel Peace Prize (posthumously awarded, 1961).

Hammerfest, town of Kvaloy Isl., N Norway, most northerly in Europe. Pop. 7000. Ice-free port, whaling, sealing. German naval base in WWII, severely damaged.

hammerhead shark, any of genus *Sphyrna* of medium-sized sharks that have hammer-like lobes on head, with eyes and nostrils at extremities.

Hammersmith, bor. of W Greater London, England. Pop. 185,000. Created 1965, former met. bor. Incl. Fulham. Olympia, White City stadium.

Hammerstein, Oscar (1895-1960), American librettist, lyricist. Famous for musicals created with composer Richard Rodgers, *eg Oklahoma, Carousel, South Pacific.*

Hammett, Dashiell (1894-1961), American author. Known for economically written 'tough guy' detective novels incl. *The Maltese Falcon, The Thin Man* (1932).

Hammond, John Hays (1855-1936), American mining engineer. Worked with Rhodes on Rand gold mines in South Africa. Involved in Jameson raid (1895); captured and imprisoned. Returned to US (1900).

Hammurabi (*fl* 18th cent. BC), king of Babylon (*c* 1792-1750 BC). Founded ancient Babylonian empire. Best remembered for his legal code, found carved in cuneiform on a diorite column (1901).

Hampden, John (*c* 1594-1643), English statesman. Became focus of resentment against Charles I through imprisonment for refusal (1636) to pay 'ship money' tax. One of five MPs whose attempted arrest by Charles (1642) was a cause of Civil War.

Hampshire, county of S England. Area 3772 sq km (1456 sq mi); pop. 1,422,000; co. town Winchester. Incl. New Forest; downs in N, SE; fertile lowland. Crops incl. cereals, root crops; livestock rearing. Indust. in ports of Southampton, Portsmouth.

Hampstead, part of Camden, NC Greater London, England. Former met. bor. until 1965. Hampstead Heath park, Parliament Hill, famous inns. Long favoured by artists, authors.

Hampton, port of SE Virginia, US; on Hampton Roads harbour. Pop. 121,000. Oyster, fish packing, export. Settled 1610.

Hampton Court, English palace on R. Thames, built by Cardinal Wolsey (1514) as his private residence. Later passed to Henry VIII and became royal residence. Partially rebuilt by Christopher Wren. Site of conference (1604) authorizing King James Bible.

hamster, rat-like burrowing rodent of Europe and W Asia, with internal cheek pouches to carry food. Common hamster, *Cricetus cricetus,* is grey or brown. Golden hamster, *Mesocricetus auratus,* is popular pet; also used for medical research.

Hamsun, Knut Pederson (1859-1952), Norwegian novelist. Work, *eg Hunger* (1899), *The Growth of the Soil* (1917), affirms elemental values of nature, condemns modern life. Awarded Nobel Prize for Literature (1920).

Han, dynasty of China (202 BC-AD 220), broken by Hsin dynasty (AD 9-25). Noted for territ. expansion and artistic development; ink and paper came into use, making of porcelain began. Buddhism introduced.

Han, river of EC China. Length *c* 1130 km (700 mi). Rises in Shensi prov., flows E to join Yangtze at Wuhan. Navigable *c* 480 km (300 mi) upstream. Fertile valley.

Hancock, John (1737-93), American revolutionary statesman. First signer of Declaration of Independence (1776). President of Continental Congress (1775-7).

hand, prehensile extremity of arm. Human hand contains 27 bones: 8 carpal bones in wrist, 5 long metacarpals, and 14 phalanges forming the fingers and thumb (3 in each finger, 2 in thumb).

handball, eleven-a-side team game played by catching, passing and throwing an inflated round ball. Aim is to score by throwing ball into goal. First played in Germany, *c* 1890. Olympic event since 1932.

George Frideric Handel

Handel, George Frideric (1685-1759), German composer. Settled in England under patronage of George I, having studied in Italy. Tried to introduce Italian opera to London, then turned to oratorio. Numerous works incl. *concerti grossi,* keyboard suites, oratorios *Messiah* (1742), *Judas Maccabaeus,* miscellaneous orchestral music, *eg Water Music.* Greatly influenced English choral tradition.

Hangchow, cap. of Chekiang prov., E China. Pop. 1,100,000. Port on R. Tsientang. Famous for silk weaving. Indust. centre, producing iron and steel, chemicals, *etc.* Cap. of S China during 12th and 13th cent., it was centre of learning and trade. Destroyed (1861) by Taiping rebels.

Hanging Garden of Babylon, terraced building planted with gardens, constructed by Nebuchadnezzar II (d. 562 BC). One of the Seven Wonders of the World.

Hanko (Swed. *Hangö*), town of SW Finland, on Gulf of Bothnia. Pop. 10,000. Port, resort. Hanko penin. leased to USSR as naval base 1940-4.

Hankow, *see* WUHAN.

Hanna, Marcus Alonzo (Mark) (1837-1904), American capitalist, politician. Active in politics, urging economic policy favourable to big business. Supported McKinley for governor of Ohio (1891, 1893), ran his presidential campaign (1896). Dominated Republican party until death.

Hannibal (247-182 BC), Carthaginian soldier. Commander in Spain (221), his capture of Saguntum led Rome to declare war on Carthage (218). Crossed Alps to invade Italy; defeated Romans at L. Trasimene (217) and Cannae (216), but had insufficient support to capture Rome. Recalled (203) to defend Carthage, defeated by Scipio Africanus at Zama (202). After peace, became ruler of Carthage; Romans forced him to flee to Syria (196). Took poison in Bithynia to avoid being surrendered to the Romans.

Hanno (*fl* 500 BC), Carthaginian navigator. Founded colonies in Morocco and explored coast of NW Africa.

Hanoi, cap. of North Vietnam. Pop. 920,000. Port on R. Red; rail jct.; agric., indust., cultural centre. Hist. cap. of Annam and Indo-China. Heavily damaged in US air raids during Vietnam war.

Hanover (*Hannover*), city of N West Germany, on R. Leine, cap. of Lower Saxony. Pop. 517,000. Indust., commercial centre; univ. (1879). Hanseatic League member from 1386; cap. of electorate of Hanover from 1692 (electors became kings of UK from 1714). Badly damaged in WWII.

Hanover, House of, British royal house. Succession claimed through Sophia, granddaughter of James I and wife of Elector Ernest Augustus of Hanover. ACT OF SETTLEMENT (1701) made their son, George, heir to Queen Anne, thus excluding Catholic Stuart line. Hanoverian monarchs were George I, II, III and IV and William IV. Lost right to British crown with Victoria (1837) because of Salic law of succession barring women from throne of Hanover.

Hansard, popular name for official report of British parliamentary proceedings. Luke Hansard began (1774) printing accounts of debates. Made official in 1803, remained in family to 1889. Now pub. by Her Majesty's Stationery Office.

Hanseatic League, medieval trading organization of N German towns. From groups of individual *hansa*, and association of merchants trading to foreign countries, league became a great confederation by 14th cent., with companies at most seaports on the Baltic and North seas. Provided trading privileges and protection of its own army. Declined steadily until dissolution in 17th cent.

Hanukkah or **Festival of Lights,** Jewish festival commemorating the rededication of the Temple by Judas Maccabaeus in 165 BC. Celebrated for 8 days in December with the lighting of special candles.

Hanyang, see WUHAN.

Hapsburg, see HABSBURG.

hara-kiri, traditional Japanese honourable suicide. Involves ritual self-disembowelment with dagger. Originally practised among warrior class to avoid dishonour of capture; *c* 1500 became privileged alternative to execution. Still occasionally practised, *eg* by officers at end of WWII. Also known as *seppuku*.

Harappa, one of the twin centres of the INDUS VALLEY CIVILIZATION.

Harar or **Harrar,** town of EC Ethiopia. Pop. 42,000. Trade in coffee, cereals, hides. Walled town founded 14th cent.; hist. centre of Ethiopian Islam, has many mosques.

Harbin, cap. of Heilungkiang prov., NE China. Pop. 2,750,000. Main port on R. Sungari; major jct. on Chinese Eastern and S Manchurian railways. Railway engineering; aircraft, tractor mfg. Developed by Russians (1896-1924).

Hardanger Fjord, inlet of North Sea, SW Norway. Length *c* 183 km (114 mi); many mountains, waterfalls. Tourist area.

Harden, Sir Arthur (1865-1940), English biochemist. Shared Nobel Prize for Chemistry (1929) for investigations into role of enzymes in sugar fermentation; showed that inorganic phosphates were involved in process.

Hardenberg, Friedrich von, see NOVALIS.

Hardenberg, Karl August, Fürst von (1750-1822), Prussian statesman. Foreign minister (1804-6), chancellor (1810-22). Followed STEIN's reforms, *eg* abolition of trade monopolies, emancipation of Jews. Influenced Frederick William III to join alliance (1813) against Napoleon.

Hardie, [James] Keir (1856-1915), British socialist, b. Scotland. Founder, 1st president (1893-1900) of Independent Labour Party. Influential in formation (1906) of Labour Party, leading it in House of Commons (1906-7).

Harding, Warren Gamaliel (1865-1923), American statesman, president (1921-3). Admin. known for inefficiency, corruption. Died before exposure of TEAPOT DOME SCANDAL.

hardness, in mineralogy, resistance a substance offers to being scratched. Measured by Mohs scale ranging from softest (1) to hardest (10), each number being represented

Keir Hardie

by a standard mineral, *eg* calcite (3), topaz (8), diamond (10).

hard water, water containing dissolved calcium and magnesium salts which interfere with lathering and cleansing properties of soap. Fatty acids in soap form insoluble precipitates (scum) with these salts. Temporary hardness, caused by dissolved bicarbonates, can be removed by heating; permanent hardness, caused by sulphates, is removed by addition of soda (sodium carbonate) or ZEOLITE.

Thomas Hardy

Hardy, Thomas (1840-1928), English novelist, poet. Novels, set in native 'Wessex' (SW England), *eg Far from the Madding Crowd* (1874), *The Mayor of Casterbridge* (1886), *Tess of the D'Urbervilles* (1891), *Jude the Obscure* (1896), reflect vision of human possibilities destroyed through malevolent destiny. Also wrote poetry, incl. *The Dynasts* (1903-8).

Hare, William, see BURKE, WILLIAM.

hare, swift rabbit-like mammal, but non-burrowing and with longer ears and hind legs than rabbit. Formerly classed as rodent, now put with rabbits in order Lagomorpha. Species incl. European brown hare, *Lepus europaeus,* and mountain hare, *L. timidus,* whose coat turns white in winter.

harebell, see BLUEBELL.

harelip, congenital cleft of one or both lips, but usually only the upper one; often occurs with associated cleft palate. May be corrected by early surgery.

Harfleur, town of Normandy, N France, at mouth of R. Seine. Pop. 16,000. Major French port until 16th cent., declined due to silting. Scene of successful siege (1415) by Henry V of England.

Hargeisa, town of NW Somalia. Pop. 50,000. Trading centre for nomadic herdsmen. Cap. of British Somaliland (1941-60).

Hargreaves, James (c 1720-78), English engineer. Built 'spinning jenny' (1764) enabling one person to spin several threads simultaneously.

Haringey, bor. of N Greater London, England. Pop. 237,000. Created 1965 from mun. bors. of Middlesex. Incl. Highgate.

Hariri, Abu Mohammed al-Qasim (1054-1122), Arabian writer. Collection of 50 *maqamat*, adventure tales in rhymed prose, have remained popular to present day.

Harlech, village of Gwynedd, W Wales. Seaside resort. Former co. town of Merionethshire. Has ruined 13th cent. castle.

Harlem, *see* NEW YORK CITY.

Harlequin, stock character of COMMEDIA DELL'ARTE, became buffoon of French, then English pantomime. Traditionally wears mask, particoloured tights.

Harley, Robert, 1st Earl of Oxford (1661-1724), British statesman. Tory lord treasurer (1711-14), became chief minister to Queen Anne. Instrumental in Peace of Utrecht (1713). Lost office to St John (Bolingbroke), imprisoned (1715) over dealings with Jacobites. Manuscript collection, Harleian Library, now in British Museum.

Harlow, Jean, orig. Harlean Carpentier (1911-37), American film actress. Famous as wise-cracking platinum blonde of 1930s, Hollywood's 1st great sex symbol. Films incl. *Public Enemy* (1931), *Red Dust* (1932), *Bombshell* (1933).

harmonica or **mouth organ,** simple musical instrument consisting of enclosed box containing tuned metal reeds with holes through which air is blown or sucked. Originated in China, not reaching the West until early 1800s.

harmonium, small organ in which the sound is produced by forcing air through reeds. Pressure is raised by pumping bellows with the feet.

harmony, in music, the combining of notes to form CHORDS in ways that are musically correct or interesting. It is a dominant feature of Western music, often of great emotional significance, but much less important in Eastern music.

Harmsworth, Alfred, *see* NORTHCLIFFE, ALFRED CHARLES WILLIAM HARMSWORTH, VISCOUNT.

Harnack, Adolf von (1851-1930), German theologian. Known for *The History of Dogma* (1886-90), an influential study of Christian theology.

harness racing or **trotting,** horse race in which horse pulls 2-wheeled sulky in which driver sits. Two forms of standard bred horse used: trotter, which raises alternately diagonally opposite hind and foreleg; pacer, which raises left legs together, then right. Popular in North America since 19th cent. and in Australia since 1920s.

Harold (c 1022-66), king of England (1066). Son of GODWIN, was recognized as heir to throne by Edward the Confessor, but had earlier been forced to swear to support William of Normandy's claim. On death of Edward, defeated and killed brother Tostig and Harold III of Norway, who invaded N England, but was defeated and killed himself by William at Hastings.

Harold Harefoot (d. 1040), king of England (1037-40). Bastard son of Canute, he claimed throne on father's death (1035), and was elected king after conflict with half-brother Harthacanute.

Harold [III] Hardrada (d. 1066), king of Norway (1046-66). Ruled jointly with Magnus I for a year, became sole ruler on Magnus's death. Joined with Tostig to invade England (1066), and was killed by Harold of England at Stamford Bridge.

harp, stringed musical instrument, with triangular frame; player plucks the strings. Modern orchestral harp has range of 6½ octaves and each string can play any of 3 notes at the touch of a pedal.

Harpers Ferry, small resort town of E West Virginia, US; at confluence of Potomac and Shenandoah rivers. Pop. 430. Site of John Brown's raid on military arsenal (1859). Captured by Confederate forces under Jackson (1862).

Harpies, in Greek myth, repellent birds with the faces of women. Associated with the powers of the underworld and believed to carry off people who disappeared without trace.

harpsichord, string keyboard musical instrument, in which the strings are plucked mechanically. Popular from about 1550 to 1800, but then replaced by the piano. Now revived for authentic performances of Baroque music.

Harrar, *see* HARAR, Ethiopia.

harrier, hawk of genus *Circus*. Hen harrier, *C. cyaneus*, once common in Europe but now rare, is also called marsh hawk.

Harrington, James (1611-77), English political theorist. Wrote utopian *Commonwealth of Oceana* (1656), envisaging power resting with landed gentry. Influenced democratic ideas in pre-revolutionary America.

Harris, Sir Arthur Travers (1892-), British airforce officer. Acquired the nickname 'Bomber Harris' as commander-in-chief of Bomber Command (1942-5), in which capacity he organized the saturation raids on German indust. centres.

Harris, Joel Chandler (1848-1908), American author. Known for 'Brer Rabbit' Negro folk collections in authentic dialect, eg *Uncle Remus: His Songs and His Sayings* (1880). Also wrote novels.

Harris, *see* LEWIS WITH HARRIS, Scotland.

Harrisburg, cap. of Pennsylvania, US; on Susquehanna R. Pop. 68,000. Railway jct.; in coal mining region. Steel, bricks, clothing mfg. Settled c 1715.

Harrison, William Henry (1773-1841), American statesman, president (1841). Opened Indiana, Ohio to white settlement while governor of Indiana Territ. (1800-12). Defeated TECUMSEH at Tippecanoe (1811). Whig presidential candidate (1840), died after month in office.

Harrogate, mun. bor. of North Yorkshire, N England. Pop. 62,000. Spa from 1596; holiday centre.

Harrow-on-the-Hill or **Harrow,** bor. of NW Greater London, England. Pop. 203,000. Created 1965 from former mun. bor. Has 11th cent. church on hill; public school (1571).

Hart, Basil Henry Liddell, *see* LIDDELL HART.

Harte, [Francis] Brett (1836-1902), American short story writer. Known for stories of prospectors, gamblers, prostitutes collected in *The Luck of Roaring Camp* (1870), *Mrs Skagg's Husbands* (1873).

hartebeest, large red-brown African antelope with short curved horns. Cape hartebeest, *Alcelaphus caama,* found in S Africa.

Hartford, cap. of Connecticut, US; on Connecticut R. Pop. 158,000; state's largest city. Commercial, insurance centre. Industs. incl. firearms, typewriters mfg. Settled 1635-6.

Hartford Foundation, fund estab. (1942) by John A. and George L. Hartford to finance medical research. Initiated use of various lifesaving machines in treatment of heart and kidney disease.

Harthacanute (d. 1042), king of Denmark (1035-42) and of England (1040-2). Son of Canute, gained English throne on death of Harold Harefoot, leaving it to Edward the Confessor.

Hartlepool, co. bor. of Cleveland, NE England, on Hartlepool Bay. Pop. 97,000. United with West Hartlepool 1967. Fishing, shipbuilding industs. Grew around 7th cent. convent.

Hartley, L[eslie] P[oles] (1895-1972), English novelist. Works, eg *Eustace and Hilda* (trilogy pub. 1958), *The Go-Between* (1953), depict innocence overwhelmed by society and experience.

Hartmann, [Karl Robert] Eduard von (1842-1906), German philosopher. Influenced by Hegel, Schopenhauer. Wrote *Philosophy of the Unconscious* (1869) on conflict between impulse and reason.

Hartmann, Nicolai (1882-1950), German philosopher. Worked on metaphysical problems. Believed ontology to be primary study of philosophy.

Hartmann von Aue (c 1170-c 1220), German poet. Wrote epics *Erec* and *Iwein*, based on CHRÉTIEN DE TROYES, 1st on ARTHURIAN LEGEND in German. Also wrote didactic religious poems, lyrics.

Harun al-Rashid (c 763-809), Abbasid caliph of Baghdad. Faced by many insurrections in the empire throughout his reign, he lost all but nominal control of N Africa. Made Baghdad centre of Arab culture; idealized in *Thousand and One Nights.*

Harvard University, Cambridge, Massachusetts, US. Oldest American coll. (founded 1636), became univ. 1780. Affiliated with Radcliffe Coll. for women; graduate and professional schools are coeducational. Noted for business studies, law, also has great library and Fogg Museum of Art.

harvestman, any of order Phalangida of spider-like arachnids with 8 long thin legs, small body. Diet of insects, plant juices.

harvest mouse, *Micromys minutus,* small red-brown European field mouse that builds its nest among stalks of plants, esp. growing grain.

William Harvey

Harvey, William (1578-1657), English anatomist, physiologist. Discovered circulation of blood; demonstrated flow of blood from heart through arteries and back to heart through veins. Pub. findings in *Exercitatio anatomica de motu cordis et sanguinis in animalibus* (1628). Pioneer in description of embryology of chicks.

Harwich, mun. bor. of Essex, SE England. Pop. 15,000. Port; ferry services to N Europe.

Haryana, state of N India. Area c 44,000 sq km (17,000 sq mi); pop. 9,971,000; cap. Chandigarh. Mainly flat, dry and barren. Formed (1966) from Hindi-speaking parts of Punjab.

Harz Mountains, forested range of C Germany, in both German republics. Highest peak BROCKEN. Former silver, lead mining. Tourism (mineral springs).

Hasdrubal (d. 207 BC), Carthaginian soldier. Took command in Spain after his brother, Hannibal, invaded Italy. After long campaign against the Scipios, crossed Alps with reinforcements for Hannibal. Defeated and killed at Metaurus.

Hašek, Jaroslav (1883-1923), Czech author. Known for classic satire of military bureaucracy, *The Good Soldier Svejk* (1923).

hashish, see HEMP.

Hasidism, beliefs of Jewish mystical movement founded (18th cent.) in Poland by BAAL-SCHEM-TOV. Spread rapidly among uneducated; still exerts some influence in Jewish life and also in modern Christian theology through MARTIN BUBER.

Hassall, John (1868-1948), English artist. Famous for his posters, *eg* the 'Skegness is so bracing' poster which featured the Jolly Fisherman.

Hassan II (1929-), king of Morocco (1961-). Introduced constitutional monarchy (1963); survived coups, assassination attempts. Led civilian 'army' in march into N of Spanish Sahara (1975) to estab. Morocco's claims to territ.

Hasselt, town of NE Belgium, on R. Demer, cap. of Limburg prov. Pop. 39,000. Brewing, distilling. Scene of Dutch victory (1831) over Belgians.

Hassi Messaoud, town of EC Algeria, in Sahara desert. Oil producing centre, refinery built 1961. Pipelines to Bejaïa, Oran, Algiers.

Hastings, James (1852-1922), Scottish biblical scholar. Known for *Dictionary of the Bible* (1898-1904) and *Encyclopaedia of Religion and Ethics* (1908-22).

Hastings, Warren (1732-1818), British colonial administrator. First governor-general of India (1773-1784). In spite of financial, admin., judicial reforms and strengthening British position in India, he met opposition in Britain. After return (1785), impeached (1787) on charges of malpractice. Acquitted (1795), made privy councillor (1814).

Hastings, co. bor. of East Sussex, SE England. Pop. 72,000. Seaside resort. Norman victory over Saxons nearby at Battle (1066). Chief of Cinque Ports.

Hastings, town of E North Isl., New Zealand. Pop. 30,000. Centre of fruit and vegetable growing, dairying region. Settled from 1864; rebuilt after 1931 earthquake.

Hastings, Battle of, confrontation between invading William, duke of Normandy (William the Conqueror), and Harold, king of England (14 Oct. 1066). Fought at Senlac Hill, near Hastings, England, until Harold was killed. First, most decisive and celebrated victory of Norman Conquest.

Hathaway, Ann (1556-1623), English farmer's daughter. Married Shakespeare in 1582.

Hatshepsut (d. c 1470 BC), Egyptian queen. Held real power during reigns of Thutmose II and Thutmose III. Concentrated on maintaining peace and building economy. Built great temple at Deir el-Bahri, near Thebes.

Hatteras, Cape, promontory of E North Carolina, US; on isl. between Pamlico Sound and Atlantic. Hazard to shipping; lighthouse (1798).

Hauptmann, Gerhart (1862-1946), German author. Early plays, *eg Before Dawn* (1889), *The Weavers* (1892), estab. German naturalism. Later works reflect more mystical interest, esp. *The Sunken Bell* (1896); novel, *The Fool in Christ, Emanuel Quint* (1910). Awarded Nobel Prize for Literature (1912).

Hauraki Gulf, inlet of Pacific Ocean, NE North Isl., New Zealand. Great Barrier Isl. near mouth; Auckland stands on SW shore. Popular fishing, water sport area.

Hausa, people of N Nigeria, S Niger. Farmers and far-ranging traders. Hausa languages are basically Hamitic but people mainly Negroid. Predominantly Moslem.

Haushofer, Karl (1869-1946), German geographer. Originator of geopolitics of Nazi expansionism. Close associate of Hitler. Committed suicide.

Haussmann, Georges Eugène, Baron (1809-91), French politician, city planner. Prefect of the Seine (1853-70). Reshaped Paris; laid out boulevards and parks (*eg* Bois de Boulogne), improved water supply and sewage system.

Havana (*La Habana*), cap. of Cuba, on Gulf of Mexico. Pop. 1,131,000. Port with excellent harbour; exports sugar, cotton, tobacco. Commercial centre; textiles, cigars, chemicals, rum mfg. Founded 1514; cap. from 1552. Blowing up of battleship *Maine* in harbour resulted in war with US and American occupation (1898-1902). Tourism declined after Castro's coup. (1959). Has 18th cent. cathedral.

Havelock, Sir Henry (1795-1857), British army officer. Rose to fame in the Indian Mutiny by capture of Kanpur (1857) and relief of Lucknow, shortly after which he died of dysentery.

Haverfordwest, mun. bor. of Dyfed, SW Wales. Pop. 9000. Former co. town of Pembrokeshire. Has ruined 12th cent. castle, priory.

Havering, bor. of NE Greater London, England. Pop. 247,000. Created 1965 from Romford, Hornchurch (both in Essex).

Havre, Le, *see* LE HAVRE, France.

Hawaii, volcanic isl. group and state of US; in C Pacific. Area 16,706 sq km (6450 sq mi); pop. 770,000; cap. Honolulu. Incl. Hawaii (area 10,456 sq km/4037 sq mi), Oahu, Maui, Kauai, Molokai isls. Coral reefs, several large active volcanoes. Extensive fishing. Agric. incl. sugar cane, pineapple production. Important tourist industs. International air and shipping base; naval base at Pearl Harbor, Oahu (attacked by Japanese in 1941 bringing US into WWII). Pop. of Japanese, Caucasian, Polynesian origin. Known as Sandwich Isls. after discovery by Cook in 1778; native rule until annexed by US (1898); was territ. (1900-59). Admitted to Union as 50th state (1959).

Haw-Haw, Lord, *see* JOYCE, WILLIAM.

Hawick, town of Borders region, SE Scotland, on R. Teviot. Pop. 16,000. Sheep market; woollen, tweed mfg.

hawk, name for several birds of prey with short, rounded wings, hooked beak and claws. Incl. kites, buzzards, harriers, falcons, caracaras.

Hawke, Edward Hawke, 1st Baron (1705-81), British admiral. Defeated French squadron off Cape Finisterre (1747) and by annihilation of French fleet at Quiberon Bay (1759) removed threat of invasion.

Hawke's Bay, region of E North Isl., New Zealand. Area 11,030 sq km (4260 sq mi); pop. 134,000; main town Napier. Mainly hilly; lowlands around Hawke Bay. Sheep, cattle rearing, dairying, fruit and vegetable growing.

hawking or **falconry,** sport of hunting game, using trained hawks or falcons. Practised in Arabia, Persia, India since ancient times, became popular in medieval Europe. Trained bird is carried on gloved wrist of falconer; unhooded and released on sight of prey.

Hawkins, Sir Anthony Hope, *see* HOPE, ANTHONY.

Hawkins or **Hawkyns, Sir John** (1532-95), English privateer. Made very profitable slaving expeditions (1562-7) to Guinea. Treasurer and comptroller of navy (1573), rear admiral in defeat of Spanish Armada (1588). Died at sea in expedition under Drake.

hawk moth, any of Sphingidae family of moths with thick body and long pointed forewings. Long proboscis used to suck flower nectar. Species incl. DEATH'S HEAD HAWK MOTH.

Hawks, Howard (1896-), American film director. Known for comedies, action films, incl. *Scarface* (1932), *Bringing up Baby* (1938), *The Big Sleep* (1946), *Rio Bravo* (1958).

hawksbill turtle, *Eretmochelys imbricata,* tropical marine turtle, whose shell provides commercial tortoiseshell.

Hawksmoor, Nicholas (1661-1736), English architect. Collaborated with Wren on St Paul's and Greenwich Hospital, with Vanbrugh on Blenheim Palace. His own work in very personalized Baroque style incl. Christchurch, Spitalfields (1723-9).

Hawley-Smoot Tariff Act (1930), most highly protective tariff legislation in US history. Retaliatory action by foreign govts. led to sharp decline in US foreign trade. Policy reversed by Trade Agreements Act (1934).

Haworth, Sir Walter Norman (1883-1950), English chemist. Shared Nobel Prize for Chemistry (1937) for work on structure of sugars and synthesis of vitamin C (which he named ascorbic acid).

Haworth, village of West Yorkshire met. county, N England. Incorporated with Keighley 1938. Has Parsonage, home of the Brontë family.

hawthorn, any of genus *Crataegus* of thorny shrubs or small trees of rose family. Native to Eurasia and North America, unknown S of equator. Clusters of fragrant white or pink flowers, small red fruits called haws.

Hawthorne, Nathaniel (1804-64), American author. Known for novel, *The Scarlet Letter* (1850), on themes of Puritanism, secret sin. Other works incl. *Twice-told Tales*

(1837), *The House of Seven Gables* (1851) and, *Tanglewood Tales* (1853) a collection of Greek myths re-told for children.

Hay, Ian, pseud. of John Hay Beith (1876-1952), Scottish writer. Known for humorous novels, *eg Pip* (1907), *A Safety Match* (1911), *A Knight on Wheels* (1914).

Joseph Haydn

Haydn, [Franz] Joseph (1732-1809), Austrian composer. Estab. classical forms of the sonata and symphony. Prolific composer, wrote over 100 symphonies, 84 string quartets, piano sonatas, operas and choral works, *eg The Creation, The Seasons.* Musical director for the Esterhazy family (1761-90).

Haydon, Benjamin Robert (1786-1846), English historical painter. Attempted to revive painting of historical and religious subjects in 'Grand Manner' of Reynolds. Largely responsible for purchase of Elgin Marbles. Wrote autobiog. memoirs.

Hayes, Helen, née Brown (1900-), American stage, film actress. Stage performances incl. *Dear Brutus, Victoria Regina.* First London appearance (1948) in *The Glass Menagerie.*

Hayes, Rutherford Birchard (1822-93), American statesman, president (1877-81). Republican presidential candidate (1876) at time of Democratic revival; returns disputed, electoral commission gave Hayes victory by 1 electoral vote.

hay fever, inflammation of mucous membranes of eyes or nose. Usually caused by allergic reaction to plant pollen. Characterized by sneezing, watering of eyes.

hazel, any of genus *Corylus* of shrubs and trees of birch family. Native to Eurasia. Yields useful elastic wood. Twigs traditionally used in water divination. Edible fruit variously known, according to variety, as hazelnut, cob, filbert, Barcelona nut.

Hazlitt, William (1778-1830), English essayist. Known for perceptive criticism of Romantic poets, Elizabethan drama, *eg Characters of Shakespeare's Plays* (1817), *Lectures on the English Poets* (1818). Noted prose stylist.

head, part of body uppermost in humans, apes, *etc* and foremost in most other animals. Bony structure in higher animals containing brain and incl. eyes, mouth, nose, jaws.

Healey, Denis Winston (1917-), British politician. Labour chancellor of exchequer (1974-). Attempted to reduce rate of inflation with 'social contract' between TUC and govt., restricting wage increases.

health insurance, pay by prior payment to provide services or cash for medical care in times of illness or disability. Can be part of voluntary or compulsory national insurance scheme connected with SOCIAL SECURITY scheme. Early forms were in Germany (1883), most comprehensive scheme coming in UK (*see* NATIONAL HEALTH INSURANCE ACT). In US, amendments (1965) to Social Security Act estab. scheme for old age persons (Medicare), for low-income persons (Medicaid).

hearing aid, device worn to compensate for hearing loss. Battery-operated electronic aids incorporate receiver and transistor amplifier. Two main types: those which transmit sounds through bone of skull and those which conduct sounds through air to stimulate ear drum.

Hearst, William Randolph (1863-1951), American journalist, publisher. Founded vast newspaper empire, was most sensational of all 'yellow press' publishers. Influential in politics, advocated extreme isolationism.

heart, muscular organ which maintains blood circulation in vertebrate animals. Human heart is divided into 2 halves by muscular wall; each half is divided into 2 chambers, upper atrium and lower ventricle. Oxygenated blood from lungs enters left atrium and is pumped into left ventricle by contraction of heart, then into arteries. Venous blood enters right atrium, is pumped into right ventricle and then into lungs to regain oxygen.

heart attack, sudden instance of heart failure, esp. that associated with coronary thrombosis.

heat, internal energy of substances produced by vibrations of constituent molecules and which passes from places of higher temperature to those of lower temperature. Transmitted by conduction, convection and radiation. SI unit of heat is joule; quantity of heat held by body is product of its mass, specific heat and temperature. Increase in heat of a body may result in increase in temperature or change of state. *See* LATENT HEAT.

Edward Heath

Heath, Edward Richard George (1916-), British statesman, PM (1970-4). Elected leader of Conservative Party in 1965. Successfully pursued policy of British entry into EEC (achieved 1973). Admin. marked by bad relations with trade unions culminating in miners' strike. Replaced as party leader (1975) after leadership election.

heath or **heather,** any of genera *Erica* and *Calluna* of shrubs of Ericaceae family. Found on temperate moorlands throughout world. Plants have bell-shaped hanging flowers. Species incl. common or Scotch heather, *C. vulgaris,* and bell heather, *E. cinerea.*

Heathrow, Greater London (Hounslow), SE England. Site of London's main airport, one of world's busiest, 24 km (15 mi) from city centre.

heatstroke, illness caused by exposure to excessive heat. May cause cramp and collapse from salt loss, or fainting. Extreme rise in body temperature may result if body's temperature-regulating mechanism breaks down.

heaven, in Judaeo-Christian theology, dwelling place of God and his angels, where the blessed will live after death. Similar beliefs exist in Islam, Mahayana Buddhism and Hinduism.

Heath (Erica tetralix)

Heaviside, Oliver (1850-1925), English physicist. His work on increasing inductance of telephone wires made long distance telephony practicable. Independently of Kennelly, predicted existence of gaseous ionized layer in upper atmosphere (Kennelly-Heaviside layer) from which electromagnetic waves are reflected.

heavy spar, see BARITES.

heavy water (D_2O), water composed of deuterium and oxygen, found in ordinary water at concentration of 1 part in 5000. Used as moderator in nuclear reactors. Name also applies to water containing substantial quantities of D_2O or HDO.

Hebbel, [Christian] Friedrich (1813-63), German dramatist. Known for realistic tragedies, esp. *Maria Magdalena* (1844), reflecting Hegelian view of historical turning points.

Hebe, in Greek myth, goddess of youth. Daughter of Zeus and Hera, wife of Heracles after his deification. Cupbearer of the gods before GANYMEDE. Identified with Roman Juventas.

Hébert, Jacques René, (1757-94), French revolutionary, journalist. Had nickname derived from paper *Le Père Duchesne,* in which he expressed radical republicanism. Led CORDELIERS, active in Paris Commune; enemy of Girondists. Earned enmity of Robespierre, arrested with followers, guillotined.

Hebrew, NW Semitic language of Afro-Asiatic family. From 586 BC to 19th cent., preserved by Jews in religion, learning, their vernacular languages being Aramaic, Yiddish. Rise of Zionism in 19th cent. caused adoption as national language, which it became with estab. of Israel (1948).

Hebrew literature, literature of Jews. Earliest works were OT, *Apocrypha,* parts of *Pseudepigraphia,* and Dead Sea Scrolls. *Talmud, Midrash* and *Targum* date from 2nd–4th cent. *Masora* developed in Palestine (6th–7th cent.), Babylonian Talmudic commentaries written 6th–11th cent. Post-11th cent. writing shifted to Spain, incl. poetry, philosophy. In 14th cent. *Zohar,* principal text of CABALA, appeared. Medieval Hebrew writers incl. Ibn Gabirol, Rashi, Maimonides and Caro. Moses Mendelssohn began modern Hebrew literature, which incl. work of Sforim (pseud. of Abramovich), Bialik, Agnon and Moshe Shamir.

Hebrews, epistle of NT, traditionally ascribed to St Paul but not now accepted as his. Written before AD 90. Exhorts Christians not to return to Judaism under pressure of persecution.

Hebrides, *c* 500 isls. off NW Scotland. Formerly admin. by Argyllshire, Inverness-shire, Ross and Cromarty. Mild, wet climate; crofting, fishing, tourism, tweed mfg. Depopulation (*c* 100 isls. inhabited). Under Norwegian rule 6th-13th cents. **Inner Hebrides** incl. Coll, Colonsay, Iona, Islay, Jura, Mull, Rhum, Skye, Tiree. **Outer Hebrides** incl. Barra, Benbecula, Lewis with Harris, St Kilda, North and South Uist. Now admin. by WESTERN ISLES isl. authority.

Hebron (Arab. *Al Khalil*), town of W Jordan. Pop. 43,000. Trade centre in vine, cereal region at alt. of 910 m (3000 ft). Sacred to Jews and Moslems; Cave of Machpelah is traditional site of tomb of Abraham and his family.

Hecate, in Greek myth, goddess of witchcraft, ghosts, with power to conjure phantoms and dreams. Worshipped at crossroads. Sometimes represented with three bodies.

Hecht, Ben (1894-1964), American journalist, film scriptwriter and critic. Scripts incl. *The Front Page* (1931), *Soak the Rich* (1936), *Spellbound* (1945).

hectare, metric unit of area, equal to 10,000 square metres; 1 hectare = *c* 2.47 acres.

Hector, in Greek legend, eldest son of King Priam and husband of Andromache. Greatest hero of Trojan troops during Trojan War. Killed by Achilles in revenge for his killing of Patroclus.

Hecuba, in Greek legend, wife of King Priam of Troy and mother of Hector, Paris, Troilus, Cassandra. To save him from the Greeks sent her youngest son, Polydorus, to King Polymestor of Thrace. As captive of Odysseus, she discovered that Polymestor had murdered Polydorus and in revenge blinded him.

Hedgehog (Erinaceus frontalis)

hedgehog, any of Erinaceidae family of spiny-backed insectivores widely distributed in Old World. Protects itself by curling up into ball with spines standing outwards. Hibernates in winter.

hedge sparrow, *Prunella modularis,* small European bird with reddish-brown back, grey head and white-tipped wings. Also called dunnock.

Hedin, Sven Anders (1865-1952), Swedish explorer. Made many expeditions to C Asia between 1885-1908; discovered sources of Brahmaputra, Indus, Sutlej rivers. Wrote accounts of travels, *eg Transhimalaya* (1912), *The Conquest of Tibet* (1934).

hedonism, in ethics, theory that pleasure or happiness of self or society is object of actions. Exponents incl. Aristippus, Epicurus, J. S. Mill.

Hegel, Georg Wilhelm Friedrich (1770-1831), German philosopher. Formulated concept of historical dialectic: fusion (synthesis) of opposite concepts (thesis and antithesis). Activating principle is 'world spirit' (*Volksgeist*) in universe of continuous self-creation. Works incl. *Phenomenology of Mind* (1807), *Science of Logic* (1812-16). Greatly influenced subsequent philosophers of history, esp. Marx.

hegemony, leadership or dominance, esp. of one state or nation over another. Usage in 20th cent. extended by Gramsci through development of Marxist theory of superstructure to incl. cultural dimension.

hegira or **hejira,** the flight of Mohammed from Mecca to Medina in AD 622. The Mohammedan era is dated from 16 July of that year, with (in West) AH after year number, *ie* After Hegira.

Heidegger, Martin (1889-1976), German philosopher. Link between Kierkegaard and later existentialists. Concerned with 'problem of being' and Western man's lost sense of being. Major work, *Being and Time* (1927).

Hegel

Heidelberg, city of WC West Germany, on R. Neckar. Pop. 122,000. Precision instruments, printing industs.; wine, fruit, tourism. Residence of Electors Palatine 13th-18th cent. Famous univ. (1386) centre of German Reformation (16th cent.); ruined 13th cent. castle. Remains of prehist. 'Heidelberg man' found nearby.

Heifetz, Jascha (1901-   ), American violinist, b. Russia. Exhibited prodigious ability, even as a child, and rose rapidly to international reputation.

Heike-monogatari ('Tales of the Heike'), Japanese historical romance. Composed in early 13th cent., tells of 12th cent. conflict between 2 great families, Minamoto (Genji), and Taira (Heike), leading to latter's downfall. Important influence on later literature, stories providing material for NO and later drama, and prose style looking forward to that of novel.

Heilbronn, city of SW West Germany, on R. Neckar. Pop. 102,000. River port, railway jct., indust. centre. Name derived from Holy Spring (*Heiligbronn*) near 11th cent. church.

Hellungkiang, prov. of NE China. Area *c* 705,000 sq km (272,000 sq mi); pop. (est.) 21,000,000; cap. Harbin. Wheat, soya beans grown; major timber indust. Indust. centres in S, minerals (oil, coal, gold). Contiguous with USSR.

Heine, Heinrich, pseud. of Chaim Harry Heine (1797-1856), German poet. Attracted by spirit of July Revolution (1830), settled in Paris (1831). Wrote in German, French. Known for travel sketches, *Trip in the Harz Mountains* (1826), romantic lyric poetry in *Book of Songs* (1827), incl. treatment of 'Lorelei' myth. Subsequently critical of Romanticism.

Heinkel, Ernst (1888-1958), German aircraft designer. Developed jet aircraft (*c* 1939) independently of Whittle. His company was Germany's largest producer of warplanes in WWII.

Heisenberg, Werner Karl (1901-76), German physicist. Developed form of quantum theory based on matrix methods. His uncertainty principle states that certain pairs of quantities (*eg* position and momentum of particle) cannot both be measured completely accurately. Awarded Nobel Prize for Physics (1932).

Hejaz, region of NW Saudi Arabia. Area *c* 388,500 sq km (150,000 sq mi); pop. 2,000,000; Mountainous plateau with coastal strip. Contains Mecca (cap.), Medina. United with Nejd (1932) to form Saudi Arabia.

Hekla, volcano of S Iceland. Height 1520 m (5000 ft). Many eruptions recorded from 12th cent., incl. disaster of 1766; most recent 1970.

Hel, in Norse myth, goddess of the underworld, daughter of Loki. Ruled the home of dead not killed in battle.

Helen, in Greek myth, beautiful wife of King Menelaus of Sparta; daughter of Zeus by Leda. Her abduction to Troy by Paris instigated Trojan War. Reconciled to Menelaus after fall of Troy.

Helena, cap. and tourist resort of Montana, US. Pop. 23,000. Ranching, mining region. Founded after gold strike (1864).

Helena, St (d. *c* 330), mother of Constantine I. Made pilgrimage to Jerusalem, where she is said to have found a relic of the True Cross.

Helensburgh, town of Strathclyde region, W Scotland, on Firth of Clyde. Pop. 10,000. Resort, at SW end of 'Highland line'.

helicopter, aircraft with horizontal rotating wings (rotors) which enable it to take off and land vertically, to move in any direction (by inclining axis of rotor) and to hover. Mainly used for short-range transportation, air-sea rescue, firefighting. *See* SIKORSKY.

Heligoland (*Helgoland*), isl. of West Germany, in North Sea, off W Schleswig-Holstein. Exchanged (1890) by UK for Zanzibar. Fortified by Germans in both WWs, submarine base in WWII.

Heliogabalus (*c* AD 205-22), Roman emperor (218-22). Cousin of the emperor Caracalla, he was priest in temple of sun god, Elagabalus, at Emesa. Chosen emperor by troops in Syria, under name Marcus Aurelius Antoninus. Reign was notorious for debauchery and cruelty. He and his mother were murdered by Praetorian Guard.

Heliopolis, ancient ruined city of N Egypt. Centre of sun-worship; schools of philosophy, astronomy. Original site of 'Cleopatra's Needles', removed 19th cent. to London, New York.

Helios (Gk.,=sun), in Greek myth, sun god, son of TITANS Hyperion and Theia. Crossed the sky daily from east to west in chariot drawn by 4 horses. Kept herd of sacred oxen on Thrinacia (Sicily). Later identified with Apollo.

heliotrope, any plant that turns to face the sun, esp. genus *Heliotropium* of plants of borage family with clusters of white or purple flowers.

helium (He), inert gaseous element; at. no. 2, at. wt. 4.003. Found in natural gas in Texas and in atmosphere. Used in balloons and airships because of lightness and non-flammability; low boiling point makes it useful in cryogenics. First discovered in Sun (1868), abundant in stars.

Hell, in Christian theology, dwelling place of devils to which sinners are doomed to eternal punishment after death. Often represented with images of fire. Similar concepts occur in Greek myths (Hades), Islam, Judaism.

hellebore, any of genus *Helleborus* of winterblooming perennials of the buttercup family. Found in Europe and Asia, frequently cultivated as ornamental, esp. Christmas rose, *H. niger.*

Hellen, in Greek myth, son of DEUCALION and Pyrrha; father of Aeolus, Dorus and Xuthus and hence eponymous ancestor of the Hellenic peoples, *ie* Aeolians, Dorians and Ionians.

Heller, Joseph (1923-), American author. Best known for *Catch-22* (1961), a novel using black humour to satirize bureaucracy in the army.

Hellespont, *see* DARDANELLES.

Hellman, Lillian (1905-), American dramatist. Works, incl. *The Children's Hour* (1934), *The Little Foxes* (1939), *Toys in the Attic* (1960), often reflect left-wing political interests.

Helmand, chief river of Afghanistan. Rises in Hindu Kush, flows *c* 1400 km (870 mi) into Lake Hamun-i-Helmand on Iran border.

Helmholtz, Hermann von (1821-94), German physician, scientist. Developed concept of conservation of energy. Pioneer of physiological optics and acoustics; extended Young's theory of colour vision. Invented ophthalmoscope (1851).

Helmont, Jan Baptista van (1577-1644), Flemish scientist. Believed that physiological processes are due to chemical reactions; held that water could be converted into living matter. Distinguished between air and other gases; first to use word 'gas'.

Helpmann, Sir Robert [Murray] (1909-), Australian choreographer, dancer, actor. Principal dancer of Sadler's Wells Ballet, choreographed such ballets as *Miracle in the*

Gorbals. Theatre work incl. leading Shakespearian roles, directing of plays; director of Australian Ballet.

Helsingborg, *see* HÄLSINGBORG, Sweden.

Helsingfors, *see* HELSINKI, Finland.

Helsingör or **Elsinore,** town of NE Zealand, Denmark, on Oresund. Pop. 42,000. Port, ferry service to Hälsingborg (Sweden). Kronborg Castle is scene of Shakespeare's *Hamlet.*

Helsinki (Swed. *Helsingfors*), cap. of Finland, on Gulf of Finland. Pop. 627,000. Admin., cultural centre; univ. (moved from Turku 1828). Chief port, kept open in winter by ice-breakers, exports timber, paper, wood products. Founded 1550, cap. from 1812. Largely rebuilt after fire (1808). Scene of 1952 Olympics.

Helvellyn, mountain of Lake Dist., Cumbria, NW England. Height 950 m (3118 ft).

Helvetia, region now within W Switzerland, formerly occupied by Celtic Helvetii (2nd cent. BC-5th cent. AD). Name still used poetically for Switzerland, and on Swiss postage stamps.

Helvétius, Claude Adrien (1715-71), French philosopher, Wrote *De l'esprit* (1758), expressing doctrine that differences in ability are not innate but caused by experience, and that all ideas derive from sensations. Utilitarian ethics influenced Bentham, Mill.

hematite, *see* HAEMATITE.

Hemel Hempstead, mun. bor. of Hertfordshire, EC England. Pop. 69,000. Designated new town 1946; light industs.

Hemichordata (hemichordates), subphylum of primitive marine animals with gill slits and small notochord in front region of body. Incl. ACORN WORM.

Ernest Hemingway

Hemingway, Ernest Miller (1899-1961), American author. Member of 'lost generation' of expatriates as described in *The Sun Also Rises* (1926). Works, *eg A Farewell to Arms* (1929), *For Whom the Bell Tolls* (1940), novella *The Old Man and the Sea* (1952), celebrate physical courage in terse, dramatic understatement. Nobel Prize for Literature (1954).

Hemiptera, order of insects incl. bugs, lice, aphids. Mouthparts adapted for sucking. Divided into suborders Homoptera and Heteroptera according to wing structure; wingless forms also exist.

hemlock, *Conium maculatum*, biennial umbelliferous herb of N hemisphere. Source of alkaloid poison coniine used medicinally and by ancient Greeks as instrument of capital punishment, notably in case of Socrates. Also, any of genus *Tsuga* of North American and Asiatic evergreen trees of the pine family; bark is used in tanning.

Hémon, Louis (1880-1913), Canadian writer, b. France. Best known for popular novel of farm life in Québec, *Maria Chapdelaine* (1916).

hemp, *Cannabis sativa*, tall Asiatic herb of nettle family. Male and female flowers on separate plants. Stems yield fibre for rope, coarse cloth, paper. Seeds used as birdfood

Hemlock (*Conium maculatum*)

and oil extracted from them as base of paints and soaps. Resin from female flower yields intoxicating drug cannabis or marijuana, or whole flower may be processed as hashish. These, when smoked or eaten, may cause mild hallucinations and sense of euphoria.

Henbane

henbane, *Hyoscyamus niger,* poisonous plant of nightshade family, native to Old World. Source of alkaloid drugs scopolamine and hyoscamine.

Henderson, Alexander (1583-1646), Scottish churchman. Leading Presbyterian. Prepared National Covenant (1638), Solemn League and Covenant (1643, *see* COVENANTERS). Intermediary between Church of Scotland and Charles I.

Henderson, Arthur (1863-1935), British statesman. As Labour foreign secretary (1929-31) worked for international peace, supporting League of Nations, attempting to ease Franco-German relations. President of World Disarmament Conference (1932-5). Nobel Peace Prize (1934).

Hendon, part of Barnet, W Greater London, England. Mun. bor. until 1965. Has Univ. of London observatory; site of former airfield.

Hengyang, city of Hunan prov., SC China; formerly Hengchow. Pop. 240,000. Communications centre (rail, road) on R. Siang. Lead and zinc mining.

Henie, Sonja (1913-69), Norwegian skater. Three times winner of Olympic figure-skating championships (1928, 1932, 1936). Highly successful as a professional, did much to popularize skating by her showmanship and film appearances.

Henley, William Ernest (1849-1903), English journalist, poet. Editor of imperialist *National Observer* (1889-94), influencing Kipling, Wells. Poems (collected 1898) incl. jingoistic *Invictus.*

Henley-on-Thames, mun. bor. of Oxfordshire, C England, on R. Thames. Pop. 11,000. Scene of annual rowing regatta from 1839.

henna, *Lawsonia inermis,* small Old World tropical shrub. Fragrant white or red flowers; leaves yield reddish-brown dye used as hair or body dye.

Henri, Robert (1865-1929), American painter, teacher. Leader of ashcan school, attempted to introduce contemporary French technique to portray American scene. Influential teacher, emphasized social role of art.

Henrietta Maria (1609-69), queen consort (1625-49) of Charles I of England. Daughter of Henry IV of France. Aroused popular resentment against Charles through attempts to aid Catholic cause.

Henry [I] the Fowler (*c* 876-936), king of Germany (919-36), duke of Saxony (912-36). He advanced German frontiers in wars with France and the Magyars. Married to St Matilda.

Henry III (1017-56), Holy Roman emperor (1046-56). Son of Conrad II, with whom he was joint king of Germany from 1028, later sole king from 1039. The empire reached the peak of its power during his reign with Henry 3 times choosing who was to be pope.

Henry IV (1050-1106), Holy Roman emperor (1084-1105). Succeeded his father, Henry III, as king of Germany (1056). Conflict with Pope Gregory VII over his right to elect bishops led to his excommunication (1075); absolved at Canossa (1077). Again excommunicated (1080), he invaded Italy and deposed Gregory (1084). Crowned emperor by antipope, Clement III. Forced to abdicate.

Henry V (1081-1125), Holy Roman emperor (1111-25). Became king of Germany (1105) after forcing abdication of his father, Henry IV. Continued father's struggle with papacy over election of bishops until compromise reached in Concordat of Worms (1122).

Henry I (1068-1135), king of England (1100-35). Youngest son of William I, seized crown on death of brother, William II, excluding his elder brother Robert II, duke of Normandy. Later seized Normandy (1105) and imprisoned Robert for life. Attempted to secure throne for daughter MATILDA.

Henry II (1133-89), king of England (1154-89). By marriage with Eleanor of Aquitaine, gained huge tracts of land in France. Named as successor by mother Matilda, invaded England and forced Stephen to name him as heir. Estab. power of throne by subduing barons, strengthening royal courts. Attempted to extend power over Church; entered long controversy with Thomas à Becket, ending in Becket's murder. Struggles with sons ended in defeat by son, Richard I.

Henry III (1207-72), king of England (1216-72). Son of John, came to power (1227) after regency. Expensive, unsuccessful campaign in France and autocratic rule led to Barons' War (1263). Simon de MONTFORT, barons' leader, defeated Henry at Lewes and summoned Parliament. Order restored by Henry's son, later Edward I.

Henry IV (1367-1413), king of England (1399-1413). Son of John of Gaunt; exiled 1398-9 by Richard II. Returned and forced Richard to abdicate; claim to throne upheld by Parliament. Reign, marked by barons' uprisings and revolt in Wales, left crown in serious debt.

Henry V (1387-1422), king of England (1413-22). Son of Henry IV; claiming French throne, reopened Hundred Years War. Defeated French at Agincourt (1415) and seized Normandy. Married Catherine of Valois; recognized as heir to French throne by her father, Charles VI.

Henry VI (1421-71), king of England (1422-61, 1470-1). Succeeded father Henry V in infancy. His claims to French throne were unrecognized by the French, whose victories under Joan of Arc and Charles VII drove English from France. Dominated by his wife Margaret of Anjou. Subject to insanity after 1453, became pawn in struggle between Houses of York and Lancaster. Deposed by Edward IV (1461). Briefly restored 1470. Imprisoned in the Tower, where he died.

Henry VII (1457-1509), king of England (1485-1509); until accession, Henry Tudor, Earl of Richmond. Head of house of Lancaster after death of Henry VI (1471), fled to France. Invaded England (1485), seized throne from Richard III after victory at Bosworth Field. United houses of York and Lancaster by marrying (1486) Elizabeth, daughter of Edward IV. Defeated Yorkist impostors Lambert Simnel, Perkin Warbeck. Centralized govt. and finances, estab. Tudor tradition of autocratic rule.

Henry VIII (1491-1547), king of England (1509-47). Son of Henry VII. Married (1509) brother's widow, Catherine of

Aragon. Govt. dominated by WOLSEY until he failed to secure annulment of marriage from pope. This initiated split from Rome, culminating in estab. of Henry as 'supreme head' of Church of England (1534). With chief minister T. CROMWELL, carried out dissolution of monasteries, confiscating wealth. Executed 2nd wife, Anne Boleyn (1536) on charge of adultery, married Jane Seymour (1537) who bore him Edward VI. Successive marriages were to Anne of Cleves (1540), Catherine Howard (1542), Catherine Parr (1543). Wars with Scotland, Ireland, France left crown in debt.

Henry II (1519-59), king of France (1547-59). Son of Francis I. Dominated by Montmorency, his mistress Diane de Poitiers and de Guise family. Continued wars against Emperor Charles V, England (winning Calais, 1558), Spain. Married (1533) Catherine de' Medici.

Henry III (1551-89), king of France (1574-89). Reign marked by continuing Catholic-Huguenot strife and conflict with Catholic League led by de Guise. Expelled from Paris (1588) by revolt inspired by de Guise. Made alliance with Huguenot leader, Henry of Navarre (later Henry IV), to regain city. Had de Guise murdered; assassinated by fanatic monk.

Henry IV, orig. Henry of Navarre (1553-1610), king of France (1589-1610), king of Navarre (1572-89). Became leader of Huguenots (1569) and legal heir to French throne (1584); fought 10 year war to estab. rule after death of Henry III. Became Catholic as political move (1593). Estab. religious tolerance with Edict of Nantes (1598). Married (1600) Marie de' Medici after marriage to Margaret of Valois annulled. In final years (1600-10), avoided war, encouraged agric., indust., reformed finances. Assassinated by fanatic.

Henry, Joseph (1797-1878), American physicist. Independently of Faraday, discovered principle of electromagnetic induction. Developed electromagnet and invented electromagnetic telegraph. Discovered self-inductance and invented an electric motor. First secretary of Smithsonian Institution.

Henry, O., pseud. of William Sidney Porter (1862-1910), American short-story writer. Known for sentimental tales with surprise endings. Collections incl. *Cabbages and Kings* (1904), *The Four Million* (1906).

Henry, Patrick (1736-99), American revolutionary. Renowned orator, led opposition to British rule; advocate of individual liberty. Prominent supporter of first 10 amendments to Constitution (Bill of Rights).

Henry the Navigator (1394-1460), Portuguese prince, son of John I. Patron of navigation and exploration of W Africa, laying basis for development of Portuguese overseas empire.

Henryson, Robert (*c* 1430-*c* 1505), Scottish poet. Best known for *Testament of Cresseid*, a severe moral treatment of 'Troilus' story.

Henslowe, Philip (d. 1616), English theatre manager. With 'Ned' Alleyn, owned Rose and Fortune theatres. Diary valuable to theatrical historians.

Henze, Hans Werner (1926-), German composer. Much of his early work was highly abstract and used 12-note technique; now concentrates on music concerned with social values. His operas incl. *The Bassarids, The Young Lord.*

hepatica, see LIVERWORT.

hepatitis, inflammation of liver. Two common forms, transmitted by viruses: serum hepatitis, conveyed by traces of blood on hypodermic needles used in transfusions, *etc*, and infectious hepatitis.

Hepburn, Katharine (1907-), American stage and film actress. Known for clipped voice, cool acting; long associated with Spencer Tracy. Films incl. *Morning Glory* (1933), *Bringing up Baby* (1938), *Adam's Rib* (1949), *The African Queen* (1951).

Hephaestus, in Greek myth, god of fire, son of Zeus and Hero, patron of smiths and craftsmen. Represented as mighty, usually bearded and comic figure. Made Achilles' armour. Identified by Romans with Vulcan.

Henry VIII: engraving after Holbein

Hepplewhite, George (d. 1786), English cabinet maker, furniture designer. Known for designs appearing in *The Cabinet-maker and Upholsterer's Guide* (pub. 1788). Developed light elegant style, esp. in his chairs, often with shield or heart-shaped backs.

Barbara Hepworth

Hepworth, Dame Barbara (1903-75), English abstract sculptor. Early work was carved directly in stone and wood; experimented with piercing holes in sculpture. Later work in bronze shows attempt to achieve perfection of form.

Hera, in Greek myth, daughter of Cronus and Rhea; sister and wife of Zeus. Patron of sexual life of women and marriage. Jealous, she persecuted Zeus' mortal offspring. Sometimes identified with Roman Juno.

Heracles, in Greek myth, son of Zeus and Alcmene. Popular Greek hero famed for strength and courage. Driven mad by Hera, he killed his wife and children. To expiate this crime served King Eurystheus of Tiryns for 12 years, achieving 12 labours: (1) brought back skin of Nemean lion, (2) killed the Hydra, (3) captured the Cerynean hind and (4) the Erymanthian boar, (5) cleaned the stables of Augeas, (6) destroyed the Stymphalian birds, (7) captured the Cretan bull and (8) the man-eating mares of Diomedes, (9) stole the girdle of Queen Hippolyte of the Amazons, (10) brought back the cattle of Geryon, (11) stole the apples of the Hesperides, (12) captured Cerberus from Hades. Also involved in many other adventures incl.

Argonauts' quest. On death he obtained immortality, married Hebe. Known as Hercules by the Romans.

Heraclitus (c 535–c 475 BC), Greek philosopher. Believed that all things imply their opposites, that change is the only reality, permanence an illusion. Held fire to be underlying universal substance.

Herakleion, see IRÁKLION, Greece.

heraldry, system of inherited symbols (traditionally displayed on shield, surcoat) used for identification of individuals, families, institutions. Prob. originated in Germany (12th cent.); in Middle Ages, rules for personal devices such as coats of arms, badges, crests, were regularized. See HERALD'S COLLEGE.

Herald's College or **College of Arms,** body chartered (1483) by Richard III of England to regularize system of HERALDRY. Traces lineage and makes grants of arms.

Herat (anc. Aria), city of NW Afghanistan, on R. Hari Rud. Pop. 109,000. Carpet, textile mfg. Ancient city on trade route from India to Persia; dominated by earthworks of citadel.

herb, any seed plant whose stem withers back to the ground after each season's growth, as distinguished from a tree or shrub whose woody stem lives from year to year. Also any plant used as a medicine or seasoning, eg thyme, basil.

Herbart, Johann Friedrich (1776-1841), German philosopher, educator. Explained nature of change in terms of altering relationships of co-existent 'reals'. In education, stressed relating new concepts to experience of learner.

Herbert, Sir A[lan] P[atrick] (1890-1971), English writer, politician. Known for humorous Misleading Cases in the Common Law (1st series 1927) reflecting legal training. Secured reform of English divorce laws. Also wrote light verse, novel The Water Gipsies (1930).

Herbert, George (1593-1633), English poet. Best known for collection of metrically, typographically inventive metaphysical poems The Temple (1633) covering all facets of the religious life. His brother, **Edward Herbert, 1st Baron Herbert of Cherbury** (1583-1648), was a philosopher, diplomat; sought rational basis for religion in De Veritate (1624).

herbivore, name applied to any animal, esp. mammal, which feeds entirely or mainly on vegetation.

Hercegovina, see BOSNIA AND HERCEGOVINA.

Herculaneum (Ital. Ercolano), ancient city of SW Italy, near Naples. Roman resort, buried (AD 79) with POMPEII in eruption of Vesuvius. Site discovered 1709.

Hercules, Roman name of HERACLES.

Hercules beetle, Dynastes herculeus, giant green and black beetle of Central and South America, with long horn on thorax. Reaches length of 15 cm/6 in.

Herder, Johann Gottfried von (1744-1803), German philosopher, poet. Known for collection Folk Songs (1778-9) influencing STURM UND DRANG movement. Also wrote Outlines of the Philosophy of Man (1784-91) taking evolutionary approach to history.

heredity, process whereby characteristics of living organisms are transmitted from parents to offspring by means of genes carried in chromosomes. Mutation in chromosomes can result in changes in inherited characteristics. Studied scientifically as genetics.

Hereford and Worcester, county of W England. Area 3927 sq km (1516 sq mi); pop. 577,000; co. town Worcester. Created 1974, comprises former Herefordshire, Worcestershire.

Herefordshire, former county of W England. Malvern Hills in E; Wye Valley in C; Black Mts. in SW. Hereford beef cattle; fruit growing, esp. apples, pears. Co. town was **Hereford,** city on R. Wye. Pop. 47,000. Agric. market. Has 11th cent. cathedral displaying many architectural styles.

Herero, nomadic BANTU people of South West Africa (Namibia). Noted for their large cattle herds. Majority of pop. massacred by Germans c 1908.

Hereward the Wake (fl 1070), English chieftain. Led Anglo-Saxon rebellion against William the Conqueror (1070-1). Took Isle of Ely as his stronghold but was defeated (1071).

hermaphrodite, animal or plant possessing both male and female reproduction systems, eg earthworms. Name sometimes applied to humans possessing physical characteristics of opposite sex due to hormone imbalance.

Hermes, in Greek myth, messenger of the gods; son of Zeus and Maia. Patron of merchants, travellers, roads and thieves. Represented with staff, winged shoes and broad hat. Associated with milestones and signposts (herms). Identified by Romans with Mercury.

Hermes Trismegistus, Greek name for Egyptian god THOTH, supposed author of the 17 treatises of Corpus Hermeticum. Prob. compiled in 3rd cent., they describe the mystical harmonies of the universe, eg astrology, alchemy. Influenced neoplatonists and became centre of cults in 17th cent. England.

Hermitage, museum and art gallery in Leningrad. Collection was built up by Catherine the Great; opened to public 1852. Its holdings of French art are esp. fine.

Hermit crab

hermit crab, type of crab of Paguridae family that protects its soft abdomen by living in empty mollusc shell which it drags around when walking.

Hermon, Mount, scenic mountain, alt. 2814 m (9232 ft), in Anti-Lebanon range. On Syria-Lebanon border.

Hermosillo, town of NW Mexico, cap. of Sonora state, on Sonora R. Pop. 207,000. Commercial centre in agric. (maize, cotton, fruit), mining region (gold, silver). Winter resort.

Hernández, José (1834-86), Argentinian poet. Known for epic Martín Fierro (1872-9), protesting about treatment of 'gauchos', incl. conscription to fight Indians.

Herne, city of W West Germany, on Rhine-Herne canal, in Ruhr. Pop. 104,000. Coalmining, iron, textiles industs.

hernia or **rupture,** abnormal protrusion of an organ through a tear in wall of surrounding structure, esp. loop of intestine into top of thigh. Usually treated by surgery.

Hero, in Greek myth, priestess of Aphrodite at Sestos. Her lover, Leander, used nightly to swim the Hellespont to visit her. She allowed the light with which she guided him to blow out and he drowned. In despair she threw herself into the sea.

hero, in Greek religion, man of proven strength and courage favoured by the gods, often having divine ancestor, and worshipped as quasi-divine. Also 'faded' gods who had been demoted to human status, or real or imaginary ancestors. Hero cults centred on reputed place of hero's tomb. Notable exception was HERACLES who was worshipped as a full god.

Hero or **Heron of Alexandria** (fl AD 2nd cent.), Greek mathematician, inventor. Developed double force pump, water organ and steam devices. Investigated operations of screws, wheels, levers and pulleys.

Herod Antipas (d. c AD 40), tetrarch of Galilee and Peraea. Married Herodias, mother of Salome; banished by Caligula (AD 39) after seeking title of king. Responsible for execution of John the Baptist; ruled at time of Jesus' death.

Herodotus (c 484–c 424 BC), Greek historian, called the 'Father of History'. Travelled widely through known world, observing and recording customs and beliefs. Major work, *History of Graeco-Persian Wars*, combines colourful anecdotes with critical style.

Herod the Great (*c* 74-4 BC), king of Judaea. Declared king of Judaea through Mark Antony's influence (40). Estab. his cap. at Jerusalem (37), where he rebuilt Great Temple. According to St Matthew, ordered massacre of male infants in Bethlehem to prevent survival of Jesus.

heroic couplet, English verse form with pair of rhymed lines, each with 5 iambic feet. Used esp. by Dryden, Pope.

heroin or **diacetyl morphine,** white crystalline powder derived from morphine. Introduced as supposed non-addictive painkilling substitute for morphine, it proved to be a powerful habit-forming narcotic.

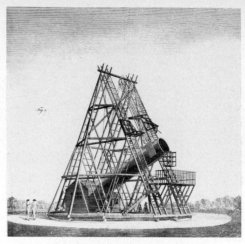

F.W.Herschel's 40ft telescope

Great blue heron (*Ardea herodias*)

heron, long-legged, long-necked wading bird of Ardeidae family. Breeds in colonies or heronries high in trees.

Herophilus (*fl* 300 BC), Greek anatomist, physician. Contemporary of Erasistratus at Alexandria; pioneer of dissection. Investigated nervous system and distinguished between motor and sensory nerves.

herpes, name given to 2 different virus diseases, characterized by eruption of small blisters on skin and mucous membranes. *Herpes simplex* is group of inflamed blisters (cold sores) often around mouth. *H. zoster* or shingles is painful infection of sensory nerves around spinal cord.

Herrick, Robert (1591-1674), English poet. Known for collection, *Hesperides* (1648), incl. religious verse, love lyrics influenced by Classical poets and Jonson.

herring, *Clupea harengus,* common food fish of N Atlantic. Once fished in great numbers, stocks greatly depleted in some areas. Related species in N Pacific.

herring gull, *Larus argentatus,* common marine bird of N hemisphere. Scavenger around harbours; feeds on fish.

Herriot, Edouard (1872-1957), French statesman. Radical Socialist leader, premier (1924-5, 1932), president of National Assembly (1947-54). Imprisoned by Germans (1940-5). Advocated conciliatory foreign policy, payment of war debts to US.

Herschel, Sir Frederick William (1738-1822), British astronomer, b. Germany. Considered founder of modern astronomy, he discovered planet Uranus (1781), 2 of its satellites (1787), and 2 satellites of Saturn. Constructed powerful reflecting telescopes and discovered numerous nebulae and double stars. His son, **Sir John Frederick William Herschel** (1792-1871), extended his study of heavenly bodies and made observations in southern hemisphere.

Hersey, John Richard (1914-), American novelist, journalist. Best known for account of effects of 1st atomic bomb, *Hiroshima* (1946). Novels incl. *A Bell for Adano* (1944), *Too Far to Walk* (1966).

Herstmonceux or **Hurstmonceux,** village of East Sussex, SE England. Castle (15th cent.) has housed Royal Observatory from 1950; has 249 cm (98 in) telescope.

Hertfordshire, county of EC England. Area 1634 sq km (630 sq mi); pop. 940,000. Low-lying; Chiltern Hills in NW. Cereals, market gardening, dairy farming. Co. town **Hertford,** mun. bor. on R. Lea. Pop. 20,000. Important hist. Saxon town.

Hertz, Heinrich Rudolf (1857-94), German physicist. Confirmed (1888) existence of electromagnetic waves predicted by Maxwell and showed that they obey same laws as light.

Hertzog, James Barry Munnik (1866-1942), South African soldier, politician, PM (1924-39). Organized anti-British National party (1913). Advocated neutrality in WWI, WWII.

Hertzsprung-Russell diagram, in astronomy, graph obtained by plotting absolute luminosity of stars against their spectral type (determined by colour or temperature). Most stars lie in diagonal band stretching from top left hand corner (main sequence); white dwarfs and giant stars form separate groups. Has proved useful in theories of stellar evolution.

Herzegovina, alternative form of Hercegovina; *see* BOSNIA AND HERCEGOVINA.

Herzen, Aleksandr Ivanovich (1812-70), Russian revolutionary, writer. Left (1847) Russia to write on it from abroad, *eg* in journal *Kolokol* (1857-62).

Herzl, Theodor (1860-1904), Hungarian writer. Founded ZIONISM after Dreyfus affair. Wrote famous pamphlet *Der Judenstaat* (1896).

Hesiod (*fl c* 8th cent. BC), Greek poet. Earliest of Greek poets after Homer. Prob. Boeotian farmer, wrote didactic poem *Works and Days* on farming. May have written *Theogony.*

Hesperides (Gk., = in the west), in Greek myth, daughters of Evening who, with the help of dragon Ladon, guarded the golden apples of the tree given by Gaea to Hera on her marriage to Zeus. Heracles killed Ladon, stole apples as his 11th labour.

Hess, Rudolf (1894-), German Nazi leader, b. Egypt. Hitler's deputy from 1933. In apparent peace bid, flew stolen plane to Scotland (1941); imprisoned. Sentenced to life imprisonment at Nuremberg trials (1946).

Hesse, Hermann (1877-1962), German author. Influenced by Romanticism, *eg Romantic Songs* (1899). Best-known novels incl. *Demian* (1919), *Steppenwolf* (1927), *The Glass-Bead Game* (1943), reflect interest in Indian mysticism, psychoanalysis. Swiss citizen from 1921. Nobel Prize for Literature (1946).

Hesse (*Hessen*), state of WC West Germany, cap. Wiesbaden. Mainly forested uplands; agric., vine growing, minerals. Resorts incl. several spas, *eg* Bad Homburg. Region incl. parts of former Hesse-Nassau prov. and Hesse-Darmstadt duchy.

Hestia, in Greek myth, goddess of the hearth; daughter of Cronus and Rhea. Regarded as kindest of the gods representing security of the home. Identified by the Romans with Vesta.

heterocyclic compounds, organic compounds with cyclic molecular structure in which atoms of carbon and at least one other element are joined in a ring, *eg* pyridine C_5H_5N.

Hevesy, Georg von (1885-1966), Hungarian biophysicist, chemist. Used radioactive isotopes to study chemical processes and in medical research; awarded Nobel Prize for Chemistry (1943). Co-discoverer of element hafnium (1923).

Heyerdahl, Thor (1914-), Norwegian ethnologist. Known for practical demonstrations of feasibility of early racial migrations. Works incl. *Kon Tiki* (1950) on voyage from Peru to Tuamotu Isls., *The Ra Expeditions* (1971) on crossing Atlantic by papyrus boat.

Heysham, *see* MORECAMBE AND HEYSHAM, England.

Heywood, Thomas (*c* 1574-1641), English actor, dramatist. Known for classic domestic tragedy *A Woman Killed with Kindness* (1603). Other works incl. defence of stage against Puritans, *The Apology for Actors* (1612).

Hezekiah, king of Judah (*c* 720-*c* 699 BC). Rebelled against the Assyrians, but he and his Egyptian allies were defeated by Sennacherib (*c* 700). Reign was marked by prophecies of Isaiah and Micah.

Hialeah, town of SE Florida, US; suburb of Miami. Pop. 102,000. Has famous Hialeah racecourse.

hibernation, winter sleep of certain animals in temperate regions. Complete hibernation involves temperature drop, no food, spring awakening; practised by some mammals, most amphibians. Partial hibernation, practised by *eg* bats, involves periodic awakening for food.

Hibiscus: flower-of-an-hour (*Hibiscus trionum*)

hibiscus, genus of ornamental plants of mallow family, comprising *c* 150 herbs, shrubs and trees. Found in tropical and warm temperate areas. Some species cultivated for food and fibre products.

hiccup or **hiccough,** involuntary spasm of diaphragm followed by intake of air which is halted by sudden closing of glottis. Most hiccup attacks pass quickly but some may last for weeks.

hickory, any of genus *Carya* of timber and nut-producing trees of walnut family. Native to E Canada and US. Species incl. PECAN.

Hideyoshi Toyotomi (1536-98), Japanese general, statesman. Became leader (1582) on death of Nobunaga, then military dictator (1585). United Japan under his rule (1590). Suppressed Jesuits.

hieratic, Egyptian cursive script derived from hieroglyphics for purpose of writing on papyrus. Gave way to DEMOTIC from 7th cent. BC but survived longer as religious script.

hieroglyphics, ancient Egyptian pictographic writing developed in pre-dynastic times, *ie* before 3100 BC. Used 3 classes of symbol: ideograms or pictograms, representing

Hieroglyphic carving on limestone stele from Thebes (*c* 2150 BC)

words in pictorial form; phonograms, representing sounds of words; determinatives, to indicate sense.

higher education, *see* COLLEGE; UNIVERSITY.

Highgate, part of Haringey, N Greater London, England. Site of stone, allegedly where Dick Whittington heard Bow Bells sound 'turn again'.

Highland games, sports meeting, often professional, originating in N Scotland in early 19th cent. Events incl. caber tossing, hammer throwing, Highland dancing and bagpipe playing.

Highlands, area of Scotland, N of line joining Helensburgh and Stonehaven. Mainly uplands, mountains rising to 1342 m (4406 ft) on Ben Nevis; many sea, freshwater lochs; bisected by Great Glen. Crofting, fishing, distilling, tourist industs. Oil discovered off N, E coasts; h.e.p. **Highland,** region of N Scotland. Area 25,141 sq km (9709 sq mi); pop. 175,000. Created 1975, incl. former Sutherland, Caithness, Ross and Cromarty, Inverness-shire, Nairnshire.

high school, *see* SECONDARY SCHOOL.

highway, in British law, any road over which right of way has been estab., as by 21 years' uninterrupted use. In US, any of national trunk roads, controlled and partly sponsored by federal govt. *See also* MOTORWAY.

highwayman, formerly, robber on horseback, who robbed travellers on highway. Esp. prevalent in UK 17th-18th cent., leading to estab. of Bow Street Runners. Claude Duval, Dick Turpin among best known.

High Wycombe, mun. bor. of Buckinghamshire, SC England. Pop. 59,000. Mainly residential; furniture indust.

hijacker, originally, one who steals goods, esp. truck and contents, in transit. Term applied from late 1960s to one who forces pilot of aircraft to fly to non-scheduled landing point. Became tactic of international guerrilla warfare, esp. by Palestinian Liberation Front.

Hilbert, David (1862-1943), German mathematician. Made significant contributions to many branches of mathematics, incl. geometry, number theory and integral equations. Gave 1st consistent axiomatic treatment of

Euclidean geometry; attempted to find consistent basis for mathematics.

Hildebrand, *see* GREGORY VII, ST.

Hildesheim, town of NE West Germany, on R. Innerste. Pop. 94,000. Radio, television mfg., rubber goods. Archbishopric from 815, Hanseatic League member. Medieval buildings (incl. 11th cent. cathedral) badly damaged in WWII.

Hill, Archibald Vivian (1886-1977), English physiologist. Shared Nobel Prize for Physiology and Medicine (1922) for his discoveries in generation of heat in muscles. Showed that oxygen is used up after muscle's contraction.

Hill, Charles, Baron Hill of Luton (1904-), British physician, broadcaster, politician. Known first as 'radio doctor' in WWII, held govt. posts during 1950s. Chairman of Governors, BBC (1967-72).

Hill, James Jerome (1838-1916), American railway builder, b. Canada. He extended the St Paul and Pacific Railroad to Seattle and estab. (1890) the Great Northern Railway.

Hill, Sir Rowland (1795-1879), English educator. As school headmaster in Birmingham, estab. self-govt. system. Also responsible for introduction of pre-paid post (1840).

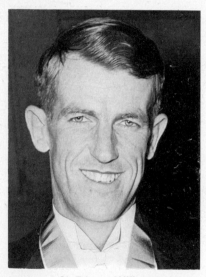

Sir Edmund Hillary

Hillary, Sir Edmund Percival (1919-), New Zealand mountaineer, explorer. He and **Tensing Norkay** (1914-), were first to reach summit of Mt. Everest (May, 1953), as part of British Everest Expedition. Hillary journeyed to South Pole (1958) by overland route.

Hillel (*fl* 30 BC-AD 10), Jewish scholar, b. Babylon. President of the SANHEDRIN; estab. systematic interpretation of the law in Hebrew Scripture. Taught moderation, justice; many of his sayings resemble teachings of Jesus, *eg* 'Do not unto others that which is hateful unto thee'.

hill figure, large monumental figure, usually a horse or man, cut from turf to show underlying chalk. Found mainly in downs of S England. Oldest is White Horse of Uffington, dating from Late Iron Age.

Hilliard, Nicholas (*c* 1547-1619), English painter, goldsmith. First true miniaturist in England, he was court painter to Elizabeth I and James I. Works incl. portraits of Queen Elizabeth, Raleigh, Drake, Sidney.

Hillingdon, bor. of W Greater London, England. Pop. 235,000. Created 1965 from Middlesex towns incl. Uxbridge.

Hilton, Conrad Nicholson (1888-'), American hotel owner. From buying 1st hotel (1919), he went on to estab. the largest world chain.

Nicholas Hilliard: portrait-miniature of James I

Hilton, James (1900-54), English novelist. Known for *Lost Horizon* (1933), best-seller *Good-Bye, Mr Chips* (1934) on the life of an English schoolmaster.

Hilversum, town of WC Netherlands. Pop. 97,000. Summer resort; textiles, electrical goods. Chief Dutch radio, television broadcasting centre.

Himachal Pradesh, state of N India. Area *c* 56,000 sq km (21,600 sq mi); cap. Simla (in Punjab). Pop. 3,424,000. In W Himalayas, bordering on Tibet. Forests yield softwood timber. Formed (1948) from former Hill States; more areas from Punjab added in 1966.

Himalayas, world's highest mountain system, stretching *c* 2400 km (1500 mi) across C Asia; forms natural barrier between Tibet and India, Nepal, and Bhutan. Peaks incl. Mt. Everest, Kanchenjunga, Nanga Parbat.

Himeji, city of Japan, SW Honshu isl. Pop. 408,000. Cotton textile mfg. Has restored 14th cent. castle.

Heinrich Himmler

Himmler, Heinrich (1900-45), German Nazi leader. Became head of SS (1929), commander of entire police force (1936), minister of interior (1943). Responsible for enforcement of extermination policies. Committed suicide.

Hindemith, Paul (1895-1963), German composer, violinist and viola player. Output large, varied, modern in style. Works incl. symphonies and operas, *eg Mathis der Maler.* Also a noted music theorist, basing much of his music on his theoretical work. Music banned by Nazis, after 1940 lived in US, Switzerland.

Hindenburg [und Beneckendorff], Paul von (1847-1934), German military, political leader. Became supreme commander of Central Forces (1916), directing German war effort until end of WWI. Elected president of Reich (1925-32) with Junkers' support. Re-elected (1932), appointed Hitler chancellor (1933).

Hindi, Indic language in Indo-Iranian branch of Indo-European family. Official language of India. Variant of Hindustani. Divided into Western and Eastern dialect groups, latter being vehicle of major literature.

Hinduism, Western term for the religion and social system of loosely-related related sects which incl. most of India's pop. Has no single founder but grew over period of *c* 5000 years, assimilating many beliefs. All Hindus traditionally subscribe to CASTE system and the sacredness of VEDA scriptures.

Hindu Kush, mountain range, mainly in NE Afghanistan, separated from W Himalayas by Indus valley. Tirich Mir in Pakistan, height 7692 m (25,236 ft), is highest peak. Has passes used by Alexander the Great and Tamerlane.

Hindustani, group of Indic languages in Indo-Iranian branch of Indo-European family. Some use term only for spoken forms of Hindi and Urdu, others incl. N Indian vernaculars. Developed from PRAKRIT. Used as lingua franca in modern India. Has 3rd largest number of speakers in world after Chinese and English.

hinny, *see* ASS.

Hinshelwood, Sir Cyril Norman (1897-1967), English chemist. Authority on chemical kinetics, esp. of gaseous reactions and chemical reactions in living organisms. Shared Nobel Prize for Chemistry (1956) with N.N. Semenov.

hinterland, area behind a coastal port which supplies most of its exports and provides a market for most of its imports. Often extended to mean area serving and served by an inland market town. First used by Germans in 1880s concerning region behind their occupied coastal territ. in N Africa.

hip, *see* BRIAR.

Hipparchus, tyrant of Athens. *See* HIPPIAS.

Hipparchus (2nd cent. BC), Greek astronomer. A founder of systematic astronomy, he made catalogue of hundreds of stars and discovered precession of equinoxes; first to use trigonometry. His findings influenced Ptolemy.

Hippias, tyrant of Athens (527-510 BC). Son of Pisistratus, shared rule of Athens with his brother Hipparchus, until latter's murder. Deposed by Alcmaeonidae family with aid of Sparta.

Hippocrates (*c* 460-*c* 370 BC), Greek physician, known as the 'Father of Medicine'. Leader of school of medicine on isl. of Cos, whose members emphasized scientific basis of medicine, distinguishing it from philosophy and religion. *Corpus Hippocraticum* (72 books) represents their teaching. Hippocratic oath, taken by medical graduates, said to represent his ethical ideas.

Hippolyte, *see* AMAZONS.

Hippolytus, St (d. *c* 236), Roman theologian. After split with Church, became 1st antipope (*c* 217). Died in exile although reconciled with Church.

Hippolytus, *see* PHAEDRA.

Hippomenes, *see* ATALANTA.

hippopotamus, heavy thick-skinned herbivorous mammal common to rivers of Africa. Large tusks in lower jaw source of ivory. Two species: *Hippopotamus amphibius,* of C Africa, and pygmy hippopotamus, *Choeropsis liberiensis,* of Liberia.

Hippopotamus *(Hippopotamus amphibius)*

hire purchase, system whereby goods are bought on payment, over a stated period, of equal instalments. Usually financed by specialist company. Buyer has use of, but does not own, goods until agreed terms have been fulfilled.

Hirohito

Hirohito (1901-), emperor of Japan (1926-). Reign marked by increase in militarism, with Sino-Japanese war (beginning 1937) and pact (1940) with Germany, Italy in WWII. Surrendered (1945). Allowed by Allies to remain as constitutional emperor, renounced (1946) claims to imperial divinity.

Hiroshima after dropping of atomic bomb

Hiroshima, seaport of Japan, SW Honshu isl. Pop. 542,000. Shipbuilding, car and textile mfg. Devastated by 1st atomic bomb (6 Aug. 1945), with loss of *c* 80,000 lives.

Hirudinea, class of annelids consisting of leeches. Body segmented, with sucker at each end; most species suck blood, using anticoagulant (hirudin) to keep blood liquid. Lives in water or wet earth. *Hirudo medicinalis* once used medicinally to bleed patients.

Hispaniola, isl. of Greater Antilles, West Indies, lying between Cuba and Puerto Rico. Area 76,483 sq km (29,530 sq mi). Comprises Haiti in W, Dominican Republic in E. Discovered by Columbus in 1492.

Hiss, Alger (1904-), American public official. Accused (1945) of conveying govt. secrets to agents of USSR, indicted on 2 counts of perjury. After 2 trials, found guilty (1950), imprisoned. Released 1954 still denying charges.

histamine, white crystalline substance found in animal tissue. Released when tissue is injured or during allergic reactions. Dilates blood vessels and stimulates gastric secretion.

history, branch of knowledge which deals systematically with the past, recording, analyzing, correlating and interpreting past events. Sources incl. buildings, artifacts as well as chronicles, contemporary written records. Herodotus considered 1st historian; Thucydides, in record of Peloponnesian War, was more limited in scope but began tradition of accuracy, continued by Tacitus in Roman period. Story-telling element stressed by Xenophon, Livy. Medieval historians preoccupied with theological interpretation of world's history, or with simply chronicling events (as by Saxo Grammaticus, Matthew of Paris), although Moslem chronicles maintained literary quality. Secular histories emerged in 12th cent., and Renaissance brought emphasis on textual criticism, esp. in 16th-17th cent. by, *eg*, Bodin. Accuracy was again combined with moral, social concern with 18th cent. writers, incl. Voltaire, Montesquieu. 19th cent. saw emergence of archaeology, philology, and development of history into academic discipline. Philosophy of history influenced by HEGEL, MARX, TOYNBEE. Other linked disciplines incl. anthropology, sociology, economics, psychology.

Hitchcock, Alfred [Joseph] (1899-), British film director. Famous for suspense thrillers. Films incl. *Blackmail* (1929), *The Thirty-Nine Steps* (1935), *The Lady Vanishes* (1938), *Rebecca* (1940), *Psycho* (1960).

Hitchcock, Lambert (1795-1852), American chair maker. Created 'Hitchcock chair', painted black, with rush, cane or wooden seat. Sometimes decorated with gilt stencils or painted designs.

Adolf Hitler

Hitler, Adolf (1889-1945), German dictator, b. Austria. Founded (1921) National Socialist (Nazi) Party. During imprisonment (1923) for attempted coup (beer hall 'putsch') in Munich, wrote *Mein Kampf* (my struggle), statement of ideology. Economic depression after 1929 brought mass support, making (1932) Nazis largest party in Reichstag. Hitler was appointed chancellor (Jan. 1933), estab. dictatorship (March, 1933) by attributing Reichstag fire to Communists. Estab. (1934) Third Reich, assuming title of Führer. Political opponents, Jews, socialists were persecuted or killed. Aggressive foreign policy and Anglo-French 'appeasement' led to MUNICH PACT (1938). Invaded Poland (1939) beginning WWII. Personal command of Russian campaign (1941) led to Stalingrad defeat. Survived assassination attempt (1944) by high-ranking officers. Faced with total defeat, committed suicide (April, 1945) with his wife, Eva Braun.

Hittites, people inhabiting Asia Minor and Syria from 3rd to 1st millennium BC. At peak of power 1450-1200, when they challenged Assyria and Egypt. Spoke one of earliest recorded Indo-European languages. Thought to be among 1st peoples to smelt iron.

hives, popular name for URTICARIA.

hoatzin, *Opisthocomus hoazin,* crested olive-coloured South American bird. Presence of wing claws on young indicates reptilian ancestry.

Hobart, cap. of Tasmania, Australia, on Derwent estuary. Pop. 153,000. Admin. centre; port with fine natural harbour, exports fruit, timber, metals; food processing, metal refining; univ. of Tasmania (1890). Founded 1804.

Hobbema, Meindert (1638-1709), Dutch painter. Considered last great 17th cent. Dutch landscape master. Influenced by Jacob van Ruisdael, he painted quiet landscapes, specializing in watermills and woodland scenes. Work incl. *Avenue at Middelharnis* (1689).

Hobbes, Thomas (1588-1679), English philosopher. Best-known work, *Leviathan* (1651), argued that humans are naturally violent, self-seeking, only to be controlled in totalitarian state, ruled by absolute monarch. Theories attacked by Locke.

Hobbs, Sir John Berry ('Jack') (1882-1963), English cricketer. Leading batsman of his times (1905-34), he exceeded 61,000 runs, incl. 197 centuries, in first-class cricket.

hobby, *Falco subbuteo,* small European falcon with long wings, short tail. Preys on insects and birds such as swallow, lark.

Hobhouse, Leonard Trelawney (1864-1929), English philosopher, sociologist. Combining history, anthropology, held that development of mind is paralleled by development of societies. Works incl. *The Metaphysical Theory of the State* (1918).

Hobson, John Atkinson (1858-1940), English economist. Anticipated post-Keynesian economics. Held that theory could be used to uncover causes of social ills. Revealed economic bases of colonization in *Imperialism* (1902).

Hochhuth, Rolf (1931-), Swiss dramatist. Known for controversial plays, *eg The Deputy* (1963) accusing Pope Pius XII of connivance in Nazi war crimes, *Soldiers* (1967) suggesting Churchill's implication in plot to kill General Sikorski.

Ho Chi Minh

Ho Chi Minh, orig. Nguyen That Thanh (1890-1969), Vietnamese political leader. Helped found French

Communist Party (1920) and Vietnamese Communist Party (1930). Organized and led Viet Minh, fighting guerrilla war against Japanese in WWII; headed provisional govt. after war. Gained complete control of North Vietnam after Indo-Chinese War (1946-54) against French. Geneva settlement divided Vietnam, Ho given control N of 17th parallel. Pursued militant policy in effort to reunite Vietnam through guerrilla war (VIET CONG) with South in 1960s.

Ho Chi Minh City. cap. and chief city of South Vietnam; formerly Saigon. Pop. *c* 1,805,000. Indust. centre with neighbouring Cholon, with canal link to R. Mekong. French colonial cap. from 1887 until independence in 1954. Hq. of US and South Vietnamese forces in Vietnamese war; seriously damaged in guerrilla fighting.

Ho Chi Minh Trail, supply route through E Laos used by North Vietnamese forces in Vietnam war, esp. after US-South Vietnamese invasion of Cambodia (1970) closed alternatives.

hockey, game played on field or ice. Field hockey, an eleven-a-side game played with ball and stick, developed in England, becoming popular in 1870s. Olympic event since 1908, now played widely in Commonwealth countries, Germany, Netherlands, *etc.* Ice hockey, six-a-side game played with stick and rubber puck, originated in Canada in 1870s. Professional National Hockey League teams (US and Canada) compete annually for Stanley Cup.

Hockney, David (1937-), English artist. Early work, using commercial imagery, is related to pop art. Later style is more realistic and colourful; excels in depiction of water. Works incl. *Mr and Mrs Clark and Percy.*

Hodgkin, Dorothy Mary Crowfoot (1910-), British biochemist, b. Egypt. Used X-rays to determine structure of vitamin B_{12} and cholesterol iodide (antidote for pernicious anaemia). Won Nobel Prize for Chemistry (1964).

Hoek van Holland, *see* HOOK OF HOLLAND.

Hofei, cap. of Anhwei prov., EC China. Pop. 400,000. Commercial, communications centre of agric. region; cotton, food processing. Univ.

Hoffa, James Riddle (1913-), American labour leader. Elected (1957) president of International Brotherhood of Teamsters (transport union), which was expelled in same year from AFL-CIO for corruption. Hoffa repeatedly tried for corruption, imprisoned (1967-72). Disappeared (1975), presumed murdered.

Hoffmann, E[rnst] T[heodor] A[madeus] (1776-1822), German author, composer. Influential during Romantic period through literary style; stories used by Offenbach for libretto of *Tales of Hoffmann.*

Hoffmann, Friedrich (1660-1742), German physician. Introduced Hoffmann's anodyne or compound spirit of ether; one of first to describe appendicitis and German measles. Believed disease to be disruption of body's tonus (giving rise to word tonic for his remedies).

Hofmannsthal, Hugo von (1874-1929), Austrian writer. Abandoned lyric poetry for mythological drama *eg Death and the Fool* (1899), *Elektra* (1903), *The Tower* (1925). Wrote libretti for Richard Strauss's operas, incl. *Rosenkavalier* (1911).

Hofstadter, Robert (1915-), American physicist. Investigated internal structure of atomic nuclei by bombardment with high energy electron beams; results showed existence of meson shells about protons and neutrons. Shared Nobel Prize for Physics (1961) with R.L. Mössbauer.

hog, name applied to several members of pig family. Species incl. red river hog, *Potamochoerus porcus,* of C and S Africa, pygmy hog, *Sus salvanius,* of Nepal, and WART HOG.

Hogan, Ben (1912-), American golfer. Winner of 9 major championships, incl. 4 US and 1 British Open titles. Seriously injured in 1949, made famous comeback.

Hogarth, William (1697-1764), English painter, engraver. Painted series of morality pictures, incl. *The Harlot's Progress, The Rake's Progress, Marriage à la Mode,* which satirized social abuses; engravings of these were popular successes. Portraits incl. *Captain Coram* and *The Shrimp Girl.*

James Hogg

Hogg, James (1770-1835), Scottish author. Known as 'The Ettrick Shepherd'. Wrote *The Private Memoirs and Confessions of a Justified Sinner* (1824) dealing with Calvinist doctrine of predestination. Also wrote poetry, *eg The Mountain Bard* (1807).

Hoggar Mountains, *see* AHAGGAR MOUNTAINS.

Hohensalza, *see* INOWROCLAW, Poland.

Hohenstaufen, German princely family, originating as dukes of Swabia. Holy Roman emperors (1138-1208, 1214-54); kings of Sicily (1194-1268).

Hohenzollern, German dynasty, founded by Frederick of Hohenzollern in Nuremberg (1192). His sons estab. 2 lines of family in Prussia and Bavaria, adding (1415) electorate of Brandenburg. Duchy of Prussia estab. by Albert of Brandenburg (1525). Territs. extended (1640-88) by Frederick William to become (1701) kingdom of Prussia under Frederick I. Emperors of Germany (1871-1918).

Hokan-Siouan, North American Indian linguistic stock. Incl. Hokan-Coahuiltecan, Iroquoian, Keresan, Natchez-Muskogean, Siouan families.

Hokkaido, isl. of N Japan, separated from Honshu isl. by Tsugaru Str. Area *c* 78,000 sq km (30,000 sq mi). Forested, with mountainous interior; harsh climate in winter. Fishing main indust.; produces coal, timber. Originally inhabited by aboriginal Ainus, settled by Japanese in 16th cent.; called Yezo until 1869.

Hokusai: *The Great Wave off Kanagawa*

Hokusai, Katsushika (1760-1849), Japanese painter and designer. Master of Japanese wood-block print (*ukiyo-e*), he is famous for his imaginative landscapes; his simplified design and dramatic composition influenced Western art. Works incl. series *36 Views of Mount Fuji.*

Hans Holbein: detail of a self-portrait

European holly

Holbein, Hans, ('the Younger') (c 1497-1543), German painter. Leading realist portrait painter of the N European Renaissance, he illustrated Luther's Bible and produced woodcut series *The Dance of Death*. Court painter to Henry VIII, his portraits incl. many of Erasmus, *Georg Gisze* and the *Ambassadors*.

Holborn, part of Camden, NC Greater London, England. Met. bor. until 1965. Has British Museum; 2 Inns of Court.

Hölderlin, [Johann Christian] Friedrich (1770-1843), German poet. Lyric poetry, *eg Bread and Wine* (1800-3), combines classical style with Romantic inspiration. Epistolary novel *Hyperion* (1797-9) reflects yearning for values of ancient Greece. Became insane in 1803.

Holguín, town of E Cuba. Pop. 193,000. Commercial centre in agric. region. Tobacco, coffee, maize, sugar cane exports; furniture, tile mfg.

Holinshed, Raphael (d. c 1580), English chronicler. Wrote *Chronicles of England, Scotland and Ireland* (1577), used as source for plots by Elizabethan dramatists, incl. Shakespeare.

Holland, Sir Sidney George (1893-1961), New Zealand statesman, PM (1949-57). Leader of National Party from 1946.

Holland, hist. region of W. Netherlands. County from 10th cent., held Zeeland, part of Friesland during Middle Ages. Prosperity at height 15th-16th cents. through commerce, cloth indust. Led Dutch independence struggle, chief of United Provs. 1579-1795. Divided 1840 into North Holland, prov. incl. some Frisian Isls. Area 2631 sq km (1016 sq mi); cap. Haarlem, chief city Amsterdam. South Holland, prov., area 2810 sq km (1085 sq mi); cap. The Hague, chief towns Rotterdam, Leiden.

Holland, Parts of, former admin. region of Lincolnshire, E England. Co. town was Boston.

Hollar, Wenceslaus (1607-77), Bohemian etcher. A leading engraver of topographical views of 17th cent. Europe. His views of London before the Great Fire are historically valuable.

Holliday, Billie, orig. Eleanora Fagan (1915-59), American jazz singer. Remembered for her subtle rendition of such songs as 'Strange fruit' and 'Am I blue?'. Autobiog. *Lady Sings the Blues* describes her difficult life.

holly, any of genus *Ilex* of evergreen, smooth-leaved trees and shrubs. Species incl. American holly *I. opaca,* and European holly *I. aquifolium* with red berries. Traditional Christmas decoration.

hollyhock, *Althaea rosea,* biennial plant of mallow family. Native to China, now widely cultivated garden plant. Large showy flowers on long spikes. Grows up to c 3 m/10 ft.

Hollywood, see LOS ANGELES, California.

Holmes, Oliver Wendell (1809-94), American writer, physician. Best known for wide-ranging prose dialogues, *eg The Autocrat of the Breakfast Table* (1858). Also wrote novels, poetry, *eg The Chambered Nautilus* (1858). His son, **Oliver Wendell Holmes** (1841-1935), was associate chief justice of US Supreme Court (1902-32). Dissented from

view that law has fixed universal power over society. Wrote *The Common Law* (1881).

holmium (Ho), metallic element of lanthanide group; at. no. 67, at. wt. 164.93. Discovered spectroscopically (1878).

Holocene or **Recent epoch,** second and current geological epoch of Quaternary period. Began c 11,000 years ago. When Pleistocene glaciers melted, climate was for a time warmer than now; present landscape formed, *eg* lakes, deserts. Man dominant; culture developed through Mesolithic and Neolithic, Bronze and Iron Ages to present level of civilization. Also see GEOLOGICAL TABLE.

holography, means of producing 3-dimensional images without use of lenses. Light from a laser is split into 2 beams, one of which falls directly onto photographic plate. Other beam illuminates subject to be reproduced and then recombines with reference beam to form interference pattern (hologram) on plate. A 3-dimensional virtual image can be seen by shining laser light through developed film.

Holothuroidea, class of echinoderms comprising sea cucumbers. Elongated cylindrical body without arms; mouth surrounded by tentacles. Moves horizontally by means of tube feet.

Gustav Holst

Holst, Gustav (1874-1934), British composer. His music is often eclectic but contains original rhythmic and harmonic devices. Work incl. opera *The Perfect Fool,* choral work *Hymn of Jesus,* orchestral suite *The Planets.*

Holt, Harold Edward (1908-67), Australian statesman, Liberal Party leader and PM (1966-7). Increased number of Australian troops in South Vietnam. Drowned.

Holtby, Winifred (1898-1935), English novelist. Advocate of women's rights. Known for novel *South Riding* (1936) set in native Yorkshire.

Holy Alliance, treaty signed (1815) by emperors of Russia, Austria, Prussia, with all European sovereigns eventually signing except George IV of Britain, pope, and sultan of Turkey. Estab. to preserve 1815 status quo, suppressed revolutions until Revolution of 1848 rendered it ineffective.

Holy Communion, see EUCHARIST.

Holy Ghost, see TRINITY.

Holy Grail, see GRAIL.

Holyhead, urban dist. of Gwynedd, NW Wales, on Holy Isl. Pop. 11,000. Tourist resort; has ferry services to Irish Republic.

Holy Island, see LINDISFARNE, England.

Holy Land, see ISRAEL.

Holy Loch, see DUNOON, Scotland.

Holyoake, Sir Keith Jacka (1904-), New Zealand statesman, PM (1957, 1960-72). Succeeded Sidney Holland as National Party leader and PM.

Holy Roman Empire, revival of ancient Roman Empire of the West, founded by CHARLEMAGNE (800). After period of decline and disunity, empire was revived by coronation of OTTO I (962), who united Lombardy with Germany. Dominions incl. Germany, Austria, Bohemia, Belgium and, until 1648, Switzerland and Netherlands. Habsburgs became hereditary rulers after 1438. Opposed Protestant Reformation in 16th cent. Influence declined after Thirty Years War (1618-48), power thereafter being wielded by Spanish and Austrian branches. Dissolved (1806) after Napoleon's conquests.

Holyrood House, royal palace in Edinburgh, Scotland, built c 1500 by James IV on site of 12th cent. abbey. Almost destroyed by fire (1650) and rebuilt by Charles II in 1670s. Scene of Rizzio murder (1566).

Holy Week, in Christian calendar, week preceding Easter, commemorating Jesus' passion and death.

Homburg vor der Höhe, town of WC West Germany, at foot of Taunus Mts. Pop. 38,000. Health resort, mineral springs. Seat (1622-1866) of landgraves of Hesse-Homburg.

Home, Sir Alec Douglas-, see DOUGLAS-HOME, ALEXANDER FREDERICK.

Home, Daniel Dunglas (1833-86), Scottish spiritualist medium. Known for levitations, séances before crowned heads, etc. Never successfully discredited.

Home Guard, in UK, originally the Local Defence Volunteers, formed (1940) as makeshift anti-invasion force, became efficient army of c 2 million by 1945.

homeopathy, system of therapeutics introduced by German physician Samuel Hahnemann (1755-1843). Based on belief that cure of disease is effected by minute doses of drugs capable of producing in a healthy individual symptoms of the disease being treated.

Homer (fl c 8th cent. BC), Greek epic poet. Traditionally regarded as author of ILIAD and ODYSSEY, although opinions differ over single authorship, with some doubt over his existence. Said to have been blind wanderer. Epics were models for all later European epics.

Homer, Winslow (1836-1910), American artist. After working as an illustrator, he devoted himself to painting pictures of outdoor life, expressing the American spirit. Best known for his depiction of the Maine coast; works incl. The Gulf Stream.

Home Rule, in Irish history, slogan used by Irish nationalists in 19th cent. who wished to obtain self-govt. for Ireland within British empire. Home Rule movement began in 1870s under leadership of PARNELL. Gladstone's 1st Home Rule Bill (1886) defeated; 2nd (1893) thwarted by House of Lords; 3rd (1912) never put into effect because of WWI and Irish pressure for independent republic.

Homestead Act (1862), law passed by US Congress permitting settlers to own up to 160 acres of previously unoccupied land after 5 year residence. Encouraged settlement of West.

Homo erectus, extinct species of man, incl. JAVA MAN and PEKING MAN. Skeletal remains c million years old have been found at OLDUVAI GORGE but more recent finds suggest that Homo erectus may have existed more than 2 million years ago in E Africa.

homosexuality, sexual attraction towards individuals of same sex. In women, commonly called lesbianism. Acceptance varies from culture to culture, male homosexual practices being illegal until recently in UK, and may be considered pathological abnormality.

Homs (anc. Emesa), city of WC Syria. Pop. 215,000. Agric. centre; oil refining, textile mfg. Had ancient temple devoted to sun god.

Honan, prov. of EC China. Area 168,350 sq km (65,000 sq mi); pop. 50,000,000; cap. Chengchow. Sparsely pop. in mountainous W, agric.; indust. in E; cereals, cotton, coal mining. Crossed by Hwang Ho.

Honduras, republic of Central America, incl. off-shore Bay Isls. Area 112,088 sq km (43,277 sq mi); pop. 2,800,000; cap. Tegucigalpa. Language: Spanish. Religion: RC. Humid Caribbean coast (US-owned banana plantations); Mosquito Coast in NE; mainly forested mountains in interior with important silver mines. Visited by Columbus (1502), colonized by Spanish; gained independence 1821; member of Central American Federation 1825-38. Disastrous floods in 1974.

Honecker, Erich (1912-), East German political leader. Secretary of Communist Party (1971-), succeeding Ulbricht.

Honegger, Arthur (1892-1955), Swiss composer, one of 'les Six'. Works incl. chamber and orchestral music, operas Judith, Le Roi David, and music for films. His best-known piece is Pacific 231, an orchestral evocation of a locomotive.

honesty or **moonwort,** Lunaria annua, European flowering plant with distinctive silver moon-shaped seed pods. Purple or white flowers in spring.

honey, sweet sticky fluid manufactured by honey bees from nectar taken from flowers, and stored in honeycombs as food. Consists of various sugars produced by action of enzymes on sucrose in nectar. Colour and flavour depends on type of flower from which nectar was collected.

honey bee, Apis mellifera, social bee of Old World origin. Builds nests of wax, storing honey in hexagonal cells; often kept in hives by man to supply honey.

honey eater, any of Meliphagidae family of brightly coloured Australasian birds. Tongue is brush-tipped for extracting nectar and insects from flowers. Species incl. wattlebird and bellbird.

honey guide, any bird of Indicatoridae family of tropical Africa and Asia. Feeds on honey, bee larvae; said to lead men and animals to bees' nests. Parasitic; young have hooks on beaks for disposing of hosts' young.

honey locust, Gleditsia triacanthos, North American tree of Leguminosae family. Bears seed pods with edible pulp; thorny branches. Grows up to c 45 m/140 ft.

honeymouse or **honey opossum,** Tarsipes spenserae, long-tailed mouse-like marsupial of SW Australia. Long pointed snout and bristly tongue used for sucking nectar.

Common honeysuckle (Lonicera periclymenum)

honeysuckle, any of genus Lonicera of wild and cultivated, erect or climbing shrubs. L. periclymenum, best-known in Europe, has fragrant yellow or white flowers. Name often used for family Caprifoliaceae, incl. viburnums, elder, as well as true honeysuckle.

Hong Kong, British crown colony of SE Asia, connected to S China. Area 1034 sq km (398 sq mi); pop. 4,160,000; cap. Victoria. Incl. Hong Kong isl., Kowloon penin., joined by tunnel (1972), and New Territ. (leased from China for 99 years in 1898). Major textile, garment industs.; shipbuilding, electrical equipment mfg. Important link for Chinese trade. Free port, with fine harbour.

Honolulu, cap. and chief port of Hawaii, US; on SE Oahu isl. Pop. 325,000. Has international airport. Financial, tourist centre; sugar processing, pineapple canning. Cap. from 1845.

Honshu, chief isl. of Japan. Area c 230,000 sq km (89,000 sq mi). Mountainous (Fujiyama), little arable land; rivers

Hong Kong

short and rapid. Densely populated; indust. centres incl. Tokyo, Yokohama, Nagoya, Osaka.

Honthorst, Gerard van (1590-1656), Dutch artist. Influenced by Caravaggio, he painted biblical, mythological and genre scenes. Noted for his candlelight effects, as in *Christ before the High Priest*.

Hooch or **Hoogh, Pieter de** (1628-*c* 1684), Dutch genre painter. Remembered for his depiction of interiors and courtyards; his rendering of effects of light is esp. fine.

Hood, Samuel Hood, 1st Viscount (1724-1816), British naval officer. Outmanoeuvred French fleet off St Kitts (1782), shared with Rodney victory off Dominica (1782). Blockaded Toulon (1793) and captured Corsica (1794).

Hood, Thomas (1799-1845), English poet, humorist. Wrote sentimental, comic verse. Serious works incl. *The Dream of Eugene Aram* (1829), *The Song of the Shirt* (1843) protesting against sweated labour.

Hooghly or **Hugli,** river of W Bengal, NE India; *c* 260 km (160 mi) long. Most westerly and most important arm of Ganges. Constant dredging of it maintains Calcutta's access to ocean.

Hooke, Robert (1635-1703), English physicist. A noted experimenter, he formulated Hooke's law of elasticity and invented the spiral spring for watches. His *Micrographia* (1665) contains numerous drawings of biological specimens observed by microscope.

Hooker, Richard (*c* 1554-1600), English theologian, clergyman. Known for *Of the Laws of Ecclesiastical Polity* (1594, 1597), dealing with concept of govt. (civil and ecclesiastical) and codifying principles of Anglicanism.

Hook of Holland (*Hoek van Holland*), town of SW Netherlands, on North Sea. Pop. 3000. Linked to Rotterdam by New Waterway. Ferry to Harwich (England).

hookworm, minute parasitic roundworm infecting humans, common in tropics. Larvae in soil penetrate skin and migrate to intestine; blood-sucking causes anaemia. *Ancylostoma duodenale* is common species.

hoopoe, *Upupa epops,* insectivorous bird of Old World, with slender bill and erectile headcrest. Solitary, timid; noted for fouling its own nest.

Hoover, Herbert Clark (1874-1964), American statesman, president (1929-33). Electoral success as Republican candidate for presidency (1928) followed by loss of public confidence on stock-market crash and subsequent Depression.

Hoover, J[ohn] Edgar (1895-1972), American public official. As autocratic director of Federal Bureau of Investigation (1924-72), made it a major force. Criticized for hostility to left-wing dissenters.

Hoover Dam, on Colorado R., US; on Arizona-Nevada border. Built 1931-6; one of world's largest dams, forming L. Mead. Supplies h.e.p. and irrigation over large area. Formerly named Boulder Dam.

hop, *Humulus lupulus,* perennial climbing vine of hemp family. Grown for the cone-like female flowers (hops), which are dried and used in flavouring beer.

Hope, Anthony, pseud. of Sir Anthony Hope Hawkins (1863-1933), English novelist. Known for popular adventure story *The Prisoner of Zenda* (1894).

Hoopoe

Hop

Hope, Bob, orig. Leslie Townes Hope (1903-   ), American comedian, b. Britain. Estab. himself as film star in 1940s, usually as comic but likeable coward. Associated with Bing Crosby, Dorothy Lamour in 'Road' films, *eg Road to Morocco* (1942), other films incl. *The Cat and the Canary* (1939), *The Paleface* (1948).

Hopeh, Hopei or **Chihli,** prov. of NE China on Pohai gulf. Area *c* 194,250 sq km (75,000 sq mi); pop. (est.) 47,000,000; cap. Shihkiachwang. Cereals, cotton, stock raising. Indust. around Peking. One of earliest areas of settlement, contains many prehistoric sites.

Hopi, *see* PUEBLO INDIANS.

Hopkins, Sir Frederick Gowland (1861-1947), English biochemist. Discovered amino acids which must be present in diet of mammals as they cannot be synthesized by body. Shared Nobel Prize for Physiology and Medicine (1929).

Hopkins, Gerard Manley (1844-89), English poet. Works, displaying metrical inventiveness, *eg* 'sprung rhythm', highly-worked language, deal with religion, nature. *Poems* (pub. 1918) incl. 'The Wreck of the Deutschland'. Jesuit convert (1868).

Hopkins, Johns (1795-1873), American financier, philanthropist. Estab. a free hospital (1867) and Johns Hopkins Univ., Baltimore (1876).

Horace, full name Quintus Horatius Flaccus (65-8 BC), Roman lyric poet, satirist. Early verse brought friendship of Vergil, patronage of Maecenas. Achieved fame with *Satires, Epodes,* but best known for *Odes, Epistles* and *Ars Poetica*.

Horae, in Greek and Roman myth, goddesses who controlled the cycle of the seasons. Also known as Peace, Justice, Order.

horehound or **hoarhound,** *Marrubium vulgare,* herb of mint family with bitter aromatic juice. Grows wild in Europe, Asia and US. Used as flavouring and for cough mixtures and lozenges.

hormone, substance formed in endocrine glands of higher animals. Carried by blood to other organs and tissues to control the body's metabolism. May be a steroid, *eg* oestrogen, a protein, *eg* insulin, or simple organic compound, *eg* adrenaline.

Hormuz, Strait of, passage off S Iran, connecting Gulf and Gulf of Oman. Also called Strait of Ormuz.

horn, a brass instrument with a funnel-shaped mouthpiece and a long, conical tube wound into a coil with a flaring bell. A natural horn or hunting horn sounds only the notes of hunting calls; FRENCH HORN has valves to produce all notes.

Horn, Cape, rocky headland of S Chile in Tierra del Fuego, most S point of South America. Notorious for stormy seas. Discovered by Dutch explorer Schouten (1616).

hornbeam, any of genus *Carpinus* of small trees of birch family. Found in US, Europe and Asia. Bears clusters of light-green nuts and yields very hard white wood.

hornbill, any bird of Bucerotidae family of Asian and African tropics. Has large curved bill with brightly coloured horny growth.

hornblende, dark green or black mineral of amphibole group. Glassy in appearance; found widely among igneous and metamorphic rocks. Major sources in Scotland, US, Canada.

hornet, name given to several species of large social wasps, esp. European *Vespa crabro.*

Horney, Karen (1885-1952), American psychiatrist, b. Germany. Founded (1941) American Institute of Psychoanalysis. Modified orthodox Freudian analysis to take account of environmental pressures on people in the development of neuroses.

Hornung, Ernest William (1866-1921), English novelist. Creator of gentleman-burglar, Raffles, in *The Amateur Cracksman* (1899) as criminal counterpart to his brother-in-law Conan Doyle's Sherlock Holmes.

horoscope, *see* ASTROLOGY.

Horse: palomino stallion

horse, *Equus caballus,* herbivorous hoofed mammal. Earliest known ancestor is dog-sized *Eohippus* of c 50 million years ago. *E. c. przewalskii* of Mongolia only surviving wild horse. Horses are classed as draught, light and ponies. Light horses such as Arabian and racehorses used for driving or riding.

horse chestnut, *Aesculus hippocastanum,* deciduous tree, native to temperate Eurasia. Large leaves, white flowers followed by glossy brown seeds ('conkers') growing in green spiky burrs.

horsefly, large fly of Tabanidae family, the female of which sucks blood of livestock. Also called cleg or gadfly.

horsepower, British unit of power; equals rate of working at 550 foot-pounds/sec; 1 horsepower = 745.7 watts.

horse racing, contest of speed between horses over designated course. Saddle racing incl. flat or thoroughbred races and steeplechases (over obstacles). HARNESS RACING

Horse chestnut

performed by horses trained to trot. In England, Jockey Club (founded 1750) controls horse racing. Famous events are Epsom Derby, St Leger Stakes, One and Two Thousand Guineas, Oaks and Grand National. American 'Triple Crown' comprises Kentucky Derby, Preakness and Belmont Stakes.

horseradish, *Armoracia rusticana,* perennial herb of mustard family, native to S Europe and naturalized in North America. Grated, pungent root is used as relish.

horseshoe bat, bat of Europe and Asia, of Rhinolophoidae family. Has horseshoe-shaped membranous outgrowths of skin (nose-leaves) around nose, used for navigation.

Giant horsetail (*Equisetum giganteum*)

horsetail, any of genus *Equisetum* of rush-like plants related to fern and club moss. Survivor of primitive, once abundant group of vascular plants.

Horta, Victor, Baron (1861-1947), Belgian architect. Early exponent of art nouveau, he is known for flowing decorative ironwork. Works incl. Maison du Peuple, Brussels (1896-9), now destroyed.

Horthy [de Nagybánya], Nicholas (1868-1957), Hungarian statesman, admiral. Led counter-revolutionary 'white' forces against Béla Kun's Communist govt. (1919-20). Became (1920) regent of Hungary. Forced to resign, deported by occupying Germans (1944).

horticulture, science of growing flowers, fruits, vegetables and shrubs, esp. in gardens and orchards.

Horus, in ancient Egyptian religion, god of the sun, light and goodness; son of Osiris and Isis. Represented with head of falcon. Known as Horus the child (Harpocrates) by Greeks and Romans, and represented as small boy with finger held to his lips and worshipped as god of silence.

Hosea, prophetic book of OT written by Hosea (8th cent. BC). Largely a sermon against moral decadence in N kingdom of Israel.

Hospitallers, *see* KNIGHTS HOSPITALLERS.

Hot Springs, resort town of C Arkansas, US; in Ouachita Mts. Pop. 36,000. In National Park which has many hot mineral springs.

Hottentot, people of South West Africa (Namibia) and NW Cape Prov. Pastoral nomads prob. related to Bushmen. Numbers diminished since Dutch settlement, pop. (est. 1963) 24,000.

Houdini, Harry, pseud. of Erich Weiss (1874-1926), American escapologist. Renowned for spectacular escapes from ropes, handcuffs, *etc.* Exposed fraudulent spiritualism by demonstrating how phenomena could be produced mechanically.

Houdon, Jean Antoine (1741-1828), French sculptor. Famous for his portrait sculptures, he received numerous commissions to portray leading figures of his time. Works incl. *Voltaire, Franklin, Diderot.*

Hounslow, bor. of W Greater London, England. Pop. 206,000. Created 1965 from Middlesex towns. Has Heathrow airport.

Houphouët-Boigny, Félix (1905-), African statesman, president of Ivory Coast (1960-). Instrumental in estab. universal suffrage, autonomy of French dependencies (1956-7). First African to become French minister of state (1957).

House fly on meat

house fly, *Musca domestica,* two-winged fly of worldwide distribution. Vomits digestive juice on food before eating it, spreading disease germs. Breeds in manure or decaying matter.

house mouse, *see* MOUSE.

House of Commons, lower chamber of British PARLIAMENT. Composed of members (MPs) popularly elected by single-ballot system, each representing specific constituency of UK; presided over by Speaker. More powerful of 2 Houses, govt. (*see* CABINET) depending on majority in it and answerable to it for all actions. Initiates all major legislation, controls national finance.

House of Lords, upper chamber of British PARLIAMENT. Composed largely of hereditary peers, with Anglican archbishops, bishops, number of life peers. Derived from medieval king's council. Presided over by Lord Chancellor. Powers curtailed by PARLIAMENT ACTS (1911, 1949). Also acts as UK's final court of appeal.

House of Representatives, lower house of US CONGRESS. Composed of members elected by populace for 2 year terms on proportional basis; presided over by Speaker. Originates revenue bills, has power to impeach president.

housing, living accommodation available to a community. Provision of housing of reasonable standard is one of the most pressing problems facing the world. It results mainly from rural-urban migration, lowering of death rate due to medical advances, and insufficient allocation of resources by govts. to housing. In developed countries this migration has now slowed, though much housing remains unfit; in developing nations it continues, leading to overcrowding, growth of ramshackle 'shanty towns' peripheral to cities, *eg* La Paz, Bolivia, and Caracas, Venezuela.

Housman, A[lfred] E[dward] (1859-1936), English poet, scholar. Known for collection of pessimistic lyric poems, *A Shropshire Lad* (1896).

Houston, Sam[uel] (1793-1863), American statesman, frontiersman. Led Texan defeat of Mexicans at San Jacinto (1836), capturing Santa Anna. First president of independent Texas (1836-8, 1841-4), state governor (1859-61) after Texas joined Union. Removed for refusal to join Confederacy.

Houston, port of SE Texas, US; on canal with access to Gulf of Mexico. Pop. 123,000. In important oil, sulphur mining region; exports cotton, chemicals, petroleum. Nearby victory at San Jacinto estab. Texas independence (1836). Cap. of Texas republic (1837-9). Has NASA space centre; Rice Univ. (1912).

Hove, mun. bor. of East Sussex, SE England. Pop. 73,000. Resort, adjoins Brighton.

hovercraft or **air-cushion vehicle,** amphibious vehicle developed (1959) in UK. Supports itself on cushion of air, usually generated by horizontal fan; forward motion provided by propellers or jets. First commercial service was Rhyl to Wallasey (UK) passenger ferry (1962).

hover fly, any of Syrphidae family of 2-winged insects. Resembles wasp with yellow and black bands on abdomen. Larvae feed on aphids, performing useful control.

Howard, Catherine, *see* HOWARD, THOMAS.

Howard, Sir Ebenezer (1850-1928), English town planner. Founder of GARDEN CITY concept, expounded in *Tomorrow: a Peaceful Path to Reform* (1898), repub. as *Garden Cities of Tomorrow* (1902). Founded Garden Cities Association (1899).

Howard, Leslie, orig. Leslie Stainer (1890-1943), British film actor. Typically cast as romantic intellectual, *eg Intermezzo* (1939), other films incl. *The Scarlet Pimpernel* (1935), *Gone with the Wind* (1939).

Howard, Luke (1772-1864), English meteorologist. His *Essay on the Modification of Clouds* (1804) estab. cloud classification still in use, defined terms *cirrus, cumulus, stratus. Climate of London* (1820) prob. influenced cloud studies by Constable.

Howard, Thomas, 2nd Duke of Norfolk (1443-1524), English nobleman. Defeated Scots at Flodden (1513). His son, **Thomas Howard, 3rd Duke of Norfolk** (1473-1554), a Catholic, had influence at Henry VIII's court through niece, Anne Boleyn, Henry's 2nd wife. Avoided execution for treason (1547) only by death of Henry; imprisoned throughout reign of Edward VI. His other niece, **Catherine Howard** (*c* 1521-42), was Henry's 5th wife; she was executed primarily to remove Howard family influence. His son, **Henry Howard, Earl of Surrey** (*c* 1517-47), was a poet, introducing sonnet forms, also iambic blank verse. Arrested with his father and executed. His son, **Thomas Howard, 4th Duke of Norfolk** (1536-72), favourite of Elizabeth I, was executed after failure of plot to free Mary Queen of Scots. His cousin, **Charles Howard, 1st Earl of Nottingham** (1536-1624), became lord high admiral (1585), commanding English fleet against Spanish Armada (1588).

Howe, Elias (1819-67), American inventor. Acquired 1st patent on lock-stitch sewing machine (1846).

Howe, Gordon (1928-), Canadian ice hockey player. Held almost every career record, incl. most goals (786) and most games played, at retirement (1971) from Detroit club in National Hockey League.

Howe, Joseph (1804-73), Canadian journalist, statesman. Editor of *Nova Scotian,* advocated responsible govt. but opposed confederation with Canada. Premier of Nova Scotia (1860-3).

Howe, Richard Howe, 1st Earl (1726-99), English admiral. Commanded Channel fleet in Seven Years War, British fleet during American Revolution. Defeated French off Ushant ('First of June', 1794). His brother, **William Howe, 5th Viscount Howe** (1729-1814), became British commander-in-chief in America after victory at Bunker Hill (1775). Defeated Washington at Brandywine (1777). Resigned 1778.

Howells, William Dean (1837-1920), American author. Known for realistic novels, *eg A Modern Instance* (1881), *The Rise of Silas Lapham* (1885), *Indian Summer* (1886). Also wrote life of Lincoln, criticism, poetry.

howler monkey, largest of New World monkeys, genus *Alouatta,* of forests of tropical America. Noted for howling noise; has prehensile tail.

Howrah, city of West Bengal, NE India. Pop. 740,000. On R. Hooghly, connected by bridge to Calcutta on opposite side. Indust. centre; textile, jute, glass mfg.

Hoxha, Enver (1908-), Albanian statesman. Led radical resistance against Italians (1939-44), founded Albanian Communist Party (1941). First secretary of party (1943-), premier of Albanian Republic (1944-54). Supported China during and after Sino-Soviet split (1961).

Hoy, isl. of Orkney, N Scotland. Has 'Old Man of Hoy' rock stack (137 m/450 ft high).

Hoyle, Edmond (1672-1769), English writer on games. Drew up rules for whist in *A Short Treatise on the Game of Whist* (1742); writings on backgammon, piquet have remained authoritative.

Hoyle, Sir Fred (1915-), English astronomer, author. Developed mathematical form of steady-state theory of universe. Author of *The Nature of the Universe* (1950) and *Galaxies, Nuclei and Quasars* (1965).

Hradec Králové (Ger. *Königgrätz*), town of N Czechoslovakia, at confluence of Elbe and Orlice. Pop. 70,000. Railway jct.; textiles; engineering. Nearby is SADOWA battlefield.

Hrdlicka, Ales (1869-1943), American anthropologist, b. Bohemia. Investigated theory of the Asiatic origin of North American Indians. Founded (1918) *American Journal of Physical Anthropology.*

Hsüan-tsang or **Hiouentang** (*c* 605-64), Chinese Buddhist scholar. Made extended pilgrimage to India collecting religious literature and writing accounts of his travels. Translated Buddhist scriptures.

Hua Kuo-feng in 1976

Hua Kuo-feng (*c* 1921-), Chinese political leader. Deputy premier and minister of public security (1975-6), appointed premier (April, 1975) on death of Chou En-lai. Succeeded Mao Tse-tung as party chairman.

Huambo, *see* NOVA LISBOA, Angola.

Huascarán, highest mountain of Peru; in W Andes. Height 6768 m (22,205 ft). Avalanche in 1962 killed 20,000 people in foothill villages.

Huayna Capac (d. 1525), Peruvian Inca emperor. Inca empire reached apogee under him, but civil war resulted from division of empire between sons Atahualpa and Huáscar, weakening resistance to Pizarro's subsequent invasion.

Hubble, Edwin Powell (1889-1953), American astronomer. Discovered large galaxies beyond the Milky Way. Formulated law that distant galaxies are receding with velocities proportional to their distances following observations of red shift in their spectra; this expansion of universe is explained by big-bang theory.

Hubli, town of Karnataka state, SW India. Pop. 380,000. Incl. town of Dharwar. Cotton trade.

huckleberry, any of genus *Gaylussacia* of North American shrubs of heath family. Dark-blue berries, resembling blueberries, but with 10 large seeds.

Huddersfield, co. bor. of West Yorkshire met. county, N England. Pop. 131,000. Woollens, carpets mfg; textile machinery.

Hudson, Henry (*c* 1550-1611), English explorer. In search of Northwest Passage, explored (in Dutch service) Hudson R. and (in English service) Hudson Bay. Disappeared after being cast adrift by mutinous crew.

Hudson, W[illiam] H[enry] (1841-1922), English author, naturalist, b. Argentina. Known for romances of South America, *eg The Purple Land* (1885), *Green*

Mansions (1904), celebrating wildlife of forests. Also wrote on ornithology, autobiog. *Far Away and Long Ago* (1918).

Hudson, river of E New York, US. Rises in Adirondack Mts. Flows S 510 km (*c* 315 mi) to New York City harbour. Chief tributary Mohawk R. Major commercial route linked to Great Lakes, St Lawrence Seaway.

Hudson Bay, inland sea of EC Canada, in SE Northwest Territs. Area 1,230,000 sq km (*c* 475,000 sq mi). James Bay in S. Discovered 1610 by Henry Hudson. Fur trade; exploration sponsored by Hudson's Bay Co. Churchill is main port. **Hudson Strait** provides access to the Atlantic.

Hudson's Bay Company, chartered 1670 for purpose of obtaining furs for the English market. Its vast territories, known as Rupert's Land, incl. all land drained by rivers flowing into Hudson Bay, were sold to Canadian govt. (1869). In 20th cent. its operations were diversified into retailing and mfg.

Hué, city of N South Vietnam. Pop. 200,000. Market centre; cement mfg. Cap. of hist. kingdom of Annam. Palaces and tombs of Annamese kings destroyed during North's Tet offensive of 1968.

Huelva, town of SW Spain, on penin. between mouths of Odiel and Tinto, cap. of Huelva prov. Pop. 97,000. Port, exports copper, iron ores; fishing, tourism. Nearby is monastery where Columbus planned his 1st voyage.

Huerta, Victoriano (1854-1916), Mexican general, president (1913-14). Supported Madero before overthrowing him, and estab. military dictatorship. Corruption, brutality provoked counter-revolutions, incl. those by Villa, Zapata. Forced to resign.

Huesca, town of NE Spain, cap. of Huesca prov. Pop. 33,000. Agric. market, pottery mfg. Site of Roman school (77 BC); cap. of Aragón 1096-1118. Cathedral (13th cent.), royal palace.

Huggins, Sir William (1824-1910), English astronomer. Pioneer of astronomical spectroscopy, he showed that certain nebulae are gaseous; developed photographic methods of recording spectra. First to apply Doppler principle to determine radial motion of stars.

Hughes, Richard Arthur Warren (1900-76), English novelist, poet. Known for novels, esp. *A High Wind in Jamaica* (1929), *In Hazard* (1938). Also wrote short stories, poetry, *eg Confessio Juvenis* (1926).

Hughes, Thomas (1822-96), English author. Known for novel *Tom Brown's Schooldays* (1857) expounding doctrine of 'muscular' Christianity. Also wrote on religion, life of David Livingstone.

Hughes, William Morris (1864-1952), Australian statesman, b. England, PM (1915-22). Headed Labor, then National wartime govts.

Hugh of Lincoln or **of Avalon, St** (d. 1200), English churchman, b. France. Called to England (*c* 1176) by Henry II, he was created bishop of Lincoln (1186). Sided with barons in refusing money for Richard I. Famed for piety, championing the poor.

Hugo, Victor Marie (1802-85), French poet, dramatist, novelist, leader of Romanticism. Introduced flexibility, melody into French verse, *eg* in play *Hernani* (1830), verse collections *Odes et ballades* (1826), *Chants du crépuscule* (1835), *Les Rayons et les ombres* (1840). Novels incl. *Notre Dame de Paris* (1831), *Les Misérables* (1862), *Les Travailleurs de la mer* reflect compassion for common man.

Huguenots, Calvinist Protestants of France, protagonists in Wars of Religion (1562-98), ending with Edict of Nantes. Many emigrated after its revocation (1685).

Huhehot, cap. of Inner Mongolia auton. region, N China. Pop. 700,000. Centre of caravan routes to Mongolian People's Republic; chemicals, motor vehicle mfg. Mongolian religious centre.

Hulagu Khan (1217-65), Mongol military leader, grandson of Genghis Khan. Sent to put down revolt in Persia, where he destroyed the Assassin sect (1256). Overthrew Abbasid caliphate with capture of Baghdad (1258). Invaded Syria, but was defeated there by Mamelukes of Egypt (1260).

Hull, Cordell (1871-1955), American statesman. Secretary of state (1933-44). Awarded Nobel Peace Prize (1945) for work leading to UN's creation.

Hull, town of S Québec, Canada; opposite Ottawa at confluence of Gatineau and Ottawa rivers. Pop. 64,000. Pulp and paper centre (matches); h.e.p. Founded 1800.

Hull or **Kingston-upon-Hull,** city and co. town of Humberside, NE England, on Humber estuary. Pop. 285,000. Port; ferry services to Europe; fishing. Has 13th cent. church; univ. (1954).

Hulme, T[homas] E[rnest] (1883-1917), English philosopher, poet. Anti-romantic, influenced Pound, Eliot, IMAGISTS. Poetry pub. in Pound's *Ripostes* (1915), essays in *Speculations* (1924).

humanism, movement in thought and literature, originally applied to Italian Renaissance. Involved reaction against medieval religious authority, rediscovery of secular Classical ideals and attitudes. Notable humanists incl. Sir Thomas More, Colet, Irving Babbitt.

Humayun or **Homayun** (1507-56), Mogul emperor of India (1530-56). Defeated and deposed (1540) by Sher Khan. Invaded India (1555), re-estab. Mogul rule.

Humber, estuary of NE England, of rivers Trent, Ouse. Length *c* 60 km (37 mi); ports incl. Hull, Grimsby.

Humberside, county of NE England. Area 3512 sq km (1356 sq mi); pop. 847,000; co. town Hull. Created 1974, comprising former East Riding of Yorkshire, N Lincolnshire.

humble bee, *see* BUMBLE BEE.

Alexander von Humboldt

Humboldt, [Friedrich Heinrich] Alexander von (1769-1859), German explorer, scientist, geographer. Expedition to Central and South America (1799-1804) resulted in greater understanding of scientific factors in geography. Explored Russia and C Asia (1829). Wrote *Kosmos* (1845-62), physical description of the Earth. His brother, **Wilhelm von Humboldt** (1767-1835), was govt. official and philologist. Prussian education minister (1809-10), reformed school system. Made pioneering study of Kawi language of Java.

Humboldt Glacier, glacier of NW Greenland, flowing into Kane Basin. Largest in N hemisphere, *c* 100 km (60 mi) wide at mouth.

Hume, David (1711-76), Scottish philosopher. Took ideas of Locke, Berkeley to logical extension of SCEPTICISM. Held that reason could only be subject to passions and rejected any rational theology. Works incl. *Treatise of Human Nature* (1739), *An Enquiry Concerning Human Understanding* (1748), *History of Great Britain* (1754).

humidity, *see* RELATIVE HUMIDITY.

hummingbird, any of Trochilidae family of small brightly coloured New World birds. Feeds on insects and nectar, hovering over flowers with rapidly-vibrating wings. Bee hummingbird, *Mellisuga helenae,* of Cuba is world's smallest bird.

Humperdinck, Engelbert (1854-1921), German composer and teacher. Friend of Wagner. His chief work was the opera *Hansel and Gretel* (1893).

Humphrey, Hubert Horatio (1911-), American politician, vice-president (1965-9). First Democrat from Minnesota to be elected (1948) to Senate. Democratic presidential candidate (1968), narrowly lost to Nixon.

humus, amorphous, black organic matter in soil. Humification is process of decomposition of plants and animals into elements useful in maintaining soil fertility. Sometimes extended to incl. partially decomposed matter in soil.

Hunan, prov. of SC China. Area *c* 207,000 sq km (80,000 sq mi); pop. (est.) 38,000,000; cap. Changsha. Leading rice producer. Major lead, zinc, antimony mines.

Hundred Years War (1337-1453), conflict between England and France, resulting from commercial and territ. rivalries. Begun when EDWARD III claimed French throne (1337). English successes at Sluis, Crécy, Poitiers were countered by later French victories under du GUESCLIN; French recovered most of their lost territ. by 1377. War was renewed by HENRY V who conquered much of Normandy after victory at Agincourt (1415). JOAN OF ARC began French recovery after 1429; by 1453 Calais was only English possession in France.

Hungary

Hungary (Magyar *Népköztársaság*), republic of EC Europe. Area 93,012 sq km (35,912 sq mi); pop. 10,449,000; cap. Budapest. Language: Magyar. Religions: RC, Protestant. Danube runs N-S; to E is Alföld plain; to W is Bakony Forest (hilly), L. Balaton. Agric. (esp. cereals) on collective system; indust. developing (coal, petroleum, bauxite). Kingdom estab. by St Stephen (11th cent.); ruled by Ottoman Turks until 1683; part of Habsburg empire until 1848 revolt; part of 'dual monarchy' (Austria-Hungary) 1867-1918, then independent republic. Joined Axis in WWII. Communist govt. estab. 1948. Revolt (1956) suppressed by USSR.

Huns, nomadic pastoralists of NC Asia who invaded E Europe *c* 370, forcing the Ostrogoths and Visigoths to migrate westwards. Under their leader Attila, overran Balkans and forced Emperor Theodosius to pay tribute. When tributes ceased Huns invaded Gaul but were defeated at Châlons (451). Subsequent invasion of Italy was abandoned (452).

Hunt, Sir Henry Cecil John (1910-), English soldier, mountaineer, explorer. Led British Everest Expedition (1953) on which Hillary and Tensing became first to reach summit. Wrote *The Ascent of Everest* (1953).

Hunt, [James Henry] Leigh (1784-1859), English poet, essayist. Wrote essays on music, painting, Italian literature. Imprisoned for attacking Prince Regent in *The Examiner* (1813). Poetry incl. 'Abou Ben Adhem' (1834), 'Jenny Kissed Me' (1844).

Hunt, William Holman (1827-1910), English painter. Founder member of Pre-Raphaelite Brotherhood with Rossetti and Millais; work is noted for its detail, harsh colour and laboured symbolism. Travelled to Palestine and Egypt to paint biblical scenes with accurate local settings. Works incl. *Light of the World.*

Hunter, John (1728-93), Scottish surgeon, physiologist. Made studies in comparative anatomy and introduced new techniques in surgery. His collection of anatomical specimens was acquired by Royal College of Surgeons, London. His brother, **William Hunter** (1718-83), was an obstetrician, known as a lecturer in anatomy. His collections formed basis of Hunterian Museum in Glasgow Univ.

Huntingdonshire, former county of EC England, now part of Cambridgeshire. Low-lying, Fens in NE; pasture, market gardening, cereals. Co. town was **Huntingdon (and Godmanchester),** mun. bor. on R. Great Ouse. Pop. 17,000. On Roman Ermine St.; bridge (14th cent.). Birthplace of Oliver Cromwell.

Huntington, Ellsworth (1876-1947), American geographer. Travelled extensively, esp. throughout Asia; evolved theories on the relationships between climate and development of civilizations. Works incl. *The Pulse of Asia* (1907), *Civilization and Climate* (1915).

Huntsville, town in N Alabama, US. Pop. 138,000. Space flight, rocket research centre. Agric. implements, textile mfg.

Hunyadi, János (*c* 1387-1456), Hungarian national hero. Won series of victories against Turks (1441-3) but was defeated with King Ladislaus at Varna (1444). Regent of Hungary (1446-52). Victory at Belgrade (1456) checked Turkish invasion of Hungary for 70 years.

Hupeh or **Hupei,** prov. of EC China. Area *c* 186,000 sq km (72,000 sq mi); pop. (est.) 32,000,000; cap. Wuhan at jct. of Yangtze and Han rivers. C part is low-lying, with many lakes and rivers. Grains, cotton, rice grown. Steel complexes.

hurling, fifteen-a-side team game played with sticks and ball, mainly in Ireland. Played for several cents. prior to formation of Gaelic Association standardized rules (1884).

Huron, confederation of 4 North American Indian tribes of Hokan-Siouan linguistic stock. Lived in Ontario in 17th cent. Numbered *c* 20,000. Farmers, crops incl. tobacco. Defeated and dispersed by Iroquois in 1649. Remaining members settled near Detroit and in Ohio where they became known as Wyandot. Later settled in Oklahoma (1867).

Huron, Lake, 2nd largest of Great Lakes, C Canada-US border. Area 59,596 sq km (23,010 sq mi). Bounded by Ontario (Canada), Michigan (US). Georgian Bay is NE extension; Saginaw Bay in S. Trade route connecting L. Superior, L. Michigan with L. Erie, used by oceangoing and lake vessels. Main cargoes iron ore, grain, limestone, coal. Ice-bound in winter.

hurricane, violent cyclonic storm occurring in tropical areas. Consists of high-speed wind system revolving around a calm, low pressure centre or 'eye'. Common in Caribbean, Gulf of Mexico areas; occur in Pacific as 'typhoons' or 'tropical cyclones'. Term also used to describe winds of velocity over 120 kmh (75 mph), *ie* force 12 on Beaufort Scale.

Hurstmonceux, see HERSTMONCEUX, England.

Hurtado de Mendoza, Diego (1503-75), Spanish writer. Diplomat under Charles V, exiled to Granada by Philip II. Wrote poetry, famous history of Moorish war of 1568-71, *Guerra de Granada* (pub. 1627) modelled on works of Tacitus.

Hus or **Huss, Jan** (*c* 1370-1415), Bohemian religious reformer. Influenced by views of Wycliffe, his preaching against clerical privilege attracted popular support and led to his excommunication (1410). Granted safe conduct to explain views to Council of Constance (1414), he was tried and condemned for heresy. Death by burning led to HUSSITE WARS.

Husein (*c* 626-680), Shiite Moslem saint, grandson of prophet Mohammed. Led unsuccessful insurrection in support of claim to succeed as CALIPH. Died in attempt. His claim is upheld by the SHIITES.

Husein ibn Ali (1856-1931), Arabian political, religious leader. Led (1916) successful revolt against Turks, proclaimed himself king of Hejaz. Deposed (1924) by Ibn Saud, exiled (1924-30). Son Feisal I founded Iraqi royal line.

Hu Shih (1891-1962), Chinese philosopher. Adviser of Chiang Kai-shek. Analyst of Chinese culture, promoted vernacular literature. Settled in Taiwan.

hussars, originally Hungarian cavalry in the 15th cent., the name was later applied to light horse regiments in many European armies.

Hussein I (1935-   ), king of Jordan (1952-   ). Moderate pro-Westerner, but led Jordan against Israel in 1967 Arab-Israeli war. After loss of Jordan W of R. Jordan, conflict arose with Palestinian guerrillas, leading to 1970 war. Although victorious, ceded W Bank to PLO (1974).

Husserl, Edmund (1859-1938), Austrian philosopher. Founder of phenomenology, *ie* belief that external data have no priority over imagination. Works incl. *Logical Inquiries* (1901), *Thoughts toward a Pure Phenomenology* (1913). Influenced later existentialists.

Hussites, followers of Jan Hus in Bohemia and Moravia who demanded religious freedoms and ending of clerical privilege; radical Taborite group, drawn mainly from peasantry, also sought social equality. Moderate Utraquist group accepted compromise settlement with Church drawn up at Council of Basle. Civil war resulted when Taborites rejected settlement, but they were defeated by Utraquists at Lipany (1434).

Hussite Wars, conflicts in Bohemia and Moravia begun when HUSSITES opposed succession of SIGISMUND as king of Bohemia (1419). Under Zizka and PROKOP, Hussites defeated crusading forces sent against them. Peace treaty (Compactata) drawn up at Council of Basle was accepted by moderate Hussites. Conflict broke out again during regency of George of Podebrad after Compactata was revoked (1462).

Huston, John (1906-   ), American film director. Films incl. *The Maltese Falcon* (1941), *Treasure of the Sierra Madre* (1947), *The African Queen* (1951), *Fat City* (1972).

Hutcheson, Francis (1694-1746), Scottish philosopher, b. Ireland. Developed theory of a 'moral sense'. Anticipated utilitarians in doctrine of 'greatest happiness for the greatest numbers'. Also wrote on aesthetics.

Hutchins, Robert Maynard (1899-   ), American educator. Promoted adult education through 'great books' programme (1946). President (1929-45) of Chicago Univ. Books incl. *Education for Freedom* (1943), *The Learning Society* (1968).

Hutchinson, Anne (*c* 1591-1643), English religious leader in New England. After banishment for antinomianism from Massachusetts Bay Colony (1637), helped found Portsmouth, Rhode Isl.

Hutten, Ulrich von (1488-1523), German scholar, soldier, poet, political reformer. Wrote *Gesprächbüchlein* (1521), anti-Italian satirical dialogues, originally written in Latin. Supported Luther, joined von Sickingen's revolt (1523), died in exile.

Hutton, James (1726-97), Scottish geologist. Originated several basic principles of modern geology, notably theory of UNIFORMITARIANISM. This belief that Earth's surface has been shaped since its origin by unchanging processes of denudation and deposition aroused much controversy; later simplified by Playfair. Wrote *Theory of the Earth* (1795).

Huxley, Elspeth Josceline, née Grant (1907-   ), English writer, b. Kenya. Known for books on African affairs, novels *eg The Walled City* (1948), *I Don't Mind if I Do* (1951).

Huxley, Thomas Henry (1825-95), English biologist. Foremost British exponent of Darwin's theory of evolution; his writings deal with conflict of traditional religion and science. Also studied physiology, anatomy, vertebrate skull and coelenterates. His grandson, **Sir Julian Sorell Huxley** (1887-1975), English biologist and author, was active in popularizing science. Works incl. *Heredity, East and West* (1949). First director-general of UNESCO (1946-8). His brother, **Aldous Leonard Huxley** (1894-1963), was a novelist and essayist. Known for novels of ideas, *eg Point Counter Point* (1928), anti-Utopian *Brave New World* (1932), *Eyeless in Gaza* (1936). Essays on religion, philosophy incl. *Heaven and Hell* (1956).

T.H. Huxley

French until defeat by British (1781). Succeeded by his son, Tippoo Sahib.

Hydra, in Greek myth, many-headed monster. When 1 head was cut off 2 grew in its place. The 2nd labour of Heracles was to kill the monster, which he did by burning the stump of neck after cutting off each head.

hydra, solitary freshwater coelenterate polyp, class Hydrozoa, which lacks free-swimming medusa stage. Tube-like body with tentacles around mouth; reproduces asexually by budding.

Hydrangea (*Hydrangea macrophylla*)

Huygens, Christiaan (1629-95), Dutch mathematician, physicist, astronomer. Invented pendulum clock. Discovered nature of Saturn's rings. Developed Huygens' principle in wave theory of light which explained polarization, reflection and refraction.

Huysmans, Joris-Karl (1848-1907), French novelist. Known for decadent novels, esp. *Against Nature* (1884), describing the restless quest for new sensation.

Hvar (Ital. *Lesina*), Adriatic isl. of Yugoslavia, off Dalmatian coast. Area 290 sq km (112 sq mi); main town Hvar. Fishing, fruit, tourism. Founded *c* 390 BC by Greeks as Pharos.

Hwainan, city of Anhwei prov., E China. Pop. 350,000. Centre of major coal mining region.

Hwang Ho or **Yellow,** river of N China. Flows *c* 4800 km (3000 mi) from Tsinghai prov. into Pohai gulf. Millennia of silting have resulted in North China Plain, which despite frequent flooding is agric. heart of country.

Hwangshih, city of Hupeh prov., EC China; on Yangtze. Pop. 200,000. Iron and steel centre built after 1950.

hyacinth, any of genus *Hyacinthus* of plants of lily family. Native to Mediterranean and S African regions. Narrow, channelled leaves, spikes of bell-shaped flowers.

hyaena, carnivorous wolf-like mammal of Africa and Asia, with bristly mane, short hind legs and powerful jaws. Feeds on carrion but will attack other animals. Species incl. spotted hyaena, *Crocuta crocuta,* of E and S Africa.

Hyatt, John Wesley (1837-1920), American inventor. Developed celluloid. Devised filter for chemical purification of water in motion.

hybrid, offspring produced by crossing 2 individuals of unlike genetic constitution, *eg* those of different race or species. Hybrid may be fertile or infertile. Hybridization is used in agric. to achieve greater vigour, growth in off-spring, *eg* mule, hybrid corn.

Hyde, Douglas, known in Irish as An Craoibhin Aoibhinn (1860-1949), Irish scholar, statesman, president of Irish Republic (1938-45). Instrumental in revival of Irish language; 1st president of Gaelic League (1893-1915).

Hyde, Edward, see CLARENDON, EDWARD HYDE, 1ST EARL OF.

Hyde Park, in Westminster, London; area 146 ha (361 acres). Incl. Serpentine lake and Rotten Row, famous riding track. Site of Great Exhibition (1851).

Hyderabad, cap. of Andhra Pradesh, SC India. Pop. 1,799,000. Transportation centre; textile mfg. Wall encloses old city containing Four Minarets (1591) and Great Mosque. Cap. of former princely state of Hyderabad (1724-1948).

Hyderabad, city of SE Pakistan. Pop. 624,000. Textile, machinery mfg. Cap. of Sind (1768-1843) until taken by British.

Hyder Ali (1722-82), Indian military leader, ruler of Mysore (1766-82). In Anglo-French conflict sided with

hydrangea, genus of flowering shrubs of saxifrage family, native to Americas. White, blue or pink flowers.

hydraulic press, device consisting of 2 liquid-filled cylinders of unequal diameter connected by a pipe and fitted with pistons. By Pascal's law, a force exerted on smaller piston will result in a greater force (proportional to quotient of the surface areas of pistons) on larger piston. Invented by J. BRAMAH.

hydraulics, branch of ENGINEERING dealing with mechanical properties of water and other liquids. Divided into hydrostatics dealing with liquids at rest, *eg* in hydraulic presses, and hydrokinetics dealing with problems of friction and turbulence in moving liquids.

hydrocarbon, organic compound containing hydrogen and carbon only.

hydrocephalus, enlargement of an infant's head caused by accumulation of fluid in the cranium. Damage to the brain and mental retardation may result.

hydrochloric acid, strong corrosive acid formed by dissolving hydrogen chloride HCl in water. Used in ore extraction, metal cleaning and as chemical reagent.

hydrocyanic acid (HCN), weak, highly poisonous acid with smell of bitter almonds, formed by dissolving hydrogen cyanide in water. Used as fumigant and in organic synthesis. Also called prussic acid.

hydro-electric power, electrical energy obtained from generators driven by water-turbines. Source of water may be natural (waterfall) or artificial (river-damming). Amount of power is proportional to rate of water flow and vertical distance through which it falls. During periods of low demand excess electricity is used to pump water back to source.

hydrofoil, wing-like device which produces upward lift when moved through water. Watercraft which use such devices to lift hull above water are capable of high speeds because of low drag.

hydrogen (H), colourless gaseous element; at. no. 1, at. wt. 1.008. Lightest known substance, its molecule consists of 2 atoms. Burns in oxygen to form water. Occurs in water, organic compounds, petroleum, coal, *etc.* Obtained by electrolysis, decomposition of hydrocarbons, or from water gas. Used in manufacture of ammonia, margarine and synthetic oils. Deuterium and tritium are isotopes important in nuclear research.

hydrogen bomb, nuclear weapon operating on principle of nuclear FUSION. Consists of atomic bomb surrounded by layer of lithium deuteride; intense heat produced by atomic fission causes nuclei of hydrogen isotopes to fuse into helium nuclei, with resultant release of enormous quantity of energy.

hydrogen ion concentration, in chemistry, number of grams of hydrogen ions per litre in an aqueous solution. The pH-value of a solution is the common logarithm of the

Hydrofoil craft

reciprocal of the hydrogen ion concentration and acts as a measure of acidity or alkalinity. Pure water has pH-value of 7; acids have values from 0 to 7, alkalis from 7 to 14.

hydrogen peroxide (H_2O_2), viscous liquid, often used in aqueous solution as a bleach and disinfectant. Powerful oxidizing agent; in concentrated form, used as rocket propellant.

hydrology, study of water upon, under and above the Earth's surface. Evaporation, precipitation, and flow through and over the Earth's surface together constitute the 'hydrological cycle'.

hydrolysis, in chemistry, decomposition by water. Hydrolysis of organic compounds may be effected by aqueous alkalis or dilute acids, *eg* esters of higher fatty acids are hydrolyzed in presence of alkalis to form soap. Inorganic salts undergo hydrolysis into acids and bases through action of hydrogen and hydroxyl ions in water.

hydrometer, instrument for measuring specific gravity of a liquid. Liquid is placed in graduated tube, which is then immersed in water. Depth to which tube sinks shows the specific gravity.

hydrophobia, see RABIES.

hydroponics, science of growing plants in solutions of the necessary minerals instead of in soil. Developed by J. von Sachs and W. Knop *c* 1860. Increasingly used commercially since 1930s.

hydroxide, compound consisting of element or radical joined to hydroxyl (OH) radical, *eg* potassium hydroxide KOH.

Hydrozoa, class of coelenterates usually showing alternation between colonial polyps and free-swimming medusae. Incl. hydra, without medusa stage, and Portuguese man-of-war, a floating colony of polyps and medusae.

Hyères, town of Provence, SE France, near Mediterranean Sea. Pop. 29,000. Resort, market gardening. Isl. group of same name offshore.

Hygeia, in Greek myth, daughter of ASCLEPIUS; goddess of health.

hygrometer, instrument for measuring RELATIVE HUMIDITY of atmosphere.

Hymen or **Hymenaeus,** in Greek myth, beautiful youth; personification of marriage.

Hymenoptera, order of insects, incl. ants, wasps, bees, with 2 pairs of wings coupled together in flight. Most species social, organized into colonies. Two suborders: Apocrita, those with narrow waist between thorax and abdomen; Symphyta, those without narrow waist.

Hymettus (*Imittos*), mountain group of Attica, SE Greece. Highest point Mt. Hymettus (1027 m/3370 ft). Famous honey; marble quarries.

hymn, song in praise or honour of a deity. Christian hymn developed as metrical form in 4th cent.; polyphonic settings evolved in 13th-16th cents. Lutheran CHORALE developed after Reformation. Dissenters of 18th cent. began English hymn tradition with collections such as those of Isaac Watts, John Wesley.

hyperbola, in geometry, curve traced by point which moves so ratio of its distance from a fixed point to distance from fixed line is a constant greater than 1. Curve has 2 branches; it is also a conic section.

Hyperboreans, in Greek myth, inhabitants of region of sunshine and everlasting spring in far north. Associated with cult of Apollo.

Hyperion, in Greek religion, one of the TITANS. Husband of his sister Theia, and by her, father of Helios, Selene and Eos. Sometimes appears as a sun god.

hypermetropia or **long sight,** defect of eye in which images are focused behind the retina, so that distant objects are seen more clearly than near objects. Caused because lens of eye is too short or its refractive power too weak. Corrected by glasses with convex lenses. Called far sight in US.

hyperons, in physics, elementary particles of baryon group with mass intermediate between that of neutron and deuteron. Decay rapidly into neutrons and protons.

hypertension, abnormally high blood pressure. May be symptom of disease, *eg* kidney disease, arteriosclerosis, but cause is sometimes unknown.

hypnosis, sleep-like condition induced in subject by monotonous repetition of words and gestures. Subject responds only to operator's voice and returns to normal consciousness when told to. Sometimes used to treat neurosis as repressed memories can be recalled under hypnosis.

hyrax, any of order Hyracoidea of rabbit-sized hoofed mammals of Africa and SW Asia. Two genera: rock-dwelling *Procavia* and arboreal *Dendrohyrax*.

hyssop, *Hyssopus officinalis*, small perennial aromatic plant, native to Mediterranean region. Blue flowers. Used in folk medicine as tonic.

hysteresis, in magnetism, lag in magnetization when ferromagnetic body is magnetized. Body retains residual magnetism when external field is removed. Graph of magnetizing field against magnetic induction in body is closed loop which indicates this lag.

hysteria, form of neurosis in which sustained anxiety expresses itself as bodily disturbance. May result in apparent paralysis of a limb or simulation of blindness.

Hythe, mun. bor. of Kent, SE England. Pop. 12,000. One of Cinque Ports, harbour now silted up.

I

iambus or **iamb,** metrical foot of 2 syllables, 1st unstressed, 2nd stressed. Term usually followed by word denoting number of feet in line, *eg* iambic pentameter (5 feet).

Iapetus, in Greek myth, one of the TITANS. Father of Atlas, Prometheus, Epimetheus and Menoetius.

Iaşi (Ger. *Jassy*), city of NE Romania. Pop. 202,000. Industs. incl. textiles, metal goods. Cultural centre; univ. (1860). Scene of German massacre of Jews (1941).

Ibadan, city of SW Nigeria. Pop. 758,000. Admin., indust. centre on Lagos-Kano railway; trade in cacao, cotton, palm oil; univ. (1962). Centre of Yoruba culture.

Ibaqué, town of WC Colombia, in C Andes. Pop. 172,000. Coffee trade centre; flour milling, brewing industs. Founded 1550.

Iberia, penin. of SW Europe, comprising Spain and Portugal, separated from rest of Europe by Pyrenees. Name derived from Greek for people living beside R. Iberus (mod. *Ebro*).

Ibert, Jacques (1890-1962), French composer. Style light and unpretentious. Wrote concertos, suites, *eg Escales,* also operas and ballets.

Nubian ibex (*Capra ibex nubiana*)

ibex, any of several species of mountain goats with backward-curving horns, found in Europe and Asia. Incl. Alpine ibex, *Capra ibex,* with short legs, powerful horns.

ibis, wading bird of Threskiornithidae family, related to stork, found mainly in tropical regions. Species incl. sacred ibis of ancient Egypt, *Threskiornis aethiopica*.

Ibiza, *see* IVIZA, Spain.

Ibn Batuta (1304-77), Arab traveller, b. Tangier. Most widely travelled person known from medieval times, journeyed for *c* 30 years in N Africa, Middle and Far East; left many reliable accounts.

Ibn Ezra, Abraham ben Meir (1098-1164), Jewish poet, mathematician, philosopher, b. Spain. Pioneered critical commentaries of biblical scriptures. Inspiration of Browning's 'Rabbi Ben Ezra'.

Ibn Gabirol, Solomon ben Judah (*c* 1020-1058), Jewish poet, also known as Avicebron. Wrote religious poetry and philosophical *The Well of Life,* a subsequent influence on Christian theology.

Ibn Khaldun (1332-1406), Arab historian, b. Tunis. Among first to develop a philosophy of history, his universal

history *Kitab al-Ibar* contains pioneering sociological material. Considered greatest Arab historian.

Ibn Saud (*c* 1880 - 1953), king of Saudi Arabia. Leader of WAHABI movement in Islam, captured Riyadh (1902) and took control of Nejd. Defeated rival Husein ibn Ali (1924) and annexed his kingdom of Hejaz. United Nejd and Hejaz (1932) to form kingdom of Saudi Arabia.

Ibn Sina, *see* AVICENNA.

Ibo, people of SE Nigeria. Number *c* 7 million. One of most advanced tribes in country, active in struggle for independence. Constitute most of pop. of BIAFRA.

Ibsen, Henrik Johan (1828-1906), Norwegian dramatist. Works stress importance of individuals' joy in living rather than conventional society's needs. Best-known plays incl. verse *Peer Gynt* (1867); social tragedies *A Doll's House* (1879), *Ghosts* (1881), *Hedda Gabler* (1890); symbolic dramas *The Wild Duck* (1884), *When We Dead Awaken* (1899) dealing with spiritual death through denial of love.

Icarus, *see* DAEDALUS.

ice, water in solid state, formed by cooling below freezing point. As water expands on freezing, ice is less dense than liquid water.

Ice ages, glaciations of PLEISTOCENE EPOCH when ice sheets and glaciers periodically advanced to cover large areas of America, Asia and Europe. Four major advances normally distinguished, most recent ending *c* 11,000 years ago. Greatly affected landscape formation. Believed to have been caused by perturbations in Earth's orbit about Sun.

iceberg, mass of ice broken off from a glacier or ice barrier and floating in the sea. Normally only *c* 1/9th total mass is visible above the surface. Hazard to shipping, *eg* sinking of *Titanic* (1912).

ice hockey, *see* HOCKEY.

Içel, *see* MERSIN.

Iceland

Iceland (*Island*), isl. republic of Europe, in N Atlantic. Area 102,950 sq km (39,750 sq mi); pop. 212,000; cap. Reykjavik. Language: Icelandic. Religion: Lutheran. Uninhabited C plateau; over 100 volcanoes (many active), hot springs, icefields (incl. Vatnajökull). Rugged coastline; mild, wet climate, stunted vegetation. Fishing (esp. cod, herring), h.e.p., grazing. Colonized 9th cent. by Norwegians; first parliament in Europe (930); united with Denmark (1380-1918). Independent republic from 1944.

Icelandic, *see* GERMANIC LANGUAGES.

Icelandic literature, best known for early works (*c* 1000-1300), EDDAS and SAGAS closely linked to OLD NORSE. Chivalric romances written from *c* 1300 on; after Reformation strong religious influence seen in hymns, *etc*, poems of Einar Sigurdsson. Only with romantic revival of mid-19th cent. did literature reach peak of pre-1300, creating new classical Icelandic style. Notable figures of 19th–20th cent. incl. Thoroddsen, Sigurdsson, Brandes, Gunnarsson, Kamban, Gudmundsson, and Nobel laureate Laxness.

Iceland moss, *Cetraria islandica,* Arctic LICHEN. Light brown, *c* 10 cm/4 in. high. Can be processed as food.

Iceland spar, colourless, transparent variety of calcite. Used in optical instruments. Found mainly in Iceland, also US, Mexico.

ice plant, *Cryophytum crystallinum,* succulent Old World plant whose thick leaves are covered with thin cells which glisten like ice.

Ichang, port of Hupeh Prov., EC China. Pop. 160,000. Ocean terminus of Yangtze, *c* 1600 km (1000 mi) from sea.

Ichikawa, Kon (1915-   ), Japanese film director. Films incl. *The Burmese Harp* (1955), *Alone on the Pacific* (1966).

I Ching or **Book of Changes,** one of five Chinese Confucian classics, originally written *c* 1027-256 BC. Contains system of divination based on 64 hexagrams.

ichneumon, *Herpestes ichneumon,* riverside-dwelling mongoose found in S Spain and throughout Africa. Sacred in ancient Egypt, often mummified.

ichneumon fly, parasitic wasp-like insect of Ichneumonidae family. Lays eggs in or near bodies of other insects. Hatched larvae devour host.

ichthyology, branch of zoology dealing with fish, their structure, classification and life history. Fish are divided into 3 main classes: jawless fish (Cyclostomata), incl. lampreys and hagfish; cartilaginous fish (Chondrichthyes), incl. sharks and rays; bony fish (Osteichthyes), comprising majority of fish. Over 20,000 living species exist.

ichthyosaur, large extinct aquatic reptile, known from fossils of Jurassic period. Dolphin-like, with 4 paddle-shaped flippers and long snout.

Icon

icon, image or picture of Christ, Virgin Mary or a saint, venerated in Eastern Orthodox church. In common use by end of 5th cent., few survived outbreak of iconoclasm in 8th and 9th cents. Following fall of Constantinople, icon-making *fl* in Russia until the Revolution.

Iconium, *see* KONYA.

Ictinus (*fl* 5th cent. BC), Greek architect. Leading Athenian architect of time of Pericles, collaborated with Callicrates on building of the Parthenon (447-432 BC). Temple of Apollo at Bassae attributed to him.

id, term used by Freud to denote that part of personality which is unconscious, primitive, instinctual, dynamic, as opposed to the EGO and SUPEREGO.

Ida, Mount (*Psiloríti*), mountain of C Crete, Greece. Height 2455 m (8058 ft).

Idaho, state of NW US. Area 216,413 sq km (83,557 sq mi); pop. 713,000; cap. Boise. Dominated by Rocky Mts.;

crossed by Snake, Salmon rivers. Timber, agric. in S (potato, wheat, sugar beet production); silver, lead, antimony mines. Settled in 1860s. Admitted to Union as 43rd state (1890).

idealism, in philosophy, theory that nothing outside ideas has any reality. The only reality of objects is in the impression they make on the mind. Normally implies the existence of absolutes, *eg* good, truth. Developed along separate lines by *eg* Plato, Berkeley, Kant, Hegel.

Idomeneus, in Greek legend, king of Crete. Led his subjects against Troy in Trojan War. During a storm on the return journey, he vowed to sacrifice to Poseidon the 1st living thing he met on landing. This turned out to be his son, whom he slew.

Idrisi or **Edrisi** (*c* 1099-*c* 1166), Arab geographer, b. Ceuta. Journeyed in Europe, Asia Minor, Mediterranean area before settling in Sicily under Roger II. Wrote a description of the Earth (1154), most important geographic work of the period.

If, Château d', fortress, formerly used as prison, on isl. of If, off Marseilles, S France. Built 16th cent., scene of imprisonment in Dumas' *The Count of Monte Cristo.*

Ife, city of SW Nigeria. Pop. 157,000. Trade in cacao, palm and kernels; univ. (1961). Hist. religious centre of Yoruba tribe.

Ifni, region of SW Morocco. On edge of Sahara; fruit growing, coastal fishing. Overseas prov. of Spain from 1860, cap. Sidi Ifni; returned to Morocco 1969.

Igarka, town of USSR, NW Siberian RSFSR; port on R. Yenisei in Arctic Circle. Pop. 16,000. Exports timber; sawmilling. Founded 1928.

Ignatius of Antioch, St (d. *c* 107), bishop of Antioch, Christian martyr. Known for 7 letters to churches in Rome and Asia Minor. Stressed importance of Virgin birth.

Ignatius of Loyola, St, (1491-1556), Spanish monk. Gave up military career after severe wounds, became religious (1521). Planned and organized Jesuit order, approved by pope (1540) on basis of *Formula* (revised as *Constitutions,* pub. at his death). Elected (1541) 1st general of order. Also wrote devotional *Spiritual Exercises.*

igneous rocks, rocks formed by cooling and solidification of molten magma. Consist of mass of interlocking crystals due to different rate of cooling of constituent minerals. Those formed after reaching Earth's surface, *ie* EXTRUSIVE ROCKS, are commonly finely crystalline; those formed at depth, *ie* INTRUSIVE ROCKS, are commonly coarsely crystalline.

Iguaçu or **Iguassú,** river of S Brazil. Flows W 1200 km (750 mi) to join Paraná at Argentina border. H.e.p. at Iguaçu Falls (joint Brazil-Argentina control).

Marine iguana *(Amblyrhynchus cristatus) of Galápagos Islands*

iguana, any lizard of Iguanidae family of tropical America. Common species is *Iguana iguana* of Mexico and N South America; greenish, with row of spines from neck to tail. Many species can change colour.

iguanodon, two-legged herbivorous dinosaur, reaching lengths of 7.6 m/25 ft. Fossils found in Cretaceous rocks esp. in Belgium.

Ijmuiden, part of Velsen, WC Netherlands, on North Sea. Fishing port at W end of North Sea canal; large steel works.

Ijsselmeer or **Ysselmeer,** shallow freshwater lake of NW Netherlands, fed by R. Ijssel. Created from former ZUIDER ZEE by dam (31 km/19 mi long) completed 1932. Four polders reclaimed, giving rich agric. land; also fishing.

ikebana, Japanese art of arranging cut flowers into aesthetically pleasing designs. Originating in practice of making offerings of flowers in Buddhist temples, it became popular pastime of the nobility in 15th cent.

Ikhnaton or **Akhenaton,** orig. Amenhotep IV (d. *c* 1354 BC), Egyptian pharaoh (*c* 1372–*c* 1354 BC), husband of Nefertiti. Built Akhetaton (modern AMARNA) as centre of his new religion devoted to worship of sun god Aton, in whose honour he changed his name.

Ile-de-France, hist. region of France, in centre of Paris basin. Agric. area, providing Paris with food; drained by rivers Seine, Oise, Marne; forests at Fontainebleau, Compiègne. Power base of 1st kings of France.

Ilhéus, port of E Brazil, in Bahía state; on inlet of Atlantic. Pop. 108,000. Important cacao, timber exports.

Iliad, Greek epic in 24 books, attributed to Homer, prob. written *c* 6th cent. BC, composed *c* 8th cent. BC. Set in Trojan War (Ilium = Troy), theme is wrath of Achilles and course of war.

Ilium, *see* TROY.

Illinois, state of NC US. Area 146,676 sq km (56,400 sq mi); pop. 11,114,000; cap. Springfield; major city Chicago. Mississippi R. forms W border. Mainly plains; agric. important esp. livestock, corn, maize, wheat. Large mineral resources in S *eg* coal, oil. Mfg. and indust. concentrated on L. Michigan shore around Chicago (meat packing, oil refining). French estab. missions in 17th cent.; passed to British 1763; taken by US in Revolution. Admitted to Union as 21st state (1818).

Illuminati (Lat.,=enlightened), mystic sects claiming special knowledge of God, esp. order founded (1776) in Germany by Adam Weishaupt. Aims were republican and anti-Catholic. With close affinities with Freemasonry, it was denounced and suppressed by Bavarian govt. (1785).

illumination of manuscripts, decoration of hand-written books with coloured pictures, esp. initial letters and marginal decorations. Early Christian examples incl. Irish *Book of Kells* (8th cent.); later ones incl. *Très Riches Heures du Duc de Berri* by Limbourg brothers (15th cent.).

Illyria, region on Adriatic coast of Yugoslavia and N Albania. Ancient tribal kingdom estab. 3rd cent. BC, partly conquered (34 BC) by Romans. Name revived by Napoleon (1809), Austria (1816-49).

ilmenite, black mineral, consisting of iron titanium oxide. Found mainly in basic igneous rocks; recently discovered to exist in quantity on the Moon. Chief source of titanium. Major sources in US, Canada, Australia, Norway.

Iloilo, seaport of Philippines, S Panay isl. Pop. 233,000. Commercial centre; exports sugar, rice and corn.

Ilorin, city of W Nigeria. Pop. 252,000. Agric. trade centre; pottery, cloth mfg. Former cap. of a Yoruba kingdom, taken 1825 by the Fulani.

image, in optics, visual likeness of object produced by reflection from a mirror or refraction by a lens. Real image is formed by light rays actually meeting at a point and entering observer's eye; may be shown on a screen. Virtual image is seen at point from which rays appear to come and cannot be shown on a screen.

imagists, group of poets incl. Richard Aldington, T.S. Eliot, Hilda Doolittle, Amy Lowell, who followed leadership of T.E. HULME, EZRA POUND in reacting against stultified Georgian romanticism. Works characterized by total precision in presentation of each image within short, free verse form. Active 1910-18 but had great influence.

imam (Arab.,=leader), in Islam, any recognized leader incl. successors of Mohammed. Esp. used by SHIITES for the unknown descendants of HUSEIN, *ie* the hidden imamate. *See* MAHDI. Imam also refers to leader of prayers in mosque.

immanence, in theology, the presence throughout natural universe of a spiritual principle. Opposed to transcendence, *ie* the existence of a spiritual principle outside the natural universe. Three main monotheistic religions believe that God is both immanent and transcendent.

Immermann, Karl Leberecht (1796-1840), German author. Known for social novel *The Late-Comers* (1836). Experimental work, *Münchhausen* (1838-9), develops 2 main plots in alternate episodes. Also wrote Romantic drama *Merlin* (1832).

immunity, natural resistance of an organism to specific infections. Presence of microbes in body stimulates formation of antibodies which provide temporary immunity for subsequent attacks of a particular disease. Can be induced by use of vaccines.

impala, *Aepyceros melampus,* medium-sized reddish antelope of S and E Africa. Male has long lyre-shaped horns. Noted for extraordinary leaping ability.

impeachment, bringing of public official before proper tribunal on charge of wrong-doing. In UK, trial is before House of Lords on Commons' accusation. Rare, although much used 1640-2. WARREN HASTINGS case (1788-95) was one of last in Britain. In US, House of Representatives has right of impeachment, Senate tries cases. Best-known case that of President A. Johnson (1868), who was acquitted. Impeachment procedure begun (1974) against Nixon, who resigned.

Imperial Conference, *see* COMMONWEALTH, BRITISH.

imperialism, extension of rule or influence by one country over another by diplomatic, military or economic means; manifested in empire. Esp. applied to European expansion (late 19th cent.) into Asia and Africa. Modern concept of neo-imperialism refers to economic or political domination of affairs of less developed countries.

impetigo, contagious disease of the skin caused by staphylococci. Characterized by eruption of isolated pus-filled blisters on hands, neck, face. Treated by antibiotics.

Imphal, cap. of Manipur state, NE India. Pop. 101,000. Agric. centre. Allied base in Burma campaign of WW II.

impressionism, school of painting, which originated in France in 1860s; name is derived from painting *Impression, Sunrise* by Monet shown at first Impressionist Exhibition (1874). Main exponents were Monet, Pissarro, Sisley, but Cézanne, Manet, Renoir and Degas were originally associated with movement. Their aim was to capture a momentary glimpse of a subject, reproducing changing effects of light in short strokes of pure colour.

impressment, practice of forcibly seizing recruits for military or naval duty. In UK, declared illegal in respect of soldiers (1641); legitimately used for naval recruitment down to early 19th cent. *See* PRESS-GANG.

incarnation, the assumption of human form by a god. Concept occurs in many religions, *eg* ancient Egyptian and Indian beliefs that certain kings were divine incarnations; also Greek belief that gods used human forms to communicate with men. Christians believe Jesus to be both wholly divine and human.

Incas, name ordinarily given to the pop. of Peru before conquest by Pizarro (1533), but properly restricted to ruling caste, ruler himself being the Inca. Civilization, centred at Cuzco, may go back to 1200. Achieved high level of culture as shown by social system, knowledge of agric., roadmaking, ceramics, textiles, buildings, *eg* Temple of the Sun at Machu Picchu.

incendiary bomb, canister containing highly inflammable substance such as thermite. Often dropped from aircraft in conjunction with explosive bombs.

incest, sexual relations between people of close kinship. Prohibited by law or custom in most societies although exceptions can be found in royal households of ancient Egypt and the Incas. Definitions of kinship, often complex, vary among societies.

Inchon, seaport of NW South Korea. Pop. 646,000. Ice-free harbour on Yellow Sea. Commercial and indust. centre; produces steel, textiles, chemicals, coke. Formerly called Chemulpo.

inclosure, alternative spelling of ENCLOSURE.

income tax, govt. tax on individual or corporate incomes. Modern form introduced in Britain by Pitt (1799) to raise funds for Napoleonic Wars; permanent tax adopted (1874). In US first levied during Civil War, present form adopted (1913). Now major source of revenue.

incubus, male demon which, in folklore, has intercourse with sleeping women, so fathering demons, witches, deformed children. Stories of them esp. common in Middle Ages. Female counterpart is succubus.

incunabula (Latin, = cradle), books printed before 1500, in infancy of printing. Printers incl. Gutenberg, Jenson, Caxton, Aldus Manutius.

Independence, town of W Missouri. Pop. 112,000. Agric. machinery mfg. Hist. starting point on Santa Fé and Oregon trails.

Independence, American War of, see AMERICAN REVOLUTION.

Independence, Declaration of, formal statement adopted (4 July, 1776) by 2nd Continental Congress declaring the 13 American colonies free and independent of Britain. Almost entirely written by Thomas Jefferson, document sets out principle of govt. under theory of natural rights.

Independent Treasury System, estab. (1846) in US out of distrust of banks after President Jackson's refusal to recharter Bank of the US. Public revenues placed in Treasury, held independently of banking system in attempt to reduce Treasury's speculation in money market. Inconsistent govt. policy led to termination (1920) after enactment of FEDERAL RESERVE SYSTEM.

Index [librorum prohibitorum], list of publications that the RC church forbade its members to read, except by special permission, as dangerous to faith or morality. First pub. in 1559; put in care of Holy Office (1917). Abolished by 2nd Vatican Council (1962).

India

India (*Bharat*), republic of SC Asia. Area *c* 3,268,000 sq km (1,262,000 sq mi); pop. 574,368,000; cap. New Delhi. Official language: Hindi; religions: Hinduism, Islam. Indian penin. bounded by Himalayas, Pakistan and Bangladesh. Largely plains, cut by Ganges, Brahmaputra, Godavari. Climate mainly tropical monsoon; agric. economy (esp. rice, cotton, tea, timber). Divided into 22 states and 9 union territs. Major cities Bombay, Calcutta. Hinduism estab *c* 1500 BC, Buddhism and Jainism introduced in 6th cent. BC. Country united under Moguls (16th-18th cent.); East India Co. rule (1757-1858) transferred to Britain after Indian Mutiny. Independence struggle led by Gandhi; independence achieved (1947) with partition of Pakistan; republic estab. 1950. Member of British Commonwealth.

Indiana, state of NC US. Area 93,994 sq km (36,290 sq mi); pop. 5,194,000; cap. Indianapolis. Mainly rolling plains; agric. esp. maize, wheat, livestock, coal mining, limestone quarrying. Settled by French; ceded to British 1763; captured by US 1779; became territ. 1800 when Indians were dispossessed of their land. Admitted to Union as 19th state (1816).

Indianapolis, cap. of Indiana, US; on White R. Pop. 743,000. Transport jct.; grain, livestock market. Meat packing; produces motor car and aircraft parts. Annual speedway races ('500').

Indian corn, see MAIZE.

Indian literature, vernacular writings of Indian subcontinent. Only extensively produced after 1500, but ancient VEDA, PALI, and Prakrit (Jainist) religious literature existed previously. Hindu pietistic movements encouraged popularization of Sanskrit, leading language of great classics, *eg Ramayana, Bhagavad-Gita,* in popular verse form. Urdu verse written for Mogul court in Persian tradition. Modern literature incl. works in English and major languages of subcontinent. Writers incl. Tagore, Iqbal, Narayan, Ghose, Naidu.

Indian Mutiny or **Sepoy Rebellion** (1857-8), revolt of native soldiers (sepoys) in Bengal army of British East India Co. Troops resented annexation of Oudh (1856), homeland of many of them, and were angered by issue of cartridges coated with fat of cows (sacred to Hindus) and of pigs (forbidden to Moslems). Revolt, beginning Feb. 1857, spread over NC India; Delhi captured, Lucknow besieged, British garrison massacred at Kanpur. Mutiny subdued by March, 1858. Resulting reforms incl. transfer of rule from East India Co. to British Crown.

Indian National Congress, Indian political party, founded (1885) to increase Indian involvement in formation of British policy in India. Soon split into opposing groups seeking dominion status or complete independence. Became more militant after 1919, adopting policy, advocated by Gandhi, of civil disobedience and passive resistance to British rule. Under Nehru, became ruling party of India and maintained power until 1977 elections.

Indian Ocean, smallest of 3 world oceans, lying between Antarctica, Africa, Asia and Australia. Area *c* 73,430,000 sq km (28,350,000 sq mi). Reaches greatest depth in Java Trench (7725 m/ 25,344 ft). Main isls. Madagascar, Sri Lanka. Arms incl. Arabian Sea, Bay of Bengal. Seasonal winds (monsoons) yield rain in S and SE Asia.

Indian paintbrush, any of genus *Castilleja* of plants of figwort family. Brilliantly coloured orange flowers and red or yellow upper leaves.

Indian pipe, *Monotropa uniflora,* leafless, fleshy, white saprophytic plant of North American and Asian woodlands. Each stem bears single white flower.

Indians, American, see AMERICAN INDIANS.

Indian shot, see CANNA.

India rubber tree, see RUBBER PLANT.

Indic, largest group of languages in Indo-Iranian branch of Indo-European family. Incl. ancient forms Vedic, Sanskrit, Prakrit; modern Punjabi, Sindhi, Hindi, Urdu, Assamese, Bengali, Gujarati, Singhalese, Marathi.

indicator, in chemistry, substance used to indicate completion of chemical reaction by sharp changes in colour. Indicators, *eg* litmus, often used to test for acidity or alkalinity, esp. during titration. Colour change indicates when neutralization has occurred. In ecology, species of plant or animal, or a community, whose occurrence serves as evidence that certain environmental conditions exist.

indictment, in law, formal written accusation charging specific persons with commission of a crime. In US, presented by grand jury to the court when jury has found, after examining presented evidence, that there is a valid case.

indigo, any plant of genus *Indigofera* of Leguminosae family. *I. tinctoria* is source of colourless indican which is oxidized to blue dye, indigo; it was used in ancient India and Egypt.

indium (In), soft metallic element; at. no. 49, at. wt. 114.82. Found in traces in zinc ores. Used in dental alloys and to protect bearings. Discovered spectroscopically (1863).

Indo-China, former federation of SE Asian states, comprising French colony of Cochin China and French protects. of Laos, Cambodia, Tonkin and Annam. Republic of Vietnam formed from Cochin China, Tonkin and Annam in 1949.

Indo-Chinese War, conflict fought (1946-54) between Viet Minh (coalition of nationalist and Communist groups under HO CHI MINH) and the French after failure of negotiations for Vietnamese independence. Decisive battle fought at Dienbienphu (1954) broke French resistance.

Subsequent GENEVA CONFERENCE divided Indo-China into North and South Vietnam, Laos and Cambodia.

Indo-European, language family with more speakers than any other, *ie c* half of world's pop. Similarities in vocabulary and grammar point to ancient parent language, originating pre-2000 BC. Differences postulated to have arisen as migration separated groups speaking it. Major branches are Anatolian, Baltic, Celtic, Germanic, Greek, Indo-Iranian, Italic, Slavic, Thraco-Illyrian, Thraco-Phrygian, Tokharian.

Indonesia

Indonesia, republic of SE Asia. Area *c* 1,904,000 sq km (736,000 sq mi); pop. *c* 129,000,000; cap. Djakarta. Official language: Bahasa Indonesian. Religion: Islam. Comprises former Dutch East Indies, consisting of *c* 3000 isls., incl. Java, Sumatra, Borneo, Lesser Sundas, Moluccas, Irian Jaya. Most islands mountainous; equatorial climate with heavy rainfall. Rice main crop; exports rubber, spices, petroleum. Hinduism and Buddhism introduced under Indian influence; Islam dominant by end of 16th cent. Colonized by Dutch East India Co. (17th cent.). Independence proclaimed 1945, sovereignty transferred 1949.

Indore, city of Madhya Pradesh, C India. Pop. 573,000. Chemical, textile mfg. Cap. of former princely state of Indore.

Indra, in early Hindu religion, god of war and storms. Represented as an amoral, boisterous god. Ruler of Amaravati, an inferior heaven.

indris, *Indri indri,* largest of lemurs, found in Madagascar. Lives in family groups in trees; vegetarian diet.

inductance, electrical, property of an electric circuit by which a changing electric current in it produces varying magnetic field. This magnetic field may induce voltages in same circuit (self-induction) or in neighbouring circuits (mutual induction).

induction, in physics, name given to 3 phenomena in electricity and magnetism. Electrostatic induction is production of charge on a body when another charged body is brought near. Magnetic induction is production of a magnetic field in ferromagnetic material by external magnetic field. *See* also ELECTROMAGNETIC INDUCTION.

inductive method, logical procedure formulated by Francis Bacon of arguing from particular observations to general principles. Opposite of deduction which argues from known principles to particular applications. Whereas deduction is infallible if original proposition is true, induction can only attain a high degree of probability. Both methods central to scientific research.

indulgence, in RC Church, total or partial remission of temporal or purgatorial punishment for sin. Granted by the Church providing the sin has already been forgiven and sinner is in a state of grace. System was once notoriously abused with sale of indulgences, and violently opposed by Luther. Council of Trent (1563) outlawed sale of indulgences but approved the system in moderation.

Indus, river of SC Asia. Rises in SW Tibet, flows *c* 2700 km (1700 mi) SW through Kashmir and Pakistan to Arabian Sea. Irrigates plains of Sind; little used for navigation. Centre of early civilization (Indus Valley) *fl* 2500 BC.

industrial democracy, sharing of power in an indust. organization among the workers. Involves their participation in making decisions affecting them, an area previously considered the prerogative of directors. May lead to estab. of WORKS COUNCIL or placing of a few workers' representatives on the board. Both are legal requirements in large companies in West Germany, Netherlands, Sweden. West Germany has 2-tier structure, with at least ⅓ of supervisory board being workers' representatives but with management board still appointed by shareholders. By mid-1970s EEC had plans for introduction of indust. democracy similar to West German model. Also *see* WORKERS' CONTROL.

Industrial Relations Act, in UK, legislation passed (1971) by Conservative govt., aimed to regulate labour relations by legal sanctions. Provisions incl. making collective agreements legally enforceable, registering trade unions, giving individual workers right not to join union in CLOSED SHOP. Repealed by Labour govt. (1974).

Industrial Revolution, social and economic change resulting from replacement of hand tools by machine and power tools and the development of large-scale indust. production; applied esp. to this change in Britain (from about 1760). Founded on widening overseas markets, development of banking, and invention of machines and new processing methods. Expansion of production took place, esp. in iron and steel, coal, textile and pottery industs. Accompanied by population increase and transport developments, it turned Britain from predominantly agric. country into leading indust. nation of world. Rapid change spread to Germany, US (after 1860), Japan, USSR, and others in 20th cent.

Industrial Workers of the World (IWW), revolutionary labour union estab. (1905) in Chicago, its leaders incl. Eugene Debs, Daniel De Leon. Aims based on SYNDICALISM. Effective mainly in US, leading 150 strikes. Declined during WWI, large numbers leaving to join Communist Party in 1917. Members known as 'Wobblies'.

Indus Valley civilization, ancient culture which *fl c* 2500-1500 BC in valley of R. Indus (area now in Pakistan). Two chief towns were Harappa, in Punjab, and Mohenjo-Daro in Sind; excavations carried out at these sites since 1920s have found evidence of organized agric., flourishing art and well-planned architecture.

Indy, Vincent d' (1851-1931), French composer. Studied under Franck. Works incl. *Symphony on a French Mountain Air,* chamber music and songs. A founder of Schola Cantorum, Paris, where he taught composition.

inert gases, the elements helium, neon, argon, krypton, xenon, radon. As their external electron shells are complete, they are virtually chemically inert, but compounds with fluorine have been produced. Also called noble or rare gases.

inertia, in physics, the tendency of bodies to resist changes in motion.

infancy, stage of human development covering first 2 years of life. In law, term infant denotes person under age of 18 (21 in some countries), though girls from age 12 and boys from age of 14 more commonly known as minors.

infantile paralysis, see POLIOMYELITIS.

infantry, branch of the army trained, equipped and organized to fight on foot. Became dominant in European warfare after invention of firearms.

infection, in medicine, invasion of body by micro-organisms, *eg* bacteria, viruses, protozoa. After period of incubation, inflammation of tissue follows and more widespread effects may result from toxins released by bacteria.

inferiority complex, in psychiatry, neurotic state resulting from real or imagined physical or social inadequacy. Behavioural patterns may be dictated by attempts to compensate for it. Basis of ADLER's psychiatric theories.

infinity, in mathematics, term used loosely to denote numerical value of a non-finite quantity. A sequence is said to 'tend to infinity' if it increases beyond all bounds.

inflammation, in medicine, defensive reaction of body to injury, infection or irritation. Heat, redness, swelling and pain are signs of inflammation, caused by increased flow of blood and lymph fluid. White blood cells engulf and destroy invading bacteria, forming pus when they die.

inflation, in economics, increase in amount of money in circulation resulting in a sudden and relatively sharp fall in its value and hence rise in price of goods and services. Wars have been common cause; govt. borrows and issues paper money, domestic production is incapable of meeting consumer demand thus causing prices to rise. Other instances of inflation incl. hyper-inflation in Germany in 1923, worldwide inflation in 1970s caused by limited supply of oil-related products. Its opposite is **deflation,** condition characterized by decline in prices, business and employment.

influenza, virus infection, usually of mucous membranes of air passages. Accompanied by muscular pains, weakness and fever. Sometimes occurs in worldwide epidemics; different strains of influenza virus minimize possibility of gaining immunity.

information theory, mathematical study of processes of communication and transmission of messages; deals esp. with information content of messages and probability of signal recognition in presence of electrical noise, *etc.* Formulated mainly by Claude E. Shannon (1948).

infrared radiation, electromagnetic radiation whose wavelength is longer than that of the red part of the visible spectrum but shorter than that of radio waves. Emitted by hot bodies; it has penetrating heating effect. Film sensitive to infrared radiation is used to photograph in total darkness or in haze.

Inge, William Ralph (1860-1954), English churchman. Dean of St Paul's Cathedral (1911-34). Works, *eg Christian mysticism* (1897), *Christian Ethics and Modern Problems* (1930), reflect interest in mysticism and the pessimism which earned him name 'gloomy dean'.

Ingolstadt, town of SC West Germany, on R. Danube. Pop. 70,000. Textiles, machinery, vehicle mfg. Resisted siege (1632) by Gustavus Adolphus in Thirty Years' War. Univ. (1472-1800) now in Munich.

Ingres, Jean Auguste Dominique (1780-1867), French painter. Pupil of David, he upheld rigid classicism against the Romantic movement led by Delacroix. Works incl. portraits, nudes and Oriental scenes, *eg Vow of Louis XIII, Bain Turc, Madame Moitessier.*

initiation, in anthropology, magical or religious ceremony among primitive peoples to mark transition from one status in society to another, *eg* from boy to man. Often involves ordeal to test subject's worthiness, or ritual representation of death and resurrection.

initiative, the right of a group of citizens to introduce a matter for legislation either to the legislature or to the voters. A **referendum** is a submission of that matter to direct vote of people; ensues automatically in latter case, and on legislature's so deciding in former. Laws passed by legislature may be submitted to referendum. Switzerland pioneered these techniques, now used in most states in US.

injection, method employed in medicine to introduce liquid into body. Usually administered by means of fine needle and syringe. May be subcutaneous (into skin), intravenous (into vein), intramuscular (into muscle), spinal (into spinal tissue).

injunction, in law, formal written order of court ordering or prohibiting some action. Courts have broadened interpretation from original prohibitive injunction to incl. positive commands.

ink, coloured liquid used in printing and writing. Blue and black writing inks usually consist of tannin extract with iron salts added; coloured writing inks use dissolved dyes. Printing ink consists of pigment mixed with linseed varnish, resins, *etc.*

Inkerman, suburb of Sevastopol, USSR, Ukrainian SSR; on Crimean penin. Scene of French and British victory over Russians in Crimean War (1854).

Inland Sea, sea between Japanese isls. of Honshu (on N) and Kyushu and Shikoku (on S). Notably scenic region, rich in fish.

Inner Hebrides, *see* HEBRIDES, Scotland.

Inner Mongolia, auton. region of N China. Area *c* 425,000 sq km (164,000 sq mi); pop. (est.) 13,000,000; cap. Huhehot. Mainly steppe, becoming increasingly arid towards Gobi Desert in W. Stockraising; cereals grown in bend of Hwang Ho. Valuable mineral deposits.

Inner Temple, *see* INNS OF COURT.

innocence, *see* BLUET.

Innocent III, orig. Giovanni Lotario di Segni (1161-1216), Italian churchman, pope (1198-1216). Estab. papal supremacy over temporal rulers by asserting will in political affairs. Named Stephen LANGTON as archbishop of Canterbury (1206) in defiance of King John; excommunicated John, and forced him to submit to papal authority. Proclaimed 4th Crusade (1202-4) and crusade against Albigensians (1208). Presided over Fourth Lateran Council (1215).

Innsbruck

Innsbruck, city of W Austria, on R. Inn, cap. of Tyrol prov. Pop. 115,000. Tourist centre, esp. winter sports. Castle (15th cent.), Hofkirche (1563), univ. (1677).

Inns of Court, four London legal societies having exclusive right to admit persons to practise at the bar in England (*see* BARRISTER). They are Lincoln's Inn, Gray's Inn, Inner Temple, Middle Temple. Date from before 14th cent.

inoculation, method of immunization against disease. Active inoculation consists of injection of weak strain of infecting microbe and consequent formation of antibodies to provide immunity. Passive inoculation, used to gain short-term immunity when antibodies have not been built up, consists of injection of antitoxins from previously infected subjects.

Inonu, Ismet (1884-1973), Turkish statesman. Chief of staff in war against Greece (1919-22). Premier under Ataturk, succeeded him as president (1938-50). Returned to power as premier (1961-5) after military coup.

Inowroclaw (Ger. *Hohensalza*), town of NC Poland. Pop. 53,000. Resort with saline springs. Agric. machinery, glass, chemical industs.; salt mines nearby. Under Prussian rule 1772-1919.

inquest, in law, any inquiry, but esp. coroner's investigation, into cause of a death. Only necessary in cases in which cause is in doubt, or is sudden or violent.

Inquisition, in RC Church, general tribunal estab. (1233) by Gregory IX for the discovery and suppression of heresy and punishment of heretics (at that time ALBIGENSIANS). Notorious for torture of the accused and other abuses esp. when secular rulers used system to their own gain. Continued until 19th cent. The Spanish Inquisition was an independent institution estab. (1478) by Ferdinand V and Isabella of Spain and controlled by the Spanish kings. Infamous for its rigour under TORQUEMADA.

insanity or **lunacy,** legal and colloquial terms, rather than medico-scientific, used for those forms of mental disorder which relieve individual of responsibility for certain acts, and which may lead to his being confined in an institution.

Insecta (insects), largest class of arthropods, with *c* 800,000 species. Adult has body divided into head, thorax and abdomen. Head bears pair of antennae; thorax has 3 segments with 3 pairs of legs and usually 2 pairs of wings. Usually 3-stage life history involving egg, larva and pupa before adulthood.

insecticide, chemical used to destroy insect pests. In 19th cent. inorganic compounds, esp. of arsenic and copper, used. Modern organic chemicals, incl. DDT, highly effective; use sometimes restricted because of cumulative toxic effect on animals and contamination of food.

Insectivora (insectivores), order of small insect-eating mammals, incl. shrews, hedgehogs and moles.

insectivorous plants, plants which supplement nitrogen supply by digesting small insects caught in cavities of plant, *eg* PITCHER PLANT, by viscidity of leaves, *eg* Portuguese fly catcher, or by movement, *eg* VENUS' FLYTRAP. Mainly found in bogs where nitrogen content of soil is low.

insemination, artificial, *see* ARTIFICIAL INSEMINATION.

instalment buying, *see* HIRE PURCHASE.

instinct, innate, often complex behaviour pattern of animals, developed without any learning process; common to all members of species. Example is nest-building behaviour of birds.

Institut de France, collection of learned academies, state controlled, founded in 1795. Incl. L'Académie Française, L'Académie des Inscriptions et Belles-Lettres, L'Académie des Sciences, L'Académie des Beaux Arts, and L'Académie des Sciences Morales et Politiques.

insulation, electrical, resistance to passage of electric current exhibited by certain substances, *eg* dry air, rubber, wax.

insulin, hormone formed in pancreas and secreted into bloodstream. Regulates amount of glucose in blood; lack of insulin causes glucose to accumulate and spill over into urine. *See* DIABETES.

insurance, system of compensating individuals or companies for loss arising, *eg* by accident, fire, theft, *etc.* Payment is made from fund to which those who are exposed to similar risks have made payments (premiums) in return for cover. System practised from ancient times, *eg* in Phoenician trade. Shipping insurance almost universal in Europe by 14th cent., dominated by LLOYD'S of London by 17th cent.; fire insurance arose in Germany (15th cent.); life insurance in England (16th cent.). Since late 19th cent. the state has been prominent in social insurance (*see* SOCIAL SECURITY).

intaglio, design or figure carved, incised or engraved into a hard material so that it is below the surface. Commonest example is engraved seal-ring.

integer, in mathematics, any positive or negative whole number or zero, *eg* 3 or -5.

integral calculus, mathematical study inverse to differential calculus; involves reconstruction of a function given form of its derivative. Used in finding areas, volumes, *etc*, and solving differential equations.

integrated circuit, electronic circuit consisting of several circuit elements and amplifying devices formed on single chip of semiconducting material. Used in calculators, computers, *etc.*

intelligence, ability of organisms to learn from experience and adapt responses to new situations; capacity to understand and relate concepts; measurement of general factor underlying individual's performance on varied specific mental tasks. Product of genetic potential and influence of environment, but relative importance of these factors is matter of controversy. BINET first developed intelligence tests enabling measurement over range of intellectual problems, with scales based on norms for specific age groups. Tests since adapted and used as predictive, diagnostic instrument in education, army, *etc.*

intelligence quotient (IQ), ratio of mental age, as measured by intelligence tests, to chronological age, expressed as a percentage.

interest, money paid for use of borrowed capital. Usually at fixed percentage rate paid yearly, half-yearly or quarterly. May be simple or compound (*ie* interest on accumulated interest). Usury, in legal terms, is interest charged on a loan above specified level, first legislated against in England (1545).

interference, in physics, interaction of 2 combining wave motions of same frequency. Waves reinforce or neutralize one another according to their relative phases on meeting. Two light beams can combine to give alternate light and dark bands (interference fringes); two sounds of nearly equal frequency can produce beats (alternate increases and decreases in loudness).

interior decoration, treatment of interior of buildings in style reflecting contemporary architecture. Thus French classical styles in 17th cent. were reflected in 'Louis XIV' interiors. In Britain, the Adam brothers pioneered the design of buildings as integrated wholes during 18th cent.

Interlaken, town of WC Switzerland, on R. Aare. Pop. 6000. Tourist centre of Bernese Oberland, between Lakes Thun (W), Brienz (E).

intermezzo (Ital., = in the middle), an instrumental interlude in the middle of an opera. Term also applied to free and short instrumental composition, and to comic opera developed from comic interlude in 17th cent. opera or ballet.

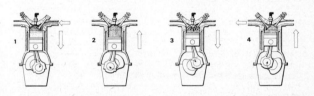

Four stroke cycle in internal combustion engine: 1.induction stroke; 2.compression stroke; 3.power stroke; 4.exhaust stroke

internal combustion engine, engine which derives its power from the explosion of a fuel-air mixture in a confined space. In typical 4 stroke automobile engine, fuel-air mixture is drawn into cylinder by downward movement of reciprocating piston (connected to a crank) and compressed as piston returns upwards. At top of stroke SPARKING PLUG ignites mixture and the rapid expansion drives piston downwards giving power stroke. The burnt gases are exhausted from cylinder by upward return of piston and the cycle begins again. Arrangement of valves, opened and closed by engine-driven cam shaft, allows mixture to be drawn in, compressed and exhausted. Two stroke engine has arrangement of valves allowing power stroke every two instead of four strokes. *See* DIESEL ENGINE, WANKEL ROTARY ENGINE.

International Atomic Energy Agency, agency of UN, estab. (1957) to promote peaceful use of atomic energy. Provides technical assistance, training and maintains research laboratories.

International Bank for Reconstruction and Development (World Bank), agency of UN, estab. 1945; hq. Washington. Funded by UN members, serves as loan agency for member states and private investors. Aims to facilitate investments, foreign trade, discharge international debts.

International Brigade, volunteer force, largely drawn from Communist sympathizers, which fought for the Republicans during Spanish Civil War (1936-9).

International Civil Aviation Organization (ICAO), agency of UN estab. (1947) at Montréal. Promotes international safety codes and symbols and investigates accidents.

International Court of Justice, court estab. (1945) as advisory or arbitrational judicial organ of UN. Replaced Permanent Court of International Justice. Comprises 15 justices; normally sits at The Hague. Renders decisions binding on member states on matters of international law. Advises on request of General Assembly.

International Criminal Police Commission (INTERPOL), organization estab. (1923) to coordinate police activities of participating nations. Has Paris hq.

international date line, imaginary line drawn N and S through Pacific Ocean, roughly following 180° meridian of longitude. Used to mark start of calendar day; 24 hours are lost when crossing it W to E and gained E to W.

Internationale, international Communist anthem, used as national anthem of USSR until 1944. Words written by a French woodworker Eugène Pottier in 1871, music composed by Belgian composer Pierre Degeyter in 1888.

International Finance Corporation (IFC), agency of UN, estab. 1956 as an affiliate of INTERNATIONAL BANK FOR RECONSTRUCTION AND DEVELOPMENT to encourage growth of productive enterprise in member states, esp. in under-developed areas.

International Labour Organization (ILO), agency concerned with conditions of work in its member countries. Estab. by Treaty of Versailles, affiliated to League of Nations (1919-45), then to UN (1946).

international law, rules generally observed and regarded as binding in relations between nations. By late 19th cent., Hague conferences were frequently resorted to for arbitration of disputes. **Institute for International Law** set up (1875) at Ghent, Belgium, for research, recording such arbitration. Awarded Nobel Peace Prize (1904). Reorganized (1961).

International Monetary Fund (IMF), agency of UN, estab. 1945; hq. Washington. Facilitates discharge of international debt by enabling member states to buy foreign currencies.

International Red Cross Committee, see RED CROSS.

International [Workingmen's Association], called First International, organization estab. (1864) in London under leadership of MARX; aimed to unite workers and achieve political power according to principles of *Communist Manifesto.* Dissolved (1876) after conflict with anarchists. Second or Socialist International (estab. 1889) was dominated by German and Russian Social Democrat parties; broke up during WWI. Third International (*see* COMINTERN) created in 1919.

Interpol, *see* INTERNATIONAL CRIMINAL POLICE COMMISSION.

Interstate Commerce Commission (ICC), US govt. agency regulating commercial transport between states. Estab. (1887) after public outcry against railway malpractices. In 1906 and 1910 its range was extended from railways to incl. other means of communication, *eg* ferries, pipelines, wireless, cable. In 1950s and 1960s, enforced desegregation of passenger transport after Supreme Court decision.

intestine, lower part of alimentary canal extending from stomach to anus, where latter stages of digestion and collection of waste products take place. Consists of convoluted upper part (small intestine), shorter but wider large intestine, and rectum.

Intolerable Acts, American revolutionaries' name for 5 acts (incl. QUEBEC ACT) passed 1774 by British Parliament. Limited geographical, political freedom. Four of acts retribution for BOSTON TEA PARTY.

introversion, *see* EXTROVERSION.

intrusive rock, any rock formed by solidification of molten material below the Earth's surface. All intrusive rocks are thus igneous rocks, forced into or between solid rocks while molten. May be formed at great depth, *ie* plutonic, or moderate depth, *ie* hypabyssal.

intuitionism, in philosophy, doctrine that man can perceive truth and ethical principles without assistance of intellect or experience. Common among medieval Christian mystics.

Inuvik, town of NW Mackenzie Dist., Northwest Territs., Canada; on Mackenzie R. Pop. 3000. Built on frozen subsoil (permafrost) as new town. Uranium mines; airport.

Inveraray, town of Strathclyde region, W Scotland, on Loch Fyne. Pop. 1000. Former royal burgh and co. town of Argyllshire. Herring fishing. Has 18th cent. castle, seat of dukes of Argyll.

Invercargill, city of S South Isl., New Zealand, on inlet of Foveaux Str. Pop. 47,000. Fishing, food processing, sawmilling; outport at Bluff Harbour.

Inverness-shire, former county of N Scotland, now in Highland region. Mainly mountainous (Ben Nevis), crossed by Great Glen; incl. S Outer Hebrides, Skye. Livestock rearing, forestry, fishing, h.e.p., tourist industs. Co. town was **Inverness,** at NE end of Great Glen. Pop. 35,000. Distilling, woollens, tourism.

invertebrate, any animal without a vertebral column.

Io, in Greek myth, daughter of King Inachus of Argos. Loved by Zeus who changed her into a white heifer to conceal her from Hera. Hera tormented Io with a gadfly which drove her across Europe and Asia until she came to Egypt where Zeus restored her to human form.

Ioánnina or **Yannina,** town of Epirus, NW Greece, on L. Ioánnina, cap. of Ioánnina admin. dist. Pop. 35,000. Agric. trade. Seat of Ali Pasha ('Lion of Yannina') 1787-1822.

iodine (I), non-metallic element of halogen family; at. no. 53, at. wt. 126.9. Consists of grey-black crystals which sublime to form violet vapour. Compounds found in seaweed and Chile saltpetre. Essential to functioning of thyroid gland. Compounds used in medicine, photography and organic synthesis.

ion, electrically charged atom or group of atoms; positively charged ion (cation) results from loss of electrons, negatively charged ion (anion) from electron gain. Ions can be created by collisions with charged particles, high energy radiation (X-rays, gamma rays) or by dissolving suitable compounds (electrolytes) in water.

Iona, small isl. of Inner Hebrides, W Scotland, in Strathclyde region. Centre of Celtic Christianity after St Columba founded monastery (563). Has 13th cent. cathedral (restored 20th cent.), reputed royal burial ground.

Ionesco, Eugène (1912-), French playwright, b. Romania. Leading exponent of ABSURD in plays, *eg The Bald Prima Donna* (1950), *Rhinoceros* (1959).

ion exchange, chemical process by which ions held on porous solid material (usually synthetic resin or ZEOLITE) are exchanged for ions in a solution surrounding the solid. Used in water softening, desalination of sea water, extraction of metals from ores.

Ionia, region of W coast of Asia Minor, incl. Aegean Isls. Colonized by ancient Greeks (Ionians) *c* 1000 BC; based on a religious league of 12 cities, prospered commercially. Conquered by Persians (6th cent. BC), revolt of cities (500 BC) led to Persian Wars. Important part of Roman and Byzantine empires, declined under Turks.

Ionian Islands, isl. chain of W Greece, in Ionian Sea. Incl. Corfu, Cephalonia, Levkas, Zakinthos. Mainly mountainous; wine, fruit olives. Venetian 15th-18th cent.; British protectorate until 1864. Devastated by earthquake 1953.

Ionian Sea, part of Mediterranean Sea, between SW Greece and SE Italy. Connected to Adriatic by Strait of Otranto.

Ionic order, one of the Greek orders of architecture, characterized by its slender column and 2 ornamental scrolls (spiral volutes) on the front of the capital and 2 on the back. Developed in Greek colonies of Asia Minor in 6th cent. BC.

ionization chamber, device used to measure intensity of ionizing radiation, *eg* gamma rays, or disintegration rate of radioactive substances. Usually consists of gas-filled chamber containing 2 electrodes between which electric potential is maintained; current flows when gas is ionized by incoming radiation.

ionosphere, region of upper atmosphere, starting *c* 50 km above ground, in which an appreciable concentration of ions and electrons is produced by solar radiation. Divided into 3 layers, incl. Kennelly-Heaviside and Appleton. Important to radio transmission as it reflects radio waves back to Earth.

Iowa, state of NC US. Area 145,791 sq km (56,290 sq mi); pop. 2,825,000; cap. Des Moines. Mainly rolling plains; lying between Missouri, Mississippi rivers; hilly in NE. Major agric. region; wheat, dairy, livestock farming. Region explored by French fur traders in 17th cent.; purchased by US as part of Louisiana Purchase (1803). Admitted to Union as 29th state (1846).

Ipatieff, Vladimir Nikolayevich (1867-1952), American chemist, b. Russia. Worked on catalytic reactions, refining petroleum and synthesizing artificial rubber. Invented process for mfg. high octane fuel.

ipecac, *Cephaelis ipecacuanha,* tropical South American shrub. Roots contain the alkaloid emetine used as emetic and to relieve coughs.

Iphigenia, in Greek myth, daughter of Agamemnon and Clytemnestra. Sacrificed by her father in order to end the contrary winds which were delaying the Greek ships heading for the Trojan War. In Euripedes' *Iphigenia in Tauris,* she survives to save life of brother, Orestes.

Ipin, city of Szechwan prov., C China. Pop. 275,000. Last port for upstream traffic on Yangtze. Commercial centre.

Ipoh, cap. of Perak state, NW West Malaysia. Pop. 248,000. Tin mining centre. Rubber plantations nearby.

Ipswich, co. town and co. bor. of Suffolk, E England, on R. Orwell. Pop. 123,000. Agric. machinery; food processing industs, brewing. Saxon *Gipeswic;* 16th cent. ecclesiastical centre.

Iqbal, Sir Mohammed (1873-1938), Indian poet, philosopher. Early advocate of Hindu-Moslem unity in fight for Indian independence, later supported formation of separate state for Indian Moslems. Wrote *Reconstruction of Religious Thought in Islam.*

Iquique, port of N Chile, on Pacific at edge of Atacama desert. Pop. 65,000. Nitrates, iodine, exports; fish canning, sugar, oil refining industs.

Iquitos, town of NE Peru, at head of navigation on Amazon R. Pop. 74,000. Coffee, cotton, timber exports. *Fl* during early 20th cent. rubber boom.

IRA, see IRISH REPUBLICAN ARMY.

Iráklion: the fortress

Iráklion (*Herakleion*) or **Candia,** town of NC Crete, Greece, cap. of Iráklion admin. dist. Pop. 64,000. Port, exports olive oil, wine. Museum of Minoan antiquities.

Iran, kingdom of SW Asia; formerly Persia. Area 1,648,000 sq km (636,000 sq mi); pop. 31,955,000; cap. Tehran. Language: Persian. Religion: Shia Islam. Consists of C plateau surrounded by Elburz Mts. in N, Zagros Mts. in S and W. Produces wool for carpet mfg., rice, cotton; economy based on rich oil resources. Divided into 13 provs. Centre of ancient Persian empire under Cyrus; conquered by Alexander the Great (*c* 330 BC). Object of British-Russian rivalry (19th-20th cent.), intensified by oil finds. Pahlevi dynasty founded (1925); name changed to Iran 1935.

Iran

Iranian, group of languages belonging to Indo-Iranian branch of Indo-European family. Divided into East and West subgroups, incl. Baluchi, Pashtu, Kurdish, Persian. Spoken in Iran, Afghanistan, Pakistan, parts of USSR.

Iraq (Arab. *Iraqia*), republic of SW Asia. Area *c* 435,000 sq km (168,000 sq mi); pop. 10,413,000; cap. Baghdad. Language: Arabic. Religion: Islam. Drained by R. Tigris, R. Euphrates. Mountainous N rich in oil; cotton and dates grown in irrigated SE. Borders correspond to ancient MESOPOTAMIA. Ottoman domination until WWI. Kingdom (1921- 58); became republic after military coup.

Ireland, John (1879-1962), British composer. Works incl. varied orchestral and choral works, delicate music for piano, and attractive songs, *eg* 'Sea Fever'.

Ireland

Ireland, isl. of British Isls., separated from Great Britain by Irish Sea. Area *c* 84,000 sq km (32,450 sq mi); pop. 4,576,000. Fertile C lowland with highland rim (Mourne, Wicklow, Kerry, Ox mountains). Main rivers Shannon, Erne, Foyle. Irregular W coast incl. many isls., inlets. Mild, damp climate favours vegetation, esp. grass; led to name 'Emerald Isle'. Partitioned (1921) into NORTHERN IRELAND, and **Republic of Ireland** (*Eire*). Area *c* 70,000 sq km (27,000 sq mi); pop. 3,029,000; cap. Dublin. Languages: Irish, English. Religion: RC. Comprises 26 counties in 4 provs. (Connacht, Leinster, Munster, Ulster). Main towns Cork, Limerick. Mainly agric., esp. dairying; fishing; tourism. Long struggle for independence from UK ended with estab. of Irish Free State (1921). Republic proclaimed (1949), left Commonwealth. Joined EEC (1973).

Irene (*c* 752-803), Byzantine empress. Appointed regent to her son Constantine VI (780-90) on death of her husband Leo IV. Ruled jointly with Constantine until latter was deposed and blinded (797); exiled 802. Canonized by Orthodox Church for restoring icon worship.

Irene, in Greek myth, goddess of peace, one of the HORAE. Identified by Romans with Pax.

Ireton, Henry (1611–51), English parliamentary army officer in Civil War. Fought at Edgehill (1642) and Naseby (1645). Married Cromwell's daughter (1646); as lord-deputy in Ireland (1650) assisted in Cromwell's repressive measures before dying there of plague.

Irian Jaya (West Irian), prov. of Indonesia, occupying W half of New Guinea. Area *c* 414,000 sq km (160,000 sq mi); cap. Djajapura. Exports timber, oil. Known as Netherlands New Guinea until transfer to Indonesia (1963), when named Irian Barat. Present name dates from 1973.

iridium (Ir), brittle metallic element; at. no. 77, at. wt. 192.2. Hard and chemically resistant; found in platinum ores. Alloys used in pen points, watch and compass bearings.

Wild iris or yellow flag (Iris pseudacorus)

Iris, in Greek myth, goddess of the rainbow and a messenger of the gods.

iris, in anatomy, round pigmented membrane in front of eye, between cornea and lens. Its muscles adjust width of pupil, which it surrounds, and regulate amount of light entering eye.

iris, genus of perennial plants of Iridaceae family, native to temperate regions. Sword-shaped leaves, flowers composed of 3 petals and 3 drooping sepals. Many varieties grown as garden flowers.

Irish language, see GAELIC.

Irish Republican Army (IRA), para-military organization which developed after Dublin Easter Rebellion (1916), pressing for an Irish republic which would incl. Ulster. After being declared illegal by De Valéra (1936) became underground terrorist movement. Sectarian militancy and 'civil rights' disturbances in 1969 sparked off resurgence of activity by the IRA, now with 2 wings, 'official' and 'provisional', the latter for some years source of systematic terrorist campaign in Northern Ireland. See SINN FEIN.

Irish Sea, between Ireland and Great Britain. Connected to Atlantic Ocean by North Channel (N), St George's Channel (S).

Irish wolfhound

Irish wolfhound, breed of large hound with rough grey coat. Tallest of dogs, stands *c* 86 cm/34 in. at shoulder.

Irkutsk, city of USSR, SC Siberian RSFSR; port at confluence of Angara and Irkut. Pop. 473,000. Indust.; produces aircraft, automobiles, machine tools. Founded 1652 as Cossack fortress.

iron (Fe), malleable ductile metallic element, easily magnetized; at. no. 26, at. wt. 55.85. Occurs in various ores, incl. magnetite, haematite and pyrites. Manufactured in blast furnace from oxide ores, limestone and coke. Usually converted (*see* BESSEMER) into wrought iron or steel, their properties depending on amount of carbon present. Compounds essential to higher forms of animal life.

Iron Age, archaeological period following Bronze Age, characterized by use of iron to make tools, weapons. Iron-working techniques were developed by Hittites in 2nd millennium BC but prob. kept secret. Knowledge spread to Middle East and Europe on collapse of Hittite empire (1200 BC). In Europe, iron-working is associated with HALLSTATT (*c* 800-500 BC) and LA TÈNE cultures.

Iron Gate, gorge of R. Danube on Romanian-Yugoslav border, between Orşova and Turnu-Severin; length *c* 3 km (2 mi).

iron lung, device used to maintain artificial respiration in a person who has difficulty in breathing, *eg* as a result of poliomyelitis. Effects expansion and contraction of lungs by mechanical changes in air pressure *c* 12 times per min.

iron pyrites, *see* PYRITE.

Ironside, William Edmund Ironside, 1st Baron (1880-1959), British general. Commanded anti-Bolshevik Archangel expedition (1918). Chief of Imperial General Staff at outbreak of WWII. Promoted to field-marshal in 1940, he was put in charge of home forces.

ironwood, any of various trees with extremely hard, heavy wood, esp. HORNBEAM.

Iroquoian, North American Indian linguistic family, Hokan-Siouan stock. Found in NE America, incl. Cherokee, Erie (dead), Mohawk, Oneida, Seneca.

Iroquois, five North American Indian tribes (Mohawk, Oneida, Onondaga, Cayuga, Seneca) of Hokan-Siouan linguistic stock. Iroquois Confederacy founded (*c* 1570) by Onondaga, led by Hiawatha and prophet Deganawidah. Estab. advanced culture in New York state. Settled hunters and farmers; lived in palisaded long houses. Dispersed Huron tribes in 1649. Strongly hostile to French but pro-British even during American Revolution. There were *c* 25,000 Iroquois left by 1970s.

Irrawaddy, chief river of Burma. Rises in NW and flows through Mandalay to Andaman Sea; *c* 2100 km (1300 mi) long. Of great economic importance; its delta is major rice growing area.

irredentism, policy of Italian nationalist movement, founded 1878, which sought to recover for Italy adjacent regions, *eg* Trentino, inhabited largely by Italians but under Austrian control. Main reason for Italy's entry into WWI. Term now refers to any similar nationalist policy.

irrigation, artificial distribution of water to soil to sustain plant growth in areas of insufficient rainfall. Methods used incl. sprinkler systems, flooding areas from canals and ditches, and running of water between crop rows. Irrigation has been used extensively in China, India and Egypt since ancient times and is now important in other countries, incl. US, USSR.

Irtysh, river of C Asia. Rises in Altai Mts. of Sinkiang-Uighur (NW China), flows *c* 2900 km (1800 mi) NW to join R. Ob in NW Siberia.

Irving, Edward (1792-1834), Scottish clergyman. Expelled (1833) from Church of Scotland for emphasizing supernatural phenomena and imminence of the second coming of Christ. Followers formed Catholic Apostolic Church (Irvingites).

Irving, Sir Henry, orig. John Henry Brodribb (1838-1905), English actor-manager. Estab. reputation with 1874 performance of Hamlet; played Mathias in melodrama, *The Bells*. Became manager of Lyceum Theatre, London (1878). First actor to be knighted (1895).

Irving, Washington (1783-1859), American author. Known for comic essays, tales, *eg History of New York* by 'Diedrich Knickerbocker' (1890), 'Rip Van Winkle', 'Sleepy Hollow'. Wrote lives of J.J. Astor, Washington.

Isaac, in OT, only son of ABRAHAM and Sarah. Offered by his father as sacrifice to God but saved by divine intervention. Father by Rebecca of Esau and Jacob.

Isaacs, Jorge (1837-95), Colombian poet, novelist. Known for sentimental novel, *María* (1867), giving picture of life in Cauca Valley.

Isabella (1296-1358), queen consort of England. Daughter of Philip IV of France, married Edward II. Badly treated by Edward, she raised an army in France with lover Roger de MORTIMER and invaded England. Deposed Edward and ruled as regent for son Edward III (1327-30) until deposed by him.

Isabella I (1451-1504), queen of Castile (1474-1504). Married (1469) Ferdinand II of Aragón, who ruled both Aragón and Castile with her as FERDINAND V.

Isabella II (1830-1904), queen of Spain (1833-68). Dispute with her uncle Don Carlos over succession led to civil war (1833-9), ending with defeat of CARLISTS. Her rule continued to be one of insurrections and political instability until she was deposed.

Isaiah, prophetic book of OT, attributed to Isaiah (*fl* 710 BC), possibly incl. other writings. Warns of the power of Assyria and foretells the destruction and redemption of Israel.

Ischl or **Bad Ischl,** spa of EC Austria. Pop. 13,000. Saline, iodine baths. Habsburg summer residence from 1822.

Ise, city of Japan, on Ise Bay, S Honshu isl. Pop. 105,000. Shinto religious centre; three shrines, one of which is sacred to imperial family.

Iseult, *see* TRISTAN AND ISOLDE.

Isfahan or **Esfahan** (anc. *Aspadana*), city of C Iran, cap. of Isfahan prov. Pop. 575,000. Carpet, textile mfg; notable silver filigree work. Cap. of Persia (17th cent.); magnificent architecture incl. Masjid-i-Shah (royal mosque).

Isherwood, Christopher [William Bradshaw] (1904-   ), English author. Known for novels depicting decadence of Weimar Republic, *eg Mr Norris Changes Trains* (1935), *Goodbye to Berlin* (1939) using filmic narrative techniques. Collaborated with Auden in expressionist plays, *eg The Ascent of F.6* (1937).

Ishmael, in OT, son of Abraham and Hagar. Exiled in desert with mother through his wife Sarah's jealousy. Regarded by Moslems as ancestor of Arabs.

Ishtar, Babylonian and Assyrian goddess of fertility, love and war. Went to the underworld to recover her lover TAMMUZ, during which time all fertility ceased on earth. Cult was widely assimilated throughout W Asia.

Isis, local name for upper stretches of R. Thames, England.

Isis, ancient Egyptian nature goddess. Sister and wife of OSIRIS; mother of Horus. Represented with cow's head. Her cult (having spread throughout Mediterranean) persisted in Roman Empire and resisted early Christian teachings.

Iskandarîya, El, see ALEXANDRIA, Egypt.

Iskenderun, port of S Turkey. Pop. 69,000. Naval base; railway terminus. Part of Syria (1920-39). Founded (333 BC) by Alexander the Great to commemorate battle of Issus; formerly known as Alexandretta.

Islam or **Mohammedanism,** monotheistic religion in which supreme deity is Allah and chief prophet and founder is MOHAMMED. Based on revelations of Mohammed in *Koran*. Concepts of god, heaven and hell akin to Judaeo-Christian beliefs, with recognition of OT prophets and Jesus. Religious duties incl. sincere profession of the creed, prayer 5 times daily, generous alms-giving, observance of Ramadan fast and pilgrimage to Mecca. Main sects are Sunnites and Shiites who are divided over caliphate. Faith spread rapidly after foundation (7th cent.) and today incl. N Africa, the Middle East, Iran, Pakistan, Indonesia and isolated pockets of SE Europe, USSR, China and S Pacific. There are *c* 350 million faithful, called Moslems or Muslims.

Islamabad, cap. of Pakistan, NW of Rawalpindi. Pop. 77,000. Built in 1960s as new cap.

island, land mass surrounded by water. Island-forming processes incl. upward movement of Earth's crust, lowering of sea level, volcanic action, deposition of sediments, coral formation. Sea isls. may be continental, *ie* formed by separation from mainland, or oceanic, *ie* formed

in the ocean. Two isls., Australia and Antarctica, are continents; largest true isl. is Greenland.

Islay, isl. of Inner Hebrides, W Scotland, in Strathclyde region. Area 609 sq km (235 sq mi); main town Port Ellen. Agric., fishing, distilling.

Islington, bor. of N Greater London, England. Pop. 199,000. Met. bor. until 1965. Incl. Finsbury; has Holloway, Pentonville prisons.

Ismailia, city of NE Egypt, on L. Timsah. Pop. 168,000. Commercial centre on Cairo-Port Said railway. Founded 1863 as construction base for Suez Canal. Badly damaged in 1967 war.

Ismail Pasha (1830-95), khedive of Egypt (1863-79). Encouraged building of Suez Canal; after incurring serious debt, forced to sell his canal shares to Britain (1875). Placed country's finances under Anglo-French management (1876). Abdicated in favour of son, Tewfik Pasha.

isobar, line on a map connecting points of equal atmospheric pressure. Since pressure varies with altitude, pressure values used for weather charts are reduced to sea-level equivalents before isobars are drawn.

Isocrates (436-338 BC), Athenian orator. Pupil of Socrates; founded a school in Athens (392), where many orators were taught. Urged Athens and Sparta to unite against Persia in his greatest oration *Panegyricus* (380).

isogamy, biological term to describe condition in a species where sexual cells (gametes) are alike, in contrast to male-female differentiation in higher organisms. Characterizes certain algae and protozoa.

Isolde, *see* TRISTAN AND ISOLDE.

isomerism, in chemistry, existence of 2 or more compounds with same molecular formula whose physical and chemical properties differ through distinct arrangements of atoms in the molecule.

isostasy, theory of equilibrium between high and low parts of Earth's crust. Continental land masses, composed of thicker layers of lighter rocks, 'float' above heavier ocean floor. Flow of molten material at depth corresponds to land movement at surface to maintain equilibrium.

isotherm, line on a map connecting points of equal temperature. May represent value at one time or average readings over a period. Since temperature varies with altitude, values are normally reduced to sea-level equivalents before isotherms are drawn.

isotopes, atoms of same element which differ in mass number, possessing different numbers of neutrons in their nuclei. Have essentially similar chemical properties, but may differ in physical properties. Most elements consist of mixtures of various isotopes.

Israel

Israel, in OT, name given to JACOB as eponymous ancestor of the Israelites.

Israel, republic of SW Asia, on Mediterranean. Area, *c* 21,000 sq km (8100 sq mi); pop. 3,252,000; cap. Jerusalem. Language: Hebrew. Religion: Judaism. Fertile coastal plain (citrus fruit) rises in N to Galilee (grain) and in S to Negev desert (irrigation schemes, co-operative farms *kibbutzim*). Part of hist. PALESTINE, region disputed by neighbours after Hebrews consolidated it (*c* 1000 BC). Subsequent occupations incl. Roman (70 BC-AD 636), Ottoman (1516-1917). British mandate (1920-48) ended in estab. of Israel as

Jewish home. Fought Arabs in wars of 1948, 1956, 1967, 1973; occupied Sinai from 1967; parts were returned to Egypt after 1973 war.

Issyk Kul, lake of USSR, Kirghiz SSR. Area c 6220 sq km (2400 sq mi); alt. 1620 m (5300 ft). Slightly saline.

Istanbul, city of NW Turkey, on both sides of Bosporus, at entrance to Sea of Marmara. Pop. 2,376,000. Major port; cultural, indust. and trade centre; starting point of Baghdad railway. Anc. *Byzantium* founded 658 BC by Greeks. Rebuilt as Constantinople by Constantine I (4th cent. AD) as new Roman imperial cap. Later cap. of Byzantine empire; often attacked, fell to soldiers of 4th Crusade (1204) and finally to Turks (1453). Ottoman and Turkish cap. until 1923; name changed 1930. Harbour is in Golden Horn. Notable architecture incl. Church of St Sophia, built by Justinian in 6th cent.; became a mosque after Turkish conquest.

Istria (*Istra*), penin. of NW Yugoslavia, in Adriatic Sea. Main towns Pula, Opatija. Agric., fishing, tourism. Ceded to Italy after WWI; all except Trieste to Yugoslavia 1947.

Italian, Romance language in Italic branch of Indo-European family. Official language of Italy, and one of Switzerland's. Developed from Latin, Florentine dialect becoming dominant in 14th cent., giving rise to modern standard Italian.

Italic, branch of Indo-European family of languages. Subdivided into 2 groups: ancient Italian, incl. Latin; ROMANCE LANGUAGES, all developed from Latin.

italic, form of type in which characters slope upwards to the right. Introduced 1501 by ALDUS MANUTIUS. Used to distinguish certain sets of words, *eg* book titles, foreign language words.

Italy

Italy (*Italia*), republic of S Europe. Comprises penin., isls. incl. Sardinia, Sicily. Area 301,165 sq km (116,280 sq mi); Pop. 55,121,000; cap. Rome. Language: Italian. Religion: RC. Chief cities Milan, Naples, Turin, Genoa. Member of EEC. Alps in N, fertile Po basin in NE, Apennines run NW-SE. Indust. based in N and Po basin, using h.e.p. from Alps. Barren S has some agric. (fruit, wine, olives), slow indust. growth. Major tourist indust. Settled by Etruscans, Greeks before rise of Imperial ROME 5th cent. BC; fell to Ostrogoths AD 5th cent. Part of Holy Roman Empire from 962; later medieval growth of city republics, *eg* Florence, Venice, *fl* in Renaissance period. United by Cavour, Garibaldi as kingdom (1861). Fascist rule under Mussolini led to expansion (Abyssinia, Albania) and alliance with Germany in WWII. Colonies lost, republic created 1946.

Ithaca (*Itháki*), isl. of W Greece, one of Ionian Isls. Area 85 sq km (33 sq mi); main town Ithaca. Home of Homer's Odysseus.

Ito, Hirobumi, Prince (1841-1909), Japanese statesman. Premier 4 times between 1886 and 1901. Achievements incl. drafting of constitution of 1890 and Anglo-Japanese alliance (1902). Assassinated at Harbin by a Korean.

Iturbide, Agustín de (1783-1824), Mexican revolutionary, emperor (1822-3). Originally a general in Spanish imperial army, later secured Mexican independence from Spain (1821). Proclaimed emperor, his oppressive rule provoked revolution. Deposed by Santa Anna, exiled, and executed on return.

Ivan [III] the Great (1440-1505), Russian ruler, grand duke of Moscow (1462-1505). Conquered Novgorod (1478) and expanded territ. of Muscovy by conquest and treaty. Threw off domination of Tartars of the Golden Horde (1480). Married Zoe, niece of last Byzantine emperor, who introduced Byzantine customs to his court.

Ivan [IV] the Terrible (1530-84), Russian tsar (1547-84). In 1533, became grand duke of Moscow on death of his father Vasily III; regency held by his mother until 1538, then by various boyars, until he was crowned tsar (1547). Began eastward expansion with conquest of Kazan (1552) and Astrakhan (1556). Unbalanced after 1560, became a harsh tyrant; in a rage, killed his son Ivan (1581). Broke political power of boyars in reign of terror.

Ivanovo, city of USSR, C European RSFSR. Pop. 434,000. Hist. centre of cotton textile indust. Founded 14th cent.

Ives, Charles Edward (1874-1954), American composer. Anticipated many later developments in music, incl. complex combinations of rhythms and keys. Successful insurance broker, he gained little musical recognition in his lifetime. Works incl. orchestral piece *The Unanswered Question*.

Iviza (*Ibiza*), third largest of Balearic Isls., Spain. Area 572 sq km (221 sq mi); main town Iviza. Tourism, agric.

ivory, hard white substance, a form of dentine, making up tusks of elephants, walruses, *etc.* Used for piano keys, cutlery handles, decorative carvings.

Ivory Coast (Fr. *Côte d'Ivoire*), republic of W Africa, on Gulf of Guinea. Area 322,500 sq km (124,500 sq mi); pop. 5,897,000; cap. Abidjan. Official language: French. Religions: native, Islam. Savannah in N, tropical forest in C, coastal swamps in S. Railway link with Upper Volta. Produces coffee, cotton, bananas, tropical hardwoods. Former centre of slave, ivory trade. French colony from 1893, part of French West Africa from 1904; independent 1960.

Ivy

ivy, *Hedera helix,* evergreen climbing shrub of Araliaceae family, native to Europe. Woody stem, greenish flowers in autumn, poisonous berries in spring. Climbs walls and trees by tiny roots. See POISON IVY.

Iwo, city of SW Nigeria. Pop. 192,000. Agric. centre, esp. cocoa, coffee, palm products; cotton mfg. Former cap. of Yoruba kingdom, *fl* 17th-19th cent.

Iwo Jima, see VOLCANO ISLANDS.

Ixion, in Greek myth, king of Thessaly. Murdered his father-in-law; Zeus then took him to Olympus to purify him. Attempted to seduce Hera but Zeus created phantom of her, by which Ixion fathered Centaurs. Punished by being eternally chained to a fiery, revolving wheel in Hades.

Izhevsk, city of USSR, cap. of Udmurt auton. republic, E European RSFSR. Pop. 456,000. Metallurgical centre; steel mills and ammunition factories estab. early 19th cent.

Izmir, port of W Turkey, on Gulf of Izmir; formerly Smyrna. Pop. 591,000. Naval base; exports tobacco, cotton. Colonized by Ionians, prosperous under Roman rule; early Christian centre. Taken by Turks in 1424. Held by Greeks (1919-22); Greek pop. expelled (1923).

Izmit (anc. *Nicomedia*), city of NW Turkey, on Sea of Marmara. Pop. 142,000. Situated in rich tobacco region. Built (264 BC) by Nicomedes of Bithynia as his cap.

Izvestia (Russ., = news), official daily newspaper of USSR. Founded (1917) after the February Revolution.

J

Jabalpur, city of Madhya Pradesh state, C India. Pop. 534,000. Railway jct. and indust. centre; armaments mfg.

Jablonec (Ger. *Gablonz),* town of NW Czechoslovakia. Pop. 34,000. Glass indust.

jaborandi, dried leaflets of various South American plants of genus *Pilocarpus* which yield the alkaloid pilocarpine, used to stimulate sweat or contract pupil of eye.

jacamar, any of Galbulidae family of brightly coloured insectivorous birds of humid forests of tropical America.

jacana, any of Jacanidae family of tropical and subtropical birds. Has long toes enabling it to walk on floating plants, *eg* lily leaves. Also called lilytrotter or lotus bird.

Jacaranda (*Jacaranda acutifolia*)

jacaranda, genus of tropical American trees of bignonia family. Finely divided foliage, large clusters of lavender flowers. Introduced into Australia.

Jáchymov (Ger. *Joachimsthal),* town of W Czechoslovakia, in Erzgebirge. Pop. 8000. Pitchblende mining; radium, uranium production. Health resort, thermal springs. Silver mining centre in 16th cent.

Black-backed jackal (*Canis mesomelas*)

jackal, wolf-like wild dog. Hunts nocturnally in packs, taking carrion or living prey. Species incl. oriental jackal, *Canis aureus,* of N Africa and S Asia.

jackdaw, *Corvus monedula,* black bird of crow family, found in Europe and W Asia.

jack-in-the-pulpit, *Arisaema triphyllum,* North American plant of arum family with upright, club-shaped flower spike, sheathing leaves and scarlet berries.

jack rabbit, large North American hare, genus *Lepus.*

Jackdaw

Jackson, Andrew (1767-1845), American general and statesman, president (1829-37). Gained victory over British at New Orleans (1815) after formal conclusion of War of 1812. Narrowly defeated as Democratic presidential candidate (1824), successful in 1828. Estranged South in conflict with South Carolina over taxation rights (NULLIFICATION crisis, 1832). Successfully opposed attempts to re-charter Bank of the United States. Jacksonian democracy brought SPOILS SYSTEM of political rewards and strengthened the executive.

Jackson, Thomas Jonathan ('Stonewall') (1824-63), American Confederate general. Fought in Civil War, victorious in Shenandoah Valley campaign (1862) and 2nd battle of Bull Run (1862). Mortally wounded at Chancellorsville.

Jackson, cap. of Mississippi, US; on Pearl R. Pop. 154,000. Railway jct., indust. and commercial centre; cotton, textiles mfg. Estab. as cap. 1821.

Jacksonville, deep-water port of NE Florida, US; on St John's R. Pop. 513,000; state's largest city. Commercial, transport centre; timber, fruit exports. Tourist resort.

Jack the Ripper, popular name for notorious murderer, never identified, of 6 women prostitutes in E London in 1888.

Jacob, in OT, twin brother of Esau. Gained Esau's birthright and their father's dying blessing by trickery. Fled to escape his brother's anger. During flight, had vision of angels ascending and descending ladder to heaven. On return, after marrying Leah and Rachel, wrestled with angel, received name Israel. The 12 tribes of Israel were descended from his sons.

Jacobean, term applied to English architecture and decoration characteristic of reign of James I. Classical features were used more widely and elaborate ornamental wood and plaster decoration employed.

Jacobean drama, term used for plays written in, and reflecting spirit of, reign of James I. Comedies were generally satires of human folly, *eg* Jonson's *Volpone.* Tragedies characterized by emphasis on human, esp. sexual, corruption, often with revenge theme, *eg* Webster's *The White Devil, The Duchess of Malfi,* Tourneur's *The Revenger's Tragedy.*

Jacobins, French society of radical democrats, formed 1789. Originally incl. GIRONDISTS, whose support of war throughout Europe later caused split. Became increasingly radical and, under Robespierre, instituted REIGN OF TERROR. Influence ended by Robespierre's fall and execution (1794).

Jacobite Church, Christian church of Iraq, Syria, parts of India. Founded (6th cent.) by Jacob Baradaeus. Regarded as heretical by RC and Orthodox churches (*see* MONOPHYSITISM).

Jacobites, supporters of claims of house of STUART to English throne after 1688. Sought restoration of James II and his descendants. Aided by France and Spain, raised rebellion of 1715 in support of James Edward Stuart. Charles Edward Stuart led last Jacobite rebellion from Scotland, defeated at Culloden (1746).

Jacobsen, Arne (1902-71), Danish architect. Noted for the elegance of his work and relating buildings to landscape. Designed St Catherine's College, Oxford and Town Hall at Rødovre.

Jacob's ladder, any plant of genus *Polemonium* of phlox family. Blue-flowered perennial. Species found in Europe and North America.

Jacquard, Joseph Marie (1752-1834), French inventor. Developed (1801-6) Jacquard loom, first to weave figured patterns; used system of punched cards.

Jacquerie, French peasants' uprising (1358), begun in Normandy. Suppressed by Charles II of Navarre with great brutality.

jade, either of 2 silicate minerals used as gem. Jadeite, a pyroxene, is rarer and more valuable than nephrite, an amphibole. Normally green in colour, may be white, yellow, pink. Used in ornamental carving, jewellery. Major sources in China, Japan, USSR, New Zealand.

Jadida, El, town of W Morocco, on Atlantic Ocean. Pop. 40,000. Port, exports agric. produce. Founded by Portuguese (1502), taken by Morocco (1769). Formerly called Mazagan.

Jadotville, *see* LIKASI, Zaïre.

jaeger, *see* SKUA.

Jaén, town of S Spain, cap. of Jaén prov. Pop. 79,000. Produces olive oil, wine, leather goods; lead mines nearby. Moorish kingdom until 1246. Cathedral (16th cent.).

Jaffa, *see* TEL AVIV.

Jagan, Cheddi Berrat (1918-   ), Guyanan statesman. Led independence movement in British Guiana after becoming premier (1961-4). After independence (1966), led Socialist opposition until 1973.

Jaguar

jaguar, *Panthera onca,* large cat of Central and South America. Resembles leopard, with black spots and yellow coat; nocturnal hunter.

Jainism, Indian religion. Arose (6th cent. BC) with Buddhism as protest against formalism of Hinduism. Doctrine based on belief in eternity of all living things, stresses asceticism, respect for all forms of life. The soul retains identity through transmigration and eventually attains NIRVANA. Adhered to by c 2 million Indians.

Jaipur, cap. of Rajasthan state, NW India. Pop. 613,000. Commercial centre; famous for jewellery. Enclosed by wall, has maharajah's palace. Cap. of former princely state of Jaipur.

Jakarta, *see* DJAKARTA.

James I, king of England, Scotland and Ireland

Jamaica, independent isl. state of West Indies, member of British Commonwealth. Area 10,962 sq km (4232 sq mi); pop. 2,000,000, mainly Negro; cap. Kingston. Language: English. Religion: Protestant. Blue Mts. in E (coffee growing). Tropical climate. Agric. economy (sugar, fruit, spice, tobacco growing); bauxite exports. Important tourism. Discovered by Columbus (1494); captured from Spanish by English (1655); slavery abolished (1833). Gained independence after it seceded from Federation of West Indies (1962).

James [the Elder], St (d. *c* AD 44), one of the Twelve Disciples, son of Zebedee. In NT, put to death with brother John by Herod Agrippa. Traditionally, body moved to Santiago de Compostela, Spain, site of famous shrine.

James I (1208-76), king of Aragón (1213-76). Conquered Balearic Isls. (1229-35) and Valencia (1238). Fought long against Moors in Murcia. Called 'El Conquistador' (the conqueror).

James I (1566-1625), king of England, Scotland and Ireland (1603-25). Succeeded to Scottish throne (1567) as James VI on abdication of mother, Mary Queen of Scots, and to English throne on death of Elizabeth I. Reign marked by conflict with Parliament, influence of his favourites (*eg* BUCKINGHAM), exercise of royal prerogative, raising of revenue. Antagonized Puritans at Hampton Court Conference (1604), which commissioned translation of Bible (Authorized Version).

James II (1633-1701), king of England, Scotland and Ireland (1685-8). A convert to Catholicism, subject to Whig attempts to exclude him from succession, which were frustrated by his brother, Charles II. After succession, put down Monmouth's rebellion; alienated subjects by autocratic rule, pro-Catholic policies. Fled country after William of Orange had been invited to become king. His restoration bid was foiled by defeat at the Boyne in Ireland (1690).

James I (1394-1437), king of Scotland (1424-37). Sent by his father to France (1406), he was captured by English and held until 1424. Tried to suppress power of his nobles and maintain peace; murdered by group of nobles.

James IV (1473-1513), king of Scotland (1488-1513). Reign marked by stability and beginnings of prosperity. As part of alliance with France, invaded England but was defeated and killed at Flodden. Marriage to Margaret Tudor (1503) formed basis of Stuart claims to English throne.

James, Jesse [Woodson] (1847-82), American outlaw. With brother, **[Alexander] Frank[lin] James** (1843-1915), led notorious outlaw gang which robbed banks and trains in midwest during 1870s. Jesse was killed by a gang member.

James, Thomas (c 1593-c 1635), English navigator. In search of Northwest Passage, explored James Bay, Canada (1631). Wrote *Strange and Dangerous Voyage* (1633).

James, William (1842-1910), American philosopher, psychologist. Opposed 'pure' metaphysical philosophy, argued for practical philosophy, *ie* pragmatism, and relativity of truth. Works incl. *The Principles of Psychology* (1890). His brother, **Henry James** (1843-1916), was a novelist. Novels deal with social relationships between Old World and New, *eg The Europeans* (1878), *The Portrait of a Lady* (1881), *The Bostonians* (1886). Short stories incl. *The Turn of the Screw* (1898). Settled in England (1877), became British national (1915).

James, two rivers of US. **1,** rises in C North Dakota, flows 1143 km (710 mi) across Dakotas to Missouri R. **2,** formed in SW Virginia, flows E 547 km (340 mi). On its lower course was Jamestown, 1st permanent English settlement in America (1607).

James, in NT, epistle traditionally ascribed to St James the Less. Propounds general points of practical morality.

James Bay, arm of SE Hudson Bay, Canada; between Ontario and Québec Has many isls., largest Akimiski. Trading posts; oil development. Explored (1631) by Thomas James.

Jameson, Sir Leander Starr (1853-1917), British colonial administrator. Led unauthorized Jameson raid (1895) into Boer colony of Transvaal to support 'Uitlanders' (largely British settlers); captured, briefly imprisoned by British. Premier of Cape Colony (1904-8).

Jesse James

Henry James

Jamestown, Virginia, US, *see* JAMES, river (2).
Jami, Nur al-Din 'Abd al-Rahman (1414–92), Persian poet, scholar, mystic. Best known for *Haft Awrang* (7 thrones), incl. poem 'Yûsuf and Zulaykhâ'. Also wrote short stories, biographies, mystical works.

Jammu and Kashmir, state of N India. Area *c* 142,000 km (55,000 sq mi); pop. 4,615,000; cap. Srinagar (summer), Jammu (winter). Almost entirely mountainous. Famous for goats' wool (cashmere). At 1947 partition this Hindu-ruled Moslem region disputed by Pakistan and India. Jammu and Kashmir declared part of India 1956; Pakistan retained Azad Kashmir.

Jamnagar, port of Gujarat state, NW India. Pop. 215,000. Textile mfg. Cap. of former princely state of Nawanagar.

Jamshedpur, city of Bihar state, NE India. Pop. 465,000. Major iron and steel works. Founded 1909 by industrialist Tata family.

Janáček, Leoš (1854-1928), Czech composer. Wrote music in national style. Works incl. rhapsody *Taras Bulba* and operas, *eg Jenufa, The Cunning Little Vixen.* Orchestral works incl. *Sinfonietta.*

Jane, Frederick (1870-1916), English naval officer, journalist. Founder, 1st editor of annuals *Jane's Fighting Ships* (1898), *All the World's Aircraft* (1910).

Janina, *see* IOANNINA, Greece.

Janissaries, elite corps of the Turkish army formed in the 14th cent. from press-ganged Christians and prisoners of war. Liquidated by Mahmud II (1826) after a mutiny.

Jan Mayen, isl. of Norway, in Arctic Sea between Iceland and Spitsbergen. Area 373 sq km (144 sq mi); has extinct volcano (2280 m/7470 ft). Meteorological station. Discovered *c* 1610, annexed 1929 to Norway.

Jansen, Cornelis (1585-1638), Dutch theologian. Attempted to reform RC church by returning to teachings of St Augustine. Attacked orthodox Jesuit teaching in *Augustinus* (pub. 1642), advocating austerity, belief in predestination similar to Calvin's but within Catholicism. Leading followers (Jansenists) set up community at Port Royal, France. Condemned in papal bulls of 1705 and 1713. Noted Jansenists incl. ARNAULD, Pascal.

Jansenism, *see* JANSEN, CORNELIS.

Janus, in Roman religion, god of doorways and hence of the beginnings of enterprises. One of principal gods, regarded as custodian of the universe. Represented with double-faced head so that he could look to front and back.

Japan (*Nippon*), country of E Asia, archipelago with 4 main isls. Honshu, Hokkaido, Kyushu and Shikoku, separated from mainland by Sea of Japan. Area *c* 372,000 sq km (142,000 sq mi); pop. 109,671,000; cap. Tokyo. Language: Japanese. Religion: Shinto, Buddhism. Mountainous with active volcanoes, frequent earthquakes; monsoon climate, abundant rainfall. Intensive cultivation yields rice, cereals, soya beans; major fisheries. Buddhism, Chinese culture introduced 6th cent AD; was feudal society under warrior leaders (shoguns) until 19th cent. European contacts estab. in 16th cent. Became world power after defeating China (1894-5), Russia (1904-5); 2nd Chinese war merged with WWII after Japanese attack on Pearl Harbor (1941). Surrendered 1945; imperial power curtailed (1947).

Japanese, language of Japan and Ryukyu Isls. Appears to be unrelated to any other language, although grammar similar to Korean. Written language adapted from Chinese since 3rd–4th cent., with simplified phonetic characters added since WWII.

Japanese beetle, *Popillia japonica,* shiny green and brown beetle; accidentally brought from Japan to US, major pest of fruit and crops.

Japanese literature, in poetry, traditional verse forms are *tanka* (5-line stanzas of 5,7,5,7,7 syllables), *haiku* (3-line stanzas of 5,7,5 syllables). In drama, the NO PLAY developed (14th cent.) from religious ceremony. The *kabuki* theatre, dating from 17th cent., is more popular form allowing greater freedom of expression. In the novel, influences have been mainly European, esp. Russian. Also *see* HEIKE-MONOGATARI, MURASAKI SHIKIBU.

japonica or **flowering quince,** spiky Asiatic shrub of genus *Chaemoneles.* Pink or red flowers, hard yellow fruit used in preserves.

Japurá, river of NW South America. Rises in Colombia as Caquetá, flows SE into Brazil to Amazon. Length *c* 2100 km (*c* 1300 mi).

Jaques-Dalcroze, Emile (1865-1950), Swiss educator, composer. Invented Dalcroze system of eurhythmics, system of musical interpretation in dance and mime, which influenced ballet, acting and physical education.

Jarrah, *Eucalyptus marginata,* large Australian eucalyptus tree. Hard wood used in flooring, fencing, *etc.*

Jarrow, mun. bor. of Tyne and Wear met. county, NE England, on Tyne estuary. Pop. 29,000. Shipbuilding; oil indust. Site of Bede's monastery. Severe unemployment after WWI.

Winter jasmine (*Jasminum nudiflorum*)

jasmine, any of genus *Jasminum* of shrubs of olive family. Native to Asia, South America and Australia. Popular as garden plant for fragrant flowers of yellow, red or white. Used in perfumes or for scenting tea.

Jason, in Greek myth, leader of the ARGONAUTS. Promised his right to throne of Iolcus by the usurper Pelias if he could recover the GOLDEN FLEECE. Secured the fleece from King Aeëtes of Colchis, whose daughter MEDEA helped him in return for promise of marriage. On return to Iolcus, Medea tricked Pelias' daughters into murdering their father, but Jason failed to retain kingdom. Reigned with Medea over Corinth until he broke faith with her. For this, condemned to exile by gods. Died when prow of *Argo* crushed him as he was resting in its shade.

jasper, impure, cryptocrystalline QUARTZ used as gem. Opaque, usually red, yellow or brown in colour.

Jaspers, Karl (1883-1969), German philosopher. Influenced by Kierkegaard. Interpreter of German EXISTENTIALISM. Held man to be encompassed in continual struggle of love and hate. Works incl. *Man in the Modern Age* (1931), *Reason and Existence* (1935).

jataka, genre of Buddhist literature. Moral tale in which principal character is afterwards identified with Buddha in previous incarnation. Large collection in PALI literature.

jaundice, condition characterized by yellow discoloration of skin, mucous membranes and urine. Caused by excess bile pigment in blood. May result from infectious hepatitis, blockage of bile ducts.

Jaurès, Jean Léon (1859-1914), French politician. Advocated democratic socialism and international pacifism. Founded socialist journal *L'Humanité* (1904). Assassinated while trying to prevent outbreak of WWI.

Java, most important isl. of Indonesia. Area *c* 132,000 sq km (51,000 sq mi). Narrow, crossed by volcanic mountains; humid, tropical vegetation. Produces rice, rubber, coffee. Densely populated; has ⅔ of Indonesian pop. and cap. Djakarta.

Java man, forerunner of modern man whose fossilized remains were found in Java by Eugène Dubois (1891). Originally classified as *Pithecanthropus erectus,* Java man now considered to be an example of *Homo erectus.*

jaw, either of 2 bones which hold the teeth and frame the mouth in most vertebrates. Upper jaw (maxilla), a component of skull, does not move; lower jaw (mandible), hinged to skull, is movable.

Jawlensky, Aleksei (1864-1941), Russian painter. Worked in Germany, where he was associated with Blaue Reiter group. Early work in expressionist style, using simplified forms and flat areas of colour; later concentrated on representations of human head.

Jay, John (1745-1829), American statesman, first chief justice (1789-95). Signed Anglo-American settlement (Jay's Treaty, 1794), authorizing negotiation by joint commission of boundary disputes in North America.

Jay (*Garrulus glandarius*)

jay, brightly coloured bird of crow family. Eurasian jay, *Garrulus glandarius,* has pinkish-brown body, blue-back wings. Blue jay, *Cyanocitta cristata,* of US has blue plumage.

jazz, music that originated in US at turn of 19th cent., deriving from American Negro music. Has now spread through much of world, esp. Europe and Japan. Key features are use of improvisation (*eg* Louis Armstrong) and rhythmic drive. Several styles are still current, *eg* traditional or New Orleans jazz, but contemporary jazz is merging both with rock and avant-garde music.

Jean Paul, see RICHTER, JOHANN PAUL.

Jeans, Sir James Hopwood (1877-1946), English astronomer, physicist. Worked on theory of rapidly spinning bodies and applied results to problem of stellar evolution. Wrote many popular scientific works incl. *The Universe Around Us* (1929).

Jedburgh, town of Borders region, SE Scotland. Pop. 4000. Former royal burgh and co. town of Roxburghshire. Tweed, woollen, rayon mfg. Has ruined 12th cent. abbey. Hist. notorious for 'Jeddart justice' (trial followed hanging).

Jeddah, see JIDDAH.

jeep, four-wheel drive military motor vehicle with ¼ ton carrying capacity; used for reconnaissance, passengers and light cargo. Developed by US in WWII.

Jefferies, [John] Richard (1848-87), English author. Best known for *Bevis: The Story of a Boy* (1882), *The Story of My Heart* (1883) describing rural Wiltshire in terms of a personal mysticism.

Jeffers, [John] Robinson (1887-1962), American poet. Collections incl. *Tamar* (1924), *Cawdor* (1928), *Dear Judas* (1929), based on biblical, classical sources, asserting Nietzschean individualism.

Jefferson, Thomas (1743-1826), American statesman, president (1801-9). Wrote much of Declaration of Independence (1776). As secretary of state (1790-3) in Washington's cabinet, opposed centralizing Federalists led by ALEXANDER HAMILTON. Elected president by House of Representatives after tie with Aaron Burr. Admin. highlighted by Louisiana Purchase (1803). Much of subsequent Democratic Party doctrine derived from Jeffersonian Republicans.

Jeffreys, George, 1st Baron Jeffreys of Wem (*c* 1645-89), English judge. Notorious for harshness at 'Bloody Assizes' after Monmouth's rebellion (1685), hanging *c* 200 and flogging, transporting many more. Lord chancellor under James II.

Jehovah, mistaken reconstruction of the ineffable name of God (YHWH) in OT. The form *Yahweh* is now regarded as more correct.

Thomas Jefferson

Lord Jeffreys

Jehovah's Witnesses, *see* RUSSELL, CHARLES TAZE.
Jellicoe, John Rushworth Jellicoe, 1st Earl (1859-1935), British admiral. Commanded Grand Fleet (1914-16), notably in battle of Jutland (1916); first sea lord (1916-17). Governor-general of New Zealand (1920-4).

Jellyfish (*Chrysaora isosceles*)

jellyfish, free-swimming medusa form of certain coelenterates. True jellyfish, class Scyphozoa, have gelatinous bell-shaped bodies and tentacles with stinging cells for capturing prey.

Jemappes, town of S Belgium. Pop. 13,000. Coalmining, iron, steel mfg. Site of battle (1792) in which French Revolutionary forces defeated Austrians.
Jena, town of SW East Germany, on R. Saale. Pop. 84,000. Precision engineering, incl. Zeiss optical instruments. Univ. (1558). Scene of Napoleon's victory (1806) over Prussians.
Jenghiz Khan, *see* GENGHIS KHAN.
Jenkins, Roy Harris (1920-), British politician. Chancellor of exchequer (1967-70), home secretary (1974-6) in Labour govts. Resigned to become (1977) president of European Commission (executive of European Community).
Jenkins' Ear, War of (1739-41), conflict between Britain and Spain, which merged into the WAR OF AUSTRIAN SUCCESSION. Robert Jenkins, a master mariner, claimed to have had his ear cut off by the Spanish; his story so aroused public opinion that Walpole was forced to declare war.
Jenné, *see* DJENNÉ, Mali.

Edward Jenner

Jenner, Edward (1749-1823), English physician. Made 1st successful vaccination (1796) against smallpox by immunizing patient with cowpox virus. Described work in *Inquiry into the Cause and Effects of the Variolae Vaccinae* (1798).
Jensen, Johannes Vilhelm (1873-1950), Danish author. Known for prose epic, *The Long Journey* (1908-22), tracing Teutonic race from baboon stage to 16th cent. in Darwinian terms. Nobel Prize for Literature (1944).
Jenson or **Janson, Nicolas** (d. *c* 1480), Venetian printer, b. France. Started publishing in Venice (1470), where he produced many beautiful editions. His elegant Roman typeface influenced many subsequent printers.
Jerba, *see* DJERBA, Tunisia.

Egyptian jerboa

jerboa, fawn-coloured nocturnal rodent of Dipodidae family from desert regions of N Africa and Asia. Uses very long back legs for jumping. Species incl. Egyptian jerboa, *Jaculus jaculus.*
Jeremiah, prophetic book of OT, taking place during reign of Josiah. Tells story of priest Jeremiah who was imprisoned for foretelling fall of Jerusalem. Went into

Egypt with the remaining Jews when prophecy fulfilled (586 BC).

Jerez (de la Frontera), city of Andalusia, S Spain. Pop. 150,000. Produces wine, sherry (named after town); bottle and cask mfg., horse breeding. Held by Moors 711-1264.

Jericho, ancient city of NW Jordan, at N end of Dead Sea, near modern village of Ariha. Thought to date from *c* 8000 BC. Canaanite city captured by Joshua and Israelites; often destroyed, rebuilt.

Jerome, Jerome K[lapka] (1859-1927), English author. Known for comic novels, esp. *Three Men in a Boat* (1889). Also wrote modern morality play. *The Passing of the Third Floor Back* (1908).

Jerome, St, full name Sophronius Eusebius Hieronymus (*c* 347-*c* 419), Dalmatian churchman, scholar. Served Pope Damasus I in Rome before retiring (386) to monastery in Bethlehem. Latin translations of Bible from Hebrew served as basis for the VULGATE.

Jersey, largest of Channel Isls., UK. Area 116 sq km (45 sq mi); pop. 73,000; cap. St Helier. Tourism; Jersey cattle; potato, tomato growing. Origin of woollen 'jerseys'.

Jersey City, in NE New Jersey, US; opposite New York City on Hudson R. Pop. 261,000. Shipping terminal; meat packing, oil refining; foundry and paper products, chemicals mfg. Settled by Dutch in 1620s.

Jerusalem, cap. of Israel, hist. cap. of Palestine. Pop. 305,000. Partitioned 1948 between Israel (new city) and Jordan (old city). Latter contains most of Jewish, Christian, Moslem holy sites. Enclosed by Turks (16th cent.). Sacred are Wailing Wall, Mosque of Omar, Church of Holy Sepulchre, monasteries, Mt. of Olives. Old city occupied by Israelis after 1967.

Jerusalem artichoke, *see* ARTICHOKE.

Jervis, John, Earl of St Vincent (1735-1823), British naval officer. Commanded the Mediterranean fleet in victory (1797), aided by Nelson, over a larger Spanish fleet off Cape St Vincent. As first lord of the admiralty (1801-6) he instituted important reforms.

Jervis Bay, inlet of Tasman Sea, SE Australia. Shore area (73 sq km/28 sq mi) became federal territ. 1915; proposed as port for Australian Capital Territory. Naval base.

Jespersen, Otto (1860-1943), Danish philologist. Known first for work on phonetics, later wrote more general works, incl. *A Modern English Grammar on Historical Principles* (1909-31).

Jesse, in OT, father of David. Name later symbolized royal line and its Messianic associations, *eg* Jesse's Rod (Jesus) and Jesse's Root (Virgin Mary).

Jesselton, *see* KOTA KINABALU.

Jesuit Martyrs of North America, eight Jesuit missionaries canonized 1930 for having suffered martyrdom (1648-9) at hands of Iroquois Indians.

Jesuits, *see* JESUS, SOCIETY OF.

Jesus, Society of, or **Jesuits,** RC religious order for men founded (*c* 1534) by IGNATIUS OF LOYOLA. Approved by pope (1540). Original aims were educational and missionary work (*eg* in Japan, India, North and South America). Characterized by disciplined organization and long, rigorous training. Political involvement (18th cent.) resulted in expulsion from France, Portugal, Spain and its dominions. Suppressed by Pope Clement XIV (1773). Revived (1814) as worldwide order.

Jesus Christ (*c* 4 BC-*c* AD 29), Jewish religious leader, central figure of Christianity. Born in Bethlehem to Mary, wife of Joseph of Nazareth. Lived at time when Jews were eager for deliverance from Roman domination. After baptism by his cousin, John the Baptist, Jesus became a wandering teacher accompanied by band of disciples. Attracted great crowds with preaching. Govt.'s fear of his power led to arrest in Jerusalem during Passover after betrayal by Judas Iscariot. Tried and convicted of blasphemy by the ecclesiastical court. Crucified by order of Pontius Pilate. According to Gospels, arose 3 days later. Book of Acts relates that, 40 days later, in sight of his disciples, he ascended to Heaven. *See* TRINITY.

jet, hard, black variety of LIGNITE. May be highly polished and used in jewellery. Major sources in England, US, France.

jet propulsion, forward movement achieved by reaction caused by expanding gases ejected rearwards. Usually air is compressed, mixed with fuel and burnt. This combustion provides rapid expansion of the gas which produces the rearward jet and also drives the intake compressor.

Jevons, William Stanley (1835-82), English economist, logician. Developed theory that value was determined by utility in *The Theory of Political Economy* (1871).

Jewish Autonomous Region, *see* BIROBIDZHAN.

Jews, people regarded as descended from the ancient Hebrews of Biblical times, whose religion is JUDAISM. In OT, lineage traced from Abraham and 12 tribes of Israel. Originally in Canaan, then Egypt; persecution resulted in Exodus led by Moses. Resettled in Canaan under Saul after period of wandering in desert. First Temple built by Solomon. Kingdom then split into Israel and Judah. Temple destroyed by Babylonians (586 BC), people exiled until their return was allowed by Cyrus the Great and Temple rebuilt (516 BC). Jerusalem destroyed by Romans (AD 70). After fall of Roman Empire, Jews appeared in W Europe but were widely persecuted from 12th-18th cent. Capitalism and 19th cent. revolutionary movements improved their conditions. Emancipation led to cultural assimilation and ZIONISM. New wave of persecution spread from Russia after assassination (1881) of Alexander II. Rise to power of Nazis in Germany resulted in extermination of 6 million Jews before and during WWII. Refuge sought in Palestine, resulting in formation of Jewish state of Israel (1948) by UN.

Jezebel (d. *c* 846BC), wife of Ahab, king of Israel. Introduced worship of Baal into Israel and persecuted the prophets. Vigorously denounced by Elijah, who prophesied her death; executed after Jehu's defeat of Ahab.

Jhelum (anc. *Hydaspes*), river of SC Asia. Rises in Kashmir, flows *c* 770 km (480 mi) SW into R. Chenab, N Pakistan.

Jibuti, *see* DJIBOUTI.

Jiddah or **Jeddah,** port of W Saudi Arabia, on Red Sea coast of Hejaz. Pop. 300,000. Provides sea access for Mecca for thousands of pilgrims.

Jiménez, Juan Ramón (1881-1958), Spanish poet. Works, *eg Sonetos Espirituales* (1917), prose-poem *Platero and I* (1917) noted for concentration of form. Nobel Prize for Literature (1956).

Jinja, town of SE Uganda, on N shore of Victoria Nyanza at outlet of Victoria Nile. Pop. 47,000. Indust. centre, grew rapidly after opening of nearby Owen Falls h.e.p. scheme; copper smelting, sugar refining, textile mfg.

Jinnah, Mohammed Ali (1876-1948), Indian statesman. President of Moslem League after 1934, successfully advocated partition of India into separate Hindu and Moslem states at independence (1947). First governor-general of Pakistan.

jinni or **djinni,** in Moslem literature, Arab folklore, human-like being with powers to change size, shape, place. May be good or evil.

Jivaro, several South American Indian tribes inhabiting E Andes of Ecuador. Renowned for former practice of head shrinking. Many killed in tribal wars. Long resisted civilization.

Joachim, Joseph (1831-1907), Hungarian violinist. Friend of Schumann, Mendelssohn, Brahms. He founded Joachim Quartet (1869) and was renowned for his interpretation of Beethoven and Brahms.

Joanna the Mad (1479-1555), Spanish queen of Castile and Léon (1504-55). The wife of Philip I, she became insane after his death (1506) and never ruled alone.

Joan of Arc, St (*c* 1412-31), French national heroine. Claimed to hear voices urging her to aid the dauphin in struggle against English. Led army which raised siege of Orléans (1429), then persuaded the dauphin to be crowned as Charles VII at Rheims. Captured at Compiègne (1430) by the Burgundians and delivered to the English. Tried and condemned by court of French ecclesiastics at Rouen as heretic and sorceress; burned at stake.

João Pessoa, port of NE Brazil, cap. of Paraíba state; near mouth of Paraíba R. Pop. 197,000. Cotton, sugar exports; cement, footwear, cigar mfg.

Job, poetical book of OT, of unknown authorship, prob. written 600-400 BC. Criticizes the association of sin with suffering by telling of the sufferings inflicted on the righteous Job by God.

Jodhpur, city of Rajasthan, NW India. Pop. 319,000. Trade in cotton; textile mfg. Walled city dominated by fort containing maharajah's palace. Cap. of former princely state of Jodhpur.

Jodrell Bank radio telescope

Jodrell Bank, site of large radio telescope, near Macclesfield, Cheshire. Has steerable parabolic dish, 76m in diameter.

Joel, prophetic book of OT, predicting plague of locusts in Judah. Promises the forgiveness of God upon repentance of sin.

Joffre, Joseph Jacques Césaire (1852-1931), French marshal. Commanded French armies on Western Front (1914-16) until outmoded strategy (notably at Verdun, 1916) led to his replacement. Chairman of Allied War Council (1916-18).

Jogjakarta, city of SC Java, Indonesia. Pop. 342,000. Centre of rice growing region. Provisional cap. of Indonesia (1945-50).

Augustus John: detail of a self-portrait

Johannesburg, city of S Transvaal, South Africa, in Witwatersrand. Pop. 1,433,000, country's largest city. Major indust., commercial centre in world's richest goldmining region; engineering, chemical mfg., diamond cutting. Two univs., stock exchange. Founded (1886) as mining settlement.

John [the Divine] or **[the Evangelist], St** (AD 1st cent.), one of Twelve Disciples, son of Zebedee and brother of James the Elder. Traditionally regarded as the unnamed disciple 'whom Jesus loved' and to whom he entrusted the care of his mother on his death. Regarded as author of 4th Gospel and *Revelations.*

John XXIII, orig. Angelo Giuseppe Roncalli (1881-1963), Italian churchman, pope (1958-63). Promoted reform within Church, reconciliation with other Christian churches and world peace. Despite opposition to Communism, advocated socialist reforms. Summoned influential 2nd Vatican Council.

John XXIII, antipope, *see* COSSA, BALDASSARRE.

John (1167-1216), king of England (1199-1216). Tried to usurp his brother, Richard I, during his absence on 3rd Crusade. Lost most of his French dominions to king of France in dispute over right to succeed Richard. Had to yield to papal authority in dispute over Stephen LANGTON. Forced to sign MAGNA CARTA (1215).

John II [the Good] (1319-64), king of France (1350-64). Captured at Poitiers (1356), he was released after his ransom was fixed by Treaty of Brétigny (1360). Unable to raise all his ransom, returned to England (1364) where he died.

John III [Sobieski] (1624-96), king of Poland (1674-96). Leader of Christian campaigns against Turks; acclaimed a hero after relieving Turkish siege of Vienna (1683). Last years of reign marked by opposition from nobles.

John I (c 1357-1433), king of Portugal (1385-1433). Secured Portuguese independence from Spanish hegemony with victory at battle of Aljubarrota. Reign marked by formation of Anglo-Portuguese alliance (1386) and beginnings of overseas exploration.

John II [the Perfect] (1455-95), king of Portugal (1481-95). Broke power of the feudal nobility, executing their leader, duke of Braganza. Concluded Treaty of Tordesillas (1494) with Spain, which estab. limits of each country's colonization of New World. Encouraged African exploration of Diaz.

John, Augustus Edwin (1878-1961), Welsh painter. Influenced by post-impressionism and Rembrandt, he painted portraits of many leading personalities of his day; later society portraits failed to realize his early promise. Works incl. *The Smiling Woman* and portraits of Shaw and Hardy. His sister, **Gwen John** (1876-1939), was also a painter; specialized in single figure compositions in greyish colour.

John, Gospel according to St, fourth of NT gospels, traditionally attributed to St John the Divine. Prob. written c AD 100. Most philosophical of gospels, propounding concept of LOGOS.

John, three epistles of NT, ascribed to apostle John the Divine; discourses setting forth the nature of Christian fellowship.

John Birch Society, extreme right-wing American anti-Communist organization (founded 1958). Named after John Birch, an intelligence officer killed by Chinese Communists (1945).

John Chrysostom, St (c 347-407), Greek churchman, theologian, patriarch of Constantinople (398-403). Deposed as result of court intrigues. Renowned preacher; author of influential commentaries, esp. on Paul's epistles.

John dory, see DORY.

John of Austria, Don (1545-78), Spanish soldier, illegitimate son of Emperor Charles V. Commanded Venetian and Spanish fleets which defeated Turks at Lepanto (1571). He conquered Tunis (1573), after which Philip II, suspicious of his intention to set up as ruler there, sent him to the Netherlands as viceroy.

John of Damascus, St (c 675-c 749), Syrian theologian. Entered monastery near Jerusalem c 726 after period as court official. Wrote standard defence against iconoclasm, incl. a history of heresies, *The Fountain of Wisdom.*

John of Gaunt, Duke of Lancaster (1340-99), English nobleman. Fourth son of Edward III, became effective ruler of England during last years of Edward and minority of Richard II. Claimed throne of Castile through his wife

Constance; withdrew claim after unsuccessful invasion of Castile (1386).

John of Leiden, orig. Jan Bockelson (*c* 1509-36), Dutch preacher. Anabaptist leader in Münster, overthrew religious and civil authorities and estab. (1534) theocracy, featuring polygamy and collective ownership of property. Tortured and executed after city was retaken.

John of Salisbury (*c* 1110-80), English scholastic philosopher. Secretary to Becket. Gathered current knowledge in *Metalogicus*; advocated separation of church and state in *Polycraticus*. Studied in France; advocate of realism.

John of the Cross, St, orig. Juan de Yepis y Alvarez (1542-91), Spanish mystic, poet. Friend of St Theresa of Avila. A founder of reformed order of Discalced Carmelites. Known for mystical poetry, *eg Spiritual Canticle,* written in prison, and treatises on mystical theology.

John O'Groats, in Highland region, N Scotland. Point of mainland Britain furthest from LAND'S END, England.

Johns, Jasper (1930-), American artist. Precursor of pop art, he is known for his attempts to transform everyday objects into art. Work incl. series of targets, flags and bronze cast *Beer Cans* (1961).

Johns Hopkins University, Baltimore, US, privately funded univ. founded in 1867. Noted for medical school, graduate research.

Johnson, Andrew (1808-75), American statesman, president (1865-9). A Democrat, elected vice-president (1864); became president on Lincoln's assassination. Post-Civil War RECONSTRUCTION programme impeded by radical Republicans. Narrowly acquitted in Senate vote over impeachment charge arising from attempt to remove secretary of war, EDWIN STANTON, from office (1868).

Johnson, John Arthur ('Jack') (1878-1946), American boxer. First black boxer to win world heavyweight title (1908), which he held until 1915. His controversial personality led to widespread desire for a 'white hope' to beat him.

Johnson, Lyndon Baines (1908-73), American statesman, president (1963-9). Achieved power in Senate as Democratic majority leader (1955-60). Elected vice-president (1960), became president on Kennedy's assassination. Legislative record of social reform offset by escalation of Vietnam war. Term also marked by race riots, anti-war movement.

Johnson, Samuel (1709-84), English writer. Known for *A Dictionary of the English Language* (1755), *Rasselas* (1759), *Lives of the Poets* (1783), many miscellaneous essays in the *Rambler* and the *Idler.* Edited Shakespeare with critical prefaces. In 1763 met Boswell who wrote his biog. Founded (1764) famous Literary Club. Tour of Hebrides produced *A Journey to the Western Islands of Scotland* (1775).

Johnston, Sir Harry Hamilton (1858-1927), English colonial administrator, explorer, naturalist. Led expedition to Kilimanjaro area (1884). In colonial service, explored C Africa (1889). Secured much territ. for UK; advocated British-controlled route 'from Cape to Cairo'.

Johnston, Joseph Eggleston (1807-1901), Confederate general. In US Civil War, he was victor at 1st battle of Bull Run. Subsequently failed to relieve Vicksburg (1863) and lost the Atlanta campaign to Sherman.

John the Baptist, St (d. *c* AD 29), Jewish prophet. In NT, son of priest of the Temple, Zacharias; cousin of Jesus. Called on people to repent in preparation for the Messiah whom he recognized in Jesus and baptized. Condemnation of Herod Antipas for his marriage to Herodias led to his beheading at her and her daughter Salome's instigation.

John the Fearless, Duke of Burgundy (1371-1419), French nobleman. Struggled for power with Louis d'Orléans, brother of insane king Charles VI; had Louis assassinated (1407). Civil war broke out (1411) between his supporters (Burgundians) and those of Orléans (Armagnacs). Murdered during attempt at reconciliation with the dauphin.

Samuel Johnson

Johore Bahru, cap. of Johore state, S West Malaysia. Pop. 136,000. Trade centre for rubber. Connected by causeway to Singapore.

joint, in anatomy, place of union between 2 bones, usually one which admits of motion of one or both bones. Joints are particularly susceptible to diseases such as gout and arthritis.

Joinville, Jean, Sire de (1225-1317), French chronicler. Wrote biog. of St Louis (Louis IX) from viewpoint of friend, companion on his 1st crusade, giving valuable picture of character of king, contemporary France.

Joliot-Curie, Irène (1897-1956), and her husband **Jean Frédéric Joliot-Curie** (1900-58), French scientists. Discovered artificial radioactivity by producing radioactive phosphorus isotope by alpha particle bombardment of aluminium; shared Nobel Prize for Chemistry (1935).

Jolson, Al, pseud. of Asa Yoelson (1886-1950), American singer, entertainer, b. Russia. Long known on Broadway, famous for appearance in 1st 'talkie', *The Jazz Singer* (1927), and for singing, with blackened face, such songs as 'Mammy', 'Swannee River'.

Jonah, prophetic book of OT, relating story of Jonah's missionary journey. Incl. story of Jonah being swallowed by a fish. A parable to warn Jews of the dangers of being inward-looking.

Jones, Henry (1831-99), *see* CAVENDISH.

Inigo Jones: Queen's House, Greenwich

Jones, Inigo (1573-1652), English architect. Influenced by Palladio, he brought Italian classicism to England. Designed Queen's House, Greenwich (1616-35) and Banqueting House, Whitehall (1619-22). Also designed scenery and costumes for court masques under James I and Charles I.

Jones, James (1921-), American novelist. Works incl. best-seller *From Here to Eternity* (1951) dealing with army life before Japanese attack on Pearl Harbor.

Jones, John Luther ('Casey') (1864-1900), American locomotive engineer, folk hero. Saved passengers in crash of *Cannon Ball* express (1900) in Mississippi, but was himself killed.

Jones, John Paul (1747-92), American naval officer, b. Scotland. During American Revolution, raided coast of Britain. Sailing in *Bon Homme Richard*, defeated British ship *Serapis* in famous engagement (1779). Later served as admiral in Russian navy.

Jones, LeRoi (1934-), American writer. Works incl. poetry, *eg The Dead Lecturer* (1964), plays, *eg The Slave* (1964). Autobiog. novel, *The System of Dante's Hell* (1965), explores stylistic innovation.

Jones, Robert Tyre ('Bobby') (1902-71), American golfer. In his 8-year golfing career, he won 13 major championships. Only man to achieve 'grand slam' (1930), winning US Open and Amateur, British Open and Amateur titles.

Jongkind, Johan Barthold (1819-91), Dutch landscape painter. Precursor of impressionism, his handling of light and atmosphere in his marine and port views strongly influenced the young Monet.

Jönköping, town of SC Sweden, at S end of Lake Vättern. Pop. 81,000. Match mfg.; paper mills; iron foundries. Chartered (1284).

jonquil, *see* NARCISSUS.

Jonson, Ben (1572-1637), English author. Known for 'comedies of humours', *eg Everyman in His Humour* (1599), *Volpone* (c 1605), *The Alchemist* (1610). Also wrote tragedy *Sejanus* (1603), court masques, classical verse.

Jordaens, Jacob (1593-1678), Flemish painter. Influenced by Rubens, he is remembered for boisterous genre scenes of drinking peasants, *eg The King Drinks*. Also painted portraits, religious and allegorical subjects.

Jordan

Jordan, kingdom of SW Asia. Area *c* 98,400 sq km (38,000 sq mi); pop. 2,418,000; cap. Amman. Language: Arabic. Religion: Sunni Islam. Mountains, arid desert; limited cultivation (wheat, fruit). Part of Ottoman empire (16th cent.-1918), mandated to Britain as Transjordan; full independence 1946. Defeated by Israelis (1967), who subsequently occupied territ. W of R. Jordan.

Jordan, river of Palestine. Length *c* 320 km (200 mi). Rises in Anti-Lebanon Mts., flows S to Sea of Galilee and Dead Sea. Not navigable but used in irrigation schemes. After 1967 Israeli victory formed part of *de facto* border with Jordan.

Joseph, St (*fl* 1st cent. BC - AD 1st cent.), Jewish carpenter, husband of Virgin Mary. Patron of RC church and of dying.

Joseph II (1741-90), Holy Roman emperor (176590). One of the 'benevolent despots', ruled solely after death (1780) of his mother, MARIA THERESA. Cut feudal power of nobles by abolishing serfdom, restricted Church's power, extended education. Attempt to annex Bavaria thwarted by Frederick II of Prussia.

Joseph (*c* 1840-1904), American Indian leader. Led Nez Percé Indians in attempt to reach Canada (1877) after they were about to be removed from land fraudulently ceded to US. Defeated US forces at Big Hole but forced to surrender before reaching Canada.

Joseph, in OT, favourite son of Jacob and Rachel. Sold into slavery in Egypt by his envious brothers where he rose to position of governor under the pharaoh. Saved his father and brothers when they were driven by famine into Egypt.

Joseph, Father, orig. François Leclerc du Tremblay (1577-1638), French Capuchin monk, known as 'Eminence Grise'. Confidant of Richelieu, advocated anti-Habsburg policy.

Josephine, full name Marie Josèphe Tascher de la Pagerie (1763-1814), empress of France, b. Martinique. First husband, Alexandre de Beauharnais, was guillotined (1794). Married Napoleon (1796), who had marriage annulled (1809) because of her alleged sterility.

Joseph of Arimathea, St (*fl* AD 1st cent.), wealthy member of Jewish Sanhedrin who, according to NT, provided tomb for Jesus. Traditionally visited Glastonbury, England.

Josephus, Flavius, orig. Joseph ben Matthias (AD 37-*c* 95), Jewish historian, soldier. Governor of Galilee during war with Rome. When his stronghold fell he won Vespasian's favour, adopting name Flavius. Works incl. *The Jewish War*, *Antiquities of the Jews*.

Joshua, historical book of OT, describing invasion and occupation of Palestine by the Hebrews under Moses' successor as leader, Joshua. Incl. story of the fall of Jericho.

Joshua tree, *see* YUCCA.

Josiah, king of Judah (*c* 639-*c* 609 BC). Reformed religious worship after discovery of lost book of the law (possibly Deuteronomy) in the Temple. Forbade all provincial sanctuaries and concentrated worship of Yahweh alone in Jerusalem.

Josquin Desprez, *see* DES PRÉS, JOSQUIN.

Jostedalsbre, snowfield of SW Norway, largest on European mainland. Area *c* 880 sq km (340 sq mi), highest point 2082 m (6834 ft). Source of many glaciers.

Jotunheim Mountains, range of WC Norway. Rises to Galdhöpiggen and Glittertind (both *c* 2465 m/8100 ft). Name from Norse 'Home of the Giants'.

Joubert, Petrus Jacobus (1834-1900), Boer general. Won battles at Laing's Nek and Majuba Hill against British (1891) and commanded Boer forces at the outbreak of Boer war.

Jouhaux, Léon (1879-1954), French trade union leader. Leader of Confederation générale du Travail (1909-47). A founder of anti-communist International Confederation of Free Trade Unions (1949). Awarded Nobel Peace Prize (1951).

Joule, James Prescott (1818-89), English physicist. Discovered law describing heating effect of electric current. Worked on interchangeability of mechanical energy and heat energy. Calculated mechanical equivalent of heat: 4.18×10^7 ergs produce 1 calorie of heat.

joule, SI unit of work or energy, defined as work done on an object by force of 1 newton acting through distance of 1 metre. Also measured as work done per sec by current of 1 ampère flowing through resistance of 1 ohm. Named after James Prescott Joule.

journalism, gathering, writing, editing, and publishing of news, through newspapers, magazines, radio, TV, film, *etc.* Developed first as offshoot of politics, business, at end of 18th cent. With technological advances, emphasis on quick reporting of events rather than polemic has encouraged growth of news agencies, wire services, *etc.*

Jouvet, Louis (1887-1951), French actor, producer. Estab. own company, Théâtre de l'Athénée, in 1934. Known for highly stylized productions of Molière, Giraudoux.

Jove, *see* JUPITER.

Jowett, Benjamin (1817-93), British scholar, educator. As master of Balliol Coll., Oxford, vice-chancellor of Oxford, greatly influenced pupils. Wrote outstanding translation of Plato's dialogues (1871).

Joyce, James Augustine Aloysius (1882-1941), Irish novelist. Works incl. greatly influential *Portrait of the Artist as a Young Man* (1916), *Ulysses* (1922), *Finnegans Wake* (1939). Used complexly allusive language combining

James Joyce

naturalism, symbolism. Leading prose innovator of 20th cent.

Joyce, William (1906-46), British Nazi propagandist, b. US. Went to Germany at outbreak of WW II and regularly broadcast German propaganda to Britain, gaining nickname Lord Haw-Haw. Hanged for treason.

Juan Carlos

Juan Carlos (1938-   ), king of Spain (1975-   ). Heir-designate from 1969, assumed monarchy on Franco's death.

Juan Fernández Islands, small isl. group of Chile, 640 km (c 400 mi) W of Valparaiso. Lobster fishing. Believed to be scene of Daniel Defoe's *Robinson Crusoe.*

Juárez, Benito Pablo (1806-72), Mexican statesman. After overthrow of Santa Anna (1855), revised law to restrict power of church and army. Became president in 1858. Thwarted Napoleon III's attempt to re-estab. empire under Maximilian (1864-7). Died while resisting revolution of Díaz.

Juárez, border town of N Mexico, on Rio Grande, opposite El Paso, Texas. Pop. 436,000. Commercial, agric. centre; cotton processing, tourism. Formerly El Paso del Norte, renamed 1888.

Juba, river of E Africa. Flows c 1600 km (1000 mi) S from SC Ethiopia across Somali Republic to Indian Ocean near Kismayu.

Judaea, see JUDAH.

Judah, hist. kingdom of S Israel ruled by house of David (931 BC-586 BC). At time of Jesus, it was Roman prov. of Judaea.

Judaism, religious beliefs and observances of the JEWS; oldest of the monotheistic religions and fundamental to Christianity and Islam. Based primarily on OT, TALMUD and TORAH. Observances incl. male circumcision, daily services in Hebrew, observance of Sabbath (7th day of week) and the 3 principal festivals, Passover, Pentecost and Tabernacles. Movements in Judaism have incl. Pharisees, Sadducees and Essenes of NT times; Karaites (8th cent.), Hasidism (18th cent.). In West, the 3 modern branches (Orthodox, Conservative, Reform) evolved in Germany (19th cent.). Festivals celebrated in SYNAGOGUE or in home. Priest known as rabbi.

Judas Iscariot (fl 1st cent. AD), Disciple of Jesus. According to NT, in return for a bribe, betrayed Jesus by kissing him, thus identifying him to Romans. Hanged himself after the Crucifixion.

Judas tree, see REDBUD.

Jude, epistle of NT. Traditionally ascribed to Disciple St Jude, brother of James the Younger, between AD 65-80. Warns against false prophets and heresy.

judge, public official with authority to hear legal disputes, pronounce sentence in court of law. In UK, appointed by lord chancellor on govt. nomination; must be barrister of several years' standing. In US, usually chosen by popular election, can be appointed by state governor or legislature.

Judges, historical book of OT. Describes govt. of the 'judges' (ie tribal leaders) who ruled Israel before union of the tribes. Recounts repeated apostasy of Israel from God, consequences at hands of alien nations and God's eventual creation of a deliverer in Saul.

judiciary, in politics, that part of govt. concerned with admin. of justice, comprising judges and law courts. Also *see* SEPARATION OF POWERS.

Judith, Apocryphal book of OT. Describes attack on Jewish city of Bethulia by Holofernes. Judith, a widow of beauty, enters enemy camp and kills Holofernes.

judo, combat sport developed (1882) in Japan by Jigoro Kano, based on practices of JU-JITSU. A coloured belt worn indicates level of proficiency (black being highest). Olympic event since 1964.

Judson, Adoniram (1788-1850), American Baptist missionary. Pioneered foreign missions in Asia. Compiled Burmese-English dictionary and Burmese translation of Bible.

Juggernaut or **Jaganath,** in Hindu religion, an incarnation of VISHNU. Cult centres on Puri, India, where his image is annually hauled through the streets. Devotees reputedly threw themselves under wheels of the cart. Has come to denote any irresistible force.

Jugoslavia, see YUGOSLAVIA.

jugular vein, either of 2 large veins in the neck. Larger internal jugular vein carries most blood from brain back to heart; smaller external jugular vein receives blood from face and scalp.

Jugurtha (d. 104 BC), king of Numidia. Inherited joint rule of Numidia with his 2 cousins (118), whom he later usurped. His actions led to war with Rome (111-106). Captured (106), died in prison in Rome.

Juiz de Fora, town of SE Brazil, on Paraibuna R. Pop. 238,000. Textile mfg. esp. knitwear; sugar refining, brewing; coffee, tobacco exports.

ju-jitsu or **jiu-jitsu,** method of weaponless self-defence, from which JUDO is derived, developed in ancient Japan. Systematized forms date from 16th cent. Strength and weight of opponent are used against him.

jujube, edible, date-like fruit of several trees and shrubs of genus *Zizyphus,* esp. *Z. jujuba*; known when preserved in syrup as Chinese dates. Used to make confectionery.

Jujuy, town of NW Argentina, cap. of Jujuy prov. Pop. 44,000. In cattle-rearing region; maize, wheat, livestock trade. Founded 1593.

Juliana (1909-   ), queen of Netherlands (1948-   ). Succeeded on abdication of mother, Queen Wilhelmina. Married Prince Bernhard of Lippe-Biesterfeld (1937). Her daughter Beatrix is heir apparent.

Julian calendar, see CALENDAR.

Julianehaab, town of S Greenland. Pop. 2000. Sheep trade centre.

Julian the Apostate (c AD 331-63), Roman emperor (361-3). Influenced by the Athenian philosophy of his teachers, renounced Christianity in favour of paganism. Proclaimed emperor by his troops (360), became sole ruler on death of Constantius I. Attempted to reintroduce paganism.

Julius II, orig. Giuliano della Rovere (1443-1513), Italian churchman, pope (1503-13). Restored Papal States to Church. Joined League of Cambrai in Italian Wars. Called 5th Lateran Council (1512) to counter French influence. Patronized Raphael, Michelangelo, Bramante.

Julius Caesar, see CAESAR, GAIUS JULIUS.

Jullundur, city of Punjab, N India. Pop. 296,000. Textile, hosiery mfg. Cap. of Punjab until Chandigarh built (1953).

July Revolution or **Revolution of 1830,** French coup d'état which deposed Charles X. Liberal opposition to reactionary govt. led POLIGNAC to issue July Ordinances, dissolving chamber of deputies and restricting press freedom. Ensuing fighting led to Charles' abdication and Louis Philippe's succession.

Jumna, river of NC India. Rises in Himalayas of Uttar Pradesh, flows c 1370 km (850 mi) through Delhi and Agra to join Ganges near Allahabad.

Junagadh or **Junagarh,** town of Gujarat state, NW India. Pop. 96,000. Trade in cotton, sugar cane. Cap. of formerly princely state of Junagadh on Kathiawar penin.

Juneau, cap. of Alaska, US; in Alaskan Panhandle. Pop. 14,000. Ice-free port; salmon canning indust., sawmilling. Settled in 1880s gold rush; became cap. 1906.

Carl Gustav Jung

Jung, Carl Gustav (1875-1961), Swiss psychologist. One of founders of analytical psychology, worked with Freud until Jung's divergent view of libido as asexual, primal energy, forced split. Later diverged further from Freud in postulating 'collective unconscious', ie innate 'memory' common to all, revealed in dreams, myths, and containing archetypal features. Also formulated extrovert, introvert types.

Jungfrau, mountain of WC Switzerland, in Bernese Oberland. Height 4156 m (13,642 ft); first climbed 1811. Highest railway in Europe to Jungfraujoch.

juniper, any of genus Juniperus of small evergreen shrubs of cypress family. Native to temperate regions throughout world. Needle-like foliage, aromatic wood; small berry-like cones used to flavour gin.

Junkers, privileged land-owning class in Prussia, who formed large part of the military elite in Prussian army.

Juno, in Roman religion, wife and sister of Jupiter. Like Greek Hera, patron of women, esp. in their sexual life.

Later became major goddess of the state, worshipped (with Jupiter and Minerva) on Capitol.

junta, name given to group of military men in power after coup d'état. Name was applied to military regimes in Greece (1967), Chile (1973).

Jupiter or **Jove,** in Roman religion, the supreme god in the pantheon, identified with Greek Zeus. Originally god of rain and agriculture, later became prime patron of state with temple on Capitol.

Jupiter, largest planet of solar system, c 778,340,000 km from Sun; diameter 142,800 km; circles Sun in 11 years 315 days; 12 known satellites. Surface temperature c –125° C; shrouded in clouds, only permanent feature is oval marking, 'Great Red Spot'. Largely or entirely composed of gases (hydrogen, helium, ammonia and methane).

Jura, limestone mountain range of E France, W Switzerland, SW West Germany. Part of Alpine system; source of Doubs, Ain rivers. Forests, pastures; tourism, h.e.p., watchmaking. Gives name to Jurassic period.

Jurassic period, second geological period of Mesozoic era; began c 195 million years ago, lasted 60 million years. Extensive limestone formation. Flora incl. conifers, ferns, cycads. Fauna incl. ammonites, brachiopods, lamelli-branchs, insects; dinosaurs reached max. size, 1st birds evident. Also see GEOLOGICAL TABLE.

Juruá, river of NW South America. Rises in Peru, flows NE 2400 km (c 1500 mi) through Brazil to join Amazon.

jury, in law, group of people (usually 12) sworn to hear evidence, inquire into facts in a case, and give decision on basis of findings. Has origin in Germanic custom, introduced into England by Normans. By 18th cent., took form known today, was incl. in US Constitution. Jurors selected from voters' roll, with certain excepted classes.

Jussieu, Bernard de (1699-c1777), French botanist. Devised system of plant classification based on natural affinities, which was elaborated by his nephew, **Antoine Laurent de Jussieu** (1748-1836), in Genera plantarum (1789). Antoine organized botanical collection of Museum of Natural History, Paris.

justice of the peace (JP), in England, local magistrate appointed by special commission to try minor cases, commit others to higher courts, grant licences to publicans, etc. In US, elected by people to try minor cases, conduct marriages.

Justinian I (483-565), Byzantine emperor (527-65). Recovered N Africa from the Vandals and Italy from Ostrogoths by victories of his generals Belisarius and Narses. Codified Roman law in Corpus Juris Civilis, basis of much European jurisprudence. Built many churches, incl. HAGIA SOPHIA in Constantinople.

Justin Martyr, St (c 100-c 165), Samarian Christian apologist. Opened school of Christian philosophy at Rome. Apology defends Christians against charges of sedition. Martyred, with some of his pupils, under Marcus Aurelius.

jute, natural fibre from tropical annual plants of genus Corchorus. Main sources are 2 species grown in valleys of Ganges and Brahmaputra. Known in W since c 1830. Coarse fibre used for sacking, rope, carpet backing, etc.

Jutes, Teutonic people originally inhabiting areas around mouths of the Rhine. Settled in 5th cent. in S England, esp. Kent, Isle of Wight.

Jutland (Jylland), penin. of N Europe, incl. parts of Denmark, N Germany. Main towns Aarhus, Aalborg. Low-lying, sand dunes in W. Agric., esp. dairying, in E. Scene of WWI naval battle (1916).

Juvenal, full name Decimus Junius Juvenalis (AD c 60-c 130), Roman poet. Famous for Satires attacking degenerate Rome for criminality, sexual corruption and tyranny.

juvenile courts, law courts estab. in US (1899), UK (1908) to deal with cases involving children under certain age (ranges from 14-21 years).

K

K₂ or Mount Godwin-Austen, N Kashmir, world's second highest mountain, height 8611 m (28,250 ft). Surveyed by Godwin-Austen, officer of British Army (1851-77). First climbed by Italian expedition (1954).

Kaaba, in Islam, the most sacred of all Moslem shrines, in the Great Mosque at Mecca. Small cubic building enclosing Black Stone said to have been given to Abraham by the angel Gabriel. Centre of Moslem world and prime goal of pilgrimage, towards which believers face when praying.

kabbala, *see* CABALA.

Kabul, cap. of Afghanistan, on R. Kabul. Pop. 315,000. Indust. and cultural centre; 1800 m (5900 ft) above sea level. Of strategic importance, many great invading forces have passed through. Became cap. 1773.

Kabwe, town of C Zambia. Pop. 43,000. Formerly called Broken Hill. Mining centre, esp. lead, zinc, vanadium.

Kachin, Mongol people of Assam and N Burma. Mainly agricultural. Tribal social structure, animistic religion. Kachin language is of the Sino-Tibetan stock.

Kádár, János (1912-), Hungarian political leader. First secretary of Hungarian Socialist Workers' party from 1955, he was also twice premier (1956-8, 1961-5). Formed pro-Soviet govt. during 1956 revolt and later had revolt's leaders executed.

Kaduna, city of N Nigeria. Pop. 181,000. Commercial and indust. centre, railway jct.; agric. market esp. for cotton, groundnuts. Former cap. of Northern Region.

Kaesong, town of S North Korea. Pop. 140,000. Commercial centre noted for porcelain, export of ginseng root. Cap. of Korea from 10th to 14th cents. Devastated during Korean War.

kaffir corn, *see* SORGHUM.

Kaffirs or **Kafirs,** name applied by Europeans to members of certain Bantu-speaking tribes of SE Africa. Name often used contemptuously by Europeans for all black Africans.

Kafka, Franz (1883-1924), German author, b. Czechoslavakia. Novels, *eg The Trial* (1925), *The Castle* (1926), short story *Metamorphosis* (1915), depict world, both real and dream-like, of threatening absurdity, futility.

Kafue, river of C Zambia. Flows *c* 960 km (600 mi) from Zambia-Zaïre border near Lubumbashi to R. Zambezi on Zambia-Rhodesia border. Provides water for copperbelt; great h.e.p. potential.

Kagoshima, port of Japan, SW Kyushu isl. Pop. 403,000. Naval yard; produces Satsuma porcelain, textiles. Damaged by volcanic eruption (1914).

kagu, *Rhynochetos jubatus,* rare nocturnal bird of New Caledonia, resembling heron, with long orange legs, greyish plumage.

Kaieteur Falls, spectacular falls on Potaro R., Guyana. Height 226 m (741 ft). In national park.

Kaifeng, former cap. of Honan prov., EC China. Pop. 330,000. Major indust., cultural centre; Imperial cap. 10th-12th cent. Suffered from flooding by Hwang Ho.

Kairouan, town of NC Tunisia. Pop. 82,000. Rug and carpet indust., leather goods. Founded 670; seat of Arab governors of W Africa until 800, of Aghlabid dynasty until 909. Moslem holy city, has 9th cent. Sidi Okba mosque.

Kaiser, Georg (1878-1945), German dramatist. Wrote expressionist plays of ideas, *eg From Morn till Midnight* (1916), trilogy *Gas* (1917-20), indicting mechanization of society.

Kaiserslautern, city of WC West Germany, on R. Lauter. Pop. 101,000. Iron works, textiles, machinery mfg. Named after castle (built by Charlemagne) enlarged in 12th cent. by Emperor (Kaiser) Frederick Barbarossa.

kakapo, *Strigops habroptilus,* flightless New Zealand parrot with green body, yellow markings. Climbs trees in search of food.

Kalahari, desert of Botswana and NE South Africa. Av. height over 920 m (3000 ft); mainly grass, scrubland. Peopled by nomadic hunters; cattle and sheep rearing, national park in SW.

Kalamazoo, town of SW Michigan, US; on Kalamazoo R. Pop. 86,000. Agric. products, paper mfg.

kale or **cole,** *Brassica oleracea acephala,* hardy variety of CABBAGE with curly leaves which do not form a head. Grown as winter vegetable; also used as animal fodder.

kaleidoscope, optical device composed of tube containing 2 mirrors that meet each other at angle, reflecting coloured chips of glass enclosed in one end. Symmetric design seen through eyepiece can be changed by rotation.

Kalemie, town of E Zaïre, on L. Tanganyika. Pop. 87,000. Port, trade centre; railway to Kabalo (on R. Lualaba), steamer to Kigoma (Tanzania). Known as Albertville until 1966.

Kalevala, Finnish national epic. Once thought to date from 1st millennium BC, prob. created in Middle Ages. Fragments first collected by Elias Lönnrot and pub. in 1835. Contains Creation myth, accounts of cosmic disaster and heroic wars.

Kalgan, *see* CHANGKIAKOW.

Kalgoorlie, town of SC Western Australia. Pop. 21,000. Mining centre, grew rapidly after gold discovered (1893); railway jct.

Kali, in Hindu myth, black goddess of death and destruction; as Parvati, she is consort of Siva. Personifies mother goddess devouring life she has produced. Represented as garlanded with skulls and bearing bloody sword. Patron of THUGS.

Kalidasa (*fl c* 5th cent.), Indian poet, dramatist. Excelled in drama, *eg Sakuntala,* 1 of 3 extant dramas, also in epic, *eg Raghuvamśa.* Also wrote lyrics.

Kalimantan, Indonesian part of BORNEO. Area *c* 539,000 sq km (208,000 sq mi). Occupies C and S region of isl.

Kalinin, Mikhail Ivanovich (1875-1946), Russian revolutionary, 1st president of the USSR (1919-38). He founded (1912) the newspaper *Pravda,* prominent in the October Revolution.

Kalinin, city of USSR, WC European RSFSR; port on R. Volga. Pop. 367,000. Rolling stock, machinery, textile mfg. Founded in 12th cent. as Tver, rivalled Moscow in importance in 14th cent.; renamed (1931) after M. I. Kalinin.

Kaliningrad (Ger. *Königsberg*), city of USSR, in W European RSFSR enclave on Baltic. Pop. 315,000. Naval base; indust. centre. Founded 1255 as fortress of Teutonic Knights. Hist. cap. of East Prussia. Birthplace of Kant, who taught at univ. (founded 1544). Suffered heavy damage in WWII. Transferred to USSR 1945.

Kalisz (Ger. *Kalisch*), town of WC Poland, on R. Prosna. Pop. 79,000. Textile mfg., tanning. Ancient settlement, identified with Ptolemy's *Calissia* (2nd cent.). Under Russian rule 1815-1919.

Kalmar, town of SE Sweden, on Kalmar Sund opposite Oland Isl. Pop. 35,000. Port, shipbuilding; match mfg. Kalmar Union (1397) joining Sweden, Norway, Denmark, signed in 12th cent. castle.

Kaluga, city of USSR, W. European RSFSR; on R. Oka. Pop. 224,000. Sawmilling, machine mfg. Founded 14th cent.

Kama, river of USSR. Flows generally S *c* 1930 km (1200 mi) through E European RSFSR to join Volga below Kazan. Chief tributary of Volga; used to transport timber.

Kamakura, city of Japan, C Honshu isl. Pop. 139,000. Site of *Daibutsu,* 13th cent. bronze statue of Buddha. Cap. of Minamoto and Hojo shogunates 1192-1333. Declined with rise of Tokyo.

Kamchatka Peninsula

Kamchatka Peninsula, arm of extreme E USSR, between Bering Sea and Sea of Okhotsk. Mountainous, with active volcanoes; fishing and fur trapping main occupations.

Kamenev, Lev Borisovich, orig. Rosenfeld (1883-1936), Soviet political leader. Member of ruling triumvirate with Stalin and Zinoviev after Lenin's death (1924); supported his brother-in-law Trotsky against Stalin. Executed with Zinoviev in purges.

Kamet, Himalayan peak of NW Uttar Pradesh, N India; height 7756 m (25,447 ft). First climbed 1931.

kamikaze (Jap., = divine wind), name given to Japanese suicide pilots, who during WW II, intentionally crashed bomb-laden planes on their targets.

Kamloops, town of SC British Columbia, Canada; on Thompson R. Pop. 26,000. Railway jct. Agric. (fruit), lumbering, mining region. Founded 1812.

Kampala, cap. of Uganda, on N shore of Victoria Nyanza. Pop. 331,000. Admin., commercial, educational, communications centre (Entebbe airport nearby); food processing, clothing mfg.; Makerere Univ. (1961). Former seat of kings of Buganda; cap. of Uganda from 1962.

Kananga, city of SC Zaïre, on R. Lulua, cap. of Kasai prov. Formerly called Luluabourg. Pop. 506,000. Cotton market, on Port Francqui-Lubumbashi railway. Stronghold of Luba tribe; rebel cap. (1960-1) during secession of Kasai prov.

Kanazawa, seaport of Japan, C Honshu isl. Pop. 361,000. Silk, porcelain, lacquer ware mfg. Notable landscape gardens.

Kanchenjunga, world's third highest mountain, in Himalayas on Nepal-Sikkim border; height 8579 m (28,146 ft). First climbed 1955 by British expedition.

Kanchipuram, city of Tamil Nadu, SE India. Pop. 110,000. Silk and cotton mfg. Sacred to Hindus, has many temples dedicated to Siva and Vishnu. Formerly called Conjeeveram, renamed 1949.

Kandahar, city of S Afghanistan. Pop. 140,000. In fruit growing region; has fruit processing plants. Occupied by many forces throughout its history, incl. British (1879-81). National cap. in 18th cent.

Kandinsky, Wassily (1866-1944), Russian painter. Credited with painting 1st purely abstract work (1910). A founder of Blaue Reiter group (1911); expounded his ideas on analogy between painting and music in *On the Spiritual in Art* (1912). Later work was more geometric and explored basic elements of design; taught at Bauhaus (1922-33).

Kandy, city of C Sri Lanka. Pop. 93,600. Centre of tea trade. Has Temple of Tooth, said to contain a tooth of Buddha; original tooth possibly destroyed by Portuguese in 16th cent. Formerly called Candy.

kangaroo, large herbivorous marsupial of Australasia with short forelegs, large hind legs and thick tail. Great grey kangaroo, *Macropus major,* reaches heights of 1.8 m/6 ft.

Young do not leave mother's pouch for first 6 months. Hunted relentlessly in some areas for hide and flesh.

kangaroo rat, *Dipodomys deserti,* small nocturnal jumping rodent of desert regions of SW US. Has cheek pouches, long hind legs.

Kanishka (*fl* 2nd cent. AD), Indian king. Domains stretched from Madura in S to Kabul and Bukhara in NW. Converted to Buddhism, he erected many Buddhist monuments and helped spread the religion into C Asia.

Kannada, *see* DRAVIDIAN.

Kano, city of N Nigeria. Pop. 357,000. Indust. centre on railway to S, has international airport; agric. market, esp. for groundnuts, cotton, hides. Ancient Hausa city state, hist. caravan route centre. Taken (1903) by British.

Kanpur or **Cawnpore,** city of Uttar Pradesh, NC India, on R. Ganges. Pop. 1,273,000. Important transport jct. Indust. centre; textile, chemical mfg. Ceded to British (1801), scene of massacre of British garrison (1857) during Indian Mutiny.

Kansas, state of C US. Area 213,064 sq km (82,264 sq mi); pop. 2,249,000; cap. Topeka; other major city Wichita. Mainly prairie; major wheat production, also sorghum, cattle. Oil, natural gas, coal resources; quarrying. Region disputed by French, Spanish until bought by US as part of Louisiana Purchase (1803). Admitted to Union as 34th state (1861).

Kansas City, two cities of C US, opposite each other in Kansas (pop. 168,000) and Missouri (pop. 507,000) at jct. of Kansas and Missouri rivers. Railway yards; grain, livestock market and distribution centre; meat packing, flour milling industs.

Kansas-Nebraska Bill, in US, legislation introduced by Stephen A. Douglas (1854), by which territs. of Kansas and Nebraska were created out of that part of Louisiana Purchase closed to slavery by MISSOURI COMPROMISE (1820). Territs. had right of self-determination on slavery which intensified conflict between North and South.

Kansu, prov. of NC China. Area *c* 777,000 sq km (300,000 sq mi); pop. 13,000,000; cap. Lanchow. Mountainous; fertile soil but little rain. Oil, coal, ores. Strategic importance in communications with USSR.

Immanuel Kant

Kant, Immanuel (1724-1804), German philosopher. Wrote *Critique of Pure Reason* (1781), *Foundations of the Metaphysics of Ethics* (1785). Distinguished between the world of objects as we know them (phenomena) and world of objects in themselves (noumena). In ethics, posited 'categorical imperative' (*ie* that one should act as if the maxim on which one acts were to become a universal law) as basis of moral action. Profoundly influenced 19th cent. philosophy.

Kaohsiung, chief seaport of S Taiwan. Pop. 915,000. Exports sugar, rice, salt. Indust. centre; produces textiles, petroleum products. Developed rapidly from fishing village under Japanese rule.

kaolin, see CHINA CLAY.

kapok, silky fibres around seeds of several tropical trees of bombax family, esp. *Ceiba pentandra*. Used for stuffing sleeping bags, life jackets, *etc.*

Kapuas, river of Kalimantan, Indonesia. Flows *c* 1100 km (700 mi) SW to South China Sea at Pontianak.

Karachi, chief seaport of Pakistan, on Arabian Sea. Pop. 3,469,000. Exports cotton, hides. Commercial, transport and mfg. centre. Became British (1843) with capture of Sind. Cap. of Pakistan (1947-59).

Karafuto, see SAKHALIN.

Karaganda, city of USSR, C Kazakh SSR. Pop. 541,000. Coalmining centre; iron and steel mfg. Developed after 1928 to supply coal to Urals indust. region.

Karageorge, orig. George Petrovich (*c* 1766-1817), Serbian nationalist, founder of Karageorgevich dynasty. Led independence movement against Turks from 1804, gaining many victories. Ruled (1808-13) until defeated after loss of Russian support. Murdered on orders of MILOSH.

Karajan, Herbert von (1908-   ), Austrian conductor. Has conducted Berlin Philharmonic Orchestra from 1955. Known for opera performances at Salzburg Festival.

Karakoram Range, mountain system of Kashmir, N India. Separated from W Himalayas by R. Indus, extends *c* 480 km (300 mi) NW-SE. Its peaks incl. K$_2$.

Karakorum, ruined city of C Mongolia. Founded *c* 1220 when Genghis Khan made it his capital. Abandoned 1267 by Kublai Khan. Discovered (1889) by N. M. Yadrintsev, who found 8th cent. Orkhon Inscriptions, earliest known examples of Turkic language.

Kara Kum, desert of S USSR, Turkmen SSR, between Caspian Sea and R. Amu Darya. Agric., esp. cotton growing, possible through irrigation by Kara Kum canal.

Karaman, town of S Turkey, N of Taurus Mts. Pop. 22,000. Cap. of independent state of Karamania in 13th cent.; fell to Ottoman Turks (1473). Has 2 notable mosques and ruined castle.

Karamanlis, Constantinos (1907-   ), Greek politician. Premier 3 times between 1955 and 1963. In exile after 1963, opposed military junta estab. in 1967. Returned as premier 1974 after restoration of democratic govt. following Turkish invasion of Cyprus.

Karamzin, Nikolai Mikhailovich (1766-1826), Russian historian, novelist. Author of *History of the Russian State* (1818-24). Also wrote sentimental tale 'Poor Liza' (1792). Made reforms in Russian literary language.

Kara Sea, part of Arctic Ocean, lying N of Siberia. Bounded by Severnaya Zemlya in E, Novaya Zemlya in W. Receives R. Ob through Gulf of Ob.

karate, method of unarmed self-defence developed in Japan. Involves use of hands and feet to deliver sharp blows to vulnerable parts of body. Considered part of the discipline of Zen Buddhism, modern form introduced to Japan from Okinawa in 1922.

Karbala or **Kerbala,** city of C Iraq. Pop. 83,000. Site of the tomb of Husain, grandson of Mohammed; important Shiite Moslem pilgrimage centre.

Karelia, auton. republic of NW European RSFSR, USSR. Area *c* 172,000 sq km (67,000 sq mi); pop. 714,000; cap. Petrozavodsk. Has numerous lakes, marshes; heavily forested. Lumbering, wood product mfg. and fishing main occupations. Iron ore mined; h.e.p. derived from rivers. Karelians, known since 9th cent., are of Finnish origin; region annexed by Russia (1721), increased by land ceded by Finland (1940).

Karens, people of Kayah state, E Burma. Renowned as soldiers under British rule. Sino-Tibetan linguistic stock.

Kariba, Lake, artificial lake on Rhodesia-Zambia border, along R. Zambezi. Length *c* 280 km (175 mi). Created by construction of Kariba Dam, built 1955-9, height 128 m (420 ft); provides h.e.p. for Rhodesia and Zambia.

Karlfeldt, Erik Axel (1864-1931), Swedish poet. Works incl. *Fridolins visor* (1898), *Hösthorn* (1927), based in folklore, written in archaic style. Refused Nobel Prize (1918) arguing that his work was only known in Sweden. It was awarded posthumously (1931).

Karl-Marx-Stadt, city of S East Germany, known as Chemnitz until 1954. Pop. 300,000. Textile centre; mining (coal, lignite). Badly damaged in WWII.

Karloff, Boris, pseud. of William Henry Pratt (1887-1969), British film actor. Famous as the monster in *Frankenstein* (1931), became stereotyped in horror parts, as in *Bride of Frankenstein* (1935), *The Body Snatcher* (1945).

Karlovy Vary (Ger. *Karlsbad, Carlsbad*), town of NW Czechoslovakia, on R. Ohře. Pop. 44,000. Spa, spring water exported. Scene of Carlsbad Decrees (1819) against liberal trends in German univs.

Karlskrona, town of SE Sweden, on Baltic Sea. Pop. 34,000. Port, harbour incl. dry docks cut out of granite. Quarrying, shipbuilding. Chief Swedish naval base from 1680.

Karlsruhe, city of SW West Germany. Pop. 258,000. Indust., admin. centre; has Federal Court of Justice, univ. (1825). Founded 1715, cap. of duchy of Baden from 1771.

Karlstad, town of WC Sweden, on Lake Vänern. Pop. 52,000. Timber indust., textiles. Union of Sweden and Norway ended by treaty (1905).

karma, in Indian religion and philosophy, sum of an individual's actions which are carried forward from one existence to next, determining incarnation for good or bad. Differing interpretations are found in Hinduism, Buddhism and Jainism.

Karmathians or **Carmathians,** Moslem sect of 9th and 10th cents. Estab. independent community in Mesopotamia. Instigated rebellions in Syria and conquered Yemen. Carried off the Black Stone from the KAABA (*c* 930; returned *c* 940). Power diminished after 1000.

Karnak, village of C Egypt, on R. Nile. Occupies part of site of ancient city of THEBES. Noted for temple of Amon (14th cent. BC).

Karnataka, maritime state of SW India. Area *c* 192,000 sq km (74,000 sq mi); pop. 29,260,000; cap. Bangalore. Formerly known as Mysore state, renamed 1973. Mainly on S Deccan plateau, with coastal plain on Arabian Sea. Largely agric. economy; coffee, rice, cotton. Forests provide sandalwood. Iron and manganese ore; major goldmining region.

Károlyi, Mihaly, Count (1875-1955), Hungarian statesman. Premier of Hungary (1918-19), then briefly 1st president of new Hungarian republic (1919). Handed over power to Communists under BELA KUN, went into exile.

Karpinsky, Aleksandr Petrovich (1846-1936), Russian geologist. Contributed much to mineralogy, palaeontology, petrology; created 1st geological map of European Russia. President of Soviet Academy of Sciences (1916-36).

karri, *Eucalyptus diversicolor*, Australian gum tree, found in SW Western Australia. Grows to *c* 85 m/250 ft. Strong, even timber used in building.

Karroo, semidesert plateau of Cape Prov., South Africa. Little Karroo (S) rises to 610 m/2000 ft; Great Karroo (C) rises to 915m/3000 ft; Northern Karroo (N), alternative name for High Veld, rises to 1830 m/6000 ft. Sheep, goat rearing; fruit, cereal growing.

Kars, town of NE Turkey, in Armenia. Pop. 41,000. Woollen goods, carpet mfg. Cap. of Armenian principality in 9th and 10th cent. Taken 3 times by Russians in 19th cent. and held by them (1878-1921) after Congress of Berlin.

Karsh, Yousuf (1908-   ), Canadian photographer, b. Armenia. Famous for portraits using high contrast, esp. 'bulldog' portrait of Churchill in WWII. Estab. (1933) studio in Ottawa.

Karst (*Kras*), arid limestone plateau of NW Yugoslavia, in Dinaric Alps. Area of ridges, potholes, caves (*eg* POSTOJNA), underground channels. Name also generally applied to all limestone areas with similar topography.

karting, sport of driving and racing low tubular-framed vehicle powered by a small-capacity engine. Speeds of 160 km/hr (100 mph) may be reached. Developed 1956 in US.

Karviná, town of NE Czechoslovakia. Pop. 76,000. Coalmining; gas, coke, chemicals, iron industs. Held by Poland (1938-45).

Kasai (Port. *Cassai*), river of Angola and Zaïre. Flows *c* 2090 km (1300 mi) from C Angola to R. Congo. Trade artery; rich in alluvial diamonds. Forms part of Angola-Zaïre border; main S tributary of R. Congo.

Kasavubu, Joseph (1917-69), Congolese political leader. First president of independent Congo (1960-5), he was involved in power struggle with LUMUMBA. Deposed in MOBUTU's 2nd coup.

Kashgar, city in Sinkiang-Uighur autonomous region, NW China. Pop. 175,000. Trade centre on caravan route to India, Afghanistan; produces rugs, sheepskins, jewellery.

Kashmir, see JAMMU AND KASHMIR.

Kassala, town of E Sudan. Pop. 81,000. Cotton market on Sennar-Port Sudan railway. Founded (1840) as Egyptian military post.

Kassel or **Cassel,** town of EC West Germany, on R. Fulda. Pop. 215,000. Railway engineering, optical instrument mfg. Formerly cap. of Hesse-Kassel electorate and of Hesse-Nassau prov. Aircraft, tank production in WWII, heavily bombed.

Kassem, Abdul Karim (1914-63), Iraqi politician. Led military coup (1958) which deposed monarchy and became premier. Executed after Baathist coup.

Kästner, Erich (1899-1974), German writer. Known for children's story *Emil and the Detectives* (1928). Also wrote satirical verse, novel *Fabian* (1931).

Katanga, region of SE Zaïre, main town Lubumbashi. Fertile plateau, rich in minerals (esp. cobalt, copper, uranium). Seceded (1960-3) after independence of Congo, rejoined after UN intervention. Prov. from 1967, renamed Shaba (1972).

Katayev, Valentin Petrovich (1897-), Russian author. Known for novels, *eg The Embezzlers* (1927), *Time, Forward!* (1932). Plays incl. marriage comedy, *Squaring the Circle* (1928).

Kathiawar, penin. of Gujarat state, W India, between Kutch and Gulf of Cambay.

Katmai, Mount, active volcano of S Alaska, US; in Aleutian Range. Height 1128 m (3700 ft). Erupted 1912 when top collapsed. National Monument estab. 1918.

Katmandu, cap. of Nepal. Pop. 210,000. Has 16th cent. wooden temple (Katmandu means 'wooden temple'). Captured (1768) by Gurkhas; became their cap.

Katowice (Ger. *Kattowitz*), city of SC Poland, cap. of Katowice prov. Pop. 306,000. Mines produce coal, iron, lead, zinc; engineering, metal industs. Chartered 1865; passed from Germany to Poland 1921.

Katrine, Loch, lake of Central region, C Scotland, on N edge of TROSSACHS. Source of Glasgow's water supply from 1859. Scene of Scott's *Lady of the Lake*.

Kattegat, str. between Denmark and Sweden. Connects with North Sea via Skagerrak (N), with Baltic Sea via Oresund (S).

katydid, insect of long-horned grasshopper family, common in tropics and E US. In evening, males attract females with sound produced by rubbing forewings together.

Kauffman, Angelica (1741-1807), Swiss decorative painter. In London from 1766-81, she designed small-scale history pieces which were often used to decorate houses designed by the Adam brothers.

Kaufman, George S[imon] (1889-1961), American playwright. Known for collaborations in popular Broadway plays, *eg The Royal Family* (1927), *Dinner at Eight* (1932) with Edna Ferber; *The Solid Gold Cadillac* (1952) with Howard Teichman.

Kaunas (Russ. *Kovno*), city of USSR, Lithuanian SSR; on R. Neman. Pop. 322,000. Founded 11th cent.; provisional cap. of Lithuania (1918-40) following Polish seizure of Vilnius.

Kaunda, Kenneth David (1924-), Zambian statesman. Founded (1960) United National Independence party; successfully opposed inclusion of Northern Rhodesia (Zambia) in Federation of Rhodesia and Nyasaland. Elected president (1964) at independence. Leader in African opposition to white rule in Rhodesia.

kauri, *Agathis australis,* pine tree of New Zealand. Straight trunk reaches *c* 30 m/100 ft. Valued for timber and gum used in varnishes and adhesives.

Kenneth Kaunda

Kautsky, Karl Johann (1854-1938), German politician. Influential in adoption of Marxist principles in Erfurt Programme for German Social Democrat party (1891); opposed revisionist policies of EDUARD BERNSTEIN. Condemned Russian Revolution as bourgeois and non-Marxist.

Kaválla or **Kavala** (anc. *Neapolis*), town of NE Greece, on Aegean Sea, cap. of Kaválla admin. dist. Pop. 44,000. Port; centre of tobacco indust.

Kawabata, Yasunari (1899-1972), Japanese novelist. Known for *Snow Country* (1935), *Thousand Cranes* (1955). Nobel Prize for Literature (1968).

Kawasaki, city of Japan, on Tokyo Bay, SE Honshu isl. Pop. 973,000. Shipbuilding, engineering, steel and textile mfg. Has Heigenji temple.

Kay, John (1704-64), English inventor. Patented (1733) flying shuttle, designed to increase working speed of handloom weaver.

kayak, an Eskimo canoe made of skins, esp. sealskins, stretched over a frame of wood to cover it completely except for opening where paddler sits. This allows vessel to capsize with less risk of sinking.

Kaye, Danny, pseud. of Daniel Kominski (1913-), American stage, film comedian. Known for films incl. *The Secret Life of Walter Mitty* (1946), *Hans Christian Andersen* (1952).

Kayseri, city of C Turkey. Pop. 183,000. Agric. centre; carpet, textile mfg. As *Caesarea Mazaca* was cap. of ancient kingdom of Cappadocia.

Kazakh Soviet Socialist Republic, constituent republic of SC USSR. Area 2,720,000 sq km (1,050,000 sq mi); pop. 12,850,000; cap. Alma-Ata. Mainly dry steppe land, rising to Altai Mts. in E and S. Wheat in N, sheep and cattle raising in C; mineral resources incl. coal, oil, copper. Came under Russian rule (1730-1820); constituent republic (1936).

Kazan, Elia (1909-), American stage and film writer-director, b. Turkey. On stage, directed *Death of a Salesman*. Films incl. *On the Waterfront* (1954), *East of Eden* (1955).

Kazan, city of USSR, cap. of Tatar auton. region, E European RSFSR; on Volga. Pop. 904,000. Indust. and cultural centre. Cap. of Tartar khanate in 15th cent.; taken by Ivan the Terrible in 1552. Suyumbeka tower of its kremlin and mosques reflect Moslem influences.

Kazantzakis, Nikos (c 1883-1957), Greek author. Works, incl. novel *Zorba the Greek* (1946), long epic poem *The Odyssey: A Modern Sequel* (1938), deal with duality of man as flesh and spirit.

Kazvin, see QAZVIN.

kea, *Nestor notabilis,* yellowish-green parrot of mountainous regions of New Zealand. Feeds on carrion, insects, berries; can injure sheep while pecking at blowfly larvae living in wool.

Kean, Edmund (*c* 1788-1833), English tragic actor. Best-known roles incl. Shylock, Richard III, Othello, which he played with wild emotion.

Buster Keaton in *Go West*

Keaton, Buster, pseud. of Joseph Francis Keaton (1895-1966), American silent film comedian. Famous for unsmiling persistence in face of disaster. Acted in, directed classics *Our Hospitality* (1923), *The General* (1926); other films incl. *The Navigator* (1924).

John Keats

Keats, John (1795-1821), English poet. Leading Romantic lyricist. Works incl. sonnets, *eg* 'On First Looking into Chapman's Homer', Horatian odes, *eg* 'Ode on a Grecian Urn', unfinished blank-verse epic *Hyperion*. 'La Belle Dame Sans Merci', 'The Eve of Saint Agnes' reflect medieval influence. Died of tuberculosis.

Keble, John (1792-1866), English clergyman, poet, hymn writer. Inspired OXFORD MOVEMENT with his 'National Apostasy' sermon (1833), expressing alarm at suppression of 10 Irish bishoprics. Works incl. devotional verse, *eg The Christian Year* (1827), and hymns.

Kebnekaise, mountain of Kjölen Mtns., N Sweden. Highest in Sweden (2122 m/6965 ft).

Kecskemét, town of C Hungary. Pop. 74,000. Agric., fruit, cattle market. Wine, preserves mfg.

Keeling Islands, *see* COCOS ISLANDS.

Keelung, *see* CHILUNG.

Keewatin, admin. dist. of SE Northwest Territs., Canada. Area 590,934 sq km (228,160 sq mi). Incl. E mainland, Hudson Bay isls., James Bay. Indian, Eskimo pop. Fur trapping.

Keflavik, town of SW Iceland, on Faxa Bay. Pop. 6000. Fishing port; international airport from WWII, US air Force base.

Keighley, mun. bor. of West Yorkshire met. county, N England, on R. Aire. Pop. 55,000. Woollens, worsteds mfg.

Kekkonen, Urho Kaleva (1900-), Finnish statesman. Three times PM before becoming president (1956). Fourth term of office as president began 1974.

Kekulé [von Stradonitz], Friedrich August (1829-96), German chemist. His work on composition of carbon compounds was of basic importance to modern chemistry. Devised theory that structure of benzene is hexagonal ring.

Keller, Gottfried (1819-90), Swiss novelist. Known for autobiog. novel *Green Henry* (1854, radically revised 1879-80), novella cycle *The People of Seldwyla* (1856-71).

Keller, Helen [Adams] (1880-1968), American author, lecturer. Blind and deaf from age of two, she was taught to read, write and speak by companion, Anne Sullivan Macy. She graduated from Radcliffe Coll. (1904), and became famous for work for handicapped.

Kellermann, François Christophe de, Duc de Valmy (1735-1820), French army officer. Saved Paris by victory against Prussians at Valmy (1792). Created marshal by Napoleon (1804).

Kellogg, Frank Billings (1856-1937), American statesman. Secretary of state (1925–9), advocated peaceful settlement of international disputes. Promoted Kellogg-Briand Pact against war, signed by 15 nations in 1928. Awarded Nobel Peace Prize (1929).

Kells (*Ceanannus Mór*), town of Co. Meath, E Irish Republic. Pop. 2000. Monastery founded in 6th cent. by St Columba, dissolved (1551). *Book of Kells,* illustrated 8th cent. manuscript, found here; now in Trinity Coll. library, Dublin.

Kelly, Edward ('Ned') (1854-80), Australian bushranger. Notorious for bank robberies in SE region, captured (1880) and hanged.

Kelly, Gene (1912-), American singer, dancer, actor, choreographer. Famous for 'Singin' in the Rain' sequence from film of same name (1952), other films incl. *On the Town* (1949), *An American in Paris* (1951).

Kelly, Grace [Patricia] (1928-), American film actress. Had star roles in 1950s as icy blonde, retired to marry Prince Rainier of Monaco. Films incl. *Rear Window* (1954), *High . Society* (1956).

kelp or **tangle,** general terms for large seaweeds of the BROWN ALGAE. Used as source of alginates and formerly of iodine. Name also applies to ashes of seaweed from which potassium salts were once obtained.

kelpie, *see* COLLIE.

Kelvin, William Thomson, Baron (1824-1907), British physicist. Formulated 2nd law of thermodynamics; supported Joule's theories of interchangeability of heat and mechanical energy. Introduced absolute scale of temperature, named Kelvin scale in his honour. Estimated age of Earth by calculations involving rate of cooling. Later years spent in perfecting Atlantic submarine telegraph cable.

Kemal, Yashar (1922-), Turkish author. Known for novels incl. *Memed, my Hawk* (1961), *The Wind from the Plain* (1963), dealing with Anatolian peasant life. Also wrote poetry, folklore collections.

Kemal Pasha, Mustafa, *see* ATATURK, KEMAL.

Kemble, Roger (1722-1802), English actor-manager. Toured with wife, children as strolling company. Daughter was SARAH KEMBLE SIDDONS. His son, **John Philip Kemble** (1757-1823), was manager of Drury Lane and Covent Garden. Important roles incl. Hamlet, Brutus, Coriolanus. Another son, **Charles Kemble** (1775-1854), was known in Shakespearian supporting roles. His daughter, **Frances Anne ('Fanny') Kemble** (1809-93), was highly successful in tragedy, comedy, *eg* as Juliet. Toured America with father (1832).

Kemerovo, city of USSR, SC Siberian RSFSR. Pop. 404,000. Centre of coalmining region of Kuznetsk Basin; chemical, fertilizer mfg.

Kempe, Margery (d. *c* 1438), English mystic. Known for *The Book of Margery Kempe* (discovered 1934), relating events of spiritual development and pilgrimages to Italy, Spain, Holy Land; earliest known English autobiog.

Kempis, *see* THOMAS À KEMPIS.

Kemsley, James Gomer Berry, 1st Viscount (1883-1968), British newspaper proprietor. With his brother Viscount Camrose (1879-1954) estab. large newspaper chain. Editor of *Sunday Times*, until holdings acquired by Roy Thomson.

Ken, Thomas (1637-1711), English churchman, bishop of Bath and Wells (1684-91). Lost see for refusing to swear allegiance to William and Mary. Author of well-known hymns incl. 'Praise God from whom all blessings flow'.

Kendal, William Hunter, orig. Grimston (1843-1917), English actor. Known for performances in Shakespearian comedies with wife, 'Madge' Kendal, née Margaret Robertson (1849-1935).

Kendal, mun. bor. of Cumbria, NW England. Pop. 22,000. Once noted for coarse cloth ('Kendal Green').

Kendall, Edward Calvin (1886-1972), American biochemist. Identified and isolated over 20 hormones secreted by adrenal cortex; prepared cortisone and investigated its effect on rheumatoid arthritis. Shared Nobel Prize for Physiology and Medicine (1950) with Hench and Reichstein.

Kenilworth, urban dist. of Warwickshire, C England. Pop. 20,000. Ruined 12th cent. castle described in Scott's *Kenilworth*.

Kénitra, city of NW Morocco, on R. Sebou. Pop. 134,000. River port, railway to Rabat; exports grain, cork. Formerly called Port Lyautey and Mina Hassan Tani.

John F. Kennedy

Kennedy, John Fitzgerald (1917-63), American statesman, president (1961-3). Son of diplomat and industrialist, Joseph Kennedy, who was US ambassador to Great Britain (1937-40). Successful Democratic candidate in 1960 election. Formed Alliance for Progress with Latin America and Peace Corps. Criticized for allowing abortive invasion of Cuba by Cuban exiles (1961); forced Soviet withdrawal of nuclear weapons from Cuba (1962). Expanded American military role in Vietnam. Assassinated in Dallas (Nov. 1963), allegedly by Lee Harvey Oswald. His brother, **Robert Francis Kennedy** (1925-68), was attorney general (1961-4). Assassinated in Los Angeles while campaigning for Democratic presidential nomination. Another brother, **Edward Moore Kennedy** (1932-), was Democratic senator for Massachusetts after 1962 election.

Kennedy, Cape, *see* CANAVERAL, CAPE.

Kennelly, Arthur Edwin (1861-1939), American electrical engineer, b. India. Predicted existence of layer of ionized particles in upper atmosphere (1902), independently of Heaviside. This layer was discovered by Appleton.

Kennelly-Heaviside Layer, layer of IONOSPHERE, between 90 and 150 km above Earth's surface, from which radio waves can be reflected. Electron concentration decreases during night and reaches maximum at noon.

Kensington and Chelsea, royal bor. of WC Greater London, England. Pop. 184,000. Created 1965 from met. bors. Has Kensington Palace; Albert Hall; museums incl. Victoria and Albert.

Kent, William (1685-1748), English architect, painter and landscape gardener. Associated with Earl of Burlington in development of neo-Palladianism in England. His naturalistic gardens were designed to harmonize with the country house.

Kent, county of SE England. Area 3732 sq km (1440 sq mi); pop. 1,435,000; co. town Maidstone. N Downs in N, curving SE to Dover; Weald in SW; elsewhere low-lying. Orchards, hops, market gardening ('Garden of England'). Chalk, gravel industs.; ports incl. Chatham, Dover; resorts incl. Margate, Broadstairs. Roman conquest 55 BC; Anglo-Saxon kingdom; Christianity estab. at Canterbury (AD 597).

Kentucky, state of EC US. Area 104,623 sq km (40,395 sq mi); pop. 3,219,000; cap. Frankfort; major city Louisville. Ohio R. forms N border. Bluegrass region (horse breeding); hilly plains; tobacco, corn; coal mining; bourbon whisky distilling. British claimed region from French (1763); frontier explored by Daniel Boone. Admitted to Union as 15th state (1792); slave state, remained in Union in Civil War (1861-5).

Kentucky and Virginia Resolutions, in US history, resolutions passed by legislatures of Kentucky and Virginia (1798). Kentucky Resolution, written by Jefferson, denied to Federal govt. powers over states not delegated to it by the Constitution. Virginia Resolution, written by Madison, similar, though milder. Regarded as 1st clear statement of STATES' RIGHTS doctrine.

Kentucky Derby, American horse race held annually since 1875 at Churchill Downs, Louisville, Kentucky. Run in May over course $1\frac{1}{4}$ mi (2 km) long.

Kenya

Kenya, republic of E Africa. Area 583,000 sq km (225,000 sq mi); pop. 12,482,000; cap. Nairobi. Languages: Swahili, English. Religions: native, Christian. Coastal strip; arid plains in N, highlands in W; incl. Great Rift Valley, part of Victoria Nyanza. Produces coffee, tea, sisal, grain, cattle; large game reserves (*eg* Tsavo); unexploited minerals. Coast controlled by Portuguese, then Arabs, until British trade exploration 19th cent.; leased by UK from Zanzibar 1887, became Kenya Protect. 1920. Interior became crown colony 1920. Discontent among Kikuyu natives led to Mau Mau terrorism 1952-6. Coast and interior united at independence 1963; republic from 1964. Member of British Commonwealth.

Kenya, Mount, peak of C Kenya. Snow-capped extinct volcano with many glaciers; height 5197 m (17,058 ft). First climbed 1899.

Kenyatta, Jomo (*c* 1893-), Kenyan statesman. Imprisoned (1953-9) for alleged involvement in Mau Mau revolt. Elected president of Kenya African National Union (1960). Became PM (1963) at Kenyan independence and president in 1964.

Kepler, Johannes (1571-1630), German astronomer. A founder of modern astronomy, he deduced 3 laws of planetary motion from Brahe's detailed observations. These laws were basis of Newton's law of universal

Jomo Kenyatta

gravitation and showed that the Sun controls motion of planets.

Kerala, maritime state of SW India on Malabar Coast. Area c 38,850 sq km (15,000 sq mi); pop. 21,280,000; cap. Trivandrum. Largely plains, with hills in E; grows rice, rubber, coconuts. Created (1956) out of Travancore-Cochin state.

keratin, tough protein forming principal matter of hair, nails, horns, wool, *etc.*

Kerbala, see KARBALA.

Kerch, city of USSR, Ukrainian SSR; at E end of Crimea. Pop. 136,000. Seaport; exports iron ore; iron and steel mfg. Founded as *Panticapaeum* by Greeks from Miletus in 6th cent. BC; many antiquities found nearby.

Kerensky, Aleksandr Feodorovich (1881-1970), Russian politician. A moderate socialist, he succeeded Prince Lvov as premier (July, 1917); supported Russian role in WW I. His indecisive policies ended in overthrow by Bolsheviks in Nov. 1917. Lived in US after 1940.

Kerguelen Islands, group of isls. in S Indian Ocean, forming part of French Southern and Antarctic Territs. Area c 7000 sq km (2700 sq mi). Comprises one large volcanic isl. (Kerguelen or Desolation), which rises to 1865 m (6120 ft), and over 300 small isls.

Kerman, city of EC Iran, cap. of Kerman prov. Pop. 100,000. Shawl, carpet mfg. Surrounded by clay walls; has mosque dating from 11th cent.

Kermanshah, city of W Iran. Pop. 239,000. Market centre for rich agric. area; oil refinery. Founded by Sassanids (4th cent.). BEHISTUN is nearby.

Kern, Jerome (1885-1945), American composer. Remembered for his musical comedies, esp. *Show Boat.* Songs incl. 'Ol' Man River', 'Smoke Gets in Your Eyes'.

kerosene, see PARAFFINS.

Kerouac, Jack (1922-69), American author. Leading figure of BEAT GENERATION. Novels, *eg On the Road* (1957), came to represent contemporary youth. *Big Sur* (1963), set in California, used similar frenetic style.

Kerr, Sir John Robert (1914-), Australian lawyer, public official. Governor-general from 1974, precipitated constitutional crisis (1975) by dismissing Whitlam as PM after refusal by Senate to work with Labor govt. Replaced him with MALCOLM FRASER.

Kerr effect, phenomenon by which an applied electric field makes certain transparent media capable of double refraction. Effect utilized in Kerr cell, a high-speed shutter capable of opening or closing in 10^{-8} seconds.

Kerry, county of Munster prov., SW Irish Republic. Area 4701 sq km (1815 sq mi); pop. 113,000; co. town Tralee. Mountains incl. Macgillicuddy's Reeks; Lakes of Killarney inland; indented coast incl. Dingle Bay. Agric., fishing, tourism.

Kesey, Ken (1935-), American novelist. Best known for *One Flew over the Cuckoo's Nest* (1962), using experience as nurse in mental hospital to satirize the dehumanization of American society.

Kesselring, Albert (1885-1960), German army officer. Commanded the Luftwaffe (1939-40) and the German armies in Italy (1943-5). Sentenced to life imprisonment (1946), he was released in 1952.

Kesteven, Parts of, former admin. county of Lincolnshire, EC England. Co. town was Sleaford.

kestrel, *Falco tinnunculus,* small brown and grey European hawk. Hovers against wind before swooping on prey of mice, insects.

Keswick, urban dist. of Cumbria, NW England. Pop. 5000. In Lake Dist.; tourism.

ketone, organic compound containing divalent carbonyl group (CO) and 2 hydrocarbon radicals. Formed by oxidation of secondary alcohols. Simplest ketone is ACETONE.

kettledrums, see DRUM.

Kew Gardens, site of Royal Botanic Gardens, S London, England. Area c 117 ha/288 acres. Founded 1761, opened to public 1841. Has botanical research centre.

key, see SCALE.

keyboard instruments, musical instruments which produce sound when player depresses levers set in a row at front. Group incl. pipe and reed organs, harpsichord (virginals and spinet), clavichord, pianoforte and celesta.

Lord Keynes

Keynes, John Maynard Keynes, 1st Baron (1883-1946), English economist. Outlined economic fallacies of Versailles treaty in *The Economic Consequences of the Peace* (1919). After Depression (1929), advocated govt. planned spending and intervention in market to stimulate employment and national purchasing power. *The General Theory of Employment, Interest, and Money* (1936) profoundly affected capitalist economic attitudes.

Key West, see FLORIDA KEYS.

KGB (Komitet Gosudarstvennoye Bezhopaztnosti), security police or intelligence agency of USSR, estab. 1954 to replace notorious NKVD, known for terror tactics in carrying out security operations.

Khabarovsk, city of USSR, indust. centre of SE Siberian RSFSR; on R. Amur. Pop. 462,000. Fur trade; oil refining. Founded (1652) as fort by explorer Khabarov.

Khachaturian, Aram Ilich (1903-), Russian composer. Influenced by Armenian folk music. Works incl. ballets *Gayaneh* (with 'Sabre Dance') and *Spartacus,* piano and violin concertos.

khaki (Hindi, = dust coloured), term first applied to uniform worn by British army in Indian Mutiny (1857). Similar uniform came into general use during the Boer War.

Khama, Sir Seretse (1921-), Botswanan politician. Returned from exile to Bechuanaland (1956) after renouncing claims to tribal chieftaincy. Became (1965) premier of Bechuanaland and president (1966) of new Botswana republic.

Kharga, largest oasis of Egypt, in Libyan Desert. Main town El Kharga. Produces cereals. dates; railway link to Nag Hammadi. Has ruins of ancient temples.

Khartoum (*El Khartûm*), cap. of Sudan, at confluence of Blue Nile and White Nile. Pop. 648,000. Admin., commercial centre, railway jct., cotton trade, univ. (1951). Founded (1822) by Mohammed Ali. Destroyed after siege (1885) by Mahdists, in which Gordon was killed; recovered (1898) by Kitchener. **Khartoum North** lies opposite Khartoum, across Blue Nile. River port, dockyards; cotton trade. Conurbation also incl. OMDURMAN; combined pop. 648,000.

Kherson, city of USSR, SW Ukrainian SSR; port near mouth of Dnepr. Pop. 283,000. Shipbuilding; produces machinery, textiles. Founded in 1778 as naval base.

Khingan, Great, mountain range of Inner Mongolia, NE China. Connected to Little Khingan range (mainly in Heilungkiang). Heavily forested, source of timber.

Khiva, town of USSR, Uzbek SSR; in oasis region of R. Amu Darya. Pop. 22,000. Carpet, textile mfg. Cap. of khanate of Khiva (16th-20th cent.); taken by Russia in 1873.

Khmer Republic, alternative name for CAMBODIA.

Khoisan or **Click,** African language family. Divided into 3 branches: Khoisan, languages of Bushmen; Khoikhoi (Hottentots); Sandawe and Hatsa (E Africa). Distinguishing characteristic is extensive use of click sounds.

Nikita Khrushchev

Khrushchev, Nikita Sergeyevich (1894-1971), Soviet political leader. Emerged as dominant figure in Soviet leadership following Stalin's death (1953); became first secretary of Communist Party (1953). Consolidated power by becoming premier (1958). Denounced Stalin and his repressive internal policies (1956); adopted policy of peaceful co-existence with West. Withdrew missiles from Cuba after confrontation with US (1962). Policies embittered China. Deposed 1964.

Khufu or **Cheops** (*fl c* 2900 BC), Egyptian pharaoh, founder of 4th dynasty. Famous for building of Great Pyramid at Giza.

Khulna, city of S Bangladesh. Pop. 452,000. Trade centre of Sundarbans near Ganges delta. Rice and jute processing.

Khyber, mountain pass, between Afghanistan and NW Pakistan, linking Peshawar and Kabul. Hist. route for invading armies and trade, *c* 45 km (28 mi) long; now carries a railway and road.

Kiamusze (*Chiamussu*), city of Heilungkiang prov. NE China. Pop. 275,000. Port on R. Sungari. Coal, aluminium, farm machinery industs.

Kiangsi, prov. of SE China. Area *c* 171,000 sq km (66,000 sq mi); pop. (est.) 22,000,000; cap. Nanchang. Mountainous, drained by many rivers incl. navigable Kan

Khyber Pass

flowing NE to L. Poyang. Major rice producer; silk cultivation. Produces tungsten, kaolin for porcelain.

Kiangsu, prov. of E China, on Yellow Sea. Area *c* 106,000 sq km (41,000 sq mi); pop. (est.) 47,000,000; cap. Nanking. Rich agric. region consisting mainly of alluvial plain of R. Yangtze. Silk mfg., cotton. Densely populated, with many large cities, incl. Shanghai.

Kicking Horse Pass, in Rocky Mts., Canada; on British Columbia-Alberta border. Height 1627 m (5339 ft). Route of Canadian Pacific Railway over Continental Divide.

Kidd, William (*c* 1645-1701), British pirate, known as Captain Kidd. Commissioned by governor of New York (1695) to protect English ships from pirates, he turned to piracy himself. Arrested (1699), he claimed his actions had official support. Tried and convicted (1701), hanged.

Kidderminster, mun. bor. of Hereford and Worcester, WC England, on R. Stour. Pop. 47,000. Carpet mfg., begun 18th cent. by Flemish immigrants.

kidnapping, illegal seizure and detention or removal of person by force or fraud, often for ransom. In US, public reaction over Lindbergh case led to federal, state reform of legislation.

kidneys, in vertebrates, pair of excretory organs; in humans, located near vertebral column in small of the back. Separate waste products, *eg* urea, toxins, from the blood and excrete them as urine through the bladder. Also regulate acidity of body fluids and secrete a hormone.

Kiel, city of NE West Germany, at E end of Kiel Canal, cap. of Schleswig-Holstein. Pop. 269,000. Shipbuilding, engineering, fishing; univ. (1665). Hanseatic League member from 1284, major German naval base 1871-1945.

Kiel Canal, Schleswig-Holstein, N West Germany. Waterway 98 km (61 mi) long, from North Sea to Baltic Sea. Built 1887-95 as Kaiser Wilhelm Canal.

Kielce (Russ. *Keltsy*), city of EC Poland, cap. of Kielce prov. Pop. 129,000. Railway jct.; food processing; marble quarries nearby. Founded 1173; under Russian rule 1815-1919.

Kierkegaard, Sören Aabye (1813-55), Danish philosopher. Attacked organized religion, believing that man must work out own relationship with God. Influenced 20th cent. existentialists. Works incl. *Either/Or* (1843), *Stages on Life's Way* (1845).

Kiesinger, Kurt Georg (1904-), West German statesman. Chancellor (1966-9) at head of coalition of Christian Democrat and Social Democrat parties. Defeated in 1969 by Brandt's Social Democrats.

Kiev, city of USSR, cap. of Ukrainian SSR; on Dnepr. Pop. 1,764,000. Indust. and cultural centre. Cap. of powerful medieval Kievan state (*fl* 10th-13th cent.); early centre of Greek Church in Russia. Under Russian control in 17th cent. Hist. buildings incl. 11th cent. cathedral of St Sophia, monastery of St Michael. City devastated in WWII.

Kigali, cap. of Rwanda. Pop. 60,000. Admin. centre; trade in cattle, hides, coffee.

Kigoma-Ujiji, town of W Tanzania, on L. Tanganyika. Pop. 33,000. Terminus of railway to Dar-es-Salaam; trade with Burundi, Zaïre. Former slave and ivory centre. Stanley met Livingstone at Ujiji (1871).

Kikuyu, African people, belonging to Bantu group. Largest Kenyan tribal group. Led by Jomo Kenyatta, fought British in Mau Mau uprising. Mainly agric. economy.

Kildare, county of Leinster prov., EC Irish Republic. Area 1694 sq km (654 sq mi); pop. 72,000; co. town Naas. Mainly agric., incl. Bog of Allen, Curragh (racecourse, horse-training). Main rivers Liffey, Barrow. **Kildare,** market town, pop. 3000. Cathedral, abbey ruins.

Kilimanjaro, mountain of NE Tanzania, highest in Africa. Permanently snow-capped extinct volcano, rises to 2 peaks (Mt. Kibo 5892 m/19,340 ft, Mt. Mawenzi 5270 m/17,300 ft). First climbed 1889 by Hans Meyer.

Kilindini, see Mombasa, Kenya.

Kilkenny, county of Leinster prov., SE Irish Republic. Area 2062 sq km (796 sq mi); pop. 62,000. Hilly; main rivers Nore, Barrow. Coalmining; black marble quarrying; agric. Co. town **Kilkenny,** on R. Nore. Pop. 10,000. Ancient cap. of Ossory. Castle (12th cent.), abbeys (13th cent.), Protestant, RC cathedrals.

Killarney, town of Co. Kerry, SW Irish republic. Pop. 7000. Lakes of Killarney nearby; tourist centre.

killdeer, *Charadrius vociferus,* North American bird of plover family, with penetrating cry.

killer whale or **grampus,** *Orcinus orca,* largest of dolphin group, reaching length of 9.1 m/30 ft. Voracious predator on seals, porpoises, birds; will attack other whales. Worldwide distribution.

Killiecrankie, Pass of, in Tayside region, C Scotland. Scene of battle (1689) in which William III's forces were defeated by Claverhouse (who was killed).

Kilmarnock, town of Strathclyde region, W Scotland. Pop. 49,000. Coalmining area; engineering, carpets, distilling. Burns Memorial museum.

Kilvert, [Robert] Francis (1840-79), English clergyman, diarist. Known for *Diary 1870-9* (1938), giving picture of life in rural parishes.

Kimberley, city of NE Cape Prov., South Africa. Pop. 104,000. Major diamond-mining and cutting centre, metal working; railway jct. Founded 1870; besieged 1899-1900 by Boers.

Kincardineshire or **The Mearns,** former county of E Scotland, now in Grampian region. Hilly in W (sheep); fertile along coast and Howe of the Mearns (cereals, root crops). Fishing; whisky distilling. Co. town was Stonehaven.

kindergarten (Ger., = garden of children), a school or class for children before official school age (usually 3-5), using informal games, exercises, crafts to prepare them for later school. Theory and 1st kindergarten formed by Froebel.

kinetic art, term referring to sculptured works which involve moving parts, shifting light, *etc.* Examples incl. mobiles of Calder and complex machines of Jean Tinguely.

kinetic theory of gases, explanation of behaviour of gases, which assumes that gas molecules are elastic spheres in continuous motion; their kinetic energy depends on the gas temperature. Impact of molecules on walls of containing vessel accounts for gas pressure. Theory explains all experimental gas laws (Boyle's law, Charles' law, *etc*).

King, Billie Jean, née Moffitt (1943-   ), American tennis player. Wimbledon champion 5 times between 1966 and 1973, US champion 4 times, she is known for her efforts to obtain equal prize money for women.

King, Martin Luther (1929-68), American clergyman, civil rights leader. Founded Southern Christian Leadership Council after leading successful boycott of segregated buses in Montgomery (1955-6). Chief advocate of non-violent action against segregation of blacks. Awarded Nobel Peace Prize (1964). Assassinated in Memphis.

King, William Lyon Mackenzie (1874-1950), Canadian statesman, Liberal PM (1921-6, 1926-30, 1935-48). Helped draw up Statute of Westminster (1931) which recognized complete autonomy of Commonwealth dominions.

kingbird, New World bird of Tyrannidae (tyrant flycatcher) family. Species incl. black and white Eastern kingbird, *Tyrannus tyrannus,*of US.

Billie Jean King

King Charles spaniel, see Spaniel.
king cobra, see Cobra.
kingcrab, see Xiphosura.

European kingfisher

kingfisher, any of Alcedinidae family of fish-eating birds with long sharp bill, short tail. European kingfisher, *Alcedo atthis,* has iridescent blue-green plumage.

Kings, book of OT, called 1st and 2nd Kings in Authorized Version. Relates history of Hebrews from death of David until fall of Judah. Incl. reign of Solomon, division of kingdom into Israel and Judah, and lives of prophets, Elijah and Elisha.

King's [or Queen's] Bench, in UK, one of three divisions of High Court of Justice. Formerly, supreme court of common law.

King's Counsel, see Barrister.

Kingsley, Charles (1819-75), English clergyman, author. Known for historical romances *Westward Ho!* (1855), *Hereward the Wake* (1866), moral fantasy *The Water Babies* (1863). Christian socialist, involved in controversy with J.H. Newman.

King's Lynn or **Lynn Regis,** mun. bor. of Norfolk, E England, on R. Great Ouse. Pop. 30,000. Market town, food processing. Medieval port; church (12th cent.); Greyfriars Tower (13th cent.).

king snake, non-poisonous constrictor snake of North America. Species incl. Eastern king snake, *Lampropeltis getulus,* which eats rodents.

Kingston, port of SE Ontario, Canada; at NE end of L. Ontario. Pop. 62,000. Locomotives mfg., textiles. Founded as Fort Frontenac (1673); destroyed 1758, resettled 1782; cap. of United Canada (1841-4). Has Queen's Univ. (1841) and Royal Military Coll.

Kingston, cap. of Jamaica, on the Caribbean. Pop. 112,000. Port with deep harbour. Hq. of coffee ·trade; tobacco produce, exports; textile, brewing, food processing industs. Founded 1692; became official cap. (1872).

Kingston-upon-Hull, *see* HULL, England.

Kingston-upon-Thames, royal bor. of SW Greater London, England, on R. Thames. Pop. 140,000. Created 1965 from Surrey residential bors. Saxon kings crowned here.

Kingstown, cap. of ST VINCENT.

King-te-chen, *see* FOWLIANG.

kinkajou, *Potos flavus,* nocturnal arboreal mammal from forests of Central and South America. Short woolly hair, long prehensile tail.

Kinross-shire, former county of E Scotland, now in Tayside region. Important agric. area. Co. town was **Kinross,** on Loch Leven. Pop. 3000. Textile mills.

Kinshasa, cap. of Zaïre, on R. Congo. Pop. 1,624,000. Admin., commercial centre, univ. (1954). River port, railway to Matadi, airport. Founded (1881) by Stanley as Léopoldville; cap. of Belgian Congo from 1929; renamed 1966.

Kintyre, penin. of Strathclyde region, W Scotland. Extends 68 km (40 mi) SSW from Tarbert. Hilly; main town is Campbeltown.

Kioga or **Kyoga, Lake,** lake of SC Uganda, on Victoria Nile. Area *c* 2600 sq km (1000 sq mi). Shallow, swampy; allows water transport in cotton-growing area.

Kiowa, North American Indian tribe. Inhabited Montana in 17th cent., later spread S. Typical nomadic Plains culture but unique linguistic stock. Allied with Comanche, Cheyenne, Apache in 19th cent. and waged war on eastern Indians and settlers. Forcibly settled in Oklahoma.

Kipling, [Joseph] Rudyard (1865-1936), English author, b. India. Works incl. novels, *eg The Light that Failed* (1891), *Kim* (1901), poetry, *eg* 'Mandalay', 'Gunga Din', 'If', in *Barrack Room Ballads* (1892), popular children's books, *eg The Jungle Book* (1894), *Puck of Pook's Hill* (1906). Reflected British imperialism in India. Nobel Prize for Literature (1907).

Kirchhoff, Gustav Robert (1824-87), German physicist. Known for his laws of electrical circuit theory. With Bunsen, developed spectroscopy and explained Fraunhofer lines in solar spectrum. Used spectroscopy to discover several elements in Sun. Devised means of investigating BLACK BODY radiation.

Kirchner, Ernst Ludwig (1880-1938), German artist. An originator of the Brücke group, he was influenced by Oceanic and primitive art; painted in an expressionist style employing bright colour and simplified form. Also made many powerful woodcuts.

Kirghiz Soviet Socialist Republic, constituent republic of SC USSR. Area *c* 199,000 sq km (76,500 sq mi); pop. 2,933,000; cap. Frunze. Mountainous, with Tien Shan range along Chinese border. Stock raising, esp. sheep; cotton, wheat grown in valleys. Annexed to Russia by 1876.

Kirin, prov. of NE China. Area *c* 186,500 sq km (72,000 sq mi); pop. (est.) 17,000,000; cap. Changchun. On fertile Manchurian plain; soya beans, grain grown. Major source of timber, coal, iron, *etc.* Cities incl. Kirin, pop. 1,200,000.

Kirk, Norman Eric (1923-74), New Zealand politician. PM at head of Labour govt. (1972-4), also served as foreign minister.

Kirkcaldy, town of Fife region, E Scotland, on Firth of Forth. Pop. 50,000. Port; linoleum, textiles mfg.; engineering indust.

Kirkcudbrightshire, former county of SW Scotland, now in Dumfries and Galloway region. Uplands in N, W; slopes S to Solway Firth. Cattle, sheep rearing; tourism. Co. town was **Kirkcudbright,** former royal burgh. Pop. 3000. Market town.

Kirkintilloch, town of Strathclyde region, C Scotland. Pop. 25,000. Iron founding, engineering. Site of Roman fort.

Kirkuk, town of NE Iraq. Pop. 208,000. Oilfield centre, linked by pipeline to ports on Mediterranean and Persian Gulf.

Kirkwall, town of Orkney, N Scotland, on Mainland isl. Pop. 5000. Fishing port, exports agric. produce; whisky distilling. Has St Magnus' cathedral (1137).

Kirov, Sergei Mironovich (1888-1934), Soviet political leader. Close aide of Stalin and member of Politburo from 1930, his assassination was excuse for massive Communist Party purges and trials during 1930s.

Kirov, city of USSR, E European RSFSR. Pop. 349,000. Railway jct.; machinery, textile mfg. Formerly called Vyatka, renamed 1934 after S. M. Kirov.

Kirovabad, town of USSR, WC Azerbaijan SSR. Pop. 195,000. Centre of fruit growing region; produces textiles, wine. Formerly called Gandzha, renamed 1935.

Kirovograd, city of USSR, SC Ukrainian SSR. Pop. 201,000. Agric. centre. Founded 1754 as Elisavetgrad; present name dates from 1939.

Kiruna, town of N Sweden. Pop. 23,000. Mining centre of high-grade iron ore, transported by rail to Luleå (Sweden), Narvik (Norway).

Kisangani, city of NC Zaïre, on R. Congo. Pop. 261,000. River port, trade in cotton, rice; univ. (1963). Founded (1883) as Stanleyville, renamed 1966. Rebel govt. estab. here briefly during civil war (1960-4).

Kisfaludy, Károly (1788-1830), Hungarian dramatist. Known for *The Tartars in Hungary* (1819), 1st genuine Hungarian drama.

Kishinev (Romanian *Chişinău*), city of USSR, cap. of Moldavian SSR. Pop. 400,000. Centre of rich agric. region; food processing. Scene of pogrom (1903). Part of Romania (1918-40).

Kissinger, Henry Alfred (1923-), American govt. official, b. Germany. Secretary of state (1973-7), he negotiated withdrawal of American troops from Vietnam, end of Arab-Israeli war (1973) and Israeli withdrawals from Arab territ. captured in 1967. Awarded Nobel Peace Prize (1973).

Kisumu, town of W Kenya, on Kavirondo Gulf of Victoria Nyanza. Pop. 31,000. Port, fishing, agric. trade centre. Formerly called Port Florence.

Kitakyushu, indust. city of Japan, N Kyushu isl. Pop. 1,042,000. Produces iron and steel, textiles, machinery, chemicals. Formed (1963) from 5 towns (Kokura, Wakamatsu, Yawata, Moji and Tobata).

Kitasato, Shibasaburo (1852-1931), Japanese bacteriologist. Authority on infectious diseases, discovered plague bacillus (1894). Also isolated bacilli of tetanus and developed antitoxin for diphtheria.

Lord Kitchener

Kitchener, Horatio Herbert Kitchener, 1st Earl (1850-1916), British field marshal, statesman, b. Ireland. After reconquering Sudan, became its governor-general (1898). As commander-in-chief (1900-2), introduced successful tactics against Boers, negotiated peace. Secretary of state for war (1914-16), supervised expansion of British army. Drowned en route to Russia.

Kitchener, town of S Ontario, Canada; on Grand R. Pop. 112,000. Tanning, meat packing; mfg. industs. Settled by Germans c 1824 (then named Berlin); renamed 1916.

kite, bird of hawk family, with long pointed wings and forked tail. Feeds on carrion and small animals. Species incl. European red kite, *Milvus milvus.*

kithara or **cithara,** lyre-like musical instrument of the ancient Greeks, with 5 to 7 strings stretched between a crossbar at the top and a sound box at the bottom. Played by plucking.

Kitimat, port of W British Columbia, Canada; on Douglas Channel. Pop. 12,000. Has deep water anchorage. Pulp and paper industs.; has world's largest aluminium smelter.

kittiwake, *Rissa tridactyla,* gull of Arctic and N Atlantic. Inhabits open sea, breeding on cliff faces.

Kitwe, city of NC Zambia. Pop. 290,000. Indust. and commercial centre in copperbelt mining region. Founded 1936.

Kiukiang, river port in Kiansi prov., SE China. Pop. 120,000. Major processing, shipping, marketing centre. Treaty port in 19th cent., with British concession.

Kivu, region of E Zaïre, main town Bukavu. Coffee, cotton, rice growing; gold, tin mining. Incl. Albert (or Virunga) National Park, Ruwenzori Mts.; rain forest (W). Scene of heavy fighting in civil war (1960-4).

Kiwi (Apteryx australis)

kiwi, nocturnal insectivorous New Zealand bird, genus *Apteryx,* with small functionless wings, hair-like feathers, and long curved bill.

Kizil Kum, *see* KYZUL KUM.

Klagenfurt, town of S Austria, at E end of Wörthersee, cap. of Carinthia prov. Pop. 74,000. Winter sports centre in mountain lakeland. Produces textiles and leather goods.

Klaipeda, city of USSR, Lithuanian SSR; port on Baltic. Pop. 155,000. Known as Memel, was Prussian possession from 17th cent. Part of Memel Territ. after WWI, which was seized by Lithuania (1923) and became auton. region of Lithuania (1924-39).

Klaproth, Martin Heinrich (1743-1817), German chemist. A founder of quantitative analysis in chemistry, influenced by ideas of Lavoisier. Discovered zirconium and uranium.

Klee, Paul (1879-1940), Swiss painter. Began as a graphic artist; later associated with Blaue Reiter group. Works, characterized by love of fantasy and calligraphic line, incl. *Twittering Machine* (1922). Taught at Bauhaus for many years.

Kleist, [Bernt] Heinrich [Wilhelm] von (1777-1811), German author. Known for plays, *eg* comedy *The Broken Jug* (1803), tragedy *Prinz Friedrich von Homburg* (1821), novella *Michael Kohlhaas* (1808).

Klemperer, Otto (1885-1973), German conductor. Left Nazi Germany and settled in US in 1933, where he became conductor of Los Angeles Symphony Orchestra. Toured Europe, America extensively; best known for interpretations of Beethoven.

Kleve (Eng. *Cleves*), town of NW West Germany. Pop. 23,000. Food processing, footwear mfg. Castle (11th cent.) associated with *Lohengrin* legend. Birthplace of Anne of Cleves.

Klimt, Gustav (1862-1918), Austrian painter. Leading exponent of art nouveau in Vienna and co-founder of Vienna Secession group, he is known for his richly ornamented decorative work, incl. female portraits and murals.

Klipspringer

klipspringer, *Oreotragus oreotragus,* small African antelope of mountainous regions of E and S Africa.

Klondike, *see* DAWSON, Canada.

Klopstock, Friedrich Gottlieb (1724-1803), German poet. Patriotic, neo-classical verse incl. *Der Messias* (1773). Also wrote prose *The German Republic of Letters* (1774).

knapweed, any of genus *Centaurea* of perennial plants of composite family, esp. *C. nigra,* with purple flowers resembling those of thistle.

knee, joint formed between lower end of femur and upper end of tibia, protected by kneecap or patella. Powerful ligaments and muscles maintain stability.

Kneller, Sir Godfrey, orig. Gottfried Kniller (c 1646-1723), English painter, b. Germany. Court painter from time of Charles II to George I. Employed large studio to produce numerous fashionable portraits; best-known work is series of portraits of 42 members of Kit Cat Club.

knighthood, form of feudal tenure involving both a property qualification and code of conduct termed CHIVALRY. Reached zenith at time of Crusades (12th–13th cents.). Feudal landholders who held land directly of the crown were required to provide given number of knights for service in field (in England, normally 40 days per year). Military or religious orders of knighthood, independent of feudal obligations, also existed, *eg* Knights Templars, Knights Hospitallers.

Knights Hospitallers, members of religious military order founded in Jerusalem during 1st Crusade to protect pilgrims. Driven from Holy Land (1291), they estab. themselves in Rhodes (1310), which they held against Turks until 1522. Moved to Malta (1530) where they continued their wars against Turks. Expelled from Malta (1798) by Napoleon.

Knights of Labor, American labour organization. Estab. 1869 in Philadelphia, quickly grew to national importance. Organized on industrial lines, aided strikers, *etc*; aims incl. 8-hour day, ban on child labour. Declined rapidly from 1890.

Knights Templars, members of military order founded c 1118 to protect pilgrims to Holy Land. Driven from Jerusalem (1187), they estab. their hq. in Acre, which they held until 1291. Resentment over their powerful banking role in Europe led to their persecution and dissolution (1314).

knitting, method of making fabric by looping yarn with special needles. Developed in 15th cent.; a knitting machine was invented in 1589 to produce hosiery.

knocking, in internal combustion engine, noise caused by explosion before sparking of over-compressed mixture of air and petrol vapour.

Knossos or **Cnossus,** ancient city of N Crete, Greece, near Iráklion. Centre of MINOAN CIVILIZATION. In Greek legend, home of King Minos and site of labyrinth.

knot, *Calidris canutus,* small wading bird of sandpiper family, common on European shores; breeds in Arctic.

Know-Nothing movement, in American history, popular name for American party (*fl* 1850s) which sought exclusion of RCs and foreigners from public office. Influence declined after split over slavery question (*c* 1855). So called because members professed ignorance of party's activities and leadership.

John Knox

Knox, John (1505 or 1515-72), Scottish religious leader. Converted to Protestantism under influence of GEORGE WISHART. Exiled in Geneva (1544) where he conferred with Calvin. Invited to lead Reformation in Scotland (1559), succeeded in estab. Presbyterianism after abdication of Mary Queen of Scots. Proposed organization of CHURCH OF SCOTLAND in *The First Book of Discipline* (1560).

Knox, Ronald Arbuthnot (1888-1957), English RC priest, author. Known for officially approved translation of the Bible (1945-50). Also wrote commentaries, devotional works and detective novels.

Knox, Fort, *see* LOUISVILLE.

Knoxville, port of E Tennessee, US; on Tennessee R. Pop. 175,000. In coal, iron, zinc mining region; livestock, tobacco market. Marble quarrying nearby. State cap. (1796-1812, 1817-19). Hq. of Tennessee Valley Authority.

Knut, *see* CANUTE.

Koala

koala, *Phascolarctos cinereus,* arboreal bear-like Australian marsupial with large ears, grey fur. Tailless, *c* 60 cm/2 ft long; diet of eucalyptus leaves. Protected since 1936, following intensive hunting.

Kobarid (Ital. *Caporetto*), village of Slovenia, NW Yugoslavia, on R. Isonzo. Ceded by Italy 1947. Scene of victory (1917) of Austro-German forces over Italians.

Kobe, seaport of Japan, on Osaka Bay, SW Honshu isl. Pop. 1,289,000. Produces iron and steel, textiles, ships, chemicals. Expanded rapidly after 1868, absorbing old port of Hyogo.

København, *see* COPENHAGEN, Denmark.

Koblenz or **Coblenz,** city of W West Germany, at confluence of Rhine and Moselle. Pop. 120,000. Centre of wine trade; furniture, piano mfg. Roman *Confluentes,* founded *c* 10 BC. Held by archbishops of Trier 1018-1794; cap. of Rhine prov. 1824-1945.

Robert Koch

Koch, Robert (1843-1910), German bacteriologist. Developed methods of identifying, classifying and growing bacteria which estab. modern science of bacteriology. Discovered (1876) anthrax bacillus and studied its life cycle. Discovered (1882) tubercule bacillus causing tuberculosis, for which work he received Nobel Prize for Physiology and Medicine (1905).

Zoltán Kodály

Kodály, Zoltán (1882-1967), Hungarian composer. With Bartók, collected Hungarian folk tunes. Works, national in idiom, incl. *Háry János, Psalmus Hungaricus, Dances of Galanta.*

Kodiak Island, off S Alaska, US; in Shelikof Str. Area 13,890 sq km (5363 sq mi). Hilly and forested, indented coastline. Salmon fishing, canning.

Kodok, town of SC Sudan, on White Nile. Formerly called Fashoda, scene of 'Fashoda incident' (1898) when French occupation caused diplomatic crisis between UK and France.

Koestler, Arthur (1905-), British writer, b. Hungary. Works, incl. essays, *eg Spanish Testament* (1937), novels, *eg Darkness at Noon* (1940), studies in history of ideas, *eg The Sleepwalkers* (1959), reflect scientific background, disillusionment with Communism.

Koffka, Kurt (1886-1941), American psychologist, b. Germany. Author of seminal *Principles of Gestalt Psychology* (1935).

Koh-i-noor (Persian, = mountain of light), large diamond possibly found at Golconda, India. Acquired by Queen Victoria (1850), re-cut and placed among British crown jewels.

kohlrabi, *Brassica oleracea caulorapa,* plant of cabbage family. Grown for edible, bulbous portion of stem.

Kokand, city of USSR, E Uzbek SSR. Pop. 139,000. Centre of fertile cotton growing region. Cap. of khanate in 18th cent.; taken by Russia (1876).

Koko Nor (*Tsinghai*), salt lake of Tsinghai prov., WC China. Area *c* 4210 sq km (1625 sq mi). In Tibetan highlands at alt. of 3205 m (10,515 ft); brackish, of little economic use.

Kokoschka, Oskar (1886-), Austrian painter, dramatist. Early work incl. violent expressionist landscapes and portraits expressing psychological tension. Has travelled extensively, painting colourful views of towns, which attempt to capture the spirit of the place.

Kokura, *see* KITAKYUSHU.

kola, *see* COLA.

Kola Peninsula, region of USSR, N European RSFSR, between Barents and White seas. Tundra in NE, forested in SW. Rich mineral resources. Chief town Murmansk.

Kolar Gold Fields, city of Karnataka state, S India. Pop. 168,000. Chief Indian goldmining centre.

Kolarovgrad, town of NE Bulgaria. Pop. 59,000. Wine, grain trade. Hist. strategic fortress; Moslem architecture. Known as Shumen until 1950.

Kolchak, Aleksandr Vasilyevich (1874-1920), Russian naval officer. Commanded the Black Sea fleet in WWI. After the Revolution (1917), organized anti-Bolshevik resistance in Siberia. He was captured and executed by the Bolsheviks.

Kolhapur, city of Maharashtra state, W India. Pop. 259,000. Textiles, pottery mfg. Important Buddhist centre with hist. remains. Cap. of former princely state of Kolhapur in Deccan.

Kollwitz, Käthe (1867-1945), German graphic artist. Work depicted harshness and suffering of proletarian life; specialized in woodcuts and lithographs. Mother and child theme was favourite subject.

Köln, *see* COLOGNE, West Germany.

Kolomna, city of USSR, C European RSFSR. Pop. 138,000. Railway engineering centre. Founded in 12th cent., was outpost for defence of Moscow against Tartars.

Kolyma, river of USSR, NE Siberian RSFSR. Rises in Kolyma Range; flows N *c* 2550 km (1600 mi) to East Siberian Sea. Passes through important goldfields.

Komodo dragon, *Varanus komodoensis,* world's largest lizard, reaching lengths of 3.7 m/12 ft. Discovered (1912) on Indonesian island of Komodo.

Komsomolsk-on-Amur, city of USSR, SE Siberian RSFSR. Pop. 226,000. Shipbuilding, sawmilling, steel mfg. Founded (1932) by Communist Youth League (Komsomol).

Konakry, *see* CONAKRY, Guinea.

Königsberg, *see* KALININGRAD.

Kon-tiki, legendary sun king supposed to have migrated from Peru to the Pacific Isls. *See* HEYERDAHL.

Konya (anc. *Iconium*), city of SC Turkey, in rich agric. region. Pop. 228,000. Textile, carpet mfg. Cap. of sultanate of Iconium or Rum under Seljuk Turks in 11th cent. Religious centre of Whirling Dervishes from 13th cent.; has tomb of their founder Celaleddin Rumi.

kookaburra, *Dacelo gigas,* large Australian kingfisher, with loud laughing cry. Also called laughing jackass.

Kooning, Willem de (1904-), American artist, b. Netherlands. Major abstract expressionist in 1940s, he is

known for his figurative series of 'women', begun in early 1950s. Later reverted to more abstract style.

Kootenai, *see* KUTENAI.

Köppen, Wladimir Peter (1846-1940), German meteorologist and climatologist, b. St Petersburg. Worked in Hamburg 1875–1918; formulated standard world climatic regions still in use.

Koran (Arab., *quran,* = recitation), sacred book of Islam. Written in classical Arabic, regarded as word of God revealed to MOHAMMED by angel Gabriel. Derived to some extent from Jewish scripture. The canonical version was estab. *c* 652.

Korçë, *see* KORITSA, Albania.

Korda, Sir Alexander (1893-1956), British film producer-director, b. Hungary. Made great contribution to British film indust. Films incl. *The Private Life of Henry VIII* (1932), *Things to Come* (1935).

Kordofanian, lesser branch of Niger-Kordofanian language family. Divided into 5 small groups of languages spoken in Sudan: Koalib, Tegali, Talodi, Tumtum, Katla.

Korea

Korea (*Choson*), historical country of E Asia, divided (1948) into North and South Korea. Mountainous penin., forested in N (gold, iron deposits), agric. in S (rice, barley) with tungsten, coal resources. Language: Korean. Religion: Confucianism. Kingdom 1392-1910 until Japanese annexation. Liberation after WWII led to Russian (N), US (S) occupation and Korean War (1950-3). **North Korea** (People's Republic of Korea) estab. under Communist govt. Area *c* 120,500 sq km (47,000 sq mi); pop. 14,900,000; cap. Pyongyang. **South Korea** (Republic of Korea) dependent on US aid after invasion by North Korea (1950). Area *c* 98,500 sq km (38,000 sq mi); pop. 33,400,000; cap. Seoul.

Korean, language of Korea and part of Japan. Appears to be unrelated to any other language, although syntax similar to Japanese. Literature dates from 7th cent. AD.

Korean War, conflict fought (1950-3) between Communist and non-Communist forces in Korea. Invasion of South Korea by North Korean troops (later backed by Chinese) led UN to authorize support for South Korea by international military force under US command. Ceasefire negotiations (begun 1951) led to 1953 agreement ending war.

Kórinthos, *see* CORINTH.

Koritsa (*Korçë*), town of SE Albania. Pop. 46,000. Agric. market, food processing (sugar, flour, brewing). Occupied by Greeks in Balkan and World Wars.

Kortrijk (Fr. *Courtrai*), town of SW Belgium, on R. Lys. Pop. 45,000. Textile centre from middle ages. Church (13th cent.). Scene of 'Battle of the Spurs' (1302) in which burghers of Ghent, Bruges defeated French.

Kos, *see* COS, Greece.

Kosciusko, Tadeusz (1746–1817), Polish national hero. Led nationalist revolutionaries against Russian invasion (1794), was captured but freed (1796) to live in exile.

Kosciusko, Mount, highest peak of Australia, in Snowy Mts., S New South Wales. Reaches 2229 m/ 7316 ft. Surrounded by Kosciusko State Park; tourism, winter sports.

kosher (Heb., = fit for use), term for food complying with Jewish dietary laws. Meat must be that of animals which chew cud and have cloven hooves; must be slaughtered by specially trained Jew and cleansed of all traces of blood, and must not be cooked or eaten with milk products. Strict observation of these laws distinguishes a Jew as orthodox.

Košice, city of E Czechoslovakia. Pop. 146,000. Indust. centre, esp. machinery, textiles, food processing. Gothic cathedral (14th cent.). Part of Hungary until 1920.

Köslin, see KOSZALIN, Poland.

Kossuth, Louis (1802-94), Hungarian revolutionary hero. Instrumental in precipitating Hungarian nationalist uprising against Austria (1848). President of short-lived republic (1849); fled to Turkey after Russia came to Austria's aid. Lived in exile in England and Italy.

Kostroma, city of USSR, NC European RSFSR; on Volga, Pop. 231,000. Famous for linen mfg. since 16th cent. Has 13th cent. cathedral.

Kosygin, Aleksei Nikolayevich (1904-), Soviet politician. Succeeded (1964) Khrushchev as premier and chairman of council of ministers, sharing power with Leonid Brezhnev, secretary of Communist Party.

Koszalin (Ger. *Köslin*), town of NW Poland, cap. of Koszalin prov. Pop. 61,000. Agric. machinery, fish processing. Founded 1188; in Prussian prov. of Pomerania until 1945.

Kotabaru, see DJAJAPURA.

Kota Kinabalu, cap. of Sabah state, N East Malaysia. Pop. 42,000. Rubber exporting port. Formerly called Jesselton.

Kotor (Ital. *Cattaro*), town of Montenegro, SW Yugoslavia, on Gulf of Kotor. Pop. 6000. Port, resort. Venetian until 1797, then Austrian naval base; ceded 1918. Medieval fortress, 16th cent. cathedral.

Kottbus or **Cottbus,** town of EC East Germany, on R. Spree. Pop. 73,000. Woollens, carpets, machinery.

Koussevitzky, Serge (1874-1951), Russian conductor. Settled in US and conducted Boston Symphony Orchestra (1924-49). Conducted 1st performances of many important works by Stravinsky, Ravel, Bartók and Prokofiev. The Koussevitzky Music Foundation, founded 1943, has encouraged many composers.

Kovno, see KAUNAS.

Kowloon, seaport and penin. of Hong Kong. Pop. (city) 2,195,000. Adjoins Kwangtung prov., S China. Main indust. area of Hong Kong; linked by rail to Kwangchow.

Kozhikode, seaport of Kerala state, SW India, on Malabar Coast. Pop. 334,000. Exports coconut goods. Formerly called Calicut, once renowned for calico. Site of many European trading posts 16th-18th cent.; ceded to British 1792.

Kra, Isthmus of, narrowest part of Malay penin., in S Thailand.

krait, venomous snake of genus *Bungarus,* found in SE Asia. Species incl. dangerous blue krait, *B. caeruleus.*

Krakatoa, small Indonesian isl., between Java and Sumatra. Violent volcanic eruption in 1883 caused much destruction; thousands killed by resulting tidal waves.

Kraków (Eng. Cracow), city of S Poland, on R. Vistula, cap. of Kraków prov. Pop. 590,000. Iron, steel industs.; trades in timber, agric. produce; educational and cultural centre, univ. (1364). Founded 8th cent., cap. of Poland 1305-1609. Under Austrian rule 1795-1919, except 1815-46 (independent republic). Cathedral (14th cent.) contains royal tombs.

Krasnodar, city of USSR, S European RSFSR; on R. Kuban. Pop. 491,000. Food processing, oil refining, steel and machinery mfg. Founded in 1794 as Cossack fort; called Ekaterinodar until 1920.

Krasnoyarsk, city of USSR, indust. centre of C Siberian RSFSR. Pop. 688,000. Railway engineering, textiles; centre of goldmining region; major h.e.p. plant on R. Yenisei.

Krebs, Sir Hans Adolf (1900-), British biochemist, b. Germany. Described Krebs or citric acid cycle, series of biochemical reactions governing the oxidation of foodstuffs and release of energy. Shared Nobel Prize for Physiology and Medicine (1953).

Krefeld or **Crefeld,** city of W West Germany, on R. Rhine. Pop. 223,000. Textile centre, formerly linen (estab. by Huguenots), now silk and rayon. Also produces steel.

Kreisky, Bruno (1911-), Austrian political leader, chancellor (1970-). Helped negotiate treaty (1955) achieving Austrian independence and neutrality. Formed (1970) 1st single party govt. in Austria since WWII after socialist electoral victory.

Kreisler, Fritz (1875-1962), Austrian violinist. Famous for his brilliant playing. Created cadenza now usually played in Beethoven's violin concerto; also wrote pastiche pieces. Settled in US during WWII.

kremlin, fortified citadel in several Russian towns. Best known is that in Moscow, much of it dating from 15th cent. Contains palaces, cathedrals, bell towers. Now centre of Soviet govt.

Kreutzer, Rodolphe (1766-1831), French violinist, composer. Works incl. 19 violin concertos, over 40 operas and violin studies still in use. Beethoven's Kreutzer sonata is dedicated to him.

krill, small shrimp-like crustacean, main food of toothless whales.

Krishna, in Hindu religion, eighth incarnation of VISHNU. As adolescent, represented as erotic, often sporting with milkmaids. As adult, he is hero of epic *Mahabharata.*

Krishna Menon, Vengalil Krishnan (1897-1974), Indian politician. First Indian high commissioner in Britain (1947-52). Indian delegate to UN (1952-62); defence minister (1957-62).

Krishnamurti, Jiddu (1895-), Indian religious leader. Toured England and US (1926-7) as protegé of ANNIE BESANT. Repudiated messianic claims made on his behalf, but continued to write and teach. Works incl. *The Songs of Life* (1931). Settled in US (1969).

Krivoi Rog, city of USSR, SC Ukrainian SSR; on R. Ingulets. Pop. 600,000. Iron mining centre; produces iron and steel, chemicals.

Kronstadt, port and naval base of USSR, on Kotlin Isl. in Gulf of Finland, W European RSFSR. Pop. *c* 50,000. Taken from Sweden (1703) by Peter the Great and later fortified. Served as port for St Petersburg but importance declined after canal built to latter (1875-85).

Kropotkin, Piotr Alekseyevich, Prince (1842-1921), Russian anarchist. Arrested for spreading nihilist propaganda in Russia (1874). Fled Russia (1876); lived in England for 30 years until returning to Russia after 1917 Revolution. In his *Mutual Aid* (1902), he argued that cooperation is essential to human survival.

Krüdener, Julie de (1764-1824), Russian novelist. Wrote popular, autobiog. novel, *Valérie* (1804), recounting love affair. Converted to Moravian PIETISM, travelled widely preaching faith.

Kruger, [Stephanus Johannes] Paul (1825-1904), South African statesman. Secured independence of Transvaal (1881) in the Pretoria Agreement with Britain. As president (1883-1900), opposed Rhodes's policies of unifying South Africa under British rule. Tried to maintain Boer supremacy by excluding non-Boers from franchise.

Kruger National Park, large wildlife sanctuary of NE Transvaal, South Africa. Area *c* 20,720 sq km (8000 sq mi). Founded (1898) as Sabi Game Reserve; renamed 1926. Tourism.

Krugersdorp, town of S Transvaal, South Africa, in Witwatersrand. Pop. 91,000. Gold, manganese, uranium mining; metal, chemical industs.

Krupp, Alfred (1812-87), German industrialist. Built up his father's small forge into the famous iron and steel works at Essen where from 1847 he manufactured arms. His son, **Friedrich Alfred ('Fritz') Krupp** (1854-1902), specialized in armaments but also built warships. His daughter Bertha married **Gustav von Bohlen und Halbach** (1870-1950), who adopted the name Krupp and manufactured almost the entire output of German armaments in WWI. Krupp works was centre for German rearmament in period after 1933. Gustav's son, **Alfred Felix Krupp** (1907-), was imprisoned as a war criminal for using slave labour; he subsequently rebuilt the organization into an international concern.

krypton (Kr), inert gaseous element; at. no. 36, at. wt. 83.80. Found in minute traces in atmosphere (*c* 1 part per million). Used in fluorescent lights. Discovered (1898) in residue of liquid air.

Kuala Lumpur, cap. of Malaysia and Selangor state, West Malaysia. Pop. 452,000, mainly Chinese. Commercial, transport centre for tin mining and rubber growing area.

Kuban, river of USSR. Rises in Caucasus Mts., flows N and NW *c* 900 km (560 mi) to enter Sea of Azov and Black Sea by broad delta. Kuban area was controlled by Kuban Cossacks from mid-18th cent. to 1920.

Kublai Khan (1216-94), Mongol emperor of China. Grandson of Genghis Khan; succeeded to empire on death of his brother Mangu Khan (1259). Completed Mongol conquest of China with defeat of Sung dynasty (1279). Invasions of Java and Japan were unsuccessful. Visited by Marco Polo.

Kubrick, Stanley (1928-), American film writer, producer-director. Independent maker of popular films, varied in style, subject, *eg Lolita* (1962), *Dr Strangelove* (1964), *2001: A Space Odyssey* (1968), *A Clockwork Orange* (1971).

Kuching, cap. of Sarawak state, East Malaysia. Pop. 63,000. Port on R. Sarawak, exporting sago flour, pepper.

Kuchuk Kainarji, Treaty of, peace treaty between Russia and Turkey (1774). Ceded certain Black Sea ports to Russia, thus facilitating annexation of the Crimea (1783), and gave Russia rights as protector of Christians in Ottoman Empire.

Kudu

kudu, *Strepsiceros strepsiceros,* large African antelope, with long spiral horns and striped grey coat.

Kuibyshev, city of USSR, E European RSFSR; port on Volga. Pop. 1,094,000. Indust. centre; aircraft, tractor, textile mfg. Founded (1586) as Samara to protect trade on Volga; renamed 1935.

Kukai or **Kobo-Daishi** (774-835), Japanese scholar, artist. Influenced by Chinese learning, founded Shingon Buddhist sect. Invented phonetic symbols for Chinese ideographs. Many paintings and sculptures attributed to him.

Ku Klux Klan, in US history, 2 distinct secret societies; original Ku Klux Klan founded (1866) to maintain white supremacy in South. Disbandment ordered (1869), but local organizations continued. Second Ku Klux Klan (founded 1915) added intense hatred of foreigners, anti-Catholicism, anti-Semitism to its white supremacy policy. At its peak in 1920s, influence has declined, even in South.

Kulturkampf, struggle in Germany to restrict power of Catholic church in politics, as represented through Centre party. Govt. under Bismarck passed series of laws from 1872, incl. measures to remove church control of school system and introduction of civil marriage. Ceased when Bismarck, fearing rise of Socialism, rescinded anti-Catholic policies.

Kumamoto, city of Japan, C Kyushu isl. Pop. 440,000. Agric. market town; bamboo ware, pottery mfg. Founded in 16th cent. around great castle.

Kumasi, city of SW Ghana, cap. of Ashanti region. Pop. 345,000. Commercial centre; market town in cocoa-producing dist., railway to coast; univ. (1961). Former cap. of Ashanti confederation, captured (1896) by British.

Nagami kumquat *(Fortunella margarita)*

kumquat, any of genus *Fortunella* of shrubs native to China and Japan. Bear small citrus fruits with soft pulp and sweet rind, often candied as sweetmeat.

Béla Kun

Kun, Béla (1886-*c* 1937), Hungarian politician. After becoming Bolshevik in Russia, headed short-lived Communist dictatorship in Hungary (1919). Fell from power after defeat by Romanian troops intervening in counter-revolution (1919). Returned to USSR where he is thought to have died in party purges.

kung-fu, Chinese system of self-defence, similar to KARATE, but emphasizing circular rather than linear movements.

Kunlun, mountain range of C Asia between Tien Shan and Himalayas along Tibet border. Length *c* 1600 km (1000 mi). Highest point 7724 m (25,340 ft) at Ulugh Muztagh.

Kunming, cap. of Yunnan prov., S China. Pop. 1,700,000. Commercial, transport centre; coal, steel complex. Ancient walled city. Bronze temple of Ming dynasty nearby. Prosperity dates from building of rail link to Hanoi (1910).

Kuomintang, Chinese nationalist political party, organized (1912) in accordance with principles of SUN YAT-SEN. Strengthened (1922-4) with aid of Communists. Under leadership of CHIANG KAI-SHEK, Kuomintang troops captured Peking (1928) and set up govt. in Nanking. Engaged in civil war with Communists after 1927. Authoritarian rule lasted until Communist victories forced Chiang and Nationalists to set up govt. in Taiwan (1950).

Kupka, František (1871-1957), Czech painter. Influenced by orphic cubism of Delaunay, he pioneered pure geometric abstraction. Explored relationship between colour and musical harmony in pictures such as *Vertical Planes.*

Kuprin, Aleksandr Ivanovich (1870-1938), Russian author. Known for short novels, *eg The Duel* (1905), *The Pit* (1909), collection *The River of Life* (1916).

Kura (anc. *Cyrus*), river of SE Europe. Flows E from Turkish Armenia *c* 1450 km (900 mi) through Georgian and Azerbaijan SSR to enter Caspian Sea S of Baku.

Kurdish, *see* IRANIAN.

Kurdistan, hist. region of SE Turkey, and parts of Iran, Iraq, Syria. Inhabited by pastoral nomads. Revolts in Turkey suppressed (1920s, 1946); Kurdish revolt in Iraq, begun in 1960s, collapsed 1975 following withdrawal of Iranian assistance.

Kure, seaport of Japan, on Hiroshima Bay, SW Honshu isl. Pop. 235,000. Naval base; shipbuilding, machinery, steel production.

Kurgan, city of USSR, W Siberian RSFSR; jct. on Trans-Siberian railway. Pop. 263,000. Agric. trade; agric. machinery mfg. Ancient burial mounds nearby.

Kuril or **Kurile Islands,** isl. chain of USSR, stretching from Kamchatka penin. to Hokkaido isl. (Japan). Area *c* 15,600 sq km (6000 sq mi). Of volcanic origin, with several active volcanoes; main occupations lumbering, fishing. Japanese possession (1875-1945).

Kurosawa, Akira (1910-), Japanese film director. Known for dramatic treatments of historical, legendary stories, *eg Rashomon* (1950), *The Seven Samurai* (1954), and *Throne of Blood* (1957), a version of *Macbeth.*

Kuro Shiwo or **Japan Current,** warm ocean current of W Pacific. Flows N past E Taiwan and Japan, moderating climate of both.

Kursk, city of USSR, SC European RSFSR. Pop. 300,000. Railway jct., agric. market; machinery and chemical mfg.

Kut (Arab. *Kut-al-Amara*), town of E Iraq, cap. of Kut prov. Pop. 42,000. Port on R. Tigris (grain, dates). Scene of C. Townshend's inconclusive campaign against Turks (1915).

Kutaisi, city of USSR, W Georgian SSR. Pop. 166,000. Centre of fruit growing area; textile, chemical mfg. Cap. of ancient Colchis in 8th cent. BC.

Kutch, Rann of, salt marsh region of Gujarat state, W India. Area disputed by India and Pakistan; scene of fighting between their forces (1965).

Kutenai or **Kootenai,** group of North American Indian tribes of unique linguistic stock. In N Montana, N Idaho in 18th cent. but driven W by Blackfoot to Kootenai R., Oregon. Now settled on Flathead Reservation, Montana.

Kutná Hora (Ger. *Kuttenberg*), town of WC Czechoslovakia. Pop. 15,000. Silver mining from 13th cent., damage in Thirty Years War and flooding of mines caused decline.

Kutuzov, Mikhail Ilarionovich (1745-1813), Russian army officer. Superseded Barclay de Tolly as commander after the defeat at Smolensk (1812), and devised the tactics which reversed the French advance and turned it into the disastrous retreat from Moscow.

Kuwait, independent sheikdom of SW Asia, at head of Persian Gulf. Area *c* 18,000 sq km (6950 sq mi); pop. 883,000. Mainly desert; major oil producer. British protect.

(1899-1961). Shares control of Neutral Territory with Saudi Arabia. **Kuwait** or **Al-Kuwait** is cap. and port. Pop. 80,000.

Kuznetsk Basin, see KEMEROVO.

Kwa, subgroup of Niger-Congo branch of Niger-Kordofanian language family. Incl. Ibo (Nigeria), Yoruba (S Sahara), Ashanti (Ghana).

Kwajalein, atoll in Ralik Chain of Marshall Isls., W Pacific Ocean. Incl. many islets. Dist. hq. of US trust territ. of the Pacific Isls.; missile station. Japanese base in WWII, taken by US (1944).

Kwakiutl, North American Indian tribe of Algonquian linguistic stock. Became known through field study by Franz BOAS.

Kwangchow or **Canton,** cap. of Kwangtung prov., S China. Pop. 2,300,000. Major port on R. Chukiang delta. International airport. China's centre for external trade, site of twice-yearly trade fair. Shipyards, textile mfg., steel complex. Centre of Sun Yat-sen's Kuomintang movement (1911).

Kwangju, city of SW South Korea. Pop. 503,000. Agric., commercial centre; rice milling, textiles.

Kwangsi (-Chuang), auton. region of S. China. Area *c* 220,000 sq km (85,000 sq mi); pop. (est.) 24,000,000; cap. Nanning. Mainly hills with basin of Si Kiang. Major producer of sugar cane, manganese, tin.

Kwangtung, maritime prov. of S China, incl. Hainan isl. Area *c* 231,500 sq km (89,400 sq mi); pop. (est.) 40,000,000; cap. Kwangchow. Coast has enclaves MACAO, HONG KONG. Fishing, agric., major sugar cane producer, oil refining.

Kweichow, prov. of SC China. Area *c* 171,000 sq km (66,000 sq mi); pop. (est.) 17,000,000; cap. Kweiyang. High plateau region. Produce incl. rice, cereals, timber. Minerals incl. mercury, coal.

Kweilin, city of Kwangsi autonomous region, S China. Pop. 235,000. Transport centre; produces paper; tin mining. In beautiful limestone region.

Kweiyang, cap. of Kweichow prov., SC China. Pop. 1,500,000. Rail, indust. centre. Important coalfields nearby. Textile and fertilizer mfg.

Kyd, Thomas (1558-94), English playwright. Estab. vogue for revenge tragedy with *The Spanish Tragedy.* Also wrote early version of *Hamlet.*

Kyoga, see KIOGA, Uganda.

Kyoto, city of Japan, SC Honshu isl. Pop. 1,419,000. Centre of Japanese art, it retains many craft industs. Founded in 8th cent., hist. cap. of Japan 794-1868 (political power resided in Tokyo after 1603). Buddhist centre with many shrines and temples; has old imperial palace. Univ. (1897).

Kyrie eleison (Gk.,=Lord have mercy), in several Christian churches, invocation forming part of the Mass. Only Greek part of RC liturgy, an English version is used in Anglican services.

Kyushu, isl. of SW Japan. Area *c* 35,600 sq km (13,800 sq mi). Mountainous; mild subtropical climate favours agric. Indust. concentrated in N around country's largest coalfield.

Kyzyl Kum or **Kizil Kum,** desert of USSR, in Uzbek SSR and Kazakh SSR, between Amu Darya and Syr Darya. Name means 'red sands'.

L

Laaland or **Lolland,** isl. of Denmark, in Baltic Sea. Area 1241 sq km (479 sq mi). Fertile lowland; cereals, sugarbeet.

labelled compound, compound in which radioactive isotope of an element replaces normal stable atom. Used to trace paths of compound through mechanical or biological systems.

Labiatae, family of flowering plants. Characterized by square stem, hairy leaves, grouping of flowers on stem, hooded petals, *eg* lavender, thyme, sage, MINT.

Labor Day, in US, Canada, 1st Monday in September, legal holiday in honour of labour.

labour, in economics, factor of PRODUCTION. In perfect competition, price of labour (wages) is elastic and depends on demand.

labour, division of, *see* DIVISION OF LABOUR.

Labour Party, in UK, political party organized to implement socialist policies, as advocated by Fabian Society, on evolutionary basis, supported by most of trade union movement. Formed (1906), adopted socialist programme (1918) and set up local branches, admitting individual members. Rose rapidly in elections, sharing major party status with Conservatives from 1922. Prominent figures incl. MacDonald, Attlee, Bevan, Wilson. Elsewhere, grouping of socialists and trade unions characterize labour parties, *eg* N Europe, Australia, New Zealand. Labour links with European SOCIAL DEMOCRACY reflect similar policies and means of implementation.

labour relations, *see* INDUSTRIAL RELATIONS ACT; NATIONAL LABOUR RELATIONS BOARD.

Labrador, mainland territ. of Newfoundland, E Canada. Area 292,000 sq km (*c* 113,000 sq mi). Separated from Newfoundland Isl. by Str. of Belle Isle. Tundra in N; forests in S. Cod fishing, iron ore industs. H.e.p. supplies from Churchill R. Inhabited by Eskimos in N. British gained control (1763); joined Newfoundland 1809.

Labrador Current, cold ocean current of W Atlantic. Flows S past W Greenland, E Canada, meets Gulf Stream off Newfoundland. Frequent fogs where currents meet.

La Bruyère, Jean de (1645-96), French writer. Known for misanthropic social satire, esp. *Les Caractères* (1688), combining portraits of types, individuals with general maxims, after model of Theophrastus.

Labuan, isl. of N East Malaysia, admin. with Sabah since 1946. Area *c* 98 sq km (38 sq mi). Main town, Victoria (pop. *c* 4000) is a shipping centre of North Borneo.

laburnum, genus of deciduous trees of Leguminosae family. Native to S and C Europe, widely grown in US. Clusters of yellow flowers followed by pods of poisonous seeds.

Laccadive, Minicoy and Amindivi Islands, union territ. of India, comprising group of 27 isls. in Arabian Sea off coast of Kerala state. Area 32 sq km (12 sq mi); pop. *c* 32,000; cap. Kavaratti Isl. Territ. renamed Lakshadweep (1973).

lace, openwork fabric woven in ornamental designs. Finest lace is made from linen. Lace became fashionable in 16th cent. and reached height of production in Flanders in 18th cent. Machine-made lace first appeared *c* 1760. Chief modern centres are France, Belgium, England, Ireland and Italy.

lacewing, insect of order Neuroptera, with delicate lace-like wings, whose larvae devour aphids and other small insects. Chrysopidae family are green, Hemerobiidae brown; Osmylidae family consists of larger lacewings.

Lachesis, *see* FATES.

Lace: *point de France* (late 17th century)

Lachlan, river of S New South Wales, Australia. Flows *c* 1480 km (920 mi) from Great Dividing Range via Wyangala Dam to Murrumbidgee R. Provides irrigation.

lac insect, scale insect, esp. *Laccifer laca* of India; secretes resinous material on trees, used as source of lacquer and shellac.

Laclos, Pierre [Ambroise François] Choderlos de (1741-1803), French artillery officer, author. Known for epistolary novel, *Les Liaisons dangereuses* (1782), dealing with power of evil to corrupt innocence.

lacquer, solution of film-forming substances dissolved in volatile solvents, applied to decorate or protect surfaces. Commonest forms use cellulose esters. Lacquer work was highly developed in art of China and Japan.

lacrosse, ten-a-side outdoor sport played with ball and netted stick. Originated by North American Indians, it was named by French settlers; 1st games played by white men date from 1840s. Adopted as Canada's national sport 1867.

lactic acid, *see* LACTOSE.

lactose, white crystalline sugar found in mammalian milk; less sweet than cane sugar. Bacterial fermentation of lactose in milk produces lactic acid. Lactic acid also formed by splitting of glucose in animal cells, with consequent release of useful bodily energy.

Ladakh, region of NE Kashmir, India, bordering on Tibet. Incl. highest of Karakoram Mts.; traversed by upper reaches of Indus. Claimed by Chinese, who occupied parts in 1962.

Ladoga, Lake, largest lake in Europe, in USSR, NW European RSFSR. Area *c* 18,200 sq km (7000 sq mi). Outlet is R. Neva, flowing to Gulf of Finland. Originally divided between Finland and USSR; passed into Soviet control (1940).

ladybird or **ladybug,** any of Coccinellidae family of small beetles; red or yellow with black spots. Larvae and adults feed on aphids.

Lady Day, *see* ANNUNCIATION, FEAST OF THE.

Lady of the Lake, *see* ARTHURIAN LEGEND.

Ladysmith, town of W Natal, South Africa. Pop. 33,000. Railway jct., engineering, textiles. Besieged 1899-1900 by Boers, relieved by British force under Buller.

lady's slipper, any of various plants of ORCHID family whose flowers resemble a slipper, esp. of genus *Cypripedium* native to Americas.

Lae, town of Papua New Guinea, E New Guinea isl. Pop. 32,000. Transportation centre.

Laënnec, René Théophile Hyacinthe (1781-1826), French physician. Invented stethoscope, which he used to diagnose disorders of the chest. Authority on tuberculosis and heart disease.

La Farge, Oliver (1901-63) American anthropologist, novelist. Known for novels, incl. *Laughing Boy* (1929), *Sparks Fly Upward* (1931), reflecting great understanding of Indian culture gained through field work amongst tribes of Arizona, Mexico.

La Fayette, Comtesse de, née Marie Madeleine Pioche de la Vergne (1634-92), French novelist. Known for psychological novel, *La Princesse de Clèves* (1678).

Lafayette, Marie Joseph Paul Yves Roch Gilbert du Motier, Marquis de (1757-1834), French soldier. Went to America in 1777 to fight for the colonists. Elected to the French National Assembly (1789) and commanded the French National Guard (1789-92), but his moderate views antagonized the Jacobins and he fled the country. Imprisoned by the Austrians, he was released by Napoleon. Led moderates in the July Revolution (1830).

La Follette, Robert Marion (1855-1925), American statesman. As governor of Wisconsin (1901-6), introduced progressive reforms known as Wisconsin Idea. As a senator (1906-25), he opposed US entry into WWI. Progressive Party presidential nominee (1924).

La Fontaine, Jean de (1621-95), French author. Known for *Fables choisies* (1668-94), adaptations of ancient fables affectionately ridiculing human folly. Also wrote *Contes et nouvelles* (1664-74) derived from tales of Ariosto, Boccaccio and others.

Laforgue, Jules (1860-87), French poet. Associated with symbolists. Works, *eg Les Complaintes* (1885), *Le Concile féerique* (1886), influenced T.S. Eliot's early poetry in form, subject matter.

Lagash, ancient Sumerian city, in Iraq. Excavated (1877) by Ernest de Sarzec, revealing *c* 30,000 clay tablets detailing temple administration.

lager, a light beer, stored for several months for ageing. Most beers in Europe, many in America are lagers.

Lagerkvist, Pär Fabian (1891-1974), Swedish author. Known for novels, *eg The Dwarf* (1944), *Barabbas* (1950). Also wrote poetry, experimental dramas *eg Let Man Live* (1949). Nobel Prize for Literature (1951).

Lagerlöf, Selma (1858-1940), Swedish author. Novels incl. *Gosta Berlings saga* (1891), *Jerusalem* (1901). Also wrote children's classic *The Wonderful Adventures of Nils* (1906). Nobel Prize for Literature (1909).

Lagos, cap. of Nigeria, on Bight of Benin. Pop. 1,477,000. Built on several isls. and mainland, linked by bridges. Admin., indust. centre; railway terminus and port, exports palm produce, groundnuts, cocoa; univ. (1962). Formerly notorious slave market; ceded (1861) to UK, became colony (1886) until merged with Southern Nigeria (1906).

Lagrange, Joseph Louis, Comte (1736-1813), French mathematician. Famed for *Mécanique analytique* (1788), purely analytic study of mechanics; contributed to calculus of variations. Advocated adoption of metric system in France.

La Guardia, Fiorello Henrico (1882-1947), American politician. Mayor of New York (1934-45), instituted major welfare programme and reduced political corruption.

Lahore, city of N Pakistan. Pop. 2,148,000. Indust., transport centre; railway engineering. Cap. of Mogul, then Sikh empires; captured by British (1846). Has Shah Jehan's Shalamar gardens (1637), tomb of Sikh ruler Ranjit Singh; univ. (1882).

Lahti, town of S Finland, on L. Paijanne waterway. Pop. 88,000. Lake port, sawmills, furniture mfg.; winter sports centre.

Laibach, see LJUBLJANA, Yugoslavia.

Laing, Ronald David (1927-   ), Scottish psychiatrist. Work, notably *Sanity, Madness and the Family* (1964), assumes mental illness does not exist clinically.

laisser-faire or **laissez-faire,** in economics, doctrine that economic system functions best without govt. interfer-

Lahore: gate into the old city

ence and that, unregulated by artificial means, natural economic order tends to favour maximum good of individual and community as a whole. First formulated by PHYSIOCRATS in reaction to MERCANTILISM, later adapted by Adam Smith, Bentham and Mill. Basis of Western economic activity in 19th cent., but development of monopolies led to govt. regulation in 20th cent.

lake (Scot. *loch*, Irish, *lough*), body of water surrounded by land. May form naturally in depression caused by glacial, volcanic or tectonic action, or artificially by damming. Normally freshwater; high evaporation causes salt lakes (sometimes, if large, called seas, *eg* Caspian, Dead Sea). Some lakes disappear in dry season, *eg* L. Eyre, Australia.

Lake District, Cumbria, NW England. National Park (area 2242 sq km/866 sq mi) of lakes (incl. Windermere, Coniston, Ullswater, Derwent) and mountains (incl. Scafell Pike, Helvellyn, Skiddaw). Literary connections *eg* Wordsworth, Coleridge, Southey ('Lake Poets').

lake dwelling, in archaeology, habitation built on artificial platform, usually supported by piles driven into lake bottom. Examples incl. one at Glastonbury, England, important for information about Iron Age in Britain, also Neolithic and Bronze Age sites in Switzerland, Germany. See also CRANNOG.

Lakshadweep, see LACCADIVE, MINICOY AND AMINDIVI ISLANDS.

lalique, art nouveau style of glassware, decorated with figures in relief. Introduced by René Lalique (1860-1945), French jeweller.

Lally, Thomas Arthur, Comte de (1702-66), French general of Irish parentage. Governor of French India (1758-61). He was executed for alleged treason after surrender to British at Pondicherry (1761), ending French presence in India.

Lalo, [Victor Antoine] Edouard (1823-92), French composer. Works incl. *Symphonie espagnole* for violin and orchestra, opera *Le Roi d'Ys.*

Lamaism, form of Buddhism practised in Tibet, Bhutan and Mongolia. Derived from Mahayana Buddhism but incorporating erotic mysticism, many animistic elements. Introduced into Tibet in 8th cent. Monastery estab. near Lhasa (*c* 750). Spiritual head, DALAI LAMA, ruled in Tibet until 1959.

Lamarck, Jean Baptiste, Chevalier de (1744-1829), French naturalist. Proposed evolutionary theory (Lamarckism) that modifications induced in an individual by the environment are transmitted to individual's descendants. His *Histoire naturelle des animaux sans vertèbres* (1815-22) founded modern invertebrate zoology.

Lamartine, Alphonse Marie Louis de (1790-1869), French poet, statesman. Major Romantic. Wrote *Les Méditations poétiques* (1820) incl. 'Le Lac'. Other works incl. narrative poem *La Chute d'un ange* (1838), *Histoire des Girondins* (1847). One-time Royalist politician, led provisional govt. of Revolution (1848).

Lamas, Carlos Saavedra, see SAAVEDRA LAMAS.

Lamarck

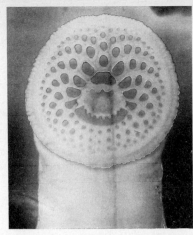

Mouth of Atlantic lamprey

La Matanza, city of E Argentina, indust. suburb of BUENOS AIRES.

Lamb, Caroline, see MELBOURNE, WILLIAM LAMB, 2ND VISCOUNT.

Lamb, Charles (1775-1834), English essayist. Works incl. *Specimens of English Dramatic Poets* (1808), collection *Essays of Elia* (1823) incl. 'A Dissertation on Roast Pig'. Children's books incl. *Tales from Shakespeare* (with sister, 1807), *Beauty and the Beast* (1811). Friend of Coleridge and other Romantics.

Lambaréné, town of W Gabon, on R. Ogooué. Pop. 18,000. Site of hospital founded (1913) by Schweitzer.

Lambert, Constant (1905-51), English composer. Known for his concert work *The Rio Grande,* and for his book *Music Ho!* (1934), a penetrating yet idiosyncratic evaluation of music of the time.

Lambert, John (1619-83), English soldier. Led the parliamentary cavalry at Marston Moor (1644) and was second-in-command to Cromwell in Scotland (1650-1). Though he supported Cromwell as protector, he opposed attempts to extend his powers. At Restoration, was arrested and banished.

Lambeth, bor. of SC Greater London, England. Pop. 303,000. Created 1965 from met. bor., incl. part of Wandsworth. Has 5 Thames bridges; National Theatre (Old Vic), Royal Festival Hall; Lambeth Palace.

Lamennais or **La Mennais, Felicité Robert de** (1782-1854), French RC apologist. Believing that the Church could have no freedom under royal govt., fervently attacked GALLICANISM. Took quarrel with French clergy to pope but was condemned in encyclical and died excommunicate.

Lamentations, prophetic book of OT, traditionally attributed to Jeremiah but written after fall of Jerusalem (*c* 586 BC). Consists of 5 poems mourning the fall of the city. Stanzas in Chapters 1-4 form Hebrew alphabetical acrostic.

Lamia, in Greek myth, woman loved by Zeus. A jealous Hera robbed her of her children. Lamia then stole or killed every child she could. In Roman legend, the name was used for women who enticed young men and fed on their blood.

lammergeier, *Gypaetus barbatus,* bird of vulture family, found in remote mountain ranges of Europe and Asia. Also called bearded vulture.

Lammermuir Hills, range of SE Scotland, runs SW-NE through Lothian, Borders regions. Rise to 533 m (1749 ft) at Says Law.

lamprey, primitive marine or freshwater CYCLOSTOME. Atlantic lamprey, *Petromyzon marinus,* has penetrated Great Lakes, becoming serious pest of fishing.

lamp shell, see BRACHIOPODA.

Lanarkshire, former county of SC Scotland, now in Strathclyde region. Lowther Hills in S (sheep); low-lying, fertile in C (market gardening); heavy industs. based on iron, coal deposits in N. Chief city Glasgow. Co. town was

Lanark, former royal burgh on R. Clyde. Pop. 9000. Market town; textiles mfg. Owen's New Lanark model town (1784) nearby.

Lancashire, county of NW England. Area 3043 sq km (1175 sq mi); pop. 1,363,000; co. town Preston. Pennine moors in N, E; fertile lowlands in C, SW. Coal mining; textile indust. (once famous for cotton); engineering. County palatine from 1351.

Lancaster, Joseph (1778-1838), English educator. A Quaker, he developed monitorial system of teaching adopted by Nonconformists. Later went to US.

Lancaster, city of Lancashire, NW England, former co. town on R. Lune. Pop. 50,000. Textiles, furniture mfg. Has univ. (1964); 13th cent. castle on site of Roman camp.

Lancaster, market town of SE Pennsylvania, US; on Conestoga R. Pop. 58,000. In fertile agric. region; related industs.; electrical goods, watch mfg. State cap. 1799-1812.

Lancaster, House of, English royal family. Founded by Edmund ('Crouchback'), son of Henry III, who was granted title of earl of Lancaster in 1267. John of Gaunt became duke (1362) through marriage into Lancaster family and his son became 1st Lancastrian king as Henry IV. Others were Henry V and Henry VI. Rivalry with House of York led to Wars of the Roses.

lancelet, see AMPHIOXUS.

Lancelot, see ARTHURIAN LEGEND.

lancers, originally light cavalry regiments armed with lances, survived until WWI, after which they were mechanized, becoming mainly armoured car units.

Lanchow, cap. of Kansu prov., NC China. Pop. 1,500,000. On Hwang Ho. Major oil refinery, plutonium processing plant. Hist. and modern transport hub. Petrochemical, plastic and fertilizer industs.

Landau, Lev Davidovich (1908-68), Soviet physicist. Worked on development of Soviet atom bomb. Awarded Nobel Prize for Physics (1962) for mathematical theory of superfluidity of liquid helium.

Landes, coastal region of SW France, between Médoc and R. Adour. Formerly wasteland of dunes, lagoons, moorland; pine forests now yield lumber, resins *etc.*

Land League, Irish organization, formed 1879 under leadership of PARNELL and Michael Davitt, which sought to improve conditions of land ownership for Catholics and to fight evictions. By operation of boycott, influenced passage of Gladstone's Land Act (1881), which fixed fair rents and secured tenure.

Landor, Walter Savage (1775-1864), English poet. Works, *eg Gebir* (1798), *Hellenics* (1847), draw on Classical, Arabic material. Also wrote prose *Imaginary Conversations of Literary Men and Statesmen* (1824-8).

Landowska, Wanda (1877-1959), French harpsichordist, b. Poland. She renewed interest in the harpsichord, and became an authority on old music, particularly that of Bach. Lived in US from 1940.

Landsberg-an-der-Warthe, *see* GORZÓW WIELKOPOLSKI, Poland.

Landseer, Sir Edwin Henry (1802-73), English painter. Specialized in sentimental paintings of animals, esp. dogs displaying human characteristics. Modelled the group of lions at base of Nelson's Column in Trafalgar Square, London. Works incl. *The Monarch of the Glen.*

Land's End, granite headland of Cornwall, SW England. Most W point of England.

Landskrona, town of SW Sweden, on Oresund. Pop. 30,000. Port, shipbuilding; food processing; tanning. Scene of naval battle (1677) in which Swedes defeated Danes.

landslide, mass movement of earth and rock down a slope. Normally occurs along definite interface, when water-saturated material detaches from impermeable material underneath. Also caused by earth tremors, undercutting of cliff face, *etc.*

Landsteiner, Karl (1868-1943), American pathologist, b. Austria. Identified 4 main human blood groups whose incompatibility is important in transfusions; awarded Nobel Prize for Physiology and Medicine (1930). Co-discoverer (1940) of Rh (Rhesus) blood factor.

Lane [Williams], Sir Allen (1902-70), British publisher. Founded Penguin Books Ltd. (1936), pioneering paperback book indust.

Lanfranc (d. 1089), Italian churchman and scholar. Quarrelled with tutor, Berenger of Tours. Archbishop of Canterbury (1070-89), instituted many church reforms incl. replacing English bishops with Normans, subjugating archbishop of York to Canterbury.

Lang, Andrew (1844-1912), Scottish poet, mythographer. Known for his multi-coloured *Fairy Books.* Poetry incl. *Ballads in Blue China* (1880), *Grass of Parnassus* (1888). Anthropological works incl. *Myth, Ritual and Religion* (1887), *The Making of Religion* (1898).

Lang, Cosmo Gordon (1864-1945), English churchman, b. Scotland. Archbishop of Canterbury (1928-42). Influential in abdication of Edward VIII.

Lang, Fritz (1890–1976), American film director-producer, b. Vienna. Known for expressionist silent films made in Germany, *eg Nibelung Saga* (1923-4), *Metropolis* (1926), and esp. *M* (1931), study of child molester. Went to US (1934), fleeing Nazis, to make more conventional melodramas, *eg Fury* (1936), *The Big Heat* (1953).

Langevin, Paul (1872-1946), French physicist. Developed electron theory of paramagnetism and diamagnetism. Studied ultrasonic sound to facilitate submarine detection, basis of modern sonar.

Langland, William (*c* 1331-*c* 1400), English poet. Probable author of *Piers Plowman,* Middle English religious allegory; long, ambitious poem exploring human predicament in relation to God.

Langley, Samuel Pierpont (1834-1906), American scientist, aeronautics engineer. Invented bolometer for recording variations in heat radiation. Built and flew (1896) heavier-than-air, powered, model aircraft; full scale version flown successfully (1914) after his death.

Langmuir, Irving (1881-1957), American chemist. Developed gas-filled tungsten light bulb and atomic hydrogen welding. Awarded Nobel Prize for Chemistry (1932) for work on surface chemistry. Experimented in production of rain by seeding clouds with silver iodide.

Langton, Stephen (d. 1228), English churchman, theologian. Elected archbishop of Canterbury, in defiance of King John, through influence of Pope Innocent III (1207). Assumed see (1213) after John submitted to papal authority. Supported barons in struggle leading to Magna Carta.

Langtry, Emilie Charlotte ('Lillie') (1853-1929), English actress, known as 'Jersey Lily'. Famous for beauty, friendship with Prince of Wales (later Edward VII).

language, systematically differentiated sounds used in significant sequences as means of communication. May be represented by further system of written signs (*see* ALPHABET). Considered a defining attribute of mankind. *See* LINGUISTICS.

langue and **parole,** *see* SAUSSURE, FERDINAND DE.

Languedoc, region and former prov. of S France, hist. cap. Toulouse. Cévennes in E; fertile Garonne plain in W. Agric., vineyards. Under medieval counts of Toulouse until incorporated (1271) into France. Name derived from *Langue d'oc* (medieval Provençal dialect).

Lanier, Sidney (1842-81), American poet. Works, *eg* 'The Symphony' (1875). 'The Marshes of Glynn' (1878), attempt to combine techniques of music with those of poetry. Also wrote novel, *Tiger-Lilies* (1867), criticism, *eg The Science of English Verse* (1880).

Lansbury, George (1859-1940), English politician. Helped found *Daily Herald* newspaper (1912) and edited it until 1922. Led parliamentary Labour Party (1931-5) but resigned leadership because of pacifist views.

Lansdowne, Henry Charles Keith Petty-Fitzmaurice, 5th Marquis of (1845-1927), British statesman. Governor-general of Canada (1883-8). As foreign secretary (1900-6), he negotiated alliances with Japan (1902) and France (1904), thus abandoning British isolationist policy.

Lansing, cap. of Michigan, US; on jct. of Grand and Cedar rivers. Pop. 132,000. Railway centre; has important motor car indust. Cap. from 1847.

lantern fish, any of Myctophidae family of deep-sea fish, with light-producing organs on body and head.

lanthanides or **rare earths,** group of rare metallic elements with atomic numbers from 57 to 71 inclusive. Have similar chemical properties and are difficult to separate.

lanthanum (La), metallic element of lanthanide series; at. no. 57, at. wt. 138.91. Discovered (1839) by Mosander.

Laocoön, in Greek legend, Trojan priest of Apollo. He warned against admitting the Greek wooden horse within the city walls. Angered Apollo (Athena in some versions) who sent sea serpents to strangle him and his 2 sons. Death represented in famous 1st cent. BC statue (now in Vatican).

Laodicea, ancient city of Asia Minor, now in SW Turkey near Denizli. Early Christian centre, it was one of the Seven Churches in Asia. Roman ruins incl. theatres and aqueduct.

Laoighis or **Leix,** county of Leinster prov., C Irish Republic. Area 1720 sq km (664 sq mi); pop. 45,000; co. town Port Laoighise. Mainly flat, with Slieve Bloom Mts. in N. Agric., dairying. Formerly called Queen's County.

Laon, town of N France, cap. of Aisne dept. Pop. 29,000. Railway jct., metals indust., printing. Gothic cathedral (12th cent.).

Laos, republic of SE Asia. Area *c* 236,800 sq km (91,500 sq mi); pop. 3,140,000; cap. Vientiane. Languages: Laotian, French. Religion: Buddhism. Forested (teak), mountainous terrain apart from Mekong valley; principal crop rice; maize, tobacco, coffee grown. French protect.1893-1949. Communist Vietminh forces invaded, withdrew with French 1954. Civil war from 1960; neutral govt. estab. 1962; fighting resumed 1967 with involvement of North Vietnamese forces. Ceasefire (1973). Monarchy abolished 1975 and Communist control estab.

Lao-tze or **Lao-tzu** (*fl* 6th cent. BC), Chinese philosopher. Traditionally held to be founder of Taoism and author of *Tao Te Ching.*

La Paz, admin. cap. of Bolivia, cap. of La Paz dept.; near L. Titicaca. Pop. 562,000. Seat of govt. Has airport at 3960 m (*c* 13,000 ft). Tanning, brewing, flour milling; textile, chemical mfg. Founded by Spanish (1548).

lapis lazuli, silicate mineral, a semi-precious gemstone. Opaque, azure blue in colour; consists mainly of lazurite (sodium aluminium silicate). Used in production of vases, bowls, beads, *etc.* Major sources in Afghanistan, Chile, US.

Laplace, Pierre Simon, Marquis de (1749-1827), French mathematician and astronomer. His *Mécanique céleste* (1799-1825) demonstrated stability of solar system and confirmed Newton's theory of gravitation. Formulated nebular hypothesis of origin of solar system (planets formed by shrinkage of gaseous nebula surrounding Sun).

Lapland, region of Arctic Europe, in N Norway, Sweden, Finland, NW USSR. Forest in S, tundra in N. Nomadic Lapps form indigenous pop.; reindeer herding, fishing,

La Paz

hunting. Area has rich mineral resources, esp. iron ore at Kiruna, Gällivare (Sweden).

La Plata, city of E Argentina, cap. of Buenos Aires prov. Pop. 408,000. Exports agric. produce from pampas region through its port, Ensenada. Meat packing, oil refining. Called Eva Perón (1952-5).

Lapps, N Scandinavian people, concentrated largely in Norway (called Finns there). Semi-nomadic reindeer herdsmen, hunters, some fishers. Origins believed to be C Asian, then pushed N. Speak Finno-Ugric language. Pop. *c* 30,000.

Laptev Sea, part of Arctic Ocean, lying N of Siberia. Bounded by Severnaya Zemlya in W, New Siberian isls. in E. Receives R. Lena.

Lapwing

lapwing, *Vanellus vanellus,* large greenish-black and white plover of Europe and C Asia, noted for erratic flight during breeding season. Also called peewit.

Larache (Arab. *El Araish*), town of NW Morocco, on Atlantic Ocean. Pop. 42,000. Port, exports fruit, vegetables, cork. Founded by Phoenicians; held by Spanish (1610-91, 1911-56).

Laramie, town of SE Wyoming, US; on Laramie R. Pop. 23,000. Commercial, transport centre in livestock rearing region.

larceny, in law, unlawful taking away of another's property without his consent, with intention of depriving person of it. In UK, replaced by Theft Act (1968). In US, it remains, with division into 'grand' and 'petty' (abandoned in UK 1827).

larch, any of genus *Larix* of tall deciduous coniferous trees of pine family. Found mainly in N hemisphere. European *L. decidua* and American *L. occidentalis* are used in building.

Lardner, Ring[gold Wilmer] (1885-1933), American humorist. Known for *You Know Me, Al* (1916), *The Love*

Nest and Other Stories (*1926*), satirizing dullness of his characters, usually baseball players, typists, chorus girls.

Laredo, border town of S Texas, US; opposite Nuevo Laredo (Mexico) on Rio Grande. Pop. 69,000. Oil refining, meat packing. Tourist resort on Inter-American Highway. Founded 1751 by Spanish; taken by US in Mexican War (1846).

lares and penates, Roman gods of the home. Lares represented ancestral spirits and were associated with fields, boundaries and crossroads. Penates were guardians of the store-cupboard.

Largo Caballero, Francisco (1869-1946), Spanish politician. Led propaganda campaign against rightist govt. from 1933. Premier of Loyalist govt. (1936-7), presided at outbreak of Spanish Civil War. Died in exile in France.

Largs, town of Strathclyde region, W Scotland, on Firth of Clyde. Pop. 10,000. Tourist resort. Scene of battle (1263) in which Alexander III of Scotland defeated Haakon IV of Norway.

Larisa or **Larissa,** town of E Greece, on R. Peneus, cap. of Larisa admin. dist. Pop. 56,000. Railway jct., agric. market. Cap. of ancient Thessaly.

lark, any of Alaudidae family of mainly Old World songbirds. Skylark, *Alauda arvensis,* noted for song as it hovers or ascends.

Larkin, Philip Arthur (1922-   ), English poet. Known for collections, *eg The Less Deceived* (1955), estab. 'new poetry' as reaction against romanticism, political enthusiasms, *The Whitsun Weddings* (1964), *High Windows* (1975).

larkspur, *see* DELPHINIUM.

Larne, port of E Northern Ireland. Pop. 18,000. In former Co. Antrim. Bauxite refining; linen mfg.; has ferry service to Stranraer (Scotland). **Larne,** district; area 340 sq km (131 sq mi); pop. 30,000. Created 1973, formerly part of Co. Antrim.

La Rochefoucauld, François, Duc de (1613-80), French author. Known for *Maximes* (1665), bitter epigrams illustrating belief that self-interest is main human motivation.

La Rochelle, town of W France, on Bay of Biscay, cap. of Charente-Maritime dept. Pop. 76,000. Port, fishing, ship-building. Huguenot stronghold in 16th-17th cent., successfully besieged (1627-8) by Richelieu. Medieval buildings, 18th cent. cathedral.

Larousse, Pierre Athanase (1817-75), French grammarian and lexicographer. Best known for his *Grand Dictionnaire universel du XIXe Siècle* (1866-76) which continues in revised form.

larva, free-living form of animal emerging from egg, usually distinct from adult and incapable of sexual reproduction. Undergoes metamorphosis into adult, *eg* tadpole into frog or caterpillar into butterfly.

larvae, *see* LEMURES.

larynx, organ of speech at entrance to windpipe (trachea); contains vocal cords; visible on outside as Adam's apple. Composed mainly of cartilage and muscle. Inflammation of lining causes laryngitis; accompanied by hoarseness, coughing and sore throat.

La Salle, René Robert Cavelier, Sieur de (1643-87), French explorer. Went to New France (1666); built forts and developed fur trade. Claimed Mississippi valley for France after journeying down river (1682); later attempt to reach its mouth from sea ended in mutiny and murder by his own men.

Las Casas, Bartolomé de (1474-1566), Spanish Dominican missionary and historian. Worked in Latin America to aid and protect the Indians, attempting to abolish slavery. Through his efforts, new laws were passed (1542) to limit forced labour. Compiled important *Historia de las Indias*.

Lascaux, site of caves in SW France decorated with animal paintings of Upper Palaeolithic Age, dating from *c* 20,000-14,000 BC. Discovered 1940, cave had to be closed following deterioration of paintings.

laser (light amplification by stimulated emission of radiation), source of intense narrow beam of coherent light.

Atoms of gas or crystalline solid (*eg* ruby) are stimulated into excited states by light beams. They return to ground state with emission of pulses or continuous beams of highly coherent light. Used in cutting and welding metals, in surgery and holography.

Lashio, town of EC Burma. Pop. 5000. Rail terminus. Linked to China by Burma road.

Laski, Harold Joseph (1893-1950), British political scientist. Influential Fabian, he taught at London School of Economics from 1920. Chairman of Labour Party (1945-6). Works incl. *Liberty in the Modern State* (1930), *Democracy in Crisis* (1933), *The American Democracy* (1948).

Laski, Jan (1499-1560), Polish Protestant reformer. Friend of Erasmus. Forced to relinquish archbishopric of Warsaw because of Calvinistic beliefs, settled in England. After 1556 led Calvinistic reformation in Poland.

Las Palmas, *see* PALMAS, LAS, Spain.

La Spezia, *see* SPEZIA, LA, Italy.

Lassa fever, acute virus disease endemic to W Africa. Symptoms incl. high fever, pains in the back and ulcers in the throat; frequently fatal. Transmitted by rodents.

Lassalle, Ferdinand (1825-64), German socialist and writer. Influenced by Marx, he advocated form of state socialism in series of speeches and pamphlets. Founded General German Workers' Union (1863), forerunner of Social Democratic party. Died after a duel.

Lassus, Orlandus or **Orlando di Lasso** (*c* 1530-94), Flemish composer. Produced over 2000 vocal works, both secular and religious, in high polyphonic style. Choirmaster at St John Lateran in Rome (1553-4), settled in Munich after travelling widely in Europe.

Last Supper, *see* EUCHARIST.

Las Vegas, resort of S Nevada, US. Pop. 126,000; state's largest town. In ranching area; entertainment centre with famous gambling casinos. First settled by Mormons.

Latakia (*El Ladhiqiya*), port of NW Syria, on Mediterranean. Pop. 126,000. Exports famous tobacco, cotton. Prospered under Romans and Crusaders, but declined 16th cent. Revived with tobacco trade.

La Tène, shallows at E end of L. Neuchâtel, Switzerland. Site of discovery of Iron Age remains of Celtic people; name now given to European Iron Age (2nd period), *c* 5th cent. BC- 1st cent. AD.

latent heat, heat required to change state of a substance from solid to liquid, or from liquid to gas, without increase in its temperature. During a change of state the addition of heat causes no rise in temperature until the change of state is complete.

Lateran Treaty, agreement signed (1929) between Church and state in Italy. Confined papal sovereignty to independent Vatican City and specified extra-territorial buildings. Recognized Roman Catholicism as state religion and guaranteed religious teaching in schools.

laterite, reddish soil composed mainly of hydrated iron oxide. Formed by decomposition of underlying rocks, *eg* granite, basalt, in areas with distinct wet and dry seasons. Used as building material, source of iron. Found in India, Malaya, tropical Africa.

latex, milky fluid found in several plants, *eg* rubber tree, poppy. Consists of an emulsion of various resins and proteins. Latex of Pará rubber tree is worked into various types of rubber.

Latimer, Hugh (*c* 1485-1555), English churchman. Supported Cranmer's rejection of papal authority under Henry VIII. Appointed bishop of Winchester (1535); resigned over Act of Six Articles (1539). Under Edward VI, preached against corruption among clergy. With Ridley, burned at stake for heresy under Mary I.

Latin, language in Italic branch of Indo-European family. Standard language of Roman empire. Divided into Classical Latin and Vulgar (vernacular) Latin. Latter gave rise to Romance languages. Now dead, but Classical form still used in Roman Catholic church, and read as vehicle of great literature.

Latin America, term denoting countries of Central and South America, S of US-Mexico border; excl. British West Indies. Refers esp. to Spanish, Portuguese-speaking countries.

Latin American Free Trade Association (LAFTA), economic organization formed (1961) by Argentina, Brazil, Chile, Colombia, Ecuador, Mexico, Paraguay, Peru, Uruguay. Venezuela joined later in 1960s. Elimination of tariffs eventual goal. 1967 Punta del Este conference agreed to work towards joining LAFTA with Central American Common Market to create Latin American Common Market.

Latini, Brunetto (*c* 1220-94), Italian writer. May have been Dante's teacher. Known for *Trésor* (written in French, *c* 1265), 1st vernacular encyclopedia.

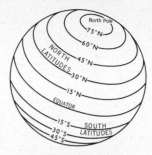

Parallels of latitude

latitude, in geography, angular distance north or south of the Equator of any point on Earth's surface, measured from Earth's centre. Parallels are lines of latitude encircling the Earth parallel to the Equator (0°).

Latium (*Lazio*), region of C Italy, cap. Rome. Coastal plain in W, Apennine foothills in E; much reclaimed marshland, *eg* Pontine Marshes. Agric., fishing, tourism, h.e.p. Ancient Latium fell to Romans 3rd cent. BC.

La Tour, Georges de (1593-1652), French painter. Worked all his life in Lorraine. Specialized in nocturnal religious and genre scenes dramatically illuminated by concealed source of light. Works incl. *St Sebastian mourned by St Irene*.

La Trappe, *see* TRAPPISTS.

Latrobe, Benjamin Henry (1764-1820), American architect, b. England. Contributed to Classical revival in American building. Work incl. Bank of Pennsylvania in Philadelphia, based on a Greek Ionic temple, and Baltimore Cathedral (1804-18), 1st cathedral in US.

Latter Day Saints, *see* MORMONS.

Latvian Soviet Socialist Republic, constituent republic of W USSR. Area *c* 66,600 sq km (25,600 sq mi); pop. 2,365,000; cap. Riga. Mainly low-lying plain with extensive forests; dairy products, timber, textiles produced. Hist. controlled by Sweden, Poland and Russia (from 1721); independent (1918-40) until annexed by USSR.

Laud, William (1573-1645), English churchman, archbishop of Canterbury (1633-45). Supported Charles I in struggle with Parliament. Attempted to eradicate Puritanism, favouring instead High Church ritual and doctrine. Attempt to impose the Prayer Book on Scotland (1638) was resisted by force. Impeached by Parliament (1640), imprisoned and executed.

Lauder, Sir Hugh MacLennan ('Harry') (1870-1950), Scottish music-hall singer. Known for comic or sentimental Scots songs, *eg* 'Roamin' in the Gloamin'.

Laue, Max Theodor Felix von (1879-1960), German physicist. Awarded Nobel Prize for Physics (1914) for prediction that atomic lattice of a crystal would act as diffraction grating for X-rays.

laughing gas, *see* NITROUS OXIDE.

laughing jackass, *see* KOOKABURRA.

Laughton, Charles (1899-1962), British film actor. Known for roles in, *eg*, *The Private Life of Henry VIII* (1933), *Mutiny on the Bounty* (1935), *Advise and Consent* (1962).

William Laud

Launceston, city of N Tasmania, Australia, at head of Tamar estuary. Pop. 35,000. Port, exports agric. produce, timber; textile mfg.

Bay laurel

laurel, any of genus *Laurus* of evergreen trees or shrubs; esp. bay laurel, *L. nobilis,* with greenish flowers, black berries, glossy leaves used as flavouring (as bay leaves) and in wreaths. Name also applied to certain similar trees and shrubs, *eg* cherry laurel, *Prunus laurocerasus,* spurge laurel, *Daphne laureola,* and American trees of Rhododendron and Magnolia families and Australian shrubs of *Anopterus* genus.

Laurens, Henri (1885-1954), French sculptor. Influenced by cubist painters, he created geometric compositions based on natural forms. Later work, based on female figure, was more naturalistic.

Laurentian Plateau, mainly in N Ontario, C Canada. Oldest rock formation of North America with dotted lake pattern formed by glacial action. Tundra in N; forested areas in S. Has rich mineral, timber, fur resources.

Laurier, Sir Wilfrid (1841-1919), Canadian statesman. First French-Canadian PM of Canada (1896-1911); influential in defining Liberal Party policy. Estab. principle of choosing regionally representative cabinet. Supported imperial preference.

Lausanne, city of SW Switzerland, on L. Geneva, cap. of Vaud canton. Pop. 137,000. Printing, woodworking, leather, tourism. Cathedral (12th cent.); coll. (1537) became univ.(1890).

Lausanne Conference, peace treaty (1922-3) between Allies and Turkey resolving problems raised by Treaty of SÈVRES, which had not been recognized by new Turkish govt. under Ataturk. Status of Dardanelles was decided and E Thrace recovered by Turkey.

lava, molten rock from interior of Earth which has reached surface through volcanic vents and fissures. 'Acid lavas', with high silica content, are thick and slow moving; 'basic lavas', with low silica content, are very fluid. Rock froth formed on surface of lava flow is called pumice.

Laval, François Xavier de (1623-1708), French churchman in Canada. First bishop of Québec (1674-88), he gave Church a strong base in colony. Opposed royal governors and traders whom he considered to be corrupting the Indians.

Laval, Pierre (1883-1945), French politician. Premier and foreign minister (1931-2, 1935-6). Created vice-premier of Pétain's Vichy govt. (1940) and all-powerful premier (1942). Collaborated with Germans, sending French workers to Germany. Executed for treason after summary trial following liberation.

Laval, town of NW France, on R. Mayenne, cap. of Mayenne dept. Pop. 49,000. Hist. textile centre (esp. linen), cheese mfg. Castle (12th cent.).

Lavalleja, Juan Antonio (*c* 1786-1853), Uruguayan revolutionary. Led independence movement, securing freedom from Brazil (1827) after victory at Ituzaingo.

La Vallière, Louise de (1644-1710), French noblewoman. Mistress of Louis XIV, she gave birth to 4 children before he transferred his affections to Mme de Montespan. Entered a Carmelite convent in 1674.

lavender, any of genus *Lavandula* of fragrant European plants of mint family, esp. *L. officinalis,* with spikes of pale purple flowers used in making perfumes.

Laver, Rod[ney] (1938-   ), Australian tennis player. Winner of 'grand slam' (British, US, Australian, French open titles) as an amateur (1962) and as a professional (1969).

Lavoisier, Antoine Laurent (1743-94), French chemist. A founder of modern chemistry, he introduced rational nomenclature, distinguished between elements and compounds, and made quantitative investigations of reactions. Explained role of oxygen in combustion and respiration, thus invalidating phlogiston theory. Estab. composition of water.

Law, Andrew Bonar (1858-1923), British statesman, b. Canada. Elected leader of Conservative Party (1911), he served in coalitions under Lloyd George (1915-21). PM (1922-3) after withdrawing from coalition; resigned because of poor health.

Law, John (1671-1729), Scottish financier. Founded Banque générale (1716) in Paris, which became royal bank (1718), issued paper currency. He acquired (1717) monopoly of trade in Louisiana, estab. vast stock company, merging (1720) it with bank. Excessive speculation led to frenzied selling and ruin of thousands, incl. Law.

Law, William (1686-1761), English clergyman, writer. Known for devotional *A Serious Call to a Devout and Holy Life* (1728), which influenced the Wesleys and promoted evangelical revival.

law court, *see* COURT.

Lawes, Sir John Bennet (1814-1900), English agriculturist. Patented (1842) artificial superphosphate fertilizer. Founded Rothamsted Experimental Station (1843).

Lawler, Raymond Evenor (1921-   ), Australian playwright. Known for *The Summer of the Seventeenth Doll* (1955) dealing with crisis in lives of 2 sugar-cane cutters.

lawn tennis, *see* TENNIS.

Lawrence, St (d. 258), Roman deacon and martyr. Traditionally put to death by being roasted on a gridiron.

Lawrence, D[avid] H[erbert] (1885-1930), English novelist, poet. Works reflect belief in sex, primitive subconscious, and nature as cures for destructive effects of modern indust. society. Novels incl. semi-autobiog. *Sons and Lovers* (1913), *Women in Love* (1920), *Lady*

Chatterley's Lover (1928). Also wrote short stories, plays, art criticism.

Lawrence, Ernest Orlando (1901-58), American physicist. Invented (1930) cyclotron, accelerator used to produce high energy proton beams for bombarding atomic nuclei. Awarded Nobel Prize for Physics (1939).

Lawrence, Gertrude (1898-1952), English actress. Appeared with Noel Coward in his plays incl. *Tonight at 8.30* and *Blithe Spirit*.

Lawrence, Sir Thomas (1769-1830), English painter. Succeeded Reynolds as painter to the king (1792); leading portraitist of his time. Commissioned to paint portraits of heads of state and military leaders concerned in the defeat of Napoleon (1818).

T.E. Lawrence

Lawrence, T[homas] E[dward] (1888-1935), British soldier, scholar, b. Wales. Known as 'Lawrence of Arabia'. Joined Arab revolt against Turks (1916), secured Arab cooperation for Allenby's campaign. As colonial adviser on Arab affairs, failed to realize his pro-Arab objectives and withdrew into obscurity. His experiences are recalled in *Seven Pillars of Wisdom* (1926).

Lawrence, town of NE Massachusetts, US; on Merrimack R. Pop. 67,000. Important woollen textiles mfg. since 19th cent. H.e.p.

lawrencium (Lr), transuranic element of actinide series; atomic no. 103, mass no. of most stable isotope 256. Lawrencium 257 first prepared (1961) by bombarding californium with boron nuclei.

Laxness, Halldór Kiljan (1902-), Icelandic novelist. Known for lyrical social novels set in fishing village, *Salka Volka* (1931), *Independent People* (1935), *The Light of the World* (1937). Nobel Prize for Literature (1955).

Layamon (fl c 1200), English poet. Known for long verse-chronicle *Brut*, on early British history. First prominent Middle English poet.

Layard, Sir Austen Henry (1817-94), English archaeologist, diplomat, b. Paris. Excavated in Mesopotamia (1845-7, 1849-51). Found Assyrian reliefs at Nimrud, which, with rest of collection, form great part of Assyrian remains at British Museum.

Lazarists, popular name for the Congregation of Priests of the Mission, an RC teaching order founded by St Vincent de Paul (1626). Named from its 1st priory, St Lazare, Paris.

Lazio, *see* LATIUM, Italy.

Leacock, Stephen Butler (1869-1944), Canadian humorist, b. England. Works, *eg Literary Lapses* (1910), *Sunshine Sketches of a Little Town* (1912), draw out everyday problems with perverse logic.

lead (Pb), soft metallic element; at. no. 82, at. wt. 207.19. Occurs as galena (PbS); obtained by roasting this ore. Used in accumulators, alloys, plumbing and roofing, and as shield against radiation; compounds used in paint. Lead tetraethyl used to prevent knocking in petrol.

leaf, outgrowth of stem of plant. Usually consists of broad blade, petide (stalk), and stipules. Functions incl. food mfg. through assimilation of carbon dioxide and absorption of light, *see* PHOTOSYNTHESIS, releasing water to atmosphere, *see* TRANSPIRATION. Chlorophyll gives green colour. Evergreen leaves are termed persistent, those which fall annually, deciduous.

leaf beetle, any of Chrysomelidae family of brightly coloured shiny beetles. Larvae are stem borers, root and leaf eaters. Species incl. Colorado beetle.

leaf-cutting bee, solitary insect of Megachilidae family. Nests in ground, building thimble-shaped egg cells from fragments bitten from leaves, petals.

leaf hopper, any of Cicadellidae family of long-bodied insects, resembling aphids. Jumps from plant to plant, sucking sap; agent of virus disease.

leaf insect, tropical insect of same family (Phasmidae) as stick insect. Wings shaped and coloured to resemble leaves among which it lives.

League of Nations, first major organization of world's countries dedicated to preservation of peace and international cooperation; hq. Geneva. Founded (1920) as part of TREATY OF VERSAILLES, largely on initiative of Woodrow Wilson. Members incl. (at some time) all major nations except US; Germany and Japan withdrew 1933. Although successful in humanitarian actions, it failed to act against aggression by some of its members, *eg* Japan (1931), Italy (1935). Dissolved itself (1946) and transferred services and property to UN.

Leakey, Louis Seymour Bazett (1903-72), British anthropologist, b. Kenya. Discovered fossil remains in East Africa, incl. those of *Zinjanthropus,* proto-man *c* 1,750,000 years old, estab. man to have existed earlier than previously supposed. Works incl. *Unveiling Man's Origins* (1969).

Leamington Spa, Royal, mun. bor. of Warwickshire, C England. Pop. 45,000. Engineering; saline springs, popular health resort from 18th cent. Visited by Queen Victoria (1838).

Leander, *see* HERO.

Edward Lear

Lear, Edward (1812-88), English humorist, artist. Famous for nonsense verse, esp. limericks, sometimes reflecting alienation and melancholy, *eg* 'The Jumblies', *A Book of Nonsense* (1846), *The Owl and the Pussycat* (1871), illustrated by himself.

leather, durable material prepared from hide or skin of animals by removal of flesh and hair and subsequent tanning. Tanning helps prevent decay and gives leather flexibility and toughness.

leatherjacket, *see* CRANEFLY.

leathery turtle or **luth,** *Dermochelys coriacea,* largest marine turtle, weighing up to 540 kg/ 1200 lbs; common in tropics. Carapace is heart-shaped, with leathery appearance. Also called leatherback.

Leavis, F[rank] R[aymond] (1895-), English literary critic. Editor of influential periodical *Scrutiny* (1932-53). Works, *eg The Great Tradition* (1948), *The Common Pursuit* (1952), reflect belief that literature should have moral value and meet standards of intellectual elite.

Lebanon, republic of SW Asia, E Mediterranean. Area *c* 10,000 sq km (3860 sq mi); pop. 2,963,000; cap. Beirut. Language: Arabic. Religions: Islam, Maronite Christian. Fertile Beqa valley (grain, fruit) lies between Lebanon Mts. and Anti-Lebanon. Centre of ancient Phoenician empire; part of Syria under Romans, Byzantines, Turks until French mandate (1920); independent 1945. Destructive religious and civil strife in mid-1970s.

Leblanc, Nicolas (1742-1806), French chemist. Invented Leblanc process for large scale production of soda from salt; important in 19th cent. indust.

Lebrun, Albert (1871-1950), French statesman. Last president of Third Republic (1932-40), he was deprived of power by Pétain after armistice with Germany.

Lebrun, Charles (1619-90), French painter. Studied with Poussin in Rome; became court painter to Louis XIV and director of reorganized Gobelins tapestry works. One of leaders in foundation of French Academy of Painting and Sculpture (1648), later became its director. Responsible for much of decoration at Versailles palaces.

Le Carré, John, pseud. of David John Moore Cornwell (1931-), English author. Known for realistic, low-key thriller fiction frequently based on experience as diplomat in cold war West Germany, incl. *The Spy Who Came in from the Cold* (1963).

Lecce, town of Apulia, SE Italy, cap. of Lecce prov. Pop. 85,000. Olives, tobacco market; ceramics, toy mfg. Many baroque buildings, *eg* cathedral.

Lech, river of C Europe. Flows 282 km (175 mi) from Vorarlberg (W Austria) past Augsburg to R. Danube at Donauwörth (West Germany).

Leconte de Lisle, Charles Marie René (1818-94), French poet. Leading PARNASSIEN. Wrote austere, pessimistic poetry, *eg Poèmes antiques* (1852), *Poèmes tragiques* (1884), verse drama *L'Apollonide* (1888).

Le Corbusier, *see* CORBUSIER, LE.

Lecouvreur, Adrienne (1692-1730), French actress. Popular at Comédie Française, Paris, particularly in tragedy.

Le Creusot, town of Burgundy, EC France. Pop. 34,000. Coalmining, Schneider iron and steel works, armaments mfg. Badly damaged in WWII.

Leda, in Greek myth, wife of Tyndareus. Seduced by Zeus who visited her in form of a swan. She bore 2 eggs; one contained DIOSCURI, other Helen and Clytemnestra.

Ledru-Rollin, Alexandre Auguste (1807-74), French politician. One of instigators of 1848 Revolution; member of Lamartine's provisional govt. Defeated by Louis Napoleon in 1849 presidential election; fled to England after failure of insurrection against Napoleon (1849). Advocated universal suffrage.

Le Duc Tho (*c* 1912-), Vietnamese political leader. Shared Nobel Peace Prize (1973) with Kissinger for negotiating 1973 ceasefire. Rejected award.

Lee, Robert E[dward] (1807-70), American army officer, commander of the Confederate forces in the Civil War. Frustrated McClellan's campaign in the Seven Days battles (June-July, 1862). Won 2nd battle of Bull Run (1862) and Chancellorsville (1863), but was defeated at Gettysburg (July, 1863) and, ultimately outnumbered, surrendered to Grant (April, 1865). Became a symbol of Southern resistance.

Lee, Tsung-Dao (1926-), American physicist, b. China. Shared Nobel Prize for Physics (1957) with C.N. Yang for prediction that PARITY is not conserved during certain interactions between elementary particles. They devised experiments which confirmed this.

leech, *see* HIRUDINEA.

Leeds, city of West Yorkshire met. county, N England, on R. Aire. Pop. 495,000. Textiles; engineering industs. Has

Robert E. Lee

univ. (1904). Woollen indust. from 14th cent.; St John's Church (17th cent.).

leek, *Allium porrum,* biennial plant of same genus as ONION. Cylindrical stem and flat leaves. Used as vegetable and in soups. National emblem of Wales.

Lee Kuan Yew (1923-), Singapore statesman. Became 1st PM of Singapore (1959). Withdrew country from Federation of Malaysia (1965) which it had joined in 1963. Expanded economic base of country.

Leeuwarden, town of N Netherlands, cap. of Friesland prov. Pop. 88,000. Railway, canal jct., cattle market, clothing mfg. Gold, silver working indust. in 16th-18th cents.

Leeuwenhoek, Antony van (1632-1723), Dutch naturalist. Developed single lens microscope, which enabled him to discover protozoa, spermatozoa and bacteria and study red blood cells.

Leeward Islands, archipelago of E West Indies, N Lesser Antilles. Extend SE from Puerto Rico to Windward Isls. Incl. Virgin Isls. (US); ex-British colonies Antigua, St Kitts-Nevis-Anguilla, Montserrat, British Virgin Isls.; Guadeloupe (French); St Eustatius (Dutch), St Martin. Isls. discovered by Columbus (1493). Disputed by Britain and France; ownership resolved 1815.

Le Fanu, Joseph Sheridan (1814-73), Irish novelist. Known for mystery and occult suspense stories, *eg The House by the Churchyard* (1863), *Uncle Silas* (1864), *In a Glass Darkly* (1872).

Legaspi, seaport of Philippines, SE Luzon isl. Pop. 61,000. Exports copra, hemp. Founded 1639 as Albay.

Legendre, Adrien Marie (1752-1833), French mathematician. Noted for work on number theory and elliptic integrals. His *Eléments de géometrie* (1794) was widely used as textbook.

Léger, Alexis Saint-Léger, *see* ST-JOHN PERSE.

Léger, Fernand (1881-1955), French painter. Associated with cubism, he later created a style employing machine-like forms and flat bands of pure colour. Designed ballet sets and decorative murals.

Leghorn (*Livorno*), town of Tuscany, NW Italy, on Ligurian Sea. Cap. of Livorno prov. Pop. 78,000. Port, exports wine, olive oil, marble; resort; naval academy. Created free port 1590. Many buildings, *eg* cathedral, destroyed in WWII.

legion, fighting unit of Roman army varying from 3000 to 4000 foot soldiers (divided into 10 cohorts) with additional cavalrymen. Organization attributed to Marcus Camillus (d. *c* 365 BC). Tended to be vulnerable to cavalry, archers and guerrilla tactics.

legislature, in politics, that part of govt. empowered to make laws for a country or state, usually comprising elected representatives. British Parliament and US

Congress were important in development of legislatures as check on judiciary and executive. Also *see* SEPARATION OF POWERS.

legitimation, giving of legitimate status to child born out of wedlock. In UK, since 1926, resulted on marriage of parents. In US, law similar in most states.

Legnica (Ger. *Liegnitz*), town of SW Poland. Pop. 75,000. In vegetable-growing area; textile, chemical industs. Ducal cap. until 1675; under Prussian rule 1742-1945.

Leguminosae, family of flowering plants and trees. Characterized by having seed pods and nitrogenous nodules on roots which allow NITROGEN FIXATION in soil. Incl. laburnum, gorse, CLOVER. Many species have tendrils which twine around supports, *eg* PEA.

Lehár, Franz (1870-1948), Hungarian composer. Works, mostly operettas, incl. *The Merry Widow* (1905).

Le Havre, city of N France, at mouth of R. Seine. Pop. 200,000. Major port with passenger and cargo traffic. Oil refining, pipeline to Paris. Founded in 1576 by Francis I. Heavily bombed in WWII.

Leibnitz

Leibnitz, Gottfried Wilhelm, Baron von (1646-1716), German philosopher, mathematician. In *Monadology* (1714) posited universe of units (monads) which cannot act independently but which follow a harmony estab. by God. Thus this becomes the 'best of all possible worlds'. Devised form of calculus independently of Newton.

Leicester, Robert Dudley, Earl of (c 1532-88), English courtier. Favourite of Elizabeth I, he was once considered her most likely choice of husband. From c1564 advocated strong measures against Catholics and Spain. Led unsuccessful expedition to assist revolt of United Provinces against Spanish rule in Netherlands (1585-7).

Leicestershire, county of EC England. Area 2553 sq km (986 sq mi); pop. 824,000. Mainly low-lying; uplands in E. Dairying (Stilton cheese); coal mining in W. Co. town **Leicester,** co. bor. on R. Soar. Pop. 287,000. Hosiery, shoe mfg. Has univ. (1957); Roman *Ratae,* remains incl. Jewry Wall; Norman castle (12th cent.); cathedral (1926).

Leichhardt, [Friedrich Wilhelm] Ludwig (1813-48), German explorer, scientist. Explored N and E Australia; journeyed from SE Queensland to Port Essington, Northern Territ. (1844-5), gaining useful knowledge of region. Disappeared on trans-continental expedition (1848).

Leiden or **Leyden,** city of WC Netherlands, on R. Old Rhine. Pop. 100,000. Produces textiles, machinery. Univ. (1575) was centre of learning in 17th and 18th cents. Survived Spanish siege (1574) by cutting dykes, flooding surrounding land. Birthplace of Rembrandt.

Leif Ericsson (*fl c* 1000), Norse explorer, son of Eric the Red. Thought to have reached North America; the 'Vinland' he discovered has not been precisely delimited, perhaps New England or Newfoundland.

Leigh, Vivien, née Hartley (1913-67), British actress. Famous in film roles incl. *The Skin of Our Teeth, A Streetcar Named Desire, Anna Karenina.* Also played on stage, esp. in *Antony and Cleopatra* with husband, Sir Laurence Olivier.

Leighton, Frederick, Baron Leighton of Stretton (1830-96), English painter. His work employed themes taken from mythology and the ancient world, executed in an academic style; also worked as a sculptor. Paintings incl. *Cimabue's Madonna carried in procession.*

Leinster, prov. of E Irish Republic. Area 20,331 sq km (7850 sq mi); pop. 1,495,000. Comprises cos. Carlow, Dublin, Kildare, Kilkenny, Laoighis, Longford, Louth, Meath, Offaly, Westmeath, Wexford, Wicklow. Ancient kingdom, former cap. Naas.

Leipzig, city of S East Germany, at confluence of Pleisse, White Elster. Pop. 581,000. Indust. centre, annual trade fair; centre of German fur trade and publishing until WWII. Univ. (1409). Medieval town, has tavern featured in Goethe's *Faust.* Badly damaged in Thirty Years War and WWII; scene of Napoleon's defeat (1813) in Battle of the Nations.

Leith, town of Lothian region, E Scotland, on Firth of Forth. Part of Edinburgh from 1920. Major Scottish seaport; fishing, whisky distilling.

Leitrim, county of Connacht prov., NW Irish Republic. Area 1526 sq km (589 sq mi); pop. 28,000; co. town Carrick-on-Shannon. Many lakes; hilly in N. Poor soil, climate. Cattle, dairying.

Leix, see LAOIGHIS, Irish Republic.

Leixões, see OPORTO, Portugal.

Lely, Sir Peter (1618-80), Anglo-Dutch painter, b. Germany. Painted for Charles I and later became court painter to Charles II. Maintained large studio to produce numerous portraits; best known for his flattering *Beauties,* depicting the women of the court.

Leman, Lac, see GENEVA, LAKE, Switzerland.

Le Mans, city of NW France, on R. Sarthe, cap. of Sarthe dept. Pop. 143,000. Railway jct., agric. market, engineering. Annual 24-hour motor race. Hist. cap. of Maine. Site of final French defeat by Prussia (1871). Cathedral (11th cent.).

Lemberg, see LVOV.

Collared lemming (*Dicrostonyx torquatus*)

lemming, small thick-furred rodent, resembling vole, of Arctic and subarctic regions. Norwegian lemming, *Lemmus lemmus,* noted for mass migration during times of overpopulation and food scarcity.

Lemnos (*Limnos*), isl. of Greece, in N Aegean Sea. Area 482 sq km (186 sq mi); main town Kastron. Fertile valleys; fruit, cereals. Traditionally sacred to Hephaestus.

lemon, *Citrus limon,* evergreen tree bearing bitter yellow fruit. Grown in Mediterranean regions, S US and South Africa. Juice used in cooking, rind in candied peel.

lemon balm, *see* BALM.

lemon sole, *Microstomus kitt,* edible flatfish of eastern N Atlantic.

lemur, primitive arboreal primate, found mainly in Madagascar. Usually nocturnal, with large eyes and long

Lemon

Ring-tailed lemur

non-prehensile tail. Diet of insects, fruit. Species incl. ring-tailed lemur, *Lemur catta.*

lemures or **larvae,** in Roman religion, malevolent ghosts of the dead. Propitiated in Lemuria rites.

Lena, longest river of USSR. Rises in Baikal Mts. W of L. Baikal, flows NE *c* 4250 km (2650 mi) through EC Siberian RSFSR to Laptev Sea. Gold and other minerals obtained along its course.

Le Nain, Antoine (*c* 1588-1648), **Louis** (*c* 1593-1648), and **Mathieu** (1607-77), family of French painters, all brothers. Series of paintings are attributed to them, esp. realistic genre scenes of peasant life, painted in greyish tones.

Lenclos, [Anne] Ninon de (*c* 1620-1705), French beauty, leader of fashion. Famous for her many distinguished lovers incl. Condé and La Rochefoucauld. Later gave fashionable receptions at her Paris salon.

Lend-Lease Act, legislation passed (1941) by US Congress, empowering president to sell, lend or lease US war supplies to countries whose defence was considered vital to defence of US. Countries such as Britain provided reciprocal programmes.

Lenglen, Suzanne (1899-1938), French tennis player. Won Wimbledon title 6 times (1919-23, 1925), French title (1920-3, 1925-6). Her exciting play did much to promote the status of women's tennis.

Lenin, Vladimir Ilyich, orig. Ulyanov (1870-1924), Russian revolutionary. Exiled twice for anti-govt. activity, engineered split (1903) between BOLSHEVIKS and Mensheviks in Social Democrats. Returned to Russia after outbreak of RUSSIAN REVOLUTION to overthrow Kerensky's govt. (Nov. 1917), estab. Council of People's Commissars. Civil war (1918-20) ended with founding of the Soviet Union. Exercised dictatorial powers as chairman of the council and chairman of the Communist Party. Instrumental in creation of COMINTERN world socialist movement. Differed from orthodox MARXISM in his actions and writings, *eg What is to be done?* (1902), advocating

Lenin

violent revolution, instigated by disciplined professional revolutionaries.

Leningrad, city of USSR, W European RSFSR; at mouth of R. Neva. Pop. 4,066,000. Major port; cultural and indust. centre; shipbuilding, exports timber. Founded (1703) as St Petersburg by Peter the Great. Intersected by numerous canals; spaciously planned, buildings incl. Winter Palace and cathedral; has Hermitage art gallery and univ. (1819). Scene of revolutions (1905,1917). Replaced as cap. by Moscow (1918). Called Petrograd (1914-24).

Leno, Dan, pseud. of George Galvin (1860-1904), English comedian. Began as clog-dancer, became famous pantomime 'dame' at Drury Lane (1888-1904).

Lenôtre, André (1613-1700), French landscape gardener. Designed parks and gardens for Louis XIV, in particular those at Versailles. His formal designs were highly influential until the growth of more naturalistic approach in 18th cent.

Lens, town of Nord, NE France. Pop. 42,000. Major coalmining centre, iron, steel and chemicals industs. French victory (1648) over Spain was last major battle of Thirty Years War. Severely damaged in both WWs.

lens, portion of transparent medium, *eg* glass, bounded by curved or plane surfaces, which causes light rays to converge or diverge on passing through it. Convex lens causes parallel beam of light to converge and produce real image, concave lens causes divergence of light and produces virtual image. ABERRATION is defect of lens.

Lent, Christian period of 40 days of penance and fasting before Easter (Ash Wednesday to Easter Sunday). Observance dates from 4th cent.

lentil, *Lens culinaris,* small branching plant of Leguminosae family. Cultivated for its round flat seeds which are dried and used in cooking. Native to Old World.

Leo I, St (*c* 400-461), Italian churchman, pope (440-61). Estab. authority over bishops. Author of *Tome of Leo* defining the 2 natures of Christ. Dissuaded (452) Attila from sacking Rome.

Leo III, St (d. 816), Italian churchman, pope (795-816). Crowned Charlemagne emperor (800) marking start of Holy Roman Empire and estab. papal right to consecrate emperor.

Leo IX, St (1002-54), Alsatian churchman, pope (1049-54). Related to Emperor Conrad II. Reformed clerical abuses. Excommunicated (1054) Michael Cerularius, patriarch of Constantinople, initiating split of Church into East and West.

Leo X, orig. Giovanni de' Medici (1475-1521), Italian churchman, pope (1513-21). Patron of Raphael, continued rebuilding of St Peter's, Rome. Excommunicated Luther (1521).

Leo XIII, orig. Gioacchino Vincenzo Pecci (1810-1903), Italian churchman, pope (1878-1903). Issued important encyclicals, moulding RC beliefs to the conditions of secular democratic states, *eg Rerum novarum* (1891). Declared Thomism official philosophy of Church and encouraged wide-ranging scholarship.

Leo [III] the Isaurian (*c* 680-741), Byzantine emperor. Seized power from Theodosius III (717). Successfully defended Constantinople against Saracen siege (718); defeated 2 later invasions (726, 739). His attempt to suppress icon worship led to struggle over iconoclasm.

Leo, see ZODIAC.

Leoben, town of SE Austria, on R. Mur. Pop. 36,000. Centre of Styrian coalmining; iron founding, brewing.

León, city of C Mexico, in Guanajuato state; alt. 1700 m (*c* 5600 ft). Pop. 454,000. Agric., mining centre; shoe, textiles, cement mfg. Founded 1576.

León, city of W Nicaragua. Pop. 91,000. Cultural, agric. and trade centre. National cap. until 1855. Destroyed by earthquake, moved to present site (1610). Has part of National Univ.

León, region and former kingdom of NW Spain. Chief cities Salamanca, Valladolid. Cantabrian Mts. in N, elsewhere plateau; drained by R. Douro. Agric., stock raising, mining, forests. Formed, with Asturias, Christian kingdom from 866; united with Castile 1230. Hist. cap. **León,** pop. 105,000, cap. of modern León prov. Agric., commercial centre. Gothic cathedral (13th cent.).

Leonardo da Vinci (1452-1519), Italian artist, scientist, engineer. Regarded as epitome of Renaissance creativity, his extant works are few and often unfinished. Paintings incl. *Adoration of the Magi, Last Supper* fresco, *Mona Lisa, Virgin of the Rocks.* His commission to decorate the Council Chamber of Florence was abandoned after 2 years work. Served as military engineer to Cesare Borgia (*c* 1500); last years were spent in service of Francis I of France. Produced notebooks covering problems in hydraulics, mechanics, anatomy, *etc.*

Leoncavallo, Ruggiero (1858-1919), Italian operatic composer. Known for *I Pagliacci* (1892), but his other operas have not survived in the repertory.

Leonidas (d. 480 BC), Spartan king. Although heavily outnumbered, he and his Spartan troops defended pass of Thermopylae (480 BC) against Persians under Xerxes; defeated and killed.

Leonov, Leonid Maksimovich (1899-), Russian author. Known for stylistically complex psychological novels, *eg The Badgers* (1925), *The Thief* (1927), reflecting reservations about Soviet Communism.

Leopard

leopard or **panther,** *Panthera pardus,* mammal of cat family, found in Africa and Asia. Yellow-buff coat, with black markings.

Leopardi, Giacomo, Conte (1798-1837), Italian poet. Belief that cosmos is inevitably hostile reflected in melancholic lyrics, *eg Versi* (1826), *Canti* (1836), philosophical essay *Le Operette Morali* (1824), aphorisms *Pensieri* (1834-7).

Leopold I (1640-1705), Holy Roman emperor (1658-1705). Reign was marked by almost continual conflict with Louis XIV of France; opposed French territ. ambitions in Low Countries, Germany and Spain in series of wars. Campaigns against Turks incl. relief of siege of Vienna (1683) and victory at Zenta (1697).

Leopold II (1747-92), Holy Roman emperor (1790-2). Succeeded his brother Joseph II. Allied with Prussia to restore Louis XVI to French throne, but died before French Revolutionary Wars broke out.

Leopold I (1790-1865), king of Belgium. Having refused Greek throne (1830), he was elected king of Belgium on its separation from Netherlands (1831). Known as the 'Uncle of Europe'.

Leopold II (1835-1909), king of Belgium (1865-1909). Financed Stanley's explorations (1879-84) in the Congo, leading to formation of Congo Free State (1885) which Leopold ruled personally. His ruthless exploitation of the territ., by which he amassed a fortune, drew much hostility.

Leopold III (1901-), king of Belgium (1934-51). Led Belgian resistance to the German occupation in WWII. Surrendered unconditionally in 1940; imprisoned until 1945. Accused of cooperating with the Germans, he remained in exile until 1950; abdicated in favour of his son Baudouin.

Léopoldville, see KINSHASA, Zaïre.

Leo [VI] the Wise (*c* 862-912), Byzantine emperor (886-912). Reorganized civil admin. of empire, notably his *Basilica* (887-93), completion of digest of Justinian code.

Lepanto, see NAUPAKTOS, Greece.

Lepidoptera, order of insects, comprising moths and butterflies, with *c* 150,000 species.

Lepidus, Marcus Aemilius (d. *c* 12 BC), Roman politician. Formed 2nd Triumvirate with Antony and Octavian. After attempting to take Sicily, Octavian deprived him of office.

Le Play, [Pierre Guillaume] Frédéric (1806-82), French sociologist, mining engineer. Known for analysis of family as unit in society, using data from extensive travels to formulate 3 basic types of family.

leprosy, chronic infectious disease of the skin and nerves, caused by bacterium *Mycobacterium leprae.* Lepromatous form causes ulcerous blotches on face; tuberculoid form causes loss of sensation in skin. Advanced leprosy may result in loss of fingers, toes. Most prevalent in tropical regions. Treated with sulphone drugs.

leptons, elementary particles which do not experience strong nuclear interaction. At present, those known are electron, muon, 2 types of neutrino and corresponding antiparticles.

Le Puy (en Velay), town of SC France, cap. of Haute-Loire dept. Pop. 30,000. Liqueur mfg., hist. lace indust. Medieval pilgrimage centre. Romanesque cathedral (12th cent.).

Lérida (anc. *Ilerda),* town of NE Spain, on R. Segre, cap. of Lérida prov. Pop. 91,000. Textile mfg., tanning. Strategic site, esp. in Civil War. Two cathedrals (13th, 18th cent.).

Lermontov, Mikhail Yurevich (1814-41), Russian author. Wrote lyric poetry influenced by Byron, *eg The Demon* (1829-41), classic novel of 'superfluous man' *A Hero of Our Time* (1840), anticipating work of 19th cent. realists.

Lerner, Alan Jay (1918-), American lyricist, librettist. Collaborated with composer Frederick Loewe in musicals incl. *Brigadoon* (1947), *Paint Your Wagon* (1951), *My Fair Lady* (1956).

Lerwick, port of Shetland, N Scotland, on Mainland isl. Pop. 6000. Fishing, knitwear, offshore oil industs.

Le Sage, Alain René (1668-1747), French author. Best known for picaresque novel of manners, *Gil Blas* (1715-35). Also wrote many farces, comedies.

lesbianism, see HOMOSEXUALITY.

Lesbos or **Mytilene,** isl. of Greece, in E Aegean Sea. Area 1632 sq km (630 sq mi); cap. Mytilene. Wheat, olives, fruits. Cultural centre *c* 6th cent. BC, home of Aristotle, poets Sappho, Alcaeus. Member of Delian League.

Lescot, Pierre (*c* 1510-78), French architect. Considered a founder of French Classicism, he built earliest part of palace which later became the Louvre. All his works were decorated by Jean Goujon.

Lesina, see HVAR, Yugoslavia.

Leslie, Alexander, 1st Earl of Leven (*c* 1580-1661), Scottish army officer. Fought in the Swedish army and was made field marshal. Returning to Scotland (1639), he organized the Covenanting army which he commanded in

N England (1644) and against the Royalists in the Civil War. Accepted Charles I's surrender at Newark (1646).

Lesotho, kingdom of S Africa, surrounded by Republic of South Africa. Area 30,300 sq km (11,700 sq mi); pop. 1,081,000, mainly Basuto tribe; cap. Maseru. Languages: Sesotho, English. Religions: native, Christian. Drakensberg Mts. in E, elsewhere tableland; main rivers Orange, Caledon. Main occupation stock rearing; exports wool, mohair, diamonds. Many Basuto tribesmen work in South African mines. British Protect. of Basutoland from 1868, independent from 1966. Member of British Commonwealth.

Lesseps, Ferdinand Marie, Vicomte de (1805-94), French diplomat, engineer. Negotiated concession for Suez Canal and supervised its construction (1859-69). Began work on Panama Canal (1881), but company went bankrupt.

Lessing, Doris May, née Taylor (1919-), English author, b. Persia. Known for semi-autobiog. 'Children of Violence' novel sequence incl. *Martha Quest* (1952), *A Proper Marriage* (1954), *The Four Gated City* (1969), dealing with her African childhood, political activism, psychological development.

Lessing, Gotthold Ephraim (1729-81), German aesthetician, dramatist. Known for theoretical works, *eg Laokoon* (1766) demarcating subject matter of painting, poetry, *Hamburg Dramaturgy* (1767-8) attacking neo-classical formalism, *Education of the Human Race* (1780) taking rationalist view of theology. Best-known dramas incl. *Emilia Galotti* (1772), *Nathan the Wise* (1779).

Letchworth, urban dist. of Hertfordshire, S England. Pop. 31,000. Printing; rubber goods. First English 'garden city' (1903).

Lethbridge, town of S Alberta, Canada; on Oldham R. Pop. 41,000. In coal mining, agric. (esp. cattle, wheat) region. Founded in 1870s as Coalbanks; renamed 1885.

Lethe, in Greek myth, one of rivers of HADES. Water drunk by the dead to gain forgetfulness of previous existence.

Leto, in Greek myth, daughter of Titans Coeus and Phoebe; mother by Zeus of Apollo and Artemis. Consequently Hera sent the serpent Python to persecute her until it was killed by Apollo. *See* PYTHIAN GAMES.

Lettish or **Latvian,** *see* BALTIC.

lettre de cachet, in French law under *ancien régime*, official, sealed communication from the king to individual or group, usually giving notice of exile or imprisonment without trial. Abolished during French Revolution.

lettuce, *Lactuca sativa*, vegetable widely grown for its crisp leaves used raw in salads. Varieties incl. asparagus lettuce (*angustana*), cabbage lettuce (*capitata*) and Cos (*longifolia*).

Leuckart, Karl Georg Friedrich Rudolf (1823-98), German zoologist. Pioneer in parasitology; worked on classifying invertebrates. Recognized parthenogenesis in insects.

leucocyte, *see* BLOOD.

leukaemia, cancer-like disease of white blood cells resulting from disorder of bone marrow and other blood-forming tissue. Accompanied by anaemia and enlargement of lymph nodes, liver, spleen. Incurable, but may be relieved or controlled by X-rays and drugs.

Levant, name given to coastlands of E Mediterranean in Turkey, Syria, Lebanon and Israel.

Levellers, extreme republican and democratic party in English Civil War period. Advocated religious and social equality, sovereign House of Commons elected by universal manhood suffrage. Gained some support in army rank and file from 1647; suppressed by Cromwell (1649) after fomenting several mutinies.

Leven, Loch, two lochs of Scotland. **1,** in Highland region, extends 14 km (9 mi) E from Loch Linnhe to Kinlochleven. **2,** in Fife region, with isl. castle in which Mary Queen of Scots was imprisoned (1567-8).

Leverhulme, William Hesketh Lever, 1st Viscount (1851-1925), English industrialist. Founded Lever Bros. Ltd. (1886), international soap manufacturers, which later became Unilever. Estab. (1888) model village, Port Sunlight, as part of benefits to employees.

Leverkusen, city of W West Germany, on R. Rhine. Pop. 109,000. Indust. centre esp. chemicals, textiles, machinery.

Leverrier, Urbain Jean Joseph (1811-77), French astronomer and mathematician. Independently of Adams, he explained irregularities in motion of Uranus by existence of previously unknown planet Neptune. Galle identified Neptune (1846) in position predicted by Leverrier.

Lévesque, René (1922-), Canadian politician. Left Liberal Party to found Parti Québecois (1967) with aim of Québec's secession from Canada. Became premier of Québec (1976) after party's election victory.

Lévi-Strauss, Claude (1908-), French anthropologist, b. Belgium. Founded 'structural' method of analyzing cultures. Works incl. *Totemism* (1962), *The Raw and the Cooked* (1969).

Levites, in OT, descendants of Levi, son of Jacob and Leah. Hereditary religious caste, bearers of the Ark of the Covenant.

Leviticus, in OT, third book of Pentateuch, detailing duties and ceremonies of priests and Levites.

Lewes, George Henry (1817-78), English miscellaneous writer. Wrote on philosophy, introducing Comte's positivism to England. Works incl. *Life and Works of Goethe* (1855), *Problems of Life and Mind* (1874-9). Lived with Mary Ann Evans (George Eliot) after 1854.

Lewes, mun. bor. and co. town of East Sussex, SE England. Pop. 14,000. Has ruined 11th cent. priory, Norman castle. Scene of defeat of Henry III by Simon de Montfort (1264). Glyndebourne (opera festival) nearby.

Lewis, C[ecil] Day, *see* DAY-LEWIS, C[ECIL].

Lewis, C[live] S[taples] (1898-1963), English author, b. Ireland. Known for criticism, *eg The Allegory of Love* (1936) on medieval literature, allegorical fantasy fiction, *eg Out of the Silent Planet* (1938), Christian apologetics, esp. *The Screwtape Letters* (1942), children's books, *eg The Lion, the Witch, and the Wardrobe* (1950).

Lewis, [Harry] Sinclair (1885-1951), American novelist. Known for satires of American life, *eg Main Street* (1920), *Babbitt* (1922), *Arrowsmith* (1925), *Elmer Gantry* (1927). *It Can't Happen Here* (1935) speculates about possibilities of fascist dictatorship in US. Nobel Prize for Literature (1930).

Lewis, John L[lewellyn] (1880-1969), American labour leader. President of United Mine Workers of America (1920-60). Helped found and headed (1935-40) Congress of Industrial Organizations, which aimed to unionize large mass production industs.

Lewis, Matthew Gregory ('Monk') (1775-1818), English author. Earned nickname for Gothic novel, *The Monk* (1796), extravagant mixture of brutality, sensuality, and supernatural. Also wrote autobiog. *Journal of a West Indian Proprietor* (1834).

Lewis, Meriwether (1774-1809), American soldier, explorer. Secretary to President Jefferson (1801-3). With William Clark, led successful expedition (1803-6) in search of route across Rocky Mts. to the Pacific. Governor of Louisiana (1807-9).

Lewis, [Percy] Wyndham (1884-1957), English painter, author, b. US. Leader of vorticist painting movement. Edited magazine *Blast* (1914-15) with Ezra Pound. Wrote novels, *eg The Apes of God* (1930), attacking cultural fashions of 1920s, *The Childermass* (1928).

Lewis, *see* LEWIS WITH HARRIS, Scotland.

Lewis and Clark Expedition, exploring expedition (1803-6) across North America led by Meriwether LEWIS and William Clark. They followed Missouri R. to its source, crossed continental divide, and explored Columbia R. from its source to Pacific.

Lewisham, bor. of SE Greater London, England. Pop. 265,000. Created 1965 from former met. bor. and Deptford. Incl. Blackheath, where Tyler (1381), Cade (1450) mustered rebel peasant forces.

Lewis with Harris, largest isl. of Outer Hebrides, NW Scotland, in WESTERN ISLES. Area 2137 sq km (825 sq mi); main town Stornoway. Mainly peat bog, moorland. Crofting, fishing industs.; Harris Tweed mfg.

Lexington, *see* BOSTON, Massachusetts.

Lexington, town of NC Kentucky, US. Pop. 108,000. In bluegrass region (horse breeding). Electrical equipment, furniture mfg. Market for tobacco and bluegrass seed.

Leyden, see LEIDEN, Netherlands.

Leyton, see WALTHAM FOREST, England.

Lhasa, cap. of Tibet auton. region, SW China. Pop. 175,000. Alt. 3600 m (11,800 ft). Trade, religious centre; Lamaist temple, monasteries, palace of Dalai Lama.

Liaoning, maritime prov. of NE China. Area c 230,500 sq km (89,000 sq mi); pop. 28,000,000; cap. Shenyang. Heavily industrialized; major coal, iron ore, paper producer. Soya beans major crop. Incl. hist. disputed LU-TA at end of Liaotung penin.

Liaotung, penin. of NE China, Liaoning prov.

Liaoyang, city of Liaoning prov., NE China. Pop. 250,000. Iron and coalmining, textile mfg. Has Buddhist temples (11th cent.). Scene of major Japanese victory in Russo-Japanese war (1904).

Liaoyuan, city of Kirin prov., NE China. Pop. c 300,000. Coalmining, iron and steel plants.

Liaquat Ali Khan (1895-1951), Pakistani politician. Led Moslem League (1936-46); PM at creation of new state of Pakistan (1947). Murdered by a fanatic.

Libau, see LIEPAJA.

Libby, Willard Frank (1908-), American chemist. Developed technique to find age of carbon-containing materials by measuring content of radioactive carbon 14. Awarded Nobel Prize for Chemistry (1960).

libel, in law, one of two types of defamation (exposure to hatred, contempt, ridicule or material loss), other being slander. Libel must take permanent form, eg writing, picture, tape, film, whereas slander consists in utterance (by speech, gesture, etc) of defamatory statement. Both, to be actionable, must affect living individual (eg relative of defamed deceased). Slander is a civil offence, libel may be criminal, eg if likely to cause breach of the peace. Defences incl. truth, fair comment, qualified privilege.

Liber, in Roman religion, god of fertility and wine. Often identified with Bacchus or Greek Dionysus.

liberalism, philosophy or movement advocating individual freedom. Theory based on LOCKE's doctrine involving freedom from restraint on life, health, liberty, property. In politics, manifested in parties pressing for democratic govt. and gradual reform of social institutions. Influence of utilitarians (esp. Bentham, Mill) enabled movement to promote state-controlled social measures in early 19th cent. Economic policies founded on opposition to state regulation. In UK, **Liberal Party** developed from WHIG PARTY after Reform Bill (1832), declining in 20th cent. with rise of Labour Party. Prominent leaders incl. Palmerston, Gladstone, Lloyd George. Liberalism in W Europe associated with nationalist movements in 19th cent. In British Commonwealth, Liberal parties achieved major party status, often forming govts., eg Canada (formed in 1850s) and Australia (founded 1944).

Liberec (Ger. *Reichenberg*), town of N Czechoslovakia, on R. Neisse. Pop. 73,000. Cloth, textile centre from 16th cent.

Liberia

Liberia, republic of W Africa. Area 111,300 sq km (43,000 sq mi); pop. 1,669,000; cap. Monrovia. Languages: tribal, English. Religions: native, Islam. Coastal plain, inland plateaux; extensive rain forest. Main food crop rice; exports iron ore, gold, diamonds. Major rubber-producing indust. from 1925; large merchant fleet using 'flag of convenience'. Founded (1822) as colony for freed American slaves; independent republic from 1847.

Liberty, Statue of, landmark dominating harbour of New York City in form of colossal female figure holding up torch. Stands on Liberty Island. Presented by Franco-American Union to commemorate alliance during American Revolution, it was constructed in 1884. Designed by F.A. Bartholdi; 46 m (152 ft) high.

libido, in psychology, term used by Freud to denote energy of sexual and creative instincts, as opposed to death instinct, destructive drive.

Libra, see ZODIAC.

library, organized collection of books and other written material. Earliest known library was collection of clay tablets in Babylonia (21st cent. BC). Noted ancient examples incl. that of Assurbanipal (d. c 626 BC) at Nineveh and those at Alexandria and Pergamum. Public libraries estab. in Greece (330 BC) and at Rome. Oldest existing public library of Europe is that of Vatican (15th cent.) with many univ. libraries estab. earlier, eg Sorbonne (1257). Modern libraries incl. Bodleian (Oxford), Bibliothèque Nationale (Paris), British Library (London), LIBRARY OF CONGRESS.

Library of Congress, public, national library of US, at Washington DC, estab. 1800. Act of 1870 provided that a copy of any book copyrighted in US must be deposited in it. Library of Congress catalogue number is given to every book published in US.

Libreville, cap. of Gabon, on estuary of R. Gabon. Pop. 73,000. Port, exports timber, palm oil; commercial, admin. centre. Founded (1848) by freed slaves.

Libya

Libya, republic of N Africa. Area 1,759,500 sq km (679,350 sq mi); pop. 2,257,000; cap. Tripoli. Language: Arabic. Religion: Islam. Fertile coastal strip; interior mainly desert (Libyan, Sahara) with some oases. Grain, fruit growing; major producer of oil, natural gas. Under Turkish rule from 16th cent.; taken by Italy 1912. Scene of heavy fighting in WWII; under Franco-British military govt., then UN rule, 1943-51. Federal kingdom of Libya estab. 1951, comprising Cyrenaica, Fezzan, Tripolitania provs.; unitary state from 1963. Republic proclaimed (1969) after military coup.

lichee, see LITCHI.

Lichen

lichen, any of large group (Lichenes) of dual plants composed of a particular alga (blue-green or green) and particular fungus growing in SYMBIOSIS. The algal cells manufacture food sugars while the fungus forms a protective shell. Typically greyish-green, grows on rocks or trees from Arctic to tropical regions.

Lichfield, mun. bor. of Staffordshire, WC England. Pop. 23,000. Has 13th cent. cathedral with 3 spires. Home of Samuel Johnson.

Lichtenstein, Roy (1923-), American painter, sculptor. A leading exponent of pop art, uses subjects of commercial art and its techniques, *eg* magnification of coarsely screened picture to bring out round dots and primary colours. Works incl. *Whaam!,* based on comic strips.

licorice, *see* LIQUORICE.

Liddell Hart, Sir Basil Henry (1895-1970), British military historian and strategist. Wrote official training manuals and histories of WWI and II. He was an early advocate of air power and mechanized warfare, greatly influencing German planning before WWII.

Lidice, village of W Czechoslovakia. Wholly destroyed in Nazi massacre after assassination of local Nazi leader (1942). Rebuilt after war.

Lie, Trygve Halvdan (1896-1968), Norwegian statesman. First secretary-general of the UN (1946-53). Denounced by Communist bloc for supporting UN action in Korea.

Liebermann, Max (1847-1935), German painter. Influential in introducing impressionism into Germany, he turned from academic genre scenes to painting in a lighter, more atmospheric manner. His subjects were scenes of outdoor life.

Liebig, Justus von (1803-73), German chemist. Developed methods of quantitative organic analysis. Pioneer of chemical methods in physiology and agric., he experimented in use of artificial fertilizers.

Liebknecht, Wilhelm (1826-1900), German politician. In exile in England (1849-62), where he was influenced by Marx. Founded (with August Bebel) German Social Democratic Labour Party (1869). His son, **Karl Liebknecht** (1871-1919), formed communist Spartacus party (1916). Imprisoned for anti-war demonstrations (1916-18); on release led, with Rosa LUXEMBURG, Spartacist insurrection against Social Democratic govt. Killed after arrest by army officers.

Liechtenstein

Liechstenstein, independent principality of WC Europe, in Rhaetian Alps. Area 166 sq km (64 sq mi); pop. 21,000; cap. Vaduz. Language: German. Religion: RC. Cereals, wine; tourism. Created 1719 from union of Vaduz, Schellenberg countships; independent 1866; joined Swiss customs union 1923.

Liège (Flem. *Luik*), city of E Belgium, on R. Meuse and Albert Canal, cap. of Liège prov. Pop. 150,000. Coal region; machinery, arms mfg.; univ. (1817). Centre of Walloon culture.

Liegnitz, *see* LEGNICA, Poland.

Liepaja (Ger. *Libau*), town of USSR, on Baltic coast of Latvian SSR. Pop. 88,000. Ice-free seaport; exports timber; steel, paper mfg. Passed to Russia 1795; became important emigration port in 19th cent.

Lifar, Serge (1905-), Russian ballet dancer. Joined Diaghilev's Ballets Russes (1923); created title role in Prokofiev's *Prodigal Son* and choreographed Stravinsky's *Renard* (1929). Principal dancer and ballet-master at Paris Opéra (1947-58); had important influence on French ballet.

Liffey, river of E Irish Republic, flows 80 km (50 mi) from Wicklow Mountains via Dublin to Dublin Bay; 3 power stations on river.

Lifford, co. town of Donegal, N Irish Republic, on R. Foyle. Pop. 1000.

ligament, short band of tough fibrous tissue connecting 2 bones at a joint, or holding an organ, *eg* liver, spleen, in position.

Ligeti, György (1923-), Hungarian composer. Works, *eg Atmosphères,* use masses of intricate detail to produce overall blend of sound.

light, electromagnetic radiation which is detectable by the eye; variation in its wavelength produces sensation of colour. According to quantum theory, light consists of discrete bundles of energy (photons) and the energy of each photon is proportional to frequency of the light. In this theory, light exhibits both wave-like and particle-like properties.

Lighthouse off Land's End

lighthouse, structure in or adjacent to navigable waters, equipped to give optical or, more recently, radio-electrical guidance to ships (*see* RADIO RANGE). Identified by characteristic light flashes, fog sirens, radio signals. Now largely automatic.

lightning, electrical discharge in the atmosphere. May be from one part of cloud to another, from cloud to cloud, or from cloud to Earth. Types incl. forked, sheet lightning; both are accompanied by thunder. Much rarer ball lightning sometimes seen as moving luminous ball, which may disintegrate explosively.

light year, distance travelled by light in 1 year; equals c 9.46×10^{12} km (5.88×10^{12} mi). Measure of distance in astronomy.

lignite or **brown coal,** soft, brownish-black fossil fuel intermediate between peat and COAL. Has low carbon content, burns with smoky flame and has low heat-producing capacity. Dates mainly from Carboniferous period and later.

lignum vitae, hard wood of tropical American evergreen trees of genus *Guaiacum.* Used for pulleys, chopping boards; contains resin used medicinally.

Liguria, region of NW Italy, cap. Genoa. Alps in W, Apennines in E, Italian Riviera in S. Olives, vines, fruit, flowers; shipbuilding, chemicals. Celtic inhabitants conquered by Romans 2nd cent. BC; dominated by Genoa in Middle Ages; annexed by Sardinia 1815.

Ligurian Sea, arm of Mediterranean Sea, between Liguria, Tuscany, and Corsica. Incl. Gulf of Genoa; Italian Riviera on N shores.

Li Hung-chang (1823-1901), Chinese statesman. Fought with General Gordon in suppression of Taiping Rebellion (1861-4). Directed foreign affairs for Empress Tzu Hsi. Negotiated treaty ending Sino-Japanese War (1895).

Likasi, city of SE Zaïre. Formerly called Jadotville. Pop. 146,000. Centre of Katanga cobalt and copper production; mineral refining.

Lilac

lilac, any of genus *Syringa* of trees or shrubs of olive family, esp. *S. vulgaris* native to Europe and Asia. Has cone-shaped clusters of blue, pink or white fragrant flowers and very hard wood.

Lilburne, John (*c* 1614-57), English politician. After resigning from position of lieutenant-colonel in army (1645), he devoted himself to pamphleteering on behalf of the LEVELLERS. Frequently imprisoned for political beliefs.

Lilienthal, Otto (1848-96), German aeronaut. Built glider in which he made *c* 2000 flights. Killed when it crashed.

Lilith, Jewish female demon, prob. derived from Babylonian fertility goddess Ninlil. In some traditions, 1st wife of Adam; later folklore makes her a vampire child-killer.

Lille, city of N France, cap. of Nord dept. Pop. 191,000. Forms conurbation with Roubaix, Tourcoing; major textile mfg., engineering centre; coalfield nearby. Cap. of French Flanders from 1668. Citadel, 17th cent. Bourse, art gallery, univ. (1808). Birthplace of De Gaulle.

Lillehammer, town of SE Norway, on L. Mjösa. Pop. 20,000. Tourist and commercial centre for Gudbrandsdal. Open-air museum.

Lillie, Beatrice (1898-), English comedian, b. Canada. Known in revues, on radio, television.

Lilongwe, cap. of Malawi. Pop. 20,000. Admin. centre, agric. coll. Founded 1947; has replaced Zomba as cap.

lily, any of genus *Lilium* of perennial, bulbous plants. Native to N temperate zones. Showy, trumpet-shaped flowers. Species incl. white madonna lily, *L. candidum.* Name also used for many unrelated lily-like flowers esp. of AMARYLLIS genus.

lily of the valley, *Convallaria majalis,* perennial plant of lily family. Native to Europe, N Asia and US. Dark green leaves with bellshaped, fragrant, white flowers.

lilytrotter, see JACANA.

Lima, cap. of Peru, with Pacific port at Callao. Pop. 2,416,000. Commercial, indust. centre; oil refining, textile mfg. Founded by Pizarro (1535), centre of Spanish colonial power in South America until 19th cent. Has numerous churches, cathedral, colonial buildings; San Marcos Univ., founded 1551, is oldest univ. on continent.

lima bean, *Phaseolus limensis,* annual fast-climbing plant, native to South America. Cultivated for broad, flat, edible seed used as vegetable.

Limassol, port of S Cyprus. Pop. 52,000. Exports grapes, raisins, wine. Tourist resort.

Limavady, dist. of NW Northern Ireland. Area 589 sq km (228 sq mi); pop. 23,000. Created 1973, formerly part of Co. Londonderry.

Limbe, see BLANTYRE, Malawi.

Limbo, in some Christian theologies, region bordering on hell, where unbaptized children and righteous people who lived before Jesus dwell after death.

Limbourg, Pol de (active *c* 1400 - *c* 1416), Franco-Flemish miniature painter. With his 2 brothers, worked for Duke of Berri, for whom they produced famous manuscript *Très Riches Heures du Duc de Berri* in International Gothic style.

Limburg (Fr. *Limbourg*), regions of NE Belgium and SE Netherlands. Coalmining in Campine, agric. Former duchy, divided 1648 between United and Spanish Netherlands. Present division dates from 1839; prov. caps. Hasselt (Belgium), Maastricht (Netherlands).

lime or **linden,** any of genus *Tilia* of tall deciduous trees native to N temperate regions. Heart-shaped leaves, white fragrant flowers. Common lime, *T. europaea,* yields white-wood used in furniture. Also, small, thorny, semitropical tree, *Citrus aurantifolia,* bearing small, lemon-shaped, greenish-yellow citrus fruit rich in vitamin C.

lime, quicklime or **calcium oxide** (CaO), white solid made by heating calcium carbonate (limestone). Combines with water to form calcium hydroxide (slaked lime). Used to make mortar, cement and to neutralize acidic soil.

Limerick (*Luimneach*), county of Munster prov., SW Irish Republic. Area 2686 sq km (1037 sq mi); pop. 140,000. Galty Mountains in SE; has part of fertile Golden Vale. Agric., salmon fishing. Co. town **Limerick,** on Shannon estuary. Pop. 57,000. Port, shipbuilding; tanning, curing industs. Once cap. of Munster kingdom. Norman castle; Protestant, RC cathedrals; site of Treaty (1691) after siege by William III of England.

limerick, humorous, usually epigrammatic poem of 5 lines of mixed iambic and anapestic metre with rhyme scheme aabba. Popularized by Edward Lear *c* 1820.

limestone, sedimentary rock composed wholly or mainly of calcium carbonate. Formed from remains of marine organisms, *eg* shells, skeletons, by chemical precipitation, or by mechanical deposition. Varieties incl. chalk, dolomite, marble; used as building stone, in lime and cement mfg.

Lim Fjord, shallow str. of N Jutland, Denmark. Links North Sea with Kattegat; many isls.

Limoges, city of C France, on R. Vienne, cap. of Haute-Vienne dept. Pop. 133,000. Enamelling indust. (estab. 13th cent.); porcelain mfg. (estab. 18th cent.) using local kaolin. Hist. cap. of Limousin. Sacked (1370) by Black Prince. Cathedral (13th cent.), ceramics museum, univ.

limonite, iron ore mineral, any of several mixtures of iron oxides and iron hydroxides. Normally brownish with yellow streak; formed by weathering of iron-rich minerals. Types incl. gossan, bog iron ore, ochre. Used as source of ochre pigment, iron.

limpet, marine gastropod mollusc with flattened cone-shaped shell. Uses fleshy foot to adhere to rocks. Used for bait and food.

Limpopo or **Crocodile,** river of SE Africa. Flows *c* 1600 km (1000 mi) from Transvaal, South Africa to Indian Ocean in SE Mozambique. Forms part of South Africa-Botswana border, all of South Africa-Rhodesia border.

Linacre, Thomas (*c* 1460-1524), English humanist, physician. Founder of Royal College of Physicians (1518); instituted lectureships at Oxford and Cambridge. Translated works of Greek physician Galen into Latin.

Abraham Lincoln

Lincoln, Abraham (1809-65), American statesman, president (1861-5). Gained prominence in campaign for senatorship for Illinois during debates with STEPHEN DOUGLAS on slavery issue. Elected president shortly before secession of Southern states and outbreak of CIVIL WAR. Tenure marked by conflicts over policies, but he eventually acquired almost dictatorial control. Morally justified Union cause with EMANCIPATION PROCLAMATION freeing slaves and GETTYSBURG ADDRESS (1863). After re-election (1864), opposed by Republican radicals for policy seeming to favour leniency towards the South. Assassinated (April, 1865) by John Wilkes Booth.

Lincoln, cap. of Nebraska, US. Pop. 150,000. In prairie region; industs. incl. food processing, flour milling. Important insurance centre. Became cap. 1867.

Lincolnshire, county of E England. Area 5885 sq km (2272 sq mi); pop. 513,000. Wolds in E; Fens in S; elsewhere fertile lowland. Agric., livestock; fishing; iron, steel industs. Co. town **Lincoln,** on R. Witham. Pop. 74,000. Agric. processing, machinery. Was Roman *Lindum;* 11th cent. cathedral with 'Great Tom' bell.

Lincoln's Inn, *see* INNS OF COURT.

Lind, Jenny (1820-87), Swedish soprano, known as the 'Swedish Nightingale'. Abandoned early career in opera for the concert platform, and toured widely with enormous success. Settled in England, becoming singing teacher at Royal Coll. of Music (1883).

Lindbergh, Charles Augustus (1902-74), American aviator. Made 1st solo transatlantic, non-stop flight (1927). His son died (1932) in prominent kidnapping. Criticized for isolationist speeches before US entry into WWII.

linden, *see* LIME.

Lindisfarne or **Holy Island,** off Northumberland, NE England. Causeway to mainland. Monastery estab. 635 by St Aidan; priory (1083); Lindisfarne Gospels (7th cent.) now in British Museum.

Lindsay, [Nicholas] Vachel (1879-1931), American poet. Attempted to find distinctively American rhythm drawing on folk tales, ballads. Works incl. *General William Booth Enters into Heaven* (1913), *The Congo* (1914), 'In Praise of Johnny Appleseed' (1921).

Lindsey, Parts of, former admin. county of Lincolnshire, E England. Co. town was Lincoln.

Line Islands, group of coral isls. in C Pacific Ocean. Christmas, Fanning, Washington isls. part of Gilbert and Ellice Isls. colony. Kingman Reef, Jarvis, Palmyra isls. admin. by US. Remainder disputed by US, UK.

linen, fabric made from fibre of FLAX plant. Uneven texture, durable and crisp. Introduced to N Europe by Romans, widely used in Middle Ages. Ireland is chief producer of fabric; Belgium produces finest fibre.

ling, large edible fish of cod family. Common ling, *Molva molva,* found in European waters. Name also applied to burbot.

lingam, phallic symbol used in worship of Hindu god Siva. *See* YONI.

lingua franca, spoken language allowing communication between people of mutually unintelligible languages. Originally applied to hybrid language (incl. Turkish, French, Spanish, Arabic elements) used by traders in E Mediterranean. Modern examples incl. use of Latin in RC church and French by diplomats.

linguistics, science of LANGUAGE, concerned both with its structure (synchronic analysis) and its hist. development (diachronic). In 19th cent., comparative philology estab. generic relations between languages, *eg* Indo-European family. SAUSSURE developed structural, synchronic approach to language which has subsequently predominated. *See* CHOMSKY, PHONETICS, SEMANTICS.

Linklater, Eric Robert Russell (1899-1974), Scottish novelist. Works incl. picaresque *Juan in America* (1931), *Ripeness is All* (1935), short stories, *Sealskin Trousers* (1947).

Linköping, town of SE Sweden. Pop. 77,000. Railway jct., engineering; textiles; tobacco. Romanesque-Gothic cathedral (13th cent.).

Linlithgow, town of Lothian region, EC Scotland. Pop. 6000. Former royal burgh and co. town of West Lothian. Paper mfg., whisky distilling. Has ruined palace, birthplace of Mary Queen of Scots.

Linnaeus

Linnaeus, Carolus, orig. Karl von Linné (1707-78), Swedish taxonomist. Estab. binomial nomenclature principle of botanical classification in *Species plantarum* (1753). *Systema naturae* (1758) extends system to animals.

linnet, *Acanthis cannabina,* small songbird of finch family, found in open countryside of Europe and W Asia.

linotype, typesetting machine, patented (1884) by Ottmar Mergenthaler (1854-99). Operated by keyboard, it composes an entire line of type in one metal bar or slug.

Lin Piao (1908-71), Chinese military and political leader. Became defence minister (1959). Ranked second to Mao Tse-tung in Communist Party hierarchy; considered Mao's political successor. Said to have died in mysterious plane crash in Mongolia; may have been removed in party purge.

linseed, seed of common FLAX plant which yields an oil used in paint, varnish and linoleum. After oil extraction, residue is used in cattle feed as linseed cake.

Linz, city of N Austria, on R. Danube, cap. of Upper Austria prov. Pop. 203,000. River port; produces iron, steel, machinery. Roman *Lentia;* prov. cap. in Holy Roman Empire. Neo-Gothic cathedral (1924).

Lion

lion, *Panthera leo,* large carnivore of cat family; once widespread, now found in Africa S of Sahara and NW India. Yellow to brown in colour; male usually has black or tawny mane. Social, lives in group called pride. Hunts zebras, wildebeeste, *etc*; old or wounded animals may attack man.

Lions, Gulf of (*Golfe du Lion*), bay of Mediterranean Sea, extending from NE Spain to Toulon (S France).

Lipari Islands or **Aeolian Islands**, isl. group of SW Italy, in Tyrrhenian Sea. Incl. active volcanoes (Stromboli, Vulcano). Exports pumice stone, wine. Traditional home of Aeolus, the wind god.

Lipchitz, Jacques (1891-1973), French sculptor, b. Lithuania. Early work was in cubist style; in 1920s became interested in open forms and evolved a 'transparent' style. Settled in US after 1941.

Lipetsk, city of USSR, WC European RSFSR. Pop. 312,000. Iron-mining centre; steel, tractor mfg. Health resort, with mineral springs.

Lippe, river of NW West Germany. Flows *c* 240 km (150 mi) via Hamm to R. Rhine at Wesel. Agric. region with deciduous forests.

Lippi, Fra Filippo (*c* 1406-69), Italian painter. Master of colour and line, as shown in *Coronation of the Virgin*; masterpiece is fresco series in the choir of Prato Cathedral (1452-*c* 1465). His son, **Filippino Lippi** (*c* 1457-1504), was also a Florentine painter. Work incl. frescoes in Florence and Rome.

Lippmann, Gabriel (1845-1921), French physicist. Discovered a method of photographic colour reproduction, for which he was awarded Nobel Prize for Physics (1908).

liquefaction of gases, process of changing gases to liquid state. Gases can be liquefied by application of pressure provided their CRITICAL TEMPERATURE is not exceeded. Methods of cooling gas incl. Joule-Thomson effect, in which gas loses temperature by expanding through porous plug.

liquid, state of matter intermediate between gas and solid. In a liquid, molecules are free to move with respect to each other but are restricted by cohesive forces from unlimited expansion as in a gas.

liquorice or **licorice,** dried root of leguminous plant, *Glycyrrhiza glabra,* of Europe and Asia. Used in confectionery and medicine.

Lisbon (*Lisboa*), cap. of Portugal, at mouth of R. Tagus. Pop. 1,034,000. Indust., commercial centre; port, exports wine, olive oil, cork. Taken from Moors 1147; cap. from 1260. Rebuilt after 1755 earthquake; floods 1967. Univ. (1290), Hieronymite monastery; Salazar suspension bridge (1966).

Lisburn, town of W Northern Ireland, on R. Lagan. Pop. 29,000. In former Co. Antrim. Linen mfg. Has 17th cent. Protestant cathedral. **Lisburn,** district; area 447 sq km (172 sq mi); pop. 73,000. Created 1973, formerly part of Cos. Antrim, Down.

Lisieux, town of Normandy, N France. Pop. 25,000. Textile mfg., dairy trade. Shrine of St Thérèse is a place of pilgrimage.

Lismore, town of Co. Waterford, S Irish Republic, on R. Blackwater. Pop. 900. Monastery founded 7th cent., medieval ecclesiastical centre. Castle (1185); Protestant, RC cathedrals.

Lismore, isl. of Strathclyde region, W Scotland, at mouth of Loch Linnhe. Has restored 13th cent. cathedral. Gaelic poetry collection made here 16th cent.

List, Friedrich (1789-1846), German economist. Imprisoned for advocating reform while professor at Univ. of Tübingen. Works, *eg The National System of Political Economy* (1840) advocated commercial association of German states.

Lister, Joseph, 1st Baron Lister (1827-1912), English surgeon. Founded antiseptic surgery; used carbolic acid (1865) and heat to sterilize instruments to prevent septic infection of wounds. Introduced many surgical techniques, incl. absorbable ligature and drainage tube.

Liszt, Franz (1811-86), Hungarian pianist, composer. Foremost pianist of his time; protégés incl. Wagner, who married his daughter Cosima. His music is highly romantic and incl. many virtuoso piano pieces, *eg* 'Hungarian Rhapsodies', as well as songs, choral and orchestral music (esp.

Joseph Lister

Franz Liszt

symphonic poems). Took minor religious orders (1865), becoming known as Abbé Liszt.

Li Tai Po or **Li Po** (*c* 700-62), Chinese poet. Wrote great number of poems (mostly lost) celebrating natural beauty, wisdom found in drunkenness, rejection of duty, preferment. According to tradition died trying to embrace reflection of moon in river.

litchi, lychee or **lichee,** *Litchi chinensis,* Chinese tree, now grown in Florida and California. Cultivated for pulpy fruit enclosed in thin, brittle shell.

literature, all writings in prose or verse, esp. those of imaginative or critical character, often distinguished from scientific writing, news reporting, *etc*. Sometimes denotes only such writings considered to be of permanent value, but use can be extended to incl. printed matter of any kind, *eg* campaign leaflets, promotional material, or to writings in particular subject area, *eg* medical literature. Historically chief vehicle for transmitting and conserving culture of society, enabling much more complex and complete records to be kept than society relying on oral, pictorial transmission. CHINESE LITERATURE prob. 1st in world. In West literature founded on writings of Greeks, Romans.

lithium (Li), soft metallic element, lightest metal known; at. no. 3, at. wt. 6.94. Chemically similar to sodium, but less active. Used in alloys; compounds used in nuclear research.

lithography, process of printing from a flat stone or metallic plate. Design is applied to surface with greasy material and surface is then wetted. Greasy ink is applied and is absorbed by greasy parts of surface but repelled by wet parts. Prints are then taken from the surface. Most modern lithography is offset, design being transferred from metal plate to rubber-covered cylinder, then to the paper.

Lithuanian, *see* BALTIC.

Lithuanian Soviet Socialist Republic, constituent republic of W USSR. Area *c* 65,200 sq km (25,200 sq mi); pop.3,129,000; cap. Vilnius. Largely flatland, drained by R. Neman; formerly mainly agric., indust. development from 1940. In 13th cent. was grand duchy formed to oppose Teutonic knights; became powerful and expanded in 14th cent. Merged with Poland (1569); passed to Russia after Polish partition (1795). Independent (1918-40) until incorporated into USSR.

litmus, colouring matter obtained from various lichens. Used as acid-base indicator in chemical analysis; acids turn it red, bases blue.

litre, unit of liquid capacity in metric system. Originally defined as volume occupied by 1 kilogram of water at 4° C; now defined as 1000 cubic cm; 1 litre = *c* 1.76 pints.

Little Belt, *see* BELT, GREAT and LITTLE, Denmark.

Little Bighorn, *see* BIGHORN.

Little Rock, cap. of Arkansas, US; on Arkansas R. Pop. 132,000. Commercial centre; cotton, bauxite, coal trade centre; clothing mfg. Federal troops enforced school integration (1957) during race riots.

Liuchow, city of Kwangsi auton. region, S China. Pop. *c* 250,000. Paper, steel, textiles mfg.

Liu Shao-chi (*c* 1898-*c* 1974), Chinese political leader. Chairman of Chinese People's Republic (1959-68), he was heavily criticized for revisionism during Cultural Revolution (1966-9) and removed from all political offices in 1968.

liver, large gland of vertebrates. In man, opens off beginning of small intestine. Functions incl. formation and secretion of bile, storage of glucose in form of glycogen, synthesis of blood proteins, storage of iron, and breakdown of haemoglobin from worn-out red blood cells.

Liverpool, Robert Banks Jenkinson, 2nd Earl of (1770-1828), British statesman, PM (1812-27). Early years of his Tory admin. were marked by introduction of Corn Laws and repressive measures against unrest (1815-20). Later took more liberal line, repealing anti-trade union laws. Abolished sinecures, took moderate line on Catholic Emancipation issue.

Liverpool, city of Merseyside met. county, NW England, on R. Mersey. Pop. 607,000. Major seaport; indust. centre; road tunnel to Birkenhead. Has Anglican, RC cathedrals; univ. (1903).

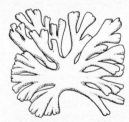

Liverwort (Riccia frostii)

liverwort, any plant of class Hepaticae of flowerless, moss-like plants. Grows on moist ground or tree-trunks. *Marchantia* and *Riccia* are 2 common genera. Name is also applied to unrelated flowering plants of buttercup family of genus *Hepatica*.

Livingstone, David (1813-73), Scottish missionary and explorer. Journeyed extensively in C and S Africa; believed in ending slave trade by estab. Christianity and legitimate commerce in its place. Reached L. Ngami (1849), R. Zambezi (1851); led 3 expeditions, discovering Victoria

David Livingstone

Falls (1855), L. Nyasa (1859). Set out (1866) to seek Nile's source; met by H.M. Stanley at Ujiji (1871). Wrote *Missionary Travels* (1857).

Livingstone, town of S Zambia, on R. Zambezi near Victoria Falls. Pop. 52,000. Tourist, commercial and trade centre. Cap. of Northern Rhodesia 1911-35. Livingstone-Rhodes museum. Renamed Maramba 1972.

Livonia, region of NE Europe, comprising modern Estonian SSR and N Latvian SSR. Conquered by Livonian Brothers of the Sword in 13th cent., later disputed by Sweden, Russia and Poland; ceded to Russia in 1721.

Livorno, *see* LEGHORN, Italy.

Livy, full name Titus Livius (59BC–AD17), Roman historian. Wrote *History of Rome* in 142 volumes, covering period from arrival of Aeneas to death of Drusus (9BC). Only 35 volumes survive, with summaries of others. Sacrificed accuracy for patriotic effect, but works are noted for style.

lizard, reptile of suborder Lacertilia, incl. gecko, iguana, monitor. Scaly skin, long body and tail; usually 4-legged, but some species legless, *eg* snake-like slow-worm.

Lizard Point, headland of Cornwall, SW England. Most S point in England.

Ljubljana (Ger. *Laibach*), city of NW Yugoslavia, on R. Sava, cap. of Slovenia. Pop. 174,000. Cultural, indust. centre; univ. (1595). Under Habsburgs from 1277; cap. of Austrian Illyria 1816-49, of Carniola until 1918.

llama, *Lama peruana*, South American hoofed mammal of camel family. Humpless, stands *c* 1.2 m/4 ft high. Used as pack animal and for wool, meat. Vicuña and guanaco are related species.

Llandrindod Wells, urban dist. of Powys, C Wales. Pop. 3000. Spa resort from 17th cent.

Llandudno, urban dist. of Gwynedd, N Wales. Pop. 19,000. Seaside resort.

Llanelli, mun. bor. of Dyfed, S Wales, on Carmarthen Bay. Pop. 26,000. Exports coal; indust. centre, esp. tinplate mfg.

Llanfairpwll (gwyngyllgogerchwyrndrobwlltysiliogogogoch), village of Gwynedd, NW Wales, in Anglesey. Longest UK placename.

Llanos, prairie of C Venezuela and E Colombia, in Orinoco basin. In famous cattle-raising region.

Llewelyn ap Gruffydd (d. 1281), prince of North Wales. Succeeded his uncle as ruler (1246). Recovered much of South and North Wales during Barons' War in England; recognized as prince of Wales (1267). Lost most of his lands in invasion of Edward I (1277).

Lleyn Peninsula, penin. of Gwynedd, NW Wales, W of Snowdonia. Main town Pwllheli. Pastoral region; fishing.

Lloyd, Harold (1893-1971), American silent film comedian. Famous as timid, bespectacled victim of accidents, hair-raising stunts in many two-reelers. Full-length films incl. *The Freshman* (1925).

Lloyd, Marie, pseud. of Matilda Alice Victoria Wood (1870-1922), English music-hall entertainer. Popularized songs 'Oh, Mr Porter!', 'My Old Man Said Follow the Van'.

Lloyd George: drawing by Max Beerbohm

Lloyd George, David, 1st Earl Lloyd-George of Dwyfor (1863-1945), British statesman, PM (1916-22). Liberal chancellor of the exchequer (1908-15). Rejection by House of Lords of his 1909 budget, seeking to finance old-age pensions, led to Parliament Act (1911) curtailing power of Lords; also introduced health and unemployment insurance (*see* NATIONAL INSURANCE ACT). As PM of wartime coalition, unified Allied war command; worked with Clemenceau and Wilson to draw up TREATY OF VERSAILLES (1919). Achieved victory in 1918 election, but reliance on Conservatives led to disintegration of his support. Remained in Parliament until 1944.

Lloyd's, association of English insurance underwriters, originally covering marine risks only, now issuing many types of insurance policy. Name derived from the coffee house, kept by Edward Lloyd in 18th cent., used as meeting place. *Lloyd's Register of Shipping* is annual publication detailing information on world shipping.

loach, any of Cobitidae family of small freshwater fish with several barbels around mouth. Found in Europe, Asia, N Africa. Species incl. stone loach, *Nemacheilus barbatula*.

loam, type of soil, composed of sand, silt, clay and humus. Porous, retains moisture well, has good air circulation. Easily worked and fertile.

Lobachevski, Nikolai Ivanovich (1793-1856), Russian mathematician. Independently of Gauss and Bolyai, discovered a form of non-Euclidean geometry. Works incl. *Pangéométrie* (1855).

lobelia, genus of annual or perennial plants of bellflower family. Native to temperate regions. Small, rounded leaves with blue, red, yellow or white irregular flowers.

Lobito, town of W Angola, on Atlantic Ocean. Pop. 98,000. Port, built mainly on reclaimed land, exports minerals, coffee, maize. Terminus of trans-African railway from Mozambique, completed 1929.

Lob Nor, *see* LOP NOR.

Lobos or **Seal Islands,** group of small isls. off NW Peru. Have valuable guano deposits.

lobotomy, surgical operation to treat certain severe psychoses. Consists of severing fibres between prefrontal lobes and rest of brain. Devised by Portuguese physician Egas Moniz (1874-1955) who shared Nobel Prize for Physiology and Medicine (1949).

lobster, edible marine crustacean of Homaridae family with 5 pairs of jointed legs, 1st pair having pincer-like jaws. Greenish or grey when alive, turns red when boiled. Species incl. common European lobster, *Homarus vulgaris*.

lobworm, *see* LUGWORM.

Locarno, town of S Switzerland, on L. Maggiore. Pop. 14,000. Tourism. Locarno Conference (1925) guaranteed post-WWI territ. boundaries.

Locarno Pact, series of treaties concluded among European nations (1925) at Locarno, Switzerland, guaranteeing German borders in W, as designated by Treaty of Versailles (1919). Germany also agreed to demilitarize Rhineland and was promised League of Nations membership. Chief architects of Pact were Stresemann, Briand and Austen Chamberlain.

John Locke

Locke, John (1632-1704), English philosopher. Leading empiricist, wrote *Essay concerning Human Understanding* (1690), holding knowledge to be based on sense experience, not innate ideas. Opposed Hobbes in belief in equality of men and happiness of original natural state. *Two Treatises on Government* (1689) influenced framers of US Constitution.

Lockhart, John Gibson (1794-1854), Scottish editor, biographer. Editor of *Quarterly Review* (1825-53). Known for vicious reviews of Keats's work, uncritical lives of Burns (1828) and father-in-law Scott (1837).

lockjaw, *see* TETANUS.

lockout, refusal by employers to allow employees to come in to work until they agree to employers' terms. Famous example is lockout of British coalminers by mine owners which provoked General Strike (1926).

Lockyer, Sir Joseph Norman (1836-1920), English astronomer. Pioneer of spectroscopic analysis of solar prominences and sunspots. Discovered helium in Sun (1868) before its discovery on Earth.

Locomotive: *The Flying Scotsman*

locomotive, powered vehicle designed to push or pull railway train. First practical example built by Trevithick (1804); other early models incl. Stephenson's *Rocket* (1829), Cooper's *Tom Thumb* (1830), all with steam as driving force. Electric locomotives (introduced *c* 1895) obtain power from 3rd rail or overhead wire. Diesel electric locomotives (*c* 1925), in which electric generator is driven by diesel engine, have extensively replaced steam locomotives.

Swarm of locusts in Africa

locust, insect of short-horned grasshopper family (Acrididae). Often migrates in swarms, devastating large areas of crops. Species incl. migratory locust, *Locusta migratoria,* of Africa and S Asia.

Lodge, Henry Cabot (1850-1924), American politician. Republican senator for Massachusetts (1893-1924), he led opposition to America's joining the League of Nations.

Lodi, town of Lombardy, N Italy, on R. Adda. Pop. 39,000. Dairying centre; linen, silk mfg. Scene of battle (1796) in which Napoleon defeated Austrians.

Lódź, city of C Poland, cap. of Lódź prov. Pop. 764,000. Major textile centre; electrical, metal industs.; univ. (1945). Village until *c* 1830; rapid growth based on weaving indust. Under Russian rule 1815-1919.

loess, fine-grained, yellowish soil transported and deposited by wind. Originates as dust from arid areas or margins of ice-sheets; forms porous, well-graded, very fertile soils. Major deposits in N China, C Europe, C US. With high humus content, forms BLACK EARTH soils of USSR.

Lofoten Islands, isl. group of NW Norway, incl. Vesteralen Isls. Within Arctic Circle; chief town Svolvaer. Rich cod, herring fisheries.

Logan, Sir William Edmond (1798-1875), Canadian geologist. Working in Wales, discovered answer to origin of coal. Head of Geological Survey of Canada (1843-69); became authority on Precambrian geology, esp. of Laurentian Shield.

Logan, Mount, in St Elias Mts., SW Yukon, Canada. Highest mountain in Canada rising to 6050 m (19,850 ft).

loganberry, hybrid BLACKBERRY, *Rubus loganobaccus,* developed from American blackberry and raspberry. Acid, purplish-red fruit.

logarithm, power to which a given number b (base of logarithm) must be raised to produce that number; thus if $b^n = c$, n is said to be logarithm of c to base b, written $\log_b c$. Tables of logarithms used extensively to reduce problems in multiplication and division to easier problems in addition and subtraction; base of common logarithms is 10. Invented by John Napier.

loggerhead, *Caretta caretta,* large-headed carnivorous sea turtle.

logic, the science of correct reasoning. Aristotle founded systematic logic using SYLLOGISM and deductive method (reasoning from general to particular). His system still finds general acceptance, although attacked by medieval nominalists who argued that logic merely reflects structure of mind, not reality. Formal logic is not to be confused with truth as it requires no reference to content. More recent

developments have been made by *eg* Boole, Russell, Wittgenstein.

logical positivism, modern school of philosophy which believes that the work of the philosopher is to clarify concepts rather than to make metaphysical speculations. Holds that for a proposition to be meaningful, it must be scientifically testable. Originated in Vienna Circle of 1920s. Exponents incl. Carnap, WITTGENSTEIN. *See* POSITIVISM.

logistics, branch of military operations concerned with supply and maintenance of equipment. Strategic implications involve personnel movement, evacuation and hospitalization.

logos (Gk.,=word), in Greek philosophy, any immanent ordering principle in universe. In Christian theology, the link between God and man manifested in God's word becoming flesh in Jesus. Specifically stated in St John's Gospel.

Lohengrin, in medieval German legend, knight of HOLY GRAIL who is led by a swan to save Princess Elsa from an unwanted suitor. Story is basis of Wagner's opera (1850).

Loire, longest river of France. Flows *c* 1005 km (625 mi) from Cévennes Mts. via Orléans, Tours, Nantes to Bay of Biscay at St Nazaire. With tributaries, incl. Allier, Cher, Vienne, drains much of France; limited navigation, seasonal flooding. Loire valley famous for wines and hist. châteaux.

Loki, in Norse myth, personification of evil and trickery. Constantly warred against gods of Asgard. It was prophesied he would cause their final downfall.

Lolland, *see* LAALAND, Denmark.

Lollards, followers of JOHN WYCLIFFE. Sect in England who anticipated some Reformation doctrines, *eg* the individual's direct responsibility to God, use of vernacular Bible as only reliable guide to faith. Attacked ecclesiastical wealth and monasticism; denied transubstantiation. Their persecution led to a minor rebellion in 1414, but movement had declined by 16th cent.

Lombardo, Pietro (*c* 1435-1515), Italian artist. He and his 2 sons were leading sculptors and architects in Venice. Executed many tombs, incl. that of Doge Pietro Mocenigo and Dante's tomb in Ravenna. Also responsible for church of Santa Maria dei Miracoli.

Lombards, Germanic people who originally inhabited lower basin of the Elbe. Under ALBOIN, invaded N Italy (568) and estab. kingdom of Lombardy. After threatening the power of the popes, they were conquered by Charlemagne, who took control of Italy.

Lombardy, region of N Italy, cap. Milan. Mountains, lakes, Alpine passes in N; tourism, h.e.p. Lombard Plain (Po basin) in S; irrigated agric. esp. maize, wheat, rice, flax; dairying. Italy's main indust. area, esp. textiles, chemicals, iron and steel. Taken by Romans 3rd cent. BC, by Charlemagne 774. Cities formed Lombard League in 12th cent., defeated Frederick I at Legnano (1176). Later ruled by Spain, France, Austria; annexed 1859 by Sardinia.

Lombok, isl. of Indonesia, in Lesser Sundas. Area *c* 4700 sq km (1800 sq mi). Wallace's Line marking division between fauna of Orient and Australia passes through Lombok.

Lombroso, Cesare (1835-1909), Italian criminologist, physician. Known for theory of criminal 'type', distinguishable by physical features. Wrote *L'uomo deliquente* (1889).

Lomé, cap. of Togo, on Bight of Benin. Pop. 193,000. Port, exports cocoa, coffee, copra; univ. of Benin (1970).

Loménie de Brienne, Etienne Charles (1727-94), French politician, churchman. Became Louis XVI's minister of finance (1787); opposition to his tax reforms led to calling of Estates-General (1789). Made a cardinal on retiring from office (1788). Arrested (1793); died in prison.

Lomond, Loch, largest lake of Scotland, between Central, Strathclyde regions. Length 35 km (22 mi); tourist and recreation area.

Lomonosov, Mikhail Vasilyevich (1711-65), Russian scientist, writer. Founder of Russian science, he anticipated later theories, incl. conservation of mass, kinetic theory of gases and heat as a form of motion.

London, Jack, pseud. of John Griffith London (1876-1916), American author. Known for adventure novels incl. *The Call of the Wild* (1903), *White Fang* (1906), reflecting Darwinian view of natural laws. Also wrote anti-Utopia, *The Iron Heel* (1907).

London: Big Ben and the Houses of Parliament

London, cap. city of England and UK, on R. Thames. Greater London area 1579 sq km (610 sq mi); pop. 7,349,000. Major admin., commercial, indust., cultural centre; has univ. (1836). Governed from 1965 by Greater London Council; comprises City of London (pop. 5000), 32 bors.; incl. Middlesex, parts of Kent, Essex, Surrey, Hertfordshire. Roman *Londinium;* chief English city from reign of Alfred. Buildings incl. Tower of London, Westminster Abbey, St Paul's Cathedral (1710), Buckingham Palace (1703), Houses of Parliament (1852), GPO Tower (1964). Extensively rebuilt after Great Plague, Fire (1665-6); damaged in WWII air raids.

London, town of SW Ontario; on Thames R. Pop. 223,000. Railway jct.; indust. and commercial centre; food produce, textile mfg. Settled 1826. Seat of Univ. of Western Ontario.

Londonderry or **Derry,** former county of N Northern Ireland. Hilly in S incl. Sperrin Mts.; rivers incl. Foyle, Bann. Agric., distilling, fishing. Co. town was **Londonderry,** on R. Foyle. Pop. 52,000. Port; shipbuilding; clothing mfg. Has Protestant, RC cathedrals. Withstood siege (1688-9) by James II. Scene of religious conflict from 1969. **Londonderry,** district; area 387 sq km (149 sq mi); pop. 82,000. Created 1973, formerly part of Co. Londonderry.

Long, Huey Pierce (1893-1935), American politician. As governor of Louisiana (1928-31), he dominated state politics, using corruption and force to achieve his ends. As senator (1932-5), gained national following as potential presidential candidate advocating 'share-the-wealth' policy. Assassinated.

Long Beach, port of S California, US. Pop. 359,000. Major oil, defence industs. Tourist resort; liner *Queen Mary* is an attraction.

long-eared bat, *Plecotus auritus,* common European bat with ears almost as long as its body. Found in lofts and belfries.

Longfellow, Henry Wadsworth (1807-82), American poet. Known for sentimental lyrics, narrative poems, *eg* 'The Village Blacksmith', *Evangeline* (1847), *Song of Hiawatha* (1855), *The Courtship of Miles Standish* (1858).

Longford, county of Leinster prov., C Irish Republic. Area 1044 sq km (403 sq mi); pop. 28,000. Low-lying, peat bogs. Cattle, dairying. Co. town **Longford,** pop. 3000. Castle (17th cent.), RC cathedral.

longhorn beetle or **longicorn,** any of Cerambycidae family of widely-distributed beetles with long antennae. Larvae are forest pests, boring holes in trees in which they pupate.

Long Island, SE New York, US, separated from mainland by Long Isl. Sound. Length 190 km (118 mi); width 19-32 km (12-20 mi). Extends E from New York City (incl. Brooklyn, Queen bors., Coney Isl. resort). Mainly residential and resort area, esp. in E. Has Kennedy, La Guardia airports.

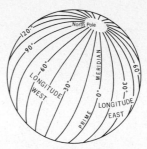

Degrees of longitude

longitude, in geography, angular distance east or west of prime meridian of any point on Earth's surface, measured from Earth's centre. By international agreement, prime meridian (0˚) runs through Greenwich, England.

Long March, journey from Kiangsi prov. to Shensi prov., *c* 9600 km (6000 mi), made (1934-5) by *c* 90,000 Chinese Communist soldiers, women and children. Under constant threat of attack from Nationalist forces, less than half of them survived. Mao Tse-tung estab. himself as Communist leader during march.

Long Parliament, name given to English Parliament (1640-60) whose opposition to Charles I led to Civil War. After expulsion of Presbyterian members (Pride's Purge, 1648), was known as Rump Parliament. Dissolved (1653) by Cromwell; reassembled (1659) and finally dissolved at Restoration (1660).

long sight, see HYPERMETROPIA.

loofah, skeleton of dishcloth gourd of genus *Luffa*. Used as bath sponge.

loom, frame machine used for weaving cloth. Power loom was introduced (1785-7) by Cartwright. An attachment invented by J. M. Jacquard (1804), using punched cards and needles, made it possible to weave intricate patterns.

loon, see DIVER.

Lope de Vega, see VEGA [CARPIO, FELIX] LOPE DE.

López, Francisco Solano (*c* 1826-70), Paraguayan politician. President (1862-70), sought to enhance Paraguayan prestige in South America by making war on Brazil, Argentina and Uruguay (1865). Disastrous campaign led to loss of much of Paraguayan pop.; he was killed in battle.

Lop Nor or **Lob Nor,** depression in Sinkiang auton. region NW China. Once filled by large lake, now covered by small shifting lakes, marshes. Site of Chinese nuclear test explosions.

loquat, *Eriobotrya japonica,* small evergreen tree of rose family, native to China and Japan. Yellow fruit known as Japanese plum.

Lorca, Federico García, see GARCÍA LORCA.

Lords, House of, see HOUSE OF LORDS.

Lord's Prayer or **Pater Noster,** most widely known and used Christian prayer. Taught by Jesus to his disciples; part of Sermon on the Mount (Matthew 6: 9-13).

Lord's Supper, see EUCHARIST.

Lorelei, rock on E bank of Rhine, West Germany, midway between Bingen and Koblenz. In legend, home of a siren who lured sailors onto reef below.

Lorentz, Hendrick Antoon (1853-1928), Dutch physicist. Shared Nobel Prize for Physics (1902) with Zeeman for explaining widening of spectral lines under influence of magnetic field. Lorentz transformation, which he introduced to explain negative results of MICHELSON-Morley experiment, was fundamental in Einstein's 1905 theory of relativity.

Lorenz, Konrad (1903-   ), Austrian zoologist. Estab. science of ethology, *ie* study of group behaviour patterns in animals. Works incl. *On Agression* (1966). Nobel Prize for Physiology and Medicine (1973).

Lorenzetti, Ambrogio (active 1319-48), and his brother **Pietro** (active 1320-48), Italian painters of Sienese school. Influenced by Duccio and Giovanni Pisano, they continued movement towards naturalism. Pietro's work incl. *Birth of the Virgin* at Siena; Ambrogio is known for allegorical fresco of *Good and Bad Government* at Siena.

Loreto, town of the Marches, EC Italy. Pop. 9000. Centre of pilgrimage based on the Holy House (*Santa Casa*) of the Virgin Mary miraculously transported here from Nazareth in late 13th cent.

Lorient, town of Brittany, NW France, on Bay of Biscay. Pop. 69,000. Port, fishing indust. Founded 1664 by French East India Co.; naval base estab. by Napoleon I. German submarine base in WWII, heavily bombed.

Slender loris

loris, tailless arboreal mammal of lemur group, found in SE Asia, India and Sri Lanka. Nocturnal, with large eyes and furry body. Species incl. slender loris, *Loris tardigradus,* and slow loris, *Nycticebus coucang.*

Lorrain, Claude, see CLAUDE LORRAIN.

Lorraine (Ger. *Lothringen*), region and former prov. of E France, hist. cap. Nancy. Low plateau, rising to Vosges Mts. in E. Main rivers Meuse, Moselle. Rich iron ore deposits; coalmining in Saar basin. French prov. from 1766. Ceded with Alsace to Germany (1871), returned (1918). Again annexed during WWII.

lory or **lorikeet,** small brightly coloured parrot of Australasia with brush-tipped tongue used to gather nectar.

Los Alamos, see SANTA FÉ.

Los Angeles, Victoria de (1923-   ), Spanish soprano. Active in opera and on the concert platform. Has done much to popularize Spanish songs, *eg* those of Falla.

Los Angeles, city of S California, US; near Pacific. Pop. 2,810,000; state's largest city with extensive suburbs. Shipping, communications centre; agric. trade, business centre; defence, film industs. Founded by Spanish Franciscan monks (1781). Became cap. of Mexican California (1845); captured by US forces (1846). Growth boosted with railway development and oil discovery. Has part of Univ. of California (1919).

Losey, Joseph (1909-   ), American film director, British resident from 1952. Films incl. *The Servant* (1963), *Accident* (1967), *The Go-Between* (1971).

Lot, river of S France. Flows *c* 480 km (300 mi) from Cévennes via Cahors to R. Garonne. Fertile valley; vineyards.

Lothair I (795-855), Holy Roman emperor (840-55). From 817 ruled as joint emperor with his father, Louis I, on whose death empire was divided between Lothair and his brothers, Charles and Louis the German. Lothair's attempts to reunite empire were resisted by his brothers.

Lothian, region of EC Scotland. Area 1753 sq km (677 sq mi); pop. 742,000; chief city Edinburgh. Created 1975, incl. former East Lothian, Midlothian, West Lothian.

Loti, Pierre, pseud. of Louis Marie Julien Viaud (1850-1923), French novelist. Known for romantic adventure stories in exotic settings, *eg Aziyadé* (1879), *Le Mariage de Loti* (1880). Also wrote novels of Breton life, *eg Pêcheur d'Islande* (1886).

Lotto, Lorenzo (*c* 1480-1556), Italian artist. Influenced by Giovanni Bellini and Titian, his best work combines Venetian colour and northern sentiment. Painted portraits, altarpieces, frescoes.

Egyptian lotus

lotus, various tropical African and Asiatic water or pond lilies. Species incl. Egyptian lotus, *Nymphaea lotus,* with white flowers and American lotus, *Nelumbo lutea,* with yellow flowers, and Indian lotus, *Nelumbo nucifera.* Blossom symbolic in Indian art and religion.

Loughborough, mun. bor. of Leicestershire, EC England. Pop. 46,000. Engineering; hosiery; bell foundry. Technological univ. (1964); teachers' coll.

Louis [I] the Pious (778-840), Holy Roman emperor (814-40). Succeeded father, Charlemagne. Reign marked by conflict between his sons (Pepin, Lothair, Louis the German, Charles the Bald) over his attempts to divide the empire between them.

Louis [VI] the Fat (1081-1137), king of France (1108-37). Consolidated power of monarchy by suppressing robber barons around Paris. Granted favours to clergy. Thwarted Henry I of England's invasions from Normandy.

Louis VII (*c* 1120-80), king of France (1137-80). Led disastrous 2nd Crusade (1147-9). Annulled marriage to wife, Eleanor of Aquitaine, whose subsequent marriage to Henry II of England provoked continual warfare for her possessions.

Louis [IX], St (1214-70), king of France (1226-70). Led 7th Crusade to Egypt, but was captured (1250) and did not return to France until 1254. Reign noted for bringing of peace and prosperity, building of great Gothic churches, *eg* Chartres, Sainte Chapelle.

Louis XI (1423-83), king of France (1461-83). Successfully curtailed power of great nobles, led by Charles the Bold of Burgundy, by mixture of cunning and force. Gained Burgundian dominions in France by Treaty of Arras (1482).

Louis XIII (1601-43), king of France (1610-43). Assumed power in 1617 following regency of mother, Marie de' Medici. Policy controlled by her protégé, Richelieu, from 1624; exiled mother (1630) after she had attempted to dismiss Richelieu.

Louis XIV (1638-1715), king of France (1643-1715). During his minority, France was ruled by MAZARIN. Known as the 'Sun King', Louis assumed absolute control after 1661; rule, epitomized by remark, *L'état, c'est moi,* marked by territ. expansion with development of army and economic reform until death of COLBERT. Louis' ambitions in Europe led to numerous wars (1683-1715), esp. with Spain, Holland and England. War of Spanish Succession (1701-14), by which he secured Spanish throne for his grandson, led to military weakness and huge debts. Under his patronage, arts and sciences flourished; had magnificent palace built at Versailles.

Louis XV (1710-74), king of France (1715-74). During minority, left govt. to duke of Orléans (d. 1723) and

Cardinal Fleury. After Fleury's death (1743), attempted to rule alone but was dominated by mistresses such as Mme de Pompadour, whose influence proved disastrous. Lost possessions in Canada and India after Seven Years War (1756-63). Personal extravagance and expenditure on war left France on verge of bankruptcy.

Louis XVI (1754-93), king of France (1774-92). Dismissed 2 ablest ministers, Turgot and Necker, who had tried to reorganize country's disastrous finances. Dominated by wife, Marie Antoinette, and his court. Forced to recall Estates-General (1789), opening way for French Revolution. At first still popular with the people, weakened his position by attempting to flee country (1791); recaptured at Varennes; agreed to become constitutional monarch. Deposed (Sept. 1792) after failures in war against Austria; tried for treason and guillotined.

Louis XVII (1785-c 1795), titular king of France. Son of Louis XVI, he was imprisoned from 1792 until his death. Proclaimed king by royalist exiles.

Louis XVIII (1755-1824), king of France (1814-24). Lived in exile (1791-1814); assumed royal title on death of Louis XVII. On fall of Napoleon (1814), ascended throne through influence of Talleyrand; expelled (1815) during Hundred Days. Restored by allies (June, 1815). Ruled moderately until 1820, after which he fell under control of reactionary ultra-royalists.

Louis I [the Great] (1326-82), king of Hungary (1342-82). Ruled at height of Hungarian power. Fought successfully against Turks in the Balkans, secured Dalmatia from Venice (1381). Succeeded to Polish throne on death of his uncle, Casimir the Great.

Louis, Joe, orig. Joseph Louis Barrow (1914-   ), American boxer. World heavyweight champion (1937-49), he made record 25 successful defences of his title. Retired 1949; defeated in comeback attempt (1950, 1951).

Louisiade Archipelago, volcanic isl. group in SW Pacific, SE of New Guinea isl.; part of Papua New Guinea.

Louisiana, state of S US, on Gulf of Mexico. Area 125,675 sq km (48,523 sq mi); pop. 3,643,000; cap. Baton Rouge; chief city New Orleans. Coastal plain dominated by Mississippi delta (subject to floods). Forestry; agric. incl. cotton, rice, sugar cane; salt, petroleum, sulphur mining. Claimed by France in 17th cent.; part of Louisiana Purchase by US in 1803. Admitted as 18th state (1812).

Louisiana Purchase, land bought from France by US in 1803 for 15 million dollars. Extended from Mississippi to Rocky Mts., and from Gulf of Mexico to Canada.

Louis Napoleon, see NAPOLEON III.

Louis Philippe (1773-1850), king of France (1830-48), known as the Citizen King. Lived in exile (1793-1814) after serving in French Revolutionary army. As Duc d'Orléans, supported deposition of Charles X (1830) and was chosen king. Reign, known as 'July Monarchy', characterized by middle-class ideals. Increasing opposition turned him from liberalism to absolutism. Reform movements forced abdication after Revolution of 1848. Fled to England.

Louisville, city of N Kentucky, US; on Ohio R. Pop. 362,000. Tobacco, whisky processing; meat packing, chemical mfg. Supplied with h.e.p. from falls on Ohio R. Has annual Kentucky Derby horse race. Nearby is Fort Knox (US gold bullion stores).

Lourdes, town of SW France, at foot of Pyrenees. Pop. 18,000. Site of St Bernadette's vision of the Virgin (1858); now major pilgrimage centre.

Lourenço Marques, see MAPUTO, Mozambique.

louse, small wingless insect with sucking mouthparts. Divided into 2 orders: Anoplura, blood-sucking lice, parasitic on most mammals; Mallophaga, biting lice, parasitic mainly on birds. Species incl. *Pediculus capitis,* human head louse.

Louth, county of Leinster prov., NE Irish Republic. Area 821 sq km (317 sq mi); pop. 75,000; co. town Dundalk. Smallest Irish county; flat, low-lying. Dairying, fishing.

Louvain (Flem. *Leuven*), town of C Belgium, on R. Dyle. Pop. 32,000. Brewing, lace mfg. Medieval cloth centre, cap. of Brabant 11th-15th cents. RC univ. (1426), library.

Louvois, François Michel le Tellier, Marquis de (1641-91), French politician. Minister of war under Louis XIV from 1666, his reorganization of the army enabled France to achieve military supremacy in Europe.

Louvre, former French royal palace in Paris, opened to the public as an art museum in 1793. Contains one of the finest collections in world, incl. *Venus de Milo;* particularly strong in Italian Renaissance paintings incl. da Vinci's *Mona Lisa.*

love bird, small Old World parrot, esp. African genus *Agapornis.* Frequently kept as cage bird.

Love-in-a-mist

love-in-a-mist, *Nigella damascena,* annual garden plant of buttercup family. Feathery leaves, blue or white flowers.

Lovelace, Richard (1618-58), English poet. Known for Cavalier lyrics, esp. 'To Lucasta, Going to the Wars', 'To Althea, from Prison'.

Lovell, Sir [Alfred Charles] Bernard (1913-   ), English astronomer. Helped in development of radar. Director of Jodrell Bank Observatory, site of radio telescope, after 1951.

Low, Sir David (1891-1963), British political cartoonist, b. New Zealand. Created 'Colonel Blimp', caricature of conservative Englishman, TUC horse, among other characters.

Low Countries, region of NW Europe. Incl. NETHERLANDS, BELGIUM, LUXEMBOURG; also *see* BRABANT, FLANDERS, HOLLAND.

Lowell, prominent American family of New England. **Francis Cabot Lowell** (1775-1817), pioneered cotton mfg., building factory which processed raw cotton to cloth. His nephew, **James Russell Lowell** (1819-91), was a poet. Wrote *Biglow Papers* (1848) in Yankee dialect, *The Vision of Sir Launfal* (1848), *A Fable for Critics* (1848) satirizing his contemporaries. Also wrote criticism, *eg Among My Books* (1870, 1876). **Percival Lowell** (1855-1916) was an astronomer. Founded Lowell Observatory, Arizona (1894) to study planet Mars; contended that 'canals' seen on Mars were waterways constructed by intelligent life. Predicted existence of planet Pluto, discovered 1930. His sister, **Amy [Lawrence] Lowell** (1874-1925), was a poet, a member of the IMAGISTS. Works incl. *Sword Blades and Poppy Seed* (1914), *Pictures of the Floating World* (1919), *What O'Clock?* (1925).

Lowell, Robert [Traill Spence] (1917-   ), American poet. Works incl. *Lord Weary's Castle* (1946), *The Mills of the Kavanaughs* (1951), verse, prose autobiog. *Life Studies* (1959).

Lowell, town of NE Massachusetts, US; at jct. of Merrimack and Concord rivers. Pop. 94,000. Textile mfg. *fl* in 19th cent. Settled 1653.

Lower California, see BAJA CALIFORNIA.

Lower Hutt, city and indust. centre of SW North Isl., New Zealand, on Port Nicholson. Pop. 59,000. Engineering, food processing, car assembly; fruit, vegetable growing in nearby Hutt R. valley.

Lowestoft, mun. bor. of Suffolk, E England. Pop. 52,000. Port, resort on North Sea. Fishing, yachting.

Lowry, [Clarence] Malcolm (1909-57), English author. Best known for *Under the Volcano* (1947) portraying the disintegration of personality through alcoholic delirium. Other works incl. *Ultramarine* (1933), *Hear Us O Lord from Heaven Thy Dwelling Place* (1961).

L.S. Lowry

Lowry, Laurence Stephen (1887-1976), English artist. Known for his paintings of the industrial landscape and its inhabitants; employed seemingly naive style, depicting people almost as matchsticks.

Loyalists, in American Revolution, those who supported British cause. Many emigrated to Canada, where they became known as United Empire Loyalists.

Loyalty Islands (Fr. *Iles Loyauté*), isl. group of SW Pacific Ocean, dependency of New Caledonia. Area *c* 2070 sq km (800 sq mi); main isls. Lifu, Maré, Uvéa. Chief crops copra, rubber, sugar cane.

Loyang, city of Honan prov., EC China on R. Lo. Pop. 750,000. Transport centre; heavy engineering, tractor and ball bearing mfg. Ancient cap. of Tang dynasty (AD 618-906).

Loyola, St Ignatius of, see IGNATIUS OF LOYOLA, ST.

LSD, see LYSERGIC ACID DIETHYLAMIDE.

Luanda, São Paulo de, cap. of Angola, on Atlantic Ocean. Pop. 475,000. Admin., commercial centre; port, exports coffee, cotton, minerals; oil refining. Founded 1575, former slave trade centre.

Luang Prabang, royal cap. of Laos. Pop. 25,000. River port at Mekong-Kahn confluence. Trade centre (rice, rubber, teak).

Lubbock, John, Baron Avebury (1834-1913), English banker, politician, naturalist. MP from 1870, promoted banking reforms. Works incl. *Origin and Metamorphoses of Insects* (1874).

Lubbock, town of NW Texas, US. Pop. 149,000. Ranching centre; produce incl. cotton, cattle, grain. Founded 1891.

Lübeck, city of N West Germany, on R. Trave. Pop. 240,000. Linked by canal (1900) to R. Elbe; port, shipbuilding, food processing. Chief city of Hanseatic League (1241-1630). Medieval buildings incl. cathedral, town hall.

Lubitsch, Ernst (1892-1947), German film director. Known for sophisticated sex comedies, with the 'Lubitsch touch', made in Hollywood from 1922, *eg The Love Parade* (1929), *Ninotchka* (1939), *Heaven Can Wait* (1943).

Lublin, city of SE Poland, cap. of Lublin prov. Pop. 239,000. Railway jct., agric. machinery, textile mfg.; univ. (1944). Under Russian rule 1815-1919; seat of provisional govts. 1919, 1944.

lubricants, substances used to reduce friction between moving surfaces. May be liquid (oil), semi-solid (grease), solid, *eg* colloidal graphite in water (aquadag) or oil (oildag). Since 19th cent. mostly derived from mineral oil but adapted to many specialist uses. Recently gas at pressure has been used in high speed machinery.

Lubumbashi, city of SE Zaïre, cap. of Shaba region. Pop. 357,000. Mineral refining centre in Katanga mining dist.;

food processing, RC cathedral. Founded (1910) as Elisabethville, renamed 1966. Scene of heavy fighting during Katanga secession (1960-3).

Lucan, full name Marcus Annaeus Lucanus (AD 39-65), Roman poet, b. Spain. Enjoyed patronage of Nero, but was forced to commit suicide after unsuccessful republican plot against latter. His epic *Bellum Civile* (or *Pharsalia*) deals with war between Caesar and Pompey.

Lucas van Leyden (1494-1533), Dutch painter, engraver. Influenced by Dürer in woodcuts and engravings, he was a brilliant draughtsman; paintings reflect beginnings of Dutch genre art.

Lucca, town of Tuscany, W Italy, cap. of Lucca prov. Pop. 91,000. Olive oil, wine; silk mfg. from Middle Ages. Roman settlement; medieval republic, scene of Guelph-Ghibelline conflict. Cathedral (11th cent.).

Luce, Henry Robinson (1898-1967), American magazine editor and publisher. Founded *Time* (1923), *Fortune* (1930), *Life* (1936). His wife, **Clare Boothe Luce** (1903-   ), wrote plays, books, edited *Vanity Fair* (1933-4), later served as member of Congress and US ambassador to Italy (1953-7).

Lucerne (Ger. *Luzern*), town of C Switzerland, on L. Lucerne, cap. of Lucerne canton. Pop. 70,000. Tourism, printing, machinery. Lion of Lucerne monument to Swiss Guard. Joined Swiss Confederation 1332.

Lucerne, Lake (Ger. *Vierwaldstättersee*), in C Switzerland, bordering on the four forest cantons. Area 111 sq km (43 sq mi). Tourism.

lucerne, see ALFALFA.

Luchow, city of Szechwan prov., SC China. Pop. 300,000. Indust. centre, river port on Yangtzekiang, To-kiang jct.

Lucian (*fl* 2nd cent.), Greek prose writer. Wrote scathing indictments of contemporary conditions, beliefs. Of *c* 80 80 works, best known are dialogues, *eg Dialogues of the Dead*, *Dialogues of Courtesans*.

Lucifer, in OT book of Isaiah, figurative reference to king of Babylon, misconstrued to mean fallen angel; hence became a term for Satan. Also Roman name for Venus as morning star.

Lucknow, cap. of Uttar Pradesh, NC India. Pop. 826,000. Railway engineering; paper, carpet mfg. Cap. of Oudh kingdom (1775-1856). British besieged city for 5 months during Indian Mutiny until relieved in Nov, 1857.

Lucretius, full name Titus Lucretius Carus (*c* 95-*c* 55 BC), Roman poet. Known for *De rerum natura* expounding Epicurean philosophy. Concerned with nature of physical world, arguing against supernatural origin of universe, and with liberating mankind from fear of gods and death.

Lucullus, Lucius Licinius (*c* 110-56 BC), Roman statesman, soldier. Appointed consul (74); fought successfully against Mithradates (73-72) in Asia. Mutinies later in his Asian campaigns led to his recall (66). Famous for luxurious living in his retirement.

Luddites, in English history, name given to those taking part in machine-wrecking riots (1811-16). Rioters were protesting against low wages and unemployment attributed to introduction of textile-making machines. Named after mythical Ned Ludd.

Ludendorff, Erich (1865-1937), German general. Chief of staff in WWI, ably supporting Hindenburg's military successes. Backed Hitler's 'beer-hall putsch' (1923).

Lüderltz, town of South West Africa, on Atlantic Ocean. Pop. 7000. Railway terminus; port, exports diamonds; lobster fishing.

Ludhiana, city of Punjab, N India. Pop. 401,000. Railway jct. Hosiery, cotton textile mfg. Founded in 15th cent.

Ludlow, town of Shropshire, W England. Pop. 7000. Medieval strategic post on Welsh border; has 11th-16th cent. castle.

Ludwigshafen, city of W West Germany, on R. Rhine, opposite Mannheim. Pop. 176,000. River port, major chemical indust., dyes, plastics.

Lugano, town of S Switzerland, on L. Lugano, near Italian border. Pop. 22,000. Tourist centre.

Lugansk, see VOROSHILOVGRAD.

Lugard, Frederick John Dealtry, 1st Baron (1858-1945), English soldier, colonial administrator. Raised and led West African Frontier Force (1897-9); commissioner of Northern Nigeria (1900-6). Governor of united Nigeria (1914-19). Advocated doctrine of 'indirect rule' through native institutions.

Lugones, Leopoldo (1874-1938), Argentinian poet. Leading modernist in early works, *eg Lunario sentimental* (1909); *Odas seculares* (1910) is more traditional, celebrating rustic values. Prose works incl. *La guerra gaucha* (1905), *Las fuerzas extrañas* (1906).

lugworm or **lobworm,** tube-dwelling annelid worm with bristly appendages on body; burrows into mud and sand. Used as bait. Species incl. common European *Arenicola marina*.

Lu Hsun, pseud. of Chou Shujen (1881-1936), Chinese author. Leader in movement to overthrow Ch'ing government. Short stories collected in *Ah Q and others* (1941).

Luik, see LIÈGE, Belgium.

Lukács, György (1885-1971), Hungarian literary theorist. Leading Marxist aesthetician. *History and the Class Consciousness* (1923) links artistic creativity with social struggle. Other works incl. *The Destruction of Reason* (1954), *The Historical Novel* (1955).

Luke, St (*fl* AD 1st cent.), Gentile physician, friend of St Mark and St Paul. Credited with authorship of 3rd Gospel of NT and Acts of the Apostles.

Luke, Gospel according to St, third of NT Gospels, attributed to St Luke. Longest and historically most detailed of the Gospels.

Luleå, town of NE Sweden, on Gulf of Bothnia at mouth of R. Lule. Pop. 37,000. Exports iron ore from Kiruna and Gällivare; timber, reindeer hides.

Lull, Ramon or **Raymond Lully** (*c* 1232-1315), Catalan scholar. Authority on Moslem culture; from Christian standpoint, held public disputes with leading Moslem scholars. Taught that all articles of faith could be demonstrated by logic. Stoned to death in N Africa.

Lully, Jean Baptiste (1632-87), French composer, b. Italy. Court composer to Louis XIV. Pioneered introduction of opera in France; operas incl. *Alceste* and *Cadmus et Hermione*. Also helped to estab. ballet in his comedy-ballets, in association with Molière.

Luluabourg, see KANANGA, Zaïre.

lumbago, pain in the small of the back, often associated with pain down the leg. May be caused by back strain or pressure on nerves by a 'slipped disc'.

Lumière, Louis Jean (1864-1948), French cinema pioneer. With his brother, **Auguste Marie Louis Nicholas Lumière** (1862-1954), invented cinematograph in 1895, 1st device to project moving pictures onto screen.

luminosity, in astronomy, measure of actual quantity of light emitted by a star, irrespective of its distance from Earth. *See* MAGNITUDE.

luminous paint, paint containing a phosphorescent sulphide, usually of barium or calcium. After exposure to light it appears luminous in dark. The type used on watch faces is excited radioactively and does not need exposure to light.

lumpsucker, *Cyclopterus lumpus,* bottomdwelling fish of N Atlantic, with sucker disc on underside.

Lumumba, Patrice Emergy (1925-61), Congolese politician. Became premier at independence of Congo. Involved in power struggle with KASAVUBU; each dismissed the other during civil war. Arrested by MOBUTU and taken to Katanga, where he was murdered.

lunacy, see INSANITY.

Lund, town of SW Sweden. Pop. 52,000. Paper, furniture mfg.; printing, publishing. Cathedral (12th cent.) with medieval astronomical clock. Univ. (1668).

Lüneburg, town of NE West Germany, on R. Ilmenau. Pop. 61,000. Spa with saline springs; saltworks, chemicals. Hanseatic League member. Medieval churches, town hall.

Lüneburg Heath (*Lüneburger Heide*), sandy heath of NE West Germany, between Elbe and Aller rivers. Sheep grazing, potato growing.

Lunéville, town of Lorraine, NE France, on R. Meurthe. Pop. 25,000. Textiles, porcelain mfg. Palace (18th cent.).

African lungfish (*Protopterus dollei*)

lungfish, any of various fish which have lungs as well as gills. Six freshwater species known, considered living fossils. Australian lungfish, *Neoceratodus forsteri,* found in Queensland, uses lungs during droughts. Other species in S America, Africa.

lungs, respiratory organs in air-breathing vertebrates. In humans, occupy most of thorax and are separated by heart. Carbon dioxide in blood is exchanged for oxygen as blood circulates through the air sacs (alveoli) of the lungs.

Lunt, Alfred, see FONTANNE, LYNN.

Lupercalia, ancient Roman fertility festival held on 15 Feb. in honour of Faunus. Goats were sacrificed and 2 male youths ran through the city slapping passers-by with lashes of the goatskin. Persisted into 6th cent.

White lupin (*Lupinus albus*)

lupin, any of genus *Lupinus* of plants of Leguminosae family. Native to Mediterranean region and North America. Flowers, borne on long spike, may be a variety of colours. Russell lupin is popular garden hybrid.

Lurgan, town of E Northern Ireland. Pop. 24,000. In former Co. Antrim. Linen, nylon mfg.

Luristan, mountainous region of SW Iran, bordering on Iraq. Rises to 4330 m (14,200 ft). Large petroleum deposits; sheep raising.

Lusaka, cap. of Zambia. Pop. 348,000. Admin., commercial, communications centre; agric. market; univ. of Zambia (1966). Replaced Livingstone as cap. of Northern Rhodesia (1935).

Lusatia (Ger. *Lausitz*), forested region of SE East Germany and SW Poland, between Elbe and Oder rivers. Part of Saxony until 1815, passed to Prussia. Present division, along R. Neisse, dates from 1945.

Lushun, see LU-TA.

Lusitania, British liner sunk without warning off Irish coast by German submarine on 7th May, 1915. Almost 1200 people were killed, over 100 of them American. This act aroused considerable American hostility to Germany and helped bring US into WWI.

Lu-ta or **Lushun-Talien,** municipality of Liaoning prov., NW China comprising Lushun (formerly Port Arthur) and Talien. Pop. 4,000,000. Soya bean, grain, coal exports; oil refining. Important naval base and ice-free port at end of Liaotung penin. Part of Kwanfung lease (1898-1945) under Japanese; finally reintegrated into China 1955.

lute, string instrument shaped like half pear, with fretted finger-board; the strings, usually 6 in number, are plucked. Popular domestic instrument (15th-17th cents.), both as a solo instrument and for accompanying singers.

lutetium (Lu), metallic element of lanthanide series; at. no. 71, at. wt. 174.97. Discovered (1907) in sample of ytterbium.

luth, see LEATHERY TURTLE.

Luther, Martin (1483-1546), German religious leader. Augustinian friar, teacher at Univ. of Wittenberg.

Campaigned against sale of indulgences; nailed 95 theses to Wittenberg church door (regarded as start of Protestant Reformation). Initially sought reform within Church but excommunicated in 1521. Fled to Wartburg after refusing to retract statements at Diet of Worms. Translated NT into German. Endorsed Melanchthon's Augsburg Confession (1530), basis of Lutheranism.

Lutheranism, Protestant doctrine founded on teachings of MARTIN LUTHER and formulated in confessional Book of Concord (1580). Regards the Bible as only necessary guide to faith; holds the individual to be directly responsible to God and salvation to come through faith alone. Rejects transubstantiation and has no unified liturgical order. Flourishes primarily in Germany, Scandinavia and US.

Luthuli, Albert John (1899-1967), South African political leader. Openly opposed *apartheid*, advocating non-violent resistance. Kept under restriction after 1952; arrested for treason (1956) but acquitted (1959). Awarded Nobel Peace Prize (1960).

Luton, mun. bor. of Bedfordshire, C England, on R. Lea. Pop. 161,000. Engineering, esp. car indust.; airport. Former centre of strawplaiting.

Lutoslawski, Witold (1913-   ), Polish composer. Has written music in wide range of styles, incl. symphonies, songs, choral works. Compositions incl. *Concerto for Orchestra.*

Luxembourg

Luxembourg, grand duchy of NW Europe. Area 2587 sq km (999 sq mi); pop. 353,000. Language: Letzeburgesch (Ger. dialect). Religion: RC. Agric., cattle; iron mining. Duchy from 1354 (Habsburg from 15th cent.); grand duchy within Netherlands from 1815; independent 1890. Occupied by Germans in both WWs. In Benelux customs union from 1948; member of EEC. Cap. **Luxembourg,** on R. Alzette. Pop. 76,000. Cultural centre. Iron, steel indust. Hq. of ECSC, European Court of Justice. Palace (16th cent.); cathedral.

Luxembourg, prov. of SE Belgium, in the Ardennes, cap. Arlon. Mainly wooded, some agric. Iron ore mined in S.

Luxembourg, Palais du, Renaissance palace in Paris, France; constructed 1615-20 for Marie de' Medici, it was enlarged in 19th cent. Surrounded by famous gardens.

Luxemburg, Rosa (1870-1919), German revolutionary, b. Poland. A Marxist, she founded the Spartacus League (1916) with Karl LIEBKNECHT. Arrested and killed after leading Spartacist insurrection.

Luxor, town of C Egypt, on R. Nile. Pop. 30,000. Occupies part of site of ancient city of THEBES.

Luzern, see LUCERNE, Switzerland.

Luzon, largest isl. of Philippines. Area *c* 105,000 sq km (40,400 sq mi). Largely mountainous, rising to 2928 m (9606 ft) at Mt. Pulog. Rich agric. areas produce rice, sugar cane, hemp; minerals incl. chromite, nickel, copper. Cap. is Quezon City, chief city Manila. Scene of heavy fighting in WWII.

Lvov, Prince Georgi Evgenyevich (1861-1925), Russian statesman. Led provisional govt. (Feb.–July, 1917) after February uprising. Succeeded by Kerensky.

Lvov (Ger. *Lemberg*), city of USSR, W Ukrainian SSR. Pop. 579,000. Indust. centre; oil refining, machinery mfg. Taken

by Poles (1349), became cap. of Austrian Galicia (1772-1919). Returned to Poland, ceded to USSR (1945).

Lyallpur, city of NE Pakistan. Pop. 136,000. Wheat trade centre; cotton mfg. Named after founder, Sir James Lyall (1895).

lycanthropy, originally, in folklore, the transformation of humans into wolves or other carnivorous animals. Common to many cultures, described by Vergil, Pliny. Used now by psychologists to denote mental disorder through which patient believes he is an animal. Subject of study by Freud.

lyceum, originally, the grove in Athens where Aristotle taught, so-called from neighbouring temple of *Apollōn Lykeios.* Now public hall for lectures, performances of music, *etc,* or an organization providing such services.

lychee, *see* LITCHI.

Lycurgus (*c* 7th cent. BC), Spartan lawgiver, said by some to be mythical. Supposed to have framed Spartan constitution, educational system.

Lydda (Arab. *Ludd*), town of C Israel. Pop. 18,000. Rail jct. International airport. Traditional birthplace of St George. Destroyed by Saladin 1191, rebuilt by Richard I of England.

Lydgate, John (*c* 1370-*c* 1452), English poet, monk. Very famous in own time but now eclipsed by his friend Chaucer. Prolific writer, works incl. *The Fall of Princes.*

Lydia, *see* SARDIS.

Lyell, Sir Charles (1797-1875), Scottish geologist. Author of standard text *The Principles of Geology* (1830-3), expounding uniformitarianism theory of James HUTTON.

Lyly or **Lilly, John** (*c* 1554-1606), English author. Known for *Euphues, the Anatomy of Wit* (1578), *Euphues and His England* (1580) written in elaborately rhetorical style known as 'euphuistic' when taken up by school of prose-romancers. Also wrote courtly entertainments, *eg Alexander and Campaspe* (1584).

lymph, colourless fluid derived from blood plasma which has filtered through the capillary walls. Carried by lymphatic vessels to various parts of body where it distributes nutrients and oxygen to the tissues. Lymph nodes are organs in lymphatic vessels which collect bacteria from lymph; also produce lymphocytes, class of white blood cells important in formation of antibodies.

Lynch, John ('Jack') (1917-   ), Irish politician. Was finance minister in Fianna Fáil cabinet before succeeding Sean Lemass as PM (1966-73); re-elected PM (1977).

Lynchburg, town of C Virginia, US; on James R. Pop. 54,000. Hist. tobacco indust. Settled 1757. Confederacy surrendered at nearby Appomattox Courthouse (April, 1865).

lynching, murder of accused person by mob action, without lawful trial. Term possibly derives from Captain William Lynch (1742-1820), member of vigilante group in Virginia (1780). Practice of pioneers in US before rule of law as penalty for, *eg,* horse-stealing, rape. Common in S US after Civil War.

Lynd, Robert Staughton (1892-1970), American sociologist. Co-author (with wife, Helen Merrell) of *Middletown, A Study in Contemporary American Culture* (1929), analysis of Muncie, Indiana.

Lynn, town of E Massachusetts, US; N of Boston. Pop. 90,000. Important shoe mfg. Settled by Pilgrims in 1629.

Lynn (Regis), *see* KING'S LYNN, England.

lynx, any of genus *Lynx* of wildcats with short tail, tufted ears. European lynx, *L. lynx,* found in N Europe and Siberia, now rare. Largest North American variety is Canadian lynx, *L. canadensis. See* BOBCAT.

Lyons, Sir Joseph (1848-1917), British businessman. Founded (1894) J. Lyons and Co., Ltd., catering firm of tea-shops which became British institution *c* WWI.

Lyons, Joseph Aloysius (1879-1939), Australian statesman, PM (1932-9). Helped estab. United Australia party (1931), headed coalition govt.

Lyons (*Lyon*), city of EC France, at confluence of Rhône and Saône, cap. of Rhône dept. Pop. 528,000. River port, transport jct.; banking centre, major textile indust. (esp. silk, rayon), univ. (1808). Roman *Lugdunum,* founded *c* 43

BC; hist. cap. of Lyonnais. Cathedral (12th cent.), stock exchange (1506).

lyre, ancient Greek stringed musical instrument, like a small portable harp but played with a plectrum. Also known in other ancient civilizations, incl. Assyria and Egypt, and in medieval Europe.

lyrebird, brightly coloured Australian bird, genus *Menura*. Male displays lyre-shaped tail during courtship dance, performed on specially built mound. Renowned mimics.

Lysander (d. 395 BC), Spartan general. Commanded fleet which inflicted final defeat on Athens at Aegospotamos (405); captured Athens (404).

Lysenko, Trofim Denisovich (1898-1976), Russian agronomist. Leading exponent of theory that characteristics acquired through influences of environment can be inherited; his genetic views became official Soviet policy in 1948 but were repudiated after Stalin's death.

lysergic acid diethylamide or **LSD,** alkaloid synthesized from lysergic acid, which is found in the fungus ergot. Powerful hallucinogenic drug, capable of inducing delusions resembling those occurring in psychotic state.

Lysippus (4th cent. BC), Greek sculptor. Leader of Sicyon school, he was prolific worker in bronze. Made many portraits of Alexander the Great. Credited with introduction of new scheme of proportions for human figures.

Lyrebird

Lytton, 1st Baron, *see* BULWER-LYTTON, EDWARD GEORGE EARLE LYTTON.

M

Maas, *see* MEUSE.

Maastricht, city of SE Netherlands, on R. Maas, cap. of Limburg prov. Pop. 112,000. Railway, canal jct.; produces textiles, ceramics. Pop. massacred by Spanish 1579. Site of oldest Dutch church (6th cent.).

Mabinogion, collection of medieval Welsh prose tales, from *mabinogi* (youth, tale of youth). Some contain ancient mythological material, show evidence of oral transmission, others much more literary. Three on parts of ARTHURIAN LEGEND.

Mabuse, Jan, orig. Jan Gossaert (*c* 1478-*c* 1533), Flemish painter. Following visit to Italy in 1508, he adopted style based on Italian Renaissance forms; introduced classical subjects with nude figures into Flemish art.

McAdam, John Loudon (1756-1836), Scottish engineer. Introduced (*c* 1815) improved roads made of crushed stone; known as 'macadam' roads.

Macao, Portuguese colony of SE Asia on Chukiang (Pearl) estuary. Area 15 sq km (6 sq mi); pop. *c* 300,000. Chief town Macao is largely coextensive with colony. Free port; trade, tourism centre; textile indust., gambling casinos. Leased by Portuguese (1557), *fl* as trade post until rise of neighbouring Hong Kong.

Macapá, town of N Brazil, cap. of Amapá territ; on N arm of Amazon delta. Pop. 86,000. Manganese mining nearby.

macaque, monkey of genus *Macaca* found mainly in India and SE Asia. Species incl. barbary ape of Gibraltar and rhesus monkey.

macaroni, preparation of glutinous wheat (semolina) and eggs originating in Italy. Other forms of same material are spaghetti and vermicelli.

MacArthur, Douglas (1880-1964), American general. Chief of general staff (1930-5). Commanded US and Allied forces in SE Asia during WWII. Directed post-war occupation of Japan. Recalled (1951) from post as UN commander in Korea for public disagreement with President Truman over strategy.

Macarthur, John (1767-1834), Australian farmer, merchant, b. England. Leader in estab. New South Wales wool indust. through use of better breeds of sheep. Also introduced viniculture.

Macaulay, Rose (1881-1958), English novelist. Known for witty, mildly satirical novels, *eg Potterism* (1920), *Told by an Idiot* (1923). *The Towers of Trebizond* (1956) reflects author's Christian belief.

Macaulay, Thomas Babington, Baron Macaulay of Rothley (1800-59), English historian. Known for Whig interpretation of history in *The History of England from the Accession of James the Second* (1849-61). Also wrote poetry, *Lays of Ancient Rome* (1842) and numerous essays, notably one on Milton (1825).

macaw, brightly coloured long-tailed parrot of tropical Central and South America. Species incl. scarlet macaw, *Ara macao*.

Macbeth (d. 1057), king of Scotland. Killed Duncan I and took crown (1040). Defeated and killed by Duncan's son, Malcolm III. Principal character of Shakespeare's *Macbeth*.

Macbride, Sean (1904-   ), Irish diplomat, b. South Africa. Secretary-general of International Commission of Jurists (1963-70). UN Commissioner for Namibia from 1974. Shared Nobel Peace Prize (1974).

Maccabees, Jewish family (*fl* 2nd cent. BC) founded by priest Mattathias (d. 166 BC). With sons, led opposition against Syrians. Judas Maccabeus (d. 161 BC) reoccupied Jerusalem, rededicated the Temple. Simon Maccabeus (d. 135 BC) estab. peace in Palestine.

Maccabees, last two books of OT Apocrypha. Covers history of MACCABEES family.

McCarthy, Joseph Raymond (1909-57), American politician. As Republican senator for Wisconsin (1947-57), he claimed (1950) that state dept. had been infiltrated by Communists. Held Senate investigations of people suspected of subversion, accused many of Communist sympathies. Censured by Senate (1954).

McCarthy, Mary (1912-   ), American writer. Best known for novel *The Group* (1963), sharply-observed, coldly witty view of contemporary social and sexual mores. Other works incl. autobiog. *Memories of a Catholic Girlhood* (1957).

Macclesfield, mun. bor. of Cheshire, W England. Pop. 44,000. Textiles mfg., esp. silk.

McCormick, Cyrus Hall (1809-94), American inventor. Devised reaping machine and manufactured it in Chicago from 1847. His grand-nephew, **Robert Rutherford McCormick** (1880-1955), owned Chicago *Tribune,* through which he attacked labour unions and US intervention in world affairs.

McCullers, Carson, neé Smith (1917-67), American novelist. Works, *eg The Heart is a Lonely Hunter* (1940), short stories *The Ballad of the Sad Café* (1951), deal with spiritual isolation in Southern US setting.

McCulloch v Maryland (1819), case decided by US Supreme Court in dispute between federal and state authority over control of currency. Decision upheld federal govt.'s supremacy over states.

McDiarmid, Hugh, pseud. of Christopher Murray Grieve (1892-   ), Scottish poet. Attempted to create a contemporary Scots poetic in *A Drunk Man Looks at the Thistle* (1926). 'Hymns to Lenin' (1931, 1935) reflect Marxist views.

Macdonald, Flora (1722-90), Scottish heroine. After Jacobite defeat at Culloden (1746), she aided Prince Charles Edward Stuart's escape to France by disguising him as her Irish maidservant and escorting him to Skye. Briefly imprisoned afterwards.

Macdonald, George (1824-1905), Scottish novelist, poet. Known for children's books, *eg At the Back of the North Wind* (1871), *The Princess and the Goblin* (1872). Also wrote adult fantasies, verse, novels attacking Calvinism.

Macdonald, Sir John Alexander (1815-91), Canadian statesman, b. Scotland, PM (1867-73, 1878-91). Premier of Upper Canada (1857), he was leading figure in promoting Canadian Confederation; became 1st PM of Dominion of Canada. Scandal over contract for Canadian Pacific Railway forced resignation of his Conservative govt. (1873).

MacDonald, [James] Ramsay (1866-1937), British statesman, PM (1924, 1929-35). Leader of parliamentary Labour Party (1911-14) until removed over pacifist stand at outbreak of WW I. First Labour PM (1924), lost ensuing election after publication of ZINOVIEV letter. PM of minority govt. (1929), split in cabinet led to formation of Conservative-dominated National govt. (1931) with MacDonald as nominal head.

Macdonnell Ranges, mountain system of S Northern Territory, Australia. Highest peak Mt. Zeil (1510 m/4955 ft). Cut by many gorges; Alice Springs built near gap in E mountains.

Ramsay MacDonald in 1931

MacDowell, Edward Alexander (1861-1908), American composer. Chief works incl. piano sonatas and concertos, *Indian Suite,* and *Woodland Sketches.*

mace, *see* NUTMEG.

Macedonia, region of SE Europe, in Greece, Yugoslavia, Bulgaria. Mainly mountainous, rising to over 2450 m (8000 ft). Sheep, goats; wheat, tobacco. Ancient Macedon reached imperial zenith under Philip II, Alexander the Great (4th-3rd cent. BC). Later held by Romans, Slavs, Turks until 1912. Hist. cap. of Greek Macedonia is Salonika. Yugoslav Macedonia is autonomous republic, cap. Skopje.

Maceió, Atlantic port of NE Brazil, cap. of Alagôas state. Pop. 264,000. Sugar, cotton processing; textile, soap mfg. Has old colonial buildings and lighthouse near town centre.

Macgillicuddy's Reeks, range of Co. Kerry, SW Irish Republic, near Lakes of Killarney. Incl. CARRANTUOHILL.

McGonagall, William (1830-1902), Scottish poet. Known for doggerel verse displaying unconsciously ludicrous rhyme, disregard for rhythm, unintentional bathos. Work collected in *Poetic Gems* (1890).

Mach, Ernst (1838-1916), Austrian physicist and philosopher. Emphasized that scientific laws are generalizations of numerous observations, not *a priori* truths. Rejected ideas of absolute space and time implicit in Newtonian mechanics; his views were vindicated by Einstein's theory of relativity.

Machado de Assis, Joaquim Maria (1839-1908), Brazilian author. Considered Brazil's greatest writer. Known for pessimistic, ironic novels, *eg Epitaph for a Small Winner* (1881), *Helena* (1876), *Dom Casmurro* (1899). Also wrote short stories, poetry.

Machault, Guillaume de (*c* 1300–77), French poet, composer. Chief of school of lyric poets which incl. Froissart, estab. rigid forms of *ballade, chant royal, rondel* and *lai,* introduced elements of personal life into poems. Works incl. long narrative poems, *eg Jugement du Roy de Navarre.* Wrote 1st known setting of Mass by a single composer (*Messe de Notre Dame*).

Machel, Samora (1933-), Mozambican politician. A founder of Mozambique Liberation Front (FRELIMO), dedicated to freedom from Portugal by armed struggle. Returned to Mozambique (1975) after 13 years exile to become 1st president of independent country.

Machen, Arthur Llewellyn (1863-1947), Welsh novelist. Known for *The Great God Pan* (1894), *The Hill of Dreams* (1907), *Angel of Mons* (1915), reflecting interest in supernatural.

Machiavelli, Niccolò (1467-1527), Italian writer, statesman. Prominent figure in Florentine republic from 1498, he learnt much of politics in several diplomatic missions. Ruined by restoration of the Medici (1512).

Retired to country estate where he wrote *The Prince* (*c* 1517), an objective analysis of means to achieve power; had enormous influence.

machine gun, firearm with mechanism allowing rapid and continuous fire. R.J. Gatling developed multi-barrel type in US (1862) but earliest in general use was belt-fed, recoil-powered Maxim (1884) issued to British army in Boer War. In WWI, Lewis light machine gun was a standard infantry weapon, while specialized machine gun tasks were allotted to the medium, water-cooled Vickers. Lewis still in use in WWII, although superseded by the Bren.

machine tools, term for large power-driven tools esp. lathe, drill, planer. Operate by removing material from object being machined, *eg* in turning (shaping cylindrical external contours), milling (shaping flat surfaces), drilling, boring, threading (cutting external screw thread) and tapping (cutting internal screw thread).

Mach number, ratio of speed of a body in some medium (*eg* air) to speed of sound in same medium. Mach number greater than 1 indicates supersonic speed.

Machu Picchu, ruined Inca city, *c* 80 km (50 mi) NW of Cuzco, Peru. Discovered 1911; terraced slopes descend to Urubamba R.; major tourist attraction.

Macias Nguema Biyoga, isl. of Equatorial Guinea, in Gulf of Guinea. Area 2020 sq km (780 sq mi); cap. Rey Malabo. Of volcanic origin, rises to 3007 m (9870 ft). Hot, wet climate; produces cocoa. Formerly called Fernando Póo.

Macintosh, Charles (1766-1843), Scottish chemist. Developed waterproof fabric ('mackintosh') and improved bleaching powder.

Mackay, town of E Queensland, Australia, on Pioneer R. Pop. 28,000. Port, exports sugar, timber; tourist centre.

Macke, August (1887-1914), German painter. Influenced by Delaunay and futurism, his work is noted for colour and prismatic patterns, although remaining figurative. Associated with Marc and Kandinsky in Blaue Reiter group.

Mackenzie, Sir Alexander (*c* 1755-1820), Scottish explorer, fur trader. Journeyed in Canada from Great Slave L. via Mackenzie R. to Arctic Ocean (1789). Became 1st European to cross continent N of Mexico (1793).

Mackenzie, Alexander (1822-92), Canadian statesman, b. Scotland. First Liberal PM (1873-8) of Canada.

Mackenzie, Sir Compton, orig. Edward Montague Compton (1883-1972), British author. Works incl. *Sinister Street* (1913), comic novel *Whisky Galore* (1947), autobiog. *My Life and Times* in 8 'octaves' (1963-9).

Mackenzie, Henry (1745-1831), Scottish author. Estab. cult of 'sensibility' with *The Man of Feeling* (1771). Also known for essays in periodicals esp. *Mirror* (1779-80), *Lounger* (1785-7).

Mackenzie, William Lyon (1795-1861), Canadian journalist, b. Scotland. Organized short-lived Rebellion of 1837, failing in attempt to seize Toronto. Fled to US, where he set up provisional govt. on isl. in Niagara R., thus provoking international incident between US and Canada. Imprisoned for violating neutrality laws; returned to Canada (1849).

Mackenzie, admin. dist. of W mainland Northwest Territs., Canada. Area 1,366,200 sq km (527,490 sq mi); chief city Yellowknife. Mackenzie Mts. in W; drained by Mackenzie R., Great Bear and Great Slave lakes. Indian, Eskimo pop. Mineral resources (esp. oil, gold); fishing, fur trapping. Large areas are wildlife reserves.

Mackenzie, river of Mackenzie Dist., Northwest Territs., Canada. Flows NW from Great Slave L. 1800 km (1120 mi) to Beaufort Sea. Tributaries incl. Liard, Athabaska, Peace, Slave. With Slave, Peace, Finlay rivers, forms the longest river system in Canada. Natural gas fields in delta region. Explored (1789) by Alexander Mackenzie.

mackerel, *Scomber scombrus,* food fish of N Atlantic and Mediterranean. Swims in large schools near surface, often inshore.

Mackinder, Sir Halford John (1861-1947), English geographer. Works incl. paper on *Geographical Pivot of History* (1904), advancing concept of Eurasian 'heartland' later adopted and modified by Germans before WWII.

McKinley, William (1843-1901), American statesman, president (1897-1901). Elected (1896) on gold-standard platform. Republican admin. dominated by expansionist policy; Philippines acquired after Spanish-American War (1898) and Hawaii annexed. Shot by anarchist in Buffalo.

McKinley, Mount, mountain of SC Alaska, US; in Alaska Range and Mt. McKinley National Park. Height 6194 m (20,320 ft). Highest peak in North America.

Mackintosh, Charles Rennie (1868-1928), Scottish artist, architect, furniture designer. Influenced by Celtic art, he was a major exponent of art nouveau. Buildings, noted for their lack of ornament and bold geometry, incl. Glasgow School of Art and Hill House, Helensburgh.

MacLeish, Archibald (1892-), American poet, statesman. Known for verse plays, eg *The Fall of the City* (1937), *Air Raid* (1938), *J.B.* (1958), poetry in *Collected Poems 1917-52* (1952). Also wrote essays on poetry, politics.

McLuhan, [Herbert] Marshall (1911-), Canadian writer, academic. Known for controversial communication theories, eg 'the medium is the message'. Works incl. *The Gutenberg Galaxy* (1962), *Understanding Media* (1964).

MacMahon, Marie Edmé Patrice Maurice de (1808-93), French army officer, statesman. Defeated Austrians at Magenta (1859). Defeated and captured by Prussians at Sedan (1870); on release, suppressed Paris Commune (1871). A monarchist, chosen president of the republic (1873); forced to resign through antagonism with republicans (1879).

McMillan, Edwin Mattison (1907-), American physicist. Shared Nobel Prize for Chemistry (1951) with Seaborg for discovery of transuranic elements neptunium and plutonium. Made improvements in particle accelerators.

Harold Macmillan in 1963

Macmillan, [Maurice] Harold (1894-), British statesman, PM (1957-63). Foreign secretary (1955), chancellor of the exchequer (1955-7); headed Conservative govt. after Eden's resignation. Famous for slogan 'You've never had it so good' in 1959 election campaign. Period of office marked by recognition of many colonies as independent states, failure of attempt to join EEC. Resigned soon after PROFUMO affair.

McNamara, Robert Strange (1916-), American politician, diplomat. Secretary of defence (1961-8), reorganized Defence Dept. using modern management techniques; resigned over handling of Vietnam War. President of World Bank (1968-).

MacNeice, Louis (1907-63), English poet, b. Ireland. Works incl. *Blind Fireworks* (1929), *Solstices* (1961), allegorical radio play *The Dark Tower* (1947). Also translated Aeschylus, Horace, Goethe.

Mâcon, town of Burgundy, EC France, on R. Saône. Cap. of Saône-et-Loire dept. Pop. 35,000. Burgundy wine trade. Huguenot stronghold in 16th cent.

Macon, town of C Georgia, US; on Ocmulgee R. Pop. 122,000. Transport jct.; cotton, clay products.

Macpherson, James (1736-96), Scottish poet. Known for *The Works of Ossian* (1765), which he claimed were translations from 3rd cent. bard. His sources were never produced but work considerably influenced Romantic movement in Britain, Germany.

Macquarie, Lachlan (1761-1824), British colonial administrator, governor (1809-21) of British colonies in Australia. Reduced corruption, estab. humane admin.

Macquarie Island, volcanic isl. of Australia, in SW Pacific Ocean c 1600 km (1000 mi) SE of Tasmania. Uninhabited except for meteorological station.

Macready, William Charles (1793-1873), English actor-manager. Known for Shakespearian tragic roles. Rival of Edwin Forrest.

Macrobius (fl c 400), Latin writer, philosopher. Known for 7-book *Saturnalia*, symposium of scholars whose discussions preserve fragments of much earlier writers.

Madagascar, see MALAGASY REPUBLIC.

Madang, town of Papua New Guinea, on NE coast of New Guinea isl. Pop. 15,000.

Madariaga, Salvador de (1886-), Spanish poet. Exiled after Civil War. Known for efforts to make Spanish literature known abroad. Works incl. novels, eg *The Heart of Jade* (1944), history, eg *España* (1942).

madder, any of genus *Rubia* of perennial herbs, esp. Eurasian vine, *R. tinctorum,* cultivated for red madder dye extracted from root.

Madeira, river of W Brazil, formed by jct. of Beni and Mamoré rivers, near Bolivian border. Flows NE 1450 km (c 900 mi) to join Amazon R. E of Manáus.

Madeira Islands, archipelago of N Atlantic, forming Funchal dist. of Portugal. Area 790 sq km (305 sq mi); cap. Funchal. Only 2 inhabited isls.: Madeira, Porto Santo. Largest isl. is Madeira, rising to 1860 m (6106 ft). Health, tourist resort. Madeira wine, fruit, fishing.

Madeira wine, dark brown fortified wine produced on isl. of Madeira. Four main types: sercial, a dry wine, and verdelho, bual and malmsey, all dessert wines. Matured for several years.

Madero, Francisco Indalecio (1873-1913), Mexican statesman. An advocate of democracy and social reform, he led successful revolution against Díaz (1910-11). As president (1911-13), failed to achieve significant reform. Shot after insurrection led by Huerta.

Madhya Pradesh, state of C India. Area c 443,400 sq km (171,200 sq mi); pop. 41,650,000; cap. Bhopal. Mainly on N Deccan plateau; monsoon climate aids largely agric. economy; dense forests provide teak. Coalmining; major source of manganese.

Madison, James (1751-1836), American statesman, president (1809-17). Leading figure in drafting US Constitution (1787), promoting its adoption through *The Federalist Papers* (1787-8). Democratic-Republican secretary of state (1801-9). War of 1812 main event of his presidency.

Madison, cap. of Wisconsin, US; on isthmus between Monona and Mendota lakes. Pop. 172,000. Centre of farming region. Founded as territ. cap. (1836). Has Univ. of Wisconsin (1848).

Madras, cap. of TAMIL NADU, SE India. Pop. 2,470,000. Major seaport, exports cotton, hides. Textile, clothing mfg. Founded as Fort St George by British (1639). Neaby is traditional site of martyrdom of St Thomas. University (1857).

Madrid, cap. of Spain and Madrid prov., on R. Manzanares. Pop. 3,146,000. Admin., indust., transport centre on the Castile plateau. Fortress, taken from Moors by Castile (1083); cap. from 1561. Besieged 1936-9 by Nationalists in Civil War. Buildings incl. Bourbon palace, Prado art gallery; univ. (1508).

madrigal, musical composition written for two or more singers and usually performed unaccompanied. First flourished in Italy in 14th cent., and then again in Italy and England in more elaborate form in 16th and 17th cents.

Madura, isl. of Indonesia, off NE coast of Java. Area 4560 sq km (1760 sq mi). Salt production, cattle rearing.

Madurai, city of Tamil Nadu, S India. Pop. 548,000. Textile, brassware mfg. Dates from 5th cent. BC. Ceded to British (1801). Has many temples, famous for festivals.

Maecenas, Gaius (d. 8 BC), Roman patron of writers. Adviser and friend of Augustus, encouraged Horace, Vergil, Propertius. Name now synonym for wealthy patron of arts.

Maelström, channel off NW Norway, in S Lofoten Isls. Area of whirlpools, dangerous currents. Term now applied to all whirlpools.

Maeterlinck, Maurice, Count (1862-1949), Belgian author. Known for anti-naturalistic dramas, *eg Pelléas et Mélisande* (1892), *L'Oiseau bleu* (1909). Also wrote dream-like verse incl. *Serres chaudes* (1889), studies of plant, animal life, *eg La Vie des abeilles* (1901). Nobel Prize for Literature (1911).

Mafeking, town of NE Cape Prov., South Africa. Pop. 8000. Agric. trade centre. Scene of 7-month siege of British by Boers 1899-1900. Extra-territ. cap. of Bechuanaland until 1965.

Mafia, originally, name given to secret groups in Sicily and S Italy, opposed to landowners and process of law. Esp. powerful 19th-early 20th cent., suppressed by Fascist govt. in 1920s, turned to industry, commerce after WWII. Brought to US by immigrants, long suspected of controlling illegal operations. Also known as 'Cosa Nostra'.

Magadha, ancient Indian kingdom, situated in modern Bihar state. Prominent in 7th cent. BC, came under Mauryan empire *c* 320 BC; recovered importance in 5th cent. AD under Gupta dynasty. Scene of development of Buddhism and Jainism.

Magadi, Lake, lake of S Kenya, in Great Rift Valley near Tanzania border. Length *c* 48 km (30 mi). Extensive sodium carbonate deposits.

Magdalena, river of Colombia. Rises in W Andes, flows N 1600 km (*c* 1000 mi) to Caribbean near Barranquilla. Important trade route, navigable to Neiva. Large oilfield in middle valley.

Magdalene, *see* MARY MAGDALENE.

Magdalenian, in archaeology, final phase of Upper Palaeolithic Age, centred on SW France; lasted from *c* 15,000 to 10,000 BC. Magdalenians are known for their cave art (*eg* that at Altamira) and refined tools, weapons.

Magdeburg, city of WC East Germany, on R. Elbe. Pop. 272,000. Railway jct., canal link with R. Weser; industs. incl. sugar refining, textiles, glass, chemicals. Former Hanseatic League member, with town law code widely copied in middle ages. Badly damaged in Thirty Years War, WWII.

Magellan, Ferdinand, English form of Fernão de Magelhães (*c* 1480-1521), Portuguese navigator. In service of Spain, sailed W (1519) to find S passage to Pacific. Explored Rio de la Plata estuary; rounded South America via Str. of Magellan (1520). Killed by natives in Philippines. One of ships, under del Cano, completed 1st global circumnavigation (1522).

Magellan Strait

Magellan Strait, narrow channel of extreme S Chile, between mainland and Tierra del Fuego. Connects Atlantic and Pacific. Discovered by Magellan (1520).

Magenta, town of Lombardy, N Italy. Pop. 18,000. Scene of battle (1859) in which French and Sardinians defeated Austrians.

Maggiore, Lake, Lombardy, NW Italy, N tip in Switzerland. Area 212 sq km (82 sq mi); incl. Borromean Isls. In mountainous region; vines, olives. Resorts incl. Locarno, Stresa.

maggot, legless worm-like larva of certain insects, *eg* house fly.

Magherafelt, dist. of C Northern Ireland. Area 562 sq km (217 sq mi); pop. 30,000. Created 1973, formerly part of Co. Londonderry.

Maghreb or **Maghrib,** Arabic term for NW Africa. Incl. N areas of Morocco, Algeria, Tunisia and, sometimes, Libya. During Moorish occupation incl. Spain.

Magi, priestly caste in ancient Media and Persia, reputed to possess supernatural powers. ZOROASTER was prob. a Magus. Term also refers to Wise Men of the East in NT who brought gifts to newborn Jesus.

magic (from MAGI), attempt to manipulate world by supernatural means. Practice depends on theory of under-lying, unseen forces. Concept occurs in many cultures, incl. fetishism, totemism, necromancy. Malevolent magic called 'black' magic.

Maginot Line, a fortification system built in 1930s along French frontier, begun by André Maginot (1877-1932), minister of war. It failed to deter German flanking action (1940) in WWII.

Maglemosian, Mesolithic culture of N Europe, dating from *c* 8000 to 5000 BC. Named after site in Denmark where bone tools, fishing gear and dugout canoes, *etc,* were found.

magma, molten material beneath the solid crust of the Earth. Solidifies when cooled to form IGNEOUS ROCKS, occasionally reaching surface as lava.

Magna Carta, charter signed by King John of England (1215) in face of demands by barons. Secured feudal rights and estab. areas over which king had no jurisdiction. Interpreted throughout English history as guaranteeing certain political and civil liberties.

magnesite, white, compact mineral, composed of magnesium carbonate. Found among serpentine, and where magnesium has replaced calcium in dolomites, limestones. Used in production of cement, furnace linings.

magnesium (Mg), light silver-white metallic element; at. no. 12, at. wt. 24.31. Burns with intense white flame. Occurs in magnesite, dolomite and sea water. Used in lightweight alloys, photographic flash bulbs; compounds used in medicine.

magnetic pole, either of 2 points on a magnet where its magnetism appears to be concentrated and from which magnetic lines of force emanate. Magnetic poles exist only in pairs (north and south poles); freely suspended magnet turns so that its south pole points N (principle used in compass). Like poles repel each other, unlike poles attract. Force acting between poles is inversely proportional to the square of the distance between them.

magnetic poles, in geography, 2 points on Earth's surface corresponding to poles of a magnet, towards which needle of magnetic compass points and where magnetic force is vertically downwards. N and S magnetic poles do not coincide with geographical poles; positions vary, following circular paths.

magnetic tape, thin plastic ribbon coated with ferromagnetic particles (usually an oxide of iron or chromium). In TAPE RECORDER particles are aligned in varying degrees according to amplitude and frequency of signal. Also used to store information in computers.

magnetism, branch of physics dealing with magnets and magnetic phenomena. Magnetic force results from electricity in motion. Magnetic properties of materials such as iron result from unbalanced electron spin in the atom, giving rise to magnetic moment of atom. Overall magnetism follows when individual magnetic moments of atoms are aligned together.

magnetite (Fe₃O₄), iron ore mineral. Hard, black in colour; consists of magnetic iron oxide (variety called lodestone is natural magnet). Major sources in Sweden, USSR, US.

Magnitogorsk, town of USSR, W Siberian RSFSR. Pop. 373,000. Major metallurgical centre based on magnetite ore; iron and steel, coke, chemical mfg. Built 1929-31.

magnitude, in astronomy, measure of star's apparent brightness. Stars of any one magnitude are 2.512 times brighter than stars of next magnitude; thus stars of 1st magnitude are brightest and are 2.512 times brighter than those of 2nd. Faintest stars visible are approximately of 6th magnitude.

Magnolia *(Magnolia denudata)*

magnolia, genus of trees and shrubs with showy, fragrant flowers. Native to North America and Asia. Species incl. southern magnolia or bull bay, *Magnolia grandiflora,* with large white flowers, and umbrella tree, *M. tripetala,* with white flowers grouped in umbrella forms at end of branches.

Common magpie

magpie, long-tailed, black and white bird of crow family, genus *Pica.* Common magpie *P. pica* found in North America, Europe.

Magritte, René (1898-1967), Belgian surrealist painter. His work examines nature of reality, often depicting familiar objects in disturbing juxtapositions or unfamiliar settings. Work incl. *Time Transfixed* (1930).

Magyars, people constituting main ethnic group of Hungary. Originally nomadic, migrated from Urals to Caucasia (5th cent.). Forced W, settled in Hungary in 9th cent. Magyar language belongs to Finno-Ugrian group.

Mahábhárata, great Sanskrit epic of India, compiled *c* 400 BC-AD 200. Main story is struggle for succession to kingdom of Bháratas. Incl. BHAGAVAD-GITA and an abridgment of RAMAYANA. Rest of book contains mix of folklore, myth, philosophy.

Mahalla el Kubra, city of N Egypt, on Nile delta. Pop. 256,000. Cotton mfg. centre in cotton, rice, cereal growing area.

Mahan, Alfred Thayer (1840-1914), American naval historian. Left US navy with rank of rear-admiral and wrote classic *The Influence of Sea Power upon History, 1660-1783* (1890).

Maharashtra, state of WC India. Area *c* 307,000 sq km (118,500 sq mi); pop. 50,335,000; cap. Bombay. Mainly on Deccan plateau, with coastal plain on Arabian Sea. Mainly agric. economy; cotton, rice, groundnuts. Textile mfg.

Mahayana, branch of BUDDHISM which arose in NW India before 6th cent. Stresses disinterested love, salvation of others as route to the individual's own salvation. Developed extensive pantheon and changed concept of NIRVANA to denote salvation or damnation in afterlife resulting from nature of one's actions. *See* BODHISATTVA.

Mahdi, leader and prophet expected by Moslems to appear on earth before the world ends to restore justice. In Sunnite Islam he is a descendant of Mohammed's daughter Fatima. In Shiite Islam he is a hidden IMAM. There have been many claimants, notably **Mohammed Ahmed** (1848-85), who led rebellion against Egyptian rule in Sudan. Died after capturing Khartoum. His followers, the Mahdists, were defeated (1898) by British.

Mahler, Gustav (1860-1911), Austrian composer. Wrote music often classic in form but highly romantic and expressive in style. Works incl. 9 symphonies, song cycle *Das Lied von der Erde.* Also renowned as a conductor, esp. in Vienna and New York.

Mahmud II (1784-1839), Ottoman sultan (1808-39). Used Egyptian troops to subdue revolt in Greece but had to accept Greek independence after battle of Navarino (1827). Forced to rely on Russian help to maintain power. Suppressed Janissaries (1826).

Mahmud of Ghazni (*c* 971-1030), Afghan ruler. Extended Afghan rule into Persia and N India. Frequently invaded India where, as a fervent follower of Islam, he campaigned against Hindu idolatry. Destroyed famous temple at Somnath in Gujarat (1025).

Mahogany

mahogany, any of genus *Swietenia* of tropical trees. Dark, heavy wood valued for furniture, esp. that of *S. mahogani* of tropical America. Name also applied to various similar woods, *eg* African mahogany of genus *Khaya,* Australian red mahogany of genus *Eucalyptus.*

Mahrattas or **Marathas,** people of WC India who speak Marathi language. Supplanted Moguls in 18th cent., controlling the Deccan and much of S India. Lost most of their territ. to the British by 1818.

Maiden Castle, well-preserved site of Iron Age hill fort near Dorchester, Dorset, England. Occupied from 3rd cent. BC, it became stronghold of Durotriges, a Belgic tribe. Captured by Romans under Vespasian (AD 43).

maidenhair, any of genus *Adiantum* of ferns native to tropical and warm temperate regions. Delicate, brown fronds.

maidenhair tree, *see* GINKGO.

Maidenhead, mun. bor. of Berkshire, SC England, on R. Thames. Pop. 45,000. Boating centre; electronic equipment mfg.

Maidstone, mun. bor. and co. town of Kent, SE England, on R. Medway. Pop. 71,000. Hops market, brewing. Has All Saints' Church (14th cent.).

Maiduguri, city of NE Nigeria. Pop. (incl. nearby Yerwa) 169,000. Railway terminus; agric. market, esp. for groundnuts, cotton; leather goods mfg.

Maikop, city of USSR, cap. of Adygei auton. region, SW European RSFSR. Pop. 119,000. Centre for nearby oil fields; timber, food-processing industs.

Mailer, Norman (1923-   ), American author. Novels incl. *The Naked and the Dead* (1948) in WWII setting, *An American Dream* (1964). Also wrote political essays, *eg The Presidential Papers* (1963). Concerned with moral and political analysis, using unconventional prose, of contemporary US.

Maillol, Aristide (1861-1944), French sculpter. Devoted himself almost totally to female nude; influenced by classical Greek sculpture, he stressed monumental quality of human form. Work incl. *Monument to Cézanne.*

Maimonides or **Moses ben Maimon** (1135-1204), Jewish philosopher and physician, b. Spain. Codified Jewish law in Mishna Torah. His philosophical *Moreh Nevukhim* influenced Aquinas.

Main, river of C West Germany. Flows *c* 500 km (310 mi) from N Bavaria via Würzburg, Frankfurt to R. Rhine at Mainz. Navigable for *c* 355 km (220 mi); canal link to R. Danube.

Maine, region and former prov. of NW France, cap. Le Mans. Agric., stock raising. County from 10th cent., united with Anjou (1126). Returned to French crown (1584).

Maine, state of extreme NE US. Area 86,027 sq km (33,215 sq mi); pop. 994,000; cap. Augusta; chief town Portland. Forested lakeland; hilly in W; crossed by many rivers esp. St John, Kennebec, Penobscot. Main occupations lumbering, farming, fishing (esp. lobsters); some mining (stone, clay). Part of Massachusetts colony in 17th-18th cent. Admitted to Union as 23rd state (1820).

Mainland, two isls. of N Scotland. **1,** also called Pomona, largest of Orkney isls.; main town Kirkwall. Wartime naval base at Scapa Flow, to S. Has important prehist. remains *eg* Skara Brae. **2,** largest of Shetland isls.; main town Lerwick.

Maintenon, Françoise d'Aubigné, Marquise de (1635-1719), second wife of Louis XIV. Married Louis XIV secretly (*c* 1685). A convert to Catholicism, she had considerable influence over him in matters of morality.

Mainz (Fr. *Mayence*), city of WC West Germany, at confluence of Rhine and Main, cap. of Rhineland-Palatinate. Pop. 179,000. River port, chemicals, engineering; major wine centre. Roman camp; 1st German archbishopric (747). Early printing centre, home of Gutenberg. Univ. (1477-1798, 1946).

maize or **Indian corn,** *Zea mays,* cultivated American cereal plant of grass family. Grain borne on cobs enclosed in husks. Naturalized in S Africa, India, China, S Europe and Australia. Cobs may be roasted or boiled. When coarsely milled, called hominy or polenta; with gluten removed becomes cornflour.

majolica or **maiolica,** variety of pottery which grew to prominence in 15th cent. Italy, after being introduced from Spain. Produced by applying tin enamel to earthenware; on firing it forms white opaque surface, on which design is painted. Object is then glazed and fired again.

Majorca (*Mallorca*), largest of Balearic Isls., Spain. Area 3639 sq km (1405 sq mi); cap. and chief port Palma. Mountainous in NW. Tourism, fruit growing, wine mfg.; fishing. Kingdom from 1276, united with Aragón 1343.

Majuba Hill, mountain of NW Natal, South Africa, in Drakensberg Mts. Height 1980 m (6500 ft). Scene of Boer victory (1881) over British.

Makarios III, orig. Michael Christedoulos Mouskos (1913-77), Cypriot churchman, political leader. Leader of Greek Cypriot movement for union with Greece (Enosis); exiled by British (1956-7). Elected president on estab. of republic

Majolica peacock by Minton

Archbishop Makarios

(1959). Deposed by Greek-inspired coup (1974) but took up presidency again after Turkish invasion.

Makassar, *see* UJUNG PANDANG.

Makemie, Francis (*c* 1658-1708), American clergyman, b. Ireland. Travelled and preached on E seaboard; estab. 1st presbytery in Philadelphia. Regarded as founder of Presbyterianism in US.

Makeyevka, city of USSR, SE Ukrainian SSR. Pop. 396,000. Metallurgical and coalmining centre. Founded 1899 as Dmitriyevsk.

Makhachkala, city of USSR, cap. of Dagestan auton. republic, SE European RSFSR; port on Caspian Sea. Pop. 200,000. Linked by pipeline to Grozny oilfields; oil refining, shipbuilding.

Malabar Coast, coastal region of SW India extending from Goa to Cape Comorin. Now mainly in Kerala state.

Malabo, cap. of Equatorial Guinea, on Macias Nguema Biyoga isl. Pop. 37,000. Commercial, admin. centre; port, exports cacao, coffee; fish processing. Formerly called Santa Isabel.

Malacca, cap. of Malacca state, SW West Malaysia. Pop. 86,000. Seaport on Str. of Malacca. Trade declined after rise of Singapore. Held by Portuguese, then Dutch, until ceded to Britain (1824).

Malachi, prophetic book of OT, sometimes attributed to Ezra. Castigates priests and the people for their laxity. Foretells judgment and coming of a Messiah.

malachite, copper ore mineral. Soft, green in colour; consists of basic copper carbonate. Found in oxidized zones of copper deposits, sometimes as cement in sandstones. Used as gem, source of pigment. Major sources in US, Chile, USSR.

Malachy, St (1095-1148), Irish churchman. Archbishop of Armagh (1134-7), estab. territorial hierarchy in Church of Ireland in place of hereditary system which dated from St Patrick, began religious revival. Died at Clairvaux while visiting St Bernard.

Malacostraca, subclass of crustaceans, incl. lobster, crab, shrimp. Has 19 segments (5 head, 8 thorax, 6 abdomen); carapace often covers thorax.

Málaga, city of S Spain, on Mediterranean Sea, cap. of Málaga prov. Pop. 374,000. Resort; port, exports wine, fruit. Founded 12th cent. BC by Phoenicians; chief port of Moorish Granada, taken by Spain 1487. Moorish citadel, 16th cent. cathedral. Birthplace of Picasso.

Malagasy Republic

Malagasy Republic, isl. republic of W Indian Ocean, separated from Africa by Mozambique Channel. Area 587,000 sq km (226,600 sq mi); pop. 6,750,000; cap. Tananarive. Languages: Malagasy, French. Religions: Christian, native. Pop. divided into Indonesian and black African ethnic groups. Main isl. Madagascar, also incl. Nossi-Bé, Sainte-Marie Isls. Narrow coastal strip; mainly C highland, now largely deforested. Unique flora and fauna. Crops incl. sugar, coffee, rice; cattle raising. French colony from 1896 until independence in 1960. Member of French Community.

Malamud, Bernard (1914-   ), American novelist. Known for novels incl. *The Natural* (1952), *The Fixer* (1966), short story collections, *eg Idiots First* (1963), dealing with Jewish themes.

Malan, Daniel François (1874-1959), South African politician, PM (1948-54). Leader of Nationalist Party (1933-54), advocated white supremacy and republicanism. His govt. enacted 1st *apartheid* laws.

Malang, city of E Java, Indonesia. Pop. 422,000. On plateau surrounded by volcanoes. Commercial centre, dealing in coffee, rice.

malaria, infectious disease caused by parasitic protozoon, genus *Plasmodium*, which feeds on red blood cells. Transmitted by bite of female mosquito of *Anopheles* group. Characterized by intermittent attacks of fever and shivering. Formerly treated by quinine, now by synthetic drugs.

Malatya (anc. *Melitene*), city of EC Turkey. Pop. 144,000. Commercial centre; trade in opium, grain. Military hq. of Romans and important city of Cappadocia.

Malawi, republic of EC Africa. Area *c* 118,000 sq km (45,250 sq mi); pop. 4,900,000; cap. Lilongwe. Languages: Bantu dialects, English. Religions: native, Christian. Great Rift Valley runs N-S, filled by L. Malawi; elsewhere plateau, incl. Shiré Highlands (SW). Produces tea, cotton, tobacco, sugar cane, groundnuts. Area of L. Malawi visited by Livingstone (1859); British protect. estab. 1891; called Nyasaland (1907-64). Formed federation with Rhodesia

(1953-62); independent 1964, republic 1966. Member of British Commonwealth.

Malawi, Lake, lake of EC Africa, between Malawi, Tanzania, Mozambique. Length *c* 580 km (360 mi); part of Great Rift Valley. Drained to S by R. Shiré into Zambezi. Major trade artery. Explored (1859) by Livingstone; called L. Nyasa until Malawi's independence (1964).

Malay, major language in MALAYO-POLYNESIAN family, with *c* 10 million speakers in Malaya and Straits settlements.

Malaya, region of SE Asia, comprising former British colonies of Malay penin.; corresponds to West Malaysia. Area *c* 131,400 sq km (51,000 sq mi). Mountainous interior flanked by plains; densely forested. Equatorial climate. World's leading rubber, tin producer. Called Federation of Malaya (1948-63); independence from Britain 1957.

Malayalam, see DRAVIDIAN.

Malay Archipelago, group of isls. between SE Asia and Australia. Incl. Indonesia, Philippines.

Malayo-Polynesian, widespread family of languages, covering vast area of Pacific incl. Madagascar, Taiwan, Papua and New Guinea, Hawaii, *etc.*

Malaysia

Malaysia, federated state of SE Asia in British Commonwealth. Area *c* 332,650 sq km (128,500 sq mi); pop. 10,424,000; cap. Kuala Lumpur. Language: Malayan. Religion: Islam. Formed (1963) from MALAYA (West Malaysia) and SABAH, SARAWAK (East Malaysia). Singapore seceded in 1965.

Malcolm III [Canmore] (d. 1093), king of Scotland (1057-93). Defeated and succeeded MACBETH (1057). Married (1070) St Margaret of Scotland, by whose influence Celtic culture of Scotland was gradually replaced by English ways. Killed while invading England.

Malcolm X, orig. Malcolm Little (1925-65), American Negro leader. Became a Black Muslim (1952); suspended from movement by Elijah Muhammad (1963). Founded Organization of Afro-American Unity (1964), dedicated to black nationalism. Assassinated.

Maldive Islands, republic in N Indian Ocean, SW of Sri Lanka; comprises *c* 2000 coral isls. Area 298 sq km (115 sq mi); pop. 119,000; cap. Malé. Language: Divehi. Religion: Islam. Agric. economy based on coconuts, fruit. British protect. from 1887, independent in 1965; became republic (1968).

Malebranche, Nicolas (1638-1715), French philosopher. Attempted to resolve Cartesian dualism and Christian theology by positing a divine will which allows the otherwise distinct realms of mind and matter to interact.

Malenkov, Georgi Maksimilianovich (1902-   ), Soviet political leader. Succeeded Stalin as premier (1953-5). Forced to resign over failure of agric. policy. Succeeded by Khrushchev. Expelled from Communist Party (1961).

Malevich, Casimir (1878-1935), Russian artist. Founder of suprematist movement, which stressed absolute geometric abstraction. His *White on White,* white square on a white background, summed up the movement.

Malherbe, François de (1555-1628), French poet. Literary arbiter of early 17th cent. Advocated classical standards of simplicity, rationality.

Mali, republic of W Africa. Area 1,240,000 sq km (478,000 sq mi); pop. 5,561,000; cap. Bamako. Languages: French, various African. Religions: Islam, native. Desert in N, elsewhere semidesert; main rivers Senegal, Niger. Swamp, marsh SW of Timbuktu; irrigation at Ségu. Main crops groundnuts, cotton, rice, maize; cattle raising. Economy severely affected by drought in early 1970s. Occupied by French in late 19th cent.; became colony (1904), called French Sudan from 1920. Part of Mali Federation (1959-60) with Senegal; independent 1960.

Malindi, town of E Kenya, on Indian Ocean. Pop. 6000. Visited 1498 by da Gama, who built monument still standing; nearby is ruined city of Gedi.

Malines, see MECHELEN, Belgium.

Malinowski, Bronislaw (1884-1942), British social anthropologist, b. Poland. Estab. 'participant observer' technique of examining culture, esp. writings on Trobriand isls. One of founders of functionalist sociology.

mallard, *Anas platyrhynchos,* wild duck of N hemisphere, from which most domestic ducks are descended. Male has green head and white band around neck.

Mallarmé, Stéphane (1842-98), French poet. Formulated theories of SYMBOLISTS. Works incl. *Hérodiade* (1869), *L'Après-midi d'un faune* (1876) which inspired Debussy's orchestral piece.

mallee, any of Australian shrubs of *Eucalyptus* genus with numerous spreading trunks and ability to withstand arid conditions and to regenerate after bush fire. Species incl. peppermint box, *E. odorata,* blue mallee, *E. fructicetorum,* green mallee, *E. viridis.*

Mallorca, see MAJORCA, Spain.

Common mallow (Malva sylvestris)

mallow, any of genus *Malva* of herbs native to N temperate regions. Large dissected leaves, purple, pink or white flowers.

Malmaison, see RUEIL-MALMAISON, France.

Malmédy, see EUPEN AND MALMÉDY, Belgium.

Malmö, city of SW Sweden, on Oresund. Pop. 265,000. Port, exports timber, grain, dairy produce; shipbuilding. Ferry to Copenhagen. Church (14th cent.), Malmöhus castle (15th cent.). Held by Denmark until 1658.

malnutrition, deficiency of essential component of diet. May be caused by inadequate food or insufficient vitamins in food. May also be caused by failure to assimilate food during illness.

Malory, Sir Thomas (d. 1471), English writer. Known for *Le Morte d'Arthur* (*c* 1469), last medieval English treatment of the ARTHURIAN LEGEND. Still read for vivid characterization, vigorous prose, varied stories.

Malpighi, Marcello (1628-94), Italian anatomist. Discovered capillaries which connect arteries and veins, confirming Harvey's description of blood circulation. Extended science of embryology by his use of microscope.

Malplaquet, village of Nord, N France. Scene of battle (1709) in which Marlborough defeated French in War of Spanish Succession.

Malraux, André (1901-76), French author, politician. Novels, incl. *La Condition humaine* (1933), *L'Espoir* (1937), deal with struggle for meaning in political setting. Also wrote *The Psychology of Art* (1947-50), depicting history of man's search for the absolute.

malt, grain, chiefly barley, which has been partially germinated and then dried in kilns. Used in brewing. Contains nutritional carbohydrates and protein.

Malta, republic of S Europe, in Mediterranean Sea S of Sicily, comprising isls. of Malta, Gozo, Comino. Area 316 sq km (122 sq mi); pop. 322,000; cap. Valletta. Languages: Maltese, English. Religion: RC. Tourist resort; agric. incl. cereals, potatoes, fruit. Taken by Norman Sicily 1090; given to Knights Hospitallers 1530. Annexed by Britain 1814; independent from 1964. Formerly major naval base; heavily bombed during WWII. Member of British Commonwealth, UN.

Malthus, Thomas Robert (1766-1834), English economist, churchman. Suggested in *An Essay on the Principle of Population* (1798) that poverty is inevitable as population increases geometrically while food supply increases arithmetically. Theory influenced Ricardo.

Maluku, see MOLUCCAS.

Malvern, urban dist. of Hereford and Worcester, W England, on E slopes of Malvern Hills. Pop. 29,000. Resort, spa; has annual drama festival associated with Shaw's plays.

Malvinas, Islas, see FALKLAND ISLANDS.

mamba, large arboreal snake, genus *Dendraspis,* of C and S Africa. Aggressive, with large fangs; venom can be fatal. Species incl. green mamba, *D. viridis,* and black mamba, *D. angusticeps.*

Mamelukes, members of military caste, originally made up of slaves, used as soldiers of caliphate. Mameluke sultanate was estab. in Egypt (1250) and dominated Middle East until absorbed into Ottoman empire (1517). Mamelukes retained actual control of Egypt until 1811.

mammals (Mammalia), class of warm-blooded vertebrates with hair on body, lungs for respiration, 4-chambered heart. Offspring fed on milk secreted by female mammary glands. Divided into 3 subclasses: primitive egg-laying monotremes, pouch-bearing marsupials and more advanced placentals.

Mammoth

mammoth, extinct large elephant of Eurasia and North America, with hairy skin and long upward-curving tusks. Known from fossil remains of Pleistocene period, frozen corpses in Siberia and cave paintings.

Mammoth Cave National Park, in S Kentucky, US. Has one of world's largest caves (area 20,783 ha./51,354 acres); limestone formations.

Mamoré, river of C Bolivia. Rises in E Andes, flows N *c* 965 km (*c* 600 mi) to join Beni, forming Madeira R.

man, *Homo sapiens,* sole surviving member of the hominid family. Precise evolution of modern man from more primitive forms, *eg* AUSTRALOPITHECUS and HOMO ERECTUS, is unclear and subject to controversy. NEANDERTHAL and CRO-MAGNON man are considered early forms of *H. sapiens.*

Man, Isle of, isl. of UK, in Irish Sea. Area 588 sq km (227 sq mi); pop. 56,000; cap. Douglas. Hilly (Snaefell, 620 m/2034 ft); mild climate. Crops, livestock; tourism. Hist. dependency of Norway, Scotland; passed to UK 1828. Parliament ('Tynwald'); Manx language now little used.

Manada or **Mendado,** cap. of N Sulawesi prov. (Celebes), Indonesia. Pop. 170,000. Seaport in extreme NE of isls.; exports coffee, copra.

Managua, cap. of Nicaragua, on L. Managua. Pop. 374,000. Admin., indust., trade centre; textiles, cement, cigarette mfg. Became cap. 1855. Evacuated 1972 after severe earthquake.

Manama, cap. of Bahrain. Pop. 88,000. Free transit port. Commercial centre; oil refining, pearl fishing base.

Manasseh ben Israel (1604-57), Jewish scholar, b. Portugal. Urged readmission of Jews into England; gained Cromwell's unofficial assent. Started 1st Hebrew press in Holland.

manatee, herbivorous aquatic mammal, genus *Trichechus*, with rounded tail and 2 front flippers. Found in shallow coastal waters of West Indies, South America, W Africa. Numbers reduced by over-hunting.

Manáus, inland port of NC Brazil, cap. of Amazonas state; on Negro R. near jct. with Amazon. Pop. 312,000. Timber, rubber, nuts exports; jute milling, oil refining. Grew during early 20th cent. rubber boom. Buildings incl. opera house; famous botanical gardens.

Mancha, La, arid treeless plateau of S New Castile, Spain. Made famous by Cervantes in *Don Quixote de la Mancha*.

Manche, La, see ENGLISH CHANNEL.

Manchester, city of Greater Manchester met. county, NW England. Met. county pop. 2,730,000; city 541,000. Linked to sea by Ship Canal (1894); major seaport. Textiles (hist. cotton mfg.), chemicals mfg. Has grammar school (1519), univ. (1880). Roman *Mancunium;* medieval wool trade. Scene of Peterloo massacre (1819).

Manchester, town of S New Hampshire, US; on Merrimack R. Pop. 88,000; state's largest town. Textile, leather, electrical equipment mfg. Major hist. cotton mfg. town.

Manchester Ship Canal, NW England, canal for ocean-going vessels, 56 km (35 mi) long. Links Manchester with Mersey estuary, Irish Sea. Opened 1894.

Manchukuo, puppet state set up in Manchuria (1932) by the Japanese after their occupation of country (1931). Ruled by Pu-yi, last emperor of all China. Manchukuo returned to China after WWII.

Manchuria, region of NE China. Comprises Liaoning, Kirin, Heilungkiang provs. Mountains surround fertile C plain, drained by Liao, Sungari rivers; major agric. and mfg. centre of China. Important timber and mineral resources. Occupied by Japanese 1931-45.

Manchu-Tungus or **Tungusic,** language group within E Altaic family. Spoken in China, USSR; incl. Manchurian.

Mandaeans, ancient Gnostic sect still extant in Iran and S Iraq. Beliefs drawn from Babylonian astrology and cults of the Magi. Principal rite is frequent baptism based on concern for ritual cleanliness and belief in water as life principle. Scripture, the *Ginza Rba* is fragmentary collection of legend, astrological and cosmogonal lore.

Mandalay: the Golden Kyoung

Mandalay, city of C Burma, on the Irrawaddy. Pop. 401,000. Transport and commercial centre. Old walled city largely destroyed by Japanese (1942); numerous pagodas.

Mandarin, see CHINESE.

Mande, subgroup of Niger-Congo branch of Niger-Kordofanian language family. Languages within it spoken in Niger valley, Liberia, Sierra Leone, incl. Mende (Liberia), Malinke (Mali).

Mandeville, Sir John (*fl* 14th cent.), English author. Wrote *The Travels of Sir John Mandeville* (*c* 1356), part genuine, part vividly imagined, record of travels in Near and Far East. Authorship disputed.

mandoline or **mandolin,** musical instrument of lute family, with 4 or 5 pairs of strings, each pair tuned to same note. Played with a plectrum.

Mandrake

mandrake, *Mandragora officinarum,* poisonous plant of nightshade family. Short stem, purple flowers. Fleshy, forked root thought to resemble a human form, long believed to have supernatural properties. Used as narcotic in Middle Ages.

mandrill, *Mandrillus sphinx,* large fierce baboon of W Africa with red nose, blue cheeks. Drill, *M. leucophaeus,* less colourful.

manes, in Roman religion, deified souls of the dead. Associated with LARES AND PENATES and LEMURES.

Manet, Edouard (1832-83), French painter. Influenced by Spanish art and Hals, his portrayal of commonplace scenes, using light and dark shadows, pioneered a new style; he greatly influenced the impressionists. In 1870s, adopted a lighter, more colourful manner. Works incl. *Déjeuner sur l'herbe,* which created a scandal on exhibition, and *Bar at the Folies-Bergère.*

mangabey, any of genus *Cercocebus* of long-tailed monkeys from equatorial Africa. Lives in small groups in treetops.

manganese (Mn), hard brittle metallic element; at. no. 25, at. wt. 54.94. Occurs as pyrolusite (MnO_2), from which it is obtained by reduction with aluminium. Used in making alloys, esp. very hard manganese steel. Manganese dioxide is used in dry cells, in glass manufacture and as an oxidizing agent.

mango, *Mangifera indica,* tree bearing fleshy yellowish-red fruit, native to Malaya and West Indies. Eaten ripe, preserved or pickled.

mangold or **mangel-wurzel,** *Beta vulgaris,* variety of beet, native to Europe. Formerly cultivated as cattle food.

Mangrove

mangrove, any of genus *Rhizophora* of tropical evergreen trees found in swampy areas and on river banks. American mangrove, *R. mangle,* common in Florida, is important in land reclamation.

Manhattan, see NEW YORK CITY.

manic-depressive psychosis, form of severe mental disturbance, characterized by alternate bouts of mania and depression. Patient is abnormally excited in manic phase, lethargic and withdrawn in depressive. Treatment incl. shock therapy for depression, lithium compounds for mania.

Manichaeism, dualist religious philosophy (*fl* 3rd cent.-7th cent.) based on teachings of Mani (b. Persia, *c* 216-76). Combined elements of Zoroastrianism, Gnostic Christianity and Platonism. Persecuted by orthodox Zoroastrians. Term came to be used in medieval Church for all dualist heresies.

Manila, chief seaport of Philippines, SW Luzon isl. Pop. 1,436,000. Exports hemp, sugar; cigarette, textile mfg. Founded 1571; national cap. until 1948. Divided by R. Pasig into old Spanish walled city (*Intramuros*) and modern section. Has Univ. of St Thomas (1611). Spanish fleet destroyed by US under Dewey (1898) in Manila Bay.

Manila hemp, strong cord-like fibre obtained from abacá (Manila hemp plant); used to make rope, paper, clothing.

Manin, Daniele (1804-57), Italian statesman. President of newly-formed Venetian republic (1848). Led resistance to 5-month siege by Austrians; surrendered 1849. Lived in exile in France.

manioc, see CASSAVA.

Manipur, state of NE India. Area *c* 22,300 sq km (8600 sq mi); pop. 1,070,000; cap. Imphal. Bounded on E by Burma; largely mountainous. Forests provide teak.

manito or **manitou,** name used by Algonquian North American Indians for supernatural forces inherent in objects. May be of either good or evil influence.

Manitoba, Prairie prov. of WC Canada. Area 638,466 sq km (246,512 sq mi); pop. 988,000; cap. Winnipeg. Tundra in N (Laurentian Shield); lakes in C; farmland in S watered by Red, Assiniboine rivers. Mainly agric. (esp. wheat, oats, barley growing); timber; mining (gold, copper, zinc). Meat packing, flour milling industs. Chartered 1670 to Hudson's Bay Co.; British control from 1763; became prov. 1870 after purchase by Canada.

Manitoba, Lake, SW Manitoba, Canada. Area 4076 sq km (1817 sq mi). N end is connected to L. Winnipegosis; drained by Dauphin R. into L. Winnipeg.

Manitoulin Islands, chain of Canada-US, in N L. Huron. Most are in Canada, incl. Manitoulin Isl., the world's largest lake isl. Summer tourist resorts on most isls.

Manizales, city of WC Colombia, in Andes; alt. *c* 2100 m (7000 ft). Pop. 220,000. Railway jct.; commercial, agric. centre (esp. coffee); textile mfg.

Manley, Norman Washington (1893-1969), Jamaican politician, PM (1959-62). Founded socialist People's National Party (1938), leader while Jamaica was in West Indies Federation (1958-62). His son, **Michael Norman Manley** (1924-), was PM from 1972. Programme incl. widespread socialist reform, closer ties with other Third World states, esp. Cuba.

Manlius Capitolinus, Marcus (d. *c* 384 BC), Roman politician. According to legend, on being aroused by sacred geese, he repulsed the invading Gauls (*c* 389) from the Capitol. Later accused of seeking kingly power, he was executed for treason.

Mann, Thomas (1875-1955), German author. Preoccupied with duality of artistic and practical life. Novels incl. *Buddenbrooks* (1901), *Death in Venice* (1913), *The Magic Mountain* (1924), *Dr Faustus* (1948). Settled in US (1939). Nobel Prize for Literature (1929). His brother, **Heinrich Mann** (1871-1950) wrote *Professor Unrat* (1905), basis of von Sternberg's film *The Blue Angel.*

Mann, Tom (1856-1941), English labour leader. Organized London dock strike (1889) with John Burns. Helped organize Australian Labor Party. A founder of British Communist Party (1920).

manna, in OT, food provided by God for the Israelites in the wilderness. Various natural explanations proposed, *eg* edible lichen, *Lecanora esculenta.*

Mannerheim, Carl Gustav Emil, Baron (1867-1951), Finnish field marshal, statesman. Led Finnish forces which drove Bolsheviks from Finland (1918); regent (1918-19). Headed army in war with Soviet Union (1939-44). President of Finland (1944-6).

mannerism, in art and architecture, 16th cent. style, originating in Italy as reaction against classical perfection of high Renaissance style of Raphael, *etc.* Painting characterized by contorted figures, lack of classical balance, vivid colour. Exponents incl. Parmigianino, Tintoretto, Pontormo.

Mannheim, Karl (1893-1947), Hungarian sociologist. In Germany, developed from Marxist theory a 'sociology of knowledge', stated in *Ideology and Utopia* (*1929*).

Mannheim, city of WC West Germany, at confluence of Rhine and Neckar, opposite Ludwigshafen. Pop. 331,000. Vehicles, machinery mfg. Seat of Electors Palatine from 1720, became centre of music, theatre (*eg* Mannheim orchestra). Has baroque buildings, palace.

Manning, Henry Edward (1808-92), English churchman. At first Anglican, was converted (1851) to RC faith through influence of OXFORD MOVEMENT. Archbishop of Westminster from 1865; created cardinal 1875. Worked for social reform, settled London dock strike of 1889.

Manolete, orig. Manuel Rodríguez y Sánchez (1917-47), Spanish matador. Considered leading matador of his time, with superb technique, he was fatally gored at height of his career.

manometer, instrument used to measure pressure of gases. Simplest type consists of U-shaped tube partially filled with liquid.

manor, see FEUDALISM.

Manresa, town of Catalonia, NE Spain. Pop. 58,000. Textile mfg. Below Jesuit convent is grotto of St Ignatius; place of pilgrimage.

Mans, Le, see LE MANS, France.

Mansard or **Mansart, François** (1598-1666), French architect. Considered outstanding exponent of French 17th cent. Classicism. His Hôtel de la Vrillière served as model for Parisian town house for many years; surviving work incl. château of Maisons Lafitte. Type of roof designed to give higher interior space named after him.

Mansfield, Katherine, pseud. of Kathleen Mansfield Beauchamp (1888-1923), British author, b. New Zealand. Known for short stories with New Zealand setting, *eg Bliss* (1920), *The Garden Party* (1922). Married Middleton MURRY.

Mansfield, mun. bor. of Nottinghamshire, NC England. Pop. 58,000. Coal dist.; clothing mfg.

manslaughter, unlawful killing of human being, distinguished from murder in being without premeditated malice. Usually divided into voluntary (intentional killing but done in heat, *eg* in sudden affray) and involuntary (unintentional; resulting from culpable negligence, *eg* reckless driving).

Mansur or **Al-Mansur** (*c* 941-1002), Moslem regent of Andalusia. Took over regency for caliph Hisham II (981) and assumed title of king (996). Restored Omayyad control of Moslem Spain.

Mansûra, city of N Egypt, on Nile delta. Pop. 212,000. Cotton mfg. centre, railway jct. Scene of Mamelukes' victory (1250) over Crusaders under St Louis.

Mantegna, Andrea (*c* 1431-1506), Italian painter. Influenced by Donatello, his figures have sculptural quality and display extreme foreshortening. Paintings reflect interest in classical antiquity, derived from archaeological studies. Works incl. frescoes in Mantua in honour of Gonzaga family.

mantis or **mantid,** any of Mantidae family of elongated slender insects. Seizes insect prey with pincer-like forelegs, often held up together as if praying.

mantis shrimp, see STOMATOPODA.

Mantua (*Mantova*), town of Lombardy, N Italy, cap. of Mantova prov. Pop. 67,000. Renaissance cultural centre

Mantis

under Gonzaga family; ducal palace (14th cent.). Birthplace of Vergil nearby.

Manu, in Hindu myth, survivor of great flood and ancestor of mankind. Traditional author of *Laws of Manu* (prob. written *c* AD 100), detailing the codes of ritual and daily life for Brahman caste. Used by Warren Hastings in formulating laws for India.

Manuel I (1469-1521), king of Portugal (1495-1521). During his reign, Portugal reached height of its commercial and colonial activities. Sea route to India was discovered by Vasco da Gama and Brazil was claimed (1500).

Manutius, Aldus, *see* ALDUS MANUTIUS.

Manx, *see* GAELIC.

Manx cat, short-haired tailless variety of domestic cat.

Manzala or **Menzaleh, Lake,** coastal lagoon of N Egypt. Area 1710 sq km (660 sq mi); extends from Damietta to Suez Canal.

Manzini, town of Swaziland. Pop. 16,000. Agric. market on railway to Mozambique. Formerly called Bremersdorp.

Manzoni, Alessandro (1785-1873), Italian author. Known for romantic historical novel, *The Betrothed* (1827), depicting divine intervention in everyday life. Death inspired Verdi's *Requiem*.

Maori, aboriginal inhabitants of New Zealand, of Polynesian stock. Traditional economy based on agric., fishing, hunting, gathering. Originally divided into tribes, with frequent intertribal wars. On British colonists' attempts to settle large tracts of land, began Maori Wars (1861-71). Now comprise 10% of pop., with 4 Maori electorates sending representatives to Parliament.

Mao Tse-tung c 1937

Mao Tse-tung (1893-1976), Chinese political leader. Helped found Chinese Communist Party; after Communist split with KUOMINTANG (1927), organized Red Army and consolidated authority during LONG MARCH (1934-5). Prolonged civil war of 1930s and 1940s ended in triumph over Chiang Kai-shek's Nationalists and estab. of People's Republic of China (1949) with Mao as chairman of govt.

council (1949-59). Retained post as Party chairman, instigating CULTURAL REVOLUTION in 1966, purging leadership in effort to recreate revolutionary spirit. Widely influential, esp. in his writings, as exponent of revolution and guerrilla warfare.

map, two-dimensional representation of the Earth's surface or part of it. Sphere cannot be represented on flat surface without some distortion of shape, area or direction. Various map projections may be used to preserve one of these qualities at expense of others; types incl. conic, cylindrical, azimuthal. Also *see* CARTOGRAPHY.

maple, any of genus *Acer* of deciduous trees or shrubs, native to N temperate regions. Various species cultivated as ornamentals, for timber or for sap which is source of maple syrup. Leaf is emblem of Canada. Also *see* SYCAMORE.

Maputo, cap. of Mozambique, on Delagoa Bay. Pop. 355,000. Admin., commercial centre; port, exports hardwoods, cotton, sugar, tobacco, mineral ores; transit trade, rail links with South Africa, Rhodesia (closed 1976), Swaziland; univ. (1962). Cap. from 1907; formerly called Lourenço Marques, renamed after Mozambique's independence (1975).

maquis (Ital. *macchia,* Span. *mattoral*), term applied to robber bands widespread in Corsica until early 20th cent., later to French underground resistance movement during German occupation of WWII. Originally word for drought-resistant scrub vegetation of W Mediterranean region.

marabou, *Leptoptilus crumeniferus,* large-billed stork of Africa, SE Asia, Green back plumage, bald head; tail feathers highly prized. Also called adjutant stork.

Maracaibo, port of NW Venezuela, on outlet of L. Maracaibo. Pop. 666,000. Coffee exports; major oil refining industs. Founded 1571, grew with exploitation of oil resources after 1917.

Maracaibo, Lake, NW Venezuela, connected by waterway with Gulf of Venezuela. Area 13,210 sq km (*c* 5100 sq mi). Major oil deposits (discovered 1917), led to deepening of channel to Caribbean.

Maracay, town of Venezuela, at NE end of L. Valencia. Pop. 193,000. Textile mfg. Has military training centre. Town modernized 1909-35, when opera house, bull ring were built.

Marajó, isl. of N Brazil, in Amazon delta. Length 240 km (*c* 150 mi). Swampy rainforest in W (timber, rubber products); grassland in E (cattle rearing). Prehist. pottery found here.

Maramba, *see* LIVINGSTONE.

Maranhão, state of NE Brazil. Area 328,663 sq km (126,897 sq mi); pop. 2,948,000; cap. São Luis. Savannah and rainforest on low coastal plain; cattle rearing in S; agric. in valleys (cotton, sugar cane).

Marañon, river of Peru, headstream of Amazon R. Rises in C Andes, flows NE 1600 km (*c* 1000 mi) joining Ucayali R. to form Amazon headstream.

***The Death of Marat* by David**

Marat, Jean Paul (1743-93), French revolutionary, b. Switzerland. Founded and edited journal *L'Ami du Peuple* (1789), in which he denounced those in power. Elected to National Convention (1792), he led campaign against

Girondists. Stabbed to death while in his bath by Charlotte Corday, a Girondist sympathizer.

Marathi, Indic language in Indo-Iranian branch of Indo-European family. Spoken mainly in Maharashtra state.

Marathon, village of SE Greece, on Plain of Marathon. Here Athenians defeated (490 BC) Persians under Darius. Soldier's run to Athens with news of victory commemorated in Olympic marathon race.

marathon race, long distance race derived from run of Pheidippides from Marathon to Athens to announce defeat of Persians (490 BC). Olympic event since 1896; distance standardized to 42.18 km (26 mi 385 yd).

marble, crystallized variety of LIMESTONE. Formed by metamorphism under heat and pressure; colour varies due to different impurites. Can take on high polish; used in building and sculpture. Major sources in Italy, Greece, Ireland.

Marburg, town of NC West Germany, on R. Lahn. Pop. 48,000. Chemicals, precision instruments mfg., univ. (1527). Church (13th cent.) has tomb of St Elizabeth. Castle was scene of debate (1529) between Luther and Zwingli.

Marc, Franz (1880-1916), German painter. Leading member of the Blaue Reiter group; attempted to describe a mystical animal world in an expressionist style employing distortion and colour symbolism. Work incl. *Blue Horses.*

Marcel Marceau

Marceau, Marcel (1923-   ), French mime. Known as creator of clown Bip. Films incl. *Un jardin public* (1955).

March, urban dist. of Isle of Ely, Cambridgeshire, EC England. Pop. 14,000. Market town. Has 14th cent. timber-roofed church.

Marchand, Jean Baptiste (1863-1934), French explorer, army officer. Occupied Fashoda in S Sudan (1898), thus precipitating major diplomatic incident between Britain and France. Forced to withdraw to avoid possible war between the 2 countries.

Marches, The (*Marche*), region of EC Italy, cap. Ancona. Apennines in W (h.e.p.); cereals, vines, livestock in river valleys, coastal plain. Name derives from frontier (march) fiefs estab. here (10th cent.) by Holy Roman Empire.

Marcionites, first heretical Christian group, founded by Marcion of Sinope (*fl* 2nd cent.). Posited 2 gods: creator and lawgiver of OT, and merciful, loving God of NT. Rejected OT and much of Gospels. Position forced Church to show fulfilment of the OT law in NT and to promulgate a canonical Gospel.

Marconi, Guglielmo, Marchese (1874-1937), Italian physicist. Famous for development of wireless telegraphy; made use of an aerial to improve transmission. Transmitted long-wave signals (1895), transatlantic signals (1901). Shared Nobel Prize for Physics (1909).

Marcos, Ferdinand Edralin (1917-   ), Philippine political leader. President of Philippines from 1965. Suppressed political opposition; declared martial law (1972) in face of alleged Communist subversion.

Marcus Aurelius Antoninus, orig. Marcus Annius Verus (AD 121-80), Roman emperor (161-80), Stoic philosopher. Defended empire against Parthians and Germans. Persecuted Christians as enemies of empire. Wrote *Meditations,* an expression of his Stoic philosophy.

Marcuse, Herbert (1898-   ), American philosopher, b. Berlin. Has applied theories of Marx and Freud to analyze modern indust. society, holding that new revolutionary elite will be drawn from skilled technical workers. Works incl. *Eros and Civilization* (1955), *One Dimensional Man* (1964).

Mar del Plata, resort of E Argentina, on Atlantic coast. Pop. 317,000. Tourist industs.; fish canning, meat packing.

Mardi Gras, French name for SHROVE TUESDAY. Last day before fasting of Lent, hence celebrated in festivals, notably in New Orleans, Rio de Janeiro, Nice.

Marduk, chief god of Babylonian pantheon. Creator of mankind, god of fertility. Identified with Bel in OT.

Marengo, village of Piedmont, NW Italy, near Alessandria. Scene of battle (1800) in which French under Napoleon defeated Austrians.

mare's tail, *Hippuris vulgaris,* aquatic perennial herb with erect stem, whorls of slender leaves and minute green flowers. Native to Europe, Asia and N Africa.

Margaret, St (c 1045-93), Scottish queen. Through her influence, Roman form of Christianity replaced earlier Celtic rites in Scotland. Helped introduce English ways into Scotland.

Margaret (1353-1412), queen of Denmark, Norway and Sweden. Married Haakon VI of Norway (1363). Became regent of Denmark (1375-87) and Norway (1380-7) for son Olaf, taking control of both kingdoms on his death (1387). Invaded Sweden (1389) and deposed Albert of Mecklenburg. United (1397) the 3 nations, ruling through grand-nephew, Eric of Pomerania.

Margaret, Maid of Norway (1283-90), queen of Scotland. Daughter of Eric II of Norway, inherited throne on death (1285) of her grandfather Alexander III. Marriage was arranged between her and Edward, prince of Wales. Died on crossing to Scotland, provoking war over succession.

Margaret of Anjou (c 1430-82), queen consort of England. Married Henry VI (1445); when Henry became insane, she opposed the protector, Richard, duke of York. Strengthened her position with birth of son Edward (1453), whose cause she supported during conflict between houses of York and Lancaster (beginning 1455). Captured (1471) at Tewkesbury; returned to France.

Margaret of Navarre or **Angoulême** (1492-1549), queen of Navarre, sister of Francis I of France. Influenced political life, religion and letters, patronizing Marot, Rabelais. Wrote French Renaissance classic *Heptaméron,* version of Boccaccio's *Decameron.*

Margaret of Valois (1553-1615), queen of Navarre and France. Wife of Henry of Navarre, later Henry IV of France. Notorious for promiscuity. Centre of literary circle during enforced retirement at Usson (1587-1605). Marriage annulled (1599).

Margaret [Rose], Countess of Snowdon (1930-   ), British princess. Second daughter of George VI. Married (1960) Antony Armstrong-Jones. Has 2 children, David (1961-   ) and Sarah (1964-   ). Obtained legal separation from husband (1976).

margarine, butter substitute prepared from hydrogenated vegetable oils and skim milk; vitamins A and D are usually added. Developed in France in 1860s using animal fats.

Margarita, isl. off NE Venezuela. Area 1150 sq km (444 sq mi). Pearl fishing; tourist resort. Discovered by Columbus (1498).

Margate, mun. bor. of Isle of Thanet, Kent, SE England. Pop. 50,000. Seaside resort.

margin requirement, in commerce, part of a security which must be paid for in cash, the balance being temporarily supplied by broker. Excessive speculation may result if requirement is too low, thus in US, Federal Reserve Board fixes percentage (usually 50-90%).

marguerite, several cultivated flowers of genus *Chrysanthemum* of composite family, esp. *C. frutescens* (Paris daisy) with single flower of white petals surrounding yellow centre.

Mari, auton. republic of EC European RSFSR, USSR; in middle Volga valley. Area *c* 23,300 sq km (8960 sq mi); pop. 685,000; cap. Yoshkar-Ola. Extensively forested; main indust. lumbering, wood product mfg. The Mari, a Finno-Ugrian people, were conquered by Ivan the Terrible in 16th cent.

Mariana Islands, isl. group of W Pacific Ocean. Main isls. GUAM, Saipan, Tinian; all except Guam part of US trust territ. of the Pacific Isls. Produce copra, sugar cane. Discovered (1521) by Magellan; all except Guam, which was ceded to US, sold by Spain to Germany (1899). Japanese from WWI, taken by US (1944).

Mariana Trench, deepest known depression on Earth's surface (11,033 m/36,198 ft), in W Pacific. Lies to E of Mariana isls. Bottom has been reached by bathyscaphe.

Mariánské Lázně (Ger. *Marienbad*), town of W Czechoslovakia. Pop. 9000. Spa popular since late 18th cent.

Maria Theresa (1717-80), Austrian empress. Ruled (1745-65) through husband, Emperor Francis I, and (1765-80) through son, Joseph II. Succeeded (1740) to Habsburg lands by terms of PRAGMATIC SANCTION. Right to do so was opposed by European alliance in War of Austrian Succession (1740-8); lost Silesia to Prussia. Alliance with France to regain Silesia led to SEVEN YEARS WAR.

Maribor (Ger. *Marburg*), town of Slovenia, N Yugoslavia, on R. Drava. Pop. 97,000. Agric. market (grain, wine), leather, textiles. Has cathedral (12th cent.), castle (15th cent.).

Marie Antoinette (1755-93), Austrian princess, queen consort of Louis XVI of France. Her Austrian origin, extravagance, involvement in scandal, attempts to influence policy in favour of Austria, opposition to economic reform, all made her unpopular. Sought Austrian military intervention (1792) in French Revolution. Convicted of treason, guillotined.

Marie Byrd Land or **Byrd Land,** region of Antarctica, E of Ross Sea and S of Amundsen Sea. Claimed for US by R.E. Byrd (1929).

Marie de France (*fl* 1185), French poet, living in England. Known for *lais,* poems of adventure and love, often with background of Celtic Arthurian romance. Also wrote *Fables* (after Aesop).

Marie de' Medici, see MEDICI.

Marie Louise (1791-1847), Austrian princess. Married (1810) Napoleon I, after he had divorced Josephine. She bore him a son (1811) before returning to Austria after his 1st abdication (1814).

Marienbad, see MARIÁNSKÉ LÁZNE.

Mariette, Auguste Edouard (1821-81), French archaeologist. Discovered (1851) the Serapeum at Saqqara, containing mummified remains of sacred bulls of Apis. Directed excavations at Memphis and Karnak. Founded Egyptian national museum.

marigold, several plants of genus *Calendula* with orange or yellow flowers. *C. officinalis* is pot marigold. So-called African marigold, *Tageteserecta,* is unrelated species, native to Mexico.

marijuana, see HEMP.

marimba, musical instrument, resembling a xylophone, but with larger resonators and usually made of metal. Played with soft-headed mallets. Of African origin, it is popular in South America.

Marin, John (1870-1953), American painter. Known for his seascapes and city scenes, painted in watercolour and employing the broken planes of cubism. Works incl. *Maine Islands* and *Lower Manhattan.*

marines, troops trained and organized for service at sea or on land. In UK, Royal Marines (founded 1664) constitute main commando force of army, as do Marine Corps (1775) in US. Traditional roles incl. spearheading beach attacks.

Marinetti, Filippo Tommaso (1876-1944), Italian author. Known as formulator of FUTURISM in *Manifeste du Futurisme* (1909).

Marini, Marino (1901-), Italian sculptor. Influenced by primitive art, he is best known for works in bronze on *Horse and Rider* theme.

Maritain, Jacques (1882-1973), French philosopher. Converted to Catholicism; related teachings of Aquinas to aspects of modern life, *eg Art and Scholasticism* (1920), *True Humanism* (1936).

Maritimes, region in E Canada. Comprise Atlantic provs. of New Brunswick, Nova Scotia, Prince Edward Isl.

Maritsa (Gk. *Evros*), river of SE Europe. Flows *c* 480 km (300 mi) from C Bulgaria via NW Turkey, NE Greece to Aegean Sea. Irrigation, h.e.p.

Maritzburg, see PIETERMARITZBURG, South Africa.

Mariupol, see ZHDANOV.

Marius, Gaius (*c* 155-86 BC), Roman soldier, politician. His rivalry with Sulla over the command against Mithradates led to civil war (88). Forced by Sulla to flee Rome, he later seized the city (87) with help of Cinna during Sulla's absence and ruthlessly destroyed his enemies.

Marivaux, Pierre Carlet de Chamblain de (1688-1763), French dramatist. Known for stylized comedies of love, *eg Le Jeu de l'amour et du hasard* (1730), *Les Fausses Confidences* (1737). Also wrote fanciful mythological plays, novels.

marjoram, several plants of mint family of genera *Origanum* or *Marjorana,* esp. *M. hortensis* (sweet marjoram), grown for its aromatic leaves used in cooking.

Mark, St, orig. John Mark (*fl* 1st cent. AD), disciple of Jesus, friend of St Peter and St Paul. Traditional author of 2nd Gospel and 1st bishop of Alexandria. Patron saint of Venice.

Mark, Gospel according to St, second of NT Gospels, attributed to St Mark; written *c* AD 70. Shortest of Gospels, recounts life of Jesus. Only Gospel in which every passage is paralleled in another Gospel.

Mark Antony, see ANTONY, MARK.

markhor, *Capra falconeri,* largest of wild goats, found in Afghanistan and Himalayas. Shaggy coat and corkscrew-spiralling horns.

Markiewicz, Constance Georgine, Countess, née Gore-Booth (*c* 1868-1927), Irish patriot. Active in Easter Rebellion (1916), she was sentenced to death; released (1917) after sentence commuted. First woman elected to British Parliament (1918), but did not take her seat.

Marks, Simon, 1st Baron Marks of Broughton (1888-1964), British businessman. Inherited father's business (Marks and Spencer), developed it into chain famous for quality clothes at low prices.

marl, calcareous mudstone, consisting of clay with calcium carbonate. Sedimentary, laid down by fresh or sea water. Crumbles easily; 'marling' is spreading marl on poor soils to reduce acidity, promote nitrification.

Marlborough, John Churchill, 1st Duke of (1650-1722), English army officer, statesman. Second-in-command of James II's army which crushed Monmouth's rebellion (1685). Supported William of Orange in deposing James. Gained power through influence of his wife, Sarah Jennings (1660-1744), over Queen Anne. Famed for victories at Blenheim (1704), Ramillies (1706) and Malplaquet (1709). Dismissed from office (1711) after wife's quarrel with Anne and return of Tories to power. Reinstated on George I's accession.

Marlborough, region of NE South Isl., New Zealand. Area 10,930 sq km (4220 sq mi); pop. 32,000; main town Blenheim. Largely mountainous; sheep rearing, dairying, wheat and barley growing, tourism.

marlin, large oceanic gamefish with spear-like snout. Species incl. blue marlin, *Makaira nigricans,* and white marlin, *Tetrapturus albidus,* of American Atlantic coast.

Marlowe, Christopher (1564-93), English dramatist, poet. Powerful plays, *eg Tamburlaine the Great, The Jew of Malta, Dr Faustus, Edward II,* estab. blank verse as Elizabethan dramatic form. Lyrics incl. famous 'Come live with me and be my love'. Life ended mysteriously in tavern brawl.

Marmara or **Marmora, Sea of** (anc. *Propontis*), sea between European and Asiatic Turkey. Links Black Sea (by Bosporus) to Aegean Sea (by Dardanelles).

Marmoset

marmoset, small squirrel-like social monkey of Callithricidae or Hapalidae family, found in Central and South America. Non-prehensile tail, claws on fingers and toes. Species incl. pygmy marmoset, *Cebuella pygmaea,* smallest monkey.

Marmot

marmot, any of genus *Marmota* of squirrel-like rodents found in mountainous areas of temperate N hemisphere. Short legs, coarse thick fur; lives in burrows. Species incl. Alpine marmot, *M. marmota,* and North American woodchuck, *M. monax.*

Marne, river of NE France. Flows *c* 525 km (325 mi) from Langres Plateau via Châlons, Epernay to R. Seine near Paris. Linked by canals to many rivers, incl. Aisne, Rhine. Scene of unsuccessful German WWI offensives (1914, 1918).

Maronites, Christian sect chiefly in Lebanon, with patriarch recognized by the pope. Distinct community since 7th cent. when they adopted MONOTHELETISM; re-entered Roman communion in 12th cent.

Maros, see MURES, Romania.

Marot, Clement (*c* 1496-1544), French poet. Introduced into French poetry elegy, epigram, eclogue, epithalamion, prob. wrote 1st French sonnet. Translated Psalms, creating new metric forms. Also wrote *rondeaux, ballades.*

Marprelate controversy, 16th cent. English religious argument. Seven Puritan-inspired pamphlets, pub. (1588-9) under pseudonym Martin Marprelate, scurrilously attacked authoritarianism of Church of England.

Marquand, J[ohn] P[hillips] (1893-1960), American novelist. Created Japanese detective 'Mr Moto' in short stories. Other works incl. comedies of upper-class manners, *eg The Late George Apley* (1937).

Marquesas Islands, archipelago of C Pacific Ocean, part of French Polynesia. Comprise N group (Washington Isls.) and S group (Mendaña Isls.); main isl. Hiva Oa. Mountainous; fertile, produce fruit, copra, cotton. Acquired by France (1842).

Marquet, Albert (1875-1947), French painter. Exhibited with the fauves in 1905; evolved a quiet clear style of depicting landscapes and port and harbour scenes.

Marquetry

marquetry, decorative technique in which ornamental woods, bone, metal, tortoiseshell, *etc,* are inlaid in veneer and then fixed to surface of furniture. Characteristic of work of A.C. Boulle.

Marquette, Jacques (1637-75), French Jesuit missionary. Accompanied Louis Jolliet on voyage from L. Michigan to the Mississippi, by way of Wisconsin R. (1673). Wrote journal of expedition (pub. 1681).

Marquis, Don[ald Robert Perry] (1878-1937), American author. Known for humorous works, *eg* satire of Greenwich Village, *Hermione and Her Little Group of Serious Thinkers* (1916), *archy and mehitabel* (1927).

Marrakesh (Fr. *Marrakech*), city of C Morocco, in foothills of Atlas Mts. Pop. 330,000. Commercial centre, agric. market; carpets, leather goods mfg.; tourist indust. Founded 1062, *fl* in Middle Ages as terminus of Saharan caravan routes. Has Koutoubiya mosque and tower (1195).

marram grass, coarse perennial grass of genus *Ammophila* grown on sandy shores to bind sand. Species incl. American *A. arenaria* and European *A. baltica.*

Marranos, Spanish term for Jews who (after 1391) had been forced to profess Christianity to escape death or persecution. They were suspected of secretly practising Judaism and were targets of the Spanish Inquisition.

marriage, union, sanctioned by custom and religion, of persons of the opposite sex as husband and wife. In most societies, sanctified by rite or sacrament. Normally limitations are placed on choice of mate, *eg* exogamy (marriage outside group), or endogamy (marriage within group). Exchange of property is often a concomitant of marriage. *See* POLYGAMY.

marrow, soft pulp in interior cavities of bones. Red marrow, in which blood cells originate, fills all bones at birth. Replaced in long bones of adults by yellow marrow, containing mainly fat.

Marryat, Frederick (1792-1848), English author. Wrote sea adventure novels, *eg Mr Midshipman Easy* (1836), children's historical novel, *The Children of the New Forest* (1847).

Mars: photograph of surface taken by Viking II spacecraft (1976)

Mars, in Roman religion, god of war, identified with Greek Ares. Father of Romulus and greatest god after Jupiter. Represented as fully-armed warrior. Honoured in several festivals in March, named for him.

Mars, planet 4th in distance from Sun; mean distance from Sun c 227.9 × 10⁶ km; diameter 6790 km; mass c 11% that of Earth. Solar orbit takes 687 days; period of axial rotation 24 hrs 37 mins. Thin atmosphere composed mainly of carbon dioxide; temperature varies from -70° C to 30° C during day. Viking space mission (1976) showed polar caps were ice but found no evidence of life.

Marsala (anc. *Lilybaeum*), town of W Sicily, Italy. Pop. 79,000. Fishing; Marsala wine. Major Carthaginian fortress from 4th cent. BC; Roman naval base. Garibaldi began Sicilian campaign here (1860).

Marseillaise, La, French national anthem. Words and music written by Rouget de Lisle (1792). Name was gained when troops from Marseilles sang the anthem on entering Paris later the same year.

Marseilles (Fr. *Marseille*, anc. *Massilia*), city of Provence, SE France, on Gulf of Lions. Cap. of Bouches-du-Rhône dept. Pop. 889,000. Major port and naval base, linked to Rhône by tunnel; soap, margarine mfg., chemicals, oil refining. Founded c 600 BC by Greeks; free city until passing to France in 1481.

Marsh, Ngaio Edith (1899-), New Zealand author. Known for detective stories incl. *A Man lay Dead* (1934), *Enter a Murderer* (1935), *Death in a White Tie* (1938).

Marshall, Alfred (1842-1924), English economist. Updated formulations of classical economists, developed marginal utility theory. Chief work, *Principles of Economics* (1890).

Marshall, George Catlett (1880-1959), American army officer, statesman. Army chief of staff (1939–45). As secretary of state (1947–9), he initiated (1947) European Recovery Program (Marshall Plan) giving economic aid to European countries. Awarded Nobel Peace Prize (1953).

Marshall, John (1755-1835), American jurist. Chief justice of Supreme Court (1801-35), helping to define its role and interpret constitution. Important decisions, incl. MCCULLOCH V MARYLAND, set precedents on Supreme Court's right to review constitutionality of legislation in appeal cases.

Marshall Islands, archipelago of W Pacific Ocean, part of US trust territ. of the Pacific Isls. Area 180 sq km (70 sq mi); comprise Ralik (W), Ratak (E) chains; main town Jaluit. Produce coffee, copra, sugar cane. German from 1885; occupied by Japanese from WWI. Taken (1944) by US; BIKINI ATOLL site of US atomic bomb tests.

Marshall Plan, see MARSHALL, GEORGE CATLETT.

marsh gas, see METHANE.

marsh mallow, *Althaea officinalis,* perennial herb with pink flowers, native to Europe, Asia and N Africa. Found in marshes. Root yields mucilage used in confectionery.

marsh marigold, *Caltha palustris,* perennial herb of buttercup family with yellow flowers and round leaves. Native to Europe, Asia and North America.

Marsilius of Padua (d. c 1342), Italian political theorist. Author of controversial *Defensor pacis,* written (1324) on behalf of Emperor Louis IV who was in dispute with Pope John XXII. Its advocacy of secular power against ecclesiastical was condemned by papacy.

Marston, John (1576-1634), English dramatist, satirist. Known for *The Malcontent* (1604), *The Dutch Courtesan* (1605).

Marston Moor, Yorkshire, England. Scene of battle (1644) in which Parliamentarians defeated Royalists in Civil War.

marsupial mole, *Notoryctes typhlops,* mole-like Australian marsupial with silky golden hair. Lives underground, burrowing for insects.

marsupials (Marsupialia), subclass of primitive mammals incl. kangaroo, wombat, found mainly in Australasia but with species, *eg* opossum, in America. Young, born small and underdeveloped, are nourished by mammary glands in female's pouch.

Marsyas, in Greek myth, Phrygian satyr. Found flute invented by Athena. Challenged Apollo to musical contest; the Muses judged in favour of Apollo who flayed Marsyas alive. The R. Marsyas sprang from his blood.

martello towers, circular forts, modelled on one at Mortella in Corsica, built around S and E coasts of England as defence against Napoleon's projected invasion.

marten, any of genus *Martes* of weasel-like arboreal carnivores with long body, short legs and valuable fur. Pine marten, *M. martes,* is European variety, with dark brown coat.

Martha's Vineyard, isl. off SE Massachusetts, US. Area 260 sq km (c 100 sq mi). Atlantic summer resort. Settled 1643; hist. important whaling, fishing industs.

Marti, José (1853-95), Cuban poet, nationalist. Known for individual, direct verse expressing belief in ordinary people, *eg Versos Libres* (written 1882), also articles, letters. Founded Cuban Revolutionary Party, killed during military expedition to Cuba.

Martial, full name Marcus Valerius Martialis (AD c 40-c 104), Roman poet, b. Spain. Known for epigrams, modern concept of which derives from his. Based works on sharply observed contemporary society.

Martin, St (c 316-397), bishop of Tours, b. Illyria. Originally a soldier, traditionally left army giving his cloak to a beggar. Evangelized Gaul, estab. many monastic communities.

Martin V (1368-1431), Roman churchman, pope (1417-31). His election during Council of Constance ended GREAT SCHISM (1378-1417). Worked to restore Church unity and rebuild Rome.

Martin, Archer John Porter (1910-), English biochemist. With R.L. Synge, shared Nobel Prize for Chemistry (1952) for developing partition chromatography, method of separating and identifying chemical mixtures. Technique used to analyze amino acids occurring in protein molecules.

Martin, John (1789-1854), English painter. Known for his enormous paintings of visionary, usually over-dramatized, religious scenes and landscapes, which brought him short-lived international fame. Works incl. *Belshazzar's Feast.*

Martin, [Basil] Kingsley (1897-1969), English journalist. Edited *New Statesman* (1931-60). Also wrote *The Press the Public Wants* (1947), *The Crown and the Establishment* (1962).

Martin, Richard, see ROYAL SOCIETY FOR PREVENTION OF CRUELTY TO ANIMALS.

martin, small bird of swallow family that feeds on insects caught in flight. Species incl. house martin, *Delechon urbica,* which builds mud nest under eaves, and sand martin, *Riparia riparia.*

Martineau, Harriet (1802-76), English author. Known for fiction illustrative of economic theories of Mill, Ricardo, *eg Illustrations of Political Economy* (1832-4). Also wrote children's stories collected in *The Play Fellow* (1841).

House martin

Martinet, Jean (d. 1672), French military engineer. Devised pontoons, assault boats and other fighting aids, but name has become household word for harsh disciplinarian, which he notoriously was.

Martinez Ruiz, José, *see* AZORÍN.

Martini, Simone (*c* 1284-1344), Italian painter of Sienese school. Pupil of Duccio, he developed his decorative linear style and colour harmonies. Works incl. mural *The Virgin in Majesty* in Siena and equestrian portrait of Guidoriccio da Fogliano.

Martinique, overseas dept. of France; isl. of SE West Indies; in Windward Isls. Area 1100 sq km (425 sq mi); pop. 343,000; cap. Fort-de-France (pop. 1600). Mountainous (Mont Pelée); of volcanic origin. Agric. incl. sugar cane, coffee; rum mfg. Colonized by French 1635; overseas dept. from 1946.

Martinů, Bohuslav (1890-1959), Czech composer. Prolific writer, sometimes employing extreme dissonance. Works incl. 13 operas, 6 symphonies, chamber music. Lived mainly in France and US after 1932.

martyr (Gk.,=witness), in Christian church, one who chooses to die rather than give up the Christian faith; 1st recorded Christian martyr is St Stephen (Acts 6: 7).

Marvell, Andrew (1621-78), English poet. Known for metaphysical lyrics incl. 'To his Coy Mistress', 'The Garden', 'The Definition of Love', 'The Nymph Complaining for the Death of her Fawn'. Also wrote political pamphlets.

marvel of Peru, *see* FOUR O'CLOCK.

Marx, Karl Heinrich (1818-83), German philosopher. Journalist and radical leader; with ENGELS, pub. *Communist Manifesto* (1848). After Revolution of 1848, spent much of his life in London and helped found (1864) association which became First INTERNATIONAL. In his theory of social change adapted Hegel's thesis to produce DIALECTICAL MATERIALISM, involving conflict of economic classes, first expressed in *The German Ideology* (1846). Major work, *Das Kapital* (1867; vols. II, III edited by Engels 1885-94), was basis for much subsequent doctrine of modern COMMUNISM and SOCIALISM. Also *see* MARXISM, SOCIAL DEMOCRACY.

Marx Brothers, American comedians, originally in vaudeville, but best known for films. They were Leonard ('Chico') (1891-1961), Adolph ('Harpo') (1893-1964), Julius ('Groucho') (1895-), and Herbert ('Zeppo') (1901-), who left after 1st 5 films. Anarchic, wise-cracking films incl. *Duck Soup* (1933), *A Night at the Opera* (1936), *A Day at the Races* (1937).

Marxism, political and economic system of thought, developed from philosophy of Karl MARX; also known as economic determinism. Method of analysis is DIALECTICAL MATERIALISM, from which was derived assertion that social change results from class struggle over control of means of

Karl Marx

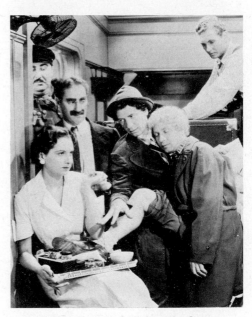

Marx Brothers in *A Night at the Opera*

production with the working class (proletariat) ultimately triumphing and leading to classless society. Marxism spread in late 19th cent. Europe through INTERNATIONALS and socialist parties (*see* SOCIAL DEMOCRACY), eventually dividing between those who believed struggle would be evolutionary and those led by Lenin advocating violent revolution if necessary. Success of Russian Revolution (1917) made permanent split between Socialists and Communists (*see* COMMUNISM, MODERN). Orthodox Marxism subsequently esp. influential in Third World countries with mainly agrarian workers.

Mary, the Virgin (1st cent. BC-1st cent. AD), mother of Jesus, wife of Joseph of Nazareth. RC, Orthodox and Anglican churches teach doctrine of her perpetual virginity. In RC church she is regarded, with Christ, as co-redeemer of mankind.

Mary I (1516-58), queen of England (1553-8). Daughter of Henry VIII and Catherine of Aragon; accession was resisted by NORTHUMBERLAND. Restored papal supremacy in England and married Philip II of Spain (1554). Sanctioned persecution of Protestants, incl. Cranmer, Latimer, Ridley, thus earning nickname 'Bloody Mary'.

Mary II (1662-94), queen of England (1689-94). Daughter of James II, she married (1677) William of Orange (William III of England). After 'Glorious Revolution' (1688), they ruled jointly until her death from smallpox.

Mary, town of USSR, Turkmen SSR; in oasis of Kara Kum desert. Pop. 61,000. Cotton grown by irrigation. Formerly known as Merv. Nearby old city of Merv, centre of medieval Moslem culture under Arab rule. In Hindu and Arab tradition, believed to be source of Aryan race.

Maryborough, city of E Queensland, Australia, on Mary R. Pop. 20,000. Agric. market, esp. fruit, sugar, dairy produce; sawmilling; engineering. Deepwater port at nearby Urangan.

Maryland, state of E US, on Atlantic. Area 27,394 sq km (10,577 sq mi); pop. 3,922,000; cap. Annapolis; chief city Baltimore. Almost divided by Chesapeake Bay; rolling upland in interior. Agric. (esp. poultry rearing); food processing, metals, shipbuilding industs.; fishing in Chesapeake Bay. Settled early 17th cent.; one of original 13 colonies of US.

Marylebone Cricket Club (MCC), London cricket club, founded 1787; responsible for original rules of game. Located at Lord's ground.

Mary Magdalene or **Magdalen** (1st cent. AD), Christian saint. In NT, demoniac healed by Jesus; present at Crucifixion and one of those who found the tomb empty and to whom the risen Christ appeared. Traditionally identified with the repentant prostitute who anointed Jesus' feet in Luke's Gospel.

Mary of Burgundy (1457-82), Burgundian noblewoman. Daughter of Charles the Bold, she married (1477) Maximilian of Austria, thus adding the Low Countries to the Habsburg empire. This alliance was opposed by the French.

Masai warrior

Masai, nomadic E Africa people, of Hamitic origin. Mainly in Kenya and Tanzania. Noted for physical courage. Livelihood depends largely on cattle rearing.

Masaryk, Thomas Garrigue (1850-1937), Czech statesman, philosopher. As member of parliament, strongly opposed Austrian policy. At outbreak of WWI, travelled widely making propaganda for Czech independence from Austria. Became president (1918) of new republic; resigned 1935, succeeded by Beneš. His son, **Jan Masaryk** (1886-1948), was foreign minister (1945-8). Said to have committed suicide after Soviet-organized coup of 1948.

Mascagni, Pietro (1863-1945), Italian composer, conductor. Known for *Cavalleria Rusticana*, which won an opera competition in 1889. Wrote several other operas, but none achieved its fame.

Mascara, town of NW Algeria. Pop. 37,000. Wine producing centre; grain trade, tobacco mfg.

Mascarene Islands, group of isls. in W Indian Ocean, E of Madagascar. Incl. Réunion, Mauritius, Rodriguez.

Mary Queen of Scots: drawing by François Clouet

Mary Queen of Scots (1542-87), queen of Scotland (1542-67). Daughter of James V, she was brought up in France. Married Francis II of France; returned to Scotland (1561) after his death. Married her cousin DARNLEY (1565), who was murdered (1567). Mary then married BOTHWELL, suspected of being Darnley's murderer. Ensuing civil war forced her abdication in favour of son by Darnley, James VI. Fled to England after defeat at Langside (1568); imprisoned by Elizabeth. Involved in several Catholic plots to place her on English throne. Executed for implication in Babington's plot.

Masaccio, orig. Tommaso Guidi (1401-*c* 1428), Italian painter. His revolutionary handling of perspective and use of light to define forms profoundly influenced subsequent painters of the Renaissance. His major extant work is fresco series in Brancacci Chapel, Florence.

John Masefield

Masefield, John [Edward] (1878-1967), English poet, playwright. Works incl. *Salt Water Ballads* (1902), containing 'Sea Fever', 'Cargoes', narrative poems, *eg The Everlasting Mercy* (1911), *Dauber* (1913). Also wrote verse dramas, sea adventure stories. Poet laureate (1930-67).

maser (microwave amplification by stimulated emission of radiation), device for creation of intense, narrow beam of high frequency radio waves; waves produced have same frequency and are in phase. Depends on excitation of atoms of a crystal or gas by incoming radiation. Hydrogen maser is basis of highly accurate atomic clock. LASER is maser operating at optical frequencies.

Maseru, cap. of Lesotho, on R. Caledon. Pop. 29,000. Admin. centre; railway links with South Africa.

Mashhad or **Meshed,** city of NE Iran, cap. of Khurasan prov. Pop. 562,000. Site of tomb of Imam Riza and pilgrimage centre for Shiite Moslems. Cap. of Persia in 18th cent.

Mashonaland, region of NE Rhodesia. Fertile plain and tableland, inhabited mainly by Mashona tribe; chief city Salisbury. Part of Southern Rhodesia from 1923.

Masolino da Panicale (c 1383-c 1447), Italian painter. Influenced by Masaccio during their collaboration on the frescoes of Brancacci Chapel, Florence. In later work, reverted to more decorative style of International Gothic.

Mason, A[lfred] E[dward] W[oodley] (1865-1948), English novelist. Works incl. *Four Feathers* (1902), *The Broken Road* (1907) with Eastern settings, and detective novels, *eg At the Villa Rose* (1910), featuring hero Hanaud of the Sûreté.

Mason-Dixon Line, boundary between Maryland and Pennsylvania, US, fixed (1763-7) by Charles Mason and Jeremiah Dixon to resolve border disputes. Regarded, before Civil War, as separating free states from slave states and now North from South.

Masons, see FREEMASONRY.

mason wasp, see POTTER WASP.

Masorah, collection of Jewish annotations concerning the correct Hebrew text of the Holy Scriptures. Involved the creation of system of vowels for pronunciation of text (Hebrew alphabet has only consonants). Compilation ceased in 15th cent.

masque, form of dramatic entertainment in which spectacle, music are emphasized, usually based on mythological, allegorical theme. Reached height with court masques contrived by partnership of Ben Jonson, Inigo Jones for James I.

Mass, liturgical service of RC church, incl. celebration of EUCHARIST. Low Mass is spoken; High Mass is more elaborate ritual, chanted and sung. Term also used by Anglo-Catholics; in Eastern churches the terms 'Holy Liturgy' or 'Offering' are used for a similar service. Formerly RCs used medieval Latin liturgy; vernacular adopted since 2nd Vatican Council.

mass, in physics, the quantity of matter in a body. More precisely, inertial mass of body is determined by acceleration produced in it by applied force. Mass is distinct from weight, which is measure of gravitational force of attraction on body. By theory of relativity, inertial mass increases as velocity increases, so that a given force produces smaller acceleration with increasing velocity (only appreciable at velocities approaching that of light). Einstein's equation $E = mc^2$ shows that mass and energy are equivalent.

Massachusetts, New England state of US. Area 21,386 sq km (8257 sq mi); pop. 5,689,000; cap. Boston. Berkshire Hills in W; Atlantic resort area (Cape Cod, Martha's Vineyard, Nantucket). Agric., livestock rearing, fisheries. Main industs. shipbuilding, machinery, textile, paper mfg. Education, research centre. Pilgrim Fathers landed at Plymouth Rock in *Mayflower* (1620); Puritan theocracy estab. Focus of pre-Revolution protest (1776). One of original 13 colonies of US.

Massachusetts Institute of Technology (MIT), Cambridge, Massachusetts, US, scientific and technical school, coeducational, chartered 1861. Famous for research, facilities incl. 70 special laboratories.

Massawa, town of Eritrea, N Ethiopia, on Red Sea. Pop. 27,000. Port and naval base, exports coffee, hides; pearl fishing. Cap. of Italian colony of Eritrea 1890-1900.

Masséna, André (1756-1817), French marshal. Noted for tactical abilities, victorious in Napoleon's Austrian campaigns (1800-9). Failed to dislodge Wellington in Peninsular War, recalled (1811) by Napoleon.

Massenet, Jules Emile Frédéric (1842-1912), French composer. Best known for lyrical operas, esp. *Manon* (1884) and *Thaïs* (1894). Also wrote oratorios, orchestral suites.

Massey, Vincent (1887-1967), Canadian statesman, diplomat. Canadian high commissioner to Britain (1936-46). First Canadian-born governor-general of Canada (1952-9). Brother of actor, Raymond Massey.

Massey, William Ferguson (1856-1925), New Zealand statesman, b. Ireland, PM (1912-25). Estab. 'Reform Party' (1903), offshoot of Conservative Party supported mainly by farmers. Headed WWI coalition govt.

Massif Central, large plateau region of SC France. Area c 85,000 sq km (33,000 sq mi); highest peak Puy de Sancy (1885 m/6187 ft). Incl. volcanic Auvergne, limestone Cévennes. Stock rearing; coal,, kaolin mining. Source of many rivers, incl. Allier, Dordogne, Loire.

Massine, Léonide (1896-   ), American ballet dancer, choreographer, b. Russia. Worked with Diaghilev. Staged *The Three-cornered Hat, La Boutique fantasque.*

Massinger, Philip (1583-1640), English dramatist. Associate of Fletcher, Dekker. Works incl. comedies *The City Madam* (1632), *A New Way to Pay Old Debts* (1625).

mass number, in chemistry, number of protons plus neutrons in atomic nucleus.

Masson, André (1896-   ), French painter. Member of surrealist group, his later work influenced American abstract expressionist painters. Evolved landscape style under influence of Chinese art.

mass spectrometer, instrument which uses electric and magnetic fields to arrange streams of ionized particles into order depending on their charge to mass ratio. Used to determine atomic weights of individual isotopes of an element and to find relative abundance of isotopes in sample of an element.

Massys or **Matsys, Quentin** (c 1466-1530), Flemish painter. Influenced by the Italian Renaissance, he is known for his genre pictures of bankers and merchants, *eg Banker and his Wife*. His many portraits incl. that of Erasmus.

mastaba, ancient Egyptian rectangular tomb. Low, flat-topped structure with sloping sides, serving as a burial place for pharaohs and nobles in the Old Kingdom.

Masters, Edgar Lee (1869-1950), American poet. Known for *Spoon River Anthology* (1915), a cycle of 'epitaphs' spoken by dead of mid-Western town. Also wrote novels, hostile life of Lincoln.

mastic, gum resin obtained from bark of evergreen shrub, *Pistacia lentiscus,* native to Mediterranean region. Used for making protective varnishes, *eg* for oil paintings.

mastiff, large powerful smooth-coated dog, used as watchdog. Stands c 76 cm/30 in. at shoulder.

mastiff bat, bat of Molossidae family of tropical regions that can walk rapidly on ground. Species incl. Californian mastiff bat, *Eumops californicus,* largest American bat.

mastodon, extinct elephant-like mammal that flourished from Oligocene epoch onwards. Differed from elephant in larger size and in structure of teeth; had 4 tusks. Term used in US for American 2-tusked mastodon of Pleistocene epoch.

Masulipatnam or **Bandar,** seaport of Andhra Pradesh, SE India. Pop. 113,000. Exports groundnuts; cotton mfg. Site of European trading posts, incl. British (1611).

Masurian Lakes, group of c 2700 lakes, Mazury region, NE Poland. Formerly part of East Prussia, passed to Poland 1945. Scene of Russian defeats in WWI (1914, 1915).

Matabeleland, region of SW Rhodesia. Inhabited mainly by Matabele tribe; chief city Bulawayo. Rich gold deposits. Part of Southern Rhodesia from 1923.

Matadi, city of W Zaïre, on R. Congo. Pop. 126,000. Head of navigation for ocean-going vessels; exports cotton, coffee, minerals. Railway to Kinshasa.

Mata Hari, orig. Margaretha Geertruida Zelle (1876-1917), Dutch-Indonesian dancer. Joined German secret service (1907). Betrayed Allied secrets to Germans in WWI. Executed by French.

matamata, *Chelys fimbriata,* turtle of swamps and rivers of South America. Cone-shaped protrusions on carapace, frill of loose skin on long neck.

Matamoros, border town of N Mexico, near mouth of Rio Grande opposite Brownsville (Texas). Pop. 183,000. Agric. industs. incl. cotton ginning, distilling, food processing. Founded 1824.

Matanzas, scenic port of NW Cuba. Pop. 86,000 In rich agric. region; sugar refining, export; textile mfg. Tourist resort with notable beaches.

Matapan, Cape, headland of Greece, S extremity of Peloponnese. Scene of British naval victory (1941) over Italians.

match, small strip of wood, cardboard, *etc,* tipped with composition which catches fire by friction. Modern match-heads contain phosphorus sulphide and oxidizing agent. Safety match-head contains antimony trisulphide and potassium chlorate; striking surface contains red phosphorus.

maté or **Paraguay tea,** dried leaves of South American evergreen tree, *Ilex paraguariensis.* Popular bitter beverage, drunk from special calabashes, is made from it.

materialism, in philosophy, system of thought which takes matter as only reality. Early materialist philosophies incl. Democritus' atomistic theory, Epicureanism, Stoicism. Subsequent exponents incl. Hobbes, Mill, Marx. Often widely held in times of scientific achievement.

mathematics, study of numbers, spatial relations and axiomatic systems. Branches of mathematics under early investigation incl. arithmetic, geometry (esp. by Greeks) and algebra. Seventeenth cent. saw beginning of standard algebraic methods and introduction of calculus, prob. most frequently applied mathematical method. Axiomatic development of mathematics began in 19th cent., which also saw perfection of techniques to solve classical problems. Twentieth cent. has seen greater subdivision of major areas of research, *eg* geometry now divided into topology, differential geometry, algebraic geometry, *etc,* as well as development of abstract mathematical systems, originally arising out of specific problems, but now studied in their own right, *eg* group theory.

Mathura or **Muttra,** town of Uttar Pradesh, N India, on R. Jumna. Pop. 140,000. Cotton, paper mfg. Hindu religious centre, revered as birthplace of Krishna.

Matilda or **Maud** (1102–67), queen of England. Daughter of HENRY I; married Emperor Henry V, and, after his death Geoffrey Plantagenet. Her cousin, Stephen, seized throne (1135) but was challenged (1139) by Matilda. Captured Stephen (1141) and was elected 'lady of the English'. Later withdrew claim to throne in favour of son, Henry II.

Matisse, Henri (1869-1954), French painter, sculptor. Leader of fauves, he developed bright, often stylized design. His characteristic decorative works, influenced by Near Eastern art, juxtaposed brilliant colours and employed distorted perspectives. He painted long series of odalisques and still lifes, incl. *The Pink Nude.*

Matlock, urban dist. and co. town of Derbyshire, C England, on R. Derwent. Pop. 20,000. Resort since 1698, mineral springs. Early cotton mill (1771).

Mato Grosso, forested area of WC Brazil. Heavy rainfall, cattle raising in SW upland; mineral resources unexploited (manganese mining near Corumba). Region mainly in Mato Grosso state. Indian pop. in Amazon basin.

matriarchy, form of social organization in which the mother is head of family or group, descent and kinship being traced through mother rather than father. Often associated with polyandry (*see* POLYGAMY). Found in South Sea Isls. and among certain North American Indians.

matrimony, *see* MARRIAGE.

matrix, in mathematics, rectangular array of numbers, arranged into rows and columns. Matrix is said to be square if it has same number of rows and columns. Used in all branches of mathematics, esp. in solution of systems of linear equations.

Matsu, isl. in Formosa Str., fortified outpost of Taiwan since 1949. Lies off Fukien prov., China.

Matisse: portrait of André Derain

Matsuyama, seaport of Japan, NW Shikoku isl. Pop. 323,000. Oil refining; textile and paper mfg. Has feudal castle (1603), park.

Matteotti, Giacomo (1885-1924), Italian political leader. Leading Socialist opponent of Fascist govt. His murder by Fascists enabled Mussolini to assume absolute dictatorship.

Matterhorn (Fr. *Mont Cervin,* Ital. *Monte Cervino*), peak of Pennine Alps, on Swiss-Italian border. Height 4475 m (14,690 ft). First climbed 1865 by Whymper.

Matthew, St (*fl* 1st cent. AD), tax gatherer of Capernaum, one of Twelve Disciples. First Gospel usually attributed to him. Traditionally said to have been martyred.

Matthew, Gospel according to St, first of NT Gospels, traditionally attributed to St Matthew since 2nd cent. Gives account of Jesus' life stressing that he was Messiah as foretold in OT.

Stanley Matthews in 1943

Matthews, Sir Stanley (1915-), English footballer. Renowned dribbler, he played 54 full international games for England as a winger. Played last first-class game at age of 50.

Matthias Corvinus (*c* 1440-90), king of Hungary (1458-90). At instigation of Pope Pius II, fought against Bohemian regent George of Podebrad. Annexed Moravia, Silesia;

proclaimed king of Bohemia (1469) but later forced to recognize Ladislaus as rightful king. Annexed parts of Austria (1482-5). Patron of learning and science; estab. fine library at Budapest.

Maudling, Reginald (1917-   ), British politician. Posts in Conservative govts. incl. chancellor of the exchequer (1962-4), home secretary (1970-2). Resigned amidst allegations of corruption.

Maugham, W[illiam] Somerset (1874-1965), English author, b. France. Novels incl. autobiog. *Of Human Bondage* (1915), *The Moon and Sixpence* (1919), *Cakes and Ale* (1930), *The Razor's Edge* (1944). Also wrote masterly short stories, plays, often using tropical setting to explore its effect on white colonialists.

Mau Mau, secret terrorist organization, active 1952-60, whose members, drawn from Kikuyu tribe, took oath to drive white settlers from Kenya. Also attacked Africans who opposed Mau Mau. Finally offered free pardon by Kenya govt. (1963).

Mauna Loa, active volcano of Hawaii, US; on Hawaii Isl. Height 4170 m (13,680 ft). Craters incl. Kilauea.

Maundy Thursday, Thursday before Easter, historically, when British sovereign distributes Maundy money to the poor. Relic of ceremony commemorating Jesus' washing Apostles' feet.

Maupassant, Guy de (1850-93), French author. Known for naturalistic short stories pessimistically depicting ironies of life, *eg* 'Boule de Suif', 'La Parure'. Also wrote novels incl. *Une Vie* (1883), *Pierre et Jean* (1888).

Mauretania, ancient region of N Africa, incl. present-day N Morocco, W Algeria. Kingdom under Numidian control in 2nd cent. BC; became Roman prov., divided (AD 42) into 2 provs. by Claudius. Overrun by Vandals in 5th cent.

Mauriac, François Charles (1885-1970), French novelist. Preoccupied with sin, salvation. Novels incl. *Thérèse Desqueyroux* (1927), *Vipers' Tangle* (1932). Nobel Prize for Literature (1952).

Maurice of Nassau (1567-1625), prince of Orange (1618-25), stadholder of Dutch Republic (1584-1625). Son of William the Silent, he continued struggle against Spanish. Secured truce (1609) giving virtual independence to United Provinces.

Mauritania

Mauritania, republic of NW Africa. Area 1,031,000 sq km (398,000 sq mi); pop. 1,290,000; cap. Nouakchott. Languages: Arabic, French. Religion: Islam. Mainly in Sahara, pop. mostly nomadic herdsmen; limited agric. (maize, millet) in S along R. Senegal. Exports iron ore, copper ore, gum arabic, dried and salted fish. French protect. from 1903; became colony (1920), admin. from St Louis (Senegal) until 1957. Independent from 1960.

Mauritius, isl. state of W Indian Ocean, part of Mascarene Isls. Has 3 dependencies incl. Rodriguez isl. Total area 1860 sq km (720 sq mi); pop. 872,000; cap. Port Louis. Languages: English, French. Religions: Hinduism, Christianity. Majority of pop. of Indian descent. Hilly, largely volcanic; economy dominated by sugar cane. Discovered (1505) by Portuguese; held by Dutch (1598-1710), by French (1715-1810), by British from 1815. Independent from 1968. Member of British Commonwealth.

Mauritius

Maurois, André, pseud. of Emile Herzog (1885-1967), French author. Known for biographies, *eg Ariel* (1923) on Shelley, *Don Juan* (1930) on Byron. Also wrote humorous novels, *Les Silences du Colonel Bramble* (1918).

Maurras, Charles (1868-1952), French writer. Ardent royalist, edited daily *L'Action Française*. Imprisoned (1945-52) for collaboration with Germans in WWII.

Mavor, Osborne Henry, *see* BRIDIE, JAMES.

Mawson, Sir Douglas (1882-1958), Australian geologist and explorer, b. England. On Shackleton's Antarctic expedition (1907-9) reached S magnetic pole. Led Australian Antarctic expedition (1911-14); mapped uncharted coasts, claiming extensive territ. for Australia.

Maxim, Sir Hiram Stevens (1840-1916), British inventor, munitions maker, b. US. Developed Maxim machine gun (1884) and a smokeless powder.

Maximilian I (1459-1519), Holy Roman emperor (1493-1519). Acquired Low Countries by marriage to Mary of Burgundy (1477). Involved in wars to defend his new territ. against French. Opposed French expansion in Italy but lost Milan to French (1516).

Maximilian I (1756-1825), king of Bavaria (1806-25). Became elector of Bavaria (1799). Received royal title and acquired new territ. through alliance with Napoleon. Remained allied to Napoleon until 1813. Granted liberal constitution (1818).

Maximilian [Joseph Ferdinand] (1832-67), emperor of Mexico (1864-7). Younger brother of Francis Joseph of Austria; accepted crown offered (1863) by French-dominated Mexican assembly. After French military support was withdrawn through American pressure, he lost power. Refused to leave country; was captured and shot.

Maxwell, James Clerk (1831-79), Scottish physicist. His 4 equations concerning electric and magnetic fields described interaction between electricity and magnetism and unified all previous observations about the 2 phenomena. Deduced that light is electromagnetic in nature and predicted existence of electromagnetic (radio) waves, detected by Hertz. Contributed to kinetic theory of gases.

May, Thomas Erskine, 1st Baron Farnborough (1815-56), English constitutional jurist. Wrote standard work, *Treatise on the Law, Privileges, Proceedings and Usage of Parliament* (1st ed. 1844; revised many times).

Maya, pre-Columbian South American civilization of Yucatán Penin., S Mexico, Guatemala and Honduras. Relics of Classic period (*c* AD 317-889) incl. pyramidal temples. Hieroglyphic inscriptions and calendars indicate knowledge of mathematics, abstract astronomy. Culture declined after 9th cent. with Spanish conquest (1546) completing its destruction.

Maya, in Hindu religion, term for goddess Devi, consort of SIVA. Also used as term for illusory world of the senses, often personified as a woman.

Mayagüez, port of W Puerto Rico. Pop. 69,000. Agric. produce (esp. sugar, coffee, tobacco); clothing mfg. (noted embroidery, needlework). Founded 1760.

Mayakovski, Vladimir Vladimirovich (1893-1930), Russian poet. Leading futurist. Works incl. propagandist

Ode to the Revolution (1918), *150,000,000* (1920). Also wrote satirical plays incl. *Mystery-bouffe* (1918), *The Bedbug* (1928).

May Day, first day of May. Important European festival, originating from pre-Christian fertility ceremonies. Traditions incl. maypoles, election of May king or queen. In Scotland, Ireland, day is called Beltane, celebrated with bonfires. May Day designated (1889) by Second Socialist International as international labour holiday.

Mayence, *see* MAINZ, West Germany.

Mayer, Louis B[urt] (1885–1957), American film executive. Formed Metro-Goldwyn-Mayer (1924) with Sam GOLDWYN. Known for flamboyant use of power over Hollywood.

Mayfair, fashionable dist. of City of WESTMINSTER, London, England. Named after fair held every May until 1809.

Mayflower, ship which carried the Pilgrims from England to America (1620). Colony was estab. at Plymouth, Mass. Agreement for govt. of colony was known as Mayflower Compact.

mayflower, name applied to several spring-blooming plants, *eg* in America the trailing arbutus, *Epigaea repens*, a trailing evergreen shrub with pink or white fragrant flowers. In Britain name given to blossoms of HAWTHORN.

Mayfly

mayfly, any of order Ephemeroptera of insects with 4 gauzy wings and 3 long tail filaments. Larvae live several years in ponds, streams, eventually changing into dull brown winged insect (subimago). Subimago moults rapidly to form shiny adult; adult dies within a few hours, being unable to feed.

Mayhew, Henry (1812-87), English author. Founded *Punch* (1841). Known for surveys of social conditions esp. *London Labour and the London Poor* (1849-62).

Maynooth, town of Co. Kildare, E Irish Republic. Pop. 1000. St Patrick's Coll. (1795), RC seminary.

Mayo, county of Connacht prov., NW Irish Republic. Area 5398 sq km (2084 sq mi); pop. 109,000; co. town Castlebar. Rugged terrain in W; more fertile E has agric., livestock.

Mays, Willie [Howard] (1931-), American baseball player. Combined batting power (660 career home runs) with speed as an outfielder with San Francisco (formerly New York) Giants.

Mazagan, *see* JADIDA, EL, Morocco.

Mazarin, Jules, orig. Giulio Mazarini (1602-61), French statesman, b. Italy. Created cardinal (1641), he succeeded his patron, Richelieu, as chief minister of France (1642). Exercised great power during Louis XIV's minority. Negotiated end of Thirty Years War at Westphalia (1648). Autocratic rule, taxation policies provoked Fronde revolt (1648-53).

Mazatlán, port of W Mexico, at S of Gulf of California. Pop. 172,000. Tobacco, fruit, mineral exports; sugar refining, textile mfg., flour milling. Popular tourist resort; game fishing.

mazurka, lively folk dance in 3/4 time. Originally from Poland, it spread to the ballrooms of W Europe and North America in 19th cent. Estab. as musical form by Chopin, who composed over 50 mazurkas.

Mazzini, Giuseppe (1805-72), Italian nationalist. Worked, primarily while in exile, to unify Italy under republican govt. by revolutionary action. Founded secret society 'Young Italy' (1830) dedicated to these aims. Headed short-lived republic in Rome (1849).

Mbabane, cap. of Swaziland. Pop. 14,000. Admin., commercial centre; railway to Mozambique. Tin, iron mining nearby.

Mboya, Thomas Joseph ('Tom') (1930-69), Kenyan politician. Influential in Kenyan independence movement. Held several posts in Kenyatta's govt. Considered potential successor to Kenyatta; assassinated.

Mdina, *see* CITTÀ VECCHIA, Malta.

Mead, Margaret (1901-), American anthropologist. Extended scope of anthropology by relating culture to personality. Works incl. *Coming of Age in Samoa* (1928), *Sex and Temperament in Three Primitive Societies* (1935).

mead, alcoholic beverage made from fermented honey and water flavoured with spices. Mead drinking was an important social activity in Anglo-Saxon communities.

meadow grass, *see* BLUEGRASS.

meadow saffron or **autumn crocus,** *Colchicum autumnale*, native to Europe and N Africa. Widely cultivated for purple crocus-like flowers in autumn. Corms yield the alkaloid colchicine used in genetic experiments and as treatment for gout.

meadowsweet, any of genus *Filipendula*, esp. *F. ulmaria*, perennial herb of rose family, native to Europe and Asia, with pink or white flowers. Name also used for several species of genus *Spiraea*.

mealybug, insect of Coccidae family, whose body is covered with waxy secretion. Some species injurious to trees and plants.

mean, in mathematics, number between smallest and largest values of some set of numbers, obtained by some prescribed method. Usually refers to arithmetic mean, *ie* sum of numbers in a group divided by number of members in the group; geometric mean of *n* positive numbers is *n*-th root of their product.

Meanders in Brazil

meander, curve in course of a river winding from side to side over flat land. By erosion, river may cut off its own meanders, forming ox-bow or mort lakes. Term derived from ancient R. Maeander (now Büyük Menderes) in Turkey.

Meany, George (1894-), American labour leader. Secretary-treasurer of American Federation of Labor (AFL) (1939-52) and later its president (1952-5). President of new federation formed by merger of AFL and Congress of Industrial Organizations (1955-).

Mearns, The, *see* KINCARDINESHIRE, Scotland.

measles, infectious viral disease spread by airborne droplets. Most common in childhood. Characterized by blotchy body rash preceded by running nose, watery eyes, fever. Incubation period 10-14 days.

meat, flesh of animals, esp. sheep, pigs and cattle, used as food. Composed mainly of muscle and connective tissue. Contains fat, vitamin B, minerals such as iron, and large amounts of protein. Cooking meat helps coagulate blood and albumen, improve flavour, soften and sterilize it. Meat packing industry concerned with slaughtering of animals and preparing their meat for marketing. Modern form dates from 1870s in US when frozen meat was transported by train; shipping of frozen meat to Europe began in 1875.

Meath, county of Leinster prov., E Irish Republic. Area 2339 sq km (903 sq mi); pop. 72,000; co. town Trim. Undulating terrain, drained by R. Boyne. Agric., livestock. Ancient kingdom (larger than present county); antiquities (*eg* at Kells, Tara).

Meaux, town of N France, on R. Marne. Pop. 31,000. Agric. trade centre of Brie. Cathedral (13th cent.) contains tomb of Bishop Bossuet.

Mecca

Mecca (*Makkah*), cap. of Hejaz region, W Saudi Arabia. Pop. 250,000. Birthplace of Mohammed. Islam's holiest city and pilgrimage centre. Goal of pilgrimage is the Kaaba, cubical stone building, contained in Great Mosque. Kaaba contains sacred Black Stone, kissed by pilgrims.

mechanical engineering, branch of ENGINEERING dealing with machines, engines and power plants. Divided into heat utilization (in engines, *etc*) and machine design.

mechanics, branch of physics dealing with effect of forces acting on bodies. Usually divided into statics and dynamics.

Mechelen (Fr. *Malines*), town of NC Belgium, on R. Dyle. Pop. 66,000. Railway jct., industs. incl. furniture, textiles, vehicles. Once famous for lace mfg. Cathedral (14th cent.), metropolitan see.

Mecklenburg, region of N East Germany. Large, low-lying fertile plain with lakes, forests. Crops incl. rye, potatoes, sugar beet. Hist. cap. Schwerin; chief ports Rostock, Wismar, Stralsund. Imperial duchy from 1348, divided into 2 duchies 1621; both joined German empire 1871. Reunited as state 1934.

medals, *see* DECORATIONS.

Medan, city of Indonesia, cap. of North Sumatra prov. Pop. 636,000. Trade centre, dealing in tobacco, rubber; tourism.

Medawar, Sir Peter Brian (1915-   ), English biologist, b Brazil. With Sir Macfarlane Burnet awarded Nobel Prize for Physiology and Medicine (1960) for showing that animals can be induced to overcome their tendency to reject transplanted tissue or organs.

Medea, in Greek myth, sorceress who helped JASON obtain Golden Fleece. When Jason wished to marry Creusa, Medea sent her a poisoned wedding dress which burned her to death. Killed her own children by Jason and married King Aegeus.

Medellín, city of NW Colombia, in Andes; alt. 1520 m (*c* 5000 ft). Pop. 1,040,000. Important textile industs., coffee exports; gold mining. Founded 1675.

Medes, ancient people of W Asia, in area now NW Iran. Subjects of Assyria in 9th cent. BC, they gained their

independence in 7th cent. BC. Defeated by Cyrus the Great *c* 550 BC, after which they merged with Persians.

Medicaid and **Medicare,** *see* HEALTH INSURANCE.

Medici, Italian family of merchants and bankers, who ruled Florence (15th-18th cent.) and were famous patrons of the arts during the Renaissance. **Cosimo de' Medici** (1389-1464) was first of family to rule Florence. Greatly extended family's banking interests; encouraged study of Greek. Patron of Donatello, Brunelleschi. His grandson, **Lorenzo de' Medici** (1449-92), called 'Il Magnifico', was a lavish patron of Greek and Latin learning, art and literature. Averted plot by Pazzi family (encouraged by Pope Sixtus IV) to overthrow Medici rule in Florence (1478). His son, Giovanni de' Medici, became pope as LEO X. Giulio de' Medici became pope as CLEMENT VII. **Alessandro de' Medici** (1510-37) was created hereditary duke of Florence after period of exile. His tyrannical rule ended in his assassination. Succeeded by **Cosimo de' Medici** (1519-74), who became grand duke of Tuscany. **Catherine de' Medici** (1519-89), consort of Henry II of France, was regent for her son Charles IX (1560-74); instigated 1572 St Bartholomew's Day massacre of French Protestants. **Marie de' Medici** (1573-1642), was queen of Henry IV of France. Acted as regent for her son, Louis XIII, after Henry's death (1610); ultimately exiled by Louis when Richelieu became his chief minister (1630).

medicine, art and science of diagnosis, treatment, curing and prevention of disease. Hippocrates (*c* 400 BC) estab. rational basis of observation in medicine, rejecting superstition and magic. Galen's anatomical writings (AD 2nd cent.), preserved by Moslem physicians in Middle Ages, dominated medical thought until more accurate studies of Vesalius appeared in 16th cent. Harvey's discovery of circulation of blood (1628) was also important. Medicine revolutionized in 19th cent. by use of antiseptics, anaesthetics and by Pasteur's findings on microbes. Advances in 20th cent. incl. use of antibiotics, inoculation with vaccine, blood transfusion, organ transplants.

Medicine Hat, indust. town of SE Alberta, Canada; on S Saskatchewan R. Pop. 27,000. In natural gas, coal mining, farming region.

Medina, city of Hejaz region, W Saudi Arabia. Pop. 80,000. Mosque contains Mohammed's tomb, pilgrimage centre. Mohammed fled here from Mecca in 622.

Mediterranean Sea

Mediterranean Sea (anc. *Mare Internum*), inland sea bounded by S Europe (N), W Asia (E), and N Africa (S). Area *c* 2,512,300 sq km (970,000 sq mi). Linked to Atlantic by Str. of Gibraltar; to Black Sea by Dardanelles; to Red Sea by Suez Canal. Main isls. Balearics, Corsica, Sardinia, Sicily, Crete, Cyprus. Focus of ancient and classical civilizations. Declined from 15th cent. until Suez Canal opened (1869). Strategic, commerical importance; tourism.

medium, *see* SPIRITUALISM.

medlar, *Mespilus germanica,* deciduous, sometimes thorny tree of rose family, native to Europe and Asia. Small, apple-shaped fruit eaten when partly decayed.

Médoc, region of SW France, between Bay of Biscay and Gironde. Famous vineyards, *eg* Château Latour, Château Margaux.

Medusa, *see* GORGONS.

Medlar

medusa, free-swimming generation of coelenterates, resembling bell or umbrella. Usually produced asexually by budding of polyps, itself reproducing sexually to form polyps. In class Scyphozoa, incl. common jellyfish, medusa stage is dominant.

Medway, river of SE England, flows 113 km (70 mi) from Surrey, Sussex through Kent to Thames estuary. Medway conurbation incl. Chatham, Gillingham, Rochester.

Meegeren, Hans van (1889-1947), Dutch painter. Known for his fake paintings in early style of Vermeer, which he claimed to be lost works. Imprisoned after WWII for selling these supposed national treasures to Goering, he proved his innocence by painting another 'Vermeer' in prison.

meerkat, see MONGOOSE.

meerschaum, soft, white clay-like mineral, consisting of hydrous magnesium silicate. Absorbent, heat-resistant; used for tobacco pipes, cigar-holders, *etc.* Major source in Asia Minor. Also called sepiolite.

Meerut, town of Uttar Pradesh, N India. Pop. 368,000. Cotton goods, flour mfg. Site of outbreak of Indian Mutiny (1857).

megalithic, form of building using large stones, common in tomb construction in Neolithic and early Bronze Age periods. Megalithic structures incl. menhirs and stone circles, *eg* those at Avebury and Stonehenge.

Megara, town of Attica, EC Greece. Pop. 15,000. Wine, olive trade. Ancient maritime trading centre under Dorians, founded colonies of Chalcedon, Byzantium. Traditional birthplace of Euclid.

Megiddo, town of N Israel, hist. Palestinian battle site. Remains date from *c* 3000 BC.

Mehemet Ali, see MOHAMMED ALI.

Meighen, Arthur (1874-1960), Canadian statesman, PM (1920-1, 1926) as leader of Conservative Party.

Meiningen, town of SW East Germany, on R. Werra. Pop. 25,000. Famous (19th cent.) for ducal theatre, orchestra. Cap. of Saxe-Meiningen 1680-1918.

meiosis, in biology, method of nuclear division in formation of gametes (sex cells) in animals and spores of most plants, by which number of chromosomes is reduced by half. Usually consists of 2 successive divisions, each resembling MITOSIS.

Meir, Golda (1898-   ), Israeli political leader, b. Russia. Settled in Palestine (1921) having previously emigrated to US. Premier (1969-74), she resigned in aftermath of 4th Arab-Israeli war.

Meissen, town of SE East Germany, on R. Elbe. Pop. 51,000. From 1710 'Dresden' china made here, from local kaolin. Castle (15th cent.).

Meistersinger (Master singers), members of German guild of poets or musicians (14th-16th cents.). Drawn from craftsmen and traders, they aimed to preserve traditions of medieval MINNESINGER.

Meitner, Lise (1878-1968), Austrian physicist, long-time resident in Sweden. Co-discoverer of element protactinium. First to interpret experimental results obtained during neutron bombardment of uranium as being due to nuclear fission, important in development of atomic bomb.

Meknès, city of N Morocco. Pop. 245,000. Trade centre in agric. region; carpets, leather goods, pottery mfg. Former cap. of Morocco, has famous 17th cent. palace.

Mekong, river of SE Asia. Rises in SC China (Tsinghai prov.), flows *c* 4180 km (2600 mi) SE along Laos border into Cambodia and forms large (*c* 194,000 sq km/75,000 sq mi) rice-growing delta in South Vietnam.

Melanchthon, orig. Philip Schwarzerd (1497-1560), German humanist scholar. Friend and follower of Luther, explained Reformation principles in *Loci communes* (1521); wrote Augsburg Confession (1530). After Luther's death, was influenced by Calvin. Helped create German school system.

Melanesia, one of three divisions of Pacific isls., S of equator. Incl. Admiralty Isls., Bismarck Archipelago, Solomon Isls., New Hebrides, New Caledonia and Fiji. Also *see* MICRONESIA, POLYNESIA.

Melanesians, peoples of S and SW Pacific isls., of Australoid stock. Language is Malayo-Polynesian. Main groups are the Papuans and taller, finer featured 'true' Melanesians.

melanin, dark brown pigment found in skin, hair and other tissues. Protects body from harmful ultraviolet solar radiation.

Melba, Dame Nellie, orig. Helen Porter Mitchell (1859-1931), Australian soprano. Went to Europe in 1886 and achieved great fame in her lyrical and coloratura roles in opera. Name survives in sweet 'peach melba' created in her honour by Escoffier.

Melbourne, William Lamb, 2nd Viscount (1779-1848), British statesman, PM (1834, 1835-41). Second Whig admin. marked by Chartist agitation, trouble in Ireland. Acted as trusted adviser to young Queen Victoria. His wife, **Lady Caroline Lamb** (1785-1828), is chiefly remembered for tempestuous love affair with Byron.

Melbourne, city of SE Australia, on Yarra R., cap. of Victoria. Pop. 2,498,000. Admin., commercial, indust. centre; exports (via Port Melbourne) minerals, agric. produce, wool; 3 univs. First settled 1835; cap. of Victoria from 1851, of Australia 1901-27. Site of 1956 Olympics. Mint, Victorian arts centre.

Melchites, Arabic-speaking Christians of Egypt, Israel and Syria. Members of part of Eastern Orthodox Church which reunited with Rome. Their head (under the pope) is patriarch of Antioch.

Meleager, in Greek myth, son of King Oeneus of Calydon and Althaea. Led hunt against boar sent by Artemis to ravage Calydon. Killed Althaea's brothers when they tried to steal hide. The Fates had told Althaea that Meleager would live while a certain log remained unburnt. She took revenge by burning log and he died.

Melilla, Spanish enclave in N Morocco, on Mediterranean Sea. Pop. 65,000. Port, exports iron ore; fishing. Spanish from 1470; held despite many assaults incl. Rif revolt 1921-6.

Melk or **Mölk,** town of N Austria, on R. Danube. Pop. 5000. Site of 1st residence of Austrian rulers. Benedictine abbey (1089) has collection of ancient manuscripts. Tourist centre.

Mellon, Andrew William (1855-1937), American financier, industrialist. Estab. leading financial institutions, held large interests in key indust. *eg* Aluminum Co. of America. Secretary of the Treasury (1921-1931), ambassador to UK (1931-32). Patron of art, helping to estab. National Gallery of Art.

melodrama, originally sensational drama with musical accompaniment. Now any play which exaggerates emotions, conflicts, at cost of psychological depth or development of characters.

melody, a sequence of notes having a distinctive musical shape. May form the tune of a song or short instrumental piece, or serve as a theme from which a longer work is developed.

melon, *Cucumis melo*, sweet juicy, edible fruit of gourd family, native to S Asia but widely cultivated in tropical and subtropical countries. Varieties incl. musk melon, honeydew and cantaloupe, a hard-shelled Mediterranean variety. *See* WATERMELON.

Melos or **Milos,** isl. of S Greece, in the Cyclades. Area 158 sq km (61 sq mi). Venus de Milo statue found here 1820.

Melpomene, in Greek and Roman myth, Muse of tragedy. Represented with tragic mask and staff of Heracles or sword.

Melrose, town of Borders region, SE Scotland, on R. Tweed. Pop. 2000. Has ruins of Cistercian abbey (1136). Scott's estate, Abbotsford, is nearby.

Melton Mowbray, urban dist. of Leicestershire, EC England. Pop. 20,000. Pork pies; Stilton cheese mfg. Fox hunting centre.

Melusine, in French legend, fairy who became a snake from the waist down on one day each week. Married Raymond of Poitiers on condition that he never saw her on that day. He spied on her and she fled.

Melville, Herman (1819-91), American author. Known for symbolic adventure novel on whaling, *Moby Dick* (1851). Also wrote *Billy Budd* (pub. 1924), short stories, poetry.

Melville Island, isl. of Northern Territ., Australia, separated from mainland by Clarence Str. Area *c* 5700 sq km (2200 sq mi); mainly wooded hills, mangrove swamp. Aboriginal reserve in N; lumbering, pearling, fishing.

Melville Island, W Franklin Dist., Northwest Territs., Canada; largest of Parry Isls. Area 42,500 sq km (*c* 16,400 sq mi). Separated from Victoria Isl. by Viscount Melville Sound. Discovered 1819.

Memel, *see* KLAIPEDA.

Memling or **Memlinc, Hans** (*c* 1430-94), Flemish painter, b. Germany. Influenced by van der Weyden, he painted pious religious subjects, lacking in dramatic intensity. Works incl. *Shrine of St Ursula* in Bruges.

memory, in psychology, term for capacity to retain and consciously recall past experience, therefore underlying all learning. Most accurate when individual is interested in subject of memory. Early childhood memories can often only be recalled in psychoanalysis, as they have been repressed.

Memphis, ancient city of N Egypt, on R. Nile. Traditionally founded by 1st pharaoh, Menes; cap. (*c* 3100-*c* 2250 BC) of united Egypt. Ruins incl. temple of Ptah, palaces, pyramids; nearby is SAKKARA.

Memphis, city of SW Tennessee, US; on Mississippi R. Pop. 624,000; state's largest city. Port, railway jct. Cotton, timber, livestock market. Settled *c* 1820, boomed as river port.

Menado, *see* MANADO.

Menai Strait, channel (24 km/15 mi long) between NW Wales coast and Anglesey. Spanned by road bridge built by Telford (1826), rail bridge by Stephenson (1850).

Menam, *see* CHAO PHRAYA.

Menander (*c* 342-291 BC), Greek comic poet. Known mainly through Latin adaptations of his plays by Plautus and Terence, through which they influenced modern European literature. Only complete play in existence is *Misanthrope,* discovered 1958.

Mencius, Latin form of Meng-tse (*c* 371-*c* 288 BC), Chinese scholar. Taught that man is innately compassionate and that only poor material conditions drive him to be self-seeking. Thus urged rulers to follow doctrines of Confucius to ensure the happiness of their subjects. Writings became fundamental in Chinese education.

Mencken, H[enry] L[ouis] (1880-1956), American journalist. Attacked America's complacent bourgeois mores as co-editor (with George Jean Nathan) of *Smart Set* (1914-23) and as founder-editor of *American Mercury* (1924-33). Compiled *The American Language* (1919, often revised).

Mendel, Gregor Johann (1822-84), Austrian monk and botanist. Pioneer of modern genetics; his experiments in cross-breeding peas led to theory of organic inheritance determined by dominant and recessive traits.

Mendeleev or **Mendelejeff, Dmitri Ivanovich** (1834-1907), Russian chemist. Developed periodic classification of elements by atomic weight (now atomic number is used);

Gregor Mendel

predicted existence and properties of then unknown elements scandium, gallium and germanium.

mendelevium (Md), transuranic element; at. no. 101, mass no. of most stable isotope 258. First prepared (1955) by bombarding einsteinium with alpha particles.

Felix Mendelssohn

Mendelssohn, Moses (1729-86), German scholar. Friend of Lessing. Advocated religious toleration and separation of religion and state in *Jerusalem* (1783). Translated Pentateuch and Psalms into German. His grandson, **[Jakob Ludwig] Felix Mendelssohn [-Bartholdy]** (1809-47), was a composer. Romantic in style but often classical in form, his music has great charm and lyricism. Works incl. overture to *A Midsummer Night's Dream,* oratorio *Elijah,* chamber music, violin concerto, 5 symphonies. Revived interest in Bach's music.

Menderes, Adnan (1899-1961), Turkish statesman. Premier (1950-60), overthrown after an army coup against his repressive measures and unsuccessful economic policies. Executed.

Mendès-France, Pierre (1907–), French political leader. Radical Socialist premier (1954-5), he negotiated French withdrawal from Indo-China. Defeated over N African policy. Anti-Gaullist leader during 1960s.

Mendicant Orders, name for 4 orders of RC church which subsist mainly on alms, *ie* Augustinian Hermits, Carmelites, Dominicans, Franciscans.

Mendip Hills, limestone range of Somerset, SW England. Extend *c* 37 km (23 mi), rising to 325 m (1068 ft) in Blackdown. Cheddar Gorge; caves with prehist. remains.

Mendoza, Antonio de (1490-1552), first viceroy of New Spain (Mexico) (1535-50). Introduced printing to colony

(1536); encouraged education and conversion of the Indians. Promoted exploration of N Mexico. Appointed viceroy of Peru (1551).

Mendoza, town of W Argentina, in Mendoza R. valley. Pop. 119,000. In wine producing region. Destroyed by earthquake (1861).

Menelaus, in Greek myth, king of Sparta, husband of Helen. Abduction of Helen by Paris instigated Trojan War. Reconciled with Helen after fall of Troy.

Menelik II (1844-1913), emperor of Ethiopia (1889-1913). Gained throne with aid of Italy. Signed treaty with Italy which he renounced after discovering Italy claimed whole country as protect. Thwarted Italian invasion (1895-6), thus ensuring Ethiopian independence.

Menes (fl 3200 BC), founder of 1st dynasty of ancient Egypt. Traditionally, united Upper and Lower Egypt and founded Memphis.

Menger, Karl (1840-1921), Austrian economist. Using empirical methods, explained phenomena of distribution and price in terms of social value. Author of *Principles of Economics* (1871).

Mengs, Anton Raffael (1728-79), German painter. Leading exponent of neo-Classicism, his best-known work is ceiling painting *Parnassus* in Rome. Court painter to Charles III of Spain, he decorated the royal palaces.

Meng-tse, *see* MENCIUS.

menhir, tall upright standing stone, found singly or in groups. Famous examples found at Carnac, Brittany. Some believed to have importance in prehist. astronomical calculations.

meningitis, inflammation of meninges, membranes surrounding brain and spinal cord. Results from infection by viruses or bacteria. Symptoms incl. fever, severe headache, muscular spasms in neck or back.

Mennonites, fundamentalist, pacifist Protestant sect. Originally Swiss, developed under influence of teachings of MENNO SIMONS. Now found chiefly in Canada, US. Amish and Herrite churches are conservative branches of Mennonites.

Menno Simons (c 1496-1561), Dutch religious leader. Left RC Church (1536) when he rejected infant baptism. Organized groups of Anabaptists in Holland, Germany. MENNONITES derive name from him.

menopause, permanent cessation of menstruation, commonly occurring between ages of 40 and 50. Results from changes in pituitary and ovarian hormones. Also called change of life or climacteric.

Menorca, *see* MINORCA, Spain.

Menotti, Gian-Carlo (1911-), American composer, b. Italy. Has written many operas, often to his own librettos and with strong theatrical sense. Works incl. *The Medium* and *Amahl and the Night Visitors* (written for television).

Menshevism, *see* BOLSHEVISM.

Menshikov, Aleksandr Danilovich (c 1660–1729), Russian field marshal, statesman. Chief adviser to Peter the Great after 1699. Involved in series of financial scandals. Ensured succession of Catherine I, acting as her chief minister. Exiled (1727) during reign of Peter II.

menstruation, discharge of cells and blood from the uterus through the vaginal opening. Occurs approximately every 4 weeks when lining of uterus is shed and regenerated. Begins in puberty and ends at menopause.

mental retardation, lack since birth of certain mental functions present in normal individual. Terms idiot (mental age of 2 or less), imbecile (3 to 6), moron (7 to 9) describe severity of retardation. Caused by infection of foetus during pregnancy, birth injury, hormone disturbance, *etc.*

menthol, white crystalline solid with characteristic smell. Found in oil of peppermint; used in medicine, cosmetics.

Menton (Ital. *Mentone*), town of SE France, on Côte d'Azur. Pop. 25,000. Resort. Part of Monaco until 1848, then independent republic until ceded to France in 1860.

Menuhin, Yehudi (1916-), American violinist. Debut made at age seven. Famed for interpretations of Elgar and Beethoven concertos.

Menzaleh, *see* MANZALA, LAKE, Egypt.

Mephistopheles, in German legend, personification of the Devil to whom FAUST sold his soul.

mercantilism, economic policy founded on principle that national wealth and power are best served by accumulating large reserves of bullion. Aim achieved by encouraging export and levying high duties on imports. Predominated during period (16th-18th cents.) of W European warfare with need to maintain armies. Supplanted during Industrial Revolution by LAISSER-FAIRE theories.

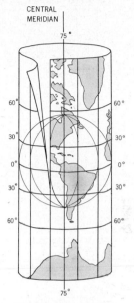

Mercator projection

Mercator, Gerardus, Latinized form of Gerhard Kremer (1512-94), Flemish cartographer, mathematician. Developed map projection (1569) named after him: modified cylindrical, all lines of latitude and longitude being straight. Produced world atlas (3 vols., 1585-94).

Mercier, Désiré Joseph (1851-1926), Belgian churchman. Leader in revival of study of Thomist philosophy. Organized institute for the study of Aquinas at Louvain. In WWI, spokesman of Belgian opposition to Germany.

Mercury, in Roman religion, god of commerce. Usually identified with Greek HERMES.

Mercury, planet nearest to Sun and smallest in Solar System. Mean distance from Sun 57.91×10^6 km; diameter 4840 km. Solar orbit takes 88 days; period of axial rotation 59 days. Almost no atmosphere; daytime temperatures reach c 430° C.

mercury or **quicksilver** (Hg), metallic element, only common metal liquid at room temperature; at. no. 80, at. wt. 200.59. Occurs as cinnabar (HgS); prepared by roasting ore in air. Used in thermometers, barometers and other scientific instruments and in mercury vapour light; alloys (amalgams) used in dentistry. Compounds, which are extremely poisonous, used in medicine, as detonators, *etc.*

Meredith, George (1828-1909), English author. Known for novels incl. *The Ordeal of Richard Feverel* (1859), *The Egoist* (1879). Also wrote poetry, *eg Modern Love* (1862).

merganser, diving sea duck of N hemisphere, with thin hooked beak. Species incl. common merganser or goosander, *Mergus merganser*, of Europe, North America, and red-breasted merganser, *M. serrator.*

Mergenthaler, Ottmar, *see* LINOTYPE.

Mérida, town of E Mexico, cap. of Yucatán state. Pop. 254,000. In sisal growing area; rope, hemp mfg. Founded (1542) on ancient Mayan site; has fine examples of 16th cent. Spanish colonial architecture.

Mérida (anc. *Emerita Augusta*), town of Estremadura, W Spain, on R. Guadiana. Pop. 40,000. Agric. market. Cap. of Roman *Lusitania; fl* under Visigoths, Moors until taken by León 1228. Roman remains incl. arch, bridge, theatre.

meridian, line of LONGITUDE. All meridians converge at the poles, cutting Equator at right-angles.

Mérimée, Prosper (1803-70), French author. Known for short novels esp. *Carmen* (1845) which inspired Bizet's opera. Also wrote literary hoaxes, *eg Théâtre de Clara Gazul* (1825) 'translated' from imaginary Spanish actress' works.

Merino

merino, breed of sheep, originally from Spain, noted for fine silky wool. Comprises 70% of Australian sheep population. Rams have spiral horns.

Merionethshire, former county of NW Wales, now in Gwynedd. On Cardigan Bay, drained by R. Dee. Mainly mountainous, many lakes *eg* Bala. Livestock rearing; slate quarrying. Co. town was Dolgellau.

Merlin, *see* ARTHURIAN LEGEND.

merlin, *Falco columbarius,* small falcon of N hemisphere. Male slate-blue above with reddish striped underparts. Called pigeon hawk in America.

mermaid, in folklore, sea creature with head and upper body of a beautiful woman and tail of a fish. Often represented as luring sailors to their death.

Merope, in Greek myth, daughter of Atlas and wife of Sisyphus. She and her sisters were changed by Zeus into stars (PLEIADES). Merope was the faintest because of her shame at having married a mortal.

Merovingians, Frankish dynasty (5th-8th cents.). First important member was CLOVIS (*c* 466-511), who estab. Frankish monarchy (481). Kingdom divided at his death. Childeric III, last Merovingian king, deposed (751) by PEPIN THE SHORT.

Merseburg, town of SC East Germany, on R. Saale. Pop. 54,000. Tanning, brewing, paper mfg. Medieval cathedral; bishop's palace (15th cent.).

Mersey, river of NW England. Flows 113 km (70 mi) to Irish Sea. Estuary 26 km (16 mi) long, incl. ocean ports of Liverpool, Birkenhead; Ship Canal to Manchester.

Merseyside, met. county of W England. Area 652 sq km (252 sq mi); pop. 1,621,000. Created 1974, comprises Liverpool and suburbs; incl. N Wirral penin.

Mersin or **İçel,** port of S Turkey, on Mediterranean. Pop. 130,000. Exports cotton, chrome, copper. Excavations show it was site of ancient city.

Merthyr Tydfil, co. bor. of Glamorgan, S Wales, on R. Taff. Pop. 55,000. Coalmining, light industs. former iron, steel centre.

Merton, Thomas (1915-68), American poet, religious writer, b. France. Became Trappist monk (1941). Known for meditations and poetry, *eg Figures for an Apocalypse* (1947), influenced by St Augustine and Blake. *The Seven Storey Mountain* (1948) is a spiritual autobiog.

Merton, bor. of S Greater London, England. Pop. 177,000. Created 1965 from residential N Surrey; incl. Wimbledon (tennis championships). Has ruined 12th cent. priory.

Merv, *see* MARY.

Meryon, Charles (1821-68), French architectural etcher. Remembered for his series of views of Paris, some of which combine architectural accuracy with outlandish fantasy, *eg Ministry of Marine with flying Devils.*

mesa (Span., = table), flat-topped, tableland area with steep sides. Formed by hard-capped, horizontal strata resisting denudation. Over time, erosion of sides of mesa produces a butte. Both are common in SW US.

Mesa Verde, plateau of SW Colorado, US. Has well-preserved cliff dwellings; Mesa Verde National Park created 1906.

mescal or **peyote,** *Lophophora williamsii,* species of cactus native of N Mexico and SW US. Button-like tops are source of hallucinogenic drug mescaline.

Meshed, *see* MASHHAD.

Mesmer, Friedrich Anton (1734-1815), German physician. Developed theory of animal magnetism (mesmerism) for curing disease. His cures of psychosomatic ailments by suggestion caused brief sensation, but were soon discredited.

Mesolithic, transitional period between Palaeolithic and Neolithic, beginning with withdrawal of ice sheets *c* 10,000 years ago. Nomadic hunting and collecting economy was replaced by localized, specialized methods. Lasted longest in N Europe.

mesons, group of unstable elementary particles with mass intermediate between that of electron and proton. Existence predicted by Yukawa to explain forces holding atomic nucleus together; first observed in cosmic rays (1947), several different types are now known.

Mesopotamia, region of SW Asia, between R. Tigris and R. Euphrates; mainly in modern Iraq. Cradle of several ancient civilizations esp. at Ur, Babylon, Nineveh.

Mesozoic or **Secondary era,** geological era intermediate between Palaeozoic and Cenozoic eras. Duration *c* 160 million years. Comprises Triassic, Jurassic, Cretaceous periods. Extensive deposition of limestone and chalk; fauna incl. molluscs, ammonites, brachiopods, giant reptiles; 1st mammals and birds. Also *see* GEOLOGICAL TABLE.

Mesquite (*Prosopis juliflora*)

mesquite, any of genus *Prosopis* of thorny shrubs of Leguminosae family. Native to SW US and Mexico. Roots may reach depth of 20 m/70 ft. Seed pods used as animal fodder.

Messiaen, Oliver (1908-), French composer. Works, sometimes based on bird song, Oriental percussion or Indian music, are often expressive of his religious mysticism. Works incl. *Turangalila* symphony, *Vingt Regards sur l'enfant Jésus* for piano.

Messiah (Heb.,=the anointed), in Judaism, the leader promised by God to restore the kingdom of David. Christians regard Jesus as Messiah.

Messina (anc. *Zancle*), town of NE Sicily, Italy, on Str. of Messina. Cap. of Messina prov. Pop. 262,000. Port, exports olive oil, wine, fruit; univ. (1549). Greek colony founded 8th cent. BC. Badly damaged by earthquakes 1783, 1908.

Messina, Strait of, channel between Italy and Sicily, linking Tyrrhenian and Ionian Seas. Length *c* 32 km (20 mi). Currents, whirlpools gave rise in ancient times to legends of Scylla and Charybdis.

Meštrović, Ivan (1883-1962), Yugoslav sculptor. Used simplified classical forms, frequently depicting biblical characters or legendary heroes of his homeland. Lived in US from 1947.

metabolism, chemical processes associated with living organisms, largely controlled by enzymes. Divided into 2 parts: catabolism, breaking down of complex substances into simpler ones or waste matter, with release of energy for vital processes; anabolism, building up of complex substances from simpler material, with storage of energy.

metallurgy, science of metals, incl. their extraction from ores and purification, formation of alloys, and study of their properties and behaviour.

metamorphic rocks, igneous or sedimentary rocks transformed in character and appearance by any of the processes of METAMORPHISM. Examples incl. granite into gneiss, limestone into marble, shale into slate.

metamorphism, in geology, processes causing change in character and appearance of rocks in Earth's crust. Caused by heat, pressure, or chemically active fluids. Commonest types of metamorphism are thermal (heat only), dynamic (pressure only), regional (heat and pressure, always associated with mountain-building).

metamorphosis, period of transformation of animal from larval to adult form. Insects placed in 2 divisions according to type of metamorphosis: Endopterygota, those undergoing complete metamorphosis with pupal stage, and Exopterygota, without pupal stage. *See* NYMPH.

metaphor, figure of speech in which word or phrase ordinarily denoting one thing is made to stand for another, *eg* 'My love is a red, red rose', whereas **simile** states the comparison explicitly by using 'like' or 'as', *eg* 'My love is like a red, red rose'.

metaphysical poetry, term first applied by Dr Johnson to early 17th cent. English verse genre, marked by complexity, compression, use of puns, paradox, unusual imagery and syntax. Poets incl. John DONNE, Richard CRASHAW, George HERBERT, Andrew MARVELL.

metaphysics, branch of philosophy which deals with first principles and seeks to explain the nature of being (ontology). Epistemology (the study of the nature of knowledge) is a major part of most metaphysical systems. The foundations were laid by Plato, Aristotle, with one of the most complete structures being estab. by St Thomas Aquinas. Since Comte many have regarded metaphysical problems as insoluble. *See* POSITIVISM, LOGICAL POSITIVISM.

Metaxas, Joannis (1871-1941), Greek army officer, statesman. Active in restoration of monarchy (1935), he was premier from 1936; exercised dictatorial powers. Led successful resistance against Italian invasion (1940).

Metchnikoff, Elie (1845-1916), Russian bacteriologist. Developed theory of phagocytosis on destruction of bacteria by white blood cells. Shared Nobel Prize for Physiology and Medicine (1908) for study of immunology.

meteor, small body which enters Earth's atmosphere from outer space; becomes incandescent (shooting star) through friction with air, leaving bright streak as it passes. Most are consumed but some, called meteorites, consisting of metal or stone, reach Earth's surface.

Meteor Crater, hole *c* 1280 m (4200 ft) wide and 180 m (600 ft) deep, in Arizona, US; formed by meteorite impact.

meteorology, study of phenomena in all levels of atmosphere. Incl. WEATHER, one branch of meteorology confined to lower levels. Earliest work is Aristotle's *Meteorologica* (*c* 340 BC); later inventions *eg* thermometer, barometer increased accuracy of observations. Advances incl. V. and J. Bjerknes' polar front theory (1917), and use of satellites.

methane (CH_4), colourless inflammable gas, 1st hydrocarbon of paraffin series. Given off by decaying vegetable matter (marsh gas); found in coal mines (firedamp). Occurs in natural gas and coal gas.

methanol or **methyl alcohol** (CH_3OH), colourless liquid, originally obtained by destructive distillation of wood. Used as a solvent, in organic synthesis; as it is poisonous, used to denature ethyl alcohol.

Methodism, Protestant religious denomination. Originated as part of Church of England revival (*c* 1729) led by JOHN WESLEY. Doctrines, influenced by those of ARMINIUS, stress repentance, salvation for all and thus evangelism and lay preaching. Separated from Church of England (1791); now has *c* 13 million followers, mainly in UK and US.

Methodius, St, *see* CYRIL, ST.

Methuselah, in OT, an antediluvian patriarch credited with having lived 969 years.

metre, SI unit of length; 1 metre = *c* 39.37 in., 1000 metres = 1 kilometre = *c* 0.62 miles

metric system, decimal system of weights and measures in which kilogram, metre and litre are basic units of weight, length and liquid capacity, respectively. Devised in France during revolutionary period (1791-5).

metronome, mechanism used to indicate the exact pace of music, indicated in beats per minute. Consists of a pendulum driven by clockwork and carrying a sliding weight that is set to the required pace. Electronic metronomes also exist.

Metropolitan Museum of Art, civic museum of New York. Founded 1870, it is supported by private endowment and membership fees. Contains European and American paintings and sculpture, also Greek, Egyptian, Oriental and medieval works of art.

Metropolitan Opera House, principal American opera house, in New York City. Opened in 1883 and rehoused in Lincoln Center in 1966.

Metsu, Gabriel (1629-67), Dutch painter. Specialized in interiors and genre scenes, depicting middle-class life. Works incl. *Mother and Sick Child.*

Metternich [-Winneburg], Clemens Wenzel Lothar, Fürst von (1773-1859), Austrian statesman, b. Germany. Foreign minister (1809-48), negotiated Napoleon's marriage to Marie Louise of Austria (1810); kept Austria out of Franco-Russian war (1812-13). Later formed alliance with Prussia and Russia against France. Chief figure at Congress of VIENNA (1814-15); advocated maintenance of 'balance of power' in Europe. Repressive measures within Austria led to enforced abdication during Revolution of 1848.

Metz, city of NE France, on R. Moselle, cap. of Moselle dept. Pop. 108,000. Centre of Lorraine iron mining; metals, textiles industs. Important city of Roman Gaul; powerful medieval bishopric. Annexed by France in 1552; part of Germany (1871-1918). Gothic cathedral (13th cent.).

Meunier, Constantin Emile (1831-1905), Belgian painter and sculptor. Known for his work expressing the dignity of labour, his subjects incl. stevedores, miners and factory workers. His major work, *Monument to Labour,* was unfinished.

Meuse (Flem. *Maas*), river of NE France, S Belgium, and Netherlands. Flows 933 km (580 mi) from Langres Plateau via Namur, Liège, Maastricht to join Rhine delta. Heavy traffic on lower course.

Mewar, *see* UDAIPUR.

Mexicali, town of NW Mexico, cap. of Baja California state; on US border. Pop. 390,000. Commercial centre in agric. region producing cotton, dates, alfalfa, wine. Border resort.

Mexican War, conflict (1846-8) between US and Mexico. Immediate cause was annexation of Texas by US (1845); war declared when Mexico declined to negotiate over border dispute and American claims in California. Taylor defeated Mexicans under Santa Anna at Buena Vista (1847). Mexico City captured by Scott after march from Veracruz. Settlement reached under Treaty of GUADALUPE HIDALGO.

Mexico (Span. *Mejico*), federal republic of SW North America. Area 1,972,544 sq km (761,600 sq mi); pop. 48,377,000; cap. Mexico City. Languages: Spanish, Indian dialects. Religion: RC. Pacific and Gulf of Mexico coastlines rise to high C plateau dominated by Sierra Madre range. Varied climate. Limited agric. concentrated in irrigated region (many of foodstuffs imported). Mineral wealth incl. silver, lead, iron, coal; tourism. Had ancient Maya, Toltec, Aztec civilizations; Spanish conquest (1519) under Cortés. Independence struggle (1810-21); in Texas revolt (1836) and war with US (1846-8), Mexico ceded all

Mexico

land N of Rio Grande to US. Revolution (1910); civil war estab. new constitution (1917).

Pyramid of the Sun at Teotihuácan, near Mexico City

Mexico, Gulf of, extensive arm of Atlantic, bounded by US, Mexico. Connected to Atlantic by Str. of Florida, and to Caribbean by Yucatán Channel. Receives Mississippi, Grande rivers.

Mexico City, cap. of Mexico and Federal Dist.; on C plateau, alt. 2380 m (*c* 7800 ft). Pop. 3,026,000. Transport, financial, cultural, indust. centre. Textile, glass mfg.; automobile indust.; gold, silver refining. Built on site of ancient Aztec cap. Tenochtitlán (1521). Has Central Plaza, Palace, National Univ. (1551), cathedral (1573); famous bull ring. Nearby shrine of Our Lady at Guadalupe Hidalgo is pilgrimage centre; also ancient site of Teotihuacán, with famous pyramids and temples. Held Olympic Games in 1968.

Meyerbeer, Giacomo (1791-1864), German composer. Operas incl. *Robert le Diable, Les Huguenots,* written for Paris Opéra.

Miami, city of SE Florida, US; on Biscayne Bay. Pop. 335,000. Famous tourist and holiday resort. Suburbs incl. Coral Gables, Miami Beach. Has international airport. Grew with 1920s land boom.

mica, group of minerals consisting of silicates of aluminium and potassium. Crystallize into thin plates; flexible and heat resistant. Types incl. muscovite (colourless), phlogopite (yellow to brown); used in insulators, paints, tiles.

Micah, prophetic book of OT, attributed to prophet Micah (8th cent. BC). Denounces social injustice and hypocrisy but foretells Messianic deliverance.

Michael VIII (*c* 1224-82), Byzantine emperor (1259-82). Usurped throne of John IV, whom he had blinded; crowned at Nicaea. Regained Constantinople (1261). Agreed to unite Eastern and Western Churches under papal supremacy (1274); union broken 1281. Helped plot Sicilian Vespers.

Michael (1596-1645), tsar of Russia, founder of Romanov dynasty. Election as tsar (1613) ended confusion in finding successor to Boris Godunov caused by series of usurpers (false Dmitris).

Michael I (1921-), king of Romania (1927-30, 1940-7). Ruled (1927-30) under regency until replaced by his father, Carol II. When Carol abdicated, regained throne. Overthrew dictatorship of Atonescu (1944) and concluded armistice with Allies. Abdicated in favour of Communist republic (1947).

Michael, archangel in Jewish, Christian and Islamic tradition, guardian of Israel. His feast (Michaelmas) is celebrated on 29th September.

Michaelmas daisy, *see* ASTER.

Michelangelo: detail of *The Creation of Adam* in the Sistine Chapel

Michelangelo (Buonarroti) (1475-1564), Italian artist, architect and poet, a major figure of the Renaissance. First great sculptures incl. *Pietà* (St Peter's, Rome), *David* (Florence). His tomb of Pope Julius II was much delayed and a greatly reduced version was substituted; only colossal *Moses* was completed. Painted fresco cycle on Old Testament themes (1508-12) and *Last Judgment* (1536-41) in Sistine Chapel, Rome. Also did frescoes *Conversion of St Paul* and *Crucifixion of St Peter* for Pauline Chapel in the Vatican, and designed sepulchral chapel of Medici in Florence. Architect of St Peter's from 1546.

Michelet, Jules (1798-1874), French historian. Professor at Collège de France (1838-51). His life-work was *Histoire de France* (1833-67); deeply researched, it displays idiosyncratic religious and political prejudices.

Michelozzo di Bartolommeo (1396-1472), Italian architect, sculptor. One of the founders of the Renaissance architectural style; built Medici-Riccardi palace for Cosimo de' Medici in Florence. Worked with Donatello and Ghiberti.

Michelson, Albert Abraham (1852-1931), American physicist, b. Germany. Devised apparatus incl. interferometer for accurate measurement of wavelength and velocity of light. Devised experiment with Morley to measure Earth's velocity through ETHER; negative results were later explained by Einstein. Awarded Nobel Prize for Physics (1907).

Michigan, state of NC US. Area 150,779 sq km (58,216 sq mi); pop. 8,875,000; cap. Lansing; chief city Detroit. Upper and Lower penins. separated by L. Michigan. Agric., dairying and livestock raising, lumbering in S; iron ore, copper, peat, bromine exploitation in N. Leading motor vehicles mfg., machinery, heavy industs. French settlement in 17th cent.; ceded to British 1763; passed to US 1783; became separate territ. 1805. Admitted to Union as 26th state (1837).

Michigan, Lake, third largest of Great Lakes, entirely within NC US. Area 57,441 sq km (22,178 sq mi). Chief ports Chicago, Milwaukee. Main cargoes incl. coal, grain, iron ore.

Mickiewicz, Adam (1798-1855), Polish poet. Wrote national epic, *Pan Tadeusz* (1834). Organized underground resistance against Russia; arrested (1823) and deported, but later allowed to travel abroad. Died in Constantinople attempting to raise Polish corps to fight against Russia in Crimea.

microbe, microscopic organism, esp. any of the bacteria which cause disease.

microfilm, film on which documents, printed pages, *etc* are photographed in a reduced size for convenience in storage. Enlarged prints may be made or film may be projected on ground glass screen in special viewer. A microfiche is a sheet of microfilm (10 cm × 15 cm) on which several pages may be recorded.

micrometer, scientific instrument for making very accurate measurement of distances and angles.

Micronesia, one of three divisions of Pacific isls., N of equator. Incl. Caroline, Mariana, Marshall and Gilbert isls. and Nauru. Also *see* MELANESIA, POLYNESIA.

Micronesians, peoples of Pacific isls. N of Melanesia. Of Australoid stock, language is Malayo-Polynesian.

microphone, device for converting sound waves into an electrical signal. Type used in telephone consists of diaphragm in close contact with loosely packed carbon grains; sound waves cause diaphragm to vibrate and compress grains. Motion of grains causes variation in current flow through associated electric circuit.

microscope, optical instrument used to obtain enlarged images of small objects. Simple microscope uses single convex lens to produce virtual image; compound microscope uses 2 convex lenses (objective and eyepiece) mounted at opposite ends of tube. *See* ELECTRON MICROSCOPE.

microwave heating, form of high-frequency radiation which may be used in very high speed cooking. Heat is immediately generated throughout an object rather than passing in from surface by conduction. Also used in pasteurization, insect destruction.

microwaves, electromagnetic radiation with wavelength between 1 mm and 30 cm. Ranges from short radio waves almost to infrared rays.

Midas, in Greek myth, king of Phrygia. Dionysus gave him power of turning everything he touched to gold. Begged relief of this power when even his food turned to gold. In another legend, given ass's ears as punishment for preferring Pan's music to Apollo's.

Middelburg, town of SW Netherlands, on Walcheren Isl., cap. of Zeeland prov. Pop. 28,000. Market town; canal link with Flushing. Hanseatic town, 12th cent. abbey. Badly damaged in WWII.

Middle Ages, period in W European history considered to have begun with fall of Roman Empire (5th cent.) and ended with early Renaissance in 15th cent. Period marked by unity of W Europe within RC church and prevalence of feudal system.

Middle English, see ENGLISH.

Middlesbrough, co. town of Cleveland, NE England. Port; iron, steel indust.; chemicals mfg. From 1968 part of co. bor. of TEESSIDE.

Middlesex, former county of SE England. Mainly absorbed by Greater London 1965, small parts joined to Surrey, Hertfordshire.

Middle Temple, see INNS OF COURT.

Middleton, Thomas (1580-1627), English dramatist. Works incl. comedies, *eg The Roaring Girl* (1611, with Dekker), tragedies, *eg The Changeling* (*c* 1623, with T. Rowley), *Women Beware Women* (*c* 1625).

Midgard, in Norse myth, region between the lands of dwarfs and giants. Incl. Mannheim, the world of men. Regarded as being encircled by the serpent Jormungard.

midge, small 2-winged insect of Ceratopogonidae family with sucking mouthparts. Some species blood-suckers, *eg Culicoides impunctatus.*

Mid Glamorgan, see GLAMORGAN, Wales.

Midlands, term used for central counties of England, incl. Derby, Nottingham, Leicester, Northampton, Warwick, Stafford.

Midlothian, former county of E Scotland, now in Lothian region. Previously called Edinburghshire. Moorfoot Hills (SE), Pentland Hills (SW); low-lying in N. Chief city Edinburgh. Sheep, dairy farming; market gardening; coal-mining; fishing.

midnight sun, feature of high latitude regions where, during midsummer period, Sun remains visible above horizon throughout 24 hours. Caused by tilting of Earth's axis.

Midrash, collection of rabbinical commentaries and explanatory notes on the Scriptures. Compiled between *c* 400 BC and *c* AD 1200.

midsummer, the summer solstice, *ie* in N hemisphere *c* 21 June. Midsummer day is 24 June, feast of St John the Baptist. Night before has been occasion for solar ceremonies since ancient times, with vestiges (*eg* bonfires, merrymaking, association with love, lovers) remaining in Europe to present day.

Midway Islands, two isls. of NC Pacific Ocean, admin. by US Dept. of Interior. Area 5 sq km (2 sq mi); comprise Eastern, Sand Isls. Discovered by US (1859), annexed (1867). Naval air base estab. 1941; site of US victory (1942) over Japan.

Midwest or **Middle West,** C region of US. Incl. prairie states of Illinois, Indiana, Ohio, Iowa, Kansas, Nebraska, Minnesota, Wisconsin, North and South Dakota, and E Montana. Mainly agric. esp. grain production. Large indust. cities concentrated in Great Lakes area.

midwife toad, *Alytes obstetricans,* small dark European toad. After female spawns, male twists strands of eggs round his hind legs, carrying them until tadpoles hatch.

Mies van der Rohe, Ludwig (1886-1969), German architect. Produced designs for all-glass skyscrapers (1921); his German pavilion for 1929 Barcelona exhibition was influential example of pure geometric architecture. Director of Bauhaus (1930-3), later worked in US. Designed Seagram Building, New York.

Garden mignonette

mignonette, any of genus *Reseda* of annual or perennial herbs native to Mediterranean and E Africa. Garden variety *R. odorata* has small spikes of fragrant, whitish flowers.

migraine, extremely severe prolonged headache, often affecting only one side of head. May be accompanied by nausea and disturbed vision. Believed to be caused by excessive expansion and contraction of blood vessels of brain.

migration, movement of animals from one place to another for breeding or finding new food supplies. Some animals, *eg* lemmings, undertake spontaneous migrations resulting from overpopulation. Certain birds and fish migrate seasonally.

Mikhailovich, Draja or **Dragoliub** (1893-1946), Yugoslav military leader. Led guerrilla warfare in Serbia against Germans. Appointed minister of war by Yugoslav govt. in exile. Opposed to Tito's Communist partisans, he was executed for treason.

Mikoyan, Anastas Ivanovich (1895-   ), Soviet political leader. Supported Khrushchev in power struggle after Stalin's death. Deputy premier (1955-7, 1958-64), president (1964-5). Retired from public office 1974.

Milan (*Milano*), city of N Italy, cap. of Lombardy and of Milan prov. Pop. 1,725,000. Indust., commercial centre, major railway jct., agric. market. Roman *Mediolanum;*

member of Lombard League (12th cent.), later medieval duchy under Visconti then Sforza families. Under Habsburgs 1713-1861, passed to Sardinia. Cathedral (1386), La Scala opera house (1778), many art galleries. Badly damaged in WWII.

mildew, any fungus, esp. of families Peronosporaceae and Erysiphaceae that attacks various plants or appears on organic matter, *eg* leather, fabrics, *etc*, when exposed to damp. Characterized by whitish, powdery coating on surface.

mile, unit of linear measure, equal to 1760 yds or 1.609 km.

Miletus, ancient port of Asia Minor, in W Turkey on R. Menderes (Maeander). Most important of 12 Ionian Cities; major trade city and centre of learning. Led revolt against Persia (499 BC). Prosperity declined when harbour silted up in early Christian times.

milfoil, *see* YARROW.

Milford Haven, Louis Alexander, 1st Marquess of, orig. Prince Louis of Battenberg (1854-1921), British naval officer, b. Germany. Director of naval intelligence (1902); 1st sea lord (1912). Resigned at outset of war because of anti-German public feeling.

Milford Haven, urban dist. of Dyfed, SW Wales. Pop. 14,000. Fishing port; oil importing and refining.

Milhaud, Darius (1892-1974), French composer. Member of 'les Six' group. Numerous works, often lighthearted in style, were variously influenced by jazz, Latin American rhythms, *etc*. Compositions incl. ballet *La Création du monde, Scaramouche* for 2 pianos.

militia, an organized military force of civilians called upon in national emergency. Known in Europe before formation of regular armies; again raised in Britain when Napoleonic invasions threatened, it later merged with the TERRITORIAL ARMY; in US it merged with the NATIONAL GUARD.

Milk, river of W US-Canada. Rises in NW Montana, flows 1175 km (730 mi) into Alberta, then SE back to Montana. Joins Missouri R. below Fort Peck Dam. Many dams on river provide irrigation over large area.

milk, fluid secreted by mammary glands of female mammals for nourishment of young. Almost a complete food, containing fat, carbohydrates, lactose sugar, vitamins A, B, D. Source of calcium and phosphorus.

milkweed, any of genus *Asclepias* of perennial plants. Native to South America and Africa. Yields LATEX and has pods which release silkenhaired seeds sometimes used as kapok substitute.

milkwort, any of genus *Polygala* of herbs native to Europe and North America. Common European milkwort, *P. vulgaris,* with small blue flowers was supposed to increase milk production of cows. American milkwort, *P. senega,* was reputed cure for snakebite.

Milky Way, belt of faint stars encircling the heavens, seen as an arch across sky at night. Now known to be a galaxy containing *c* 10^{11} stars, incl. the Sun.

J.S. Mill

Mill, James (1773-1836), English philosopher. An associate of Bentham, and advocate of UTILITARIANISM. Also wrote *History of India* (1817). His son, **John Stuart Mill** (1806-73), was also a philosopher. Introduced more humanitarian ideas into utilitarian theory, favouring democracy and social reform. Emphasized importance of quality, as well as quantity, of pleasure as motivating force in life. Works incl. *Essay on Liberty* (1859), *Utilitarianism* (1863), *Autobiography* (1873).

Millais, Sir John Everett (1829-96), English painter. Founder member of the Pre-Raphaelite Brotherhood with Hunt and Rossetti; early work was richly coloured and detailed. Later painted trivial genre scenes and fashionable portraits. Works incl. *Christ in the House of his Parents.*

Millay, Edna St Vincent (1892-1950), American poet. Known for sophisticated, witty verse incl. *A Few Figs from Thistles* (1920), *The Harp-Weaver* (1923), *The Buck in the Snow* (1928).

Miller, Arthur (1915-), American playwright. Known for committedly liberal plays, *eg Death of a Salesman* (1947), *The Crucible* (1953) using 17th cent. Salem witch hunt as metaphor for McCarthy investigations, *The Price* (1968). Also autobiog. *After the Fall* (1964), perhaps portraying second wife, Marilyn Monroe.

Miller, Henry (1891-), American author. Many works mainly fictionalized autobiog. incl. *Tropic of Cancer* (1934), *Nexus* (1960). Also many essays on literature, painting.

miller's thumb, *see* BULLHEAD.

Milles, Carl (1875-1955), Swedish sculptor. Influenced by Rodin, he is noted for sculpture complementing public architecture, esp. fountains. Work incl. the fountain *Meeting of the Waters* in St Louis.

Millet, Jean François (1814-75), French painter. Worked at Barbizon after 1849, where he specialized in painting peasant life and rustic scenes. Works incl. *The Gleaners* (1857) and *The Angelus* (1859).

millet, name for several cereal and forage grasses, *eg* common millet, *Panicum miliaceum,* grown in Asia, N Africa and S Europe as food crop. North American foxtail millet, *Setaria italica,* is used for fodder.

Millikan, Robert Andrews (1868-1953), American physicist. Awarded Nobel Prize for Physics (1923) for determining charge on an electron and experimental verification of Einstein's predictions about photoelectric effect.

Millipede

millipede, any of class Diplopoda of many-legged arthropods. Cylindrical, segmented body; herbivorous. Differs from centipede in having 2 pairs of legs on each segment and no poisonous bite.

Milne, A[lan] A[lexander] (1882-1956), English author. Known for children's books originally written for son, Christopher Robin, incl. *Winnie-the-Pooh* (1926) and verse collection, *When We Were Very Young* (1924). Also wrote plays, detective story *The Red House Mystery* (1922).

Milos, *see* MELOS, Greece.

Milosh [Obrenovich] (1780-1860), Serbian ruler. Led Serbian rebellion against Turks (1815-17). Prob. had his rival KARAGEORGE murdered. Assumed title of prince

(1817); recognized by sultan (1830). Despotic ruler, forced to abdicate (1839) in favour of son; reinstated 1858.

Miltiades (d. 489 BC), Athenian army commander. Defeated Persians at Marathon (490 BC), then marched his troops to Athens and defended city against naval attack.

Milton, John (1608-74), English poet. Early works incl. 'L'Allegro', masque *Comus* (1634), pastoral elegy *Lycidas* (1637). Blind after 1652, wrote his masterpiece, blank verse epic *Paradise Lost* (1667), attempting to 'justify the ways of God to men'. Also wrote classical drama, *Samson Agonistes* (1671), prose pamphlets, *eg Areopagitica* (1644) on censorship, *Of Education* (1644). Latin secretary to Commonwealth (1649-60).

Milton Keynes, area of Buckinghamshire, SC England, designated new town. Present pop. 46,000; planned 250,000. Site of Open Univ.

Milwaukee, port of SE Wisconsin, US; on L. Michigan. Pop. 717,000; state's largest city. Shipping centre; important brewing, meat packing industs.; heavy machinery, electrical equipment mfg. Trade post estab. 1795; grew after German refugee influx (1848).

mimicry, in zoology, protective resemblance of one species to another. In Batesian mimicry, harmless animal resembles poisonous or dangerous animal and thus gains protection from predators; in Müllerian mimicry, 2 harmful or distasteful species resemble each other and each gains protection from other's predators.

mimosa, genus of trees, shrubs and herbs of Leguminosae family, mostly native to tropical and subtropical America. Several species respond to light and touch, *eg Mimosa pudica,* the sensitive plant. Related species incl. ACACIA of Africa and Australia.

Mina Hassan Tani, see KÉNITRA, Morocco.

minaret, slender tower attached to corner of Islamic mosque from which muezzin calls the faithful to prayer 5 times a day. Oldest minarets were 4 Greek watchtowers at corners of ancient temple which became Great Mosque at Damascus.

Minas Gerais, inland state of E Brazil. Area 587,171 sq km (226,707 sq mi); pop. 11,498,000; cap. Belo Horizonte. Dry climate. Rich mineral resources esp. iron ore. Agric. incl. cattle rearing, maize, coffee, cotton, tobacco growing.

Minch, channel off NW Scotland, separating Outer Hebrides from mainland. Little Minch to S separates Inner and Outer Hebrides.

mind, presumed seat of consciousness. In philosophy, the concept has been interpreted in various ways. Materialists explaining it in terms of matter, dualists holding that the mind exists independently alongside matter, idealists that the mind is the only reality and apparent matter the creation of the imagination.

Mindanao, isl. of S Philippines. Area *c* 94,600 sq km (36,500 sq mi). Mountainous, rising to 2954 m (9690 ft) at Mt. Apo; heavily forested. Produces pineapples, hemp, rice, coffee; gold mined. Underwent rapid population growth in 1960s; scene of fighting against terrorists belonging to large Moslem minority in 1970s.

Minden, town of N West Germany, on R. Weser. Pop. 49,000. Chemicals, soap mfg., engineering. Bishopric founded *c* 800 by Charlemagne; medieval cathedral destroyed in WWII. Hanseatic League member.

Mindoro, isl. of Philippines, S of Luzon. Area 9740 sq km (3760 sq mi). Mountainous, with little arable land. Timber produced.

Mindszenty, Jozsef (1892-1975), Hungarian churchman. Primate of Hungary (1945-74); arrested (1948), sentenced to life imprisonment for opposing Communist rule. Released during 1956 rising; took refuge in US legation, Budapest, after rising suppressed. Moved to Rome (1971). Removed from primacy (1974).

mine, originally explosive-filled tunnel dug under an enemy position, used in static situations as in WWI. Later, took form of buried canister, detonated by pressure or remote control, laid in systematic patterns as defence against armoured fighting vehicles. Anti-personnel version scatters shrapnel. Naval mine is larger container of explosive detonated by contact, magnetically or by remote control.

mineral, naturally occurring inorganic solid of homogeneous structure and definite composition expressible as a chemical formula. ROCKS are usually a mixture of minerals.

mineralogy, branch of geology dealing with the study of minerals. Early works incl. Theophrastus' *On Stones* (*c* 315 BC), Pliny's *Natural History* (*c* AD 77); advances in classification made by Agricola (16th cent.). Emphasis in 19th-20th cent. on chemical composition and crystallographic features.

mineral water, water naturally impregnated with metallic salts or gases, often held to have medicinal value. Sulphates, phosphates, carbonates of such metals as iron, magnesium, sodium, barium, or gases such as carbon dioxide or hydrogen sulphide, occur in mineral waters. Famous spas incl. Bath, Vichy, Aachen.

Minerva, in Roman religion, goddess of arts, craftsmen and wisdom. Identified with Greek ATHENA. Worshipped with Jupiter and Juno.

Ming, Chinese dynasty (1368-1644), founded by Chu Yuan-chang. Empire extended from Korea to Burma at its height. First contacts with Europeans, esp. missionaries, began in Ming period. Noted for literary excellence, fine porcelain. Supplanted by Manchu dynasty.

Minho (Span. *Miño*), river of NW Spain and N Portugal. Flows *c* 340 km (210 from Galicia to Atlantic Ocean in N Portugal.

miniature, very small painting, usually a portrait, executed in gouache or watercolour. Early miniatures on card or vellum developed from medieval manuscript illumination; form *fl* in 16th and 17th cent. in hands of such practitioners as Holbein, Hilliard and Cooper.

mining, process of extracting metallic ores and minerals from Earth's crust. When mineral deposits lie near surface, opencast (open cut) and strip mining are used. Subterranean system of shafts and galleries is used to extract minerals which lie deeper.

American mink

mink, semi-aquatic carnivore of weasel family, genus *Mustela*. Species incl. European mink, *M. lutreola* and larger North American, *M. vison,* bred for its soft, thick fur.

Minneapolis, city of E Minnesota, US; contiguous with St Paul ('Twin Cities'), on Mississippi R. Pop. 432,000; state's largest city. Financial, commercial, indust. centre of agric. region; processes grain and dairy produce, clothing mfg. Seat of Univ. of Minnesota (1851).

Minnesinger, poet and musician of Germany in 12th-13th cents. who sang of courtly love; incl. Walther von der Vogelweide, Wolfram von Eschenbach. Corresponded to TROUBADOURS. *See* MEISTERSINGER.

Minnesota, state of N US. Area 217,736 sq km (84,068 sq mi); pop. 3,805,000; cap. St Paul; largest city Minneapolis. N borders with Canada; prairies in S (grain, dairy farming esp. butter production); iron ore, granite mining in Mesabi Range. Drained by Hudson, St Lawrence, Mississippi river systems. Region ceded to British by French (1763); obtained by US from British (1783) and French (1803). Admitted to Union as 32nd state (1858).

minnow, *Phoxinus phoxinus,* smallest fish of carp family, common in European fresh water. Males brightly coloured at spawning time.

Miño, see MINHO.

Minoan civilization, Bronze Age civilization of Crete revealed by excavations of ARTHUR EVANS. During Middle

Minoan period (*c* 2000-1600 BC), great palaces were built at Knossos, Phaistos, Mallia, urbanization began and metal-working reached high point. Two pictographic scripts, Linear A and later Linear B (deciphered 1952), were used. Destruction of Knossos *c* 1400 BC marks decline of civilization and growth of Mycenaean power.

Minorca (*Menorca*), second largest of Balearic Isls., Spain. Area 702 sq km (271 sq mi); main town and port Mahón. Mainly low-lying. Tourism, cereals, fruit growing, livestock.

Minos, in Greek myth, king of Crete, son of Zeus and Europa. Had Labyrinth built to house the monstrous Minotaur, offspring of wife Pasiphaë by a bull. Minotaur was slain by THESEUS. Minos became a judge in Hades after his death.

Minotaur, *see* MINOS.

Minsk, city of USSR, cap. of Byelorussian SSR. Pop. 996,000. Indust. and cultural centre; tractor, automobile, textile mfg. Passed from Poland to Russia (1793). Large Jewish community (40% of pop.) decimated during German occupation (1941-4).

Spearmint

mint, any of genus *Mentha* of aromatic herbs native to Mediterranean area but now widespread. Species incl. garden mint, *M. rotundifolia*, used for sauces; peppermint, *M. piperita*, used in confectionery and medicines and spearmint, *M. spicata*, used in chewing gum and sauces.

Minton bone china plate

Minton, Thomas (1765-1836), English potter. Estab. small pottery at Stoke-on-Trent (1789). Created celebrated Willow Pattern ware and produced good bone china. His son, **Herbert Minton** (1793-1858), developed pottery, estab. reputation of company.

minuet, French dance in triple time. Originally rustic, became fashionable court dance in 18th cent. Used by Haydn, Mozart in sonatas.

Minyâ, El, city of C Egypt, on R. Nile. Pop. 122,000. River port; sugar refining, cotton ginning, flour milling.

Miocene epoch, fourth geological epoch of Tertiary period. Alpine mountain building continued; withdrawal of seas, formation of extensive plains. Mammals still dominant. Decrease in temperature continued from Oligocene. Also *see* GEOLOGICAL TABLE.

Miquelon, *see* ST PIERRE AND MIQUELON.

Mirabeau, Honoré Gabriel Riqueti, Comte de (1749-91), French statesman. A leader in National Assembly (1789), he sought to create constitutional monarchy on lines of British one. Aimed to become chief minister of the king and began to advise him in secret. This role was not discovered until after his death.

miracle, event which apparently transcends laws of nature and is thus thought to be due to supernatural intervention, esp. that of God. Concept only occurs where natural laws and divine will have been clearly distinguished, *eg* in the 3 major monotheistic religions. Many miracles of Jesus recorded in Gospels. In RC church, attestation of miracles required in process of canonization.

miracle play or **mystery play,** medieval religious drama. Began as simple dramatization of religious stories, later presented with contemporary social realism, humour. Developed into full cycles, performed on feast-days by town guilds on movable wagons. French, German, English works extant.

mirage, optical illusion in the atmosphere. Caused by refraction and reflection of light rays in layers of air of different temperature and density. Occurs most often in deserts, polar seas.

Mirandola, *see* PICO DELLA MIRANDOLA.

Miró, Joan (1893-   ), Spanish painter. Joined surrealist group in 1925; work has become more abstract and is noted for its use of amoeba-like shapes and bright colours. Executed murals in UNESCO building, Paris.

miscarriage, in medicine, *see* ABORTION.

misdemeanour, minor crime, distinguished from FELONY. In UK, distinction no longer maintained. In US, penalty is summary fine and imprisonment for less than year.

Mishima, Yukio, pseud. of Kimitake Hiraoka (1925-70), Japanese author. Works, *eg Confessions of a Mask* (1949), *Sound of Waves* (1954), *The Sailor Who Fell from Grace with the Sea* (1963) celebrate the beauty and violence of traditional Japanese life. Committed ritual suicide after haranguing a demonstration.

Mishnah, *see* TALMUD.

Miskolc, city of NE Hungary, on R. Sajó. Pop. 186,000. Iron, steel indust., railway engineering. Cattle, wine, tobacco market. Medieval church, buildings. Univ. (1949).

missile, *see* GUIDED MISSILE.

missions, organizations with aim of spreading religious knowledge. Early dissemination of Christianity undertaken by missionaries, *eg* St Paul; in early Middle Ages by St Patrick, St Augustine, St Boniface. Further wave of activity (esp. by Jesuits) with opening up of New World. Protestant missions incl. Society for Promoting Christian Knowledge (1698), Baptist Missionary Society (1792). Since 19th cent., missions have emphasized medical care and education.

Mississippi, state of SE US. Area 123,584 sq km (47,716 sq mi); pop. 2,217,000; cap. Jackson; other major town Meridian. W border formed by Mississippi R.; mainly on Gulf of Mexico coastal plain. Cotton, soya beans, poultry, livestock farming. Some oil resources, fishing, lumbering. Taken by British from French (1763); gained by US after Revolution. Admitted to Union as 20th state (1817).

Mississippi, river of C US. Rises in N Minnesota, flows S 3780 km (*c* 2350 mi) forming many natural state boundaries. Enters Gulf of Mexico forming delta in SE Louisiana. Tributaries incl. Ohio, Missouri, Arkansas rivers; main ports St Louis, New Orleans. Region explored by French in 17th cent.; US control after Louisiana Purchase 1803; important in 19th cent. W expansion.

Mississippian period, earlier of 2 subdivisions of Carboniferous period in North America. Began *c* 345 million years ago, lasted 20 million years. Time of large shallow seas, deposition of limestones, sandstones, shales. Typified by brachiopods, crinoids, corals; increasing amphibians, fish, insects; mosses, ferns. Also *see* GEOLOGICAL TABLE.

Missolonghi (*Mesolóngion*), town of WC Greece, on Gulf of Patras. Pop. 11,000. Fish, tobacco trade. Greek stronghold in independence struggle against Turks (1822-6), Byron died here (1824).

Missouri, state of C US, on W bank of Mississippi R. Area 180,487 sq km (69,686 sq mi); pop. 4,677,000; cap. Jefferson City; other major city St Louis. Mainly rolling prairie, crossed by Missouri R. Livestock, grain, dairy farming; lead, barytes mining. Explored by French in 17th cent.; bought by US as part of Louisiana Purchase (1803). Admitted to Union as 24th state (1821). Slave state, remained in Union in Civil War.

Missouri, river of WC US; longest in North America. Rises in SW Montana (Rocky Mts.); flows E 4130 km (*c* 2565 mi), then SE across C plains through North and South Dakota, Missouri to join Mississippi near St Louis. Hist. fur trade route until railway boom. Provides h.e.p., irrigation.

Missouri Compromise, legislation (1820-1) passed by US Congress, providing for Missouri's entry into Union as a slave state but prohibiting slavery in rest of Louisiana Purchase N of Missouri's S boundary. *See* KANSAS-NEBRASKA BILL.

Mistinguett, pseud. of Jeanne Marie Bourgeois (1875-1956), French actress, dancer. Appeared at Folies-Bergère and Moulin Rouge in Paris, often with Maurice Chevalier.

Mistletoe

mistletoe, *Viscum album,* European evergreen plant. Parasitic on trees, has yellowish flowers and white, poisonous berries. Traditional Christmas decoration. Name also used for similar and related plants of genera *Phoradendron* of North America and *Loranthus* of Africa.

mistral, cold, dry, often strong N or NW wind which blows in S France, esp. Rhône valley and delta, in winter.

Mistral, Gabriela, pseud. of Lucila Godoy Alcayaga (1889-1957), Chilean poet, educationist. Works deal with love, suffering, religious experience, *eg Desolación* (1922). Nobel Prize for Literature (1945).

Mitchell, John Newton (1913-), American govt. official. Attorney-general (1969-72). Headed committee to re-elect Nixon (1972). Involvement in 'Watergate affair' led to conviction (1975) for conspiracy and obstruction of justice.

Mitchell, Margaret (1900-49), American novelist. Known for only book, best-selling romantic novel about Georgia during Civil War, *Gone with the Wind* (1936).

Mitchell, William Lendrum ('Billy') (1879-1936), American general, b. France. Commanded air-force units in WWI and developed ideas on strategy of aerial warfare (*eg* strategic bombing), which were later vindicated in WWII but antagonized general staff. Court-martialled (1925) and forced to resign.

Mitchell, Mount, peak of W North Carolina, US; in Black Mts. Highest mountain in E US. Height 2037 m (6684 ft).

mite, tiny arachnid of order Acarina, with 4 pairs of legs and rounded body. Often parasitic on animals or destructive of food. Species incl. itch mite, *Sarcoptes scabiei,* which lays eggs under skin surface, causing scabies.

Mitford, Nancy Freeman (1904-73), Known for ironic, satirical novels of upper-class manners, *eg The Pursuit of Love* (1945). With Professor Alan Ross edited comic study of social distinctions, *Noblesse Oblige* (1956), coining terms 'U', 'non-U'. Her sister, **Jessica Mitford** (1917-), wrote autobiog. *Hons and Rebels* (1960), *The American Way of Death* (1963).

Mithra, originally, in ancient Zoroastrian myth, god of light and wisdom; by 5th cent. BC principal Persian god. Cult spread into Europe; by 2nd cent. AD major religion of Roman Empire. Mithras (Latin form) worshipped by legions as ideal comrade and soldier. Cult involved rigorous ethics and secret ritual; declined in 3rd cent.

Mithradates [VI] the Great (*c* 132-63 BC), king of Pontus. Expansion of his empire over Asia Minor and into Greece led to series of 3 wars with Rome (88-84, 83-81, 74-63). In last war, defeated by Lucullus and driven into Armenia. Later recovered Pontus but was defeated by Pompey (66).

Mitla, religious centre of Zapotec Indians, near Oaxaca, Mexico. Prob. built 13th cent., incl. many low buildings with stucco and mosaic representations of sky serpent Quetzalcoatl.

mitosis, in biology, method of division of nucleus of body cells, prior to division into 2 new cells. Chromosomes are formed in nucleus and, when nuclear membrane breaks up, they migrate to equator of cell and divide lengthways. The 2 halves move to opposite ends of the cell where 2 new nuclei are assembled around them.

Mitre, Bartolomé (1821-1906), Argentinian statesman, soldier, journalist. Involved in secession of Buenos Aires from Argentinian confederation (1859). Defeated Urquiza at Pavón (1861) and brought about national unity as president (1862-8). Founded Buenos Aires newspaper, *La Nación.*

Mitterrand, François Maurice Marie (1916-), French politician. Head of Socialist Party from 1971. Narrowly defeated in presidential elections (1965 against De Gaulle, 1974 against Giscard d'Estaing) as candidate of Combined Left.

Mizoguchi, Kenji (1898-1956), Japanese film director. Long known in Japan, best known to Western audiences for *Ugetsu Monogatari* (1952), critically acclaimed.

Mnemosyne, in Greek myth, personification of memory. A Titan, mother of Muses by Zeus.

moa, any of Dinornithidae family of extinct flightless birds of New Zealand, hunted by Maoris *c* 500 years ago. Resembled ostrich, reaching heights of 3.7 m/12 ft.

Moab, ancient country of Jordan, in uplands E of Dead Sea. Moabite stone is 9th cent. BC record, in language similar to Biblical Hebrew, of successful revolt against Israel. Discovered 1868, now in Louvre.

Mobile, seaport of SW Alabama, US, on Mobile Bay. Pop. 190,000. Shipbuilding indust.; exports cotton, timber. Founded by French (1710). Seized from Spanish by US (1813).

mobile, form of moving abstract sculpture invented by Alexander Calder (1932). Consists of series of thin metal or wood shapes connected by wire or rods, and set in motion by air currents.

Mobutu, Joseph Désiré (1930-), Zaïrian army officer, politician. Led army coup against 1st Congolese govt. (1960); arrested Lumumba, who was later murdered by Mobutu's troops. In 2nd coup (1965), deposed Kasavubu and Tshombe, becoming head of state. Changed name to Mobutu Sese Seko (1972).

Moçambique, *see* MOZAMBIQUE.

Moçâmedes, town of SW Angola, on Atlantic Ocean. Pop. 8000. Port, railway from interior; exports iron ore, cotton, tobacco; fish processing.

Mocha, seaport of S Yemen on Red Sea. Pop. 5000. Gave name to former exports of Arabian coffee and Mocha stones (agates used in jewellery). Declined in 19th cent.

mock heroic, satirical poem in which insignificant people and events are treated in an epic framework, *eg* Pope's *The Rape of the Lock.*

mockingbird, *Mimus polyglottos,* American bird noted for melodious song and mimicry of other birds.

mock orange, *see* SYRINGA.

Model Parliament, parliament summoned (1295) by Edward I of England, so called because it estab. general type of future parliaments. First attempt to be representative, as it drew on all 3 estates.

Modena (anc. *Mutina*), city of Emilia-Romagna, NC Italy, cap. of Modena prov. Pop. 173,000. Agric. machinery, vehicles; univ. (1678). Ruled by Este family 13th-19th cent. Medieval cathedral, ducal palace.

moderator, in physics, substance, *eg* graphite or heavy water, used to slow down high energy neutrons produced during fission in nuclear reactor, thus making them more likely to cause further fission.

modern art, term used loosely to describe painting and sculpture of late 19th and 20th cent., esp. abstract work.

modernism, in religion, term for movement in late 19th and 20th cents. which tries to redefine Christian teachings in light of modern science, historical research. In RC Church referred to specific movement condemned by Pius X in 1907 when its adherents denied divine sanction of the sacraments.

Modigliani: *The Little Peasant*

Modigliani, Amedeo (1884-1920), Italian painter, sculptor. Influenced by African sculpture, cubism and Italian masters such as Botticelli, he was a superb draughtsman. His distinctive elongated portraits incl. *The Little Peasant.*

modulation, in physics, alteration of characteristics, *eg* frequency or amplitude, of a wave in accordance with characteristics of another wave. Amplitude modulation, in which amplitude of radio wave is changed in accordance with signal to be broadcast, is principal mode of radio transmission. Frequency modulation provides radio transmission with reduced noise and outside interference.

Mogadishu (Ital. *Mogadiscio*), cap. of Somalia, on Indian Ocean. Pop. 230,000. Admin., commercial centre; port, exports livestock, bananas. Founded 9th cent. by Arabs. Taken by sultan of Zanzibar (1871); sold to Italy (1905), became cap. of Italian Somaliland.

Mogilev, city of USSR, E Byelorussian SSR. Pop. 220,000. Indust. and transport centre. Annexed to Russia (1772) after Polish partition.

Mogul, dynasty of Moslem emperors of India. Founded (1526) by BABER. Achieved greatest power under AKBAR. Weakened by wars against MAHRATTAS in 18th cent., later emperors were under control of the British, who dissolved empire in 1857.

Mohács, town of S Hungary, on R. Danube. Pop. 20,000. Scene of defeat of Hungary by Turkey (1526) and of defeat of Turks by Charles of Lorraine (1687).

Mohammed (*c* 570-632), Arab prophet, founder of ISLAM. A rich merchant, b. in Mecca, where he had vision (*c* 610) calling on him to found a monotheistic religion. Plot to kill him led to flight (HEGIRA) to Medina (622), where he estab. Islamic theocracy. Conquered Mecca (630), estab. basis for Mohammedan empire.

Mohammed Ahmed, *see* MAHDI.

Mohammed Ali or **Mehemet Ali** (*c* 1769-1849), pasha of Egypt, b. Albania. Suppressed power of MAMELUKES in Egypt (1811). Intervened successfully in Greek war of independence until defeated by European allies at Navarino (1827). Invaded Syria (1831) after MAHMUD II denied him its governorship. Revolted against sultan in Asia Minor (1839), but European intervention prevented sultan's overthrow. Granted hereditary rights to governorship of Egypt, founding royal line.

Mohammedanism, *see* ISLAM.

Mohammed II (1429-81), Ottoman sultan (1451-81), founder of Ottoman empire. After 50 day siege, captured Constantinople (1453), which he made his cap. Conquered Greece, Serbia, Albania and the Crimea. Noted linguist and patron of arts and learning.

Mohammed V (1844-1918), Ottoman sultan (1909-18). Dominated by ENVER PASHA, reign saw loss of Tripoli to Italy (1911-12), loss of most European territ. in Balkan Wars (1912-13) and defeat in WWI.

Mohammed VI (1861-1926), Ottoman sultan (1918-22). After Turkey's defeat in WWI, he retained power with Allied support through Treaty of Sèvres. Deposed and exiled by ATATURK.

Mohawk, *see* IROQUOIS.

Mohegan or **Mohican,** North American Indian tribe of Algonquian linguistic stock. In SW Connecticut, broke away from Pequot tribe. Supported by British became one of most powerful tribes in S New England. Increase of white settlement led to virtual extinction by 19th cent.

Mohenjo-Daro, one of two centres of INDUS VALLEY CIVILIZATION.

Mohican, *see* MOHEGAN.

Mohl, Hugo von (1805-72), German botanist. Working in plant physiology and histology, discovered and named protoplasm. Expert on microscopy.

Moholy-Nagy, László (1895-1946), Hungarian artist. Influenced by constructivism, he experimented with kinetic art and photography, and made use of new materials such as plexiglass. Founded (1937) Institute of Design in Chicago.

Mohorovičić Discontinuity or **Moho,** boundary line between Earth's crust and mantle, av. depth below land surface *c* 35 km (22 mi). Discovered by Andrija Mohorovičić (1857-1936), Croatian geologist, during his investigation of earthquakes.

Mohs, Friedrich (1773-1839), German mineralogist. Devised Mohs scale for classifying minerals according to HARDNESS.

Moissan, Henri (1852-1907), French chemist. Developed electric arc furnace to produce rare metals from their ores; attempted to manufacture artificial diamonds. First to isolate fluorine. Awarded Nobel Prize for Chemistry (1906).

Mojave or **Mohave,** desert of S California, US; S of Sierra Nevada. Area 38,850 sq km (*c* 15,000 sq mi). Death Valley in N, Mojave R. in S. Arid region with wide valleys and mountain ranges.

Mol, town of NE Belgium. Pop. 28,000. Founded 9th cent. Nuclear research centre.

molasses, syrup obtained from drainings of raw sugar cane or from sugar during refining (latter syrup being called treacle in Britain). Used in making rum, confectionery and as cattle feed.

Mold, urban dist. and co. town of Clwyd, N Wales. Pop. 8000. Livestock market; coal mining.

Moldau (*Vltava*), river of Czechoslovakia. Flows *c* 435 km (270 mi) from Böhmerwald via Prague to R. Elbe. H.e.p.

Moldavia (*Moldova*), region of NE Romania, fertile plain between rivers Prut, Siret. Principality founded 14th cent., formerly incl. Bukovina, Bessarabia. United with Walachia to form Romania (1859).

Moldavian Soviet Socialist Republic, constituent republic of W USSR, bounded by Ukrainian SSR and Romania. Area *c* 33,800 sq km (13,000 sq mi); pop. 3,572,000; cap. Kishinev. Largely flat, with fertile black-earth soil; extensive vineyards. Created (1940) by merger of former Moldavian ASSR with parts of Bessarabia ceded by Romania.

mole, small burrowing insectivore of Talpidae family, with small weak eyes, pointed snout, clawed feet. European common mole, *Talpa europaea,* has black velvety fur, eats mainly earthworms. *Scalopus aquaticus* is North American variety.

mole cricket, any of Gryllotalpidae family of insects, with front legs adapted for burrowing. Eats plant roots, insects.

molecular weight, sum of atomic weights of all atoms in a molecule of a substance.

molecule, smallest portion of a substance able to exist independently and retain properties of original substance.

mole rat, burrowing rodent of E Africa, genus *Tachyoryctes,* with very large incisors, strong paws, small eyes.

Molière, pseud. of Jean Baptiste Poquelin (1622-73), French dramatist. Known for comedies of manners involving caricatures of human folly, pretentiousness, *eg Tartuffe* (1664), *Le Misanthrope* (1666), *Le Bourgeois Gentilhomme* (1670), *Les Femmes savantes* (1672), *Le Malade imaginaire* (1673). Founded Illustre Théâtre company in 1643.

Molinos, Miguel de (1640-*c* 1697), Spanish priest, mystic. Author of *Guida spirituale* (1675), estab. principles of QUIETISM based on contemplation and passivity. Condemned (1687) by Inquisition; died in prison.

Mölk, see MELK, Austria.

Mollusca (molluscs), phylum of soft-bodied unsegmented animals often with hard shell. Usually move by means of single muscular foot. Incl. snail, slug, octopus (no shell), squid (small internal shell).

Moloch, pagan Semitic god of fire. Practice of sacrificing first-born children to him condemned by OT prophets.

moloch, *Moloch horridus,* agamid lizard of Australian deserts. Brown body covered with spines; feeds on ants. Also called spiny lizard or thorny devil.

Molotov, Vyacheslav Mikhailovich, orig. Skriabin (1890-   ), Soviet political leader. As foreign minister (1939-49, 1953-6), he negotiated Non-aggression Pact with Germany (1939). Influence declined during Khrushchev's rise, which he opposed. Expelled from party (1964).

Moltke, Helmuth Bernhard, Graf von (1800-91), Prussian army officer. As chief of staff (1858-88) reorganized Prussian army, facilitating victories against Denmark (1864), Austria (1866), France (1870). His nephew, **Helmuth Johannes Ludwig von Moltke** (1848-1916), became chief of staff (1906) but was relieved of his post after the loss of the battle of the Marne (1914).

Moluccas, group of isls., forming Maluku prov. of Indonesia. Area *c* 84,000 sq km (32,000 sq mi). Incl. Amboina, Ceram, Halmahera, Aru and Tanimbar Isls. Formerly called Spice Isls., nutmeg and cloves originated here. Under Dutch control from 1667 to WWII.

molybdenite, molybdenum ore mineral. Soft, blue-grey in colour; consists of molybdenum disulphide. Major sources in US, Mexico, Chile.

molybdenum (Mo), metallic element; at. no. 42, at. wt. 95.94. Occurs as molybdenite (MoS_2); obtained by reducing oxide with carbon. Used to harden steel; molybdenum disulphide used as a lubricant.

Mombasa, city of E Kenya, on Indian Ocean. Pop. 255,000. Port at Kilindini to SW exports coffee, sisal, hides, tea; handles major part of Kenya, Uganda, Tanzania's trade. Oil refining, cement, glass mfg. Arab trade centre from 11th cent.; held by Portugal 16th-17th cent. Ceded to UK by Zanzibar 1887. Oriental influence still evident; mosques, bazaars.

moment of force, measure of tendency of a force to cause rotation of a body about a point or axis. Measured as product of magnitude of force and perpendicular distance from its line of action to axis of rotation.

momentum, in physics, the product of mass and velocity of a body. In Newtonian mechanics, total momentum of system of bodies on which no external forces act is constant.

Mommsen, Theodor (1817-1903), German historian. Author of *History of Rome* (1854-6), a work of authoritative scholarship. Awarded Nobel Prize for Literature (1902).

Monaco, independent principality of S Europe, enclave within SE France. Area 149 ha. (368 acres); pop. 25,000; cap. Monaco. Commercial centre La Condamine; tourism in MONTE CARLO. Ruled by Genoese Grimaldi family from 13th cent. Part of France (1793-1814), Sardinia (1815-61). Constitutional monarchy from 1911-59 (restored 1962). Customs union with France.

Monadhliath Mountains, range of NC Scotland, in Highland region; rise to 941 m (3087 ft).

Monaghan, county of Ulster prov., NE Irish Republic. Area 1290 sq km (498 sq mi); pop. 46,000. Undulating terrain; oats, livestock. Co. town **Monaghan,** on Ulster Canal. Pop. 5000. RC cathedral.

monasticism, system of organized community life for those who have retired from world under religious vows. Vows of celibacy, poverty and obedience are typical. Feature of Christianity, Buddhism, Jainism and Islam. Middle Ages in Europe saw rise of great monastic orders, *eg* Benedictines, Cistercians, Carthusians.

Monastir, see BITOLJ, Yugoslavia.

monazite, yellow to reddish-brown mineral, consisting of phosphate of cerium and other metals. Commercial source of rare elements, *eg* thorium, yttrium. Major sources in US, Australia, Brazil.

Monck or **Monk, George, 1st Duke of Albemarle** (1608-70), English soldier. Fought for Charles I in Scotland, captured at the battle of Nantwich (1644) and in 1646 turned parliamentarian. In the unrest which followed Cromwell's death, he intervened with an army from Scotland and engineered Charles II's restoration (1660) by inducing him to make Declaration of Breda.

Moncton, town of SE New Brunswick, Canada, on Petitcodiac R. Pop. 48,000. Railway jct.; engineering indust., clothes mfg. Tidal bore is feature of river.

Mond, Ludwig (1839-1909), British chemist, b. Germany. Perfected Solvay process for manufacture of alkali. Devised method for extraction of nickel from its ores using carbon monoxide (Mond process). His son, **Alfred Moritz Mond, 1st Baron Melchett** (1868-1930), was an industrialist. Merged (1926) Brunner-Mond with other companies to form Imperial Chemical Industries (ICI).

Mondale, Walter Frederick (1928-   ), American politician, vice-president (1977-   ). Senator from Minnesota (1964-77), successful Democratic vice-presidential candidate in 1976 election.

Mondrian, Piet (1872-1944), Dutch painter. Chief exponent of neo-plasticism, a strict form of geometric abstraction. Works are characterized by use of straight line grids and rectangles of primary colours. *Broadway Boogie-woogie* was in more vibrant style.

Monet: *Poplars on the Epte*

Monet, Claude (1840-1926), French painter. Leading member of the impressionists, he evolved a broken-colour technique to catch the changing effects of light. In later work, he ceased painting directly from nature; series of waterlily paintings culminated in almost abstract vision of nature. Works incl. *Impression, Sunrise* (1872) and *Rouen Cathedral* series.

money, in economics, unit of value or means of payment. Cattle often used as unit of value in ancient societies with more convenient objects as means of payment. Subsequently both these roles merged in durable, intrinsically valuable metals. State coinage prob. originated in Lydia (7th cent. BC), thus allowing govt. to use currency of higher face value than its commodity value. Paper currency (widely in use since 17th cent.) usually backed by a precious metal until 1930s (*see* FIDUCIARY ISSUE).

Mongolia, republic of C Asia, formerly Outer Mongolia. Area *c* 1,566,000 sq km (605,000 sq mi); pop. 1,290,000; cap. Ulan Bator. Language: Mongolian. Religion: Lamaist Buddhism. Mainly grazing plateau land (*see* GOBI DESERT) with extremes of climate. Trade in wool, hides, cloth; mineral extraction. Economy based on stock rearing. Nomadic Mongols conquered region under Genghis Khan (*c* 1205). Republic estab. 1924 after break with China.

Mongolian, language group within E Altaic family. Incl. Chakhar, Afghanistan Mongol, Selenga, Kalmuck.

mongolism or **Down's syndrome,** congenital disease caused by fault in formation of ovum. Characterized by mental retardation and broad face, slanting eyes.

Mongols, nomadic Asiatic tribe who, under GENGHIS KHAN and his sons, conquered much of Asia, incl. China. Also invaded Europe, penetrating as far as Hungary and Poland. Power waned towards end of 14th cent.; Mongol rule in China ended 1368.

mongoose, small Old World carnivore of Viverridae family. Feeds on small mammals, birds' eggs, *etc;* often kept for killing snakes. Species incl. Indian mongoose, *Herpestes edwardsi,* Meerkat, *Suricata suricata,* is South African species.

monism, in philosophy, doctrine that there is only one ultimate substance or principle, whether matter (materialism) or mind (idealism) or some third thing which unifies both.

monitor, any of Varanidae family of large carnivorous lizards of Africa, Asia, Australia. Elongated snout, long neck and extensible forked tongue. Largest species is KOMODO DRAGON.

monitor, a class of warship designed for coastal bombardment, named after the Union turret-ship *Monitor* in the American Civil War. British monitors were used off German-occupied Channel ports in WWI.

Moniz, Egas, *see* LOBOTOMY.

Monk, George, *see* MONCK, GEORGE, 1ST DUKE OF ALBEMARLE.

monkey, group of long-tailed primates; divided into platyrrhines (New World monkeys) of South America and catarrhines (Old World monkeys) of African and Asian tropics. Incl. capuchin, marmoset, macaque.

monkey puzzle, *see* ARAUCARIA.

Monkshood

monkshood or **aconite,** any of genus *Aconitum* of perennial herbs of buttercup family, esp. *A. napellus,* native to N temperate regions, with hoodshaped flowers. All species are poisonous.

Monmouth, James Scott, Duke of (1649-1685), claimant to English throne. Illegitimate son of Charles II by Lucy Walter, he became figurehead for Whig supporters of Protestant succession in opposition to Catholic duke of York. Fled to Holland after RYE HOUSE PLOT (1683). On accession of James II (1685), returned to England and raised rebellion against him. Defeated at Sedgemoor and executed.

Monmouthshire, former county of SE Wales, on English border, now called Gwent. Hilly in W, incl. part of S Wales coalfield. Main town Newport. Coalmining; iron, steel works; light industs. Co. town was **Monmouth,** mun. bor. at confluence of Wye and Monnow. Pop. 7000. Has remains of town walls; 12th cent. castle.

Monnet, Jean (1888-   ), French economist. Produced Monnet Plan for revival of French indust. and agric. (1947). President of European Coal and Steel Community (1952-5).

monocotyledon, plant of subclass Monocotyledoneae with one seed-leaf (cotyledon). Stems usually hollow or soft, *eg* palms, bamboos, grasses; foliage leaves parallel-veined.

Monod, Jacques (1910-   ), French molecular biologist. Shared Nobel Prize for Physiology and Medicine (1965) with François Jacob and André Lwoff for work on the way in which body cells synthesize protein. Writings incl. *Chance and Necessity* (1971).

Monophysitism, Christian heresy of 5th and 6th cents. Taught that Jesus had only one nature (divine), opposed at Council of Chalcedon (451). Adhered to by Coptic, Jacobite and Armenian churches.

monopoly, in economics, virtual control of supply of commodity or service by one producer, enabling producer to fix price at which consumer must purchase product. Legislation places restraints on monopolistic tendencies; in US began with Sherman Anti-Trust Act (1890), subsequently reinforced; in UK, Monopolies Commission set up 1948. Govt. monopolies (*eg* postal system) operated to facilitate public services. Socialist doctrine extends monopoly principle to all basic industries, *eg* nationalization of steel by British Labour govt. *See* OLIGOPOLY.

monorail, railway with single rail. Usually the rail is elevated with cars suspended from it or running above it. Driving wheels may rotate horizontally making contact with side of rail.

monosodium glutamate, white soluble crystalline salt extracted from grains or beets. Intensifies flavours, used widely in tinned food.

monotheism, belief that there is only one god, as in Judaism, Christianity and Islam.

Monotheletism, Christian heresy of 7th cent. Taught that Christ operated with one will although he had 2 natures. Arose as compromise between MONOPHYSITISM and orthodoxy. Adopted (622) by Emperor Heraclius I as official form of Christianity in Byzantine Empire. Died out except among MARONITES.

monotremes (Monotremata), subclass of primitive egg-laying mammals showing many reptilian features. Echidna and duckbilled platypus only living species, found in Australia and New Guinea.

monotype, typesetting machine which produces separate letters. Consists of composing machine, operated by a keyboard, which perforates a paper roll. The roll is fed into and used to govern a casting machine which casts each letter and assembles the type.

Monroe, James (1758-1831), American statesman, president (1817-25). Negotiated Louisiana Purchase (1803). His 2-term admin. marked by acquisition of Florida from Spain (1819), entry of Missouri into Union as slave state (1821). Promulgated Monroe Doctrine (1823), opposing European attempts to interfere in affairs of American countries or to recolonize recently independent American colonies; provided basis for much subsequent American foreign policy.

Monroe, Marilyn, orig. Norma Jean Baker or Mortenson (1926-62), American film actress. Known for sex goddess image which frustrated her real talent for comedy, revealed

Marilyn Monroe

in, *eg Gentlemen Prefer Blondes* (1953), *The Seven-Year Itch* (1955), *Some Like It Hot* (1959). Committed suicide.

Monroe Doctrine, *see* MONROE, JAMES.

Monrovia, cap. of Liberia, near mouth of R. St Paul. Pop. 110,000. Admin., commercial centre; port, exports rubber, iron ore. Founded (1822) for freed American slaves.

Mons (Flem. *Bergen*), town of SW Belgium, cap. of Hainaut prov. Pop. 28,000. Coalmining, textiles, chemicals. Battleground in both WWs. Town hall (15th cent.), cathedral (16th cent.).

Monsarrat, Nicholas (1910-), English author. Known for novels of war at sea, *eg The Cruel Sea* (1951), *The Ship That Died of Shame* (1959). Also wrote war reminiscences, *Corvette Command* (1944).

monsoon, wind system involving seasonal reversal of prevailing wind direction. Found most often within tropics, esp. SE Asia. In India, winter monsoon (Nov.-April) is cold, dry N wind; summer monsoon (May-Sept.) is warm, wet SW wind.

Montagu, Lady Mary Wortley, neé Pierrepont (1689-1762), English letter-writer. Member of circle of Pope, Addison. Known for lively descriptions of Turkish life from viewpoint as wife of British ambassador. Introduced inoculation to England from Turkey.

Montaigne, Michel Eyquem, Seigneur de (1533-92), French writer. Creator of modern essay form. *Essais* (complete edition, 1595) reflect personal scepticism, philosophical interests. Greatly influenced European thought.

Montale, Eugenio (1896-), Italian poet. Known for pessimistic 'hermetic' poetry, *eg Ossi di seppia* (1925), *Le occasioni* (1940). Awarded Nobel Prize for Literature (1975).

Montana, state of NW US, in Rocky Mts. Area 381,087 sq km (147,138 sq mi); pop. 694,000; cap. Helena. Bounded in N by Canada; Bitterroot Range in W; plains in E. Main occupations cattle, grain farming; lumbering; copper, zinc, silver, gold mining. Explored by fur traders in 18th, 19th cents.; developed with gold, silver, copper strikes. Admitted to Union as 41st state (1889).

Montanism, movement in Christian church (2nd cent.). Arose in Phrygia under leadership of Montanus. Followers believed in imminent Judgment Day; encouraged ecstatic prophecy. Survived in isolated pockets in Phrygia until 7th cent.

Montauban, town of S France, on R. Tarn, cap. of Tarn-et-Garonne dept. Pop. 49,000. Agric. market, engineering. Former stronghold of Albigensians (13th cent.), Huguenots (16th cent.). Fortress (12th cent.), brick bridge (14th cent.).

Mont Blanc, peak of Savoy Alps, SE France. Highest in Alps (4808 m/15,781 ft). Part of Mont Blanc massif extending into Italy, Switzerland; incl. several peaks, glaciers (*eg* Mer de Glace). First ascended 1786. Road tunnel (11.3 km/7 mi long) opened 1965, links France with Italy.

montbretia, any of genus *Tritonia* of flowering plants native to S Africa. European garden varieties incl. *T. crocosmiflora* with orange-crimson flowers.

Montcalm, Louis-Joseph de Montcalm - Gozon. Marquis de (1712-59), French general. Commanded French forces in Canada after 1756, capturing Fort William and defending Ticonderoga (1758). Killed in defeat at Québec by British forces under Wolfe.

Monte Carlo, town of Monaco, on Riviera. Resort, gambling casino. Annual car rally and motor racing grand prix.

Monte Cassino, see CASSINO, Italy.

Monte Cervino, see MATTERHORN.

Monte Cristo, isl. of Italy, in Tyrrhenian Sea, made famous by Alexandre Dumas' *The Count of Monte Cristo.*

Montego Bay, port of NW Jamaica, on Gulf of Mexico. Pop. 43,000. Banana, sugar exports. Scenic winter resort with excellent beach.

Montenegro (*Crna Gora*), autonomous republic of SW Yugoslavia. Area 13,838 sq km (5343 sq mi); cap. Titograd. Mountainous, except around L. Scutari; sheep, goats. Mineral resources. Medieval prov. of Zeta, within Serbia; independent after 1389, resisted Turks 14th-19th cent. Yugoslav prov. from 1918, republic from 1946.

Monte Rosa, mountain group of SW Switzerland and N Italy, in Pennine Alps. Highest is Dufourspitze (4636 m/15,217 ft), first climbed 1855.

Monterrey, city of NE Mexico, cap. of Nuevo León state. Pop. 1,180,000. Indust. and rail centre; lead, iron, steel, textile, glass mfg. Founded 1579. Has notable 18th cent. cathedral.

Montesquieu, Charles Louis de Secondat, Baron de la Brède et de (1689-1755), French political theorist. Wrote ironic *Lettres persanes* (1721), satirizing French contemporary life and institutions. His comparative analysis of govt. in *L'Esprit des Lois* (1748) influenced formulation of American Constitution.

Montessori, Maria (1870-1952), Italian educator, doctor. Developed Montessori Method, emphasizing importance for children of 3-6 years of freedom of choice and action and use of exercises and games in growth of coordination, perceptual skills.

Monteux, Pierre (1875-1964), French conductor. Conductor of Diaghilev's Ballets Russes, with which he premiered Stravinsky's *Rite of Spring* and Ravel's *Daphnis and Chloe*. Later, conducted several major orchestras, incl. London Symphony.

Monteverdi, Claudio Giovanni Antonio (1567-1643), Italian composer. Leading figure in early development of opera with such works as *Orfeo* (1607). Wrote 9 books of madrigals and much church music, incl. 2 sets of Vespers.

Montevideo, cap. of Uruguay, on Río de la Plata estuary. Pop. 1,280,000. Major seaport, handles most of Uruguay's trade. Wool, hides, meat exports. Meat packing, tanning, flour milling industs. Founded 1726. Became cap. 1828. Has National Univ. (1849). Tourism, in scenic area.

Montez, Lola, real name Maria Gilbert (1818-61), Irish adventuress. Great beauty and would-be Spanish dancer, she became mistress of Ludwig I of Bavaria. Greatly influenced his policy until banished (1848). After travelling widely, died in US.

Montezuma II (*c* 1480-1520), Aztec emperor of Mexico (1502-20). Captured by Cortés (1519) during Spanish conquest and held hostage in Mexico City (Tenochtitlán). Persuaded by Cortés to quell an Aztec uprising, he was killed by his own subjects.

Montfort, Simon de, Earl of Leicester (*c* 1208-65), English statesman. Led baronial opposition to Henry III, securing Provisions of Oxford (1258), which set up council of 15 to advise the king. Led baronial side in Barons' War (1263-7). Victory at Lewes (1264) followed by the Great Parliament estab. precedent of representation in England. Defeated and killed at Evesham.

Montgolfier, Joseph Michel (1740–1810), French inventor. With his brother, **Jacques Etienne Montgolfier** (1745-99), invented 1st practical hot-air balloon, in which they made 1st manned flight (1783).

Montgomery, Bernard Law, 1st Viscount Montgomery of Alamein (1887-1976), British field marshal. Given command of British 8th Army in N Africa in 1942, restored morale after German successes and won the victory of El Alamein, followed by successful penetration into Tunisia and final defeat of Axis forces. Commanded land forces in Normandy invasion (1944) and was made chief of Imperial General Staff after war.

Montgomery, L[ucy] M[aud] (1874-1942), Canadian novelist. Known for *Anne of Green Gables* (1908), based on childhood memories.

Montgomery, cap. of Alabama, US; on Alabama R. Pop. 133,000. Railway jct.; cotton, livestock produce. First cap. of Confederacy (1861).

Montgomeryshire, former county of C Wales, now in Powys. Mountainous. moorland; fertile valleys in E. Sheep rearing, oats; slate, stone quarrying. Co. town was **Montgomery,** mun. bor. Pop. 1000. Agric. market.

Montherlant, Henry de Millon (1896-1972), French author. Known for novels celebrating masculine 'superiority', eg *Les Bestiaires* (1926), *Les Célibataires* (1934), *Les Jeunes Filles* (1936). Also wrote plays, eg *La Reine morte* (1942).

Montluçon, town of C France, on R. Cher. Pop. 60,000. Indust. centre, esp. steel, chemicals; Commentry coalfield nearby. Many 15th-16th cent. houses.

Montmartre, see PARIS, France.

Montpelier, cap. of Vermont, US; on Winooski R. Pop. 9000. Agric. market. Cap. from 1805.

Montpellier, city of Languedoc, S France, cap. of Hérault dept. Pop. 162,000. Resort, wine trade, chemicals mfg. Purchased (1349) from Aragón; former Huguenot stronghold. Botanic gardens (1593); univ. (1289).

Montréal or **Montreal,** largest city of Canada, in SE Québec; on isl. at confluence of St Lawrence, Ottawa rivers, at foot of Mt. Royal. Pop. 1,214,000; mainly French-speaking. Major seaport, commercial, transport, financial centre. Leading grain exports; railway equipment mfg.; iron and steel industs.; fur trade centre. Settled by French (1642); surrendered to British (1760). Seat of McGill Univ. (1821), Montréal Univ. (1876). Site of Expo 1967 fair, 1976 Olympic Games.

Montreux, town of SW Switzerland, on L. Geneva. Pop. 20,000. Tourism; woodworking; mountain railway. Castle of CHILLON nearby.

Montrose, James Graham, Marquess of (1612-50), Scottish soldier. Leader of Covenanters in Bishops' War (1639-40). Changed sides in Civil War and successfully led Highland army for Charles I against Presbyterians. Defeated by Leslie at Philiphaugh (1645) and fled abroad. On return, hanged after attempt to raise rebellion.

Montrose, town of Tayside region, E Scotland, Pop. 10,000. On penin. between North Sea and Montrose Basin (lagoon). Port, tourist resort; fishing; flax, jute mills.

Montserrat, isl. of E West Indies, in Leeward Isls. Area 98 sq km (38 sq mi); pop. 12,000; cap. Plymouth. Cotton, fruit exports. Discovered by Columbus (1493). British colony from 17th cent. Volcanic and rugged; subject to earth tremors.

Montserrat or **Monserrat,** mountain of Catalonia, NE Spain. Height 1235 m (4054 ft). On ledge is Benedictine Monastery and church containing shrine of black Virgin.

Mont-St-Michel, rocky isl. of NW France, in Bay of Mont-St-Michel. Tourist centre, linked to mainland by causeway. Abbey (founded 708), used as prison in 19th cent.

Monza, city of Lombardy, NW Italy. Pop. 116,000. Textiles, carpets, hats. Cathedral contains iron crown of Lombardy. Scene of assassination (1900) of Umberto I. Motor racing track.

Moody, Dwight Lyman (1837-99), American evangelist. With Ira David Sankey (1840-1908) made notable revivalist tours of US and UK. Also known for collections of hymns.

Moon, only natural satellite of Earth; diameter 3476 km (2160 mi). Revolves around Earth at mean distance of 384,000 km once in c 27⅓ days (with reference to stars) or c 29½ days (with respect to Sun). Shines by reflected light from Sun; said to be full when opposite Sun and new when

Mont-St-Michel

between Earth and Sun and partly visible. Without atmosphere or water; first visited by American spacemen July, 1969.

moonfish or **opah,** *Lampris guttatus,* widely distributed large fish, with red fins and side, blue back and white-spotted body.

moonstone, semi-precious gemstone. Blue-white, translucent; a variety of feldspar. Major sources in Sri Lanka, Burma.

moonwort, see HONESTY.

Moore, George (1852-1933), Irish author. Novels, eg *Esther Waters* (1894), reflect influence of French naturalism. Also wrote several volumes of autobiog., plays, art criticism championing impressionism.

Moore, G[eorge] E[dward] (1873-1958). English philosopher. Known mainly as rigorous expounder of philosophical problems rather than deviser of a system. Concerned with language, epistemology. Works incl. *Principia Ethica* (1903).

Henry Moore: *Reclining Figure* (1951)

Moore, Henry (1898-   ), English sculptor. Advocate of direct carving, his work is based on natural forms expressed in stone, wood or bronze. Themes incl. mother and child, reclining figures; drawings incl. studies of underground air raid shelters.

Moore, Sir John (1761-1809), British army officer, b. Scotland. Commander of expedition sent by Wellington (1808) to assist Spanish army in dislodging Napoleon, was mortally wounded at battle of Corunna, which he had won though greatly outnumbered.

Moore, Marianne [Craig] (1887-1972), American poet. Witty, meticulous verse incl. *What Are Years?* (1941), *Collected Poems* (1951), translation of La Fontaine's *Fables* (1954).

Moore, Thomas (1779-1852), Irish poet. Remembered for lyrics incl. 'The Harp That Once through Tara's Halls', 'Oft in the Stilly Night', in *Irish Melodies* (1808-34). Also wrote *Lalla Rookh; an Oriental Romance* (1817).

moorhen, *Gallinula chloropus,* olive green water bird of Europe and North America, found near ponds, marshes. Called gallinule in America.

Moors, nomadic people of N Africa of mixed Arab and Berber descent. Became Moslem in 8th cent.; conquered Spain (711) but were defeated in France by Charles Martel (732). Founded caliphate in Spain famed for learning and architectural splendour. Gradually expelled from Spain by Christians, their last stronghold, Granada, falling in 1492.

moose, *Alces americanus,* largest of deer family, found in Alaska, Canada, N US. Huge branching antlers spanning up to 1.8 m/6 ft. Elk is related European species.

Moose Jaw, town of SC Saskatchewan, Canada; W of Regina. Pop. 32,000. Railway jct., grain market; flour milling, oil refining industs.

Moradabad, town of Uttar Pradesh, N India. Pop. 272,000. Ornamental brassware, cotton mfg. Founded 1625, has Great Mosque (1631).

moraine, accumulation of ungraded debris, ranging from clay to boulders, transported and deposited by glacier. Types incl. lateral, medial, ground and terminal moraines, classification being dependent on which part of glacier laid them down.

morality plays, didactic late medieval, early Renaissance verse dramas. Developed from MIRACLE PLAYS, Biblical characters of which gave place to personifications of vice, virtues, as in EVERYMAN.

Moral Re-Armament or **MRA,** movement started (1938) by F. BUCHMAN. Followers believe in national spiritual reconstruction starting with the individual. They base evangelical work on informal meetings, group confessions.

Moravia, Alberto, pseud. of Alberto Pincherle (1907-   ), Italian novelist. Known for realistic novels, *eg The Time of Indifference* (1929), *Mistaken Ambitions* (1935), *Two Women* (1957).

Moravia (*Morava*), region of Czechoslovakia, between Bohemia (W) and Slovakia (E). Main towns Brno, Ostrava. Drained by R. Morava. Agric., coalmining. Habsburg domain until 1918, became prov. of Czechoslovakia. Combined with Silesia (1927); abolished as political unit (1949).

Moravian Church, evangelical Protestant episcopal sect, founded in Bohemia (1457) among followers of JAN HUS. Persecuted and driven out of Bohemia; revived in Saxony (18th cent.). Active in all Americas; missionary work continues.

Moraviantown, Battle of, encounter (Oct. 1813) near Thames R., S Ontario, during War of 1812. American forces defeated retreating British and Indian troops. Indian leader, Tecumseh, was killed. Also known as Battle of the Thames.

Moray, James Stuart, 1st Earl of, *see* MURRAY.

moray eel, any of Muraenidae family of widely distributed marine eels. Aggressive carnivore, laterally compressed, often brightly coloured; hides in rock crevices. *Muraena helena* found in Mediterranean and E Atlantic.

Morayshire, former county of NE Scotland, now in Grampian region. Previously called Elginshire. Cromdale Hills in S; low-lying, fertile in N. Livestock rearing, salmon fishing, whisky distilling. Co. town was Elgin. **Moray Firth,** inlet of North Sea, between former Morayshire, Nairnshire and Ross and Cromarty.

mordant, substance used in dyeing to fix colouring matter. Usually consists of basic metal hydroxide (*eg* aluminium hydroxide), which combines with dye to form insoluble coloured compound (lake) in fibres of fabric.

Mordvinia, auton. republic of E European RSFSR, USSR. Area *c* 26,160 sq km (10,100 sq mi); pop. 1,030,000; cap. Saransk, Forested steppe; agric., lumbering and wood product mfg. Mordvinians, a Finno-Ugrian people, were conquered by Russians in 16th cent.

More, Hannah (1745-1833), English author, reformer, philanthropist. Known for religious tracts incl. 'The Shepherd of Salisbury Plain'. Also wrote domestic tragedy, *Percy* (1777), novel of ethical instruction, *Coelebs in Search of a Wife* (1808).

More, Henry (1614-87), English philosopher. Leading Cambridge Platonist. Attempted to reconcile rational and mystical. Works incl. *The Mystery of Godliness* (1660), *Divine Dialogues* (1668).

More, Sir Thomas (1478-1535), English statesman, scholar. Friend of Erasmus, who exerted strong influence on More's humanist ideas. Succeeded Wolsey as lord chancellor (1529-32); resigned over Henry VIII's divorce from Catherine of Aragon. Refused (1534) to recognize Henry as head of Church; executed for treason. Most famous work, *Utopia* (1516), depicts ideal state ordered by reason.

Moreau, Gustave (1826-98), French painter. Painted religious and mythological fantasies in an ornate detailed style. Taught at Ecole des Beaux-Arts, Paris, where his pupils incl. Matisse and Rouault.

Moreau, Jean Victor Marie (1763-1813), French general. Won actions against Austrians on the Rhine and Moselle front but after reverses was superseded (1797) by Joubert, on whose death he was recalled. After victory at Hohenlinden (1800) he fell out with Napoleon and joined allies (1813). Killed at Dresden.

Morecambe (and Heysham), mun. bor. of Lancashire, NW England, on Morecambe Bay. Pop. 42,000. Resort; port, ferry to Belfast; oil refinery.

Morel (*Morchella esculenta*)

morel, any of genus *Morchella* of edible mushrooms resembling a sponge on a stalk. *M. esculenta,* the commonest, is found in deciduous woods and pastures of Europe and North America. Used in soups and sauces.

Morelia, town of WC Mexico, cap. of Michoacán state. Pop. 210,000. Processing centre of agric. and cattle rearing area. Founded as Valladolid (1541); renamed after Mexican patriot, Morelos.

Morgagni, Giovanni Battista (1681-1771), Italian anatomist. Considered founder of pathology, he attempted to explain effects of disease anatomically. Pub. (1761) book describing his numerous post-mortem dissections.

Morgan, Sir Henry (*c* 1635-88), Welsh buccaneer. Led pirates in West Indies against Spaniards; made daring march across Panama isthmus to capture Panama City (1671). Called to England to answer charges of piracy, he gained royal favour and was later made governor of Jamaica.

Morgan, Junius Spencer (1813-90), American financier. Head of international banking enterprise handling British funds in US. Made notable loan to French govt. during Franco-Prussian War. His son, **J[ohn] Pierpont Morgan** (1837-1913), enlarged family fortunes, esp. in railway holdings; formed (1901) US Steel Corporation. Became a symbol of wealth, renowned philanthropist. His son, **J[ohn] Pierpont Morgan** (1867-1943), helped raise Allied funds during WWI.

Morgan, Lewis Henry (1818-81), American anthropologist. Recorded social patterns and evolution of Iroquois Indians of upper New York state in *Systems of Consanguinity and Affinity of the Human Family* (1870) and *Ancient Society* (1877).

Morgan, Thomas Hunt (1866-1945), American biologist. Awarded Nobel Prize for Physiology and Medicine (1933) for genetic research on laws and mechanism of heredity, following studies of fruit fly *Drosophila.*

morganatic marriage, form of marriage in which man of royalty marries a woman of inferior social status with provision that although children of the marriage will be legitimate, neither they nor the wife may lay claim to his rank or property.

Moriscos, name given to Spanish Moslems who accepted Christian baptism. Edict of 1568 demanded abandonment of all remaining Moorish customs; led to revolt and persecution of Moriscos. Finally expelled from Spain in 1609.

Morland, George (1763-1804), English painter. Painted numerous landscapes and genre scenes, esp. of cottage interiors and taverns. Works were much popularized by engravings.

Morley, Thomas (1557-1603), English composer. Organist at St Paul's Cathedral. Wrote *A Plaine and Easie Introduction to Practicall Musicke* (1597) on composition. Works incl. madrigals, consort pieces.

Mormons or **Church of Jesus Christ of Latter-Day Saints,** evangelical religious sect founded in US (1830) by JOSEPH SMITH after divine revelations. Settled in communities in W Missouri but came into conflict with their neighbours. After death of Smith, BRIGHAM YOUNG became leader and transferred centre of movement to Salt Lake City, Utah. Now worldwide membership of *c* 3 million as result of extensive proselytizing.

morning glory, common name for various twining vines of convolvulus family esp. of genus *Ipomoea;* incl. American *I. purpurea,* widely cultivated for its purple flowers. Seeds of some varieties contain hallucinogens.

Morocco

Morocco (Arab. *Al-Mamlaka al-Maghrebia*), kingdom of NW Africa. Area 447,000 sq km (172,500 sq mi); pop. 16,880,000; cap. Rabat. Language: Arabic. Religion: Islam. Largely desert; Atlas Mts. run SW-NE; fertile coast. Produces cereals, fruit, olives, cattle. Minerals incl. phosphates, petroleum, iron ore. Part of Roman MAURETANIA: Arabs brought Islam 7th cent., *fl* under Berber dynasties 11th-14th cents. Settled by Portuguese (1415-1769); became Barbary pirate base. Disputed in 19th cent.; French, Spanish protects. estab. 1912, Tangier internationalized (1923). Independent 1956, constitutional monarchy from 1962.

Moroni, Giovanni Battista (*c* 1525-78), Italian painter. Best known for his portraits, which combine realism of Holbein with Venetian style. Works incl. *The Tailor* (London).

Morpheus, in Greek and Roman myth, shaper of dreams.

morphine, white crystalline alkaloid derived from opium. Used in medicine to relieve pain; continued use leads to addiction.

Morris, William (1834-96), English artist, writer, decorator, printer. Founded firm of Morris and Company to produce stained glass, tapestry, furniture, in an attempt to raise standard of Victorian design. Founded Kelmscott Press (1890) to revive standards of printing. Believed in possibility of improving quality of working life through craftsmanship (*see* ARTS AND CRAFTS MOVEMENT); his socialist beliefs are reflected in writings such as *Dream of John Ball* (1888).

Morris, William Richard, *see* NUFFIELD, WILLIAM RICHARD MORRIS, VISCOUNT.

Morris Jesup, Cape, *see* PEARY LAND.

Morrison, Herbert Stanley, Baron Morrison of Lambeth (1888-1965), British statesman. Leader of London County Council (1934-40). Home secretary in

William Morris

National govt. (1940-5). Defeated by Gaitskell in vote for Labour Party leadership (1955).

Morse, Samuel Finley Breese (1791-1872), American inventor, painter. Devised one form of electric telegraph and system of communication, Morse Code, using short and long taps to represent letters of alphabet.

mortar, short-barrelled, large-bore cannon, used in early siege warfare for lobbing missiles over city walls at short range. In WWI and II modern version projected 2 or 3 in. finned bombs (explosive or smoke) as infantry support.

Mortimer, Roger de, 1st Earl of March (*c* 1287-1330), English nobleman. Opposed EDWARD II in baronial wars (1321-2) but was captured (1322); escaped to France (1324) where Edward's wife, ISABELLA, became his mistress. Together they invaded England, forced Edward's abdication (1326). Ruled England until Edward III had him executed.

Mosaic at Moulay Idriss, Morocco

mosaic, surface ornamentation by laying small pieces of stone, tile, metal or glass on a bed of cement. Used principally for decoration of floors and walls. Art was first developed by the Romans and perfected by Byzantines (6th cent.); revived by the Italians in 13th cent., it declined with introduction of fresco.

Mosaic Law, laws by which the Jewish people were governed, contained mainly in Pentateuch and stated in Ten Commandments given to Moses on Mt. Sinai.

Mosan, North American linguistic family, of Algonquian-Mosan stock. Incl. Chimakuan, Salishan and Wakashan groups.

moschatel, *see* MUSK.

Moscow (*Moskva*), cap. of USSR and RSFSR; on R. Moskva. Pop. 7,300,000. Indust., cultural and political centre; metal goods, textile mfg. Founded 12th cent.; became national cap. (1547) under 1st tsar Ivan the Terrible; remained so until 1712. Burned during occupation by Napoleon (1812). Cap. again after Revolution (1918).

Kremlin (fortified citadel) contains 15th cent. Uspenski and 16th cent. Arkhangelski cathedrals, Grand Palace. Lenin's tomb and 16th cent. St Basil's Cathedral in Red Square. Theatres incl. Moscow Arts, Bolshoi.

Moseley, Henry Gwyn-Jeffreys (1887-1915), English physicist. His work on frequencies of atomic spectra led him to equate charge on atomic nucleus with atomic number; this resolved problems in Mendeleev's periodic table.

Moselle (Ger. *Mosel*), river of NE France and NW West Germany. Flows c 550 km (340 mi) from Vosges via Metz, Thionville to R. Rhine at Koblenz. Canalized for much of course. Vineyards below Trier produce Moselle wines.

Moses (*fl c* 13th cent. BC), Jewish lawgiver, OT prophet. Led Jews out of captivity in Egypt (Exodus); received Ten Commandments on Mt. Sinai. Estab. organized Jewish religion. Traditional author of Pentateuch.

Moses, Anna Mary Robertson ('Grandma') (1860-1961), American painter. A modern primitive, she is remembered for her popular scenes of rural life, which evoke nostalgia for old world simplicity.

Moslem League, political organization estab. (1906) to safeguard rights of Moslems in India. Under leadership of Jinnah, demanded creation of separate Moslem state in 1940s; achieved in founding (1947) of Pakistan.

Moslem religion, see ISLAM.

Mosley, Sir Oswald (1896-), British politician. Held office in Labour govt. of 1929; resigned over economic policy. Organized (1932) British Union of Fascists; led agitation against Jews. Detained 1940-3, attempted to revive movement after WW II.

mosque, building for Moslem worship. Main features are: *qibla* wall, with its central *mihrab* or prayer niche which indicates direction of Mecca; a *dikka* (platform for services); a minaret. Early mosques were adaptations of Christian basilicas, *eg* Great Mosque at Damascus. Domed mosques incl. Hagia Sophia in Istanbul.

mosquito, any of Culicidae family of 2-winged insects. Female uses skin-piercing mouthparts to suck blood of animals, often transmitting diseases through its saliva, *eg* *Anopheles* carries malaria parasite.

Mosquito Coast, belt of land on Caribbean coast, in NE Honduras and E Nicaragua. Sparse pop.; lumbering, banana industs. British protect. (1678-1860), S part annexed by Nicaragua (1894).

moss, any of class *Musci* of small primitive plants. Worldwide distribution. Grows in tufts on moist ground, tree trunks. Important as pioneers of rock surfaces, holding moisture and producing humus, mosses allow seeds of other plants to germinate.

Mossadegh, Mohammed (1880-1967), Iranian statesman. Premier (1951-3), nationalized (1951) British-owned oil indust.; dispute led to breaking-off of diplomatic relations between Iran and Britain. Imprisoned after attempt to overthrow shah.

Mossamedes, see MOCÂMEDES, Angola.

moss animal, see POLYZOA.

Mössbauer, Rudolf Ludwig (1929-), German physicist. Awarded Nobel Prize for Physics (1961) for discovery of Mössbauer effect in which gamma rays emitted by certain radioactive isotopes maintain unvarying wavelength if radiating nuclei are held in crystal form. Effect has been widely used.

Mostaganem, town of NW Algeria, on Gulf of Arzew. Pop. 64,000. Port, exports wine, fruit, wool. *Fl* 16th cent. under Turks. Gas pipeline from Hassi Messaoud.

Mostar, town of Bosnia-Hercegovina, WC Yugoslavia, on R. Neretva. Pop. 35,000. Fruit, wine trade. Former cap. of Hercegovina. Has mosques, cathedral, 16th cent. bridge.

Mosul (*Al Mawsil*), city of N Iraq, on R. Tigris. Pop. 293,000. Agric. trade centre; rich oilfields nearby. Near ruins of Nineveh. A centre of Nestorian Christianity.

motet, relatively short, freely contrapuntal piece of vocal music, usually unaccompanied, with Biblical or similar prose text. Early motets were based on plainsong.

moth, insect of order Lepidoptera. Distinguished from butterfly by different antennae, wing venation, and night flight.

mother-of-pearl, hard iridescent lining of certain marine shells, *eg* pearl oyster, abalone. Used for decoration, jewellery.

Motherwell, Robert (1915-), American painter, theorist. Proponent of abstract expressionism, his work is characterized by undefined shapes painted in strong colours.

Motherwell (and Wishaw), town of Strathclyde region, C Scotland. Pop. 74,000. Towns united 1920. Coalmining; iron, steel industs.

motion pictures, see CINEMA.

motion sickness, nausea and vomiting caused by effect of motion on balance organ of inner ear; experienced on ships, motor vehicles, aircraft, *etc.* Relieved by drugs, *eg* hyoscine, which often cause drowsiness.

motor, see ELECTRIC MOTOR.

motor car, see AUTOMOBILE.

Motorcycle racing

motorcycle, two-wheeled vehicle propelled by an internal combustion engine. Prob. first built by Gottlieb Daimler (*c* 1885). Engines are usually air-cooled, often 2-stroke (cycle) and generally range from 50-1000 cc. Their popularity has revived greatly since 1960s through technical innovations of Japanese manufacturers.

motorcycle racing, sport dating from introduction of reliable motorcycles in early 1900s. Events incl. annual TT races held in Isle of Man since 1907 and American National Jack Pine 500 mi (805 km) championships.

motor racing, competitive sport for motor cars, introduced in France (1894). Present-day international Formula One championship is decided on results of Grand Prix races in over 10 countries. Other events incl. Indianapolis 500 (805 km) in US and Le Mans 24-hr race.

motorway [UK], road designed to link major centres of pop.; restrictions of use facilitate speed and obviate congestion. Modelled on Italian autostrada, German autobahn. US equivalent is turnpike, networked to form Interstate Highway System.

moufflon, *Ovis musimon*, rare wild sheep of rocky areas of Corsica and Sardinia. White muzzle and rusty short coat. Male has long curved horns.

mould, name for various minute fungi forming furry coating mostly on dead organic matter. Common forms incl. black bread mould, *Rhizopus nigricans*. The blue mould often found on cheese is of *Penicillium* genus, source of penicillin.

Moulins, town of C France, on R. Allier, cap. of Allier dept. Pop. 27,000. Railway jct.; tanning, textile mfg. Hist. cap. of Bourbonnais. Cathedral (15th cent.).

Moulmein (*Maulamyaing*), seaport of S Burma, near mouth of R. Salween. Pop. 175,000. Exports rice, teak.

mountain, natural elevation of Earth's surface, raised relative to surrounding area to height over 305 m/1000 ft. Distinguished from plateau by summit being small in proportion to base. Formed by volcanic action, differential erosion of high land, earth movements, esp. folding and faulting, or combination of all factors. A major mountain-building period is called an orogeny (*see* GEOLOGICAL TABLE).

Mountain ash (*Sorbus americana*)

mountain ash or **rowan,** any of genus *Sorbus* of small trees and shrubs of rose family. Native to N temperate regions. Compound leaves, white flowers followed by red berries. Common European species is *S. aucuparia*.

mountain beaver, *Aplodontia rufa,* primitive burrowing rodent of coastal regions of W US. Rabbit-sized, with reduced tail. Also called sewellel.

mountaineering, sport of climbing mountains. Modern form dates from 1850s when British climbers scaled most of the Alpine peaks; Alpine Club founded in London (1857) did much to popularize sport. Ten highest mountains in world had been climbed by 1964.

Mountbatten, Louis Francis Albert Victor Nicholas, 1st Earl Mountbatten of Burma (1900-), British admiral. In WWII, supreme Allied commander in SE Asia (1943–6). Last viceroy of India (1947), governor-general (1947–8) after partition. Admiral of fleet (1955–9) and chief of defence staff (1959–65).

Mount Isa, town of W Queensland, Australia, in Selwyn Ranges. Pop. 25,000. Mining centre, esp. copper, lead, zinc, silver, uranium; railway to Townsville.

Mount Vernon, Virginia, home of George Washington from 1747 until his death in 1799. Preserved as US national monument.

Mourne Mountains, range of SE Northern Ireland. Highest peak Slieve Donard (852 m/2796 ft). Scenic area.

Fieldmouse

mouse, small omnivorous rodent of same family (Muridae) as rat, vole. Species incl. house mouse, *Mus musculus,* found worldwide near human habitation, and wood or field mouse, *Apodemus sylvaticus,* of W European countryside.

mouse deer, *see* CHEVROTAIN.

mousefish or **beaked salmon,** *Gonorhynchus gonorhynchus,* bottom-dwelling fish of Indian and Pacific oceans. Pointed snout, body covered with rough-edged scales.

Mousterian, middle Palaeolithic culture represented by flint indust. of Neanderthal man. Takes name from cave of Le Moustier in SW France where remains of flint tools were found.

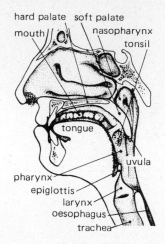

Human mouth

mouth, in anatomy, front opening of the alimentary canal. Roof is formed of hard palate, muscular tongue rests on floor; lined with mucous membrane. Process of digestion is begun in mouth by enzyme in saliva which helps convert starch to sugar.

mouth organ, *see* HARMONICA.

Moyle, dist. of N Northern Ireland. Area 494 sq km (191 sq mi); pop. 15,000. Incl. Rathlin Isl. Created 1973, formerly part of Co. Antrim.

Mozambique

Mozambique or **Moçambique,** republic of SE Africa. Area 783,000 sq km (302,300 sq mi); pop. 9,029,000; cap. Maputo. Languages: Bantu, Portuguese. Religions: native, Christianity. Coastal lowlands; mountains in interior, N and W; main rivers Limpopo, Zambezi. Produces sugar cane, cashew nuts, tea, copra, sisal; h.e.p. at Cabora Bassa. Transit trade with C, S Africa. Reached (1498) by Vasco da Gama; Portuguese settlement followed 15th-19th cent. Became Portuguese East Africa colony (1907). Overseas prov. from 1951. Intense guerrilla warfare by 'Frelimo' nationalists from mid-1960s and fall of govt. in Portugal (1974) resulted in independence (1975).

Mozambique or **Moçambique,** town of NE Mozambique, on Mozambique Channel. Pop. 15,000. Port, exports cashew nuts, timber. Cap. of Portuguese East Africa until 1907.

Mozarabs, term for Spanish Christians who were permitted to practise their religion in a modified form during the Islamic domination. Briefly persecuted in 11th cent.

Mozart

Mozart, Wolfgang Amadeus (1756-91), Austrian composer. Began to perform in public and compose at age of six. Prolific composer, raised classical music to great heights in his elegance of style and beauty of form. Died in poverty. Over 600 compositions incl. 41 symphonies, 21 piano concertos, string quartets, operas, *eg Marriage of Figaro, Don Giovanni, Così fan tutte, The Magic Flute.*

Muallaqat, collection of Arabic poems compiled *c* 8th cent. Contains 7-10 odes depending on text, composed by 6th-7th cent. pre-Islamic Bedouin poets.

mucous membrane, skin-like layer lining alimentary canal and air passages. Secretes mucus, which has protective and lubricating function.

mudpuppy, aquatic North American salamander, genus *Necturus.* Retains certain larval characteristics, *eg* external gills, underdeveloped legs.

mudskipper, fish of goby family, genus *Periophthalmus* or *Boleophthalmus,* found in tropics. Lives in mud of mangrove swamps, using pectoral fins to hop over mud surface or climb mangrove roots.

mufti, in Islamic countries, legal adviser consulted in applying religious laws. Also, state official in Ottoman Empire.

Muhammad, alternative spelling of MOHAMMED.

Mühlhausen, town of SW East Germany, on R. Unstrut. Pop. 46,000. Textiles, machinery, furniture mfg. Former Hanseatic League member; medieval fortifications, 14th cent. churches.

Mühlheim-an-der-Ruhr, city of W West Germany, in Ruhr. Pop. 193,000. Coalmining, iron and steel mfg., textiles. Coal research institute.

Muir, Edwin (1887-1959), Scottish poet. Works, *eg* in *Collected Poems* (1952), draw on dream imagery, archetypal myth. Also translated Kafka into English, wrote prose *Autobiography* (1954).

Mujibur Rahman (1920-75), Bangladeshi political leader. Leader of Awami League in East Pakistan (later Bangladesh) which sought independence from Pakistan; imprisoned in West Pakistan (1971) after electoral victory. Returned (1972) as 1st PM of independent Bangladesh following Indian intervention in civil war. Killed in army coup.

Mukden, *see* SHENYANG.

mulberry, any of genus *Morus* of deciduous trees and shrubs, native to N temperate and subtropical regions. Fruit resembles raspberry. Leaves of *M. alba,* white mulberry, and *M. nigra,* black mulberry, used for feeding silkworms.

Muldoon, Robert David (1921-), New Zealand states-man, PM (1975-). Headed National Party elected on

White mulberry

pledges to reduce inflation, deal with problems in indust. relations.

mule, *see* ASS.

Mulhouse (Ger. *Mülhausen*), city of Alsace, E France, on R. Ill and Rhine-Rhône canal. Pop. 116,000. Textile mfg., chemicals (potash deposits nearby), engineering. Part of Swiss Confederation (1515-1798), voted to join France. Held by Germany (1871-1918).

Mull, isl. of Inner Hebrides, W Scotland, in Strathclyde region. Area 909 sq km (351 sq mi), main town Tobermory. Crofting, fishing, tourism.

Common mullein (Verbascum thapsus)

mullein, any of genus *Verbascum* of biennial herbs of figwort family. Found in Europe and Asia. *V. thapsus* has woolly leaves and spike of yellow flowers. *V. phoenicium* is purple mullein.

Müller, Paul Herman (1899-1965), Swiss chemist. Discovered (1939) DDT's use as insecticide; its large-scale production was begun in WW II. Awarded Nobel Prize for Physiology and Medicine (1948).

mullet, any of Mugilidae family of grey edible freshwater or marine fish. Feeds on debris in shallow water. Unrelated red mullet or goat fish of Mullidae family is important food fish.

Mullingar, co. town of Westmeath, C Irish Republic. Pop. 6000. Agric. market, tanning. RC cathedral.

mullion, in architecture, slender vertical division of a window. Often associated with Gothic architecture.

Mulock, Dinah Maria, *see* CRAIK, DINAH MARIA.

Multan, city of C Pakistan. Pop. 544,000. Agric. centre; textile, carpet mfg. Ancient city, taken by Alexander the Great.

multinational corporation, company or group of commonly-owned companies operating in a number of countries, usually involving extensive financial and indust. interests. As policy decisions are made in international context, they often conflict with local interests in countries where particular operations take place. Thus demands have been made for legislation to enable national interests to prevail, both in West and Third World.

multiple sclerosis, chronic disease of nervous system, resulting in degeneration of nerve sheaths of brain and spinal cord. Symptoms incl. speech disorder, loss of muscular coordination; cause unknown.

Mumford, Lewis (1895-), American writer. Concerned with man and his environment; has written on history of technology, architecture, town planning. Works incl. *The Golden Day* (1926), *Technics and Civilization* (1934), *The City in History* (1961).

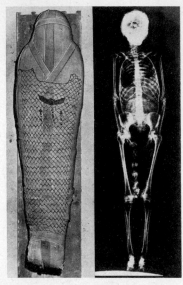

Egyptian mummy with X-ray picture of enclosed body

mummy, dead body preserved by embalming, esp. associated with ancient Egypt. Usual method was removal of internal organs, drying of body with natron and wrapping in linen bandages. Human mummies often placed in human-form coffins.

mumps, infectious disease caused by airborne viruses. Symptoms incl. fever and painful swelling of parotid salivary glands. Usually childhood disease; may cause sterility in adult men. Incubation period 2-4 weeks.

Munch, Edvard (1863-1944), Norwegian painter, graphic artist. Forerunner of expressionism; his neurotic works, characterized by distortion and vivid colour, depict anguish and themes of love and death. Works incl. *The Scream, The Sick Child* and numerous woodcuts, lithographs, *etc.*

München, see MUNICH, West Germany.

München-Gladbach, city of W West Germany. Pop. 151,000. Centre of cotton indust., also produces paper. Grew around abbey founded 972. Badly damaged in WWII.

Münchhausen, Karl Friedrich Hieronymus, Baron von (1720-97), German soldier. Fought for Russians against Turks. Best known as hero of many fantastic adventures, collected and pub. in 1785 by Rudolf Erich Raspe and subsequently expanded by others.

Muncie, town of E Indiana, US; on White R. Pop. 69,000. Agric. processing, market; glassware, electrical equipment mfg.

Munich (*München*), city of S West Germany, on R. Isar, cap. of Bavaria. Pop. 1,338,000. Cultural, indust. centre; publishing, brewing industs. Tourism, annual *Oktoberfest.* Under Wittelsbachs from 1255, cap. of Bavaria from 1506. Nazi hq. from 1919; scene of Hitler's *Putsch* (1923), Munich Pact (1938). Has museums, art galleries, English Garden (1832), univ. (moved from Landshut 1826). Site of Olympics 1972.

Munich Pact, agreement (Sept. 1939) signed by Germany, Italy, Britain and France, sanctioning Hitler's annexation of Sudetenland, Czechoslovakia. Represented height of Western appeasement policy towards Nazi Germany; agreement thought then to have averted world war.

Munro, H[ector] H[ugh], see SAKI.

Munster, prov. of SW Irish Republic. Area 24,126 sq km (9315 sq mi); pop. 880,000. Comprises cos. Clare, Cork, Kerry, Limerick, Tipperary, Waterford. Ancient kingdom, former cap. Cashel.

Münster, city of NW West Germany, on Dortmund-Ems canal. Pop. 198,000. Metal goods, brewing; univ. (1773). Hanseatic League member; scene of experimental Anabaptist govt. (1533-5) under John of Leiden. Treaty of Westphalia (1648) signed here. Medieval appearance destroyed in WWII.

Muntjac

muntjac, small deer with short antlers, genus *Muntiacus,* found in forests of India and SE Asia. Also called barking deer.

muon or **mu-meson,** elementary particle of lepton family with mass 207 times that of electron and either positive or negative charge. Decays rapidly into electron, neutrino and anti-neutrino.

mural painting, decoration of walls or ceilings by oil paint, ceramics, tempera, fresco, encaustic wax, *etc.*

Murasaki Shikibu (*c* 978-*c* 1030), Japanese novelist and diarist. Famous for novel *Genji-monogatari* (*The Tale of Genji,* translated by Arthur Waley, 1935).

Murat, Joachim (1767-1815), French marshal, king of Naples (1808-15). Grew to favour with Napoleon as leader of cavalry; married Napoleon's sister, Caroline (1800). Made king of Naples (1808). Joined Allies (1814) in attempt to retain throne, but fought for Napoleon during Hundred Days; defeated by Austrians. Shot after unsuccessful invasion to recover Naples.

Murcia, city of SE Spain, on R. Segura, cap. of Murcia prov. Pop. 244,000. Textiles (hist. silk mfg.), food processing; univ. (1915). From 11th cent. cap. of Moorish kingdom of Murcia, conquered by Castile 1266. Gothic cathedral (14th cent.).

murder, unlawful killing of human being, distinguished from MANSLAUGHTER in that it is malicious, premeditated; also, any killing done while committing another serious crime, *eg* rape, robbery. In some countries, premeditated murder still receives CAPITAL PUNISHMENT. In US, some statutes grade seriousness of murder, *eg* 1st degree receives harshest penalty.

Murdoch, [Jean] Iris (1919-), English author, b. Ireland. Known for sensitive, intricate, intellectual novels, *eg Under the Net* (1954), *The Bell* (1958), *The Unicorn* (1963). Also wrote *Sartre, Romantic Rationalist* (1953).

Murdock, William (1754-1839), Scottish engineer. Discovered and demonstrated use of coal gas in lighting (1792).

Mureş (Hung. *Maros*), river of E Europe, flows *c* 800 km (500 mi) from Romanian Carpathians via Târgu-Mureş, Arad to R. Tisza in Hungary.

Murfreesboro, town of C Tennessee, US; on Stones R. Pop. 26,000. State cap. 1819-25; scene of destructive Civil War battle (1862-3).

Murger, Henri (1822-61), French author. Known for *Scènes de la vie de Bohème* (1851), which formed basis for Puccini's opera *La Bohème.*

Murillo, Bartolomé Estéban (1617-82), Spanish painter. Known for his idealized religious paintings, *eg The Immaculate Conception,* and sentimental genre scenes; his work was enormously popular into the 19th cent.

Murmansk, city of USSR, N European RSFSR; on Barents coast of Kola penin. Pop. 329,000. Ice-free port; exports timber; fisheries. Founded 1915, important base in WWII.

Murnau, F. W., pseud. of Friedrich Wilhelm Plumpe (1889-1931), German silent film director. Known for 'subjective' use of camera to tell story without subtitles, *eg* in *Sunrise* (1927).

Murray, [George] Gilbert [Aimé] (1866-1957), British scholar, b. Australia. Known for verse translations of Aristophanes, Sophocles, Euripides, Aeschylus. Also wrote *Four Stages of Greek Religion* (1912) giving picture of religious, social background to plays.

Murray or **Moray, James Stuart, 1st Earl of** (*c* 1531-70), Scottish nobleman. One of leaders in Scottish Reformation. Adviser to half-sister, Mary Queen of Scots, on her return to Scotland; appointed regent after her abdication (1567). Assassinated.

Murray, chief river of Australia, flows *c* 2575 km (1600 mi) from Snowy Mts. via Albury, Murray Bridge to Indian Ocean at L. Alexandrina. Main tributaries Darling, Goulburn, Murrumbidgee. Forms most of Victoria-New South Wales border. Provides extensive irrigation, h.e.p.

Murrow, Edward Roscoe (1908-65), American news broadcaster. First noted for reports from London to US for CBS during WWII, later for influential news analysis, in-depth interviews. Director of US Information Agency 1961-4.

Murrumbidgee, river of S New South Wales, Australia. Flows *c* 1600 km (1000 mi) W from Snowy Mts. to Murray R. Main tributary Lachlan. Murrumbidgee Irrigation Area (M I A) permits high-yield fruit, rice, livestock farming.

Murry, [John] Middleton (1889-1957), English author. Known for biographical literary criticism, *eg Keats and Shakespeare* (1925), *Son of Woman, the Story of D.H. Lawrence* (1931), *William Blake* (1933). Also wrote *Life of Jesus* (1926) reflecting his Christian Marxism.

Muscat, cap. of Oman. Pop. 25,000. Port on Gulf of Oman. Exports dates, dried fish, mother-of-pearl.

Muscat and Oman, *see* OMAN.

muscle, body tissue consisting of bundles of cells in the form of fibre which contract or expand under suitable stimulation. Three types of muscle exist: striated or voluntary muscle, which forms flesh and is under conscious control; smooth or involuntary, which is found in walls of alimentary canal, blood vessels, *etc,* and is under control of nervous system; cardiac or heart muscle.

Muscle Shoals, town of NW Alabama, US. Pop. 7000. Centre of Tennessee Valley Authority redevelopment irrigation project (estab. 1933).

muscovite, *see* MICA.

muscular dystrophy, condition which produces progressive wasting of the muscles, esp. in males. Cause unknown; no method of treatment or cure.

Muses, in Greek myth, nine daughters of Zeus and Mnemosyne, goddesses of the arts and literature. Worshipped at Pieria in Thessaly and Mt. Helicon in Boeotia.

mushroom, fleshy, edible fungi esp. those of family Agaricaceae. Species incl. field mushroom *Agaricus campestris,* horse mushroom, *A. arvensis,* and wood mushroom, *A. silvicola.*

music, art of combining sounds made by musical instruments or human voice. In Europe up to 17th cent., vocal music was dominant form (*see* PLAINSONG; POLYPHONY). In 17th cent., instrumental music developed independent style and OPERA emerged. CONCERTO form dates from early 18th cent.; beginnings of classical SYMPHONY were estab. by STAMITZ and form developed to great heights by Haydn, Mozart and Beethoven. Music of 20th cent. has moved away from conventional harmony and tonality, under influence of such innovators as SCHOENBERG. Musical instruments can be divided into 6 main groups: string, wind (woodwind, brass), percussion, keyboard, electric, electronic. Recent developments incl. use of chance and electronic methods.

music, electronic, music produced by electronic circuits. In electronic instruments, *eg* electronic organ and synthesizer, signals are produced by such devices as oscillators, amplified and then fed into loudspeakers. Keyboard of electronic instrument serves as group of switches. Electronic music can be performed 'live' or may be prerecorded on tape, processed in the studio, and replayed at any time.

musicology, academic study of music, *eg* history, analysis, acoustics, music appreciation and music education.

musk, various plants with musky scent esp. *Mimulus moschatus* of figwort family, with yellow flowers, and moschatel, *Adoxa moschatellina,* with greenish flowers.

musk deer, *Moschus moschiferus,* small solitary deer from highlands of C Asia. Hunted for glandular secretion (musk) from abdomen of male, used in perfumery.

muskellunge, *Esox masquinongy,* large North American game fish related to pike, found esp. in Great Lakes. Reaches lengths of 1.8 m/6 ft.

musket, muzzle-loading handgun with matchlock action used by infantry from late 15th cent., later (from *c* 1680) with flintlock, esp. 'Brown Bess' musket. Superseded by breech-loading magazine rifle in 19th cent.

Musk ox

musk ox, *Ovibos moschatus,* hoofed ruminant intermediate between ox and sheep, found in tundra of Canada and Greenland. Long coarse hair, downward curving horns, musky smell.

muskrat or **musquash,** *Ondatra zibethica,* North American aquatic rodent with musky odour. Cultivated for glossy brown fur; introduced *c* 1905 into Europe, proved to be pest.

musk turtle, North American freshwater turtle, genus *Sternotherus,* with strong musky odour.

Muslim religion, *see* ISLAM.

muslin, group of plain woven cotton fabrics, believed to be named after Mosul, Iraq. Introduced into England in late 17th cent.

musquash, *see* MUSKRAT.

mussel, marine or freshwater bivalve mollusc. Marine mussels, usually of Mytilidae family, attach themselves to rocks, *etc,* by thread-like secretions. Freshwater mussels of Unionidae family sometimes source of mother-of-pearl and pearls. Species incl. edible common mussel, *Mytilus edulis,* of N Atlantic coasts, and freshwater pearl mussel *Unio margaritiferus.*

Musselburgh, town of Lothian region, EC Scotland; a suburb of Edinburgh. Pop. 17,000. Paper, rope mfg.

Musset, [Louis Charles] Alfred de (1810-57), French poet. Known for introspective love lyrics, *Les Nuits* (1835-40). Also wrote comedies of manners, *eg On ne badine pas avec l'Amour* (1834), novels. Lover of George Sand.

Mussolini, Benito (1883-1945), Italian dictator. Originally a Socialist, he founded (1919) *Fasci di Combattimento,* dedicated to aggressive nationalism and suppression of Socialism and Communism. Organized Fascism into political party (1921). Directed march on Rome (Oct. 1922) which led to his appointment as premier. Assumed dictatorial powers by 1926; reformed govt. according to Fascist principles. Conquered Ethiopia (1935-6), annexed Albania (1939). Entered WW II (1940) in Axis alliance with Hitler. Resigned 1943 after Allied invasion of Italy; rescued from custody by German paratroopers. Shot by partisans.

Mussorgsky, Modest Petrovich (1839-81), Russian composer. Member of 'the Five'. Musical output was restricted by alcoholism. Famed for opera *Boris Godunov* (revised by Rimsky-Korsakov), and piano work *Pictures at an Exhibition* (orchestrated by Ravel).

Mustafa Kemal, *see* ATATURK.

Black mustard

mustard, various annual plants of genus *Brassica* with yellow flowers and slender seed pods. Native to Europe and W Asia. Main types are black mustard, *B. nigra,* and white mustard, *B. hirta,* both used in condiment mustard. Indian mustard is *Bijuncea.*

mutation, in heredity, sudden change in number or chemical composition of chromosomes. Mutation in gametes can produce inherited change in characteristics of organisms which develop from them and is basis of evolution. Mutations occur naturally at slow rate but can be accelerated, *eg* by exposure to radiation.

mute swan, *see* SWAN.

Muttra, *see* MATHURA.

Mwanza, town of NW Tanzania, on Victoria Nyanza. Pop. 35,000. Port, railway terminus; trade with Kenya, Uganda. Gold and diamond mining.

Mycenae, ancient city of Greece, in NE Peloponnese, near modern Mikínai. Centre of MYCENAEAN CIVILIZATION.

Mycenaean civilization, late Bronze Age Greek civilization with its centre at Mycenae, which *fl* 1600-1200 BC. Deriving their culture in part from the Minoans of Crete, Mycenaeans gained ascendancy over Crete by 1450 BC and achieved commercial and cultural dominance in Greece (1400-1200 BC). Built strongly-walled cities at Mycenae, Tiryns, Pylos, and noted beehive tombs. Overthrown by Dorian invaders.

Myers, Frederic William Henry (1843-1901), English psychic investigator. Co-founder and 1st president of the Society for Psychical Research. Wrote *The Human Personality and its Survival of Bodily Death* (1903).

Myitkyina, town of N Burma, on the Irrawaddy. Pop. 7000. Northern terminus of railway from Rangoon.

My Lai, small village of South Vietnam, scene of massacre of over 300 civilians by US troops, who alleged that it was a Viet Cong base. Commanding officer, W.C. Calley, was convicted of murder (1971, conviction overturned 1974); incident contributed to growing disillusionment over US involvement in Vietnam War.

mynah, Asiatic starling found mainly in India and Sri Lanka. Hill mynah, *Gracula religiosa,* noted for mimicking human speech, has black plumage; often kept as pet.

Indian mynah

myopia or **short sight,** condition in which images are focused in front of retina, so that distant objects are seen unclearly. Caused because lens of eye is too long or its refractive power too great. Corrected by glasses with concave lenses. Called near sight in US.

Myrdal, Gunnar (1898- ‘), Swedish economist. Wrote *Asian Drama* (1968) analyzing how social and economic factors affect govt. in Asia. Expert on economic problems of developing countries. Shared Nobel Prize for Economics with Friedrich von Hayek (1974).

Myriapoda (myriapods), obsolete term for class of arthropods comprising millipedes and centipedes. Now divided into 2 classes, Diplopoda (millipedes) and Chilopoda (centipedes).

Myrmidons, ancient Greek warrior tribe of Thessaly. In legend, descendants of ants changed by Zeus into fighting men. In Homer, warriors of Achilles.

Myron (5th cent. BC), Greek sculptor. Worked mainly in bronze; famed for the realism of his animals. Created the *Discobolus* (discus thrower); it survives in Roman copies.

myrrh, aromatic gum resin extracted from small tree, *Commiphora myrrha,* native to Arabia and Ethiopia.

Common myrtle

myrtle, any of genus *Myrtus* of evergreen shrubs native to Asia. Common Mediterranean myrtle, *M. communis,* has oval leaves, white flowers, purple berries. Yields extract used in perfumery.

Mysore, city of Karnataka state, SW India. Pop. 356,000. Silk and cotton goods mfg. Former state cap. Has maharajah's palace with notable throne.

mysteries, in Greek and Roman religion, various secret cults. Most important among the Greeks were the Eleusinian (*see* ELEUSIS) and Orphic. Esp. important from 5th cent. BC. Several Asiatic cults were incorporated by the Romans, *eg* those of Isis and Mithras. Possibly many of the cults derived from earlier fertility rituals.

mystery plays, *see* MIRACLE PLAYS.

mysticism, belief that person can intuitively understand spiritual truths beyond the comprehension of the intellect, *eg* that individual can form a direct relationship with God. Has incl. such movements as neoplatonism, Gnosticism; influenced Quakers.

myth, traditional story of unknown authorship, usually relating supernatural events, actions of gods. May be associated with religious ceremony or offer explanations of natural phenomena, customs, origin of a people, *etc.* Modern myth interpretation regarded as beginning with Max Müller, who took linguistic approach; Sir James Frazer's *The Golden Bough* (1890) linked myth with birth, death, resurrection cycle in nature. Today authropologists tend to reject interpretations of the concept of myth and concentrate on the various myths of a given people.

Mytilene (*Mitilini*), cap. of Lesbos isl, Greece. Pop. 26,000. Port; fruit, olive trade.

myxomatosis, infectious virus disease of rabbits spread by mosquitoes and fleas. Characterized by growth of soft tumours in connective tissue. Artificially introduced into Britain and Australia to reduce rabbit population.

N

Naas, co. town of Kildare, EC Irish Republic. Pop. 5000. Hunting, horseracing. Former cap. of Leinster.

Nabis, les, name taken by group of French artists, incl. Bonnard, Vuillard and Denis, during 1890s. Influenced by Gauguin, work is characterized by flat areas of pure colour and heavy outlines.

Nabokov, Vladimir, pseud. of Vladimir Sirin (1899-), American author, b. Russia. Works, incl. *Laughter in the Dark* (1938), *The Real Life of Sebastian Knight* (1941), *Lolita* (1958), *Pale Fire* (1962), use idiosyncratic verbal games.

nacre, *see* PEARL.

Nadene, North American Indian linguistic stock, spreading from Alaska to New Mexico. Incl. Athabascan, Pacific, and Southern groups, which incl. Chipewyan, Hupa, Apache, Navaho.

nadir, in astronomy, point on celestial sphere directly opposite ZENITH and directly below observer.

Naevius, Gnaeus (*c* 270-*c* 201 BC) Roman dramatist, poet. Most important work was epic *Bellum Punicum*, which influenced Vergil and Ennius. Also wrote outspoken comedies.

Nagaland, state of NE India on Burma border. Area 16,500 sq km (6400 sq mi); pop. 515,600; cap. Kohima. Wild, forested region inhabited by Nagas, headhunters until recently. Formed in 1962 following nationalist agitation, which lasted until 1964.

Nagasaki, major port of Japan, W Kyushu isl. Pop. 421,000. Shipbuilding and engineering indust.; fisheries. Opened to foreign trade in 16th cent.; kept open to Dutch (1641-1858) when rest of Japan closed to foreigners. Devastated by 2nd atomic bomb (9 Aug. 1945), with loss of 25,000 lives.

Nagoya, major port of Japan, SC Honshu isl. Pop. 2,036,000. Engineering, chemical and textile mfg.; produces pottery and porcelain. Has Atsuta Shinto shrine (2nd cent.), Buddhist temple (1692) and castle (1612).

Nagpur, city of Maharashtra state, C India. Pop. 866,000. Railway jct.; cotton goods, hosiery mfg. Former cap. of Nagpur Mahratta kingdom; passed to British (1853).

Nagy, Imre (1896-1958), Hungarian political leader. As Communist premier (1953-5), he introduced reforms to hard-line Stalinist Communism. Critical of Soviet influence in Hungary, removed from office. Recalled to lead new govt. after revolution (1956). Executed after Soviet military occupation.

Naha, port of Okinawa, Japan; hq. of former US military govt. of Ryuku Isls. Pop. 276,000. Pottery, textile mfg.; exports sugar.

Nahum, prophetic book of OT, written *c* 650 BC; of unknown authorship. Foretells fall of Nineveh (612 BC).

Naiads, in Greek myth, NYMPHS of springs, lakes and rivers.

nail, in anatomy, horny outgrowth of the outer layer of skin (epidermis) growing at tips of fingers and toes. Grows from fold in skin at base of nail; composed of keratin.

Naipaul, V[idiadhar] S[urajprasad] (1932-), English novelist, b. Trinidad. Known for comic novels with Caribbean setting, *eg The Mystic Masseur* (1957), *A House for Mr Biswas* (1961). His brother, Shiva Naipaul, is known for novel *Fireflies* (1971).

Nairnshire, former county of NE Scotland, now in Highland region. Hilly in S; low-lying, fertile in N. Agric., livestock rearing; fishing. Co. town was **Nairn,** former royal burgh on Moray Firth. Pop. 8000. Fishing port, tourist resort.

Nairobi, cap. of Kenya, in E African highlands. Pop. 535,000. Admin., commercial, tourist centre on Uganda-Mombasa railway; exports coffee, sisal, hides; has coll., part of Univ. of E Africa. Nairobi National Park (game reserve) nearby. Founded 1899.

Nakhichevan, town of USSR, cap. of Nakhichevan auton. republic, Azerbaijan SSR. Pop. 33,000. Wine making, cotton ginning. As Naxuana, disputed by Turks, Armenians and Persians.

Nakuru, town of C Kenya. Pop. 48,000. Trade centre in agric. region. On N shore of L. Nakuru (area 90 sq km/35 sq mi) with famous bird, esp. flamingo, sanctuary.

Nalchik, city of USSR, cap. of Kabardino-Balkar auton. republic, S European RSFSR. Pop. 171,000. Food-processing, furniture, oilfield equipment mfg. Health resort on N slope of Greater Caucasus.

Namaqualand, coastal desert of South West Africa and Cape Prov., South Africa; divided by R. Orange. Source of copper, tungsten, alluvial diamonds. Pop. mainly Nama Hottentots.

Namibia, *see* SOUTH WEST AFRICA.

Namur (Flem. *Namen*), town of SE Belgium, at confluence of Meuse and Sambre, cap. of Namur prov. Pop. 33,000. Leather goods, cutlery, glass mfg. Battleground in many wars; badly damaged in WWII. Cathedral (18th cent.).

Nanaimo, town of British Columbia, Canada; on E Vancouver Isl. Pop. 15,000. Lumber, fishing (esp. herring), agric. industs.

Nana Sahib, orig. Dandhu Panth (*c* 1820-*c* 1859), Indian insurgent, adopted son of hereditary chief of Mahrattas. Hostile to British after they refused to continue to him a pension granted to his father. Led Sepoy massacre of British at Kanpur (1858). Fled to Nepal after defeat.

Nanchang, cap. of Kiangsi prov., SE China. Pop. 900,000. Transport, indust. centre on R. Kan; tractor mfg., engineering, large silk complex. First Chinese soviet estab. here briefly (1927).

Nancy, city of NE France, on R. Meurthe and Marne-Rhine canal, cap. of Meurthe-et-Moselle dept. Pop. 123,000. Iron and steel mfg., engineering; univ. (1768). Cap. of duchy of Lorraine from 12th cent.; model of 18th cent. planning under Stanislas I.

Nanga Parbat, Himalayan peak in N India, near Kashmir-Pakistan border; height 8126 m (26,660 ft). First climbed 1953.

Nanking, cap. of Kiangsu prov., E China. Pop. 2,000,000. Rail jct. on Yangtze; textiles, oil refining, iron and steel mfg. Treaty of Nanking (1842) opened China to foreign trade. Cultural centre; Ming imperial tombs. Cap. of Nationalist govt. (1928-37), until captured by Japanese.

Nanning, cap. of Kwangsi auton. region, S China. Pop. 375,000. Mfg. town on Si Kiang in fertile farming area; sugar refining, fertilizer mfg.

Nansen, Fridtjof (1861-1930), Norwegian explorer, scientist and statesman. Crossed Greenland icefields (1888); attempted to reach North Pole by drifting in ship *Fram* (1893-5), reached further N than anyone before. Awarded Nobel Peace Prize (1922) for work with post-WWI refugees.

Nantes, city of Brittany, NW France, on R. Loire. Cap. of Loire-Atlantique dept. Pop. 259,000. Outport at St Nazaire; oil refining, food processing. Seat of dukes of Brittany (10th-16th cent.). Edict of Nantes (1598), giving Huguenots freedom, signed here. Ducal castle, cathedral; univ. (1460).

Nantes, Edict of, decree issued (1598) by Henry IV of France granting religious freedom and civil rights to Huguenots (French Protestants). Its terms were gradually nullified in 17th cent.; revoked 1685.

Nantucket, isl. off SE Massachusetts, US; separated from Cape Cod by Nantucket Sound. Atlantic summer resort. Settled 1659. Hist. whaling centre.

Nantung, port of Kiangsu prov. on Yangtze estuary, E China. Pop. 300,000. Centre of major cotton growing area. Textile mfg.

napalm, incendiary material made from petrol or oil and a thickening agent (soap or polymer). Used in warfare as it sticks to target while burning.

naphtha, mixture of light hydrocarbons obtained by distillation of petroleum, coal tar, *etc.* Inflammable and volatile; used as cleaning solvent and in making varnish.

naphthalene ($C_{10}H_8$), white crystalline solid with penetrating smell. Obtained from distillation of coal tar. Used in moth balls and manufacture of dyes.

Napier, Sir Charles James (1782-1853), British army officer. Sent to India (1841) to subdue the emirs of Sind, whom he finally defeated at Hyderabad (1843) after which he was made governor. Returned to England (1847) after disagreements with govt.

Napier, John (1550-1617), Scottish mathematician. First to publish table of logarithms (1614); introduced calculating rods ('Napier's bones') to facilitate arithmetic computations. Also produced religious writings.

Napier, city of E North Isl., New Zealand, on Hawke's Bay. Pop. 40,000. Major wool trade centre; textile, tobacco, food processing industs. Founded 1855; rebuilt after 1931 earthquake.

Naples (*Napoli,* anc. *Neapolis*), city of S Italy, on Bay of Naples. Cap. of Campania and of Napoli prov. Pop. 1,259,000. Major port, indust. centre; tourism. Greek colony founded 6th cent. BC, Roman resort. Under Normans from 1139; cap. of Kingdom of Naples (1282-1860). Univ. (1224), cathedral, castles, museum (has relics of Herculaneum, Pompeii). Damaged in WWII.

Napoleon I

Napoleon I, full name Napoleon Bonaparte or Buonaparte (1769-1821), French military and political leader, emperor (1804-14), b. Corsica. Revitalized Revolutionary Army in Italian campaign (1796-7), driving out Austrians. Invaded Egypt (1798) as part of plan to take India; campaign became hopeless after Nelson's naval victory at Aboukir. Coup d'état (1799) estab. Napoleon as first consul, effectively dictator. Reorganized state, codified laws in Code Napoléon. Had himself created emperor. In Napoleonic Wars, thwarted European alliance against him by defeating Austria at Austerlitz (1805), Prussia at Jena (1806), Russia at Friedland (1807); ruled virtually entire continent after peace treaty of Tilsit, placing members of his family on several thrones (*see* BONAPARTE). Defeated by Nelson at Trafalgar (1805); failed in attempts to prevent

trade with Britain by CONTINENTAL SYSTEM (1806-12). Decline set in with failure of PENINSULAR campaign in Spain and disastrous invasion of Russia (1812), ending in retreat and loss of most of army. Defeated at Leipzig by new European alliance. Abdicated 1814, exiled to Elba. Returned to France, but Hundred Days rule ended in defeat at Waterloo (1815). Exiled to St Helena, where he died.

Napoleon III, orig. Louis Napoleon Bonaparte (1808-73), French political leader, emperor (1852-70). Nephew of Napoleon I, he spent youth in exile. Plotted 2 unsuccessful coups (Strasbourg, 1836; Boulogne, 1840). Elected president of republic after Revolution of 1848. After coup d'état (1851), dissolved legislature and assumed dictatorial powers; proclaimed emperor (1852). Rule marked by military intervention in Crimea, Mexico, Italy; annexed Nice, Savoy. Manoeuvred by Bismarck into war with Prussia (1870); defeated, taken prisoner at Sedan. Exiled to England, where he died.

Napoli, see NAPLES, Italy.

Nara, town of Japan, SC Honshu isl. Pop. 208,000. Cultural and religious centre; 1st permanent cap. of Japan 709-84. Has many Buddhist temples, one with colossal bronze statue of Buddha. Nearby is Mt. Kasuga, revered as home of gods.

Narayanganj, city of Bangladesh on R. Dhaleshwari. Pop. 425,000. River port for Dacca; jute trade.

Narbonne (anc. *Narbo Martius*), town of Languedoc, S France. Wine trade, brandy distilling, sulphur processing. Pop. 40,000 First Roman colony in transalpine Gaul, estab. 118 BC; *fl* in Middle Ages until harbour silted up (14th cent.). Palace, cathedral (both 13th cent.).

narcissism, in psychology, extreme self-love, term deriving from Greek myth of Narcissus. Regarded by psychoanalysts as early stage in normal psychosexual development, at which sexual object is self.

Narcissus, in Greek myth, beautiful youth who rejected love of others. Caused by Aphrodite to become enamoured of his own image in a mountain pool. Pined away and was changed into a flower.

Narcissus: jonquil

narcissus, genus of bulbous perennial herbs of amaryllis family. Found in Europe, Asia and North America. Erect linear leaves; yellow, white or bicolour flowers, often with trumpet-shaped corolla. Species incl. jonquil, *Narcissus jonquilla,* and DAFFODIL.

narcotic, substance which has depressant effect on nervous system. Used medicinally in small doses to relieve pain, induce sleep, *etc.* Main narcotics are opium and its derivatives (morphine, heroin). Usually addictive; overdoses may cause coma and death.

Narmada or **Narbada,** river of WC India. Flows *c* 1300 km (800 mi) from Madhya Pradesh W to Gulf of Cambay. Only navigable near its mouth. Sacred to Hindus.

Narva, town of USSR, NE Estonian SSR. Pop. 31,000. Port on R. Narva. Textile centre. Founded 1223 by Danes; member of Hanseatic League. Scene of Charles XII of Sweden's victory (1700) over Peter the Great, who later took town (1704).

Narvik, town of NW Norway, on Ofot Fjord. Pop. 13,000. Ice-free port, railway terminus; exports Swedish iron ore. Scene of heavy fighting (1940).

narwhal, *Monodon monoceros,* medium-sized arctic whale. Male has long spiralled tusk, up to 2.4 m/8 ft long, extending from upper jaw. Hunted for oil.

Naseby, village of Northamptonshire, C England. Site of Royalists' defeat by Cromwell's Parliamentarians (1645).

Nash, John (1752-1835), English architect, town planner. Achieved most noted effects in elegant classicism of his developments in London for George IV, *eg* Regent Street and Regent's Park.

Nash, Ogden (1902-71), American poet. Known for humorous verse pub. in *New Yorker*. Collections incl. *I'm a Stranger Here Myself* (1938), *Everyone But Thee and Me* (1962).

Paul Nash: *The Landscape of the Vernal Equinox*

Nash, Paul (1889-1946), English artist. Official war artist in both World Wars; poetic vision, influenced by surrealism, is revealed in his landscapes. Works incl. *Totes Meer,* painted during WWII. His brother, **John Nash** (1893-), is best known for English landscapes, less visionary than Paul's.

Nash, Sir Walter (1882-1968), New Zealand statesman, b. England. Labour Party leader and PM (1957-60).

Nashe, Thomas (1567-1601), English author. Wrote anti-Puritan pamphlets in Marprelate controversy. Known for picaresque novel, *The Unfortunate Traveller* (1594), satirical masque *Summer's Last Will and Testament* (1592) containing famous lyric, 'Adieu, farewell, earth's bliss'.

Nashville, cap. of Tennessee, US; on Cumberland R. Pop. 448,000. Road, railway jct.; cotton trade, printing and publishing industs.; centre of recording indust. Seat of Vanderbilt Univ. (1873).

Nasik, town of Maharashtra state, W India. Pop. 176,000. Brassware mfg. Hindu pilgrimage centre; legendary site of exile of Hindu god Rama.

Nassau, former duchy of WC West Germany, cap. Wiesbaden. Forested and hilly; agric., wine production, spas (*eg* Bad Homburg). Duchy from 1806; part of Prussian prov. of Hesse-Nassau from 1866, of Hesse from 1945. Branches of Orange-Nassau family rule Luxembourg, Netherlands.

Nassau, cap. and port of Bahamas, on New Providence Isl. Pop. 102,000. Famous holiday resort. Exports pulpwood, salt, crayfish.

Nasser, Gamal Abdel (1918-70), Egyptian political leader. Joined Mohammed Neguib in military coup which estab. 1952 republic; became premier (1954), president (1956). Nationalized Suez Canal (1956) and withstood Anglo-French invasion to recover it. Aggressive anti-Israel policy led to war (1967); resignation after defeat was rejected by legislature. Promoted building of Aswan dam (completed 1970).

Nasser, Lake, see ASWAN, Egypt.

nasturtium, any of genus *Tropaeolum* of plants, native to South America. Common garden variety is *T. majus* with orange spurred flowers. Leaves sometimes used in salads. Also name of genus of WATERCRESS.

Gamal Abdel Nasser in 1953

Natal, smallest prov. of South Africa, in E. Area 91,400 sq km (35,300 sq mi); pop. 2,193,000; cap. Pietermaritzburg. Coastal strip, interior plateau with Drakensberg foothills in W. Sugar, cereals, fruit growing; coalmining. Sighted 1497 and named by da Gama. Boer republic founded 1838; annexed by Britain 1843, became UK colony 1856. Absorbed Zululand 1897; prov. of Union of South Africa 1910.

Natal, port of NE Brazil, cap. of Rio Grande do Norte state; near mouth of Potengi R. Pop. 265,000. Exports sugar, cotton, salt; textile mfg. International airport nearby.

Natchez, North American Indian tribe of Hokan-Siouan linguistic stock. Sedentary farmers of SW Mississippi during 17th cent. Scattered during wars with French.

National Aeronautics and Space Administration (NASA), US govt. agency (estab. 1958) responsible for space exploration. Supervises construction of equipment and research on flights within and without Earth's atmosphere.

national anthem, patriotic hymn sung on ceremonial occasions. Some countries have had compositions created specifically to serve as anthems.

National Assembly, name adopted by Estates-General of France in 1789, marking its defiance of Louis XVI.

National Association for the Advancement of Colored People (NAACP), organization formed (1910) to end racial discrimination and segregation in US. Early campaigns were directed against lynching of blacks. Now advocates non-violent opposition to discrimination rather than methods of black power extremists.

national debt or **public debt,** indebtedness of govt. expressed in monetary terms. Calculated in many different ways, variously incl. public borrowing from individuals (*eg* loan stocks, bonds, treasury notes) or from foreign govts. or international organizations.

National Gallery, London, art gallery in Trafalgar Square containing British national picture collection. Founded 1824 with purchase of the Angerstein collection, present building was opened 1838. Holding of Italian art is esp. strong.

National Gallery of Art, Washington DC, part of the Smithsonian Institution; estab. 1937, it was opened in 1941. Fine collections of French, Italian and American paintings.

National Guard, in US, body estab. (1903) to replace state militias. Subject to state jurisdiction in peacetime. Responsible to president in national emergency.

National Health Insurance Act (1946), in UK, legislation providing for estab. of National Health Service (1948), most comprehensive medical care scheme of its time. Under it, free medical attention can be obtained from any doctor participating in service. Funded by national govt. and local taxation.

National Insurance Act (1911), in UK, legislation devised by LLOYD GEORGE, providing for estab. of compulsory national schemes in areas of old age pensions, sickness and disability insurance, and unemployment. *See* SOCIAL SECURITY.

nationalism, social and political creed expressing common heritage and culture through unification of an ethnic group, manifested either, in estab. nations, as doctrine that national welfare should prevail over international considerations, or, as basis for achieving independence as advocated by separatist groups (*eg* Spanish Basques). Nationalism was driving force behind expansionist nation-building in 19th cent. Europe, and in 20th cent. Asia and Africa. Extreme forms linked with FASCISM, as in Nazi Germany.

nationalization, transference of ownership or control of land, resources, industs., *etc.*, to national govt. Associated with socialist, communist regimes, *eg* USSR after 1918, UK and France (1945-50). Also refers to acquisition by state of foreign-owned assets, *eg* Suez Canal by Egypt (1956).

National Labor Relations Board (NLRB), US govt. agency estab. (1935) by National Labor Relations Act (Wagner Act). Regulates labour relations, assists unions in collective bargaining, investigates alleged unfair practices by employers. Amended by Taft-Hartley Act (1947) to cover employers' complaints against unions.

National League, US professional baseball league, estab. 1876. Comprises 8 members surviving from 1900 with 4 more teams added by 1969.

national liberation front, revolutionary political front, or party, working for national independence. Originated with FLN (Front de Libération Nationale) in Algeria, where independence was achieved under Ben Bella after guerrilla campaign (1955-62); only recognized party under Algerian constitution. Influenced FLQ whose terrorist activities in Québec in 1960s led Canada's PM Trudeau to impose War Measures Act, (1970). Formation of such a front in South Vietnam (1961) helped Communists infiltrate villages, leading ultimately to victory over US-supported forces in early 1970s.

national park, area of scenic beauty and scientific interest, protected from development. Main purposes are conservation of flora and fauna, and human recreation. Since estab. of Yellowstone, US (1872), many countries, *eg* Canada, South Africa, UK, Tanzania, have designated national parks.

National Socialism or **Nazism,** ideology of National Socialist German Workers' Party (Nazi Party). Formulated in part by Hitler in *Mein Kampf* (1923) and by ROSENBERG. Founded on principles of racial purity, (Aryans representing 'master race'), allegiance to *Führer* (leader), reversal of terms of Versailles Treaty, German territ. expansion, esp. into Slav lands, and eradication of Communists and Jews, who were said to have betrayed Germany in WWI. As sole legal party after Hitler's rise to power, acted with brutality in consolidating power within Germany and forced outbreak of WWII through aggressive external policies.

National Theatre Company, repertory theatre company opened (1963) in Old Vic Theatre, London, under direction of Sir Laurence Olivier. New theatre complex opened 1976 on South Bank of Thames.

National Trust, in UK, non-profitmaking organization chartered (1895) by Parliament. Aims to promote preservation for people of lands and buildings of historic or aesthetic value. Has power to acquire land, issue protective orders on private property.

native cat, carnivorous arboreal Australian marsupial of Dasyuridae family. Species incl. Eastern native cat, *Dasyurus viverrinus,* with white spots on body.

NATO *see* NORTH ATLANTIC TREATY ORGANIZATION.

Natron, Lake, lake of NE Tanzania, on border with Kenya, in Great Rift Valley. Length *c* 55 km (35 mi); soda and salt deposits.

natterjack, *Bufo calamita,* small toad of W Europe. Brownish yellow in colour; short hind legs make it poor jumper.

natural gas, mixture of gaseous hydrocarbons, esp. methane, occurring naturally as deposits in porous rock, often in association with petroleum. Used as domestic fuel.

natural selection, in evolution, process by which those individuals of a species best-fitted to their specific environment tend to leave more offspring, which inherit those characteristics in which this fitness lies, whereas those less fitted tend to leave less offspring and die out. Thus there is progressive tendency towards greater degree of adaptation. Basis of Darwin's theory of evolution described by him and A.R. Wallace (1859).

Naucratis, ancient city of N Egypt, on R. Nile, SE of Alexandria. First Greek colony in Egypt, founded 7th cent. BC. Remains incl. temples, pottery.

Naumburg, town of SC East Germany, on R. Saale. Pop. 38,000. Textiles, leather. Founded 10th cent.; cathedral (13th cent.).

Naupaktos (Ital. *Lepanto*), town of WC Greece, on Gulf of Corinth. Pop. 7000. Athenian naval base in Peloponnesian War. Scene of destruction of Turkish fleet by Holy League in battle of Lepanto (1571).

Nauplia (*Návplion*), town of Greece, in E Peloponnese, cap. of Argolis admin. dist. Pop. 9000. Port; tobacco, fruit trade. First cap. of independent Greece (1830-4).

Nauru, isl. republic of SW Pacific Ocean. Area 20 sq km (8 sq mi); pop. 7000. Extensive phosphate deposits. Discovered (1798), named Pleasant Isl.; admin. by Australia from 1947 until independence (1968). Member of British Commonwealth.

nausea, feeling of a desire to vomit. May be caused by irritation of stomach, unpleasant smells, *etc.*

Nausicaä, in Greek myth, daughter of Alcinoüs of Phaeacia. Welcomed Odysseus when shipwrecked during his wanderings after Trojan War.

nautical mile, unit of distance used in sea and air travel; equivalent to 1 minute of arc of a great circle of Earth. International nautical mile equals 1852 m (*c* 1.15 ml); UK nautical mile is slightly larger, equalling 6080 ft (1853.18 m).

nautilus, cephalopod mollusc of Indian and Pacific oceans. External coiled shell divided into chambers, animal living in outermost chamber; other chambers filled with gas, giving shell buoyancy.

Navaho Indian

Navaho or **Navajo,** North American Indian tribe of Nadene linguistic stock. Inhabited NE Arizona in 17th cent. Nomadic hunters, farmers, shepherds. Raided Pueblo and Spanish settlements in New Mexico. Settled on reservations in SW US. Largest surviving tribe.

Navarino, *see* PYLOS, Greece.

Navarre, region and former kingdom of N Spain and SW France, hist. cap. Pamplona. Mountainous, incl. pass of Roncesvalles; drained by R. Ebro. Pop. mainly Basque.

Cereals, livestock, h.e.p. Founded 9th cent.; S part annexed to Spain (1515), N part to France (1589).

nave, in architecture, central aisle of a church. Term once meant the area from the altar to main door, incl. side aisles, intended for use of the laity.

navel or **umbilicus,** scar, usually in form of depression in middle of the abdomen, marking place where the umbilical cord was joined to the foetus.

Navigation Acts, English legislation designed to restrict carrying of goods from abroad only to English-owned ships or to ships of country producing the goods. Acts of 1651 were designed to combat Dutch competition in trade with English possessions. Finally repealed 1849.

navy, branch of armed services equipped for maritime warfare. Originated among ancient nations bordering on Mediterranean. In Britain, expanded 16th-17th cents., becoming in Charles II's reign disciplined and efficient. British naval dominance challenged in early 20th cent. esp. by Germany, Japan, leading to estab. of US as a major naval power. With development of air and submarine warfare in 20th cent., size of vessels has given place to speed and mobility, the only large warships being aircraft carriers. By early 1970s most powerful navies were those of USSR and US.

Naxos, isl. of Greece, in Aegean Sea, largest of Cyclades. Area 438 sq km (169 sq mi). Fruits, wine. Ancient centre for worship of Dionysus. In legend, here Theseus abandoned Ariadne.

Nazareth, town of N Israel. Pop. *c* 23,000. Associated with early life of Jesus. Pilgrimage centre.

Nazism, see NATIONAL SOCIALISM.

Nazi-Soviet Non-aggression Pact, see NON-AGGRESSION PACT.

Ndjamena, cap. of Chad, at confluence of Logone, Shari rivers. Pop. 179,000. Admin. centre, market for salt, dates, livestock. Founded 1900, known as Fort Lamy until 1973.

Ndola, city of NC Zambia. Pop. 201,000. Indust., commercial, railway centre in copperbelt region. Scene of aircrash (1961) in which Dag Hammarskjold died.

Neagh, Lough, C Northern Ireland. Largest freshwater lake in British Isles: length 29 km (18 mi); width 18 km (11 mi).

Neanderthal man, early form of man, usually considered a representative of *Homo sapiens.* Lived between 100,000 and 40,000 years ago. Had prominent brow ridges, receding chin, sloping forehead but brain similar in size to modern man's. Remains 1st discovered (1856) in Neanderthal valley, Germany.

near sight [US], see MYOPIA.

Nebraska, state of C US; on W bank of Missouri R. Area 200,000 sq km (77,230 sq mi); pop. 1,484,000; cap. Lincoln; chief city Omaha. Mainly prairies; tableland in W. Maize, wheat, sorghum, livestock farming. Agric. related industs. Exploration by Spanish in 16th cent. Region developed after Louisiana Purchase by US (1803). Admitted to Union as 37th state (1867).

Nebuchadnezzar II (d. 562 BC), king of Babylonia (*c* 605-562 BC). Quelled revolt in Judah (597), taking many Jews into exile in Babylon. Destroyed Jerusalem (586) after 2nd revolt. Rebuilt Babylon, constructing temples, palaces and city walls.

nebula, luminous cloud-like patch seen in night sky, consisting of masses of rarefied gas and dust. Name was formerly applied to extra-galactic systems of stars.

neck, part of man or animal joining the head to the body. In man, column of 7 cervical vertebrae form bones of neck; they are surrounded by systems of muscles which move and support them.

Neckar, river of SW West Germany. Flows *c* 370 km (230 mi) from Black Forest to R. Rhine at Mannheim. Navigable to Stuttgart; canal link to Danube. Vineyards, h.e.p., tourism.

Necker, Jacques (1732-1804), French statesman, b. Switzerland. Succeeded TURGOT as finance minister (1776) and attempted fiscal reform to restore financial stability; dismissed (1781) by Louis XVI. Recalled 1788, he advised summoning of Estates-General. Subsequent dismissal led

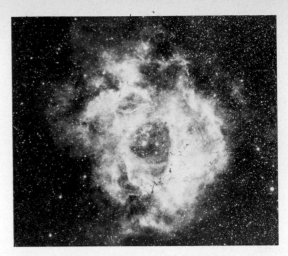

Rosette nebula in the Milky Way

to storming of Bastille (14 July, 1789) and reinstatement. Resigned 1790.

necrosis, in medicine, death of a particular area of tissue. May be caused by cessation of blood supply, bacterial poisoning, *etc.*

nectar, see AMBROSIA.

nectarine, see PEACH.

needlefish, see GARFISH.

Needles, The, three chalk stacks off W Isle of Wight, S England. Has lighthouse.

Nefertiti or **Nefretete** (*fl* 14th cent. BC), Egyptian queen, wife of Ikhnaton. Her beauty is suggested by famous portrait bust found (1912) at Amarna (now in Berlin).

Negev or **Negeb,** semi-desert of S Israel, between Mediterranean and Aqaba. Area *c* 13,310 sq km (5140 sq mi). Minerals, natural gas. Settled by immigrants on cooperative farms (*kibbutzim*).

Negri Sembilan, state of S West Malaysia. Area *c* 6700 sq km (2590 sq mi); pop. 480,000; cap. Seremban. Exports incl. rubber, tin, rice, copra.

Negro, river of NW Brazil. Rises in E Colombia, forming part of Colombia-Venezuela border. Flows SE 2250 km (*c* 1400 mi) to join Amazon near Manáus.

Negros, isl. of Philippines, NW of Mindanao. Area *c* 12,700 sq km (4900 sq mi). Mountainous, with extensively cultivated lowland. Major sugar producer.

Nehemiah, historical book of OT. Relates story of Nehemiah, cup-bearer to King Artaxerxes I of Persia. Later governed Jerusalem (from 445 BC). Rebuilt city walls and reformed temple worship.

Nehru, Jawaharlal (1889-1964), Indian statesman and writer, PM (1947-64). Influenced by Gandhi, devoted himself to obtaining Indian independence from Britain. President of Indian National Congress 4 times. Frequently in jail for civil disobedience campaigns of 1930s. First PM of independent Indian state. Maintained influential neutral stand in foreign affairs.

Neill, Alexander Sutherland (1883-1973), British educator. Known for views on progressive, child-centred education; founded Summerhill, school run according to his views, in Suffolk. Books incl. *Summerhill* (1962).

Neisse (*Nysa*), two rivers of E Europe. **Glatzer** or **Silesian Neisse** flows *c* 195 km (120 mi) NE from SW Poland to R. Oder near Brzeg. **Görlitzer** or **Lusatian Neisse** flows *c* 225 km (140 mi) N from NW Czechoslovakia via Görlitz to R. Oder near Gubin (Poland); forms part of Poland-East Germany border.

Nejd, plateau region of C Saudi Arabia. Many oases in N and E where dates are grown. Chief city Riyadh. United with Hejaz (1932) to form Saudi Arabia.

Nekrasov, Nikolai Alekseyevich (1821-77), Russian poet, editor. Published early work of Dostoyevski, Tolstoy,

Turgenev. Wrote verse reflecting social concern, *eg Frost the Rednosed* (1863).

Lord Nelson

Nelson, Horatio, Viscount Nelson (1758–1805), English admiral. Aided Jervis off Cape St Vincent and ended Napoleon's Egyptian campaign by destroying the French fleet at Aboukir Bay (1798). At Naples he put down a Jacobin revolt and formed a liaison with EMMA HAMILTON, wife of the British ambassador. In 1801 he destroyed the Danish fleet at Copenhagen, and in 1805 died of wounds at the moment of victory over a combined French and Spanish fleet at Trafalgar.

Nelson, region of NW South Isl., New Zealand. Area 17,900 sq km (6910 sq mi); pop. 69,000. Mainly mountainous; lowlands around Tasman Bay. Forestry; sheep, cattle raising; fruit, hops, tobacco growing. Main town **Nelson,** on Tasman Bay. Pop. 29,000. Port with ferry service to North Isl.; fruit, vegetables, tobacco exports; food processing, sawmilling, textile mfg. Has marble Anglican cathedral.

Neman (Polish *Niemen*), river of W USSR. Rises in Byelorussian SSR, flows generally NW *c* 900 km (550 mi) through Lithuanian SSR to Baltic. Used for transporting timber.

Nematoda (nematodes), phylum of unsegmented roundworms, *eg* threadworms, eelworms. Incl. soil-dwellers, free-swimming forms, and parasites, *eg* hookworm.

Nemean lion, in Greek myth, monstrous lion, offspring of Typhon and Echidna. Invulnerable to weapons but strangled by Heracles (1st labour).

Nemertea (nemerteans), phylum of mainly marine worms with unsegmented body and protrusible proboscis used to catch prey. Variable length, reaching 18 m/60 ft. Also called ribbon worms.

Nemesis, in Greek myth, personification of retribution, esp. in cases of human presumption towards the gods.

Nemi, Lake, small crater lake of Latium, WC Italy. Two pleasure craft of Caligula raised here (1930-1), burned by Germans (1944). Nearby are ruined temple, wood sacred to Diana.

Nennius (*fl* 796), Welsh chronicler. *Historia Britonum* attributed to him, on early British history and legends, incl. ARTHURIAN LEGEND.

neo-Classicism, artistic style of 2nd half of 18th cent. which began as reaction to Baroque and rococo styles. Inspired by antique buildings and archaeological finds, its principal theorist was Winckelmann. Noted practitioners incl. Adam brothers in architecture, Mengs in painting.

neodymium (Nd), metallic element of the lanthanide series; at. no. 60, at. wt. 144.24. Compounds used to colour glass.

Neolithic, last period of STONE AGE in which domestication of animals, farming began. Started in SW Asia 8000-6000 BC; ended at different times in different areas, *eg c* 3500 BC in Mesopotamia but later in Europe.

neon (Ne), inert gaseous element; at. no. 10, at. wt. 20.18. Found in traces in atmosphere; obtained by fractional distillation of liquid air. Produces bright reddish-orange glow when electric current is passed through it; used in neon signs.

neon fish, *Paracheirodon innesi,* small brightly coloured fish discovered in Amazon R. (1936). Popular aquarium fish.

neoplatonism, philosophy loosely derived from doctrines of Plato, expounded (3rd cent.) by Plotinus. Held that all existence, material and spiritual, emanates from transcendent One through the divine mind (*see* LOGOS) and world soul. Freedom from sin gained by the individual soul seeking reintegration with the One. Exponents incl. Porphyry and Iamblichus. Banned by Justinian I (529) but influence continued through Middle Ages, affected 17th-19th cent. writers, poets.

Neoptolemus, in Greek legend, son of Achilles. Summoned to Trojan War after death of Achilles; killed Priam and was awarded Andromache, Hector's widow, as captive. Married Hermione, daughter of Menelaus and Helen.

neoteny, in zoology, temporary or permanent retention of larval characteristics in adult animal form. When permanent, animal can breed in juvenile form; phenomenon is exhibited by AXOLOTL, which, although it retains external gills, *etc,* can produce similar offspring.

Nepal

Nepal, kingdom of SC Asia. Area *c* 140,000 sq km (54,600 sq mi); pop. 12,319,000; cap. Katmandu. Language: Nepali. Religions: Hindu, Buddhism. Formerly remote region in Himalayas, bordered by India and Tibet; rice and grain grown in Nepal valley. Under Gurkha control from 1768; sovereignty recognized by British in 1923.

nephritis, inflammation of the kidneys, often caused by bacterial infection. Form known as acute glomerulonephritis usually follows infection by streptococci; characterized by swelling under skin due to leakage of water. Chronic form involves deterioration of kidneys.

Neptune, planet 8th in distance from Sun; mean distance from Sun *c* 4500×10^6 km; diameter 44,800 km; mass *c* 17 times that of Earth. Solar orbit takes *c* 165 years. Discovered (1846) by Galle following predictions of Leverrier and Adams.

Neptune, in Roman religion, god of water. Possibly derived from an indigenous fertility god; sometimes identified with Greek POSEIDON, whose attributes he assimilated.

neptunium (Np), transuranic element; at. no. 93, mass no. of most stable isotope 237. First transuranic element, discovered (1940) by McMillan and Abelson during neutron bombardment of uranium.

Nereidae (nereids), family of free-swimming annelid worms, order Polychaeta, consisting of ragworms.

Nereids, in Greek myth, daughters of Nereus; NYMPHS of the Aegean Sea.

Nereus, in Greek myth, wise and kindly sea deity. Had attributes of prophecy and shape-changing.

Nergal, in Babylonian pantheon, god of the dead and the chase. Could be beneficent but normally associated with destruction and pestilence.

Nero [Claudius Caesar Drusus Germanicus] (AD 37-68), Roman emperor (AD 54-68). Adopted as heir to

Claudius I through intrigues of his mother Agrippina. After accession, arranged deaths of rightful heir Britannicus, Agrippina, wives Octavia and Poppaea, his adviser Seneca and many others. Suspected of starting great fire of Rome (64), began persecution of Christians, whom he accused of the crime. Committed suicide during revolt.

Neruda, Pablo, pseud. of Neftalí Ricardo Reyes (1904-73), Chilean poet. Best-known works incl. *Crepusculario* (1923), *Residencia en la tierra* (1933). Also wrote play, *The Splendour and Death of Joaquin Murieta* (1967). Nobel Prize for Literature (1971).

Nerval, Gérard de, pseud. of Gérard Labrunie (1808-55), French author. Wrote short stories, *eg* in *Les Filles du feu* (1854), sonnet series, *Les Chimères,* translation of Goethe's *Faust* (1828), spiritual autobiog. *Aurélia.*

Nervi, Pier Luigi (1891-   ), Italian architectural engineer. Known for his masterful use of reinforced concrete to create complicated new structures. Works incl. Giovanni Berta stadium in Florence (1929-32) and Turin exhibition hall (1948-9).

nervous system, network of nerves and nerve tissue in animals which conducts impulses to other parts of animal to coordinate senses and activities. Basic unit is nerve cell or neuron, consisting of nerve cell body and various thread-like processes (usually single long axon and several short dendrites). Impulses are transmitted from axons to dendrites at junctions called SYNAPSES. Certain impulses are communicated to brain and spinal cord from receptors (sensory organs inside or outside body), other impulses are communicated to effectors, *eg* muscles or glands.

Nesbit, E[dith] (1858-1924), English author. Known for anti-romantic children's fiction, *eg The Railway Children* (1906), *Five Children and It* (1902), which attempted to break with conventional middle-class mode.

Ness, Loch, lake of Highland region, N Scotland. Length 39 km (24 mi), forms part of Caledonian Canal. Home of reputed 'monster'.

Nessus, in Greek myth, centaur slain by Heracles for attempt to violate his wife, Deianira. The blood of Nessus, smeared on a robe by Deianira to regain Heracles' love, caused his death.

nest, structure prepared by animals for laying of eggs or giving birth to young. Many birds and certain reptiles, insects, fish and mammals build nests. Structure of bird's nest varies greatly, with most elaborate nests built by smallest birds. Some birds do not build nests, laying eggs on ground, *eg* ostrich.

Nestor, in Greek myth, son of Neleus and king of Pylos. In old age went with Greeks to Trojan War and was respected warrior and counsellor.

Nestorians, Christian followers of NESTORIUS. Driven into Persia after Council of Ephesus (431), they suffered persecution from Kurds and Turks. Modern Nestorian Church (mainly in Iraq) upholds Nestorius' doctrines only on the position of the Virgin Mary.

Nestorius, (d. *c* 451), Syrian churchman. Patriarch of Constantinople; objection to name 'Mother of God' for Virgin Mary led to deposition as heretic after Council of Ephesus (431).

netball, seven-a-side game for women played mainly in English-speaking countries. Introduced into England (1897) from US as form of BASKETBALL; 1st rules date from 1901.

Netherlands (*Nederland*), kingdom of NW Europe. Area 41,344 sq km (15,963 sq mi); pop. 13,504,000; cap. Amsterdam, seat of govt. The Hague. Language: Dutch. Religions: Protestant, RC. Low-lying, 25% below sea level; large reclaimed areas. Dairying, bulbs, fishing. Extensive canal system links main rivers (Scheldt, Maas, Rhine), important transit trade. Industs. centred in Amsterdam, Rotterdam (Europe's leading port), Utrecht. Member of EEC. Part of Low Countries until 16th cent.; rebelled against Spanish rule after religious repression. N provinces declared independence 1579. Estab. overseas empire 17th cent. Union with former Austrian Netherlands (Belgium) (1814-30). German occupation in WWII.

Netherlands

Netherlands Antilles, autonomous Dutch isl. groups in Caribbean. Area 394 sq km (1020 sq mi); pop. 215,000; cap. Willemstad. Language: Dutch. N group in Leeward Isls. incl. Saba, St Eustatius, S part of St Martin; S group off Venezuela, incl. Curaçao, Aruba, Bonaire. Economy depends on refining of Venezuelan oil on Curaçao and Aruba. Dutch territ. from 17th cent. (known as Curaçao until 1949); granted full autonomy (1954).

Netherlands New Guinea, *see* IRIAN JAYA.

nettle, any of genus *Urtica* of plants with stinging hairs on leaves which cause a rash (urticaria) by injecting histamine into the skin. Common stinging nettle, *U. dioica,* found in Europe and North America.

nettle rash, *see* URTICARIA.

Neuchâtel (Ger. *Neuenburg*), city of W Switzerland, on L. Neuchâtel, cap. of Neuchâtel canton. Pop. 39,000. Watch mfg.; chocolate, condensed milk. Academy (1838) now univ.

Neuilly-sur-Seine, suburb of NW Paris, France. Motor car mfg. Scene of peace treaty (1919) between Allies and Bulgaria.

Neumann, Johann Balthasar (1687-1753), German architect. Designed staircases of palaces at Würzburg and Bruchsal. Masterpiece is pilgrimage church at Vierzehnheiligen (1743) in rococo style.

neuralgia, pain felt along the course of a nerve. Trigeminal neuralgia is severe pain along the branches of the trigeminal nerve in the face.

neuritis, inflammation of a nerve or group of nerves. May be caused by viral infection (*eg* shingles) or by bacteria (*eg* leprosy), *etc.*

neuron, *see* NERVOUS SYSTEM.

neurosis, form of mental disturbance merging normal behaviour with genuine derangement. Characterized by one or more of following: anxiety, depression, phobias, compulsions and obsessions, *etc.*

Neusiedler, Lake (Hung. *Fertő Tó*), on Austria-Hungary border. Area 337 sq km (130 sq mi). Reeds supply cellulose indust.; fishing. Prehist. remains.

Neuss, city of W West Germany. Pop. 117,000. Railway jct., agric. machinery mfg. Roman settlement, close to Rhine bridge. Has Romanesque church (13th cent.).

neutrality, condition of a state abstaining from participation in a war between other states, and maintaining an impartial attitude in dealing with belligerent states.

neutralization, in chemistry, interaction of acid and base to form a salt and water. Solution is said to be neutral when there are equal numbers of hydrogen and hydroxyl ions present.

Neutral Territory, *see* KUWAIT.

neutrino, uncharged elementary particle with zero rest mass. Existence predicted by Pauli in connection with beta-decay. First detected 1956; 2 different types exist, corresponding to electron and to muon.

neutron, uncharged elementary particle, with mass slightly greater than that of proton, found in nucleus of atom (except that of hydrogen). Outside nucleus, neutron decays into proton, electron and anti-neutrino (half-life *c* 13 mins.). Discovered by Chadwick (1932); neutrons play important role in nuclear fission.

neutron star, hypothetical state of sufficiently massive star which undergoes GRAVITATIONAL COLLAPSE. Gravitational forces within star would be sufficient to compress the matter composing star into immensely dense ball of neutrons a few kilometres wide. Pulsars are believed to be rapidly rotating neutron stars.

Nevada, state of W US. Area 286,299 sq km (110,540 sq mi); pop. 489,000; cap. Carson City. Mainly within arid Great Basin region; Sierra Nevada on W border. Livestock rearing esp. cattle, sheep; important mining (iron ore, copper, gold). Resort towns incl. Las Vegas, Reno (famous for gambling casinos). Ceded to US by Mexico (1848); developed with Comstock gold, silver strikes. Admitted to Union as 36th state (1864).

Nevers, town of C France, at confluence of Loire and Nièvre, cap. of Nièvre dept. Pop. 45,000. Iron and steel, engineering, pottery mfg. Former cap. of duchy of Nivernais. Romanesque church, 13th cent. cathedral, 15th cent. ducal palace.

Nevis, isl. of E West Indies, in Leeward Isls. Area 130 sq km (50 sq mi); pop. 46,000 (with St Kitts); chief town Charlestown. Cotton, sugar cane growing. Former British colony with St Kitts, Anguilla; became associate state 1967.

Nevis, Ben, mountain of Highland region, W Scotland, near Fort William. Highest in British Isles, 1342 m (4406 ft).

New Amsterdam, port of NE Guyana, at mouth of Berbice R. Pop. 15,000. Founded by Dutch (1740).

Newark, city of NE New Jersey, US; on Newark Bay and Passaic R. Pop. 382,000; state's largest city. Commercial, indust., shipping centre. Varied mfg. industs. Founded by Connecticut Puritans (1666). Photographic film first made here.

Newark-upon-Trent, mun. bor. of Nottinghamshire, C England. Pop. 25,000. Engineering; building materials mfg. Has 12th cent. castle where King John died (1216).

New Bedford, port of SE Massachusetts, US; on Buzzard's Bay. Pop. 102,000. Resort, fishing, varied mfg. industs. Hist. important whaling in 18th, 19th cents. Settled 1652.

Newbolt, Sir Henry John (1862-1938), English poet. Wrote patriotic, nautical verse, *eg Vitai Lampada* (1908, better known as 'There's a breathless hush in the close tonight'), *Drake's Drum* (1897), *Admirals All* (1898).

New Britain, isl. in Bismarck Archipelago; part of Papua New Guinea. Area *c* 36,600 sq km (14,100 sq mi); chief town Rabaul. Mountainous, with active volcanoes. Exports copra, timber.

New Brunswick, Maritime prov. of SE Canada. Area 72,481 sq km (27,985 sq mi); pop. 635,000; cap. Fredericton; chief city St John. Mainly low-lying; major river St John. Timber, coal, gas, h.e.p. resources. Agric. esp. dairy farming. Fishing in Gulf of St Lawrence, Bay of Fundy. French settlement (1604); passed to English (1714); separated from Nova Scotia (1784). Became one of 4 original provs. of Canada (1867).

Newburgh, city of SE New York, US; on Hudson R. Pop. 26,000. Textiles, varied metal product mfg. Hist. river port. Site of disbanding of Continental army. West Point military academy is nearby.

Newbury, mun. bor. of Berkshire, S England. Pop. 24,000. Market town; brewing, flour milling. Has famous racecourse; Cloth Hall (16th cent.) now museum. Two battles of Civil War fought here (1643,1644).

New Caledonia, overseas territ. of France, in SW Pacific Ocean. Comprises New Caledonia, Loyalty, and other isls. Area 18,700 sq km (7200 sq mi); pop. 122,000; cap. Nouméa. Produces copra, coffee, cotton; deposits of nickel, iron ore, chromium. Discovered (1774) by Cook; French from 1853, used initially as penal colony.

Newcastle, Thomas Pelham-Holles, Duke of (1693-1768), British politician, PM (1754-6, 1757–62). Secretary of state (1724–54). Headed Whig admin. dominated by William PITT during Seven Years War.

Newcastle, city of E New South Wales, Australia, at mouth of Hunter R. Pop. 250,000. Major coalmining, iron and steel mfg. centre; port, exports coal, wheat, wool. Has cultural centre, cathedral, univ.

Newcastle-under-Lyme, mun. bor. of Staffordshire, WC England. Pop. 77,000. In the Potteries; tile mfg. Keele Univ. (1962) nearby.

Newcastle upon Tyne, city of Tyne and Wear met. county, NE England, on R. Tyne. Pop. 222,000. Major indust. centre; coal, shipbuilding indust., chemicals mfg.; port. Has univ. (1963). Linked by tunnel, 5 bridges to Gateshead. On Hadrian's Wall; has castle (12th cent.); St Nicholas Cathedral (14th cent.).

New Church or **Church of the New Jerusalem,** religious body estab. by followers of SWEDENBORG. First public service held in London (1788). Each congregation administers itself but with annual conventions.

Newcomen, Thomas (1663-1729), English inventor. In partnership with Thomas Savery (*c* 1650-1715), devised steam engine (1705) used to pump water from mines.

New Deal, US domestic reform programme enacted (1933) during admin. of F.D. Roosevelt. Sought recovery from Depression by centralizing under federal govt., extensive economic and social reform and public works projects. Estab. numerous emergency organizations (*eg* National Recovery Administration), passed Social Security Act. Long-term projects incl. Tennessee Valley Authority.

New Delhi, *see* DELHI.

New Democratic Party (NDP), Canadian political party, founded (1961) as union of Co-operative Commonwealth Federation (CCF) and Canadian Labour Congress (CLC). CCF estab. (1932) to represent agrarian, labour and socialist aims, formed Saskatchewan govt. (1944-64). NDP attempted to widen programme. Strongest in W, winning (early 1970s) provincial govts. in Manitoba, Saskatchewan, British Columbia.

New Economic Policy (NEP), official economic policy (1921-8) of USSR. Introduced by Lenin to counter unrest. Abolished compulsory labour service, requisition of grain. Provided open market with fixed prices and limited private enterprise. Replaced by FIVE YEAR PLAN.

New England, region of NE US, incl. Maine, New Hampshire, Vermont, Massachusetts, Rhode Isl., Connecticut. Centre of pre-American Revolution activity.

New English Art Club, society of artists founded in 1886 to oppose conventionalism of the Royal Academy and to promote naturalism in the French manner. Members incl. Steer, Sargent, Sickert, Augustus John.

New Forest, woodland heath of Hampshire, S England. National park, area 376 sq km (145 sq mi). Agric.; livestock, ponies. Royal hunting forest of Saxons; William II killed here (1100).

Newfoundland, isl. and prov. of E Canada. Area 404,519 sq km (156,185 sq mi); pop. 522,000; cap. St John's. Prov. comprises isl. (area 106,810 sq km /42,734 sq mi) and mainland Labrador which are separated by Str. of Belle Isle. Timber, iron ore, h.e.p. resources. Fisheries (esp. cod) on Grand Banks. Discovered by John Cabot (1497); British sovereignty estab. 1714; jurisdiction over Labrador 1809. Voted to join Canada as 10th prov. (1949).

Newfoundland dog, breed of large powerful dog, developed in Newfoundland. Coat dense and oily; noted for swimming prowess. Stands *c* 71 cm/28 in. high at shoulder.

New Guinea, isl. of SW Pacific, N of Australia. Area *c* 830,000 sq km (320,000 sq mi). Mountainous, rising to over 5000 m (16,500 ft); tropical rain forests. Agric. economy, minerals largely unexploited. Divided into IRIAN JAYA (West Irian) and mainland of PAPUA NEW GUINEA.

Newham, bor. of E Greater London, England. Pop. 236,000. Created 1965 from East Ham, West Ham co. bors., parts of Barking, Woolwich.

New Hampshire, New England state of US. Area 24,097 sq km (9304 sq mi); pop. 738,000; cap. Concord; largest town Manchester. White Mts. in N.; many lakes, woods. Poultry, dairy farming; granite quarrying; timber, h.e.p. resources. Mfg. industs. concentrated in S. First colonized in 1620s. Under Massachusetts jurisdiction until 1679. One of original 13 colonies of US.

New Haven, port of S Connecticut, US; on Long Island Sound. Pop. 138,000. Varied mfg. industs. Settled as Puritan theocracy. Joint cap. with Hartford (1701-1875). Seat of Yale Univ. (1701).

New Hebrides, archipelago of SW Pacific Ocean, jointly admin. by UK and France. Area *c* 14,760 sq km (5700 sq mi); pop. 93,000; cap. Vila. Produces copra, tuna fish, manganese ore. Discovered (1606) by Portuguese; UK-French condominium estab. 1906.

New Ireland, isl. in Bismarck Archipelago; part of Papua New Guinea. Area *c* 8600 sq km (3300 sq mi). Mountainous. Coconuts chief crop.

New Jersey, state of NE US; on Atlantic. Area 20,295 sq km (7836 sq mi); pop. 7,168,000; cap. Trenton; chief cities Newark, Jersey City. Indust. concentrated in N; farmlands, resorts in S. Shipbuilding, oil refining; machinery, textiles, chemicals mfg. First settled by Dutch, Swedish colonists. English gained control 1664. One of original 13 colonies of US.

New London, port of SE Connecticut, US; at mouth of Thames R. Pop. 32,000. Hist. shipbuilding, whaling industs. in 19th cent. Has US Coast Guard Academy.

Newman, Barnett (1905-71), American painter. Known for his large abstract paintings, often in almost uniform colour, but divided by vertical stripe of another colour. Works incl. series *Stations of the Cross*.

Cardinal Newman

Newman, John Henry (1801-90), English churchman. Anglican vicar, joined KEBLE in writing *Tracts for the Times* (1833), inspiring OXFORD MOVEMENT. Became RC in 1845; created cardinal in 1879. Writings, noted for lucid prose style, incl. spiritual autobiog. *Apolologia pro Vita Sua* (1865), begun as defence against attacks by Charles Kingsley.

Newmarket, urban dist. of Suffolk, E England. Pop. 13,000. Horse racing, training centre from 17th cent.; hq. of Jockey Club.

New Mexico, state of SW US. Area 315,115 sq km (121,606 sq mi); pop. 1,016,000; cap. Santa Fé; largest city Albuquerque. Arid plateau crossed by Rio Grande, Pecos R. Agric., incl. cattle, sheep, grain farming; important mining (copper, petroleum, uranium, potash). Spanish colonies opposed by Apache, Pueblo Indians. US control estab. after Mexican War (1846-8); developed with Santa Fé Trail and railway. Admitted to Union as 47th state (1912).

New Orleans, port of SE Louisiana, US; on Mississippi R. Pop. 593,000; state's largest city. Major commercial, trade centre. Sugar, oil refining; petroleum, timber, iron and steel exports. Founded by French (1718); French-Creole cultural influence still remains. Hist. cotton, slave trade. Andrew Jackson defeated British here (1815). Seat of Tulane Univ. (1884). Has annual Mardi Gras festival; traditional home of jazz.

New Plymouth, city of W North Isl., New Zealand, on North Taranaki Bight. Pop. 34,000. Port, exports dairy produce (esp. cheese); food processing. Settled from 1841.

Newport, mun. bor and co. town of Isle of Wight, S England. Pop. 22,000. Market town. Has Parkhurst prison; Carisbrooke Castle nearby.

Newport, resort and naval base of SE Rhode Isl., US. Pop. 35,000. Settled 1639; hist. shipbuilding, molasses trade. Joint cap. with Providence until 1900. Has many fashionable 19th cent. mansions.

Newport, co. bor. and co. town of Gwent, SE Wales, on R. Usk. Pop. 112,000. Extensive docks (exports coal); iron, steel indust. Old church became cathedral in 1921.

Newport News, seaport of SE Virginia, US; on Hampton Roads (James R.). Pop. 138,000. Has shipyards, drydocks. Coal, petroleum, tobacco exports. Settled by Irish colonists (1621).

Newry, port of S Northern Ireland. Pop. 11,000. In former Co. Down. Linen, rope mfg.

Newry and Mourne, dist. of SE Northern Ireland. Area 910 sq km (351 sq mi); pop. 73,000. Created 1973, formerly part of Cos. Armagh, Down.

news agency, *see* NEWSPAPER.

New Siberian Islands, archipelago of USSR, between Laptev and East Siberian seas. Incl. Kotelny, Faddeyevsky and Novaya Sibir. Remains of mammoths found here; site of meteorological stations.

New South Wales, state of SE Australia. Area 801,300 sq km (309,400 sq mi); pop. 4,590,000; cap. Sydney. Incl. Lord Howe Isl. dependency. Comprises narrow coastal lowlands; tablelands and mountains of Great Dividing Range; W slopes and plains, incl. Murray-Darling basin. Mainly pastoral, agric. incl. dairying, wheat. Indust. centred in Newcastle, Wollongong, Sydney; h.e.p. in Snowy Mts. Australian E coast called New South Wales by Cook (1770); first colonized 1788. Became federal state (1901); ceded Australian Capital Territ. (1911), Jervis Bay (1915) to federal govt.

newspaper, publication usually intended to convey news, issued regularly, *eg* daily or weekly. Developed in 17th cent. with spread of printing. In late 19th cent. achieved mass appeal with growth of literacy, better printing techniques, and newspapers attempting literary merit were joined by sensationalist 'tabloids'. Increased interest in international news gave rise to news agencies, *eg* Associated Press, Reuters. Leading newspapers incl. British *The Times* and US *New York Times*.

Smooth newt (*Triturus vulgaris*)

newt, small lizard-like amphibian of salamander family, found in Europe, North America, Asia. Crested newt, *Triturus cristatus*, is largest European species.

New Testament, second part of the Christian Bible which deals with life and teachings of Jesus Christ (4 Gospels); growth of the Church (Acts of the Apostles); letters to individuals and newly-formed Christian communities (Epistles); vision of the struggle between the Church and its enemies (Revelation). Recorded in Greek in early Christian period.

Newton, Sir Isaac (1642-1727), English physicist, mathematician. Author of *Principia* (1687), in which he enunciated 'inverse square law' of gravitation and 3 laws of motion; application of these laws enabled him to explain planetary motion for 1st time. Made discoveries in optics, incl. fact that white light is composed of colours of spectrum; invented reflecting telescope. Developed differential

Sir Isaac Newton

New York City: Brooklyn Bridge

and integral calculus, independently of Leibnitz, as tool for studies of motion.

newton, SI unit of force; defined as force required to impart an acceleration of 1 m/sec^2 in mass of 1 kilogram.

Newton Abbot, urban dist. of Devon, SW England, at head of Teign estuary. Pop. 19,000. Market town. William III proclaimed king (1688) at St Leonard's Tower.

Newtonian mechanics, mechanics described by Newton's 3 laws of motion. Its predictions prove extremely successful for describing motion of bodies at ordinary velocities but must be modified to take account of relativistic effects for velocities close to that of light.

new town, planned urban community in UK, estab. under New Towns Act of 1946. Created, like GARDEN CITIES, to reduce congestion in major conurbations *eg* Greater London, Clydeside; some completely new, some extend existing towns. Examples incl. Basildon, England and Cwmbran, Wales.

Newtownabbey, town of EC Northern Ireland. Pop. 58,000. In former Co. Antrim; suburb of Belfast.

Newtownabbey, district; area 139 sq km (54 sq mi); pop. 72,000. Created 1973, formerly part of Co. Antrim.

Newtownards, town of EC Northern Ireland, on Strangford Lough. Pop. 15,000. Linen, hosiery mfg. Has 13th cent. monastery.

New Westminster, seaport of SW British Columbia, Canada; on Fraser R. Pop. 43,000. Fishing, food processing industs. Founded 1859; was colonial cap. until 1866.

New World, name used for the continent of America, *ie* North, Central and South America.

New York, state of NE US, incl. Long Isl. in SE. Area 128,402 sq km (49,576 sq mi); pop. 18,241,000; cap. Albany; chief cities Buffalo, New York, Rochester. Appalachian Mts. in C; St Lawrence valley in N; crossed by Erie Canal, Mohawk, Hudson rivers. Agric. esp. dairy farming, fruit, cereal growing. Food produce, clothing, machinery mfg., printing and publishing. Indust., shipping concentrated in New York City. E region explored by Hudson (1609), settled by Dutch as New Amsterdam; taken by English (1664). Battleground during Revolution. One of original 13 colonies of US.

New York City, in SE New York state, US; major port on Hudson R. Pop. 7,896,000; largest city in US. Comprises bors. Bronx, Brooklyn, Manhattan, Queen's, Richmond (Staten Isl.). Rail, air, shipping terminal. Varied mfg. industs. esp. consumer goods. Financial centre (Wall Street); major US trade centre. Manhattan Isl. settled by Dutch (1625); seized by English (1664); state cap. until 1797. Harbour dominated by Statue of Liberty; has UN hq.,

Empire State Building. Notable areas Chinatown, Greenwich Village, Harlem. Seat of 5 univs. incl. Columbia (1754).

New Zealand

New Zealand, country in SW Pacific Ocean. Area 268,100 sq km (103,500 sq mi); pop. 2,860,000; cap. Wellington. Comprises North, South, Stewart, and several smaller isls. Mountain ranges run NE - SW, rising to Mt. Cook in Southern Alps; many fertile valleys, coastal lowlands, *eg* Canterbury Plains. Economy based on sheep farming, dairying; timber indust., h.e.p.; food processing, engineering in towns. Ancestors of Maoris arrived 10th cent.; Tasman was 1st white man to reach New Zealand (1642). Under UK rule from 1840; Maori freedom guaranteed by Waitangi Treaty, but land disputes led to series of wars after 1843. Gold discoveries from 1861 accelerated settlement. Dominion from 1907; independent 1931. Member of British Commonwealth.

Nexö, Martin Andersen, see ANDERSEN NEXÖ, MARTIN.

Ney, Michel (1769-1815), French army officer. Won victory of Elchingen (1805), and commanded rearguard in retreat from Moscow (1812). He supported Louis XVIII after Napoleon's abdication but changed side again to lead Old Guard at Waterloo (1815). Condemned as traitor and shot.

Nez Percé, North American Indian tribe of Penutian linguistic stock. Named for custom of a few members of tribe of wearing nose pendants. Fishers, food gatherers in 17th cent., adopted buffalo hunting after introduction of horse (*c* 1700). Now on reservation in Idaho.

Niagara Falls, resort of NW New York state, US; on Niagara R. Pop. 86,000. Indust. based on h.e.p. from Falls. Town burned by British in war of 1812.

Niagara Falls, famous waterfalls on Canada-US boundary; on Niagara R. Forms part of border between Ontario and New York State. Goat Isl. separates Canadian (Horseshoe) Falls and American Falls. Popular tourist area. H.e.p. supplies. Circumvented by Welland Ship Canal.

Marshal Ney

Chief Joseph of Nez Percé tribe

Niamey, cap. of Niger, on R. Niger. Pop. 102,000. Admin., commercial centre; trade in livestock, hides, groundnuts; bricks, cement mfg. Terminus of trans-Sahara motor route.

Nibelungenlied (The Lay of the Nibelungs), medieval German heroic epic written c 1200 from older sources. First part tells legend of Siegfried, his love for Kriemhild, wooing of Brunhild on behalf of Burgundian king Gunther, and death at hands of Hagen; second part deals with historical encounter between Burgundians (Nibelungs) and Huns. Wagner used first part for opera *Ring of the Nibelung.*

Nicaea (modern *Isnik*), ancient city of Asia Minor, in NW Turkey. Founded in 4th cent. BC as Antigonia, was Roman trade centre. Scene of ecumenical council of AD 325 called by Constantine I.

Nicaragua, republic of Central America. Area 128,410 sq km (49,579 sq mi); pop. 1,975,000; cap. Managua. Language: Spanish. Religion: RC. Mountain ranges and interior plateaux flanked by Pacific, Caribbean coasts. Main crops incl. cotton, coffee, sugar; exports timber, gold. Under Spanish rule (1522-1821); member of Central American Federation (1825-38). Earthquake damage (1972).

Nicaragua, Lake, in SW Nicaragua, largest lake in Central America. Area 8000 sq km (3089 sq mi). Commercial, sporting fisheries (esp. tuna, shark).

Nice (Ital. *Nizza*), city of Provence, SE France, on Côte d'Azur, cap. of Alpes-Maritimes dept. Pop. 322,000. Port, resort, perfume and soap mfg., fruit and flowers (has 'battle of flowers' festival). Greek colony of *Nikaia*, founded 3rd cent. BC. Ceded by Sardinia to France in 1860. Cathedral, observatory. Birthplace of Garibaldi.

Nicene Creed, statement formulated by Council of Nicaea (325); modified by 1st Council of Constantinople (381) giving orthodox doctrine of the Trinity. *See* CREED.

Nicholas, St (*fl* 4th cent.), Lycian churchman, bishop of Myra. Popular saint in Eastern churches, patron of children, mariners, pawnbrokers (his emblem is 3 golden balls). Origin of Santa Claus.

Nicholas I (1796-1855), tsar of Russia (1825-55). Crushed Decembrist revolt (1825) which arose over his succession. Ruled autocratically, suppressing dissent; introduced secret police. Militarist policies helped precipitate Crimean War (1853).

Nicholas II

Nicholas II (1868-1918), tsar of Russia (1894-1917). Suppressed Revolution of 1905 which followed defeat in Russo-Japanese war; later came under influence of RASPUTIN. Maintained autocratic rule of predecessors. Forced to abdicate after failures in WWI and held captive during Russian Revolution. He and his family said to have been shot at Ekaterinburg.

Nicholson, Jack (1937-   ), American film actor, director. Best known as actor, esp. for *One Flew Over the Cuckoo's Nest* (1976); also directed and appeared in *Five Easy Pieces* (1970).

Nicholson, Sir William (1872-1949), English painter. Collaborated with James Pryde in designing posters under name of 'The Beggarstaff Brothers'; known for woodcuts and still lifes. His son, **Ben Nicholson** (1894-   ), was influenced by cubism and Mondrian. Works are characterized by austere geometric designs and restricted colour range.

nickel (Ni), magnetic metallic element; at. no. 28, at. wt. 58.71. Extremely resistant to corrosion; used in numerous alloys, as a catalyst, in electro-plating, *etc.*

Nicklaus, Jack William (1940-   ), American golfer. Has won more major championships than any other golfer; titles incl. 2 US Amateurs, 3 US Opens, 2 British Opens, 5 Masters and 4 PGAs.

Nicobar Islands, see ANDAMAN.

Nicolai, Otto (1810-49), German composer. Best known for comic opera *The Merry Wives of Windsor.* Founded concerts (1842) which were forerunners of Vienna Philharmonic Orchestra.

Nicolson, Sir Harold George (1886-1968), British writer, diplomat. Known for biographies of poets, statesmen and *Diaries and Letters* (3 vols., 1966-8, edited by Nigel Nicolson).

Nicosia: part of the old city

Nicosia (Gk. *Levkosia*, Turk. *Lefkosha*), cap. of Cyprus. Pop. 117,000. Commercial centre, agric. market. Produces leather, textiles, cigarettes. Has 16th cent. walls built by Venetians. Scene of fighting in 1960 and during Turkish invasion (1974).

nicotiana, genus of American and Australian herbs and shrubs of nightshade family. Large leaves, whitish or purple flowers. Some species are source of nicotine. *Nicotiana tabacum* is source of commercial TOBACCO.

nicotine, colourless water soluble alkaloid found in leaves of TOBACCO plant. Extremely poisonous, used as basis of insecticides.

Niebuhr, Reinhold (1892-1971), American theologian, social historian. Works incl. *Moral Man and Immoral Society* (1932), reflect pessimistic vision of society ruled by self-interest.

Nielsen, Carl August (1865-1931), Danish composer. Works characterized by progressive tonality, esp. in his 6 symphonies. Other compositions incl. opera *Saul and David,* concertos, chamber music.

Niemen, *see* NEMAN.

Niemeyer, Oscar (1907-   ), Brazilian architect. Worked with Le Corbusier on building of Ministry of Education in Rio de Janeiro (1937-43). Directed planning of Brasilia (1950-60).

Niemöller, Martin (1892-   ), German Protestant churchman. At first sympathetic to Nazism, subsequently preached against Hitler's creation of a 'German Christian church'. Imprisoned during WWII.

Nietzsche

Nietzsche, Friedrich Wilhelm (1844-1900), German philosopher. Most influential work, *Thus Spake Zarathustra* (1883), characterized by passionate individualism, calls for race of 'supermen' to replace 'slave morality' of Christianity. Other works incl. *The Birth of Tragedy* (1872), *Beyond Good and Evil* (1886).

Niger, republic of W Africa. Area 1,267,000 sq km (489,000 sq mi); pop. 4,476,000; cap. Niamey. Language: French. Religion: Islam. Sahara desert, Aïr Mts. in N, semidesert in S; drained by R. Niger. Produces groundnuts, cotton, animal products, uranium ore. Territ. of French West Africa from 1904, became independent 1960.

Niger, river of W Africa. Flows *c* 4180 km (2600 mi) from Guinea via Mali, Niger, entering Gulf of Guinea by large delta in S Nigeria. Main tributary is R. Benue. Irrigation, h.e.p., *eg* Kainji Dam, N of Jebba, opened 1969.

Niger-Congo, vast branch of Niger-Kordofanian language family. Languages within it spoken throughout S, C Africa and most of W Africa south of Sahara. Subdivided into W Atlantic, Mande, Gur or Voltaic, Kwa, Benue-Congo and Andamawa-Eastern groups.

Nigeria

Nigeria, federal republic of W Africa, on Gulf of Guinea. Area 925,000 sq km (357,000 sq mi); pop. 61,270,000; cap. Lagos. Main languages: Hausa, English. Main religions: Islam, Christianity, native. Chief tribes Fulani, Hausa, Ibo, Yoruba. Flat semi-desert in N, savannah plateaux in C, tropical forest in S; main rivers Niger, Benue. Agric. products incl. palm oil, cocoa, groundnuts, cotton, rubber. Major petroleum exporter, found in Niger delta and offshore. Colony and protect. estab. (1914) by merging of Northern and Southern Nigeria and Lagos. Four regions created (1954); independent 1960, republic 1963. Military govt. imposed (1965); 12 states replaced regions (1967). Secession of Eastern Region (mainly Ibo) as Biafra caused civil war (1967-70). Member of British Commonwealth, UN.

nighthawk, *see* NIGHTJAR.

Nightingale, Florence (1820-1910), English nurse, hospital administrator. Took 38 nurses to Crimea (1854); estab. hospital units at Scutari and Balaklava. Greatly reduced death rate among army casualties by imposing high standards of hygiene and care. Founded (1860) nurses' training institution at St Thomas's Hospital, London.

nightingale, *Luscinia megarhynchos,* small migratory songbird of thrush family, with brown upper-parts, whitish brown under-parts. Found in woods of Europe, Asia, N Africa. Male noted for singing at night.

nightjar or **goatsucker,** any of Caprimulgidae family of small nocturnal birds. Short bill and wide mouth; feeds on insects captured in air. European nightjar, *Caprimulgus europeaus,* brown with white marks on tail. Nighthawks form New World subfamily Chordeilinae; species incl. common nighthawk, *Chordeiles minor,* of North America.

nightshade, any plant of genera *Solanum* and *Atropa* mainly native to South America and subtropical regions. Black nightshade, *S. nigrum,* has white flowers followed by black berries. Woody nightshade (bittersweet), *S. dulcamara,* has red berries. Extremely poisonous deadly nightshade, *A. belladonna,* has black berries and yields the alkaloid atropine which reduces action of parasympathetic nerves. Formerly used cosmetically to dilate pupils of eyes.

nihilism, in political history, 19th cent. Russian revolutionary movement. Rejected all estab. institutions,

Nightingale

took terrorist action, *eg* arson, assassination; culminated in tsar's murder (1881). Term (from Latin, *nihil* = nothing) coined by Turgenev in *Fathers and Sons*. In philosophy, denial of any basis for knowledge or truth; rejection of beliefs in morality, religion, *etc.*

Niigata, seaport of Japan, on W coast of Honshu isl. Pop. 384,000. Exports oil; machinery, chemical and textile mfg.

Nijinsky

Nijinsky, Vaslav (1890-1950), Russian ballet dancer. One of most famous of Diaghilev's dancers, created leading roles in *L'Après-midi d'un faune*, *Spectre de la rose*. Famed for graceful athleticism; career cut short by insanity.

Nijmegen (Ger. *Nimwegen*, Fr. *Nimègue*), city of E Netherlands, on R. Waal. Pop. 150,000. Inland port, with canal link to R. Maas; engineering, chemicals. RC univ. (1923). Scene of Treaty of Nijmegen (1678) ending Dutch wars. Remains of Charlemagne's palace (777) in Valkhof park.

Nike, in Greek myth, goddess of victory, daughter of Pallas and Styx. Usually represented as winged, carrying wreath or palm branch. Presided over all contests, athletic and military; esp. popular after Persian Wars. Identified by Romans with Victoria.

Nikolayev, seaport of USSR, SW Ukrainian SSR; at confluence of Southern Bug and Ingul. Pop. 353,000. Naval base; exports grain, metal ore; shipbuilding, flour milling.

Nikopol, town of N. Bulgaria, on R. Danube. Pop. 6000. Scene of Christian defeat by Turks (1396) during Balkan conquest.

Nile

Nile, world's longest river, in NE Africa. Flows *c* 6690 km (4160 mi) from farthest headstream, R. Luvironza (Burundi), to Mediterranean Sea. Nile proper (*c* 3015 km/1875 mi long) formed at Khartoum by union of Blue Nile (rises in Ethiopian Highlands) and White Nile (formed at L. No, Sudan, by jct. of Bahr-el-Ghazal and Bahr-el-Jebel). Drops 285 m (935 ft) in 6 cataracts between Khartoum and Aswan; joined by R. Atbara. Below Cairo enters wide delta, reaches sea via Rosetta (W), Damietta (E) channels. Seasonal flooding, due to Blue Nile, used for irrigation from *c* 4000 BC; irrigation, h.e.p. developed 20th cent. by series of dams (*eg* Aswan, Sennar, Jebel Aulia) and barrages. Nile valley was focus of ancient Egyptian civilization; its source legendary until 19th cent. explorations by Bruce, Speke, Stanley.

nilgai, *Boselaphus tragocamelus,* largest Indian antelope, standing *c* 1.2 m/4 ft at shoulder. Male is bluish-grey with short straight horns and black mane. Also called blue bull.

Nilo-Saharan, African language family, second to Niger-Kordofanian in size. Divided into 6 branches: Songhai (Mali); Saharan; Maban (E of Lake Chad); Furian (Sudan); Coman (Ethiopia and Sudan); CHARI-NILE.

Nîmes (anc. *Nemausus*), city of Languedoc, S France, cap. of Gard dept. Pop. 123,000. Tourist centre; wine, fruit, grain trade. Founded by Greek colonists; important Roman remains incl. arena, temples, nearby Pont du Gard aqueduct.

Nimitz, Chester William (1885-1966), American admiral. Commanded the US Pacific Fleet after the attack on Pearl Harbor (1941). He became director of naval operations in 1945.

Nimrud, remains of ancient town on N bank of Tigris, S of Mosul, Iraq. Founded 13th cent. BC, became Assyrian cap. under Assurnasirpal II (883-859 BC). Destroyed by Medes (612 BC). Excavated by LAYARD; identified with biblical Calah.

Nineveh, ruins of N Iraq, on R. Tigris. Cap. of ancient Assyrian empire (*fl* 9th-7th cent. BC).

Ninghsia-Hui, auton. region of NC China. Area *c* 276,000 sq km (106,000 sq mi); pop. (est.) 2,000,000; cap. Yinchuan. Mainly desert, rough grazing on Inner Mongolian plateau; agric. in SE near Hwang Ho. Largely pop. by Mongols.

Ningpo, formerly Ninghsien, town of Chekiang prov., E China. Pop. 350,000. Fishing port; textile mfg., fish processing. One of 5 original treaty ports (1842).

Niobe, in Greek myth, queen of Thebes and daughter of Tantalus. Boasted about her many children compared to Leto, whereupon Artemis and Apollo (the only 2 children of Leto), killed them all. Turned by Zeus into a stone column which wept perpetually.

niobium or **columbium** (Nb), rare metallic element; at. no. 41, at. wt. 92.91. Used in alloys which are resistant to high temperatures.

Nippur, ancient Sumerian city in Mesopotamia; religious centre for worship of god Enlil. Excavations revealed cuneiform tablets which are major source of information on Sumerian culture.

nirvana, in Buddhism and some forms of Hinduism, state of annihilation of the worldly self and thus of being free of the cycle of rebirth.

Niš (anc. *Naïssus*), city of Serbia, SE Yugoslavia, on R. Nišava. Pop. 133,000. Major railway centre, engineering, tobacco. Held by Turks 1386-1878. Medieval fortress. Birthplace of Constantine the Great.

Nishapur, market town of NE Iran. Pop. 33,000. Famous turquoise mines nearby. Birthplace and burial place of Omar Khayyam.

Nishinomiya, town of Japan, on Osaka Bay, SW Honshu isl. Pop. 377,000. Famous for brewing of rice wine (sake).

Niterói, residential town of SE Brazil, cap. of Rio de Janeiro state; on E shore of Guanabara Bay. Pop. 324,000. Shipbuilding, textile mfg. Popular tourist resort. Has ferry link with Rio de Janeiro.

nitrates, salts or esters of nitric acid, the salts being soluble in water. Nitrates in soil are source of nitrogen, needed by plants for growth; produced from nitrogen by bacteria. Metallic nitrates used to make explosives, as fertilizers and in chemical synthesis.

nitric acid (HNO_3), colourless corrosive liquid; powerful oxidizing agent. Obtained by catalytic oxidation of ammonia. Used in manufacture of fertilizers, explosives and in organic synthesis.

nitrocellulose or **cellulose nitrate,** any of various esters of nitric acid and cellulose, formed by action of mixture of nitric and sulphuric acids on cellulose. Used to make explosives (guncotton), plastics and lacquers.

nitrogen (N), colourless gaseous element, chemically inactive; at. no. 7, at. wt. 14.01. Forms $c\,4/5$ of atmosphere; occurs in Chile saltpetre (sodium nitrate) and saltpetre deposits. Essential constituent of living organisms, occurring in proteins and nucleic acids. Used in manufacture of ammonia (Haber process).

nitrogen cycle, cycle of natural processes by which nitrogen in atmosphere is made available to living organisms. Inorganic nitrogen compounds in soil are absorbed by plants and converted to proteins and nucleic acids; animals absorb proteins by eating plants. Nitrogen compounds re-enter soil by plant decay or as animal excreta; they are broken down by bacteria in soil into form suitable for plant utilization.

nitrogen fixation, conversion of atmospheric nitrogen into nitrates, which can be used by plants, by action of bacteria or blue-green algae. Bacteria are found in soil or in nodules of certain leguminous plants (peas, clover, *etc*). Part of NITROGEN CYCLE.

nitroglycerin[e], thick pale yellow oily liquid, prepared by action of concentrated sulphuric and nitric acids on glycerol. Explodes when struck; used to make DYNAMITE, cordite, *etc.*

nitrous oxide or **laughing gas** (N_2O), colourless sweet-tasting gas, used as light anaesthetic in dentistry. Obtained by heating ammonium nitrate.

Nixon, Richard Milhous (1913-), American statesman, president (1969-74). Republican vice-president (1953-61) under Eisenhower. Narrowly lost 1960 election to Kennedy. Retired from politics after failure to win governorship of California (1962). Comeback culminated in successful bid for presidency (1968). Terms marked by US withdrawal from Vietnam, rapprochement with China, economic recession. Investigations into 'Watergate affair' after 1972 revealed widespread govt. corruption in which Nixon was involved. Threatened with impeachment, he resigned; pardoned by successor, President Ford.

Nizhni Novgorod, *see* GORKY.

Nizhni Tagil, town of USSR, W Siberian RSFSR. Pop. 383,000. Metallurgical centre, based on nearby iron ore; produces copper, gold, chemicals.

Nkomo, Joshua (1917-), Rhodesian politician. President of Zimbabwe African People's Union (1961-). Imprisoned (1963-4). Placed under restriction (1964-74). On

Richard Nixon

release, entered into constitutional negotiations with Ian Smith.

Nkrumah, Kwame (1909-72), Ghanaian political leader. PM of Ghana (formerly Gold Coast) at its independence (1957), became 1st president (1960) of republic. Rule marked by extravagance and self-glorification. Overthrown by army coup (1966), went into exile in Guinea.

no or **noh play,** highly stylized form of Japanese theatre. Plays mostly written in 15th cent., *c* 800 extant. Characteristic features incl. use of chorus, wooden masks, elaborate costumes, many symbolic allusions, formal acting style using dance to express emotion, and the 'freezing' of characters in elaborate tableaux.

Noah, in OT, builder of the ark which saved human and animal life from the Flood. His sons Shem, Ham and Japheth became the eponymous ancestors of the biblical races of mankind.

Alfred Nobel

Nobel, Alfred Bernhard (1833-96), Swedish chemist, philanthropist. Invented dynamite (1866) and perfected other explosives. Bequeathed fund from which annual prizes were to be awarded for work in physics, chemistry, physiology and medicine, literature, and for work in cause of peace. Awards made annually since 1901.

nobelium (No), transuranic element; at. no. 102, mass no. of most stable isotope 255. Discovered (1957) at Nobel Institute, Stockholm, by nuclear bombardment of curium.

noble gases, *see* INERT GASES.

noble metals, metals such as gold, platinum or silver which resist corrosion and are chemically inactive.

Noctiluca, *see* DINOFLAGELLATA.

nocturne, short lyrical piece usually for piano; introduced by JOHN FIELD and much used by Chopin.

Noguchi, Hideyo (1876-1928), Japanese bacteriologist. Discovered (1913) spirochaete *Treponema pallidum* which causes syphilis. Worked on snake venoms and yellow fever.

Nolan, Sidney (1917-), Australian artist. Known for his paintings of the Australian scene in deliberately naive style; esp. concerned with myth surrounding Ned Kelly, whom he depicted clad in home-made armour in outback landscapes.

Nolde, Emil, orig. Hansen (1867-1956), German expressionist painter. Painting is characterized by violent colour, simplified form and influence of primitive art; finest works are landscapes and religious subjects.

nomad, member of a tribe of people having no permanent home, moving about constantly in search of food, pasture *etc.* Characteristic of C Asian herdsmen, Australian aborigines, African bushmen, Eskimos, some North American Indian tribes.

Nome, town of W Alaska, US; on S Seward penin. Pop. *c* 2000. Transport and tourist centre; Eskimo handicraft industs. Settled in 1898 gold rush.

nominalism, in philosophy, doctrine first current in medieval SCHOLASTICISM that universal concepts (*eg* the concept of 'table' rather than a particular table) have no general reality and are merely conveniences of classification. Concomitant of most empiricist and materialist philosophies. Opposed to REALISM.

Non-aggression Pact (Aug. 1939), secret agreement between USSR and Germany to divide Poland and E Europe into spheres of Soviet and German influence, and to foil Anglo-French moves to involve USSR in containing German aggression. Ended with German attack on USSR in 1941.

nonconformist, *see* DISSENTER.

non-Euclidean geometry, branch of geometry based on postulates different from those of Euclid. Usually Euclid's 5th or parallel postulate is rejected (that through any point only 1 line can be drawn parallel to another line). Invented independently by Lobachevski, Bolyai and Gauss.

Nonjurors, English and Scottish clergymen who, after Revolution of 1688, refused to take oath of allegiance to William and Mary. Incl. archbishop of Canterbury, 7 bishops and many others.

Nootka, North American Indian tribe of Algonquian linguistic stock, living on W coast of Vancouver Isl. in long communal wooden houses. Depend largely on fishing and whaling. Name is often given to the Aht Confederacy of *c* 20 tribes of Northwest Coast area.

Nord, region and dept. of NE France, on Belgian border. Largely low-lying, drained by Escaut (Scheldt) and Sambre, many canals. Main towns Lille, Cambrai, Douai. Incl. part of Franco-Belgian coalfield; coalmining, textile and engineering industs. Battlefield in both WWs.

Nordenskjöld, Nils Adolf Erik, Baron (1832-1901), Swedish explorer and geologist, b. Finland. Navigated Northeast Passage (1878-80) in ship *Vega*; made several expeditions to Spitsbergen and Greenland, mapping large areas.

Nördlingen, town of SC West Germany. Pop. 14,000. Scene of major battles in 1634 (Imperial victory) and 1645 (French victory) in Thirty Years War.

Norfolk, Dukes of, *see* HOWARD, THOMAS.

Norfolk, county of E England. Area 5355 sq km (2068 sq mi); pop. 624,000; co. town Norwich. Flat, low-lying; fertile soils; rich agric., poultry; fishing. In E, Norfolk Broads, area of shallow lakes, rivers; yachting.

Norfolk, seaport of SE Virginia, US; on Hampton Roads (Elizabeth R.). Pop. 308,000. Naval base (Atlantic fleet hq.), shipyards; coal, tobacco exports. Founded 1682.

Norfolk Island, territ. of Australia, in S Pacific Ocean *c* 1600 km (1000 mi) NE of Sydney. Area 34 sq km (13 sq mi). Tourist resort; whaling; exports fruit. Discovered (1774) by Cook; penal colony until 1855. Transferred from New South Wales to federal govt. 1913.

Norilsk, town of USSR, N Siberian RSFSR. Pop. 145,000. Nickel mining centre; copper, platinum, cobalt refining.

Norman architecture, form of Romanesque developed in Normandy and England (11th-12th cents.). Characterized

Norman arch in church at Kilpeck, Herefordshire

by massive construction, semi-circular arches, barrel vaults. Keep (White Tower) of Tower of London and Durham Cathedral (1st to use rib vaulting) are examples.

Normandy (*Normandie*), region and former prov. of N France, hist. cap. Rouen. Low-lying, drained by Seine, Eure, Orne: incl. Cotentin penin. Main towns Rouen, Le Havre, Cherbourg. Agric. (cattle, dairying, apples), fishing, tourism. Name derives from Norsemen who invaded area in 9th cent.; Normandy conquered England (1066), colonized S Italy (11th-12th cent.). Part of France from 1450. Scene of Allied invasion in 1944.

Normans, descendants of Viking settlers who conquered N France (Normandy) in 9th cent. Under Duke William, conquered England (1066), displaced Anglo-Saxon nobility, reformed law and social system. Also conquered S Italy and Sicily (11th cent.), on pretext of expelling Byzantine Greeks and Arabs.

Norns, FATES of Norse myth; determined destiny of gods and men. Usually represented as Urth (past), Verthandi (present), Skuld (future), who spun and wove web of life.

Norris, Frank (1870-1902), American novelist. Known for naturalistic novels incl. *McTeague* (1899) and 2 vols. of projected trilogy on wheat trade, *The Octopus* (1901), *The Pit* (1903).

Norrköping, town of SE Sweden, on inlet of Baltic Sea. Pop. 91,000. Port; textile centre; paper mfg.; h.e.p.

Norse, *see* GERMANIC LANGUAGES, OLD NORSE LITERATURE.

Norsemen, *see* VIKINGS.

Norse mythology, *see* TEUTONIC MYTHOLOGY.

North, Frederick North, 8th Baron (1732–92), British politician, PM (1770-82). Premiership was dominated by influence of George III; carried out taxation policies which led to American Revolution (1776). Resigned after British surrender.

North, Sir Thomas (*c* 1535-*c* 1601), English translator. Best known for translation of Plutarch's *Lives* (1579, from French version by Amyot) used as source by Shakespeare.

North Africa campaign, conflict (1940-3) during WWII along Egypt-Libya coastal area for control of Mediterranean and Suez Canal. Began with Italian attempts to capture Egypt. German forces under Rommel (Afrika Korps) drove British back into Egypt; advance was halted by British victory under Montgomery at El Alamein (1942). Germans retreated into Tunisia and eventually surrendered to Allies (May, 1943).

Northallerton, urban dist. and co. town of North Yorkshire, N England. Pop. 7000. Agric. market. Nearby is site of Battle of the Standard where English defeated Scots (1138).

North America, third largest continent; in W hemisphere; comprises US (incl. Alaska), Canada, Mexico. Area *c* 24,346,000 sq km (9,400,000 sq mi); pop. 327,000,000. Central plain separates E mountain ranges (Laurentian, Appalachian) from W Rocky Mts. River systems incl. Mississippi, St Lawrence-Great Lakes. Highest point Mt. McKinley. Climate varies from Arctic in N to subtropical in S. Varied agric., pastoral in plains; extensive mineral resources. Indigenous Indian pop.; Spanish settlers followed by French, British and some Germans. Thirteen British colonies gained independence after American Revolution (1776-83). Mexico gained independence from Spain in 1821. Canada settled by traders, ceded to Britain by France (1763); confederation formed 1867. Pop. now mainly of European descent with Negro, Indian minorities.

Northamptonshire, county of C England. Area 2367 sq km (914 sq mi); pop. 488,000. Wheat growing, cattle, sheep rearing; iron ore; fox hunting. Co. town **Northampton,** on R. Nene. Pop. 128,000. Footwear mfg. Has round church (12th cent.).

North Atlantic Drift, warm ocean current of N Atlantic Ocean. Continuation of Gulf Stream, flows NE from off Newfoundland. Ameliorates W European winters.

North Atlantic Treaty Organization (NATO), defence force estab. 1952 as result of pact (1949) between US, Britain, Canada, France, Benelux, Denmark, Norway, Iceland, Italy and Portugal. Later additions were Greece (1952), Turkey (1952), West Germany (1954).

North Bay, town of SE Ontario, Canada; on L. Nipissing. Pop. 49,000. Railway jct., lumber industs.

North Borneo, see SABAH.

North Brabant, prov. of S Netherlands. Area 4929 sq km (1903 sq mi); cap. 's Hertogenbosch. Textiles, electrical industs. Hist. links with N Belgium (*see* BRABANT).

North Canadian, river, see CANADIAN.

North Cape (*Nordkapp*), headland of Norway, on Magerøy Isl. Popularly taken as most N point of Europe, lat. 71° 10' N.

North Carolina, state of E US; on Atlantic. Area 136,200 sq km (52,590 sq mi); pop. 5,082,000; cap. Raleigh; largest city Charlotte. Coastal swamp rises to Piedmont and Appalachians in W (MT. MITCHELL, highest mountain in E US). Tobacco, cotton, peanut growing, mica quarrying. Settled 1650 by Virginia colonists. One of original 13 colonies of US. Joined South during Civil War.

Northcliffe, Alfred Charles William Harmsworth, Viscount (1865-1922), British journalist, publisher. With his brother Harold, later Lord ROTHERMERE, estab. world's largest newspaper enterprise, the Amalgamated Press. He founded the *Daily Mail* (1896), and *Daily Mirror* (1903), innovating use of attractive lay-out, esp. through pictures. Acquired and revived *The Times* (1908). Influential in politics, esp. in WWI.

North Dakota, state of NC US; on Canada border. Area 183,000 sq km (70,670 sq mi) pop. 618,000; cap. Bismarck. Mainly plains crossed by Missouri R. Barley, wheat, livestock farming; quarrying. Explored by French; acquired by US in Louisiana Purchase (1803). Admitted to Union, jointly with South Dakota, as 39th state (1889).

North Down, dist. of E Northern Ireland. Area 74 sq km (28 sq mi); pop. 54,000. Created 1973, formerly part of Co. Down.

Northeast Frontier Agency, see ASSAM.

Northeast Passage, passage from North Sea to Pacific, along N coast of Europe and Asia. Explored 16th-18th cent.; first navigated 1878-9 by Swede Nils Nordenskjöld. Soviet shipping route, kept open by icebreakers.

Northern Ireland, constituent part of UK. Area 14,146 sq km (5462 sq mi); pop. 1,525,000; cap. Belfast. Comprises former Cos. Antrim, Armagh, Down, Fermanagh, Londonderry, Tyrone (most of ancient ULSTER); divided into 26 dists. (1973). Agric. (cereal, potatoes, livestock); fishing; industs. incl. shipbuilding, textiles (esp. linen). Estab. 1921

after IRELAND partitioned; continuing Protestant-RC conflict led to suspension of Stormont govt. 1972. 'Power-sharing' attempted (1973-4) but direct rule from Westminster restored.

Northern Rhodesia, see ZAMBIA.

Northern Territory, territ. of N Australia. Area 1,349,000 sq km (521,000 sq mi); pop. 86,000, incl. *c* 21,000 aborigines; territ. cap. Darwin. Plains, basins in N, mountain ranges in S; tropical monsoon climate in N, arid in S. Beef cattle raising; mining, esp. copper, manganese, bauxite, iron, lead. Fifteen aboriginal reservations, largest of which is Arnhem Land. Became federal territ. 1911; divided into Central and Northern Australia 1926-31.

North Holland, see HOLLAND.

North Island, one of main isls. of New Zealand, separated from South Isl. by Cook Str. Area 114,690 sq km (44,280 sq mi); pop. 2,051,000; main cities Wellington, Auckland. C plateau has active volcanoes, hot springs, geysers, and L. TAUPO. Dairy cattle and sheep in fertile valleys, coastal lowlands.

North Korea, see KOREA.

North Ossetia, auton. republic of S European RSFSR, USSR; on N slopes of Caucasus. Area *c* 8030 sq km (3090 sq mi); pop. 552,000; cap. Ordzhonikidze. Mountainous; fruit, grain, cotton grown in valleys. Metal ore (lead, zinc) and oil deposits. Region annexed by Russia by 1806. **South Ossetia** is auton. region of Georgian SSR on S slopes of Caucasus.

North Pole, northern end of Earth's axis; first reached (1909) by Peary. Distinct from north magnetic pole, position towards which needle of magnetic compass points and location of which varies with time.

North Rhine-Westphalia (*Nordrhein-Westfalen*), state of W West Germany. Area *c* 33,930 sq km (13,100 sq mi); cap. Düsseldorf. Highly indust. area (incl. RUHR), main products iron, steel, chemicals, textiles. Formed 1946 from Westphalia, part of Rhine prov., Lippe state.

North Riding, see YORKSHIRE, England.

North Sea, between Great Britain and NW Europe, *c* 965 km (600 mi) long N-S, up to 645 km (400 mi) wide. Shallows incl. DOGGER BANK. Fishing grounds; natural gas, oil deposits off Norway, Scotland. Major ports on coasts *eg* Rotterdam.

North Star, see POLARIS.

Northumberland, John Dudley, Duke of (*c* 1502-53), English statesman. As chief minister to Edward VI, he tried to alter succession in favour of his daughter-in-law, Lady Jane Grey, a Protestant, thus excluding Mary Tudor, a Catholic. His plot, lacking popular support, failed; executed for treason.

Northumberland, county of NE England. Area 5033 sq km (1943 sq mi); pop. 283,000; co. town Newcastle. Cheviot Hills (N), Pennines (W). Sheep farming; coal, shipbuilding, engineering industs. on Tyneside. Northumberland National Park (1031 sq km/398 sq mi) incl. Hadrian's Wall.

North Vietnam, see VIETNAM.

North West Company, organization of Montréal merchants and fur traders formed (1783) to compete with Hudson's Bay Co. Its employees, incl. Thompson and Mackenzie, made pioneering explorations of W Canada. Merged with Hudson's Bay Co. (1821) following period of bitter rivalry.

Northwest Frontier Province, former province of British India on Afghanistan border, created 1901. Became part of Pakistan in 1947. Mountainous region; passes, incl. Khyber, were strategically important.

Northwest Passage, sea route linking Atlantic, Pacific oceans round N North America. Long-sought as possible short route to Orient. Frobisher, Davis, Franklin failed to discover it. First navigated by Amundsen (1903-6).

Northwest Territories, admin. region of N Canada; incl. 3 dists.: MACKENZIE (SW), FRANKLIN (N), KEEWATIN (SE). Area 3,379,699 sq km (1,304,903 sq mi); pop. 35,000, mainly Eskimo, Indian; admin. centre Yellowknife. Drained in W by Mackenzie R.; has many lakes incl. Great Bear, Great Slave. Fur trading; mineral resources in Mackenzie Dist. Exploration, trade sponsored by Hudson's Bay Co. (estab.

1670); known as Rupert's Land (incl. Prairies) until ceded to Canada (1869).

Northwich, urban dist. of Cheshire, NW England. Pop. 18,000. Centre of salt indust.

North Yorkshire, county of N England. Area 8317 sq km (3211 sq mi); pop. 645,000; co. town Northallerton. Created 1974, comprising mainly former N, W Ridings of Yorkshire.

Norton, Caroline [Elizabeth Sarah], née Sheridan (1808-77), English author. Works incl. polemics attacking social conditions, *eg Voice from the Factories* (1836). Successfully agitated for Married Women's Property Act. Notorious for accusation by husband of affair with Lord Melbourne.

Norway

Norway (*Norge*), kingdom of NW Europe, in W Scandinavia. Area 324,250 sq km (125,200 sq mi); pop. 3,971,000; cap. Oslo. Language: Norwegian. Religion: Lutheran. Nomadic Lapps in N. Deeply indented coast (ice-free due to N Atlantic Drift), mountainous; partly within Arctic Circle. Important North Sea fishing, forestry, minerals, h.e.p., limited agric.; offshore oil resources developed in 1970s. United with Denmark, Sweden 1397, ceded to Sweden 1814; independent from 1905. Occupied by Germans 1940-5.

Norwegian, N Germanic Indo-European language. Spoken in Norway and parts of US. Descended from Old Norse. Two official forms: formal *bokmål,* found in south and east, and *nynorsk* found in west and north; may be melded to form *samnorsk,* one common tongue.

Norwegian Antarctic Territory, all isls. and mainland S of 60°S and between 20°E and 45°W. Incl. Queen Maud, Princess Astrid, Princess Ragnhild, Prince Harald, Crown Prince Olav, Crown Princess Martha lands and part of Coats Land.

Norwich, city and co. town of Norfolk, E England, on R. Wensum. Pop. 122,000. Agric. market; food processing; footwear mfg. Has Univ. of East Anglia (1963). Medieval ecclesiastical centre; Norman cathedral (1096).

nose, facial organ containing openings of respiratory passages and organ of smell. Internal cavity is divided by cartilaginous septum into 2 halves which unite in nasal part of PHARYNX.

Nossi-Bé, volcanic isl. of Malagasy Republic, off NW Madagascar. Area 336 sq km (130 sq mi); main town Hellville. Produces bananas.

Nostradamus, Latin name of Michel de Nostredame (1503-66), French astrologer, physician. Wrote *Centuries* (1555), rhymed quatrains of obscure prophecies, long popular.

notochord, skeletal rod, composed of cells, lying between digestive tract and central nervous system in most primitive members of phylum Chordata. Present in embryonic stages of vertebrates, it is later surrounded and replaced by the vertebral column.

Notre Dame de Paris, cathedral church of Paris; on Ile de la Cité, isl. in R. Seine. Masterpiece of early French Gothic, begun in 1163; W front is esp. fine.

Nottinghamshire, county of C England. Area 2164 sq km (836 sq mi); pop. 982,000. Low-lying, in Trent Valley, hilly in SW. Cereals, root crops, cattle; coal mining in W. Incl. remains of Sherwood Forest. Co. town **Nottingham,** city

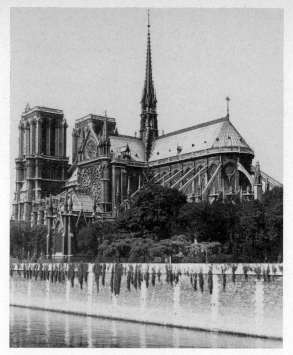

Notre Dame de Paris

on R. Trent. Pop. 300,000. Hosiery, bicycles; Danish town (9th cent.); hist. silk, lace mfg. Has univ. (1948); RC cathedral.

Nouakchott, cap. of Mauritania. Pop. 55,000. Admin., commercial centre on caravan routes; harbour nearby on Atlantic coast. Grew rapidly after selection (1957) as future cap.

Nouméa, cap. of New Caledonia. Pop. 58,000. Admin. centre; port, exports nickel, iron ore, chromium. Formerly called Port de France.

nova, in astronomy, star whose brightness suddenly increases by several thousand times and then slowly fades to its original intensity. Believed to be caused when star blows off part of its outer layer.

Novalis, pseud. of Friedrich Leopold von Hardenberg (1772-1801), German poet. Leading Romantic, *Hymns to the Night* (1800) express yearning for mystical unity in death. Also wrote unfinished novel *Heinrich von Ofterdingen* (1802).

Nova Lisboa, town of WC Angola, on Bié plateau. Pop. 50,000. Large railway repair works; trade in grain, hides. Founded 1912 as Huambo.

Novara, city of Piedmont, NW Italy, cap. of Novara prov. Pop. 103,000. Textiles, rice-milling, map-making. Scene of Austrian victory (1849) over Piedmontese under Charles Albert.

Nova Scotia, Maritime prov. of SE Canada, incl. CAPE BRETON Island. Area 55,491 sq km (21,425 sq mi); pop. 788,960; cap. Halifax. Rugged coastline has many natural harbours. Fishing (esp. cod), timber, agric. (dairy farming, fruit); coal, metals, salt mining. Settled as ACADIA by French; British gained possession (1714); joined with Cape Breton (1820). One of 4 original provs. of Canada (1867).

Novaya Zemlya, 2 isls. of USSR, between Barents and Kara seas. Area *c* 83,000 sq km (32,000 sq mi). N island permanently ice covered, tundra in S.

novel, long fictional prose narrative. Although antecedents exist in Classical Greece, Rome, medieval Italy, 1st true examples with realistic treatment of psychology incl. Cervantes' *Don Quixote,* Richardson's *Pamela,* Fielding's *Tom Jones.* Influential exponents incl. Jane Austen (domestic novel of manners), Melville, Flaubert,

Dostoyevski, Zola (naturalism), Proust, Joyce, Robbe-Grillet.

Novello, Ivor, pseud. of Ivor Novello Davies (1893-1951), Welsh actor-manager, composer. Known for songs, esp. 'Keep the Home Fires Burning', plays, *eg The Dancing Years* (1939), *Perchance to Dream* (1945).

Novgorod, city of USSR, W European RSFSR; on R. Volkhov. Pop. 135,000. One of oldest Russian cities, estab. of Rurik as Prince of Novgorod (862) regarded as foundation of Russia. Cap. of powerful trading state in 13th and 14th cent., rivalling Moscow in power. Subjugated by Ivan III and devastated by Ivan the Terrible (1570). Its kremlin has 11th cent. Cathedral of St Sophia.

Novi Pazar, town of Serbia, SC Yugoslavia, on R. Raška. Pop. 67,000. Carpets, copperware mfg. Cap. of Serbia 12th-14th cent., taken (1456) by Turks. Occupied by Austrians 1878-1908, returned to Serbia 1913.

Novi Sad (Ger. *Neusatz*), city of NE Yugoslavia, on R. Danube, cap. of Vojvodina. Pop. 142,000. River port; commercial, indust. centre. Serbian cultural, religious centre until WWI.

Novocherkassk, city of USSR, S European RSFSR. Pop. 170,000. Locomotive, machinery mfg. Founded 1805 as Don Cossack cap.

Novokuznetsk, city of USSR, SC Siberian RSFSR. Pop. 508,000. Metallurgical centre in Kuznetsk Basin; iron and steel, aluminium mfg. Developed as Stalinsk following amalgamation of old city of Kuznetsk and new indust. town (1932); renamed 1961.

Novorossiisk, port of USSR, S European RSFSR; on Black Sea. Pop. 139,000. Exports grain; oil refining, cement mfg. Formerly Turkish, taken by Russia 1808.

Novosibirsk, city of USSR, SC Siberian RSFSR; jct. of Trans-Siberian railway on R. Ob. Pop. 1,200,000. Founded 1896, grew as indust. centre based on proximity of Kuznetsk Basin; agric. machinery, textile mfg.

Noyes, Alfred (1880-1958) English poet, critic. Known for ballads, *eg* 'The Highwayman', 'Come to Kew in Lilac-time', verse epic *Drake* (1908). Criticism incl. fiercely anti-modernist *Some Aspects of Modern Poetry* (1924).

Nu, U (1907-), Burmese statesman, 1st premier (1948-56) of Republic of Burma. Twice resumed office (1957-8, 1960-2) before arrest during military coup led by Ne Win. Went into exile in Thailand.

Nubia, ancient region of NE Africa. Extended from Aswan (Egypt) to Khartoum (Sudan), boundaries poorly defined. Conquered Egypt (7th cent. BC) after being subject to it for cents.; powerful Christian kingdom 6th-14th cent. Conquered by Egypt in 19th cent. Incl. **Nubian Desert,** barren sandstone plateau of NE Sudan, between Nile valley and Red Sea; rises to over 2135 m/7000 ft near coast.

Nubian, language group within Chari-Nile branch of Nilo-Saharan language family. Remarkable among modern indigenous African languages in that it was used as written language, with extant texts, during medieval period. Spoken in Sudan.

nuclear energy, energy released from atomic nucleus during nuclear reactions, esp. FISSION or FUSION. Results from conversion of matter into energy.

nuclear fission, *see* FISSION.

nuclear forces, forces which hold together neutrons and protons in the atomic nucleus. Their range is less than 10^{-13} cm but they are immensely strong. Yukawa suggested that these forces arise from interchange of mesons between protons and neutrons.

nuclear fusion, *see* FUSION.

nuclear physics, branch of physics dealing with structure of atomic nuclei, subatomic particles, fission process, radioactive decay, *etc.*

nuclear reactor, structure in which nuclear fission chain reaction is initiated and controlled to produce energy or further fissionable material. Metal rods are used to absorb neutrons produced during fission and so control rate at which reaction proceeds.

nuclear warfare, hostilities involving use of nuclear warheads, envisaging total destruction of enemy's war potential before retaliation is possible. Strategic emphasis

is therefore on methods of delivery, which incl. low-level bombers and long range GUIDED MISSILES. Tactical weapons carrying small amounts of nuclear material have also been tested.

nucleic acids, *see* DNA, RNA.

nucleus, in biology, central body present in most plant and animal cells, enclosed by membrane which separates it from protoplasm of rest of cell. Contains hereditary material in form of chromosomes, which control reproduction, growth, *etc.*

nucleus, in physics, central part of the atom, consisting of protons and neutrons (except for hydrogen nucleus, which consists of single proton). Mass of atom is concentrated in nucleus, which bears a positive charge.

Nuevo Laredo, border town of NE Mexico, on Rio Grande opposite Laredo (Texas). Pop. 151,000. Transport centre; agric., stock trade. Point of entry for US tourists.

Nuffield, William Richard Morris, Viscount (1877-1963), English industrialist, philanthropist. Beginning in 1912, developed Morris Motors Ltd. into major mass-producer of motor cars. His benefactions incl. founding of Nuffield College, Oxford, and Nuffield Foundation for research (1943).

Nukualofa, cap. of Tonga, on Tongatabu Isl. Pop. 16,000. Admin. centre, port.

Nukus, town of USSR, cap. of Kara-Kalpak auton. republic, W Uzbek SSR; on Amu Darya delta. Pop. 74,000. Food processing, cotton goods.

Nullarbor Plain, arid limestone tableland of South and Western Australia. Extends *c* 400 km (250 mi) inland from Great Australian Bight. No surface water or trees (hence name); many subterranean caves, passages. Sheep pasture on margins; crossed by Trans-Australian Railway.

nullification, political doctrine, advocated by exponents of STATES' RIGHTS in US, that state is not bound to enforce federal legislation. Leading advocate, John Calhoun, encouraged South Carolina to nullify federal tariff acts (1832), but state rescinded (1833) after President Jackson had been empowered to use army to enforce tariffs.

numbat, *Myrmecobius fasciatus*, small rat-sized Australian marsupial anteater. Long snout and bushy tail; catches ants, termites with sticky tongue. Brown with distinctive white stripes.

Numbers, in OT, fourth book of Pentateuch. Contains two censuses of Israelites and continues history of Exodus and journey to Promised Land with rise of Joshua and Caleb as leaders.

Numidia, ancient kingdom of NW Africa, corresponding nearly to modern Algeria. United as Roman prov. after defeat (201 BC) of Carthage; *fl* 3rd-1st cent. BC. Main cities were *Cirta* (now Constantine), *Hippo Regius* (now Annaba).

numismatics, study of coins and medals. Invention of coinage is attributed to Chinese; in West, first coins were struck by Lydians of Asia Minor in electrum (mixture of gold and silver) *c* 750 BC.

nun, member of a religious community of women, esp. one living under monastic vows. *See* MONASTICISM.

Nuneaton, mun. bor. of Warwickshire, C England. Pop. 67,000. Coalmining; textiles. Has ruined 12th cent. nunnery.

Nuremberg (*Nürnberg*), city of SC West Germany, on R. Pegnitz. Pop. 480,000. Toys, precision instruments, clocks (first pocket watch made here *c* 1500). Medieval commercial centre; centre of German Renaissance. Religious Peace of Nuremberg agreed here (1532). Scene of annual Nazi rallies from 1933, and post-war crimes trials (1945-6). Birthplace of Dürer.

Nuremberg Trials, trial of Nazi leaders and military commanders after WWII by Allied Tribunal under charter agreed upon by US, UK, USSR and France. Charges incl. crimes against peace and humanity, war crimes. Those sentenced to death or long terms of imprisonment incl. Goering, Ribbentrop, Speer, Hess and Dönitz. Trial estab. principle of individual responsibility not to carry out criminal orders.

Nureyev, Rudolf (1939-), Russian ballet dancer. Lived in West after 1961. Internationally known for appearances with Dame Margot Fonteyn and others.

Nurmi, Paavo (1897-1973), Finnish athlete. Won 6 Olympic titles in running at 1500-10,000 m distances and 3 more in cross-country events. Set 20 world records (1920-31). Famous for timing himself with stopwatch while running.

nursery rhymes, short poems for children, stressing rhythm, rhyme; usually traditional. Many thought to have basis in ancient rites, *eg* 'Here we go round the mulberry bush', or more recent historical events.

nursing, care of the sick. Practised by various religious orders in the Middle Ages, it was revitalized in 17th cent. by the founding of the Sisters of Charity by St Vincent de Paul. First hospital training school was estab. at Kaiserswerth, Germany by Theodor Fliedner (1836). School estab. (1860) at St Thomas's Hospital by Florence Nightingale became model for such schools everywhere.

Nusa Tenggara, *see* SUNDAS.

nut, dry, one-seeded fruit of various trees and shrubs. Consists of kernel (often edible) in a hard woody shell which is separable from the seed itself, *eg* walnut, hazelnut.

nutcracker, *Nucifraga caryocatactes,* bird of crow family, found in coniferous forests of Europe and Asia. Brown with white speckles.

nuthatch, small sharp-beaked tree-climbing bird of Sittidae family. Nests in holes in trees; diet of insects, nuts. Species incl. European nuthatch *Sitta europaea* and North American white-breasted nuthatch *S. carolinensis.*

nutmeg, hard aromatic seed of East Indian tree, *Myristica fragrans.* Grated and used as spice, while outer covering yields the spice mace. Oil derived from seed and covering used in medicine and cosmetics.

nutria, name applied to COYPU or its fur, which is soft and brown.

nux vomica, poisonous disc-shaped seed of Asiatic deciduous tree, *Strychnos nux-vomica,* of logania family. Contains various alkaloids, incl. strychnine.

nyala, *Tragelaphus angasi,* medium-sized antelope of S and E Africa, related to bush buck.

Nyasa, Lake, *see* MALAWI, LAKE.

Nyasaland, *see* MALAWI.

Nyerere, Julius Kambarage (1921-), Tanzanian statesman. Became PM at independence (1961) of Tanganyika, then president upon estab. of republic (1962). Pursued socialist policies, with Chinese aid. Negotiated union with Zanzibar which created Tanzania, becoming president (1964).

Nyköping, town of E Sweden, on Baltic Sea. Pop. 31,000. Port; textiles; furniture.

nylon, name given to group of synthetic long-chain polymeric amides, made into fibres, yarn, moulded plastics, *etc.* Fibre, characterized by strength, elasticity and low absorbency of moisture, is used in mfg. of hosiery and textiles.

nymph, larva of insect undergoing incomplete metamorphosis (without pupal stage). Resembles adult, but without wings and sexually immature. Winged adult emerges after series of moults.

nymphs, in Greek myth, generic name for large number of minor female deities associated with natural objects. Usually represented as young, beautiful and amorous, *eg* NAIADS, NEREIDS, DRYADS, OREADS.

Nysa, *see* NEISSE.

O

Oahu, volcanic isl. of Hawaii, US. Area 1540 sq km (595 sq mi); main city HONOLULU. Tourism; extinct volcanoes Diamond Head, Punchbowl.

oak, any of genus *Quercus* of hardwood trees and shrubs of beech family bearing nuts called ACORNS. Widely distributed in N temperate regions. Wood used in furniture. Bark of cork oak, *Q. suber,* is used commercially as source of cork.

Oakham, urban dist. of Leicestershire, EC England, former co. town of Rutland. Pop. 5000. Market town; hosiery, shoe mfg.

Oakland, port of W California, US; on San Francisco Bay. Pop. 362,000. Naval base; electrical equipment, chemicals. shipbuilding. Incl. residential areas overlooking Bay. Connected by bridge with San Francisco.

Oak Ridge, town of E Tennessee, US. Pop. 28,000. Has nuclear research station estab. 1943 as site for atom bomb project. Pop. then *c* 70,000.

oarfish, marine fish, genus *Regalecus,* with long ribbon-like body and mane-like crest behind head. Reaches lengths of 6.1 m/20 ft.

oasis, fertile area in a desert, caused by presence of water. May be natural spring or made by sinking artesian well. Date palm is commonest vegetation. Some oases very extensive, *eg* Kufra Oasis, Libya.

oat, *Avena sativa,* hardy, widely grown cereal grass, native to Asia. Cultivated as food for man, *eg* oatmeal, and for horses.

Oates, Titus (1649-1705), English Protestant conspirator. Fabricated and testified to 'Popish Plot' (1678), said to involve murder of Charles II, burning of London, and reintroduction of Catholicism. Resulting panic caused judicial murder and persecution of many Catholics. Imprisoned for perjury (1685); pardoned (1688).

Oaxaca, town of S Mexico, cap. of Oaxaca state. Pop. 98,000, mainly Indian. In high valley, built on Aztec city. Handicrafts *eg* gold, silver, pottery; agric. industs. Founded 1486 by Aztecs; fine examples of colonial architecture.

Ob, river of USSR. Formed by union of Biya and Katun rivers, flows *c* 3500 km (2200 mi) N and NW through W Siberian RSFSR to Gulf of Ob. Middle course extensively flooded during spring thaw. Trade route in summer; h.e.p. near Novosibirsk.

Obadiah or **Abdias,** shortest prophetic book of OT. Foretells triumph of Israel over Edom. Prob. written before 550 BC.

Oban, town of Strathclyde region, W Scotland. Pop. 7000. Port, tourist resort; fishing industs. Ferry services to Inner Hebrides.

obbligato, musical term originally denoting essential part of composition, usually a particular instrumental line, as opposed to an optional part. Mainly found in baroque music. Subsequent misunderstanding has reversed meaning.

obeah or **obi,** form of witchcraft or magic practised by Negroes in some parts of Africa and in West Indies. Combines elements of Christianity and fetishism.

Obeid, El, town of C Sudan. Pop. 66,000. Railway terminus, road jct., trade in gum arabic, cereals, cattle. Scene of Mahdi's victory (1883) over Egyptians.

obelisk, in ancient Egypt, four-sided monolithic slender shaft, tapering towards top, with pyramidical apex. Dedicated to the sun god, they were often placed in pairs about temples. Examples have been removed to London, New York, Paris. London and New York examples called Cleopatra's Needles.

Oberammergau, town of S West Germany, on R. Ammer, in Bavarian Alps. Pop. 5000. Woodcarving, tourism, winter sports. Passion Play performed every 10 years (begun 1634) is thanksgiving for deliverance from plague.

Oberhausen, city of W West Germany, on Rhine-Herne canal, in Ruhr. Pop. 245,000. Coalmining, oil refining, zinc smelting. Founded 19th cent.

obesity, excess of body fat. Usually results from over-eating of carbohydrate foods. Obesity can usually be reduced by eating less sugar and starch and taking more exercise.

obi, *see* OBEAH.

oboe, woodwind instrument with double reed and conical bore, developed from medieval shawm or pommer. Attained its present form in France in *c* 1650. Cor anglais or English horn is similar, but a fifth lower in pitch.

Obote, [Apollo] Milton (1924-), Ugandan political leader, PM (1962-6). Seized presidency (1966); while absent abroad, deposed by Amin (1971).

O'Brien, Conor Cruise (1917-), Irish statesman, writer. Represented UN in Katanga, during province's secession from Congo (1961). Labour member of Irish parliament from 1969; minister of posts and telegraphs from 1973. Sought to restrict IRA activities in the republic.

observatory, building designed for observation of astronomical or meteorological phenomena, *eg* Mt. Palomar and Mt. Wilson observatories in California.

obsidian, hard, usually black, volcanic glass. Formed by viscous acid lava cooling too quickly for minerals to crystallize. Used esp. in prehist. times for weapons, ornaments. Major sources in Mediterranean isls., Iceland, Mexico, US.

obstetrics, branch of medicine concerned with childbirth and treatment of mother before and after delivery.

ocarina, musical instrument, elongated oval in shape, with 5 finger holes for each hand and mouthpiece. Produces flute-like sound.

Sean O'Casey

O'Casey, Sean (1880-1964), Irish dramatist. Works, reflecting early life in Dublin slums, incl. tragi-comedies *Juno and the Paycock* (1924), *The Plough and the Stars*

(1926). Also wrote expressionist anti-WWI drama, *The Silver Tassie* (1929).

occasionalism, see GEULINCX.

occultism, belief in hidden powers and forces, esp. supernatural. Designates alleged mystic arts, *eg* alchemy, astrology, magic, spiritualism.

ocean, large expanse of salt water on Earth's surface. Five usually distinguished: Antarctic or Southern, Arctic, Atlantic, Indian and Pacific, the largest. Together, oceans cover 71% of Earth's surface.

Oceania, general term for isls. of Pacific belonging to Melanesia, Micronesia and Polynesia groups, and sometimes those of Australasia.

Ocean Island or **Banaba,** part of Gilbert and Ellice Isls. colony. Area 5 sq km (2 sq mi). Phosphate deposits. Former cap. of colony until WWII.

Oceanus, in Greek myth, the great outer stream which encircled the earth. Personified as a TITAN who was father of river gods and sea nymphs (Oceanids).

ocelot, *Felis pardalis,* wild cat of Central and South America; body length *c* 76 cm/30 in. Yellow or grey coat with black spots. Valued for its fur.

ochre or **ocher,** natural earth, mixture of hydrated iron oxide and clay. Ranges in colour from yellow to brown and red. Used as pigment in paints. Major sources in US, France, Italy.

Ochrida or **Okhrida** (*Ohrid*), town of Macedonia, SW Yugoslavia, on L. Ochrida. Pop. 13,000. Resort, fishing, trade centre. Turkish architecture; church (11th cent.). **Lake Ochrida** (area 347 sq km/134 sq mi) forms part of Yugoslav-Albanian border. Picturesque, famed for clear water.

O'Connell, Daniel (1775-1847), Irish nationalist leader. Founded (1823) Catholic Association to further Catholic emancipation. Elected to Parliament (1828), although unable to take oaths necessary to assume seat; Catholic Emancipation Act (1829) was passed as a result. After 1841, worked for repeal of union with Britain but his conservative ways lost him popular support.

Octavian, see AUGUSTUS.

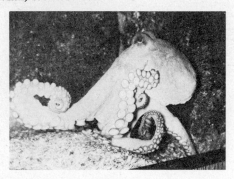

Octopus

octopus, cephalopod mollusc with rounded sac-like body, no shell and 8 sucker-bearing arms. Lives mainly on sea bottom, ejecting inky fluid for protection. Species incl. common octopus, *Octopus vulgaris,* of Atlantic and Mediterranean.

ode, originally Greek poem sung to musical accompaniment. Either for single voices, *eg* those of Sappho, Alcaeus, Anacreon; or choral, *eg* Pindar. In modern period, revived in 16th cent. France by Ronsard; 17th cent. English poets influenced chiefly by Horace, also by Pindar, *eg* Milton, Cowley, Dryden.

Odense, city of Fyn Isl., Denmark. Pop. 137,000. Port, exports dairy produce; shipbuilding; textiles. Founded 10th cent., cathedral (rebuilt in 13th cent.). Birthplace of Hans Christian Andersen.

Oder (Czech and Pol. *Odra*), river of E Europe. Flows 900 km (560 mi) from NC Czechoslovakia through Poland to Baltic Sea at Szczecin. Forms N Part of Polish-East German border. Navigable below Racibórz, canals to Katowice indust. region.

Odessa, city of USSR, SW Ukrainian SSR; on Black Sea. Pop. 941,000. Port; exports grain, timber; indust. centre. Taken in 1789 from Turks by Russia. Scene of workers' revolution led by mutineers from *Potemkin* (1905). Under Romanian occupation (1941-3); large Jewish pop. decimated.

Odets, Clifford (1906-63), American playwright. Known for committedly socialist plays, *eg Waiting for Lefty* (1935), *Awake and Sing!* (1935), *Golden Boy* (1937).

Odin, in Norse myth, the supreme god, creator of earth, sky and mankind. Associated with war and learning. Sometimes identified with Roman Mercury.

Odovacar or **Odoacer** (*c* 435–93), German chieftain, 1st barbarian ruler of Rome. Proclaimed king by the German mercenaries he led in service of Rome, he deposed the emperor Romulus Augustulus (476), thus ending Western Roman Empire. Defeated by invading Ostrogoths under Theodoric and treacherously murdered at latter's instigation.

Odysseus, in Greek myth, king of Ithaca. A leader of Greeks in TROJAN WAR, noted for his cunning. Devised Wooden Horse scheme. Hero of Homer's ODYSSEY. Known as Ulysses by Romans.

Odyssey, Greek epic in 24 books attributed to Homer. Tells story of ODYSSEUS. After fall of Troy, attempted to return to kingdom Ithaca, but incurred curse of Poseidon which led to 10 years of wandering before homecoming, having lost all companions; rid palace of wife Penelope's suitors with aid of son Telemachus before estab. rule again.

oedema or **dropsy,** abnormal accumulation of fluid in body tissues, resulting in swelling. Caused by heart failure, obstruction of lymphatic vessels, kidney disease, *etc.*

Oedipus, in Greek myth, king of Thebes. Abandoned on Mt. Cithaeron when it was prophesied that he would kill his father Laius and marry his mother Jocasta. Brought up in Corinth ignorant of his true parentage; fled upon learning of prophecy from Delphic oracle. Killed Laius in chance encounter on way to Thebes and married Jocasta after saving kingdom by answering riddle of the Sphinx. Later learned truth, blinded himself; Jocasta committed suicide. Succeeded by Creon and died at Colonus. Children were POLYNICES, Eteocles, ANTIGONE and Ismene. Hero of Sophocles' *Oedipus Rex, Oedipus at Colonus.*

Oedipus complex, in psychoanalytic theory, sexual desire of son for mother and conflict with father. May be openly expressed at age 4-5 years, later repressed as son realizes sanctions against incest, but persists in unconscious. Concept developed by Freud, using the Greek legend, and was fundamental not only to psychoanalysis but to his theory of culture and religion. Daughter's desire for father called Electra complex.

Oersted, Hans Christian (1777-1851), Danish scientist. Estab. relationship between electricity and magnetism (1819) by discovery that magnet takes up right-angled position to direction of electric current.

oesophagus or **gullet,** part of alimentary canal connecting the PHARYNX with the stomach. Carries food to stomach by muscular contraction of its walls.

oestrogen, any of group of female hormones, produced synthetically or secreted in ovaries of mammals. Responsible for development of female secondary sexual characteristics and stimulation of ovulation.

oestrus, period of heat (maximum sexual receptivity) in female mammals.

Offa (d. 796), Anglo-Saxon chieftain, king of Mercia (757-96). Estab. Mercian supremacy over most of England S of the Humber. Had defensive earthwork, Offa's Dyke, built on Welsh border. Recognized as an equal by Charlemagne, with whom he drew up a trading treaty (796).

Offaly, county of Leinster prov., C Irish Republic. Area 1997 sq km (771 sq mi); pop. 52,000; co. town Tullamore. Flat, low-lying, has part of Bog of Allen; Slieve Bloom Mts. in SE. Agric., cattle; peat. Formerly called King's County.

Offa's Dyke, ancient earthworks between England and Wales, from R. Dee to R. Severn. Built (8th cent.) by Offa, king of Mercia; parts still form border.

Offenbach

Offenbach, Jacques (1819-80), French composer, b. Germany. Wrote popular light operas, *eg Orpheus in the Underworld,* and serious *Tales of Hoffmann.*

Offenbach, city of WC West Germany, on R. Main. Pop. 120,000. Major leather indust., begun by Huguenots (17th cent.); leather museum.

O'Flaherty, Liam (1897-), Irish novelist. Works incl. *Thy Neighbour's Wife* (1923) set in Aran Islands, *The Informer* (1925) depicting Republican terrorism.

ogam or **ogham,** alphabetic system of writing developed in Ireland in 5th cent. AD. Letters are represented by combinations of lines and notches carved along edges of memorial stones.

Ogbomosho, city of SW Nigeria. Pop. 387,000. Trade centre for agric. region, esp. cotton, yams, cassava.

Ogden, C[harles] K[ay] (1889-1957), English psychologist, linguist. With I. A. Richards originated BASIC ENGLISH, collaborated in *The Meaning of Meaning* (1923).

ogham, see OGAM.

Oglethorpe, James Edward (1696-1785), English army officer, philanthropist. Estab. (1733) colony of Georgia as refuge for imprisoned debtors. Accompanied 1st colonists, founded Savannah; organized defence against Spaniards.

Ogowé or **Ogooué,** river of WC Africa. Flows *c* 1095 km (680 mi) from Congo Republic via Gabon to Atlantic Ocean S of Port Gentil. Major trade route of Gabon.

O'Higgins, Bernardo (1776-1842), Chilean revolutionary. Led opposition to Spanish rule from 1810; defeated at Rancagua (1814), fled to Argentina. Returned with San Martín's army, became ruler after victory at Chacabuco (1817). Exiled to Peru after overthrow (1823).

Ohio, state of N US. Area 106,765 sq km (41,222 sq mi); pop. 10,652,000; cap. Columbus; chief cities Cleveland, Cincinnati. Mainly flat with L. Erie in NE, Ohio R. in S, Allegheny Mts. in E, prairies in W. Important agric. esp. wheat, livestock; mining incl. coal, oil; indust. concentrated in iron and steel, machinery, rubber, motor car, paper mfg. Control of fur trade estab. by British (1763); ceded to US after Revolution (1783). Admitted to Union as 17th state (1803).

Ohio, river of NC US. Flows from W Pennsylvania SW 1579 km (981 mi) to Mississippi R. Forms 5 state borders; drains indust. region of Pittsburgh, Cincinnati, Louisville. Navigable from Pittsburgh; subject to flooding.

Ohm, Georg Simon (1787-1854), German physicist. His work on electrical circuits led him to formulate Ohm's law: potential difference between ends of a conductor is proportional to current flowing. Unit of electrical RESISTANCE named after him.

oil beetle, small beetle, esp. of genus *Meloe,* that discharges evil-smelling oily substance from glands on legs when disturbed.

oil bird, *Steatornis caripensis,* nocturnal cave-dwelling bird of N South America. Young, fed on oily fruit, accumulate fat which may be boiled down for lighting oil. Also called guacharo.

oils, group of liquids divided into 3 main classes: (1) fatty oils, consisting of mixtures of glycerides of fatty acids, found in animals and plants; (2) mineral oils, consisting of mixtures of hydrocarbons, obtained from petroleum, shale or coal; (3) ESSENTIAL OILS.

Oise, river of N France. Flows *c* 305 km (190 mi) from Belgian Ardennes via Compiègne to R. Seine NW of Paris. Heavy river traffic, canal links with Sambre, Somme, Escaut (Scheldt).

Ojibwa or **Chippewa,** group of North American Indian tribes of Algonquian linguistic stock. Inhabited L. Superior region (17th cent.). Hunters, farmers largely dependent on wild rice, over which they warred with Sioux. Now on reservations W of Great Lakes.

Ojos del Salado, peak in Chilean Andes, on Argentina-Chile border. Height 6870 m (22,539 ft); 2nd highest peak in Andes.

Ojukwu, Chukwuemeka Odumegwu (1933-), Nigerian general. Leader of Biafra secessionist govt. (1967-70) in Nigerian civil war. Escaped into exile after defeat.

Oka, 2 rivers of USSR. **1,** flows *c* 1450 km (900 mi) through C European RSFSR to join Volga at Gorky. Used to carry wheat, timber. **2,** flows *c* 800 km (500 mi) through SC Siberian SSR from E Sayan Mts. to join R. Angara.

okapi, *Okapia johnstoni,* rare mammal of giraffe family, from Congo forests. Stands *c* 1.5 m/5 ft at shoulder; red-brown in colour, white bands on legs.

Okavango (Port. *Cubango*), river of SW Africa. Flows *c* 1600 km (1000 mi) SE from C Angola to Botswana, forming Okavango swamp. Forms part of Angola-Namibia border.

Okayama, port of Japan, SW Honshu isl. Pop. 375,000. Railway and indust. centre; cotton goods, porcelain mfg.

Okefenokee Swamp, marsh of SE US, in SE Georgia and N Florida. Area 1550 sq km (*c* 600 sq mi). Wildlife reserve estab. 1937.

Okhotsk, Sea of, arm of NW Pacific, on E Siberian RSFSR. Enclosed by Kamchatka penin., Kuril and Sakhalin Isls.

Okhrida, see OCHRIDA, Yugoslavia.

Okinawa, largest of Ryuku Isls., W Pacific. Area 1176 sq km (454 sq mi); cap. Naha. Sugar cane, rice, sweet potatoes grown. Scene of intense fighting between Japan and US (1945). Placed under US military control until returned to Japan in 1972.

Oklahoma, state of SC US. Area 181,090 sq km (69,919 sq mi); pop. 2,559,000; cap. Oklahoma City; other major city Tulsa. Mainly prairie, mountainous in E; chief rivers Red on S border, Arkansas and tributaries. Main occupations wheat growing, livestock rearing esp. cattle; oil, natural gas resources. First explored by Spanish; part of Louisiana Purchase (1803); reserved for Indians, redistributed (1889) for white settlers. Admitted to Union as 46th state (1907).

Oklahoma City, cap. of Oklahoma, US; on North Canadian R. Pop. 369,000. Indust., commercial centre in agric., oil producing region; related industs. incl. oil refining, food processing. Founded 1889; became cap. 1910.

Okra

okra or **gumbo,** *Hibiscus esculentus,* aromatic bean of mallow family, native to Africa. Grown extensively in S US, India. Used as vegetable and in soups.

Olaf II [Haraldsson] (*c* 995-1030), king of Norway (1015-28). Attempted to convert Norway to Christianity and unify country under his rule. Exiled after rebellion in favour of CANUTE (1028). Killed during invasion to regain crown. Patron saint of Norway.

Olaf V (1903-), king of Norway (1957-). Succeeded his father, Haakon VII. His son, Harald, is heir to throne.

Oland Island, Baltic isl. of SE Sweden, separated from mainland by Kalmar Sund. Area 1347 sq km (520 sq mi); main town Borgholm. Agric.; limestone quarrying; tourism.

Olbers, Heinrich Wilhelm (1758-1840), German astronomer. Known for Olbers' paradox: night sky should be uniformly bright if there are infinitely many stars evenly distributed in space. Paradox now explained by expansion of universe causing red shift of light emitted by stars.

Old Bailey, street in City of London. Name used popularly for Central Criminal Court, sited there.

Old Catholics, Christian church estab. by German clergy who rejected decrees of the 1870 Vatican Council, esp. dogma of papal infallibility. Priests are allowed to marry; confession is optional. Survives in Germany, Netherlands, US.

Oldenburg, Claes (1929-), American sculptor, b. Sweden. Works, derived from advertising and display techniques, are usually classed as pop art; most famous are large, soft renditions of everyday objects, *eg Giant Hamburger.*

Oldenburg, city of NW West Germany, on R. Hunte. Pop. 132,000. Railway jct., agric. market, textiles, dyes. Cap. of former county (duchy from 1777). Source of Danish rulers (1448-1863); part of Denmark 1676-1773.

Old English, *see* ENGLISH.

Oldham, bor. of Greater Manchester met. county, NW England. Pop. 106,000. Textile indust., esp. cotton spinning.

Old Moore's Almanac, annual British publication containing predictions of events of coming year. First published (1700) as *Vox Stellarum* by Francis Moore (1657-*c* 1715) as vehicle to advertise his patent medicines.

Old Norse literature, literature of Northmen, or Norsemen, *c* 850-*c* 1350. Little survives outside ICELANDIC LITERATURE, which incl. Edda, ancient lays on gods, goddesses; Scaldic poetry, subjective songs of love, sorrow, triumph; sagas, heroic prose narratives; also noteworthy hist. writing, *eg* by SNORRI STURLUSON.

Old Prussian, *see* BALTIC.

Old Testament, Christian term for Hewbrew part of the Bible. Relates story of the Jews from time of Moses to (with APOCRYPHA) cent. before birth of Jesus. Largely based on 3rd cent. BC translation into Greek (SEPTUAGINT). W Churches adopted the Latin version (VULGATE).

Olduvai Gorge, archaeological site in Tanzania where remains of tool-making precursors of man, *c* 1.8 million years old, were discovered by the LEAKEYS in 1959. Other fossil hominids have since been found there.

Old Vic, London theatre. Opened (1818) as Coburg. Renamed (1880) as Royal Victoria Hall (hence 'Old Vic'). Famous for productions of Shakespeare (1914-39) under management of Lilian Baylis. Became home of National Theatre Company (1963-76).

Old World, name used for the continents of Europe, Asia and Africa.

oleander, *Nerium oleander,* poisonous evergreen shrub native to Mediterranean region. Lance-shaped leathery leaves, large pink flowers.

oleaster, common name for plants of genus *Elaeagnus*; incl. *E. angustifolia,* ornamental shrub, native to S Europe and W Asia. Yellow flowers and olive-like fruit.

Oligocene epoch, third geological epoch of Tertiary period. Alpine mountain building continued. Mammals dominant; rise of true carnivores, erect primates. Decrease in temperature from Eocene epoch. Also *see* GEOLOGICAL TABLE.

Oleander

Oligochaeta, order of annelid worms, class Chaetopoda. Few bristles (chaetae) on body and no definite head. Mainly freshwater but some species terrestrial, *eg* earthworm.

oligopoly, in economics, virtual control of supply of commodity or service by a few producers. While privately-controlled MONOPOLY is rare, oligopoly is relatively usual in form of CARTEL or interlocking directorates. Also *see* MULTI-NATIONAL CORPORATION.

Oliphant, Sir Marcus Laurence Elwin ('Mark') (1901-), Australian physicist. Studied nuclear disintegration of lithium; designed Australian proton synchrotron.

Olivares, Gaspar de Guzmán, Conde de (1587-1645). Spanish statesman. Chief minister to Philip IV (1621-43); his foreign policy incl. renewal of war in Netherlands and entry of Spain into Thirty Years War. Taxation policy led to secession of Portugal (1640).

olive, *Olea europaea,* European evergreen tree, native to Asia Minor. Cultivated since ancient times for fruit, eaten either unripe (green) or ripe (black), or used as source of oil. Wood prized for ornamental work.

Olives, Mount of or **Olivet,** ridge E of Jerusalem visited many times by Jesus. Garden of Gethsemane on W slope.

Olivier, Laurence [Kerr], Baron Olivier of Brighton (1907-), English actor, director. Famous for appearances at Old Vic and in films, *eg Rebecca, Richard III, Hamlet.* Director of UK's National Theatre (1962-73).

olivine, green, usually transparent mineral. Consists of silicate of iron and magnesium. Used in refractories; also as a gem called peridot. Major sources in Red Sea area, Burma, US.

Olomouc (Ger. *Olmütz*), town of C Czechoslavakia, on R. Morava. Pop. 80,000. Food processing. Former cap. of Moravia. Cathedral (14th cent.); town hall (15th cent.) with astronomical clock. Univ. (1573).

Olsztyn (Ger. *Allenstein*), town of NE Poland, cap. of Olsztyn prov. Pop. 90,000. Railway jct.; agric. machinery, tanning. Founded 1348 by Teutonic Knights; under Prussian rule 1772-1945.

Olympia, ancient city of Greece, in W Peloponnse. Founded *c* 1000 BC; centre for worship of Zeus, temple had Phidias' statue of Zeus. OLYMPIC GAMES first held here.

Olympia, cap. and port of Washington, US; at end of Puget Sound. Pop. 23,000. Exports fish, timber. Tourism in Olympic Mts. to N. Founded 1850; became territ. cap. 1853.

Olympian gods, in Greek myth, the twelve major gods who lived on Mt. Olympus. Succeeded the TITANS as rulers of universe. Headed by Zeus and his sister and wife, Hera.

Olympic games, ancient Greek festival consisting of contests in athletics, poetry and music held every 4 years at Olympia. First records kept from 776 BC; abolished AD 393. Games were revived (1896) by Pierre de Coubertin; women participated from 1912. Winter Olympics estab. 1924.

Olympus (*Olimbos*), mountain range of NE Greece, near Aegean coast. Rises to 2915 m (9570 ft), highest point in Greece. Legendary home of ancient gods.

Omagh, town of WC Northern Ireland. Pop. 12,000. Former co. town of Tyrone. Agric. market; dairy produce. **Omagh,** district; area 1125 sq km (434 sq mi); pop. 39,000. Created 1973, formerly part of Co. Tyrone.

Omaha, city of E Nebraska, US; on Missouri R. Pop. 347,000; state's largest city. Railway, insurance centre. Livestock market, meat packing, machinery mfg. Supply base for mid-19th cent. W expansion. Founded 1854; territ. cap. 1855-67.

Oman, independent sultanate of SW Asia, SE Arabian penin., along Gulf of Oman. Area *c* 212,000 sq km (82,000 sq mi); pop. 743,000; cap. Muscat. Coastal plain (dates) backed by mountains, arid plateau. Linked by treaty with Britain. Called Muscat and Oman until 1970.

Omar (*c* 581-644), Arab ruler. One of Mohammed's ablest advisers, he succeeded Abu Bakr (634) as 2nd caliph. Greatly extended Islamic empire with victories in Persia, Syria, Egypt.

Omar Khayyam (*fl* 11th cent.), Persian poet, mathematician. Famous in West for *Rubáiyát* through Edward Fitzgerald's English translation (1859); series of independent epigrammatic stanzas. Famous in East as astronomer and mathematician, assisted calendar reform.

Omayyads, Arab dynasty of caliphs. Founded 661 by Muawiya, whose cap. was Damascus. Overthrown by Abbasids (750), who massacred Omayyad family. A survivor escaped to Spain, where he founded emirate of Córdoba (756-929) later a caliphate (929-1031).

ombudsman, public official appointed to investigate citizens' complaints against local or national govt. agencies for infringement of rights of individual. Introduced into Sweden (1809). Appointed in New Zealand (1962), UK (1966), Hawaii (1969).

Omdurman, city of C Sudan, on White Nile opposite Khartoum. Pop. 230,000. Noted for native markets, trade in livestock, hides, cotton goods. Mahdi's cap. 1884, site of his tomb. Scene of Kitchener's victory (1898) over Khalifa's forces.

Omphale, in Greek myth, queen of Lydia in whose service Heracles, dressed as a woman, did womanly tasks for 3 years to appease the gods.

Omsk, city of USSR, W Siberian RSFSR; at confluence of Om and Irtysh. Pop. 876,000. Automobile, agric. machinery mfg; oil refining. Founded 1716 as fort.

Onager

onager, *Equus hemionus onager,* wild ass of India and Persia.

Onassis, Aristotle Socrates (1906-75), Greek shipping magnate, b. Turkey. Known as 'the golden Greek', amassed vast fortune in shipping, real estate. Married Jacqueline Bouvier Kennedy (1968).

Onega, Lake, second largest lake of Europe, in USSR, NW European RSFSR. Area *c* 9840 sq km (3800 sq mi). Outlet is R. Svir, flowing into L. Ladoga. Important fisheries.

O'Neill, Eugene [Gladstone] (1888-1953), American dramatist. Experimented with technique, combining myth, symbolism, expressionism. Plays incl. trilogy *Mourning Becomes Electra* (1931), *The Iceman Cometh* (1946), *Long Day's Journey into Night* (pub. 1956). Nobel Prize for Literature (1936).

onion, *Allium cepa,* biennial plant of lily family, native to SW Asia. Widely cultivated for edible bulb with pungent smell and flavour. Used as vegetable since ancient times.

Onitsha, city of S Nigeria, on R. Niger. Pop. 197,000. River port, trade centre; road bridge across river links E and W Nigeria.

Onion

Ontario, prov. of C Canada. Area 1,068 587 sq km (412,582 sq mi); pop. 7,703,000; cap. Toronto; other major cities Ottawa, Hamilton. Forests, lakes in N (Laurentian Plateau) with nickel, uranium, iron, copper resources. Indust., agric., pop. concentrated in S around Great Lakes (trade, transport focus of Canada). French fur traders settled region in 17th cent., British control from 1763; area named Upper Canada (1791); became one of 4 original provs. of Canada (1867).

Ontario, Lake, smallest of Great Lakes, EC Canada-US. Connects L. Erie with St Lawrence Seaway. Area 19,529 sq km (7540 sq mi); chief port Toronto. Important trade link; commercial fishing (affected by recent pollution).

onyx, semi-precious form of CHALCEDONY. Differs from agate only in having straight, parallel, regular bands of colour. Used by Romans for cups, vases, *etc*, now in cameos, ornaments.

oolite, sedimentary rock composed of spherical nuclei surrounded by concentric layers, normally of calcium carbonate. Oolitic LIMESTONE is chemically precipitated; term formerly applied to upper Jurassic period in Europe.

Oostende, *see* OSTEND, Belgium.

opah, *see* MOONFISH.

opal, hydrated amorphous form of silica. Impurities determine colour; gem opals pearly and translucent, with red, green and blue tints. Major sources of gem opals in Australia, Mexico.

op or **optical art,** style of abstract painting developed in 1960s which uses geometric patterns to create optical illusions of movement. Exponents incl. Bridget Riley and Vasarely.

Opava (Ger. *Troppau*), town of NE Czechoslovakia. Pop. 50,000. Food processing, textiles. Former cap. of Austrian Silesia. Scene of Congress of Troppau (1820).

Open University, Milton Keynes, UK, estab. 1969 to provide tuition for non-qualified part-time adult students through correspondence courses integrated with radio, TV broadcasts, summer schools, and counselling and tutorial system. Has over 50,000 students.

opera, stage drama in which singing largely or totally takes place of speech. Developed in West as Italian court entertainment from *c* 1600 (MONTEVERDI being earliest master of form). Rigidity of resulting conventions led to reaction in favour of dramatic expression *c* 1750. In 19th cent., grand opera, spectacular and serious, contrasted with entertaining light operas. Most operas of 20th cent. retain earlier musical forms, but are often more subtle or symbolic in content.

operetta, short light OPERA, usually with some spoken dialogue, esp. works of Offenbach, Johann Strauss, Gilbert and Sullivan.

Ophion, in Greek myth, serpent who ruled world before Cronus. See EURYNOME.

Ophiuroidea, *see* BRITTLE STAR.

Opisthobranchiata, order of gastropod molluscs incl. sea hare, sea slug, with reduced shells or no shell.

opium, narcotic drug obtained from unripe seed capsules of OPIUM POPPY. Derivatives incl. morphine, heroin, codeine, used medicinally as sedative, but strictly controlled as they are addictive.

opium poppy, *Papaver somniferum,* annual plant native to Asia and Asia Minor. Cultivated as source of OPIUM.

Opium Wars (1839-42, 1856-8), wars between China and Britain, resulting from Chinese refusal to allow importation of opium from India. Hong Kong ceded by China after British victory (1842). British-French victory in 2nd war estab. free trade in Chinese ports and legalization of opium trade.

Opole (Ger. *Oppeln*), town of S Poland, on R. Oder, cap. of Opole prov. Pop. 85,000. River port, agric. market. Ducal cap. 1163-1532. Prussian from 1742; cap. of German Upper Silesia 1919-45.

Oporto (*Pôrto*), city of W Portugal, on R. Douro. Pop. 693,000. Seaport, exports port wine; artificial harbour for large ships at nearby Leixões; textiles, pottery mfg. Univ. (1911); Torre dos Clerigos is famed landmark (75 m/246 ft high); 2-storey bridge (1887). Roman *Portus Cale,* gave name to Portugal.

opossum, any of Didelphidae family of mainly arboreal American marsupials with long prehensile tails. Noted for habit of feigning death when in danger - 'playing possum'. Species incl. nocturnal rat-like Virginia opossum *Didelphis virginiana* found from Argentina to N US. Name also applied to Australian HONEY MOUSE.

Oppeln, see OPOLE, Poland.

Oppenheimer, J[ohn] Robert (1904-67), American physicist. Directed research at Los Alamos (1942-5) leading to production of 1st atomic bomb; opposed decision to develop hydrogen bomb. Considered security risk, he was deprived of membership of US Atomic Energy Commission (1953).

Ops, in Roman religion, wife of Saturn; mother of Jupiter and Juno. Goddess of the harvest. Identified with Greek Rhea.

optical fibres, see FIBRE OPTICS.

optics, science of light and principles underlying phenomena of light and vision, divided into physical and geometrical optics. Former studies nature of light and its wave properties, latter treats reflection, refraction, *etc,* by ray aspect of light.

oracle, in Greek religion, answer given by particular gods, usually through priest or priestess, to human questioner. Name also applied to shrine where such responses were given. Most famous were those of Zeus at Dodona and of Apollo at Delphi. Apart from Sibylline Books, oracles at Rome were much less important than those in Greece.

Orádea (Hung. *Nagyvárad*), city of NW Romania. Pop. 149,000. Indust. centre in wine-making region. Bishopric from 1080; ceded by Hungary to Romania (1919).

Oran, city of NW Algeria, on Gulf of Oran. Pop. 328,000. Port, exports wine, wheat, wool; food processing. Founded 10th cent.; alternated between Spain, Turkey after 1509, taken by France (1831). Severely damaged by earthquake (1791). Scene of British destruction of French fleet (1940), to prevent capture by Germans.

Orange, House of, ruling family of the Netherlands. Name derives from principality in SE France inherited (1544) by William the Silent, of house of Nassau. His successors were stadholders of Dutch republic. William VI, prince of Orange, became 1st king of Netherlands in 1815.

Orange, town of Provence, SE France. Pop. 26,000 Tourist centre. Hist. cap. of Orange principality, rulers united (16th cent.) with House of Nassau; descendants form Dutch royal family. Roman remains incl. arch, amphitheatre.

Orange, river of S Africa. Flows *c* 2100 km (1300 mi) W from N Lesotho via South Africa to Atlantic Ocean at Alexander Bay. Forms part of South Africa-South West Africa border. Large irrigation, h.e.p. scheme; alluvial diamond deposits.

orange, evergreen tree of genus *Citrus*, bearing round, reddish-yellow fruit. Native to China but widely cultivated. Species incl. *C. sinensis*, common sweet orange used esp. in production of orange juice, and *C. aurantium*, bitter or Seville orange used in marmalade.

Orange Free State, prov. of EC South Africa. Area 129,250 sq km (49,900 sq mi); pop. 1,652,000; cap. Bloemfontein. Mainly plateau, bounded by R. Orange (S), R. Vaal (N). Sheep rearing, fruit, cereal growing; mines produce gold, diamonds, coal. Settled after 1836 Trek by Boers; republic created 1854. Annexed by Britain in Boer War, became Orange River Colony 1900. Prov. of Union of South Africa from 1910.

orange hawkweed, same as DEVIL'S PAINTBRUSH.

Orange Society, militant Irish Protestant organization; named after William of Orange, whose victory at battle of Boyne (1690) estab. Protestant succession. Formed (1795) to maintain Protestant supremacy over Catholics.

Orangutan

orangutan, *Pongo pygmaeus,* large anthropoid ape of forests of Borneo and Sumatra. Long arms, short legs and reddish-brown hair; male up to 1.5 m/5 ft tall. Mainly arboreal; vegetarian diet.

oratorio, musical setting of text (usually religious) for soloists, chorus and orchestra, first introduced by St Philip Neri at his Oratory in Rome *c* 1550. Examples are Handel's *Messiah* and Schütz's *Christmas Oratorio.*

oratory, art of eloquence. Originated in ancient Greece and Rome as branch of rhetoric concerned with effective delivery of speeches. Noted classical exponents incl. Demosthenes and Cicero; Aristotle and Quintilian wrote on theory of oratory. Classical models influenced medieval sermons, and with rising importance of parliaments, 18th cent. political speakers.

Orcagna, orig. Andrea di Cione (*c* 1308-68), Italian painter, sculptor, architect. Leading Florentine artist after Giotto, his style represents reversion to monumental Byzantine figure type. Few extant works incl. frescoes and marble tabernacle at Orsanmichele, Florence.

orchestra, large group of players of musical instruments, usually under direction of a conductor. Developed in West from *c* 1600. Modern symphony orchestra evolved in course of 18th and early 19th cents. and consists of 4 sections: strings, brass, woodwind and percussion. Except in string section, where several players play same part to increase volume, players have separate parts to play.

Tropical Asian orchid of genus *Dendrobium*

orchid, any of family Orchidaceae of perennial plants. Worldwide distribution but most of *c* 450 genera native to humid tropical regions. Some species are epiphytic. Flowers usually showy and of all colours, esp. genus *Cattleya* of tropical America, used in decoration.

Orczy, Emmuska, Baroness (1865-1947), English author, b. Hungary. Remembered for romantic adventure story of French Revolution, *The Scarlet Pimpernel* (1905), and many sequels.

ordeal, ancient method of trial. Accused exposed to physical dangers, *eg* fire. If he survived, was thought to have done so through divine intervention and therefore was innocent.

order in council, in UK, govt. decree of the sovereign issued with advice of the Privy Council. Survival of sovereign's sole power to govern. Used by Victoria to abolish (1870) purchase of army commissions, thereby avoiding opposition of House of Lords. Still used as subordinate legislation to issue new constitution for overseas territ.

orders of architecture, several classical styles of structure distinguished chiefly by the type of column (incl. base, shaft, and capital) and entablature. The 5 orders are IONIC, DORIC and CORINTHIAN, developed in Greece, and Tuscan and Composite, developed in Italy.

Ordnance Survey, official UK mapping agency. Estab. 1791 under Board of Ordnance, produced 1st map 1801. Also *see* CARTOGRAPHY.

Ordovician period, second geological period of Palaeozoic era; began *c* 500 million years ago, lasted *c* 65 million years. Extensive seas; beginning of Caledonian mountain building period. Typified by graptolites, trilobites, crinoids, corals; earliest vertebrates (fish) in North America. Also *see* GEOLOGICAL TABLE.

Ordzhonikidze, city of USSR, cap. of North Ossetian auton. republic. S European RSFSR; in N Caucasus. Pop. 252,000. Zinc, lead and silver refining; food processing. Founded 1784 as Vladikavkaz.

ore, mineral or rock from which one or more metals may be profitably extracted.

Oreads, in Greek myth, NYMPHS of the mountains.

Orebro, town of SC Sweden, at W end of Lake Hjalmaren. Pop. 87,000. Railway jct.; shoe mfg. Isl. castle scene of many hist. diets *eg* when Bernadotte chosen king of Sweden (1810).

Oregon, state of NW US, on Pacific. Area 251,181 sq km (96,981 sq mi); pop. 2,091,000; cap. Salem; largest city Portland. Columbia R. forms N border, Willamette R. divides W Coast and Cascade ranges. Important timber production, industs. Agric. in valleys (wheat, fruit, vegetables, livestock). Contested by Britain, US until 1846; territ. 1848, settlement began in 1840s via Oregon Trail. Admitted to Union as 33rd state (1859).

Orel or **Oryol,** city of USSR, SW European RSFSR; on R. Oka. Pop. 247,000. Market centre; textile machinery mfg. Founded 1564 as outpost against Tartars. Birthplace of Turgenev.

Orellana, Francisco de (*c* 1490-*c* 1546), Spanish explorer. Sailed down the Amazon from the Andes to its mouth. River derives its name from his story of meeting female warriors (Amazons) along its course.

Orenburg, city of USSR, E European RSFSR; on R. Ural. Pop. 370,000. Agric. and flour milling centre. Developed with opening of railway to Tashkent (1905). Named Chkalov (1938-57) after Soviet aviator.

Orense, town of NW Spain, on R. Miño, cap. of Orense prov. Pop. 73,000. Agric. market; sulphur springs known from Roman times. Gothic cathedral, 13th cent. bridge.

Orestes, in Greek myth, only son of AGAMEMNON and Clytemnestra. Avenged father's murder by killing Clytemnestra and her lover, Aegisthus, with aid of sister Electra. Pursued by Eumenides to Athens. Acquitted of matricide by the Areopagus. Married Hermione, daughter of Menelaus and Helen. Story is treated by Aeschylus, Sophocles and Euripides.

Oresund (Eng. The Sound), str. between Denmark and Sweden, links Kattegat with Baltic Sea. Minimum width 5 km (2 mi).

Orff, Carl (1895-), German composer. Known for his highly rhythmic compositions, frequently for the stage. Works incl. *Carmina Burana* (1937), based on medieval Latin verse.

organ, keyboard instrument, sound of which is produced by air forced through a pipe or past a metal reed (*see* HARMONIUM). Modern instruments generally have 2 or 3 keyboards (great, swell and choir) controlling different sets or ranks of pipes, and a set of foot pedals. The electronic organ contains electrical circuits that create electric signals when the keys are pressed; signals are amplified and fed to a loudspeaker to produce sound.

Organization for Economic Cooperation and Development (OECD), body of 24 nations, founded 1961; hq. in Paris. Aims incl. promotion of economic growth among its member countries, expansion of world trade, coordination and improvement of development aid.

Organization of African Unity (OAU), group of 30 African states estab. 1963 in Addis Ababa. Aims incl. African solidarity, elimination of colonialism, coordination of economic, cultural, health, defence policy. Now has over 40 member states.

Organization of American States (OAS), body of 24 American countries, estab. 1948; hq. in Washington. Aims incl. promotion of peace and economic development. Expelled Cuba (1962) and began trade boycott against it; some member countries have resumed trade with Cuba.

Organization of Petroleum Exporting Countries (OPEC), body of 11 countries which export large quantities of crude oil. Founded 1960 in Baghdad; aims to unify petroleum policies of member countries, which incl. Saudi Arabia, Iran, Libya, Algeria. Imposed fivefold increase in price of oil in 1974.

organ-pipe cactus, *Pachycereus marginatus,* tree-like cactus of Mexico. Brownish-purple flowers.

organ-pipe coral, coral composed of blood-red upright tubes resembling set of organ pipes, genus *Tubipora.*

Orientale, region of N Zaïre, main town Kisangani. Goldmining; cotton, coffee growing. Secession attempted after independence of Congo, became centre of rebel forces (1960-3). Renamed Haut-Zaïre 1972.

orienteering, sport combining cross-country running with navigation by map and compass. Introduced (1918) in Sweden, it is most popular in Scandinavia.

Origen [Adamantius] (*c* 185-*c* 254), Egyptian theologian. Head of catechetical school of Alexandria. Compiled parallel text of 6 Hebrew and 2 Greek versions of Bible. Wrote defence of Christianity, *Contra Celsum.*

original sin, in Christian theology, tendency to sin considered innate in mankind as a result of Adam's sin of rebellion. Thus salvation can only be obtained through divine GRACE.

Orinoco, river of Venezuela. Rises in Guiana Highlands, flows NW to Colombia, then NE across Venezuela into Atlantic creating wide delta. Length 2735 km (1700 mi). Navigable for 435 km (*c* 270 mi) as far as Ciudad Bolívar.

oriole, any of Oriolidae family of brightly coloured songbirds of Europe and Asia. Species incl. golden oriole, *Oriolus oriolus*; male yellow with black wings. Name also applied in US to genus *Icterus,* incl. BALTIMORE ORIOLE.

Orion, in Greek myth, giant and hunter of Boeotia loved by Artemis. She accidentally killed him and in grief placed him in heavens as a constellation.

Orion, in astronomy, constellation located at celestial equator, containing bright stars Rigel and Betelgeuse. Incl. gaseous Orion nebula, visible to unaided eye as faint patch of light.

Orissa, maritime state of E India. Area *c* 156,000 sq km (60,000 sq mi); pop. 21,935,000; cap. Bhubaneswar. Mainly hilly with fertile coastal strip; agric. economy based on rice. Iron and manganese ore, coalmining. Under British control (1803).

Orizaba, resort town of EC Mexico. Pop. 93,000. Agric. industs., major textile mfg. centre. To N is volcanic

Orizaba, highest mountain in Mexico. Height 5700 m (18,700 ft). Tourist resort, with magnificent scenery.

Orkney, isl. authority of N Scotland, comprising Orkney Isls. Area 975 sq km (376 sq mi); pop. 17,000; main town Kirkwall. Only 20 of *c* 70 isls. inhabited, incl. Mainland, South Ronaldsay, Hoy. Low-lying, treeless. Dairy, poultry farming; fishing. Have prehist. remains. Isls. passed from Norway to Scotland 1471.

Orlando, resort town of C Florida, US. Pop. 99,000. In citrus fruit growing, market gardening region; related packing, canning industs.

Orlando, Vittorio Emmanuele (1860-1952), Italian statesman, premier (1917-19). Left Paris Peace Conference (1919) after failing to obtain territ. in Dalmatia promised to Italy. Opposed Fascist takeover of govt. (1925); withdrew from politics until end of WWII.

Orléans, Charles, Duc d' (1391-1465), French nobleman and poet. Taken prisoner at Agincourt (1415) and held in captivity in England for 25 years until ransomed. Devoted himself to poetry on return to France. His son became Louis XII.

Orléans, Philippe, Duc d' (1674-1723), French nobleman. Acted as regent for Louis XV after annulling terms of Louis XIV's will. Rule was noted for corruption; notorious for his profligacy. Encouraged financial methods of John Law. His great-grandson, **Louis Philippe Joseph, Duc d'Orléans** (1747-93), known as Philippe Egalité, achieved prominence as liberal during French Revolution. Guillotined after eldest son (later Louis Philippe) deserted French army.

Orléans, town of Orléanais, NC France, on R. Loire, cap. of Loiret dept. Pop. 96,000. Road and railway jct., wine and grain trade, textile mfg., univ. (1312). From 10th cent. second residence after Paris of French kings; duchy from 1344. Besieged by English (1428-9), saved by Joan of Arc; again by Catholics (1563) as Huguenot stronghold. Gothic cathedral.

Ormandy, Eugene (1899-), American conductor, b. Hungary. Succeeded Stokowski as conductor of Philadelphia orchestra (1936), a position he still holds. Known for interpretation of 19th cent. classics.

ormer, see ABALONE.

ormolu, copper and zinc alloy used in imitation of gold. Much used in France in 18th cent. to decorate furniture and clocks.

Ormonde, James Butler, 1st Duke of (1610-88), Irish soldier. Appointed lieutenant-general of troops in Ireland (1640), he fought against Irish rebels. As lord lieutenant of Ireland, came to terms with rebels (1647). Left for France after Cromwell's conquest of Ireland (1649). Lord lieutenant twice more; finally removed from office (1684) by intrigue.

Ormuz, see HORMUZ.

ornithology, branch of zoology dealing with birds.

orogenesis, process of mountain building, resulting in formation of mountain ranges. See also MOUNTAIN.

Orpheus, in Greek myth, poet and musician, son of muse Calliope by Apollo. His music charmed animals, trees and rivers. After wife Eurydice's death, went to Hades to recover her. The gods, persuaded by his music, released her on condition that he should not look at her until they reached upper world. He could not resist and she vanished. He was later torn to pieces by Thracian women; head floated, still singing, down R. Hebrus and reached Lesbos.

Orphic mysteries, religious cult of ancient Greece, traditionally founded by Orpheus. Followers believed in dual nature of man; Dionysian (divine) and Titanic (evil). Stressed strict ethical code.

Orr, John Boyd, see BOYD ORR, JOHN, 1ST BARON.

orris root or **orrice,** root of *Iris florentina,* a European IRIS. Powdered and used in perfumery, dentifrices.

Orsk, city of USSR, E European RSFSR; on R. Ural. Pop. 231,000. Mining centre for copper, nickel; metal refining. Terminus for pipeline from Emba oilfield.

Ortega y Gasset, José (1883-1955), Spanish essayist, philosopher. Author of *Revolt of the Masses* (1930), demonstrating decay of art under mob control.

Ortelius, Abraham (1527-98), Flemish cartographer, b. Antwerp. Friend of Mercator; pub. *Theatrum orbis terrarum* (1570), uniform series of 70 maps covering the world.

orthoclase, pinkish-red mineral, consisting of potassium feldspar. Found among granitic rocks. Used in porcelain mfg.; gemstone form is called MOONSTONE.

Orthodox Church, see EASTERN ORTHODOX CHURCH.

orthopaedic surgery, branch of surgery concerned with diagnosis and treatment of injuries, deformities and diseases of bones, joints, muscles, *etc.*

Orthoptera, order of insects, incl. crickets, locusts, grasshoppers. Thickened forewings cover membranous hind wings in most species; biting mouthparts. Metamorphosis proceeds by series of moults.

Oruro, town of W Bolivia, cap. of Oruro dept. Pop. 120,000. Commercial and railway centre in mining area. Important tin, copper, tungsten mines; hist. silver mining. Founded in 17th cent.

Orvieto, town of Umbria, WC Italy. Pop. 25,000. Market town, wine, pottery. Cathedral (13th cent.) with marble facade, palace has Etruscan relics.

Orwell, George, pseud. of Eric Arthur Blair (1903-50), English author, b. India. Known for novels reflecting independent socialist commitment, esp. allegory of Russian Revolution *Animal Farm* (1946), anti-Utopia *1984* (1949). Also wrote many important literary, political essays.

Oryol, see OREL.

oryx, any of genus *Oryx* of long-horned African and Asian antelopes, inhabiting semi-desert areas. Species incl. Arabian oryx, *O. leucoryx,* nearing extinction, and *O. gazella* of Kalahari.

Osage, North American Indian tribe of Hokan-Siouan linguistic stock. Originally warlike nomads, moved from central US plains to Oklahoma reservation. Oil discoveries have made them wealthiest tribe in US.

Osaka, major seaport of Japan, on Osaka Bay, SW Honshu isl. Pop. 2,980,000. Indust. and commercial centre; exports cotton goods, machinery. Textiles, chemical and steel mfg. Has rebuilt 16th cent. castle, Buddhist and Shinto temples. Univ. (1931).

Osborn, Henry Fairfield (1857-1935), American palaeontologist, geologist. Noted for work on fossil vertebrates, esp. as curator at American Museum of Natural History from 1891.

Osborne, Dorothy (1627-95), English letter writer. Known for series of letters (1652-4, pub. 1888) written to Sir William Temple (1628-99), whom she married in 1655.

Osborne, John [James] (1929-), English playwright. Plays incl. *Look Back in Anger* (1956), creating archetype of the 'angry young man', *The Entertainer* (1957).

'Oscar', see ACADEMY AWARDS.

oscillograph, instrument for displaying or recording, in form of curve, waveforms of alternating currents and high frequency oscillations, *eg* sound waves. Oscilloscope is type of oscillograph which displays waveforms on fluorescent screen of cathode ray tube.

Oshawa, port of SE Ontario, Canada; on N shore of L. Ontario. Pop. 92,000. Car mfg., leather goods, plastics industs.

Oshogbo, city of SW Nigeria, on R. Oshun. Pop. 253,000. Trade centre on Lagos-Kano railway, esp. for cocoa, palm oil, cotton.

osier, see WILLOW.

Osijek (Ger. *Esseg),* town of Croatia, NE Yugoslavia, on R. Drava. Pop. 94,000. Chief town of Slavonia; river port, agric. market. Roman *Mursa,* colony and fortress.

Osiris, ancient Egyptian god of underworld; husband and brother of Isis. Treacherously slain by brother, Set. Associated with fertility and immortality; represented as wearing mummy wrappings.

Osler, Sir William (1849-1919), Canadian physician. Noted for work on diseases of the blood and spleen. Influential teacher, wrote *Principles and Practice of Medicine* (1892).

Oslo, cap. of Norway, on Oslo Fjord. Pop. 477,000. Admin., commercial centre; ice-free port; timber, electrical, clothing industs., shipbuilding. Founded 1048, medieval Hanseatic town. Rebuilt after fire (1624), called Christiania 1624-1925. Seat of Nobel Institute. Buildings incl. Storting (parliament), Akershus fortress (13th cent.).

Osman or **Othman I** (1259–1326), Turkish sultan, founder of Ottoman dynasty. Asserted his independence from Seljuk Turks by estab. own sultanate (*c*1299). Conquered NW Asia Minor.

osmium (Os), hard metallic element; at. no. 76, at. wt. 190.2. Densest substance known; occurs in natural alloy osmiridium with iridium. Forms hard alloys with platinum and iridium, used in pen points.

osmosis, tendency of solvent to pass through a semi-permeable membrane (permeable to solvent but not to dissolved substance) into solutions of higher concentrations. Makes possible absorption of water by plant roots and cells of animal bodies.

Osnabrück, city of NW West Germany, on R. Hase. Pop. 143,000. River port, metal goods mfg., engineering. Bishopric founded 783 by Charlemagne; Hanseatic League member, *fl* 15th cent.

Osprey

osprey, *Pandion haliaetus,* large bird of hawk family of Europe, Asia, North America. Dark plumage with white underparts. Found near water; feeds on fish.

Ossetia, *see* NORTH OSSETIA.

Ossian or **Oisin,** semi-legendary Irish bard of 3rd cent. Supposedly son of Finn MacCumhaill who lived to tell tales of his father to St Patrick. *See* MACPHERSON, JAMES.

Ossietzky, Carl von (1889-1938), German pacifist. Imprisoned (1932) for writings exposing German rearmament. Placed in concentration camp (1933-6). Award of 1935 Nobel Peace Prize to him prompted Hitler to forbid acceptance of any further Nobel Prizes by Germans.

Ossining, village of SE New York, US; on Hudson R. Pop. 22,000. Originally named Sing Sing; renamed 1901. Site of Sing Sing state prison, once noted for severe discipline procedures.

Ostend (Flem. *Oostende*), town of W Belgium, on North Sea. Pop. 58,000. Resort; port, ferry to Dover, canal to Bruges, Ghent. Fishing, fish processing, shipbuilding.

osteoarthritis, *see* ARTHRITIS.

osteomyelitis, infection of bone, with formation of pus in the marrow. Usually caused by bacteria carried in the bloodstream; treated by antibiotics.

osteopathy, medical practice based on theory that ailments result from 'structural derangements' of bones and muscles, which can be corrected by manipulation. Pioneered by Andrew Still (1828-1917).

Ostia, ancient city of WC Italy. Once port for Rome, at mouth of Tiber, *fl c* AD 100-300. Now 5 km (3 mi) from sea. Extensive ruins excavated from 1854.

ostracism, in ancient Athens, temporary banishment of citizen by popular vote. Votes recorded on shells (Gk., *ostrakon*= shell, potsherd).

Ostrava or **Moravská Ostrava,** city of E Czechoslovakia, on Moravian side of R. Ostravice. Iron, steel indust., railway engineering. Opposite is Slezská Ostrava, on Silesian side, coalmining centre. Combined pop. 279,000.

ostrich, *Struthio camelus,* fast-running flightless bird of Africa and Arabia. Long sparsely-feathered neck, long legs with 2 toes on each foot; largest of all birds, *c* 2.4 m/ 8 ft tall. Male is black with white wing and tail feathers.

Ostrogoths, branch of GOTHS who were conquered by the Huns *c* 370. Gained their independence *c* 450 and settled in Pannonia (modern Hungary). Under Theodoric, invaded

Ostia

Ostrich

and conquered Italy (488-93). Lost their separate identity after defeat by Byzantine forces of Justinian (552).

Ostrovski, Aleksandr Nikolayevich (1823-86), Russian dramatist. Known for realistic plays depicting merchant class of Moscow, *eg The Bankrupt* (1847), *The Storm* (1860).

Ostwald, Wilhelm (1853-1932), German chemist, b. Latvia. For work on catalysis, chemical equilibrium and rate of reactions, awarded Nobel Prize for Chemistry (1909). Developed process for synthesis of nitric acid from ammonia.

Oswald, Lee Harvey (1939-63), American accused of assassination (Nov. 1963) of President J.F. Kennedy. Shot while under arrest in Dallas by Jack Ruby. Held to be responsible for crime by Warren Commission (1964).

Oswego tea, *see* BERGAMOT.

Oswiecim (Ger. *Auschwitz*), town of S Poland. Pop. 39,000. Railway jct.; agric. machinery, chemical indust. Site of Nazi concentration camp in WWII, where *c* 4 million people died.

Otago, region of S South Isl., New Zealand. Area 66,120 sq km (25,530 sq mi); pop. 294,000; chief city Dunedin. Southern Alps, glacial lakes, fjords in W; valleys, coastal lowlands in E. Sheep, dairy farming, tourism, h.e.p. Pop. rose rapidly during gold rush of 1860s.

Otaru, seaport of Japan, SW Hokkaido isl. Pop. 192,000. Exports coal, timber; fishing indust.

Othman I, *see* OSMAN I.

Otranto (anc. *Hydruntum*), town of Apulia, SE Italy, on Str. of Otranto. Pop. 5000. Roman port; destroyed 1480 by Turks, never recovered.

Ottawa, cap. of Canada, in SE Ontario; on Ottawa R. Pop. 302,000. Connected to L. Ontario by Rideau Canal. Political, social, cultural centre. Important lumber indust.; major pulp and paper mills. Founded 1827 as Bytown, renamed 1854; chosen as cap. by Queen Victoria (1858). Has Parliament buildings, National Gallery, Ottawa Univ. (1866), Carleton Univ. (1942).

Ottawa: Parliament buildings

Ottawa, river of EC Canada. Flows from W Québec, SE 1130 km (c 700 mi) to St Lawrence R. near Montréal. Forms extensive part of S Québec-Ontario border. Many lakes, rapids along its course. Connected with L. Ontario by Rideau Canal.

Otter

otter, any of genus *Lutra* of aquatic carnivorous mammals, of worldwide distribution. Long flattened tail, webbed feet used for swimming. Usually lives beside fresh water, feeding on fish; SEA OTTER is marine variety. Species incl *L. lutra,* European otter, and American *L. canadensis.*

otter shrew, *Potamogale velox,* large amphibious mammal of forests of W Africa. Resembles otter, using flattened tail for swimming; diet of fish, insects.

Otto [I] the Great (912-73), king of Germany (936-73) and Holy Roman emperor (962-73). Succeeded his father Henry the Fowler. Extended realm over much of Germany and Lombardy. Defeated Magyars at Lechfeld (955). Crowned emperor by Pope John XII (962). Deposed John (963) and had his own choice elected pope.

Otto, Nikolaus August (1832-91), German engineer. Developed 4-stroke (or Otto) cycle (1876), widely used in INTERNAL COMBUSTION ENGINE.

Ottoman Empire, Islamic empire estab. in Asia Minor by OSMAN I and his descendants following collapse of Seljuk Turk empire. Under Mohammed II, Constantinople captured (1453). Under Suleiman the Magnificent, empire reached its peak, incl. Turkey, Syria, Hungary, Egypt, Persia, most of Greece and Balkans. After unsuccessful siege of Vienna (1683), its European power declined. Gradually dismembered by Russia and European powers (19th–early 20th cent.).

Otway, Thomas (1652-85), English playwright. Wrote Restoration tragedies, *eg The Orphan* (1680), *Venice Preserved* (1682).

Ouagadougou, cap. of Upper Volta. Pop. 125,000. Admin., commercial centre. Railway to Abidjan (Ivory Coast); trade in groundnuts, millet, livestock. In Ivory Coast (1933-47).

Oudenaarde (Fr. *Audenarde*), village of W Belgium, on R. Scheldt. Scene of French defeat (1708) by British and Austrians in War of Spanish Succession.

Oudh, former province of British India, now part of Uttar Pradesh. Annexation by Britain (1856) a cause of Indian Mutiny (1857-8).

Oudjda, *see* OUJDA, Morocco.

Ouessant, *see* USHANT, France.

Ouida, pseud. of Marie Louise de la Ramée (1839-1908), English novelist. Known for romantic novels, incl. *Under Two Flags* (1867), *Moths* (1880). Also wrote *Bimbi: Stories for Children* (1882).

Ouija (from French, *oui,* German, *ja,* both = 'yes'), trademark for device consisting of a planchette and a board inscribed with the alphabet. Used in spiritualist séances to convey messages supposedly from spirits.

Oujda or **Oudjda,** city of NE Morocco. Pop. 156,000. Railway jct., agric. trade centre for E Morocco, W Algeria. Occupied by French 1907-56.

Oulu (Swed. *Uleåborg*), town of W Finland, on Gulf of Bothnia. Pop. 85,000. Port, exports timber products; shipbuilding. Univ. (1958), cathedral.

ounce, *see* SNOW LEOPARD.

Our Father, *see* LORD'S PRAYER.

Ourique, village of SE Portugal. Traditionally, scene of victory of Alfonso I over Moors (1139).

Ouro Prêto, town of E Brazil, former cap. of Minas Gerais state. Pop. 46,000. In iron, manganese mining area; textile mfg. Focus of 18th cent. gold rush. Retains many colonial buildings; became national monument (1933).

Ouse, rivers of England. **1,** in Yorkshire, flows 97 km (60 mi) to R. Trent, forming Humber estuary. **2,** in Sussex, flows 48 km (30 mi) through S Downs to English Channel at Newhaven. **3,** Great Ouse, flows 257 km (160 mi) from Northamptonshire across the Fens to the Wash.

Outer Hebrides, *see* HEBRIDES, Scotland.

Outer Mongolia, *see* MONGOLIA.

outlawry, originally deprivation by law of person's legal rights, property, protection, as punishment for crime. Killing of outlaw was not an offence.

ouzel, name applied to birds of DIPPER family and RING OUZEL.

ovary, in zoology, either of 2 female reproductive organs (ductless glands) which produce germ cells or ova, and, in vertebrates, sex hormones.

ovenbird, *Seiurus aurocapillus,* North American bird of wood warbler family, that builds oven-shaped grass nest on ground. Name also applied to birds of Furnariidae family from Central and South America that build similar clay nests, incl. spinetails, canasteros.

Overijssel, prov. of E Netherlands. Area 3810 sq km (1471 sq mi); cap. Zwolle. Drained by R. Ijssel. Textiles, dairying.

overture, prelude for orchestra before opera or choral work, or independent orchestral work in similar style, *eg* Brahms' *Tragic Overture.*

Ovid, full name Publius Ovidius Naso (43 BC–c AD 18), Roman poet. Known for erotic *Ars Amatoria,* and *Metamorphoses,* series of tales from ancient mythology. Latter profoundly influenced European literature from medieval times on. Later wrote poems of exile, *Tristia,* after banishment.

Oviedo, city of N Spain, cap. of Oviedo prov. Pop. 154,000. Indust. centre in coal and iron mining area; armaments mfg., chemicals; univ. (1604). Cap. of Asturias 9th-10th cent. Gothic cathedral; 9th cent. Cámara Santa contains famous relics.

ovum or **egg,** in biology, female gamete or reproductive cell. Once fertilized by male sperm, develops into new member of same species.

Owen, Robert (1771-1858), British social reformer. Estab. model indust. community for mill workers at New Lanark, Scotland. Improved housing and working conditions, opened schools and shops. Similar scheme at New Harmony, Indiana, unsuccessful. In 1830s, advocated that trade unions should run industs. along cooperative lines.

Owen, Wilfred (1893-1918), English poet. Known for *Poems* (1920, collected by Sassoon) expressing horror of war. Killed in WWI.

Owen Falls, waterfall of SE Uganda, on Victoria Nile near Victoria Nyanza. Site of dam (1954) which controls floods, supplies h.e.p. to Uganda and Kenya.

Jesse Owens

Owens, John Cleveland ('Jesse') (1913-   ), American athlete. Only man to win 4 track and field gold medals (100m, 200m, long jump, 4 × 100m relay) in single Olympics (1936). In an athletics meeting in 1935 he broke 6 world records within 45 mins.

owl, any of order Strigiformes of widely distributed nocturnal birds of prey. Broad head and forward-facing eyes surrounded by disc of stiff feathers; short hooked beak. Feeds on rodents and small birds, regurgitating pellets of fur and feathers.

owlet moth, any of Noctuidae family of dull-coloured moths, often attracted to lights. Larvae, incl. cutworms and army worms, most active by night, damage plants.

ox, name for several members of Bovidae family. Name specifically applies to castrated bull of domesticated breeds, esp. *Bos taurus.*

oxalic acid, white crystalline poisonous solid occurring in small quantities in sorrel and rhubarb leaves. Used in ink manufacture, dyeing and bleaching.

Oxalis: European wood sorrel

oxalis or **wood sorrel,** any of genus *Oxalis* of creeping plants with five-parted flowers, cloverlike leaves. European wood sorrel, *O. acetosella,* contains oxalic acid.

ox bow lake, *see* MEANDER.

Oxenstierna, Count Axel Gustafsson (1583-1654), Swedish statesman. Appointed chancellor (1612), administered country during Gustavus Adolphus' absence at war. Continued Swedish involvement in Thirty Years War after Gustavus' death; made alliance with France after defeat at Nördlingen (1634). Virtual ruler of Sweden during minority of Queen Christina.

Oxfam, British organization, estab. 1942 to raise funds for relief of poverty, suffering in Third World or disaster-hit areas. Name originally Oxford Committee for Famine Relief, changed in 1965.

Oxford, Edward de Vere, Earl of (1550-1604), English poet. Claimed by some to be true author of Shakespeare's plays.

Oxford, town of C Mississippi, US. Pop. 14,000. Has Univ. of Mississippi; scene of race riots when 1st Negro student enrolled (1962).

Oxford, Provisions of, programme of political reform, drawn up (1258) by Simon de Montfort and forced upon Henry III of England. Provided for advisory council of 15 and attempted to limit king's taxation powers. Repudiation by Henry (1261) precipitated Barons' War (1263-7).

Oxford Movement, term for movement (from 1833) to revive Church of England through a return to practices of early Christianity. Held Anglicanism to be middle ground between Roman Catholicism and evangelicalism. First led by NEWMAN who wrote, with Keble and Pusey, *Tracts for the Times* (1833-41). Controversial in its emphasis on ritual. Movement lost ground with entry of Newman and others into RC church. Also called Tractarianism, Anglo-Catholicism.

Oxfordshire, county of SC England. Area 2611 sq km (1008 sq mi); pop. 530,000. Cotswolds in W, Chilterns in SE; elsewhere fertile clay vale. Cereals, livestock. Co. town **Oxford,** on R. Thames (Isis). Pop. 114,000. Cars, electrical goods industs. Univ. grew as medieval centre of learning from 1249. Buildings incl. Bodleian Library, Ashmolean Museum. Scene of several medieval parliaments, esp. 1258 (Provisions of Oxford). Royalist hq. in Civil War.

Oxford University, oldest univ. in UK, estab. in early 12th cent. Has grown to comprise 28 undergraduate colleges, 5 of which are women's. Centre of medieval learning, has more recently led in classics, theology, political science. Incl. Ashmolean Museum and BODLEIAN LIBRARY.

oxidation, in chemistry, originally, process by which oxygen combines with or hydrogen is removed from a substance. More generally, process in which electrons are removed from atoms or ions.

oxlip, *Primula elatior,* perennial plant of primrose family. Yellow flowers in spring.

Oxus, *see* AMU DARYA.

oxygen (O), gaseous element; at. no. 8, at. wt. 16.00. Forms *c* 1/5 of atmosphere; most abundant of all elements on Earth. Chemically active, it combines with most elements. Necessary in respiration and combustion. Obtained by fractional distillation of liquid air; used in welding flames; liquid oxygen used as rocket propellant.

oyster, edible marine bivalve mollusc, esp. of genera *Ostrea* and *Crassostrea.* Shell made of 2 unequal halves with rough outer surface. Lives on sea bed or adheres to rocks in shallow water. May be cultivated as food in artificial beds.

Ozark Mountains, plateau of SC US; mainly in S Missouri and NW Arkansas. Average height 610 m (2000 ft). Important lead, barytes deposits; many mineral springs. Tourist area.

ozone (O_3), unstable allotropic form of oxygen, with 3 atoms in molecule rather than usual 2. Pale blue gas with penetrating odour; powerful oxidizing agent. Formed by silent electrical discharge through oxygen or, naturally, by action of ultraviolet light; used as bleaching agent or germicide.

ozonosphere, layer of upper atmosphere, between 15 and 30 km above Earth's surface, in which there is an appreciable concentration of ozone. It absorbs much of Sun's ultraviolet radiation, which would be harmful to animal life.

P

Paarl, town of SW Cape Prov., South Africa. Pop. 49,000. Wine-making centre, tobacco indust. Settled (1690) by Huguenots, who introduced vine.

pacemaker, electronic device connected to the wall of the heart which provides small regular electronic shocks to restore normal heartbeat.

Pachuca de Soto, town of C Mexico. cap. of Hidalgo state. Pop. 85,000. Important silver mining, refining; leather mfg., woollen goods. Founded 1534 on ancient Toltec site.

Pacific, War of the, war (1879-84) between Chile and Bolivia, allied to Peru. Precipitated by rescinding of Chilean mining contract in Bolivian prov. of Atacama. War declared after Chile took port of Antofagasta. Separate treaties with Peru (1883) and Bolivia (1904) gave victorious Chile provs. of Tacna, Arica and Atacama.

Pacific Islands, Trust Territory of the, isls. of Pacific Ocean, held from 1947 by US under trusteeship from UN. Incl. Caroline, Mariana (except Guam), Marshall isls. Area *c* 1800 sq km (700 sq mi); pop. 114,000; cap. Saipan (Marianas).

Pacific Ocean, world's largest and deepest ocean; stretches from Asia-Australia (W) to the Americas (E), from Antarctica to the Bering Strait. Area *c* 180,000,000 sq km (70,000,000 sq mi). Reaches depth of 11,033 m (36,198 ft) in Mariana Trench. Many volcanic and coral isls. in S and W, esp. Polynesia, Melanesia and Micronesia. Ocean currents circulating in Pacific incl. Equatorial, Kuroshio, East Australia, Humboldt, California.

Pacific scandal (1873), Canadian political issue which hastened fall of Conservative govt. of Sir John Macdonald. Charge was made that Macdonald accepted campaign funds for awarding Hugh Allan's syndicate a contract to build Canadian Pacific Railway.

pacifism, individual or collective opposition to the use of armed force, esp. between nations; more generally, opposition to any violence. Religious reasons for pacifism found in Christianity, Buddhism, Confucianism, *etc.* Noted exponents incl. Gandhi, Bertrand Russell.

pack rat, North American rodent, genus *Neotoma,* often with bushy tail. Noted for habit of collecting shiny objects to decorate nest.

Padang, town of Indonesia, cap. of West Sumatra prov. Pop. 196,000. Seaport; exports coal, coffee, rubber. Estab. by Dutch 1663.

Paddington, *see* WESTMINSTER, CITY OF, England.

paddlefish, either of 2 large fish with elongated paddle-shaped snouts: *Polyodon spathula,* found in Mississippi, and *Psephurus gladius* in Yangtze.

paddy or **padi field,** intensively irrigated or lightly flooded area of land in which rice is cultivated. Common throughout India, China, SE Asia. Derived from *padi,* Malay term for unhusked rice.

Paderborn, town of N West Germany. Pop. 42,000. Agric. market, cement mfg. Bishopric estab. *c* 800 by Charlemagne, who convened some important diets here. Univ. (1614-1819). Badly damaged in WWII.

Paderewski, Ignacy Jan (1860-1941), Polish pianist, statesman. Famed performer, esp. of Chopin. Best-known composition is *Minuet in G.* Active in cause for Polish independence, became premier for 10 months in 1919.

Padua (*Padova*), city of Venetia, NE Italy, cap. of Padova prov. Pop. 238,000. Indust., transport centre. Roman *Patavium; fl* in Middle Ages under Carrara family and Venice. Galileo taught *c* 1600 at univ. (1222), basilica (13th cent.), botanical gardens (1545). Birthplace of Livy.

View of Padua

Paeonius (*fl* 5th cent. BC), Greek sculptor. Known for his marble statue *Nike* (Victory) which survives at Olympia.

Páez, José Antonio (1790-1873), Venezuelan revolutionary. Led guerrilla band against Spaniards from 1810. Assisted Bolívar in victories (1821, 1823) which drove out Spaniards. Secured separation of Venezuela from Greater Columbia (1830). President (1831–5, 1839–43); dictator (1861-3).

Paganini

Paganini, Niccolò (1782-1840), Italian violinist, composer. His virtuoso playing revolutionized violin technique. Compositions feature brilliant effects that he discovered; incl. 4 violin concertos, *Perpetual Motion,* and 24 caprices for solo violin.

Page, Sir Earle Christmas Grafton (1880-1961), Australian statesman, PM (1939). Leader of Country Party (1920-39). Minister for health (1937-9, 1949-55), estab. national health scheme (1953).

pagoda, Buddhist temple in form of pyramidal tower, built in superimposed stories tapering towards top. Common in India and China, they were imitated in 18th cent. European architecture.

Shwedagon pagoda, Rangoon

Pago Pago or **Pango Pango,** main town of American Samoa, on Tutuila Isl. Pop. 2000. Admin. centre, port, international airport. US naval base, coaling station (1878-1951).

Pahang, state of West Malaysia. Area *c* 36,000 sq km (13,900 sq mi); pop. 503,130; cap. Kuala Lipis. Largely jungle with mountainous interior. Rubber, rice, tin mining.

Pahlevi, Reza or **Riza Khan** (1877–1944), shah of Iran (1925-41). Led military coup d'état (1921); became premier (1923). Deposed Ahmad Mirza, last of Qajar dynasty and became shah (1925). Enacted many reforms. Abdicated in favour of son, Mohammed Reza.

pain, sensation arising from excessive stimulation of sensory nerve ends and conveyed by nerve fibres to the brain, where it is perceived. Relieved by analgesics, narcotics, *etc.*

Thomas Paine

Paine, Thomas (1737-1809), American writer, b. England. Argued for immediate independence of American colonies in pamphlet *Common Sense* (1775); promoted patriot cause in series of pamphlets *The American Crisis.* Defended French Revolution in *The Rights of Man* (1791-2). Accused of treason in England, fled to France (1792).

paint, pigment in suspension with oil, water or other medium (often with additional thinners) used to decorate or protect a surface. After application, dries to adhesive film by evaporation of thinner or oxidation of medium. One of commonest media is linseed oil with turpentine as thinner, but many specialized synthetic paints increasingly used.

painted lady, *Vanessa cardui,* widely distributed butterfly with brownish-black and orange wings.

painting, one of the fine arts, practised from earliest times. Examples of palaeolithic animal paintings survive at Lascaux. Frescoes were important in art of ancient Egypt and Rome. Oil colour, portraiture and use of perspective were developed in 15th cent., landscape in 16th and 17th cents. Abstract painting began in early 20th cent.

Paisley, town of Strathclyde region, WC Scotland. Pop. 95,000. Textiles industs. esp. thread; once famous for Paisley shawls. Has 12th cent. abbey.

Pakistan

Paiute or **Piute,** North American Indian tribes of Uto-Aztecan linguistic family. N group of Idaho and Nevada opposed white settlers of 1860s. S group of Great Basin, Nevada were sedentary root gatherers. Originators of GHOST DANCE religion.

Pakistan, republic of SC Asia, on NW India boundary. Area *c* 804,000 sq km (311,000 sq mi); pop. 65,000,000; cap. Islamabad. Language: Urdu. Religion: Islam. Mountains in N and W; population concentrated in plains watered by Indus and its tributaries; desert in SW. Agric. economy (esp. grains, rice, cotton). Major cities Karachi, Lahore. Divided into 4 provs. (Baluchistan, Punjab, Sind, Northwest Frontier). Created 1947 out of India following Moslem agitation led by Jinnah; became republic 1956. Long-standing dispute with India over possession of Kashmir led to fighting (1965). East Pakistan became independent republic of BANGLADESH (1972) following civil war and Indian military intervention.

Palaeocene epoch, first geological epoch of Tertiary period. Beginning of Alpine mountain building. Replacement of dinosaurs by primitive mammals, ancestors of cat, dog, horse, elephant; modern vegetation *eg* seed-bearing plants. Also *see* GEOLOGICAL TABLE.

palaeography or **paleography,** study of ancient writing. Concerned with deciphering, describing and dating of scripts.

Palaeolithic or **Old Stone Age,** prehist. period beginning *c* 1.8 million years ago during which modern man, *Homo sapiens,* evolved from 1st tool-making predecessors, *eg* AUSTRALOPITHECUS. Usually subdivided into Lower, Middle and Upper periods. Lower period, earliest division, saw development of simple stone tools, *eg* hand axes. Middle period, represented by culture of Neanderthal man, saw introduction of flint tools. In Upper period, *H. sapiens* emerged, and specialized tools, *eg* burins, were developed.

Palaeologus, last dynasty to rule Byzantine Empire (1260-1453). First of dynasty was Michael VIII (d. 1282), last was CONSTANTINE XI.

palaeontology, branch of geology dealing with the study of prehist. life, based on fossil remains. Incl. palaeobotany, palaeozoology; yields information on evolution, adaptation of organisms to changing environment. Early works incl. Agricola's *De natura fossilium* (1558); foundations laid in 19th cent. by Cuvier, Darwin, Smith, Osborne.

Palaeozoic or **Primary era,** geological era intermediate between Precambrian and Mesozoic eras. Duration c 350 million years. Cambrian, Ordovician, Silurian periods form Lower Palaeozoic; time of trilobites, graptolites, brachiopods, earliest fish. Devonian, Carboniferous, Permian periods form Upper Palaeozoic; time of amphibians, reptiles, corals, crinoids, earliest terrestrial flora. Also see GEOLOGICAL TABLE.

Palafox [y Melzi], José de (c 1780-1847), Spanish general. Leader of the heroic defence of Saragossa (1808-9) in the Peninsular War; imprisoned by French victors. Given the duchy of Saragossa (1836).

Palamedes, in Greek legend, one of Greek heroes in Trojan War. Discovered Odysseus' deceit in trying to evade service. Odysseus in revenge had him executed on false evidence of treachery.

palate, term for roof of human mouth. Front portion, hard palate, joins tooth ridge; back portion, soft palate, is fibrous muscular arch which closes back of nose during swallowing. Uvula projects from centre of arch.

Palatinate (*Pfalz*), two regions of West Germany, hist. linked under Wittelsbach family (1214-1918). **Lower** or **Rhenish Palatinate** (*Rheinpfalz*), lies between R. Rhine and French border; now part of Rhineland-Palatinate state. Fertile, produces wines; main towns Neustadt, Kaiserslautern. **Upper Palatinate** (*Oberpfalz*), now part of Bavaria prov. Agric., cattle raising. Counts Palatine were imperial electors from 1356; territ. called Electoral Palatinate (*Kurpfalz*).

Palau Islands, isl. group of W Pacific Ocean, part of Caroline Isls. Japanese base in WWII, taken (1944) by US.

Palawan, isl. of W Philippines. Area c 11,800 sq km (4550 sq mi). Little arable land; produces timber, chromite.

pale, hist. term for restricted region within a country, where different system of law and govt. prevailed. In Irish history, denotes region around Dublin where English rule was enforced (12th-17th cent.).

Palembang, city of Indonesia, cap. of South Sumatra prov., port on R. Musi. Pop. 583,000. Trade centre for nearby oilfields; exports petroleum products, rubber. Cap. of sultanate until abolished by Dutch in 1825.

Palencia, town of N Spain, on R. Carrión, cap. of Palencia prov. Pop. 58,000. Engineering, textile mfg. Residence of king of León; had 1st univ. in Spain (1208, moved to Salamanca).

Palermo (anc. *Panormus*), town of N Sicily, Italy, on Tyrrhenian Sea. Cap. of Sicily and Palermo prov. Pop. 657,000. Port, exports fruit, wine, olive oil; indust. centre; univ. (1805). Founded by Phoenicians, later held by Carthage, Rome, Byzantium. *Fl* under Arabs, Normans (esp. 12th-13th cents.). Cathedral (12th cent.).

Palestine, see ISRAEL.

Palestrina, Giovanni Pierluigi da (c 1525-94), Italian composer. Director of Julian Chapel choir in St Peter's, Rome. Wrote mainly sacred works for unaccompanied voices, incl. over 100 Mass settings. Considered master of counterpoint and polyphony.

Paley, William (1743-1805), English theologian. Author of standard utilitarian work on ethics, *Principles of Moral and Political Philosophy* (1785), and popular *A View of the Evidences of Christianity* (1794).

Pali, vernacular dialect of classical SANSKRIT. The language of S Buddhist scriptures, has become religious language of Buddhism.

Palissy, Bernard (c 1510-89), French potter. Originated richly coloured, smooth-glazed pottery known as Palissy ware. Specialized in rustic pottery, incl. plates, dishes and vases, with realistic figures of fish, reptiles, *etc.*

Palladio, Andrea (1508-80), Italian architect. Known for theoretical writings on harmonic proportion in architecture, esp. Roman, as exemplified by *Quattro Libri dell'Architettura* (1570). Designed many villas in or near Vicenza, *eg* Villa Rotonda, which display classical temple front. Greatly influenced neo-Classical work of 17th and 18th cents. throughout Europe.

Palladium, in ancient Greece and Rome, any statue of Pallas ATHENA, esp. legendary statue in Troy on the preservation of which the safety of the city was supposed to depend. Stolen by Diomedes and Odysseus during Trojan War. The Romans claimed to have the true Palladium, brought by Aeneas from Troy.

palladium (Pd), white metallic element; at. no. 46, at. wt. 106.4. Occurs with platinum and iridium. Used as catalyst in hydrogenization and in alloys with gold, platinum, silver.

Pallas, one of the minor planets, or asteroids, revolving about the Sun between Mars and Jupiter. Discovered (1802) by Olbers.

Pallas Athena, see ATHENA.

palm, any of family Palmae of tropical and subtropical trees or shrubs. Woody, branchless trunk, large evergreen feather-like or fan-shaped leaves growing in bunch at top. Economically important species incl. date, coconut, raffia and sago palms.

Palma (de Mallorca), cap. of Majorca and Baleares prov., Spain, on Bay of Palma. Pop. 234,000. Chief city and port of Balearic Isls., exports agric. produce; tourist resort. Roman colony; held by Moors 8th-13th cent. Moorish palace, 13th cent. cathedral; Lonja exchange.

Palmas, Las, city of Grand Canary, Canary Isls., Spain, cap. of Las Palmas prov. Pop. 287,000. Tourist resort, in fertile valley noted for palms; outport at Puerto de la Luz, exports fruit, wine; fishing. Cathedral (18th cent.).

Palme, [Sven] Olof [Joachim] (1927-), Swedish politician, premier (1969-76). Succeeded Erlander as Social Democratic leader and premier. Defeat in 1976 election marked end of 44 years of Social Democrat rule in Sweden.

Palmer, Arnold (1929-), American golfer. Winner of 4 US Masters, 1 US Open, 2 British Open championships. His exciting play helped make golf a major spectator sport.

Samuel Palmer

Palmer, Samuel (1805-81), English painter. Influenced by Blake, he is remembered for the visionary landscapes of his 'Shoreham Period' (1826-35).

Palmerston, Henry John Temple, 3rd Viscount (1784-1865), English statesman, PM (1855-8, 1859-65). As Whig foreign secretary (1830-41, 1846-51), secured Belgian independence and supported Turkish territ. integrity against plans of Russia and France to take control of Bosporus and Egypt. As PM, continued Crimean War, supported Italian nationalism, put down Sepoy revolt in India (1857-8).

Palmerston North, city of S North Isl., New Zealand, on Manawatu R. Pop. 57,000. Market town and railway jct. for large dairying, sheep farming region; woollen mills; timber indust.

palm oil, fatty, orange-red oil obtained from fruit of many palms, incl. oil palm *Elaeis guineensis*. Used in manufacture of soap, candles, *etc.*

Palm Sunday, Christian holy day commemorating Jesus' entry into Jerusalem. Celebrated on Sunday before Easter.

Palmyra, ancient city of C Syria. Rose to prominence (AD 130-270) until destroyed by Romans in 273. Has ruins of temple devoted to sun worship.

Oil palm, source of palm oil

Giant panda

Palomar, Mount, mountain of S California, US; near San Diego. Height 1867 m (6126 ft). Has world's largest reflecting telescope, 508 cm (200 in.) in diameter.

Pamirs, mountainous region of C Asia, mainly in USSR, E Tadzhik SSR, but extending into Afghanistan and China. Consists of high mountain valleys bordered by mountain ranges; peaks incl. Mt. Communism.

Pampas, large grassy plain of NC Argentina, mainly given over to cattle raising, dairy farming; wealth from related industs., eg meat packing.

pampas grass, several giant perennial South American grasses of genera *Cortaderia* and *Gynerium.* Grown as ornamentals.

Pamplona, city of N Spain, at foot of Pyrenees, cap. of Navarra prov. Pop. 147,000. Agric. market, iron, lead-smelting. Annual festival when bulls run through streets. Basque kingdom founded 824, was cap. of kingdom of Navarre until union with Castile (1515). Cathedral (14th cent.).

Pan, in Greek myth, god of flocks and shepherds. Represented as partly goat-like in form. Played musical pipes in memory of nymph Syrinx, who had been changed into a reed when he was pursuing her. Worshipped originally in Arcadia, believed to inspire lonely travellers with terror (panic). Identified with Faunus by Romans.

Panama, republic of Central America, enclosing Panama Canal Zone. Area 75,650 sq km (29,210 sq mi); pop. 1,428,000; cap. Panama City. Language: Spanish. Religion: RC. Volcanic mountains in W and E; fertile lowlands in C (bananas, coffee, mahogany exports). Also important fishing industs., esp. shrimps. Pop. mainly mestizo (mixed). Explored by Balboa (1513); became part of Colombia after break with Spain (1821); independence after Colombia's refusal to allow US to build Canal (1903).

Panama Canal, waterway across Isthmus of Panama, connecting Caribbean and Pacific; 64 km (40 mi) long. Incl. artificial Gatun L. (area 422 sq km/163 sq mi). Built by US (1904-14), admin. as part of Panama Canal Zone.

Panama Canal Zone, admin. region of US comprising *c* 16 km (10 mi) wide canal strip in C Panama. Area 1432 sq km (553 sq mi); admin. hq. Balboa. Incl. ports Cristóbal (Atlantic), Balboa (Pacific).

Panama City, cap. of Panama, on Gulf of Panama. Pop. 420,000. Prosperous from building of Panama Canal. Clothing, shoes, beer mfg. Founded 1519; rebuilt 1673 after destruction by pirates under Henry Morgan. Became cap. 1903.

Pan-Americanism, movement for economic and political cooperation among countries of North and South America. Sporadic 19th cent. attempts to formulate policy frustrated by suspicions of US imperialism. Series of 20th cent. meetings culminated in formation of ORGANIZATION OF AMERICAN STATES.

Panay, isl. of Philippines, S of Luzon. Area *c* 11,500 sq km (4450 sq mi). Lowlands in E produce rice, corn, copra.

Panchen Lama, Tibetan spiritual leader, regarded as reincarnation of Amitabha, the Buddha of light. Holds responsibility for spiritual matters under DALAI LAMA.

pancreas, gland found in mesentery, near duodenum, of vertebrates. Secretes alkaline mixture of digestive enzymes through a duct into duodenum. Cell groups (islets of Langerhans) also secrete hormones insulin and glucagon.

panda, arboreal, mainly vegetarian mammal of order Carnivora. Giant panda, *Ailuropoda melanoleuca,* found in Tibet and SW China, feeds mostly on bamboo shoots; black and white, resembles bear. Lesser panda, *Ailurus fulgens,* of Himalayas, resembles raccoon; reddish-brown fur, long bushy tail.

Pandarus, in Greek legend, a Trojan warrior. Broke truce in Trojan War by wounding Menelaus. Killed by Diomedes. In medieval romance, name given to the intermediary between the lovers Troilus and Cressida.

Pandit, Vijaya Lakshmi (1900-), Indian diplomat, sister of Nehru. Prominent in Indian National Congress before independence. Held several diplomatic posts after Indian independence; high commissioner in London (1955-61).

Pandora, in Greek myth, first woman on earth. Fashioned from clay by Hephaestus at command of Zeus as vengeance on man because of Prometheus' stealing of fire from the gods. Endowed with charm and deceit by the gods. Sent to Epimetheus, brother of Prometheus, carrying box which she opened, releasing all evils on world, while hope alone remained in box.

Tree pangolin (*Manis tricuspis*)

pangolin or **scaly anteater,** any of order Pholidota of toothless mammals of Africa and tropical Asia. Body and tail protected by horny scales; feeds on ants, termites caught by sticky tongue. Species incl. giant pangolin, *Manis gigantes.*

Pango Pango, *see* PAGO PAGO.

Panipat, town of Haryana state, NW India. Pop. 88,000. Sugar processing, brassware mfg. Scene of 3 great battles, incl. victory of Akbar the Great over king of Bengal (1556).

Panjim, cap. of union territ. of Goa, Daman and Diu, W India. Pop. 35,000.

Emmeline Pankhurst

Pankhurst, Emmeline, née Goulden (1858-1928), English suffragette. Founded Women's Social and Political Union (1905), whose members used militant methods in cause of women's suffrage. Imprisoned (1912-13) and released after hunger strikes. Supported by daughters, **Christabel Pankhurst** (1880-1958) and **Sylvia Pankhurst** (1882-1960).

panpipes, ancient musical instrument made of several pipes of different length bound together and played by blowing across open upper ends. Used in folk music, *eg* that of Romania.

Pan-Slavism, doctrine of 19th cent. urging political and cultural unity of all Slavs. First Pan-Slav conference, held (1848) in Prague, favoured Austrian protection of Slavs. Russia later seen as champion of Pan-Slavism, but widely believed to use doctrine for expansion into Austrian and Turkish empires.

pansy, *see* VIOLET.

pantheism, system of belief which identifies God in all things. Found in all periods, *eg* in Brahmanism and philosophy of Xenophanes, and in much nature poetry, *eg* Wordsworth's.

pantheon, originally building for worship of all gods. Pantheon at Rome was built by Agrippa (27 BC) and rebuilt *c* AD 120 by Hadrian. Preserved almost intact, it has great hemispherical dome. Term also denotes building in which illustrious men are buried, *eg* Panthéon, Paris.

panther, *see* LEOPARD.

pantomime, originally type of drama without speech. In 18th cent. term used for mimed scenes, spectacles, based on Italian *commedia dell'arte.* Now a typically British Christmas entertainment, with comedy, songs, dancing.

Panzer (Ger., = armour), a mechanized unit of the German army, organized for rapid attack, Panzer divisions were highly successful in WWII, esp. in N Africa.

Paotow, city of Inner Mongolia auton. region, N China. Pop. 800,000. Port and trade centre on Hwang Ho. Iron and steel indust., chemical and fertilizer mfg.

papacy, office of the pope as bishop of Rome and head of RC church. Estab., according to RC doctrine, when Jesus gave Peter primacy of Church.

Papadopoulos, George (1919-　), Greek political leader. Became premier after leading 1967 military coup. Abolished monarchy (1973) and became president. Overthrown by military coup amidst popular unrest (1973). Sentenced to death for treason (1975); sentence commuted.

Papal States, former independent territ. of C Italy, cap. Rome. Originated in 'Patrimony of St Peter' given to popes in 4th cent.; grew to max. extent 16th cent. (incl. Latium, Umbria, the Marches, E Emilia-Romagna). Italian unification (1861) absorbed all but Rome (annexed 1870). Also *see* VATICAN CITY.

papaw, *see* PAWPAW

papaya, *Carica papaya,* tropical American tree. Large, edible melon-like fruit.

Papeete, cap. of Tahiti and French Polynesia. Pop. 28,000. Admin. centre; international airport, port (exports copra, vanilla, pearl shell); tourist centre.

Papen, Franz von (1879-1969), German politician. Member of Catholic Centre Party, made chancellor by Hindenburg (1932). On resignation, helped secure Hitler's chancellorship and served as his deputy (1933-4). Acquitted of war crimes at Nuremberg.

paper, thin material consisting of sheets of cellulose derived from vegetable fibres. Most paper is made from wood pulp freed from non-cellulose material; higher grade made from cotton rags. Invented in China *c* AD 105, it was spread to rest of world by the Arabs in 8th cent.; paper mfg. in Europe began in Spain in 12th cent. Leading producers incl. Canada, USSR, Scandinavia.

Papineau, Louis Joseph (1786-1871), French-Canadian insurgent. Helped precipitate Rebellion of 1837 after British failures to implement financial and constitutional reform in Lower Canada. Fled to US, then lived in France; returned after general amnesty (1845).

paprika, *see* PEPPER.

Papua New Guinea, country of SW Pacific, member of British Commonwealth. Area 463,000 sq km (178,000 sq mi); pop. 2,490,000; cap. Port Moresby. Consists of E part of New Guinea isl., Bismarck Archipelago, Bougainville and other isls. Timber exports; minerals incl. gold, copper. Country formed from Australian territ. of Papua and former German colony of New Guinea, mandated to Australia by League of Nations in 1920. Became independent 1975.

Papyrus

papyrus, *Cyperus papyrus,* tall sedge of Africa and Asia. Ancient Egyptians used stem for boats, cloth and to make sheets of writing material, also called papyrus.

Pará, state of N Brazil. Area *c* 1,230,000 sq km (475,000 sq mi); pop. 2,160,000; cap. Belém. Largely unexploited tropical rain forest. Produces nuts, rubber, hardwood. Transportation mainly by river steamers.

Pará, river of N Brazil, wide arm of Amazon delta. Separates Marajó Isl. from mainland. Length 320 km (*c* 200 mi).

parable, term used in Gospels for brief narrative illustrating a religious teaching, esp. those of Jesus.

parabola, in geometry, curve described by a point which moves so that its distance from a fixed point (focus) equals its distance from fixed line (directrix). Also described by intersection of cone with plane parallel to one side.

Paracelsus, Philippus, orig. Theophrastus von Hohenheim (*c* 1493-1541), Swiss physician, alchemist, chemist. Forerunner of scientific medicine, advocated use of experiment, study of anatomy, specific drugs. Wrote many medical and occult works.

parachute, umbrella-shaped nylon or silk canopy (developed 18th cent.) reducing speed of falling body through air. Used in military and sporting activity; also as brake for aircraft and spacecraft during landing.

Paraclete, in Christian theology, the Holy Spirit, considered as comforter, intercessor or advocate.

Paradise, term denoting Garden of Eden before the Fall; also used to denote heaven or intermediate stage for righteous souls between death and final judgement.

paraffins, hydrocarbons of general formula C_nH_{2n+2}; chemically inactive. First 4 members of paraffin series, incl. methane, are gases, used as fuels. Next 11 are liquids which form principal constituents of paraffin oil (kerosene), a fuel obtained in distillation of petroleum. Other members are wax-like solids, chief constituents of paraffin wax.

Paráiba, state of NE Brazil. Area 56,371 sq km (21,765 sq mi); pop. 2,385,000; cap. João Pessoa. Narrow coastal plain, hilly interior. Agric. incl. cotton, sugar cane, tobacco; cattle rearing.

parakeet, any of several small parrots with long tails. BUDGERIGAR is common species.

parallax, in astronomy, apparent difference in position of heavenly body with reference to some point on surface of Earth and some other point, *eg* centre of Earth (diurnal parallax) or centre of Sun (annual parallax). Caused by Earth's rotation and revolution about Sun. Used to measure distance from Earth to heavenly body.

parallel, in mapping, *see* LATITUDE.

paralysis, loss of voluntary movement, usually caused by disorders of nervous system. Damage to spinal cord or brain, stroke, poliomyelitis may result in paralysis.

paramagnetism, property of certain materials, *eg* platinum and aluminium, of being weakly attracted by magnets (magnetic permeability of such material is slightly greater than 1). Degree of paramagnetism may be increased in some substances by decrease of temperature.

Paramaribo, cap. of Surinam, port near mouth of Surinam R. Pop. 111,000. Rum, bauxite, coffee exports. Many canals give it a Dutch appearance.

Paraná, port of EC Argentina, cap. of Entre Ríos prov. on Paraná R. Pop. 190,000. Grain, cattle produce. Cap. of Argentina 1853-62. Has cathedral; famous Urquiza Park.

Paraná, river of S Brazil. Formed by Paranaíba-Rio Grande rivers, flows SW 3200 km (*c* 2000 mi) along Paraquay border, through Argentina to Uruguay R. at La Plata estuary.

Paranaguá, Atlantic port of S Brazil. Pop. 52,000. Ocean access for Curitiba, connected by road with Asunción (Paraguay). Important coffee exports. Founded *c* 1600.

paranoia, in psychiatry, mental disorder associated with delusions of persecution or grandeur. Often occurs with schizophrenia; true paranoia, in which personality remains intact, is rare.

Paraguay, republic of SC South America. Area 406,752 sq km (157,047 sq mi); pop. 2,396,000; cap. Asunción. Languages: Spanish, Guaraní. Religion: RC. Unexploited Chaco in W; concentration of pop. and indust. between Paraguay, Paraná rivers. Cotton, maté growing; cattle rearing (meat packing). Settled in 16th cent. by Spanish; gained independence 1811. Extended Chaco frontier in war (1932-5) with Bolivia; political instability, economic under-development from late 1940s.

Paraguay, river of SC South America. Rises in E Mato Grosso (W Brazil), flows S 2100 km (*c* 1300 mi) through Paraguay to join Paraná R. Forms part of Argentina-Brazil border.

parasite, plant or animal that lives on or in an organism of another species from which it derives nourishment or protection without benefiting the host and usually harming it. Ectoparasites, *eg* lice, live on surface of host; endoparasites, *eg* tapeworms, inside host's body.

parathyroid, one of usually four small glands on or near the thyroid gland. They secrete a hormone, parathormone, which regulates calcium and phosphate concentration of blood.

Parcae, *see* FATES.

parchment, writing material prepared from stretched untanned animal skins. First used in Pergamum (*c* 150 BC).

Pardubice (Ger. *Pardubitz*), town of C Czechoslovakia, on R. Elbe. Pop. 72,000. Railway jct.; indust. centre (oil refining, brewing). Cathedral (13th cent.).

Pareto, Vilfredo (1848-1923), Italian economist, sociologist, b. France. Attempted to develop economics as scientific study, sociology and psychology to be concerned with non-rational elements in human behaviour. Best known for theory of development and fall of elites. Wrote *Mind and Society* (1916).

Paris, in Greek myth, son of Priam of Troy. Exposed on Mt. Ida when it was prophesied that he would cause fall of Troy. Brought up by shepherds and returned to the city. Chosen to settle dispute over APPLE OF DISCORD thus instigating Trojan War. In War, killed Achilles and was killed by Philoctetes.

Paris, Matthew (d. 1259), English monk and historian. His *Chronica majora* is major source of knowledge on European history from 1235 to 1259. Used his influential friends, *eg* Henry III, to supply him with information.

Paris (anc. *Lutetia*), cap. and dept. of France, on R. Seine. Pop. 2,591,000, greater Paris 8,187,000. River port, transport focus; admin., commercial, indust. centre (esp. luxury goods, clothing); tourism. Dominates France culturally and economically. Gaulish, then Roman settlement; made cap. of France in 987 by Capet. Medieval scholastic, religious centre; *fl* as literary, artistic centre 17th-18th cent. Focus of revolutions in 1789, 1830, 1848, 1871. Places of interest incl. Ile de la Cité (site of 1st

Paris: the Eiffel Tower

settlement) with Notre Dame Cathedral (12th - 13th cent.), Palais de Justice, Sainte-Chapelle; Arc de Triomphe, Eiffel Tower (300 m/984 ft), Montmartre (artistic quarter), Palais d'Elysée (president's residence), Sorbonne univ. (12th cent.), Louvre art gallery. Modern Paris planned (19th cent.) by Haussmann.

Paris, Congress of, conference held (1856) to negotiate settlement of Crimean War. Russian-Turkish boundary restored to pre-war status, Black Sea declared neutral, Moldavia and Walachia (later Romania) became auton.

Paris, Treaty of, name of several treaties signed in Paris. That of 1763, signed by Britain, France and Spain, ended Seven Years War. By treaty of 1783, Britain acknowledged independence of US. Treaty of 1814 gave France favourable settlement of Napoleonic wars after Napoleon's abdication but that of 1815, after French defeat at Waterloo, was much harsher.

Paris, University of, France's largest univ. Dates from 13th cent., but re-estab. (1808) after Revolution in grounds of SORBONNE. General council of faculties estab. 1885. Now occupies many sites around Paris and incl. several specialized institutes *eg* military, agricultural, artistic.

Paris Peace Conference, *see* VERSAILLES, TREATY OF.

parity, conservation of, in physics, principle that there is no fundamental difference between left and right; thus laws of physics should be valid for both left-handed and right-handed systems of coordinates. Lee and Yang showed (1956) principle was violated by certain types of beta-decay of atomic nuclei.

Mungo Park

Park, Mungo (1771-1806), Scottish explorer. Explored and estab. much of course of R. Niger (1795-6); drowned on 2nd expedition after attack by natives. Wrote *Travels in the Interior of Africa* (1799).

Park Chung Hee (1917-), South Korean political leader. Seized power in army coup (1961); became president (1963). Estab. dictatorial powers, ostensibly to withstand threats of North Korean invasion. Suppressed critics of his govt.

Parker, Charlie ('Bird'), orig. Charles Christopher Parker (1920-55), American jazz musician. Noted for his saxophone improvisations, he was a leader in the movement away from swing to the 'bop' style of the late 1940s.

Parker, Matthew (1504-75), English churchman. Archbishop of Canterbury (1559-75). Revised (1562) the Thirty-nine Articles, basic Anglican creed.

Parkes, town of EC New South Wales, Australia. Pop. 9000. Agric. market; former goldmining centre. Nearby is 64 m (210 ft) radiotelescope (1961).

Parkinson, Cyril Northcote (1909-), British historian, author. Known for humorous study of business world, *Parkinson's Law* (1958), stating that 'work expands to fill the time available for its completion'.

Parkinson's disease, disturbance of voluntary movements caused by degeneration of the basal ganglia of the brain. Characterized by rhythmic body tremors and muscular rigidity. Usually occurs in later life. First described by English physician James Parkinson (1755-1824).

Parliament, bicameral legislature of UK, consisting of HOUSE OF LORDS, HOUSE OF COMMONS. Executive power rests in sovereign, who in reality acts only on advice of ministers, *ie* PRIME MINISTER and CABINET. Modern development began in 13th cent. with frequent assemblies, influence of DE MONTFORT; MODEL PARLIAMENT esp. important. Its political power grew under Plantagenets, marked by deposition of 2 kings and growth of Parliament's control of national finance. Commons' drafting of statutes replaced petitions (1414). Tudors generally dominated both Houses, but under Charles I traditional conflict between sovereign's prerogative and parliamentary privilege exaggerated into absolutism *v* popular govt. Led to CIVIL WAR. Parliament's power affirmed by BILL OF RIGHTS (1689). Party system developed after Civil War, became important in 19th cent. Reform Bill (1832) reconstituted Commons, extended

SUFFRAGE. Parliament Acts (1911, 1949) estab. predominance of Commons, esp. with power in finance bills.

Parliament Act (1911), legislation restricting veto power of House of Lords. Arose from rejection of 1909 finance bill by Lords. In case of financial legislation, Lords stripped of rights to amend or reject; right to delay other legislation limited to two years, reduced to one year under 1949 Parliament Act.

Parma, city of Emilia-Romagna, NC Italy, cap. of Parma prov. Pop. 177,000. Agric. market, textiles, Parmesan cheese mfg. Medieval cultural centre; under Farnese family 1545-1731. Romanesque cathedral (11th cent.), univ. (1502), wooden Farnese theatre (1618).

Parmigianino, orig. Francesco Mazzola (1503-40), Italian painter, etcher. An early mannerist, his elegant graceful work is marked by its elongation of figures. Paintings incl. *Madonna with the Long Neck.*

Parnaíba, river of NE Brazil. Flows N 1300 km (*c* 800 mi) to Atlantic, near town of Parnaíba. Export route for river valley area.

Parnassiens, les, school of French poets (*c* 1870), incl. Leconte de Lisle, Mallarmé, Verlaine, who published their work in journal *Parnasse Contemporain* (1866-76). They reacted against ROMANTICISM, advocating emotional detachment, 'art for art's sake'.

Parnassus, Mount, peak of Boeotia, C Greece. Height 2456 m (8061 ft). Sacred to Apollo, Dionysus, the Muses. Fountain of Castalia and Delphic oracle lie on slopes.

Parnell, Charles Stewart (1846-91), Irish nationalist leader. Led obstructive tactics of Irish nationalists in Parliament from 1877. Directed campaign for land reform in Ireland; imprisoned (1881) for obstructing provisions of new land act; released (1882). Supported Gladstone's Home Rule bill (1886). Career ruined after involvement in divorce scandal with Katharine O'Shea (1889-90).

Páros, isl. of Greece, in Aegean Sea, one of Cyclades. Area 166 sq km (64 sq mi). Tourism. Famous from ancient times for Parian marble.

Parr, Catherine (1512-48), English queen consort, 6th wife of Henry VIII. Married Henry in 1543; acted as regent during his absence (1544). After Henry's death, married Lord Thomas Seymour (1547).

Parrot

parrot, hook-billed, often brilliantly coloured bird of Psittacidae family. Widely distributed, esp. in Australasia and South America. Noted for speech mimicry. Species incl. cockatoo, macaw, parakeet, lory.

Parry, Sir William Edward (1790-1855), English explorer, naval officer. Led several expeditions (1818-25) in search of Northwest Passage; attempted to reach North Pole by sledge (1827). Wrote valuable records.

Parry Islands, archipelago of C Franklin Dist., Northwest Territs., Canada. Incl. Melville, Bathurst, Devon Isls.

Parseeism, see ZOROASTRIANISM.

Parsifal, figure in ARTHURIAN LEGEND, sometimes called Percival, often identified with Gawain. Story basis of medieval poems, eg Parzival by Wolfram von Eschenbach.

parsley, Petroselinum hortense, biennial herb with aromatic curled leaves, used as flavouring, yellow umbelliferous flowers. Also see UMBELLIFERAE.

Parsnip

parsnip, Pastinaca sativa, biennial plant of parsley family. Long, fleshy edible root.

Parsons, Sir Charles Algernon (1854-1931), English engineer. Invented a form of steam TURBINE and demonstrated its many applications.

parthenogenesis, biological reproduction from unfertilized ovum. Occurs naturally in some organisms; male drones of ants, bees and wasps are produced by parthenogenesis. Can be artificially induced in rabbits, frogs, etc, but resulting offspring rarely reach maturity.

Parthenon, temple of Athena on Acropolis, Athens. Built by Callicrates and Ictinus (447-432 BC) in Doric style; Phidias supervised the sculpture. Middle section destroyed by Venetian bombardment 1687. Part of sculptured frieze was acquired by Lord Elgin (1801-3) and is now in British Museum.

Parthia, ancient kingdom of SW Asia, corresponding to Khurasan, NE Iran. Once part of Assyrian and Persian empires, Parthian kingdom founded in 248 BC. Reached greatest power under Mithradates I and II, controlling regions between Euphrates and Indus. Soldiers were noted horsemen and archers.

Partridge, Eric Honeywood (1894-), English literary critic, lexicographer, b. New Zealand. Best known for A Dictionary of Slang and Unconventional English (1937), and Dictionary of the Underworld, British and American (1950).

partridge, medium-sized European game bird with plump body, short tail. Common European partridge, Perdix perdix, mottled brown above with grey speckled breast, successfully introduced into North America.

Pasadena, residential town of S California, US; near Los Angeles. Pop. 113,000. Education centre, has California Institute of Technology; annual Tournament of Roses and football game in Rose Bowl stadium.

Pascal, Blaise (1623-62), French philosopher, scientist. Worked on mathematical theory of probability and differential calculus. Developed hydraulic press, formulating law on application of pressure on contained fluids. Religious writings incl. Lettres provinciales (1656) defending Jansenism, and famous collection, Pensées, stating his belief in inadequacy of reason.

pasha or **pacha,** title formerly used in Turkey and N Africa for military leaders and provincial governors. Abolished in Turkey (1934), in Egypt (1952).

Pashtu or **Pushtu,** see IRANIAN.

Pašić or **Pashitch, Nikola** (1846–1926), Serbian statesman. Five times premier of Serbia and, later, of Yugoslavia. Negotiated union (1917) of Serbia, Croatia and Slovenia to form state of Yugoslavia.

Pasiphaë, see MINOS.

Pasolini, Pier Paolo (1922-75), Italian film director, poet, novelist. Known for films concerned with Marxism, religion, myth, eg The Gospel according to St Matthew

(1964); later turned to adaptations of story-sequences, eg The Arabian Nights (1974).

pasqueflower, see ANEMONE.

passacaglia, type of musical composition in slow 3/4 time, in which series of variations are constructed over a repeated theme. Very similar to chaconne, in which theme occurs in bass.

Passau, town of SE West Germany, at confluence of Danube, Ilz and Inn rivers. Pop. 31,000. River port, railway jct. Episcopal see from 738; scene of religious Treaty of Passau (1552).

Passchendaele, village of W Belgium. Scene of battle (1917) forming part of unsuccessful British offensive; many casualties.

passenger pigeon, Ectopistes migratorius, extinct North American pigeon; once numerous, ruthlessly slaughtered by man in 19th cent.

Passeriformes, order of perching birds with first toe pointing backward, other 3 toes forward. Contains more than half known species of bird. Group incl. sparrows, thrushes, tits, finches.

Passionflower (Passiflora caerulea)

passionflower, any of genus Passiflora of climbing vines native to tropical America. Showy flowers; small, edible, yellow or purple egg-like fruits.

Passion play, dramatic representation of the suffering, death and resurrection of Jesus; a form of miracle play. Most famous staged at Oberammergau, Bavaria, every 10 years from 1634.

Passover, Jewish religious festival commemorating deliverance of Israelites from Egypt (although based on much older festival). Celebrated late March or early April; lasts 7 days. Meals of first 2 evenings known as Seders, observed with traditional foods and ceremonies.

pastel, painting medium consisting of powdered pigment mixed with just enough gum to bind it; usually moulded into sticks. Used in Italy in 15th cent.; major exponents of medium incl. Chardin and Degas.

Pasternak, Boris Leonidovich (1890-1960), Russian author. Wrote lyric, narrative poetry, novel Dr Zhivago (pub. in West, 1958). Forced to refuse Nobel Prize for Literature (1958).

Louis Pasteur

Pasteur, Louis (1822-95), French chemist. Showed that fermentation is caused by micro-organisms and that similar micro-organisms present in air are responsible for infection of wounds. Pasteurization process for sterilization of food is based on his work on fermentation of beer and wine. Eliminated disease of silkworms; produced vaccines against rabies and anthrax.

Pasto, town of SW Colombia; alt. 2594 m (8510 ft) in volcanic region. Pop. 88,000. Founded 1539; hist. Spanish colonial centre.

Paston Letters, collection of correspondence of Paston family of Norfolk (1422-1509), now largely in British Museum. Provide hist. material on customs of England towards end of Middle Ages.

pastoral, in literature, work idealizing rustic life. The supposedly simple life of a shepherd is contrasted with complexity, hypocrisy of court or city life. Form developed by Theocritus. Used by others incl. Vergil, Spenser, Milton, Shelley.

Patagonia, region of S Argentina, from Colorado R. to Tierra del Fuego (incl. S Chile). Mainly semi-arid grassy plateau; sheep rearing, some cattle in W; oil, gas resources, iron ore deposits S of Río Negro.

Patan, town of SC Nepal. Pop. 195,000 Cap. of Nepali kingdom until capture by Gurkhas (1768).

patent, govt. document conferring MONOPOLY right to produce, sell, or get profit from an invention for a certain number of years. Rights extend only within state granting patent, but since first signing (1883) of International Convention for the Protection of Industrial Property, many countries give rights outside original country.

Pater, Walter [Horatio] (1839-94), English scholar, critic. Support for humanist values in art reflected in *Studies in the History of the Renaissance* (1873), *Marius the Epicurean* (1885), *Plato and Platonism* (1893). Noted prose stylist.

Pater Noster, *see* LORD'S PRAYER.

Paterson, William (1658-1719), Scottish financier. Advised (1691) foundation of Bank of England, which Parliament approved in 1694. Helped organize Darien Scheme (1695) to estab. Scottish trading colony in Panama; accompanied disastrous expedition of 1698, returned home 1699.

Paterson, town of N New Jersey, US; on Passaic R. Pop. 144,000. Textile industs., esp. silk weaving, dyeing. H.e.p. supplies from falls on river. Estab. 1791. Scene of early US factory strike.

Pathans, semi-nomadic Moslem people of W Pakistan and Afghanistan. Noted as fierce fighters. Former occupants of Northwest Frontier Prov.; absorbed within Pakistan but continue to press for autonomy.

pathology, branch of medicine concerned with structural and functional changes in the body, their causes and effects.

Patmore, Coventry [Kersey Dighton] (1823-96), English poet. Associate of Pre-Raphaelites. Works incl. celebration of conjugal love, *The Angel in the House* (1854-62), collection of odes *The Unknown Eros* (1877).

Patmos, isl. of Greece, in Aegean Sea, in the Dodecanese. Area 34 sq km (13 sq mi). St John the Divine wrote the Revelation here. Monastery (11th cent.).

Patna, cap. of Bihar state, NE India. Pop. 490,000. Railway jct.; centre of rice growing region. Dates from 6th cent. BC. Has famous mosques, Sikh temple.

Paton, Alan [Stewart] (1903-), South African novelist. Known for works indicting regime, *eg Cry, the Beloved Country* (1948), *Too Late the Phalarope* (1953).

Patras (*Pátrai*), town of W Greece, in NW Peloponnese, on Gulf of Patras. Pop. 112,000. Cap. of Patras admin. dist. Port; exports currants, olive oil, wine. Greek War of Independence began here (1821).

patriarch, in OT, one of the founders of the ancient Jewish families, *eg* Abraham, Jacob. Also bishops of Eastern Orthodox Church who hold authority over other bishops, *eg* Alexandria, Antioch, Constantinople.

patricians, members of privileged class of ancient Rome, descended from original citizens. Unlike the plebeians, they were entitled to hold public office. By 3rd cent. BC, almost all public offices were open to plebeians, and term patrician became an honourable title.

Patrick, St (*c* 385-461), patron saint of Ireland. Prob. born in Britain but captured in youth and enslaved in Ireland. Escaped and returned as Christian missionary, effected conversion of country from Tara. Writings incl. *Confessions*. Buried at Downpatrick. Feast day is 17 Mar.

patristic literature, term for Christian writings up to 8th cent. Mainly in Greek and Latin, incl. works of St Clement I, Origen, St Augustine, St John of Damascus.

Patroclus, in Greek legend, intimate friend of Achilles. In Trojan War slain by Hector, thus causing Achilles to be reconciled with Agamemnon and return to battle.

Patterson, American family of journalists. **Robert Wilson Patterson** (1850-1910), was chief editor of the Chicago *Tribune.* His son, **Joseph Medill Patterson** (1879-1946), acquired part control of the *Tribune,* and later founded (1919) the *Daily News,* 1st successful tabloid, achieving top US circulation through sensationalism. His sister, **Eleanor Medill Patterson** (1884-1948), edited Hearst's *Washington Herald,* later merging it (1939) with the Washington *Times.*

Patton, George Smith (1885-1945), American general. Commanded 3rd Army playing leading role in liberation of France (1944), C Europe (1945).

Pau, town of SW France, cap. of Pyrénées-Atlantiques dept. Pop. 74,000. Resort, wine trade, textile mfg., univ. (1724). Hist. cap. of Béarn; residence from 1512 of kings of Navarre.

Paul, St, Jewish name Saul (d. *c* AD 67), Christian missionary, b. Tarsus. Jewish nationalist. Was converted while on road to Damascus to help suppress Christianity (prob. *c* AD 35). Became 'Apostle to the Gentiles'; travelled as missionary throughout Greek world and Near East. Prob. martyred in Rome under Nero. Epistles, attributed to him, contain fundamental statements of Christian doctrine.

Paul III, orig. Alessandro Farnese (1468-1549), Italian churchman, pope (1534-49). During his pontificate, Catholic Reformation began. Attempted to introduce reforms into the church; convened Council of TRENT (1545). Approved founding of Jesuit order (1540).

Paul VI, orig. Giovanni Battista Montini (1897-), Italian churchman, pope (1963-). First pope to leave Italy in 150 years, visited Holy Land, US, India and Far East; improved relations with communist countries. Reconvened 2nd Vatican Council and implemented its reforms. Reaffirmed Church's ban on contraception in encyclical *Humanae Vitae* (1968).

Paul I (1754-1801), tsar of Russia (1796-1801). Mentally unbalanced, he ruled despotically, attempting to curb power of the nobles. Assassinated by disaffected army officers.

Pauli, Wolfgang (1900-58), Austro-American physicist. Awarded Nobel Prize for Physics (1945) for discovery of Pauli exclusion principle of quantum theory: no 2 electrons in atom can have same 4 quantum numbers. Principle has been extended to other elementary particles (fermions).

Pauling, Linus Carl (1901-), American chemist. Awarded Nobel Prize for Chemistry (1954) for work on nature of chemical bond; also worked on structure of protein molecules. Widely known for advocacy of vitamin C in treatment of common cold. Awarded Nobel Peace Prize (1962) for opposition to nuclear tests.

Paulist Fathers, American society of RC priests; officially Society of Missionary Priests of St Paul the Apostle. Founded (1858) in New York by Isaac Hecker to convert Americans in ways appropriate to US society.

Paulus, Friedrich von (1890-1957), German army officer. Besieged and captured by Russians at Stalingrad (1943).

Pausanias (*fl* AD 2nd cent.), Greek traveller, geographer. Compiled description of Greece, incl. topography, local history, legends *etc.*

Pavia (anc. *Ticinum*), town of Lombardy, NW Italy, on R. Ticino. Cap. of Pavia prov. Pop. 90,000. Agric. market, textiles. Scene of victory (1525) of Emperor Charles V over Francis I of France. Law school (9th cent.) became univ. 1361. Carthusian monastery (Certosa di Pavia) nearby.

Pavlodar, city of USSR, NE Kazakh SSR; on R. Irtysh. Pop. 208,000. In rich agric. region; food processing. Rapid growth from WWII.

Pavlov, Ivan Petrovich (1849-1936), Russian physiologist. His experiments on stimulation of salivation in dogs by ringing of bells led to theory of the conditioned reflex. Awarded Nobel Prize for Physiology and Medicine (1904) for work on digestion, esp. secretion of digestive juice in the stomach.

Pavlova, Anna Matveyevna (c 1882-1931), Russian ballet dancer. Danced in Diaghilev's Ballets Russes. Famous in *The Dying Swan,* created for her by Fokine, and *Giselle,* among other ballets.

Pawnee, North American Indian tribe of Hokan-Siouan linguistic stock. Moved from Texas to S Nebraska in 16th cent. Warlike tribe but allied to US govt.; moved to reservation in Oklahoma (1876).

pawpaw or **papaw,** *Asimina triloba,* tree native to S US. Oblong, yellowish, edible fruit with many seeds. Name also applied to PAPAYA.

Pawtucket, town of NE Rhode Isl., US; on Blackstone R. Pop. 77,000. Textiles mfg.; had first US water-power cotton mill (1790).

Pax, in Roman religion, goddess of peace. Identified with Greek Irene.

Paxton, Sir Joseph (1803-65), English architect, landscape gardener. His greenhouses built for Duke of Devonshire served as model for his innovatory design of the Crystal Palace, built for 1851 Great Exhibition.

Paysandú, port of W Uruguay, on Uruguay R. Pop. 60,000. Meat packing centre; soap, leather, textile mfg.

Paz, Octavio (1914-), Mexican poet. Works, *eg Sun Stone* (1957), reflect concern for nature of Mexican culture. Also wrote literary essays.

pea, *Pisum sativum,* annual climbing leguminous herb, widely cultivated for edible pod-borne seeds, used as vegetable. Also *see* CHICKPEA, SWEET PEA.

Peabody, George (1795-1869), American financier, philanthropist. After successful broking career in London, founded Peabody Trust to house London poor, and Peabody Education Fund to promote education in S states of US, among other charities.

Peace, river of Canada. Rises in N British Columbia, Canada; flows NE 1923 km (1195 mi) through Alberta to join Slave R. near L. Athabaska. Extensive agric. in river valley.

Peace Corps, agency of US govt. Estab. (1961) to send trained workers to Third World with expressed aim of helping in education, health care, agric. and technology.

Peach

peach, *Prunus persica,* small tree of rose family with decorative pink blossom and sweet, velvety-skinned, stone fruit. Native to China, now cultivated throughout warm temperate regions. The nectarine, *P. persica nectarina,* is a smooth-skinned variety.

Peacock, Thomas Love (1785-1866), English author. Known for novels satirizing intellectual fashions of his day, *eg Nightmare Abbey* (1818), *Crotchet Castle* (1831), *Gryll Grange* (1861). Also wrote verse parodies, pastiches.

peacock, *Pavo cristatus,* male game bird native to India and SE Asia, introduced elsewhere as ornamental bird. Erects long iridescent tail feathers into fan shape as courtship display.

Peak District, national park of S Pennines, C England, mainly in Derbyshire. Area 1404 sq km (542 sq mi). Limestone in S, many caves.

Peake, Mervyn (1911-68), English author, illustrator, b. China. Known esp. for trilogy of Gothic fantasies, *Titus Groan* (1946), *Gormenghast* (1950), *Titus Alone* (1959).

peanut or **groundnut,** *Arachis hypogaea,* spreading annual vine of Leguminosae family. Yellow flowers, underground seedpods. Native to Brazil but widely cultivated in tropical and subtropical regions for seeds which are eaten raw or roasted and salted, and also used to make oil and peanut butter.

Pear

pear, any of genus *Pyrus* of rose family, esp. European *P. communis* and Oriental *P. pyrifolia,* widely cultivated in temperate regions for edible apple-like fruit.

Pearl, river of China, *see* CHUKIANG.

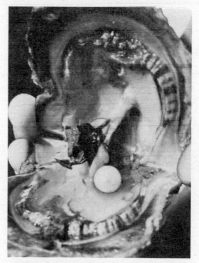

'Cultured' pearl in Japanese oyster

pearl, hard, rounded secretion found in certain shellfish, esp. pearl oyster and pearl mussel; used as a gem. Colours incl. white, pink, black. Formed by layers of calcite or aragonite encircling an irritant, *eg* grain of sand, parasite; composition same as flat 'mother-of-pearl', or nacre, layer on inside of shell. Major sources of natural pearls incl. Persian Gulf, Pacific isls.; 'cultured' pearls mostly from Japan.

Pearl Harbor, *see* HAWAII.

Pears, Peter (1910-), English tenor. Long associated with Britten, who created many vocal works and operatic roles, *eg Peter Grimes, Serenade* and *War Requiem,* for him.

Pearse, Patrick Henry (1879-1916), Irish patriot, educator. Leading figure in revival of Gaelic language, esp. in schools. Led Irish forces in Easter Rebellion (1916); executed after surrendering.

Pearson, Sir Cyril Arthur (1866-1921), British newspaper proprietor. Founded *Daily Express* (1900), bought (1904) *Evening Standard.* Blind himself after 1910, made his house, St Dunstan's, hospital for blinded servicemen in 1915.

Pearson, Lester Bowles (1897-1972), Canadian statesman, PM (1963-8). Secretary of state for external affairs (1948-57) before becoming Liberal leader. Led Canadian delegation to UN General Assembly (1946-57). Awarded Nobel Peace Prize (1957) for negotiating compromise to Suez crisis.

Peary, Robert Edwin (1856-1920), American explorer, naval officer. Led expeditions (1886-95) to N Greenland, proving it to be an island. From 1898 made several attempts to reach North Pole, became 1st man to succeed (April, 1909).

Peary Land, penin. of N Greenland. Mountainous, terminates at Cape Morris Jesup, world's most N point of land (710 km/440 mi from N Pole).

Peasants' Revolt, rising of English peasants (1381), led by Wat TYLER and John BALL, resulting from low wages, heavy taxes and desire to reform feudal system. Rebels entered London and, after meeting Richard II, were promised end of serfdom. Rebellion quickly suppressed after Tyler's murder.

Peasants' War (1524-5), rising of peasants in S and C Germany against loss of feudal rights and extortionate demands of princes and landowners. Inspired partly by preaching of Luther, who, however, condemned violence and advised peace. Rising ruthlessly suppressed.

peat, partly decomposed vegetable matter, found in marshy lands in temperate zones, mainly where there is no limestone to neutralize the acids formed by decomposition. Early stage in formation of coal. Used dried as fuel in Ireland, W Scotland, Scandinavia, and as mulch in horticulture.

pecan, *Carya illinoensis,* hickory tree of S and C US, producing edible nut similar to walnut.

peccary, small New World wild pig, genus *Tayassu,* with scent glands and sharp tusks. Two species, collared peccary, *T. angulatus,* found from SW US to Argentina, and white-lipped peccary, *T. pecari.*

Pechenga, ice-free port of USSR, NW European RSFSR; on Barents Sea near Norwegian border. Centre for fishing and metal ore mining. As Petsamo, under Finnish control (1920-44).

Pechora, river of USSR, N European RSFSR. Rises in N Urals, flows *c* 1750 km (1100 mi) N and W to enter Gulf of Pechora on Barents Sea by extensive delta. Coal mining in its basin.

Peckinpah, Sam (1926-), American film director. Known for extreme violence of his films, *eg The Wild Bunch* (1969), *Straw Dogs* (1971).

Pecos, river of S US. Rises in N New Mexico, flows SE 1480 km (926 mi) through SW Texas to join Rio Grande. Extensive water supplies for irrigation from dams.

Pécs (Ger. *Fünfkirchen*), city of S Hungary. Pop. 154,000. Indust. centre in coalmining area; leather, tobacco, wine. Cathedral (11th cent.); 1st Hungarian univ. (1367-1526, 1921). Under Turkish rule (1543-1686).

Pedro I (1798-1834), emperor of Brazil (1822-31). Son of John VI of Portugal, escaped with family to Brazil on Napoleon's invasion; remained as regent on father's return to Portugal. Proclaimed Brazil independent (1822); abdicated 1831. Succeeded by his son, **Pedro II** (1825-91), who ruled benevolently (1831-89) until eventually forced to abdicate in favour of republic. Abolished slavery (1888).

Peeblesshire or **Tweeddale,** former county of S Scotland, now in Borders region. In Southern Uplands; sheep rearing; woollen goods mfg. Co. town was **Peebles,** former royal burgh on R. Tweed. Pop. 6000. Textile mfg. Has 13th cent. Cross Kirk.

Peel, Sir Robert (1788-1850), British statesman, PM (1834-5, 1841-6). As home secretary, secured Catholic Emancipation Act (1829), created London police force (1829); opposed Reform Bill of 1832. Statement of policy in his Tamworth Manifesto (1834) held to mark beginning of

Conservative Party. Split party over removal of import duties and repeal of Corn Laws (1846).

Peele, George (*c* 1558-97), English dramatist. Wrote pastoral, *The Arraignment of Paris* (1582), comedy *The Old Wives' Tale* (1595), tragedy *David and Bethsabe* (pub. 1599), pamphlets, commemorative verse, lyrics.

peewit, *see* LAPWING.

Pegasus, in Greek myth, winged horse sprung from blood of Medusa when she was slain by Perseus. From imprint of hoof flowed spring, Hippocrene, sacred to Muses. Captured by BELLEROPHON.

pegmatite, very coarse-grained, igneous rock. Composition similar to granite; contains large crystals of quartz, mica, feldspar. Source of rare elements, tin, tungsten, gemstones. Major sources in Norway, Brazil, India, US.

Pegu, city of S Burma, on R. Pegu. Pop. 125,000. Cap. of united Burma in 16th cent. Many temples incl. Shwe Mawdaw pagoda.

Péguy, Charles Pierre (1873-1914), French author. Wrote polemics in defence of Catholicism, socialism, Dreyfus. In poetry, *eg Le Mystère de la charité de Jeanne d'Arc* (1897), attempted to fuse Catholicism, nationalism.

Peiping, *see* PEKING.

Peipus, Lake (*Chudskoye Ozero*), lake of USSR, on Estonian-RSFSR border. Area *c* 3540 sq km (1360 sq mi). S extension called L. Pskov. Outlet is R. Narova flowing to Gulf of Finland. Scene of Alexander Nevsky's victory (1242) over Livonian Knights.

Pekinese or **Pekingese,** Chinese breed of small dog introduced to Europe in 1860. Long silky coat, pug nose; stands 15-23 cm/6-9 in. at shoulder.

Peking or **Peiping,** cap. of China, special municipality (area *c* 17,000 sq km, 6564 sq mi) of Hopeh prov. Pop. 8,000,000. Financial, political hub of country. Indust., transport centre; international airport. Imperial centre (Forbidden City), cap. 1421-1911; again after Communist victory (1949). Noted Ming and Ching architecture; several univs.

Peking man, fossil remains of proto-human *Homo erectus* found at Choukoutien near Peking (1927). Originally dated as 350,000 years old. Recent finds of almost identical fossils in E Africa, dated as 1.5 million years old, have introduced new problems into study of man's evolution.

Pelagius (*c* 360-*c* 420), British monk. Rejected predestination; denied existence of original sin and individual's need of GRACE. Spread teachings in N Africa, Palestine. These, regarded as heresy (Pelagianism), were condemned at Council of Ephesus (431).

Pelasgians, name given by ancient Greeks to aboriginal inhabitants of Greece, Asia Minor and Aegean isls.

Pelé

Pelé, real name Edson Arantes do Nascimento (1940-), Brazilian footballer. Considered one of the greatest forwards ever, he scored his 1000th first-class goal in 1969. Played major part in Brazil's World Cup wins of 1958, 1962, 1970.

Pele, Hawaiian volcano goddess.

Peleus, in Greek myth, king of the Myrmidons; father of Achilles by nymph Thetis. *See* APPLE OF DISCORD.

Pelham, Henry (1696-1754), British statesman, PM (1743-54). Served in Walpole's govt. from 1721, then headed Whig admin. until his death.

Dalmatian pelican *(Pelecanus crispus)*

pelican, any of Pelecanidae family of gregarious web-footed water birds. Very large bill with pouch suspended underneath where it stores fish. Species incl. *Pelecanus onocrotalus,* white pelican of Africa, Asia.

Pella, ancient town of N Greece. Cap. of Macedon under Philip II; birthplace of Alexander the Great. Also modern admin. dist., cap. Edessa.

pellagra, disease caused by lack of niacin, vitamin of B group. Symptoms incl. sore tongue, diarrhoea, skin rash, disturbance of nervous system. Occurs in areas where diet consists mainly of maize.

Peloponnese (*Peloponnisos*), penin. of S Greece, joined to C Greece by Isthmus of Corinth. Formerly called Morea. Main towns Patras, Corinth. Largely mountainous; rugged coast. Currants, vines, olives; livestock; tourism. Dominated by Sparta until defeat by Thebes (4th cent. BC).

Peloponnesian War (431-404 BC), struggle between Athens and Peloponnesian Confederacy led by Sparta. Chief events in 1st 10 years were Athenian successes at Pylos and Sphacteria (425) and Spartan victory at Amphipolis (422). Peace was negotiated by Nicias (421) but only partially observed. Spartans gained important victory at Mantinea (418). Athenian expedition against Sicily (415), urged by Alcibiades, ended in disastrous destruction of fleet and army (413). Athenians rebuilt fleet but despite naval victories (411, 410, 406) were finally defeated by Lysander at Aegospotamos (405), and obliged to accept Spartan terms (404).

Pelops, in Greek myth, son of Tantalus. Murdered and served as food to the gods by his father. They punished Tantalus and restored Pelops to life. Won Hippodamia in marriage by defeating her father Oenomaus in chariot race. Bribed and murdered Oenomaus' charioteer who cursed house of Pelops. Curse fell on sons ATREUS and THYESTES.

pelota, name for several games played with ball and racket, glove, hand or bat. Originating in the Basque provs. of Spain and France, it is popular in Latin America and Florida.

Pelotas, port of S Brazil, on São Gonçalo Canal at S end of Lagôa dos Patos. Pop. 208,000. Meat packing, tanning; meat, wool, hides exports.

pelvis, basin-shaped bony structure composed of lower part of backbone and 2 hip bones. Hip bone consists of pubis, ilium and ischium, on which body rests when sitting. Female pelvis is larger to aid childbirth.

Pemba, isl. of Tanzania, in Indian Ocean. Area 980 sq km (380 sq mi); cap. Chake Chake. Exports cloves, copra. Part of sultanate of Zanzibar from 1822; former slave trade.

Pembrokeshire, former county of SW Wales, now in Dyfed. Co. town was Haverfordwest. Hilly NE; rugged coast is national park. Potato growing, dairy farming; fishing; tourism. Early centre of Celtic Christianity. **Pembroke,** with Pembroke Dock, is mun. bor. Pop. 14,000. Has ruined 11th cent. castle priory; WWII naval base.

Penal Laws, legislation enacted after English Reformation banning Roman Catholics from civil office and penalizing them for not conforming to Church of England. Laws were extended to Nonconformists after Restoration. Ended by Catholic Emancipation Act (1829).

penance, in RC and Eastern Orthodox churches, sacrament involving confession of sin, repentance and submission to the satisfaction imposed, followed by absolution by a priest.

Penang or **George Town,** cap. of Penang state, NW West Malaysia. Pop. 270,000. Leading seaport of Malaysia, on Penang Isl.

penates, *see* LARES AND PENATES.

Penda (d. 654), king of Mercia (*c* 632-54). Defeated Edwin of Northumbria (632), making himself king of Mercia. Defeated and killed Oswald of Northumbria (*c* 641). Took control of Wessex and East Anglia. Killed in battle against Oswy of Northumbria.

Penelope, in Greek myth, wife of Odysseus. Despite many suitors, she remained faithful during Odysseus' absence. Agreed to marry only when she had finished weaving Laertes' shroud, which she unravelled nightly.

King penguin

penguin, any bird of order Sphenisciformes, of S hemisphere. Flightless, wings form strong flippers for swimming and diving; nests in large colonies. Species incl. emperor penguin, *Aptenodytes forsteri,* and king penguin, *A. patagonica.*

penicillin, group of antibiotic substances produced by *Penicillium* moulds, esp. *P. chrysogenum* and *P. notatum.* Anti-bacterial effect noted by A. Fleming (1929); purified and used medicinally (1941).

Peninsular War, campaign fought (1808-14) against French in Iberian penin. by Britain, Portugal and Spanish guerrillas. Began when Napoleon invaded Portugal (1807) and then provoked revolts in Spain by placing his brother Joseph on Spanish throne (1808). British intervened in Portugal, defeated French at Vimeiro and then invaded Spain. Following Sir John Moore's retreat, Sir Arthur Wellesley (later Duke of Wellington) took command in Portugal. After defensive campaign centred on Torres Vedras, he invaded Spain and routed French at Vitoria

(1813). Napoleon abdicated after British advanced into France (1814).

penis, in males of higher vertebrates, organ which emits sperm in copulation. In mammals, also provides a urinary outlet. Human penis consists of 3 columns of erectile tissue.

Penki, city of Liaoning prov., NE China. Pop. 750,000. Metallurgical centre; iron and coal mines. Founded 1915.

Penn, William (1644-1718), English religious leader, founder of Pennsylvania. Became a Quaker (1667), then preached and wrote in favour of religious toleration. Obtained charter to estab. colony in Pennsylvania, (1682). As its governor, drew up liberal constitution and made exemplary treaty with Indians.

Pennine Range or **Pennines,** England. Hills running N-S from Cheviots to Peak Dist. Watershed of N English rivers; rises to 893 m (2930 ft) in Cross Fell. Rough pasture; tourism. 'Pennine Way' footpath 400 km (250 mi) long, opened in 1965

Pennsylvania, state of NE US. Area 117,412 sq km (45,333 sq mi); pop. 11,794,000; cap. Harrisburg; chief cities Philadelphia, Pittsburgh. Mainly in Appalachian Mts. Drained by Ohio R. in W, Susquehanna R. in E. Agric.; mineral wealth, esp. coal, oil, iron ore (related iron and steel, heavy industs.). Settled by Dutch, Swedish, English colonists. English colony estab. under William Penn (1682). Centre of activity in Revolution, Civil War. One of original 13 colonies of US.

Pennsylvanian period, later of 2 subdivisions of Carboniferous period in North America. Began *c* 325 million years ago, lasted *c* 45 million years. Fauna incl. freshwater lamellibranchs, 1st reptiles, giant dragonflies, spiders. Luxuriant vegetation, formation of vast swamps; development of European, North American coal measures. Also *see* GEOLOGICAL TABLE.

pennyroyal, small perennial plant of mint family. Two varieties: European *Mentha pulegium* and North American *Hedeoma pulegioides.* Bluish flowers; yields aromatic oil.

Pensacola, port of NW Florida, US; on Gulf of Mexico. Pop. 60,000. Naval air base. Paper products, fish canning. Contested by Spanish, French, British. US gained control (1821).

pension, payment made regularly to a person, or dependants, who has fulfilled certain conditions of service or reached a certain age. Pension plan is paid for prior to retirement and can be part of voluntary scheme or compulsory national scheme, connected with SOCIAL SECURITY provisions.

Pentagon, the, building in Arlington, Virginia in which main offices of US Department of Defense are situated. Consists of 5 concentric buildings connected by corridors; completed 1943.

Pentateuch, first five books of OT. Known in Judaism as the Torah.

pentathlon, five-event athletic contest for women comprising 100 m hurdles, shot put, high jump, long jump and 200 m. Olympic event from 1964.

Pentecost (Gk., *pentekoste* = 50th), Jewish religious festival celebrating end of grain harvest which takes place 50 days after Passover. Also Christian festival celebrating descent of the Holy Ghost upon the Disciples on the 50th day after Jesus' resurrection. Sometimes known as Whit Sunday from the white garments of neophytes baptized on this day.

Penthesilea, in Greek myth, queen of the Amazons who fought against Greeks in Trojan War. Killed by Achilles who mourned beauty of her corpse.

Pentland Firth, strait off N Scotland, separating former Caithness from Orkney Isls. Notorious for rough seas.

penumbra, partly lighted area surrounding complete shadow of a body. Observed when light emanates from large source. Term generally used in connection with eclipses.

Penutian, NW American, Central American indigenous linguistic stock. Main groups within it are Californian Penutian, Chinook, Mayan, Mixe-Zoque, Oregon Penutian, Sahaptin, Totonacan and Tsimshian.

Penza, city of USSR, EC RSFSR. Pop. 383,000. Centre of fertile region; sawmilling, engineering. Founded as fortress (1666).

Penzance, mun. bor. of Cornwall, SW England, on Mount's Bay. Pop. 19,000. Fishing port; resort.

Peony (*Paeonia officinalis*)

peony or **paeony,** any of genus *Paeonia* of perennial herbs or shrubs of buttercup family. Native to Eurasia and W US. Large scarlet, pink or white flowers.

Peoria, town of C Illinois, US; on Illinois R. Pop. 127,000. Grain, livestock market; agric. machinery mfg., food processing. Focus of territ. settlement in early 19th cent.

Pepin the Short (*c* 714-68), king of Franks (751-68). Son of Charles Martel, he deposed last Merovingian king, Childeric III, thus founding Carolingian dynasty. Father of Charlemagne.

pepper, *Piper nigrum,* tropical vine yielding fruit dried as condiment; ground as black pepper or (without seed cover) as white pepper. Also condiments (sometimes known as paprika) prepared in similar way from tropical American *Capsicum frutescens* or chili. *See* CAYENNE, PIMENTO.

peppermint, *see* MINT.

pepper tree, *Schinus molle,* South American evergreen tree. Cultivated as ornamental; yellow flowers followed by aromatic red berries.

pepsin, digestive enzyme produced in the stomach. In presence of hydrochloric acid, converts proteins into peptones, which are absorbed by body.

peptic ulcer, erosion of lining of stomach (gastric ulcer) or duodenum (duondenal ulcer). Aggravated by action of acidic gastric juices. Symptoms incl. stomach ache, nausea, heartburn. Cause unknown; possibly related to stress.

Samuel Pepys

Pepys, Samuel (1633-1703), English diarist, naval official. Famous for his *Diary* (pub. 1825), recording, in cipher, personal life, public affairs of 1660s.

Perak, state of West Malaysia. Area *c* 20,800 sq km (8030 sq mi); pop. 1,562,600; cap. Ipoh. Consists largely of R. Perak basin. Tin mining; rubber, coconuts, rice grown.

Perceval, Spencer (1762-1812), British statesman, PM (1809–12). Tory chancellor of exchequer (1807–9) before succeeding Portland as PM. Assassinated in lobby of House of Commons.

European perch

perch, any of genus *Perca* of freshwater food fish with spiny dorsal fins. Species incl. yellow perch *P. flavescens* of North America and European *P. fluviatilis.*

percussion instruments, musical instruments struck to produce sound. Most produce no definite notes and their function is chiefly rhythmic, *eg* drum, triangle, cymbals, though some do produce notes of definite pitch, *eg* xylophone, timpani, glockenspiel.

Percy, Henry, 1st Earl of Northumberland (1342-1408), English nobleman. Helped secure throne for Henry IV from Richard II. Later, took part in plot led by his son, **Sir Henry Percy** (1366-1403) (known as 'Hotspur') and Owen Glendower to overthrow king. Plan to crown Edmund de Mortimer ended with Hotspur's death at Shrewsbury. **Thomas Percy, 7th Earl of Northumberland** (1528-72), plotted release of Mary Queen of Scots and restoration of Roman Catholicism to England; beheaded after revolt failed.

Percy, Thomas (1729-1811), English antiquary, poet. Known for *Reliques of Ancient English Poetry* (1765), a collection of ballads which stimulated Romantic writers' interest in medieval verse.

peregrine falcon, *Falco peregrinus,* swift falcon of Europe, Asia, North America; much used in falconry. Male has slate-grey upper-parts, buff under-parts. Feeds on birds, *eg* pigeon.

Pereira, town of W Colombia, in Andes. Pop. 216,000. Coffee, cattle trade; gold, silver processing; clothing mfg. Founded 1863.

perennial, *see* ANNUAL.

Pérez Galdós, Benito (1843-1920), Spanish author, b. Canary Isles. Known for novels, *eg* historical cycle of 46 vols., *Episodios nacionales* (1873-1912), dialogue novel *Realidad* (1892).

perfume, fragrant essence prepared from essential oils of plants or synthetic compounds, mixed with fixatives such as musk or ambergris. The ingredients are generally dissolved in alcohol. Favoured plant oils are found in flowers of lavender, roses, jasmine, fruit of bergamot and citrus fruit.

Pergamum or **Pergamus** (modern *Bergama*), ancient city of Asia Minor, now in W Turkey on R. Caicus. Cap. of kingdom of Pergamum (3rd-2nd cent. BC); under Roman rule (133 BC). Famous remains incl. alter of Zeus, temple of Athena and library. Early Christian centre; one of Seven Churches in Asia.

Pericles (*c* 495-429 BC), Athenian statesman. Dominant figure in Athens from *c* 460, at time of city's political and cultural zenith. Created empire out of Delian league, successfully defending it against Persia, Sparta. Patronized arts and literature; responsible for building of Parthenon. Onset of Peloponnesian War brought his overthrow (430); reinstated before he died.

peridotite, coarse-grained igneous rock. Consists of mixture of olivine and pyroxene.

perigee, in astronomy, point nearest Earth in orbit of celestial bodies, *eg* Moon and artificial satellites. Opposite is apogee.

Périgueux, town of SW France, on R. Isle, cap. of Dordogne dept. Pop. 40,000. Tobacco trade, food processing esp. pâté, truffles. Hist. cap. of Périgord (incorporated into France 1589). Roman remains incl. amphitheatre, tower.

perihelion, in astronomy, point nearest Sun in orbit of celestial bodies, *eg* planets and comets. Opposite is aphelion.

Perim, isl. of Southern Yemen, in Bab-el Mandeb Str. off SW Yemen. Area *c* 13 sq km (5 sq mi); pop. 1700. Barren isl. formerly important as coaling station.

periodical, publication issued regularly, distinct from a newspaper in that it contains authors'/editors' opinions on news, *etc,* rather than factual accounts. Term incl. magazines, scholarly reviews, journals.

periodic table, arrangement of chemical elements according to their atomic numbers to illustrate periodic law: properties of elements are in periodic dependence upon their atomic numbers. Formulated by MENDELEEV (1869-71). Law reflects way in which successive electron shells are filled; elements with same number of electrons in their outer shell have similar properties, *eg* alkali metals have one such electron. *See* VALENCY.

periscope, optical instrument which enables observer to see objects not directly visible from his position, esp. those above eye level. Consists of long tube at each end of which is a prism or mirror, which reflects light to observer's eye. Used esp. in submarines.

peritoneum, membrane lining abdominal cavity and enclosing in its folds the internal organs. Also forms double-thickness membrane (mesentery) enfolding and supporting small intestine. Peritonitis is inflammation of peritoneum, usually caused by bacteria.

periwinkle, small marine mollusc with conical spiral shell, genus *Littorina.* Species incl. European edible periwinkle, *L. littorea.*

European periwinkle

periwinkle, any of genus *Vinca* of mostly trailing, evergreen plants of dogbane family, esp. European *V. minor* with light lilac-blue, pink or white flowers.

Perkin, Sir William Henry (1838-1907), English chemist. Founded aniline dye indust. after discovering 1st synthetic dye (mauve). Discovered Perkin reaction for synthesis of aromatic acids.

Perm, city of USSR, E European RSFSR; railway jct. and port on R. Kama. Pop. 880,000. Centre of Urals indust. area; agric. machinery, timber products. Developed with estab. of copper-smelting plant in 18th cent.

permafrost, permanently frozen subsoil. Found in high latitudes where rainfall is low and mean annual temperature is below 0°C. Topsoil may thaw for part of year.

Permian period, final geological period of Palaeozoic era; began *c* 280 million years ago, lasted *c* 55 million years. Increasing aridity; swamps dried up, salt beds formed, marls, sandstones, evaporites developed. Increasing reptiles, ammonites, more advanced conifers; last trilobites. Also *see* GEOLOGICAL TABLE.

Pernambuco, state of NE Brazil. Area 98,280 sq km (37,946 sq mi); pop. 5,167,000; cap. Recife. Has humid coastal zone; arid interior. Mainly agric. (sugar, fruit, cotton).

Pernik, town of W Bulgaria, on R. Struma. Pop. 76,000. Indust. centre of coalmining dist. Known as Dimitrovo 1949-1962.

Perón, Juan Domingo (1895-1974), Argentinian political leader. Elected president (1946) after taking part in military coup (1943). Made series of reforms based on nationalism,

Juan Perón

populism and state socialism (known as *peronismo*). Career aided by popularity of 2nd wife, **Eva Duarte Perón** (1919-52), who had great political following. Lost support after her death; deposed by army coup (1955), went into exile. Returned 1973, re-elected president. His 3rd wife, **María Estela ('Isabel') Martínez 'de' Perón** (1931-), succeeded him as president on his death. Deposed by military junta (1976).

perpendicular, name given to final phase of English Gothic architecture (late 14th-middle 16th cent.) Characterized by vertical tracery for walls and windows, fan vaulting. King's College Chapel, Cambridge, is example of style.

Perpignan, city of S France, on R. Têt, cap. of Pyrénées-Orientales dept. Pop. 102,000. Wine, fruit trade; tourist centre. Cap. of Spanish Roussillon (17th cent.). Cathedral (14th cent.), castle.

Perry, Fred[erick John] (1909-), English lawn tennis and table tennis player. World table tennis champion (1929). Won Wimbledon title 3 times in succession (1934-6) and lawn tennis titles of US (1933), Australia (1934) and France (1935).

Perse, St-John, see ST-JOHN PERSE.

Persephone, in Greek myth, daughter of Zeus and Demeter. Abducted by Pluto to underworld and required to spend winter months of year there. Return symbolized start of vegetative growth. Her cult was celebrated in the Eleusinian mysteries; also worshipped at Rome as Proserpina.

Persepolis, cap. of ancient Persian empire, now ruined, in SC Iran. Has ruined palaces of Darius and his successors. Nearby are royal tombs. Partially destroyed by Alexander the Great in 331 BC. Shiraz nearest modern town.

Perseus, in Greek myth, son of Zeus and Danaë. Slew Medusa, used her head to turn ATLAS into a mountain. Married Andromeda. Accidentally killed his grandfather, Acrisius, in discus contest thus fulfilling a prophecy at his birth.

Pershing, John J[oseph] (1860-1948), American army officer, commander-in-chief of American Expeditionary Force in WWI (1917-8).

Persia, see IRAN.

Persian, see IRANIAN.

Persian cat, small domestic cat with long silky hair, originally raised in Persia and Afghanistan.

Persian Gulf, arm of Indian Ocean, between Iran and Arabian penin. Connected to Arabian Sea by Str. of Hormuz and Gulf of Oman.

Persian Gulf States, see UNITED ARAB EMIRATES; BAHRAIN; QATAR.

Persian Wars, struggles (500-449 BC) between Greek city states and Persian Empire. Begun by Greek support for revolt of Ionian cities of Asia Minor against Persian rule.

Persian Gulf

Persian expedition under Darius I was defeated at Marathon (490). Later expedition led by Xerxes I, son of Darius, successfully invaded Greece but Persian fleet was destroyed at Salamis (480) and army crushed at Plataea (479). Wars dragged on but Greek cities had estab. their freedom.

persimmon, see EBONY.

perspective, system of representing 3-dimensional space in spatial recession on flat surface. Geometric system based on converging lines was formulated by Alberti and Brunelleschi in 15th cent. and developed by Uccello, Piero della Francesca, *etc.* Aerial perspective uses changes of tone and colour to suggest distance; used early in Far Eastern art.

perspex [UK] or **plexiglass** [US], trademark for transparent polyacrylic plastic. May be moulded while hot.

perspiration, see SWEAT.

Perth, city of SW Australia, on Swan R., cap. of Western Australia. Pop. 739,000. Admin., commercial centre; W terminus of Trans-Australian Railway; exports (via Fremantle) agric. produce, minerals, esp. gold. Founded 1829; has Univ. of Western Australia (1911), Anglican and RC cathedrals, many parks.

Perthshire, former county of C Scotland, now in Central and Tayside regions. Grampian Mts., Trossachs; lochs incl. Earn, Tay, Katrine; fertile lowland. Agric.; deer forest, sheep rearing; h.e.p. at Pitlochry; tourist indusls. Co. town was **Perth,** former royal burgh on R. Tay. Pop. 43,000. Insurance centre; whisky distilling. Cap. of Scotland (12th-15th cents.).

Peru

Peru, republic of W South America. Area 1,285,210 sq km (496,220 sq mi); pop. 14,640,000; cap. Lima. Languages: Spanish, Quechua, Aymará (Indian). Religion: RC. Pacific coastal plain in W rises to 2 Andean ranges in interior. Important mineral resources (zinc, silver, copper); subsistence agric. esp. cotton; sheep, llamas, alpacas raised for wool. Anchovy, fish meal indusls. Well-organized Inca empire was destroyed by Spanish following Pizarro's invasion (1532); independence obtained under Bolívar, Sucre (1824). S region lost in war with Chile (1879-84).

Perugia, city of Umbria, C Italy, cap. of Perugia prov. Pop. 132,000. Indust. centre, chocolate mfg. Etruscan, Roman remains. Centre of Umbrian school of painting (13th-16th cents.). Univ. (1276).

Perugino, orig. Pietro di Vannucci (c 1445-1523), Italian painter of Umbrian school. Executed fresco *Christ Giving the Keys to St Peter* in Sistine Chapel. His repetitive style caused his reputation to fade. Raphael was his pupil.

Perutz, Max Ferdinand (1914-), British biochemist, b. Austria. Shared Nobel Prize for Chemistry (1962) for discovery of structure of haemoglobin using X-ray diffraction.

Pesaro, town of the Marches, EC Italy, on Adriatic Sea. Cap. of Pesaro prov. Pop. 86,000. Port, resort; ceramics mfg. from 15th cent. Music academy, endowed by Rossini (born here).

Pescara, city of Abruzzi e Molise, EC Italy, on Adriatic Sea at mouth of R. Pescara. Cap. of Pescara prov. Pop. 122,000. Port, resort; mfg.

Peshawar, town of N Pakistan, near Khyber Pass. Pop. 273,000. Centre for trade between Pakistan and Afghanistan. Taken by British (1848), was outpost for operations against Afghans.

Pestalozzi, Johann Heinrich (1746-1827), Swiss educational reformer. Laid foundation of modern educational theory, stressing importance of relating words, ideas to concrete things, through pupil activities, instruction tailored to age-groups and individuals.

Marshal Pétain in May, 1940

Pétain, Henri Philippe (1856-1951), French military, political leader. In WWI, halted German advance at Verdun (1916); created marshal of France (1918). Premier at time of France's collapse in WWII, concluded armistice with Germans. Headed Vichy govt., serving as figurehead for LAVAL after 1942. Death sentence for collaboration (1945) commuted to life imprisonment.

Peter, St orig. Simon (d. c AD 67), leader of Twelve Disciples. He and brother, St Andrew, were fishermen in Galilee when called by Jesus. Given charge of Church by Jesus after resurrection. Prob. martyred during Nero's rule; traditionally buried on site of St Peter's Church, Rome.

Peter [I] the Great (1672-1725), tsar of Russia (1682-1725). Joint tsar with brother Ivan V, became sole ruler on Ivan's death (1696). Introduced policy of westernizing Russia; toured Europe to gain knowledge of indust. techniques. Reorganized army and civil admin., encouraged trade, indust. and science. Gained access to Baltic through war with Sweden (1700-21). Built new cap. at St Petersburg.

Peter III (1728-62), tsar of Russia (1762). Forced to abdicate in face of plot led by the Orlovs, favourites of his wife and successor, Catherine II. Assassinated, prob. at behest of Aleksey Orlov.

Peter III (c 1239-85), king of Aragón (1276-85). Claimed Naples and S Italy through his marriage to Constance of Sicily, thus antagonizing Charles of Anjou. Took possession of Sicily after SICILIAN VESPERS (1282).

Peter I (1844-1921), king of Serbia (1903-21). Called to throne after assassination of Alexander Obrenovich. Chosen as ruler of new kingdom of Serbs, Croats, Slovenes (later Yugoslavia).

Peter II (1923-70), king of Yugoslavia (1934-45). Succeeded under regency after murder of his father, Alexander. Assumed power after overthrow of regency (1941); fled to England during Nazi invasion. Deposed by Tito; died in US.

Peter 1 and **2,** epistles of NT, traditionally ascribed to St Peter.

Peterborough, town of SE Ontario, Canada; on Otonabee R., NE of Toronto. Pop. 58,000. Railway and indust. centre. Has Canada's largest cereal and flour mills.

Peterborough, city of Cambridgeshire, E England, on R. Nene. Pop. 70,000. Railway jct; engineering, bricks mfg. Has remains of Saxon village; ruined abbey (655); cathedral (12th cent.).

Peterhead, town of Grampian region, NE Scotland, on North Sea. Pop. 14,000. Herring indust.; granite quarries; offshore oil service industs. Former whaling port.

Peter the Great

Peter Lombard (c 1100-60), Italian churchman. Parts of his collection of theological opinions, *Sententiarum libri,* became official RC doctrine, esp. on sacraments.

Peterloo Massacre, incident at St Peter's Field, Manchester, England (1819). Large meeting, petitioning for parliamentary reform, dispersed by yeomanry and hussars; 11 people killed. Resulting indignation accelerated reform movement.

Peter's pence, annual tax of one penny paid to papal see by English households before Reformation. Now annual voluntary donation made by Roman Catholics to papal see.

Peter the Hermit (c 1050-1115), French preacher. Induced many to go on 1st Crusade and became one of its leaders. Founded monastery at Liège.

Petition of Right (1628), document containing constitutional demands presented by English Parliament to Charles I. Declared taxation without parliamentary approval illegal, reaffirmed principle of habeas corpus, *etc.* Acceptance by Charles resulted in restoration of subsidies to him.

Petöfi, Sándor (1823-49), Hungarian poet. Wrote semi-autobiog. poem, 'The Apostle' expressing patriotism, revolutionary ideals. Killed at Segesvár fighting Austrians.

Petra, ancient city of SW Jordan. Edomite cap. from 4th cent. BC until capture by Romans in AD 106. Ruins, discovered 1812 by Burckhardt, incl. temples and tombs carved in pink rock.

Petrarch or **Francesco Petrarca** (1304–74), Italian poet. First Renaissance humanist, began revival of spirit of antiquity, profound influence on later European writers. Famous for Italian songs and sonnets expressing love for Laura in *Canzoniere,* also allegorical poem *Trionfi.*

petrel, one of various small seabirds of 2 families: Hydrobatidae, storm petrels; Pelecanoididae, diving petrels. Noted fliers, returning to land only to breed. Species incl. storm petrel, *Hydrobates pelagicus,* of NE Atlantic and Mediterranean.

Petrie, Sir [William Matthew] Flinders (1853-1942), English archaeologist. Excavated at Memphis, Thebes and discovered 1st dynasty tombs at Abydos. Advanced methods of archaeology by exhaustive study of commonplace objects, meticulous technique.

petroleum, naturally occurring liquid mixture of hydrocarbons, with varying amounts of sulphur and nitrogen compounds. Fractional distillation yields petrol (gasoline), paraffin oil (kerosene), diesel oils, heavy fuel oils and bitumens, *etc.* Formed millions of years ago from remains of animals and plants buried and compressed. Main petroleum producing areas are in Middle East, USSR and US.

petrology, branch of geology dealing with study of all aspects of rocks. Incl. study of origins (petrogenesis), systematic description of rocks (petrography).

Petronius Arbiter, Gaius (d. AD 66), Roman satirist. Author of *Satyricon,* huge picaresque novel, of which only parts of Books XV and XVI are extant. Favourite of Nero.

Petropavlovsk, city of USSR, N Kazakh SSR; jct. on Trans-Siberian railway. Pop. 180,000. Meat packing, flour milling. Centre for caravan trade between Russia and C Asia in 18th cent.

Petropavlovsk(-Kamchatski), city of USSR, E Siberian RSFSR; on SE Kamchatka coast. Pop. 171,000. Naval base; fisheries, shipbuilding, sawmilling.

Petrópolis, mountain tourist resort of SE Brazil, N of Rio de Janeiro. Pop. 189,000. Brewing; textiles, chemicals mfg. Has Gothic cathedral, Imperial Museum.

Petrozavodsk, city of USSR, cap. of Karelian auton. republic, NW European RSFSR; on L. Onega. Pop. 193,000. Shipyards, fisheries, sawmilling. Named after ironworks founded here (1703) by Peter the Great.

Petsamo, see PECHENGA.

Petunia (Petunia hybrida)

petunia, genus of perennial herbs of nightshade family, with funnel-shaped flowers of various colours. Native to tropical America. Esp. *Petunia hybrida,* cultivated widely in temperate regions as garden flower.

Pevensey, village of East Sussex, SE England. William the Conqueror's landing place (1066); former port.

Pevsner, Antoine (1886-1962), Russian sculptor. Influenced by cubism, collaborated with brother Naum Gabo on manifesto of constructivism (1920). Later developed abstract and constructional sculpture.

pewter, any of several alloys of tin, with lead, copper or antimony added to improve malleability. Used from Roman times to make domestic utensils until replaced by china in 18th and 19th cents.

peyote, see MESCAL.

Pforzheim, town of SW West Germany, on R. Enz, at N edge of Black Forest. Pop. 90,000. Jewellery, watchmaking centre. Devastated (1689) by French.

Phaedra, in Greek myth, daughter of Minos and wife of Theseus. Fell in love with stepson Hippolytus, but was rejected by him and hanged herself.

Phaëthon, in Greek myth, son of Helios (the sun). Attempted to drive father's chariot, but unable to control horses. Killed by Zeus' thunderbolt.

phagocyte, blood cell, esp. a leucocyte, which engulfs and destroys bacteria, dead cells, foreign particles.

phalanger, arboreal Australasian marsupial of Phalangeridae family. Thick fur, prehensile tail; nocturnal. Flying phalangers use membrane stretched between limbs to glide through trees. Also called possum.

phalarope, small aquatic bird of Phalaropodidae family. Male, smaller and less brightly coloured than female, incubates eggs. Species incl. Wilson's phalarope, *Phalaropus tricolor,* of North American prairies.

phallicism or **phallism,** worship of image of male reproductive organ as symbol of regenerative powers of nature. Occurs in many primitive societies, also in cult of Priapus in classical Greece and of Cybele and Attis in Rome. In India, the deity Siva is often represented as a phallic symbol or lingam. Also see FERTILITY RITES.

Phanerozoic eon, all geological time from beginning of the Palaeozoic era to the present. Contrasts with Precambrian times in possessing sedimentary accumulations in which are found abundant remains of plants and animals. Also see GEOLOGICAL TABLE.

Pharisees, one of two main Jewish sects which originated in Maccabean age (other being their opponents, SADDUCEES). Insisted on strictest observance of Mosaic Law. Advocated democratization of religious observances.

pharmacopoeia, list of approved drugs, describing their preparation, properties, dosage, standards of purity. First appeared in 16th cent.; now published by medical councils, designating recognized legal standards.

pharmacy, preparation and dispensing of medicines and drugs. Pharmacology is the scientific study of drugs, their chemistry, effects on the body; it incl. research into new drugs.

Pharos of Alexandria, lighthouse which stood on an isl. off Alexandria, Egypt. Completed *c* 280 BC under Ptolemy II, it was destroyed in 14th cent. by earthquake. One of the Seven Wonders of the ancient World.

Pharsala, ancient city of Thessaly, EC Greece. Here in 48 BC Caesar defeated Pompey, recorded in Lucan's *Bellum Civile* or *Pharsalia.*

pharynx, muscular cavity of alimentary canal leading from mouth and nasal passages to the oesophagus. Top part, nasopharynx, is concerned only with breathing; middle part, oropharynx, is passage for food and air; lower part, laryngeal pharynx, is for swallowing only.

Impeyan pheasant or Himalayan monal (Lophophorus impejanus)

pheasant, game bird of Phasianidae family. Males brilliantly coloured, with long tapering tail. Mainly terrestrial, building nest on ground. Species incl. ring-necked pheasant, *Phasianus colchicus,* and Lady Amherst's pheasant, *Chrysolophus amherstiae,* of Chinese origin.

phenols, aromatic compounds having hydroxyl (OH) radicals directly attached to benzene ring. Commonest is carbolic acid (C_6H_5OH), white crystalline solid produced from coal tar; used as disinfectant and in manufacture of plastics.

phenomenology, movement in philosophy founded by HUSSERL. Aims to study objects of consciousness without any preconceptions about the objects themselves and thus apprehend phenomena directly. Influential in early development of EXISTENTIALISM.

Phidias (active c 475-430 BC), Athenian sculptor, architect. Greatly admired by his contemporaries, none of his original work remains. Works incl. colossal statues of Athena on the Parthenon, Athens, and Zeus at Olympia, one of Seven Wonders of the ancient World.

Philadelphia, port of SE Pennsylvania, US; on Delaware R. Pop. 1,950,000, state's largest city. Shipping, commercial centre. Exports coal, grain, timber. Imports raw materials. Varied industs. incl. oil refining, shipbuilding. Founded 1682 by Quakers. Focus of activity in Revolution; federal state cap. in 18th cent. Has many hist. famous buildings esp. Independence Hall, scene of Constitutional Convention (1787); Philharmonic Orchestra, Univ. of Pennsylvania (1740).

Philae, small isl. of S Egypt, in R. Nile above Aswan High Dam. Submerged Nov.–June; site of ancient ruins (incl. temple of Isis), most removed before dam completed.

philately, collection and study of postage stamps. Collecting began after issue of first stamps in 1840s; 1st catalogues printed c 1861. Important collections in British Museum, London, and Smithsonian Institute, Washington.

Philby, Harry St John Bridges (1885-1960), English explorer, writer. Led mission to C Arabia (1917-18). Wrote *The Empty Quarter* (1933), *Forty Years in the Wilderness* (1957). Became Moslem. Father of Soviet-British 'double agent' Harold ('Kim') Philby.

Philemon, Epistle to, NT epistle written by St Paul. Consists of request to Philemon asking him to forgive his slave, Onesimus, for escaping.

Philemon and Baucis, in Greek myth, an aged couple of Phrygia. Showed such hospitality to the disguised Zeus and Hermes that their cottage was made a temple. On death, became trees whose branches intertwined.

Philip, St (fl AD 1st cent.), one of Twelve Disciples. Possibly preached in Phrygia.

Philip [II] Augustus (1165-1223), king of France (1180-1223). Abandoned 3rd Crusade after quarrel with Richard I of England. Gained English possessions in France at expense of King John (1202-6). Defeated alliance of Germans, Flemings and English formed against him at Bouvines (1214).

Philip [IV] the Fair (1268-1314), king of France (1285-1314). Quarrel with Boniface VIII over right to tax clergy ended in pope's deposition by Philip, who secured Clement V's election (1305) and transfer of see to Avignon (1309). Supplemented treasury by persecution of KNIGHTS TEMPLARS (1308-14), who held powerful banking role in France.

Philip VI (1293-1350), king of France (1328-50). Elected regent on death of cousin, Charles IV, invoking Salic law to exclude claims of Edward III of England (1328). Crowned first of Valois kings (1328). Disputes with Edward led to Hundred Years War and English victory at Crécy (1346).

Philip II (382-336 BC), king of Macedonia (359-336 BC). Seized throne from his cousin; reorganized army, introducing formidable phalanx formation. Began conquest of Greece, culminating in defeat of Athens and Thebes at Chaeronea (338). Assassinated while preparing for war against Persia.

Philip II (1527-98), king of Spain (1556-98). Succeeded his father, Emperor Charles V. His dominions incl. Netherlands, Naples, Sicily, and much of New World. Championed orthodox Catholicism, persecuting heretics. His repression and introduction of Inquisition provoked major revolt in Netherlands (1567). Annexed Portugal (1580). Economy drained by wars, Spanish power declined after destruction of Armada (1588).

Philip V (1683-1746), king of Spain (1700-46). Grandson of Louis XIV, his accession as 1st Bourbon king of Spain provoked War of Spanish Succession. Policies dominated by his wives and Cardinal ALBERONI.

Philip Mountbatten, *see* EDINBURGH, PHILIP MOUNTBATTEN, DUKE OF.

Philip Neri, St (1515-95), Italian reformer. Known as 'apostle of Rome' for work among poor of city. Founded lay brotherhood.

Philip the Bold (1342-1404), duke of Burgundy (1363-1404). Virtual ruler of France during Charles VI's minority. His struggle for power with Louis d'Orléans during period of king's insanity (beginning 1392) was continued by his son, JOHN THE FEARLESS.

Philip the Good (1396-1467), duke of Burgundy (1419-67). Allied with the English during their attempts to secure French throne for Henry V and his heirs, but later supported Charles VII of France. Made Low Countries centre of commerce and culture.

Philippi, ancient city of Macedonia, N Greece. Here Octavian and Antony defeated (42 BC) Brutus and Cassius.

Philippians, epistle of NT, written by St Paul from captivity in Rome to Christians at Philippi, Macedonia.

Philippines, republic of SE Asia, isl. group incl. Luzon, Mindanao. Area c 300,000 sq km (115,000 sq mi); pop. 41,457,000; cap. Quezon City. Language: Filipino. Religion: RC. Mountainous, densely forested; tropical monsoon climate on larger isls. Mainly agric. economy; produces rice, corn, hemp, sugar, timber; minerals incl. chromite, gold. Discovered by Magellan (1521); under Spanish control (1564-1898) until ceded to US after Spanish-American War. Total independence gained in 1946. Occupied by Japanese in WWII.

Philippines

Philistines, non-Semitic people, prob. of Cretan origin, who inhabited S Palestine from 12th cent. BC. Constantly at war with Israelites; conquered by David and under Solomon incorporated into kingdom of Israel. Regained independence, finally accepted Assyrian domination (8th cent. BC).

Phillip, Arthur (1738-1814), British colonial administrator. First governor of New South Wales (1786-92), estab. penal settlement at Sydney (1788). Promoted agric., colonization.

Phillips, J[ohn] B[ertram] (1906-), English churchman. Known for translation, *The New Testament in Modern English* (1958). Other works incl. *God our Contemporary* (1960).

Philo Judaeus (c 20 BC-c AD 50), Jewish philosopher, native of Alexandria. Attempted to reconcile Bible with works of Greek philosophers, esp. Plato. Related infinite God with finite world by means of the concept of the intermediary *logos*.

philology, *see* LINGUISTICS.

Philomela, in Greek myth, daughter of King Pandion of Attica. Seduced by her brother-in-law, Tereus, who cut out her tongue. She embroidered the story in some cloth and sent it to her sister, Procne, who murdered her own son by Tereus. To save the sisters from Tereus' revenge, the gods turned Philomela into a swallow, Procne into a nightingale (Latin version reverses these).

philosopher's stone, substance sought by alchemists, who believed it would turn base metals into gold.

philosophy (Gk., = love of wisdom), theory or logical analysis of principles underlying the ultimate nature of the universe (ontology, metaphysics) and related fields, incl. conduct (ethics), thought (logic), knowledge (epistemology). In the West, tradition springs from classical Greece (esp. Plato, Aristotle) and was reinterpreted in Christian terms by medieval scholastics mainly from Arabic editions. Modern rationalism begins with Descartes; modern empiricism with Locke. Other disciplines are critically examined for basic principles and concepts, *eg* philosophy of science, philosophy of history. Eastern philosophy, though often rigorous, tends to be regarded as part of mystical theology.

Phiz, *see* BROWNE, HABLOT KNIGHT.

phlebitis, inflammation of a vein, usually associated with blockage of vein by blood clots (thrombophlebitis). May occur after childbirth or surgery; use of oral contraceptives sometimes disposes women to thrombophlebitis. Blood clots, usually in leg, may dislodge and travel to lungs.

phloem, vascular tissue of a plant which distributes synthesized foods, *eg* proteins and sugars.

phlogiston theory, proposition advanced in 17th cent. that all combustible material contained phlogiston which escaped when material was burned, leaving ash or calx that represented true material. Theory refuted by Lavoisier.

phlox, genus of herbs native to North America, esp. various hybrids of *Phlox drummondi*, cultivated for showy flowers.

Phnom Penh or **Pnom Penh,** cap. of Cambodia. Pop. 470,000. Trade centre, port on R. Mekong. Stronghold of loyalist forces during civil war (1970-5). Became cap. of Cambodia 1867.

phobia, irrational fear of a particular thing or situation, creating state of anxiety.

Phocis or **Fokis,** region of C Greece, on Gulf of Corinth; modern admin. dist., cap. Amphissa. Mountainous, incl. Mt. Parnassus; sheep, goats. Ancient Phocis fought 3 'Sacred Wars' to retain Delphi; fell to Thebes 4th cent. BC.

Phoenicians, Semitic people descended from the Canaanites who occupied the coastal areas of modern Syria and Lebanon (Phoenicia). Exercised maritime and commercial power *c* 1200-600 BC throughout the Mediterranean area, founding colonies in Cyprus, N Africa and Spain. Chief cities were Tyre and Sidon.

Phoenix, cap. of Arizona, US; on Salt R. Pop. 581,000. Commercial centre in irrigated agric. region producing fruit, cotton. Health resort. Has Pueblo Indian ruins, excavated 1927. Became cap. 1889.

phoenix, in ancient Egyptian myth, beautiful lone bird which lived in the Arabian desert for 500 years and then consumed itself in fire, new phoenix arising from ashes. Used in religion as symbol of death, resurrection.

Phoenix Islands, group of 8 coral isls. in C Pacific Ocean. Canton and Enderbury Isls. jointly admin. by US, UK; other 6 part of Gilbert and Ellice Isls. colony.

phonetics, study of system of LANGUAGE sounds. Branches incl. study of speech sounds using written symbols to transcribe accurately their differences, and phonemics, the study of significant differences between groups of roughly similar sounds.

phonograph, *see* GRAMOPHONE.

phosphates, salts or esters of phosphoric acid (H_3PO_4). Calcium superphosphate used as fertilizer, sodium phosphate (Na_3PO_4) used in detergents.

phosphorescence, property of certain substances of giving off lingering emission of light following excitation by radiation, *eg* light or X-rays. Causes certain minerals, *eg* zinc sulphide, to glow in dark.

phosphorus (P), non-metallic element; at. no. 15, at. wt. 30.97. Occurs in various allotropic forms: white form is waxy poisonous solid which ignites spontaneously in air; red form is non-poisonous and less reactive, obtained by heating white form. Occurs widely in phosphate minerals; essential to life, occurs in blood, bones, *etc*. Compounds used in fertilizers, detergents, matches, *etc*.

photochemistry, study of influence of light and other radiant energy on chemical reactions; photochemical effects are utilized in photography and photosynthesis.

photoelectric effect, emission of electrons from surface of certain substances when exposed to light of suitable frequency. Photoelectric cell uses effect to convert light into electrical energy. Commonest type contains electric circuit with 2 electrodes separated by light-sensitive semi-conductor; current flow in circuit increases when light strikes semiconductor. Used to open automatic doors, as burglar alarm, *etc*.

photoengraving, photomechanical process used for printing illustrations. Subject to be reproduced is photographed and its image is transferred through the negative to a metal plate coated with light-sensitive chemical. Coating unaffected by light is removed and underlying metal plate etched away. Half-tone is form of photoengraving using dots of varying size to obtain variations in tone.

photography, process of reproducing optical image on light-sensitive substance (silver bromide or chloride) under controlled conditions in camera. Developer produces metallic silver on those parts of photographic plate previously exposed to light. Fixing agent, *eg* 'hypo', dissolves remaining silver salts, leaving negative image. Positive image is obtained by placing negative on light-sensitive paper and then repeating developing and fixing process.

photon, fundamental quantum of electromagnetic energy, the energy of light. Sometimes regarded as uncharged elementary particle of zero rest mass, travelling at speed of light. Its energy is product of Planck's constant and frequency of electromagnetic wave.

photosynthesis, process by which plants make food by transformation of carbon dioxide and water into carbohydrates. Occurs in green part of plants and utilizes energy from sunlight. The green pigment CHLOROPHYLL is necessary for the reaction.

Phuket, isl. of SW Thailand, off W Malay penin. Area *c* 520 sq km (200 sq mi). Rich tin ore deposits; also produces rubber.

pH-value, in chemistry, *see* HYDROGEN ION CONCENTRATION.

phylacteries, two small leather cases holding parchment inscribed with passages from Scripture (Exodus and Deuteronomy). One is worn on the forehead, other on left arm by Orthodox Jews during morning prayers as a reminder of God.

phylloxera, plant louse of genus *Phylloxera*. Grape phylloxera, *P. vitifoliae*, attacks leaves and roots of grape vines in US and Europe; it almost destroyed wine industry in France after its accidental introduction in 1860s.

physical anthropology, branch of ANTHROPOLOGY concerned with physical characteristics of peoples. Studies evolution of body types and development of racial groups using statistical methods.

physics, science concerned with fundamental relationships between matter and energy. Classical physics, developed in 19th cent., deals with electricity, magnetism, heat, optics, mechanics, *etc*. Quantum physics of 20th cent., which assumes that energy exists in discrete bundles, explains atomic and nuclear phenomena.

physiocrats, group of 18th cent. French economic theoreticians headed by FRANCOIS QUESNAY. Among first to study economics systematically. Saw land and agric. as basis of wealth. Believed in natural economic laws which must be allowed to operate freely. Influenced Adam Smith and other laisser-faire economists.

physiology, study of functions and vital processes of living organisms, both plants and animals.

physiotherapy, method of treating illness and injury by physical means such as massage, exercise, heat and electricity.

pi (π), symbol used to denote ratio of circumference of a circle to its diameter; $\pi = 3.14159$ (to 5 decimal places).

Piacenza (anc. *Placentia*), city of Emilia-Romagna, NW Italy, on R. Po. Cap. of Piacenza prov. Pop. 109,000. Agric. machinery, pasta mfg. Member of Lombard League (12th cent.). Part of duchy of Parma and Piacenza (under Farnese family) from 1545.

Piaf, Edith, orig. Edith Giovanna Gassion (1915-63), French singer, known as 'the Little Sparrow'. Renowned for her passionate songs of troubles and unhappiness, *eg* 'Je ne regrette rien'.

Piaget, Jean (1896-   ), Swiss psychologist. Known for unique contributions to theories of cognitive development, postulating genetically determined stages through which children pass to reach abstract reasoning ability. Later abandoned these theories for application of structuralism to behavioural sciences.

piano or **pianoforte,** keyboard instrument having compass of 7 octaves, keys of which operate hammers which strike the strings. First appeared mid-18th cent. Many 19th cent. composers were also virtuoso pianists (*eg* Beethoven, Chopin, Liszt, Grieg and Brahms).

Picardy (*Picardie*), region and former prov. of N France, hist. cap. Amiens. Fertile area, drained by R. Somme; agric., textile indust. Part of France from 1477. Battlefield in WWI.

Picasso

Picasso, Pablo [Ruiz y] (1881-1973), Spanish artist. Dominant figure in many 20th cent. art movements. In his 'blue' period (1901-4), painted expressive scenes of human poverty and degradation; in 'rose' period (1905-7), painted circus scenes. Influenced by Cézanne and negro sculpture, evolved cubist style with Braque in Paris; *Les Demoiselles d'Avignon* marks beginning of cubist phase. Later turned to monumental classical nudes, sculptures, pottery. Famous work *Guernica* (1936) expresses his horror at outrages of Spanish Civil War.

Piccard, Auguste (1884-1962), Belgian physicist, b. Switzerland. Made 1st balloon ascents into stratosphere (1931). Constructed bathyscaphe to explore ocean; reached depth of 10,900 m (35,800 ft).

piccolo, small woodwind instrument; pitched an octave higher than FLUTE.

Pickering, Edward Charles (1846-1919), American astronomer, physicist. Devised instruments to measure light of stars and studied stellar spectra. His brother, **William Henry Pickering** (1858-1938), predicted location of planet Pluto before its discovery; discovered 9th satellite of Saturn.

Pickford, Mary, orig. Gladys Smith (1893-   ), American film actress, b. Canada. Became famous as 'America's sweetheart' through silent films, incl. *Pollyanna* (1919), *Little Lord Fauntleroy* (1921). Co-founded United Artists Films.

Pico della Mirandola, Giovanni, Conte (1463-94), Italian philosopher, humanist. Sought to reconcile Platonism and Christianity in series of theses, prefaced by *On the Dignity of Man.* Also wrote *Heptaplus.*

Picts, Iron Age people inhabiting Scotland, N Ireland. First described by Romans in AD 297, they resisted Roman conquest and maintained their independence until absorbed into kingdom of the Scots *c* 850.

pidgin, lingua franca, not 1st language of speakers, with restricted vocabulary, simple syntax. Originally applied to variety of English spoken by Chinese trading with English, extended to incl. pidgins developed from Portuguese, French, Spanish, Malay *etc,* in Africa, West Indies, as well as Far East.

Piedmont (*Piemonte*), region of NW Italy, cap. Turin. H.e.p., livestock in mountainous W; wheat, rice in fertile Po valley. Ruled by house of Savoy from 12th cent; part of Sardinia from 1720 to unification (1860). Annexed to France 1798-1814. Battleground in many wars.

piedmont, area of land lying at foot of mountains or upland. May also describe particular feature *eg* piedmont plain, piedmont glacier.

Pierce, Franklin (1804-69), American statesman, president (1853-7). Unexpected Democratic presidential nominee in 1852, elected on policy of appeasing the South on slavery issue. Alienated North by authorizing KANSAS-NEBRASKA BILL (1854).

Piero della Francesca (*c* 1420-92), Italian painter. Known for the geometric perfection of his forms, his mastery of perspective and subtle colour harmonies, work incl. fresco series *The Legend of the True Cross* at Arezzo, and *Flagellation of Christ* at Urbino.

Pierre, cap. of South Dakota, US; on Missouri R. Pop. 10,000. Livestock market, shipping industs. Founded 1880; became cap. 1889.

Pietermaritzburg or **Maritzburg,** cap. of Natal, South Africa. Pop. 113,000. Admin., indust., railway centre in stock rearing area; produces wattle extract for tanning; has part of univ. of Natal (1909). Founded (1838) by Boer leaders. Two cathedrals, Voortrekker museum, many gardens.

Pietism, movement in Lutheran church favouring devotion rather than dogmatism. First leader was German theologian, Philip Jakob Spener (1635-1705), who in *Pia desideria* (1675) stressed study of Bible and participation of lay members in spiritual control of Church. Attacked as unorthodox; declined in late 18th cent. Influenced Kant, Kierkegaard.

piezoelectric effect, property exhibited by certain crystals of developing electric charge on their surface when subjected to pressure. Crystals also expand and contract in response to alternating current. Piezoelectric crystals are used in microphones, loudspeakers, record player pick-ups, *etc.*

Domestic pig (large white)

pig, any of Suidae family of hoofed mammals. Omnivorous, canine teeth often lengthened into tusks. Domestic pig developed from wild boar, *Sus scrofa;* source of pork, lard. Wild species incl. babirussa, wart hog.

pigeon, bird of Columbidae family, widely distributed in tropical and temperate regions. Wood pigeon or ring dove, *Columba palumbus,* with greyish plumage, is largest European species. Domesticated breeds derived from rock dove, *C. livia;* noted for homing ability.

Pigmy, *see* PYGMY.

Pigs, Bay of, inlet of S Cuba. Scene of unsuccessful invasion by Cuban exiles backed by US forces in attempt to overthrow Communist Castro regime (1961).

pika, small tailless mammal, genus *Ochotona,* of same order (Lagomorpha) as rabbit. Found in rocky mountains of Asia and North America.

Pike (with eel)

Pike, Zebulon Montgomery (1779-1813), American soldier, explorer. Led expedition to discover source of Mississippi (1805). Sighted mountain named after him (Pikes Peak) on expedition up Arkansas R. into Colorado.

pike, *Esox lucius,* carnivorous freshwater fish of N temperate regions. Voracious predator, feeding on fish, water birds, *etc.* Reaches lengths of 1.5 m/5 ft.

pike, obsolete infantry weapon with long shaft and iron point, often used defensively in rows braced against the ground. Superseded by the bayonet.

Pikes Peak, mountain of C Colorado, US. Height 4301 m (14,110 ft). Most famous peak in Rocky Mts. Colorado Springs is at foot. Tourist region.

Pilate, Pontius (*fl* AD 1st cent.), Roman procurator of Judaea (*c* 26-36). Fearing Jewish religious and popular recrimination, allowed execution of Jesus. Traditionally, committed suicide in Rome.

pilchard, *Sardina pilchardus,* small marine food fish of herring family, common in Mediterranean and off Portuguese coast. Sardine is young pilchard. Other species incl. Californian and South African pilchard.

Pilcomayo, river of Bolivia. Rises in Andes near L. Poopó; flows SE 1130 km (*c* 700 mi) across the Chaco to join Paraquay R. near Asunción. Forms part of Paraguay-Argentina border.

piles, *see* HAEMORRHOIDS.

pilgrimage, journey made to a shrine or holy place as a religious act. Occurs in many religions, *eg* in Hinduism to Ganges, in Islam to Mecca, in Judaism to Temple at Jerusalem, in Christianity to Jerusalem, Bethlehem, Nazareth. Important in medieval Europe, with major centres at Canterbury (England), Santiago de Compostela (Spain). In RC church, pilgrimage is still fostered with Rome being the major centre.

Pilgrimage of Grace (1536), rising of English Roman Catholics, esp. in Lincolnshire and Yorkshire, protesting against abolition of papal supremacy and suppression of monasteries by Henry VIII. Rebels dispersed peacefully, but many were executed after further rebellion in 1537.

Pilgrim Fathers, name given to those English emigrants who sailed in *Mayflower* (1620) to found Plymouth Colony in Massachusetts. About ⅓ of them had previously migrated to Holland in search of religious freedom.

Pill, the, popular name for oral contraceptive which interferes with menstrual cycle, preventing ovulation by hormone action.

Pillars of Hercules, *see* GIBRALTAR, STRAIT OF.

Pillnitz, Declaration of, statement (1791) calling on European powers to restore Louis XVI of France to his former power; issued by Prussia and Austria.

pilot fish, *Naucrates ductor,* spiny-finned marine fish, often found accompanying sharks, turtles.

Pilsen *see* PLZEŇ, Czechoslovakia.

Pilsudski, Joseph (1867-1935), Polish military and political leader. Active in cause of Polish independence from Russia before WWI. Led Polish troops against Russia

in support of Austria in WWI. Became head of state of independent Poland (1919). Retired 1922, returned as virtual dictator (1926-35) after coup d'état.

Piltdown man, human skull fragment found with ape-like jaw at Piltdown, Sussex (1912). Believed to be oldest human species found in Europe until proved to be a hoax (1953). Fragments had been tampered with and were of modern origin.

pimento, *Pimenta officinalis,* tree of myrtle family, native to West Indies. Dried fruits used as spice.

pimpernel, any of genus *Anagallis* of annual herbs of primrose family; esp. scarlet pimpernel, *A. arvensis,* with red, white or blue, star-like flowers which close in bad weather.

Pindar (518-438 BC), Greek poet. Wrote choral lyrics, incl. odes celebrating athletic victories, *Epinikia.*

Pindus Mountains (*Pindhos*), range of NC Greece, runs N-S between Epirus (W), Thessaly (E). Highest point Smólikas (2636 m/8652 ft).

pine, any of genus *Pinus* of evergreen conifers, widely distributed in N hemisphere. Needle-shaped leaves. Certain varieties yield timber, turpentine, resin. Species incl. stone pine, *P. pinea,* Austrian pine, *P. nigra,* pitch pine, *P. rigida* and Scots pine, *P. sylvestris.*

pineal body, small cone-shaped projection from centre of brain of all vertebrates. In certain amphibians and reptiles, it is sensitive to light and is remnant of central eye. Function in humans unknown, but believed to secrete hormone which influences sexual development.

pineapple, *Ananas comosus,* plant native to tropical America, now grown chiefly in Hawaii. Edible, juicy fruit develops from flower spike.

Pine marten

pine marten, *Martes martes,* nocturnal carnivore of forests of N Europe and W Asia. Omnivorous, often catching squirrels. Has dark brown fur, bushy tail.

Pinero, Sir Arthur Wing (1855-1934), English playwright. Wrote skilful farces, *eg Dandy Dick* (1887), problem plays, *eg The Second Mrs Tanqueray* (1893), sentimental comedies, *eg Trelawny of the Wells* (1898).

Pines, Isle of, isl. off W Cuba. Area 3056 sq km (1180 sq mi). Fishing, agric., marble quarrying; covered by pine forests Has large prison for political prisoners. Discovered by Columbus (1494). Awarded to Cuba over US claims (1925).

ping-pong, *see* TABLE TENNIS.

pink, any of genus *Dianthus* of annual or perennial plants native to temperate regions. White or red flowers with ragged edges. Species incl. garden pink, *D. plumarius,*

Sweet William

maiden pink, *D. deltoides* and sweet william, *D. barbatus*. *See* CARNATION.

Pinkerton, Allan (1819-84), American detective, b. Scotland. Founded Pinkerton National Detective Agency (1850), active in tracing train robbers. Directed espionage operations for Union in Confederate States during Civil War.

Pinkie, Battle of, Scottish defeat by English forces under duke of Somerset (1547). Caused Scots to send Mary (later Mary Queen of Scots) to France to avoid marriage to Edward VI. Battle site is near Musselburgh.

Pinnipedia (pinnipeds), order of aquatic carnivorous mammals. Three families: true or earless seals (Phocidae); eared seals (Otariidae); walruses (Odobenidae).

Pinochet [Ugarte], Augusto (1916–), Chilean political leader. Took control of govt. after overthrowing Marxist regime of Allende (1973). Suppressed left-wing opposition; declared Marxist parties illegal.

Pinter, Harold (1930-), English dramatist. Known for menacing comedies, *eg The Caretaker* (1959), *The Homecoming* (1964), one-act plays incl. *The Dumb Waiter* (1957), screenplays, *eg Accident* (1967).

pion or **pi-meson,** elementary particle with mass *c* 270 times that of electron. Discovered (1947) in cosmic radiation; plays important role in forces which bind atomic nucleus.

Piozzi, Hester Lynch, neé Salusbury (1741-1821), English writer, b. Wales. Known (as Mrs Thrale) as friend of Dr JOHNSON. Wrote *Anecdotes of the Late Samuel Johnson* (1786), *Letters to and from the late Samuel Johnson LL.D.* (1788).

pipa, aquatic South American toad, genus *Pipa*. Female carries fertilized eggs in small pockets on her back. Young emerge almost identical to adults. Also called Surinam toad.

pipal, *see* BO TREE.

Great pipe fish

pipe fish, small elongated marine fish of Syngnathidae family. Long tubular snout, bony plates on skin. Male broods eggs in pouch on body. Species incl. great pipe fish, *Syngnathus acus*, common in E Atlantic.

pipistrelle, small insectivorous bat of wide distribution, genus *Pipistrellus*. Species incl. eastern pipistrelle, *P. subflavus*, smallest North American bat, and *P. pipistrellus*, smallest British bat.

pipit, small songbird of Motacillidae family, genus *Anthus*. Brown plumage; insectivorous. Species incl. European meadow pipit, *A. pratensis*, and North American Sprague's pipit *A. spragueii*.

piracy, taking of ship or contents on the high seas, distinct from privateering in that pirate holds no commission, does not fly national flag. Formerly common, esp. in Spanish Main, Barbary coast, Chinese and Malay waters. Famous pirates incl. Henry Morgan, Edward Teach (Blackbeard). *See* also HIJACKER.

Piraeus, *see* ATHENS, Greece.

Pirandello, Luigi (1867-1936), Italian author. Known for plays dealing with relationship between illusion, reality incl. *Right You Are If You Think You Are* (1917), *Six Characters in Search of an Author* (1921), *Henry IV* (1922). Also wrote novels, short stories. Nobel Prize for Literature (1934).

Piranesi, Giovanni Battista (1720-78) Italian architect, engraver. His numerous etchings of Roman antiquities greatly influenced Romantic concept of Rome. Famous for *Carceri d'Invenzione* (reworked 1761), series of fantastic imaginary prisons.

piranha, South American freshwater fish with sharp teeth and powerful jaws. Lives in schools which can attack large animals. Species incl. *Pigocentrus piraya*, up to 60 cm/2 ft in length.

Pisa, city of Tuscany, WC Italy, on R. Arno. Cap. of Pisa prov. Pop. 112,000. Medieval maritime republic, warred with Florence, defeated (1284) by Genoa. Centre of Pisan school of sculpture (13th-14th cent.). Cathedral (12th cent.), leaning tower (1173, height 55m/180 ft). Birthplace of Galileo.

Pisa, Council of, council summoned (1409) to try to end Great SCHISM. Supporters of Gregory XII and Benedict XIII agreed to depose them both and elect Alexander V pope. Various claims were not finally settled until 1417.

Pisanello, orig. Antonio Pisano (*c* 1395-1455), Italian artist. Leading exponent of International Gothic style in Italy in succession to Gentile da Fabriano, he was an accomplished draughtsman and portraitist. His portrait medals are valuable historical records.

Pisano, Andrea (*c* 1290-1348), Italian sculptor, architect. Continued Giotto's work on cathedral and campanile in Florence; most famous work is bronze doors of Baptistery at Florence, begun 1330.

Pisano, Nicola (*c* 1220-*c* 1280), Italian architect, sculptor. Leading figure in rebirth of sculpture in Italy. His works, incl. pulpits in Baptistery at Pisa and in Siena cathedral, are marked by synthesis of Gothic and classical styles. His son, **Giovanni Pisano** (*c* 1250-*c* 1314), assisted his father and continued revival of sculpture. Works incl. pulpit of Pisa cathedral.

Pisces, *see* ZODIAC.

Pisistratus (*c* 605-527 BC), tyrant of Athens. Leader of popular party, he seized power *c* 560. Twice exiled, he returned (541) and estab. his personal rule until his death. Encouraged building, poetry.

Pissarro, Camille (1830-1903), French painter, b. West Indies. A leading member of the impressionists, he participated in all 8 impressionist exhibitions. Enormously prolific, he influenced early work of Cézanne and Gauguin.

Pistachio

pistachio, *Pistacia vera*, small tree native to Mediterranean region and Asia. Fruit contains greenish, edible nut eaten salted or used in cookery and confectionery.

Pistoia, town of Tuscany, NC Italy, cap. of Pistoia prov. Pop. 94,000. Catiline defeated, killed here (62 BC). Cathedral (13th cent.).

pistol, small, short-barrelled firearm designed to be fired with one hand. Originally made in Italy (16th cent.); REVOLVER made in 19th cent. and 'automatic' repeating pistols in 20th cent.

Pitcairn Island, isl. of SC Pacific Ocean, admin. by UK. Area 5 sq km (2 sq mi). Fruit growing. Colonized (1790) by mutineers from HMS *Bounty* and Tahitian women; pop. removed 1856, some later returned.

pitch, dark sticky substance, liquid when heated, solid when cold. Obtained as residue from distillation of petroleum, coal tar, wood tar. Used in waterproofing, road construction.

pitch, quality of a musical sound dependent on rate of vibrations producing it. The greater the number of vibrations per second, the higher the note. Instruments are tuned to a standard pitch in which the A above middle C is equal to 440 vibrations per second.

pitchblende, uranium ore mineral, a form of uraninite. Consists of uranium oxide with various impurities. Source of uranium; also radium, lead, thorium, some rare-earth elements. Major sources in US, Canada, Australia, Zaïre.

pitcher plant, any of genus *Sarracenia,* insectiverous bog herbs of North America. Leaves in form of pitcher.

Pitlochry, town of Tayside region, C Scotland, on R. Tummel. Pop. 3000. Control point of Highland h.e.p. system. Annual drama festival; tourism.

Pitman, Sir Isaac (1813-97), English inventor. Developed improved system of phonetic shorthand, expounded in *Stenographic Soundhand* (1837); adapted for use in many languages.

Pitt, William, 1st Earl of Chatham (1708-78), English statesman, known as the 'Great Commoner'. Chief figure in coalition with duke of Newcastle (1757-61), architect of military defeat of French in India and Canada (1759). Forced to resign by George III. Retired because of ill health from 2nd coalition (1766-8). Broke with Whigs over colonial policy in America, favouring conciliation. His son, **William Pitt** (1759-1806), was Tory PM (1783-1801, 1804-6). Reformed finances to help fund national debt, introduced new taxes. Failed to anticipate war with revolutionary France; his various coalitions had little success on land against French. Took strong measures to suppress political reformers. Solved Irish question by passing Act of Union (1800), but resigned when George III vetoed Catholic emancipation. Second ministry ended with his death soon after defeat of Allies by Napoleon at Austerlitz.

Pitt-Rivers, Augustus Henry Lane-Fox (1827-1900), English soldier, archaeologist. Advanced archaeological technique by recording in detail excavations on his Wiltshire estate; recognized importance of apparently trivial finds. Pub. *Excavations in Cranborne Chase* (1887-98).

Pittsburgh, city of SW Pennsylvania, US; at point where Allegheny and Monongahela rivers form Ohio R. Pop. 520,000. In rich coal mining region. Iron and steel, oil refining, machinery mfg. industs. Settled in 1760 as Fort Pitt (formerly French Fort Duquesne). Has Carnegie Institute of Technology.

pituitary gland, endocrine gland situated at base of brain. Composed of anterior and posterior lobes. Anterior lobe secretes important hormones whose functions incl.: maintenance of growth, stimulation of thyroid and sex organs, *etc.* Posterior lobe secretes hormone which regulates flow of urine.

pit viper, any of Crotalidae family of venomous snakes, incl. rattlesnake, sidewinder, *etc,* with heat-sensory pits on each side of head. Found in Asia and New World.

Pius V, St, orig. Michele Ghislieri (1504-72), Italian churchman, pope (1566-72). Furthered the Catholic Reformation by implementing the decrees of the Council of Trent. Organized alliance between Venice and Spain against the Turks, which led to victory at Lepanto (1571).

Pittsburgh

Pius VI, orig. Angelo Braschi (1717-99), Italian churchman, pope (1775-99). Opposed attempts of Emperor Joseph II and subsequently of French Revolution to subject church to state. Taken prisoner (1798) during French occupation of Rome. Died in captivity.

Pius VII, orig. Barnaba Chiaramonti (1740-1823), Italian churchman, pope (1800-23). Signed Concordat (1801) with Napoleon to re-estab. Church in France. Taken prisoner (1809-14) by French on occupation of papal states. Worked to restore Church in Europe on return to Rome.

Pius IX, orig. Giovanni Mastai-Ferretti (1792-1878), Italian churchman, pope (1846-78). Refused to recognize new kingdom of Italy and in 1870 retired to Vatican. Proclaimed dogma of Immaculate Conception (1854); convened 1st Vatican Council which enunciated papal infallibility.

Pius XI, orig. Achille Damiano Ratti (1857-1939), Italian churchman, pope (1922-39). Responsible for Lateran Treaty (1929) estab. Vatican City state. Condemned Nazism in 1937 encyclical.

Pius XII, orig. Eugenio Pacelli (1876-1958), Italian churchman, pope (1939-58). Worked to limit extension of WWII, while taking ambiguous stand towards Axis powers. Attempted to reduce Communist power (excommunicated Hungary, Romania, Poland in 1953).

Piute, see PAIUTE.

Pizarro, Francisco (*c* 1476-1541), Spanish conquistador. With partner, Almagro, led expedition to Peru (1530) in search of fabulous wealth of Incas. Seized Inca ruler Atahualpa (1532) and had him murdered after receiving his enormous ransom (1533). Captured Cuzco (1533), completing conquest of Peru. Founded Lima (1535). Dispute between Almagro and Pizarro and his brothers led to conflict and execution of Almagro (1538). Almagro's followers later assassinated Pizarro.

Place, Francis (1771-1854), English radical. Successfully campaigned (1814-24) for repeal of Combination Acts, forbidding trade unions. Vigorous organizer of movement for political reform.

placenta, organ consisting of embryonic tissue by which the embryo of viviparous animals is nourished. Attached to lining of mother's uterus. Oxygen and dissolved nutrients are carried to placenta by mother's blood.

plague, contagious disease caused by bacterium *Pasteurella pestis*; carried by fleas from infected rats. Form known as bubonic plague is characterized by swollen lymph nodes (buboes); pneumonic plague infects lungs. Occurred sporadically in Europe, notably in Black Death (1346-9) and Great London Plague (1665).

plaice, *Pleuronectes platessa,* marine flatfish, commercially important in Europe. Light brown body with orange spots.

Plaid Cymru, see WELSH NATIONALIST PARTY.

plain, large area of relatively flat land usually at low altitude. Commonest types are glacial plains, flood plains, coastal plains. Often grass-covered *eg* pampas (South America), steppes (USSR), savannah (tropics).

plainsong, religious chant that developed in early Christian church and survives in RC liturgy. Consists of single melodic line sung in unison, usually unaccompanied. Developed into POLYPHONY in late Middle Ages. Also known as Gregorian chant.

Max Planck

Planck, Max Karl Ernst Ludwig (1858-1947), German physicist. Attempts to explain distribution of black-body radiation led to his hypothesis that vibrating atoms absorb or emit radiant energy only in discrete bundles (quanta) whose magnitude is product of Planck's constant and frequency of radiation. Founder of modern quantum theory. Nobel Prize for Physics (1918).

plane, any of genus *Platanus* of deciduous trees native to temperate regions. Palmate leaves, pendulous burr-like fruit. Species incl. Oriental plane, *P. orientalis,* London plane, *P. acerifolia,* with 3-lobed leaves, and American sycamore or buttonwood, *P. occidentalis.*

planet, heavenly body in orbit round the Sun, which shines by reflected sunlight. Minor planet is called an ASTEROID. *See* SOLAR SYSTEM.

planetarium, arrangement for projecting images of heavenly bodies on inside of large hemispherical dome by means of system of optical projectors which is revolved to show celestial motion. Name also applied to building in which system is housed.

plankton, general term for minute organisms found drifting near surface of sea or lakes. Incl. protozoa, crustacea, algae and other invertebrates.

plant, member of vegetable group of living organisms. Generally manufactures own food by PHOTOSYNTHESIS (but *see* FUNGUS); has an unlimited growth (*ie* old tissue remains in place and new tissue grows away from it); has cells with more or less rigid walls; has no means of independent locomotion. Divided into 4 main divisions: Thallophyta (algae, lichens, fungi); Bryophyta (mosses, liverworts); Pteridophyta (ferns, club mosses, horsetails); Spermophyta (conifers, flowering plants). *See* CLASSIFICATION.

Plantagenet, name applied to English royal house, whose monarchs were Henry II, Richard I, John, Henry III, Edward I, II, III, Richard II. After Richard II's deposition (1399), house divided into houses of York and Lancaster.

plantain, *Musa paradisiaca,* tropical plant. Produces long yellow-green fruit-like banana. Name also applies to any of genus *Plantago* of plants with rosettes of leaves and spikes of greenish flowers.

Plantin, Christophe (1514-89), French printer. Considered greatest printer of his time, he set up his press in Antwerp (1555). Pub. polyglot Bible (8 vols., 1569-73).

Plantain (*Plantago media*)

His printing works continued in operation until 1867, and is now a museum.

plant louse, see APHID.

plasma, in biology, clear fluid forming 55% of blood. Composed mainly of water, with dissolved proteins, inorganic salts, urea and sugar.

plasma, in physics, high-temperature ionized gas, composed almost entirely of equal numbers of electrons and positive ions. Excellent electrical conductor and responsive to magnetic fields; study of plasma is important to achievement of controlled thermonuclear reactions.

Plassey, village of West Bengal, NE India. Scene of Clive's victory over Nawab of Bengal (1757) giving Britain control of Bengal.

plaster of Paris, fine white powder produced by heating gypsum. When mixed with water, forms paste which sets and hardens. Used for casts, moulds, *etc.*

plastics, materials which are stable in normal use but are plastic in some part of their production and can be moulded by heat and pressure. Most plastics are synthetic polymers. The 2 main groups are thermoplastic materials, which can be melted and reset many times, and thermosetting materials, which cannot be remoulded.

plastic surgery, surgery dealing with repair of lost or damaged tissue or with making cosmetic improvements. Skin grafting is used to cover extensive burns or other injuries, both to improve final appearance and prevent infection.

Plata, Rio de la (River Plate), wide estuary of SE South America, formed at confluence of Uruguay and Paraná rivers. Chief ports Buenos Aires, Montevideo. Explored by Magellan (1520). Scene of naval battle (1939) in which German battleship *Graf Spee* was scuttled.

Plataea, ancient city of Boeotia, SE Greece. Scene of Greek naval victory (479 BC) over Persians. Sacked by Spartans (427 BC), Thebans (373 BC), rebuilt by Alexander the Great.

plateau, elevated area of land with relatively level surface. Causes incl. basalt lava flows (*eg* Deccan of India), faulting, erosion. Types incl. tableland, bordered by steep sides all around, and dissected plateau, where different rates of erosion eventually leave only isolated peaks.

plate tectonics, study of the main structural features of the Earth's crust in terms of several great crustal regions, or plates, which change their positions through time. Mountain ranges, faults, trenches, mid-oceanic ridges result from plate movements. CONTINENTAL DRIFT theory derives from plate tectonics, continents being embedded in shifting plates.

Plath, Sylvia (1932-63), American poet. Known for intense, highly personal verse, *eg* in collections *The Colossus* (1960), *Ariel* (1965). Also wrote a novel, *The Bell Jar* (1971), a fictionalized account of her nervous breakdown.

platinum (Pt), metallic element; at. no. 78, at. wt. 195.09. Malleable and ductile; resists corrosion by air and acids; excellent conductor of electricity. Used in electrical apparatus, jewellery and chemical catalysis.

Plato (*c* 427-*c* 347 BC), Greek philosopher, pupil of Socrates. Founded (387 BC) Academy near Athens to educate ruling elite. Author of *Republic* advocating ideal state based on rational order, ruled by philosopher kings. Propounded independent reality of universal ideas (esp.

idea of the good), and ideal forms which man could come to perceive through dialectic method of inquiry. Held that virtue, reason, happiness were one. Dialogues incl. *Apology, Crito, Protagoras, Phaedo, Timaeus, Laws.* Most noted student was Aristotle.

Platte, river of Nebraska, US. Formed by North and South Platte rivers, flows E 500 km (*c* 310 mi) to Missouri R. S of Omaha.

Plattensee, see BALATON, Hungary.

Platyhelminthes (flatworms), phylum of bilaterally symmetric invertebrates. Reproduction by complex hermaphroditic system. Divided into 3 classes: Cestoda, tapeworms; Trematoda, parasitic flukes; Turbellaria, free-swimming aquatic worms.

platypus, see DUCKBILLED PLATYPUS.

Plauen, town of S East Germany, on R. White Elster. Pop. 81,000. Textile indust. (curtains, lace) from 15th cent. Branch of Teutonic Knights based here from 1224.

Plautus, Titus Maccius (*c* 254–184 BC), Roman comic poet. Adapted Greek New Comedy for Roman stage; noted for boisterous humour, gift for dialogue, song, as in *Aulularia, Miles Gloriosus.* Profound influence on later European literature.

playing cards, cards used in gaming, divination and conjuring. Originated in the Orient, reaching Europe in 14th cent. Symbols for the 4 suits and 52-card deck were introduced in France in 16th cent.

plebeians, members of unprivileged class of ancient Rome, originally excluded from holding public office. Secured political equality with the patricians in years from *c* 500-300 BC.

plebiscite, expression of people's will by direct ballot on political issue, as in referendum. Since 18th cent., used for deciding between independent nationhood or affiliation with another nation.

Pléiade, la, group of 16th cent. French poets led by Ronsard, du Bellay. Aimed to enrich, purify French language, create national literature through imitation of classical forms.

Pleiades, in Greek myth, seven daughters of Atlas and nymph Pleione. Pursued by Orion and turned into constellation which bears their name.

Pleiades, star cluster in constellation Taurus. Six stars are readily visible but cluster contains several hundred.

Pleistocene epoch, first geological epoch of Quaternary period. Began *c* 2 million years ago, lasted until *c* 11,000 years ago. Incl. 4 major glaciations, or Ice ages, accompanied in warmer equatorial regions by high rainfall (pluvial) periods. Fauna incl. mastodons, mammoths, sabre-tooth carnivores, wolves, bison. During this epoch, man evolved from primitive ape-like creatures, *eg* Java, Peking man, to present form; time of Palaeolithic culture. Also *see* ICE AGES, and GEOLOGICAL TABLE.

Plekhanov, Georgi Valentinovich (1857-1918), Russian revolutionary. Influential in introducing Marxist thought to Russia. Broke with Bolsheviks after 1903 split in Social Democratic Party; his view that Russia was not ready for Socialism was adopted by Mensheviks.

plesiosaur, extinct marine reptile of Jurassic period and later, order Plesiosauria. Long thin neck, 4 paddle-like limbs, long tail. Reached lengths of 15 m/50 ft.

pleurisy, inflammation of pleura, the membrane enclosing the lung. Usually caused by infection by bacteria or viruses; often occurs with pneumonia. Characterized by difficulty in breathing and sometimes collection of fluid around lungs.

Pleven or **Plevna,** city of N Bulgaria. Pop. 108,000. Agric. centre; textiles; wine. Taken by Russia from Turks after siege (1877).

plexiglass, see PERSPEX.

Pliny the Elder, full name Gaius Plinius Secundus (AD *c* 23-79), Roman scholar. Wrote *Historia, naturalis,* encyclopedic collection of scientific knowledge in 37 books; some of the fanciful information he relates was long held as scientific fact. His nephew, **Pliny the Younger,** full name Gaius Plinius Caecilius Secundus (AD *c* 62-*c* 113), was consul. Wrote letters of literary and historical importance.

Pliocene epoch, final geological epoch of Tertiary period. End of Alpine mountain building. Continuing decrease in temperature caused extinction of many mammals, migration of others. Beginning of Lower Palaeolithic culture. Also see GEOLOGICAL TABLE.

Plock, town of NC Poland on R. Vistula. Pop. 66,000. Oil refining (pipeline from USSR), agric. market. Under Russian rule 1815-1921. Cathedral (12th cent.) contains royal tombs.

Ploeşti, city of SC Romania. Pop. 186,000. Petroleum indust., pipelines to Bucharest, Constanza. Bombed in WWII.

Plotinus (*c* AD 205-70), Greek philosopher, b. Egypt. Settled (AD 244) in Rome, founding neoplatonist school. Developed concept of creation by Emanation from God rather than directly by God.

plough, farm implement used to cut, break and turn over the soil. First ploughs consisted of wooden wedge tipped with iron, pushed or pulled by men or oxen. Modern plough incorporates: coulter, blade or disc, which makes vertical cuts in soil; share, which cuts horizontally through undersoil; mouldboard, which turns over soil.

Plovdiv (anc. *Philippopolis*), city of C Bulgaria, on R. Maritsa. Pop. 262,000. Agric. centre, esp. cereals, wine, attar of roses; textiles; tobacco. Taken by Philip II of Macedonia, renamed; cap. of Roman Thracia, and of 19th cent. Eastern Rumelia.

Ringed plover (Charadrius hiaticula)

plover, wading bird of Charadriidae family. Species incl. golden plover, *Pluvialis dominica,* which breeds in North America and NW Asia, and American KILLDEER.

plum, small tree or shrub of genus *Prunus,* native to Asia Minor. Oval, smooth-skinned, edible fruit with flattened stone. Commercially cultivated species incl. damson, *P. domestica,* and varieties of *P. salicina.*

Plutarch (AD *c* 46-*c* 120), Greek biographer, essayist. Best known for *Parallel Lives,* paired biographies of Greeks and Romans, with vivid characterization, anecdotes. Popular in Elizabethan England through translation by Sir Thomas North, source for Shakespeare's Roman plays.

Pluto, in Greek myth, son of Cronus and Rhea; ruler of HADES. Worshipped as god of dead and of earth's fertility. Identified with Roman Orcus or Dis Pater.

Pluto, planet 9th in distance from Sun; mean distance from Sun *c* 5900 × 10^6 km; diameter *c* 5800 km; period of rotation about Sun *c* 248 years. First detected 1930. Has surface of frozen methane.

plutonic rock, igneous rock formed at great depth below Earth's surface. Commonly occurs as INTRUSIVE ROCK; slow cooling produces coarsely crystalline texture, *eg* granite.

plutonium (Pu), transuranic element; at. no. 94, mass no. of most stable isotope 244. Plutonium 239, produced by irradiating uranium 238 with neutrons, is used as fuel in nuclear reactors and in nuclear weapons.

Plymouth, city of Devon, SW England, at head of Plymouth Sound. Pop. 239,000. Seaport, naval base; boatbuilding, fishing. Medieval *Sutton,* hist. seafaring base (Drake, Raleigh, 'Pilgrim Fathers'). Has RC cathedral. Damaged in WWII air raids.

Plymouth, town of SE Massachusetts, US; on Plymouth Bay. Pop. 19,000. Fishing, tourist industs. Site of Pilgrim landing in 1620 after sailing from England on *Mayflower,* marked by Plymouth Rock.

Plymouth Brethren, evangelical sect founded in Dublin by John Nelson Darby (1827). Spread to Europe and North

America. Movement follows literal interpretation of Bible, has no ordained ministers.

Plzeň (Ger. *Pilsen*), city of W Czechoslovakia. Pop. 148,000. Agric. market; breweries; metallurgy, munitions.

pneumoconiosis, disease of the lungs resulting from inhalation of mineral dust, esp. asbestos and silica. Usually affects miners, sand-blasters, *etc.* Causes lung inflammation and growth of fibrous scar tissue.

pneumonia, inflammation of the air sacs (alveoli) of the lungs, caused by bacterial or viral infection. Bronchial pneumonia is confined to area close to air passages, lobar pneumonia affects whole lobe. Bacterial form characterized by fever, pain in chest, blood-stained sputum; treated by antibiotics.

Pnom Penh, see PHNOM PENH.

Po (anc. *Padus*), river of N Italy. Flows *c* 650 km (405 mi) E from Alps to delta on Adriatic Sea. Po basin is most fertile region of Italy.

Pocahontas (*c* 1595-1617), American Indian princess, daughter of Powhatan. Said to have saved John Smith, English colonist in Jamestown, Virginia, from execution. Married another colonist, James Rolfe (1614). Died in England.

pochard, *Aythya ferina,* European diving duck found on lakes, *etc.* Male has black chest, grey body, chestnut head and neck. Name also applied to several other diving ducks, incl. CANVASBACK.

Po Chu-i (772-846), Chinese poet. Extremely prolific, known for lucid language use in short, topical poems.

pocket borough, in Great Britain before Reform Bill (1832), borough in which representation in Parliament was controlled by one family or person.

Podgorica, see TITOGRAD, Yugoslavia.

Podgorny, Nikolai Viktorovich (1903-), Soviet politician. Became president (head of state) in 1965, succeeding Mikoyan. Removed from office (1977) to allow constitutional changes redefining role of president.

Edgar Allan Poe

Poe, Edgar Allan (1809-49), American author. Known for short stories creating atmosphere of suspense, *eg* in *Tales of the Grotesque and Arabesque* (1840) incl. 'The Fall of the House of Usher'. Poetic works incl. *The Raven and Other Poems* (1845) which influenced Baudelaire. Also wrote detective stories, *eg The Murders in the Rue Morgue* (1841), literary criticism.

poet laureate, office of court poet in Britain. Ben Jonson first held position although Dryden first held title. Poets laureate incl. Wordsworth, Tennyson, Robert Bridges, John Masefield, John Betjeman.

poetry, in literature, term for imaginative, concentrated writing esp. using metrical and figurative language. Verse may be rhymed or un-rhymed (blank).

Pogonophora, phylum of marine invertebrates discovered off Indonesia (1900). Thread-like body contained in chitinous tube; bottom dwelling. Called beard worms because of beard-like tentacles around head.

pogrom, Russian word, originally denoting a riot; later applied to organized attacks on Jews, often carried out with connivance of tsarist govt. Pogroms of 1881-2 and 1903 were esp. severe.

Pohai, Gulf of, arm of Yellow Sea. Indents NE China coast. Bordered by Hopeh, Liaoning, Shantung provs. Formerly called Gulf of Chihli.

Poincaré, Raymond Nicolas Landry (1860-1934), French statesman, president (1913-20). Demanded strict treatment of Germany after WWI. As premier (1922-4, 1926-9), ordered armed occupation of Ruhr to enforce payment of war reparations (1923). His cousin, **Jules Henri Poincaré** (1854-1912), was a mathematician. Did pioneering research on topology of surfaces. Anticipated parts of relativity theory.

poinsettia, *Euphorbia pulcherrima,* plant native to Mexico and tropical America. Yellow flowers surrounded by tapering red leaves resembling petals.

Pointe Noire, city of Congo Republic, on Atlantic Ocean. Pop. 150,000. Port, railway from Brazzaville; exports timber, rubber, palm products.

pointer, short-haired hunting dog; usually white with brown spots. Hunts by scent and will 'point' to game with tail and muzzle outstretched. Stands *c* 66 cm/26 in. at shoulder.

pointillism, technique of painting in which a white ground is covered with tiny dots of pure colour which blend together to form intense colour effects when seen at a distance. Developed by the neo-impressionists, incl. Seurat and Signac; they preferred term 'divisionism'.

poison, substance having a dangerous or fatal effect on living things when drunk, absorbed, *etc.* Some are corrosive, *eg* acids, disinfectants; others interfere with body chemistry, *eg* cyanide.

poison gas, substance of corrosive or poisonous nature, in form of gas or vapour-forming liquid or solid. First employed in WWI. Incl. chlorine which affects lungs, mustard gas which affects skin, and nerve gases which attack central nervous system.

poison ivy, any of genus *Toxicodendron* of cashew family. Leaves of 3 leaflets, greenish flowers, ivory-coloured berries. Can cause severe rash on contact with skin.

Poitiers, town of W France, cap. of Vienne dept. Pop. 75,000. Wine and wool trade; metal, chemical industs., univ. (1431). Gaulish religious centre; hist. cap. of Poitou. Scene of victory (1356) of Black Prince over John II of France. Baptistery (4th cent.), cathedral (12th cent.).

poker, card game, with two basic variations, draw and stud poker; usually played for financial stakes. Originated in US, growing popular after 1870.

Pokeweed

pokeweed, *Phytolacca americana,* tall, coarse, perennial herb of North America. Dark purple berries contain poisonous seeds and yield emetic and purgative extracts.

Pola, see PULA, Yugoslavia.

Poland (*Polska*), republic of EC Europe. Area *c* 312,600 sq km (120,700 sq mi); pop. 33,600,000; cap. Warsaw. Language: Polish. Religion: RC. Forested N Carpathians in S, elsewhere fertile plain; main rivers Oder, Vistula. Agric. incl. cereals, livestock. Indust. centred in Silesia, Warsaw, Lódź; coal, iron, lead mining, textile mfg., engineering. First

Poland

Polecat

united 10th cent., medieval colonization by Teutonic Knights whom the Poles defeated at Tannenberg (1410). Disappeared completely after partitions (1772, 1793, 1795) between Austria, Prussia, Russia; re-formed 1918-21. Conflict with Germany over Danzig led to WWII; occupied by Germans and Russians, Jewish pop. almost wholly exterminated. Territ. lost to USSR, gained from Germany after WWII. From 1947 ruled by communist govt.; member of COMECON.

Polanski, Roman (1933-), Polish film director. Gained reputation for taut, intense films with touch of macabre, eg *Repulsion* (1965), *Rosemary's Baby* (1968).

Polar bear

polar bear, *Thalarctos maritimus,* large creamy white bear of Arctic Circle. Good swimmer, lives on floating ice; preys on seals, young walruses. Reaches lengths of 2.7 m/9 ft.

Polaris, star of constellation Ursa Minor, less than 1° from the north celestial pole and thus important navigationally. Also called North Star or Pole Star.

polarized light, light whose transverse vibrational pattern is confined to a single plane. Polarizing agents incl. crystals and nicol prism.

polaroid, trade name for transparent material containing embedded crystals which polarizes light passing through it. Used in spectacles to prevent glare.

polder, Dutch term for land reclaimed from sea or fresh water. Normally flat, lying below sea level; protected by dykes, drained by pumps. Makes fertile agric. land, eg N Holland polders reclaimed from Zuider Zee.

Pole, Reginald (1500-58), English churchman. Lived in Rome after Henry VIII's break with pope. Returned to England after Mary's accession and worked to restore RC church. Archbishop of Canterbury (1556-8).

pole, in geography, extremity of Earth's axis. *See* NORTH POLE, SOUTH POLE, MAGNETIC POLES.

polecat, *Mustela putorius,* carnivorous mammal of N Europe and Asia, related to weasel. Dark brown outer fur; feeds on rodents, reptiles. Scent glands emit fetid odour for protection. Ferret is domesticated polecat.

Pole Star, *see* POLARIS.

Poliakoff, Serge (1906-69), Russian artist. Worked in Paris; developed abstract style, using mosaic form of interlocking shapes and colour harmonies.

police, force, or body of persons, estab. and maintained for keeping order, enforcing law and preventing, detecting and prosecuting crimes. First instituted as official body in Britain by Peel (1829) with reorganization of SCOTLAND YARD. In UK, police administered by Home Office in England, Scottish Office in Scotland. In US, first local police force estab. in New York (1844).

Polignac, Jules Armand, Prince de (1780-1847), French statesman, premier (1829-30). Leader of ultra-royalists during reigns of Louis XVIII and Charles X. As premier, issued July Ordinances to counter liberal Chamber of Deputies; provoked July Revolution (1830). Imprisoned (1830-6).

poliomyelitis or **infantile paralysis,** virus infection of the grey matter of spinal cord. Affects nerve cells which control muscular contraction, sometimes causing paralysis. Immunity became possible with Salk vaccine (1955) and Sabin vaccine (1961).

Polish Corridor, strip of land, lying between East Prussia and rest of Germany, which gave Poland access to Baltic. Formerly German territ., awarded to Poland (1919). German agitation to recover it led to invasion of Poland, precipitating WWII (1939).

Polish Succession, War of the, war arising out of competition for Polish throne (1733-5). On death of Augustus II, Stanislaus I sought to recover throne lost in 1709; opposed by Augustus' son, Augustus III. France, with Spain and Šardinia, supported Stanislaus; Russia and Emperor Charles VI supported Augustus III. By Treaty of Vienna, Augustus kept Poland, Stanislaus received Lorraine.

Politburo, policy-making committee of Soviet Communist Party, the effective govt. of USSR. Called presidium of Central Committee (1952-66).

Politian, see POLIZIANO, ANGELO.

Poliziano, Angelo or **Politian,** pseud. of Angelo Ambrogini (1454-94), Italian poet, humanist. One of foremost Latin and vernacular poets of time, known for *Stanze per la Giostra.*

Polk, James Knox (1795-1849), American statesman, president (1845-9). A Democrat, he achieved many of stated aims, incl. reduction of tariffs. Annexation of Texas led to Mexican War (1846-8), by which California and much of SW were acquired.

polka, lively Bohemian dance in 2/4 time, originating c 1830. Popular in Europe for about 50 years.

pollack, *Pollachius virens,* marine food fish of cod family, found in N Atlantic. Also called coalfish or saithe. Related to European pollack, *P. pollachius.*

Pollaiuolo, Antonio (c 1432-98), Italian artist. Reputedly first to dissect corpses to study anatomy; his anatomical knowledge is displayed in engraving *Battle of the Nude Gods.* Executed statues in bronze and collaborated with his brother, **Piero Pollaiuolo** (c 1443-96), in paintings, eg *St Sebastian.*

pollen, fine, yellowish dust, produced in anthers of flowering plants. Mature grains containing male element unite with female element in ovule to produce embryo which becomes SEED.

pollination, process allowing FERTILIZATION in seed plants. Pollen is transferred to stigma by wind, bees or other insects.

Pollock, Jackson (1912-56), American painter. Leading abstract expressionist; developed 'action painting', influenced by surrealist theories of automatism. Typical works, prepared by dripping paint on large canvases, incl. *Blue Poles.*

pollution, harm caused to environment as a result of man's activities, esp. by emission of substances which are non-biodegradable, or which, when broken down, become dangerous. Became matter of international concern in 1960s, although has been problem since Industrial Revolution. Atmospheric pollutants incl. sulphur gases, hydrocarbons and solid waste from smoke and automobile emissions, which become esp. dangerous in smog; also fluorocarbons, used as aerosol propellants, which reduce OZONOSPHERE's capacity to protect Earth from ultraviolet radiation. Water pollutants incl. sewage, indust. effluent (often containing poisonous heavy metals, *eg* mercury, cadmium, lead), detergents, pesticides (*see* DDT), oil spills. Any may kill living things in water by poisoning or deoxygenation, or be ingested and passed to higher organisms, incl. man, in food-chain. Pollution of seas now one of concerns of UN Environmental Programme which also admins. international monitoring, controls on heavy indust. Pollution protection is responsibility of Environmental Protection Agency in US, Dept. of Environment in UK. Also *see* GREENHOUSE EFFECT.

Pollux, in classical myth, *see* DIOSCURI.

Polo, Marco (*c* 1254-*c* 1324), Venetian traveller. Journeyed with father and uncle to Far East (1271-5). Reached court of Kublai Khan, who later employed him on diplomatic missions. Returned to Venice (1292-5), captured while fighting Genoa. While in prison, dictated valuable accounts of his travels.

Polo: Prince Charles aiming for the ball

polo, outdoor game, prob. originating in Persia, played between teams of 4 on horseback. Long-handled sticks used to hit wooden ball into the opponents' goal. Brought by British army officers from India to England, where it was first played competitively in 1871.

polonaise, stately Polish dance in 3/4 time at a moderately fast tempo. Best known are those by Chopin.

polonium (Po), radioactive element; at. no. 84, mass no. of most stable isotope 209. Formed by decay of radium; discovered (1898) in pitchblende by the Curies. Powerful source of alpha particles.

Poltava, city of USSR, NC Ukrainian SSR. Pop. 239,000. Centre of fertile agric. region producing sugar beet, fruit, grain. Peter the Great defeated Charles XII of Sweden nearby (1709).

poltergeist, name given to force, often supposed to be supernatural, responsible for unexplained rappings,

movement of furniture, flying about of small objects in house.

polyandry, *see* POLYGAMY.

polyanthus, *Primula polyantha,* hardy perennial herb of primrose family. Derived from hybrid of common primrose and cowslip. Grown as garden plant.

Polybius (*c* 201-*c* 120 BC), Greek historian. Taken as a prisoner to Rome (168), he enjoyed patronage of the Scipio family. Wrote history of years 220-146 BC in 40 books, 5 of which survive.

Polychaeta, order of marine annelid worms with numerous bristles on body. Free-swimming, burrowing and tube-dwelling varieties incl. lugworm, ragworm.

Polyclitus (*fl* 5th cent. BC), Greek sculptor. Famous for his *Doryphorus* (Spear Bearer) which exemplified his ideal of physical perfection. No original works survive.

polygamy, state or practice of having 2 or more husbands (polyandry) or wives (polygyny) at same time. Polyandry is found in South Sea Isls. and among some North American Indian and Eskimo tribes. In Tibet, takes form of marriage to several brothers. Often associated with MATRIARCHY. Polygyny is more widespread esp. among hunting peoples, *eg* in Africa. Often confined to ruling caste, as in ancient Egypt. Has occurred in certain Christian sects.

polygon, in geometry, closed plane figure bounded by 3 or more sides; triangle is 3-sided polygon. Designated a regular polygon if all sides have equal length.

polyhedron, solid figure having polygons for its faces. Designated a regular polyhedron if faces are all congruent regular polygons; only those with 4, 6, 8, 12 and 20 faces can exist (formerly called the 'Platonic solids').

polymer, chemical compound consisting of giant molecules formed by linkage of smaller molecules (monomers). In addition polymerization, giant molecules are multiples of monomer molecule; in condensation polymerization, they are formed from monomers by chemical reaction involving elimination of some by-product, *eg* water. Cellulose is natural polymer; nylon and rayon are synthetic.

polymorphism, in zoology, condition in which species has 2 or more different morphological forms, *eg* various castes of social insects such as ants.

Polynesia, one of three major divisions of Pacific isls., to E of Melanesia and Micronesia. Bounded by New Zealand, Hawaii and Easter Isl., incl. Samoa, Tonga, Line, Cook, Ellice, Phoenix isls. and groups forming French Polynesia.

Polynesians, people of Pacific isls. between Hawaii, New Zealand and Easter Isls., of Malayo-Polynesian linguistic stock. May have come from Malaysia or South America.

Polynices or **Polyneices,** in Greek myth, son of Oedipus. After banishment of father, agreed to rule Thebes alternately with brother Eteocles. When Eteocles refused to relinquish throne Polynices led 'Seven against Thebes' expedition. All were killed except Adrastus, king of Argos. Story basis of tragedies by Aeschylus, Euripides.

polyp, sedentary form of coelenterate with tube-like body and mouth surrounded by tentacles. Either solitary (*eg* Hydra) or colonial (*eg* coral-forming polyps). Some reproduce asexually, forming free-swimming medusae by budding; others reproduce sexually to form new polyps.

polyp, in medicine, tumour growing from mucous membrane, to which it is attached by a stalk. Found in intestines, uterus, *etc*; removed if malignant. Polyps in nose are swellings caused by allergy or infection.

Polyphemus, in Greek myth, a Cyclops, son of Poseidon. In Homer's *Odyssey,* imprisoned Odysseus and his men in cave. They escaped under Polyphemus' sheep after Odysseus had blinded him with burning stake.

polyphony, style of musical composition in which inter-related *eg* in a round. Developed in West in medieval times, when extra parts were added to plainsong. Reached great heights in music of Bach and Palestrina.

polyptych, set of 2 or more panels bearing pictures, carvings, often hinged for folding together; frequently used as an altarpiece. Two panels form a diptych, three a triptych, *etc.*

polytheism, belief in or worship of more than one god. Usually each god is distinguished by a particular function but is represented in myth as related to other members of cosmic family. Prob. development of primitive ANIMISM.

polythene or **polyethylene,** thermoplastic material made by polymerization of ethylene. Used to make translucent plastic film, moulded objects and in electrical insulation.

polyvinyl chloride (PVC), colourless thermoplastic material formed by polymerization of vinyl chloride. Resistant to water, acid, alcohol. Used for flooring, coated fabrics, cable covering.

Polyzoa or **Bryozoa,** phylum of small sedentary animals; usually colonial, with external resemblance to coelenterate polyps. Mainly marine, found attached to rocks, seaweed. Known also as moss animals.

Pombal, Sebastião José de Carvalho e Melo, Marquês de (1699-1782), Portuguese statesman. Foreign affairs minister (1749-77), chief minister from 1756, he exercised complete control over King Joseph. Encouraged indust., colonization; expelled Jesuits. Exiled under Maria I.

Pomegranate

pomegranate, *Punica granatum,* small tree native to subtropical Asia. Scarlet flowers followed by many-seeded, pulpy, edible fruit.

Pomerania (Pol. *Pomorze,* Ger. *Pommern*), region of NC Europe, on Baltic coast, extending from Stralsund (East Germany) in W to R. Vistula (Poland) in E; incl. Rügen isl. Flat, low-lying; agric., livestock, forestry. In 1945, all Pomerania E of R. Oder, incl. Stettin, passed to Poland.

Pomeranian, breed of small dog with long silky hair, erect ears, tail curved over back. Stands *c* 15 cm/6 in. at shoulder.

Pomona, *see* MAINLAND, Orkney Isls.

Pompadour, Antoinette Poisson, Marquise de (1721-64), mistress of Louis XV of France. Her beauty and wit enabled her to rise to great power with Louis; encouraged alliance with Austria, leading to French involvement in Seven Years War. Patron of Voltaire.

Pompeii, ancient city of Campania, S Italy, near Bay of Naples. Roman port, resort; buried (AD 79) with Herculaneum in eruption of Vesuvius. Site discovered 1748. Many public buildings and villas, with well-preserved murals, have been uncovered.

Pompey, full name Gnaeus Pompeius Magnus (106-48 BC), Roman soldier. Made consul (70), he cleared the Mediterranean of pirates (67) and defeated Mithradates in Asia Minor (66). Joined Caesar and Crassus in 1st Triumvirate (60). Later opposed Caesar and championed senatorial party. Defeated by Caesar in civil war at Pharsala (48); fled to Egypt, where he was murdered.

Pompidou, Georges Jean Raymond (1911-74), French statesman, president (1969–74). Premier (1962–8), dismissed by De Gaulle soon after 1968 student-labour unrest. Elected president after De Gaulle's resignation, pursued similar policies.

Ponce, seaport of S Puerto Rico. Pop. 128,000. Sugar, tobacco produce; textile, rum mfg. Named after Juan Ponce de León who conquered Puerto Rico (1509).

Ponce de León, Juan (*c* 1460-1521), Spanish soldier and explorer. Conquered Puerto Rico (1508), where he was appointed governor (1510), and discovered Florida (1513).

Pondicherry, union territ. of S India. Area 474 sq km (183 sq mi); pop. 471,000; cap. Pondicherry. Comprises former French India (founded 1674); transferred to India (1954). Became union territ. 1962.

pond lily, *see* LOTUS.

pondskater or **waterstrider,** any of Gerridae family of narrow-bodied insects with long middle and hind legs. Moves rapidly over pond surfaces seeking insect prey, supported by surface tension of water.

pondweed, any of genus *Potamogeton* of aquatic plants. Submerged or floating leaves, spikes of inconspicuous flowers, Species incl. *P. crispus* of US. Name also applied to similar *Elodea canadensis* native to Canada. *See* WATERWEED.

Ponta Delgada, *see* AZORES, Portugal.

Pontefract or **Pomfret,** mun. bor. of West Yorkshire met. county, N England. Pop. 31,000. Famous liquorice confections. Ruined 11th cent. castle where Richard II imprisoned, murdered (1400).

Pontevedra, town of NW Spain, on Atlantic Ocean, cap. of Pontevedra prov. Pop. 52,000. Fishing port, agric. market. Roman bridge (*Pons Vetus*).

Pontiac (*fl* 18th cent.), American Indian chief. Led uprising (1763-6) against British, who had gained control of Indian lands after defeating French. Besieged Detroit and destroyed British outposts before rebellion was quelled and peace signed.

Pontianak, city of Indonesia, cap. of West Kalimantan prov. (Borneo), on R. Kapuas delta. Pop. 218,000. Exports coconuts, rubber and some gold. Almost exactly on equator.

Pontine Marshes, area of WC Italy, between Tyrrhenian Sea and Apennines. Fertile, populous in Roman times; abandoned due to malaria. Drainage completed 1920s, agric. settlement followed.

Pontius Pilate, *see* PILATE, PONTIUS.

pontoon, card game. *See* VINGT-ET-UN.

Pontormo, Jacopo, orig. Jacopo Carrucci (1494-1556), Italian painter. Style represents transition between late classicism and early mannerism. His *Deposition* in Florence is masterpiece of early Florentine mannerism.

Pontus, region of Asia Minor, now in NE Turkey. Became kingdom *c* 300 BC and *fl* under Mithradates until defeat by Romans under Pompey (66 BC).

Pontypool, urban dist. of Gwent, SE Wales. Pop. 37,000. Coalmining; tinplate mfg. (first made here 17th cent.).

Pontypridd, urban dist. of Glamorgan, S Wales, on R. Taff. Pop. 34,000. Coalmining; iron, brass founding.

pony express, mail service running from St Joseph, Missouri to Sacramento, California, US. Riders covered distance of *c* 3200 km (2000 mi) in 8 days. Inaugurated 1860, replaced by telegraph in 1861.

poodle, breed of dog probably developed in Germany. Thick frizzy or curly coat usually trimmed in standard style (introduced in France). Stands over 38 cm/15 in. at shoulder. Miniature poodles are 25-38 cm/10-15 in. at shoulder and toy poodles are under 25 cm/10 in.

pool, *see* SNOOKER.

Poole, mun. bor. of Dorset, S England, on Poole Harbour. Pop. 107,000. Port, resort; boatbuilding; pottery mfg. (from local clay).

Poona, city of Maharashtra state, W India. Pop. 853,000. Cotton, paper mfg. Military centre. Under British rule was summer residence of Governor of Bombay.

Poor Laws, legislation providing public relief and assistance for poor. English law (1601), 1st state intervention on behalf of destitute, made them responsibility of parish. Poorhouses built, work provided, local levies raised. Workhouses estab. (18th cent). Speenhamland System (1795) attempted to help by subsidizing low wages. Abuses aroused discontent in agric. workers and employers, led to Poor Law amendment (1834). This act granted relief only to able-bodied poor in strictly regulated workhouses, introduced strong central authority. Harsh effects helped rise of CHARTISM. Complete reform finally achieved 1930. Poor Law abolished, replaced by National Assistance Board (1948). In US, states had separate systems until 1930s introduced federal relief, with Social Security Act (1935).

pop art, realistic art style, appearing in late 1950s, which uses subjects and techniques derived from commercial art and popular culture. Subject matter incl. assemblages of cans, replicas of food, enlarged photographs and comic book characters. American exponents incl. Warhol, Oldenburg, Lichtenstein.

Pope, Alexander (1688-1744), English poet. Known for skilled use of heroic couplet, poems incl. discussion of classical values, *An Essay on Criticism* (1711), mock heroic *The Rape of the Lock* (1714), satirical *Dunciad* (1728), deistic *Essay on Man* (1733-4), 'Epistle to Dr Arbuthnot' (1735). Translated *Iliad, Odyssey.*

pope, *see* PAPACY.

Popish Plot, name given to story, fabricated (1678) by Titus OATES, of Jesuit-inspired plan to assassinate Charles II and restore Catholicism.

Poplar, *see* TOWER HAMLETS, England.

Lombardy poplar

poplar, any of genus *Populus* of trees of willow family. Native to N temperate regions. Soft fibrous wood, flowers in catkins. Species incl. Lombardy poplar. *P. nigra,* North American cottonwood, *P. deltoides.*

Popocatépetl, dormant volcano of C Mexico, overlooking Mexico City. Height 5452 m (17,887 ft). Has unexploited sulphur deposits. Another volcano, **Ixtacihuatl,** is nearby. Height 5286 m (17,342 ft).

Popper, Sir Karl Raimund (1902-), British philosopher, b. Austria. Wrote classic *The Logic of Scientific Discovery* (1935) on the problem of induction and demarcation of science. Other works incl. *The Open Society and Its Enemies* (1945) attacking Marxist doctrine, *The Poverty of Historicism* (1961). Settled in UK after 1946.

Iceland poppy *(Papaver nudicaule)*

poppy, any of genus *Papaver* of annual and perennial plants. Showy red, violet, yellow or white flowers. Incl. commercially important OPIUM POPPY. Corn poppy, *P. rhoeas,* is found in Europe; Californian poppy, *P. californium,* is state flower of California.

Popular Front, in French history, term for alliance in 1930s between left-wing political parties. Socialists, Communists, and Radical Socialists united under Léon Blum and formed Popular Front govt. (1936-8) which carried out series of social reforms, incl. introduction of 40-hour working week.

Populism, American agrarian political movement of late 19th cent. Discontent among farmers of Northwest and South led to formation (1891) of Populist Party, whose presidential candidate polled over 1 million votes in 1892 election. Majority of populists had joined Democrats under W.J. Bryan by 1896.

porcelain, hard, white, non-porous variety of pottery which is translucent; made of kaolin, feldspar and quartz or flint. First made by the Chinese during T'ang period, it was refined during Sung period. European varieties incl. Sèvres and Limoges (France), Chelsea, Bow and Staffordshire (England), Meissen and Dresden (Germany).

Porcupine, river of Canada-US. Rises in C Yukon, flows N, then W 721 km (448 mi) to join Yukon R. in E Alaska.

Crested porcupine

porcupine, rodent covered with sharp erectile spines in addition to hair. Two families: New World Erethizontidae (partly arboreal) and Old World Hystricidae (mainly terrestrial). Species incl. Canadian porcupine, *Erethizon dorsatum,* and crested porcupine, *Hystrix cristata,* of N Africa and S Europe.

porgy, marine fish of Sparidae family, also called sea bream, common in Mediterranean and West Indies. Species incl. European red sea bream, *Pagellus bogaraveo.*

Pori (Swed. *Björneborg*), town of SW Finland, on Gulf of Bothnia. Pop. 71,000. Port, exports timber products; copper refining.

Porifera, phylum of sessile aquatic animals, consisting of the sponges. Body-wall usually supported by skeleton of either lime, silica or spongin (used in bath sponges). Sponge feeds by drawing water through pores on body surface.

porphyry, igneous rock comprising large crystals, called phenocrysts, embedded in fine-grained groundmass. Term refers to any such texture, not composition. Red porphyry, *ie* feldspar crystals in purplish groundmass, was valued by ancient Egyptians.

porpoise, small toothed whale of Phocaenidae family. Common porpoise, *Phocaena phocaena,* found in N Atlantic, is smallest species, reaching lengths of 1.8 m/6 ft. Feeds on fish, crustaceans.

port, sweet fortified wine made in Douro valley of Portugal. May be ruby, tawny or white; vintage port is matured in the bottle after spending 2 or 3 years in casks.

Port Adelaide, port for Adelaide, South Australia, on St Vincent Gulf. Exports wheat, wool, fruit; also iron, steel, chemicals industs.

Portadown, town of EC Northern Ireland. Pop. 21,000. In former Co. Armagh. Railway jct., clothing mfg.; rose nurseries.

Port Arthur, *see* THUNDER BAY, Canada.

Port Arthur, China, *see* LU-TA.

Port Arthur, port of SE Texas, US; on Sabine L. Pop. 57,000. Oil refining, exports via canal to Gulf of Mexico.

Port Augusta, city of SE South Australia, at head of Spencer Gulf. Pop. 12,000. Port, exports wool, wheat; thermal power station; salt works.

Port-au-Prince, cap. of Haiti, major port on Gulf of Gonaïves. Pop. 494,000, mostly Negro, mulatto. Rum distilling, sugar refining, brewing. Founded 1749; became cap. 1770. Has Univ. of Haiti (1944); 18th cent. cathedral.

Port Bouet, see ABIDJAN, Ivory Coast.

Port Darwin, inlet of Beagle Gulf, Northern Territ., Australia. Name also applied to port and indust. area of city of Darwin.

Port Elizabeth, city of S Cape Prov., South Africa, on Algoa Bay. Pop. 469,000. Port, exports minerals, fruit, wool; car assembly works. Founded (1820) by British.

Porter, Cole (1893-1964), American composer of musicals. Songs, of which he wrote both words and music, incl. 'Night and Day', 'Anything Goes'. Renowned for clever internal rhymes in lyrics.

Porter, Katherine Anne (1890-   ), American author. Works incl. short story collections *Flowering Judas* (1930), *Pale Horse, Pale Rider* (1939), novel *Ship of Fools* (1962).

Port Gentil, town of W Gabon, on Cape Lopez Bay. Pop. 48,000. Port, exports timber; petroleum refinery estab. 1967.

Port Glasgow, town of Strathclyde region, W Scotland, on R. Clyde. Pop. 22,000. Shipbuilding; rope, canvas mfg. Built (1668) as port for Glasgow, declined after Clyde channel deepened.

Port Harcourt, city of SE Nigeria, on Niger delta. Pop. 217,000. Railway terminus and port, exports palm oil, groundnuts, cocoa; commercial and indust. centre, esp. oil refining, metal products, tyre mfg., vehicle assembly. Founded (1912) by British.

Port Kembla, see WOLLONGONG, Australia.

Portland, William Bentinck, 1st Earl of (1649-1709), Dutch statesman. Adviser to William of Orange, he came to England after 'Glorious Revolution' (1688). Negotiated Treaty of Ryswick (1697) for French recognition of William as king of England. **William Henry Cavendish Bentinck, 3rd Duke of Portland** (1738-1809), headed coalition govt. of North and Fox in 1783; again PM (1807-9).

Portland, urban dist. on Isle of Portland penin., Dorset, SW England. Pop. 12,000. Limestone quarries; naval base; Portland Bill lighthouse. Has 16th cent. castle.

Portland, port of SW Maine, US; on Atlantic inlet. Pop. 65,000; state's largest town. Timber, fishing; paper and textile mfg. Settled in 1630s; was state cap. 1820-31.

Portland, port of NW Oregon, US; on Willamette R. Pop. 381,000; state's largest city. Railway jct.; shipyards. Timber, grain exports, wood industs.

Port Laoighise, co. town of Laoighis, C Irish Republic. Pop. 4000. Formerly called Maryborough.

Port Louis, cap. of Mauritius. Pop. 137,000. Admin. centre; port, exports sugar; international airport. Founded 1735; has citadel, Anglican and RC cathedrals.

Port Lyautey, see KÉNITRA, Morocco.

Port Moresby, cap. of Papua New Guinea, in SE New Guinea isl. Pop. 66,000. Exports rubber, gold. Air traffic centre.

Pôrto, see OPORTO, Portugal.

Pôrto Alegre, city of S Brazil, cap. of Rio Grande do Sul state; at N end of Lagôa dos Patos. Pop. 886,000. Meat, hides, wool exports. Settled by German, Italian immigrants in 19th cent. Modern city with 2 univs.

Port of Spain, cap. of Trinidad and Tobago, on NW Trinidad isl. Pop. 68,000. Sugar produce, oil refining, rum distilling. Receives iron, bauxite shipments from Venezuela, Guianas. Has many parks; mosque, Anglican, RC cathedrals. Became cap. 1783.

Porto Novo, cap. of Benin, on coastal lagoon near Bight of Benin. Pop. 85,000. Admin. centre; port, exports palm oil, kapok, cotton. Former seat of a native kingdom, became colonial cap. 1900.

Port Phillip Bay, inlet of Bass Str., SE Australia. Ports incl. Melbourne and Geelong; resorts on sandy E shores.

Port Pirie, city of South Australia, on Spencer Gulf. Pop. 16,000. Port with bulk wheat terminal, lead smelting works; exports ores from Broken Hill.

Port Said (*Bûr Saîd*), city of NE Egypt, at Mediterranean entrance to Suez Canal. Pop. 313,000. Major port and fuelling station, exports cotton; salt, chemical industs.; railways to Cairo, Suez. Founded 1859, named after Said Pasha. Has statue of Ferdinand de Lesseps, planner of Canal.

Portsmouth, Louise Renée de Kéroualle, Duchess of (1649-1734), mistress of Charles II of England. Encouraged English alliance with France from 1671 until Charles's death (1685). Greatly disliked in England, she fled to France.

Portsmouth, city on Portsea Isl., Hampshire, S England. Pop. 197,000. Main UK naval base. Has Cathedral of St Thomas (12th cent.); Nelson's flagship *Victory,* Dickens' birthplace, both now museums.

Portsmouth, port of SE New Hampshire, US; at mouth of Piscataqua R. Pop. 26,000. Summer resort, naval base with shipyards. Colonial cap. 1679-1776. Treaty ending Russo-Japanese War signed here (1905).

Portsmouth, port of SE Virginia, US; on Hampton Roads (Elizabeth R.). Pop. 111,000. Naval depot; shipyards (has important Norfolk Navy Yard). Exports cotton, tobacco; varied mfg.

Port Sudan, city of NE Sudan, on Red Sea. Pop. 110,000. Sudan's chief port, exports cotton, gum arabic, hides, salt; railway terminus.

Port Sunlight, see BEBINGTON, England.

Port Talbot, mun. bor. of Glamorgan, S Wales, on Swansea Bay. Pop. 51,000. Ore terminal, new harbour (1970) serve large steelworks. Formed 1921 from union of Aberavon, Margam.

Portugal

Portugal, republic of SW Europe, on W Iberian penin. Incl. Azores, Madeira Isls. Area 92,000 sq km (35,500 sq mi); pop. 8,564,000; cap. Lisbon. Language: Portuguese. Religion: RC. Mountainous in N, E; main rivers Minho, Douro, Tagus. Agric., wine, cork, fishing (sardines, tuna). Subtropical in S (tourism). Part of Roman *Lusitania,* fell to Visigoths, Moors. Independent from 12th cent.; acquired overseas empire 15th-16th cent. Under Spanish rule 1580-1668. Suffered in War of Spanish Succession, Peninsular War; lost Brazil 1822. Republic estab. 1910; dictatorships followed, esp. Salazar (1928-68). Political unrest followed military uprising 1974; decolonization policy led to independence of Portuguese Guinea (1974), Angola and Mozambique (1975).

Portuguese East Africa, see MOZAMBIQUE.

Portuguese Guinea, see GUINEA-BISSAU.

Portuguese man-of-war, *Physalia physalis,* colonial marine coelenterate of open Atlantic. Floating bladder bears medusae and polyps with diverse functions, *eg* reproduction, feeding. Long tentacles with poisonous stinging organs dangerous to swimmers.

Portuguese Timor, see TIMOR.

Portuguese West Africa, see ANGOLA.

Posadas, town of NE Argentina, cap. of Misiones prov.; on Alto Paraná R. Pop. 104,000. Agric. trade (maté, tobacco, rice); meat packing, flour milling industs.

Poseidon, in Greek myth, brother of Zeus and god of the sea; sons incl. Pegasus, Polyphemus, Orion. Represented as vengeful god carrying a trident with which he could cause earthquakes. Identified by Romans with Neptune.

Posen, see POZNAŃ, Poland.

positivism, system of philosophy basing knowledge solely on observable scientific facts and their relations to each other. Rejects metaphysics. Founded by Auguste Comte. *See* LOGICAL POSITIVISM.

positron, anti-particle of electron, possessing same mass but positive electric charge. Positron-electron pairs can be produced by conversion of energy into matter, but the 2 particles annihilate each other.

possum, *see* OPOSSUM.

Post, Emily, née Price (1873-1960), American writer. Arbiter of American manners. Works incl. *Etiquette* (1922), *How to Behave Though a Debutante* (1928).

postal service, arrangement for delivery of mail to members of public. Early systems estab. in Persian, Roman empires. In Britain, Charles I estab. acceptance of public mail, extending services of royal couriers; flat-rate penny post instituted by Rowland Hill in 1840. In US, penny postage began 1839. Pony express took mail to West (1860-61), rail service then took over, with air mail starting in 1918. Universal Postal Union regulates international harmony (estab. 1875).

post-impressionism, term used to describe work of those French painters who rejected impressionism in favour of greater emphasis on the subject or the formal structure and style of the painting. Most important exponents were Gauguin, van Gogh, Cézanne.

Postojna (Ital. *Postumia*), town of Slovenia, N Yugoslavia, Karst region. Pop. 4000. Has stalagmite/stalactite caves, largest in Europe.

potash or **potassium carbonate** (K_2CO_3), compound used as fertilizer and in manufacture of glass and soap.

potassium (K), soft metallic element; at. no. 19, at. wt. 39.10. Highly reactive; combines with water to produce strong alkali potassium hydroxide. Occurs in wide variety of silicate rocks and mineral deposits; essential to life processes. Compounds used in manufacture of soap, glass and fertilizers.

potato, *Solanum tuberosum,* plant of nightshade family. Native to South America but widely cultivated for starchy, edible tubers. Introduced into Europe *c* 1570.

Potchefstroom, town of SW Transvaal, South Africa. Pop. 68,000. In cattle raising and goldmining dist.; univ. coll., agric. coll. First cap. of Transvaal (1838-60).

Potemkin, Grigori Aleksandrovich, Prince (1739-91), Russian army officer. Took part in the annexation (1783) of the Crimea, where he governed ably. He reformed the army, built the Black Sea fleet, estab. the port of Sevastopol. Favourite of Catherine II.

Potemkin Mutiny, *see* RUSSIAN REVOLUTION.

potential, in physics, work done against force exerted by field in bringing unit physical quantity (*eg* mass, electric charge, magnetic pole) from infinity to some specified point. Used as measure of strength of field at any point.

Potomac, river of E US; forms Maryland's S border. Flows E 460 km (285 mi) past Washington DC to Chesapeake Bay. Shenandoah R. (Civil War battleground) is main tributary. George Washington's Mount Vernon estate is on S shore.

Potosí, town of SW Bolivia, cap. of Potosí dept. Alt. 4200 m (*c* 13,780 ft). Pop. 64,000. Leading mining centre; tin, copper, tungsten (silver once important). Founded 1545. Has 19th cent. cathedral; univ. (1571).

Potsdam, city of C East Germany, on R. Havel. Pop. 112,000. Produces precision instruments, chemicals. Residence successively of Brandenburg, Prussian, German rulers. Palaces incl. Sans Souci, built 1747 for Frederick II. Scene of Potsdam Conference (1945) on Allied control of post-war Germany.

Potsdam Conference, meeting (July, 1945) of Allied leaders to implement agreement of YALTA CONFERENCE. Estab. American, British, French and Soviet occupation zones in Germany, to be supervised by Allied Control Council. Redistributed German territ. to Poland and USSR; laid economic and political basis of post-WWII Germany.

Potter, [Helen] Beatrix (1866-1943), English author and illustrator of children's books incl. *The Tale of Peter Rabbit* (1902), *The Tale of Jemima Puddle-Duck* (1908).

Potter, Stephen (1900-70), English writer. Known for humorous works, esp. *The Theory and Practice of Gamesmanship* (1947). Also wrote literary criticism.

Beatrix Potter

Potteries, The, area of Staffordshire, NC England, in Trent Valley. Pottery indust. founded 1769 by Wedgwood. Incl. Stoke-on-Trent, Newcastle-under-Lyme.

potter wasp, solitary wasp of subfamily Eumeninae which builds vase-like nests of mud. Also called mason wasp.

pottery, general term for objects made of clay and baked hard. Originally hand made, pottery was fashioned on wheels in Egypt before 4000 BC; glazes were also developed in Egypt in 2nd millennium BC. Red and black figured vases produced in Greece *c* 600-450 BC represent high point of art and provide valuable historic record. Chinese independently developed advanced pottery techniques which inspired potters to emulate them when Chinese pottery was introduced into Europe in 16th cent. Islamic potters of Syria, Persia, Turkey produced brilliantly coloured and glazed work from 9th-16th cents., which also influenced European style.

potto, *Periodictus potto,* small slow-moving nocturnal primate of loris family. Arboreal; found in forests of W Africa.

Poughkeepsie, town of SE New York, US; on Hudson R. Pop. 32,000. Iron and steel industs., business machinery mfg. Settled by Dutch (1687). Vassar Coll. is nearby.

Poulenc, Francis (1899-1963), French composer, pianist. Member of 'les Six' group of composers. Works, often witty in nature, incl. ballet music, *eg Les Biches,* and piano, orchestral, chamber works.

Pound, Ezra Loomis (1885-1972), American poet, lived in Europe after 1907. Influenced modern poetry as imagist, vorticist and friend, patron, of younger poets. Works incl. allusive, erudite *Hugh Selwyn Mauberley* (1920), *Cantos* (1925-69). Also wrote prose, *eg ABC of Reading* (1934), *Essays* (1954, edited by T.S. Eliot). Fascist sympathizer during WWII.

pound, in measurement, British unit of weight; equal to *c* 0.4536 kilograms.

Poussin, Nicolas (1594-1665), French painter. Dominant influence on French classical painting, he stressed intellectual discipline in art. Developed classical landscape in 1640s, austere and constructed with geometric precision. Works incl. 2 series of *Seven Sacraments* and *Landscape with Diogenes;* spent most of his life in Rome.

Powell, Anthony Dymoke (1905-   ), English novelist. Known for 12 vol. roman-fleuve 'A Dance to the Music of Time' from *A Question of Upbringing* (1951) to *Hearing Secret Harmonies* (1975), portraying a comic vision of structure of English social life. Other works incl. *Afternoon Men* (1931); biog. of John Aubrey (1948).

Powell, Cecil Frank (1903-69), English physicist. Awarded Nobel Prize for Physics (1950) for developing photographic method by which he discovered the pi-meson particle in cosmic radiation (1947).

Powell, Enoch (1912-   ), British politician. Conservative minister of health (1960-3). Controversial views on immigration, incl. repatriation of non-white immigrants, led to dismissal from shadow cabinet (1968). Re-entered Parliament as an Ulster Unionist (1974).

power, in physics, the rate of doing work. SI unit of power is the watt.

Powys, John Cowper (1872-1963), English novelist. Wrote mystical novels, *eg Wolf Solent* (1929), *A Glastonbury Romance* (1932), *Porius* (1951), expressing highly personal philosophy. Discursive works incl. *The Meaning of Culture* (1929), *In Defence of Sensuality* (1930). His brother, **Theodore Francis Powys** (1875-1953), also wrote novels, *eg Mr Weston's Good Wine* (1927).

Powys, inland county of E Wales. Area 5077 sq km (1960 sq mi); pop. 100,000; co. town Brecon. Created 1974, incl. former Breconshire, Montgomeryshire, Radnorshire.

Poyang Hu, lake of Kiangsi prov., SE China. Area *c* 2600 sq km (1000 sq mi), varying with season. Connected to Yangtze by canal. Rice grown in basin.

Poynings' Law, act of Irish Parliament (1494). Stated that approval of English legislature was required for summoning of Irish Parliament and for passing of any legislation. Repealed 1782.

Poznań, (Ger. *Posen*), city of W Poland, on R. Warta, cap. of Poznań prov. Pop. 473,000. Railway jct.; engineering and chemical industs.; univ. (1919). Seat of Polish primate from 1821. Under Prussian rule 1793-1919. Heavily bombed in WWII.

Prado, Spanish national museum of painting and sculpture, in Madrid, opened to the public in 1819. Nucleus of collection derives from royal collections; holdings of Spanish, Flemish and Venetian painting are outstanding.

Praetorians, body guard of Roman emperors, first organized in reign of Augustus. Played important part in accession of certain emperors. Disbanded by Constantine I.

Praetorius, Michael, orig. Michael Schultheiss (1571-1621), German composer. Prolific composer, esp. of choral works. Also wrote on musical instruments and theory of his day in *Syntagma Musicum* (3 vols.).

Pragmatic Sanction, 1) decree issued (1438) by Charles VII of France, limiting papal authority over Church in France; 2) decree issued (1713) by Emperor Charles VI, extending right of succession in Austrian Empire to female line. On death of Charles, led to War of Austrian Succession (1740-8).

pragmatism, movement in philosophy which determines the validity of concepts by their practical results. Opposed to RATIONALISM. Exponents incl. C. S. Peirce, William James, John Dewey.

Prague: the old town square

Prague (*Praha*), cap. of Czechoslovakia, on R. Moldau. Pop. 1,082,000. Admin., commercial centre. Metal working; textiles; food processing; printing, publishing. Univ (1348); Hradčany Palace, St Vitus cathedral. Centre of 15th cent. Hussite movement. Czech cap. from 1918. German occupation 1939-45. Focus of 1968 liberalization movement, suppressed by Soviet forces.

prairie, area of gently undulating, treeless natural grassland. Applies esp. to such areas in North America between Rockies and Great Lakes, former grazing land now extensively cultivated for cereals.

prairie chicken, brown and white hen-like grouse of North American plains, genus *Tympanuchus*. Species incl. greater prairie chicken, *T. cupido,* and lesser prairie chicken, *T. pallidicinctus.*

prairie dog, *Cynomys ludovicianus,* burrowing squirrel-like rodent of North American plains. Lives in large colonies; barks like a dog.

Prairies, region of WC Canada, incl. Alberta, Saskatchewan, Manitoba provs. Flat agric. region; major wheat, oats, barley growing. Also describes Mississippi valley region of US.

prairie wolf, *see* COYOTE.

Prakrit, languages other than Sanskrit and Vedic of Indic group of Indo-Iranian branch of Indo-European family. Incl. modern vernaculars. Some scholars hold PALI to be a Prakrit. Literature mainly Jainist.

Prasad, Rajendra (1884-1963), Indian statesman. Headed Indian National Congress several times. Followed Gandhi's policy of non-cooperation with British; imprisoned (1942-5). Became 1st president of India (1950-62).

praseodymium (Pr), metallic element of lanthanide series; at. no. 59, at. wt. 140.91. Compounds used to colour glass and enamel. First isolated 1904.

pratincole, any of genus *Glareola* of long-winged wading birds. Gregarious, breeding in colonies; insectivorous. Common pratincole, *G. pratincola,* found in S Europe, Africa, S Asia.

Prato, city of Tuscany, NC Italy. Pop. 143,000. Textiles, hist. centre of woollen indust. Medieval town hall; cathedral contains works by Donatello and Filippo Lippi.

Pratt, E[dwin] J[ohn] (1883-1964), Canadian poet. Known for heroic narrative verse, *eg* 'The Titanic' (1935), 'Brébeuf and His Brethren' (1940), 'Dunkirk' (1941).

Pravda (Russ., = truth), Russian daily newspaper, founded in 1912. State-controlled since Revolution, represents Communist party line, while *Izvestia* represents govt.

prawn, any of various edible shrimp-like crustaceans, widely distributed in fresh and salt waters. Common prawn, *Palaemon serratus,* is 7.5-10 cm/3-4 in. long.

Praxiteles (*fl c* 350 BC), Athenian sculptor. With Phidias, considered greatest sculptor of ancient Greece. Marble *Hermes with the Infant Dionysus* at Olympia is only surviving work. Copies of other statues incl. *Aphrodite of Cnidus.*

Precambrian or **Archaean era,** earliest geological era, incl. all time from consolidation of Earth's crust to beginning of Palaeozoic era. Duration *c* 4000 million years. Sometimes divided into Early and Late Precambrian. Largely metamorphic rock, exposed as continental shields, *eg* Canadian, African, Australian. Rare traces of rudimentary life; forerunners of trilobites, worms, sponges, jelly fish; some algae, fungi. Also *see* GEOLOGICAL TABLE.

precession of the equinoxes, westward movement of equinox along the ecliptic. Caused by gravitational pull of Sun and Moon on Earth's equatorial bulge; Earth's axis describes cone returning to original position every 26,000 years. Noted by Hipparchus (*c* 120 BC); explained by Newton (1687).

precious stone, *see* GEMSTONE.

predestination, in Christian theology, doctrine that God foreordained all events, esp. the salvation of certain souls. Follows from belief in omniscience and omnipotence of God; formulated by St Augustine. RC doctrine allows the co-existence of free will, while Calvin taught absolute predestination of souls. Occurs also in Judaism and Islam.

pregnancy, period of development of fertilized ovum in the uterus. In humans, lasts on average 40 weeks (dated from time of last menstrual period).

premier, *see* PRIME MINISTER.

Preminger, Otto [Ludwig] (1906-), American film producer-director, b. Austria. Known for craftsmanship, serious treatment of intricate stories, as in *Anatomy of a Murder* (1959), *Exodus* (1961), *Advise and Consent* (1961).

Pre-Raphaelite Brotherhood, society, nucleus of which was 3 English artists, D.G. Rossetti, Millais and Holman Hunt, formed 1848 to revive painting with a fidelity to nature they considered characteristic of Italian art before Raphael. Violently attacked by the critics, movement was defended by Ruskin; dissolved by 1853.

Presbyterianism, system of Christian church govt. by elders (presbyters), elected by the congregation rather than by bishops. Instituted by JOHN CALVIN it is the system of most reformed churches. The Church of Scotland is the only Presbyterian church estab. by law.

president, chief EXECUTIVE of a republic, acting as both head of state and govt. In republic with parliamentary govt. has little or no executive power, head of govt. usually being prime minister or premier. In US, president has substantial powers defined in constitution. In 5th republic of France, president also has substantial executive powers despite having a premier as head of CABINET.

Presley, Elvis (1935-77), American singer. Leading exponent of rock-and-roll in 1950s with such songs as 'Heartbreak Hotel', 'Blue Suede Shoes' and 'Hound Dog'.

press-gang, a naval party empowered by law to force men to serve in British fleet. Initiated by Edward III, it was chief method of naval recruitment from Elizabethan times down to Napoleonic wars, after which it was discontinued though still legal.

pressure, in physics, force per unit area acting on a surface. Atmospheric pressure is pressure due to weight of Earth's atmosphere; at sea level, this pressure supports column of mercury c 76 cm high.

Presteigne, urban dist. of Powys, EC Wales. Pop. 1000. Former co. town of Radnorshire.

Prester John, legendary Christian priest and ruler of a great empire, originally thought to be in Asia, later associated with Ethiopia. Legend first arose in 12th cent. chronicles.

Preston, co. bor. and co. town of Lancashire, NW England, on R. Ribble. Pop. 97,000. Port; textiles esp. cotton; engineering.

Prestonpans, town of Lothian region, EC Scotland. Pop. 3000. Scene of battle (1745) in which Jacobite forces defeated English.

Prestwick, town of Strathclyde region, SW Scotland. Pop. 13,000. Tourist resort. Has international airport.

Pretender, Old, see STUART, JAMES FRANCIS EDWARD.

Pretender, Young, see STUART, CHARLES EDWARD.

Pretoria, admin. cap. of South Africa and cap. of Transvaal. Pop. 562,000. Admin., indust. centre; railway engineering, large steelworks; univ. (1930). Founded 1855; cap. of Boer confederation from 1860, of Union of South Africa from 1910.

Prévost d'Exiles, Antoine François (1697-1763), French author, known as Abbé Prévost. As gentleman-adventurer, wrote *Mémoires et aventures d'un homme de qualité* (1728-3) incl. *Manon Lescaut* (1731), basis of operas by Massenet, Puccini.

Priam, in Greek legend, king of Troy during Trojan War. Chief wife was Hecuba; among 50 sons and many daughters were Hector, Paris, Cassandra. Slain by Neoptolemus at fall of Troy.

Priapus, in Greek myth, son of Dionysus and Aphrodite. Fertility god of gardens. Statues of him as misshapen little man with enormous phallus were used as scarecrows.

Pribilof Islands, four isls. off SW Alaska, US; in Bering Sea. Seal fur trading. Convention of 1911 prevented extinction of local seals through estab. of breeding grounds.

prickly pear, common name for various species of genus *Opuntia* of cacti with flattened, jointed, spiny stems. Native to Mexico. Pear-shaped fruits of several species are edible. Introduced into Australia, has proved to be a pest.

Pride, Thomas (d. 1658), English soldier. Colonel on Parliamentary side during Civil War. Carried out purge (1648) of Presbyterian members of House of Commons (believed to be royalist sympathizers). Resulting Rump Parliament pursued prosecution of Charles I.

Priestley, J[ohn] B[oynton] (1894-), English author, critic. Known for novels incl. *The Good Companions*

Prickly pear (Opuntia tuna)

(1929), *Angel Pavement* (1930). Also wrote plays experimenting with treatment of time, *eg Time and the Conways* (1937).

Priestley, Joseph (1733-1804), English chemist, theologian. Improved methods for studying gases by collecting them over mercury; prepared and studied various gases incl. sulphur dioxide, ammonia and oxygen. Adopted Unitarian views; his sympathy for French Revolution provoked popular resentment and he emigrated to US (1794).

primary school, institution at which children of up to c 11 years old are taught basic subjects, *eg* reading, arithmetic. In US, known as elementary school.

primates, order of mammals, incl. monkeys, apes, man. Primarily arboreal, with 5 digits on hands and feet; well-developed vision and large brain. Order incl. more primitive lemurs and tarsiers.

prime minister or **premier,** chief member of CABINET, responsible to parliament. In UK and Commonwealth, holds executive power; appoints cabinet and is leader of governing party.

prime number, integer that can be evenly divided only by itself and 1. Each integer can be written as a product of prime numbers.

Primo de Rivera, Miguel (1870-1930), Spanish military and political leader. Estab. military dictatorship (1923) with support of Alfonso XIII. Continued as leader of civil admin. from 1925. Resigned 1930. His son, **José Antonio Primo de Rivera** (d. 1936), founded FALANGE party. Executed by Loyalists.

primrose, see PRIMULA.

primula, large genus of perennial herbs with white, yellow and pink flowers, found in temperate regions of N hemisphere. Main European varieties are common primrose, *Primula vulgaris,* COWSLIP. OXLIP and cultivated POLYANTHUS. Himalayan primrose, *P. denticulata,* has lilac-coloured flowers on long stem.

Prince Albert, town of C Saskatchewan, Canada; on N Saskatchewan R. Pop. 28,000. Commercial centre in mixed farming region. Fur, lumber trade.

Prince Edward Island, Maritime isl. prov. of SE Canada. Area 5657 sq km (2184 sq mi); pop. 112,000; cap. Charlotte-town. Agric.; stock raising, dairy farming; fishing (esp. lobsters). Settled in 17th cent. by French; ceded to Nova Scotia 1763; became separate colony 1769; prov. 1873.

Prince George, town of C British Columbia, Canada; on Fraser R. Pop. 33,000. Railway jct.; lumber, mining centre. Founded 1807 as fur trading post.

Prince Rupert, seaport of W British Columbia, Canada; on isl. near mouth of Skeena R. Pop. 16,000. Mining, lumber, grain exports. In agric. region. Important fishing indust. (esp. salmon, halibut).

Princeton, residential bor. of W New Jersey, US; on Millstone R. Pop. 13,000. Has Princeton Univ. (1756). Settled 1696 by Quakers.

Principe, see SÃO TOMÉ AND PRINCIPE.

printed circuit, electronic circuit in which wiring is printed on an insulating base. May be prepared by attaching copper foil to base, drawing circuit pattern on foil with wax and then etching away untreated foil.

printing, method of reproducing words or illustrations in ink on paper or other material by mechanical means. Block printing was used in China in 8th cent. and movable type was introduced there in 11th cent. GUTENBERG is credited with the European invention of movable type. In England, Caxton set up 1st printing press in London (1476). Modern commercial printing uses such processes as LITHOGRAPHY and PHOTOENGRAVING.

Prior, Matthew (1664-1721), English poet, diplomat. Wrote parodies, eg *The City Mouse and the Country Mouse* (1687) burlesquing Dryden; graceful 'society' verse. Helped draft Treaty of Utrecht (1713).

Pripet Marshes, forested marshland of USSR, C Byelorussian SSR. Formerly natural defence barrier between Poland and Russia. Crossed by R. Pripet, which rises in NW Ukrainian SSR and flows *c* 800 km (500 mi) to join R. Dnepr.

prism, in optics, transparent body whose ends are congruent triangles in parallel planes and whose 3 sides are parallelograms. Glass prisms change direction of light passing through them; triangular prisms disperse white light into colours of spectrum.

prison, place where convicted criminals are confined. Became important in late 18th cent., replacing capital punishment, mutilation, *etc*, in response to BECCARIA, JOHN HOWARD. Howard's work influenced reform, esp. in US, where 1st cellular prison estab. (1790), and Pennsylvania system of discipline developed. In UK, Quaker group, esp. ELIZABETH FRY, led reform. Modern prisons seek rehabilitation, *eg* by use of specialist staff, open prisons, although punitive treatment, *eg* chain gangs, solitary confinement still exists. *See* PROBATION.

prisoners of war, members of the regular or irregular armed forces of a nation at war held captive by the enemy. Hague Conference of 1907 and Geneva Conventions of 1929 and 1949 laid down rules governing their treatment.

privateers, privately owned war vessels having govt. commission to seize enemy shipping (1589-1815). The system was subject to much abuse as a cover for piracy and was abolished by the Declaration of Paris (1856).

privet, any of genus *Ligustrum* of shrubs and small trees of olive family. Widely cultivated for hedges, esp. common privet, *L. vulgare.*

privy council, body of advisors or counsellors appointed by or serving head of state, esp. in UK and Commonwealth. Comprises cabinet, members of judiciary (in UK incl. archbishops). Acted as executive arm of govt. until 1688, superseded by cabinet.

probability theory, mathematical study of laws of chance. Event whose probability is 0 will never occur, one whose probability is 1 is certain to occur. Probability that tossed coin will fall as a head is $\frac{1}{2}$.

probation, in penology, system whereby sentence on convicted offender is suspended on condition of good behaviour, regular reporting to probation officer. Used first in US (1878).

process engraving, *see* PHOTOENGRAVING.

Proconsul, extinct primate of Miocene period, known from fossils found in Kenya. Possible ancestor of chimpanzee, gorilla.

Procrustes, in Greek myth, highwayman who forced travellers to lie on either a short or a long bed. Stretched them or cut off their legs to make them fit. Killed in like manner by Theseus.

production, in economics, creation of economic value, *eg* farming or extraction of raw materials and imparting utility to them. Factors of production are regarded as land, labour, capital.

profit, in economics, return on CAPITAL. Classical economics distinguished between profit of entrepreneur and that of capitalist.

Profumo, John Dennis (1915-), British politician. Conservative secretary of state for war, he resigned after his involvement in prostitution scandal was revealed. 'Profumo affair' prob. contributed to Conservatives' electoral defeat (1964).

programme music, instrumental music intended to portray a scene or a story in its mental associations. Examples incl. Berlioz' *Symphonie fantastique,*

Mendelssohn's *Fingal's Cave,* Mussorgsky's *Pictures at an Exhibition.*

progression, in mathematics, series of numbers, each formed by a specific relationship to its predecessor. In arithmetic progression, successive terms differ by a fixed amount (common difference); in geometric series, ratio of successive terms is constant (common ratio).

Progressive party, in US, name of three 20th cent. political organizations, active at different presidential elections. First was 'Bull Moose' party, estab. (1911) by Republicans dissatisfied with W.H. Taft; supported (1912) THEODORE ROOSEVELT. Second had socialist programme, supported LA FOLLETTE in 1924 campaign. Third was again left-wing, challenged Democrats in 1948 election, nominating Henry Wallace.

prohibition, method of legally regulating manufacture, sale and transporting of alcoholic beverages. In US, refers to period (1920-33) of absolute ban on such manufacture and sale by federal law (18th Amendment, 1919). Widespread bootlegging led to repeal (21st Amendment, 1933).

Prokofiev, Sergei Sergeyevich (1891-1953), Russian composer. His music has an individual harmonic quality often allied to great lyricism. Works incl. operas, *eg Love for Three Oranges,* symphonies, satirical film music *Lieutenant Kije*; wrote orchestral fairy tale *Peter and the Wolf.*

Prokop (*c* 1380-1434), Czech religious leader, called 'Procopius the Great'. Led radical Hussites (Taborites) to victory over anti-Hussite crusaders at Ustinad-Labem (1426). Invaded Hungary, Silesia, Saxony; won further battles over Catholic forces before his death at Lipany.

Prokopyevsk, city of USSR, SC Siberian RSFSR. Pop. 270,000. Mining centre in Kuznetsk basin. Founded in 20th cent.

proletariat, in socialist theory, term used for class of wage earners existing on their own labour, esp. in indust. environment; derived from word for propertyless class in ancient Rome. In Marxist theory, proletariat is exploited by capitalist class, from which it must take power to achieve classless society.

Prometheus, in Greek myth, stole fire from the gods and gave it to mankind. Chained by Zeus to rock in Caucasus, where his liver was eternally devoured by an eagle. Released by Heracles; in some versions submitted to Zeus. Subject of Aeschylus' *Prometheus Bound.*

promethium (Pm), radioactive element of lanthanide series; at. no. 61, mass no. of most stable isotope 145. Obtained in nuclear reactors from fission of uranium.

pronghorn or **prongbuck,** *Antilocapra americana,* antelope-like North American ruminant, only member of Antilocapridae family. Hollow branched horns cast annually. Long persecuted by man, now protected.

proof spirit, alcoholic spirit containing 49.28% ethanol by weight or 57.1% by volume. Spirit said to be 70° proof or 30° under proof contains $0.7 \times 57.1 = 39.97\%$ ethanol by volume.

propaganda, technique of moulding public opinion by spreading true or false information through all media to gain religious, social or political ends in area of controversy. Important in dissemination of information by political parties in both democratic and totalitarian countries.

prophets, in OT, Jewish religious leaders regarded as chosen by God to guide the people, esp. during kingdom of Palestine and the Captivity. Incl. Isaiah, Jeremiah, Ezekiel and Daniel. Term applied collectively to the books of OT bearing their names.

proportional representation (PR), system of voting giving numerical reflection of voting strength of each party in representative assembly. Advocated by J.S. MILL, in order to allow minorities voice in govt. Best-known system is **single transferable vote,** in which elector has only one vote, but may indicate order of preference on list of candidates. Candidate elected on minimum quota of votes, after which surplus votes goes to next on list, *etc.*

Propylaea, portal and entrance to W end of Acropolis, Athens. Built (437-432 BC) by Mnesicles.

prose, ordinary form of spoken or written language, without metrical structure, as opposed to poetry or verse. Usual form of expression in novel, biography, essay. Earliest extant European prose work is Herodotus' *History of the Persian Wars* (5th cent. B.C.).

Proserpine, *see* PERSEPHONE.

prostate gland, partially muscular gland surrounding urethra at base of urinary bladder in males. Secretes part of seminal fluid. Enlargement of prostate is common disorder of middle and old age; removal by surgery allows free flow of urine.

prostitution, offering oneself, or another, for sexual intercourse for money, material gain. Legal definitions vary; in UK, only women defined as prostitutes; in some states in US, prostitute is any indiscriminately sexually active woman. In many societies, prostitution was religious act, *eg* in ancient Babylon, W Asia. Tolerated in Middle Ages, became problem with spread of venereal disease (16th cent), and legally suppressed by Protestant reformers. Police regulation, attempt to close or license brothels in 19th cent. Subsequent concern more with suppression of associated crimes, diseases, *eg* West German emphasis on medical checks.

protactinium (Pa), radioactive element of actinide series; at. no. 91, mass no. of most stable isotope 231. Occurs in uranium ores. Discovered 1918 by Hahn and Meitner.

Proteaceae, family of flowering shrubs and trees, mostly native to S Africa and Australia, incl. popular garden plant, *Protea bolussii,* with coneshaped flower heads.

Protectorate, govt. of England (1653-9) estab. by Cromwell after he had dissolved Rump Parliament. Cromwell assumed title of lord protector and, with army support, ruled as dictator. His son, Richard Cromwell, succeeded him as lord protector (1658); resigned 1659.

proteins, large group of complex nitrogen containing organic substances essential to living organisms. Made up of 20 amino acids, linked together in numerous ways to form large molecules. Synthesis of protein from amino acids is essential to growth and tissue maintenance.

Protestantism, religion of all Christian churches except RC and Eastern Orthodox, most of which originated during REFORMATION. Stresses individual responsibility to God rather than to ecclesiastical authority.

Proteus, in Greek myth, wise old man of the sea with power of assuming various forms to escape questioning. If caught and held would foretell the future.

Protochordata, subphylum of simple chordates, incl. amphioxus, acorn worms, sea squirts. Without true brain, jaws, vertebrae or paired limbs.

Protocols of the Elders of Zion, document purporting to give details of Jewish plot to take control of world govt. First appeared in Russia (1905). Later shown to have been invented by Russian secret police, using a French satire as basis.

proton, stable elementary particle possessing charge equal in magnitude but opposite in sign to that of electron; c 1836 times heavier than electron. Occurs in nucleus of all atoms, usually joined with neutrons.

protoplasm, essential living matter of plant and animal cells, consisting of colloidal solution of proteins, lipoids, carbohydrates and inorganic salts. Carries out essential processes of reproduction, absorption of food, waste excretion, *etc.* In cell, differentiated into central nucleoplasm and surrounding cytoplasm.

Protozoa, phylum of all unicellular animals, consisting of naked mass of protoplasm surrounded by membrane. Reproduction often by fission but some parasitic varieties, *eg* malaria parasite, have complicated life cycle involving several hosts.

Proudhon, Pierre Joseph (1809-65), French social theorist. Condemned private property in *What is Property?* (1840) for maintaining inequality and injustice. Favoured theory of mutualism, whereby association of owner-producers cooperate for common good.

Marcel Proust

Proust, Marcel (1871-1922), French novelist. Influenced by Bergson's theory of subjective nature of time. Known for semi-autobiog. roman-fleuve, *A la recherche du temps perdu* (16 vols., 1913-27), detailing narrator's changing reactions to experience.

Prout, William (1785-1850), English chemist, physiologist. Discovered existence of hydrochloric acid in stomach digestive juices. Known for Prout's hypothesis that atomic weights of elements are whole number multiples of atomic weight of hydrogen. This, although untrue, was an important contribution to atomic theory.

Provençal, variety of French. Considered by some to be dialect(s), others a separate language. Spoken in Provence and other areas of S France. Developed as *langue d'oc* of Middle Ages, vehicle of troubadour literature. *Langue d'oc* unsuccessfully revived in 19th cent. by literary movement.

Provence, region and former prov. of SE France, hist. cap. Aix. Largely mountainous, Rhône valley in W, coastal plain (incl. Camargue) in S. Wine, fruit, silk, cattle, h.e.p. Tourism, esp. along Riviera. Settled 7th cent. BC by Greeks, became Roman prov. Part of France from 1486. Provençal language widely used until 16th cent., revived 19th cent.; distinctive culture, esp. literature.

Proverbs, poetic book of OT, collection of moral maxims traditionally attributed to Solomon. Prob. from various sources and collected 9th-2nd cent. BC.

Providence, seaport and cap. of Rhode Isl., US; on arm of Narragansett Bay. Pop. 179,000. Machinery, jewellery, silverware mfg. Founded by Roger Williams on free worship basis (1636). Joint cap. with Newport until 1900. Has famous 18th cent. buildings. Seat of Brown Univ. (1764).

Provo, town of NC Utah, US; on Provo R. Pop. 53,000. Commercial centre in agric. and mining area. Settled by Mormons (1849). Has Brigham Young Univ. (1875).

Prudhoe Bay, inlet of Arctic Ocean, N Alaska; E of Colville R. delta. Large oil reserves discovered (1968); climate, terrain make extraction difficult.

Prud'hon, Pierre-Paul (1758-1823), French painter, interior designer. Patronized by both Napoleon's empresses, he designed bridal suite for Empress Marie Louise. Paintings, *eg Venus and Adonis,* influenced the Romantics.

prune, plum that has been dried without fermentation taking place. Prepared mainly on Pacific coast of US.

Prussia (*Preussen*), hist. region and former state of Germany. Comprised much of NE Germany, cap. Berlin. Teutonic Knights conquered heathen Prussians in 13th cent.; their territ. became hereditary duchy in 16th cent. and passed to electors of Brandenburg (1618). Kingdom of Prussia was created from Brandenburg dominions in 1701. Frederick the Great (1740-86) began period of expansion, acquiring Silesia and W parts of Poland. Further territ.

Prussia

gains made after Napoleonic Wars. Under Bismarck, assumed leadership of German states (1860s); William I of Prussia became 1st emperor of Germany (1871). Reduced in size after WWI. Dissolved (1947) after WWII.

prussic acid, see HYDROCYANIC ACID.

Przemyśl, town of SE Poland, on R. San. Pop. 52,000. Food processing, engineering, timber indust. Founded 8th cent.; under Austrian rule 1772-1919. Strategic fortress in WWI, withstood Russian siege (1914-15).

Przewalski's horse

Przewalski's horse, *Equus caballus przewalskii,* only surviving wild horse, confined to Mongolia and Sinkiang. Tan coloured with black mane; stands *c* 1.4m/4.5 ft at shoulders.

Psalms, poetical book of OT, traditionally attributed to David. Prob. by many authors and collected 6th-1st cent. BC.

pseudepigrapha, group of early writings not incl. in Biblical canon or Apocrypha, some of which were falsely ascribed to Biblical characters. Composed *c* 200 BC-*c* AD 400 in Hebrew, Aramaic and Greek. Incl. fragments allegedly written by Jesus, most of the Disciples, Pilate among others.

Pskov, city of USSR, W European RSFSR; near L. Peipus. Pop. 131,000. Centre of flax-growing region; linen mfg. Important medieval town; cap. of powerful commercial city state (1348-1510) until annexed by Moscow. Scene of abdication of Nicholas II (1917).

psoriasis, chronic skin disease, characterized by scaly red patches on scalp, back and arms. Cause unknown; relieved by ultraviolet light.

Psyche, in Greek myth, a beautiful girl and the personi-fication of human soul, loved by Cupid. He forbade her to look at him but she disobeyed and he left her. After a long search, she was made immortal and united with him forever.

psychiatry, medical study and treatment of disorders of the mind, incl. psychosis, neurosis. Gained prominence in late 19th cent., esp. with Freud's development of psychoanalysis.

psychical research, study of supernormal phenomena. Estab. as serious study by British Society for Psychical Research (founded 1882), which investigated mediums,

poltergeists, *etc.* Extra-sensory perception (ESP), *ie* telepathy, precognition, has been subject of research in 20th cent., *eg* by J.B. RHINE.

psychoanalysis, term coined by Freud to denote system of psychology and method of treatment of mental disorders (*see* NEUROSIS). Lays emphasis on importance of unconscious mind, inducing its expression and evading conscious mind's censorship through analytic techniques of free association, dream interpretation.

psychology, science of the mind, more specifically the studies of all interactions between living organisms (esp. humans) and the environment. Allied to biological and sociological sciences, but distinguished by its concentra-tion on individual's behaviour, both through mental and emotional processes. Specific concerns are abnormal behaviour, cognition and cognitive development, *etc*; modes of approach incl. PSYCHOANALYSIS, BEHAVIOURISM, GESTALT.

psychosis, name given to certain severe mental disorders which involve loss of contact with reality. Functional psychoses, without apparent organic cause, are mainly of schizophrenic or manic-depressive type; organic psychoses are caused by brain damage or disease.

psychosomatic disease, physical disorder of body resulting from disturbance of the mind. Asthma, duodenal ulcers, high blood pressure, certain heart disorders, *etc,* are considered partly psychosomatic in origin.

psychotherapy, treatment of mental disorder by psychological means, involving communication between trained person and patient. Methods incl. suggestion, hypnosis and psychoanalysis.

Ptah, ancient Egyptian god worshipped at Memphis, creator of universe. Represented as a smith, assimilated into Greek Hephaestus.

ptarmigan, bird of grouse family, genus *Lagopus,* of mountains of N hemisphere. Toes and legs feathered; winter plumage is white. Species incl. willow ptarmigan, *L. lagopus,* and rock ptarmigan, *L. mutus.*

Pteridophyta, division of plants comprising FERN, HORSETAIL and CLUB MOSS groups. Incl. many ancient fossil varieties.

pterodactyl, any of order Pterosauria of extinct flying reptiles of Mesozoic era. Membranous wings stretched between hind limb and greatly elongated fourth digit of forelimb.

Ptolemy I [Soter] (d. 284 BC), Macedonian general under Alexander the Great. Given control of Egypt during partition of Alexander's empire, he held it against rival DIADOCHI. Estab. new Egyptian dynasty (305). Descendant, **Ptolemy XII** (d. 47 BC), ruled Egypt jointly with sister (and wife) Cleopatra. Forced by Caesar to accept her reinstatement after he had deprived her of power. Drowned in Nile. His brother, **Ptolemy XIII** (d. 44 BC), was then made joint ruler with Cleopatra by Caesar. She had him murdered.

Ptolemy or **Claudius Ptolemaus** (*fl* AD 140), Greco-Egyptian astronomer. Systematized work of Greek astronomers, esp. Hipparchus, in his *Almagest.* Described geocentric solar system in which Sun and planets revolved in circular orbits about stationary Earth; influential until superseded by works of Copernicus.

puberty, stage of child's development when sexual maturity begins. Generally, age 11-14 in girls and 12-16 in boys. Hormones from pituitary gland stimulate gonads to form fertile sperm or ova and to secrete hormones which control secondary sex characteristics. In girls, 1st menstrual period signifies onset of puberty.

public debt, see NATIONAL DEBT.

public ownership, another term for NATIONALIZATION.

public school, in UK, secondary school, run on fee-paying (private) basis and having academic curriculum. Famous examples incl. boys' boarding schools Eton, Harrow, Winchester. Elsewhere, public schools are free to all pupils at primary or secondary levels. Financed usually by public taxes and supervised by local authorities.

publishing, trade concerned with creation and distribution of books and other reading matter. Closely allied to printing and bookselling. Narrowly defined, involves preparation of author's work for chosen market. Introduction of movable type (15th cent.) facilitated large-scale distribution of reading material.

Puccini

Puff adder

Puffin

Puccini, Giacomo (1858-1924), Italian composer. Renowned for operas *Manon Lescaut, La Bohème, Tosca, Madame Butterfly* and *Turandot.* Combined great dramatic expression with strong melody to create some of the most moving operas ever written.

Puebla, city of C Mexico, cap. of Puebla state. Pop. 522,000. Onyx quarrying, cotton milling, pottery industs. Has one of finest cathedrals in Mexico (1649); Teatro Principal (one of oldest Latin American theatres); univ. (1537).

Pueblo, town of SC Colorado, US; on Arkansas R. Pop. 97,000. Large iron and steel indust., meat packing.

Pueblo, group of North American Indian tribes of various language families, living in SW US. Distinguished by custom of living in adobe communal longhouses (*pueblos*). Reached highest level of civilization N of Mexico, esp. in agric., sand paintings, pottery *etc.* Successfully resisted Spanish colonization in 17th cent. Groups incl. Hopi, Zuni. Some 20,000 still live on reservations in Arizona, New Mexico.

puerperal fever, infection by bacteria of womb after childbirth. Caused many deaths in 19th cent. until Ignaz Semmelweis introduced disinfection of midwives' hands.

Puerto Rico, isl. territ. of US, E West Indies, in Greater Antilles. Area 8871 sq km (3425 sq mi); pop. 2,712,000, one of highest pop. densities in world; cap. San Juan. Languages: Spanish, English. Religion: RC. Mainly mountainous; tropical climate. Fertile agric. soil (sugar cane, tobacco growing). Settled by Spanish (1508), ceded to US after 1898 war. Became 'Commonwealth' 1952. Much emigration to US because of unemployment.

Pufendorf, Samuel, Baron von (1632-94), German jurist, historian. Known for *De jure naturae et gentium* (1672), maintaining priority of natural law, underlying all rational legal systems.

puff adder, *Bitis arietans,* highly poisonous viper common in tropical Africa. Short tail, yellow markings on body; reaches lengths of *c* 1.2 m/4 ft.

puffball or **smokeball,** spherical fungus which breaks open when ripe to emit dust-like spores. Common puffball is *Lycoperdon perlatum.*

puffer, tropical fish of Tetraodontidae family. Skin covered with small prickles erected when body is inflated with air or water. Edible if expertly prepared; otherwise poisonous.

puffin, *Fratercula arctica,* small marine bird with black and white plumage. Triangular beak banded with blue, red and yellow. Breeds colonially on Atlantic coasts, nesting in burrows.

pug, breed of small dog, probably of Chinese origin. Broad flat nose, curled tail; stands *c* 28 cm/11 in. at shoulder.

Pugachev, Yemelian Ivanovich (d. 1775), Russian Cossack leader. Claiming to be Tsar Peter III, led revolt of Cossacks and peasants against Catherine II. Defeated near Volgograd, betrayed and beheaded in Moscow.

Pugin, Augustus Welby Northmore (1812-52), English architect, writer. Influential advocate of Gothic revival in writings, *eg Contrasts* (1836). Designed fittings and ornamental details for Barry's Houses of Parliament.

Puglia, *see* APULIA, Italy.

Pula (Ital. *Pola*), town of Croatia, NW Yugoslavia, on Istria penin. Pop. 37,000. Port, resort. Austrian naval base from 1797; under Italy as cap. of Istria 1919-47. Roman remains, incl. amphitheatre.

Pulitzer, Joseph (1847-1911), American newspaper owner, b. Hungary. Acquired and built up New York *World,* owned *Post-Dispatch,* which was maintained by his son and grandson in liberal tradition. Founded (1903) the School of Journalism at Columbia Univ., left funds for the **Pulitzer Prizes,** awarded each year since 1917 for achievements in journalism, letters and musical compositions.

Pullman dispute, strike over wage cuts (1894) by railway sleeping car workers at Pullman model community (now a Chicago suburb). Union leader Eugene Debs jailed; President Cleveland sent federal troops to quell strike despite opposition from Illinois govt.

Pulmonata, order of gastropod molluscs, incl. snails, slugs, that breathe through lung-like chamber.

pulsar, heavenly body which emits short pulses of radio waves at regular intervals. First detected 1967. An optical pulsar is in Crab nebula. Believed to be a rotating neutron star, remnant of supernova explosion.

pulse, in physiology, wave of arterial expansion caused by beating of heart. Normal rate in adults is *c* 60–70 beats per min.

puma, *Felis concolor,* large member of cat family, ranging from Argentina to Canada. Yellowish-brown short fur, slender build. Called cougar or mountain lion in North America.

pumice, *see* LAVA.

pump, machine for raising, transferring or increasing the pressure of water or other fluids (incl. gases). In ancient times the screw type was used for irrigation purposes. Various types exist now, incl. reciprocating, gear and centrifugal pumps.

Pumpkin

pumpkin or **squash,** *Cucurbita pepo,* annual vine with large, round, edible fruit. Native to North America, widely cultivated. Name also given to similar plants of genus *Cucurbita,* eg *C. maxima* and musk pumpkin, *C. moschata.*

Punch and Judy, puppet play introduced to England in 17th cent., prob. derived from Italian *commedia dell'arte.* Characters incl. murderous hunchback, Punch, and nagging wife, Judy.

Punic Wars, series of conflicts between Rome and Carthage for dominance of Mediterranean. First Punic War (264-241 BC) resulted in acquisition of Sicily by Rome. During 2nd Punic War (218-201 BC), Hannibal invaded Italy but could not capture Rome. Forced to return to Carthage, he was defeated at Zama by Scipio Africanus Major (202). Third Punic War (149-146 BC), instigated by Roman fears of Carthaginian commercial power, led to total destruction of Carthage by Scipio Africanus Minor.

Punjab, state of N India. Area *c* 75,600 sq km (29,200 sq mi); pop; 13,473,000; cap. Chandigarh. Hist. region of Punjab dominated by Sikhs in 19th cent.; annexed by Britain after Sikh Wars (1845-9). At partition, W Punjab became Pakistani prov. Indian prov. of E Punjab later divided (1966) into states of Haryana (Hindi-speaking) and Punjab (Punjabi-speaking).

Punjabi, Indic language in Indo-Iranian branch of Indo-European family. Spoken in NW India and Pakistan. Close to W Hindi, Urdu.

Punta Arenas, port of S Chile, on Magellan Str. Pop. 65,000. World's most S city. Wool, lamb exports. Coal mining nearby.

pupa, third stage of development of insect undergoing complete metamorphosis. Involves anatomical changes, often occurring in cocoon or cell. Adult emerges after pupa stage.

pupil, in anatomy, circular opening in centre of iris of eye. Size of pupil varies with intensity of light and is affected by adrenaline in the blood and drugs such as belladonna.

puppet, small figure of human or animal made to perform on miniature stage by unseen operator who speaks dialogue. Types incl. marionette, controlled by wires, and 'glove' puppet. Puppet shows have great antiquity, being familiar in 5th cent. BC Greece. Now mainly restricted to performances for children.

Purbeck, Isle of, penin. of Dorset, S England. Purbeck marble (limestone) quarried.

Purcell, Henry (1659-95), English composer, organist of Chapel Royal. Works incl. opera *Dido and Aeneas,* music

Henry Purcell

for *The Fairy Queen, King Arthur,* as well as songs, instrumental and church music (esp. anthems).

Purchas, Samuel (*c* 1575-1626), English compiler of travel books. Known for *Purchas his Pilgrimage* (1613), *Hakluytus Posthumus* (1625), based on papers left by Richard HAKLUYT.

purgative, drug given to induce bowel movement. Vegetable purgatives incl. senna, rhubarb, bran; mineral salts used incl. magnesium sulphate (Epsom salts).

purgatory, in RC and Eastern Orthodox theology, place where those who have died in grace of God expiate their unatoned sins by suffering. Suffering can be lessened by prayers of living. Protestants reject this doctrine.

Puri, resort town of Orissa state, E India. Pop. 61,000. Famous for 12th cent. temple of Jagannath (Juggernaut). Image of god drawn through streets annually by pilgrims.

Purim, Jewish festival commemorating deliverance of Jews by Esther from a massacre. Celebrated on 14 Adar (usually mid-March) with carnivals and feasting.

Puritanism, social and theological movement in Protestantism in Britain and America. Arose out of pressure for reform of religious establishment (16th cent.). Influenced by Calvinist theory and aimed at less ritualistic forms of worship. By 17th cent., had separated from Church of England, and opposed Charles I, precipitating Civil War (1640s). Puritanism taken by colonists to New England, where it exerted a great influence on society.

Puritan Revolution, conflict (1603-49) between English kings James I, Charles I and predominantly Puritan Parliament. Arose partly out of kings' advocacy of govt. by 'divine right', disputed by Parliament, which itself claimed sovereignty. Culminated in Civil War, execution of Charles and estab. of Protectorate.

Purple Heart, Order of the, oldest US military award. Instituted by George Washington (1782).

purslane, *Portulaca oleracea,* annual herb native to India. Fleshy, succulent leaves sometimes used as salad or pot herb.

Purus, river of NC South America. Rises in E Peru, flows NE 3380 km (*c* 2100 mi) across Brazil through tropical rain forest to the Amazon SW of Manáus.

pus, thick yellowish-white substance produced as result of bacterial inflammation. Composed of white blood cells, tissue fluid, bacteria and dead tissue.

Pusan, seaport of SE South Korea, on Korea Str. Pop. 1,881,000. Largest Korean port; indust., commercial centre; railway engineering, shipbuilding; produces iron and steel, textiles. UN supply base in Korean War.

Pusey, Edward Bouverie (1800-82), English clergyman, leader in OXFORD MOVEMENT. Helped Newman and Keble with *Tracts for the Times* from 1834. Remained Anglican, delivering sermons that checked moves to RC church.

Aleksandr Pushkin

Pushkin, Aleksandr Sergeyevich (1799-1837), Russian author. Best-known works incl. verse-novel *Eugene Onegin* (1831), tragedy *Boris Godunov* (1831). Poetry incl. Byronic lyrics, narrative poem, *The Bronze Horseman* (1833). Also wrote short story cycle, *Tales of Belkin* (1830). Had great influence on subsequent Russian literature.

Pushkin, town of USSR, W European RSFSR. Pop. 55,000. Founded as Tsarkoye Selo (tsar's village) by Peter the Great; has summer palaces of Catherine II and Alexander I and extensive parks.

Pushtu or **Pashtu,** *see* IRANIAN.

Puskas, Ferenc (1927-), Hungarian footballer. Outstanding forward in Honved and Hungarian national teams in mid-1950s. Joined Real Madrid, for whom he scored 4 goals in 1960 European Cup final against Eintracht Frankfurt.

puss moth, *Cerura vinula,* large white moth of Notodontidae family. Caterpillar protects itself by ejecting formic acid. Cocoon resembles tree bark.

Putney, *see* WANDSWORTH, England.

Putumayo, river of NW South America. Rises in Colombian Andes, flows E 1600 km (*c* 1000 mi) forming Colombia-Peru border, then into Brazil to join Amazon as the Içá.

Puvis de Chavannes, Pierre (1824-98), French painter. Developed style of monumental decorative painting. Specialized in allegorical themes or subjects from antiquity. Decorated many public buildings in France; admired by Gauguin, Seurat.

Puy, Le, *see* LE PUY, France.

Puy-de-Dôme, extinct volcano of Auvergne Mts., SC France. Height 1464 m (4806 ft). Ruined Roman temple, observatory on summit.

Pu-Yi, Henry (1906-67), last Chinese emperor (1908-12). Member of Ch'ing dynasty, he ruled as Hsuan Tung. Later, served as emperor (1934-45) of Japanese puppet state of Manchukuo. Handed over to Chinese Communists (1950), he was imprisoned until 1959.

Pygmalion, in Greek myth, king of Cyprus. Made ivory statue, Galatea. When he fell in love with it Aphrodite brought statue to life and he married her.

Pygmy or **Pigmy,** diminutive, *c* 1.5 m (5 ft), Negroid people of Africa, Malaysia and New Guinea. Sometimes called Negrillos (Africa) or Negretos (Far East). Generally hunters and food gatherers living in small nomadic bands in scrub regions.

pygmy hippopotamus, *see* HIPPOPOTAMUS.

Pylos (*Pilos*), town of Greece, in SW Peloponnese. Scene of Athenian victory (425 BC) over Sparta and of battle of Navarino (1827) in which British, French and Russian fleet defeated Turks, Egyptians. Ruined Mycenaean palace (13th cent. BC).

Pygmies in Congo basin

Pym, John (*c* 1583-1643), English politician. Led Puritan opposition to Charles I in Parliament; instrumental in drawing up Petition of Right (1628). In the Long Parliament, moved impeachment of Strafford and Laud. One of the five members of Commons whom Charles tried to arrest (1642).

Pynchon, Thomas (1937-), American novelist. Works, *eg V.* (1963), *The Crying of Lot 49* (1966), *Gravity's Rainbow* (1973), use wide-ranging erudition to communicate a paranoid fictive world.

Pyongyang, cap. of North Korea. Pop. 1,500,000. Indust. centre of coal, iron region. Mfg., heavy engineering. Rebuilt after destruction of Korean War.

pyorrhoea, any discharge of pus. Name usually applies to *Pyorrhoea alveolaris*, infection of gums and teeth sockets, usually leading to loosening of teeth.

pyralid moth, any of Pyralidae family of small or medium-sized moths found largely in tropics. Species incl. CACTUS MOTH, flour moth, sugarcane moth.

Khafre Pyramid from top of Great Pyramid

pyramid, in ancient Egypt, monumental stone structure with square base and triangular sides, meeting at an apex. Erected as tombs for kings of Egypt, great period of pyramid building was *c* 2700-2300 BC. Three famous pyramids at Giza incl. Great Pyramid of Khufu (Cheops), one of Seven Wonders of the ancient World.

Pyramids, Battle of the, defeat by Napoleon (July, 1798) soon after his invasion of Egypt, of an army of 60,000 Mamelukes. Briefly gave him control of the area until Nelson destroyed his fleet at Aboukir.

Pyramus and **Thisbe,** in classical myth, Babylonian lovers. Pyramus, mistakenly thinking Thisbe had been killed by a lion, killed himself. When Thisbe found his body, she took her own life with his sword.

Pyrenees (Sp. *Pirineos*), mountain range of SW France, NE Spain. Extend from Bay of Biscay to Mediterranean. Higher in C, E, rise to 3403 m (11,168 ft) at Pico de Aneto. Passes incl. Roncesvalles. Incl. Andorra enclave. tourism, h.e.p.

Pyrenees, Peace of the, treaty ending fighting between France and Spain (1659). By its terms, Louis XIV was to marry daughter of Philip IV of Spain; Spain gave Roussillon and parts of Flanders to France. Franco-Spanish border estab. at Pyrenees.

pyrethrum, *Chrysanthemum coccineum,* perennial plant native to Persia and Caucasus. Widely cultivated in temperate regions for red, pink or white flowers and commercially for insecticide pyrethrum powder extracted from dried flower heads.

pyrite or **iron pyrites** (FeS$_2$), yellow mineral, consisting of iron sulphide. Most widespread sulphide mineral; often mistaken for gold (nicknamed 'fool's gold'). Source of iron and sulphur.

pyroclastic rock, fragmented volcanic material thrown into atmosphere by explosive activity. May be solid when ejected or liquid solidified by contact with air. Size ranges from dust to large blocks; incl. pumice.

pyrometer, instrument used to measure temperatures beyond range of normal thermometers. Various types incl. platinum resistance thermometer which utilizes change in resistance with temperature.

pyroxenes, group of rock-forming minerals, composed mainly of silicates of calcium, iron and magnesium. Types incl. augite.

Pyrrho (*c* 365-270 BC), Greek philosopher. Founder of SCEPTICISM. Taught that every proposition could be maintained or contradicted with equal plausibility, thus knowledge must always be in question.

Pyrrhus (*c* 318-272 BC), king of Epirus (295-272 BC). Invaded Italy (281) to aid Tarentum against Rome. Sustained heavy losses in 2 victories over Romans (hence term 'Pyrrhic victory') before defeat at Beneventum (275).

Pythagoras (*c* 582-*c* 507 BC), Greek philosopher, b. Samos. Founded religious brotherhood at Crotona. Held that all relationships could be expressed in numbers. Made

Indian python *(Python molurus)*

discoveries in musical intonations. Influenced subsequent work of Euclid. Believed Earth revolved around fixed point ('hearth') of universe.

Pythia, in Greek religion, priestess and oracular prophetess of Apollo at Delphi. Uttered prophecies in a trance. These were interpreted to the questioner by a priest.

Pythian games, in ancient Greece, games held at Delphi every 4 years in honour of Apollo. Incl. athletic, literary and musical contests.

python, any of Pythonidae family of constrictor snakes, of Old World tropics. Reaches lengths of 9.1 m/30 ft. Lays eggs, unlike boas.

'Q', see QUILLER-COUCH, SIR ARTHUR THOMAS.

Qaddhafi or **Gadafy, Muammar al-** (1942-   ), Libyan political leader. Gained power after military coup overthrowing King Idris (1969). Fostered Arab unity; failed in attempt to unite Egypt and Libya (1973). Used Libyan oil wealth to support revolutionary movements, esp. Palestinian guerrillas.

Qâhira, El, see CAIRO, Egypt.

Qatar, penin. of E Arabia, in Persian Gulf. Area c 11,400 sq km (4400 sq mi); pop. 160,000; cap. Doha (pop.95,000). Oil reserves. Sheikdom under British protection until 1971. Allied with United Arab Emirates.

Qattara Depression, arid region of N Egypt, in Libyan Desert. Area c 18,130 sq km (7000 sq mi); falls to 133 m (436 ft) below sea level, lowest point in Africa. Has extensive salt marsh. Formed S part of Allied defence line at El Alamein (1942).

Qazvin, city of NC Iran. Pop. 88,000. Carpet and textile mfg. Founded in 4th cent. AD, became national cap. in 16th cent. Also called Kazvin.

Qom or **Qum,** city of NC Iran. Pop. 164,000. Transport centre; oil deposits. Has shrine of Fatima (d. 816); Shiite Moslem pilgrimage centre.

Quadruple Alliance, 1) league formed (1718) by Britain, France, Austria and Netherlands to prevent Spain from nullifying terms of Peace of Utrecht. Spain renounced claims to Austrian territ. in Italy in settlement of 1720. 2) alliance formed (1814) by Austria, Britain, Prussia and Russia to strengthen coalition against Napoleon.

quagga, Equus quagga, extinct South African zebra. Excessively hunted for hide in 19th cent.

quail, any of various small migratory game birds. Only European species is Coturnix coturnix, which winters in Africa. North American species incl. BOBWHITE.

Quakers, see SOCIETY OF FRIENDS.

Quant, Mary (1934-   ), English fashion and cosmetic designer. Revolutionized fashion in 1960s, making London a leading fashion centre. Popular lines, made for a youthful market, incl. 'mini' skirt.

quantum theory, physical theory introduced by Planck that radiation is emitted and absorbed not continuously but only in multiples of indivisible units (quanta). Extended by Einstein to explain photoelectric effect and by Bohr to explain atomic spectra. In 1920s, developed into mathematical theory of wave mechanics which explains many phenomena of atomic physics.

quarantine, restriction of movements on people and animals who may have been exposed to infectious diseases. Arose in 14th cent. Europe as an attempt to control spread of plague through ports such as Venice and Rhodes. Often applied to animals to prevent spread of foot-and-mouth disease, rabies, etc.

quarks, hypothetical elementary particles, introduced by M. Gell-Mann and G. Zweig, which serve as building blocks for all strongly-interacting elementary particles (hadrons). Originally 3 quarks, bearing charges which are fractions of that on electron, were introduced; more may be needed to explain new phenomena.

Quarles, Francis (1592-1644), English poet. Known for Emblems (1635), verses illustrating symbolic pictures.

quarrying, removal of building stone, granite, marble, slate, etc, from surface deposits. Stone in broken or crushed form, used for cement, road making and concrete aggregate, is removed by drilling and blasting. Blocks of stone suitable for building and ornamental work are machine cut.

quartz, commonest mineral, consisting of silicon dioxide (SiO_2). Hard, normally colourless and transparent; coloured by impurities. Varieties incl. agate, amethyst, chalcedony, onyx. Used in jewellery, electronics, lenses and prisms.

quartzite, hard metamorphic rock, consisting of firmly cemented quartz grains. Normally light-coloured; may be darker due to mineral impurities. Formed by metamorphism of pure quartz sandstone.

quasars (quasi stellar radio sources), extragalactic sources of immense quantities of light or radio waves. Observed red shift of their spectral lines suggests they are receding at velocity close to that of light.

Quasimodo, Salvatore (1901-68), Italian poet. Early works, eg Waters and Land (1929), reflect occult, hermetic interests. The Promised Land and Other Poems (1958) marks preoccupation with social, political issues. Nobel Prize for Literature (1959).

quassia, genus of small trees and shrubs native to tropics. Esp. Quassia amara, yielding a medicinal extract. Name also used for Picrasma excelsa of West Indies, yielding a similar extract.

Quaternary period, second and current geological period of Cenozoic era. Began c 2 million years ago. Comprises Pleistocene and Holocene (or Recent) epochs. Deterioration of climate, begun in Tertiary, led to extensive glaciations; followed by warmer climate, formation of modern landscape eg lakes, deserts. Development of man from primitive ape-like creature to present form. Also see GEOLOGICAL TABLE.

Quathlamba, see DRAKENSBERG MOUNTAINS.

Québec or **Quebec,** prov. of E Canada, incl. Anticosti, Magdalen isls. in Gulf of St Lawrence. Area 1,553,640 sq km (594,860 sq mi); pop. 6,028,000; cap. Québec; largest city Montréal. Bounded in N by Hudson, Ungava bays. Resources in Laurentians (timber, asbestos, aluminium, iron ore, h.e.p.). St Lawrence R. valley is agric., indust. base. French landed 1534; settled region as New France in 17th cent.; British gained control 1763; named Lower Canada 1791; became one of original 4 provs. of Canada (1867). French language and customs retained. Separatist movement grew from 1960s.

Québec or **Quebec City,** cap. and major port of Québec prov., Canada; on St Lawrence R. Pop. 186,000, mainly French speaking. Timber produce and exports, shipbuilding, clothing mfg. Port icebound in winter. French settlement under Champlain (1608); cap. of New France until British defeat of French on Plains of Abraham (1759); cap. of Lower Canada (1791). Has Citadel, Laval Univ. (1852).

Quebec Act, legislation passed (1774) by British parliament. Extended W boundaries of Québec, estab. French civil law in Québec and granted religious freedom to French-Canadians. Intended to estab. permanent British admin. in Canada; opposed by American colonies.

Québecois, Parti, see LÉVESQUE, RENÉ.

quebracho, name for several South American hardwood trees. Esp. Aspidosperma quebracho-blanco, yielding medicinal alkaloids and Schinopsis lorentzii, yielding an extract used in tanning.

Quechua, Kechua or **Quichua,** South American group of languages, belonging to Andean-Equatorial stock. Incl.

languages spoken in parts of Peru, Ecuador, Bolivia, Argentina. Incas' language was of this group.

Quedlinburg, town of WC East Germany, on R. Bode. Pop. 31,000. Horticulture, agric. market. Fortified (922) by Henry I, 12th cent. church contains his tomb.

Queen Anne's lace, see CARROT.

Queen Charlotte Islands, archipelago of W British Columbia, Canada; separated from mainland by Hecate Str. Timber, fishing industs. Haida Indian pop. Largest of group is Graham Isl.; area 6436 sq km (2485 sq mi).

Queen Maud Land, see NORWEGIAN ANTARCTIC TERRITORY.

Queen's, see NEW YORK CITY.

Queensberry, John Sholto Douglas, 8th Marquess of (1844-1900), Scottish nobleman. Patron of the rules of modern gloved boxing drafted by John Chambers (1867).

Queen's Counsel, see BARRISTER.

Queensland, state of NE Australia. Area 1,727,500 sq km (667,000 sq mi); pop. 1,823,000; cap. Brisbane. Great Dividing Range parallels coast, incl. Darling Downs (S), Atherton Tableland (N); Great Artesian Basin in SW; Barrier Reef off shore. Sugar cane, fruit growing; timber indust.; beef cattle raising; mining, esp. copper, lead, bauxite, oil. Penal settlement estab. 1824 at Moreton Bay; Queensland became colony (1859), federal state (1901).

Queenston Heights, Battle of, decisive confrontation in War of 1812 in which American invasion force was defeated by British on Niagara frontier, Canada. British commander, Isaac Brock, was killed in action.

Quelimane, town of E Mozambique, on Indian Ocean. Pop. 66,000. Railway terminus and port, exports copra, sisal, palm products. Former slave trade centre.

Queneau, Raymond (1903-76), French author. Known for humorous novels, *Skin of Dreams* (1944), *Zazie* (1959); surrealist-inspired verse, *eg Petite Cosmogonie portative* (1950).

Quesnay, François (1694-1774), French economist. Founder of the PHYSIOCRATS. Wrote *Tableau économique* (1758).

Quetta, town of WC Pakistan, near Bolan Pass. Pop. 156,000. Centre for trade with Afghanistan. Taken by British (1876), it became a military station. Almost destroyed (1935) by earthquake.

quetzal, crested bird of Trogonidae family, of forests of Central America. Green and red plumage, with long tail feathers. Species incl. resplendent quetzal, *Pharomachrus mocino.*

Quetzalcoatl, principal god of Toltecs, and subsequently, Aztecs. Credited with discovery of arts and sciences. Represented as plumed serpent.

Quevedo [y Villegas], Francisco Gómez de (1580-1645), Spanish author. Known for cynical picaresque novel *Vida del Buscón,* (1626), satires in *Los Sueños* (1627). Also wrote many short verse satires.

Quezaltenango, town of SW Guatemala, alt. 2286 m (7500 ft). Pop. 54,000. In agric. region, producing coffee, sugar; flour milling. Destroyed by eruption of Santa Maria volcano (1902).

Quezon, Manuel Luis (1878-1944), Philippine statesman. Leader in drive for independence of Philippines from US. Became 1st president of Commonwealth of Philippines (1935).

Quezon City, cap. of Philippines, C Luzon isl. Pop. 896,000. Replaced nearby Manila as cap. 1948. Largely residential; textile mfg.

quicksand, deposit of loose, fine-grained saturated sand particles. May engulf heavy object. Often found near river mouths, along sea shores.

quicksilver, see MERCURY.

quietism, form of Christian mysticism which holds that union with God is achieved through complete passivity of soul, annihilation of will and cessation of self-consciousness. Founded (1675) by Spanish priest, MOLINOS. Condemned (1687) by Pope Innocent XI.

Quiller-Couch, Sir Arthur Thomas (1863-1944), English author. Wrote short stories, novels, *eg The Ship of Stars* (1899), under pseud. 'Q'. Edited *Oxford Book of English Verse* (1900). Known for literary criticism, *eg On the Art of Reading* (1920).

Quimper, town of Brittany, NW France, cap. of Finistère dept. Pop. 58,000. Pottery (Quimper or Brittany ware), tourism. Cathedral (13th cent.).

Quince

quince, *Cydonia oblongata,* small tree native to Asia. Bears bitter, yellow, pear-shaped fruit used in preserves.

Quincy, town of E Massachusetts, US; on Boston Bay. Pop. 88,000. Granite quarrying, shipbuilding. Settled 1634.

quinine, crystalline alkaloid extracted from cinchona bark. Introduced into Europe from South America, it was formerly used in treatment of malaria.

Quintilian, full name Marcus Fabius Quintilianus (*c* AD 35-*c* 95), Roman rhetorician, b. Spain. Author of instruction course on public speaking, *Institutio oratoria,* in 12 books. First 2 books give much information on Roman education.

Quisling, Vidkun (1887-1945), Norwegian fascist leader. Collaborated in German invasion of Norway (1940); headed subsequent puppet govt. after 1942. Shot for treason after War. Name became synonymous with traitor.

Quito, cap. of Ecuador at foot of Pichincha volcano, near the equator. Alt. 2850 m (9350 ft). Pop. 528,000. Brewing, flour milling, major textile mfg. Indian settlement before Spanish conquest (1534). Has univ. (1787); many famous churches.

Qum, see QOM.

Qumran, W Jordan, site of discovery of Dead Sea Scrolls (1947). Originally iron-age fort, occupied (2nd cent. BC) by monastic community until AD 68. Scrolls comprise their library.

quoits, outdoor game in which an iron ring is thrown at a peg in an attempt to encircle it. Known in England since 14th cent. Horseshoe pitching, popular in US, is a similar game.

R

Ra, ancient Egyptian sun god. Represented as hawk, lion. Sailed across sky in barge during day. Early Egyptian kings claimed descent from him.

Rabat, cap. of Morocco, at mouth of Bou Regreg. Pop., incl. nearby Salé, 534,000. Admin. centre; textile, carpet industs. Ancient walled town with 12th cent. Hassan Tower. Former cap. of French Morocco (1912-56).

Rabaul, port of NE New Britain, Bismarck Archipelago. Pop. 11,000. Exports copra, cocoa, timber.

rabbi (Heb., = my master), originally a scholar and teacher of the Jewish law. Now refers to those trained and ordained as spiritual heads of congregations. Duties incl. deciding matters pertaining to marriage and kosher laws.

rabbit, *Oryctolagus cuniculus,* burrowing European mammal of hare family, order Lagomorpha. Smaller and less swift than hare; lives in large groups. Serious pest of farmland, its great fertility makes control difficult. Domestic varieties sometimes bred for fur.

Rabelais, François (c 1494-1553), French author. Wrote satirical romance, *Gargantua and Pantagruel* (5 vol., 1532-64, last 2 vol. perhaps not by Rabelais), narrating adventures of giant and son in search of wisdom, experience. Also contain passages on education, politics, philosophy.

Rabi, Isidor Isaac (1898-), American physicist, b. Austria. Awarded Nobel Prize for Physics (1944) for study of molecular beams resulting in highly accurate calculation of magnetic properties of atoms.

rabies or **hydrophobia,** infectious virus disease of mammals, affecting brain and spinal cord. Transmitted in saliva of infected animals, usually by biting; symptoms incl. fever, delirium, muscle spasms, inability to drink, paralysis. Incubation period 10 days to several months. No known treatment; early administration of vaccine usually effective.

Raccoon

raccoon, *Procyon lotor,* medium-sized North American mammal, with mask-like facial markings and black ringed tail. Nocturnal, largely arboreal; classed as carnivore, it is omnivorous, immersing all food in water before eating.

race, in biology, term used to denote subspecies or variety of species, differing slightly in characteristics from typical species member.

Rachel, pseud. of Elisa Félix (1820-58), French actress. Noted in tragedy, esp. works of Racine.

Rachmaninov, Sergei Vasilyevich (1873-1943), Russian composer, pianist. Works, highly romantic in style, incl. symphonies, concertos, piano music, *eg*

Rachmaninov

Preludes. The *Rhapsody on a Theme of Paganini* for piano and orchestra is esp. popular. Lived mainly in US after 1917.

Racibórz (Ger. *Ratibor*), town of S Poland, on R. Oder. Pop. 39,000. River port; engineering. In Prussian Silesia 1745-1945.

Racine, Jean (1639-99), French dramatist. Famous for classical tragedies of passion, *Andromaque* (1007), *Iphigénie en Aulide* (1674), *Phèdre* (1677). Also wrote comedy satirizing legal system, *Les Plaideurs* (1668).

Racine, port of SE Wisconsin, US; on L. Michigan. Pop. 95,000. Agric. machinery, electrical equipment mfg. Grew after railway link and harbour were improved.

rackets or **racquets,** ball-and-racket game played on enclosed court by 2 or 4 persons. Ball is struck against endwall. Modern form developed in England in 19th cent.; SQUASH RACKETS is variant played on smaller court.

Rackham, Arthur (1867-1939), English watercolour painter and illustrator. Known for his illustrations of books, esp. children's books, *eg Peter Pan* (1906), *Alice in Wonderland* (1907).

radar, system employing transmitted and reflected radio waves to detect presence of objects and determine their position, distance, height or speed. Also used for navigation in ships, aircraft.

Radcliffe, Ann, née Ward (1764-1823), English novelist. Known for 'gothick' romances, esp. *The Mysteries of Udolpho* (1794).

Radcliffe-Brown, Alfred Reginald (1881-1955), British social anthropologist. Attempted to develop general laws for social investigation using concept of 'function'. Wrote *The Andaman Islanders* (1922).

Radek, Karl (1885-c 1939), Soviet political leader, journalist, b. Poland. Helped reorganize German Communist Party after abortive revolution of 1918. Returned to USSR, became member of Comintern executive; wrote for *Izvestia*. Prob. died in prison following Stalinist purge (1937).

radiant energy, energy which is transmitted in form of electromagnetic energy, *eg* heat, light, X-rays. Radiant heat can be communicated from source to observer through a vacuum or intervening medium without heating it.

radiation, see ELECTROMAGNETIC RADIATION.

radiation sickness, disease resulting from exposure to uncontrolled radiation, esp. X-rays or that resulting from nuclear explosions. Effects incl. genetic damage, cancer of skin and blood cells, *etc.*

Radić, Stefan (1871-1928), Yugoslav politician. After WWI, supported Croatian unity with Serbia and Montenegro. Later opposed Serbian domination of Yugoslavia; assassinated in legislature.

radical, in chemistry, group of 2 or more atoms that acts as single unit and maintains its identity in chemical reactions; usually incapable of independent existence.

Radiguet, Raymond (1903-23), French novelist. Known esp. for novel of adolescence, *Le Diable au corps* (1923).

radio, transmission of electric signals by means of electromagnetic radiation generated by high-frequency alternating current. Maxwell postulated existence of radio waves (1873) and Hertz demonstrated their existence (1888); Marconi demonstrated their use in communication (1895).

radioactive dating, determination of age of objects or materials by estimation of its content of radioactive isotopes. Radioactive carbon 14, produced in the atmosphere by action of cosmic rays and absorbed into living tissue, is used to estimate age of archaeological specimens.

radioactivity, spontaneous disintegration of atomic nuclei of certain elements said to be radioactive, *eg* radium, uranium, thorium. Accompanied by emission of alpha or beta particles and possibly gamma rays. Radioactivity can be induced in elements not naturally radioactive by neutron bombardment in nuclear reactor.

radio astronomy, study of heavenly bodies by analysis of radio waves which they emit. These radio waves were first detected by Jansky (1932). Emission sources incl. bodies too distant for optical observation as well as non-luminous or dark stars, and larger bodies in Solar System, *eg* Sun, Jupiter.

radiography, use of X-rays to produce images on photographic material. Used in medicine and industry.

radiology, use of radiation in diagnosis and treatment of disease. X-rays are used to photograph living bone and tissue and also to destroy abnormal cells (*eg* cancer cells). Gamma rays from cobalt 60 also used to cure cancer.

radio range, system of application of radio to marine and air navigation. Usually consists of unattended 'beacons' emitting a constant, identifiable radio signal. Ships and aircraft may take bearings on the beacon (using a receiver with a directionally sensitive antenna) and plot their position.

Radish

radish, *Raphanus sativus,* annual plant of mustard family, native to Europe and Asia. Pungent, fleshy root eaten raw as relish.

Radisson, Pierre Esprit (*c* 1632-1710), French fur trader in North America. Explored Lake Superior and Minnesota. Later worked for the English, voyaging to Hudson Bay for furs (1668). His successful mission led to formation of Hudson's Bay Co. (chartered 1670).

radium (Ra), naturally occurring radioactive element; at. no. 88, mass no. of most stable isotope 226. Occurs in pitchblende and other uranium ores; formed by disintegration of uranium 238. Discovered (1898) by the Curies. Used to treat cancer and in luminous paints.

Radnorshire, former county of EC Wales, now in Powys. Mountainous, incl. Radnor Forest. Sheep rearing; reservoirs. Co. town was Presteigne.

Radom, city of EC Poland. Pop. 161,000. Railway jct., agric. machinery mfg. Ancient settlement, New Radom founded 14th cent. by Casimir the Great; seat of Polish diets 14th-16th cent. Under Russian rule 1815-1919.

radon (Rn), radioactive gaseous element; at. no. 86, mass no. of most stable isotope 222. Formed as immediate disintegration product of radium; one of the inert gases.

Raeburn, Sir Henry (1756-1823), Scottish painter. Influenced by Reynolds, he portrayed many of the leading personalities of Scotland. Works incl. *The Macnab* (1803-13).

Raeder, Erich (1876-1960), German admiral. Commander of German navy from 1928; planned invasion of Norway, Greece. Dismissed by Hitler (1943). Imprisoned for war crimes (1946-55).

Raffles, Sir Thomas Stamford (1781-1826), British colonial official. Served with East India Co.; masterminded capture of Java from the Dutch (1811). As lieutenant governor of Java (1811-16), reorganized its admin. and commerce. Acquired Singapore (1819) and began its settlement.

Ragged robin

ragged robin, *Lychnis flos-cuculi,* slender perennial herb native to Europe and N Asia. Pink flowers with ragged-looking petals. Also called cuckoo flower.

Raglan, Fitzroy James Henry Somerset, 1st Baron (1788-1855), British army officer. Served on Wellington's staff at Waterloo (1815). Commanded the British expeditionary force in the Crimea, where he won the battle of Inkerman (1854); blamed for the failure to take Sevastopol.

Ragnarok, in Norse myth, destruction of world in last great battle between the Gods and forces of chaos led by Loki and giants. Would start with ice age and lead to new golden age.

ragtime, style of piano music using syncopated melodic lines over rigid march-like bass. Introduced in 1890s, became widely popular; lost popularity to jazz in 1920s. Principal composer of rags was Scott Joplin.

Ragusa, town of SC Sicily, Italy, cap. of Ragusa prov. Pop. 59,000. Oil production, asphalt mining. Ancient ruins of *Hybla Heraea.*

ragweed, any of genus *Ambrosia* of plants of daisy family, native to North America. Pollen of common ragweed or hogweed, *A. artemisiifolia,* and great ragweed, *A. trifida,* is a major cause of hay fever.

ragworm, annelid worm of Nereidae family, order Polychaeta. Largely marine, living under stones or burrowing in mud and sand. Commonly used for bait.

ragwort, see GROUNDSEL.

Rahman [Putra], Tunku Abdul (1903-   ), Malaysian politician, PM (1963-70). First PM of Malaya at independence (1957). Advised formation of Malaysia federation (created 1963).

Raikes, Robert (1735-1811), English philanthropist. Estab. 1st Sunday school in Gloucester (1780) for poor children, starting movement which spread throughout England, later US.

Common ragweed

rail, marsh bird of Rallidae family, with short wings and tail. Species incl. water rail, *Rallus aquaticus,* of Europe and Asia, noted for piercing cry.

railway, transport system running on fixed rails. Early railways were developed for use in mines. Important innovations incl. introduction of iron rails in 18th cent. and building of 1st locomotive to run on rails (Trevithick, 1804). Stockton-Darlington line (1825) was 1st to carry passengers regularly, and Liverpool-Manchester line (1830) was 1st to use steam locomotives exclusively. In US, Baltimore and Ohio Railroad (1830), operated at first by horses, was 1st public railway. Railway had important part in development of W North America. In 20th cent., steam gave way to electric and diesel power. Modern developments incl. high-speed trains, *eg* those running between Tokyo and Osaka in Japan.

rain, drops of condensed atmospheric water vapour brought to earth by force of gravity. Varieties incl.: orographic, found in mountain areas; cyclonic, associated with depressions; convectional, common in equatorial regions. Rain can be artificially produced by 'seeding' clouds with silver iodide crystals.

rainbow, arc of colours of SPECTRUM seen in sky during rainy weather. Caused by reflection and refraction of sunlight through raindrops. Primary rainbow has red on outside, violet on inside. Secondary rainbow, in which colours are reversed, formed by 2 internal reflections.

Raine, Kathleen Jessie (1908-   ), English poet. Works, *eg Stone and Flower* (1943), *The Pythoness* (1949), reflect belief in poetry as spiritual mythology. Also known for Blake criticism.

Rainier III, orig. Rainier de Grimaldi (1923-   ), ruling prince of Monaco (1949-   ). Married American film actress Grace Kelly (1956).

Rainier, Mount, peak of W Washington, US; highest in Cascade Range, at 4392 m (14,410 ft). In Mt. Rainier National Park.

Rainy Lake, on Ontario-Minnesota border, C Canada-US. Area 890 sq km (345 sq mi). Drained by Rainy R. into Lake of the Woods. Has many isls. Tourist resort.

Rais or **Retz, Gilles de Laval, Seigneur de** (1404-40), French soldier. Fought with distinction against English, accompanying Joan of Arc in her campaigns. Confessed in ecclesiastical court to abusing and murdering over 100 children. Hanged on witchcraft charge. Thought to be original Bluebeard.

raised beach, strip of flat land, formerly beach, raised above sea level by land rising or sea level falling. May be several, producing step-like landscape near coast.

raisin, sun-dried fruit of certain varieties of sweet white grape. Varieties incl. sultana and currant. California, Australia and Mediterranean region are main production centres.

Rajagopalachari, Chakravarti (1878-1972), Indian statesman. Prominent in Indian National Congress after WWI; backed Gandhi's policy of non-cooperation with British. Supported formation of separate state for Indian Moslems. Governor-general of independent India (1948-50).

Rajasthan, state of NW India. Area c 342,000 sq km (132,000 sq mi); pop. 25,724,000; cap. Jaipur. Thar Desert in W borders on Pakistan. Mainly agric. economy; grain, cotton.

Rajkot, city of Gujarat state, W India. Pop. 300,000. Railway jct.; grain trade, flour milling. Cap. of formerly princely state of Rajkot in Kathiawar penin.

Rajputs, land-owning warrior caste, formerly dominant in Rajputana (roughly coextensive with Rajasthan, N India). After British conquest of India, many Rajput princes retained independent states.

Rákóczy, Francis (1676-1735), Hungarian nobleman. Led unsuccessful uprising, supported by Hungarian Calvinists, against Habsburg rule in Hungary (1703-11). Died in exile. Commemorated in 'Rákóczy March', used by Berlioz.

Raleigh or **Ralegh, Sir Walter** (c 1552-1618), English courtier, navigator, writer; favourite of Elizabeth I. Made unsuccessful attempt to estab. 'Virginia' colony in North America. Introduced tobacco, potatoes into Britain. Under James I, convicted of treason and imprisoned in the Tower (1603), where he began his *History of the World.* Beheaded on original treason charge after failure of voyage to the Orinoco in search of gold (1616).

Raleigh, cap. of North Carolina, US. Pop. 124,000. Tobacco trade; electrical and textile industs. Cap. from 1788.

Ramadan, ninth month of Moslem year; period of daily fasting from sunrise to sunset. Commemorates first revelation of the Koran.

Raman, Sir Chandrasekhara Venkata (1888-1970), Indian physicist. Awarded Nobel Prize for Physics (1930) for study of scattering of light; Raman effect describes change in frequency of light passing through transparent medium.

Ramat Gan, town of C Israel. Pop. 117,000. Textiles, food processing. Founded 1921.

Ramayana, Indian epic. Written c 3rd cent. BC, tells story of Rama in 7 books. Immense popularity in India caused adaptation in most vernacular languages, incl. 2 famous medieval versions in Hindi and Tamil.

Rameau, Jean Philippe (1683-1764), French composer. Wrote pioneering treatises on theory of harmony. Began career as opera writer with *Hippolyte et Aricie* (1733), but his style was later considered obsolete. Noted for harpsichord pieces.

Ramée, Marie Louise de la, see OUIDA.

Rameses or **Ramses II** (d. 1225 BC), Egyptian king (1292-1225 BC). Fought for 15 years against Hittites, concluding peace treaty with them in 1272. Splendour of his reign marked by building of temples at Karnak and Thebes; temple at Abu Simbel bears 4 colossal figures of him.

ramie or **China grass,** *Boehmeria nivea,* perennial plant of nettle family, native to SE Asia. Cultivated for strong, silky fibre of stems used in cloth mfg.

Ramillies, village of C Belgium. Scene of French defeat (1706) by British, Dutch and Danish (under Marlborough) in War of Spanish Succession.

Ramsay, Allan (c 1685-1758), Scottish poet. Known for pastoral comedy, *The Gentle Shepherd* (1725), collections of Scots songs, ballads, *eg The Tea Table Miscellany* (1724-37). His son, **Allan Ramsay** (1713-1784) was a noted portrait painter.

Ramsay, Sir William (1852-1916), Scottish chemist. Discovered, with various collaborators, the 5 inert gases in the atmosphere. Awarded Nobel Prize for Chemistry (1904).

Ramsey, [Arthur] Michael (1904-   ), English churchman, archbishop of Canterbury (1961-74). A leading advocate of ECUMENISM.

Ramsey, town of Isle of Man, UK. Pop. 5000. Port; seaside resort.

Ramsgate, mun. bor. of Isle of Thanet, Kent, SE England. Pop. 39,000. Resort; fishing, yachting.

Rancagua, town of C Chile; indust. and agric. centre in Andean foothills. Pop. 95,000. Important copper mines nearby. Flour milling, fruit canning. Has railway link with Teniente copper mine.

Rand, The, see WITWATERSRAND, South Africa.

Rangoon, cap. and main port of Burma, near mouth of R. Rangoon. Pop. 3,187,000. Exports rice, teak, petroleum. Dominated by gold-spired Shwe Dagon pagoda, major Buddhist shrine. Cap. of region from 1753. Taken by British (1824, 1852); cap. of united Burma (1886). Severely damaged during WWII Japanese occupation.

Ranjitsinhji, Jam Sahib (1872-1933), English cricketer, b. India. A stylish batsman, he was first man to score over 3000 runs in a season. Was maharajah of Nawanagar.

Rank, Otto (1884-1939), Austrian psychoanalyst. Early disciple of Freud, but held birth trauma, rather than Oedipus complex, to be source of neurosis. Used Freudian analysis to interpret myth.

Ranke, Leopold von (1795-1886), German historian. First to employ objective technique in historical analysis; made extensive use of contemporary material in official archives. Works incl. histories of Germany, France, also world history *Weltgeschichte* (1881–8).

Ransom, John Crowe (1888-1974), American critic, poet. Founded influential *Kenyon Review.* Wrote philosophical literary criticism, *eg The New Criticism* (1941). Poetry in *Selected Poems* (1945).

Ransome, Arthur Mitchell (1884-1967), English author. Known for realistic children's adventure stories, *eg Swallows and Amazons* (1931), usually with Lake District, Norfolk Broads setting. Also wrote criticism, travel books.

Ranunculaceae, family of dicotyledonous plants with characteristic divided leaves. Incl. buttercup, anemone, delphinium.

Raoult, François Marie (1830-1901), French chemist. Formulated law stating that in liquid, change in vapour pressure in a solution is proportional to ratio of number of solvent molecules to solute molecules; law useful in finding molecular weights.

Rapallo, town of Liguria, NW Italy. Pop. 21,000. Port, resort on Riviera di Levante. Treaties between Italy and Yugoslavia (1920), Russia and Germany (1922) signed here.

rape, several plants of genus *Brassica,* esp. *B. napus* and *B. campestris.* Widespread in N hemisphere. Grown extensively for forage. Seeds yield edible oil and mustard substitute.

Raphael: *Plato,* detail of *The School of Athens*

Raphael, archangel in Apocryphal OT book of Tobit.

Raphael, real name Raffaello Sanzio (1483-1520), Italian painter. One of the creators of the High Renaissance, his works are known for their calm perfection of line and colour. Works incl. *The Betrothal of the Virgin, Sistine Madonna.* Executed Vatican murals, notably *The School of Athens* and the *Disputa.*

rare earths, oxides of the lanthanide series of elements; much alike in physical and chemical properties. Name also applied to LANTHANIDES themselves.

Rarotonga, main isl. of Cook Isls., SC Pacific Ocean. Area 67 sq km (26 sq mi); main town Avarua. Produces fruit, copra. Discovered 1823, admin. by New Zealand from 1901.

Ras Addar, see BON, CAPE, Tunisia.

Rashid, *see* ROSETTA, Egypt.

Rasht or **Resht,** city of N Iran, cap. of Gilan prov. Pop. 170,000. In fertile region near Caspian Sea; produces rice, silk.

Rasmussen, Knud Johan Victor (1879-1933), Danish explorer, ethnologist, b. Greenland. Sought to prove that Eskimo originated in Asia. Crossed the Northwest Passage by dog sled. Works incl. *Across Arctic America* (1927).

European raspberry

raspberry, various shrubs of genus *Rubus* of rose family. Grown in temperate regions for soft, edible berries. European *R. idaeus* and North American and Asian *R. strigosus* yield red fruit, North American *R. occidentalis* yields black.

Rasputin

Rasputin, Grigori Yefimovich (1872-1916), Russian monk. Gained power over the tsarina who believed he could cure her son, Alexis, of hæmophilia. His corrupting influence over state affairs led to his murder by a group of noblemen.

rat, one of many long-tailed rodents of Muridae family, of worldwide distribution. Species incl. BLACK RAT, BROWN RAT.

Ratel

ratel, nocturnal carnivorous mammal, genus *Mellivora,* with grey pelt above and black below. Resembles badger, but larger. Species incl. African *M. capensis* and Indian *M. indica.* Also called honey badger.

Rathenau, Walther (1867-1922), German industrialist, statesman. A founder of Democratic Party in 1918, he became minister of reconstruction (1921) and foreign minister (1922). Murdered by anti-Jewish nationalists.

Rathlin, isl. off N Northern Ireland, in former Co. Antrim. Has 6th cent. church founded by St Columba. Traditional scene of Robert the Bruce's encounter with spider (1306).

Ratibor, *see* RACIBÓRZ, Poland.

rationalism, in philosophy, doctrine that truth comes wholly from reason without aid from senses or intuition. Opposed to EMPIRICISM. Implies belief in mind's ability to read the true order of the outside world. Exponents incl. Descartes, Leibnitz, Spinoza.

rational number, number expressed as a quotient of 2 integers; integers are rational numbers whose denominators are 1. Also called fraction.

Ratisbon, *see* REGENSBURG, West Germany.

rattan, climbing palms of genera *Calamus* and *Daemonorops* native to tropical Asia. Long stems used for Malacca canes and in wickerwork.

Rattigan, Terence Mervyn (1911-), English playwright. Known for popular narrative dramas, *eg French without Tears* (1936), *The Winslow Boy* (1946), *Separate Tables* (1954), film scripts.

rattlesnake, venomous New World snake of pit viper family. Loose horny tail segments produce characteristic rattle when shaken. Diamondback, *Crotalus adamanteus,* is largest and most dangerous.

Rauschenberg, Robert (1925-), American artist. A formative influence on pop art; has used collage, silk screen printing, and combinations of disparate objects. Works incl. *Monogram,* a stuffed goat encircled by a tyre.

Ravel, Maurice (1875-1937), French composer. His early works are often poetic and atmospheric. Master of orchestration; works incl. ballet *Daphnis et Chloé,* orchestral pieces, *eg Bolero, Rhapsodie espagnole,* chamber music, piano pieces, *eg Miroirs.*

Raven

raven, *Corvus corax,* large bird of crow family, found on cliffs and mountains of N hemisphere. Glossy black plumage, large pointed bill.

Ravenna, city of Emilia-Romagna, NC Italy, cap. of Ravenna prov. Pop. 133,000. Indust. centre, agric. market. Cap. of Western Empire from AD 402, Ostrogothic cap. under Odoacer, Theodoric. Many Byzantine buildings, mosaics, *eg* church of St Vitale. Tomb of Dante.

Rawalpindi, city of N Pakistan. Pop. 615,000. Railway engineering, chemical mfg; Pakistani army hq. Interim cap. of Pakistan from 1959 until completion of nearby Islamabad.

Rawlinson, Sir Henry Creswicke (1810-95), English orientalist. Copied (1835) cuneiform inscription at Behistan (in modern Iran) making possible decipherment of Assyrian text.

Ray, Satyajit (1921-), Indian film director. First known for 'Apu' trilogy, incl. *Pather Panchali* (1954); continued to experiment with story, technique, as in *The Adventures of Goopy and Bagha* (1968), *Distant Thunder* (1973).

ray, any of various cartilaginous fish of order Hypotremata, with flattened body, huge pectoral fins and whip-like tail. Many species carry stinging organs. Families incl. sting rays, eagle rays and mantas or devil rays.

ray, in physics, straight line along which light or other radiation is regarded as propagating from its source. Name also applied to streams of particles emitted by radioactive substances or of electrons in vacuum tubes.

Rayleigh, John William Strutt, 3rd Baron (1842-1919), English physicist. Contributed to many branches of physics, incl. sound, optics, elasticity, radiation. Awarded Nobel Prize for Chemistry (1904) for discovery with Ramsay of argon.

rayon, synthetic fibre made from cellulose, usually obtained from wood pulp. Two most important forms are made either by forcing cellulose acetate through fine holes and allowing solvent to evaporate in warm air or by VISCOSE PROCESS.

Razin, Stenka (d. 1671), Russian Don Cossack leader. Led marauding band of Cossacks who pillaged lower Volga (1670); captured Volgograd and Astrakhan. Later joined by oppressed peasants in revolt against govt.; defeated and executed.

Razorbill

razorbill, *Alca torda,* seabird of auk family. Plumage black above, white below; bill crossed by white band. Nests colonially on Atlantic coasts.

razorshell, marine bivalve mollusc with long razor-shaped shell. Burrows rapidly in sand when disturbed. Species incl. *Solen marginatus.*

Read, Sir Herbert Edward (1893-1968), English critic. Known for essays on art, poetry incl. *Reason and Romanticism* (1926), *To Hell with Culture* (1963). Also wrote poetry, novel reflecting anarchist beliefs, *The Green Child* (1935).

Reade, Charles (1814-84), English author. Known for historical romance of Reformation, *The Cloister and the Hearth* (1861). Also wrote social propaganda novels, *eg Hard Cash* (1863) on corrupt asylums.

Reading, co. bor. and co. town of Berkshire, S England, at confluence of Thames, Kennet rivers. Pop. 132,000. Railway jct.; biscuits; seed nurseries. Noted agric. work at univ. (1926).

Reading, town of SE Pennsylvania, US; on Schuylkill R. Pop. 88,000. Railway centre; iron and steel products. Hist. munitions indust.

Reagan, Ronald Wilson (1911-), American politician. Film actor before entering politics. Governor of California (1967-75), narrowly defeated by Ford for Republican presidential candidacy (1976).

realism, in medieval philosophy, theory that universal concepts have a real existence and are not merely conveniences of classification. Opposed to NOMINALISM. In scholasticism, St Thomas Aquinas is main exponent. Also has specialized use in modern epistemology to denote theory that objects exist independently of our perception, *ie* opposite of IDEALISM.

real number, any number expressible as a possibly infinite decimal. Those expressed by non-repeating decimal are called irrational (*eg* π); those expressed by repeating decimal are called rational (*eg* $\frac{1}{3}$ = 0.333....).

Réaumur, René Antoine Ferchault de (1683-1757), French scientist. Invented alcohol thermometer and devised temperature scale in which boiling point of water is 80°. Worked on methods of making steel and wrote on insect natural history.

Rebellion of 1837, short-lived uprising in Upper and Lower Canada protesting against British admin. policies in Canada. Insurgents advocated that office holders be elected rather than appointed by Crown. Most of leaders, incl. W.L. MACKENZIE and L.J. PAPINEAU, escaped to US.

recall, type of referendum, device intended to give electorate direct control over its representative by voting for his resignation. Used first in Switzerland, adopted by some states in US.

Récamier, Jeanne Françoise Julie, née Bernard (1777-1849), French literary hostess. Her circle incl. Mme de Staël, Sainte-Beuve, Chateaubriand.

Recife, Atlantic port of NE Brazil, cap. of Pernambuco state. Pop. 1,061,000. Sugar, coffee, cotton exports. Canals link 3 parts of city (named 'Venice of Brazil'). Founded 1548, has many notable churches, naval station, airport.

Recklinghausen, city of W West Germany, in Ruhr. Pop. 125,000. Coalmining, iron founding, brewing.

reclamation of land, conversion of unproductive land into land suitable for human settlement, cultivation or indust. development. Methods incl. drainage (*eg* Dutch polders), irrigation and flood control (*eg* Al Jazirah scheme, Sudan), control of soil erosion.

Reconstruction, term applied to US post-Civil War era, during which programme to reorganize defeated states and reintegrate them into Union was adopted. To enforce Negro enfranchisement in South, Reconstruction Act (1867) passed by Congress estab. 5 military districts. Structure broke down as South was overrun by CARPETBAGGERS. Civil govt. restored by 1876.

recorder, wind instrument of flute type. Blown from end through whistle mouthpiece; usual sizes are descant or soprano, treble or alto, tenor and bass. Developed in medieval times and popular in 16th-18th cents. until replaced by flute. Revived in 20th cent.

rectifier, in electronics, device for converting alternating current into direct current. Types in use incl. thermionic valve and semiconductors.

rector, in Church of England, clergyman in charge of parish who formerly held rights to all its tithes, unlike a vicar who is paid a stipend.

rectum, in anatomy, terminal part of large intestine, opening into the anal canal.

Red, river of SE Asia. Rises in S China (Yunnan prov.), flows *c* 1175 km (730 mi) SE through North Vietnam to Gulf of Tonkin. Delta forms economic centre of North Vietnam.

Red, river of C US and Canada. Formed at river jct. in North Dakota. Flows N 500 km (310 mi) through Minnesota into L. Winnipeg, Manitoba. Flows through fertile wheat region.

Red, river of SC US. Flows 1967 km (1222 mi) from N Texas to Oklahoma border, then SE through Arkansas, Louisiana to join Mississippi R.

red algae, any of division Rhodophyta of ALGAE that contain a red pigment which masks the green chlorophyll. Distinguished by their sexual reproduction. Mostly found as shrubby masses in depths of warm oceans.

Red Army [Worker-Peasant Red Army], official name (1918-45) of Soviet Army. Set up to combat White Armies of counter-revolutionary forces after Bolshevik seizure of power (1917).

red blood cell, see BLOOD.

Redbridge, bor. of NE Greater London, England. Pop. 239,000. Created 1965 from Ilford, Wanstead, Woodford, part of Dagenham (all in Essex).

Redbud (*Cercis siliquastrum*)

redbud or **Judas tree,** any of genus *Cercis* of mainly North American trees of Leguminosae family. Species incl. common redbud, *C. canadensis*. Traditionally, Judas hanged himself on Old World species.

red bug, one of various red insects of tropical areas. Incl. cotton stainer, genus *Dysdercus*, of S US which pierces cotton bolls, staining fibres.

Red Cross, international society for relief of suffering in time of war or disaster. International Committee of Red Cross founded (1863) on advocacy of J.H. Dunant (1828-1910). Delegates from 14 countries adopted Geneva Convention (1864), providing for neutrality of personnel treating wounded, *etc.* Over 100 national Red Cross societies now exist. Awarded Nobel Peace Prize (1917, 1944, 1963).

Red deer stag

red deer, *Cervus elaphus*, deer of temperate Europe and Asia. Branched antlers shed annually, reddish coat; fairly common game animal.

red giant, large star with relatively low surface temperature, between 10 and 100 times larger than Sun and *c* 100 times brighter. Most normal stars are believed to evolve into red giants as their hydrogen fuel is consumed.

Redgrave, Sir Michael Scudamore (1908-   ), English actor. Played at Old Vic, notably in Shakespearian roles. Has also appeared in films. His daughter, **Vanessa Redgrave** (1937-   ), actress, known for stage, film roles.

Red Guard, in China, Communist youth organization mobilized 1966-7 by Mao Tse-tung to enforce CULTURAL REVOLUTION. Declined following indust. strikes opposing their violent methods.

red-hot poker, herb of genus *Kniphofia*, native to S Africa. Bright red or orange poker-shaped flowers. *K. uvaria* is garden species.

Redi, Francesco (*c* 1626-*c* 1698), Italian naturalist, poet. Disproved theory of spontaneous generation by showing that no maggots form on protected meat. Poetry incl. ode *Bacchus in Tuscany* (1685).

Red Indians, see AMERICAN INDIANS.

Redmond, John Edward (1856-1918), Irish political leader. Leader of Irish Nationalists in Parliament after 1900. Supported Home Rule bill (1912). Opposed Easter Rebellion (1916); lost power to more radical Sinn Fein.

redpoll, *Acanthis flammea,* small grey-brown finch with crimson forehead. Found throughout N temperate areas.

Red River Rebellion (1869-70), revolt of Métis (French-Canadian halfbreeds) and Indians after transfer of Red River Settlement from Hudson's Bay Co. to Canada. Provisional govt. set up under RIEL. Revolt collapsed when troops sent against it.

Red Sea, narrow sea between NE Africa and SW Arabia, in Great Rift Valley. Length *c* 2400 km (1500 mi). Linked to Mediterranean by Gulf of Suez and Suez Canal; to Gulf of Aden by Str. of Bab-el-Mandeb.

redshank, *Tringa totanus,* wading bird, related to sandpiper, of Eurasia and N Africa. Long red legs.

red shift, in astronomy, displacement of spectral lines towards longer wavelengths at red end of spectrum of light from distant galaxies. Explained as a DOPPLER effect due to recession of galaxies; leads to Hubble's law that velocity is proportional to distance of source.

redstart, *Phoenicurus phoenicurus,* European bird of Turdinae family, with red tail and black throat. Name also applied to American warbler *Setophaga ruticilla;* male black and orange above, white below.

reduction, in chemistry, reaction opposite to oxidation. Originally denoted removal of oxygen from a substance or addition of hydrogen; now incl. reactions adding one or more electrons to atom or ion.

redwood, see SEQUOIA.

Reed, Sir Carol (1906-76), British film director. Best known for films in 1940s using screenplays by Graham Greene, eg *The Third Man* (1949).

Reed, John (1887–1920), American journalist. Worked for radical magazine *The Masses* after 1913, covered revolt of Pancho Villa. Best known for eye-witness account of Bolshevik coup in Petrograd (1917), *Ten Days that Shook the World* (1919). Buried at the Kremlin.

reed, several grasses, esp. of genus *Phragmites.* Cosmopolitan common reed, *P. communis,* is tall, stout aquatic grass. Dried stems used in thatching.

reed instrument, musical instrument in which sound derives from vibrating reed. In double reed instruments, eg oboe, bassoon, wind is blown between 2 reeds. Clarinet has single reed laid against wind aperture.

reed mace, see CATTAIL.

re-entry, return of missile or space vehicle into Earth's atmosphere. Enormous quantities of heat are generated by friction between molecules of air and speeding vehicle; a heat shield is designed to give protection from this heat.

Reeves, William Pember (1857-1932), New Zealand politician, writer. Minister for education and justice in Liberal govt. (1891-6). Estab. 1st compulsory state arbitration system in world. Wrote classic study of New Zealand, *The Long White Cloud* (1898).

referendum, see INITIATIVE.

refining, process by which impurities are removed from metals, petroleum, sugar, *etc.* Petroleum is refined by factional distillation and catalytic cracking; metals by electrolysis (*eg* for copper), amalgamation with mercury (*eg* for silver), leaching with cyanide (*eg* for gold).

reflex, in physiology, involuntary response to a stimulus, *eg* a sneeze, determined by nervous impulses. Stimulated receptor area causes sensory neurons to transmit nervous impulses to nerve cells in brain and spinal cord; these in turn transmit impulses to motor neurons which determine action of muscles, glands, *etc.*

Reformation, religious revolution in W Europe in 16th cent. Began as reform movement in RC church, evolved into doctrines of Protestantism. Begun in Germany by LUTHER and in Geneva by CALVIN. KNOX introduced Calvinism to Scotland. Spread of Reformation also implemented by church-state political conflict and rise of middle class, commerce. In England, Henry VIII rejected papal control and formed Church of England.

Reformation, Catholic, reform movement in RC church in 16th cent. as response to Protestant REFORMATION; popularly known as Counter-Reformation. Attempted to reform abuses within Church in order to protect traditional Roman Catholicism against Lutheranism. Implemented by Council of Trent (1545).

Reform Bills, in British history, legislation passed to liberalize House of Commons' representation. Whigs' **1832** bill enfranchised large indust. towns previously unrepresented, abolished numerous 'rotten boroughs' and extended vote to middle-class men. Derby-Disraeli's **1867** bill more than doubled franchise by giving vote to working men in towns. Gladstone's **1884** bill relaxed rural qualifications.

Reformed Church in America, founded by Dutch Protestant settlers in New Netherland colony; formerly known as Dutch Reformed Church. Gave civil allegiance to England after her conquest of colony (1664). Remains a major denomination.

refraction, in physics, change in direction of ray of light passing from one medium to another; caused by light travelling at different velocities in different media. Snell's law states that ratio of sine of angle of incidence to sine of angle of refraction is a constant called refractive index of that pair of media. The refractive index of a medium is usually given in relation to a vacuum.

refrigeration, process of reducing temperature of substances. In refrigerators, vaporized refrigerant, usually ammonia or Freon, is compressed and forced through a condenser, where it loses heat and liquefies. It vaporizes in coils of refrigeration compartment and draws heat from materials placed there. Refrigerant returns to compressor and cycle is repeated.

Regency, in British history, last 9 years (1811-20) of reign of George III. Because of king's periodic insanity, govt. conducted in name of Prince of Wales, later George IV. Period of social unrest, much literary and artistic activity.

regeneration, regrowth or restoration of damaged tissue. In higher mammals, incl. man, regeneration is limited to healing of wounds, production of blood cells and scar tissue. In lower animals, entire new limbs, tails, *etc,* can be grown.

Regensburg or **Ratisbon,** city of SE West Germany, at confluence of Danube and Regen. Pop. 132,000. River port, railway jct. Roman *Castra Regina*; episcopal see from 739. Prosperous medieval centre until 15th cent. Armaments mfg. during WWII, heavily bombed.

Reggio di Calabria (anc. *Rhegium*), city of SW Italy, on Str. of Messina, cap. of Reggio di Calabria prov. Pop. 162,000. Port, resort, agric. market. Scene of riots (1970) following removal of Calabrian cap. to Catanzaro. Badly damaged by earthquakes 1783, 1908.

Reggio nell'Emilia, city of Emilia-Romagna, NC Italy, cap. of Reggio nell'Emilia prov. Pop. 130,000. Agric., indust. centre, aero engines. Renaissance buildings.

Regina, prov. cap. of Saskatchewan, Canada; on Wascana Creek. Pop. 139,000. Railway jct., wheat trade centre; agric. machinery, car mfg., oil refining. Founded 1882. Cap. of Northwest Territs. (1883-1905). W hq. of Royal Canadian Mounted Police.

Regulus, Marcus Atilius (d. *c* 250 BC), Roman soldier. In 1st Punic War, invaded Africa, but was defeated and captured by Carthaginians (255). Sent to Rome to propose peace, but advised continuing war. Returned to Carthage as promised, where he was put to death.

Rehoboam, Hebrew king (*c* 931-*c* 914 BC), son of Solomon. During his reign, N tribes rebelled and formed new kingdom of Israel under Jeroboam I. He remained king of Judah in S.

Reich, Wilhelm (1897-1957), Austrian psychiatrist, resident in US after 1939. Works, incl. *The Function of the Orgasm* (1927), stress the importance of frequent sexual release to avoid neurosis. Ideas on therapeutic properties of all-pervading orgone energy led to imprisonment, in which state he died.

Reichenberg, *see* LIBEREC, Czechoslovakia.

Reichstag, name given to lower chamber of federal German legislature (1871–1945). Grew in power after 1919, but could be dissolved by the president. Under Hitler's regime, only National Socialist party was represented. Fire in Reichstag building (1933) gave Hitler pretext to suppress Communists.

Reid, Sir George Houston (1845-1918), Australian statesman, b. Scotland, PM (1904-5). Leader of Free Trade Party. First Australian high commissioner to London (1910-16).

Reid, Thomas (1710-96), Scottish philosopher. Sought to escape Hume's scepticism by positing self-evident knowledge. Founder of common sense or Scottish school. Works incl. *An Inquiry into the Human Mind* (1764).

Reigate, mun. bor. of Surrey, S England. Pop. 56,000. Incorporates Redhill.

Reign of Terror (1793-4), final period of French Revolution. Committee of Public Safety, led by Robespierre, controlled France; effected ruthless elimination of counter-revolutionaries (*c* 2500 guillotined). Ended with overthrow of Robespierre by National Convention.

Reims, *see* RHEIMS, France.

reincarnation or **metempsychosis,** belief common to several religions that, after death, soul of human being enters another body, human or animal. In Hinduism and Buddhism, moral conduct determines quality of subsequent incarnations. Also occurs in Greek thought, *eg* in Pythagoras, Plato.

reindeer, *Rangifer tarandus,* large deer of Arctic regions of Europe and Asia. Both sexes have long branched antlers. Can be domesticated; milk, flesh and skin valued. Caribou is related species. Numbers greatly reduced by hunting.

reindeer moss, LICHEN of genus *Cladonia.* Grey, tufted *C. rangiferina* of Arctic regions is eaten by reindeer and caribou.

Reinhardt, Max, pseud. of Max Goldmann (1873-1943), Austrian stage director. Pioneered several theatrical techniques, incl. mechanical effects, lighting. Settled in US (1933).

Lord Reith

Reith, John Charles Walsham, 1st Baron Reith of Stonehaven (1889-1971), British public official. First director-general of British Broadcasting Corporation, creating and developing radio services and world's first regular TV transmissions. Stamped BBC with own personality, ideals.

Réjane, pseud. of Gabrielle Réju (1857-1920), French actress. Best known as Catherine in Sardou's *Madame Sans-Gêne* (1893). Played leading roles in *Zaza, La Passerelle.*

relative humidity, measure of moisture of atmosphere. Equals ratio of mass of water vapour per unit volume of air to maximum mass of water vapour same volume of air could contain at same temperature; usually expressed as percentage.

relativity theory, physical theory of space, time, energy and gravitation formulated by Einstein. Special theory of 1905 is limited to observers in state of uniform motion relative to each other. It assumes that the laws of physics take same form for all observers and that speed of light is same for all observers, irrespective of their own motion. Its consequences incl. principle that mass and energy are interchangeable, that it is impossible to travel at speed faster than that of light and that measurement of time depends on observer's motion (there is no absolute time). General theory of 1916 deals with observers not in state of uniform motion and is a geometric interpretation of gravitation. Its consequences incl. fact that light rays are deflected towards large gravitating bodies.

relay, electrical, device by which variations in one electric circuit control switching on and off of current in another circuit. May be mechanical switch operated by electromagnet; used in telegraphy and electrical control.

relics, objects associated with Jesus or saint, venerated in RC and Eastern Orthodox churches. Notable examples incl. pieces of the True Cross, Holy Nails of the iron crown of Lombardy, relics of St Edward the Confessor in Westminster Abbey. Medieval traffic in relics led to their cult being condemned by Protestant reformers.

religion, expression of belief in powers higher than man. Often involves attempts to explain origin and nature of universe, evolution of techniques to make the inexplicable more acceptable. Ethical concepts were introduced by BUDDHISM, JUDAISM, CHRISTIANITY, ISLAM. Religions are divided into 'revealed' *eg* Christianity where Jesus revealed word of God, and 'natural' *eg* Buddhism which is result of human speculation alone. *See* POLYTHEISM, MONOTHEISM.

Religion, Wars of, general term for series of civil wars in France (1562-98), fought between Huguenots (Protestants) and Catholics. After Huguenot leader, Henry of Navarre, became king of France (1589) and was converted to Catholicism, wars ended with Edict of NANTES (1598).

Remarque, Erich Maria (1898-1970), German novelist. Known for classic anti-war novels, *All Quiet on the Western Front* (1929), *A Time to Live and a Time to Die* (1954). Settled in US (1937).

Rembrandt: detail of self-portrait

Rembrandt [Harmensz van Rijn], (1606-69) Dutch painter, etcher. Estab. himself as successful portrait painter with *Anatomy Lesson of Dr Tulp.* Business declined with death of his wife in 1642; declared bankrupt 1656. His later series of portraits, esp. self-portraits, are masterpieces of psychological insight. Best known for *Night Watch* (1642). Enormous output incl. over 300 etchings, of which form he was a great master.

Remington, Eliphalet (1793-1861), American inventor. Estab. small-arms factory (1828), later expanded to make agricultural implements (1856). His son, **Philo Remington** (1816-89), perfected Remington breech-loading rifle and initiated manufacture of sewing machines (1870) and typewriters (1873).

Remonstrants, followers of ARMINIUS who presented a remonstrance in 1610 setting forth their differences from the Calvinism of the Dutch Reformed Church. Originally suppressed, recognized as independent church in 1795.

remora, any of Echeneidae family of marine fish. Dorsal fin modified to form oval sucking disc by which remora attaches itself to sharks, turtles, *etc.*

Remscheid, city of W West Germany, on R. Wupper. Pop. 137,000. Steel mfg., machine tools, cutlery.

Remus, see ROMULUS.

Renaissance (Fr., = rebirth), period of cultural and intellectual revival in W Europe (14th-16th cent.). Originated in Italy, where scholarship was stimulated by classical manuscripts, foundation of libraries and academies. Under patronage of popes and nobles, *eg* Medici, men of genius were encouraged to create works of an individuality and humanism unknown in Middle Ages. Study of classical models influenced architecture of Alberti, Brunelleschi; discoveries of laws of perspective by Donatello, Masaccio, *etc,* made painting, sculpture more realistic. Later masters incl. Leonardo da Vinci, Michelangelo, Raphael. Learning spread to other countries in 15th cent., hastened by invention of printing. Other major Renaissance figures incl. Josquin des Prés in music, Erasmus in humanism, Machiavelli in politics, Cervantes and Shakespeare in literature.

Renan, [Joseph] Ernest (1823-92), French philosopher, religious historian. Held that just society could only be attained through development of small elite. Took relativistic approach to religions. Best known for *Vie de Jésus* (1883).

Renault, Mary, pseud. of Mary Challans (1905-   ), English historical novelist. Known for novels on legend of Theseus *The King Must Die* (1958), *The Bull From the Sea* (1962). Other works incl. *The Charioteer* (1953), *The Last of the Wine* (1956).

Renfrewshire, former county of WC Scotland, now in Strathclyde region. Hilly in W, SE; elsewhere lowland. Dairying; oats, potatoes. Industs. incl. engineering, chemicals, textile mfg., whisky distilling, centred in Paisley, Greenock (shipbuilding). Co. town was **Renfrew,** port and former royal burgh on R. Clyde. Pop. 19,000. Engineering indust.

Reni, Guido (1575-1642), Italian painter of Bolognese school. Early exponent of Classicism, his sentimentalized religious works were highly regarded in 17th and 18th cents. Best-known work is fresco *Aurora* in Rome. Opened an academy in Bologna.

Rennes, city of NW France, at confluence of Ille and Vilaine, cap. of Ille-et-Vilaine dept. Pop. 181,000. Agric. trade centre, textile mfg.; univ. (1735). Hist. cap. of Brittany. Law courts were scene of Dreyfus case. Badly damaged by fire (1720) and during WWII.

rennet, substance extracted from membrane lining stomach of unweaned mammals, esp. calves. Contains enzyme rennin which curdles milk; used to make cheese and junkets.

Reno, resort of W Nevada, transport route on Truckee R. Pop. 73,000. Cattle, mining centre. Famous for legal gambling, quick divorces.

Renoir, Pierre Auguste (1841-1919), French artist. Leading impressionist, he was a noted figure painter, specializing in children and beautiful young women. Later returned to more classical style, devoting himself to well-rounded nudes. His son, **Jean Renoir** (1894-   ), is film director. Works incl. *La Grande Illusion* and *La Règle du jeu.*

reparations, payment made by defeated nation to victorious, to compensate for material losses incurred in war. After WWI, Dawes Plan (1924) awarded loan to Germany which had fallen behind in payments to Allies. Young Plan (1929) sought to ensure payment by mortgaging German railways and estab. Bank for International Settlements. After WWII, payment by Germany to Allies was to be effected by confiscation of assets and equipment.

Representatives, House of, *see* HOUSE OF REPRESENTATIVES.

repression, *see* DEFENCE MECHANISM.

reprieve, legal postponement of penalty, esp. death. In UK, prerogative of Crown, which acts on home secretary's advice. In US, prerogative of state governors, or president in federal cases, *eg* treason.

reproduction, process by which all living organisms produce new individuals. May be sexual or asexual. Asexual reproduction found in plants and lower animals; simplest form is by division of single cell (fission). Sexual reproduction involves union of male and female gamete to form a zygote.

Reptilia (reptiles), class of cold-blooded scaly-skinned vertebrates. Mainly terrestrial, with some aquatic varieties; oviparous. Dominant animal group in Mesozoic period; fossils show links between birds, mammals. Incl. turtles, tortoises, lizards, snakes, crocodiles, tuatara.

republic, state or nation in which supreme power rests in electorate and is exercised by elected representatives. Govt. of republic may be centralized (*eg* France), or federated (*eg* US).

Republican Party, in US, one of the two major political parties. Hist. linked with Hamilton's Federalists. Founded (1854) in opposition to slavery, consolidated with Lincoln's election (1860). Held power during RECONSTRUCTION, became party of business interest in late 19th cent.; T. ROOSEVELT split party (1912). Conservative policies resulted in blame for Depression (1929), after which held presidency twice (1953-61, 1969-77) and dominated by Democrats in Congress.

Requiem, in RC church, Mass for the repose of the souls of the dead. Consists of 8 sections, derived in part from ordinary Mass. Performed on All Souls' Day and at funerals. Has inspired notable musical settings, *eg* by Mozart, Verdi.

Resht, see RASHT.

resin, substance exuded from various plants, esp. pines and firs. Used in varnish, lacquer and medicines. Synthetic resins are used extensively in plastics indust.

resistance, electrical, property of conductor by which it resists flow of electric current, and converts part of the electrical energy into heat. From Ohm's law, resistance is measured by ratio of potential difference between ends of conductor to size of current flowing.

Resnais, Alain (1922-   ), French film director. Best known for *nouvelle vague* approach; experimented with time in *Last Year at Marienbad* (1961), also made *Hiroshima Mon Amour* (1959).

resolving power, in optics, measure of smallest distance between 2 points in image of an optical system (microscope or telescope) when the 2 points can be distinguished as separate.

resonance, in physics, sympathetic vibration of body in response to vibrations of some external source. Effect is greatest when natural frequency of body is reached by the exciting source.

Respighi, Ottorino (1879-1936), Italian composer. Produced bright, lyrical music, *eg Fountains of Rome,* but best known for arranging Rossini's music for the ballet *La Boutique fantasque.*

respiration, process by which living organisms take in oxygen from air or water, use it to oxidize carbohydrates, fats, *etc,* with subsequent release of energy, and give off products of oxidation, esp. carbon dioxide. Process describing taking in of oxygen and giving out of carbon dioxide is more properly called breathing.

Restif de la Bretonne, Nicolas Edmé (1734-1806), French author. Known for novels detailing low life of Paris, *eg Le Paysan perverti* (1775), *La Vie de mon père* (1779), *Aventures des jolies femmes* (1780-5).

Restoration, in English history, name given to re-estab. of monarchy on accession in 1660 of Charles II following collapse of Protectorate. Name also applies to entire period of Charles' reign.

Restoration, in French history, period of Bourbon rule, under Louis XVIII and Charles X, from abdication of Napoleon I (1814) to July Revolution (1830). Excluded return of Napoleon (Hundred Days) in 1815.

Restoration drama, name given to 2 types of play popular in England in late 17th cent.: the heroic play, partly inspired by French classical tragedy, *eg* Dryden's *Conquest of Granada,* and witty, often immoral comedies of manners, *eg* Congreve's *The Way of the World.*

resurrection, rising from death to life. Used esp. for rising of Jesus from the tomb and for rising of all dead at Last Judgment. Belief in resurrection of body also a tenet of Moslem belief.

retina, membrane lining back cavity of eyeball. Light-sensitive nerve endings (rods and cones) convey impulses to the brain via the optic nerve. Visual purple in rods makes them sensitive to dim light, but it is inactivated by bright light. Cones function in bright light and are responsible for colour vision and detailed vision.

Retz, Gilles de, see RAIS, GILLES DE.

Réunion, isl. in WC Indian Ocean, overseas dept. of France. Area *c* 2510 sq km (970 sq mi); pop. 477,000; cap. St Denis. Of volcanic origin, with one active volcano; rises to 3069 m (10,069 ft) at Piton des Neiges. Sugar cane leading crop; exports sugar, rum. Settled by French in 1642.

Reuter, Paul Julius, Baron de, orig. Israel Beer Josaphat (1816-99), British news agency founder-owner, b. Germany. Founded Reuters, world news agency based in London.

Reuther, Walter Philip (1907-70), American labour leader. Instrumental in organizing United Automobile Workers of America (UAW) in 1930s, became president (1946). Vice-president of AFL-CIO (1955-68), led UAW dispute with GEORGE MEANY.

Reval, see TALLINN.

Revelation, Apocalyptic book of NT, traditionally written by St John the Divine. Consists of prophetic vision of triumph of God and martyrs over evil.

Revere, Paul (1735-1818), American silversmith. Famous for ride (1775) from Charlestown to Lexington to warn Massachusetts patriots of advance by British troops at outbreak of American Revolution.

Revolution of 1848, series of revolts in Europe provoked by February Revolution in France, in which Louis Philippe was overthrown and republic estab. In Germany, popular uprising for united country quelled by Prussian army. In Hungary, attempts to estab. independence from Austria were unsuccessful; led to overthrow of Metternich. In Italy, 1st attempts to expel Austrians and unite country (*see* RISORGIMENTO) were defeated.

revolver, PISTOL with cylindrical breech rotated mechanically and bored with chambers for bullets which are fired in succession. Developed by Samuel Colt (1836).

revue, type of stage show consisting of loosely connected sketches, songs, often with satirical content.

Reykjavik

Reykjavik, cap. of Iceland, on Faxa Bay. Pop. 82,000. Admin., cultural centre. Port, fishing indust. (esp. cod, herring), textiles, publishing; univ. (1911). Founded 874. Natural hot water supply from nearby springs. Lutheran, RC cathedrals.

Reymont, Wladyslaw Stanislaw (1868-1925), Polish novelist. Best known for prose epic of village life, *The Peasants* (1902-9). Nobel Prize for Literature (1924).

Reynaud, Paul (1896-1966), French statesman. Succeeded Daladier as premier (1940), resigned in opposition to Pétain's acceptance of armistice with Germans; imprisoned 1940-5.

Reynolds, Sir Joshua (1723-92), English painter. Historically the most important British painter, he did much to raise status of artists in Britain. First president of the Royal Academy (1769); his *Discourses* delivered to the Academy enshrine his advocacy of the Grand Manner, style of history painting practised in 17th cent. academies. Painted numerous portraits.

Rhadamanthus, in Greek myth, son of Zeus and Europa, so renowned for his justice that he was made judge of dead in Hades.

Rhaeto-Romanic, Romance group of dialects in Italic branch of Indo-European family. Incl. Romansh, Ladin, Friulian. Former is one of four official languages of Switzerland, latter two spoken in Italian Tyrol, NE Italy.

Rhazes or **Rasis** (*c* 860-*c* 925), Persian physician, alchemist. First to distinguish between measles and smallpox. Writings describing careful observations of disease were widely distributed in Greek and Arabic.

Rhea, in Greek myth, a Titan; wife and sister of CRONUS. Helped Zeus overthrow Cronus.

rhea, any of Rheidae family of flightless South American birds, similar to ostrich. Three-toed feet, partially feathered head and neck. Species incl. common rhea, *Rhea americana.*

Rhee, Syngman (1875-1965), Korean statesman. Leader of drive for independence during Chinese, Japanese occupations. President of South Korea (1948-60) until exiled. Rule noted for corruption and repression.

Rheims (*Reims*), city of Champagne, NE France, on R. Vesle. Pop. 153,000. Centre of Champagne wine indust. (nearby caves provide storage), textile mfg.; univ. (1547). Clovis baptized here (496); coronation place of many French kings. Scene of surrender (1945) of Germany. Cathedral (13th cent.) badly damaged in WWI.

rhenium (Re), hard metallic element; at. no. 75, at. wt. 186.2. Very rare; found in molybdenum ores. Used in thermocouples and as a catalyst. Discovered 1925.

rheostat, instrument introduced into electric circuit to vary its resistance and control flow of current. Used to regulate brightness of electric lights, *etc.*

rhesus factor (Rh factor), protein present in red blood cells of 85% of people. Those having factor are said to be Rh positive, those without Rh negative. Transfusion of blood from Rh positive person to Rh negative person causes antibodies to form in latter's blood, resulting in agglutination of red blood cells. An Rh negative mother who has a positive baby may experience problems with later pregnancies, unless suitably treated.

rhesus monkey, *Macaca mulatta,* light brown long-haired macaque of SE Asia. Much used in medical and biological research.

rhetoric, see ORATORY.

rheumatic fever, acute inflammatory disease of lining and valves of the heart and of larger joints. Usually affects children and adolescents. Cause unknown, but is always preceded by infection with haemolytic streptococci.

rheumatoid arthritis, see ARTHRITIS.

Rheydt, city of W West Germany. Pop. 102,000. Textiles, machinery, chemicals mfg. Part of München-Gladbach (1929-33).

Rh factor, *see* RHESUS FACTOR.

Rhine, Joseph Banks (1895-   ), American investigator of extra-sensory perception. Known for work seeming to prove telepathy, precognition.

Rhine

Rhine (Ger. *Rhein*, Dutch *Rijn*), river of WC Europe. Flows 1320 km (820 mi) from SE Switzerland through W West Germany, Netherlands, joining R. Meuse before entering North Sea at Hook of Holland. Tributaries incl. Main, Moselle, Neckar. Forms parts of several national borders, esp. Franco-German. W Europe's main waterway, navigable below Basle; heavy barge traffic; linked to Ruhr indust. area. Vineyards; tourism in Rhine Gorge (Bingen to Bonn; incl. Lorelei). Former E frontier of Roman Gaul; picturesque medieval castles.

Rhine, Confederation of the, league of German princes formed (1806) under Napoleon. Disintegrated after Napoleon's retreat from Russia (1812-13).

Rhineland, area of W West Germany, on both sides of R. Rhine. Incl. parts of North Rhine-Westphalia, Rhineland-Palatinate, Hessen, Baden Württemberg. Occupied by Allies after WWI; demilitarized under treaty of Locarno within 50 km E of Rhine. Refortified by Hitler from 1936.

Rhineland-Palatinate, see PALATINATE, West Germany.

Black rhinoceros

rhinoceros, any of Rhinocerotidae family of massive thick-skinned herbivorous mammals of tropical Africa and Asia. One or two upright horns composed of matted hair on snout. Species incl. Indian rhinoceros, *Rhinoceros unicornis,* with 1 horn and black African rhinoceros, *Diceros bicornis,* with 2 horns. Numbers greatly reduced by hunting.

rhinoceros beetle, beetle of Dynastinae subfamily, male of which has rhinoceros-like horn on head. Species incl. *Dynastes tityus* of E US.

rhizome, creeping stem lying at or under the surface of soil. Differs from root in having scale leaves and leaves or shoots near tip. Produces roots from underside. Unlike root, does not die if cut and may become new plant. Rhizomatous plants incl. common iris, ginger.

Rhizopoda, class of Protozoa, incl. amoeba. Characterized by possession of pseudopodia (temporary protrusion of cell by movement of protoplasm), used for feeding and locomotion.

Rhode Island, New England state of US. Area 3144 sq km (1214 sq mi); pop. 950,000; cap. Providence. Smallest US state, named after isl. in Narragansett Bay. Mainly low-lying; important farming esp. poultry; fishing, tourist,

textile industs. Hist. rum, slave, molasses trade. Last of original 13 colonies to ratify US Constitution (1790).

Cecil Rhodes

Rhodes, Cecil John (1853-1902), British capitalist, colonial administrator. Acquired fortune through control of Kimberley diamond mines. As part of plan to estab. British rule in Africa from Cape to Cairo, advised annexation of Bechuanaland (1885), then formed British South Africa Co. (1889) to exploit area known later as Rhodesia. PM of Cape Colony (1890-5), supported British in Transvaal. Resigned over complicity in JAMESON Raid. Endowments incl. Rhodes Scholarships to Oxford Univ.

Rhodes (*Rhodos*), isl. of Greece, in SE Aegean Sea, largest of Dodecanese. Area 1404 sq km (542 sq mi); main town Rhodes. Ancient Rhodes *fl* 4th-3rd cent. BC, built 'Colossus of Rhodes' (destroyed by earthquake 224 BC). Held by Knights Hospitallers (1309-1523), ceded to Greece by Italy 1947.

Rhodesia

Rhodesia, republic of SC Africa. Area 391,000 sq km (151,000 sq mi); pop. 5,900,000; cap. Salisbury. Languages: Bantu, English. Religions: native, Christianity. Largely plateau, drained by Limpopo, Zambezi river systems. Tobacco growing, stock raising; rich in gold, asbestos, chrome, coal; h.e.p. from Kariba Dam. Admin. by British South Africa Co. (estab. by Rhodes) from 1889; became colony of Southern Rhodesia 1923. United federally (1953-63) with Northern Rhodesia (now ZAMBIA), Nyasaland (now MALAWI). Declared independence (UDI) 1965, republic from 1970. Regime not recognized by UN; increasing political and military pressure in mid-1970s to allow black majority rule.

rhodium (Rh), hard metallic element of the platinum group; at. no. 45, at. wt. 102.91. Occurs with and resembles platinum. Resists corrosion; used in alloys, electrical contacts, thermocouples and as a catalyst.

Rhododendron

rhododendron, genus of trees and shrubs of heath family, native to Asia but widely cultivated in N temperate regions. Mainly evergreen with red, purple or white flowers. See AZALEA.

Rhodope Mountains, range of N Greece and S Bulgaria. Runs NW-SE, rising to 2924 m (9596 ft) in Rila Mts., Bulgaria.

Rhondda, mun. bor. of Glamorgan, S Wales. Pop. 89,000. Coalmining; light industs. Severely hit by Depression (1930s).

Rhône, river of W Switzerland and SE France. Flows *c* 810 km (505 mi) from Rhône glacier (Switzerland) via L. Geneva, Lyons, Avignon to delta (Camargue) on Gulf of Lions. H.e.p. from Génissiat Dam (1948). Vine, fruit, olive growing in fertile valley. Canal link with Rhine. Rhône-Saône corridor a hist. route between N and S France.

rhubarb, any of genus *Rheum* of perennial, large-leaved plants with edible reddish stalks, esp. *R. rhaponticum* and *R. hybridum.* Leaves of all varieties contain poisonous oxalic acid, stalks yield cathartic extract.

Rhum or **Rum,** isl. of Inner Hebrides, W Scotland. Area 109 sq km (42 sq mi). Mainly mountainous. Nature reserve.

rhyme or **rime,** identity or similarity of sound of final accented syllables of words, esp. in vowels and succeeding consonants. Used in poetry esp. at line endings to form audible patterns. First became popular in medieval Latin poetry.

rhyolite, fine-grained acid volcanic rock. Composition similar to granite, but richer in silica. Occurs as highly viscous lava, explosively ejected through Earth's surface.

Rhys, Jean (*c* 1894-), English novelist, b. Dominica. Early works, *eg After Leaving Mr Mackenzie,* deal with loneliness in Parisian bohemia. *Wide Sargasso Sea* (1966) reconstructs the early life of Mr Rochester's mad wife in *Jane Eyre.*

rhythm, in music, pattern produced by relative stress and duration of notes. Its use to produce a sense of uplift in both performer and listener is very important.

rib, any of the arched bones attached to the vertebral column and enclosing the chest cavity. In man, there are 12 pairs of ribs, attached to the thoracic vertebrae.

Ribbentrop, Joachim von (1893-1946), German diplomat. As Hitler's foreign minister (1938-45), helped negotiate Russo-German Non-aggression Pact (1939). Hanged as war criminal.

Ribble, river of NW England. Flows 121 km (75 mi) from Pennines via Preston to Irish Sea.

ribbon fish, marine fish of Trachipteridae family, with long laterally-compressed body resembling ribbon. Species incl. deal fish, *Trachipterus arcticus,* of N Atlantic.

ribbon worm, *see* NEMERTEA.

Ribe, town of SW Jutland, Denmark, on R. Ribe. Pop. 8000. Romanesque cathedral (*c* 1135).

Ribeirão Prêto, town of SC Brazil, in São Paulo state. Pop. 212,000. Agric. market (esp. coffee); cotton milling, distilling; agric. machinery mfg.

Ribera, José or **Jusepe** (1591-1652), Spanish painter. Spent his working life in Naples; influenced by Caravaggio, his work is characterized by dramatic contrasts in light and shade and an often gruesome naturalism. Works incl. *The Martyrdom of St Bartholomew.*

riboflavin or **vitamin B₂,** vitamin of B group found in yeast, liver, milk, *etc.* Lack of riboflavin in diet causes stunted growth, loss of hair, skin lesions, *etc.*

Ricardo, David (1772-1823), English economist. Having amassed fortune as stockbroker, wrote influential *Principles of Political Economy and Taxation* (1817) setting out theory correlating rent, profit, wages, taxation.

Rice, Elmer (1892-1967), American dramatist. Known for portrayal of social injustice, *eg The Adding Machine* (1923), *Street Scene* (1929). Also wrote novels, *eg* utopian satire *A Voyage to Purilia* (1930).

rice, grain of cereal grass *Oryza sativa.* Grown extensively in tropical and subtropical regions of China, India, Japan, Indonesia and SE Asia, which produce *c* 90% of world's rice. Also cultivated in US and Europe. Rich in carbohydrate; brown rice, retaining outer husk, has more protein and vitamin value than polished white rice.

Richard [I] the Lion Heart (1157-99), king of England (1189-99). Twice rebelled against father, Henry II, before accession. Leader of 3rd Crusade with PHILIP II of France (1190); helped capture Acre (1191). Captured in Austria during return to England; turned over to custody of Emperor Henry VI and released on payment of great ransom (1194). Killed while fighting Philip in France.

Richard II (1367-1400), king of England (1377-99). Son of Edward the Black Prince, effectively quelled PEASANTS' REVOLT (1381). Power threatened by nobles led by Gloucester until John of Gaunt returned from Spain (1389). Had Gloucester murdered (1397). Deposed after rebellion led by Henry Bolingbroke (HENRY IV). Imprisoned at Pontefract where he died.

Richard III (1452-85), king of England (1483-5). On death of Edward IV, he seized Edward's heir, Edward V, and assumed the crown when Parliament declared Edward illegitimate. Suspected of arranging Edward's murder after he had him imprisoned in the Tower. Defeated and killed at Bosworth by Henry Tudor (HENRY VII).

Richards, Frank, pseud. of Charles Hamilton (1875-1961), English author. Known as creator of Billy Bunter in comic book schoolboy stories for *Magnet* and *Gem.*

Richards, Sir Gordon (1904-), English jockey. Champion jockey 26 times from 1925 to 1953. Rode 269 winners in 1947 season.

Richards, I[vor] A[rmstrong] (1893-), English critic. Known for study of relationship of language, thought, *The Meaning of Meaning* (1923, with OGDEN), theoretical works on criticism, *eg Principles of Literary Criticism* (1925), *Practical Criticism* (1929).

Richardson, Henry Handel, pseud. of Ethel Florence Robertson, née Richardson (1870-1946), Australian novelist. Known for naturalistic trilogy *The Fortunes of Richard Mahony* (1917-29) dealing with mental degeneration of hero.

Richardson, Sir Ralph David (1902-), English actor. Actor-director of Old Vic (1944-7). Noted roles incl. Sir Toby Belch in *Twelfth Night,* in *Flowering Cherry, Home*; film *Oh! What a Lovely War!.*

Richardson, Samuel (1689-1761), English novelist. Helped develop novel form with epistolary works, *eg Pamela* (1740), *Clarissa* (1748), *Sir Charles Grandison* (1754). Deals with moral struggles in sentimental terms.

Richelieu, Armand Jean du Plessis, Duc de (1585-1642), French statesman, churchman. Created cardinal 1622. With help of regent Marie de' Medici, became chief minister to Louis XIII (1624) and virtual ruler of France. Sought to reduce Habsburg power by aiding Protestants in Thirty Years War, then brought France into war as ally of Sweden (1635). In France, strengthened royal power to detriment of Huguenots and nobility; captured Huguenot stronghold of La Rochelle (1628).

Richmond, cap. of Virginia, US; at head of navigation on James R. Pop. 249,000. Financial, cultural, shipping centre. Tobacco, grain, coal exports; tobacco processing. Settled 1637; cap. from 1779. Strategic as cap. of Confederacy during Civil War.

Richmond-upon-Thames, bor. of SW Greater London, England, on R. Thames. Pop. 174,000. Formerly Sheen, created 1965 from Barnes, Twickenham mun. bors. Has Richmond Park, Kew Gardens; Hampton Court Palace.

Richter, Johann Paul Friedrich, pseud. Jean Paul (1763-1825), German author. Wrote formally experimental novels, *eg Life of the Complacent Little Schoolmaster Maria Wuz* (1790), *Quintus Fixlein* (1796). Other works incl. theoretical *Introduction to Aesthetics* (1804).

Richthofen, Manfred, Baron von (1892-1918), German airman, known as the 'Red Baron'. Credited with shooting down 80 aircraft during WWI. Died in action.

Rickenbacker, Edward Vernon (1890-1973), American airman. US and French hero during WWI.

rickets, disease resulting from vitamin D deficiency, affecting calcium metabolism and causing softening and bending of bones. Caused by insufficient exposure to sunlight or inadequate diet.

Rideau Canal, SE Ontario, Canada; connects Ottawa with L. Ontario (at Kingston). Length 203 km (126 mi).

Ridgway, Matthew Bunker (1895-), American general. Commander of US 8th Army in Korea (1950), became supreme commander of Allied forces in Europe (1952-3), US chief of staff (1953-5).

Ridley, Nicholas (*c* 1500-55), English clergyman. Worked with Cranmer on Book of Common Prayer; became bishop of London (1550). After accession of Mary I, burned at stake with Latimer.

Riefenstahl, Leni (1902-), German film director. Best known for her brilliant propaganda films for Nazis, *Triumph of the Will* (1934), *Olympische Spiele 1936.*

Riel, Louis (1844-85), Canadian rebel. Led unsuccessful RED RIVER REBELLION (1869-70). In 1884, led revolt of Indians and Métis in Saskatchewan. Defeated and executed for treason.

Riemann, Georg Friedrich Bernhard (1826-66), German mathematician. Developed theory of analytic functions of complex variable and their representation by Riemann surfaces. Riemannian geometry, which describes non-uniform space, has important applications in relativity theory.

Rienzi, Cola di (*c* 1313-54), Italian political leader. Used popular support to estab. short-lived Roman republic, but was soon expelled under papal pressure. Sponsored by new pope, Innocent VI, returned (1353) to Rome, but his dictatorial rule ended in his murder.

Riesman, David (1909-), American sociologist. Known for study of post-war American character, *The Lonely Crowd* (1950).

Rif or **Riff, Er,** mountain region of N Morocco; extends from Ceuta (W) to Melilla (E). Rises to over 2450 m/8000 ft. Stronghold of Berber tribes who revolted against French and Spanish rule (1921-6).

rifle, firearm with spiral-grooved barrel which imparts spin to bullet. Usually fired from shoulder. *See* SMALL ARMS.

rift valley or **graben,** natural trough formed by sinking of land between two approximately parallel faults. Associated with volcanic activity. Examples incl. Great Rift Valley of E Africa, Rhine valley, Scottish central lowland valley.

Riga, city of WC USSR, cap. of Latvian SSR; on Gulf of Riga. Pop. 755,000. Port; exports timber, flax, paper; indust. centre. Founded 12th cent., became centre of Livonian Knights and prosperous Hanseatic trading town. Held by Poland, Sweden and finally Russia (1710). Cap. of independent Latvia (1919-40) until Soviet occupation.

Rights, Bill of, in British history, statute (1689) confirming rights of Parliament and the people previously violated during reign of James II. Estab. political supremacy of Parliament. Embodied terms by which William and Mary succeeded to throne and provided for Protestant succession.

Rights, Bill of, in American history, *see* CONSTITUTION OF THE UNITED STATES.

Rights of Man, Declaration of the, hist. French document, drafted by Sieyès (1789); became preamble of French Constitution of 1791. Influenced by Rousseau and American Declaration of Independence, it asserted equality of all men, sovereignty of the people, inalienable rights of the individual to 'liberty, property, security'.

right whale, whalebone whale of Balaenidae family, found in polar waters. Toothless, with large head. Species incl. Greenland whale, *Balaena mysticetus,* reaching lengths of 21 m/70 ft. Now very rare, due to uncontrolled hunting.

rigor mortis, progressive stiffening of muscles of body which occurs several hours after death (depending on atmospheric conditions and state of body). Ended by onset of decomposition after *c* 24 hrs.

Rig-Veda, *see* VEDA.

Rijeka-Sušak (Ital. *Fiume*), town of Croatia, NW Yugoslavia, on the Adriatic. Pop. 133,000. Country's largest port; indust. centre, oil refining, shipbuilding; tourism. Hungarian from 1779, seized (1919) by D'Annunzio; annexed (1924) by Italy, ceded (1947) to Yugoslavia. Sušak, E suburb, Yugoslav from 1919. Roman arch, cathedral (14th cent.).

Rijksmuseum, Dutch national museum in Amsterdam, founded 1808 by Louis Napoleon Bonaparte; present building opened 1885. Collection of Dutch art particularly good, esp. of 17th cent. masters.

Rijswijk or **Ryswick,** town of W Netherlands, near The Hague. Pop. 49,000. Treaty of Ryswick (1697) ended War of Grand Alliance against France.

Bridget Riley: *Fall*

Riley, Bridget (1931-), English painter. Leading exponent of op art, early work, *eg Fall* (1963), was confined to repetitive geometric patterns in black and white. More colour introduced into later work.

Rilke, Rainer Maria (1875-1926), German poet, b. Prague. Early lyrics subjective, *eg Book of Hours* (1905), later works more philosophical, *eg Duino Elegies* (1923) recounting reactions to existentialism, *The Sonnets to Orpheus* (1923). Also wrote novel based on parable of Prodigal Son, *The Notebooks of Malte Laurids Brigge* (1910).

Rimbaud, [Jean Nicolas] Arthur (1854-91), French poet. Known for decadent verse written between 15 and 19. Intimate of VERLAINE. Works incl. 'Le Bateau ivre' (1871), prose piece detailing his spiritual development *Une Saison en enfer* (1873).

Rimini (anc. *Ariminum*), city of Emilia-Romagna, EC Italy, on Adriatic Sea. Pop. 120,000. Port, resort, railway jct. Founded 3rd cent. BC, donated (AD 754) to Papacy. Siezed (13th cent.) by Malatesta family. Arch of Augustus (27 BC); Renaissance church, designed by Alberti.

Rimsky-Korsakov, Nikolai Andreyevich (1844-1908), Russian composer, one of 'the Five'. Music, strongly influenced by folk tunes, displays brilliant orchestration. Works incl. orchestral piece *Scheherezade*, opera *Le Coq*

Rainer Maria Rilke

d'or. Revised Borodin's *Prince Igor,* Mussorgsky's *Boris Godunov.*

rinderpest or **cattle plague,** acute infectious disease of cattle, sheep, *etc.* Characterized by fever and lesions of skin and mucous membrane. Common in C Africa, SE Asia, India.

ring ouzel, *Turdus torquatus,* European bird of thrush family. Male has black plumage with white band on chest.

ringworm, contagious skin disease caused by infection with certain microscopic fungi. Characterized by formation of ring-shaped eruptive patches and itching. Common sites are between the toes (athlete's foot), scalp and groin.

Rio Branco, town of W Brazil, cap. of Acre state, on Acre R. Pop. 84,000. Rubber, Brazil nuts exports. Important river transport link.

Río Bravo, Mexican name for RIO GRANDE.

Río Cuarto, town of C Argentina, in Córdoba prov. Pop. 164,000. In agric. region (esp. cereal growing). Commercial centre; garrison town.

Rio de Janeiro, major port of Brazil, cap. of Guanabara state, on SW shore of Guanabara Bay. Pop. 4,252,000. Transport and communication centre. Coffee, sugar, iron ore exports; flour milling, sugar refining, railway engineering. Tourist attractions incl. Sugar Loaf Mt., Corcovado peak (with statue of Christ), Copacabana beach, botanical gardens. Has shanty towns on adjacent hills. First settled by French; Portuguese occupation 1567; cap. of Brazil (1763-1960). Seat of Univ. of Brazil (1920).

Río de la Plata, *see* PLATA, RÍO DE LA.

Rio Grande (Mex. *Río Bravo*), river of S US. Flows S 3000 km (1885 mi) from SW Colorado through New Mexico, then SE along Texas-Mexico border to Gulf of Mexico.

Rio Grande do Sul, state of SE Brazil. Area 282,183 sq km (108,951 sq mi); pop. 6,670,000; cap. Pôrto Alegre. Stock rearing; cereals, fruit, wine production.

Río Muni, mainland area of Equatorial Guinea. Area 26,000 sq km (10,040 sq mi); main town Bata. Narrow coastal plain, interior plateau. Hot, wet climate; main products coffee, hardwoods.

Rio Negro, *see* NEGRO.

Riopelle, Jean Paul (1924-), Canadian artist. Known for his dense abstract paintings in rich blobs of paint, worked with palette knife into interlocking bars.

Riot Act, legislation passed (1714) in face of widespread rioting over accession of George I. Under its terms, if an unlawful assembly of 12 or more persons fails to disperse within an hour of reading of prescribed proclamation by a magistrate, those present are guilty of felony and may be dispersed by force.

Río Tinto or **Minas de Riotinto,** town of Andalusia, SW Spain, in Sierra de Aracena. Pop. 9,000. Rich copper mines, also iron and manganese deposits.

Riouw Islands, group of isls. off E coast of Sumatra, Indonesia, at S entrance of Str. of Malacca. Area *c* 5900 sq km (2300 sq mi). Largest isl., Bintan, has tin and bauxite mines.

Ripley, George (1802-80), American writer. Left Unitarian ministry; set up (1841) transcendentalist community, Brook Farm. Contributed to *Dial* (1842-4), outlining social, religious theories of transcendentalists.

Ripon, town of North Yorkshire, N England. Pop. 11,000. Tanning, brewing; paint mfg. Has cathedral (12th-16th cent.); Fountains Abbey ruins nearby.

Risorgimento (Ital., = resurgence), movement in 19th cent. Italy for liberation and national unification. Despite failure of 1848-9 insurrections under MAZZINI and CAVOUR, French military intervention against Austria and Garibaldi's conquest of Naples and Sicily enabled Victor Emmanuel of Sardinia to become 1st king of Italy (1861). Unification completed with acquisition of Venetia (1866) and Papal States (1870).

Ritter, Karl (1779-1859), German geographer. A founder of modern geography; emphasized relationships between nature and man's development. Wrote *Die Erdkunde* (1817-18).

river, natural stream of fresh water draining into sea, lake, inland depression or another river. May flow only intermittently in arid regions. Rising at a source, river normally possesses 'youth', 'maturity' and 'old age' stages in upper, middle and lower courses respectively.

Rivera, Diego (1886-1957), Mexican artist. Influenced by Communism while in Europe. Depicted Mexican social problems on large fresco murals commissioned for decoration of public buildings in Mexico.

Riverina, area of S New South Wales, Australia, between Murray, Murrumbidgee and Lachlan rivers. Fertile, irrigated; produces wheat, sheep, fruit, rice.

Rivers, William Halse Rivers (1864-1922), English anthropologist, psychologist. Wrote *Kinship and Social Organization* (1914) after expeditions to Australasia. Fused ethnological data and psychoanalytic theory. Other works incl. *Medicine, Magic and Religion* (1924), *History of Melanesian Society* (1914).

Riverside, residential town of S California, US; near Los Angeles. Pop. 140,000. Citrus fruit packing, trade centre. Has part of Univ. of California.

Riviera, narrow coastal strip extending from Hyères (SE France) to La Spezia (NW Italy). Italian Riviera divided by Genoa into E and W sections; French Riviera also called 'Côte d'Azur'. Many fashionable resorts *eg* Cannes, Monte Carlo. Vine, flower, fruit growing; fishing.

Riyadh, cap. of Saudi Arabia. Pop. 300,000. Oasis trade centre of Nejd region. Centre of Wahabi Islam since 19th cent. Many modern buildings date from oil boom.

Rizal, José (1861-96), Philippine author. Exiled after writing novel, *Noli me tangere* (*The Lost Eden,* 1886), attacking Spanish rule in Philippines. Convicted of inciting rebellion and executed.

Rizzio, David (*c* 1533-66), Italian musician, favourite of Mary Queen of Scots. Became Mary's personal secretary. Influence with Mary aroused enmity of group of nobles, incl. her husband, Darnley; stabbed to death at their command.

RNA or **ribonucleic acid,** fundamental genetic material found esp. in protein-making ribosomes in cytoplasm of cells. Molecule consists of long chains of ribose sugar, phosphate groups and nitrogenous bases. One form, messenger RNA, whose synthesis is controlled by DNA in cell nucleus, migrates to ribosomes where it builds up protein molecules. Another form, transfer RNA, arranges sequence of amino acids which determine structure of a particular protein to be built by messenger RNA.

roach, *Rutilus rutilus,* freshwater fish of carp family, found in N Europe. Silvery white with reddish fins.

road, man-made semi-permanent route for wheeled vehicles. Constructed in ancient Persia *c* 500 BC; art developed by Romans, many of whose examples still exist. European road-building neglected from fall of Roman Empire until 19th cent. when TELFORD and McADAM improved surfaces. *See* MOTORWAY.

roadrunner, *Geococcyx californianus,* long-tailed, crested desert bird, related to cuckoo, found in SW US. Poor flier, runs with great speed. Also called chaparral cock.

Roanoke, town of SW Virginia, US; on Roanoke R. Pop. 92,000. Transport, indust. centre. Railway engineering, textiles, chemical industs.

Roanoke, river of E US. Formed in S Virginia, flows SE 660 km (410 mi) through N Carolina to Albemarle Sound. Roanoke Island, off coast of North Carolina, was site of Raleigh's unsuccessful colonies (1585, 1587).

Robbe-Grillet, Alain (1922-), French author. Formulated critical theory of *nouveau roman* dispensing with many familiar devices of novel. Works incl. *Les Gommes* (1953), *Dans le Labyrinthe* (1959), film scenario *L'Année dernière à Marienbad* (1960).

robber fly, any of Asilidae family of 2-winged hairy flies. Prominent eyes; large proboscis used to suck body fluids of insects seized in flight.

robbery, in law, illegal taking of another's property from his person or in his immediate presence by use of violence or intimidation.

Robbia, Luca della (*c* 1399-1482), Florentine sculptor. Head of family workshop which produced glazed terracotta sculpture; specialized in small figures in white set against a blue background.

Robbins, Jerome (1918-), American choreographer, director, dancer. Staged ballets, musicals, *eg The King and I, West Side Story.*

Robbins, Lionel Charles Robbins, Baron (1898-), English economist. Chaired govt. committee on higher education which produced report (1963) recommending extending student numbers.

Robert [I] the Bruce (1274-1329), king of Scotland (1306-29). Fought to recover Scottish territ. from English after assuming throne. Forced to flee after defeat at Methven (1307). His courage allegedly derived from watching a spider spinning its web. Successfully resumed campaign after death of Edward I, ultimately defeating Edward II at Bannockburn (1314). Treaty of Northampton (1328) acknowledged Scottish independence.

Robert II [Curthose] (*c* 1054-1134), duke of Normandy. Eldest son of William the Conqueror, on whose death he inherited Normandy (1087). Claimed English throne from brother Henry I but was defeated at Tinchebrai (1106) and imprisoned for rest of life.

Robert Guiscard (*c* 1015-85), Norman nobleman. Duke of Apulia, Calabria and Sicily, ousted Arabs, Byzantines and Lombards from these lands. Captured Rome (1084) to free Pope Gregory VII from Emperor Henry IV.

Roberts, Sir Charles George Douglas (1860-1943), Canadian author. Known for poetry, *eg Orion and Other Poems* (1880), *Songs of the Common Day* (1893). Also wrote nature studies and tales.

Roberts of Kandahar, Frederick Sleigh Roberts, 1st Earl (1832-1914), British field marshal. Successful campaign in Afghanistan (1879) incl. relief of Kandahar. Commander-in-chief (1899-1900) against Boers in South Africa.

Robertson, Thomas William (1829-71), English dramatist. Known as originator of 'cup and saucer' school of domestic realism. Plays incl. *Society* (1865), *Caste* (1867).

Robeson, Paul (1898-1976), American singer, leading exponent of Negro spirituals. Also an actor, his roles incl. Othello. His left-wing political views aroused hostility in US and he lived abroad for some years.

Robespierre, Maximilien François Marie Isidore de (1758-94), French revolutionary. Jacobin leader, member of Committee of Public Safety, which instituted Reign of Terror (1793-4). Ousted rivals Hébert and Danton, exercised dictatorial power through Revolutionary Tribunal. Overthrown by the Convention, tried and guillotined. Had reputation of incorruptibility.

Robey, Sir George, pseud. of George Edward Wade (1869-1954), English comedian. Known as 'Prime Minister of Mirth'. Famous in songs incl. 'Tempt Me Not!', 'In Other Words'.

American robin

robin, *Erithacus rubecula,* songbird of thrush family found in Europe and W Asia. Brownish plumage with orange-red face and breast. American robin, *Turdus migratorius,* is larger thrush with dull-red breast.

Robin Hood, legendary hero of medieval England. Idealized outlaw, lived in Sherwood Forest with Little John, Friar Tuck, Maid Marian and his band. Robbed the rich to help the poor.

Robinson, Edwin Arlington (1869-1935), American poet. Known for melancholy, ironic verse, *eg The Children of Night* (1897), *Man against the Sky* (1916), verse novels 'Tristram' (1927), 'King Jasper' (1935), often reflecting small-town gloom.

Robinson, [William] Heath (1872-1944), English graphic artist. Known for his book illustrations and humorous drawings of complex machinery which performed simple tasks.

Robinson, Lennox (1886-1958), Irish playwright. Manager of Abbey Theatre, Dublin (1910-23); director (1923-58). Introduced realistic drama. Works incl. *The Whiteheaded Boy* (1920), *The White Blackbird* (1925).

Robinson, Sir Robert (1886-1975), English biochemist. Awarded Nobel Prize for Chemistry (1947) for work on structure and synthesis of alkaloids, incl. morphine and strychnine.

Robinson, ('Sugar') Ray, real name Walker Smith (1920-), American boxer. Rated as one of the best boxers ever, he became middleweight champion (1951). Retired 1952; returned to boxing and won title 3 more times (1955, 1957, 1958).

robot, mechanical device constructed to perform human tasks. Term popularized by Karel Capek in play, *RUR* (*Rossum's Universal Robots*) in 1921. *See* AUTOMATION.

Rob Roy, real name Robert Macgregor (1671-1734), Scottish outlaw. Member of proscribed Macgregor clan, led cattle-stealing raids against duke of Montrose. Submitted voluntarily; sentenced to transportation, was pardoned (1727).

Robson, Dame Flora (1902-), English actress. Roles incl. Mary Paterson in *The Anatomist,* Miss Tina in *The Aspern Papers.*

Roca, Julio Argentino (1843-1914), Argentinian statesman, president (1880-6, 1898-1904). Began colonization of Patagonia by defeating native Indians (1878-9). His foreign minister, Drago, devised Drago Doctrine (1902) to protect South American states from coerced repayment of debts.

Rochdale, bor. of Greater Manchester met. county, NW England. Pop. 91,000. Cotton mfg. (esp. spinning). English co-operative movement founded here (1844).

Rochefort (-sur-Mer), town of W France, on R. Charente. Pop. 35,000. Port, fishing indust. Formerly important naval base, built 17th cent. Napoleon surrendered nearby (1815).

Rochelle, La, see LA ROCHELLE, France.

Rochester, John Wilmot, 2nd Earl of (1647-80), English poet, courtier. Known mainly for satires incl. sceptical *A Satyr against Mankind* (1675). Also wrote scurrilous epigrams.

Rochester, city of Kent, SE England, on Medway estuary. Pop. 55,000. Indust. centre; engineering. Has Roman *Durobrivae* (fort); cathedral (11th cent.); Norman castle (12th cent.); Dickens' home nearby.

Rochester, town of SE Minnesota, US. Pop. 54,000. Agric. market; dairy products. Has Mayo Clinic (estab. 1889).

Rochester, port of NW New York, US; on L. Ontario. Pop. 296,000. Fruit, market gardening, flower nurseries. Optical, photographic equipment. H.e.p. supplies from Genesee R.

rock, naturally occurring substance forming Earth's crust. Consists of one or more types of mineral; may also contain natural glass, decayed organic material, *etc.* Basic types are IGNEOUS, METAMORPHIC and SEDIMENTARY.

rock dove, see DOVE.

John D. Rockefeller, the elder

Rockefeller, John D[avison] (1839-1937), American industrialist, philanthropist. Ruthlessly built his Standard Oil Co. into largest refining company in US. Philanthropies incl. founding Univ. of Chicago (1892), and Rockefeller Foundation (1913). His son, **John D[avison] Rockefeller, Jr** (1874-1960), carried on father's businesses and philanthropies, estab. Rockefeller Center. His son, **Nelson Aldrich Rockefeller** (1908-), entered public service (1940). Governor of New York (1958-73); vice-president (1974-7).

rocket, popular name for several biennial or perennial plants of mustard family. Esp. dame's violet, *Hesperis matronalis,* with white or purple flowers and rocket salad, *Eruca sativa,* with leaves eaten in salads.

rocket, projectile driven by its reaction to stream of hot gases it produces by burning propellant. By carrying its own source of oxygen, it operates independently of Earth's atmosphere and can be used in outer space. Propellants used incl. liquid hydrogen and liquid oxygen.

Rockford, town of N Illinois, US; on Rock R. Pop. 147,000. Agric. trade centre, shipping; tools and machinery mfg. Founded 1834.

Rockhampton, city of E Queensland, Australia, on Fitzroy R. Pop. 48,000. Trade centre for large stock raising, dairying, gold and copper mining region; exports wool, meat, minerals via Port Alma.

Rockingham, Charles Watson-Wentworth, 2nd Marquess of (1730-82), British Whig statesman, PM (1765-6, 1782). Headed coalition that repealed Stamp Act (1766). Favoured independence of American colonies.

rock music, form of music popular from mid-1950s. Derives in part from American rhythm and blues, gospel, and country and western music. Early exponents incl. Bill Haley, Elvis Presley, Chuck Berry. Status of rock music as vehicle for artistic expression was enhanced by such performers as the Beatles, Rolling Stones and Bob Dylan in mid-1960s. Modern rock music has absorbed such influences as Eastern music, jazz, electronic and classical music.

Rocky Mountain goat, *Oreamnos americanus,* ruminant mammal intermediate between goat and antelope, found in remote mountains of NW North America. Thick white coat, short black horns in both sexes.

Rocky Mountains, extensive mountain system of W North America, from Alaska to SW US, E of Coast Ranges. Canadian Rockies form British Columbia-Alberta border (glaciers, resorts). In US incl. scenic Grand Teton Range; Sawatch Mts. rise to Mt. Elbert (4399 m/14,431 ft). Many national parks, *eg* Banff (Canada), Glacier (US).

Rocky Mountain sheep, see BIGHORN.

rococo, style of architecture and decoration developed in early 18th cent. France from the Baroque. Characterized by elaborate and profuse ornamentation imitating foliage, shell work, scrolls, *etc.* Became popular in Germany, Austria and Italy.

Rodentia (rodents), order of gnawing mammals with large chisel-like incisors which grow continuously. Incl. mouse, rat, squirrel, beaver, porcupine, guinea pig.

rodeo, competitive exhibition of the skills of cowboys. Events incl. bronco-riding (saddled or bareback), bull-riding, calf-roping and steer-wrestling. First rodeo charging admission money took place in Arizona (1888). Most famous is annual Calgary Stampede.

Rodgers, Richard Charles (1902-), American composer. Collaborated with Lorenz Hart on musicals *eg Pal Joey,* and with Oscar Hammerstein on *Carousel, South Pacific, The King and I, The Sound of Music.*

Rodin, Auguste (1840-1917), French sculptor. Most famous sculptor of late 19th cent., his powerful realistic sculpture was influenced by Michelangelo and Gothic art. Works incl. *The Age of Bronze, The Thinker, The Kiss, The Burghers of Calais.*

Rodney, George Brydges Rodney, 1st Baron (1718-92), British admiral. Captured Martinique (1762) in Seven Years War. Famous for victory (1782) over French fleet under de Grasse in American Revolution.

Rodrigo, Joaquin (1902-), Spanish composer. Blind from age of 3. Best known for *Concerto d'Aranjuez* for guitar and orchestra.

Rodriguez, isl. of Mascarene Isls., W Indian Ocean, a dependency of Mauritius. Area 104 sq km (40 sq mi); main town Port Mathurin. Produces fruit, tobacco, maize. Discovered (1645) by Portuguese; taken (1810) by British.

Roebling, John Augustus (1806-69), American engineer, b. Germany. One of first to manufacture steel cable. Built suspension bridges, notably Brooklyn Bridge (completed by son, 1883), during which project he lost his life.

roe deer, *Capreolus capreolus,* small Eurasian deer found in woodland. Male has short 3-tined antlers.

Roeselare (Fr. *Roulers*), town of W Belgium. Pop. 40,000. Textiles (esp. linen), carpet mfg. Damaged in WWI.

Rogation Days, in RC calendar, 4 days (25th April and 3 days preceding Ascension Day) observed by processions asking God's mercy. Adaptation of Roman pagan ceremony seeking blessing for crops.

Roger II (*c* 1095-1154), Norman king of Sicily (1130–54). Crowned by Antipope Anacletus, he was opposed by forces drawn together by Pope Innocent II; forced Innocent to acknowledge him as king (1139). Court at Palermo was cultural centre.

Rogers, Bruce (1870-1957), American typographer, book designer. Gained reputation as leading American book designer while acting as adviser to Cambridge and Harvard Univ. presses. Designed Centaur typeface.

Roget, Peter Mark (1779-1869), English physician, lexicographer. One of founders of Univ. of London. Best known for *Thesaurus of English Words and Phrases* (1852, constantly revised).

Röhm, Ernst (1887-1934), German political leader. Organized Nazi storm troops (SA), who enabled him to rival Hitler for political power in 1930s. Executed in Hitler's purge.

Roland (d. 778), French national hero. His death at hands of Basques while commanding rearguard of Charlemagne's retreating army at Roncesvalles became subject of legend, notably in *Chanson de Roland* (11th cent.)

Roland, Chanson de, 11th cent. French epic. Oldest and most famous of extant CHANSONS DE GESTE. Poem, part of Charlemagne cycle, describes Roland's heroic death. Noted for characterization, *eg* contrast of Roland and Oliver, and simple, evocative style.

Roland de la Platière, Manon Jeanne, née Phlipon (1754–93), French revolutionary. Made her home intellectual centre of the Girondists during French Revolution; guillotined after their fall. Her husband, **Jean Marie Roland de la Platière** (1734-93), achieved prominence with Girondists through her influence. Killed himself after her execution.

Rolfe, Frederick William, see CORVO, BARON.

Rolland, Romain (1866-1944), French author, musicologist. Known for novel series *Jean Christophe* (1904-12, 10 vol.) satirizing modern society. Also wrote plays on revolutionary heroism, *eg Les Loups* (1898), *Robespierre* (1938), music criticism. Nobel Prize for Literature (1915).

roller, jay-like bird of Coraciidae family, found esp. in S Europe and Africa. Noted for tumbling flight in nuptial display. Species incl. Eurasian common roller, *Coracias garrulus.*

roller skating, *see* SKATING.

Rolling Stones, English rock music group formed in early 1960s. Estab. wide following in Europe, North America with songs displaying aggressive rhythm *eg* 'Satisfaction'. Group featured personality of Mick Jagger, music of Jagger and Keith Richard.

Rolls, Charles Stewart (1877-1910), English pioneer motorist, aviator. Drove in many of the European classic races. First to fly across English channel and back non-stop (1910). Killed in flying accident. With **Sir [Frederick] Henry Royce** (1863-1933), English engineer, formed Rolls-Royce Ltd. (1906), automobile and aeroplane engine manufacturers.

Romains, Jules, pseud. of Louis Farigoule (1885-1972), French author. Founded Unanimism, doctrine that artist can find significance only within group. Wrote novel cycle *Les Hommes de bonne volonté* (1932-47, 27 vol.), prose poems *Puissance de Paris* (1911), verse. *See* ABBAYE.

Roman Catholicism, major division of Christianity. Main tenets incl. recognition of pope as spiritual leader of the church, belief in apostolic succession, conveyance of God's grace through sacraments. Largest Christian denomination with hundreds of millions of adherents around the world. Centre of RC community is Vatican City, Rome.

romance, in Middle Ages, narrative poem (*roman*) on chivalry, love, adventure, derived from short episodes from epics, condensed *chansons de geste.*

Romance languages, only surviving group of Italic branch of Indo-European language family. Spoken mainly in Europe, present and past European colonies. Incl. French, Italian, Portuguese, Romanian, Spanish. Developed from Latin vernacular (Vulgar Latin), after fall of Roman Empire.

Romanesque, style of architecture prevalent throughout Europe from mid-11th to mid-12th cents. Based on Roman forms, style is characterized by rounded arches, massive walls, interior square bays. Church of St Etienne at Nevers is representative example.

Romania or **Rumania,** republic of SE Europe. Area 237,428 sq km (91,671 sq mi); pop. 21,029,000; cap. Bucharest. Language: Romanian. Religion: Eastern Orthodox. Crossed N-S by Carpathians, E-W by Transylvanian Alps. Incl. lower Danube. Agric. mainly grain (lowlands), livestock (highlands), vines. Indust. development rapid, esp. petroleum. Corresponds to Roman *Dacia*; formed by union of MOLDAVIA, WALACHIA (1859);

Romania

independent from 1878. Gained Transylvania (1920); internal strife, lost territ. (1940). Communist govt. estab. 1948. Large minorities in pop., esp. Hungarian, German, Jewish.

Romanian or **Rumanian,** Romance language in Italic branch of Indo-European family. Official language of Romania used in USSR, Albania, Greece, *etc.*

Roman law, code of laws of ancient Rome, basis for modern legal system of many countries. Formulated first (*c* 450 BC) as 12 Tables, achieved final form in Tribonian's *Corpus juris civilis,* compiled (AD 528-34) under Justinian I. Outstanding in clarity, comprehensiveness; incl. *jus gentium,* code of international law, and is basis of all European civil law.

Romanov, ruling house of Russia (1613-1917). Dynasty estab. by Michael, descendant of Ivan IV. Ceased to rule with enforced abdication of Nicholas II.

Roman religion, religious beliefs and practices of Roman state. Derived from animistic cults of indigenous Italic tribes. These were associated with family, home and harvests. During development of republic (from *c* 500 BC) many foreign elements were absorbed, *eg* from Etruscans, Greeks and various Oriental cults. Old Roman gods became identified with Greek equivalents. By end of republic 3 religions existed: old rural cults, upper-class Greco-Roman religion, new Oriental cults of people. New cults reflected demand for more emotionally satisfying beliefs, later shown in spread of Christianity.

Romans, epistle of NT, written by St Paul to Christians at Rome (*c* AD 58). Fundamental statement of Pauline theology; stresses justification by faith and universality of God's love.

Romansh, see RHAETO-ROMANIC.

Romanticism, in the arts, movement emphasizing imagination, emotions rather than intellect and formal restraint. Romantic characteristics incl. philosophic idealism, interest in primitive cultures, revolt against social and cultural conventions esp. in treatment of love. Grew in Europe as revolt against 18th cent. neo-CLASSICISM.

Romany, *see* GYPSY.

Rome (*Roma*), cap. of Italy and of Latium, on R. Tiber. Pop. 2,843,000. Admin., indust., commercial, transport centre; film-making; tourism. Traditionally founded (753 BC) on 7 hills by Romulus. Etruscan rulers overthrown *c* 500 BC; republic estab., expanded *eg* by Punic Wars. Empire estab. (31 BC) by Octavian; declined after AD 2nd cent., divided (last Western emperor deposed 476), overrun by Goths, Vandals. Cap. of Papal States throughout Middle Ages; annexed to Italy 1870. Ancient ruins incl. Forum, Colosseum. Many churches, incl. St Peter's, St John in the Lateran. Also *see* VATICAN CITY.

Rome, Treaty of (1957), *see* EUROPEAN COMMUNITIES.

Romford, see HAVERING, England.

Romilly, Sir Samuel (1757-1818), English lawyer. From 1807, worked on reform of criminal law, esp. harsh penal laws.

Rommel, Erwin (1891-1944), German army officer. Commanded a panzer division in the invasion of France (1940); as leader of the Afrika Corps (1941-3) showed brilliant qualities in desert warfare. Suspected of

Rommel

implication in the plot to kill Hitler (1944), he was forced to commit suicide by the Nazis.

Romney, George (1734-1802), English painter. With Gainsborough and Reynolds, one of the leading portraitists of his time. Known for his fashionable portraits of women and children, notably Lady Hamilton.

Romney Marsh, low-lying drained coastal marshland of Kent, SE England. Sheep pasturage. Reclamation from Roman times.

Romulus, legendary founder of Rome; son of Mars and Rhea Silvia, daughter of Numitor, king of Alba Longa. With his twin brother Remus, cast into R. Tiber by Amulius, usurper of Numitor's throne. Survived and suckled by she-wolf. Killed Remus in quarrel when building walls of Rome. Procured wives for Roman citizens by rape of Sabine women. Vanished in thunderstorm, worshipped as god Quirinus.

Romulus Augustulus, last Roman emperor in West (475-6). Proclaimed emperor by his father Orestes, who had deposed Julius Nepos. Deposed by German mercenary ODOVACAR.

Roncesvalles (Fr. *Roncevaux*), village of Navarre, NE Spain, in Pyrenees. Mountain pass, height 1056 m (3468 ft), is traditionally scene of defeat of Charlemagne and death of Roland (778).

Ronda, town of Andalusia, SW Spain, in Sierra de Ronda. Pop. 31,000. Olive, wine trade; tanning. Deep gorge divides old Moorish town from new (15th cent.) town.

Ronsard, Pierre de (c 1524-85), French poet. Leader of Pléiade group who sought to revitalize French poetry by imitating classical models. Works incl. patriotic *Discours des misères de ce temps* (1562), melancholic love poetry *Sonnets pour Hélène* (1578).

Röntgen or **Roentgen, Wilhelm Konrad** (1845-1923), German physicist. Discovered X-rays while experimenting with cathode rays; showed that these rays affect photographic plates and pass through substances opaque to light. Awarded Nobel Prize for Physics (1901).

Roodepoort-Maraisburg, city of S Transvaal, South Africa. Pop. 114,000. Goldmining and residential centre in Witwatersrand.

rood screen, in medieval church architecture, ornamental screen serving as partition between nave and chancel. Above it was rood beam which bore wooden crucifix (rood) flanked by figures of St John and the Virgin.

rook, *Corvus frugilegus,* gregarious European bird of crow family. Glossy black plumage with bare whitish face.

Roon, Albrecht Theodor Emil, Graf von (1803-79), Prussian army officer. As war minister (1859-73) reorganized army, facilitating victories over Austria (1866), and France (1870-1).

Wilhelm Röntgen

Franklin D. Roosevelt

Roosevelt, Franklin Delano (1882-1945), American statesman, president (1933-45). Partially crippled by poliomyelitis 1921. Governor of New York (1929-33), successful Democratic presidential candidate (1932). Countered Depression with NEW DEAL legislation to aid labour, agriculture, unemployed. Attempted to reorganize Supreme Court which had invalidated several New Deal measures. Elected for unprecedented 3rd term (1940), kept US out of WWII until Japan attacked Pearl Harbor (Dec. 1941). Laid basis for post-war Europe in meetings with Churchill, Stalin. Died after election for 4th term. Wife, **[Anna] Eleanor Roosevelt** (1884-1962), served as US delegate at UN (1945-53, 1961), worked for social reform.

Roosevelt, Theodore (1858-1919), American statesman, president (1901-9). Popular hero after serving in Cuba, elected (1898) governor of New York. Republican vice-president (1901), succeeded McKinley at latter's death. Vigorously regulated big business by 'trust busting' under Sherman Anti-Trust Act. Pursued militant Latin American policy; secured independence of Panama (1903) to allow building of Panama Canal. Re-elected 1904, awarded Nobel Peace Prize (1906) after mediating to end Russo-Japanese War. Picked successor, W.H. TAFT, whom he later ran against as Progressive candidate (1912).

Root, Elihu (1845-1937), American politician. Secretary of war (1899-1904), improved admin. of War Dept.; secretary of state (1905-9). Member of Permanent Court of Arbitration at The Hague. Awarded Nobel Peace Prize (1912).

root, that part of a plant which absorbs moisture and food, provides anchorage and support. May store food. Usually penetrates soil but can grow in air or water.

Theodore Roosevelt

Rose

root, in mathematics, solution of an algebraic equation. Square root of a number is that number which when multiplied by itself gives original number, *eg* 3 and -3 are square roots of 9.

Roraima, Mount, peak on border jct. of Venezuela, Brazil, Guyana. Height 2810 m (9219 ft).

rorqual, toothless whale of worldwide distribution, genus *Balaenoptera*. Small pointed head, well-developed dorsal fin. Species incl. common rorqual, *B. physalus,* and blue whale, *B. musculus.*

Rorschach, Hermann (1884-1922), Swiss psychiatrist. Devised test to analyze personality, in which patient describes his interpretations of 10 standardized ink blot designs. His responses are then analyzed and interpreted.

Rosa, Salvator (1615-73), Italian painter, satiric poet, b. Naples. Known for his landscapes, representing wild and savage scenes, and battle pieces. Enormously popular in 18th and 19th cent. England.

Rosaceae, large family of flowering herbs, shrubs and small trees. Incl. rose, bramble, apple, plum and cherry.

Rosario, port of EC Argentina, on Paraná R. Pop. 798,000. Large railway jct., export depot for wheat, beef from Pampas; sugar refining, meat packing, flour milling industs.

rosary, in RC church, series of prayers, counted as they are said on a string of beads. Usually 5 or 15 sets (decades) of 1 large and 10 small beads. Prayers used are Lord's Prayer, Gloria Patri and Ave Maria.

Rosas, Juan Manuel de (1793-1877), Argentinian political leader. Governor of Buenos Aires prov. (1829-32, 1835-52), extended tyrannical dictatorship over most of Argentina. Forced into exile by Brazilian-backed revolt under URQUIZA.

Roscellinus or **Roscelin, Johannes** (*c* 1050-*c* 1120), French philosopher. Delineated problem of universal concepts; defended extreme NOMINALISM. Accused of heresy of tritheism at Soissons (1092).

Roscius, Quintus (*c* 126–62 BC), Roman actor, greatest of his day. Taught elocution to Cicero.

Roscommon, county of Connacht prov., WC Irish Republic. Area 2463 sq km (951 sq mi); pop. 53,000. Bounded in E by R. Shannon; lakes, bogland. Cattle, sheep pasture. Co. town **Roscommon,** pop. 2000. Agric. market; castle (1269), priory.

rose, any of genus *Rosa* of shrubs native to N temperate regions. Spiny stems, five-parted, usually fragrant flowers of various colours. Many varieties, widely cultivated, are derived from wild sweetbriar, *R. rubiginosa* and dog-rose, *R. canina.*

Rosebery, Archibald Philip Primrose, 5th Earl of (1847-1929), British statesman, PM (1894-5). Succeeded Gladstone as PM. His advocacy of imperialist policies in Africa estranged him from much of Liberal Party.

rosemary, *Rosmarinus officinalis,* evergreen shrub of mint family, native to Mediterranean region. Used as culinary herb and in cosmetics.

Rosenberg, Alfred (1893-1946), German Nazi ideologist. Wrote *Der Mythus des 20 Jahrhunderts* (1930) to provide quasi-scientific basis for Hitler's racist policies. Convicted, hanged as war criminal.

Rosenberg, Julius (1917-53), American spy. With his wife Ethel, was executed for passing atomic secrets to USSR during WWII. Their accomplices, Ethel's brother David Greenglass and Harry Gold, received long prison sentences.

rose of Jericho, *Anastatica hierochuntica,* Asiatic desert shrub. Curls up when dry and expands when moist.

rose of Sharon, *Hibiscus syriacus,* Asian ornamental plant, and *Hypericum calycinum,* evergreen European shrub with large yellow flowers.

Roses, Wars of the, civil wars (1455-85) fought between Houses of Lancaster and York for the English throne. Their badges were red rose and white rose, respectively. Lancastrian king Henry VI was forced to recognize duke of York as his heir but York's claims were set aside on birth of king's son (1454). Fighting began at 1st battle of St Albans (1455). York was defeated and killed at Wakefield (1460) but his son deposed Henry after 2nd battle of St Albans (1461), becoming Edward IV. Henry was briefly restored (1470-1) but was defeated by Edward at Barnet and Tewkesbury. Wars ended when Henry Tudor, a Lancastrian, assumed power as Henry VII after defeating Richard III at Bosworth (1485).

Rosetta (*Rashid*), town of N Egypt, near mouth of Rosetta branch of Nile delta. Pop. 75,000. Port, fishing, rice milling. ROSETTA STONE found nearby (1799).

Rosetta stone

Rosetta stone, ancient Egyptian basalt slab, now in the British Museum, discovered during Napoleon's occupation of Egypt. Bears a decree of Ptolemy V (196 BC) written in hieroglyphics, demotic and Greek. Knowledge of Greek version enabled CHAMPOLLION to decipher hieroglyphics.

rose window, in ecclesiastical architecture, circular window divided by mullions radiating from centre or filled with tracery, suggesting rose form. Famous example at Notre Dame, Paris.

rosewood, hard reddish wood obtained from various tropical trees, esp. Brazilian rosewood or jacaranda, *Dalbergia nigra*. Used for cabinet-making, veneering.

Rosicrucians, members of 17th and 18th cent. occult groups claiming ancient Egyptian origins for their movement. Symbols incl. rose, cross, swastika, pyramid. Prob. derives from works of Johan Andreä (1586-1654) who took pseud. Christian Rosenkreuz. Modern US movement adheres to theosophical doctrines.

rosin, residue from distillation of crude turpentine. Hard, brittle resin, usually light-yellow or amber. Used in making varnishes, soaps, and for treating violin bows, *etc.*

Roskilde, town of E Zealand, Denmark. Pop. 44,000. Port, fishing; tanning. Danish cap. until 1443; cathedral (13th cent.) has royal tombs. Peace of Roskilde between Denmark and Sweden signed here (1658).

Ross, Sir John (1777-1856), Scottish explorer, naval officer. In search of Northwest Passage, discovered Boothia Penin. and King William Land (1829–33). His nephew, **Sir James Clark Ross** (1800-62), made several Arctic expeditions from 1818; located N magnetic pole (1831). Led Antarctic voyage (1839-43), discovered Ross Sea, Ross Isl., Victoria Land.

Ross, Sir Ronald (1857-1932), British physician, b. India. Awarded Nobel Prize for Physiology and Medicine (1902) for discovery of the malaria-causing parasite in the *Anopheles* mosquito.

Ross and Cromarty, former county of N Scotland, incl. some of Hebrides, now in Highland region. Mountains, moorland, lochs (incl. Broom, Carron, Maree); lowland in E (Black Isle). Agric., crofting, sheep farming, deer forests; fishing, tourism. Co. town was Dingwall.

Ross Dependency, New Zealand Antarctic territ., lying S of 60°S and between 160°E and 150°W. Incl. Ross Sea, coastal areas of Victoria, Edward VII and Marie Byrd lands, Ross Isl. (site of Mt. Erebus).

Rossellini, Roberto (1906-77), Italian film director. Became known for film on post-war Rome, *Open City* (1945), went on to make other classic neo-realist films.

Dante Gabriel Rossetti: self-portrait (1847)

Rossetti, Dante Gabriel (1828-82), English painter, poet. Founded Pre-Raphaelite Brotherhood (1848) with Millais and Hunt; pub. journal *Germ* in which appeared poem 'The Blessed Damozel'. Subjects of paintings were taken from Dante and medieval romance; works incl. *Girlhood of Mary Virgin*. His poems were attacked on grounds of morality. His sister, **Christina Georgina Rossetti** (1830-94), was also a poet. Wrote religious, often melancholy poetry; works incl. *Goblin Market and Other Poems* (1862).

Rossini, Gioacchino Antonio (1792-1868), Italian composer. Noted for melodic and humorous qualities. Wrote 36 operas from 1810-29, incl. *The Barber of Seville, William Tell*. Then virtually abandoned composition, although producing *Stabat Mater*.

Rossini

Ross Sea, inlet of S Pacific Ocean, E of Victoria Land, Antarctica. Ross Ice Shelf forms S section. Explored *c* 1841 by Sir James Ross.

Rostand, Edmond (1868-1918), French poet, dramatist. Best known for *Cyrano de Bergerac* (1897), drama of rhetoric, high adventure, lyrical feeling. Also wrote allegory *Chantecler* (1910).

Rostock, town of N East Germany, at head of Warnow estuary. Pop. 201,000. Port; fisheries, shipbuilding, machinery. Hanseatic League member (14th cent.); univ. (1418). Aircraft works bombed in WWII.

Rostov-on-Don, city of USSR, SW European RSFSR; near mouth of Don on Sea of Azov. Pop. 823,000. Port, exports grain, wool; shipbuilding, agric. machinery mfg. Founded 1761, grew in 19th cent. as grain centre. Damaged in WWII.

Rotary International, organization of business, professional men, founded 1905 (US), 1914 (UK). Professed aim to promote standards in business, professions. Supports charities.

Roth, Philip (1933-), American author. Novels, *eg Goodbye Columbus* (1959), *When She Was Good* (1967), *Portnoy's Complaint* (1969), frequently treat the tension between Jewish and Gentile cultures in middle-class America.

Rothamsted, *see* ST ALBANS, England.

Rothenburg ob der Tauber, town of SC West Germany, on R. Tauber. Pop. 11,000. Well-preserved medieval walled town; tourist centre.

Rothenstein, Sir William (1872-1945), English painter. Known for his pictures of famous personalities and Jewish subjects; official war artist in WWI. Book *Men and Memories* gives lively picture of artistic life in London and Paris.

Rotherham, bor. of South Yorkshire met. county, N England. Pop. 85,000. Iron and steel indust. 15th cent. bridge over R. Don (rebuilt 1930).

Rothermere, Harold Sidney Harmsworth, 1st Viscount (1868–1940), English publisher. Provided financial direction in his brother NORTHCLIFFE's publishing firm, at whose death he took control. Founded (1915) *Sunday Pictorial.*

Rothesay, town and small port of Strathclyde region, W Scotland, on Isle of Bute. Pop. 7000. Tourist resort.

Rothko, Mark (1903-70), American painter, b. Russia. Known for his large abstract works which consist of rectangles of luminous colour merging into each other. Committed suicide.

Rothschild, Mayer Amschel (1743-1812), German banker. Founded family fortune as financial agent in Frankfurt. His sons opened branches in Paris, Vienna and London, where **Nathan Meyer Rothschild** (1777-1836) estab. family branch (1798), supplying British govt. with finances in struggle against Napoleon and making loans to European and South American countries. His son, **Baron Lionel Nathan de Rothschild** (1808-79), further extended family's influence. First Jewish MP.

Rotifera, phylum of microscopic animals found mainly in fresh water. Characterized by ring of cilia at top of body, used for swimming and feeding.

Rotorua, town of NC North Isl., New Zealand, on L. Rotorua. Pop. 31,000. Major health and tourist centre based on hot springs, geysers, Maori culture; also timber, fishing industs.

rotten borough, in English history, parliamentary constituencies which continued to return representatives to Parliament despite virtual disappearance of electorate. Most notorious was Old Sarum. Abolished by 1832 Reform Act.

Rotterdam, city of W Netherlands, on R. Nieuwe Maas. Pop. 670,000. Chief European seaport, canal links via R. Rhine with NW Germany; entrepôt trade. Indust. centre, incl. shipbuilding, oil refining. Chartered 1328, expanded 19th cent. Development of Europoort (1960s), massive port, indust. complex. City centre destroyed in WWII. Birthplace of Erasmus.

Rouault, Georges (1871-1958), French painter. Trained as a stained glass maker; his early paintings, employing heavy black outlines, depict injustice and suffering; subjects incl. prostitutes, clowns, judges. Later turned to religious painting.

Roubaix, city of Nord, N France. Pop. 113,000. Textile centre, esp. woollens, carpets. Forms conurbation with Lille and Tourcoing.

Rouen, city of N France, on R. Seine, cap. of Seine-Maritime dept. Pop. 120,000. Major port, indust. centre (esp. metals, chemicals, textiles); univ. (1966). Hist. cap. of Normandy. Held by English (1419-49); Joan of Arc burned here (1431). Notable Gothic architecture, esp. 13th cent. cathedral. Birthplace of Corneille, Flaubert. Badly damaged in WWII.

Rouget de Lisle, Claude Joseph (1780-1836), French poet, musician, army officer. Although a royalist, wrote words and music of *La Marseillaise,* French national anthem.

Roulers, see ROESELARE, Belgium.

roulette, gambling game played by rolling a small ball around a shallow bowl with an inner disc revolving in the opposite direction. Ball comes to rest in one of 36 numbered compartments, coloured alternately red and black, determining winning bets.

rounders, nine-a-side English outdoor game played with bat and ball. Similar to baseball, which is prob. derived from it.

Roundheads, name given to members of Parliamentary or Puritan party during English Civil War. So called because of their close-cropped hair.

Round Table, see ARTHURIAN LEGEND.

roundworm, see NEMATODA.

Rousseau, Henri (1844-1910), French painter, known as 'le Douanier'. Employed a seemingly naive, but direct, imaginative style to depict jungle scenes, exotic subjects, *etc.* Works incl. *The Sleeping Gypsy.*

Rousseau, Jean Jacques (1712-78), French philosopher, b. Geneva. Wrote *Discours sur l'origine de l'inégalité des hommes* (1754), an attack on property and the state as causes of inequality. His *Contrat social* (1762) describes ideal state with sovereignty held inalienably by people as a whole; individual retains freedom by submitting to 'general will'. Other works incl. novel on education, *Emile* (1762), autobiog. *Confessions.* Had great influence on later thinkers and 19th cent. Romanticism.

Rousseau, [Pierre Etienne] Théodore (1812-67), French painter. Leading member of Barbizon school of landscape painters, work noted for its handling of atmospheric effects.

Rouyn, mining town of W Québec, Canada; on L. Osisko. Pop. 18,000. With nearby Noranda has important copper, gold, zinc mines.

Henri Rousseau: *Tropical Storm with a Tiger*

Rovaniemi, town of N Finland, on R. Kemi. Pop. 28,000. Admin. centre for Finnish Lapland; starting point of Great Arctic Highway. Timber, fur trade; winter sports.

rowan, see MOUNTAIN ASH.

Rowe, Nicholas (1674-1718), English dramatist. Wrote tragedies, *eg Jane Shore* (1714). Edited Shakespeare (1709), influencing change from Elizabethan staging. Poet laureate (1715).

rowing, sport of propelling a boat by means of oars. Competitive rowing dates from early 19th cent. in England; Leander Club, London, was formed in 1818, similar clubs formed in US in 1830s. Annual boat races between Oxford and Cambridge (estab. 1829) and Harvard and Yale (estab. 1852) are major rowing events in UK and US. Olympic sport since 1908.

Rowlandson, Thomas (1756-1827), English caricaturist. Known for satires on the social scene; his *Tours of Dr Syntax* was very popular.

Rowley, William (*c* 1585-1642), English actor, dramatist. Best known for collaboration with Thomas Middleton on *The Changeling* (presented 1621). Also worked with Dekker and Ford (*The Witch of Edmonton*, 1621).

Roxana (d. 311 BC), Bactrian princess, wife of Alexander the Great. Gave birth to son after Alexander's death (323). Imprisoned in Macedonia by CASSANDER, who had her and her son murdered.

Roxburghshire, former county of SE Scotland, now in Borders region. Mainly hilly, Cheviots in S. Teviot, Tweed rivers. Sheep rearing; woollens, tweed mfg. Co. town was Jedburgh.

Royal Academy [of Arts], institution founded (1768) in London by George III to encourage painting, sculpture and architecture; moved to present site at Burlington House in 1867. Holds annual summer exhibition of contemporary art and maintains a free school.

Royal Air Force, junior of 3 fighting services in UK, formed (1918) by merging Royal Flying Corps and Royal Naval Air Service.

Royal Canadian Mounted Police, federal law-enforcement agency of Canada. Estab. (1873) as North West Mounted Police, early duties incl. protecting settlers, preventing Indian disorders. Renamed 1920.

Royal Marines, see MARINES.

Royal Navy, see NAVY.

royal prerogative, see CROWN.

Royal Society (Royal Society of London for Improving Natural Knowledge), British scientific society, founded (1660) to encourage scientific research. Eminent scientists are elected as fellows (FRS).

Royal Society for the Prevention of Cruelty to Animals (RSPCA), British organization founded (1824) in London to promote humane treatment of animals and provide free veterinary treatment. Founder, Richard

Martin (1754-1834), was Irish landowner, known as 'Humanity' Martin. American SPCA was estab. in 1866.

Royce, Sir [Frederick] Henry, *see* ROLLS, CHARLES STEWART.

Royce, Josiah (1855-1916), American philosopher. Leading American idealist. Held that reality is in the world mind, that this includes a moral order. Works incl. *The World and the Individual* (1901).

RSFSR, *see* RUSSIAN SOVIET FEDERATED SOCIALIST REPUBLIC.

Ruanda-Urundi, *see* RWANDA; BURUNDI.

Ruapehu, Mount, active volcano of New Zealand, in Tongariro National Park. Highest peak of North Isl. (2975 m/9175 ft); has warm crater lake. Tourist area; timber on lower slopes.

Rub-al-Khali, desert region of S Arabia, mainly in Saudi Arabia. Area *c* 582,750 sq km (225,000 sq mi). Also known as 'empty quarter'.

rubber, elastic substance produced from latex, esp. of *Hevea brasiliensis* tree. Most rubber articles are made by treating latex chemically, *eg* by mixing with sulphur and heating (vulcanization). Rubber can be produced synthetically as polymer of isoprene.

rubber plant, *Ficus elastica,* Asian tree of mulberry family. Large, glossy, leathery leaves. Often grown indoors as ornamental where it may reach height of 3 m (10 ft). Also called India rubber tree.

Rubber tree

rubber tree, various tropical and subtropical trees producing LATEX. Chief source is *Hevea brasiliensis,* native to Amazon but cultivated in SE Asia. Latex is collected from cuts made in bark.

Rübbra, Charles Edmund (1901-   ), English composer. His music is influenced by early English polyphonic music and is often traditional in form. Works incl. 9 symphonies, vocal music.

rubella or **German measles,** infectious virus disease, common in childhood. Characterized by pink rash, swelling of lymph nodes behind the ears. In pregnant women, may cause damage to the embryo if contracted before 4th month of pregnancy.

Rubens, Peter Paul (1577-1640), Flemish painter. Court painter to duke of Mantua, then to Archduke Albert in Antwerp. Travelled widely as diplomat and painter, carrying out commissions in Madrid, London and Paris. Work in exuberant Baroque style is fluent in colour and texture; paintings incl. *Descent from the Cross, Peace and War* and series *Life of Marie de' Medici.*

Rubicon, small river of EC Italy, flowing into Adriatic Sea N of Rimini. In ancient times marked border of Italy and Cisalpine Gaul; crossing (49 BC) by Julius Caesar represented declaration of war on Pompey and Senate.

rubidium (Rb), soft metallic element; at. no. 37, at. wt. 85.47. Extremely reactive member of alkali metal group; ignites spontaneously in air and reacts vigorously with water. Used in photocells.

Rubinstein, Artur (1887-   ), American pianist, b. Poland. Noted for interpretation of Chopin, Beethoven, Schubert. Has performed worldwide into his old age.

ruby, precious gemstone, a variety of CORUNDUM. Deep red and transparent; used in jewellery. Finest rubies come from Burma, Thailand.

Rude, François (1784-1855), French sculptor. Leading French sculptor of early 19th cent.; most famous work is

Rubens: detail of self-portrait (with his wife)

relief on Arc de Triomphe, Paris, *The Departure of the Volunteers* (called *La Marseillaise*).

Rudolf, Lake, lake of NW Kenya and SW Ethiopia, in Great Rift Valley. Length *c* 275 km (170 mi). Has no outlet; gradually diminishing. Now called L. Turkana.

Rudolph I (1218-91), Holy Roman emperor (1273-91). Originally count of HABSBURG, he was founder of the imperial dynasty. Defeated Bohemians (1278) and made his sons dukes of Austria and Styria, thus strengthening empire.

Rudolph (1858-89), crown prince of Austria, only son of Emperor Francis Joseph. Found dead at Mayerling with mistress, Maria Vetsera, in mysterious circumstances.

rue, *Ruta graveolens,* European perennial herb. Yellow flowers, blue-green leaves with pungent taste formerly used in medicine.

Rueil-Malmaison, suburb of W Paris, France, on R. Seine. Metal, chemical industs., photographic equipment. Nearby is Château Malmaison, once residence of Napoleon I and Josephine.

ruff, *Philomachus pugnax,* Eurasian sandpiper, related to plover, male of which has ruff of erectile feathers during breeding season.

Rugby, mun. bor. of Warwickshire, C England. Pop. 59,000. Railway jct.; engineering; cattle market, cement mfg. Public school (1567), where rugby football originated (1823). Major radio communications centre nearby.

rugby football, fifteen-a-side team game, played with oval leather ball which may be kicked and handled. Said to have originated at Rugby School, England, in 1823; 1st rules drawn up in 1871. Differences over payment of players led to formation of professional Rugby League (1895), whose members play thirteen-a-side variation of game.

Rügen, isl. of N East Germany, in Baltic Sea. Area 927 sq km (358 sq mi); main town Bergen. Agric., fishing, resorts; ancient remains. Joined to mainland by causeway.

Ruhr, major indust. area of NW West Germany, based on R. Ruhr (length *c* 230 km/145 mi). Duisburg, Essen, Gelsenkirchen, Bochum, Dortmund form vast conurbation served by extensive system of canals, roads, railways. Major industs. incl. coalmining, iron and steel, chemicals. Developed in 19th cent. Heavily bombed in WWII, but rapid recovery aided post-war revival of German economy.

Ruisdael or **Ruysdael, Jacob van** (*c* 1628-82), Dutch painter. Major Dutch landscape painter of 17th cent., his realist work influenced 19th cent. artists. Frequently depicted overcast skies with light breaking through the clouds; works in more romantic later style incl. *The Jewish Cemetery.*

Ruíz, Juan (*c* 1283-*c* 1350), Spanish poet, archpriest of Hita. Named as author of *Libro de buen amor,* set of fables within story framework, giving vignettes of everyday Castilian life in richly decorated style.

Rum, see RHUM, Scotland.

rum, spirit distilled from fermented cane sugar by-products, chiefly molasses. Naturally colourless; brown colour results from storage in casks or addition of caramel. Most export rums are produced in West Indies.

Rumania, see ROMANIA.

Rumelia, area of S Balkan Penin. Incl. Thrace, Macedonia. Hist. part of Ottoman Empire; Eastern Rumelia (cap. Plovdiv) autonomous from 1878, annexed by Bulgaria (1885).

Rumford, Benjamin Thompson, Count (1753-1814), British scientist, administrator, b. US. Known for investigations into mechanical production of heat; his belief that heat is produced by motion of particles helped undermine earlier caloric theory of heat.

ruminant, cloven-hoofed cud-chewing mammal. Four-chambered stomach; food passes first 2 chambers, then is re-chewed and passes to last 2 chambers. Incl. cattle, sheep, goats, deer, giraffes.

rummy, card game played by two or six players. Variations incl. gin rummy and CANASTA.

Rump Parliament, name given to members of Long Parliament remaining after exclusion of army's opponents, carried out in Pride's Purge (1648). Dissolved by Cromwell (1653), who later instituted PROTECTORATE.

Runcorn, urban dist. of Cheshire, NW England, on R. Mersey and Manchester Ship Canal. Pop. 36,000. River port; chemicals indust.

Rundstedt, [Karl Rudolf] Gerd von (1875-1953), German field marshal. Commanded in Polish (1939) and French (1940) campaigns. Commanded all German occupation forces in Europe from 1942 until Allied invasion (1944), when he was superseded; reinstated to organize Ardennes offensive.

Runeberg, Johan Ludvig (1804-77), Finnish poet. Leader of national literary movement. Wrote epics, eg *The Elk Hunters* (1832), long romances, eg *Tales of Ensign Stal* (1848) which incl. Finnish national anthem.

runes, ancient alphabet, prob. derived from Greek script; used by Scandinavians and other early Germanic peoples from *c* AD 300. Letters consist of oblique, perpendicular and a few curved lines. Carved on wood or stone.

Runnymede, meadow of Egham, Surrey, S England, on S bank of R. Thames. Probable site of sealing of MAGNA CARTA (1215) by King John. National Memorial to President Kennedy (1965).

Runyon, Damon (1884-1946), American short story writer. Known for humorous works, eg *Guys and Dolls* (1932), detailing lives of Broadway characters in racy vernacular.

Prince Rupert of the Rhine

Rupert (1619-82), German prince in military service of uncle, Charles I of England. Commanded Royalist cavalry in Civil War; defeated by Cromwell at Marston Moor (1644). Returned to England after Charles II's Restoration, sponsored founding of Hudson's Bay Co. (1670).

Rupert's Land, hist. territ. of N Canada, held by Hudson's Bay Co. (1670-1869). Comprised drainage basin of Hudson Bay, embracing large areas of many modern Canadian provs. Sold to Canada (1869).

rupture, in physiology, see HERNIA.

Rurik (d. 879), traditional founder of first Russian dynasty. Leader of a band of Scandinavian traders (Varangians), he estab. himself as prince of Novgorod (*c* 862). His heirs eventually ruled all Russia.

Ruse (Turk. *Ruschuk*), city of N Bulgaria, on R. Danube. Pop. 163,000. Indust., commercial centre, exports cereals. Fortified Roman town; developed as port by Turks. Ceded to Bulgaria (1877).

rush, any of genus *Juncus* of long-stemmed plants with small, greenish flowers. Found in marshes of temperate and cold regions. Stems used for making mats, baskets, *etc.* Name also applied to similar plants, *eg* BULRUSH, CATTAIL.

Rush-Bagot Convention, settlement (1817) of US-Canadian border negotiated by US secretary of state, Richard Rush, and British minister in Washington, Charles Bagot. Limited armaments along border and estab. precedent of peaceful relations between US and Canada.

Rushmore, Mount, see BLACK HILLS.

Ruskin, John (1819-1900), English critic. His *Modern Painters* (1843-60) started as a defence of Turner but later dealt with politics, social reform, architecture; his *Stones of Venice* (1851-3) reflects advocacy of Gothic architecture as an uncorrupted style. Believed in possibility of reviving artistic standards by a return to freedom of medieval craftsmanship.

Russell, Countess, see ARNIM, ELIZABETH VON.

Bertrand Russell in 1962

Russell, Bertrand Arthur William, 3rd Earl Russell (1872-1970), English philosopher, mathematician, b. Wales. Collaborated with A. N. Whitehead on *Principia Mathematica* (1910-13) attempting to estab. logical basis of mathematics. Developed symbolic logic. Other works incl. *The ABC of Relativity* (1925), *History of Western Philosophy* (1945). Leading pacifist spokesman. Nobel Prize for Literature (1950).

Russell, Charles Taze (1852-1916), American clergyman. Founded (1872) evangelical Jehovah's Witnesses (originally called Russellites). Doctrine centres on belief in imminent 2nd coming of Christ and a millennial period when repentent sinners may be redeemed. Members refuse to participate in warfare or govt. Publications incl. *The Watch Tower.*

Russell, George William (1867-1935), Irish poet, patriot. Known for mystical verse under pseud. 'AE', eg *The Earth Breath* (1897), *House of the Titans* (1934). Also wrote prose work on mysticism *The Candle of Vision* (1918). Associated with Abbey Theatre, Dublin, editor of *The Irish Statesman.*

Russell, John Russell, 1st Earl (1792-1878), British statesman, PM (1846-52, 1865-6). Supported Catholic Emancipation (1829) and helped draft Reform Bill of 1832. As foreign secretary under Palmerston (1859–65), advocated British neutrality in American Civil War.

Russia, see UNION OF SOVIET SOCIALIST REPUBLICS.

Russian, language in E Slavic branch of Indo-European family. Spoken by c140 million as 1st language in USSR, one of official languages of UN. Uses Cyrillic alphabet.

Russian Orthodox Church, branch of EASTERN ORTHODOX CHURCH. Originally headed by patriarch of Constantinople, patriarchate of Moscow estab. 1589. National church of Tsarist Russia, power and influence declined after Russian Revolution, esp. 1925-43 (when new patriarch appointed).

Russian Revolution: disorder following Leninists' siege of the duma (July, 1917)

Russian Revolution, national uprisings (1905, 1917) against tsarist autocracy. Discontent over agric. and indust. conditions resulted in series (1905) of strikes, mutinies (eg battleship *Potemkin* at Odessa); led to limited concessions, such as estab. of *duma* parliament. Further opposition arose after continued Russian losses during WWI. February Revolution (1917) led to estab. of provisional govt. in defiance of tsar, who then abdicated. Socialist opposition to War, led by LENIN and BOLSHEVIKS, culminated in October Revolution. Communist Party estab.; private ownership abolished, Russia withdrew from WWI. Ensuing civil war (1918-20) between Red Army, organized by TROTSKY, and White Army, supported by European nations, ended with Communist consolidation of power and founding (1921) of USSR.

Russian Soviet Federated Socialist Republic (RSFSR), largest constituent republic of USSR. Area c 17,070,000 sq km (6,590,000 sq mi); pop. 130,090,000; cap. Moscow. Admin. subdivisions incl. 16 auton. republics and 5 auton. regions. Stretches from Baltic in W to Pacific in E and N to Arctic. Mountain ranges incl. Urals, which divide European plain from Siberia. Economy, history and culture is that of USSR.

Russo-Japanese War (1904-5), conflict provoked by Russian penetration into Manchuria and Korea. Japan attacked and captured Port Arthur, destroyed Russian fleet at Tsushima. Peace settlement reduced Russian role in E Asia.

Russo-Turkish Wars, series of wars (18th–19th cent.) in which Russia sought to control Black Sea and gain access to Mediterranean at expense of Ottoman Empire. Russian expansion checked by European allies during Crimean War (1853-6). Final settlement dictated at Congress of Berlin (1878).

rust, disease of various plants caused by parasitic fungi whose spores have appearance of spots of rust.

rust, reddish-brown coating formed on surface of iron or steel exposed to atmosphere. Consists mainly of ferric oxide (Fe_2O_3) and hydroxide. Caused by action of oxygen and moisture.

Ruth, George Herman ('Babe') (1895-1948), American baseball player. Member of New York Yankees team, he dominated the sport with his colourful personality and many records incl. 60 home runs in 1927. His career total of 714 home runs was not beaten until 1974 (by Henry Aaron).

Ruth, book of OT. Relates story of Ruth, Moabite widow who accompanied her Jewish mother-in-law to Bethlehem and married Boaz. Ancestress of David.

Ruthenia, region of C Europe, in S Carpathian Mts.; now largely in USSR (Ukraine). Part of Austro-Hungarian empire until 1918, then held by Czechoslovakia until 1939. Ceded to USSR in 1945.

ruthenium (Ru), hard brittle metallic element of platinum group; at. no. 44, at. wt. 101.07. Used to make hard alloys with platinum and palladium and as a catalyst.

Rutherford, Ernest Rutherford, 1st Baron (1871-1937), British physicist, b. New Zealand. Estab. existence of alpha and beta particles given off during radioactive decay and developed theory of radioactivity with F. Soddy; awarded Nobel Prize for Chemistry (1908). Work with alpha particles led to his description of atom as central positively charged nucleus surrounded by orbiting electrons. Experimented in nuclear transmutation of elements induced by alpha particle bombardment.

Rutherford, Dame Margaret (1892-1972), English actress. Noted in comedy roles, eg Mme Arcati in *Blithe Spirit,* Miss Prism (1939), later Lady Bracknell (1947) in *The Importance of Being Earnest.*

rutile, titanium ore mineral. Reddish-brown in colour; consists of titanium dioxide, iron normally also present. Occurs as prismatic crystals among igneous and metamorphic rocks. Found in Switzerland, Norway, Brazil, US.

Rutland, former county (smallest) of England, now part of Leicestershire. Co. town was Oakham. Agric., esp. wheat, barley market.

Ruusbroec or **Ruysbroeck, Jan van** (1293-1381), Flemish monk, mystic. Known for mystical treatises, incl. *The Seven Steps of the Ladder of Spiritual Love.*

Ruwenzori, mountain range of Uganda and Zaïre, between lakes Albert and Edward. Peaks incl. Stanley, Margherita, Alexandra, all c5120 m (16,800 ft). Discovered (1889) by Stanley. Possibly the ancient 'Mountains of the Moon', once supposed to be source of Nile.

Ruyter, Michiel Andriaánszoon de (1607–76), Dutch naval officer. In 2nd Dutch war, saved fleet after defeat by English at North Foreland (1666). Soon after (1667) led spectacular raid up the Thames and Medway. Killed in 3rd Dutch war whilst leading Spanish-Dutch fleet against French off Sicily.

Rwanda

Rwanda, republic of EC Africa. Area 26,400 sq km (10,200 sq mi); pop. 3,984,000; cap. Kigali. Languages: Bantu, French. Religions: native, Christian. Mainly high plateau, L. Kivu in W. Cattle rearing, tin mining, exports coffee. Former kingdom, part of German East Africa from 1899; part of Belgian colony of Ruanda-Urundi after WWI; independent as republic from 1962. Invasion by Tutsi émigrés from Burundi ended in massacre of Tutsi pop. 1964.

Ryazan, city of USSR, C European RSFSR. Pop. 378,000. Trade in agric. produce; agric. machinery mfg. Old town, c

50 km (30 mi) distant, was cap. of principality from 11th cent. until destroyed by Mongols 1237.

Rybinsk, city of USSR, C European RSFSR; port on Volga. Pop. 224,000. Shipyards, sawmilling; site of dam and h.e.p. station. Linked to Leningrad by canal system.

Rye, mun. bor. of East Sussex, SE England, on R. Rother. Pop. 4000. Resort; market town. Has Ypres Tower (12th cent.); former Cinque Port.

rye, *Secale cereale,* tall Eurasian annual grass grown extensively in Eurasia and North America. Black grain used in making black rye bread, rye whiskey and for livestock feed.

Rye House Plot, conspiracy (1683) to assassinate King Charles II and brother James on London road in Hertfordshire. Plot uncovered, used as excuse to execute several of Charles' opponents.

Rykov, Aleksei Ivanovich (1881-1938), Soviet political leader. Supported Stalin against Trotsky after death of Lenin; premier (1924-30). Politically suspect after opposing Stalin's collectivization policy. Executed during party purges.

Ryle, Gilbert (1900-76), English philosopher. Known for influential *The Concept of Mind* (1949), attempting to show that the Cartesian distinction between inner and outer world is false.

Ryle, Sir Martin (1918-), British radioastronomer, astronomer royal (1972). Shared Nobel Prize for Physics (1974) with Antony Hewish for work on detection of pulsars.

Ryswick, Treaty of, settlement of War of Grand Alliance (1688-97) thwarting French territ. ambitions; signed (1697) at Ryswick, Netherlands. Dutch gained commercial concessions. Savoy's independence and William III's rule of England acknowledged.

Ryukyu Islands, archipelago of W Pacific Ocean, between Taiwan and Japan. Area 2200 sq km (850 sq mi); pop. 1,235,000; main isl. Okinawa. Sweet potatoes, sugar cane, pineapples, fishing. Part of Japan from 1879, under US jurisdiction from 1945. N group returned to Japan (1953), remainder returned (1972).

Rzeszów, town of SE Poland, cap. of Rzeszów prov. Pop. 77,000. Railway jct., engineering. Founded 14th cent. by Casimir the Great; under Austrian rule 1772-1919.

S

Saale or **Thuringian (Saxonian) Saale,** river of Germany. Flows *c* 425 km (265 mi) from NE Bavaria (West Germany) to R. Elbe near Magdeburg (East Germany).

Saarbrücken (Fr. *Sarrebruck*), city of W West Germany, on R. Saar; cap. of Saarland. Pop. 128,000. Coalmining; machinery, instrument mfg. Site of Roman bridge. Ceded to Prussia by France 1815.

Saarinen, Eero (1910-61), American architect, b. Finland. Designed Trans World Airlines terminal at Kennedy Airport, New York, whose soaring concrete vaults suggest flight.

Saarland, state of West Germany. Area 2567 sq km (991 sq mi); cap. Saarbrücken. Mainly hilly and forested, incl. R. Saar valley. Rich coalfield, major iron and steel indust. Returned after plebiscites to Germany (1935, 1957) following French occupation.

Saavedra Lamas, Carlos (1880-1959), Argentinian lawyer, diplomat, statesman. Expert in international law, presided over Buenos Aires conference (1935) ending Gran Chaco War. Awarded Nobel Peace Prize (1936).

Sabadell, city of Catalonia, NE Spain. Pop. 159,000. Textile mfg. from medieval times; also timber, dye industs.

Sabah, state of East Malaysia. Area *c* 76,500 sq km (29,500 sq mi); pop. 656,000; cap. Kota Kinabulu. Largely mountainous, rising 4100 m (13,455 ft) at Mt. Kinabulu; densely forested. Produces rubber, copra, timber. Was British protect. of North Borneo (1882-1963) until it joined Malaysia.

Sabbatai Zevi (1626-76), Jewish çabalist, b. Smyrna. Proclaimed himself messiah (1648); proclaimed year 1666 as date of millennium. Eventually embraced Islam to escape death.

Sabbath (Heb., = rest), day of rest and worship. Observed by Jews from sunset on Friday to sunset on Saturday, by most Christian denominations on Sunday (except ADVENTISTS). Friday is Islamic day of public worship.

Sabin, Albert Bruce (1906-), American microbiologist, b. Russia. Developed live-virus vaccine, taken orally, to provide long-term immunity against poliomyelitis.

Sabines, ancient people of C Italy, from earliest times connected with Rome. According to legend, wives were taken from the Sabines for unmarried followers of Romulus ('rape of Sabine women'). Constantly warred with Romans, but by 3rd cent. BC had amalgamated with them.

sable, *Martes zibellina,* carnivorous mammal of marten family, found in N Asia. Cultivated for valuable fur.

Sable, Cape, S Florida, most S point of US mainland. In Everglades National Park.

sable antelope, *Hippotragus niger,* large dark-coloured antelope of S Africa. Long ringed backward-curving horns.

sabre-toothed tiger, extinct cat of Machairodontidae subfamily, with tusk-like canine teeth in upper jaw. Existed between Oligocene and Pleistocene epochs.

saccharin, white crystalline powder produced synthetically from toluene. Slightly soluble in water; *c* 500 times sweeter than sugar. Used as sugar substitute in diabetic diets and as calorie-free sweetener.

Sacco, Nicola (1891–1927) and **Bartolomeo Vanzetti** (1888-1927), Italian anarchists. Tried and convicted (1921) for murder in Massachusetts; case became *cause célèbre* in US, many believing conviction resulted from their reputation as radicals. Decision upheld despite appeals, both were executed.

Sacher-Masoch, Leopold von (1836-95), Austrian novelist. Famous as source of term 'masochism', the sexual abnormality portrayed in his novels, *eg False Ermine* (1873), *The Legacy of Cain* (1877).

Sacheverell, Henry (*c* 1674-1724), English clergyman. Accused Whig govt. of neglecting Anglican church and tolerating religious dissenters. His suspension (1710) from preaching led to downfall of Whigs.

Sachs, Hans (1494-1576), German poet, cobbler. Prolific writer, known as Meistersinger portrayed by Wagner in *The Mastersingers of Nuremberg*, but best works in *Schwänk, Fastnachtspiel* forms, producing realistic scenes of everyday life.

Sachs, Nelly (1891-1970), Swedish poet, b. Berlin. Wrote expressionist lyrics, poetic drama often concerned with suffering of Jews. Shared Nobel Prize for Literature (1966) with Shmuel Agnon.

Sackville, Thomas, 1st Earl of Dorset (1536-1608), English poet, statesman. Collaborated with Thomas Norton on *Gorboduc* (1561), regarded as 1st English tragedy. Also wrote famous 'Induction' to 1563 edition of *The Mirror for Magistrates*.

Sackville-West, Victoria Mary (1892-1962), English author. Known for novels, *eg The Edwardians* (1930), poetry, *eg The Land* (1927). Model for hero/heroine of Virginia Woolf's *Orlando*.

sacrament, in Christianity, religious act or ceremony considered esp. sacred and distinct from other rites through institution by Jesus. In RC and Eastern Orthodox churches, 7 sacraments (Eucharist, baptism, penance, confirmation, ordination, matrimony, extreme unction) held to bestow God's grace on man. Most Protestant denominations observe Holy Communion (EUCHARIST) and baptism, but only as symbols of God's grace.

Sacramento, cap. of California, US; on Sacramento R. Pop. 257,000. Railway jct.; food processing, packing. First settled 1839; expanded with 1848 gold rush; became cap. 1854. Terminus of 1st transcontinental railway, Pony Express.

sacred ibis, see IBIS.

sacrifice, the offering of a person, animal or object in homage to a deity. In Bible, occurs in OT, *eg* in story of Cain and Abel; in Greek and Roman religion, among Maya and Aztecs, and many primitive cultures. In NT, Jesus is symbolized as sacrificial lamb. Eucharist is regarded as a form of commemorative sacrifice.

Sadat, Anwar el- (1918-), Egyptian political leader. Succeeded Nasser as president (1970); favoured American diplomacy to gain concessions from Israel after 1973 war. Reduced Soviet influence in country.

Sadducees, smaller of two main Jewish sects which originated in Maccabean age (other being opponents, PHARISEES). Opposed all doctrines not taught in Torah, *eg* resurrection and immortality.

Sade, Donatien Alphonse François, Comte de, known as Marquis de Sade (1740-1814), French author. Cruel sexual practices reflected in novels, *eg Justine* (1791), *Juliette* (1797), *Les 120 Journées de Sodome* (1931-5). Gave name to sadism.

Sadi or **Saadi** (*c* 1184-1291), Persian poet, Sufi moralist. Wrote *Gulistan* (Rose Garden, 1258), rhyming prose masterpiece, also much occasional verse.

Sadowa, village of N Czechoslovakia, near Hradec Králové. Scene of battle (1866) in which Prussians defeated Austrians.

safety lamp, oil lamp for use in mines, designed not to explode firedamp (methane). First successful type usually attributed to Humphrey Davy (*c* 1816). Uses metal-gauze screen to dissipate heat of flame. Also indicates presence of methane when flame has blue halo. Largely replaced by electric lighting and gas sensing equipment.

saffron, *see* CROCUS.

Saffron Walden, mun. bor. of Essex, SE England. Pop. 10,000. Centre of saffron crocuses indust. (14th-18th cents.).

saga, in Old Norse literature, long prose narrative written 11th–13th cent., usually relating story of historical or legendary hero or important family, incl. battles, legends, *etc, eg Sturlunga Saga, Heimskringla, Njala, Volsungsaga.*

Sagan, Françoise, pseud. of Françoise Quoirez (1935-   ), French author. Known for novels, esp. *Bonjour Tristesse* (1954), dealing with feminine psychology. Plays incl. *Château en Suède* (1960).

Sagasta, Práxedes Mateo (*c* 1827-1903), Spanish statesman. Many times premier; founded Liberal Party (1880). Blamed for mismanagement of Spanish-American War in Cuba (1898).

sage, *Salvia officinalis,* aromatic herb of worldwide distribution. Grey-green leaves used as seasoning in cookery.

sagebrush, several bushy, deciduous plants of genus *Artemisia,* common in arid regions of W US. Big sagebrush, *A. tridentata,* is used as forage plant.

Saginaw, town of C Michigan, US; on Saginaw R. Pop. 92,000. Commercial, indust. centre in agric. region. Oil, salt deposits nearby. Oil refining.

Sagittarius, *see* ZODIAC.

sago, edible starch extracted from pith of various palms esp. *Metroxylon sago* found mainly in Far East. Important food source.

Saguenay, river of C Québec, Canada. Flows S 200 km (125 mi) through L. St John to St Lawrence R. at Tadoussac. Main tributary Peribonca R. Navigable to Chicoutimi. H.e.p.

Sagunto (anc. *Saguntum*), town of Valencia, E Spain. Pop. 27,000. Formerly called Murviedro. Agric. market, iron and steel indust. Taken by Hannibal (218 BC) at start of 2nd Punic War. Roman remains incl. theatre.

Sahara

Sahara, desert of N Africa. Largest in world, area *c* 9,065,000 sq km (3,500,000 sq mi); extends from Atlantic Ocean to Red Sea. Largely stony with some sandy areas; interior ranges incl. Ahaggar, Tibesti Mts. Extremely arid climate; inhabited by Sudanese, Negroes, Berbers, Tuaregs. Oases produce dates, fruit; mineral resources incl. salt, iron ore, phosphates, oil and gas.

Saida, seaport of S Lebanon, on Mediterranean. Pop. 22,000. Ancient Sidon of Phoenicia. Famous for its purple dyes and glassware; excavations have revealed many sarcophagi.

Saigon, *see* HO CHI MINH CITY.

sail, area of strong material spread from ship's mast to harness force of the wind as means of propulsion. Sails of papyrus used by ancient Egyptians. Flax and cotton, formerly used in sailmaking, have been replaced by synthetics. Square-rig sail arrangement largely replaced by fore-and-aft rig.

sailfish, any of genus *Istiophorus* of large marine fish. Related to swordfish, has sail-shaped dorsal fin and spear-like upper jaw. Popular as game fish.

sailing, sport, *see* YACHTING.

sailing ships, wind-propelled vessels prob. first used by ancient Egyptians, later by Greeks and Romans. With introduction of mariner's compass, use of sails in place of oars became general. Rivalry between Britain and America in Chinese and Indian tea trade led to the construction of the clippers, most famous being the British *Cutty Sark* and American *Ann McKim.* Introduction of steamship (19th cent.) led to gradual disappearance of sailing ships, both as commercial and naval vessels.

Saimaa, lake system of SE Finland, comprising *c* 120 lakes draining into L. Ladoga. Area *c* 4790 sq km (1850 sq mi). Connected to Gulf of Finland at Vyborg, USSR by Saimaa Canal (length 58 km/36 mi; built 1856, reconstructed 1968).

saint, *see* CANONIZATION.

St Albans, mun. bor. of Hertfordshire, EC England. Pop. 52,000. Printing; electronics. Roman *Verulamium,* many remains; St Alban martyred here (*c* 303); has 8th cent. abbey; Norman cathedral. Rothamsted agric. station nearby.

St Andrews, town and resort of Fife region, E Scotland. Pop. 12,000. Woollens mfg. Has Royal and Ancient Golf Club (1754); 12th cent. ruined cathedral; 13th cent. castle; oldest Scottish univ. (1411).

St Augustine, resort of NE Florida, US. Pop. 12,000. Main occupation shrimp fishing. Oldest town in US (founded 1565 by Spanish).

St Austell (with Fowey), mun. bor. of Cornwall, SW England. Pop. 32,000. Centre of china clay indust. Combined with Fowey from 1968.

Saint Bartholomew's Day Massacre, massacre of French Huguenots, instigated by Henri de Guise and Catherine de'Medici; began in Paris on 24th Aug. 1572. Number killed est. at 50,000, incl. Huguenot leader Admiral Coligny. Led to resumption of French Wars of Religion.

St Bernard

St Bernard, breed of large dog with dense short hair. Once kept by monks of St Bernard's Hospice in Swiss Alps to rescue travellers. Stands *c* 71 cm/28 in. at shoulder.

St Bernard Passes, two Alpine passes. Great St Bernard (height 2471 m/8110 ft) links Valais canton (Switzerland) with Valle d'Aosta (Italy). Road tunnel tunnel, 5.6 km (3.5 mi) long, opened 1964. Little St Bernard (height 2187 m/7178 ft) links Valle d'Aosta with French Savoy. Each pass has hospice founded (11th cent.) by St Bernard of Menthon to aid travellers.

St Boniface, town of SE Manitoba, Canada; on Red R. opposite Winnipeg. Pop. 47,000, mainly French-Canadian. Oil refineries, stockyards, meat packing. Founded by missionaries (1818).

St Catharines, town of S Ontario, Canada; on Welland Ship Canal. Pop. 110,000. In important fruit-growing region. Engineering, food canning industs. Founded 1790.

St Christopher, see ST KITTS.

St Clair, Lake, on EC US-Canada border, N of Detroit. Area 1270 sq km (490 sq mi). Connects rivers between L. Huron and L. Erie. St Clair R. has deepened shipping channel.

St Cloud, suburb of W Paris, France. Horse racing, porcelain mfg. Palace (17th cent., destroyed 1870).

St Cyr, towv of N France, near Versailles. Pop. 17,000. Site of military school, founded 1808 by Napoleon, destroyed in WWII.

St Davids, village of Dyfed, SW Wales. Has 12th cent. cathedral and shrine of St David; medieval pilgrimage centre. Ruined 14th cent. bishop's palace.

St Denis, suburb of N Paris, France. Engineering, chemical industs. Site of Benedictine abbey (626). First Gothic cathedral built here (12th cent.), contains many royal tombs.

St Denis, cap. and seaport of Réunion, WC Indian Ocean. Pop. 86,000. Exports sugar, rum, tobacco.

Sainte-Beuve, Charles Augustin (1804-69), French literary critic. Wrote criticism stressing biog. detail of author, historical, social background. Criticism collected in *Causeries du Lundi* (1851-62).

Sainte Chapelle, former chapel in Paris, built by Louis IX (1243-8) to house relics brought from Holy Land. Richly decorated with stained glass windows, it is a masterpiece of Gothic art. Now part of Palais de Justice.

Saint Elmo's fire, visible electric discharge seen at wingtips of aircraft or masts of ships. Caused by static electricity in atmosphere; often observed during electric storms.

St Etienne, city of EC France, cap. of Loire dept. Pop. 213,000. Coalmining centre, iron and steel mfg. Hist. armaments and textiles (esp. silk) industs. School of mining (1816).

Saint-Exupéry, Antoine de (1900-44), French author, aviator. Novels, eg *Vol de nuit* (1931), *Terre des hommes* (1939), reflect humanistic philosophy of endeavour. Also wrote whimsical fantasy *Le Petit Prince* (1943).

St Gall (Ger. *Sankt Gallen*), town of NE Switzerland, cap. of St Gall canton. Pop. 81,000. Indust. centre, esp. silk, cotton. Medieval centre of learning; abbey (8th cent.) library has valuable documents.

Saint-Gaudens, Augustus (1848-1907), American sculptor, b. Ireland. Foremost American sculptor of his day, his public monuments incl. Lincoln Memorial in Chicago and statue of General Sherman in New York.

St George's Channel, British Isles; between Irish Sea and Atlantic, separating Wales from Ireland. Width 74 km (46 mi) at narrowest point.

St Germain, Treaty of, post-WWI settlement (1919) between Austria and Allies. Austro-Hungarian empire dissolved, Austria gave up parts of its German-speaking territ. to Italy and Czechoslovakia. Independence of Hungary, Yugoslavia, Poland and Czechoslovakia recognized.

St Germain (-en-Laye), suburb of W Paris, France, on R. Seine. Residential area with forest park. Renaissance château; scene of treaty (1919) between Allies and Austria.

St Gotthard Pass, mountain pass of S Switzerland, height 2107 m (6916 ft). Road built 1830; railway tunnel (length 14.9 km/9.25 mi; height 1153 m/3786 ft) built 1880.

St Helena, isl. of S Atlantic, British crown colony. Area 122 sq km (47 sq mi); pop. 5000; cap. Jamestown. Napoleon's final place of exile (1815-21). Became crown colony 1834.

St Helens, bor. of Merseyside met. county, NW England. Pop. 105,000. Major glass indust.; iron; chemicals mfg.

St Helier, town of Jersey, Channel Isls., UK. Pop. 28,000. Resort; agric. market. Elizabeth Castle (16th cent.) nearby.

St Ives, mun. bor. of Cornwall, SW England, on St Ives Bay. Pop. 10,000. Fishing port; resort long favoured by artists.

St James's Palace, in Pall Mall, London, was built by Henry VIII and served as royal residence 1698-1837. Foreign ambassadors are still accredited to Court of St James's.

St John, ice-free port of S New Brunswick, Canada; on Bay of Fundy at mouth of St John R. Pop. 89,000. Railway terminus; has large dry docks. Major timber exports, pulp and paper industs. Estab. as fort in 17th cent.

St John, river of E Canada-US. Rises in N Maine, flows SE 673 km (418 mi) through New Brunswick to Bay of Fundy. Transport link to coast; navigable to Fredericton. In fertile valley. Strong tides of Bay of Fundy cause river to reverse its flow at Reversing Falls during high tides.

St John, Henry, see BOLINGBROKE, HENRY ST JOHN, VISCOUNT.

St-John Perse, pseud. of Alexis Saint-Léger Léger (1887-1975), French poet, diplomat. Exotic, mysterious poetry incl. *Eloges* (1911), *Anabase* (1924), *Neiges* (1944). Served in French Foreign Service (1914-40); settled in US (1940). Nobel Prize for Literature (1960).

St John's, cap. of ANTIGUA.

St John's, cap. and seaport of Newfoundland, Canada; on Avalon penin. Pop. 88,000. Railway terminus; naval and fishing base; cod, herring industs. One of oldest settlements in North America. Starting point of first transatlantic flight (1919).

St John's wort, any of genus *Hypericum* of plants native to Asia and Europe. Speckled leaves, yellow flowers.

St Joseph, town of NW Missouri, US; on Mississippi R. Pop. 73,000. Railway jct.; livestock, grain market; meat packing, flour milling. E terminus of Pony Express (1860).

Saint-Just, Louis Antoine de (1767-94), French revolutionary. Leading member of Committee of Public Safety during Reign of Terror (1793-4). Arrested and guillotined with his close associate, Robespierre.

St Kilda, small isl. of Outer Hebrides, W Scotland. Uninhabited from 1930; bird sanctuary.

St Kitts or **St Christopher,** isl. of E West Indies, in Leeward Isls. Area 176 sq km (68 sq mi); pop. 46,000 (with Nevis); cap. Basseterre (pop. 14,000). Former British colony with Nevis, Anguilla from 1783; became associate state (1967).

St Laurent, Louis Stephen (1882-1973), Canadian statesman. Liberal PM (1948-57), succeeding Mackenzie King.

St Lawrence, river of E Canada. Flows NE 1197 km (744 mi) from L. Ontario to Gulf of St Lawrence. Main tributaries incl. Ottawa, Saguenay, St Maurice rivers. Forms numerous lakes along course. Major shipping route. Canal system (St Lawrence Seaway) links Great Lakes to Atlantic. Has wide estuary.

St Lawrence, Gulf of, extension of Atlantic, SE Canada; between Québec and Newfoundland. At mouth of St Lawrence R. Has important fishing grounds (esp. cod).

St Louis, town of NW Senegal, on R. Senegal. Pop. 48,000. Port, exports groundnuts, hides; railway to Dakar. Founded 1659; 1st cap. of French West Africa (1895-1902). Cap. of Senegal until 1958.

St Louis, city of E Missouri, US; on Mississippi near mouth of Missouri R. Pop. 622,000; state's largest city. Commercial, trade, transport centre. Furs, livestock, grain market, meat packing; motor vehicles, aircraft, chemical mfg. Estab. 1764 by French; became river port in 19th cent. Boomed with Mississippi steamship traffic.

St Lucia, isl. of SE West Indies, in Windward Isls. Area 616 sq km (238 sq mi); pop. 101,000; cap. Castries (pop. 40,000). Scenic mountains with forest covered slopes. Fruit, coconut exports. Former British colony; became associate state 1967.

St Malo, town of Brittany, NW France, at mouth of R. Rance. Pop. 44,000. Port, exports agric. produce to England; fishing, tourism. Fl 15th-18th cent. as base for privateers. Badly damaged in WWII.

St Martin (*Sint Maarten*), isl. of N Leeward Isls., divided between French (Guadeloupe dependency) and Dutch (Netherlands Antilles). Area 96 sq km (37 sq mi). Has little agric. land. Main export is salt from coastal lagoons.

St Marylebone, *see* WESTMINSTER, CITY OF.

St Maurice, river of SC Québec, Canada. Rises in Laurentian Mts., flows S 520 km (325 mi) to St Lawrence R. at Trois Rivières. Lumber transportation.

St Moritz, town of SE Switzerland, on R. Inn in Engadine Valley. Pop. 3000. Spa from 16th cent.; winter sports.

St Nazaire, town of W France, at mouth of R. Loire. Pop. 63,000. Port, outport of Nantes; shipbuilding, food processing. German submarine base in WWII, heavily bombed.

St Niklaas (Fr. *St. Nicolas*), town of NC Belgium, in Flanders. Pop. 49,000. Textiles (carpet) mfg., bricks, pottery.

St Omer, town of Nord, N France. Pop. 20,000. Metals, textile mfg. Grew around monastery founded 7th cent. by St Omer. British hq. in WWI. Gothic basilica (13th cent.).

St Pancras, *see* CAMDEN, England.

St Paul, uninhabited isl. in S Indian Ocean, forming part of French Southern and Antarctic Territs.

St Paul, cap. of Minnesota, US; contiguous with Minneapolis ('Twin Cities') on Mississippi R. Pop. 310,000. Commercial, indust. centre in agric. region. Livestock trade; automobile, tapes, computers, electronic instrument mfg. Has RC cathedral.

Saint Paul's Cathedral, London, was built (1675-1710) by Sir Christopher Wren on site of old St Paul's which had been severely damaged in Great Fire (1666). Has famous classical dome.

St Peter Port, town of Guernsey, Channel Isls., UK. Pop. 16,000. Port for agric. exports. Has castle (partly 12th cent.).

Saint Peter's, Rome, patriarchal basilica of St Peter, in Vatican City. Built mainly between 1506 and 1626, it replaced 4th cent. basilica built by Constantine over supposed tomb of St Peter. Designed chiefly by Bramante and Michelangelo, with piazza added by Bernini (1629-62). Largest Christian church in world.

St Petersburg, *see* LENINGRAD.

St Petersburg, winter resort of W Florida, US; on Tampa Bay. Pop. 216,000. Important recreation centre with associated tourist industs.

Saint-Pierre, Jacques Henri Bernardin de, *see* BERNARDIN DE SAINT-PIERRE.

St Pierre, town of S Réunion, WC Indian Ocean. Pop. 45,000.

St Pierre and Miquelon, overseas isl. territ. of France; off S Newfoundland, Canada. Area 241 sq km (93 sq mi); pop. 6000, cap. St Pierre. Has ice-free harbour; important fishing industs. (esp. cod). Suffers from fogs. Settled by French in 17th cent.

St Quentin, town of N France, on R. Somme. Pop. 66,000. Textile mfg. (esp. muslin, lace, curtains), engineering. Scene of French defeat by Prussians (1871), and of German counter-offensive (1918).

Saint-Saëns, [Charles] Camille (1835-1921), French composer. Best known for *The Carnival of the Animals* for 2 pianos and orchestra. Also wrote symphonies, piano concertos.

Saintsbury, George Edward Bateman (1845-1933), English critic. Known for historical literary criticism, *eg Short History of English Literature* (1898), *Scott* (1897), *The Peace of the Augustans* (1916). Works subjective but had great influence.

Saint-Simon, Claude Henri, Comte de (1760–1825), French social theorist. Advocated indust. state directed by science and universal association for common good. Writings incl. *Du Système industriel* (1821), *Nouveau Christianisme* (1825). Followers continued his theories in system called Saint-Simonianism.

Saint-Simon, Louis de Rouvroy, Duc de (1675-1755), French courtier, author. Wrote bitter account of personalities of Louis XIV's court, pub. as *Mémoires* (1829).

Saint-Saëns

St Thomas, one of Virgin Isls. Area 83 sq km (32 sq mi); cap. Charlotte Amalie. Mountainous, of volcanic origin. Settled by Danish from 1672.

St Tropez, town of Provence, SE France, on Côte d'Azur. Pop. 6000. Fishing port, fashionable resort.

St Vincent, isl. of SE West Indies, in Windward Isls. Area 388 sq km (150 sq mi); pop. 90,000; cap. Kingstown (pop. 17,000). Mountainous, well forested. Cotton growing, banana exports. British colony from 1763; became associate state 1969.

St Vincent, Cape, headland of SW Portugal. Scene of naval battle (1797) when British under Jervis defeated Spanish fleet.

St Vincent Gulf, shallow inlet of Indian Ocean, South Australia, between Yorke Penin. and Adelaide. Many resorts; fishing, salt production.

Saint Vitus' dance or **chorea,** condition characterized by irregular involuntary movements of any part of the body. Most common among children. Cause unknown but closely associated with rheumatic fever.

Saipan, main isl. of Mariana Isls., W Pacific Ocean. Admin. hq. of US trust territ. of the Pacific Isls. Major WWII air base after taken by US (1944).

Sakai, indust. city of Japan, on Osaka Bay in SW Honshu isl. Pop. 594,000. Machinery, chemical and textile mfg. Major port in 15th and 16th cents.; declined when harbour silted up.

saké, alcoholic beverage made from fermented rice. National drink of Japan, where it is served warm.

Sakhalin, isl. of USSR, off E coast of Siberian RSFSR. Area *c* 76,400 sq km (29,500 sq mi). Mountainous, with cold climate; fishing and lumbering main occupations; oil and coal fields. Settled by Russians in 19th cent.; S half, called Karafuto, occupied by Japan (1905-45).

Sakharov, Andrei Dmitryevich (1921-), Soviet physicist, dissident. Leader in development of Soviet hydrogen bomb. Vigorous advocate of civil liberty and democratic reform in USSR. Awarded Nobel Peace Prize (1975), but refused permission to receive award.

Saki, pseud. of H[ector] H[ugh] Munro (1870-1916), British author, b. Burma. Known for humorous, often macabre short stories in *The Chronicles of Clovis* (1912), novel *The Unbearable Bassington* (1912). Killed in WWI.

saki, monkey of South America, genera *Pithecia* and *Chiropotes*. Long bushy tail, long rough hair.

Sakkara or **Saqqâra,** village of N Egypt, SW of Cairo. Site of main necropolis for ancient MEMPHIS with step pyramids.

Saladin (*c* 1137-93), Moslem military and political leader, b. Mesopotamia. Gained prominence in conquest of Egypt from Fatimid dynasty (1164-74); became sultan of Egypt (1175). Extended control over Syria (1174-86); led Saracen capture of Jerusalem after defeating Christians at Hattin

(1187). Repelled 3rd Crusade led by Richard I of England (1190-2).

Salado, river of NC Argentina. Rises in Andes as Juramento R., flows SE 2010 km (*c* 1250 mi) to join Paraná R. at Santa Fé.

Salamanca, city of W Spain, on R. Tormes, cap. of Salamanca prov. Pop. 125,000. Transport jct.; univ. (*c* 1230) was centre of Arabic learning. Taken from Moors 1085; medieval cultural, religious centre. Scene of Wellington's victory (1812) over French in Peninsular War. Two cathedrals (12th, 16th cent.); colonnaded Plaza Mayor.

salamander, tailed amphibian of order Urodela. Scaleless with soft, moist skin; teeth in both jaws, no gills. Regenerates lost limbs or tail. Species incl. giant salamander of Japan, *Megalobatrachus japonicus,* reaching length of 1.5 m/5 ft.

Salamis, isl. of Greece, in Saronic Gulf. Area 93 sq km (36 sq mi). Scene of naval battle (480 BC) in which Greeks under Themistocles defeated Persians under Xerxes.

Salazar, António de Oliveira (1889-1970), Portuguese statesman. Stabilized country's economy as finance minister before becoming premier (1932-68). Exercised dictatorial power after introducing (1933) new constitution, *Novo Estado.* Suppressed political opposition in Portugal and independence movements in colonies.

Salé (Arab. *Sla*), suburb of Rabat, NW Morocco, on Atlantic Ocean. Port; carpets, pottery mfg. Base of Barbary pirates ('Sallee Rovers') in 17th cent.

Salem, city of Tamil Nadu, S India. Pop. 308,000. Iron and manganese mining; textile mfg.

Salem, port of NE Massachusetts, US. Pop. 41,000. Settled 1626. Notorious for witchcraft trials of 1692. Important in sailing clipper era. Hist. buildings incl. Custom House (1819).

Salem, cap. of Oregon, US; on Willamette R. Pop. 68,000. In farming, cattle region; varied agric. related industs., metal goods, paper mfg. Cap. from 1851.

Salerno, city of Campania, SW Italy, on Gulf of Salerno. Cap. of Salerno prov. Pop. 158,000. Port, agric., commercial centre. Medical school founded 9th cent., cathedral (11th cent.). Scene of Allied landings (1943).

Salford, bor. of Greater Manchester met. county, NW England, on R. Irwell and Manchester Ship Canal. Pop. 131,000. Extensive docks; indust. centre; RC cathedral (1848).

Salic law, law adopted in Middle Ages by certain noble and royal European families, excluding female succession to offices and titles. Name derives from erroneous supposition that it was part of 6th cent. *Lex Salica* of Salian Franks, which excluded women from inheriting land. Applied mainly in France and Spain.

salicylic acid, white crystalline solid obtained from willow bark or phenol. Used in manufacture of aspirin, in food preservation, and as an antiseptic.

Salinger, J[erome] D[avid] (1919-), American novelist. Known for *The Catcher in the Rye* (1951) dealing with adolescent hero's resistance to adult 'phoniness'; novels dealing with Glass family, *eg Franny and Zooey* (1961).

Salisbury, Robert Arthur Talbot Gascoyne-Cecil, 3rd Marquess of (1830-1903), British statesman, PM (1885, 1886-92, 1895-1902). Pursued cautious imperialist policy, trying to arrange territ. expansion in Africa by agreement with European powers; retired at end of Boer war.

Salisbury, Robert Cecil, 1st Earl of (1563-1612), English statesman. Succeeded father, Lord Burghley, as Elizabeth's chief minister (1598); arranged James I's accession to throne and admin. his govt.

Salisbury, town of Wiltshire, SW England, on R. Avon. Pop. 35,000. Market town. Built as 'New Sarum' (near ancient 'Old Sarum' fortress). Famous cathedral (13th cent.) has highest spire in England (123 m/ 404 ft).

Salisbury, cap. of Rhodesia. Pop. 490,000. Admin., commercial, transport centre in agric. and gold mining region; tobacco indust.; univ. Founded 1890 as Fort

Salisbury; cap. of Federation of Rhodesia and Nyasaland 1953-63.

Salisbury Plain, chalk downs of Wiltshire, SW England. Military training area. Incl. STONEHENGE.

Salish, *see* FLATHEAD.

saliva, watery secretion of 3 pairs of salivary glands situated around mouth. Contains enzyme ptyalin which begins process of breaking down starch into sugar. Also cleanses mouth and makes sense of taste possible.

Salk, Jonas Edward (1914-), American microbiologist. Developed vaccine, prepared from dead viruses, used against poliomyelitis.

Sallust, full name Gaius Sallustius Crispus (86-*c* 34 BC), Roman historian. After retiring from public office, he wrote histories of the Catiline conspiracy and the wars against JUGURTHA.

salmon, food and game fish, genus *Salmo* or *Oncorhynchus,* which breeds in fresh water. After feeding period of up to 6 years, young migrate to open sea, remaining up to 4 years. Adults return to birthplace to spawn. All Pacific salmon, *Oncorhynchus,* die after spawning but some females of Atlantic salmon, *Salmo salar,* survive.

salmonella, genus of bacteria which incl. causes of typhoid fever and various forms of food poisoning in man and domestic animals.

Salome, traditional name for the daughter of Herodias. In NT, story of how her dancing pleased Herod so much that he granted her request for the head of John the Baptist.

Salonika (*Thessaloníki*), town of NE Greece, on Gulf of Salonika, cap. of Macedonia. Pop. 346,000. Founded 4th cent. BC. St Paul addressed 2 epistles to the Thessalonians. Taken by Turks 1430; Greek from 1912. Base for Allied campaigns against Bulgaria in WWII. Has Byzantine churches. Birthplace of Kemal Ataturk.

Salop, county of W England. Area 3490 sq km (1347 sq mi); pop. 348,000; co. town Shrewsbury. Hilly in SW (cattle, sheep); flat in N, E (agric., dairying). Formerly known as Shropshire; reconstituted 1974.

salsify, vegetable oyster or **oyster plant,** *Tragopogon porrifolius,* plant native to S Europe, also grown in North America. Purple flowers, white roots with oyster-like flavour used as vegetable.

salt, in chemistry, compound formed when hydrogen of an acid is wholly or partly replaced by a metal. Salts are formed by reaction of bases with acids. Common salt, sodium chloride ($NaCl$), occurs in sea water and mineral deposits; used in manufacture of chlorine and sodium compounds.

Salta, town of NW Argentina, in Lerma valley; cap. of Salta prov. Pop. 183,000. In rich agric. region; meat packing, tanning industs. On railway to Antofagasta (Chile). Founded 1582.

saltbush, various plants of genus *Atriplex* mainly native to Australia. Cultivated in arid, saline soils as forage. *A. semibaccato* has been introduced commercially into California.

Saltillo, town of NE Mexico, cap. of Coahuila state. Pop. 192,000. Railway jct., mining centre. Textile, ceramics mfg. Famous woollen shawls. Founded 1586. Has 18th cent. cathedral.

Salt Lake City, cap. of Utah, US; SE of Great Salt L. at foot of Wasatch Range. Pop. 176,000. Transport, commercial, indust. centre. Oil refining, copper smelting; textile, food mfg. Founded 1847 by Brigham Young; Mormon Temple (1893).

Salto, port of NW Uruguay, at head of navigation on Uruguay R. Pop. 58,000. Commercial and indust. centre in fruit-growing region; meat packing, trade in agric. produce.

saltpetre or **potassium nitrate** (KNO_3), white crystalline salt. Used in fertilizers, gunpowder, glass manufacture, *etc.* Chile saltpetre is sodium nitrate.

Saluki, breed of slender hound of ancient origin. Long ears, silky coat; stands up to 71 cm/28 in. at shoulder.

Salut, Iles du, small isl. group off French Guiana. Had notorious penal colony on Devil's Isl. (1854-1938).

Salvador, Atlantic port of E Brazil, cap. of Bahia state. Pop. 1,008,000. Cocoa, sugar, tobacco exports; sugar refining, flour milling. Founded 1549, cap. of Portuguese territ. until 1763. Formerly named Bahia.

Salvador, see EL SALVADOR.

salvage, in maritime law, term used either for act of rescuing life or property from destruction at sea, or for reward to which rescuers are entitled.

salvarsan, trade name for ARSPHENAMINE.

Salvation Army, international evangelical and philanthropic movement. Estab. (1865) in London, UK, by WILLIAM BOOTH, given present name in 1878. Aims to bring Christian religion to those it does not normally reach, as well as bringing practical relief to poor, eg soup kitchens, hostels for homeless. Organized on military lines, with uniforms, ranks.

Salween, river of S China and Burma. Rises in Tibet, flows through deep gorges c 2800 km (1750 mi) to Gulf of Martaban. Navigable only 120 km (75 mi) upstream.

Salzburg, city of NC Austria, on R. Salzach, cap. of Salzburg prov. Pop. 129,000. Cultural, tourist centre. Annual music festival (birthplace of Mozart). Archbishopric from 8th cent.; monastery (8th cent.), medieval castle, cathedral (17th cent.). Univ. (1623), opera house (1960).

Salzgitter, see WATENSTEDT-SALZGITTER, West Germany.

Samar, isl. of Philippines, SE of Luzon. Area c 13,100 sq km (5050 sq mi). Produces bananas, hemp, coconuts. Subject to typhoons.

Samara, see KUIBYSHEV.

Samaria, hist. cap. of kingdom of Israel, during 10th-8th cent. BC. Excavations begun in 1908 have revealed extensive ruins.

Samaritans, descendants of non-Jewish colonists from Babylonia, Syria and elsewhere who were settled in Samaria when Israelites were deported (722 BC). Small number remain in Israel at Nablus and Jaffa. Traditional enemies of Jews; recognized only the Pentateuch.

Samaritans, the, in UK, voluntary organization estab. (1953) by Chad Varah to help potential suicides. Members man telephones to offer counselling, friendship.

samarium (Sm), metallic element of lanthanide series; at. no. 62, at. wt. 150.35. Discovered 1879 by spectroscopy; isolated 1901.

Samarkand, city of USSR, E Uzbek SSR. Pop. 278,000. Silk and cotton centre. Ancient city, destroyed by Alexander the Great (329 BC); centre of Arab culture in 8th cent. AD, on trade route between Europe and China. Cap. of Tamerlane's empire 14th cent.; its buildings incl. his mausoleum. Later held by emirs of Bukhara until taken by Russia (1868).

Samarra, town of E Iraq, on R. Tigris. Pop. c 8000. Site of ancient settlement. Gave name to type of Neolithic pottery of c 5000 BC. Noted mosque (17th cent.).

Samoa, isl. group of C Pacific. Mainly volcanic and mountainous. Discovered (1722) by Dutch; formerly called Navigators Isls. Divided (1899) between US and Germany. **American Samoa** is overseas territ. Area 200 sq km (77 sq mi); pop. 31,000; cap. Pago Pago. Fruit growing, tuna fishing. **Western Samoa,** comprising Savaii, Upolu, and smaller isls. is independent state. Area 2850 sq km (1100 sq mi); pop. 155,000; cap. Apia. Produces fruit, copra, cocoa. Taken from Germans by New Zealand in WWI, held by them as UN trust territ. until independence 1962.

Sámos, isl. of Greece, in E Aegean Sea. Area 492 sq km (190 sq mi); cap. Vathi. Mountainous; wine, fruit, tobacco. Ancient Sámos fl 6th cent. BC under Polycrates. Birthplace of Pythagoras.

Samothrace (Samothráki), isl. of Greece, in NE Aegean Sea. Area 181 sq km (70 sq mi). Sponge fishing, goats. Famous Nike or Winged Victory of Samothrace statue (306 BC) found here 1863.

Samoyed, breed of Siberian dog with thick white or cream coat. Used to pull sleds; stands up to 60 cm/23.5 in. at shoulder.

samphire, Crithmum maritimum, European seashore plant of parsley family. Yellowish flowers, pointed, aromatic leaves used in salads.

Samson, one of judges who ruled Israel before estab. of monarchy. Renowned for great strength which depended on his unshorn hair, symbolizing his vows to God. Story of his betrayal to Philistines by Delilah in OT book of Judges.

Samsun, port of N Turkey, on Black Sea. Pop. 151,000. Situated in major tobacco growing region; exports tobacco. Founded as Greek colony of Amisus; important in Pontic and Roman empires.

Samuel, Herbert Louis Samuel, 1st Viscount (1870-1963), British statesman. First Jewish cabinet minister (1909). High commissioner in Palestine (1920-5).

Samuel 1 and **2,** books of OT dealing with estab. of Israel as monarchy and its struggle against Philistines. Covers lives of Samuel, Saul, David. Samuel was last of judges who ruled Israelites; Saul and David were 1st kings.

Samuelson, Paul Anthony (1915-), American economist. Advocate of Keynesian theory; presidential adviser in 1960s. Wrote standard introductory textbook Economics (1948); awarded Nobel Prize for Economics (1970).

samurai, aristocratic warrior class of feudal Japan with a strict code (BUSHIDO) of chivalry. Rose to power in 12th cent. during period of weak govt. and held influence until the Meiji restoration (1868).

Sana, cap. of Yemen. Pop. 125,000. Marketing centre. Noted buildings, esp. Great Mosque; palace of former Imam.

San Antonio, city of SC Texas, US; on San Antonio R. Pop. 654,000. Railway jct., commercial, indust. centre. Cattle, cotton market, oil refining, food processing, brewing. Spanish mission estab. 1718. Taken by Texas (1835); heroic Alamo defence 1836.

Sancho III [the Great] (c 970-1035), king of Navarre (c 1000-35). Inherited Navarre and Aragón; expanded kingdom to incl. most of Christian Spain. At his death, kingdom was divided among his 4 sons.

San Cristóbal, town of W Venezuela. Pop. 157,000. Commercial, route centre in coffee-growing region; tanning, distilling, cement mfg. Founded 1561.

sanctions, in international politics, coercive measures adopted in an attempt to enforce a country's fulfilment of its treaty obligations or compliance with international law. Usually economic measures are applied, esp. partial or complete trade boycott. UN banned trade with Rhodesia after unilateral declaration of independence (1965).

George Sand

Sand, George, pseud. of Amandine Lucile Aurore Dudevant, Baronne de, née Dupin (1804-76), French novelist. Left husband, formed liaisons with Musset, Chopin and others. Novels advocating free love incl. Indiana (1832), Lélia (1833), Elle et lui (1859).

sand, sediment composed of rock particles, precisely defined in geology as having particle size between 1/16mm and 2mm. Major constituent is quartz; used in production of glass, building materials, abrasives.

sandalwood, several trees of genus *Santalum* incl. Indian *S. album,* white sandalwood. Hard, fragrant wood used for ornamental carving and burned as incense. East Indian red sandalwood, *Pterocarpus santalinus,* yields dye.

Sandburg, Carl (1878-1967), American poet. Known for free verse celebrating common man, *eg Chicago Poems* (1916), *The People, Yes* (1936), *Honey and Salt* (1965). Also wrote *Life of Abraham Lincoln* (1926-39).

sand dollar, round flat sea urchin that lives on sandy sea bed. Species incl. *Dendraster excentricus* of Pacific coast of North America.

sand fly, small 2-winged fly, genus *Phlebotomus,* whose bite spreads diseases, *eg* oriental sore, sand fly fever.

sandgrouse, any of Pteroclidae family of pigeon-like birds, found in sandy areas of S Europe, Africa, S Asia. Short, feathered legs, long pointed wings and tail. Species incl. pin-tailed sandgrouse, *Pterocles alchata.*

sandhopper, small crustacean with body modified for hopping. Common sandhopper, *Talitrus saltator,* abundant in tidal seaweeds.

Sandhurst, village of Berkshire, S England. Has Royal Military Academy (1799); National Army Museum.

San Diego, seaport of S California, US; on San Diego Bay. Pop. 697,000. Naval base, defence industs.; fish, cotton, agric. exports. Tuna fishing and canning; aerospace and electronic industs. Spanish mission estab. 1769.

sand lizard, *Lacerta agilis,* lizard of sandy regions in C and W Europe.

Common sandpiper

sandpiper, small long-billed shore bird of Scolopacidae family. Species incl. common sandpiper *Tringa hypoleucos,* of Old World, and spotted sandpiper *T. macularia* of North America.

Sandringham, village of Norfolk, E England. Sandringham Hall is a private residence of royal family (acquired 1863).

sandstone, porous sedimentary rock composed mainly of sand grains cemented together. Sand grains usually composed of quartz; cementing material may be calcium carbonate, silica, or iron oxides. Widely distributed; used as building stone.

sandstorm, strong, dry wind carrying clouds of coarse sand. Sand particles rarely raised above 30m/100ft or transported far from source, but may obscure sun. Common in desert areas, esp. N Africa, Arabia, SW US.

Sandusky, port of NC Ohio, US; on Sandusky Bay in L. Erie. Pop. 33,000. Has natural harbour; ships coal, sand, salt. Fishing indust.

Sandwich, John Montagu, 4th Earl of (1718-92), British politician. Maintained corrupt ministry as first lord of the Admiralty (1771-82); generally blamed for British naval failures of American Revolution. Sandwich Isls. named after him, as are sandwiches.

Sandwich, mun. bor. of Kent, SE England, on R. Stour. Pop. 4000. Former Cinque Port; hist. wool indust. estab. by Flemish immigrants.

Sandwich Islands, see HAWAII.

San Fernando, seaport of Trinidad, on Gulf of Paria. Pop. 37,000. Sugar refining, petroleum exports.

San Francisco, seaport of W California, US; on penin. between San Francisco Bay and Pacific. Pop. 716,000. Financial, cultural centre. Exports iron and steel, agric.

produce; shipbuilding, oil refining, printing and publishing industs. Founded 1776; grew after 1849 gold rush; destroyed by 1906 earthquake. Known for Golden Gate Bridge, Latin quarter, Chinatown, cable-cars. Has parts of Univ. of California.

Sanger, Frederick (1918-), English biochemist. Awarded Nobel Prize for Chemistry (1958) for research on amino acid sequence in protein structure of insulin.

Sanhedrin, highest court and council of the ancient Jewish nation, with religious and civil functions. Ended with destruction of Temple (AD 70).

San Jacinto, see HOUSTON, Texas.

San José, cap. of Costa Rica, on C plateau. Pop. 199,000. Commercial, indust. centre; coffee, cacao industs., flour milling, fruit canning. Founded 1738. Has univ. (1843); cathedral; National Museum.

San José, city of W California, US. Pop. 446,000. In fruit-growing area; dried fruit processing, packing; varied mfg. industs. Founded 1777; prospered during gold rush.

San Juan, town of W Argentina, cap. of San Juan prov.; on San Juan R. Pop. 113,000. Wine production. Founded 1562. Devastated by earthquake (1944).

San Juan, cap. of Puerto Rico, seaport on NE coast. Pop. 453,000. Sugar refining; cigar, textile, drug mfg. Founded 1521. Has govt. residence La Fortaleza (built 1529), cathedral (1512).

Sankey, Ira David, see MOODY, DWIGHT LYMAN.

San Luis, town of WC Argentina, cap. of San Luis prov. Pop. 59,000. Grain, wine, cattle market; onyx quarrying nearby. Founded 1596.

San Luis Potosi, town of NC Mexico, cap. of San Luis Potosi state. Pop. 207,000. Railway jct.; clothes, leather mfg. Smelting, metal refining. Founded 1576.

San Marino

San Marino, independent republic of S Europe, enclave within E Italy. Area 62 sq km (24 sq mi); pop. 19,000; cap. San Marino. Silk mfg.; agric. (exports wine, cattle). Quarrying on Mt. Titano. World's smallest republic; claims to be oldest in Europe; traditionally founded 4th cent.

San Martín, José de (1778-1850), Argentinian revolutionary. Organized army in struggle for Argentinian independence from Spain (1812-16). Invaded Chile and defeated Spanish at Chacabuco (1817), securing Chilean independence. Broke off advance into Peru after meeting with Bolívar at Guayaquil (1822).

San Miguel de Tucumán, city of NW Argentina, cap. of Tucumán prov. Pop. 326,000. Railway jct.; in irrigated agric. region in Andean foothills, producing sugar, rice, grain. Cathedral and many colonial buildings.

San Pedro Sula, town of NW Honduras. Pop. 102,000. Banana, sugar export centre; flour milling, soap, cigar mfg. Founded 1536.

San Remo, town of Liguria, NW Italy, on Riviera. Pop. 63,000. Resort; fruit, flower growing. Cathedral (13th cent.). Damaged in WWII.

San Salvador, small isl. of Bahamas. First sighted by Columbus in discovering Americas (1492). Also known as Watling or Watlings Isl.

San Salvador, cap. of El Salvador. Pop. 359,000. Commercial, indust. centre; meat packing, flour milling, textile industs. Founded 1521; cap. of Central American Federation (1831-8). Has National Univ. Has suffered repeated earthquakes.

sans-culottes, term applied during French Revolution to poorer classes, who wore trousers instead of knee breeches worn by aristocracy and bourgeoisie; by extension name was given to extreme republicans.

San Sebastián, city of N Spain, on Bay of Biscay, cap. of Guipúzcoa prov. Pop. 166,000. Port, resort, fishing indust. Former royal summer residence.

Sanskrit, ancient Indic language in Indo-Iranian branch of Indo-European family. Oldest known form is Vedic Sanskrit, language of the Veda (c 1500 BC). Became (c 400 BC) court language as well as literary, religious. Used for Hindu literature until AD 1100, still used in liturgy. Many modern Indic languages developed from it. Comparison of Sanskrit with European languages in 18th cent., esp. by Sir William Jones, initiated scientific study of languages.

San Stefano, Treaty of, settlement (1878) ending war between Russia and Turkey. Concessions to Russia amounting to virtual disintegration of Turkish empire led to treaty's revision at Congress of BERLIN.

Santa Ana, town of W El Salvador. Pop. 105,000. Coffee (one of world's largest coffee mills), sugar industs.; cattle market. Has Gothic cathedral.

Santa Anna, Antonio López de (1794-1876), Mexican military, political leader; president (1833-6, 1841-4, 1846-7, 1853-5). Helped overthrow Iturbide (1823); gained power in lengthy struggle. Attempt to suppress Texas revolt ended in his capture (1836). Defeated in Mexican War (1848). In exile 1848-53, 1855-74.

Santa Barbara, resort town of S California, US; on the Pacific. Pop. 70,000. Centre of citrus fruit growing region. Founded by Spanish (1782); buildings, incl. hist. Santa Barbara Mission (1820), retain a Spanish air.

Santa Barbara Islands, group of 8 isls. off S California, US. Incl. Santa Catalina Isl. resort.

Santa Catarina, state of SE Brazil. Area 95,985 sq km (37,060 sq mi); pop. 2,903,000; cap. Florianópolis. Coastal lowlands in S, offshore isls.; plateaux in W; forests in N. Agric. incl. maize growing, pig rearing. Coal mining in SE.

Santa Clara, town of C Cuba. Pop. 132,000. Commercial, transport centre; sugar, tobacco produce. Founded 1689.

Santa Cruz, town of C Bolivia, cap. of Santa Cruz dept. Pop. 135,000. Agric., commercial centre; trade in rice, sugar cane. Development boosted by transport links. Settled in 1590s.

Santa Cruz de Tenerife, city of Tenerife isl., Canary Isls., Spain; cap. of Santa Cruz de Tenerife prov. Pop. 151,000. Port, exports agric. produce; resort, refuelling station.

Santa Fé, town of EC Argentina, cap. of Santa Fé prov. Pop. 312,000. Linked by canal to Paraná R., transport jct. for grain, livestock trade. Founded 1573. Has cathedral.

Santa Fé, cap. and tourist resort of New Mexico, US. Pop. 41,000. Commercial centre in agric. region. Founded by Spanish (1609); noted buildings incl. 17th cent. Palace of Governors. W terminus of Santa Fé trail, important 19th cent. caravan route. Los Alamos atomic research centre is c 40 km (25 mi) away.

Santa Isabel, see MALABO.

Santa Marta, port of N Colombia, on Caribbean. Pop. 129,000. Has deep harbour; banana, coffee exports. Founded 1525, frequently sacked in colonial period.

Santander, Francisco de Paula (1792-1840), Colombian revolutionary. Banished 1828 for opposing Bolívar, his former colleague in revolt against Spain. Returned as president of New Granada (1832-6) after break-up of Greater Columbia at Bolívar's death.

Santander, city of N Spain, on Bay of Biscay, cap. of Santander prov. Pop. 150,000. Port, resort; iron works, shipbuilding. Largely rebuilt after fire (1941). Nearby is ALTAMIRA.

Santarém, town of C Portugal, on R. Tagus. Pop. 17,000. Cap. of Ribatejo prov.; olives, wine trade. Taken from Moors 1147; medieval walls, castle.

Santayana, George (1863-1952), American philosopher, poet, b. Spain. Lived in Europe from 1912 to escape American Puritanism. Philosophy reflects scepticism, materialism, eg The Life of Reason (1905-6), The Realms of Being (1940). Also wrote novel The Last Puritan (1935), sonnets.

Santiago, cap. of Chile, at foot of Andes; alt. 520 m (c 1700 ft). Pop. 2,662,000 (with suburbs). Commercial, indust. centre; textile, clothing, iron and steel, chemical mfg. Has railway link with Valparaiso. Founded 1541. Chilean independence achieved under San Martín nearby at Maípu. Has National Univ. (1842); cathedral (1619).

Santiago (de Compostela), town of Galicia, NW Spain. Pop. 71,000. Tourist resort, pilgrimage centre from 9th cent.; univ. (1501). Cathedral (11th cent.) contains relics claimed to be those of St James.

Santiago de Cuba, major port of SE Cuba. Pop. 292,000. Sugar, tobacco produce; mineral exports. Founded 1514. Has cathedral.

Santiago del Estero, town of NC Argentina, cap. of Santiago del Estero prov., on Río Dulce. Pop. 119,000. Health resort. Cattle produce; flour milling, tanning, textile mfg. Founded 1553.

Santiago (de los Caballeros), town of NC Domincan Republic. Pop. 155,000. In fertile agric. region; commercial centre for coffee, rice, tobacco produce. Settled in 16th cent.

Santo Domingo, cap. of Dominican Republic, port on S coast. Pop. 671,000. Sugar, coffee, cacao exports; distilling, brewing, soap mfg. Founded 1496; called Ciudad Trujillo (1936-61). Has univ. (1538); 16th cent. cathedral (reputed tomb of Columbus). Badly damaged in 1930 hurricane.

Santos, Atlantic port of SE Brazil, in São Paulo state. Pop. 346,000. Major coffee, sugar, fruit exports. Ocean access for São Paulo.

São Francisco, river of E Brazil. Rises in SW Minas Gerais plateau, flows NE 2900 km (c 1800 mi) to enter Atlantic ocean NE of Aracajú. H.e.p. supplies from Afonso Falls.

São Luís, seaport of N Brazil, cap. of Maranhão state; on São Luís Isl. Pop. 266,000. Cotton, sugar industs. Founded by French (1612).

Saône, river of E France. Flows c 450 km (280 mi) from Vosges via Chalon, Mâcon to R. Rhône at Lyons. Rhône-Saône corridor is hist. route between N and S France; canal links with many rivers, eg Rhine, Seine.

São Paulo, city of SE Brazil, cap. of São Paulo state. Pop. 5,922,000 (with suburbs). Leading commercial, transport centre. Exports farm produce via port of Santos. Heavy machinery, motor vehicles, chemicals, textiles mfg. Founded by Jesuits (1554). Has many notable modern buildings, 4 univs., law school; Butanta Institute (snake serum). Underwent rapid growth in late 19th cent.

São Tomé and Principe, republic off W coast of Africa, comprising 2 isls. in Gulf of Guinea. Area 964 sq km (372 sq mi); pop. 75,000; cap. São Tomé (pop. 8000). Exports coffee, cacao, coconut products. Prov. of Portugal from 1522, became independent 1975.

sap, fluid in plants consisting of inorganic salts from soil and carbohydrates manufactured by plant in an aqueous solution. See TRANSPIRATION.

Sapir, Edward (1884-1939), American anthropologist and linguist, b. Pomerania. Known for ethnological and linguistic studies of Indians of NW US. Wrote Language, an Introduction to the Study of Speech (1921).

Sapper, pseud. of [Herman] Cyril McNeile (1888-1937), English author, soldier. Known for adventure story Bulldog Drummond (1920) and sequels.

sapphire, precious gemstone, a variety of CORUNDUM. Deep blue and transparent; used in jewellery and gramophone styli. Major sources in Burma, Thailand, India (esp. Kashmir), Australia.

Sappho (*fl* 6th cent. BC), Greek poet. Famous from own period as lyric poet of love, poems are intensely personal, passionate, metrically versatile. Began tradition of subjective love lyric. Verse survives only in fragments.

Sapporo, city of Japan, indust. centre of SW Hokkaido isl. Pop. 1,010,000. Flour milling, woodworking and printing industs. Tourist centre; site of 1972 Winter Olympics.

saprophyte, any organism which lives on dead organic matter, *eg* certain fungi, bacteria, *etc.*

Saracens, name applied by the Christians during the Middle Ages to their Moslem enemies. Name originally applied to nomadic Arabs inhabiting frontier land between Roman and Persian empires.

Saragossa (*Zaragoza*), city of NE Spain, on R. Ebro, cap. of Saragossa prov. Pop. 480,000. Agric. market; indust., commercial centre; univ. (1587). Roman *Caesarea Augusta*; held by Moors until 1118; cap. of Aragón 12th-15th cent. Surrendered to French after heroic defence (1808-9) in Peninsular War. Moorish castle, 2 cathedrals (12th, 17th cent.).

Sarajevo, city of C Yugoslavia, cap. of Bosnia and Hercegovina. Pop. 244,000. Railway jct.; indust. centre, esp. carpets, tobacco, chemicals. Under Turkish rule 15th-19th cent. Scene of assassination (June 1914) of Archduke Francis Ferdinand, led to WWI. Has mosques (Islamic centre); RC, Orthodox cathedrals.

Saratoga Springs, health resort of E New York, US. Pop. 19,000. Has spa, horse racecourse. Scene of heavy fighting in American Revolution (1777).

Saratov, city of USSR, SC European RSFSR; on Volga. Pop. 790,000. Indust. centre, producing agric. machinery, chemicals, locomotives. Oil refining; natural gas fields nearby.

Sarawak, state of East Malaysia. Area *c* 125,000 sq km (48,000 sq mi); pop. 977,000; cap. Kuching. Produces oil, bauxite, rubber. Ceded to James Brooke (1841), whose family ruled as rajahs until 1946; British protect. 1888; joined Malaysia 1963.

sarcoma, malignant tumour arising in the connective tissue, bones or muscles. Spreads by extension into neighbouring tissue or by way of bloodstream.

sarcophagus, stone or terracotta coffin, often elaborately carved and inscribed. Oldest known examples are Egyptian; famous example is that of Tutankhamen (from 14th cent. BC). Well-preserved Greek examples were found at Sidon in Phoenicia.

sardine, see PILCHARD.

Sardinia (*Sardegna*), isl. of Italy, separated from mainland by Tyrrhenian Sea, from Corsica by Str. of Bonifacio. Area 24,092 sq km (9302 sq mi); cap. Cagliari. Mountainous, rising to over 1830 m (6000 ft); pasturage, fishing; zinc, lead mining. Carthaginian, taken by Rome 238 BC; contested by Pisa, Genoa from 11th cent.; papal award to Spain 14th cent. Ruled as Kingdom of Sardinia by Savoy from 1720 until it led move to Italian unification (1861).

Sardis or **Sardes,** ancient city of W Asia Minor, now village in Turkey. Cap. of kingdom of Lydia in 7th cent. BC. Early Christian centre; one of Seven Churches in Asia. Sacked by Tamerlane (1402).

sardonyx, semi-precious gemstone, a variety of CHALCEDONY. Consists of alternate layers of brownish-red sard or carnelian and white chalcedony or onyx. Used in jewellery, esp. in cameos.

Sardou, Victorien (1831-1908), French playwright. Known for light comedies of manners, *eg Les Pattes de mouche* (1860), *La Famille Benoîton* (1865). Also wrote historical plays, *eg La Tosca* (1887), basis of Puccini's opera.

Sargasso Sea, area of still water at centre of ocean currents in N Atlantic between West Indies and Azores. Abundant seaweed covers its surface. Of great biological interest.

Sargent, John Singer (1856-1925), American painter, b. Florence. Resident in London after 1884, he painted fashionable society portraits with brilliant virtuosity. Also painted impressionistic watercolour landscapes.

Sargent, Sir [Harold] Malcolm (1895-1967), English conductor. Conducted BBC Symphony Orchestra (1951-7). Achieved great popularity as conductor-in-chief of Promenade Concerts (1951-67).

Sargon II (772-705 BC), king of Assyria (722-705 BC). Extended and consolidated Assyrian empire. Conquered N kingdom of Israel, carrying Jews into captivity. Subdued Babylon (710).

Sark (Fr. *Sercq*), one of Channel Isls., UK. Area 5sq km (2sq mi); comprises Great and Little Sark connected by isthmus. Isl. governed by hereditary 'seigneur' or 'dame'.

Sarnia, port of SW Ontario, Canada; on St Clair R. at S end of L. Huron. Pop. 58,000. Connected by pipeline to Alberta oil fields, has major oil refineries. Synthetic rubber mfg.

Saronic Gulf or **Gulf of Aegina,** inlet of Aegean Sea, SE Greece. Chief port Piraeus. Joined to Gulf of Corinth by canal (1881-93).

Saroyan, William (1908-), American author. Known for short story collections, *eg The Daring Young Man on the Flying Trapeze* (1934), plays, *eg The Time of Your Life* (1939). Also wrote novels incl. *Boys and Girls Together* (1963), an indictment of American marriage.

Sarraute, Nathalie, née Tcherniak (1902-), French novelist, b. Russia. Early exponent of *nouveau roman*. Works incl. *Tropismes* (1939), *Portrait d'un inconnu* (1947), *Le Planétarium* (1959).

sarsaparilla, several climbing or trailing tropical American vines of genus *Smilax*. Toothed, heart-shaped leaves; large, fragrant roots used as flavouring in a soft drink and formerly in medicine.

Sarto, Andrea del (1486-1531), Florentine painter. Noted for his rich colour and painterly qualities, he specialized in religious subjects; works incl. fresco *Nativity of the Virgin* and painting *Madonna of the Harpies*.

Jean-Paul Sartre

Sartre, Jean-Paul (1905-), French philosopher. Leading figure in EXISTENTIALISM. Works incl. novels *eg La Nausée* (1938), trilogy *Les Chemins de la liberté* (1945-9), plays *Les Mouches* (1943), *Huis Clos* (1944), philosophical *L'Etre et le néant* (1943). Nobel Prize for Literature (1964).

Sarum, Old and **New,** see SALISBURY, England.

Sasebo, seaport of Japan, W Kyushu isl. Pop. 248,000. Naval base; shipbuilding, engineering.

Saskatchewan, Prairie prov. of WC Canada. Area 651,903 sq km (251,700 sq mi); pop. 926,000; cap. Regina; other major city Saskatoon. Drained in N by Churchill R. Forests, lakeland in N, prairies in S. Mineral resources in N (esp. uranium at Athabaska); timber in C parkland; major wheat production in S. Fur trading area purchased by Canada from Hudson's Bay Co. (1869). Became prov. in 1905.

Saskatchewan, river of C Saskatchewan, Canada; formed by confluence of N Saskatchewan and S Saskatchewan rivers. Flows E 550 km (340 mi) through Cedar L. to L. Winnipeg. Provides h.e.p., irrigation for large area.

Saskatoon, city of SC Saskatchewan, Canada; on S Saskatchewan R. Pop. 126,000. Agric. distribution centre; meat packing, oil refining.

Sassafras

sassafras, *Sassafras albidum,* North American tree of laurel family with yellow flowers, dark blue fruits and aromatic bark and foliage. Various extracts formerly used in manufacture of medicines, foods, drinks (root beer) but now regarded as possible carcinogen.

Sassanids or **Sassanians,** last dynasty of native Persian rulers (AD *c* 226-*c* 641). Founded by chieftain Ardashir, who estab. his cap. at Ctesiphon and overthrew kingdom of Parthia. Fought frequent wars with Rome and Byzantium. Conquered by Arabs (*c* 641).

Sassoon, Siegfried Lorraine (1886-1967), English author. Experiences in WWI inspired anti-war *Counter-attack and Other Poems* (1918). Wrote semi-autobiog. novels, *Memoirs of a Fox-Hunting Man* (1928), *Memoirs of an Infantry Officer* (1930).

Satan, in Judaism, Christianity and Islam, the enemy of God and humanity, *ie* a unified personification of evil as opposed to that of good. Also called the Devil. NT developed idea of Satan as prince of demons, enemy of Christ, and describes war in heaven. Central figure of many popular legends, in literature appears as Mephistopheles (*eg* Goethe's *Faust*), Lucifer (*eg* Milton's *Paradise Lost*). During medieval and early modern period, conceived of as everpresent enemy of Christians, esp. saints.

satellite, in astronomy, celestial body in orbit about larger body, usually a planet; Moon is a satellite of the Earth. Russians placed 1st artifical satellite (sputnik) in orbit about Earth (1957). Many have been launched since for communication purposes and to study upper atmosphere, radiation from outer space, *etc.*

Satie, Erik (1866-1925), French composer. Produced clear and simple music, often ironic or satirical in character. Works incl. ballets, *eg Parade,* songs, and many piano pieces, *eg Gymnopédies.*

satin, silk or rayon fabric having a smooth finish, glossy on the face and dull on the back. First made in China, popularized in Europe during Middle Ages.

satinwood, close-grained, hard, yellow wood of East Indian tree *Chloroxylon swietenia* and West Indian *Zanthoxylum flavum.* Used in veneers, marquetry, *etc.*

satire, literary work, in prose or poetry, or work of art, *etc,* which ridicules individuals, situations, ideas, esp. with aim of correcting vice. Uses mockery, wit, parody or irony; may be humorous or serious.

Sato, Eisaku (1901-75), Japanese statesman. Premier (1964-72) at head of Liberal Democratic govt. Negotiated treaty normalizing relations between South Korea and Japan (1965). Awarded Nobel Peace Prize (1974).

Satsuma, penin. of SW Kyushu isl., Japan. Famous porcelain made in area from 16th cent. Scene of revolt against imperial govt. in 1877.

Saturn, in Roman religion, god of harvests, later identified with Greek Cronus. Husband of Ops, father of Jupiter, Juno, Ceres, Pluto, Neptune. His festival, Saturnalia, was celebrated near the winter solstice with feasting, revelry and licence for slaves, and was prototype for modern Christmas.

Saturn, in astronomy, 2nd largest planet of Solar System, 6th in distance from Sun; mean distance from Sun *c* 1427 million km; diameter 119,300 km; revolves about Sun with period of *c* 29½ years. Has 10 natural satellites and system of 3 concentric rings of small particles. Has dense atmosphere containing hydrogen, ammonia and methane.

satyr, in Greek myth, minor woodland deity; attendant of Dionysus. Represented with pointed ears, short horns, head and body of man, legs of a goat. Given to riotous merriment and lechery. Similar to Roman faun.

Saudi Arabia, kingdom of SW Asia, occupying most of ARABIA. Area *c* 2,149,690 (830,000 sq mi); pop. 8,443,000; cap. Riyadh. Language: Arabic. Religion: Sunnite Islam. Mainly desert; agric., pastoral economy; great wealth derived from rich oil deposits in E. Has Islamic holy cities Mecca, Medina in Hejaz. State formed 1932 following unification of Nejd and Hejaz under Ibn Saud in 1925.

Saul (d. *c* 1012 BC), first king of Israel. The Bible relates how he was consumed by jealousy for his rival David, whose patron he had previously been. Killed himself after defeat by Philistines at Mt. Gilboa.

Sault Ste Marie, port of SC Ontario, Canada; on international canal link between L. Superior and L. Huron. Pop. 80,000. Timber, steel industs. Estab. as French mission in 17th cent.; became fur trade post. Opposite is **Sault Ste Marie,** town of Michigan, US; on St Mary's R. Pop. 15,000.

Saumur, town of Anjou, W France, on R. Loire. Pop. 23,000. Produces brandy and sparkling wines, medallions. Huguenot stronghold in 16th cent. Church (12th cent.), cavalry school (1768).

Saussure, Ferdinand de (1857-1913), Swiss linguist, regarded as father of structural LINGUISTICS. Clearly demarcated synchronic and diachronic ways of studying language. Held that language must be studied as social phenomenon. Distinguished between total structure of a language (*langue*) and individual acts of speaking (*parole*). Theories contained in *Cours de linguistique générale* pub. (1916).

Saussure, Horace Benedict de (1740-99), Swiss physicist and geologist. Studied meteorology, botany, geology of Alpine regions. Wrote *Voyages dans les Alpes* (1779-96).

Sava or **Save,** river of N Yugoslavia. Flows *c* 940 km (585 mi) from Julian Alps via Zagreb to Danube at Belgrade. Fertile basin used for agric.

Savage, Michael Joseph (1872-1940), New Zealand statesman, b. Australia. First Labour PM (1935-40). Term notable for social legislation, *eg* Social Security Act (1938).

Savaii, isl. of Western Samoa. Area 1750 sq km (675 sq mi). Mountainous but fertile, produces bananas, coconuts, cocoa. Formerly called Chatham Isl.

savanna or **savannah,** natural grassland containing scattered trees and bushes. Found in tropical and subtropical areas with distinct rainy season. Most extensive in Africa; occurs also in *llanos* and *campos* of South America.

Savannah, port of E Georgia, US; near mouth of Savannah R. Pop. 118,000. Naval supplies, cotton exports; shipbuilding, sugar refining, varied mfg. industs. Strategic in American Revolution and Civil War.

savings and loan association, *see* BUILDING SOCIETY.

Savoie, see SAVOY, France.

Savona, town of Liguria, NW Italy, on Gulf of Genoa. Cap. of Savona prov. Pop. 81,000. Port; iron, steel, pottery industs. Hist. rival of Genoa, defeated 1528.

Savonarola, Girolamo (1452-98), Italian Dominican monk. Gained power in Florence through his powerful sermons and prophetic visions. Inspired expulsion of Pietro de' Medici from Florence (1494) and ruled as virtual dictator, advocating a return to ascetic Christian values. Denounced corruption of papal court but was excommunicated by Alexander VI (1497). Ordered to stop preaching by city govt., he was arrested, convicted of heresy and executed.

savory, any of genus *Satureia* of aromatic herbs of mint family. Species incl. summer savory, *S. hortensis,* and winter savory, *S. montana,* both native to Europe and used in cooking.

Savoy (*Savoie*), region of SE France, hist. cap. Chambéry. Incl. Savoy Alps, Graian Alps, Mont Blanc massif. Agric., esp. dairying, tourism, h.e.p. Medieval county; duchy from 1416. Ruled by House of Savoy, lost much territ. to France, Switzerland in early 16th cent. Part of Kingdom of Sardinia from 1720; ceded to France (1860).

Savoy, House of, European royal family, sometime rulers of Piedmont, Valois, Bresse, Nice. Acquired Sicily under Peace of Utrecht (1714) and exchanged it for Sardinia (1720). Reign of CHARLES ALBERT, king of Sardinia, saw beginnings of RISORGIMENTO; his son VICTOR EMMANUEL II was 1st king of united Italy. Ruling Italian dynasty lasted from 1861 until abdication of Humbert II (1946).

sawbelly, see ALEWIFE.

sawfish, cartilaginous fish with flattened shark-like body, genus *Pristis,* common in tropical seas. Elongated flattened snout with pointed teeth on side used to dig for food.

sawfly, any of suborder Symphyta of hymenopterous insects. Female has saw-like ovipositor used to lay eggs in leaves or stems of plants. Caterpillar-like larvae are herbivorous; often garden pests.

Sax, [Antoine Joseph] Adolphe (1814-94), Belgian musical instrument maker. Designed saxophone and saxhorn family of wind instruments.

Saxe, Maurice, Comte de (1696-1750), German soldier in French service. In the War of the Austrian Succession, gained a brilliant victory over European Allies at Fontenoy (1745).

Saxe-Coburg-Gotha (*Sachsen-Coburg-Gotha*), region of West Germany, former duchy created 1826 by union of Saxe-Coburg and Gotha under Ernest I. Ernest's house came to rule Belgium (under his brother, Leopold) and England (under his son, Albert, consort of Victoria). Duchy dispersed (1920) into Thuringia and Bavaria.

Saxe-Weimar (*Sachsen-Weimar*), region of C Germany. Former duchy, cap. Weimar, ruled by Wettin dynasty from 15th cent. United 1741 with Eisenach, became rich cultural centre in 18th cent. Grand duchy from 1815, incorporated (1920) into Thuringia.

saxhorn, family of conical-bore brass wind instruments with valves. Designed in 1840s by Adolphe Sax; played in brass bands.

saxifrage, any of genus *Saxifraga* of mainly perennial plants of N temperate and Arctic regions. Most species grow wild as low, rock plants. Garden varieties incl. London pride, *S. umbrosa,* and rockery variety, *S. aizoon.*

Saxo Grammaticus (*c* 1150-*c* 1206), Danish historian. Wrote Latin *Gesta Danorum* (English translation, 1894), incl. Norse legends, Germanic history.

Saxons, Teutonic people originally inhabiting what is now Schleswig (S Jutland). Spread during 5th–6th cent. through NW Germany, N coast of Gaul, S England (in area of later kingdoms of Sussex, Wessex and Essex). Continental Saxons became known as Old Saxons; fought periodically with Franks until subjugation and conversion by Charlemagne (9th cent.).

Saxony (Ger. *Sachsen*), region of East Germany, hist. cap. Dresden. Main cities Chemnitz, Leipzig. Duchy from 9th cent.; electorate from 14th cent.; kingdom from 1806, joined German empire 1871. Became East German prov. after WWII (dissolved 1952). Name also applied to region of West Germany, corresponding to state of Lower Saxony (*Niedersachsen*).

saxophone, family of musical wind instruments, varying in range and size but all having single reed and conical tube of brass. Used in military bands, jazz groups and orchestras. Developed by Adolphe Sax in 1840s.

Say, Jean Baptiste (1767-1832), French economist. Recognizing work of Adam Smith, evolved theory of markets (supply creates demand) in *Treatise on Political Economy* (1803).

Sayers, Dorothy L[eigh] (1893-1957), English author. Known for detective novels featuring erudite hero, Lord Peter Wimsey, *eg Clouds of Witness* (1926). Also wrote religious radio play, *The Man Born to be King* (1941), translations of Dante.

scabies, skin disease caused by parasitic mite *Sarcoptes scabiei.* Female burrows under skin, esp. around elbows and groin, to lay eggs. Main symptom is intense itch.

Devil's bit scabious (Scabiosa succisa)

scabious, any of genus *Scabiosa* of annual or perennial herbs native to Europe, Asia and Africa. Species incl. sweet scabious, *S. atropurpurea,* with white, pink or purple flowers and field scabious, *S. arvensis,* with purple flowers.

Scafell Pike, mountain of Lake Dist., Cumbria, NW England. Highest in England (978 m/3210 ft); part of Scafell mountain group. Tourist area.

Scala, Teatro alla, famous opera house in Milan, Italy, usually known as La Scala. Opened 1778; built on site of church Santa Maria della Scala.

scalawags, term used in South after US Civil War to refer to white Southern Republicans who aided RECONSTRUCTION programme.

scale, in music, progression in ascending or descending order of related groups of notes. Most pieces of music are based on specific scale, the key of any piece being given by starting note (tonic note) of scale.

scale insect, small insect of Coccidae family. Female body covered with 'scale' made of cast-off skin and glutinous secretion. Many parasitic on plants, poisoning them with saliva. Others commercially useful, yielding shellac or carmine dye.

scallop, any of Pectinidae family of bivalve molluscs. Two fan-shaped, radially-ribbed shells with wavy outer edge; swims by snapping shells together. Adductor muscle is edible.

scalp, skin covering top and back of head. Attached to an underlying muscle (occipitofrontalis) which in turn covers a layer of loose tissue and blood vessels.

scalytail, any of Anomaluridae family of arboreal rodents of tropical Africa. Resembles flying squirrel, with gliding membrane stretched between limbs.

Scandinavia, penin. of NW Europe, comprising Norway, Sweden; bounded by Arctic Ocean, Atlantic, Baltic, Gulf of Bothnia. Culturally and hist. also incl. Denmark, Finland, Iceland, Faeroe Isls.

Scandinavian, see GERMANIC LANGUAGES.

scandium (Sc), rare metallic element; at. no. 21, at. wt. 44.96. Occurs in several minerals; discovered (1879) by spectroscopic analysis.

Scapa Flow, sea area of Orkney Isls., N Scotland. UK naval base in WWI and II. Interned German fleet scuttled (1919).

Scaphopoda, class of marine molluscs, comprising tusk shells. Curved tapering shell open at both ends, powerful foot used for burrowing in sand.

scarab beetle, any of Scarabaeidae family of large beetles with club-ended antennae. Incl. dung beetles and chafers. Name particularly applies to Egyptian sacred dung beetle *Scarabaeus sacer* whose image appears on seals or charms.

Scaramouche, stock character in COMMEDIA DELL'ARTE, a cowardly braggart.

Scarborough, mun. bor. of North Yorkshire, NE England. Pop. 44,000. Spa, resort; fishing port. Has remains of 12th cent. castle.

Alessandro Scarlatti

Schiller

Scarlatti, Alessandro (*c* 1660-1725), Italian composer. Pioneer of Italian opera, developed *aria da capo;* wrote masses, cantatas, oratorios. His son, **[Giuseppe] Domenico Scarlatti** (1685-1757), was also a composer. His harpsichord sonatas, over 500 in number, show great originality in use of the keyboard.

scarlet fever or **scarlatina,** contagious disease, esp. of children, caused by bacterium *Streptococcus pyogenes.* Characterized by fever, sore throat, and a scarlet rash. Treated by antibiotics, *eg* penicillin.

scepticism or ' **skepticism,** in philosophy, theory contending that range of knowledge is limited by capacity of mind or inaccessibility of object. Exponents incl. Democritus, Pyrrho, Kant.

Schacht, Hjalmar Horace Greeley (1877–1970), German financier. As president of Reichsbank (1923-30, 1933-9), stabilized currency after disastrous inflation of 1923; helped finance rearmament under Hitler. Acquitted at Nuremberg trials over role in rearmament.

Schaffhausen, town of N Switzerland, on R. Rhine, cap. of Schaffhausen canton. Pop. 37,000. Indust. centre using h.e.p. from Schaffhausen Falls. Romanesque minster (11th cent.).

Scheele, Karl Wilhelm (1742-86), Swedish chemist. Discovered numerous compounds, incl. chlorine, oxygen, nitrogen and many acids.

scheelite, tungsten ore mineral. Consists of calcium tungstate; brown, yellow or white in colour, always fluorescent in ultraviolet light. Major source of US tungsten, found also in Italy, Germany, England.

Scheldt (Fr. *Escaut*; Dutch, Flem. *Schelde*), river of W Europe. Flows 435 km (270 mi) from N France via Belgium (Tournai, Antwerp) to estuary in Netherlands. Connected to many canals.

Schelling, Friedrich Wilhelm Joseph von (1775-1854), German philosopher. Influential in German Romanticism. Sought to solve problem of knowledge by positing unity of mind and nature. Works incl. *The Ages of the World* (1854).

Schenectady, town of E New York, US; on Mohawk R. Pop. 77,000. General Electric Company hq.; chemical mfg. Founded by Dutch (1661).

Schick test, test to determine immunity to diphtheria. Diluted dose of diphtheria toxin is injected into skin; if area of inflammation appears, patient is not immune.

Schiedam, town of W Netherlands, on R. Nieuwe Maas. Pop. 83,000. Port; famous gin indust., glass mfg.

Schiehallion, mountain of Tayside region, C Scotland. Almost conical in shape; height 1081 m (3547 ft). Density of Earth calculated here in 1774.

Schiele, Egon (1890-1918), Austrian painter. Influenced by Klimt and Freudian psychology, he is known for his expressionist linear style of depicting figures.

Schiller, [Johann Christoph] Friedrich von (1759-1805), German poet, dramatist, historian. Associate of Goethe, began with Sturm und Drang prose dramas, *eg The Robbers* (1781). Later works more realistic, classical in form, *eg Wallenstein* (1798-9), *Maria Stuart* (1800), *The Maid of Orleans* (1801), *Wilhelm Tell* (1804). Also wrote didactic poems, *eg* 'The Artists' (1789), scholarly *History of the Thirty Years' War* (1791-3).

Schism, Great, split in RC church (1378-1417) after death of Gregory XI, resulting in rival lines of popes in Avignon and Rome. Following Council of Pisa (1409), there were 3 rival claimants to papacy, Gregory XII, Benedict XIII and John XXIII. Concluded by Council of Constance, when Martin V was elected pope.

schist, metamorphic rock, composed of thin, parallel layers of constituent minerals. Mineral crystals are finer than gneiss, coarser than slate. Types distinguished by dominant mineral *eg* mica schist, hornblende schist, talc schist.

schistosomiasis, see BILHARZIA.

schizophrenia, severe mental disorder characterized by separation of thought processes from reality, fragmentation of personality, withdrawal from human contact, bizarre behaviour, delusions and hallucinations. Treated by electric shocks, tranquilizer drugs such as chlorpromazine, psychotherapy.

Schlegel, August Wilhelm von (1767-1845), German scholar. Known for translations of Shakespeare (1797-1810, completed by others). Edited periodical *Athenaeum* with brother, Friedrich. Critical works influenced German Romantic movement.

Schleiermacher, Friedrich Daniel Ernst (1768-1834), German philosopher. Protestant theologian, attacked rationalism and orthodoxy in *The Christian Faith* (1821-2).

Schlesinger, John (1926-), British film director. Became known in early 1960s, esp. for *Billy Liar* (1963); later made *Midnight Cowboy* (1969) in US.

Schleswig-Holstein, state of N West Germany, in S Jutland penin. Area 15,656 sq km (6045 sq mi); cap. Kiel. Low-lying; main rivers Elbe, Eider, crossed by Kiel Canal. Cereals, potatoes, livestock production; industs. centred in Kiel, Lübeck, Flensburg. Duchies associated with Denmark from 15th cent.; annexed by Prussia (1866) after Austro-Prussian War. N Schleswig returned (1920) to Denmark after plebiscite.

Schlieffen, Alfred, Graf von (1833-1913), German army officer. As chief of general staff (1891-1906), devised the 'Schlieffen plan' for a hinge-like flanking movement across Holland and France; used in modified form in WWI.

Schliemann, Heinrich (1822-1890), German archaeologist. Amassed a fortune in business, then devoted himself to locating Homer's Troy. Began excavating (1871) at Hissarlik near Dardanelles and discovered 9

Heinrich Schliemann

superimposed sites which he identified as Troy. His excavations at Mycenae (1874-6) revealed remarkable MYCENAEAN CIVILIZATION.

Schmidt, Helmut (1918-), West German politician. Posts in Social Democratic govt. incl. finance minister from 1972 until succeeding Brandt as chancellor (1974).

schnauzer, breed of short-haired German terrier with blunt nose, erect ears. Standard schnauzer, used as guard dog, stands 43-51 cm/17-20 in. at shoulder.

Schnitzler, Arthur (1862-1931), Austrian author. Known for wittily erotic works portraying Viennese society, *eg* plays *Anatol* (1893), *Reigen* (1900), novels, many short stories.

Schoenberg, Arnold (1874-1951), Austrian composer. Early music was romantic, *eg Transfigured Night* (1899). Later developed ATONALITY of composition, which dispensed need for a key, as in *Pierrot Lunaire* (1912). From 1921, organized this into system of 12-note composition based on manipulation of rows of notes of the chromatic scale. Lived in US from 1933.

scholasticism, philosophical system of medieval European theologians, esp. Robert Grosseteste, St Thomas Aquinas and Albertus Magnus. Constituted synthesis of Aristotelian philosophy and Christian revelation, influenced by neoplatonism. Central problem that of universal concepts (*see* NOMINALISM, REALISM). Major scholastic works incl. Peter Lombard's *Sentences,* Aquinas' *Summa Theologica*.

Schopenhauer, Arthur (1788-1860), German philosopher. Influenced by Kant. Believed man's irrational will to be the only reality, and release from suffering and discord to be achieved only by negation of will. Works incl. *The World as Will and Representation* (1818), *Will in Nature* (1836).

Schreiner, Olive, pseud. Ralph Iron (1855-1920), South African author. Wrote *The Story of an African Farm* (1883), *Trooper Peter Halket of Mashonaland* (1897) and feminist tracts.

Schrödinger, Erwin (1887-1961), Austrian physicist. Following work of de Broglie on wave nature of matter, he developed mathematical form of quantum theory as wave mechanics. Shared Nobel Prize for Physics with Dirac (1933).

Schubert, Franz Peter (1797-1828), Austrian composer. Noted for his lyrical melody, his work is often underlaid by melancholy. Foremost exponent of German *Lieder;* famous song cycles incl. *Die schöne Müllerin* and *Die Winterreise*. Wrote masterly string quartets, piano pieces. Best-known symphonies are 9th ('Great C major') and 8th ('The Unfinished').

Schuman, Robert (1886-1963), French statesman, premier (1947-8). As foreign minister (1948-53), evolved plan (1950) for European Coal and Steel Community, basis of later European Community.

Schubert

Schumann

Schumann, Robert Alexander (1810-56), German composer. Works incl. collections of piano pieces, *Carnaval* and *Kreisleriana,* Piano Concerto in A Minor, and *Spring* and *Rhenish* symphonies. Encouraged appreciation of works of Chopin and Brahms. His wife, **Clara Schumann,** née Wieck (1819-96), was renowned pianist and leading interpreter of her husband's work.

Schuschnigg, Kurt von (1897-), Austrian statesman. Succeeded Dollfuss as chancellor (1934). Resisted Hitler's attempts to incorporate Austria into Germany; forced to resign after Nazis had occupied Austria (March, 1938). Imprisoned 1938-45.

Schütz, Heinrich (1585-1672), German composer. Studied in Italy, where he was influenced by Giovanni Gabrieli and Monteverdi. Introduced Italian techniques of vocal writing into Germany. Works incl. madrigals, series of *Symphoniae Sacrae, Christmas Oratorio.*

Schwarzkopf, Elisabeth (1915-), German singer. Formerly principal soprano at Vienna State Opera and Royal Opera House, Covent Garden. Excelled in Mozart and Richard Strauss. Noted interpreter of *Lieder.*

Schwarzwald, *see* BLACK FOREST, West Germany.

Schweitzer, Albert (1875-1965), Alsatian physician, missionary, theologian. From 1913, devoted himself to medical mission at Lambaréné, Gabon. Noted organist; wrote biog. of Bach and edited his organ music. In philosophy, believed in 'reverence for life', respecting all living creatures. Awarded Nobel Peace Prize (1952).

Schwerin, town of NW East Germany, on L. Schwerin. Pop. 91,000. Chemicals, pharmaceticals mfg. Founded 1160; hist. cap. of Mecklenburg.

Schwitters, Kurt (1887-1948), German artist. Invented *Merz*, collage form using bits of paper and rubbish. Made large constructions (*Merzbau*) of scrap metal, wood, *etc.*

Schwyz, town of C Switzerland, cap. of Schwyz canton. Pop. 12,000. Tourist centre near L. Lucerne.

sciatica, pain along the course of the sciatic nerve, esp. affecting back of thigh, calf and foot. Often caused by pressure exerted on spinal nerves by invertebral discs.

science, system of knowledge, founded on formal axioms or theories constructed from observation and experiment. Sciences such as physics and chemistry, which try to describe and account for natural phenomena, are often studied by theories which express mathematically a principle underlying numerous observations. Ideally, such theories encompass all previous knowledge on the phenomena and can be used to make testable predictions; they are discarded or suitably modified if they are found to be too inaccurate or at a variance with experimental evidence.

science fiction, literary genre drawing on scientific knowledge or speculation to present fantasy. Typical motifs incl. interplanetary travel, artificial intelligence, global cataclysm. Early exponents incl. Jules Verne, H.G. Wells; developed by Isaac Asimov, Ray Bradbury, Arthur C. Clarke.

scientology, religio-scientific movement estab. in US (*c* 1950) by Lafayette Ronald Hubbard (1911-   ). From 1959 world hq. at East Grinstead, England. Members use process similar to psychoanalysis to release energy of subconscious drives. Controversial practices have led to official inquiries in some countries.

Scilly Isles, archipelago off Cornwall, SW England. Incl. *c* 140 granite isls., 5 inhabited (St Mary's, Tresco, St Martin's, St Agnes, Bryher). Area 16 sq km (6 sq mi); pop. 2000; cap. Hugh Town. Mild climate; tourism; early flowers indust. Prehist. barrow on Samson Isl.

Scipio, Publius Cornelius ('Africanus Major') (*c* 234-183 BC), Roman soldier. Routed Carthaginian armies in Spain (210-206). Invaded Carthage (204), forcing Hannibal to return from Italy. Defeated Hannibal at Zama (202). His son's adopted son, **Publius Cornelius Scipio ('Africanus Minor')** (*c* 185-129 BC), commanded destruction of Carthage, ending 3rd Punic War (146).

Scone, village of Tayside region, C Scotland. Old Scone was site of Scottish coronations. Coronation Stone ('Stone of Destiny') moved (1297) to Westminster Abbey.

Scopes trial, in US legal history, trial (1925) of school teacher John T. Scopes for teaching Darwinian theory of evolution, then contrary to Tennessee state law. He was convicted but later released on a technicality.

Scorpio, see ZODIAC.

Scorpion

scorpion, any of order Scorpionida of arachnids of warm and tropical regions. Two large pincers in front, long segmented tail with venomous sting.

scorpion fish, spiny-rayed marine fish of Scorpaenidae family. Tropical varieties often have poisonous dorsal fins.

scorpion fly, any of order Mecoptera of small carnivorous flies. Curled-over abdomen of male resembles scorpion tail.

Scotland, constituent country of UK, in N part of GREAT BRITAIN. Area 78,749 sq km (30,405 sq mi); pop. 5,228,000;

Scotland

cap. Edinburgh; largest city Glasgow. Comprises 9 regions, 3 isl. authorities. Main rivers Clyde, Forth, Tay, Dee. Highlands, isls. in N, W (crofting, fishing, forestry, tourism); uplands in S (sheep rearing). Pop. and industs. mainly concentrated in C lowlands, incl. coalmining, shipbuilding, engineering industs. Offshore oil, gas in E. Christianity spread from 6th cent.; hist. warring with England until union of Crowns under James VI (1603), politically united with England from 1707; Jacobite rebellions in 1715, 1745. Resurgence of nationalism in 20th cent.

Scotland, Church of, established national church in Scotland, presbyterian in govt. Jurisdiction of RC church abolished by Parliament in act of 1560. Under influence of KNOX, reformed church created on self-governing units after Geneva models. Two *Books of Discipline* (1560, 1581) laid out church organization. Development complicated by periods of episcopacy under Stuart rulers leading to National Covenant (*see* COVENANTERS). Established status confirmed in Act of Settlement (1690) and Act of Union (1707). Secessionary groups incl. Free Church of Scotland (1843).

Scotland Yard, hq. of Metropolitan London police, UK. Name derives from original site in street near Whitehall. Used esp. for Criminal Investigation Dept. (CID) which it houses.

R.F. Scott

Scott, Sir George Gilbert (1811-78), English architect. Active in Gothic revival, his numerous works incl. St Pancras Station and Albert Memorial, London. Carried out controversial restorations to many churches, *eg* Westminster Abbey. His grandson, **Sir Giles Gilbert Scott** (1880-1960), designed unfinished Liverpool Cathedral.

Scott, Robert Falcon (1868-1912), English naval officer, explorer. Led expedition (1901-4) in *Discovery* to explore Ross Sea; discovered King Edward VII Land. Led 2nd expedition in *Terra Nova*, reached South Pole (Jan. 1912)

35 days after Amundsen. He and 4 companions died on return journey.

Scott, Sir Walter (1771-1832), Scottish author. Kindled interest in Scots folklore in ballad collection *The Minstrelsy of the Scottish Border* (1802-3), narrative poems, eg *Lay of the Last Minstrel* (1805), *Lady of the Lake* (1810). Romantic historical novels incl. *Waverley* (1814), *Old Mortality* (1816), *Rob Roy* (1818), *The Heart of Midlothian* (1818), *Ivanhoe* (1820), *Kenilworth* (1821).

Scott, Winfield (1786-1866), American general. Supreme army commander (1841-61), he headed the push into Mexico, ending Mexican War (1846-8) with the capture of Mexico City.

Scottish Gaelic, see GAELIC.

Scottish Nationalist Party (SNP), political party evolved from Scottish Home Rule Association (formed 1886). Advocates self-govt. for Scotland. Made significant electoral gains in 1970s.

Scottish terrier, breed of dog developed in Scotland in 19th cent. to hunt game. Stands *c* 25 cm/10 in. at shoulder.

Scotus, see DUNS SCOTUS, JOHN.

Scranton, town of NE Pennsylvania, US; on Lackawanna R. Pop. 102,000. Indust. centre of anthracite mining region; textile and chemical mfg.

screamer, any of Anhimidae family of long-legged birds of South American forests and rivers. Two sharp spurs on each wing. Species incl. horned screamer, *Anhima cornuta,* with large bony horn on head.

scree, see TALUS.

screech owl, New World owl, genus *Otus.* Species incl. North American *O. asio* with grey or reddish brown body, ear tufts and wailing cry.

Scriabin, Aleksandr Nikolayevich (1872-1915), Russian composer and pianist. Works, often mystical, incl. tone poems *Prometheus, Divine Poem, Poem of Ecstasy.* Used personal harmony based on a special 'mystic chord'.

scribes, term for officials learned in Jewish law. First applied to Ezra (*c* 444 BC); last to Simeon the Just (4th-3rd cent. BC). Work developed into Oral Law of TALMUD.

Scripps, Edward Wyllis (1854-1926), American newspaper publisher. With brother George and M.A. McRae formed Scripps-McRae League, influential radical newspaper chain. Estab. United Press Association (1907). His son, R.P. Scripps, controlled chain with R.W. Howard after 1922, and it was renamed Scripps-Howard chain.

scrofula, tuberculosis of lymph nodes of neck. Characterized by swelling of nodes and ulceration of overlying skin. Formerly called the King's evil, it was believed to be cured by royal touch.

scrub, thick, stunted vegetation found on tracts of poor, semi-arid land. Types incl. maquis of W Mediterranean area, mallee and mulga scrub of Australia, cactus scrub of E Africa.

Scudéry, Madeleine de (1607-1701), French author, also known as 'Sapho'. Wrote discursive sentimental romances, eg *Artamène, ou le Grand Cyrus* (1649-53), *Clélie* (1654-60), containing portraits of her circle.

Scullin, James Henry (1876-1953), Australian statesman, PM (1929-31). United Labor Party (1928), and was its leader (1928-35). Advocated public spending cuts, deflation to deal with Depression.

sculling, sport of propelling a boat by means of sculls (light oars) held in each hand. Competitive sculling races date from 1840s. Single and double sculling are Olympic events.

sculpin, see BULLHEAD.

sculpture, art of producing 3-dimensional representations of forms. Techniques used incl. carving in wood or stone and modelling in wax or clay for eventual casting in plaster, lead or bronze. Field of sculpture has expanded in 20th cent. to incl. kinetic sculpture, assemblages, welded structures, *etc.*

Scunthorpe, mun. bor. of Humberside, E England. Pop. 71,000. Iron and steel indust., developed from local iron ore deposits.

scurvy, disease resulting from deficiency of vitamin C in diet. Characterized by weakening of capillaries, haemorrhages in tissue, bleeding from gums. Formerly a problem on long sea voyages when fresh fruit was unavailable, it was treated in 18th cent. by issuing of lime juice.

Scutari (*Shkodër*), town of NW Albania, on L. Sartari. Pop. 50,000. Wool, grain, tobacco. RC cathedral; Venetian citadel. Cap. of ancient Illyria until 168 BC.

Scutari, Turkey, see ISTANBUL.

Scylla, in Greek myth, daughter of Hecate, loved by Poseidon and turned into a monster by Amphitrite. Devoured sailors who passed her cave in Straits of Messina, S Italy. Opposite was **Charybdis**, a monster who had been thrown into sea by Zeus for stealing Hercules' cattle. A whirlpool was created as she sucked and spewed water.

Scyphozoa, class of coelenterates, consisting of true jellyfish, in which polyp stage is minute or absent.

Scythians, nomadic tribe inhabiting the steppes N of Black Sea between the Danube and Don. (7th-2nd cents. BC). Known from their trading contacts with the Greeks. Their expansion was resisted by Persians under Darius (*c* 512 BC). By 4th cent. BC, a declining power and by 2nd cent. BC, had been overwhelmed by Sarmatians.

sea anemone, sedentary marine coelenterate of class Actinozoa. Columnar body without skeleton; mouth surrounded by circles of petal-like tentacles. Found attached to rocks, weeds.

Seaborg, Glenn Theodore (1912-), American chemist. Shared Nobel Prize for Chemistry (1951) with E.M. McMillan for discoveries in chemistry of transuranic elements; co-discoverer of americium, curium, berkelium and several other elements.

sea bream, see PORGY.

sea cow, name applied to DUGONG or MANATEE.

sea cucumber, see HOLOTHUROIDEA.

sea elephant, *Mirounga leonina,* large seal, largest of pinnipeds; reaches lengths of 6 m/20 ft. Male has inflatable proboscis.

sea gooseberry, see CTENOPHORA.

seagull, common name for many species of GULL.

sea hare, slug-like marine gastropod mollusc, genus *Aplysia,* with small internal shell. Moves by beating 2 lateral lobes (parapodia).

Seahorse

seahorse, small fish of Syngnathidae family, esp. genus *Hippocampus.* Elongated snout and prehensile tail; male has pouch for brooding eggs. *H. ramulosus* is commonest European species.

seal, carnivorous marine mammal, order Pinnipedia. True seal (Phocidae family) has no external ears and rudimentary hind limbs united to tail. Seals of Otariidae family, incl. sea lion, have external ears and hind limbs used for locomotion. Hunted for skins and oil-yielding blubber.

sea leopard, *Hydrurga leptonyx,* large earless seal of Antarctic. Aggressive predator, feeding on penguins and young seals.

sea lily, flower-like marine echinoderm, class Crinoidea. Sedentary, attached to sea bottom by stalk.

Sea lion

sea lion, eared seal of Otariidae family with smooth coat and no under-fur. Californian sea lion, *Zalophus californianus,* noted for agility, is commonest; lives in colonies on N Pacific coast and Galapagos.

Seal Islands, *see* LOBOS ISLANDS.

Sealyham, breed of terrier developed in Wales in 19th cent. Coat mainly white; stands 25 cm/ 10 in. at shoulder.

séance, *see* SPIRITUALISM.

sea otter, *Enhydra lutris,* web-footed marine carnivore of N Pacific coast. Larger than common otter, with long tail; dark brown fur valued commercially.

sea pen, any of order Pennatulacea of feather-like colonial marine coelenterates. Colony consists of central stalk-like polyp with secondary polyps budded off from top. Base of stalk burrows in mud.

sea perch, carnivorous fish of Serranidae family found mainly in tropical seas. Spiny dorsal fin, toothed scales; reaches weights of 450 kg/1000 lb.

sea robin, *see* GURNARD.

sea sickness, *see* MOTION SICKNESS.

sea snake, any of Hydrophidae family of poisonous snakes of Indian and Pacific oceans. Flattened oar-like body, small eyes.

sea spider, any of class Pycnogonida of marine arthropods with very long legs and minute abdomen. Uses large sucking proboscis to feed on sea anemones, *etc.*

sea squirt, any of class Ascidiacea of sedentary marine tunicates. Cylindrical or globular body enclosed in skin of cellulose-like material. Contracts body and squirts water when disturbed.

Seattle, seaport of W Washington, US; on Puget Sound between Olympic and Cascade Mts. Pop. 531,000. Indust., commercial centre; timber, fish, fruit exports; shipbuilding, aircraft mfg. Settled in 1850s. Boomed in Alaska gold rush (1899) and after opening of Panama Canal (1914).

sea urchin, any echinoderm of class Echinoidea. Globular or disc-shaped; body covered with calcareous plates studded with spines.

seaweed, common name for all types of marine ALGAE, esp. BROWN ALGAE.

Sebastian, St (*fl c* 3rd cent.), Roman martyr. Traditionally, a favourite of Diocletian who turned against him by embracing Christianity. Shot with arrows and left for dead; wounds healed but he was eventually battered to death. Frequently represented in Renaissance art.

Sebastopol, *see* SEVASTOPOL.

secondary school, institution providing for the education of children over the age of 11 years; attendance normally compulsory until age of 14-16 years. Types incl. GRAMMAR SCHOOL and secondary modern for less academic pupils, both of these being superseded by COMPREHENSIVE EDUCATION. In US, secondary school also known as high school, divided into junior and senior, offering academic or vocational subjects.

Second Empire (1852-70), period in French history when Louis Napoleon, after overthrowing Second Republic,

St Sebastian by Dürer

ruled as emperor NAPOLEON III. Terminated by Franco-Prussian War.

secretary bird, *Sagittarius serpentarius,* long-legged S African bird of prey with head crest resembling quill pens. Feeds on snakes, insects.

securities, evidence of property, *eg* bonds or stock certificates.

Securities and Exchange Commission (SEC), govt. agency of US. Estab. by Securities Exchange Act (1934) to supervise stock exchange dealings, administer govt. regulations on investments.

Security Council, *see* UNITED NATIONS ORGANIZATION.

Sedan, town of NE France, on R. Meuse. Pop. 24,000. Textile mfg., metal goods. Huguenot stronghold in 16th-17th cent., passed to France (1642). Scene of decisive Prussian victory (1870) over France; German breakthrough (1940) in WWII.

sedative, drug administered to diminish excitement, nervousness or irritation. Among widely used types are barbiturates. Large doses induce sleep, making patient drowsy.

Seddon, Richard John, known as 'King Dick' (1845-1906), New Zealand statesman, PM (1893-1906), b. England. Minister in John Ballance's Liberal govt., succeeding him as PM. Continued social reforms, *eg* factory acts, old age pensions.

sedge, any of family Cyperaceae of grass-like plants found on wet ground or in water. Genera incl. *Carex, Cyperus* and *Scirpus,* used in making paper.

Sedgemoor, former marsh of Somerset, SW England. Scene of James II's victory over Duke of Monmouth (1685).

sedimentary rocks, rocks formed by deposition and compaction of sediments. Consist of sand, gravel *etc,* laid down by seas, lakes, rivers, glaciers or wind, and compressed into layers, or strata, of varying thickness. Types incl. limestone, sandstone, shale.

sedum, genus of mainly perennial herbs native to N temperate regions. Found on rocks and walls; fleshy stalks and leaves, white, yellow or pink flowers. Species incl. wall pepper, *Sedum acre,* insipid stonecrop, *S. sexangulare.*

Seebeck effect, in physics, production of current in a circuit when junctions of unlike metals have different temperatures. Also called thermoelectric effect.

seed, fertilized ovule which forms reproductive structure of seed plants. Consists of embryo, stored food and protective covering.

Segovia, Andrés (1893-), Spanish virtuoso guitarist. Pioneered use of guitar as concert instrument. Author of many arrangements of classical pieces for guitar.

Segovia, town of NC Spain, cap. of Segovia prov. Pop. 42,000. Tourist centre, pottery mfg. Roman aqueduct still supplies water; Moorish alcazar, Gothic cathedral (16th cent.).

Segrè, Emilio (1905-), American physicist, b. Italy. Discovered (1937) element technetium by bombarding molybdenum with deuterons. With Owen Chamberlain (1920-) shared Nobel Prize for Physics (1959) for work with bevatron confirming existence of the antiproton.

segregation, policy or practice of compelling different racial groups to live apart from each other, go to separate schools, use separate social facilities, *etc.* In Southern states of US, segregation was extensively enforced by 1920; Supreme Court rulings and legislation in 1950s and 60s banned most forms of segregation. Known as APARTHEID in South Africa.

Ségu or **Ségou,** town of SC Mali, on R. Niger. Pop. 31,000. River port; market town, centre of large agric. irrigation project (begun 1932). Founded 17th cent., taken by French (1890).

Seine, river of N France. Flows *c* 770 km (480 mi) from Langres Plateau via Troyes, Paris, Rouen to English Channel at Le Havre. With tributaries (incl. Aube, Marne, Oise), drains most of Paris Basin; navigable by ocean-going vessels to Rouen.

seismology, study of earthquakes and related phenomena. Occurrence and severity of tremors are recorded on a seismograph. Seismological techniques are also used in *eg* mineral prospecting, measuring thickness of ice sheets, depth and shape of ocean floors.

Sekondi-Takoradi, city of SW Ghana, on Gulf of Guinea, cap. of Western Region. Pop. 161,000. Port, exports cocoa, timber, manganese, bauxite. Sekondi was Gold Coast's chief port, superseded by Takoradi deepwater harbour (completed 1928). Towns merged 1946.

Selachii (selachians), order of cartilaginous fish, incl. sharks and rays.

Selangor, state of West Malaysia. Area *c* 8160 sq km (3150 sq mi); pop. 1,629,400; cap. Kuala Lumpur. Tin mined; rubber, rice, pineapples grown. British protect. 1874. Joined Federation of Malaya (1948).

Selden, John (1584-1654), English jurist, scholar. Wrote legal histories, *eg England's Epinomis* (1610); noted Orientalist. Elected to Parliament (1623), supported parliamentary rights and privileges; helped draft Bill of Rights (1628).

Selene, in Greek myth, moon goddess; daughter of Titans Hyperion and Theia, sister of Helios (the sun). Sometimes identified with Hecate and Artemis.

selenium (Se), non-metallic element of sulphur group; at. no. 34, at. wt. 78.96. Occurs in several allotropic forms; obtained from flue dust produced by burning sulphide ores. Grey metallic form used in photoelectric cells as its conductivity varies with intensity of light. Used in glass and ceramic indust. to impart red colour.

Selfridge, Harry Gordon (1857-1947), American businessman. After career in retailing in US, founded (1909) Selfridges Store, London, 1st big dept. store in Britain.

Selim I (1467-1520), Ottoman sultan (1512-20). Conquered parts of Persia (1514), Egypt and Syria (1517). Succeeded to Islamic caliphate, gaining control of holy cities of Islam.

Seljuks, Turkish ruling dynasty, who conquered and controlled most of Near East (11th–13th cents.). Power decayed in 13th cent. and Mongols captured most of their territs.

Selkirk, Alexander (1676-1721), Scottish sailor. Marooned on Juan Fernández isl. for 4 years. Episode suggested Defoe's *Robinson Crusoe.*

Selkirkshire, former county of SE Scotland, now in Borders region. In Southern Uplands; sheep rearing; woollens, tweed mfg. Co. town was **Selkirk,** former royal burgh. Pop. 6000. Tweed mfg. Once famous for 'souters' (shoemakers).

Selma, town of SC Alabama, US; on Alabama R. Pop. 27,000. Agric. market, food processing. Scene of anti-racial segregation marches (1965).

Selznick, David O[liver] (1902-65), American film producer. Formed (1936) Selznick International Pictures after working for RKO and MGM. Films incl. *A Star is Born* (1937), *Gone with the Wind* (1939).

semantics, study of the relations between words and meaning. Divided into empirical study of how words are used, philosophic study of nature of meaning itself and the generation of symbolic formal languages. *See* SEMIOTICS.

Semarang, city of Indonesia, cap. of Central Java prov., on Java Sea. Pop. 647,000. Shipbuilding and mfg. centre. Exports sugar, tobacco, copra.

Semele, in Greek myth, daughter of Cadmus and Harmonia. Loved by Zeus in human form, whom she asked to appear as a god, but was consumed by lightning when he did. Zeus took her unborn son, Dionysus, from ashes and nurtured him in his thigh.

semiconductor, substance whose electrical conductivity is low at normal temperatures but which increases with rising temperature. Conductivity also increases by addition of minute quantities of special impurities. Those in use incl. germanium, silicon and gallium arsenide; important in transistors, rectifiers and photoelectric cells.

Seminole, North American Indian tribe of Hokan-Siouan linguistic stock. Separated from Creek in 18th cent. and settled in Florida. Fought US govt. (1835-42). Majority (*c* 2000) now in Oklahoma, some 850 remain in Everglades, Florida.

semiotics or **semiology,** science of signs in general, incl. SEMANTICS and pragmatics, the study of relationship of signs to their users.

Semipalatinsk, town of USSR, E Kazakh SSR. Pop. 251,000. Transport centre; food processing, tanning, textiles.

Semiramis, legendary queen of Assyria. Reputedly founded Babylon. Noted for her beauty, wisdom, sexual excesses. Changed into dove after death.

Semite, etymologically a descendant of Shem, son of Noah in Old Testament. Term now used for a linguistic category which incl. Hebrews, Arabs, Syrians, Ethiopians and ancient peoples of Babylon, Assyria, Canaan, Phoenicia.

Semitic, one of two major language groups making up Afro-Asiatic family. Divided into E and W branches, incl. Aramaic, Hebrew, Arabic, Ethiopic.

Semmering Pass, E Austria, between Lower Austria and Styria. Height 980 m (3215 ft); site of oldest mountain railway in the world (1848-55).

semolina, cereal food consisting of coarsely ground particles of durum wheat produced during making of fine flour. Used in making macaroni, puddings, *etc.*

Senanayake, Don Stephen (1884-1952), Ceylonese statesman. First PM (1947-52) of independent Ceylon (now Sri Lanka). Succeeded by his son, **Dudley Shelton Senanayake** (1911-73) who was PM (1952-3, 1960, 1965-70).

Senate, in US, upper house of CONGRESS. Composed of senators (2 from each state) serving 6-year terms; presided over by vice-president. Senators were chosen by state legislatures until 17th Amendment (1913) estab. direct popular election. In addition to passing legislation, Senate must ratify treaties and confirm presidential appointments.

senate, governing body in ancient Rome. In early years of republic, censors chose its members, usually from ex-magistrates. During 3rd and 2nd cent. BC, it controlled foreign affairs, the army, finances, *etc.* Power first challenged by the Gracchi, resulting in division into senatorial and popular parties, and by military leaders, *eg* Sulla, Pompey, Julius Caesar. Its authority diminished after Caesar's death, lessening still further during empire.

Sendai, city of Japan, N Honshu isl. Pop. 545,000. Produces chemicals, metal goods, silk. Seat of Tohoku Univ. (1907).

Seneca, [Lucius Annaeus] (*c* 4 BC-AD 65), Roman philosopher, dramatist, statesman. Tutor to Nero, briefly virtual ruler of Rome; later ordered to commit suicide, doing so in manner suited to his philosophy, Stoicism. Best known as writer of tragedies, incl. *Medea, Phaedra, Oedipus,* which greatly influenced Renaissance and later literature.

Senefelder, Aloys (1771-1834), German engraver, b. Prague. Invented (1796) printing technique of lithography, using limestone as his printing surface.

Senegal

Senegal, republic of W Africa. Area 196,000 sq km (76,000 sq mi); pop. 4,315,000; cap. Dakar. Language: French. Religion: Islam. Mainly low-lying savannah; stock rearing; exports groundnuts, phosphates. Coastal settlements disputed by France, Portugal 18th-19th cents.; centre of slave trade. Part of French West Africa from 1895; part of Mali Federation 1959-60; independent 1960. Member of French Community.

Senegal, river of W Africa. Flows *c* 1690 km (1050 mi) NW from Fouta Djallon highlands to Atlantic at St Louis. Forms Senegal-Mauritania border; provides irrigation.

Senghor, Léopold Sédar (1906-), Senegalese statesman, writer. Writings reflect belief in importance of African heritage (*negritude*). Elected president of Senegal at break-up of Mali Federation (1960).

senility, mental deterioration associated with old age. Characterized by loss of memory, confusion, *etc.* Causes incl. degeneration of brain cells and inadequate blood flow to the brain resulting from hardened arteries.

Sennacherib (d. 681 BC), king of Assyria (705-681 BC), son of Sargon II. Captured and destroyed Babylon (689). Restored Nineveh as his cap. and built splendid palace there. Murdered, prob. by his sons.

Sennar, town of EC Sudan, on Blue Nile. Pop. 8000. Railway jct., cotton trade. Dam (completed 1925) irrigates Gezira region. Nearby Old Sennar was cap. of a Moslem kingdom 16th-19th cent.

Sennett, Mack, orig. Michael Sinnott (1888-1960), American film director. Famous for slapstick silents of 1920s, creating the Keystone Kops, using Charlie Chaplin, Fred Mace.

Sens, town of N France, on R. Yonne. Pop. 25,000. Market town, tanning. Part of France from 1055. Scene of condemnation (1140) of Abelard's teachings; massacre of Huguenots (1562) began Wars of Religion. Gothic cathedral (12th cent.).

sensationalism, in philosophy, belief that all knowledge is acquired through the senses. Central to the philosophies of *eg* Hobbes, Locke, Hume.

sensitive plant or **humble plant,** *see* MIMOSA.

Senta (Hung. *Zenta*), town of Vojvodina, N Yugoslavia, on R. Tisza. Pop. 25,000. Agric. market. Scene of decisive defeat (1697) of Turks by Prince Eugene of Savoy.

Seoul, cap. of South Korea. Pop. 5,536,000. Indust. centre on R. Han; railway engineering; textile mfg. Historical cap. of Korea from 14th cent. Seat of Japanese occupation govt. (1910-45). UN hq. (severely damaged) during Korean War, it was rebuilt on modern lines.

separation of powers, in political theory, principle that excecutive, legislative and judicial functions of govt. should be independent of each other. Principle formulated by Montesquieu, served as basis for framers of US Constitution.

Sephardim, *see* ASHKENAZIM.

sepia, dark brown pigment, originally prepared from inky secretion of cuttlefish.

Sepoy Rebellion, *see* INDIAN MUTINY.

Sept-Iles, port of E Québec, Canada; on St Lawrence R. Pop. 24,000. Railway terminus from Schefferville iron ore mines. Exports iron ore.

Septuagint (Lat.,= seventy), most ancient and celebrated Greek version of the Hebrew Scriptures. Traditionally written in 72 days by 72 translators employed by Ptolemy II. Prob. made *c* 250-100 BC from versions of texts now lost.

Sepulchre, Holy, site NW of Calvary, Jerusalem. Traditional site of Jesus' tomb, now covered by Church of the Resurrection, shared by Orthodox, Coptic, Syrian, Armenian and RC churches.

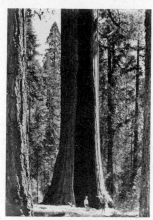

Sequoia: redwood

sequoia, two species of large coniferous trees of W US coast. Redwood, *Sequoia sempervirens,* and big tree *Sequoiadendron giganteum.* Both grow to *c* 100 m (300 ft). Some big trees are *c* 4000 years old.

Seraing, town of SE Belgium, on R. Meuse. Pop. 41,000. Coalmining area; iron works (locomotives, machinery), glass mfg.

seraphim, *see* ANGEL.

Serbia (*Srbija*), autonomous republic of E Yugoslavia, incl. Vojvodina autonomous prov., Kosovo autonomous region. Area 88,337 sq km (34,107 sq mi); cap. Belgrade. Mountainous in S; fertile Danubian plain in N (wheat, flax, fruit growing). Medieval kingdom, defeated (1389) by Turks. Independent from 1878, kingdom 1882. Expansionist policy led to Balkan Wars (1912-13), conflict with Austria led to WWI. Nucleus of Yugoslavia 1918, reorganized as republic 1946.

Serbo-Croat, language in S Slavic branch of Indo-European family. Chief official tongue of Yugoslavia.

serenade, in music, a set of movements for chamber orchestra or wind instruments, lighter than orchestral suite.

Serengeti National Park, area of N Tanzania, E of Victoria Nyanza. Game reserve, mainly grass-covered plain; area 13,000 sq km (5000 sq mi).

serfdom, condition of hereditary semi-bondage characteristic of most peasants under FEUDALISM. Serf usually worked on land of his master, but unlike a slave, retained certain rights and could not be sold. Widespread practice developed throughout Europe during Middle Ages. Disappeared in England towards end of Middle Ages; abolished in France by French Revolution; remained in Russia until Edict of Emancipation (1861).

serialism, *see* DUNNE, JOHN WILLIAM.

Seringapatam, town of S India. Pop. 14,000. On isl. in R. Cauvery. Former cap. of Mysore (Karnataka). Has mausoleum of Tippoo Sahib and his father. Fortress captured and Tippoo killed by British (1799).

serotine bat, *Eptesicus serotinus,* large European bat. Lives in small colonies.

Serowe, town of E Botswana. Pop. 34,000. Agric. market; cap. of Bamangwato tribe.

serpent, ancient bass wind musical instrument shaped like coiled snake. Usually made of wood with finger-holes and sometimes keys, and played with a cup mouthpiece like that of brass instruments.

serpentine, green or brownish-green mineral, consisting of hydrous magnesium silicate. Chrysotile, a fibrous variety, is major source of asbestos. Name also applied to rock, a mixture of serpentine and other minerals, which may be cut and polished for ornaments.

Sérrai or **Serres** (anc. *Serrae),* town of Macedonia, NE Greece, cap. of Sérrai admin. dist. Pop. 40,000. Trade centre in fertile plain (called 'Golden Plain' by Turks). Cap. of medieval Serbia.

serum, clear yellowish liquid which separates from blood after clotting. Name also applies to blood fluid containing antibodies of immunity taken from an animal immunized against a specific disease; used as an antitoxin.

Servetus, Michael (1511-53), Spanish theologian. Gained renown as physician in Vienne, France. Entered into correspondence with Calvin over radical religious views; denied doctrine of Trinity. Fled from Inquisition to Geneva after pub. of *Christianismi Restitutio* (1553), arrested on Calvin's orders and burnt at stake.

Service, Robert William (1874-1958), Canadian poet, b. England. Known for popular ballads of Yukon gold rush, *eg* 'The Shooting of Dan McGrew'. Also wrote novels.

servomechanism, automatic device in which small input power controls much larger output power. Output is compared with input through feedback so that difference between the 2 quantities can be used to achieve desired amount of control. Used in aircraft and mfg. machinery.

sesame, *Sesamum indicum,* Asian plant whose flat seeds are used in flavouring and yield edible oil.

Set or **Seth,** in ancient Egyptian religion, god of evil and darkness. Brother and murderer of OSIRIS.

set, in mathematics, collection of objects, *eg* numbers, with some defining property to tell whether a particular object is member of this collection. Operations with sets and their study are important in modern mathematics and logic.

Sète, town of Languedoc, S France, on Gulf of Lions. Pop. 41,000. Port (terminus of Canal du Midi) with wine, salt, fish trade, oil refining; tourist resort. Formerly called Cette.

Sétif, town of NE Algeria. Pop. 98,000. Grain and livestock market, on Algiers-Tunis railway. Roman *Sitifis,* remains incl. mausoleum.

Seton, Elizabeth Ann, née Bayley (1774-1821), American religious leader. After her husband's death, she became RC. Opened 1st Catholic free school at Emmitsburg, Maryland (1809). Formed 1st US congregation of Daughters of Charity. Canonized in 1975.

setter, large gun dog trained to find game and point its position. Breeds incl. English, Irish and Gordon setter.

Settlement, Act of, act of English Parliament (1701) regulating succession to throne. Provided that succession should pass to house of Hanover (which it did in 1714) if William III and Anne died without heir. Also declared that only Protestants can succeed to throne.

Setúbal, town of S Portugal, on Bay of Setúbal. Pop. 45,000. Port, exports oranges, wine, cork; fishing. Castle (16th cent.).

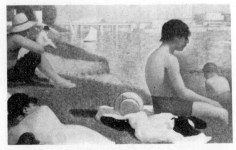
Seurat: detail of *Une Baignade, Asnières*

Seurat, Georges (1859-91), French painter. Devised divisionist technique of painting in small dots of colour; his works have a classical rigour of draughtsmanship and composition. Works incl. *Un Dimanche à la Grande Jatte,* most complete exposition of his theories.

Sevastopol or **Sebastopol,** seaport of USSR, Ukrainian SSR; on S Crimea coast. Pop. 246,000. Naval base and shipbuilding centre; seaside resort. Site of 5th cent. BC Greek colony. Captured after 11 month siege (1854-5) by French, British and Turkish troops in Crimean War. Fell to Germans after 8 month siege (1942).

Seven, Group of, group of Canadian landscape painters, incl. A.Y. Jackson and J.E.H. MacDonald, formed in Toronto *c* 1913. Inaugurated nationalist movement in Canadian painting. Renderings of N Canadian landscape characterized by brilliant colour and bold form.

Seven against Thebes, *see* POLYNICES.

seven deadly sins, in RC theology, capital sins (pride, covetousness, lust, anger, gluttony, envy, sloth). Frequently portrayed by artists, writers.

Seventh Day Adventists, *see* ADVENTISTS.

Seven Weeks War, name for AUSTRO-PRUSSIAN WAR.

Seven Wonders of the World, in antiquity, held to be Great Pyramid of Khufu, Hanging Gardens of Babylon, Statue of Zeus at Olympia, Temple of Artemis at Ephesus, Mausoleum at Halicarnassus, Colossus of Rhodes, Pharos (lighthouse) at Alexandria.

Seven Years War, conflict (1756-63) resulting from formation of coalition by France, Austria, Russia and allies to reduce power of Prussia. Also involved French-British colonial wars in North America (called French and Indian Wars) and India. Campaigns by Frederick II of Prussia in Bohemia, Saxony and Silesia thwarted by Austria and Russia. Peace treaty of Hubertusburg, although restoring status quo, marked emergence of Prussia as European power. Britain's colonial supremacy settled by Treaty of Paris after victories at Québec (1759) and Plassey (1757).

Severn, river of SW UK. Flows *c* 338 km (210 mi) from C Wales via Worcester, Gloucester to Bristol Channel. Has tidal bore as far as Tewkesbury. Road suspension bridge (1966).

Severus, Septimius (146-211), Roman emperor (193-211), b. Africa. Seized throne after murder of emperor Pertinax, overthrowing rival claimants in Rome (193), Syria (194) and Gaul (197). Built famous triumphal arch in Old Forum at Rome.

Sévigné, Marquise de, née Marie de Rabutin-Chantal (1626-96), French noblewoman. Letters to her daughter and intimates survive as lively account of Louis XIV's reign.

Seville: the Giralda tower of the cathedral

Seville (*Sevilla*), city of SW Spain, on R. Guadalquivir, cap. of Seville prov. Pop. 548,000. River port, fruit, wine trade, mfg. industs.; univ. (1502). Chief city of S Spain under Romans (anc. *Hispalis*), Visigoths; *fl* under Moorish rule 712-1248; New World trade centre (15th-17th cents.). School of painting (Murillo, Velázquez). Moorish tower and palace, 15th cent. cathedral contains tomb of Columbus.

Sèvres, suburb of SW Paris, on R. Seine. Porcelain works (Sèvres ware) estab. 1756. Treaty of Sèvres (1920) between Allies and Turkey signed here.

Sèvres, Treaty of, peace settlement (1920) signed at Sèvres, N France, between Turkey and Allies. Abolished Ottoman Empire, created new Turkish frontiers. Rejection of treaty by Kemal Ataturk led to LAUSANNE CONFERENCE.

sewage disposal, system for removal and disposal of (mainly liquid) indust. and domestic wastes and excess rainwater. Frequently, toxic indust. wastes are disposed of separately. Domestic sewage treatment is dependent on aerobic bacteria feeding on organic material. Sludge may be processed as plant fertilizer. Early sewers incl. Cloaca Maxima in Rome (*c* 6th cent. BC), but most effective systems date from 19th cent.

Seward, William Henry (1801-72), American statesman. Secretary of state (1861–9), resolved Civil War incident involving seizure of British ship *Trent*. Negotiated purchase of Alaska (1867).

Sewell, Anna (1820-78), English author. Known for children's story *Black Beauty, the Autobiography of a Horse* (1877).

sewing machine, device with mechanically driven needle for sewing of cloth, leather, *etc.* First successful model built (1846) by Elias Howe; developed by Isaac Singer. Two basic types; chain stitch uses single thread, lock stitch has second thread fed to underside of cloth.

sex, either of 2 divisions, male and female, into which animals are divided, with reference to their reproductive functions.

sex chromosome, chromosome present in germ cells of most animals and some plants. Such chromosomes are usually designated by letters X and Y. In humans, ova carry an X chromosome, spermatozoa either an X or a Y. An ovum receiving an X chromosome at fertilization develops into a female, and into a male if it receives a Y. Inherited characteristics, *eg* colour blindness, determined by genes on the X chromosome are said to be sex-linked.

sextant, instrument for measuring angular distance of celestial bodies from the horizon. Used in navigation, surveying. Developed independently by John Hadley in England and Thomas Godfrey in US during 18th cent.

sexton beetle, *Necrophorus humator,* bluish-black burying beetle. Larvae feed on corpses of buried vertebrates.

Seychelles, volcanic isl. group (*c* 90) in W Indian Ocean; member of British Commonwealth. Area *c* 380 sq km (150 sq mi); pop 56,000; cap. Victoria (pop. 12,000) on Mahé Isl. Coconuts, fish, copra, cinnamon, guano exports. French territ. 18th cent., ceded to British 1814. Became independent 1976.

Seymour, Jane (*c* 1509-37), English noblewoman, 3rd wife of Henry VIII. Died after birth of son, Edward VI. Her brother, **Edward Seymour, Duke of Somerset** (*c* 1506-52), became Edward's protector (1547). Sponsored Protestant reforms of Cranmer. Beheaded after losing power to NORTHUMBERLAND. **Thomas Seymour, Baron Seymour of Sudeley** (*c* 1508-49), secretly married Catherine Parr (1547). Rivalled brother for king's favour before execution for treason.

Sfax, city of E Tunisia, on Gulf of Gabès. Pop. 215,000. Port, exports phosphates, olive oil, sponges; fishing. Former Phoenician then Roman colony; stronghold of Barbary pirates.

Sforza, Ludovico (1451-1508), Italian nobleman. Succeeded to duchy of Milan (1494). Driven from power (1499) by Louis XII of France, he died in captivity. Famous for his lavish expenditure on arts and sciences. Patron of Leonardo da Vinci.

's Gravenhage, *see* HAGUE, THE, Netherlands.

Shaba, *see* KATANGA.

Sir E.H. Shackleton

Shackleton, Sir Ernest Henry (1874-1922), British explorer, b. Ireland. Accompanied Scott to Antarctic (1901-4); led expedition (1907-9) which located S magnetic pole. Lost ship *Endurance* on expedition (1914-16), journeyed *c* 1300 km (800 mi) overland to safety. Died on expedition to Enderby Land.

shad, migratory saltwater fish of herring family, genus *Alosa,* that spawns in rivers or estuaries. Species incl. American shad, *A. sapidissima,* once abundant food fish.

Shadwell, Thomas (*c* 1642-92), English dramatist. Wrote comedies incl. *Epsom Wells* (1672), *The Squire of Alsatia* (1688). Now remembered as butt of Dryden's satire *MacFlecknoe.* Succeeded Dryden as poet laureate (1689).

Shaftesbury, Anthony Ashley Cooper, 1st Earl of (1621-83), English statesman. Gained favour of Charles II after supporting Restoration. Member of CABAL cabinet; opposed to king's pro-Catholic policy. Dismissed as lord chancellor after supporting anti-Catholic Test Act (1673). Sought to exclude James II from succession, backing claims of Monmouth instead; forced to flee to Holland (1682). His grandson, **Anthony Ashley Cooper, 3rd Earl of Shaftesbury** (1671-1713), wrote philosophical essays, many collected in *Characteristics of Men, Manners, Opinions and Times* (1711). **Anthony Ashley Cooper, 7th Earl of Shaftesbury** (1801-85), was social reformer. Tory MP from 1826, promoted factory legislation forbidding employment of women and children in coal mines (1842), introducing 10-hour working day (1847).

Shag

shag, *Phalacrocorax aristotelis,* green-black seabird of cormorant family, found in Europe and N Africa. Nests on cliffs in colonies. Also called green cormorant.

Shah Jehan (*c* 1592-1666), Mogul emperor (1628-58). Conquered much of the Deccan. Reign considered golden age of Mogul architecture; built TAJ MAHAL at Agra. Deposed and imprisoned by his son Aurangzeb until his death.

Shahn, Ben (1898-1969), American artist, b. Lithuania. Early works were realistic and politically engaged, *eg The Passion of Sacco and Vanzetti* (1931); art shows interest in life of poor people and uses photographs, advertisements, *etc.*

Shakers, popular name for ecstatic religious sect, United Society of Believers in Christ's Second Appearing. Originated among Quakers in England *c* 1747, taken to US (1774) by group under Ann Lee. Practised separation from society in closed, communal group. Now largely extinct.

William Shakespeare

Shakespeare, William (1564-1616), English dramatist, poet, b. Stratford-upon-Avon. Spent early years in London as actor, becoming a partner in Globe Theatre (1599). Early plays (written before 1596) incl. histories, *Henry VI* (parts I, II, III), *Richard III;* comedies, *eg Two Gentlemen of Verona, A Midsummer Night's Dream;* tragedy, *Titus Andronicus.* Tragedy, *Romeo and Juliet* (*c* 1595), indicates more developed treatment of character as in later comedies, *eg The Merchant of Venice* (1596), *Much Ado About Nothing* (1598), *As You Like It* (1599), *Twelfth Night* (1599); histories *Henry IV* (parts I, II, 1597), *Henry V* (1598). The 4 great tragedies, *Hamlet* (1600), *Othello* (1602), *King Lear* (1605), *Macbeth* (1606) and classical plays, *eg Julius Caesar* (1599), *Coriolanus* (1608), represent the height of his work. Last period incl. problematic *Measure for Measure* and *The Tempest* (1611). Verse incl. sonnets, narrative poems, *eg Venus and Adonis* (1593), *The Rape of Lucrece* (1594). The 'First Folio' of 1625 is the first reliable text of his work.

Shakhty, city of USSR, SW European RSFSR. Pop. 211,000. Anthracite mining centre of Donbas. Founded 1829.

shale, fine-grained, sedimentary rock. Consists mainly of clay compressed or cemented into thin, parallel layers which readily separate. Some shales are sources of oil *eg* in Scotland, US.

shallot, *Allium ascalonicum,* small edible onion with violet-coloured roots and green leaves used as flavouring.

shamanism, religious beliefs and practices of Siberian tribes of N Asia; term also applied to similar practices among Eskimos and North American Indians. Central figure is shaman (priest-magician) who is held to have innate ability to communicate with spirit world and thus protect the tribe from any destructive influences.

Shamash, Assyrian and Babylonian sun god. Responsible for success of crops, symbol of justice.

Shallot

shamrock, common name for several trifoliate plants, esp. a clover, *Trifolium dubium.* National emblem of Ireland and symbol of Trinity in Christianity.

Shan, people of Shan state. Linguistically and ethnically close to Thais, Laotians. Mainly Buddhist, with agric. economy. Dominated Burma 13th–16th cent.

Shanghai, seaport and largest city of China, special municipality of Kiangsu prov. Pop. 11,000,000. Steel mfg., shipbuilding, heavy engineering, textiles. International airport. Open port (1843-1946) with European, American concessions; International Settlement now in modern section. Univs. incl. Futan (1905). Japanese occupation (1937-45).

Shannon, river of Irish Republic, longest in British Isls. Flows 360 km (224 mi) from Cavan via Lough Derg to Limerick. Long estuary to Atlantic. Provides h.e.p. Shannon airport is in Co. Clare.

Shansi, prov. of NC China. Area *c* 155,000 sq km (60,000 sq mi); pop. (est.) 18,000,000; cap. Taiyuan. High plateau region; low rainfall limits agric. Lumber; coal, iron deposits.

Shantung, prov. of E China on Yellow Sea. Area *c* 140,000 sq km (54,000 sq mi); pop. (est.) 57,000,000; cap. Tsinan. Mountainous in E and C, Hwang Ho delta in W. Agric. limited by low rainfall; wheat, cotton grown. Coal, iron, oil, silk mfg., fishing.

shanty, work song of sailors dating from days of sailing ships. Verse sung by shantyman gave rhythm, chorus was sung by group hauling on rope, or performing other task.

Shapley, Harlow (1885-1972), American astronomer, astrophysicist. Investigated size of Milky Way and showed that the Sun is not at its centre; studied Cepheid variable stars. Wrote *Galaxies* (1943), *Beyond the Observatory* (1967).

shares, in finance, capital holdings in business enterprise, ownership of which certified by possession of stocks. Bonds are similar certification of ownership but with guaranteed payment if company is liquidated.

Shari (Fr. *Chari*), river of NC Africa. Flows *c* 960 km (600 mi) from N Central African Republic via Ndjamena (Chad) to L. Chad, entering by broad delta. Floods over wide area in rainy season.

Great white shark or man-eater

shark, cartilaginous marine fish with slender torpedo-shaped body. Crescent-shaped mouth with numerous pointed teeth. Several families incl. dogfish, whale sharks (largest known fish) and hammerhead sharks. Mainly fish-eating, some species will attack man.

Sharp, Cecil James (1859-1924), English collector of folk music. Revived English folk song and dance after collecting material in England and Appalachian Mts. of US.

Sharp, James (1613-79), Scottish churchman. Sent to London (1660), he was converted to supporting restoration of episcopacy in Scotland. As reward, created archbishop of St Andrews (1661). Persecuted the Covenanters, a group of whom murdered him.

Sharpville, town of S Transvaal, South Africa, near Vereeniging. Scene of civic disturbances (1960) after police fired shots into black African crowd demonstrating against 'Pass Laws', *c* 70 killed.

Shastri, Lal Bahadur (1904-66), Indian statesman, PM (1964-6). Took office as PM after Nehru's death. Died in Tashkent after signing peace agreement with Pakistan.

Shatt-al-Arab, river of SE Iraq, formed at Tigris-Euphrates confluence. Length *c* 193 km (120 mi). Flows into Persian Gulf. Navigable by ocean-going vessels to Basra.

George Bernard Shaw

Shaw, George Bernard (1856-1950), British dramatist, critic, b. Dublin. Prominent member of Fabian Society. Early work attacks intellectually complacent London theatre, *eg Plays Pleasant and Unpleasant* (1898) incl. *Candida, Mrs Warren's Profession.* Notable plays with recurring theme of social satire incl. *The Devil's Disciple* (1896), *Caesar and Cleopatra* (1899), *Man and Superman* (1903), *Major Barbara* (1905), *Pygmalion* (1912), *Saint Joan* (1924). Also wrote many socialist polemics in prefaces to plays and in longer works, *eg The Intelligent Woman's Guide to Socialism and Capitalism* (1928). Nobel Prize for Literature (1925).

Shawinigan, town of SC Québec, Canada; on St Francis R. Pop. 28,000, mainly French speaking. Falls on river provide h.e.p. for paper mills, aluminium smelting.

Shawnee, North American Indian tribe of Algonquian linguistic stock. Settled in Ohio in 18th cent. Warrior tribe. Now settled in Oklahoma.

Shays, Daniel (*c* 1747-1825), American soldier. Led armed uprising of debt-burdened small farmers (1786-7) in Massachusetts. Insurgents defeated by state troops; Shays later pardoned (1788).

shearwater, any of genus *Puffinus* of oceanic birds, related to petrel. Slender bill, tube-like external nostrils. Species incl. Cory's shearwater, *P. diomedea,* found mainly in Mediterranean.

sheathbill, white Antarctic seabird, genus *Chionis,* with horny sheath on upper bill. Two species are snowy sheathbill, *C. alba,* and black-faced *C. minor.*

Sheba, OT name for region of S Arabia, incl. Yemen and the Hadramaut. Inhabitants, Sabaeans, estab. highly developed culture *c* 6th-5th cents. BC. The queen of Sheba who visited Solomon (1 Kings) *fl* 10th cent. BC.

Shechem, town of ancient Palestine, now in Nablus, W Jordan. Traditional burial place of Joseph. Site (1918) of Allenby's defeat of Turks, completing conquest of Palestine.

sheep, ruminant mammal of Bovidae family, esp. genus *Ovis.* Domestic sheep, *O. aries,* reared for wool, leather, mutton. Breeds incl. Cotswold and Merino, known for wool; Southdown and Shropshire, kept for wool, mutton. Wild species incl. bighorn, moufflon.

sheepdog, dog trained to herd and guard sheep. Popular breeds incl. old English sheepdog with shaggy blue-grey and white coat; stands 53-64 cm/21-25 in. at shoulder.

Sheerness, town of Kent, SE England. Port; former royal dockyard; fortified to protect Thames entrance. From 1968 part of Queenborough-in-Sheppey.

Sheffield, city of South Yorkshire met. county, N England, at confluence of Don and Sheaf rivers. Pop. 520,000. Iron and steel indust. (1st to use Bessemer process), long estab. stainless steel cutlery mfg. Has 15th cent. church now cathedral; univ. (1905).

Shelburne, William Petty Fitzmaurice, 2nd Earl of (1737-1805), British statesman, PM (1783). Tory foreign secretary under both Pitts. Headed ministry that granted US independence at Treaty of Paris.

shellac, refined form of lac, resin secreted by female lac insects on certain Indian trees. Dissolved in alcohol, used as varnish and surface coating; also used in electrical insulation.

Percy Bysshe Shelley

Shelley, Percy Bysshe (1792-1822), English poet. Romantic works, reflecting radical views on society and religion, incl. *Queen Mab* (1813), *Prometheus Unbound* (1820), *Adonais* (1821, elegy on death of Keats). Now best known for short lyrics, *eg* 'Ozymandias', 'To a Skylark', 'Ode to the West Wind', 'The Cloud'. Drowned while sailing in Italy. His 2nd wife, **Mary [Wollstonecraft] Shelley,** née Godwin (1797-1851), wrote Gothic novel *Frankenstein* (1818).

shell shock, obsolete term for severe form of anxiety neurosis which occurred among soldiers in WWI after prolonged exposure to attack.

Shenandoah, *see* POTOMAC, US.

Shensi, prov. of NC China. Area *c* 197,000 sq km (76,000 sq mi); pop. (est.) 21,000,000; cap. Sian. Wheat, cotton grown; rich coal and iron deposits, oil. Seat of Communists (1935-49).

Shenyang or **Mukden,** cap. of Liaoning prov., NE China. Pop. 3,750,000. Rail jct.; heavy engineering; aircraft, machine tools mfg., chemicals. Developed indust. after seizure by Japanese (1931). Taken by Communists (1948) after 10 months' siege.

shepherd's purse, *Capsella bursa-pastoris,* annual plant of mustard family. Wide distribution in temperate zones. White flowers followed by seed pods. Regarded as troublesome weed.

Sheppard, Jack (1702-24), English criminal. Notorious for many robberies, escapes, until hanged. Subject of popular stories, plays.

Shepparton, city of N Victoria, Australia, on Goulburn R. Pop. 19,000. Centre of rich, irrigated fruit and vegetable growing dist.; canning indust.

Sheppey, Isle of, off Kent, SE England, in Thames estuary. Separated from mainland by the Swale. Sheep rearing, cereals, vegetable growing. From 1968 part of Queenborough-in-Sheppey.

Sheraton, Thomas (1751-1806), English furniture designer. Wrote *The Cabinet Maker's and Upholsterer's Drawing Book* (1791-4), an influential source of designs. Work characterized by simplicity, straight vertical lines, neo-Classical motifs, use of inlay.

Sherborne, urban dist. of Dorset, S England. Pop. 6000. Once cap. of Wessex; had bishopric 705-1075; abbey (15th cent.); public school (16th cent.).

Sherbrooke, town of SE Québec, Canada; on St Francis R. Pop. 81,000. Agric. market; clothing, machinery mfg.

Sheridan, Philip Henry (1831-88), American general. Union cavalry commander in Civil War, destroyed (1864) Confederate supply lines in Shenandoah. Cut off Lee's retreat, forcing South's surrender.

Sheridan, Richard Brinsley (1751-1816), British dramatist, politician, b. Ireland. Known for satirical comedies of manners, *eg The Rivals* (1775) containing Mrs Malaprop, *The School for Scandal* (1777), *The Critic* (1779). Instrumental in impeachment of Warren HASTINGS.

sheriff, in England, officer appointed by Crown to administer county or shire (now honorary), whearas is legal official in Scotland. In US, chief law-enforcement officer of county; duties are keeping the peace, executing court orders.

General Sherman

Sherman, William Tecumseh (1820-91), American general. During Civil War, commanded Union push through Georgia (1864); burned Atlanta, devastated countryside. Early advocate of 'total' warfare tactics. His brother, **John Sherman** (1823-1900), was senator from Ohio. Sponsored Anti-Trust Act (1890).

Sherman Anti-Trust Act (1890), legislation passed by US Congress to regulate interstate, foreign trade. Attempted to outlaw restraints, *eg* monopolies, on such trade. Theodore Roosevelt was first to use it successfully to break up Standard Oil, American Tobacco Co. in 1911.

Sherriff, R[obert] C[edric] (1896-1975), English author. Wrote play *Journey's End* (1929) reflecting WWI experiences of trench life. Also wrote novels, *eg The Fortnight in September* (1931), film scripts, *eg Goodbye Mr Chips.*

Sherrington, Sir Charles Scott (1857-1952), English physiologist. Studied the action of the nervous system, incl. the function of synapses, and introduced a theory of reflex action. Shared Nobel Prize for Physiology and Medicine (1932).

sherry, fortified wine, originating in Jerez de la Frontera region of Spain. Three main types: fino, dry and light yellow; oloroso, richer and darker in colour; amontillado, darker than fino and less rich than oloroso.

's Hertogenbosch or **Den Bosch,** town of SC Netherlands, cap. of North Brabant prov. Pop. 83,000. Railway jct., cattle market. Fortress city until 1876. Birthplace of Hieronymus Bosch.

Sherwood, Robert E[mmet] (1896-1955), American playwright. Plays, mainly concerned with showing horrors of war, totalitarianism incl. *The Petrified Forest* (1934), *The Best Years of Our Lives* (1946). Speechwriter for F.D. Roosevelt.

Sherwood Forest, ancient royal forest of Nottinghamshire, C England, now largely cleared. Traditional home of Robin Hood.

Sheshawen see XAUEN, Morocco.

Shetland, isl. authority of N Scotland, comprising Shetland Isls. Formerly Zetland county. Incl. *c* 100 isls.; area 1429 sq km (552 sq mi); pop. 18,000; main town Lerwick. Main isls. are MAINLAND, Yell, Unst. Sheep rearing, Shetland ponies; fishing, knitwear mfg. Offshore oil service industs. Acquired from Norway 1472.

Shetland pony, small breed of pony with thick, shaggy coat, mane and forelock. Noted for strength and endurance; stands 1 m/40 in. at shoulder.

shibboleth, in OT, test word used by Gileadites to detect the escaping Ephraimites who could only pronounce it as 'sibboleth'. Now means watchword or party phrase.

shieldbug, any of Pentatomidae family of large, often brightly coloured insects. Large triangular thoracic plate and 5-segmented antennae. Largely herbivorous, some species are pests. Foul-smelling varieties known as stinkbugs.

Shigatse, town of Tibet auton. region, SW China. Pop. 20,000. On R. Tsangpo (Brahmaputra). Trade centre on caravan route from Lhasa to Nepal.

Shihkiachwang, cap. of Hopeh prov., NE China. Pop. 1,500,000. Rail jct.; produces textiles, pharmaceuticals. Grew rapidly with coming of railway in early 20th cent.

Shiites or **Shiahs,** members of the smaller of the 2 main Moslem sects, who upheld right of ALI to succeed Mohammed as 1st caliph and supported later claims of his sons Hasan and HUSEIN to caliphate. Also reject the Sunna, traditional law based on teachings of Mohammed. Predominate in Iran.

Shikoku, isl. of SW Japan, smallest of the 4 major isls. Area 18,770 sq km (7240 sq mi). Mountainous interior, rising to *c* 1980 m (6500 ft); heavily forested. Produces rice, tobacco, tea.

Shillong, cap. of Assam, NE India. Pop. 84,000. Resort, trade centre. Destroyed by earthquake (1897) and rebuilt.

Shiloh, Battle of, US Civil War encounter (April, 1862), fought in S Tennessee, in which the Confederates, at first superior, were defeated after the arrival of Union reinforcements.

Shimonoseki, seaport of Japan, extreme SW Honshu isl. Pop. 258,000. Shipbuilding, engineering, fishing industs. Connected to Kitakyushu by road and rail tunnels. Treaty ending Sino-Japanese War signed here (1895).

shingles, in medicine, see HERPES.

Shinto, term used for native Japanese religious beliefs and practices. Based on ancient oral myths (collected in the *Kojiki,* AD 712). Modified under influence of Buddhism and Confucianism, developed as patriotic state Shinto (stressing divinity of emperor, disavowed by Hirohito 1946) and sectarian churches (stressing veneration of ancestors).

shinty, twelve-a-side stick and ball game played in Scottish Highlands. Resembles HURLING, from which it is derived. Revival of game and formulation of rules date from 1880s.

ship, term for large sea-going vessel. Used in ancient times by Egyptians, Greeks, Phoenicians and Chinese (propelled by sails and oars). Discovery of Americas led to increase in ship-building. One of first successful steamships was Fulton's *Clermont* on Hudson R. (1807). Steel replaced wood in construction from *c* 1840s. Subsequent developments incl. steam turbines, diesel engine, nuclear power.

Shipka Pass, through Balkan Mts., C Bulgaria. Height *c* 1265 m (4150 ft). Battleground in Russo-Turkish war (1877-8).

ship money, in English history, tax for upkeep of navy and coastal defences. Legality of writs issued by Charles I, levying ship money in peace time and on inland as well as maritime counties, was challenged by John HAMPDEN. Declared illegal 1641.

shipworm, worm-like marine bivalve mollusc, esp. of genus *Teredo*. Uses its small shell to bore into submerged timber; pest to boats and piers.

Shiraz, city of SC Iran, cap. of Fars prov. Pop. 356,000. Produces wines, brocades, rugs. Cap. of Persia at various times, lastly under Karim Khan in 18th cent.

shire horse, breed of powerful draft horse common on farms. Bred in Middle Ages to carry knight in full armour.

shittim, close-grained, yellowish wood of shittah tree used for the Ark of the Covenant in Old Testament. Now generally identified with several Asian *Acacia, eg A. segal* and *A. tortils*. Name also used for North American false buckthorn, *Bumelia lanuginosa.*

Shiva, see SIVA.

Shizuoka, port of Japan, SC Honshu isl. Pop. 416,000. Centre of tea growing area; trade in oranges, tea. Centre of Tokugawa shogunate.

Shkodër, see SCUTARI, Albania.

shock, in medicine, disorder resulting from inadequate blood circulation to the tissues. Symptoms incl. decrease in blood pressure, rapid pulse. Causes may be internal bleeding, widening of blood vessels, heart damage.

shock absorber, device for damping motion of elastic suspension system such as that of a vehicle. Retards sudden motion hydraulically or by friction.

Shockley, William Bradford (1910-), American physicist, b. Britain. His studies in semiconductors led to the invention of the transistor, important development in miniaturization of electronic devices. Shared Nobel Prize for Physics (1956) with W. Brattain and J. Bardeen.

shock therapy, method of treating certain mental disorders by chemical agents, *eg* insulin, or by applying electric currents to the brain. Sometimes effective in treating depression.

shoebill or **whale-headed stork,** *Balaeniceps rex,* stork-like wading bird with broad shoe-shaped bill. Lives along banks of White Nile; feeds on marsh animals, lungfish.

shogun, title given to hereditary military rulers who controlled Japanese feudal system (12th–19th cent.). Held real power under nominal rule of emperors. Shogunate system of govt. displaced by Meiji restoration (1868).

Sholapur, city of Maharashtra state, SC India. Pop. 398,000. Major textile centre; cotton indust., carpets, glass. Has Moslem fort (14th cent.).

Sholokhov, Mikhail Aleksandrovich (1905-), Russian novelist. Known for stories of native region *Don Stories* (1926) and masterpiece *And Quiet Flows the Don* (1928-40). Nobel Prize for Literature (1965).

shooting, sport of firing with pistol, rifle or shotgun at moving or stationary targets. Organizations such as British National Rifle Association (formed 1860) and American NRA (formed 1871) standardized rules and held competitions in 19th cent. Olympic sport since 1896; events incl. trap or clay pigeon, skeet and small-bore rifle shooting.

shooting star, any of genus *Dodecatheon* of North American herbs of primrose family. *D. meadia* is common garden species.

shooting star, see METEOR.

Shoreditch, see HACKNEY, England.

short circuit, connection, either accidental or deliberate, between 2 points in electrical circuit by path of low resistance, instead of normal high resistance path. Excessive current flow may cause permanent damage to circuit; fuses are designed to avoid effects of short circuit.

shorthand, method of rapid handwriting using strokes, abbreviations or symbols to denote letters, words, phrases. Early systems were orthographic (*ie* using abbreviations for groups of letters but retaining standard spelling and usually applicable to a single language). Phonetic system developed (1837) by Isaac PITMAN allows *c* 280 words per minute to be recorded.

short sight, see MYOPIA.

Shoshone: Chief Washakie

Shoshone, North American Indian tribe of Uto-Aztecan linguistic stock. Spread across NW US in 19th cent. E group were buffalo hunters of N Great Plains, in W the tribe were settled food gatherers. Now *c* 4000 live on reservations in California, Idaho, Wyoming.

Shostakovich, Dmitri (1906-75), Russian composer. Works employ modern musical devices, often in traditional forms, and incl. 15 symphonies, string quartets. Twice encountered official disapproval of his music, tried to recover favour with 5th symphony (1937).

shoulder, in man, joint connecting the head of the humerus (bone of upper arm) with the scapula or shoulder blade.

shoveler, freshwater duck with large broad bill, genus *Anas*. Species incl. *A. clypeata* of N hemisphere; male has green-glossed head, white and brown underparts.

Shovell, Sir Cloudesley (*c* 1650-1707), British naval officer. Shared with Rooke the capture of Gibraltar (1704), commanded the fleet which took Barcelona (1705) but failed at Toulon (1707) and was lost with his ship off the Scillies.

show jumping, see EQUESTRIANISM.

Shrapnel, Henry (1761-1842), British general. Developed shot-filled shell with bursting charge, adopted by British army in 1803.

Shreveport, town of NW Louisiana, US; on Red R. Pop. 182,000. Oil, natural gas resources; railway engineering, varied mfg. industs.

shrew, any of Soricidae family of small, solitary, insectivorous mammals, widely distributed in N hemisphere and Africa. Long snout, musk glands; some species secrete poison. Species incl. WATER SHREW and common shrew, *Sorex araneus,* of Europe and N Asia.

Shrewsbury, mun. bor. and co. town of Salop, WC England, on R. Severn. Pop. 56,000. Market town; tanning, brewing. Strategic site in medieval Welsh border conflict. Has public school (1552).

shrike, any of Laniidae family of largely Old World birds. Strong hooked bill; feeds on insects and small animals, impaling bodies on thorns. Species incl. great grey shrike, *Lanius excubitor,* called northern shrike in North America.

shrimp, small free-swimming marine crustacean. Slender elongated body with 5 pairs of legs; many species edible.

Species incl. common European brown shrimp, *Crangon vulgaris.*

Shropshire, former county of WC England. Now known as SALOP; scene of hist. English-Welsh border conflict.

Shrove Tuesday, in Christian calendar, day before Lent begins. Named after practice of receiving absolution (shriving). In England, celebrated by eating pancakes. *See* MARDI GRAS.

shrub, low, perennial woody plant, smaller than TREE and with several permanent stems branching from or near ground rather than single trunk. Usually less than 6 m (20 ft) high at maturity.

Shumen, *see* KOLAROVGRAD, Bulgaria.

Shute, Nevil, pseud. of Nevil Shute Norway (1899-1960), English novelist. Wrote popular novels, *eg A Town Like Alice* (1950), *On the Beach* (1957).

Si or **Si-kiang,** river of S China. Length *c* 2000 km (1250 mi). Rises in Yunnan prov., flows E to South China Sea near Kwangchow, forming fertile delta. Navigable most of its length.

sial, in geology, upper, discontinuous layer of Earth's crust underlying the continents. Consists of relatively light rocks, *eg* granite; named from *si*lica and *al*uminium, the main constituents. Also *see* SIMA.

Sialkot, town of N Pakistan. Pop. 212,000. Sports goods, textile mfg. Has 12th cent. fort; mausoleum of Guru Nanak, founder of Sikh religion, is pilgrimage centre.

Siam, *see* THAILAND.

Siam, Gulf of, arm of South China Sea, between Malay penin. and Indo-China.

Siamese cat, breed of short-haired cat with slanting blue eyes. Fawn-coloured coat with darker colour at face and legs.

Siamese twins, twins born with bodies joined by tissue in some way. Term derived from male twins, Chang and Eng, b. 1811 in Siam.

Sian, cap. of Shensi prov,, NC China. Pop. 1,900,000. Commercial centre. Iron, steel production, textile mfg. Ancient imperial cap. (3rd cent. BC) and religious centre. Has city wall and numerous pagodas.

Siangtan, city of Hunan prov., SC China. Pop. 300,000. Manganese ore, cement production. Mao Tse-tung born nearby.

Sibelius

Sibelius, Jean Julius Christian (1865-1957), Finnish composer. Music, traditional in form, was often inspired by legends and scenery of Finland. Works incl. tone-poem *Finlandia,* violin concerto, 7 symphonies. Govt. grant enabled him to devote himself to composition from 1897.

Siberia (*Sibir*), region of C and E USSR, approximating Asiatic part of RSFSR. Area *c* 12,700,000 sq km (4,900,000 sq mi). Plains in W, drained by Ob, Irtysh; plateau in C and S; tundra in N along Arctic Ocean; mainly mountainous in E, incl. Kamchatka Penin. Agric. concentrated in fertile SW plains (main crop wheat); mineral resources incl. oil, coal,

Siberia

gold, iron. Indust., *eg* Kuznetsk basin, has grown rapidly since 1920s. Russian conquest led by Cossacks (16th-17th cent.). Used as political exile colony under tsars; colonization began with Trans-Siberian railway (1892-1905); economic development began in 20th cent.

Sibiu (Ger. *Hermannstadt*), city of C Romania, in Transylvania. Pop. 127,000. Textiles, machinery, brewing. Roman colony, resettled 12th cent. by Germans; retains medieval appearance.

Sibylline Books, collection of oracular utterances, written in Greek hexameters, thought to have been brought from Greece to Cumae, then to Rome. Traditionally, 3 volumes bought by Tarquinius Superbus from Sibyl of Cumae. Consulted by Romans in cases of calamities, *eg* earthquakes. Destroyed in burning of capitol, 83 BC.

sibyls, name given by Greeks and Romans to prophetesses of Apollo. Most famous was Sibyl of Cumae, Italy. *See* SIBYLLINE BOOKS.

Sicilian Vespers, rebellion (1282) in Sicily against French rule of Charles of Anjou; began at time of vespers on Easter Tuesday. Most of French were massacred. Resulted in estab. of Peter III of Aragón as king of Sicily.

Sicily (*Sicilia*), isl. of Italy, separated from mainland by Str. of Messina. Largest Mediterranean isl., area 25,708 sq km (9926 sq mi); cap. Palermo. Mountainous, incl. Mt. Etna; agric., fishing, sulphur, oil. Phoenician, then Greek colony, taken by Rome 241 BC. Under Normans (12th-13th cent.) before forming with Naples, Kingdom of the Two Sicilies (1815); liberated from Bourbons by Garibaldi (1860).

Sickert, Walter Richard (1860-1942), British artist, b. Munich. His sub-impressionist paintings are sombre in tone; helped introduce French ideas into English art. Painted music hall scenes and views of Venice, Dieppe and London.

Siddons, Sarah Kemble (1755-1831), English actress, daughter of ROGER KEMBLE. Renowned in tragic roles, *eg* Lady Macbeth, Ophelia, Desdemona.

sidewinder, *Crotalus cerastes,* desert rattlesnake of SW US. Moves by sideways spiralling action.

Sidgwick, Henry (1838-1900), English philosopher. Worked on ethics. Formulated system combining intuitionism and utilitarianism. Works incl. *Methods of Ethics* (1874), *The Principles of Political Economy* (1883).

Sidi-bel-Abbès, town of NW Algeria, on R. Mekerra. Pop. 101,000. Agric. market. Walled town, French military post from 1843, hq. of Foreign Legion until 1962.

Sidmouth, Henry Addington, 1st Viscount (1757-1844), English statesman, PM (1801-4). Headed Tory govt. which concluded Treaty of Amiens (1802) with Napoleon. Known for repressive policy as home secretary (1812–21) under Liverpool.

Sidney, Sir Philip (1554-86), soldier, writer, leading figure at Elizabeth I's court. Died in battle of Zutphen. Works incl. romance *Arcadia* (pub. 1590), sonnet sequence *Astrophel and Stella* (1591), critiques, *eg The Defence of Poesie* (1595). Considered archetype of Renaissance courtier.

Sidon, *see* SAIDA.

Siegfried or **Sigurd,** hero of N European mythology. Appears in German epics, esp. *Nibelungenlied,* as dragon-

Sir Philip Sidney

killer, lover of Kriemhild, conqueror of Brunhild. Earliest account in Norse Volsungsaga (13th cent.).

Siemens, [Ernst] Werner von (1816-92), German industrialist, inventor. Founded (1847) Siemens und Halske, which became one of most important electrical firms in world. Invented many commonly-used techniques, *eg* Siemens armature. His brother, **Sir William Siemens,** orig. Karl Wilhelm (1823-83), was known for his innovatory work in electricity and application of heat, utilized in British business from 1844 on; estab. (1865) firm of Siemens Bros. Developed Siemens-Martin steel-making process.

Siena, town of Tuscany, WC Italy, cap. of Siena prov. Pop. 69,000. Marble, wine; tourism. Medieval cultural, banking centre. Sienese school of painting (13th-14th cent.). Gothic cathedral, town hall. Horse race held annually in Piazza del Campo.

Sienkiewicz, Henryk (1846-1916), Polish author. Known for novel, *Quo Vadis?* (1895), about Christianity in Nero's Rome. Also wrote national novels, *eg With Fire and Sword* (1890). Nobel Prize for Literature (1905).

Sierra Leone

Sierra Leone, republic of W Africa. Area 71,700 sq km (27,700 sq mi); pop. 2,861,000; cap. Freetown. Official language: English. Religions: native, Christianity, Islam. Coastal swamps, rising inland to wooded plateau. Main food crop rice; exports diamonds, iron ore, bauxite, palm products. Minor slave trade 17th-18th cent. Freetown area became colony (1808); hinterland incl. in protect. created (1896). Independent from 1961.

Sierra Madre, mountain system of Mexico, dominating much of country except Yucatán penin. Comprises Sierra Madre Oriental in NE, Occidental in W and del Sur in S. Rises to 5700 m (18,700 ft) at highest point, Orizaba.

Sierra Maestra, mountain range of SE Cuba rising to 2000 m (6560 ft). Focus of Castro's revolt in 1950s. Rich in minerals, incl. iron, copper, manganese.

Sierra Morena, mountain range of SC Spain. Extends *c* 600 km (375 mi) E-W, separating Andalusia from C, N Spain. Rises to *c* 1310 m (4300 ft). Rich in minerals, esp. copper, lead, mercury.

Sierra Nevada, mountain range of S Spain; extends *c* 100 km (60 mi) E-W from Granada to Almeria. Incl. Mulhacén, highest peak in Spain at 3479 m (11,420 ft).

Sierra Nevada, mountain range of E California. Incl. Mt. Whitney (highest mountain in US outside Alaska) and Sequoia, Yosemite, Kings Canyon national parks.

Sieyès, Emmanuel-Joseph (1748–1836), French revolutionary. Originally a priest, grew to prominence with pamphlet *What is the Third Estate?* (1788). Became a leader in Estates-General of 1789. Supported Napoleon in coup d'état (1799) which estab. Consulate.

Siger de Brabant (*fl* 1260-77), French theologian. Leader of Latin Averroism movement, adopting Averroe's concept of 'double truth' to reconcile reason and faith. Attacked by Aquinas.

Sigismund (1368-1437), Holy Roman emperor (1433-7). Became king of Hungary (1387), Germany (1411). Persuaded the pope to call Council of Constance (1414) to end Great Schism. Granted safe conduct for Jan HUS to attend Council, but Hus was condemned to death there for heresy. Led crusade against Hussites in Bohemia (1420) but was defeated.

Sigismund [II] Augustus (1520-72), king of Poland (1548-72). United Poland and Lithuania by Union of Lublin (1569). Reign saw Reformation, which he opposed, at its height in Poland.

Sigismund III (1566-1632), king of Poland (1587-1632). Inherited Swedish throne (1592) from father, John III of Sweden; opposed by Swedish Protestants, deposed (1599) after defeat at Stängebro.

Signac, Paul (1863-1935), French painter. Disciple of Seurat, he adopted the divisionist technique; expounded theories of neo-impressionism in book *De Delacroix au Néo-Impressionisme* (1899).

Sihanouk, Norodom (1922-   ), Cambodian statesman, king (1941-55). Abdicated in favour of father, but continued as premier (1951-70), leading Popular Socialists. Went into exile in China after rightist coup d'état (1970).

sika, *Cervus nippon,* small Japanese deer, introduced into Europe. Chestnut brown coat, white-spotted in summer.

Sikhs, Indian religious community mostly in Punjab. Founded (*c* 1500) by Nanak. Aiming to unite Hindus and Moslems, taught basic identity of all religions. Developed as military power in early 18th cent. against Mogul empire and Islam. Today Akali Dal movement seeks to estab. Sikh state in NW India.

Sikh Wars, conflicts (1845-6, 1848-9) between Sikhs and British, resulting in annexation of Punjab. First war resulted from Sikh invasion of British territ. following disorder in Punjab. After British had estab. protect. in Punjab, rioting led to 2nd war.

Si-kiang, river of China, *see* SI.

Sikkim, state of India, in Himalayas between Nepal and Bhutan. Area 7100 sq km (2700 sq mi); pop. 206,000; cap. Gangtok. Constitutional monarchy under British protection until 1947, became Indian protectorate 1950. Independence and power of king virtually ended 1974, when it became Indian associate state. Became 22nd state of India (1975).

Sikorski, Wladyslaw (1881-1943), Polish general, statesman. After German invasion of Poland (1939), became premier of Polish govt. in exile and commander-in-chief of Polish troops fighting with Allies. Killed in air crash.

Sikorsky, Igor Ivanovich (1889-1972), American aeronautical engineer, b. Russia. Built and flew 1st multi-engined plane (1913). Designed, manufactured 1st successful helicopter (1941).

silage, green fodder preserved in airtight silos, used as supplementary feed for cattle, sheep, *etc.* During storage, fermentation processes are set up which generate heat and give off gases.

Silenus, in Greek myth, leader of satyrs and sometimes regarded as foster father and tutor of Dionysus. Represented as inspired, musical and drunken old man. He might be induced to prophesy if caught when asleep.

Silesia (Pol. *Slask,* Ger. *Schlesien,* Czech. *Slezsko*), region of EC Europe, now mainly in Poland; smaller areas in NW Czechoslovakia, SE East Germany. Incl. basin of upper Oder; coal, iron, zinc mining. Chief cities Gliwice, Katowice, Wroclaw. Polish until 14th cent., passed to Bohemia, then to Habsburgs. Annexed by Prussia 1742; divided into Upper, Lower Silesia. Former returned to Poland 1921, latter returned 1945.

silica or **silicon dioxide** (SiO_2), hardy glassy mineral; found free as sand, quartz, flint and as silicates in rocks. Used in manufacture of glass and ceramics.

silicates, salts of silicic acid (H_2SiO_3). Most rocks and many minerals consist of silicates of calcium, magnesium, aluminium and other metals.

silicon (Si), non-metallic element; at. no. 14, at. wt. 28.09. Exists as brown powder and grey crystals; 2nd most abundant element on Earth, occurring in silica and silicate rocks. Obtained by reduction of silica with carbon in electric arc furnaces. Used in alloys, glass making, semiconductor devices.

silicones, group of polymerized organic compounds containing alternate oxygen and silicon atoms with various organic radicals attached to the chain. Characterized by chemical inertness, resistance to electricity and heat; used as lubricants, polishes, waterproofing compounds.

silk, natural fibre produced by silkworms. Usually obtained from cocoon spun by larva of *Bombyx mori* which feeds on mulberry leaves. Silk production began in ancient China, then in 6th cent. spread throughout Asia into Europe (esp. Italy and France).

silk screen printing, method of stencil printing in which paint is squeezed through a piece of fine silk. Parts of design not to be printed are masked by paper or film of lacquer. Developed for commercial purposes, now used for obtaining large numbers of artists' prints.

silkworm, larva of Chinese silkworm moth, *Bombyx mori.* Spins cocoon of silk fibre, cultivated commercially as source of silk.

Sillanpää, Frans Eemil (1888-1964), Finnish author. Wrote sensitive psychological novels, *eg Meek Heritage* (1919), *The Maid Silja* (1931). Nobel Prize for Literature (1939).

Sillitoe, Allan (1928-), English novelist. Wrote regional working-class novels, *eg Saturday Night and Sunday Morning* (1958), short story collection *The Loneliness of the Long Distance Runner* (1959).

Silone, Ignazio, pseud. of Secondo Tranquilli (1900-), Italian novelist. Wrote anti-totalitarian novels, *eg Fontamara* (1933), *Bread and Wine* (1937).

silt, sediment composed of rock particles, precisely defined in geology as having particle size between 1/256mm and 1/16mm. Commonest constituent is quartz.

Silurian period, third geological period of Palaeozoic era. Began *c* 435 million years ago, lasted *c* 40 million years. Extensive seas; Caledonian mountain building period continued. Typified by graptolites, trilobites, brachiopods, cephalopods; jawless fish, 1st land plants. Also *see* GEOLOGICAL TABLE.

Silvanus, in Roman religion, spirit of woodlands and uncultivated fields. Sometimes identified with Pan and Faunus. Cult regarded as very ancient.

silver (Ag), white metallic element; at. no. 47, at. wt. 107.87. Malleable and ductile; best-known conductor of electricity; resists corrosion by air. Used in coinage, jewellery, mirrors; halogen compounds used extensively in photography as they are light-sensitive.

silverfish, *Lepisma saccharina,* bristletail insect of silvery-white appearance. Found indoors, often attracted by sugary food.

silverside, small fish of Atherinidae family, with silvery stripe along sides. Widely distributed; some fished commercially. Species incl. Californian grunion, *Leuresthes tenuis.*

sima, in geology, lower continuous layer of Earth's crust underlying ocean floors and continental SIAL. Consists of relatively heavy rocks, *eg* basalt; named from *si*lica and *ma*gnesium, the main constituents.

Simcoe, Lake, in S Ontario, Canada; forms part of Trent Canal system. Area 1396 sq km (539 sq mi). Resort area.

Simenon, Georges (1903-), French author, b. Belgium. Known for detective novels featuring Inspector Maigret, *eg La Maison du Canal* (1933). Also wrote psychological novels, *eg La Neige était sale* (1948).

Simeon I (d. 927), Bulgarian ruler (893-927). Defeated Leo VI, emperor of Byzantium (897); conquered Serbia. Proclaimed himself 1st tsar of Bulgaria (925). Known for cultural splendour of his court; patron of Church Slavonic literature.

Simeon Stylites, St (*c* 390-459), Syrian hermit. Traditionally lived for 36 years on top of pillar from which he taught.

Simferopol, town of USSR, Ukrainian SSR; in S Crimea. Pop. 262,000. Centre of orchard and vineyard region; fruit and vegetable canning. Site of cap. of ancient Scythia.

simile, see METAPHOR.

Simla, cap. of Himachal Pradesh state, N India. Pop. 43,000. In Himalayas, at height of 2100 m (700 ft). Summer residence of viceroy and govt. during British rule.

Simmel, Georg (1858-1918), German philosopher, sociologist. Attacked models of society as reality external to individuals; developed analysis of social interaction in small units, allowing for coexistence of order and conflict.

Simon, St (*fl* 1st cent. AD), one of Twelve Disciples; also called Cananaean, Zealot. Traditionally, martyred with St Jude.

Simon, John Allsebrook Simon, Viscount (1873–1954), British politician. Posts in National govt. incl. foreign secretary (1931–5), home secretary (1935–7). Favoured disarmament and appeasement of Germany.

Simonides of Ceos (*c* 556-*c* 468 BC) Greek poet. Rival of Pindar, achieving concentration of epigrammatic verse in lyrics. Extant fragments show power to evoke pathos, tolerance of human failings; incl. epitaphs on Marathon, Thermopylae heroes.

Simonov, Konstantin Mikhailovich (1915-), Russian author. Novels incl. *Days and Nights* (1945) on defence of Stalingrad, *Victims and Heroes* (1959) criticizing handling of Soviet-German conflict.

Simonstown, town of SW Cape Prov., South Africa, on False Bay. Pop. 10,000. Resort, port, major naval base. Founded (1741) by Dutch; ceded to UK (1898), to South Africa (1957).

Simplon Pass, Alpine pass between S Switzerland and N Italy, height 2008 m (6592 ft). Road built by Napoleon (1800-7). Railway tunnel, world's longest (19.7 km/12.25 mi), opened 1906.

Simpson, Sir James Young (1811–70), Scottish obstetrician. Pioneered use of anaesthetics (chloroform, ether) in childbirth (1847).

Sir James Simpson

Simpson, N[orman] F[rederick] (1919-), English dramatist. Plays, *eg A Resounding Tinkle* (1957), *One Way*

Pendulum (1959), depict the development of logic to level of absurdity.

Simpson, Wallis, *see* WINDSOR, WALLIS WARFIELD, DUCHESS OF.

sin, in Judaism, Christianity and Islam, any transgression of the will of God. Concept does not occur in religions where there is no personal God, *eg* Buddhism. In RC theology, sins are mortal if committed with intent in a serious matter. *See* ORIGINAL SIN, SEVEN DEADLY SINS.

Sinai, barren penin. between Gulf of Suez (W) and Gulf of Aqaba (E). Main town El Arish. Coastal plain in N, El Tih plateau in C; mountainous in S. Nomadic pastoralism, oil drilling, manganese, iron mining. Jebel Musa (possibly Mt. Sinai) has famous Greek Orthodox monastery. Part of Egypt; occupied by Israelis from 1967 war, partly restored 1974-5.

Sinatra, Francis Albert ('Frank') (1917-   ), American singer, film actor. Rose to fame as singer with bands of Harry James and Tommy Dorsey; singing idol of 'bobby-soxers' in 1940s. Films incl. *From Here to Eternity.*

Sinclair, Upton [Beall] (1878-1968), American novelist. Polemic novels of social protest incl. *The Jungle* (1906) exposing conditions in Chicago's stockyards, *Boston* (1928) on Sacco and Vanzetti case. Also wrote Lanny Budd adventure stories.

Sind, region of SE Pakistan and former province of British India. Mainly flat, arid land lying in lower Indus valley. Agric. economy. Taken by British under Sir Charles Napier (1843).

Singapore, island republic off S end of Malay penin.; in British Commonwealth. Area 583 sq km (225 sq mi); pop. 2,070,000, predominantly Chinese. British colony 1824-1963; joined Malaysia 1963, seceded 1965. City of **Singapore** (pop. 1,240,000) is a major seaport, former British naval base. Commercial centre; exports rubber, tin and copra from Malaysia. Occupied by Japanese 1942-5.

Singer, Isaac Merritt (1811-75), American inventor. Patented (1851) practical sewing machine; became leading manufacturer. Later added many improvements.

Singhalese, Indic language in Indo-Iranian branch of Indo-European family. Spoken on Sri Lanka. Separated from other Indic languages by region of DRAVIDIAN speakers, which has influenced its vocabulary.

singing, use of human voice for production of music with or without words. Voices range from female or boy soprano, mezzo-soprano, contralto, male and female alto, to male countertenor, tenor, baritone and bass. Classical style of singing, developed in Italy in 17th-18th cent., demands special voice production.

single tax, in economics, doctrine advanced by PHYSIOCRATS, advocating collection of revenue based only on land. Most successful exponent was H. GEORGE.

Sing Sing, *see* OSSINING, US.

Sining, cap. of Tsinghai prov., NC China. Pop. 250,000. Trade centre (wool, hides, salt) on caravan route to Tibet. Chemical and textile mfg.

Sinkiang(-Uighur), auton. region of NW China, bordering on Mongolia, USSR. Area *c* 1,709,400 sq km (660,000 sq mi); pop. (est.) 8,000,000; cap. Urumchi. Peopled mainly by Turkic Uighurs (Moslems). Grazing on Dzungaria plateau in N. Taklamakan desert covers S. Low rainfall but irrigation schemes allow agric. (cereals, cotton). Mineral, oil resources. Scene of frontier incidents with USSR (1969).

sinking fund, sum of govt. or business income set aside; its accumulation eventually allows repayment of outstanding debts. First estab. in Britain (1786).

Sinn Fein (Irish, = ourselves alone), Irish separatist national movement founded by Arthur Griffith (1899). Gained popular political support under leadership of DE VALÉRA; set up Irish assembly in Dublin (1918) and declared independence. Influence declined with formation of Fianna Fáil (1926). Name now applies to political wing of Irish Republican Army.

Sino-Japanese War, First (1894-5), struggle between China and Japan for control of Korea. Japanese victory consolidated by Treaty of Shimonoseki by which China ceded Taiwan and other islands and Liaotung penin.; Korea awarded nominal independence.

Sino-Japanese War, Second (1937-45), Struggle prompted by growing Japanese domination of China. Japan annexed Manchuria (1931), set up puppet state of Manchukuo. Hostilities began 1937; Japanese captured most of large Chinese cities and ports by 1938. Chinese, driven W, continued guerrilla warfare. Allies aided China after Japan's entry into WWII. After Japanese surrender (Sept. 1945), Cairo Declaration restored Taiwan, Manchuria to China.

Sinop (anc. *Sinope*), town of N Turkey, on Black Sea. Founded 8th cent. BC; became important port, exporting cinnabar. Cap. of Pontic empire (2nd cent. BC); prospered under Roman and Byzantine rule.

Sino-Tibetan, major language family with 3 branches, Chinese, Thai, and Tibetan-Burman.

Sintra, *see* CINTRA, Portugal.

Sinuiju, town of NW North Korea. Pop. 130,000. Chemical and aluminium mfg., based on h.e.p. from Supung Dam. Connected by bridge across R. Yalu to Antung, China.

sinus, name given to any of the various air cavities of the skull opening into the nasal passage. Inflammation of mucous membranes of the sinuses (sinusitis) may occur as a result of colds, allergies; blockage of sinuses by mucus causes headache.

Sioux or **Dakota,** seven North American tribes, dominant group of Hokan-Siouan linguistic stock. Gradually driven W, they settled (late 18th cent.) in N Great Plains area. Invasion of their reservation by gold prospectors in 1870s led to uprising in which General Custer perished.

Sioux City, city of NW Iowa, US; on Missouri R. jct. Pop. 86,000. Agric., livestock market; shipping indust., clothing mfg., meat packing.

Sioux Falls, town of SE South Dakota, US; on Big Sioux R. Pop. 72,000; state's largest town. Livestock, grain trade, meat packing. Named after falls on river.

siphon, bent tube used to transfer liquid from higher container to lower one by pressure of atmosphere acting on liquid surface. Tube must be filled with liquid before flow will start.

Siqueiros, David Alfaro (1898-1974), Mexican painter. Works, mainly murals and frescoes, reflect support of revolutionary socialism.

siren, any of Sirenidae family of aquatic eel-like amphibians, found in North American swamps. Retains certain larval characteristics: gills, lidless eyes, no hind limbs.

Sirens, in Greek myth, sea nymphs represented as part woman and part bird who, by their beautiful singing, lured sailors to their death on rocks. Argonauts were saved by the more beautiful music of Orpheus, while Odysseus stopped ears of his crew with wax.

Sirius or **Dog Star,** brightest star in sky, located in constellation Canis Major. In 1862, observed to have a companion, Sirius B, a white dwarf star.

sirocco, hot, dust-laden S wind originating in Sahara Desert and affecting N Africa, Sicily, S Italy. Occurs mainly in spring; withers vegetation. Called *khamsin* in Egypt.

sisal, strong fibre obtained from leaves of an agave, *Agave sisalana,* native to S Mexico, but now grown throughout the tropics. Used for making rope, sacking.

Sisley, Alfred (1839-99), French painter of English descent. Member of the impressionist group, he devoted himself to landscape. Noted for his fine sense of colour and tonal values.

Sistine Chapel, private chapel of the pope in the Vatican. Built (1473) under Sixtus IV, it is renowned for frescoes of the Creation, Deluge and Last Judgment by Michelangelo.

Sisyphus, in Greek myth, king of Corinth, renowned for his cunning. For his disrespect to Zeus, condemned in Tartarus to roll repeatedly a heavy stone to top of hill; when stone reached top, it rolled down again.

Sitka, town of SE Alaska, US; on Baranof Isl. Pop. *c* 3500. Main occupation fishing. Cap. of Russian America until 1867; cap. of Alaska until 1906.

Sitter, Willem de (1872-1934), Dutch astronomer, mathematician. Using Einstein's general theory of relativity, he developed idea of an expanding universe containing essentially no matter.

Sitting Bull

Sitting Bull (*c* 1831-90), American Indian chief. Led Sioux at battle of Little Bighorn (1875) in which Custer and his troops were wiped out. Later settled on reservation; opposed selling of Sioux land, shot by Indian police.

Sitwell, Dame Edith (1887-1964), English author. Works incl. poetry, *eg Façade* (1922) set to music by William Walton, *Green Song* (1944), essays, *eg A Poet's Notebook* (1943). Her brother, **Sir Osbert Sitwell** (1892-1969), wrote series of family memoirs incl. *Left Hand, Right Hand!* (1944), poetry. Their brother, **Sir Sacheverell Sitwell** (1897-   ), poet and art critic, wrote histories of art incl. books on Baroque.

SI units (Système International d'Unités), internationally agreed coherent system of units, which has replaced c.g.s. and f.p.s. systems for scientific purposes. Based on 7 units: metre (m), kilogram (kg), second (s), ampère (A), kelvin (K), mole (mol) and candela (cd). Numerous other units incl. newton, joule, watt, volt, ohm, are derived from these.

Siva as Lord of the Dance

Siva or **Shiva,** in Hinduism, god of destruction and reproduction; one of the supreme trinity. In destructive role, represented with garland of skulls and surrounded by demons. As Natarajah, regarded as Lord of the Cosmic Dance; consort was KALI. Anciently associated with phallic worship.

Sivas, city of C Turkey. Pop. 150,000. Textile and carpet mfg.; copper mines nearby. Nationalist movement leading to revolution begun here by Ataturk (1919). Has notable 13th cent. buildings of Seljuk sultans.

Six, les, group of six French composers, said to have been influenced by Satie and Cocteau. Comprised MILHAUD,

POULENC, HONEGGER, AURIC, Louis Durey and Germaine Tailleferre.

Sjaelland, *see* ZEALAND, Denmark.

Skagerrak, str. between SE Norway and NW Denmark, linking North Sea and Kattegat. Width *c* 130 km (80 mi).

Skagway, town of SE Alaska, US; at foot of White Pass. Pop. 675. Railway terminus on route for Klondike. Pop. *c* 15,000 during gold rush of 1897-8.

Skåne or **Scania,** region of S Sweden, chief city Malmö. Held by Denmark until conquered by Charles X (1658). Many prehist. and medieval remains.

Skara Brae, Neolithic village in Orkney, Scotland, uncovered from a sand dune by a storm (1851). Comprises stone houses linked by a roofed-over alleyway.

skate, large ray, esp. of genus *Raja,* often used as food. Species incl. European skate, *R. batis,* found in deep water.

skating, sport of gliding on ice by means of specially-designed metal blades fitted to boots. Originally, blades made from bone or wood, and iron by 17th cent. Used in ice HOCKEY. Olympic event since 1924, incl. pair, free, figure and speed skating. Another form, **roller skating,** uses specially-constructed metal skates bearing 4 small roller wheels to glide on smooth surfaces. James Plympton introduced modern roller skates into US in 1863.

Skegness, urban dist. of Lincolnshire, E England. Pop. 14,000. Seaside resort; extensive beaches.

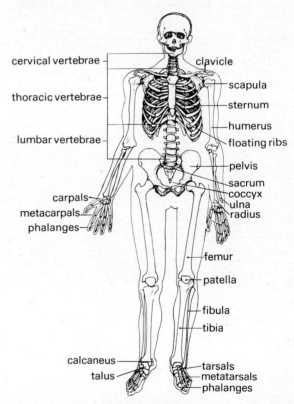

Human skeleton

skeleton, solid framework which supports and protects soft tissue of an animal body. Vertebrates have skeletal structures composed of bone and cartilage entirely within the organism (endoskeleton); other animals, *eg* arthropods, coelenterates, have skeletons external to living tissue (exoskeletons).

Skelton, John (*c* 1464-1529), English poet. Known for artless verse, *eg* mock-dirge *Philip Sparrow*, crudely comic *Tunning of Eleanor Rumming*; also wrote verse attacking Scots, lampooning Wolsey. Used 'Skeltonics', short, usually 3-stressed lines.

skepticism, *see* SCEPTICISM.
Skiddaw, mountain of Lake Dist., Cumbria, NW England. Height 930 m (3054 ft).

Alpine skiing

skiing, method of gliding over snow using elongated wooden or metal runners fastened to the feet. Sport of skiing is divided into 2 sections: Alpine, in which competitors race down prepared slopes; Nordic, which incl. cross-country and ski-jumping events. Competitive skiing began in 19th cent. and was esp. developed in Norway. Skiing was introduced into 1924 Olympics.

Skikda, town of NE Algeria, on Gulf of Stora. Pop. 85,000. Formerly called Philippeville. Outport for Constantine, exports incl. fruit, wine, iron ore. Founded (1838) by French on site of Carthaginian colony.

skimmer, any of Rhynchopidae family of tropical wading birds, found near river estuaries. Skims water using mandible to scoop up fish. Species incl. Indian skimmer, *Rhynchops albicollis.*

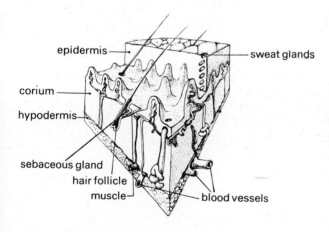

Structure of human skin

epidermis — sweat glands

corium —

hypodermis —

sebaceous gland

hair follicle

muscle — blood vessels

skin, flexible external covering of body. In humans, consists of outer epidermis and inner dermis. Former is covered by layer of dead cells which are constantly replaced. Latter contains blood vessels, nerve endings, hair follicles, sweat and sebaceous glands. Main functions are to protect, to regulate body temperature and to serve as organ of sense and excretion.

skink, any of Scincidae family of snake-like lizards, found mainly in desert regions. Elongated body, scaly tongue; limbs reduced or absent. Largest lizard family, with *c* 600 species, incl. common skink, *Scincus scincus,* of African desert.

Skinner, B[urrhus] F[rederick] (1904-), American psychologist. Known for extreme behaviourism, completely rejecting the unobservable; developed theory of programmed and social learning based on conditioning. Books incl. *Science and Human Behavior* (1953), *Beyond Freedom and Dignity* (1971).

skipper, any of Hesperiidae family of primitive moth-like butterflies. Noted for bursts of swift erratic flight. Larvae feed on grass.

skittles, game played with pins and balls or discs. Nine pins are set up in diamond pattern and missile is hurled at the pins with object of knocking them over.

Skopje, city of S Yugoslavia, on R. Vardar, cap. of Macedonia. Pop. 312,000. Transport, indust. centre (iron, steel), univ. (1946). Cap. of Serbia in 14th cent.; under Turks 1392-1913, called Uskub. Badly damaged by earthquake 1963.

Great skua

skua, any of Stercorariidae family of large gull-like sea birds. Will chase other birds, stealing their food. Species incl. great skua, *Stercorarius skua,* of both polar regions. Some species called jaeger in US.

skull, bony framework of the head comprising cranium, or brain case, and facial skeleton. Contains more than 20 tightly interlocked bones. Protects brain and sense organs, *ie* nose, eyes and ears.

skunk, bushy-tailed North American carnivore of Mustelidae family. Glossy black fur, usually with white stripe on back; ejects foul-smelling contents of 2 glands at back of tail for defence. Species incl. striped skunk, *Mephitis mephitis.*

skunk cabbage, *Symplocarpus foetidus,* low, fetid, broad-leaved plant of E North America. Grows in moist ground.

skydiving, sport of jumping from an aircraft and executing free-fall manoeuvres before opening the parachute, often as late as possible.

Skye, largest isl. of Inner Hebrides, W Scotland, in Highland region. Area 1665 sq km (643 sq mi); main town Portree (pop. 1000). Hilly in S (Cuillins). Sheep rearing, crofting; tourist centre. Has Dunvegan Castle, home of chief of Clan McLeod, in NW.

Skye terrier, terrier originally bred in Skye for hunting. Long silky coat, short legs, long body; stands 25 cm/10 in. at shoulder.

skylark, *see* LARK.

Skyros (*Skiros*), isl. of Greece, in Aegean Sea. Area 205 sq km (79 sq mi). Agric., fishing; chromite. In legend, Theseus killed here. Burial place of Rupert Brooke.

skyscraper, popular name for many-storeyed building. Originally designed in the US in order to save space, 1st examples were built in Chicago in 1880s. Tallest is Sears Building, Chicago, with 110 stories (473 m/1472 ft high).

slander, *see* LIBEL.

slate, dense, fine-grained metamorphic rock. Formed by compression of SHALE over long period; splits readily into thin, smooth plates. Used as roofing material.

slavery, ownership of a human being by another. Fundamental to social system of Greek city states and

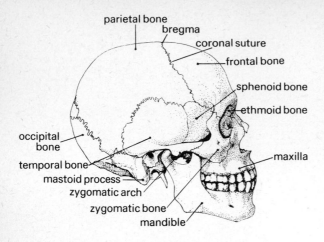

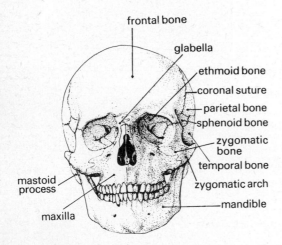

Side and front views of human skull

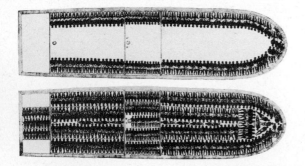

Slavery in America: plan of a slave ship

Roman empire. Largely replaced in Europe by serfdom under feudal system, but large numbers of African slaves were introduced to Americas as agric. labourers. Attempts at abolition on humanitarian grounds date from early 19th cent. (slave trade banned by UK 1807; slavery in British West Indies abolished 1833). Major issue in US Civil War,

being basis of South's plantation economy. Lincoln's Emancipation Proclamation (1863) and the North's victory abolished slavery in principle.

Slavic or **Slavonic,** branch of Indo-European family of languages, close to BALTIC. Divided into 3 groups: E Slavic, incl. Russian, Ukrainian; W Slavic, incl. Polish, Czech, Slovak; S Slavic, incl. Serbo-Croat, Slovenian, Bulgarian.

Slavonia, region of N Yugoslavia, between Drava and Sava rivers. Main town Osijek. Low-lying, fertile; cereals, vegetable growing. Passed (1699) from Turkey to Hungary; united with Croatia 1868.

Slavs, Indo-European linguistic group, originally from N Carpathian region. Incl. Russians, Poles, Czechs, Slovaks, Bulgars, Slovenes and Serbo-Croats.

sleep, bodily state of rest when there is little or no conscious thought or voluntary movement. Electrical waves recorded from brain show sleep occurs in cycles of *c* 2 hours; in a cycle there is a period of intense electrical brain activity and rapid movement of eyes under lids (REM) followed by longer session without REM. Dreaming occurs during REM and appears to be necessary mental process.

sleeping sickness, infectious disease of tropical Africa caused by either of 2 trypanosomes transmitted by bite of tsetse fly. Symptoms incl. fever, swollen lymph nodes; lethargy follows later when trypanosomes invade nervous system, and death may follow.

slide rule, mathematical instrument consisting of a ruler with central sliding piece, both being marked with logarithmic scales; used in making rapid calculations by adding and subtracting logarithms.

Sligo, county of Connacht prov., NW Irish Republic. Area 1797 sq km (694 sq mi); pop. 50,000. Indented Atlantic coast; rugged, Ox Mts. in W. Cattle, potatoes; fishing. Co. town **Sligo,** pop. 14,000. Port, resort; food processing. Abbey, RC cathedral, megalithic remains nearby.

Slim, William Joseph Slim, 1st Viscount (1891-1970), British field marshal. During WWII, commanded repulse of Japanese in Burma. Governor-general of Australia (1953-60).

slime mould, saprophytic fungus of class Myxomycetes. Widely distributed, living in moist places on wood or other plant material undergoing decomposition.

Sliven, town of EC Bulgaria. Pop. 68,000. Woollens, carpets; wine centre. Hist. strategic site, often involved in Balkan conflicts.

Sloane, Sir Hans (1660-1753), British physician. Made extensive collection of plants, discovering over 800 new species in Jamaica. His library and cabinet of curiosities formed nucleus of British Museum collection (founded 1753).

sloe, *see* BLACKTHORN.

Two-toed sloth (*Choloepus didactylus***)**

sloth, slow-moving herbivorous mammal of Bradypodidae family, found in tropical forests of Central and South America. Long coarse hair, often coloured green by algae; lives upside down in trees, using hooked claws to walk along branches. Two genera; *Bradypus,* three-toed sloth; *Choloepus,* two-toed sloth.

sloth bear, *Melursus ursinus,* long-snouted bear of S India and Sri Lanka. Uses long tongue to feed on ants.

Slough, mun. bor. of Buckinghamshire, SC England. Pop. 87,000. Industs. incl. chemicals; vehicle, aircraft parts; radio, television mfg.

Slovakia (*Slovensko*), region of E Czechoslovakia; main town Bratislava. Mountainous, incl. Tatra. Agric., mining. Part of Hungary (10th cent.-1918), became prov. of Czechoslovakia. Independent ally of Axis in WWII, reunited (1945). Distinctive Slovak language, culture.

Slovenia, autonomous republic of NW Yugoslavia. Area 20,246 sq km (7817 sq mi); cap. Ljubljana. Julian Alps in NW, main rivers Drava, Sava. Agric., forestry, mining. Under Habsburgs until became (1918) part of Yugoslavia. Occupied by Axis in WWII; awarded (1947) part of NE Italy.

slow-worm, *Anguis fragilis,* legless snake-like lizard, widely distributed in Europe and Asia. Found in woods, damp meadows; diet of insects, worms. Also called blindworm.

Black slug (Arion ater)

slug, terrestrial gastropod mollusc, order Pulmonata, with reduced plate-like shell enclosed by its mantle. Herbivorous, often destructive of plants; moves on muscular foot leaving trail of slime.

Sluis or **Sluys** (Fr. *L'Ecluse*), town of SW Netherlands, near Belgian border. Port, founded 13th cent. Scene of offshore naval battle (1340) in which Edward III of England defeated French. Held by Spanish 1587-1604.

Sluter, Claus (*c* 1350-*c* 1406), Flemish sculptor. Worked for Philip the Bold of Burgundy in Dijon; his masterpiece, *Well of Moses* in Dijon, marks transition from International Gothic style towards greater realism.

smallpox, infectious virus disease characterized by prolonged fever and red spots which develop into pus-filled blisters. May cause permanent scarring of the skin. Largely controlled by vaccination, it is now endemic only in parts of Ethiopia.

smell, one of five senses, less developed in humans than sight, touch, hearing. Perceived through stimulation of olfactory nerves of the nose by particles given off by substances.

smelt, small silvery marine food fish of Osmeridae family; spawns in fresh water. Species incl. common smelt, *Osmerus eperlanus,* of Europe, North America; also found landlocked in lakes.

smelting, process of obtaining metal from its ores by action of heat. Usually involves reduction of metal oxide with carbon.

Smetana, Bedřich (1824-84), Czech composer. Leader of nationalist Czech music. Works incl. opera *The Bartered Bride,* orchestral cycle *Ma Vlast* ('My Country'), string quartet 'From my Life'. Deaf for last 10 years of his life, continued to compose.

Smiles, Samuel (1812-1904), Scottish writer. Known for didactic, popular books, *Self Help* (1859). Also wrote biogs. of successful industrialists, *eg* Josiah Wedgwood.

Smirke, Sir Robert (1781-1867), English architect. Noted practitioner of neo-Classical style, his works incl. front façade of British Museum.

Smith, Adam (1723-90), Scottish economist. Formulated theory of division of labour, defined value as labour expended to make object. Advocated free trade, rejecting MERCANTILISM. His influential *Wealth of Nations* (1776) was 1st systematic formulation of economic theory, became basis of 19th cent. LAISSER-FAIRE doctrine.

Smetana

Smith, David (1906-65), American sculptor. Used forged and welded steel to make large abstract constructions. Later work was more geometric, *eg Cubi* series.

Smith, Frederick Edwin, *see* BIRKENHEAD, 1ST EARL OF.

Smith, Ian Douglas (1919-   ), Rhodesian statesman, PM (1964-   ). Issued Unilateral Declaration of Independence from Britain (1965). Set up republic under constitution perpetuating white minority rule (1969). Under pressure from US, entered into discussion with nationalist leaders on question of majority rule and transfer of power (1976).

Smith, Jedediah Strong (1799-1831), American explorer. Opened up trapping in West. Led small force on pioneering expedition across Great Salt Desert to San Diego and back (1825-7).

Smith, John (*c* 1580-1631), English colonist. Leader in settlement (1606-9) of Jamestown, Virginia. Supposedly saved from execution at order of Indian chief, Powhatan, by intervention of Powhatan's daughter, Pocahontas (1607).

Smith, Joseph (1805-44), American religious leader. Claimed to have vision directing him to sacred writings, transcribed as *Book of Mormon* (1829). Founded church (1830) based on revelations. Murdered by mob at Carthage, Illinois. Followers formed MORMONS.

Smith, Sydney (1771-1845), English clergyman, writer. Helped found literary *Edinburgh Review* (1802). Wrote *The Letters of Peter Plymley* (1807) supporting Catholic Emancipation. Celebrated wit, conversationalist.

Smith, William (1769-1839), English geologist. Estab. principle that all geological strata contain characteristic groups of fossils, which aid dating of strata. Constructed geological map of British Isles (1815).

Smith, William Robertson (1846-94), Scottish scholar. Dismissed from professorship in Aberdeen (1881) for modernist views in articles on religion and anthropology in *Encyclopaedia Britannica* (9th edition), which he later edited. Author of *Religion of the Semites* (1889).

Smithson, James (1765-1829), English scientist, b. France. Left fortune to found Smithsonian Institution, Washington (1846), to encourage scientific research.

Smithsonian Institution, Washington, DC, US, scientific institution, estab. (1846) by Congressional act. Conducts research in all aspects of science relevant to US. Controls National Gallery of Art, museums of history and natural history.

smoke, suspension of solid particles in a gas, esp. particles of carbon and hydrocarbon in atmosphere derived from combustion of carbonaceous fuels. When combined with fog, forms smog. Considered health risk, therefore controlled by govt. measures advocating clean air and smokeless zones.

smokeball, *see* PUFFBALL.

Smoktunovsky, Innokenti (1925-   ), Russian stage, film actor. Known to West for starring roles in films, *eg Hamlet* (1964).

Smolensk, town of USSR, railway jct. of W European RSFSR; port on R. Dnepr. Pop. 225,000. Linen and textile mfg. Founded 9th cent.; became commercial centre, trading with Constantinople. Cap. of principality 12th-14th cent. Occupied by Napoleon (1812) and Germans (1941-3).

Smollett, Tobias [George] (1721-71), Scottish writer, surgeon. Known for energetic picaresque novels *Roderick Random* (1748), *Peregrine Pickle* (1751), *Humphrey Clinker* (1771).

smuggling, offence of importing or exporting goods illegally, esp. those requiring payment of duty. Esp. prevalent in 18th cent. with imposition of duties in UK, North America, Europe; goods smuggled incl. spirits, lace, tobacco, tea. Modern smuggling incl. drugs, illegal immigrants.

smut or **bunt,** various parasitic fungi of order Ustilaginales. Appear as black sooty spores on host plant. Serious threat to cereal crops. Treatment with compounds of sulphur and mercury.

Field Marshal Smuts

Smuts, Jan Christiaan (1870-1950), South African soldier, statesman, PM (1919-24, 1939-48). Commanded Boer forces (1901-2) in war against UK, later sought co-operation with British. Joined Botha in creating (1910) Union of South Africa. Member of British war councils during both WWs.

Smyrna, see IZMIR.

snail, gastropod mollusc of order Pulmonata with spiral protective shell. Marine, freshwater and terrestrial varieties. Species incl. common garden snail, *Helix aspersa,* and edible or Roman snail, *H. pomatia.*

Snake, river of NW US, rising in Yellowstone National Park (Wyoming). Flows SW 1670 km (1038 mi) through Idaho, then NW along Oregon border to Washington to join Columbia R.

snake, any of suborder Ophidia of limbless elongated reptiles. Horny scales on body, forked tongue; mouth opens wide for swallowing large prey. Poisonous snakes carry venom in salivary glands; venom acts either as nerve poison, paralysing victim, or as tissue poison, destroying cells and causing haemorrhages.

snakeroot, name for various North American plants formerly reputed to be cure for snakebites, *eg* black snakeroot, *Cimicifuga racemosa,* and white snakeroot, *Eupatorium rugosum.*

snapdragon, any of genus *Antirrhinum* of perennial plants native to Mediterranean region, esp. garden variety *A. majus* with showy white, crimson or yellow flowers.

snapper, any of Lutjanidae family of marine fish. Red snapper, *Lutjanus sebae,* found in Indian and Pacific oceans, is valuable food fish.

snapping turtle, any of Chelydridae family of turtles, found in North American swamps and rivers; species incl. *Chelydra serpentina,* aggressive predator with powerful jaws.

snare drum, percussion instrument. Consists of side drum with catgut strings to produce rattling sound.

sneeze, reflex action consisting of brief indrawn breath followed by forcible expulsion of air through nose. Initiated by irritation of lining of nose.

Snellius or **Snell, Willebrord** (1591-1626), Dutch physicist, mathematician. Discovered law governing REFRACTION of light, connecting sines of angles of incidence and refraction.

snipe, wading bird of Scolopacidae family, with long narrow bill used for digging. Species incl. common snipe, *Gallinago gallinago,* of Europe and Asia, and South American noble snipe, *G. nobilis.*

snooker, game played on billiard table with 15 red balls, 6 coloured balls and white cue ball. Derived from BILLIARDS. Similar to US game of pool.

Snorri Sturluson (1179-1241), Icelandic historian, politician. Wrote *Edda* (pre-1223), handbook on poet's art which uses myths as examples; *Heimskringla* (*c* 1223-35), history of Norwegian kings, incl. *Saga of Saint Olaf, King Harold's Saga.* Writing noted for characterization, dialogue and rhetoric, and narrative skill.

Snow, C[harles] P[ercy], Baron Snow of Leicester (1905-   ), English author, scientist. Known for long novel sequence incl. *Strangers and Brothers* (1940), *The Light and the Dark* (1947), *The Masters* (1951), *Corridors of Power* (1963), dealing with ethics of power. Wrote controversial essay, *The Two Cultures* (1959).

snow, precipitation consisting of delicate, hexagonal ice crystals, formed in atmosphere at temperatures below freezing point. Lower limit of permanent snow cover is called 'snow-line'; it reaches sea level at poles.

snowball, see GUELDER ROSE.

snowberry, *Symphoricarpos albus,* North American shrub of honeysuckle family. Tubular, small, pink flowers and soft, white berries.

snow bunting, *Plectrophenax nivalis,* small bird of N regions; in spring, male's plumage is white with black back and tail. Breeds in Arctic, migrating to Europe and America in winter.

Snowdon, Anthony Armstrong-Jones, 1st Earl of (1930-   ), British designer, photographer. Married (1960) Princess Margaret; separated in 1976. Designs incl. aviary at London Zoo.

Snowdon, mountain of Gwynedd, NW Wales. Highest in England and Wales (1085 m/3560 ft). Rack Railway from Llanberis. Snowdonia national park in surrounding area.

snowdrop, any of genus *Galanthus* of early-blooming, bulbous perennials native to Europe. Garden varieties incl. common snowdrop, *G. nivalis.*

snow goose, *Anser caerulescens,* white North American goose with black-tipped wings, dark pink bill and legs. Breeds colonially in Arctic.

snow leopard or **ounce,** *Uncia uncia,* large cat of mountains of C Asia; reaches lengths of 2.1 m/7 ft. Coat whitish with dark blotches in summer, almost pure white in winter. Feeds on sheep, goats, ibex.

Snowy Mountains, range of SE New South Wales, Australia, in Australian Alps. Highest point Mt. KOSCIUSKO. Snowy Mts. scheme estab. 1949 to provide h.e.p., irrigation from Snowy, Tumut, Eucumbene and other rivers.

snowy owl, *Nyctea scandiaca,* large owl of Arctic and subarctic regions. Largely diurnal and solitary; white plumage with dark brown markings. Feeds on hares, lemmings, fish.

snuff, powdered tobacco sniffed into nostrils or rubbed on to teeth and gums. Snuff-taking was widespread in 18th cent. when elaborately decorated snuff boxes were made.

Soane, Sir John (1753-1837), English architect. Evolved individual style, based on neo-Classicism; most important work was at Bank of England (now destroyed). His house in London is now a museum.

soap, mixture of sodium salts of fatty acids (esp. oleic, palmitic and stearic acids) or of potassium salts of these acids (soft soaps). Prepared by boiling fats and oils with alkali. Acts most effectively in soft water; hard water causes scum (precipitated calcium or magnesium salts) to form.

soapberry, any of genus *Sapindus* of tropical trees and shrubs. Fruit, containing saponin, formerly used as soap.

soapstone or **steatite,** soft, grey mineral, composed mainly of TALC with other minerals *eg* chlorite, mica, quartz. Used in sculpture and electrical insulators.

Soapwort

soapwort or **bouncing Bet,** *Saponaria officinalis,* European annual or perennial herb widely naturalized in North America as garden plant. Clusters of pink flowers; sap forms lather with water.

Soares, Mario (1924-), Portuguese political leader. Imprisoned in 1960s for socialist opposition to Salazar regime, exiled (1970-4). Returned after military coup (1974) to become minister for foreign affairs (1974-5). Became PM after elections (1976).

Sobers, Sir Garfield St Aubrun ('Gary') (1936-), Barbadian cricketer. Leading West Indies' all-rounder of 1960s, he scored over 8000 runs in test cricket, incl. 26 centuries. Hit record 365 in test match against Pakistan (1957-8).

Sobieski, John, see JOHN III [SOBIESKI], king of Poland.

soccer, *see* ASSOCIATION FOOTBALL.

Sochi, resort of USSR, SW European RSFSR; on E Black Sea coast. Pop. 236,000. Food, tobacco produce.

social class, category or grouping of people according to economic, occupational or social status. In Marxist terms, refers exclusively to those persons with common relationship to material production. Traditionally, society divided into upper, middle and working (lower) classes, according to socio-economic grouping; its study may involve aspects on health, crime rates, racial, political attitudes, mobility between classes, life styles.

social contract, theory that society originated out of voluntary association, bringing with it mutual obligations. Formulated by Hobbes and Locke, expanded by Rousseau, had great influence on subsequent development of responsible govt. in democracies.

Social Credit, economic programme, developed from theories of economist C.H. DOUGLAS. Calls for redistribution of purchasing power by issuing dividends (based on estimate of nation's wealth) to all persons to counter economic depression. Adopted by Social Credit Party of Alberta, Canada; elected (1935) under William Aberhart. Later achieved power in British Columbia.

social democracy, advocacy of socialism within democratic framework, adhering to evolutionary means of achieving power; esp. important in Europe. Split in German Social Democratic party (SPD) at start of 20th cent. reflected dilemma of other European Socialist parties, whether or not to cooperate with bourgeois govts. to achieve gradual reform; E. BERNSTEIN leading proponent of this 'revisionism', opposing use of violent revolution to gain power for proletariat (*see* MARXISM). Collapse of Internationals during WWI led to increase of reform-conscious Social Democratic parties in Europe, some forming govts., *eg* in Scandinavian countries and Britain (*see* LABOUR PARTY), between WWs. In Germany, SPD revived after WWII; gained power under Brandt (1969). In France, Socialist groups under Blum formed Popular Front govt. in 1930s; formed major opposition party in Fifth Republic.

socialism, any of various economic and political theories or systems advocating transfer of means of production and distribution from private ownership to community as a whole, with all sharing work, produce. In this sense, can incl. SOCIAL DEMOCRACY as well as MARXISM. Early socialist theorists (eg OWEN, SAINT-SIMON) believed in reform of existing society to achieve utopian ideal. Attacked by Marx, who taught inevitability of revolution. By 1870s, Marxist ('scientific') socialism was strong political force in Europe, but internally split into 2 main factions, gradualists and revolutionaries. Schism made permanent with triumph of revolutionary COMMUNISM in Russia (1917).

social realism, in art, depiction of contemporary scene, usually with some social or political content. In Britain, Bratby is an exponent; in US, Ben Shahn. Distinct from **socialist realism,** official art of Communist countries, which glorifies the worker, peasant and Party.

social security, system by which govt. provides for nation's wage earners and dependants, esp. for their protection in health, old age or unemployment. First estab. 1883 in Germany with HEALTH INSURANCE and PENSION SCHEMES. In UK, NATIONAL INSURANCE ACT (1911) added unemployment insurance. In US, Social Security Act (1935) embodied principles.

Society Islands, archipelago of SC Pacific Ocean, part of French Polynesia. Comprise Windward Isls. (incl. Tahiti) and Leeward Isls. Produce copra, pearl shell, vanilla. Acquired by France (1843).

Society of Friends or **Quakers,** Christian sect founded (*c* 1650) in England by GEORGE FOX. Hold that understanding and guidance come directly from 'inward light' of Holy Spirit and that sacrament, and formal worship are unnecessary for Christian life. Colony estab. (1682) in Pennsylvania, US, by PENN. American Friends Service Committee and Service Council of the British Society of Friends awarded Nobel Peace Prize (1947).

Society of Jesus, *see* JESUS, SOCIETY OF.

Socinus, Laelius, Latin form of Lelio Sozzini (1525-62), Italian theologian. Writings questioned orthodox concept on Trinity. Developed by his nephew, Fausto Sozzini (1539-1604), as Socinianism. Pronounced heretical, but provided basis of belief of Polish Brethren.

sociology, study of human society, and of social relations, organization and change; specifically the study of the beliefs, values, interrelationships, *etc*, of social groups and of the principles and processes governing social phenomena. Systematic discipline since 19th cent., esp. through work of Auguste Comte, and later Durkheim and Max Weber.

Socotra, isl. of Southern Yemen, in Arabian Sea. Area *c* 3630 sq km (1400 sq mi). Barren plateau with mountainous interior. Part of British protect. of Aden after 1886. Former coaling station.

Socrates

Socrates (469-399 BC), Greek philosopher. Believed knowledge could be approached by question-and-answer sequence (dialectic method), and wisdom to be based on recognition of one's ignorance. Ideas on weakness of democratic govt. unpopular in Athens. Assembly tried and condemned him on charge of corrupting youth; died by drinking poison. Teachings preserved in writings of disciple Plato, and subsequently Aristotle.

soda, name applied to various sodium compounds, incl. sodium carbonate, bicarbonate and hydroxide. Sodium carbonate, manufactured on large scale from common salt, is used to make soap, glass, paper and to soften water. Sodium bicarbonate is used in baking powder and medicine.

Soddy, Frederick (1877-1956), English chemist. Evolved theory of radioactive decay with Rutherford. Predicted existence of isotopes to explain the many intermediate products occurring during radioactive decay; awarded Nobel Prize for Chemistry (1921).

Söderblom, Nathan (1866-1931), Swedish churchman, primate of the Lutheran Church of Sweden. Leading ecumenist, awarded Nobel Peace Prize (1930).

sodium (Na), soft silvery-white metallic element; at. no. 11, at. wt. 22.99. Reacts violently with water to form strong alkali sodium hydroxide. Occurs combined as chloride (common salt), nitrate (Chile saltpetre); prepared by electrolysis of fused chloride. Used in organic syntheses, *eg* of lead tetraethyl; yellow sodium vapour light used in street lighting.

Sodom and Gomorrah, in OT, two of the cities of the plain, destroyed by God because of their wickedness. Possibly situated SW of Dead Sea.

Sofia (anc. *Sardica*), cap. of Bulgaria. Pop. 928,000. Major route centre in W Balkans. Indust. centre, esp. machinery, textiles. Univ. (1880), Black Mosque. Colonized by Romans; sacked by Huns (447). Cap. of former Turkish Rumelia, of Bulgaria from 1879.

soft-shelled turtle, freshwater turtle of Trionychidae family of Africa, Asia and North America. Bones of shell encased in leathery tissue; long beak with soft lips. Species incl. North American *Trionyx spinifera.*

Sogne Fjord, inlet of Atlantic Ocean, SW Norway. Longest (*c* 180 km/110 mi) and deepest (1220 m/ 4000 ft) fjord in Norway, reaches inland to Jotunheim Mts. Tourist area.

Soho, dist. of City of WESTMINSTER, London, England. Has many foreign restaurants; theatres, nightclubs; film co. offices. Origin of name prob. old hunting cry.

soil, loose accumulation of material forming topmost layer of Earth's land surface. Consists of organic material (humus) and inorganic material (weathered rock, incl. clay, silt, sand) together with air and water. Types incl. BLACK EARTH, LOAM, LOESS. Study of soil is called pedology.

Soissons, town of N France, on R. Aisne. Pop. 28,000. Agric. market for Soissonais. Cathedral (12th cent.); ruined abbey contains tombs of Merovingian kings.

Sokoto, town of NW Nigeria, on R. Kebbi. Pop. 50,000. Trade centre, esp. in groundnuts, hides. Cap. of vast Moslem Fulani empire of Sokoto estab. early 19th cent.; fell to British (1903).

Solanaceae, family of plants native to tropical and temperate regions, esp. tropical America. Incl. deadly nightshade, tobacco, potato. Many species contain poisonous alkaloids.

solan goose, see GANNET.

solar energy, energy liberated by thermonuclear reactions in Sun and radiated in form of radio waves, X-rays and light. May be utilized by solar cells to generate electricity or by solar furnaces to produce high temperatures.

solar flare, short-lived eruption of Sun's surface, usually associated with sunspots. Accompanied by emission of particles, X-rays, *etc*; causes magnetic and radio disturbances on Earth.

Solar System, name for Sun and collection of bodies in orbit about it. Comprises Sun, 9 major planets (Mercury, Venus, Earth, Mars, Jupiter, Saturn, Uranus, Neptune, Pluto), their satellites, minor planets, comets and meteors.

solar wind, stream of ionized particles, mainly protons and electrons, emitted from Sun's surface, esp. during solar flares and sunspot activity. Particles reaching Earth are trapped by its magnetic field to form Van Allen radiation belt; others cause auroral displays around the poles.

solder, alloy used in joining metal. Soft solders, which have low melting point, contain lead and tin in varying proportions with some antimony.

sole, edible flatfish of Soleidae family, with worldwide distribution. European *Solea solea* is commercially valuable; sold as Dover sole.

Solent, The, channel between Hampshire, S England, and Isle of Wight. Shipping route to Southampton, Portsmouth; yachting.

sol-fa, tonic, *see* TONIC SOL-FA.

Solferino, village of N Italy, near Mantua. Scene of indecisive battle (1859) between French and Austrians which inspired Dunant to form Red Cross.

solicitor, in England, member of legal profession who is not member of the bar; may not plead cases in superior courts. Advises clients in legal cases, engages barristers for them, *etc.*

solid, state of matter in which constituent molecules or ions possess no translatory movement. Solids possess definite crystalline structure and retain their shape unless deformed by external forces; certain amorphous non-crystalline solids, *eg* glass, may be considered as supercooled fluids.

solid-state physics, branch of physics dealing with matter in solid state. Often refers specifically to study of semiconductors and their use in electronic devices without moving parts or heated filaments.

Solingen, city of W West Germany, in Ruhr. Pop. 177,000. Steel mfg. (esp. cutlery) begun in Middle Ages with production of sword blades.

Solna, town of EC Sweden, now suburb of Stockholm. Pop. 58,000. Hq. of Swedish film indust. Scientific institutes, incl. Nobel.

Solo, see SURAKARTA.

Sologub, Feodor, pseud. of Feodor Kuzmich Teternikov (1863-1927), Russian author. Wrote novel *The Petty Demon* (1907) about a grotesquely evil schoolmaster. Also wrote short stories, symbolist poetry.

Solomon (d. *c* 932 BC), king of Israel, son of David and Bathsheba. His peaceful reign was marked by growth of trade and building of the Temple in Jerusalem. The heavy taxes he imposed led to a revolt in N Israel. Famous for his wisdom.

Solomon Islands, state of SW Pacific, member of British Commonwealth. Area *c* 29,800 sq km (11,500 sq mi); pop. 163,000; cap. Honiara. Consists of all isls. of Solomon Isls. archipelago (incl. Guadalcanal), except Bougainville and Buka, which belong to Papua New Guinea. Formerly known as British Solomon Isls. Protect. (estab. by 1899), independent 1977.

Solon (*c* 639-*c* 559 BC), Athenian statesman. Revised constitution to create limited form of democracy. Extended basis of membership of the sovereign assembly. Improved the conditions of debtors and poor people.

Solothurn (Fr. *Soleure*), town of NW Switzerland, on R. Aare, cap. of Solothurn canton. Pop. 18,000. Watches, precision instruments. Medieval buildings; cathedral (18th cent.).

solstice, time of year when Sun appears directly overhead at the line marking its furthest distance N or S of the Equator. For N hemisphere, summer solstice (21 June) occurs when Sun reaches Tropic of Cancer, winter solstice (22 Dec.) when Sun reaches Tropic of Capricorn. Day is at max. length at summer solstice, night at winter solstice.

solution, homogeneous molecular mixture of 2 or more substances, *eg* of solid or gas in liquid. Some alloys are solutions of one metal in another.

Solutrean, Upper Palaeolithic culture dating from *c* 19,000 BC; characterized by flint spearheads shaped like laurel leaves. Named after site at Solutré, near Mâcon, France.

Solway Firth, inlet of Irish Sea, between SW Scotland and NW England. Fishing.

Solzhenitsyn, Aleksandr Isayevich (1918-), Russian author. Known for novels critical of Soviet regime, *eg First Circle* (1964), *Cancer Ward* (1966), *August 1914* (1972), *The Gulag Archipelago* (1974). *One Day in the Life of Ivan Denisovich* (1962) is a short novel detailing conditions in labour camp. Nobel Prize for Literature (1970). Exiled in 1974.

soma, legendary intoxicating liquor possibly derived from juice of Indian plant, *Sarcostemma acidum,* of milkweed family. Referred to in Vedic texts.

Somalia

Somalia or **Somali Democratic Republic,** republic of E Africa. Area 637,700 sq km (246,200 sq mi); pop. 3,003,000; cap. Mogadishu. Language: Somali. Religion: Islam. Coastal lowland, arid interior plateau. Nomadic pastoralism; exports bananas, livestock, hides. Formed 1960 from union of British Somaliland (created 1884, cap. Hargeisa) and Italian Somaliland (created 1889, cap. Mogadishu; from 1950 a UN trust territ.).

Somaliland, French, see AFARS AND THE ISSAS, FRENCH TERRITORY OF THE.

Somers, John Somers, Baron (1651-1716), English statesman, jurist. Presided over committee which drafted BILL OF RIGHTS (1689). Gained favour as confidential adviser to William III; lord chancellor (1697-1700). Successfully defended himself against impeachment charge.

Somerset, Edward Seymour, Duke of, see SEYMOUR, JANE.

Somerset, county of SW England. Area 3458 sq km (1335 sq mi); pop. 399,000; co. town Taunton. Exmoor in W; Mendips in NE; plain in C. Dairying (esp. Cheddar cheese), sheep, cider apples.

Somme, river of N France. Flows *c* 240 km (150 mi) from near St Quentin via Amiens, Abbeville to English Channel. Canal links to Oise, Scheldt. Scene of heavy fighting in WWI (1916).

Somoza, Anastasio (1896-1956), Nicaraguan political leader, president (1937-47, 1950-6). Ruthless rule after gaining dictatorial power in coup (1936). Assassinated.

sonar or **asdic,** method of detecting and locating underwater objects, esp. submarines or shoals of fish, by projecting soundwaves through water and registering the vibrations reflected back. Also used in measuring depths.

sonata, piece of instrumental music so named to distinguish it from a cantata for voices and instruments. Developed from *c* 1600 as a composition for a single instrument, esp. a keyboard one, with or without accompaniment. Usually in several movements, first of which is in sonata form containing 2 themes subjected to statement, development and recipitulation.

Sönderborg, town of SE Denmark; mainly on Als isl., partly on mainland. Pop. 25,000. Port, resort. Part of Schleswig until 16th cent.

song, vocal form of musical expression, normally setting of lyric. Earliest documented European song dates from 10th cent. Early practitioners were TROUBADOURS, MINNESINGER. Developed by such masters as MACHAUT, DUFAY, LASSUS and English lutanists of 16th-17th cents. Reached peak as vehicle of romantic expression in work of Schubert, Schumann and Brahms in 19th cent. Folk song has survived with little change for centuries.

Song of Solomon, poetical book of OT, traditionally attributed to Solomon, but sometimes dated as late as 3rd cent. BC. Primarily a glorification of pure love or an allegory of God's love for Israel.

songthrush, *Turdus philomelos,* common European songbird with brown back and spotted breast.

sonic boom, noise created by shock waves set up by aircraft travelling faster than sound. Waves are transmitted as variations in atmospheric pressure; when waves touch ground, characteristic double bang is heard.

sonnet, poem of 14 lines, expressing single complete thought or idea, generally written in iambic pentameter. Most common rhyme schemes are the Italian form (*eg* Keats's *On First Looking into Chapman's Homer*) with 8 lines (octave) followed by group of 6 lines (sestet), and Shakespearian form with 3 quatrains followed by couplet.

Soochow or **Wuhsien,** city of Kiangsu prov., E China. Pop. 1,300,000. On Grand Canal; rail jct. Famous silks, weaving. Former treaty port, opened 1896. Has many canals, gardens and pagodas.

Sophists, term applied in Athens (middle 5th cent. BC) to persons giving lessons in rhetoric, politics and mathematics in return for money. Later Sophists emphasized rhetoric rather than substance of knowledge, becoming known for their ability to conduct specious argument. Condemned by Socrates and Plato. Leading Sophists incl. Protagoras, Gorgias.

Presumed head of Sophocles

Sophocles (*c* 496–406 BC), Greek tragic poet. One of three great masters of tragedy, other two being contemporaries Aeschylus and Euripides. Known for use of dialogue rather than lyric, introducing 3rd actor to increase dialogue's importance, complexity; also use of dramatic irony. Extant plays are *Oedipus Rex, Oedipus at Colonus, Antigone, Electra, Ajax, Women of Trachis, Philoctetes.*

Sophonias, see ZEPHANIAH.

soprano, highest singing voice in women and boys, latter also known as treble. Term sometimes applied to high-pitched member of a family of instruments, *eg* soprano saxophone.

Sopron (Ger. *Odenburg*), town of NW Hungary. Pop. 42,000. Railway jct., textiles, chemicals. Medieval churches.

Sopwith, Sir Thomas Octave Murdoch (1888-   ), British aircraft designer. Flew across English Channel (1910). Founded (1912) company which built WWI aeroplanes.

Sorbonne, traditional name for Univ. of Paris, France, from 1st college estab. (1253) by Robert de Sorbon; reorganized in 19th cent. Early known for theological studies.

Sorel, Albert (1842-1906), French historian, diplomat. Major work was *L'Europe et la révolution française* (8 vols., 1895-1904). Made use of diplomatic documents in foreign ministry archives.

Sorel, Georges (1847-1922), French social philosopher. Introduced Marxist ideas into France, later becoming anarcho-syndicalist, then Leninist, regarding Marxism, like all extremist social doctrines, as world-changing myth, not science. Known for *Reflections on Violence* (1908), defending role of violence in revolution.

Sorghum

sorghum, genus of grasses with solid stems native to Africa; esp. *Sorghum vulgare,* widely cultivated as forage crop. Variously known as Kaffir corn, durra, Guinea corn, Indian millet.

Sorokin, Pitirim Aleksandrovich (1889-1968), American sociologist, b. Russia. Known for theory of social, cultural change developed in *Social and Cultural Dynamics* (3 vols., 1937-41).

sorrel, see DOCK, OXALIS.

Sorrento, town of Campania, SW Italy, on Bay of Naples. Pop. 29,000. Scenic cliff-top resort; long famous for wine.

Sosnowiec, city of S Poland. Pop. 145,000. Iron and steel industs., engineering. Rapid growth from late 19th cent. based on coalmining. Under Russian rule 1815-1919.

Sotheby, John (1740-1807), English auctioneer, antiquarian. Director of saleroom for prints, manuscripts; developed auction house, Sotheby's of London, which bought Parke-Bernet Gallery, New York City (1964).

soul, concept of non-material, immortal life-essence or spiritual identity of individual. Mind and body conceived as its vehicle. Occurs in most religions either as individual attribute (Christianity, Islam) or as general principle or world soul (Hinduism, Buddhism). Denied by materialists.

Sound, The, see ORESUND, Denmark.

sound, vibrations in air or some other medium which stimulate the auditory nerves and give sensation of hearing. Travels at *c* 330 m/sec (760 mph) in air; velocity varies with temperature and is greater in solids. Pitch of sound depends on number of vibrations per second; lowest normally audible sound has frequency of *c* 20 cycles/sec, highest *c* 20,000.

Sousa, John Philip (1854-1932), American composer, band leader. Best known for marches, *eg The Stars and Stripes Forever,* of which he composed more than 100.

Sousse or **Susa,** town of E Tunisia, on Gulf of Hammamet. Pop. 83,000. Tourist resort; port, exports olive oil. Ancient *Hadrumetum,* founded 9th cent. BC by Phoenicians. Mosque, fortress (both 9th cent.).

South Africa

South Africa, republic of S Africa. Area 1,221,000 sq km (471,500 sq mi); pop. 23,724,000; caps. Pretoria (admin.), Cape Town (legislative), Bloemfontein (judicial).

Languages: Afrikaans, English. Religion: Christianity. Comprises Cape Prov., Natal, Orange Free State, Transvaal; controls South West Africa despite withdrawal of UN mandate (1966). Mainly plateau, fringed by mountains (*eg* Drakensberg); main rivers Orange, Vaal. Cereals, fruit, sugar cane, vines; great mineral wealth, esp. in Witwatersrand. Dutch settlement estab. 1652 at Table Bay; Cape annexed by UK 1806. Boer dislike of British rule led to 'Great Trek' 1836 to Orange Free State, Transvaal; Boer republics estab. 1850s. Boer War (1899-1902) ended in British victory; Union of South Africa estab. 1910. Republic from 1960, withdrew from British Commonwealth 1961. Follows controversial policy of separate development (*apartheid*) of blacks and whites; incl. 9 Bantu 'homelands' eventually to become partly independent (*eg* TRANSKEI).

South African War, see BOER WAR.

South America, S continent of W hemisphere, bounded by Pacific in W and Atlantic in E. Area *c* 17,819,000 sq km (6,880,000 sq mi); pop. 195,000,000. Dominated in W by Andean cordillera; C plateau incl. Mato Grosso, Pampas; drained by Amazon, Plata, Orinoco river systems. Hist. highly developed Indian civilizations (esp. Incas) *fl* before Spanish, Portuguese exploration and colonization for mineral wealth in 16th cent. Nine Spanish-speaking republics estab. under Bolívar, San Martín in 19th cent.; Brazil is Portuguese-speaking. Guiana Highlands comprise Surinam, Guyana, French Guiana. Much political instability in all republics after independence.

Southampton, Henry Wriothesley, 3rd Earl of (1573-1624), English courtier. Patron of Shakespeare and other poets; Shakespeare's *Venus and Adonis* is dedicated to him. Imprisoned by Elizabeth I for involvement in Essex's rebellion (1601); pardoned by James I.

Southampton, city of Hampshire, S England, on Southampton Water. Pop. 215,000. Chief English passenger seaport; transatlantic services. Also cargo port; large graving dock (1933). Oil refinery at Fawley. Medieval walls, churches; univ. (1952). Damaged in WWII bombing.

Southampton Island, in E Keewatin Dist., Northwest Territs., Canada; at entrance to Hudson Bay. Area 40,700 sq km (15,700 sq mi). Scattered communities, mainly Eskimo.

South Arabia, Federation of, see SOUTHERN YEMEN.

South Australia, state of S Australia. Area 984,500 sq km (380,100 sq mi); pop. 1,173,000; cap. Adelaide. Mainly low-lying, incl. Nullarbor Plain in SW, L. Eyre in N; has Musgrave (N), Flinders and Mt. Lofty (SE) ranges. Produces sheep, wheat, fruit, wine; minerals incl. iron ore, salt. First settled 1836; became crown colony 1842, federal state 1901. Controlled Northern Territ. 1863-1911.

South Bend, town of N Indiana, US; on St Joseph R. Pop. 126,000. Farm machinery mfg., agric. processing. Estab. as fur trading post. Has Univ. of Notre Dame (1842).

South Carolina, state of SE US, on Atlantic coast. Area 80,432 sq km (31,055 sq mi); pop. 2,591,000; cap. Columbia. Low coastal plain, Savannah R. on S border; plateau in NW. Important agric. (tobacco, cotton, soya beans, maize, stock rearing), related industs.; stone, clay mining. First settled by Spanish (1526); then by English (1670). One of original 13 colonies of US. First secessionist state before Civil War (1860).

South China Sea, part of Pacific Ocean enclosed by SE China, Indo-China, Malay penin., Borneo, Philippines and Taiwan.

Southcott, Joanna (1750-1814), English visionary. Prophecies (after 1792) gained many followers. Claimed she would be mother of new messiah (never born).

South Dakota, state of NC US. Area 199,552 sq km (77,047 sq mi); pop. 666,000; cap. Pierre. Mainly agric. (grains, livestock rearing); plains in E divided from Black Hills in SW (gold mines) by Missouri R. Acquired by US as part of Louisiana Purchase (1803). Territ. estab. (1861); Sioux Indians resisted white settlement (1868-90), deprived of land. Admitted to Union, jointly with North Dakota, as 39th state (1889).

Southeast Asia Treaty Organization (SEATO), alliance, estab. 1954 at Manila, Philippines. Charter

South Dakota: The Badlands

members incl. Australia, France, New Zealand, UK and US; formed for collective defence against aggression.

Southend-on-Sea, co. bor. of Essex, SE England, on N side of Thames estuary. Pop. 162,000. Electrical goods mfg. Resort, famous pier (2 km/1.25 mi long).

Southern Alps, mountain range of South Isl., New Zealand. Runs SW-NE, highest point MT. COOK. Many snowfields, glaciers *eg* Tasman Glacier; source of many rivers, *eg* Clutha, Waitaki. Tourist area, snow sports.

Southern Cross (Crux), small constellation in S hemisphere whose 4 brightest stars appear to form tips of a cross.

Southern Rhodesia, *see* RHODESIA.

Southern Yemen

Southern Yemen, republic of SW Asia. Area *c* 287,500 sq km (111,000 sq mi); pop. 1,400,000; cap. Aden. Coastal strip in S borders Arabian Sea; mountains and plateau in interior. History dates from 1963 estab. of Federation of South Arabia out of states of Aden protect. Southern Yemen proclaimed 1967.

Southey, Robert (1774-1843), English author. One of 'Lake poets'. Known for short poems, *eg* 'The Battle of Blenheim', 'Inchcape Rock', and biog. of Nelson (1813). Poet laureate (1813).

South Georgia, *see* FALKLAND ISLANDS.

South Glamorgan, *see* GLAMORGAN, Wales.

South Holland, *see* HOLLAND.

South Island, one of main isls. of New Zealand, separated from North Isl. by Cook Str. Area 150,480 sq km (58,100 sq mi); pop. 810,000; chief cities Christchurch, Dunedin. Plateau in SW; Southern Alps form W backbone. Coastal lowland incl. Canterbury Plains. Grain, sheep farming; timber; h.e.p.

South Korea, *see* KOREA.

South Orkney Islands, group of isls. in S Atlantic, SE of Cape Horn, forming part of British Antarctic Territ. from 1962. Area *c* 620 sq km (140 sq mi). Discovered 1821; also claimed by Argentina.

South Pole, point at S end of Earth's axis, latitude 90°S. First reached 1911 by Roald Amundsen.

Southport, co. bor. of Merseyside met. county, NW England. Pop. 84,000. Clothing mfg. Seaside resort. Has Royal Birkdale golf course.

South Sea Bubble, popular name for financial scheme in which South Sea Co. (founded 1711 with monopoly in South American trade) took over British national debt, exchanging its stock for govt. bonds. After widespread speculation, company became bankrupt (1720); resulting investigation revealed govt. corruption.

South Shetland Islands, group of isls. in S Atlantic, NW of Graham Land, forming part of British Antarctic Territ. from 1962. Area *c* 4700 sq km (1800 sq mi). Discovered 1819; formerly base for sealers and whalers.

South Shields, co. bor. of Tyne and Wear met. county, NE England, on S side of Tyne estuary. Pop. 101,000. Shipbuilding, engineering, chemicals industs.

South Vietnam, *see* VIETNAM.

Southwark, bor. of SC Greater London, England. Pop. 260,000. Created 1965 from Bermondsey, Camberwell, Southwark met. bors. Hist. famous for inns; has former Clink prison for heretics; Globe Theatre; Guy's Hospital (1721).

South West Africa or **Namibia,** territ. of SW Africa, admin. by Republic of South Africa. Area 824,000 sq km (318,000 sq mi); pop. 673,000; cap. Windhoek. Languages: Bantu, Afrikaans, English. Religions: native, Christianity. Namib Desert along coast, plateau inland; salt pans in N. Stock raising, rich in minerals; exports skins, diamonds, copper, lead, manganese. German colony from 1892; admin. after WWI by South Africa under League of Nations mandate. Revocation 1966 by UN disputed by South Africa.

South Yorkshire, met. county of NC England. Area 1560 sq km (602 sq mi); pop. 1,319,000; admin. centre Barnsley. Created 1974 from part of former S Riding of Yorkshire.

Soutine, Chaim (1894-1943), Lithuanian painter, resident in Paris after 1911. Painted tormented, heavily impasted works in violent expressionist style; noted for his portraits of cooks and page-boys, studies of carcasses, and landscapes.

sovereignty, in politics, supreme independent power held by state or other govt. unit. Sovereign state can conduct diplomacy, make treaties, war, peace. Internally, it makes laws, controls finances and the military.

Sovetsk, town of USSR, W European RSFSR; port on R. Neman. Pop. 60,000. Woodworking and cheese mfg. As Tilsit, site of treaty between Russia, Prussia and France (1807), leading to loss of Prussian territ. Passed to USSR (1945) and renamed.

soviet (Russ., = council), in USSR, any of various governing councils, local, intermediate, national, elected by and representing people. Each forms part of a pyramid govt. structure, with village, town soviets at base, Supreme Soviet at apex. Organized first (1905) as strike committees. Re-estab. 1917 by workers, soldiers, became govt. instruments under Lenin (1918).

Soviet Union, *see* UNION OF SOVIET SOCIALIST REPUBLICS.

sowbug, *see* WOODLOUSE.

Soweto, township of S Transvaal, South Africa, near Johannesburg. Black African pop. Scene of anti-govt. riots (1976) following protests against use of Afrikaans language in schools for black African children; *c* 150 killed.

soybean, soyabean or **soja bean,** *Glycine max,* annual plant of Leguminosae family. Native to China and Japan but widely cultivated for seeds which are rich in protein and oil used in glycerine and rubber substitutes.

Soyinka, Wole (1934-   ), Nigerian author. Has attempted to create an indigenous Nigerian theatre in plays, *eg The Swamp Dwellers* (1963), *The Road* (1965), using themes from Nigerian folklore. His novels incl. *The Interpreters* (1965).

Soybean

Spa, town of SE Belgium, in the Ardennes. Pop. 9000. Resort, mineral springs discovered 14th cent. Name now given to all such health resorts.

Spacecraft: Apollo X command module

spacecraft, vehicle designed for travelling in outer space. Pioneered by USSR and US. Early craft were artificial satellites put into orbit round Earth. Subsequent developments incl. manned capsules, docking vehicles steered by rockets, *Skylab* orbiting space station with living quarters for 3 astronauts. Planned developments incl. space shuttle capable of re-landing on Earth and being used many times.

space exploration, navigation in manned spacecraft in regions beyond Earth's atmosphere. Unmanned artificial satellites carried out 1st explorations, relaying to Earth information about atmospheric conditions. Orbital flight by manned vehicle first achieved by YURI GAGARIN. Subsequent extended flights have incl. manned flights to Moon (US), *eg* that of Apollo XI (1969), and unmanned probes to Venus and Mars sending back data to Earth.

space-time continuum, four-dimensional description of the universe, blending three space dimensions with dimension of time. Necessitated by theory of relativity in which time is no longer absolute but depends on relative motion of the observer. The geometry of space-time continuum is determined by gravitation; large gravitating bodies affect its curvature.

spade-foot toad, toad of Pelobatidae family; uses horny spurs on hind legs to burrow into sand. Species incl. European *Pelobates cultripes*.

spaghetti, *see* MACARONI.

Spahis, Moslem cavalry of Ottoman army. Employed by Sultan Mahmud II (1826) to crush JANISSARIES. Name also refers to native Algerian cavalrymen in French army.

Spain (*España*), kingdom of SW Europe, occupying most of Iberian penin.; incl. Balearic, Canary Isls. Area 505,000 sq

Spain

km (195,000 sq mi); pop. 35,857,000; cap. Madrid. Language: Spanish. Religion: RC. Distinct languages and cultures in Basque Provs. and Catalonia. Pyrenees in NE; large C plateau between Cantabrian Mts. (N), Sierra Morena (S). Main rivers Douro, Ebro, Tagus. Agric. incl. fruit, olives, wine (S), livestock (N); rich in minerals, tourism. Inhabited from prehist. times, part of Roman Empire after defeat of Carthage. Germanic invasion 5th cent.; Moorish conquest 8th cent. Christian reconquest completed 1492, led by Aragón and Castile (united 1479). Exploration led to colonizing Americas, empire *fl* under Habsburgs, colonies lost 19th cent. Republic proclaimed 1931; Civil War (1936-9) resulted in fascist state under Franco; monarchy restored 1975.

Spalato, *see* SPLIT, Yugoslavia.

Spandau, suburb of West Berlin, West Germany, at confluence of Havel and Spree rivers. Fortress built (1594) by electors of Brandenburg; used as prison in 19th cent. and after WWII (1945-6).

spaniel, one of various breeds of dog with drooping ears and silky coat. Breeds incl. King Charles spaniel, with black and tan coat; stands 25 cm/10 in. at shoulder.

Spanish, Romance language in Italic branch of Indo-European family. Spoken as 1st language in Spain and 18 countries in Central, South America. Developed from Latin, Castilian dialect becoming dominant in early Middle Ages.

Spanish-American War (1898), conflict between US and Spain occasioned by US intervention in Cuban struggle for independence from Spain. Mysterious sinking of US battleship *Maine* in Havana heightened pro-war sentiments in US. Spanish fleet destroyed in Manila by Dewey; Spanish forces surrendered after defeat at Santiago de Cuba. Treaty of Paris granted Cuba independence under US protection; US acquired Guam, Puerto Rico, Philippines.

Spanish Armada, *see* ARMADA, SPANISH.

Spanish Civil War, conflict (1936-9) precipitated by military opposition to liberal govt. of Spanish republic (proclaimed 1931). Conservative interests, merged under FRANCO, won early victories over Republican (or loyalist) forces. International non-intervention pact (signed 1936) broken; Germany and Italy supplied arms to Franco's Insurgents, USSR supported Republicans. Triumph by Insurgents (Madrid captured, Mar. 1939) led to estab. of Franco's dictatorship.

Spanish Guinea, *see* EQUATORIAL GUINEA.

Spanish Inquisition, *see* INQUISITION; TORQUEMADA.

Spanish Sahara, former overseas prov. of Spain, in NW Africa. Area 266,000 sq km (102,700 sq mi); pop. 86,000; cap. El-Aaiún. Mostly desert, pop. largely nomadic; livestock, dates, fishing, rich phosphate deposits. Spanish colony from 1884, became prov. 1958. In 1975, Spain withdrew, leaving Morocco and Mauritania in joint control until future is decided; territ. also claimed by Algeria. Interim name is Western Sahara.

Spanish Succession, War of the (1701-14), European conflict over succession to Spanish throne; claimants were Philip, grandson of Louis XIV, and Charles, son of Emperor Leopold I of Austria. England, Holland and Austria, seeking to prevent potential union of Spain and France, allied against France, Spain and Bavaria. Hostilities ended by treaties of Utrecht (1713), Rastaat (1714); Philip recognized as king (Philip V).

Spanish Town, town of S Jamaica. Pop. 15,000. Replaced as cap. by Kingston (1872).

Spark, Muriel Sarah (1918-   ), Scottish novelist. Known for *The Ballad of Peckham Rye* (1960), *The Prime of Miss Jean Brodie* (1961).

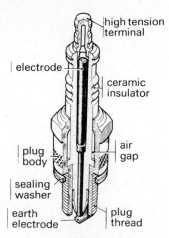

Sparking plug

sparking plug or **spark plug,** device used in internal combustion engine to ignite fuel-air mixture. Consists of 2 electrodes with a gap of *c* 0.38 mm–1.02 mm between them. When a high voltage is impressed on electrodes a spark is discharged.

sparrow, one of various small short-beaked seed-eating birds, esp. of genus *Passer*. House sparrow, *P. domestious,* has streaked brown and grey plumage; native of N Europe and Asia, introduced into North America, Australia, New Zealand.

sparrow hawk, *Accipiter nisus,* small Old World hawk with short rounded wings and long tail. Male has slate-grey upper parts, red-brown barred lower parts. American sparrow hawk, *Falco sparverius,* is a falcon.

Sparta (*Spárti*), town of Greece, in SC Peloponnese, on R. Eurotas. Pop. 10,000. Founded 1834; fruit, olive trade. Nearby are ruins of ancient Sparta (*Lacedaemon*) militaristic city state at zenith after defeating Athens in Peloponnesian War. Defeated by Thebes (371 BC), Philip II of Macedon.

Spartacists, radical German Socialist group, founded 1916. Led by Karl Liebknecht and Rosa Luxemburg. Became (1918) German Communist Party. Uprising (Jan. 1919) ruthlessly suppressed by Berlin govt.

Spartacus (d. 71 BC), Roman gladiator, b. Thrace. Organized revolt of escaped slaves in S Italy and defeated 2 Roman armies sent against him. Defeated and killed in battle with Crassus. Many of his followers were crucified along Rome-Capua road.

spastic paralysis, condition in which certain muscles are kept permanently taut, causing loss of voluntary movement and spasms of affected muscles. Congenital form (cerebral palsy) is caused by brain damage and may be accompanied by mental retardation.

species, in biology, *see* CLASSIFICATION.

specific gravity, ratio of material's density to density of water at 4˚C.

specific heat, in physics, quantity of heat required to raise the temperature of unit mass of a substance by one degree. Expressed in calories per gm per ˚C.

spectacles, lenses worn to correct or help defective vision. Concave lenses correct short sight (myopia), convex lenses long sight (hypermetropia), cylindrical lenses astigmatism. Earliest European spectacles date from 13th cent.

spectroscope, optical instrument designed to study spectrum of light. Light is introduced through a slit, its rays made parallel by a collimator, dispersed by a prism or grating, and viewed through a telescope eyepiece. Used to determine chemical composition of substances by examination of spectral lines in light emitted or absorbed, and in astronomy to determine physical and chemical nature of stars. The spectral lines of a substance are fundamental characteristics of it and thus a means of identification.

spectrum, in physics, originally name for coloured bands produced by white light passing through a prism or diffraction grating. Colours seen are red (longest wavelength), orange, yellow, green, blue and violet (shortest wavelength). Now refers to resolution of any electromagnetic radiation into its constituent wavelengths.

Spee, Maximilian, Graf von (1861-1914), German naval officer. Defeated Cradock at Coronel (Nov. 1914) but lost and was drowned at battle of Falkland Isls. (Dec. 1914).

speedwell, *see* VERONICA.

Speer, Albert (1905-   ), German architect, Nazi leader. Official architect to Nazi party. Became minister of armaments (1942); organized major indust. output in last months of war. Pleaded guilty to war crimes (1946); sentenced to 20 years' imprisonment.

J.H. Speke

Speke, John Hanning (1827-64), English soldier, explorer. Accompanied R.F. Burton on 2 African expeditions (1854, 1857-9). Discovered L. Victoria (1858), returning (1862) to confirm it as source of Nile.

Spemann, Hans (1869-1941), German embryologist. Discovered 'organizer effect' of certain chemicals which determine manner in which the various areas of an embryo develop. Awarded Nobel Prize for Physiology and Medicine (1935).

Spence, Sir Basil Urwin (1907-76), Scottish architect. Designed Coventry Cathedral, buildings for Sussex Univ., Knightsbridge Cavalry Barracks.

Spencer, Herbert (1820-1903), English philosopher. Stated theory of evolution was of universal application, that all change within any structure was of increasing differentiation and, at same time, of increasing integration. Works incl. *The Principles of Psychology* (1855), *First Principles* (1862).

Spencer, Sir Stanley (1891-1959), English painter. Painted religious scenes set in familiar environment of his native village; work, incl. several interpretations of Resurrection theme.

Spencer Gulf, inlet of Indian Ocean, South Australia, between Eyre and Yorke penins. Ports incl. Port Augusta, Port Pirie, Whyalla.

Spender, Stephen Harold (1909-   ), English poet, critic. Associated with Auden, Day-Lewis in 1930s. Later poems

Herbert Spencer

indicate more liberal than left-wing attitudes. *Collected Poems* pub. 1955.

Spengler, Oswald (1880-1936), German philosopher, historian. Author of *The Decline of the West* (1922); postulated existence of life cycles through which all human cultures pass. Held that Western civilization was in unavoidable decline.

Edmund Spenser

Spenser, Edmund (*c* 1552-99), English poet. Works incl. *Amoretti* (1595) on his courtship, *Epithalamion* (1595) on his marriage, *The Shepheardes Calender* (1579). Developed Spenserian stanza for masterpiece, *The Faerie Queene* (1590, 1596), an allegorical epic of moral development, praising Elizabeth I.

spermaceti, white wax-like substance solidifying from colourless oil in head of sperm whale; significance unknown, but may assist in diving. Used in making cosmetics, candles, *etc.*

Spermatophyta, in botany, term for seed-bearing plants. Subdivided into GYMNOSPERM and ANGIOSPERM.

sperm whale or **cachalot,** *Physeter catodon,* large whale of worldwide distribution, much hunted by whalers. Enormous head, one cavity of which contains SPERMACETI oil; teeth in lower jaw. Feeds on molluscs; reaches lengths of 18.3 m/60 ft.

Spey, river of NE Scotland, flows 172 km (107 mi) from Highland region to Moray Firth at Spey Bay. Salmon fishing.

Speyer or **Spires,** town of WC West Germany, on R. Rhine. Pop. 41,000. River port; textiles, paper mfg. Romanesque cathedral (11th cent.) has emperors' tombs. Scene of Diet of Speyer (1529).

Spezia, La, city of Liguria, NW Italy, on Ligurian Sea. Cap. of La Spezia prov. Pop. 128,000. Port, oil refining; main Italian naval base. Shelley drowned nearby. Badly damaged in WWII.

sphagnum, bog moss or **peat moss,** genus of soft mosses. Found mainly on surface of bogs. Used for potting and packing plants and in absorbent dressings.

sphalerite or **zincblende,** zinc ore mineral. Black, brown or yellow in colour; consists of zinc sulphide. Often found in association with galena. Major source of zinc.

The Sphinx at Giza

sphinx, in ancient Egyptian art, sculptural representation of recumbent lion with head of man, ram or hawk. Often taken to symbolize pharaoh as descendant of Ra. Many built, most famous near Gîza, Egypt. In Greek myth, destructive agent of gods, represented as winged woman with body of lion or dog.

spice, aromatic vegetable product, *eg* pepper, ginger, nutmeg, cinnamon, clove, used in cookery to season or flavour food.

Spice Islands, *see* MOLUCCAS.

Spider

spider, any of order Araneida of arachnids. Abdomen bears 2 or more pairs of spinnerets; silk thread produced used for web-making and to enclose cocoons. Most species possess poison glands for killing prey; venom of black widow and Australian funnel-web is dangerous to man.

spider crab, sea crab of Majidae family with triangular body and long thin legs. *Macrocheira kaempferi,* found off Japan, is largest crustacean; leg span of *c* 2.4 m/8 ft.

spider monkey, long-legged South American monkey with long prehensile tail, genus *Ateles.* Diet of fruit. Species incl. black-faced spider monkey, *A. ater.*

spider wasp, solitary long-legged wasp of Pompilidae family. Paralyses spiders with sting and carries them to underground burrows; lays eggs on spiders, larvae later feed on corpses.

spikenard, *Nardostachys jatamansi,* Asian perennial aromatic herb. Rhizomes formerly used to make ointment.

spin, in nuclear physics, intrinsic angular momentum of an elementary particle or photon, produced by rotation about its own axis. Quantum considerations restrict the value of spin.

spina bifida, congenital defect of the vertebrae in which one or more of the vertebral arches does not develop. Resulting damage to spinal cord causes varying amounts of paralysis. Treated by immediate surgery.

spinach, *Spinacia oleracea,* widely cultivated annual plant, native to SW Asia. Dark-green edible leaves are rich in iron and eaten cooked as vegetable.

spinal column, *see* VERTEBRA.

spinal cord, portion of central nervous system extending from brain and enclosed in spinal canal formed by vertebral arches. Consists of outer layer of white matter (nerve fibres), inner layer of grey matter (nerve cells) and central canal containing cerebrospinal fluid. Spinal nerves (31 pairs) connected to it convey sensory and motor impulses to and from brain.

spindle tree, any of genus *Euonymus* of shrubs and trees. Species incl. *E. europaeus* native to Europe. Orange seeds, white wood formerly used to make spindles.

spinel, hard crystalline mineral consisting mainly of magnesium aluminium oxide. Found in various colours, red variety used as a gem. Major sources in Burma, Sri Lanka.

spinet, small harpsichord, popular in 17th cent. Usually triangular in shape, with strings at an angle of 45° to keyboard. Replaced rectangular virginals, in which strings are parallel to keyboard.

spinning, process of drawing out and twisting fibre into continuous thread. Simplest tools used were distaff, a rod on which fibre was wrapped, and spindle, a weighted rod on which fibre drawn from distaff was twisted. Later developments incl. spinning wheel, which revolved spindle, often by means of a treadle. In 18th cent. spinning was mechanized by efforts of Hargreaves, Crompton, Arkwright, *etc.*

Spínola, António Sebastião Ribeiro de (1910-   ), Portuguese soldier, political leader. Wrote influential *Portugal and the Future* (1974), asserting that Portugal could not win military victory against rebels in its African colonies. Led coup which overthrew Caetano govt. (April, 1974). Headed provisional govt., went into exile 1975.

Spinoza

Spinoza, Benedict or **Baruch** (1632-77), Dutch philosopher. Influenced by Descartes, developed system chiefly contained in *Ethics* (1677), in which all life is embraced by infinite God (or Nature). Excommunicated (1656) from native Jewish sect for unorthodoxy of thought.

spiny anteater, *see* ECHIDNA.

spiraea, genus of herbs of rose family found in temperate regions. Dense clusters of small pink or white flowers. Species incl. European willow spirea, *Spiraea salicifolia.*

spiral galaxy, galaxy with spiral structure; 2 or more spiral arms, composed mainly of dust, gas and relatively young stars, emerge from central nucleus and swirl round it. Milky Way is spiral galaxy.

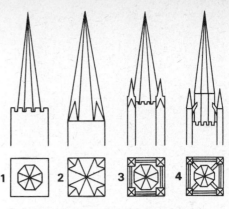

Spires: 1. needle; 2. broach; 3. octagonal; 4. buttress

spire, steeply pointed tapering structure topping a tower. First examples appeared in Romanesque architecture of 12th cent.; elaborate spires were developed in Gothic period in England, Germany and France.

Spires, *see* SPEYER, West Germany.

spiritual, religious folk song of American Negroes. Created by black singers and choirs in 19th cent.

spiritualism, popularly, belief and practice of communication with spirits of the dead. Common to many cultures, *eg* Haiti, North American Indians. Became popular in West during 19th cent., originally in US. Practice usually involves a medium, who (sometimes in trance) acts as intermediary between living and dead, at meeting called séance. Physical phenomena incl. unexplained noises, movement of objects, levitation, *etc.*

Spithead, anchorage in the SOLENT, off Portsmouth, S England. Scene of fleet mutiny (1797).

Spitsbergen (*Svalbard*), isl. group of Norway, in Arctic Ocean. Area *c* 62,150 sq km (24,000 sq mi); main town Longyearbyen. Ceded to Norway 1920. Coalfields shared with USSR. Hist. starting point for polar expeditions, whaling station.

Spitteler, Carl [Friedrich Georg], pseud. Felix Tandem (1845-1924), Swiss author. Known for verse epics, *eg Prometheus und Epimetheus* (1881), *Olympian Spring* (1910), dealing with problem of ethics. Also wrote naturalistic novel *Conrad the Lieutenant* (1898). Nobel Prize for Literature (1919).

spittle bug, *see* FROGHOPPER.

Spitz, Mark (1950-   ), American swimmer. Won record 7 Olympic gold medals (1972) with victories in 100m and 200m freestyle and butterfly events, and 3 relays.

spleen, large lymphatic organ on left hand side of abdominal cavity. Destroys old red blood cells and forms certain white cells; acts as reserve blood supply in emergencies. Removable without risk.

Split (Ital. *Spalato*), town of Croatia, W Yugoslavia, on Adriatic Sea. Pop. 152,000. Port, fishing, resort. Estab. 7th cent. by refugees from nearby Salona. Ruled by Venice from 1420, by Austria 1815-1918. Has cathedral, baptistery, remains of Roman palace.

Spock, Benjamin McLane (1903-   ), American pediatrician. Best known for enormously popular *The Common Sense Book of Baby and Child Care* (1945), which influenced parents worldwide.

Spode, Josiah (1754-1827), English potter. Took over pottery firm founded (1770) by his father (of same name) at Stoke-on-Trent. Originated type of bone china, bearing his name, which became standard in England.

Spohr, Ludwig (1784-1859), German composer, violinist, conductor. Wrote over 15 violin concertos and many operas, symphonies now seldom performed. His nonet remains popular. One of 1st conductors to use a baton.

spoils system, practice developed in US of rewarding loyal supporters by appointing them to political offices.

First used on large scale by President Jackson. Corruption incurred by system led to civil service reform in late 19th cent.

Spokane, town of E Washington, US; at falls on Spokane R. Pop. 171,000. Commercial centre in agric., cattle rearing region; aluminium mfg.

Spoleto (anc. *Spoletium*), town of Umbria, C Italy. Pop. 40,000. Agric. market, textiles. Cap of medieval duchy, passed to Papal States (13th cent.). Roman remains; cathedral (12th cent.).

sponge, see PORIFERA.

spontaneous combustion, sudden burning of substance of low ignition point, caused by heat produced through slow oxidation of substance.

White spoonbill (Platalea leucorodia)

spoonbill, wading bird with beak flattened and spoon-shaped at tip, genus *Platalea*. Species incl. roseate spoonbill, *P. ajaja,* of Florida and South America.

Spooner, William Archibald (1844-1930), British scholar. Best known for tendency to transpose initial consonants of adjacent words (*eg* 'town drain' for 'down train') from which term 'spoonerism' was coined.

Sporades, isls. of Greece, in Aegean Sea. N Sporades, NE of Euboea, incl. Skyros. S Sporades, or Dodecanese, incl. Sámos, Ikaría.

spore, in botany, non-sexual reproductive cell produced by flowerless plants. Capable of giving rise to new plant which may or may not resemble parent.

Sporozoa, class of parasitic protozoa whose life cycle usually has sexual and asexual phases involving reproduction by spore formation. Incl. malaria parasite, transmitted to host by mosquito bite.

sprat, *Sprattus sprattus,* small European food fish of herring family. Pale green back with silver underside; lives in large coastal shoals, exploited commercially.

Spree, river of East Germany. Flows 397 km (247 mi) from Lusatian Mts. via Berlin to R. Havel at Spandau. Runs through Spree Forest (*Spreewald*), resort area.

spring, natural outlet at ground surface for accumulated underground water. Where WATER TABLE intersects sloping ground surface, 'spring line' occurs; springs also common in limestone areas. Mineral springs may contain sulphur, salt, *etc*; hot springs, *eg* GEYSERS, occur mainly in volcanic areas.

springbok, *Antidorcas marsupialis,* antelope of S Africa, noted for high, stiff-legged leaps in air.

Springfield, cap. of Illinois, US; on Sangamon R. Pop. 92,000. Agric. machinery mfg., food products. Home, burial place of Abraham Lincoln.

Springfield, town of SW Massachusetts, US; on Connecticut R. Pop. 164,000. Plastics, chemical mfg.; printing and publishing industs. US armoury here (1794-1966) developed Springfield army rifle.

Springfield, town of SW Missouri, US; in Ozark resort area. Pop. 120,000. Dairy, poultry, livestock produce; railway engineering, light industs.

Springs, city of S Transvaal, South Africa. Pop. 104,000. Gold, coal and uranium mining centre in Witwatersrand.

springtail, any of order Collembola of minute wingless insects. Often found in damp soil; when disturbed, can leap great distances.

spruce, any of genus *Picea* of evergreen trees of N temperate zones. Cultivated as ornamentals and for straight-grained, lightweight timber. Varieties incl. Norway spruce, *P. abies,* white spruce, *P. glauca,* Colorado spruce, *P. pungens.* Most species yield pulp for paper-making.

spurge, any of genus *Euphorbia* of subtropical marsh and woodland plants. Flowers without petals or sepals. Yields milky juice.

Spurgeon, Charles Haddon (1834-92), English preacher. Minister of Baptist Metropolitan Tabernacle, London, built for him (1861). Pub. influential sermons.

sputnik, see SATELLITE.

Squamata, order of reptiles, comprising lizards (suborder Lacertilia) and snakes (suborder Ophidia).

squash, see PUMPKIN.

squash rackets, game similar to RACKETS, played in 4-walled court, normally by 2 people. Originated at Harrow School, England, before 1850.

squid, marine cephalopod mollusc with torpedo-shaped body. Ten tentacles, 2 being much longer than others, with suckers at ends. Giant squid, genus *Architeuthis,* reaches lengths (incl. tentacles) of 15 m/50 ft.

squill, any of genera *Scilla* and *Urginea* of lily family. Garden varieties incl. Siberian squill, *S. sibirica.* Sea onion, *U. maritima,* yields extract from bulbs used as diuretic and rat poison.

squint, disorder of muscles of eye in which both eyes cannot be focused on same point at same time. Concomitant squint, affecting both eyes equally, is due to muscle imbalance. Treatment incl. corrective glasses and exercise of eye muscles.

American red squirrel (Tamiasciurus hudsonicus)

squirrel, small, usually arboreal, rodent of Sciuridae family. Species incl. European red squirrel, *Sciurus vulgaris,* which hides food (acorns, nuts) in ground; North American grey squirrel, *S. carolinensis,* now common in Europe.

Sri Lanka, isl. republic, off SE coast of India; member of British Commonwealth. Area 65,600 sq km (25,300 sq mi); pop. 12,711,000; cap. Colombo. Chief language: Sinhalese. Religion: Buddhism. Mountainous centre with broad coastal plain. Agric. economy (rice, rubber, coconuts, tea). Under Dutch control from mid 17th cent. to late 18th cent; annexed by British (1815). Independent as Ceylon (1948), republic (1956); native name adopted in 1972.

Srinagar, summer cap. of Jammu and Kashmir, N India. Pop. 404,000. Resort on R. Jhelum, with many canals and wooden bridges linking different parts of town.

Staël, Madame de, née [Anne Louise] Germaine Necker (1766-1817), French woman of letters, b. Switzerland.

Sri Lanka

Stalin

Introduced German Romanticism into France in *De l'Allemagne* (1810). Known for influential salons incl. Chateaubriand, Constant. Also wrote novels, *eg Delphine* (1802).

Staffordshire, county of WC England. Area 2716 sq km (1049 sq mi); pop. 985,000. POTTERIES in N; BLACK COUNTRY in S; R. Trent plain in C. Large coalfields; iron ore, clay also extracted. Co. town **Stafford,** on R. Sow. Pop. 55,000. Footwear mfg.

stag beetle, any of Lucanidae family of beetles with branched antler-like mandibles. Larvae feed on rotting wood. *Lucanus cervus* is large European species.

stained glass, coloured glass used in making windows. Designs or figures are made from panes of many colours held together by lead strips which themselves form part of design. Art is of Byzantine origin; introduced into W Europe in 11th cent., best work was executed in medieval Gothic cathedrals, *eg* Chartres, Canterbury and York.

Stair, James Dalrymple, 1st Viscount (1619-95), Scottish jurist. Lord advocate under William III. Wrote *Institutions of the Law of Scotland* (1681).

Stalactites and stalagmites

stalactite, icicle-shaped deposit hanging from ceiling of cave in limestone area. Consists mainly of calcium carbonate, transported to cave in water solution and left behind as water drips from ceiling to floor. Outstanding examples found *eg* in Carlsbad Caverns, New Mexico, US. Also *see* STALAGMITE.

stalagmite, icicle-shaped deposit rising from floor of cave in limestone area. Consists mainly of calcium carbonate, transported to cave in water solution and left behind as water drips onto floor from ceiling. Also *see* STALACTITE.

Stalin, Joseph, orig. Joseph Vissarionovich Dzhugashvili (1879-1953), Soviet political leader. Returned (1917) from exile during Russian Revolution. Elected Communist Party general secretary (1922); shared leadership after Lenin's death (1924) until 1927, when he engineered removal of TROTSKY and Zinoviev. Consolidated power through series of purges in 1930s, becoming premier 1941. Initiated

indust. and agric. collectivization with Five Year Plans. Assumed military leadership after Germany invaded USSR (1941). Expanded Soviet power in E Europe in meetings with other Allied leaders and by aggressive post-war foreign policy. His tyrannical methods and personality cult were denounced by Khrushchev (1956).

Stalinabad, see DUSHANBE.

Stalingrad, see VOLGOGRAD.

Stalinsk, see NOVOKUZNETSK.

Stambul, Turkish name for old part of ISTANBUL.

stamen, male organ of flower. Consists of pollen-bearing anther on filament.

Stamford, mun. bor. of Lincolnshire, EC England, on R. Welland. Pop. 14,000. Agric. market. Has Burghley House (art collection).

Stamitz, Johann (1717-57), German musician, composer, b. Bohemia. Became musical director at court of Mannheim (1745); largely responsible for reputation of Mannheim orchestra. His numerous symphonies helped estab. classical form of symphony.

Stamp Act, measure passed by British Parliament (1765), requiring all legal documents in American colonies to bear a revenue stamp. Violently opposed in America on grounds that Parliament did not have right to impose taxation without corresponding representation. Act repealed 1766.

Stanhope, Charles Stanhope, 3rd Earl of (1753-1816), English statesman, inventor. A radical in Parliament, supported French Revolution and parliamentary reform. Invented a printing press and lens. His daughter, **Lady Hester Lucy Stanhope** (1776-1839), was Pitt's private secretary. Settled in Lebanon (1810); gained reputation as prophetess with local tribesmen.

Stanislaus I, surname Leszczynski (1677-1766), king of Poland (1704-9, 1733-5). First elected king with aid of Charles XII of Sweden, on whose defeat at Poltava, Stanislaus lost throne to Augustus II. Return from exile as king precipitated WAR OF POLISH SUCCESSION; defeated, renounced rights to throne. Awarded duchy of Lorraine.

Stanislaus II [Augustus Poniatowski] (1732-98), king of Poland (1764-95). Elected king through Russian influence, which remained strong in Poland throughout his reign. Series of 3 partitions of Poland by Prussia, Russia and Austria (1772, 1793, 1795) led to end of country's separate existence.

Stanislavsky, Konstantin, pseud. of Konstantin Sergeyevich Alekseyev (1863-1938), Russian actor, producer, dramatic theorist. With Nemirovich-Danchenko, founded (1898) Moscow Art Theatre, where he implemented influential 'method' theory of production, sometimes called 'Stanislavsky system'.

Stanley, Edward George Geoffrey Smith, see DERBY, 14TH EARL OF.

Stanley, Sir Henry Morton, adopted name of John Rowlands (1841-1904), British explorer and journalist, b. Wales. Sent by New York *Herald* to Africa (1871) to find David LIVINGSTONE. In service of Belgium, explored and organized Congo Free State (1879-84).

Sir H.M. Stanley

Stanley Falls, series of cataracts on R. Lualaba, NE Zaïre. Extends *c* 88 km (55 mi) between Ubundi and Kisangani; river drops *c* 60 m (200 ft). Interrupts navigation; towns linked by railway. Recently renamed Boyoma Falls.

Stanleyville, see KISANGANI, Zaïre.

Stanovoy Range, mountain system of USSR, SE Siberian RSFSR. Rises to 2482 m (8143 ft) at Mt. Skalisty. Forms watershed between rivers flowing to Arctic and Pacific.

Stanton, Edwin McMasters (1814-69), American statesman. His opposition to President Johnson's reconstruction plans in Southern states after Civil War led Johnson to suspend him from office of secretary of war (1868). This led to Johnson's impeachment by Congress; Stanton resigned after failure of impeachment proceedings.

Stanton, Elizabeth Cady (1815-1902), American suffragette. First president of National Woman Suffrage Association (1869-92). Helped compile 3 volumes of *History of Woman Suffrage* (1881-6).

staphylococcus, any of the genus *Staphylococcus* of spherical bacteria, usually occurring in clusters. *S. aureus* causes boils, abscesses and infection in wounds. Can cause food poisoning by release of toxins.

star, self-luminous gaseous body similar to the Sun, whose energy is derived from thermonuclear reactions which convert hydrogen into helium. Nearest star, other than Sun, is Proxima Centauri, *c* 4 light years away. Stars are grouped into galaxies, those visible from Earth being part of Milky Way. They appear to be fixed, but in fact are in motion about the galaxy. *See* STELLAR EVOLUTION.

Stara-Zagora, city of C Bulgaria. Pop. 118,000. Railway jct., trade centre. Food processing, fertilizers; textiles; attar of roses. Turkish Eski-Zagora until ceded to Bulgaria in 1877.

starch, polymeric carbohydrate derived from glucose, found in grain, potatoes, rice, *etc.* Produced in plants by photosynthesis, it serves as food store. Starch in plants is converted into glucose by animals and is major energy source. Used as stiffener in laundering and in adhesives, foods, *etc.*

Star Chamber, room in king of England's palace, Westminster, so named for stars on ceiling. Name used from 15th cent. for tribunal comprising king's councillors, judges, which met there. Important under Tudors as regular part of law enforcement, became hated when Stuarts used it to enforce unpopular policies, esp. religious. Abolished (1641) by Long Parliament.

starfish, any of class Asteroidea of echinoderms with 5 or more arms radiating from central disc. Skin covered with calcareous plates and spines; moves by tube-feet on underside of arms. Species incl. common *Asterias rubens,* predator of oysters and mussels.

Starfish

stargazer, marine fish of Uranoscopidae family, with venomous spine and eyes at top of head. Burrows in sea bed to await prey.

Starhemberg, Ernst Rüdiger, Graf von (1638-1701), Austrian army officer. Gallantly held Vienna against Turks (1683) until relieved by John Sobieski of Poland.

Starling

starling, *Sturnus vulgaris,* gregarious European bird with dark metallic plumage. Roosts in woods and city buildings, where it is often regarded as a pest. Introduced into North America, now common in E US.

star-of-Bethlehem, *Ornithogalum umbellatum,* bulbous plant of lily family. Native to Mediterranean region but widely cultivated. Narrow leaves, white star-shaped flowers with green markings.

Star-spangled Banner, national anthem of US from 1931. Words written by Francis Scott Key, after witnessing British assault of Fort McHenry (1814). Music by John Stafford Smith, adapted from an English song.

Staten Island, see NEW YORK CITY.

States-General, see ESTATES-GENERAL.

states' rights, constitutional doctrine advocated by exponents of decentralized govt. in US. Arose over interpretation of 10th Amendment of Constitution. Manifested in KENTUCKY AND VIRGINIA RESOLUTIONS, NULLIFICATION crisis and ultimately in secession of Southern states leading to Civil War (1861-5). Invoked in 20th cent. by states opposed to civil rights programme.

static electricity, electric charge at rest, usually produced by friction or electrostatic induction.

statics, in physics and engineering, branch of mechanics dealing with bodies and forces at rest or in equilibrium.

statistics, science of collecting, classifying and interpreting numerical facts and data. Used as method of analysis in sciences, social science, business, *etc.* Concerned both with description of actual events and predictions of likelihood of an event occurring.

statute, law passed by legislature and formally placed on record. In UK, statutes make up written law, distinct from COMMON LAW; in Europe, almost all law is statutory. Term used by international jurists to denote whole body of law of a state.

Stavanger, town of SW Norway, on Stavanger Fjord. Pop. 81,000. Port, fishing, shipbuilding, offshore oil service indust. Founded 8th cent., cathedral (12th cent.).

Stavisky affair (1934), French financial and political scandal. Serge Alexander Stavisky (1886-1934), floated fraudulent companies, sold forged bonds, gained control of several newspapers, became associate of public figures. When exposed (1933), he fled and was either shot by police or committed suicide. Scandal caused fall of govt. and riots (Feb. 1934), crushed by Daladier.

Stavropol, city of USSR, cap. of Stavropol territ., S European RSFSR. Pop. 211,000. Agric. machinery mfg., textiles. Natural gas pipeline to Moscow.

steady-state theory, in cosmology, theory that universe is in steady state. Although the universe is expanding, matter is continously created and so no overall change can be detected. In this theory, universe has no beginning or end. Rival theory is BIG-BANG THEORY.

steam engine, engine using steam under pressure to supply mechanical energy. When water is converted to steam, it expands *c* 1600 times, producing force capable of mechanical work either on piston or in TURBINE. Experiments first recorded (*c* 130 BC) by Hero of Alexandria. James Watt produced 1st practical version (1769) using separate condenser and valves allowing steam to exert force on piston in both directions.

stearic acid, colourless wax-like fatty acid, found in animal and vegetable fats. Used in manufacture of soap, candles, cosmetics and medicine.

steatite, *see* SOAPSTONE.

steel, iron containing up to 1.5% carbon. Its properties can be varied by changes in quantity of carbon and other metals present and by heat treatment. Manufactured by Bessemer and open-hearth processes. Corrosion-resistant stainless steel contains up to 25% chromium.

Steele, Sir Richard (1672-1729), English author, b. Ireland. Founded *The Tatler* (1709) and, with ADDISON, *The Spectator* (1711-12), writing witty essays, creating character of Sir Roger de Coverley. Plays incl. *The Conscious Lovers* (1722). Became (1714) manager of Drury Lane Theatre.

Steen, Jan (1626-79), Dutch painter. Known for his depiction of peasant life and scenes of merriment in taverns and homes. Works incl. *The Game of Skittles.*

Stefansson, Vilhjalmur (1879-1962), Canadian explorer, anthropologist. Led longest polar expedition, staying N of Arctic Circle (1913-18) by adopting Eskimo way of life. Works incl. *The Friendly Arctic* (1921).

Steffens, Joseph Lincoln (1866-1936), American editor, author. One of 1st 'muckrakers', he wrote exposés of corruption in politics and business, collected *eg* in *The Shame of the Cities* (1904).

Stein, Gertrude (1874-1946), American author, settled in Paris (1903). Attempted to create 'cubist' literature, *eg Tender Buttons* (1914). Best known for *Autobiography of Alice B. Toklas* (1933). Leader of American expatriate 'lost generation' in Paris.

Stein, Heinrich Friedrich Karl, Freiherr vom (1757-1831), Prussian statesman. Premier (1807-8), abolished serfdom and opened up occupations to all classes; dismissed on pressure by Napoleon. Helped form Russian alliance against Napoleon (1813).

Steinbeck, John Ernst (1902-68), American author. Concerned with struggle of poor within dehumanized society. Works incl. short stories, *eg The Red Pony* (1937), novels *Of Mice and Men* (1937), *The Grapes of Wrath*

John Steinbeck

(1939), *Cannery Row* (1944), *East of Eden* (1952), screenplays. Nobel Prize for Literature (1962).

Steiner, Rudolf (1861-1925), German occultist, b. Austria. Originally leading theosophist, subsequently developed own system of 'anthroposophy' attempting to explain world through nature of man. Works incl. *Philosophy of Spiritual Activity* (1922).

Steinmetz, Charles Proteus (1865-1923), American electrical engineer, b. Germany. Discovered law of magnetic hysteresis, which helped to minimize power loss in electric generators; developed mathematical method to describe alternating current phenomena.

stellar evolution, description of life-history of a star. Stars are believed to condense from clouds of gas, mainly hydrogen, which contract under internal gravitational forces. Thermonuclear reactions take place and create energy by fusion of hydrogen into helium; as hydrogen is used up, star expands to become red giant. It then contracts, its final state depending on its size.

Stellenbosch, town of SW Cape Prov., South Africa. Pop. 30,000. Agric. trade, residential and educational centre; univ. (1918).

Stendhal, pseud. of Marie Henri Beyle (1783-1842), French novelist. Wrote novels treating melodramatic subjects with intense realism, *eg Le Rouge et le noir* (1830), *La Chartreuse de Parme* (1839). Also wrote criticism, *eg Racine et Shakespeare* (1823) dealing with Classicism and Romanticism.

sten gun, light sub-machine gun, working on recoil principle. Used as close-range infantry weapon in WWII.

Stephen, St (d. *c* AD 36), one of seven deacons of early Church. Stoned to death at Jerusalem, becoming 1st Christian martyr.

Stephen [I], St (*c* 975-1038), king of Hungary (1001-38). His coronation with crown sent to him by the pope marks beginning of Hungarian kingdom. Continued his father's policy of converting Magyars to Christianity.

Stephen (*c* 1097-1154), king of England (1135-54). Usurped throne from Henry I's daughter, MATILDA, whose invasion (1130) of England to regain throne began long period of civil strife. She reigned briefly after Stephen's capture (1141) but he regained throne on release. After death of his son (1153), forced to name Matilda's son, Henry II, as successor.

Stephen, Sir Leslie (1832-1904), English man of letters. First editor of *Dictionary of National Biography* from 1882. Wrote studies of rationalist thinkers, *eg English Thought in the Eighteenth Century* (1876-81), biogs. incl. *Pope* (1880), *Swift* (1882). Father of Virginia Woolf.

Stephen Báthory (1533-86), king of Poland (1575-86). Elected prince of Transylvania (1571); elected king of Poland, married daughter of last Jagiello king. Acquired Livonia in war against Ivan IV of Russia (1582).

Stephen Dushan (c 1308-55), king of Serbia (1331-55). By conquest, extended Serbian empire to its greatest extent. Had himself crowned tsar of Serbs, Greeks, Bulgars and Albanians (1346). Empire crumbled on his death.

Stephens, James (1882-1950), Irish author. Helped found *Irish Review* (1911). Works incl. poetry, *eg Insurrections* (1909), prose fantasy *The Crock of Gold* (1912), mythological romances, *eg Deirdre* (1923).

Stephenson, George (1781-1848), English engineer. Built his 1st locomotive (1814) and 1st locomotive to use steam blast (1815). His famous *Rocket* (1829) was used on Liverpool-Manchester railway. Devised a type of miner's safety lamp.

Stepney, see TOWER HAMLETS, England.

Stepniak, pseud. of Sergei Mikhailovich Kravchinski (1852-95), Russian author. Exiled as revolutionary (1878). Works incl. profile of revolutionaries *Underground Russia* (1882), novel *The Career of a Nihilist* (1889).

steppe, level, treeless grasslands extending from SE Europe to C Asiatic USSR. Used for grazing, extensive wheat growing. Term also applied to similar mid-latitude grasslands in other continents and to semi-arid areas bordering hot deserts.

stereochemistry, branch of chemistry dealing with arrangement in 3-dimensional space of the atoms which make up a molecule, and the effect of the arrangement on physical and chemical properties of molecule.

stereophonic sound, sound recorded simultaneously by microphones at various distances from sound source. In playback sound emanates from several speakers situated in roughly similar relative positions as original microphones. Gives impression of depth of original sound. Quadrophonic sound uses 4 channels of sound.

sterility, inability to reproduce sexually. Causes in humans incl. glandular imbalance, disease and psychological problems.

sterilization, method of rendering substances free from contamination by bacteria. Immersion in boiling water or alcohol solution, or exposure to radiation are methods used. Term also used for rendering of sexual organs incapable of reproduction; in male, sealing of vas deferens is used, in female, blocking of Fallopian tubes.

Stern, Otto (1888-1969), American physicist, b. Germany. Awarded Nobel Prize for Physics (1943) for developing molecular beam to measure magnetic properties of atom and atomic nuclei.

Sterne, Laurence (1713-68), English author, b. Ireland. Known for idiosyncratic treatment of thought, feeling, time, as in *The Life and Opinions of Tristram Shandy* (1759-67). *A Sentimental Journey* (1768) burlesques the cult of sentiment.

steroids, group of organic compounds incl. vitamin D, bile acids, male and female sex hormones, adrenal cortex hormones.

stethoscope, instrument used in medicine to detect sounds made by heart and lungs. Consists of chest piece connected by rubber tubes to 2 ear pieces. Devised (1816) by Laënnec to aid diagnosis.

Stettin, see SZCZECIN, Poland.

Stevenage, urban dist. of Hertfordshire, SC England. Pop. 67,000. First 'new town'; furniture mfg.

Stevens, John (1749-1838), American inventor. Helped estab. 1st US patent laws. Built (1806-8) *Phoenix* steamboat, which later shuttled between Philadelphia and Trenton. Developed locomotive after receiving 1st US railroad charter. His son, **Robert Livingston Stevens** (1787-1856), improved design and building of steamboats, railway track. Another son, **Edwin Augustus Stevens** (1795-1868), designed Stevens plough. Built ironclad warships.

Stevens, Thaddeus (1792-1868), American politician. Republican Congressman from Pennsylvania (1849-53, 1859-68), fought to emancipate slaves; helped write 14th Amendment. Led attempt to impeach President Johnson (1868).

Stevens, Wallace (1879-1955), American poet. Known for stylish, philosophically speculative verse, *eg Harmonium* (1923), *The Man with the Blue Guitar* (1937), *Collected Poems* (1954). Also wrote prose essays on aesthetics, *The Necessary Angel* (1951).

Stevenson, Adlai Ewing (1900-65), American politician. Governor of Illinois (1949-53). Defeated by Eisenhower as Democractic presidential candidate (1952, 1956). Ambassador to the UN (1961-5).

Robert Louis Stevenson

Stevenson, Robert Louis [Balfour] (1850-94), Scottish author. Works incl. travel books, *eg Travels with a Donkey in the Cévennes* (1879), popular novels incl. *Treasure Island* (1883), *Kidnapped* (1886), *The Strange Case of Dr Jekyll and Mr Hyde* (1886), poetry in *A Child's Garden of Verses* (1885). Suffered from tuberculosis, spent last years in Samoa.

Stewart, House of, see STUART, HOUSE OF.

Stewart, James (1908-), American film actor. Known for drawl, starring roles from 1935. Films incl. *Destry Rides Again* (1939), *Broken Arrow* (1950), *Anatomy of a Murder* (1959).

Stewart, John ('Jackie') (1939-), Scottish motor racing driver. Won 27 world championship Grand Prix victories, taking world championship 3 times. Retired 1973.

Stewart Island or **Rakiura,** volcanic isl. of S New Zealand, separated from South Isl. by Foveaux Str. Area 1375 sq km (670 sq mi); largely mountainous. Summer resort; fishing, esp. for oysters.

Steyr, town of NC Austria, at confluence of Enns and Steyr rivers. Pop. 41,000. Iron, steel indust. Castle (10th cent.).

stibnite, antimony ore mineral. Soft, lead-grey in colour; consists of antimony trisulphide. Major source of antimony; powdered stibnite used in ancient times as cosmetic.

stick insect, insect of Phasmidae family, commonest in tropical forests. Elongated wingless body resembles twig and matches surroundings. Species incl. North American walking stick, *Diapheromera femorata.*

Three-spined stickleback

stickleback, any of Gasterosteidae family of small spiny-backed fish; found in fresh and salt water of N hemisphere. Species incl. three-spined stickleback, *Gasterosteus aculeatus*; male builds nest for eggs and guards young.

Stieglitz, Alfred (1864-1946), American photographer. Opened (1905) his '291' gallery in New York to exhibit photography as a fine art; made innovations in methods of photography. Helped introduce work of European artists to US by exhibitions at his gallery.

Stilicho, Flavius (*c* 359-408), Roman soldier. Vandal by birth, defended Gaul against Barbarians. Regent of West (395-408) for Honorius, who had him murdered.

Black-necked stilt *(Himantopus mexicanus)*

stilt, wading bird of Recurvirostridae family, inhabiting mainly marshes. Black-winged stilt, *Himantopus himantopus,* with black upper-parts, white under-parts, is found in S Europe, Africa, Asia. *H. mexicanus* is American species.

Stilwell, Joseph Warren (1883-1946), American army officer. An authority on China, chief of staff to Chiang Kaishek, commanded Chinese force helping Allies in Burma (1942), and US forces in China (1943). Recalled after dispute with Chiang (1944).

sting ray, *see* RAY.

stinkbug, *see* SHIELDBUG.

stinkhorn, *Phallus impudicus,* foul-smelling mushroom. Spores borne in jelly and dispersed by insects attracted by smell.

stinkwood, tree with foul-smelling wood, esp. *Ocotea bullata* native to South Africa. Hard durable wood used in cabinet making.

Stinnes, Hugo (1870-1924), German industrialist. Built up huge combine of coal mines, iron and steel foundries, shipping firms. During WWI, he was chief supplier of war materials to German govt.

Stirling, James Frazer (1926-), Scottish architect. His projects, noted for their extensive use of glass, incl. Engineering Building, Leicester Univ. and History Faculty Building, Cambridge Univ.

Stirling, William Alexander, Earl of (1567-1640), Scottish poet, statesman. Wrote love lyrics, *Aurora* (1604), and *Four Monarchicke Tragedies* (1603-7). Member of court of James I.

Stirlingshire, former county of C Scotland, now in Central region. Mountainous in S and W incl. Campsies; fertile lowlands. Agric., coalmining; industs. centred in Falkirk, Grangemouth (oil refining). Scene of many battles in independence wars 13th-14th cents. Co. town was **Stirling,** former royal burgh and market town on R. Forth. Pop. 30,000. Has univ. (1965); royal castle, Wallace Monument (1869).

stoat, *Mustela erminea,* small carnivore, resembling weasel, with short legs, long body. Reddish-brown coat with black-tipped tail. Found in N Europe, C Asia, North America. Northern varieties turn white in winter, being known as ermine (name also applies to white fur).

stock, any of genus *Matthiola* of annual or perennial plants of mustard family. Native to Mediterranean region and S Africa. Showy, fragrant blossoms. Name also used for several unrelated plants, *eg* Virginia stock, *Malcomia maritima.*

stock exchange, organized market for trading in stocks and bonds. Only open to members (brokers) who conduct trade for customers on commission. Board of governors stipulate requirements before stock may be listed for trading. Exists in every major financial centre.

Stoat

Stockhausen, Karlheinz (1928-), German composer. Early exponent of electronic music, *eg Mikrophonie.* Later work has favoured indeterminacy and oriental mysticism. Compositions incl. *Gruppen* for 3 orchestras, *Stimmung* for 6 voices.

Stockholm, cap. of Sweden, between L. Mälaren and Baltic Sea. Pop. 973,000. Admin., commercial centre; port; engineering; food processing; chemicals. Founded 1255; associated with Hanseatic League; built partly on isls. ('Venice of the North'). Staden Isl. has royal palace (1754). Mainly modern, planned city, incl. Olympic stadium (1912), city hall (1923).

Stockport, bor. of Greater Manchester met. county, NW England. Pop. 140,000. Textiles, esp. cotton; machinery.

stocks, *see* SHARES.

Stockton-on-Tees, *see* TEESSIDE, England.

Stoicism, school of philosophy founded by Zeno of Citium (*c* 315 BC). Exponents incl. Cleanthes, Chrysippus. Saw world as material whole with God as shaping force. Man's true end is active life in harmony with Nature, *ie* God's will. Universal benevolence and justice conceived of as duty, necessitating control of emotion and passions. Followers of stoic doctrine in Rome incl. Seneca, Epictetus, Marcus Aurelius.

Stoke Newington, *see* HACKNEY, England.

Stoke-on-Trent, city of Staffordshire, WC England, on R. Trent. Pop. 265,000. In POTTERIES dist.; formed 1910 from Burslem, Hanley, Fenton, Longton, Tunstall. Pottery indust. (Wedgwood, Minton, Spode); also coalmining, engineering.

Stoker, 'Bram' (Abraham) (1847-1912), Irish author. Known for horror story of vampires, *Dracula* (1897), which became basis of many films.

Stokes, Sir George Gabriel (1819-1903), Irish mathematician, physicist. Investigated viscosity of fluids; did notable study of fluorescence. Worked on wave theory of light.

Stokowski, Leopold Anton Stanislaw (1882-), American conductor, b. England. Conducted Philadelphia Orchestra (1913-36). Orchestrated Bach's organ music. Championed cause of modern music.

Stolypin, Piotr Arkadevich (1863-1911), Russian political leader. Premier (1906-11); suppressed revolutionaries by mass exile and execution. Tried to institute agrarian reform. Assassinated.

Stomatopoda (stomatopods), order of burrowing marine crustaceans, sometimes called mantis shrimps. Strong clasping claws on 2nd pair of legs used to crack shells of crabs, *etc.*

Stone, Lucy (1818-93), American suffragette. Advocate of emancipation of slaves, women's rights; helped found *Woman's Journal* (1870), organ of American Woman Suffrage Association. Kept maiden name after marriage to H.B. Blackwell.

Stone Age, period of human culture when stone implements were first used. Usually divided into PALAEOLITHIC, MESOLITHIC and NEOLITHIC periods.

stonefish, highly venomous tropical fish, genus *Synanceja.* Lies motionless in reefs, camouflaged to resemble stone or coral; dorsal fins inject dangerous poison. *S. trachynis* is common Australian species.

stonefly, any of order Plecoptera of soft-bodied 4-winged insects. Long antennae and cerci; weak flier, found near water. Nymphs are aquatic, breathing through thread-like gills.

Stonehaven, resort town and small port of Grampian region, NE Scotland, former co. town of Kincardineshire. Pop. 5000.

Stonehenge

Stonehenge, prehist. monument on Salisbury Plain, England. Outer circle of sarsen stone blocks connected by lintels surrounds horseshoe formation of 5 trilithons, each trilithon consisting of 2 upright stones connected by a lintel. This structure dates from *c* 1500-1400 BC. Within it is ovoid structure, which surrounds Altar Stone. A circle of bluestone menhirs was later set between outer circle and trilithons. Believed to have religious or astronomical significance.

White stork

stork, any of Ciconiidae family of large migratory wading birds. Long legs, neck and bill; tree or roof nesting. Species incl. Old World white stork, *Ciconia ciconia.*

Stormont, parliament of Northern Ireland, formerly responsible for internal affairs. Estab. 1920 at Stormont, near Belfast. Suspended 1972 in favour of direct rule by UK Parliament during civil strife.

Stornoway, main town of Lewis with Harris, NW Scotland, in Western Isles. Pop. 5000. Fishing port; Harris tweed mfg.

stout, dark beer made from roasted malt. Similar to porter, but containing higher percentage of hops.

Stowe, Harriet Beecher (1811-96), American novelist. Known for anti-slavery novel, *Uncle Tom's Cabin* (1851-2).

Strabane, town of NW Northern Ireland, at confluence of Finn and Mourne rivers. Pop. 9000. Clothing mfg., salmon fishing. **Strabane,** district; area 862 sq km (333 sq mi); pop. 35,000. Created 1973, formerly part of Co. Tyrone.

Strabo (*c* 63 BC–*c* AD 24), Greek geographer and historian, b. Asia Minor. Only surviving work is *Geographia,* survey of known world in 17 vols.

Strachey, [Giles] Lytton (1880-1932), English biographer. Member of BLOOMSBURY GROUP. Rejected panegyrics for psychological, critical biogs., *eg Queen Victoria* (1921), *Eminent Victorians* (1918) debunking Dr Arnold, Florence Nightingale, General Gordon.

Stradivari, Antonio or **Antonius Stradivarius** (1644-1737), Italian violin maker. Studied under Niccolò Amati; founded renowned Cremona workshop continued by sons. Often considered greatest of violin makers.

Strafford, Thomas Wentworth, 1st Earl of (1593-1641), English statesman. Became supporter of king's policy in Parliament in response to royal favour (1628). Took efficient, but repressive, measures as lord deputy of Ireland (1632-9), then became Charles I's chief adviser. Impeached by Parliament after unsuccessful campaign against Scots; convicted and beheaded.

Stralsund, town of N East Germany, on Baltic Sea. Pop. 68,000. Port, fishing, shipbuilding. Causeway to Rügen Isl. Founded 1209, former Hanseatic League member. Many medieval buildings.

strangeness, in nuclear physics, property of certain elementary particles of decaying much more slowly than would be expected. These particles are created in strong nuclear interactions but decay by weak interactions.

Stranraer, market town of Dumfries and Galloway region, SW Scotland. Pop. 10,000. Fishing industs. Ferry service to Larne, Northern Ireland.

Strasberg, Lee (1901-), American theatrical director, b. Austria. Co-founder of influential Group Theatre, New York (1931), where he taught Stanislavsky's acting method. Director of Actor's Studio, New York, from 1948.

Strasbourg (Ger. *Strassburg*), city of E France, at confluence of Ill and Rhine, cap. of Bas-Rhin dept. Pop. 254,000. Indust., commercial centre of Alsace; major river port. Metal goods, oil refining; tanning, wine trade, pâté mfg. Free city from 13th cent., taken by Louis XIV (1681); part of Germany (1871-1919). Cathedral (11th cent.) with famous astronomical clock; univ. (1567). Site of European Parliament.

Strassburg, Gottfried von, *see* GOTTFRIED VON STRASSBURG.

Strategic Arms Limitations Talks (SALT), series of discussions between US and Soviet Union to limit size of defence forces of the 2 countries. Accord reached in 1972 agreed to restrict antiballistic missile systems. Second round of talks in 1974 failed to achieve purpose.

Stratford, town of SW Ontario, Canada; on Avon R. Pop. 25,000. Textiles, food processing. Has annual Stratford Shakespearian festival.

Stratford-upon-Avon, mun. bor. of Warwickshire, WC England, on R. Avon. Pop. 19,000. Tourist centre, associations with Shakespeare (birthplace, grave, *etc*), annual festival at Memorial Theatre (1932).

Strathclyde, region of W Scotland. Area 13,849 sq km (5347 sq mi); pop. 2,578,000; chief city Glasgow. Created 1975, incl. former Argyllshire, Ayrshire, Dunbartonshire, Lanarkshire, Renfrewshire. Site of ancient kingdom.

Strathcona and Mount Royal, Donald Alexander Smith, 1st Baron (1820-1914), Canadian statesman, financier, b. Scotland. Governor of Hudson's Bay Co. (1889-1914). Instrumental in construction of Canadian Pacific Railway (1880-5). High commissioner in UK (1896-1914).

stratification, in geology, arrangement of SEDIMENTARY ROCKS in strata, or layers. Strata are separated by surfaces called 'bedding planes'. Strata need not be horizontal; angle determined by earth movements.

stratosphere, second lowest layer of Earth's ATMOSPHERE, immediately above troposphere. Begins between *c* 9.5 km (6 mi) and 16 km (10 mi) above surface. Temperature low, varies little with height (hence sometimes called 'isothermal layer'); no clouds or dust. Incl. ozone layer.

stratus cloud, *see* CLOUD.

Johann Strauss, the younger

Strauss, Johann (1804-49), Austrian composer, conductor. Toured many countries with his own orchestra playing Viennese waltzes and other dances. Composed *Radetzky March.* His son, **Johann Strauss** (1825-99), was also a composer and conductor. Wrote over 400 waltzes, such as *Blue Danube, Emperor Waltz,* and operetta *Die Fledermaus* ('The Bat').

Strauss, Richard Georg (1864-1949), German composer. Continued Romantic style of the 19th cent. well into the 20th cent., but with great dramatic and orchestral gifts. Works incl. symphonic poems *Don Juan, Till Eulenspiegel,* operas *Salomé* and *Der Rosenkavalier.*

Stravinsky

Stravinsky, Igor Fedorovich (1882-1971), Russian composer. Music is noted for original use of harmony and rhythm. Worked with Diaghilev early in career, for whom he wrote ballets *Rite of Spring, The Firebird, Petrouchka.* In 1920s, wrote such works as *Pulcinella* in neo-Classical style. Took up serial music in 1950s, using this method to compose *Requiem Canticles.* Left Russia in 1914, eventually settling in US (1939).

strawberry, any of genus *Fragaria* of low perennial herbs of rose family. Native to temperate regions. Valued for fruit. *F. vesca* is the wild strawberry; cultivated strawberry is hybrid between *F. virginiana* of E North America and *F. chiloensis* of Chile.

strawflower, *Helichrysum bracteatum,* annual plant of daisy family, native to Australia. Cultivated for colourful blossoms and dried as an everlasting flower.

Wild strawberry

stream of consciousness, in literature, narrative technique of presenting thoughts and images as they occur to a character rather than in logical external sequence. First used in Edouard Dujardin's *Les Lauriers sont coupés* (1887) which influenced Joyce in writing *Ulysses.* Virginia Woolf adapted technique, *eg* in *Mrs Dalloway.*

Streicher, Julius (1885-1946), German political leader of Nazi era. Edited pornographic periodical *Der Stürmer,* vehicle for his fervent anti-Semitism. *Gauleiter* of Franconia from 1933. Hanged after conviction at Nuremberg trials.

streptococcus, any of the genus *Streptococcus* of spherical bacteria, usually occurring in chains. Some species cause infection, *eg* sore throats, and pus formation in wounds. Also release toxins which can destroy blood cells and tissue.

Stresemann, Gustav (1878-1929), German statesman, chancellor (1923). As foreign minister (1923-9), negotiated LOCARNO PACT (1925) with European powers. Obtained French evacuation of Ruhr (1924). Accepted terms of Dawes and Young plans for payment of reparations. Shared Nobel Peace Prize (1926) with Briand.

strike, total withdrawal of labour by employees. Chief weapon of labour unions, first used in UK in early 19th cent., *eg* by Luddites, and in US in late 19th cent., with first national strike (1877) by rail workers. Strike follows union authorization to make it official. Unofficial strike, often local, also known as 'wildcat' strike. Inter-union demarcation disputes led to passing of TAFT-HARTLEY ACT (1947). GENERAL STRIKE weapon of European labour, esp. in Russia (1905), UK (1926), France (1968), Italy (1970s).

Strindberg, [Johan] August (1849-1912), Swedish author. Paranoid sensibility reflected in short stories, novels, naturalistic dramas, incl. *The Father* (1887), *Miss Julie* (1888), *Dance of Death* (1901). Later works, *eg A Dream Play* (1901), reflect interest in inner life, mysticism. Autobiog. *Inferno* (1897) recounts an emotional crisis.

string[ed] instruments or **strings,** group of musical instruments which produce sound from vibrating strings. Strings may be plucked (*eg* harp, guitar, lute), stroked with horsehair bow (*eg* violin, viola) or struck with hammer (*eg* dulcimer, piano, clavichord).

stroboscope, flashing lamp whose frequency can be synchronized with frequency of a rotating object so that the object will appear at rest when illuminated by stroboscope light. Used to study periodic or varying motion.

Stromboli, see LIPARI ISLANDS, Italy.

strong nuclear interaction, nuclear force acting between certain elementary particles, *eg* protons, neutrons and certain mesons, when they are less than 10^{-13} cm apart. It lasts *c* 10^{-23} secs and is the strongest known force in nature.

strontium (Sr), metallic element, resembling calcium in its chemical properties; at. no. 38, at. wt. 87.62. Occurs in strontianite and celestine. Compounds impart crimson colour to flames; used in fireworks. Radioactive strontium 90 occurs in fall-out; dangerous as it replaces calcium in bones.

structuralism, methodology, originating in linguistics, whose advocates hold that systems, esp. of myths, language, can be regarded as structures which are stable, whole, self-regulating (by a process of exclusion), and which obey internal 'transformation laws' by which the whole structure can be deduced from separate elements. Stemming from work of F. de SAUSSURE, developed by LÉVI-STRAUSS, CHOMSKY, Roland Barthes, Michel Foucault. Subsequently extended to other areas incl. biology, mathematics.

Struensee, Johann Friedrich, (1737-72), Danish statesman, b. Germany. As physician to the insane Christian VII, became chief minister (1771) and exercised dictatorial powers. Arrested, confessed to adultery with queen consort; beheaded.

Strutt, Jedediah (1726-97), English inventor, manufacturer. Patented (1759) knitting machines for ribbed fabric. Partner of Arkwright.

Struve, Friedrich Georg Wilhelm von (1793-1864), German astronomer. Catalogued numerous double stars and determined parallax of star Vega; founded and directed Pulkovo Observatory in Russia. His son, **Otto Wilhelm von Struve** (1819-1905), succeeded him at Pulkovo. Discovered 500 double stars and a satellite of Uranus (1847).

Stuart or **Stewart, House of,** ruling family of Scotland (after 1371) and of England (after 1603) until death of Anne (1714). James VI of Scotland succeeded to English throne as James I. Two crowns united by Act of Union (1707). Subsequent Hanoverian rule challenged by JACOBITES.

Stuart, Charles Edward, see STUART, JAMES FRANCIS EDWARD.

Stuart, Gilbert (1755-1828), American painter. Best known for his portraits of George Washington, which exist in 3 main types and numerous versions.

Stuart or **Stewart, James Francis Edward** (1688-1766), son of James II, known as the 'Old Pretender'. Claim to English throne frustrated by Act of Settlement (1701) which guaranteed succession to House of Hanover. Accession of 1st Hanoverian, George I, resulted in series of uprisings by his Jacobite supporters; landed briefly in Scotland during 1715 Jacobite rebellion. His son, **Charles Edward Stuart** (1720-88), called 'Bonnie Prince Charlie' and the 'Young Pretender', led Jacobite rebellion of 1745. Won victory at Prestonpans; reached Derby in march on London. Retreated into Scotland, defeated at Culloden Moor (1746). Fled to France. His brother, **Henry Benedict Maria Stuart** (1725-1807), was last direct male Stuart heir. Made RC cardinal (1747).

Stuart, John McDouall (1815-66), Scottish explorer, surveyor. Emigrated to Australia (1838), joined Sturt's expedition to C Australia (1844-6). Made 6 expeditions to interior from 1858, finally reached Van Diemen's Gulf (1862).

Stubbs, George (1724-1806), English painter. Studied human and animal anatomy; pub. *Anatomy of the Horse* (1766) for which he made the engravings. Known for his paintings of animals, esp. horses, and sporting scenes.

Stubbs: *Mares and Foals in a Landscape*

Stubbs, William (1825-1901), English churchman, historian. Author of *The Constitutional History of England in its Origins and Development* (1874-8), long an authoritative work.

stucco, plaster or cement, used for surfacing inside or outside walls or for moulded decoration.

sturgeon, fish of Acipenseridae family found in N hemisphere; usually migratory, feeding in sea and breeding in fresh water. Long pointed head, toothless mouth; rows of spiny plates on body. Valued as source of caviare and isinglass.

Sturm und Drang (Ger., = storm and stress), literary movement originating in late 18th cent. Germany. Name from lyric drama *Die Wirrwarr: oder, Sturm und Drang* (1776) by Maximilian Klinger. Emphasized genius of individual as opposed to rationalistic ideal of the Enlightenment. Exponents incl. Goethe, Schiller, Lenz. Great influence in development of ROMANTICISM.

Sturt, Charles (1795-1869), English soldier and explorer, b. India. Explored Murray, Darling, Murrumbidgee river area of SE Australia (1828-30). On 3rd expedition (1844-6), accompanied by J. McD. Stuart, journeyed to interior via L. Eyre and Cooper's Creek.

Stuttgart, city of SW West Germany, on R. Neckar, cap. of Baden-Württemberg. Pop. 633,000. Railway jct.; publishing, precision instruments, motor vehicle mfg. Badly damaged in WWII. Birthplace of Hegel.

Stuyvesant, Peter (d. 1672), Dutch colonial administrator. Governed despotically as director-general (1647-64) in Dutch colony of New Netherlands (New York). Lost colony in surprise attack by English (1664).

Stymphalian birds, in Greek myth, man-eating birds with brazen claws and beaks. Lived in woods around L. Stymphalus in Arcadia. Destroyed by Heracles (6th labour).

styrene, colourless aromatic liquid, which polymerizes to polystyrene, a thermoplastic material used as electrical and heat insulator. Styrene is used to make synthetic rubber.

Styria (*Steiermark*), prov. of SE Austria. Area 16,384 sq km (6326 sq mi); cap. Graz. Largely mountainous, main rivers Mur, Enns. Forestry, mining (lignite, iron ore), tourism. S part ceded to Yugoslavia 1919.

Styx, in Greek myth, see HADES.

Suárez, Adolfo (1932-), Spanish politician. Following Franco's death, appointed premier of interim govt. by Juan Carlos (1976). Won 1977 election as head of Centre Democratic Union, forming 1st democratically-elected govt. since 1930s.

subconscious, in psychology, term used for processes of same kind as conscious processes, but occurring outside individual's awareness. Often used loosely as synonym of UNCONSCIOUS.

sublimation, in chemistry, process of changing a substance directly from solid to vapour, by-passing liquid stage.

sublimation, in psychology, term employed, originally by Freud, for an unconscious transformation of socially or personally unacceptable impulse, esp. sexual, into acceptable expression.

submarine, warship that submerges and travels under water. Usually equipped with torpedoes or missiles. In use since 19th cent. Latest are nuclear-powered.

submersible, small underwater research vessel, with pressurized hull, self-contained air supply, power system *etc.* Bathysphere is lowered from deck of ship by winch. Largely replaced by bathyscaphe (developed 1954 by A. Piccard) which is free-moving, using petrol for buoyancy, iron shot for ballast. In 1960 a bathyscaphe took 2 men to depth of 35,800 ft (10,900 m) in Mariana trench.

Subotica (Hung. *Szabadka*), town of Vojvodina, N Yugoslavia. Pop. 88,000. Food processing, railway jct. Part of Hungary until 1920.

subway, see UNDERGROUND.

succubus, see INCUBUS.

Suchow, city of Kiangsu prov., E China. Pop. 1,500,000. Rail jct; commercial, indust. centre; produces machine tools, textiles. Called Tungshan (1912-45). Civil war battle (1948).

sucker, freshwater fish of Catostomidae family, of North America and E Asia. Mouth adapted for sucking up food.

Suckling, Sir John (1609-42), English poet. Wrote Cavalier love lyrics, *eg* in *Fragmenta Aurea* (1646), plays, *eg* tragedy *Aglauria* (1637), comedy *The Goblins*.

Sucre, Antonio José de (1795-1830), South American revolutionary. Assisted Bolívar in revolution against Spain; won decisive victory at Ayacucho (1824). First president of Bolivia (1826-8). Assassinated.

Sucre, cap. of Bolivia, in Chuquisaca dept. Pop. 49,000. Agric. market. Scene of outbreak of South American independence revolt (1809). Founded 1538. Has cathedral, archbishopric; univ. (1624).

sucrose, sugar obtained from sugar cane, sugar beet, maple syrup, *etc.* Consists of glucose and fructose joined together in single molecule.

Sudan

Sudan, republic of NE Africa. Area 2,505,800 sq km (967,500 sq mi); pop. 16,901,000; cap. Khartoum. Language: Arabic. Religions: Islam, native. Nubian Desert in NE; savannah in C; forest, swamps in S. Main rivers Nile and tributaries. Agric. incl. millet, livestock; exports cotton, gum arabic. Unified (1820-2) by Egyptians; scene of Mahdist revolt (1883-5). Taken by Kitchener (1898); ruled as Anglo-Egyptian condominium until independence (1956).

Sudbury, town of EC Ontario, Canada. Pop. 91,000. Railway jct. In world's major nickel mining region; related smelting, refining industs. Also processes lead, silver, gold.

Sudeten (Czech *Sudety*), mountain range of N Czechoslovakia, rising to 1602 m (5258 ft). Minerals, timber; spas. German pop. in NW used to justify Hitler's annexation of region (Munich Pact, 1938). Restored to Czechoslovakia (1945).

Suess, Eduard (1831–1914), Austrian geologist, b. England. Noted for study of structural geology, esp. of mountains. Wrote *The Face of the Earth* (1883-1901).

Suetonius [Tranquillus], Gaius (AD *c*70-*c*130), Roman biographer. Extant works are *De vita Caesarum,* describing lives of the Caesars from Julius Caesar to Domitian, and *De viris illustribus.*

Suez (*El Suweis*), city of NE Egypt, at head of Gulf of Suez and S end of Suez Canal. Pop. 315,000. Port; oil refining, pipeline to Cairo; railways to Cairo, Port Said. Damaged in Arab-Israeli wars (1967, 1973).

Suez Canal

Suez Canal, waterway linking Mediterranean (at Port Said) with Red Sea (at Suez); 166 km (103 mi) long. Built 1859-69 by Ferdinand de Lesseps; formerly managed by Suez Canal Co., in which Britain held majority of shares. Nationalization (1956) by Egypt precipitated SUEZ CRISIS. Closed 1967 after Arab-Israeli war; reopened June, 1975. At S end is Gulf of Suez, NW arm of Red Sea.

Suez Crisis, international incident (1956) begun when Egypt nationalized Suez Canal. In combined operation, Israel invaded Egypt and French and British troops occupied canal area. Under US pressure, invading forces withdrew and were replaced by UN emergency force. Disagreement over British role led to resignation of PM, Anthony Eden.

Suffolk, county of E England. Area 3800 sq km (1467 sq mi); pop. 562,000; co. town Ipswich. Flat, low-lying, with marshy coasts. Crops incl. wheat, barley, sugar beet. Racehorse training, breeding at Newmarket.

suffrage, right of voting, or exercising of that right. Universal adult suffrage is system whereby every national has vote on reaching age of majority, usually 18 or 21 years. In UK, achieved with Representation of the People (Equal Franchise) Act (1928), which included women over 21 in franchise; culmination of process begun by REFORM BILL of 1832. In US, 14th-15th Amendments provided for Negro enfranchisement, 19th Amendment for women (1920). *See* also ELECTION; WOMEN'S SUFFRAGE.

suffragettes, name given to those who campaigned for women's right to vote (*see* WOMEN'S SUFFRAGE). Often adopted measures, esp. in UK (early 20th cent.), putting themselves at physical risk.

Sufism, mystical movement of Islam; developed (10th cent.) among Shiites with Neoplatonic, Buddhist and Christian influences. Rejects ritual, emphasizing personal union with God. Influenced many Persian poets, *eg* Omar Khayyam, who developed rich symbolism of soul's relation with God.

sugar, any of class of sweet soluble crystalline carbohydrates, comprising monosaccharides, *eg* fructose, glucose, and disaccharides, *eg* sucrose, lactose, maltose. Name is most commonly applied to sucrose, obtained from juice of sugar beet and sugar cane.

sugar beet, *see* BEET.

Sugar cane

sugar cane, *Saccharum officinarum,* tall, perennial, tropical grass. Cultivated as main source of sugar (*c* 65% of world production). By-products incl. molasses and rum.

Suharto, T.N.J. (1921-), Indonesian military, political leader. Took power after leading army coup that deposed Sukarno (1966). Became president 1968.

suicide, act of voluntary, intentional self-destruction. In UK, until 1961 regarded as crime if committed while of sound mind. In US, rarely so regarded, though assistance in act may be counted as criminal. Many religions count suicide as murder, although considered honourable in India (SUTTEE), Japan (HARA-KIRI).

Sukarnapura, *see* DJAJAPURA.

Sukarno, Achmed (1901-70), Indonesian political leader, president (1945-66). Active in Indonesian nationalist movement before WWII. Became 1st president of independent republic (1945). His pro-Communist sympathies led to an army coup under Suharto.

Sukhumi (anc. *Dioscurias*), port of USSR, cap. of Abkhazian auton. republic, Georgian SSR. Pop. 107,000. Resort with sulphur baths. Trade in fruit, tobacco. Site of ancient Greek colony.

Sukkur, town of SC Pakistan. Pop. 159,000. Commercial centre; textile, hosiery mfg. Nearby Sukkur Barrage dam across Indus controls extensive irrigation scheme.

Sulawesi, *see* CELEBES.

Suleiman I (1494-1566), Ottoman sultan (1520-66), known as 'the Magnificent'. Brought Ottoman empire to peak of its power; captured Belgrade, Rhodes; annexed much of Hungary. Entered into long-lasting alliance with France (1536). Patronized arts, introduced legal and admin. reforms.

Sulla, Lucius Cornelius (138-78 BC), Roman soldier and political leader. Campaigned successfully against MITHRADATES in Pontus. His return to Italy precipitated civil war with followers of popular party (originally led by MARIUS). Captured Rome and ruled as dictator (82-79). Proscribed members of popular party and had them killed; made constitutional reforms.

Sir Arthur Sullivan

Sullivan, Sir Arthur Seymour (1842-1900), English composer. Songs incl. 'Onward Christian Soldiers', 'The Lost Chord'. With W.S. GILBERT, wrote numerous popular light operas.

Sullivan, Louis (1856-1924), American architect. Formative influence in development of modern style; pioneered steel-frame construction, coined dictum, 'form follows function'. Worked mainly in Chicago.

Sully, Maximilien de Béthune, Duc de (1560-1641), French statesman. A Protestant, he supported Huguenots in French Wars of Religion. Became Henry IV's superintendent of finances (1598), restored country's prosperity by encouraging agric. and extending system of roads, canals.

Sully-Prudhomme, pseud. of René François Armand Prudhomme (1839-1907), French poet. Member of PARNASSIENS. Works incl. *La Justice* (1878), *Le Bonheur* (1888). Nobel Prize for Literature (1901).

sulphates, salts or esters of sulphuric acid. Calcium sulphate in form of gypsum used in building or casting. Magnesium sulphate sold as Epsom salts.

sulphur (S), non-metallic element, occurring in several allotropic forms; at. no. 16, at. wt. 32.06. Common form is rhombic sulphur, pale yellow solid; occurs free and as sulphide and sulphate minerals. Burns with blue flame to form sulphur dioxide. Used in manufacture of sulphuric acid, carbon disulphide, gunpowder, matches, in vulcanizing rubber and in medicine.

sulphuric acid (H_2SO_4), oily colourless corrosive liquid. Manufactured by catalytic oxidation of sulphur dioxide.

Wide indust. use in manufacture of explosives, fertilizers, detergents, dyes and in lead ACCUMULATOR.

Sumac

sumac or **sumach,** any of genus *Rhus* of subtropical and temperate trees. Pinnate leaves, large, cone-shaped clusters of hairy red fruits. Dried bark and leaves yield extract used in tanning. Species incl. staghorn sumac, *R. typhina,* of E US.

Sumatra, isl. of Indonesia, SW of Malay penin. Area *c* 474,000 sq km (183,000 sq mi). Barisan Mts. run parallel to W coast, jungle lowlands in E. Equatorial climate, with heavy rainfall. Produces rice, rubber, tobacco, petroleum. Hindu kingdom estab. 8th cent, Islam introduced by Arab traders in 13th cent. Dutch control started in 17th cent.

Sumerians, people inhabiting S Mesopotamia between 4th and 2nd millennia BC. Began world's 1st urban civilization at such cities as Ur, Lagash and Erech, developed pottery and metalwork. Credited with the invention of cuneiform writing. Eventually conquered by rival Semitic cities.

summer time, *see* DAYLIGHT SAVING TIME.

Sumner, William Graham (1840-1910), American sociologist. Held extreme laisser-faire position in economics and believed social customs to be so entrenched that reform was impossible. Wrote *Folkways* (1907).

Sumter, Fort, *see* CHARLESTON, US.

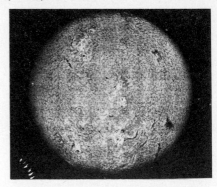

Sun in hydrogen light

Sun, central body of Solar System around which planets revolve in orbit; it is star nearest Earth, an incandescent sphere composed mainly of hydrogen and helium. Mean distance from Earth *c* 150 million km; diameter *c* 1.4 million km. Temperature at visible surface (photosphere) 6000° C; temperature at its interior, between 10 and 20 million° C, enables fusion of hydrogen into helium to take place and supply Sun's energy. Chromosphere, av. temperature *c* 20,000° C, surrounds the photosphere, and the corona, region of extremely high temperature and low density, forms outermost part of Sun's atmosphere.

sun bear, *Helarctos malayanus,* smallest of bears, found in SE Asia. Harmless; agile tree climber. Also called Malayan bear.

sunbird, brilliantly coloured songbird of Nectariniidae family, found mainly in Africa.

sunbittern, *Eurypyga helias,* solitary wading bird of tropical America. Long orange legs, long neck; seldom flies.

Sundas, Greater, isl. group of Indonesia. Comprises Borneo, Sumatra, Java, Celebes, and adjacent isls. **Lesser Sundas** or **Nusa Tenggara,** E of Java, incl. Bali, Lombok, Sumba, Flores and Timor.

Sunday school, organization for giving religious instruction to children, usually attached to church. Robert Raikes began movement in UK, estab. 1st school in 1780; by 1785 over 1000 schools had been founded. Movement introduced (1786) into US by Francis Asbury; American Sunday-School Union estab. in 1824, using British curriculum *etc.* At height by end of 19th cent., with founding (1889) of World Sunday School Convention, later (1947) World Council of Christian Education. Movement had immense influence on spread of popular education in UK.

Sunderland, bor. of Tyne and Wear met. county, NE England, at mouth of R. Wear. Pop. 217,000. Port (coal exports from 14th cent.); shipbuilding, engineering industs. Has remains of monastery (674).

Common sundew (*Drosera rotundifolia*)

sundew or **dew plant,** any of genus *Drosera* of INSECTIVOROUS PLANTS. Worldwide distribution. Catches and digests prey by sticky tentacles on cup-shaped leaves.

sundial, instrument indicating time of day by position of shadow of upright centre pin (gnomen) cast by Sun on graduated surface. Earliest extant example is Egyptian (*c* 1500 BC).

Ocean sunfish

sunfish, any of various large oceanic fish of Molidae family, esp. ocean sunfish, *Mola mola.* Name also applied to some North American freshwater fish of Centrarchidae family.

sunflower, any of genus *Helianthus* of plants of daisy family. Native to New World. Large, yellow daisy-like flowers with dark central discs containing edible seeds from which oil is extracted. Species incl. common sunflower, *H. annuus,* state flower of Kansas.

Sung, Chinese imperial dynasty (960-1279). Period noted for improvement in commercial facilities, growth of large cities, intensive scholarship and development of fine arts. Overthrown by Mongols.

Sungari, river of NE China. Length *c* 1850 km (1150 mi). Rises in Changpai Mts., Kirin prov., flows N to meet Amur

Common sunflower

at USSR border. Important trade artery in fertile region. H.e.p. at Fengman Dam.

Sunnites or **Sunnis,** members of the larger and more orthodox of the 2 main Moslem sects. They accept historical order of 1st 4 caliphs as rightful line of succession to Mohammed and admit the authority of the Sunna, law based on Mohammed's traditional teachings (as opposed to SHIITES).

sunspider, any of order Solpugida of large arachnids with powerful pincers (chelicerae). Voracious predator found in hot dry regions.

sunspot, dark spot appearing on surface of Sun, caused by solar magnetic fields; its temperature is lower than surrounding points on surface. Periods of sunspot activity usually follow cycles of *c* 11 years; associated with magnetic storms on Earth.

Sun Yat-sen (1866-1925), Chinese revolutionary, national hero. Worked outside China from 1895 to bring about revolution. Adopted 'Three People's Principles' of nationalism, democracy, people's livelihood, as his political philosophy (basis of KUOMINTANG party which he led). Returned to China (1911) to serve briefly as president (1912). Set up unofficial govt. of S China at Kwangchow (1921) to oppose warlords in N. Agreed to cooperate with Chinese Communists despite misgivings.

superconductivity, phenomenon exhibited by certain pure metals and alloys, *eg* mercury, cadmium, aluminium, of having almost no electrical resistance at temperatures near absolute zero. Current induced in superconductor will flow almost indefinitely after current source is removed.

superego, in psychoanalysis, that part of the mind which acts as a form of conscience, critical of EGO, and causing guilt and anxiety when ego's thoughts and acts oppose it. At UNCONSCIOUS level, censors unacceptable impulses of ID.

superfluidity, phenomenon exhibited by liquid helium at temperatures below 2.18° Kelvin of flowing without friction and having high thermal conductivity. Helium in superfluid state will flow upwards out of a container, along an invisible film of liquid.

Superior, port of NW Wisconsin, US; shares harbour with Duluth at W end of L. Superior. Pop. 32,000. Important grain, iron ore exports from US Middle West.

Superior, Lake, largest, deepest and most W of Great Lakes, C Canada-US. Area 82,414 sq km (31,820 sq mi). Drained by L. Huron. Important trade route; main cargoes are grain, timber, metal ore. Canals at Sault Ste Marie enable ships to enter and leave lake. Commercial fishing.

supernova, exploding star whose brightness suddenly increases by up to 10^8 times and then fades away. Only 3 have been observed in our galaxy recently, in 1054, 1572 (Tycho's nova), 1604 (Kepler's nova). Believed to occur when sufficiently massive star undergoes gravitational collapse as its store of hydrogen becomes depleted.

supply and demand, in classical economics, factors determining price. Supply refers to the amount of a commodity that producers will supply at varying prices (supply falls as price decreases); demand refers to the desire for the commodity (falls as price increases). In perfect competition, price will stabilize at equilibrium of these 2 values.

suprematism, movement in abstract art founded by Malevich in 1913; based on the use of squares, circles, triangles, it was earliest form of pure geometric abstract art.

supreme court, highest organ of JUDICIARY in federal systems of govt. US Supreme Court is composed of 9 judges, of whom one acts as chief justice. Estab. (1789) by Constitution with status independent of Congress. Greatest bulk of work is as appeal court, also rules on disputes between states, between state and and central govts. Interprets Constitution, its function as reviewer of acts of Congress estab. by JOHN MARSHALL; later extended to state legislation. Has functioned to regulate economy, civil liberties in 20th cent.

Supreme Soviet, highest legislative body of USSR. Consists of 2 equal chambers, Soviet of the Union (members elected on basis of population), and Soviet of Nationalities (members elected on basis of voting by the various republics and auton. regions).

Surabaya or **Surabaja,** of E Java prov., Indonesia. Pop. 1,556,000. Seaport and major export centre; naval base. Shipbuilding, oil refining, textile mfg.

Surakarta or **Solo,** town of C Java, Indonesia. Pop. 414,000. Goldwork, batik cloth mfg. Has notable walled palace of former sultan.

Surat, city of Gujarat state, W India, on Gulf of Cambay. Pop. 472,000. Important port in 17th cent.; English trading post (1612). Textile, paper mfg.

surface tension, force tending to contract surface area of a liquid, due to unequal cohesive forces between molecules near surface. Causes surface to behave like elastic membrane, capable of supporting light objects; also responsible for shape of water droplets and soap bubbles.

surfing, sport of gliding in towards the shore on the crest of a wave, usually on a surfboard. Prob. originated in Polynesia and Hawaii. Developed in early 20th cent. by Hawaiian Duke Kahanamoku, who introduced sport to Australia in 1915.

surgeon fish, any of Acanthuridae family of tropical fish, with sharp-pointed blade-like spine on each side of tail.

surgery, branch of medicine concerned with treatment of injury, deformity and disease by means of manual operations with or without instruments. Although practised from ancient times, major advances in this field were not made until the introduction of aseptic techniques and anaesthetics in 19th cent.

Surinam

Surinam, republic of NE South America. Area 63,037 sq km (163,266 sq mi); pop. 385,000; cap. Paramaribo. Coastal lowlands rise to forested highlands in S. Coffee, rum, timber, bauxite production, exports. Indian Negro, Indonesian, European pop. Region disputed by English, Dutch; resolved 1815. Named Dutch Guiana; renamed 1948. Ceased being colony (1954), fully independent 1975.

surrealism, in literature and art, movement (esp. 1920s-30s) attempting to draw symbols and images from subconscious mind, influenced by Freud. Founded (1924) by French author André Breton in his *Manifeste du surréalisme*. In literature, confined almost entirely to France. In painting, international figures incl. Salvador Dali, Max Ernst, Joan Miró; in films, Luis Buñuel.

Surrey, Henry Howard, Earl of, *see* HOWARD, THOMAS.

Surrey, county of SE England. Area 1654 sq km (639 sq mi); pop. 994,000; co. town Kingston-upon-Thames. Crossed E-W by North Downs (sheep rearing); dairying, market gardening. London suburbs in NE.

Surtsey, isl. of Iceland, formed 1963-5 by eruption of underwater volcano. Area *c* 325 ha. (800 acres). Nature reserve.

surveying, science of determining relative position of points on the Earth's surface. Such data may then be presented as maps by techniques of cartography. Land surveying incl. both GEODESY and plane-surveying, latter not taking account of Earth's curvature; other branches incl. hydrographic (*ie* water) surveying, topographic (*ie* relief) surveying. Surveying by use of air photographs is called photogrammetry.

Susa, *see* SOUSSE, Tunisia.

Suslov, Mikhail Andreyevich (1902-), Soviet political leader. Communist Party's principal ideologist; member of Politburo from 1955.

suspension, in chemistry, system in which small solid particles are dispersed, but not dissolved, in a fluid medium. Differs from a COLLOID in that particles are larger.

Sussex, former county of SE England. South Downs in S, ending at Beachy Head; Vale of Sussex in C; Weald in N. Agric., livestock; extensive woodlands. Coastal resorts incl. Brighton, Worthing. From 1974 divided into **East Sussex** (area 1795 sq km/693 sq mi; pop. 658,000; co. town Lewes) and **West Sussex** (area 2016 sq km/778 sq mi; pop. 630,000; co. town Chichester).

Sutherland, Graham Vivian (1903-), English painter. Known for his landscapes and studies of natural forms, *eg* thorns, trees. Works incl. portraits *Maugham* and *Churchill*; also tapestry for Coventry Cathedral.

Sutherland, former county of N Scotland, now in Highland region. Mountains, moorland; rocky indented coast. Cape Wrath in NW. Deer forest, sheep farming, crofting, fishing, tourism. Co. town was Dornoch.

Sutlej, river of SC Asia. Longest of five rivers of Punjab, rises in Tibet. Flows *c* 1450 km (900 mi) SW through Himachal Pradesh and Indian Punjab to join Indus in Pakistan.

suttee, Hindu custom involving voluntary cremation of widow on husband's funeral pyre. Abolished by British colonial govt. (1829).

Suttner, Bertha, Baroness von (1843-1914), Austrian author. Known for pacifist novel *Lay Down Your Arms* (1889). Influenced Nobel in estab. Nobel Peace Prize which she received (1905).

Sutton, bor. of S Greater London, England. Pop. 169,000. Created 1965 from N Surrey towns, incl. Carshalton.

Sutton Hoo: gold buckle from site

Sutton Hoo, site in Suffolk, England, of Saxon ship-burial, dating from *c* AD 650. Excavated in 1939, superb examples of jewellery, coins and weapons were found.

Su Tung-po or **Su Shih** (1036-1101), Chinese poet, essayist, painter. Considered greatest poet of Sung dynasty, although equally famous for prose in own time. Poems typically descriptive or lyrical; also wrote satires.

Suva, cap. of Fiji Isls., on Viti Levu isl. Pop. 63,000. Admin. centre; port, exports fruit, sugar, copra, gold; seat of Univ. of South Pacific (1968).

Suvarov, Aleksandr Vasilyevich, Count (1729-1800), Russian army officer. Fought with distinction in Russo-Turkish wars (1773-4, 1787-92); suppressed Polish rebellion (1794). Routed French Revolutionary army in N Italy (1799) but forced to retreat through lack of Austrian support.

Suwannee, river of SE US. Rises in Okefenokee swamp, SE Georgia, flows S 390 km (c 240 mi) to Gulf of Mexico (Florida). Made famous in Stephen Foster's 'Swanee River' song.

Suzdal, town of USSR, C European RSFSR. Pop. c 9000. Founded in 11th cent., became important city of duchy of Vladimir-Suzdal in 12th cent. Has ancient kremlin containing 13th cent. monastery and cathedral.

Suzuki, Daisetz Teitaro (1870-1966), Japanese scholar. Authority on Zen, contributed much to exchange of religious ideas between East and West. Works incl. *An Introduction to Zen Buddhism* (1949), *Mysticism: Christian and Buddhist* (1957).

Svalbard, see SPITSBERGEN, Norway.

Sverdlovsk, city of USSR. W Siberian RSFSR; railway jct. and indust. centre in E Ural foothills. Pop. 1,073,000. Metallurgical plants process iron, gold, copper from Ural Mts.; chemical and machinery mfg. Founded in 1721 as Ekaterinburg; expanded with coming of Trans-Siberian railway (1895). Scene of execution of Tsar Nicholas II and his family (1918).

Svevo, Italo, pseud. of Ettore Schmitz (1861-1928), Italian novelist. Friend of Joyce. Wrote psychological novel *The Confessions of Zeno* (1923). Other works incl. *Senility* (1898).

Swabia (*Schwaben*), hist. region of SW West Germany, now in S Baden-Württemberg and SW Bavaria. Incl. source of Danube, Black Forest, Swabian Jura. Duchy under Hohenstaufens from 1079, divided 1268. Cities, incl. Augsburg, formed several Swabian leagues 14th-16th cent.

Swahili, Bantu language of Niger-Congo branch of Niger-Kordofanian language family. Spoken as native tongue in Tanzania, Kenya, Zaïre, Burundi, Uganda, also used as lingua franca by non-indigenous peoples, *etc.* Since beginning of 18th cent. has been used for literature. Term also used for many inhabitants of EC Africa, not united ethnic group but defined by common cultures, livelihood, esp. trade, use of language.

swallow, small long-winged migrating bird of Hirundinidae family. Long forked tail; weak feet; feeds on insects caught in flight. Species incl. *Hirundo rustica,* summer visitor to Europe; builds mud and straw nest on buildings.

Swallowtail butterfly

swallowtail butterfly, *Papilis machaon,* yellow and black European butterfly whose rear wings have tail-like points. Related species found worldwide.

Swammerdam, Jan (1637-80), Dutch naturalist. Pioneer in use of compound microscope; detected red blood cells. His *Biblia Naturae* (pub. 1737-8) contains descriptions and illustrations of insect anatomy.

swamp, tract of water-saturated land, normally with abundant vegetation. Found in low-lying coastal plains,

river flood plains. Temperate swamps contain grasses, rushes, sphagnum moss; tropical swamps contain cypresses, mangroves.

Swan, Sir Joseph Wilson (1828-1914), English inventor. Made electric lamp (1860). In photography, invented carbon printing, a dry plate process and bromide paper.

swan, large web-footed aquatic bird, genus *Cygnus.* Long slender neck, adult plumage generally white. Species incl. European mute swan, *C. olor,* North American trumpeter swan, *C. buccinator,* and Australian black swan, *C. atratus.*

Swansea (*Abertawe*), co. bor. and port of Glamorgan, S Wales, on R. Tawe. Pop. 173,000. Exports coal, metal goods, imports ore for iron, steel industs. Oil refining. Has coll. of Univ. of Wales (1920). Famous blue pottery.

swastika, decorative mystic symbol consisting of cross with right-angle extensions at points. Of great antiquity, occurs in many cultures. Adopted as symbol of German Nazi party and Third Reich.

Swatow, seaport of Kwangtung prov., SE China, on Han delta. Pop. 400,000. Fishing, shipbuilding. Opened to foreign trade in 1858.

Swaziland, kingdom of SE Africa. Area 17,350 sq km (6700 sq mi); pop. 478,000; cap. Mbabane. Languages: SiSwati, English. Religions: Christianity, native. High, middle and low veld areas from W to E; main rivers Komati, Usutu. Crops incl. maize, fruit, sugar, cotton; cattle rearing; iron ore and asbestos mining. Independent from Zulus in 19th cent.; British protect. from 1906 until independence 1968. Member of British Commonwealth.

sweat, weak solution of salt secreted by sweat glands in skin. Heat lost in evaporation of sweat from body helps regulate body temperature.

swede or **rutabaga,** see TURNIP.

Sweden

Sweden (*Sverige*), kingdom of N Europe, in E part of Scandinavian penin. Incl. Baltic isls., Gotland, Oland. Area 449,748 sq km (173,648 sq mi); pop. 8,150,000; cap. Stockholm. Language: Swedish. Religion: Lutheranism. Mountains in N, W; lakes in S. Mainly agric. (wheat, dairying); timber indust.; iron ore; h.e.p. Settled by Germanic tribes, Christianity estab. by 11th cent. United with Norway, Denmark at Kalmar (1397). Independent kingdom from 1523; *fl* under Gustavus Adolphus (17th cent.). United with Norway 1814-1905; neutral in WWs. Increasingly indust.; advanced social welfare system.

Swedenborg, Emanuel, orig. Emanuel Swedberg (1688-1772), Swedish theologian, mystic. Scientific investigations led him to pursue religious studies, believing Second Coming of the Lord had occurred. After his death NEW CHURCH organized by his followers. Works incl. *Heaven and Hell* (1758).

Swedish, N Germanic language of Indo-European family. Spoken in Sweden, S Finland, Estonia. Descended from Old Norse. Historically divided into Old Swedish (9th–16th cent.), New Swedish (from 16th cent.).

sweetbriar, see BRIAR.

sweet gum, *Liquidambar styraciflua,* tall, pyramidal tree native to North America. Hard, red wood used in furniture. Exudes balsam used in medicine and perfumery.

Emanuel Swedenborg

sweet pea, *Lathyrus odoratus,* climbing annual plant of Leguminosae family, native to Europe. Butterfly-shaped, fragrant flowers.

sweet potato, batata or **long potato,** *Ipomoea batatas,* tropical American trailing, perennial plant. Widely cultivated for edible, reddish, sweet-tasting tubers. Used as vegetable, dessert or preserved.

sweet william, *see* PINK.

Sweyn (d. 1014), king of Denmark (*c* 986-1014). Partitioned Norway with Swedish allies after victory over Olaf I (1000). Led series of raids against England, exacting tribute; accepted as king of England (1013). Succeeded by his son, CANUTE.

Jonathan Swift

Swift, Jonathan (1667-1745), English author, b. Ireland. Tory pamphleteer. Known for political, moral satire *Gulliver's Travels* (1726). Also wrote religious satire *Tale of a Tub* (1704), *The Battle of the Books* (1704) on merits of ancient *v* modern writers, *The Drapier's Letters* (1724) and *A Modest Proposal* (1729) on Irish question. Dean of St Patrick's, Dublin (1713-45).

swift, any of Apodidae family of migratory swallow-like birds. Long scythe-like wings, short tail; spends most of time in flight. Species incl. common European swift, *Apus apus,* with black plumage and white throat patch, and North American chimney swift, *Chaetura pelagica.*

swift moth, any of Hepialidae family of primitive rapid-flying moths. Larvae often injurious to plants and trees; adults, without functional mouthparts, cannot feed.

swimming, recreation and competitive sport of self-propulsion through water. Four basic swimming styles: front crawl, developed in Australia and US; backstroke;

Common European swift

breaststroke; butterfly, classed as new stroke in 1952. Olympic event since 1896.

Swinburne, Algernon Charles (1837-1909), English poet. Works notable for technical skill, radical fervour, sensuality, *eg* classical verse play *Atalanta in Calydon* (1865), poetry *Songs before Sunrise* (1871), *Tristram of Lyonesse* (1882).

Swindon, mun. bor. of Wiltshire, S England. Pop. 91,000. British Rail workshops; has railway museum (1962).

swine, name given to members of Suidae family, esp. domestic pig.

swine fever or **hog cholera,** infectious, often fatal, virus disease of swine. Characterized by fever, vomiting, diarrhoea.

swing music, style of jazz played by big bands consisting of brass, saxophone and rhythm sections. Originated in US in 1930s and remained popular to 1950s. Exponents incl. Benny Goodman, Count Basie.

Swithin or **Swithun, St** (d. 862), English churchman, bishop of Winchester. According to tradition, weather on his feast day (15 July) guarantees same weather on succeeding 40 days.

Switzerland

Switzerland (Fr. *Suisse,* Ger. *Schweiz,* Ital. *Svizzera*), federal republic of WC Europe. Area 41,285 sq km (15,940 sq mi); pop. 6,435,000; cap. Bern. Main cities Basle, Geneva, Zürich. Languages: German, French, Italian. Religions: Protestant, RC. Plateau in C (lakes incl. Geneva, Zurich, Constance); Alps in S, E. Dairy produce (cheese, milk), confectionery; watches, optical instruments; banking, tourism. Part of Holy Roman Empire from 1033, Confederation estab. 1291 for defence against Habsburgs, now comprises 22 cantons. Centre of 16th cent. Reformation. Full independence from 1648; French occupation (1798-1815). Neutrality estab. by Treaty of Paris (1815). Hq. of many international agencies, *eg* League of Nations (1920-46), WHO (1946).

swordfish, *Xiphias gladius,* large food and game fish (up to 4.6 m/15 ft long), related to tunny, widely distributed in warm seas. Upper jaw extended into flat sword-like structure.

sycamore, *Acer pseudoplatanus,* Eurasian maple tree. Large and deciduous with yellow flowers; planted as shade tree. Name also used for several American PLANE trees. *Ficus sycamorus,* a FIG tree is sycamore of the Bible.

Sydney, city of SE Australia, on Port Jackson, cap. of New South Wales. Pop. 2,800,000. Admin., commercial centre;

major port, exports wool, wheat, meat; industs. incl. coalmining, iron and steel mfg., food processing, car assembly. Settled (1788) as penal colony. Has harbour bridge (1932), opera house (1973), 3 univs.

Sydney, seaport of E Nova Scotia, Canada; on Cape Breton Isl. Pop. 33,000. In important coal mining area; has steel mills, shipbuilding indust. Founded 1783; cap. of Cape Breton 1784-1820.

syenite, coarse-grained igneous rock. Consists of feldspars plus any of various ferromagnesian minerals, *eg* augite, hornblende; similar to granite but contains no quartz. Major sources in US, Germany, Norway.

Syktyvkar, city of USSR, cap. of Komi auton. republic, NE European RSFSR. Pop. 136,000. Timber centre; wood pulp and paper mfg; shipyards.

syllogism, in logic, method of argument drawing a conclusion from 2 premises. Described by Aristotle, remains principal instrument of traditional deductive logic. Most common form is categorical, made up of 3 statements of fact, *eg* all dogs have 4 feet; a pug is a dog; therefore a pug has 4 feet. The 2 other types are hypothetical (conditional proposition and 2 statements of fact); and disjunctive (alternative proposition and 2 statements of fact).

symbiosis, in biology, living together of 2 dissimilar organisms by which each benefits, *eg* cellulose-digesting bacteria present in stomach of cows.

symbolists, group of French poets esp. Rimbaud, Verlaine, Mallarmé, active in late 19th cent., who reacted against realism in literature, feeling that poetry should evoke inexpressible subjective states.

Symons, Arthur (1865-1945), English poet, critic, b. Wales. Known for influential critical work *The Symbolist Movement in Literature* (1899). Also wrote decadent poetry, *eg Silhouettes* (1892), *Images of Good and Evil* (1899).

symphony, orchestral composition generally in similar form to SONATA. Classical symphony was estab. by Haydn and perfected by Mozart in 18th cent. In 19th cent., composers who developed the form incl. Beethoven, Schubert, Berlioz and Mahler. Symphony has been less dominant in 20th cent. music; noted 20th cent. symphonists incl. Sibelius, Shostakovich.

synagogue, in Judaism, building designed for public prayer, religious education and other communal activities. Prob. originated *c* 6th cent. BC among Jews in exile in Babylon, unable to visit TEMPLE in Jerusalem.

synapse, junction between nerve cells where nervous impulses are transmitted from one cell to another. Impulses usually travel down conducting nerve fibre (axon) of nerve cell and, on reaching end of fibre, stimulate release of ACETYLCHOLINE. This excites dendrites of adjacent cell and passes on the impulses.

synchroton, particle accelerator used to obtain high energy protons, electrons, *etc,* by combination of magnetic field, whose intensity is modulated cyclically, and high frequency electric field.

syncopation, in music and poetry, shifting of stress from normal beat. Rhythmic suspension, unaccented beat, rest, or silence on beat are types of syncopation. Characteristic of modern music and of verse using speech rhythms.

syndicalism, revolutionary doctrine and plan for post-revolutionary society. Adherents advocate abolition of central govt., replacement by trade unions as decision-makers on production and distribution. Influenced by Proudhon, SOREL.

Synge, J[ohn] M[illington] (1871-1909), Irish dramatist. A leading figure in Irish Renaissance. Known for controversial presentation of peasant life in plays, *eg Riders to the Sea* (1904), *The Playboy of the Western World* (1907).

Synoptic Gospels, *see* GOSPELS.

synthesis, in chemistry and biology, formation of compounds from their constituent elements or simpler materials.

synthetic fibres, artificial, chemically produced fibres,

usually derived from long-chain polymers. Woven as fabrics which are generally quick-drying, resistant to creasing and chemical damage; less pleasant to wear than natural fibres as they absorb less moisture and are not so warm. Incl. nylon, rayon, Dacron and Orlon.

syphilis, infectious disease caused by spirochaete (spiral bacterium) *Treponema pallidum.* Usually transmitted by sexual intercourse or acquired congenitally. In later stages, can affect almost any organ or tissue of the body, esp. mucous membranes, skin and bone, nervous system. Treatment by penicillin effective if applied early enough.

Syracuse (*Siracusa*), city of SE Sicily, Italy, cap. of Siracusa prov. Pop. 109,000. Port; fishing, salt, wine. Founded *c* 734 BC by Greeks, *fl* 5th-3rd cent. BC; taken by Rome 212 BC. Many remains, esp. on Ortygia Isl. (original site).

Syracuse, town of C New York, US; on Barge Canal. Pop. 197,000. Electrical equipment, typewriter mfg. Hist. salt indust. declined *c* 1870.

Syr Darya (anc. *Jaxartes*), river of SC USSR. Rises as R. Naryn in E Kirghiz SSR and joins Kara Darya in Fergana valley, Uzbek SSR; flows *c* 2100 km (1300 mi) through Kazakh SSR to Aral Sea.

Syria

Syria, republic of SW Asia. Area 185,000 sq km (71,000 sq mi); pop. 7,121,000; cap. Damascus. Language: Arabic. Religion: Islam. Bounded by Anti-Lebanon Mts. in W and Syrian desert in S. Agric. in fertile valleys of Euphrates and Orontes; cotton main export; pipelines carrying Iraqi oil provide revenue. Conquered by many peoples, was part of Ottoman Empire (1516-1918). Mandated to France (1920), became completely independent 1944. Joined Egypt in UAR (1958-61).

syringa, genus of the LILAC. Name also given to North American mock orange, genus *Philadelphus,* shrub of saxifrage family, with fragrant white flowers resembling those of the orange.

Syros (*Síros*), isl. of Greece, in Aegean Sea, most populous of Cyclades. Area 85 sq km (33 sq mi); cap. Syros (Hermoupolis), port, pop. 17,000.

Szczecin (Ger. *Stettin*), city of NW Poland, on R. Oder, cap. of Szczecin prov. Pop. 340,000. Port; shipbuilding, indust. centre; formerly port for Berlin. Hanseatic League member from 1360. Part of Prussian Pomerania 1720-1945. Birthplace of Catherine the Great.

Szechwan, prov. of SC China. Area *c* 570,000 sq km (220,000 sq mi); pop. (est.) 70,000,000; cap. Chengtu. Isolated region. High mountains in W crossed by Yangtze. Fertile Red basin in C is densely populated and major source of rice, sugar cane, cotton

Szeged, city of SE Hungary, on R. Tisza. Pop. 130,000. Port in agric. area, food processing; light industs. Partly destroyed by flood (1879).

Székesfehérvár (Ger. *Stuhlweissenburg*), town of W Hungary. Pop. 68,000. Tobacco, wine; aluminium complex. Roman *Alba Regia*; coronation and burial place of Hungarian kings to 16th cent.

Szymanowski, Karol (1882-1937), Polish composer. Works incl. operas, *eg King Roger,* symphonies, 2 violin concertos, and much piano music.

T

tabasco, trademark for extremely spicy sauce made from *Capsicum conoides,* a pepper native to Mexico.

Tabernacle, in OT, portable sanctuary carried by the Jews in their wanderings from Egypt to Palestine. Contained Ark of the Covenant.

Tabernacles, Feast of, Jewish festival (Sukkoth), celebrated 15th-22nd of Tishri (late October). Marks end of harvest season and celebrated by taking meals in tents or huts in memory of wanderings during Exodus.

Table Bay, inlet of Atlantic Ocean, SW Cape Prov., South Africa; *c* 9.7 km (6 mi) across. First Dutch settlement in S Africa estab. 1652 on shores. Overlooked by **Table Mountain,** height 1087 m (3567 ft). Flat-topped; ascended by cable railway (built 1929).

table tennis or **ping-pong,** indoor game played on a rectangular table with hollow celluloid ball and rubber-covered bats. Prob. originated in 1880s and 1890s in England. International Table Tennis Federation was formed (1926) to arrange championships and standardize rules.

taboo or **tabu,** prohibition, common among primitive peoples, of certain words and actions, usually on religious grounds. Also refers to certain objects set aside for religious use. Practice occurs esp. in Polynesia.

Tabora, town of C Tanzania. Pop. 21,000. Railway jct.; agric. market, trade in cotton, millet, groundnuts. Former slave trade centre.

Tabriz, city of NW Iran, cap. of E Azerbaijan prov. Pop. 493,000. Market centre for fertile agric. area; textile and rug mfg. Often devastated by earthquakes, has ruined 15th cent. Blue Mosque.

Tacitus (AD *c* 55–*c* 120), Roman historian. Author of *Germania,* giving valuable hist. information on Germanic tribes. Wrote biography of Agricola, his father-in-law and governor of Britain. His history of the empire from reign of Galba to Domitian (69-97) gives picture of Roman life.

Tacna, town of Peru in Andean foothills, alt. 548 m (1800 ft). Pop. 34,000. Centre of irrigated region producing tobacco, cotton, sugar cane. Railway link with Arica (Chile). Held by Chile 1883-1929.

Tacoma, port of W Washington, US; on Puget Sound, S of Seattle. Pop. 155,000. Exports timber, grain, flour, phosphates; shipyards, lumber, flour mills, copper smelting.

Tadoussac, village of SC Québec, Canada; at confluence of Saguenay and St Lawrence rivers. Pop. *c* 1000. Earliest French settlement in Canada (1600); estab. as fur trading post.

Tadzhik Soviet Socialist Republic, constituent republic of SC USSR. Area *c* 143,000 sq km (55,200 sq mi); pop. 2,900,000; cap. Dushanbe. Largely mountainous, containing Pamir and Alai systems; lowlands in Amu Darya valley. Crops incl. cotton, wheat, fruit; sheep and cattle raising. Region under Russian control by 1895; constituent republic (1929).

Taegu, city of SE South Korea. Pop. 1,083,000. Commercial centre of agric. region (grains, tobacco); textiles produced.

Taejon, city of W South Korea. Pop. 415,000. Rail jct.; food processing, silk and textile mfg.

Tafawa Balewa, Alhaji Sir Abubakar (1912-66), Nigerian statesman, 1st PM (1957-66). Assassinated in military coup.

taffeta, light plain-weave fabric with high sheen, originally made of silk. Used in ribbons and umbrellas.

Tafilelt or **Tafilalet,** oasis of SE Morocco. Largest in Sahara, area *c* 1375 sq km (530 sq mi). Produces dates, leather. Rich independent kingdom 8th-10th cent.; original home of Morocco's ruling dynasty.

Taft, William Howard (1857-1930), American statesman, president (1909-13). Republican secretary of war under T. Roosevelt, whom he succeeded. Defeated in 1912 election after Roosevelt split Republican vote by running as Progressive candidate. His son, **Robert Alphonso Taft** (1889-1953), was Senator from Ohio. Sponsored TAFT-HARTLEY LABOR ACT.

Taft-Hartley Labor Act, common name for Labor-Management Relations Act (1947). Attempted to regulate labour disputes in US, with sanctions against 'wildcat'(unofficial) and demarcation strikes, extended govt. mediation, and prohibited CLOSED SHOP. Also *see* INDUSTRIAL RELATIONS ACT.

Tagalog or **Tagal,** second major ethnic group in population of Philippine Islands. Language is one of Malayo-Polynesian family, an official language of Philippines since 1940.

Taganrog, port of USSR, SE European RSFSR; on Gulf of Taganrog (arm of Sea of Azov). Pop. 265,000. Exports grains and coal; metallurgy; heavy machinery mfg. Founded as fortress (1698) by Peter the Great; twice taken by Turks in 18th cent.

Taglioni, Maria (1804-84), Italian ballet dancer. Known esp. for *La Sylphide* (Paris, 1832), created for her by her father. May have introduced *sur les pointes* technique.

Rabindranath Tagore

Tagore, Sir Rabindranath (1861-1941), Indian author, educator. Founded Santiniketan (1901), forerunner of Visva-Bharati Univ. Wrote love lyrics, *eg* collection *Gitanjali* (1912), and philosophical *Sadhana* (1913). Nobel Prize for Literature (1913).

Tagus (Span. *Tajo,* Port. *Tejo*), river of Spain and Portugal. Flows *c* 910 km (565 mi) from Teruel prov., EC Spain to Atlantic Ocean by estuary at Lisbon. Forms part of Spain-Portugal border.

Tahiti, main isl. of French Polynesia, in Windward group of Society Isls. Area 1040 sq km (402 sq mi); cap. Papeete. Mountainous; produces fruit, sugar, copra, vanilla. Home of Gauguin for many years.

Taichung, city of WC Taiwan. Pop. 490,000. Centre of region producing rice, sugar cane, bananas.

Taimyr Peninsula, most N projection of USSR mainland, on Arctic coast of Siberian RSFSR. N extremity is Cape Chelyuskin. Covered mainly by tundra; inhabited by nomadic Samoyeds.

Tainan, port of SW Taiwan, on Formosa Str. Pop. 495,000. Agric. centre for rice, sugar cane; produces textiles, machinery. Cap. of isl. in 17th cent., retained political power until 1885.

taipan, *Oxyuranus scutellatus,* large brown dangerously poisonous snake, up to 3 m/10 ft in length. Found in NE Australia and New Guinea.

Taipei, cap. of Taiwan, commercial and indust. centre. Pop. 1,922,000. Founded in 18th cent., replaced Tainan as cap. in 1885. Developed under Japanese rule.

Taiping Rebellion (1850-64), revolt in China against Manchu dynasty. Led by Hung Hsiu-chuan who declared himself leader of Taiping (Great Peace) dynasty. After initial success, incl. capture of Nanking (1853), crushed with help of Western troops under C. G. GORDON.

Taiwan (*Formosa*), isl. republic of E Asia, separated from China by Formosa Str. Area c 36,000 sq km (13,900 sq mi); pop. 15,000,000; cap. Taipei. Language: Mandarin Chinese. Religion: Buddhism. Crossed N-S by mountain range, reaching c 4000 m (13,100 ft); tropical climate, with abundant rainfall. Produces rice, timber, sugar. Settled in 17th cent. by Chinese after expulsion of Dutch. Ceded to Japan (1895-1945). Seat of Chiang Kai-shek's nationalist govt. after 1949; under threat of Chinese invasion, has developed under US economic and military aid. Withdrew from UN (1971), on entry of China.

Taiyuan, cap. of Shansi prov., NC China. Pop. 2,725,000. In major iron and coal area; iron and steel plants, heavy machinery and chemical mfg. Ancient walled city.

Tajamulco, Mount, inactive volcano of SW Guatemala. Highest peak in Central America rising to 4211 m (13,816 ft).

Taj Mahal

Taj Mahal, white marble mausoleum beside R. Jumna, near Agra, India. Built 1630-48 by Shah Jehan as tomb for his favourite wife.

Tajo, *see* TAGUS.

Takahashi, Korekiyo (1854-1936), Japanese banker, statesman; 4 times finance minister between 1913 and 1936. Opposed army appropriations; assassinated in unsuccessful military coup.

Takamatsu, port of Japan, N Shikoku isl. Pop. 274,000. Wood pulp and paper ware mfg. Notable landscape gardens in Ritsurin Park.

Takamine, Jokichi (1854-1922), Japanese chemist. Founded 1st fertilizer works in Japan. First to isolate adrenalin (1901). Settled in US (1890).

Taklamakan, desert region of Sinkiang auton. region, NW China. Area c 323,750 sq km (125,000 sq mi). Uninhabited; oases on its edges.

Takoradi, *see* SEKONDI-TAKORADI, Ghana.

Talbot, William Henry Fox (1800-77), English photographic pioneer. Patented various processes for making negative and positive prints ('talbotypes'). Wrote

The Pencil of Nature (1844), illustrated with his own photographs.

talc, softest common mineral; consists of hydrated magnesium silicate. Main constituent of SOAPSTONE. Used in electrical insulators, lubricants, paper mfg., also as talcum powder. Major sources in Austria, Italy, US.

Talca, town of SC Chile, in agric. region. Pop. 103,000. Wine, wheat production. Founded 1692. Scene of proclamation of Chilean independence (1818). Destroyed by earthquake (1928).

Talcahuano, *see* CONCEPCIÓN, Chile.

Talien, *see* LU-TA.

Tallahassee, cap. of Florida, US. Pop. 73,000. Lumber produce. Indian, Spanish settlement prior to territ. cap. (1824).

Talleyrand [-Périgord], Charles Maurice de (1754-1838), French statesman. Bishop of Autun (1789-91), represented clergy in Estates-General (1789); supported moderate reform. Fled abroad on fall of monarchy. Foreign minister under Directory (1797-9) and under Napoleon (1799-1807). On Napoleon's exile to Elba, secured accession of Louis XVIII and favourable peace terms for French at Congress of Vienna (1814-15). Ambassador to London (1830-4) under Louis Philippe.

Tallien, Jean Lambert (1767-1820), French revolutionary. A leader in the Convention which overthrew Robespierre (1794). Influenced by his wife, **Thérèsa Tallien** (1773-1835), known as 'Notre Dame de Thermidor', who was originally one of his political prisoners. She became a social leader in Directory period.

Tallinn (Ger. *Reval*), city of USSR, cap. of Estonian SSR; on Gulf of Finland. Pop. 378,000. Port; exports timber, paper; shipbuilding; wood products and textile mfg. Founded by Danes (1219); member of Hanseatic League (1285). Taken by Russia from Sweden (1710). Cap. of Estonia (1919-40).

Tallis, Thomas (c 1505-1585), English composer. Joint organist with Byrd of Chapel Royal. Compositions, noted for contrapuntal skill, incl. motets, *eg Spem in Alium* and *Cantiones sacrae,* anthems, keyboard music.

tallow, solid fat extracted from animals, esp. cattle and sheep. Used to make candles and soap.

Talma, François-Joseph (1763-1826), French actor. Major tragic actor. Instituted reforms in style of declamation. Advocated realism in costume, scenery.

Talmud, collection of writings constituting Jewish civil and religious law. Consists of 2 parts, Mishnah (text), and Gemara (commentary). Passages devoted to law itself are known as halakah; those which contain illustrative parables, legends, *etc,* as haggadah. Regarded as Oral Law as distinct from Written Law of the TORAH.

talus or **scree,** accumulation of rock fragments formed at foot of steep slope. Results from weathering of rock face above.

Tamale, town of N Ghana, cap. of Northern Region. Pop. 99,000. Road jct.; agric. market, trade in groundnuts, cotton, livestock.

tamandua, *Tamandua tetradactyla,* arboreal anteater of tropical America. Elongated snout and sticky tongue for catching insects; prehensile tail. Also called three-toed anteater.

tamarind, *Tamarindus indica,* large evergreen tree of Leguminosae family, native to tropical Africa. Pod contains seeds enclosed in juicy acid pulp, used in beverages and food.

tamarisk, any of genus *Tamarix* of shrubs and small trees native to Mediterranean region and C Asia. Feathery leaves, pink or white flowers. Often cultivated as windbreak near salt water.

Tamatave, town of NE Malagasy Republic, on Indian Ocean. Pop. 57,000. Deepwater port, exports coffee, rice, sugar; railway to Tananarive.

tambourine, hand-held percussion instrument consisting of circular frame and single drumhead, with circular metal plates or jingles in frame.

Tambov, town of USSR, SC European RSFSR. Pop. 240,000. Indust. centre of fertile agric. region; machinery, chemical mfg. Founded in 1636 as outpost against Tartars.

Tamarisk *(Tamarix gallica)*

Tamburlaine, *see* TAMERLANE.

Tamerlane or **Timur Leng** (*c* 1336–1405), Mongol conqueror. Estab. himself as ruler of Turkestan with his cap. at Samarkand (1369). Conquered Persia, S Russia, India as far as Delhi. Defeated Ottoman Turks at Angora (1402) and captured the sultan Beyazid. Patron of learning; notorious for his cruelty. Subject of Marlowe's play *Tamburlaine.*

Tamil, *see* DRAVIDIAN.

Tamil Nadu, maritime state of S India; formerly Madras, renamed 1969. Area *c* 130,000 sq km (50,000 sq mi); pop. 41,103,000; cap. Madras. Plain along Coromandel Coast in E; mountainous in W, reaching alt. of 2400 m (8000 ft) in Nilgiri Hills. Agric. economy; rice, cotton, groundnuts. Under British control by 1800 after wars against French and Tippoo Sahib.

Tammany, powerful Democratic political organization of New York City, incorporated 1789. Historically associated with corruption under such leaders as 'Boss' Tweed. Declined in power during La Guardia admin. (1933-45); ceased to exist after 1965.

Tammuz, in Babylonian and Assyrian religion, god of nature, personification of recreative power of spring. Loved by fertility goddess ISHTAR; killed and restored to life by her.

Tampa, resort and port of W Florida, US; on Tampa Bay. Pop. 247,000. Citrus fruit canning indust., phosphates export; breweries, cigar mfg.

Tampere (Swed. *Tammerfors*), city of SW Finland, between Lakes Näsi and Pyhä. Pop. 154,000. Railway jct.; indust. centre, esp. textiles, timber, using h.e.p. from nearby rapids. Has cathedral (20th cent.).

Tampico, port of NE Mexico, near mouth of Pánuco R. Pop. 196,000. Oil refining, petroleum exports; important fishing indust., sawmilling, chemical mfg.

Tamworth, city of E New South Wales, Australia, on Peel R. Pop. 25,000. Road and rail centre; market town for large agric. region; food processing, timber mills.

Tamworth, mun. bor. of Staffordshire, WC England, on R. Tame. Pop. 40,000. Cars, clothing industs.; bricks, tiles mfg. Has castle; 14th cent. church.

Tamworth Manifesto, election address by ROBERT PEEL at Tamworth, Staffordshire (1834). Considered manifesto for emerging Conservative Party; accepted Reform Bill of 1832 and proposed careful social and economic reform.

Tana or **Tsana, Lake,** largest lake of Ethiopia, in NW. Area 3625 sq km (1400 sq mi); alt. 1830 m (6000 ft). Source of Blue Nile.

tanager, small songbird found mainly in New World tropics; male usually brightly coloured. North American species incl. scarlet tanager, *Piranga olivacea.*

Tanagra, ancient town of Boeotia, EC Greece. Famous 4th cent. BC terracotta figurines found in graves.

Tanaka, Kakuei (1918-), Japanese politician. Premier of Liberal Democratic govt. (1972-4), resigned in corruption scandal.

Tananarive, cap. of Malagasy Republic, in C Madagascar highlands. Pop. 378,000. Admin., commercial centre; univ.; railway to port at Tamatave. Founded 17th cent., taken (1895) by French.

Taney, Roger Brooke (1777-1864), American lawyer. Cabinet member (1831-4), helped President Jackson in struggle to curb powers of Bank in the US. Chief justice of Supreme Court (1836-64), upheld state sovereignty in maintaining slavery in DRED SCOTT CASE (1857).

Tanga, town of NE Tanzania, on Indian Ocean. Pop. 61,000. Railway terminus; port, exports sisal, coffee, copra.

Tanganyika, *see* TANZANIA.

Tanganyika, Lake, lake of EC Africa, in Great Rift Valley. Borders on Burundi (NE), Tanzania (E), Zambia (S), Zaïre (W). Area 32,900 sq km (12,700 sq mi); second deepest (1432 m/4700 ft) in world. Reached 1858 by Burton and Speke.

tangerine, small, thin-skinned variety of ORANGE belonging to mandarin orange species, *Citrus reticulata.* Native to SE Asia, now widely grown in tropical and subtropical regions.

Tangier (anc. *Tingis*), city of N Morocco, on Str. of Gibraltar. Pop. 186,000. Port, commercial and tourist centre. Focus of dispute over Morocco in 19th cent., estab. (1923) as international zone. Part of Morocco from 1956, declared free port 1961.

tangle, *see* KELP.

tango, dance of Spanish-American origin, internationally popular since *c* 1915. Tempo is moderately slow and rhythm similar to Cuban habanera.

Tangshan, city of Hopeh prov., NE China. Pop. (pre 1976) 1,200,000. Coalmining centre. Iron and steel works, motor vehicle and chemical mfg. Devastated by earthquake (1976), est. 500,000 killed.

Tanizaki, Junichiro (1886-1965), Japanese novelist. Works incl. modernized version of Murasaki Shikibu's *The Tale of Genji* (1941), *The Makioka Sisters* (1943-8).

Tanjore, *see* THANJAVUR.

Sherman tank used in WWII

tank, heavily armoured vehicle, moving on tracks, mounting a field gun or smaller armament. First used by the British in the Somme (1916). Became major weapon of land warfare in WWII, esp. in N Africa.

Tannenberg (Pol. *Stebark*), village of Olsztyn prov., NE Poland. Scene of defeat (1410) of Teutonic Knights by Poles and Lithuanians under Ladislaus II, and defeat (1914) of Russians by Germans under Hindenburg.

tannin or **tannic acid,** astringent compound present in many plants, *eg* tea, walnut, gall nuts, hemlock and oak bark. Used in tanning, making of inks, as a fixative in dyeing and for clarifying solutions in medicine.

tanning, process by which animal skins are turned into leather. Skins are usually soaked in tannin obtained from vegetable material. Alum and chrome salts or fats and oils (for chamois leather) are also employed.

Tansy

tansy, *Tanacetum vulgare,* common European flowering herb of daisy family now naturalized in North America. Formerly used as stimulant in medicine, now cultivated as garden plant.

Tanta, city of N Egypt, on Nile delta. Pop. 254,000. Railway and commercial centre, cotton indust. Noted for Moslem festivals and fairs.

tantalum (Ta), rare metallic element; at. no. 73, at. wt. 180.95. Occurs with niobium in certain minerals. Corrosion resistant, malleable and ductile. Used in surgical instruments, manufacture of hard alloys, and electronic equipment.

Tantalus, in Greek myth, son of Zeus and father of Pelops and Niobe. For angering the gods, eternally punished in Tartarus by being set in pool of water, hungry and thirsty, but unable either to drink from the pool, or to reach fruit tree.

Tantra, group of post-Vedic Sanskrit treatises. Consist of dialogues between SIVA and his consort. Basis of various secret and erotic cults which worshipped female divinities. Influenced Hindu erotic art.

Tanzam Railway, line, operational from 1976, between Zambia and Dar-es-Salaam, Tanzania. Length *c* 1870 km (1160 mi); built with Chinese assistance. Also called Great Uhuru ('Freedom') railway.

Tanzania

Tanzania, republic of E Africa. Area 945,000 sq km (364,900 sq mi); pop. 14,372,000; cap. Dar-es-Salaam. Languages: Swahili, English. Religions: native, Islam, Christianity. Narrow coastal plain; interior plateau, with volcanic peaks (*eg* Kilimanjaro), cut by Great Rift Valley. Bordered by L. Tanganyika (W) Victoria Nyanza (N). Exports coffee, cotton, sisal, diamonds; Tanzam railway links Zambia with Dar-es-Salaam. Explored 16th cent. by Portuguese; ivory, slave trade under Arabs 18th-19th cent. Part of German East Africa from 1884; mandated to Britain 1916. Independent 1961. Tanzania formed 1964 by union of Tanganyika with Zanzibar.

Taoism, Chinese religion and philosophy. Based on book, *Tao-teh-king,* traditionally ascribed to Lao-tse (6th cent. BC) but prob. written 3rd cent. BC. By AD 5th cent., developed into religious system with influences from Mahayana Buddhism. Emphasized effortless action, cessation of all striving. Condemned social philosophy of Confucius.

Tapajós, river of WC Brazil. Rises in Mato Grosso, flows NE 970 km (*c* 600 mi) to join Amazon at Santarém.

tape recorder, electromagnetic instrument which records speech and music by interpreting sounds as variations in magnetic field which act on MAGNETIC TAPE. On playback, magnetic patterns reconverted into electrical impulses, in turn converted into audible sound waves.

tapestry, ornamental fabric for covering walls, furniture and for curtains. Made by interweaving of plain warp threads with silk or wool of varying colour and texture. European wool tapestries are extant from 10th cent. Noted centres were Arras (from 14th cent.), Brussels, Aubusson, Beauvais and Gobelins factory, Paris.

tapeworm, long ribbon-shaped segmented parasitic flatworm of class Cestoda. Adults infest intestines of man and other vertebrates, absorbing nutrients through body; life cycle may involve several hosts.

tapioca, *see* CASSAVA.

Malayan tapir

tapir, nocturnal timid pig-like ungulate of tropical America and SE Asia. Flexible snout, resembling small trunk; herbivorous. Species incl. Malayan tapir, *Tapirus indicus,* with black limbs and forequarters, white hindquarters.

tar, dark brown or black viscous liquid obtained from distillation of wood, coal and similar substances. Pitch is more solid form. Used for road-making, as protective coating for wood, *etc.* Distillation of coal tar yields bases for aniline dyes.

Tara, Hill of, Co. Meath, E Irish Republic. Seat of Irish kings until 6th cent. Earthworks.

Taranaki, region of W North Isl., New Zealand. Area 9710 sq km (3750 sq mi); pop. 101,000; main town New Plymouth. Sheep farming in E hills; dairying (butter, cheese mfg.) on W lowlands.

Taranto (anc. *Tarentum*), town of Apulia, SE Italy, on Gulf of Taranto. Cap. of Ionio prov. Pop. 236,000. Port, naval base; major steelworks. Founded 8th cent. BC by Greeks, taken by Rome 272 BC. Byzantine castle, medieval cathedral.

tarantula, name given to various large hairy spiders of Theraphosidae family, with poisonous but rarely fatal bite. Name originally applied to S European *Lycosa tarantula* whose bite was believed to lead to dancing mania in Middle Ages.

Tarawa, atoll in C Pacific Ocean, cap. of Gilbert and Ellice Isls. colony. Pop. 13,000. Admin. centre; port, exports copra, phosphates.

Tarbes, town of SW France, on R. Adour, cap. of Hautes-Pyrénées dept. Pop. 60,000. Tourist resort; livestock trade. Romanesque cathedral.

tarboosh or **fez,** brimless cap of cloth or felt, shaped like a truncated cone; worn in Moslem countries. Once a badge of Turkish citizenship, proscribed (1925) by Kemal Pasha.

Tardigrada (tardigrades), phylum of minute animals with segmented body and 4 pairs of legs. Often found in water surrounding moss. Sometimes considered as primitive arthropods.

tare, *see* VETCH.

Târgoviste, town of SC Romania. Pop. 47,000. Oil refining. Cap. of Walachia until 1698. Noted 16th cent. church.

Târgu-Mureş, town of C Romania, on R. Mureş. Pop. 92,000. Agric. market, grain, wine, timber trade. Medieval cultural centre.

tariffs or **customs,** duties on imported goods intended to protect domestic producers by increasing prices of imports in relation to home-produced goods. Used as protectionist policy by most countries, EEC is leading example of international cooperation on tariffs. Opposed to FREE TRADE.

Tarik ibn-Ziyad (*fl* 711), Moslem general. Led Moorish invasion of Spain, after crossing from N Africa to Gibraltar (named after him). Defeated (711) Roderick, last king of Visigoths, and conquered much of Iberia.

Tarim, river of Sinkiang auton. region, NW China. Length *c* 2100 km (1300 mi). Flows E along N edge of Taklamakan desert to Lop Nor salt lake.

Tarkington, [Newton] Booth (1869-1946), American author. Wrote realistically of social changes of Indiana in

The Magnificent Ambersons (1918), about youth in *Penrod* (1914). Also wrote plays, dramatized novels, *eg* historical romance *Monsieur Beaucaire* (1900).

Tarn, river of S France. Flows *c* 370 km (230 mi) from Cévennes via Albi, Montauban to R. Garonne. Limestone gorges attract tourists.

Tarnów, town of SE Poland. Pop. 84,000. Railway jct., chemicals indust. Under Austrian rule 1772-1919. Gothic cathedral (14th cent.).

Taro

taro, *Colocasia esculenta,* large, tropical Asiatic plant of arum family. Shield-shaped leaves. Cultivated for edible corms.

tarot, oldest surviving card game, using esoteric designs; now used mainly for fortune-telling.

tarpan, wild horse, once common in Europe and Asia, closely related to Przewalski's horse. Became extinct *c* 1900; attempts since made in Poland to regenerate species by selective breeding.

Tarpeia, in Roman legend, daughter of officer commanding Romans against Sabines. Betrayed citadel for gold bracelets worn by Sabines, who then killed her.

tarpon, *Tarpon atlanticus,* large primitive fish found in warm Atlantic waters; reaches lengths of 1.8 m/6 ft. Popular game fish.

Tarquinius Superbus, Lucius (*fl* 6th cent. BC), last king of Rome. Expelled from Rome (510 BC) because of his despotism; enlisted the aid of Etruscan Lars Porsena to restore himself to throne. Although Porsena captured Rome, Tarquinius was not made king.

tarragon, *Artemisia dracunculus,* European perennial WORMWOOD. Long, slender aromatic leaves used as seasoning, esp. in vinegar.

Tarragona, town of NE Spain, on Mediterranean Sea, cap. of Tarragona prov. Pop. 78,000. Port, exports wine; Chartreuse liqueur mfg. from 1903. Cap. of Roman *Tarraconensis.* Roman walls, aqueduct. Cathedral (12th cent.).

Tarrasa, city of Catalonia, NE Spain. Pop. 139,000. Major textile centre, esp. woollens, cotton.

Tarsier

tarsier, small arboreal primate of Tarsiidae family, related to lemur; found in Philippines and East Indies. Rat-sized, with large eyes and ears; long feet and hands equipped with sucker-like discs. Nocturnal, feeds on lizards, insects, *etc.*

Tarsus, town of S Turkey. Pop. 57,000. Agric. trade centre. Has extensive ruins of ancient Tarsus, cap. of Cilicia. Birthplace of St Paul.

tartan, woollen cloth woven in pattern of coloured checks. Tartan kilts and plaids were worn by Scottish clans from 15th cent., each clan having distinctive pattern. Illegal (1746-82) after 1745 Jacobite uprising.

tartaric acid, crystalline organic acid, found in vegetable tissue and fruit juices. Salt, potassium hydrogen tartrate, present in grape juice, is deposited as argol in wine casks; used in baking powder (cream of tartar).

Tartars or **Tatars,** name given to peoples who invaded Russia (13th cent.) under Mongol leadership. Known as GOLDEN HORDE, they overran and dominated parts of Eurasia until their empire was lost to Ottomans and dukes of Moscow (15th–16th cents.). In USSR, there are *c* 5 million Tartars, who are Moslems and speak a Turkic language.

Tartarus, in Greek myth, abyss below HADES where Zeus hurled Titans. Place of punishment of wicked after death.

Tartu (Ger. *Dorpat*), town of USSR, Estonia SSR. Pop. *c* 84,000. Metalworking, textile, cigarette mfg. Founded in 1030 as Yuryev; Hanseatic town. Disputed by Poland, Sweden and Russia; passed to Russia (1704). Has univ. founded by Gustavus Adolphus of Sweden (1632).

Tashkent, city of USSR, cap. of Uzbek SSR; in oasis of R. Chirchik. Pop. 1,460,000. Cotton textile mfg.; fruit and cotton grown by irrigation. Founded 7th cent.; conquered by Genghis Khan and Tamerlane. Taken by Russia in 1865.

Tasman, Abel Janszoon (1603-59), Dutch navigator. Discovered Tasmania (named it Van Diemen's Land), New Zealand, Friendly Isls. (1642–3); proved Australia not united to polar continent.

Tasmania, isl. state of Australia, separated from SE mainland by Bass Str. Area incl. King Isl. and Furneaux Isls. 67,900 sq km (26,200 sq mi); pop. 390,000; cap. Hobart. Large forested C plateau with many lakes and valleys; narrow coastal plains. Fruit (esp. apples) and vegetable growing, wool, dairying; timber indust.; h.e.p.; minerals incl. copper, zinc. Discovered (1642) and named Van Diemen's Land by Tasman. First settled (1803) as penal colony, part of New South Wales until 1825; federal state from 1901.

Tasmanian devil, *Sarcophilus harrisii,* burrowing nocturnal carnivorous marsupial of Tasmania. Much hunted because of attacks on domestic animals, now rare.

Tasmanian wolf or **thylacine,** *Thylacinus cynocephalus,* wolf-like carnivorous marsupial; red-brown coat with dark stripes on back. Confined to Tasmania, is almost extinct.

Tasman Sea, area of SW Pacific Ocean, between SE Australia and NW New Zealand. Named (1890) after Abel Tasman.

Tasso, Torquato (1544-95), Italian poet, one of most famous of Renaissance. Known for *Gerusalemme Liberata* (*Jerusalem Delivered,* 1575), religious epic on 1st Crusade, and *Aminta* (1573), hedonistic pastoral play. Also wrote lyrics.

taste, sensation caused by stimulation of sensory organs (taste buds) in mucous membranes of tongue and palate. Four basic tastes: bitter, salt, sour and sweet. Flavour depends more on smell than taste.

Tatars, *see* TARTARS.

Tate, Nahum (1652-1715), English author, b. Ireland. Remembered for version of Shakespeare's *King Lear* with happy ending which was generally produced until mid-19th cent. Made Poet laureate (1692).

Tate Gallery, art gallery in London, containing British national collection of modern foreign art and British art. Opened 1897 following donation of pictures and money by Sir Henry Tate (1819-99).

Tati, Jacques (1908-   ), French actor. Originally in music hall, later known for writing, directing and acting in films, incl. *Monsieur Hulot's Holiday* (1952), *Playtime* (1968), *Traffic* (1971).

Tatra Mountains (Czech *Tatry*), range on Czech-Polish border, part of Carpathians. High Tatra (N) reach 2662 m (8737 ft); Low Tatra (S) reach 2044 m (6709 ft). Tourism; winter sports.

Tattersall, Richard (1724-95), English auctioneer. Opened Tattersall's thoroughbred racehorse auction (1766) at Hyde Park, London. Firm transferred its auctions to Newmarket (1965).

Tatung, city of Shansi prov., NC China. Pop. 300,000. Railway and indust. centre; major coal mine.

Taunton, mun. bor. and co. town of Somerset, SW England. Pop. 37,000. Clothing mfg. Scene of Judge Jeffreys' 'Bloody Assize' after Monmouth's rebellion (1685).

Taupo, Lake, largest lake in New Zealand, in volcanic region of C North Isl. Area 620 sq km (240 sq mi). Used as h.e.p. reservoir; tourist area, with hot springs.

Tauranga, city of N North Isl., New Zealand, on Bay of Plenty. Pop. 28,000. Port, exports dairy produce, meat; centre of citrus fruit growing area. First settled *c* 1830.

Taurus, see ZODIAC.

Taurus Mountains, range of S Turkey, running parallel to Mediterranean. Rises to 3734 m (12,251 ft) at Ala Dag; crossed by Cilician Gates N of Tarsus. Extends NE as Anti-Taurus. Has important mineral deposits (chromium, copper).

tautomerism, in chemistry, existence of certain compounds as a mixture of 2 isomeric forms in equilibrium; each form may be converted into the other but the equilibrium will tend to be maintained in the mixture.

Taverner, John (*c* 1490-1545), English composer. Wrote polyphonic church music in elaborate Tudor vocal style. Works incl. 8 Masses, 3 Magnificats, motets. Believed to have abandoned music to work as paid agent of Thomas Cromwell.

Tawney, R[ichard] H[enry] (1880-1962), English economic historian, b. India. Best known for *Religion and the Rise of Capitalism* (1926), relating Protestant ethic and early capitalism.

tawny owl, *Strix aluco,* woodland bird of Europe and Asia; black eyes, no ear-tufts, tawny-brown upper-parts.

taxation, govt. levy to provide revenue. Oldest form is land tax; other means of taxation developed as scope of govt. responsibilities widened, esp. in 19th-20th cent. Direct taxes, graduated according to individual's ability to pay, incl. INCOME TAX (major source of internal revenue), death duties or inheritance tax, rates, corporation tax. Forms of indirect taxation incl. sales, purchase and value-added taxes, based on stipulated percentage of retail cost. All levels of govt. have designated taxation powers. Income tax is levied by national govt., *eg* by Inland Revenue in UK and by Internal Revenue in US.

taxidermy, art of skinning and preserving animals in life-like state, mostly for exhibition. Fur or feathers are cleaned with special preservative preparation and hide is stretched over artificial framework.

Tay, longest river of Scotland, flows 193 km (120 mi) from Central region via Loch Tay, Firth of Tay, to North Sea. Estuary crossed by road, rail bridges at Dundee. Salmon fishing.

Taylor, A[lan] J[ohn] P[ercivale] (1906-   ), English historian. Works incl. *The Origins of the Second World War* (1961). Noted popularizer through his TV lectures and newspaper articles.

Taylor, Henry Osborn (1856-1941), American historian. Authority in ancient and medieval studies, he wrote *The Medieval Mind* (1911).

Taylor, Jeremy (1613-67), English churchman, writer. Chaplain to Archbishop Laud and Charles I. Received Irish bishopric of Down and Connor (1660). Known for sermons and devotional works incl. *Holy Living* (1650), *Holy Dying* (1651).

Taylor, John (1753-1824), American political philosopher. One of early formulators of doctrine of STATES' RIGHTS, wrote *An Inquiry into the Principles and Policy of the Government of the United States* (1814).

Taylor, Zachary (1784-1850), American statesman, president (1849-50). Renowned Indian fighter; won decisive victory at Buena Vista (1847) in Mexican War. Successful Whig presidential candidate (1848). Died in office.

Tayside, region of EC Scotland. Area 7501 sq km (2896 sq mi); pop. 397,000; chief city Dundee. Created 1975, incl. former Angus, Kinross-shire, most of Perthshire.

Tbilisi (Russ. *Tiflis*), city of USSR, cap. of Georgian SSR; route centre on R. Kura. Pop. 927,000. Agric. trade centre;

textile, machinery mfg. Founded 4th cent.; prospered on trade route between Europe and Asia. Under Russian rule from 1800. Old section incl. Zion cathedral (5th cent.) and Armenian cathedral (15th cent.).

Tchaikovsky

Tchaikovsky, Piotr Ilich (1840-93), Russian composer. His music is melodious and romantic; orchestral compositions particularly popular. Works incl. *Pathétique* symphony, ballets *Swan Lake, The Sleeping Beauty,* and fantasies, *eg Romeo and Juliet.* Also wrote *1812* overture, operas, *eg Eugene Onegin,* and songs.

Tea

tea, *Thea sinensis,* shrub with fragrant white flowers, extensively cultivated in China, Japan, India, Sri Lanka, *etc.* Bitter, aromatic beverage is prepared by infusion of dried leaves in boiling water. Tea drinking became popular in Britain in 17th cent.

Teach, Edward (d. 1718), English pirate, called 'Blackbeard'. Gained notoriety through his raids on West Indies and coasts of Virginia and the Carolinas. Killed by force sent by governor of Virginia.

teak, *Tectona grandis,* large East Indian timber tree of family Verbenaceae. Now cultivated in W Africa and tropical America. Hard, yellowish wood used in shipbuilding and furniture.

teal, small freshwater duck, genus *Anas.* Species incl. green-winged teal, *A. crecca,* smallest European duck, and North American blue-winged teal, *A. discors.*

Teapot Dome scandal, incident arising out of lease (1922) of US naval oil reserve, Teapot Dome, in Wyoming. Secretary of Interior, Albert Fall, convicted for accepting bribes to lease land without competitive bidding. Senate investigations led to allegations of govt. corruption.

tear gas, aerosol, usually bromide compound, inducing temporary loss of sight through excessive flow of tears. Used in warfare and civil disturbances.

teasel, any of genus *Dipsacus* of biennial or perennial herbs native to Europe, Asia and N Africa. Fuller's teasel, *D. fullonum,* is cultivated for its prickly flower heads, used for raising the nap on woollen cloth.

Fuller's teasel

technetium (Tc), radioactive metallic element; at. no. 43, mass no. of most stable isotope 97. First artificially made element, prepared 1937; now obtained as fission product of uranium.

technology, study of methods used in application of science in industry. First technological univ., Ecole Polytechnique, Paris (1794). US institutes incl. Massachusetts (1861) and California (1913).

tectonics, study of the main structural features of the Earth's crust. Current theories on changing formation of Earth's surface centre on PLATE TECTONICS.

Tecumseh (c 1768-1813), American Indian chief. Led Shawnees in revolt against loss of Indian land in Indiana; defeated by Harrison at Tippecanoe (1811). Killed while aiding British in War of 1812.

Tedder, Arthur William Tedder, 1st Baron (1890-1967), British air force officer. In WWII, organized Middle East air campaign against Rommel. Deputy Supreme Commander, Europe, under Eisenhower (1943-5).

Tees, river of N England. Flows 113 km (70 mi) from Pennines to North Sea at Middlesbrough.

Teesside, bor. of Cleveland, NE England, at mouth of R. Tees. Pop. 395,000. Heavy industs. Formed 1968 from Middlesbrough, Redcar, Stockton-on-Tees, etc.

teeth, in most vertebrates, hard bone-like structures embedded in upper and lower jaws, serving to bite, tear and chew. Tooth consists of pulp-filled central cavity, surrounded by shell of dentine (ivory) which is coated on crown by enamel and on root by softer cement. In man, early set of 20 deciduous (or milk) teeth is replaced by 32 permanent teeth, beginning in c 6th year. On each side of jaw, there are 2 incisors, 1 canine, 2 premolars and 3 molars.

Tegucigalpa, cap. of Honduras, on Choluteca R. Pop. 219,000. Food processing, distilling, cigarette, textile mfg. Founded 1578 as gold, silver mining centre. Became cap. 1880. Has univ. (1847); 18th cent. cathedral.

Tehran or **Teheran,** cap. of Iran, S of Elburz Mts. Pop. 3,858,000. Industrial, commercial and transport centre. Became cap. 1788 under Aga Mohammed Khan. In royal palace is Peacock Throne, brought from India. City centre modernized after 1925 by Riza Shah. Univ (1935). Scene of Allied Conference (1943).

Tehran Conference, meeting (Nov.-Dec. 1943) held at Tehran between Allied leaders Churchill, F.D. Roosevelt and Stalin during WWII. Outlined plans for invasion of Europe and role of UN in peace settlement.

Tehuantepec, isthmus of E Mexico between Campeche and Tehuantepec gulfs. Narrowest part of Mexico.

Teilhard de Chardin, Pierre (1881-1955), French theologian, palaeontologist. A Jesuit, he attempted controversial reconciliation of Christian theology with evolutionary theory. Evolved concept of interaction of psychic and physical energy. Works, pub. posthumously, incl. *The Phenomenon of Man* (1955), *The Divine Milieu* (1957).

Tejo, see TAGUS.

Tel Aviv, city of WC Israel, on Mediterranean. Pop. 362,000. Financial, indust. centre; textiles, metals, chemicals. Incorporated neighbouring Jaffa 1949. Univ. (1953). International airport.

telecommunications, long-distance communication by radio, TELEGRAPH, TELEPHONE, etc. Formerly relied on long distance cables, now increasingly uses microwaves reflected from artificial satellites. First of these was *Telstar* (launched July, 1962).

telegraph, method of sending messages in form of electrical impulses by radio or wire. First practicable system developed by Samuel Morse (c 1837). Traditionally, message carried by opening and closing circuit at a distance; sophistications incl. simultaneous transmission of several messages, reception of messages in printed form (teleprinter), and transmission of photographs (facsimile machine).

Tel-el-Amarna or **Tell-el-Amarna,** site of N Egypt, N of Asyût. City of Akhetaton built here c 1365 BC by IKHNATON as new cap. and centre of reformed religion. Ruins, rock tombs; inscribed tablets discovered 1887.

Telemachus, in Greek myth, son of Odysseus and Penelope. Set out to search for his father, returned in time to help in massacre of Penelope's suitors.

Telemann, Georg Philipp (1681-1767), German composer. Director of music for several churches in Hamburg from 1721. Wrote numerous compositions, incl. motets, 44 passions, oratorios, 600 overtures, 40 operas, keyboard and chamber music.

telepathy, see PSYCHICAL RESEARCH.

telephone, device for conveying speech over distances by converting sound into electrical impulses. Invented by Alexander Bell (1876).

telephoto lens, combination of convex and concave lens, used to increase effective focal length of camera and thus magnify images, without increasing distance between film and camera lens.

Replica of Newton's reflecting telescope

telescope, optical instrument for viewing distant objects. Refracting telescope uses 2 convex lenses, objective and eyepiece; reflecting telescope uses concave mirror and eyepiece. A further lens or prism is needed for upright image. Invented (c 1608) in Holland, first used for astronomy by Galileo (1609).

television, transmission and reception of visual images using electromagnetic radiation. Pattern of electric impulses from camera reconstructed in receiver to form picture on luminous screen. First developed in UK by John Logie Baird (1926) using mechanical scanning system; later replaced by electronic scanning. TV has become a major form of media communication, profoundly affecting esp. Western lifestyles. Also see BROADCASTING.

Telford, Thomas (1757-1834), Scottish civil engineer. Built Caledonian Canal (1803-23), c 1000 miles of roads in Scotland. Constructed (1826) Menai Suspension Bridge, Anglesey.

Telford's suspension bridge over the Menai Strait

Tell, William (*fl c* 1300), Swiss hero. Traditionally, forced to shoot apple off son's head as punishment for failure to recognize Austrian authority. After his success, he instigated revolt by shooting Austrian bailiff, Gessler.

Teller, Edward (1908-), American physicist, b. Hungary. Authority in nuclear physics, aided atomic bomb research during WWII. Called 'father of hydrogen bomb' for contributions to development of H-bomb.

tellurium (Te), semi-metallic element, with properties similar to sulphur; at. no. 52, at. wt. 127.6. Appears as brittle white crystalline solid or amorphous powder. Used to colour glass and ceramics, in vulcanizing rubber and in alloys.

Telugu, *see* DRAVIDIAN.

Tema, town of S Ghana, on Gulf of Guinea. Pop. 27,000. New harbour completed 1961, exports cocoa; oil refining, aluminium smelting.

Temesvár, *see* TIMISOARA, Romania.

Tempe, Vale of (*Témbi*), scenic gorge of Thessaly, NE Greece. Valley of R. Peneus, between Mt. Olympus and Mt. Ossa. Sacred to Apollo.

tempera, method of painting in which pigments are mixed with size, casein or egg, esp. egg yolk. Egg tempera was commonest mode of painting easel paintings until 15th cent.; paint dries quickly to produce dull finish.

temperance movement, movement with aim of persuading people against, or preventing by laws, the consumption of alchoholic beverages. Became powerful in 19th cent., leading to estab. in US of Women's Christian Temperance Union (1874), Anti-Saloon League (1893), Prohibition Party, instrumental in securing PROHIBITION.

temperature, measure of degree of hotness of a body, referred to some scale. Celsius (centigrade) scale takes freezing point of water as 0°, boiling point of water as 100°. Fahrenheit scale takes freezing point as 32° and boiling point as 212°. Kelvin or absolute scale takes ABSOLUTE ZERO as its zero point. Kelvin and Celsius degrees are equal, Fahrenheit degree equals 5/9 of Celsius degree.

Temple, Sir William (1628-99), English diplomat, essayist. Negotiated Triple Alliance with Holland and Sweden against France (1668) and William of Orange's marriage to Mary. Devoted himself to writing after 1681. Husband of DOROTHY OSBORNE.

Temple, William (1881-1944), English churchman. Archbishop of York (1929-42), of Canterbury (1942-4). First president of Workers' Educational Association (1908-24). Works incl. *Nature, Man and God* (1934).

Temple, three centres of worship successively built by the Jews in ancient Jerusalem: Solomon's, destroyed by Nebuchadnezzar; Zerubbabel's, built after exile in Babylon; and Herod's, destroyed by Romans (AD 70). Wailing Wall survives as part of the last.

tempo, in music, indication of speed at which piece should be played. A description is given often in Italian, *eg largo, andante, allegro, presto,* or a metronome number is given indicating number of beats per minute.

Temuco, town of SC Chile. Pop. 146,000. Agric., timber industs.; tanning, flour milling, sawmilling. Peace treaty with Araucanian Indians signed nearby (1881).

tench, *Tinca tinca,* European freshwater fish of carp family. Bronze-brown with red eyes.

Ten Commandments or **Decalogue,** in OT, summary of law of God as given to Moses in form of 10 statements on Mt. Sinai. Basis of ethical code of Judaism, Christianity and Islam. Divided into 3 groups dealing with duty to God, personal integrity, proper treatment of others.

tendon, cord of tough fibrous tissue which connects muscle with bone. Achilles tendon attaches muscles of the calf to the heel bone.

Tenerife, largest of Canary Isls., Spain. Area 2060 sq km (795 sq mi); cap. Santa Cruz. Rises to 3712 m (12,192 ft) in volcanic Pico de Teide. Tourist resort; banana, tomato growing.

Teng Hsiao-ping (1904-), Chinese political leader. General secretary of Communist Party (1956-67); removed from office during Cultural Revolution. Restored to office (1973), influence declining with death of Chou En-lai (1975) and increasing after death of Mao Tse-tung (1976).

Teniers, David (1610-90), Flemish painter. Court painter to Archduke Leopold Wilhelm, governor of Austrian Netherlands, and curator of his great art collection. Known for his genre scenes of peasant life and paintings of the archduke's collection.

Tennant Creek, town of C Northern Territ., Australia, on Stuart Highway. Pop. 1000. Founded (1872) with estab. of overland telegraph station; now mining centre for nearby gold, copper, silver deposits.

Tennessee, state of EC US. Area 109,412 sq km (42,244 sq mi); pop. 3,924,000; cap. Nashville; largest city Memphis. Mississippi R. forms W border; agric. plain rises to Cumberland Plateau and Appalachians in E. Cotton, tobacco, maize, livestock farming; coal, stone and zinc, phosphate mining; industs. incl. textiles, chemical mfg. Economic development under Tennessee Valley Authority. British estab. claim 1763; admitted to Union as 16th state (1796). Joined Confederacy in Civil War; important battlegrounds.

Tennessee, river of EC US. Formed in E Tennessee, flows 1050 km (650 mi) SW through Tennessee, Kentucky to Ohio R. Series of dams created by Tennessee Valley Authority (estab. 1933) control flooding and provide h.e.p.

Tennessee Valley Authority (TVA), independent, govt.-supported agency, created (1933) by US Congress, empowered to develop Muscle Shoals, Alabama, and integrate power and irrigation projects of Tennessee R. basin. Widespread programme arrested flood damage, soil erosion, provided stimulus for growth of region.

Tenniel, Sir John (1820-1914), English caricaturist. Cartoonist of *Punch* for 50 years (1851-1901). Illustrated *Alice in Wonderland* (1866) and *Through the Looking-Glass* (1870).

tennis or **lawn tennis,** ball-and-racket game played by 2 or 4 players on prepared surface, either indoors or outdoors. Descended from royal game (real tennis) played in France and England in 14th cent. Modern game devised by Major Wingfield in England (1873); 1st Wimbledon championships held 1877. International tournaments restricted to amateur players until late 1960s, esp. popular in US, Australia, England, Europe.

Alfred Tennyson

Tennyson, Alfred Tennyson, 1st Baron (1809-92), English poet. Wrote short lyrics, *eg* 'Ulysses' 'Break, Break, Break', elegies incl. *In Memoriam* (1850). Longer narrative poems incl. *The Charge of the Light Brigade* (1855), *Idylls of the King* (1859-88) on Arthurian legends. Created poet laureate (1850).

tenor, in singing, high male voice, below alto but above baritone. Also member of family of instruments of similar range, *eg* tenor trombone.

tenrec, nocturnal insectivorous mammal of Tenrecidae family, found in Madagascar. Species incl. hedgehog tenrec, *Setifer setosus,* with spines on back; rolls into ball for protection.

Tensing Norkay, *see* HILLARY, SIR EDMUND.

tent caterpillar, hairy moth caterpillar, genus *Malacosoma,* that lives colonially in tent-like webs spun in trees. Causes serious defoliation; common in North America.

tepee or **tipi,** *see* WIGWAM.

tequila, Mexican spirit distilled from fermented juice of various agaves.

terbium (Tb), metallic element of lanthanide series; at. no. 65, at. wt. 158.92. Occurs in gadolinite; difficult to isolate.

Ter Borch, Gerard (1617-81), Dutch painter. Known for his small portraits and scenes of prosperous middle-class life. Most famous work is *Peace of Münster.*

terebinth, *Pistacia terebinthus,* small European tree. Bark yields turpentine.

Terence, full name Publius Terentius Afer (*c* 195-159 BC), Roman comic poet. After Plautus, leading adapter of Greek New Comedy for Roman stage. Influenced modern comedy of manners. Works incl. *Andria, Hecyra, Eunuchus* and *Adelphi.*

Teresina, town of N Brazil, cap. of Piauí state; on Parnaíba R. Pop. 221,000. Agric., livestock market, sugar refining; textiles, soap mfg.

Terman, Lewis Madison (1877-1956), American psychologist. Known for Stanford Revision of Binet-Simon Intelligence Tests (1916; 2nd revision 1937), application of intelligence tests to school children, and studies of genius.

Terminus, in Roman religion, god of boundaries and landmarks.

Termites

termite, any of order Isoptera of soft-bodied social insects. Lives in colonies composed of several castes: fertile winged forms, sterile workers and soldiers, *etc.* Builds or tunnels large nests; feeds on wood, destroying trees and wooden structures. Most species are tropical.

Arctic tern (Sterna macrura)

tern, migratory seabird of Laridae family, related to gull. Species incl. common tern, *Sterna hirundo,* of Europe and North America; slender body, forked tail, graceful flight.

Terni, city of Umbria, C Italy, cap. of Terni prov. Pop. 106,000. Railway jct., iron and steel, munitions; h.e.p. from nearby waterfalls. Founded 7th cent. BC. Birthplace of Tacitus.

terpenes, in chemistry, series of unsaturated hydrocarbons, found in resins and essential oils. Used in perfumes and medicine.

Terpsichore, in Greek myth, Muse of dancing. Represented with lyre and plectrum.

terracotta, hard reddish brick-like earthenware, porous and unglazed. Used since antiquity for statues, figures, vases, *etc.*

terrapin, name applied to several species of edible aquatic turtles. Species incl. diamond back terrapin, *Malaclemys terrapin,* found in salt marshes of S and E US.

terrier, breed of dog originally used to dig out burrowing animals. Breeds incl. Boston, bull, cairn, fox, Scottish and Skye terriers.

Territorial Army, British volunteer force. Estab. under Territorial and Reserve Forces Act of 1907. Replaced in 1967 by a smaller Territorial and Army Volunteer Reserve.

Terry, Dame Ellen Alice (1847-1928), English actress. Acted opposite Henry Irving, accompanying him on American tours. Notable in Shakespearian roles.

Tertiary period, first geological period of Cenozoic era; began *c* 65 million years ago, lasted *c* 63 million years. Comprises Palaeocene, Eocene, Oligocene, Miocene,

Pliocene epochs. Alpine, Himalayan mountain-building period. Evolution of primitive mammals, ancestors of modern fauna, *eg* mammoths, man-like apes; had modern birds. Deterioration of climate toward end of period. Also *see* GEOLOGICAL TABLE.

Tertullian (*c* 160- *c* 230), Roman theologian. Converted to Christianity (*c* 197). Wrote powerful defences of faith. Followed MONTANISM, latterly estab. Tertullianist sect.

Tesin (Ger. *Teschen,* Pol. *Cieszyn*), town of S Poland and N Czechoslovakia, divided by border. Pop. 24,000. In former duchy of Tesin; under Austrian rule until 1919. Disputed (1920) by Poland, Czechoslovakia. E part given to former, W part (incl. coalfield) to latter.

Test Act, legislation passed (1673) by English Parliament to exclude from office those who refused to take oaths of supremacy and allegiance and to receive communion according to Church of England. Repealed (1828).

test-ban treaty, *see* DISARMAMENT.

testis or **testicle,** either of two oval male sex glands which are suspended in the scrotum. Secretes spermatozoa and sex hormone testosterone.

testosterone, male steroid sex hormone, obtained as white crystalline substance from animal testes. Promotes development of male secondary sex characteristics.

tetanus or **lockjaw,** acute infectious disease caused by toxin released by bacterium *Clostridium tetani,* which usually enters body through wounds. Toxin disturbs motor nerve cells, causing muscular spasms, esp. in jaw, face and neck. Prevented by vaccination, treated with tetanus antitoxin.

tetracycline, any of group of broad-spectrum antibiotics derived from bacteria of genus *Streptomyces.*

Tetuán or **Tétouan,** city of N Morocco. Pop. 137,000. Textile, leather industs.; Mediterranean outport at Río Martín exports agric. produce. Former cap. of Spanish Morocco (1912-56).

Tetzel, Johann (*c* 1465-1519), German monk, preacher. Dominican, licensed to sell indulgences. Arrival in Saxony (1517) provoked attack by Luther in 95 theses.

Teutonic Knights, members of medieval German military and religious order, founded *c* 1190 in Holy Land. Undertook conquest of pagan E Prussia (13th cent.), where they estab. their rule. Gradually lost power to the Poles after defeat at Tannenberg (1410).

Teutonic mythology, pre-Christian religious mythology of tribes of Germany and Scandinavia. Originally 2 groups of gods: Aesir, Vanir; Vanir was absorbed by Aesir. Chief gods incl. Woden (ODIN), Tiw, Thor, Frey and Freyja; all lived in the palace of Valhalla in ASGARD. Gods were not immortal and most were doomed to die at RAGNAROK. Related stories, with some Christian influence, found in Icelandic Norse myths.

Tewkesbury, mun. bor. of Gloucestershire, SW England, on R. Severn. Pop. 9000. Has Norman abbey (12th cent.). Scene of Yorkist victory ending Wars of the Roses (1471).

Texas, state of SC US; on Gulf of Mexico. Area 692,408 sq km (267,339 sq mi); pop. 11,197,000; cap. Austin; main cities Houston, Dallas, San Antonio. Prairies in N Panhandle, plains in W, Rio Grande separates Texas from Mexico, Red R. forms NE border. Greatest agric. yield in US. Livestock, major cotton crop, rice, grains; minerals esp. oil, natural gas. Space research indust. Spanish settlement in 18th cent. Americans ousted Mexicans (1835-6). Republic until annexed by US (1845), precipitating Mexican War. Admitted to Union as 28th state (1845). Joined Confederacy in Civil War.

Texel, NW Netherlands. Largest of West FRISIAN ISLANDS, area 181 sq km (70 sq mi). Summer resort; sheep rearing.

Thackeray, William Makepeace (1811-63), English author, b. India. Masterpiece *Vanity Fair* (1847-8) uses self-seeking adventuress as heroine to expose hypocrisy of social code. Other novels incl. *Pendennis* (1850), *Henry Esmond* (1852), *The Newcomes* (1853-5).

Thai, Sino-Tibetan language group. Incl. Laotian, Shan, Thai.

Thailand, kingdom of SE Asia. Area *c* 514,000 sq km (198,500 sq mi); pop. 41,023,000; cap. Bangkok. Language:

Thailand

Thai. Religion: Hinayana Buddhism. C plain watered by R. Chao Phraya, major rice producing area; S is narrow strip extending down Malay penin. Mainly agric. economy; produces tin, tungsten, rubber, teak. Siamese kingdom dates from 14th cent.; frequent wars with Burmese; lost territ. to British and French in 19th-20th cent. Constitutional monarchy (1932). Formerly Siam, name changed 1939.

Thales (*c* 636-*c* 546 BC), Greek philosopher, mathematician, astronomer. Regarded as first Western philosopher. Believed water to be fundamental matter of Nature.

Thalia, in Greek myth, Muse of comedy. Represented with comic mask, shepherd's staff or wreath of ivy.

thalidomide, drugs used as a sedative in Europe (1958-61). Withdrawn when found to cause defects of limbs in unborn children if taken during 1st 12 weeks of pregnancy. Discovery led to adoption of stricter regulations in testing of new drugs.

thallium (Tl), rare soft metallic element, similar to lead; at. no. 81, at. wt. 204.37. Obtained from flue dust during processing of pyrites ores. Thallium and its compounds are poisonous; used in insecticides, rat poison, and alloys.

Thames, river of S England. Flows 338 km (210 mi) from Cotswolds via Oxford, Reading, London to North Sea. Tidal to Teddington, W London; hist. major waterway, serving port of London. Boating, angling above London.

Thanet, Isle of, Kent, SE England. True isl. until 16th cent. Resorts incl. Ramsgate, Margate.

Thanjavur, city of Tamil Nadu, SE India. Pop. 140,000. Silks, jewellery, brassware mfg. Has temple to Siva (11th cent.). Formerly Tanjore.

Thanksgiving Day, US national holiday. Commemorates 1st harvest of Plymouth Colony and celebration feast held by Pilgrims and neighbouring Indians. Celebrated 4th Thursday in Nov.; also observed in Canada.

Thant, U (1909-74), Burmese diplomat. Succeeded Dag Hammarskjöld as UN secretary-general (1961-72); granted wider emergency powers. Sought to bring stability to Middle East.

Thásos, isl. of Greece, in N Aegean Sea. Area 399 sq km (154 sq mi). Olives, vines. Famous goldmines, exploited by Phoenicians. Turkish from 1455, passed to Greece 1913.

Thatcher, Margaret Hilda, née Roberts (1925-), British politician. Succeeded Edward Heath as leader of Conservative Party (1975), becoming 1st woman ever to head major UK party.

theatre, building for presentation of dramatic performances. Originally an outdoor auditorium for Greek drama, first recorded *c* 5th cent. BC. In Middle Ages, European religious drama performed in churches and in open. Palladio's Teatro Olimpico (1580) was 1st indoor secular theatre. English Elizabethan theatres used courtyard plan, open to the air. By 17th-18th cent., audience separated from performers by raised stage, lights, curtains. 'Theatre in the round', with actors entirely surrounded by audience, is 20th cent. innovation.

Thebes, ancient city of C Egypt, site now occupied by Karnak and Luxor. *Fl* between XI and XX dynasties (2134-1085 BC) as cap. of Upper Egypt, centre of Amon worship.

Many remains, incl. Tutankhamen's tomb (discovered 1922) in nearby Valley of the Kings.

Thebes (mod. *Thívai*), ancient city of Boeotia, SE Greece. Led Boeotian League; fought against Athens in Persian, Peloponnesian Wars. Defeated Sparta, at Leuctra (371 BC). Defeated and destroyed (336 BC) by Alexander the Great.

theft, *see* LARCENY.

Theiss, *see* TISZA, Hungary.

Themis, in Greek myth, a Titan; goddess of law and order. Mother by Zeus of HORAE and FATES.

Themistocles (*c* 525-*c* 460 BC), Athenian statesman. Responsible for the building of a strong Athenian navy. During Persian invasion of Greece (480), planned both the evacuation of Athens and Greek naval victory at Salamis. Exiled by his opponents (471), fled to Persia.

Thénard, Louis-Jacques (1777-1857), French chemist. Discovered hydrogen peroxide and blue porcelain stain. Collaborated with Gay-Lussac in many discoveries.

Theocritus (*fl* 270 BC), Greek poet. Regarded as founder of pastoral poetry, using own background of Sicily which, when imitated later, became artificial, set form for genre. Poems known as idylls.

Theodora (*c* 508-48), Byzantine empress. An actress and prostitute before her marriage to Justinian I (523), she exerted a strong influence over Justinian. Ordered BELISARIUS to suppress the Nika revolt (532) when Justinian was about to flee Constantinople.

Theodorakis, Mikis (1925-), Greek composer. Noted for, esp. through his melodious songs, revival of Greek popular music in 1960s. Imprisoned for Communist sympathies; music banned during military dictatorship in Greece.

Theodoric the Great (*c* 454-526), king of Ostrogoths (*c* 474-526). Encouraged by Roman emperor of the East, Zeno, to invade Italy (488), he completed his conquest with defeat of ODOVACAR at Ravenna (493). Ruled ably after having Odovacar murdered.

Theodosian Code, Roman legal code issued (AD 438) by Theodosius II, emperor of the East. Was collection of imperial constitutions for benefit of public officials. Used in compiling *Corpus juris civilis.*

Theodosius [I] the Great (*c* 346-95), Roman emperor in the East (379-95). Proclaimed emperor in the East by Gratian, he defeated the puppet emperor in the West, Eugenius, and replaced him by his own son Honorius. Empire remained split after his death.

theology, the study of God, his attributes and relation with universe. Systematic theology concerns specific doctrine, *eg* Christianity.

theosophy, term for various systems which claim direct mystical contact with divine principle. Esp. doctrines of the Theosophical Society founded by Mme BLAVATSKY to promote study of comparative religions and philosophies.

Theresa of Avila, St, orig. Teresa de Cepeda y Ahumada (1515-82), Spanish nun, mystic. Founded (1562) reformed order of (Discalced) Carmelite nuns. Inspired revival and Catholic Reformation. Devotional works incl. *The Way of Perfection* (*c* 1565).

Theresa of Lisieux, St, orig. Thérèse Martin (1873-97), French Carmelite nun, called 'Little Flower of Jesus'. Spiritual autobiog. *The Story of a Soul* (1897) with account of 'little way' of humble goodness became immensely popular.

thermae, in Roman architecture, public baths, often elaborately decorated and of great architectural splendour. Earliest date from *c* 25 BC; surviving examples incl. Thermae of Caracalla (AD 217) at Rome.

Thermidor, eleventh month of French Revolutionary calendar. Revolution of 9 Thermidor, year 2, (27 July, 1794) saw overthrow of ROBESPIERRE and end of Reign of Terror; those responsible were called Thermidorians.

thermionic valve, electronic device consisting of heated cathode which emits electrons, an anode which attracts the electrons, and possibly further perforated grids which control electron flow. Arrangement is placed in glass or metal envelope, usually evacuated or containing gas at low pressure. *See* DIODE, TRIODE.

thermit, mixture of aluminium powder and metal oxide (*eg* iron oxide). Emits tremendous heat when ignited by magnesium ribbon. Used esp. in welding and for incendiary bombs.

thermocouple, device used to measure temperature. Consists of pair of different metals joined at each end; one end is kept at fixed temperature, other is placed at point whose temperature is to be found. Temperature difference causes thermoelectric current to flow which is measured by suitably calibrated galvanometer.

thermodynamics, mathematical study of relation between heat and other forms of energy, and the conversion of one form into another. Based on 3 laws, concerning conservation of energy principle and concept of entropy. Applied to theory of heat engines and chemical reactions.

thermometer, instrument used to measure temperature. Common type consists of graduated sealed glass tube with bulb containing mercury or coloured alcohol. Other types used incl. thermocouple, platinum resistance thermometer.

thermonuclear reaction, nuclear fusion reaction between atomic nuclei whose energy is derived from thermal agitation. Principle is employed in hydrogen bomb. Controlled thermonuclear reaction as means of energy production involves problem of containing deuterium and tritium gas at temperatures as high as $5 \times 10^{9°}$ C.

Thermopylae, pass of EC Greece. Here Leonidas' 300 Spartans heroically resisted Persians under Xerxes (480 BC).

Theseus slaying the Minotaur (design on red Attic bowl)

Theseus, in Greek myth, son of Aegeus, king of Athens, or of Poseidon. Heroic deeds incl. killing of Minotaur of Crete (with help of ARIADNE). Abducted Queen Hippolyte who bore him Hippolytus. Married Phaedra, sister of Ariadne. Helped Pirithous abduct Persephone; sent to Hades, but rescued by Heracles. Returned to Athens, found his kingdom in rebellion; sailed to Skyros where he was murdered by King Lycomedes.

Thespis (*fl* 6th cent. BC), Greek poet. Traditionally regarded as inventor of tragedy. First to appear in tragedy as actor replying to chorus, thereby introducing dialogue into hitherto choral performance.

Thessalonians, two epistles of NT, written (*c* AD 52) by St Paul from Corinth to church at Thessalonica. Praises faith of Thessalonians but corrects false ideas about general resurrection and the Second Coming.

Thessaloniki, see SALONIKA, Greece.

Thessaly (*Thessalía*), region of EC Greece. Mountains flank central fertile lowland drained by R. Peneus. United under Jason (374 BC), fell (344 BC) to Philip II of Macedon; part of Roman Macedonia. Turkish from 1355, passed to Greece 1881.

Thetford, mun. bor. of Norfolk, E England. Pop. 14,000. Market town. Has Castle Hill mound (6th cent.); ruined priory (1104).

Thetford Mines, town of S Québec, Canada. Pop. 22,000. Major asbestos mining centre.

Thetis, in Greek myth, one of Nereids and mother of Achilles. Loved by Zeus and Poseidon but given by them in marriage to mortal Peleus because of prophecy that her son would be greater than his father.

thiamin or **vitamin B₁,** vitamin of B group, found in milk, liver, beans, peas, *etc.* Essential to carbohydrate metabolism; deficiency results in beriberi.

Thibault, Jacques Anatole François, see FRANCE, ANATOLE.

Thiers, [Louis] Adolphe (1797-1877), French statesman. Writings in journal *National* helped precipitate July Revolution (1830); held various offices under Louis Philippe. Later, led opposition in legislature to Napoleon III's policies. Negotiated peace after Franco-Prussian War (1871), suppressed Paris Commune. First president of Third Republic (1871-3). Written works incl. *History of the French Revolution* (1823-7).

Thieu, Nguyen van (1923-), South Vietnamese political leader, president (1967-75). Rose to prominence in army, helped overthrow Diem (1963). Nominal president (1965), exercised near-dictatorial powers after official election. Fled country shortly before capitulation of South Vietnam to Communist forces (April, 1975).

Thimbu, see BHUTAN.

Thionville (Ger. *Diedenhofen*), town of Lorraine, NE France, on R. Moselle. Pop. 39,000. Iron and steel centre. Taken by Prussia after siege (1870), returned (1919).

Third Reich, name given by Hitler to German state under his dictatorship (1933-45). Supposed to last 1000 years.

Third World, name given to those technologically underdeveloped nations of Africa, Asia and Latin America. Distinguished from technologically advanced Western nations and those of Soviet bloc. China not usually considered Third World country.

Thirteen Colonies, name applied to British colonies of North America that fought American Revolution and founded United States. They were Massachusetts, New Hampshire, Rhode Island, Connecticut, New York, New Jersey, Pennsylvania, Delaware, Maryland, Virginia, North Carolina, South Carolina and Georgia.

Thirty-nine Articles, basic CREED of Church of England. Originally drawn up (1551-3), revised and adopted by Convocation (1562). Estab. by Act of Parliament (1571).

Thirty Years War, European conflict (1618-48), fought mainly in Germany, involving religious and territ. struggle between German princes, variously supported by external powers, and Holy Roman Empire. War precipitated by refusal of Protestant nobles in Bohemia to elect Emperor Ferdinand II king; revolt crushed (1620). War continued in Palatinate; imperial victories led to Danish intervention (1625), effectively crushed by WALLENSTEIN and TILLY (1626-9). Victories of Gustavus Adolphus of Sweden (1631-2) recovered N Germany for Protestants; imperial cause improved with death of Gustavus (1632). War spread beyond Germany after France allied with Sweden (1635). Eventual settlement came with PEACE OF WESTPHALIA, which broke power of Empire and confirmed French ascendancy.

Thisbe, see PYRAMUS AND THISBE.

thistle, any of genera *Onopordum, Cirsium* and *Cnicus* of spiny-leaved plants of composite family. Heads consist of many small, purple, yellow, pink or white flowers followed by wind-borne seeds (thistledown). Species incl. Scotch thistle, *O. acanthium,* the emblem of Scotland, bull thistle, *Cirsium lanceolatum,* and Canada thistle, *Cirsium arvense.*

Thistlewood, Arthur (1770-1820), English conspirator. Active in trying to bring about revolution in Britain. Leader in Cato Street conspiracy to assassinate cabinet ministers; after plot failed, he and 4 others hanged for treason.

Thomas, St (*fl* 1st cent. AD), one of the Twelve Disciples, also known as Didymus (Gk.,=twin). Doubted

Scotch thistle

Resurrection of Christ until he saw Jesus, touched his side. Traditionally, went to S India or Parthia.

Dylan Thomas in 1946

Thomas, Dylan Marlais (1914-53), Welsh poet. Wrote intricate life-affirming verse, *eg Deaths and Entrances* (1946), radio play *Under Milk Wood* (1954). Also wrote prose autobiog. *Portrait of the Artist as a Young Dog* (1940).

Thomas, [Philip] Edward (1878-1917), English author. Writing reflects love of English countryside. Works incl. prose nature studies, *eg The Heart of England* (1906), biogs., *eg* of Richard Jefferies (1909), *Collected Poems* (1920).

Thomas à Becket, St (*c* 1118-70), English churchman, martyr. Befriended by Henry II, appointed chancellor (1155) and archbishop of Canterbury (1162). Opposed king over taxation. Henry's attempt in Constitutions of Clarendon (1164) to secure jurisdiction over clergy ended in Becket's flight to Rome. Quarrel after return led to murder of Becket in Canterbury Cathedral. Henry did public penance (1174), built shrine.

Thomas à Kempis (*c* 1380-1471), German monk. Augustinian; reputed author of famous devotional work, *The Imitation of Christ.*

Thomas Aquinas, St (1225-74), Italian philosopher. Major figure of SCHOLASTICISM. Member of Dominican order; pupil of Albertus Magnus. Taught at Paris. His system, known as Thomism, became official Catholic theology in 1879. Major work is *Summa theologica* (1267-73).

Thompson, David (1770-1857), Canadian geographer and explorer, b. England. Explored Rocky Mts.; 1st white man to reach source of Columbia R. (1807). Produced map of W Canada (1814).

Thompson, Francis (1859-1907), English poet. Wrote mystic, religious verse, *eg* 'The Hound of Heaven' in *Poems* (1893).

Thompson, John Taliaferro (1860-1940), American army officer. Invented (1920) .45 calibre submachine gun, known as 'tommy-gun', used in WWII.

Thomson, James (1700-48), Scottish poet. Wrote *The Seasons* (1730) depicting universal order in wide-ranging nature poetry. Also wrote social satire *The Castle of Indolence* (1748), patriotic song 'Rule Britannia'.

Thomson, Sir Joseph John (1856-1940). English physicist. Awarded Nobel Prize for Physics (1906) for study of conduction of electricity through gases exposed to X-rays. Measured charge to mass ratio of cathode rays (1897) and deduced that these rays were beams of subatomic particles (electrons). His son, **Sir George Paget Thomson** (1892-1975), also a physicist, discovered electron diffraction. Shared Nobel Prize for Physics (1937).

Thomson, Roy Herbert, 1st Baron Thomson of Fleet (1894-1976), British newspaper owner, b. Canada. Controlled newspapers, radio and TV stations in Britain and Canada. Acquired Times Newspapers Ltd. (1966).

Thonburi, city of SC Thailand, on R. Chao Phraya opposite Bangkok. Pop. 628,000. Rice milling and sawmilling. Has Wat Arun temple. Cap. of Siam (1767-82).

Thor, in Norse and Teutonic myth, god of thunder, patron of peasants and warriors. Attributes incl. hammer which returned when he threw it and belt of strength. Sometimes identified with Roman Jupiter, thus Jove's day became Thor's day (Thursday).

thorax, in higher vertebrates, part of body between neck and abdomen, containing heart and lungs, protected by ribs. In mammals, diaphragm separates it from abdomen. In insects, thorax consists of 3 segments bearing legs and wings.

Thoreau, Henry David (1817-62), American poet, naturalist. Associate of EMERSON. Wrote *Walden* (1854) recording observations of nature, thoughts about society, after 2 years spent in isolated cabin. Other works incl. essay 'Civil Disobedience' (1849) which influenced Gandhi.

Thorfinn Karlsefni (*fl* 11th cent.), Icelandic navigator. Led colonizing expedition from Greenland to NE North America (*c* 1010); project later abandoned.

thorium (Th), radioactive metallic element; at. no. 90, at. wt. 232.04. Occurs in monazite sands. Used in filaments and as nuclear fuel; oxide used in gas mantles.

Thorndike, Dame [Agnes] Sybil (1882-1976), English actress. Known for leading roles in works of Shakespeare, Shaw.

Thornhill, Sir James (1675-1734), English decorative painter. Only English decorator in European Baroque tradition, he painted panels for dome of St Paul's Cathedral and decorated hall of Greenwich Hospital.

Thorpe, James ('Jim') (1888-1953), American athlete. All-American football player at Carlisle Indian School (1911-12). Forced to give up gold medals in pentathlon and decathlon events in 1912 Olympics after discovery of earlier professional activity in baseball.

Thorshavn, see FAEROES, Denmark.

Thorwaldsen, Bertel (1768-1844), Danish sculptor. A leader of the neo-Classical movement, much of his work is modelled on antique Greek sculpture; enormously successful, he employed a large workshop. Works incl. *Jason* and *Lion of Lucerne*.

Thoth, ancient Egyptian god of wisdom and magic. Credited with invention of hieroglyphics, geometry, *etc.* Represented as human with ibis head. Identified by Greeks with HERMES TRISMEGISTUS.

Thousand and One Nights, see ARABIAN NIGHTS.

Thousand Islands, group of *c* 1800 isls. on Canada-US border in St Lawrence R., at E end of L. Ontario. Popular summer resort area.

Thrace (*Thráki*), region of NE Greece. Main town Komotíni. Tobacco, wheat, cotton. Formerly much larger, incl. S Bulgaria to R. Danube, European Turkey. Did not accept Greek culture; Greek colonies traded gold, silver. Subdued (342 BC) by Philip II of Macedon; *fl* under

Romans. Hist. battleground; present borders fixed after Balkan Wars, WWI.

Thrale, Hester Lynch, *see* PIOZZI.

thrasher, North American songbird of Mimidae family. Species incl. thrush-like brown thrasher, *Toxostoma rufum,* with long tail, curved bill, chestnut upper-parts.

Three Age system, scheme devised (1816-19) by Danish archaeologist C. Thomsen for dividing prehist. into Stone, Bronze and Iron Ages, which followed each other in this order. Scheme was gradually elaborated by further subdivisions of the 3 ages.

Three Emperors' League, informal agreement (1872) between Germany, Russia and Austria-Hungary to maintain social order and ensure peace between Russia and Austria-Hungary. Superseded by TRIPLE ALLIANCE.

Three Rivers, see TROIS RIVIÈRES, Canada.

thrift, any of genus *Armeria,* esp. *A. maritima,* common thrift or sea pink found on sea cliffs and salt marshes. Cultivated for globe-shaped, papery flowers which may be dried as EVERLASTING FLOWERS.

thrips, any of order Thysanoptera of minute black or yellowish insects. Feeds on juice of plants. *Heliothrips haemorrhoidalis* is common greenhouse variety.

throat, passage leading from arch of the palate to upper openings of trachea and oesophagus. Incl. PHARYNX.

thrombosis, clotting of blood in an artery or vein. In coronary thrombosis, clot forms in coronary artery or its branches; loss of blood supply may cause death (infarction) of heart tissue. Also *see* APOPLEXY.

European mistle thrush

thrush, widely distributed songbird of Turdidae family, with dark spots on light breast. Species incl. European mistle thrush, *Turdus viscivorus,* which feeds on mistletoe berries, and American robin, *T. migratorius.*

Thucydides (*c* 460-400 BC), Greek historian. After an unsuccessful command against the Spartans in the Peloponnesian War, he went into exile from Athens (424-404). During his exile, wrote *History of the Peloponnesian War,* an objective and analytical account of war until 411.

Thugs or **Phansigars,** secret Indian religious sect, incl. both Hindus and Moslems. Worshipped Hindu goddess Kali, strangling victims as sacrifices to her. Suppressed by British (1829-48).

Thule, name given by ancients to most N land of Europe, variously identified as Norway, Iceland, Shetland Isls. Modern Thule is settlement (pop. *c* 550) of NW Greenland, founded 1910. Major US air base nearby.

thulium (Tm), metallic element, rarest of lanthanide series; at. no. 69, at. wt. 168.93.

Thun, town of WC Switzerland. Pop. 37,000. Metal goods, pottery; castle (12th cent.). On R. Aare at NW end of L. Thun (Ger. *Thunersee*), length 18 km (11 mi); boating, tourist area.

thunder, sound following lightning flash. Caused by rapid expansion of air produced by heat of lightning.

Thunder Bay, port of SW Ontario, Canada; on NW shore of L. Superior. Pop. 108,000. Shipping terminus of Great

Lakes; exports grain, iron ore. Has many grain elevators; pulp and paper, flour milling industs. Formed (1970) after amalgamation of Fort William and Port Arthur.

thunderstorm, storm accompanied by thunder, lightning, and often violent gusts of wind, heavy rain or hail. Strong upward currents of moist, rapidly cooling air form deep *cumulonimbus* clouds which produce rain, static electricity. Commonest over land areas of equatorial regions.

Thurber, James [Grover] (1894-1961), American humorist. Known for elegant pieces for *New Yorker,* eg 'The Secret Life of Walter Mitty', illustrated by himself. Collaborated on parody of 'scientific' sex articles, *Is Sex Necessary?* (1929). Collections of work incl. *The Seal in the Bedroom* (1932), *Men, Women, and Dogs* (1943).

Thuringia, region of SW East Germany. Main towns Erfurt, Mühlhausen. Hilly, crossed NW-SE by Thuringian Forest; main rivers Saale, White Elster. Agric., esp. cereals, sugar beet. Divided (1485) into several duchies; part of German empire from 1871. East German prov. after WWII (dissolved 1952).

Thurrock, urban dist. of Essex, SE England, on Thames estuary. Pop. 125,000. Formed 1936, incl. Port of London docks, Tilbury; oil refineries. Road Tunnel to Dartford (1963).

Thurso, town of Highland region, N Scotland. Pop. 9000. Dounreay nuclear power station nearby.

Thutmose III (d. *c* 1436 BC), Egyptian pharaoh. Extended his empire as far as the Euphrates. Enriched Egypt with the spoils of his campaigns. Built many temples dedicated to god Amon.

Thyestes, in Greek myth, son of Pelops and brother of ATREUS. Seduced Atreus' wife, Aerope. Regained throne of Mycenae with help of his son AEGISTHUS.

Common garden thyme

thyme, any of genus *Thymus* of shrubby plants or aromatic herbs of mint family. White, pink or red flowers used in seasoning. European *T. vulgaris* is a common garden variety.

thymus gland, ductless gland-like body found in base of neck. Shrinks in size after puberty, becoming vestigial. Plays important role in development of infant's immune system.

thyroid gland, ductless gland in front of neck, consisting of 2 lobes on each side of trachea connected by thin tissue. Secretes iodine-containing hormone thyroxine which accelerates carbohydrate metabolism and release of energy.

Tiber (*Tevere*), river of C Italy. Flows 405 km (252 mi) from Tuscan Apennines via Rome to Tyrrhenian Sea at Fiumicino and Ostia.

Tiberias, town on sea of Galilee. Pop. 24,000. Trade centre; holiday resort noted for hot springs.

Tiberias, Lake, see GALILEE, SEA OF.

Tiberius [Claudius Nero] (42 BC–AD 37), Roman emperor (AD 14-37). Succeeded his stepfather Augustus. Improved finances of the empire by reforming taxation system and imposing economies. Lived as recluse in Capri towards end of life, becoming cruel, tyrannical.

Tibesti Mountains, mountain range of Sahara desert, NC Africa, in N Chad and S Libya. Volcanic in origin, rise to Emi Koussi (3412 m/ 11,200 ft).

Tibet, auton. region of SW China. Area *c* 1,221,700 sq km (471,700 sq mi); pop. (est.) 1,400,000; cap. Lhasa. High

plateau, *c* 4880 m (16,000 ft), lying between Kunlun Mts. in N and Himalayas in S. Agric. in Tsangpo valley; rough grazing. Largely unexploited mineral resources. Chief religion: Lamaism. Theocratic kingdom under Dalai Lama from 7th cent. Often claimed by China; absorbed 1950. Dalai Lama fled to India after suppression of 1959 revolt.

Tibetan, language group within Tibetan-Burman branch of Sino-Tibetan family. Spoken in Tibet, Tsinghai and Kansu provs. of China, and in Bhutan, Nepal, Sikkim and part of Kashmir.

Tibetan-Burman, one of three main branches of Sino-Tibetan family of languages.

Tibullus, Albius (*c* 48–19 BC), Roman poet. Known for elegies, esp. on erotic themes.

Ticino (Ger. *Tessin*), canton of S Switzerland. Area 2813 sq km (1086 sq mi); cap. Bellinzona. Mainly mountainous; lakes incl. Maggiore, Lugano. Tourism, vines, tobacco. Pop. is Italian-speaking, RC. Joined Swiss Confederation (1803). Source of R. **Ticino,** flows 257 km (160 mi) via L. Maggiore to R. Po near Pavia (Italy).

tick, parasitic wingless arachnid of order Acarina. Sucks blood of mammals and birds; may spread diseases, incl. forms of typhus.

tide, alternate rise and fall of surface of oceans, seas, bays and rivers. Caused by gravitational pull of Moon and Sun; level rises and falls twice per lunar day (24 hrs., 50 mins.). Spring tides occur when Moon and Sun act together, giving higher high tide, lower low tide; neap tides occur when they act in opposition, reducing amplitude.

Tieck, [Johann] Ludwig (1773-1853). German author. Leading Romantic. Known for dramatization of folk tales, *eg* satirical comedy *Puss in Boots* (1797). Also wrote novel *Franz Sternbald's Wanderings* (1798), translated *Don Quixote.*

Tien Shan, mountain range of C Asia, in Kirghiz SSR and Sinkiang auton. region, China. Reaches 7439 m (24,406 ft) at Mt. Pobeda.

Tientsin, city of NE China in Hopeh prov., admin. directly by central govt. Pop. 4,500,000. International port on Grand Canal and Hai Ho. Chemical, metallurgical, textile industs. Has Nankai Univ. (1919). Treaty port for French and British (1860); walls razed by Europeans during Boxer Rebellion (1900). Japanese occupation 1937-43.

Tiepolo, Giovanni Battista (1696-1770), Italian painter. Leading exponent of Venetian rococo style, he is renowned for his fresco decorations, *eg* in episcopal palace at Würzburg and royal palace in Madrid.

Tierra del Fuego, archipelago of extreme S South America, separated from mainland by Magellan Str. Divided between Chile and Argentina. Main isl. consists of flat tableland (sheep, timber production). Cape Horn is in S. Frequent high winds and heavy rainfall on coast.

Tiffany, Louis Comfort (1848-1933), American artist, designer. Famous for invention of Favrile glass, characterized by iridescent colour and flowing shapes. Founded decorating firm of Tiffany Studios.

Tiflis, *see* TBILISI.

tiger, *Panthera tigris,* large lion-sized cat, widely distributed in Asia. Coat usually orange-yellow striped with black; no mane. Hunts at night.

tiger beetle, any of Cicindelidae family of brightly-coloured carnivorous beetles. Active predator, found in sandy places; commonest in tropics. Larvae burrow in soil and seize passing prey.

tiger moth, any of Arctiidae family of moths with brightly striped or spotted wings. Larvae (woolly bears) are brown hairy caterpillars. Species incl. common tiger moth, *Arctia caia,* of N hemisphere.

Tigris, river of SW Asia. Length *c* 1850 km (1150 mi). Rises in E Turkey, flows through Iraq, merges with Euphrates to form Shatt-al-Arab. Watered ancient Mesopotamia. Large flood control and irrigation scheme near Baghdad. Navigable to Baghdad for shallow draught vessels.

Tihwa, *see* URUMCHI.

Tijuana, resort of NW Mexico, in Baja California. Pop. 335,000. Varied tourist industs.; gambling casinos, racecourses, bull rings.

Tiger

Tilburg, city of S Netherlands, in North Bribant. Pop. 155,000. Railway jct.; textile centre, dyeing.

Tilbury, see THURROCK, England.

Tilden, Samuel Jones (1814-86), American politician. Took leading part in breaking corrupt 'Tweed Ring' which dominated New York City politics. Governor of New York (1875-6). Defeated as Democratic presidential candidate (1876), although electoral returns of 4 states were in error.

till, see BOULDER CLAY.

Tillett, Benjamin (1860-1943), English labour organizer. Co-leader, with Tom Mann, John Burns, of 1889 dock strike, important step towards British unionization. Labour MP after WWI.

Tilly, Jan Tserklaes, Count von (1559-1632), Flemish army officer. Commanded Catholic army in Thirty Years War, won victories at White Mt. and Prague (1620), took Magdeburg (1631) but lost to Gustavus Adolphus at Breitenfeld (1631). Died of wounds after defeat at the Lech (1632).

Tilsit, see SOVETSK.

Timaru, city of E South Isl., New Zealand, on Caroline Bay. Pop. 28,000. Port, market town in sheep raising, wheat growing area; exports meat, wool, grain; fishing; tourist resort.

timber wolf, see WOLF.

Timbuktu (Fr. *Tombouctou*), town of C Mali, near R. Niger. Pop. 10,000. First settled 11th cent.; long famous as centre of caravan trade routes, slave market. Fl 14th-16th cent. as Moslem commercial, educational centre. Taken by French (1893).

Times, The, British national daily newspaper. Founded (1785) by John Walter, called *The Times* after 1788. Reputation for serious reporting, comment, as well as letters page. Name also used for renowned *New York Times* founded (1851) by H.J. Raymond.

Timgad, ruined city of NE Algeria. Ancient Roman *Thamugadi,* founded AD 100 by Trajan; destroyed (7th cent.) by Berbers. Excavation began 1881, remains incl. forum, baths, arch.

Timişoara (Hung. *Temesvár*), city of W Romania. Pop. 205,000. Railway jct., indust. centre; univ. (1945), 2 cathedrals. Former cap. of the BANAT OF TEMESVÁR; annexed by Hungary, Turkey, Savoy; passed to Romania (1920).

Timor, isl. of Malay Archipelago, most E of Lesser Sundas. Indonesian Timor in W part of isl. forms prov. of E Nusa Tenggara. Area *c* 15,000 sq km (5700 sq mi); pop. 823,000. Passed to Indonesia from Dutch 1950. **Portuguese Timor** comprises E half of isl. and an enclave on NW coast. Area *c* 19,000 sq km (7300 sq mi); pop. 610,000; cap. Dili (pop. 7000). Indonesian intervention in civil war (1975) led to its forcible annexation by Indonesia.

Timoshenko, Semyon Konstantinovich (1895-1970), Russian marshal. Instrumental in victory over Finland (1939-40). In WWII, recaptured Rostov (1941), helped relieve Moscow.

Timothy

timothy or **timothy grass,** *Phleum pratense,* tall European grass with long cylindrical spikes. Grown in N US and Europe for hay.

Timothy, two epistles of NT, traditionally ascribed to St Paul. Prob. addressed to Timothy, bishop of Ephesus. Gives counsel on the safeguarding of Christian faith.

timpani, see DRUM.

tin (Sn), soft metallic element; at. no. 50, at. wt. 118.69. Exists in 3 allotropic forms; malleable, ductile, unaffected by water or air at normal temperatures. Occurs as cassiterite (SnO_2) in Bolivia and Malaysia. Used in tin plating and in alloys (solder, bronze, pewter).

tinamou, any of Tinamidae family of game birds of Central and South America. Ground-living but capable of flight. Species incl. crested tinamou, *Eudromia elegans,* of open pampas.

Tinbergen, Nikolaas (1907-), British zoologist, b. Netherlands. Studied animal behaviour, incl. social signals and their ritualization; awarded Nobel Prize for Medicine and Physiology (1973).

Tindal, Matthew (*c* 1655-1733), English deist. Works, violently condemned at time, *eg Christianity as Old as the Creation* (1730), outline rationalist position.

Tintagel Head, cape of Cornwall, SW England. Tintagel Castle traditional birthplace of King Arthur. Has ruined Celtic monastery.

Tintoretto, real name Jacopo Robusti (1518-94), Venetian painter. Leading Venetian mannerist, his works are marked by brilliant brushwork and dramatic use of light and colour. Works incl. great religious cycle in Scuola di San Rocco, Venice.

Tippecanoe, see WABASH, US.

Tipperary, county of Munster prov., SC Irish Republic. Area 4255 sq km (1643 sq mi); co. town Clonmel. Mountains (Galty, Knockmealdowns); fertile Golden Vale. Admin. divisions North Riding (pop. 54,000), South Riding (pop. 69,000). Towns incl. **Tipperary,** pop. 5000. Dairy produce; lace mfg.

Tippett, Sir Michael Kemp (1905-), English composer. Music combines appreciation of early English music and folk song with that of 20th cent. advances. Works incl. *Fantasia Concertante on a Theme of Corelli,* oratorio *A Child of Our Time,* opera *The Midsummer Marriage.*

Tippoo Sahib (*c* 1750-99), Indian prince, sultan of Mysore (1782-99). Continued French-backed wars of father, Hyder Ali, against British; eventually defeated by Cornwallis at Travancore (1792). Killed when British stormed Seringapatam.

Tirana (*Tiranë*), cap. of Albania. Pop. 175,000. Cultural indust. (textiles, soap, flour) centre; univ. (1957). Founded by Turks (17th cent.); rebuilt as cap. 1920. Has mosques.

tire, see TYRE.

Tiresias, in Greek myth, Theban blinded by Hera and given long life and gift of prophecy by Zeus. Consulted by Odysseus, revealed truth about OEDIPUS and warned Creon of consequences of defiance of divine laws. Appears in many Theban myths.

Tirol, see TYROL, Austria.

Tippoo Sahib

Tirana: Skanderbeg Square

prompted stricter safety regulations and permanent iceberg patrol.

titanium (Ti), metallic element resembling iron; at. no. 22, at. wt. 47.9. Compounds widely distributed in nature, but metal difficult to extract. Corrosion resistant, strong and light. Added to various steel alloys and used in aircraft and missiles because of heat-resisting properties.

Titans, in Greek myth, 6 sons and 6 daughters of Uranus and Gaea. Overthrew their father and ruled universe but defeated by OLYMPIAN GODS.

tithes, in Church of England, originally one tenth of produce of land paid by inhabitants of parish to support parish church and its incumbent. In 1836 commuted to a cash payment. System abolished in 1936.

Titian: *Bacchus and Ariadne*

Titian, real name Tiziano Vecellio (c 1487-1576), Venetian painter. Leading Venetian artist of High Renaissance, noted for dramatic use of colour. Worked for Emperor Charles V and Philip II of Spain. Developed esp. free handling of colour and form in late paintings. Works incl. religious subjects, *eg Assumption of the Virgin,* portraits, *eg Paul III and his Nephews,* and mythological subjects, *eg Rape of Europa.*

Titicaca, Lake, in WC South America, on Peru-Bolivia border. Area 8290 sq km (3200 sq mi). Drained by Desaguadero R. Highest lake in the world, alt. 3810 m (c 12,500 ft). Its ameliorating effect on temperature makes agric. possible.

Tito, Josip Broz (1892-   ), Yugoslav military and political leader, president (1953-   ). Led partisan resistance to German occupation in WWII. Became premier of new Communist republic (1945). Accused of deviation from orthodox Communist doctrine, withdrew Yugoslavia from Cominform (1948). Favoured policy of nonalignment, resisted Soviet attempts to reimpose hegemony. Sought to maintain national unity in face of Croatian separatists.

Titograd, town of SW Yugoslavia, cap. of Montenegro. Pop. 31,000. Known as Podgorica until 1948. Tobacco, foodstuffs. Has mosque, Turkish architecture.

titration, process of finding out how much of a certain substance is contained in known volume of solution by measuring how much of a standard solution is required to produce a given reaction.

Titus, epistle of NT, traditionally ascribed to St Paul. Addressed to Titus, bishop in Crete, giving advice on church govt.

Titus [Flavius Sabinus Vespasianus] (AD 39-81), Roman emperor (79-81), son of Vespasian. Completed building of Colosseum in Rome. Captured Jerusalem (70); commemorated by building Arch of Titus by Domitian (81).

Tiverton, mun. bor. of Devon, SW England, on R. Exe. Pop. 16,000. Hist. wool trade; lace mfg. (19th cent.).

Tivoli (anc. *Tibur*), town of Latium, C Italy, on R. Aniene. Pop. 34,000. H.e.p. from nearby waterfalls. Ruins of Hadrian's villa; Villa d'Este (16th cent.).

Tiw or **Tyr,** in Teutonic myth, god of war and athletic events. Identified with Roman Mars, thus Mars' day became Tiw's day (Tuesday).

Tirpitz, Alfred von (1849-1930), German naval officer. As naval secretary (1897–1916), initiated the naval arms race in Europe and advocated unrestricted submarine warfare in WWI.

Tirso de Molina, pseud. of Fray Gabriel Téllez (c 1583-1648), Spanish dramatist. Major playwright of 'Golden Age'. Wrote prolifically, now known for *The Libertine of Seville* (1630), creating character Don Juan.

Tiruchirapalli, city of Tamil Nadu, S India. Pop. 306,000. Railway centre; jewellery, textile mfg. Ruined fort surrounds Rock of Trichinopoly, 83 m (273 ft) high. Formerly Trichinopoly.

tissue, in biology, an aggregate of cells similar in form, such as in nerve, connective, muscle and epithelial tissue in animals, and equivalents in plants.

Tisza (Ger. *Theiss*), river of C Europe. Flows c 980 km (610 mi) SW from Ukrainian Carpathians through Hungary to R. Danube near Novi Sad in Yugoslavia. Partly navigable; fisheries.

tit or **titmouse,** any of Paridae family of small short-billed songbirds. Species incl. coal tit, *Parus ater,* and blue tit, *P. caeruleus.* Widely distributed, except South America and Australia.

Titanic, English passenger liner (46,000 tons). On maiden voyage, 14th April, 1912, struck iceberg in N Atlantic and sank with loss of 1513 lives of 2224 aboard. Disaster

Tjirebon or **Cheribon,** port of NC Java, Indonesia. Pop. 179,000. Exports rubber, copra. Mfg. centre.

Tlaxcala, town of EC Mexico, cap. of Tlaxcala state. Pop. 21,000. Has oldest American church (1521) founded by Cortés. Sanctuary of Ocotlán is nearby.

Tlemcen, town of NW Algeria. Pop. 87,000. Agric. trade centre, carpet mfg. Fl 13th-16th cent. as Berber cap.; taken by Turks (1553), French (1842). Noted Moslem architecture.

TNT or **trinitrotoluene,** high explosive solid, prepared by action of sulphuric and nitric acids on toluene.

Horned bull toad (Megophrys nasuta)

toad, tailless amphibian, esp. of genus *Bufo.* Frog-like, but with drier, warty skin, from which it secretes noxious white fluid. Largely terrestrial, lays eggs in water. Species incl. giant toad, *B. marinus,* of Australia.

toadfish, any of Batrachoididae family of scaleless marine fish, with broad head and wide mouth. Some South American species have poison glands. Oyster toadfish, *Opsanus tau,* is found along Atlantic coast of US.

toadflax or **butter-and-eggs,** any of genus *Linaria* of European herbs. Esp. *L. vulgaris* with yellow and orange flowers, naturalized as weed in North America.

toadstool, see FUNGUS.

Tobacco (Nicotiana tabacum)

tobacco, any of genus *Nicotiana* of tropical American plants of nightshade family. Now widely cultivated esp. in US, India, China and USSR. Large, sticky leaves, white, greenish or purple flowers. Dried and cured leaves of *N. tabacum* may be rolled into cigars, shredded for cigarettes and pipes, processed for chewing, powdered for snuff. *N. rustica* now grown in Turkey is mainly used for cigarettes.

Tobago, see TRINIDAD AND TOBAGO.

Tobey, Mark (1890-   ), American painter. Influenced by Chinese and Japanese calligraphy and Zen; developed abstract style of 'white writing' in which white brushstrokes overlay darker tones.

tobogganing, sport of sliding down ice-covered slopes on small sleds. Perfected in Switzerland in 1880s using specially prepared runs, *eg* Cresta at St Moritz. Form known as luge tobogganing has been Winter Olympic event since 1964.

Tobolsk, town of USSR, WC Siberian RSFSR; at confluence of Irtysh and Tobol rivers. Pop. 45,000. Sawmilling; fish and fur processing. Has 18th cent. kremlin modelled on that at Moscow.

Tobruk, town of NE Cyrenaica, Libya, on Mediterranean Sea. Pop. 28,000. Supply base in WWII; scene of heavy fighting, taken by British 1942.

Tocantins, river of C Brazil. Flows N 2640 km (1640 mi) from E plateau to join Pará R. near Belém.

Tocqueville, [Charles] Alexis de (1805-59), French writer, politician. Wrote *Democracy in America* (1835), in which he foresaw triumph of democracy and social equality in Europe. Considered liberty incompatible with equality.

Todd, Alexander Robertus (1907-   ), Scottish biochemist. Awarded Nobel Prize for Chemistry (1957) for work on structure and synthesis of nucleotides, important contribution in determining structure and function of nucleic acids.

Togo, Heihachiro, Count (1847-1934), Japanese naval officer. As commander-in-chief in Russo-Japanese war, destroyed Russian fleet at Port Arthur and won the decisive battle of Tsushima (1905).

Togo

Togo, republic of W Africa. Area 57,000 sq km (22,000 sq mi); pop. 2,117,000; cap. Lomé. Official language: French. Religions: native, RC. Tropical forest in N, savannah in S. Exports cacao, coffee, copra, phosphates. Formerly French Togoland, formed (1922) from part of former German protect. of Togoland under League of Nations mandate. Independent 1960.

Togoland, British; French, see GHANA; TOGO.

Tojo, Hideki or **Eike** (1884-1948), Japanese military, political leader. Premier (1941-4), provoked US entry into WWII by bombing of Pearl Harbor (Dec. 1941); resigned after sustained losses. Hanged as war criminal after suicide attempt in 1945.

Tokaj or **Tokay,** town of NE Hungary on R. Tisza. Pop. 5000. Centre of vine-growing area, producing famous Tokay wine.

Tokyo, cap. of Japan, port on Tokyo Bay, SE Honshu isl. Pop. 8,841,000; incl. suburbs, 11,408,000. Major commercial, mfg. (textiles, cars), indust. (shipbuilding, engineering) and publishing centre. Founded 12th cent. as Edo, became cap. of Tokugawa shogunate. Replaced Kyoto as imperial cap. 1868 and renamed as Tokyo ('Eastern Capital'). Rebuilt after extensive damage from 1923 earthquake and bombing in WWII. Site of imperial palace and 4 univs.

Toland, John (1670-1722), British deist, b. Ireland. Known for *Christianity not Mysterious* (1696) attempting to show Christianity to be comprehensible to human reason.

Toledo, city of C Spain, on granite hill above R. Tagus, cap. of Toledo prov. Pop. 44,000. Famous from Moorish times for swords, steel; textile mfg. Seat of Spanish primate. Cap. of Visigothic kingdom from 6th cent., fl under Moors from 712. Taken by Castile 1085, cap. of Spain until 1561.

Cathedral (13th cent.); home of El Greco, several churches have works by him.

Toledo, port of NE Ohio, US; at W end of L. Erie. Pop. 379,000. Commercial, shipping centre; exports coal, oil, agric. produce; glass, motor vehicle, chemical mfg., oil refining.

J.R.R. Tolkien in 1966

Tolkien, J[ohn] R[onald] R[euel] (1892-1973), English author, philologist, b. South Africa. Known for imaginatively complex fantasies *The Hobbit* (1937), *The Lord of the Rings* (3 vol. 1954-5) using knowledge of Germanic, Celtic myths and language.

Toller, Ernst (1893-1939), German dramatist. Leading expressionist. Wrote abstract dramas on problems of maintaining ideals in mass movements, *eg Masses and Man* (1920), *The Machine Wreckers* (1922). Also wrote *Hurray, We're Living!* (1927) a dramatic treatment of politics of post-WWI Europe.

Tolpuddle, village of Dorset, S England. 'Tolpuddle Martyrs' were agric. labourers transported for forming a trade union (1834).

Tolpuddle Martyrs, name given to 6 farm labourers prosecuted and transported (1834) to Australia for organizing trade union branch of fellow workers. Public protest forced pardon (1836).

Tolstoy, Aleksei Nikolayevich, Count (1883-1945), Russian author. Known for trilogy of revolutionary times, *Road to Calvary* (1919-41). Also wrote science fiction, *eg Aelita* (1922) describing Russian landing on Mars.

Leo Tolstoy

Tolstoy, Leo Nikolayevich, Count (1828-1910), Russian author. Advocated social reform, passivity in opposition to evil forces. Evolved own theology of universal love, mysticism, personal deity. Best known for

great realistic novels, *eg War and Peace* (1865-9), *Anna Karenina* (1875-7). Also wrote plays, *eg The Power of Darkness* (1886), short stories, essays.

Toltec, hist. (*c* 6th-13th cent.) civilization of Mexico. Associated with archaeological sites at Teotihuacán, Cholula, Tollán. Noted as skilled metal and stoneworkers. Religion centred on deified hero, Quetzalcoatl. Southern expansion (11th-13th cent.) led to domination of Maya, but eventually supplanted by Aztecs.

Toluca, town of C Mexico, cap. of Mexico state; alt. 2670 m (*c* 8760 ft). Pop. 220,000. Famous for bull breeding; textile mfg. food processing, pottery, basket weaving.

toluene (C_7H_8), liquid hydrocarbon of benzene series. Obtained by distillation of coal tar or from petroleum. Used as solvent and in manufacture of TNT, dyes, *etc.*

Tomar, town of C Portugal. Pop. 8000. Important centre of Knights Templar and Military Order of Christ. Monastery-castle dominates town.

Tomato

tomato, *Lycopersicon esculentum,* annual plant of nightshade family. Native to tropical America but widely cultivated for edible, red or yellow, pulpy fruit. Introduced into Europe in 16th cent.

Tombouctou, see TIMBUKTU, Mali.

tommy-gun, see THOMPSON, J. T.

Tomsk, city of USSR, WC Siberian RSFSR; on R. Tom. Pop. 360,000. Machinery, ball bearing and electrical equipment mfg. Cultural centre; univ. (1888). Founded 1604; developed in 19th cent. with discovery of gold.

Tom Thumb

Tom Thumb, orig. Charles Sherwood Stratton (1838-83), American dwarf, entertainer. Exhibited first by P.T. BARNUM, later guest of European monarchs; amassed enormous fortune. Height never more than 84 cm (33 in.).

Tone, [Theobald] Wolfe (1763-98), Irish nationalist. A founder of society of United Irishmen (1791), whose members he convinced of necessity of revolution against

Britain. Enlisted French aid to invade Ireland and set up independent republic. Captured by British, convicted of treason. Committed suicide.

tone poem or **symphonic poem,** musical composition characteristic of Romantic period, intended as interpretation of literary, dramatic and pictorial elements. Introduced by Liszt.

Tonga or **Friendly Islands,** kingdom of S Pacific Ocean, comprised of Tongatabu, Vavau, Haapai isl. groups. Area 675 sq km (260 sq mi); pop. 98,000; cap. Nuku'alofa. Exports copra, fruit. Discovered (1616) by Dutch; named Friendly Isls. by Cook (1773). Under British protection from 1900, independent 1970. Member of British Commonwealth.

tongue, muscular organ attached to floor of mouth in most vertebrates. Covered by mucous membrane in which the taste buds are embedded. Minute projections (papillae) give it rough texture. Used in mastication and swallowing and, in man, articulation of speech.

tonic sol-fa, in music, notation system adapted from French *solfège* and Italian *solfeggio* systems, designed to simplify sight-reading. Notes are *doh, ray, me, fah, soh, lah, te, doh,* indicating position in major scale relative to a given key note. Signs like punctuation marks indicate duration of notes.

tonka bean, any of genus *Dipteryx* of South American trees of Leguminosae family. Fragrant, almond-shaped seed yields coumarin, formerly used as vanilla substitute and in perfumery.

Tonkin, hist. region of North Vietnam. Area *c* 103,600 sq km (40,000 sq mi). Became French protect. of Union of Indo-China in 1887. With parts of ANNAM formed North Vietnam after 1954.

Tonkin, Gulf of, arm of South China Sea bounded by S China and North Vietnam. Here, in 1964, an alleged attack by North Vietnamese torpedo boats on 2 US destroyers precipitated increased US involvement in Vietnam.

Tonlé Sap, lake of C Cambodia. Expands from *c* 2850 sq km (1100 sq mi) to *c* 10,360 sq km (4000 sq mi) in wet season. Important fisheries.

tonsil, mass of lymphoid tissue on each side of throat at back of mouth. Tonsillitis is an inflammation of tonsils, usually by streptococci; occurs mostly in childhood.

Toowoomba, city of SE Queensland, Australia. Pop. 58,000. Road and rail jct., trade centre for Darling Downs agric. region; food processing (meat, dairy produce), agric. machinery.

topaz, hard, colourless to yellow mineral; consists of silicate of aluminium and fluorine. Found among acid igneous rocks. Yellow variety used as a gem. Major sources in USSR, Brazil, Australia.

Topeka, cap. of Kansas, US; on Kansas R. Pop. 125,000. Commercial, indust. centre; wheat, cattle shipping; tyre mfg., railway engineering, printing.

topology, mathematical study of those features of surfaces which remain unchanged under continuous transformations; it is concerned with structure, rather than size.

Torah, *see* PENTATEUCH.

Torbay, co. bor. of Devon, SW England. Pop. 109,000. Created 1968 from Torquay, Paignton, Brixham.

Tordesillas, town of Valladolid prov., NC Spain, on R. Douro. Pop. 5000. Scene of treaty (1494) signed by Spain and Portugal dividing between them the New World.

Torino, *see* TURIN, Italy.

tornado, funnel-shaped, rotating column of air extending downward from *cumulonimbus* cloud. Travels at 30-66 kph (20-40 mph); small in area but very destructive. Common E of Rocky Mts., US and Australia.

Toronto, prov. cap. of Ontario, Canada; on N shore of L. Ontario at mouth of Humber R. Pop. 713,000. Natural harbour. Important transport, commercial, education centre. Food processing, printing and publishing, railway industs. Supplied with h.e.p. from Niagara Falls. Founded by French as fort 1749; called York 1793-1834. Has famous City Hall; Univ. of Toronto (1843).

torpedo, name given to various electric rays of genus *Torpedo*. Commonest Atlantic species is *T. nobiliana*.

torpedo, underwater explosive missile first developed by Robert Whitehead (1866). Early types were propelled by compressed air or electric motor, later by jet engines with sophisticated guidance systems. Discharged usually from tubes on ship or submarine, but also from aircraft.

Torquay, town of Devon, SW England, on Tor Bay. Resort, yachting. Torre Abbey (12th cent.). Part of TORBAY.

Torquemada, Tomás de (1420-98), Spanish Dominican monk. Appointed (1483) inquisitor general of Castile and Aragón. Responsible for expulsion of Jews from Spain (1492). Notorious for cruelty during INQUISITION.

Torrens, Lake, salt lake of SC West Australia, W of Flinders Range. Area *c* 5850 sq km (2250 sq mi); rarely contains any water.

Torreón, town of N Mexico, centre of agric. Laguna region. Pop. 257,000. Cotton, grain produce; textile mfg., flour milling, chemical mfg. Silver, zinc mines nearby.

Torres Strait, channel between S New Guinea and Cape York Penin., NE Australia. Width *c* 130 km (80 mi); contains many isls.

Tôrres Vedras, town of W Portugal. Pop. 6000. Medieval fortress, royal residence. Centre of Wellington's defence lines in Peninsular War.

Torricelli, Evangelista (1608-47), Italian physicist, mathematician. Invented principle of barometer, using mercury-filled tube, and demonstrated existence of air pressure with it. Obtained 1st man-made vacuum by means of his barometer.

Torstensson, Lennart (1603-51), Swedish general. In Thirty Years War, commanded victories in Saxony, Bohemia, drove Danes from Holstein (1643-4).

Galápagos giant tortoise (*Testudo elephantopus*)

tortoise, name given to various land-dwelling turtles, esp. of genus *Testudo*. Widely distributed in warm regions, may hibernate in cool climates; herbivorous. Giant tortoises live up to 150 years.

tortoise beetle, small tortoise-shaped leaf beetle of Chrysomelidae family, often brightly coloured or iridescent.

Tortosa, town of Catalonia, NE Spain, on R. Ebro. Pop. 46,000. Port; agric. market, pottery mfg. *Fl* under Moors 713-1148. Cathedral (14th cent.).

Toruń (Ger. *Thorn*), city of NC Poland, on R. Vistula. Pop. 131,000. Railway jct., river port; engineering. Founded 1231 by Teutonic Knights; Hanseatic League member. Under Prussian rule 1793-1919. Birthplace of Copernicus.

Tory, Geoffroy (*c* 1480-1533), French engraver, printer, publisher. Major influence in development of 16th cent. French style of book decoration. Helped popularize Roman type in preference to Gothic.

Tory Party, British political organization. Began (*c* 1680) as group supporting James II. Discredited for pro-Jacobite leanings after accession of George I, spent much of 18th cent. in opposition to Whigs. Traditionally favoured continued influence of Crown and Church of England; supported by country gentry. Revived under younger Pitt, held almost unbroken power until 1830. Evolved into CONSERVATIVE PARTY in 1830s.

Toscana, *see* TUSCANY, Italy.

Toscanini, Arturo (1867-1957), Italian conductor. Became musical director at La Scala, Milan (1898), then principal conductor of Metropolitan Opera, New York (1908). Also conducted New York Philharmonic and NBC Symphony orchestras. Renowned for concern with detail.

total internal reflection, in optics, reflection of light ray incident at boundary with medium in which it travels faster. Occurs when angle of refraction predicted by Snell's law exceeds 90°.

totalitarianism, system of absolute govt., in which social and economic activity of state organized hierarchically to eliminate opposition. Highly centralized govt. controlled by single official party. Doctrine usually appeals to nationalist and socialist sentiment through aggressive foreign policy. Extreme modern examples incl. Stalinist USSR and Nazi Germany.

totemism, belief of tribe or clan that its distinctive bond is symbolized by a particular animal or plant. This symbol may be represented in tattoos, carvings, *eg* in totem poles of certain North American Indian tribes. Also occurs in Melanesia, Australia.

Totila (d. 552), last king of Ostrogoths (541-52). Drove Byzantines from C and S Italy and captured Rome (546). Byzantines recovered Italy when Totila was defeated and killed by Justinian's general, Narses.

toucan, any of Ramphastidae family of fruit-eating birds, found in tropical American forests. Black body with bright throat; extremely long brightly coloured beak.

touch-me-not, any of genus *Impatiens* of Eurasian annual plants, esp. *I. noli-me-tangere.* When ripe, pods burst on being touched, scattering seeds.

touchstone, hard, black, fine-grained stone, usually basalt or chert. Formerly used to determine purity of gold and silver by examining streaks left on it when rubbed with metal.

Toulon, city of Provence, SE France, on Mediterranean Sea. Pop. 175,000. Port, shipbuilding, armaments mfg. Major naval base from 17th cent.; French fleet scuttled here (1942). Fortifications, Gothic church.

Toulouse, city of Languedoc, S France, on R Garonne. Cap. of Haute-Garonne dept. Pop. 371,000. Agric. trade centre, aeronautics indust., univ. (1230). Cap. of Visigoths; countship from 9th cent. Centre of medieval Provençal culture. Plundered during Albigensian Crusade; part of France from 1271. Romanesque church (11th cent.), Gothic cathedral (13th cent.).

Toulouse-Lautrec, Henri Raymond de (1864-1901), French artist. Influenced by Degas and Japanese prints, he painted scenes from cabarets, music halls, circuses, *etc.* Famous for his posters, *eg Jane Avril* and *Aristide Bruant.*

Toungoo, town of SC Burma, on R. Sittang. Pop. 32,000. Cap. of independent kingdom from 14th to 16th cent.

Touraine, region and former prov. of WC France, hist. cap. Tours. Fertile 'garden of France' (wine and fruit growing) drained by Loire, Indre, Cher. Many châteaux (15th-17th cent.). Under counts of Anjou from 11th cent., passed to France 1204.

Tourcoing, town of Nord, N France. Pop. 99,000. Textile centre (esp. woollens, carpets). Forms conurbation with Lille and Roubaix.

Touré, Sékou (1922-), Guinean politician. A Marxist, he rose to prominence in trade union organization. Elected president at Guinea's independence (1958).

tourmaline, crystalline mineral, consisting of complex silicate of boron and aluminium. Usually black, gem varieties are blue, green, yellow; found among granites, gneiss, schist. Major sources in Burma, Sri Lanka, Brazil, US.

Tournai (Flem. *Doornik*), town of W Belgium, on R. Scheldt. Pop. 33,000. Textiles (wool, linen), carpets. Cathedral (11th cent.).

Tournefort, Joseph Pitton de (1656-1708), French botanist. Classified plants on basis of similarity in structure of flowers and fruits. System widely accepted until superseded by Linnaeus'.

Tourneur or **Turner, Cyril** (*c* 1575-1626), English poet, dramatist. Wrote satire *The Transformed Metamorphosis* (1600). Known as probable author of typically Jacobean *The Revenger's Tragedy* (1607), *The Atheist's Tragedy* (1611).

Tours, city of WC France, on R. Loire, cap. of Indre-et-Loire dept. Pop. 128,000. Agric. market for Touraine; wine, brandy trade. Medieval centre of learning, silk indust. Gothic cathedral (12th cent.), art museum. Birthplace of Balzac. Nearby Charles Martel defeated Moors (732).

Toussaint L'Ouverture, François Dominique (*c* 1744-1803), Haitian revolutionary. Born a slave, he led successful Negro revolt to free slaves (1791-3). Drove British and Spanish from Haiti; achieved complete control of isl. by 1801. Captured by French forces sent to reintroduce slavery; died in prison in France.

Tower Hamlets, bor. of EC Greater London, England. Pop. 165,000. Created 1965 from met. bors., Bethnal Green, Poplar, Stepney. Incl. Tower of London.

Tower of London: miniature of the White Tower from a 15th century manuscript

Tower of London, fortress in London, England, on N bank of R. Thames. Enclosed by dry moat and double wall. Oldest part, the Keep or White Tower, built (1078) by Gundulf, bishop of Rochester. Formerly used as royal residence and state prison, now an armoury and museum. British Crown Jewels on display in Jewel House.

Townes, Charles Hard (1915-), American physicist. Invented MASER to produce intense microwave beams by excitation of ammonia molecules. Shared, with Basov and Prochorov, Nobel Prize for Physics (1964) for this invention and later developments.

town planning, process of arranging urban land use pattern to satisfy considerations of health, amenities, communications and attractive appearance. Planned towns often show rectangular 'gridiron' plan. Practised in ancient times, *eg* by Indus Valley, Greek, Roman civilizations; examples of recent planning incl. Paris (19th cent.), Brasilia, Canberra, Rotterdam (all 20th cent.). Also *see* GARDEN CITY.

Townshend, Charles (1725-67), British statesman. As chancellor of exchequer, introduced Townshend Acts (1767) which imposed duties on tea, glass, *etc*, imported by American colonies. Ensuing colonial unrest led to Boston Massacre (1770), Boston Tea Party (1773).

Townshend, Charles Townshend, 2nd Viscount (1674-1738), English statesman. Whig secretary of state for northern dept. (1715-16), quelled Jacobite uprising (1715). Reappointed (1721-30). Devoted himself to experimental agric. in retirement (hence nickname 'Turnip' Townshend).

Townsville, city of NE Queensland, Australia, on Cleveland Bay. Pop. 68,000. Port, serving extensive agric., mining hinterland; meat processing, copper refining; tourist resort. Has James Cook Univ. (1970).

toxaemia, *see* BLOOD POISONING.

toxin, name applied to various unstable poisonous proteins formed by bacteria, which cause diseases such as botulism and tetanus. Name also applied to various similar poisons produced by plants or animals, *eg* cobra venom.

Toyama, town of Japan, on Toyama Bay, C Honshu isl. Pop. 269,000. Patent medicine; drug and textile mfg.

Toynbee, Arnold (1852-83), English reformer, historian. Author of *Lectures on the Industrial Revolution of the 18th Centruy in England* (1884). Worked among the poor of London; 1st social settlement, Toynbee Hall, in E London, named after him. His nephew, **Arnold Joseph Toynbee** (1889-1975), was also historian. Wrote *A Study of History* (1934-54), rejecting determinism and attempting to analyze rise and fall of civilizations.

Trabzon or **Trebizond,** port of NE Turkey, on Black Sea. Pop. 66,000. Exports tobacco, nuts. Founded as Greek colony (8th cent. BC). Cap. of Greek empire of Trebizond (1204-1461) until capture by Ottomans; it was renowned for its wealth and beauty.

trace element, chemical element essential in plant and animal nutrition, but only in minute quantities, *eg* iron, copper, zinc. Some are constituents of vitamins, hormones and enzymes.

tracery, ornamental stonework in upper part of window or panel; sometimes used decoratively in vaults and arches. Characteristic of Gothic architecture from early 13th cent., its basic forms are bar and plate tracery.

trachea or **windpipe,** tube extending from larynx to its division into the 2 main bronchi. Strengthened by rings of cartilage and muscle.

Tractarianism, *see* OXFORD MOVEMENT.

Trades Union Congress (TUC), voluntary organization of British trade unions. Estab. 1868. Delegates of affiliated unions meet annually, elect General Council to negotiate with govt., international labour bodies.

trade union, *see* UNION, LABOUR.

trade winds, winds blowing constantly from subtropical high pressure belts (25°-30°N and S) to equatorial low pressure belt (doldrums). Blow from NE in N hemisphere, from SE in S hemisphere.

Trafalgar, Cape, headland of Cádiz prov., SW Spain, on Str. of Gibraltar. Scene of naval battle (1805) in which French were defeated by English under Nelson, who was killed.

tragedy, dramatic form defined by Aristotle as a representation of events in which hero of stature brings unforeseen disaster on himself by error, not accident or wickedness. Definition still used today, but seldom fully achieved even by ancient Greeks. Evolved by them in 6th cent. BC from religious ritual, reached peak in hands of Aeschylus, Sophocles, Euripides. Other conventions, *eg* violence, revenge, ghosts, transmitted by Seneca, influenced development of English tragedies, *eg* those by Marlowe, Shakespeare. French tragedy, constrained by unities of time, place and action, as in plays of Corneille, Racine. Modern tragedy much looser category. Concerned more with ordinary people, who may still display heroic attributes in conflicts, *eg* those of Ibsen, or may be 'anti-heroes', or pawns of meaninglessness, *etc,* of life, as in Miller's *Death of a Salesman.*

Traherne, Thomas (*c* 1638-74), English poet, mystic. Known for metaphysical *Poetical Works* (first pub. 1903), prose reflections *Centuries of Meditations* (first pub. 1908). Majority of works only discovered in 1896.

Trail, town of SE British Columbia, Canada; on Columbia R. just N of US border. Pop. 11,000. Lead, zinc, copper smelting.

Trajan, full name Marcus Ulpius Trajanus (AD *c*53-117), Roman emperor (98-117), b. Spain. His conquest of Dacia (106) is commemorated by Trajan's Column in Rome (erected 114). Built Forum of Trajan in Rome.

Tralee, co. town of Kerry, SW Irish Republic, on R. Lee. Pop. 12,000. Agric. market; tourism.

tranquillizer, drug used to calm the emotions. Distinct from sedative in that it does not induce sleep. Those used incl. meprobamate, chlorpromazine, rauwolfia.

transcendence, *see* IMMANENCE.

transcendentalism, in philosophy, mode of thought emphasizing intuitive and spiritual perception beyond mundane thought or experience. First associated with Kant. Developed in America in writings of Emerson, Thoreau.

transducer, device used to transform energy from one form into another, *eg* loudspeaker or electric generator.

transept, transverse section of cross-shaped church, at right angles to long main section; usually set between nave and chancel.

transformational-generative grammar, *see* CHOMSKY.

transformer, device used to change voltage of alternating current without changing its frequency. Consists of 2 coils of insulated wire wound on an iron core; current is induced in one coil by variation of magnetic field resulting from current flow in other coil. Ratio of voltages in coils is roughly equal to ratio of number of turns of wire in coils.

transistor, electronic semiconductor device used to amplify voltage and current. Invented 1948, it is smaller, requires less power and has a longer life than equivalent thermionic valve.

Transjordania, *see* JORDAN.

Transkei, Bantu homeland of South Africa, between R. Great Kei and Natal. Area 42,750 sq km (16,500 sq mi); pop. 1,751,000; cap. Umtata. Comprises Griqualand East, Pondoland, Transkei, Tembuland territs. Stock rearing; labour source for Witwatersrand mines. Separated from Cape Prov. 1963; autonomous state from 1976.

transmigration of souls, passing of soul into another body on death. *See* REINCARNATION.

transpiration, loss of water by evaporation from leaves of green plants. Promotes ascent of SAP from roots of plant allowing intake of water and minerals.

transplantation, in surgery, transfer of tissue or organs from one subject to another. Grafting usually refers to tissue transplants from one part of same subject's body to another. Main problem in transplantation is rejection of foreign tissue by action of antibodies. First human kidney transplant was performed 1950, first heart transplant 1967.

Trans-Siberian railway, line in USSR from Leningrad to Vladivostok on Pacific coast. Serves Moscow, Omsk, Novosibirsk, Irkutsk. Begun 1891, completed 1905; originally passed through Manchuria (this part now Chinese Eastern railway); now branches near Chita to remain entirely in USSR. Crucial to development of Siberia.

transubstantiation, *see* EUCHARIST.

transuranic elements, chemical elements with atomic number greater than 92 (that of uranium). Such elements are radioactive and do not normally occur naturally; prepared by nuclear reactions.

Transvaal, prov. of NE South Africa. Area 286,000 sq km (110,500 sq mi); pop. 8,717,000; cap. Pretoria. Mainly high veld, lies between R. Limpopo (N), R. Vaal (S). Produces grain, fruit; great mineral wealth, esp. in WITWATERSRAND. Boer state estab. 1837 after Great Trek; became South African Republic 1856. Discovery of gold (1886) led to influx of British prospectors, resulting in Boer War (1899-1902). UK colony from 1902; prov. of Union of South Africa from 1910.

Transylvania, region and former prov. of N Romania. Main towns Cluj, Brasov. Mainly forested plateau *c* 450 m (1500 ft) high, crossed by R. Mureş. Incl. S Carpathians, known as Transylvanian Alps, rising to *c* 2530 m (8300 ft). Part of Roman *Dacia*; independent (1526-1699). Pop. Romanian, Magyar, German.

Trapani (anc. *Drepanum*), town of W Sicily, Italy, cap. of Trapani prov. Pop. 70,000. Port; tuna fishing, wine, salt. Carthaginian naval base, taken by Rome 241 BC.

trapdoor spider, spider, esp. of Ctenizidae family, which makes silk-lined burrow with tight-fitting hinged lid.

Trappists, in RC church, order of CISTERCIANS of the Stricter Observance. Founded (17th cent.) at La Trappe, France. Monks normally observe silence, are vegetarian.

travel sickness, *see* MOTION SICKNESS.

treacle, *see* MOLASSES.

treason, crime of attacking safety of sovereign state or its head. In US (as declared in Constitution) consists only in levying war against US, or in giving aid, comfort, to its enemies. In UK, Statute of Treasons (1351) distinguished

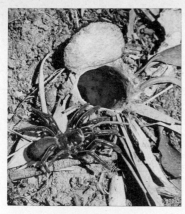

Trapdoor spider

high treason (*eg* killing king, king's law officers, making war on realm) and petty treason (killing one's superior, *eg* master, husband). Reforms in 19th cent. incl. abolition of petty treason, less harsh punishment. Now punishable by death or life imprisonment in US, UK. Famous trials incl. Aaron Burr (1807) in US, and Roger Casement (1916) in UK.

treasury, dept. of state or nation controlling revenue, taxation, public finances. In UK, concerned with major aspects of fiscal policy, esp. annual BUDGET; does not admin. revenue. Main function that of controlling govt. expenditure. Effective chief is chancellor of exchequer. In US, federal dept., estab. 1789, does not prepare budget, but admin. revenue; initiates tax proposals, has close relationship with, although has no legal authority over, Federal Reserve System. Headed by secretary of treasury.

Trebizond, see TRABZON.

Tree, Sir Herbert Beerbohm (1853-1917), English actor-manager. Manager of Haymarket Theatre, London (1887-97) and Her Majesty's Theatre, London (1897-1917). Noted in Shakespearian and modern roles.

tree, perennial plant with permanent woody, self-supporting main stem or trunk. Usually grows to greater height than shrub, developing branches and foliage. May be either deciduous, with leaves shed at end of growing season, or evergreen.

tree creeper, small insectivorous bird esp. of Certhiidae family. Long slender curved bill, long tongue; uses sharp claws to climb trees. Species incl. common tree creeper, *Certhia familiaris,* of Europe and North America.

tree fern, any of various tropical ferns with tree-like trunk, esp. of genera *Cyathea, Alsophila* and *Hemitelia.* Mainly native to Australia.

tree frog, arboreal frog of Hylidae family. Digits end in adhesive suckers to assist climbing; strong jumpers.

treehopper, any of Membracidae family of small leaping insects, commonest in tropics. Prothorax bent back over abdomen to form long point. Feeds on plant sap.

tree shrew, any of Tupaiidae family of squirrel-like primates, found in forests of SE Asia. Solitary, nocturnal; feeds mainly on insects.

trefoil, any of various plants with leaves divided into 3 leaflets, *eg* CLOVER and similar plants of genus *Lotus* of Leguminosae family. Varieties incl. European bird's foot trefoil, *L. corniculatus,* and prairie trefoil, *L. americanus.*

Treitschke, Heinrich von (1834-96), German historian. Supported German unification under Prussian domination. Known for his extreme nationalism and anti-Semitism. Major work was *History of Germany in the Nineteenth Century* (1879-94).

Trek, Great, migration from Cape Colony, South Africa (1835-6) of Boer farmers. In protest against British rule, they moved N to found Transvaal and Orange Free State.

Trematoda, see FLUKE.

Trench, Richard Chenevix (1807-86), British clergyman, author, b. Ireland. Protestant archbishop of Dublin (1863-84). Well known for poetry, works on philology, incl. *Justin Martyr* (1835), *The Study of Words* (1851).

Trenchard, Hugh Montague Trenchard, 1st Viscount (1873-1956), British air force officer. First commander of Royal Flying Corps in WWI. As chief of air staff (1918-29), shaped offensive strategy used in WWII. Commissioner of metropolitan police (1931-5), instituted many reforms esp. in training.

trench warfare, that in which opposing forces dig systems of defensive earthworks as base for operations, reached most elaborate form in WWI. Outdated by increased mobility of mechanized warfare, esp. with introduction of TANK.

Trent, river of C England. Flows 274 km (170 mi) from Staffordshire via Stoke, Nottingham, to join R. Ouse in forming Humber.

Trent, Council of (1545-63), ecumenical COUNCIL convened by Pope Paul III, continued under Julius III and Pius IV. Discussed concessions to restore religious peace after Reformation. Protestant demands considered impracticable. Council defined RC doctrine and discipline; effected reform of many ecclesiastic abuses.

Trent Affair, diplomatic incident (1861) of American Civil War, involving removal of 2 Southern diplomats from British ship *Trent* by Union ship *San Jacinto.* After British protest, prisoners were released.

Trentino-Alto Adige, region of NE Italy, bordering Austria and Switzerland. Incl. part of Tryolean Alps, Dolomites; main river Adige. Main towns Trento, Bolzano. Forestry, h.e.p., tourism. Alto Adige largely German-speaking.

Trento (Eng. *Trent*), town of Trentino-Alto Adige, NE Italy, on R. Adige. Cap. of Trento prov. Pop. 95,000. On route to Brenner Pass. Scene of Council of Trent (1545-63). Held by Austria 1803-1919.

Trenton, cap. of New Jersey; on Delaware R. Pop. 105,000. Metal products, cable, rope, pottery mfg. Settled by Quakers (1679). Scene of Revolution battle in which Washington crossed the Delaware and defeated British (1776).

trepan or **trephine,** small crown saw used to remove circular section of bone from the skull. Trepanning is performed to relieve pressure on brain and, in primitive cultures, to release evil spirits. Trepanned skulls dating from prehist. times have been found.

Trevelyan, Sir George Otto (1838-1928), English historian, politician. Wrote *American Revolution* (1899-1907), *George the Third and Charles Fox* (1912), also biog. of his uncle, Lord Macaulay. His son, **George Macaulay Trevelyan** (1876-1962), wrote *British History in the Nineteenth Century* (1922), *History of England* (1926).

Trèves, see TRIER, West Germany.

Treviso, town of Venetia, NE Italy, cap. of Treviso prov. Pop. 95,000. Agric. centre in fertile Venetian plain. Cathedral (12th cent.). Damaged in WWII.

Trevithick, Richard (1771-1833), English engineer. Designed high-pressure steam engine (1800) for use in mines. Built (1804) 1st steam locomotive to run on rails.

Trevor-Roper, Hugh Redwald (1914-), British historian. Has written on a wide range of hist. topics; works incl. *The Last Days of Hitler* (1947), researched in Berlin at end of WWII.

Trianon, Treaty of (1920), post-WWI peace treaty between Hungary and Allies. Large amounts of Hungarian territ. ceded to Romania, Yugoslavia, Czechoslovakia, Austria; size of army reduced. Caused much resentment in Hungary.

Triassic period, first geological period of Mesozoic era; began *c* 225 million years ago, lasted *c* 30 million years. Extensive arid or semi-arid areas; conifers, ferns, tree ferns. Typified by ammonites, crinoids, lamellibranchs; earliest mammals, dinosaurs. Also see GEOLOGICAL TABLE.

tribune, name assigned to various officers of ancient Rome. Tribunes of plebs were elected defenders of the plebeians rights, protecting them from abuse by the magistrates. Office was begun in 494 BC and its influence was extended (c 130 BC) by the Gracchi.

trichina, *Trichinella spiralis,* parasitic nematode worm often transmitted to man by eating inadequately cooked pork. Reproduces in intestine; larvae may migrate to muscles, forming cysts. Cause of disease trichinosis, characterized by fever, muscular pains, *etc.*

Trichinopoly, see TIRUCHIRAPALLI.

Trier (Fr. *Trèves*), city of W West Germany, on R. Moselle. Pop. 103,000. Wine trade, textile mfg., tourist centre. Roman remains incl. amphitheatre, gate Porta Nigra; cathedral has 'Holy Coat' of Christ; univ. (1473-1797). Badly damaged in WWII. Birthplace of Karl Marx.

Trieste (Slav *Trst*), city of NE Italy, on Gulf of Venice, cap. of Friuli-Venezia Giulia and of Trieste prov. Pop. 274,000. Port from Roman times, shipbuilding, oil refining. Held by Austria (1382-1918), as freeport from 1719; passed to Italy 1918. Created Free Territ. 1947; city passed (1954) to Italy, environs to Yugoslavia.

Grey triggerfish

triggerfish, any of Balistidae family of deep-bodied tropical fish. Long spines on dorsal fin used to wedge fish into crevices of coral reefs. Species incl. grey triggerfish, *Balistes capriscus,* of European waters.

trigonometry, branch of mathematics which deals with relations between sides and angles of a triangle. Trigonometric functions, sine, cosine and tangent, express ratios of different sides of right-angled triangle. Applied in navigation, astronomy.

Trilling, Lionel (1905-75), American critic. Essay collections, *eg The Liberal Imagination* (1950), *Beyond Culture* (1965), reflect belief in literature as of primary social value. Other works incl. *E.M. Forster* (1943), novel *The Middle of the Journey* (1947).

trillium, genus of perennial plants of lily family. Native to North America and E Asia. Erect stems have whorl of 3 leaves and large solitary pink or white flower. Species incl. wake robin, *Trillium grandiflorum.*

trilobite, any of class Trilobita of extinct marine arthropods. Flattened oval body divided into 3 segments; fossils found in Cambrian rocks.

Trim, co. town of Meath, E Irish Republic, on R. Boyne. Pop. 2000. Has 12th cent. castle.

Trincomalee, port of NE Sri Lanka. Pop. 42,000. Excellent natural harbour; exports tea. Former British naval base.

Trinidad and Tobago, republic of SE West Indies, member of British Commonwealth. Area 5129 sq km (1980 sq mi); pop. 945,000; cap. Port of Spain. Language: English. Religions: Protestant, RC. Hilly in interior; tropical climate. Agric. crops incl. sugar cane, coconuts, citrus fruits. Important asphalt, oil refining industs. Trinidad discovered by Columbus (1498); ceded to Britain (1802). Seat of govt. of Federation of West Indies (1958-62). Joined by Tobago in creation of British crown colony (1888).

Trinity, in Christianity, three aspects of divine being, *ie* God the Father, Son (incarnate in Jesus), Holy Ghost. Doctrine asserted early, estab. in Nicene Creed.

triode, thermionic valve containing three electrodes: cathode, anode and control grid.

Triple Alliance, formed 1882 when Italy joined Germany and Austria-Hungary (united by Dual Alliance of 1879). Growing conflict of interest with other European states (*see* TRIPLE ENTENTE) increased diplomatic tension before WWI.

Triple Entente, diplomatic accord between France, Russia and Britain. Grew out of concern over German commercial, naval and colonial expansion, and alliance of C European powers. Dual Alliance between Russia and France announced 1895. Britain, formerly maintaining isolationist policy in Europe, entered informal alliance with France (Entente Cordiale) by 1904 and negotiated alliance with Russia in 1907.

Tripoli (Arab. *Tarabulus*), port of N Lebanon, on Mediterranean. Pop. 175,000. Oil refining; terminus of pipeline from Iraq. Founded c 700 BC; cap. of Phoenician federation of Tyre, Sidon and Aradus.

Tripoli, cap. of Libya, on Mediterranean Sea. Pop. 264,000. Admin. centre; port, exports oil, hides, dates, sponges. Founded 7th cent. BC by Phoenicians. Under Turkish rule from 16th cent., stronghold of Barbary pirates. Cap. of Italian colony of Libya (1911-43). Ruins of Roman city *Leptis Magna* nearby.

Tripolitania, region of NW Libya. Fertile coastal strip, interior desert; grain, fruit growing, stock rearing. Name derived from 3 Phoenician cities founded 7th cent. BC. Under Turkish rule from 16th cent.; colonized by Italy 1911-43. Federal prov. (cap. Tripoli) 1951-63.

Tripolitan War, war fought between US and Barbary States of N Africa (1800-15). Arose out of US refusal to pay increased tribute to Pasha of Tripoli to gain immunity from attacks by Barbary pirates on shipping.

Tripura, state of NE India. Area c 10,450 sq km (4030 sq mi); pop. 1,557,000; cap. Agartala. Hilly with dense jungle; timber, rice, jute. Became union territ. 1956, state 1972.

Tristan and Isolde or **Tristram and Yseult,** medieval legend of Celtic origin. Tells of Tristan's journey to Ireland to bring Princess Isolde to Cornwall as bride of uncle, King Mark. On ship while returning, pair drink love potion which causes irresistible, eternal love, leading to death of both. Theme of many French romances, combined with ARTHURIAN LEGEND, *eg* Malory's *Morte d'Arthur.* Used by Tennyson (*Idylls of the King,* 1859-85), Wagner (*Tristan and Isolde.*)

Tristan da Cunha, small group of isls. in S Atlantic, dependency of St Helena since 1938. Only inhabited isl. is Tristan (pop. c 280), formed by volcano rising to 2060 m (6760 ft); eruption in 1961 led to temporary evacuation of pop.

tritium, radioactive isotope of hydrogen, with mass no. 3. Found in minute quantities in natural hydrogen; can be produced from lithium in nuclear reactions. Used as radioactive tracer and in hydrogen bombs.

Triton, in Greek myth, son of Poseidon and Amphitrite. Represented as fish-shaped from waist down, blowing conch shell to calm waves.

Triumvirate, term applied in ancient Rome to govt. carried out by 3 men. First Triumvirate formed by Julius Caesar, Pompey and Crassus (60 BC), Second Triumvirate (43 BC) by Octavian, Mark Antony and Lepidus.

Trivandrum, cap. of Kerala state, S India. Pop. 410,000. Port on Arabian Sea. Coconut products, textile mfg.

Trnava (Hung. *Nagyszombat*), town of S Czechoslovakia. Pop. 38,000. Agric. market, food processing. Gothic cathedral (14th cent.).

Trnovo or **Turnovo,** town of NC Bulgaria. Pop. 37,000. Former cap. of Bulgaria (12th-14th cents.), kingdom proclaimed here (1908).

Trois Rivières or **Three Rivers,** town of S Québec, Canada; at confluence of St Maurice and St Lawrence rivers. Pop. 56,000. Important newsprint, iron and steel indust. Founded 1634.

Trojan War, in Greek legend, war waged for 10 years by the Greeks on the Trojans to recover HELEN, wife of MENELAUS, abducted by PARIS. Gods fought for both sides. Major events in the war incl.: quarrel between ACHILLES and AGAMEMNON; Achilles' refusal to fight; death of PATROCLUS,

Achilles' return to war and death of HECTOR; Trojans reinforced by Amazons and Ethiopians; death of Achilles at hands of Paris; summoning by Greeks of NEOPTOLEMUS and Philoctetes, who slew Paris. Finally, Greeks simulated departure, leaving a huge wooden effigy of a horse outside city gates. Despite warnings by CASSANDRA and LAOCOON, Trojans brought it into city, enabling Greek soldiers hidden inside it to open the gates to their army and destroy the city.

Trollhättan, town of SW Sweden, on R. Göta. Pop. 41,000. Waterfalls supply major h.e.p. station; electricity for town (chemicals, cellulose industs.) and much of S Sweden.

Trollope, Anthony (1815-82), English novelist. Known for 'Barsetshire Chronicles' incl. *The Warden* (1855), *Barchester Towers* (1857), depicting clerical life in imaginary English county. Also wrote political novel series, 'The Pallisers', incl. *Can You Forgive Her?* (1864), *The Eustace Diamonds* (1873).

trombone, brass musical instrument, formerly called sackbut. Known from 15th cent. Fitted with sliding tube which controls pitch or valves. Orchestras today usually have 1 bass and 2 tenor trombones.

Tromp, Maarten Harpertszoon (1597-1653), Dutch naval officer. Defeated Spanish fleet at Downs (1639). Won several skirmishes with English under Blake in the Channel (1652-3), but was finally defeated and killed off the Dutch coast.

Tromsö, town of NW Norway, on Tromsöy Isl. Pop. 36,000. Fishing, sealing industs. Largest town N of Arctic Circle; Arctic museum.

Trondheim, town of WC Norway, on Trondheim Fjord. Pop. 129,000. Port, fishing, shipbuilding. Founded 996 as Nidaros, cap. until 1380. German base in WWII. Cathedral (11th cent.).

tropical fish, name given to aquarium fish requiring controlled water temperature. Varieties incl. angel fish, mollys, gourami, zebra fish.

tropic bird, any of genus *Phaethon* of sea birds which breed on tropical islands. White plumage with black markings; elongated tail feathers.

tropism, natural movement of plants in response to external stimuli, *eg* a sunflower turning to face the light exhibits positive phototropism.

troposphere, lowest layer of Earth's ATMOSPHERE. Extends to *c* 9.5km (6mi) above surface. Temperature falls with increasing height; turbulent layer, containing much water vapour, dust. Separated from stratosphere by tropopause.

Troppau, see OPAVA, Czechoslovakia.

Trossachs, scenic glen of Central region, C Scotland, between lochs Achray and Katrine. Incl. Ben Venue.

Trotsky as war commissar in mid-1920s

Trotsky, Leon, orig. Lev Davidovich Bronstein (1879-1940), Russian revolutionary, journalist. In exile for Marxist activities before 1917 Revolution. Following Bolshevik triumph, organized victorious Red Army during civil war (1918-20). After Lenin's death (1924), led opposition to Stalin; expelled from Communist Party (1927), exiled 1929. Founded Communist Fourth INTERNATIONAL (1937). Assassinated in Mexico City, prob. at Stalin's instigation. His political followers (Trotskyists) maintain his policy of continuing world revolution.

trotting, see HARNESS RACING.

troubadours, poets of 11th-13th cent., who created first cultivated vernacular lyric poetry in Europe. Carefully stylized, poems were written in *langue d'oc* (Provençal) whether poets were French, German, Spanish or Italian. Subjects were love and chivalry, esp. ideals of courtly love. Poems spoken to musical accompaniment.

trout, game and food fish of salmon family, esp. of genera *Salmo* and *Salvelinus*. Found mainly in fresh water, but some varieties migrate to sea to feed. Species incl. European trout *Salmo trutta* (brown trout, sea trout and lake trout are subspecies) and N American rainbow trout *S. gairdneri*.

trouvères, poets of 11th-14th cent., N French counterparts of TROUBADOURS. Poetry incl. CHANSONS DE GESTE.

Troy

Troy (*Illum*), ancient city of Asia Minor, in NW Turkey, near mouth of Dardanelles. Excavations by Schliemann (1871-82) revealed 9 city levels; Homer's Troy, *c* 1200 BC, believed to lie at 7th level. *See* TROJAN WAR.

Troyes, town of NE France, on R. Seine, cap. of Aube dept. Pop. 75,000. Road and railway jct., textile and hosiery mfg. Cap. of Champagne from 11th cent. Scene of medieval fairs; gave name to 'troy' weight. Gothic cathedral (13th cent.).

Trst, see TRIESTE, Italy.

Trucial States, see UNITED ARAB EMIRATES.

Trudeau, Pierre Elliott (1919-), Canadian statesman, PM (1968-). Chosen by Liberals to succeed Pearson. Imposed War Measures Act after political kidnappings by Québec separatists (1970). Ardent federalist, term subsequently marked by rise of PARTI QUÉBECOIS.

Truffaut, François (1932-), French film director, critic. One of first and most popular of *nouvelle vague* directors. Films incl. *Quatre Cents Coups* (1959), *Jules et Jim* (1961).

truffle, any of genus *Tuber* of European edible fungi. Regarded as great delicacy, truffles grow underground and are sought with the aid of pigs or dogs.

Trujillo, town of NW Peru, on coastal plain. Pop. 156,000. Commercial centre in irrigated region producing sugar cane; food processing, tanning. Founded 1535. Has cathedral, univ. (1824).

Trujillo Molina, Rafael Leonidas (1891-1961), Dominican political leader, president (1930-8, 1942-52). Military coup brought him to power, which he maintained both in and out of office. Used autocratic, repressive measures to improve material welfare of country. Assassinated.

Truman, Harry S. (1884-1972), American statesman, president (1945-53). Democratic vice-president, took office at death of F.D. Roosevelt. Authorized use of 1st atomic bomb (1945) against Japan. Implemented Marshall Plan to aid recovery of post-war Europe and 'Truman Doctrine' of containing Communist expansion. Re-elected in surprise victory over Thomas Dewey (1948); 2nd term dominated by KOREAN WAR.

Harry S. Truman

trumpet, brass wind instrument. A long cylindrical tube bent twice on itself, opening out into bell. Played with cup mouthpiece. Modern trumpet has 3 valves, and is usually pitched in B flat or A.

trumpet creeper, *Campsis radicans,* high-climbing vine of S US with pinnate leaves and large red trumpet-shaped flowers.

trumpeter, any of genus *Psophia* of crane-like S American birds. Long legs, long neck; noted for loud cry.

trunkfish, any of Ostraciontidae family of tropical fish, whose bodies are encased in bony plates with spaces for eyes, mouth, gills and fins.

trusteeship, territorial, system of agreed control of non self-governing territs., administered by UN to promote welfare and preparation for self-govt. Supervised by Trusteeship Council of UN members. Replaced mandates operated by League of Nations. Only remaining trust territ. in 1976 was Pacific Isls.

trypsin, enzyme produced by vertebrate pancreas. Converts proteins into amino acids and polypeptides.

Tsamkong or **Chankiang,** port of Kwangtung prov., S China. Pop. 220,000. Formerly Fort Bagard, chief town of French territ. of Kwangchowan (regained by China 1945). Developed as sea port since 1954.

Tsana, see TANA, LAKE, Ethiopia.

tsar or **czar,** title of Russian emperors, first adopted (1547) by Ivan IV. Last tsar was Nicholas II.

Tsaritsyn, see VOLGOGRAD.

Tselinograd, city of USSR, NC Kazakh SSR; on R. Ishim. Pop. 194,000. Railway jct.; agric. machinery mfg. Founded in 19th cent. as Akmolinsk; renamed 1961.

tsetse fly, blood-sucking fly of genus *Glossina,* of C and S Africa. Bite transmits trypanosomes (flagellate protozoa) which cause sleeping sickness in man and nagana in cattle and other domesticated animals.

Tshombe, Moise Kapenda (1919-69), Congolese political leader. President (1960) of secessionist Katanga. Imprisoned 1961 after Lumumba's murder; later exiled. Returned as premier of Congo (1964-5); fled after MOBUTU'S 2nd coup; kidnapped and detained in Algiers (1967), where he died.

Tsimshian, group of North American Indian tribes speaking common language possibly of Penutian linguistic stock. Typical NW coast culture, fishing, seal hunting. Now *c* 5000 live on reservations in British Columbia and Alaska.

Tsinan, cap. of Shantung prov., E China. Pop. 1,500,000. Near Hwang Ho. Railway jct. Machinery, chemicals, textile mfg. Ancient walled city. Japanese occupation 1937-45.

Tsinghai or **Chinghai,** prov. of W China. Area *c* 647,500 sq km (250,000 sq mi); pop. (est.) 2,000,000; cap. Sining. Contains Kunlun and Nan mountains, Koko Nor salt lake, sources of Hwang Ho, Yangtze, Mekong rivers. Mainly high, desolate plateau. Rich coal, oil resources largely unexploited. Hist. part of Tibet.

Tsingtao, port of Shangtung prov., E China. Pop. 1,900,000. Naval depot, indust. centre on Yellow Sea. Railway engineering. Former treaty port, leased to Germany (1898).

Tsitsihar, city of Heilungkiang prov., NE China. Pop. 1,500,000. On R. Nen. Food processing; engineering, cement and paper mfg.

Tsushima, isl. group of Japan, in Korea Str. Scene of decisive naval victory of Japanese under Admiral Togo over Russians (1905); most of Russian ships captured or destroyed.

Tuamotu Islands, archipelago of SC Pacific Ocean, part of French Polynesia. Comprise *c* 80 atolls. Produce copra, pearl shell. Acquired by France (1844).

Tuareg, BERBER people of Sahara. Matrilinial culture in which men, rather than women, wear veil. The upper classes are nomadic traders, warriors; the lower group are partly settled farmers.

Tuatara

tuatara, *Sphenodon punctatus,* primitive lizard-like reptile found on islands in Cook Strait of New Zealand. Row of spines along head, back and tail; well-developed pineal eye. Only living representative of order Rhynchocephalia.

tuba, bass brass instrument of SAXHORN type. Used in orchestras and in most brass bands.

tuber, see BULB.

tuberculosis (TB), infectious disease caused by tubercle bacillus *Mycobacterium tuberculosis.* Similar form of disease affects cattle and can be passed to man in milk. Characterized by formation of nodular lesions (tubercles) in various parts of body, esp. lungs, lymph nodes, bones and skin. Treated by drugs such as streptomycin; BCG vaccine provides immunity. Pulmonary form formerly known as consumption.

Tübingen, town of SW West Germany, on R. Neckar. Pop. 55,000. Printing, precision instruments, textile mfg. Famous univ. (1477), scholars incl. Melanchthon.

Tubman, William Vacanarat Shadrach (1895-1971), Liberian statesman, president (1944-71). Suppressed rivalry among native tribesmen. Encouraged economic development of country.

Tubuai or **Austral Islands,** archipelago of SC Pacific Ocean, part of French Polynesia. Produce copra, coffee, tobacco. Acquired by France (1844).

TUC, see TRADES UNION CONGRESS.

Tucson, city of SE Arizona, US. Pop. 263,000. Railway jct.; mining, ranching trade centre; electronics and optics indust.; health resort. Settled by Spanish *c* 1700.

Tucumán, see SAN MIGUEL DE TUCUMÁN.

Tudor, House of, English ruling family (1485-1603). Estab. by Owen Tudor, a Welsh squire who married widow of Henry V. His grandson took throne as Henry VII, ending Wars of the Roses. Succeeded by Henry VIII, Edward VI, Mary I and Elizabeth I.

Tu Fu (712-70), Chinese poet. Considered one of greatest of Tang dynasty, poetry reflects compassion for terrible effects of civil strife. Also wrote satires.

Tuileries, former royal palace, Paris, France. Planned by Catherine de' Medici, begun (1564) in present Tuileries Gardens. Used as residence by Louis XVI and Napoleon I. Destroyed by fire (1871) during Commune of Paris.

Tula, city of USSR, C European RSFSR. Pop. 478,000. Metal goods mfg., esp. firearms and samovars; sugar refining. First Russian gun factory estab. here (1595) by Boris Godunov.

Cultivated tulips

tulip, any of genus *Tulipa* of bulbous plants of lily family. Large, cup-shaped solitary flowers of various colours. Most garden tulips are varieties of *T. gesneriana* introduced into Europe from Turkey in 16th cent.

tulip tree or **tulip poplar,** *Liriodendron tulipifera,* large tree of magnolia family. Native to E North America. Tulip-shaped, greenish-yellow flowers. Yellowish, soft wood is used in cabinet-making.

Tull, Jethro (1674-1741), English agriculturist. Known for his improvements of British agric., he invented (*c* 1701) a seed drill which sowed in rows. Wrote *Horse-hoeing Husbandry* (1733).

Tullamore, co. town of Offaly, C Irish Republic, on Grand Canal. Pop. 7000. Brewing, distilling. Nearby Durrow Abbey founded (6th cent.) by St Columba.

Tulle, town of SC France, cap. of Corrèze dept. Pop. 21,000. Produces firearms, textiles (gave name to 'tulle' fabric). Cathedral (12th cent.).

Tulsa, city of NE Oklahoma, US; on Arkansas R. Pop. 330,000. Important oil refining; oilfield equipment, aircraft mfg. Settled in 1880s as cattle town.

Tulsi Das (1532-1623), Indian poet. Wrote Hindu masterpiece, *The Lake of Rama's Deeds.*

tumbleweed, any plant which breaks away from its roots in autumn and is blown by the wind, scattering seeds. Abundant in prairie regions as Russian thistle, *Salsola kali,* and amaranth, *Amaranthus graecizans.*

tumour, swelling on some part of the body, esp. a growth of new tissue that is independent of its surrounding structures and serves no useful purpose. Said to be benign if localized and harmless; malignant tumour is a CANCER.

tuna, *see* TUNNY.

Tunbridge Wells, (Royal), mun. bor. of Kent, SE England. Pop. 45,000. Spa, discovered 1606; has 'Pantiles' promenade.

tundra, cold, treeless plains in N Eurasia and N North America. Region of PERMAFROST; mean monthly temperature below freezing point for most of year. Snow and ice cover in winter; topsoil thaws in summer, giving swampy conditions.

tungsten (W), hard metallic element; at. no. 74, at. wt. 183.85. Occurs in tungstite, scheelite, wolframite. Corrosion resistant, ductile. Used in lamp filaments, alloys, electric contact points; tungsten carbide used in drills and grinding tools. Also known as wolfram.

Tungting Hu, lake of Hunan prov., SC China. Varies in size with season *c* 3600-10,300 sq km (1400-4000 sq mi), at largest during summer rains. Connected by canal to Yangtze. Waters rice producing region.

Tunguska, name of 3 rivers of USSR, NC Siberian RSFSR; tributaries of R. Yenisei. They are **Lower Tunguska,** *c* 2550 km (1600 mi) long; **Stony Tunguska** *c* 1500 km (950 mi) long; **Upper Tunguska,** the lower course of R. Angara. All rise in Sayan Mts. near L. Baikal and flow NW into Yenisei.

Tunhwang, town of Kansu prov., N China. Pop. *c* 50,000. Near Chienfotung caves, site of discovery in 1900 of *Diamond sutra,* 1st printed book (868).

Tunicata (tunicates), subphylum of marine chordates with bodies enclosed in hard covering. Active tadpole-like larvae have notochord in tail region. *See* SEA SQUIRT.

Tunis, cap. of Tunisia, on L. of Tunis. Pop. 470,000. Canal link with Mediterranean, exports iron ore, phosphates, petroleum, dates, olive oil; textile and carpet mfg. Cap. of Berber state of Tunis from 13th cent.; taken 16th cent. by Turks. Pirate centre until French occupation 1881. Mosques, Bardo museum; nearby are ruins of CARTHAGE.

Tunisia

Tunisia, republic of N Africa. Area 164,200 sq km (63,400 sq mi); pop. 5,641,000; cap. Tunis. Languages: Arabic, French. Religion: Islam. Atlas Mts. in N, Sahara in S. Produces wheat, dates, olives, grapes; exports phosphates, petroleum, iron ore; fishing; growing tourist indust. Ruled by Carthage until 2nd cent. BC; became Roman prov. of 'Africa'. Fl 13th-16th cent. under Berbers; fell to Turks, became Barbary pirate base; occupied (1881) by France. Independent 1956, republic from 1957.

tunnel, passage cut underground to facilitate communications. Longest rail tunnel is Simplon, Switzerland (20 km/12.3 mi, completed 1922); longest road, Mont Blanc, France-Italy (11.5 km/7.2 mi, 1965). Earth tunnels normally cylindrical, lined with rings of cast iron or pre-cast concrete. Shield tunnel driving is method whereby circular ring is pressed forward by hydraulic jacks, first used by M. I. Brunel under R. Thames (1824).

tunny or **tuna,** large marine food fish of Scombridae family. Species incl. bluefin tuna, *Thunnus thynnus,* migratory fish of warm Atlantic, and albacore, *T. alalunga.* Large quantities canned.

Tupolev, Andrei Nikolayevich (1888-1972), Russian aeronautical engineer. First to design all-metal aircraft in USSR. Designed many of foremost military and commercial aircraft.

turaco or **plantain eater,** brightly coloured cuckoo-like bird of Muscophagidae family, found in African forests. Plumage contains red pigment which may be washed out by rain.

Turbellaria, class of mainly free-swimming aquatic flatworms. Body usually leaf-shaped and covered with cilia which aid movement.

turbine, rotary engine driven by pressure of a fluid (liquid or gas) against curved vanes of a wheel. Steam turbine, developed by C. PARSONS (1884), widely used in electrical generation and ship propulsion. Gas turbine, in which air is burnt with fuel to provide high pressure flow, used in aircraft propulsion.

turbot, *Scophthalmus maximus,* large flatfish of N Atlantic and Mediterranean. Both eyes on left side of head. Valuable food fish.

Turenne, Henri de la Tour d'Auvergne, Vicomte de (1611-75), French soldier. Hero of French army during Thirty Years War. Defeated Condé in Fronde (1652) and at Battle of the Dunes (1658) in subsequent war against Spain. Killed in Louis XIV's war against Dutch.

Turfan, depression of Sinkiang auton. region, NW China. Area *c* 13,000 sq km (5000 sq mi); lowest point 150 m (500 ft) below sea level. Agric. region. Contains town of Turfan (pop. 20,000).

Turgenev, Ivan Sergeyevich (1818-83), Russian novelist. Concern about serfdom produced *A Sportsman's Sketches* (1852). Masterpiece *Fathers and Sons* (1862) portrays conflict of traditionalists with new generation of

Turgenev

nihilists. Also wrote plays, short stories, *eg First Love* (1860), *Poems in Prose* (1878-82).

Turgot, Anne Robert Jacques (1727-81), French economist, statesman. Comptroller general of finances (1774-6), attempted sweeping economic reform, incl. removal of tax immunities and estab. of free trade.

Turin (*Torino*), city of NW Italy, on R. Po, cap. of Piedmont and of Torino prov. Pop. 1,188,000. Car, aircraft mfg., textiles. Under house of Savoy from *c* 1280; cap. of Kingdom of Sardinia from 1720 and Italy 1861-4. Cathedral (1492) has shroud reputedly of Christ; univ. (1404). Badly damaged in WWII.

Turkana, Lake, *see* RUDOLF, LAKE.

Turkestan or **Turkistan,** region of C Asia, now divided between USSR, China and Afghanistan. Russian sector comprises Kirghiz, Turkmen, Uzbek SSRs and S Kazakh SSR; conquered by Russia in 19th cent.

Turkey

Turkey, republic of Asia Minor and SE Europe. Area 781,000 sq km (296,000 sq mi); pop. 38,270,000; cap. Ankara, largest city Istanbul. Language: Turkish. Religion: Islam. Major part consists of Anatolia, an arid plateau crossed by Pontic Mts. in N and Taurus Mts. in S. Separated from European Turkey by Sea of Marmara, Bosporus and Dardanelles. Mainly agric. economy; produces wheat, barley, tobacco, fruit; minerals incl. coal, copper, chromium. Centre of Hittite civilization in 2nd millennium BC; parts colonized by Greeks; has ruins of Troy. Invaded by Seljuk Turks in 11th cent., then by Ottoman Turks. Ottoman Empire grew to incl. Balkans, Egypt, Arabia, *etc*; declined after defeat at Vienna (1683). Empire lost in series of wars, ending with WWI. Became republic (1923) under Ataturk who introduced Westernizing policy.

turkey, *Meleagris gallopavo,* large American game bird introduced into Europe from Mexico in 16th cent. Bronze-coloured plumage with bare head and neck; intensively reared for flesh.

Turkey

Turkic, language group within W Altaic family. Incl. Kirghiz, Kazakh, Turkish, Turkoman, Tatar, Uigur, Uzbek.

Turkmen Soviet Socialist Republic, constituent republic of SC USSR, on Iran border. Area *c* 488,000 sq km (188,400 sq mi); pop. 2,160,000; cap. Ashkhabad. Largely arid lowland (Kara Kum desert) in W and C; plateau in E. Agric., esp. cotton, maize and fruit growing, concentrated in oases and river valleys. Fisheries on Caspian Sea; oil fields. Conquered by Russia (1881); incorporated as republic (1924).

Turks and Caicos Islands, two isl. groups E of Bahamas; British crown colony. Area 430 sq km (166 sq mi); pop. 6000; admin. town Grand Turk (on Grand Turk Isl.). Salt, crayfish exports. Settled in 17th cent.; admin. by Jamaica (1873-1962).

Turku (Swed. *Abo*), city of SW Finland, on Baltic Sea. Pop. 152,000. Port, exports timber, butter; sawmilling, textile industs. Cultural centre; Swedish, Finnish univs., cap. of Finland until 1812. Rebuilt after fire (1827). Has cathedral (13th cent.).

turmeric or **tumeric,** *Curcuma longa,* East Indian perennial herb of ginger family. Large aromatic yellow rhizome which yields spice, colouring and medicinal agents.

Turner, Frederick Jackson (1861-1932), American historian. Known for studies on significance of the frontier in shaping American democracy. Most important work was *The Frontier in American History* (1920).

Turner: *The Fighting Temeraire*

Turner, Joseph Mallord William (1775-1851), English painter. Began as topographical painter working in watercolour; early oils were in emulation of Claude,

Poussin and Dutch marine painters. His rendering of light and dissolution of form in an attempt to capture atmospheric effects make late works almost abstract. Works incl. *Rain, Steam and Speed* and *The Fighting Temeraire.*

Turnip *(Brassica rapa)*

turnip, plant of genus *Brassica* of mustard family. Cultivated in temperate zones for edible tubers used as cattle food and vegetable. Chief varieties are *B. rapa* with white tubers and rutabaga or Swedish turnip, *B. napobrassica,* with yellow tubers.

turnpike, stretch of road paid for and maintained by fees collected from users at tollgates. Authorized in England in 1346 and in North America in 1785. Now usually state-owned.

turpentine, essential oil obtained by distillation of gum or resin from pine or other trees. Consists mainly of pinene ($C_{10}H_{16}$): used to thin paints and as solvent.

Dick Turpin and his horse Black Bess as depicted in a Victorian toy theatre

Turpin, Richard ('Dick') (1706-39), English highwayman. His famous overnight ride from London to York was an invention by Harrison Ainsworth in romance *Rockwood* (1834). Hanged at York.

turquoise, semi-precious gemstone, consisting of hydrous phosphate of aluminium plus some copper. Colour varies from sky blue to green; former most valued. Major sources in Iran, US.

turtle, any of order Chelonia of reptiles; name often applied only to aquatic species, terrestrial species being called tortoises. Soft body encased in plates of bone usually covered with horny shields; horny edged toothless jaws; retractile head, limbs and tail. Species incl. snapping turtle, hawksbill turtle, edible green turtle.

turtle dove, *see* DOVE.

Tuscaloosa, town of WC Alabama, US; on Black Warrior R. Pop. 66,000. Cotton goods, paper, tyre mfg., oil refining. State cap. 1826-46.

Tuscany *(Toscana),* region of WC Italy, cap. Florence. Incl. Elba; hilly, main river Arno. Main towns Leghorn, Pisa, Siena. Wheat, olives, wine; iron ore, mercury, Formed most of ancient Etruria; grand duchy (1567-1860). Renaissance cultural centre, esp. under Medici family. Language adopted by united Italy.

tusk shell, *see* SCAPHOPODA.

Madame Tussaud's: waxwork of *When did you last see your Father?*

Tussaud, Marie (1760-1850), Swiss wax modeller. Imprisoned during French Revolution, later founded (London, 1802) Madame Tussaud's wax museum, containing life-size models of famous hist. and contemporary figures.

Tutankhamen (*fl* 14th cent. BC), Egyptian king. Reversed policies of his father-in-law, IKHNATON, returning to worship of god Amon and restoring Thebes as cap. His tomb in Valley of Kings (excavated 1922 by H. Carter) contained many ancient Egyptian treasures.

Tuticorin, port of Tamil Nadu, S India, on Gulf of Mannar. Pop. 155,000. Cotton textiles, salt mfg. Founded by Portuguese in 16th cent., later held by Dutch.

Tutuola, Amos (1920-), Nigerian author. Known for fantasies which mingle magic, folk mythology with texture of modern life, *eg The Palm-Wine Drinkard* (1952), *Feather Woman of the Jungle* (1962).

Tuvalu, *see* ELLICE ISLANDS.

TVA, *see* TENNESSEE VALLEY AUTHORITY.

Tver, *see* KALININ.

Twain, Mark, pseud. of Samuel Langhorne Clemens (1835-1910), American humorist, novelist. Based classics *Tom Sawyer* (1876), *Huckleberry Finn* (1885) on Mississippi boyhood. Also wrote novels incl. *The Prince and the Pauper* (1881), *A Connecticut Yankee in King Arthur's Court* (1889), autobiog. *Life on the Mississippi* (1883).

Tweed, William Marcy (1823-78), American politician. Leader of TAMMANY in New York, controlled political appointments and city admin. 'Tweed Ring', consisting of Tweed and 3 others, defrauded city of millions of dollars; exposed in *New York Times* (1870). Died in prison, having been extradited from Spain.

Tweed, river of Scotland and England, flows 156 km (97 mi) from Borders region to North Sea at Berwick, forming part of national border.

tweed, rough-surfaced woollen fabric woven in various shades and patterns. Durable and almost weather-proof. Well-known types are made in Harris, Scotland and Donegal, Ireland.

Tweedsmuir, 1st Baron, *see* BUCHAN, JOHN.

Twelfth Night, eve of EPIPHANY. Celebrated as end of Christmas season.

Twelve Disciples, men chosen by Jesus to be his original followers: Andrew, Bartholomew, James (the younger, son of Alphaeus), James (the elder) and John (sons of Zebedee), Jude, Judas Iscariot, Matthew, Philip, Simon the Zealot, Simon (called Peter) and Thomas (Didymus).

twelve-tone system or **twelve-note music,** music composed by system utilizing equally all 12 chromatic notes of octave. Developed by SCHOENBERG and his followers, *eg* Berg, Webern. Also known as dodecaphonic or serial music.

Twickenham, former mun. bor. of SW Greater London, England, now part of RICHMOND-UPON-THAMES. Incl. English rugby football stadium; Hampton Court Palace.

twins, two offspring born at the same birth. Identical twins born from division of a single fertilized ovum are of same sex and closely resemble each other. Fraternal twins born of separately fertilized ova may differ in sex and appearance. In humans, twins occur once every *c* 90 births.

two-stroke (cycle) engine, *see* INTERNAL COMBUSTION ENGINE.

Tyche, in Greek myth, personification of chance. Represented with ship's rudder and cornucopia. *See* FORTUNA.

Tyler, John (1790-1862), American statesman, president (1841-5). Joined Whigs in protest against Democrats' federalist and fiscal policies. His own cabinet resigned after he vetoed Whig bank proposals.

Tyler, Wat (d. 1381), English rebel. Led impoverished serfs in PEASANTS' REVOLT (1381). Captured Canterbury and entered London. After his murder by Lord Mayor of London, uprising was crushed.

Tyndale or **Tindale, William** (*c* 1494-1536), English humanist, reformer. Began translation of NT in England; continued work in exile after meeting Luther. Pub. edition of NT from 1526. Copies denounced and suppressed in England. Convicted of heresy and executed at Antwerp.

Tyne, river of NE England. Formed by union of N, S Tyne rivers near Hexham, flows 48 km (30 mi) in Northumberland to North Sea via indust. Tyneside (Newcastle, South Shields).

Tyne and Wear, met. county of NE England. Area 540 sq km (208 sq mi); pop. 1,198,000; admin. centre Newcastle. Created 1974 to incl. area around mouth of R. Tyne.

Tynemouth, co. bor. of Tyne and Wear met. county, NE England. Pop. 69,000. Shipbuilding, engineering industs.

type, rectangular piece of metal used for printing. European invention of movable type is attributed to Gutenberg. Designers of widely-used typefaces incl. Jenson, Aldus Manutius, Caslon, Bodoni, Baskerville. Mechanized methods of typesetting incl. MONOTYPE, LINOTYPE. More recent methods of letterpress typesetting use photocomposition and computer (rather than hot metal).

typewriter, writing machine with a keyboard for reproducing letters, figures, *etc*, that resemble printed ones. When the keys are struck, raised characters are pressed against an inked ribbon, making an impression on an inserted piece of paper. First practical, commercial machine patented (1868) by C.L. Sholes (1819-90). Subsequent developments incl. electric machines requiring minimum effort (*c* 1935), 'golf-ball head' in which the characters are carried on quickly interchangeable globes (1961).

typhoid fever, acute infectious disease caused by bacillus *Salmonella typhosa*, usually found in contaminated food and water. Affects intestine, spleen and bones. Treated by chloramphenicol, *etc*.

typhoon, *see* HURRICANE.

typhus, acute infectious disease caused by rickettsia, micro-organisms transmitted by bite of lice, fleas. Characterized by eruption of red spots, prostrating fever.

Tyr, *see* TIW.

tyrannosaur, *Tyrannosaurus rex*, ferocious 2-legged carnivorous dinosaur; *c* 6 m/20 ft tall, with short forelimbs and sharp teeth. Existed in Cretaceous period.

tyrant flycatcher, any of Tyrannidae family of New World flycatchers; *c* 360 species, incl. kingbirds. Usually olive-green or dark with white markings; many species crested.

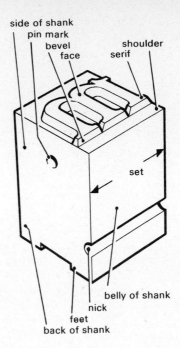

Type

Tyre (Arab. *Sur*), port of S Lebanon, on Mediterranean. Pop. 12,000. Ancient Phoenician centre, founded *c* 1500 BC on an island. Commercial centre, famous for purple dye. Destroyed 1291 by Arabs, it never recovered.

tyre or **tire,** pneumatic, rubber tube, filled with air, fixed about wheel of vehicle to absorb shocks and provide traction. First invented by R.W. Thomson (1845) but largely ignored until DUNLOP patented bicycle tyre (1888). First fitted to automobiles by Michelin company in France. Recent developments incl. radial ply tyres giving longer life and better handling on road.

Tyrol (*Tirol*), prov. of W Austria. Area 12,650 sq km (4884 sq mi); cap. Innsbruck. Alpine region, highest peak GROSSGLOCKNER; main river Inn. Tourism, dairying, forestry, salt mining. S Tyrol ceded to Italy 1919.

Tyrone, former county of WC Northern Ireland. Hilly, Sperrin Mts. in N. Agric., dairying. Co. town was Omagh.

Tyrrhenian Sea, part of W Mediterranean Sea, bounded by Italy, Sicily, Sardinia, Corsica. Named after Tyrrhenoi (ancient Etruscans).

Tyumen, city of USSR, W Siberian RSFSR; on R. Tura. Pop. 291,000. Sawmilling; shipyards. Centre of oil and natural gas producing region. Founded 1586, oldest Russian settlement in Siberia.

Tzepo or **Tzupo,** city of Shantung prov., E China. Pop. 850,000. Formed by merger of coalmining towns.

Tzu Hsi or **Tsu Hsi** (1834-1908), dowager empress of China (1861-1908). Served as regent 3 times (1861-73, 1874-89, 1898-1908). Fostered anti-foreign feeling which led to unsuccessful BOXER REBELLION (1898-1900).

U

UAR, see EGYPT.

Ubangi, river of WC Africa. Formed by confluence of Mbomu and Uele, flows *c* 1125 km (700 mi) via Bangui to R. Congo W of L. Tumba. Former part of Zaïre-Central African Republic and Zaïre-Congo Republic borders.

Ubangi-Shari, see CENTRAL AFRICAN REPUBLIC.

U-boat, abbreviation of German *Unterseeboot,* SUBMARINE.

Ucayali, river of E Peru. Flows N 1600 km (*c* 1000 mi) to join Marañón R., forming mainstream of Amazon.

Uccello, Paolo, orig. Paolo di Dono (*c* 1396-1475), Florentine painter. Early exponent of perspective and foreshortening; works incl. fresco *The Flood* and 3 scenes of *Rout of San Romano.*

Udaipur, city of Rajasthan, NW India. Pop. 163,000. Agric. centre. Cap. of former princely state of Udaipur or Mewar (1568-1948).

Udall, Nicholas (1505-56), English dramatist. Known for *Ralph Roister Doister* (*c* 1553), 1st known English comedy.

udder, mammary gland of cow, goat and other mammals. Mammary tissues manufacture liquids and solids forming milk for feeding of young.

Udine, city of Friuli-Venezia Giulia, NE Italy, cap. of Udine prov. Pop. 110,000. Produces machines, textiles. Gothic town hall, cathedral (13th cent.) in arcaded square. Damaged in earthquake (1976).

Udmurt, auton. republic of E European RSFSR, USSR. Area 42,100 sq km (16,250 sq mi); pop. 1,417,000; cap. Izhevsk. Forested area in W foothills of Urals; grain, flax, potatoes cultivated. Indust. centred on Izhevsk. Udmurts, a Finno-Ugrian people, colonized by Russia in 16th cent.

Ufa, city of USSR, cap. of Bashkir auton. republic, E European RSFSR; at confluence of Ufa and Belaya rivers. Pop. 821,000. Oil refining centre, connected by pipeline to Volga-Ural oilfield; chemical mfg. Founded 1574.

Uffizi Gallery, art museum in Florence, Italy. Building is 16th cent. palace built by Giorgio Vasari for Cosimo I de' Medici. Nucleus of collection derives from Medici family collection; esp. strong holding of Italian Renaissance painting and sculpture.

Uganda

Uganda, republic of EC Africa. Area 236,000 sq km (91,100 sq mi); pop. 11,170,000; cap. Kampala. Languages: Bantu, English. Religions: native, Christianity, Islam. Mainly plateau, bordered by lakes Albert, Edward, Victoria, and Ruwenzori Mts. Tropical savannah; cotton, coffee growing, forestry; industs. based on copper ores, Owen Falls Dam h.e.p. Explored by Speke (1862); Buganda (native kingdom) became British protect. (1894), other territ. added (1896). Independent from 1962 under the kabaka of Buganda, who became president. Coups by Obote (1966) and Amin (1971). Asian pop. mostly expelled 1973. Member of British Commonwealth.

Ugarit, ancient cap. of Ugarit kingdom, W Syria, near modern Latakia. Excavated in 1929; remains dating from 5th millennium BC found. Commercial centre in 15th and 14th cent. BC. Finds of Cuneiform tablets in Ugaritic language aided study of Semitic culture.

Ugaritic, ancient Semitic language, related to classical Hebrew. Discovered on clay tablets excavated from Ugarit, Syria. From 14th cent. BC, they are written in cuneiform script, one of earliest known alphabets.

UHF, see VHF.

Uhland, [Johann] Ludwig (1787-1862), German poet. Known for folk-style ballads, *eg* 'The Minstrel's Curse'. Also compiled scholarly folklore collection *Old South and North German Folk Songs* (1844-5).

Uigurs or **Uighurs,** Turkic people of C Asia. Rulers of Mongolia (744-840). Founded empire (*fl* 9th-13th cent.) in present-day Sinkiang-Uigur Auton. Region, still inhabited by their descendants.

Uist, North and **South,** isls. of Outer Hebrides, NW Scotland, in Western Isles. Separated by Benbecula. Main occupations crofting, fishing.

Ujiji, see KIGOMA-UJIJI.

Ujjain, city of Madhya Pradesh, C India. Pop. 209,000. One of the 7 holy cities of Hindus; pilgrimage centre. Cap. of former Gwalior state in 18th cent.

Ujung Pandang, cap. of S Sulawesi prov. (Celebes), Indonesia. Pop. 435,000. Seaport; exports coffee, spices, resins. Formerly known as Makassar.

ukelele, small four-stringed guitar of Portuguese origin. Easy to play, it became popular in Hawaii and spread to Europe and US after WWI.

Ukrainian or **Little Russian,** language in E Slavic branch of Indo-European family. Close to Russian, spoken in Ukrainian SSR.

Ukrainian Soviet Socialist Republic, constituent republic of SW USSR. Area *c* 601,000 sq km (232,000 sq mi); pop. 47,136,000; cap. Kiev. Largely steppeland covered with fertile blackearth soil; major agric. region, producing grain, sugar beet. Indust. based on coal of Donets basin, iron ore of Krivoi Rog, manganese of Nikopol. N and W part of Kievan principality until Tartar conquest in 13th cent.; passed to Poland, then to Russia by 1795. Independent (1918-20) during civil war. Territ. increased after WWII.

Ulan Bator, cap. of Mongolia. Pop. 282,000. Indust., commercial centre; linked to Trans-Siberian railway. Produces woollen goods, leather, footwear. Founded 17th cent.; has residence of Living Buddha, former spiritual leader of Mongolia. Called Urga until 1924.

Ulanova, Galina (1910-), Russian prima ballerina. Became leading ballerina of USSR, known esp. for performances in *Swan Lake, Giselle.*

Ulan-Ude, city of USSR, cap. of Buryat auton. republic, SC Siberian RSFSR; route centre on Trans-Siberian railway. Pop. 269,000. Railway engineering, wood products, textiles. Formerly called Verkhne-Udinsk.

Ulbricht, Walter (1893-1973), East German political leader, head of state (1960-71). In exile in USSR during Nazi regime. First secretary of Communist party (1953-71). Hard-line Stalinist, had Berlin Wall built (1961).

ulcer, break in skin or mucous membrane which does not heal. May be caused by infection (*eg* syphilitic ulcer),

Walter Ulbricht

defective blood supply (*eg* varicose ulcer) or irritation (*eg* peptic ulcer).

Uleåborg, *see* OULU, Finland.

Ullswater, scenic lake of Lake Dist., Cumbria, NW England. Length 12 km (7.5 mi).

Ulm, town of S West Germany, on R. Danube. Pop. 93,000. Railway jct.; metal goods, food processing. Scene of victory (1805) of Napoleon over Austrians. Cathedral (14th cent.) has tower 161 m (528 ft) high. Birthplace of Einstein.

Ulster, ancient prov. of NE Ireland. Comprises 6 counties of Northern Ireland, with Cavan, Donegal, Monaghan of Irish Republic. Scene of 17th cent. 'Plantations' of English, Scottish settlers.

ultramontanism, term for party in RC church which advocated doctrine of papal supremacy, *ie* opposed to GALLICANISM.

ultrasonics, science of sound vibrations of frequencies higher than those normally audible to human ear. Used to detect flaws in metals, detect underwater objects, *etc.*

ultraviolet rays, electromagnetic radiation with wavelength ranging from 4×10^{-5} to 5×10^{-7} cm, between visible light and X-rays. Radiation from Sun contains c 5% ultraviolet rays; these are mainly absorbed by oxygen and ozone in atmosphere, and glass. Produced by mercury vapour lamp; action on skin produces vitamin D.

Ulyanovsk, town of USSR, EC European RSFSR; Volga port. Pop. 382,000. Motor vehicle and machine tool mfg.; food processing. Formerly Simbirsk, renamed (1924) after Lenin (V. I. Ulyanov), who was born here.

Ulysses, *see* ODYSSEUS.

Umbelliferae, large family of hollow-stemmed, herbaceous plants with compound flowerheads radiating from point at top of stem. Incl. carrot, parsley, hemlock.

umbilical cord, fleshy structure uniting abdomen of foetus with placenta in mother's womb, through which shared blood circulates. Severed at birth, resulting scar is navel.

umbrella bird, any of genus *Cephalopterus* of black Central and South American birds, related to the cotinga. Male has umbrella-like head crest which covers bill.

umbrella tree, *see* MAGNOLIA.

Umbria, region of C Italy, chief cities Perugia, Terni. Mainly mountainous, incl. L. Trasimeno. Cereals, wine, olive oil; h.e.p., chemicals. Many Etruscan, Roman remains. School of painting (15th-16th cent.) incl. Perugino, Raphael.

Umtali, town of E Rhodesia. Pop. 54,000. Commercial centre, on Salisbury-Beira railway. Tobacco indust.; gold mining nearby.

Umtata, cap. of Transkei, S Africa, on R. Umtata. Pop. 25,000. Admin. centre, railway to East London. Anglican cathedral.

Unamuno [y Jugo], Miguel de (1864-1936), Spanish author. Philosophy concentrates on problems of freedom, *eg* in *The Tragic Sense of Life in Men and in Peoples* (1913). Also wrote formally experimental philosophical novels, *eg Mist* (1914).

Unanimism, *see* ROMAINS, JULES.

uncertainty principle, law of quantum theory stated by Heisenberg, that it is impossible to measure simultaneously and exactly 2 suitably related quantities, *eg* position and momentum of particle such as an electron. This uncertainty may be neglected for measurements other than those on an atomic scale.

'Uncle Sam', popular personification of US. Came into existence during War of 1812, origin uncertain. Depicted as tall, spare man with chin whiskers, dressed in red, white and blue swallow-tailed coat, striped trousers, tall hat with band of stars.

unconscious, in psychology, term used for dynamic elements of personality, both structures and processes, of which individual is temporarily or permanently unaware. According to Freud, unconscious processes are distinct from rational thought, allowing mutually contradictory wishes to co-exist. Jung postulated existence of racial or collective unconscious as well as individual one, from which derive archetypes, or collective symbols.

underground [UK] or **subway** [US], subterranean railway forming part of city rapid transport system. First was in London, England (1863); others incl. Boston (1898), Paris (1900). Moscow's is famous architecturally.

Underground Railroad, in US history (mid-19th cent.), system enabling Southern slaves to reach Northern states and Canada. Fugitive slaves were guided and sheltered by abolitionists on journey N.

Undset, Sigrid (1882-1949), Norwegian novelist, b. Denmark. Wrote medieval trilogy *Kristin Lavransdatter* (1920-2). Modern works reflect concern with social, psychological problems, author's conversion to Catholicism (1924). Nobel Prize for Literature (1928).

undulant fever or **brucellosis,** infectious disease of man and animals caused by bacteria of genus *Brucella.* Contracted by handling diseased animals or from milk. Frequently causes recurrent fever in man and abortion in animals.

unemployment, state in which work is unavailable to large number of people requiring it. Called structural if caused by decline or change in processes of given industry. Widespread during period 1918-39. Industrialized nations attempt to control economy in order to balance supply with demand of labour. Supposedly eliminated in China and USSR through public ownership of means of production and distribution. Also *see* SOCIAL SECURITY.

UNESCO *see* UNITED NATIONS EDUCATIONAL, SCIENTIFIC AND CULTURAL ORGANIZATION.

Ungaretti, Giuseppe (1888-1970), Italian poet, b. Egypt. Leading member of hermetic school of occult poets. Works incl. *L'Allegria* (1919), *Il Dolore* (1947), dealing with personal suffering.

Ungava Bay, inlet of NE Québec, Canada; extending S from Hudson Str. Area rich in iron ore deposits.

ungulate, herbivorous hoofed mammal. Two orders: Perissodactyla, odd-toed ungulates incl. horse, rhinoceros; Artiodactyla, even-toed ungulates, incl. sheep, cattle.

unicorn, legendary horse-like animal, usually pure white, with a single horn growing from the centre of its forehead. Believed by Greeks to exist in India. In medieval literature and heraldry, symbolizes virginity.

unified field theory, projected mathematical theory which attempts to describe in single set of equations properties and interactions of the 4 fundamental forces of nature: gravitation, electromagnetism, strong and weak nuclear interactions.

uniformitarianism, in geology, theory that features of Earth's crust evolve by means of process unchanged through geologic time. Opposes CATASTROPHISM theory.

First advanced (1795) by James Hutton; supported by John Playfair (1802) and LYELL (1830-3). Initially caused much controversy, now widely accepted.

Uniformity, Acts of, four acts of English Parliament (1549, 1552, 1559, 1662) aimed at enforcing standard reformed practices. Last act reestab. Church of England rites, prescribed use of Book of Common Prayer.

Union, Acts of, in British history, two acts, first (1707) uniting parliaments of England and Scotland, second (1800) uniting those of Britain and Ireland.

union, labour, employees' association with aims of self-protection, better pay and working conditions. Developed in Britain in 19th cent., achieving guaranteed legal recognition (1871) and joining (1893) Independent Labour Party. British unions organized on craft lines, called therefore 'trade unions'; in US and rest of Europe, unions are based within their indust. Achieve aims by COLLECTIVE BARGAINING and STRIKE.

Unionist Party, British political party formed (1886) to maintain parliamentary union between Britain and Ireland. Consisted of coalition of Liberal Unionists, who seceded from Liberal Party, and Conservatives. Later identified with Conservative Party.

Union of South Africa, see SOUTH AFRICA.

Union of Soviet Socialist Republics (USSR), federal state of E Europe and N Asia, world's largest country. Area, c 22,402,000 sq km (8,649,000 sq mi); pop. 245,066,000; cap. Moscow; other major city Leningrad. Chief language: Russian. Religion: Russian Orthodox. Comprises 15 constituent republics and 20 auton. republics stretching from Baltic to Pacific and N to Arctic. Hist. Russia founded by Rurik at Novgorod (862); Kievan state dominant 10th-12th cent.; Greek form of Christianity estab. 988. Overrun by Mongols in 13th cent.; Muscovite princes became dominant in 14th and 15th cents. after period of disunity. Expansion into Siberia began with first tsar, Ivan the Terrible. Romanov dynasty estab. 1613, Westernization policy introduced by Peter I; under his rule and that of Catherine II, became European power, taking territ. from Poland, Turkey, Sweden. Desire for reform of reactionary rule led to abolition of serfdom (1861); social unrest and military defeats led to Revolution (1905, 1917) and estab. of USSR under Lenin. Underwent enormous indust. growth under Stalin. Emerged as a dominant world power after WWII.

Union Pacific Railroad, railway system in US. Main line built (1865-9) W from Omaha, Nebraska, joined Central Pacific Railroad at Ogden, Utah, forming 1st US transcontinental railway. Early history marked by financial scandals. Now operates c 16,100 km (10,000 mi) of track in 13 states.

Unitarianism, form of Protestantism which rejects orthodox doctrine of Trinity. Accepts moral teachings of Jesus but denies his divinity. Holds that God exists only in one person. Arose during Reformation; estab. in England by JOHN BIDDLE. Taken to US by JOSEPH PRIESTLEY.

United Arab Emirates, group of 7 sheikdoms, SE Arabia, on Persian Gulf (Abu Dhabi, Ajman, Dubai, Fujairah, Ras al- Khaimah, Sharjah, Umm al-Qaiwain). Area c 84,000 sq km (32,400 sq mi); pop. 208,000; temporary cap. Abu Dhabi. Pearls, dried fish; oil at Abu Dhabi. British protect. (1892-1971), known as Trucial States at independence.

United Arab Republic, see EGYPT.

United Empire Loyalists, name given to colonists who remained loyal to Britain during American Revolution and migrated to Canada, esp. in 1783-4. Extensive settlement in Nova Scotia and Québec led to estab. of new prov. of New Brunswick (1784) and of Upper Canada (1791).

United Irishmen, see TONE, WOLFE.

United Kingdom (of Great Britain and Northern Ireland), kingdom of NW Europe. Area 244,750 sq km (94,500 sq mi); pop. 55,745,000; cap. London. Language: English. Religions: Anglican, Presbyterian, RC. Incl. England, Scotland, Wales, Northern Ireland, Channel Isls., Isle of Man. Constitutional monarchy (2-chamber parliamentary govt.); member of British Commonwealth,

EEC. After 1801 called UK of GREAT BRITAIN and Ireland; present name derived from Irish partition (1921).

United Nations [Organization] (UN), international body (hq. in New York), estab. 1945 to maintain peace and security and to promote cooperation between nations in solving social, economic and cultural problems. Charter, drawn up at San Francisco conference, designated admin. functions to Secretariat (headed by secretary-general), deliberative functions to General Assembly (comprising delegates from all member nations) and policy decision functions to Security Council (15 members, 5 permanent - UK, US, USSR, France, China - 10 non-permanent). Other principal organs are International Court of Justice, Trusteeship Council, Economic and Social Council. Also sponsors special agencies such as UNESCO, World Health Organization, International Monetary Fund, Universal Postal Union. As arbiter of international disputes, UN has had limited success, as in Arab-Israeli wars (1948, 1956, 1967, 1973), Korea (1951-3), Cyprus (1974).

United Nations Educational, Scientific and Cultural Organization (UNESCO), special agency of UN, estab. 1946 to contribute to peace and security by promoting collaboration among nations through education, science and culture. Trains teachers, encourages scientific research and cooperation.

United Nations General Assembly, see UNITED NATIONS [ORGANIZATION].

United Nations High Commissioner for Refugees, office estab. 1951 to protect refugees, seek solution of their problems by repatriation or resettlement and to provide emergency relief. Awarded Nobel Peace Prize (1954).

United Nations International Children's Emergency Fund (UNICEF), agency estab. (1946) to assist child health, nutrition and welfare, esp. in devastated areas and underdeveloped countries. Financed by voluntary contributions. Awarded Nobel Peace Prize (1965).

United States (of America), federal republic occupying most of S North America. Area 9,363,353 sq km (3,615,191 sq mi); pop. 210,000,000; cap. Washington; major cities New York, Chicago, Los Angeles, Philadelphia, Detroit, Houston. Language: English. Religions: Protestant, RC. Comprises 50 states, incl. outlying Alaska, Hawaii; mainland stretches from Pacific to Atlantic, Great Lakes to Gulf of Mexico. Rocky Mts. divide W interior; grain-producing Great Plains in C, drained by Mississippi system, S of which is oilrich region (esp. Texas). SE US primarily agric. Great Lakes, Atlantic coast, California centres of indust. and pop. Colonial struggle begun in 16th cent., ended with English victory over French (1756-63). Republic estab. by Thirteen Colonies after AMERICAN REVOLUTION (1776-83). W expansion facilitated by Louisiana Purchase (1803), Mexican War (1846-8). South's secession over slavery issue ended with defeat by Union in CIVIL WAR (1861-5). Indigenous Indians almost exterminated by colonists. Leading indust., agric., mineral producer; political power estab. in 20th cent.; challenged by USSR after WWII.

United States Air Force Academy, founded 1954 for officer training at Denver, Colorado, US; permanent site at Colorado Springs estab. 1958.

United States Military Academy, founded 1802 at West Point, New York State, to train military engineers. Extended (1866) to train officers of all branches of army.

United States Naval Academy, founded 1845 at Annapolis, Maryland, to train officers.

Universal Postal Union, international agency of UN, hq. at Bern, Switzerland. Founded 1875, passed to UN (1947). Facilitates international exchange of mail.

universe, all space and all matter contained in space. Distant galaxies are believed to be moving away from each other at high speeds and thus the universe is expanding. See COSMOLOGY.

university, institute of highest level of education. Generally has one or more undergraduate colleges, together with programme of graduate studies and number of professional schools. Has authority to confer degrees, eg

United States of America

bachelor's, master's, doctor's. Earliest were in Italy (Salerno, Bologna), France (Paris). In Middle Ages, developed under royal or ecclesiastical patronage, among most famous being Oxford, Cambridge. By late 19th cent., univs. had secular admin. and curricula (UK in 1871); in most Western states, univs. funded either by private endowment or govt. assistance, or both.

Unknown Warrior, body of unidentified soldier buried in Westminster Abbey (1920) as memorial to dead of WWI. Similar tombs exist at Arlington (US), Paris, Berlin.

Unruh, Fritz von (1885-1970), German author. Major figure in expressionism. Known for anti-militaristic works, *eg* prose epic *The Way of Sacrifice* (1916) on Verdun, novel *The End is Not Yet* (1945).

Untouchables, *see* CASTE.

Upanishads, in Hinduism, group of late Vedic metaphysical treatises. *See* VEDANTA.

upas, *Antiaris toxicaria,* large tree of mulberry family, native to Java. Bark yields juice used as arrow poison.

Updike, John Hoyer (1932-), American author. Works incl. poetry collections, *eg Hoping for a Hoopoe* (1959), short stories, *eg The Same Door* (1959), novels, *eg Rabbit Run* (1960), *Couples* (1968), *Beck: A Book* (1970).

Upolu, isl. of Western Samoa. Area 1100 sq km (430 sq mi); cap. Apia. Volcanic; fertile, produces bananas, coconuts, cocoa.

Upper Palatinate, *see* PALATINATE.

Upper Volta (Fr. *Haute-Volta*), republic of W Africa. Area 274,300 sq km (105,900 sq mi); pop. 5,737,000; cap. Ouagadougou. Official language: French. Religions: native, Islam, RC. Landlocked plateau, mainly savannah and semidesert; maize, millet, groundnuts, livestock. French colony from 1919; divided between Ivory Coast, Sudan, Niger (1933). Recreated (1947) as territ. of French West Africa, until independence (1960).

Uppsala, city of EC Sweden. Pop. 93,000. Cultural centre, incl. Sweden's oldest univ. (1477), library with precious

manuscripts (*eg* 6th cent. *Codex Argenteus*). Cathedral (13th cent.) has tombs of Gustavus Vasa, Linnaeus.

Ur, ruins of SE Iraq. Cap. of ancient Sumerian empire (*fl* 4th millennium BC).

Ural, river of WC USSR. Rises in S Ural Mts., flows S and W *c* 2250 km (1400 mi) to enter Caspian Sea near Guryev. Navigable to Orenburg.

Uralic, family of languages, main groups of which are FINNO-UGRIC and Samoyedic.

Ural Mountains, range of WC USSR, extending from Arctic Ocean to Kirghiz steppe region of Kazakh SSR; part of natural boundary between Europe and Asia. Rise to 1894 m (6214 ft). C part densely forested and rich in minerals (iron, manganese, nickel, copper). Urals indust. area, based on local coal and mineral resources, developed in 1930s; incl. towns of Chelyabinsk, Magnitogorsk and Sverdlovsk.

Urania, in Greek myth, Muse of astronomy. Represented with staff pointing to globe.

uranium (U), hard radioactive metallic element; at. no. 92, at. wt. 238.03. Occurs combined in pitchblende, carnotite, *etc.* Uranium 235, capable of sustaining chain reaction, is used in nuclear reactors; more plentiful uranium 238 is used to make plutonium, another nuclear fuel.

Uranus, in Greek myth, personification of heavens; according to Hesiod, son and husband of Gaea, the earth. Father of Titans, incl. Cronus (father of Zeus); emasculated and overthrown by Cronus.

Uranus, in astronomy, planet 7th in distance from Sun. Revolves about Sun at mean distance of *c* 2870 million km in 84 yrs; diameter 47,000 km; mass 14.5 times that of Earth. Has 5 satellites and dense atmosphere containing hydrogen, methane and ammonia. Discovered (1781) by William Herschel.

Urban II, orig. Odo of Lagery (*c* 1042–99), French churchman, pope (1088-99). His sermon (1095) at Clermont urging Christians to fight for Holy Sepulchre helped launch 1st Crusade.

Urbino, town of the Marches, E Italy. Pop. 23,000. Agric. centre; hist. majolica mfg. Cultural centre under Montefeltro family (12th-16th cent.). Has ducal palace (15th cent.), univ. (1506). Birthplace of Raphael.

Urdu, Indic language in Indo-Iranian branch of Indo-European family. Official language of Pakistan. Written variant of Hindustani. Used by Moslems, written in modified Arabic alphabet, contains many Persian, Arabic loan-words.

urea, crystalline organic compound, found in urine, blood, bile, *etc,* of all mammals. First organic compound to be prepared synthetically (by Wöhler 1828). Used in making fertilizers and resins.

Urey, Harold Clayton (1893-), American chemist. Awarded Nobel Prize for Chemistry (1934) for discovery of deuterium, isotope of hydrogen. Devised methods to separate isotopes, particularly uranium 235 from uranium 238.

Urfa (anc. *Edessa*), city of SE Turkey. Pop. 119,000. Market town. Christian centre until capture by Arabs (638); taken by Ottomans (1637). Scene of massacres of Armenian Christians in late 19th cent.

Urga, *see* ULAN BATOR.

urial, *Ovis vignei,* reddish-brown wild sheep of mountains of N India and Tibet.

uric acid, crystalline organic acid, found in urine and excreta of birds and reptiles. Gout is caused by deposits of uric acid salts in the joints.

urinary bladder, flexible muscular sac acting as temporary reservoir for urine.

urine, fluid formed in kidneys of man and some other vertebrates. Composed of water and waste products, incl. urea, uric acid, mineral salts. Stored in urinary bladder and discharged via the urethra.

Urmia, Lake, shallow saltwater lake of NW Iran, at alt. of 1300 m (4250 ft). Area varies between 3900 sq km (1500 sq mi) and 6000 sq km (2300 sq mi).

Urquiza, Justo José de (1801-70), Argentinian political leader. Governor of Entre Rios prov. from 1842. Gained federal power after defeating ROSAS at Monte Caseros (1852); president of Argentinian confederation (1854-60). Lost power in defeat by MITRE (1861).

Ursa Major or **Great Bear,** constellation of N hemisphere, whose 7 brightest stars form the Plough or Big Dipper.

Ursa Minor or **Little Bear,** constellation of N hemisphere; brightest star is Polaris or North Star, near N celestial pole.

urticaria, skin irritation caused by allergy. Characterized by itching, burning and formation of blotches. Also called nettle rash and hives.

Uruguay, , republic of SE South America. Area 177,508 sq km (68,536 sq mi); pop. 2,900,000; cap. Montevideo. Language: Spanish. Religion: RC. Fertile plains (wheat growing) rise to N grasslands (sheep, cattle rearing). Temperate climate. Spanish-Portuguese struggle for possession in 16th, 17th cents.; liberated with Argentina (1810); gained independence under Artigas (1825). Repression under military dictatorships in 20th cent.

Uruguay, river of SC South America. Rises in S Brazil, flows W, then S 1610 km (c 1000 mi) to join Paraná R., together with which it forms Rio de la Plata. Forms Argentina-Uruguay, Brazil-Argentina borders. Navigable to Paysandú.

Urumchi (*Tihwa*), cap. of Sinkiang auton. region, NW China. Pop. 500,000. On trade route to USSR; indust. centre, iron and steel works, cotton mills.

Usedom or **Uznam,** isl. of Bay of Pomerania, Baltic Sea. Area 445 sq km (172 sq mi). Divided from 1945 between Poland and East Germany; chief town Swinoujście (Poland). Agric., fishing, tourism.

Ushant (*Ile d'Ouessant*), rocky isl. off Brittany, NW France. Fishing, sheep raising. Scene of 2 naval battles between French and English (1778, 'Glorious First of June' 1794).

Usher, James, *see* USSHER, JAMES.

Usküb, *see* SKOPJE, Yugoslavia.

Usküdar, *see* ISTANBUL.

Uspallata Pass, route 3800 m (c 12,500 ft) high through Andes. Connects Santiago (Chile) and Mendoza (Argentina). 'Christ of the Andes' statue built here (1904).

Ussher or **Usher, James** (1581-1656), Irish churchman. Archbishop of Armagh from 1625; showed Calvinist tendencies. Known for long- accepted chronology of events in Bible, placing creation at 4004 BC.

USSR, *see* UNION OF SOVIET SOCIALIST REPUBLICS.

Ussuriisk, city of USSR, SE Siberian RSFSR; Pop. 135,000. Jct. of Trans-Siberian railway. Railway engineering, agric. machinery mfg. Formerly called Voroshilov.

Usti-nad-Labem (Ger. *Aussig*), town of NW Czechoslovakia, on R. Elbe. Pop. 72,000. River port, railway jct.; chemicals, textiles.

Ust-Kamenogorsk, city of USSR, E Kazakh SSR; on R. Irtysh. Pop. 241,000. Mining centre; lead, zinc smelting; h.e.p. station nearby.

Ust Urt, desert plateau of USSR, SW Kazakh SSR and NW Uzbek SSR; between Caspian and Aral seas. Area c 235,000 sq km (90,000 sq mi).

Usumbura, *see* BUJUMBURA, Burundi.

usury, *see* INTEREST.

Utah, state of W US. Area 219,932 sq km (84,916 sq mi); pop. 1,059,000; cap. Salt Lake City. Arid Great Basin in W, Great Salt L. in N; scenic Wasatch Range runs N-S. Limited agric., mainly livestock, wheat; rich copper, gold mines. Settled by Mormons in 1847; ceded to US after Mexican War (1848). Admitted to Union as 45th state (1896).

Colourprint by Utamaro

Utamaro, Kitagawa (1753-1806), Japanese colourprint artist. Famous for his depiction of women, distinguished by graceful line and colour. Also produced drawings for book *Insects* (1788), innovatory in naturalism.

uterus or **womb,** hollow muscular organ in female mammals in which the foetus develops. Usually c 7.6 cm (3 in.) long in humans, but greatly enlarged during pregnancy. Situated in pelvis; lower end opens via the cervix into the vagina, upper part opens at each side into a Fallopian tube leading to an ovary.

Utica, town of C New York, US; on Mohawk R. Pop. 92,000. Textiles, clothing industs. developed in 19th cent.

utilitarianism, philosophical school founded by Jeremy Bentham and later developed by J.S. Mill, who incorporated it into 19th cent. LIBERALISM. Doctrine based on concepts that man's needs are dictated by pleasure and the state's concern should be 'greatest happiness for the greatest number'.

Uto-Aztecan, *see* AZTECO-TANOAN.

Utrecht

Maurice Utrillo: *A Village Street*

Utrecht, prov. of C Netherlands. Area 1362 sq km (526 sq mi); cap. **Utrecht,** city on Lower Rhine. Pop. 275,000. Railway jct., indust. centre (chemicals, machinery, clothing). Union of Utrecht (1579) united 7 provs. of N Netherlands against Spanish rule. Peace of Utrecht (1713) ended War of Spanish Succession. RC archiepiscopal see, cathedral (14th cent.); univ. (1636).

Utrecht, Treaty of, settlement (1713) ending WAR OF SPANISH SUCCESSION, supplemented by French-Austrian agreements of 1714. Philip V, having renounced claim to French throne, recognized as king of Spain. Spanish possessions in Low Countries and Italy ceded to Austria. France recognized Hanoverian claim to British throne. Britain received Gibraltar, parts of North America and was granted commercial advantages.

Utrillo, Maurice (1883-1955), French painter. Known for his Parisian street scenes, often painted from picture postcards. Best work, marked by predominance of white, was done between 1908 and 1916.

Uttar Pradesh, state of N India. Area *c* 294,000 sq km (113,000 sq mi); pop. 88,365,000; cap. Lucknow. Most of state in Ganges plain, with Himalayas in NW. Agric. economy; grains, sugar cane. Formed (1950) from United Provinces of Agra and Oudh and 3 princely states.

uvula, *see* PALATE.

Uzbek Soviet Socialist Republic, constituent republic of SC USSR. Area *c* 449,500 sq km (173,500 sq mi); pop. 11,963,000; cap. Tashkent. Largely plain and desert (Kyzyl Kum), watered by Amu Darya and Syr Darya. Agric. in oases and Fergana valley possible through irrigation; cotton and rice grown; stock raising. Minerals incl. coal, oil. Centre of Tamerlane's 14th cent. empire. Settled by remnants of Golden Horde in 16th cent. Conquered by Russia by 1873; constituent republic of USSR (1924).

V

Vaal, river of South Africa. Flows *c* 1125 km (700 mi) SW from SE Transvaal to R. Orange in N Cape Prov. Forms most of Transvaal-Orange Free State border. Provides irrigation, h.e.p. for WITWATERSRAND.

Vaasa (Swed. *Vasa*), town of W Finland, on Gulf of Bothnia. Pop. 49,000. Formerly called Nikolainkaupunki. Port; textiles, food processing. Founded 1606, destroyed by fire (1852); rebuilt nearer sea.

vaccine, preparation of weakened or killed micro-organisms introduced into the body to produce immunity against a specific disease by causing formation of antibodies. Introduced by E. Jenner (1795) to immunize against smallpox.

vacuum, in physical theory, an enclosed space containing no matter. In practice, perfect vacuum unobtainable because of vapour emitted by container itself.

Vaduz, cap. of Liechtenstein, near R. Rhine. Pop. 4000. Agric. market; cotton indust.

vagina, in female mammals, passage leading from the uterus to the exterior at the vulva.

vagus nerve, either of 10th pair of cranial nerves. Arises in brain stem; its branches reach heart, lungs, oesophagus and digestive organs. Conveys sensory impulses from heart and lungs and motor impulses to stimulate digestive organs and slow the heart.

Vaihinger, Hans (1852-1933), German philosopher. Leading Kant scholar. In *The Philosophy of 'As If'* (1924) argued that, as reality cannot be known, man creates systems and acts 'as if' they represented reality.

Valais (Ger. *Wallis*), canton of SW Switzerland. Area 5234 sq km (2021 sq mi); cap. Sion. Mountainous, incl. Matterhorn, Monte Rosa (alpine resorts, h.e.p., forests on lower slopes); Rhône valley (cereals, vines). Pop. is French-speaking, RC. Joined Swiss Confederation 1813.

Valdivia, Pedro de (*c* 1500-54), Spanish conquistador. Commissioned by Pizarro to conquer Chile (1540); appointed governor (1549). Massacred with his men at Tucapel in Indian revolt.

Valdivia, town of SC Chile, on Valdivia R. Pop. 91,000. Indust. centre (beer, shoes). Founded 1552; influx of German immigrants in 19th cent. Suffered severe damage in 1960 earthquake.

Valence, town of S France, on R. Rhône, cap. of Drôme dept. Pop. 64,000. Textile (esp. silk, rayon) mfg., agric. market. Romanesque cathedral (11th cent.).

Valencia, region and former kingdom of E Spain. Mountainous in NW (sheep rearing), irrigated fertile coastal plain (fruit growing, esp. oranges). Moorish emirate; held by El Cid 1094-9; part of Aragón from 1238. Hist. cap. **Valencia,** cap. of modern Valencia prov. Pop. 654,000. Port, exports fruit, wine; shipyards, tobacco mfg., textile indust.; univ. (1501). Cathedral (13th cent.), silk market (15th cent.).

Valencia, town of N Venezuela, W of L. Valencia. Pop. 232,000. In leading agric. region producing sugar cane, cotton. Motor vehicles, chemicals, textile mfg. Founded 1555.

Valenciennes, town of Nord, N France, on R. Escaut (Scheldt). Pop. 47,000. Indust. centre, esp. coalmining, textile mfg.; noted for lace. Formerly in Hainaut, passed to France 1678.

valency or **valence,** in chemistry, capacity of an element or radical to combine with another to form molecules, measured by number of hydrogen atoms which one radical or atom of element will combine with or replace. Valency is explained in terms of electrons in outermost shell of atom which take part in reactions.

Valentine, St (*fl* 3rd cent.), Roman martyr. Traditionally patron saint of lovers; declaration of love on feast day (14 Feb.) originated in medieval times but may derive from earlier pagan festival.

Rudolph Valentino in *The Sheik*

Valentino, Rudolph, orig. Rodolpho d'Antonguolla (1895-1926), American film actor, b. Italy. Idolized in 1920s as great screen lover, sudden death brought personality cult. Films incl. *The Four Horsemen of the Apocalypse* (1921), *The Sheik* (1921), *Blood and Sand* (1922).

Valera [y Alcalá Galiano], Juan (1824-1905), Spanish novelist, critic, diplomat. Noted for great urbanity of style in novels, eg *Pepita Jiménez* (1874), *Doña Luz* (1879).

Valéry, [Ambroise] Paul [Toussaint Jules] (1871-1945), French poet. Main themes reflect concern with conflict between detached reason against involved passion, eg in dramatic monologues *La Jeune Parque* (1917), *Le Cimetière marin* (1920). Also wrote prose, essays.

Valhalla, in Norse myth, banqueting hall in ASGARD where Odin received souls of dead heroes.

Valkyries, in Norse and Teutonic myth, warrior hand-maidens of ODIN who fly over field of battle, choosing those to be slain and escorting them to Valhalla.

Valladolid, city of NC Spain, on R. Pisuerga, cap. of Valladolid prov. Pop. 236,000. Textile mfg., agric. market; univ. (1346). Castilian royal residence in 15th cent.; scene of marriage of Ferdinand and Isabella. Cathedral (16th cent.).

Valle d'Aosta, region of NW Italy, bordering France and Switzerland, cap. Aosta. Pop. mainly French-speaking. Main river Dora Baltea; h.e.p., forestry, tourism.

Valletta or **Valetta,** cap. of Malta, NE Malta. Pop. 16,000. Port, indust., commercial centre; univ. (1769). Founded 16th cent. by Knights Hospitallers; former British naval base, heavily bombed in WWII. Cathedral (1577).

valley, elongated depression in Earth's surface, between uplands, hills or mountains. Valleys cut by rivers are typically V-shaped, those cut by glaciers U-shaped. Also *see* RIFT VALLEY.

Valmy, village of Marne dept., NE France. Scene of French victory (1792) over Austro-Prussian army in Revolutionary Wars.

Valois, Dame Ninette de, orig. Edris Stannus (1898-), British prima ballerina, choreographer, b. Ireland. Founder of The Royal Ballet School (1931), director of the Royal Ballet (1931-63). Wrote autobiog. *Come Dance with Me* (1957).

Valona (*Vlonë*), town of SW Albania, on Adriatic. Pop. 50,000. Port, exports petroleum (pipeline from Kuçovë oilfield); fishing. Albanian independence from Turkey proclaimed here (1912).

Valparaiso, port of C Chile. Pop. 251,000. Indust. centre; sugar, textiles mfg. Settlement began 1554. Resort town of Viña del Mar (pop. 184,000) is suburb. Damaged in earthquake of 1906.

value, in economics, worth of commodity or service in terms of money or goods at a certain time. Depends on scarcity and desirability.

value-added tax, form of indirect sales tax paid on products at each stage of production or distribution, based on value added at that stage and incl. in cost to ultimate consumer. Originally introduced in France (1954), in UK (1973). Important element in tax structure of EEC.

vampire, in folklore, a corpse which becomes reanimated, leaving grave at night to suck blood of sleeping persons. Traditional method of killing vampire is to drive wooden stake through its heart.

vampire bat, small blood-sucking bat of genus *Desmodus* or *Diphylla* found in Central and South America. Feeds nocturnally on vertebrate blood; transmits rabies virus in saliva.

Van, for names not listed thus below, *see* 2nd constituent of surname.

Van, Lake, salt lake of E Turkey. Alt. 1700 m (5600 ft); area 3760 sq km (1450 sq mi). Salt and soda extracted by evaporation.

vanadium (V), rare hard metallic element; at. no. 23, at. wt. 50.94. Used to provide heat resistance, tensile strength and elasticity in steel alloys.

Van Allen radiation belts, 2 layers of charged particles (electrons and protons) trapped in outer atmosphere by Earth's magnetic field. Named after J.A. Van Allen (1914-), who suggested their existence following satellite explorations (1958). Inner belt believed to be caused by cosmic rays, outer belt by solar wind.

Vanbrugh, Sir John (1664-1726), English dramatist, architect. Late Restoration comedies of manners incl. *The Relapse* (1696), *The Provok'd Wife* (1697). Later associated with Wren as an architect; designed Blenheim Palace, Castle Howard.

Van Buren, Martin (1782-1862), American statesman, president (1837-41). Vice-president under Andrew Jackson. Advocated treasury system independent of all banks. Unsuccessful Democratic candidate in 1840 presidential election.

Vancouver, George (1757-98), English naval officer, explorer. Commanded expedition (1791-4) to explore coast of NW North America, reached via Australia. Vancouver Isl. named after him.

Vancouver, chief port of SW British Columbia, W Canada. Pop. 426,000. Natural harbour on Pacific. Transport terminus, commercial centre. Lumber, mineral, sawmilling, fishing, shipbuilding industs. Tourist resort, overlooked by mountains. Has Univ. of British Columbia (1908).

Vancouver Island, SW British Columbia, Canada; largest isl. off W North America. Area 32,137 sq km (12,408 sq mi). Has rugged coastline, mainly mountainous, forested. Agric. incl. dairy, fruit farming; mining incl. coal, gold, copper; fishing, lumbering, tourism. Pop. concentrated in E. Became crown colony (1849), part of British Columbia (1866).

Vandals, ancient Germanic people who settled in Spain (409). Under their leader GAISERIC, they invaded Africa (429) and conquered most of Roman territ., incl. Carthage. Controlled most of Mediterranean with their powerful fleet; sacked Rome (455). Defeated by Byzantine forces under BELISARIUS (534).

Van de Graaff generator, electrostatic generator, using a moving belt to accumulate charge in hollow metal sphere. Produces potentials of millions of volts; used to accelerate charged particles, *eg* electrons, to high energies.

Vanderbilt, Cornelius (1794-1877), American railway magnate. Known as 'Commodore' Vanderbilt because of large shipping interests, he amassed a fortune in railways after Civil War. Controlled (1867) New York Central Railroad. Endowed Vanderbilt Univ. (1875), Nashville, Tennessee.

Van der Post, Laurens Jan (1906-), South African novelist. Known for travel books, *eg Venture to the Interior* (1952), *The Lost World of the Kalahari* (1958), novels, *eg The Heart of the Hunter* (1961), short story cycle *Seed and the Sower* (1963).

Vandyke: detail of self-portrait

Vandyke or **Van Dyck, Sir Anthony** (1599-1641), Flemish painter. Assistant to Rubens in his teens, he later worked in Italy, painting pictures of Genoese nobility. Court painter to Charles I of England from 1632, he profoundly influenced subsequent English portraiture.

Vane, Sir Henry (1613-62), English statesman. Governor of Massachusetts Bay Colony (1636-7). Elected to Parliament (1640); member of council of state (1649-53). Negotiated Solemn League and Covenant with Scotland. Executed for treason after Restoration.

Vänern, largest lake of Sweden, in SW. Area 5545 sq km (2141 sq mi). Drained by R. Göta into Kattegat. Linked to L. Vättern by Göta Canal.

vanilla, genus of climbing tropical American orchids. Fragrant greenish-yellow flowers. Pod-like capsule of some species yields flavouring extract. *Vanilla planifolia* native to Mexico is widely cultivated.

Vannes, town of Brittany, NW France, on Gulf of Morbihan. Cap. of Morbihan dept. Pop. 41,000. Shipbuilding, textile mfg. Many megaliths nearby. Celtic and Roman antiquities, 13th cent. cathedral.

Van't Hoff, Jacobus Hendricus (1852-1911), Dutch chemist. Received 1st Nobel Prize for Chemistry (1901) for relating chemical reactions to thermodynamics and discoveries in osmotic pressure. Pioneer of stereochemistry.

Vanua Levu, isl of Fiji Isls., SW Pacific Ocean. Area 5540 sq km (2140 sq mi). Gold mining; sugar cane.

Vanzetti, Bartolomeo, see SACCO, NICOLA.

vapour pressure, pressure of a vapour in equilibrium with its solid or liquid form at any given temperature.

Varanasi, city of Uttar Pradesh, NC India. Pop. 583,000. On Ganges, in which Hindu pilgrims bathe to gain absolution from sin. Many mosques, incl. Golden Temple, and *c* 1500 Hindu temples. Formerly known as Benares.

Varangians, Viking warriors and merchants of 9th cent. who founded colonies in Russia and carried out raids as far S as Constantinople. One of their leaders, RURIK, was legendary founder of Russian royal house.

Varenius, Bernardus, Latinized form of Bernhard Varen (1622-50), Dutch geographer, b. Germany. Author of *Geographia generalis* (1650), standard work for over 100 years.

Varèse, Edgard (1885-1965), American composer, b. France. Wrote experimental music, often employing unusual combinations of instruments and powerful rhythmic effects. Compositions incl. *Ionisation* for percussion instruments and siren, *Déserts* for orchestra and magnetic tape.

Vargas, Getúlio Dornelles (1883-1954), Brazilian statesman, president (1930-45, 1951-4). Seized power, estab. benevolent dictatorship to enact social reform, improve agric., and begin industrialization. Re-elected president (1950), again forced to resign; committed suicide.

variable star, star whose brightness varies, either periodically or irregularly. Variation of Cepheid stars follows law relating period and luminosity, enabling their distance to be determined.

varicose veins, abnormal and irregular swelling of veins, usually in the legs. Caused by defects in the valves which keep blood circulating towards heart. Results from ageing, prolonged standing, pregnancy, *etc.*

Varna, city of E Bulgaria, on Black Sea. Pop. 252,000. Port, resort, trade centre (fish, grain). Univ. (1920). Founded by Greeks in 6th cent. BC; Thracian, Roman centre. Ceded to Bulgaria (1878); known as Stalin (1949-56).

varnish, solution of gum or resin in oil (oil varnish) or in volatile solvent (spirit varnish). On drying, forms hard, usually glossy, protective coating.

Varro, Marcus Terentius (116-27 BC), Roman scholar. A prolific writer, his few surviving works incl. *De re rustica,* on farming, and *De lingua latina,* treatise on Latin grammar.

Vasa, see VAASA, Finland.

Vasari, Giorgio (1511-74), Italian artist, biographer. Painted frescoes in Florence and Rome and designed Uffizi Palace in Florence. Fame rests on his *Lives of the Artists,* series of biogs. of artists, which serves as basic source of knowledge about Renaissance art.

vasectomy, method of male sterilization by sealing of vas deferens, the duct which conveys sperm away from the testicle.

Västerås, city of EC Sweden, on Lake Mälaren. Pop. 99,000. Västeras Recess (1527) brought Reformation to Sweden. Gothic cathedral, castle (12th cent.).

Vatican City, independent papal state within Rome, WC Italy. Area 44 ha. (109 acres); pop. 1000. Created 1929 by Lateran Treaty; has own citizenship. Seat of govt. of RC church. Buildings incl. Vatican Palace, St Peter's. Libraries, museums contain priceless collections.

Vatican Councils, two ecumenical councils of RC church. First (1869-70), enunciated doctrine of papal infallibility. Second (1962-5), convened by Pope John XXIII, revised church's role in modern society.

Vatnajökull, icefield of SE Iceland. Largest in Europe, area *c* 8160 sq km (315 sq mi), highest point Oraefajökull (2117 m/6950 ft). Incl. several active volcanoes.

Vättern, picturesque lake of S Sweden. Area 1898 sq km (733 sq mi). Linked to Vänern by Göta Canal; to Baltic Sea by R. Motala.

Vauban, Sébastien le Prestre, Marquis de (1633-1707), French army officer and military engineer. Famed for defensive fortifications around French frontier, revolutionized siege warfare.

Vaud (Ger. *Waadt*), canton of W Switzerland. Area 3209 sq km (1239 sq mi); cap. Lausanne. Mountainous in SE; fertile elsewhere. Wine indust.; lakeside resorts. Joined Swiss Confederation 1803.

Vaughan, Henry (*c* 1622-95), Welsh poet. Known as 'Silurist'. Works incl. metaphysical religious verse *Silex Scintillans* (1650-5).

Vaughan Williams, Ralph (1872-1958), English composer. Works were influenced by folk song (which he collected) and Tudor polyphony. Wrote 9 symphonies incl. *London Symphony,* orchestral works, choral works, *eg Sancta Civitas,* operas.

Ralph Vaughan Williams

vault, in architecture, arched ceiling or roof built with stone or brick. Romans developed barrel or tunnel vault, continuous semi-cylinder of masonry, which enabled them to build rigid structures. Medieval vaults, developed from Roman styles, incl. Gothic ribbed vault.

Vavilov, Nikolai Ivanovich (1887-*c* 1943), Russian plant geneticist. Postulated principle that original locale of plant is the area where greatest diversity of species is found. Died in Soviet concentration camp.

Veblen, Thorstein Bunde (1857-1929), American social theorist. Best known for interpretative rather than empirical surveys of social institutions, *eg The Theory of the Leisure Class* (1899), examining roles of businessman, technologist, academic bureaucrats.

vector, physical quantity possessing both magnitude and direction, *eg* velocity, momentum.

Veda, general term for scriptures of Hinduism. Oldest, Rig-Veda, incl. *c* 1000 hymns in praise of gods; Sama-Veda incl. stanzas extracted from the former Yajur-Veda has liturgical formulas and Atharva-Veda incantations to appease demons.

Vedanta, philosophic writings forming commentaries of the VEDA; incl. Upanishads. Hold that ultimate reality is not accessible to experience but only to direct intuition. Term is also applied to this system of thought.

Vega, Garcilaso de la (1539-1616), Peruvian historian. Son of Spanish knight and Inca princess. Wrote account of Inca empire and its conquest by Spain in *Royal Commentaries* (1609).

Vega [Carpio], Lope [Félix] de (1562-1635), Spanish poet, dramatist. Major poet of 'Golden Age'. Wrote *c* 1800 plays incl. religious dramas, 'cloak and sword' plays. Other works incl. lyrics, prose romance *La Dorotea* (1632).

vegetarianism, practice of restricting diet to foods of vegetable origin, for religious, humanitarian or health reasons. Strict vegetarians abstain from all food of animal origin, *eg* eggs, milk, butter.

vein, in anatomy, blood vessel which carries de-oxygenated blood from the tissues to the heart. Veins have thinner walls than arteries but greater diameters. Provided with valves to prevent back-flow of blood.

Velasco Ibarra, José Maria (1893-   ), Ecuadorian statesman. Four times president between 1934 and 1961, encouraged social and economic reforms. Re-elected (1968), became dictator (1970); replaced by military junta (1972).

Velázquez, Diego de (*c* 1460-*c* 1524), Spanish conquistador. Accompanied Columbus on his 2nd voyage to Hispaniola. Conquered Cuba (1511-14) and made himself its 1st governor. Commissioned Cortés to conquer Mexico (1519).

Velázquez: detail of boy's head from *An Old Woman cooking Eggs*

Velázquez, Diego Rodríguez de Silva y (1599-1660), Spanish painter. Court painter to Philip IV, whom he painted frequently; work is noted for its superb colour values and use of plain grey backgrounds. Famous works incl. *Surrender of Breda, Maids of Honour, Rokeby Venus.*

veld or **veldt,** open grassy plateau of E and S Africa. Types distinguished by height *eg* High, Middle, Low Veld, or by vegetation *eg* bush, grass, karoo veld. Used for potato and maize growing, cattle herding.

Velde, Henri van de (1863-1957), Belgian architect, decorator. A leading exponent of art nouveau; influenced by philosophy of William Morris and English arts and crafts movement, he founded Weimar School of Arts and Crafts (1902) to improve the practical arts.

vellum, fine parchment made from specially treated calf, lamb or kid skins. Used as writing surface and in bookbinding.

velocity, rate of change of position. Velocity is vector quantity, distinct from speed, which is a scalar quantity measuring magnitude of velocity.

Velsen, town of NW Netherlands, on North Sea Canal. Incl. port of Ijmuiden, joint pop. 67,000. Produces chemicals, steel. Damaged in WWII.

velvet, fabric woven with short thick pile on one side, often made of silk or rayon. Used for drapery, furniture upholstery. Modern grades incl. velveteen and corduroy.

Vendée, region and dept. of Poitou, W France, cap. La Roche-sur-Yon. Agric. (esp. cattle, cereals), forests. Scene of peasant-royalist uprising (1793-6) against Revolutionary govt.

Vendôme, Louis Joseph, Duc de (1654-1712), French army officer. In War of the Spanish Succession, campaigned against the European allies in Italy, Flanders, Spain; was relieved of command after defeat at Oudenarde (1708) but recalled to win victories at Brihuega and Villaviciosa (1710).

venereal disease (VD), infectious disease usually transmitted by sexual contact with infected person. Incl. gonorrhoea, syphilis. Prompt medical treatment with antibiotics and sulphonamides usually effective but delay may cause irreparable damage.

Venetia (*Veneto*), region of NE Italy, cap. Venice. Hilly, incl. Dolomites in N; fertile plain in S. Wheat, vines, sugar beet, hemp. Conquered by Romans 2nd cent. BC; ruled by Austria 1814-66.

Venezia, see VENICE, Italy.

Venezuela

Venezuela, republic of N South America, on Caribbean. Area 912,050 sq km (352,143 sq mi); pop. 11,300,000; cap. Caracas. Language: Spanish. Religion: RC. Coast (valuable oil production) rises to E Andes (agric., esp. coffee, cacao); cattle raising in Llanos of Orinoco basin; rain forest on Guiana Highlands. Major oil, gold, diamond exports. Settled by Spanish in 16th cent.; independence struggle (1811-21) under Bolívar. Part of Greater Columbia until secession (1830). Subsequent rule mainly by dictatorship. Influx of immigrants in 20th cent.

Venice: Bridge of Sighs

Venice (*Venezia*), city of NE Italy, on Gulf of Venice, cap. of Venetia and of Venezia prov. Pop. 378,000. Port, naval base; oil refining, glass; tourist centre. Built on 118 isls., with 170 canals (incl. Grand Canal), 400 bridges (incl. Rialto, Bridge of Sighs). Rich medieval maritime republic, *fl* 14th-15th cent.; defeated Genoa 1380. St Mark's Sq., Doge's Palace, Academy of Fine Arts are major attractions.

Venizelos, Eleutherios (1864-1936), Greek statesman, b. Crete. Premier 6 times between 1910 and 1933, brought Greece into WWI on Allied side after abdication of pro-German king, Constantine I (1917). Favoured creation of republic (approved by 1924 plebiscite). Led opposition to restoration of monarchy; died in exile.

Ventris, Michael George Francis (1922-56), English architect, archaeologist, linguist. Worked on examples of Mycenaean scripts, esp. Linear B (found near Pylos, Greece), identifying them as primitive form of Greek. With John Chadwick, wrote *Documents in Mycenaean Greek* (1956).

Venus, in Roman religion, perhaps orig. goddess of gardens, but became goddess of love, identified with Greek Aphrodite. Venus Genetrix regarded as mother of Aeneas.

Venus, in astronomy, planet 2nd in distance from Sun; revolves about Sun at mean distance of *c* 108 million km in

225 days; diameter 12,300 km; mass *c* 0.8 that of Earth. Has dense cloud layer containing carbon dioxide and surface temperature of 425° C. Seen as 'evening star' in W.

Venus flower basket, deep-sea sponge of genus *Euplectella.* Skeleton consists of lattice of small spines of silica.

Venus' flytrap

Venus' flytrap, *Dionaea muscipula,* perennial insectivorous herb native to North Carolina and Florida. Hinged leaves close when touched; insects trapped in leaves are digested.

Venus' slipper, *see* LADY'S SLIPPER.

Veracruz, port of EC Mexico. on Gulf of Mexico. Pop. 242,000. Major export centre esp. coffee, vanilla, tobacco; chemicals, textile, soap mfg. Estab. 1599. Tourist resort with fine beaches.

verbena, genus of plants chiefly native to tropical America. Showy spikes or clusters of red, white or purplish flowers. Widely cultivated as ornamental. European vervain, *Verbena officinalis,* was held sacred by ancient Greeks, Romans and Druids.

Vercingetorix (d. 46 BC), Gallic chieftain. Led revolt in Gaul against Roman occupation (58-51 BC). After initial success, he was besieged in Alesia by Caesar and he and his allies defeated. Put to death in Rome.

Verde, Cape, penin. of Senegal; most W point of Africa. Dakar is on S coast.

Verdi

Verdi, Giuseppe (1813-1901), Italian composer. Renowned for operas, incl. *Il Trovatore, La Traviata, Rigoletto, Aïda,* and later, based on Shakespeare's plays, *Otello* and *Falstaff.* Also wrote *Requiem* and *Stabat Mater.*

verdigris, greenish deposit formed on copper, brass or bronze surfaces exposed to atmosphere. Consists of basic copper carbonate or sulphate.

Verdun, town of Lorraine, NE France, on R. Meuse. Pop. 25,000. Textile mfg., food processing. Treaty of Verdun (843) divided Charlemagne's empire into 3 parts. Fortified 17th cent.; fortress was scene of long German assault (1916) resisted by French. War cemeteries.

Vereeniging, city of S Transvaal, South Africa, on R. Vaal. Pop. 170,000. Indust. centre in coalmining dist. Treaty ending Boer War signed here (1902).

Vergil or **Virgil,** full name Publius Vergilius Maro (70-19 BC), Roman poet. Famous for *Aeneid,* epic in 12 books on wanderings of Aeneas, reflecting preoccupations with greatness of Rome, virtues of a leader, nature of human existence and destiny. Also wrote pastoral poems, *Eclogues* (37 BC), didactic poems on rural life, *Georgics* (30 BC). To early medieval writers he was the supreme poet; influence remained profound up to 17th cent.

Verhaeren, Emile (1855-1916), Belgian poet. Pre-WWI verse characterized by faith in human brotherhood, progress. *Les Ailes Rouges de la Guerre* (1917) marks failure of his hopes.

Verlaine, Paul (1844-1896), French poet. Prominent among SYMBOLISTS. Encouraged in debauchery by RIMBAUD. Graceful, musical verse collections incl. *Fêtes galantes* (1869), *Romances sans paroles* (1874), *Sagesse* (1881).

Vermeer, Jan (1632-75), Dutch painter, b. Delft. Known for the calm perfection of his subtly-lit interiors, with 1 or 2 figures engaged in domestic or recreational activities. Works incl. *Allegory of Painting* and *Woman with a Water Jug.*

Vermigli, Pietro Martire (1500-62), Italian preacher, scholar; known as Peter Martyr. Augustinian monk, left Italy after expressing Protestant views on Eucharist. Worked in England with Cranmer on revision of Book of Common Prayer until restoration of Roman Catholicism by Queen Mary (1553).

Vermont, New England state of US. Area 24,887 sq km (9609 sq mi); pop. 445,000; cap. Montpelier; largest town Burlington. Canada on N border; L. Champlain in NW; Green Mts. cross N-S; chief river Connecticut. Agric. incl. dairy farming, fruit, maple syrup; marble quarrying, tourism. Settled in 18th cent.; part of New York until 1777. Admitted to Union as 14th state (1791).

vermouth, fortified white wine flavoured with aromatic herbs. Made chiefly in France and Italy.

Verne, Jules (1828-1905), French author. Early exponent of SCIENCE FICTION in novels, *eg Twenty Thousand Leagues Under the Sea* (1870), *Around the World in Eighty Days* (1873).

Verner, Karl Adolf (1846-96), Danish comparative philologist. Known for Verner's law, explaining sound changes in Germanic languages which had seemed exceptions to Grimm's law.

vernier, graduated scale that slides along longer graduated instrument and is used to indicate fractional parts of divisions.

Verona, city of Venetia, NE Italy, on R. Adige. Cap. of Verona prov. Pop. 264,000. On route to Brenner Pass; agric. market, printing. Joined (1167) Lombard League, *fl* 13th-14th cent. under della Scala family. Austrian fortress 1797-1866. Roman amphitheatre, Gothic town hall.

Veronese, real name Paolo Caliari (*c* 1528-88), Italian painter, b. Verona. Worked in Venice from 1553; specialized in huge allegorical, religious and historical scenes. Works, characterized by splendid colour, incl. *Feast in the House of Levi, Marriage Feast at Cana.*

veronica or **speedwell,** any of genus *Veronica* of perennial plants native to temperate regions. Many species cultivated as garden flowers incl. blue flowered speedwell, *V. persica.*

Verrocchio, real name Andrea di Cioni (*c* 1435-88), Italian sculptor, painter. Ran large workshop in Florence, where many artists, incl. Leonardo da Vinci, were trained. Executed famous equestrian statue of Bartolomeo Colleoni in Venice.

Versailles, town of N France, W of Paris, cap. of Yvelines dept. Pop. 95,000. Tourist centre, noted for palace and gardens built late 17th cent. for Louis XIV. Site of many treaties, *eg* between France and Prussia (1871), after WWI (1919).

Versailles, Treaty of, peace treaty at end of WWI signed by Allies (Britain, France, US and Italy) and Germany (1919). Germany, which took no part in negotiations, forced to accept terms, incl. loss of colonies, return of Alsace-Lorraine to France, loss of territ. to Denmark, Poland, Belgium, demilitarization of Rhineland, restrictions on armaments, payment of reparations. Treaty also contained covenant of LEAGUE OF NATIONS.

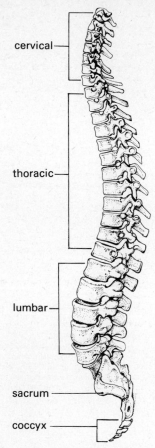

cervical

thoracic

lumbar

sacrum

coccyx

Human vertebral column

vertebra, segment of spinal column or backbone of vertebrates. Man has 33 vertebrae: 7 cervical in neck, 12 thoracic (each carrying pair of ribs), 5 lumbar; last 9 are fused to form sacrum and tail-like coccyx. Flexible discs unite the vertebrae; pressure on nerve fibres caused by bulges in discs is condition known as 'slipped disc'.

vertebrate, any of subphylum Vertebrata of chordate animals, with segmented spinal column and skull containing well-developed brain. Incl. mammals, birds, amphibians, reptiles.

vertigo, giddiness with associated feeling of whirling movement. Caused by disturbance in balance mechanism of the inner ear or eyes.

vervain, see VERBENA.

Verwoerd, Hendrik Frensch (1901-66), South African statesman, b. Netherlands. As minister of native affairs (1950-8), enacted harsh APARTHEID laws. As premier (1958-66), took South Africa out of Commonwealth and estab. republic (1961). Assassinated.

Vesalius, Andreas (1514-64), Flemish anatomist. His dissections and experiments on human body mark start of scientific anatomy; his findings overthrew accepted teachings of Galen. Wrote *De humani corporis fabrica* (pub. 1543), illustrated by remarkable van Calcar drawings.

Vespasian, full name Titus Flavius Vespasianus (AD 9-79), Roman emperor (AD 69-79). Fought in Britain where he conquered Isle of Wight. Chosen emperor by his troops while campaigning in Palestine. During his reign, Agricola made major conquest in Britain. Built Colosseum.

Vespucci, Amerigo (1454-1512), Italian navigator, b. Florence. In service of Spain, made many voyages to New World; explored mouth of Amazon (1499). Proved South America not part of Asia; American continent named after him.

Vesta, in Roman religion, goddess of the hearth, worshipped in every house. Sacred fire of state kept ever burning in Temple of Vesta, tended by 6 **Vestal Virgins,** daughters of noble families. Returned to private life after serving 30 years. Penalty for breaking vow of chastity was burial alive.

Vesteralen Islands, *see* LOFOTEN ISLANDS.

Vestmannaeyjar (Eng. *Westman Islands*), isl. group of Iceland, off SW coast; largest isl. Heimaey. Fishing, waterfowl breeding grounds. Volcanic eruption (1973) caused evacuation.

Vesuvius, SW Italy, on Bay of Naples, only active volcano on European mainland. Height now *c* 1185 m (3890 ft). Vines (for 'Lacrima Christi' wine) on lower slopes. Seismological observatory, chairlift. Many eruptions, incl. AD 79 when Pompeii, Herculaneum buried.

vetch, any of genus *Vicia* of weak-stemmed herbs of Leguminosae family, native to N temperate regions and South America. Common vetch or tare, *V. sativa,* is cultivated for forage and soil improvement.

veterinary science, branch of medicine dealing with diseases of animals, esp. domestic varieties.

veto, order prohibiting proposed act, esp. by person in authority. Term used specifically for constitutional right of ruler or branch of govt. to reject bills passed by another branch of govt. In US, president has power of veto over bill passed by Congress; can be overruled by two-thirds majority vote in Congress. Governors of states have similar power. In UN, any of 5 permanent members of Security Council have power of veto on action other than procedural.

V H F (Very High Frequency), electromagnetic radiation at frequency of 30×10^6 - 30×10^7 cycles per second. Used in frequency MODULATION radio transmission. UHF (Ultra High Frequency) is from 30×10^7 - 30×10^8 cycles per second.

viaduct, long bridge to carry a road or railway line over a valley or gorge. Usually consists of series of short, concrete or masonry spans supported on piers or towers.

Vian, Boris (1920-59), French author. Influenced by surrealism, used fantasy to pierce through accepted social values and semantic confusion. Novels incl. *L'écume des jours* (1947), *L'herbe rouge* (1950).

Viborg, town of NC Jutland, Denmark. Pop. 27,000. Iron founding; textiles; distilling. Cathedral (12th cent.).

vibraphone, percussion instrument having metal bars and resonators with rotating lids driven by an electric motor to simulate a vibrato. Also called vibraharp in US.

viburnum, genus of shrubs and small trees of honeysuckle family. Native to Europe, Asia and N Africa. Species incl. wayfaring tree, *Viburnum lantana.* White flowers used as decoration.

Vicente, Gil (*c* 1470-1536), Portuguese dramatist. Known for innovatory interest in characterization, fluent verse, portrayal of contemporary society. Very influential on Spanish, Portuguese drama.

Vicenza, city of Venetia, N Italy, cap. of Vicenza prov. Pop. 121,000. Railway jct., agric. market, machinery. Many buildings by Palladio (born here). Medieval cathedral, damaged in WWII.

Vichy, town of C France, on R. Allier. Pop. 34,000. Spa resort from Roman times; exports Vichy water. Seat of pro-German 'Vichy govt.' of France (1940-4).

Vichy government, govt. of unoccupied France, with seat at Vichy, set up under Pétain after Franco-German armistice (1940). Became tool of Germany under P. LAVAL (1942); powerless after German occupation of all France (Nov. 1942).

Vicksburg, town of W Mississippi, US; near jct. of Mississippi, Yazoo rivers. Pop. 25,000. Cotton, cattle trade centre. Scene of strategic victory by Union during Civil War after lengthy siege (1863).

Vico, Giovanni Battista (1668-1744), Italian philosopher. Originated scientific approach to history in *Scienza nuova* (1725), developing modified cyclical theory of civilization in place of history viewed as development of God's will. Often seen as 1st modern historian.

Victor Emmanuel II (1820-78), king of Italy (1861-78). Succeeded his father, Charles Albert, as king of Sardinia (1849). Acted as figurehead for policies of Italian unification of his premier, CAVOUR; enlisted support of Britain and France for cause. Proclaimed king of Italy following unification of most of country under Sardinian auspices.

Victor Emmanuel III (1869-1947), king of Italy (1900-46). Asked Mussolini to form govt. after declining to oppose his march on Rome; effectively deprived of power under Fascist regime. Made armistice (1943) with Allies in WWII. Abdicated.

Queen Victoria

Victoria (1819-1901), queen of Great Britain and Ireland (1837-1901). Married Prince Albert of Saxe-Coburg-Gotha (1840); guided by him in matters of policy. On Albert's death (1861), spent several years in seclusion. Influenced by personal charm of Disraeli; became empress of India (1876) under his guidance. Reign marked by indust. and colonial expansion, domestic reform.

Victoria, Tomás Luis de (c 1548-1611), Spanish composer. Worked in Rome for many years, then served as choirmaster to Empress Maria in Madrid. Compositions, all written for church, show masterly handling of polyphony.

Victoria, state of SE Australia. Area 227,700 sq km (87,900 sq mi); pop. 3,496,000; cap. Melbourne. Narrow coastal lowlands; uplands incl. C plateau, Australian Alps (SE); Murray basin in NW. Agric. (irrigated in NW) incl. wheat, fruit, vegetable growing, sheep and cattle raising; timber indust.; minerals incl. coal, oil, natural gas, gypsum. Industs. incl. petro-chemicals, car assembly, paper mfg. Settled from 1834; independent from New South Wales (1851). Pop. grew rapidly after 1851 gold discoveries. Federal state from 1901.

Victoria, seaport and cap. of British Columbia, Canada; on Vancouver Isl. Pop. 62,000. Timber, fishing, tourist industs. Esquimalt naval base is suburb. Founded 1843 by Hudson's Bay Co. as fur trading post.

Victoria, cap. of Hong Kong, on Hong Kong Isl. Pop. 849,000.

Victoria Cross, highest British military decoration. Instituted by Queen Victoria (1856).

Victoria Falls, massive waterfall of R. Zambezi, on Rhodesia-Zambia border. Width 1.6 km (1 mi); max. height 128 m (420 ft). Tourist centre; h.e.p. Discovered 1855 by Livingstone.

Victoria Island, SW Franklin Dist., Northwest Territs., Canada; part of Arctic archipelago. Area 212,200 sq km (81,930 sq mi). Has weather station at Cambridge in SE.

Victoria Land, region of Antarctica, divided between Ross Dependency and Australian Antarctic Territ.

Victoria Nyanza or **Lake Victoria,** freshwater lake of EC Africa, 2nd largest in world. Borders on Uganda (N), Kenya (E), Tanzania (S). Area 69,490 sq km (26,830 sq mi); source of White Nile. Originally called L. Ukerewe; Speke was 1st European to reach it (1858).

vicuña, *Lama vicugna,* wild llama found in South American Andes. Hunted by man for wool; numbers much reduced.

Vidal, Gore (1925-), American author. Known for sophisticated satirical novels incl. *Messiah* (1954), *The City and the Pillar* (1948), *Myra Breckinridge* (1968), *Burr* (1974). Also wrote plays, *eg The Best Man* (1960).

Vidal de la Blache, Paul (1845-1918), French geographer. Founder of French school of human geography; emphasized environmental effects of man's activity, links between geography and history. Founded *Annales de Géographie* (1891).

Vienna (*Wien*), cap. and prov. of Austria, on R. Danube. Pop. 1,615,000. River port, admin., commercial centre. Cap. and cultural centre of Austria from 12th cent. Home of Beethoven, Mozart, Strauss. Univ. (1365) famous for medicine, psychiatry (Freud). Buildings incl. Hofburg (imperial palace), cathedral of St Stephen, Houses of Parliament, opera house; also museums, parks. Resisted Turkish sieges 1529, 1683. Congress of Vienna (1814-15) rearranged Europe after Napoleon's defeat. German-occupied in WWII, Jewish pop. wiped out. Occupied by Allies 1945-55.

Vienna, Congress of, meeting (1814-15) of European powers (foremost being Austria, Prussia, Russia, Britain and France) to settle problems arising out of defeat of Napoleon. Resolved boundary disputes, reallocated control of many small states, estab. 'balance of power' principle in international politics.

Vienne, town of SE France, on R. Rhône. Pop. 30,000. Agric. market, textiles (esp. silk mfg.), tanning. Hist. seat of kings of Burgundy. Council (1312) suppressed Knights Templar. Roman remains incl. temple, theatre.

Vienne, river of WC France. Flows *c* 355 km (220 mi) from Corrèze dept. via Limoges to R. Loire.

Vientiane, admin. cap. of Laos. Pop. 174,000. Commercial centre on R. Mekong; timber, textiles. Cap. of kingdom 1707-1827. Became cap. of French protect. of Laos 1899. Noted for houses on stilts, pagodas, palaces.

Vierwaldstättersee, *see* LUCERNE, LAKE, Switzerland.

Viet Cong, Communist military force engaged in guerrilla warfare in South Vietnam during 1960s and 1970s. Following withdrawal of US troops (1973), Communist offensive of 1975 led to surrender of South Vietnam (April, 1975).

Vietnam

Vietnam, country of SE Asia. Area *c* 333,000 sq km (128,000 sq mi); pop. *c* 43,198,000; cap. Hanoi. Language: Vietnamese. Religion: Taoism. Forested mountains and plateau with Mekong delta in S. Rice chief crop. Part of French ruled INDO-CHINA until estab. of republic from Annam, Tonkin, Cochin China; dispute with France over independence led to INDO-CHINESE WAR, ending with Geneva conference (1954) which divided country into 2 states, North and South Vietnam. **North Vietnam,** area *c* 159,000 sq km (61,000 sq mi); pop. 23,244,000; cap. Hanoi. **South Vietnam,** area *c* 174,000 sq km (67,000 sq mi); pop. 19,954,000; cap. Ho Chi Minh (Saigon). North Vietnam's attempts (*see* HO CHI MINH) to reunify country under Communist rule led to US military intervention (1960s). US withdrew following 1973 ceasefire. South Vietnam fell to Communist forces in 1975 and gradual political reintegration followed.

Vietnam War, conflict in SE Asia, fought mainly in South Vietnam from 1954 between US-backed go͞vt. forces and VIET CONG guerrillas supported by North Vietnam and Soviet armaments. US support of South with economic, military aid began 1961, and intensified from 1964, when alleged Tonkin gunboat attacks prompted bombing of North. Tet offensive (1968) discredited US reports of ultimate victory. After President Johnson withdrew from 1968 election, peace talks involving both Vietnams, US and NLF began in Paris. Despite formal conclusion of war (1973), guerrilla activities continued in South, which capitulated with capture of Saigon (April, 1975). Length of war, high US casualties, corruption of South Vietnam govt. contributed to opposition of war within US.

Vignola, Giacomo Barozzi da (1507-73), Italian architect. Architect to Pope Julius III, he worked mainly in Rome. His work on Il Gesù (1568), mother-church of Jesuits, greatly influenced church architecture. Wrote *Treatise on the Five Orders of Architecture* (1562).

Vigny, Alfred Victor, Comte de (1797-1863), French author. Leading Romantic. Works incl. restrained, stoical *Poèmes antiques et modernes* (1826), play *Chatterton* (1835), historical novel *Cinq Mars* (1826).

Vigo, city of Galicia, NW Spain, on Bay of Vigo. Pop. 197,000. Port; shipbuilding, oil refining, fishing. Twice attacked by Drake (1585, 1589); scene of naval victory (1702) of British and Dutch over French and Spanish.

Viipuri, *see* VYBORG.

Vijayavada, city of Andhra Pradesh, SE India. Pop. 344,000. Railway jct.; hq. of Krishna canal irrigation system. Formerly known as Bezwada.

Vikings, Scandinavian sea-warriors who raided coasts of Europe (9th-11th cents.) in their oar-powered longships. Colonized Iceland, Normandy, parts of Britain and Ireland. Thought to have reached North America (*see* LEIF ERICSSON). Traded S and E to Persia, Spain, Russia. Also called Norsemen.

Francisco Villa

Villa, Francisco ('Pancho') (*c* 1877-1923), Mexican revolutionary. Took part in 1910 revolution. Involved in power struggle with Carranza from 1914. Raided New Mexican border towns in retaliation against US recognition of Carranza (1915); escaped capture in subsequent US incursion into Mexico. Assassinated.

Villa-Lobos, Heitor (1887-1959), Brazilian composer. Works show influence of Brazilian folk song and South American Indians. Compositions incl. *Chôros* (serenades) for various instruments and *Bachianas Brasileiras*, series of pieces intended to invoke spirit of Bach in Brazilian styles.

Villarrica, market town of SE Paraguay, in Guaira dept. Pop. 17,000. Cattle, maté, tobacco, cotton trade.

Villars, Claude Louis Hector, Duc de (1653-1734), French army officer. Commanded French troops aiding elector of Bavaria in War of the Spanish Succession. Won battle of Friedlingen (1702). In charge of main force confronting Marlborough, lost at Malplaquet (1709) but defeated Albemarle at Denain (1712). Negotiated Peace of Rastatt (1714).

Villehardouin, Geoffroi de (*c* 1160-*c* 1212), French soldier. Wrote *La Conquête de Constantinople* (pub. 1585), a chronicle of 4th Crusade.

villein, peasant of W Europe under medieval manorial system. Did not own land, but owed services to lord. Unlike serf, was personally free. Villeinage system declined in England by 14th cent. but survived elsewhere until 19th cent.

Villeneuve, Pierre Charles Jean Baptiste Sylvestre de (1763-1806), French naval officer. Consistently unsuccessful in battles with Nelson, from Nile (1798) to Trafalgar (1805). On his way home after captivity in England he committed suicide.

Villiers, George, *see* BUCKINGHAM, GEORGE VILLIERS, 1ST DUKE OF.

Villiers de L'Isle-Adam, [Jean Marie Mathias Philippe] Auguste, Comte de (1838-89), French author. Forerunner of SYMBOLISTS. Known for macabre short stories *Contes cruels* (1883), also wrote plays, incl. visionary *Axël* (1890).

Villon, François (1431-after 1463), French poet. Violent, criminal life reflected in verse, expressing compassion for human suffering, piety, alongside biting satire, ribaldry. Wrote *Lais* or *Petit Testament* (1456), containing lighthearted 'bequests' to friends, *Grand Testament* (1461), review of past life into which are set famous *ballades, eg* 'Ballades des dames du temps jadis' with refrain 'Where are the snows of yester-year?'

Vilnius (Russ. *Vilna*), city of USSR, cap. of Lithuanian SSR. Pop. 395,000. Railway jct.; food processing, sawmilling, agric. machinery mfg. Cap. of Lithuania (1323-1795); passed to Russian control. Intended cap. of independent Lithuania but seized (1920) by Poland and held until 1939. Large Jewish pop. decimated by Germans (1941-4). RC cathedral; univ. (1579).

Vilyui, river of USSR, NC Siberian RSFSR. W tributary of R. Lena, *c* 2400 km (1500 mi) long.

Viña del Mar, *see* VALPARAISO.

Vincennes, suburb of E Paris, France. Engineering, chemical industs. Royal residence from 12th cent., château near Bois de Vincennes used as state prison (17th-18th cent.).

Vincent de Paul, St (*c* 1580-1660), French priest. Founded secular Congregation of the Mission or 'Lazarists' (1625) and Sisters of Charity (1634), dedicated to work in orphanages, schools, hospitals.

vine, climbing or trailing plant, either woody or herbaceous, *eg* grape vine, ivy, Virginia creeper.

vinegar, sour liquid consisting of dilute and impure acetic acid, obtained by action of bacteria on beer (producing malt vinegar), wine, cider, industrial alcohol, *etc.* Used as preservative in pickling and as a condiment.

vingt-et-un, gambling game at cards, in which each player's aim is to obtain from dealer cards totalling 21 points or as near as possible to that total without exceeding it. Also known as blackjack and pontoon.

Vinland, hist. portion of North American coast discovered by Leif Ericsson (*c* AD 1000). Location of his landing disputed, most likely on S coast of New England. Also known as Wineland.

Vinnitsa, city of USSR, agric. centre of W Ukrainian SSR. Pop. 237,000. Sugar and fertilizer mfg. Part of Poland (1569-1793). Large Jewish pop. until German occupation (1941-3).

vinyl group, univalent chemical radical CH_2 : CH derived from ethylene. Various vinyl compounds, incl. chloride and acetate, may be polymerized to form plastics and resins.

viol, family of six-stringed instruments with fretted fingerboards, played with bow; popular esp. 16th-17th cent. Held on or between player's knees. Superseded by violin family; revived for performances of old music.

viola, member of violin family, between violin and cello in range. Pitched an octave above cello. Held under chin.

viola da gamba, member of viol family with similar range to cello.

Garden pansy

violet, any of genus *Viola* of small plants native to N temperate zones. White, blue, purple or yellow irregular flowers with short spurs. Species incl. *V. odorata* with small purple flowers and *V. tricolor* or garden pansy.

violin family, string instruments of which the four strings are bowed or plucked. Strings are stretched across a wooden bridge which transfers their vibrations to a sound chamber forming body of instrument. Fingerboard is fretless. Members are violin, viola and violoncello (CELLO), double bass. Evolved in 16th cent. and perfected by Italian violin makers, *eg* Amati, Stradivari, in 17th cent.

Viollet-le-Duc, Eugène Emmanuel (1814-79), French architect. Leading exponent of Gothic revival in France, he studied medieval architecture extensively. In *Dictionnaire raisonné de l'architecture française* (1858-74), emphasized engineering aspect of Gothic building. Numerous restorations incl. work on Notre Dame, Paris.

violoncello, *see* CELLO.

viper, any of Viperidae family of Old World venomous snakes, incl. adder, *Vipera berus,* and asp, *V. aspis.* Name also applied to New World pit vipers, incl. rattlesnake, bushmaster, fer-de-lance.

Virgil, *see* VERGIL.

virginals, *see* SPINET.

Virginia, Atlantic state of E US. Area 105,711 sq km (40,815 sq mi); pop. 4,648,000; cap. Richmond; largest city Norfolk. Low coastal plain (partly swamp) rises to Appalachians in W. Chief rivers Potomac, James, Rappahannock. Agric. esp. tobacco growing; fisheries, shipbuilding, mfg. industs. First permanent English colony estab. at Jamestown (1607). One of original 13 colonies of US. Major battleground in Revolution, Civil War.

Virginia bluebell, *see* BLUEBELL.

Virginia creeper, *Parthenocissus quinquefolia,* North American tendril-climbing vine widely cultivated in Europe as ornamental. Palmate leaves of 5 leaflets, green flowers followed by inedible blue berries.

Virgin Islands, group of *c* 100 isls. in West Indies, E of Puerto Rico. Discovered and named (1493) by Columbus. **British Virgin Islands** incl. Tortola, Anegada, Virgin Gorda isls. Area 153 sq km (59 sq mi); pop. 11,000; cap. Road Town (on Tortola). Colony from 17th cent. **Virgin Islands of the United States** incl. St Thomas, St Croix, St John isls. Area 345 sq km (133 sq mi); pop. 65,000; cap. Charlotte Amalie (on St Thomas). Purchased (1917) from Denmark.

Virgin Mary, *see* MARY, THE VIRGIN.

Virgo, *see* ZODIAC.

virus, disease-producing micro-organism, capable of multiplication only within living cells. Essential constituent is a nucleic acid (DNA, RNA), surrounded by a protein coat. Typical virus attaches itself to a cell of host and introduces its nucleic acid. Cell is forced to synthesize further nucleic acid and protein, enabling virus to reproduce itself. Cause of diseases such as measles, influenza, smallpox.

Visby, town of Sweden, cap. of Gotland Isl. Pop. 19,000. Port, resort. Early Hanseatic centre; prosperous medieval town, declined in 14th cent. Ruined fortifications, 12th cent. cathedral.

Visconti, Gian Galeazzo (*c* 1350-1402), Italian nobleman. Bought title of Duke of Milan (1395) from Holy Roman emperor Wenceslaus, then thwarted German imperial ambitions in N Italy with victory in 1401. Campaign to unify Italy ended when he died of plague near Florence. Founded Milan Cathedral.

Visconti [de Modrone], Luchino (1906-76), Italian film writer-director. Known as father of neo-realism for *Ossessione* (1942). Later films incl. studies of decadence, *eg The Damned* (1969), and passion in old age, *eg Death in Venice* (1970).

viscose process, method of making rayon from viscose, a brown liquid prepared by treating cellulose with sodium hydroxide and carbon disulphide. Yarn is made by forcing viscose through fine holes into acid solution. Discovered in 1892.

viscosity, internal friction of a fluid, caused by molecular attraction, making it resist tendency to flow. Viscosity of liquids decreases with rising temperature.

Vishakhapatnam, seaport of Andhra Pradesh, E India, on Bay of Bengal. Pop. 362,000. Exports manganese ore, groundnuts. Oil refinery; India's major shipyards.

Vishinsky, Andrei, *see* VYSHINSKY, ANDREI.

Vishnu, in Hinduism, one of three supreme gods. Early myth associates him with solar deities of Rig-Veda. Many incarnations incl. Rama, Krishna, Buddha. Represented as dark blue and holding conch, discus, mace and lotus.

Visigoths or **West Goths,** branch of GOTHS who were driven into Thrace and the Balkans by the Huns (*c* 375). Under ALARIC, they invaded Italy and sacked Rome (410). Later conquered much of S France and Spain. Forced to retreat into Spain by Clovis (507). Their kingdom in Spain was overrun during Moorish conquest (711).

vision, *see* EYE; RETINA.

Vistula (Pol. *Wisla,* Ger. *Weichsel*), river of Poland. Flows *c* 1080 km (670 mi) from N Carpathians via Kraków, Warsaw, Toruń to Gulf of Gdańsk near Gdańsk. Major trade route; canal links with other rivers *eg* Oder, Dnepr.

vitamin A, fat-soluble vitamin, found in fish-liver oil, milk, butter, *etc.* Can be synthesized in body from carotene found in green plants and carrots. Deficiency causes night blindness.

vitamin B complex, group of unrelated water-soluble vitamins, found in liver, yeast, wheat-germ, *etc.* Incl. THIAMIN, RIBOFLAVIN and vitamin B_{12}, a deficiency of which causes pernicious anaemia.

vitamin C, *see* ASCORBIC ACID.

vitamin D, any of group of fat-soluble vitamins, found in fish-liver oil, milk, *etc.* Formed in skin by action of ultraviolet radiation from Sun. Essential to formation of bones and teeth.

vitamin K, fat-soluble vitamin found in certain green leaves of plants and synthesized by bacteria in the intestines. Promotes blood clotting.

vitamins, group of complex organic compounds essential in small amounts to normal body metabolism. Some can be synthesized in body from other substances found in food, *eg* vitamin A; others, *eg* vitamin C, must be present in diet. Vitamin deficiencies cause various diseases, which can be cured by taking appropriate vitamin.

Vitebsk, city of USSR, N Byelorussian SSR; on W Dvina. Pop. 250,000. Agric. machinery, textile mfg. Chief town of Polotsk principality before coming under Lithuanian rule in 14th cent. Annexed to Russia in 1772.

Viterbo, town of Latium, C Italy, cap. of Viterbo prov. Pop. 59,000. Agric.; pottery, furniture. Medieval papal residence. Cathedral (12th cent.).

Viti Levu, largest of Fiji Isls., SW Pacific Ocean. Area 10,400 sq km (4010 sq mi); cap. Suva. Volcanic, largely mountainous. Produces sugar, fruit, coconuts.

Vitim, river of USSR, EC Siberian RSFSR. Rises in Vitim plateau (goldmining area), flows *c* 1750 km (1100 mi) to join R. Lena at town of Vitim.

Vitória, Atlantic port of E Brazil, cap. of Espírito Santo state. Pop. 124,000. Iron ore, coffee exports; sugar refining. On an isl., linked to mainland by bridge.

Vitoria, city of N Spain, cap. of Alava prov. Pop. 137,000. Agric. market, tanning. Scene of Wellington's decisive victory (1813) over French in Peninsular War. Cathedral (12th cent.).

vitriol, name given to various sulphate salts and sulphuric acid. Green vitriol is ferrous sulphate, blue vitriol copper sulphate, oil of vitriol concentrated sulphuric acid.

Vitruvius [Pollio, Marcus] (*fl* 1st cent. AD), Roman architect, engineer. Author of 10 vol. *De architectura,* treatise dealing with all aspects of building, town planning, *etc.* Source much used by Renaissance architects.

Vivaldi, Antonio (*c* 1675-1741), Italian composer. Known for more than 450 concertos, mainly *concerti grossi* for several instruments, but also for solo instruments, esp. violin, *eg The Four Seasons.* Influenced Bach, who rearranged some of Vivaldi's concertos.

Vivekananda (1863-1902), Indian mystic. Founded Ramakrishna Mission, travelled widely in Europe and US lecturing on VEDANTA.

vivisection, use of living animals for medical research into causes and prevention of diseases, esp. of man.

Vlaardingen, town of SW Netherlands, on R. Nieuwe Maas. Pop. 79,000. Fishing; fish processing, esp. herring and cod.

Vladimir, city of USSR, C European RSFSR. Pop. 248,000. Textiles, tractor mfg. Cap. of Vladimir principality (12th-14th cent.) until court removed to Moscow. Kremlin contains restored Uspenski and Demetrius cathedrals (12th cent.).

Vladivostok

Vladivostok, city of USSR, SE Siberian RSFSR. Pop. 472,000. Port and naval base (kept ice-free in winter) on Pacific coast. Exports timber, soya bean oil; shipbuilding, sawmilling; fishing, whaling. Settled 1860, developed after completion of Chinese Eastern railway (1903). Terminus of Trans-Siberian railway.

Vlaminck, Maurice de (1876-1958), French painter. One of the original fauves, early work is characterized by exuberant colour. Later specialized in darker, more expressionistic landscapes.

Vlissingen, *see* FLUSHING, Netherlands.

Vlonë, *see* VALONA, Albania.

Vltava, *see* MOLDAU, Czechoslovakia.

vodka, unaged colourless spirit distilled from barley, rye, maize, or potatoes. Originally made in Russia, Poland and Baltic states.

voice, sound produced by vibration of vocal cords, 2 pairs of membranous cords in larynx. Air from lungs causes lower pair to vibrate; pitch of sound is controlled by tension of cords and volume by regulation of air passing through larynx. Sinuses act as resonators, and muscles of the tongue and cheek articulate the sound.

Vojvodina, autonomous prov. of N Yugoslavia, in Serbia. Area 21,500 sq km (8300 sq mi); cap. Novi Sad. Fertile, low-lying, drained by Danube, Sava, Tisza; large amounts of cereals, vegetables, fruit grown. Part of Hungary until 1920.

Volcanic island of San Benedicto in the Pacific

volcano, vent in Earth's crust through which lavas, gases, *etc* are ejected. May be on land or submarine. Solidified material around outlet gives conical shape. Volcanoes may be active, *ie* subject to frequent eruption, dormant, *ie* undergoing long period of inactivity, or extinct, *ie* no longer liable to erupt.

Volcano Islands, group of 3 volcanic isls. in W Pacific, S of Japan. Area 29 sq km (11 sq mi); main isl. Iwo Jima. Annexed by Japan 1887. Captured by US forces in WWII and administered by US until 1968.

Bank vole (*Clethrionomys glareolus*)

vole, small rat-like burrowing rodent with blunt nose and short tail. Species incl. field vole, *Microtus agrestis*, and water vole, *Arvicola amphibius*.

Volga, river of USSR, European RSFSR; longest river of Europe. Rises in Valdai hills, flows *c* 3850 km (2400 mi) generally SE into wide Caspian delta. Connected by canals to Moscow, Leningrad and R. Don; major transportation system. Used for irrigation, h.e.p.; fishing in lower course.

Volgograd, city of USSR, SE European RSFSR; port on lower Volga. Pop. 852,000. Transport and indust. centre; oil refining, shipyards, steel and heavy machinery mfg. Founded 1589 as Tsaritsyn; Stalingrad (1925-61). Became commercially important in 19th cent. Scene of decisive Soviet victory in WWII after German siege (1942-3).

volleyball, six-a-side team game played on a rectangular court. Players hit a ball with their hands, attempting to

Volga

return it over net without its touching ground. Originated (1895) in US by W.G. Morgan. Olympic event since 1964.

Vologda, town of USSR, N European RSFSR. Pop. 190,000. Railway jct.; trade in dairy produce, railway engineering. Founded 1147 as a colony of Novgorod.

Volstead Act, legislation sponsored by Andrew Volstead (1860-1947) and passed (1919) by US Congress over President Wilson's veto. Provided for enforcement of PROHIBITION of alcoholic beverages under 18th Amendment. Repealed 1933.

volt, SI unit of electric potential, defined as difference in potential between 2 points on a conductor carrying constant current of 1 ampère when power dissipated between points is 1 watt.

Volta, Alessandro, Conte (1745-1827), Italian physicist. Invented electrophorus to produce electric charge. His attempts to refute Galvani's idea of 'animal electricity' led to discovery of voltaic pile (battery) which produced steady electric current. Unit of electromotive force, volt, named after him.

Volta, river of W Africa. Black and White Volta rivers from Upper Volta unite to form Volta in C Ghana; flows S to Gulf of Guinea at Ada. Volta River Scheme provides h.e.p., irrigation; Akosombo Dam (1966) formed L. Volta (area 4920 sq km/1900 sq mi).

Voltaic Republic, see UPPER VOLTA.

Voltaire: bust by Houdon (1781)

Voltaire, pseud. of François Marie Arouet (1694-1778), French philosopher, writer. Attacked organized religion, superstition, intolerance, civil repression. Influenced by English thought esp. by Newton, Locke, ideas influenced movement culminating in French Revolution. Wrote immense number of works, incl. tragedy (inspired by Shakespeare's *Othello*) *Zaïre* (1732), *Letters Concerning the English Nation* (1733). Best known for philosophical novel, *Candide* (1759), satirizing LEIBNITZ. Conducted stormy friendship with Frederick the Great.

Volta Redonda, town of SE Brazil, on Paraíba R. Pop. 121,000. Major steel mfg. plant. Model indust. town on railway link between Rio de Janeiro, São Paulo.

voltmeter, instrument for measuring potential difference between 2 points. Usually consists of galvanometer in series with a high resistance.

volvox, genus of small chlorophyll-bearing organisms forming hollow, spherical colonies common in ponds. Regarded by zoologists as flagellate protozoans, by botanists as green algae.

Von Braun, Wernher (1912-77), American rocket expert, b. Germany. Helped develop German V-2 military rocket. Director (from 1960) of Space Flight Center which developed *Apollo* rockets. Administrator of National Aeronautics and Space Administration (NASA) from 1970.

Vonnegut, Kurt (1922-), American author. Novels, *eg Player Piano* (1952), *Cat's Cradle* (1963), *Slaughterhouse Five* (1969), use the apparatus of science fiction and black humour to convey mistrust of human institutions.

Von Neumann, John (1903-57), American mathematician, b. Hungary. Made significant contributions to quantum theory, mathematical logic, continuous groups, *etc.* Founder of game theory; influential in development of high-speed computers, which aided production of the atomic bomb.

Von Sternberg, Josef, orig. Josef Stern (1894-1969), Austrian director, settled in US in 1920s. Known for creation of Marlene Dietrich's image, as in *The Blue Angel* (1930), *Shanghai Express* (1932).

von Stroheim, Erich, orig. Hans Erich Maria Stroheim von Nordenwall (1885-1957), Austrian film actor, director. Went to US (1909); known as director in 1920s, esp. for *Greed* (1923). As actor, remembered for Prussian officer roles, esp. in *La Grande Illusion* (1937).

voodoo, religious beliefs, practices of West Indian, S US and South American Negroes. Derived from W African snake worship, fetishism. Esp. prevalent in Haiti.

Voronezh, city of USSR, SC European RSFSR; near confluence of Voronezh and Don rivers. Pop. 693,000. Indust. centre of black-earth region; synthetic rubber and machinery mfg. Rebuilt after fires in 18th cent.

Voroshilov, Kliment Yefremovich (1881-1969), Soviet general. Active in October Revolution (1917). Armed forces commissar (1925-40), reorganized Red Army. Commanded defence of Leningrad against Germans (1941). Chairman of presidium (1953-60).

Voroshilov, see USSURIISK.

Voroshilovgrad, town of USSR, E Ukrainian SSR; in Donbas mining area. Pop. 404,000. Locomotives, coalmining equipment. Iron foundry estab. here 1795. Formerly Lugansk.

Vorster, Balthazar Johannes (1915-), South African political leader, PM (1966-). Succeeded Verwoerd, whose APARTHEID policies he upheld. Having sustained Rhodesia after UDI, later put pressure on it to accept black majority rule.

vortex, term used to describe rapid rotatory movement of a fluid. Used mainly of liquids (whirlpools) and of air (tornadoes, whirlwinds).

vorticism, English art movement founded (1913) by Wyndham Lewis; stimulated by futurism, and influenced by cubism, it sought to revitalize English art by introducing modern industrial forms. Adherents incl. Gaudier-Brzeska, Nevinson, Wadsworth. Journal, *Blast,* published literary work by, *eg* Ezra Pound, T. S. Eliot.

Vosges, mountain range of E France. Extends *c* 240 km (150 mi) NE from Belfort Gap, separates Alsace (E) from Lorraine (W), highest peak Ballon de Guebwiller (1423 m/4672 ft). Forests, vineyards, resorts. Source of Moselle, Sarre rivers.

vote, see ELECTION, PROPORTIONAL REPRESENTATION, SUFFRAGE, CIVIL RIGHTS.

Voysey, Charles Francis Annesley (1857-1941), English architect, designer. His country houses, built before WWI, were influential in their small size, simplicity and lack of period imitations.

Vries, Hugo de (1848-1935), Dutch botanist. One of three investigators who independently rediscovered Mendel's work on heredity; he discovered role of mutation in evolution.

Vuillard, Edouard (1868-1940), French painter. Member of the Nabis, he is known for intimate interiors, which display his feeling for texture and detail.

Vulcan, in Roman religion, fire god, perhaps god of the smithy. Became identified with Greek Hephaestus.

Vulgate, Latin version of Bible prepared (late 4th cent.) by St JEROME from Hebrew (OT) and Old Latin (NT) texts. Chosen by Council of Trent (1546) as official version in RC church.

vulture, large carrion-eating bird with hooked beak, strong claws, and featherless neck and head. True vultures, found only in C Europe, Africa and parts of Asia, incl. LAMMERGEIER and griffon vulture, *Gyps fulvus.* New World vultures incl. ANDEAN CONDOR.

Vyborg (Finn. *Viipuri,* Swed. *Viborg*), port of USSR, NW European RSFSR; on Gulf of Finland. Pop. 63,000. Exports timber, wood products. Site of Swedish castle (1293); Hanseatic port. Ceded to Russia by Sweden (1721); part of Finland (1812-1947).

Vyshinsky or **Vishinsky, Andrei** (1883-1954), Soviet diplomat. Chief prosecutor at treason trials following Stalin's purges (1936-8). Foreign minister (1949-53); frequently represented USSR at UN.

W

Waals, Johannes Diderik van der (1837-1923), Dutch physicist. Devised gas equation, taking size of molecules and their attractive forces into account, which gave better description of real gases than 'perfect gas equation'. Awarded Nobel Prize for Physics (1910).

Wabash, river of WC US. Rises in W Ohio, flows W 765 km (475 mi) through Indiana, then S to Ohio R. Its jct. with Tippecanoe R. (WC Indiana) is near site of decisive US defeat of Indians (1811).

Waco, town of EC Texas, US; on Brazos R. Pop. 95,000. Important cotton trade, cattle market. Glass, tyre, textile mfg. Has Baylor Univ. (1845).

wadi, watercourse in desert regions of N Africa and Arabia. Normally dry; formed by water torrents which accompany infrequent heavy rainfall.

Wadi Halfa, town of N Sudan, on R. Nile. Pop. 11,000. Railway terminus from Khartoum, steamer services from Egypt; transshipment point for Sudan-Egypt trade.

Wad Medani, town of EC Sudan, on Blue Nile. Pop. 71,000. Cotton market; centre of Gezira irrigation scheme. Agric. research station.

wages, in economics, share of total product of industry that goes to labour as distinct from share taken by capital. May be in money, goods or services. Real wages determined by amount of goods monetary wages will buy. Wage theorists incl. Ricardo, Marx.

Wagga Wagga, city of SE New South Wales, Australia, on Murrumbidgee R. Pop. 28,000. Trade centre for dairying, stock raising, wheat growing region. Agric. coll.; RC cathedral.

Wagner

Wagner, Richard (1813-83), German composer. Developed romantic music to great heights, using musical motifs in continuously evolving form to underline drama. Founded festival theatre at Bayreuth where he presented 4-opera cycle *Ring of the Nibelung* (1876); this work embodied his operatic theories. Other operas incl. *Die Meistersinger, Tannhäuser, Tristan und Isolde.*

Wagram, village of NE Austria. Scene of battle (1809) in which Napoleon defeated Austrians.

wagtail, small, chiefly European, bird of Motacillidae family. Slender body with long tail that wags up and down. Species incl. black and white pied wagtail, *Motacilla alba.*

Wahabi, followers of Mohammed ibn Abd al-Wahab (*c* 1703-91), who founded strict Moslem religious sect. Stress austerity in worship and living. Religion of ruling family of Saudi Arabia, where it predominates.

Waikato, longest river of New Zealand. Flows *c* 320 km (200 mi) NW from C volcanic plateau into Tasman Sea S of Auckland. Provides h.e.p. Scene of fighting (1863-5) against Maoris.

Wain, John Barrington (1925-), English poet, novelist. Works incl. collections of dryly witty verse, *eg A Word Carved on a Sill* (1956), novels, *eg Hurry on Down* (1953), criticism.

Wajda, Andrzej (1926-), Polish film director. Known for trilogy *A Generation* (1954), *Kanal* (1955), *Ashes and Diamonds* (1958), on growing up in war-torn Poland.

Wakamatsu, *see* Kitakyushu.

Wakayama, town of Japan, on Inland Sea, SW Honshu isl. Pop. 365,000. Iron and steel, textile mfg. Has 16th cent. castle.

Wakefield, Edward Gibbon (1796-1862), British statesman. Advocated sale of colonial land to finance further immigration. Helped found South Australia (1836). Managed colonization scheme of New Zealand Land Co. (1839).

Wakefield, city and co. town of West Yorkshire met. county, N England, on R. Calder. Pop. 60,000. Agric. market; woollens; coalmining. Has 14th cent. cathedral; grammar school (16th cent.). Scene of battle (1460) of Wars of the Roses in which Richard of York killed.

Wake Island, atoll with 3 islets, C Pacific Ocean, dependency of US. Area 8 sq km (3 sq mi). US naval, air base. Visited and named (1796) by British, annexed (1898) by US. Occupied by Japanese in WWII.

wake robin, *see* Trillium.

Waksman, Selman Abraham (1888-1973), American biologist, b. Russia. Awarded Nobel Prize for Physiology and Medicine (1952) for discovery of antibiotic streptomycin.

Walachia or **Wallachia,** region of S Romania. Chief city Bucharest. Comprises hist. provs. of Muntenia (Greater Walachia) in E, Oltenia (Lesser Walachia) in W. Agric., oilfields. Principality founded 1290; Turkish rule from 14th cent. until united with Moldavia (1859) to form Romania.

Walbrzych (Ger. *Waldenburg*), city of SW Poland. Pop. 125,000. Coalmining, porcelain mfg. In German Lower Silesia until 1945.

Walburga, St, *see* Walpurgis, St.

Walcheren, region of SW Netherlands, at mouth of Scheldt estuary. Main towns Middelburg, Flushing. Lowland, protected by North Sea dykes; agric., tourism. German occupation in WWII ended by bombing dykes.

Waldemar IV (*c* 1320-75), king of Denmark (1340-75). Recovered the parts of his kingdom occupied by foreign rulers by 1361. His victory over Hanseatic cities (1362) voided by Treaty of Stralsund (1370) which restored Hanseatic trading privileges in Denmark. Father of Margaret.

Waldenburg, *see* Walbrzych, Poland.

Waldenses or **Waldensians,** Christian sect formed (1170) by Peter Waldo (d. 1217). Dedicated to poverty and meditation, with Bible as sole authority. Forbidden to preach by Pope Alexander III (1179); declared heretical

(1215). Persecuted 15th-17th cent.; recognized 1848 by Charles Albert of Savoy.

Waldheim, Kurt (1918-   ), Austrian govt. official, UN secretary-general (1972-   ). Led Austria's 1st delegation to UN (1958); served as Austrian foreign minister (1968-70).

Waldo, Peter, see WALDENSES.

Wales

Wales (*Cymru*), principality of UK, in W part of Great Britain. Area 20,761 sq km (8006 sq mi); pop. 2,724,000; cap. Cardiff. Languages: English, Welsh. Religion: Methodist groups. Comprises 8 counties. Main rivers Severn, Wye, Taff. Crossed N-S by Cambrian Mts. (highest point Snowdon). Mainly pastoral; indust. based on S Wales coalfields (Swansea, Merthyr Tydfil, Rhondda). Originally inhabited by Celts. English conquest by Edward I (1282), but fierce fighting continued; politically united from 1536. Resurgence of nationalism in late 20th cent.

Wales, Prince of, title created (1301) by Edward I of England for his eldest son after conquest of Wales; since conferred on eldest son of monarch.

Waley, Arthur (1889-1966), English orientalist. Known for influential translations of Chinese, Japanese works incl. *The Tale of Genji* (6 vols., 1925-32).

Walker, William (1824-60), American adventurer. Invaded Lower California (1853), declared republic but forced to withdraw. Leading guerrilla band to assist Nicaraguan rebels (1855), captured Granada; became president, expelled (1857). Invasion of British-controlled Honduras (1860) ended in capture and execution.

wallaby, common name applied to small kangaroo when hind foot of adult is less than 25 cm/10 in. long; widely distributed in Australia and Tasmania. Species incl. agile rock-wallaby, genus *Petrogale,* and rare hare-wallaby, genus *Lagorchestes.*

Wallace, Alfred Russel (1823-1913), English naturalist. Researched on geographical distribution of animals; described imaginary (Wallace) line, running between Borneo, Celebes, Bali and Lombok, which marks division between Asian and Australian animal species. Developed theory of natural selection independently of Darwin.

Wallace, [Richard Horatio] Edgar (1875-1932), English author. Known for series of light novels with West African setting, *eg Sanders of the River* (1911), detective thrillers, *eg Green Archer* (1923).

Wallace, George Corley (1919-   ), American politician. Known for his espousal of segregationist policies as governor of Alabama (1962-6) which led to federal intervention. Won several states as Independent Party's presidential candidate (1968). Paralysed after assassination attempt (1972); re-elected governor in 1974.

Wallace, Henry Agard (1888-1965), American politician. An authority on farming methods, he was secretary of agric. (1933-4); vice-president under Roosevelt (1941-5). Progressive party presidential candidate (1948) after split with Democrats.

Wallace, Lew[is] (1827-1905), American soldier, author. Served as general in Union army. Remembered as author of *Ben Hur: A Tale of the Christ* (1880).

Wallace, Sir Richard (1818-90), English art collector. Son of 4th Marquess of Hertford, whose collection of paintings, *etc,* he inherited. **Wallace Collection** was presented to British nation by his widow in 1897; it is esp. rich in 18th cent. French painting.

Wallace, Sir William (*c* 1272-1305), Scottish patriot. Led forces which defeated Edward I's army at Stirling (1297), then drove English across border. Ruled Scotland briefly as guardian of kingdom. Defeated (1298) by English at Falkirk. Captured (1305), executed in London.

Wallach, Otto (1847-1931), German chemist. Awarded Nobel Prize for Chemistry (1910) for study of alicyclic organic compounds; investigated structure of terpenes, important in perfumery and essential oils.

Wallachia, see WALACHIA, Romania.

Wallasey, bor. of Merseyside met. county, NW England, on Wirral penin. Pop. 97,000. Resort, residential; ferry to Liverpool.

wallcreeper, *Tichodroma muraria,* small grey-black bird of Sittidae family, with crimson wing patches. Inhabits cliffs and rocky places of S Europe, N Africa and Asia.

Wallenstein, Albrecht von (1583-1634), Bohemian soldier, commander of forces of Emperor Ferdinand II. Fought successfully for Catholic League against the Danes in early years of THIRTY YEARS WAR. Dismissed after failure to capture Stralsund (1628). Recalled to counter Swedish threat, defeated by Gustavus Adolphus at Lützen (1632). Murdered, prob. for carrying out secret peace negotiations.

Waller, Edmund (1606-87), English poet. Wrote polished occasional poems, love lyrics, *eg* 'On a Girdle', 'Go, Lovely Rose' from *Poems* (1645). Banished from England (1643-52) for involvement in a Royalist plot.

walleye, *Stizostedion vitreum,* North American freshwater food and game fish of perch family, *c* 90 cm/3 ft long. Large staring eyes.

wallflower, *Cheiranthus cheiri,* European plant with sweet-scented yellow or orange flowers. Many garden varieties cultivated.

Wallis, Sir Barnes Neville (1887-   ), English aeronautical engineer. Designed R 100 airship and bouncing bombs used against Möhne and Eder dams (1943). Invented swing-wing aeroplane.

Wallis and Futuna Islands, overseas territ. of France, in SC Pacific Ocean. Area 272 sq km (105 sq mi); pop. 9000; main isl. Uvéa. Produce timber. Acquired by France (1842); dependency of New Caledonia until 1959.

Walloons, people of S provs. of Belgium who speak Walloon, a dialect of French. Walloon regions are centres of mining and heavy indust., unlike Flemish-speaking N provs. Friction between Walloons and Flemings remains element of Belgian politics.

Wall Street, New York street in lower Manhattan. As centre of great financial district, name has become synonymous with American finance.

English walnut

walnut, any of genus *Juglans* of deciduous trees of N temperate zones. Edible nut; timber valued for cabinet making. Species incl. Persian or English walnut, *J. regia,* and black walnut, *J. nigra,* of E US.

Walpole, Horace or **Horatio, 4th Earl of Orford** (1717-97) English author. Wrote prototypical 'gothick' novel, *The Castle of Otranto* (1765). Rebuilt villa, Strawberry Hill, at Twickenham, making 'gothick' taste fashionable. Also known for letters (3000 of them).

Walpole, Sir Hugh Seymour (1884-1941), English novelist, b. New Zealand. Wrote popular novels, *eg Mr*

Perrin and Mr Traill (1911), *The Herries Chronicle* (1930-3), criticism.

Walpole, Robert, 1st Earl of Orford (1676-1745), British statesman. Led Whig admin. (1721-42) as first lord of treasury and chancellor of exchequer, effectively acting as 1st PM. Restored economic stability after SOUTH SEA BUBBLE (1720). Encouraged free trade, cooperation with France; tried to keep Britain out of European wars. Estab. principle of CABINET responsibility to Parliament.

Walpurgis or **Walburga, St** (d. 779), English missionary in Germany. *Walpurgisnacht,* eve of her feast on 1 May, is traditional witches' sabbath.

walrus, either of 2 species of seal-like carnivores of Odobenidae family. Large upper canines form tusks used for scraping shellfish from sea bottom. Males up to 4.5 m/15 ft long may weigh over 1000 kg/1 ton. *Odobenus rosmarus* inhabits NW Atlantic, Arctic and *O. divergens* the Bering Sea.

Walsall, bor. of West Midlands met. county, WC England. Pop. 185,000. In BLACK COUNTRY; coal, iron industs.; leather goods.

Walsingham, Sir Francis (*c* 1532-90), English statesman. Employed on diplomatic missions to bring about Anglo-French alliance against Spain. Secretary of state after 1573, directed far-reaching spy ring. Discovered Babington's plot which implicated Mary Queen of Scots (1587).

Walsingham, Little, village of Norfolk, E England. Shrine (11th cent.) of Our Lady of Walsingham, centre of medieval pilgrimage.

Walter, Hubert (d. 1205), English churchman, archbishop of Canterbury (1193-1205). As justiciar (1193-8), he was virtual ruler of England during Richard I's absence. Carried out reforms in admin. and taxation.

Waltham Abbey or **Waltham Holy Cross,** urban dist. of Essex, SE England. Pop. 15,000. Govt. explosives research centre. Remains of 11th cent. abbey. King Harold said to have been buried here after Battle of Hastings.

Waltham Forest, bor. of NE Greater London, England. Pop. 234,000. Created 1965 from Chingford, Leyton, Walthamstow (all in Essex).

Walther von der Vogelweide (*c* 1170-*c* 1230), German poet. Famous for lyric poems, many on courtly love, religion; also moral and political lyrics.

Walton, Izaak (1593-1683), English writer. Wrote *The Compleat Angler* (1653) on pleasures of fishing. Also wrote biogs. of Donne, Wotton and others, *Lives* (1670).

Walton, Sir William Turner (1902-), English composer. Works incl. setting of poems by Edith Sitwell, *Façade.* Also wrote *Viola Concerto,* film scores, *eg Hamlet,* opera *Troilus and Cressida,* 2 symphonies and oratorio *Belshazzar's Feast.*

waltz, dance in triple time developed from German *Ländler.* Popularity spread from Vienna in 19th cent. through compositions of Strauss family.

Walvis Bay, town of South West Africa, on Atlantic Ocean. Pop. 16,000. Railway terminus, port, fishing and whaling industs. With hinterland (area *c* 970 sq km/375 sq mi) forms exclave of Cape Prov., Republic of South Africa.

wandering Jew, various trailing or creeping ornamental plants, esp. *Zebrina pendula* and *Tradescantia fluminensis.*

Wandsworth, bor. of SC Greater London, England. Pop. 299,000. Created 1965 from Battersea, Wandsworth met. bors. Incl. Putney area; Wandsworth prison.

Wanganui, city of SW North Isl., New Zealand, on Wanganui R. Pop. 36,000. Market town in large dairying, sheep and cattle raising area. Founded 1842.

Wang Ching-wei (1883-1944), Chinese politician. Leader of left wing of Kuomintang after Sun Yat-sen's death (1925); later turned to right. Split with Chiang Kai-shek's nationalists (1938). Headed pro-Japanese Nanking puppet govt. (1940-1).

Wankel rotary engine, type of INTERNAL COMBUSTION ENGINE invented by Felix Wankel (1902-). Derives power from rotor rather than reciprocating pistons. Successfully adapted to automobile.

Wankie, town of W Rhodesia. Pop. 24,000. Coalmining centre serving Zambian Copperbelt.

Wanstead, *see* REDBRIDGE, England.

wapiti, *Cervus canadensis,* American elk; largest North American deer, related to European red deer.

waratah, any of genus *Telopea* of trees and shrubs native to Australia. *T. speciosissima* has large red composite flowerheads; floral emblem of New South Wales.

Warbeck, Perkin (*c* 1474-99), pretender to English throne, b. Flanders. Under Yorkist influence, claimed to be Richard, son of Edward IV (who had prob. been murdered in the Tower). Invaded Cornwall and proclaimed himself king (1497); captured and hanged.

warble fly, two-winged fly of Oestridae family. Larvae are endoparasites of cattle, forming swellings (warbles) in skin when they emerge to pupate.

warbler, small insectivorous songbird. Old World warblers of large subfamily Sylviinae have mainly grey and brown plumage. Species incl. garden warbler, *Sylvia borin.* American wood warblers of Parulidae family are brightly coloured; species incl. yellow warbler, *Dendroica petechia.*

war crimes, actions which contravene rules of war laid down by Hague Convention (1907), UN War Crimes Commission (1943), *etc.* Crimes incl. mass extermination (as in post-WWII Nuremberg trials of Nazi leaders), slave labour, murder of prisoners.

Ward, Mrs Humphrey, née Mary Augusta Arnold (1851-1920), English novelist, philanthropist, b. Australia. Wrote didactic novels, *eg Robert Elsmere* (1888). Grand-daughter of Thomas Arnold.

Warhol, Andy (1930-), American artist, film producer. Leading exponent of pop art, uses silk screen printing techniques to obtain repeated images of familiar objects, *eg* soup cans, and popular personalities, *eg* Marilyn Monroe. Films incl. *Chelsea Girls.*

Warner, Rex (1905-), English author. Works incl. novels portraying evils of capitalist society, *eg The Professor* (1938), *The Aerodrome* (1941); translations of Aeschylus, Euripides.

War of 1812, conflict (1812-15) between US and Britain. US claimed rights of neutral shipping to trade with France, disputed by Britain. Campaign saw early US naval successes, US attempts to capture Canada thwarted by Britain, British naval blockade of US coast and burning of Washington (1814). War ended officially by Treaty of Ghent (1814) before defeat of British forces at New Orleans (1815).

Warren, Earl (1891-1974), American politician, jurist. As chief justice of Supreme Court (1953-69), made many important decisions on civil rights. Headed investigation into President Kennedy's assassination (1964-5); its conclusion that Oswald acted alone has been disputed.

Warren, Robert Penn (1905-), American author. Works incl. poetry, *eg Selected Poems 1923-43* (1944), *Brother to Dragons* (1953), novels, *eg All the King's Men* (1946), *World Enough and Time* (1950), explore problems of the South. Criticism incl. *Understanding Poetry* (1938, with Cleanth Brooks).

Warrington, co. bor. of Cheshire, NW England, on R. Mersey. Pop. 68,000. Iron founding; chemicals, soap mfg. Dates from Roman times.

Warsaw (*Warszawa*), cap. of Poland and of Warszawa prov., on R. Vistula. Pop. 1,317,000. Admin., indust., cultural centre; engineering, food processing; univ. (1818). Cap. of Poland from 16th cent.; under Russian rule 1815-1917. Occupied in WWII by Germans, severely damaged (incl. destruction of Jewish ghetto 1943); rebuilt on old pattern. Scene of Warsaw Treaty (1955).

Warsaw Treaty Organization, military alliance estab. (1955) through defence pact signed in Warsaw between Albania, Bulgaria, Czechoslovakia, East Germany, Hungary, Poland, Romania, Soviet Union. Diplomatic counter to acceptance of West Germany's entry to NATO.

wart, small, usually hard, tumour on skin, caused by a virus. May disappear spontaneously, only to reappear later; treated by application of acid and cauterization.

wart hog, *Phacochoerus aethiopicus,* wild African pig with large incurved tusks and warty skin on face. Capable of running quickly when alarmed.

Warton, Thomas (1728-90), English literary historian, poet. Known for *History of English Poetry* (1774-81) seminal in modern appreciation of medieval literature. Created poet laureate (1785).

Warwick, Richard Neville, Earl of (1428-71), English military, political leader, known as 'Kingmaker'. Supported York's claim to protectorship of Henry VI, then fought on Yorkist side in Wars of the Roses. Virtual ruler of England during early years of Edward IV's reign, but superseded by the Woodvilles. Joined Lancastrians and invaded England from France; defeated Edward and restored Henry as king (1470). Killed at Barnet by Edward's forces.

Warwick, residential town of C Rhode Isl., US; S of Providence. Pop. 84,000. Textiles mfg. (cotton, rayon, silk). Settled 1642.

Warwickshire, county of WC England. Area 1980 sq km (765 sq mi); pop. 468,000. Major indust. area in NW (esp. metal working); coal in NE; agric., fruit in S. Stratford, Forest of Arden associated with Shakespeare. Co. town **Warwick,** mun. bor. of R. Avon. Pop. 18,000. Castle (14th cent.) has art collection.

Wash, The, shallow inlet of North Sea, E England. Indents Lincoln-Norfolk coast; subject to silting, increasing reclamation. Two navigable channels (Boston, Lynn Deeps).

Washington, Booker T[aliaferro] (1856-1915), American black educator, reformer. First principal of Tuskegee Institute (1881-1915), travelled across US to promote technical education for blacks. Wrote autobiog., *Up from Slavery* (1901).

George Washington

Washington, George (1732-99), American statesman, president (1789-97). Given command of Continental Army at outset of American Revolution (1775); after victories at Trenton and Princeton, defeated at Brandywine (1776); survived difficult winter at Valley Forge (1778). With French support, gained victories culminating in British surrender at Yorktown (1781). Presided at Constitutional Convention (1787), later becoming 1st president. Admin. marked by split between HAMILTON and JEFFERSON, latter resigning 1793. Set precedent by refusing 3rd term in office. Warned against foreign entanglements in Farewell Address.

Washington, state of NW US, borders on Pacific and Canada. Area 176,617 sq km (68,192 sq mi); pop. 3,409,000; cap. Olympia; largest city Seattle. Cascade Range divides E plateau from Puget Sound; chief rivers Columbia, Snake. Agric. esp. fruit, vegetables; fishing, timber industs., aircraft mfg. H.e.p. supplies boosted industs. (Grand Coulee, Bonneville dams). Region disputed by British; boundary fixed 1846. Territ. estab. 1853. Admitted to Union as 42nd state (1889).

Washington, cap. of US, in DISTRICT OF COLUMBIA (DC) on Potomac R. Pop. 757,000. Built 1790-1800 as cap. Buildings incl. White House (president's residence), Capitol (Congress), Pentagon (military admin.); Library of Congress, National Gallery, Lincoln memorial. Arlington cemetery nearby.

Wasp nest

wasp, winged insect of order Hymenoptera, with worldwide distribution. Social wasps have caste system of queens, workers, and male drones. Colonies make nest of chewed wood pulp; in temperate climates only queen survives winter. Queens and workers have sting which can be used repeatedly. Solitary wasps incl. POTTER WASP.

Wassermann, August von (1866-1925), German bacteriologist. Devised complement fixation test (Wassermann test) for syphilis which determines presence of syphilitic antibodies in patient's blood serum.

Wassermann, Jakob (1873-1934), German novelist. Wrote psychologically realistic novels, *eg Caspar Hauser* (1908), *The World's Illusion* (1919), *The Maurizius Case* (1928).

Wast Water, lake of Lake Dist., Cumbria, NW England. Deepest in England (79 m/258 ft).

Watenstedt-Salzgitter, city of NE West Germany. Pop. 118,000. Iron, potash mining; chemicals, gas mfg., steel mills. Incorporated 1942, formed from many small towns.

water (H_2O), colourless liquid, compound of hydrogen and oxygen. Poor conductor of heat and electricity; important solvent. Reaches its maximum density at *c* 4° C.

water beetle, name given to various aquatic beetles, esp. of Dytiscidae family. Back legs bearing bristles function as oars.

water boatman, name given to aquatic insects of 2 families: Notonectidae, greater water boatmen or BACKSWIMMERS; Corixidae, lesser water boatmen. Latter are herbivorous, swimming with back uppermost. Both are strong fliers.

waterbuck, *Kobus ellipsiprymnus,* large shaggy brown antelope, with lyre-shaped horns on male. Found in swamps of S, W and E Africa.

water buffalo, *Bubalus bubalis,* buffalo with large crescent-shaped horns, found wild in S Asia and Borneo. Often wallows in mud. Domesticated varieties widely distributed in Europe and Asia; used as draught animals, source of milk. Also called Indian buffalo.

Waterbury, town of W Connecticut, US; on Naugatuck R. Pop. 108,000. Brass indust. dating from *c* 1800. Incorporated 1686.

watercolour, method of painting with pigment ground up with water-soluble gums, *eg* gum arabic.

watercress, *Nasturtium officinale,* white-flowered European herb of mustard family. Naturalized in North America. Found in or around water; pungent leaves used as garnish and in salads.

Waterbuck

Watermelon

water cricket, any of Veliidae family of predaceous insects found on water surfaces. Feeds on insects and spiders.

waterfall, abrupt descent of stream or river. Caused normally by bed of soft rock in river bed being more easily eroded than adjacent hard rock. Waterfalls impede navigation but provide water power. Examples incl. Angel Falls, Victoria Falls, Niagara Falls.

water flea, any of order Cladocera of small freshwater crustaceans. Swims by jerky movement of 2 forked antennae. Genera incl. *Daphnia* and *Leptodora*.

Waterford, county of Munster prov., S Irish Republic. Area 1839 sq km (710 sq mi); pop. 77,000. Mountain ranges incl. Comeragh, Knockmealdowns. Agric., dairying; fishing. Co. town **Waterford,** on R. Suir. Pop. 32,000. Exports dairy produce; hist. glass indust. Protestant, RC cathedrals.

water gas, mixture of hydrogen and carbon monoxide, formed by action of steam on white hot coke. Used as industrial fuel.

Watergate affair, in US history, scandals involving President Nixon's admin. arising out of break-in (June, 1972) at Democratic Party hq. in Watergate apartments, Washington, DC. Conviction of burglars (Jan. 1973) was followed by revelations of widespread conspiracy in campaign to re-elect Nixon in 1972 election and massive cover-up of those who had known of the break-in. White House counsel John Dean implicated attorney general MITCHELL and presidential advisers John Ehrlichman, Bob Haldeman. Nixon's involvement gradually became apparent, esp. after taperecordings of his conversations were made public by Supreme Court order. Faced with impeachment proceedings, Nixon resigned (Aug. 1974) and was succeeded by Ford.

water glass, sodium silicate (Na_2SiO_3), usually dissolved in water to form syrupy liquid; used in fireproofing, as preservative for eggs, *etc.*

waterhen, name applied to various birds of rail family, incl. grey moorhen, *Gallinula chloropus.*

water hyacinth, *Eichhornia crassipes,* tropical American aquatic plant. Floating leaf stalks, violet funnel-shaped flowers. Troublesome river weed.

water lily, see LOTUS.

Waterloo, village of C Belgium, S of Brussels. After actions at Ligny and Quatre Bras, British (under Wellington) and Prussians (under Blücher) here defeated Napoleon (June, 1815); ended Napoleonic Wars.

water louse, freshwater crustacean resembling wood louse, found in weedy streams and ponds. Species incl. *Asellus aquaticus,* common in N hemisphere; walks on plants or pond bottom.

watermark, design impressed into paper during mfg., usually by means of a rubber roller. Used in banknotes and stamps to prevent forgery.

watermelon, *Citrullus vulgaris,* annual trailing vine native to tropical Africa. Widely cultivated for large globular or elongated fruits with hard green rind and pink, sweet, watery pulp.

water moccasin or **cottonmouth,** *Agkistrodon piscivorus,* large poisonous pit viper of SE US. Olive-brown in colour; found in swamps or by rivers.

water ouzel, see DIPPER.

water polo, game played with inflated ball by 2 teams of 7 swimmers. Goals scored by forcing ball into opponents' goal net. Originated in Britain in 1870s. Olympic event since 1900.

water rat, name applied to various rodents that live near water, esp. European water vole, *Arvicola amphibius* and North American muskrat, *Ondatra zibethica.*

water scorpion, any of Nepidae family of aquatic insects. Flattened leaf-like body, powerful forelegs resembling scorpion's pincers; long sting-like tube at end of abdomen for breathing.

watershed, elevated land separating river systems. Headwaters of adjacent CATCHMENT AREAS flow in opposite directions on either side of watershed. Major examples incl. Rocky Mts., US, and Andes Range, South America. Term used in US to mean drainage basin itself.

water shrew, *Neomys fodiens,* largest European shrew; semi-aquatic, found on river banks. Hind feet and long tail fringed with stiff hairs to aid swimming.

water skiing, sport of gliding over water surface on ski-like boards while being pulled by motor boat. Competitions date from 1930s. World Water Ski Union (founded 1949) organizes world championships.

watersnake, name applied to various aquatic or semi-aquatic snakes, esp. of genus *Natrix.* Species incl. *N. sipedon* of E US, similar in habits to European GRASS SNAKE.

water spider, *Argyoneta aquatica,* European freshwater spider. Constructs underwater bell-shaped silk structure filled with air bubbles brought from surface in its body hairs. Only spider known to live under water.

waterstrider, see PONDSKATER.

water table, level below which soil and rock are saturated with ground water. Uneven and variable, may rise in wet weather. Where water table intersects ground surface, a SPRING results.

waterweed, various water plants with inconspicuous flowers, *eg* PONDWEED. Esp. North American *Anacharis canadensis* with white flowers. Commonly used in aquaria.

Watford, mun. bor. of Hertfordshire, S England, on R. Colne. Pop. 78,000. Printing, engineering, brewing industs.

Watling Island, see SAN SALVADOR.

Watling Street, Roman road running *c* 160km (100 mi) from London via St Albans to Wroxeter in Shropshire, England. Used throughout Middle Ages; parts still in good condition.

Watson, J[ohn] B[roadus] (1878-1958), American psychologist. First formulator of BEHAVIOURISM, emphasized study of learning, need for operational definition of concepts. Wrote *Behaviorism* (1925).

Watson-Watt, Sir Robert Alexander (1892-1973), Scottish physicist. Evolved method of radiolocation of aircraft (1935), developed into radar prior to WWII.

Watt, James (1736-1819), Scottish engineer. Manufactured an improved form (patented 1769) of

Newcomen's steam engine, developed method of converting reciprocating motion into rotary. Unit of power, watt, named after him.

watt, SI unit of power, equal to 1 joule/sec or power developed in a circuit by current of 1 ampère flowing through potential difference of 1 volt.

Watteau: detail of *Fêtes Venitiennes*

Watteau, [Jean] Antoine (1684-1721), French painter of Flemish descent. Noted for fanciful yet poignant pastoral scenes featuring courtiers or depiction of sad figures from French and Italian comedies. Works incl. *Gilles* and *Embarkation for Cythera*.

wattle, name for various Australian shrubs of genus *Acacia*.

Watts, George Frederick (1817-1904), English artist. Known for his portraits of contemporary celebrities, *eg Gladstone, Tennyson*, and large allegorical pictures, *eg Hope*. His sculpture incl. *Physical Energy*, executed for Cecil Rhodes Memorial, Cape Town.

Watts, Isaac (1674-1748), English hymn writer. A nonconformist clergyman, he wrote such popular hymns as 'O God, our help in ages past' and 'When I survey the wondrous cross'.

Waugh, Evelyn Arthur St John (1903-66), English novelist. Known for comic novels satirizing upper-class English manners, *eg Decline and Fall* (1928), *Brideshead Revisited* (1945), war trilogy *Men at Arms* (1952-61).

wave, in physics, periodic disturbance in a medium or space. May involve actual displacement of medium (mechanical waves) or periodic change in some physical quantity, *eg* strength of electromagnetic field. Distance between peaks of disturbance is called wavelength and number of crests per second is frequency.

Wavell, Archibald Percival Wavell, 1st Earl (1883-1950), British army officer. Commander-in-chief in Middle East (1939-41), defeated Italians in N Africa. Viceroy of India (1943-7).

wave mechanics, branch of quantum theory which associates mathematical function (wave function) with atomic particles. Manipulation of this function gives probability of finding position, momentum, *etc,* of particle at any time.

wax, substance composed mainly of esters of higher fatty acids with alcohols. Beeswax is secreted by bees for building honeycombs; carnauba wax, obtained from Brazilian wax palm, is used in polishes, lipsticks, *etc.* Paraffin wax is mineral wax obtained from petroleum.

waxbill, African bird of Estrildidae family, esp. genus *Estrilda*. Species incl. black-rumped waxbill, *E. troglodytes*, tiny sparrow-like bird with crimson bill.

waxwing, songbird of forests of North America and Eurasia, genus *Bombycilla*. Brown silky plumage and scarlet wax-like wing tips. Species incl. common or Bohemian waxwing, *B. garrulus*.

wayfaring tree, *see* VIBURNUM.

Common waxwing

Wayne, John, orig. Marion Michael Morrison, (1907-), American film actor. One of best known Hollywood stars, esp. for roles in Westerns as tough hero. Appeared in films from 1929, typically in *Stagecoach* (1939), *The Alamo* (1960); later more genial films incl. *True Grit* (1969).

Waziristan, mountainous region of Pakistan bordered on W by Afghanistan. Peopled by Waziri and Mahsud tribesmen, given to feuds and banditry. Centre of resistance to British rule in 19th cent.

weak nuclear interaction, nuclear force responsible for decay of all unstable elementary particles, c 10^{12} times weaker than strong nuclear interaction. Predicted by Pauli to explain beta decay of radioactive nuclei.

Weald, The, region of SE England, between North and South Downs. Grazing; hops, fruit, vegetables. Once forested, provided charcoal for 16th-17th cent. iron indust.

Wear, river of NE England. Flows 105 km (65 mi) through Tyne and Wear into North Sea at Sunderland.

European weasel

weasel, small carnivorous mammal, genus *Mustela,* found in temperate and cold regions of N hemisphere. Resembles small stoat, similar habits; feeds on voles, mice. *M. nivalis* is European species; reddish-brown above, white below.

weather, local atmospheric conditions at a given time or over short period. Factors incl. atmospheric pressure, temperature, humidity, cloud cover, rainfall, wind. Forms part of subject matter of meteorology. Weather conditions over many years give CLIMATE.

weathering, process of disintegration of rock on Earth's surface by atmospheric forces. With erosion and transportation, forms one of constituent processes of denudation. Rain, frost and temperature changes all gradually destroy rocks, aiding soil formation.

weaverbird, bird of Ploceidae family, found mainly in Africa. Weaves elaborate hanging nest of sticks, grass, *etc,* large numbers often together in one tree.

weaving, interlacing of yarns to form a fabric, usually done on a loom. Warp yarn runs lengthwise and weft crosswise, being carried across the loom by a shuttle. Basic weaves are plain, twill and satin.

Webb, Matthew (1848-1883), English swimmer. First man to swim the English Channel (1875), covering distance

Weaverbird's nest

from Dover to Calais in 21 hrs 45 mins. Drowned attempting to swim rapids above Niagara Falls.

Webb, Sidney James, Baron Passfield (1859-1947), English economist. With his wife, **Beatrice Webb**, née Potter (1858-1943), and other Socialists formed early nucleus of Fabian Society (founded 1884), influential in development of British labour movement. Their works incl. *History of Trade Unionism* (1894), *English Local Government* (1906); founded *New Statesman* (1913).

Carl Maria von Weber

Weber, Carl Maria Friedrich Ernst von (1786-1826), German composer, pianist. Developed romantic German opera. Works incl. *Der Freischütz, Euryanthe, Oberon,* and piano music.

Weber, Max (1864-1920), German sociologist. Set up non-Marxist framework for empirical analysis of institutional bases in Western capitalist society. Best-known work is *Protestant Ethic and the Spirit of Capitalism* (1920), demonstrating connection between Calvinism and capitalism.

Webern, Anton von (1883-1945), Austrian composer. Pupil of Schoenberg, he developed 12-note music with great intellectual rigour while retaining sensitivity to tone colour and expression. Works, *eg Five Orchestral Pieces,* are usually very short but highly concentrated.

Webster, Daniel (1782-1852), American lawyer, statesman. Senator from Massachusetts (1827-41, 1845-50); famed for eloquent oratory. As Whig secretary of state (1841-3), negotiated Webster-Ashburton Treaty settling Maine-New Brunswick boundary dispute (1842).

Webster, John (c 1580-c 1638), English dramatist. Known for typically Jacobean revenge tragedies, *The White Devil* (1612), *The Duchess of Malfi* (c 1613).

Webster, Noah (1758-1843), American scholar, lexicographer. Sought to standardize American spelling and pronunciation; compiled *American Dictionary of the English Language* (1828, frequently revised). Advocated centralized govt. in *Sketches of American Policy* (1785).

Weddell Sea, extension of S Atlantic, bordered by Antarctic Peninsula and Coats Land. Lies within British Antarctic Territ.

Wedekind, Frank (1864-1918), German dramatist. Forerunner of theatrical expressionism. Wrote plays on sexual themes, *eg Spring's Awakening* (1891), *Pandora's Box* (1903), creating heroine Lulu as archetypical amoral woman.

Wedgwood, Josiah (1730-95), English potter. Developed Staffordshire pottery indust. with new cream-coloured earthenware ('queen's ware'), and black basalt, used for reproduction of ancient Greek vases. Pottery most famous for jasper ware, unglazed porcelain in blue, decorated with white relief.

weever, small European marine fish of Trachinidae family. Poisonous spines on dorsal fin and head can inflict painful wound; often lies hidden on sea bottom. Species incl. greater weever, *Trachinus draco.*

weevil, small beetle of Curculionidae family, with worldwide distribution. Head prolonged into beak-like snout used to bore into grain, fruit, *etc.* Many species, incl. BOLL WEEVIL.

Wegener, Alfred Lothar (1880-1930), German geologist, meteorologist. Suggested theory of CONTINENTAL DRIFT. Made several expeditions to Greenland, on one of which he died.

weigela, genus of E Asian deciduous shrubs of honeysuckle family. Clusters of bell-shaped white or pink flowers. *Weigela florida* is widely cultivated species with dark crimson flowers.

weight, in physics, gravitational force of attraction of the Earth or other planet on a given MASS.

weightlessness, in physics, state experienced by body in absence of gravitational force or when falling freely.

Weihai, seaport of Shantung prov., NE China. Pop. c 60,000. Leased to Britain as naval base (1898-1930). Summer resort on Pohai gulf.

Weil, Simone (1909-43), French writer on philosophical, mystical subjects. Of Jewish parentage but attracted by Christianity. Advocated political quietism. Works incl. *Waiting for God* (1949).

Weill, Kurt (1900-50), German composer. Worked with BRECHT on satirical, jazz-influenced operas, *eg The Threepenny Opera* (based on Gay's *Beggar's Opera*). Wrote musicals in US from 1935.

Weimar, town of SW East Germany, on R. Ilm. Pop. 64,000. Textiles, printing. Former cap. of grand duchy of Saxe-Weimar-Eisenach. Cultural centre in 18th, 19th cents. (Bach, Goethe, Liszt, Schiller). Scene of declaration (1919) of Weimar Republic. Badly damaged in WWII.

Weimar Republic, name given to German Republic (1919-33). Created by constitutional assembly at Weimar (1919). Dissolved by Hitler.

Weismann, August (1834-1914), German biologist. Formulated continuity of germ plasm theory to explain heredity and natural selection; proposed that germ plasm is transmitted from generation to generation and controls development of organism.

Weiss, Peter (1916-), German author, film director, painter. Best known as author of plays *Marat/Sade* (1964), *The Investigation* (1965).

Weizmann, Chaim (1874-1952), Jewish statesman, chemist, b. Russia. Active in Zionist causes in Britain, helped secure Balfour Declaration favouring estab. of Jewish homeland in Palestine; 1st president of Israel (1949-52). Discovered method of producing acetone for explosives in WWI.

welding, process of joining metal surfaces together by heating sufficiently for them to melt and fuse together.

Required temperature is obtained by oxyacetylene flame or electric arc.

Welensky, Sir Roy (1907-), Rhodesian politician, PM of Federation of Rhodesia and Nyasaland (1956-63).

Welkom, city of NC Orange Free State, South Africa. Pop. 132,000. Commercial centre in goldmining dist. Founded 1947.

well, hole bored into Earth's crust for purpose of bringing substances, usually water or oil, to surface. Such substances may require pumping, or flow upward by underground pressure as in ARTESIAN WELL.

Welland, canal port of S Ontario, Canada. Pop. 44,000. In fruit-growing area. Steel, agric. machinery mfg. Welland Ship Canal bypasses Niagara Falls, connecting L. Ontario with L. Erie. Length 44 km (28 mi). Part of St Lawrence Seaway canal system.

Welles, [George] Orson (1915-), American film actor, writer, director, producer. After stage and radio experience (in 1938 panicked US with radio version of *The War of the Worlds*), turned to films. Best known for *Citizen Kane* (1941), *The Third Man* (1949).

Wellesley, Richard Colley Wellesley, Marquess of (1760-1842), British colonial administrator. Assisted by his brother (later WELLINGTON), checked power of native princes, notably Tippoo Sahib, as governor in India (1797-1805). Greatly extended British colonial power in India. Later served as foreign secretary (1810-12).

Wellington, Arthur Wellesley, 1st Duke of (1769-1852), British army officer, statesman; PM (1828-30). Aided his brother Richard Wellesley in Indian campaigns (1796-1805). Commanded British troops in PENINSULAR WAR (1809-13), eventually driving French from Spain; ultimately defeated Napoleon at Waterloo (1815). Although opposed to Catholic Emancipation, saw necessity of his Tory govt. legislating to avoid conflict in Ireland; govt. fell after his declaration against parliamentary reform.

Wellington, cap. of New Zealand, at S tip of North Isl., on Cook Str. Pop. 136,000. Admin., commercial centre; port, exports dairy produce, wool, meat. Founded 1840; replaced Auckland as cap. 1865. Has Parliament House, National Museum, Victoria Univ. (1897). Chief city of **Wellington** region. Area 28,150 sq km (10,870 sq mi); pop. 553,000. Largely mountainous; coastal lowlands in W. Dairying, sheep rearing.

Wells, H[erbert] G[eorge] (1866-1946), English author. Early exponent of SCIENCE FICTION in novels, *eg The Time Machine* (1895), *The War of the Worlds* (1898). Other works incl. fictionalized naturalistic social commentary, *eg Kipps* (1905), *The History of Mr Polly* (1910), discursive *The Outline of History* (1919).

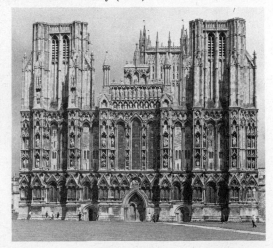

Wells cathedral

Wells, city of Somerset, SW England. Pop. 7000. Cheese; paper mfg. Has medieval city wall, cathedral (12th cent.). Nearby is Wookey Hole limestone cave.

Wels, town of NW Austria. Pop. 47,000. Railway jct.; engineering. Natural gas from nearby wells. Gothic church (14th cent.), castle.

Welsh, *see* CELTIC.

Welsh Nationalist Party (Plaid Cymru), political organization dedicated to obtaining Welsh independence by constitutional methods.

Welwyn Garden City, urban dist. of Hertfordshire, SE England. Pop. 40,000. Light industs.; food processing, chemicals. Planned (1920) by Howard, designated new town 1954.

Wembley, part of BRENT, W Greater London, England. Incl. English national soccer stadium.

Wenceslaus, St (d. 929), duke of Bohemia. Promoted spread of Christianity in Bohemia. Murdered by his brother Boleslav. Remembered as 'Good King Wenceslaus' of the Christmas carol.

Wenceslaus (1361-1419), Holy Roman emperor (1378-1400). Succeeded his father Charles IV as emperor, but was never crowned; later deposed by German nobles, who elected Rupert in his place. Wenceslaus was reconciled when his brother SIGISMUND became king of Germany (1411). King of Bohemia (1378-1419), he supported early reforms of JAN HUS.

Wenchow, seaport of Chekiang prov., E China. Pop. 250,000. On Wu Kiang. Trade in tea, cotton, oranges.

Wentworth, William Charles (1793-1872), Australian lawyer, politician. Leader in self-govt. movement which achieved Representative Council (1842). Helped draft constitution, passed (1855).

Werfel, Franz (1890-1945), Austrian author. Religious works incl. novel *The Song of Bernadette* (1941), expressionist plays, *eg Goat Song* (1921), *Jacobowsky and the Colonel* (1944).

Weser, river of N West Germany. Formed by union of Fulda and Werra rivers at Münden, flows *c* 480 km (300 mi) via Minden, Bremen to North Sea at Bremerhaven. Connected by Mittelland canal to Elbe, Ems, Rhine rivers.

Wesker, Arnold (1932-), English playwright. Known for committedly socialist plays, *eg Chicken Soup with Barley* (1958), *Roots* (1959), *Chips With Everything* (1962).

John Wesley

Wesley, John (1703-91), English evangelical preacher. Anglican churchman, founded METHODISM. Visited American colonies (1735). Began to preach (in open air) salvation through faith in Christ alone. Estab. framework for Methodist societies. Sermons became standard for Wesleyans. His brother, **Charles Wesley** (1707-88), was preacher and founding Methodist. Opposed any movement to separate from Church of England. Wrote *c* 6500 hymns, incl. 'Hark! the Herald Angels Sing'.

Wessex, *see* WILTSHIRE, England.

West, Benjamin (1738-1820), American painter, resident in London after 1763. Historical painter to George III after 1772; a founder member of the Royal Academy, became its president in 1792. His paintings, *eg The Death of Wolfe,* broke convention by clothing figures in contemporary clothes.

Mae West and W.C. Fields in *My Little Chickadee*

West, Mae (1892-   ), American stage, film actress, writer. Famous for wit, sexual innuendo, in comedies, *eg She Done Him Wrong* (1933), *I'm No Angel* (1933), and in films with W.C. Fields.

West, Nathanael, pseud. of Nathan Wallenstein Weinstein (1904-40), American novelist. Known for blackly comic indictments of American success myth, *eg Miss Lonelyhearts* (1933), *A Cool Million* (1934), *Day of the Locust* (1939).

West, Rebecca, pseud. of Dame Cicily Isabel Fairfield (1892-   ), British author, b. Ireland. Works incl. psychological novels, *eg The Return of the Soldier* (1918), *The Birds Fall Down* (1966), travel book on Yugoslavia, *Black Lamb and Grey Falcon* (1942), criticism, biogs.

West Atlantic, subgroup of Niger-Congo branch of Niger-Kordofanian language family. Many languages within it, incl. Wolof (Senegal), Temne (Sierra Leone), Fulani (WC Africa).

West Bengal, state of NE India. Area *c* 88,000 sq km (33,000 sq mi); pop. 44,440,000; cap. Calcutta. Heavy indust. based in Ganges delta; coal, petroleum deposits. Formed at 1947 partition of Bengal between India and Pakistan.

West Bromwich, bor. of West Midlands met. county, C England. Pop. 167,000. In BLACK COUNTRY; coalmining, metal industs.

westerlies, prevailing winds of mid-latitude areas in both hemispheres. Normally blow from SW in N hemisphere, from NW in S hemisphere. Bring continual procession of depressions and anticyclones.

Westermarck, Edward Alexander (1862-1939), Finnish philosopher, anthropologist. Noted historian of marriage customs. Works incl. *The History of Human Marriage* (1891), *Christianity and Morals* (1939).

Western Australia, state of W Australia. Area 2,537,900 sq km (979,900 sq mi); pop. 1,027,000; cap. Perth. Kimberley plateau in N, Hamersley Range in NW; vast desert tableland, salt lakes in interior; fertile area in SW; Nullarbor Plain in SE. Agric. incl. beef cattle, sheep, wheat, fruit. Minerals incl. gold, iron ore. Industs., incl. oil refining, iron and steel mfg., centred in Perth and Fremantle. Settled from 1826; became federal state (1901).

Western European Union (WEU), economic, social, cultural and defensive association of Belgium, France, West Germany, Italy, Luxembourg, Netherlands and UK. Estab. 1955 as extension of Brussels Treaty Organization (1948).

Western Isles, isl. authority of W Scotland. Area 2898 sq km (1119 sq mi); pop. 31,000. Created 1975; incl. Outer

Hebrides isls., formerly part of Inverness-shire and Ross and Cromarty.

Western Sahara, *see* SPANISH SAHARA.

Western Samoa, *see* SAMOA.

Western Union Telegraph Company, world's largest cable and telegraph company. Completed 1st transcontinental telegraph line (1861) across North America.

West Germany, *see* GERMANY.

West Glamorgan, *see* GLAMORGAN, Wales.

West Ham, *see* NEWHAM, England.

West Indies

West Indies, archipelago between North and South America, separating Caribbean and Atlantic Ocean. Incl. Hispaniola, Cuba, Jamaica, Puerto Rico (Greater Antilles); Barbados. Leeward and Windward Isls., Trinidad and Tobago (Lesser Antilles); also Bahamas, Virgin Isls. Cuba, Haiti, Dominican Republic are independent. Remainder are dependencies of UK, US, France, Netherlands or members of British Commonwealth. European settlement followed Columbus' visit in 1492.

West Indies, Federation of, short-lived union (1958-62) of British Caribbean territs. Incl. Jamaica, Trinidad and Tobago, Barbados, most of Leeward and Windward Isls.

West Irian, *see* IRIAN JAYA.

Westland, region of W South Isl., New Zealand. Area 15,560 sq km (6010 sq mi); pop. 23,000; main town Greymouth. Narrow coastal plain, rising to Southern Alps in E. Coalmining, timber, fishing industs. Pop. rose rapidly during 1860s gold discoveries.

West Lothian, former county of EC Scotland, now in Lothian region. Formerly called Linlithgowshire. Coal, iron, oil shale deposits; rich agric. Co. town was Linlithgow.

Westman Islands, *see* VESTMANNAEYJAR, Iceland.

Westmeath, county of Leinster prov., C Irish Republic. Area 1764 sq km (681 sq mi); pop. 54,000; co. town Mullingar. Low-lying, extensive bogland, lakes incl. Lough Ree. Livestock, dairying; fishing (esp. trout).

West Midlands, met. county of C England. Area 899 sq km (347 sq mi); pop. 2,785,000. Created 1974, incl. Birmingham and suburbs, Coventry.

Westminster, City of, bor. of C Greater London, England. Pop. 233,000. Created 1965 from Westminster, Paddington, St Marylebone met. bors. Incl. Piccadilly, Soho, West End, Mayfair, Hyde Park, Trafalgar Sq. Buildings incl. Westminster Abbey, palaces (Buckingham, St James's, Westminster), Parliament, Royal Albert Hall, Covent Garden, National Gallery.

Westminster, Statute of (1931), British parliamentary enactment recognizing independence of dominions of British Commonwealth. Implemented decision of previous Imperial Conferences which had met from 1887.

Westminster Abbey, national shrine and scene of coronation of almost all English monarchs since William I. Norman church consecrated under Edward the Confessor (1065); rebuilding in Gothic style begun in 1245 and finished 1528; additions made in 18th cent. by Wren and Hawksmoor.

Westminster Assembly (1643-9), convocation summoned by Long Parliament to estab. liturgy and govt. of the Church in England. Strongly influenced by

Presbyterian members. Issued Westminster Confession of Faith, creed of most Presbyterian churches.

Westmorland, former county of NW England, now part of Cumbria. Co. town was Appleby. Incl. much of Lake Dist.

Weston-super-Mare, mun. bor. of Avon, SW England. Pop. 51,000. Resort on Bristol Channel.

Westphalia (*Westfalen*), region of W West Germany, now part of North Rhine-Westphalia state. Mainly low-lying, chief rivers Ems, Lippe, Ruhr. Incl. RUHR coalfield and indust. region; main cities Dortmund, Cologne, Düsseldorf, Essen. Duchy created 12th cent.; made kingdom (1807) by Napoleon; prov. of Prussia from 1816. Treaty of Westphalia (1648), agreed at Münster and Osnabrück, ended the Thirty Years War.

Westphalia, Peace of (1648), settlement ending THIRTY YEARS WAR. Power of Habsburgs diminished; Holy Roman Empire dissolved into sovereign states, rulers of which could grant religious toleration to their subjects.

West Point, *see* NEWBURGH, US.

West Riding, *see* YORKSHIRE, England.

West Sussex, *see* SUSSEX, England.

West Virginia, state of E US. Area 62,629 sq km (24,181 sq mi); pop. 1,744,000; cap. Charlestown. In Allegheny plateau, has 2 panhandles in N and E. Chief rivers Ohio, Potomac. Important mining incl. bituminous coal, natural gas; glass and chemical industs. Chief agric. crops hay, maize, fruit. Region settled in 1730s. Part of Virginia until Civil War. Admitted to Union as 35th state (1863).

West Yorkshire, met. county of NC England. Area 2039 sq km (787 sq mi); pop. 2,080,000; admin. centre Wakefield. Created 1974, incl. most of former W Riding of Yorkshire.

Wexford, county of Leinster prov., SE Irish Republic. Area 2352 sq km (908 sq mi); pop. 86,000. Mainly low-lying (except Mt. Leinster), fertile; drained by R. Barrow (SW). Cereals, dairying; fishing. Co. town **Wexford,** on Wexford Harbour. Pop. 12,000. Fishing port; agric. market. Sacked by Cromwell (1649).

Weyden, Roger van der (*c* 1400-64), Flemish artist. Major Flemish painter of mid-15th cent.; his religious works, combining dramatic power and spirituality, incl. *The Deposition*. His portraits incl. *Charles the Bold*.

Weygand, Maxime (1867-1965), French general, b. Belgium. Chief of staff to Foch in WWI. Supreme Allied commander (1940) his outmoded tactics failed to halt German BLITZKRIEG. Served Vichy regime until interned by Germans (1942-5).

Weymouth (and Melcombe Regis), mun. bor. of Dorset, S England. Pop. 42,000. Resort; has ferry service to Channel Isls.

whale, large marine fish-like mammal, order Cetacea. Whales divided into 2 groups: toothed whales (Odontoceti), incl. sperm whales, porpoises, dolphins; whalebone or baleen whales (Mystacoceti), in which teeth are replaced by whalebone plates used to strain plankton from water. Whalebone whales incl. blue whale, largest of mammals, rorqual and right whale.

whale shark, *Rhincodon typus,* largest living fish, reaching lengths of 15 m/50 ft, found in tropical waters. Harmless to man, feeds on plankton and small fish.

whaling, industry of catching whales for food, oil, *etc.* Organized first by Dutch at Spitsbergen in 17th cent. Developed on large scale with invention of explosive harpoon (*c* 1856) and building of factory ships for extraction of oil. Decline in whale pop. through over-hunting has led to international controls.

Whangarei, city of N North Isl., New Zealand, on Whangarei Harbour. Pop. 31,000. Port, exports dairy produce, fruit, meat; oil refining; coalmining nearby.

Wharton, Edith Newbold, née Jones (1862-1937), American novelist. Wrote novels of manners depicting New York society, *eg The House of Mirth* (1905), *The Age of Innocence* (1920). Became prominent in American expatriate circles in Paris, depicted in autobiog. *A Backward Glance* (1934).

wheat, any of genus *Triticum* of cereal grasses with dense, erect spikes. *T. aestivum* is widely cultivated in temperate regions. Yields grain which is processed into flour or meal and used chiefly in breadmaking. Comprises *c* 40% of world's cereal acreage. Leading producers are Canada, US, China and USSR.

wheatear, small migratory thrush-like bird with white rump, genus *Oenanthe*. Species incl. *O. oenanthe* of North America, N Europe and Asia.

Wheatley, Dennis Yates (1897-), English author. Known for occult thrillers, *eg The Devil Rides Out* (1935). Other works incl. 'Roger Brook' espionage series.

Wheatstone, Sir Charles (1802-75), English scientist. Pioneer of telegraphy, he invented an electric telegraph (1837), following advice of Henry. Popularized 'Wheatstone bridge', device to measure electrical resistance. Credited with invention of concertina.

wheel, name given to any disc-shaped device used as part of machine or vehicle. When fitted to an axle gives mechanical advantage equal to ratio of wheel radius to axle radius. Earliest vehicular wheel dates from Bronze Age (*c* 3500 BC).

Wheeler, Sir [Robert Eric] Mortimer (1890-1976), English archaeologist. Made excavations at MAIDEN CASTLE, Caerleon; helped reveal the INDUS VALLEY CIVILIZATION. Did much to popularize archaeology by his television appearances.

Wheeling, town of West Virginia, US; on Ohio R., in N panhandle. Pop. 48,000. In coal, natural gas producing region; major iron and steel indust. Settled 1769.

whelk, marine gastropod mollusc with spiral shell, esp. of genus *Buccinum*. Species incl. common edible whelk, *B. undatum.*

whidah, *see* WHYDAH.

Whig Party, British political party, predecessor of present Liberal Party. Name, originally denoting rebel Scottish Covenanters, applied to upholders of exclusion of James, Duke of York, from throne (1679). Supported Glorious Revolution (1688), held power (1714-60). Disorganized in early years of George III's reign, revived in opposition to newly-dominant Tory Party under Pitt. In early 19th cent., advocated parliamentary reform, culminating in Reform Bill (1832), after which Whigs became known as Liberals.

Whig party, US political party. Composed of groups originally formed (1824) in opposition to Andrew Jackson, *eg* National Republican party, Anti-Masonic party. Leaders incl. Henry Clay, Daniel Webster. Successful in election of W.H. HARRISON as president (1840). Break-up began 1848, despite Zachary Taylor's victory in presidential election.

whippet, breed of slender hound developed in England from greyhound in 18th cent. Once used for hare coursing, now mainly for racing; stands 46-57 cm/18-22 in. at shoulder.

whip-poor-will, *Caprimulgus vociferus,* nocturnal North American bird of nightjar family. Brown plumage mottled with black and cream; name derived from its call.

whip scorpion, any of order Uropygi of nocturnal arachnids of warm regions. Powerful pincers in front and long whip-like tail at rear of abdomen; no sting, secretes acetic acid for defence. Also called vinegaroon in US.

Whipsnade, village of Bedfordshire, SC England. Zoological park (2 sq km/500 acres) opened 1931.

whirligig beetle, any of Gyrinidae family of blue-black aquatic beetles. Whirls in circles about water surface; has broad hair-fringed swimming legs.

whirlpool, circular, revolving eddy in river, lake or sea. Caused by meeting of opposing tides or currents, wind action, irregular formation of river or sea bed, or waterfalls. Examples incl. Maelstrom off Norway.

whirlwind, rotating column of air with low atmospheric pressure at centre. Produced by atmospheric instability; in arid areas may cause dust or sand storms.

whisky or **whiskey,** spirit distilled from fermented mash of grain, *eg* barley, rye. Flavour of Scotch whisky derives from quality of water used and curing of malt over peat fires. US and Canadian whiskies are mostly made with rye; some, *eg* bourbon, are made from corn (maize). Whisky is stored for several years in wooden casks where it acquires characteristic brown colour.

whist, card game for 4 players. Of English origin, its popularity derives in part from writings of HOYLE and CAVENDISH. Gave rise to bridge in 19th cent.

Whistler: *Old Battersea Bridge*

Whistler, James [Abbott] McNeill (1834-1903), American artist, resident in France, England. Influenced by Velazquez and Japanese prints, he was a master of tone and colour, and superb etcher. Works incl. series of *Nocturnes* and *The White Girl.* Fought famous lawsuit against Ruskin following Ruskin's criticism of *The Falling Rocket.*

Whitby, urban dist. of North Yorkshire, N England, at mouth of R. Esk. Pop. 13,000. Resort, fishing port, boatbuilding; jet ornaments mfg. Abbey founded 656. Home of Capt. Cook, his ships built here. Synod of Whitby (664) estab. Roman rather than Celtic forms for English church.

White, Gilbert (1720-93), English clergyman, naturalist. Author of classic *Natural History and Antiquities of Selborne* (1789), based on record of observations.

White, Patrick Victor Martindale (1912-), Australian novelist, b. London. Known for symbolic, poetic novels incl. *The Tree of Man* (1955), *Voss* (1957), *Riders in the Chariot* (1961), *The Solid Mandala* (1966). Nobel Prize for Literature (1973).

White, T[erence] H[anbury] (1906-64), English author, b. India. Known for erudite, idiosyncratic treatment of Arthurian legend in tetralogy *The Once and Future King* (1938-58); basis of musical and film *Camelot.*

whitebait, young of several European herrings, esp. common herring, *Clupea harengus,* and sprat. In US incl. young silverside. Esteemed as food.

white blood cell, see BLOOD.

white collar, grouping of workers engaged in non-manual labour. American in origin, term derives from white shirts typically worn by clerical, professional, and managerial employees. Meaning developed esp. by C. Wright Mills in *White Collar* (1951).

white dwarf, small, extremely dense star of low luminosity, typically with mass of Sun but radius no larger than Earth's. Represents stage of star's evolution as its store of hydrogen is used up.

Whitefield, George (1714-70), English evangelist. Joined WESLEY's group. Preached in America contributing to revivalist 'Great Awakening'. Opposed Wesley's view on predestination, estab. (*c* 1741) independent Calvinistic Methodists.

whitefish, fish of salmon family, esp. genus *Coregonus,* found mainly in lakes and rivers of N Europe and North America. Silvery, with small jaws, minute teeth.

whitefly, any of Aleyrodidae family of minute insects. Wings and body coated with white powdery wax. Many species, incl. cabbage whitefly, *Aleyrodes proletella,* are crop pests.

Whitehaven, mun. bor. of Cumbria, NW England. Pop. 27,000. Port; coalmining; flour milling.

Whitehead, Alfred North (1861-1947), English philosopher, mathematician. Collaborated with Russell on *Principia Mathematica* (1910-13). Formulated an idealist 'philosophy of organism' holding that universal concepts give a useful interpretation of experience. Rejected notion of omnipotent God.

Whitehorse, cap. of Yukon territ., Canada; on Lewes (Upper Yukon) R. Pop. 11,000. Copper mining region; hunting centre. Cap. from 1952.

White Horse, Vale of the, valley of R. Ock, Berkshire, SC England. Named after White Horse (114 m/374 ft long) cut into chalk hillside of Berkshire Downs to S. In tradition, commemorates Alfred's victory over Danes (871).

White House, official residence of the President of the US, in Washington, DC. White-painted building, designed by James Hoban (1792); first occupied 1800. Rebuilt after being burnt by British (1814).

White Nile, see NILE.

White Russia, see BYELORUSSIAN SOVIET SOCIALIST REPUBLIC.

White Russians, name given to anti-Communist groups who opposed Bolsheviks in Russian civil war (1918-20). Supported by Allied intervention.

White Sea, inlet of Barents Sea, between Kola and Kanin penins., N European USSR. Connected to Baltic by canal. Chief port Archangel.

white-tailed deer, *Odocoileus virginianus,* common American deer whose tail is white underneath. In summer, has red coat with white spots.

whitethroat, Old World warbler with white throat, genus *Sylvia.* Species incl. lesser whitethroat, *S. curruca.*

Whitgift, John (*c* 1530-1604), English churchman. Archbishop of Canterbury (1583-1604). Worked to estab. uniformity within Church of England under Elizabeth I. Severely repressed Puritans.

whiting, *Merlangus merlangus,* common European marine food fish of cod family. Found in inshore waters, esp. of North Sea. Name also applied to Australian fish of genus *Sillago.*

Whitlam, [Edward] Gough (1916-), Australian statesman, PM (1972-5). Headed 1st Labor govt. in more than 20 years, improving Australia's relations with Communist countries of Far East, until economic crisis led to opposition's refusal to cooperate in Senate. Dismissed by governor-general, Sir John Kerr, who appointed Malcolm Fraser as PM.

Walt Whitman

Whitman, Walt[er] (1819-92), American poet. Best known for stylistically unconventional collection, *Leaves of Grass* (1855), celebrating fertility, sensuality, comradeship. Other works incl. collection, *Drum Taps* (1865), elegy for Lincoln, 'When Lilacs Last in the Dooryard Bloom'd' (1867), prose collection, *Specimen Days and Collect* (1882).

Whitney, Eli (1765-1825), American manufacturer. Invented cotton gin, facilitating separation of fibre and seed. Produced 1st muskets with standard interchangeable parts.

Whitney, Mount, mountain of E California, US; in Sequoia National Park in Sierra Nevada. Second highest peak in US (4418 m/14,494 ft).

Whitsunday, *see* PENTECOST.

Whittier, John Greenleaf (1807-92), American poet. Wrote anti-slavery poems in *Voices of Freedom* (1846). Other works incl. Civil War verse, *eg* classic 'Barbara Frietchie', 'Yankee pastoral' New England nature poetry, *eg Snow-Bound* (1866).

Whittington, Richard (d. 1423), English merchant, 3 times mayor of London. Made large fortune as a mercer, which he left to charities at his death. Subject of story of Dick Whittington and his cat.

Whittle, Sir Frank (1907-), English aeronautic engineer. Patented (1930) designs for turbo-jet engine, forerunner of modern jet aircraft engine.

whooping cough or **pertussis,** infectious disease, usually of children, caused by bacillus *Haemophilus pertussis.* Characterized by repeated coughing ending in forced intake of air or whoop.

Whorf, Benjamin Lee (1897-1941), American engineer, linguist. Formulated Sapir-Whorf hypothesis (based on arguments first stated by SAPIR) that any language imposes a conceptual framework on its users.

whortleberry, *see* BILBERRY.

Whyalla, city of S South Australia, on Spencer Gulf. Pop. 32,000. Port, exports iron ore from Eyre Penin.; iron and steel works, shipbuilding.

whydah or **whidah,** small African bird of Viduinae subfamily. Male, normally all black, has long tail and red breast in breeding season. Species incl. paradise whydah, *Vidua paradisea.*

Whymper, Edward (1840-1911), English mountaineer. First man to climb the Matterhorn (1865), succeeding at his 7th attempt; during descent, 4 of his party fell to their deaths.

Wichita, city of S Kansas, US; at jct. of Arkansas and Little Arkansas rivers. Pop. 277,000; state's largest city. Railway jct., commercial, indust. centre in wheat growing, oil producing region. Livestock, grain trade; aircraft, chemical mfg.

Wick, port of Highland region, E Scotland. Pop. 8000. Whisky distilling, glass mfg. Former co. town of Caithness.

Wicklow, county of Leinster prov., E Irish Republic. Area 2025 sq km (782 sq mi); pop. 66,000. Scenic Wicklow Mts. (Lugnaquillia 926 m/3039 ft), Glendalough. Cattle rearing; h.e.p. on Liffey. Co. town **Wicklow,** pop. 3000. Port; ruined castle (12th cent.), priory (13th cent.).

widgeon, *see* WIGEON.

Widnes, mun. bor. of Cheshire, NW England, on R. Mersey. Pop. 57,000. Chemicals indust. Bridge connection to Runcorn.

widow bird, African bird of Ploceinae subfamily, genus *Euplectes.* Parasitic on waxbill; eggs and throat markings of young resemble those of host.

Wieland, Christoph Martin (1733-1813), German poet, novelist. Wrote satirical novels, *eg The Abderites, a Very Probable Story* (1774). Poetic works incl. epic, *Oberon* (1780), basis of Weber's opera.

Wien, *see* VIENNA, Austria.

Wiener, Norbert (1894-1964), American mathematician. Contributed to probability theory, Fourier transforms, quantum theory, *etc.* Founded science of cybernetics; contributed to development of electronic computers. Wrote *Cybernetics* (1948).

Wiesbaden, city of W West Germany, at foot of Taunus Hills, cap. of Hesse. Pop. 252,000. Wine trade, chemicals, film studios. Spa resort from Roman times. Cap. of duchy

of Nassau 1815-66; seat of Allied Rhineland Commission 1918-29.

Wigan, bor. of Greater Manchester met. county, NW England. Pop. 81,000. Food processing, engineering industs.

Wigeon

wigeon or **widgeon,** migratory duck, genus *Anas.* Male of Eurasian wigeon, *A. penelope,* has chestnut head, grey body, pinkish breast.

Wiggin, Kate Douglas, née Smith (1856-1923), American author, educator. Pioneer of kindergartens. Wrote *Rebecca of Sunnybrook Farm* (1903).

Wight, Isle of, isl. county of S England. Area 381 sq km (147 sq mi); pop. 109,000; co. town Newport. Separated from mainland by SOLENT. Chalk hills run E-W, end in Needles. Resorts; yachting.

Wigner, Eugene Paul (1902-), American physicist, mathematician, b. Hungary. Shared Nobel Prize for Physics (1963) for work on structure of atomic nucleus; helped in development of atomic bomb in WWII.

Wigtownshire, former county of SW Scotland, now in Dumfries and Galloway region. Indented coast; incl. Rhinns of Galloway penin. in W. Rich agric., dairy farming, livestock. Co. town was **Wigtown,** former royal burgh on Wigtown Bay. Pop. 1000.

wigwam, ALGONQUIAN name loosely applied to dwellings of E North American Indians. Originally referred to dome-shaped huts made of skins or matting stretched over poles. Now confused with portable, conical tepee of Plains Indians.

Wilberforce, William (1759-1833), British reform politician. Campaigned for abolition of slavery. Sponsored passage (1807) of bill abolishing slave trade. Died month before slavery was abolished throughout British Empire. His son, **Samuel Wilberforce** (1805-73), was a churchman; bishop of Winchester (1869-73). Defended Anglican orthodoxy against Tractarians; known for opposition to Darwinism.

Wilbur, Richard (1921-), American poet, critic. Works, *eg The Beautiful Changes* (1947), *Walking to Sleep* (1969), reflect formal aestheticism, polished manner of academic poet.

Wild, Jonathan (*c* 1682-1725), English criminal. Built up immense business, organizing London thieves, selling stolen goods in 'lost property office'. Hanged at Tyburn.

wild boar, *see* BOAR.

wild carrot, *Daucus carota,* common biennial weed. See CARROT.

wildcat, *see* BOBCAT.

Wilde, Oscar [Fingal O'Flahertie Wills] (1854-1900), British author, b. Dublin. Noted decadent wit, aesthete. Works incl. novels, *eg The Picture of Dorian Grey* (1891), satirical social comedies, *eg Lady Windermere's Fan* (1892), *The Importance of Being Earnest* (1895). Accused of homosexual practices, imprisoned (1895-7). Wrote most famous poem, *The Ballad of Reading Gaol* (1898), in exile.

wildebeest, *see* GNU.

Wilder, Samuel ('Billy') (1905-), Austrian film writer-director, in US from 1934. Known for comedies, suspense dramas, incl. *Double Indemnity* (1944), *The Lost Weekend* (1945), *Some Like it Hot* (1959).

Wilder, Thornton Niven (1897-1975), American author. Known for undidactic philosophical novels, *eg The Bridge of San Luis Rey* (1927), plays, *eg Our Town* (1938), *The Skin of Our Teeth* (1942).

Oscar Wilde

Wilhelmina (1880-1962), queen of Netherlands (1890-1948). Lived in England during WWII. Abdicated in favour of daughter Juliana.

Wilhelmshaven, city of NW West Germany, on Jade Bay. Pop. 103,000. Port; oil refining, chemical mfg. Chief German North Sea naval base from opening of harbour (1869). Heavily bombed in WWII; dismantled by Allies, rebuilt.

Wilkes, Charles (1798-1877), American naval officer, explorer. Led expedition (1838-42) to Antarctic, isls. of Pacific and NW American coast; Wilkes Land named after him. While commanding *San Jacinto*, caused 'Trent Affair' diplomatic incident (1861).

Wilkes, John (1727-97), English politician. Founded periodical *North Briton*; attacked George III's speech from throne, for which he was briefly imprisoned (1763). Expelled from Parliament on seditious libel charge (1764), fled to France. Re-elected (1768), frequently prevented from taking seat in Commons through royal pressure; gained great popular support. Admitted to Commons (1774), championed parliamentary reform, American colonial cause.

Wilkins, Sir [George] Hubert (1888-1958), British explorer and aviator, b. Australia. Flew from Alaska to Spitsbergen (1928). Took part in many polar expeditions, esp. with Stefansson (1913-16), Shackleton (1921-2); explored Arctic in submarine *Nautilus* (1931).

will, in law, legal statement of person's wishes concerning disposal of property after death; document containing this. In UK, US, must be witnessed, testator (person making will) must be of sound mind and not under undue influence of another. Testator usually appoints executor to administer will. In US, wills must be submitted to probate, *ie* to legal validation.

will, in philosophy, inner force motivating a person's conscious actions. Existence denied by some philosophers (*eg* in DETERMINISM), defined by others (*eg* Plato, Descartes, Kant) on intuitive grounds as motive force of personality, yet others (*eg* Leibnitz, Hume) have seen it as the resultant of conflicting elements.

willemite, zinc ore mineral. Usually yellow-green in colour; consists of zinc silicate. Found among crystalline limestones. Major sources in Congo, Rhodesia, Greenland, US.

Willemstad, cap. of Netherlands Antilles, on Curaçao Isl. Pop. 44,000. Shipping and tourist centre. Refining of Venezuelan oil.

William I (1797-1888), 1st emperor of Germany (1871-88), king of Prussia (1861-88). Dominated by chancellor BISMARCK, whose policies led to creation of German Empire.

William II (1859-1941), emperor of Germany (1888-1918). Dismissed Bismarck (1890), thereafter pursuing aggressive colonial and military policy. Antagonized Britain by supporting Boers, promoting German naval expansion. Influence declined after outbreak of WWI; fled to Holland day before armistice, abdicated.

William [I] the Conqueror (*c* 1027-87), king of England (1066-87). Succeeded to duchy of Normandy (1035). Prob. promised succession to English throne by Edward the Confessor; forced HAROLD to swear support for his claim. Pursued claim by invading England and defeating Harold at Hastings (1066). Consolidated Norman power by building castles, granting land to his followers, introducing foreign clergy; introduced hierarchical FEUDAL SYSTEM. Commissioned survey of England in *Domesday Book*.

William [II] Rufus (*c* 1058-1100), king of England (1087-1100), b. Normandy. Involved in disputes with brother Robert Curthose over rule of Normandy. His extravagant and covetous rule was unpopular. Found slain by arrow in New Forest.

William III (1650-1702), king of England, Scotland and Ireland (1689-1702), prince of Orange. Became stadholder of Holland (1672), successfully defended country against France. Married (1677) Mary, daughter of duke of York (later JAMES II). Invited to become king of England by opponents of James; proclaimed joint sovereign with Mary after James was deemed to have abdicated (*see* GLORIOUS REVOLUTION). Defeated Catholic force under James at Battle of Boyne (1690).

William IV (1765-1837), king of Great Britain and Ireland (1830-7). Third son of George III; succeeded his brother, George IV. Agreed to create enough peers to assure passage of Reform Bill of 1832.

William I (1772-1843), 1st king of Netherlands (1815-40). Created king after Napoleonic Wars; ceded German possessions to Prussia. Anti-Catholic policies precipitated revolt leading to Belgian independence (1831). Abdicated in favour of his son William II.

William of Malmesbury (d. *c* 1143), English historian. Author of *Gesta regum Anglorum* (*c* 1125) and *Historia novella*, latter of which describes contemporary events after 1126.

William of Occam or **Ockham** (*c* 1285-1349), English Franciscan philosopher. Major nominalist (*see* NOMINALISM). Held that thought is not a measurement of reality. Demarcated philosophy and theology. Summoned to answer charges of heresy by Pope John XXII.

William of Tyre (*c* 1130-*c* 1185), historian and churchman, b. Palestine. Chancellor of Latin Kingdom of Jerusalem (1174-83) and archbishop of Tyre (1175). Wrote important account of Crusades from 1095 to 1184.

William of Wykeham (1324-1404), English churchman. Bishop of Winchester (1366-1404), he was twice lord chancellor (1367-71, 1389-91). Founded New College, Oxford (1379), and Winchester College school (1378).

Williams, Sir George, *see* YOUNG MEN'S CHRISTIAN ASSOCIATION.

Williams, Roger (*c* 1603-83), American clergyman, b. England. Banished from Massachusetts, founded (1636) colony of Providence, Rhode Island. Advocated complete religious freedom.

Williams, Tennessee, pseud. of Thomas Lanier Williams (*c* 1914-), American dramatist. Plays frequently centre on insecure, neurotic woman, sustained by illusion, confronted with reality of male violence, *eg The Glass Menagerie* (1945), *A Streetcar Named Desire* (1947), *Cat on a Hot Tin Roof* (1955), *Night of the Iguana* (1961). Also wrote novels, poetry.

Williams, William Carlos (1883-1963), American poet, novelist. Known for poetry which extracts detail from everyday objects, speech patterns, *eg Spring and All* (1923), *Collected Later Poems* (1950). Novels incl. *White Mule* (1937) and sequels.

Williamsburg, town of SE Virginia, US. Pop. 9000. Settled 1632, hist. cap. of Virginia (1699-1779). Yorktown campaign fought nearby ending American Revolution

(1781). Has many hist. colonial buildings esp. Colonial Palace, Capitol; restoration began 1927.

William the Lion (1143-1214), king of Scotland (1165-1214). After capture at Alnwick (1174), forced to pay homage to Henry II of England by terms of Treaty of Falaise. Treaty was rescinded (1189) by Richard I in exchange for money.

William the Silent, Prince of Orange (1533-84), Dutch statesman. Appointed stadholder of Holland, Zeeland and Utrecht by Philip II of Spain (1559). Opposed Spanish tyranny and religious intolerance in Netherlands. Led armies in struggle for Dutch independence from Spain (1568-76). Became stadholder of 7 N provs. (1579), which declared their independence from Spain (1581). Assassinated by Catholic fanatic.

will-o'-the-wisp or **jack-o'-lantern,** pale, flickering light seen over marshland at night. Prob. caused by spontaneous combustion of methane.

Pussy willow (Salix discolor)

willow or **osier,** any of genus *Salix* of trees and shrubs of N temperate and subarctic regions. Narrow leaves, male and female catkins borne on separate plants. Tough, pliable twigs used in basketwork, *etc.* Common species incl. *S. viminalis* of Europe. Cricket bats made from white willow, *S. alba.*

willowherb, any of genus *Epilobium* of plants, esp. *E. angustifolium* or fireweed, a North American shrub with narrow leaves, reddish-purple flowers. Grows in fireswept areas.

willow pattern, design in blue and white, incorporating bridge, pagoda, willow trees and figures, used to decorate chinaware. Developed after 1780 in Staffordshire, England; design is attributed to Thomas Minton.

Wilmington, port of NE Delaware, US; on Delaware R. Pop. 80,000; state's largest town. Important chemical indust. (Dupont), textile mfg. First settled 1638 by Swedish.

Wilson, Angus Frank Johnstone (1913-), English novelist, critic, b. Scotland. Satirical works incl. *Such Darling Dodos* (1950), *Hemlock and After* (1952), *Anglo-Saxon Attitudes* (1956), *No Laughing Matter* (1967).

Wilson, Charles Thomson Rees (1869-1959), Scottish physicist. Developed CLOUD CHAMBER to study ionized subatomic particles by making their paths visible (1911). Awarded Nobel Prize for Physics (1927).

Wilson, Colin (1931-), English author. Known for popular critical work *The Outsider* (1956) reflecting mid-50s cult of existentialist anti-hero.

Wilson, Edmund (1895-1972), American author, critic. Known for erudite cultural study, *To the Finland Station* (1940), classic work on symbolism, *Axel's Castle* (1931). Other works incl. *The Scrolls from the Dead Sea* (1955).

Wilson, Sir [James] Harold (1916-), British statesman, PM (1964-70, 1974-6). Elected Labour Party leader (1963), succeeding Gaitskell. First term highlighted by Rhodesia's UDI (1965) ; both admins. dominated by serious inflation, civil strife in Northern Ireland. Resigned from office.

Wilson, Henry Maitland Wilson, 1st Baron (1881-1964), British field marshal. In WWII commander-in-chief in Middle East (1943-4); supreme Allied commander in Mediterranean (1944-5). Head of British joint staff mission in Washington (1945-7).

Woodrow Wilson

Wilson, [Thomas] Woodrow (1856-1924), American statesman, president (1913-21). Governor of New Jersey (1911-13), successful Democratic presidential candidate (1912). Kept US out of WWI until 1917, then entered to make 'world safe for democracy'. Negotiated armistice of 1918 on basis of his 'Fourteen Points' previously enunciated in Jan. 1918; secured League of Nations covenant at TREATY OF VERSAILLES (1919). Awarded Nobel Peace Prize (1919).

Wilton, mun. bor. of Wiltshire, S England. Pop. 4000. Sheep market; carpet mfg. from 16th cent. Wilton House associated with many Elizabethan poets.

Wiltshire, county of S England. Area 3481 sq km (1344 sq mi); pop. 501,000; co. town Salisbury. Chalk uplands incl. Marlborough Downs (N), Salisbury Plain (S). Fertile vales. Wheat, sheep; military training grounds. Prehist. remains incl. Stonehenge, Avebury. Centre of Saxon kingdom of Wessex.

Wimbledon, see MERTON, England.

Winchester, city and co. town of Hampshire, S England, on R. Itchen. Pop. 31,000. Roman *Venta Belgarum;* Saxon cap. of Wessex. Has cathedral (11th cent.), Norman castle. Famous English public school (1382).

Winckelmann, Johann Joachim (1717-68), German art historian and archaeologist. In his *History of Ancient Art* he described history of Greek art and principles on which it was based; it laid foundations of modern art history.

wind, natural current of air parallel to Earth's surface. Caused by differences in air pressure within atmosphere; air flows from high pressure to low pressure areas. Many sectors of globe have almost continuous prevailing winds, *eg* mid-latitude westerlies, tropical trade winds. Localized winds incl. MISTRAL, SIROCCO. Wind velocity measured by anemometer, classed on BEAUFORT SCALE.

Windermere, Lake, largest lake of England, in Lake Dist., Cumbria. Length 17 km (10.5 mi). Tourism, steamer service in summer. Resort of Windermere (pop. 7000) on E bank.

windflower, common name for wild varieties of ANEMONE.

Windhoek, cap. of South West Africa. Pop. 61,000. Admin. centre, railways to Walvis Bay and South Africa; trade in skins, minerals. Formerly called Windhuk as cap. of German colony.

wind instruments, name given to woodwind and brass families of instruments. Sound is produced when player sets column of air vibrating inside the instruments. Woodwind instruments incl. clarinet, saxophone, oboe, bassoon, flute. Brass instruments incl. horn, trumpet, trombone, bugle, tuba.

windmill, apparatus which harnesses wind power for pumping water, grinding corn, generating electricity, *etc.*

Windmill in Suffolk

Usually consists of tower with revolving arms at top bearing sails to catch wind. Introduced to Europe prob. during 12th cent, widely used esp. in Holland.

Windsor, House of, name of royal family of Great Britain. Adopted by George V (1917) in place of House of Saxe-Coburg-Gotha. Subsequent monarchs Edward VIII, George VI, Elizabeth II.

Windsor, Wallis Warfield, Duchess of (1896-), American-born wife of Edward, duke of Windsor. Married Edward Simpson (1927), from whom she obtained a divorce (Oct. 1936). Her association with EDWARD VIII led him to abdicate British throne; married him (June, 1937).

Windsor, indust. city of SW Ontario, Canada; on Detroit R. Pop. 203,000. Linked with Detroit (US) by road and rail tunnels. Major auto indust.; salt and chemicals mfg. Settled by French (1749).

Windsor, New, mun. bor. of Berkshire, S England, on R. Thames. Pop. 30,000. Castle estab. by William I, still royal residence; St George's Chapel, parks. Town hall designed by Wren.

Windward Islands, archipelago of SE West Indies, in S Lesser Antilles. Extends S from Leeward Isls. Incl. Dominica, St Lucia, St Vincent, Grenada; Martinique (French possession). Of volcanic origin; equable tropical climate. French, British contested ownership, resolved 1815.

wine, alcoholic beverage made from fermented grape juice. Fortified wine, *eg* sherry, port, has brandy added to it; sparkling wine, *eg* champagne, is made by inducing secondary process of fermentation in bottle. Dry wine is obtained by allowing all grape sugar to be converted to alcohol, sweet wine by arresting process of fermentation. In red wines, entire grape is used; in white, only juice is used. Leading and best-known wine producers are France, Italy, Germany.

Wingate, Orde Charles (1903-44), British army officer. In WWII, defeated Italians in Ethiopia (1941). Organized Chindits for guerrilla operations against Japanese in Burma (1942-3). Killed in air accident.

winkle, marine snail of genus *Littorina,* found on rocky shores. Destroys oysters by drilling shell and rasping away the flesh. Species incl. common edible winkle, *L. littorea.* Also called periwinkle.

Winnipeg, cap. of Manitoba, Canada; at confluence of Red, Assiniboine rivers. Pop. 246,000. Railway jct., commercial centre. Chief wheat market of Prairie provs. Meat packing, flour milling, agric. machinery mfg. Settled as Fort Rouge; renamed (1873). Seat of Manitoba Univ. (1877).

Winnipeg, Lake, SC Manitoba, Canada. Area 24,514 sq km (9465 sq mi). Receives Red, Winnipeg, Saskatchewan rivers. Drained by Nelson R. to Hudson Bay. In lumbering, fishing, tourist region.

Winston-Salem, town of W North Carolina, US. Pop. 133,000. Major tobacco mfg. centre. Formed 1913 by union of 2 towns (Winston and Salem). Salem founded as Moravian colony 1766.

winterberry, various hollies of North America, esp. *Ilex verticillata,* deciduous shrub with oval serrated leaves and red berries.

wintergreen, several creeping evergreen plants of genus *Gaultheria,* esp. *G. procumbens* of North America. Yields medicinal and flavouring oil. Red berries are called checkerberries.

Winterthur, town of NE Switzerland. Pop. 93,000. Indust. centre, textiles; railway jct., locomotive mfg.

Winthrop, John (1588-1649), English colonist. Governed Massachusetts Bay Colony, helping to estab. theocratic structure. Banished Anne Hutchinson on charge of heresy.

wireworm, *see* CLICK BEETLE.

Wirral Peninsula, area of Merseyside met. county, NW England, between Dee and Mersey estuaries. Birkenhead, Wallasey in NE. Former royal forest.

Wisbech, mun. bor. of Isle of Ely, Cambridgeshire, EC England, on R. Nene. Pop. 17,000. Agric. market; flowers, bulbs, fruit, vegetables.

Wisconsin, state of NC US. Area 145,439 sq km (56,154 sq mi); pop. 4,418,000; cap. Madison; largest city Milwaukee. Bordered by L. Superior in N, L. Michigan in E, Mississippi R. in W. Mainly low-lying. Leading dairy producer, also grains; iron ore mining; industs. incl. meat packing, brewing. Explored in 17th cent. by French; ceded to British 1763. Part of US from 1787. Admitted to Union as 30th state (1830).

Wise, Isaac Mayer (1819-1900), American rabbi, b. Bohemia. Estab. Reform JUDAISM in US. His innovations incl. sermons in English.

Wiseman, Nicholas Patrick Stephen (1802-65), English RC churchman, b. Spain. Created cardinal and 1st archbishop of Westminster (1850). Worked to allay anti-Catholic feeling in England.

wisent, *Bison bonasus,* European bison, almost extinct in wild. Smaller head and less shaggy body than American bison.

Wishart, George (*c* 1513-46), Scottish religious reformer. Achieved conversion of John Knox to Protestantism. Burned for heresy at St Andrews.

Wismar, town of NW East Germany, on Baltic Sea. Pop. 55,000. Oil, fishing port; shipbuilding, sugar refining. Important Hanseatic centre; held by Sweden 1648-1803.

wisteria, genus of climbing shrubs of Leguminosae family. Native to E US and E Asia. Showy clusters of white, blue, pink or voilet drooping flowers.

witan, *see* WITENAGEMOT.

Witbank, town of E Transvaal, South Africa. Pop. 51,000. Indust. centre in coalmining dist.; chemicals indust.

witchcraft, the working of magic. Common to most cultures. In Europe, may be survival of Palaeolithic fertility cults. Features incl: holding of 'Sabbaths' 4 times a year; district groupings into 'covens' of 13; use of spells, charms; supposed transformation into animals, ability to fly, worship of devil. Condemned as heresy (14th cent.) by Christian church; subject of widespread persecution 16th-17th cent. In US, most noted persecution occurred (1692) at Salem.

witch hazel, any of genus *Hamamelis* of small trees and shrubs. Native to North America and Asia. *H. virginiana* of E North America has yellow flowers. Medicinal lotion is derived from bark.

witenagemot or **witan,** aristocratic assembly of nobles and high churchmen in Anglo-Saxon England. Appointed by king to advise him on questions of law, tax, foreign policy.

Witch hazel

Timber wolf

Witt, Jan de (1625-72), Dutch statesman. Leader of Republican party and virtual ruler of Holland, he obtained successful conclusion to war with England (1667). Resigned after William of Orange had gained popular support. Killed by mob.

Wittenberg, town of C East Germany, on R. Elbe. Pop. 47,000. Machinery, soap mfg. Here Luther nailed (1517) his 95 Theses to Schlosskirche (which contains his tomb). First Lutheran bible (1534) printed here. Univ. (1502) incorporated into Halle univ. 1817.

Wittgenstein, Ludwig Josef Johann (1889-1951), Austrian philosopher. Worked mainly in England. *Tractatus Logico-Philosophicus* (1919) helped develop LOGICAL POSITIVISM. Later work, in *Philosophical Investigations* (pub. 1953), on the false problems created by the ambiguity of language.

Witwatersrand or **The Rand,** area of S Transvaal, South Africa, centred on gold-bearing ridge (alt. *c* 1830 m/6000 ft). Gold discovered 1886; now produces 33% world's output. Also coal, manganese deposits. Main cities Johannesburg, Germiston, Benoni.

woad, any of genus *Isatis* of plants of mustard family, esp. *I. tinctoria* with yellow flowers. Leaves yield blue dye used by ancient Britons as body paint; widely used to dye clothes until advent of aniline dyes.

Wodehouse, (Sir) P[elham] G[renville] (1881- 1975), English novelist. Known for novels, short stories caricaturing English upper-class world of 1920s in stylized slang. Created characters Bertie Wooster, his man Jeeves. Settled in US *c* 1920.

Woden, Germanic name for ODIN.

Woffington, Margaret ('Peg') (*c* 1714-60), English actress, b. Ireland. Best known playing aristocratic women, 'breeches' roles. Notorious for affairs, esp. with Garrick.

Wöhler, Friedrich (1800-82), German pioneer of organic chemistry. His synthesis of urea (1828) helped refute doctrine of 'vital force' necessary for manufacture of organic compounds. Devised methods of isolating metallic aluminium.

Wolf, Friedrich August (1759-1824), German scholar, philologist. In *Prolegomena ad Homerum* (1795), claimed Homer's *Iliad* and *Odyssey* were written by several people.

Wolf, Hugo (1860-1903), Austrian composer. Wrote numerous romantic *lieder,* incl. settings of poems by Goethe, *Spanish Songbook* and *Italian Songbook*. Also wrote *Italian Serenade* for string quartet, later orchestrated.

wolf, carnivorous, intelligent, dog-like mammal, genus *Canis,* found in remote areas of N hemisphere. Hunts in packs; can attack more powerful animals. North American timber or grey wolf considered subspecies of European *Canis lupus*.

Wolfe, James (1727-59), British army officer. Given command of expedition to take Québec (1759). Victory over French under Montcalm on Plains of Abraham secured Canada for Britain. Fatally wounded.

Wolfe, Thomas Clayton (1900-38), American novelist. Known for vast, intensely realistic, autobiog. cycle, incl. *Look Homeward, Angel* (1929), *Of Time and the River* (1935).

Wolfe, Tom, pseud. of Thomas Kennerly (1931-), American journalist. Known for chronicles of various American alternative cultures, *eg The Kandy-Kolored Tangerine-Flake Streamline Baby* (1965), *Radical Chic and Mau-mauing the Flak Catchers* (1970).

Wolfenbüttel, town of NE West Germany, on R. Oker. Pop. 40,000. Agric. machinery, food processing. Seat of dukes of Brunswick until 1753; famous ducal library (17th cent.).

wolfhound, large dog originally used for hunting wolves. Breeds incl. Irish wolfhound and borzoi.

wolfram, *see* TUNGSTEN.

Wolfram von Eschenbach (*fl* early 13th cent.), German poet. Known for Holy Grail epic *Parzival* (basis of Wagner's *Parsifal*), also wrote epics *Titurel, Willehalm,* lyrics. One of greatest of the MINNESINGER.

Wolfsburg, town of NE West Germany. Pop. 89,000. Founded 1938; centre of Volkswagen automobile indust.

wolf spider, spider of Lycosidae family that hunts prey on ground rather than trapping it in webs. Species incl. S European tarantula, *Lycosa tarantula*.

Wollongong, city of SE New South Wales, Australia, on Tasman Sea. Pop. 250,000. Originally dairying, cedar exporting centre; now major coalmining, iron and steel industs. Coal exported via suburb of Port Kembla.

Wollstonecraft, Mary (1759-97), English miscellaneous writer. Member of group of Radicals which incl. GODWIN, by whom she had daughter who became SHELLEY'S second wife. Best-known work, *Vindication of the Rights of Women* (1792).

Wolseley, Garnet Joseph Wolseley, 1st Viscount (1833-1913), British general. Commanded expedition against Red River rebellion in Canada (1870). Known for attempt to relieve Gordon at Khartoum (1884-5). Commander-in-chief of army (1895-1901).

Wolsey, Thomas (*c* 1473-1530), English churchman, statesman. Created (1515) cardinal and lord chancellor by Henry VIII. Had charge of English foreign and domestic policy; attempted to mediate for peace in Europe. Achieved great personal wealth; founded Cardinal College, Oxford (Christchurch) and had Hampton Court built. Failure to arrange Henry's divorce from Catherine of Aragon led to his dismissal and arrest (1530).

Wolverhampton, bor. of West Midlands met. county, WC England. Pop. 269,000. In BLACK COUNTRY; metal working incl. cars, bicycles, locks; rayon, chemicals. Hist. wool trade, until 16th cent.

wolverine or **glutton,** *Gulo gulo,* carnivorous bear-like mammal, largest of weasel family, found in Arctic and subarctic regions of Europe, Asia, North America. Short-legged, with bushy tail and shaggy coat; voracious predator, it will attack most animals.

womb, *see* UTERUS.

wombat, burrowing nocturnal Australian marsupial, esp. of genus *Vombatus*. Rodent-like, with stocky body and continuously growing incisors; herbivorous. Species incl. common wombat, *V. hirsutus*. All species becoming rarer.

women's rights, *see* CIVIL RIGHTS.

Wombat *(Vombatus ursinus)*

women's services, auxiliary corps of navy, army and air force employing women to release manpower for fighting. In UK and US, women first served in large numbers in WWII, *eg* Women's Royal Naval Service (UK, 1939), Women's Auxiliary Air Force (UK, 1939), Women's Army Corps (US, 1942). Nursing services, incl. Women's Voluntary Services (UK, 1938), also performed important duties.

women's suffrage, right of women to vote. In UK, first proposed by Mary Wollstonecraft in *A Vindication of the Rights of Women* (1792). First women's suffrage committee formed (1865) in Manchester. Local committees united (1897) in National Union of Women's Suffrage Societies. More militant Women's Social and Political Union formed (1903), led by Emmeline Pankhurst and daughters. Used arson, bombing; many arrested, went on hunger strike when imprisoned. Achieved right to vote for married women over 30 (1918); extended to cover all women over 21 (1928). In US, women's participation in Anti-Slavery movement led to women's rights demand; advocates incl. Elizabeth Stanton, Lucretia Mott, Susan B. Anthony. National Woman Suffrage Association formed (1869) to agitate for constitutional amendment. Acquired (1918) equal suffrage in 15 states. WWI accelerated progress, leading to 19th Amendment (1920) making denial of women's right to vote unconstitutional.

Wonsan, port of SE North Korea, on sea of Japan. Pop. 125,000. Railway engineering, oil refining, fishing.

Wood, Mrs Henry, née Ellen Price (1814-87), English novelist. Wrote many popular novels of middle-class life. Now known for bestseller *East Lynne* (1861), basis of several melodramas.

Wood, Sir Henry Joseph (1869-1944), English conductor. Began Promenade Concerts in London (1895) and conducted them until his death. Helped introduce many new works to British audiences.

Wood, John (1704-54), English architect, town planner. Influenced by Palladian theories; known as 'Wood of Bath' for work, *eg* the Circus, in planning that city.

wood, hard, fibrous substance which makes up greater part of stems and branches of trees and shrubs beneath the bark. Composed of XYLEM and PHLOEM intersected by transverse vascular rays.

woodbine, name for HONEYSUCKLE and VIRGINIA CREEPER.

woodchuck or **ground hog,** *Marmota monax,* burrowing North American marmot with coarse red-brown hair. Frequents woodland and farms; hibernates underground in winter.

woodcock, woodland game bird, chestnut or brown in colour, genus *Scolopax.* Feeds largely on insect larvae. Species incl. Eurasian woodcock, *S. rusticola,* and American woodcock, *S. minor.*

woodcut and **wood engraving,** terms applied to prints made from wood blocks cut by hand. Earliest dated woodcut is Chinese *Diamond Sutra* of AD 868. Woodcuts appeared in Europe in early 15th cent.; great practitioners of art incl. Dürer and Holbein.

woodlouse, small terrestrial crustacean of suborder Oniscoidea. Flattened elliptical body with 7 pairs of legs;

Woodchuck

dull brown or grey in colour. Lives in damp places, *eg* under stones. Also called sowbug or slater.

wood mouse, *see* MOUSE.

Green woodpecker

woodpecker, widely distributed tree-climbing bird of Picidae family. Wedge-shaped bill used to bore holes, long tongue for catching insects; stiff tail aids climbing. Species incl. European green woodpecker, *Picus viridis,* and American red-headed woodpecker, *Melanerpes erythrocephalus.*

wood pigeon, *see* PIGEON.

Woods, Lake of the, on Manitoba-Ontario border with Minnesota, C Canada-US. Area 3846 sq km (1485 sq mi). In forested region. Popular tourist area.

wood sorrel, *see* OXALIS.

Woodstock, mun. bor. of Oxfordshire, SC England. Pop. 2000. Glove mfg. Site of old palace where Elizabeth I imprisoned (1554). Blenheim Palace (1724) designed by Vanbrugh.

Woodville, Elizabeth (*c* 1437-92), English queen, consort of Edward IV. After her secret marriage to Edward, Woodville family grew powerful at court to detriment of

WARWICK. Her sons Edward and Richard were seized by Gloucester (RICHARD III) on her husband's death and declared illegitimate. Daughter married Henry VII.

wood-wasp, any of Siricidae family of large wasp-like insects. Uses ovipositor to bore into conifers to make holes for eggs; larvae bore further, causing much damage. Also called horntail.

woodwind, group of musical instruments in which a sound is obtained by blowing through a mouthpiece, and pitch varied by closing keys or holes with fingers.

woodworm, larva of beetles of Anobiidae family. Beetle lays eggs in cracks in wood and larvae burrow into wood; adults emerge leaving holes. Most common is furniture beetle, *Anobium punctatum.* Preservatives have been developed to combat woodworm.

wool, curly fibrous hair of sheep and other animals, *eg* goat, llama and alpaca. Absorbent, strong, warm, crease resistant and able to hold dye; spun into yarn and used extensively in mfg. of clothing. Major wool producers are Australia, USSR, New Zealand and Argentina.

Virginia Woolf

Woolf, Virginia Adelaine, née Stephen (1882-1941), English novelist, critic. Prominent in BLOOMSBURY GROUP. Known for sensitive novels of inner experience, experimental in form, *eg Mrs Dalloway* (1925), *To the Lighthouse* (1927), *The Waves* (1931), *Between the Acts* (1941). Essays incl. two series, *The Common Reader* (1925, 1932).

Woolley, Sir [Charles] Leonard (1880-1960), English archaeologist. Led excavations at Ur, where he found treasures in Royal Cemetery and evidence of a flood similar to that of Genesis and the Gilgamesh epic. Wrote *Ur of the Chaldees* (1929), a popular account of his work.

woolly monkey, monkey of genus *Lagothrix* from Amazon forests. Grey woolly coat, prehensile tail; moves about in troops.

Woolman, John (1720-72), American religious leader. Quaker preacher, one of 1st opponents of slavery. Known for *Journal* (1774).

Woolwich, *see* GREENWICH, England.

Woolworth, Frank Winfield (1852-1919), American merchant. Founded 'dime-store' chain with first (1879) in Pennsylvania. Extended chain to Britain (1910).

Woomera, town of SC South Australia. Pop. 5000. Base for weapons-testing range, rocket launching and tracking facilities; estab. 1947 by Australian, UK govts. on part of aboriginal reserve.

Worcester, town of C Massachusetts, US; on Blackstone R. Pop. 177,000. Machinery, electrical equipment mfg. Blackstone Canal to Providence built 1828. Annual music festival.

Worcestershire, former county of WC England, now part of Hereford and Worcester. Incl. valleys of Severn and Warwickshire Avon. Vale of Evesham (orchards) in SE; BLACK COUNTRY (indust.) in NE. **Worcester,** city on R. Severn, co. town of Hereford and Worcester. Pop. 73,000. Gloves, china, 'Worcester Sauce' mfg. Has hospital (11th cent.), cathedral (14th cent.). Scene of battle (1651) in which Cromwell defeated Charles II.

William Wordsworth

Wordsworth, William (1770-1850), English poet. Romantic lyrics noted for radically new simplicity of language in depicting nature. Wrote *Lyrical Ballads* (1798) with Coleridge, incl. 'Tintern Abbey'. *Poems in Two Volumes* (1807) incl. 'Ode to Duty', 'Intimations of Immortality', 'The Idiot Boy', 'Michael', 'The Daffodils'. Other works incl. verse autobiog. *The Prelude.* Poet laureate from 1843. His sister, **Dorothy Wordsworth** (1771-1835), kept noted journals.

work, in physics, product of a force and displacement in line of action of force. SI unit of work is joule; other units incl. erg.

workers' control, holding of exclusive decision-making rights by workers in an indust. organization, incl. right to hire and dismiss management. In socialist theory, involves total restructuring of relationships within indust. and, in effect, overthrow of capitalism by placing means of production, distribution and exchange in workers' hands.

workhouse, British institution for maintenance of poor. *See* POOR LAW.

works council, consultative body within an indust. organization, in which workers' representatives participate in decisions affecting the work force. Workers' views are taken into account by a board retaining decision-making responsibility. Legal requirement in large companies in West Germany, Netherlands, Sweden, Italy. *See* INDUSTRIAL DEMOCRACY.

World Bank, *see* INTERNATIONAL BANK FOR RECONSTRUCTION AND DEVELOPMENT.

World Council of Churches, organization assembled (1948) at Amsterdam of representatives from 150 Protestant and Orthodox churches. By 1970s had over 260 member churches from *c* 90 countries. Has no legislative power, provides opportunity for practical co-operation and discussion.

World Federation of Trade Unions (WFTU), body formed (1945) to represent trade union organizations in more than 50 countries. All non-Communist trade unions had withdrawn by 1951. Meets every 4 years.

World Health Organization (WHO), agency of UN (estab. 1948) set up with the aim of attaining highest possible level of health for all peoples. Activities incl. medical research and training in care of sick and prevention of disease.

World Meteorological Organization (WMO), agency of UN (estab. 1951), hq. at Geneva. Aims to standardize, coordinate and improve meteorological services around the world.

World War I, conflict (1914-18) precipitated by assassination (June, 1914) of Francis Ferdinand of Austria-

Hungary in Serbia. By Aug., Europe was involved in total warfare, opposing alliances being Central Powers (Germany, Austria-Hungary and Turkey) and Allies (Britain, France, Russia, Belgium, Serbia, Montenegro and Japan). Rapid German advance in W thwarted near Paris; followed by prolonged stalemate with concentrated trench warfare. In E, German victories contributed to success of RUSSIAN REVOLUTION (1917) and Russian withdrawal from war. In 1915, Bulgaria joined Central Powers, Italy joined Allies. Unrestricted German submarine attacks (1916-17) led to US entry on Allied side and eventual end to stalemate. Successful counter-attack by Allies in 2nd battle of the Marne followed by surrender of all Central Powers except Germany. After internal revolt, Germany signed armistice (11 Nov. 1918) at Compiègne. Subsequent peace treaties, esp. TREATY OF VERSAILLES, radically altered political boundaries of Europe at expense of Central Powers. Overwhelming loss of life (est. 10 million dead) led to international search for peace, initially through LEAGUE OF NATIONS.

World War II, conflict (1939-45) climaxing aggressive policies of AXIS powers (Germany, Italy and Japan) and attempts to counter them by W European nations (UK and France). Hitler's success in Bohemia (*see* MUNICH PACT) and NON-AGGRESSION PACT signed with USSR opened way for attack (Sept. 1939) on Poland. Britain (with Commonwealth) and France declared war on Germany. Hitler's quick victory in Poland followed by occupation of Denmark, Norway and Low Countries; crushed France (surrendered June, 1940) after Allies were forced to evacuate DUNKIRK. Britain, led by W. CHURCHILL, resisted German air offensive in 'Battle of Britain'. German and Italian successes in N Africa and Balkans (1940-1) preceded invasion of USSR (June, 1941). Japanese attack on Pearl Harbor (Dec. 1941) brought US into war; Japan then occupied much of SE Asia. Axis triumphs halted in N Africa (*see* NORTH AFRICA CAMPAIGN) by Allied landings in Algeria and S Italy, US naval victories in Pacific and USSR's defeat of German forces at Stalingrad (1943). Italy surrendered (Sept. 1943), but Germany continued to resist Allies. Russian drive through E Europe and Allied invasion of Normandy under EISENHOWER (June, 1944) brought eventual German collapse and surrender (May, 1945). American 'island-hopping' strategy in Pacific and dropping of atomic bombs on Hiroshima and Nagasaki led to Japan's surrender (Sept., 1945). Need to ensure international peace led to formation of UNITED NATIONS; however, problems of post-war Europe remained unresolved, difficulty increasing with development of COLD WAR between East and West.

worm, name given to members of several phyla of elongated creeping animals, esp. common earthworm. *See* ANNELIDA, NEMATODA.

worm lizard, any of Amphisbaenidae family of worm-like burrowing lizards. Vestigial eyes; no limbs except in genus *Bipes,* which retains forelimbs. Found mainly in tropics.

Worms, town of W West Germany, on R. Rhine. Pop. 77,000. Wine trade. Scene of Synod of Worms (1076) which deposed Pope Gregory VII and of Diet of Worms (1521) which tried and outlawed Luther.

Worms, Concordat of (1122), agreement between Pope Calixtus II and Emperor Henry V after dispute over investiture of clergy. Emperor conceded right of free elections of bishops, abbots. Pope granted Henry right to be present at elections and to invest those elected with lay rights before consecration.

Worms, Diet of (1521), meeting of theologians and officials of RC church called by Emperor Charles V at Worms. Martin Luther appeared under safe conduct to defend his doctrines. On refusal to retract, he was outlawed, together with his followers.

wormwood, *Artemesia absinthium,* Eurasian perennial plant. Silvery-grey leaves, small yellow flowers. Yields intensely bitter oil used in flavouring, *eg* in absinthe.

Worthing, mun. bor. of West Sussex, S England. Pop. 88,000. Resort; horticulture. Prehist. Cissbury Ring nearby; Roman remains.

Wotton, Sir Henry (1568-1639), English poet. Prominent member of circle of Donne, Izaac Walton. Poetry, miscellaneous writings collected in *Reliquiae Wottonianae* (1651).

Wrangel, Ferdinard Petrovich, Baron von (1794-1870), Russian naval officer, Arctic explorer. Surveyed Siberian coastline and Arctic ocean. First governor of Russian colony in Alaska (1829-35).

Wrangel, Piotr Nikolayevich, Baron (1878-1928), Russian army officer. Succeeded Denikin as White Army commander, eventually forced back into Crimea by Red forces (1920); exiled to Belgium.

Wrangel Island, Arctic isl. off NE Siberian RSFSR coast. Area *c* 4700 sq km (1800 sq mi). Largely tundra. Discovered 1867 by American whaler T. Long. Claimed by USSR (1924).

wrasse, brightly coloured marine fish of Labridae family, found worldwide. Some species pick parasites from bodies of larger fish.

Wrath, Cape, promontory of Highland region, Scotland, most NW point on mainland.

Sir Christopher Wren

Wren, Sir Christopher (1632-1723), English architect, mathematician. His plan to rebuild London after Great Fire (1666) was not adopted, but he designed St Paul's Cathedral and 51 City churches, noted for their spires. Other buildings incl. parts of Greenwich Hospital, Sheldonian Theatre (Oxford), Trinity College Library (Cambridge). Works characterized by engineering skill, imaginative use of classical orders.

Wren, P[ercival] C[hristopher] (1885-1941), English novelist. Known for bestselling romantic adventure tales of Foreign Legion, esp. *Beau Geste* (1924).

wren, any of Troglodytidae family of small slender-billed, dull-coloured songbirds. Species incl. European *Troglodytes troglodytes,* with brown plumage and erect tail, and North American house wren, *T. aedon.*

wrestling, sport in which two contestants struggle hand-to-hand to throw or force one another to the ground. Of ancient origin, wrestling was incl. in Olympics of 704 BC. Two styles are incl. in modern Olympics: freestyle and Graeco-Roman.

Wrexham, mun. bor. of Clwyd, NE Wales. Pop. 39,000. Indust. centre; coalmining; metal goods, chemicals mfg. Seat of RC bishopric.

Wright, Frank Lloyd (1869-1959), American architect. Evolved 'organic' concept to integrate building and environment; innovator in use of industrial materials, *eg* reinforced concrete. Greatly influenced course of 20th cent. architecture. Works incl. Johnson admin. building, Racine, Wisconsin, and Guggenheim Museum, New York.

Wright, Judith (1915-   ), Australian poet. Works, *eg The Moving Image* (1946), *The Gateway* (1953), *The Two Fires*

Frank Lloyd Wright in 1955

(1955), reflect introspective, mystical search for true values.

Wright, Orville (1871-1948), American aviator. With his brother, **Wilbur Wright** (1867–1912), developed engine for use in glider and made 1st sustained power-driven aeroplane flight (1903) near Kitty Hawk, North Carolina.

Wright, Richard (1908-60), American author. Works deal with role of negro in American society, *eg* short stories in *Uncle Tom's Children* (1938), novels *Native Son* (1940), *The Long Dream* (1958), autobiog. *Black Boy* (1945).

writing, art of forming symbols on surface of some medium to record and communicate ideas. Pictographic writing developed independently in Egypt, China, Mesopotamia and among the Maya. For development of phonemic writing, *see* ALPHABET.

Wroclaw (Ger. *Breslau*), city of SW Poland, on R. Oder, cap. of Wroclaw prov. Pop. 528,000. Railway jct., river port; engineering, food processing; univ. (1702). Cap. of medieval duchy of Silesia, Hanseatic League member; under Habsburgs from 1526, Prussia from 1742; cap. of German Lower Silesia until 1945. Cathedral (13th cent.).

Wuchang, *see* WUHAN.

Wuhan, cap. of Hupeh prov., EC China. Pop. 4,250,000. Port at jct. of Han and Yangtze rivers. Transport, indust. centre (shipbuilding, cotton mills, major steel complex) formed by union of Hankow, Hanyang, Wuchang. Major road-rail bridge across Yangtze links towns.

Wuhsien, *see* SOOCHOW.

Wuhu, city of Anhwei prov., E China. Pop. 300,000. Deepwater port on Yangtze. Major rice market; processing centre for agric. produce.

Wundt, Wilhelm Max (1832-1920), German physiologist, psychologist. Estab. 1st experimental psychology laboratory in Leipzig (1878).

Wuppertal, city of W West Germany, on R. Wupper. Pop. 417,000. Textile mfg., pharmaceuticals, brewing. Formed 1929 by union of several towns, incl. Elberfeld (noted in 19th cent. for Elberfeld system of poor relief). Badly damaged in WWII.

Württemberg, region of SW West Germany, hist. cap. Stuttgart. Hilly, crossed by Swabian Jura, Black Forest in W; main rivers Danube, Neckar. Duchy from 1495, kingdom 1806-1918. Became part of Baden-Württemberg state 1952.

Würzburg, city of C West Germany, on R. Main. Pop. 116,000. Indust. centre, esp. wine, printing; univ. (1582). Bishopric founded 741; Marienberg fortress was residence of bishops 13th-18th cent. Has cathedral (11th cent.), baroque palace.

Wusih, city of Kiangsu prov., E China. Pop. 900,000. On Tai lake and Grand Canal. Food processing; produces silk, machinery. Still makes famous figurines of dramatic characters.

Wyatt, Sir Thomas (1503-42), English poet, courtier. With Surrey, introduced sonnet form into English. Works incl. translations of Plutarch, Petrarch, love lyrics posthumously published in *Tottel's Miscellany*.

Wycherley, William (1640-1716), English dramatist. Known for licentious Restoration comedies. *eg The Gentleman Dancing Master* (1672), *The Country Wife* (1675), creating misanthropic picture of society.

John Wycliffe

Wycliffe, Wyclif or **Wickliffe, John** (c 1328-84), English religious reformer. Gained support of John of Gaunt by denying Church's authority in temporal affairs. Rejected Church doctrine, *eg* transubstantiation, penances, absolution; held Scriptures to be supreme authority. Condemned as heretic but never sentenced. Made 1st English translation of Bible with help of friends. Followers, called Lollards, spread his teachings, influencing Jan Hus and other reformers.

Wye, river of Wales and England, flows 210 km (130 mi) from C Wales to Severn estuary near Chepstow. Attractive scenery.

Wyoming, state of W US. Area 253,597 sq km (97,914 sq mi); pop. 334,000; cap. Cheyenne. Great Plains in NE, Rocky Mts. dominate W, semi-desert in SW. Chief rivers Yellowstone, Snake, Green. Livestock, wool, grain production; oil, uranium mining. First explored in early 19th cent.; part of Louisiana Purchase (1803). Grew with gold strike (1867) and cattle boom. Became territ. 1869. Admitted to Union as 44th state (1890).

Wyss, Johann David (1781-1830), Swiss author. Known for children's story of shipwrecked family *The Swiss Family Robinson* (1813). Also wrote Swiss national anthem, collected folklore.

XYZ

Xánthi or **Xanthe,** town of Thrace, NE Greece, cap. of Xánthi admin. dist. Pop. 26,000. Tobacco trade centre. Large Moslem minority.

Xauen or **Sheshawen,** town of Morocco, in Rif mountains. Pop. 14,000. Moslem holy city; noted for craft indust. Founded 15th cent. by Moors from Granada.

Xavier, St Francis, see FRANCIS XAVIER, ST.

xenon (Xe), rarest element of inert gas family; at. no. 54, at. wt. 131.3. Found in minute traces in atmosphere (1 part per 170 million); produced commercially from liquid air. Forms compounds with fluorine. Used in bubble chambers, thermionic valves, *etc.*

Xenophon (*c* 430-*c* 355 BC), Greek historian, pupil of Socrates. Joined Greek expedition to aid Cyrus of Persia against his brother Artaxerxes. Wrote *Anabasis,* relating heroic retreat after defeat at Cunaxa (401). Later banished from Athens for siding with Sparta. Other works incl. *Memorabilia* on Socrates and history of Greece.

xerography, commercial process of copying printed material without using light-sensitive paper. Electrostatic image of original is formed by action of light on selenium-coated plate. Oppositely-charged mixture of thermoplastic and carbon powder is dusted on to plate and adheres to charged areas; image formed is transferred to copying paper and fixed by heat.

Xerxes I (d. 465 BC), Persian king (486-465 BC). Succeeded father Darius the Great whose punitive wars against Greece he continued. Defeated Greeks at Thermopylae (480) and razed Athens. Fleet was destroyed at Salamis and army defeated at Plataea after his return to Persia (479). Murdered by one of his guard.

Xingu, river of C Brazil. Rises on Mato Grosso, flows N 1980 km (1230 mi) to Amazon delta. Has rapids in middle course.

Xiphosura, order of aquatic arachnids consisting of kingcrabs; considered living fossils. Brown horse-shoe shaped carapace, long spiny tail. *Limulus polyphemus* found on American Atlantic coast.

Xochimilco, lake of Mexico, near Mexico City. Soil-covered rafts placed in lake by ancient Indians still supply vegetables to the city.

X-rays, electromagnetic radiation of short wavelength, varying from c 5×10^{-9} m to 10^{-11} m. Produced by bombardment of matter, usually heavy metals, by high-speed electrons (*eg* cathode rays). Detected by ionizing properties or by affecting photographic plates and fluorescent screens. Penetrate substances opaque to light to a varying degree dependent on density and at. wt. of substance; widely used in medicine to photograph internal organs, bones, and to destroy diseased tissue.

xylem, woody vascular tissue of a plant which conducts water and mineral salts in the stem, roots and leaves and gives support to the softer tissues. In mature trees, constitutes majority of trunk.

xylene, or **xylol** (C_8H_{10}), colourless liquid hydrocarbon, existing in 3 isomeric forms. Occurs in coal tar, wood tar; used in manufacture of polyester fibres, dyes and as a solvent.

xylophone, percussion instrument consisting of a set of resonant wooden bars, tuned to different pitches, which are struck with hammers.

yachting or **sailing,** sport of racing or cruising in yachts. Modern form was developed in Holland in 17th cent. and popularized in England by Charles II. In US organized racing dates from foundation (1844) of New York Yacht Club. Olympic event since 1908. International ocean-racing contests incl. AMERICA'S CUP, Fastnet Cup.

Yahya Khan, Agha Mohammed (1917-   ), Pakistani general, president (1969-71). Headed martial law govt. Tried to suppress independence movement in East Pakistan by military intervention, precipitating civil war (1971). Resigned after defeat by combined Indian and East Pakistani forces.

yak, *Poephagus grunniens,* hardy wild ox of Himalayas and Tibet. Shaggy brown hair, short legs. Domesticated yak is source of milk and meat; also used as beast of burden.

Yakutsk, city of USSR, E Siberian RSFSR; summer port on R. Lena. Pop. 120,000. Trade in furs and hides; tanning, sawmilling.

Yale, Elihu (1648-1721), English merchant, b. New England. A chief benefactor of New Haven Collegiate School, renamed (1718) Yale College (now Yale Univ.).

Yale University, New Haven, Connecticut, US, privately endowed univ., founded in 1701, becoming univ. in 1887. Incl. Peabody Museum of National History, art gallery, large library. Press estab. 1908.

Yalta, town of USSR, S Ukrainian SSR; Black Sea health resort of S Crimea. Pop. 34,000. Scene of Allied conference between Stalin, Roosevelt and Churchill (Feb. 1945), resolved post-WWII fate of Germany and agreed on founding of UN.

Yalu, river on China-North Korea border. Rises in Kirin prov., flows 800 km (500 mi) SW into Bay of Korea; h.e.p. source. Used to transport timber.

yam, any of genus *Dioscorea* of tropical climbing plants. Edible starchy tuberous roots. Cultivated for human and animal consumption.

Yamagata, Aritomo, Prince (1838-1922), Japanese statesman. As war minister, modernized Japanese army. Twice premier, insisted on military domination over the cabinet. Virtual ruler of Japan as president of privy council (1909-22).

yang, see YIN AND YANG.

Yangtze, river of China. At 5550 km (3450 mi), longest in Asia. Rises in Tsinghai prov., flows E into East China Sea near Shanghai. Navigable to ocean-going ships as far as Ichang, 1600 km (1000 mi) upstream. Major commercial waterway.

Yankee or **Yank,** term used within US for natives of New England, outside, for any American. In Civil War, used for Northerners.

Yannina, see IOÁNNINA, Greece.

Yaoundé, cap. of Cameroon. Pop. 178,000. Admin., commercial centre; market town on Douala-Chad railway, trades in coffee, cocoa, rubber; univ. of Cameroon (1962). Former cap. of colony of French Cameroons.

Yaqui, American Indian tribe of Uto-Aztecan linguistic stock. Settled agriculturalists on Yaqui R. of Sonora, Mexico. They do not recognize sovereignty of Mexican govt.

Yarkand, town of Sinkiang auton. region, W China. Pop. c 80,000. Oasis at edge of Taklamakan desert, on R. Yarkand. Trade centre for goods travelling to USSR and India. Inhabited by Moslems, has 120 mosques.

Yarmouth, see GREAT YARMOUTH, England.

Yaroslavl, city of USSR, NC European RSFSR; port on upper Volga. Pop. 538,000. Motor vehicles, textiles, synthetic rubber mfg. Founded 1024; cap. of principality until annexed by Moscow in 15th cent.

Yarrow

yarrow or **milfoil,** any of genus *Achillea* of perennial plants of daisy family, esp. *A. millefolium* native to Eurasia but naturalized in North America. Strong-smelling, feathery leaves, clusters of small, pink or white flowers.

Yawata, *see* KITAKYUSHU.

yaws or **framboesia,** acute infectious tropical disease caused by spirochaete *Treponema pertenue.* Transmitted by insects and direct contagion. Similar to syphilis in early stages; characterized by skin eruptions and later lesions in skin and bone.

Yazd or **Yezd,** city of C Iran. Pop. 93,000. Textile and carpet mfg. Old Zoroastrian centre, with sizable Zoroastrian pop.

year, term used for period taken by Earth to revolve once around the Sun, usually computed at 365 days 5 hrs 48 mins 46 secs. Sidereal year, interval in which Sun appears to complete 1 revolution with respect to fixed stars, is *c* 20 mins longer; difference is due to precession of equinoxes. Calendar year is fixed at 365 days with an extra day every 4 years (leap year).

yeast, microscopic single-celled fungus, esp. of genus *Saccharomyces.* Lives on sugars, producing alcohol and carbon dioxide. Used in fermentation of alcoholic beverages and industrial alcohol. Also used in baking, as yeast acts upon carbohydrates in dough, producing carbon dioxide and causing mixture to 'rise'.

W.B. Yeats

Yeats, William Butler (1865-1939), Irish poet, dramatist. Prominent in Celtic Revival, helped found ABBEY THEATRE. Poetry draws on mystical, symbolist influences. Works incl. 'The Lake Isle of Innisfree', 'Byzantium', 'Easter 1916', collection *Last Poems* (1940). Plays incl. *Countess Cathleen* (1899), *Deirdre* (1907). Member of Irish Senate (1922-8). Nobel Prize for Literature (1923).

Yellow, river of China, *see* HWANG HO.

'Yellow Book', quarterly magazine pub. in London (1894-7) by John Lane. Contributors incl. Lionel Johnson, Henry James, Arthur Symons and Aubrey Beardsley (illustrations).

yellow fever, infectious tropical disease caused by virus transmitted by *Aedes* mosquito. Characterized by jaundice, vomiting. Prevented by vaccination, mosquito control.

yellowhammer, *Emberiza citrinella,* European bird of bunting family. Male has yellow head and under-parts, chestnut rump. Name also given to yellow flicker, *Colaptes auratus,* woodpecker of E America.

Yellowknife, cap. and admin. centre of Northwest Territs., Canada; on N Great Slave L. in S Mackenzie Dist. Pop. 6000. Gold mining, transport centre. Founded 1935 after discovery of gold in region.

yellowlegs, shore bird of genus *Tringa,* related to sandpiper, found in N and S America. Black and white plumage, long yellow legs. The 2 species are greater yellowlegs, *T. melanoleuca,* and lesser yellowlegs, *T. flavipes.*

Yellow Sea (*Hwang Hai*), arm of Pacific between China and Korea.

Yellowstone, river of W US. Rises in NW Wyoming, flows N 1080 km (671 mi) through Montana to Missouri R. in W North Dakota. Traverses scenic Yellowstone National Park on high plateau. Wildlife reserve, many hot springs, geysers (incl. Old Faithful).

yellowwood, *Cladrastis lutea,* tree of Leguminosae family, native to SE US. Clusters of fragrant white flowers. Hard yellow wood yields dye. Name applied to other trees yielding yellow wood, *eg* West Indian satinwood, *Zanthoxylum flavum.*

Yemen

Yemen, republic of SW Asia, at S end of Arabian penin. Area *c* 195,000 sq km (75,300 sq mi); pop. 6,500,000; cap. Sana. Language: Arabic. Religion: Sunnite Islam. Coastal strip in W; mountainous, desert in interior; grains, fruits, coffee grown. Historically similar to Arabia. Under Turkish rule (1849-1918); boundaries estab. 1934. Member of UAR (1958-61), became republic 1962.

Yemen, Southern, *see* SOUTHERN YEMEN.

Yenisei, river of USSR, C Siberian RSFSR. Formed by union of 2 headstreams at Kyzyl; flows *c* 3850 km (2400 mi) W, then N, to enter Arctic Ocean via Yenisei Gulf. Used for timber, grain transport.

Yentai, *see* CHEFOO.

yeomen, term in English social history for class of small landowner who worked own farms. Esp. characteristic of period between disintegration of feudal system and beginning of agrarian, Industrial revolutions.

Yeomen of the Guard, royal bodyguard of England, now restricted to ceremonial functions at Tower of London. Instituted (1485) by Henry VII. Also called 'Beefeaters'.

Yerevan (Russ. *Erivan*), city of USSR, cap. of Armenian SSR; on R. Zanga. Pop. 818,000. Textiles, chemical mfg.; h.e.p. derived from Zanga. Founded 8th cent.; alternately Persian and Turkish until ceded to Russia (1828). Buildings incl. Blue Mosque; Armenian state univ. (1921).

Yesenin or **Esenin, Sergei Aleksandrovich** (1895-1925), Russian poet. Wrote lyric poetry, led notoriously debauched life. Other works incl. verse tragedy *Pugachov* (1922). Married dancer Isadora Duncan.

yeti or **abominable snowman,** animal resembling man, said to live in Himalayas. Tracks found have been ascribed to it. Existence disputed, but believed by some to be a remnant of Neanderthal man.

Yevtushenko, Yevgeny Aleksandrovich (1933-   ), Russian poet. Known for youthful, rebellious poetry critical of Soviet regime. Works incl. *Stalin's Heirs* (1961), *A Precocious Autobiography* (1963).

English yew

yew, any of genus *Taxus* of evergreen coniferous trees and shrubs. Native to Eurasia and North America. Dark green, flattened needles, red, cup-like, waxy cones containing single poisonous seed. Yields fine-grained elastic wood. Species incl. English yew, *T. baccata,* and North American ground hemlock, *T. canadensis.* Wood once used to make longbows.

Yezd, *see* YAZD.

Yezidis, religious sect living mainly around Mosul, Iraq. Combines elements of Islam and Christianity. Incorporates worship of devil as an agent of God.

Yezo, *see* HOKKAIDO.

Yggdrasill, in Norse myth, tree of universe. Eagle (heaven) at top, serpent (hell) at bottom; squirrel between was symbolic of strife.

Yiddish, language in West Germanic group of Indo-European languages. Non-national but 1st language of Jews all over the world. Vocabulary contains loan-words from HEBREW, Slavic, Romance languages and English. Alphabet Hebrew. Has important literature dating from late 19th cent.

yin and yang, in Chinese philosophy, terms for contrasting and complementary forces or principles of universe. Yin is passive, negative, feminine; yang is active, positive, masculine, source of light and heat.

Yingchuan, cap. of Ninghsia-Hui auton. region, NC China. Pop. *c* 90,000. Port on Hwang Ho. Textile mfg; coal mines nearby.

yoga (Sanskrit, = union), in Hinduism, system of spiritual discipline by which believers seek union with supreme being or ultimate principle through liberation of the self. Involves exercises in self-control, meditation, breathing, posture.

yogurt or **yoghourt,** semi-solid dairy product prepared by curdling action on milk of bacterium *Lactobacillus bulgaricus.* Easily digested, highly nutritious.

Yokohama, seaport of Japan, on Tokyo Bay, SE Honshu isl. Pop. 2,238,000. Exports silk, canned fish; shipbuilding; motor vehicle and textile mfg. Small fishing village when visited by Perry (1854); opened to foreign trade (1859). Rebuilt after extensive damage suffered in 1923 earthquake and bombing in WWII.

Yokosuka, seaport of Japan, naval base on Tokyo Bay, SE Honshu isl. Pop. 348,000. Major shipbuilding centre. Has tomb of English navigator William Adams (d. 1620).

Yom Kippur, *see* ATONEMENT, DAY OF.

yoni, representation of the vulva, a symbol used in worship of Hindu god Shakti. *See* LINGAM.

Yonkers, residential town of SE New York; suburb of New York City on Hudson R. Pop. 204,000. Elevators, chemicals, cable mfg. First settled 1646 by Dutch.

Yoritomo Minamoto (1148-99), Japanese warrior ruler. Became (1192) 1st shogun (military dictator of feudal system) and set up system of centralized govt. Encouraged Zen Buddhism, BUSHIDO.

York, House of, English royal family. Claimed throne through Edmund of Langley (1341-1402), 5th son of Edward III, who was created (1385) duke of York. Wars of the Roses arose from rivalry between Richard, Duke of York (1411-60) and Lancastrians. Edward IV, Edward V, Richard III were Yorkist kings before 2 houses united under Henry. VII.

York, Richard, Duke of (1411-60), English nobleman. Recognized by Henry VI as his heir, York's claims were set aside on birth of Henry's son (1454). Appointed protector (1453-4) during Henry's insanity, his dismissal on Henry's recovery precipitated Wars of the Roses (1455). Reinstated as protector and heir to the throne after Yorkist victories, he was defeated and killed at Wakefield.

Yorke Peninsula, penin. of SE South Australia, between Spencer and St Vincent gulfs. Sheep and grain farming; salt, copper deposits.

Yorkshire, former county of N England. Was divided in 3: East Riding (co. town Beverley); North Riding (co. town Northallerton); West Riding (co. town Wakefield). Pennines, Dales in W; Vale of York in C; Moors, Wolds in E. Iron, steel, woollen industs. based on W coalfield, centres incl. Sheffield, Leeds, Bradford. Fishing at Hull; resorts incl. Harrogate, Scarborough, Whitby. Co. town was **York,** city on R. Ouse. Pop. 105,000. Railway jct.; confectionery; univ. (1963). Roman *Eboracum,* Constantine proclaimed Emperor here (306); ecclesiastical centre, archbishopric from 7th cent. Cathedral (12th cent.), many medieval buildings.

Yorkshire terrier, English breed of toy terrier. Dark steel blue on back, tan on head, chest and legs; stands 23 cm/9 in. at shoulder.

Yorktown, *see* WILLIAMSBURG, US.

Yoruba, African people within Kwa group of Niger-Congo branch of Niger-Kordofanian language family. Originated in SW Nigeria, spread throughout W Africa. Tend to live in towns. Use as slaves has led to cultural influence being found in Brazil, Cuba.

Yosemite, region of C California, US; in Sierra Nevada. National Park, has mountains, canyons (esp. Yosemite Valley), highest waterfall in North America (739 m/2425 ft), rivers, sequoia groves.

Yoshkar-Ola or **Ioshkar-Ola,** town of USSR, cap. of Mari auton. republic, EC European RSFSR. Pop. 180,000. Pharmaceuticals, agric. machinery mfg.

Youghal, town of Co. Cork, S Irish Republic, on Blackwater estuary. Pop. 5000. Port, resort; carpet, lace mfg. Occasional home of Raleigh, who introduced potato, tobacco to Ireland.

Young, Arthur (1741-1820), English agricultural writer. Travelled extensively, recording his observations of farming techniques in series of *Tours.* Founded monthly periodical *Annals of Agriculture* (1784).

Young, Brigham (1801-77), American religious leader. Converted to Mormon faith; became member of Council of Twelve (1835). After assassination (1844) of Joseph Smith, led W migration; settled Salt Lake City as co-operative theocracy.

Young, Owen D. (1874-1962), American public official. Drew up Young Plan for payment of German reparations after WWI. Adopted 1930, Plan was to specify exact debt and reduce annual payments; thwarted by German economic depression.

Young, Thomas (1773-1829), English physicist, physician. Discovered phenomenon of interference of light and revived wave theory to explain it; made calculations of wavelength of light. Conceived 3-colour theory of colour vision, later extended by Helmholtz. Pioneer in decipherment of Egyptian hieroglyphics.

Younghusband, Sir Francis Edward (1863-1942), British explorer, b. India. Explored mountains between China and Kashmir (1886-7), crossing Gobi Desert. Commissioner to Tibet (1902-4), led British expedition into Lhasa (1904).

Young Men's Christian Association (YMCA), international organization providing young men with accommodation, education, recreational facilities. Estab. 1844 in UK by Sir George Williams, spread to North America (1851-4). Originally solely didactic Christian movement. Has Geneva hq. **Young Women's Christian Association (YWCA)** founded (1855) with similar aims in Britain and US.

Youngstown, city of E Ohio, US; on Mahoning R. Pop. 140,000. In coal, iron ore mining region; steel mfg., other related industs. First settled 1796.

Young Turks, reformist and nationalist movement of Ottoman Empire in early 20th cent. Organized revolt which deposed Abdul Hamid II (1909). Its leader, ENVER PASHA, became virtual dictator in 1913.

Ypres (Flem. *Ieper*), town of W Belgium. Pop. 18,000. Textile centre from Middle Ages. Gothic cathedral, Cloth Hall (14th cent.), both restored after extensive damage in WWI. Scene of 3 WWI battles, incl. extensive use of gas by Germans.

Ypsilanti, Alexander (1792-1828), Greek revolutionary. Led revolt in Moldavia (1821) and proclaimed Greek independence from Turkey; uprising put down by Turkish overlords. His brother, **Demetrios Ypsilanti** (1793-1832), was a leader in simultaneous uprising in the Peloponnese (1821). Helped secure Greek independence.

Yseult, see TRISTAN AND ISOLDE.

Ysselmeer, see IJSSELMEER, Netherlands.

ytterbium (Yb), rare metallic element of lanthanide series; at. no. 70, at. wt. 173.04. Occurs with yttrium and lutetium in gadolinite. Isolated 1907.

yttrium (Y), rare metallic element; at. no. 39, at. wt. 88.91. Occurs with other rare metals in gadolonite, *etc.* Isolated (1843) by C.G. Mosander.

Yuan Shih-kai (1859-1916), Chinese military, political leader. Supported imperial regime until 1912, then advised abdication of last emperor. Succeeded Sun Yat-sen as head of provisional govt.; dictatorial methods led to revolts. Attempt to make himself emperor thwarted (1916).

Yucatán, penin. separating Gulf of Mexico from Caribbean. Area 181,000 sq km (*c* 70,000 sq mi). Mainly limestone plateau in E Mexico, incl. N Guatemala, Belize. Forests in S, savannah in NW. Centre of ancient Mayan civilization with many archaeological ruins.

Yucca (Yucca filamentosa)

yucca, genus of plants native to Mexico and S US. Pointed, usually rigid leaves, white waxy flowers on erect spike. Species incl. Joshua tree, *Yucca brevifolia,* of desert regions.

Yugoslavia (*Jugoslavija*), federal republic of SE Europe. Area *c* 255,750 sq km (98,750 sq mi); pop. 21,101,000; cap. Belgrade. Main language: Serbo-Croat. Religions: Orthodox, RC, Islam. Comprises Bosnia and Hercegovina, Croatia, Macedonia, Montenegro, Serbia, Slovenia republics. Julian Alps, Karst in NW; Dinaric Alps run NW-SE; fertile lowlands in NE. Drained by Danube and tributaries. Cereals, forestry, livestock; coal, iron, copper; tourism, esp. on Adriatic. Kingdom of Serbs, Croats and Slovenes created 1918, renamed Yugoslavia 1929. Partisans resisted German occupation 1941-5; People's Republic estab. 1945 under Tito, remaining independent from Soviet Communism after 1948. Gained territ. (1947) from Italy.

Yugoslavia

Yukawa, Hideki (1907-   ), Japanese physicist. Predicted existence of meson, particle of mass *c* 200 times that of electron, to explain powerful forces binding atomic nuclei. Awarded Nobel Prize for Physics (1949).

Yukon, territ. of NW Canada. Area 536,327 sq km (207,076 sq mi); pop. 18,000; cap. Whitehorse. Mainly uninhabited in N Arctic; mountainous in SW with Mt. Logan (Canada's highest peak). Important mining area esp. gold, silver, lead, zinc; fur trading. Dramatic increase in pop. during Klondike gold rush (1896).

Yukon, river of Canada-US. Formed in SC Yukon by jct. of Lewes and Pelly rivers. Flows NW 3220 km (*c* 2000 mi) to Alaska, then SW to Bering Sea. Salmon fishing, h.e.p. resources. Major route to goldfields during Klondike gold rush.

Yumen, city of Kansu prov., NC China. Pop. 325,000. Leading oil extraction, refining centre. Great Wall runs nearby.

Yunnan, prov. of S China. Area *c* 419,600 sq km (162,000 sq mi); pop. (est.) 23,000,000; cap. Kunming. Mountain ranges in W drained by many rivers incl. Mekong; plateau in E. Great metal resources, esp. tin. Agric. limited by terrain.

Zaandam, town of NW Netherlands. Pop. 69,000. Sawmilling, chemicals. Here Peter the Great of Russia studied shipbuilding (1697).

Zabrze, city of S Poland. Pop. 197,000. Coalmining, iron and steel indust.; grew rapidly from late 19th cent. Under Prussian rule 1742-1945; known as Hindenburg 1915-45.

Zadar (Ital. *Zara*), town of Croatia, NW Yugoslavia, on Adriatic Sea. Pop. 25,000. Port, resort; liqueur, tobacco mfg. Cap. of Austrian Dalmatia 1815-1918, became Italian enclave 1920. Ceded to Yugoslavia 1947. Roman remains, 9th cent. church.

Zadkine, Ossip (1890-1967), French sculptor, b. Russia. Influenced by cubism, he developed a semi-abstract style of representing human form. Works incl. memorial to destruction of Rotterdam, *The Destroyed City.*

Zagazig, city of N Egypt, on Nile delta. Pop. 173,000. Railway and canal jct. in cotton, cereal growing dist.

Zagorsk, town of USSR, C European RSFSR. Pop. 74,000. Famous for 14th cent. Troitsko-Sergievskaya monastery, containing 15th and 16th cent. cathedrals, bell tower and Boris Godunov tomb; formerly pilgrimage centre, now museum. Called Sergiev until 1930.

Zagreb (Ger. *Agram*), city of NW Yugoslavia, on R. Sava, cap. of Croatia. Pop. 566,000. Transport, indust. centre esp. chemicals, metal goods. Croatian cultural centre, univ. (1669). Old town ('Kaptol') has RC cathedral (11th cent.), palace (18th cent.).

Zagros Mountains, range forming SW edge of Iranian plateau. Rise to 4548 m (14,920 ft) at Zard Kuh.

Zaharoff, Sir Basil, orig. Basileios Zacharias (1849-1936), Turkish financier, munitions manufacturer. Through dealings in arms and financial aid, had great unofficial influence in international affairs, esp. after WWI.

Zaïmis, Alexander (1855-1936), Greek statesman. Kept Greece neutral as premier in WWI until 1917. President (1929-35) until restoration of monarchy. Term marked by conflict between republicans and monarchists. Died in exile.

Zaïre

Zaïre, republic of C Africa. Area 905,400 sq km (345,000 sq mi); pop. 23,563,000; cap. Kinshasa. Languages: Bantu, French. Religions: native, Christian. Occupies most of R. Congo basin; rain forest in N, savannah in S. Produces cotton, coffee, palm oil, timber; cobalt, copper from Katanga; indust. diamonds from Kasai. Source of slaves 17th-19th cent. Explored by Livingstone, Stanley; Congo Free State estab. 1885 by Leopold II of Belgium, became Belgian Congo colony (1908). Independent (1960) as Republic of the Congo; disunity, incl. secession of Katanga, and civil war followed, ended by UN intervention. Renamed Zaïre (1971).

Zaïre, river of C Africa, *see* CONGO.

Zákinthos (Ital. *Zante*), isl. of W Greece, one of Ionian Isls. Area 409 sq km (158 sq mi); cap. Zante. Currants, olive oil. Held by Venice 1482-1797. Site of many earthquakes.

Zama, ancient village of N Tunisia. Scene of defeat (202 BC) of Hannibal of Carthage by Scipio Africanus of Rome, which ended 2nd Punic War.

Zambezi, river of SC and SE Africa. Flows *c* 2250 km (1700 mi) from NW Zambia via Victoria Falls and Kariba Dam to Mozambique Channel near Chinde. Navigable stretches separated by rapids.

Zambia, republic of SC Africa. Area 753,000 sq km (290,500 sq mi); pop. 4,635,000; cap. Lusaka. Languages: Bantu, English. Religions: native, Christian. Mainly plateau, mountainous in N, NE; main rivers Zambezi, Kafue. Savannah; agric. incl. maize, tobacco, coffee, livestock. Rich copper deposits, h.e.p. from Kariba Dam; 'Tan-Zam' railway to Dar-es-Salaam. Explored 1850s-60s by Livingstone; admin. by British South Africa Co. from 1889. Northern Rhodesia created (1911); part of Federation of Rhodesia and Nyasaland (1953-63). Independent as Zambia (1964). Member of British Commonwealth.

Zamboanga, port of Philippines, SW Mindanao isl. Pop. 221,000. Centre of iron and timber producing area; exports copra, hemp. Inhabitants mainly Moslems (Moros).

Zamenhof, *see* ESPERANTO.

Zamość (Russ. *Zamostye*), town of SE Poland. Pop. 30,000. Agric. trade centre, univ. (1773). Under Russian rule 1815-1919.

Zamyatin, Yevgeny Ivanovich (1884-1937), Russian author. Best known for anti-Utopian novel, *We* (1929), which strongly influenced Orwell's *1984*.

Zanzibar, isl. of Tanzania, in Indian Ocean. Area 1660 sq km (640 sq mi); cap. Zanzibar. Exports cloves, copra. With PEMBA, under Portuguese rule from 1503; taken by sultan of Oman 1698, became independent sultanate 1856. British protect. from 1890; independent 1963. United 1964 with Tanganyika to form Tanzania.

Zapata, Emiliano (*c* 1879-1919), Mexican revolutionary. Seeking agrarian reform, led Indian revolt in S (1911-16). Occupied Mexico City 3 times. Killed by agent of CARRANZA.

Zaporozhye, city of USSR, S Ukrainian SSR; on Dnepr. Pop. 697,000. Metallurgical centre; motor vehicle, machinery mfg. Expanded with building of Dneproges dam and h.e.p. station in 1930s. Nearby Khortitsa isl. was home

Emiliano Zapata

of Zaporozhye Cossacks, important in history of Ukraine (16th-18th cent.).

Zapotec, Indian people of Oaxaca and Isthmus of Tehuantepec, Mexico. Highly-developed civilization *c* 100 BC. Culturally akin to Maya, but religion different. Conquered by Spanish (1522-6) after resisting Aztec domination. Culture now predominantly Spanish, although strong vestiges of original remain.

Zara, *see* ZADAR, Yugoslavia.

Zaragoza, *see* SARAGOSSA, Spain.

Zarathustra, *see* ZOROASTER.

Zaria, city of N Nigeria. Pop. 201,000. Railway jct., trade centre in cotton-growing dist.; Ahmadu Bello Univ. (1962). Former Hausa city state; fell to Sokoto empire (19th cent.), to British (1901).

Zarqa, city of N Jordan. Pop. 225,000. Rail jct.

Zatopek, Emil (1922-), Czech runner. Greatest long-distance runner of his time, he won 5000 m, 10,000 m and marathon titles in 1952 Olympics.

Zealand (*Sjaelland*), largest isl. of Denmark, between Kattegat and Baltic, separated from Sweden by Oresund. Area 7016 sq km (2709 sq mi); chief city Copenhagen. Livestock, dairying, fishing. Road, rail bridge to Falster.

Zealots, Jewish party (*c* 37 BC–AD 70) formed in opposition to idolatrous practices of Herod the Great. Revolted against Romans (AD 6) and continued intermittent violence until Jerusalem was destroyed by Romans (AD 70). Zealots disappeared as Jews left Palestine.

zebra, African mammal of horse genus, *Equus*. White or buff coloured with dark stripes; attempts to domesticate it have been unsuccessful. Species incl. common or Burchell's zebra, *E. burchelli,* of E and S Africa, and Grévy's zebra, *E. grevyi,* the largest species.

zebra fish, any of various unrelated tropical fish with barred zebra-like markings. Species incl. Indian danio, *Brachydanio rerio,* popular aquarium fish.

zebu, *Bos indicus,* species of domesticated Asiatic cattle, notably resistant to heat and disease. Long pendulous ears, large dewlap, fatty hump over shoulders. Also called humped or brahman cattle.

Zechariah, prophetic book of OT. First part by Zechariah, dated 519-517 BC. Later part, by another author, prob. *c* 2nd cent. BC. Consists of visions of destruction of Jerusalem and subsequent redemption under Messiah.

Zeebrugge, town of W Belgium, on North Sea. Port, canal to Brugge; produces chemicals, cake and glass. German naval base in WWI.

Burchell's zebra

Zeeland, prov. of SW Netherlands, incl. Walcheren, North and South Beveland isls. Area 1772 sq km (684 sq mi); cap. Middelburg. Chief port Flushing. Mainly agric.; land reclamation in Scheldt estuary. Joined United Provs. 1579.

Zeeman, Pieter (1865-1943), Dutch physicist. Discovered Zeeman effect (1896), involving splitting of single spectral lines into groups of lines when radiation source is placed in magnetic field. Shared Nobel Prize for Physics (1902) with H. A. Lorentz.

Zeiss, Carl (1816-88), German industrialist. With Ernst Abbe, developed outstanding optical instrument factory. Developed many new lenses, heat-resisting glasses. Firm later famous for cameras.

Zelaya, José Santos (1853-1919), Nicaraguan statesman, president (1894-1909). Tried to unite Central America under his rule; fomented revolution in neighbouring countries to this end. Ambitions provoked US to help depose him.

zemstvo, Russian local assemblies estab. (1864) to supervise public services, *eg* transport, health, education. In spite of land owners' relative majority, achieved liberal reforms. Functions taken over by soviet.

Zen Buddhism, form of Buddhism developed in India and widely adopted in Japan from 12th cent. Holds that good works, intellectual effort, *etc,* are of no value without ultimate insight (*satori*). This is sought through meditation, esp. on paradoxes to throw doubt on conventional logic.

Zend-Avesta, *see* AVESTA.

zenith, in astronomy, point on celestial sphere vertically above any place on Earth, directly opposite NADIR.

Zenobia, queen of Palmyra from AD 267. Ruled as regent for her son and extended her empire in the East at the expense of Rome. Defeated (272) by Aurelian who took her to Rome as part of his triumph.

Zeno of Citium (*c* 334-*c* 262 BC), Greek philosopher, b. Cyprus. In Athens, studied under the Cynics. Taught that logic must serve ethics. Founder of Stoicism.

Zenta, *see* SENTA, Yugoslavia.

zeolites, group of natural hydrated aluminosilicates of sodium, calcium, *etc,* found in igneous rocks, characterized by ability to take up and lose water of hydration. Used to soften hard water by ion exchange and in purification processes.

Zephaniah or **Sophonias,** prophetic book of OT. Dated 7th cent. BC. Denounces sins of the people but ends with prediction of salvation and Jews' return to God's grace.

Zeppelin, Ferdinand, Graf von (1838-1917), German army officer, inventor. Built 1st rigid-frame motor-driven airship (1900); subsequent models named after him.

Zermatt, town of S Switzerland. Pop. 3000. Resort, mountaineering centre at foot of Matterhorn. Rack-and-pinion railway to summit of the Gornergrat alt. 3100 m (10,280 ft).

Zernike, Frits (1888-1966), Dutch physicist. Awarded Nobel Prize for Physics (1953) for developing phase contrast microscope, useful in biological and medical research.

Zetland, *see* SHETLAND, Scotland.

Zeus, in Greek myth, chief of the OLYMPIAN GODS; son of CRONUS and Rhea. Overthrew Cronus, became ruler of heaven. Husband of Hera who bore him Hebe, Ares; also fathered many children by goddesses, nymphs, mortals. Dispensed good and evil to men, protected law, order, justice. Manifested authority with thunderbolt; made earth fertile with rain. Identified with Roman Jupiter.

Zhdanov, port of USSR, SE Ukrainian SSR; on Sea of Azov. Pop. 435,000. Exports grain, coal. Steel, machinery, chemical mfg. Formerly Mariupol, renamed 1948 after Soviet statesman.

Marshal Zhukov

Zhukov, Georgi Konstantinovich (1896-1974), Soviet army officer. In WWII, led counter-attack at Stalingrad and relief of Leningrad (1943); captured Berlin (1945) and received German surrender. Defence minister (1955-7).

Ziegfeld, Florenz (1869-1932), American theatre manager. His 'Ziegfeld Follies', based on Folies-Bergère of Paris, estab. American theatrical revue. Employed leading entertainers of the day.

Ziegler, Karl (1898-1973), German chemist. His work on use of catalysts to control polymerization of chemicals was important in manufacture of plastics. Shared Nobel Prize for Chemistry (1963) with G. Natta.

Zimbabwe, ruined city of EC Rhodesia. Granite ruins of Bantu culture date from 14th-15th cent., incl. temple, acropolis, dwellings; discovered 1868. Term adopted as African name for Rhodesia.

zinc (Zn), hard metallic element; at. no. 30, at. wt. 65.37. Occurs as zincblende (sulphide), calamine (carbonate, silicate), *etc;* obtained by roasting and reducing ore. Used as protective coating for iron and steel, in alloys (*eg* brass) and dry cell batteries.

zincblende, *see* SPHALERITE.

Zinder, town of S Niger. Pop. 15,000. Trades in livestock, hides, groundnuts; at S end of trans-Sahara route to N Africa. Cap. of Niger colony until 1926.

Zinjanthropus, *see* AUSTRALOPITHECUS.

zinnia, genus of plants of daisy family. Native chiefly to Mexico but widely cultivated for variously coloured daisy-like flowers. *Zinnia elegans* is state flower of Indiana.

Zeppelin: the *Schwaben*

Zinoviev, Grigori Evseyevich (1883-1936), Soviet political leader. President of Comintern after 1919. Opposed Stalin in struggle for Communist Party leadership after Lenin's death. Executed in Stalinist purge. Name linked to forged 'Zinoviev letter' involving alleged Communist uprising in Britain; its publication contributed to Labour govt. defeat (1924).

Zion, originally fortress in Jerusalem captured by David and known as 'City of David'. Later term used for hill in Jerusalem on which Temple was built, and for symbolic centre of Judaism.

Zionism, political and cultural movement seeking to re-estab. Jewish national state in Palestine. First World Zionist Congress, organized by HERZL, convened 1897. Played important part in setting up Israel (1948), esp. by securing BALFOUR DECLARATION. Now promotes emigration to Israel and donations to support Israeli armed forces.

zircon, hard mineral, consisting of zirconium silicate. Found as tetragonal crystals among acid igneous and sedimentary rocks. May be yellow, brown or red; transparent varieties used as gems.

zirconium (Zr), metallic element; at. no. 40, at. wt. 91.22. Occurs in zircon (silicate). Used as structural material in nuclear reactors; compounds used in manufacture of ceramics and refractory materials.

zither, folk musical instrument of Austria and S Germany with 30-45 strings stretched over sounding box. Has 4 or 5 melody strings which are fretted, other strings provide accompaniment. Played with plectrum and the fingertips.

Zlatoust, city of USSR, W Siberian RSFSR. Pop. 183,000. Metallurgical centre of S Ural Mts. since 18th cent.; produces special steels, agric. machinery.

Zlín, see GOTTWALDOV, Czechoslovakia.

Zodiac (from Gk., *zodiakos kyklos* = circle of animals), in astronomy and astrology, imagined belt in heavens within which lie paths of Sun, Moon, and major planets. Stars in belt arranged in 12 constellations, originally corresponding to 12 equal divisions of the belt. Divisions therefore named

Signs of the zodiac: 1. Capricorn; 2. Aquarius; 3. Pisces; 4. Aries; 5. Taurus; 6. Gemini; 7. Cancer; 8. Leo; 9. Virgo; 10. Libra; 11. Scorpio; 12. Sagittarius

after constellations, and distinguished by signs. In order east from vernal equinox, these are Aries (Ram), Taurus (Bull), Gemini (Twins), Cancer (Crab), Leo (Lion), Virgo (Virgin), Libra (Balance), Scorpio (Scorpion), Sagittarius (Archer), Capricorn (Goat), Aquarius (Water Bearer), Pisces (Fish). The 1st 6 lie N of the equator, the 2nd, S. Defined by Babylonians (c 2000 BC), precession of equinoxes has since caused misalignments of named divisions and constellations, but astrologers still use Zodiac to predict individual's fate from state of heavens at time of birth.

Zog, orig. Ahmed Zogu (1895-1961), king of Albania (1928-43). Became president (1925) before being proclaimed king. Granted concessions to Italy in exchange for financial aid. Fled abroad on Italian invasion (1939). Died in exile.

Zola, Emile (1840-1902), French author. Leader of naturalists, advocating novel of social determinism with close attention to detail, detached narration, in essay *Le*

Roman expérimental (1880). Novels incl. *Nana* (1880) *Germinal* (1885), part of 20 vol. series *Les Rougon-Macquart* (1871-93). Advocate of social reform, defended DREYFUS in pamphlet *J'Accuse* (1898); prosecuted for libel, fled to England.

Zollverein, customs union among German states in 19th cent. Began (1818) in Prussia, gradually absorbed other German tariff unions. Contributed to political unity, achieved by creation (1871) of German Empire.

Zomba, town of S Malawi, in Shiré Highlands. Pop. 20,000. Centre of coffee, cotton, tobacco growing region. Former cap. of Nyasaland protect. of Malawi until replaced by Lilongwe.

zoology, branch of biology concerned with study of animals. Systematic classification of animals into species, genera, orders, *etc,* introduced by Linnaeus; later codified by international agreement. Field of zoology expanded by study of embryology, physiology, ecology and genetics.

Zorn, Anders (1860-1920), Swedish artist. Popular portrait painter, esp. in US, he also painted nudes and peasant scenes. His etchings are more highly regarded now.

Zoroaster or **Zarathustra** (*c* 628-*c* 551 BC), Persian prophet. Founder of ZOROASTRIANISM. Little known of his life.

Zoroastrianism, dualistic religion derived from Persian pantheism of *c* 8th cent. Instituted by Zoroaster. Doctrines stated in *Zend-Avesta* scriptures: universe dominated by warring forces of good (Ahura Mazdah or Ormuzd) and evil (Ahriman), in which good will triumph. Ceremony centres on purification rites. Survives in Iran and India (known as Parseeism).

Zouaves, corps of French infantry raised in Algeria in 1831 from like-named Berber tribe; later became purely French. Noted for discipline and colourful uniform.

zucchini, see COURGETTE.

Zuckmayer, Carl (1896-1977), German playwright. Known for satirical comedy *The Captain of Köpenick* (1931), anti-Nazi drama *The Devil's General* (1946) written in exile in US.

Zug, town of N Switzerland, on L. Zug, cap. of Zug canton. Pop. 23,000. Printing, woodworking, electrical equipment.

Zugspitze, highest mountain of West Germany, in Bavarian Alps. Height 2963 m (9721 ft); ascended by cable railways from Garmisch-Partenkirchen and Ehrwald (Austria).

Zuider Zee, former inlet of North Sea, NW Netherlands. Divided by dam, completed 1932, into Ijsselmeer (S) and Waddenzee (N). Large-scale reclamation since 1920.

Zulu, African people, belonging to BANTU group. Now settled in Zululand (N South Africa). Agric. primarily cattle-raising. Most Zulu live in enclosures (kraals) of beehive huts, each kraal containing community based on close kinship. Ties becoming weaker as many men leave to work in south. Zulu became powerful in early 19th cent. under Chaka; later, chief Dingaan continued clashes with Boers, and later still Cetewayo warred with British, finally defeated in 1879.

Zululand, hist. region of NE Natal, South Africa, cap. Eshowe. Coastal plain (cotton, sugar plantations), interior plateau (cattle raising), several game reserves. Zulus became powerful early in 19th cent., resisted Boer settlers (1830s). Finally defeated (1879) by British; part of Natal from 1897. Partly corresponds to Kwazulu homeland (area 31,000 sq km/12,000 sq mi; cap. Ulundi) estab. 1959.

Zurbarán, Francisco de (1598-1664), Spanish painter. Influenced by Caravaggio, he developed naturalistic style and sculpturesque form to express religious devotion in paintings of saints, monks, *etc.* Works incl. *Adoration of the Shepherds.*

Zürich, city of N Switzerland, on L. Zürich, cap. of Zürich canton. Pop. 423,000. Cultural, commercial (esp. banking), indust. centre; printing, publishing; univ. (1833). Joined Swiss Confederation 1351. Centre (under Zwingli) of 16th cent. Reformation. Protestant churches, town hall.

Zweibrücken (Fr. *Deux-Ponts),* town of W West Germany. Pop. 33,000. Textiles, leather, metal goods. Seat of counts (later dukes) palatine of Zweibrücken from 1410. French 1801-14.

Zweig, Stefan (1881-1942), Austrian author. Humanistic view of European culture expressed in biogs., *eg Three Masters* (1920) on Balzac, Dickens, Dostoyevski, *Maria Stuart* (1935). Psychological novels incl. *Beware of Pity* (1938).

Zwickau, town of S East Germany, on R. Mulde. Pop. 126,000. Coalmining, textiles, paper mfg. Anabaptist movement founded here by Thomas Münzer (1520).

Zwingli, Ulrich or **Huldreich** (1484-1531), Swiss religious reformer, humanist. Estab. Protestantism in Zurich in 1520s; set forth doctrines opposed to monasticism, worship of images. Believed in republican basis for church, subsequently influenced Calvin. Killed in war with anti-Protestant Swiss cantons.

Zwolle, town of C Netherlands, cap. of Overijssel prov. Pop. 73,000. Railway, canal jct.; cattle market, chemicals. Thomas à Kempis lived (15th cent.) at nearby monastery.

Zworykin, Vladimir Kosma (1889-), American physicist, b. Russia. Developed cathode-ray tube for television receiver and 1st practical television camera. Perfected electron microscope.

CHEMICAL ELEMENTS

With International Atomic Weights. Carbon at 12 is the standard.
Figures in parentheses give mass number of most stable isotope

	Symbol	Atomic Number	Atomic Weight		Symbol	Atomic Number	Atomic Weight
actinium	Ac	89	(227)	mercury	Hg	80	200.59
aluminium	Al	13	26.9815	molybdenum	Mo	42	95.94
americium	Am	95	(243)	neodymium	Nd	60	144.24
antimony	Sb	51	121.75	neon	Ne	10	20.183
argon	Ar	18	39.948	neptunium	Np	93	(237)
arsenic	As	33	74.9216	nickel	Ni	28	58.71
astatine	At	85	210(?)	niobium	Nb	41	92.906
barium	Ba	56	137.34	nitrogen	N	7	14.0067
berkelium	Bk	97	(247)	nobelium	No	102	(255)
beryllium	Be	4	9.0122	osmium	Os	76	190.2
bismuth	Bi	83	208.980	oxygen	O	8	15.9994
boron	B	5	10.811	palladium	Pd	46	106.4
bromine	Br	35	79.909	phosphorus	P	15	30.9738
cadmium	Cd	48	112.40	platinum	Pt	78	195.09
caesium	Cs	55	132.905	plutonium	Pu	94	(244)
calcium	Ca	20	40.08	polonium	Po	84	(209)
californium	Cf	98	(251)	potassium	K	19	39.102
carbon	C	6	12.01115	praseodymium	Pr	59	140.907
cerium	Ce	58	140.12	promethium	Pm	61	(145)
chlorine	Cl	17	35.453	protactinium	Pa	91	(231)
chromium	Cr	24	51.996	radium	Ra	88	(226)
cobalt	Co	27	58.9332	radon	Rn	86	(222)
copper	Cu	29	63.546	rhenium	Re	75	186.2
curium	Cm	96	(247)	rhodium	Rh	45	102.905
dysprosium	Dy	66	162.50	rubidium	Rb	37	85.47
einsteinium	Es	99	(254)	ruthenium	Ru	44	101.07
erbium	Er	68	167.26	samarium	Sm	62	150.35
europium	Eu	63	151.96	scandium	Sc	21	44.956
fermium	Fm	100	(257)	selenium	Se	34	78.96
fluorine	F	9	18.9984	silicon	Si	14	28.086
francium	Fr	87	(223)	silver	Ag	47	107.868
gadolinium	Gd	64	157.25	sodium	Na	11	22.9898
gallium	Ga	31	69.72	strontium	Sr	38	87.62
germanium	Ge	32	72.59	sulphur	S	16	32.064
gold	Au	79	196.967	tantalum	Ta	73	180.948
hafnium	Hf	72	178.49	technetium	Tc	43	(97)
helium	He	2	4.0026	tellurium	Te	52	127.60
holmium	Ho	67	164.930	terbium	Tb	65	158.924
hydrogen	H	1	1.00797	thallium	Tl	81	204.37
indium	In	49	114.82	thorium	Th	90	232.038
iodine	I	53	126.9044	thulium	Tm	69	168.934
iridium	Ir	77	192.2	tin	Sn	50	118.69
iron	Fe	26	55.847	titanium	Ti	22	47.90
krypton	Kr	36	83.80	tungsten	W	74	183.85
lanthanum	La	57	138.91	uranium	U	92	238.03
lawrencium	Lr	103	(256)	vanadium	V	23	50.942
lead	Pb	82	207.19	xenon	Xe	54	131.30
lithium	Li	3	6.939	ytterbium	Yb	70	173.04
lutetium	Lu	71	174.97	yttrium	Y	39	88.905
magnesium	Mg	12	24.312	zinc	Zn	30	65.37
manganese	Mn	25	54.9380	zirconium	Zr	40	91.22
mendelevium	Md	101	(258)				

Census

Census

All population figures in this book have been taken from the latest census figures or from later official estimates when these are available. Populations given for towns are, wherever possible, those of the towns proper, excluding suburbs. In China, the populations of towns under 500,000 are largely estimates based on the 1957 census. The following list of countries gives the date of the latest census or estimate available before the book went to print.

Afghanistan	1973	India	1971
Albania	1971	Indonesia	1971
Algeria	1967	Iran	1972
Angola	1970	Iraq	1970
Argentina	1970	Ireland	1971
Australia	1973	Israel	1972
Austria	1971	Italy	1973
Bahamas	1970	Ivory Coast	1969
Bahrain	1971	Jamaica	1971
Bangladesh	1974	Japan	1972
Belgium	1971	Jordan	1973
Belize	1970	Kenya	1970
Benin	1969	North Korea	1967–70
Bolivia	1973	South Korea	1970
Brazil	1970	Kuwait	1970
Brunei	1971	Laos	1973
Bulgaria	1973	Lebanon	1971
Burma	1970–73	Lesotho	1972
Burundi	1970	Liberia	1971
Cambodia	1973	Libya	1970
Cameroon	1970	Luxembourg	1972
Canada	1971–72	Macao	1971
Central African Republic	1971	Malagasy Republic	1971
Chad	1973	Malawi	1971
Chile	1970	Malaysia	1970
China	1957, 1970	Mali	1970
Colombia	1972–73	Malta	1970
Congo	1970–72	Martinique	1972
Costa Rica	1972	Mauritania	1972
Cuba	1970	Mauritius	1973
Cyprus	1973	Mexico	1973
Czechoslovakia	1974	Monaco	1970
Denmark	1970–72	Mongolia	1971
Dominican Republic	1970	Morocco	1971
Equador	1974	Mozambique	1970
Egypt (UAR)	1970	Nepal	1971
El Salvador	1971	Netherlands	1974
Equatorial Guinea	1960	Netherlands Antilles	1971
Ethiopia	1973	New Caledonia	1971
Fiji	1966	New Zealand	1973
Finland	1973–74	Nicaragua	1971
France	1975	Niger	1972
French Guiana	1967	Nigeria	1971
French Polynesia	1971	Norway	1974
French Territ. of Afars & Issas	1970	Pakistan	1972
Gabon	1970	Panama	1970
Gambia	1973	Papua/New Guinea	1971
East Germany	1973	Paraguay	1972
West Germany	1973	Peru	1972
Ghana	1970	Philippines	1973
Gibraltar	1973	Poland	1973
Greece	1971	Portugal	1970–72
Guadeloupe	1972	Puerto Rico	1970
Guam	1970	Qatar	1971
Guatemala	1973	Réunion	1972
Guinea	1967	Rhodesia	1973
Guinea-Bissau	1960	Romania	1973
Guyana	1970	Rwanda	1970
Haiti	1971	Saudi Arabia	1967
Honduras	1973	Senegal	1969
Hong Kong	1971	Sierra Leone	1970
Hungary	1973	Singapore	1972
Iceland	1972	Somalia	1972

South Africa	1970
Sothern Yemen (Aden)	1970
South-West Africa	1970
Spain	1970
Sri Lanka	1971
Sudan	1971
Surinam	1971
Sweden	1970
Switzerland	1970–72
Syria	1970
Taiwan	1970–73
Tanzania	1970
Thailand	1970
Togo	1970
Trinidad & Tobago	1970
Tunisia	1966
Turkey	1973
Uganda	1969
USSR	1973
United Arab Emirates	1972
United Kingdom	1974
United States	1970
Upper Volta	1970
Uruguay	1969
Venezuela	1970
North Vietnam	1966
South Vietnam	1971
Western Samoa	1971
Yemen	1970
Yugoslavia	1971
Zaïre	1972
Zambia	1972

Illustration Acknowledgements

American History Picture Library, Brentwood, Essex: 32c, 104b, 159a, 374b, 514, 522b, 621b.
Ardea, London: 274 (photograph by I. Beames), 187a, 267, 335a (photographs by C. Haagner), 156c, 421a (photographs by A. Lindau), 161a (photograph by McDougal Tiger Tops), 59a (photograph by P. Morris), 600a (photograph by R. T. Smith), 512a (photograph by R. Taylor), 10, 281a (photographs by A. Warren), 25, 207a, 259a, 505a, 622a (photographs by A. Weaving).
Peter Baker: 285, 405a.
Barnaby's Picture Library: 6b, 50a, 91.
Courtesy of the Trustees, the British Museum: 36c, 67, 121a, 145b, 187b, 262a, 266b, 269b, 485c, 489b, 527b, 546b, 560, 569a.
J. Allan Cash: 5c, 20, 27, 51b, 53b, 64b, 70b, 90, 104, 109, 135, 150b, 152a, 173b, 174, 183b, 200a, 231b, 299b, 320, 323b, 328b, 340a, 368a, 384a, 386c, 388b, 390b, 422a, 424a, 425a, 433c, 444b, 450b, 450c, 456, 464, 476, 481, 493b, 498b, 510b, 535b, 566a, 594c, 602c, 611; 203a, 204c, 212a, 217c, 237a, 241d, 243, 292c, 311b, 351b, 360a, 402b, 406a, 453c, 498a, 523a, 536c, 538b, 539b, 548c, 554b, 561a, 602b, 608, 613c (photographs by John Markham).
Peter A. Clayton: 13a, 26a, 40b.
The Duke of Sutherland: 474b.
Mary Evans Picture Library: 73, 77c, 184b, 276a, 329c, 405b, 459, 610b.
Fitzwilliam Museum: 107b, 583.
Glasgow Art Gallery: 177 (© S.P.A.D.E.M., Paris, 1977), 584b (© S.P.A.D.E.M., Paris, 1977).
Courtesy of the Glasgow Herald: 5a.
Historical Picture Service, Brentwood, Essex: 577b.
Courtesy of the Imperial War Museum: 160a, 224c, 244, 267c, 268a, 484a, 552b.
Courtesy of the National Film Archive/Stills Library: 37, 64a (© United Artists), 167b (© U.F.A.), 169a (© Walt Disney Productions Ltd.), 362c (© M.G.M.), 383 (© Twentieth Century Fox Film Co. Ltd.), 585, 605a (© Universal).
Courtesy of the Trustees, the National Gallery, London: 61, 101a, 198a, 236a, 487 (© S.P.A.D.E.M., Paris, 1977), 510a, 565c, 576d.
The National Gallery of Scotland: 118b, 225b, 381 (© S.P.A.D.E.M., Paris, 1977), 588a.
The National Portrait Gallery, London: 13b, 33, 39, 40b, 41a, 46b, 48b, 54b, 57, 59c, 62b, 75, 78, 87a, 88, 89b, 92, 106c, 108a, 118c, 122b, 140, 158a, 159b, 164b, 169b, 173a, 207d, 212b, 214b, 233b, 239, 252, 253, 269a, 278a, 294b, 296b, 298b, 299a, 301a, 307b, 309b, 312, 326a, 336a, 338a, 376a, 403a, 413, 425b, 426, 428a, 430a, 436b, 455, 462b, 486a, 511a, 512a, 513a, 513b, 517a, 544a, 548b, 558a, 586, 600a, 614a, 614b, 615, 618b.
Pictorial Press Ltd.: 136b.
Picturepoint Ltd.: 58c, 153a, 314b.
Popperfoto: 5b, 6c, 8a, 18, 19, 21b, 31a, 36a, 36b, 38, 45b, 50b, 51a, 51c, 53a, 54a, 56a, 58a, 63a, 66a, 66b, 71, 74a, 74b, 46a, 80, 82a, 83a, 83b, 85, 87b, 89a, 93a, 94a, 96b, 99a, 104c, 106b, 111a, 115b, 115c, 117a, 121b, 124a, 125, 129, 130, 132b, 132c, 134b, 143b, 149c, 153b, 157a, 160b, 161b, 165, 167a, 172a, 173c, 176a, 176b, 181a, 181b, 183a, 184a, 190b, 192, 200b, 201, 203b, 204b, 208, 209a, 209b, 210, 214a, 217b, 218a, 218b, 221a, 221b, 223b, 224a, 225c, 230, 232a, 232b, 234, 235a, 235b, 245b, 247a, 249, 251, 256, 259b, 260, 262, 263, 265b, 266a, 266c, 267b, 268b, 270a, 270c, 272c, 275, 279, 280a, 281a, 288a, 289b, 292b, 293a, 293b, 295b, 296c, 296e, 298a, 301b, 302, 304b, 306, 308a, 309a, 310a, 311a, 313a, 313b, 314a, 317a, 321a, 321b, 323a, 325a, 326b, 328a, 333b, 336b, 337b, 338c, 339, 341a, 343, 344, 346, 348, 349, 352a, 355a, 356c, 358, 360b, 361, 362a, 362b, 363a, 363b, 363c, 367a, 367b, 370a, 370b, 372a, 376b, 377, 386b, 389a, 390a, 391, 392b, 395a, 396b, 398, 399a, 402a, 404a, 404c, 406b, 407b, 408, 410b, 414, 415a, 417a, 418a, 421b, 421c, 422b, 423a, 424b, 427c, 429, 434, 435a, 438a, 439a, 440b, 443a, 443b, 444, 445b, 446, 447a, 448, 460b, 461a, 461c, 463a, 463b, 470c, 470d, 471a, 471b, 477b, 477c, 480, 484b, 484c, 485a, 486b, 488b, 489b, 495, 497, 500, 503a, 503b, 504a, 504b, 504c, 505c, 506, 507a, 509b, 511b, 516a, 521a, 521c, 522c, 523b, 529a, 530b, 532b, 532c, 534a, 534b, 536b, 537, 539a, 540a, 540b, 541a, 541b, 545b, 550, 551, 553b, 555a, 556b, 558b, 558c, 562, 564a, 565b, 568a, 572a, 574a, 574b, 576a, 576c, 577c, 580, 584a, 587, 588c, 589a, 589b, 591a, 592, 594a, 594b, 597, 601a, 602a, 603b, 607b, 612b, 613a, 613b, 616b, 622b.
Radio Times Hulton: 23, 24a, 48a (© S.P.A.D.E.M., Paris, 1977), 109b, 111b, 114, 120a, 120b, 123a, 127, 133c, 138, 161c, 178, 185a, 187c, 193, 194, 215, 223a, 225a, 226, 227, 238, 241a, 245a, 248, 254a, 296a, 296d, 307a, 314c, 317c, 327, 334b, 338b, 354b, 357b, 365b, 374c, 427b, 430b, 431c, 435b, 439b, 467a, 470a, 474a, 482, 490a, 507b, 518, 524, 525b, 531b, 532a, 533a, 535c, 536a, 538a, 548a, 561b, 565a, 567b, 567d, 573a, 604b.
Courtesy of the Science Museum: 9, 45a, 62c, 156b, 170a, 264b, 544c, 557, 623a.
The Scottish National Gallery of Modern Art: 396a.
The Scottish National Portrait Gallery: 314a.
Spectrum Colour Library: 264a, 356a, 403b, 437a, 547a (photograph by T. Boxall), 238b (photograph by R. Chapman), 233a (photograph by I. Fresson), 451 (photograph by W. J. Howes), 146b (photograph by I. Mayo-Smith), 604a (photograph by Col. J. S. Mennell, Rtd.), 147b (photograph by C. S. Milkins), 532d (photograph by M. Roberts), 189c (photograph by A. Smith).
The Tate Gallery, London: 151b (© S.P.A.D.E.M., Paris, 1977), 356a (© S.P.A.D.E.M., Paris, 1977), 380 (© A.D.A.G.P., Paris, 1977), 479, 542, 607.
Sally Anne Thompson: 3, 16d, 45c, 77b, 133a, 231a, 273a, 330, 461b, 603a.
Topix: 98, 108b, 126b, 258a, 352b, 407a, 567a.
Universal Pictorial Press: 6a, 32b, 62a, 86b, 118a, 146a, 616a.
Crown Copyright, Victoria and Albert Museum: 100b, 131b, 189a, 189b, 319, 360c, 520b, 595b, 609.
Western Americana Picture Library, Brentwood, Essex: 122c, 134a, 136b, 294a, 397, 404b, 515, 520a.

Maps by Kazia L. Kram.

The letters a, b, c, d, e following the page numbers indicate the order on pages with more than one illustration; the illustrations are ordered from the top of the left hand column to the bottom of the right hand column.